THE ANNU

American Bed & Breakfasts

1993 Edition

THE ANNUAL DIRECTORY OF

American Bed & Breakfasts

1993 Edition

Julia M. Pitkin, *Editor*

RUTLEDGE HILL PRESS
NASHVILLE, TENNESSEE

The editor would like to thank Stephen R. Woolverton for his heroic efforts in bringing this volume to completion. I also thank the following people for their participation in the production of this book:

Sharon R. Arnold	Jennifer L. Bruer
Alice Ewing	Eliot Houser
Tracey C. Menges	Ronald E. Pitkin

And lastly, I thank Laura Thomas, the proofreading team, and all of the people who helped with the many technical and production aspects.

Julie M. Pitkin

Published in Nashville, Tennessee, by Rutledge Hill Press, Inc. 513 Third Avenue South, Nashville, Tennessee 37210

Cover design and book design by Harriette Bateman
Maps and selected illustrations by Tonya Pitkin Presley

Photograph on front cover of Vermont Marble Inn courtesy of Vermont Marble Inn, Fair Haven, Vermont and used by permission.

Photograph on back cover of Inn at Buckeystown courtesy of Inn at Buckeystown, Buckeystown, Maryland, copyright © 1992 by Tom Bagley and used by permission.

Manufactured in the United States of America
1 2 3 4 5 6 — 95 94 93 92

Contents

Introduction

Another year, another directory, you're thinking. Not so. The 1993 edition of *The Annual Directory of American Bed & Breakfasts* includes more than one thousand new entries, making this directory one of the most comprehensive on the bookstore shelves.

Whether you are planning your honeymoon, a family vacation or reunion, or a business trip (many bed and breakfasts provide conference facilities), you will find what you are looking for at a bed and breakfast. From the restored sea captain's home in Maine to the antebellum plantation in Mississippi. From the adobe hideaway in Santa Fe to the working farm in Iowa. From the lavish Victorian in San Francisco to the rustic cabin near the glaciers in Alaska. They are all here just waiting to be discovered.

Once you have chosen your destination, look for it, or one close by, to see what is available. Each state has a general map with city locations to help you plan your trip efficiently. There are listings in all 50 states, Canada, Puerto Rico, and the Virgin Islands. Don't be surprised to find even the remotest spot you thought only you knew about. Even if your favorite hideaway isn't listed, you're sure to discover a new one.

How to Use This Guide

The sample listing below is typical of the entries in this directory. Each bed and breakfast is listed alphabetically by city and establishment name. The description provides an overview of the bed and breakfast and may include nearby activities and attractions. Note: The descriptions were written by the hosts. The publisher has not visited these bed and breakfasts and is not responsible for any inaccuracies.

GREAT TOWN _____

Favorite Bed and Breakfast

123 Main Street, 10000
(800) 555-1234

This quaint bed and breakfast is surrounded by five acres of award-winning landscaping and gardens. There are four guestrooms, each individually decorated with antiques.

It is close to antique shops, restaurants, and outdoor activities. Breakfast includes homemade specialties and is served in the formal dining room at your leisure.

Hosts: Sue and Jim Smith
Rooms: 4 (2 PB; 2 SB) $65-80
Full Breakfast
Credit Cards: A, B
Minimum stay: 2 nights
Notes: 2, 5, 8, 10, 11, 12, 13

Following the description are notes that are designed for easy reference. Looking at the sample, a quick glance tells you that this bed and breakfast has four guest rooms, two with private baths (PB), and two that share a bath (SB). In most cases, the rates are for two people sharing one room. Tax may or may not be included. The specifics of "Credit Cards" and "Notes" are listed on the bottom of each page. For example, the letter A means that the hosts accept MasterCard. The number 10 means that tennis is available on the premises or within 10 to 15 miles.

In many cases, the bed and breakfast name is listed with a reservation service that represents several houses in one area. This service is responsible for bookings and can answer other questions you may have. They also inspect each listing and can help you choose the best place for your needs.

Before You Arrive

Now that you have chosen the bed and breakfast that interests you, there are some things you need to find out. While you are making reservations, which are often recommended, ask about the local tax. City taxes can be surprising. Make sure your children will be welcome. If you have dietary needs or prefer nonsmoking rooms, find out if these requirements can be accommodated. Ask about check-in times and cancellation policies. Get specific directions. Most bed and breakfasts are conveniently situated, but many are a little out of the way.

When You Arrive

Remember that in many cases you are visiting someone's home. Be respectful of their property, their schedules, and requests. Don't smoke if they ask you not to, and don't show up with pets without prior arrangement. Be tidy in shared bathrooms, and be prompt. Most places have small staffs or may be run single-handedly and cannot easily adjust to surprises.

With a little effort and a sense of adventure you will learn firsthand the advantages of bed and breakfast travel. You will rediscover hospitality in a time when kindness seems to have been pushed aside. And with the help of this directory, you will find accommodations that are just as exciting as your traveling plans.

THE ANNUAL DIRECTORY OF

American Bed & Breakfasts

1993 Edition

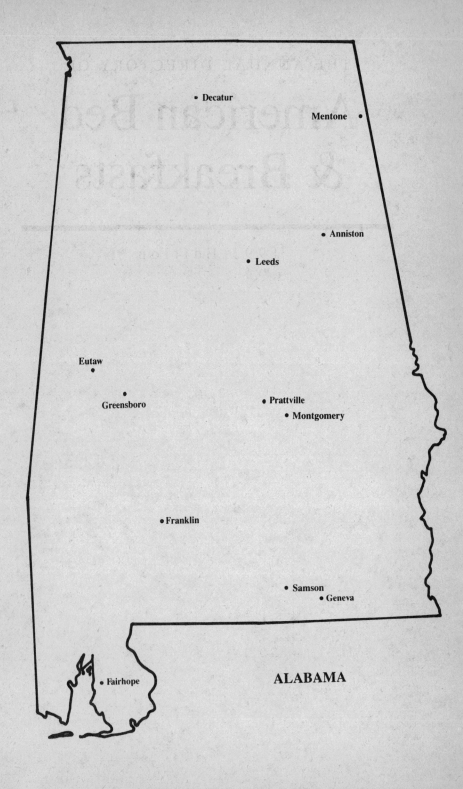

• Decatur

Mentone •

• Anniston

• Leeds

Eutaw
•

• Prattville

• Greensboro

• Montgomery

• Franklin

• Samson

• Geneva

• Fairhope

ALABAMA

Alabama

ANNISTON

The Noble-McCaa-Butler House

1025 Fairmont, 36201
(205) 236-1791

This Victorian house in the historic district is the home of Anniston's founding family and has been restored to period, circa 1886; decorated in Victorian revival with antiques, and fireplaces in every room. Listed on the National Register of Historic Places, it is open for tours. Twenty miles from Talladega Speedway and Cheaha State Park, and minutes from the Anniston Museum of Natural History and Community Theater. Antique malls are nearby, with the Boaz Outlet Center just an hour's drive.

Hosts: Robert and Prudence Johnson
Rooms: 6 (3 PB; 3 SB) $85-95
Full Breakfast
Credit Cards: A, B, C, E
Notes: 2, 5, 9, 10, 11, 12, 14

BIRMINGHAM

The Pickwick Hotel

1023 20th Street South, 35205
(800) 255-7304

The Pickwick Hotel is in the heart of Five Points South. The area is the focal point of the metropolitan area's business and entertainment activities. At the Pickwick Hotel, amenities are not extras. Fresh coffee is available on each floor along with the morning newspaper. Afternoon tea and evening wine and cheese are served in the sitting room. A complimentary continental breakfast is served each morning and features home-baked goods, fresh fruit, and various breakfast items.

Rooms: 63 (PB)
Continental Breakfast
Credit Cards: A, B, C, E
Notes: 2, 5, 6 (small), 7, 8, 9, 10, 11, 14

DECATUR

Hearts and Treasures

911 7th Avenue Southeast, 35601
(205) 353-9562

Beautiful antiques, wood floors, high ceilings, and pretty woodwork grace this newly decorated 1920s home that offers guests privacy in a comfortable and nostalgic setting. The two spacious bedrooms have high antique beds, period pieces, and an airy feel. Relax before the livingroom fireplace

The Noble-McCaa-Butler House

and listen to a player piano serenade. Full breakfast in the elegant formal dining room begins your day. Lunch and dinner available upon request. Just like home, but you're so pampered.

Host: Lukie Pressley
Rooms: 2 (SB) $48
Full Breakfast
Credit Cards: A, B
Notes: 2, 5, 8 (over 12), 9, 10, 11, 12

Kirkwood, 1860 Bed and Breakfast

EUTAW

Kirkwood, 1860 Bed and Breakfast

111 Kirkwood Drive, 35462
(205) 372-9009

Come enjoy this bed and breakfast in an antebellum plantation home. There are many antebellum homes in this small town. Kirkwood construction began in 1857 and was completed in 1860. The Swayzes purchased the home in 1972, and 15 years were spent in restoration work.

Host: Mary B. Swayze
Rooms: 2 (SB) $75 plus tax
Full Breakfast
Credit Cards: None
Notes: 2, 5, 8, 10, 11

FAIRHOPE

Mershon Court Bed and Breakfast Inn

203 Fairhope Avenue, 36532
(205) 928-7398

Mershon Court is a charming and friendly place where you can relax in old-fashioned comfort. Situated in beautiful and peaceful Fairhope, one block from the shopping district and two blocks from beautiful Mobile Bay. The area is known for its interesting shops and restaurants, and this turn-of-the-century home is a Fairhope landmark and has maintained much of its original character.

Hosts: Betty Jo and Rufus Bethea
Rooms: 4 (2 PB; 2 SB) $59-69
Continental Breakfast
Credit Cards: A, B
Notes: 2, 5, 9, 11

FRANKLIN

The Rutherford-Johnson House

Bed and Breakfast Montgomery
P. O. Box 1026, Montgomery, 36101
(205) 264-0056; FAX (205) 262-1872

Original period pieces and antiques grace the four large guest bedrooms with 14-foot ceilings. The bedrooms, parlor, and dining room were added about 100 years ago to the original antebellum structure. For a longer stay, river excursions, nature walks, and picnics enhance its charm. Reservations well in advance. $65.

GENEVA

Live Oaks of Geneva

307 South Academy Street, 36340
(205) 684-2489

Beautifully restored 1918 home situated

NOTES: Credit cards accepted: A Master Card; B Visa; C American Express; D Discover Card; E Diner's Club; F Other; 2 Personal Checks accepted; 3 Lunch available; 4 Dinner available; 5 Open all year;

one block from downtown Geneva in southeast Alabama, this bed and breakfast offers comfortable bedrooms with private baths and TV. Enjoy the large porch, sun room, and living room as a family member. A guest entrance allows you to come and go as you wish. Smoking is restricted to the porch. No pets in bedrooms. Children welcome.

Hosts: Horace and Pamela Newman
Rooms: 3 (PB) $40
Continental Breakfast
Credit Cards: None
Notes: 2, 5, 8, 12

GREENSBORO

Blue Shadow

Bed and Breakfast Montgomery
P. O. Box 1026, Montgomery, 36101
(205) 264-0056; FAX (205) 262-1872

A country setting on 320 acres, nature trail, private fish pond, elegant accommodations, afternoon tea; Indian mounds, antebellum homes, Judson College, Marion Institute, and the University of Alabama nearby. $50.

LEEDS

Bed and Breakfast Birmingham

Route 2, Box 275, 35094
(205) 699-9841

Reservation service for the whole state of Alabama. Hosts in Huntsville, Birmingham, Anniston, Decatur, Arab, Tri City area, Spanish Fort Mobile area, Franklin, Mt. Brook.

Full Breakfast
Credit Cards: None
Notes: 2, 3, 4, 5, 11, 14

Country Sunshine

Route 2, Box 275, 35094
(205) 699-9841

A four and one-half-acre secluded retreat with a quiet country atmosphere. Barn and pasture to board your horses. Ranch-style house with four bedrooms and four baths, TV den, fireplace, formal dining room, country dining room, outside screened patio. Guided fishing, camping, horseback riding in the area. Twenty minutes south of Birmingham, near the Botanical Gardens, Vulcan Park, and Oak Mountain State Park.

Host: Kay Rice
Rooms: 4 (PB and SB) $50-65
Full Breakfast
Credit Cards: None
Notes: 2, 3, 4, 5, 8 (over 13), 14

Live Oaks of Geneva

MENTONE

Mentone Inn Bed and Breakfast

Highway 117, Box 284, 35984
(205) 634-4836

In an old-fashioned, relaxing town near DeSoto Falls. Good hospitality; rock on the front porch and watch the world go by.

Host: Amelia Kirk
Rooms: 12 (PB) $55-65
Full Breakfast
Credit Cards: None
Notes: 2, 3, 4, 8, 11, 12, 14

6 Pets welcome; 7 Smoking allowed; 8 Children welcome; 9 Social drinking allowed; 10 Tennis available; 11 Swimming available; 12 Golf available; 13 Skiing available; 14 May be booked through travel agents.

MOBILE

Stickney's Hollow

1605 Springhill Avenue, 36604
(205) 456-4556

Lovely old Victorian home nestled in the
shade of ancient oak trees and surrounded
by azaleas. The guest house is adjacent to
the main house. It is a private one- or two-
bedroom apartment with living room, dining room, kitchen, and bath. The refrigerator is stocked for your convenience and privacy.

Rooms: 2 (1 PB; 1 SB) $50
Self-serve Breakfast
Credit Cards: None
Notes: 2, 5, 7, 9

MONTGOMERY

Cloverdale

Bed and Breakfast Montgomery
P. O. Box 1026, 36101
(205) 264-0056; FAX (205) 262-1872

Friendly, retired hostess serves delicious
breakfasts in a very comfortable home in
one of Montgomery's loveliest areas. Its
tree-shaded, quiet street is near some of

Red Bluff Cottage

Montgomery's best restaurants and quite
accessible from interstates and both the
central and new business districts. Private
entrance, private bath. $44.

Red Bluff Cottage

551 Clay Street, P. O. Box 1026, 36101
(205) 264-0056

The Waldos built Red Bluff Cottage in
1987 high above the Alabama River in
Montgomery's historic Cottage Hill
District. A raised cottage, all guest rooms
are on the ground floor, with easy access to
off-street parking, gazebo, and fenced play-
yard. Upstairs, guests will enjoy pleasantly
light and airy public rooms, including dining, living, music (piano and harpsichord),
and sitting (TV) rooms, plus a deep porch
overlooking downtown, the state capitol,
and river plain.

Hosts: Ann and Mark Waldo
Rooms: 4 (PB) $55
Full Breakfast
Credit Cards: None
Notes: 2, 5, 8, 9, 14

MT. MEIGS

East Fork Farm

Bed and Breakfast Montgomery
P. O. Box 1026, Montgomery, 36101
(205) 264-0056; FAX (205) 262-1872

"The Colonel's Rest" describes accurately
the rural vistas of this beautifully designed
country contemporary on 60 acres east of
Montgomery, two minutes from I-85 and
convenient to the Alabama Shakespeare
Festival. All seven guest rooms have private baths and kitchenettes. Breakfast is
served in the central "keeping room" that
truly deserves the modern label "great
room!" $48.

PRATTVILLE

Plantation House

Bed and Breakfast Montgomery
P. O. Box 1026, Montgomery, 36101
(205) 264-0056; FAX (205) 262-1872

Four and one-half acres of lawn and woods surround this 1830s Prattville mansion, an oasis of serenity and history in the midst of this booming commercial area. Your hosts, among many other interests, raise tropical fish. The master guest bedroom has a private bath with a Jacuzzi and a fireplace. The other two guest rooms have fireplaces and share a bath. Within minutes of downtown Montgomery.

SAMSON

Jola Bama Guest House

201 South East Street, 36477
(205) 898-2478

This comfortable clapboard Victorian boasts a collection of interesting antiques. Located 85 miles south of Montgomery, "The Cradle of the Confederacy." North Florida beaches and the Fort Rucker Army Aviation Museum are nearby. Your host, a tree farmer and cattle rancher, looks forward to welcoming you.

Host: Jewel M. Armstrong
Rooms: 2 (PB or SB) $20-29
Continental Breakfast
Credit Cards: None
Notes: 5, 6, 7, 8 (over 15), 9, 14

---

6 Pets welcome; 7 Smoking allowed; 8 Children welcome; 9 Social drinking allowed; 10 Tennis available; 11 Swimming available; 12 Golf available; 13 Skiing available; 14 May be booked through travel agents.

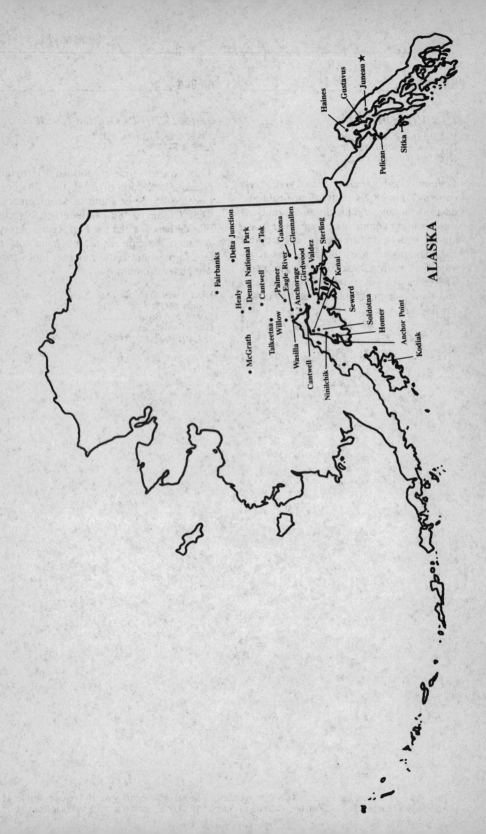

Alaska

Accommodations Alaska Style Stay with a Friend-TNN-ALASKA

3605 Arctic Boulevard #173, 99503
(907) 278-8800; FAX (907) 272-8800

Part of the Bed and Breakfast National Network, Accommodations Alaska Style offers bed and breakfast not only in Alaska, but also in many other cities and states across the country. The members of this network adhere strictly to the standards set by TNN, such as getting to know the hosts personally, having an established cancellation and refund policy, and following a thorough inspection and approval process for all properties rented. This is because each member of the network is dedicated to ensuring your comfort, pleasure, and personal needs while you are staying at one of our "homes away from home."

Accommodations Alaska Style Stay with a Friend 1D

3605 Arctic Boulevard #173, 99503
(907) 278-8800; FAX (907) 272-8800

As close as you can get to Cook Inlet on land by a small park and in view of the scenic coastal walking/bike trail, only a minute from excellent restaurants. Two bedrooms share a bath; family room with TV and Hide-a-bed. Glorious views of Mount Susitna and the Alaska Range with Mount McKinley some 250 road miles away. Full breakfast. No smoking. $65.

Accommodations Alaska Style Stay with a Friend 4D

3605 Arctic Boulevard #173, 99503
(907) 278-8800; FAX (907) 272-8800

Twenty-minute walk to historic Government Hill area and two-minute drive to Elmendorf Air Force Base. Split-level home has self-contained apartment, separate entrance. Two rooms share bath. Enjoy delicious full breakfast upstairs with hosts or prepare your own from stocked kitchen. Living room has TV and phone. $55.

Accommodations Alaska Style Stay with a Friend 5D

3605 Arctic Boulevard #173, 99503
(907) 278-8800; FAX (907) 272-8800

Nicely decorated room on ground level of modern home two blocks from Cook Inlet and 14 blocks to city center. Private bath, color TV, phone. Enjoy the water view when you breakfast upstairs or pioneer Alaskan homesteader hostess will provide continental breakfast in room. No smoking. $70.

Accommodations Alaska Style Stay with a Friend 6D

3605 Arctic Boulevard #173, 99503
(907) 278-8800; FAX (907) 272-8800

NOTES: Credit cards accepted: A Master Card; B Visa; C American Express; D Discover Card; E Diner's Club; F Other; 2 Personal Checks accepted; 3 Lunch available; 4 Dinner available; 5 Open all year; 6 Pets welcome; 7 Smoking allowed; 8 Children welcome; 9 Social drinking allowed; 10 Tennis available; 11 Swimming available; 12 Golf available; 13 Skiing available; 14 May be booked through travel agents.

Apartment suite in Anchorage's premier neighborhood, right on Cook Inlet. Two bedrooms, full bath, livingroom, and kitchen in lower level of large home. No view from rooms but step outside and walk to Coastal Trail or see the sunset over Mount Susitna. Self-serve breakfast from stocked refrigerator. $70; $120 family of four. Off-season weekly rates.

Accommodations Alaska Style Stay with a Friend 7D

3605 Arctic Boulevard #173, 99503
(907) 278-8800; FAX (907) 272-8800

Large home in Bootlegger Cove neighborhood has three-bedroom apartment with separate entrance. Hostess is wild about fishing and has been known to share her catch. Full bath, color TV, phone, and kitchen stocked for self-serve breakfast. $70; $120 family of four.

Accommodations Alaska Style Stay with a Friend 8D

3605 Arctic Boulevard #173, 99503
(907) 278-8800; FAX (907) 272-8800

Charming Government Hill home with warm hospitality and a full cookie jar. Guest rooms are up one flight and share baths. Separate kitchen and sitting room, but most guests are drawn to the hostess' kitchen for lavish full breakfast. $60.

Accommodations Alaska Style Stay with a Friend 22A

3605 Arctic Boulevard #173, 99503
(907) 278-8800; FAX (907) 272-8800

Charming home with many windows and large yard with trees and flowers. Breakfast of your choice served by hosts who are anxious to share Alaskan experiences. Queen-size bed with private bath, $75; queen bed and double bedrooms share a bath, $65.

Accommodations Alaska Style Stay with a Friend 23A

3605 Arctic Boulevard #173, 99503
(907) 278-8800; FAX (907) 272-8800

Ground-level guest room equipped with microwave, refrigerator, pots and pans for light cooking, TV, phone, private bath. Hostess can make second room available for extra guests. Continental breakfast upstairs with Campbell Lake and Chugach Mountain views. No smoking. $65.

Accommodations Alaska Style Stay with a Friend 26A

3605 Arctic Boulevard #173, 99503
(907) 278-8800; FAX (907) 272-8800

Warm and inviting split-level home with many Alaskan artworks has two bedrooms sharing a bath and relaxing family room (with small refrigerator, wet bar, and TV). Homemade berry jams a feature of the delicious breakfast upstairs. No smoking. $60.

Accommodations Alaska Style Stay with a Friend 31E

3605 Arctic Boulevard #173, 99503
(907) 278-8800; FAX (907) 272-8800

Large, split-level family home with many fascinating collectibles, including Alaskan and African hunting and fishing trophies in bedrooms. Beautiful mountain view from dining table where you may enjoy full breakfast with fresh jam from the garden. All welcome in large family room with TV, refrigerator, phone. Wheelchair access can be arranged. Some pets OK in fenced yard. Resident cat. No smoking. $55; $70 family of three.

NOTES: Credit cards accepted: A Master Card; B Visa; C American Express; D Discover Card; E Diner's Club; F Other; 2 Personal Checks accepted; 3 Lunch available; 4 Dinner available; 5 Open all year;

Accommodations Alaska Style Stay with a Friend 50M

3605 Arctic Boulevard #173, 99503
(907) 278-8800; FAX (907) 272-8800

Cozy, red house about a 20-minute hike to city center. Small room with double bed, half-bath, and garden view. Another room shares bath with hostess. Guests have own sitting room for TV and reading. Breakfast to order with fruit, juice, croissants, muffins, cereal. Crib, high chair. Resident dog. No smoking. $50.

Accommodations Alaska Style Stay with a Friend 51M

3605 Arctic Boulevard #173, 99503
(907) 278-8800; FAX (907) 272-8800

A few blocks from University shopping mall in quiet subdivision, a split-level home with two guest rooms sharing bath and recreation room with TV. All ages welcome to share hosts' hobbies of skiing, fishing, flying, gardening, sewing. Continental breakfast. No smoking. $50.

Accommodations Alaska Style Stay with a Friend 52M

3605 Arctic Boulevard #173, 99503
(907) 278-8800; FAX (907) 272-8800

Five minutes by car from airport, downtown, or the Coastal Trail. Spacious home with two guest rooms by main entrance, up one flight of stairs. Rooms are decorated with antiques, Laura Ashley linens, have TV's. Shared bath. Continental breakfast in dining room, kitchen, or on the deck if weather permits. Resident dog. $65.

Accommodations Alaska Style Stay with a Friend 54M

3605 Arctic Boulevard #173, 99503
(907) 278-8800; FAX (907) 272-8800

Hosts live across the street from this cozy cottage decorated in Alaskan country decor. Sitting room with fireplace/stove has Hide-a-bed for additional guests; bedroom plus loft. Full kitchen with appliances. Continental breakfast in refrigerator. $95; $150 four guests.

Accommodations Alaska Style Stay with a Friend 58M

3605 Arctic Boulevard #173, 99503
(907) 278-8800; FAX (907) 272-8800

Garden-view efficiency apartment in quiet neighborhood. Kitchen fully equipped, and breakfast materials are in the refrigerator for you. TV, phone, and extra sleeping. Sauna and Jacuzzi tub in private bathroom. German, Swiss, French, Italian, and English spoken. Children over ten welcome. No smoking. $75; $90 family of three.

Accommodations Alaska Style Stay with a Friend 80H

3605 Arctic Boulevard #173, 99503
(907) 278-8800; FAX (907) 272-8800

Separate two-bedroom apartment on ground level of home near Diamond Center Mall. Kitchen equipped for self-serve continental breakfast or cook yourself a feast any time. Livingroom has TV, phone. Shared bath. $65.

6 Pets welcome; 7 Smoking allowed; 8 Children welcome; 9 Social drinking allowed; 10 Tennis available; 11 Swimming available; 12 Golf available; 13 Skiing available; 14 May be booked through travel agents.

Accommodations Alaska Style Stay with a Friend 81H

3605 Arctic Boulevard #173, 99503
(907) 278-8800; FAX (907) 272-8800

Very special and beautiful tri-level home with private suite (has separate entrance) decorated with antiques and country collectibles. Sitting room has wood-burning fireplace and writing nook; outdoor hot tub on a deck overlooking the Chugach State Forest. Delicious breakfast of your choice. Honeymoon suite with refinished antiques to add to the total Alaska experience. Resident children and dogs. No smoking. $90.

Accommodations Alaska Style Stay with a Friend 82H

3605 Arctic Boulevard #173, 99503
(907) 278-8800; FAX (907) 272-8800

Separate apartment in beautiful home with panoramic view of the city, Cook Inlet, the Alaska Range, Mount McKinley. Unit has a small herb and flower garden and deck and lots of privacy. Full kitchen with refrigerator stocked by hostess for breakfast, or you may talk her into cooking. She is a gourmet caterer. $100.

Accommodations Alaska Style Stay with a Friend 83H

3605 Arctic Boulevard #173, 99503
(907) 278-8800; FAX (907) 272-8800

Situated in south Anchorage. Large room with queen-size bed, private bath, and sitting room. Continental breakfast. $70.

Accommodations Alaska Style Stay with a Friend 85H

3605 Arctic Boulevard #173, 99503
(907) 278-8800; FAX (907) 272-8800

Executive home on bluff above Turnagain Arm. Elegant sitting room with fireplace and piano, formal dining room, deck. Whale watching, moose, migratory water fowl, and mountain view. European breakfast served on fine china and Swedish crystal. Newlywed special champagne breakfast. No smoking. $98-125.

Accommodations Alaska Style Stay with a Friend 89H

3605 Arctic Boulevard #173, 99503
(907) 278-8800; FAX (907) 272-8800

Spacious home on a lake that has swans, loons, ducks, and geese. Panoramic view of Cook Inlet and surrounding mountains. Full breakfast. Cat in home. Queen-size bed with private bath, $75; queen bedroom and twin bedroom share a bath, $65.

Accommodations in Alaska AC

The Friendly Choice Lodge
P.O. Box 100624, 99511-0624
(907) 345-4761

You will enjoy the solitude and landscaping of this spacious yard brimming with summer flowers. This traditional homestay is situated in a quiet, exclusive neighborhood close to downtown. Three guest rooms are offered with queen or double beds, one with private bath. Situated near health and fitness facilities, shopping, and restaurants. Christian hostess serves a variety of breakfasts, choice of full or continental. Resident dog. Free parking. Outdoor smoking. $75-90

NOTES: Credit cards accepted: A Master Card; B Visa; C American Express; D Discover Card; E Diner's Club; F Other; 2 Personal Checks accepted; 3 Lunch available; 4 Dinner available; 5 Open all year;

Accommodations in Alaska AF

The Friendly Lodge Choice
P. O. Box 100624, 99511-0624
(907) 345-4761

This custom-built home nestled in the trees on three landscaped acres offers a variety of accommodations. Rooms with king, queen, or double beds, shared or private bath, two with Jacuzzis, one with a VCR, rock fireplace, and sauna. Personable hostess serves delicious full breakfasts in the formal dining room. Furnished with Alaskan artifacts and trophies, this traditional homestay offers intriguing opportunities to learn more about the area. Free parking. Outdoor smoking. $95-175.

Accommodations in Alaska AH

The Friendly Choice Lodge
P.O. Box 100624, 99511-0624
(907) 345-4761

Your innkeepers enjoy watching the moose and bald eagles from their large sun deck. Tall evergreens surround this traditional homestay in south Anchorage. The two guest rooms share a bath. A family room adjoins the guest rooms complete with cable TV, VCR, rock fireplace, and minikitchen. Guests may also enjoy the electric sauna. Weather permitting, full breakfasts are served on the deck. Free parking. Outdoor smoking. Resident dog. $75-100

Accommodations in Alaska AK

The Friendly Lodge Choice
P. O. Box 100624, 99511-0624
(907) 345-4761

Between downtown and the airport, this large home has facilities for outdoor pets on approval. Recently remodeled, this traditional homestay fits the needs of many visitors to Alaska. Near parks, a free tennis court and popular fitness trail. Accommodations are on the lower level and offer private and shared baths. Twin or double beds. Full breakfast. Sauna. Resident dogs. Free parking. Outdoor smoking. $75-90.

Accommodations in Alaska AL

The Friendly Lodge Choice
P. O. Box 100624, 99511-0624
(907) 345-4761

A breathtaking view of greater Anchorage awaits you at this secluded custom-built home. Beautifully furnished traditional homestay has many resident pets and an active, well-traveled family of six. Exercise equipment, Jacuzzi tub, and sauna for guests' pleasure. Rooms with twin, double, queen, and king beds. Hostess is an accomplished cook, serving sumptuous full breakfasts in an elegant formal dining room. Suite has microwave, refrigerator, separate entrance, and private bath. Free parking. Smoking permitted. $75-95.

Accommodations in Alaska AN

The Friendly Lodge Choice
P. O. Box 100624, 99511-0624
(907) 345-4761

You'll have two knowledgeable hostesses at this traditional homestay near the Chugach foothills. Hostesses enjoy restoring antique furniture. Situated in a family-oriented neighborhood, with library, restaurants, theaters, and supermarket nearby. Twin with shared bath or suite with private bath. The wilderness of Chugach State Park is just blocks away. Return from your expedition to a cozy fire and hot cocoa. Continental breakfast. Resident dog. Free parking. Outdoor smoking. $65-85.

6 Pets welcome; 7 Smoking allowed; 8 Children welcome; 9 Social drinking allowed; 10 Tennis available; 11 Swimming available; 12 Golf available; 13 Skiing available; 14 May be booked through travel agents.

Accommodations in Alaska AP

The Friendly Lodge Choice
P. O. Box 100624, 99511-0624
(907) 345-4761

Your hostess is well traveled and interested in meeting visitors from around the world. The oversize livingroom affords a good view of the Chugach Mountains to the east. Visitors interested in sporting events will appreciate the proximity to Anchorage's major sports complex. A traditional homestay offering king and queen beds, suites or shared bath. Hostess enjoys scuba diving and cooking; host is an amateur radio operator. Resident dog. Free parking. Outdoor smoking. $70-85.

Accommodations in Alaska AT

The Friendly Lodge Choice
P. O. Box 100624, 99511-0624
(907) 345-4761

Your hostess is a native-born Alaskan. Her renowned traditional homestay features full breakfasts accompanied by generous helpings of tall tales. Designed as a bed and breakfast, this rustic establishment is decorated in Alaskana and treasures collected from all corners of the world. Year-round outdoor hot tub and wood-burning sauna. 360-degree view on five wooded acres is at 1,100 feet elevation, overlooking everything. Outdoor dogs and cats. Free parking. Outdoor smoking. $85-125.

Accommodations in Alaska BB

The Friendly Choice Lodge
P.O. Box 100624, 99511-0624
(907) 345-4761

This Christian family offers a traditional homestay with your privacy in mind. This is a popular accommodation, as families can economize. Your suite includes two bedrooms with queen-size beds, a double Hide-a-bed, and private bath. There is also a TV, microwave, and refrigerator. Free parking is provided in the carport near your private entrance. Free tennis and basketball courts are nearby. Hostess, a professional baker, serves heavenly breakfasts. Resident dog. Outdoor smoking. $85.

Accommodations in Alaska BG

The Friendly Lodge Choice
P. O. Box 100624, 99511-0624
(907) 345-4761

Guest rooms are named after bear species in this traditional homestay near both military bases. Two rooms have half-baths, and one room has a three-quarter-bath. Innkeepers have an amazing collection of old Alaskana for you to enjoy. The family practices a self-sufficient lifestyle and enjoys gathering wild berries, gardening, hunting, fishing, and clamming. Full breakfast including wild game may be served at your request. Free parking. Outdoor smoking. $75-80.

Accommodations in Alaska CA

The Friendly Lodge Choice
P. O. Box 100624, 99511-0624
(907) 345-4761

An abundance of summer vegetables and flower gardens enhances this traditional homestay, situated in a quiet neighborhood. A stream borders this oversize property. Two professionally decorated suites, each with a private bath. Each suite has room for four guests, with a queen-size bed and two twin beds. Near health care facilities, the university, and shopping. Easy access to major highway routes. Full breakfast is served with fresh Alaska honey. Free parking. Outdoor smoking. $75-85.

NOTES: Credit cards accepted: A Master Card; B Visa; C American Express; D Discover Card; E Diner's Club; F Other; 2 Personal Checks accepted; 3 Lunch available; 4 Dinner available; 5 Open all year;

Accommodations in Alaska CE

The Friendly Lodge Choice
P. O. Box 100624, 99511-0624
(907) 345-4761

You'll be just 100 feet from the shoreline at this traditional homestay in a quiet downtown neighborhood, a few steps from the popular Coastal Trail. Enjoy sunsets from the deck. Two nicely appointed guest rooms with queen or twin beds share a bath. The cozy suite has a queen bed, private entrance, private bath, and kitchenette. The innkeeper of this 7,500-square-foot home is a professional chef. Gourmet continental breakfast. Free parking. Outdoor smoking. $85-100.

Accommodations in Alaska CG

The Friendly Lodge Choice
P. O. Box 100624, 99511-0624
(907) 345-4761

This modest homestay is near Merrill Field, a popular small-plane airport near downtown Anchorage. Two friendly outdoor German shepherds and their professionally employed hostesses enjoy company and look forward to your visit. Their location is also close to health care facilities and the university. The guest room has a double bed and shared bath. Continental breakfast. Free parking. Outdoor smoking. $65.

Accommodations in Alaska CM

The Friendly Lodge Choice
P. O. Box 100624, 99511-0624
(907) 345-4761

Three shy house cats assist in hosting this elegant home filled with quality furnishings. Both guest rooms have private baths. The hostess serves a full breakfast in the formal dining room. This traditional homestay has easy access to all major highways, yet is isolated from traffic noise. You are sure to enjoy the unobstructed view of the Chugach Mountains from the sun deck. Outdoor smoking. Free parking. $85-100.

Accommodations in Alaska CR

The Friendly Lodge Choice
P. O. Box 100624, 99511-0624
(907) 345-4761

Your hosts enjoy getting acquainted with visitors from around the world in this traditional homestay a few blocks south of major hotels. Three guest rooms with queen, double, and twin beds reflect varied traveling experiences of this professionally employed couple. Flowers abound in the landscaped yard. A popular fitness trail is nearby. Full secretarial services complete with computers, FAX, laser printer, and copier. Continental breakfast. Free parking. Outdoor smoking. $85.

Accommodations in Alaska CW

The Friendly Lodge Choice
P. O. Box 100624, 99511-0624
(907) 345-4761

The innkeepers at this cozy Cape Cod-style home serve homemade jams and jellies with the tasty continental breakfast. This traditional homestay caters to hiker's, cyclists, pilots, rafters, and all types of outdoor adventurers. Three rooms with shared baths. Twin, queen, or king size beds. Situated in an older neighborhood convenient to Merrill Field, Sears Mall, theaters, recreational facilities, the university, and restaurants. Easy freeway access. Free parking. Outdoor smoking. $75.

6 Pets welcome; 7 Smoking allowed; 8 Children welcome; 9 Social drinking allowed; 10 Tennis available; 11 Swimming available; 12 Golf available; 13 Skiing available; 14 May be booked through travel agents.

Accommodations in Alaska FX

The Friendly Lodge Choice
P. O. Box 100624, 99511-0624
(907) 345-4761

One of the prettiest lawns in Anchorage surrounds this traditional homestay near the Chugach Mountains. Your oversize room has a double bed and private bath. Hosts enjoy Alaska's great outdoors and have traveled extensively in Latin America. Continental breakfast includes homemade breads. Resident dogs. Free parking. Outdoor smoking. $75.

Accommodations in Alaska GH

The Friendly Choice Lodge
P.O. Box 100624, 99511-0624
(907) 345-4761

This guest room has a king size bed, private bath, and sauna. The friendly hostess prepares a delicious full breakfast and serves it with a smile. This traditional homestay is a custom redwood home, nestled on 1.5 wooded acres. You are sure to appreciate the large yard offering a chance to relax and enjoy the flowers. This quiet established neighborhood is convenient to the airport, downtown, and all the local attractions. Free parking. Outdoor smoking. $100.

Accommodations in Alaska HO

The Friendly Lodge Choice
P. O. Box 100624, 99511-0624
(907) 345-4761

Guests are invited to join the family around the antique pump organ for musical interludes at this traditional homestay. All beds are queen-size, one bedroom with a private bath. Your delicious Alaskan breakfast may include fresh salmon or many other house specialties. Hungarian and Polish spoken. Free parking. Outdoor smoking. $60-85.

Accommodations in Alaska HS

The Friendly Lodge Choice
P. O. Box 100624, 99511-0624
(907) 345-4761

Your pioneer hosts are weekend gold prospectors and invite you to share their modern custom home near the airport. This traditional homestay is out of the flight path, situated on an oversize lot with plenty of lawn and flower gardens to enjoy. Families are welcome. Variety of beds with shared bath, and queen-size bed with private bath and Jacuzzi. Full breakfast. Free parking in garage. Outdoor smoking. $85-125.

Accommodations in Alaska LS

The Friendly Lodge Choice
P. O. Box 100624, 99511-0624
(907) 345-4761

Your accommodations on the ground floor of this custom-designed home include a private entrance, laundry facilities, fireplace, TV, VCR, microwave, refrigerator, queen bed, shower, bidet, and oversize Jacuzzi. The 14-foot picture windows overlook the Chugach Mountains and 150 feet of private lake frontage. Situated in an exclusive neighborhood near shopping, restaurants, and recreational facilities. Continental breakfast is served to your suite each morning. Resident dog. Free parking. Outdoor smoking. $100.

Accommodations in Alaska MB

The Friendly Lodge Choice
P. O. Box 100624, 99511-0624
(907) 345-4761

NOTES: Credit cards accepted: A Master Card; B Visa; C American Express; D Discover Card; E Diner's Club; F Other; 2 Personal Checks accepted; 3 Lunch available; 4 Dinner available; 5 Open all year;

A creek meanders through six wooded acres of this 1953 log homestead. Twenty minutes south of Anchorage on a peaceful hillside, this traditional homestay is popular with travelers who appreciate quiet adult atmosphere. Both suites have a private entrance, private bath, and queen-size bed. The upper suite has a kitchenette, romantic wood stove, and queen Hide-a-bed for a party of four. Friendly hostess serves full breakfast. Free parking. Outdoor smoking. $85-100.

Accommodations in Alaska MN

The Friendly Lodge Choice
P. O. Box 100624, 99511-0624
(907) 345-4761

You'll think you stepped into yesterday when you enter this modern home decorated with three generations of antiques. Gothic stained-glass windows enhance the romantic living-room, which sometimes serves as a wedding chapel. Two rooms, one with balcony and Jacuzzi. Close to tourist attractions, shopping, and restaurants. Full breakfast served by knowledgeable hostess. Resident dog and cat. Free parking, Outdoor smoking. $85-100.

Accommodations in Alaska PC

The Friendly Lodge Choice
P. O. Box 100624, 99511-0624
(907) 345-4761

These innkeepers have lived in Alaska for 45 years and welcome families. This homestay offers four accommodations, shared bath to private suite with private entry, deck, and laundry and cooking facilities. All have queen beds. Convenient to both military bases. Easy access to Fairbanks and Denali Highway. Host provides freshly caught seafood as part of your full breakfast. Resident dog. Free parking. Outdoor smoking. $75-95.

Accommodations in Alaska RH

The Friendly Lodge Choice
P. O. Box 100624, 99511-0624
(907) 345-4761

Your Christian hostess is an accomplished seamstress and craftswoman. This homestay is decorated in tasteful and sometimes whimsical antiques, as well as her own clever creations. Hillside location offers a respite from downtown hustle and bustle. Three guest rooms with double and queen beds, private or shared bath. Close to wilderness hiking trails. Easy freeway access for guests traveling either direction. Continental breakfast. Outdoor dog. Free parking. Outdoor smoking. $75-95.

Accommodations in Alaska SF

The Friendly Lodge Choice
P. O. Box 100624, 99511-0624
(907) 345-4761

This modest home has one room with shared bath and queen bed. This traditional homestay offers a fenced back yard that can accommodate friendly traveling canines. Hostess enjoys many crafts and has added loving touches to the guest room. Situated within walking distance of shopping and dining. Also close to health-care facilities and the university. Convenient to city bus routes. Continental breakfast. Resident dogs. Free parking. Outdoor smoking. $75.

Accommodations in Alaska SH

The Friendly Lodge Choice
P. O. Box 100624, 99511-0624
(907) 345-4761

You'll want to bring your bathing suits no matter what the season. This homestay

6 Pets welcome; 7 Smoking allowed; 8 Children welcome; 9 Social drinking allowed; 10 Tennis available; 11 Swimming available; 12 Golf available; 13 Skiing available; 14 May be booked through travel agents.

offers magnificent views of the Chugach Mountains from the large Jacuzzi spa in the sun room. Enjoy a game of billiards on the antique table. Or just relax by the fireplace and browse through the library. Three guest rooms with twins, doubles, or queen, all with private baths. Resident dog. Free parking. Outdoor smoking. $85-100.

Accommodations in Alaska SL

The Friendly Lodge Choice
P. O. Box 100624, 99511-0624
(907) 345-4761

You're sure to appreciate easy access to the major airports at this homestay near the Coastal Trail, a paved hiking and biking trail about three miles from downtown. Relaxation comes easy in the spacious living room enhanced by a 30-foot-wide stone fireplace that reaches the vaulted ceiling. Three guest rooms with queen beds and shared bath. Continental breakfast. Resident cats and dogs. Free parking. Outdoor smoking. $85.

Accommodations in Alaska SN

The Friendly Lodge Choice
P. O. Box 100624, 99511-0624
(907) 345-4761

Fishing and swimming ponds are in walking distance to this homestay with easy access to all freeways. Situated near Anchorage airports, yet out of the flight path, four guest rooms share two baths. One suite with a private bath. Guests are invited to use the family recreation room, complete with microwave, refrigerator, TV, VCR, and wet bar. Full breakfast is served—eggs Benedict is a house specialty. Resident dog. Free parking. Outdoor smoking. $65-85.

Accommodations in Alaska SP

The Friendly Lodge Choice
P. O. Box 100624, 99511-0624
(907) 345-4761

The spacious sun deck catches the evening sun. You may want to grill your dinner on the barbecue at this homestay and enjoy the midnight summer sunsets. Accommodations include queen bed and private bath. Private sitting area has TV and bookcase filled with literature on Alaska and travel. Continental breakfast is served. Free parking. Smoking permitted. $75.

Accommodations in Alaska SW

The Friendly Lodge Choice
P. O. Box 100624, 99511-0624
(907) 345-4761

This custom home is designed to resemble a swan in flight. Guests will find the history and design fascinating; from the 127 windows to the jade and black walnut fireplace mantle, nothing is left unaddressed. Offering three distinctive guest rooms with private or shared bath, this traditional homestay overlooks downtown. Hot tub, gourmet continental breakfast. Indoor dog. Free parking. Outdoor smoking. $100-195.

Accommodations in Alaska TS

The Friendly Lodge Choice
P. O. Box 100624, 99511-0624
(907) 345-4761

A world away, tucked into treetops on two secluded acres, this hideaway is the top floor of a private home. This traditional homestay can comfortably accommodate a party of six. There's a wood stove, full kitchen, laundry facilities, and private bath. Full breakfast is served in your suite, or you may dine on your sun deck overlooking the abundant gardens. Outdoor smoking. Free parking. $125.

Accommodations in Alaska 419

The Friendly Lodge Choice
P. O. Box 100624, 99511-0624
(907) 345-4761

This downtown cottage has a colorful past that reaches back into the 1920s. Your suite includes a minikitchen, three-quarter-bath, bedroom and livingroom. Breakfast at this traditional homestay includes nutritional whole foods and good coffee. Your hostess is interested in Alaskan wildflowers, therapeutic massage, and natural health. Free parking. Outdoor smoking. $100.

Alaskan Bed and Breakfast

320 East 12th Avenue, 99501
(907) 279-3200

Cottage with both TV and phone; two rooms with TV and phone with shared bath. View of downtown Anchorage. Walking distance to central business district. Visit Portage Glacier, Alyeska Ski Resort. Tour of historic Anchorage. Fishing, wildlife bird sanctuary, Mount McKinley, bicycling, sightseeing, or just relaxing.

Host: Joy Young
Rooms: 3 (SB) $55-65
Continental Breakfast
Credit Cards: A, B, C, D, E, F
Notes: 2, 5, 8, 9, 11, 13, 14

All the Comforts of Home

12531 Turk's Turn Street, 99516-3309
(907) 345-4279; FAX (907) 345-4761

Your arrival receives a warm welcome at this renowned establishment. Retreat just ten minutes beyond urban bustle to a secluded slice of country living. Five wooded acres at 1,100-foot elevation provide magnificent views of greater Anchorage, Mount McKinley, active volcanos, and distant glaciers. Pioneer hostess serves full breakfast in a 14-foot bay window that overlooks it all. The outdoor hot tub is heated year-round, sheltered by towering evergreens.

Host: Sydnee Mae Stiver
Rooms: 3 (1 PB; 2 SB) $85-125
Full Breakfast
Credit Cards: A, B, C, D, E, F
Notes: 2, 5, 7 (outside), 8, 9, 10, 11, 12, 13, 14

All the Comforts of Home

Arctic Loon Bed and Breakfast

P.O. Box 110333, 99511
(907) 345-4935

Elegant accommodations await guests in this exquisite 6,500 square-foot Scandinavian home on the hillside area of South Anchorage. Breathtaking, spectacular views of Mount McKinley and Anchorage Bowl. An eight person Jacuzzi hot tub, sauna, and rosewood grand piano provide relaxation after a full gourmet breakfast. Fully licensed, quiet mountain setting near golf course, zoo, and Chugach State Park hiking trails.

Hosts: Janie and Lee Johnson
Rooms: 3 (1 PB; 2 SB) $75-85
Full Breakfast
Credit Cards: A, B
Notes: 2, 5, 8, 9, 10, 11, 12, 13, 14

6 Pets welcome; 7 Smoking allowed; 8 Children welcome; 9 Social drinking allowed; 10 Tennis available; 11 Swimming available; 12 Golf available; 13 Skiing available; 14 May be booked through travel agents.

Bed and Breakfast by Putman

2903 West 29th, 99517-1702
(907) 248-4255

Comfortable, homey atmosphere. Six minutes from airport. Near bus stop, hiking trails, restaurants, and shopping. Plenty of paved off-street parking. Full breakfast served. Laundry facilities, storage, and freezer space for fish available. No smoking.

Hosts: Mary and Russ Putman
Rooms: 2 (SB) $70
Full Breakfast
Credit Cards: None
Notes: 2, 5, 9, 10, 11, 12, 13, 14

Bed and Breakfast on the Park

602 West 10th Avenue, 99501
(907) 277-0878

Converted log cabin church in downtown Anchorage. Three rooms with private baths. Beautiful setting. Rec room, free local phone service.

Rooms: 3 (PB)
Credit Cards: None
Notes: 5

Cardigan House

Alaska Sourdough Bed and Breakfast Association
889 Cardigan Circle, 99503
(907) 563-6244

Situated in a quiet, wooded residential setting, just five minutes from the International Airport and Lake Hood float plane service. Ten minutes from downtown by auto or bus, and one block from a park with tennis courts and jogging trails. Excellent restaurants and bus service to downtown sightseeing and tour connections are a pleasant three blocks away. Fine traditional furnishings and plush carpeting. Spring pastel color warms a guest room with a private bath. A lovely sitting room with a fireplace, television, and herbal teas is also for guest enjoyment.

Host: Wanell Ekemo
Rooms: 3 (1 PB; 2 SB) $35 winter; $50 summer
Full Breakfast
Credit Cards: A, B, C
Notes: 2, 5, 8, 9, 10, 14

Green Bough Bed and Breakfast

3832 Young Street, 99508
(907) 562-4636

Anchorage's oldest independent bed and breakfast home was opened in 1981. Your hosts have developed the art of complementing spacious, smoke-free lodgings with warm hospitality. Slip into freshly ironed sheets at night and awaken to aromas of coffee and cinnamon. Guests represent the world and most walks of life. Freezer space, storage, public transportation, a convenient location, and on-site laundry.

Hosts: Jerry and Phyllis Jost
Rooms: 3 (SB) $45-60
Continental Breakfast
Credit Cards: None
Notes: 2, 5, 8, 10, 11, 12, 13, 14

Lakeway Villa

6614 Lakeway Drive, 99502
(907) 243-6655

Interim living condo with lake privileges including swimming, fishing, sailing, and ice skating. Fully equipped kitchen and washing facilities, close to airport. Area offers Portage Glacier, Alyeska Ski Resort, tours of historic Anchorage, fishing, wildlife bird sanctuary, Mount McKinley, bicycling, sightseeing, or just relaxing.

Host: Terry Harding
Rooms: 3 (1 PB; 2 SB) $55-80
Breakfast on request
Credit Cards: A, B, C, D, E, F
Notes: 2, 5, 9, 11, 13, 14

McCarthy Wilderness Bed and Breakfast

P.O. Box 111241, 99511
(907) 277-6867

NOTES: Credit cards accepted: A Master Card; B Visa; C American Express; D Discover Card; E Diner's Club; F Other; 2 Personal Checks accepted; 3 Lunch available; 4 Dinner available; 5 Open all year;

Nestled in the mountains of the Wrangell-St. Elias National Park, this bed and breakfast offers rustic accommodations in the Mother Lode Powerhouse, circa 1917. A peaceful retreat without telephones or electricity. Outdoor plumbing. Guided glacier hikes, tours of the copper mining ghost town of Kennicott, and nature walks to the major mountaineering, backpacking, and white- water rafting expeditions.

Host: Babbie Jacobs
Rooms: 5 (SB) $60
Full Breakfast
Credit Cards: None
Notes: 2, 8, 14

View Point Manor

10800 Stroganof, P.O. Box 202482, 99520-2482
(907) 346-2612

High on the south Anchorage hillside with a spectacular view overlooking the city from a 2,000-foot level, this comfortable bed and breakfast is on the border of Chugach State Park. The Park abounds with wildlife (bears, moose, squirrels, and many other animals), and it offers camping, hiking, ski trails, horseback riding, and much more. The location is convenient— only fifteen minutes from restaurants, shopping, theaters, and a zoo.

Hosts: Irene and Jay Jemison
Rooms: 3 (PB) $80-120
Full Breakfast
Credit Cards: A, B, C
Notes: 5, 8, 13, 14

ANCHOR POINT

Accommodations in Alaska OF

The Friendly Lodge Choice
P. O. Box 100624, Anchorage, 99511-0624
(907) 345-4761

This homestay sits on seven wooded acres near the best fishing in the state. Two guest rooms are offered, one with private bath. Each has room for four guests. Christian hostess can provide information about her favorite fishing and beachcombing spots. Wood-burning sauna. Complimentary laundry facilities. Freshly caught crab, scallops, shrimp, halibut, and salmon are for sale. Full breakfast. Resident dog and cat. Free parking. Outdoor smoking. $60-80.

BETHEL

Bentley's Porter House Bed and Breakfast

624 First Avenue, P. O. Box 529, 99559
(907) 543-3552

On the beautiful Kuskokwim River in southwest Alaska, offering comfortable rooms with cable TV. Full, elegant breakfast is served on fine china and includes great sourdough waffles and bread! Special dietary accommodations with advance notice. Reservations advisable; brochure available.

Hosts: Bette Goodwine and Millie Bentley
Rooms: 9 (SB) $90
Full Breakfast
Credit Cards: A, B (for reservations)
Notes: 2, 5, 7, 8, 9

CANTWELL

Adventures Unlimited Lodge

P.O. Box 89, 99729
No telephone

Remotely located in the heart of Alaska's Denali Valley among timbered valleys, rolling tundra, glaciers, and towering snow-capped mountains. The closest neighbor is thirty-five miles away. Trout and grayling fishing is abundant; commonly seen wildlife includes caribou, moose, wolves, foxes, grizzly bears, and varied species of birds.

Hosts: Doug and Michelle Hamrick
Rooms: 5 (2 PB; 3 SB) $50
Full Breakfast
Credit Cards: None
Notes: 2, 3, 4, 5, 7, 8, 11, 13 (XC), 14

6 Pets welcome; 7 Smoking allowed; 8 Children welcome; 9 Social drinking allowed; 10 Tennis available; 11 Swimming available; 12 Golf available; 13 Skiing available; 14 May be booked through travel agents.

DELTA JUNCTION

Accommodations in Alaska TB

The Friendly Lodge Choice
P. O. Box 100624, Anchorage, 99511-0624
(907) 345-4761

This homestay is midway between Tok and Fairbanks. Wildlife abounds in the black spruce, willow, and birch forest surrounding this modern log home. Two guest rooms are offered; one has shared bath, the other private. Your choice of bed sizes. The innkeepers enjoy relaxing around their outdoor fireplace in the evenings. Your hostess cooks "heart healthy" full breakfasts and serves them by the wood stove. Outdoor dogs. Free parking. Outdoor smoking. $75-90.

DENALI NATIONAL PARK

Accommodations Alaska Style Stay with a Friend 90N

3605 Arctic Boulevard #173, Anchorage, 99503
(907) 278-8800; FAX (907) 272-8800

Cozy log cabins situated only eight minutes from entrance of park in prime wildlife habitat viewing area. All cabins are heated, carpeted, furnished with table, chairs, linens. Enjoy two large outdoor redwood hot tubs, a sauna, picnic grills and tables, walking trails. There is a gift shop, gas station with some groceries, and small diner. Some share bath. Overnight tour 95 miles into park to newly constructed cedar log cabins. $110.

Accommodations in Alaska DH

The Friendly Lodge Choice
P. O. Box 100624, Anchorage, 99511-0624
(907) 345-4761

Healy, a community of 500, is situated 12 miles north of Denali Park. This homestay is a unique structure: a four-story geodesic dome on two and one-half wooded acres. This active family of five invites you to enjoy mountain views from livingroom windows. Two guest rooms with queen beds are available, each with a private bath. Indoor sauna. Continental breakfast features tasty homemade cinnamon rolls. Resident dog. Free parking. Outdoor smoking. $60-80.

Kantishna Roadhouse

P. O. Box 130, 99755
(907) 733-2535; (800) 942-7420

Kantishna Roadhouse is a modern full-service lodge with all the amenities you would expect from a first-class wilderness resort. Packages include transportation to and from Kantishna, three home-cooked meals a day, and a wide range of activities.

Host: Roberta L. Wilson
Cabins: 27 (PB)
Full Breakfast, Lunch, and Dinner
Credit Cards: Summer only
Open June 5 - Sept. 10
Notes: 2, 3, 4, 7, 8, 9, 14

McKinley/Denali Cabins and Breakfast

P. O. Box 90-BB, 99755
(907) 683-2258

Private cabins situated one mile north of the park entrance. Free shuttle from train depot, raft trips, and wildlife tours. Restaurant, gift shop, and grocery/produce store on premises. Seasonal service from mid-May to mid-September. A full sourdough breakfast is provided. Call or write for free brochure.

Host: Kevin Helwig
Rooms: 16 (3 PB; 13 SB) $65-110
Full Breakfast
Credit Cards: A, B, C
Notes: 2, 3, 4, 6, 7, 8, 9, 14

NOTES: Credit cards accepted: A Master Card; B Visa; C American Express; D Discover Card; E Diner's Club; F Other; 2 Personal Checks accepted; 3 Lunch available; 4 Dinner available; 5 Open all year;

North Face Lodge

Denali National Park, 99755
(907) 683-2290

Country inn situated in the heart of Denali National Park, with view of Mount McKinley. Vacation price includes: all meals, lodging, round-trip transportation from park entrance (180 miles), hiking, canoeing, fishing, cycling, nature photography, wildlife observation, and evening natural-history programs. Naturalists on staff.

Hosts: Wallace and Jerryne Cole
Doubles: 13 (PB) $250/person; $188/youth
10% discount for 3 or more family members in
    same room
Triples: 1 (PB)
Family Suite: (sleeps 4) (PB)
Full Breakfast
Minimum stay: 2 or 3 nights; fixed arrival and
    departure dates
Credit Cards: None
Closed early Sept.-early June
Notes: 2, 3, 4, 8, 14

EAGLE RIVER

Accommodations Alaska Style Stay with a Friend 50N

3605 Arctic Boulevard #173, Anchorage, 99503
(907) 278-8800; FAX (907) 272-8800

Bed and breakfast home looks ordinary from street but special decor and charm is evident as you step inside. A small museum for your pleasure with a variety of collections. Rooms are attractively furnished and decorated. Private and shared baths. Complete European continental breakfast. Outdoor ducks and geese, indoor cats. $60.

Accommodations in Alaska AW

The Friendly Lodge Choice
P. O. Box 100624, Anchorage, 99511-0624
(907) 345-4761

This lovely log home at 2,000-foot elevation has an impressive view of mountains, valleys, water, islands, and volcanoes. Just 12 miles north of Anchorage, this homestay has two guest rooms with private baths. Free laundry. Limited German spoken. Well-traveled hosts serve continental breakfast. Resident dog and cat. Free parking. Outdoor smoking. $85.

Accommodations in Alaska CC

The Friendly Lodge Choice
P. O. Box 100624, Anchorage, 99511-0624
(907) 345-4761

You'll appreciate a soak in the stainless steel hot tub after a day of business or pleasure. This homestay is in an exclusive neighborhood of custom-built homes. The Christian family of six welcomes children. One room with space for four has a queen-size bed, futon, and private bath. Full breakfast with 65-year-old sourdough starter. Resident dog. Free parking. Outdoor smoking. $85.

Accommodations in Alaska CH

The Friendly Lodge Choice
P. O. Box 100624, Anchorage, 99511-0624
(907) 345-4761

This traditional homestay, just twelve miles north of Anchorage, offers privacy from the host family if you prefer. New in 1992, your accommodations include a private bath with an oversize Jacuzzi, a wood stove, kitchen, living and dining room. The hostess, who is fluent in German, serves a lovely full breakfast. This bed and breakfast can comfortably host a party of six. Resident dog. Free parking. Outdoor smoking. $80-125.

6 Pets welcome; 7 Smoking allowed; 8 Children welcome; 9 Social drinking allowed; 10 Tennis available; 11 Swimming available; 12 Golf available; 13 Skiing available; 14 May be booked through travel agents.

Accommodations in Alaska LH

The Friendly Lodge Choice
P. O. Box 100624, Anchorage, 99511-0624
(907) 345-4761

A cozy log lodge with a view overlooking the surrounding countryside. Custom-built with a spectacular native stone fireplace, this traditional homestay offers a choice of two rooms with private or shared bath and a generous full breakfast. The 1.5 acre yard abounds with blooming flowers, which means moose visit often. You may want to grill your catch of the day on the stone barbeque. Resident dog. Free parking. Outdoor smoking. $85-100.

Homestays at the Homestead

Box 771283, 99577
(907) 272-8644

The Homestead group offers bed and breakfasts in Anchorage, Seward, Homer, Fairbanks, Matanuska Valley, Seldonia, Haines, Juneau, and Sitka. Tours, fishing, transportation, hiking, winter and summer outdoor activities, and other information are all available through the service. Private and shared baths; full and continental breakfast. No smoking. $65-98.

FAIRBANKS

Accommodations Alaska Style Stay with a Friend 60N

3605 Arctic Boulevard #173, Anchorage, 99503
(907) 278-8800; FAX (907) 272-8800

Walk easily to downtown attractions, but the temptation is to linger over full breakfast and visit with this gold mining family of Fairbanks pioneers. Enjoy the lovely flower and vegetable gardens. $55 shared bath; $65 private bath.

Accommodations Alaska Style Stay with a Friend 62N

3605 Arctic Boulevard #173, Anchorage, 99503
(907) 278-8800; FAX (907) 272-8800

Friendly home within walking distance to downtown attractions, close to Chena River. Full breakfast cheerfully cooked when you wish. Private and shared baths. $60-70.

Accommodations Alaska Style Stay with a Friend 63N

3605 Arctic Boulevard #173, Anchorage, 99503
(907) 278-8800; FAX (907) 272-8800

Downtown home with queen bedrooms share a bath. Full breakfast. $65.

Accommodations Alaska Style Stay with a Friend 64N

3605 Arctic Boulevard #173, Anchorage, 99503
(907) 278-8800; FAX (907) 272-8800

Country home with animals has two queen bedrooms and one twin room, shared bath, sitting room, and full breakfast. $65.

Accommodations Alaska Style Stay with a Friend 65N

3605 Arctic Boulevard #173, Anchorage, 99503
(907) 278-8800; FAX (907) 272-8800

Modern home on the Fort Wainwright side of town on Chena River, about two miles from downtown with river view. Vegetable gardens. Full or continental breakfast. No smoking. Private and shared baths. $55-65.

NOTES: Credit cards accepted: A Master Card; B Visa; C American Express; D Discover Card; E Diner's Club; F Other; 2 Personal Checks accepted; 3 Lunch available; 4 Dinner available; 5 Open all year;

Accommodations Alaska Style Stay with a Friend 64N

3605 Arctic Boulevard #173, Anchorage, 99503
(907) 278-8800; FAX (907) 272-8800

Country home with animals has two queen bedrooms and one twin room, shared bath, sitting room, and full breakfast. $65.

Accommodations Alaska Style Stay with a Friend 65N

3605 Arctic Boulevard #173, Anchorage, 99503
(907) 278-8800; FAX (907) 272-8800

Modern home on the Fort Wainwright side of town on Chena River, about two miles from downtown with river view. Vegetable gardens. Full or continental breakfast. No smoking. Private and shared baths. $55-65.

Accommodations Alaska Style Stay with a Friend 67N

3605 Arctic Boulevard #173, Anchorage, 99503
(907) 278-8800; FAX (907) 272-8800

Two miles from downtown on the Chena River. Queen room and twin rooms share a bath. Continental breakfast. $50.

Accommodations in Alaska BV

The Friendly Lodge Choice
P. O. Box 100624, Anchorage, 99511-0624
(907) 345-4761

You'll get plenty of midnight sun on the deck of this spacious home right on the river. Three guest rooms—one with private bath, two share a bath. The friendly hostess of this homestay serves a full breakfast. Resident dog. Free parking. Outdoor smoking. $75-80.

Accommodations in Alaska MD

The Friendly Lodge Choice
P. O. Box 100624, Anchorage, 99511-0624
(907) 345-4761

The first level of this homestay is dedicated to the guest rooms. Three rooms share baths. You'll appreciate the central location, convenient to all downtown attractions, shopping, and restaurants. The 20 hours of summer sunshine help keep the yard filled with blooming flowers. Innkeepers are longtime Alaskans with a desire to assist in making your visit special. Continental breakfast. Free parking. Outdoor smoking. $65-80.

Alaska's 7 Gables Bed and Breakfast

P. O. Box 80488, 99708
(907) 479-0751

Historically, Alaska's 7 Gables was a fraternity house within walking distance to the UAF campus, yet near the river and airport. The spacious 10,000-square-foot, Tudor-style home features a floral solarium, antique stained glass in the foyer with an indoor waterfall, cathedral ceilings, a wedding chapel, wine cellar, and rooms with dormers. A gourmet breakfast is served daily. Other amenities include cable TV and phone in each room, laundry facilities, Jacuzzi, bikes, and canoes.

Hosts: Paul and Leicha Welton
Rooms: 12 (5 PB; 7 SB) $40-110
Full Breakfast
Credit Cards: A, B, D, E
Notes: 2, 5, 8, 9, 13, 14

6 Pets welcome; 7 Smoking allowed; 8 Children welcome; 9 Social drinking allowed; 10 Tennis available; 11 Swimming available; 12 Golf available; 13 Skiing available; 14 May be booked through travel agents.

with your hosts, who have lived several years in the Alaskan bush as well as in Fairbanks. Full sourdough breakfasts feature delicious items such as sourdough pancakes, reindeer sausage, home-ground wheat bread, and lowbush cranberry muffins. Established in 1987.

Hosts: Tim and Debra Vanasse
Rooms: 2 (SB) $45-55
Full Breakfast
Credit Cards: None
Notes: 2, 5, 6, 8, 14

Joan's Bed and Breakfast

5101 Electra, 99709
(907) 479-6918

Comfortable rooms three minutes from the airport, this bed and breakfast is near the riverboat Discovery and the University of Alaska. Free pick-up on advance reservations, and senior citizen discount is offered.

Rooms: 4 (SB) $40-50
Full Breakfast
Credit Cards: A, B, C, D
Notes: 2, 5, 7, 8 (over 8), 9, 14

A Pioneer Bed & Breakfast

1119 2nd Avenue, 99701
(907) 452-4628; (907) 452-5393

Stay in your own restored 1906 log cabin. A complete breakfast is provided, and you cook it at your own convenience in your fully stocked kitchen. There is also a bedroom with a double bed and the livingroom has a queen-size Hide-a-bed, telephone, and TV. Pets allowed upon approval. Located within walking distance to downtown.

Hostess: Nancy Williams
Rooms: 1 (PB) $65
Full Breakfast
Credit Cards: B
Notes: 2, 6 (with prior approval), 7 (limited), 8, 9, 14

GAKONA

Accommodations in Alaska BC

The Friendly Lodge Choice
P.O. Box 100624, Anchorage, 99511-0624
(907) 345-4761

Enjoy a view of the Wrangell Mountains from ten acres of natural wilderness. This traditional homestay is twelve miles from Glenallen, a major crossroad in Alaska's highway system. A full breakfast is served in this two story saltbox by the friendly host who will pester you with his incessant airplane banter. Walking distance to fishing spots and the Alyeska Pipeline. Two rooms share a bath. German spoken. Free parking. Outdoor smoking. Freezer available. $75.

GIRDWOOD

Alyeska View Bed and Breakfast

P.O. Box 234, 99587
(907) 783-2747

Situated 45 minutes south of Anchorage along the magnificent Turnagain Arm of Cook Inlet. En route watch for Beluga whales, Dall sheep, moose, eagles, and other wildlife. At mile 90 on the Seward Highway, turn to Girdwood in the scenic Glacier Valley. Enjoy your stay in our two-story home with Austrian-Alaskan hospitality. Within walking distance of Alyeska Ski Resort and with Portage Glacier and Whittier ferry connection only ten minutes south of Girdwood, this bed and breakfast is sure to make your stay in Alaska memorable.

Hosts: Heinrich and Emmy Gruber
Rooms: 3 (SB) $60-70
Full Breakfast
Credit Cards: A, B
Notes: 2, 5, 6, 8 (over 6), 9, 13

NOTES: Credit cards accepted: A Master Card; B Visa; C American Express; D Discover Card; E Diner's Club; F Other; 2 Personal Checks accepted; 3 Lunch available; 4 Dinner available; 5 Open all year;

GLENNALLEN

Accommodations Alaska Style Stay with a Friend 99N

3605 Arctic Boulevard #173, Anchorage, 99503
(907) 278-8800; FAX (907) 272-8800

Ranch house with casual family atmosphere is home to long-time Alaskans. Full breakfast featuring Alaskan specialties; freezer space for fish. $60; $95 family of three.

Glacier Bay Country Inn

GUSTAVUS

Glacier Bay Country Inn

P. O. Box 5, 99826
(907) 697-2288; FAX (907) 697-2289
Winter: (801) 673-8480; FAX (801) 673-8481

Peaceful storybook accommodations away from the crowds in a wilderness setting. Cozy comforters, warm flannel sheets. Superb dining features local seafood, garden-fresh produce, home-baked breads, spectacular desserts. Enjoy fishing, whale watching, sightseeing, hiking, bird watching, photography. Rates include three meals, airport transfers, and use of bicycles. Glacier Bay boat/plane tours.

Hosts: Al and Annie Unrein
Rooms: 9 (8 PB; 1 SB) $120-198 (American Plan)

Full Breakfast, Lunch, Dinner
Credit Cards: None
Notes: 2, 3, 4, 8, 9, 14

Good Riverbed and Breakfast

Box 37, 99826
(907) 697-2241

Enjoy a warm welcome in this elegant, spacious log home with comfy beds, patchwork quilts, two modern bathrooms (tub and shower), and a rustic yet sophisticated atmosphere. A hearty breakfast includes fresh home-baked breads, wild berry jams, locally smoked salmon, and lots more. This is the perfect Gustavus base to explore Glacier Bay, go fishing or kayaking, or just take one of the bikes provided for your pleasure. Glacier Bay tours arranged.

Host: Sandy Burd
Rooms: 5 (SB) $50-75
Continental Breakfast
Credit Cards: None
Notes: 2, 5, 14

Gustavus Inn

Gustavus Inn

Box 60, 99826
(907) 697-2254

Glacier Bay's historic homestead, newly renovated, full-service inn accommodates 26. Family-style meals, seafood, garden produce, wild edibles. Boat tours of Glacier Bay, charter fishing, and air transportation from Juneau arranged. Bikes and airport transfers included in the daily rates. American Plan only.

Hosts: David and Jo Ann Lesh
Rooms: 12 (7 PB; 5 SB) $120
Full Breakfast
Credit Cards: A, B, C
Closed Sept. 20-May 1
Notes: 2, 3, 4, 7, 8, 9, 14

A Puffin's Bed and Breakfast

1/4 Mile Logging Road, Box 3, 99826
(907) 697-2260

Your own modern cottage on a five-acre, partially wooded homestead carpeted in wildflowers and berries. Full country breakfast served in new picturesque lodge with private meeting room. Covered picnic area with barbeque. Coin-op laundry. Lunch and dinner available within walking distance. Special diets accommodated. Hike beaches or bicycle miles of country roads. See marine life from a charter cruiser or kayak. Courtesy transportation; Glacier Bay tours, travel services available.

Hosts: Chuck and Sandy Schroth
Cottages: 3 (PB) $40-65; children under 12: $8,
    under 2: free; 5 percent senior citizen discount
Full Breakfast
Credit Cards: A, B
Closed Sept. 30-May 1
Notes: 6, 7 (outside), 8, 9 (cabins), 14

HAINES

Accommodations Alaska Style Stay with a Friend 113P

3605 Arctic Boulevard #173, Anchorage, 99503
(907) 278-8800; FAX (907) 272-8800

Historical house near downtown, with nice views of the Lynn Canal. Rooms share baths. Start your day with homemade sourdough pancakes and ham, French toast, or eggs, and lots of good coffee and conversation. The bed and breakfast was built in 1912 by a member of the Soapy Smith Gang, but you should leave town alive. No smoking. $70.

Officer's Inn Bed and Breakfast

P. O. Box 1589, 99827
(907) 766-2000; (800) 542-6363
FAX (907) 766-2445

Former officer's quarters of Fort Seward, the first permanent army post in Alaska. Grand Victorian structure established in 1904. Stately design in Jeffersonian architecture boasting gable slate roofs, ten-foot ceilings, two open verandas, Greek Doric columns. Original period radiators accent each room with individual heating controls. Many rooms are graced with turn-of-the-century Belgian tile fireplaces and classic claw foot bathtubs. Each room offers TV and phone. Walking distance to restaurants, shops, and entertainment. Free parking, courtesy transfers, Avis car rental, and next door to area bus terminal.

Hosts: Joyce and Arne Olsson
Rooms: 14 (12 PB; 2 SB) $50-74
Continental Breakfast
Credit Cards: A, B, C, D, E
Notes: 2, 7, 8, 9, 14

HATCHER PASS

Accommodations in Alaska HP

The Friendly Lodge Choice
P. O. Box 100624, Anchorage, 99511-0624
(907) 345-4761

You may have dreamed of visiting Alaska and staying in your very own log cabin. These little charmers are newly constructed, warm, and cozy. They have individual heat and electricity and are decorated with artifacts reminiscent of yesteryear, right down to the functional water pitchers and basins. Each of the three cabins has indoor chemical toilets. Running water for showers at main home. Outdoor summer hot tub. Full breakfast. Resident dog. Free parking. Outdoor smoking. $55-70.

NOTES: Credit cards accepted: A Master Card; B Visa; C American Express; D Discover Card; E Diner's Club; F Other; 2 Personal Checks accepted; 3 Lunch available; 4 Dinner available; 5 Open all year;

HEALY

Accommodations Alaska Style Stay with a Friend 95N

3605 Arctic Boulevard #173, Anchorage , 99503
(907) 278-8800; FAX (907) 272-8800

Thoreau would love this spot. A 15-minute drive from Denali National Park and situated on a ridge overlooking a valley with the Alaska Range in the background. Peaceful dirt roads to hike or run and sunset view that takes your breath away. Continental breakfast upstairs with hosts. A two-story chalet cabin with full bath, livingroom and kitchen available. Lovely handmade family quilts add to the charm. Next door a smaller cedar cottage has a sleeping loft with private bath, living-room, and kitchen; large deck. Cottages offer self-serve breakfast. Children over 12 welcome. No smoking. $80-100.

Accommodations in Alaska HH

The Friendly Lodge Choice
P. O. Box 100624, Anchorage, 99511-0624
(907) 345-4761

Situated in Healy, a community twelve miles north of Denali's entrance is a unique bed and breakfast offering. You may select a traditional homestay with innkeepers or choose one of their new cabins on a nearby ridge. These units are self-contained with full utilities and kitchens stocked and equipped for you to prepare breakfast at your leisure. Free parking. Outdoor smoking. Fully licensed. $90-180.

HOMER

Accommodations Alaska Style Stay with a Friend 73S

3605 Arctic Boulevard #173, Anchorage, 99503
(907) 278-8800; FAX (907) 272-8800

Sip a cool drink on the deck of this large home while you enjoy a panoramic view of Kachemak Bay, the Spit, and Kenai Mountain. About two miles from town, spacious rooms with private and shared baths. Suite with recreation room with pool table. Full continental breakfast with fruits, juice, cereal, rolls, and beverages. $60-85.

Accommodations in Alaska BR

The Friendly Lodge Choice
P. O. Box 100624, Anchorage, 99511-0624
(907) 345-4761

Year-round travelers have come to rely on this downtown homestay for good value and friendly hospitality. An outdoor hot tub was recently added for the enjoyment of guests. Five guest rooms with a variety of sleeping arrangements share two baths in this log home. A full breakfast is served in the spacious kitchen and may feature fresh seafood. Free parking. Outdoor smoking. $75-85.

Accommodations in Alaska RB

The Friendly Lodge Choice
P. O. Box 100624, Anchorage, 99511-0624
(907) 345-4761

Two acres of tall spruce surround this three-story cedar home, 15 minutes from downtown. Observation windows span 36 feet for Kachemak Bay views. This homestay offers two suites with color TV, phone, and private baths. Ground-floor suite has wood stove and kitchenette. Third-story guest room offers a private balcony and king-size bed. Continental breakfast features homemade breads. Resident dog. Free parking. Outdoor smoking. $75-100.

Magic Canyon Ranch

40015 Waterman Road, 99603
(907) 235-6077

6 Pets welcome; 7 Smoking allowed; 8 Children welcome; 9 Social drinking allowed; 10 Tennis available; 11 Swimming available; 12 Golf available; 13 Skiing available; 14 May be booked through travel agents.

Custom private home sits on 75 acres overlooking Kachemak Bay and glaciered Kenai Mountain. Four rooms furnished in country manor style offer private or shared bath. Full gourmet breakfast features renowned recipes. Sun deck hot tub, hiking, pony rides. Children welcome. Hostess is an ornithologist and museum curator.

Hosts: Davis and Betsy Webb
Rooms: 4 (1 PB; 2 SB) $75-85
Full Breakfast
Credit Cards: None
Notes: 2, 8, 9, 14

Seekins Bed and Breakfast

Box 1264, 99603
(907) 235-8996

Fantastic view of bay, mountains, and glaciers. Enjoy the outside wood-heated sauna, wildflowers, and an occasional moose. Suite has sliding glass doors and private deck overlooking bay and mountains. Guest house, cabin, and apartment have kitchens completely furnished with pots, pans, dishes, appliances, freezer space for halibut and salmon, and barbecue grill. Fishing trips and sightseeing by land, float plane, helicopter, or boat, are arranged.

Hosts: Floyd and Gert Seekins
Rooms: 8 (6 PB; 2 SB) $60-70
Expanded Continental Breakfast
Credit Cards: A, B
Notes: 2, 5, 8, 9, 13, 14

JUNEAU

Bed and Breakfast Inn

1801 Old Glacier Highway., 99801
(907) 463-5855

Enjoy the peace and serenity of our bed and breakfast overlooking the Gastineau Channel at the foot of Mt. Juneau. We offer six rooms with shared baths and one room with a private bath, and guests can choose between double or single beds. A large and comfortable lounge room with a TV is available for guests to enjoy, and laundry facilities are available also. The entire inn

is decorated with pieces done by Alaska's most popular artists, and every piece is for sale, should something catch your eye. Our full breakfast is always a plentiful treat, and downtown shopping and dining are within walking distance.

Host: Ronda Flores
Rooms: 7 (1 PB; 6 SB) $50-65
Full Breakfast
Credit Cards: A, B, C
Notes: 2, 5, 8, 9, 14

The Lost Chord

2200 Fritz Cove Road, 99801
(907) 789-7296

The hosts' music business has expanded to become a homey bed and breakfast on an exquisite private beach. Breakfast is with the proprietors, who have been in Alaska since 1946. Situated in the country 12 miles from Juneau; a car is suggested.

Hosts: Jesse and Ellen Jones
Rooms: 4 (1 PB; 3 SB) $35-65
Full Breakfast
Credit Cards: None
Notes: 2, 5, 6 (by arrangement), 7 (on deck), 8, 9, 10, 11, 12, 13, 14

Pearson's Pond Luxury Bed and Breakfast

4541 Sawa Circle, 99801
(907) 789-3772

Alaskan luxury invites you to watch wild mallards landing on a glacial pond as you relax in a steaming spa tucked in a forest just steps from your deck. Deluxe suites with all amenities, including private entries, phones, VCR, stereo, and extra space, beckon you to enjoy a long, leisurely stay. Barbeque, rowboat, bikes, freezer, wildlife, and majestic views of Mendenhall Glacier, and close to airport, ferry, shopping, and trails. Self-serve breakfast provided in adjoining kitchenette. Free travel/tour arrangements.

Hosts: Steve and Diane Pearson
Rooms: 3 (1 suite PB; 2 SB) $79-149

NOTES: Credit cards accepted: A Master Card; B Visa; C American Express; D Discover Card; E Diner's Club; F Other; 2 Personal Checks accepted; 3 Lunch available; 4 Dinner available; 5 Open all year;

Full/Self-serve Breakfast
Credit Cards: A, B, E, F
Notes: 2, 5, 8 (over 3), 9, 13, 14

Pot Belly Bed and Breakfast

5115 North Douglas Street, 99801
(907) 586-279

The stove is an original made to be used for a mail box. Inside homemade furniture, moose horn chair, burrough tables, wagon wheel table. Bowls and planters out of burrough—all Alaskan made. Homey atmosphere. Sit, have coffee, watch the eagles, enjoy yourself. Come see.

Host: Elaine Powell
Rooms: 2 (PB) $60
Full Breakfast
Closed Sept. 30-May 30
Credit Cards: None
Notes: 2, 4

KENAI

Accommodations Alaska Style Stay with a Friend 72S

3605 Arctic Boulevard #173, Anchorage, 99503
(907) 278-8800; FAX (907) 272-8800

Chalet home with queen beds and private bath, full breakfast, $75; two bedroom cabin, fully equipped, $125, for four.

Daniel's Lake Lodge

P.O. Box 1444-AD, 99611
(907) 776-5578

Christian establishment with a fantastic lake view in a private, serene, smoke-free environment. Abundant wildlife in the area including moose, eagles, loons, beaver, and spawning salmon. Fish for the native Rainbow trout, hike, and pet the ducks. Private entrance into the living and dining rooms. Fully equipped kitchen and laundry for guests. Alaska reindeer sausage and fresh duck eggs for self-serve breakfast. Boat and canoe rentals. Twenty-one miles

north of Kenai in a secluded cove on the edge of sparsely populated Daniel's Lake.

Host: Karen Walters
Rooms: 4 (1 PB; 3 SB) $45-75
Full Self-serve Breakfast
Credit Cards: None
Notes: 5, 8, 9, 11, 13, 14

KODIAK

Kodiak Bed and Breakfast

308 Cope Street, 99616
(907) 486-5367

Visitors enjoy a spectacular view of Kodiak's busy fishing fleet in a location just above the boat harbor. Mary's home is easy walking distance from a historic Russian church, art galleries, Baronof Museum, and downtown restaurants. Enjoy this fishing city with its Russian heritage, stunning beaches and cliffs, and abundant fish and bird life. Fresh local fish is often a breakfast option.

Host: Mary A. Monroe
Rooms: 16 (13 PB; 3 SB) $78
Full Breakfast
Credit Cards: A, B
Notes: 2, 5, 6, 8, 9, 12, 13, 14

Northland Ranch Resort

P. O. Box 2376, 99615
(907) 486-5578

Northland Ranch Resort is a cozy little lodge on a very large cattle, horse, and bison ranch. Set amidst beaches, mountains, and salmon streams, Northland Ranch offers hiking and horseback riding opportunities along with beach combing, fishing, and seasonal hunting. Informal, comfortable, and friendly.

Hosts: Omar and Meldonna Stratman
Rooms: 11 (4 PB; 7 SB) $150-290
all meals included
Full Breakfast, Lunch, and Dinner
Credit Cards: A, B, C
Notes: 2, 3, 4, 5, 7, 8, 9, 14

6 Pets welcome; 7 Smoking allowed; 8 Children welcome; 9 Social drinking allowed; 10 Tennis available; 11 Swimming available; 12 Golf available; 13 Skiing available; 14 May be booked through travel agents.

MCGRATH

Accommodations in Alaska FO

The Friendly Lodge Choice
P. O. Box 100624, Anchorage, 99511-0624
(907) 345-4761

Depending on the season, your complimentary pickup at the airstrip may be by truck, 3- or 4-wheeler, or dog sled! Situated on the Iditarod Trail, this unique lodging experience is a small cabin right on the Kuskokwim River. The innkeepers live next door. Double bed, propane stove. Running water for laundry, showers across the street. Full breakfast. Outdoor dogs. Outdoor smoking. $75.

NINILCHIK

Accommodations Alaska Style Stay with a Friend

3605 Arctic Boulevard #173, Anchorage, 99503
(907) 278-8800; FAX (907) 272-8800

Log home near Deep Creek. Small goats and kids in the large yard. Flowers, trees, and peaceful walks. Cat in home. Queen bed with private bath, $75.

NOME

Ocean View Manor

490 Iron Street, Box 65, 99762
(907) 443-2133

Spacious home with large private room with private bath, TV and phone, plus two bedrooms with shared bath. Spectacular view of Bering Sea and surrounding mountains. Two blocks to central business district and restaurants, but only ten miles to pristine wilderness. Activities include gold panning, fishing, sightseeing, tours of historic homes, bird watching, wildlife reservation, canoeing, hiking, relaxing. Call or write for price information.

Host: Joy Young
Rooms: 3 (1 PB; 2 SB)
Continental Breakfast
Credit Cards: A, B, C, D, E, F
Notes: 2, 5, 8, 9, 10, 11, 12, 13, 14

PALMER

Accommodations Alaska Style Stay with a Friend 93N

3605 Arctic Boulevard #173, Anchorage, 99503
(907) 278-8800; FAX (907) 272-8800

Beautifully decorated traditional European country home tucked in a quiet pine forest, with friendly llamas to gaze on from your guest room windows. Flowers and quiet paths are also inviting. Shared bath. Jacuzzi tub available. Full continental breakfast. German spoken, Dutch understood. Visit Tannenhof and walk the llamas; then read by a cozy fire in the great room. A short drive to the Musk Ox farm. Llama pack trips and day hikes can be arranged. No smoking. $75.

Hatcher Pass Bed and Breakfast

H.C.-01, Box 6797-D, 99645
(907) 745-4210

You may have dreamed of visiting Alaska and staying in your very own log cabin. These cozy charmers offer the best of Alaskan living. They have heat and electricity and are decorated with artifacts reminiscent of yesteryear, right down to the functional water pitchers and basins. Each cabin has indoor chemical toilets. Showers are at the main house, as well as breakfast. We look forward to visiting with you over breakfast. Open year round. One hour north of Anchorage.

Host: Roxanne Anderson
Rooms: 3 cabins; $55
Full Breakfast
Credit Cards: A, B, E
Notes: 2, 5,7, 8, 9, 14

PELICAN

Lisianski Inlet Lodge Bed and Breakfast

Box 776, 99832
(907) 735-2266

Wilderness, waterfront log cabin homestead; access by boat or plane only. Alpine hiking, both saltwater and freshwater sport fishing. Fishing/touring charters arranged. Trips to Glacier Bay and Chichagof-Yakobic Wilderness. Beach cabin for five; accommodations for eight in log homestead. Menu specialties are salmon, halibut, crab, and berry pies. Housekeeping accommodations in the cabin.

Host: Gail Corbin
Rooms: 5 (2 SB) $65-95
Full Breakfast
Credit Cards: None
Notes: 2, 3, 4, 5, 8, 9, 14

SELDOVIA

Annie McKenzie's Boardwalk Bed and Breakfast

P. O. Box 72, 99663
(907) 234-7816

Lovely waterfront lodge in small fishing town. Wilderness and fishing just five minutes out your door. Plush, clean, quiet. Private baths. Faces Seldovia Harbor for lovely view. Rustic decks for lounging. Hostess provides bicycles and berry buckets.

Host: Annie McKenzie
Rooms: 13 (PB) $106-120
Continental Breakfast
Credit Cards: None
Notes: 2, 5, 7, 8, 9, 14

SEWARD

Accommodations Alaska Style Stay with a Friend 71S

3605 Arctic Boulevard #173, Anchorage, 99503
(907) 278-8800; FAX (907) 272-8800

Bungalow conveniently situated within walking distance of harbor has ground-level room with bay window, TV, private shower. Breakfast includes juice, muffins, French toast, eggs, coffee and tea served by hosts. Bed and breakfast not available most weekend nights. Children over 12 welcome. No smoking. $65.

Swiss Chalet Bed and Breakfast

P. O. Box 1734, 99664
(907) 224-3939

Pioneer Alaskans offer gracious hospitality in a nonsmoking environment catering to adults only. Shared or private baths. Situated a block off the Seward Highway, it is near the road to Seward's spectacular Exit Glacier and a short ride to the small boat harbor in magnificent Resurrection Bay where tours and charters originate.

Hosts: Stan and Charlotte Freeman-Jones
Rooms: 4 (2 PB; 2 SB) $50-65
Full Breakfast
Credit Cards: None
Notes: 2, 9, 14

The White House Bed and Breakfast

P. O. Box 1157, 99664
(907) 224-3614

Nestled in a mountain panorama. The home's intrigue is country charm—quilts and hand-crafts abound. Breakfast is self-serve buffet in guest kitchen. Cable TV in guest common area. Attractions close by: Resurrection Bay/Kenai Fjords National Park, historical Iditarod Trail (cross-country skiing or dog mushing), Exit Glacier.

6 Pets welcome; 7 Smoking allowed; 8 Children welcome; 9 Social drinking allowed; 10 Tennis available; 11 Swimming available; 12 Golf available; 13 Skiing available; 14 May be booked through travel agents.

Hosts: Tom and Annette Reese
Rooms: 5 (3 PB; 2 SB) $45.90-76.50.
Continental Breakfast
Credit Cards: A, B
Notes: 2, 5, 8, 13 (XC), 14

SITKA

Accommodations Alaska Style Stay with a Friend 111P

3605 Arctic Boulevard #173, Anchorage, 99503
(907) 278-8800; FAX (907) 272-8800

Elegant home on the hillside on Cascade Creek overlooking Sitka Sound, Mount Edgecumbe, with Pacific Ocean sunset views, within walking distance to downtown. Rooms are tastefully furnished with antiques and reproductions. Continental breakfast. No smoking. $55-75.

Bed Inn 518

518 Monastery, 99835
(907) 747-3305

Spacious, comfortable, friendly, and affordable. Conveniently situated within walking distance of shopping, restaurants, museums, and an abundance of interesting sites of Alaskan, Russian, and local history. Hiking trails. Nestled in the foothills of the Sitka Mountains. You'll enjoy the spectacular view of Alaska's natural beauty, from breathtaking mountains to soaring eagles.

Hosts: Margaret and Fred Hope
Rooms: 2 (1 PB; 1 SB) $43 plus
Continental Breakfast
Credit Cards: None
Notes: 2, 5, 7, 8, 9, 10, 11, 14

SOLDOTNA

Accommodations Alaska Style Stay with a Friend 75S

3605 Arctic Boulevard #173, Anchorage, 99503
(907) 278-8800; FAX (907) 272-8800

Large log house on the edge of a small lake which has loons that return to nest each summer. Friendly hospitality and big breakfasts here—not a lot of privacy as the fisher folk rise early in the morning. Variety of bed sizes and rooms share bath. Lunches can be ordered for fishing, hiking trips. New cabin with private bath available. $45-75.

Accommodations in Alaska LV

The Friendly Lodge Choice
P. O. Box 100624, 99511-0624
(907) 345-4761

This spacious log home is on a lake near the heart of the Kenai Peninsula. The full breakfast includes homemade cinnamon buns, and upon request your breakfast may include wild game. This traditional homestay is furnished with many trophies won by the host. Sauna and freezer space for registered guests. Three rooms. The dormitory is popular with local fisherman. Indoor cats and dogs. Free parking. Outdoor smoking. $75-100.

Eagle's Nest Bed and Breakfast

Box 23, 386 Monte Drive, 99669
(907) 262-5396

An original homestead house, quiet, secluded, and only a five-minute drive from the Kenai River with some of the world's best salmon fishing. Charters arranged for offshore fishing in Kachemak Bay or Cook Inlet, renowned for their giant halibut, crab, shrimp, clams, and salmon. "Arrive as a guest and leave as a friend."

Hosts: Pat and David Fay
Rooms: 4 (SB) $70
Continental Breakfast
Credit Cards: None
Notes: 2, 5, 7, 8, 9, 11, 12, 14

NOTES: Credit cards accepted: A Master Card; B Visa; C American Express; D Discover Card; E Diner's Club; F Other; 2 Personal Checks accepted; 3 Lunch available; 4 Dinner available; 5 Open all year;

Posey's Kenai River Hideaway B & B Lodge

Posey's Kenai River Hideaway Bed and Breakfast Lodge

P. O. Box 4094-ABB, 99669
(907) 262-7430; FAX (907) 262-7430

Situated on the bank of the Kenai River with its world-record king salmon. Good, wholesome breakfast served before you go fishing. Will arrange your guided salmon or halibut charter, also fly-out fishing or sightseeing trips. After catching your fish, relax on the sun deck built out over the river and swap fish stories. Will freeze and pack your fish for your return trip home.

Hosts: Ray and June Posey
Rooms: 10 (3 PB; 7 SB) $110-130
Full Breakfast
Credit Cards: A, B
Notes: 2, 3, 4, 5, 7, 9, 12, 13, 14

STERLING

Accommodations in Alaska SR

The Friendly Lodge Choice
P. O. Box 100624, Anchorage, 99511-0624
(907) 345-4761

A real Alaskan log home close to the Kenai National Wildlife Refuge and popular Kenai River. On 15 acres with a nice view of the Chugach Mountains, this homestay offers five guest rooms with twins or dou-

bles, and shared baths. One room has a king-size bed with a private bath. There is a place to clean your catch and freeze a few. Full breakfast is served. No alcohol. Free parking. Outdoor smoking. $65-80.

TALKEETNA

Accommodations in Alaska BA

The Friendly Lodge Choice
P. O. Box 100624, Anchorage, 99511-0624
(907) 345-4761

Three miles from beautiful downtown Talkeetna is this brand new log home with stone fireplace. A breathtaking view of Mount McKinley, which is just a few minutes away. This homestay offers three guest rooms on the upper level with rustic open log-beam ceilings throughout. Two shared baths. Innkeepers are eager to share the beauty of Alaska with you. Continental breakfast. Free parking. Outdoor smoking. $75.

Alaska Log Cabin Bed and Breakfast

P. O. Box 19, 99676
(907) 733-2668

Lodging and cooking facilities in a charming, custom-crafted log cabin located on a quiet, wooded acre just two blocks from the Talkeetna River. A leisurely 1/4-mile walk along the river brings you to the old historic town site. Easy access to the shops, restaurants, museums, park, riverboat services, Alaska Railroad, and post office. Sorry, no indoor plumbing. Showers available in town. Cabin can sleep six.

Host: Susie Tallman
Cabin: 1 (PB—outhouse) $45
Continental Breakfast
Credit Cards: None
Notes: 2, 5, 6, 7, 8, 9, 13, 14

6 Pets welcome; 7 Smoking allowed; 8 Children welcome; 9 Social drinking allowed; 10 Tennis available; 11 Swimming available; 12 Golf available; 13 Skiing available; 14 May be booked through travel agents.

TOK

Accommodations in Alaska
ST

The Friendly Lodge Choice
P. O. Box 100624, Anchorage, 99511-0624
(907) 345-4761

Rough edges on this rustic setting fool travelers. Log buildings are surrounded by barrels and buckets of colorful blooming plants. A full bath is shared by two guest rooms with queen- and king-size beds. The guest cabin is a non-threatening "wilderness experience." Breakfasts are home-cooked and delicious. The innkeeper of this unique homestay also boards horses. Resident dog. Free parking. Outdoor smoking. $55-85.

The Stage Stop

P. O. Box 69, 99780
(907) 883-5338

For horses and people. This charming log home offers a private cabin and two large rooms with king and queen beds. Full country breakfast. New log barn and corrals for horses. New room with private bath. Quiet location just off Tok Cutoff Highway.

Host: Mary Dale Underwood
Rooms: 3 (1 PB; 2 SB) $45-75
Full Breakfast
Credit Cards: None
Notes: 2, 5, 6, 8, 9, 14

VALDEZ

Accommodations in Alaska
BZ

The Friendly Lodge Choice
P. O. Box 100624, Anchorage, 99511-0624
(907) 345-4761

One of the best breakfasts in town is elegantly served at this homestay near downtown and the ferry terminal. You're sure to appreciate the hosts' attention to your needs and the memorable meals they serve. Three rooms with shared baths. Near indoor pool, tennis, hiking, and shopping. Resident dog. Free parking. Outdoor smoking. $75-95.

Alaskan Flower Forget-Me-Not Bed and Breakfast

P. O. Box 1153, 99686
(907) 835-2717

Prince William Sound hospitality at its best. You will enjoy your visit as you relax in one of the luxurious guest rooms. Enjoy the complimentary informal breakfast from 6:30-9:00 AM. Walk to nearby cruise ships, the ferry, and downtown area.

Host: Betty Schackne
Rooms: 4 (1 PB; 3 SB) $60-75
Continental Breakfast
Credit Cards: None
Notes: 2, 5, 9, 11, 13, 14

Christian Bed & Breakfast

P.O. Box 1629, 99686
(907) 835-2609

This bed and breakfast offers four non-smoking rooms with king-size beds and private baths. Located within walking distance of shops, tourist information and movie theaters. Alyeska Pipeline Terminal, Columbia Glacier, Keystone Canyon (river rafting), Mineral Creek Canyon (hiking and biking), berry picking, and fishing spots are also nearby. Courtesy pickup from airport and state ferry with arrangements. Reservation deposit required.

Host: Darryll and Judith Sumner
Rooms: 4 (PB) $65
Continental Breakfast
Credit Cards: None
Notes: 2, 5, 8, 13

Johnson House
Bed and Breakfast

P. O. Box 364, 99686
(907) 835-5289

NOTES: Credit cards accepted: A Master Card; B Visa; C American Express; D Discover Card; E Diner's Club; F Other; 2 Personal Checks accepted; 3 Lunch available; 4 Dinner available; 5 Open all year;

Four rooms share three baths. Cable TV in rooms; sauna; large-screen TV. Tennis, indoor swimming pool nearby. Free airport and ferry transfers.

Host: Brian K. Johnson
Rooms: 5 (PB) $55-75
Continental Breakfast
Credit Cards: None
Notes: 2, 5, 8, 9, 10, 14

WARD COVE

North Tongass Bed and Breakfast

P.O. Box 879, 99928
(907) 247-0879

Friendly Alaskan hospitality, just minutes from Ketchikan. Near fine restaurants, grocery stores, and boat harbors. Lovely beach home with private guest quarters, entry, deck, and sitting room. Also includes kitchenette, barbecue, and freezers for your catch of the day.

Host: Lynn and Judy Freels
Rooms: 10 (SB) $50-70
Continental Breakfast
Credit Cards: None
Notes: 2, 5, 8, 9, 11, 14

WASILLA

Accommodations Alaska Style Stay with a Friend 97N

3605 Arctic Boulevard #173, Anchorage, 99503
(907) 278-8800; FAX (907) 272-8800

A 100-cow barn converted to a beautiful guest house. Wonderful rooms finished as individual log cabins, each with a special theme, share two full baths in common hall. Continental breakfast is served in the Alaska room. The barn offers a 270-degree view. Your host will organize hunting, fishing parties; arrange weddings and meetings. No smoking. $60-70.

Accommodations in Alaska CL

The Friendly Lodge Choice
P. O. Box 100624, Anchorage, 99511-0624
(907) 345-4761

This active family includes your host, combination bread baker/chief pilot at this home-stay and sightseeing operation. Floatplanes are docked at the front door on a quiet canal of Lake Wasilla. Two guest rooms share a bath. Two acres provide many bird watching opportunities. This just may be the "Alaskan Experience" you are seeking. Full breakfast includes freshly baked bread. Resident dogs and cats. Free parking. Outdoor smoking. $65.

Yukon Don's

HC 31 5086, 99654
(907) 376-7472

Yukon Don's is an extraordinary bed and breakfast inn. Each room is decorated in a specific Alaskan theme (Iditarod, fishing, hunting, Klondike, etc.). The 900 square foot Alaska room is the guest lounge, furnished with an Alaskan collection, pool table, darts, Alaska video library, and more. The 270-degree view of the Chugach and Talkeetna mountains is unequaled.

Hosts: Art and Diane Mongeau
Rooms: 5 (1 PB; 4 SB) $63-84
Continental Breakfast
Credit Cards: None
Notes: 2, 5, 7 (on deck), 8, 9, 11, 12, 13, 14

WILLOW

Accommodations Alaska Style Stay with a Friend 94N

3605 Arctic Boulevard #173, Anchorage, 99503
(907) 278-8800; FAX (907) 272-8800

Cabins can sleep up to six or eight, and some have modern conveniences; others

6 Pets welcome; 7 Smoking allowed; 8 Children welcome; 9 Social drinking allowed; 10 Tennis available; 11 Swimming available; 12 Golf available; 13 Skiing available; 14 May be booked through travel agents.

use a central wash and flushhouse. Great fishing, hiking, berry picking, and friendly hostesses serve continental breakfast in the adjoining small lodge. Ski, skate, or canoe, depending on the season. Near small lake with view of Mount McKinley. Cabins are immaculate, charming, warm and cozy near small lake. Central bath $45; cabin with private bath $75; three-bedroom house $125.

Accommodations in Alaska WC

The Friendly Lodge Choice
P. O. Box 100624, Anchorage, 99511-0624
(907) 345-4761

Your accommodations are on 90 acres surrounding a portion of Willow Creek. The original homestay has been in the family for three generations. Comfortable homes of varying architecture and size have been constructed in this peaceful wilderness. Prepare breakfast at your leisure from the stocked and furnished kitchens. You might catch your trout or grayling dinner right in your own front yard. Free parking for all size vehicles. Smoking permitted. $100-150.

Arizona

AJO

Bed and Breakfast Scottsdale and the West 104

P. O. Box 3999, Prescott, 86302-3999
(602) 776-1102

Enjoy this 1925 mining corporation executive home near Organ Pipe Cactus National Monument, just 50 minutes from Mexico. Three guest rooms with private baths. Full breakfast. No smoking. $59-69.

APACHE JUNCTION

Mi Casa Su Casa #306

P. O. Box 950, Tempe, 85280-0950
(602) 990-0682; (800) 456-0682

Situated on the Western face of the Superstition Mountains, this 10-acre ranch blends the seclusion of a desert mountain retreat with a variety of recreational activities. The guest cottage units are on the second story of a building built in 1991. One room has a view of the mountains, queen-size bed, queen Hide-a-bed, microwave, and small coffee service. The other room has a view of the city, queen bed, two twin beds, private bath, and redwood deck. Seven-person spa and campfire area available. $71; both units available for $125.

BISBEE

Mi Casa Su Casa #2552

P. O. Box 950, Tempe, 85280-0950
(602) 990-0682; (800) 456-0682

Newly renovated home built around the turn of the century and situated in the Warren area of town. Step back in time as you enjoy the art collection and antiques. Two guest rooms share a bath. A family room with TV, VCR, and many books, and a sun room decorated in antique wicker and green plants are available for entertainment and reading. Breakfast might include eggs Benedict, berry muffins, or Belgian waffles, and is served in the dining room, sun room, or on the patio. $50-$65, plus tax.

Park Place Bed and Breakfast

Old Pueblo Homestays
P. O. Box 13603, Tucson, 85732
(800) 333-9RSO

No visit to Arizona is complete without seeing the historical old mining town of Bisbee some 25 miles from Tombstone. Cool in the summer and far enough south to have mild winters. Park Place is a 1920-vintage, well-cared for, two-story Mediterranean-style home with spacious bedrooms, balconies, terraces, library, and sun room. Two guest rooms have queen beds and adjoining baths. Two other bedrooms share hall bathroom. Minimum stay is two nights. $50-70.

School House Inn

818 Tombstone Canyon, P. O. Box 32, 85603
(800) 537-4333

NOTES: Credit cards accepted: A Master Card; B Visa; C American Express; D Discover Card; E Diner's Club; F Other; 2 Personal Checks accepted; 3 Lunch available; 4 Dinner available; 5 Open all year; 6 Pets welcome; 7 Smoking allowed; 8 Children welcome; 9 Social drinking allowed; 10 Tennis available; 11 Swimming available; 12 Golf available; 13 Skiing available; 14 May be booked through travel agents.

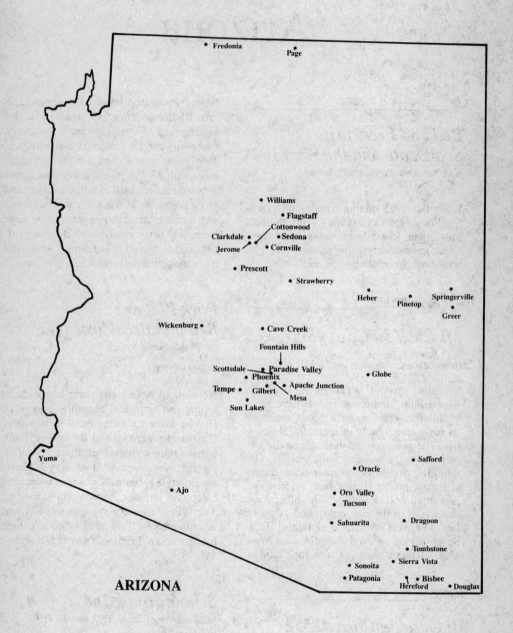

ARIZONA

An old schoolhouse built in 1918 and converted into lovely large rooms and suites with twelve-foot ceilings and private baths. Situated high up Tombstone Canyon, the 5,400 foot elevation provides spectacular scenery, clean air, and a relaxing retreat. A full breakfast is served on the shaded patio or in a spacious family room. The inn is close to mine tours, art galleries, antique shops, hiking, bird watching, and much more.

Hosts: Marc and Shirl Negus
Rooms: 9 (PB) $40-60
Full Breakfast
Credit Cards: A, B , C
Notes: 2, 5, 8

CAVE CREEK

Bed and Breakfast Scottsdale and the West 072

Box 3999, Prescott, 86302-3999
(602) 776-1102

Stay on ten acres of lush desert with cactus and trees, and hike to old Indian sites. This bed and breakfast has a queen bed and private bath. Continental breakfast is served; no smoking. Minimum stay is two nights. $50.

Mi Casa Su Casa #286

P. O. Box 950, Tempe, 85280-0950
(602) 990-0682; (800) 456-0682

Rustic Frank Lloyd Wright home is a five-acre, working ranch in a picturesque setting of saguaro cactus, Continental Mountain, Skull Mesa, and Elephant Butte. Large suite with connecting full bath, queen bed, one double bed, one twin bed. Rustic apartment with private entrance, bath, kitchenette, and two double beds also available. Near local sites. Pool available. Cook-outs, barbecues, and hay rides available by appointment. Continental breakfast weekdays; full breakfast on weekends. $40-$70.

CLARKDALE

Mi Casa Su Casa #145

P. O. Box 950, Tempe, 85280-0950
(602) 990-0682; (800) 456-0682

This secluded country ranch house with separate guest house is a short walk to the nearby Verde River, and is situated near Tuzigoot Indian ruin site, Ft. Verde, Sedona, and Jerome. One guest room has a queen bed and shares a bath with another guest room with one twin bed. The cottage has air conditioning, queen bed, private shower. Hot tub available. Full breakfast. No smoking. $35-55.

CORNVILLE

Pumpkinshell Ranch Bed and Breakfast

HC 66, Box 2100, 86325
(602) 634-4797

New solar home in secluded country setting. Two large bedrooms, one with twin beds, one with a queen-size brass bed. Each has a private bath. Modern, elegant decor. Decks overlooking a twelve-foot waterfall in backyard. Large library; generous gourmet breakfasts with homemade muffins and jams.

Hosts: Kay and Terry Johnson
Rooms: 2 (PB) $65-70
Full Breakfast
Credit Cards: A, B
Notes: 2, 5, 7 (outside), 8, 9

COTTONWOOD

Mi Casa Su Casa #284

P. O. Box 950, Tempe, 85280-0950
(602) 990-0682; (800) 456-0682

This small country estate is nestled beside the Verde River. Master bedroom has a queen bed, private bath, and air conditioning. Easily accessible for wheel-chaired guests. Three hours to the Grand Canyon, two hours from Phoenix, and a short drive to the small planes airport. Full breakfast served in the Garden Room, which overlooks a well-manicured lawn and flower beds. $55.

DOUGLAS

Mi Casa Su Casa #1628

P. O. Box 950, Tempe, 85280-0950
(602) 990-0682; (800) 456-0682

This ranch is on the northeastern slope of the Chiricahua Mountains near many historical sites, museums, and Old Mexico. Daily trail rides are available for 4-20 people, and the ranch can supply pack animals for heavy packs. One- or two-room bunk houses have baths; an apartment includes a kitchenette and private patio. Camper and trailer hook-ups nearby. Three meals daily included in the price. Swimming pool and three-acre catfish pond on premises. Rates include room/meals/horse. $85-160.

DRAGOON

Mi Casa Su Casa #307

P. O. Box 950, Tempe, 85280-0950
(602) 990-0682; (800) 456-0682

Situated between the Texas Canyon and the Dragoon Mountains, the main house is a rammed-earth, passive solar structure. Two bedrooms share a bath; one has a queen bed, and the other has two twin beds. A full breakfast is served each morning in the dining room next to twelve-foot windows overlooking the mountains. Private sun deck, gas grill, and spa available. $45-55 plus tax.

FLAGSTAFF

Arizona Mountain Inn

685 Lake Mary Road, 86001
(602) 774-8959

The Old English Tudor-style inn and cottages are situated about three miles from Flagstaff. There are 13 wooded acres surrounded by national forest. The rooms are decorated in antiques, crystal, and lace in a beautiful mix of European charm and classic southwestern elegance.

Hosts: The Wanek family
Rooms: 5 (1 PB; 4 SB) $50-100
Full Breakfast
Credit Cards: A, B, D
Notes: 2, 5, 9, 13

Bed and Breakfast Scottsdale and the West 107

Box 3999, Prescott, 86302-3999
(602) 776-1102

Situated in quiet neighborhood backing onto the forest. Accommodations include bedroom, family room, kitchenette, and private bath. Continental breakfast is served, and spa is available. $75.

Bed and Breakfast Scottsdale and the West 113

Box 3999, Prescott, 86302-3999
(602) 776-1102

Three private cottages, each with two bedrooms, kitchen, bath, living room. wood burning stove, washer/dryer, cable TV, and bicycles. Continental breakfast is provided. No smoking. $80; $100 for three or more.

Dierker House

423 West Cherry Street, 86001
(602) 774-3249

NOTES: Credit cards accepted: A Master Card; B Visa; C American Express; D Discover Card; E Diner's Club; F Other; 2 Personal Checks accepted; 3 Lunch available; 4 Dinner available; 5 Open all year;

Charming old house with spacious antique-filled rooms, private entrance, sitting room, and guest kitchen. An excellent breakfast is served at 8:00 A.M. in the downstairs dining room; continental breakfast for late risers.

Host: Dorothea Dierker
Rooms: 3 (SB) $40
Full Breakfast
Credit Cards: None
Notes: 2, 5, 9, 10, 11, 12, 14

Mi Casa Su Casa #100

P. O. Box 950, Tempe, 85280-0950
(602) 990-0682; (800) 456-0682

Very nice split-level house built in 1967 in a pretty residential neighborhood. The guest rooms are on the first level, and both rooms have king-size beds. A full-size bath is across the hall, and on the same floor is a recreation room with TV, VCR, books, refrigerator, coffeemaker, fireplace, and double sofa bed. Only one party accepted at a time. $45-60.

Mi Casa Su Casa #247

P. O. Box 950, Tempe, 85280-0950
(602) 990-0682; (800) 456-0682

Contemporary, trilevel home situated in the forest has multiple spacious decks and extra large rooms with tongue-in-groove wood ceilings. The house is decorated with Grand Canyon and Navajo art. The guest area on the first level has a private entrance, king-size bed, double-size futon, small flip chair, playpen, and a large bedroom/sitting area with a private hall bath. Family room with a wet bar, microwave, small refrigerator, TV, VCR, private telephone, and a wood-burning stove. $55-65.

Mi Casa Su Casa #257

P. O. Box 950, Tempe, 85280-0950
(602) 990-0682; (800) 456-0682

Apartment attached to a house makes very private accommodation arrangement with a dining area with wet bar, refrigerator, TV, and wood-burning stove. Roll-away bed available. Small kitchen area stocked with juice, fresh fruit, muffins, coffee cake, yeast rolls, cold cereal, milk, and coffee. Minimum stay is two nights. $85.

Mi Casa Su Casa #259

P. O. Box 950, Tempe, 85280-0950
(602) 990-0682; (800) 456-0682

Restored home built circa 1917 with wrap-around porch contains five guest rooms. Two rooms share one bath, and most rooms have queen-size beds. One room contains a king-size bed and a private bath. A full breakfast is served each morning, and tea is served in the late afternoon. A phone and TV are available on the first floor. Bicycles and VCR are also available. $60-75.

Mi Casa Su Casa #339

P. O. Box 950,Tempe, 85280-0950
(602) 990-0682; (800) 456-0682

This two-story modern-style home has country decor and is on a quiet residential cul-de-sac two miles from the Butler Avenue exit on I-40. Two guest rooms, each with a queen-size bed, share a hall bath. Guests are welcome to use the TV in the common room, and complimentary refreshments are served. Full breakfast. Children over six. No smoking. $65.

FOUNTAIN HILLS

Bed and Breakfast Scottsdale and the West 070

Box 3999, Prescott, 86302-3999
(602) 776-1102

Enjoy this luxurious 6,500-square-foot Spanish contemporary home with lush tropical courtyard, gazebo, and 40-foot pool. Three magnificent levels and a tennis court. Full breakfast; private bath. Fireplace. $110.

Mi Casa Su Casa #318

P. O. Box 950, Tempe, 85280-0950
(602) 990-0682; (800) 456-0682

A lovely territorial duplex situated in a residential area. One guest room has a queen bed, TV, connecting private bath with double sink and sit-down shower. A full gourmet breakfast features homemade baked breads, muffins, and sticky buns. Near The World's Tallest Fountain and Mayo Clinic. Fountain Hills was incorporated and carved out of the desert in the early 1970s. $30-50.

FREDONIA

Mi Casa Su Casa #340

P. O. Box 950, Tempe, 85280-0950
(602) 990-0682; (800) 456-0682

Built in the early 1900s, this two-story house was one of the first homes in Fredonia, a town within one and one-half hours of the Grand Canyon and the center of the Grand Circle. Five guest rooms offer a variety of bed sizes, and both shared and private baths are available. Guests are welcome to use the TV in the livingroom. Breakfast is included. $40-45.

GILBERT

Mi Casa Su Casa #283

P. O. Box 950, Tempe, 85280-0950
(602) 990-0682; (800) 456-0682

Rural-style ranch home has a quiet park setting with large, mature trees, Arabian horses, and peacocks. When in season, an orchard supplies some of the fruit for the full breakfast served each morning. One room has a twin bed; the other has a king-size bed. No smoking. $45-60.

GLOBE

Mi Casa Su Casa #302

P. O. Box 950, Tempe, 85280-0950
(602) 990-0682; (800) 456-0682

Ranch-style, seven-acre horse farm has separate guest house with two guest rooms. Both the main house and the guest house are decorated in southwestern style. One room has a queen-size bed; the other room has two twin beds with a connecting full bath. Large common kitchen and living-room area; the livingroom is equipped with phone, cable TV, VCR, and dining area, and the kitchen is stocked so guests can help themselves. $50-65.

GREER

Mi Casa Su Casa #303

P. O. Box 950, Tempe, 85280-0950
(602) 990-0682; (800) 456-0682

Meadowview is a ten-room house that combines the feel of a traditional log cabin with modern convenience and luxury. Master suite on the first floor includes a queen-size bed, full bath with Jacuzzi, and a fireplace. Another guest room contains two twin trundle beds and has a private full bath across the hall. There is a private guest entrance and a front deck. Light kitchen facilities are offered, and full breakfast is available upon request. $45-75.

HEBER

Mi Casa Su Casa #258

P. O. Box 950, Tempe, 85280-0950
(602) 990-0682; (800) 456-0682

NOTES: Credit cards accepted: A Master Card; B Visa; C American Express; D Discover Card; E Diner's Club; F Other; 2 Personal Checks accepted; 3 Lunch available; 4 Dinner available; 5 Open all year;

Rustic home adjoining the Sitgreaves National Forest has a large guest suite on the first level. Suite includes king-size bed, queen sofa bed, private full bath, private entrance, private deck, microwave, refrigerator, satellite TV, VCR, washer/dryer, outside cooker, combination wood-burning stove/fireplace. Near many attractions and recreational facilities. Panoramic views. $35-55, seasonal.

HEREFORD

Ramsey Canyon Inn

31 Ramsey Canyon Road, 85615
(602) 378-3010

Capture the romantic spirit of country living with a warmth and graciousness that is traditionally Arizona. Situated in the Huachuca Mountains at an elevation of 5,400 feet, Ramsey Canyon is truly a hummingbird haven with fifteen recorded species. The inn is on a winding mountain stream and surrounded by sycamore, maple, juniper, oak, and pine trees. Wildlife abounds, and the average summer temperature is 75 degrees. Discover the rich history of Cochise County.

Hosts: Ronald and Shirlene De Santis
Rooms: 6 (PB) $75-105
Cottages: 2 (PB)
Full Gourmet Breakfast
Credit Cards: None
Notes: 2, 5,7 (outside), 8 (over 12), 10, 11, 12 (all nearby)

JEROME

Mi Casa Su Casa #144

P. O. Box 950, Tempe, 85280-0950
(602) 990-0682; (800) 456-0682

Originally a Mexican miner's home, this bed and breakfast has been remodeled and restored. The guest room features a private entrance, double bed, and full bath and dressing room. The entry room has a sofa bed. A full breakfast is served each morning. Smokers are welcome. $50-95.

Mi Casa Su Casa #285

P. O. Box 950, Tempe, 85280-0950
(602) 990-0682; (800) 456-0682

This two-story home is on the side of Minges Mountain and has a spectacular view. Two guest rooms on the second floor share a full bath and a livingroom. Guest rooms are near the porch that looks out over the mountains. Full breakfast is served each morning. No smoking. $45-95.

Ramsey Canyon Inn

MESA

Mi Casa Su Casa #001

P. O. Box 950, Tempe, 85280-0950
(602) 990-0682; (800) 456-0682

Nestled in a large citrus grove is a self-contained guest cottage built in 1975 to match the design of the handsome ranch-style main house. One guest room in the main house offers a queen-size bed, cable TV, private hall bath, and full breakfast. The guest cottage has a livingroom with TV and phone, complete kitchen, twin beds, dressing room, full bath, and enclosed garage. Hosts invite guests to pick all the fruit they can eat. Minimum stay in the cottage is three nights. No children. No smoking. $40-65.

---

6 Pets welcome; 7 Smoking allowed; 8 Children welcome; 9 Social drinking allowed; 10 Tennis available; 11 Swimming available; 12 Golf available; 13 Skiing available; 14 May be booked through travel agents.

Mi Casa Su Casa #002

P. O. Box 950, Tempe, 85280-0950
(602) 990-0682; (800) 456-0682

Large contemporary Spanish home is close
to shopping, golf, and spring baseball training. Guest suite has double bed, double
Hide-a-bed, private bath, dining area, sink
and refrigerator, private entrance, and TV.
Large breakfasts include homemade breads
and jams, and fresh eggs produced right on
the premise. Handicapped access is available. $30-40.

Mi Casa Su Casa #220

P. O. Box 950, Tempe, 85280-0950
(602) 990-0682; (800) 456-0682

Spacious Spanish-style home is one mile to
the golf course, three miles to the Cub's
spring training, and an easy drive to
Superstition Mountains and Apache Trail.
One guest room has a queen-size bed and
shares a full hall bath with another guest
room that has a double bed. Light kitchen
privileges and laundry facilities are available. Full breakfast. No smoking. $30-40.

Mi Casa Su Casa #229

P. O. Box 950, Tempe, 85280-0950
(602) 990-0682; (800) 456-0682

Spacious new home is 1.5 blocks from
where the Chicago Cubs have spring training. Hostess features homemade sticky
buns, breads, jams, jellies, and thanks to
her southern heritage, offers homemade
biscuits and gravy on Saturdays or by
request. First floor guest room has a double
bed, and a private hall bath with a shower.
Second floor guest room includes a king-
size bed with a full private bath in the hall.
Minimum stay is two nights. No smoking.
$40-50.

Mi Casa Su Casa #230

P. O. Box 950, Tempe, 85280-0950
(602) 990-0682; (800) 456-0682

Modest patio home within walking distance
of the Mesa Country Club. Full breakfast
and kitchen privileges for lunch or dinner
available. The master guest suite has a connecting bath with a shower and a queen-
size bed. The second guest room has two
twin beds and shares a bath with the hostess. Minimum stay is two nights. $40.

Mi Casa Su Casa #236

P. O. Box 950, Tempe, 85280-0950
(602) 990-0682; (800) 456-0682

Spacious stucco Mediterranean-looking
home has a view of the Superstition
Mountains. Near many sites and recreations. Three guest rooms are available;
one has a double bed, another has a twin
day bed, and the third has a king-size or
pair of twin beds. Guests have use of a
family room with stereo and fireplace, and
a separate livingroom that has cable TV
and VCR. Bedtime snacks and a pool are
available. $35-45.

MUNDS PARK

Mi Casa Su Casa #342

P. O. Box 950, Tempe, 85280-0950
(602) 990-0682; (800) 456-0682

This two-story cottage in a heavily wooded
area near the Pinewood Country Club is
charmingly decorated in chintz. Two guest
rooms on the second floor share a full hall
bath; one room has a king-size bed, and the
other room has a pair of twin beds. Guests
are welcome to use the cable TV in the liv-
ing- room. Tennis courts, 18-hole golf
course, and heated pool available. Full,
healthy breakfast. Minimum stay is two
nights. No children. No smoking. $65.

NOTES: Credit cards accepted: A Master Card; B Visa; C American Express; D Discover Card; E Diner's
Club; F Other; 2 Personal Checks accepted; 3 Lunch available; 4 Dinner available; 5 Open all year;

ORACLE

Villa Cardinale

Old Pueblo Homestays
P. O. Box 13603, Tucson, 85732
(800) 333-9RSO

A Spanish hideaway with red tile roofs and courtyard with fountain. Just 35 minutes from Tucson but a world away from the city's fast pace. Catalina Mountain country with spectacular views and clear, starry nights. Spacious rooms, private entrance, fireplace, baths. A full country breakfast is included as part of your stay. Minimum stay is two nights. Children over 16. $45.

ORO VALLEY

Desert Adventure

Old Pueblo Homestays
P. O. Box 13603, Tucson, 85732
(800) 333-9RSO

Large adobe ranch-style home on one acre in northwest foothills. Fenced yard with pool and mountain views. Two large bedrooms with private bath. Tiled and carpeted. Guest sitting room with fireplace and TV. Kitchen privileges on the weekdays with breakfast supplies provided. Resident cat. Minimum stay is two nights. Children welcome. $45.

PAGE

Bed and Breakfast Scottsdale and the West 112

Box 3999, Prescott, 86302-3999
(602) 776-1102

You'll love the cliffside views of Lake Powell and canyonlands. On the quiet edge of town, this bed and breakfast has a shared bath, pool, and Jacuzzi. Full breakfast is provided. Seven miles to Wahweap Marina. $60.

Mi Casa Su Casa #248

P. O. Box 950, Tempe, 85280-0950
(602) 990-0682; (800) 456-0682

New home overlooking Lake Powell with a panoramic view of the Navajo Reservation. Two guest rooms share a private bath in the guest wing. Both rooms have two twin beds. Pool and whirlpool spa available. Breakfasts are served on the patio so that guests can enjoy the view. Minimum stay is two nights. $40-60.

PARADISE VALLEY

Mi Casa Su Casa #272

P. O. Box 950, Tempe, 85280-0950
(602) 990-0682; (800) 456-0682

Near shopping, tennis, golf, and the Camelback and Squaw Peak Mountains, this luxury home is a statement of warmth. TV in every guest room, pool, large open spaces and windows, robes to wear to the pool, and soft drinks served poolside available. Both private and shared baths available. Full breakfast is served. $100 for master suite; extra $50 for a third person in the room.

PATAGONIA

Little House

P. O. Box 461, 341 Sonoita Avenue, 85624
(602) 394-2493

Situated in the heart of southeast Arizona's birding and naturalist area at a comfortable 4,000 feet, Little House offers two rooms in a private adobe guest house. Both queen bed and twin rooms have patios, fireplaces, private baths, and sitting areas. Complimentary gourmet breakfasts feature homemade breads, sausages, and eggs from local hens. Always fresh fruit and juices accompany select teas and freshly ground coffees.

Hosts: Don and Doris Wenig
Rooms: 2 (PB) $60
Full and Continental Breakfast
Credit Cards: None
Notes: 2, 5, 7 (outside), 9

PAYSON

Mi Casa Su Casa #47

P. O. Box 950, Tempe, 85280-0950
(602) 990-0682; (800) 456-0682

Three miles south of Payson, a very large
A-frame house adjoins the National Forest.
Queen bedroom with private full bath and a
large balcony with trundle beds overlook-
ing the livingroom. Easy drive to Mogollon
Rim, Zane Grey cabin, and Tonto Natural
Bridge. Continental breakfast is served.
Minimum stay is two nights. No smoking,
and no alcoholic beverages. $45-50.

Mi Casa Su Casa #305

P. O. Box 950, Tempe, 85280-0950
(602) 990-0682; (800) 456-0682

This handsome new two-story home surrounded by large pines is decorated with a
mix of antiques, traditional, and contemporary furnishings. Situated one and one-half
miles east of downtown Payson. L-shaped
apartment accommodations offer a private
entrance, veranda, double bed, queen-size
sofa bed, kitchen, and full bath. The
kitchen is stocked so guests can enjoy a
self-catered, continental breakfast. No pets.
$65.

PHOENIX

Bed and Breakfast Scottsdale and the West 053

Box 3999, Prescott, 86302-3999
(602) 776-1102

Large home in prime Arcadia area north of
the Arizona Country Club. Guest accommodations include choice of rooms or
suites, pool, and full breakfast. Close to
golf. $40-60; $75 for suites; $5 surcharge
for one-night stays.

Bed and Breakfast Scottsdale and the West 105

Box 3999, Prescott, 86302-3999
(602) 776-1102

This is a popular home with bed and breakfast travelers. Featured in Arizona
Highways Magazine and highlighted by
antiques and glass, it has a spa and private
bath. Full breakfast. Near golf and tennis.
$55; $5 surcharge for one-night stays.

Maricopa Manor

15 West Pasadena Avenue, 85013
(602) 274-6302

Five luxury suites, spacious public rooms,
patios, decks, and the gazebo spa offer an
intimate Old World atmosphere in an elegant urban setting. Maricopa Manor is in
the heart of the Valley of the Sun, convenient to shops, restaurants, museums,
churches, civic and government centers.
The Spanish-style manor house, built in
1928, houses beautiful art, antiques, and a
warm southwestern hospitality. Advance
reservations required.

Hosts: Mary Ellen and Paul Kelley
Suites: 5 (PB) $69-99
Expanded Continental Breakfast
Credit Cards: None
Notes: 2, 5, 7, 8, 9, 14

Mi Casa Su Casa #82

P. O. Box 950, Tempe, 85280-0950
(602) 990-0682; (800) 456-0682

Handsome large home situated near
Biltmore has an extra-large yard with a
pool. Separate guest wing has a large bedroom with a king-size bed, private bath
with a shower, sitting and writing area, and
a private entrance. Full breakfast served.
Minimum stay is three nights. $50-60.

NOTES: Credit cards accepted: A Master Card; B Visa; C American Express; D Discover Card; E Diner's
Club; F Other; 2 Personal Checks accepted; 3 Lunch available; 4 Dinner available; 5 Open all year;

Maricopa Manor

Mi Casa Su Casa #86

P. O. Box 950, Tempe, 85280-0950
(602) 990-0682; (800) 456-0682

Patio home is in a quiet area near the Heard Museum, Phoenix library, and Phoenix art museum. Two bedrooms and two baths are situated on opposite ends of the house. Both bedrooms contain two sets of twin beds, with a private full bath across the hall. Continental breakfast. $50.

Mi Casa Su Casa #127

P. O. Box 950, Tempe, 85280-0950
(602) 990-0682; (800) 456-0682

This upscale patio home is within easy access to downtown Phoenix and Scottsdale. The guest room is by the front door, has a double bed, large closet with mirrored doors, and a private bath next door. Guests may use pool, heated spa, and tennis court. Minimum stay is two nights . $40-50.

Mi Casa Su Casa #155

P. O. Box 950, Tempe, 85280-0950
(602) 990-0682; (800) 456-0682

Situated in the historic district of Phoenix, this home was built circa 1930 and has been renovated and furnished in 1930s

style. The beamed livingroom ceilings and arched doorways lend quaint charm to the Spanish-style home. One room includes a queen-size bed, lace curtains from England, and overlooks the garden and gazebo. A room with a twin bed is available for a companion. Full breakfast. Minimum stay is two nights. $40-50.

Mi Casa Su Casa #165

P. O. Box 950, Tempe, 85280-0950
(602) 990-0682; (800) 456-0682

Spanish-style house in a residential neighborhood sits at the foot of a mountain and is situated 10 minutes from downtown Phoenix, and 20 minutes from downtown Scottsdale. Large bedroom has extra-long twin beds or king bed, bath with Roman tub and shower, small refrigerator, microwave, TV, telephone, dressing room, and sitting area with a private entrance. Continental breakfast. Minimum stay is three nights. $45-55.

Mi Casa Su Casa #207

P. O. Box 950, Tempe, 85280-0950
(602) 990-0682; (800) 456-0682

Situated on a street known for large houses, yards and old trees, this old Spanish-style home has been restored and furnished with English Victorian and Louis XIV antiques. Three guest rooms offer a choice of king, queen, or twin beds, and all are equipped with full baths. Pool and spa available. An abundant breakfast includes fresh-squeezed orange juice from two acres of citrus trees adjoining the property. $45-60.

Mi Casa Su Casa #226

P. O. Box 950, Tempe, 85280-0950
(602) 990-0682; (800) 456-0682

Condominium in the Biltmore area has two bedrooms, two baths, and overlooks the golf course from a balcony. The hostess lives in one of the bedrooms, and the guest room has a queen-size bed, cable TV, and connecting full bath. Two heated swimming pools, Jacuzzi, four tennis courts, and an exercise room are available to guests. Continental breakfast. Minimum stay is two nights. $45-55.

Mi Casa Su Casa #254

P. O. Box 950, Tempe, 85280-0950
(602) 990-0682; (800) 456-0682

Adobe town house situated on a 60-year-old date ranch features a bedroom with a Safari decor, queen bed, and private connecting bath. Pool and heated spa with a view of Camelback Mountain are available to guests. Continental breakfast, and walking distance to to some fine area restaurants. $50-60.

Mi Casa Su Casa #268

P. O. Box 950, Tempe, 85280-0950
(602) 990-0682; (800) 456-0682

1974 Southwest stucco ranch-style house offers gracious accommodations in a handsome neighborhood. Centrally situated to nearby public golf courses. Handsome new two-story house has an L-shaped apartment with private entrance and veranda. The room includes a double bed, and queen sofa bed; kitchen has a small refrigerator, microwave, toaster oven, and coffee pot. Lighted tennis courts, riding stables, and Turf Paradise. One guest room has a queen-size bed and full hall bath; another guest room has two twin beds, TV, and shares the full hall bath. (Only one party is accepted at a time.) Full breakfast and complimentary refreshments. Pool and family room with fireplace, VCR, and cable available. $50-55.

Mi Casa Su Casa #269

P. O. Box 950, Tempe, 85280-0950
(602) 990-0682; (800)456-0682

Large new home with four bedrooms and two baths is situated near diverse activities. One guest room is a large master bedroom with a queen bed, sitting area, TV, and arcadia doors opening to the back yard. The other guest room also has a queen-size bed and shares a full hall bath. An optional third bedroom has a twin bed and shares the hall bath. Light kitchen and laundry privileges, RV and/or boat parking, bicycles, barbecue pit, and large livingroom with sofa bed, TV, and fireplace available. Continental breakfast. Minimum stay is two nights. $40-45.

Mi Casa Su Casa #270

P. O. Box 950, Tempe, 85280-0950
(602) 990-0682; (800) 456-0682

Traditional ranch home with 3,200 square feet is situated in the "green belt" of central Phoenix. Private guest wing has two large guest rooms with king-size beds, TVs, and phones. One guest room has a connecting bath with a shower, and the other guest room has a private full hall bath. Hostess is professional baker and cake decorator. Full breakfast on weekends, continental on weekdays. $40-55.

Mi Casa Su Casa #282

P. O. Box 950, Tempe, 85280-0950
(602) 990-0682; (800) 456-0682

This 1955 ranch-style home is in a beautiful older neighborhood with large, mature trees. Conveniently situated to airport, diverse activities, and interstates. Photographic exhibit in the sun room. Two hall bedrooms share a hall bath. One bedroom has a queen-size bed with a private entrance opening to the patio and pool; another room has two trundle beds ideal for children, and two doors that open onto the sunroom. Hosts have been residents of Phoenix for 22 years. Full, heart-healthy breakfasts. $40-45.

Mi Casa Su Casa #293

P. O. Box 950, Tempe, 85280-0950
(602) 990-0682; (800) 456-0682

A 650-square-foot cottage with private entrance and parking faces heated pool and attractive, landscaped back yard. Centrally situated to everything. One bedroom has a king-size bed, and the other has a pair of twin beds. Livingroom-kitchen area has a TV, VCR, refrigerator, and microwave. Kitchen is stocked, so guests can eat when they want. Minimum stay is three nights. Visa and Master Card accepted. $75.

Mi Casa Su Casa #313

P. O. Box 950, Tempe, 85280-0950
(602) 990-0682; (800) 456-0682

Recently remodeled home with Camelback Mountain in the background. Guest room has queen-size bed, TV, phone, and connecting bath with a shower. Swimming pool available. Full breakfast. $40-45.

Mi Casa Su Casa #315

P. O. Box 950, Tempe, 85280-0950
(602) 990-0682; (800) 456-0682

Contemporary two-story town house, overlooking a bridge and pond and set in the middle of a grapefruit grove. Near Camelback Mountain, airport, Biltmore shopping center, and public transportation. Guest room is up a spiral staircase on the second floor and includes a phone, TV, and private bath. Pool is situated next door. Resident cat. Minimum stay is two nights. $45-55.

Mi Casa Su Casa #319

P. O. Box 950, Tempe, 85280-0950
(602) 990-0682; (800) 456-0682

This southwestern two-story house built in 1987 is Spanish-style with stucco interior and a tile roof. Situated next to South Mountain, it is 500 feet higher than Phoenix. Near South Mountain Park, hiking, biking, tennis, and golf. The guest room is on the second floor. It has a queen-size bed, TV, private hall bath, and phone in the room. Full breakfast with homemade bread. Minimum stay is two nights. $55.

Mi Casa Su Casa #329

P. O. Box 950, Tempe, 85280-0950
(602) 990-0682; (800) 456-0682

This California-style bungalow is in the historic Willo neighborhood, where the homes were built between 1910 and 1930. Evaporative cooling and air conditioning cool the guest room. A double bed is built into an alcove wall. Private guest bath is in the hall. A full gourmet breakfast is served each morning. No children. Resident cats. No smoking. $45.

Mi Casa Su Casa #332

P. O. Box 950, Tempe, 85280-0950
(602) 990-0682; (800) 456-0682

Gracious hostess welcomes guests into her home near a beautiful, top quality golf course with a view of Camelback Mountain. Two guest rooms share a full hall bath; one room offers a queen-size bed, and the other room has a pair of twins. Many resort facilities are available for an extra charge, and this bed and breakfast is near fine dining, shopping, and film complexes. Full breakfast is served. No pets. Resident dog. Handicapped access possible. No smoking. $75-85.

6 Pets welcome; 7 Smoking allowed; 8 Children welcome; 9 Social drinking allowed; 10 Tennis available; 11 Swimming available; 12 Golf available; 13 Skiing available; 14 May be booked through travel agents.

Mi Casa Su Casa #337

P. O. Box 950, Tempe, 85280-0950
(602) 990-0682; (800) 456-0682

Large oleander bushes and tall old tamarisk trees conceal this gracious adobe home and 1920s guest cottage situated on three acres. Featured in *Phoenix House and Garden Magazine* as their Designer Show House in October 1991, the house features a conservatory suite with four-poster European-style, queen bed with step stool, full private bath, sitting room, view of the garden, and private entrance. A guest house has a library, livingroom, minikitchen, two bedrooms, each with a king bed, and private bath and entrances. Gourmet breakfast. Minimum stay is two nights. Meeting facilities for 30 people and wedding facilities for up to 200 guests. No children. No pets. No smoking. $150.

Mi Casa Su Casa #338

P. O. Box 950, Tempe, 85280-0950
(602) 990-0682; (800) 456-0682

On one acre of flowering shrubs, palm, citrus, and pomegranates, the house was built in 1924, and the guest cottage, which is separate from the main house, was built in the 1950s. The cottage was redecorated four years ago and offers a kitchen, French doors separating the bedroom from the rest of the area, a connecting bath with claw-footed tub, and a porch with a view of the pool. A full breakfast is served in the main house, FAX and laundry facilities are available for an extra charge, and the bed and breakfast is ten minutes from Heard Airport, twenty minutes to Sky Harbor Airport, and two blocks from Central Avenue. Minimum stay is two nights. Children over five. $50-75, seasonal rates apply.

Mi Casa Su Casa #341

P. O. Box 950, Tempe, 85280-0950
(602) 990-0682; (800) 456-0682

Midwestern transplants welcome guests to their one-story white house surrounded by olive, queen palm, citrus, and ornamental orange trees. Two rooms share a hall bath; one room has a pair of twin beds, and the other has a double bed, TV, and telephone. Breakfast includes homemade bread, cinnamon rolls, pecan rolls, and homemade jams. Just one mile from I-17, two miles from ASU West, and three miles from Metro Center. No pets. Handicapped access possible. No smoking. $30-40.

Westways "Private" Resort Inn

Valley of the Sun, Box 41624, 85080
(602) 582-3868

In northwest Phoenix, Westways is a jewel situated among executive estate homes, surrounded by mountain preserve, convenient to I-17, Thunderbird Park, and Arrowhead Country Club. Arizona room with large-screen TV, VCR, games, library, and fireplace; guest wet bar/refrigerator, and microwave available. Radio, TV, and sitting area in each deluxe queen-bed guest room; diving pool, whirlpool, courtyard for guest use. Use of country club facilities. Casual western comfort with a touch of class where guests preserve their privacy. Rated as one of the fifty best inns in America. Reservations necessary.

Host: Darrell Trapp
Rooms: 6 (PB) $49-122; special rates available
Full or Continental Breakfast
Credit Cards: A, B, C
Notes: 2, 4, 5, 9, 10, 11, 12, 14

PINE TOP

Mi Casa Su Casa #113

P. O. Box 950, Tempe, 85280-0950
(602) 990-0682; (800) 456-0682

NOTES: Credit cards accepted: A Master Card; B Visa; C American Express; D Discover Card; E Diner's Club; F Other; 2 Personal Checks accepted; 3 Lunch available; 4 Dinner available; 5 Open all year;

Log-sided ranch-style house is built on a secluded mountain lot with pines. Decorated in American primitive antiques, one guest room has a queen-size bed, Jacuzzi tub, and cable TV. Another guest room has a king-size bed with a connecting bath. A third guest room has a queen bed and shares a bath with a fourth guest room with a double bed. Bicycles available, full breakfast, and complimentary refreshments. Minimum stay is two nights. No smoking. $35-75.

PRESCOTT

Bed and Breakfast Scottsdale and the West 083

Box 3999, 86302-3999
(602) 776-1102

Rural luxury with a 25-acre lot. Decks, spa, and volleyball available. Full breakfast is provided. Private baths. $55-65; $85 suites.

Bed and Breakfast Scottsdale and the West 084

Box 3999, 86302-3999
(602) 776-1102

Magnificently restored historic register home on Nob Hill near Courthouse Plaza and Whiskey Row. Full breakfast. $85-130.

The Cottages at Prescott Country Inn Bed and Breakfast

503 South Montezuma, U.S. Highway 89, 86303
(602) 445-7991

Relax in one of twelve enchanted, charmingly appointed country cottages, each with private entrance, bath, refrigerator, coffee brewer, phone, color cable TV, king- or queen-size bed with quilted comforters,

live plants, collectibles, works of art, and separate heating and cooling controls. Three units with fireplaces available. Your breakfast is brought to your cottage, porch, or patio, or you can join other guests in the plant solarium. Guests have free use of Prescott's most complete health club, which offers indoor/outdoor pool, spa, sauna, racquet ball, and tennis courts. Prescott is one mile high, surrounded by tall pines, and removed from smog, freeway traffic, and stress. Reservations advised.

Hosts: Morris and Sue Faulkner
Rooms: 12 (PB) $49-119
Continental Plus Breakfast
Credit Cards: A, B
Notes: 2, 5, 7 , 8, 9, 10, 11, 12, 14

Lynx Creek Farm Bed and Breakfast

P. O. Box 4301, 86302
(602) 778-9573

Secluded country hilltop setting with great views overlooking Lynx Creek. Spacious suites in separate guest house filled with antiques and "country" decor. Organic garden and orchard supply fresh fruit, produce, and homemade apple cider for full gourmet breakfasts. Jacuzzi, billiard table, croquet, volleyball, horseshoes, gold panning, animals, exotic birds. Light cocktails and hors d'oeuvres each evening. Also available for weddings and cooking classes.

Hosts: Greg and Wendy Temple
Rooms: 4 (PB) $85-125
Full Breakfast
Credit Cards: A, B
Notes: 2, 5, 6, 7 (limited), 8, 9, 10, 11, 12, 14

Mi Casa Su Casa #1061

P. O. Box 950, Tempe, 85280-0950
(602) 990-0682; (800) 456-0682

Spacious cedar two-story home built on a hill that gives the illusion of living in the treetops. Large windows are everywhere so that a visitor can take advantage of the

6 Pets welcome; 7 Smoking allowed; 8 Children welcome; 9 Social drinking allowed; 10 Tennis available; 11 Swimming available; 12 Golf available; 13 Skiing available; 14 May be booked through travel agents.

beautiful piney surroundings of the house. The master guest suite is on the second level and includes a king-size waveless waterbed, a large living- room, a private full hall bath, and a queen Hide-a-bed. The first floor has two guest rooms that share a private hall bath, one has a king-size waterbed, and the other has twin trundle beds. Full breakfast. Resident dog. No smoking. Open summers only. $35-95.

Mi Casa Su Casa #1065

P. O. Box 950, Tempe, 85280-0950
(602) 990-0682; (800) 456-0682

Contemporary redwood home with open floor plan and three decks is situated in a setting of granite boulders, rolling hills, and forests. Easy drive to various local activities and recreation. One guest room has a king-size bed, or two twins, with a private bath, a microwave, and an adjacent covered patio. Another room has a queen-size bed, and is ideal for a third or fourth party sharing a bath with the other guest room. Full breakfast. $30-70, seasonal rates.

Mi Casa Su Casa #1066

P. O. Box 950, Tempe, 85280-0950
(602) 990-0682; (800) 456-0682

Western Victorian built around 1900 is furnished with antiques and offers a spectacular view of Thumbe Butte. Three guest rooms are on the second floor and share a hall bath. One room has a queen bed and cable TV, another room has a pair of twin beds and cable TV, and a third room has a day bed. Hall bath has a newly tiled shower. Guests are invited to use the livingroom and dining room and help themselves to herb tea and homemade cookies. Continental breakfast. $50-55.

Prescott Pines Inn: Bedand Breakfast

901 White Spar Road, 86303
(602) 445-7270; (800) 541-5374 reservations

Formerly the Haymore Dairy in the early 1900s, the inn is now a haven for those seeking fresh air, rest, and "welcome home" surroundings. Thirteen "elegant country" guest rooms are in one of four guest houses around the main house. Each guest room has a private bath and entry, eight have kitchens, four have fireplaces. Relax under the veranda overlooking rose gardens and a fountain, or read a book on the tree swing in the patio area. A full breakfast is served at 8:00 or 10:00 a.m. in the dining room. Smoking in designated rooms only.

Hosts: Jean Wu and Michael Acton
Rooms: 13 (PB) $60-90
Full Breakfast
Credit Cards: A, B
Notes: 2, 5, 7, 10, 11, 12, 13, 14

SAFFORD

Mi Casa Su Casa #322

P. O. Box 950, Tempe, 85280-0950
(602) 990-0682; 1-800-456-0682

Western Colonial-style brick house built in 1890 has wide verandas that run across the front of the house. Three large, old-fashioned guest rooms all share a large hall bath. One room has a double bed, a twin bed, and a old-fashioned pedestal sink. Another room has a double bed, dressing room, and a large window that overlooks two old, large pecan trees. A third room has an antique armoire, double bed, French doors to the balcony, and two twelve-foot pocket doors to the sitting room. A guest cottage is also available. Full breakfast. No smoking. Visa and MasterCard. $65.

NOTES: Credit cards accepted: A Master Card; B Visa; C American Express; D Discover Card; E Diner's Club; F Other; 2 Personal Checks accepted; 3 Lunch available; 4 Dinner available; 5 Open all year;

SAHUARITA

Mi Casa Su Casa #265

P. O. Box 950, Tempe, 85280-0950
(602) 990-0682; (800) 456-0682

Small A-frame cottage is at the 5,500-foot level of the Madera Canyon. The living area is about 600 square feet, complete with a great room that includes the kitchen, living- room area, wood-burning stove, dining room, and bath. A loft houses a double bed and a TV, and a barbecue is in the small back yard. Self-catering (you bring your own food). No smoking. $52.50, plus $5.00 booking fee.

SASABE

Mi Casa Su Casa #1627

P. O. Box 950, Tempe, 85280-0950
(602) 990-0682; (800) 456-0682

3,800 feet high in the Sonoran Desert, this fascinating 250-year-old ranch is one of the last great Spanish haciendas still standing in the United States. There are 16 full modernized guest rooms, each with its own private bath and fireplace. Heated pool, spa, hot tub, variety of recreational activities on site, including horseback riding. Three meals are served a day. $60-75, non-riding package; $90-105, includes horse, tack, and trail rides.

SCOTTSDALE

Bed and Breakfast in Arizona

P. O. Box 8628, 85252
(602) 995-2831; (800) 266-STAY

Representing private homes, bed and breakfasts, guest houses, and inns across Arizona, we offer over seventy individual bed and breakfasts, which total more than 200 rooms. All inspected and monitored for quality of stay, hospitality, and cleanliness, we represent the best of Arizona and New Mexico. One call puts all of our rooms at your fingertips. We take care of the reservations for you at no additional fee.

Contact: Stephanie Osterlitz
Credit Cards: A, B , C, D
Notes: 2, 5, 7, 8, 10, 11, 12, 14

Bed and Breakfast Scottsdale and the West 060

Box 3999, Prescott, 86302-3999
(602) 776-1102

This charming guest house is near Camelback corridor and golf club. Hosts raise Arabians and Beagles. Private baths; continental breakfast; pool. $50.

Bed and Breakfast Scottsdale and the West 067

Box 3999, Prescott, 86302-3999
(602) 776-1102

This two-level contemporary home is in northeastern Scottsdale near biking and jogging track. Enjoy the private upper deck overlooking the pool. Pool table available. Private bath; full breakfast. $75; $10 surcharge for one-night stays.

Bed and Breakfast Scottsdale and the West 068

Box 3999, Prescott, 86302-3999
(602) 776-1102

There is plenty of living space in this large Spanish-style home in northeastern Scottsdale. The entry to the guesthouse is from the pool patio. Private bath; continental breakfast; near the golf course. $55.

6 Pets welcome; 7 Smoking allowed; 8 Children welcome; 9 Social drinking allowed; 10 Tennis available; 11 Swimming available; 12 Golf available; 13 Skiing available; 14 May be booked through travel agents.

Bed and Breakfast Scottsdale and the West 095

Box 3999, Prescott, 86302-3999
(602) 776-1102

This charming bed and breakfast is near Scottsdale Fashion Square and the Phoenician Golf Club. Large four-poster canopy beds and French doors to the pool make it special. Private bath; continental breakfast. $75, seasonal; $10 surcharge for one-night stays.

Bed and Breakfast Scottsdale and the West 110

Box 3999, Prescott, 86302-3999
(602) 776-1102

This guest house is a great value. Near Scottsdale and Lincoln, walk to the Borgata, Hilton Village, and new Crazy Gold center. Private bath; continental breakfast; pool. Near golf and tennis. $75; $10 surcharge for one-night stays.

Mi Casa Su Casa #46

P. O. Box 950, Tempe, 85280-0950
(602) 990-0682; (800) 456-0682

Ranch-style home with Canadian hostess is near Desert Botanical Gardens, Phoenix Zoo, hiking, airport. Small guest room downstairs has private bath and double bed. No smoking; continental breakfast. Minimum stay is two nights. $40.

Mi Casa Su Casa #66

P. O. Box 950, Tempe, 85280-0950
(602) 990-0682; (800) 456-0682

One-story patio home is near golf courses, Hilton Village, Borgata, and a short walk to lighted tennis courts, spa, and pool. Master guest suite has queen bed with connecting bath. Continental breakfast on weekdays; full breakfast on weekends. Hostess smokes outside when guests are present. $40-45.

Mi Casa Su Casa #189

P. O. Box 950, Tempe, 85280-0950
(602) 990-0682; (800) 456-0682

Spacious trilevel condo is situated in a nice complex with a parklike setting, and is close to everything. One room is a large bedroom-sitting room with a private bath situated eight steps up the stairwell and a refrigerator and snack corner. Another guest room has a double Hide-a-bed and shares the host's bath. Full breakfast served until 9AM; afterward, coffee and rolls available. $35-50.

Mi Casa Su Casa #204

P. O. Box 950, Tempe, 85280-0950
(602) 990-0682; (800) 456-0682

Contemporary ranch-style house is minutes from PGA driving range, world-class golf courses, and paths by the canal for jogging or walking. Master guest suite with king-size bed, dressing area and sitting area with TV and phone, and private bath. Bicycles and golf clubs available; gas grill on the porch. Full country breakfast and complimentary refreshments. $45, summer rates; $55, all others.

Mi Casa Su Casa #227

P. O. Box 950, Tempe, 85280-0950
(602) 990-0682; (800) 456-0682

Southwestern adobe home on two acres of land has a panoramic view of the McDowell Mountains. Conveniently situated near Taliesen West, Carefree, Mayo Clinic, Rawhide, and fine dining and golf courses. Cozy guest room has a pair of twin beds with handmade quilts, TV, private full bath, private exit to the pool, patio, and parking areas. Full gourmet breakfast. No smoking. Minimum stay is two nights. $55-65.

NOTES: Credit cards accepted: A Master Card; B Visa; C American Express; D Discover Card; E Diner's Club; F Other; 2 Personal Checks accepted; 3 Lunch available; 4 Dinner available; 5 Open all year;

Mi Casa Su Casa #245

P. O. Box 950, Tempe, 85280-0950
(602) 990-0682; (800) 456-0682

Attractive ranch-style house is situated on one acre of tall palms, pines, and native plants. Lush resort landscaping surrounds the pool. Large private guest suite includes a sitting room, office area with a FAX, private bath with a shower, and smaller second bedroom with a twin bed. Private tennis/health club facilities accessible (for a small extra fee). Breakfast and complimentary refreshments are served. $65-75.

Mi Casa Su Casa #273

P. O. Box 950, Tempe, 85280-0950
(602) 990-0682; (800) 456-0682

Large adobe-style luxury home has an outstanding view of the McDowell Mountains, a large covered patio, beautiful pool, and minutes to Carefree, Mayo Clinic, and Rawhide. One guest room has a twin bed and TV, and another has a double bed and TV. Private bath in the hall. Only one party accepted at a time. Hostess is a gifted cook and makes wonderful full breakfasts. No smoking. Minimum stay is two nights. $65.

Mi Casa Su Casa #279

P. O. Box 950, Tempe, 85280-0950
(602) 990-0682; (800) 456-0682

Large adobe-style luxury home offers an outstanding view of the McDowell Mountains. Convenient to Mayo Clinic, downtown Scottsdale, Rawhide, Carefree, shopping, and restaurants. Two rooms available, with either a twin or double beds. Full bath in the hall (Only one party accepted at a time.) Children over 14. Full breakfast. No smoking. Minimum stay is two nights. $65.

Mi Casa Su Casa #287

P. O. Box 950, Tempe, 85280-0950
(602) 990-0682; (800) 456-0682

Ranch-style home on a quiet cul-de-sac. Close to public golf courses, tennis courts, paracourse walking path, "urban" fishing, and shopping. One bedroom has twin beds; another bedroom has twin trundle beds. Both have a large full bath with a double sink. There is a large covered patio, pool, and family room with TV, fireplace, and VCR. Hostess loves to cook and smokes outside when guests are present. Full breakfast. Minimum stay is three nights. $40-45.

Mi Casa Su Casa #288

P. O. Box 950, Tempe, 85280-0950
(602) 990-0682; (800) 456-0682

Spacious regional ranch-style home is conveniently situated near Taliesen West, Carefree, Cave Creek, Westworld, Mayo Clinic, outstanding golfing, and upscale shopping. One guest area has a four-poster queen bed, luxury full bath, and Arcadia doors leading to the pool. Another guest area is a two-bedroom suite with separate hall bath. (Only one party is booked into these two rooms.) One bedroom has a double bed and cable TV, and the second, smaller room has a pair of twin beds. Complimentary use of facilities at nearby fitness club is available. Full breakfast. Minimum stay is two nights in the master suite. Master suite-$75; one room in two bedroom suite-$55; both rooms-$110. Seasonal rates also apply.

Mi Casa Su Casa #301

P. O. Box 950, Tempe, 85280-0950
(602) 990-0682; (800) 456-0682

Guest cottage is situated opposite the main house with the pool in-between. Cottage

6 Pets welcome; 7 Smoking allowed; 8 Children welcome; 9 Social drinking allowed; 10 Tennis available; 11 Swimming available; 12 Golf available; 13 Skiing available; 14 May be booked through travel agents.

has air conditioning, pair of twin beds in bedroom, TV, phone, kitchen stocked with breakfast food, and water and air purifiers. Resident dog. No smoking. $60-65.

Mi Casa Su Casa #312

P. O. Box 950, Tempe, 85280-0950
(602) 990-0682; (800) 456-0682

Luxury home has beautifully landscaped back yard with a pool and citrus trees, and is situated in the McCormick Ranch area of Scottsdale. The guest area is situated by itself on one end of the house. The bedroom adjoins a sitting area, has a queen-size bed, and a large private luxury bath. From the sitting area, French doors open to a private patio with chaise longes for relaxing. Full breakfast. Minimum stay is two nights. $85.

Mi Casa Su Casa #327

P. O. Box 950, Tempe, 85280-0950
(602) 990-0682; (800) 456-0682

Handsome, 7,500-square-foot adobe-style main house has beautiful, resort-style grounds and is near Carefree and Taliesen West. One room has a four-poster queen-size bed, fireplace, connecting bath, and TV, and adjoins another guest room, which has a brass double bed, TV, and shares the other guest room's bath. The guest house has a California king-size bed, livingroom with TV and fireplace, kitchen, and small dining area. Private tennis court, pool and spa on premises. Full breakfast. Smoking outside. $100-150.

Mi Casa Su Casa #328

P. O. Box 950, Tempe, 85280-0950
(602) 990-0682; (800) 456-0682

Spacious stucco home is in the McCormick Ranch area and looks out toward the lakes. One room has a king-size bed, connecting bath, TV, and lake view. Another room has

a queen-size bed, connecting bath with whirlpool tub, and TV. Lap swimming pool and game pool on property. Tennis courts nearby. Canoe or bicycles available. Full breakfast on weekends, continental on weekdays. No smoking. Minimum stay is two nights. $100-150.

Mi Casa Su Casa #331

P. O. Box 950, Tempe, 85280-0950
(602) 990-0682; (800) 456-0682

Sociable host couple welcomes guests into their luxurious home near fine shopping and restaurants. Guest room has a queen bed, romantic decor, and bath with a shower. Beautiful pool and landscaping. Full, health-conscious breakfast. Resident dog. No smoking. Minimum stay is two nights. $100.

SEDONA

Bed and Breakfast Scottsdale and the West 097

Box 3999, Prescott, 86302-3999
(602) 776-1102

This large home offers a choice of four separate rooms or a private suite. A large buffet breakfast is served. $68-$98, plus tax; $5 surcharge for one-night stays.

Country Elegance Bed and Breakfast

P. O. Box 1257, 86336
(602) 634-4470

Country Elegance Bed & Breakfast offers French ambience in a beautiful, secluded country setting outside of Sedona. Ideally situated between majestic Sedona and historic Jerome, the inn's elegant decor is the work of designer innkeeper, Rita Sydelle. It features well-appointed rooms with mountain views that allow guests to retreat to the understated luxury and tranquility of country life. A private library and the Arizona Room offer relaxation after a day of touring. Country Elegance is also a minifarm with egg-laying chickens, organic vegetable gardens, and fruit and nut trees. A full gourmet country breakfast is served that can include crepes, stuffed French toast, quiche, blintzes, garden egg dishes, breads and muffins, and triple chocolate brownies.

Hosts: Rita Sydelle
Rooms: 3 (2 PB; 1 SB) $65-85
Full Breakfast
Credit Cards: F (travelers checks)

The Cozy Cactus

80 Canyon Circle Drive, 86336-8673
(602) 284-0082

Cozy Cactus Bed and Breakfast is situated at the foot of Castle Rock between Sedona's red rock cliffs and Wild Horse Mesa. Cozy Cactus is a ranch-style home comfortably furnished with family heirlooms and theatrical memorabilia. Each room has a private bath, and each pair of bedrooms shares a sitting room with a fireplace. Breakfasts are served in the great room. Guests have direct access into Coconino National Forest for hiking, birdwatching, and photography.

Hosts: Bob and Lynne Gillman
Rooms: 4 (PB) $90
Full Breakfast
Credit Cards: A, B
Notes: 2, 5, 8 (over 6), 9, 10, 12, 13, 14

Garland's Oak Creek Lodge

P. O. Box 152, 86336
(602) 282-3343

What a delightful surprise this lodge is, tucked away in Oak Creek Canyon eight miles north of Sedona. An oasis of green lawns, gardens, and fruit trees, this bed and breakfast offers fifteen log cabins. Fabulous fresh food graces the tables of the elegant, rustic dining hall. Dinner and breakfast are included in the daily rate.

Hosts: Gary and Mary Garland
Rooms: 15 (PB) $142-162
Full Breakfast
Credit Cards: A, B
Closed Nov. 15-March 30
Notes: 2, 4, 7, 8, 9, 10

The Graham
Bed and Breakfast Inn

150 Canyon Circle Drive, 86336
(602) 284-1425

The Graham Bed and Breakfast Inn was built specifically as an inn, and is situated with views of the red rock formations that have made Sedona famous. There are six unique guest rooms, all with private balconies and baths, some with Jacuzzi and fireplace. Sculptures and painting by local artists add to the beauty of the inn. The beautifully landscaped grounds with pool, spa, and fountain invite you to enjoy the outdoors. Guests experience comfortable elegance and memorable breakfasts.

Hosts: Carol and Roger Redenbaugh
Rooms: 6 (PB) $98-198
Full Breakfast
Minimun stay weekends: 2 nights; Holdays 2-3
  nights
Credit cards: A, B, D
Notes: 2, 5, 8, 9, 10, 11, 12, 14

6 Pets welcome; 7 Smoking allowed; 8 Children welcome; 9 Social drinking allowed; 10 Tennis available; 11 Swimming available; 12 Golf available; 13 Skiing available; 14 May be booked through travel agents.

Lantern Light Inn

3085 West Highway 89A, 86336
(602) 282-3419

Convenient easy-to-find highway location at far end of business district
across from Thunder Mountain.
Walking distance to restaurants, close
to hiking trails and galleries. Buildings
set back from road on tree-lined
grounds in quiet, private environment.
All rooms are on ground floor, and
each has a private entry and bath. Two
have a shared deck. Spacious suite has
kitchenette. Decor is country French.
Library and den for guests' use. Full
breakfasts. No smoking. Caring and
congenial hosts.

Hosts: Ed and Kris Varjean
Rooms: 3 (PB) $70-90
Full Breakfast
Credit Cards: None
Notes: 2, 5, 10, 11, 12, 13

Mi Casa Su Casa #186

P. O. Box 950, Tempe, 85280-0950
(602) 990-0682; (800) 456-0682

German hosts invite guests into their
large, one-story, ranch-style home.
The master guest suite is called
Honeymoon Suite and has a king-size
bed, view of Sedona's red rocks, and
private bath with a whirlpool tub.
Another guest room has a queen-size
bed, and connecting bath, and a third
guest room, decorated with memorabilia from the host's native land, has a
pair of twin beds and a full bath across
the hall. A full breakfast features
homemade baked goods. No smoking.
Minimum stay is two nights. $50-75.

Mi Casa Su Casa #244

P. O. Box 950, Tempe, 85280-0950
(602) 990-0682; (800) 456-0682

Lovely two-story home is built with a view
of Sedona's red rocks. One room has a
queen-size four-poster bed and an adjacent
bath with a shower. Another guest room
has a queen bed and a day bed, and private
full bath across the hall. Guest area has a
private entrance and is removed from the
rest of the house. Full breakfast. Minimum
stay is two nights. $75.

Mi Casa Su Casa #261

P. O. Box 950, Tempe, 85280-0950
(602) 990-0682; (800) 456-0682

Two acres of high desert with beautiful
views of the red rocks and mesas surround
this ranch-style home with matching stable.
Near the national forest, hiking and riding
trails, and golf. One room has a queen bed,
views of the red rocks, and private hall
bath. The other guest room has a queen bed
and private bath as well. Full breakfast.
Room for two horses in the stables.
Minimum stay is two nights on the weekend. $75-80.

Mi Casa Su Casa #309

P. O. Box 950, Tempe, 85280-0950
(602) 990-0682; (800) 456-0682

Four-bedroom inn made from a triplex
ranch- style house built in 1983 is situated
at the foot of Castle Rock overlooking the
valley between Wild Horse Mesa and the
red rock cliffs. All four bedrooms have
their own connecting baths with large
windows. Full breakfast is served in the
great room at a large knotty pine table
overlooking Bell Rock. Handicapped
facilities. Minimum stay is two nights.
$85-95.

Mi Casa Su Casa #317

P. O. Box 950, Tempe, 85280-0950
(602) 990-0682; (800) 456-0682

Ranch-style house has a view of the Sugar Loaf red rock formation. Accommodations include one guest room in the main house and a separate guest house. The guest room in the main house has a queen-size bed and a private hall bath. The guest house has air conditioning, a full kitchen stocked with breakfast foods, an upstairs bedroom with a queen bed, TV, and full hall bath; a futon is available for a third adult. Full breakfast is served in the main house; the apartment is self-catering. No smoking. Minimum stay is two nights. $40-55.

Rose Tree Inn
376 Cedar Street, 86336
(602) 282-2065

Small, quaint, private, quiet. Three units with fully furnished kitchenettes. Beautiful property situated in a lovely English garden environment. Within walking distance of "Old Town" Sedona. One hundred miles north of Phoenix; two and one-half hours to the Grand Canyon. Reservations a must.

Host: Rachel Gillespie
Rooms: 4 (PB) $69-96
Coffee and Tea in room
Credit Cards: A, B
Notes: 2, 5, 7, 8, 9, 10, 12, 14

Sipapu Lodge
P. O. Box 552, 86336
(602) 282-2833

Red rock, ranch-style house is nestled among natural vegetation. Each spacious room reflects influence of Anasazi Indian culture and Lea's family history. Hosts are knowledgeable about local history and special hiking in the Red Rock country. Vincent is a massage technician and potter. Unique, original recipes from Lea's kitchen are a speciality.

Hosts: Lea Pace and Vincent Mollan
Rooms: 5 (3 PB; 2 SB) $74-108
Full Breakfast
Credit Cards: None
Notes: 2, 5, 6, 7 (outside), 8, 9, 10, 11, 12, 14

A Touch of Sedona Bed and Breakfast
595 Jordan Road, 86336
(602) 282-6462

Eclectic elegance, furnished with stained-glass lamps and antiques, but with a mix of contemporary. Generous hospitality and old-fashioned breakfasts with home-baked bread await you in lavish accommodations within walking distance of uptown.

Hosts: Dick and Doris Stevenson
Rooms: 4 (PB) $85-95
Full Breakfast
Credit Cards: A, B
Notes: 5, 7 (limited), 9, 10, 11, 12, 14

SIERRA VISTA

Mi Casa Su Casa #30
P. O. Box 950, Tempe, 85280-0950
(602) 990-0682; (800) 456-0682

Small ranch at a 5,000-foot elevation is situated in the foothills of the beautiful Huachuca Mountains, two miles from the Mile High Nature Conservancy, and an easy drive to Tombstone, Bisbee, Chiricahua Mountains, and Cochise Stronghold. One guest room has a queen bed, connecting bath, TV, and phone. Another guest room has a pair of twin beds, connecting full bath, TV, and phone. Pool, spa, and light kitchen privileges. Full breakfast. No smoking. Minimum stay is two nights. $45-55.

SONOITA

Mi Casa Su Casa #1623
P. O. Box 950, Tempe, 85280-0950
(602) 990-0682; (800) 456-0682

This working ranch offers luxury accommodations in Arizona's high grass country. There are facilities for 16 people in both the main house and

---

6 Pets welcome; 7 Smoking allowed; 8 Children welcome; 9 Social drinking allowed; 10 Tennis available; 11 Swimming available; 12 Golf available; 13 Skiing available; 14 May be booked through travel agents.

guest house, and sizes of beds range from king to twin. For those wanting more privacy, the entire house can be rented. Ranch is next to the National Forest, foothills, and Santa Rita Mountains. Guests are not waited on hand and foot, because the hosts believe that most people want privacy, seclusion, and the freedom to choose their own mealtimes. Kitchen privileges, partial maid service, bed linens, pool, and tennis court are all available. Minimum stay is two nights. $75-300.

SPRINGERVILLE

Mi Casa Su Casa #325

P. O. Box 950, Tempe, 85280-0950
(602) 990-0682; (800) 456-0682

Carefully restored Colonial Revival home circa 1910 allows a visitor to step back in time. Enjoy antiques such as an original soda fountain, two old operable jukeboxes, and Coca-Cola signs. Four bedrooms with private baths are furnished with antiques, handmade quilts, and goosedown pillows. Full breakfast is served with antique crystal, china, and table linens. Smoking outside only. $75-125.

STRAWBERRY

Mi Casa Su Casa #294

P. O. Box 950, Tempe, 85280-0950
(602) 990-0682; (800) 456-0682

Country warmth and hospitality characterize this two-story home. Guests have a private entrance on the second floor, where two bedrooms share a full hall bath and a redwood deck. Host is a native of Arizona. Continental breakfast. $39-44.

SUN LAKES

Bonna Casa

Old Pueblo Homestays
P. O. Box 13603, Tucson, 85732
(800) 333-9RSO

Enjoy a lakeside continental breakfast in this modern home. Professional hostess makes you comfortable in one of two bedrooms. One room has a queen bed with a private hall bath, and the master suite has a king-size bed with sitting area, fireplace, and private bath. Spa and barbecue, and wet bar on the patio. Golf cart, clubs, and bikes available from the hosts. No pets. Children over ten. Smoking outside. $65-85.

TEMPE

Mi Casa Su Casa Reservation Service

P. O. Box 950, 85250-0950
(602) 990-0682; (800) 456-0682

Over 150 approved friendly homestays, guest cottages, ranches, and inns in Arizona, Utah, and New Mexico. Some of the listings are situated in Ajo, Bisbee, Cave Creek, Dragoon, Flagstaff, Greer, Jerome, Madera Canyon, Mesa, Oracle, Page, Paradise Valley, Patagonia, Phoenix, Pinetop, Prescott, Scottsdale, Sedona, Sierra Vista, Tempe, Tombstone, Tuscon, Wickenburg, Yuma; Albuquerque, New Mexico; Salt Lake City, Utah; and others.

Coordinator: Ruth Young
Rooms: 290 (275 PB; 15 SB) $40-150
Full, Continental, and Self-serve Breakfast
Credit Cards: None
Notes: 2, 5, 6, 7, 8, 9, 10, 11, 12, 13, 14

NOTES: Credit cards accepted: A Master Card; B Visa; C American Express; D Discover Card; E Diner's Club; F Other; 2 Personal Checks accepted; 3 Lunch available; 4 Dinner available; 5 Open all year;

Mi Casa Su Casa #131

P. O. Box 950, 85280-0950
(602) 990-0682; (800) 456-0682

Chosen as one of the 100 best bed and breakfasts by their guests, this bed and breakfast is minutes from the recreation centers, shopping, ASU, and Mesa Community College. One guest room has a king-size bed, connecting private bath, and glass doors to the patio area; the other guest room has a double bed and shares the hall bath with the hosts. Full breakfast features homemade muffins and bagels. $45-55.

Mi Casa Su Casa #290

P. O. Box 950, 85280-0950
(602) 990-0682; (800) 456-0682

Single-family residence is situated near public transportation to Phoenix, Mesa, and ASU, with many golf courses, tennis and handball courts, and fitness centers in the vicinity. One room has a queen-size bed, TV, and private hall bath with whirlpool jets. Another room has a double bed and shares a bath with the other room. A sofa bed with a private bath is also available and is situated in the lower level family room. Full breakfast. No smoking. Minimum stay is two nights. $40-55.

Mi Casa Su Casa #314

P. O. Box 950, 85280-0950
(602) 990-0682; (800) 456-0682

Built in 1939, the main house features red oak floors and solid panel doors and is on a street less than two blocks from ASU and one-half mile from renovated downtown Tempe. The guest cottage, a new addition that remains consistent with the main house, has 475 square feet, a sitting room with TV, VCR, microwave, and refrigerator, whirlpool tub, king-size bed. Minimum stay is two nights. $65.

TOMBSTONE

Mi Casa Su Casa #330

P. O. Box 950, Tempe, 85280-0950
(602) 990-0682; (800) 456-0682

This historic site built around 1880 has been carefully restored, with refinished hardwood floors, white stucco on the outside, and Victorian furnishings, including a baby grand piano in the parlor. Six guest rooms, all with private baths, are in the main house, and one guest room is in the miners' cabin. Most rooms have double beds; one queen-size bed is also available. Full breakfast. Smoking outside. Handicapped accessible. $45-65.

The Jeff Milton House

Old Pueblo Homestays
P. O. Box 13603, Tucson, 85732
(800) 333-9RSO

The 100-year-old Jeff Milton House is one block from Tombstone's famous OK Corral. The house is Western style, and antiques include an old-fashioned Singer sewing machine and a Tiffany lamp. Your room has a queen-size bed, a twin bed, and a futon. Private bath. Breakfast is homey and satisfying. Smoking outside. No pets. Children are $10 extra. Minimum stay is two nights. $45.

TUCSON

Adobe House

Old Pueblo Homestays
P. O. Box 13603, 85732
(800) 333-9RSO

This home is in the foothills between the Santa Catalina Mountains and midtown Tucson. Private bath and sitting room with TV and radio. Outside is a covered porch complete with swing

6 Pets welcome; 7 Smoking allowed; 8 Children welcome; 9 Social drinking allowed; 10 Tennis available; 11 Swimming available; 12 Golf available; 13 Skiing available; 14 May be booked through travel agents.

and a patio. Beautiful mountain views can be enjoyed during the day. Continental breakfast served outside, weather permitting, and includes freshly squeezed juice. Minimum stay is two nights. No children. Smoking outside. $60.

Bed and Breakfast Scottsdale and the West 073

Box 3999, Prescott, 86302-3999
(602) 776-1102

Luxury Santa Fe adobe inn built in 1929. Five custom-designed suites are available. Gourmet breakfast and afternoon tea are served. Private bath. Close to golf and tennis. $90-110, plus tax.

Bed and Breakfast Scottsdale and the West 088

Box 3999, Prescott, 86302-3999
(602) 776-1102

You'll find gracious Southwest living in this restored 1870s home in El Presidio historic district. There is a garden courtyard with fountains. Private bath; continental breakfast. $85-95, plus tax; $10 surcharge for one-night stays.

Bed and Breakfast Scottsdale and the West 089

Box 3999, Prescott, 86302-3999
(602) 776-1102

Private home in residential northeast Tucson. Featuring a garden patio and private entrance. Private bath; continental breakfast. $50; $5 surcharge for one-night stays.

Bed and Breakfast Scottsdale and the West 102

Box 3999, Prescott, 86302-3999
(602) 776-1102

There are several rooms to choose from in this spacious hacienda-style home with central courtyard. Near the University of Arizona and three miles northeast of the City Center. Private bath; continental breakfast; pool. Close to golf and tennis. $75; $5 surcharge for one-night stays.

Bed and Breakfast Scottsdale and the West 114

Box 3999, Prescott, 86302-3999
(602) 776-1102

You can choose from accommodations in an adobe-style hacienda built in the 1870s, or one with a Japanese hot tub. Convenient for downtown walking and shopping. Full breakfast. $70-120, plus tax; $10 surcharge for one-night stays.

Casa Alegre Bed and Breakfast Inn

316 East Speedway, 85705
(602) 628-1800

This distinguished 1915 home is between the University of Arizona and downtown Tucson has four uniquely decorated guest rooms with private baths. A scrumptious breakfast is served in the formal dining room or poolside on the serene patio. Casa Alegre allows easy access to Tucson's many historic, cultural, and recreational attractions, state and national parks, as well as great shopping and fantastic eateries.

Host: Phyllis Florek
Rooms: 4 (PB) $70-80
Full Breakfast
Credit Cards: A, B
Notes: 2, 5, 9, 10, 11, 12, 14

NOTES: Credit cards accepted: A Master Card; B Visa; C American Express; D Discover Card; E Diner's Club; F Other; 2 Personal Checks accepted; 3 Lunch available; 4 Dinner available; 5 Open all year;

Casa Tierra
Bed and Breakfast Inn
11155 West Calle Pima, 85743
(602() 578-3058

Casa Tierra is on five acres of beautiful
Sonoran desert thirty minutes west of
Tucson. This secluded area has hundreds of
saguaro cactus, spectacular mountain
views, and brilliant sunsets. The rustic
adobe house features entryways with vaulted brick ceilings, an interior arched courtyard, Mexican furnishings, and a hot tub
overlooking the desert. Great hiking and
birding. Near Desert Museum, Saguaro
National Monument, and Old Tucson.

Hosts: Karen and Lyle Hymer-Thompson
Rooms: 3 (PB) $60-75
Full Breakfast
Credit Cards: None
Notes: 2, 8, 9, 14

The Desert Yankee
Old Pueblo Homestays
P. O. Box 13603, 85732
(800) 333-9RSO

Family residence is in a quiet neighborhood. Five rooms, all with private baths,
offer a variety of bed sizes. Lovely courtyard, great room, and pool available.
Continental breakfast served in the dining
room or courtyard. Withing walking distance of the university. Smoking on the
patio only. Pets are allowed, as there are
two cats in residence. Children are $10
extra. $65-85.

Double K Ranch
Old Pueblo Homestays
P. O. Box 13603, 85732
(800) 333-9RSO

Bird watcher's paradise! Private guest
facility with Ben Franklin stove, private
shower, and patio. Color TV, radio, tape
player, phone, western books, and games.

Jacuzzi and pool available. Experience
splendid bird watching, explore ancient
Hohokam sites on private trail, or venture
off on nearby national forest trails. The
ranch is home to many animals. Tennis is
five minutes away, and bicycles are loaned
to guests. Children welcome. $55.

El Presidio Bed and Breakfast
297 North Main Street, 85701
(602) 623-6151

A Victorian adobe, this inn is a splendid
example of American-Territorial style and
is listed on the National Register of
Historic Places. Close to downtown and
within walking distance of the best restaurants, museums, and shopping. Guests
enjoy true southwestern charm in spacious
suites, two with kitchens that open onto
large courtyards and gardens, fountains,
and lush floral displays. A tranquil oasis
with the ambiance of Old Mexico. Three-
star rating in the Mobile Travel Guide,
1991, 1992.

Host: Patti Toci
Rooms: 4 (PB) $85-105
Full Breakfast
Credit Cards: None
Notes: 2, 5, 9, 10, 11, 12, 14

Ford's Bed and Breakfast
Old Pueblo Homestays
P. O. Box 13603, 85732
(800) 333-9RSO

A warm welcome awaits you at this non-
smoking, air-conditioned home situated in
a residential cul-de-sac on Tucson's northeastern side. Guests enjoy a bird's-eye
view of the mountains from their own private patio. Suite consists of two bedrooms,
small sitting room with TV, refrigerator,
private bath, and separate entrance.
Expanded continental breakfast served.
Visit Saguaro Monument East, Sabino
Canyon, Colossal Cave, and scenic drives.
Minimum stay is two nights. Children over
12. $50.

6 Pets welcome; 7 Smoking allowed; 8 Children welcome; 9 Social drinking allowed; 10 Tennis available; 11
Swimming available; 12 Golf available; 13 Skiing available; 14 May be booked through travel agents.

Fort Escalante

Old Pueblo Homestays
P. O. Box 13603, 85732
(800) 333-9RSO

A mile from Sahuaro National Monument, this French Chateau-styled home offers you a breathtaking, unobstructed view of the beautiful Sonoran Desert. Guest quarters feature a furnished livingroom with a TV, satellite, VCR, radio and phone, full bath, separate bedroom with a double bed, and a sofa that will turn into a king-size bed or two twin beds. Also available in the main house is a bedroom decorated in blue with a king-size bed. Smoking limited to the patio. No pets. Children over 12. $45-50.

Katy's Hacienda

Old Pueblo Homestays
P. O. Box 13603, 85732
(800) 333-9RSO

Charming home filled with antiques. Hostess entertains with home privileges. Colorful, restful back yard. A choice breakfast is served. Within walking distance of Park Mall, theaters,and many fine restaurants. Close to bus line. One room with private bath. Resident dog. Minimum stay is two nights. Children over 12. $45.

La Casita

Old Pueblo Homestays
P. O. Box 13603, 85732
(800) 333-9RSO

Town house set in lush desert growth area. Hostess is a former travel agent. One room with a king-size waterbed and private bath. Pool adjacent to the house for enjoyment in the hot summer, and another pool is heated during the winter. Jacuzzi is heated year-round. Continental breakfast. Near La Paloma, Vantana Canyons, and resort golf courses. Minimum stay is two nights. $50.

Las Naranjas

Old Pueblo Homestays
P. O. Box 13603, 85732
(800) 333-9RSO

Restored Spanish Colonial circa 1900 is conveniently situated in the West University area close to Fourth Avenue and city bus lines. The Rebecca Room and the Canopy Room feature exquisite antiques and private baths. Enjoy the working fireplace, covered front porch, breakfast room with large bay window, laundry and kitchen facilities, and Edgar, the bed and breakfast cat. Continental breakfast features lots of homemade goodies, and the hostess stocks a cookie jar full of homemade chocolate chip cookies. Smoking allowed; children and some pets allowed. $40-50.

La Posada Del Valle

1640 North Campbell Avenue, 85719
(602) 795-3840

An elegant 1920s inn nestled in the heart of the city with five guest rooms with private baths and outside entrances. Mature orange trees perfume the air as guests enjoy a gourmet breakfast and sip tea each afternoon on the patio overlooking the garden.

Hosts: Charles and Debbi Bryant
Rooms: 5 (PB) $87.50-125
Full Breakfast weekends; Continental Breakfast
week-days

La Posada Del Valle

Credit Cards: A, B
Notes: 2, 4, 5, 8 (over 12), 9, 10, 11, 12, 14

The Lodge on the Desert

306 North Alvernon, 85711
(602) 325-3366; (800) 456-5634
FAX (602) 327-5834

A small resort hotel providing the finest in food and accommodations. The lodge has been under the same family ownership for over 50 years. Close to golf, tennis, and shopping. One-half hour from Arizona-Sonora Living Desert Museum, Old Tucson movie location, Coronado National Forest. Three miles from the University of Arizona.

Host: Schuyler W. Lininger
Rooms: 40 (PB) $48-135
Continental Breakfast
Credit Cards: A, B, C, D, E, F
Notes: 2, 3, 4, 5, 6 (call), 7, 8, 9, 10, 11, 12, 14

Mesquite Retreat

Old Pueblo Homestays
P. O. Box 13603, 85732
(800) 333-9RSO

Offering desert quiet near the base of Mount Lemmon, yet easy access to the city—five minutes to fine dining. This spacious ranch-style home is decorated with a blend of traditional and many antiques. Two guest rooms feature antique beds and share a bath. Living area shared with host has TV and fireplace. Mountain view patio with pool and spa. Full or light breakfast served. Resident dog. Children over 12. $50.

Mi Casa Su Casa #22

P. O. Box 950, Tempe, 85280-0950
(602) 990-0682; (800) 456-0682

The Catalina foothills are behind this ranch house with abundant wildlife and trails to the Pima Canyon leading from the back yard. Bedrooms are in a private guest wing. One room has a pair of twin beds, sitting area, private full bath and a view of the mountains. Another room is smaller and also has a pair of twin beds, small TV, and private hall bath. $30-50.

Mi Casa Su Casa #142

P. O. Box 950, Tempe, 85280-0950
(602) 990-0682; (800) 456-0682

Guests have called this architect-designed 1,100-square-foot guest cottage a home away from home. Near 127 acres of natural desert. Dining room, kitchen, bedroom with two twin beds, private phone, washer/dryer, double doors leading to a pool. Hostess fixes breakfast first thing in the morning; afterward, guests help themselves. Minimum stay is three nights. $65-75.

Mi Casa Su Casa #161

P. O. Box 950, Tempe, 85280-0950
(602) 990-0682; (800) 456-0682

Two-story Mediterranean style town house is near Colossal Cave, Sabino Canyon, Saguaro National Monument, and downtown Tucson. First-floor guest room has queen-size bed, large closet, TV, and connecting bath with a shower. The second-floor suite has a queen bed, a sitting area with a queen sofa bed, full bath in between the suite and the host's bedroom, cable TV, and a phone. Two pools available. Full breakfast with homemade breads and gourmet coffee. $35-55.

Mi Casa Su Casa #169

P. O. Box 950, Tempe, 85280-0950
(602) 990-0682; (800) 456-0682

This two-story Mediterranean style town house looks out on a large, grassy mall with pine trees. The home has contemporary, Oriental, and antique decor. Near Colossal Cave, Sabino Canyon, Saguaro National Monument East, and downtown

Tucson. First floor guest room has a queen-size bed, large closet, TV, radio, and connecting bath with a shower. The second floor suite has a queen-size bed, sitting area, and a full bath that connects between the suite and the host's bedroom. Two swimming pools available. Breakfast features homemade breads with gourmet coffee. No pets. Children over 14. Airport pickup available. Resident cat. $45-55.

shops, restaurants, and bohemian atmosphere, as well as the University of Arizona and the University Medical Center. One room has a roomy bedroom/sitting room with a queen bed and a private bath. Another room is on the second floor and has a canopied double bed and shared hall bath with the hostess. Continental breakfast. Light kitchen privileges, and laundry facilities available. $35-50.

Mi Casa Su Casa #277

P. O. Box 950, Tempe, 85280-0950
(602) 990-0682; (800) 456-0682

Handsome two-level home in the Catalina Foothills is situated near Sabina Canyon with its spectacular mountain tram tour. Four guest rooms are decorated with American antiques and southwestern furnishings, and all have their own entrance coming from the pool-patio area. Private and shared baths. Continental and full breakfast. $55-65.

Mi Casa Su Casa #304

P. O. Box 950, Tempe, 85280-0950
(602) 990-0682; (800) 456-0682

Luxury town house in a beautifully landscaped green area is one block from malls, theatres, good restaurants, and the University of Arizona. One room has a king bed, TV, phone, and a connecting full bath. Another room is moderate size, has twin beds, TV, phone, and shares full hall bath. Pool, spa, and tennis courts on complex. Complimentary refreshments and continental breakfast. $60-70.

Mi Casa Su Casa #316

P. O. Box 950, Tempe, 85280-0950
(602) 990-0682; (800) 456-0682

Spanish Colonial built in 1900 is close to eclectic Fourth Avenue, known for its

Mi Casa Su Casa #320

P. O. Box 950, Tempe, 85280-0950
(602) 990-0682; (800) 456-0682

Large ranch house situated in the Catalina Mountain foothills preserves the desert setting surrounding this upscale neighborhood and is five minutes from Sabino Canyon. One room has a queen bed, TV, and private bath, and another room has two twin beds, TV, and a private bath. Handicapped facilities available. Continental breakfast. Minimum stay is two nights. $55-60.

Mi Casa Su Casa #324

P. O. Box 950, Tempe, 85280-0950
(602) 990-0682; (800) 456-0682

This homestay is in a quiet neighborhood in the Catalina foothills. The stucco guest house is in a contemporary southwest style and has a private entrance. Two rooms adjoin a small kitchen area and spacious bathroom that opens onto the pool/patio area. Electric heat and air conditioning provide climate control, and two guest rooms in the main house offer a queen-size bed, a view of the Catalina Mountains, and a pair of twin beds with a glass door leading to the pool and patio. Answering machine, computer/printer, and bicycles are available for guests to use. Full, self-catered breakfast. Smoking outside only. Children over five. Minimum stay is two nights. $65-85, seasonal rates.

NOTES: Credit cards accepted: A Master Card; B Visa; C American Express; D Discover Card; E Diner's Club; F Other; 2 Personal Checks accepted; 3 Lunch available; 4 Dinner available; 5 Open all year;

Mi Casa Su Casa #326

P. O. Box 950, Tempe, 85280-0950
(602) 990-0682; (800) 456-0682

Contemporary stucco home built in 1990 is
in the mountain foothills in a quiet residential neighborhood. One room has a king
bed, or two twin beds with an adjoining
private full bath. Another room is available
for guests in the same party and has a double or queen sofa bed. Both rooms have
private use of the livingroom with a TV
and an adjoining dining room. Neighborhood has tennis courts, heated swimming
pool, Jacuzzi, health club, massages, and an
eighteen-hole golf course. Full breakfast.
Handicapped facilities available. Hosts are
nonsmoking, but guests are welcome to
smoke. $75.

Mi Casa Su Casa #336

P. O. Box 950, Tempe, 85280-0950
(602) 990-0682; (800) 456-0682

This home is a picturesque mixture of
Santa Fe Pueblo Indian and Mexican influences. Situated on an acre lot in a quiet residential neighborhood, this home was
where Clark Gable lived in the early 1940s.
All bedrooms have king-size beds and TVs,
and one room offers a private bath and a
fireplace. Continental plus breakfast. No
smoking. Children over six. $40-70.

O'Desert Dream

825 Via Lucitas, 85718
(602) 297-1220

Designed to complement its Catalina
Mountains setting, this adobe ranch-style
home commands a spectacular view of the
city in the valley below. The Desert
Museum, Sabino Canyon, Pima Air
Museum, and the San Xavier Mission are
but a few of the not-to-be-missed nearby
sights. You are welcome to use the kitchen
for light snacks and the spacious patio for
relaxing.

Hosts: Ken and Nell Putnam
Rooms: 1 (PB) $40
Continental Breakfast
Credit Cards: None
Notes: 9

The Open Door

Old Pueblo Homestays
P. O. Box 13603, 85732
(800) 333-9RSO

If you're looking for just plain, old-fashioned hospitality, this is it. A nice view of
the mountains from the bedrooms and a
very special brand of friendliness.
Conveniently situated with easy access to
airport. Seven miles from the University of
Arizona. Close to bus lines and restaurants.
Full breakfast. Resident dog and cat.
Minimum stay is two nights. $40.

Peppertree Bed and Breakfast Inn

724 East University Boulevard, 85719
(602) 622-7167

A 1905 Victorian Territorial house just two
blocks west of the main gates of the
University of Arizona. The house, which is
furnished with family antiques, is within
walking distance of the university, museums, shops, restaurants, theaters, and
downtown. There are five guest rooms, one
of which has a private bath. The other four
guest rooms are situated in two guest houses across the flower-filled patio. Each guest
house contains a liv-ingroom, dining room,
full kitchen with washer/dryer, and private
patio. This situation is ideal for families or
couples traveling together. Your hostess is
a published cookbook author and is
renowned for her gourmet breakfasts and
afternoon tea.

Host: Marjorie Martin
Rooms: 5 (1 PB; 4 SB) $65-80
Full Breakfast
Credit Cards: A, B
Notes: 2, 5, 8, 9, 14

---

6 Pets welcome; 7 Smoking allowed; 8 Children welcome; 9 Social drinking allowed; 10 Tennis available; 11
Swimming available; 12 Golf available; 13 Skiing available; 14 May be booked through travel agents.

Prickly Pear Casa

Old Pueblo Homestays
P. O. Box 13603, 85732
(800) 333-9RSO

Your hostess from England and her Ohio-born husband welcome you to their spacious ranch-style house on four desert acres. All rooms have cable TV and share a large hall bath, plus two powder rooms. Enjoy the view of the Catalina Mountains or relax by the pool. Close to fine dining, shopping, and Catalina State Park. Two cats and two dogs in residence. Smoking outside. Choice of king, queen, or twin beds. No children. $65-75.

Quail's Nest

Old Pueblo Homestays
P. O. Box 13603, 85732
(800) 333-9RSO

A comfortable midtown home in a quiet residential neighborhood. Two rooms, one with private bath, one with shared bath. Full breakfast is served on the patio in warm weather. Easy access to sightseeing, University of Arizona Medical Center, shopping, golf, and tennis. Close to bus lines. Minimum stay is two nights. Children over four. $45.

Quail's Vista

Old Pueblo Homestays
P. O. Box 13603, 85732
(800) 333-9RSO

Panoramic view of the Catalina Mountains makes this Santa Fe-style, rammed-earth solar structure home give guests the feeling of true desert living. Guest room has a queen-sized bed with private full hall bath. Swim-stream spa, and hostess' membership at private country club with golf, tennis, and aerobics available to guests. Continental breakfast. Smoking outside. No pets or children. $60.

Redbud House

Old Pueblo Homestays
P. O. Box 13603, 85732
(800) 333-9RSO

In a quiet neighborhood within walking distance to parks, shops, and good restaurants, as well as transportation. Cozy atmosphere with mountain views, use of livingroom with fireplace. Two cheerful bedrooms with private bath and TV. Full or light breakfast offered. Use of barbecue, patio, books, games, and bicycles. Minimum stay is two nights. $45.

Rimrock West

Old Pueblo Homestays
P. O. Box 13603, 85732
(800) 333-9RSO

A southwestern hacienda of two talented artists situated on twenty acres in the foothills of the Santa Catalina Mountains, two miles from city limits. Two rooms in main house with private baths open onto courtyard with fountain. Separate adobe guest house near pool area has livingroom, full kitchen, bedroom. Breakfast is informal and plentiful, including freshly baked muffins and interesting conversation. Minimum stay is two nights. $85-105.

Roadrunner

Old Pueblo Homestays
P. O. Box 13603, 85732
(800) 333-9RSO

Stay in a home with a spectacular view of the mountains. The great room provides reading material, TV, and piano for guests. All rooms are light and cheerful, tastefully furnished with antiques and Oriental rugs. Private baths, one with Jacuzzi. Full gourmet breakfast with a special of cracked broiled whole-wheat served with delicious desert honey and syrup. Four rooms available. $45-90.

NOTES: Credit cards accepted: A Master Card; B Visa; C American Express; D Discover Card; E Diner's Club; F Other; 2 Personal Checks accepted; 3 Lunch available; 4 Dinner available; 5 Open all year;

The SunCatcher

105 North Avenida Javalina, 85748
(602) 885-0883; (800) 835-8012

Our rooms are named for and decorated in the style of the world's best hotels; The Connaught, London; The Regent, Hong Kong; The Oriental, Bangkok; and The Four Seasons, Chicago. Guests enjoy complimentary newspapers, fresh roses, TV/VCRs, fine linens, and bath soaps at the SunCatcher. Gourmet breakfast, afternoon poolside hors d'oeuvres, and bottled waters refresh guests, and our location offers unsurpassed views of both the Catalina and Rincon Mountains.

Hosts: Dave Williams
Rooms: 4 (PB) $110-130 plus tax
Full Breakfast
Credit Cards: A, B, C
Notes: 2, 4, 5, 9, 10, 11, 12, 14

Sunnyside

Old Pueblo Homestays
P. O. Box 13603, 85732
(800) 333-9RSO

In the foothills of the Santa Catalina Mountains. Enjoy our sumptuous continental plus breakfast while watching desert birds flock to our feeders. All rooms have their own TV and private bath, and beds range from a pair of twins to a queen or king. Top resorts and Sabino Canyon tram tour five minutes away. Minimum stay is two nights. Smoking outside. Children over nine. $60.

The Swedish Guest House Bed and Breakfast

941 West Calle Dadivoso, 85704
(602) 742-6490

Situated in Tucson at the beginning of the Catalina Foothills, the guest house offers spacious 1,100-square-foot guest quarters. Fireplace, phone with private number, TV, radio, air conditioning, parking in garage, own patio overlooking the swimming pool. Plush bathroom has bathtub, extra large shower. Wheelchair accessible. Nearby are golf courses, hiking, horseback riding. Eighteen minutes from the University of Arizona. Hosts are transplanted Swedes from Stockholm, Sweden, and Tucson residents since 1977. Smoking outside only. Weekly rates available. Valkommen!

Hosts: Lars and Florence Ejrup
Guest house: 1 (PB) $85
Full Breakfast on weekends; Self-serve weekdays
Credit Cards: None
Closed July
Notes: 9, 11, 14

Timrod

Old Pueblo Homestays
P. O. Box 13603, 85732
(800) 333-9RSO

Desert living at its best. Beautiful home set in a lovely rural area with mountain vistas. A self-contained four-room suite. Private bath, full kitchen, separate entrance. Hostess stocks refrigerator with breakfast foods. Second suite with two bedrooms and bath. Pool is heated at additional charge. Pottery lessons available by hostess. Resident dog. Minimum stay is two nights. Children over 15. $60-80.

Travelers Rest

Old Pueblo Homestays
P. O. Box 13603, 85732
(800) 333-9RSO

A neighborhood park surrounded by pleasant homes is the setting for this inviting offering. One room with twin beds, private bath, and separate entrance. Private patio for relaxing. Close to shopping, restaurants, churches, theaters, and doctors. Neighborhood pool available late spring and summer. Three miles to University of Arizona. Resident dog. Minimum stay is two nights. $40.

6 Pets welcome; 7 Smoking allowed; 8 Children welcome; 9 Social drinking allowed; 10 Tennis available; 11 Swimming available; 12 Golf available; 13 Skiing available; 14 May be booked through travel agents.

Tucson Mountain Hideaway

Old Pueblo Homestays
P. O. Box 13603, 85732
(800) 333-9RSO

This home offers a relaxed, friendly atmosphere. Three rooms with shared bath. Queen bedroom with private bath. Hostess sets out a very special continental breakfast. Easy access to desert and mountain trails, community center, downtown Tucson, and the University of Arizona. Share family room, TV, and pool. Minimum stay is two nights. Children over 12. $40-50.

Vista Montana

Old Pueblo Homestays
P. O. Box 13603, 85732
(800) 333-9RSO

An unobstructed view of the Santa Catalina Mountains beckons from this charming private home in the foothills. The luxurious bedroom has twin beds, phone, and TV. Adjoining bath has private access to an enclosed patio with lap pool that can be used most of the year. Luscious breakfast of your choice is served in the shade of a ramada by the pool. This adobe brick home is 15 minutes from the University of Arizona, and close to shopping centers, outstanding art galleries, and restaurants. Resident dog. Minimum stay is two nights. $65.

WICKENBURG

Mi Casa Su Casa #263

P. O. Box 950, Tempe, 85280-0950
(602) 990-0682; (800) 456-0682

Historic ranch with ten acres of land offers spectacular views of the Vulture Peak and Bradshaw Mountains. Private guest wing has two large bedrooms that share a bath.

Rental horses in the vicinity and inexpensive horse boarding available. Tennis and golf available in nearby resorts. Heated pool. Full breakfast. $60.

Mi Casa Su Casa #1626

P. O. Box 950, Tempe, 85280-0950
(602) 990-0682; (800) 456-0682

Homesteaded at the turn of the century and a guest ranch since 1926, this working ranch is listed on both the state and national historic registers. The handmade adobe buildings are snuggled close by the Hassayampa River, and the food is worth a letter home. Three meals a day are included, and guests can choose from a variety of lodging choices. Horseback riding, heated pool. Minimum stay is two nights. Visa and MasterCard accepted. $95-355.

WILLIAMS

The Johnstonian Bed and Breakfast

321 West Sheridan Avenue, 86046
(602) 635-2178

As you cross the threshold of the century-old, two-story Victorian home, your hosts will welcome you into a relaxed family atmosphere in keeping with the same spirit of hospitality that pervaded the Victorian era. Your senses will transport you to the turn of the century when you see the quaint rooms furnished with antiques and smell fresh bread baking. Enjoy breakfast in the dining room at the round oak table.

Hosts: Bill and Pidge Johnston
Rooms: 4 (1 PB; 1 SB) $50-65
Full Breakfast
Credit Cards: None
Notes: 2, 5, 8, 9, 13

NOTES: Credit cards accepted: A Master Card; B Visa; C American Express; D Discover Card; E Diner's Club; F Other; 2 Personal Checks accepted; 3 Lunch available; 4 Dinner available; 5 Open all year;

Mi Casa Su Casa #1631

P. O. Box 950, Tempe, 85280-0950
(602) 990-0682; (800) 456-0682

This two-story inn is situated conveniently in the center of Williams, two blocks from the Grand Canyon Railroad station. Each of the nine rooms is decorated differently. Continental-plus breakfast. $45-75.

YUMA

Mi Casa Su Casa #110

P. O. Box 950, Tempe, 85280-0950
(602) 990-0682; (800) 456-0682

Handsome old adobe-style home decorates its guest room with fine antiques. Breakfast is served on fine china, crystal, and table linens, and hostess is a native of Yuma. Pool. $55.

6 Pets welcome; 7 Smoking allowed; 8 Children welcome; 9 Social drinking allowed; 10 Tennis available; 11 Swimming available; 12 Golf available; 13 Skiing available; 14 May be booked through travel agents.

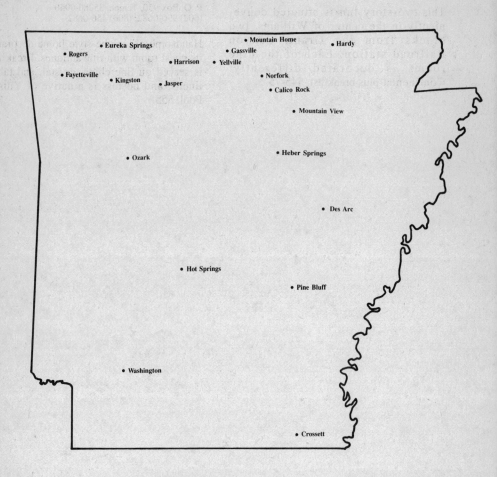

ARKANSAS

Arkansas

CALICO ROCK

Arkansas and Ozarks Bed and Breakfast ACR01

HC 61, Box 72, 72519
(501) 297-8764; (501) 297-8211

Contemporary home in a secluded woodland setting offers a full delicious breakfast, large family room, satellite TV and games, a hot tub in the sunroom, and pool table. Beautiful stained-glass creations by the hostess and collectibles from around the world make this a delightful setting. Garage parking is available, and children are welcome. $35.

Arkansas and Ozarks Bed and Breakfast ACR02

HC 61, Box 72, 72519
(501) 297-8764; (501) 297-8211

Two log cabins surrounded by the Ozark National Forest, decorated with the past in mind but offering modern comforts. A sleeping loft in each cabin sleeps two; downstairs has a Hide-a-bed and wood stove in the living area, kitchen and bath. The cabins are unhosted for maximum privacy but provided with coffee, milk, cereal, and homemade fruit bread. Relax on the front porch and enjoy a panoramic view of river, forest and ever-present wildlife. Only minutes from town, the Ozark Fold Center, Blanchard Springs Caverns, antique shops, and live music shows or dinner theaters. $42.50.

Arkansas and Ozarks Bed and Breakfast ACR03

HC 61, Box 72, 72519
(501) 297-8764; (501) 297-8211

Original 1923 hotel within walking distance of two boat docks, one block from Main Street. Continental breakfast provided. Furnishings include antiques and collectibles of the 1920s. Handmade jewelry shop on premises. $25-45.

Arkansas and Ozarks Bed and Breakfast ACR04

HC 61, Box 72, 72519
(501) 297-8764; (501) 297-8211

Forest home lodge is perched on a 300-foot bluff overlooking the beautiful, clear White River. A large country breakfast, including homemade breads and a hearty main dish, is served on a deck outside your room. The contemporary home, decorated with stained glass, has a large three-keyboard organ, satellite TV, and video games in the spacious living room for the guests' enjoyment. The Ozark Folk Center, Blanchard Caverns, craft shops, antique shops, and hiking trails are only minutes away. $35.

CLARKSVILLE

The May House

101 Railroad Avenue, 72830
(501) 754-6851

NOTES: Credit cards accepted: A Master Card; B Visa; C American Express; D Discover Card; E Diner's Club; F Other; 2 Personal Checks accepted; 3 Lunch available; 4 Dinner available; 5 Open all year; 6 Pets welcome; 7 Smoking allowed; 8 Children welcome; 9 Social drinking allowed; 10 Tennis available; 11 Swimming available; 12 Golf available; 13 Skiing available; 14 May be booked through travel agents.

The May House

Lovely Victorian home overlooking downtown historic Clarksville, offering turn-of-the-century charm. Features spacious bedrooms with beautiful antiques, finest amenities, and the Ozark Ritz Tea Room. Situated on I-40 at Highway 64 and scenic Highway 21 (the gateway to the Ozarks), the area is a mountain lovers' paradise.

Host: Pat Moody
Rooms: 4 (2 PB; 2 SB) $55-65
Full Breakfast
Credit Cards: A, B
Notes: 2, 3, 4, 5, 8, 10, 11, 12

CROSSETT

The Trieschmann House Bed and Breakfast

707 Cedar, 71635
(501) 364-7592

Built in 1903 for an official of the Crossett Company, this lovely bed and breakfast is nine miles from the Felsenthal Refuge for good fishing and hunting. Front porch with wicker swing and furniture; common room with a wood-burning stove, cable television, and games. Full breakfast is served in the kitchen, and the home is furnished with furniture from the past. We invite you to go back in time with us.

Hosts: Pat and Herman Owens
Rooms: 3 (1 PB; 2 SB) $40-45
Full Breakfast
Credit Cards: A, B
Notes: 2, 5, 12

DES ARC

Arkansas and Ozarks Bed and Breakfast ADA01

HC 61, Box 72, Calico Rock, 72519
(501) 297-8764; (501) 297-8211

Antiques and collectibles decorate this four-square Colonial Revival home recorded on National Register of Historic Places. Situated 14 miles north of I-40 half-way between Memphis and Little Rock, and only two blocks from the White River. Wildlife management areas, lakes, bayous, and duck hunting are all nearby. Private suite, private or shared bath, and an unhosted garage apartment with stocked breakfast makings. Full breakfast is served with advance notice. No smoking. $32.50-40 single.

EUREKA SPRINGS

Bridgeford House Bed and Breakfast

263 Spring Street, 72632
(501) 253-7853

Nestled in the heart of Eureka Springs' historic residential district, Bridgeford House is an 1884 Victorian delight. Outside are shady porches that invite you to pull up a chair and watch the world go by on Spring Street. Each room has a private entrance, antique furnishings, and private bath. Fresh coffee in your suite, a selection of fine teas, color TV, air conditioning, and a mouth-watering breakfast.

Hosts: Michael and Denise McDonald
Rooms: 4 (PB) $70-90
Full Breakfast
Credit Cards: A, B
Notes: 2, 5, 7 (outside), 9, 10, 11, 12, 14

NOTES: Credit cards accepted: A Master Card; B Visa; C American Express; D Discover Card; E Diner's Club; F Other; 2 Personal Checks accepted; 3 Lunch available; 4 Dinner available; 5 Open all year;

Brownstone Inn

75 Hillside, 72632
(501) 235-7505

The inn was built in 1890 and for 70 years served as the site of the Ozarks Water Co. The limestone structure maintains the original facade, while the interior has been converted to two large suites and two smaller units. All are decorated in unique Victorian fashion filled with many antiques. The inn sits directly across from the ES&NA Railroad and 1880s steam train lunch and dinner excursion. The inn is situated in a cool valley surrounded by a brick patio on the ground level and wood terrace for the upper level.

Host: Connie
Rooms: 4 (PB) $75-85
Full Breakfast
Credit Cards: A, B
Notes: 2, 4, 6, 7, 8, 9

Crescent Cottage Inn

211 Spring Street, 72632
(501) 253-6022

Famous Painted Lady on the National Register of Historic Places, this Victorian House was built in 1881 for the first Arkansas governor after the Civil War. Two veranda porches overlook mountains for the best view in town. Two sleeping

Crescent Cottage Inn

areas have separate double Jacuzzi spas and their own verandas. One two-room suite is also available. All accommodations have private baths. Walk to town on historic loop lined with maples and flowers. Superb antiques throughout this home, and truly memorable breakfasts. Located near the trolley stop.

Hosts: Ralph and Phyllis Becker
Rooms: 4 (PB) $65-95
Full Breakfast
Credit Cards: None
Notes: 2, 8 (over 15), 9, 11, 12

Dairy Hollow House

515 Spring Street, 72632
(501) 253-7444; (800) 562-8650

Welcome to Dairy Hollow House, a tiny, irresistible country inn and restaurant nestled in a serene, wooded valley. Just one mile from Eureka's historic downtown, there are two houses, each with the prettiest rooms and suites imaginable. Waiting for you are fireplaces, landscaped hot tub, fresh flowers, regional antiques, and Ozark wildflower soaps. Uncle Ben's Best Inn of the Year, 1989, 1990, and 1991 and Mobile Two-Star inn. There is also a murder mystery weekend four times a year. The restaurant serves a six-course "Nouveau 'Zarks Haute Country Cuisine" dinner each night at 7:00 p.m. Members of Independent Innkeepers' Association.

Hosts: Crescent Dragonwagon and Ned Shank
Rooms: 6 (PB) $115-165
Full Breakfast
Credit Cards: A, B, C, D, E
Notes: 2, 4, 5, 8, 9, 10, 11, 12, 14

Heart of the Hills Inn

5 Summit Street, 72632
(501) 253-7468

This historic home was built in the 1800s and offers three rooms with air conditioning, refrigerator, TV. Private baths, tubs with showers, and one suite has a two-person Jacuzzi with a shower. There is also

6 Pets welcome; 7 Smoking allowed; 8 Children welcome; 9 Social drinking allowed; 10 Tennis available; 11 Swimming available; 12 Golf available; 13 Skiing available; 14 May be booked through travel agents.

one completely equipped cottage with deck overlooking the woods. Eureka Springs is noted for its Passion play, outstanding restaurants, fine museums, and trolley system.

Host: Jan Jacobs Weber
Rooms: 3 (PB) $60-99
Cottage 1 (PB)
Full Breakfast
Credit Cards: A, B
Notes: 2, 8, 9, 10, 11, 14

The Heartstone Inn and Cottages

35 Kings Highway, 72632
(501) 253-8916

Nine rooms and two charming guest cottages in historic district of Eureka Springs. Turn-of-the-century charm, plus modern conveniences. Antiques, air conditioning, private entrances, limited smoking.

Hosts: Iris and Bill Simantel
Rooms: 9 (PB) $58-105
Cottages: 2 (PB)
Full Breakfast
Minimum stay holidays: 3 nights; weekends: 2 nights
Credit Cards: A, B, C
Closed Christmas
Notes: 2, 9, 11, 12, 14

The Heartstone Inn and Cottages

Ozark Mountain Country Bed and Breakfast A301

Box 295, Branson, Missouri, 65616
(800) 321-8594

This gardener's cottage is located in the historic district. It offers privacy, a kitchen, livingroom, skylights, antique furnishings, a double iron bed, bath with a tub. No breakfast is served. Minimum stay is two nights. $65-75.

Ozark Mountain Country Bed and Breakfast A302

Box 295, Branson, Missouri, 65616
(800) 321-8594

This 1891 Queen Anne mansion offers 12,000 square feet of antique furnishings. Four guest rooms and two suites offer private and shared baths. Snacks are served and an indoor hot tub is available. No breakfast is served, but lunch is included at The Victorian Sampler. (Winter rates do not include lunch.) $65-125.

Ozark Mountain Country Bed and Breakfast A315

Box 295, Branson, Missouri, 65616
(800) 321-8594

These luxury Victorian accommodations include seven suites with private baths, fireplaces, individually controlled heat/air, TV's, VCR's, and continental breakfast baskets delivered to your suite in the morning. No smoking. $125-145.

Ozark Mountain Country Bed and Breakfast A316

Box 295, Branson, Missouri, 65616
(800) 321-8594

NOTES: Credit cards accepted: A Master Card; B Visa; C American Express; D Discover Card; E Diner's Club; F Other; 2 Personal Checks accepted; 3 Lunch available; 4 Dinner available; 5 Open all year;

The Pearl Tatman House gives guests exclusive use of 1,500 square feet, including fully equipped kitchen, three bedrooms, cable TV upstairs and downstairs, and an antique claw footed tub. Breakfast baskets are delivered to guests for an extra $10. Available all year. $109.

Ozark Mountain Country Bed and Breakfast A317

Box 295, Branson, Missouri, 65616
(800) 321-8594

Miss Priscilla's offers three luxurious suites with antiques, TVs, and microwave ovens. The retreat sleeps two in a four room suite that has a kitchen, double bed, hand-painted murals. An additional suite sleeps four, offers five rooms, and an equipped kitchen and Murphy bed. The Somewhere in Time suite sleeps two people, and offers three rooms with a claw foot tub, brass bed, small refrigerator. Open all year. $85-95.

Ozark Mountain Country Bed and Breakfast A318

Box 295, Branson, Missouri, 65616
(800) 321-8594

The Ridgeway House is a classic 1908 home lovingly restored and beautifully decorated. Situated on a quiet Eureka Springs street, just a five minute walk downtown. Antiques, cable TV/ VCR in the living room, full breakfast served in the dining room, and evening snacks before bedtime. Three upstairs rooms, with a complete kitchen, queen-size bed, private bath with a shower. Two room suite with queen and twin beds and a private bath and shower also available. A suite with a private entrance, bedroom, livingroom, kitchen, bath, and TV is also available. No pets. Smoking outside only. $65-80.

RedBud Manor

7 Kings Highway, 72632
(501) 253-9649

This country Victorian bed and breakfast was built by Grover Cleveland in 1891. Furnished with antiques and situated on the historic loop, we offer off-street parking, air conditioning, private baths, and private entrances.

Host: Shari Bozeman
Rooms: 3 (PB) $85 plus tax
Full Breakfast
Credit Cards: A, B
Notes: 2, 5, 7 (restricted), 9, 14

Singleton House and Cottage

Scandia Bed and Breakfast Inn

P. O. Box 166, Highway 62 West, 72632
(501) 253-8922; (800) 523-8922

Set in the pines on the quiet side of town, Scandia offers quaint 1940s cottages featuring designer linens and draperies. Elegant breakfasts are served daily in the breakfast room where you will find the tables festively adorned with fresh flowers, china, silver, and folded linen napkins. A romantic hot tub gazebo under the dogwoods awaits at any hour. Evening room service and boat excursions on beautiful Beaver Lake are optional. Water-skiing,

6 Pets welcome; 7 Smoking allowed; 8 Children welcome; 9 Social drinking allowed; 10 Tennis available; 11 Swimming available; 12 Golf available; 13 Skiing available; 14 May be booked through travel agents.

canoeing, horseback riding, wedding services, honeymoon suite for two with Jacuzzi, and fantasy grapevine and ivy arbor are all available for guests to enjoy.

Hosts: Cynthia Barnes and Marty Lavine
Rooms: 7 (PB) $65-95
Full Breakfast
Credit Cards: A, B, C, D
Notes: 2, 4, 5, 7 (limited), 8, 9, 10, 11, 12, 14

Singleton House and Cottage

11 Singleton Street, 72632
(501) 253-9111

This country Victorian home is an old-fashioned place with a touch of magic. Each guest room is whimsically decorated with a delightful collection of antiques and folk art. Breakfast is served on the balcony overlooking the fantasy wildflower garden below, with its goldfish pond and curious birdhouse collection. A honeymoon cottage with a Jacuzzi at a separate location is also available. Situated in the historic district. Guests park and walk a secluded pathway to Eureka's shops and cafes.

Host: Barbara Gavron
Rooms: 5 (4 PB; 1 SB) $55-65
Cottage: 1 (PB) $95
Full Breakfast
Credit Cards: A, B, C, D
Notes: 2, 5, 8, 9, 14

Sunnyside Bed and Breakfast Inn

5 Ridgeway, 72632
(501) 253-6638

Come stroll back to the special Victorian Queen Anne home late in the year of 1883. Enjoy Grandmother's old lace linens on her beds of antique cherry wood. Enjoy a full four-course breakfast at Grandmother's table laden with elegant silver and the finest Haviland china, surrounded by her deep purple needlepoint chairs.

Hosts: Jamie Eccleston and Mary Capps
Rooms: 5 (PB) $80-200
Full Breakfast
Credit Cards: A, B
Notes: 2, 5, 14

EVERTON

Ozark Mountain Country Bed and Breakfast A309

Box 295, Branson, Missouri, 65616
(800) 321-8594

This early 1900s stone home is a converted corn-cob pipe factory. The three guest rooms with double beds are decorated with antiques. Chicken dinner is available. Children welcome. $42.

Hill Avenue Bed and Breakfast

FAYETTEVILLE

Hill Avenue Bed and Breakfast

131 South Hill Avenue, 72701
(501) 444-0865

This two-story older home in a residential neighborhood is the only registered bed and breakfast in Fayetteville. It is near the University of Arkansas and the town square. Guests will find comfortable, non-smoking accommodations. A hearty country breakfast is served in the dining room or on the large porch.

Hosts: Dale and Cecelia Thompson
Rooms: 3 (SB) $40
Full Breakfast
Credit Cards: None
Notes: 5

NOTES: Credit cards accepted: A Master Card; B Visa; C American Express; D Discover Card; E Diner's Club; F Other; 2 Personal Checks accepted; 3 Lunch available; 4 Dinner available; 5 Open all year;

Lace and Linen II

1753 Zion Road, Park Lake, Suite A-5, 72703
(501) 443-7517

You are welcome to relax in the living room with a cozy wood-burning fireplace during the winter months, but the lush woodlands overlooking Fayetteville Lake would be a spring and summer delight. The lake is within walking distance. Five miles away is the newly opened Walton Arts Center, donated by the late Sam Walton of Wal-mart Stores. The furnishings in this lovely inn are in delicate pastels, European pieces, and white Victorian wicker. The area is rich in arts and crafts and southern hospitality is everywhere. Fayetteville is the home of the University of Arkansas. Fayetteville.

Host: Patricia Parks
Rooms: 2 (PB) $40
Continental Breakfast
Credit Cards: None
Notes: 5, 7, 9, 10, 11, 12, 14

Oaks Manor

945 Oaks Manor Drive, 72703
(501) 443-5481

Oaks Manor is a brick ranch with white columns, shutters, porches, and a beautiful patio overlooking woodland where squirrels and rabbits play. There is antique English colonial furniture in two bedrooms and the breakfast/dining area, where old china, handmade linens, and silver pieces are used. There is also a private parlor with piano, decorated in Victorian decor. The hostess provides southern hospitality that makes guests feel welcome and comfortable.

Host: Clara Griffith
Rooms: 3 (PB) $40-45
Continental Breakfast
Credit Cards: None
Notes: 5, 7 (limited), 9, 12, 14

GASSVILLE

Arkansas and Ozarks Bed and Breakfast AGV01

HC 61, Box 72, Calico Rock, 72519
(501) 297-8764; (501) 297-8211

This 100-year-old former health lodge has been lovingly restored with added gift shop featuring the hosts' own fine handicrafts. Breakfast is served in the dining room or large, screened front porch. On 39 acres of meadows and woods, it reflects the original lodge in character. Near the White and Buffalo rivers and between Bull Shoals and Norfork dams. An ideal location. No alcoholic beverages. $37.50-40.

HARDY

Arkansas and Ozarks Bed and Breakfast AHA01

HC 61, Box 72, Calico Rock, 72519
(501) 297-8764; (501) 297-8211

This newly renovated stone house used as a boarding house in the depression is only a short walk from handicraft and antique shops and the Spring River. The rock formations in its walls and fireplace provide an interesting background for its antiques, collectibles, and locally handcrafted decor. Music shows, golfing, tennis, horseback riding, and canoeing are available nearby. $45 weekdays; $55 Friday and Saturday.

Olde Stonehouse Bed and Breakfast Inn

511 Main Street, 72542
(501) 856-2983

Native Arkansas stone house with large porches lined with jumbo rocking chairs is comfortably furnished with antiques and features central heat and air, ceiling fans,

6 Pets welcome; 7 Smoking allowed; 8 Children welcome; 9 Social drinking allowed; 10 Tennis available; 11 Swimming available; 12 Golf available; 13 Skiing available; 14 May be booked through travel agents.

queen-size beds, and private baths. One block from Spring River and the shops of old Hardy town. Three country music theaters, golf courses, horseback riding, canoeing, and fishing nearby. Local attractions include Mammoth Spring State Park, Grand Gulf, Evening Shade, Arkansas, and Arkansas Traveller Theater.

Host: Peggy Johnson
Rooms: 5 (PB) $55
Full Breakfast
Credit Cards: A, B, D
Notes: 2, 5, 9, 10, 11, 12, 14

HARRISON

Ozark Mountain Country Bed and Breakfast A311

Box 295, Branson, Missouri, 65616
(800) 321-8594

Located between Harrison and Branson, this bed and breakfast offers "million dollar views from three directions." Open all year, guest accommodation offer a private entrance, sitting area, and TV. Three areas offered. Two double beds are in one room, and 1 double and one single day bed are in the other. The rooms share a bath. Smoking is OK. Children are welcome. $50-55.

Ozark Mountain Country Bed and Breakfast OMC314

Box 295, Branson, Missouri, 65616
(800) 321-8594

This lovely restored Victorian home offers a sitting area for guests, stained glass windows, antique furnishings, big screen TV, and a full breakfast served in a glass-enclosed dining area. Four guest rooms, two of which offer private baths and two of which share a bath, are available, and a cottage with an equipped kitchenette, queen size bed and TV is also available. Children over 12 welcome. No smoking. $58-75.

Ozark Mountain Country Bed and Breakfast A318

Box 295, Branson, Missouri, 65616
(800) 321-8594

This rustic retreat is a log cabin on the side of the mountain, between Green Forest and Berryville. Hiking, swimming, fishing, a cave to explore and spectacular views of the mountain are a few of the recreations available to guests. The accommodations feature a fireplace, living area, double bed, equipped gas kitchen, bath with a shower, naturally warmed water, and breakfast delivered to your cottage. No phones, TV, or electricity. No pre-teenagers. $50.

Oak Tree Inn

HEBER SPRINGS

Oak Tree Inn

Vinegar Hill and 110 West, 72543
(501) 362-7731

An inn for nonsmoking adults, each room with its own private whirlpool bath, five have wood-burning fireplaces. Situated near 45,000-acre Greers Ferry Lake. Dessert and a full breakfast are served daily. Tennis courts, swimming pool, and hot tub. Lakeside condos and river cottage also available.

Host: Freddie Lou Lodge
Rooms: 6 (PB) $70-80
Full Breakfast
Credit Cards: None
Notes: 2, 5, 10, 11, 12, 14

HOT SPRINGS

Dogwood Manor

906 Malvern, 71901
(501) 624-0896

Dogwood Manor has been listed on the National Register of Historic Places. It is a 100-year-old Victorian, with a great array of antique furnishings. Complimentary wine, and breakfast served on a tray in bed by request. Five bedrooms can accommodate up to thirteen people, and each room has a private bath. Our hospitality makes this a home away from home.

Host: Lady Janie Wilson
Rooms: 5 (PB) $45-90
Continental Breakfast
Credit Cards: A

HOT SPRINGS NATIONAL PARK

Vintage Comfort Bed and Breakfast Inn

303 Quapaw, 71901
(501) 623-3258

Vintage Comfort Bed and Breakfast is an elegant, two-story Victorian home with warmth, graciousness, and comfort as its key ingredients. A full breakfast is served, and guests are pampered with old-fashioned hospitality. The inn is centrally located within easy walking distance of Hot Springs Bathhouse Row, art galleries, restaurants, shops, and Hot Springs National Park.

Host: Helen R. Bartlett
Rooms: 4 (PB) $60-75 plus tax
Full Breakfast
Credit Cards: A, B, C, D
Notes: 2, 5, 8 (over 5), 9, 14

JASPER

Brambly Hedge Cottage

HCR 31, Box 39, 72641
(501) 446-5849

Breakfast above the clouds at this mountaintop home right on Scenic Highway 7. Gorgeous view "clear to Missouri" overlooks Buffalo River Valley. Country French-Victorian elegance in the rugged Ozarks. "Absolutely charming," National Geographic Traveller, 1991. Thick-walled livingroom is a homestead log cabin. Lovely upstairs guest room. Minutes from Buffalo National River float trips, hiking trails, Dogpatch ARK, craft shops; short distance to Eureka Springs; Branson, Missouri; major lakes. 4.2 miles south of Jasper.

Hosts: Bill and Jacquelyn Smyers
Rooms: 3 (2 PB) $55
Full Breakfast
Credit Cards: None
Notes: 2, 5, 9

KINGSTON

Ozark Mountain Country Bed and Breakfast A308

Box 295, Branson, Missouri 65616
(800) 321-8594

This contemporary home overlooks the mountains. The spacious deck with hot tub and antiques throughout the three guest rooms add to its appeal. Country breakfast. $55.

MOUNTAIN HOME

Arkansas and Ozarks Bed and Breakfast AMH01

HC 61, Box 72, Calico Rock, 72519
(501) 297-8764; (501) 297-8211

This charming two-story Colonial is on the National Register of Historic Places and is furnished with antiques and wicker. An extended continental breakfast (featuring Belgian waffles) is served while you enjoy the country scene from the glass-enclosed breakfast room. A short drive to Norfork and Bull Shoals lakes, a variety of Ozark art and craft shops, and music shows, golfing, fishing, and swimming. $35-40.

MOUNTAIN VIEW

The Commercial Hotel: A Vintage Guest House Bed and Bakery

On the Square, P. O. Box 72, 72560
(501) 269-4383

Recommended by Gourmet, Mid-West Living, Arkansas Times, The New York Times, and others, this unpretentious bed and breakfast is situated on the historic courthouse square near the Ozark Folk Center and Blanchard Springs Caverns. The inn houses the Hearth Stone Bakery; and local musicians often gather on the porch for old-time music. Listed on the National Register of Historic Places.

Hosts: Todd and Andrea Budy
Rooms: 8 (3 PB; 5 S2B) $38-55
 Continental Breakfast
 Credit Cards: A, B, C, D
Notes: 2, 3, 5, 8, 10, 11

The Commercial Hotel

The Inn at Mountain View

West Washington Street, 72560
(800) 535-1301

On the National Register of Historic Places, the inn has been a traditional stopping place for folks since 1886. The inn has 10 guest suites, each with private bath. All rooms are furnished with antiques and air-conditioned. Breakfast is a hearty meal of homemade biscuits, sausage, gravy, eggs, Belgian waffles, fresh fruit compote, raspberry ambrosia, bacon, homemade peach and apple butters, juice, and lots of coffee. Mountain View is the world capital of folk music, with the National Folk Center just one mile from the inn. The caverns at Blanchard Springs are about nine miles from the inn. White River trout fishing is five miles away, and the Buffalo River, noted for its canoe and float trips, is a short drive.

Hosts: Bob and Jenny Williams
Rooms: 10 (PB) $52-88
Full Breakfast
Credit Cards: A, B, D
Notes: 2, 5, 9, 10, 11, 14

NORFORK

Arkansas and Ozarks Bed and Breakfast ANF01

HC 61, Box 72, Calico Rock, 72519
(501) 297-8764; (501) 297-8211

A mountain retreat with a country club setting, this lodge sits on the banks of the White River and overlooks the beauty and serenity of the Ozark National Forest. In the large, antique-furnished dining room, family-style home-cooked meals (including hand selected meats, fowl, fish, vegetables, freshly baked breads and European desserts) are served. A complete breakfast is included with your lodging. The bedrooms have their own entrances into an open-air courtyard. $62.50.

NOTES: Credit cards accepted: A Master Card; B Visa; C American Express; D Discover Card; E Diner's Club; F Other; 2 Personal Checks accepted; 3 Lunch available; 4 Dinner available; 5 Open all year;

OZARK

Ozark Mountain Country Bed and Breakfast OMC309

Box 295, Branson, Missouri, 65616
(800) 321-8594

One block from the square and the Arkansas River, this bed and breakfast offers three large rooms, two with queen-size beds and one with a full-size bed. A hearty breakfast is served, and antiques can be found everywhere. Luncheon facilities, a bakery, catering, and an antique shop can be found on premises. Smoking and non-smoking rooms available. $40-45.

Ozark Mountain Country Bed and Breakfast OMC310

Box 295, Branson, Missouri, 65616
(800) 321-8594

This little house on the river is a contemporary, rustic cottage near Ozark. The kitchen is fully equipped, the livingroom has a Hide-a-bed sofa, and the bedroom offers a full-size bed. The full bath has a tub/shower, and continental breakfast is served each morning. No pre-teenagers. Open all year. $60.

PINE BLUFF

Margland II, III, and IV Bed and Breakfast Inns

703 West Second Street, 71611
(501) 536-6000; (501) 534-0201

Southern hospitality as it was meant to be—each suite is carefully furnished for the perfect combination of atmosphere and comfort. You may savor your breakfast in the privacy of your room, in the garden, or in the formal dining room. Cable TV, private baths, VCR's and Jacuzzis. Twin, double or queen beds; conference rooms; exercise room. Maryland II is handicap-accessible. All buildings equipped with sprinkler fire protection system.

Host: Wanda Bateman
Rooms: 17 (PB) $50-100
Full Breakfast
Credit Cards: A, B, C, D, E
Notes: 2, 3 & 4 (by reservation for at least 8), 5, 7, 8, 9, 10, 11, 12, 14

ROGERS

Arkansas and Ozarks Bed and Breakfast ARO01

HC 61, Box 72, Calico Rock, 72519
(501) 297-8764; (501) 297-8211

This country charmer is nestled among oak, dogwood, and redbud trees for adult travelers. Queen-size beds, private baths, fruit and homemade candy are just a few of the features. A full breakfast is served in the spacious country dining room or on the veranda where birds, wildlife, and natural beauty may also be enjoyed. The hosts delight in providing special arrangements for birthdays, anniversaries, and other occasions. Only minutes from boating, fishing, swimming, golf, and a variety of shopping and craft areas. $40-55.

ROMANCE

Hammons Chapel Farm

271 Hammons Chapel Road, 72136
(501) 849-2819

This working cattle farm features American Brahman cattle, which originated as the sacred cows of India, and Hereford cattle. Situated in the foothills of the Ozarks a short drive from beautiful 45,000-acre Greers Ferry Lake, this attractive white stucco ranch home reflects John's love of reading, writing, and painting and Susan's love of cooking and gardening. There are no stairs to climb, and some of the antiques date back for generations.

Hosts: John and Susan Hammons
Rooms: 1 (PB) $45
Full Breakfast
Credit Cards: None
Notes: 2, 3, 4, 5, 6, 9

6 Pets welcome; 7 Smoking allowed; 8 Children welcome; 9 Social drinking allowed; 10 Tennis available; 11 Swimming available; 12 Golf available; 13 Skiing available; 14 May be booked through travel agents.

The Old Washington Jail Bed and Breakfast Inn

WASHINGTON

The Old Washington Jail Bed and Breakfast Inn

P.O. Box 179, 71862
(501) 983-2461

Situated forty miles east of Texarkana in historic Washington. The inn was a jail built in 1872 and was renovated and opened as an inn in 1982. Guest rooms are furnished in period antiques. Enjoy one of the three sitting rooms or one of the porches, as well as the tranquil setting of Old Washington State Park. Many tourist attractions are within a short drive.

Hosts: Hugh and Ruth Erwin
Rooms: 5 (PB) $50
Continental Breakfast
Credit Cards: None
Notes: 2

YELLVILLE

Arkansas and Ozarks Bed and Breakfast AYV01

HC 61, Box 72, Calico Rock, 72519
(501) 297-8764; (501) 297-8211

This elegant Victorian home is beautifully and lovingly restored to its stately charm. There are six rooms in this spacious inn, and a "honeymoon suite" for those special celebrations. Also available are sitting rooms, a large dining room with a breakfast buffet of "make-it-yourself" Belgian Waffles. Homemade cakes and other delights are served as snacks. Major credit cards accepted. Children over 5 welcome. Smoking is limited. $37; $55 honeymoon suite.

NOTES: Credit cards accepted: A Master Card; B Visa; C American Express; D Discover Card; E Diner's Club; F Other; 2 Personal Checks accepted; 3 Lunch available; 4 Dinner available; 5 Open all year;

California

ALAMEDA

Garratt Mansion

900 Union Street, 94501
(415) 521-4779

This 1893 Victorian makes time stand still on the tranquil island of Alameda. Only 15 miles to Berkeley or downtown San Francisco. The hosts will help maximize your vacation plans or leave you alone to regroup. Rooms are large and comfortable, and breakfasts are nutritious and filling.

Hosts: Royce and Betty Gladden
Rooms: 6 (3 PB; 3 SB) $80-125
Full Breakfast
Credit Cards: A, B, C, E,
Notes: 2, 5, 8, 11, 12, 14

Garratt Mansion

Webster House

1238 Versailles Avenue, 94501
(510) 523-9697

Webster House is the 22nd historical monument in the city. Quaint, enchanting 1854 Gothic revival cottage is the oldest house on the island of Alameda. Nestled in coastal redwoods and scrub oaks, with a large deck, waterfall, fountain. Afternoon tea and evening snack complimentary. Gourmet dinners available by reservation. Near beach, golf, tennis, fishing, shopping, and bicycling. Twenty minutes from San Francisco.

Hosts: Andrew and Susan McCormack
Rooms: 6 (2 PB; 4 SB) $75-105
Full Breakfast
Credit Cards: None
Notes: 2, 3, 5, 7 (restricted), 8, 9, 10, 11, 12, 14

ALBION

Fensalden Inn

Box 99, 95410
(707) 937-4042

A restored 1860s stagecoach way station with antique furnishings; several units with fireplaces. Quiet country setting with pastoral and ocean views. Enjoy strolling country lanes where grazing deer share the crisp morning air, or the evening panorama of the setting sun over a crimson-stained ocean.

Hosts: Frances and Scott Brazil
Rooms: 8 (PB) $80-135
Full Breakfast
Minimum stay weekends: 2 nights; holidays: 3
  nights
Credit Cards: A, B
Notes: 2, 5, 8 (over 11), 9, 10, 11, 12, 14

NOTES: Credit cards accepted: A Master Card; B Visa; C American Express; D Discover Card; E Diner's Club; F Other; 2 Personal Checks accepted; 3 Lunch available; 4 Dinner available; 5 Open all year; 6 Pets welcome; 7 Smoking allowed; 8 Children welcome; 9 Social drinking allowed; 10 Tennis available; 11 Swimming available; 12 Golf available; 13 Skiing available; 14 May be booked through travel agents.

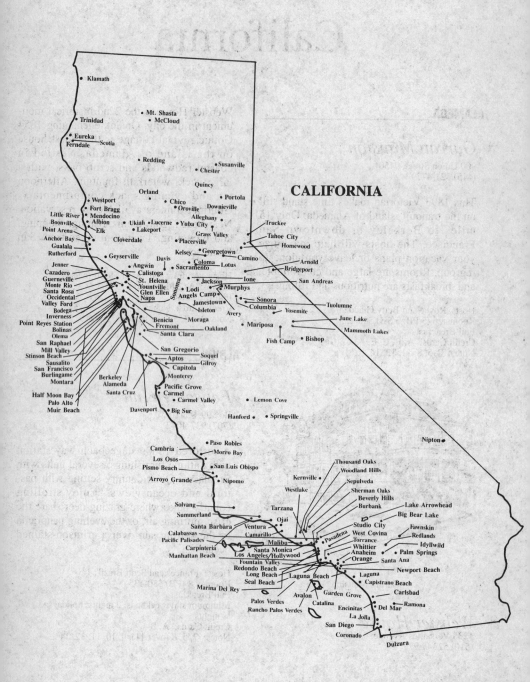

CALIFORNIA

Klamath

Mt. Shasta
McCloud

Trinidad

Eureka
Ferndale Scotia

Redding
Susanville
Chester

Quincy

Orland
Portola

Westport
Chico Downieville
Fort Bragg Oroville
Little River Mendocino Alleghany
Boonville Albion Ukiah Lucerne Yuba City Truckee
Point Arena Elk Lakeport Grass Valley Tahoe City
Anchor Bay Cloverdale Placerville Homewood
Gualala
Rutherford Geyserville Kelsey Georgetown Camino
Davis Coloma Arnold
Jenner Angwin Sacramento Lotus Bridgeport
Cazadero Calistoga Ione
Guerneville St. Helena Jackson San Andreas
Monte Rio Yountville Lodi Murphys
Santa Rosa Glen Ellen Angels Camp
Occidental Napa Jamestown Sonora
Valley Ford Isleton Columbia Tuolumne
Bodega Avery Yosemite
Inverness Benicia Moraga June Lake
Point Reyes Station Fremont Mariposa Mammoth Lakes
Bolinas Oakland
Olema Santa Clara Fish Camp Bishop
San Raphael
Mill Valley San Gregorio
Stinson Beach Aptos Soquel
Sausalito Gilroy
San Francisco Capitola
Burlingame Monterey
Montara Berkeley
Half Moon Bay Alameda Pacific Grove Lemon Cove
Palo Alto Santa Cruz Carmel
Muir Beach Carmel Valley
Davenport Big Sur Hanford Springville

Cambria Paso Robles Nipton
Los Osos Morro Bay
Pismo Beach San Luis Obispo
Arroyo Grande Nipomo
Thousand Oaks
Woodland Hills
Kernville Sepulveda
Westlake Sherman Oaks
Solvang Beverly Hills
Summerland Tarzana Burbank Lake Arrowhead
Big Bear Lake
Santa Barbara Ventura Studio City Fawnskin
Calabassas Camarillo Pasadena West Covina Redlands
Pacific Palisades Malibu Torrance Idyllwild
Carpinteria Santa Monica Whittier
Manhattan Beach Los Angeles/Hollywood Anaheim Palm Springs
Fountain Valley Orange Santa Ana
Redondo Beach Newport Beach
Long Beach Laguna
Seal Beach Laguna Beach Capistrano Beach
Marina Del Rey Carlsbad
Avalon Garden Grove Ramona
Palos Verdes Catalina Encinitas Del Mar
Rancho Palos Verdes La Jolla
San Diego
Coronado
Dulzura

ALLEGHENY

Kenton Mine Lodge

P. O. Box 942, 95910
(916) 287-3212

Take a step back in time to the site of
California's richest grade gold mining district. Furnished cabins, a nine room guest
house, large lawn, mountain stream, panning for gold, home cooked meals, sauna,
campfire, fishing, and hiking are just some
of the recreations available for guests to
enjoy. Relax in quiet rustic setting. Full bar
and group rates available.

Hosts: Rocky Rockwood
Rooms: 16 (7-PB; 9-SB) $90-120 (includes two
    meals)
Continental Breakfast; brunch and dinner available
Credit Cards: A, B
Notes: 2, 3, 4, 5, 7, 9, 11

ANAHEIM

America's B&B #14

P. O. Box 9302, Whittier, 90608
(310) 699-8427

Furnished in country antiques, this comfortable home includes a suite with complete privacy, a queen bed, as well as queen
sofa bed and facilities for light cooking. A
large country breakfast is served on antique
china. Guests are welcome to use the fireplace in the living room with color TV.
Situated halfway between Disneyland and
Knott's Berry Farm, as well as near the
Anaheim Convention Center and all
Orange County attractions. $55.

B&B International #501

P. O. Box 282910, San Francisco, 94128-2910
(415) 696-1690; FAX (415) 696-1699

Perfect location for visiting Disneyland,
Knott's Berry Farm, and other tourist
attractions in Southern California. This is a
large two-story home that is ideal for a
family. Guest room has a queen bed, private
bath, plus a queen sofa bed in an adjacent
sitting room with a fireplace and balcony.
Breakfast at this house lasts all day. $55.

Bed and Breakfast Los Angeles 7-2

730 Catalina Avenue, Seal Beach, 90740
(310) 493-6837; (800) 383-3513

This young couple invites you to to share
their newly decorated home, located just 10
minutes from Disneyland. Guest wing has
one large room with a wonderful antique
bed and private bath. A second room down
the hall can accommodate another couple
or the kids. Affordable rates.

Bed and Breakfast Los Angeles 7-6

730 Catalina Avenue, Seal Beach, 90740
(310) 493-6837; (800) 383-3513

Less than a mile from Disneyland, three
guest rooms share two baths. Your hosts
are German and Scandinavian, and family
rates are available. Affordable rates.

Bed and Breakfast Los Angeles 7-7

730 Catalina Avenue, Seal Beach, 90740
(310) 493-6837; (800) 383-3513

Just five miles from Disneyland, this beautiful, contemporary house is set on one-
quarter acre, with a view of the hills from
the pool and spa. Three nice guest rooms
share two baths. Affordable rates.

NOTES: Credit cards accepted: A Master Card; B Visa; C American Express; D Discover Card; E Diner's
Club; F Other; 2 Personal Checks accepted; 3 Lunch available; 4 Dinner available; 5 Open all year; 6 Pets
welcome; 7 Smoking allowed; 8 Children welcome; 9 Social drinking allowed; 10 Tennis available; 11
Swimming available; 12 Golf available; 13 Skiing available; 14 May be booked through travel agents.

Eye Openers Bed and Breakfast Reservations AN-A9I

P. O. Box 694, Altadena, 91003-0694
(213) 684-4428; (818) 797-2055
FAX (818) 798-3640

Beautifully restored and decorated, this 1910 Princess Anne Victorian, now a friendly bed and breakfast, is surrounded by lovely gardens and is located in a residential area convenient to most Orange County attractions with local bus service. Hearty breakfast and afternoon refreshments. No smoking. Nine guest rooms with private and shared baths. $65-125.

Eye Openers Bed and Breakfast Reservations AN-P3

P. O. Box 694, Altadena, 91003-0694
(213) 684-4428; (818) 797-2055
FAX (818) 798-3640

This bed and breakfast, with its country kitchen and full breakfast, offers comfort, convenience, economy, and good location near restaurants and public transportation. Bicycles, hot tub, and complimentary transport to Disneyland are available. Children welcome.Two guest rooms with private and shared baths. $30-50.

Eye Openers Bed and Breakfast Reservations AN-W3

P. O. Box 694, Altadena, 91003-0694
(213) 684-4428; (818) 797-2055
FAX (818) 798-3640

One mile to Disneyland and Anaheim Convention Center. Hearty breakfast served with special attention from European host in the large family room or dining room. No smoking. Three guest rooms with shared bath. $45-55 plus tax.

Eye Openers Bed and Breakfast Reservations GG-04

P. O. Box 694, Altadena, 91003-0694
(213) 684-4428; (818) 797-2055
FAX (818) 798-3640

Convenient to Orange Couny attractions, this bed and breakfast features large comfortable rooms, full breakfast, and TV room with fireplace. Four guest rooms with private and shared baths. $40-55

Eye Openers Bed and Breakfast Reservations OR-C3

P. O. Box 694, Altadena, 91003-0694
(213) 684-4428; (818) 797-2055
FAX (818) 798-3640

Enjoy a delicious country-style breakfast in a contemporary wood-and-glass bed and breakfast. Relax in the outdoor pool, Jacuzzi, living room, or interesting family room. Convenient to Disneyland, Anaheim Convention Center and Stadium. Handicapped accessible with adaptive equipment. No smoking. Three guest rooms. $60.

Eye Openers Bed and Breakfast Reservations SA-D1

P. O. Box 694, Altadena, 91003-0694
(213) 684-4428; (818) 797-2055
FAX (818) 798-3640

Older home in a lovely neighborhood has been restored by young hosts. Antique accents are featured in the guest room and the living room. One guest room with private bath is available, and generous continental breakfast served. This bed and breakfast is convenient to the Anaheim Convention Center and Disneyland. Cats in residence. No smoking. $55.

NOTES: Credit cards accepted: A Master Card; B Visa; C American Express; D Discover Card; E Diner's Club; F Other; 2 Personal Checks accepted; 3 Lunch available; 4 Dinner available; 5 Open all year;

Kids Welcome 7-5

730 Catalina Avenue, Seal Beach, 90740
(310) 493-6837; (800) 383-3513

The guest wing of this spacious house in
Anaheim has room for the entire family,
with a living room with a fireplace, balcony, kitchen, and private bath. Living
room couch converts to a bed for the kids.
Two downstairs guest rooms share a bath.
Enjoy the spa and patio, as well as your full
country breakfast. Pets welcome. Affordable rates

ANGELS CAMP

Cooper House Bed and Breakfast Inn

Box 1388, 95222
(209) 736-2145

Beautiful turn-of-the-century home in
California's historic gold country. Quiet
location surrounded by manicured gardens.
Spacious rooms with private baths and air
conditioning. Sumptuous full breakfast.
Near caverns, wineries, giant sequoias,
Columbia State Park, gourmet dining.

Host: Chris Sears
Rooms: 3 (PB) $85-90
Full Breakfast
Credit Cards: A, B, C
Notes: 2, 5, 7 (limited), 8, 9, 10, 12, 13, 14

ANGWIN

Forest Manor

415 Cold Springs Road, 94508
(707) 965-3538

Secluded 20-acre English Tudor estate
tucked among forest vineyards in famous
Napa wine country. Described as "one of
the most romantic country inns. A small
exclusive resort." Fireplaces, verandas, 53-
foot pool, spas, spacious suites (one with
Jacuzzi), refrigerators, coffee makers,

home-baked breakfast. Close to over 200
wineries, ballooning, hot springs, and a
lake.

Hosts: Harold and Corlene Lambeth
Rooms: 3 (PB) $85-195
Expanded Continental Breakfast
Credit Cards: A, B
Notes: 2, 5, 9, 10, 11, 14

APTOS

Apple Lane Inn

6265 Soquel Drive, 95003-3117
(408) 475-6868

Apple Lane Inn is a historic Victorian
farmhouse restored to the charm and tranquility of an earlier age. It is situated just
south of Santa Cruz on two and one-half
acres of grounds, with gardens, a romantic
gazebo, and fields. Explore the many miles
of beaches within walking distance. Golf,
hiking, fishing, shopping, and dining are all
close by.

Hosts: Doug and Diana Groom
Rooms: 5 (3 PB; 2 SB) $70-125
Full Breakfast
Credit Cards: A, B, D
Notes: 2, 5, 7 (limited), 9, 10, 11, 12, 14

Bayview Hotel Bed and Breakfast Inn

8041 Soquel Drive, 95003
(408) 688-8654

Vintage California Victorian in the heart of
Aptos Village built in 1878 and furnished
with original antiques. Near golf, tennis,
fishing, state beaches, and antique shops.
Only one block from the entrance to the
10,000-acre forest of Nisene Marks State
Park with 35 miles of hiking trails. Fine
restaurant, the Veranda, on the premises.

Hosts: Barry and Sue Parker
Rooms: 8 (PB) $80-115
Full Breakfast
Credit Cards: A, B, C
Notes: 2, 3, 4, 5, 8 (over 5), 10, 11, 12, 14

Mangels House

570 Aptos Creek Road, Box 32, 95001
(408) 688-7982

A large southern Colonial situated on four
acres of lawn and orchard, and bounded by
a 10,000-acre redwood forest and is only
three-fourth's mile from the beach. The
five large, airy rooms are eclectic in decor
and European in feel, reflecting the owners' background.

Hosts: Jacqueline and Ronald Fisher
Rooms: 5 (5 PB) $94-120
Full Breakfast
Credit Cards: A, B
Closed Dec. 24-26
Notes: 2, 5, 6 (outside), 7 (limited), 8 (over 12), 9,
   10, 11, 12, 14

Lodge at Manuel Mill

ARNOLD

Lodge at Manuel Mill

P. O. Box 998, 95223
(209) 795-2622

Secluded vacation retreat overlooks historic
trout-filled mill pond. Near Big Trees State
Park, the lodge is surrounded by Stanislaus
National Forest and miles of hiking and
biking trails. It features a massive stone
fireplace in open-beamed main room, and
romantic antique-appointed guest rooms
with private baths and entrances on deck.
Views of pond and sounds of waterfall lull

guests to sleep. Full ranch breakfast.
Complimentary any (California) bottle of
wine. Ideal for special occasions.

Hosts: Jerry and Pat King
Rooms: 5 (PB) $95-105
Full Breakfast
Credit Cards: None
Notes: 2, 5, 10, 11, 12, 13

ARROWHEAD

Bed and Breakfast Los Angeles 10-2

730 Catalina Avenue, Seal Beach, 90740
(310) 493-6837; (800) 383-3513

Twenty-four cottages, ranging in size from
one to three bedrooms, are open year-round
for fun and skiing. Cottages include fireplace and Jacuzzi; breakfast of your choice
is served off the dining room menu. Luxury
rates.

ARROYO GRANDE

Arroyo Village Inn

407 El Camino Real, 93420
(805) 489-5926

Romantic, award-winning Victorian offering a delightful blend of yesterday's charm
and hospitality with today's comforts and
conveniences. Spacious suites are decorated with Laura Ashley prints and antiques
with private baths, window seats and bal-
conies.Situated in the heart of California's
Central Coast, halfway between Los
Angeles and San Francisco. Near beaches,
wineries, mineral spas, San Luis Obispo;
less than one hour to Hearst Castle."The
best kept secret on the Central Coast," *Los
Angeles Times*.

Hosts: John and Gina Glass
Rooms: 7 (PB) $95-165
Full Breakfast
Credit Cards: A, B, C, D, E
Notes: 2, 5, 8 , 9, 10, 11, 12, 14

NOTES: Credit cards accepted: A Master Card; B Visa; C American Express; D Discover Card; E Diner's
Club; F Other; 2 Personal Checks accepted; 3 Lunch available; 4 Dinner available; 5 Open all year;

The Guest House

120 Hart Lane, 93420
(805) 481-9304

A charming Colonial home built in 1865 and furnished with many rare antiques of that era. Beautiful, old-fashioned gardens in which a hearty breakfast and afternoon libations are enjoyed. A short walk to the interesting shops and restaurants in the old village of Arroyo Grande.

Hosts: Mark Miller and Jim Cunningham
Rooms: 2 (SB) $45-60
Full Breakfast
Credit Cards: None
Notes: 2, 5, 7 (limited), 9, 10, 11, 12

AUBURN

Lincoln House
Bed and Breakfast Inn

191 Lincoln Way, 95603
(916) 885-8880

Charming country inn situated in historic Auburn, heart of gold country. Enter crossing a footbridge over koi-filled fishpond. Guest rooms are decorated with antiques, soft colors, and cozy quilts; all with private baths. Two fireplaces provide parlor and sitting room with just that little bit extra for quiet evenings and romantic getaways. Sumptuous full breakfast is served in the dining room where large windows frame a stunning view of Sierra Nevadas. Refreshing large swimming pool is in the garden area.

Hosts: Leslie and Stan Fronczak
Rooms: 3 (PB) $65-90
Full Breakfast
Credit Cards: A, B, C
Notes: 2, 5, 8, 10, 11, 12, 13

Powers Mansion Inn

164 Cleveland Avenue, 95603
(916) 885-1166

This magnificent mansion was built from a gold fortune in the late 1800s. It has easy access to I-80 and off-street parking. Clo. to water sports, hiking, horseback riding, skiing, ballooning, and restaurants.

Host: Anthony Verhaart
Rooms: 15 (PB) $75-160
Full Breakfast
Credit Cards: A, B, C
Notes: 2, 5, 6, 8, 9, 10, 11, 12, 13, 14

AVALON

The Garden House Inn

125 Third Street, P. O. Box 851
(310) 510-0356

1923 historic home is located 100 ft from Avalon Bay on Catalina Island. Nine lovely rooms are available, many of which have ocean views and private terraces. All have private tiled baths, queen size beds, and overstuffed upholstered furnishings. Buffet breakfast and wine hour daily. Large gardens run along the ocean side of the house, and our location is within walking distance to all of Avalon. Come and enjoy our romantic, relaxed atmosphere. Call about our mid-week SEASON discount.

Hosts: Jon and Cathy Olsen
Rooms: 9 (PB) $95-250
Continental Plus Breakfast
Credit Cards: A, B, C
Notes: 2, 5, 10, 11, 12, 14

---

6 Pets welcome; 7 Smoking allowed; 8 Children welcome; 9 Social drinking allowed; 10 Tennis available; 11 Swimming available; 12 Golf available; 13 Skiing available; 14 May be booked through travel agents.

Gull House

344 Whittley Avenue, Box 1381, 90704
(310) 510-2547

For honeymooners and those celebrating anniversaries. AAA-approved contemporary house with swimming pool, spa, barbecue, gas-log fireplaces, morning room with refrigerator, color TV. Close to bay beaches and all water activities. Deposit or full payment in advance reserves taxi pickup and return. Ask about our guest rooms.

Hosts: Bob and Hattie Michalis
Suites: 2 (PB) $130-140
Continental Breakfast
Minimum stay: 2 nights
Credit Cards: None
Notes: 2, 8, 9, 11, 12, 14

Zane Grey Pueblo Hotel

199 Chimes Tower Road, Box 216, 90704
(213) 510-0966

Hopi Indian-style pueblo built in 1926 as the private home of author Zane Grey. Panoramic ocean and mountain views from the guest rooms, each with a queen bed and private bath. Pool and view decks are surrounded by natural gardens. Original living room with fireplace, piano, and TV. Courtesy taxi. Romantic atmosphere.

Hosts: Karen Baker and Kevin Anderson
Rooms: 17 (PB) $48-125
Continental Breakfast
Credit Cards: A, B, C
Notes: 5, 7, 9, 10, 11, 12, 14

AVERY

Avery Hotel

4573 Moran Rd, 95224
(209) 795-9935

We are a 138-year-old historical hotel, restaurant and bar. Originally the Halfway House on the way to the Big Trees in the 1800s. Fun and lively on the weekends and quiet during the weekdays, we offer dinner

at reasonable price, open bar seven days a week, and restaurant open Wednesday through Sunday brunch.

Rooms: 6 (SB) $55
Continental breakfast
Credit Cards: None
Notes: 2, 4, 5, 7, 8, 9, 12 all nearby

Union Hotel

BENICIA

Union Hotel

401 First Street, 94510
(707) 746-0100

Built in 1882 and active as a 20-room bordello until the early 1950s, the Union Hotel was completely renovated in 1981 into a 12-room hotel and bed and breakfast. Each of the 12 rooms is decorated with a theme and named accordingly. Each room has a queen or king bed, individual room-temperature controls, Jacuzzi bathtub, and television. The superb stained-glass picture windows in the bar and dining room are worth a trip on their own. Restaurant on premises. Ideally situated for visiting the wine country (20 minutes) 45 minutes from San Francisco; 20 minutes from the ferry to Fisherman's Wharf.

Host: Stephen Lipworth
Rooms: 12 (PB) $74-135
Continental Breakfast
Credit Cards: A, B, C, D, E
Notes: 2, 3, 4, 5, 7, 8, 9, 14

NOTES: Credit cards accepted: A Master Card; B Visa; C American Express; D Discover Card; E Diner's Club; F Other; 2 Personal Checks accepted; 3 Lunch available; 4 Dinner available; 5 Open all year;

BERKELEY

Gramma's Rose Garden Inn

2740 Telegraph Avenue, 94705
(510) 549-2145
FAX (510) 549-1085

Two turn-of-the-century Tudor-style mansions, garden cottage, and carriage houses set amid English country gardens. Rooms furnished with antiques; many have fireplaces, decks, porches, and/or views. Near the University of California, Berkeley shops, parks, and museums.

Host: Barry Cleveland
Rooms: 40 (PB) $85-175
Full Breakfast
Credit Cards: A, B, C
Notes: 2, 5, 8, 9, 10, 11, 12, 14

BEVERLY HILLS

America's Bed & Breakfast #16

P. O. Box 9302, Whittier, 90608
(310) 699-8427

Cozy home owned by a writer, with a hot tub overlooking the back yard. Guests will enjoy talking with their host about movies from the past; he has researched the lives of many stars. The inviting fireplace offers a place to plan for the next day's outing. Two doubles, one with queen-size bed. Private bath. $65-75.

Bed and Breakfast Los Angeles 2-6

730 Catalina Avenue, Seal Beach, 90740
(310) 493-6837; (800) 383-3513

This spacious condo includes a guest room with twin beds, TV, and garden view. Great location in a delightful setting. Moderate rates.

Bed and Breakfast Los Angeles 2-7

730 Catalina Avenue, Seal Beach, 90740
(310) 493-6837; (800) 383-3513

Tucked behind the host's home, this quaint cottage features twin beds, private bath, refrigerator, and TV. Affordable rates.

Bed and Breakfast Los Angeles 2-8

730 Catalina Avenue, Seal Beach, 90740
(310) 493-6837; (800) 383-3513

This little hotel in Beverly Hills has comfy rooms, private baths, TV, phone, continental breakfast. Kids under 12 stay free. Moderate-luxury rates.

Bed and Breakfast Los Angeles 2-9

730 Catalina Avenue, Seal Beach, 90740
(310) 493-6837; (800) 383-3513

Near Beverly Hills and the museums, this charming inn is hidden in a residential neighborhood. Rooms include color TV, phones & air conditioning. Relax in the parlor or outside patio; breakfast in the dining room. Moderate rates.

Eye Openers Bed and Breakfast Reservations BH-N1

P. O. Box 694, Altadena, 91003-0694
(213) 684-4428; (818) 797-2055
FAX (818) 798-3640

Located in the heart of Beverly Hills, this bed and breakfast offers a guest cottage in the garden area for ultimate privacy and comfort. Cottage has microwave, refrigerator, and choice of continental or full breakfast. Public transportation available. Private bath. $45-50.

6 Pets welcome; 7 Smoking allowed; 8 Children welcome; 9 Social drinking allowed; 10 Tennis available; 11 Swimming available; 12 Golf available; 13 Skiing available; 14 May be booked through travel agents.

BIG BEAR LAKE—SEE ALSO FAWNSKIN

Eagle's Nest Bed and Breakfast

Box 1003, 92315
(714) 866-6465

The Eagle's Nest Bed and Breakfast is ideally situated in the heart of a four-seasons resort. The lodge offers elegance in a rustic setting. The main house is a recently built two-story log cabin lodge. Five cozily decorated rooms all have private baths, queen beds, and warm goose-down comforters. Three new cottage suites with fireplaces; two with Jacuzzis.

Hosts: James Joyce and Jack Draper
Rooms: 8 (PB) $75-150
Expanded Continental Breakfast
Credit Cards: None
Notes: 2, 5, 8, 9, 10, 11, 12, 13, 14

BIG SUR

Ventana Inn

Highway 1, 93920
(408) 624-4812; (408) 667-2331
(800) 628-6500 California

Deluxe romantic inn situated on 243 acres above Pacific, 35 miles from Monterey airport. Decorator-designed accommodations in 12 buildings with king- or queen-size bed, terrace, air conditioning, and phone; most with fireplace, some with wet bar or hot tub. All with TV's and VCR's. Three town house suites. Wheelchair accessibility. Complimentary continental breakfast and afternoon wine and cheese. Highly regarded restaurant. Fireside lounge. Two heated pools, sauna, massage, two Japanese hot baths, horseback riding and hiking. Country store. Beach nearby.

Host: R. E. Bussinger
Rooms: 60 (PB) $170-475
Expanded Continental Breakfast
Credit Cards: A, B, C, D, E
Notes: 2, 3, 4, 5, 7 (restricted), 9, 11, 14

BISHOP

1898 Chalfant House

213 Academy, 93514
(619) 872-1790

Turn-of-the-century inn standing between towering mountains just one block off Highway 395. Each of six guest rooms has private bath, antiques, and handmade quilts and comforters. The wood-burning stove in the antique-filled sitting room creates a cozy ambience to be enjoyed while reading, watching TV, or visiting with other guests. A full gourmet breakfast is generously served on china and silver service. Old-fashioned ice cream sundaes are a delightful complimentary treat in the evenings.

Hosts: Fred and Sally Maneche
Rooms: 6 (PB) $60-75
Full Breakfast
Credit Cards: C
Notes: 2, 5, 8, 12, 13

The Matlick House

1313 Rowan Lane, 93514
(619) 873-3133

A 1906 ranch house, completely renovated, nestled at the base of the eastern Sierra Nevada Mountains. Close to year-round fishing, hiking, skiing, trail rides. Telephones available, air conditioning, wine and hors d'oeuvres; antiques throughout.

Host: Nanette Robidart
Rooms: 5 (PB) $55-75
Full Breakfast
Credit Cards: None
Notes: 2, 5, 7 (limited), 8 (over 14), 9, 10, 11, 12, 13

BODEGA

The Schoolhouse Inn

17110 Bodega Lane, P. O. Box 136, 94922
(707) 876-3257

Built in 1873 as a public school, this historical landmark was seen in Hitchcock's movie The Birds. There are four charming bedrooms with private baths. A hot breakfast is served upstairs in the sitting room with cozy fireplace and panoramic views of the gentle rolling hills of northern California.

Host: Mary Leah Taylor
Rooms: 4 (PB) $75-90
Full Breakfast
Credit Cards: A, B
Notes: 2, 5

Thomas' White House Inn

BOLINAS

Kids Welcome 16-3

730 Catalina Avenue, Seal Beach, 90740
(310) 493-6837; (800) 383-3513

This cabin is on a spit of land surrounded by Bolinas Bay. P{point Reyes National Park is on one side; Stinson Beach and Mount Tamalpais is on the other side. Amenities include two bedrooms, a living room, full kitchen, and bath. The cabins are well stocked, including charcoal for the barbecue. Luxury rates.

Thomas' White House Inn

118 Kale Road, P. O. Box 132, 94924
(415) 868-0279

A New England-style inn near Point Reyes National Seashore in West Marin. Situated in one of the most beautiful areas on the California coast. Two lovely rooms with window seats offer panoramic views of the mountains and the Pacific Ocean.

Host: Jacqueline Thomas
Rooms: 2 (SB) $93.50-104.50
Continental Breakfast
Credit Cards: None
Notes: 2, 4, 5, 7, 8, 9, 10

BOONVILLE

Anderson Creek Inn

P. O. Box 217
12050 Anderson Valley Way, 95415
(707) 895-3091

The Anderson Valley is truly a peaceful setting for this spacious ranch-style Bed and Breakfast that affords ultimate privacy and lush views. Guests are treated to appetizers each evening and an elegant full breakfast in bed or in the dining room. Stroll through the gardens, sip wine by the pool, or enjoy the gentle llamas and rare lambs.

Hosts: Rod and Nancy Graham
Rooms: 4 (PB) $95-125
Full Breakfast
Credit Cards: A, B
Notes: 2, 5, 8, 9, 10, 11, 14

BRENTWOOD

Eye Openers Bed and Breakfast Reservations LA-S1

P. O. Box 694, Altadena, 91003-0694
(213) 684-4428; (818) 797-2055
FAX (818) 798-3640

Brentwood town house features lovely livingroom with appointed antiques and French doors that open onto a patio facing a green belt complete with eucalyptus grove. A quiet retreat in the midst of busy, exciting Brentwood. Continental breakfast. Public transportation available. No smoking. One guest room with private bath. $45-50.

6 Pets welcome; 7 Smoking allowed; 8 Children welcome; 9 Social drinking allowed; 10 Tennis available; 11 Swimming available; 12 Golf available; 13 Skiing available; 14 May be booked through travel agents.

BRIDGEPORT

The Cain House

11 Main Street, 93517
(619) 932-7040
(800)433-CAIN

Situated in a small valley with a view of the rugged eastern Sierras, the Cain House has blended European elegance with a western atmosphere. Every amenity has been provided for, including wine and cheese in the evenings. After breakfast, the pristine beauty of the valley, lakes, and streams await you for a day of hiking, boating, fishing, hunting, and cross-country skiing. Three-diamond AAA and Mobil approved.

Host: Chris and Marachal Gohlich
Rooms: 6 (PB) $79-130
Full Breakfast
Credit Cards: A, B, C, D, E
Notes: 2, 5, 9, 10

BURBANK

Bed and Breakfast Los Angeles 3-7

730 Catalina Avenue, Seal Beach, 90740
(310) 493-6837; (800) 383-3513

This charming cottage has a pool, barbecue, and wet bar. Guest room has trundle beds and private bath. Quarters also have handicapped facilities. Affordable rates.

BURLINGAME

Burlingame Bed and Breakfast

1021 Balboa Avenue, 94010
(415) 344-5815

Boating, swimming, fishing (bay and ocean), running, golfing, hiking, art, entertainment, sports. Near Stanford, other colleges, junior colleges, and transportation.

Hosts: Joe and Elnora Fernandez
Room: 1 (PB) $50
Continental Breakfast
Credit Cards: None
Notes: 2, 5, 7 (outside), 8, 10, 11, 12

CALABASSAS

Kids Welcome 11-1

730 Catalina Avenue, Seal Beach, 90740
(310) 493-6837; (800) 383-3513

Your friendly Scottish hostess opens her beautiful, three-level home to families with children over age seven. Just fifteen minutes from Malibu, two guest rooms on the top floor share a bath. A family room, a library, and heated pool are at your doorstep. Affordable rates.

CALISTOGA

Brannan Cottage Inn

109 Wapoo Avenue, 94515
(707) 942-4200

Six guest rooms, all with private baths, central air and heat, and private entrances. Rates include a full breakfast and complimentary evening beverages. Mud baths, glider rides, champagne, wine tasting, and bike rentals are all within a five-minute walk.

Calistoga's Wishing Well Inn

Hosts: Mary Jacobsen & Earle Mills
Rooms: 6 (PB) $110-145
Full Breakfast
Credit Cards: A, B
Notes: 2 (in advance), 5, 10, 11, 12, 14

Calistoga Country Lodge

2883 Foothill Boulevard, 94515
(707) 942-5555

This 1917 farmhouse, set among 100 year oaks, has been restored in a southwestern style. Rooms feature whitewashed pine floors, custom lodgepole furnishings, and one of a kind Navajo rug wall hangings. A large, stone fireplace and Georgia O'Keefe style artifacts draw guests to the spacious common area. A colorful breakfast buffet overlooks the patio and heated pool, where guests can relax and enjoy the views.

Host: Rae Ellen Fields
Rooms: 6 (4 PB; 2 SB) $85-115
Expanded Continental Breakfast
Credit Cards: A, B, C
Notes: 2, 5, 9, 11

Calistoga's Wishing Well Inn

2653 Foothill Boulevard, 94515
(707) 942-5534

A country estate among vineyards with elegant period interiors. Situated on four acres in a historical setting. Enjoy your country breakfast featuring homegrown fruits and preserves, and complimentary wine and hors d'oeuvres poolside with a magnificent view of Mount St. Helena or on your private sun deck. Fireplace in the common parlor; Jacuzzi under the stars; all private baths. Near mud baths, balloon rides, wineries.

Hosts: Marina and Keith Dinsmoor
Rooms: 3 (PB) $100-120
Full Breakfast
Credit Cards: A, B
Notes: 2, 5, 8, 9, 10, 11, 12, 14

Calistoga Wayside Inn

1523 Foothill Boulevard, 94515
(707) 942-0645; (800) 845-3632

Situated in a garden setting, this graceful 1920s Spanish-style hacienda offers a special hideaway in the Napa Valley. Relax on the secluded patio or in the hammock, or borrow a picnic basket and explore world-famous vineyards. In winter, curl up by the fire, sipping cider. A short walk to town. Spas and wineries nearby.

Hosts: Deborah and Leonard Flaherty
Rooms: 3 (PB) $105-135
Full Breakfast
Credit Cards: A, B, C
Notes: 2, 5, 9, 11, 14

Calistoga Wayside Inn

6 Pets welcome; 7 Smoking allowed; 8 Children welcome; 9 Social drinking allowed; 10 Tennis available; 11 Swimming available; 12 Golf available; 13 Skiing available; 14 May be booked through travel agents.

"Culvers," A Country Inn

1805 Foothill Boulevard, 94515
(707) 942-4535

A lovely Victorian residence built in 1875, filled with antiques and offering a full country breakfast. Jacuzzi and seasonal pool, indoor sauna. Within minutes of wineries, mud baths, and downtown Calistoga. Lovely view of St. Helena mountain range from the veranda. Sherry is offered in the afternoon.

Hosts: Meg and Tony Wheatley
Rooms: 6 (SB) $85-115 + tax
Full Breakfast
Credit Cards: For deposit only
Closed Dec. 24-26
Notes: 2, 9, 10, 11, 12, 14

Foothill House

3037 Foothill Boulevard, 94515
(707) 942-6933; (800) 942-6933

"The most romantic inn of the Napa Valley," according to the Chicago Tribune travel editor. In a country setting, Foothill House offers spacious suites individually decorated with antiques, each with private bath and entrance, fireplace, and small refrigerator. Private cottage also available.

Hosts: Doris & Gus Beckerx
Rooms: 3 (PB) $115-120
Expanded Continental Breakfast
Credit Cards: A, B, C
Notes: 2, 5, 9, 10, 11, 12, 14

Hillcrest

3225 Lake County Hwy, 94515
(707) 942-6334

Breathtaking view of Napa Valley countryside. Hiking and fishing on 40 acres. Family-owned since 1860. Hilltop modern country home decorated with heirlooms from family mansion. Rooms have balconies. Fireplace and grand piano, rare art work, silver, crystal, china, and Oriental rugs. Family photo albums date back to 1870s. Breakfast is served weekends on a 12-foot antique table fit for a king.

Host: Debbie O'Gorman
Rooms: 4 (1 PB; 3 SB) $55-90
Continental Breakfast
Credit Cards: None
Notes: 2, 5, 7, 9, 10, 11, 12, 13, 14

Mountain Home Ranch

3400 Mountain Home Ranch Road, 94515
(707) 942-6616

Situated in the hills above the Napa Valley, the 300-acre vacation facility has been in the same family since 1913. Quiet, restful, rejuvenating. Pool, tennis, lake fishing, wilderness walking trails. Fifteen minutes to the heart of the wine country with its hot air ballooning, spas, and golf.

Hosts: George and Joey Fouts
Rooms: 14 (PB) $50-95
Continental Breakfast
Credit Cards: A, B
Closed mid-Dec.-end Jan.
Notes: 2, 7, 8, 9, 10, 11, 12, 14

The Pink Mansion

1415 Foothill Boulevard, 94515
(707) 942-0558

A 116-year-old Victorian in the heart of the Napa Valley wine country. Within biking distance to several wineries; walking distance to Calistoga's many spas and restaurants. Fully air-conditioned; complimentary wine and cheese. Each room has a wonderful view and private bath.

Host: Jeff Seyfried
Rooms: 5 (PB) $75-155
Full Breakfast
Minimum stay weekends & holidays: 2 nights
Credit Cards: A, B
Notes: 2, 5, 8 (over 12), 9, 10, 11, 12

Quail Mountain Bed and Breakfast Inn

4455 North St. Helena Highway, 94515
(707) 942-0316

NOTES: Credit cards accepted: A Master Card; B Visa; C American Express; D Discover Card; E Diner's Club; F Other; 2 Personal Checks accepted; 3 Lunch available; 4 Dinner available; 5 Open all year;

Quail Mountain is a secluded luxury bed and breakfast situated on 26 wooded and vineyard acres. Three guest rooms, each with king bed, private bath, and private deck. Complimentary wine, pool, spa. Full breakfast. Close to Napa Valley wineries & restaurants.

Hosts: Don and Alma Swiers
Rooms: 3 (PB) $98-130
Full Breakfast
Minimum stay weekends & holidays: 2 nights
Credit Cards: A, B
Notes: 2, 5, 10, 11, 12, 14

Trailside Inn

4201 Silverado Trail, 94515
(707) 942-4106

A charming 1930s farmhouse centrally situated in the country with three very private suites. Each suite has its own entrance, porch or deck, bedroom, bath, fireplace, spa, and air conditioning. Fresh home-baked breads provided in your fully equipped kitchen.

Hosts: Randy and Lani Gray
Suites: 3 (PB) $95-120
Continental Breakfast
Credit Cards: C, D
Notes: 2, 5, 7, 8, 9, 10, 11, 12, 14

Zinfandel House

1253 Summit Drive, 94515
(707) 942-0733

Zinfandel House is in a wooded setting on a western hillside with a spectacular view of the famous Napa Valley vineyards. Halfway between St. Helena and Calistoga. Choose among three tastefully decorated rooms with a private or shared bath. Breakfast is served on the deck or in the solarium.

Hosts: Bette and George Starke
Rooms: 3 (PB or SB) $70-100
Full Breakfast
Credit Cards: None
Notes: 2, 5, 9, 10, 11, 12, 14

CAMARILLO

Kids Welcome 3-14

730 Catalina Avenue, Seal Beach, 90740
(310) 493-6837; (800) 383-3513

This four-acre ranch in Camarillo has stables, fruit trees, a spa, and hiking trails. The two guest wings have a total of five rooms, which is perfect for a large family. Affordable rates.

CAMBRIA

Beach House

6360 Moonstone Beach Drive, 93428
(805) 927-3136

The Beach House is situated on the oceanfront with beautiful views, decks, and patios. Some rooms have fireplaces. Large common room with large deck facing the ocean to watch the gorgeous sunsets. Hearst Castle six miles away. Complimentary bicycles.

Hosts: Penny Hitch and Tigg Morales
Rooms: 7 (PB) $111.30-143.10
Expanded Continental Breakfast
Credit Cards: A, B,
Notes: 2, 5, 8, 9, 10, 11, 12, 14

The Blue Whale Inn

6736 Moonstone Beach Drive, 93428
(805) 927-4647

The Inn is located six miles south of Hearst castle on scenic Moonstone Beach. The six mini-suites are decorated in "European Country", with canopy beds, fireplaces, and colorful wall hangings. Each room has its own outdoor entrance, private bath, and color television. A full gourmet breakfast featuring gingerbread pancakes with lemon sauce and whipped cream, blueberry crepes and zucchini bread are just a sample of what's in store for our guests.

6 Pets welcome; 7 Smoking allowed; 8 Children welcome; 9 Social drinking allowed; 10 Tennis available; 11 Swimming available; 12 Golf available; 13 Skiing available; 14 May be booked through travel agents.

Hosts: Nancy and John Young
Rooms: 6 (PB) $135-165
Full Breakfast
Credit Cards: A, B
Notes: 2, 5

Eye Openers Bed and Breakfast Reservations CA-P31

P. O. Box 694, Altadena, 91003-0694
(213) 684-4428; (818) 797-2055
FAX (818) 798-3640

Just south of Heast Castle at the ocean, this bed and breakfast features rooms with fireplaces, private patios, and bath en suite. A full breakfast is served with an ocean view. No smoking. Three guest rooms. Private bath. $75 plus tax.

Eye Openers Bed and Breakfast Reservations CA-B51

P. O. Box 694, Altadena, 91003-0694
(213) 684-4428; (818) 797-2055
FAX (818) 798-3640

Contemporary A-frame bed and breakfast inn on the beach has antique furnishings, ocean views, and outdoor decks. Continental breakfast. No smoking. Five guest rooms. Private bath. $105-125 plus tax.

Eye Openers Bed and Breakfast Reservations CA-D1

P. O. Box 694, Altadena, 91003-0694
(213) 684-4428; (818) 797-2055
FAX (818) 798-3640

English couple hosts an elegant bed and breakfast with a relaxed atmosphere near Hearst Castle and mid-coast beaches. First floor is guest's domain and includes a large sitting room/bedroom with a fireplace and wet bar. Continental breakfast with jams and jellies from homegrown berries. No smoking. One guest room with private bath. $90.

Eye Openers Bed and Breakfast Reservations CA-O61

P. O. Box 694, Altadena, 91003-0694
(213) 684-4428; (818) 797-2055
FAX (818) 798-3640

Each guest room in this 1873 Greek Revival-style historic inn is decorated differently, but all have antiques from the 1800s. Full breakfast. No smoking. Six guest rooms. Private bath. $85-115 plus tax.

Megan's Friends #08

1776 Royal Way
San Luis Obispo, CA 93405
(805) 544-4406

This retreat is situated in the pines above West Village. It has two bedrooms with queen or twin beds and a shared bath, and provides radios and books. Continental breakfast is served on the deck, in the dining room, or in the breakfast area. A five-minute drive to the village shops and art galleries. Pack a lunch and walk along the craggy beaches nearby off Highway 1, where picnic table are conveniently situated.

Megan's Friends #09

1776 Royal Way
San Luis Obispo, CA 93405
(805) 544-4406

Two cabins are available for guests: the Blue Cabin and the Brown Cabin, both with double beds, showers, color TV, VCR, microwave ovens, and refirgerators. Each cabin has a deck outside with a shared barbecue. Expanded continental breakfast. No children. please. $70.

NOTES: Credit cards accepted: A Master Card; B Visa; C American Express; D Discover Card; E Diner's Club; F Other; 2 Personal Checks accepted; 3 Lunch available; 4 Dinner available; 5 Open all year;

Megan's Friends #10

1776 Royal Way
San Luis Obispo, CA 93405
(805) 544-4406

Luxurious, architect-designed home close to the Pacific Ocean. Guests are provided with a spacious bedroom, king-size bed, and private bath. An extra room can be available with a shared bath. Private entrance. Refreshments upon arrival. Full breakfast. $78.

Megan's Friends #11

1776 Royal Way
San Luis Obispo, CA 93405
(805) 544-4406

Separate wing and private entrance available for guests. Two bedrooms, one with double bed, one with king-size bed and Frankilin stove. Cable TV. Private or shared bath. Self-catered continental breakfast. $75-125.

Megan's Friends #12

1776 Royal Way
San Luis Obispo, CA 93405
(805) 544-4406

Beautiful cottage in quiet area. Kitchen with refrigerator, fully suplied with coffee maker, toaster oven, utilities. Fireplace and color TV. French doors open to a deck and patio. Twenty-minute walk to Pacific Ocean. Welcome basket and continental breakfast. $75.

The Pickford House Bed and Breakfast

2555 MacLeod Way, 93428
(805) 927-8619

Only eight miles from Hearst Castle, Pickford House is decorated with antiques reminiscent of the golden age of film. Eight rooms have king or queen beds, private baths, fireplaces, and a view of the mountains. Parlor with an 1860 bar is used for wine and tea bread at 5:00 p.m. TV in rooms. All have claw-foot tubs and showers in rooms. Well-behaved children welcome. Extra person-$20 extra dollars. Crib or rollaway bed available.

Host: Anna Larsen
Rooms: 8 (PB) $85-120
Full Breakfast
Credit Cards: A, B
Notes: 5, 7 (limited), 8, 9, 14

CAMINO

Camino Hotel: The Seven Mile House

4103 Carson Road, P. O. Box 1197, 95709
(916) 644-7740

Situated in the Apple Hill region of California's Gold Country at an elevation of 3,000 feet along the historic Carson Wagon Trail, the Camino Hotel is within walking or biking distance of several apple ranches, wineries, antiques, and dining. For years, the town of Camino has been a haven for loggers and weary wayfarers. Today it continues this tradition of offering hospitality to travelers from around the world.

Hosts: Paula Nobert and John Eddy
Rooms: 10 (3 PB; 7 SB) $55-85
Expanded Continental Breakfast
Credit Cards: A, B, C, D, F
Notes: 2, 5, 8, 9, 11, 12, 13, 14

CAPISTRANO

Bed and Breakfast Los Angeles 6-8

730 Catalina Avenue, Seal Beach, 90740
(310) 493-6837; (800) 383-3513

This classic little Spanish inn sits on the beach in San Juan Capistrano. Individually decorated rooms feature wood-burning fire-

6 Pets welcome; 7 Smoking allowed; 8 Children welcome; 9 Social drinking allowed; 10 Tennis available; 11 Swimming available; 12 Golf available; 13 Skiing available; 14 May be booked through travel agents.

places, wet bars, refrigerators, and private patios. Continental breakfast includes croissants and jam. Moderate rates.

CAPITOLA

The Inn at Depot Hill
250 Monterey Avenue, 95010
(408) 462-3376

Sophistication and elegance describe The Inn at Depot Hill in the quaint Mediterranean-style, beach-side resort of Capitola. You're buying a ticket to romance, illusion, and escapism. Travel the world, make stops at Portofino, Stratford-on-Avon, Delft, Sissinghurst, or Paris. Possibly you can capture your dream in Cote d'Azur, or come home to America in the contemporary Capitola beach room. Each of the eight suites has a fireplace and private bath. All are unique—so varied that it will be difficult to decide where your journey will begin or end.

Host: Suzie Lankes
Rooms: 8 (PB) $165-265
Full Breakfast
Credit Cards: A, B, C
Notes: 2, 5, 14

CARLSBAD

Pelican Cove Inn
320 Walnut Avenue, 92008
(619) 434-5995

Pelican Cove Inn features Jacuzzi, feather beds, fireplaces, private entries, private baths, lovely antiques, a sun deck, balconies, and a gazebo. Walk to the beach and restaurants. Palomar Airport and Amtrak pick-up. Beach chairs, towels, picnic baskets available. Afternoon refreshments, flowers, fruit, and candy provided. New and beautiful.

Hosts: Bob and Celeste Hale
Rooms: 8 (PB) $85-150

Continental Breakfast
Minimum stay weekends & holidays: 2 nights
Credit Cards: A, B, C
Notes: 2, 5, 7, 8 (over 12), 9, 10, 11, 12, 14

Pelican Cove Inn

CARMEL

Bed & Breakfast International #203
P. O. Box 282910, San Francisco, 94128-2910
(415) 696-1690; FAX (415) 696-1699

Large contemporary home with several decks surrounded by hills ten minutes from Carmel. There is a studio guest house with a queen-size lodgepole pine bed, wood-burning fireplace, and private entrance. There is a hot tub on one of the decks for guests to use. Breakfast is brought to the guest house by the host. $88.

Bed & Breakfast International #205
P. O. Box 282910, San Francisco, 94128-2910
(415) 696-1690; FAX (415) 696-1699

Spacious modern home has four fireplaces, and is very contemporary in design, just minutes from downtown Carmel. The guest room has a charming and cozy decor with professional decorator touches. There is a

NOTES: Credit cards accepted: A Master Card; B Visa; C American Express; D Discover Card; E Diner's Club; F Other; 2 Personal Checks accepted; 3 Lunch available; 4 Dinner available; 5 Open all year;

private entrance, fireplace in the room, private bath, and view of Point Lobos. Breakfast is prepared by the host in the main house. $95.

Bed & Breakfast International #207

P. O. Box 282910, San Francisco, 94128-2910
(415) 696-1690; FAX (415) 696-1699

Contemporary town house with fine art and tasteful furnishings situated on the east side of Highway 1, five minutes from Carmel Beach. The guest room is large and has a queen bed and private bath. There is a pool available for guests' use. $78.

Carriage House Inn

Junipero between 7th and 8th, 93921
(800) 433-4732

Fresh flowers and country-inn flavor. Continental breakfast and newspaper delivered to your room each morning. Woodburning fireplaces, down comforters. Spacious rooms, many with open-beam ceilings and sunken tubs. Wine and hors d'oeuvres each evening in the library. Carmel's AAA four-diamond inn. A romantic getaway!

Hosts: Paul Lopez
Rooms: 13 (PB) $130-325
Continental Breakfast
Minimum stay weekends & holidays: 2 nights
Credit Cards: All Major
Notes: 2, 5, 7, 11, 12, 14

Cypress Inn

Lincoln and Seventh, P. O. Box Y, 93921
(408) 624-3871; (800) 443-7443 (US and Canada)

Carmel's landmark since 1929, the Cypress Inn combines the comfortable ambiance of a country inn with the luxury of a small hotel. Set in the heart of the village, this historic property is just around the corner from everything.

Host: Michelle McConnell
Rooms: 33 (PB) $88-190
Continental Breakfast
Credit Cards: A, B, C
Notes: 2, 5, 6, 7, 14

Eye Openers Bed and Breakfast Reservations CA-C251

P. O. Box 694, Altadena, 91003-0694
(213) 684-4428; (818) 797-2055
FAX (818) 798-3640

This country inn offers twenty-five large, nicely decorated guest rooms with fireplace, full breakfast, afternoon, and evening refreshments. Convenient to all Carmel area attractions. No smoking. Private bath. $105-180 plus tax.

Eye Openers Bed and Breakfast Reservations CA-G191

P. O. Box 694, Altadena, 91003-0694
(213) 684-4428; (818) 797-2055
FAX (818) 798-3640

Close to the beach, in a quiet neighborhood, this 1926 refurbished inn has a lush garden setting. Buffet breakfast and afternoon refreshments. No smoking. Nineteen guest rooms. Private bath. $75-150 plus tax.

Happy Landing Inn

Box 2619, 93921
(408) 624-7917

Delightful little bed and breakfast inn in the heart of downtown Carmel. Beautiful antiques, stained-glass windows, fresh flowers. Breakfast served in your room. This inn looks like a page out of a Beatrix Potter book; you'll love it.

Hosts: Robert Ballard and Dick Stewart
Rooms: 7 (PB) $90-145
European Breakfast
Minimum stay weekends: 2 nights
Credit Cards: A, B
Notes: 2, 5, 8 (over 12), 9, 10, 12

6 Pets welcome; 7 Smoking allowed; 8 Children welcome; 9 Social drinking allowed; 10 Tennis available; 11 Swimming available; 12 Golf available; 13 Skiing available; 14 May be booked through travel agents.

Holiday House

P. O. Box 782, Camino Real at 7th Avenue, 93921
(408) 624-6267

Built in 1905, this comfortable inn is a brown-shingled house on a hillside amid a colorful, well-maintained garden. Six quaint rooms, four with private baths, offer refuge and relaxation. All rooms are furnished with antiques, complimenting the slanted ceilings and dormer windows looking out onto ocean or garden. A full breakfast is served buffet-style daily. Three blocks to beach and one block off Carmel's main street. A cozy get-away right in the heart of charming Carmel.

Hosts: Dieter and Ruth Back
Rooms: 6 (4 PB; 2 SB) $80-85
Full Breakfast
Credit Cards: A, B
Notes: 2, 5, 9, 10, 11, 12

Monte Verde Inn

P. O. Box 394
Ocean Avenue and Monte Verde, 93921
(408) 625-6046; (800) 328-7707

A charming country inn nestled in the heart of Carmel and surrounded by lovely gardens and terraces as well as decks. The inn has ten uniquely furnished warm rooms with either king or queen beds, all with private baths. Some rooms have spectacular ocean views, while others have wood-burning fireplaces. Only three short blocks to the shimmering Pacific Ocean. With a courteous staff, this little inn is one many would like to keep secret.

Hosts: Willa and Ernest Aylaian
Rooms: 10 (PB) $85-145
Continental Breakfast
Credit Cards: A, B, C
Notes: 2, 5, 8, 9, 14

San Antonio House

P. O. Box 3683, 93921
(408) 624-4334

A romantic seaside country inn capturing the charm of early Carmel. Situated one block from Carmel Beach and four blocks from town. Four comfortably furnished rooms with private entrances, patios, and wood-burning fireplaces offer that restful place to get away from the hectic pace of the world. Beautiful gardens surround the inn. Close to golf.

Host: Jeanne Goodwin
Rooms: 4 (PB) $110-150
Expanded Continental Breakfast
Credit Cards: A, B
Notes: 2, 5, 12, 14

The Sandpiper Inn-at-the-Beach

2408 Bay View Avenue, 93923
(408) 624-6433

Within sight and sound of beautiful Carmel Beach. Quiet comfort and luxury in a relaxed atmosphere. Rooms and cottages are filled with antiques and fresh flowers; all have private baths. Some have glorious ocean views, others have fireplaces. Breakfast and complimentary sherry are served in the comfortable lounge. Perfect for anniversaries and special occasions.

Hosts: Graeme and Irene Mackenzie
Rooms: 16 (PB) $90-170
Continental Breakfast
Credit Cards: A, B, C
Notes: 2, 5, 9, 10, 11, 12

Sea View Inn

P. O. Box 4138
Camino Real between 11th and 12th, 93921
(408) 624-8778

The Sea View Inn, a simple country Victorian, has been welcoming guests for over 70 years. A quiet, cozy bed and breakfast, the Sea View has eight individually decorated rooms, six with private baths. Situated near the village and the beach, the Sea View provides a welcoming retreat. A generous continental breakfast and afternoon tea are complimentary.

Host: Diane Hydorn
Rooms: 8 (6 PB; 2 SB) $80-110
Expanded Continental Breakfast
Credit Cards: A, B
Notes: 2, 5, 9

NOTES: Credit cards accepted: A Master Card; B Visa; C American Express; D Discover Card; E Diner's Club; F Other; 2 Personal Checks accepted; 3 Lunch available; 4 Dinner available; 5 Open all year;

Stonehouse Inn

P. O. Box 2517, 93921
(408) 624-4569

Victorian house (1906), furnished with antiques, within walking distance of the beach, shops, restaurants. Living room with large fireplace is the gathering spot for guests to enjoy spirits and snacks before dinner. Breakfast is served in the bright and cheery dining room each morning.

Hosts: Barbara Cooke
Rooms: 6 (SB) $90-125
Full Breakfast
Credit Cards: A, B
Notes: 2, 5, 8 (over 11), 9, 10, 12, 14

Tally Ho Inn

P. O. Box 3726, 93921
(408) 624-2232

The Tally Ho is conveniently situated three blocks from a white sandy beach in the heart of the village, close to superb restaurants and shopping. A delightful buffet breakfast is served in the dining room overlooking beautiful Carmel Bay. In the evenings, an aged French brandy awaits your return from dinner. Five minutes from 17-mile drive, championship golf, and the Monterey Aquarium. Spectacular bay views.

Hosts: Barbara and Erven Torell
Rooms: 14 (PB) $105-250
Expanded Continental Breakfast
Credit Cards: A, B, C
Notes: 2, 5, 7, 8, 9, 10, 11, 12, 14

Tickle Pink Inn

155 Highland Drive, 93923
(408) 624-1244

Perched on a hillside above the Pacific, the Tickle Pink Inn offers spectacular views of the area's dramatic coastline. A favorite spot of those who are looking for a special place to relax. Many rooms have a fireplace. Continental breakfast is served in an ocean-view lounge or delivered to your room. It includes an assortment of pastries baked every day at the inn. Freshly baked cookies are served every afternoon.

Host: Elisa Frankel
Rooms: 35 (PB) $109-299
Continental Breakfast
Credit Cards: A, B, C
Notes: 2, 5, 7, 8, 9, 14

Vagabond's House Inn

P. O. Box 2747, 93921
(408) 624-7738; (800) 262-1262 Reservations only

Situated in the heart of Carmel village, Vagabond's House Inn surrounds a Carmel-stone courtyard that is dominated by large oak trees, plants, ferns, and flowers in profusion. The 11 unique guest rooms are appointed with a combination of collectibles and antiques in a mixture of European elegance and country tradition.

Hosts: Honey Spence and Jewell Brown
Rooms: 11 (PB) $79-150
Continental Breakfast
Credit Cards: A, B, C
Notes: 2, 5, 6, 7, 9, 10, 11, 12, 14

CARMEL VALLEY

Hilltop House

11685 McCarthy Road, 93924
(408) 659-3060

Peaceful, private mountain retreat overlooking sunny Carmel Valley, just 20 minutes away from Monterey Peninsula's natural attractions, cultural activities, and fine restaurants. Comfortable two-room guest suite with bath and wood-burning fireplace; 40-foot pool and hot tub, extensive rose and sculpture gardens. Delicious breakfast and afternoon refreshments in a friendly, hospitable home.

Hosts: Margaret and Richard Mayer
Rooms: 2 (SB) $75-90
Full Breakfast
Credit Cards: None
Notes: 2, 5, 9, 10, 11, 12

---

6 Pets welcome; 7 Smoking allowed; 8 Children welcome; 9 Social drinking allowed; 10 Tennis available; 11 Swimming available; 12 Golf available; 13 Skiing available; 14 May be booked through travel agents.

The Valley Lodge

Carmel Valley Road and Ford Road
P. O. Box 93, 93924
(408) 659-2261; (800) 641-4646

A quiet country inn situated on seven beautifully landscaped acres in picturesque
Carmel Valley, the sunbelt of the Monterey
Peninsula. Relax and unwind in a garden
patio room, a fireplace suite, or a cozy one
or two bedroom fireplace cottage with a
kitchen. Enjoy our heated pool, hot spa,
sauna, fitness center, and games area. Walk
to fine restaurants and quaint shops in
Carmel Valley Village, or just "listen to
your beard grow."

Host: Peter Coakley
Rooms: 31 (PB) $95-135
Expanded Continental Breakfast
Credit Cards: A, B, C
Notes: 2, 5, 6, 7, 8, 9, 11, 14

CARPINTERIA

America's Bed & Breakfast #19

P. O. Box 9302, Whittier, 90608
(310) 699-8427

An experienced hostess will share avocado
and fruit ranching activities with guests in a
comfortable condominium situated on one
of the finest beaches in the world.
Complete kitchen and comfortable beds
offer complete privacy and a place in the
sun. $75.

Carpinteria Beach Condo

1825 Cravens Lane, 93013
(805) 684-1579

Situated in a lush flower-growing valley.
Across the street from "the world's safest
beach." Unit has mountain view. Tropical
island decor has a sunset wall mural, fully
furnished kitchen, queen bed, and color
cable TV. Pool, spa, and gas barbecue on
complex. Self-catering with beverage provided and fruit from host's ranch. Sleeps
four. Eleven miles south of Santa Barbara.
Hosts available for tennis, bridge, or tour of
their semitropical fruit ranch. No smoking.

Hosts: Bev and Don Schroeder
Suite: 1 (PB) $60-65
Continental Breakfast
Credit Cards: None
Notes: 2, 5, 8, 9, 10, 11, 12

D&B Schroeder Ranch

1825 Cravens Lane, 93013
(805) 684-1579

The D&B Schroeder Ranch in the carpinteria foothills produces avocados and semitropical fruit. Located one mile from Hwy.
101 and eleven miles from Santa Barbara,
the non-smoking guest unit has a queen
size bed, color cable TV, private bath, and
ocean view decks. There is spa set in tropical flora to relax weary travellers. A full
breakfast is served, and swimming and tennis are available in town or at the Polo and
Racquet Club.

Hosts: Beverly Schroeder
Room: 1 (PB) $60-65
Full Breakfast
Credit Cards: None
Notes: 2, 5, 9, 10, 11, 12

CATALINA

Bed and Breakfast Los Angeles 5-5

730 Catalina Avenue, Seal Beach, 90740
(310) 493-6837; (800) 383-3513

Sprawling over a hillside, this house in colorful San Pedro offers three rooms with
private baths. One room has a crib. Visit
the tide pools a few blocks from your door.
Affordable rates.

CAZADERO

Cazanoma Lodge

1000 Kidd CR RD, 954221-0037
(707) 632-5255

Old World lodge situated on 147 acres of redwood and fir forest with waterfall and trout pond. All suites and cabins have private baths. Situated near the ocean and the Russian River wine country. Fine dining— German and American menu—full bar.

Hosts: Randy and Gretchen Neuman
Rooms: 5 (PB) $75-105 Cabin also available.
Continental Breakfast
Credit Cards: A, B, C
Closed Dec. 1-Feb. 20
Notes: 2, 4, 6 (cabins), 7, 8, 9, 10, 11, 12, 14

CHESTER

Cinnamon Teal

227 Feather River Drive, P. O. Box 1517, 96020
(916) 258-3993

The Cinnamon Teal is located in the town of Chester at Lake Almanor, 35 miles from Mt. Lassen. Ninety-nine miles to Sacramento, the state capitol. The Chester airport is only one and one-half miles to pick up service. No commercial flights. Old World charm. Feather beds. Area has many fine restaurants and shops.

Host: Betty Braun
Rooms: 4 (2 PB; 2 SB) $65-95
Full Breakfast
Credit Cards: None
Notes: 2, 5, 11, 12, 13

CHICO

O'Flaherty House Bed and Breakfast

1462 Aracadian and West 5th Avenue, 95926
(916) 893-5494

A 1905 Victorian situated within walking distance to California State University, Chico, Bidwell Mansion, and downtown shopping. Decorated with antiques, nostalgia, and humor. One king, two queens, and a double are available and share two bathrooms. Robes provided, large yards, phone, TV, VCR. Friendly, helpful staff and an ever-alert security dog named Rejekt greet you.

Host: Barbi Boeger Easter
Rooms: 6 (2 PB; 4 SB) $58-82
Extended Continental Breakfast
Credit Cards: A, B, C, D, E, F
Notes: 2, 5, 9, 14

O'Flaherty House Bed and Breakfast

CLEAR LAKE

Muktip Manor

12540 Lakesore Drive, 95422
(707) 994-9571

Suite consiting of bedroom, bath, kitchenette, sitting room, TV, and deck. Private beach on the largest lake in California, with canoe and bicycles available. Several golf courses are in the county. Hiking, biking, and rock hounding. Located 110 miles north of San Francisco, near five wineries.

Host: Jerry Schiffman
Room: 1 (PB) $50
Full Breakfast
Credit Cards: None
Notes: 2, 5, 6, 7, 9, 10, 11

6 Pets welcome; 7 Smoking allowed; 8 Children welcome; 9 Social drinking allowed; 10 Tennis available; 11 Swimming available; 12 Golf available; 13 Skiing available; 14 May be booked through travel agents.

CLOVERDALE

Vintage Towers Bed and Breakfast Inn

302 North Main Street, 95425
(707) 894-4535

This lovely Queen Anne Victorian mansion was built in 1901 with three architecturally unique towers that now house some of the guest suites. Situated near 52 wineries in the serene Sonoma Valley and the Russian River Basin. Gourmet breakfast prepared by a French pastry chef.

Hosts: Jim Mees and Garrett Hall
Rooms: 7 (5 PB; 2 SB) $80-115
Full Breakfast
Credit Cards: A, B, C, D
Notes: 2, 7 (limited), 8, 9, 10, 11, 12, 14

COLOMA

Coloma Country Inn

345 High Street, Box 502, 95613
(916) 622-6919

Columbia City Hotel

Surrounded by the 300-acre Gold Discovery State Park, this 1852 farmhouse provides quiet comfort and close access to Sutter's Mill, museum, and attractions. White-water rafting and ballooning with hosts. Featured in the June 1988 issue of *Country Living* magazine.

Hosts: Cindi and Alan Ehrgott
Rooms: 5 (3 PB; 2 SB) $79-89
Expanded Continental Breakfast
Credit Cards: None
Notes: 2, 5, 8 (over 6), 9

COLUMBIA

Columbia City Hotel

Box 1870, 95310
(209) 532-1479

Centrally situated in Columbia, a historic Gold Rush town preserved and protected by the state of California, this impeccable inn is surrounded by relics of the past. All rooms have been restored to reflect the 1850s. Downstairs, the highly acclaimed restaurant and always inviting What Cheer Saloon provide a haven for travelers seeking comfort and gracious hospitality. All rooms have half-baths; hall showers.

Host: Tom Bender
Rooms: 9 (PB) $70-85
Continental Breakfast
Credit Cards: A, B, C
Closed Dec. 24-25; midweek in Jan.
Notes: 2, 3, 4, 5, 7 (limited), 8, 9, 10, 11, 12, 13, 14

Fallon Hotel

Washington Street, 95310
(209) 532-1470

Since 1857, the historic Fallon Hotel has provided a home away from home to countless visitors. Authentically restored to its Victorian grandeur, most of the furnishings are original to the inn. Several rooms have private balconies, and all rooms have half-baths. Baskets of toiletries, robes and slippers are provided for the showers off the hallway. One handicapped room available. Centrally situated in a state-restored Gold Rush town. Adjacent to the Fallon Theatre which provides year-round productions. Call or write for price information.

Host: Tom Bender
Rooms: 14 (SB) $55-85
Continental Breakfast
Credit Cards: A, B, C
Notes: 2, 8

CORONADO ISLAND

Bed and Breakfast Los Angeles 8-4

730 Catalina Avenue, Seal Beach, 90740
(310) 493-6837; (800) 383-3513

Not just a bed and breakfast, but a weekend experience, this hostess also teaches fitness and dance classes. Her 1894 historic landmark home also features the Balanchine, Baryshnikov, and Fred and Ginger rooms. Breakfast includes Armenian eggs and baklava. Cooking classes available, too. Luxury rates.

DAVENPORT

New Davenport Bed and Breakfast

31 Davenport Avenue, 95017
(408) 425-1818; (408) 426-4122

Halfway between Carmel-Monterey and San Francisco, on Coast Highway 1. Small, rural, coastal town noted for whale watching, wind surfing, Ano Nuevo Elephant Seal State Reserve, hiking, bicycling, and beach exploration. Wonderful restaurant and gift store with unusual treasures and jewelry.

Hosts: Bruce and Marcia McDougal
Rooms: 12 (PB) $55-105
Full Breakfast
Credit Cards: A, B, C
Notes: 2, 3, 4, 5, 8, 9

DAVIS

University Inn Bed and Breakfast

340 A Street, 95616
(916) 756-8648

Adjacent to the University of California at Davis, this country inn offers a charming escape from a busy college town in a home-like setting. Each room has a private bath, phone, TV, and refrigerator. There are complimentary chocolates, beverages, and flowers, and a generous breakfast is served.

Hosts: Lynda and Ross Yancher
Rooms: 4 (PB) $50 plus tax
Continental Breakfast
Credit Cards: All Major
Notes: 2, 5, 6 (limited), 7 (outside), 8, 9, 10, 11, 12, 14

DEL MAR

The Blue Door

13707 Durango Drive, 92014
(619) 755-3819

Enjoy New England charm in a quiet Southern California setting. Lower-level two-room suite with king bed, private bath, and cozy sitting room opening onto bougainvillaea-splashed patio with open vista of Torrey Pines Reserve Canyon. Twenty miles north of San Diego. Creative full breakfast.

Hosts: Bob and Anna Belle Schock
Suite: 1 (PB) $50-60
Full Breakfast
Credit Cards: None
Notes: 2, 5, 8 (over 16), 9, 10, 11, 12

Eye Openers Bed and Breakfast Reservations DM-R101

P. O. Box 694, Altadena, 91003-0694
(213) 684-4428; (818) 797-2055
FAX (818) 798-3640

6 Pets welcome; 7 Smoking allowed; 8 Children welcome; 9 Social drinking allowed; 10 Tennis available; 11 Swimming available; 12 Golf available; 13 Skiing available; 14 May be booked through travel agents.

Romantic getaway in a lovely seaside village just north of San Diego offers a choice of ten rooms, many with an ocean view and one with a fireplace. Enjoy an extended continental breakfast, afternoon refreshments, a walk on the beach, or a trip to the racetrack or nearby renown flower-growing areas. Private and shared bath. $80-135 plus tax.

Gull's Nest

12930 Via Esperia, P. O. Box 1056, 92014
(619) 259-4863

Gull's Nest rustic hideaway is a contemporary wood home surrounded by pines with a beautiful ocean and bird sanctuary view from two upper decks. Home is decorated with many paintings, mosaics, and wood carvings. Five minutes from La Jolla and Del Mar. Close to I-5, and just 20 minutes from the San Diego Zoo and airport.

Hosts: Michael and Constance Segel
Rooms: 2 (PB) $60-75
Full Breakfast
Credit Cards: None
Notes: 2, 5, 7 (outside), 8 (over 5), 9, 11, 12

DORRINGTON

Dorrington Hotel and Restaurant

3431 Highway 4, P. O. Box 4307, 95223
(209) 795-5800

This 1860 hotel was originally a stage coach stop and served as a depot for stockmen and as a summer resort. Restored, the hotel provides a gracious and relaxing atmosphere. Cozy homemade quilts, brass beds and handsome antiques fill the five comfortably-elegant rooms. Fresh fruit and other amenities will make you feel at home. A continental breakfast including freshly ground, gourmet coffee and a newspaper will be left outside your door at the time of your choice. Enjoy a tastefully prepared

meal in the casual elegance of the Northern Italian-style restaurant or a leisurely glass of sherry in the sitting room.

Hosts: Bonnie and Arden Saville
Rooms: 5 (2 SB) $75
Continental Breakfast
Credit Cards: A, B
Notes: 2, 3, 4, 5, 10, 11, 12, 13

DOWNIEVILLE

Sierra Shangri-La

P. O. Box 285, 95936
(916) 289-3455

A small resort on the North Fork of the Yuba River in the Sierra Nevada Range. At 3,100 feet elevation on the site of a former mining camp. Three rooms in the main lodge, with balconies overlooking magnificent views of the river, which is known for its rainbow and German brown trout angling.

Hosts: Fran and Frank Carter
Rooms: 3 (PB) $55-70
Continental Breakfast
Credit Cards: A, B
Notes: 2, 9, 11, 13

DULZURA

Brookside Farm Bed and Breakfast Inn

1373 Marron Valley Road, 92017
(619) 468-3043

A country farmhouse furnished with collectibles, handmade quilts, and stained glass. Tree-shaded terraces by a stream, farm animals, gardens, hot tub in the grape arbor. Perfect for country walks. Close to Tecate, Mexico, and 35 minutes from San Diego.

Hosts: Edd and Sally Guishard
Rooms: 9 (7 PB; 2 SB) $48.60-81
Full Breakfast
Minimum stay holidays and some rooms: 2 nights
Credit Cards: A, B
Notes: 2, 4 (weekends), 9, 14

NOTES: Credit cards accepted: A Master Card; B Visa; C American Express; D Discover Card; E Diner's Club; F Other; 2 Personal Checks accepted; 3 Lunch available; 4 Dinner available; 5 Open all year;

ELK

Elk Cove Inn

6300 South Highway 1, 95432
(707) 877-3321

An 1883 Victorian atop a bluff with spectacular ocean views. Some cabins with fireplaces. Full gourmet breakfast is served in the ocean-view dining room. Ready access to an expansive, driftwood-strewn beach. Beds have the subtle luxury of sun-dried linens. Romantic atmosphere in rural coastal village. New addition provides dormers, window seats, and ocean-view deck.

Host: Hildrun-Uta Triebess
Rooms: 4 (PB) $98-148
Cabins: 4 (PB)
Full Breakfast
Credit Cards: None
Notes: 2, 5, 8 (over 12), 9, 11, 12

Sierra Shangri-La

ENCINITAS

Eye Openers Bed and Breakfast Reservations EN-C41

P. O. Box 694, Altadena, 91003-0694
(213) 684-4428; (818) 797-2055
FAX (818) 798-3640

Located in Encinatas, a renown flower-growing area in California, this new family-run bed and breakfast with ocean views has large rooms, a Southwest decor, and a relaxed atmosphere. Continental breakfast. No smoking. Three rooms and one suite. Private bath. $75-95 plus tax.

Inncline Bed and Breakfast

121 North Vulcan Avenue, 92024
(619) 944-0318

Encinitas's first bed and breakfast. A true find, squeaky clean. "An absolute treasure," said KABC talk radio. Features in this contemporary two-story ocean-view home are three bedrooms all with private baths, downstairs that has common sitting room with a fireplace and kitchenette, done in Southwest custom-designed handcrafted furnishings and decor. A new addition to our inn is the penthouse, a true "boudoir," with a king size bed, cable TV & VCR, whirlpool tub and shower, plus an eight foot spa on an ocean valley view balcony. Also, an upstairs one-bedroom apartment with fireplace and kitchen. There is a lovely sun deck in the front yard with a waterfall and fish pond. Make reservations early.

Hosts: Richard and Kirsten Cline
Rooms: 4 (PB) $75-95
Expanded Continental Breakfast
Credit Cards: A, B, C
Notes: 2, 5, 7, 8, 9, 10, 12, 14

EUCALYPTUS HILL

Kids Welcome 11-3

730 Catalina Avenue, Seal Beach, 90740
(310) 493-6837; (800) 383-3513

This hilltop home with ocean views has a pool, spa, and two guest rooms, both with private entrances and private baths. Breakfast is served poolside. Friendly golden retriever will greet you. Moderate rates.

6 Pets welcome; 7 Smoking allowed; 8 Children welcome; 9 Social drinking allowed; 10 Tennis available; 11 Swimming available; 12 Golf available; 13 Skiing available; 14 May be booked through travel agents.

EUREKA

Carter House and The Carter Hotel

301 L Street, 95501
(707) 444-8062

Spectacularly re-created landmark Victorians in scenic Old Town Eureka, near the famed Carson Mansion. Original art and antique appointments. Bay and marina vistas, fireplaces, whirlpool baths, featherbeds, truly elegant dining. Dinners featured in Bon Appetit. "Best breakfast in California"—California magazine.

Hosts: Mark and Christi Carter
Rooms: 27 (24 PB; 3 SB) $75-350
Full and Continental Breakfast
Credit Cards: A, B, C, E, F
Notes: 2 (on approved credit), 4, 5, 8 (over 8), 9, 10, 11, 12, 14

An Elegant Victorian Mansion

1406 C Street, 95501
(707) 444-3144; (707) 442-5594

"Victorian opulence, grace, grandeur—the most elegant house in Eureka"—The New York Times. A state landmark on the National Register of Historic Places. Features sauna, massage, croquet, Victorian ice cream sodas, French gourmet breakfasts, secured private parking, vintage classic movies, bicycles, antique cars. Near redwood parks, fishing, boating, tennis, cultural events, carriage and train rides, bay cruises. Located in a quiet Victorian neighborhood near Old Town.

Hosts: Doug and Lily Vieyra
Rooms: 4 (1 PB; 3 SB) $65-95
Full Breakfast
Credit Cards: A, B
Notes: 2, 5, 9, 10, 12, 14

Heuer's Victorian Inn

1302 E Street, 95501
(707) 442-7334

A Queen Anne Victorian built in 1893 and restored to its present splendor in 1980. Just like being transported back in time to an earlier era. For that quiet, relaxing time, it's a must.

Hosts: Charles and Ausbern Heuer
Rooms: 3 (1 PB; 2 SB) $75
Continental Breakfast
Credit Cards: A, B, C, D, E, F
Notes: 2, 5, 9, 10, 12

Old Town Bed and Breakfast Inn

1521 Third Street, 95501
(707) 445-3941

Historic 1871 Victorian in Eureka's famous Old Town district. Small, cozy, uniquely warm, plush, original art and period antiques. Tubs and showers; Teddy bears, rubber duckies; full breakfast. "The quintessence of world-class bed and breakfast."

Hosts: Leigh and Diane Benson
Rooms: 7 (5 PB; 2 SB) $75-130
Full Breakfast
Credit Cards: A, B
Notes: 2, 5, 8 (over 10), 9, 10, 11, 12, 14

A Weaver's Inn

1440 B Street, 95501
(707) 443-8119

An Elegant Victorian Mansion

NOTES: Credit cards accepted: A Master Card; B Visa; C American Express; D Discover Card; E Diner's Club; F Other; 2 Personal Checks accepted; 3 Lunch available; 4 Dinner available; 5 Open all year;

A Weaver's Inn, the home and studio of a fiber artist and her husband, is a stately Queen Anne/Colonial Revival house built in 1883 and remodeled in 1907. Placed in a spacious fenced garden, it is airy and light, but cozy and warm when veiled by wisps of fog. Visit the studio, try the spinning wheel before the fire, or weave on the antique loom before having refreshments.

Hosts: Bob and Dorothy Swendeman
Rooms: 4 (2 PB; 2 SB) $65-85
Full Breakfast
Credit Cards: A, B, C, D
Notes: 2, 5, 6, 8, 9, 14

FAWNSKIN

The Inn at Fawnskin Bed and Braekfast

880 Canyon Road, P. O. Box 378, 92333
(714) 866-3200

Beautiful custom log home nestled in its own private pine forest, just steps away from lake and forest trails. Living room with big rock fireplace, baby grand piano, comfy furniture, decks with lake and forest views. Dining room with big rock fireplace, delicious homemade breakfast. Large game room—50-inch TV screen, pool table, game table, stereo, wet bar. Gazebo with

Jacuzzi. Basketball court. Breathtaking master suite. Comforters and plush robes. Exceptional hospitality provided by owner/operators.

Hosts: G.B. and Susie Sneed
Rooms: 4 (2 PB; 2 SB) $75-155
Full Breakfast
Credit Cards: A, B
Notes: 2, 3, 4, 5, 9, 10, 11, 12, 13, 14

FERNDALE

The Gingerbread Mansion

400 Berding Street, 95536
(707) 786-4000

The Gingerbread Mansion bed and breakfast Inn is well known as one of America's most photographed homes. Its striking Victorian architecture trimmed with gingerbread, its colorful peach and yellow paint, and its surrounding English gardens all make the Gingerbread Mansion a photographer's delight. It is an understatement to say that the interiors are also spectacular.

Host: Ken Torbert
Rooms: 9 (PB) $105-175
Expanded Continental Breakfast
Credit Cards: A, B
Notes: 2, 5, 9, 10, 12, 14

The Gingerbread Mansion

Shaw House Inn

703 Main Street, P. O. Box 1125, 95536
(707) 786-9958

This 1854 Carpenter Gothic is cottage-like, very cozy and bright, like sleeping at Grandma's. There are lots of antiques and good reading in the library. This is the founder's home and is listed on the National Register of Historic Places. Afternoon tea at check-in, 3:00 to 6:00 p.m.

Hosts: Ken and Norma Bessingpas
Rooms: 5 (1 PB; 4 SB) $65-115
Expanded Continental Breakfast
Credit Cards: A, B, C
Notes: 2, 5, 7 (limited), 8 (over 8), 10, 14

FISH CAMP

Karen's Bed and Breakfast Yosemite Inn

1144 Railroad Avenue, P. O. Box 8, 93623
(209) 683-4550; (800) 346-1443

Experience the splendor of each season in Yosemite National Park. Only two miles from the south entrance, Karen's is open year-round offering you cozy country comfort. Nestled amid the towering pines and whispering cedars at 5,000 feet, it blends contemporary and country living. Your innkeepers will assist you in planning your visit while in the Yosemite area to assure maximum enjoyment during your stay.

Grey Whale Inn

Hosts: Karen Bergh and Lee Morse
Rooms: 3 (PB) $75
Full Breakfast
Credit Cards: None
Notes: 2, 5, 8, 12, 13, 14

Scotty's Bed and Breakfast

1223 Hwy 41, P. O. Box 82, 93623
(209) 683-6936

You will enjoy a cozy room with a private entrance and bath, full or queen size bed, river rock fireplace, color TV, stereo, microwave, continental breakfast, beautiful yard, barbecue, creek-side view, fishing, golf, skiing, historical train ride, back country hiking, biking, and stables. All of this and more is only two miles from Yosemite National Park.

Hosts: Scott B. Sanders
Rooms: 2 (1-PB; 1-SB) $55-75 plus tax
Continental Breakfast
Credit Cards: None
Notes: 2, 5, 8, 9, 10, 11, 12, 13

FORT BRAGG

Avalon House

561 Stewart Street, 95437
(707) 964-5555

A 1905 Craftsman house built completely of redwood and extensively remodeled in 1988, Avalon House is furnished with a mix of antiques and willow furniture. The emphasis here is on luxury and comfort: fireplaces, whirlpool tubs, down comforters and pillows, good bedside lights, as well as mood lights to create a romantic ambience. The inn is in a quiet residential area three blocks from the Pacific Ocean and one block from Highway 1. The Skunk Train depot is two blocks away.

Host: Anne Sorrells
Rooms: 5 (PB) $70-125
Full Breakfast
Credit Cards: A, B, C, D
Notes: 2, 5, 8, 9, 14

NOTES: Credit cards accepted: A Master Card; B Visa; C American Express; D Discover Card; E Diner's Club; F Other; 2 Personal Checks accepted; 3 Lunch available; 4 Dinner available; 5 Open all year;

Glass Beach Bed and Breakfast Inn

726 North Main St, 95437
(707) 964-6774

The Glass Beach Inn is a gracious guest house where we offer you elegance, relaxation and the comforts of home. Built in the 1920s as a private home, and renovated in 1980 as charming and unique inn, each room is furnished with its own distinct style. A generous breakfast is freshly prepared and served to you in our dining room, and you are a short walk to beaches, shops, restaurants, museums, and the famous Skunk Train.

Hosts: Richard Fowler and Nancy Cardenas
Rooms: 9 (PB) $62-92
Full Breakfast
Credit Cards: A, B
Notes: 2, 5, 7, 8, 9, 10, 11, 12

Grey Whale Inn

615 North Main Street, 95437
(707) 964-0640; (800) 382-7244 Reservations

Handsome four-story Mendocino Coast landmark since 1915. Cozy rooms to expansive suites, all private baths. Ocean, garden, or hill and city views. Some have fireplace, some have TV, one has whirlpool tub, all have phones. Recreation area: pool table, books, fireside lounge, TV theater. Conference room (16 persons). Complimentary buffet breakfast features

Pudding Creek Inn

Colette's Blue-ribbon coffee cakes. Friendly, helpful staff. Relaxed seaside charm, situated six blocks from beach. Celebrate your special occasion on the fabled Mendocino Coast! Mobil three-star rating. AB & BA Three crowns.

Host: Colette Bailey
Rooms: 14 (PB) $75-150
Full Breakfast
Credit Cards: A, B, C
Notes: 2, 5, 9, 10, 11, 12, 14

Noyo River Lodge

500 Casa Del Noyo Drive, 95437
(800) 628-1126

Country inn-style luxury on over two acres overlooking the famous fishing harbor and river. Eight individually decorated rooms (all with private baths) are available, and some have wood-burning fireplaces. There are also lavish suites with fireplaces. Some suites have private decks and double soaking tubs with separate showers; others offer separate sunrooms. All have fabulous views. Complimentary breakfast is served in the dining room, which has a fireplace, or on a large deck overlooking the river.

Hosts: Ellie Sinsel
Rooms: 16 (PB) $80-140
Continental Breakfast
Credit Cards: A, B, D
Notes: 2, 5, 8, 9, 12, 14

Pudding Creek Inn

700 North Main Street, 95437
(707) 964-9529

Two Victorian homes built in 1884 by a Russian count, connected by a lush enclosed garden. All rooms are comfortably decorated in Victorian style; all have private baths, and some have fireplaces. Exceptional accommodations with personal service, friendly hospitality, and yet special emphasis on privacy. Within walking distance of Glass Beach, Pudding Creek, downtown shops and restaurants, logging museum, Skunk Train depot.

6 Pets welcome; 7 Smoking allowed; 8 Children welcome; 9 Social drinking allowed; 10 Tennis available; 11 Swimming available; 12 Golf available; 13 Skiing available; 14 May be booked through travel agents.

Hosts: Garry and Carole Anloff
Rooms: 10 (PB) $65-125
Full Buffet Breakfast
Credit Cards: A, B, C
Notes: 2, 8, 9, 10, 11, 12, 14

FOUNTAIN VALLEY

Bed and Breakfast Los Angeles 7-1

730 Catalina Avenue, Seal Beach, 90740
(310) 493-6837; (800) 383-3513

This immaculate home in Fountain Valley has four guest rooms, all with private baths and TV's. Disney territory location. Affordable rates.

FREMONT

Lord Bradley's Inn

43344 Mission Boulevard, 94539
(415) 490-0520

This Victorian is nestled below Mission Peak, adjacent to the Mission San Jose. Numerous olive trees on the property were planted by the Ohlone Indians. Common room, garden, patio. Parking in rear. Take the bus or Bay Area Rapid Transit to San Francisco for a day.

American River Inn

Hosts: Keith and Anne Bradley Medeiros
Rooms: 8 (PB) $65-75
Continental Breakfast
Credit Cards: A, B, D
Notes: 2, 5, 6, 9, 14

GARDEN GROVE

Kids Welcome 7-4

730 Catalina Avenue, Seal Beach, 90740
(310) 493-6837; (800) 383-3513

Kids are really welcome in this lovely older home in Garden Grove. There are three guest rooms; one has a fireplace and a balcony, and another one has a TV and small refrigerator. All have private baths. Your hostess is a weaver and doll collector. Affordable rates.

Rent-A-Room

11531 Varna St., 92640
(714) 638-1406

This is a referral service that books private homes between Los Angeles and San Diego. No inns are on our list; our bed and breakfasts are in the British tradition. Most of our offerings are close to Southern California attractions, such as Disneyland, Knott's Berry Farm, San Diego Zoo, Sea World, Universal Studios, Anaheim Convention Center, and beaches. One to three guest rooms in each home. All rooms have private baths. Full breakfast is served in all bookings. $45-65.

GEORGETOWN

American River Inn

Orleans Street, Box 43, 95634
(916) 333-4499; (800) 245-6566 California

Located in the heart of Gold Country nine miles off Hwy. 49 between Hwy I-80 and I-50, this "Jewel of the Mother Lode" is a totally restored 1853 miners' boarding

---

NOTES: Credit cards accepted: A Master Card; B Visa; C American Express; D Discover Card; E Diner's Club; F Other; 2 Personal Checks accepted; 3 Lunch available; 4 Dinner available; 5 Open all year;

house. Each room is individually decorated with Victorian and turn-of-the-century antiques. Gorgeous natural gardens; a refreshing mountain stream; pool with Jacuzzi; a dove aviary; bicycles. Enjoy a full breakfast in the morning, local wines and treats in the evening. Antique shop on the premises. Facilities for the handicapped. Georgetown is a Sierra foothills village with real flavor and six historic buildings to explore.

Hosts: Will and Maria
Rooms: 25 (12 PB; 13 SB) $78-108
Full Breakfast
Credit Cards: A, B, C, D
Notes: 2, 5, 7, 8, 9, 10, 11, 12, 13, 14

GEYSERVILLE

Campbell Ranch Inn

1475 Canyon Road, 95441
(707) 857-3476

Thirty-five-acre country setting in the heart of Sonoma County wine country. Spectacular view, beautiful gardens, tennis court, swimming pool, hot tub, bicycles. Full breakfast served on the terrace; homemade evening dessert. Teenagers welcome. Color brochure available.

Hosts: Mary Jane and Jerry Campbell
Rooms: 5 (PB) $100-145
Full Breakfast
Minimum stay weekends: 2 nights; major holiday
    weekends: 3 nights
Credit Cards: A, B
Notes: 2, 5, 7 (limited), 9, 10, 11, 14

The Hope-Merrill House/ The Hope-Bosworth House

Box 42, 95441
(707) 857-3356

Vintage Victorian turn-of-the-century inns welcome travelers in grand style to the California wine country. Twelve rooms with private baths (two with Jacuzzi tubs), beautiful gardens, gazebo, vineyards, and heated swimming pool will make your stay a memorable experience. Featured in

Country Homes, Sunset, House Beautiful magazines.

Hosts: Bob and Rosalie Hope
Rooms: 12 (10 PB; 2 SB) $65-125
Full Breakfast
Credit Cards: A, B
Notes: 2, 3, 5, 8, 9, 10, 11, 12, 14

Bed & Breakfast

Isis Oasis Lodge

20889 Geyserville Avenue, 95441
(707) 857-3524

A classic lodge of 12 rooms, lounge with fireplace, meeting room, and game area. A pool spa and sauna in a secluded garden. Acres of land with exotic birds and animals to play with. A honeymoon cottage with fireplace and private hot tub. The Retreat House, Vineyard House, and Tower House in addition to yurts, a tipi, and a wine barrel room give guests a variety of options. Wine and country breakfasts. Group rates.

Hosts: Loreon Vigne and Paul Ramses
Rooms: 23 (7 PB; 16 SB) $50-100
Full Breakfast
Credit Cards: A, B
Notes: 2, 3, 4, 5, 11

GILROY

Country Rose Inn

P. O. Box 1804, 95021-1804
(408) 842-0441

6 Pets welcome; 7 Smoking allowed; 8 Children welcome; 9 Social drinking allowed; 10 Tennis available; 11 Swimming available; 12 Golf available; 13 Skiing available; 14 May be booked through travel agents.

An oasis 30 miles south of San Jose, 20 minutes from historic San Juan Bautista, and 45 minutes from Monterey. Experience rural grandeur. Nestled in the heart of the south Santa Clara Valley wine region. Ancient oak lofts above the bridal suite, and four other lovely rooms offer views of rural repose. Ballooning, hiking, golf. Outlet shopping, full breakfast, and driving range available.

Host: Rose Hernandez
Rooms: 5 (PB) $85-149
Full Breakfast
Credit Cards: A, B, C
Notes: 2, 5, 9, 10, 11, 12, 14

GLEN ELLEN

Glenelly Inn

5131 Warm Springs Road, 95442
(707) 996-6720

Charming country inn situated in the Sonoma wine country near Jack London Park. Restored turn-of-the-century inn with spacious lawn and oak trees. Boutique wineries and good restaurants nearby. One hour north of San Francisco.

Host: Kristi Hallamore Grove
Rooms: 8 (PB) $80-125
Full Breakfast
Credit Cards: A, B
Notes: 2, 5, 7 (outside), 8 (by arrangement), 11, 12, 14

JVB Vineyards

14335 Sonoma Highway, P. O. Box 997, 95442
(707) 996-4533

Two private little Spanish-style adobe haciendas overlooking the vineyard. Queen beds, hot tub, beautiful patio. Great waffles for breakfast. Thirty-seven wineries and champagne cellars in historic Sonoma Valley. Site of raising of the Bear Flag, author Jack London's Wolf House, last mission on the California trail, and home of General Vallejo.

Hosts: Beverly and Jack Babb
Rooms: 2 (PB) $85 & $95
Full Breakfast
Credit Cards: None
Notes: 2, 5, 9, 11, 12, 14

GRANADA HILLS

Kids Welcome 4-14

730 Catalina Avenue, Seal Beach, 90740
(310) 493-6837; (800) 383-3513

These three guest rooms in Granada Hills share two bathrooms. Hosts are friendly, and the neighborhood is lovely. Pool available. Affordable rates.

GRASS VALLEY

The Holbrooke Hotel

212 West Main Street, 95945
(916) 273-1353

The Holbrooke hotel, established in 1851, is a classic Victorian tradition. You may choose from a variety of accommodations, from the small and cozy to the elegant and luxurious D. P. Holbrooke suite. Antiques grace each of the rooms, all of which have private baths, television, and air conditioning. Enjoy the complimentary continental breakfast served each morning in the library.

Hosts: Linda Rasor
Rooms: 27 (PB) $66-145
Continental Breakfast
Credit Cards: A, B, C
Notes: 2, 3, 4, 5, 7, 8, 9, 14

GROVELAND

Bed & Breakfast International #401

P. O. Box 282910, San Francisco, 94128-2910
(415) 696-1690; FAX (415) 696-1699

Contemporary wood home with deck situated on the top of one of the hills in an area called Pine Mountain Lake. Home has a

---

NOTES: Credit cards accepted: A Master Card; B Visa; C American Express; D Discover Card; E Diner's Club; F Other; 2 Personal Checks accepted; 3 Lunch available; 4 Dinner available; 5 Open all year;

view of the lake below and the mountains of Yosemite in the distance. It is 25 miles to the entrance of Yosemite. There are three rooms with private baths. Hosts serve excellent breakfasts, sometimes with a south-of-the-border flair. $60.

GUALALA

North Coast Country Inn

34591 South Highway 1, 95445
(707) 884-4537

A cluster of rustic redwood buildings with ocean views. Rooms feature queen beds, fireplaces, kitchenettes, private baths, decks, and private entries. The inn has a hot tub and gazebo. Full breakfast is served in guest rooms. Nearby golf, hiking, horseback riding, fishing, and beaches.

Hosts: Loren and Nancy Flanagan
Rooms: 4 (PB) $126.50
Full Breakfast
Minimum stay weekends: 2 nights; holidays:
   3 nights
Credit Cards: A, B, C
Notes: 2, 5, 9, 10, 11, 12, 14

Whale Watch Inn

35100 South Highway 1, 95445
(707) 884-3667; (800) WHALE42

Romance on the rugged northern California coast. Oceanfront, cliff-side accommodations on two acres of gardens and a private stairway to the beach. Luxurious contem-

porary rooms and suites, all of which have ocean views and secluded decks, sixteen of which have fireplaces, and eight of which have a two person Jacuzzi, are available. Skylights provide moon and star viewing, and gourmet breakfast is delivered to your room. Located three hours north of San Francisco and ranked among the top fifty romantic California getaways.

Hosts: Jim and Kazuko Popplewell
Rooms: 18 (PNB) $160-275
Full Breakfast
Credit Cards: A, B
Notes: 2, 5, 9, 10, 12

GUERNEVILLE

Applewood—An Estate Inn

13555 Highway 116, 95446
(707) 869-9093

Country Inns Magazine has called this Bed and Breakfast "among the great romantic hideaways of the Pacific North Coast." This historic California Mission Revival mansion has received a Grand Hotel Award from San Francisco *Focus* Magazine's panel of top travel writers and editors. Offering an atmosphere of quiet, comfortable elegance amid redwoods, orchards, and vineyards in the beautiful Russian River Valley, this inn has inspired comments like "We found heaven...one of the most delightful, beautiful, and well-managed inns in the country." (San Francisco Examiner) This Bed and Breakfast also offers a heated pool and spa, delicious country breakfasts, and romantic, candlelit dinners.

Host: A. Darryl Notter
Rooms: 10 (PB) $100-175
Full Breakfast
Notes: 4, 5, 9, 10, 11, 12, 14

Bed & Breakfast International #304

P. O. Box 282910, San Francisco, 94128-2910
(415) 696-1690; FAX (415) 696-1699

Applewood—An Estate Inn

An estate situated among rolling hills in one of Northern California's most beautiful wine country areas. Very peaceful atmosphere, high quality decor, and full breakfasts. Nine rooms, all with private baths, and furnished in antiques and other fine pieces. Lots of fresh flowers. Swimming pool and hot tub available. $115-150.

Ridenhour Ranch House Inn

12850 River Road, 95446
(707) 887-1033

A 1906 inn on two and one-fourth acres of trees, gardens, and meadow situated in the Russian River area of Northern California. Each room is decorated in country English and American antiques, quilts, plants, and fresh flowers. The area has many restaurants, and dinner can be arranged at the inn.

Hosts: Diane and Fritz Rechberger
Rooms: 8 PB $95-130
Full Breakfast
Credit Cards: A, B
Notes: 2, 4, 5, 8 (over 10), 14

HALF MOON BAY

Bed and Breakfast Los Angeles 13-8

730 Catalina Avenue, Seal Beach, 90740
(310) 493-6837; (800) 383-3513

These British-born hosts offer complimentary wine and a wood-burning stove in their perfectly restored Queen Anne-style home. They have seven rooms, including a Garden Suite featuring an in-room hot tub, and a fridge stocked with goodies. Your hostess collects rare herbs and invites guests to share in her cuttings. Two children still live at home. Moderate-luxury rates.

Bed and Breakfast Los Angeles 13-9

730 Catalina Avenue, Seal Beach, 90740
(310) 493-6837; (800) 383-3513

This historic inn in Half Moon Bay has brass beds and hand-tooled cornices. Your hostess is a European-trained chef who provides a hearty continental breakfast and other meals at your option. Most of the twelve rooms have private baths. There is a sauna, a big redwood deck, massive fire pits where guests can sip cognac and watch the stars. Affordable-moderate rates.

Bed and Breakfast Los Angeles 13-10

730 Catalina Avenue, Seal Beach, 90740
(310) 493-6837; (800) 383-3513

The original home of the town's first city planner still stands in the town of Half Moon Bay. Sumptuous buffet is served in the morning. Beverages are served around the fire at night. Nine rooms, all of which have private baths, some with Jacuzzis and/or fireplaces, are available to guests with "well-behaved children"–or those who want to leave the children at home. Luxury rates.

Cypress Inn on Miramar Beach

407 Mirada Road, 94019
(415) 726-6002

Cypress Inn is situated 26 miles south of San Francisco and two miles north of Half Moon Bay. All eight luxury ocean-front rooms have a private deck, fireplace, and bathroom. The unique architecture and Mexican folk art decor are a perfect compliment to the beachfront location. Breakfast is outstanding, and tea is served every afternoon. Many activities and fine dining nearby.

Hosts: Cindy Granados and Michael Fogli
Rooms: 8 (PB) $135-175; $250 suite
Full Breakfast
Credit Cards: A, B, C
Notes: 2, 3, 4, 5, 9, 10, 11, 12, 14

Old Thyme Inn

779 Main Street, 94019
(415) 726-1616

This 1890s Victorian is on historic Main Street and has an herbal theme. Guests are invited to stroll in Anne's English herb garden and take cuttings. Everybody loves Simon's buttermilk scones with herb tea for breakfast. Some rooms have double-size whirlpool tubs; fireplaces and antiques are everywhere.

Hosts: Anne and Simon Lowings
Rooms: 7 (PB) $65-210
Full Breakfast
Credit Cards: A, B, C, D
Notes: 2, 5, 6, 9, 10, 12, 14

Zaballa House

324 Main Street, 94019
(415) 726-9123; (800) 77 BNB4U (772-6248)

The first house built in Half Moon Bay (1859), standing at the entrance to historic Main Street, has been carefully restored into a bed and breakfast. The inn is set in a

Zaballa House

garden across the street from shopping and two fine restaurants. Guests enjoy the Victorian decor in rooms with high ceilings and antiques, some with double-wide whirlpool tubs and fireplaces. The friendly innkeeper provides drinks in the evening and a wonderful breakfast in the morning.

Host: Sharon Tedrow and Linda Malone
Rooms: 9 (PB) $65-150
Full Breakfast
Credit Cards: A, B, C, D
Notes: 2, 5, 6, 8, 9, 10, 12, 14

HANFORD

The Irwin Street Inn

522 North Irwin St., 93230
(209) 583-8791

Four impeccably restored turn-of-the-century Victorian homes and surrounding tree-shaded lawns create a one acre sanctuary in downtown Hanford. Each of our thirty rooms and suites are different. Our outside restaurant offers French-California fare with meals served in our elegant dining room or awning covered veranda. Guests may relax by our pool or on shaded brick patios. Conference facilities are available for business meetings and banquets.

Hosts: Bruce Evans and Lucy Burnworth
Rooms: 30 (PB) $69-110
Continental Breakfast
Credit Cards: A, B, C, E
Notes: 2, 3, 4, 5, 7, 8, 9, 11, 14

HEALDSBURG

B&B San Francisco #16

P. O. Box 349, 94101
(415) 931-3083; FAX (415) 921-BBSF

Jane's place is situated in the heart of wine country, just minutes from some of California's finest wineries, close to the Russian River beaches and resorts and only one-half hour from the Pacific coast. There are three quaintly furnished rooms with private baths on an estate overlooking vineyards. Home-cooked breakfast. $75.

6 Pets welcome; 7 Smoking allowed; 8 Children welcome; 9 Social drinking allowed; 10 Tennis available; 11 Swimming available; 12 Golf available; 13 Skiing available; 14 May be booked through travel agents.

Frampton House

489 Powell Avenue, 95448
(707) 4333-5084

A stately 1908 Victorian situated in the
heart of Sonoma wine country, Frampton
House offers personalized service and privacy. All-terrain bikes, Ping-Pong, exercy-
cle, pool, spa, sauna, fireplace, wine.
Custom-made tubs for two. Relax in any
season.

Host: Paula Bogle
Rooms: 3 (PB) $75.60-97.20
Full Breakfast
Credit Cards: A, B
Notes: 2, 5, 7 (limited), 8 (over 14), 9, 10, 11, 12, 14

Grape Leaf Inn

539 Johnson Street, 95448
(707) 433-8140

A magnificently restored 1900 Queen Anne
Victorian home with seven bedrooms, each
with private bath (five with whirlpools and
skylights). All rooms are air-conditioned
and have king or queen beds. A full country breakfast is served each morning.
Afternoon complimentary premium local
wines and cheeses. Conveniently situated
near Healdsburg town center, the Russian
River, Lake Sonoma, and 53 wineries.

Hosts: Terry and Karen Sweet
Rooms: 7 (PB) $85-130
Full Breakfast
Credit Cards: A, B, D
Notes: 2, 5, 9, 10, 12, 14

Haydon House

321 Haydon Street, 95448
(707) 433-5228

Situated in a quiet residential area within
walking distance of the historic plaza,
many fine shops and restaurants. Minutes
away from 59 wineries. Beautifully
restored Victorian furnished in antiques.
Separate Gothic cottage with two rooms
and private baths with whirlpool tubs.

Hosts: Keiu and Tom Woodburn
Rooms: 8 (4 PB; 4 SB) $75-150
Full Breakfast
Credit Cards: A, B
Closed Dec. 20-31
Notes: 2, 9, 10, 11, 12, 14

Healsdburg Inn on the Plaza

116 Matheson Street, P. O. Box 1196, 95448
(707) 433-6991

A 1900 brick Victorian, formerly a Wells
Fargo stagecoach express station, now
restored and elegantly furnished as a bed
and breakfast Bay windows view old town
plaza; fireplaces; central air/ heat.
Solarium/roof garden for afternoon snacks,
popcorn, wine, music. Coffee, and cookies
available all day. Champagne breakfasts on
weekends. TV, VCR, phone, and gift certificates available. Family owned and operated, close to everything.

Hosts: Genny Jenkins and Dyanne Celi
Rooms: 9 (PB) $75-145
Full Breakfast
Credit Cards: A, B
Notes: 2, 5, 9, 10, 11, 12

Madrona Manor, A Country Inn

1001 Westside Road, 95448
(707) 433-4231; (800) 258-4003
FAX (707) 433-0703

Mardrona Manor

NOTES: Credit cards accepted: A Master Card; B Visa; C American Express; D Discover Card; E Diner's
Club; F Other; 2 Personal Checks accepted; 3 Lunch available; 4 Dinner available; 5 Open all year;

This 21-room inn in a national historic district is distinguished by its sense of homey elegance that combines the graciousness one might feel at a friend's home with luxurious European amenities: thick terrycloth robes, an expansive breakfast buffet, stately furniture, elegant decor. Nationally acclaimed restaurant.

Hosts: John and Carol Muir
Rooms: 21 (PB) $120-195 off-season; $135-210 in season
Full Breakfast
Credit Cards: A, B, C, D, E
Notes: 2, 4, 5, 6, 7, 8, 10, 11, 12, 14

The Raford House

10630 Wohler Road, 95448
(707) 887-9573

A Victorian farmhouse sitting among the vineyards in a country setting that offers seven guest rooms, most with private baths, two with fireplaces. Country historic landmark.

Hosts: The Villeneuves
Rooms: 7 (5 PB; 2 SB)
Full Breakfast
Credit Cards: A, B
Notes: 2, 5, 7 (outside), 8 (over 12), 9, 10, 11, 12, 14

HOLLYWOOD

Bed and Breakfast Los Angeles 1-2

730 Catalina Avenue, Seal Beach, 90740
(310) 493-6837; (800) 383-3513

Art Deco classicism around the corner from Mann's Chinese Theatre. Color TV and phones. Newspaper and breakfast delivered to your door. Free valet parking; two-room suites available. Moderate rates.

Bed and Breakfast Los Angeles 2-1

730 Catalina Avenue, Seal Beach, 90740
(310) 493-6837; (800) 383-3513

Just north of Sunset Boulevard, this upstairs suite has two bedrooms, two baths, and a sun deck. Hosts live downstairs and speak seven languages. Affordable rates.

Eye Openers Bed and Breakfast Reservations LA-G2

P. O. Box 694, Altadena, 91003-0694
(213) 684-4428; (818) 797-2055
FAX (818) 798-3640

This 1910 California bungalow is on a quiet palm-lined street close to Hollywood's well-known attractions. There are two second-floor guest rooms, one with a sun deck overlooking the spacious garden. Well-travelled hosts speak several languages. Continental breakfast. Good public transportation. Resident dog. No smoking. Private bath. $35-45.

Eye Openers Bed and Breakfast Reservations LA-M1

P. O. Box 694, Altadena, 91003-0694
(213) 684-4428; (818) 797-2055
FAX (818) 798-3640

Bed and Breakfast Inn lovingly decorated by host offers guest living room with fireplace, dining room, kitchen and laundry privileges. Relax in the backyard garden, or walk to nearby studios and restaurants. Good public transportation nearby. Host is a scientist who enjoys travelling and folk dancing. No smoking. Two guest rooms. Shared bath. $30-40 plus tax.

Kids Welcome 2-2

730 Catalina Avenue, Seal Beach, 90740
(310) 493-6837; (800) 383-3513

6 Pets welcome; 7 Smoking allowed; 8 Children welcome; 9 Social drinking allowed; 10 Tennis available; 11 Swimming available; 12 Golf available; 13 Skiing available; 14 May be booked through travel agents.

Kids, dogs, and cats live downstairs, and you live upstairs in this West Hollywood home near Sunset Boulevard. Hosts speak many languages. Affordable rates.

Kids Welcome 2-3

730 Catalina Avenue, Seal Beach, 90740
(310) 493-6837; (800) 383-3513

Cute three-bedroom, two-bathroom bungalow can be rented by the room or by the whole house. West Hollywood location includes livingroom (with fireplace), dining room, and kitchen. Hostess brings breakfast from the house next door. Affordable rates.

HOMEWOOD

Rockwood Lodge

5295 West Lake Boulevard, 96141-0226
(916) 525-5273; (800) Le-Tahoe (538-2463)
FAX (916) 525-5949

Old Tahoe-style home made of rock, knotty pine, and hand-hewn timbers. The lodge has been completely renovated for the enjoyment of those who appreciate fine appointments and luxury combined with the warm, friendly atmosphere of Lake Tahoe's magical west shore.

Host: Louis Reinkens
Rooms: 4 (2 PB; 2 SB) $100-150
Continental Breakfast
Credit Cards: None
Notes: 2, 5, 9, 10, 11, 12, 13, 14

IDYLLWILD

Wilkum Inn

Box 1115, 92549
(909) 659-4087

Nestled among the pines in a rustic mountain village, this two-story shingle-sided inn offers rooms that are individually furnished with the innkeepers' antiques and collectibles. Knotty-pine paneling and a river-rock fireplace enhance the hospitality of the common room.

Hosts: Annamae Chambers and Barbara Jones
Rooms: 5 (3 PB; 2 SB) $65-95
Expanded Continental Breakfast
Credit Cards: None
Notes: 2, 5, 9, 11, 14

INVERNESS

Dancing Coyote Beach

P. O. Box 98, 94937
(415) 669-7200

Four charming cottages set on a private beach surrounded by Point Reyes National Seashore, each with fireplace, decks, and bay views. Stroll along the beach, linger over breakfast in the morning sun on your private deck, walk into the village of Inverness, or simply relax by the fire.

Rooms: 4 (PB) $95-125
Full Breakfast
Credit Cards: None
Notes: 2, 5, 6, 8, 9

Fairwinds Farm Bed and Breakfast

P. O. Box 581, 94937
(415) 663-9454

Large, secluded, cozy cottage high atop Inverness Ridge surrounded by 68,000-acre National Seashore (direct access). Ocean view from hot tub. Living room, fireplace, fully equipped kitchen, full bath with tub and shower. Sleeps six comfortably. TV, stereo, VCR, movies, library, guitar. Generous country breakfast plus homemade tea treats. Private garden with ponds and swing, barnyard animals, and playhouse. A private hideaway, adjacent to hiking, biking, beaches, whale watching, horseback riding.

Host: Joyce H. Goldfield
Cottage: 1 (PB) $125
Full Breakfast
Credit Cards: None
Notes: 2, 5, 8, 9, 11

NOTES: Credit cards accepted: A Master Card; B Visa; C American Express; D Discover Card; E Diner's Club; F Other; 2 Personal Checks accepted; 3 Lunch available; 4 Dinner available; 5 Open all year;

Kids Welcome 16-2

730 Catalina Avenue, Seal Beach, 90740
(310) 493-6837; (800) 383-3513

Your hosts have thought of everything for
the perfect rural vacation. This farmhouse
has a bedroom, loft, living room, fireplace,
fully equipped kitchen, bath, private garden
(with a pond), kids' playhouse and swing,
deck-top hot tub (with ocean view), barnyard animals, TV, stereo. VCR (with
movies), library, typewriter, guitar, and
teddy bears. Luxury rates.

Rosemary Cottage

75 Balboa Avenue, Box 619, 94937
(415) 663-9338

Imagine! Romantic seclusion in a French-
style country cottage that you have all to
yourself! A wall of windows overlooks a
dramatic forest view in the Point Reyes
National Seashore. This comfortable cottage has a bedroom with queen bed, fully
equipped kitchen, and private bath. Living
room has high ceilings, wood-burning
stove, additional sleeping space for two.
Families welcome; full breakfast makings.

Host: Suzanne Storch
Cottage: 1 (PB) $125-150
Full Breakfast
Credit Cards: None
Notes: 7, 10, 11, 12, 14

Ten Inverness Way

10 Inverness Way, Box 63, 94937
(415) 669-1648

The *Los Angeles Times* calls it "one of the
niftiest inns in Northern California."
Hearty breakfasts, private baths, ebullient
garden, handmade quilts, Oriental rugs,
stone fireplace, and private hot tub. A red-
wood-shingled haven for hikers and rainy-
day bookworms.

Host: Mary Davies
Rooms: 4 (PB) $100-130
Suite: 1(PB) $140
Full Breakfast
Credit Cards: A, B
Notes: 2, 5, 9, 11, 12, 14

IONE

The Heirloom

214 Shakeley Lane, 95640
(209) 274-4468

Travel down a country lane into a romantic
English garden where a petite Colonial mansion (circa 1863) is shaded by century-old
trees and scented by magnolias and gardenias. fireplaces and balconies. Breakfast has
a French flair. enjoy gracious hospitality.

Hosts: Patricia Cross and Melisande Hubbs
Rooms: 6 (4 PB; 2 SB) $50-80
Full Breakfast
Credit Cards: None
Closed Thanksgiving, Dec. 24- 25
Notes: 2, 8 (over 10), 9, 10, 11, 12, 14

ISLETON

Delta Daze Inn

20 Main Street, P. O. Box 607, 95641
(916) 777-7777

This historic bed and breakfast offers relaxation with fun. Boat and bus tours, free
bikes, or just sitting by the river are all part
of the Delta experience. And after you have
browsed through the boutiques and art galleries, "unlax" in the parlor, or have a Delta
Delite from the old fashioned ice cream
parlor while you listen to music from the
1920s on a hand-crank Grafanola. It's all
part of living, Delta style.

Host: Shirley Russell
Rooms: 12 (PB) $90-125
Expanded Continental Breakfast
Credit Cards: A, B, C
Notes: 2, 5, 7 (limited), 9, 14

---

6 Pets welcome; 7 Smoking allowed; 8 Children welcome; 9 Social drinking allowed; 10 Tennis available; 11
Swimming available; 12 Golf available; 13 Skiing available; 14 May be booked through travel agents.

JACKSON

Court Street Inn

215 Court Street, 95642
(209) 223-0416

An 1872 Victorian inn with five rooms and a two-room cottage. Four rooms with private bath, three with semiprivate. Full breakfast. Fireplace in two rooms plus parlor and cottage. Patio with rose garden, front porch with swing, and spa. Hors d'oeuvres. Near wineries, restaurants, and shopping.

Hosts: Janet and Lee Hammond; Gia and Scott Anderson
Rooms: 7 (4 PB; 3 SB) $75-125
Full Breakfast
Credit Cards: A, B
Notes: 2, 5, 10, 11, 14

Gate House Inn

1330 Jackson Gate Road, 95642
(209) 223-3500

Charming turn-of-the-century Victorian in the country on an acre of garden property with a swimming pool. Rooms are decorated with Victorian and country furnishings. One has a fireplace, and the private cottage has a wood stove. Walk to fine restaurants and historic sites. Three-star Mobil rating.

Court Street Inn

Hosts: Stan and Bev Smith
Rooms: 5 (PB) $75-115
Full Breakfast
Credit Cards: A, B, D
Notes: 2, 5, 8 (over 12), 9, 10, 11, 12, 14

The Wedgewood

11941 Narcissus Road, 95642
(209) 296-4300; (800) 933-4393

Charming Victorian replica tucked away on wooded acreage. Antique decor, afternoon refreshments, porch swing, balcony, wood-burning stoves, full gourmet breakfast. In the heart of the gold country, close to excellent dining, shopping, and sightseeing. Gazebo and terraced English gardens. Mobil travel guide three stars.

Hosts: Vic and Jeannine Beltz
Rooms: 6 (PB) $85-130
Full Breakfast
Credit Cards: A, B
Notes: 2, 5, 7 (limited), 8 (over 12), 9

JAMESTOWN

Bed and Breakfast Los Angeles 17-3

730 Catalina Avenue, Seal Beach, 90740
(310) 493-6837; (800) 383-3513

Breakfast starts with biscuits and gravy at this old-fashioned hotel in downtown Jamestown. "Jimtown" has been the site for dozens of Hollywood movies, seeking authentic gangster-era settings. The town is a treasure trove of antique stores, restaurants, and saloons—most in continuous operation since the the 1800s. Sixteen rooms share a lesser number of baths, but private cottages are also available. Balconies, patio, barbecue, and gazebo are all at your fingertips. Very affordable.

The National Hotel

Box 502, 95327
(209) 984-3446

NOTES: Credit cards accepted: A Master Card; B Visa; C American Express; D Discover Card; E Diner's Club; F Other; 2 Personal Checks accepted; 3 Lunch available; 4 Dinner available; 5 Open all year;

Historic National Hotel bed and breakfast, an 11-room Gold Rush hotel (1859). Fully restored, with an outstanding restaurant and the original saloon. Classic cuisine and gracious service are only part of the charm.

Hosts: Stephen and Pamela Willey
Rooms: 11 (5 PB; 6 SB) $45-80
Continental Breakfast
Credit Cards: A, B
Notes: 2, 3, 4, 5, 6 (call), 7, 8 (call), 9, 10, 11, 12, 13, 14

JENNER

Bed and Breakfast Los Angeles 16-5

730 Catalina Avenue, Seal Beach, 90740
(310) 493-6837; (800) 383-3513

Jenner is a little town just north of Point Reyes. You may rent one of eleven rooms, or a whole beachfront house. The inn is furnished with some of the original antiques from the 1890s owners. Try snuggling down on a chesterfield in the main room with a good book. House rentals include linens and firewood and may accommodate groups as large as ten people. No breakfast is served. Moderate-luxury rates.

The Wedgewood Inn

JULIAN

Butterfield Bed and Breakfast

2284 Sunset Drive, P. O. Box 1115, 92036
(619) 765-2179

Nestled on a gently sloping hillside among tall pines and gentle breezes, this home is decorated with antiques and country collectibles with a history of pampering its guests. Known for our Country Gourmet Breakfast, intimate weddings, and family reunions. We are located within the Historic District of Julian just one mile from town, ideal for walking, hiking, and biking. Afternoon freshly baked goodies are served in the Billiards Room. Romantic evening dinners are available on request.

Hosts: Ray, Mary, and Steve Trimmins
Rooms: 5 (1 PB; 4 SB) $89-109
Full Breakfast
Credit Cards: None
Notes: 2, 5,7 (outside only), 9

Julian Gold Rush Hotel

2032 Main Street, P. O. Box 1856, 92036
(619) 765-0201

Built nearly 100 years ago by a freed slave and his wife, this inn still reflects the dream and tradition of genteel hospitality of the Victorian era. The "Queen of the Back Country" has the distinction of being the oldest continuously operating hotel in Southern California.

Hosts: Steve and Gig Ballinger
Rooms: 18 (5 PB; 13 SB) $64-145
Full Breakfast
Credit Cards: A, B, C
Notes: 2, 5, 7, 8, 9, 14

Julian Lodge

2427 C Street, P. O. Box 1930, 92036
(619) 765-1420; (800) 542-1420

A bed and breakfast mountain inn situated 60 miles northeast of San Diego in the gold mining town of Julian. Furnished with antiques in the 1885 style, with modern conveniences. Situated in town, close to shops, museums, and restaurants.

Hosts: Jim and Linda Huie
Rooms: 23 (PB) $72-82
Expanded Continental Breakfast
Credit Cards: A, B, C
Notes: 5, 8, 10, 14

Pinecroft Manor

2142 Whispering Pines Drive
P. O. Box 665, 92036
(619) 765-1611

Contemporary five-level English Tudor featuring English gardens; cathedral ceilings; lofty decks overlooking pines, oaks, cedars, and beautiful sunsets. Furnished in antiques and interesting old things. Evening manor hospitality served in the common room/library; wood-burning earth stove with glass doors, game room with TV, VCR and piano. Walking distance to historic gold mining town. AAA-rated and listed in California Bed and Breakfast tourism guide.

Host: Diane L. Boyer
Rooms: 2 (SB) $80-85
Full Breakfast
Minimum stay holiday weekends: 2 nights
Credit Cards: None
Notes: 2, 5, 7 (limited), 8 (over 11), 9, 14

JUNE LAKE

Bed and Breakfast Los Angeles 18-4

730 Catalina Avenue, Seal Beach, 90740
(310) 493-6837; (800) 383-3513

This large family resort in the heart of the High Sierra Mountains offers guest rooms, lake-view suites (some with multiple bedrooms and fireplaces), apartments, housekeeping cabins, and big lakefront houses. Breakfast is not included, but other amenities include recreation room with TV and fireplace, game tables, heated indoor pool, large Jacuzzi pool, and a sauna. Guests are five minutes from ski lifts. Moderate-luxury rates.

KELSEY

Mountainside Bed and Breakfast

Box 165, 95643
(916) 626-0983

This old country home is in the center of 80 acres, with a 180-degree view. The large parlor is cozy with its fireplace and piano. Three pleasant guest rooms have private baths, while the large paneled attic with its own bath and deck can sleep up to eight. A country breakfast is served in the dining room, sunny breakfast room, or breakfast deck. Guests enjoy the spa on the spa deck after a day of river rafting, hiking, or fishing.

Hosts: Mary Ellen and Paul Mello
Rooms: 4 (PB) $70-75
Full Breakfast
Credit Cards: None
Notes: 2, 5, 9, 14

Kern River Bed and Breakfast

KERNVILLE

Kern River Bed and Breakfast

119 Kern River Dr., P. O. Box 1725, 93238
(619) 376-6750

A warm, charming country-style inn on the wild and scenic Kern River in a quaint western town within Sequoia National Forest in the southern Sierra Nevada Mountains. Six individually decorated country bedrooms reflect the charm of

Kern River Valley; all offer river views, and some have fireplaces or whirlpool tubs. Breakfast features home-baked cinnamon rolls, special blend cereals, sweetheart waffles, muffins, fresh fruit, juices, coffee, and teas. Year-round activities include rafting fishing, golf, hiking, biking, and skiing. Fine restaurants, antique shops, and museum are within walking distance.

Hosts: Mike and Marti
Rooms: 6 (PB) $79-89 plus tax
Full Breakfast
Credit Cards: A, B
Notes: 5, 9, 14

KLAMATH

Requa Inn

451 Requa Road, 95548
(707) 482-8205

This inn is on the majestic Klamath River 60 miles north of Eureka in the heart of the Redwood National Park. Near hiking trails and beaches. A nature lover's paradise. Relax in the front parlor overlooking the river, or treat yourself to an unforgettable dinner in the dining room.

Hosts: Paul and Donna Hamby
Rooms: 10 (PB) $60-85
Full Breakfast
Credit Cards: A, B, C
Closed Jan.
Notes: 4, 8 (over 9), 9

LAGUNA BEACH

Bed and Breakfast Los Angeles 6-1

730 Catalina Avenue, Seal Beach, 90740
(310) 493-6837; (800) 383-3513

This getaway by the sea has a private entry, spacious room with four-poster bed, sitting room with sofa bed, TV, private bath, refrigerator, microwave, and a very large sun deck with a 180-degree ocean view. Breakfast is served on the deck or dining room. Children over eight. Moderate rates.

Bed and Breakfast Los Angeles 6-6

730 Catalina Avenue, Seal Beach, 90740
(310) 493-6837; (800) 383-3513

This rambling Spanish-style inn is set into a hillside, with elegant gardens, library, and pool. Some suites have kitchens, and others have ocean views. All are within walking distance to the beach. Luxury rates.

Bed and Breakfast Los Angeles 6-7

730 Catalina Avenue, Seal Beach, 90740
(310) 493-6837; (800) 383-3513

This hilltop home has sweeping views of the ocean. Two guest rooms share one bath. Downstairs suite includes pool table, bar, deck, and private bath. Children over eight, please.

The Carriage House

1322 Catalina Street, 92651
(715) 494-8945

The Carriage House features all private suites with living room, bedroom, bath, and some kitchen facilities. Two-bedroom suites available. All surround a courtyard of plants and flowers, two blocks from the ocean. Close to art galleries, restaurants, and shops.

The Carriage House

6 Pets welcome; 7 Smoking allowed; 8 Children welcome; 9 Social drinking allowed; 10 Tennis available; 11 Swimming available; 12 Golf available; 13 Skiing available; 14 May be booked through travel agents.

Hosts: Vern, Dee, and Tom Taylor
Suites: 6 (PB) $95-150
Continental Breakfast
Minimum stay weekends: 2; holidays: 3 nights
Credit Cards: None
Notes: 2, 5, 7, 8, 9, 10, 11, 12, 14

Casa Laguna Inn

2510 South Coast Highway, 92651
(714) 494-2996; (800) 233-0449

A Spanish mission-style inn in an ocean-view hillside setting with tropical gardens and courtyards, heated pool, aviary, observation bell tower, and cozy library. Complimentary afternoon tea, wine, and hors d'oeuvres. Near Los Angeles and Disneyland.

Host: Kevin Henry
Rooms: 20 (PB) $90-205
Continental Breakfast
Credit Cards: A, B, C, D, E
Notes: 2, 5, 7, 8, 9, 10, 11, 12, 14

Eiler's Inn

741 South Coast Highway, 92651
(714) 494-3004

Situated in the heart of Laguna, just a few steps from the Pacific Ocean. Tennis, shops, and restaurants are within walking distance. The inn offers elegant yet casual sophistication, with all rooms furnished in antiques, ocean views from the sun deck, fireplaces, and flower-scented brick courtyard with bubbling fountain.

Hosts: Henk and Annette Wirtz
Rooms: 12 (PB) $100-175
Full Breakfast
Credit Cards: A, B, C
Notes: 2, 5, 7, 8, 9, 10, 11, 12, 14

Eye Openers Bed and Breakfast Reservations LA-J1

P. O. Box 694, Altadena, 91003-0694
(213) 684-4428; (818) 797-2055
FAX (818) 798-3640

Sitting room, bedroom, bath, and large deck with panoramic ocean views makes up this suite for guests with private entrance. Suite has refrigerator, microwave, TV and VCR, and a full breakfast. Guest cottage has a living room, kitchen, loft bedroom, deck, Jacuzzi tub, and continental breakfast. Walk to the beach. No smoking. Private bath. $85-100.

Eye Openers Bed and Breakfast Reservations LG-B2

P. O. Box 694, Altadena, 91003-0694
(213) 684-4428; (818) 797-2055
FAX (818) 798-3640

Hilltop bed and breakfast has an ocean view, hot tub, and sauna. European hostess can accommodate up to eight guests. Full or continental breakfast is served. Resident dog. Two guest rooms. Shared bath. $55-90.

Eye Openers Bed and Breakfast Reservations LG-C201

P. O. Box 694, Altadena, 91003-0694
(213) 684-4428; (818) 797-2055
FAX (818) 798-3640

Charming Spanish-style bed and breakfast inn with unique guest rooms and suites provides a generous buffet breakfast and evening refreshments in the library or poolside. Nineteen guest rooms and one cottage. Private bath. $95-155 plus tax.

Eye Openers Bed and Breakfast Reservations LG-E121

P. O. Box 694, Altadena, 91003-0694
(213) 684-4428; (818) 797-2055
FAX (818) 798-3640

NOTES: Credit cards accepted: A Master Card; B Visa; C American Express; D Discover Card; E Diner's Club; F Other; 2 Personal Checks accepted; 3 Lunch available; 4 Dinner available; 5 Open all year;

Rooms in lovely continental-style bed and breakfast in the heart of Laguna are set around a courtyard, complete with fountain, flowers, tables, and chairs, where guests can enjoy breakfast and lounging. The beach is just outside the back gate. No smoking. Eleven guest rooms and one suite. Private bath. $95-150 plus tax.

Eye Openers Bed and Breakfast Reservations LG-S2

P. O. Box 694, Altadena, 91003-0694
(213) 684-4428; (818) 797-2055
FAX (818) 798-3640

Contemporary seaside getaway in Laguna offers expansive view from an outdoor deck. Self-hosted apartment. Bedroom and living room with small kitchen have ocean views. Quiet area of bustling renowned seaside art colony. Self-catered breakfast. No smoking. $110-140.

LA JOLLA

The Bed and Breakfast Inn at La Jolla

7753 Draper Avenue, 92037
(619) 456-2066

Offering deluxe accommodations in sixteen charmingly decorated rooms, The Bed and Breakfast Inn at La Jolla is listed as historical Site 179 on the San Diego Registry. Fireplaces and ocean views are featured in many rooms, and every bedroom offers either a queen size or pair of twin beds. Fresh fruit, sherry, fresh flowers, and terry robes await you in each guest room. Savor light breakfast in the dining room, on the patio, the sun deck, or your bedroom. A picnic basket to add the finishing touch to your day is available also.

Hosts: Pierette Timmerran
Rooms: 16 (15-PB; 1-SB) $85-225

Full Breakfast
Credit Cards: A, B, D
Notes: 2, 5, 7, 8, 9,, 10, 11, 12

Prospect Park Inn

1110 Prospect Street, 92037
(619) 454-0133; (800) 433-1609
FAX (619) 454-2056

Overlooking scenic La Jolla, a block from beaches, restaurants, and shops. Delightful small hotel in the European tradition. Balconies, ocean-view rooms, penthouse suites, and studios with kitchen facilities. All modern amenities, continental breakfast, and afternoon beverage. Close to all San Diego attractions. Weekly and monthly rates available.

Host: Jean Beazley
Rooms: 23 (PB) $89-229
Continental Breakfast
Credit Cards: A, B, C, D, E
Notes: 2, 5, 8, 9, 10, 11, 12, 14

LAKE ARROWHEAD—SEE ALSO SKY FOREST

Bluebelle House Bed and Breakfast

263 S. State Hwy. 173, Box 2177, 923352
(714) 336-3292

Enjoy elegance in an alpine setting. Five rooms, each decorated in its own theme. Walk to lake, village, beach, shops, restaurants. Your hosts love to pamper their guests. Evening refreshments. AAA three-stars.

Hosts: Rick and Lila Peiffer
Rooms: 5 (3 PB; 2 SB) $75-110
Expanded Continental Breakfast
Credit Cards: A, B
Closed Dec. 24-27
Notes: 2, 5, 10, 11, 12, 13

The Carriage House Bed and Breakfast

472 Emerald Drive, P. O. Box 982, 92352
(714) 336-1400

6 Pets welcome; 7 Smoking allowed; 8 Children welcome; 9 Social drinking allowed; 10 Tennis available; 11 Swimming available; 12 Golf available; 13 Skiing available; 14 May be booked through travel agents.

New England-style house hidden in the woods, with views of Lake Arrowhead. Country decor, with feather beds and down comforters. Three rooms, each with private bath. Beverages and snacks in afternoon. Large sun room and deck. Close to lake and wonderful walking trails. Returning guests rave about the warmth and hospitality of the hosts and the great breakfasts.

Hosts: Lee and Johan Karstens
Rooms: 3 (PB) $90-115
Full Breakfast
Credit Cards: A, B
Notes: 2, 5, 9, 11, 13

Chateau Du Lac

Chateau Du Lac

P. O. Box 1098, 911 Hospital Road, 92352
(714) 337-6488; FAX (714) 337-6746

The Chateau Du Lac rises on a bluff overlooking beautiful Lake Arrowhead in the San Bernardino Mountains with a spectacular view of lake and mountains. Sparkling sun in the morning, mist and gentle breezes in the afternoon make this a romantic place to be. In winter, snow and crackling fires add to the beauty and charm. Innkeepers will make your stay pleasant and memorable in the house by the lake where the four seasons come and go.

Hosts: Jody and Oscar Wilson
Rooms: 6 (4 PB; 2 SB) $95-250
Full Breakfast
Credit Cards: A, B, C
Notes: 2, 5, 13

Eagle's Landing

12406 Cedarwood, Box 1510, Blue Jay, 92317
(909) 336-2642

The interesting architecture (Mountain Gothic), tower, stained glass, 26-foot ceilings, and walls of glass with grand views of Lake Arrowhead make Eagle's Landing a landmark, but the warmth, fun, and hospitality of the hosts are what guests return for. The three beautiful rooms are decorated with art, antiques, and crafts collected from around the world. The suite is cabin-like and done in Early California style.

Host: Dorothy Stone
Rooms: 4 (PB) $95-195
Full Breakfast
Credit Cards: A, B, D
Notes: 2, 5, 9, 10, 11, 13, 14

LAKE NACINMETO

Bed and Breakfast Los Angeles 12-8

730 Catalina Avenue, Seal Beach, 90740
(310) 493-6837; (800) 383-3513

Twenty-one miles north of Paso Robles, this secluded old homestead is nestled among the meadows of Adelaida. Cabin has bedroom, living room (with twin

The FORBESTOWN INN

couch-beds and a fireplace), modern kitchen (full of goodies), and a bathroom. Fishing, hiking, and riding trails abound, along with pigs, wild turkeys, and friendly grazing cattle. Hosts live about a mile away and want you to know that "dogs, kids, horses, and boats can all be accommodated." Moderate rates.

LAKEPORT

Forbestown Inn

825 Forbes Street, 95453
(707) 263-7858

The peace, solitude, and charm of Forbestown Inn will please the senses. Built in 1869 when Lakeport was known as Forbestown, it is furnished with unique American oak antiques, fabrics by Bill Blass and Laura Ashley. Full, hearty breakfast; afternoon tea; baked goods; or wine, cheese and crackers. The inn is one block from Clear Lake, boating, Jetski, water skiing, parasailing, bicycling, fishing, wineries, antique hunting, gold mines, geothermal steam wells.

Hosts: Nancy and Jack Dunne
Rooms: 4 (1 PB; 3 SB) $60-105
Full Breakfast
Credit Cards: A, B, C
Notes: 2, 5, 7 (limited), 8 (over 12), 9, 10, 11, 12, 13 (water)

LAKE TAHOE

Bed and Breakfast Los Angeles 18-2

730 Catalina Avenue, Seal Beach, 90740
(310) 493-6837; (800) 383-3513

Pine trees and serenity surround you at this historic lodge on the west shore of Lake Tahoe. The Fireplace Room and Studio can accommodate four people. The cottage and family suites are better for three or four people. Features include a hearty breakfast,

Scandinavian sauna, and one of the nicest beaches on the lake. The main house is always open for games, piano playing, or lounging by the fire. Moderate rates.

Eye Openers Bed and Breakfast Reservations LT-C3

P. O. Box 694, Altadena, 91003-0694
(213) 684-4428; (818) 797-2055
FAX (818) 798-3640

Lakefront 1928-style Tahoe stone house bed and breakfast has contemporary decor with antique accents. Continental or full breakfast. Three rooms. Private and shared baths. No smoking. $75-95.

Eye Openers Bed and Breakfast Reservations LT-C71

P. O. Box 694, Altadena, 91003-0694
(213) 684-4428; (818) 797-2055
FAX (818) 798-3640

This 1938 Old Tahoe-style with European pine furniture offers cottage suites and large rooms, full breakfast, afternoon refreshments, private beach with a dock, and winter ski packages. Private bath. No smoking. $80-100 plus tax.

Eye Openers Bed and Breakfast Reservations LT-R41

P. O. Box 694, Altadena, 91003-0694
(213) 684-4428; (818) 797-2055
Fax (818) 798-3640

Inn decorated with Laura Ashley fabrics has pine walls and lake view. Full breakfast. Four guest rooms. Private bath. $100-150 plus tax.

6 Pets welcome; 7 Smoking allowed; 8 Children welcome; 9 Social drinking allowed; 10 Tennis available; 11 Swimming available; 12 Golf available; 13 Skiing available; 14 May be booked through travel agents.

LEMON COVE

Lemon Cove Bed and Breakfast

33038 Highway 198, 93244
(209) 597-2555

Situated near the Sequoia National Park, the Lemon Cove Bed and Breakfast is nestled in the Sierra foothills, just one mile below Lake Kaweah. A bridal suite with fireplace, whirlpool bath, and balcony is one of nine romantic rooms tastefully decorated with antiques and quilts. Off-street parking.

Hosts: Pat and Kay Bonette
Rooms: 9 (7-PB; 2-SB) $55-89
Full Breakfast
Credit Cars: A, B
Notes: 2, 5, 8, 9, 11, 12

LITTLE RIVER

Glendeven

8221 North Highway 1, 95456
(707) 937-0083

Glendeven is a delightful small country inn on a meadow headland overlooking Little River Bay. Tucked into the rural setting are the 1867 Maine-style farmhouse, the old water tower, the restored barn that holds a two-story guest suite, Gallery Glendeven, and Stevenscroft, with four elegant accommodations.

Hosts: Jan and Janet de Vries
Rooms: 10 (8 PB; 2 SB) $75-150
Expanded Continental Breakfast
Credit Cards: A, B
Notes: 2, 5, 8, 9, 10, 11, 12, 14

LODI

Wine and Roses Country Inn

2505 West Turner Road, 95242
(209) 334-6988

Converted to a romantic country inn with ten elegant suites filled with handmade comforters, antiques, and fresh flowers, the 1902 estate is secluded on five acres of towering trees and old-fashioned flower gardens. Afternoon tea and cookies, evening wine, delightful breakfast, library, "wine country" dining. Five minutes to wine-tasting, golf, tennis, health club. The 1,000-mile Delta waterway is 15 minutes away; museums, performing arts, Sacramento, and gold country within 30 minutes. Full restaurant which serves lunch Tuesday-Friday, dinner Wednesday-Saturday, and brunch on Sunday. Cocktails and full bar also available. San Francisco one and one-half hours; Lake Tahoe and Yosemite two and one-half hours.

Hosts: Kris Cromwell; Del and Sherri Smith
Rooms: 10 (PB) $79-125
Continental Breakfast 6-9 A.M.; Full Breakfast 9 A.M.
Credit Cards: A, B, C
Notes: 2, 3, 4, 5, 9, 10, 11, 12, 14

LONG BEACH

Bed and Breakfast Los Angeles 5-6

730 Catalina Avenue, Seal Beach, 90740
(310) 493-6837; (800) 383-3513

This classic box-style Victorian near downtown features two large guest rooms which share an old-fashioned bath and sitting room. Charming garden, large livingroom, and second bath downstairs. Weekly rates are available. Moderate rates.

Bed and Breakfast Los Angeles 5-8

730 Catalina Avenue, Seal Beach, 90740
(310) 493-6837; (800) 383-3513

Deep pastels swath this 1903 home on a hill in Long Beach. Two guest rooms (one with kids beds and toys) share one and one-

NOTES: Credit cards accepted: A Master Card; B Visa; C American Express; D Discover Card; E Diner's Club; F Other; 2 Personal Checks accepted; 3 Lunch available; 4 Dinner available; 5 Open all year;

half baths, a large wooden deck, a hot tub, an old-fashioned garden. Less than one mile from the airport. Affordable rates.

Eye Openers Bed and Breakfast Reservations LB-A51

P. O. Box 694, Altadena, 91003-0694
(213) 684-4428; (818) 797-2055
FAX (818) 798-3640

Newly refurbished inn with handcrafted features is centrally located in Long Beach. Nicely decorated with antiques and artwork, rooms offer comfort and privacy. Continental-plus breakfast. No smoking. Five guest rooms. Private bath. $50-70 plus tax.

Eye Openers Bed and Breakfast Reservations LB-M1

P. O. Box 694, Altadena, 91003-0694
(213) 684-4428; (818) 797-2055
Fax (818) 798-3640

Second floor of this bed and breakfast is three short blocks from the beach, with one guest room and one suite with kitchen. Continental breakfast. Weekly rates available. Private bath. $50-75.

Eye Openers Bed and Breakfast Reservations LB-XX

P. O. Box 694, Altadena, 91003-0694
(213) 684-4428; (818) 797-2055
FAX (818) 798-3640

Two bed and breakfast inns in the historic section of Long Beach are convenient to beaches, convention center and downtown Long Beach. $55-95, plus tax.

Kids Welcome 5-7

730 Catalina Avenue, Seal Beach, 90740
(310) 493-6837; (800) 383-3513

Steps to the beach, this elegant Spanish-style home has an upstairs guest suite with a large bedroom, full bath, sitting room with Hide-a-bed and small kitchen. Your seventh night is free. Affordable rates.

Lord Mayor's Inn

435 Cedar Avenue, 90802
(213) 436-0324

Originally the home of the first mayor of Long Beach, this elegant Edwardian home has been beautifully restored. The home is well kept, filled with antiques, and has been presented with an award for excellence in restoration. The inn has five rooms, all with private baths, and guests enjoy a full breakfast served in the dining room. In addition, there are covered porches and decks to enjoy Southern California weather, beaches, entertainment; Queen Mary and convention centers are nearby.

Hosts: Laura and Reuben Brasser
Rooms: 5 (PB) $85-95
Full Breakfast
Credit Cards: A, B, C
Notes: 2, 5, 7 (limited), 8, 14

LOS ANGELES

Bed and Breakfast Los Angeles 1-1

730 Catalina Avenue, Seal Beach, 90740
(310) 493-6837; (800) 383-3513

Lush gardens and a shaded patio in the Los Feliz Hills, minutes from the heart of the city. Three guest rooms, each with a balcony. One private bath; one shared. Friendly hosts donate all proceeds to United Cerebral Palsy. Moderate rates.

6 Pets welcome; 7 Smoking allowed; 8 Children welcome; 9 Social drinking allowed; 10 Tennis available; 11 Swimming available; 12 Golf available; 13 Skiing available; 14 May be booked through travel agents.

Bed and Breakfast Los Angeles 1-3

730 Catalina Avenue, Seal Beach, 90740
(310) 493-6837; (800) 383-3513

Time stands still in this 1902 mansion near downtown LA. Leaded windows, period furnishings, full breakfast, and complimentary wine. Five rooms, private baths, library, game room. Secure parking. Older children only, please. Moderate-luxury rates.

Bed and Breakfast Los Angeles 1-4

730 Catalina Avenue, Seal Beach, 90740
(310) 493-6837; (800) 383-3513

Our oldest home, located above Echo Park and built in 1887, sits on a hill in the middle of the city. Four rooms range from cozy to sumptuous, with gorgeous views and antique furnishings. Play in the game room, stroll in the gardens, or walk to the Music Center, Union Station, Olvera Street, or Chinatown. Older children only, please. Affordable luxury rates.

Bed and Breakfast Los Angeles 1-6

730 Catalina Avenue, Seal Beach, 90740
(310) 493-6837; (800) 383-3513

A whole house is available to you. Two bedrooms, one and one-half baths, kitchen, dining room, living room (with fireplace), laundry room, and deck. Mid-Wilshire location. Hosts live next door. Affordable rates.

Bed and Breakfast Los Angeles 1-7

730 Catalina Avenue, Seal Beach, 90740
(310) 493-6837; (800) 383-3513

This 1909 beauty, nestled in a residential neighborhood, is frequently used as a movie set. Every detail is designed for appreciation; wood-beamed ceilings, leaded-glass windows, antique-filled rooms, sumptuous breakfast and afternoon tea. Five rooms, including a huge attic suite. Older children only. Moderate rates.

Bed and Breakfast Los Angeles 1-8

730 Catalina Avenue, Seal Beach, 90740
(310) 493-6837; (800) 383-3513

Close to the USC campus, this 1910 Craftsman historic register home has two upstairs guest rooms, with a bath between them. There is a shaded porch in front, a sunny deck in the rear, and a smaller sun porch off one guest room. Affordable rates.

Bed and Breakfast Los Angeles 2-4

730 Catalina Avenue, Seal Beach, 90740
(310) 493-6837; (800) 383-3513

Spacious high-rise near UCLA campus has two guest rooms, each with a private bath. Hostess speaks many languages. Older children only, please. Moderate rates.

Bed and Breakfast Los Angeles 2-5

730 Catalina Avenue, Seal Beach, 90740
(310) 493-6837; (800) 383-3513

Share this third floor condo near La Cienga and Santa Monica Boulevard. Host has one guest room, underground parking, and serves a continental breakfast. Host prefers weekly rates. Affordable rates.

Bed and Breakfast Los Angeles 2-10

730 Catalina Avenue, Seal Beach, 90740
(310) 493-6837; (800) 383-3513

NOTES: Credit cards accepted: A Master Card; B Visa; C American Express; D Discover Card; E Diner's Club; F Other; 2 Personal Checks accepted; 3 Lunch available; 4 Dinner available; 5 Open all year;

The woods surround this elegant two-story redwood town house which looks out onto two acres of eucalyptus and wildlife. Decorated in Early American, there is a guest room with a private bath and TV, and a master suite with a fireplace and Jacuzzi. Older children only. Moderate rates.

Bed and Breakfast Los Angeles 2-11

730 Catalina Avenue, Seal Beach, 90740
(310) 493-6837; (800) 383-3513

Minutes from the airport, this contemporary home has two guest rooms which share a bath. Friendly, bilingual host. TV in your room is available. Affordable rates.

Bed and Breakfast Los Angeles 4-2

730 Catalina Avenue, Seal Beach, 90740
(310) 493-6837; (800) 383-3513

Cozy family home in a quiet neighborhood has two guest rooms, which share one and one-half baths. Close to the beach, and hosts will pick you up at the airport. Babies or children over five please. Affordable rates.

Bed and Breakfast Los Angeles 4-7

730 Catalina Avenue, Seal Beach, 90740
(310) 493-6837; (800) 383-3513

Ten minutes from LAX, this European-style hotel features breakfast in the courtyard; wine and cheese in the evenings. Cribs and roll-away beds are available. Luxury rates.

California Home Hospitality

P. O. Box 66662, 90066
(213) 390-1526

Situated in a quiet residential area, this hilltop home enjoys a spectacular view of the Santa Monica mountains and the entire northern portion of the city, including Beverly Hills, Westwood, and Century City. The city lights in the evening are lovely. Just 15 minutes from the beach at Santa Monica and adjacent to Marina del Rey Yacht Harbor and Santa Monica Municipal Airport. Hosts stress comfort, cleanliness, secure surroundings, and lots of TLC! For enthusiastic sight-seers, a rental car is suggested, although public transportation is within walking distance.

Hosts: Helen and Don Bourquin
Rooms: 2 (PB) $45-55
Full Breakfast
Credit Cards: None
Notes: 3, 4, 5, 7 (limited), 9

Eye Openers Bed and Breakfast Reservations LA-B1

P. O. Box 694, Altadena, 91003-0694
(213) 684-4428; (818) 797-2055
FAX (818) 798-3640

Five minutes from the Marina and LAX and walking distance to parks, tennis courts, golf, and restaurants, this cozy bed and breakfast is also near public transportation. Continental breakfast. No smoking. One guest room. Shared bath. $35-45.

Eye Openers Bed and Breakfast Reservations LA-C2

P. O. Box 694, Altadena, 91003-0694
(213) 684-4428; (818) 797-2055
FAX (818) 798-3640

Beautifully restored Craftsman-style house on the National Register of Historic Places is close to USC and civic and convention centers. Two comfortable guest rooms, lovely gardens and patio are available for guests to enjoy. No smoking. Shared and private baths. $40-50.

6 Pets welcome; 7 Smoking allowed; 8 Children welcome; 9 Social drinking allowed; 10 Tennis available; 11 Swimming available; 12 Golf available; 13 Skiing available; 14 May be booked through travel agents.

Eye Openers Bed and Breakfast Reservations LA-D1

P. O. Box 694, Altadena, 91003-0694
(213) 684-4428; (818) 797-2055
FAX (818) 798-3640

Spacious West Los Angeles apartment with elegant hospitality, interesting artifacts and a location near most West Side destinations makes this a good bed and breakfast at a modest price. Swimming pool available. Continental breakfast. No smoking. Two guest rooms. Private bath. $50-55.

Eye Openers Bed and Breakfast Reservations LA-D2

P. O. Box 694, Altadena, 91003-0694
(213) 684-4428; (818) 797-2055
FAX (818) 798-3640

Convenient to L.A. International Airport, this comfortable, homey bed and breakfast with two spacious guest rooms has full exercise equipment room and hearty American breakfast. Spanish is spoken. No smoking. Private and shared baths. $40-45.

Eye Openers Bed and Breakfast Reservations LA-E81

P. O. Box 694, Altadena, 91003-0694
(213) 684-4428; (818) 797-2055
FAX (818) 798-3640

Lovely 1887 hilltop Victorian is located in Los Angeles' first Historical Preservation Zone. The inn and neighborhood are listed in the National Register of Historic Places. Continental breakfast and evening refreshments are served, and this bed and breakfast is convenient to the civic center, Hollywood, and tourist attractions. Ten guest rooms. Shared and private baths. No smoking. $50-125 plus tax.

Eye Openers Bed and Breakfast Reservations LA-H1

P. O. Box 694, Altadena, 91003-0694
(213) 684-4428; (818) 797-2055
FAX (818) 798-3640

Quite residential area near the airport and Marina has good public transportation. Share comfortable living room with fireplace, lovely yard, and a full or continental breakfast with hosts whose interest are folk instruments and music. No smoking. One guest room. Shared bath. $32-38.

Eye Openers Bed and Breakfast Reservations LA-P1

P. O. Box 694, Altadena, 91003-0694
(213) 684-4428; (818) 797-2055
FAX (818) 798-3640

Walk to Westwood and UCLA from this attractive Wilshire Boulevard bed and breakfast. Enjoy an ample continental breakfast on the balcony prepared by French-speaking host. No smoking. Good public transportation nearby. One guest room with private bath. $60.

Eye Openers Bed and Breakfast Reservations LA-S1

P. O. Box 694, Altadena, 91003-0694
(213) 684-4428; (818) 797-2055
FAX (818) 798-3640

Centrally located, spacious 800-square-foot, three-room apartment with patios is a good location for vacationing sightseers, business people, and people interested in relocating to the Los Angeles area. Breakfast is self-catered. Weekly rates available. No smoking. Private bath. $65-75.

NOTES: Credit cards accepted: A Master Card; B Visa; C American Express; D Discover Card; E Diner's Club; F Other; 2 Personal Checks accepted; 3 Lunch available; 4 Dinner available; 5 Open all year;

Eye Openers Bed and Breakfast Reservations LA-S3

P. O. Box 694, Altadena, 91003-0694
(213) 684-4428; (818) 797-2055
FAX (818) 798-3640

Two-story Art Deco-style architect-designed bed and breakfast nestled in the beautiful Los Feliz Hills of near Griffith Park and the Greek Theatre. Offering a quiet, comfortable setting convenient to fine restaurants, entertainment, and tourist attractions. Two guest rooms and private bath. Public transportation available. $55-120.

Eye Openers Bed and Breakfast Reservations LA-S51

P. O. Box 694, Altadena, 91003-0694
(213) 684-4428; (818) 797-2055
FAX (818) 798-3640

Antique-decorated, restored 1908 Craftsman home provides the setting and mood of an earlier era. A marvelous, full gourmet breakfast and evening refreshments are served. Convenient to the University of Southern California, Civic Center, Hollywood, and tourist attractions. Five guest rooms. Shared and private bath. $65-95, plus tax.

Eye Openers Bed and Breakfast Reservations LA-T51

P. O. Box 694, Altadena, 91003-0694
(213) 684-4428; (818) 797-2055
FAX (818) 798-3640

Close to the Los Angeles Convention Center, this stately 1902 bed and breakfast inn with period furnishings offers a lovely setting. Full breakfast and afternoon tea or wine is served in the parlor or library. No smoking. Five guest rooms. Private bath. $75-105.

Kids Welcome 1-5

730 Catalina Avenue, Seal Beach, 90740
(310) 493-6837; (800) 383-3513

Five minutes from Music Center, this Silverdale apartment easily accommodates five. Full kitchen, TV, private entrance, situated in the hills above downtown. Moderate rates.

Kids Welcome 3-5

730 Catalina Avenue, Seal Beach, 90740
(310) 493-6837; (800) 383-3513

This retired couple in a quiet neighborhood has two guest rooms and one bath in their upstairs suite. Toys, crib, and TV, and you can walk to Universal Studios. Affordable rates.

Kids Welcome 8-3

730 Catalina Avenue, Seal Beach, 90740
(310) 493-6837; (800) 383-3513

This Craftsman cottage is perfect for a family of three. Turn-of-the-century decor, king-size bedroom, single bed in the living room, full bath and kitchen make it a real home. Your hostess brings breakfast to the door each morning. Affordable-moderate rates.

LOS OSOS

America's B&B #17

P. O. Box 9302, Whittier, 90608
(310) 699-8427

Lovely contemporary home with exciting view of the ocean and bay. This home is two miles from the beaches and Montana De Oro State Park. Near golf courses. Activities include boating and whale watching. This home is only 35 minutes from the Hearst Castle. Three bedrooms

6 Pets welcome; 7 Smoking allowed; 8 Children welcome; 9 Social drinking allowed; 10 Tennis available; 11 Swimming available; 12 Golf available; 13 Skiing available; 14 May be booked through travel agents.

with king, queen, or twin beds available, and private and shared baths. Children welcome. $57.

and double beds. Perfect for honeymooners and couples. A full breakfast is provided in the kitchen for guests to serve themselves. No children under 10. $60-$75.

Gerarda's Bed and Breakfast

1056 Bay Oaks Drive, 93402
(805) 528-3973

The ideal place to stop between San Francisco and Los Angeles. On the coast with ocean and mountain views. Close to Hearst Castle, Morro Bay, and San Luis Obispo; golf, tennis, hiking, and shopping. Dutch hospitality; your host speaks several languages.

Host: Gerarda Ondang
Rooms: 3 (1 PB; 2 SB) $42
Full Breakfast
Credit Cards: None
Notes: 2, 4, 5, 6, 8, 9, 10, 11, 12

Megan's Friends #06

Bed & Breakfast Reservation Service
1776 Royal Way, San Luis Obispo, 93405
(805) 544-4406

A large hillside house with a stunning view of the valley, mountains, bay, and Pacific Ocean. There is a bedroom with a queen bed and separate entrance, and a twin bedroom adjacent for two couples traveling together. Meticulous Dutch housekeeping and hospitality. Two miles from the sand dunes and Montana de Oro State Park. Full breakfast served in the dining room.

Megan's Friends #07

Bed & Breakfast Reservation Service
1776 Royal Way, San Luis Obispo, 93405
(805) 544-4406

This Austrian-style guesthouse is on the ocean bluff, with deer and racoons for neighbors. The guesthouse is a separate unit with pegged oak floors, large windows with a view of the ocean, and features king

LOTUS

Golden Lotus

1006 Lotus Rd, P. O. Box 830, 95651
(916) 621-4562

Escape the ordinary, and enter into any one of our six fantasy worlds (Westward Ho, Orient Expressed, Secret Garden, Tranquility, Pirate's Cove, Wish Upon.) Rooms offer king or queen size beds and private baths. Enjoy a full breakfast in an 1855 brick building or on the veranda. Extensive library is open to guests. River frontage, white water rafting, one mile to Gold Discovery Park. Herb and flower gardens. Separate antique store, plus garden accessories. Restaurant on premises. Reiki available.

Host: Bruce and Jill Smith
Rooms: 6 (PB) $75-95
Full Breakfast
Credit Cards: None
Notes: 2, 3, 4, 5, 14

LUCERNE

Kristalberg

P. O. Box 1629, 95458
(707) 274-8009

1985 Cape Cod 800 feet above Clear Lake. Magnificent 30-mile view of lake and countryside. Three rooms elegantly furnished with antiques; two have private baths and balcony on lake side; master bath has whirlpool tub. Breakfast in formal dining room includes fresh fruit and home-baked items. Afternoon wine and after-dinner brandy. Hiking and biking from front door. Boating, fishing, antique shops, wineries, good restaurants. German and Spanish spoken.

NOTES: Credit cards accepted: A Master Card; B Visa; C American Express; D Discover Card; E Diner's Club; F Other; 2 Personal Checks accepted; 3 Lunch available; 4 Dinner available; 5 Open all year;

Host: Merv Myers
Rooms: 3 (2 PB; 1 SB) $55-150
Expanded Continental Breakfast
Credit Cards: C
Notes: 2, 5, 9, 10, 14

MALIBU

Bed and Breakfast Los Angeles 4-10

730 Catalina Avenue, Seal Beach, 90740
(310) 493-6837; (800) 383-3513

The entire second floor of this spacious house in Malibu is reserved for guests. Master room has a king-size bed, private bath, and balcony that looks out over the mountains. Sitting room loft can accommodate the kids and two other rooms share a bath. No toddlers, please. Affordable rates.

Bed and Breakfast Los Angeles 4-11

730 Catalina Avenue, Seal Beach, 90740
(310) 493-6837; (800) 383-3513

This charming cottage has views through the canyon all the way to the ocean. Bedroom, living room, small kitchen, full bath, deck. Breakfast on weekends only. Children over 12. Moderate rates.

Bed and Breakfast Los Angeles 4-12

730 Catalina Avenue, Seal Beach, 90740
(310) 493-6837; (800) 383-3513

Rooms in this truly luxurious little hotel have ocean-view balconies, wet bars, TV's, VCR's, and fireplaces. Continental breakfast. Luxury rates.

Casa Larronde

Box 86, 90265
(213) 456-9333

This is the area of "the famous," and the locals call this beach "Millionaires' Row." The ocean suite has 40 feet of windows adjoining its deck. The amenities include: TV, phone, fireplace, kitchenette, ceiling fan over a king-size bed, floor-to-ceiling three-way mirrors in the dressing room, and a large bathroom with twin basins. Cocktails are offered in the evening, and a full American breakfast is leisurely served in the morning.

Host: Charlou Larronde
Rooms: 2 (PB) $100-115
Full Breakfast
Credit Cards: None
Notes: 2, 8, 9, 10, 11

Eye Openers Bed and Breakfast Reservations MA-L2

P. O. Box 694, Altadena, 91003-0694
(213) 684-4428; (818) 797-2055
FAX (818) 798-3640

Newly decorated Malibu bed and breakfast offers sunshine, sea air, hiking, tennis, and swimming. Private beach available. Generous continental breakfast. No smoking. Two guest rooms. Shared bath. $65-85.

Malibu Beach Inn

22878 Pacific Coast Highway, 90265
(310) 456-6444; (800) 4MALIBU

Malibu...a tiny and exclusive coastal strip just north of los Angeles, famous for its white beaches, breaking surf, natural beauty, and casual but elegant lifestyle. That's exactly what you'll find at the the beautiful Malibu Beach Inn. Built directly on the beach, the Inn offers the ultimate "California Dreamin" experience. Accommodations are designed to create the feeling of being in one's own private cottage on the beach and features private oceanfront balconies, fireplaces, and a full range of amenities.

6 Pets welcome; 7 Smoking allowed; 8 Children welcome; 9 Social drinking allowed; 10 Tennis available; 11 Swimming available; 12 Golf available; 13 Skiing available; 14 May be booked through travel agents.

Hosts: Dan Ferrante
Rooms: 47 (PB) $125-210
Expanded Continental Breakfast
Credit Cards: A, B, C, E
Notes: 3, 4, 5, 7, 9, 10, 12, 14

Malibu Country Inn

6506 Westward Beach Road, 90265
(213) 457-9622; FAX (213) 457-1349

A romantic country inn on a bluff above
one of the world's most famous and beautiful beaches. This cozy bed and breakfast
offers guests intimate accommodations in a
private, three-acre, lush garden setting.
Rooms feature privately enclosed patios,
refrigerators, coffee makers and TV. A
heated swimming pool with sun decks and
view of ocean and mountains. Beach is just
a short walk away. Receive a welcoming
fruit basket and a daily Los Angeles Times.

Hosts: Tony and Pamela Regan
Rooms: 16 (PB) $105-225
Full Breakfast
Credit Cards: A, B, C
Notes: 5, 7, 8, 9, 10, 11, 12, 14

MAMMOTH LAKES

Bed and Breakfast Los Angeles 10-1

730 Catalina Avenue, Seal Beach, 90740
(310) 493-6837; (800) 383-3513

This inn has 19 rooms and four two-
bedroom apartments. Your hostess can
arrange great ski packages and also has a
hot tub, a big social room, and an early
evening appetizer party. Moderate, seasonal rates.

MANHATTAN BEACH

Eye Openers Bed and Breakfast Reservations MB-C2

P. O. Box 694, Altadena, 91003-0694
(213) 684-4428; (818) 797-2055
FAX (818) 798-3640

Walk to the beach, shops, and restaurants
from this restored beach bungalow. Ocean
view from upstairs guest room. Continental
breakfast, and other amenities available.
No smoking. Two guest rooms. Private and
shared bath. $45-75.

Eye Openers Bed and Breakfast Reservations MB-L2

P. O. Box 694, Altadena, 91003-0694
(213) 684-4428; (818) 797-2055
FAX (818) 798-3640

Beachfront bed and breakfast is the entire
first floor of this lovely home on the
Strand. Private entrance, living/dining
room area with fireplace, wet bar and guest
parking are some of the amenities offered.
Continental breakfast. No smoking. Two
guest rooms. Private bath. $75-84.

MARINA DEL REY

Eye Openers Bed and Breakfast Reservations MR-Z1

P. O. Box 694, Altadena, 91003-0694
(213) 684-4428; (818) 797-2055
FAX (818) 798-3640

Large apartment in Marina Del Rey offers
privacy and comfort, contemporary decor,
full kitchen, living/dining room area, and
self-catered continental breakfast. Walk to
the beach, and short ten minutes from
LAX. Weekly rates available. No smoking.
Private bath. $55-75.

Eye Openers Bed and Breakfast Reservations PL-D2

P. O. Box 694, Altadena, 91003-0694
(213) 684-4428; (818) 797-2055
FAX (818) 798-3640

NOTES: Credit cards accepted: A Master Card; B Visa; C American Express; D Discover Card; E Diner's
Club; F Other; 2 Personal Checks accepted; 3 Lunch available; 4 Dinner available; 5 Open all year;

Set on a hillside near the beach, this three story Tudor-style bed and breakfast offers the first story as guest quarters with guest living room and patio. Gourmet, continental or full breakfast served. No smoking. Two guest rooms. Private bath. $60-80.

MARIPOSA

Bed and Breakfast Los Angeles 18-6

730 Catalina Avenue, Seal Beach, 90740
(310) 493-6837; (800) 383-3513

The little town of Mariposa is 38 miles from Yosemite Valley where you can visit the Ansel Adams Museum or take the kids for a mule ride. Your hosts have an old-fashioned inn with a suite consisting of a bedroom, living room, dining area, bathroom, and porch. You can also rent a room with a shared bath in one of Mariposa's elegant old homes. Amenities include a swimming pool and a hot tub.

Oak Meadows, too.

5263 Highway 140N, Box 619, 95338
(209) 742-6161

Situated in the historic Gold Rush town of Mariposa, this bed and breakfast has turn-of-the-century charm. New England architecture; rooms decorated with handmade quilts, wallpaper, and brass headboards. Close to Yosemite. Home of the California State Mining & Mineral Museum.

Hosts: Frank Ross and Kaaren Black
Rooms: 6 (PB) $59-69
Expanded Continental Breakfast
Credit Cards: A, B
Notes: 2, 5, 14

The Pelennor

3871 Highway 49 South, 95338
(209) 966-2832

Country atmosphere about 45 minutes from Yosemite National Park. After a day of sightseeing, you may want to take a few laps in the pool, unwind in the spa, enjoy the available games, relax in the sauna, and listen to an occasional tune played on the bagpipes.

Hosts: Dick and Gwen Foster
Singles: $35; Doubles: $45
Type of Beds: 2 Twin; 1 Double; 2 Queen
Full Breakfast
Credit Cards: None
Notes: 2, 5, 6, 8, 9, 11

Schlageter House

5038 Bullion Street, P. O. Box 1202, 95338
(209) 966-2471

Quiet Victorian comfort, patios, porches, and gardens for guests' enjoyment. Nearby is beautiful Yosemite and the charm of the history of the California Gold Rush. A large breakfast in a surprise tradition of the "Cousin Jack Miners of 1849" served at any time convenient in the guests' itinerary.

Hosts: Lee and Roger McElligott
Rooms: 2 (PB) $70-80
Full Breakfast
Credit Cards: None
Notes: 2, 5, 7, 8, 9, 10, 13, 14

Winsor Farms Bed and Breakfast

5636 Whitlock Road, 95338
(209) 966-5592

A country home seven miles north of Mariposa, just off Hwy. I-40 to Yosemite National Park. This peaceful hilltop retreat among majestic pines and rugged oaks offers two rooms decorated for your comfort and convenience. An extended continental breakfast is served. The town of Mariposa is the Gateway to the Mother Lode Gold Country, with museums and a history center. Yosemite National Park, a scenic wonder of the world, offers year-round activities.

6 Pets welcome; 7 Smoking allowed; 8 Children welcome; 9 Social drinking allowed; 10 Tennis available; 11 Swimming available; 12 Golf available; 13 Skiing available; 14 May be booked through travel agents.

Hosts: Donald and Janice Haag
Rooms: 2 (SB) $50
Continental Breakfast
Credit Cards: None
Notes: 2, 5

MAR VISTA

Bed and Breakfast Los Angeles 4-5

730 Catalina Avenue, Seal Beach, 90740
(310) 493-6837; (800) 383-3513

This contemporary home is near Santa Monica and has two rooms, each designed for a single guest. Two bathrooms are shared with your hosts. Nice patio and bikes are available. Children over five years old. Affordable rates.

McCLOUD

Hogin House

424 Lawndale, 96057
(916) 964-2882

Located ten miles off I-5 on Hwy 89 and situated on the southeastern slope of mount Shasta, Hogin House is a charming two story Victorian within walking distance of downtown McCloud, a company built mill town. The large, sunny guest rooms offer a variety of accommodations. Downstairs, you may relax by the fire, enjoy a book or magazine, play cards, or visit with fellow guests. A fine continental breakfast awaits you in the dining room or on the porch, when weather permits. Kitchen privileges also available.

Hosts: Angie and Richard Toreson
Rooms: 4 (2-PB; 2-SB) $50.
Expanded Continental Breakfast
Credit Cards: A, B, C
Notes: 2, 5, 14

McCloud Guest House

606 West Colombero Drive, 96057
(916) 964-3160

Built in 1907, this beautiful old country home is nestled among stately oaks and lofty pines on the lower slopes of majestic Mount Shasta. On the first floor is one of Siskiyou County's finer dining establishments. The second floor has a large parlor surrounded by five guest rooms, each individually decorated.

Hosts: Bill and Patti Leigh; Dennis and Pat Abreu
Rooms: 5 (PB) $75-90
Continental Breakfast
Minimum stay holidays: 2 nights
Credit Cards: A, B
Closed Thanksgiving and Christmas
Notes: 2, 4, 5, 11, 12, 13

Stoney Brook Inn

309 West Colombero, P. O. Box 1860, 96057
(916) 964-2300; (800) 369-6118

On the south side of majestic Mount Shasta in the heart of the Shasta Cascade wonderland is the historic Stoney Brook Inn. It is fully restored, yet retains its homey character. Enjoy its soothing atmosphere. Relax in the outdoor hot tub, sauna, or on the spacious front porch. Unwind with a therapeutic massage, or lounge by the fire in the winter. Group and individual retreats available.

Hosts: Walter and Szuszi
Rooms: 17(14 PB; 3 SB) $32-58
Hearty Breakfast
Credit Cards: A, B
Notes: 2, 3, 4, 5, 8, 12, 13, 14

MENDOCINO

Agate Cove Inn

11201 Lansing Street, Box 1150, 95460
(707) 937-0551

Agate Cove Inn is on an ocean bluff with dramatic views of the ocean and rugged coastline. There are individual cottages, each with an ocean view, a Franklin fireplace, and a private bath. Included is a full country breakfast served in the main 1860s farmhouse. Hiking, golf, and tennis are close by.

NOTES: Credit cards accepted: A Master Card; B Visa; C American Express; D Discover Card; E Diner's Club; F Other; 2 Personal Checks accepted; 3 Lunch available; 4 Dinner available; 5 Open all year;

Hosts: Sallie McConnell and Jake Zahavi
Rooms: 10 (PB) $75-175
Full Breakfast
Credit Cards: A, B, C, D
Notes: 2, 5, 9, 10, 12, 14

Bed & Breakfast Los Angeles 16-6

730 Catalina Avenue, Seal Beach, 90740
(310) 493-6837; (800) 383-3513

Your lodging at this unusual bed and breakfast may be in the Greenhouse (complete with Franklin fireplace), the Gazebo (converted children's playhouse). The Barn, or the Water Tower (really a water tower). Some guest areas are are perfect for big families. The main house is stuffed with lovingly restored antiques. Affordable rates.

Brewery Gulch Inn

9350 Coast Highway 1, 95460
(707) 937-4752

An authentic country bed and breakfast farm situated on the rugged coast just one mile from the village of Mendocino. The lovely old white farmhouse is furnished in the Victorian style with queen beds, homemade quilts, and down pillows. Each guest room window provides views of the gardens and meadows beyond.

The Headlands Inn

Host: Anne Saunders
Rooms: 5 (3 PB; 2 SB) $75-115
Full Breakfast
Credit Cards: A, B
Notes: 2, 5, 10, 11, 12

The Headlands Inn

Box 132, 95460
(707) 937-4431

The Headlands Inn is an 1868 Victorian, centrally situated within Mendocino village on California's scenic north coast minutes from redwoods and wineries. Full gourmet breakfasts are served in your room. All rooms have wood-burning fireplaces and spectacular ocean views overlooking an English-style garden. King or queen beds. Two parlors, many unusual antiques. Afternoon tea serv ice with mineral waters, cookies, and mixed nuts.

Hosts: Pat and Rod Stofle
Rooms: 5 (PB) $98-164
Full Breakfast
Minimum stay weekends: 2 nights; holidays: 3-4
    nights
Credit Cards: None
Notes: 2, 5, 9, 10, 11, 12

John Dougherty House

571 Ukiah Street, P. O. Box 817, 95460
(707) 937-5266

Historic John Dougherty House was built in 1867 and is one of the oldest houses in Mendocino. Situated on land bordered by Ukiah and Albion streets, the inn has some of the best ocean and bay views in the historic village of Mendocino; steps away from great restaurants and shopping, but years removed from 20th century reality. The main house is furnished with period country antiques and will take you back to 1867. Enjoy quiet peaceful nights seldom experienced in today's urban living.

Hosts: David and Marion Wells
Rooms: 6 (PB) $85-140
Expanded Continental Breakfast
Credit Cards: None
Notes: 2, 5, 9, 14

6 Pets welcome; 7 Smoking allowed; 8 Children welcome; 9 Social drinking allowed; 10 Tennis available; 11 Swimming available; 12 Golf available; 13 Skiing available; 14 May be booked through travel agents.

Joshua Grindle Inn

44800 Little Lake Road, P. O. Box 647, 95460
(707) 937-4143

Situated on two acres in the historic village of Mendocino overlooking the ocean, the Joshua Grindle Inn is a short walk to the beach, art center, shops, and fine restaurants. Stay in the lovely two-story Victorian farmhouse, a New England-style cottage, or a three-story water tower. Six rooms have fireplaces; all have private baths, antiques, and comfortable reading areas. Enjoy a full breakfast served around a ten-foot 1830s harvest table.

Hosts: Jim and Arlene Moorehead
Rooms: 10 (PB) $90-135
Full Breakfast
Credit Cards: A, B, D
Notes: 2, 5, 9, 10, 12, 14

Kids Welcome 16-7

730 Catalina Avenue, Seal Beach, 90740
(310) 493-6837; (800) 383-3513

These hosts raised a total of twelve children in their Victorian home before they started taking in bed and breakfast guests. They have four guest rooms, all with private baths, and the house has plenty for kids to do and all the necessities a parent could ask for. Kids stay free in parents' room. Breakfast is not included. Affordable rates.

MacCallum House Inn

45020 Albion Street, P. O. Box 206, 95460
(707) 937-0289

Unique accommodations that include the Victorian home of Daisy MacCallum, water tower, greenhouse, barn, and English gardens. In the center of the village; walk to shops, restaurants, beach.

Hosts: Melanie and Joe Reding
Rooms: 20 (7 PB; 13 SB) $45-165
Continental Breakfast
Minimum stay May-Dec. weekends: 2 nights; holidays: 2-3 nights
Credit Cards: A, B
Notes: 2, 4, 5, 8, 9, 10, 11, 12, 14

Mendocino Farmhouse

Box 247, 95460
(707) 937-0241

Mendocino Farmhouse is a small bed and breakfast with all the comforts of home, surrounded by redwood forest, beautiful gardens, a pond, and meadow. Choose from comfortable rooms decorated with country antiques for a quiet night's rest and enjoy a farmhouse breakfast in the morning.

Hosts: Margie and Bud Kamb
Rooms: 5 (PB) $75-100
Full Breakfast
Credit Cards: None
Notes: 2, 5, 8 (call), 10, 11, 12

Mendocino Village Inn

Main Street, Box 626, 95460
(707) 937-0246

A well-done bed and breakfast inn that promises hummingbirds, Picassos, French-roast coffee, fuchsias, fireplaces, Vivaldi. This 1882 Victorian is filled with everything necessary for charm and gracious living, including four-poster beds, Bokharas, fresh blackberries, and complimentary wine.

Hosts: Bill and Kathleen Erwin
Rooms: 12 (10 PB; 2 SB) $60-140
Full Breakfast
Minimum stay weekends: 2 nights; holidays:
    3 nights
Credit Cards: None
Notes: 2, 5, 8 (over 10), 9, 10, 11, 12

Rachel's Inn

P. O. Box 134, 95460
(707) 937-0088

Comfort with style in an elegantly restored 1860s house and new companion "barn." Ocean, garden, and meadow views. Wheelchair access. Adjoins state park with beaches, deer meadows, and forests. Whale and seal watching from ocean cliffs, hiking, nearby golf. Two miles from Mendocino village. Lavish breakfast.

Host: Rachel Binah
Rooms: 9 (PB) $96-165
Full Breakfast
Credit Cards: None
Notes: 2, 5, 7, 8, 9, 10, 12, 14

S.S. Seafoam Lodge

P. O. Box 68, 95460
(707) 937-1827

"The best-kept secret on the Mendocino coast." A unique Mendocino getaway in the nautical mode featuring 24 ocean-view staterooms with private decks. Nestled on six acres of gardens and forest, the lodge overlooks spectacular Buckhorn Cove with beach access. Nearby golf, tennis, hiking, fishing, and diving. Choose from a wide variety of fine restaurants in Little River and the nearby Victorian village of Mendocino with its quality art galleries and unique shops.

Host: Ed Zimmerman
Rooms: 24 plus vacation cabins (2 BR) (PB)
    $85-200
Continental Breakfast
Credit Cards: A, B
Notes: 2, 5, 6, 7, 8, 14

Stanford Inn by the Sea

P. O. Box 487
Highway 1 and Comptche-Ukiah Road, 95460
(707) 937-5615; (800) 331-8884

Elegantly rustic lodge situated on a meadow sloping to the sea. Accommodations with wood-burning fireplaces, down comforters, and the amenities expected at the finest hotels, including VCR's, remote controlled television, refrigerators, wine, coffee makers. A true country inn, the Stanford Inn is the home of California Certified Organic Big River Nurseries and Big River Llamas. The finest canoes, kayaks, and bicycles available for exploring. Indoor swimming pool, sauna, and spa.

Hosts: Joan and Jeff Stanford
Rooms: 26 (PB) $145-160
Expanded Continental Breakfast
Credit Cards: A, B, C, D, E, F
Notes: 2, 5, 6, 7 (limited), 8, 9, 11

Stevenswood Lodge

8211 North Highway 1, Little River
P. O. Box 170, 95460
(707) 937-2810; (800) 421-2810

Distinctive contemporary suites, all hand-crafted, on Mendocino's spectacular coast. Virgin "old-growth" setting off shoreline Highway 1 with beach access and forest trails. Complimentary gourmet breakfast and evening wine bar/appetizers. Ocean views, fireplaces, stocked refrigerators, 33-channel remote-control TV, library, executive conference room, VCR, art gallery, and wine cellar.

Hosts: Robert and Vera Zimmer
Rooms: 1 (PB)
Suites: 9 (PB) $90-195
Full Breakfast
Credit Cards: A, B, D
Notes: 2, 5, 8, 9, 12, 14

Whitegate Inn

Box 150, 499 Howard Street, 95460
(707) 937-4892

Everything you look for in a bed and breakfast experience: antiques, fireplaces, ocean views, and private baths. Elegant 1880 Victorian, in the center of the historic preservation village of Mendocino. Shops, galleries, and nationally acclaimed restaurants are just steps away. A perfect setting for romance, weddings, or rest and relaxation.

Hosts: Carol and George Bachtloff
Rooms: 6 (PB) $90-130
Full Breakfast
Credit Cards: None
Notes: 2, 5, 9, 10, 11, 12

MILL VALLEY

Mountain Home Inn

810 Panoramic Highway, 94941
(415) 381-9000

A romantic country inn high atop Mount Tamalpais, offering spectacular views of the Marin Hills and San Francisco Bay. Ten guest rooms await you. Some offer

6 Pets welcome; 7 Smoking allowed; 8 Children welcome; 9 Social drinking allowed; 10 Tennis available; 11 Swimming available; 12 Golf available; 13 Skiing available; 14 May be booked through travel agents.

Jacuzzi baths, private decks, and fireplaces. Just outside the front door is Mount Tamalpais State Park offering miles of hiking trails. Muir Woods National Monument, Muir Beach, and Stinson Beach are a short drive away, with downtown San Francisco only 25 minutes away. Restaurant on premises.

Rooms: 10 (PB) $121-178
Full Breakfast
Credit Cards: A, B
Notes: 2, 3, 4, 5, 7, 8, 9, 10, 11, 12, 14

MONTARA

B&B San Francisco #15

P. O. Box 349, San Francisco, 94101
(415) 931-3083; FAX (415) 921-BBSF

Twenty miles south of San Francisco on California's famous Highway 1 lies the small beach community of Montara. The hosts offer a very romantic Hide-a-away suite with a sitting room, fireplace, and ocean view. Montara is well known for its terrific beach, hiking trails, and horseback riding. Deep sea fishing and whale-watching excursions leave from nearby Princeton. Moderate-luxury rates.

The Goose and Turrets

835 George Street, Box 937, 94037
(415) 728-5451

A 1908 Italian villa in a quiet garden offers comfort and four-course breakfasts. Thirty minutes to San Francisco; 20 minutes from San Francisco airport; one-half mile to the beach. Near restaurants, horseback riding, tide pools, galleries, golf. Pick-up at local harbor and airport. French spoken.

Hosts: Raymond and Emily Hoche-Mong
Rooms: 5 (PB) $85-110
Full Breakfast
Credit Cards: A, B, C, D
Notes: 2, 8, 9, 10, 11, 12, 14

Montara Bed and Breakfast

1125 Tamarind Street, 94037
(415) 728-3946

Just 20 miles south of San Francisco on the scenic California coast. Semirural area with nearby hiking, beaches, and horseback riding. Private entrance, private bath, ocean view, fireplace, TV, stereo, telephone, sun deck. Business travelers welcome.

Hosts: Bill and Peggy Bechtell
Rooms: 1 (PB) $80
Full Breakfast
Minimum stay weekends & holidays: 2 nights
Credit Cards: A, B
Notes: 2, 5, 9, 10, 11, 12, 14

MONTEREY

B&B International #204

P. O. Box 282910, San Francisco, 94128-2910
(415) 696-1690; FAX (415) 696-1699

Three homes situated on the southern end of Monterey, all modestly priced. Two have views of the bay. There are six rooms that offer twin, queen, and double beds. All have shared baths. Excellent breakfasts are prepared by experienced hosts. $50-60.

B&B International #206

P. O. Box 282910, San Francisco, 94128-2910
(415) 696-1690; FAX (415) 696-1699

Contemporary two-story redwood home situated in one of Monterey Peninsula's most exclusive areas and one block to the ocean. The home is spacious with much glass. The breakfast room is a glass semicircle extending into the garden. There is a fireplace and a view of the ocean from the living room. Two rooms with private baths. $88-98.

Bed and Breakfast Los Angeles 12-5

730 Catalina Avenue, Seal Beach, 90740
(310) 493-6837; (800) 383-3513

NOTES: Credit cards accepted: A Master Card; B Visa; C American Express; D Discover Card; E Diner's Club; F Other; 2 Personal Checks accepted; 3 Lunch available; 4 Dinner available; 5 Open all year;

This nineteen-room inn has fireplaces, living room suites, and two bedroom units. Located in the heart of Monterey, this inn also has a pool, continental breakfast, and no charge for a child in an adult's room. Affordable rates.

Del Monte Beach Inn

1110 Del monte Avenue, 93940
(408) 649-4410

The only one of its kind on the monterey Peninsula, the del monte Beach Inn offers guests all of the charm and comfort of a quaint European Bed and Breakfast at comfortably affordable rates in an ideal location. Walk across the boulevard to the beach and the bike and walking trail, and you are only minutes from Fisherman's Wharf, Cannery Row, Historic Monterey, and the Aquarium.

Hosts: Lisa Glover
Rooms: 18 (2 PB; 16 SB) $40-75
Extended Continental Breakfast
Credit Cards: A, B
Notes: 2, 5, 8, 9, 10, 11, 12, 14

The Jabberwock

The Jabberwock

598 Laine Street, 93940
(408) 372-4777

Alice's Wonderland just four blocks above Cannery Row and the Monterey Bay Aquarium. The Jabberwock has one-half acre of lush gardens and waterfalls overlooking Monterey Bay. Each room has down pillows and comforters. Hors d'oeuvres at 5:00 P.M. and cookies and milk at bedtime.

Hosts: Jim and Barbara Allen
Rooms: 7 (3 PB; 4 S2B) $100-175
Full Breakfast
Credit Cards: None
Notes: 2, 5, 9, 10, 11, 12, 14

Old Monterey Inn

500 Martin Street, 93940
(408) 375-8284

Surrounded by more than an acre of English gardens, the award-winning Old Monterey Inn offers guests an exclusive retreat so hidden and enchanting you will lxuriate in its surroundings. Built in 1929, the grand Tudor-style manor offers private baths, sitting rooms, and fireplaces. This four-star bed and breakfast inn, in the heart of Monterey is truly an inn-lover's dream.

Hosts: Ann and Gene Swett
Rooms: 10 (PB) $160-220
Full Breakfast
Credit Cards: A, B
Notes: 2, 5, 10, 12

MONTE RIO

Highland Dell Inn

21050 River Boulevard, P. O. Box 370, 95462-0370
(800) 767-1759

Beautifully restored 1906 inn. Rich stained-glass windows, grand lobby fireplace, large living areas overlooking the Russian River, and nestled among redwoods. Ten uniquely decorated bedrooms, one suite with a river view and queen size sleigh bed, grand suite with sunken tub, wood stoves, and leaded-

6 Pets welcome; 7 Smoking allowed; 8 Children welcome; 9 Social drinking allowed; 10 Tennis available; 11 Swimming available; 12 Golf available; 13 Skiing available; 14 May be booked through travel agents.

and stained-glass windows with commanding views, both of which have television and VCR. Complimentary expanded continental breakfast. Dinners on selected Saturday evenings. Close by Sonoma's North Coast and premier wineries.

Hosts: Glenn Dixon and Anthony Patchett
Rooms: 10 (8-PB; 2-SB) $65-225
Full Breakfast
Credit Cards: A, B, C, D
Notes: 4, 5, 6, 11, 12, 14

Huckleberry Springs

P. O. Box 400, 95462
(707) 865-2683; (800) 822-2683

An upscale relaxed country inn on 56 acres offers five unique cottage with private decks, and baths. Spring water spa and pool. Regional gourmet dining. Breakfast and dinner included in the rates.

Host: Suzanne
Rooms: 5 (PB) $175
Full Breakfast
Credit Cards: A, B
Notes: 2, 4 (included), 9, 10, 11, 12, 14

MORAGA

Hallman Bed and Breakfast

309 Constance Place, 94556
(415) 376-4318

Situated on a quiet cul-de-sac in the beautiful Moraga Valley. Bed down in one of two tastefully appointed rooms that share a bath; awake refreshed; breakfast on the delightful terrace; then take off and "do" San Francisco or any other bay area attraction that interests you. Return in time for a refreshing dip in the pool or a relaxing sit in the Jacuzzi spa, both in a very private setting, before enjoying a gourmet dinner at one of the many fine restaurants nearby.

Hosts: Frank and Virginia Hallman
Rooms: 2 (SB) $50
Full Breakfast
Credit Cards: None
Notes: 2, 5, 8, 9, 11 (seasonal)

MORROW BAY

Bed and Breakfast Los Angeles 12-7

730 Catalina Avenue, Seal Beach, 90740
(310) 493-6837; (800) 383-3513

Your Dutch hostess has three bedrooms, one with a private bath and two with shared baths. Rates are very low, breakfast is sumptuous, and pets are welcome. Your hostess speaks five languages. Affordable rates.

Megan's Friends #05

Bed & Breakfast Reservation Service
1776 Royal Way, San Luis Obispo, 93405
(805) 544-4406

This beautiful home in a quiet area overlooks the bay and the Pacific Ocean. Sit on the deck and watch th sailboats on the Bay, the herons nesting in their rookery, or deer silhouetted on the dunes in the evening. There is a large upstairs room with a king-size bed, private shower, and a separate entrance. Downstairs there is a suite with a king-size bed, private bath/shower, and a second bedroom with a queen-size bed with shared bath and shower. Crib available. The state park, a golf course, and the Museum of Natural History are all close

Dunbar House, 1880

NOTES: Credit cards accepted: A Master Card; B Visa; C American Express; D Discover Card; E Diner's Club; F Other; 2 Personal Checks accepted; 3 Lunch available; 4 Dinner available; 5 Open all year;

by. Charter fishing, kayak and bicycle rentals available. It is just a half hour drive to Hearst Castle. $75; suite $125.

MOUNT SHASTA

Mount Shasta Ranch

1008 W. A. Barr Road, 96067
(916) 926-3870

This Northern California historic two-story ranch house offers affordable elegance. There are four spacious guest rooms in the main house, each with private bath. Carriage house accommodations include five rooms. Two-bedroom vacation cottage available year-round. Guests are invited to enjoy the rec room with Ping-Pong, pool tables, and piano. Relax in the Hot-Spring® spa. Close to lake, town, and ski slopes. Full country-style breakfasts each morning.

Hosts: Bill and Mary Larsen
Rooms: 9 (4 PB; 5 SB) $55-75
Full Breakfast
Credit Cards: A, B, C
Notes: 2, 5, 7, 8, 9, 10, 11, 12, 13, 14

MUIR BEACH

B&B San Francisco #22

P. O. Box 349, 94101
(415) 931-3083; FAX (415) 921-BBSF

A lovely bedroom suite with private entrance, fireplace, and private bath that overlooks the Pacific Ocean and beach. Muir Beach is a quiet community 45 minutes from downtown San Francisco. Full breakfast. $95.

Pelican Inn

10 Pacific Way, 94965-9729
(415) 383-6000

The romantic getaway over the hills to the beach, a country inn capturing the spirit of 16th-century England's West country awaits you. The hospitable Pelican nestles among pines and alders—a refuge between the ocean and redwoods of National Recreational Area. The Pelican opens its doors to you for the fellowship of its Tudor Bar, British ales, carefree feasting, and relaxation. Scarcely 20 minutes north of Golden Gate Bridge.

Host: R. Barry Stock
Rooms: 7 (PB) $135-155
Full English Breakfast
Credit Cards: A, B
Closed Christmas
Notes: 2, 3, 4, 5, 7, 8, 9

MURPHYS

Dunbar House, 1880

271 Jones Street, 95247
(209) 728-2897

Explore Gold Country during the day and enjoy a glass of lemonade or local wine on the wide porches in the afternoon. Inviting fireplaces and down comforters in your antique-filled room; cedar room has a two-person whirlpool bath. All rooms have tulvers and classic video library. Breakfast may be served in your room, the dining room, or in the century-old gardens.

Hosts: Bob and Barbara Costa
Rooms: 4 (PB) $105-145
Full Breakfast
Minimum stay weekends: 2 nights
Credit Cards: A, B
Notes: 2, 5, 8 (over 10), 9, 10, 11, 12, 13, 14

NAPA

Beazley House

1910 First Street, 94559
(707) 257-1649

You'll sense the hospitality as you stroll the walk past verdant lawns and bright flowers. The landmark 1902 mansion is a chocolate brown masterpiece. You'll feel instantly welcome as you're greeted by a smiling innkeeper. The view from each room reveals beautiful gardens. And all

6 Pets welcome; 7 Smoking allowed; 8 Children welcome; 9 Social drinking allowed; 10 Tennis available; 11 Swimming available; 12 Golf available; 13 Skiing available; 14 May be booked through travel agents.

rooms have a private bath; some a private spa and a fireplace. Napa's first bed and breakfast and still its best!

Hosts: Carol and Jim Beazley
Rooms: 10 (P.B) $105-185
Full Breakfast
Credit Cards: A, B, C
Notes: 2, 5, 9, 10, 11, 12

The Blue Violet Mansion

443 Brown Street, 94559-3348
(707) 253-BLUE

An 1886 Queen Anne Victorian mansion on one acre, this inn is listed on the National Register of Historic Places. King and queen beds. Two rooms with balcony and fireplaces; two with spas. Antique furnishings and Oriental carpets. Complimentary use of bicycles and kites. Gazebo garden. Outdoor spa. Wine and sherry available. Full breakfast served in the dining room. Situated in historic Old Town near shops, Napa Wine Train, hot air balloons, wine tasting.

Hosts: Bob and Kathy Morris
Rooms: 6 rooms and 1 suite (PB) $115-195
Full Breakfast
Credit Cards: A, B
Notes: 2, 4, 5, 8, 9, 10, 11, 12, 14

The Chateau Hotel

4195 Solano Avenue, 94558
(707) 253-9300

The Chateau is the perfect blend of the comforts and conveniences of a city hotel, but preserves the quiet warmth and elegance of a classic European country inn. There are 115 beautifully decorated rooms with six charming suites; heated pool and spa; complimentary continental buffet breakfast and evening wine social. In addition, there is an executive conference center that can seat up to 80 people theater-style or 155 people reception-style.

Rooms: 115 (PB) $80-95
Continental Breakfast
Credit Cards: A, B, C, D, E
Notes: 5, 7, 8, 9, 11, 14

Churchill Manor Bed and Breakfast Inn

485 Brown Street, 94559
(707) 253-7733

A magnificent 1889 mansion resting on an acre of beautiful gardens, Churchill Manor is listed on the National Register of Historic Places. Elegant parlors boast carved wood ceilings and columns, leaded-glass windows, Oriental rugs, brass and crystal chandeliers, four fireplaces, and a grand piano. Ten guest rooms are individually decorated with gorgeous antiques. Guests enjoy afternoon fresh-baked cookies and lemonade, evening wine and cheese reception, and a full gourmet breakfast served in a mosaic-floored sun room. Complimentary tandem bicycles and croquet.

Host: Joanna Guidotti and Brian Jensen
Rooms: 10 (PB) $75-145
Full Breakfast
Credit Cards: A, B, C
Notes: 2, 5, 9, 10, 11, 12, 14

Hennessey House

1727 Main Street, 94559
(707) 226-3774

Queen Anne Victorian situated in downtown Napa, the gateway to the historic wine country. Main house and carriage house. All rooms are furnished in antiques and have private baths. Selected rooms have fireplaces and whirlpool tubs. Full breakfast is served in unique dining room which features a beautiful hand-painted, stamped tin ceiling. Listed on National Register of Historic Places. Sauna, bike rentals on premises. Complimentary wine in evening.

Hosts: Andrea Weinstein and Lauriann Delay
Rooms: 10 (PB) $85-155
Full Breakfast
Credit Cards: A, B, C
Notes: 2, 5, 9, 12, 14

La Belle Epoque

1386 Calistoga Avenue, 94559
(707) 257-2161

NOTES: Credit cards accepted: A Master Card; B Visa; C American Express; D Discover Card; E Diner's Club; F Other; 2 Personal Checks accepted; 3 Lunch available; 4 Dinner available; 5 Open all year;

Historic Queen Anne Victorian bejeweled in stained glass. Six guest rooms furnished in period antiques, each with private bath, and one with a fireplace. Charming wine-tasting room/cellar. Within walking distance of the Wine Train Depot, restaurants, shops, and river front. Wineries nearby, as well as hot-air ballooning, mud baths, tennis, swimming, and golf.

Hosts: Merlin and Claudia Wedepohl
Rooms: 6 (PB) $105-140
Full Breakfast
Credit Cards: A, B, C, D
Notes: 2, 5, 9, 10, 11, 12, 14

La Residence Country Inn

4066 St. Helena Highway, 94558
(707) 253-0337

Accommodations, most with fireplaces, are in two structures: a Gothic Revival home, decorated in traditional American antiques, and the "French barn," decorated with European pine antiques. Two acres of grounds with hot tub and a heated swimming pool surrounded by a gazebo and trellis. Complimentary wine is served each evening.

Hosts: David Jackson and Craig Calussen
Rooms: 20 (18 PB; 2 SB) $85-170
Full Breakfast
Credit Cards: A, B
Notes: 5, 8, 9, 10, 11, 12, 14

The Blue Violet Mansion

Napa Inn

1137 Warren Street, 94559
(707) 257-1444

The Napa Inn is a beautiful Queen Anne Victorian situated on a quiet tree-lined street in the historic section of the town of Napa. The inn is furnished in turn-of-the-century antiques in the five guest rooms, large parlor, and formal dining room. Each spacious guest room has its own private bath and two suites feature fireplaces. The inn is conveniently situated to the Napa, Sonoma, and Carneros wine regions. Also many other activities: hot air ballooning, gliding, biking, hiking, golf, tennis, many fine restaurants, and the Napa Valley Wine Train.

Hosts: Doug and Carol Morales
Rooms: 5 (PB) $100-160
Full Breakfast
Credit Cards: A, B, D
Closed Christmas
Notes: 2, 10, 12, 14

The Old World Inn

1301 Jefferson Street, 94559
(707) 257-0112; (800) 966-6624

For a holiday of romance and plentiful gourmet delights, plan a stay at this charming Victorian inn. You can relax in the outdoor spa or choose a room with a sunken spa tub. You'll be pampered with home-baked treats from morning until bedtime. Make yourself at home with the afternoon tea, unwind during the wine and cheese social, treat yourself to a chocolate lover's dessert buffet, and top the morning with a gourmet breakfast.

Host: Diane Dumaine
Rooms: 8 (PB) $97-137
Expanded Continental Breakfast
Credit Cards: A, B, C, D
Notes: 2, 5, 9, 14

Sybron House

7400 St. Helena Highway, 94558
(707) 944-2785

6 Pets welcome; 7 Smoking allowed; 8 Children welcome; 9 Social drinking allowed; 10 Tennis available; 11 Swimming available; 12 Golf available; 13 Skiing available; 14 May be booked through travel agents.

Victorian inn situated on a hill in the middle of the Napa Valley, with magnificent view of surrounding wineries and vineyards. Private tennis court. Excellent restaurants nearby, as well as ballooning, biking, hiking, golf, and mud baths.

Hosts: Sybil and Cheryl Maddox
Rooms: 4 (2 PB; 2 SB) $110-150
Continental Breakfast
Credit Cards: A, B, C
Notes: 2, 5, 9, 10, 12, 14

Wine Country Reservations

P. O. Box 5059, 94581-0059
(707) 257-7757

We offer many unique accommodations in the wine country. Let us help you experience that memorable stay while visiting the many attractions the Valley has to offer. There are no fees for helping you select the bed and breakfast of your choice. Advanced reservations are advised. We also have a wedding consultant available for those of you who wish to get married in the wine country. We are open daily from 9:00 A.M. to 9:00 P.M. (PST). We are usually closed on major holidays, but we do have voice mail available so that you can leave us a message and we can return your call. We look forward to helping you with your accommodations.

Owner: Mary Foux
Rooms: Over 150 available rooms; $65-400
Continental or Full Breakfast

NAPA VALLEY

Bed and Breakfast Los Angeles 15-1

730 Catalina Avenue, Seal Beach, 90740
(310) 493-6837; (800) 383-3513

This rural 1930s farmhouse has three suites with fireplaces, kitchens and redwood decks. The family cottage can accommodate up to six. It has a refrigerator stocked with goodies and French doors that open onto the vineyards. Moderate rates.

Bed and Breakfast Los Angeles 15-2

730 Catalina Avenue, Seal Beach, 90740
(310) 493-6837; (800) 383-3513

These 1875 wooden cottages dot the hillside outside Calistoga. Some have fireplaces, and one suite can accommodate six. All are surrounded by lush foliage and gardens. Breakfast is served to your doorstep. Barbecue facilities on the decks are available. Moderate-luxury rates.

Bed and Breakfast Los Angeles 15-4

730 Catalina Avenue, Seal Beach, 90740
(310) 493-6837; (800) 383-3513

Victorian furniture and stained-glass windows adorn this elegant 1893 Queen Anne mansion. Hosts offer six rooms. Breakfast is served in the sun room, and complimentary wine tastings are available in the cellar. Babies or older children only, please. Luxury rates.

Eye Openers Bed and Breakfast Reservations NA-C91

P. O. Box 694, Altadena, 91003-0694
(213) 684-4428; (818) 797-2055
FAX (818) 798-3640

Bed and breakfast in the heart of wine country is offered in the 1889 mansion that has been designated as a national historic landmark. Each room is individually decorated. Enjoy an extended continental breakfast, and relax on the veranda with evening refreshments. No smoking. Nine guest rooms Private bath. $75-145 plus tax.

NOTES: Credit cards accepted: A Master Card; B Visa; C American Express; D Discover Card; E Diner's Club; F Other; 2 Personal Checks accepted; 3 Lunch available; 4 Dinner available; 5 Open all year;

Eye Openers Bed and Breakfast Reservations SH-D21

P. O. Box 694, Altadena, 91003-0694
(213) 684-4428; (818) 797-2055
FAX (818) 798-3640

Secluded in a forest above the vineyards, yet near the town, this small bed and breakfast offers a peaceful retreat for its guest rooms, one with a fireplace. Large continental breakfast is served, and a swimming pool is available for guests to enjoy. No smoking. Two guest rooms. Private bath. $95-125 plus tax.

Kids Welcome 15-3

730 Catalina Avenue, Seal Beach, 90740
(310) 493-6837; (800) 383-3513

This hostess truly loves and welcomes children. She has a crib and toys available, and her 1900 farmhouse overlooks Napa Valley's best vineyards. One room has a fireplace and wet bar. Breakfast is served by the pool, and wine and cheese is served in the afternoon. Luxury rates.

Tall Timbers Chalet

1012 Darms Lane, 94558
(707) 252-7810

Built in 1944, eight rustic, whitewashed cottages are located just off Highway 29. Continental breakfast is served in the breakfast nook, and walking trails, golf and bicycle rentals, wineries, and restaurants are nearby. No pets. Smoking restrictions. Reservation deposit required. Minimum stay is two nights.

Rooms: 8 (PB) $95-125
Full Breakfast
Credit Cards: None
Notes: 2, 5, 8, 9, 14

NEVADA CITY

Downey House Bed and Breakfast

517 West Broad Street, 95959
(916) 265-2815; (800) 258-2815

Eastlake Victorian, circa 1870, restored to its original elegance with lovely garden and water falling into a lily pond by new arbor with tables where guests may eat breakfast. Situated one block from fine shops and restaurants, live theater, museums, art galleries, and horse-drawn carriages. Near historic gold mines, lakes, streams, tennis, golf, skiing, horseback riding, and more,

Host: Miriam Wright
Rooms: 6 (PB) $75-95
Full Breakfast
(sound-proofed rooms)
Credit Cards: A, B
Notes: 2, 5, 8, 10, 11, 12, 13, 14

Grandmere's

449 Broad Street, 95959
(916) 265-4660

Beautiful garden, suitable for weddings or receptions. Seven rooms, each with private bath and down comforters, are decorated in elegant country French decor. A full breakfast is served at 9:00 A.M. in the dining room.

Hosts: Doug and Geri Boka
Rooms: 7 (PB) $100-150
Full Breakfast
Credit Cards: A, B
Notes: 2, 5, 8, 9, 10, 11, 12

Palley Place

12766 Nevada City Highway, 95959
(916) 265-5427

This bed and breakfast home is situated in the Sierra foothills with easy access to skiing and hiking trails. Rooms are decorated with work of local crafts people; the owner weaves and spins. A healthy buffet break-

6 Pets welcome; 7 Smoking allowed; 8 Children welcome; 9 Social drinking allowed; 10 Tennis available; 11 Swimming available; 12 Golf available; 13 Skiing available; 14 May be booked through travel agents.

fast is set out in the breakfast room, where the windows frame beautiful mountaintops in the distance. The state capital is just one hour away. Charming town has fine theater and music groups. One child welcome. Like visiting your grandmother.

Host: Meg K. Palley
Rooms: 2 (SB) $60
Buffet Breakfast
Credit Cards: None
Notes: 2, 5, 8, 11, 12, 13

The Parsonage Bed and Breakfast

427 Broad Street, 95959
(916) 265-9478

Gold Rush history comes alive in this 125-year-old Nevada City home. Located in the town's historic district, the Parsonage Bed and Breakfast Inn is within easy walking distance of many fine restaurants, boutiques, and nightlife. The parlor, dining room, and family room, as well as the three cozy guest rooms, are lovingly furnished with the innkeeper's own pioneer family antiques. Guests are served an elaborate continental breakfast in the formal dining room, and a complimentary afternoon beverage. In every way, the Parsonage evokes a gentler, bygone era when gracious hospitality prevailed.

Host: Deborah Dane
Rooms: 3 (PB) $65-90
Expanded Continental Breakfast
Credit Cards: A, B
Notes: 2, 3, 4, 5, 9, 13

Piety Hill Inn

523 Sacramento Street, 95959
(916) 265-2245

The inn consists of eight cottages surrounding a lush garden, which includes a gazebo-crowned hot tub. Featured are pre-Civil War to early 20th-century furnishings, king beds, refrigerators, wet bars, TV, and breakfast in bed. Nearby are quaint shops, theater, music, excellent restaurants, hiking, swimming, and winter sports.

Host: Linda
Rooms: 8 (PB) $75-125
Full Breakfast
Credit Cards: A, B
Notes: 2, 5, 8, 9, 10, 11, 12, 13, 14

The Red Castle Inn

109 Prospect Street, 95959
(916) 265-5135

High on a forested hillside breezes linger on wide verandas, strains of Mozart echo through lofty hallways, chandeliers sparkle, the aura of another time prevails. There are seven rooms and suites, all with private baths. In Gold Country, the four-story Gothic Revival inn "would top my list of places to stay. Nothing else quite compares with it"—Gourmet.

Hosts: Mary Louise and Conley Weaver
Rooms: 7 (PB) $70-140 plus tax
Full Breakfast
Credit Cards: A, B
Notes: 2, 5, 7 (outside), 8 (over 10), 9, 10, 11, 12, 13 (XC), 14

NEWPORT BEACH

America's B&B #11

P. O. Box 9302, Whittier, 90608
(310) 699-8427

Charming contemporary home just a short walk from the beach. Two bedrooms, each with private bath, and all facilities for barbecues. Hosts are caterers as well as creative teachers; the full breakfast is always a treat. Children welcome. Complimentary hors d'oeuvres and beverages. Spectacular ocean view. $60.

Bed and Breakfast Los Angeles 6-3

730 Catalina Avenue, Seal Beach, 90740
(310) 493-6837; (800) 383-3513

NOTES: Credit cards accepted: A Master Card; B Visa; C American Express; D Discover Card; E Diner's Club; F Other; 2 Personal Checks accepted; 3 Lunch available; 4 Dinner available; 5 Open all year;

Stained glass, bricks and wood add to the charm of this unusual house just minutes from the beach in Newport. Upstairs room is a loft with a private bath, mini kitchen, and stairs to the rooftop deck. Downstairs guest room also has a private bath. Not safe for toddlers. Moderate rates.

Bed and Breakfast Los Angeles 6-4

730 Catalina Avenue, Seal Beach, 90740
(310) 493-6837; (800) 383-3513

This luxury inn has twelve guest rooms, all with private baths, most with private decks and ocean views. Beautifully furnished with antiques, and right on the beach in Newport. Luxury rates.

Bed and Breakfast Los Angeles 6-5

730 Catalina Avenue, Seal Beach, 90740
(310) 493-6837; (800) 383-3513

Marble sunken tubs, fireplaces, ocean views, and antique decor are all part of this perfect little inn on Newport Beach. Breakfast is served in the parlor. Luxury rates.

Doryman's Inn Oceanfront Bed and Breakfast

2102 West Oceanfront, 92663
(714) 675-7300

Romance, luxury and resounding elegance await you at this exquisite oceanfront bed and breakfast. Capture picture-perfect sunsets on the Pacific Ocean, sip champagne on the a bayview patio, or have any one of the world-class concierges draw a bath with rose petals and chilled grapes. All rooms come with a complimentary bottle of champagne and a French breakfast in the morning. All rooms have imported Italian marble bathrooms with sunken tubs and French-Victorian style decor.

Hosts: Michael D. Palitz
Rooms: 10 (PB) $135-275
Full Breakfast
Credit Cards: A, B, C, D, E
Notes: 2, 3, 4, 5, 7, 8, 9, 10, 11, 12, 13, 14

Eye Openers Bed and Breakfast Reservations NP-D2

P. O. Box 694, Altadena, 91003-0694
(213) 684-4428; (818) 797-2055
FAX (818) 798-3640

Crow's-nest with 360-degree view tops this tri-level beach home. Third level is a large guest deck with barbecue and refrigerator. Stained glass is featured throughout the house. Perfectly located for beach and and bay activities; bicycle and beach chairs available. Full or continental breakfast and afternoon refreshments. Two rooms. Private bath. $50-75.

Eye Openers Bed and Breakfast Reservations NP-D101

P. O. Box 694, Altadena, 91003-0694
(213) 684-4428; (818) 797-2055
FAX (818) 798-3640

A very special beachfront bed and breakfast inn has spacious antique-decorated guest rooms, each with its own fireplace and some with Jacuzzis. Delicious continental breakfast is served in your room, on the patio, or in the parlor. Ten guest rooms. Private bath. $135-275 plus tax.

Eye Openers Bed and Breakfast Reservations NP-W2

P. O. Box 694, Altadena, 91003-0694
(213) 684-4428; (818) 797-2055
FAX (818) 798-3640

6 Pets welcome; 7 Smoking allowed; 8 Children welcome; 9 Social drinking allowed; 10 Tennis available; 11 Swimming available; 12 Golf available; 13 Skiing available; 14 May be booked through travel agents.

Stunning, well-decorated bed and breakfast on the water's edge has a guest den with retractable roof, lounge chairs, refrigerator, and grassy yard for sun bathing. Take the shuttle or bike to unique shops and restaurants. Continental breakfast. Minimum stay is two nights. Resident dog. Two guest rooms. Private bath. $80-85.

NIPOMO

Kaleidoscope Inn Bed and Breakfast

130 East Dana Street, P. O. Box 1297, 93444
(805) 929-5444

This 1886-built Victorian is furnished with antiques and offers beautiful gardens, delicious full breakfast, Jacuzzi tub in one bath, and king-size bed in one room. Located halfway between Los Angeles and San Francisco, this bed and breakfast is near local attractions, golf, beach, lakes, hot springs, great dining, theater, horseback riding, and wind surfing. This owner-operated inn loves to spoil guests.

Host: Patti Linane
Rooms: 3 (PB) $80
Full Breakfast
Credit Cards: A, B, C
Notes: 2, 5, 9, 12, 14

NIPTON

Hotel Nipton

72 Nipton Road, 92364
(619) 856-2335

Hotel Nipton, originally built in 1904, was completely restored in 1986. Situated in the east Mojave National Scenic Area 65 miles south of Las Vegas. The hotel offers a panoramic view of the New York Mountains, outside Jacuzzi for stargazing. Thirty minutes from Lake Mojave.

Hosts: Jerry and Roxanne Freeman
Rooms: 4 (SB) $48.15
Continental Breakfast
Credit Cards: A, B
Notes: 5, 7, 8, 9

NORTH HOLLYWOOD

Anna's Bed and Breakfast

10926 Hamlin Street, 91606-2711
(818) 980-6191

Small house in quiet residential area. Close to major freeways. Double bed in master bedroom, bathroom shared with owner. Patio, TV, fireplace. No smoking, no pets; children over 12 welcome. Reservation appreciated one day in advance.

Host: Anneliese Ohler
Room: 1 (SB) $40
Full or Continental Breakfast
Credit Cards: None
Notes: 5, 8 (over 12), 9

Bed and Breakfast Los Angeles 3-2

730 Catalina Avenue, Seal Beach, 90740
(310) 493-6837; (800) 383-3513

Spacious guest wing in a North Hollywood home has a lovely yard, pool, And decorator whimsy. Private bath and TV. Affordable rates.

NORTHRIDGE

Bed and Breakfast Los Angeles 3-4

730 Catalina Avenue, Seal Beach, 90740
(310) 493-6837; (800) 383-3513

Stained glass, art, and country decor grace this Northridge home on one-half acre with trees, pool, and paddle tennis court. Guest room, sitting room, private bath, and TV. Affordable rates.

NOTES: Credit cards accepted: A Master Card; B Visa; C American Express; D Discover Card; E Diner's Club; F Other; 2 Personal Checks accepted; 3 Lunch available; 4 Dinner available; 5 Open all year;

Bed and Breakfast Los Angeles 3-8

730 Catalina Avenue, Seal Beach, 90740
(310) 493-6837; (800) 383-3513

Treasures from a bygone era decorate this contemporary Northridge home. Guest room has an antique bed and shared bath. Crib available. Babies or older kids only. Affordable rates.

OAKLAND

Bayside Boat and Breakfast

77 Jack London Square, 94607
(510) 444-5858

Spend a romantic evening on a yacht! Luxurious private yachts available for overnight dockside accommodations allow a fantasy to become a reality. Yachts are available at the Jack London Square in Oakland and Pier 39 in San Francisco; charters on the bay with a captain are also available. Enjoy a magnificent yacht all to yourself for an evening.

Host: Rob Harris
Rooms: 7 yachts (PB) $95-275
Continental Breakfast
Credit Cards: A, B, C
Notes: 2, 4, 5, 7, 8, 9, 14

OCCIDENTAL

The Inn at Occidental

3657 Church Street, 95465
(707) 874-1311; (800) 551-2292

In a charming village near the spectacular Sonoma coast and wine country, The Inn at Occidental is a completely renovated 1867 Victorian with European ambience. With antique furnishings and goose-down comforters, each room features fresh flowers and a private bath. Amenites include a courtyard garden, lobby and dining room fireplaces, full service restaurant, and a sumptuous breakfast.

Rooms: 8 (PB) $95-185; Suite $225
Full Breakfast
Minimum stay weekends & holidays: 2 nights
Credit Cards: A, B, C, D
Notes: 2, 3, 4, 5, 9, 10, 11, 12, 14

OJAI

The Theodore Woolsey House

1484 East Ojai Avenue, 93932
(805) 646-9779

Once you turn off Ojai Avenue and drive down the rose-lined country driveway, time rolls back to the late 1800s. This is a time of simple pleasures and beauty. With seven rooms available, the Woolsey House provides the perfect getaway for those who seek an intimate place to spend with a loved one. The Woolsey House offers a homestyle atmosphere where you will want to stay again and again.

The Inn at Occidental

Hosts: Ana Cross
Rooms: 7 (4-PB; 3-SB) $50-110
Continental Breakfast
Credit Cards: None
Notes: 2, 5, 8, 9, 10, 11, 12, 14

OLEMA

Point Reyes Seashore Lodge

10021 Highway 1, P. O. Box 39, 94950
(415) 663-9000

6 Pets welcome; 7 Smoking allowed; 8 Children welcome; 9 Social drinking allowed; 10 Tennis available; 11 Swimming available; 12 Golf available; 13 Skiing available; 14 May be booked through travel agents.

A re-creation of a turn-of-the-century lodge offers eighteen designer coordinated rooms and three suites, many with whirlpool tubs and fireplaces. A great base for exploring the Point Reyes National Seashore Park, bird or whale watching, hiking, and biking.

Hosts: Judy and John Burkes
Rooms: 21 (PB) $85-175
Expanded Continental Breakfast
Credit Cards: A, B, C
Notes: 2, 5, 7, 9, 10, 11, 12, 14

ORANGE

Country Comfort Bed and Breakfast

5104 East Valencia Drive, 92669
(714) 532-2802

Situated in a quiet residential area, this house has been furnished with your comfort and pleasure in mind. It is handicapped accessible with adaptive equipment available. Amenities include a swimming pool, cable TV and VCR, atrium, fireplace, piano, and the use of bicycles, one built for two. Breakfast often features delicious Scotch eggs, stuffed French toast, and hash, as well as fruits and assorted beverages. Vegetarian selections also available. Disneyland and Knotts Berry Farm are less than seven miles.

Hosts: Geri Lopker and Joanne Angell
Rooms: 4 (2PB; 2SB) $50-60
Full Breakfast
Credit Cards: None
Notes: 2, 5, 7 (outside), 8, 9, 11, 14

ORLAND

The Inn at Shallow Creek Farm

Route 3, Box 3176, 95963
(916) 865-4093

A gracious two-story farmhouse offering spacious rooms furnished with antiques—a blend of nostalgia and comfortable country living. Three miles off Interstate 5. The inn is known for its orchard and fresh garden produce. Breakfast features old-fashioned baked goods and local fruits and juices.

Hosts: Kurt and Mary Glaeseman
Rooms: 4 (2 PB; 2 SB) $55-75
Full Breakfast
Credit Cards: A, B
Notes: 2, 5, 9, 11, 12, 14

OROVILLE

Jean's Riverside Bed and Breakfast

45 Cabana Drive, P. O. Box 2334, 95965
(916) 533-1413

Rustic cedar with window walls overlooking Feather River. All rooms have private baths and TV. Some have wood stoves and private Jacuzzis. Fishing, swimming, gold panning, bird watching, horseshoes, badminton, croquet on property. Quaint shops, excellent restaurants, Oroville Dam and Fish Hatchery, historical sites, hiking, and scenic drives nearby.

Host: Jean Pratt
Rooms: 15 (PB) $48.50-95
Expanded Continental Breakfast
Credit Cards: A, B
Notes: 2, 3 and 4 (catered), 5, 7 (limited), 9, 10, 11, 12, 14

PACIFIC GROVE

Bed and Breakfast Los Angeles 13-3

730 Catalina Avenue, Seal Beach, 90740
(310) 493-6837; (800) 383-3513

Soak in the hot tub of this elegant Cape Cod-style home, built originally as a convent in 1910. Hosts emphasize comfort, tranquility, and attention to every detail. Accommodations range from a canopied, double-bedded room with an ocean view and a crib to a spacious two-room cottage that can accommodate four. Breakfast includes champagne. Location is three miles from Monterey. Older kids only. Luxury rates.

Eye Openers Bed and Breakfast Reservations PG-C201

P. O. Box 694, Altadena, 91003-0694
(213) 684-4428; (818) 797-2055
FAX (818) 798-3640

Century old Victorian boarding house is a refurbished award-winning bed and breakfast inn. Beautifully decorated rooms, delicious breakfast, and afternoon refreshments. Shared and private baths. $75-175 plus tax.

Eye Openers Bed and Breakfast Reservations PG-G111

P. O. Box 694, Altadena, 91003-0694
(213) 684-4428; (818) 797-2055
FAX (818) 798-3640

1888 Queen Anne-style mansion-by-the-sea has a panoramic view of Monterey Bay. Delicious breakfast and afternoon refreshments. Shared and private baths. $95-150.

Eye Openers Bed and Breakfast Reservations PG-G211

P. O. Box 694, Altadena, 91003-0694
(213) 684-4428; (818) 797-2055
FAX (818) 798-3640

Beautifully preserved 1887 Victorian on the National Register of Historic Places can now be enjoyed as a bed and breakfast inn. Wonderful breakfast, afternoon hors d'oeuvres, and wine or tea served. $85-145.

Eye Openers Bed and Breakfast Reservations PG-G81

P. O. Box 694, Altadena, 91003-0694
(213) 684-4428; (818) 797-2055
FAX (818) 798-3640

1884 Victorian with ocean views was renovated and opened its doors in the summer of 1990 to become a Pacific Grove bed and breakfast inn close to the beach. Each room is uniquely decorated and features views or sundecks. Delicious full breakfast and afternoon refreshments are provided. No smoking. Private bath. $95-155.

Gosby House Inn

643 Lighthouse Avenue, 93950
(408) 375-1287

The Gosby House Inn sits in the heart of the quaint town of Pacific Grove. Its magnificent Queen Anne Victorian architecture will enchant you, as will its individually decorated sleeping rooms, antique doll collection, and gracious staff. A bountiful breakfast and afternoon wine and hors d'oeuvres are served. Fluffy robes, complimentary beverages, and a heaping cookie jar.

Host: Jillian Brewer
Rooms: 22 (20 PB; 2 SB) $85-130
Full Breakfast
Credit Cards: A, B, C
Notes: 2, 5, 8, 9, 10, 11, 12, 14

The Martini Inn

255 Oceanview Boulevard, 93950
(408) 373-3388

Surpassed only by the beauty of Monterey Bay, the Martini Inn complements the rugged terrain with a timeless sense of graciousness. Don and Marion Martini have filled this Victorian-turned-Mediterranean mansion, built in the 1890s, with an extensive collection of antiques. The all-private bath bedrooms offer richness in history and tradition, many of which offer incredible

---

6 Pets welcome; 7 Smoking allowed; 8 Children welcome; 9 Social drinking allowed; 10 Tennis available; 11 Swimming available; 12 Golf available; 13 Skiing available; 14 May be booked through travel agents.

ocean views or a wood-burning fireplace. As you enjoy the spectacular bay vistas, breakfast, evening wine, and hors d'oeuvres are served on Old Sheffield silver, fine china, and crystal.

Hosts: Marion and Don Martini; Tracy Harris
Rooms: 19 (PB) $115-225
Full Breakfast
Credit Cards: A, B
Notes: 2, 3, 5, 9, 10, 11, 12, 14

The Martini Inn

The Old St. Angela Inn

321 Central Avenue, 93950
(408) 372-3246; (800) 873-6523

A 1910 Cape Cod-style Victorian home overlooking Monterey Bay. Full breakfast is served daily; late afternoon refreshments are served in the garden solarium. Truly an experience in comfort. Monterey Bay Aquarium, Cannery Row, Fisherman's Wharf, and resturants are within walking distance.

Host: Barbara Foster
Rooms: 9 (6 PB; 3 SB) $90-150
Full Breakfast
Credit Cards: A, B
Notes: 5, 9, 10, 11, 12, 14

Roserox Country Inn by-the-Sea

557 Ocean View Boulevard, 93950
(408) 373-7673

Historic country mansion set on the edge of the Pacific shoreline. Built at the turn of the century, the inn is an intimate four-story inn with original patterned oak floors, high ceilings, high brass beds, imported soaps and French water, designer linens, ocean sounds, and a special gift for each guest. A full country breakfast and wine and cheer hour. The Shoreline Trail to Cannery Row, Monterey Bay Aquarium, world-renown shops and restaurants, as well as swimming beach, bicycling, and fishing, are within 30 feet of the inn.

Host: Dawn Vyette Browncroft
Rooms: 8 (S4B) $105-205
Full Breakfast
Credit Cards: None
Notes: 2, 5, 9, 10, 11, 12, 14

Seven Gables Inn

555 Ocean View Boulevard, 93950
(408) 372-4341

It is difficult to imagine a more scenic and dramatic spot than the rocky promontory occupied by Seven Gables Inn overlooking Monterey Bay. This century-old mansion is furnished throughout with elegant Victorian antiques. All guest rooms have panoramic ocean views and private baths. A generous, full, sit-down breakfast and four o'clock high tea are included. Smoking is in the garden areas only. Seven Gables is easily accessible to the Monterey Aquarium, Cannery Row, 17-Mile Drive, Carmel, and numerous other scenic sites in the Monterey area.

Hosts: The Flatley family
Rooms: 14 (PB) $95-185
Full Breakfast
Credit Cards: A, B
Notes: 2, 5

NOTES: Credit cards accepted: A Master Card; B Visa; C American Express; D Discover Card; E Diner's Club; F Other; 2 Personal Checks accepted; 3 Lunch available; 4 Dinner available; 5 Open all year;

PACIFIC PALISADES

Bed and Breakfast Los Angeles 4-9

730 Catalina Avenue, Seal Beach, 90740
(310) 493-6837; (800) 383-3513

Two guest rooms share a bath in a traditional home in this exclusive neighborhood. Private entrance, recreation room with fireplace and refrigerator. Flower-filled yard, and only one-half mile to the beach. Moderate rates.

Bed and Breakfast Los Angeles 9-1

730 Catalina Avenue, Seal Beach, 90740
(310) 493-6837; (800) 383-3513

This 1930s family-style inn, located in the center of town, has several units with kitchens, patios, and fireplaces. The courtyard has a nice pool, spa, and big, old fruit trees. Affordable rates.

Eye Openers Bed and Breakfast Reservations PP-D2

P. O. Box 694, Altadena, 91003-0694
(213) 684-4428; (818) 797-2055
FAX (818) 798-3640

Comfortable bed and breakfast in a lovely neighborhood ten minutes from Santa Monica and Getty Museum has lovely patio and backyard for guests to enjoy. Popular tennis area. Continental breakfast. Resident cat. No smoking. Two guest rooms. Private and shared bath. $50-55.

PALM SPRINGS

Casa Cody Bed and Breakfast Country Inn

175 South Cahuilla, 92262
(619) 320-9346

Romantic, historic hideaway in the heart of Palm Springs village. Beautifully redecorated in Santa Fe decor, with kitchens, wood-burning fireplaces, patios, two pools, and a spa. Close to the Desert Museum, Heritage Center, and Moorten Botanical Gardens. Nearby hiking in Indian canyons, horseback riding, tennis, golf. Polo, ballooning, helicopter, and desert Jeep tours. Near celebrity homes, date gardens, and Joshua Tree National Monument.

Hosts: Therese Hayes and Frank Tysen
Rooms: 17 (PB) $35-160
Continental Breakfast
Credit Cards: A, B, C
Notes: 2, 5, 6, 7, 8, 9, 10, 11, 12, 13, 14

Eye Openers Bed and Breakfast Reservations PB-B4

P. O. Box 694, Altadena, 91003-0694
(213) 684-4428; (818) 797-2055
FAX (818) 798-3640

Spacious, contemporary bed and breakfast offers privacy, peace and quiet, and a wonderful location. Each room has a bath in suite, and large living area and decks look onto a 400-foot pool with a fountain. Paddle tennis court available. Host is a professional photographer who offers photography workshop. Continental breakfast. No smoking. Four rooms. Private bath. $80-110.

Eye Openers Bed and Breakfast Reservations PS-C2

P. O. Box 694, Altadena, 91003-0694
(213) 684-4428; (818) 797-2055
FAX (818) 798-3640

6 Pets welcome; 7 Smoking allowed; 8 Children welcome; 9 Social drinking allowed; 10 Tennis available; 11 Swimming available; 12 Golf available; 13 Skiing available; 14 May be booked through travel agents.

The ambience of Japan characterizes the guest rooms in this bed and breakfast. Each room has a sliding glass door that leads to the patio and pool. Enjoy a continental or Japanese breakfast in the large family dining room or patio. Prints and artifacts from hostess's native Japan accent this large, contemporary home. No smoking. Two rooms. Private bath. $55-70.

Sacura, Japanese Bed and Breakfast Inn

1677 North Via Miraleste, 92262
(619) 327-0705; FAX (619) 327-6847

Experience the serene graciousness of the Japanese lifestyle. Here you'll find a Japanese garden, bedrooms that open onto a beautiful patio with pool and spa, and a striking mountain background. Provided in the rooms are kimonos, futons, and bedcovers designed and made by Fumiko. Enjoy a tour movie of Japan or a Shiatsu massage, and try an authentic Japanese breakfast. There are over 90 golf courses in the area, as well as tennis, hiking, biking, and a tramway ride. Winter daytime temperatures are between 70º and 85º. Personally planned and guided B & B tours of Japan available.

Hosts: George and Fumiko Cebra
Rooms: 6 (SB) $45-75
Full Breakfast
Notes: 2, 4, 8, 10, 11, 12, 14

PALO ALTO

Adella Villa

P. O. Box 4523, 93409
(415) 321-5195; FAX (415) 325-5121

Exclusive luxury villa on a secluded acre. Electronic gates, pool, fountains, barbecue. The 4,000-square-foot residence has three bedrooms, three private baths (two with Jacuzzi tubs), grand piano in the music foyer. Full breakfast cooked to order. Complimentary sherry and white wine; bicycles available.

Hosts: Scott and Tricia Young
Rooms: 3 (PB) $99
Full Breakfast
Credit Cards: C
Notes: 2, 5, 8 (over 12), 9, 11, 14

Hotel California

2431 Ash Street, 94306
(415) 322-7666

A unique bed and breakfast inn ideal for visiting professionals, out-of-town guests, and many foreign academic visitors. One of the most reasonably priced places to stay. Twenty comfortable rooms, each with private bathroom and attractively furnished with turn-of-the-century pieces. Close to Stanford University and shops. A great and convenient place to stay if you are visiting Stanford. Breakfast is served downstairs in the bakery.

Hosts: Mark and Mary Ann Hite; Warren Wong
Rooms: 20 (PB) $51-58
Continental Breakfast
Credit Cards: A, B, C, D, E, F
Notes: 5, 14

The Victorian on Lytton

555 Lytton Avenue, 94301
(415) 322-8555

Special amenities include down comforters, Battenberg lace canopies, botanical prints, Blue Willow china, and claw foot tubs. Wander through the English country garden with over 900 perennial plants. Five king-size and five queen-size beds available. Relax with a picture book or novel in the parlor with a cup of tea while listening to classical music.

Hosts: Maxwell and Susan Hall
Rooms: 10 (PB) $99-192.50
Continental Breakfast
Credit Cards: A, B, C
Notes: 2, 5, 9, 10, 11, 12, 14

NOTES: Credit cards accepted: A Master Card; B Visa; C American Express; D Discover Card; E Diner's Club; F Other; 2 Personal Checks accepted; 3 Lunch available; 4 Dinner available; 5 Open all year;

PALOS VERDES

America's B&B #10

P. O. Box 9302, Whittier, 90608
(310) 699-8427

Cozy, oceanfront home with a private beach. Two guest rooms, each with private bath. TV in all rooms. Full gourmet breakfast. Children welcome. $60-70.

Eye Openers Bed and Breakfast Reservations PV-E2

P. O. Box 694, Altadena, 91003-0694
(213) 684-4428; (818) 797-2055
FAX (818) 798-3640

Guests can relish a marvelous ocean view from the guest rooms of this homey bed and breakfast and gracious hosts offer beach equipment for use at a private beach. Delicious full breakfast. Resident dog. Private bath. $45-50.

Kids Welcome 5-2

730 Catalina Avenue, Seal Beach, 90740
(310) 493-6837; (800) 383-3513

This house on the Palos Verdes Peninsula has a sweeping view of the ocean and a road to a private beach and surfing cove. Two guests are available, both with TV's and private baths. One bath is connecting, and the other bath is down the hall. Hosts provide fresh robes. Two guest rooms. Affordable rates.

PASADENA

Eye Openers Bed and Breakfast Reservations AL-C2

P. O. Box 694, Altadena, 91003-0694
(213) 684-4428; (818) 797-2055
FAX (818) 798-3640

A special 1926 French Normandy farmhouse in a lovely neighborhood has two-story livingroom and open-hearth fireplace. Enjoy an elegant continental breakfast in the garden patio or dining room. Good hiking trails, museums, and libaries nearby. Short drive to Los Angeles. No smoking. Two guest rooms. Private and shared baths. $55.

Eye Openers Bed and Breakfast Reservations AL-J1

P. O. Box 694, Altadena, 91003-0694
(213) 684-4428; (818) 797-2055
FAX (818) 798-3640

View of nearby mountains from this second floor, private two-room suite provides the illusion of living in a tree house. Continental breakfast is served in the family dining room, garden, or bridge overlooking the garden. No smoking. Private bath. $75.

Eye Openers Bed and Breakfast Reservations AL-J1B

P. O. Box 694, Altadena, 91003-0694
(213) 684-4428; (818) 797-2055
FAX (818) 798-3640

Poolhouse with small kitchen offers privacy and comfort. Contempory bed and breakfast on a cul-de-sac is across from the golf course and has good local hiking. Fifteen- to twenty-minute drive to the LA Civic Center or Hollywood. Continental breakfast. No smoking. Private bath. $45-55.

6 Pets welcome; 7 Smoking allowed; 8 Children welcome; 9 Social drinking allowed; 10 Tennis available; 11 Swimming available; 12 Golf available; 13 Skiing available; 14 May be booked through travel agents.

Eye Openers Bed and Breakfast Reservations AL-M2

P. O. Box 694, Altadena, 91003-0694
(213) 684-4428; (818) 797-2055
FAX (818) 798-3640

Large Mediterranean-style home with mountain views has large guest rooms in a beautiful area with good hiking areas. Continental breakfast. Resident cat and dog. No smoking. Two guest rooms. Private and shared bath. $50-55.

Eye Openers Bed and Breakfast Reservations AL-P8

P. O. Box 694, Altadena, 91003-0694
(213) 684-4428; (818) 797-2055
FAX (818) 798-3640

Enjoy an extended continental breakfast near the fountain in this beautifully landscaped, walled garden of a stately, Spanish-style home, hosted by a yoga teacher and amateur astronomer. No smoking. Two guest rooms. Shared bath. $45-55.

Eye Openers Bed and Breakfast Reservations AL-R2

P. O. Box 694, Altadena, 91003-0694
(213) 684-4428; (818) 797-2055
FAX (818) 798-3640

Large, contemporary home with Old World wine cellar has Angeles National Forest as its backyard. Enjoy a continental or full breakfast on the deck overlooking pool and view of the valley. Host teaches wine classes and is a gourmet cook. No smoking. Two guest rooms. Private bath. $55-60.

Eye Openers Bed and Breakfast Reservations AL-S1

P. O. Box 694, Altadena, 91003-0694
(213) 684-4428; (818) 797-2055
FAX (818) 798-3640

Large, well-landscaped yard in a quiet, residential community is a wonderful retreat at the end of the day. A delicious continental breakfast is served. No smoking. One guest room. with private bath. $50-55.

Eye Openers Bed and Breakfast Reservations AR-P2

P. O. Box 694, Altadena, 91003-0694
(213) 684-4428; (818) 797-2055
FAX (818) 798-3640

Horserace and garden enthuiasts will be close to Santa Anita Racetrack and the Los Angeles County Arboretum while enjoying the hospitality at this large, well-decorated, contemporary home. Enjoy a continental breakfast by the pool or in the family room. Resident dog. Two guest rooms. Private and shared baths. $45-50.

Eye Openers Bed and Breakfast Reservations AR-W2

P. O. Box 694, Altadena, 91003-0694
(213) 684-4428; (818) 797-2055
FAX (818) 798-3640

Quiet cul-de-sac near the Santa Anita racetrack, LA County Arboretum, Huntington Library, golf courses, and the beautiful San Gabriel Mountains is the setting for this bed and breakfast. Host loves to garden, hike, and travel. Enjoy a continental breakfast on the pool patio. No smoking. Two guest rooms with private and shared baths. $35-45.

NOTES: Credit cards accepted: A Master Card; B Visa; C American Express; D Discover Card; E Diner's Club; F Other; 2 Personal Checks accepted; 3 Lunch available; 4 Dinner available; 5 Open all year;

Eye Openers Bed and Breakfast Reservations PA-G2

P. O. Box 694, Altadena, 91003-0694
(213) 684-4428; (818) 797-2055
FAX (818) 798-3640

Large two-story Spanish-style bed and breakfast in the Cal Tech area of lovely old Pasadena has a swimming pool, Jacuzzi, and full country breakfast prepared by a gourmet cook. No smoking. Two guest rooms. Private bath. $70-90.

Eye Openers Bed and Breakfast Reservations PA-H1

P. O. Box 694, Altadena, 91003-0694
(213) 684-4428; (818) 797-2055
FAX (818) 798-3640

Located near the Huntington Hotel, which is now the Ritz-Carlton, this contemporary bed and breakfast is hosted by a retired school administrator. Enjoy the lovely garden room, where an ample continental breakfast is served. Convenient to all local tourist attractions. Resident cat. No smoking. One guest room with private bath. $45-50.

Eye Openers Bed and Breakfast Reservations PA-P2

P. O. Box 694, Altadena, 91003-0694
(213) 684-4428; (818) 797-2055
FAX (818) 798-3640

Sprawling ranch-style house in Colonial style has a large livingroom and book-lined library, both with a fireplace. A full scrumptious breakfast is served on the sunny patio or formal dining room. Host is concert pianist, organist, and harpsichordist. Close to Los Angeles and most tourist attractions. No smoking. Two guest rooms. Private and shared baths. $55.

Eye Openers Bed and Breakfast Reservations PA-R2

P. O. Box 694, Altadena, 91003-0694
(213) 684-4428; (818) 797-2055
FAX (818) 798-3640

This cheerful bed and breakfast is in one of Pasadena's well-known neighborhoods of tree-lined streets and well-kept homes. Continental breakfast, hot tub, private bath. No smoking. Two guest rooms. $45-50.

Eye Openers Bed and Breakfast Reservations PA-R3

P. O. Box 694, Altadena, 91003-0694
(213) 684-4428; (818) 797-2055
FAX (818) 798-3640

Short walk to Pasadena Civic and Convention Center, this bed and breakfast is an older, well-kept California bungalow with second-floor guest accommodations, as well as a separate, private apartment. Hosts who enjoy traveling have lived abroad and speak Swedish. Continental or full breakfast. Private and shared baths. No smoking. $35-75.

Eye Openers Bed and Breakfast Reservations PA-S9

P. O. Box 694, Altadena, 91003-0694
(213) 684-4428; (818) 797-2055
FAX (818) 798-3640

Gracious hosts interested in art offer very private guest quarters which make up the entire first floor of this contemporary hillside home with guest livingroom and patio. Garden and pool lend an Oriental atmosphere, and a delicious full breakfast served along with a view of the city makes this Bed and Breakfast a special place for guests to stay. No smoking. Two guest rooms. Shared bath. $55-65.

6 Pets welcome; 7 Smoking allowed; 8 Children welcome; 9 Social drinking allowed; 10 Tennis available; 11 Swimming available; 12 Golf available; 13 Skiing available; 14 May be booked through travel agents.

Eye Openers Bed and Breakfast Reservations PA-W1

P. O. Box 694, Altadena, 91003-0694
(213) 684-4428; (818) 797-2055
FAX (818) 798-3640

Half-timbered Tudor-style home was designed and built by the host, who is a magician, yoga enthusiast, and vegetarian gourmet cook. Lovely community with good hiking is close to museums and tourist attractions. No smoking. One guest room with private bath. $55-60.

Eye Openers Bed and Breakfast Reservations SP-P1

P. O. Box 694, Altadena, 91003-0694
(213) 684-4428; (818) 797-2055
FAX (818) 798-3640

400-square-foot redwood guest house shares patio and Jacuzzi with host's home, which faces Arroyo Seco natural recreation area. Horse stable, par three golf course, racquetball, and tennis courts are within walking distance. Cottage has cooking facilities and TV. Twelve minute drive to Los Angeles. No smoking. Private bath. $55-75.

PASO ROBLES

Megan's Friends #02 Bed and Breakfast Reservation Service

1776 Royal Way, San Luis Obispo, 93405
(805) 544-4406

Early 1900s California farmhouse with modern comforts. Peace and quiet in your own separate cabin yet close to town on a well-paved country road with easy access to wineries and wine tasting rooms. Lakes Nacimiento and San Antonio, less than an hour away, for water skiing, fishing, and sailing. Cabin has two bedrooms with bath and a country kitchen supplied with breakfast foods and juices. Nature trails over 40 acres of farmland. $75.

Megan's Friends #03 Bed and Breakfast Reservation Service

1776 Royal Way, San Luis Obispo, 93405
(805) 544-4406

This is an elegant, gated hilltop estate in the Paso Robles wine country. It is a large, traditional home on more than six acres with a 360-degree view and a pool, spa, and gazebo. There are three guest rooms, one with private bth; two share a bath. Gourmet breakfast is served. Each room comes with a fruit basket and a local wine, and robes are provided. No children please. $100-125.

PLACERVILLE—SEE ALSO KELSEY

Bed and Breakfast Los Angeles 17-5

730 Catalina Avenue, Seal Beach, 90740
(310) 493-6837; (800) 383-3513

Watch white-water rafting from the deck of this contemporary inn on the American River. Three guest rooms and one larger suite available, and most rooms have private baths. There is a hot tub available, and activities include fishing, swimming, gold panning, and antique shopping in nearby Placerville. A full breakfast is served on deck or at the fireplace. Moderate rates.

The Chichester-McKee House

800 Spring Street, 95667
(916) 626-1882; (800) 831-4008

NOTES: Credit cards accepted: A Master Card; B Visa; C American Express; D Discover Card; E Diner's Club; F Other; 2 Personal Checks accepted; 3 Lunch available; 4 Dinner available; 5 Open all year;

This elegant 1892 home was built by lumber baron D.W. Chichester. Enjoy fireplaces, fretwork, stained glass, antiques,, and relaxing hospitality. A "special" full breakfast is served in the dining room, and three air-conditioned guest rooms with private baths and robes are available. Located in downtown Placerville, near Apple Hill and Gold Discovery Site.

Hosts: Doreen and Bill Thornhill
Rooms: 3 (PB) $75-80
Full Breakfast
Credit Cards: A, B, D
Notes: 2, 5, 8, 9, 10, 11, 12, 13, 14

Combellack-Blair House

3059 Cedar Ravine, 95667
(916) 622-3764

This gracious Queen Anne Victorian home has stood as a landmark to travelers and Placerville residents alike for nearly a century. When you enter the front door you will enjoy the magnificent sight of a spiral staircase that is a work of art. The front parlor is a collection of period furnishings, recalling the 1890s. The rooms are decorated in a Victorian manner. This truly is a historic home, now a bed and breakfast for you to enjoy.

Hosts: Al and Rosalie McConnell
Rooms: 2 (PB) $89-99
Continental Breakfast
Credit Cards: A, B
Notes: 5, 7 (outside), 13

River Rock Inn

1756 Georgetown Drive, 95667
(916) 622-7640

Welcome to Gold Country. The River Rock Inn offers comfortable rooms furnished with antiques (two with half-baths), a hot tub on the deck, and an uninterrupted view of the river. Go exploring, fishing, gold panning, white-water rafting, or hot air ballooning. Tour an old gold mine, visit Marshall State Park, or enjoy friendly

shops, antique stores, restaurants, and wineries that are all just minutes away. It's all here for you to enjoy.

Host: Dorothy Irvin
Rooms: 4 (2 PB; 2 SB) $72-85
Full Breakfast
Credit Cards: None
Notes: 2, 5, 8, 11, 12, 13, 14

COMBELLACK-BLAIR HOUSE
Circa 1895

POINT ARENA

Coast Guard House

695 Arena Cove, 95468
(707) 882-2442; (800) 524-9320

Located on the beautiful Mendocino Coast, this historic Coast Guard lifesaving station, built in 1901, was authentically restored by the owners/hosts. Furnishings are from the studio arts and crafts period of American design (1870-1920), a style characterized by fine craftsmanship and simple, elegant lines. Nearby beaches, whale watching, and fishing are but a few of the coastal activities available.

Hosts: Merita Whatley and Richard Wasserman
Rooms: 6 (4 PB; 2 SB) $75-145
Continental Breakfast
Credit Cards: A, B
Notes: 2, 5

6 Pets welcome; 7 Smoking allowed; 8 Children welcome; 9 Social drinking allowed; 10 Tennis available; 11 Swimming available; 12 Golf available; 13 Skiing available; 14 May be booked through travel agents.

POINT REYES STATION_____

Bed and Breakfast Los Angeles 16-1

730 Catalina Avenue, Seal Beach, 90740
(310) 493-6837; (800) 383-3513

Gather your own breakfast eggs at this bountiful cottage in Point Reyes. House is stocked with full breakfast goodies, as well as beds for four and available crib. You can walk through rolling meadows to the center of town, and the owners invite you to share in their help-yourself garden of flowers, vegetables, herbs, fruit trees, and chickens. Luxury rates.

The Country House

P. O. Box 98, 94956
(415) 663-1627

California ranch house on an acre over-looking Point Reyes Station. Three suites with queen beds and private baths. Fire-places, antiques, beautiful views, and good food. Apple orchards and cottage flower garden. Walk to village; easy drive to Point Reyes National Seashore. Minimum stay holidays and weekends. Deposit required. Suitable for vacation rentals.

Host: Ewell H. McIsaac
Suites: 3 (PB) $85-100
Full Breakfast
Credit Cards: None
Notes: 2, 5, 8, 9, 14

Cricket Cottage

P. O. Box 627, 94956
(415) 663-9139

Garden cottage with private outdoor red-wood hot tub. Franklin fireplace with wood provided. Antique decor with original art. Private garden. Pastoral, meadow setting. One queen bed, one double sofa bed. Full bath with shower and claw foot tub. Partial kitchen with appliances. Breakfast provided.

Host: Penny Livingston
Cottage: 1 (PB) $115
Full Breakfast
Credit Cards: None
Notes: 2, 5, 8

Ferrandos Hideaway

12010 Highway 1, 94956
(415) 663-1966

Rich and homey bed and breakfast one mile north of Point Reyes Station. Private cottage with fully equipped kitchen and two rooms in main house. Hot tub, private baths, wood-burning stoves, vegetable gar-den, chickens. Close to Point Reyes National Seashore, hiking, biking, birding, horseback riding, whale watching, and miles of sandy beaches.

Hosts: Greg and Doris Ferrando
Rooms: 2 plus cottage (PB) $95-120
Continental Breakfast
Credit Cards: None
Notes: 2, 5, 12, 14

Horseshoe Farm Bed and Breakfast Cottage and Cabin

39 Drake's Summit, P. O. Box 332, 94956
(415) 663-9401

Private, cozy, charming cottage and cabin, both with sunny decks, fireplaces, and pri-vate hot tubs, in the peaceful, quiet woods of Inverness Ridge, adjacent to scenic won-ders of 65,000-acre Point Reyes National Seashore. Ocean beaches, hiking trails, whale watching, year-round bird watching. Great restaurants nearby.

Host: Paki Stedwell-Wright
Rooms: 2 (PB) $105-135
Full Breakfast
Credit Cards: None
Notes: 2, 5, 6, 7

Jasmine Cottage

11561 Coast Route One, 94956
(415) 663-1166

NOTES: Credit cards accepted: A Master Card; B Visa; C American Express; D Discover Card; E Diner's Club; F Other; 2 Personal Checks accepted; 3 Lunch available; 4 Dinner available; 5 Open all year;

This charming guest cottage was built in 1879 for the original Point Reyes schoolhouse. Secluded, romantic cottage sleeps four, has a library, wood-burning stove, full kitchen, beautiful pastoral views, private patios, and gardens. Five-minute walk down the hill to town; five-minute drive to spectacular Point Reyes National Seashore. A crib and highchair are available.

Host: Karen Gray
Cottage: 1 (PB) $115 plus
Full Breakfast
Credit Cards: None
Notes: 2, 4, 5, 6, 8, 9, 11, 14

Marsh Cottage Bed and Breakfast
Box 1121, 94956
(415) 669-7168

The privacy of your own peaceful bayside retreat near Inverness and spectacular Point Reyes National Seashore. Exceptional location and views, tasteful interior, fireplace, fully equipped kitchen, complete bath. Breakfast provided in the cottage. Ideal for romantics and naturalists. Hiking nearby.

Host: Wendy Schwartz
Room: 1 (PB) $95-110
Full Breakfast
Minimum stay weekends and holidays: 2 nights
Credit Cards: None
Notes: 2, 5, 8, 9, 11

Terri's Homestay
P. O. Box 113, 94956
(415) 663-1289; (800) 969-1289

High atop the Inverness Ridge, this sunny, secluded trailside bed and breakfast offers magnificent views. Rooms feature private baths, private entrance, and private deck. Natural fiber bedding and colorful Central American themes decorate the rooms. Step outside and enjoy the extensive network of Point Reyes National Seashore trails. Relax in our ozone-purified hot tub (with 95%

less chlorine). Health-oriented, supportive staff also provides professional massage, which couples can receive simultaneously. A 1¼ hour drive north of San Francisco. Detailed map with reservation.

Hosts: Terri Elaine and Richard Lailer
Rooms: 2 (PB) $85-115
Full Breakfast
Credit Cards: A, B, C
Notes: 2, 5, 8, 9, 10, 11

Thirty-nine Cypress
39 Cypress Road, 94956
(415) 663-1709

This small redwood inn overlooking a 500-acre ranch, marshlands, and the upper reaches of Tomales Bay offers spectacular views for guests to enjoy. Furnished with family antiques, Oriental rugs, original art, and an eclectic library, each of the rooms opens onto its own private patio. An outdoor spoa overlooking the views is available, and this is a favorite spot for bird watchers. Located near Point Reyes National Seashore, with its splendid beaches and 140 miles of hiking trails.

Host: Julia Bartlett
Rooms: 3 (SB) $95-115
Full Breakfast
Credit Cards: A, B
Notes: 2, 5, 9, 14

The Tree House
P. O. Box 1075, 73 Drake Summit, 94956
(415) 663-8720

On the Inverness Ridge with a view of Point Reyes Station, and direct access to the National Seashore Park. The Tree House sits close to the beaches, the lighthouse, hiking trails; this is also a bird watcher's paradise all year round. Whale watching from Dec. through April. Horseback riding available.

Host: Lisa P. Patsel
Rooms: 3 (PB) $80-95
Full or Continental Breakfast
Credit Cards: None
Notes: 2, 5, 6, 7, 8, 9

6 Pets welcome; 7 Smoking allowed; 8 Children welcome; 9 Social drinking allowed; 10 Tennis available; 11 Swimming available; 12 Golf available; 13 Skiing available; 14 May be booked through travel agents.

POINT RICHMOND

East Brother Light Station, Inc.

117 Park Place, 94801
(510) 233-2385

Formed as a non-profit organization in 1979 for the preservation and restoration of the light station. Overnight guests will enjoy an innovative five-course dinner expertly prepared and four guest rooms comfortably appointed with Victorian furnishings, brass beds, and fresh flowers. Located on an island off the San Francisco coast. Guests are treated to a demonstration of the restored diaphone foghorn after an exquisite breakfast. Accomodations are available Thursday through Sunday nights only.

Hosts: Cliff and Ruth Benton
Rooms: 4 (2 PB; 2 SB) $295
Full Breakfast and Dinner
Credit Cards: None
Notes: 2, 3, 4, 5, 9

PORTOLA

Upper Feather Bed and Breakfast

256 Commercial Street, 96122
(916) 832-0107

Small-town comfort and hospitality in casual country style. No TV or radio, but we have board games, puzzles, and popcorn for relaxing. Walk to the railroad museum, restaurants, wild and scenic river, and national forest. Only one hour from Reno entertainment.

Hosts: Jon and Lynne Haman
Rooms: 5 (SB) $42 plus tax
Suite: 1 (SB) 63 plus tax
Full Breakfast
Credit Cards: None
Notes: 2, 5, 6, 8, 9, 10, 11, 12, 13

QUINCY

The Feather Bed

542 Jackson Street, P. O. Box 3200, 95971
(916) 283-0102

The Feather Bed is a country Victorian, circa 1893, in the small community of Quincy, a town located in the high Sierras. All seven guest rooms have private baths, queen-size beds, and private entrances. An abundant country breakfast is served each morning in the charming dining room, and during the summer months. In the Victorian patio. Guests can enjoy hiking, swimming, picnicking, and other outdoor activities nearby. Enjoy a stroll through historic downtown Quincy, dine in one of the fine restaurants, or relax on the old-fashioned veranda.

Hosts: Chuck and Dianna Gilbert
Rooms: 7 (PB) $65-95
Full Breakfast
Credit Cards: A, B, C, E
Notes: 2, 5, 8, 12, 13, 14

RAMONA

Bed and Breakfast Los Angeles 8-5

730 Catalina Avenue, Seal Beach, 90740
(310) 493-6837; (800) 383-3513

Nestled among four acres of avocado and orange groves, this home is filled with antiques and collectibles. Two guest rooms share one bath, and activities include biking, swimming, croquet, badminton, and bird watching. Affordable rates.

RANCHO PALOS VERDES

Bed and Breakfast Los Angeles 5-1

730 Catalina Avenue, Seal Beach, 90740
(310) 493-6837; (800) 383-3513

NOTES: Credit cards accepted: A Master Card; B Visa; C American Express; D Discover Card; E Diner's Club; F Other; 2 Personal Checks accepted; 3 Lunch available; 4 Dinner available; 5 Open all year;

Ocean breezes and a panoramic view are part of everyday life in this Rancho Palos Verdes home. Two comfortable guest rooms, both with private baths, are available to families. Older children only. Moderate rates.

Bed and Breakfast Los Angeles 5-3

730 Catalina Avenue, Seal Beach, 90740
(310) 493-6837; (800) 383-3513

This large guest room includes a private entrance and bath, as well as a TV, VCR, stereo, and sliding glass door to the yard. Extra room with a waterbed may be available for older children. Affordable rates.

Pacific View Bed and Breakfast

4110 Palos Verdes Drive, South
(310) 377-2860

Contemporary house with a long deck and gorgeous ocean view offers two bed and breakfast rooms, each with private bath. Quiet, cool, no smog, walking access to private beach with barbecue facilities. No pets. Children by prior arrangement. Smoking outside only. $25 reservation deposit. Flexible check-in time. Weekly rates available.

Host: Ann Booth
Rooms: 2 (PB) $60 plus tax
Expanded Continental Breakfast
Credit Cards: None
Notes: 2, 5, 7 (outside), 9, 14

RED BLUFF

The Faulkner House

1029 Jefferson Street, 96080
(916) 529-0520

An 1890's Queen Anne Victorian, furnished in antiques. Screened in porch looks out on a quiet , tree-lined street for relaxing, or let us help you discover our area.

Go hiking or skiing at Lassen Park, visit Ide Adobe, or a Victorian museum, Enjoy Sacrement0 River fishing.

Host: Harvey and Mary Klingler
Rooms: 4 (PB) $55-80
Full Breakfast
Credit Cards: A, B, C
Notes: 2, 5, 7 (limited), 9, 12, 13, 14

REDDING

Palisades Paradise Bed and Breakfast

1200 Palisades Avenue, 96003
(916) 223-5305

You'll love the breathtaking view of the Sacramento River, city, and surrounding mountains from this beautiful contemporary home with its garden spa, fireplace, wide-screen TV, VCR, and home-like atmosphere. Palisades Paradise is a serene setting for a quiet hideaway, yet conveniently situated one mile from shopping and Interstate 5, with water skiing and river rafting nearby.

Host: Gail Goetz
Rooms: 2 (SB) $55-70
Expanded Continental Breakfast weekdays;
    Full Breakfast weekends
Credit Cards: A, B, C
Notes: 2, 5, 7 (limited), 8, 9, 10, 11, 12, 13, 14

REDLANDS

Morey Mansion Bed and Breakfast Inn

190 Terracina Boulevard, 92373
(714) 793-7970

Built in 1890 by David Morey, a retired shipbuilder, this Queen Anne Victorian with a Russian dome is a landmark in historical Redlands. There are five guest rooms available, four with a private bath, and a continental breakfast is served in the morning. The downstairs area, as well as the porch and lawn, are available for weddings, receptions, and teas.

---

6 Pets welcome; 7 Smoking allowed; 8 Children welcome; 9 Social drinking allowed; 10 Tennis available; 11 Swimming available; 12 Golf available; 13 Skiing available; 14 May be booked through travel agents.

Host: Donna Norris
Rooms: 5 (3 PB; 2 SB) $109-225
Continental Breakfast
Credit Cards: A, B, C
Notes: 5, 8, 14

REDONDO BEACH

Ocean Breeze Bed and Breakfast

122 South Juanita Avenue, 90277
(310) 316-5123

Near the beach, between Los Angeles and
Long Beach, close to freeways. Private
entry, spa bathtub, and hospital beds with
heated mattress covers. Remote TV,
microwave oven, toaster, coffee maker in
large luxurious rooms.

Hosts: Norris and Betty Binding
Rooms: 2 (PB) $30-50
Continental Breakfast
Credit Cards: None
Notes: 2, 5, 7, 8 (over 5), 9, 10, 11, 12

RUTHERFORD

Rancho Caymus Inn

1140 Rutherford Road, P. O. Box 78, 94573
(707) 963-1777; (800) 845-1777

If you are looking for pure romance, this is
it! This country inn stands on land once
part of Caymus Rancho granted to the U.S.
by the governor of Mexico in 1836. It
offers twenty-six handcrafted suites, with
hand-carved walnut beds, fireplaces, and
wet bars in each suite. Some of our master
suites include kitchenettes and large
Jacuzzi tubs. All rooms encircle a series of
award-winning courtyards and are designed
to capture the rustic elegance of old California. Relaxing indoor and outdoor garden
terrace dining is available at the Garden
Grill Restaurant.

Host: Tony Prince
Rooms: 26 (PB) $115-295
Continental Breakfast
Credit Cards: A, B, C
Notes: 2, 3, 5, 7, 9, 14

SACRAMENTO

Amber House Bed and Breakfast

1315 22nd Street, 95816
(916) 444-8085; (800) 755-6526
FAX (916) 447-1548

This 1905 mansion is elegantly appointed
with antiques, original art, Oriental rugs,
and fresh flowers. Relax in front of the fireplace or enjoy the cozy library. Guest
rooms feature private baths (four with big
Jacuzzi tubs for two), private telephones,
radios, TV's. Full gourmet breakfast served
in room, dining room, or outside on the
veranda.

Hosts: Michael and Jane Richardson
Rooms: 8 (PB) $77-195
Full Breakfast
Credit Cards: A, B, C, E, F
Notes: 2, 5, 9, 10, 11, 14

B&B International #402

P. O. Box 282910, San Francisco, 94128-2910
(415) 696-1690; FAX (415) 696-1699

Historic Victorian home close to the
Capitol, Old Town, museums, and restaurants. It is on the Sacramento Old House
Tour and is furnished in antiques. There is
an upstairs sitting room with a fireplace,
one guest room with private bath, one with
shared. $50-60.

ST. HELENA

Ambrose Bierce House

1515 Main Street, 94574
(707) 963-3003

Built in 1872, this house combines history,
romance, and pampering. Queen-size beds,
claw foot tubs, and armoires decorate the
former home of the writer Ambrose Bierce.
Suites are named for historical figures
whose presence touched Bierce and Napa
Valley in the late 1800s. Convenient loca-

NOTES: Credit cards accepted: A Master Card; B Visa; C American Express; D Discover Card; E Diner's
Club; F Other; 2 Personal Checks accepted; 3 Lunch available; 4 Dinner available; 5 Open all year;

tion, walking distance to restaurants, shops, and wineries. A gourmet continental breakfast is complimentary, as is the hospitality.

Host: Jane Gibson
Rooms: 3 (PB) $89-139
Continental Breakfast
Credit Cards: None
Notes: 2, 5, 9, 14

Asplund Conn Valley Inn

726 Rossi Road, 94574
(707) 963-4614

Nestled in lush garden surroundings with views of vineyards and rolling hills—peaceful, quiet, and romantic. In-room refrigerators, air conditioning, antiques. Common room with fireplace, library, TV. Complimentary wine, fruit, cheese, and crackers. Lots of country roads for strolling or jogging. Volleyball, badminton. Close to wineries, restaurants, tennis, golf, swimming, spas, balloon rides, and glider rides.

Host: Elsie Asplund Hudak
Rooms: 3 (1 PB; 2 SB) $85-95
Expanded Breakfast
Credit Cards: A, B, C
Notes: 2, 5, 8, 9, 10, 11, 12, 14

Bartels Ranch and Country Inn

1200 Conn Valley Road, 94574
(707) 963-4001; FAX (707) 963-5100

In the heart of the world-famous Napa Valley wine country, is this secluded, romantic, elegant country estate overlooking a "100-acre valley with a 10,000-acre view." Honeymoon suite with sunken Jacuzzi, sauna, shower, stone fireplace, and TV, VCR, and stereo. The Blue Valley Room, the Sunset Room, and the Brass Room, with various amenities, are all available for guests. Expansive entertainment room, pool table, fireplace, library, and terraces overlooking the vineyard. Bicycles, refrigerator, TV, and phone available. Wineries, lake, golf, tennis, fishing, boating, and mineral spas nearby. Limousine,

hot air balloons, and helicopter available. Wine seminars with a tailored itinerary are a house special.

Host: Jami Bartels
Rooms: 4 (PB) $115-275
Expanded Continental Breakfast
Credit Cards: A, B, C, D
Notes: 2, 3, 4, 5, 9, 10, 11, 12, 14

Cinnamon Bear Bed and Breakfast

1407 Kearney Street, 94574
(707) 963-4653

Classic arts and craft house, built in 1910 and furnished in that style with lots of bears. Close to downtown shops and restaurants; air-conditioned. Afternoon socializing with snacks, beverages, TV, phone. Family-owned and operated; full breakfast.

Host: Genny Jenkins
Rooms: 4 (PB) $75-145
Full Breakfast
Credit Cards: A, B
Notes: 2, 5, 9, 10, 11, 12

Creek-side Inn

945 Main Street, 94574
(707) 963-7244

Creek-side is a beautiful and quiet country cottage in the heart of St. Helena, yet peacefully sheltered from the hustle and bustle of town by ancient oaks and the murmurs of White Sulpher Creek rippling past its secluded rear garden patio. When you walk through the door from the outside world, you enter the private world that is Creek-side.

Hosts: Jean Nicholson and Virginia Toogood
Rooms: 3 (SB) $75-95
Full Breakfast
Credit Cards: A, B
Note: 2

Deer Run Inn

3995 Spring Mountain Road, 94574
(707) 963-3794

A lovely cedar clapboard-style gem on four acres offers a guest unit in the main house, with private bath, entrance, and fireplace. Another unit, a spacious carriage room in a spearate building, offers private bath, entrance, and decking. A third accommodation choice is a cottage complete with a livingroom, bedroom, and bath, and offers the advantage of a full breakfast delivered each morning. Swimming pool, Ping-Pong, horseshoes, and tranquility are just a few of the amenities. Close to restaurants, spas, wineries, balloon rides, and glider rides

Hosts: Tom and Carol Wilson
Rooms: 3 (PB) $95-125
Full Breakfast
Credit Card: C
Notes: 2, 5, 9, 10, 11, 12, 14

Erika's Hillside

285 Fawn Park, 94574
(707) 963-2887

You will be welcomed with warm European-style hospitality when you arrive at this hillside chalet. Just two miles from St. Helena, it has a peaceful, wooded country setting and view of the vineyards and wineries. The grounds (three acres) are nicely landscaped. The rooms are spacious, bright, and airy, with private entrances and bath, fireplace and hot tub. Continental breakfast and German specialities are

Harvest Inn

served on the patio or in the garden room. More than 100 years old, the structure has been remodeled and personally decorated by German-born innkeeper.

Host: Erika Cunningham
Rooms: 3 (PB) $65-165
Continental Breakfast
Credit Cards: All Major
Notes: 2, 5, 8, 9, 10, 11, 12, 14

Harvest Inn

1 Main Street, 94574
(707) 963-WINE; (800) 950-8466

Situated in the heart of the Napa Valley wine country, this inn of courtly English Tudor architecture is surrounded by lovely gardens and a 14-acre working vineyard. Rooms are furnished with antiques, and most include fireplaces, wet bars, refrigerators, color TV, air conditioning, and telephones. A wine bar, two pools, and Jacuzzis are also available for guests of the inn.

Rooms: 54 (PB) $110-325
Continental Breakfast
Credit Cards: A, B, C, D
Note: 2, 5, 6, 8, 9, 10, 11, 12, 14

The Ink House
Bed and Breakfast

1575 St. Helena Highway, 94574
(707) 963-3890

This spacious and elegant Italianate Victorian built in 1884 is listed on the National Register of Historic Places. Country setting, antiques throughout, observatory overlooking surrounding vineyards and hills. Sherry, brandy, bicycles, pool table, soda and mineral waters. Centrally located. Seen on national TV and in major magazines.

Host: Ernie Veniegas
Rooms: 4 (PB) $95-150
Continental Breakfast
Credit Cards: None
Notes: 2, 5, 9, 10, 11, 12, 14 (Sun.-Thurs.)

Shady Oaks Country Inn

399 Zinfandel Lane, 94574
(707) 963-1190

Secluded and romantic on two acres, nestled among the finest wineries and restaurants in Napa Valley. Wine and cheese are served each evening, and the full champagne breakfast is known as "the best in the valley." The inn's reputation has been built on warm, sincere hospitality with all of your comforts in mind. Each immaculate room is spacious and furnished with antiques; elegant ambience and country tranquility.

Hosts: John and Lisa Wild-Runnells
Rooms: 4 (PB) $75-145
Full Champagne Breakfast
Credit Cards: None
Notes: 2, 5, 9, 10, 11, 12, 14

The Wine Country Inn

1152 Lodi Lane, 94574
(707) 963-7077

Perched on a knoll overlooking manicured vineyards and the nearby hills, this country inn offers 25 individually decorated guest rooms. The hosts used family-made quilts, local antiques, fireplaces, and balconies to create an atmosphere of unparalleled comfort.

Hosts: Jim Smith and Diane Horkheimer
Rooms: 25 (PB) $130-155
Continental Breakfast
Credit Cards: A, B, C
Closed Christmas
Notes: 2, 7, 9, 10, 11, 12, 14

Zinfandel Inn

800 Zinfandel Lane, 94574
(707) 963-3512

Elegant, serene, and peaceful, the Zinfandel Inn is only ninety minutes from San Francisco in the center of the Napa Valley wine country. It is the ideal place to relax and vacation, just minutes from many major Napa Valley points of interest. Refresh yourself in this country setting among the vineyards of the famous wine region. Enjoy staying in one of four accommodations, including the Zinfandel Suite with a king bed, Jaccuzzi bath, and private deck; the Chardonnay Suite, with a large stone fireplace, king-size brass bed, private bath, and private entrance; or the Chablis Room, with a queen-size oak four-poster bed and private bath.

Hosts: Terry and Diane Payton
Rooms: 4 (PB) $100-200
Full Breakfast
Credit Cards: A, B, C
Notes: 2, 5

The Wine Country Inn

SAN ANDREAS

Courtyard Bed and Breakfast

334 West St. Charles, 95249
(209) 754-1518

Master suite has fireplace, bathroom, walk-in closet, baby grand piano, and French doors leading to the hot tub and the deck. Blue Room has a double bed and coffee is served to both rooms in the morning on silver service. Beautiful gardens and rock formations. Perfect spot for weddings and garden parties. Over fifty unique birdhouses, and some lovely stained-glass windows. Hot tub and horseshoe pit available.

6 Pets welcome; 7 Smoking allowed; 8 Children welcome; 9 Social drinking allowed; 10 Tennis available; 11 Swimming available; 12 Golf available; 13 Skiing available; 14 May be booked through travel agents.

Host: Lucy Thein
Rooms: 2 (PB) $55-75
Full Breakfast
Credit Cards: none
Notes: 2, 5, 6, 7 (outside), 8, 10, 12, 13

Robin's Nest

P. O. Box 1408, 95249
(209) 754-1076

This Victorian, built in 1895, retains its dramatic character and Old World charm with modern conveniences. The inn is situated on an acre of grass and fruit trees. Nearby activities include California Caverns, art and antique shops, Big Trees State Park, wine tasting, boating, fishing, water and cross-country skiing.

Hosts: George and Carolee Jones
Rooms: 9 (7 PB; 2 SB) $65-110
Full Breakfast
Credit Cards: A, B
Notes: 2, 5, 8 , 10, 11, 12, 13, 14

Casa de Flores Bed and Breakfast

SAN CLEMENTE

Casa de Flores Bed and Breakfast

184 Avenue La Cuesta, 92672
(714) 498-1344

San Clemente's best-kept secret. Midway between Los Angeles and San Diego sits a beautiful 4,500-square-foot Spanish home

offering two two-room suites and a spectacular view of the Pacific Ocean and Dana Point Harbor. One suite features a fireplace in the bedroom and a spa in its own private enclosed patio, the other a double sofa bed in the sitting room for two additional people at an extra charge. Both suites offer TV/VCR's and in-room coffee. Beach chairs and towels, over 200 videos, pool table, washer, dryer, and iron available. Complimentary beverages. Turn-down service. Beautiful beaches and fine restaurants within one mile.

Hosts: Marilee and Robert Arsenault
Suites: 2 (PB) $75-100
Full Breakfast
Minimum stay holidays and weekends: 2
Credit Cards: None
Notes: 2, 5, 7, 8, 9, 10, 11, 12, 14

SAN DIEGO

America's B&B #18

P. O. Box 9302, Whittier, 90608
(310) 699-8427

Lovely home in a quiet residential neighborhood, minutes from Mission Bay, beaches, the zoo, and downtown. The four guest rooms feature three private baths (two shared baths), and children are welcome. The large livingroom offers guests an inviting place to enjoy the fireplace and TV overlooking a beautiful patio and large Jacuzzi. Bumper pool table is available. Hosts have traveled widely and offer airport and train pickup with prior arrangement. $57.

The Balboa Park Inn

3402 Park Boulevard, 92103
(619) 298-0823

One of San Diego's most romantic settings, a guest house in the heart of the city. The affordable difference is a suite for the price of a room. Within walking distance of the San Diego Zoo, Old Globe Theatre, museums, restaurants; ten minutes from the beach.

NOTES: Credit cards accepted: A Master Card; B Visa; C American Express; D Discover Card; E Diner's Club; F Other; 2 Personal Checks accepted; 3 Lunch available; 4 Dinner available; 5 Open all year;

Host: Ed Wilcox
Suites: 25 (PB)
Continental Breakfast
Credit Cards: A, B, C, E, F
Notes: 2, 5, 7, 8, 9, 10, 11, 12, 14

Bed and Breakfast Los Angeles 8-1

730 Catalina Avenue, Seal Beach, 90740
(310) 493-6837; (800) 383-3513

Small beachfront cottages can accommodate a family of four; the two-bedroom apartments have room for six. Kitchens are stocked with goodies for breakfast. Great weekend and monthly rates are available. Affordable rates.

The Cottage

Carole's Bed and Breakfast

3227 Grim Avenue, 92104
(619) 280-5258

A friendly home close to all major attractions. Only one and one-half miles to the San Diego Zoo and Balboa Park. This house, built in 1904, is decorated with antiques and has a large swimming pool. Complimentary wine and cheese are also served.

Hosts: Carole Dugdale and Michael O'Brien
Rooms: 8 (1 PB; 7 SB) $55-75
Continental Breakfast
Credit Cards: None
Notes: 5, 9, 10, 11, 12, 14

The Cottage

3829 Albatross Street, 92103
(619) 299-1564

Situated between the zoo and Sea World, the Cottage is a quiet retreat in the heart of a downtown residential neighborhood. The turn-of-the-century furnishings throughout evoke visions of a bygone era. Each morning you will be served a breakfast of freshly baked bread, juice, and beverage.

Hosts: Robert and Carol Emerick
Rooms: 2 (PB) $59-75
Continental Breakfast
Credit Cards: A, B, C
Notes: 2, 5, 8, 9, 14

Erene's Inn

3776 Hawk Street, 92103
(619) 295-5622

This charming, circa 1900, Mission Hills home close to Balboa Park, Gaslamp district, and Old Town, welcomes you with its pillared porch and French doors. Original paintings, enamels, and ceramics complement Greek antiques, English armoires, Oriental wares, and Turkish rugs. Coffee and tea around the fireplace or on the sunny deck, fresh flowers on the breakfast table and tiny surprises under your pillow are some of the cordial gestures you'll enjoy.

Host: Erene Rallis
Rooms: 2 (1 PB; 1 SB) $40-50
Continental Breakfast
Credit Cards: None
Notes: 4, 5, 6 (outside), 7 (outside), 8, 9, 10, 12, 14

Eye Openers Bed and Breakfast Reservations DD-P2

P. O. Box 694, Altadena, 91003-0694
(213) 684-4428; (818) 797-2055
FAX (818) 798-3640

Japanese ambience characterizes this two-bedroom guest house and numerous outdoor areas. Views of nearby mountain lakes and surrounding mountains can be

6 Pets welcome; 7 Smoking allowed; 8 Children welcome; 9 Social drinking allowed; 10 Tennis available; 11 Swimming available; 12 Golf available; 13 Skiing available; 14 May be booked through travel agents.

enjoyed from the decks, livingroom with fireplace, and upstairs bedroom. Indoor hot tub. Choice of full or continental breakfast. It is twenty minutes inland from San Diego near Escondido, and is only a short drive to several beach cities. No. smoking. $70-115.

Eye Openers Bed and Breakfast Reservations FA-B2

P. O. Box 694, Altadena, 91003-0694
(213) 684-4428; (818) 797-2055
FAX (818) 798-3640

Large country French chateau is nestled on a working avocado ranch. Relax and unwind poolside in a peaceful, hilltop setting. Antiques are throughout this pretty bed and breakfast, and the guest room overlooks the garden. Full breakfast. Wineries, antique shops, and golf courses are nearby. Resident cats and dogs. No smoking. Two guest rooms with private and shared baths. $60-75.

Eye Openers Bed and Breakfast Reservations SD-C21

P. O. Box 694, Altadena, 91003-0694
(213) 684-4428; (818) 797-2055
FAX (818) 798-3640

New Bed and Breakfast inn has two uniquely decorated guest rooms as well as guest livingroom with fireplace and dining area where a full breakfast is selected from a menu. Close to San Diego tourist attractions. Two guest rooms with shared bath. $50.

Eye Openers Bed and Breakfast Reservations SD-E1

P. O. Box 694, Altadena, 91003-0694
(213) 684-4428; (818) 797-2055
FAX (818) 798-3640

Separate guest house with turn-of-the-century furnishings assures privacy in central San Diego and offers a bedroom, sitting room with wood-burning stove, and dining area where a delicious continental breakfast is served. Additional guest room in the house is available. Private bath. $45-60 plus tax.

Eye Openers Bed and Breakfast Reservations SD-H3

P. O. Box 694, Altadena, 91003-0694
(213) 684-4428; (818) 797-2055
FAX (818) 798-3640

Self-hosted three-bedroom, beachfront home can accommodate two to eight guests. Weekly and monthly rates also available. Three guest rooms. Private baths. $120-220.

Eye Openers Bed and Breakfast Reservations SD-H41

P. O. Box 694, Altadena, 91003-0694
(213) 684-4428; (818) 797-2055
FAX (818) 798-3640

Beautifully restored, tastefully decorated inn with large rooms and views is in the Golden Hill area of San Diego, convenient to downtown and many tourist attractions. Large rooms have sitting areas, and one has a fireplace. Extended continental breakfast is served in the formal dining room. There are several outdoor areas for sunning and relaxation. No smoking. Four guest rooms with shared bath. $50-60, plus tax.

Eye Openers Bed and Breakfast Reservations SD-E1

P. O. Box 694, Altadena, 91003-0694
(213) 684-4428; (818) 797-2055
FAX (818) 798-3640

Eye Openers Bed and Breakfast Reservations SD-H61

P. O. Box 694, Altadena, 91003-0694
(213) 684-4428; (818) 797-2055
FAX (818) 798-3640

NOTES: Credit cards accepted: A Master Card; B Visa; C American Express; D Discover Card; E Diner's Club; F Other; 2 Personal Checks accepted; 3 Lunch available; 4 Dinner available; 5 Open all year;

Tri-level bed and breakfast inn with a harbor view and garden is near Balboa Park, Sea Wold, and the zoo. Continental breakfast. Six guest rooms. Private baths. $60-95.

Eye Openers Bed and Breakfast Reservations SD-H91

P. O. Box 694, Altadena, 91003-0694
(213) 684-4428; (818) 797-2055
FAX (818) 798-3640

1889 Victorian antique-furnished bed and breakfast inn is in a restored village convenient to tourist attractions. Full breakfast, candlelight dinners, and special amenities available. No smoking. Nine guest rooms. Private baths. $85-125 plus tax.

Eye Openers Bed and Breakfast Reservations SD-P1

P. O. Box 694, Altadena, 91003-0694
(213) 684-4428; (818) 797-2055
FAX (818) 798-3640

Condominium bed and breakfast near San Diego Stadium with excellent freeway access to all tourist attractions. Continental breakfast, swimmingpool, Jacuzzi, kitchen, and laundry facilities. One room with private bath. No smoking. $75.

Eye Openers Bed and Breakfast Reservations SD-Q21

P. O. Box 694, Altadena, 91003-0694
(213) 684-4428; (818) 797-2055
FAX (818) 798-3640

Converted San Diego Trolley Car and four-room guest cottage, beautifully restored and decorated with memorabilia and appointed antiques, are located near a quiet ravine in a natural setting in central San Diego close to Balboa Park. Lushly landscaped patios are a quiet retreat after a busy day of sightseeing. Self-hosted continental-plus breakfast and afternoon refreshments are provided. No smoking. Private bath. $65-75 plus tax.

Eye Openers Bed and Breakfast Reservations SD-S2

P. O. Box 694, Altadena, 91003-0694
(213) 684-4428; (818) 797-2055
FAX (818) 798-3640

Clairmont area above Misson Bay is the convenient locale of this bed and breakfast, with spacious suite and second guest room. Located near most tourist attractions, there is bus transportation nearby. A full breakfast is served in the dining room. The host, an amateur winemaker, enjoys showing off his wine cellar. Resident dog. No smoking. One guest room and suite. Private baths. $46-56.

Heritage Park Bed and Breakfast Inn

2470 Heritage Park Row, 92110
(619) 299-6832

A splendid Queen Anne in San Diego's unique setting for romantic overnight lodging, a 7.8-acre Victorian Park in the heart of historic Old Town. Accommodations include eight distinctive guest chambers, each carefully furnished with authentic period antiques, Victorian wall coverings, and nostalgic trimmings of a century ago. Full homemade breakfast buffet is served in the dining room and may be enjoyed on the veranda. Evening social hour and nightly vintage movies.

Hosts: Nancy and Charles Helsper
Rooms: 8 (4 PB; 4 SB) $80-120
Full Breakfast
Credit Cards: A, B
Notes: 2, 4, 5, 8 (over 12), 9, 14

6 Pets welcome; 7 Smoking allowed; 8 Children welcome; 9 Social drinking allowed; 10 Tennis available; 11 Swimming available; 12 Golf available; 13 Skiing available; 14 May be booked through travel agents.

Splendid Serenity

25536 Pappas Road, 92065
(619) 788-9232

Located in the historic Oaks of the Cuyamaca National Forest. Enjoy quiet relaxation after tourist attractions in the city. Guests may choose to use the services of the nearby golf, equestiran, and swimming clubs or to visit the nearby wild animal park.

Hosts: Beverly McCall-Seitz and Dr. Michael R.
  Seitz
Rooms: 3 (1 PB; 2 SB) $45
Continental Breakfast
Credit Cards: A, B

Surf Manor and Cottages

P. O. Box 7695, 92167
(619) 225-9765

Old World charm and ambience in a rarefied beach setting. Bed and breakfast accommodations are offered from September through June. A stocked refrigerator provides a continental or full English breakfast. Choose from the manor directly on the beach or a cottage in the desirable area of South Mission Beach. Close to Mission Bay, Sea World, San Diego Zoo, Balboa Park, and other sites and attractions. Weekly and monthly rates available, varying according to season.

Host: Jerri Grady
Rooms: 3 (PB) $60 plus
Full Self-Serve Breakfast
Credit Cards: None
Notes: 2, 5, 8, 11, 14

Vera's Cozy Corner

2810 Albatross Street, 92103
(619) 296-1938

This crisp white Colonial with black shutters sits in a quiet cul-de-sac overlooking San Diego Bay. Comfortable guest quarters consist of a separate cottage with private entrance across a flower-filled patio. Vera offers freshly squeezed orange juice from her own fruit trees in season as a prelude to breakfast, which is served in the dining room. The house is convenient to local shops and restaurants, beaches, and is one mile from the San Diego Zoo.

Host: Vera V. Warden
Room: 1 (PB) $50
Continental Breakfast
Credit Cards: None
Notes: 2, 5, 9, 10, 11, 12, 14

SAN FRANCISCO

America's B&B #20

P. O. Box 9302, Whittier, 90608
(310) 699-8427

Delightful home near bus transportation to most of the delights of this famous city. Bedrooms are comfortable, and hostess offers laundry facilities. Full breakfast. $55.

Amsterdam Hotel

749 Taylor Street, 94108
(415) 673-3277; (800) 637-3444
FAX (415) 673-0453

The Amsterdam Hotel reflects the charm of a small European hotel. From the spacious lobby and cozy sitting room to the beautifully decorated guest rooms, this 1909 bed and breakfast inn offers every modern convenience to discriminating business or pleasure travelers. All rooms feature color cable TV, radio, telephone, and remodeled bathrooms. The Amsterdam Hotel is just minutes away from San Francisco's historic cable cars, Union Square shopping, theaters, Chinatown, and the financial district.

Host: Harry
Rooms: 31 (26 PB; 5 SB) $45-70
Continental Breakfast
Credit Cards: A, B, C
Notes: 5, 7, 8, 9, 10, 11, 12, 14

Archbishops Mansion Inn

1000 Fulton Street, 94117
(415) 563-7872

NOTES: Credit cards accepted: A Master Card; B Visa; C American Express; D Discover Card; E Diner's Club; F Other; 2 Personal Checks accepted; 3 Lunch available; 4 Dinner available; 5 Open all year;

Centrally located on a beautiful park surrounded by much-photographed Victorian homes. All the interesting areas of the city are only minutes away. Every guest room is custom designed to create a personalized atmosphere reminiscent of the last century. Amenities include exquisite antiques, embroidered linens, and comfortable sitting area. Most rooms have fireplaces. Lovely private baths, stacks of towels, French-milled soaps, and private phones.

Host: Kathleen Austin
Rooms: 15 (PB) $139-285
Continental-plus Breakfast
Credit Cards: A, B, C
Notes: 2, 5, 7, 8, 9, 10, 11, 12, 14

Art Center and Bed and Breakfast Suites, Wamsley

1902 Filbert Street, 94123
(415) 567-1526; (800) 821-3877

The best residential area—Marina, Cow Hollow—where history stands still. Twenty-minute walk to Fisherman's Wharf. A French-New Orleans inn, with privacy and kitchens, canopied queen beds, fireplaces, and whirlpool suite. Shopping on Union Street, jogging at the marina. Day tours of Northern California's charms, nearby theater, music, cruising, and dancing on the bay—all within easy reach. Business travelers and families welcome. Commercial discounts, art classes, and gallery.

Hosts: George and Helvi Wamsley
Rooms: 5 (PB) $75-120
Continental Breakfast
Credit Cards: A, B, C, D, E, F
Notes: 2, 5, 8, 9, 10, 12, 14

Bed and Breakfast International-TNN-CALIFORNIA

P. O. Box 282910, 94128-2910
(415) 696-1690; (800) 872-4500

Part of the Bed and Breakfast National Network, Bed and Breakfast International offers bed and breakfast not only in California but also in many other cities and states across the country. The members of this network adhere strictly to the standards set by TNN, such as getting to know the hosts personally, having an established cancellation and refund policy, and following a thorough inspection and approval process for all properties rented. This is because each member of the network is deidcated to ensuring your comfort, pleasure, and personal needs while you are staying at one of our "homes away from home."

B&B International #101

P. O. Box 282910, 94128-2910
(415) 696-1690; FAX (415) 696-1699

Situated in the heart of San Francisco on Russian Hill, this charming garden apartment has a king-size bed and private entrance. It is professionally decorated and has glass doors that open onto the patio. It is in walking distance to North Beach, and a block away from the cable cars. Breakfast is left for guests to enjoy at their leisure. $85.

B&B International #102

P. O. Box 282910, 94128-2910
(415) 696-1690; FAX (415) 696-1699

Ideally situated second-floor home in a modernized Victorian building near the North Beach area on Telegraph Hill. Walking distance to Fisherman's Wharf and many restaurants. Cable car is three blocks away. Two rooms share a bath. $55-68.

B&B International #103

P. O. Box 282910, 94128-2910
(415) 696-1690; FAX (415) 696-1699

Three-story turn-of-the-century home that has been pictured in Sunset magazine. Favorite spot for many returning guests.

6 Pets welcome; 7 Smoking allowed; 8 Children welcome; 9 Social drinking allowed; 10 Tennis available; 11 Swimming available; 12 Golf available; 13 Skiing available; 14 May be booked through travel agents.

Situated only 15 minutes from Union Square and an equal distance to Ocean Beach. Within walking distance to Golden Gate Park and the Presidio and to the many shops and restaurants on Clement Street. One room with sitting area and private bath. Two rooms with shared bath. $60-70.

B&B International #104

P. O. Box 282910, 94128-2910
(415) 696-1690; FAX (415) 696-1699

Exceptionally clean and well-decorated guest room, studio, or carriage house in the back garden of an 1880 Victorian. Room has a double bed, private bath, and private entrance. Studio has queen bed, fireplace, fully equipped kitchen, and deck. Two-story carriage house has fireplace, grand piano, formal dining room, and fully equipped kitchen. Continental breakfast items are left for the guests. $65-175.

B&B International #105

P. O. Box 282910, 94128-2910
(415) 696-1690; FAX (415) 696-1699

This 1876 Victorian is "eccentrically, eclectically and very tastefully decorated." This home is truly "San Francisco" and is close to shops and restaurants in popular Pacific Heights. There is a room with private bath, mini-kitchen, and sitting room. In the back garden, there is a guest cottage that affords privacy and opens onto the patio. $80-85.

B&B International #107

P. O. Box 282910, 94128-2910
(415) 696-1690; FAX (415) 696-1699

Four homes all built around the 1920s furnished in antiques and situated near many interesting shops and restaurants on Haight Street. All homes have back decks for guests to enjoy. Situated about 15 minutes from downtown and walking distance to

Golden Gate Park. Ten rooms with all types of bed sizes. All have shared baths. Host prepares breakfast. $50-58.

Bed and Breakfast Los Angeles 14-2

730 Catalina Avenue, Seal Beach, 90740
(310) 493-6837; (800) 383-3513

This private home is located near Lombard and Chestnut streets. Your hostess offers two guest rooms with one bath and full use of her country kitchen. Parking available. Moderate rates.

Bed and Breakfast Los Angeles 14-3

730 Catalina Avenue, Seal Beach, 90740
(310) 493-6837; (800) 383-3513

This old hotel has eighteen rooms, most of which share baths. Continental breakfast is provided, and guests are welcome to use a small kitchen. Suites for 4-6 people also available. Affordable-moderate rates.

Bed and Breakfast Los Angeles 14-5

730 Catalina Avenue, Seal Beach, 90740
(310) 493-6837; (800) 383-3513

This three-story mansion has four guest rooms and two baths, all of which are upstairs. Features include full American breakfast, afternoon wine and munchies, fireplaces, antique furnishings, and off-street parking. Moderate-luxury rates.

Bed and Breakfast Los Angeles 14-6

730 Catalina Avenue, Seal Beach, 90740
(310) 493-6837; (800) 383-3513

NOTES: Credit cards accepted: A Master Card; B Visa; C American Express; D Discover Card; E Diner's Club; F Other; 2 Personal Checks accepted; 3 Lunch available; 4 Dinner available; 5 Open all year;

Secluded on a hill, but close to Golden Gate Park, this cute cottage has twin beds, a fireplace, kitchen and bath, as well as a full view of the city. Hosts require a three-night minimum stay. Moderate rates.

Bed and Breakfast Los Angeles 14-7

730 Catalina Avenue, Seal Beach, 90740
(310) 493-6837; (800) 383-3513

This 1910 Edwardian home is located near the University of California Medical Center and Golden Gate Park, and has four guest rooms which share two baths. Cribs are available. Continental breakfast is served. Affordable rates.

B&B San Francisco #03

P. O. Box 349, 94101
(415) 931-3083; FAX (415) 921-BBSF

The *Peaceful Warrior* is a 75-foot floating bed and breakfast fun and a unique way to be accommodated in San Francisco. The motor yacht has two salons, two staterooms, and two heads (bath). The master stateroom is quite large and has a queen-size bed. The other bedroom has traditional seafaring bunks. The boat is nonhosted, but full breakfast is provided. The location is in the Marina District on the bay half-way between the Golden Gate Bridge and Fisherman's Wharf. The Marina area offers wonderful rerstaurants and shopping. $200-300.

B&B San Francisco #06

P. O. Box 349, 94101
(415) 931-3083; FAX (415) 921-BBSF

One of San Francisco's most beautiful neighborhoods. The homes on Russian Hill offer wonderful views of the bay and Golden Gate Bridge. It's a wonderful walk down the hill to Fisherman's Wharf and North Beach. Cable cars are just one block away. Your host has two guests rooms, both offering a bay view. $75-85.

B&B San Francisco #07

P. O. Box 349, 94101
(415) 931-3083; FAX (415) 921-BBSF

A scenic location in San Francisco with a panoramic view. Three guest rooms, each facing west, allow a lovely sunset view overlooking the Glen Canyon Park with its beautiful eucalyptus grove. Mt. Davidson towers majestically over the canyon in full view from each guest room. Each room has a TV. Two bathrooms for guest use. Breakfast is a gourmet treat. $60.

B&B San Francisco #08

P. O. Box 349, 94101
(415) 931-3083; FAX (415) 921-BBSF

A wonderful warm San Francisco neighborhood. Lots of excellent local shops and restaurants on 24th Street. This lovely bed and breakfast is on the J-Church streetcar line only 20 minutes from downtown. Full breakfast; shared bath. $55.

B&B San Francisco #09

P. O. Box 349, 94101
(415) 931-3083; FAX (415) 921-BBSF

Quiet, spacious, tastefully decorated room with fireplace, fresh flowers, and fruit basket. Breakfast served by the bay window, king-size bed, and TV. Second room has antique double bed. Fisherman's Wharf and cable cars are only two blocks away. Full breakfast; shared bath. $55-60.

B&B San Francisco #11

P. O. Box 349, 94101
(415) 931-3083; FAX (415) 921-BBSF

6 Pets welcome; 7 Smoking allowed; 8 Children welcome; 9 Social drinking allowed; 10 Tennis available; 11 Swimming available; 12 Golf available; 13 Skiing available; 14 May be booked through travel agents.

Pines Mews, a Victorian treasure, sits in San Francisco's most prestigious neighborhood, Pacific Heights. The three accommodations, the Carriage House, the Studio, and the Guest Quarter, have been splendidly restored, and some modern amenities have been added. Full breakfast is provided. $65-$200.

B&B San Francisco #12

P. O. Box 349, 94101
(415) 931-3083; FAX (415) 921-BBSF

Buena Vista Heights offers panoramic views of downtown San Francisco. The Three Bears are three exceptional flats just minutes from the city center. Full breakfast is provided for all three sets of accommodations. $75-200.

B&B San Francisco #13

P. O. Box 349, 94101
(415) 931-3083; FAX (415) 921-BBSF

A new private addition onto a charming old San Francisco home. If you prefer privacy this nonhosted, charming and quiet bed and breakfast is most enjoyable. Large bedroom has a view of North Beach; excellent Italian restaurants in the neighborhood. Fisherman's Wharf and Chinatown are a short walk away. Crib available. Full breakfast. $125; $10-15 extra for children.

B&B San Francisco #18

P. O. Box 349, 94101
(415) 931-3083; FAX (415) 921-BBSF

The quaint town of Larkspur is where this bed and breakfast is located. The hostess offers her guests an entire floor with a livingroom, two bedrooms, bath, and a wonderful private patio. Pool available during the summer months. Muir Woods, Stenson Beach, and the rugged California coast are just a short drive away. Full breakfast. $95-115.

B&B San Francisco #19

P. O. Box 349, 94101
(415) 931-3083; FAX (415) 921-BBSF

The hosts offer San Francisco hospitality in their contemporary Russian Hill home. The quaint, quiet street offers the true flavor of the city, and cable cars, Fisherman's Wharf, and Chinatown are only a short walk away. They offer two guest rooms, one with a queen-size bed, and the other with a pair of twin beds. Both rooms share a full bath. The livingroom has a fireplace. Full breakfast is served. $65-75.

B&B San Francisco #20

P. O. Box 349, 94101
(415) 931-3083; FAX (415) 921-BBSF

High atop charming Russian Hill sits a two-bedroom Victorian flat with a beautiful view of San Francisco Bay. This is a great place for two couples or a family. Off the livingroom is a sunny solarium, a full kitchen, and a bath. One bedroom has a double bed, and the other bedroom offers a queen-size bed. A futon is available. The livingroom has a TV, fireplace, and phone. Cable cars are just around the corner, and the Wharf is just a short distance away. Special rates for stays longer than seven days. $125-$150.

Casa Arguello

225 Arguello Boulevard, 94118
(415) 752-9482

Comfortable rooms in a cheerful, spacious flat ten minutes from the center of town. Situated in a desirable residential neighborhood near Golden Gate Park and the Presidio. Restaurants and shops within walking distance. Excellent public transportation.

Hosts: Emma Baires and Marina McKenzie
Rooms: 5 (3 PB; 2 SB) $52-77
Expanded Continental Breakfast

NOTES: Credit cards accepted: A Master Card; B Visa; C American Express; D Discover Card; E Diner's Club; F Other; 2 Personal Checks accepted; 3 Lunch available; 4 Dinner available; 5 Open all year;

Credit Cards: None
Notes: 2, 5, 8, 9, 10, 11, 12, 14

Casita Blanca

330 Edgehill Way, 94127
(415) 564-9339

Casita Blanca is a guest cottage high on a
hill near Golden Gate Park. A delightful
studio nestled in the trees, it has twin beds,
private bath, and kitchen. Listen to birds
singing or curl up comfortably in front of
the fireplace.

Host: Joan Bard
Room: 1 (PB) $80
Continental Breakfast
Minimum stay: 2 nights
Credit Cards: None
Notes: 2, 5

Chateau Tivoli

1057 Steiner Street, 94115
(415) 776-5462; (800) 228-1647
FAX (415) 776-0505

The Chateau Tivoli is a landmark mansion
that was the residence of the owners of San
Francisco's world-famous Tivoli Opera
House. Guests experience a time-travel
journey back to San Francisco's golden age
of opulence, the 1890s. The chateau is furnished with antiques from Cornelius
Vanderbilt, Charles de Gaulle, J. Paul Getty,
and famous San Francisco madam Sally
Stanford.

Hosts: Rodney Karr and Bill Gersbach
Rooms: 5 (PB) $80-125
Suites: 2 (PB) $160-200
Expanded Continental Breakfast
Credit Cards: A, B, C
Notes: 2, 5, 8, 9, 10, 11, 12, 14

Cornell Hotel—Restaurant Jeanne d'Arc

715 Bush Street, 94108
(415) 421-3154

The Cornell Hotel, a six-story Victorian
under French management, offers elegant
rooms, comfortably appointed and individually decorated. All rooms are non-smoking.

Its restaurant, Jeanne d'Arc, replete with
tapestries, statues, and artifacts provides
fine French-country cuisine. Ideal low Nob
Hill location in the heart of the city.

Host: Claude H. Lambert
Rooms: 50 (40 PB; 10 SB) $60-85
Full Breakfast
Credit Cards: A, B, C, E
Notes: 4, 5, 9, 14

Country Cottage Bed and Breakfast

5 Dolores Terrace, 94110
(415) 479-1913; (800) 452-8249
FAX (415) 921-2273

A cozy country-style bed and breakfast in
the heart of San Francisco. The three guest
rooms are comfortably furnished in antiques
and brass beds. The house is at the end of a
quiet street, away from the city noise. There
is a small patio with trees and birds. A full
breakfast is served in the sunny kitchen.

Hosts: Susan and Richard Kreibich
Rooms: 4 (S2B) $65
Full Breakfast
Credit Cards: A, B, C
Notes: 2, 5, 8, 9, 10, 11, 12, 14

Dolores Park Inn

3641 17th Street, 94114
(415) 621-0482

This 1874 Italianate Victorian inn is in the
sunny part of the city near international
restaurants and transportation. A lush sub-

Casita Blanca

6 Pets welcome; 7 Smoking allowed; 8 Children welcome; 9 Social drinking allowed; 10 Tennis available; 11
Swimming available; 12 Golf available; 13 Skiing available; 14 May be booked through travel agents.

tropical garden and patio with birds and a fountain give this charming and much-photographed home a special flair. Three rooms have fireplaces. A carriage house with eight-foot spa, fireplace, kitchen, and patio is also available. Selected as one of the ten best bed and breakfasts in San Francisco.

Host: Bernie
Rooms: 6 (2 PB; 4 SB) $60-138
Continental or Full Breakfast
Minimum stay weekends and holidays: 2 nights
Credit Cards: A, B
Notes: 2, 5, 7 (limited), 8 (over 12), 9, 10, 14

Eye Openers Bed and Breakfast Reservations SF-A3

P. O. Box 694, Altadena, 91003-0694
(213) 684-4428; (818) 797-2055
FAX (818) 798-3640

Victorian with Old World decor offers friendly hospitality and excellent location in the Marina District. Good public transportation. Continental breakfast. Three guest rooms and studio. Shared and private bath. $60-100, plus tax.

Eye Openers Bed and Breakfast Reservations SF-B1

P. O. Box 694, Altadena, 91003-0694
(213) 684-4428; (818) 797-2055
FAX (818) 798-3640

Unique small cottage to the rear of the host home atop one of San Francisco's highest points near Golden Gate Park has fireplace and kitchen. Continental breakfast is self-catered. Car essential. Minimum stay is three nights. Private bath. $75-85.

Eye Openers Bed and Breakfast Reservations SF-K51

P. O. Box 694, Altadena, 91003-0694
(213) 684-4428; (818) 797-2055
FAX (818) 798-3640

Victorian bed and breakfast features three guest rooms with fireplace, rooftop deck with Jacuzzi, and full breakfast. Excellent location with good transporatation to all tourist attractions and business meetings. Five guest rooms. Private and shared baths. $75-125 plus tax.

Eye Openers Bed and Breakfast Reservations SF-L1

P. O. Box 694, Altadena, 91003-0694
(213) 684-4428; (818) 797-2055
FAX (818) 798-3640

Centrally located Victorian condo is well-decorated with period pieces and offers privacy in lovely surroundings. Continental breakfast. Five guest rooms. Self-hosted apartment. No smoking. $100.

Eye Openers Bed and Breakfast Reservations SF-M1

P. O. Box 694, Altadena, 91003-0694
(213) 684-4428; (818) 797-2055
FAX (818) 798-3640

Upstairs guest room in a well-maintained garden apartment is in a quiet neighborhood three miles from Golden Gate Park, five miles from downtown, and provides a continental-plus breakfast. No smoking. One guest room with shared bath. $45.

NOTES: Credit cards accepted: A Master Card; B Visa; C American Express; D Discover Card; E Diner's Club; F Other; 2 Personal Checks accepted; 3 Lunch available; 4 Dinner available; 5 Open all year;

Eye Openers Bed and Breakfast Reservations SF-M2

P. O. Box 694, Altadena, 91003-0694
(213) 684-4428; (818) 797-2055
FAX (818) 798-3640

1910 vintage Victorians near Golden Gate Park and UC Medical Center offer inexpensive, friendly hospitality. Good public transportation. Continental breakfast. Four guest rooms with shared baths. $39-69 plus tax.

Eye Openers Bed and Breakfast Reservations SF-M301

P. O. Box 694, Altadena, 91003-0694
(213) 684-4428; (818) 797-2055
FAX (818) 798-3640

Four-story Victorian hotel, now a Marina District bed and breakfast inn, features four poster-beds and modern amenities. Continental breakfast. Thirty guest rooms. Private bath. $65-85.

Eye Openers Bed and Breakfast Reservations SF-P261

P. O. Box 694, Altadena, 91003-0694
(213) 684-4428; (818) 797-2055
FAX (818) 798-3640

Sister inns, one French Country and the other formal English, are two blocks from Union Square and offer beautifully appointed rooms, friendly hospitality, afternoon refreshments, and wonderful breakfast. Twenty-six guest rooms. Private bath. $105-195 plus tax.

Eye Openers Bed and Breakfast Reservations SF-P3

P. O. Box 694, Altadena, 91003-0694
(213) 684-4428; (818) 797-2055
FAX (818) 798-3640

Hilltop home in Diamond Heights area has glorious view of the bay and city from the two-story livingroom. Enjoy a full breakfast in the Scandanavian furnished dining area. Each of three guest rooms has a balcony. Two shared bath. $35-45

The Golden Gate Hotel

775 Bush Street, 94108
(415) 392-3702; (800) 835-1118

The ambience, location, and price make the Golden Gate Hotel an extraordinary find in the heart of San Francisco. Dedicated to a high standard of quality and personal attention, the hosts keep fresh flowers in all the rooms, and the continental breakfast includes fresh croissants and the city's strongest coffee.

Hosts: John and Renate Kenaston
Rooms: 23 (14 PB; 9 SB) $55-89
Continental Breakfast
Credit Cards: A, B, C, E, F
Notes: 2 (prior arrangement),
5, 6 (prior arrangement), 7, 8, 9, 10, 11, 12, 14

The Grove Inn

890 Grove Street, 94117
(415) 929-0780; (800) 829-0780

The Grove Inn is a charming, intimate, and affordable bed and breakfast. Centrally situated and convenient to public transportation, it has two suites for the convenience of families with children. The owners and managers are always available for information, help in renting cars, booking shuttles to the airport, and city tours.

6 Pets welcome; 7 Smoking allowed; 8 Children welcome; 9 Social drinking allowed; 10 Tennis available; 11 Swimming available; 12 Golf available; 13 Skiing available; 14 May be booked through travel agents.

Hosts: Klaus and Rosetta Zimmermann
Rooms: 18 (14 PB; 4 SB) $45-65
Continental Breakfast
Credit Cards: A, B, C
Closed December
Notes: 2, 5, 8, 9, 10, 11, 12, 14

The Inn San Francisco

943 South Van Ness Avenue, 94110
(415) 641-0188; (800) 359-0913

Restored historic Italianate Victorian mansion, circa 1872. Ornate woodwork, Oriental carpets, marble fireplaces, and period antiques, combined with modern hotel conveniences. Relax in the redwood hot tub in the garden or reserve a room with a private spa tub—the perfect romantic escape!

Hosts: Marty Neely and Connie Wu
Rooms: 22 (17 PB; 5 SB) $75-170
Expanded Continental Breakfast
Minimum stay weekends and holidays: 2-4 nights
Credit Cards: A, B, C, D, E, F
Notes: 2, 5, 7 (limited), 8, 10, 11, 12, 14

The Inn San Francisco

Kids Welcome 14-1

730 Catalina Avenue, Seal Beach, 90740
(310) 493-6837; (800) 383-3513

Walk to Golden Gate Park from this three-story Victorian that is geared toward traveling families. Two guest rooms share one bath on each floor. Full breakfast is provided, and guests are welcome to use the kitchen, fireplace, and even the playpen. Host's teenage daughter is willing to babysit. Family rates are available. Moderate rates.

Kids Welcome 14-5

730 Catalina Avenue, Seal Beach, 90740
(310) 493-6837; (800) 383-3513

This 1920 Edwardian home is located near the University of California Medical Center and Golden Gate Park. Four guest rooms which share two baths are available. Cribs are also available. Continental breakfast is self-serve. Affordable rates.

Kids Welcome 14-4

730 Catalina Avenue, Seal Beach, 90740
(310) 493-6837; (800) 383-3513

Your hostess offers two guest rooms, one with twin beds, and the other a queen. Bath between the two is shared. Located on Knob Hill in San Francisco, Chinatown is only three blocks away. Moderate-luxury rates.

The Mansions Hotel

2220 Sacramento Street, 94115
(415) 929-9444

Two connected historic mansions in San Francisco's most prestigious neighborhood, Pacific Heights. Hideaway for the stars, guests have included Barbra Striesand, Eddie Fisher, Andre Sakharov, and others. Rates include sumptuous breakfast, fresh

---

NOTES: Credit cards accepted: A Master Card; B Visa; C American Express; D Discover Card; E Diner's Club; F Other; 2 Personal Checks accepted; 3 Lunch available; 4 Dinner available; 5 Open all year;

flowers, nightly concerts, sculpture gardens, billiard room. "Elegance to the Nth degree"—*San Francisco Examiner*. "Marvelous hospitality" —Barbra Striesand.

Host: Bob Pritikin
Rooms: 29 (PB) $89-225
Full Breakfast
Credit Cards: All major
Notes: 2, 3, 4, 5, 6, 7, 8, 9, 10, 11, 12, 14

Monica and Ed Widburg

2007 15th Avenue, 94116
(415) 564-1751

This charming home in a quiet residential area has an ocean view and ample parking. There is one bed and breakfast room, but for groups up to four guests, additional accommodations are available in an adjacent room. Queen beds in both rooms. The park, museums, and zoo are close by. Public transportation is easily available to downtown and Fisherman's Wharf. Reservations required.

Hosts: Monica and Ed Widburg
Room: 1 (PB) $65
Full Breakfast
Credit Cards: None
Notes: 2, 5, 10, 11, 12

The Monte Cristo

600 Presidio Avenue, 94115
(415) 931-1875

The elegantly restored Monte Cristo was originally built in 1875 as a saloon and hotel. It has served as a bordello, a refuge after the 1906 earthquake, and a speakeasy. Only two blocks from Victorian shops, restaurants, and antique stores on Sacramento Street; ten minutes to any other point in the city.

Host: George
Rooms: 14 (11 PB; 3 SB) $63-108
Expanded Breakfast
Minimum stay weekends and holidays: 2-3 nights
Credit Cards: A, B, C, D, E
Notes: 5, 7, 8, 14

No Name Victorian Bed and Breakfast

847 Fillmore Street, 94117
(800) 452-8249; (415) 479-1913
FAX (415) 921-2273

Situated in one of the most photographed areas of San Francisco, the historic district of Alamo Square, the No Name bed and breakfast is close to the civic center, opera house, Davies Symphony Hall, Union Square, and all the sights that make the city famous. In the evening, help yourself to wine and relax in the hot tub where many a guest has had a surpise visit from the neighborhood resident, Nosey the Raccoon. Three of the guest rooms have fireplaces.

Hosts: Susan and Richard Kreibich
Rooms: 5 (3 PB; 2 SB) $75-85
Full Breakfast
Credit Cards: A, B, C
Notes: 2, 5, 8, 9, 10, 11, 12, 14

Petite Auberge

6 Pets welcome; 7 Smoking allowed; 8 Children welcome; 9 Social drinking allowed; 10 Tennis available; 11 Swimming available; 12 Golf available; 13 Skiing available; 14 May be booked through travel agents.

Petite Auberge

863 Bush Street, 94108
(415) 928-6000

A French country inn in the heart of San Francisco. Each room is individually decorated; many have fireplaces. Guests enjoy a full buffet breakfast, afternoon wine and hors d'oeuvres, valet parking, fresh fruit, and homemade cookies. Truly romantic.

Host: Rich Revaz
Rooms: 26 (PB) $116.55-172
Full Breakfast
Credit Cards: A, B, C
Notes: 2, 5, 7 (limited), 8, 9, 10, 12, 14

The Queen Anne Hotel

1590 Sutler Street, 94109
(415) 441-2828

An 1890 landmark that has been beautifully restored with 49 individually designed rooms and suites, many of which include bay windows, fireplaces, and turn-of-the-century antiques. The Queen Anne Hotel is centrally located on the corner of Sutter and Octavia streets in lower Pacific Heights. Easy access to downtown, civic center, and Fisherman's Wharf. Complimentary continental breakfast, morning limousine to downtown (Monday through Friday), and nightly tea and sherry are only a few of the amenities provided.

Hosts: Stephen Galvan
Rooms: 49 (PB) $99-175
Expanded Continental Breakfast
Credit Cards: A, B, C, D, E
Notes: 2, 5, 8, 14

Red Victorian Bed and Breakfast Inn

1665 Haight Street, 94117
(415) 861-7264

Built at the turn of the century as a country resort hotel serving nearby Golden Gate Park, the Red Victorian enjoys an international clientele of globally minded people. From the aquarium bathroom to the Redwood Forest Room to the Peace Gallery where breakfast is served among Transformational paintings, the Red Victorian exudes color and joy.

Host: Sami Sunchild
Suite: 1 (PB) $135
Rooms: 13 (3 PB; 10 SB) $55-100
Expanded Continental Breakfast
Credit Cards: A, B, C
Notes: 2, 5, 10, 11, 12, 14

Stanyan Park Hotel

750 Stanyan Street, 94117
(415) 751-1000

A fully restored Victorian hotel on the east border of Golden Gate Park at the geographical center of San Francisco and listed on the National Register of Historic Places. Walk to the Japanese Tea Garden, DeYoung Museum, and more. Enjoy a complimentary continental breakfast each morning and coffee, teas, and cookies each evening in the dining room. All rooms have color TV's, direct-dial phones, and private baths. Excellent public transit.

Host: Brad Bihlmeyer
Rooms: 36 (PB) $78-100 rooms; suites $125-170
Continental Breakfast
Credit Cards: A, B, C, D, E
Notes: 5, 7, 8, 9, 10, 12, 14

Victorian Inn on the Park

301 Lyon Street, 94117
(415) 931-1830; (800) 435-1967

Queen Anne Victorian situated near Golden Gate Park and decorated with Victorian antiques. Many rooms have fireplaces, and the Belvedere Room features a private balcony overlooking the park. The inn features fireplaces, dining room with oak paneling, and a parlor with fireplace. Complimentary wine served nightly; freshly baked breads daily.

Hosts: Lisa and William Benau
Rooms: 12 (PB) $88-144
Expanded Continental Breakfast
Credit Cards: A, B, C, D, E
Notes: 2, 5, 7, 8, 9, 10, 11, 12, 14

NOTES: Credit cards accepted: A Master Card; B Visa; C American Express; D Discover Card; E Diner's Club; F Other; 2 Personal Checks accepted; 3 Lunch available; 4 Dinner available; 5 Open all year;

The Washington Square Inn

1660 Stockton Street, 94114
(415) 981-4220; (800) 388-0220
FAX (415) 397-7242

The Washington Square Inn is in the heart of San Francisco's historic North Beach area just one block from Telegraph Hill. Continental breakfast, afternoon tea, wine and hors d'oeuvres are served. With only 15 rooms, the inn is special for those who care about quiet and comfort with dashes of elegance. The staff has time to concentrate on the guests' individual needs and wants. No smoking.

Host: Brooks Bayly
Rooms: 15 (10 PB; 5 SB) $85-180
Continental Breakfast
Credit Cards: A, B, C
Notes: 2, 5, 8, 9, 14

White Swan Inn

845 Bush Street, 94108
(415) 775-1755

In the heart of San Francisco, a bit of London resides. Each oversize guest room has a fireplace, wet bar, sitting area, color TV, radio, bathrobes, fresh fruit, and soft drinks. Enjoy a full breakfast, afternoon wine and hors d'oeuvres, newspaper, valet parking, concierge, laundry, FAX machine, livingroom, library, and gracious service.

Host: Rich Revaz
Rooms: 26 (PB) $161-177.60
Full Breakfast
Credit Cards: A, B, C
Notes: 2, 5, 7 (limited), 8, 9, 10, 12, 14

SAN GREGORIO

Rancho San Gregorio

5086 San Gregorio Road, P. O. Box 21, 94074
(415) 747-0722

Five miles inland from the Pacific off Highway 1 in a rural valley, Rancho San Gregorio welcomes travelers to share relaxed hospitality. This country getaway has 15 acres, an old barn, creek, gardens, decks, and gazebo. Full country breakfast features home-grown specialities. Forty-five minutes from San Francisco, Santa Cruz, and the bay area.

Hosts: Bud and Lee Raynor
Rooms: 4 (PB) $65-125
Full Breakfast
Credit Cards: A, B, C
Notes: 2, 5, 7 (limited), 8, 9, 14

White Swan Inn

SAN LUIS

Bed and Breakfast Los Angeles 12-1

730 Catalina Avenue, Seal Beach, 90740
(310) 493-6837; (800) 383-3513

This little adobe inn in San Luis emphasizes family service. The rooms have small alcove beds, and a full breakfast includes cereals, muffins, juice, and hot dishes. Your hostess can point out two parks within walking distance, and the children's zoo, children's aquarium, and children's museum are not far. Affordable-moderate rates.

Bed and Breakfast
Los Angeles 12-3

730 Catalina Avenue, Seal Beach, 90740
(310) 493-6837; (800) 383-3513

Just north of San Luis, this ranch has 800 acres of hiking trails and streams meandering among the oak and pine. Wild herbs and vegetables abound, as do quail, rabbits, deer, and eagles. Your hosts have four rooms, two with private baths. Hosts also have horses for rent and suggest the moonlight trail ride. Moderate rates.

SAN LUIS OBISPO- SEE ALSO ARROYO GRANDE

Eye Openers Bed and
Breakfast Reservations
LO-03

P. O. Box 694, Altadena, 91003-0694
(213) 684-4428; (818) 797-2055
FAX (818) 798-3640

Well-traveled, multilingual host offers comfortable accommodations. Livingroom has a view of Morro Rock. Delicious breakfast. No smoking. Three guest rooms. Shared and private bath. $32-50, plus tax.

Eye Openers Bed and
Breakfast Reservations
PB-S301

P. O. Box 694, Altadena, 91003-0694
(213) 684-4428; (818) 797-2055
FAX (818) 798-3640

Contemporary inn on the beach in the midst of twenty-three miles of unspoiled sand and surf. Continental breakfast delivered to your room. Twenty-five guest rooms. Private bath. $65-165 plus tax.

Eye Openers Bed and
Breakfast Reservations
SL-G131

P. O. Box 694, Altadena, 91003-0694
(213) 684-4428; (818) 797-2055
FAX (818) 798-3640

This 1887 Italianate Queen Anne Victorian recently restored to its orginal splendor is an elegant and friendly bed and breakfast. Full breakfast served. Close to the beaches and attractions of the Central Coast. Nine guest rooms and four suites. Private bath. No smoking. $80-160, plus tax.

Garden Street Inn

1212 Garden Street, 93401
(805) 545-9802

The grace and simplicity of yesteryear prevail at the 1887 Italianate Queen Anne home situated one block from a 1772 mission and the old-fashioned downtown in one of the nation's celebrated California communities. Classic Victorian decor in nine guest rooms and four suites appointed with antiques, fireplaces, Jacuzzis, and historical , cultural, and personal memorabilia. Homemade full breakfast, spacious outside decks, and well-stocked library. Close to Hearst Castle, Pismo Beach, Morro Bay, and Cambria.

Hosts: Dan and Kathy Smith
Rooms: 9 and 4 suites (PB) $90-160
Full Breakfast
Credit Cards: A, B, C
Notes: 2, 5, 9, 10, 11, 12, 14

SAN MIGUEL

Bed and Breakfast
Los Angeles 12-4

730 Catalina Avenue, Seal Beach, 90740
(310) 493-6837; (800) 383-3513

This five-bedroom mansion is located on a Morgan horse ranch. One room has a private bath, and the other four share a bath. Game room with a pool table, a library, and a yummy breakfast. Affordable rates.

SAN RAFAEL

Casa Soldavini

531 C Street, 94901
(415) 454-3140

A charming 1932 Spanish home filled with many family antqiues. Quiet and relaxing, within walking distance of the mission, museums, parks, shopping, and recreation. Each room uniquely decorated and private. Large sitting room with piano, TV, VCR, and library. Hearty, scrumptious home-made breakfasts, afternoon tea, and snacks daily. Front porch swing. Minutes from San Francisco, beaches and redwoods, and wineries. Bicycles and picnic baskets.

Hosts: Dan Cassidy and Linda Soldavini
Rooms: 3 (1 PB; 2 SB) $65-75
Expanded Continental Breakfast
Credit Cards: None
Notes: 2, 5, 6 (limited), 9, 10, 14

SANTA ANA

America's B&B #15

P. O. Box 9302, Whittier, 90608
(310) 699-8427

Two-story Craftsman-style home, redecorated in the style of the era and furnished with American and Danish antiques. Near Disneyland, Knott's Berry Farm, South Coast Plaza, and Bowers Museum, it features two large first-floor rooms with shared bath. $60.

Bed and Breakfast Los Angeles 7-3

730 Catalina Avenue, Seal Beach, 90740
(310) 493-6837; (800) 383-3513

This marvelous Craftsman home has spacious rooms, elegant decor, patio, and pool. The two upstairs guest rooms share a bath in the hall. Moderate rates.

SANTA BARBARA

Bath Street Inn

1720 Bath Street, 93101
(805) 682-9680; (800) 788-2284

An 1873 Queen Anne Victorian in the heart of historic Santa Barbara. Scenic downtown is within walking distance. Rooms have views, balconies, and private baths. Breakfast is served in the dining room or garden; bikes are available; evening refreshments.

Host: Susan Brown
Rooms: 8 (PB) $90-125
Full Breakfast
Credit Cards: A, B, C
Notes: 2, 5, 8, 9, 10, 11, 12, 14

Bed and Breakfast Los Angeles 11-4

730 Catalina Avenue, Seal Beach, 90740
(310) 493-6837; (800) 383-3513

Set among the ancient oaks, this private little bed and breakfast has one cottage (bedroom, livingroom with roll-away bed, small bath, and refrigerator), and two guest rooms in the main house (one with a sitting room, fridge, and private bath). Guests are provided with lots of goodies for self-catered breakfast. Walk to the Mission, Botanical Gardens, and Natural History Museum. Affordable rates.

Bed and Breakfast at Valli's View

340 North Sierra Vista, 93108
(805) 969-1272

6 Pets welcome; 7 Smoking allowed; 8 Children welcome; 9 Social drinking allowed; 10 Tennis available; 11 Swimming available; 12 Golf available; 13 Skiing available; 14 May be booked through travel agents.

Just three miles from the center of Santa Barbara in the Montecito foothills, this lovely private home, with its garden setting, deck, patios, and ever-changing mountain views, has an ambience of tranquility and comfort. Enjoy lounges for sunning, a porch swing for relaxing, and all nearby tourist attractions. In the evening, enjoy a cup of cafe mocha or a glass of wine in the spacious livingroom that overlooks the mountains.

Hosts: Valli and Larry Stevens
Rooms: 3 (PB) $55-100
Full Breakfast
Minimum stay weekends: 2 nights
Credit Cards: None
Notes: 2, 5, 6 (outside), 7 (outside), 8, 9, 10, 11, 12, 14

Bed and Breakfast Los Angeles 11-2

730 Catalina Avenue, Seal Beach, 90740
(310) 493-6837; (800) 383-3513

On a perfect hill in Santa Barbara, this little bed and breakfast features one spacious guest room with room for a daybed, two decks, a porch swing, a fireplace, and a grand piano. Hosts will pick you up at the train station or airport, and they pride themselves on turning strangers into friends. Moderate rates.

Blue Quail Inn and Cottages

1908 Bath Street, 93101
(805) 687-2300; (800) 549-1622 CA
(800) 676-1622 US

Relax and enjoy the quiet country atmosphere of the Blue Quail Inn and Cottages, just three blocks to Sansum Clinic and Cottage Hospital. Linger over a delicious full breakfast including home-baked goods served on the patio or in the main house dining room. Take a picnic lunch for your day of adventure on the inn's bicycles, then return for afternoon wine and light hors d'oeuvres. Sip hot spiced apple cider in the evening before enjoying a restful sleep in your cottage, suite, or guest room.

Host: Jeanise Suding Eaton
Rooms: 9 (7 PB; 2 SB) $73.80-165
Full Breakfast
Credit Cards: A, B, C
Closed Dec. 24-25
Notes: 2, 9, 10, 11, 12, 14

Cheshire Cat Inn

36 West Valerio Street, 93101
(805) 569-1610

Victorian elegance in a Southern California seaside village. The Cheshire Cat is conveniently situated near theaters, restaurants, and shops. Decorated exclusively in Laura Ashley papers and linens, the sunny guest rooms have private baths; some with fireplaces, spas, balconies. Collectibles, English antiques, and fresh flowers enhance your stay in beautiful Santa Barbara.

Hosts: Christine Dunstan and Midge Goeden
Rooms: 14 (PB) $79-249
Full Breakfast
Credit Cards: A, B
Notes: 2, 5, 7 (outside), 9, 10, 11, 12, 14

Eye Openers Bed and Breakfast Reservations SB-B1

P. O. Box 694, Altadena, 91003-0694
(213) 684-4428; (818) 797-2055
FAX (818) 798-3640

Centrally located and filled with country charm, this inn beautiful grounds that provide a feeling of seclusion. Delicious full breakfast and evening refreshments. Bicycles available. No smoking. Eight rooms. Private and shared bath. $82-120 plus tax.

Eye Openers Bed and Breakfast Reservations SB-R1

P. O. Box 694, Altadena, 91003-0694
(213) 684-4428; (818) 797-2055
FAX (818) 798-3640

NOTES: Credit cards accepted: A Master Card; B Visa; C American Express; D Discover Card; E Diner's Club; F Other; 2 Personal Checks accepted; 3 Lunch available; 4 Dinner available; 5 Open all year;

Architect-designed contemporary home is nestled among oaks near Santa Barbara Mission and five minutes to the beach and shopping. Choice of full or continental breakfast. One room. Private bath. No smoking. $45-50.

Eye Openers Bed and Breakfast Reservations SB-C110

P. O. Box 694, Altadena, 91003-0694
(213) 684-4428; (818) 797-2055
FAX (818) 798-3640

Luxurious Victorian inn with a wide choice of uniquely decorated guest rooms is centrally located and offers and excellent breakfast. No smoking. Eleven rooms. Private bath. $108-150 plus tax.

Eye Openers Bed and Breakfast Reservations SB-H91

P. O. Box 694, Altadena, 91003-0694
(213) 684-4428; (818) 797-2055
FAX (818) 798-3640

Located near the beach, this elegant inn is decorated with French and English antiques and has a country feeling. Full breakfast and afternoon tea. Nine rooms. Private bath. $85-105, plus tax.

Eye Openers Bed and Breakfast Reservations SB-O61

P. O. Box 694, Altadena, 91003-0694
(213) 684-4428; (818) 797-2055
FAX (818) 798-3640

Delcious, elegant breakfast, comfortable rooms, and friendly hospitality are found at this conveniently located inn near beaches and Mission. 1904 Craftsman-style bunga-

low with individually decorated rooms, several with private decks. Beach towels and chairs provided. Six rooms and one guest cottage. Private bath. $85-120 plus tax.

Eye Openers Bed and Breakfast Reservations SB-R51

P. O. Box 694, Altadena, 91003-0694
(213) 684-4428; (818) 797-2055
FAX (818) 798-3640

This 1886 restored Victorian inn decorated with antiques is close to Mission and shops. Continental breakfast with homemade breads. Bikes available. Five guest rooms. Private and shared baths. No smoking. $75-100, plus tax.

Harbour Carriage House

420 West Montecito, 93101
(805) 962-8447

A renovated 1895 house, tastefully decorated in French and English antiques. Breakfast is served in the sunny solarium, and evening refreshments are served fireside. Two blocks from the harbor, the house adjoins the gardens of two historic homes.

Host: Kimberly Pegram
Rooms: 9 (PB) $76.50-175
Full Breakfast
Credit Cards: A, B, C
Closed Dec. 24-25
Notes: 2, 8, 9, 10, 11, 12, 14

Long's Seaview Bed and Breakfast

317 Piedmont Road, 93105
(805) 687-2947

Overlooking the ocean and Channel Islands. Situated in quiet neighborhood of lovely homes. Breakfast usually served on huge patio. Convenient to beach, Solvang,

6 Pets welcome; 7 Smoking allowed; 8 Children welcome; 9 Social drinking allowed; 10 Tennis available; 11 Swimming available; 12 Golf available; 13 Skiing available; 14 May be booked through travel agents.

and all area attractions. Large bedroom furnished with antiques and a king-size bed. Private entrance, private bath. Local information and maps provided. No smoking.

Host: LaVerne Long
Room: 1 (PB) $70-75
Full Breakfast
Credit Cards: None
Notes: 2, 5

Montecito Inn

1295 Coast Village Road, 93108
(805) 969-7854; (800) 843-2017

Quiet elegance with a touch of European charm in seaside community of Montecito. Two blocks from the beach, the inn has 52 Provincial-style rooms and suites with floral prints, hand-painted tiles, and ceiling fans. Complimentary continental breakfast, room service available. Heated outdoor pool, spa, sauna, and exercise room. Free sightseeing trolley passes and use of touring bicycles. Charlie Chaplin video library, cable TV with Showtime. New conference facility. Valet parking.

Host: Linda Davis
Rooms: 52 (PB) $95-245
Continental Breakfast
Credit Cards: A, B, C, D, E
Notes: 2, 3, 4, 5, 7, 8, 9, 11, 14

Ocean View House

Box 20065, 93102
(805) 966-6659

A wonderful location in Santa Barbara in a quiet, private home within walking distance of the ocean. Two rooms with antique charm, TV, interesting books, and collections. Oranges, apples, and melons are presented from the garden with breakfast on the patio.

Host: Carolyn Canfield
Rooms: 2 (PB) $50
Expanded Continental Breakfast
Credit Cards: None
Notes: 2, 5, 6, 8, 9, 10, 11, 12, 14

Old Mission House

435 East Pedregosa, 93103
(805) 569-1914

This is a Craftsman house built in 1895 with fireplaces in all rooms. Within walking distance of the Santa Barbara Mission, parks, downtown stores, museums, and ten minutes by car to the beach.

Host: Marie Miller
Rooms: 3 (1 PB; 2 SB) $45-65
Continental Breakfast
Credit Cards: None
Notes: 2, 5, 8, 9, 10, 11, 12

The Old Yacht Club Inn

431 Corona Del Mar Drive, 93103
(805) 962-1277; (800) 549-1676 (CA)
(800) 676-1676 (US)

The Old Yacht Club Inn has nine guest rooms in two houses: a 1912 California Craftsman and a 1920s Early California-style building. The inn opened as Santa Barbara's first bed and breakfast in 1980 and is now world-renowned for its hospitality and warmth in comfortable surroundings, and for its fine food. The inn is within a block of the beach and close to tennis, swimming, boating, fishing, and golf. Bikes and beach chairs available.

Hosts: Nancy Donaldson, Lu Caruso, Sandy Hunt
Rooms: 9 (PB) $65-145
Full Breakfast
Credit Cards: A, B, C, D
Notes: 2, 3 (picnic baskets), 4 (Sat.), 5, 8, 12, 14

The Olive House

1604 Olive Street, 93101
(805) 962-4902; (800) 786-6422

Enjoy quiet comfort and gracious hospitality in a lovingly restored 1904 Craftsman-style house replete with redwood paneling, bay windows, window seats, coffered ceilings, and a fireplace in the livingroom. Richly refurbished in 1990. Breakfast is served in the large, sunny dining room that also houses a studio grand piano. Enjoy mountain and ocean views from the sun deck and several guest rooms.

NOTES: Credit cards accepted: A Master Card; B Visa; C American Express; D Discover Card; E Diner's Club; F Other; 2 Personal Checks accepted; 3 Lunch available; 4 Dinner available; 5 Open all year;

Hosts: Lois Gregg
Rooms: 6 (PB) $85-125
Expanded Continental Breakfast
Credit Cards: A, B
Notes: 2, 5, 10, 11, 12, 14

The Parsonage Bed and Breakfast Inn

1600 Olive Street, 93101
(805) 962-9336

Charming 1892 Victorian, furnished beautifully with antiques and oriental rugs, is centrally situated within walking distance of the mission, shops, restaurants, and theatres. Romantic honeymoon suite with city and ocean views is available, and enjoy your breakfast on the spacious sun deck with its cozy gazebo.

Host: Holli Harmon
Rooms: 6 (PB) $85-165
Full Breakfast
Credit Cards: A, B, C
Notes: 2, 5, 9, 10, 11, 12, 14

Simpson House Inn

121 East Arrellaga, 93101
(805) 963-7067; (800) 676-1280

Elegant 1874 Victorian home, secluded on an acre of English gardens, only a five-minute walk to downtwon historic sights, theaters, restaurants, and shops. Furnished with antiques, fine art, Oriental carpets, and English lace. Complimentary wine and bikes.

Hosts: Gillean Wilson; Glyn and Linda Davies
Rooms: 10 (PB) $85-200
Full Breakfast
Minimum stay weekends and holidays: 2 nights
Credit Cards: A, B, D
Notes: 2, 5, 7 (limited), 9, 10, 11, 12, 14

The Upham Hotel and Garden Cottages

1404 De la Vina Street, 93101
(800) 727-0876

Established in 1871, this beautifully restored Victorian hotel is situated on an acre of gardens. Guest rooms and suites are decorated with period furnishings and antiques. Continental breakfast and afternoon wine and cheese. Walk to museums, galleries, historic attractions, shops, and restaurants in downtown Santa Barbara.

Host: Jan Martin Winn
Rooms: 49 (PB) $110-300
Continental Breakfast
Credit Cards: A, B, C, D, E, F
Notes: 3, 4, 5, 7, 8, 9, 10, 11, 12, 14

The Villa Rosa

15 Chapala Street, 93101
(805) 966-0851

The Villa Rosa is a classic Spanish-style, 18-room inn completely renovated. Beautifully situated in Santa Barbara only one-half block from the beach, Stearns Wharf, shops and restaurants. The Villa Rosa exudes the warmth of a bed and breakfast with the professionalism and services of a sophisticated hotel, combining such niceties as 24-hour service and the Los Angeles Times at your door each morning with roses on your pillow at night.

Host: Beverly Kirkhart
Rooms: 18 (PB) $80-190 seasonal
Continental Breakfast
Credit Cards: A, B, C
Notes: 5, 7, 9, 11, 14

SANTA CLARA

Bed and Breakfast Los Angeles 13-7

730 Catalina Avenue, Seal Beach, 90740
(310) 493-6837; (800) 383-3513

There are six guest rooms at this 1895 Queen Anne-style mansion, four with private baths. Hosts serve a full breakfast and own a film library. Moderate rates.

Madison Street Inn

1390 Madison Street, 95050
(408) 249-5541; (800) 249-5541

6 Pets welcome; 7 Smoking allowed; 8 Children welcome; 9 Social drinking allowed; 10 Tennis available; 11 Swimming available; 12 Golf available; 13 Skiing available; 14 May be booked through travel agents.

Just ten minutes from San Jose airport and five minutes from Santa Clara University, this elegant Victorian sits peacefully in the heart of Silicon Valley. Telephones in rooms.

Hosts: Ralph and Theresa Wigginton
Rooms: 7 (3 PB; 4 SB) $55-75
Full Breakfast
Credit Cards: A, B, C, E
Notes: 2, 5, 8, 9, 10, 11, 12, 14

SANTA CRUZ

Babbling Brook Inn

1025 Laurel Street, 95060
(408) 427-2437; (800) 866-1131
FAX (408) 427-2457

Waterfalls and a meanderring brook are in the gardens of this 12-room inn with French decor. Each room has a private bath, telephone, TV, fireplace, private deck, private entrance. Two have deep soaking bathtubs. Walk to beaches, the boardwalk, a garden mall, or tennis. Full breakfast and complimentary wine and cheese. Romantic garden gazebo for weddings.

Host: Helen King
Rooms: 12 (PB) $85-135
Full Breakfast
Minimum stay weekends: 2 nights
Credit Cards: A, B, C, D, E
Notes: 2, 5, 8 (over 12), 9, 10, 11, 12, 14

Bed and Breakfast Los Angeles 13-6

730 Catalina Avenue, Seal Beach, 90740
(310) 493-6837; (800) 383-3513

This beautiful mansion overlooks the ocean. Eight rooms, most with semi-private baths, are filled with unusual antiques and artwork. Guests can busy themselves by the great room fireplace, visit the Boardwalk, or walk through the redwoods. Moderate rates.

B&B San Francisco #21

P. O. Box 349, San Francisco, 94101
(415) 931-3083; FAX (415) 921-BBSF

This Frank Lloyd Wright-designed home is in the beautiful Santa Cruz mountains only seven miles from the popular Santa Cruz beach. One bedroom has a moutain view, private entrance, and private bath. Another bedroom has mountain view and shared bath. Full breakfast. Minimum stay is three nights. $65-75.

Chateau Victorian, A Bed and Breakfast Inn

118 First Street, 95060
(408) 458-9458

Chateau Victorian was built in the 1880s only one block from the beach and Monterey Bay as a family home. Opened in June 1983 as an elegant bed and breakfast inn, each room features a private bathroom, fireplace, queen-size bed, carpeting, and an individual heating system. Each room is furnished in Victorian style. Chateau Victorian is within walking distance to downtown, the municipal wharf, the Boardwalk amusement park, and fine dining.

Hosts: Franz and Alice-June Benjamin
Rooms: 7 (PB) $100-130
Expanded Continental Breakfast
Credit Cards: A, B, C
Notes: 2, 5, 9

The Darling House– A Bed and Breakfast Inn by the Sea

314 West Cliff Drive, 95060
(408) 458-1958

A 1910 oceanside architectural masterpiece designed by William Weeks, lighted by the rising sun through beveled glass, Tiffany lamps, and open hearths. The spacious lawns, rose gardens, citrus orchard, towering palms, and expansive ocean view verandas create colorful California splendor. Stroll to secluded beaches, lighthouse, wharf, and boardwalk. Soak in the hot tub spa, and fall asleep securely to the serenade of seals and surf.

NOTES: Credit cards accepted: A Master Card; B Visa; C American Express; D Discover Card; E Diner's Club; F Other; 2 Personal Checks accepted; 3 Lunch available; 4 Dinner available; 5 Open all year;

Hosts: Darrell and Karen Darling
Rooms: 8 (2-PB; 6-SB) $85-225
Expanded Continental Breakfast
Credit Cards: A, B, C, D
Notes: 2, 5, 8, 9, 10, 11, 12, 14

Jasmine Cottage

731 Riverside Avenue, 95060
(408) 429-1415

Charming and centrally located home with
all amenities, private entrance, and fresh
foods cooked to individual taste. King and
twin beds, private bath. Deposit required to
confirm booking.

Host: Dorothy Allen
Room: 1 (PB) $35-60
Full Breakfast
Credit Cards: None
Notes: 2, 5

Valley View

Box 66593, 95067
(415) 321-5195; FAX (415) 325-5121

Magnificent forest/glass house with hot spa
on the large deck that overlooks the 20,000-
acre redwood valley below. Barbecue,
stereo, cable TV, beautiful stone fireplace,
piano. Unhosted for total privacy. Very
peaceful. Only ten minutes to beaches.

Hosts: Scott and Tricia Young
Rooms: 2 (PB) $110
Full Breakfast
Credit Cards: A, B, C, E
Notes: 2, 5, 8 (over 12), 9, 10, 11, 12, 14

SANTA MONICA

B&B International #502

P. O. Box 282910, San Francisco, 94128-2910
(415) 696-1690; FAX (415) 696-1699

Designer-built addition with a deck on the
second floor of a renovated 1920 California
bungalow. Contemporary furnishings in
blue and white and natural wood. Close to
the Venice boardwalk and one mile to
Santa Monica pier, two blocks to the beach.
Beach chairs, equipment, and towels are
available. $75.

Bed and Breakfast Los Angeles 4-3

730 Catalina Avenue, Seal Beach, 90740
(310) 493-6837; (800) 383-3513

Fully restored apartments include private
baths and kitchens. Elegant decor, and only
a block to the beach and Main Street.
Luxury rates.

Bed and Breakfast Los Angeles 4-4

730 Catalina Avenue, Seal Beach, 90740
(310) 493-6837; (800) 383-3513

This sunny studio apartment looks out onto
the ocean in Santa Monica. Walk to the
shops or borrow the owner's bikes.
Moderate rates.

Bed and Breakfast Los Angeles 4-6

730 Catalina Avenue, Seal Beach, 90740
(310) 493-6837; (800) 383-3513

This perfectly restored Santa Monica mnan-
sion has fourteen guest rooms, all with prio-
vate baths and phones. Features include
ocean views, a hilltop spa, continental
breakfast, and afternoon goodies. Handicapped facilities available. Luxury rates.

6 Pets welcome; 7 Smoking allowed; 8 Children welcome; 9 Social drinking allowed; 10 Tennis available; 11
Swimming available; 12 Golf available; 13 Skiing available; 14 May be booked through travel agents.

Channel Road Inn

219 West Channel Road, 90402
(310) 459-1920

Elegant inn one block from the beach in Santa Monica. "One of the most romantic places in Los Angeles"—*LA* magazine. Views and bicycles. Two miles from the J. Paul Getty Museum.

Hosts: Kathy Jensen and Susan Zolla
Rooms: 14 (PB) $85-195
Full Breakfast
Credit Cards: A, B
Notes: 2, 5, 8, 9, 10, 11, 12, 14

Eye Openers Bed and Breakfast Reservations SM-H1

P. O. Box 694, Altadena, 91003-0694
(213) 684-4428; (818) 797-2055
FAX (818) 798-3640

Economically priced bed and breakfast in Santa Monica offers large guest room. Hosts have interesting collection of folk instruments and a large library. Good public transportation nearby. Continental breakfast. Resident cat and dog. Private bath. No smoking. $40-45.

Eye Openers Bed and Breakfast Reservations VE-V10I

P. O. Box 694, Altadena, 91003-0694
(213) 684-4428; (818) 797-2055
FAX (818) 798-3640

Turn-of-the-century beach estate is now a lovely bed and breakfast inn. Guest rooms and suites are individually decorated with antiques and hand-detailed furnishings. Large continental breakfast and evening refreshments are served. Ten guest rooms. Shared and private bath. No smoking. $75-135, plus tax.

The Sovereign Hotel at Santa Monica Bay

205 Washington Avenue, 90403
(310) 395-9921; (800) 331-0163

Built in the 1920s, the Sovereign Hotel is reminiscent of something out of a Raymond Chandler novel. The building's Mediterranean architecture has been lovingly renovated, and each room individually decorated with upgraded appointments. The Sovereign offers first-class accommodations with the charm of a bed and breakfast. Personalized service is a specialty.

Hosts: Priscilla Mora and Marie Jean De La Cruz
Rooms: 52 (PB) $69-199
Continental Breakfast
Credit Cards: None

SANTA ROSA

Gee-Gee's

7810 Sonoma Highway (Highway 12), 95409
(707) 833-6667

Lovely remodeled farmhouse on one acre in a parklike setting in the Valley of the Moon, surrounded by fine wineries, mountains, and orchards. Pleasant guest rooms, gourmet breakfasts, sitting room with TV and fireplace, decks, swimming pool, complimentary bicycles. Free RV parking for bed and breakfast guests. Gift certificates available. French and German spoken.

Host: Gerda Heaton-Weisz
Rooms: 4 (S2B) $75-95
Full Breakfast
Credit Cards: A, B
Notes: 2, 5, 10, 11, 12, 14

Hilltop House Bed and Breakfast

9550 St. Helena Road, 94574
(707) 944-0880

NOTES: Credit cards accepted: A Master Card; B Visa; C American Express; D Discover Card; E Diner's Club; F Other; 2 Personal Checks accepted; 3 Lunch available; 4 Dinner available; 5 Open all year;

Poised at the top of the ridge that separates the famous wine regions of Napa and Sonoma, Hilltop House is a country retreat with all the comforts of home. The owners built their contemporary home with this mountain panorama in mind, and the vast deck allows you to enjoy it at your leisure with a glass of wine in the afternoon, breakfast in the morning, or a long soak in the hot tub. The sunrises and sunsets are amazing. You'll cherish the natural setting, the caring hospitality, and the prize location.

Host: Annette Gevarter
Rooms: 3 (PB) $95-165
Extended Continental Breakfast
Credit Cards: A, B, C
Notes: 2, 5, 7, 8, 9, 10, 11, 12, 14

Melitta Station Inn

5850 Melitta Road, 95409
(707) 538-7712

Late 1800s restored railroad station, this American country bed and breakfast is on a country road in the Valley of the Moon in the center of wine country. Next to three state parks, hiking, biking, horseback riding, hot air balloons, gliders, hot baths, and massages. Within minutes of many fine restaurants and wineries.

Hosts: Vic Amstadter and Diane Crandon
Rooms: 6 (4 PB; 2 SB) $75-90
Full Breakfast
Credit Cards: A, B
Notes: 2, 5, 8 (over 9), 9, 10, 11, 12, 14

Pygmalion House Bed and Breakfast

331 Orange Street, 95407
(707) 526-3407

Pygmalion House, one of Santa Rosa's historic landmarks, is a fine example of Queen Anne Victorian architecture. Each morning a bountiful breakfast is served in the country kitchen. Throughout the day, complimentary bottled spring water and soft drinks are available. In the evening, guests may enjoy cheese, nuts, coffee, or tea while relaxing around the fireplace.

Host: Lola L. Wright
Rooms: 5 (PB) $50-70
Full Breakfast
Credit Cards: A, B, C
Notes: 2, 5, 9, 10, 12, 14

Vintners Inn

4350 Barnes Road, 95403
(707) 575-7350

A European-style country inn surrounded by owner's working vineyard. All rooms with antique furniture, modern private baths, many with fireplaces; complimentary breakfast. Home of the acclaimed John Ash & Co. Restaurant. AAA four-diamond rating.

Hosts: John Duffy and Cindy Young
Rooms: 44 (PB) $127.44-199.80
Continental Breakfast
Credit Cards: A, B, C, E
Notes: 2, 3, 4, 5, 8, 9, 10, 11, 12, 14

SAUSALITO

B&B International #108

P. O. Box 282910, San Francisco, 94128-2910
(415) 696-1690; FAX (415) 696-1699

Try a new way to stay at a bed and breakfast. Three houseboats docked in Sausalito, five minutes north of the Golden Gate Bridge and close to interesting shops and restaurants in downtown Sausalito. Two have beautiful views of the bay from the decks, and all are beautifully furnished in fine furniture and art. Two are unhosted leaving guests much privacy. The third comes with a home-cooked breakfast. $96-125.

B&B San Francisco #04

P. O. Box 349, San Francisco, 94101
(415) 931-3083; FAX (415) 921-BBSF

The Marin County picturesque village of Sausalito offers wonderful restaurants, quaint shops, and romantic views of San Franscisco. Stay aboard a houseboat, a permanently moored home on the bay. Decks on three sides, livingroom with a fireplace, king-size bed in the bedroom, full kitchen, and a full bath. The home is nonhosted, but all breakfast items are in the kitchen for a self-catered breakfast. Enjoy a glass of wine as you watch the city lights come on and the sun slips behind Mt. Tamalpias. $125.

The Butterfly Tree

P. O. Box 790, 94966
(415) 383-8447

At Muir Beach, you are in easy walking distance to the Pacific Ocean, Muir Woods, and the Golden Gate National Recreation Area. A secluded, fragile environment good for nature buffs, lovers, hikers, and bird watchers. Only 30 minutes from San Francisco; 20 minutes to the Sausalito ferry, shopping, and excellent dining.

Host: Karla Andersdatter
Rooms: 2 (PB) $95-115
Full Breakfast
Credit Cards: None
Notes: 2, 5, 7 (limited), 8 (under six months or over 6 years), 11, 14

Casa Madrona Hotel

801 Bridgeway, 94965
(415) 332-0502; (800) 228-0502

Nestled in the hills of Sausalito, the Casa Madrona is truly a 19th-century reminder of a less hurried time. Rooms cascade down the hillside, offering enchanting views of the harbor. Each room is individually designed and decorated. An unforgettable haven.

Host: John W. Mays
Rooms: 35 (PB) $105-225
Continental Breakfast
Credit Cards: A, B, C
Notes: 2, 3, 4, 5, 7, 8, 9, 10, 12, 14

The Sausalito Hotel

16 El Portal, 94965
(415) 332-4155

A European-style hotel decorated in Victorian antiques with all the amenities, including fresh flowers. Situated in the historic heart of Sausalito adjacent to the San Francisco ferry. Most rooms afford a harbor view. A special treat is the suite with Gen. Ulysses S. Grant's furniture and a fireplace. A warm, hospitable, and romantic atmosphere prevail in this lovely setting.

Hosts: Gene Hiller; Liz MacDonald, manager
Rooms: 15 (10 PB; 5 SB) $75-175
Continental Breakfast
Credit Cards: A, B, C, E
Notes: 2, 5, 6, 7, 8, 9, 14

SCOTIA

The Scotia Inn

P. O. Box 248, 95565
(707) 764-5683

Lovely old historic hotel with grand piano in the lobby and antiques throughout. Formal dining room, large banquet facilities, with seating up to 400, and cocktail lounge downstairs. Gorgeous lawn and trees for outdoor weddings, receptions, etc.

Rooms feature king- and queen-size beds, some with television and Hide-a-beds. Antiques, clawfoot tubs, and no phones in the rooms take you back to another era.

Host: Gerald Carley
Rooms: 11 (PB) $55-150
Continental Breakfast
Credit Cards: A, B, C, D, E, F
Notes: 2, 3, 4, 5, 8, 9, 14

SEAL BEACH

Bed and Breakfast Los Angeles 6-2

730 Catalina Avenue, Seal Beach, 90740
(310) 493-6837; (800) 383-3513

Antique furnishings and tropical plants combine to form a rich texture in this twenty-two room inn just a short walk from the beach. All rooms have a private bath; 15 rooms have kitchens. Pool, library, and lovely dining room also available. Luxury rates.

Eye Openers Bed and Breakfast Reservations SB-B2

P. O. Box 694, Altadena, 91003-0694
(213) 684-4428; (818) 797-2055
FAX (818) 798-3640

Large villa on the sand with colorful gardens beach-side beckons you to indulge in water sports, sun on the dunes, or relax on an enclosed balcony with an ocean view. Indoor Jacuzzi, continental-plus breakfast. Two guest rooms. Private bath. No smoking.

Eye Openers Bed and Breakfast Reservations SB-S241

P. O. Box 694, Altadena, 91003-0694
(213) 684-4428; (818) 797-2055
FAX (818) 798-3640

A bed and breakfast inn with the look and ambience of an elegant European inn is surrounded by lovely gardens. Inn has a brick courtyard, pool, library, and gracious dining room for large continental breakfast and evening refreshments. Twenty-four guest rooms all have individual decor and private baths. This lovely, quiet beach community is a well-kept secret. $88-155 plus tax.

Seal Beach Inn and Gardens

212 Fifth Street, 90740
(310) 493-2416

An elegant country inn by the sea, with a classic French Mediterranean appearance. The accommodations are appointed in handsome antique furnishings. Many have sitting areas and kitchens. The inn is surrounded by lush, colorful, gardens, French sculpture, fountains, and ancient garden art. An Old World-style bed and breakfast, but far more than that. This is a full-service country inn with all the conveniences, activities, and amenities of a fine hotel.

Host: Marjorie Bettenhausen
Rooms: 23 (PB) $98-155
Continental Breakfast
Credit Cards: A, B, C, E
Notes: 2, 5, 11, 14

SEQUOIA

Kids Welcome 18-3

730 Catalina Avenue, Seal Beach, 90740
(310) 493-6837; (800) 383-3513

This family cottage in the little town of Three Rivers was built by an architect for beauty and efficiency. It has a bedroom, livingroom, bath, full kitchen, and redwood deck. The splendor of the wilderness surrounds this cottage. Moderate rates.

6 Pets welcome; 7 Smoking allowed; 8 Children welcome; 9 Social drinking allowed; 10 Tennis available; 11 Swimming available; 12 Golf available; 13 Skiing available; 14 May be booked through travel agents.

Eye Openers Bed and Breakfast Reservations TR-C1

P. O. Box 694, Altadena, 91003-0694
(213) 684-4428; (818) 797-2055
FAX (818) 798-3640

Enjoy an architect designed cottage with kitchen facilities. Beautiful views of the mountains from this community near the entrance to Sequoia National Park. Hot tub available. Private bath. No smoking. $75.

SEPULVEDA

Bed and Breakfast Los Angeles 3-9

730 Catalina Avenue, Seal Beach, 90740
(310) 493-6837; (800) 383-3513

A fluffy cat named Spot lives in this cozy house. Guest room has a king-size bed and private bath down the hall. Air conditioning, family room, and full house privileges. Hosts will pick you up at the Van Nuys airport. Affordable rates.

SHERMAN OAKS

Bed and Breakfast Los Angeles 3-6

730 Catalina Avenue, Seal Beach, 90740
(310) 493-6837; (800) 383-3513

Drive through an enchanting garden to your own private suite, which includes a bedroom, sitting room, bath, TV, and refrigerator. This home also features a pool, Jacuzzi, and deck, as well as a crib, highchair, and a laundry room. Moderate rates.

SKYFOREST

Storybook Inn

P. O. Box 362, 28717 Highway 18, 92385
(714) 336-1483

Nine elegantly decorated rooms, all with baths and a separate rustic three-bedroom, two-bath cabin with stone fireplace. The inn has a spectacular 100-mile view. Full home-cooked breakfast is served in your room on white wicker trays with Bavarian china, silverplate, and crystal or in the elegant dining room with its fantastic view and fine furnishings. Social hour with complimentary wines and hors d'oeuvres nightly. Menus are planned each week around a theme. Monthly wine tasting, conference room, nearby hiking trails, and private picnics.

Hosts: Kathleen and John Wooley
Rooms: 9 plus cabin (PB) $98-200
Full Breakfast
Credit Cards: A, B
Notes: 2, 3 & 4 (for conference or picnics), 5, 8, 9, 11, 13, 14

SOLVANG

Megan's Friends #01

Bed and Breakfast Reservation Service
1776 Royal Way, San Luis Obispo, 93405
(805) 544-4406

Lovely home graciously furnished in contemporary style blended with Oriental accessories and original oil paintings is in one of the major tourist meccas nestled between the Santa Ynez and San Rafael mountain ranges. The twin-bedroom suite has a sumptuous dressing room and private bath. The patio offers a view of the Santa Ynez hills and garden. In the valley is Santa Ynez Mission with its impressive museum with a wide array of Indian artifacts, wall murals, and its Chapel of the Madonnas. $60.

NOTES: Credit cards accepted: A Master Card; B Visa; C American Express; D Discover Card; E Diner's Club; F Other; 2 Personal Checks accepted; 3 Lunch available; 4 Dinner available; 5 Open all year;

SONOMA

B&B International #301

P. O. Box 282910, San Francisco, 94128-2910
(415) 696-1690; FAX (415) 696-1699

Situated in the heart of Sonoma, in walking
distance to the plaza and wineries, is an old
stonecutter's cottage. It has a king/twin bed
with bath and large deck. There is a
Franklin stove in the cottage. In a garden
setting surrounded by countryside studded
with giant oaks. Breakfast is served in the
main house. $110-115.

B&B International #302

P. O. Box 282910, San Francisco, 94128-2910
(415) 696-1690; FAX (415) 696-1699

Contemporary, Colonial-style, two-story
home situated in the Sonoma Valley wine
country. Surrounded by 17 acres, it has
views of rolling hills and Mount St.
Helena, yet only three miles from downtown Healdsburg. Guest quarters are in a
separate building from the main house and
are furnished in antiques, quilts, and
Oriental rugs. Both rooms have double
beds and private baths. Breakfast is in main
house. $80.

B&B San Francisco #14

P. O. Box 349, San Francisco, 94101
(415) 931-3083; FAX (415) 921-BBSF

In a rural country setting among the vineyards three miles from the quaint town
square of Sonoma sits Willow Tree Farm.
The owner offers a wide variety of accommodations on her working horse farm. A
wonderful swimming pool is available for
guests during the summer months. Full
breakfast. $65-85.

El Dorado Hotel

405 First Street West, 95476
(707) 996-3030

Situated in the heart of wine country, just
sixty miles north of San Francisco, the El
Dorado overlooks Sonoma's historic
Spanish Square. Rates include complimentary wine at check-in and a European
breakfast. The El Dorado features fine
Italian cuisine at Ristyorante Platti. The
hotel's central location makes it the perfect
spot to embark on an afternoon in the tasting rooms or stroll through boutique-
studded streets. Meeting and banquet facilities available.

Rooms: 25 (PB) $80-140
Continental Breakfast
Credit Cards: A, B, C
Notes: 2, 3, 4, 5, 7, 8, 9, 10, 11, 12, 14

Eye Openers Bed and Breakfast Reservations HE-C61

P. O. Box 694, Altadena, 91003-0694
(213) 684-4428; (818) 797-2055
FAX (818) 798-3640

This 1869 Italianate Victorian town house
on one-half acre has landscaped grounds
with pool and large antique-filled guest
rooms Breakfast with fresh baked breads
and afternoon refreshments are served. Six
guest rooms. Shared and private baths. $75-
115 plus tax.

Eye Openers Bed and Breakfast Reservations HE-F2

P. O. Box 694, Altadena, 91003-0694
(213) 684-4428; (818) 797-2055
FAX (818) 798-3640

Seventy-acre grape ranch in Sonoma
County's spectacular Dry Creek Valley
near many wineries and restaurants is a

---

6 Pets welcome; 7 Smoking allowed; 8 Children welcome; 9 Social drinking allowed; 10 Tennis available; 11
Swimming available; 12 Golf available; 13 Skiing available; 14 May be booked through travel agents.

family-run bed and breakfast. Enjoy charming antique decorated guest rooms, tranquil vineyard setting, and walks, swimming pool, garden terrace, and wildlife pond. Full breakfast. Two guest rooms. Private bath. No smoking. $90.

Eye Openers Bed and Breakfast Reservations HE-G71

P. O. Box 694, Altadena, 91003-0694
(213) 684-4428; (818) 797-2055
FAX (818) 798-3640

This 1902 Queen Anne Victorian offers an elegant return to a bygone era. Upstairs rooms have roof windows and view of the lovely grounds. Full country breakfast. Seven guest rooms. Private bath. No smoking. $85-105 plus tax.

The Hidden Oak

214 East Napa Street, 95476
(707) 996-9863

The Hidden Oak is a large, two-story Craftsman bungalow in the historic neighborhood of Sonoma, one block from the plaza. There are three exquisitely decorated rooms with queen beds and private baths. Full breakfast and bicycles are complimentary. Situated near the wineries, shopping, restaurants, art galleries, and historic sites.

Host: Catherine Cotchett
Rooms: 3 (PB) $85-105
Full Breakfast
Credit Cards: A, C, D
Notes: 2, 5, 9

Sonoma Chalet

18935 Fifth Street West, 95476
(707) 938-3129

Located in the beautiful Valley of the Moon, which is truly a fascinating area, this inn is surrounded by early California history. Visit the wineries and enjoy the rich colorful vineyards and natural beauty of Sonoma Valley. The Chalet has overnight accommodations in a wonderful country farm setting. The Swiss-style farmhouse and country cottages are located on three beautiful acres just minutes away from some of the Valley's most celebrated wineries. Come visit the chalet and see why we are listed as one of the "Best Places to kiss in the bay Area."

Host: Joe Leese
Rooms: 7 (4 PB; 3 SB) $75-135
Expanded Continental Breakfast
Credit Cards: A, B, C
Notes: 2, 14

Sparrow's Nest Inn

424 Denmark Street, 95476
(707) 996-3750

Come to the Sparrow's Nest Inn for a romantic retreat in the historic town of Sonoma. We are less than two miles from the lovely town square, and the cottage's English country decor and furnishings are comfortable and pleasing in soft white, rose, and blue. The surrounding flower gardens and brick patio within the private yard makes a peaceful setting, and every effort is made to insure that the guests feel welcome and their visit is memorable.

Hosts: Kathleen and Thomas Anderson
Cottage: 1(PB) $85-105
Expanded Continental Breakfast
Credit Cards: A, B
Notes: 2, 5, 6, 8 (over 10), 10, 12

Victorian Garden Inn

316 East Napa Street, 95476
(707) 996-5339; (800) 543-5339

Lush gardens with private nooks; classic rooms from storybooks; private entrances, private baths; rooms overlooking garden paths; gourmet breakfast, lunch, and breaks; midweek conferences at competitive rates; romantic getaways, excursions, and tours; all of these and more are yours. Just one and one-half blocks from the historic Sonoma Plaza and Sebastiani Winery.

NOTES: Credit cards accepted: A Master Card; B Visa; C American Express; D Discover Card; E Diner's Club; F Other; 2 Personal Checks accepted; 3 Lunch available; 4 Dinner available; 5 Open all year;

Host: Donna Lewis
Rooms: 4 (3 PB; 1 SB) $79-139
Continental Breakfast
Credit Cards: A, B, C, E
Notes: 2, 5, 7, 8 (over 13), 9, 10, 11, 12, 14

SONORA

Bed and Breakfast
Los Angeles 17-1

730 Catalina Avenue, Seal Beach, 90740
(310) 493-6837; (800) 383-3513

Located on Gold Street in historic Sonora, this wonderful old Victorian home has five guest rooms with private baths and balconies. There is a library and music room. Lovely gardens and a big wrap-a-round porch. Just a short drive away are snow and water-skiing, fishing, hunting, horseback riding, and gold panning. Moderate rates.

Lavender Hill
Bed and Breakfast

683 South Barretta Street, 95370
(209) 532-9024

Delightfully restored 1900 Victorian with four lovely guest rooms, two with private baths. Formal parlor, dining room, antiques, porch swing, and beautiful grounds. Within walking distance of shops and restaurants in the heart of the Gold Country.

Hosts: Alice Byrnes and Carole Williams
Rooms: 4 (2 PB; 2 SB) $65-75
Full Breakfast
Credit Cards: None
Notes: 2, 5, 7 (limited), 9, 10, 12

Kids Welcome 17-2

730 Catalina Avenue, Seal Beach, 90740
(310) 493-6837; (800) 383-3513

Play with the llamas at this creek-side guest ranch in the country. Amenities include hot tub and sauna, music room/library (with lots of kids' games), and gracious Southern hospitality. Moderate rates.

Lulu Bell's
Bed and Breakfast

85 Gold Street, 95370
(209) 533-3455; (800) 538-3455

Charming 1886 Victorian with beautiful gardens and a relaxing atmosphere. Each of the five lovely guest rooms features private baths, private entrances and air conditioning. Enjoy delicious hearty breakfasts and excellent location to explore the "Gold Country." Get-away packages available for dinner/theater, river rafting, steam train excursions, and skiing.

Rooms: 5 (PB) $80-100
Full Breakfast
Credit Cards: A, B, C, D
Notes: 2, 5, 8, 9, 10, 11, 12, 13, 14

The Ryan House

153 South Shepherd Street, 95370
(209) 533-3445

Footsteps from town and a century removed, this Gold Rush home, built in 1855, has been restored to become a bed and breakfast inn. Spacious gardens and near Yosemite, Columbia State Park, hunting, fishing, river rafting, antiquing, and wineries. Queen-size beds, antiques, and handmade quilts. Theater packages arranged. Gift certificates available.

Hosts: Nancy and Guy Hoffman
Rooms: 3 plus 1 suite (PB) $80-125
Full Breakfast
Credit Cards: A, B
Notes: 2,5, 9, 10, 11, 12, 14

SOQUEL

Blue Spruce Inn

2815 Main Street, 95073
(408) 464-1137

The O'Brien's 1873 farmhouse blends the flavor of yesterday with the luxury and privacy of today. Situated on the crest of Monterey Bay. Guests can easily enjoy the beaches as well as unique shops and dining

6 Pets welcome; 7 Smoking allowed; 8 Children welcome; 9 Social drinking allowed; 10 Tennis available; 11 Swimming available; 12 Golf available; 13 Skiing available; 14 May be booked through travel agents.

in this distinctive destination. There are excellent local wineries, many antique shops, and state parks with miles of biking or hiking trails. The hosts offer a bountiful breakfast to fuel guests for the activities of the day and recommend the hot tub under the stars for the perfect day's end.

Hosts: Pat and Tom O'Brien
Rooms: 5 (PB) $80-125
Full Breakfast
Credit Cards: A, B, C
Notes: 2, 5, 8, 9, 12, 14

Blue Spruce Inn

SOULSBY

Kids Welcome 17-41

730 Catalina Avenue, Seal Beach, 90740
(310) 493-6837; (800) 383-3513

Enjoy private tennis courts, lake swimming, and evening sherry by the fire at this 1880s ranch house. Hosts promise the perfect year-round hide-a-away on a latitude below the winter snow, but above the summer heat. Moderate rates.

SPRINGVILLE

Annie's Bed and Breakfast

33024 Globe Drive, 93265
(209) 539-3827

Situated on five acres in the beautiful Sierra foothills, this inn features beautiful antiques, feather beds, and handmade quilts. Full country breakfast is prepared on an antique wood cookstove. Close to golf, tennis, river, boating, lakes, hiking, swimming, and redwoods. The host has a custom saddle shop and horse training facility on the property. Guests are welcome to come out and watch. Annie's is a great place to relax and enjoy the peace and quiet of country life.

Hosts: Annie and John Bozanich
Rooms: 3 (PB) $85-95
Full Breakfast
Credit Cards: A, B, C, E
Notes: 2, 4, 5, 9, 10, 11, 12, 14

STINSON BEACH

Casa del Mar

37 Belvedere Avenue, P. O. Box 238, 94970
(415) 868-2124

Nestled in the lap of Mount Tamalpais overlooking the ocean, a Mediterranean villa rises above a terraced garden. From the gate you'll wind through jacarandas, bananas, and fruit trees, around the fishpond, and up to the inn. You can hear the waves break all day long. Your own room has a view of the Pacific or Mount Tamalpais, its own private bath and balcony, and fresh flowers from the garden. Fantastic full breakfast and hors d'oeuvres in the evening.

Host: Rick Klein
Rooms: 5 (PB) $90-225
Full Breakfast
Credit Cards: A, B, C
Notes: 2, 5, 9, 14
Studio City

STUDIO CITY

America's B&B #13

P. O. Box 9302, Whittier, 90608
(310) 699-8427

NOTES: Credit cards accepted: A Master Card; B Visa; C American Express; D Discover Card; E Diner's Club; F Other; 2 Personal Checks accepted; 3 Lunch available; 4 Dinner available; 5 Open all year;

Ideally situated on a quiet tree-lined street close to shopping areas, movie studios and the Ventura freeway, this tree-shaded home is decorated with New England antiques. Patio and pool are available to guests. Twin-bed room with private bath and air conditioning. $55.

SUMMERLAND

Summerland Inn

2161 Ortega Hill Road, P. O. Box 1209, 93067
(805) 969-5225

The Summerland Inn "where New England meets the Pacific" is a delightful bed and breakfast with ten rooms, all with private baths, telephones, television, and with breakfast served in your room. Summerland has its own beach a short walk from the inn, antique and gift shops, and places to eat.

Host: James R. Farned
Rooms: 10 (PB) $50-120
Continental Breakfast
Credit Cards: A, B, C, D, E
Notes: 2, 5, 8, 14

SUNSET PALISADES

Megan's Friends #04 Bed and Breakfast Reservation Service

1776 Royal Way, San Luis Obispo, 93405
(805) 544-4406

Serene ocean view form the livingroom of this spacious home with beach access. Breakfast overlooking the surf from the deck. Nearby attractions: Avila Plunge, massage, spa, hot tubs. Super breakfasts (special diets on request), and dinner for $5 or $6 with wine with advance notice. Even bridge games, if your're inclined. $60.

SUSANVILLE

The Roseberry House

609 North Street, 96130
(916) 257-5675

Everything is coming up roses at the Roseberry House. Delicate rose patterns cover the walls and floors and accent the Victorian furnishings. The four upstairs bedrooms are spacious and comfortable, with queen beds and choice antiques. Early morning coffee is available in the upstairs hall, with a full breakfast served in the formal dining room. Susanville is situated on the eastern slopes of the Sierra Nevadas, with warm summer days, spectacular autumn colors, and often a white Christmas.

Hosts: Bill and Maxine Ashmore
Rooms: 4 (PB) $50-65
Full Breakfast
Credit Cards: A, B, C
Notes: 2, 5, 10, 12

TAHOE CITY

Bed and Breakfast Los Angeles 18-1

730 Catalina Avenue, Seal Beach, 90740
(310) 493-6837; (800) 383-3513

This unique lakefront house was built in 1928 by Italian stonemasons. It has a private pier, used for everything from windsurfing to parasailing. Bikes and paddleboats are rentable. Hosts have four rooms, two with private baths, and two with shared baths. They serve a scrumptious breakfast on the deck and hot drinks around the fireplace at night. Moderate-luxury rates.

The Captain's Alpenhaus

6941 West Lake Boulevard, P. O. Box 262, Tahoma, 96142
(916) 525-5000; (916) 525-5266

6 Pets welcome; 7 Smoking allowed; 8 Children welcome; 9 Social drinking allowed; 10 Tennis available; 11 Swimming available; 12 Golf available; 13 Skiing available; 14 May be booked through travel agents.

A European-style country inn and gourmet restaurant with an alpine bar, stone fireplace, rooms, and cottages with fireplaces nestled in pine woods. Cozy and quaint resort on Lake Tahoe's unspoiled west shore, five minutes from Emerald Bay, one of the scenic wonders of the world.

Hosts: Joel and Phyllis Butler
Rooms: 7 (PB) $55-115
Suites: 2; Cottages: 6
Full Breakfast
Minimum stay holidays: 2 nights
Credit Cards: A, B, C, E
Notes: 2, 3, 4, 5, 6, 7, 8, 9, 10, 11, 12, 13, 14

Chaney House

P. O. Box 7852
4725 West Lake Boulevard, 96145
(916) 525-7333

Built on the Lake Tahoe shore by Italian stonemasons, Chaney House has an almost medieval quality with its dramatic arched windows, 18-inch-thick stone walls, and enormous fireplace. The private beach and pier beckon guests. Bicycling, hiking, boating, fishing, and 19 ski areas are close at hand. Scrumptious breakfasts are served on the patio overlooking the lake on mild days.

Hosts: Gary and Lori Chaney
Rooms: 4 (2 PB; 2 SB) $85-110
Full Breakfast
Credit Cards: None
Notes: 2, 5, 8, 9, 10, 11, 12, 13, 14

Mayfield House

236 Grove Street, P. O. Box 5999, 96145
(916) 583-1001

Snug and cozy 1930s Tahoe home, one-half block from the beach. Premium skiing within ten miles. Full breakfast, homemade baked goods. Within walking distance of shops and restaurants in Tahoe City. Off-street parking.

Hosts: Cynthia and Bruce Knauss
Rooms: 6 (SB) $70-105
Full Breakfast
Credit Cards: A, B
Notes: 2, 5, 7 (limited), 8, 9, 10, 11, 12, 13, 14

TARZANA

California Houseguests International

6051 Lindley Avenue #6, 91356
(818) 344-7878

This reservation service offers comfortable accommodations in specially selected homes, condominiums, and apartments in a wide range of rates and locations. For example: an oceanfront mansion with private beach and maid; a charming flat within walking distance of UCLA, theaters, shopping; a grand Spanish hacienda with pool, garden/patios, gourmet meals; Italian Renaissance villa with formal gardens close to Los Angeles Music Center. Hosts are chosen for their hospitality, housekeeping, and dedication to make your visit memorable. Coordinator: Trudi Alexy. $45-250 plus.

TEMECULA

Bed and Breakfast Los Angeles 8-2

730 Catalina Avenue, Seal Beach, 90740
(310) 493-6837; (800) 383-3513

Rent this whole apartment for the cost of a hotel room. Apartment includes bedroom, livingroom with a sofa bed, Jacuzzi, barbecue area, and parking. Affordable rates.

Eye Openers Bed and Breakfast Reservations TE-S61

P. O. Box 694, Altadena, 91003-0694
(213) 684-4428; (818) 797-2055
FAX (818) 798-3640

Located in Southern California's wine country, this lovely bed and breakfast has six uniquely decorated guest rooms. Full country breakfast. No smoking. Six rooms. Private bath. $75-95 plus tax.

Loma Vista
Bed and Breakfast

33350 La Serena Way, 92591
(714) 676-7047

Loma Vista, in the heart of Temecula wine country, is conveniently situated to any spot in Southern California. This beautiful new mission-style home is surrounded by citrus groves and premium vineyards. All six rooms have private baths; most have balconies.

Hosts: Betty and Dick Ryan
Rooms: 6 (PB) $95-125
Full Breakfast
Credit Cards: A, B, D
Closed Thanksgiving, Christmas, New Year's
Notes: 2, 9, 10, 11, 12, 14

THOUSAND OAKS

Bed and Breakfast
Los Angeles 3-13

730 Catalina Avenue, Seal Beach, 90740
(310) 493-6837; (800) 383-3513

Overlooking a regional nature center, this beautiful Thousand Oaks home has a gorgeous view, pool, deck, and spa. Guest room has twin beds and a shared bath. Affordable rates.

Bed and Breakfast
Los Angeles 3-15

730 Catalina Avenue, Seal Beach, 90740
(310) 493-6837; (800) 383-3513

This luxury condo has a view of the hills and great recreational facilities. Retired hosts offer one guest room with a private bath. Older children only. Afffordfable rates.

TOLUCA LAKE

Bed and Breakfast
Los Angeles 3-1

730 Catalina Avenue, Seal Beach, 90740
(310) 493-6837; (800) 383-3513

This southwestern-style home in Toluca Lake features two guest rooms, private baths, private entrances, TV's, pool, decks, and spa. One room even has a full line of baby equipment. Moderate rates.

TORRANCE

America's B&B #12

P. O. Box 9302, Whittier, 90608
(310) 699-8427

Charming contemporary home with a lovely courtyard entrance. The house has a light, open feeling with an atrium that demonstrates the hostess's love of gardening. Four miles from beach. Near Los Angeles International Airport. A full breakfast is served. Children are welcome; hostess will meet guests at airport with prior arrangement. Four miles to beach. $65.

Bed and Breakfast
Los Angeles 5-4

730 Catalina Avenue, Seal Beach, 90740
(310) 493-6837; (800) 383-3513

This well-kept family house in Torrance is only a block to the park and the tennis courts. Two guest rooms share a bath in the hall; a patio with a barbecue and a TV in the family room are also available to guests. Handicapped facilities available. Affordable rates.

---

6 Pets welcome; 7 Smoking allowed; 8 Children welcome; 9 Social drinking allowed; 10 Tennis available; 11 Swimming available; 12 Golf available; 13 Skiing available; 14 May be booked through travel agents.

TRINIDAD

The Lost Whale Bed and Breakfast

3452 Patrick's Point Drive, 95570
(707) 677-3425

Unique bed and breakfast on four wooded acres with a private beach and trail. Wake to barking sea lions and a spectacular ocean view. Amenities include outdoor hot tub, afternoon tea, private baths and queen beds. Fifteen minutes from Eureka airport and the largest redwood forests in the world.

Hosts: Lee Miller and Susanne Lakin
Rooms: 6 (4 PB; 2 SB) $90-120
Full Breakfast
Credit Cards: A, B
Notes: 2, 5, 8, 14

Kids Welcome 16-4

730 Catalina Avenue, Seal Beach, 90740
(310) 493-6837; (800) 383-3513

You can watch the waves from your hot tub, while the kids are out berry-picking at this perfect family vacation spot. Hosts designed this bed and breakfast retreat for family fun and comfort. Breakfast is big and nutritious; town is nearby and full of activity; and scenic trails to tide pools are at your doorstep. The kids are provided with an enclosed playground, playhouse, barnyard animals, and storytelling. Need a night out? Childcare is available, too. Luxury rates.

Trinidad Bed and Breakfast

Box 849, 95570
(707) 677-0840

A Cape Cod-style home overlooking beautiful Trinidad Bay. The inn offers spectacular views of the rugged coastline and fishing harbor from two suites, one with a fireplace, and two upstairs bedrooms, all with private baths. Surrounded by beaches, trails, and redwood parks. Within walking distance of restaurants and shops. The suites enjoy breakfast delivered. The other two rooms enjoy breakfast at a family-style table.

Hosts: Paul and Carol Kirk
Rooms: (PB) $90-145
Expanded Continental Breakfast
Credit Cards: A, B, D
Notes: 2, 5, 9, 12

TRUCKEE

The Truckee Hotel

10007 Bridge Street, 96161
(800) 659-6921

This circa 1873 Victorian bed and breakfast is in Truckee's historical district. Begin your day with our expanded continental breakfast, and enjoy the sights and activities that our beautiful Sierra location offers. In-house dining at The Passage offers fine wine and cuisine. Relax fireside in our parlor before turning in for the night. Shopping and dining are moments from the inn, and Amtrak is close by. Come visit us by train. No smoking.

Host: Dottie Hall
Rooms: 37 (8 PB; 29 SB) $60-114
Expanded Continental Breakfast
Credit Cards: A, B, C
Notes: 2, 5, 8, 13

TUOLUMNE

Oak Hill Ranch Bed and Breakfast

P. O. Box 307, 18550 Connally Lane, 95379
(209) 928-4717

A perfect stay on 56 wooded acres, near three historic state parks and Yosemite National Park. Relish the full country breakfast and homey hospitality, private baths, fireplaces, and a private cottage. Victorian decor and Eastlake antique furniture, flower gardens, lawn, and gazebo set off this romantic setting. Close to restaurants, live theaters, ski resort, and outdoor recreation.

NOTES: Credit cards accepted: A Master Card; B Visa; C American Express; D Discover Card; E Diner's Club; F Other; 2 Personal Checks accepted; 3 Lunch available; 4 Dinner available; 5 Open all year;

Hosts: Sanford and Jane Grover
Rooms: 4 plus cottage (3 PB; 2 SB) $67-110
Full Breakfast
Credit Cards: None
Notes: 2, 5, 9, 10, 11, 12, 13, 14

UKIAH

Kids Welcome 16-8

(310) 493-6837; (800) 383-3513

The champagne baths are the center of this parklike resort at the foot of the Mendocino Hills. Twelve individually decorated rooms with private baths date from the 1860s, while the two free-standing cottages (with modern kitchens) were built in 1854. Wildlife abounds in the 700 acres of woods, meadows, streams, and falls that surround the ranch. Sailing, wind-surfing, jet-skiing, and salmon fishing are all within easy reach, and naturally carbonated hot tubs are at your doorstep. Moderate-luxury rates.

Oak Knoll Bed and Breakfast

858 Saanel Drive, 95482
(707) 468-5646

A large redwood contemporary home with spectacular views of hills, valleys, vineyards, and sheep. Spacious deck. Lovely furnishings of Orientals and chandeliers. Two rooms with shared bath, adjacent sitting room, TV and movies on a 40-inch screen in the family room. Full breakfast in the dining room or on the deck in summer. Hiking, golf, and boating are nearby.

Host: Shirley Wadley
Rooms: 2 (SB) $70
Full Breakfast
Credit Cards: None
Notes: 2, 5, 9, 10, 11, 12, 14

Vichy Springs Resort and Inn

2605 Vichy Springs Road, 95482
(707) 462-9515

Vichy Springs Resort, a delightful two-hour drive north of San Francisco, 12 rooms and two self-contained cottages that have been renovated and individually decorated. Nearby are 14 tubs built in 1860 and used by the rich and famous in California's history. Vichy features naturally sparkling, 90-degree mineral baths, a communal 104-degree pool, Olympic-size pool, 700 private acres with a waterfall, trails and roads for hiking, jogging, picnicking and mountain bicycling, and Swedish massage, reflexology, and herbal facials.

Hosts: Gilbert and Marjorie Ashoff
Rooms: 14 (PB) $110-160
Expanded Continental Breakfast
Credit Cards: A, B, C, D, E, F
Notes: 2, 3, 4, 5, 8, 9, 10, 11, 12, 14

VALLEY FORD

The Inn at Valley Ford

Box 439, 94972
(707) 876-3182

The inn is a 120-year-old farmhouse furnished with antiques. Each room commemorates an author and includes a collection of his work. Valley Ford, situated in the pastoral hills of western Sonoma County, is just minutes from the Pacific. Nearby are galleries, antiques, wineries, restaurants, bird watching, bicycling, and hiking.

Hosts: Nicholas Balashov and Sandra Nicholls
Rooms: 5 (SB) $68-78
Expanded Continental Breakfast
Credit Cards: A, B
Notes: 2, 5, 7 (outside), 9, 10, 11, 12, 14

VENICE BEACH

Bed and Breakfast Los Angeles 4-1

730 Catalina Avenue, Seal Beach, 90740
(310) 493-6837; (800) 383-3513

6 Pets welcome; 7 Smoking allowed; 8 Children welcome; 9 Social drinking allowed; 10 Tennis available; 11 Swimming available; 12 Golf available; 13 Skiing available; 14 May be booked through travel agents.

Turn-of-the-century home has a sunny livingroom where a full breakfast is served. Some private, some shared baths, and one bath has a side-by-side tub. Older children only, please. Moderate luxury rates.

VENTURA

Eye Openers Bed and Breakfast Reservations VE-B171

P. O. Box 694, Altadena, 91003-0694
(213) 684-4428; (818) 797-2055
FAX (818) 798-3640

Three blocks from the beach, this inn with Mediterranean decor offers comfort and convenience. Full breakfast and afternoon refreshments. Seventeen rooms. Private bath. $75-120, plus tax.

La Mer

411 Poli Street, 93001
(805) 643-3600

Nestled in a green hillside, this Cape Cod-style Victorian overlooks the heart of historic San Buena Ventura and the California coastline. Originally built in 1890, a historical landmark, La Mer has individually decorated, antique-filled rooms furnished to capture a specific European country, all with private baths and entrances, plus ocean view.

La Mer

Host: Gisela Flender Baida
Rooms: 5 (PB) $100-155
Full Breakfast
Minimum stay weekends and holidays: 2 nights
Credit Cards: A, B
Closed Christmas
Notes: 2, 5, 9, 10, 11, 12, 14

WESTCHESTER

Bed and Breakfast Los Angeles 2-12

730 Catalina Avenue, Seal Beach, 90740
(310) 493-6837; (800) 383-3513

This remodeled Craftsman bungalow is close to the airport with easy access to the beach. Two nice guest rooms share a bath in hall. Airport pick-up is possible. Affordable rates.

Kids Welcome 2-13

730 Catalina Avenue, Seal Beach, 90740
(310) 493-6837; (800) 383-3513

Country-style cottage near the airport in Westchester has one guest room, which shares a bath with your host. Close to restaurants, tennis, and golf. Affordable rates.

WEST COVINA

Hendrick Inn

2124 East Mercer Avenue, 91791
(810) 919-2125

This large, rambling house provides a real taste of the California lifestyle with its gorgeous deck, swimming pool, Jacuzzi. Centrally situated for visiting Disneyland, the mountains, and the desert. Only 45 minutes to airport; 20 to Ontario Airport.

Hosts: Mary and George Hendrick
Rooms: 4 (2 PB; 2 SB) $35-60
Full Breakfast
Credit Cards: None
Notes: 2, 4 (with notice), 5, 8 (over 4), 9, 10, 11, 12

NOTES: Credit cards accepted: A Master Card; B Visa; C American Express; D Discover Card; E Diner's Club; F Other; 2 Personal Checks accepted; 3 Lunch available; 4 Dinner available; 5 Open all year;

WEST LAKE

Bed and Breakfast Los Angeles 3-11

730 Catalina Avenue, Seal Beach, 90740
(310) 493-6837; (800) 383-3513

On a quiet cul-de-sac, this Spanish-style home has one guest room with a private bath. You are welcome to use their neighborhood recreation area. Affordable rates.

Bed and Breakfast Los Angeles 3-12

730 Catalina Avenue, Seal Beach, 90740
(310) 493-6837; (800) 383-3513

This large guest suite has a fireplace, private bath, and a Hide-a-away bed for the kids. Two other rooms that share a bath are available. Because of the back yard pool, hosts cannot accommodate toddlers. Family rates available. Affordable rates.

WESTPORT

Bowen's Pelican Lodge and Inn

38921 North Highway 1, P. O. Box 358, 95488
(707) 964-5588

A Victorian western inn reminiscent of the 1890s. In a remote location with the sea in front yard, the mountain in back, and miles of virtually untouched wilderness all around. The nearest town, Fort Bragg, is 15 miles away. A place to get away from it all, hike secluded beaches, explore the hills, or unwind. Full bar and restaurant; home cooking.

Host: Velma Bowen
Rooms: 6 (4 PB; 2 SB) $48.60-81
Continental Breakfast
Minimum stay holidays: 2 nights
Credit Cards: A, B
Notes: 2, 3, 4, 5, 7, 9, 14

DeHaven Valley Farm

39247 North Highway 1, 95488
(707) 961-1660

The inn, a Victorian farmhouse built in 1875, is on 20 acres of meadows, hills, and streams, across from the Pacific Ocean. Guests enjoy various farm animals, exploring tide pools, and soaking in the hot tub. Restaurant serves delicious four-course dinners complemented by home-grown herbs and vegetables. The inn is ideally situated to visit the gigantic redwoods 25 miles to the north or the artist colony of Mendocino 25 miles to the south.

Hosts: Jim and Kathy Tobin
Rooms: 8 (6 PB; 2 SB) $85-125
Full Breakfast
Credit Cards: A, B, C
Closed Jan.
Notes: 2, 4, 8, 9

DeHaven Valley Farm

Howard Creek Ranch

Box 121, 95488
(707) 964-6725

A historic 1867 farm on 20 acres, only 100 yards from the beach. A rural retreat adjoining wilderness. Suite and cabins; views of ocean, mountains, creek, or gardens; fireplace/wood stoves; period furnishings; wood-heated hot tub, sauna, pool, horseback riding nearby. Gift certificates available.

Hosts: Charles (Sunny) and Sally Grigg
Rooms: 8 (5 PB; 3 SB) $54-121
Full Breakfast
Credit Cards: A, B
Notes: 2, 5, 6 (by prior arrangement), 7 (limited), 8
  (reservation requested), 9, 11

Howard Creek Ranch

WHITTIER

Coleen's California Casa

Box 9302, 90608
(310) 699-8427

Take your children to Disneyland, Knott's
Berry Farm, and Universal Studios, then
come back to a luxurious home. Bedrooms
are decorator designed with elegant private
baths, one with Jacuzzi tub. From the deck
you can see Los Angeles, Long Beach, and
Catalina Island. Hosts will help you plan
your tours, provide baby-sitting, and pick
you up at the airport for a charge.

Host: Coleen Davis
Rooms: 3 (PB) $55-65
Full Breakfast
Minimum stay: 2 nights; holidays: 3 nights
Credit Cards: None
Notes: 2, 3, 4, 5, 7 (limited), 8, 9, 10, 11, 12, 14

WOODLAND HILLS

Kids Welcome 3-10

730 Catalina Avenue, Seal Beach, 90740
(310) 493-6837; (800) 383-3513

This traditional home is graced with a
grand piano and delightful brick patio with
a firepit. Two guest rooms share one bath;
family rates are available. Affordable rates.

YOSEMITE

Bed and Breakfast Los Angeles 18-5

730 Catalina Avenue, Seal Beach, 90740
(310) 493-6837; (800) 383-3513

This small bed and breakfast is the only
bed and breakfast in Yosemite. It consists
of one guest room in the main house and
one free-standing cottage, both with private
baths. Breakfast is full at your hostess'
cafe, and redwoods surround the area.
Moderate rates.

Eye Openers Bed and Breakfast Reservations YG-C2

P. O. Box 694, Altadena, 91003-0694
(213) 684-4428; (818) 797-2055
FAX (818) 798-3640

Get away to this large A-frame house with
open-beamed ceilings on a tree-filled hillside above a private lake twenty minutes
west of Yosemite. Loft bedroom/sitting
room and two other guest rooms available.
Full breakfast served on deck with view of
the Sierra Nevadas. Private bath. $60.

YOUNTVILLE

Bordeaux House

6600 Washington Street, 94599
(707) 944-2855

A charming English-French country inn
nestled in the heart of Napa Valley with
lush gardens. Wood-burning fireplaces, spacious rooms, wonderful continental breakfast served. All rooms air-conditioned.

NOTES: Credit cards accepted: A Master Card; B Visa; C American Express; D Discover Card; E Diner's
Club; F Other; 2 Personal Checks accepted; 3 Lunch available; 4 Dinner available; 5 Open all year;

Rooms: 6 (PB) $95-120
Continental Breakfast
Credit Cards: A, B, C, D, E
Notes: 5

Burgundy House

P. O. Box 3156, 6711 Washington Street, 94599
(707) 944-0889

Solidly built 1890 French Country stone
structure. Originally a brandy distillery
with 22-inch-thick walls of river-rock and
fieldstone. Five comfortable rooms, all
with private bath, invite you to settle in and
relax. The antique furnishings throughout
the house add to the Old World charm and
ruggedness. Colorful rose garden and lawn
invite you to picnicking or wine tasting.
Full breakfast served buffet-style every
day. Right in the center of Napa Valley's
wine region.

Hosts: Dieter and Ruth Back
Rooms: 5 (PB) $90-110
Full Breakfast
Credit Cards: A, B
Notes: 2, 5, 9, 10, 12, 14

Oleander House

7433 St. Helena Highway, 94599
(707) 944-8315

Country French charm, situated at the
entrance to the wine country. Spacious,
high-ceiling rooms done in Laura Ashley
fabric and wallpaper and antiques.
Breakfast is served in the large dining room
on the main floor. All rooms have fireplaces, private baths, and their own decks.

Hosts: The Packards
Rooms: 4 (PB) $115-160
Full Breakfast
Minimum stay weekends & holidays: 2 nights
Credit Cards: A, B
Notes: 2, 9, 10, 11, 12, 14

Vintage Inn

6541 Washington Street, P. O. Box 2536, 94599
(800) 351-1133

Vintage Inn in Napa Valley is a contemporary luxury country inn located on a historic twenty-three-acre winery estate in the
walking town of Yountville. Centered
amidst some of Napa Valley's finest vineyards, guests enjoy a unique resort atmosphere with pool, spa, tennis, cycling, and
hot air ballooning. A California champagne
buffet breakfast of pastries, assorted fruits,
cheeses, yogurt, and cereals is included
with each guest stay. The Vintage Inn
offers superb accommodations for year-
round comfort, featuring a wood-burning
fireplace, whirlpool bath, compact refrigerators, and many other extras.

Host: Nancy M. Lochmann
Rooms: 80 (PB) $134-194
Continental Breakfast
Credit Cards: A, B, C, E, F
Notes: 2, 3, 4, 5, 6, 7, 8, 9, 10, 11, 14

YUBA CITY

Harkey House
Bed and Breakfast

212 C Street, 95991
(916) 674-1942

1864 Victorian Gothic, queen beds, fireplaces, TV/VCR/CD, telephones. Breakfast
served in dining room or on patio. Spa, air
conditioning in all rooms, basketball court,
chess, game table. Library. Original art
work, piano. Near museums, hiking, and
fishing. Fresh flowers, down comforters. A
romantic getaway! Reservation deposit
required. Five-day cancellation notice. $10
cancellation fee.

Hosts: Bob and Lee Jones
Rooms: 4 (PB) $75-100 plus tax
Continental Breakfast
Credit Cards: A, B, D
Notes: 2, 5, 8, 9, 11, 12, 13, 14

6 Pets welcome; 7 Smoking allowed; 8 Children welcome; 9 Social drinking allowed; 10 Tennis available; 11 Swimming available; 12 Golf available; 13 Skiing available; 14 May be booked through travel agents.

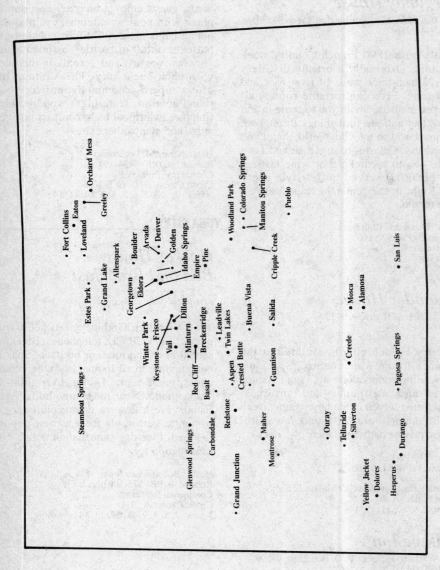

COLORADO

Colorado

ALAMOSA

Cottonwood Inn Bed and Breakfast and Gallery

123 San Juan Avenue, 81101
(719) 589-3882

Lovely turn-of-the-century Craftsman-style inn, decorated with antiques and local artwork. Near the Cumbres-Toltec Scenic Railway, Great Sand Dunes, wildlife refuges, Adams State College, cross-country skiing, llama trekking. Delicious breakfasts featuring freshly ground coffee, homemade baked goods, and fresh fruit. Famous for their green chili strata.

Hosts: Julie Mordecai and George Sellman
Rooms: 5 (2 PB; 3 SB) $40-65
Full Breakfast
Credit Cards: A, B
Notes: 2, 5, 8, 9, 10, 11, 12, 14

ALLENSPARK

Allenspark Lodge

P. O. Box 247, 80510
(303) 747-2552

A 1933 three-story, hand-hewn log lodge with a great room, game and reception room, hot tub, and the Wilderquest Room, with a selection of beverages and hors d'oeuvres. Fourteen rooms, some with private bath and deep, bear claw tubs, three cabins. Horseback riding available. Minutes from Rocky Mountain National Park. Three housekeeping cabins are also available.

Hosts: Mike and Becky Osmun
Rooms: 14 (5 PB; 9 SB) $30.95-74.95
Continental Breakfast
Credit Cards: A, B
Notes: 2, 3, 4, 5, 8, 9, 13, 14

Lazy H Guest Ranch

15747 Highway 7, P. O. Box 248, 80510
(303) 747-2532

A log-and-stone lodge built high on a mountain ridge. Guest rooms each have their own individual personality mingled with antiques, cozy country flavor, and spectacular views. Enjoy watching deer, elk, and big horn sheep. Our own rock creek has excellent fishing, and swimming and horseback riding are available in the summer. Lunch and dinner can be served by request. Amenities include a hot tub and sauna open year-round, conference rooms, and wedding facilities.

Hosts: Karen and Phil Olbert
Rooms: 14 (PB) $70-125
Full Breakfast
Credit Cards: A, B, D
Notes: 2, 3, 4, 5, 8, 9, 11, 13, 14

Wild Basin Lodge

North Star Route, 80510
(303) 747-2545

Rest and relaxation in the mountains. Situated at the southern end of Rocky Mountain National Park, with lots of hiking and walking trails. Large, spacious rooms overlooking beautiful river and up the Wild Basin Valley to snow-capped Copeland Mountain. Enjoy great home cooking in Smorgasbord Restaurant. Full breakfast with your room. Full bar available. No smoking

Hosts: Randy and Sandy Good
Rooms: 3 (PB) $65-75
Full Breakfast
Credit Cards: A, B, C
Notes: 2, 3, 4, 5, 8, 9, 14

ARVADA

On Golden Pond Bed and Breakfast

7831 Eldridge, 80005
(303) 424-22961

This custom-built, two-story brick home is situated on ten acres with dramatic views of the mountains, prairies, and downtown Denver, 15 miles to the west. It offers a fishing pond, exotic birds, and natural wildlife in peaceful surroundings. You can also savor a soak in the hot tub, swim laps in the pool, walk on the garden path, bicycle along the creek, and horseback ride into the foothills. Antique shopping and Arvada Center of Performing Arts.

Hosts: Kathy and John Kula
Rooms: 6 (PB) $40-80
Full Breakfast
Credit Card: A, B
Notes: 2, 5, 6 (outside) , 7 (outside), 8, 9, 11, 12, 14

The Tree House

6600 Simms, 80004
(303) 431-6352

A charming guest house in the middle of a ten-acre forest. Squirrels, rabbits, and birds abound, breaking the quiet serenity of the setting. Balconies on the front and back of the house provide a lovely view of the forest and a perfect spot for breakfast. Guest rooms with wood-burning fireplaces are furnished with brass beds, handmade quilts, and lovely antiques. A common area with fireplace and oak and leather furniture can be used for small meetings or just to relax. Perfect for weddings, anniversaries, and family reunions.

Host: Sue Thomas
Rooms: 5 (PB) $49-79
Full Breakfast
Credit Cards: A, B
Notes: 2, 5, 9, 11, 12, 13, 14

ASPEN

The Ambiance Inn

Bed and Breakfast-Rocky Mountains
906 South Pearl Street
Denver, 80209
(303) 744-8415; (800) 733-8415

This contemporary, chalet-style home offers one suite and three bedrooms, all with private baths and queen-sized beds. Each room is decorated with with the host's favorite destinations in mind: Sonoma, Aspen, Santa Fe, and Kauai. Year-round activities include world class alpine skiing, cross-country skiing, gold medal fishing, whitewater rafting, golf, hiking, biking, and horseback riding. Full breakfasts feature homemade jams and bread, fresh fruit, eggs, and meat dish. Smoking in designated areas only. Moderate-luxury rates.

The Aspen Bed and Breakfast

Bed and Breakfast-Rocky Mountains
906 South Pearl Street
Denver, 80209
(303) 744-8415; (800) 733-8415

You will long remember this tastefully decorated, 38-room, contemporary lodge made into a bed and breakfast. All doors enter from the spacious atrium/lounge where a thirty-foot river-rock fireplace makes an impressive centerpiece. Meeting rooms are available. Each room has a queen bed, a double fold-out, wet bar, and refrigerator; some balcony rooms have a Jacuzzi tub; outdoor, heated pool and Jacuzzi year-round. Full buffet breakfast. No pets. Moderate-luxury rates.

NOTES: Credit cards accepted: A Master Card; B Visa; C American Express; D Discover Card; E Diner's Club; F Other; 2 Personal Checks accepted; 3 Lunch available; 4 Dinner available; 5 Open all year;

Avalanche Ranch

Bed and Breakfast-Rocky Mountains
906 South Pearl Street
Denver, 80209
(303) 744-8415; (800) 733-8415

This original 1913 farmhouse has been
restored into a country inn bed and breakfast, antique shop, and restaurant. The
country inn is decorated with an eclectic
collection of early country antiques and
folk art. On 45 acres of lush countryside
overlooking the Crystal River and Elk
Mountain Range, the ranch is surrounded
by the fabulous White River National
Forest. Fourteen cozy log cabins with full
amenities. Smoking outside. Full breakfast.
Moderate-luxury rates.

Biggerstaff House

Bed and Breakfast-Rocky Mountains
906 South Pearl Street
Denver, 80209
(303) 744-8415; (800) 733-8415

Charm and coziness await you in this four
bedroom bed and breakfast. You'll love the
names of the four guest rooms: Fannie Etta,
Minnie Maude, Victoria Mae, and Nina
Melvina. Furnished with antiques, lace curtains, and stained glass, two rooms have a
private balcony with views of Mt. Sopris.
Close to all recreational facilities. Full
deluxe breakfast. No pets, no smoking.
Children over 12 welcome. Budget-moderate rates.

Boomerang Lodge

500 West Hopkins, 81611
(303) 925-3416; (800) 992-8852

Unique ski lodge located in Aspen's quiet
West End within walking distance to the
music festival or downtown. All Boomerang rooms and fireplace apartments have
a sunny patio or a balcony, thanks to the
handsome design which was influenced by
the owner-architect's teacher, Frank Lloyd

Wright. Thoughtful touches include continental breakfast, pool, whirlpool, and
sauna. Additional winter amenities include
afternoon tea and town courtesy van.
Discover why devoted guests return to
Boomerang.

Hosts: Charles and Fonda Paterson
Rooms: 35 (PB) $93-174
Continental Breakfast
Credit Cards: A, B, C, E
Notes: 2, 5, 8, 11, 13, 14

C.C.'s

Bed and Breakfast Vail Ski Areas
P. O. Box 491, 81658
(303) 949-1212; (800) 748-2666

Hot tub under a star-filled sky warms you
after a long day on the slopes. Hosts are
restauranteurs who serve a hearty breakfast.
Five minutes to Snowmass Mountain and
15 minutes to downtown Aspen. On bus
route. No smoking. $65.

Chalet Lisl

Bed and Breakfast-Rocky Mountains
906 South Pearl Street
Denver, 80209
(303) 744-8415; (800) 733-8415

Boomerang Lodge

6 Pets welcome; 7 Smoking allowed; 8 Children welcome; 9 Social drinking allowed; 10 Tennis available; 11
Swimming available; 12 Golf available; 13 Skiing available; 14 May be booked through travel agents.

Cozy studio and one-bedroom apartments offer private baths, full kitchens, TV and telephones in the rooms. They are modest, comfortable units with a happy decor. There is a hot tub under the stars. The inn is two blocks to Aspen town center. No smoking, no pets. Moderate-luxury rates.

Crestahaus Lodge

1301 East Cooper Avenue, 81611
(303) 925-7081; (800) 344-3853

Experience European charm in the heart of the Rockies. Thirty distinctive rooms feature private baths, telephones, cable TV, and most have mountain views. Lodge amenities include Jacuzzi and sauna, heated pool (open summers only) , daily house-keeping, complimentary breakfast buffet, and après ski (winter only) . Choose between rustic-traditional rooms located in the main lodge, or deluxe-contemporary rooms. Enjoy two fireplace areas, barbecue/ patio area, and year-round hospitality and comfort. Airport transportation and free shuttle downtown (1/4 mile) .

Host: Melinda Goldrich
Rooms: 30 (PB) $50-175
Continental Plus Breakfast
Credit Cards: A, B
Notes: 2, 5, 6, 7, 8, 9, 11, 13, 14

Little Red Ski Haus

118 East Cooper Street, 81611
(303) 925-3333

Charming 100-year-old Victorian three blocks from the center of town. No TV but always interesting conversation. One could travel the world just sitting in the living room. The house is very popular with Australians. Exceptionally clean and friendly, especially suited to those traveling alone. Dinner is available on Wednesdays for eight dollars.

Hosts: Marge Riley and Irene Zydek
Rooms: 16 (3 PB; 13 SB) $22-110

Full Breakfast winter; Continental summer
Credit Cards: A, B
Closed April 10-May 31
Notes: 4, 5, 8, 9, 10, 11, 12, 13, 14

Main Street

Bed and Breakfast Vail Ski Areas
P. O. Box 491, 81658
(303) 949-1212; (800) 748-2666

All rooms are richly appointed, opening up to a center room lounge. They offer wet bars, refrigerators, cable TV, and phones. On the premises is a heated pool, Jacuzzi, and parking lot. A river rock fireplace cascades the lounge where a continental breakfast and a wine and cheese party is served daily. Great for traveling couples.

Mountain House Bed and Breakfast

905 East Hopkins, 81611
(303) 920-2550

The Mountain House offers exceptional quality and service in a tranquil and peaceful setting. Our spacious guest rooms come in variety of sizes, ranging from king- and queen-size beds to larger suites, one of which (our presidential suite) has a private Jacuzzi. Each room is beautifully appointed and comes with color cable TV, refrigerator, and phones, and most have outside decks. We offer inviting fireplaces, indoor Jacuzzi, and ski lockers.

Little Red Ski Haus

Hosts: John Werning, P.J. Sullivan, and Syd Devine
Rooms: 24 (PB) $40-180
Full breakfast during ski season; Continental, other times
Credit Cards: A, B, D, E
Notes: 2, 5, 8, 9, 10, 11, 12, 13, 14

Sardy House Hotel and Restaurant

128 East Main Street, 81611
(303) 920-2525; (800) 321-3457

One of Aspen's finest historic residences, now an elegant hotel, beautifully restored and graciously appointed in the Victorian tradition. An enclosed gallery bridges a private brick mews, joining the Sardy House to its carriage house wing. Blue-green spires of Colorado spruce, among them the tallest in Aspen, rise above the hotel's landscaped grounds. At the west end of the mews are a heated swimming pool, spa, and sauna. Fine dining is offered in the Victorian dining room.

Host: Jayne Poss
Rooms: 14 plus 6 suites (PB) $160-375 summer; $240-550 winter
Full Gourmet Breakfast
Credit Cards: A, B, C, E
Notes: 2, 4, 8, 9, 10, 12, 13, 14

Slice of Heaven

Bed and Breakfast Vail Ski Areas
P. O. Box 491, 81658
(303) 949-1212; (800) 748-2666

Hot tub, snowmobile rentals, snowmobile tours atop Aspen Mountain. Airport pickup. This converted barn has open-beamed rooms individually decorated with antiques, old-fashioned claw foot tubs, and huge fireplace. Secluded, cozy, and restful. $80 summer; $120 winter.

Snow Queen Victorian Lodge

124 East Cooper Street, 81611
(303) 925-8455; (303) 925-6971

This quaint, family-operated Victorian ski lodge built in the 1880s. The charming parlor has a fireplace and color TV for guests. There is a variety of rooms with private baths, plus two kitchen units. The lodge is situated in town, within walking distance of restaurants, shops, and the ski area. A nice outdoor hot tub is available. Lower rates are available during off-season and summer.

Hosts: Norma Dolle and Larry Ledingham
Rooms: 5 (PB) $65-135
Continental Breakfast
Credit Cards: A, B, C
Closed April 15-May 15
Notes: 2, 8, 9, 10, 11, 12, 13, 14

Snowmass Village Bed and Breakfast

Bed and Breakfast-Rocky Mountains
906 South Pearl Street
Denver, 80209
(303) 744-8415; (800) 733-8415

Enjoy the country elegance of this charming home situated on five acres above the valley floor, commanding spectacular views of three ski area mountains. Backdoor access to hiking, biking, cross-country skiing, riding, and four ski areas. Lovely private double suite with private bath and cozy sitting area; elegant queen bedroom with private bath and balcony. Continental-plus breakfast. No smoking, no children, no pets. Moderate-luxury rates.

Starry Pines Bed and Breakfast

Bed and Breakfast-Rocky Mountains
906 South Pearl Street
Denver, 80209
(303) 744-8415; (800) 733-8415

Starry Pines is situated on 70 private acres in scenic Snowmass Valley. Wake up to panoramic views of Mount Sopris and Elk Mountain Range, then enjoy a continental breakfast on the deck overlooking a beautiful mountain stream. Enjoy the patio hot tub with view of nearby peaks. Resident cat. No smoking or pets. Moderate-luxury rates.

6 Pets welcome; 7 Smoking allowed; 8 Children welcome; 9 Social drinking allowed; 10 Tennis available; 11 Swimming available; 12 Golf available; 13 Skiing available; 14 May be booked through travel agents.

Ullr Lodge Inc.

520 West Main Street, 81611
(303) 925-7696

This small family-owned and operated
lodge is located in the quiet residential
West End of Aspen. Rooms with private
bath and one- and two-bedroom apartments
are available. In winter we offer a free ski
shuttle to all four mountains, and in the
summer we are a five-minute walk to the
music festival, Aspen Institute, and Given
Institute. Full breakfast for rooms only in
the winter. Continental breakfast for rooms
and apartments in the summer.

Host: Anthony Percival
Rooms: 23 (PB) $55-165
Full Breakfast, winter; Continental, summer
Credit Cards: A, B, C, E
Notes: 2, 5, 9, 11, 12, 13, 14

What A View!

Bed and Breakfast Vail Ski Areas
P. O. Box 491, 81658
(303) 949-1212; (800) 748-2666

For the feel of being in the mountains with
great view, this is it!!! A former home that
has been renovated into four units, this
apartment was the family's patio overlooking Aspen highlands and Maroon Bells.
Located within walking distance of downtown Aspen, your room offers plenty of
privacy with a lock-off master bedroom
suite and a sunken   Japanese tub in the
bathroom. A warm and comfortable stay.
$65-75.

BASALT

Altamira Ranch Bed and Breakfast

23484 Highway 82, 81621
(303) 927-3309

Beautiful ranch fifteen minutes from Aspen
on the Roaring Fork River, a gold medal
trout stream. Enjoy quiet, peaceful country

atmosphere adjacent to skiing, hiking, river
sports, and famous Glenwood Hot Springs.
Antique shop on the premises. Your home
away from home.

Host: Martha Waterman
Rooms: 2 (SB) $50-60
Full Breakfast
Credit Cards: None
Notes: 2, 5, 8 (over 6 yrs) , 9

Shenandoah Inn

0600 Frying Pan Lane, Box 578
(303) 927-4991

Contemporary western Colorado bed and
breakfast is situated on two riverboat acres
on the Frying Pan River, one of North
America's premier trout streams, in the
heart of the White River National Forest.
Twenty minutes from Aspen and
Glenwood Hot Springs; year-round access
to the best of Colorado outdoors. Fishing
and bicycling available. Warm, friendly
atmosphere, and exceptional cuisine.

Hosts: Bob and Terry Ziets
Rooms: 4 (semi-private) $60-75
Full Gourmet Breakfast
Credit Cards: None
Notes: 2, 5, 9, 10, 12, 13, 14

BOULDER

The Bluebell

Bed and Breakfast-Rocky Mountains
906 South Pearl Street
Denver, 80209
(303) 744-8415; (800) 733-8415

This bright, airy, contemporary home is
furnished with antiques collected by the
owners. The neighborhood is quiet but near
bus line, a bike path, mountain trails and
within walking distance of the University
of Colorado Stadium and the Events
Center. Two bedrooms and sitting room
privately situated upstairs. Children welcome. No smoking. Budget-Moderate rates.

NOTES: Credit cards accepted: A Master Card; B Visa; C American Express; D Discover Card; E Diner's
Club; F Other; 2 Personal Checks accepted; 3 Lunch available; 4 Dinner available; 5 Open all year;

The Blue Spruce

Bed and Breakfast-Rocky Mountains
906 South Pearl Street
Denver, 80209
(303) 744-8415; (800) 733-8415

Situated in historic Mapleton Hill, this lovely two-story home is only a six-block walk to the downtown Boulder Mall. In the summer you can enjoy a full breakfast on the outdoor deck while listening to the sounds of the creek that borders the property. Children over six welcome. No smoking. $45. magazines. Complete breakfast in dining room or breakfast in bed. Complimentary sherry, tea trays afternoons and evenings. English shortbread cookies. Casual elegance close to Boulder's best restaurants and attractions.

Hosts: Margaret and Bob Weisenbach
Rooms: 9 (6 PB; 3 SB) $53-105
Full Breakfast
Credit Cards: A, B, C, E
Notes: 2, 5, 8, 9, 14

The Bluebird Lodge

Gold Hill Star Route, 80302
(303) 443-6475

This bed and breakfast is located in a historic lodge adjacent to Gold Hill Inn Restaurant. The Finn family will make your stay a pleasure. The lodge is rustic, offers nine guest rooms, antiques, a cozy deck, and a hot tub. Breakfast includes homemade breads, fresh fruit, and yogurt. Always call for information and reservations.

The Boulder Victoria Historic Bed and Breakfast

Hosts: The Finn family
Rooms: 9 (SB) $40
Continental Breakfast
Credit Cards: None
Notes: 2, 4, 7, 8, 9

The Boulder Victoria Historic Bed and Breakfast

1305 Pine Street, 80302
(303) 938-1300

Downtown Boulder's exquisitely renovated Victorian inn offers you seven unique guest rooms that feature antique furniture, private baths, telephone, and TV. Enjoy dessert and cappuccino in the elegant parlor, luxuriate in your private steam shower, or enjoy breakfast in the bay-windowed dining room. Soak in Boulder's sun on the spacious patio. Convenient to downtown, campus, and mountain activities.

Hosts: Jackie Myers and Kristen Peterson
Rooms: 7 (PB) $95-125
Continental Breakfast
Credit Cards: A, B, C
Notes: 2, 5, 9, 10, 11, 12, 13, 14

Briar Rose Bed and Breakfast

2151 Arapahoe, 80302
(303) 442-3007

Enjoy the comfort and elegance of Boulder's first and finest bed and breakfast. All rooms are furnished with period antiques, fine linens, fresh flowers, and good books, and offer a choice of a twin, double, or queen-size bed. Enjoy afternoon and evening tea service, a complete healthy breakfast, the roaring fire, or a walk in the garden. Close to Boulder's best restaurants, fine shopping and the university of Colorado.

Host: Margaret and Bob Weisenbach
Rooms: 9 (PB) $80-105
Continental Plus Breakfast
Credit Cards: A, B, C, E
Notes: 2, 5, 8, 9, 14

The Greenwood

Bed and Breakfast-Rocky Mountains
906 South Pearl Street
Denver, 80209
(303) 744-8415; (800) 733-8415

The second floor of this home is just for you. There is a bright, sunny feeling in this home, which has been decorated with a Southwest contemporary flair. The bedrooms have a great view of the mountains, and you can relax in the private sitting room. The hostess, a Colorado native who also designed this home, serves a continental breakfast. Lovely garden for warm weather enjoyment. No smoking. Budget rates.

Magpie Bed and Breakfast

Kalmia House

Bed and Breakfast-Rocky Mountains
906 South Pearl Street
Denver, 80209
(303) 744-8415; (800) 733-8415

This contemporary home is in north Boulder. There is a grand piano just waiting to be played in the living room. A full breakfast is served in the atrium or, weather permitting, outside under the tree. The hostess is an excellent cook. No smoking. Budget-moderate rates

Magpie Bed and Breakfast

Bed and Breakfast-Rocky Mountains
906 South Pearl Street
Denver, 80209
(303) 744-8415; (800) 733-8415

Built in 1899, the Magpie Inn was one of Boulder's finer Mapleton Hill homes. Restored to its elegance, the Magpie Inn has an atmosphere reminiscent of a golden era. Ideally situated one block from the popular Pearl Street Mall. Also within walking distance are Boulder Creek and the University of Colorado. Continental breakfast. No smoking or pets. Moderate-luxury rates.

Old Grey-Stone

Bed and Breakfast-Rocky Mountains
906 South Pearl Street
Denver, 80209
(303) 744-8415; (800) 733-8415

Feel right at home in this lovely old greystone home with European flavor, just off-campus and beautifully decorated. The larger room on the second floor is bright and cheerful with a twin bed decorated in pinks and ruffles. The second room, also a twin, is decorated with antique pine furniture. Full breakfast, including fresh ground coffee and homemade bread. No pets, no smoking, available July-December only. Budget rates.

Pearl Street Inn

1820 Pearl Street, 80302
(303) 444-5584; (800) 232-5949

The Pearl Street Inn, Boulder's only downtown inn, blends the privacy and service of a country bed and breakfast with the amenities of a luxury hotel. The rooms, which encircle a garden courtyard, have antique furniture, full bath, fireplace, and TV. The inn is three blocks from a famous pedestrian mall and only a few minutes from the University of Colorado.

NOTES: Credit cards accepted: A Master Card; B Visa; C American Express; D Discover Card; E Diner's Club; F Other; 2 Personal Checks accepted; 3 Lunch available; 4 Dinner available; 5 Open all year;

Host: Theresa Schuller
Rooms: 7 (PB) $78-98
Continental Breakfast
Credit Cards: A, B, C
Notes: 2, 5, 6, 7, 8, 9, 10, 11, 12, 13, 14

Rinn's Nest

Bed and Breakfast-Rocky Mountains
906 South Pearl Street
Denver, 80209
(303) 744-8415; (800) 733-8415

Feel at home while visiting this contemporary ranch home in a country setting just 12 miles from Boulder. Large yard with flower garden and gazebo. One spacious guest room with a double bed and private bath. Full breakfast with homemade breads. Excellent location in the Boulder area. No smoking. Budget rates.

The Salina House— Historic Mountain Cabin

365 Gold Run Road, 80302
(303) 442-1494

Enjoy the serenity of Colorado's mountains in this private cabin that has been meticulously restored and historically preserved, providing 19th-century charm with 20th-

Pearl Street Inn

century comfort. This rustic yet elegant lodging provides a private, fully equipped kitchen, living/dining room, bedroom, and bath. Also sofa bed, electric heat, and wood stove. Truly a one-of-a-kind lodging. Reduced rates for longer stays.

Host: Margo Newman
Cabin: 1 (PB) $80
Continental Breakfast
Credit Cards: None
Notes: 2, 5, 7, 8, 9, 13, 14

Sandy Point Inn

6485 Twin Lakes Road, 80301
(303) 530-2939; (800) 322-2939

A unique, modern, quiet country inn with 30 studio suites with mini kitchen and private bath in each room. Laundry rooms and a central kitchen for all guests to enjoy. A complimentary breakfast buffet with fresh fruit, homemade muffins, and granola awaits each morning. Health club facilities, free skiing, restaurant discounts are all included in reasonable daily, weekly, and monthly rates. A very homey, comfortable home away from home in beautiful Boulder.

Host: Juaneta Miller
Rooms: 30 (PB) $50-73
Continental Buffet Breakfast
Credit Cards: A, B, D, E
Notes: 2, 5, 6, 7, 8, 11, 13

The Sunset House

Bed and Breakfast-Rocky Mountains
906 South Pearl Street
Denver, 80209
(303) 744-8415; (800) 733-8415

This contemporary brick home sits on a ridge that overlooks the city. The terraced back yard has a large, secluded deck with a lovely view. The hosts are a retired couple knowledgeable about the Boulder area. Full breakfast. Resident cat. No smoking. Budget-moderate rates.

The Allaire Timbers Inn

BRECKENRIDGE

The Allaire Timbers Inn

Bed and Breakfast-Rocky Mountains
906 South Pearl Street
Denver, 80209
(303) 744-8415; (800) 733-8415

Designed by the owners after three and a half years of planning, this newly constructed log inn offers comfort as well as convenience. It is close to all the sports and shopping available in Breckenridge. Eight rooms and two suites available, all with private baths and phones. Three hot tubs; ski and golf storage. Full breakfast in the winter, and continental breakfast in the summer. No smoking, children over 12. Moderate-luxury rates.

Breckenridge Inn #1

Bed and Breakfast Vail Ski Areas
P. O. Box 491, 81658
(303) 949-1212; (800) 748-2666

Two blocks from downtown shops and restaurants on the free shuttle bus during ski season, this inn offers free parking and ski storage. Located in the historic section of this Victorian mining town, this inn offers guests comfortable accommodations and use of a central livingroom with TV, games, books, and fireplace. Summer activities include hiking, backpacking, bicycling, four-wheeling, sailing, horseback riding, golf, and rafting. If meeting people and spending time with travelers who want a true bed and breakfast experience is appealing, you'll enjoy staying at this inn.

Cotten House

Bed and Breakfast-Rocky Mountains
906 South Pearl Street
Denver, 80209
(303) 744-8415; (800) 733-8415

Built circa 1886, this cozy Victorian bed and breakfast is listed in the Nnational Historic Register. Three beautiful, turn-of-the-century rooms with wester decor all have spectacular views of the slopes and fresh flowers everyday. Guest phone in the foyer. Full seven-day menu with a large variety of foods; fresh ground coffee served in the dining room at 8:00 A.M. No smoking, no pets, children welcome. Moderate-luxury rates.

Hay's Tack Bed and Breakfast

Bed and Breakfast-Rocky Mountains
906 South Pearl Street
Denver, 80209
(303) 744-8415; (800) 733-8415

This cozy bed and breakfast homestay is nestled among the mountains and pine trees of Breckenridge. Guests share two bedrooms and a bath upstairs; hosts have their living quarters downstairs. Enjoy the magnificent view, fireplace and company of the hosts. Continental breakfast. No smoking, no pets, children over 12. Minimum stay is two nights. Budget-moderate, seasonal rates.

Hi-Point Bed and Breakfast

Bed and Breakfast-Rocky Mountains
906 South Pearl Street
Denver, 80209
(303) 744-8415; (800) 733-8415

This charming two-story mountain house is nestled in the pines and has lovely views of the mountains. Three bright guest rooms on the second floor, one with a private bath. Kitchen privileges. Continental breakfast, and full breakfast on the weekends. Moderate rates.

NOTES: Credit cards accepted: A Master Card; B Visa; C American Express; D Discover Card; E Diner's Club; F Other; 2 Personal Checks accepted; 3 Lunch available; 4 Dinner available; 5 Open all year;

Hummingbird House

Bed and Breakfast-Rocky Mountains
906 South Pearl Street
Denver, 80209
(303) 744-8415; (800) 733-8415

Enjoy a beautiful mountain view from this cozy home. Two queen bedrooms with a private entrance each have a private bath, and third bedroom with two trundle beds shares a bath with one of the queen rooms. Full breakfast. Smoking permitted unless other guests object. Moderate, seasonal rates.

Longbranch Condominium

Bed and Breakfast-Rocky Mountains
906 South Pearl Street
Denver, 80209
(303) 744-8415; (800) 733-8415

Downtown condominium with shuttle to the ski slopes has two bedrooms and two baths. One queen-size bed, two twins, and a queen Hide-a-bed available for a maximum of six people. Indoor pool and sauna, underground parking, fireplace, TV, VCR, and balcony. No restrictions. Moderate, seasonal rates.

Mountain Crest

Bed and Breakfast Vail Ski Areas
P. O. Box 491, 81658
(303) 949-1212; (800) 748-2666

This lovely, contemporary cedar home sits in a large, peaceful forest one and one-half miles south of the Breckenridge ski area. With your own private entrance you have a large sitting room with a full-size pool table, color TV, and wood-burning stove. Full breakfast on weekends; continental on weekdays. Cross-country skiing available from the front door winter; hiking trails to lakes in summer. No smoking. $80-85.

One Wellington Square

Bed and Breakfast-Rocky Mountains
906 South Pearl Street
Denver, 80209
(303) 744-8415; (800) 733-8415

This newly built Victorian-style home is perfectly situated for those guests without transportation. Just minutes from downtown and the ski shuttle; less than one mile to the Breckenridge slopes. Bicycle trails, gold-medal fishing, golf, hiking. Continental breakfast. No smoking. Budget-moderate rates.

Ridge Street Inn

Bed and Breakfast-Rocky Mountains
906 South Pearl Street
Denver, 80209
(303) 744-8415; (800) 733-8415

Appreciate the cozy decor great location of this historic Victorian-style bed and breakfast. In the heart of Breckenridge, you'll be close to shops and restaurants. Two rooms share private baths and each sleeps up to four; dorm rooms available with shared bath. Kitchen use permitted. Hostess will take guests on hiking, biking, ski and fly-fishing tours. No smoking. Budget-seasonal rates.

Schloss Im Kiefer

Bed and Breakfast-Rocky Mountains
906 South Pearl Street
Denver, 80209
(303) 744-8415; (800) 733-8415

In this peaceful and quiet residential neighborhood, guests will enjoy a home away from home. Built in the lodge pole pine forest that surrounds Breckenridge, this cedar chalet is six blocks from Main Street, four blocks from the ski shuttle, five minutes by car to ski slopes. Biking, hiking, music, fishing, and golf in the summer. Full gourmet breakfast. Moderate-luxury rates.

---

6 Pets welcome; 7 Smoking allowed; 8 Children welcome; 9 Social drinking allowed; 10 Tennis available; 11 Swimming available; 12 Golf available; 13 Skiing available; 14 May be booked through travel agents.

Walker House

Bed and Breakfast-Rocky Mountains
906 South Pearl Street
Denver, 80209
(303) 744-8415; (800) 733-8415

Unique, quaint, and comfortable describes
this three story log Victorian home in the
heart of the historic district. Recently renovated to add comfort, it has retained its
Victorian flavor and rustic charm. Master
bedroom with private bath, sitting room
and queen-sized bed, and a second room
with a twin Victorian wicker day bed.
Continental breakfast. Free shuttle to ski
mountains, apres ski refreshments,
coffee/tea/hot chocolate and cookies anytime, complimentary pass to health club
within walking distance. Luxury, seasonal
rates.

Williams House Bed and Breakfast

303 North Main Street, P. O. Box 2454, 80424
(303) 453-2975

Step back in time when gold fever brought
people to Breckenridge, and enjoy this
restored historic mining home furnished
with fine antiques. Two romantic parlors,
each with mantled fireplaces, are available
for guest's use, and bedrooms have private
baths. Hearty miners' breakfast with homemade baked goods is served each morning,
and afternoon refreshments are served each
afternoon. Located in the historic district
on the trolley route. Approved by Bed and
Breakfast Innkeepers of Colorado.

Hosts: Diane Jaynes and Fred Kinat
Rooms: 4 (PB) $55-125
Full Breakfast
Credit Cards: C
Notes: 2, 9, 10, 11, 12, 13, 14

Whiskey Hill

Bed and Breakfast Vail Ski Areas
P. O. Box 491, 81658
(303) 949-1212; (800) 748-2666

If you are looking for a quiet, secluded,
romantic bed and breakfast room, here it is.
The bedroom on your own floor has a rock
fireplace, private bath, and private
entrance. Near shops, restaurants, and close
to Beaver Creek. Continental breakfast. No
smoking. $80.

BUENA VISTA

Blue Sky Inn

Bed and Breakfast-Rocky Mountains
906 South Pearl Street
Denver, 80209
(303) 744-8415; (800) 733-8415

Located in a scenic mountain area on the
river, Blue Sky Inn caters to cross country
skiers in the winter and hikers and fishermen in the summer. Beautifully decorated
with antiques, this inn provides quiet relaxation after a busy day. Full breakfast features home baked goodies, and hostess will
be glad to fix picnic lunch. Smoking
allowed on the terrace only. Moderate luxury rates.

Trout City Inn

P. O. Box 431, 81211
(719) 495-0348

Historic railway station on Trout Creek
Pass in national forest. Victorian decor and
antiques in depot rooms—plus elegant private Pullman car and Drover's caboose. Its
own railroad, trout stream, beaver ponds,
and gold mine, with grand view of canyon
and Collegiate peaks. White water rafting,
horseback riding, mountain hiking and
climbing, mountain bike trails just minutes
away—plus great eating and shopping in
historic Buena Vista. Trophy trout fishing
in river and lakes, ghost towns, caves, Jeep
tours, melodrama, antique shops all nearby.

Hosts: Juel and Irene K. Jeldsen
Rooms: 4 (PB) $32-40

NOTES: Credit cards accepted: A Master Card; B Visa; C American Express; D Diner's
Club; F Other; 2 Personal Checks accepted; 3 Lunch available; 4 Dinner available; 5 Open all year;

Full Breakfast
Credit Cards: A, B
Notes: 2, 8, 9, 11, 14

CARBONDALE

The Ambiance Inn

66 North 2nd Street, 81623
(303) 963-3597

Enjoy Aspen, Glenwood Springs, and the beautiful Crystal Valley from this spacious chalet-style home featuring vaulted ceilings throughout. The 1950s ski lodge decor of the very large Aspen Suite or the Victorian elegance of the Sonoma Room featuring a romantic four-poster bed are ideal for your getaways. The Santa Fe Room is alive with the warmth of the Southwest. All rooms adjoin the library-sitting room on the balcony.

Hosts: Norma and Robert Morris
Rooms: 4(PB) $60-80
Full Breakfast
Credit Cards: A, B
Notes: 2, 3, 4, 5, 9, 10, 11, 12, 13

CEDAR EDGE

Cedar's Edge Llamas Bed and Breakfast

2169 Highway 65., 81413
(303) 856-6836

Unique cedar home perched high on the southern slope of Grand Mesa. Peaceful, quiet atmosphere with fabulous 100-mile view. Rooms filled with handmade country decor, quilts, and plants. Breakfast on your private deck overlooking llama pastures and cedar forests. Friendly, curious llamas will charm you. Close to blue-ribbon fishing, skiing, and much more. Come, relax, and enjoy.

Hosts: Ray and Gail Record
Rooms: 2 (PB) $45-55
Full Breakfast
Credit Cards: None
Notes: 2, 5, 8, 9, 12, 13, 14

COLORADO SPRINGS

Black Forest Bed and Breakfast

Bed and Breakfast-Rocky Mountains
906 South Pearl Street
Denver, 80209
(303) 744-8415; (800) 733-8415

Picture yourself in a massive log home built on the highest point of the Rockies! This rustic mountain setting is complete with 20 rolling acres of ponderosa pines, a wonderful location for a peaceful, relaxing time away. Two guest rooms with private baths, and separate one-bedroom apartment above the log barn. Continental-plus or create your own in the guest kitchen. No smoking, no pets. Moderate rates.

Delft Haven

Bed and Breakfast-Rocky Mountains
906 South Pearl Street
Denver, 80209
(303) 744-8415; (800) 733-8415

This elegantly furnished home boasts a hillside view of Colorado Spring's twinkling lights at night and Garden of the Gods at a distance. Feel right at home in the one bedroom with canopied double bed and private bath. Extensive continental breakfast. No pets, no smoking. Moderate rates.

Eastholme

Bed and Breakfast-Rocky Mountains
906 South Pearl Street
Denver, 80209
(303) 744-8415; (800) 733-8415

Awesome mountain setting surrounds this 105 year-old Victorian home. With its breathtaking views, this inn offers variety in lodging choices, including rooms, suites, and a cozy cabin. Winner of Colorado's 1989 "Excellence in Preservation" award. Full country fare breakfast. No smoking, no pets, children over 10 welcome in the inn, any age in the separate cabin. Budget-moderate rates.

6 Pets welcome; 7 Smoking allowed; 8 Children welcome; 9 Social drinking allowed; 10 Tennis available; 11 Swimming available; 12 Golf available; 13 Skiing available; 14 May be booked through travel agents.

Glenluce

Bed and Breakfast-Rocky Mountains
906 South Pearl Street
Denver, 80209
(303) 744-8415; (800) 733-8415

The namesake for this bed and breakfast was a Scottish monastery that opened its doors to the weary traveler. Beside a cozy fireplace on cool nights, you'll be greeted with wine and cheese, or coffee and homemade cookies. With only three guest rooms, the small number of people provides the intimacy needed for fun and interesting conversation. Full gourmet breakfast. No smoking, no pets, children over 10 welcome. Budget-moderate.

Hearthstone Inn

Bed and Breakfast-Rocky Mountains
906 South Pearl Street
Denver, 80209
(303) 744-8415; (800) 733-8415

Whether you stay at the Hearthstone Inn for a romantic retreat, a family vacation, or for business, you'll enjoy the charm, elegance, panoramic views, and convenience this inn offers. National Historic Register and recipient of many awards, Hearthstone offers a variety of rooms and bed sizes with both shared and private baths and all furnished with lovely antiques. Full gourmet breakfast. No smoking, no pets. Moderate-luxury rates.

Holden House—1902 Bed and Breakfast Inn

1102 West Pikes Peak Avenue, 80904
(719) 471-3980

A 1902 storybook Victorian and a 1906 carriage house filled with antiques and heirlooms. Immaculate accommodations in a quiet area near historic district and central to the Pikes Peak region. Enjoy the parlor, living room with fireplace, or veranda with mountain views. Guest rooms boast queen beds, down pillows, and private baths. Honeymoon suites with tubs for two, fireplaces, and more. Complimentary refreshments. Friendly resident cat named Mingtoy. "Experience the romance of the past with the comforts of today." AAA and Mobile approved.

Hosts: Sallie and Welling Clark
Rooms: 2 (PB) $60
Suites: 3 (PB) $90
Full Gourmet Breakfast
Minimum stay holidays, special events & high season (Mem. Day, Labor Day) : 2-3 nights
Credit Cards: A, B, C, D
Notes: 2, 5, 9, 10, 11, 12, 14

Parkside Bed and Breakfast

Bed and Breakfast-Rocky Mountains
906 South Pearl Street
Denver, 80209
(303) 744-8415; (800) 733-8415

Holden House—1902

This lovely Mediterranean-style home in a quiet Colorado Springs neighborhood offers the comforts of home in an excellent central location. It's a wonderful opportunity to relax in peaceful, private surroundings after a full day of activity and sightseeing. One guest room has a queen-size bed. Indoor lap pool and spa. Continental-plus breakfast, featuring baked goods and healthful cereals. No smoking, no pets, children over 12. Moderate rates.

Parkside

Bed and Breakfast-Rocky Mountains
906 South Pearl Street
Denver, 80209
(303) 744-8415; (800) 733-8415

The Victorian bedroom set in this contemporary, tri-level home makes a cozy place to visit. The hostess, a Colorado native, is knowledgeable about the area and the front range. A continental breakfast of fruit and fresh pastries is featured. The quiet park across the street frames a magnificent view of Pikes Peak. Short walk to stable, golf course, and tennis. No smoking. Budget rates.

Pinehaven Lodge

Bed and Breakfast-Rocky Mountains
906 South Pearl Street
Denver, 80209
(303) 744-8415; (800) 733-8415

These unhosted lodges are in the shadow of Pikes Peak, two miles from the beginning of Pikes Peak Highway. Their close proximity to Green Mountain Falls and Manitou Springs allows for fishing, tennis, swimming, hiking, horseback riding, or cross-country skiing. Dining is convenient at nearby restaurants. Weekly rates from mid-June through August. $65-100 daily.

Tudor Manor

Bed and Breakfast-Rocky Mountains
906 South Pearl Street
Denver, 80209
(303) 744-8415; (800) 733-8415

This stately 1929 home has been lovingly updated but still retains the feeling of a bygone era. Spacious rooms, exquisitely decorated with family treasures and antiques. Guests are invited to enjoy the cozy library with its first-edition books, fireplace, and railroad memorabilia. Full gourmet breakfast with international favorites served in an elegant dining room or on the patio. Complimentary fruit, cheese, and Colorado mineral water or wine in the evening. No pets or smoking. Moderate-luxury rates.

Valley View Family Bed and Breakfast

Bed and Breakfast-Rocky Mountains
906 South Pearl Street
Denver, 80209
(303) 744-8415; (800) 733-8415

This exceptional bed and breakfast caters to the entire family with a lovely three bedroom suite. Enjoy the fireside and balcony view overlooking the 9th green of the neighboring golf course. Master bedroom features a king-size bed and private bath; other rooms have queen beds and shared baths. Enjoy the fireside and balcony view overlooking the 9th green of the neighboring golf course, next-door swimming, year-round golf, croquet, swing set, and toy room. Full and hearty western gourmet, and complimentary bedtime snack. No smoking. Budget-moderate rates.

Whispering Pines

Bed and Breakfast-Rocky Mountains
906 South Pearl Street
Denver, 80209
(303) 744-8415; (800) 733-8415

This large, comfortable home overlooks a distant mountain from a private front deck entrance. The bed and breakfast is modestly furnished, and the hosts are very friendly. Main bedroom for guests has a double bed upstairs with a shared bath just outside your door. Can accommodate three additional guests downstairs in the family room. Large playroom with games and ping-pong table downstairs. Full breakfast. Budget rates.

6 Pets welcome; 7 Smoking allowed; 8 Children welcome; 9 Social drinking allowed; 10 Tennis available; 11 Swimming available; 12 Golf available; 13 Skiing available; 14 May be booked through travel agents.

CREEDE

Creede Hotel

Box 284, 81130
(719) 658-2608

The hotel is a landmark in Creede, dating back to the wild days of the silver boom. Four rooms, all with private baths, have been individually restored. The hotel dining room is open to the public and noted for its delicious food. You'll love Creede and the hotel! "Warm hospitality. . .capturing the lure of the 1890s."

Hosts: Cathy and Rich Ormsby
Rooms: 4 (PB) $59
Full Breakfast
Credit Cards: A, B, D
Notes: 2, 3, 4

CRESTED BUTTE

Claim Jumper

Bed and Breakfast-Rocky Mountains
906 South Pearl Street
Denver, 80209
(303) 744-8415; (800) 733-8415

This beautiful old log home features six unique theme rooms and is located within walking distance of romantic restaurants, famous bars and unusual shops. Full gourmet breakfast. No smoking, children not encouraged. Moderate-luxury, seasonal rates.

Purple Mountain Lodge

Box 897, 81224
(303) 349-5888

Guests enjoy sharing their adventures and discussing plans in the living room by a fire in the massive stone fireplace. If conversation slows, cable TV is available. The spa in the sun room offers welcome relief to tired muscles. Crested Butte is situated in a high (8,885 feet) , open valley surrounded by the Elk Mountains. It has many trails and roads to explore by foot, mountain bike, horseback, or four-wheel-drive automobile. Nearby mountain lakes and streams provide canoeing, kayaking, rafting, and fishing.

Hosts: Walter and Sherron Green
Rooms: 5 (3 PB; 2 SB) $40-76
Full Breakfast
Credit Cards: A, B, E
Notes: 2, 5, 7 (limited) , 8, 9, 10, 12, 13, 14

Tudor Rose Bed and Breakfast

P. O. Box 337, 429 White Rock, 81224
(303) 349-6253

A gracious country inn offering relaxed, down home atmosphere features five unique rooms dotted with antiques and period furniture. Hot tub, comfortable beds, hearty mountain breakfasts, and plenty of warm Crested Butte hospitality. Glacier Lily room features a full kitchen, private bath, and sleeps four to five guests. Located in the historic district, within two blocks of shopping, restaurants, and free ski shuttle. Children and pets welcome.

Hosts: Sherri and Mike
Rooms: 5 (1 PB; 2 SB) $60-85
Full Breakfast
Credit Cards: A, B
Notes: 2, 5, 6, 8, 10, 12, 13

The Portland Inn

CRIPPLE CREEK

The Portland Inn

Bed and Breakfast-Rocky Mountains
906 South Pearl Street
Denver, 80209
(303) 744-8415; (800) 733-8415

Cute, cozy and quaint describes this turn-of-the-century inn. Enjoy a relaxed atmosphere with four tastefully decorated rooms featuring antique beds and feather pillows. Three rooms have double beds, one has a queen with a single day bed. Sun deck, hot tub, and legalized gambling in Cripple Creek area. Continental-plus breakfast. Budget-moderate rates.

DENVER

Balsam

Bed and Breakfast-Rocky Mountains
906 South Pearl Street
Denver, 80209
(303) 744-8415; (800) 733-8415

Feel right at home in the comfortable, relaxing atmosphere of this two-story home in a quiet, residential area. Perfect area for morning walks, or enjoy coffee on the deck with a view of the mountains. Two rooms upstairs share a bath; both have double beds, and one has a crib. Continental-plus breakfast. No smoking, no pets, children welcome. Budget rates.

Bed and Breakfast Rocky Mountain-TNN-COL-ORADO

673 Grant Street, Denver, 80203
(303) 860-8415; (800) 733-8415

Part of the Bed and Breakfast National Network, Bed and Breakfast Rocky Mountain offers bed and breakfast not only in Colorado but also in many other cities and states across the country. The members of this network adhere strictly to the standards set by TNN, such as getting to know the hosts personally, having an established cancellation and refund policy, and following a thorough inspection and approval process for all properties rented. This is because each member of the network is dedicated to ensuring your comfort, pleasure and personal needs while you are staying at one of our "homes away from home."

Castle Marne

Castle Marne

1572 Race Street, 80206
(303) 331-0621; (800) 92-MARNE

Come, fall under the spell of one of Denver's grandest historic mansions. Built in 1889, the Marne is on both the local and national his toric registers. Your stay is a unique experience in pampered luxury. Minutes from the finest cultural, shopping, sightseeing attractions, and the convention center 12 minutes from Stapleton International Airport. Ask about our candlelight dinners.

Host: The Peiker family
Rooms: 9 (PB) $80-155
Full Breakfast
Credit Cards: A, B, C, E
Notes: 2, 5, 9, 10, 11, 12, 14

---

6 Pets welcome; 7 Smoking allowed; 8 Children welcome; 9 Social drinking allowed; 10 Tennis available; 11 Swimming available; 12 Golf available; 13 Skiing available; 14 May be booked through travel agents.

Cliff House Lodge

Bed and Breakfast-Rocky Mountains
906 South Pearl Street
Denver, 80209
(303) 744-8415; (800) 733-8415

In the center of Morrison, mountain ambiance surrounds Cliff House. Originally built in 1873, the Cliff House has been awarded a National Historic title. Eleven romantic bedrooms furnished with antiques offer a variety of bed sizes, and some accommodations are cottages with kitchens and honeymoon suites with private hot tubs and wood-burning fireplaces. Full gourmet breakfast is served each morning. No pets. Moderate-luxury rates.

The Gourmet

Bed and Breakfast-Rocky Mountains
906 South Pearl Street
Denver, 80209
(303) 744-8415; (800) 733-8415

This large, English Tudor-style home in Lakewood is situated on the quiet west side of Denver, yet is less than a 15-minute drive to the downtown area and historic Larimer Square. The home has an unusual, delightful antiques collection and a thriving greenhouse. Your hostess serves a full gourmet breakfast. No pets or smoking. $45.

On Golden Pond

Bed and Breakfast-Rocky Mountains
906 South Pearl Street
Denver, 80209
(303) 744-8415; (800) 733-8415

For European hospitality and a relaxing blend of country comfort, join us at our secluded 10-acre retreat. Six rooms offer a variety of bed sizes and amenities. Outdoor deck, pool, and spa, fishing, TV, phone, horseback, and bicycle riding available. Full breakfast. No smoking indoors. Moderate rates.

The Oxford Hotel

1600 17th Street, 80202
(303) 628-5400

Built in 1891, the landmark Oxford Hotel is celebrating its 101st birthday. Renovated in 1983, the rooms are furnished in 19th-century French and English antiques. Amenities include complimentary coffee service, sherry service, shoe shine, turn-down with chocolates, morning newspaper, and limousine service. Adjacent health club and European city spa. Situated in historic lower downtown less than one block from Union train station and close to shopping, dining, and arts complex.

Host: Jill Johnson
Rooms: 80 (PB) $89-275
Continental Breakfast
Credit Cards: A, B, C, D, E
Notes: 2, 3, 4, 5, 6, 7, 8, 9, 14

Queen Anne Inn

2147 Tremont Place, 80205
(303) 296-6666; (800) 432-INNS reservations only

Award-winning 1879 Victorian in downtown historic district. The luxurious, designer-quality surroundings and upscale amenities are among the most elegant anywhere. Already named "Best bed and breakfast in Town" and "Colorado Company of the Year." Listed by several editors as one of "America's Top Ten." Horse-drawn carriage rides, museums, art galleries, shopping, restaurants, cultural events, historic districts, lakes, streams, bike paths, and parks are available.

Hosts: Ann and Chuck Hillestad
Rooms: 10 (PB) $64-124
Expanded Continental Breakfast
Credit Cards: A, B, C
Notes: 2, 4 (advance notice) , 5, 9, 10, 11, 12, 14

Suburbia South

Bed and Breakfast-Rocky Mountains
906 South Pearl Street
Denver, 80209
(303) 744-8415; (800) 733-8415

NOTES: Credit cards accepted: A Master Card; B Visa; C American Express; D Discover Card; E Diner's Club; F Other; 2 Personal Checks accepted; 3 Lunch available; 4 Dinner available; 5 Open all year;

Enjoy a view of the nearby mountains from the windows of your room in this two-story traditional home. This home is furnished with many fine Victorian pieces collected by your hostess. Second floor has two guest rooms with double beds, goose-down quilts, and private baths. Continental breakfast. No smoking, no pets. Budget rates.

The Tree House

Bed and Breakfast-Rocky Mountains
906 South Pearl Street
Denver, 80209
(303) 744-8415; (800) 733-8415

The Tree House is a charming guest house in the middle of a ten-acre forest, with sixty-foot oak trees and maple trees surrounding the house. Balconies on the front and back of the house provide a perfect spot for afternoon tea or breakfast. Five bedrooms all have private baths, and four have wood-burning fireplaces. Full breakfast. Guests are welcome to use the kitchen and laundry facilities. No pets, no smoking. Moderate-luxury rates.

Victoria Oaks Inn

1575 Race Street, 80206
(303) 355-1818

The warmth and hospitality of Victoria Oaks Inn is apparent the moment you enter this historic restored 1896 mansion. Elegant original oak woodwork, tile fireplaces, and dramatic hanging staircase replete with ornate brass chandelier set the mood for a delightful visit.

Hosts: Clyde and Rie
Rooms: 9 (1 PB; 8 SB) $49-79
Continental Breakfast
Credit Cards: A, B, C, E, F
Notes: 2, 5, 6, 7, 8, 9, 10, 11, 12, 14

The Zang Mansion

Bed and Breakfast-Rocky Mountains
906 South Pearl Street, Denver, 80209
(303) 744-8415; (800) 733-8415

Enjoy quiet, relaxed elegance within minutes of sights, events, and shopping in downtown Denver. All business amenities available. This home is listed on the National Register of Historic Places. Master bedroom with attached private bath, fireplace, and TV; another room with a queen-size bed and unattached private bath; another room with a twin bed, and unattached private bath. Continental-plus breakfast served on Wedgwood china. No smoking, no pets. Moderate-luxury rates.

Zel's Soda Bar

Bed and Breakfast-Rocky Mountains
906 South Pearl Street
Denver, 80209
(303) 744-8415; (800) 733-8415

A lovely tri-level ranch home in Greenwood Village that boasts an imported (from Kansas) full soda fountain. If you are good, your hostess will make you a sundae. Two rooms with private baths. Full breakfast. No smoking, no pets, children welcome. Budget.

DILLON

Annabelle's Bed and Breakfast

Bed and Breakfast-Rocky Mountains
906 South Pearl Street
Denver, 80209
(303) 744-8415; (800) 733-8415

This quiet home provides comfortable and economical accommodations convenient to an area full of activity. Large four-room suite with private bath, daily maid service, TV, telephone, laundry facilities, and storage space for skis. Swimming, parking, Jacuzzi and sauna available. Continental-plus breakfast includes homemade coffee cakes, bagels, fruits, yogurt, coffee, tea, espresso or cappuccino. No smoking, no pets. Budget rates.

6 Pets welcome; 7 Smoking allowed; 8 Children welcome; 9 Social drinking allowed; 10 Tennis available; 11 Swimming available; 12 Golf available; 13 Skiing available; 14 May be booked through travel agents.

Blue Valley Guest House

Blue River Route 26 R, 80435
(303) 468-5731; (800) 530-3866

A charming mountain inn on the Blue
River, a gold-medal trout stream, surrounded by majestic peaks. Close to fishing, golf,
stables, hiking, biking, fantastic skiing,
restaurants, and shopping. Convenient, yet
quiet and private. Guests enjoy the large
fireplace room, outdoor hot tub, and deck.
Comfortable sleeping is a priority. High
Country continental breakfast includes hot
breads, fresh fruit, and gourmet coffee
served from an antique tea wagon at the
window table overlooking the river.

Hosts: Alice and George Lund
Rooms: 3 (1 PB; 2 SB) $50-85
Expanded Continental Breakfast
Credit Cards: A, B
Notes: 5, 8, 9, 10, 12, 13, 14

Paradox Lodge

Gore Range
Bed and Breakfast

Bed and Breakfast-Rocky Mountains
906 South Pearl Street
Denver, 80209
(303) 744-8415; (800) 733-8415

Picture yourself having a hot, hearty breakfast in view of the Colorado Rockies' spectacular Gore Range. Warmth and personal
attention is the trademark. Situated in a
quiet, wooded residential area only minutes

away from all ski areas, walking distance to
factory outlet stores, tennis courts, fishing,
and fine restaurants. No smoking. Budget-
luxury, seasonal rates.

Paradox Lodge

Bed and Breakfast-Rocky Mountains
906 South Pearl Street
Denver, 80209
(303) 744-8415; (800) 733-8415

Paradox Lodge is situated on 37 acres
secluded on the Snake River surrounded by
national forest. From this 10,000-foot location there are vistas of mountain peaks and
alpine forests. Biking, hiking, cross-country ski trails. Access to paved road and
close to Summit County ski resorts.
Continental breakfast. Moderate-luxury
rates.

Puddin' and the Fat Cat

Bed and Breakfast-Rocky Mountains
906 South Pearl Street
Denver, 80209
(303) 744-8415; (800) 733-8415

A cozy, warm Wilderness home in the
pines. Guests have room with queen bed,
cable TV, and private bath. Cross-country
skiing, hiking, and mountain bike trail-
heads one block from home. Full, gourmet-
to-order, breakfast. No smoking. Moderate-
luxury, seasonal rates.

Snowberryhill

P. O. Box 2910, 80435
(303) 468-8010

Quiet, antique-filled, romantic getaway situated 70 miles west of Denver in Summit
County, the heart of Colorado ski country.
Lace curtains and quilts lend charm to the
private suite occupying the entire first
floor. Bedroom has antique queen-size
brass bed. Living room has two additional
twins and kitchen. Private bath. TV/VCR,

phone. Memorable full breakfasts. Central to six major ski areas, cross-country skiing, mountain biking, fishing, horseback riding, hiking, golf, tennis.

Hosts: Kristi and George Blincoe
Rooms: 1 (PB) $60-100
Full Breakfast
Credit Cards: None
Notes: 2, 5, 8, 9, 10, 11, 12, 13, 14

DOLORES

Historic Rio Grande Southern Hotel

101 South 5th Street, P. O. Box 516
(303) 882-7527

This historic railroad hotel was built in 1893. Situated on the town square, it is within walking distance to the Dolores River, McFee Reservoir, Mesa Verde National Park, Anasazi Heritage Center, Crow Canyon, and golfing. Fishing, skiing, hunting, backpacking, and bicycling. Ski Telluride half-price program available. Open year round.

Hosts: Tom and Beverly Clark
Rooms: 13 (3 PB; 10 SB) $45-60
Full Breakfast
Credit Cards: A, B, C, D
Notes: 2, 5, 7, 8, 10, 11, 12, 13

Snowberryhill

Mountain View Bed and Breakfast

28050 County Road P, 81323
(303) 882-7861

Mountain View is located in the "four corners area," and is one mile from the gateway to the San Juan Skyway, a designated national 238 mile scenic loop, and twelve miles from the entrance to Mesa Verde National Park. Mountain View includes twenty-two acres with walking trails, cottonwood-lined stream and canyon. Located on the west slope of the San Juan Mountains at an elevation of 6,500, overlooking the beautiful Montezuma Valley.

Hosts: Brenda and Cecil Dunn
Rooms: 7 (PB) $45-55
Full Breakfast
Credit Cards: A, B
Notes: 2, 5, 8, 11, 12, 13

DURANGO

Blue Spruce Trading Post

Bed and Breakfast-Rocky Mountains
906 South Pearl Street
Denver, 80209
(303) 744-8415; (800) 733-8415

A great place for families, this log, roadside inn relives the tradition of the "Old West" stage stops. Five large well-kept rooms on the second floor each have private baths, and a variety of bed sizes is available. Full breakfast is served. No smoking, no pets, children welcome. Budget rates.

Country Sunshine Bed and Breakfast

35130 Highway 550N, 81301
(303) 247-2853; (800) 383-2853

Nestled below rocky bluffs, there's a spectacular view of the San Juan Mountains from this spacious ranch home. Enjoy the

---

6 Pets welcome; 7 Smoking allowed; 8 Children welcome; 9 Social drinking allowed; 10 Tennis available; 11 Swimming available; 12 Golf available; 13 Skiing available; 14 May be booked through travel agents.

sound of the Animas River flowing or the sight of abundant wildlife from the deck. The bed and breakfast has spacious common areas, serves full hearty breakfasts, and is centrally situated to many area attractions.

Hosts: Jim and Jill
Rooms: 6 (PB) $85-100
Full Breakfast
Credit Cards: A, B
Notes: 2, 5, 8, 9, 11, 12, 13, 14

Gable House

Bed and Breakfast-Rocky Mountains
906 South Pearl Street
Denver, 80209
(303) 744-8415; (800) 733-8415

A wonderful spot for couples, this three-story Queen Anne Victorian home is located on a tree-lined street in an established neighborhood. Spacious rooms with both single and double beds available share two baths down the hall. Full breakfast. Smoking on the balconies only, no pets, children over 12 welcome. Budget rates, available July-August only.

Logwood Bed and Breakfast

35060 U.S. Highway 550, 81301
(303) 259-4396; (800) 369-4082

Logwood is a red cedar log structure designed as a home and bed and breakfast. Large windows allow the natural beauty of the upper Animas Valley to be with you indoors. The spacious deck is a place to languish on a warm afternoon, sip iced tea, and take in the mountains, river and stream, birds, trees. Logwood is a home away from home. Pamper yourselves, as others do, and come home to Logwood!

Hosts: Debbie and Greg Verheyden
Rooms: 5 (PB) $70-80
Full Breakfast
Credit Cards: A, B
Notes: 2, 5, 8 (over 6) , 9, 11, 12, 13, 14

Penny's Place

1041 County Road 307, 81301
(303) 247-8928

Penny's Place is 11 miles from Durango, situated on 26 acres in rolling countryside overlooking the spectacular La Plata Mountains. There are deer and meadowlarks visiting most days. There is a king room with a private entrance, deck, and bath. A spiral staircase joins this room to the common room with a hot tub, satellite TV, and wood-burning stove. A stay of several days is recommended to see the wonderful sites of the Durango area, including the narrow gauge train, Mesa Verde, hiking, horseback riding, fishing and more.

Host: Penny O'Keefe
Rooms: 3 (1 PB; 2 SB) $44-65
Full Breakfast
Credit Cards: A, B
Notes: 2, 5, 8, 9, 12, 13, 14

River House
Bed and Breakfast

495 Animas View Drive, 81301
(303) 247-4775

River House is a large, sprawling, southwestern home facing the Animas River. Guests eat in a large atrium filled with plants, a water fountain, and eight skylights. Antiques, art, and artifacts from around the world decorate the six bedrooms, snooker and music room, and common room with fireplace and large-screen TV. Comfort, casualness, and fun are themes.

Host: Crystal Carroll
Rooms: 6 (PB) $45-65
Full Breakfast
Credit Cards: A, B, D
Notes: 2, 5, 8, 9, 10, 11, 12, 13, 14

Scrubby Oaks
Bed and Breakfast Inn

P. O. Box 1047, 81302
(303) 247-2176

NOTES: Credit cards accepted: A Master Card; B Visa; C American Express; D Discover Card; E Diner's Club; F Other; 2 Personal Checks accepted; 3 Lunch available; 4 Dinner available; 5 Open all year;

Situated on ten acres overlooking the spectacular Animas Valley and surrounding mountains. Three miles from downtown Durango and one-half hour from Purgatory ski resort. Rooms are spacious and furnished with antiques, art works, and good books. Beautiful gardens and patios frame the inn outside, with large sitting areas inside for guest use.

Host: Mary Ann Craig
Rooms: 7 (3 PB; 4 S2B) $55-65
Full Breakfast
Credit Cards: None
Notes: 2, 5, 8, 9, 10, 11, 12, 13, 14

EATON

The Victorian Veranda Bed and Breakfast

P. O. Box 361, 515 Cheyenne Avenue
(303) 454-3890

Wood-framed, two-story Queen Anne-style house with a wraparound porch that overlooks a mountain view. All three rooms are very comfortable and furnished with antiques of the 1800s. Guests enjoy relaxing in a private whirlpool tub, riding the bicycles built for two, or listening to the baby grand player piano. One bedroom has a wood-burning fireplace and a balcony. A large picnic area is available in the backyard for guests to cook their own lunch and dinner.

Hosts: Dick and Nadine White
Rooms: 3 (1 PB; 2 SB) $40-55
Full Breakfast
Credit Cards: None
Notes: 2, 5, 8, 12

ELDORA SPRINGS

Goldminer Hotel

601 Klondyke Avenue, 80466-9542
(800) 422-4629

Built in 1897, this hotel served miners' needs through the 1920s. Situated in the middle of the Eldora National Historic District, the Goldminer offers the traveler a unique vantage point for horseback trips to the Continental Divide or legal gambling in the historic mining town of Central City just minutes to the south. Winter brings skiing at the door. Beautiful weather year-round.

Host: Carol Rinderknecht
Rooms: 6 (2 PB; 3 SB; 1 Cabin) $43-95
Full Breakfast
Credit Cards: A, B, D
Notes: 2, 5, 6, 7, 8, 9, 13, 14

EMPIRE

Mad Creek Bed and Breakfast

Bed and Breakfast-Rocky Mountains
906 South Pearl Street
Denver, 80209
(303) 744-8415; (800) 733-8415

This 1881 Gothic-style home offers both a rustic atmosphere and Victorian charm. The common area features a bay window with snow-shoe style love seat and rock fireplaces. Second floor bedrooms are furnished with antiques and cozy comforters on double beds, and include ceiling fans, knotty pine floors, fleece robes, and shared bath on the main floor. Continental-plus breakfast includes homemade granola, jam and muffins, gourmet coffee and tea. No smoking, no children, no pets. Budget rates.

ESTES PARK

Allenspark Lodge

Bed and Breakfast-Rocky Mountains
906 South Pearl Street
Denver, 80209
(303) 744-8415; (800) 733-8415

Virtually every charm and beauty of the high mountain world is your to enjoy at Allenspark Lodge. Fifteen rooms with a variety of bed sizes and amenities are avail-

6 Pets welcome; 7 Smoking allowed; 8 Children welcome; 9 Social drinking allowed; 10 Tennis available; 11 Swimming available; 12 Golf available; 13 Skiing available; 14 May be booked through travel agents.

able, and the special "Hideaway" room with brass bed, decorator linens, and a private bath with an old-fashioned bear claw tub is perfect for honeymooners. Hot tub, game room, and a wine and cheese bar with a variety of wines and beers open to guests. Continental-plus breakfast features home baked goods. No smoking, no pets, children welcome. Moderate rates.

The Anniversary Inn

1060 Mary's Lake Road, Moraine Route, 80517
(303) 586-6200

The Anniversary Inn is a turn-of-the-century log home situated one mile from Rocky Mountain National Park and one and one-half miles from the shopping area of Estes Park. The inn is convenient to a multitude of activities. Antiques and cozy country accents are a part of each of the guest rooms and common areas. Exposed log walls, beamed ceilings, and a massive moss-rock fireplace are among the inn's highlights.

Hosts: Don and Susan Landwer
Rooms: 5 (2 PB; 3 SB) $65-100
Full Breakfast
Credit Cards: A, B
Notes: 2, 5, 10, 11, 12, 13, 14

Black Dog Inn

Bed and Breakfast-Rocky Mountains
906 South Pearl Street
Denver, 80209
(303) 744-8415; (800) 733-8415

Built in 1910, this rambling mountain bed and breakfast is surrounded by towering fir and aspen on a rolling acre and has an expansive view of Lumpy Ridge and the Estes Valley. The inn has four guest rooms with both private and shared baths, and all rooms are decorated with family antiques. Complimentary bicycles, goodies with hot and cold drinks served, and full country breakfast with typical Colorado fare. No smoking, no pets, children over 15. Moderate-luxury rates.

Cottenwood House

Bed and Breakfast-Rocky Mountains
906 South Pearl Street
Denver, 80209
(303) 744-8415; (800) 733-8415

Old-fashioned hospitality awaits you at Cottenwood House, from the lemonade on the front porch in the summer and complimentary wine in the evenings to the floral-scented bath salts and handmade sachets to freshen your suitcase. Breakfast menus change daily and may include blueberry Belgian waffles, eggs Benedict or gingerbread pancakes. Situated three miles from Rocky Mountain National Park. Moderate-luxury rates.

Emerald Manor

441 Chiquita Lane, P. O. Box 3592, 80517
(303) 586-8050

This elegant estate home is in the Rocky Mountains within easy walking distance of downtown Estes Park. The home is approximately 8,000 square feet, with indoor pool and sauna, game room with pool table. Enjoy a full gourmet breakfast and look forward to meeting other guests.

Hosts: Reggie and Moira Fowler
Rooms: 5 (S3B) $59-69
Full Breakfast
Credit Cards: For deposit only
Notes: 2, 5, 9, 10, 11, 12, 13, 14

Hearthside
Bed and Breakfast Inn

Bed and Breakfast-Rocky Mountains
906 South Pearl Street
Denver, 80209
(303) 744-8415; (800) 733-8415

You'll experience more than the beauty of the Rocky Mountains when you discover the warm hospitality and European ambience of the HearthSide Inn. Pamper yourself in a jetted whirl bathtub. The unique textures, patterns, and antique furnishings are reminiscent of European country

NOTES: Credit cards accepted: A Master Card; B Visa; C American Express; D Discover Card; E Diner's Club; F Other; 2 Personal Checks accepted; 3 Lunch available; 4 Dinner available; 5 Open all year;

homes. A gazebo, reflection pond, and walking paths await your delight and pleasure. Full breakfast. No smoking. Luxury rates.

Henderson House

Bed and Breakfast-Rocky Mountains
906 South Pearl Street
Denver, 80209
(303) 744-8415; (800) 733-8415

Relax and be pampered with royal service in this inviting Victorian and cape Cod-style home. Two rooms and a master suite, all with private baths and king-size beds. Two rooms have whirlpool tubs for two. Complimentary snack baskets available on arrival. Full breakfast. Hosts are a Christian couple with over 12 years of experience. Married couples only, no smoking, no pets, no children. Luxury rates.

Inn of Glen Haven

Bed and Breakfast-Rocky Mountains
906 South Pearl Street
Denver, 80209
(303) 744-8415; (800) 733-8415

This Old English inn nestled in the Rocky Mountains offers a complete retreat for the family. No TV, no clocks, no radios. Five rooms with private baths, two suites and a cottage available. Gourmet dining in the small pub. Continental breakfast. No smoking in the rooms, no pets, well-behaved children welcome. Moderate-luxury rates.

RiverSong Inn

P. O. Box 1910, 80517
(303) 586-4666

Once the summer home of the very rich, this nine-room inn lies secluded at the end of a country road on 30 forested acres. A veritable wildlife sanctuary with its private ponds, wildflower gardens, hiking trails in the forest, the inn also has a "heart-stop-ping" view of the snow-capped peaks of Rocky Mountain National Park. All of the rooms have private baths, some with Jacuzzi whirlpool tubs in front of fireplaces. With no guest phones or TV's but only the sounds of a rushing trout stream to lull you to sleep, it's easy to see why RiverSong is so very popular as a romantic escape.

Hosts: Gary and Sue Mansfield
Rooms: 9 (PB) $85-160
Full Breakfast
Credit Cards: A, B
Notes: 2, 4, 5, 14

Rocky Pines Bed and Breakfast

Bed and Breakfast-Rocky Mountains
906 South Pearl Street
Denver, 80209
(303) 744-8415; (800) 733-8415

A contemporary mountain home on four and one-half acres of rock outcroppings, ponderosa, and fir. Ideally situated within two miles of excellent hiking in Rocky Mountain National Park. Full breakfasts are served on the deck. Homemade cinnamon sticky rolls and a variety of treats. Trail lunches for hikers at no additional charge. Children welcome. No pets or smoking. Moderate rates.

Sapphire Rose

Bed and Breakfast-Rocky Mountains
906 South Pearl Street
Denver, 80209
(303) 744-8415; (800) 733-8415

The Sapphire Rose is a beautifully restored 1909 home situated one block from the village and within minutes of scenic Rocky Mountain National Park. Awaken each morning to the fresh aroma of a special country breakfast being prepared just for you. In spring and summer: fishing, hiking, boating, golf, tennis, horseback riding. In winter: skiing, snowmobiling, sleigh rides, or ice skating. Special gourmet dinners prepared on request by host, who is a master chef. Children welcome. No smoking. Moderate-luxury rates.

Shining Mountains Inn

775 West Wonderview Avenue
P. O. Box 3100, 80517
(303) 586-5886

Special touches are what you will love about Shining Mountains Inn, from the fresh fruit and snacks available in the kitchen, to warm booties and your own cozy bathrobe. The inn, a 12-room log home more than half a century old, is friendly like its well-traveled hosts. You can curl up near the moss-rock fireplace with a book from the library, picnic on five acres, or enjoy the vast mountain views from the sun room. Breakfasts are hearty and healthful. Afternoon tea is at four o'clock with freshly baked goodies. Rocky Mountain National Park is the inn's back yard—so come share it!

Hosts: Tad and Dean Wariner
Rooms: 2 (PB) $75-85
Full Breakfast
Credit Cards: A, B
Notes: 2, 10, 11, 12, 13, 14

Valhalla Resort

Bed and Breakfast-Rocky Mountains
906 South Pearl Street
Denver, 80209
(303) 744-8415; (800) 733-8415

Tucked away from the highway next to the Rocky Mountain National Park is a quiet little paradise known as Valhalla Resort. From rustic to luxurious, Valhalla offers a wide variety of clean and comfortable accommodations surrounded by trees and mountains. Complete vacation homes with fireplace, cable TV, full kitchens, hot tubs, and laundry facilities are available. Continental breakfast. No pets. Budget-luxury, seasonal rates.

FORT COLLINS

Duck Inn

Bed and Breakfast-Rocky Mountains
906 South Pearl Street
Denver, 80209
(303) 744-8415; (800) 733-8415

Located near Colorado State University, this charming and comfortable home is surrounded by large Colorado spruce and mature landscaping. Four guest rooms with shared family bath feature heirloom antique furniture. Refrigerator for guests' beverages available, and the sun porch on the second floor has a sitting area with a TV and large selection of books. Smoking in livingroom only, no pets, well-behaved children welcome. Budget rates.

Elizabeth Street Guest House

Bed and Breakfast-Rocky Mountains
906 South Pearl Street
Denver, 80209
(303) 744-8415; (800) 733-8415

This beautifully restored 1905 house is situated in the historic district, one block from Colorado State University and within walking distance to Old Town. The turn-of-the-century ambience is enhanced with antiques, porcelain dolls, and other country handicrafts made and collected by the owner. Scenic hiking and fishing up the Poudre River 20 minutes away. Full breakfast. Children over ten welcome. No pets or smoking. $45-55; $150 for whole house, two-day minimum.

FRISCO

Finn Inn

Bed and Breakfast-Rocky Mountains
906 South Pearl Street
Denver, 80209
(303) 744-8415; (800) 733-8415

NOTES: Credit cards accepted: A Master Card; B Visa; C American Express; D Discover Card; E Diner's Club; F Other; 2 Personal Checks accepted; 3 Lunch available; 4 Dinner available; 5 Open all year;

This Frisco Country house will welcome you with a beautiful mountain view from the large, open living room and wrap-around deck. The two bedrooms and bath downstairs can form a suite. A third bedroom upstairs has one double bed, one twin, and a private half-bath. Hot tub on outside deck, and huge moss rock fireplace. Full and hearty country breakfast. Moderate, seasonal rates.

Frisco Lodge

321 Main Street, P. O. Box 1325, 80443
(303) 668-0195; (800) 279-6000

The Frisco Lodge, built in 1885, is the longest ongoing lodging facility in Summit County. It was a stagecoach stop as well as a facility serving train passengers on the D and RGW Railroad. The lodge is centrally situated in town to all the finer shops and restaurants. Outdoor hot tub, ski and bicycle tuning and storage room, free movies, phones. Great location near the extensive 50-plus mile paved bike path network.

Hosts: Susan Wentworth and Bruce Knoepfel
Rooms: 18 (10 PB; 8 SB) $25-75
Continental Breakfast
Credit Cards: A, B, C, D
Notes: 2, 5, 7, 8, 9, 10, 11, 12, 13

MarDei's Mountain Retreat

221 South 4th Avenue, 80443
(303) 668-5337

MarDei's chalet architecture is influenced by and features European design interior. Guest rooms have king, queen, and twin beds with down comforters. Hot tub and fireplaces available, and the inn is located in the center of four ski areas. Bicycle trails, rafting, fishing, and sailing are also nearby.

Hosts: Steve and Tommy Office
Rooms: 5 (2 PB; 3 SB) $35-100
Full European Breakfast
Credit Cards: None
Notes: 2, 5, 8, 9, 12, 13, 14

Naomi's Nook

Bed and Breakfast Vail Ski Areas
P. O. Box 491, 81658
(303) 949-1212; (800) 748-2666

Located in a quiet neighborhood, this one bedroom suite has a private entrance and bath with laundry facilities. Guests basically have the whole floor to themselves, although hosts enjoy talking and visiting with guests and would be happy to sit and talk in front of the wood-burning stove. Breakfast is served either upstairs or downstairs in your suite. Great central location for the wide variety of skiing mountains that Summit County offers.

Frisco Lodge

Twilight Inn

Bed and Breakfast-Rocky Mountains
906 South Pearl Street
Denver, 80209
(303) 744-8415; (800) 733-8415

The Twilight Inn is situated in downtown Frisco with convenient access to ski areas. The three-story, twelve-room inn has private and shared baths, double and queen beds. Within walking distance to shuttle stops, restaurants, night clubs, and horse-and-buggy rides. Expanded continental breakfast. Moderate-luxury, seasonal rates.

6 Pets welcome; 7 Smoking allowed; 8 Children welcome; 9 Social drinking allowed; 10 Tennis available; 11 Swimming available; 12 Golf available; 13 Skiing available; 14 May be booked through travel agents.

GEORGETOWN

The Hardy House

Bed and Breakfast-Rocky Mountains
906 South Pearl Street
Denver, 80209
(303) 744-8415; (800) 733-8415

The Hardy House is situated in the historic mining town of Georgetown, only an hour's drive from Denver. This Victorian home is one-half block from Main Street shops and a 15-minute walk to the Loop railroad station. A 10- to 45-minute drive to five major ski areas, and great fishing in Clear Creek is a stone's throw away. Full breakfast. No smoking. Budget-moderate rates.

GLENWOOD SPRINGS

Adducci's Inn Bed and Breakfast

Bed and Breakfast-Rocky Mountains
906 South Pearl Street
Denver, 80209
(303) 744-8415; (800) 733-8415

A picture setting come true, this turn-of-the-century Victorian home has been refurbished with antiques and is convenient to all Glenwood Springs has to offer. Rooms are available with private baths and common shower. Full breakfast. Hot tub. No smoking, no pets. Budget-moderate rates.

Bedsprings Bed and Breakfast

Bed and Breakfast-Rocky Mountains
906 South Pearl Street
Denver, 80209
(303) 744-8415; (800) 733-8415

This charming post-Victorian home is distinguished by its high ceiling, natural oak woodwork, large country kitchen, and big wrap-around porch. Two blocks from the railroad station, free ski bus for Sunlight ski area, shops, and restaurants. Hot Springs Pool close by. No pets or smoking. Budget-moderate rates.

The Kaiser House

932 Cooper Avenue, 81601
(303) 945-8827; FAX (303) 945-8826

In the center of the "Spa of the Rockies," The Kaiser House features turn-of-century charm with twentieth-century conveniences. Located on the corner of 10th and Cooper, The Kaiser House features seven bedrooms, each with attached baths, and each uniquely decorated in Victorian style. In the winter, before hitting the ski slopes, enjoy a gourmet breakfast in the spacious dining room or the sunny breakfast area. In the summer, enjoy brunch on the private patio. From the Kaiser House, it's an easy walk to parks, shopping, and fine restaurants, and to the Hot Springs Pool and Vapor Caves.

Hosts: Ingrid and Glen Eash
Rooms: 7 (PB) $55-115
Full Breakfast
Credit Cards: A, B
Notes: 2, 5, 9, 10, 11, 12, 13, 14

GOLDEN

The Dove Inn

711 14th Street, 80401-1906
(303) 278-2209

Charming Victorian inn situated in the foothills of west Denver, yet in the small-town atmosphere of Golden. Close to Coors tours, Rocky Mountain National Park; one hour to ski areas. No unmarried couples, please.

Hosts: Sue and Guy Beals
Rooms: 6 (4 PB; 2 SB) $44-64
Full Breakfast
Credit Cards: A, B, C, E
Notes: 2, 5, 8, 9, 10, 11, 12, 13, 14

NOTES: Credit cards accepted: A Master Card; B Visa; C American Express; D Discover Card; E Diner's Club; F Other; 2 Personal Checks accepted; 3 Lunch available; 4 Dinner available; 5 Open all year;

GRAND JUNCTION

Cedars' Edge Llamas Bed and Breakfast

Bed and Breakfast-Rocky Mountains
906 South Pearl Street
Denver, 80209
(303) 744-8415; (800) 733-8415

Unique cedar home filled with handmade decor and lots of green plants. Peaceful, quiet atmosphere with fabulous 100-mile view. Breakfast on you own private deck overlooking llama pastures and cedar forests. Two bedrooms feature queen or double beds, private baths, and your own private deck. Full breakfast, served in romantic privacy. Children welcome, smoking and pets outside only. Budget-moderate rates.

The Cider House Bed and Breakfast

1126 Grand Avenue, 81501
(303) 242-9087

The Cider House Bed and Breakfast is at home in a 1907 frame house refurbished and decorated with wallpaper and lots of lace. Antiques and French doors carry out the Victorian theme. The guest rooms are queen-size with lots of light and quiet. A full breakfast is served in the formal dining room. The hostess enjoys entertaining and welcomes the opportunity to make the guests' travel experiences memorable.

Host: Helen Mills
Rooms: 4 (1 PB; 3 SB) $38-45
Full Breakfast
Credit Cards: A, B
Notes: 2, 3, 4, 5, 7 (limited) , 8, 10, 11, 12, 13

Gate House Bed and Breakfast

Bed and Breakfast-Rocky Mountains
906 South Pearl Street
Denver, 80209
(303) 744-8415; (800) 733-8415

Built in 1899 as part of the Osgood Mansion in Redstone, this Tudor-style home also served as the south gatehouse to the Redstone Castle. In 1945 it was moved to its present location. It has been restored and offers the warmth and elegance of a fine English country inn. The grounds are perfect for outdoor weddings with fruit trees, a myriad of flowers, and a vine-covered arbor. Many outdoor sports are nearby. Full breakfast. Children over 12 welcome. No pets or smoking. Budget-moderate rates.

Junction Country Inn

861 Grand Avenue, 81501
(303) 241-2817

Lace curtains and rocking chairs, timeless memories and new friends await you in beautiful surroundings, the comfortable feeling of "coming home." Join us at the inn when you need to relax. Children welcome and provided for. The inn's non-smoking atmosphere and delicious full breakfast will fuel you for a day of recreation and sightseeing.

Hosts: The Bloom family
Rooms: 4 (20PB; 2 SB) $30-59
Full Breakfast
Credit Cards: A, B, C
Notes: 2, 5, 8, 9, 12, 13, 14

GRAND LAKE

Onahu Lodge

Bed and Breakfast-Rocky Mountains
906 South Pearl Street
Denver, 80209
(303) 744-8415; (800) 733-8415

A wonderful experience in the Colorado Rockies, this hand hewn log home offers a spectacular view of the "Never Summer Mountains" and the Rocky Mountain National Park Land. Two charming bedrooms with private and shared baths have patios that overlook the salt lick. Nearby stable for rental horses, excellent fishing,

6 Pets welcome; 7 Smoking allowed; 8 Children welcome; 9 Social drinking allowed; 10 Tennis available; 11 Swimming available; 12 Golf available; 13 Skiing available; 14 May be booked through travel agents.

hiking and boating, great for single writers and artists (special long-term rates and use of a secluded office possible.) Continental breakfast features home baked muffins. No smoking, children over 5. Moderate-luxury rates.

Peak's Point

Bed and Breakfast-Rocky Mountains
906 South Pearl Street, Denver, 80209
(303) 744-8415; (800) 733-8415

This four-level 2300-square-foot home overlooks Lake Granby, the Colorado River, and Rocky Mountain National Park. Enjoy spacious, private decks in the summer and the large indoor hot tub anytime. Two bedrooms, each with private baths and doubles. Laundry facilities available. Full and hearty breakfast. No pets, children over 6, smoking permitted. Moderate rates.

Winding River Resort Bed and Breakfast

Bed and Breakfast-Rocky Mountains
906 South Pearl Street
Denver, 80209
(303) 744-8415; (800) 733-8415

Winding River is picturesquely nestled between Rocky Mountain National Park and Arapahoe National Forest in the countryside of Grand Lake village. Start your morning with a gourmet breakfast in the home of your hosts. Horseback riding, fishing, hiking, cross-country skiing, snowmobiling, ice skating, and sleigh rides. Children welcome. No smoking. Moderate-luxury rates.

GREELEY

Sterling House Inn

Bed and Breakfast-Rocky Mountains
906 South Pearl Street
Denver, 80209
(303) 744-8415; (800) 733-8415

Enjoy the comfort and charm of this recently renovated 100-year-old Victorian, once the home of one of Greeley's pioneers. Two rooms are available, both decorated with antiques, queen beds and private baths. Many amenities for the business traveler. Full gourmet breakfast. No pets, smoking on the back porch only, children over 10 welcome. Budget-moderate rates.

Mary Lawrence Inn

GUNNISON

Mary Lawrence Inn

601 North Taylor Street, 81230
(303) 641-3343

Make this Victorian home the center of your excursions through Gunnison County. The mountains, river, and lakes are extraordinary. Golf, swimming, rafting are accessible. The inn is furnished with antiques and collectibles. Breakfasts are bountiful and imaginative. Special event weekends: fly fishing, mystery. Great ski package offered for Crested Butte skiing.

Hosts: Tom and Les Bushman
Rooms: 3 (PB) $63
Suite: 2 (PB) $78
Full Breakfast
Credit Cards: A, B
Notes: 2, 5, 8, 10, 11, 12, 13, 14

NOTES: Credit cards accepted: A Master Card; B Visa; C American Express; D Discover Card; E Diner's Club; F Other; 2 Personal Checks accepted; 3 Lunch available; 4 Dinner available; 5 Open all year;

HESPERUS

Blue Lake Ranch

16919 Highway 140, 81326
(303) 385-4537

Blue Lake Ranch has evolved from a simple homestead to a luxurious European-style country estate. Surrounded by the gardens that supply the ranch's flower seed businesses, the ranch overlooks trout-filled Blue Lake and the La Plata Mountains, offering a quiet retreat fifteen minutes from Durango. A European-style buffet breakfast and afternoon tea are complementary. A magical experience in a magnificent private setting in all four seasons.

Hosts: Shirley and David Alford
Main House: 4 BR, 4 Bath
Cottage: 1 BR, 1 Bath
Cabin: 3 BR, 2 Baths
Suites: 1 BR, 1 Bath
Suite: 2 PB $78
Full Breakfast
Credit Cards: None
Notes: 2, 5, 8, 9, 10, 11

IDAHO SPRINGS

St. Mary's Glacier Bed and Breakfast

Bed and Breakfast-Rocky Mountains
906 South Pearl Street
Denver, 80209
(303) 744-8415; (800) 733-8415

From the deck of this a mountain retreat, you can enjoy majestic views of the Continental Divide, a waterfall, and a lake. In the evening, return to your suite to be greeted by a teddy bear wrapped in a down comforter on a brass queen-size bed. Relax in a private hot tub surrounded by hearts and bears or enjoy a roaring fire in a wood-burning stove in the livingroom. Full breakfast. No smoking, no children. Moderate rates.

KEYSTONE

The Ski Tip Lodge

P. O. Box 38/ 07, Montezuma Road
(303) 468-4202; (800) 222-0188

The Ski Tip Lodge is a restored stagecoach stop dating back to the 1860s. The existing lodge was built by the Dercum family in the early 1940s. At the Ski Tip Lodge, guests enjoy comfortable, cozy rooms furnished with antiques. A fine dining experience in the restaurant, featuring American regional cuisine, is available to guests and the public year round. Ski Tip is adjacent to the Cross Country Center and Trails.

Rooms: 19 (17 PB; 2 SB) $66-250
Full Breakfast in winter; continental in summer
Credit Cards: A, B, C
Notes: 3, 4, 5, 8, 9, 10, 11, 12, 13, 14

LAKE CITY

The Adobe Bed and Breakfast

Bed and Breakfast-Rocky Mountains
906 South Pearl Street
Denver, 80209
(303) 744-8415; (800) 733-8415

Don't miss this unique custom-designed adobe home that has an exquisite art collection, many antiques, and two bedrooms that share a full and a half bath. Perched on a hillside overlooking the historic mining town of Lake City. Spacious common area with fireplace and hot tub in the solarium is available for guests. Full gourmet breakfast is served with homemade jams and muffins. No smoking or pets. Moderate, seasonal rates.

The Crystal Lodge

P. O. Box 246, 81235
(303) 944-2201

This beautiful mountain retreat offers a quiet and secluded retreat from city life.

The hosts are dedicated to good taste in accommodations, guest rooms, apartments, and cottages. As a guest, you will be served delicious foods in the charming restaurant. Enjoy the heated swimming pool, biking, and hiking. The biking and hiking trails are right outside the front door.

Hosts: Harley, Caryl, Sarah, and Katie Rudofsky
Rooms: 18 (PB) $54-95
Credit Cards: None
Notes: 2, 4, 11

The Moss Rose Bed and Breakfast

P. O. Box 910, 81235
(303) 366-4069

A remote, secluded retreat nestled in a high mountain valley at 9,700 feet. Fishing, hunting, biking, Jeeping, and just plain relaxing. Great breakfasts, queen beds, and a spectacular mountain setting. 9 miles west of Lake City-Alpine Loop Scenic route.

Hosts: Dan and Joan Moss
Rooms: 3 (1 PB; 2 SB) $50-60
Full Breakfast
Credit Cards: None
Open May 15-Nov. 1
Notes: 2, 9

Historic Delaware Hotel

The Old Carson Inn

Bed and Breakfast-Rocky Mountains
906 South Pearl Street, Denver, 80209
(303) 744-8415; (800) 733-8415

Beautiful log home blends comfort, style, and hospitality with the rustic Old West. Five rooms with private baths and a variety of bed sizes. Hot tub, complimentary coffee, tea, and desserts. Full breakfast, served family style. No pets, no smoking, children over 6 welcome. Budget-moderate rates.

LEADVILLE

Historic Delaware Hotel

700 Harrison Avenue, 80461
(719) 486-1418; (800) 748-2004

Enjoy the ambiance of this historic hotel, circa 1886. Each of the thirty-six rooms features antique furnishings and heirloom style bedspreads. Private baths and TV are in every room, and a Jacuzzi, Callaway's Restaurant, and Victorian lobby and lounge are available for guests to enjoy.

Rooms: 36 (PB) $50-90
Full Breakfast
Credit Cards: A, B, C, D, E
Notes: 2, 5, 6, 7, 8, 9, 11, 12, 13, 14

Leadville Country Inn

Bed and Breakfast-Rocky Mountains
906 South Pearl Street
Denver, 80209
(303) 744-8415; (800) 733-8415

Situated in a historic mining community, this large, 1893 Queen Anne Victorian boasts a magnificent view of Mount Massive and Mount Elbert. The inn is within walking distance of downtown Leadville. Ski Cooper is just 20 minutes away. Enjoy a complete family-style breakfast served from authentic English tea trolleys. Dinner available for groups. Also, enjoy afternoon tea with your hosts. Children welcome. No pets or smoking. Moderate rates.

Woodhaven Manor

807 Spruce, 80461
(719) 486-0109; (800) 748-2570

Woodhaven Manor is situated on Leadville's Bankers Row, a street with five turn-of-the-century Victorian houses built by famed architect Herbert Dimick for Leadville's elite. The formal entry contains an elaborate oak staircase. The main floor/common areas include a high Victorian parlor, dining room with fireplace, and cozy library. Each of the five guest rooms is furnished elegantly with antiques.

Hosts: Bob and Jolene Wood; Sid and Judy
    Clemmer
Rooms: 8 (7 PB; 1 SB) $47-87
Full Breakfast
Credit Cards: A, B, C, D
Notes: 2, 5, 9, 10, 11, 12, 13, 14

LOVELAND

The Lovelander Bed and Breakfast Inn

217 West Fourth Street, 80537
(303) 669-0798

Nestled against the Rocky Mountain foothills, minutes from Rocky Mountain National Park,the Lovelander is a rambling Victorian-style inn. Its beauty and elegance are characteristic of the turn of the century, when the home was built. Near restaurants, shops, museums, and art galleries, the Lovelander is a haven for business and recreational travelers and romantics. Meeting and reception facilities available.

Hosts: Marilyn and Bob Wiltgen
Rooms: 9 (PB) $49-105
Full Breakfast
Credit Cards: A, B, C
Notes: 2, 5, 8 (over 10) , 9, 10, 11, 12, 14

MAHER

Camp Stool Ranch Bed & Breakfast

80367 Highway 92, Box 14, 81421
(303) 921-6461

Enjoy the beautiful scenery and warm hospitality in this unique rock house built in 1912. Located in scenic western Colorado on State Highway 92 (originally the first road over Black Mesa) , this home offers guests a location close to stream fishing, water skiing, boating, river rafting, hiking, golfing, cross country and downhill skiing, snowmobiling, ice fishing and skating.

Hosts: George and Winnie Tracy
Rooms: 3 (SB) $40-50
Full and Continental Breakfast
Credit Cards: F
Notes: 2, 6, 7, 8

MANITOU SPRINGS

Gray's Avenue Hotel

711 Manitou Avenue, 80829
(719) 685-1277

This bed and breakfast is situated in the Manitou Springs Historic Preservation District. It was built in 1886 and opened as the "Avenue Hotel," one of the original seven hotels in this resort town. We are within minutes of most tourist attractions and walking distance to shops and restaurants. Children over 10, please.

Hosts: Tom and Lee Gray
Rooms: 9 rooms, 1 suite (3 PB; 6 SB) $40-65
Full Breakfast
Credit Cards: A, B, C
Notes: 2, 5, 14

Onaledge Bed and Breakfast

336 El Paso Boulevard, 80829
(719) 685-4265; (800) 530-8253

---

6 Pets welcome; 7 Smoking allowed; 8 Children welcome; 9 Social drinking allowed; 10 Tennis available; 11 Swimming available; 12 Golf available; 13 Skiing available; 14 May be booked through travel agents.

Built on a hill overlooking Manitou Springs, this 1912 English Tudor rock home speaks of romance. At the foot of Pikes Peak near all attractions. Lovely honeymoon suite featuring a private hot tub and all amenities. Lovely gardens and patios. Although within walking distance of Garden of the Gods and downtown Manitou Springs, Onaledge retains the seclusion of an English country inn.

Hosts: Mel and Shirley Podell
Rooms: 4 (PB) $70-110
Full Breakfast
Credit Cards: A, B, C, D
Notes: 2, 5, 7, 9, 10, 11, 12, 13, 14

Onaledge Bed and Breakfast

Redstone Castle

Bed and Breakfast-Rocky Mountains
906 South Pearl Street
Denver, 80209
(303) 744-8415; (800) 733-8415

Magnificently restored and graciously appointed, this Victorian mansion is one of Colorado's finest historic residences. The spectacular castle sits on a twenty-acre estate overlooking the National Historic District of Manitou Springs and has commanding views of the Garden of the Gods and Iron and Red Mountains. The third floor features two guest rooms with queen beds, luxurious private bath, turret sitting room, and loft balconey. Full breakfast includes fresh fruit, homemade cinnamon rolls, breads and muffins. No smoking, no pets, children welcome. Luxury rates.

Sunnymede Bed and Breakfast

106 Spencer Avenue, 80829
(719) 685-4619

This 105-year-old Victorian on a quiet hillside overlooks Manitou Springs in the heart of Pikes Peak country. Many family heirlooms and antiques. Quilts made by greatgrandmother will keep you warm on even the coldest of winter nights. Guests are welcomed as temporary family. Within walking distance of unique shops.

Hosts: Bill and Chris Power
Rooms: 3 (1 PB; 2 SB) $50
Full Breakfast
Credit Cards: None
Notes: 2, 5, 7 (limited) , 8, 9

Two Sisters Inn

Bed and Breakfast-Rocky Mountains
906 South Pearl Street
Denver, 80209
(303) 744-8415; (800) 733-8415

Gracious bed and breakfast nestled at the base of Pike's Peak mixes the charm of the Victorian past with the comfort of the present. Built in 1919 as a boardinghouse, this rose-colored bungalow has four main house bedrooms and a honeymoon cottage in the back. Complimentary beverages available to guests, and gourmet breakfast served in the dining room features home baked muffins, freshly ground coffee, fresh fruits, and a delectable hot entree. No smoking, no pets, well-behaved children welcome. Moderate-luxury rates.

MINTURN

Eagle River Inn

145 North Main Street, Box 100, 81645
(303) 827-5761; (800) 344-1750

NOTES: Credit cards accepted: A Master Card; B Visa; C American Express; D Discover Card; E Diner's Club; F Other; 2 Personal Checks accepted; 3 Lunch available; 4 Dinner available; 5 Open all year;

Lovely 12-room inn decorated in the south-western style. All guest rooms have private baths. Enjoy a full gourmet breakfast in our sunny breakfast room; in the evenings, relax in front of the fireplace while you enjoy wine, cheese, and classical music, or enjoy the outdoor hot tub overlooking the Eagle River. Situated seven miles from the Vail ski resort.

Hosts: Beverly Rude and Richard Galloway
Rooms: 12 (PB) $79-155
Full Breakfast
Minimum stay Christmas: 5 nights
Credit Cards: A, B, C
Closed May and October
Notes: 2, 8 (over 12) , 9, 10, 11, 12, 13, 14

MONTROSE

Fifth Street Bed and Breakfast

448 South 5th, 81401
(303) 249-4702

A turn-of-the-century-style, three-story Victorian home situated in the older residential area of Montrose and within walking distance of the downtown shops and restaurants. Choices include three rooms, a double bed, queen waterbed, or twin beds all tastefully decorated to enhance the charm of the Victorian decor. A delightful stay with a native Colorado couple who serve a full breakfast in the formal dining room.

Hosts: Norm and Dena Brooks
Rooms: 3 (SB) $35-40
Full Breakfast
Credit Cards: None
Notes: 2, 5

MOSCA

Great Sand Dunes Country Club

5303 Highway 150, 81146
(719) 378-2356

In the beautiful San Luis Valley, at the foot of the south central Colorado's Sangre De Cristo Mountains, lies this historic ranch nestled among 100-year-old cottonwood trees. Newly renovated log buildings, comfortable rooms, handmade quilts, comforters, private baths, 18-hole championship golf course, sauna, Jacuzzi, well-equipped exercise room, heated swimming pool, horseback rides, mountain bikes, massages and tours on the Buffalo Ranch. Come relax, enjoy golf and health spa. Get away from all the rush and stress of everyday life—leave feeling rejuvenated!

Host: Tianne Tanner
Rooms: 15 (PB) $130-150
Expanded Continental Breakfast
Credit Cards: A, B, C, D
Notes: 2, 3, 4, 8, 9, 11, 12, 14

ORCHARD MESA

The Orchard House

Bed and Breakfast-Rocky Mountains
906 South Pearl Street, Denver, 80209
(303) 744-8415; (800) 733-8415

Picture yourself relaxing on the porch with spectacular views of the mountains. Complete guest house with a private entrance, living room, full bath and kitchen offers one bedroom with a king-size bed, and another bedroom with a pair of twins. Full gourmet breakfast, and complimentary refreshments. Smoking in limited areas, children with well-behaved parents welcome. Moderate rates.

Fifth Street Bed and Breakfast

6 Pets welcome; 7 Smoking allowed; 8 Children welcome; 9 Social drinking allowed; 10 Tennis available; 11 Swimming available; 12 Golf available; 13 Skiing available; 14 May be booked through travel agents.

OURAY

The Damn Yankee
Bed and Breakfast Inn

P. O. Box 709, 100 6th Avenue, 81427
(800) 845-7512

Eight uniquely appointed rooms await,
each with a private bath and entrance. Drift
off to the soothing music of a mountain
stream from your luxurious queen-size bed.
Snuggle under a plush down comforter. Sit
back and watch your favorite film on cable
television. Drink in the fresh mountain air,
relax in our hot tub, or gather around the
parlor with friends to play the piano. Feast
your senses, enjoy complimentary sodas,
fresh fruit, and afternoon in our towering
observatory, and savor a hearty breakfast as
you watch the sun glint over the mountaintops.

Host: Joyce and Mike Manley
Rooms: 8 (PB) $58-145
Full Gourmet Breakfast
Credit Cards: A, B, C
Notes: 2, 5, 9, 10, 11, 13, 14

Main Street
Bed and Breakfast

322 Main Street, P. O. Box 641, 81427
(303) 325-4871

Two superbly renovated, turn-of-the-century residences offer three suites, three
rooms, and a two-story cottage. All accommodations have private baths, queen-size
beds, and cable TV. Five of the units have
decks with spectacular views of the San
Juan Mountains. Three units have fully
equipped modern kitchens. Guests who
stay in rooms without kitchens are served a
full breakfast on antique china. Guests also
have exclusive use of a landscaped courtyard and play area.

Hosts: Lee and Cathy Bates
Rooms: 7 (PB) $53-80
Full Breakfast
Credit Cards: A, B
Notes: 2, 8, 9, 11

The Manor
Bed and Breakfast

Bed and Breakfast-Rocky Mountains
906 South Pearl Street
Denver, 80209
(303) 744-8415; (800) 733-8415

The Manor is nestled 7,800 feet high in the
San Juan Mountains. This 1890 manor
house offers polished Victorian charm in a
quiet setting within walking distance to
Ouray's unique shops and restaurants.
Relax in the natural hot springs pool. Jeep,
hike, backpack, cross-country ski, skate,
and climb ice. Parlor with TV and fireplace; balcony, patio, croquet courts, and
manicured grounds. Buffet-style continental breakfast. Budget-moderate rates.

St. Elmo Hotel

426 Main Street, P. O. Box 667, 81427
(303) 325-4951

Listed in the National Registry of Historic
Places, established in 1898 as a miners'
hotel, and now fully renovated with stained
glass, antiques, polished wood, and brass
trim throughout. An outdoor hot tub and an
aspen-lined sauna are available, as well as a
cozy parlor and a breakfast room.

Hosts: Sandy and Dan Lingenfelter
Rooms: 9 (PB) $54-78
Full Breakfast
Credit Cards: A, B, D
Notes: 3, 4, 5, 7 (limited) , 9, 10, 11, 13 (XC) , 14

PAGOSA SPRINGS

Davidson's Country Inn
Bed and Breakfast

Box 87, 81147
(303) 264-5863

A three-story log inn decorated in antiques
and family heirlooms, situated on a 32-acre
ranch on Highway 160 in the foothills of
the Rocky Mountains. Game room, outdoor
activities, children's corner. Full country

NOTES: Credit cards accepted: A Master Card; B Visa; C American Express; D Discover Card; E Diner's
Club; F Other; 2 Personal Checks accepted; 3 Lunch available; 4 Dinner available; 5 Open all year;

breakfast. Hiking, stream and lake fishing, rafting, skiing, and beautiful scenic drives are all nearby. Two-bedroom cabin also available.

Hosts: Gilbert and Evelyn Davidson
Rooms: 9 (PB and SB) $44-62
Full Breakfast
Credit Cards: A, B
Notes: 2, 5, 6, 8, 10, 11, 13, 14

Echo Manor Inn

3366 Highway 84, 81147
(303) 264-5646

Beautiful country Dutch Tudor manor with towers, turrets, and gables. Set in the majestic San Juan Mountains and described by many as a "fairy tale castle", this lovely bed and breakfast offers a honeymoon suite, full country breakfast, hot tub, horseback riding, rafting, snow mobiling, fishing, hunting, and boating. Located across the street from beautiful Echo Lake. Guests are invited to enjoy cozy wood stoves and fireplaces.

Hosts: Sandy and Ginny Northcutt
Rooms: 10 rooms, 1 large suite (6 PB; 4 SB) $49-125
Full Country Breakfast
Credit Cards: F
Notes: 2, 5, 8, 9, 10, 11, 12, 13, 14

Royal Pine Inn

4760 W. Highway 60, 81157
(303) 731-4179

This inn is an eight-year-old building designed in the old Tudor fashion. Offering five bedrooms, three with private baths. Two bedrooms share an extra large full bath with a half bath across the hall. Bedrooms are large and spacious and decorated in Laura Ashley style. All rooms have their own TV and breathtaking views. During winter months, we serve a full breakfast of waffles, french toast, and eggs to order, June through September we serve our continental breakfast that features freshly baked pastries, jams, fresh fruit, and cold cereal. Coffee, juice, and herbal tea are always available.

Hosts: Kathy and Roy
Rooms: 5 (3 PB; 2 SB) $45-60
Full Breakfast October-May; Continental Plus
 June-September
Credit Cards: A, B
Notes: 2, 5, 7(downstairs only) , 8, 13

PAONIA

Agape Inn

P. O. Box 640, 206 Rio Grande, 81428
(303) 527-4004

Restored turn-of-the-century home situated in the beautiful north fork of the Gunnison River. Large yard with large elm trees. Plenty of off-street parking. Excellent fishing and hunting nearby. Paonia is known for its Cherry Days Celebration over the Fourth of July. There are many fruit orchards in the valley. Snowmobiling in the winter.

Hosts: Jim and Norma Shutts
Rooms: 3 (2 PB; 1 SB) $45
Full Breakfast
Credit Cards: None
Notes: 2, 5, 8, 10, 12

PINE

Meadow Creek
Bed and Breakfast

Bed and Breakfast-Rocky Mountains
906 South Pearl Street, Denver, 80209
(303) 744-8415; (800) 733-8415

6 Pets welcome; 7 Smoking allowed; 8 Children welcome; 9 Social drinking allowed; 10 Tennis available; 11 Swimming available; 12 Golf available; 13 Skiing available; 14 May be booked through travel agents.

This rustic mountain retreat on 35 acres was built in 1929 from stone found on the property and served as a private residence until its renovation in 1988. Large parlor with native stone fireplace, outdoor deck, hot tub, and sauna room. A hearty full breakfast is served in the sunny dining area or in your room. Candlelight dinner may be ordered two days in advance except Sunday. Perfect for weddings, small family reunions, corporate workshops. Minimum stay two nights. Budget-moderate rates.

PUEBLO

Abriendo Inn

300 West Abriendo Avenue, 81004
(719) 544-2703

A classic bed and breakfast on the National Register of Historic Places, situated in the heart of Pueblo and one mile off the interstate. Bask in the comfort, style, and luxury of the past in rooms delightfully decorated with antiques, crocheted bedspreads, brass and four-poster beds. Restaurants, shops, galleries, golf, tennis, and other attractions are all within five minutes of the inn.

Host: Kerrelyn Trent
Rooms: 7 (PB) $48-85
Full Breakfast
Credit Cards: A, B, C, E
Notes: 2, 5, 8 (over 7) , 9, 10, 11, 12, 13, 14

KK Ranch

Bed and Breakfast-Rocky Mountains
906 South Pearl Street
Denver, 80209
(303) 744-8415; (800) 733-8415

Two creeks run through the 67 acres of the 1870 homestead. A 600-acre mountain park adjoins the property with hiking trails and streams. Fishing at Lake Isabel and the famed Royal George and Old West theme park and movie town of "Buckskin Joe." Both rooms have double bed and share baths. Continental breakfast. No smoking. Budget rates.

RED CLIFF

The Pilgrim's Inn

P. O. Box 151, 101 Eagle Street, 81649
(303) 827-5333

The Pilgrim's Inn is a quiet bed and breakfast in a turn-of-the-century Victorian home, newly restored and filled with books, antiques, Asian art, and the work of local painters and photographers. Situated just 15 miles from Vail in the small mining town of Red Cliff, the inn is a perfect base camp or retreat. Four charming rooms available, one with private bath complete with claw foot tub and skylights. Complimentary vegetarian breakfast served. Hot tub on back deck with spectacular mountain views.

Hosts: Molly and Michael Wasmer
Rooms: 4 (2 PB; 2 SB) $60-85
Full Breakfast
Credit Cards: A, B
Notes: 2, 4, 5, 8, 9, 13, 14

REDSTONE

Avalanche Ranche Country Inn & Cabins

12863 Highway 133, 81623
(303) 963-2846

The 1913 farmhouse has been restored to a country inn bed and breakfast and antique shops. The inn is decorated with an eclectic collection of early country antiques and folk art. Fourteen cozy log cabins feature different amenities. Each cabin is fully equipped with a kitchen and bathroom. Avalanche Ranch provides an ideal setting for romantic getaways, family reunions, and weddings. In accordance with an emphasis on health, smoking is not permitted in the ranch building. While the hosts have taken great care to create an interesting yet comfortable atmosphere for their guests, it is their philosophy that "The ornament of a house is the friends who frequent it" (Emerson) .

NOTES: Credit cards accepted: A Master Card; B Visa; C American Express; D Discover Card; E Diner's Club; F Other; 2 Personal Checks accepted; 3 Lunch available; 4 Dinner available; 5 Open all year;

Hosts: Sharon and Jim Mollica
Rooms: 4 (2 PB; 2 SB) $75-90
Cabins: 14 (PB) $70-110
Continental Breakfast
Credit Cards: A, B, D
Notes: 2, 5, 6 (in cabins) , 8 (in cabins) , 9, 13, 14

Cleveholm Manor: The "Historic" Redstone Castle

0058 Redstone Boulevard, 81623
(303) 963-3463; (800) 643-4837

Cleveholm Manor is a majestic 42-room manor home built at the turn of the century by coal and steel baron John Cleveland Osgood. The finest quality craftsmanship, furnishings, and decoration lend charm and grace to transport a guest back in time to an era of solitude and serenity. Cleveholm operates today as a bed and breakfast mountain inn, and as a host for special events, retreats, weddings, concerts, elegant dinners, and conferences.

Hosts: Rose Marie Johnson and Cyd Lange
Rooms: 16 (8 PB; 8 SB) $78-167
Continental Plus Breakfast
Credit Cards: A, B, C
Notes: 2, 4, (most Friday and Saturday evenings), 5, 6, 7(designated areas only) , 8, 9, 14

SALIDA

The Poor Farm Inn

Bed and Breakfast-Rocky Mountains
906 South Pearl Street
Denver, 80209
(303) 744-8415; (800) 733-8415

The Poor Farm is rich with history. Built in 1892 to serve the county's poor and later purchased by the city for a grange hall. Grace and old-time homeyness are seen in the 12-foot ceilings, a library with books dating from 1863, unique "warming" radiators, and family photos. Close to Monarch ski area, hot springs pool and mineral bath. Full breakfast. Children welcome. Budget-moderate rates..

Victorian Manor

Bed and Breakfast-Rocky Mountains
906 South Pearl Street
Denver, 80209
(303) 744-8415; (800) 733-8415

This restored English Victorian home is in the center of Colorado's largest historic district. Your hosts invite you to relax in

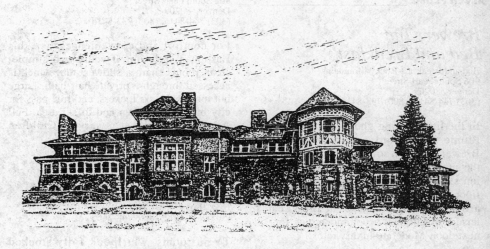

Cleveholm Manor: The "Historic" Redstone Castle

6 Pets welcome; 7 Smoking allowed; 8 Children welcome; 9 Social drinking allowed; 10 Tennis available; 11 Swimming available; 12 Golf available; 13 Skiing available; 14 May be booked through travel agents.

the Labelle, Victoriana, or Mountain Peaks rooms. Nearby activities include kayaking, horseback riding, hot springs swimming, and touring ghost towns and mines. Full gourmet, home-cooked breakfast. Budget rates.

SAN LUIS

El Convento
Bed and Breakfast

Bed and Breakfast-Rocky Mountains
906 South Pearl Street
Denver, 80209
(303) 744-8415; (800) 733-8415

El Convento was originally built as a school in 1905 by Fr. José Samuel Garcia. It has now been transformed into a cozy, luxurious inn for weary travelers. Each guest room is decorated with handcrafted and antique furniture made by local artisans. Gourmet breakfast is served in the dining room. Library and gallery on the premises. Moderate rates.

SILVER PLUME

Brewery Inn
Bed and Breakfast

Bed and Breakfast-Rocky Mountains
906 South Pearl Street
Denver, 80209
(303) 744-8415; (800) 733-8415

In the little "living ghost town" of Silver Plume there's only one place to stay: Brewery Inn. A cozy Victorian home on the site of the historic Busch brewery. The inn sleeps 12 and has a suite on the main floor with a fireplace. Home-baked goodies are served for breakfast at the guests' leisure. Additional accommodations for 12 next door. Moderate-luxury rates.

SILVERTON

Christopher House
Bed and Breakfast

821 Empire Street, P. O. Box 241, 81433
(303) 387-5857 (June-Sept)
(904) 567-7549 (Oct-May)

Traditional Irish bed and breakfast hospitality amid the scenic splendor of the Rocky Mountains. The charming 1894 Victorian home features original woodwork and fireplace, sturdy antiques. Comfortable, carpeted rooms with mountain view and fresh flowers. Within walking distance of shops, restaurants, riding stable, stage coach, and narrow-gauge train station. Reasonable rates.

Hosts: Eileen and Howard Swonger
Rooms: 4 (1 PB; 3SB) $42-52
Full Breakfast
Credit Cards: None
Closed Sept. 16-May 30
Notes: 2, 8, 9, 10, 14

STEAMBOAT SPRINGS

The Clermont Inn

Bed and Breakfast-Rocky Mountains
906 South Pearl Street
Denver, 80209
(303) 744-8415; (800) 733-8415

For comfort and convenience, visit this European-style inn. Twenty-two simple, clean rooms share a shower/ tub, which is accessed through a private half-bath. Large hot tub inside, ski lockers, and free pass for city bus around town and to ski area. Full American breakfast is served. Children welcome. Budget-moderate rates.

Easy Access

Bed and Breakfast Vail Ski Areas
P. O. Box 491, 81658
(303) 949-1212; (800) 748-2666

TV in rooms, whirlpool, fully stocked library, bumper pool, or movie watching are just a few of the amenities offered here. Simply decorated and affordable, this is great for skiers wanting comfortable accommodations. Within walking distance to downtown shops and restaurants, this bed and breakfast is located three miles from the ski area.

Inn Town

Bed and Breakfast Vail Ski Areas
P. O. Box 491, 81658
(303) 949-1212; (800) 748-2666

In the heart of downtown with restaurants, shops; hot mineral springs within walking distance. Each room has unique antique decor. Phone, TV, HBO. Kids stay free. Continental breakfast. $57-119 seasonal.

Iris House

Bed and Breakfast-Rocky Mountains
906 South Pearl Street
Denver, 80209
(303) 744-8415; (800) 733-8415

This rugged post-and-beam house is set in an aspen grove overlooking Steamboat and the Yampa Valley. It is furnished with heirlooms, art work, lots of books, and comfortable furniture. Japanese soaking tub in the bathroom. Full breakfast is served family-style. Hiking trails, cross-country, and downhill skiing nearby. Resident cats. No smoking. $65 summer; $85 winter.

The Log Cabin

Bed and Breakfast-Rocky Mountains
906 South Pearl Street
Denver, 80209
(303) 744-8415; (800) 733-8415

The spectacular Elk River Valley is the setting for this newly built guest cabin constructed of whole logs and river rock. Its wood stove, library, large shower, microwave, and tiny refrigerator ensure comfort and privacy. Fifteen miles from the Steamboat ski area and close to national forest and wilderness area. Resident cats, dogs, and horses. Moderate rates.

Scandinavian Lodge

2883 Burgess Creek Road
P. O. Box 774484, 80477
(800) 233-8102

Enjoy a relaxing vacation amid the pine and aspen groves in the Colorado Mountains. The Scandinavian Lodge, situated on Mount Werner ski area in Steamboat Springs, is away from traffic and busy streets and has easy access to town and other recreational activities. The lodge, with its pleasant European atmosphere, has bed and breakfast rooms, a lounge, and an authentic Swedish restaurant. An outdoor heated pool, sauna, tennis court, soccer field, and access to ski slopes will enhance your visit.

Host: The Olsson family
Rooms: 18 (PB) $49-96
Full Breakfast
Credit Cards: None
Notes: 2, 4, 6, 7, 8, 9, 10, 11, 12, 13, 14

Shamrock Ranch

Bed and Breakfast-Rocky Mountains
906 South Pearl Street
Denver, 80209
(303) 744-8415; (800) 733-8415

A wonderful location for the whole family, this rustically elegant log "lodge" is built of native spruce and furnished with antiques. Originally a homestead in the 1930s, this ranch sits on 400 acres and is adjacent to the national forest. Three bedrooms with shared baths and two bedroom cabins with full baths and living areas are available. Full breakfast is served. Gold medal trout fishing, ranch animals, and an eagle's nest nearby. Gourmet dinners by reservation. Luxury rates.

6 Pets welcome; 7 Smoking allowed; 8 Children welcome; 9 Social drinking allowed; 10 Tennis available; 11 Swimming available; 12 Golf available; 13 Skiing available; 14 May be booked through travel agents.

Steamboat Bed and Breakfast

Bed and Breakfast-Rocky Mountains
906 South Pearl Street
Denver, 80209
(303) 744-8415; (800) 733-8415

Enjoy Victorian elegance in Old Steamboat. The inn is a renovated church school attractively decorated with antiques, a music conservatory, a deck overlooking the gardens, and the quaint older part of town. Within walking distance of retail stores, the hot springs pool, and restaurants; two miles to the ski resort. Full breakfast. Fishing, golfing, hiking, kayaking, hot air ballooning. No smoking. Budget-moderate rates.

Vista Verde Guest Ranch, Inc.

P. O. Box 465, 80477
(303) 879-3858; (800) 526-7433

Our small, highly regarded western guest and cattle ranch offers a secluded, picturesque setting and an active program of riding, hiking, rock climbing, rafting, and more. In winter, we offer ski touring, sleigh rides, dog sleds, and other similar activities. In all seasons enjoy superbly prepared cuisine served family style. Relax in the authentic, elegantly furnished log cabins with fireplaces or in our hot tub and sauna. Minimum stays required by season.

Rooms: 8 cabins (PB) $240-360
Full Breakfast
Credit Cards: None
Notes: 2, 3, 4, 8, 9, 10, 11, 12, 13, 14

TELLURIDE

Alpine Inn Bed and Breakfast

P. O. Box 2398, 440 West Colorado Avenue, 81435
(303) 728-6282

This restored Victorian Inn built in 1907 is located in historic downtown Telluride. The Inn has seven rooms with both shared and private baths. Within walking distance of ski lifts and summer festival activities, the inn is furnished with antiques, Victorian accents and quilts. Full breakfast is served daily in the large sunroom, which offers a panoramic view of the mountains. Hot tub with a mountain view is also available for guests to use. Under new management as of May, 1992

Hosts: Johnnie and Jay Weaver
Rooms: 7 (3-PB; 4 SB) $60-155
Full Breakfast
Credit Cards: A, B, C
Notes: 2, 5, 13, 14

Bear Creek Bed and Breakfast

221 East Colorado, P. O. Box 1797, 81435
(303) 728-6681; (800) 338-7064

A mountain style, contemporary bed and breakfast offering affordable charm, gracious service, and a view from every room. Located on Main Street, the inn is steps away from dining, shopping, ski slopes, and adjacent to town park and summer festivals. Rooms have queen beds, phones, private baths, and HBO. Enjoy the large sauna and steam room, fireplace, and roof deck.

Hosts: Tom and Colleen Whiteman
Rooms: 8 (PB) $45-115
Full Breakfast
Credit Cards: A, B, C
Closed April 12-May 6 and Oct. 25-Nov. 18
Notes: 2, 9, 10, 11, 12, 13, 14

Johnstone Inn

403 West Colorado, Box 546, 81435
(303) 728-3316; (800) 752-1901

A true, 100-year-old restored Victorian boarding house, this bed and breakfast is in the center of Telluride and the spectacular San Juan Mountains. Rooms are warm and romantic, with Victorian marble and brass, and private baths. Full breakfast is served each morning, and the winter season includes après ski refreshments. A sitting room fireplace and outdoor hot tub complete your amenities. Nordi and Alpine skiing, jeep tours, and loafing are within walking distance of the Inn.

Rooms: 8 (PB) $70-145
Full Breakfast
Credit Cards: A, B, C
Notes: 2, 9, 12, 13, 14

Pennington's Mountain Village Inn

P. O. Box 2428, 100 Pennington Court, 81435
(303) 728-5337; (800) 543-1437

A luxurious bed and breakfast located on the twelfth fairway of the Telluride Golf Course. The large rooms and suites enjoy spectacular views of the San Juan Mountains, private baths, and decks. Amenities include a whirlpool spa, steam room, game room, guest lockers, fireplace lounge, library, and free laundry facilities. A gourmet breakfast is served daily, as well as a complimentary happy hour with spirits, beer, soft drinks, and a variety of hot and cold hors d'oeuvres.

Bear Creek Bed and Breakfast

Hosts: Michael and Judy Maclean
Rooms: 12 (PB) $140-275
Full Breakfast
Credit Cards: A, B, C, D
Notes: 2, 5, 7(very limited) , 8, 9, 10, 11, 12, 13, 14

San Sophia

330 West Pacific Avenue, P. O. Box 1825, 81435
(800) 537-4781

Elegant, luxurious accommodations for the discriminating traveler. Indoor and outdoor dining areas, huge bathtubs for two, brass beds, handmade quilts, dramatic view of the surrounding 13,000-foot mountains. Common areas include an observatory, library, and gazebo with Jacuzzi. "One of the most luxurious and romantic inns in America"—*Inside America*. Complimentary refreshments each afternoon.

Hosts: Dianne and Gary Eschman
Rooms: 16 (PB) $85-175
Full Breakfast
Credit Cards: A, B, C
Closed April 8-May 4 and Oct. 25-Nov. 24
Notes: 2, 9, 10, 11, 12, 13, 14

TWIN LAKES

Mt. Elbert Lodge

Bed and Breakfast-Rocky Mountains
906 South Pearl Street
Denver, 80209
(303) 744-8415; (800) 733-8415

This historic lodge combines country charm with American frontier tradition. Located just on the other side of Independence Pass and surrounded by Mt. Elbert, Mt. Massive, French and LaPlata Peaks. Six rooms are available with queen, double, and single beds and share two full baths. Hearty continental breakfast with homemade goodies, cereals, fruits, and yogurt. Smoking in designated areas only. Budget-moderate rates.

6 Pets welcome; 7 Smoking allowed; 8 Children welcome; 9 Social drinking allowed; 10 Tennis available; 11 Swimming available; 12 Golf available; 13 Skiing available; 14 May be booked through travel agents.

VAIL

Alpen Haus

Bed and Breakfast Vail Ski Areas
P. O. Box 491, 81658
(303) 949-1212; (800) 748-2666

This Austrian-flavored home is one bus stop from Vail village on the golf course. Great views from each bedroom, one overlooking the Gore Range and Vail village; the other looks out on tall pines and aspens. Common gathering room available for après ski with TV, VCR, and library. Kitchenette with microwave and refrigerator. No smoking. $105-115.

Aspen Haus

Bed and Breakfast Vail Ski Areas
P. O. Box 491, 81658
(303) 949-1212; (800) 748-2666

If you would like to be pampered, then this is the house for you. Set on a hillside, surrounded by trees, your suite has a delightful, homey feeling with a great view. There is a TV, phone, and large couch to snuggle into when you want to relax. The bath is located in the suite for extra privacy. Breakfast is served upstairs in the European decorated home. High ceilings and wonderful German artifacts grace the sunny kitchen area. Your hosts offer a ski locker in town at the base of the the mountain, as well as an athletic club membership, discounted parking tickets, and ski tickets (limited availability) . Wine and cheese are served each afternoon. $125.

Aunt Em's Bed and Breakfast

Bed and Breakfast Vail Ski Areas
P. O. Box 491, 81658
(303) 949-1212; (800) 748-2666

Just short three miles from the base of Beaver creek snuggled on the Eagle River is this Victorian town house full of warmth and comfort. A cozy, homey feeling is what you feel when you walk in the door. Aunt Em's is appointed with turn of the century antiques, homemade quilts, and a wood-burning stove that will entice any guest in the winter. In summer, exercise at the athletic facility. Your room has an outdoor deck, and is finely decorated with an antique sleigh bed, TV, VCR, microwave, and private bath. Each night before you turn in, choose your breakfast from the menu provided. Discounted Vail parking and young children welcome. $60-75.

BB Inn

Bed and Breakfast Vail Ski Areas
P. O. Box 491, 81658
(303) 949-1212; (800) 748-2666

This inn is everything you would expect from a Rocky mountain getaway. Located on Gore Creek, this handcrafted log inn with an enormous main room has a cozy fire, great views, and warmth beyond compare. Breakfast features baked breads, rolls, muffins, fruits in season, and a daily gourmet creation. Apres-ski snacks and appetizers are also served daily. $80-175.

Black Bear Inn

Bed and Breakfast-Rocky Mountains
906 South Pearl Street
Denver, 80209
(303) 744-8415; (800) 733-8415

Located on the banks of Gore Creek on its own secluded parcel of land, this inn is everything you would expect to find in a Rocky Mountain getaway. Close enough to the slopes and other amenities to make your stay enjoyable, the handcrafted log inn has 12 distinct rooms, each with its own tiled bath. Full, mountain breakfast includes a daily gourmet chef's creation. No smoking, no pets, well-supervised children welcome. Luxury, seasonal rates.

NOTES: Credit cards accepted: A Master Card; B Visa; C American Express; D Discover Card; E Diner's Club; F Other; 2 Personal Checks accepted; 3 Lunch available; 4 Dinner available; 5 Open all year;

Bluebird

Bed and Breakfast Vail Ski Areas
P. O. Box 491, 81658
(303) 949-1212; (800) 748-2666

This wonderful mountain home offers warmth and charm to all guests who stay here. Your hostess offers quaint rooms, each of which has its own decor. Additional children are welcome in the room or on the futon for an extra $10-15. Microwave and refrigerator are available for guests to use. Views of Vail and surrounding mountains are spectacular. In summer, relax on the outside sunny deck while feasting on breakfast. Bus stops at the end of the street, and free shuttle to downtown. $80-95.

Brown Palace

Bed and Breakfast Vail Ski Areas
P. O. Box 491, 81658
(303) 949-1212; (800) 748-2666

Great breakfasts! Situated on free bus route, ten minutes from Vail. Skiing family offers one bedroom with twin beds and shared bath. $65-75.

Colorado Comfort

Bed and Breakfast Vail Ski Areas
P. O. Box 491, 81658
(303) 949-1212; (800) 748-2666

This comfortable two story town house offers beautiful views of Aspen and the pine trees while overlooking a challenging golf course. Your room is high vaulted with an electric blanket, humidifier, TV, and bathroom in the room. Cross country ski outside you back door in the winter, and golf in the summer. Guests are welcome to relax in the home when shopping and touring are finished. $8-11 discount lift tickets and Vail parking is available. (excluding Christmas and New Year's) $80-85.

Columbine Chalet
Bed and Breakfast of Vail

P. O. Box 1407, 81658
(303) 476-1122

Stay in this American style chalet nestled in the pines of an exclusive neighborhood at the edge of the Vail golf course. Enjoy a hearty breakfast, afternoon refreshments, outdoor hot tub, games, books, and puzzles. A recreation path outside the front door serves cross country skiers in the winter and bicyclist and hikers in the summer. Just one bus stop away from the town of Vail bus are the award-winning slopes of Vail.

Hosts: Pat Funk and Ruthie Bopes
Rooms: 3 (PB) $40-150
Full Breakfast
Credit Cards: A, B
Notes: 2, 5, 8, 9, 10, 12, 13, 14

Cottonwood Falls

Bed and Breakfast Vail Ski Areas
P. O. Box 491, 81658
(303) 949-1212; (800) 748-2666

Sunny, secluded location conveniently situated on free bus route; cross-country skiing and bike path nearby; tennis courts within walking distance. Rock fireplace, kitchen, private entrance, parking, VCR available. Fully stocked kitchen, but gourmet breakfast is served with hosts. $125-150.

Dave's Domain

Bed and Breakfast Vail Ski Areas
P. O. Box 491, 81658
(303) 949-1212; (800) 748-2666

Situated on Vail's free bus shuttle, this self-contained apartment is perfect for two traveling couples or a family of four. Full kitchen, private entrance, TV, small living room. Host lives upstairs. Five minutes from downtown Vail and close to shopping and skiing. $90-125.

6 Pets welcome; 7 Smoking allowed; 8 Children welcome; 9 Social drinking allowed; 10 Tennis available; 11 Swimming available; 12 Golf available; 13 Skiing available; 14 May be booked through travel agents.

Eagle River Inn

Bed and Breakfast-Rocky Mountains
906 South Pearl Street
Denver, 80209
(303) 744-8415; (800) 733-8415

Romance combines with Southwestern style to create the perfect mountain atmosphere in this twelve room country inn. The rooms all have private baths, cable TV, and king-size beds. Amenities include an outdoor Jacuzzi, wine and cheese served downstairs by the fireplace, and new conference room for small meetings. Full breakfast features fresh baked goods, homemade granola, fresh fruit, daily hot special, coffee, tea, and fresh squeezed orange juice. No smoking, no pets. Moderate-luxury, seasonal rates.

Elk View

Bed and Breakfast Vail Ski Areas
P. O. Box 491, 81658
(303) 949-1212; (800) 748-2666

This gorgeous townhome is nestled on the hillside of Beaver creek is six levels with breathtaking view of Beaver Creek Mountain. Beautifully decorated, each room has a charm of its own, and the house is impeccably furnished. In summer, breakfast can be enjoyed on one of the three outside decks, and in the winter, after a long day of skiing, relax in the outside hot tub. This property is perfect for honeymoon couples and guests wanting to relax with the locals. $85 and up.

Fairway House

Bed and Breakfast Vail Ski Areas
P. O. Box 491, 81658
(303) 949-1212; (800) 748-2666

This beautiful rustic mountain home lies very close to the ski mountain. Your room is cozy, with a stucco fireplace and magnificent view of Gore Range. Adjoining living room with fireplace, TV, VCR, wet bar, library, pool table. Two blocks from free bus route. Continental breakfast. $100.

Game Creek House

Bed and Breakfast Vail Ski Areas
P. O. Box 491, 81658
(303) 949-1212; (800) 748-2666

Situated between Vail and Beaver Creek, this private home is situated on nine acres and is surrounded on three sides by forest service land. Near four local favorite restaurants. Refrigerator, laundry, fireplace, TV, VCR. Many outdoor activities. Breakfast is served in the kitchen with beautiful mountain view. $75.

Hi-Country Auberge

Bed and Breakfast Vail Ski Areas
P. O. Box 491, 81658
(303) 949-1212; (800) 748-2666

This is a true luxury mountain resort. Elegant condominium home overlooking Vail Mountain. Private lower level with two bedrooms and private bath. Fireplace, TV, kitchen, and dining area. Pool and hot tub are just steps from front door. Full homemade breakfast. $130-155 winter; $100-125 summer.

Kay's Corner

Bed and Breakfast Vail Ski Areas
P. O. Box 491, 81658
(303) 949-1212; (800) 748-2666

This brand-new home, nestled in a corner lot, offers a great view and serenity. Bedroom is spacious with TV, refrigerator, and a great view. Host is a ski instructor. Continental breakfast. $80.

Matterhorn

Bed and Breakfast Vail Ski Areas
P. O. Box 491, 81658
(303) 949-1212; (800) 748-2666

NOTES: Credit cards accepted: A Master Card; B Visa; C American Express; D Discover Card; E Diner's Club; F Other; 2 Personal Checks accepted; 3 Lunch available; 4 Dinner available; 5 Open all year;

TV's in rooms, phone nearby, snow tires suggested for driveway. Enjoy a hearty breakfast with a magnificent view of the Gore Valley. A European family (all speak German—daughter is bilingual) offers a comfortable, cozy home. Box lunch is provided for early rising convention attendants. Great for single travelers. $60-75.

Minturn Meadows

Bed and Breakfast Vail Ski Areas
P. O. Box 491, 81658
(303) 949-1212; (800) 748-2666

Your upstairs room in this private home is cozy, bright, and private. Hosts share the general living area and offer genuine warmth and care. Perfect for avid skiers. Full breakfast. No smoking. Resident pets. $60-65.

Mountain Chalet

Bed and Breakfast Vail Ski Areas
P. O. Box 491, 81658
(303) 949-1212; (800) 748-2666

Ski out your front door to cross-country terrain, or summers, just walk on the Vail golf course. This beautiful Bavarian mountain chalet is wonderfully decorated with antiques. Large moss-rock fireplace and sitting room with TV and stereo. On bus route. Full breakfast. $185 for two rooms.

Mountain Hideaway

Bed and Breakfast Vail Ski Areas
P. O. Box 491, 81658
(303) 949-1212; (800) 748-2666

Bring your bathing suits so that you can sooth your weary bones in the hot tub while sipping on a glass of wine or cappuccino while enjoying apres-ski refreshments. Located on a wooded lot overlooking a creek, this spacious mountain home beckons you. Newly renovated with high vaulted ceilings and a beautiful glassed-in kitchen nook, you will find countless hours of relaxation here. Close to the village on the free bus route, your host family hospitality is incomparable. Discounted Vail parking is available. $90-125.

Mt. Retreat

Bed and Breakfast Vail Ski Areas
P. O. Box 491, 81658
(303) 949-1212; (800) 748-2666

If you are looking for an out-of-the-way spectacular home with an unsurpassed view, this bed and breakfast will meet your needs. You will need a car to get there, because it is not on any of the bus routes, but once you arrive, you will never want to leave. Your hostess pampers your every need with breakfast served on fine china and crystal. A hot tub room is available so you can soak while enjoying the views of Beaver Creek and Arrowhead mountains. Your room is impeccably decorated and offers another great view. $100-125.

Mountain Weavery

Bed and Breakfast Vail Ski Areas
P. O. Box 491, 81658
(303) 949-1212; (800) 748-2666

This spacious, child-free, single family home on the fourth fairway of the Vail Golf Course offers great hospitality, magnificent views and is steps away from the free bus shuttle, Your hostess is an nationally known designer and weaver and welcomes guests into her studio. Guests are also offered use of the microwave to make evening dinner and snacks.

Mr B's

Bed and Breakfast Vail Ski Areas
P. O. Box 491, 81658
(303) 949-1212; (800) 748-2666

The location and the cost cannot be beat for a stay at this wonderful mountain, located

6 Pets welcome; 7 Smoking allowed; 8 Children welcome; 9 Social drinking allowed; 10 Tennis available; 11 Swimming available; 12 Golf available; 13 Skiing available; 14 May be booked through travel agents.

just five minutes from cross country and downhill skiing. Bright and airy, guests enjoy a room with a private entrance and a bath with a fridge in the room. The bus stop is only two houses away. For comfort and easy access, you'll love this home.

Outdoorsman

Bed and Breakfast Vail Ski Areas
P. O. Box 491, 81658
(303) 949-1212; (800) 748-2666

Overlooking a lake and the majestic mountains, this beautifully appointed condo is decorated with an abundance of antiques and special color blends. Full breakfast. No smoking. $65-75.

Plum House

Bed and Breakfast Vail Ski Areas
P. O. Box 491, 81658
(303) 949-1212; (800) 748-2666

This small, cozy mountain home is at the base of Shrine Mountain Pass, a favorite of cross-country skiers. Relax in the hot tub, enjoy the library, or warm up in front of the wood-burning stove. Hostess is a gourmet chef. Full breakfast. No smoking. $60.

Sis's

Bed and Breakfast Vail Ski Areas
P. O. Box 491, 81658
(303) 949-1212; (800) 748-2666

This comfortable condo, located on the creek and a wooded lot, will meet all your needs. The free bus stops right outside your door, and you are whisked into the village in no time. Your hostess, a ski instructor, loves to entertain, and her warmth and home are unmatched anywhere. Relaxing in the living room with the fireplace and overlooking the creek will sooth tired bones after a hard day of skiing or hiking. Perfect for travelling couples or a family of four.

The Ski Stop

Bed and Breakfast-Rocky Mountains
906 South Pearl Street
Denver, 80209
(303) 744-8415; (800) 733-8415

Situated in East Vail, Ski Stop is within two blocks of the shuttle bus and three miles to lifts and parking. A full breakfast is served. Guests are free to use the hot tub, laundry, and common room. Spectacular views to the south and west. $50 summer; $85 peak ski season.

Sportsman's Haven

Bed and Breakfast Vail Ski Areas
P. O. Box 491, 81658
(303) 949-1212; (800) 748-2666

Surrounded by pine trees and nestled on a creek, this home is a warm, spacious mountain home that beckons guests to snuggle in in during the winter, or lounge on the sunny, private sun decks in summer. Your hosts offer a ski home with two rooms. One is bright and cheery with pine trees outside every window, and the downstairs room has a private bath with a sauna and offers an adjoining family room with TV, pool table, shuffleboard, and fireplace. Your home is easy walking distance from the free bus. Discounted parking tickets available if you should decide to drive. $70-80.

Streamside

Bed and Breakfast Vail Ski Areas
P. O. Box 491, 81658
(303) 949-1212; (800) 748-2666

This town house is conveniently located just a few minutes west from Vail Village. The bus stop is only a few steps away so you don't even need a car. Your hosts are a young couple and avid skiers, and are eager to share their life in Vail with guests. On cold afternoons, you can look forward to a warm or cold apres-ski drink, heat some popcorn in the microwave, or store drinks in the fridge. Upstairs, you can relax by the fire in the main living room to watch TV or read a book. This property is perfect for two couples travelling together or for a young family. $70-85.

Tortilla Flats

Bed and Breakfast Vail Ski Areas
P. O. Box 491, 81658
(303) 949-1212; (800) 748-2666

Bordered by forest land with a spectacular view of Meadow Mountain, this bed and breakfast has immediate access to cross-country, hiking, and mountain biking trails. This cozy suite features a sitting room and bedroom with a private bath and is furnished with antique oak and brass. An extra day bed is also available for a family with a child. Continental breakfast is served in your private dining area. Within walking distance to Minturn's restaurants and galleries. Private parking and entrance allow for secluded, quiet retreat. $85.

Vail View Bed and Breakfast

Bed and Breakfast Vail Ski Areas
P. O. Box 491, 81658
(303) 949-1212; (800) 748-2666

Begin your morning with a spectacular view of the Gore Range while sipping on your coffee. Check out the weather, and decide your course of action as you stare into the mountains. What a way to start the day! Your hosts and cats welcome you to their home, offering comfortable home away from home accommodations. Your room has a TV and stereo for days that you prefer to stay at home and relax, and breakfasts at this terrific bed and breakfast are great. $70-75.

Village Artist

Bed and Breakfast Vail Ski Areas
P. O. Box 491, 81658
(303) 949-1212; (800) 748-2666

Centrally situated, on the free bus route, right in the heart of Vail. You are within walking distance of the village, slopes, Vail's nightlife, Vista Bahn, and Lionshead Gondola. Share the living area, TV, fireplace, and kitchen with hostess. Full or continental breakfast. $75.

WINTER PARK

Alpen Rose
Bed and Breakfast

244 Forest Trail, P. O. Box 769, 80482
(303) 726-5039

Surrounded by aspen and pine trees with a spectacular view of the front range. Situated in a sporting paradise, two miles from nation's fifth largest ski area and 40 minutes from Rocky Mountain National Park, the Alpen Rose reflects the owners' love of Austria and feels like an Austrian chalet. Five rooms with Austrian furnishings, down puffs, and handmade quilts make you feel at home. A memorable breakfast with Austrian specialties awaits you in the morning; crackling fire, hot tea, and cookies beckon you home after an enjoyable day in the Rockies.

Hosts: Robin and Rupert Sommerauer
Rooms: 5 (PB) $65-95
Full Breakfast
Credit Cards: A, B, C
Notes: 2, 9, 13, 14

Angle Mark
Bed and Breakfast

50 Little Pierre Avenue, P. O. Box 161, 80482
(303) 726-5354

A beautiful mountain home off the beaten path provides the guest with a safe, quiet stay.International collections decorate the roomy suites. Full gourmet breakfast served in the Colorado room while birds and squirrels perform on feeders just outside. Complimentary hors d'oeuvres served

6 Pets welcome; 7 Smoking allowed; 8 Children welcome; 9 Social drinking allowed; 10 Tennis available; 11 Swimming available; 12 Golf available; 13 Skiing available; 14 May be booked through travel agents.

each evening. The area offers all amenities of a small, family-oriented mountain resort town.

Hosts: Bob and Jeanenne Temple
Rooms: 3 (PB) $75-95
Full Breakfast
Credit Cards: A, B
Notes: 2, 5, 9, 10, 11, 12, 13

Arapahoe Ski Lodge

Bed and Breakfast-Rocky Mountains
906 South Pearl Street
Denver, 80209
(303) 744-8415; (800) 733-8415

Feel right at home in this comfortable, cozy, and homey ski lodge located in the heart of Winter Park. All rooms have two beds and a private bath. Indoors pool and sauna, and free transportation to and from the Winter Park slopes. Full breakfast, and dinner included in winter stays. No smoking in public areas. No pets. Budget to moderate rates.

Engelmann Pines Bed and Breakfast

P. O. Box 1305, 80482
(303) 726-4632

Engelmann Pines is a contemporary mountain home furnished with European and American antiques, Oriental rugs, and art. Beds have European down comforters and handmade quilts. Our spacious home provides a TV room, reading room, and kitchen for guests to use. We serve a full gourmet breakfast, which includes Swiss specialities. We are nestled among the pines, high in the Rocky Mountains, close to Winter Park Ski Resort, Pole Creek Golf Course, and Rocky Mountain National Park.

Hosts: Margaret and Heinz Engel
Rooms: 6 (2 PB; 4 SB) $55-95
Full Gourmet Breakfast
Credit Cards: A, B, C
Notes: 2, 5, 8, 9, 10, 11, 12, 13, 14

The Other Woman

Bed and Breakfast-Rocky Mountains
906 South Pearl Street
Denver, 80209
(303) 744-8415; (800) 733-8415

Secluded in a wooded area near Winter Park, this beautiful solar home provides a lovely and relaxing environment with a fabulous fireplace and archway. Two second floor rooms each have a balcony opening onto a greenhouse and hot tub below. Both have a queen-size bed and a semiprivate bath. Full gourmet breakfast. No smoking, no pets, children over 12, snow tires in ski season needed. Moderate-luxury rates.

WOODLAND PARK

Pikes Peak Paradise

P. O. Box 5760, Pinecrest Rd, 80866
(719) 687-6656; (800) 728-8282

Luxury accommodations in National Forest, and only thirty minutes to Colorado Springs, this bed and breakfast offers a hot tub, gourmet breakfast, fireplace and love seat in a peaceful, quiet, romantic setting.

Hosts: Tim Stoddard, Martin Meier, Priscilla Arthur
Rooms: 5(PB) $85-125
Full Breakfast
Credit Cards: A, B, C, D, E, F
Notes: 2 (in advance only) , 5, 9, 13, 14

YELLOW JACKET

Wilson's Pinto Bean Farm

House No. 21434, Road 16, 81335
(303) 562-4476

The Wilson's farm is in Montezuma County, 40 miles from the Four-Corners where the four western states join. Waving wheat, fragrant alfalfa, pinto beans, and mountains are visible in every direction. The farmhouse sits among elm trees, with orchards and gardens around. There are

NOTES: Credit cards accepted: A Master Card; B Visa; C American Express; D Discover Card; E Diner's Club; F Other; 2 Personal Checks accepted; 3 Lunch available; 4 Dinner available; 5 Open all year;

farm animals to enjoy, home-cooked meals, eggs to hunt, and fruits to pick in season. Children of all ages can see the delights of farm animals and country living.

Hosts: Arthur and Esther M. Wilson
Rooms: 2 (SB) $33 + $6.00 each for supper
Full Breakfast
Credit Cards: None
Notes: 2, 3, 4, 6, 8, 9, 11

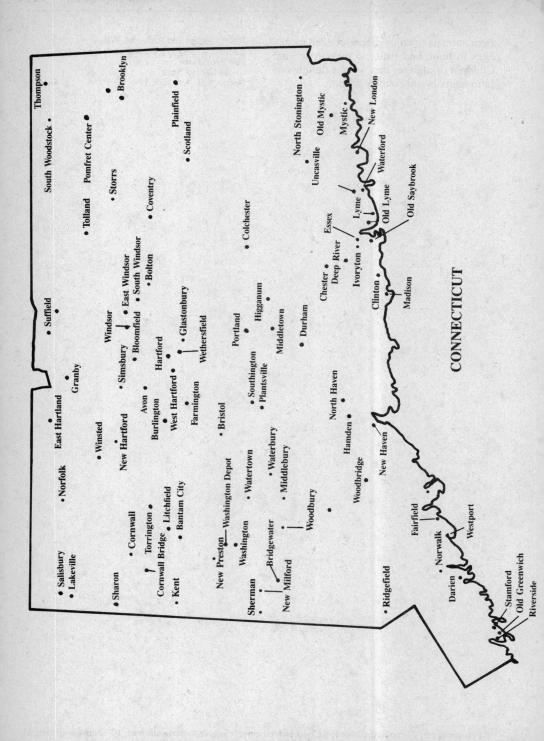

CONNECTICUT

Connecticut

AVON

Nutmeg Bed and Breakfast Agency #414

P. O. Box 1117, West Hartford, 06107
(203) 236-6698

This bright, spacious contemporary has a solarium, deck, and lovely grounds including a Japanese garden with a pond and a waterfall. One room has a cathedral ceiling and skylight; adjacent studio. Six languages spoken here. Continental breakfast and afternoon tea served. Children welcome—baby-sitting available. No smoking.

BANTAM

Nutmeg Bed and Breakfast Agency #319

P. O. Box 1117, West Hartford, 06107
(203) 236-6698

Deer Island Guest house on Bantam Lake with a lake view in back, front on road; rustic but comfortable. One bedroom with three twin beds, fireplace, chairs, table for dining in a completely equipped kitchen, bath with a shower; kitchen stocked for breakfast; canoe rentals nearby, restaurant nearby. Continental breakfast, children allowed, no smoking, no pets in the guest house.

BARKHAMSTED

Covered Bridge

P. O. Box 447, Norfolk, 06058
(203) 542-5944

Rustic Victorian lake lodge features fireside concerts on the antique grand piano, wrap-around porch with a commanding view of woods, and crystal clear lake. Feel free to borrow the canoe, relax on the private beach, or enjoy a country walk. Three guest rooms, one with a balcony overlooking the lake, share a bath and a half. $80-95.

BARLINGTON

Four Seasons International Bed and Breakfast Service

11 Bridlepath Road, West Simsbury, 06092
(203) 651-3045

Rambling, comfortable Dutch Colonial on 12 wooded acres with trails to explore in Barlington. Full breakfast. Private home offers twin beds or double in three rooms. $38 single; $65 double.

BLOOMFIELD

Nutmeg Bed and Breakfast Agency #407

P. O. Box 1117, West Hartford, 06107
(203) 236-6698

NOTES: Credit cards accepted: A Master Card; B Visa; C American Express; D Discover Card; E Diner's Club; F Other; 2 Personal Checks accepted; 3 Lunch available; 4 Dinner available; 5 Open all year; 6 Pets welcome; 7 Smoking allowed; 8 Children welcome; 9 Social drinking allowed; 10 Tennis available; 11 Swimming available; 12 Golf available; 13 Skiing available; 14 May be booked through travel agents.

A 1920s farmhouse, this bed and breakfast has its own duck pond. Three guest rooms share one full bath and two half baths. Guests enjoy country English living room with a lovely deck. Private apartment available for long-term guests. Continental breakfast. Children ten and over welcome.

Nutmeg Bed and Breakfast Agency #450

P. O. Box 1117, West Hartford, 06107
(203) 236-6698

Hospitality rules here, with a den, refrigerator and ice, and a sociable resident cat. Four guest rooms with private and shared baths. One has connecting playroom with TV and phone. Convenient to West Hartford and Hartford and across the road from Penwood State Forest for walking, jogging, or cross-country skiing. Full breakfast. Children welcome.

Nutmeg Bed and Breakfast Agency #467

P. O. Box 1117, West Hartford, 06107
(203) 236-6698

This 1958 ranch-style house has spacious rooms, wide hallways, and wheelchair accommodations. There are three rooms

Chimney Crest Manor

with a choice of king, double, or single beds. All share a bath. Convenient to he University of Hartford, Loomis Shaffee, the University of Connecticut, and the airport. Three minutes to public transportation, off-street parking available. Continental breakfast served to the room if desired, Children allowed. No smoking, no resident pets.

BOLTON

Jared Cone House

25 Hebron Road, 06043
(203) 643-8538

Enjoy the charm of this historic country home. It has spacious bedrooms with queen beds and scenic views of the countryside. Bicycle and canoe available. Hosts serve a full breakfast featuring homemade maple syrup. Fine dining nearby, and a short distance from berry farms, antiques, herb farms, and parks.

Hosts: Jeff and Cinde Smith
Rooms: 3 (SB) $45-70
Full Breakfast
Credit Cards: None
Notes: 2, 5, 8, 10, 11, 12

BRISTOL

Chimney Crest Manor

5 Founders Drive, 06010
(203) 582-4219

Experience quiet elegance in this splendid 32-room Tudor mansion. Chimney Crest was built in 1930 in the Federal Hill Historic District, just minutes away from the Litchfield Hills, where you will find antiques, wineries, parks, art galleries, museums, and restaurants. Stay in the spacious suites, for pleasure or on business. You will be treated with warm, attentive hospitality set in the splendor and style of a bygone era.

NOTES: Credit cards accepted: A Master Card; B Visa; C American Express; D Discover Card; E Diner's Club; F Other; 2 Personal Checks accepted; 3 Lunch available; 4 Dinner available; 5 Open all year;

Hosts: Dan and Cynthia Cimadamore
Suites: 5 (PB) $69.89-112
Full Breakfast
Credit Cards: A, B, C
Notes: 5, 8, 10, 11, 12, 13, 14

Nutmeg Bed and Breakfast Agency #433

P. O. Box 1117, West Hartford, 06107
(203) 236-6698

Visitors to Bristol's clock museum and history lovers will especially enjoy a stay in the Dutch Colonial home of the city historian. Large lawns and gardens surround this lacy home in a residential area. One guest room with private bath. Full breakfast. No smoking.

BRIDGEWATER

Sanford/Pond House

P. O. Box 306, Main St, 06752
(203) 355-4677

A gracious Federal Greek revival mansion with stately, uniquely decorated bedrooms with sitting rooms or sitting areas and private baths. Relax in elegant style. "The Versailles of the region's bed and breakfast's"—*Travel and Leisure* magazine. Excellent restaurants, antique shops, art galleries, and boutiques in the area.

Host: George and Charlotte Pond
Rooms: 5 (PB) $85-115
Continental Plus Breakfast
Credit Cards: A, B
Notes: 2, 5, 8, 10, 11, 12, 13, 14

BROOKLYN

Tannerbrook

329 Pomfret Road (Route 169), 06234
(203) 774-4822

Restored 1750 Colonial saltbox with 12 beautiful acres, including private spring-fed fishing lake, towering sugar maples, and hiking paths. Brooklyn is central for touring New England by way of nearby expressways. Boston and Hartford, one hour; Cape Cod, one and one-half hours; New York, two and one-half hours.

Hosts: Jean and Wendell Burgess
Rooms: 2 (PB) $65
Full Breakfast
Credit Cards: A, B
Notes: 2, 5, 7, 8, 9, 10, 11, 12

BURLINGTON

Nutmeg Bed and Breakfast Agency #478

P. O. Box 1117, West Hartford, 06107
(203) 236-6698

This ranch-style home has a screened porch, pool, and lovely gardens. There is a room with twin beds, private bath, living room, porch, and deck for guests' use. Convenient to Avon Old Farms, Miss Porter's, and the University of Connecticut Medical Center. Full breakfast. No children. No smoking. Dogs on premises.

CHESTER

Chester Village Bed and Breakfast

Box 370, 123 Main Street, 06412
(203) 526-9770

Relaxing retreat located in a charming New England village. Walk to the area's finest dining, antiques, and artisan shops. Enjoy Connecticut River activities, beaches, hiking trails, theater nearby. Midway between Boston and New York City. Day trips to Mystic Village, Thimble Islands, and Gillette Castle.

Hosts: Michael Momparler and Thayer Quoos
Rooms: 5 (3 PB; 2 SB) $55-85
Full Breakfast
Credit Card: C
Notes: 2, 5, 8, 10, 11

6 Pets welcome; 7 Smoking allowed; 8 Children welcome; 9 Social drinking allowed; 10 Tennis available; 11 Swimming available; 12 Golf available; 13 Skiing available; 14 May be booked through travel agents.

CLINTON

Captain Dibbell House

221 Commerce Street, 06413
(203) 669-1646

This 1866 Victorian, located on a historic residential street, is two blocks from the harbor and features a century-old, wisteria-covered iron truss bridge. Rooms are furnished with a comfortable mix of heirlooms, antiques, auction finds, and a growing collection of original art by New England artists. Bicycles are available.

Hosts: Helen and Ellis Adams
Rooms: 4 (PB) $75-85
Full Breakfast
Credit Cards: A, B, C
Closed Jan.
Notes: 2, 8 (over 14), 9, 10, 11, 12, 13, 14

Captain Dibble House

COLCHESTER

The Hayward House Inn

35 Hayward Avenue, 06415
(203) 537-5772

A 1767 home on the National Register of Historic Places; a Federal Colonial furnished with antiques. All rooms have private baths. The Goodspeede Opera house, shops, beaches, golf, biking, and tennis are all within a short distance. Come experience small-town New England at its best. Massage therapy on the premises. Lunch, dinner, and tea are served at an extra charge in the tea room on the premises.

Hosts: Bettyann and Stephen Possidento
Rooms: 6 (PB) $75-95
Continental Plus Breakfast
Credit Card: A, B
Notes: 2, 3, 4, 5, 8, 9, 10, 11, 12, 13 (XC), 14

Nutmeg Bed and Breakfast Agency #438

P. O. Box 1117, West Hartford, 06107
(203) 236-6698

Located on the town green, this 1776 home is on the historic register. Four rooms with private baths, one with Jacuzzi. Two carriage house apartments available. Biking, a picnic, and good restaurant meal can be arranged. Country American antique shop is open in the barn. Continental breakfast. Children over eight welcome. No smoking.

CORNWALL

Cornwall Inn

Route 7, 06754
(800) 786-6884

Nestled in the northwest hills of Connecticut, an inn for all seasons. Antique-decorated inn rooms and the country motel-type rooms all have private baths. Enjoy the pool and patio in the summer or the roaring fireplace in the dining room in the winter.

Hosts: Lois and Emily
Rooms: 13 (12 PB; 1 SB) $50-110
Full Breakfast
Credit Cards: A, B
Notes: 2, 3, 4, 5, 6, 7, 8, 9, 11, 13, 14

NOTES: Credit cards accepted: A Master Card; B Visa; C American Express; D Discover Card; E Diner's Club; F Other; 2 Personal Checks accepted; 3 Lunch available; 4 Dinner available; 5 Open all year;

Covered Bridge 1C

P. O. Box 447, Norfolk, 06058
(203) 542-5944

1808 Colonial farmhouse set on 20 acres adjoin Mohawk State Forest. The guest living room has a large old Colonial fireplace and wood stove. Breakfast is served in the country kitchen, or in the summer, on the terrace. Three bedrooms decorated in period antiques with shared full and half baths. $85.

Covered Bridge 2C

P. O. Box 447, Norfolk, 06058
(203) 542-5944

Enjoy warm, quiet hospitality at this custom-designed stone home set on a 64-acre private estate with breathtaking views of the countryside. Hearty full breakfasts are served before the library fireplace or on the terrace. All of the rooms are decorated in antiques. Two guest rooms with private baths. $95.

CORNWALL BRIDGE

Nutmeg Bed and Breakfast Agency #344

P. O. Box 1117, West Hartford, 06107
(203) 236-6698

Recently renovated small inn/motel has 5 rooms on the second floor of inn; 3 rooms have private baths, 2 share and are rented to families or to couples traveling together; also second floor sitting room with TV, books, and games. Motel rooms have queen or king beds (some have 2 queen), private baths, TV. Breakfast included; inn also has restaurant serving lunch and dinner, and a bar. Full breakfast, children allowed (5 years and younger free), smoking allowed, dog and cat on premises, pets accepted. Check-in 2 P.M.. Check-out 11A.M.

COVENTRY

Nutmeg Bed and Breakfast Agency #458

P. O. Box 1117, West Hartford, 06107
(203) 236-6698

Pink towered Victorian with a well-travelled hostess who collect antique toys; shop and museum in addition to Bed and Breakfast dining area with picture windows and skylights, solarium with potted plants. House is AC; two guest rooms have private baths, one has a queen-size bed and the other a pair of twin beds; both have access to large guest balcony overlooking the garden. Another twin bedded room shared a bath with hosts. Full breakfast, children allowed, no smoking, no pets.

Nutmeg Bed and Breakfast Agency #461

P. O. Box 1117, West Hartford, 06107
(203) 236-6698

Circa 1845 restored two story colonial, pool, hot tub and cabana. Quiet area with a pond and river a short walk away. Two second floor guest rooms, one with a queen, one with a double sleigh bed; both with private baths. Best suited for one couple or four members of one family since two bedrooms are joined. Continental breakfast. Children allowed. Smoking allowed. No resident pets. Long term only.

Nutmeg Bed and Breakfast Agency #463

P. O. Box 1117, West Hartford, 06107
(203) 236-6698

Fully modernized colonial built in 1731 on 3 1/4 acres with a pool, Jacuzzi, maple trees with hammocks, 3 fireplaces, 4 guest rooms with double beds share 1 upstairs and 1 downstairs bath. Rollaway available. Full breakfast, infants and over 5 allowed, no smoking, dog in residence.

6 Pets welcome; 7 Smoking allowed; 8 Children welcome; 9 Social drinking allowed; 10 Tennis available; 11 Swimming available; 12 Golf available; 13 Skiing available; 14 May be booked through travel agents.

DARIEN

Nutmeg Bed and Breakfast Agency #103

P. O. Box 1117, West Hartford, 06107
(203) 236-6698

Originally built in the late 1800s as a stable and barn, this house was converted to a home in the 1920s. Two guest rooms share a bath. Views of Long Island Sound are breathtaking. Continental breakfast. Children welcome. $60-85.

DEEP RIVER

Riverwind Inn

209 Main Street, 06417
(203) 526-2014

With its eight wonderfully appointed guest rooms, rambling common areas, and informal country atmosphere, Riverwind is more than just a place to stay; it's a destination. Relax, step back in time, and enjoy a stay amid an enchanting collection of New England and southern country antiques. Each morning starts with the inn's complimentary southern buffet breakfast.

Hosts: Barbara Barlow and Bob Bucknall
Rooms: 8 (PB) $85-145
Full Breakfast
Credit Cards: A, B, C
Notes: 2, 5, 7, 9, 10, 11, 12, 14

DURHAM

Nutmeg Bed and Breakfast Agency #516

P. O. Box 1117, West Hartford, 06107
(203) 236-6698

Enjoy the swimming pool and the rural setting of this two-story Colonial. It has a large entrance hall downstairs and a lovely sitting room. Three guest rooms share a bath and are comfortably furnished. A roll

away and crib are available. Air-conditioned. Continental breakfast. Children welcome. No smoking.

EAST HARTLAND

Nutmeg Bed and Breakfast Agency #480

P. O. Box 1117, West Hartford, 06107
(203) 236-6698

Guest house adjacent to colonial farmhouse built in 1700s. Private entrance to sitting room with working fireplace, double Murphy bed, complete kitchen, full bath, and beautiful setting with horses, stone fences, and hills beyond. Full breakfast served in antique-filled main dining room or in guest house. 20 minutes from airport; hiking, skiing, biking, fishing minutes away. Children allowed. No smoking. No pets in guest house.

EAST LYME

Nutmeg Bed and Breakfast Agency #517

P. O. Box 1117, West Hartford, 06107
(203) 236-6698

This 1760 Colonial has exposed beams, wide, oak floor boards, seven fireplaces, a root cellar, an original goose pen, and a host and hostess who bake and make jelly. One guest room with private bath, and one guest room with a shared bath. Afternoon tea or apple cider is served in season. Full breakfast is served on the outdoor deck in good weather. No smoking.

EAST WINDSOR

Nutmeg Bed and Breakfast Agency #410

P. O. Box 1117, West Hartford, 06107
(203) 236-6698

NOTES: Credit cards accepted: A Master Card; B Visa; C American Express; D Discover Card; E Diner's Club; F Other; 2 Personal Checks accepted; 3 Lunch available; 4 Dinner available; 5 Open all year;

This beautifully restored 1837 home has a pond and two goats. Four guest rooms, one with private oak bathroom and Jacuzzi. Antiques, family art, and stenciled walls and floors make this the perfect country getaway. Full breakfast and afternoon tea are served. Children over nine welcome.

The Stephen Potwine House

84 Scantic Road, 06088
(203) 623-8722

A charming, old country farmhouse overlooking a pond, flowers, and willow trees. The house is situated on picturesque open property surrounded by acres of farm land and fields. The historic house today is a homestead decorated in country decor with antiques and collectibles. Country atmosphere, a rural setting, and East Windsor's convenient location near many attractions make this a unique place to visit with access to major cities, Hartford and Springfield.

Hosts: Vangi and Bob Cathcart
Rooms: 3 (1 PB; 2 SB) $55-75
Full Breakfast
Credit Cards: None
Notes: 2, 5

ESSEX

Nutmeg Bed and Breakfast Agency #508

P. O. Box 1117, West Hartford, 06107
(203) 236-6698

If you're a boating enthusiast, your entertaining hostess, whose family shares your passion, would love to trade some sailing stories with you. This special home, right on the bank of the Connecticut River, is convenient to many attractions of the area, 20 miles from Mystic, and close to Hammonasset public beach in Madison. Theaters and fine restaurants are nearby. Two rooms share a bath. Full breakfast can be served on the glass porch overlooking the river. Children welcome.

FAIRFIELD

Nutmeg Bed and Breakfast Agency #110

P. O. Box 1117, West Hartford, 06107
(203) 236-6698

Nestled in two acres of woods, this English cottage is the perfect spot for a cozy getaway. Guest room with private bath is furnished with a blend of country English and antiques. In nice weather, continental breakfast is served on patio overlooking a pond. No smoking.

Nutmeg Bed and Breakfast Agency #112

P. O. Box 1117, West Hartford, 06107
(203) 236-6698

This early 1950s custom-built ranch has a large screened porch, comfortable antique furnishings, and off-street parking or garage. There are two double bedrooms, or one double and one single as needed. Both rooms share a bath. A full breakfast is served. No smoking, no children, no pets on premises.

FARMINGTON

Four Seasons International Bed and Breakfast Service

11 Bridlepath Road, West Simsbury, 06092
(203) 651-3045

Architect-designed and owned contemporary home nestled in a wooded setting in the historic town of Farmington. Just five miles from I-84. Full breakfast often includes homemade bread. Two rooms, private half bath, queen bed. $40 single; $65 double.

6 Pets welcome; 7 Smoking allowed; 8 Children welcome; 9 Social drinking allowed; 10 Tennis available; 11 Swimming available; 12 Golf available; 13 Skiing available; 14 May be booked through travel agents.

Nutmeg Bed and Breakfast Agency #406

P. O. Box 1117, West Hartford, 06107
(203) 236-6698

This elegant estate is now a gracious small inn with beautifully landscaped grounds, pool, tennis court, conference room, and lounge. There are seven rooms with TV's, phones, and private baths. A short drive from Hartford. Perfect for the business traveler. Continental breakfast. Children welcome.

Nutmeg Bed and Breakfast Agency #415

P. O. Box 1117, West Hartford, 06107
(203) 236-6698

This is a luxurious new inn with 56 suites complete with kitchens, fireplaces, and bathrooms with all the amenities. Enjoy complimentary racquet club privileges with pools and tennis courts. Continental breakfast. Children welcome.

Nutmeg Bed and Breakfast Agency #472

P. O. Box 117, West Hartford, 06107
(203) 236-6698

This single-story home in a quiet setting is convenient to Avon Old Farms, Miss Porter's, St. Joseph's College, and West Hartford and Hartford colleges. A two-room suite has a double bed, and both the bedroom and and the sitting room open onto a private deck with view of the woods. A full breakfast is served. Children allowed, smoking allowed, and there is a dog and cat in residence.

GLASTONBURY

Butternut Farm

1654 Main Street, 06033
(203) 633-7197

An 18th-century architectural jewel that is furnished in museum-quality period antiques. Estate setting with ancient trees, herb gardens, prize dairy goats, barnyard chickens, and pigeons. Ten minutes from Hartford. All Connecticut is within one and one-half hours.

Host: Don Reid
Rooms: 5 (3 PB; 2 S2B) $65-85
Full Breakfast
Credit Cards: A, B, C
Notes: 2, 5, 8, 9, 10, 11, 12, 13, 14

Udderly Woolly Acres

581 Thompson Street, 06033
(203) 633-4503

Stay the night in a suite of rooms in an 1820 farmhouse set on 20 acres in East Glastonbury. Look out on a pastoral scene with sheep, goats, and geese on a working homestead. Farm-fresh vegetables, fruit, milk, eggs, and cheese in season. Lodging includes breakfast.

Hosts: Joan and Tom Kemble
Suite: 1 (PB) $75
Full Breakfast
Credit Cards: None
Notes: 2, 5, 8, 9

GRANBY

Nutmeg Bed and Breakfast Agency #442

P. O. Box 1117, West Hartford, 06107
(203) 236-6698

There is a sophisticated country atmosphere to this stone house. The separate guest wing includes a sitting room with TV, two guest rooms with private baths. Convenient to Bradley International Airport, state parks, historic Old Newgate Prison, and local attractions. Guests enjoy wine, cheese, and crackers in the afternoon, and a continental breakfast is served. Your horses can be boarded for a nominal fee. Children welcome. No smoking.

NOTES: Credit cards accepted: A Master Card; B Visa; C American Express; D Discover Card; E Diner's Club; F Other; 2 Personal Checks accepted; 3 Lunch available; 4 Dinner available; 5 Open all year;

GREAT BARRINGTON

Nutmeg Bed and Breakfast Agency #332

P. O. Box 1117, West Hartford, 06107
(203) 236-6698

100-year-old Victorian with porch, deck, and hot tub, has one bedroom with private. bath, double. bed, two rooms with double. beds share bath; sitting area in all rooms, TV in 2 rooms. Continental breakfast, children allowed, smoking allowed. One cat, two dogs, on premise.

HAMDEN

Nutmeg Bed and Breakfast Agency #205

P. O. Box 1117, West Hartford, 06107
(203) 236-6698

Come home to this two-story Colonial located just outside New Haven. Decorated in Early American furnishings, your accommodations include a first-floor bedroom with a double bed and private bath. Nearby bus stop. Continental breakfast. Children welcome.

Nutmeg Bed and Breakfast Agency #207

P. O. Box 1117, West Hartford, 06107
(203) 236-6698

A pool and lovely deck add to your enjoyment of this comfortable home. Situated right outside New Haven, this house has one guest room with shared bath, perfect for the single traveler. Continental breakfast. Children welcome. No smoking.

HARTFORD

Nutmeg Bed and Breakfast Agency #428

P. O. Box 1117, West Hartford, 06107
(203) 236-6698

Classical musician husband and wife host this elegant late Victorian bed and breakfast. Authentic stained glass and hand-done stenciling add charm to this city home. One guest room with shared bath. Pull-out bed for children. Close to Trinity, the Bushnell, the Civic Center, and the bus line. Enjoy a continental breakfast with hosts or privately. Children welcome. No smoking. German and some French spoken.

Nutmeg Bed and Breakfast Agency #453

P. O. Box 1117, West Hartford, 06107
(203) 236-6698

Lovely Victorian home in an exclusive residential section has a third floor room with king bed, private bath with shower, seating area with sofa which opens into queen bed, TV, clock radio, terry robe, 2 telephone jacks; second floor room with double bed and bath shared with hosts, small TV. Kitchen and laundry privileges for long-term stay. Two-night minimum for weekends in summer and fall (Memorial Day through end of October). Continental plus breakfast, no children, smoking allowed, cat and dog in residence.

Nutmeg Bed and Breakfast Agency #477

P. O. Box 1117, West Hartford, 06107
(203) 236-6698

High rise condo built in the mid 60s; 24-hour doorman, close to insurance companies, St. Francis Hospital, Mark Twain

House, downtown Hartford. Ninth floor unit has balcony off one room; guest bedroom with double bed, desk, TV, phone, private bath next to bedroom. Handicapped accessible and convenient. Outdoor pool, exercise room in building. Continental plus breakfast, no children, no smoking, three well-behaved cats in residence.

HIGGANUM

Nutmeg Bed and Breakfast Agency #521

P. O. Box 117, West Hartford, 06107
(203) 236-6698

This Dutch Colonial home is in a very secluded setting on a wooded two-acre lot. There is a second floor king bedroom with a private bath across the hall, and a single bed is available in the next room for a child. There is a sauna and shower in the basement. Full breakfast is served. Children are allowed. No smoking. No pets.

IVORYTON

The Copper Beech Inn

46 Main Street, 06442
(203) 767-0330

Gracious gardens and rustic woodlands set the stage for this handsome inn. A gallery offers antique Oriental porcelain, and the dining room is noted for fine country French cuisine. Beautiful countryside, quaint villages, museums, antique shops, theater, and water sports distinguish the area.

Hosts: Eldon and Sally Senner
Rooms: 13 (PB) $112-179.20
Buffet Breakfast
Minimum stay weekends and holidays: 2 nights
Credit Cards: A, B, C, E
Closed Mondays, Christmas, New Year's Day
Notes: 2, 4, 5, 8 (over 8), 10, 11, 12

KENT

Covered Bridge 1K

P. O. Box 447, Norfolk, 06058
(203) 542-5944

Charming 18th-century house is one of the oldest in Kent and is a splendid example of Federal architecture and decor. Living room with fireplace is available for guests; upstairs suite has an ornately carved four-poster canopy bed and private bath. Continental breakfast. $85-120.

Covered Bridge 2K

P. O. Box 447, Norfolk, 06058
(203) 542-5944

This 1860 Colonial set on two acres is close to Kent Falls. The owner, who also has an antique shop on the grounds, has decorated all of the rooms with period furniture. There is a living room and a den with a fireplace and TV. Continental breakfast. Three guest rooms, shared and private bath. $85-95.

Nutmeg Bed and Breakfast Agency #322

P. O. Box 1117, West Hartford, 06107
(203) 236-6698

Friendly hospitality awaits you at the 1860s colonial bed and breakfast home. Unwind in the romantic rose stenciled room with beamed ceiling or the country blue room with carved Victorian headboard, both with private baths. Relax by the fireplace in the cozy den or walk the lovely grounds and view St. John's Ledges. After a continental breakfast in the charming dining room, visit the adjoining antique shop. Nearby to hiking, skiing, canoeing, museums and many fine restaurants. Children over 12 welcome. No smoking.

NOTES: Credit cards accepted: A Master Card; B Visa; C American Express; D Discover Card; E Diner's Club; F Other; 2 Personal Checks accepted; 3 Lunch available; 4 Dinner available; 5 Open all year;

Nutmeg Bed and Breakfast Agency #351

P. O. Box 1117, West Hartford, 06107
(203) 236-6698

Guest cottage suitable for a couple and 2 children on 7 acres of land a has loft with double bed, room with foldout double bed, private bath. Continental breakfast. Children allowed. No smoking. No pets.

LAKEVILLE

Nutmeg Bed and Breakfast Agency #320

P. O. Box 1117, West Hartford, 06107
(203) 236-6698

The smell of blueberry muffins and warm hospitality await you when you stay at this bed and breakfast. The three comfortable guest rooms have private and semi-private baths. Enjoy the screened in porch in the evenings or sit before the cozy fireplace in the sitting room. Nearby to Lime Rock, private schools and many fine restaurants. Children over 10 are welcome. No smoking.

The Copper Beach Inn

Nutmeg Bed and Breakfast Agency #327

P. O. Box 1117, West Hartford, 06107
(203) 236-6698

A quiet contemporary home on beautiful Lake Wononscopomuc, this bed and breakfast is only one and a half miles from town and fine restaurants. The three guest rooms feature king- and queen-size beds and private and semi-private baths. Watch the sunset form the boathouse dock; sit by the fireplace for a cozy chat; or watch the sailboats go by as you eat your full country breakfast in the dinning room. "The Captain" welcomes you aboard. Children over 12 are also welcome. No smoking.

Nutmeg Bed and Breakfast Agency #328

P. O. Box 1117, West Hartford, 06107
(203) 236-6698

Set along a lovely lake, this fifteen room turn of the century bed and breakfast is filled with antiques and charm. You may choose guest rooms with a Sleigh or a Spool bed, each with its own private bath. After a sumptuous continental breakfast enjoy some of the areas many attractions: Lime Rock Park, Music Mountain, and Mohawk Ski Area. Children over 8 are welcome. No smoking.

Nutmeg Bed and Breakfast Agency #329

P. O. Box 1117, West Hartford, 06107
(203) 236-6698

Built nearly 100 years ago, this charming house is surrounded by cliffs and gardens and has a beautiful view of Lake Wononscopomuc. The guest rooms, which share a bath, are furnished with antiques and family heirlooms. Enjoy your full breakfast (complete with homemade coffee cake). Savor the old fashioned front porch when the weather is warm. Or snuggle by the parlor fireplace if the weather is snowy! Children over 3 and smoking are allowed.

Nutmeg Bed and Breakfast Agency #330

P. O. Box 1117, West Hartford, 06107
(203) 236-6698

High on a peaceful hill this stately home sits on beautifully landscaped acreage. You will find flowers in your room, fresh from the greenhouse, and terry cloth robes to snuggle in after you bathe in an old-fashioned claw-foot tub. The three guest rooms are lovingly furnished with antiques and have private and semi-private baths. Guests have a private entrance and share their own sitting room with fireplace. Children over 10 are welcome. No smoking.

Host: Henri J. P. Manassero

LITCHFIELD

The Covered Bridge

P. O. Box 447, Norfolk, 06058
(203) 542-5944

Pre-Revolutionary War Colonial set on over 200 acres. In summer, guests can enjoy a full breakfast overlooking a rolling view towards a wooded brook. There are three guest rooms, one on the first floor with a queen bed and private bath, and two king bedrooms on the second floor with a bath between the rooms. $90.

Nutmeg Bed and Breakfast Agency #333

P. O. Box 1117, West Hartford, 06107
(203) 236-6698

Situated on a quiet country road outside the historic village of Litchfield, this bed and breakfast features three guest rooms: one with private entrance, queen-size bed, and private bath and two with king-size beds which share a bath. The house is a pre-Revolutionary Colonial, shaded by century-old sugar maples. Horses and sheep graze in the pasture. Guests will enjoy their full breakfast on the stone terrace or the covered porch in warm weather where they can overlook a rolling view of a wooded brook. Children over 12 welcome.

LYME

Covered Bridge -LY

P. O. Box 447, Norfolk, 06058
(203) 542-5944

A 1765 Colonial set on four acres and surrounded by stone walls, gardens, and terraces. Relax in the living room with fireplace and the original beehive oven or choose a book from the library. Full breakfast. Two guest rooms with private bath. $95.

The Covered Bridge -2LY

P. O. Box 447, Norfolk, 06058
(203) 542-5944

European charm and antiques make this Colonial set on fourteen acres a very special retreat. A full breakfast is served in the elegant dining room or in the sitting room that has a wood burning stove and offers a lovely view of the grounds. Several pieces of furniture have been hand-painted by the hostess, reflecting her Swiss heritage, and both of the queen guest rooms, each with a private bath, have handmade quilts. $85.

Nutmeg Bed and Breakfast Agency #512

P. O. Box 117, West Hartford, 06107
(203) 236-6698

NOTES: Credit cards accepted: A Master Card; B Visa; C American Express; D Discover Card; E Diner's Club; F Other; 2 Personal Checks accepted; 3 Lunch available; 4 Dinner available; 5 Open all year;

This new center-chimney Colonial is on several acres of woods and has its own walking trail and horseshoe court. Two guest rooms with private baths are accented by family pieces and European furnishings. Convenient to the Old Lyme Art Center, all the shoreline attractions, and many restaurants. Full breakfast. No smoking.

MADISON

Madison Beach Hotel

94 West Wharf Road, 06443
(203) 245-1404

Built in the early 1800s, the Madison Beach Hotel is nestled on a private beach on Long Island Sound. Distinctly Victorian in style and decor. Many rooms have private balconies overlooking the water. Antique oak bureaus, wainscotting, wicker and rattan furniture, along with old-fashioned wallpaper, complete the Victorian feeling. Restaurant serves lunch and dinner.

Hosts: Betty and Henry Cooney; Roben and Kathy
  Bagdasarian
Rooms: 35 (PB) $55-195
Continental Breakfast
Credit Cards: A, B, C
Closed Jan.and Feb.
Notes: 2, 3, 4, 7, 8, 9, 10, 11, 14

Nutmeg Bed and Breakfast Agency #518

P. O. Box 1117, West Hartford, 06107
(203) 236-6698

This is a three-story Colonial inn, built circa 1890, but completely renovated and updated. Near Hammonasset State Beach, this small inn combines hospitality and convenience. Beach passes are available to guests. Ten guest rooms have private baths and lovely Early American and early 19th-century furnishings. Continental breakfast. Children welcome.

Nutmeg Bed and Breakfast Agency #520

P. O. Box 1117, West Hartford, 06107
(203) 236-6698

Lovely center chimney Colonial about 20 years old, large livingroom for guests, lovely dining room, pool, comfortably large eat-in kitchen, fireplace in family room, pool, patio for breakfast on nice days; about 5 minutes from beach. Two second-floor guest rooms share bath; one has double spool bed, wicker chaise, chest, large closet, shuttered windows overlooking pool; one has twin beds, bedroom chair, chest, large closet. Continental breakfast. No children. No smoking. No resident pets.

Tidewater Inn

949 Boston Post Road, 06443
(203) 245-8457

Located in the beautiful shoreline town of Madison. With New England Colonial charm and picture post-card vistas, this bed and breakfast offers ten guest rooms, all with a private bath and different furnishings with a colorful variety of wall coverings and flower arrangements. Guest rooms offer bed sizes ranging from king to twin, and all rooms have cable TV and air-conditioning. Some rooms have working fireplaces. Continental breakfast is served in the great room by the bay window or in front of the large, traditional fireplace.

Rooms: 10 (PB) $85-115
Continental Breakfast
Credit Cards: A, B, C
Notes: 5, 7, 14

MIDDLEBURY

Tucker Hill Inn

96 Tucker Hill Road, 06762
(203) 758-8334

6 Pets welcome; 7 Smoking allowed; 8 Children welcome; 9 Social drinking allowed; 10 Tennis available; 11 Swimming available; 12 Golf available; 13 Skiing available; 14 May be booked through travel agents.

Tucker Hill Inn is a large center-hall Colonial just down from the village green in Middlebury. It was built around 1920 and was a restaurant and catering house for almost 40 years. The period rooms are spacious. Nearby are antiques, country drives, music and theater, golf, tennis, water sports, fishing, hiking, and cross-country skiing.

Hosts: Richard and Susan Cabelenski
Rooms: 4 (2 PB; 2 SB) $55-80
Full Breakfast
Credit Cards: A, B, C
Closed Christmas Day
Notes: 2, 7 (limited), 8, 9, 11, 12, 14

MIDDLETOWN

Nutmeg Bed and Breakfast Agency #471

P. O. Box 1117, West Hartford, 06107
(203) 236-6698

1920 Colonial, two upstairs guest rooms, each with queen beds. Fresh, light, colorful decor, semi-private bath. Two blocks from Wesleyan, 20 minutes to Hartford, 20 minutes to New Haven. Full breakfast. Children over 10 allowed. Smoking restricted. Dog and cat in residence.

MYSTIC

The Adams House

382 Cow Hill Road, 06355
(203) 572-9551; (800) 321-0433

Charming 1790-era home offers a homey colonial atmosphere year-round with three old-fashioned fireplaces; six bedrooms, all with private baths; two bedrooms have a fireplace. Continental breakfast. The carriage house is a separate building with sauna and can accommodate up to four people.

Hosts: Ron and Maureen Adams
Rooms: 7 (PB) $65-135

Continental Breakfast
Credit Cards: A, B
Notes: 2, 11

Covered Bridge -1M

P. O. Box 447, Norfolk, 06058
(203) 542-5944

This 150-year-old restored Victorian farmhouse is situated on two acres of lovely, landscaped grounds with old stone walls, fruit trees, and an outdoor eating area for guests' enjoyment. A full breakfast is served in the dining room, and a Scottish tea is served in the afternoon. There are five guest rooms, one with a fireplace and a private bath. $75-125.

Covered Bridge-2M

P. O. Box 447, Norfolk, 06058
(203) 542-5944

This 1800s Colonial in a village setting offers a quiet retreat only minutes from the center of Mystic. There is a pleasant living-room with a fireplace and a large dining room where a full breakfast is served. There are four guest rooms in the main house, three with fireplaces, and four guests rooms in the carriage house, two with whirlpool tubs. All rooms have queen-size beds and private baths. $98-125.

Comolli's House

36 Bruggeman Place, 06355
(203) 536-8723

Ideal for vacationers touring historic Mystic or the business person who desires a homey respite while traveling. This immaculate home, situated on a quiet hill overlooking the Mystic Seaport complex, is convenient to Olde Mistick Village and the aquarium. Sightseeing, sporting activities, shopping, and restaurant information is provided by your hosts. Off-season rates are available.

NOTES: Credit cards accepted: A Master Card; B Visa; C American Express; D Discover Card; E Diner's Club; F Other; 2 Personal Checks accepted; 3 Lunch available; 4 Dinner available; 5 Open all year;

Host: Dorothy M. Comolli
Rooms: 2 (PB) $95
Continental Breakfast
Credit Cards: None
Notes: 2, 5

Nutmeg Bed and Breakfast Agency #513

P. O. Box 1117, West Hartford, 06107
(203) 236-6698

Built in 1837, this large farmhouse is surrounded by fruit trees and strawberry beds. Five guest rooms, one with private bath, four sharing two baths. There is also a spacious dining room and a warm family room. The home-cooked breakfast with specialty muffins is amply satisfying. Full breakfast. Children over 11 welcome. No smoking.

Nutmeg Bed and Breakfast Agency #522

P. O. Box 1117, West Hartford, 06107
(203) 236-6698

Lovely, bright house convenient to downtown Mystic and Seaport but in a nice residential neighborhood. Guest bedroom on the first floor with double spool bed, private full bath. Small upstairs room available for child. Living room available for guests. Continental breakfast. Children allowed. No smoking. Cat in residence

NEW CANAAN

The Maples Inn

179 Oenoke Ridge, 06840
(203) 966-2927; (800) 959-6477

The Maples Inn combines a friendly atmosphere, accommodations of taste and elegance, and a wide choice of charming and spacious bedrooms, all enhanced by the serene ambience of a turn-of-the-century New England mansion. Next to one of Connecticut's foremost gourmet restaurants

and one of New England's most beautiful nature centers, this inn is only fifty miles from everything Manhattan has to offer.

Host: C.T. Haas
Rooms: 15 (11 PB; 4 SB) $50-150
Continental Breakfast
Credit Cards: A, B, C

NEW HARTFORD

Covered Bridge -1NH

P. O. Box 447, Norfolk, 06058
(203) 542-5944

A grand, 14-gabled Victorian in a very secluded setting yet not far from a very charming village on the Farmington River. There is a sitting room with TV and also a livingroom with a fireplace that guests are welcome to enjoy. A continental breakfast is served in the elegant dining room or in the summer on the huge porch overlooking the grounds. All four guest rooms are tastefully decorated in antiques. The guest rooms can be taken as suites with a bath in between two rooms, or two rooms with a private bath. $75-95

Covered Bridge - 2NH

P. O. Box 447, Norfolk, 06058
(203) 542-5944; (800) 488-5690

Featured in *Country Living*, this 1700s Colonial farmhouse is set on 40 acres. The grounds include a spring-fed pond for swimming and fishing, a barn for horses, chickens and pigs, and beautiful flower gardens. Enjoy old brick fireplaces, living room with sun porch, and country kitchen. Full breakfast. Five guest rooms. $95-125.

Four Season International Bed and Breakfast Service

11 Bridlepath Road, West Simsbury, 06092
(203) 651-3045

6 Pets welcome; 7 Smoking allowed; 8 Children welcome; 9 Social drinking allowed; 10 Tennis available; 11 Swimming available; 12 Golf available; 13 Skiing available; 14 May be booked through travel agents.

A historic Victorian private home with 14 gables high on a hilltop in New Hartford. Overlooking Ski Sundown. Breakfast alfresco in warmer weather. Four rooms. $45 single; $70-95 double.

Nutmeg Bed and Breakfast Agency #319

P. O. Box 1117, West Hartford, 06107
(203) 236-6698

Stay at this charming 1818 Colonial that sits high on a hill overlooking acres of meadows and the Berkshire Mountains. This home is furnished in period antiques and reproductions and has two spacious guest rooms, one with a private sun room with wicker furniture. The second guest room has a working fireplace, kitchenette and eating area, all with a wonderful view. Located near skiing, swimming, golf, boating, fishing and fine dining.

Nutmeg Bed and Breakfast Agency #334

P. O. Box 1117, West Hartford, 06107
(203) 236-6698

Built in 1879, this bed and breakfast is truly a grand old Victorian graced with flair. There are two guest rooms with semiprivate bath. A hearty breakfast is served. Located in the quaint village of New Hartford on a secluded hilltop, it is minutes from skiing, hiking, horseback riding and antiquing. Children over 12 welcome.

NEW HAVEN

Bed and Breakfast, Ltd.

P. O. Box 216, 06513
(203) 469-3260 after 5 P.M., weekdays, Sept.-June, and anytime weekends and July-August

Bed and Breakfast, Ltd offers over 125 listings of selected private homes and small inns throughout Connecticut, from elegantly simple to simply elegant. We provide personal service and great variety to the budget conscious traveler. A quick phone call assures you up-to-the-minute availability, and descriptions are all designed to meet your needs and price range.

Host: Jack M. Argenio, Director
Rooms: 125 (60 PB; 65 SB) $55-75
Continental Breakfast or Full Breakfast

Nutmeg Bed and Breakfast Agency #208

P. O. Box 1117, West Hartford, 06107
(203) 236-6698

Catch a game at the Yale Bowl or the bus downtown from this bed and breakfast in the Westville section. This English Tudor has two guest rooms with shared bath. Help yourself to continental breakfast. Children welcome.

Nutmeg Bed and Breakfast Agency #210

P. O. Box 1117, West Hartford, 06107
(203) 236-6698

Walk to Yale from this gracious Victorian home set in the residential section of New Haven. A newly decorated third-floor suite consists of a bedroom with a large private bath and a smaller bedroom. A guest room is also available on the second floor. Continental breakfast. Children welcome.

Nutmeg Bed and Breakfast Agency #211

P. O. Box 1117, West Hartford, 06107
(203) 236-6698

Built in 1902, this Federal-Georgian home is only a ten-minute walk from Yale. A separate entrance leads to three guest rooms that share two baths. Enjoy tennis or swimming at a nearby club. Full breakfast. Children welcome.

Nutmeg Bed and Breakfast Agency #212

P. O. Box 1117, West Hartford, 06107
(203) 236-6698

This beautiful home has a livingroom with grand piano, fireplace, central air. One guest room has twin pineapple four-poster beds, large closet, balcony, view of East Rock, and feather comforters; the other guest room has a single bed and sofa, TV and VCR, large closet, beautiful printed coverlet; both rooms share a bath. Continental breakfast. Infants and children over 5 allowed. No smoking. No resident pet.

Nutmeg Bed and Breakfast Agency #214

P. O. Box 1117, West Hartford, 06107
(203) 236-6698

A 1926 Colonial style with large porch; master bedroom with private bath (Jacuzzi and shower shared with hosts); cable TV, private deck, king bed; two blocks from public transportation. Continental breakfast, children allowed. No smoking. No pets.

NEW LONDON

The Queen Anne Inn

265 Williams Street, 06320
(203) 447-2600; (800) 347-8818

This spectacular turn-of-the-century home features rich oak woodwork and nautical art displayed throughout the inn. Relax by the fire in the parlor, enjoy the wraparound porch, or unwind in the Jacuzzi. Retire to one of the ten antique-filled rooms with brass, canopied, or four-poster beds. The inn serves a full gourmet breakfast and afternoon tea. Minutes from Mystic, Ocean Beach, antiquing, and performing arts. Convenient access to I-95. No smoking.

Hosts: Ray and Julie Rutledge
Rooms: 10 (8 PB; 2 SB) $78-155
Full Gourmet Breakfast
Credit Cards: A, B, C, D, E
Notes: 2, 5, 14

NEW MILFORD

Heritage Inn of Litchfield County

34 Bridge Street, 06776
(203) 345-8883

This historic landmark building, which dates back to the 1800s, was once a warehouse for some of Litchfield County's finest tobacco plants. The Heritage Inn is a country hotel that combines personal comfort with a relaxed atmosphere. Here, you'll find amenities you expect, like air conditioning, private bath, and telephones. In addition, you can look forward to the *New York Times* every morning, and a full breakfast.

Host: Deana Berry
Rooms: 20 (PB) $69-94
Full Breakfast
Credit Cards: A, B, C
Notes: 5, 7, 8, 14

Covered Bridge 1NM

P. O. Box 447, Norfolk, 06058
(203) 542-5944

Vista for viewing, woods for walking, hills for cross-country skiing, streams for fishing, flower gardens, and a pool are some of the attractions of this sprawling estate three miles outside of town. First-floor guest room with private bath and an upstairs guest room. $60-95.

The Homestead Inn

5 Elm Street, 06776
(203) 354-4080

Enjoy warm hospitality in this charming Victorian inn located near the village green

6 Pets welcome; 7 Smoking allowed; 8 Children welcome; 9 Social drinking allowed; 10 Tennis available; 11 Swimming available; 12 Golf available; 13 Skiing available; 14 May be booked through travel agents.

in the heart of the Litchfield Hills. Stroll to the village and enjoy the shops, restaurants, and movie theater. Eight inn rooms and six motel rooms, all recently redecorated. Most have country antiques, private bath, color TV, air conditioning, and phone. AAA approved.

Hosts: Rolf and Peggy Hammer
Rooms: 14 (PB) $68-88
Expanded Continental Breakfast
Credit Cards: A, B, C, D
Notes: 2, 5, 7, 8, 9, 10, 11, 12, 13 (XC), 14

Nutmeg Bed and Breakfast Agency #315

P. O. Box 1117, West Hartford, 06107
(203) 236-6698

A delightfully restored reverse wood tobacco barn, this bed and breakfast is beautifully landscaped with a pool and tennis court. Private and shared bath. Continental breakfast includes homegrown berries, homemade jams, popovers, and muffins prepared by former chef. Children welcome.

NEW PRESTON

Nutmeg Bed and Breakfast Agency #335

P. O. Box 1117, West Hartford, 06107
(203) 236-6698

Enjoy one of Litchfield County's most beautiful lakes at this Victorian bed and breakfast with a beautiful suite. Available on a nightly or weekly basis, the suite features a livingroom, a bedroom, kitchen, and bath with private entrance. Enjoy a quiet afternoon on the porch or swim off the private dock and boat-house. Near many fine restaurants, hiking, skiing, antiquing. Children over 3 welcome. Pets and smoking are also allowed.

NORFOLK

Blackberry River Inn

Route 44, 06058
(203) 542-5100

A 225-year-old Colonial inn located in rural northwestern Connecticut with 18 guest rooms, some with working fireplaces. Fine food and drink. Cross-country skiing, swimming, trout fishing, tennis, the Norfolk Chamber Music Festival, Lime Rock Race Track and antiques nearby.

Hosts: Kim and Bob Zuckerman
Rooms: 18 (10 PB; 8 SB) $65-150
Expanded Continental Breakfast
Credit Cards: A, B, C, E, F
Notes: 2, 3, 4, 5, 7, 8, 9, 10, 11, 12, 13 (XC), 14

Covered Bridge - 2N

P. O. Box 447, Norfolk, 06058
(203) 542-5944

Early 1900s Victorian estate on five acres in a very secluded setting. There is a large living room with fireplace and a spacious sun porch for guests' use. A full breakfast is served in each of the three guest rooms. Two guest rooms have fireplaces, and one includes a living room. $90-150.

Manor House

Maple Avenue, P. O. Box 447, 06058
(203) 542-5690

Victorian elegance awaits you at this historic Tudor/Bavarian estate. Antique-decorated guest rooms, several with fireplaces, canopies, and balconies, offer a romantic retreat. Enjoy a sumptuous breakfast in the tiffany-windowed dining rooms or treat yourself to breakfast in bed. Designated Connecticut's Most Romantic Hideaway, and included in *Fifty Best Bed and Breakfast's in the USA*.

Host: Hank and Diane Tremblay
Rooms: 9 (PB) $85-160
Full Breakfast
Credit Cards: A, B, C
Notes: 2, 5, 8 (over 12), 9, 10, 11, 12, 13, 14

NOTES: Credit cards accepted: A Master Card; B Visa; C American Express; D Discover Card; E Diner's Club; F Other; 2 Personal Checks accepted; 3 Lunch available; 4 Dinner available; 5 Open all year;

NORTH HAVEN

Nutmeg Bed and Breakfast Agency #202

P. O. Box 1117, West Hartford, 06107
(203) 236-6698

Golfers will love this two-story frame home with a six-hole putting green on the grounds. Two guest rooms: one with shared bath, one a suite. French and Spanish spoken. Continental breakfast. Children welcome.

NORTH STONINGTON

Antiques and Accommodations

32 Main Street, 06359
(203) 535-1736

A warm welcome awaits you at this beautifully restored 1861 Victorian home furnished in the Georgian manner with formal antique furniture and accessories, canopy beds, and private baths. Begin the day with a four-course candlelight breakfast, relax on the porches and patios, and stroll among the extensive gardens. The 1820 house has two suites, each with three bedrooms, living room, and kitchen; it is ideal for families or groups traveling together. A small antique shop is located in the Victorian barn. Easy access from I-95.

Hosts: Tom and Ann Gray
Rooms: 4 (3 PB; 1 SB) $95-145
Suites: 2 $125 midweek; $185 weekends
Full Breakfast
Credit Cards: None
Notes: 2, 5, 8, 9, 10, 11, 12, 14

Covered Bridge 1NS

P. O. Box 447, Norfolk, 06058
(203) 542-5944

Two 1861 and 1820 Victorian houses are linked by a courtyard and set in a charming, historic seacoast town close to Mystic.

The hosts furnished their home in the Georgian manner with formal antique furniture and accessories, many of which are offered for sale. The four guest rooms in the 1861 house have four-poster canopy beds. Full English breakfast. $90-150.

Nutmeg Bed and Breakfast Agency #506

P. O. Box 1117, West Hartford, 06107
(203) 236-6698

This beautiful village Victorian, built in 1861, has a covered porch and lovely flower and herb gardens. The rooms are beautifully furnished, and a gourmet breakfast is served in the elegant dining room with silver and china. There are four guest rooms; two with private baths, some with four-poster canopy beds. Mystic Seaport is just ten minutes away, and Rhode Island beaches are close by, as are Stonington Village and local vineyards. Full breakfast. No smoking.

NORWALK

Nutmeg Bed and Breakfast Agency #115

P. O. Box 1117, West Hartford, 06107
(203) 236-6698

50 year old Cape Cod with two-room suite, private entrance, bedroom with double bed, private bath, livingroom with color TV; air conditioning for summer and electric blanket for winter. Phone and small refrigerator in livingroom, cot available. Continental breakfast, children allowed. No smoking, no resident pets.

Nutmeg Bed and Breakfast Agency #118

P. O. Box 1117, West Hartford, 06107
(203) 236-6698

6 Pets welcome; 7 Smoking allowed; 8 Children welcome; 9 Social drinking allowed; 10 Tennis available; 11 Swimming available; 12 Golf available; 13 Skiing available; 14 May be booked through travel agents.

Contemporary home with private first floor guest room with high rise bed, desk, TV, and ample storage space. Full private bath with tub and shower. Continental breakfast, no children, no smoking, no dogs on premises.

OLD GREENWICH

Nutmeg Bed and Breakfast Agency #120

P. O. Box 1117, West Hartford, 06107
(203) 236-6698

On Long Meadow Creek, an open, airy beach house with a dock on the tidal inlet off Greenwich Cove. Walking distance to the village and train to NYC, and about a mile off I-95. First floor room with queen-size sofa bed (open when quests arrive), wicker sofa, TV, private bath with shower. Full breakfast, ask about children, no smoking, cats on premises.

OLD LYME

Old Lyme Inn

85 Lyme Street, P. O. Box 787, 06371
(203) 434-2600; FAX (203) 434-5352

Outside, wildflowers bloom all summer; inside, fireplaces burn all winter, beckoning you to enjoy the romance and charm of this 13-room Victorian country inn with an award-winning, three-star *New York Times* dining room. Within easy reach of the state's attractions, yet tucked away in an old New England art colony.

Host: Diana Field Atwood
Rooms: 13 (PB) $95-140
Continental Breakfast
Credit Cards: A, B, C, D, E
Closed first two weeks in Jan.
Notes: 2, 3, 4, 6, 7, 8, 9, 10, 11, 12, 14

OLD MYSTIC

Red Brook Inn

P. O. Box 237, 06372
(203) 572-0349

Enjoy Colonial hospitality in a real country inn. Located in southeastern Connecticut. Seven acres of wooded hillside provide seclusion and serenity. Early American antiques, fireplaces, and down comforters are among the many amenities offered to the traveler. The inn is near Mystic Seaport Museum, the Mystic Aquarium, the Nautilus Submarine Museum, and Foxwood's casino.

Host: Ruth Keyes
Rooms: 11 (PB) $95-179
Full Breakfast
Credit Cards: A, B
Notes: 2, 4, 5, 8, 9, 10, 11, 12

OLD SAYBROOK

Nutmeg Bed and Breakfast Agency #503

P. O. Box 1117, West Hartford, 06107
(203) 236-6698

A lovely southern hostess greets guests at this 1740 Colonial on the historic register. This house is seven blocks from the Long Island Sound. There are two guest rooms sharing a bath, plus a suite with a private entrance and a kitchenette. High tea is served in the afternoon upon request. Continental breakfast. Children welcome. No smoking.

PLAINFIELD

French Renaissance House

550 Norwich Road, 06374
(203) 564-3277

This lovely historic home, built in 1871 by a wealthy Victorian gentleman, is one of

NOTES: Credit cards accepted: A Master Card; B Visa; C American Express; D Discover Card; E Diner's Club; F Other; 2 Personal Checks accepted; 3 Lunch available; 4 Dinner available; 5 Open all year;

the finest examples of French Renaissance Second Empire architecture in Connecticut. It is near Plainfield Greyhound Park, within reasonable driving distance of Mystic Seaport, Hartford and Providence; and Newport, Rhode Island, and Sturbridge Village, Massachusetts. Near Foxwood Indian Casino.

Host: Lucile Melber
Rooms: 4 (1 PB; 3 S2B) $50, winter rates
Full Breakfast
Credit Cards: A, B, E
Notes: 2, 5, 8, 9, 10, 11, 12

PLANTSVILLE

Nutmeg Bed and Breakfast Agency #465

P. O. Box 1117, West Hartford, 06107
(203) 236-6698

This eleven-room central-chimney Colonial circa 1740 is situated on a beautifully land-scaped acre with a pool and surrounded by centuries-old maple trees. There are four fireplaces and a Dutch oven in the great room. One guest room has a king-size bed and a private bath; another has queen-size bed, shared bath, and working fireplace. Both rooms are air-conditioned. Full breakfast is served. Children are allowed, smoking is restricted, and there is a cat and dog on the premises.

POMFRET

The Covered Bridge

P. O. Box 447, Norfolk, 06058
(203) 542-5944

Set on over 6 acres, this 18-room Victorian cottage offers a very secluded country get-away. All of the common rooms and guest rooms are exquisitely decorated with Oriental rugs and antiques. There is a large living room with a fireplace and a very ele-gant dining room. There are two quest rooms with private baths and a two-bedrom suite with a bath. Several rooms also have fireplaces. A full breakfast and afternoon tea are served. $75-110

PORTLAND

The Croft

7 Penny Corner Road, 06480
(203) 342-1856

An 1822 Colonial in central Connecticut situated on four picturesque acres. with barns, an herb garden, and a picnic grove. One- and two-bedroom non-smoking suites, each with a private entrance, bath, telephone, television, and refrigerator. One has a complete kitchen. Golf and skiing nearby. Convenient to Wesleyan Univer-sity.

Host: Elaine Hinze
Suites: 2 (PB) $55-75
Full Breakfast
Credit Cards: None
Notes: 2, 5, 8, 9, 10, 11, 12, 13, 14

RIDGEFIELD

Nutmeg Bed and Breakfast Agency #119

P. O. Box 1117, West Hartford, 06107
(203) 236-6698

Contemporary cottage with oriental archi-tectural accents beside a rushing stream and two small waterfalls. The guest room has a livingroom/bedroom with two glass walls overlooking the stream. The kitchen has a deck beside the waterfall. Private bath in cottage; guests have use of the heated spa/sunroom. Two pullout beds. Full break-fast, children allowed, smoking allowed, no resident pets.

6 Pets welcome; 7 Smoking allowed; 8 Children welcome; 9 Social drinking allowed; 10 Tennis available; 11 Swimming available; 12 Golf available; 13 Skiing available; 14 May be booked through travel agents.

Nutmeg Bed and Breakfast Agency #301

P. O. Box 117, West Hartford, 06107
(203) 236-6698

Combine a trip into history with the pleasures of an active getaway at this 200-year-old bed and breakfast. Complimentary tickets to Keeler Tavern, the historical society's showcase, and bicycles for a tour of the nearby nature trails. Two guest rooms with a shared bath. Wine and cheese served upon arrival. Robes, heated spa, and Jacuzzi provided. Children welcome.

Nutmeg Bed and Breakfast Agency #352

P. O. Box 1117, West Hartford, 06107
(203) 236-6698

An elegant historical home on three and a half beautifully landscaped acres, pool, sun room available for guests. Two guest rooms with queen beds and private baths. Rooms may be booked together as a suite. Convenient to NYC and airports; swimming, hikinzg, cycling, golfing nearby. Full breakfast, children allowed, no smoking, 2 dogs on premises.

West Lane Inn

22 West Lane, Route 35, 06877
(203) 438-7323

The West Lane Inn offers colonial elegance in overnight accommodations. Also close to museum, points of interest, and shopping.

Host: M. M. Mayer
Rooms: 20 (PB) $120-160
Continental Breakfast
Credit Cards: A, B, C, E
Notes: 3, 5, 7, 8, 9, 10, 11, 12, 13, 14

RIVERSIDE

Nutmeg Bed and Breakfast Agency #105

P. O. Box 1117, West Hartford, 06107
(203) 236-6698

These active hosts have decided to share their lovely country-style Cape home. Guest room has private bath. New York City is only one hour away. Full breakfast. Children welcome. No smoking.

SALISBURY

Covered Bridge 1S

P. O. Box 447, Norfolk, 06058
(203) 542-5944

An 1810 Colonial set on two private, landscaped acres in the center of town. There is a large living room with a fireplace and a study with a TV for guests. A full breakfast is served. Two guest rooms. $85.

Nutmeg Bed and Breakfast Agency #324

P. O. Box 117, West Hartford, 06107
(203) 236-6698

Among the oldest in Salisbury, this attractive home is a fine example of early Federal period architecture. There are three guests rooms with private and semi-private baths. A continental breakfast is served in the dining room. There is a special Sunday half-day option for those who want to stretch their weekend. No children, no smoking. Pets on the premises.

Nutmeg Bed and Breakfast Agency #337

P. O. Box 117, West Hartford, 06107
(203) 236-6698

NOTES: Credit cards accepted: A Master Card; B Visa; C American Express; D Discover Card; E Diner's Club; F Other; 2 Personal Checks accepted; 3 Lunch available; 4 Dinner available; 5 Open all year;

This 1813 Colonial is in the historic district of Salisbury, one of Connecticut's most charming villages. There are three guest rooms with private and semi-private baths. Enjoy breakfast in the dining room or the stone terrace in warm weather. Walk to fine restaurants, shopping, and antiquing. Convenient to Lime Rock and the Appalachian Trail. Children welcome, no smoking. Pets on the premises.

Nutmeg Bed and Breakfast Agency #338

P. O. Box 117, West Hartford, 06107
(203) 236-6698

An elegant country retreat perched on top of a high hill. Watch the geese land on beautiful Lake Wononscopomuc while you eat your full home-made breakfast. The guest room has twin beds and a private bath. No children, no smoking. Pets on the premises.

Nutmeg Bed and Breakfast Agency #339

P. O. Box 117, West Hartford, 06107
(203) 236-6698

A restored 1774 home with period furnishings that has three guest rooms with a shared bath. Full gourmet breakfasts are served. Near Music Mountain, antique shops, boating, hiking, and skiing. Children are welcome. No smoking. No pets on the premises.

Yesterday's Yankee

Route 44 East, 06068
(203) 435-9539

A restored 1744 home with period furnishings sets the scene for comfortable air-conditioned guest rooms, complete gourmet breakfasts featuring home baking, and

warm hospitality. Summer theater, auto racing, music centers, hiking, independent schools, antique shops, boating, swimming, and skiing are nearby.

Hosts: Doris and Dick Alexander
Rooms: 3 (SB) $65-75
Full Breakfast
Credit Cards: A, B, C
Notes: 2, 5, 8, 9, 10, 11, 12, 13, 14

SCOTLAND

Nutmeg Bed and Breakfast Agency #454

P. O. Box 1117, West Hartford, 06107
(203) 236-6698

A 1797 Colonial-style country inn with a large sitting room for guests, keeping room, and kitchen for breakfast. Also a TV room with fireplace. double bedroom, and queen bedroom with fireplace. Both share a bath. Full breakfast, children over 10 allowed, no smoking, cat in residence.

SHARON

Covered Bridge 1SH

P. O. Box 447, Norfolk, 06058
(203) 542-5944

Beautifully situated in a secluded setting, this lovely contemporary home is decorated throughout with antiques. Guests are welcome to enjoy the large living room, sun porch, and deck. Within walking distance of the village green and the Sharon Playhouse. Reserve a suite or just ask for the bedroom. $85-125.

Covered Bridge 2SH

P. O. Box 447, Norfolk, 06058
(203) 542-5944

An 1890 Colonial on the main street in Sharon is set on beautifully landscaped grounds. There is a large living room and

6 Pets welcome; 7 Smoking allowed; 8 Children welcome; 9 Social drinking allowed; 10 Tennis available; 11 Swimming available; 12 Golf available; 13 Skiing available; 14 May be booked through travel agents.

sun porch for guests. A large lake is nearby for swimming, and several areas for skiing in the winter. Four guest rooms with private baths, two with microwave and refrigerator. Full breakfast. $90.

SHERMAN

Barnes Hill Farm Bed Breakfast

29 Route 37 East, 06784
(203) 354-4404

An elegantly restored historic 1835 colonial farmhouse situated on acres of unspoiled land in the Litchfield hills of Connecticut. One-half mile from Candlewood Lake. Featured in *Yankee Travel Guide*, *Connecticut* magazine, and *Glamour*.

Rooms: 3 (PB) $60-85
Full Breakfast
Credit Cards: A, B
Notes: 2, 5, 9, 10, 11, 12, 13

Covered Bridge 1SHR

P. O. Box 447, Norfolk, 06058
(203) 542-5944

Circa 1835, this restored bed and breakfast was a rest stop for travelers throughout the 1800s. There is a pleasant living room for guest use and a Jacuzzi on the deck overlooking the secluded grounds. Acres of woods and fields for hiking or cross-country skiing. Three guest rooms with private baths. Full breakfast. $85-95.

Nutmeg Bed and Breakfast Agency #321

P. O. Box 1117, West Hartford, 06107
(203) 236-6698

This superbly restored 1835 Colonial farmhouse has three air-conditioned guest rooms which are furnished with antiques and have private baths. After a full country breakfast, guests are invited to enjoy the outdoor Jacuzzi, game room or sitting room with television. One mile from Candlewood Lake, boating, fishing, swimming, and cross country skiing nearby. Children over 10 are welcome. No smoking.

SIMSBURY

Four Seasons International Bed and Breakfast Service

11 Bridlepath Road, West Simsbury, 06092
(203) 651-3045

A charming Colonial in Simsbury's historic district, this private home has been lovingly restored by its owners. Full breakfast. Two rooms: single $40; queen $60.

Simsbury 1820 House

731 Hopmeadow Street, 06070
(203) 658-7658

An authentic early 19th-century country inn with 34 individually designed guest rooms with private baths. Fine dining daily in our restaurant. Within walking distance of the charming town of Simsbury; 20 minutes to downtown Hartford and Bradley International Airport.

Host: Kelly Hohengarten
Rooms: 34 (PB) $85-125
Suite: 1 (PB) $135
Continental Breakfast
Credit Cards: A, B, C, D, E
Notes: 2, 3, 4, 5, 7, 8, 9, 10, 11, 12, 13, 14

SOUTHINGTON

Nutmeg Bed and Breakfast Agency #461

P. O. Box 1117, West Hartford, 06107
(203) 236-6698

A two-story Colonial-style farmhouse with a large wraparound pillared veranda, 70 acres of grounds with a fish pomd, pine grove, and rolling hills. Traditional furnishings in two upstairs bedrooms, each with double beds and shared full bath at the end of the hall. Full continental, or low-cal breakfast, also special diets if necessary. Long term preferred. Children allowed on premises

SOUTH WOODSTOCK

The Inn at Woodstock Hill

94 Plaine Hill Road, 06267-0098
(203) 928-0528

"Romance in the country." Circa 1816, situated on 14 beautiful acres, this charming inn affords breathtaking views of verdant hills and meadows. Its 19 suites and guest rooms are uniquely decorated in floral chintz fabrics, have private bath, television, telephone, and air conditioning. Four-poster beds, wood-burning fireplaces enhance special ambience. Candlelight, soft music, fine linens, and polished silver are reminiscent of the finest Old World hotels. Treat someone you care for to something unforgettable.

Hosts: Sheila and Richard Naumann
Rooms: 19 (PB) $70-140
Continental Breakfast
Credit Cards: A, B
Notes: 2, 3, 4, 5, 6, 7, 8, 9, 11, 12

SOUTH WINDSOR

Cumon Inn

130 Buckland Drive, 06074
(203) 644-8486

This beautiful old farm house is hosted by Krawski Klan, a speciality building material business owner, a working farmer and a former fighter pilot. This bed and breakfast is open all year. Relax in any of the eight guests rooms with six shared baths in this saltbox Colonial on 20 acres. Featured in *House Beautiful.*

Host: Krawski Klan
Rooms: 8 (SB) $75-100
Full Breakfast
Credit Cards: A, B
Notes: 5, 7, 11, 14

STAMFORD

Nutmeg Bed and Breakfast Agency #116

P. O. Box 1117, West Hartford, 06107
(203) 236-6698

This Nantucket Colonial 50 to 60 years old and has 4 bedrooms, two and a half baths on the sandy beach, Shippan Point. Ten minutes from railroad station. Tastefully furnished, gorgeous water view, breakfast on sun porch. One double bedroom with built-in bunk beds, one single bedroom with shared bath with double room, one queen bedroom with private bath. Full breakfast. One child allowed. No smoking. No pets on premises.

Nutmeg Bed and Breakfast Agency #117

P. O. Box 1117, West Hartford, 06107
(203) 236-6698

1960s ranch-style inn has a family room with fireplace, country kitchen, screened porch. The first floor bedroom trundle bed can be single or double. Private bath, TV. Continental breakfast. No children. No smoking. One dog on premises.

STONEY CREEK

Nutmeg Bed and Breakfast Agency #201

P. O. Box 1117, West Hartford, 06107
(203) 236-6698

You will love having your own log cabin with large bedroom, living room, bath-

6 Pets welcome; 7 Smoking allowed; 8 Children welcome; 9 Social drinking allowed; 10 Tennis available; 11 Swimming available; 12 Golf available; 13 Skiing available; 14 May be booked through travel agents.

room, and stocked kitchenette. Wood-burning stove, stereo, TV, and all the amenities you need for a perfect weekend. Continental breakfast. Children welcome.

STORRS

Storrs Farmhouse on the Hill

418 Gurleyville Road, 06268
(203) 429-1400

An elegant farmhouse located near the University of Connecticut. The Kollets raise Columbia sheep. Sturbridge and Worcester, Massachusetts; Mystic, Hartford, and New London are less than an hour away. Don't forget to try Elaine's muffins! Cribs, high chairs, and carriages available for children. Hot tub and exercise equipment in the new addition.

Hosts: Bill and Elaine Kollet
Rooms: 5 and apartment (PB) $35 plus
Full Breakfast
Credit Cards: None
Notes: 2, 5, 7, 8, 9, 10, 11, 12, 13, 14

SUFFIELD

Nutmeg Bed and Breakfast Agency #427

P. O. Box 1117, West Hartford, 06107
(203) 236-6698

This large, custom-built ranch house about a mile from Suffield Academy is immaculate and quiet, with an attentive, hospitable hostess. Private, spacious first floor guest room with bath, TV, phone, and private entrance. Full breakfast. Fruit and snacks always available.

Nutmeg Bed and Breakfast Agency #474

P. O. Box 1117, West Hartford, 06107
(203) 236-6698

An 1825 Federal Colonial near the town green on Main Street; it is a five-minute walk to the grocery, library, pharmacy, movies, and restaurants. There is a chioice of a bedroom with attached bath with tub and shower, double four-poster bed, chest, easy chair, and a large built-in closet, or a bedroom not attached to bath with old Victorian double bed, princess dresser, easy chair, bookcase, two closets, sink. Will rent either room but not both; guests have use of living room, dining room, kitchen, and yard. There is a TV with HBO in one room. It is ten minutes to Bradley; host will provide transportation to and from airport with advance notice. Long term only. No children. No smoking. No resident pets.

Nutmeg Bed and Breakfast Agency #480

P. O. Box 1117, West Hartford, 06107
(203) 236-6698

This two-bedroom condo has a bedroom with private bath, cable TV, washer, dryer, use of the whole apartment, patio, pool, and tennis court. On the Connnecticut River, minutes from the highway. Long-term only. No children. No smoking. No pets on premises.

THOMPSON

Lord Thompson Manor

Route 200, P. O. Box 428, 06277
(203) 923-3886

If you are in search of the ultimate in gracious hospitality, here is the country estate you've longed for. A baronial manor house set on 62 acres, lost amid gently rolling hills, shaded by towering trees, in northeastern Connecticut's quiet corner. Crackling fires, candlelit rooms, intimate dinners, enchanting music, and elegant

NOTES: Credit cards accepted: A Master Card; B Visa; C American Express; D Discover Card; E Diner's Club; F Other; 2 Personal Checks accepted; 3 Lunch available; 4 Dinner available; 5 Open all year;

overnight accommodations. Come experience the magic of romance. The memories you'll create are forever.

Host: Jacqueline Sherman
Rooms: 9 (5 PB; 4 SB) $65-110
Full Breakfast
Credit Cards: None
Notes: 2, 3, 4, 5, 6, 7, 8, 9

Nutmeg Bed and Breakfast Agency #468

P. O. Box 1117, West Hartford, 06107
(203) 236-6698

A new post-and-beam two-story home in a wooded area with lake frontage, three acres, a picnic and swimming area, and within walking distance to convenience store and antique furnishings. The inn offers cable TV, VCR, telephone. Two bedrooms, one double one twins, share a bath and large sitting room, private entrance, queen Hide-a-bed in the sitting room, rollaways, and a refrigerator available to guests. Convenient to Sturbridge Village, Woodstock Fair, Thompson Raceway. Pets welcome. Full breakfast, children welcome, no smoking, dogs in residence.

TOLLAND

The Tolland Inn

63 Tolland Green, 06084-0717
(203) 872-0800

Built in 1800, the Tolland Inn stands in the northwest corner of the Tolland village green, one-half mile from I-84. Located midway between Boston and New York City, the inn is convenient to the University of Connecticut, Old Sturbridge, Caprilands, Hartford, and Brimfield Fair.

Hosts: Susan and Stephen Beeching
Rooms: 7 (5 PB; 2 SB) $56-78.40
Suites: $78.40-100.80
Full Breakfast
Credit Cards: A, B, C
Notes: 2, 5, 8 (over 10), 9, 10, 11, 12

TORRINGTON

Yankee Pedlar Inn

93 Main Street, 06790
(203) 489-9226; (800) 777-1891

Step back 100 years to the charm and gracious warmth of this unique 1891 hotel. Each of the 60 rooms reflects its own dis-

Yankee Pedlar Inn

6 Pets welcome; 7 Smoking allowed; 8 Children welcome; 9 Social drinking allowed; 10 Tennis available; 11 Swimming available; 12 Golf available; 13 Skiing available; 14 May be booked through travel agents.

tinctive flavor, with Hitchcock furniture, stenciled walls, or four-poster beds. Yet all have been restored with modern conveniences to make your stay more comfortable. Fireplace in the lobby, and dining rooms complete the perfect setting. Directly across from the Warner Theatre and surrounded by shopping, skiing, and foliage. Stop by and tour this area landmark. Group and weekend packages available.

UNCASSVILLE

1851 Guest House

1851 Route 32, 06382
(203) 848-3649

Our recently remodeled, ninety-year-old house offers two suites and two spacious guest rooms with fireplaces. Each accommodation is tastefully decorated and includes private outside entrance, queen-size bed, color cable TV, phone, private bath, complimentary stocked refrigerator, fat soaps, fluffy towels, embroidered linens, long-stemmed glasses, and other amenities. Continental breakfast is elegantly served in our white Victorian gazebo surrounded by herb and perennial flower gardens. If they desire, guests are offered breakfast in their suites at no additional charge.

Hosts: Al Fernaud and Sandra Samolis
Rooms: 4 (PB) $70-120
Continental Breakfast
Credit Cards: A, B
Notes: 2, 5, 7, 8, 9, 10, 11, 12, 14

WASHINGTON

Covered Bridge 1WA

P. O. Box 447, Norfolk, 06058
(203) 542-5944

Cozy Cape Cod cottage surrounded by woods and fields in nicely landscaped setting. There is a living room with a grand piano and a sitting room with a TV for guests. Two guest rooms with private baths. Continental breakfast. $85.

Nutmeg Bed and Breakfast Agency #313

P. O. Box 1117, West Hartford, 06107
(203) 236-6698

This serene bed and breakfast is a true working farm. There is a brook, a small lake, a pool, and cross-country skiing on the property. Nearby you'll find canoeing, hiking, and good biking trails. Relax over a glass of wine before retiring to one of three guest rooms. A single loft room is also available. Full breakfast of farm-fresh eggs and homemade breads starts the day. Children welcome. No smoking.

WASHINGTON DEPOT

Nutmeg Bed and Breakfast Agency #348

P. O. Box 1117, West Hartford, 06107
(203) 236-6698

A lovely contemporary home overlooking lawns, fields, woodlands, and a small pond has a completely private guest house with nicely furnished sitting room (cable TV and VCR), spacious double bedroom, private bath with shower, separate sleeping alcove with built-in single bed, and small porch. There is a small refrigerator in the guest house and picnic table in pine grove next to the pond. Continental breakfast. Children allowed. Smoking outside only. Cat on premises.

WATERBURY

Covered Bridge 1WAT

P. O. Box 447, Norfolk, 06058
(203) 542-5944

An 1888 Victorian house on the National Register of Historic Places set on an acre in a historic district. There are several common rooms, including an antique-decorated living room with a fireplace. All of the guest rooms are decorated with antiques. Full breakfast and high tea are served. $75-150.

House on the Hill Bed and Breakfast

92 Woodlawn Terrace, 06710-1929
(203) 757-9901

A gracious 1888 Victorian listed on the National Register of Historic Places and beautifully furnished with antiques and flowers, House on the Hill is perched on an acre and a half of gardens and woodlands. Six fireplaces, sunny wraparound porches, and renowned breakfasts have made this inn the choice of experienced business and leisure travelers. Elegant setting for weddings, corporate entertaining, and special events. Featured in *Victoria Magazine*, *Yankee Magazine*, *Connecticut Magazine*, and *Fodor's Guide*. One mile from I-84.

Host: Marianne Vandenburgh
Rooms: 5 (4 PB; 1 SB) $65-100 plus tax
Full Breakfast
Notes: 2, 4 (by arrangement), 5, 8, 9, 14

WATERTOWN

The Graham House

1002 Middlebury Road, 06795
(203) 274-2647

A candle glows in every window as a sign of welcome to this charming 1840 Colonial farmhouse nestled in the foothills of Litchfield County. Close to historic district and Main Street. Near area antique shops. Quilts and dolls adorn the three country-decorated guest rooms. Wonderful continental and full breakfasts. All rooms non-smoking.

Hosts: George and Judy Graham
Rooms: 3 (1 PB; 2 SB) $55-65
Full Breakfast
Notes: 2, 5,

WEST HARTFORD

Nutmeg Bed and Breakfast-TNN-CONNECTICUT

P. O. Box 1117, 06127-1117
(203) 236-6698; (800) 727-7592

Part of the bed and breakfast National Network, Nutmeg bed and breakfast offers bed and breakfast not only in Connecticut, but also in many other cities and states across the country. The members of this network adhere strictly to the standards set by TNN, such as getting to know the hosts personally, having an established cancellation and refund policy, and following a thorough inspection and approval process for all properties rented. This is because each member of the network is dedicated to ensuring your comfort, pleasure and personal needs while you are staying at one of our "homes away from home."

Nutmeg Bed and Breakfast Agency #441

P. O. Box 1117, West Hartford, 06107
(203) 236-6698

The single-story home is furnished with a blend of modern, traditional, and antique. One guest room with TV and private bath. Continental breakfast. Hungarian spoken. Children welcome. No smoking.

Nutmeg Bed and Breakfast Agency #455

P. O. Box 1117, West Hartford, 06107
(203) 236-6698

This center hall Colonial has a year-round sunroom. On the bus line and within walking distance to University of Connecticut, West Hartford branch, and St. Joseph's College. Small child in house. Second floor bedroom with double bed and bath shared with the family. Long term preferred. Continental breakfast. Children allowed. No smoking. No pets.

Nutmeg Bed and Breakfast Agency #462

P. O. Box 1117, West Hartford, 06107
(203) 236-6698

This charming home in a convenient location has a second floor room facing lovely gardens with a double canopy bed and private bath. The third floor suite has a double bed, desk, sitting room, private bath. Continental breakfast. Children allowed. No smoking. Resident dog and cat.

Nutmeg Bed and Breakfast Agency #473

P. O. Box 1117, West Hartford, 06107
(203) 236-6698

This apartment is located on the first floor in back of the house with private entrance, bedroom with two closets and queen bed, sitting room with TV, and table for dining, fully equipped kitchen with storage, bath with tub and shower, and small hallway. Central air, weekly laundering of linens, periodic cleaning with cleaning fee. Long term only; no breakfast, no children, no smoking, no pets on premises.

Nutmeg Bed and Breakfast Agency #482

P. O. Box 1117, West Hartford, 06107
(203) 236-6698

Ranch-style home with facilities for handicapped. Guest bedroom with private bath,

attractive furnishings, three windows, carpeted, queen bed, ample storage; second bedroom with twin beds, a full bath (both used for a family traveling together). Continental breakfast (full on request), children allowed, no smoking, no pets on premises.

WESTPORT

Nutmeg Bed and Breakfast Agency #111

P. O. Box 1117, West Hartford, 06107
(203) 236-6698

Breathtaking setting overlooking Long Island Sound, this home combines rural beauty with metropolitan sophistication. Guest wing is private with its own sitting room, fireplace, and entrance. Three guest rooms with private and shared bath. Enjoy the beach during summer. Continental breakfast. Children welcome. No smoking. $60 plus.

Nutmeg Bed and Breakfast Agency #113

P. O. Box 1117, West Hartford, 06107
(203) 236-6698

An Italianate Victorian on 3 acres. Formal garden, grape arbor, brook, terrace, sculpture studio (hosts are professional artists). Double bed, private bath with tub and shower, beautiful furnishings. Full breakfast. No children. No smoking. Dogs on premises.

Nutmeg Bed and Breakfast Agency #114

P. O. Box 1117, West Hartford, 06107
(203) 236-6698

A large Colonial surrounded by many old trees on hilly, wooded acre just outside of

NOTES: Credit cards accepted: A Master Card; B Visa; C American Express; D Discover Card; E Diner's Club; F Other; 2 Personal Checks accepted; 3 Lunch available; 4 Dinner available; 5 Open all year;

town. The original part of the house was built in 1740; guest quarters with separate entrance, bedroom with separate sitting room, double bed, Hide-a-bed in sitting room. Full private bath; parking in front lot. Pool and spa for guests, dog pen available. Continental breakfast. Children allowed. No smoking. Dogs on premises.

WETHERSFIELD

Chester Bulkley House Bed and Breakfast

184 Main Street, 06109
(203) 563-4236

Enjoy the New England charm of this historic village settled in 1634. Walk to shops, restaurants, museums, and church. Take a stroll along the cove at sunset. Newly renovated inn boasts warm and friendly hospitality, generous full breakfast, period antiques, fireplaces, and five large guest rooms (suite available). Convenient location between New York and Boston, only minutes from Hartford. Open year-round for business and holiday travelers. Member AAA.

Hosts: Frank and Sophie Bottaro
Rooms: 5 (3 PB; 2 SB) $65-75
Full Breakfast
Credit Cards: A, B, C
Notes: 2, 5, 8, 10, 11, 12, 14

Nutmeg Bed and Breakfast Agency #408

P. O. Box 1117, West Hartford, 06107
(203) 236-6698

Nestled in the historic village of Old Wethersfield, this classic Greek Revival brick house has been lovingly restored to provide a warm and gracious New England welcome to all travelers. Built in 1830, it boasts five airy guest rooms furnished with period antiques. Three rooms have private baths; two rooms share a bath. Fresh flow-

ers, cozy living room and parlor, afternoon tea, and elegant continental breakfast buffet. Children over 11 welcome.

Nutmeg Bed and Breakfast Agency #429

P. O. Box 1117, West Hartford, 06107
(203) 236-6698

This attractive Colonial home is rich in the history of the town. The hostess, a member of the historical society, offers one guest room with private bath. A small room suitable for a child available. Close to a park and safe for walking. Full breakfast. Children welcome.

WINDSOR

Nutmeg Bed and Breakfast Agency #469

P. O. Box 1117, West Hartford, 06107
(203) 236-6698

Charming Victorian home dating to 1860s, renovated with an addition in 1890. Lovely antique furniture, large front porch, three second floor bedrooms, 2 with extra long double beds, one with extra long twin beds, all with private baths. Convenient to airport, University of Hartford, Loomis Chaffee. Full breakfast. Children over 12. No smoking. Dog on premises.

Nutmeg Bed and Breakfast Agency #479

P. O. Box 1117, West Hartford, 06107
(203) 236-6698

A 10-year-old Colonial in a nice residential neighborhood. Bright first floor room with private front and rear entrances; private bath with stall shower. Tiny kitchenette for snacks. Two twin four-poster beds. Private phone line for local or calling card calls. Access to screened porch overlooking the garden and woods. Airport transportation if pre-arranged; heart-saver continental.plus breakfast upon request. Continental breakfast. Children over 12 allowed. No smoking. Cat on premises.

This bi-level contemporary home is situated on more than two acres of land. The guest suite has cable TV, sitting room, private bath, refrigerator, phone, air conditioning. Living room with fireplace opens onto patio. Continental breakfast. Children welcome. $60-85.

WINSTED

Nutmeg Bed and Breakfast Agency #325

P. O. Box 1117, West Hartford, 06107
(203) 236-6698

Rustic turn-of-the century lake lodge-style home with wraparound porch affording commanding views of the encircling woods as well as Connecticut's cleanest lake, well stocked with fish. Abundant couches and chairs for relaxation, use of private beach, canoe, fishing boat; large lattice-covered dock where breakfast can be served. TVs available in rooms, VCR in livingroom. One double bed room has private bath and balcony overlooking lake; one twin, one double, and another double with two or three child-size rollaways share a bath. Continental breakfast, children welcome, smoking allowed, cat in residence.

WOODBRIDGE

Nutmeg Bed and Breakfast Agency #102

P. O. Box 1117, West Hartford, 06107
(203) 236-6698

WOODBURY

Curtis House

506 Main Street, 06798
(203) 263-2101

Connecticut's oldest inn, in operation since 1754, in a quaint New England town famous for antique shops. The inn features canopied beds and a popular restaurant serving regional American fare, amply portioned and moderately priced.

Host: The Hardisty family
Rooms: 18 (12 PB; 6 SB) $30-70
Continental Breakfast
Credit Cards: A, B
Closed Christmas Day and Monday lunch
Notes: 2, 3, 4, 5, 7, 9, 10, 11, 12, 13

Nutmeg Bed and Breakfast Agency #312

P. O. Box 1117, West Hartford, 06107
(203) 236-6698

Here's a 1730 Colonial, home to a warm couple who have restored their own early period furniture. Two second-floor rooms share a bath. Plenty of antiquing nearby. Hearty breakfast includes homemade breads.

NOTES: Credit cards accepted: A Master Card; B Visa; C American Express; D Discover Card; E Diner's Club; F Other; 2 Personal Checks accepted; 3 Lunch available; 4 Dinner available; 5 Open all year;

Delaware

BETHANY BEACH

The Addy Sea

99 Ocean View Parkway, 19930-0275
(302) 539-3707

The Addy Sea is a charming Victorian inn on the pristine shores of the Atlantic Ocean, built in 1901 by John Addy. Beautiful antique furnishings against period wallcoverings and original woodwork make this bed and breakfast extra special. The Addy Sea is perfect for fresh sea air, relaxing on the front porch or beside the original fireplace. Proprietor Leroy Gravatte, III and family remain true to the Addy Sea's tradition and dignity. Restoration is beautifully focused, and The Addy Sea has been nominated for the National Historic Register.

Host: Leroy T. Gravatte, III
Rooms: 16 (2 PB; 14 SB) $80-110
Continental Breakfast
Credit Cards: None
Notes: 2, 7, 9

DAGSBORO

Bed and Breakfast of Delaware #30

P. O. Box 177, Wilmington, 19810
(302) 479-9500

This is the oldest existing residence in Dagsboro, circa 1850. Parkhurst, the original builder or owner was also a postmaster, with the post office located in the inn. The rooms have a warm, comfortable country theme. Guests can relax with a book or have a friendly conversation in front of the two fireplaces. There are three guest rooms with private baths.

DOVER

Bed and Breakfast of Delaware #23

P. O. Box 177, Wilmington, 19810
(302) 479-9500

The charm of Historic Dover's Victorian era is found in this 1880s home filled with antiques. There are four bedrooms with private baths. Full breakfast is served.

LAUREL

Bed and Breakfast of Delaware #25

P. O. Box 177, Wilmington, 19810
(302) 479-9500

Step back in time and enjoy the charm of this 18th-century country manor listed in the National Register of Historic Places. There are four spacious rooms and one suite with authentic period furnishings and fireplaces. Bicycles and picnic lunches are available to explore the Eastern Shore.

LEWES

Bed and Breakfast of Delaware #26

P. O. Box 177, Wilmington, 19810
(302) 479-9500

NOTES: Credit cards accepted: A Master Card; B Visa; C American Express; D Discover Card; E Diner's Club; F Other; 2 Personal Checks accepted; 3 Lunch available; 4 Dinner available; 5 Open all year; 6 Pets welcome; 7 Smoking allowed; 8 Children welcome; 9 Social drinking allowed; 10 Tennis available; 11 Swimming available; 12 Golf available; 13 Skiing available; 14 May be booked through travel agents.

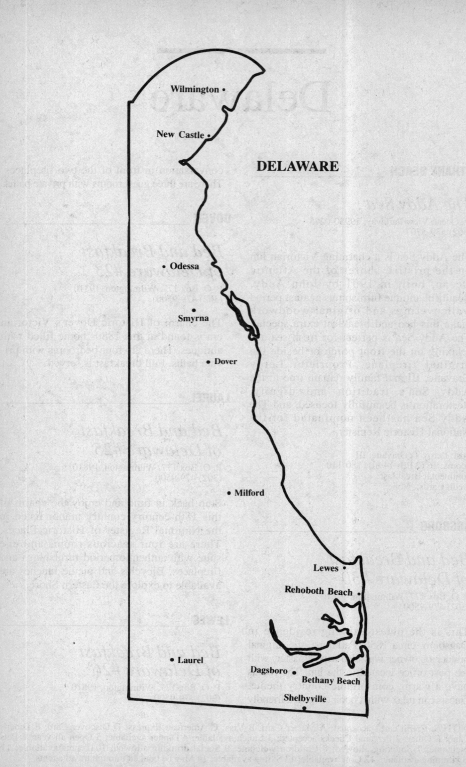

DELAWARE

Wilmington •

New Castle •

• Odessa

• Smyrna

• Dover

• Milford

Lewes •

Rehoboth Beach •

• Laurel

Dagsboro •

Bethany Beach •

Shelbyville •

This cottage is about 150 years old. All rooms have pieces from the 17th, 18th, and 19th centuries. The bathrooms are totally modern, and there is a large screened porch comfortably furnished in rattan and old pine. One mile from the Delaware bay and 5 minutes by car from the Atlantic Ocean. Continental breakfast is served.

The New Devon Inn

142 Second Street, 19958
(302) 645-6466

Reminiscent of the charming pensions of the Continent, this elegant but informal, historic bed and breakfast occupies a corner in the old market section of the maritime town of Lewes; 24 standard rooms, two suites decorated with original antiques; fine linens and fluffy towels; private baths; individually controlled heat and air conditioning; private telephones; conference rooms; steps to antiquing, dining, shopping. Beach under a mile. Mobil three-star rated. Nightly turndown service.

Host: Ms. D. Dale Jenkins
Rooms: 26 (PB) $70-140
Expanded Continental Breakfast
Credit Cards: A, B, C, E
Notes: 2, 3, 4, 5, 7, 9, 10, 11, 12, 14

Savannah Inn Bed and Breakfast

330 Savannah Rd., 19958
(302) 645-5592

Quaint village location is near ocean and bay beaches, state park, and resorts. Casual, comfortable bedrooms with fans, books, piano, backyard, and airy porch and delicious vegetarian breakfast create an atmosphere for a relaxing stay. Hosts enjoy nature, outdoor sports, and organize gardening. Resident cat. Minimum stay is two nights. Weekly discount for extended stays. Breakfast served Memorial Day through Sept. 30.

Hosts: Dick and Susan Stafursky
Rooms: 7 (SB) $37-53
Continental Breakfast
Credit Cards: None
Notes: 2, 7 (limited), 8, 9, 10, 11

MILFORD

Bed and Breakfast of Delaware #31

P. O. Box 177, Wilmington, 19810
(302) 479-9500

This Greek Revival mansion, built in 1763 and on the National Register of Historic Places, has been home to two former governors, Rogers (1797-1799) and Causey (1855-1859). It is situated on three and one-half acres in downtown Milford. The original slave quarters are still on the property. There are queen and twin bedrooms. A full country breakfast is served.

NEW CASTLE

Bed and Breakfast of Delaware #20

P. O. Box 177, Wilmington, 19810
(302) 479-9500

This bed and breakfast is on the Delaware River just southeast of Wilmington. The cobblestone streets date from the Colonial era. This historic home has four lovely rooms with queen-size beds and all with private baths. Decorated in Laura Ashley prints, with Oriental rugs. A gourmet continental breakfast is served.

Jefferson House Bed and Breakfast

The Strand at the Wharf, 19720
(302) 323-0999; (302) 322-8944

Packed with charm and history, Jefferson House is an elegant 200-year-old river-

6 Pets welcome; 7 Smoking allowed; 8 Children welcome; 9 Social drinking allowed; 10 Tennis available; 11 Swimming available; 12 Golf available; 13 Skiing available; 14 May be booked through travel agents.

front hotel-residence. Located on a cobble-stone street in the center of New Castle's historic district, just a few feet from all the historic buildings, museums, shops, and parks. Antique furnishings, hot tub, air conditioning, fireplace, screened porch, efficiencies (long- or short-term). Private parking. Brochure available.

Host: Chris Bechstein
Rooms: 3 (PB) $49-85
Full Breakfast
Credit Cards: A, B
Notes: 2, 3, 5, 7, 8, 9, 10, 11, 12, 14

The Terry House Bed and Breakfast

130 Delaware Street, 19720
(302) 322-2505

The Terry House, located in the center of historic New Castle, is an 1860s Federal town house. It offers four large bedrooms with private baths and cable TV. The rooms overlook the Delaware River and Battery Park, and the porches are the perfect spot to sit and relax after a day of shopping and sightseeing.

Host: Brenda Rogers
Rooms: 5 (PB) $60-80
Continental Breakfast
Credit Cards: A, B, C, D
Notes: 2, 5, 14

William Penn Guest House

206 Delaware Street, 19720
(302) 328-7736

Choose one of three rooms in this beautifully restored 1682 guest house in the center of historic New Castle, 20 minutes from museum and public gardens.

Hosts: Richard and Irma Burwell
Rooms: 3 (SB) $45
Continental Breakfast
Credit Cards: None
Notes: 2, 5, 8 (over 9), 9, 10

ODESSA

Bed and Breakfast of Delaware #22

P. O. Box 177, Wilmington, 19810
(302) 479-9500

This circa 1840 home has been beautifully restored and furnished with period antiques. There are two bedrooms with private baths, and a suite with a queen-size bed, whirlpool bath, and lovely view of the town.

Cantwell House

107 High Street, 19730
(302) 378-4179

Odessa was an important trading port on the Delaware River until the 1890s. The town contains fine examples of Colonial, Federal, and Victorian architecture, including three museums owned by Winterthur. Cantwell House (circa 1840) has been completely restored and furnished in country antiques.

Host: Carole F. Coleman
Rooms: 3 (1 PB; 2 SB) $50-75
Continental Breakfast
Credit Cards: None
Notes: 2, 5, 7 (limited), 8, 9, 10, 14

REHOBOTH BEACH

Barry's Gull Cottage

P. O. Box 843, 19971
(302) 227-7000

A special retreat for those who want to get away. Gull Cottage, decorated in wicker and offering modern conveniences, centers around pampering its guests. The beaches and bay are within walking distance, and you can plan your day while enjoying a healthy gourmet breakfast. Nearby shopping includes a large number of factory outlets, and dining in the area ranges from French cuisine to the eastern seaboard's finest seafood. Fresh fruit abounds in nearby orchards and vegetable stands. Afternoon tea. Hot tub available. Minimum stay is two nights.

Hosts: Bob and Vivian Barry
Rooms: $65-95
Full Gourmet Breakfast
Credit Card: B
Note: 2

The Royal Rose Inn Bed and Breakfast

41 Baltimore Avenue, 19971
(302) 226-2535

A charming and relaxing 1920s beach cottage, this bed and breakfast is tastefully furnished with antiques and a romantic rose theme. A scrumptious breakfast of homemade bread, muffins, egg dishes, and much more is served on a large screened-in porch. Air-conditioned bedrooms, guest refrigerator, and off-street parking are real pluses for guests. Centrally located one and a half blocks from the "Avenue," shops, boutiques, and restaurants are everywhere. Midweek special, weekend packages, gift certificates. Open May through October.

Hosts: Kenny and Cindy Vincent
Rooms: 8 (2 PB; 6 SB) $35-110
Hearty Continental Breakfast
Credit Cards: A, B
Notes: 2, 9, 10, 11, 12

Tembo Bed and Breakfast

100 Laurel Street, 19971
(302) 227-3360

Tembo, situated 750 feet from the beach in a quiet, residential area offers a casual atmosphere with warm hospitality. Relax among Early American furnishings, antiques, oil paintings, waterfowl carvings, and Gerry's elephant collection. Clean bedrooms are with firm beds.

Hosts: Don and Gerry Cooper
Rooms: 6 (1 PB; 5 SB) $81-108
Continental Breakfast
Minimum stay weekends: 2 nights; holidays: 3
  nights

Credit Cards: None
Notes: 2, 5, 6 (11/31-3/31), 8 (over 12), 9, 10, 11, 12

SELBYVILLE

Bed and Breakfast of Delaware #28

P. O. Box 177, Wilmington, 19810
(302) 479-9500

This turn-of-the-century Victorian home displays family heirlooms, Oriental carpets, crystal chandeliers and antiques. Enjoy the cozy Victorian parlor or read a book in a rocking chair on the breezy verandas. The guest rooms have high ceilings. Located nine miles from Ocean City or Fenwick Island, the estate is close enough to get to the beach, but far enough away to avoid the hustle.

Bed and Breakfast of Delaware #29

P. O. Box 177, Wilmington, 19810
(302) 479-9500

This Irish bed and breakfast is in a lovely quiet area and offers a swimming pool, two adult bicycles, tennis courts, and raquets. There are five bedrooms with two shared baths. Five miles to Bethany Beach and Fenwick Island. Convenient to state and national parks.

SMYRNA

The Main Stay

41 South Main Street, 19977
(302) 653-4293

This early 1800s white clapboard Colonial town house is in the heart of the downtown historic area. It is furnished with Oriental rugs and antique furniture and is accented with needlework and handmade quilts.

6 Pets welcome; 7 Smoking allowed; 8 Children welcome; 9 Social drinking allowed; 10 Tennis available; 11 Swimming available; 12 Golf available; 13 Skiing available; 14 May be booked through travel agents.

Each bedroom has twin beds and shares a bath. Breakfast may include homemade muffins, bread, scones, or hot cakes.

Host: Phyllis E. Howarth
Rooms: 3 (SB) $50
Continental Breakfast
Credit Cards: None
Closed June 1-Nov. 1
Notes: 7 (limited), 8, 9, 10, 12

WILMINGTON

Bed and Breakfast of Delaware: A Reservation Service

3650 Silverside Road, P. O. Box 177, 19810
(302) 479-9500

Accommodations in private homes and small historic inns throughout Delaware, Maryland, and Virginia's Chesapeake Bay, Pennsylvania's Brandywine Valley Wyeth, Hagley, Winterthur, Nemours Museum, and Longwood Gardens.

Host: Mille Alford, director
Rooms: 45 homes in registry; $60-160
Full or Continental Breakfast
Credit Cards: A, B
Notes: 2, 5, 8, 10, 11, 12, 14

Bed and Breakfast of Delaware #21

P. O. Box 177, Wilmington, 19810
(302) 479-9500

A lovely Cape Cod in a quiet suburban neighborhood, this inn has beautiful award-winning landscaped grounds and three double rooms with private baths furnished with fresh flowers and fruit. In the winter the mature hedges and unusual shrubs are decorated for the holidays. Five minutes north of downtown Wilmington, 27 miles south of the center of Philadelphia. Minutes to Brandywine Valley museums, colleges, and industry. A full breakfast is served.

NOTES: Credit cards accepted: A Master Card; B Visa; C American Express; D Discover Card; E Diner's Club; F Other; 2 Personal Checks accepted; 3 Lunch available; 4 Dinner available; 5 Open all year;

District of Columbia

Adams Inn

1744 Lanier Place, NW, 20009
(202) 745-3600

Convenient, comfortable, home-style
atmosphere in a neighborhood with over
forty ethnic restaurants to choose from.
Near the bus lines, shopping, Metro, museums, government buildings, and convention
sites. Economical for the tourist and business traveler. Both private and shared
rooms available.

Hosts: Gene and Nancy Thompson; Anne Owens
Rooms: 25 (12 PB; 13 SB) $55-95
Continental Plus Breakfast
Credit Cards: A, B, C, D, E
Notes: 2, 5, 8, 14

Bed and Breakfast About Town

P. O. Box 34791, 20043
(202) 234-0923

There are over 150 bed and breakfasts,
inns, and guest houses with Bed and
Breakfast About Town. The accommodations range from budget to luxury. In the
larger cities, many are near public transportation, tourist sights, and convention
areas. For escape weekends and special
occasion trips, there are many in areas such
as Harper's Ferry, West Virginia; the
Eastern Shore of Chesapeake Bay; and the
back roads of Virginia's Shenandoah
Valley. Contact: Michael Dale. All major
credit cards accepted. $50-195.

Bed and Breakfast Ltd. of Washington D.C.-TNN-DC

P. O. Box 12011, 20005
(202) 328-3510

Part of the Bed and Breakfast National
Network, Bed and Breakfast Ltd. of
Washington D.C. offers bed and breakfast
not only in the District of Columbia, but
also in many other cities and states across
the country. The members of this network
adhere strictly to the standards set by TNN,
such as getting to know the hosts personally, having an established cancellation and
refund policy, and following a thorough
inspection and approval process for all
properties rented. This is because each
member of the network is dedicated to
ensuring your comfort, pleasure, and personal needs while you are staying at one of
our "homes away from home."

The Bed and Breakfast League, Ltd. #1

P. O. Box 9490, 20016
(202) 363-7767

The Park House is a late Victorian house
that overlooks the Folger Park, three blocks
from the U.S. Capitol and the Capitol
South Metro stop. The master bedroom has
a king bed, sitting area with TV, desk,
phone, and private bath. Two other bedrooms share a bath. The hostess, a lobbyist,
serves a help-yourself continental breakfast. No smoking. Children over 12 welcome. $65-100.

NOTES: Credit cards accepted: A Master Card; B Visa; C American Express; D Discover Card; E Diner's
Club; F Other; 2 Personal Checks accepted; 3 Lunch available; 4 Dinner available; 5 Open all year; 6 Pets
welcome; 7 Smoking allowed; 8 Children welcome; 9 Social drinking allowed; 10 Tennis available; 11
Swimming available; 12 Golf available; 13 Skiing available; 14 May be booked through travel agents.

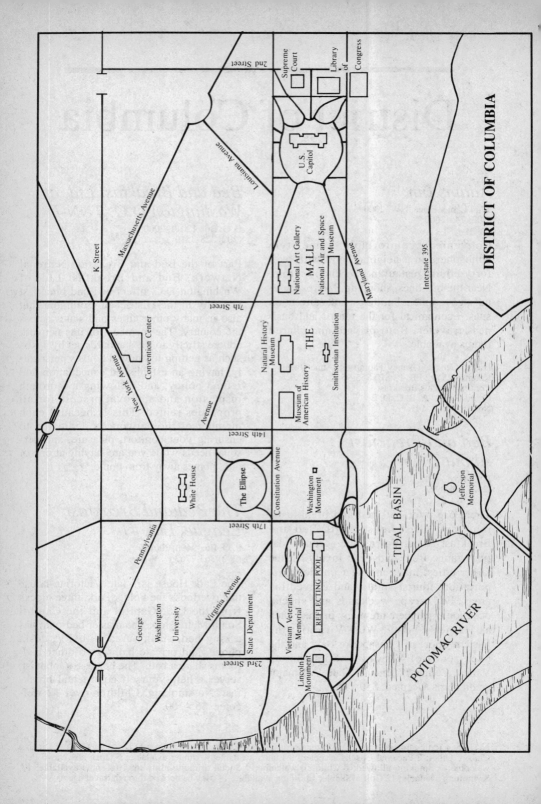

DISTRICT OF COLUMBIA

The Bed and Breakfast League, Ltd. #2

P. O. Box 9490, 20016
(202) 363-7767

The Madison House, just across the street-from the Madison Building of the Library of Congress, was built in 1850 and retains its original woodwork and mantels. It is elegantly decorated with antiques and reproductions. Two suites and a master bedroom with private bath and Jacuzzi are available. Breakfast is served in the dining room with a fireplace or on the deck in good weather. No smoking. Children welcome in some rooms. $70-160.

The Bed and Breakfast League, Ltd. #3

P. O. Box 9490, 20016
(202) 363-7767

The charming turn-of-the-century Victorian was lovingly rescued and restored by the hostess. It is decorated with period furnishings, beautiful wallpaper and linens, and some antiques. Six guest rooms share three baths. Relax in the parlor or library, or on the deck in good weather. A five-minute walk to all the shops and restaurants of Connecticut Avenue, and a ten-minute walk to the DuPont Circle Metro stop. Full breakfast. No smoking. Children over 11 welcome. $65-70.

The Bed and Breakfast League, Ltd. #4

P. O. Box 9490, 20016
(202) 363-7767

This Federal-style Victorian house is hosted by an independent film producer, an energy consultant, and their children. The third-floor guest area consists of two bedrooms, a shared bath, and a small kitchen. Breakfast is served in the dining room with

a fireplace. A number of antiques, Oriental rugs, and an art collection decorate the house. A 10- to 12-minute walk to the Woodley Park/Zoo Metro stop and to major hotels. No smoking. Children welcome. $55-60.

The Bed and Breakfast League, Ltd. #5

P. O. Box 9490, 20016
(202) 363-7767

The Inver House is an elegant Georgian home in an area close to many embassy residences. A short walk from two major convention hotels and the Woodley Park-Zoo Metro stop, the house is decorated with antique furniture, Oriental rugs, and porcelains. The spacious guest rooms include a master bedroom with a king bed, private attached bath, and private deck. Other guest rooms have either a king or queen bed and private or shared baths, depending on the room. All rooms include color TV and private telephone lines. No smoking. Children over 12 welcome. Ample free parking. $65-150 plus tax.

The Bed and Breakfast League, Ltd. #6

P. O. Box 9490, 20016
(202) 363-7767

The Capitol Hill Suite is part of a Victorian house located on one of the prettiest blocks in the Capitol Hill District. It is three blocks from the Eastern Metro stop and eight blocks east of the US Capitol, the Supreme Court, and the Library of Congress. The guest area contains a bedroom/sitting room with a queen bed, dining area, private bath, kitchen, and private deck. The suite is beautifully and comfortably decorated and includes color TV and private telephone. Parking is on the street and easily available. No smoking. $60-85, plus tax.

6 Pets welcome; 7 Smoking allowed; 8 Children welcome; 9 Social drinking allowed; 10 Tennis available; 11 Swimming available; 12 Golf available; 13 Skiing available; 14 May be booked through travel agents.

The Bed and Breakfast League, Ltd. #7

P. O. Box 9490, 20016
(202) 363-7767

Georgetown is the oldest section of the city, home of some of the city's best restaurants, and renown for its world class shopping. After a full day of touring, return to this quiet and secluded suite and relax in the sitting room before walking out for dinner. In addition to the sitting room with color TV, there is a wet bar, bedroom with queen bed, and private bath. The host stocks the wet bar for a continental breakfast. All the shops and restaurants are within easy walking distance, as are Georgetown University and Dumbarton Oaks Museum and Gardens. No smoking. $70-80, plus tax.

Bed 'n' Breakfast Ltd. of Washington, D.C. #100

P. O. Box 12011, 20006
(202) 328-3510

This 100-year-old Victorian was built by John Shipman as his personal residence and has been carefully and extensively restored by its present owners who have added exterior landscaping, gardens, terrace, and fountains to the existing townhouse. The house has been featured on the Logan Circle House Tour and was written up in *Washington Gardener Magazine, The Washington Post,* and *The Philadelphia Inquirer.* Accommodations offer either a queen or double bed, and have both shared and private baths. Parking must be arranged in advance. $55-85.

Bed 'n' Breakfast Ltd. of Washington, D.C. #111

P. O. Box 12011, 20006
(202) 328-3510

Located on General's Row, a row of townhouses constructed in the late 1880s. This house is just three blocks from Dupont Circle, second only to Georgetown as a neighborhood for the trendy. Dupont Circle offers good restaurants, boutiques, and theaters, and the Dupont Circle Metro Subway is three blocks away . Four guest rooms have either double or pair of twin beds, and both shared and private baths are available. Your hostess is an artist with a MA from the University of Alabama. Resident cat. $60-75.

Bed 'n' Breakfast Ltd. of Washington, D.C. #120

P. O. Box 12011, 20006
(202) 328-3510

This upper Northwest Washington residence is tastefully appointed with crafts, flowers, and comfortable furniture. The fashionable neighborhood offers elegant shopping, close access to all the attractions in downtown Washington, and other major activity areas in Maryland. Your host family has lived in Washington D.C. for 25 years, and he is an urban planner, which makes him an excellent source on Washington attractions. $55-65.

Bed 'n' Breakfast Ltd. of Washington, D.C. #122

P. O. Box 12011, 20006
(202) 328-3510

This unhosted apartment is located at a prestigious address set back from Wisconsin Avenue in its own park-like environment. Located in the upper Georgetown, it is close to major atrtractions, yet posses an air of being miles from city life. The efficiency has a double-size, fold-out sleep sofa, a kitchen with microwave, dishwasher, and European-styled cabinetry, TV, telephone, and washer and dryer. $70-75.

NOTES: Credit cards accepted: A Master Card; B Visa; C American Express; D Discover Card; E Diner's Club; F Other; 2 Personal Checks accepted; 3 Lunch available; 4 Dinner available; 5 Open all year;

Bed 'n' Breakfast Ltd. of Washington, D.C. #123

P. O. Box 12011, 20006
(202) 328-3510

Designed in 1891 by famous Washington architect Franklin Schneider, this house was recently renovated by its prersent owner, an attorney who has traveled all over the United States, Europe, and the Far East. Accommodations include a queen-size reproduction of a Victorian iron and brass bed, private hall bath, and separate sitting room. There is also a front study with extensive bookcases and a sun porch that guests are welcome to use. $75-85.

Bed 'n' Breakfast Ltd. of Washington, D.C. #125

P. O. Box 12011, 20006
(202) 328-3510

This Victorian townhouse was built in 1990 and is filled with an eclectic mix of period pieces, Oriental, and contemporary art. Four gracefully appointed bedrooms share two baths on the second floor. A third floor two room suite adjoins a private bath and can accommodate up to four people. Conveniently located in the heart of the city, this home is located one mile north of the White House and six blocks of Dupont Circle Metro stop on the red line. No smoking, no children. $65-75.

Bed 'n' Breakfast Ltd. of Washington, D.C. #126

P. O. Box 12011, 20006
(202) 328-3510

This house is a Georgian-style brick Colonial with a slate roof. Located on a wide, tree-lined avenue in a residential neighborhood, Tenley Circle is convenient-ed situated between Georgetown and Chevy Chase, Maryland. Guests have easy access to downtown business areas and major bus routes, and within two blocks are many restaurants, shops, movie theaters, tennis courts and an indoor pool. Two large guest room each have a private bath with a tiled shower. Pets and smoking are not permitted. $70-80.

Bed 'n' Breakfast Ltd. of Washington, D.C. #129

P. O. Box 12011, 20006
(202) 328-3510

This red-brick, former schoolhouse, circa 1880, was converted about four years ago into condominiums. It features enormous windows and fifteen foot ceilings. Located four and one-half blocks from Union Station. The guest room was designed by your hostess, an avid collector of antiques. It has an Old World-style bed built into an existing alcove, and an entertainment center and appliances are all operated by remote control so that a tired guest can prop himself against a pillow and never have to move. Walking distance to charming cafes and restaurants that line Massachuttes Avenue. $60, single only.

Bed 'n' Breakfast Ltd. of Washington, D.C. #130

P. O. Box 12011, 20006
(202) 328-3510

Built in 1892, this home was one of the early gracious row houses of Capitol Hill. The house has been renovated, but the original architectural details have been retained. A spacious guest room on the English Basement level has a comfortable queen-size, half cherry poster bed, comfortable sitting chairs, a bookshelf full of American history books, cable TV, and a private entrance. Located two blocks from your host's home is Capitol South Metro (Blue Line) and many good restaurants. $75-85.

6 Pets welcome; 7 Smoking allowed; 8 Children welcome; 9 Social drinking allowed; 10 Tennis available; 11 Swimming available; 12 Golf available; 13 Skiing available; 14 May be booked through travel agents.

Bed 'n' Breakfast Ltd. of Washington, D.C. #131

P. O. Box 12011, 20006
(202) 328-3510

This Federal-style brick home was custom-designed by the owners and built in 1982. The house has two guest rooms, each with a private bath and double bed. Between Conneticut and Wisconsin Avenues, the house is convenient to numerous restaurants, movie theaters, and elegant shopping. The Metro subway is a brief three and one-half blocks away, and buses arrive regularly at stops on Wisconsin and Connecticut Avenues. $65-75.

Bed 'n' Breakfast Ltd. of Washington, D.C. #136

P. O. Box 12011, 20006
(202) 328-3510

This unhosted apartment on a quiet residential street of three-story townhouses is only a few blocks away from Metro stops to the White House, Woodley Park/Zoo, excellent area shops and restaurants, and the Sheraton Washington and Connecticut Avenue. This completely self-contained one-bedroom apartment occupies one floor of the townhouse. It has been professionally decorated, has a queen-size bed, full bath, fully equipped kitchen and living room with cable TV, VCR, stereo, and private patio. Roll-away bed, laundry facilities, and weekly maid service available. $90-100.

Bed 'n' Breakfast Ltd. of Washington, D.C. #137

P. O. Box 12011, 20006
(202) 328-3510

Seven blocks behind the Capitol, walking distance to the Supreme Court and Library of Congress, and a ten-minute walk to both Eastern Market Metro and Union Station.

This house, built in 1902, has been restored to its present condition by the owner, a fashion designer whose renovations have been featured in *Better Homes and Gardens* and *The Washington Post*. Two guest rooms are available, each with a double bed, color TV, telephone, and shared bath. $65-75.

Bed 'n' Breakfast Ltd. of Washington, D.C. #145

P. O. Box 12011, 20006
(202) 328-3510

This quintessentially Washington-style townhouse is located in a prestigious district on Captiol Hill. The elegant restorations and decor of this thirteen-room residence has four guest accommodations with a variety of bed sizes and both private and shared baths. All rooms have a color TV and a telephone. This home is original and exudes great warmth and hospitality. Resident cats. $65-85.

Bed 'n' Breakfast Ltd. of Washington, D.C. #155

P. O. Box 12011, 20006
(202) 328-3510

A 19th century inn located in historic Virginia just 45 minutes from downtown, the inn has been lovingly restored as a beautiful, cozy bed and breakfast. There are fourteen unique rooms furnished with antiques and reproductions, and each is named for a noteworthy Virginian. The dining room was inspired by Belvoir, the home of William Fairfax. Gardens designed to reflect the era when the inn was constructed have been added to both the front and back of the building. Full breakfast and high tea are both served. $115-250.

Bed 'n' Breakfast Ltd. of Washington, D.C. #171

P. O. Box 12011, 20006
(202) 328-3510

NOTES: Credit cards accepted: A Master Card; B Visa; C American Express; D Discover Card; E Diner's Club; F Other; 2 Personal Checks accepted; 3 Lunch available; 4 Dinner available; 5 Open all year;

This split-level home is locatred in a country seting, with a county park across the street that has a nature trail leading to the Potomac River. Two guest rooms, both with double bed and a shared bath, are available. Iron, laundry facilities, parking, telephone, and color TV with VCR and cable are offered as well. Smoking is permitted, and pets can be accommodated in the garage. $40-60.

Bed 'n' Breakfast Ltd. of Washington, D.C. #196

P. O. Box 12011, 20006
(202) 328-3510

This house, a new Victorian-style, has a wrap-around porch and decks for sitting or sunning. Located in Silver Springs, an old established community adjacent to Washington, D.C. The guest rooms are comfortably furnished and share one large bathroom. Guests will also enjoy relaxing in the huge spa on the deck that looks out toward the woods. The general area has a large variety of interesting restaurants and shopping malls, and major downtown attractions are only thirty minutes away via Metro, which is three miles away with ample parking. Resident dog. $60-70.

Embassy Inn

1627 16th Street Northwest, 20009
(202) 234-7800; (800) 423-9111

A European-style inn nine blocks north of the White House and within short walking distance to Metro subway transportation. Features a charming and relaxed atmos-phere, personalized service, and extras such as continental breakfast, evening sherry, and snacks each day. Economical rates in a nice neighborhhod.

Host: Susan Stiles
Rooms: 38 (PB) $78-100
Continental Breakfast
Credit Cards: A, B, C, E, F
Notes: 2, 5, 7, 8, 9, 14

Henley Park Hotel

926 Massachusetts Avenue, NW, 20001
(202) 638-5200; FAX (202) 638-6740

An intimate 96-room luxury property reminiscent of a traditional European country inn specializes in personalized services, such as mini-bars, VCRs, and 24-hour room service. Our restaurant offers award-winning cuisine, and has been named in the top five most romantic restaurants, with its sun-filled atrium. Marley's lounge offers live jazz. The Wilkes Room has a traditional tea with scones and Devonshire cream in a cozy atmosphere of fresh flowers and a fireplace. Located near Union Station, Capitol, Smithsonian Museums, and the Metro.

Host: Michael Pawson, general manager
Rooms: 96 (PB)

Kalorama Guest House at Woodley Park

2700 Cathedral Avenue Northwest, 20008
(202) 328-0860

This turn-of-the-century Victorian town house offers you a downtown residential home away from home. Decorated in period antiques, the guest house is a short walk to the underground Metro, restaurants, and

THE EMBASSY INN · THE WINDSOR INN

Smithsonian and White House, yet offering you the relaxation and hospitality of a country inn. Enjoy a complimentary continental breakfast and evening apéritif.

Host: Michael Gallagher
Rooms: 19 (12 PB; 7 SB) $40-85
Continental Breakfast
Credit Cards: A, B, C, E
Notes: 2, 5, 7, 8, 9, 14

Morrison-Clark Inn

Massachusetts and L Street, 20001
(202) 898-1200

The newly restored Morrison-Clark Inn preserves the elegance of Victorian design and creates the feel of an elegant turn-of-the-century Washington home. The guest rooms and suites are individually decorated with authentic period furnishings. Lunch and dinner are served in the restaurant, one of the best in Washington. The inn is just six blocks from the White House near downtown shopping, Chinatown, Techworld and the convention center. Weekend rates are available.

Host: Lorraine Lucia
Rooms: 54 (PB) $115-195
Continental Breakfast
Credit Cards: A, B, C, E
Notes: 2, 3, 4, 5, 7, 8, 9, 14

The Reeds

P. O. Box 12011, 20005
(202) 328-3510

A 100-year-old Victorian mansion that has been carefully and extensively restored. Original wood paneling, stained glass, chandeliers, porch. Each room has a color TV and phone; laundry facilities are available. Adjoins Logan Circle Historic District, with excellent transportation and easy parking. This beautiful home was selected as a part of the "Christmas at the Smithsonian" festivities, and was featured in the Washington Post in December when it was decorated for Christmas. Ten blocks from the White House. Your hosts speak English and French.

Hosts: Charles and Jackie Reed
Rooms: 5 (SB) $55-82.50
Continental Breakfast
Credit Cards: A, B, C, E
Notes: 2 (two weeks in advance), 5, 8, 9

Windsor Inn

1842 16th Street Northwest, 20009
(202) 667-0300; (800) 423-9111

A charming inn located 11 blocks from the White House in the heart of Washington, D.C. Features a relaxing and friendly atmosphere as well as personalized service from the staff. Complimentary continental breakfast, evening sherry, and snacks are available daily. Economical rates; suites; nice neighborhood.

Host: Susan Stiles
Rooms: 46 (PB) $89.19-168
Continental Breakfast
Credit Cards: A, B, C, E, F
Notes: 2, 5, 7, 8, 9, 14

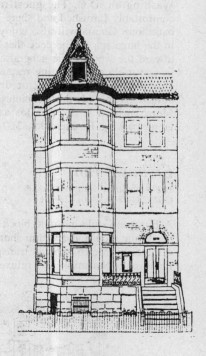

The Reeds

NOTES: Credit cards accepted: A Master Card; B Visa; C American Express; D Discover Card; E Diner's Club; F Other; 2 Personal Checks accepted; 3 Lunch available; 4 Dinner available; 5 Open all year;

Florida

Elizabeth Pointe Lodge

98 South Fletcher Avenue, 32034
(904) 277-4851

Seaside lodge of an 1890s Nantucket shingle-style architecture. Large porches. Overlook ocean with rockers and lemonade. Great room with fireplace/library. Oversize tubs, remote color cable TV, fresh flowers, newspaper delivered to room. Wine at 6:00 p.m. Homemade snacks/desserts always available. Baby-sitting, laundry/room service, concierge assistance. Historic seaport of Fernandina nearby. Bikes available for touring the island.

Hosts: David and Susan Caples
Rooms: 20 (PB) $85-115
Full Breakfast
Credit Cards: A, B, C
Notes: 2, 3, 4, 5, 7, 8, 9, 10, 11, 12, 14

The 1735 House

584 South Fletcher Avenue, 32034
(904) 261-5878; (800) 872-8531

An oceanfront country inn. Antique nautical decorations enhance your private ocean view. Full suites, private bath, freshly baked pastries, and morning newspaper. One suite in a lighthouse, with two bedrooms, bath, galley, working light, and observation deck.

Hosts: Gary and Emily Grable
Suites: 6 (PB) $55-125
Continental Breakfast
Credit Cards: A, B, C, D
Notes: 2, 5, 7, 8, 9, 10, 11, 12, 14

Florida House Inn—1857

20-22 South Third Street, P. O. Box 688, 32034
(904) 261-3300; (800) 259-3301
FAX: (904) 277-3831

Florida House Inn—1857

NOTES: Credit cards accepted: A Master Card; B Visa; C American Express; D Discover Card; E Diner's Club; F Other; 2 Personal Checks accepted; 3 Lunch available; 4 Dinner available; 5 Open all year; 6 Pets welcome; 7 Smoking allowed; 8 Children welcome; 9 Social drinking allowed; 10 Tennis available; 11 Swimming available; 12 Golf available; 13 Skiing available; 14 May be booked through travel agents.

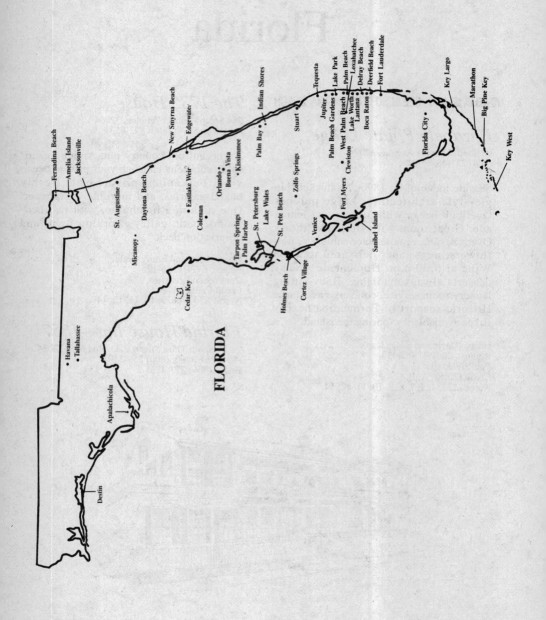

Situated on Amelia Island in the heart of the 50-block historic district of Fernandina. Built in 1857 as a tourist hotel; today's guests can enjoy the same large porches and 11 rooms, some with fireplaces, all with private baths. Country pine and oak antiques, cheerful handmade rugs and quilts found in each room. Airport pickup available; bikes; FAX machine; handicapped access.

Hosts: Bob and Karen Warner
Rooms: 11 (PB) $65-125
Full Breakfast
Credit Cards: All Major
Notes: 2, 3, 4, 5, 7 (limited), 8 (limited), 9, 10, 11, 12, 14

APALACHICOLA

The Gibson Inn

P. O. Box 221, 32320
(904) 653-2191

All rooms are decorated with period furnishings: four-poster beds, ceiling fans, antique armoires, and pedestal lavatories with wide basins and porcelain fixtures. Shelling, boating, and fishing are close, plus four barrier islands to explore. Apalachicola is a seafood lover's paradise.

Hosts: Michael Koun and Charlene Carter
Rooms: 30 (PB) $60-80
Full Breakfast on weekends; Continental breakfast Monday through Friday
Credit Cards: A, B
Notes: 2, 4, 5, 6, 7, 8, 9, 14

The Barnacle

BIG PINE KEY

The Barnacle

Route 1, Box 780A, 33043
(305) 872-3298

Enjoy the ambience of a home-stay bed and breakfast, along with every amenity. A unique experience on the ocean, surrounded by lush, verdant foliage, where you can enjoy peace and quiet, yet be only 30 miles from the attractions of Key West.

Hosts: Wood and Joan Cornell
Rooms: 4 (PB) $70-100
Full Breakfast
Credit Cards: None
Notes: 2, 5, 7, 9, 11

Bed and Breakfast on the Ocean "Casa Geande"

P. O. Box 430378, 33043
(305) 872-2878

This spaectacular Spanish-style home was designed to suit the natural beauty of the keys. Breakfast is served on the landscaped garden patio that has panoramic views of the beach and ocean. There is a hot tub/Jacuzzi for relaxing by day or under a moonlit sky. The large guest rooms are comfortably cooled by Bahama fans or air conditioning. Key deer and birds around. From your private beach you may swim, snorkel, sunbathe, or fish.

Hosts: Jon and Kathleen Threlkeld
Rooms: 3 (PB) $75-85
Full Breakfast
Credit Cards: None
Notes: 2, 5, 7 (restricted), 11

Canal Cottage

P. O. Box 262, 33043
(305) 872-3881

Relax in the private apartment of this quaint, natural-wood stilt home. Nestled in the treetops, cooled by island breezes and Bahama fans. Enjoy the bicycles, cable TV, gas grill, and fully furnished kitchen. Near a nature trail and the Key Deer Refuge.

6 Pets welcome; 7 Smoking allowed; 8 Children welcome; 9 Social drinking allowed; 10 Tennis available; 11 Swimming available; 12 Golf available; 13 Skiing available; 14 May be booked through travel agents.

Hosts: Dean and Patti Nickless
Rooms: 2 (PB) $85
Continental Breakfast
Credit Cards: None
Notes: 2, 5, 7, 8, 9, 11, 14

Deer Run

Long Beach Road, Box 431, 33043
(305) 872-2015; (305) 872-2800

Deer Run is a Florida Cracker-style house nestled among lush native trees on the ocean. Breakfast is served on the large veranda overlooking the ocean. Dive at Loo Key National Marine Sanctuary, fish the Gulf Stream, or lie on the beach. A nature lovers paradise and a birdwatchers heaven.

Host: Sue Abbott
Rooms: 2 (PB) $85-95
Full Breakfast
Minimum stay: 2 nights
Credit Cards: None
Notes: 2, 5, 9, 11

BOCA RATON

Bed & Breakfast Co. BR317

P. O. Box 262, South Miami, 33243
(305) 661-3270

Attractively furnished unit in small condo. Conveniently situated; overlooks the golf course of the Boca Raton Hotel and Club; a ten-minute walk to the beach; and just around the corner to Mizner Park. Choice of restaurants, theater, boutiques. Decorator furnishings. Heated pool. $60.

Camino Real #10

Open House Bed and Breakfast Registry
P. O. Box 3025, Palm Beach, 33480
(407) 842-5190

This neoclassic home is a decorator's delight. From your king-size bedroom, the sliding glass doors open to the landscaped patio and pool. Enjoy your ample breakfast with the morning newspaper. Other amenities include TV with remote control, room telephone, and an electric tea kettle in your room for tea, coffee, or soup any time. Five-minute drive to the ocean. $75.00

Suburban Ranch #11

Open House Bed and Breakfast Registry
P. O. Box 3025, Palm Beach, 33480
(407) 842-5190

A comfortable home west of Florida's Turnpike and near mall restaurants and shopping. Guests are welcome to use the barbecue and refrigerator on the patio. From the pool, relax and enjoy looking at the lush greens of a local golf course. Choose between a corner queen-size bedroom or a single bedroom. $40-60.

BRADENTON

B & B Suncoast Accommodations #6

8690 Gulf Boulevard
St. Petersburg Island, 33706
(813) 360-1753

This home offers a pool, spa, king-size bed, and private bath to guests. Situated on the Canal, the Gulf beach is ten minutes away. Seventh night free. $65-85.

B & B Suncoast Accommodations #7

8690 Gulf Boulevard
St. Petersburg Island, 33706
(813) 360-1753

This home offers two guest rooms, both of which have a private bath. Pool on premises, and ten minutes to the beach. Seventh night free. $55-70.

NOTES: Credit cards accepted: A Master Card; B Visa; C American Express; D Discover Card; E Diner's Club; F Other; 2 Personal Checks accepted; 3 Lunch available; 4 Dinner available; 5 Open all year;

CEDAR KEY

The Historic Island Hotel

P. O. Box 460, 32625
(904) 543-5111

Pre-Civil War Jamaican-style architecture, rustic "tabby-walled" building on the National Register of Historic Places. Award-winning hotel and gourmet natural foods dining room. Like stepping back in time, with muraled walls, paddle fans, French doors, verandas, and gulf breezes. A cozy lounge bar completes a perfect place to get away from it all.

Host: Marcia Rogers
Rooms: 10 (6 PB; 4 S2B) $80-104
Full Breakfast
Credit Cards: A, B, D
Notes: 2, 4, 5, 8, 9, 10, 11, 14

CLEWISTON

Clewiston Inn

108 Royal Palm Avenue, 33440
(813) 983-8151

The Clewiston Inn is different. Its unique Colonial styling is no accident. The old southern Colonial plantation is known for its hospitality. Southern cuisine and relaxing atmosphere. Delightfully different from any other hotel, the Clewiston Inn offers comfort and relaxation for the business traveler or vacationing family. The inn has become famous for its Colonial dining room and the Everglades Lounge. It is conveniently situated in the heart of sugar country on Highways 27 and 80, on the south shore of Lake Okeechobee.

Rooms: 52 (PB)
Full Breakfast
Credit Cards: A, B, C, D, E
Notes: 3, 4, 5, 7, 8, 9, 10, 12, 14

COLEMAN

The Son's Shady Brook Bed and Breakfast

P. O. Box 551, 33521
(904) PIT-STOP (748-7867)

A refreshing change. This modern home has comfortable beds with private baths. Overlooks spring-fed creek on 21 secluded, wooded acres. A relaxing retreat for elderly, handicapped, newlyweds, and others. Air conditioning, heat, sound system throughout rooms, piano, library, and more. Solitude and tranquility with therapeutic, scenic, picturesque surroundings. Rural setting, easy to find. Within 100 miles of Central Florida attractions. Good fishing nearby. Brochure available.

Host: Jean Lake Martin
Rooms: 4 (PB) $50-60
Full Breakfast
Credit Cards: A, B, C
Notes: 2, 3 (prior arrangement), 4 (prior arrangement), 5, 10, 12

DAYTONA BEACH

Captains Quarters Inn

3711 South Atlantic Avenue, 32127
(904) 767-3119

The inn features new oceanfront suites with private balconies overlooking the Atlantic Ocean and heated swimming pool. Daily maid service, old English charm with poster beds. Only minutes from Disney World. Enjoy old-fashioned coffee shop and Rebecca's Place, full of gifts and antiques. Wine and cheese; and daily newspaper is delivered to your door. AAA-rated excellent.

Hosts: Beckey Sue Morgan and family
Rooms: 25 (PB) $75-110
Credit Cards: A, B, C, D
Notes: 2, 3, 5, 7, 8, 9, 10, 11, 12

6 Pets welcome; 7 Smoking allowed; 8 Children welcome; 9 Social drinking allowed; 10 Tennis available; 11 Swimming available; 12 Golf available; 13 Skiing available; 14 May be booked through travel agents.

Coquina Inn

544 South Palmetto Avenue, 32114
(904) 254-4969

Daytona Beach's beautification award-winning inn offers brightly enameled woodwork, polished wood floors accented with Oriental rugs. Cozy rooms where romance abounds with floral prints, fireplaces, and antique soaking tubs. Awaken each morning to a gourmet candlelit breakfast served on fine china. Picnic lunches and private dinners available upon request. All the finest amenities.

Hosts: Jerry and Susan Jerzykowski
Rooms: 4 (PB) $69-99
Full Breakfast
Credit Cards: A, B
Notes: 2, 3, 4, 5, 9, 10, 11, 12, 14

Live Oak Inn

448 South Beach Street, 32114
(904) 252-4667

The two oldest homes in Daytona, circa 1871 and 1881, are only one mile to the beach. Sixteen rooms, most of which have Jacuzzis, overlook the marina and gardens, and robes and rocking chairs are just a few of the amenities available for guests. Afternoon tea, meeting rooms, and special services are available for business travelers, and sunset and river cruises, performing artists program, golf packages and gourmet packages, are also available. AAA rated excellent. Voted best in Daytona for a rendezvous.

Hosts: Vinton and Sandra Fisher
Rooms: 16 (PB)
Continental Plus Breakfast
Credit Cards: A, B, C
Notes: 2, 3, 4, 5, 9, 10, 11, 12, 14

DEERFIELD BEACH

Parkside #14

Open House Bed and Breakfast Registry
P. O. Box 3025, Palm Beach, 33480
(407) 842-5190

A country home in the suburbs on 1 1/4 acres invites you to sun by the pool or stroll across the ground to the private pond. A footbridge and waterfall are part of the garden landscape. Some French is spoken by your hosts, a professional couple. They will prepare extra breakfast treats on weekends. A small dog will greet you. $45-55.

DELRAY BEACH

The Lanai #13

Open House Bed and Breakfast Registry
P. O. Box 3025, Palm Beach, 33480
(407) 842-5190

A Bermuda-style home furnished with old English antiques, convenient to the beach and sophisticated dining. The guest suite includes a pair of twin beds, a bath, and a private sitting room facing the swimming pool. Fruit trees abound on the sequestered lawn. There is even a tree house with a sunset view. Full breakfast. You will be greeted by family pets, four lovable pups. $55

A Petit Salon #12

Open House Bed and Breakfast Registry
P. O. Box 3025, Palm Beach, 33480
(407) 842-5190

The name accurately describes this artist's home. Your hostess' talents carry through to her lush tropical garden. Double or twin bedrooms, each with a private bath, are available. One and one-half miles from the beach. Children welcome, bikes provided. Resident cats. $55

DESTIN

Henderson Park Inn— A Beachside Bed and Breakfast

2700 Hwy 98E-Beach Route, 32541
(800) 336-4853

NOTES: Credit cards accepted: A Master Card; B Visa; C American Express; D Discover Card; E Diner's Club; F Other; 2 Personal Checks accepted; 3 Lunch available; 4 Dinner available; 5 Open all year;

Destin's first and only beachside bed and breakfast combines the charm of a Queen Anne-style inn with the amenities of a modern resort. Perfect for couples and romantics, rooms are decorated with cozy Impressionistic themes, antique hand-crafted reproductions, high ceilings, fire-places, four-poster canopy beds, fine linens, private balconies and baths, some of which have gulfside Jacuzzis. Villas are perfect for families up to six. Continental beachside breakfast, beach and maid service, evening social receptions, heated pool, veranda, palm grove, and restaurant. Dedicated conference/meeting facilities for up to eighty.

Host: Carl Rush
Rooms: 19 rooms; 18 villas (PB) $46-300
Continental Breakfast
Credit Cards: A, B
Notes: 2, 3, 4, 5, 7, 8, 9, 11, 12, 14

EASTLAKE WEIR

Lakeside "Country" Bed and Breakfast

P. O. Box 71, 32133
(904) 288-1396; (904) 732-0000

The Lakeside "Country" Bed and Breakfast was built as a hunting lodge for wealthy Canadians and has been in existence for 110 years. The walls are knotty cypress in the living area, which gives the lodge a rustic ambience with a Victorian flair. Lake Weir is a 5,600-acre recreational, spring-fed lake with all water sports and fishing available. A canoe is available for guests to use, and the inn, while old-fashioned, does offer modern conveniences. Guest basket with drinks and snacks and fresh flowers await you. Breakfast is served on the second floor veranda overlooking the lake (when weather permits.) Private lakeview suite available for long weekends or weekly stays.

Hosts: Sandy and Bill Bodner
Rooms: 6,and 1 suite (3 PB; 3 SB) $40-80
Full CountryuBreakfast
Credit Cards: None
Notes: 2, 9, 11, 12, 14

EDGEWATER

The Colonial House

110 East Yelkca Terrace, 32132
(904) 427-4570

Situated on Florida's east coast between Daytona Beach and Cape Canaveral. Guests enjoy fine European hospitality in a quiet family atmosphere. Rooms have air conditioning, TV, refrigerator, and private bath. Enjoy solar-heated swimming pool and Jacuzzi. Nearby beaches, golf, deep-sea fishing, the Space Center, Disney World.

Host: Eva Brandner
Rooms: 3 (PB) $45
Full Breakfast
Minimum stay: 2 nights
Credit Cards: None
Notes: 2, 5, 8 (over 4), 9, 10, 11, 12, 14

FERNANDINA BEACH

The Phoenix' Nest

619 South Fletcher Avenue, 32034
(904) 277-2129

On Amelia Island, a seaside retreat in the bed and breakfast tradition. Suites 200 feet from the Atlantic. Wide, unobstructed ocean views. Beautiful, private, gracious, rich in color and texture. Fascinating books and magazines spanning 250 years are so enthralling you may hope it rains. Bikes, hammock, surf fishing gear, videos from Chaplin to Napolean, Koko to O'Keefe.

6 Pets welcome; 7 Smoking allowed; 8 Children welcome; 9 Social drinking allowed; 10 Tennis available; 11 Swimming available; 12 Golf available; 13 Skiing available; 14 May be booked through travel agents.

Host: Harriett Johnston Fortenberry
Suites: 4 (PB) $75-85
Continental Breakfast
Credit Cards: A, B
Notes: 2, 5, 7, 9, 10, 11, 12, 14

FLORIDA CITY

Grandma Newtons Bed and Breakfast

40 Northwest Fifth Avenue, 33034
(305) 247-4413

Visit Grandma and the relaxed country atmosphere of her historic 1914 two-story, renovated country home. Minutes from Everglade and Biscayne National Parks, the Florida Keys, and Miami. Spacious rooms with air conditioning ensure a peaceful rest that sets your appetite for a huge country breakfast.

Host: Mildred T. Newton
Rooms: 8 (4 PB; 4 SB) $39.20-67.20
Full Breakfast
Minimum stay holidays: 2 nights
Credit Cards: None
Notes: 2 (deposit only), 5, 7, 8, 9, 10, 11, 12, 14

FORT LAUDERDALE

The Dolan House

1401 Northeast 5 Court, 33301
(305) 462-8430

Centrally situated for the beach, shopping, businesses, and full park exercise facilities. Each room is equipped with ceiling fans and individual air conditioners. The garden and patio areas are great for enjoying the Florida sun, or you may want to slip into the hot tub spa. A 20 percent discount summer months, May through October.

Hosts: Tom and Sandra Dolan
Rooms: 4 (2 PB; 2 SB) $59.95-65.40
Continental Breakfast
Minimum stay: 2
Credit Cards: None
Closed Aug. & Sept.
Notes: 2, 7 (limited), 9, 10, 11

FORT MYERS

Embe's Hobby House

5570-4 Woodrose Court, 33907
(813) 936-6378

This town house is designed to be your home away from home during your stay. The bright, spacious suite is cheery and comfortable, with combined sleeping and living areas, including private bath with dressing room. There is a resident cat. Situated just 15 minutes from the beaches, Sanibel and Captiva islands, fine shopping, good restaurants, and the Edison and Ford homes.

Host: Embe Burdick
Room: 1 (PB) $55
Continental Breakfast
Credit Cards: None
Notes: 2, 5, 9, 10, 11, 12

HAVANA

Gaver's Bed and Breakfast

301 East Sixth Avenue, 32333
(904) 539-5611

Circa 1907 restored house with a screened porch, cable TV, central air conditioning, ceiling fans, ten-foot ceilings. Licensed by the state of Florida and the town of Havana. Off-street, lighted parking. Situated in the center of town, two blocks from ten antique stores. Twelve miles north of I-10 and Tallahassee on U.S. 27. Exit 29 off I-10.

Hosts: Shirley and Bruce Gaver
Room: 1 (PB) $55
Continental Breakfast
Credit Cards: None
Notes: 2, 5, 8, 9, 12, 14

Harrington House Bed and Breakfast

5626 Gulf Drive, 34217
(813) 778-5444

The charm of old Florida architecture and the casual elegance of beachfront living are beautifully combined at the Harrington House, a one-of-a-kind bed and breakfast guest house on Anna Maria Island. Built in 1925, this lovingly restored home has seven charming bedrooms, each with private bath. Most rooms have French doors leading to balconies overlooking the pool, the beach, and the blue-green Gulf of Mexico. Guests are served a full breakfast in the dining room as they enjoy stimulating conversation with other guests. Relax by the pool, take a moonlit stroll on the beach, or listen to the surf. AAA rated, Mobil Guide rated; American Bed and Breakfast Association rated.

Hosts: Frank and Jo Adele Davis
Rooms: 8 (PB) $79-139
Full Breakfast
Credit Cards: A, B
Notes: 2, 5, 9, 11, 14

JACKSONVILLE

House on Cherry Street

1844 Cherry Street, 32205
(904) 384-1999

Historic restored home on the St. Johns River near downtown Jacksonville, featuring antiques, elegant breakfasts, wine, snacks, and bicycles for guest use.

Host: Carol Anderson
Rooms: 4 (PB) $66.40-88.52
Full Breakfast
Credit Cards: A, B
Notes: 2, 5, 8 (over 9), 9, 10, 12, 14

Judge Gray's House

2814 St. Johns Avenue, 32205
(904) 388-4248; (800) 654-3095

Built in 1911, this beautiful Queen Anne-style home is furnished with antiques and lots of art. Each queen-size bedroom has its own private bath, TV, and phone. The exterior features three verandas, with swing, hammock, and patio furniture for guest use. Off-street parking. Convenient to down-town, I-10, I-95, shopping centers, parks, tennis, golf. Rates include complimentary wine or tea, continental plus breakfast.

Host: Bill Edmonds
Rooms: 3 (PB) $45-60
Continental Breakfast
Credit Cards: None
Notes: 2, 5, 7 (limited), 8 (older), 9, 14

Plantation Manor Inn

1630 Copeland Street, 32204
(904) 384-4630

Completely restored in 1992, this gracious 1905 plantation mansion rises more than three stories and sits high on a corner lot two blocks from the St. John's River in historical Riverside. Crystal and brass chandeliers glow above antique furnishings and Oriental carpets. Cable TV and business telephones can be found in all eight accommodations. Heated swimming pool and spa and close proximity to I-95, Convention Center, churches, art museum, parks, and hospitals.

Hosts: Jerry and Cathy Ray
Rooms: 8 (PB) $75-135
Continental Breakfast
Credit Cards: A, B, C
Notes: 2, 5, 7, 8, 9, 11, 14

JUPITER

Innisfail

134 Timber Lane, 33458
(407) 744-5905

A contemporary ranch framed by palm trees is the home gallery of the VanNoorden sculptors. While you don't have to be an art lover to visit, it helps to be a pet lover, as the four-footed family consists of three dogs and two cats. Enjoy a relaxing poolside continental breakfast before exploring the lovely beaches of Jupiter and the many sights and activities of the Palm Beach area.

Host: Katherine VanNoorden
Rooms: 1 (PB) $60 Nov.-May; $50 June-Oct.
Continental Breakfast

6 Pets welcome; 7 Smoking allowed; 8 Children welcome; 9 Social drinking allowed; 10 Tennis available; 11 Swimming available; 12 Golf available; 13 Skiing available; 14 May be booked through travel agents.

Credit Cards: None
Notes: 2, 4, 5, 6, 8, 9, 11

Ocean Villa #3

Open House Bed and Breakfast Registry
P. O. Box 3025, Palm Beach, 33480
(407) 842-5190

This location is perfect for a quiet getaway retreat. Enjoy long walks on the beach and take your choice between a dip in the ocean or the private, heated swimming pool. The elegant guest room boasts its own private walled garden. An ample breakfast is served poolside. Tennis on premises and golf nearby. $75.

The Ridge #15

Open House Bed and Breakfast Registry
P. O. Box 3025, Palm Beach, 33480
(407) 842-5190

A colony of contemporary resort homes offers guests a panoramic view of the Atlantic Ocean. Enjoy the spacious, cathedral-ceilinged livingroom, or stroll down to the beach or nearby swimming pool. Tennis also on premises. Choice of restaurants nearby. Two queen-size bedrooms, private baths. Children welcome. Kitchen privileges. $60.

KEY LARGO

Jules' Undersea Lodge

51 Shoreland Drive
P. O. Box 3330, 33037
(305) 451-2353

Dive, dine, and dream at five fathoms in "the world's first and only underwater hotel." Situated at Key Largo Undersea Park in Florida. Resort courses available for non-certified divers, packages for $195 to $295 per person. Includes dinner, breakfast, unlimited diving, refreshments, 42-inch windows, TV, VCR, CD player, tape deck, refrigerator, and global communications.

Host: Neil Monney and Ian Koblick
Rooms: 2 (SB) $195-295
Full Breakfast and Dinner
Credit Cards: A, B, F
Notes: 2, 4, 5, 11, 14

KEY WEST

Andrew's Inn

Zero Walton Lane, 33040
(305) 294-7730

Central Old Town Key West and down a shaded lane off Duval Street. Each queen deluxe room is distinctive and beautiful. All have private entrances, full bath, remote control TV, air conditioning, and phone. You'll be served a hot, full breakfast each morning, and cocktails are on the house. Overlooking the Hemingway estate.

Hosts: Tim Gatewood and Andrew Cleveland
Rooms: 7 (PB) $89-139
Full Breakfast
Credit Cards: A, B, C
Notes: 2, 5, 6, 7, 8, 9, 11, 12, 14

Artist House

534 Eaton Street, 33040
(305) 296-3977; (800) 582-7882

Turn-of-the-century Victorian mansion completely renovated to its original standing. Furnished with antiques and period reproductions. Centrally situated in Old

Plantation Manor Inn

NOTES: Credit cards accepted: A Master Card; B Visa; C American Express; D Discover Card; E Diner's Club; F Other; 2 Personal Checks accepted; 3 Lunch available; 4 Dinner available; 5 Open all year;

Town, one-half block from Duval Street shopping and dining. Four blocks from Mallory Square. Complimentary breakfast served in the tropical garden. Six large rooms to choose from, one including a turret as the play room. Reservations strongly suggested.

Host: Ed
Rooms: 6 (PB) $85-225
Continental Breakfast
Credit Cards: A, B, C, D, E
Notes: 5

The Banyan Resort

323 Whitehead Street, 33040
(305) 296-7786; FAX (305) 294-1107

The Banyan Resort is located in the the heart of Old Town Key West within easy walking distance to shops, restaurants, and museums and galleries. The Resort consists of six historic homes on the National Register of Historic Places, with two pools and an outdoor Jacuzzi. Weekly rates are available. No pets.

Host: Martin J. Bettercourt
Rooms: 38 (PB) $115-265, seasonal rates apply
Kitchen in every room; coffee by the pool
Credit Cards: A, B, C, D
Notes: 2, 3, 5, 7, 9, 11, 14

Artist House

Duval House

Colours Key West— The Guest Mansion

410 Fleming Street, 33040
(305) 294-6977; (800) 284-5622

Circa 1889, this Victorian mansion has been renovated and has maintained all the original architectural detail, including 14-foot ceilings, chandeliers, polished wood floors, and graceful verandas. The host states the mansion is for the liberal-minded adult only.

Host: James Remes
Rooms: 12 (10 PB; 2 SB) $72-185
Continental Breakfast
Credit Cards: A, B, C, D, F
Notes: 5, 7, 9, 10, 11, 12, 13, 14

Duval House

815 Duval Street, 33040
(305) 294-1666

Restored century-old Victorian house with charm and deluxe amenities. Large swimming pool and quiet tropical gardens. Walk to restaurants and all attractions. AAA and Mobil Travel Guide approved.

Host: Richard Kamradt
Rooms: 28 (25 PB; 3 SB) $64-145
Continental Breakfast
Credit Cards: A, B, C
Notes: 5, 7, 9, 10, 11, 12

6 Pets welcome; 7 Smoking allowed; 8 Children welcome; 9 Social drinking allowed; 10 Tennis available; 11 Swimming available; 12 Golf available; 13 Skiing available; 14 May be booked through travel agents.

Garden House of Key West

329 Elizabeth Street, 33040
(305) 296-5368; (800) 6956453
FAX (305) 292-1160

Situated in the historic district and within walking distance to everything. Tropical gardens, spa with waterfall, and sun deck. Air-conditioned, rooms with both private and shared bath. Complimentary continental buffet breakfast and wine hour daily under the covered patio.

Host: David Mayne
Rooms: 10 (8 PB; 2 SB) $63-120
Expanded Continental Breakfast
Credit Cards: A, B, C, D, E
Notes: 5, 7, 9

Heron House

512 Simonton Street, 33040
(305) 294-9227

Heron House consists of three homes. One, built in 1856, represents the few remaining classic conch houses. Location is in the very heart of the historic district, one block from the main tourist street and three blocks from the nearest beach.

Host: Fred Geibelt
Rooms: 17 (PB) $49.95-194.25
Continental Breakfast
Credit Cards: A, B, C
Notes: 2 (for deposit), 5, 7, 9, 10, 11, 12, 14

Key West Bed and Breakfast: The Popular House

415 William, 33040
(305) 296-7274

A classically restored turn of the century three-story Victorian. Built by Bahamian Shipbuilders and located on a quiet tree-shaded street. The house is decorated in Caribbean style. Four porches, sundeck, tropical gardens, Jacuzzi, and sauna for your immediate relaxation. Located in the heart of the historic preservation district within walking distance to restaurants, beaches, and shops.

Host: Jody Carlson
Rooms: 8 (4 PB; 4 SB) $59-165
Expanded Continental Breakfast
Credit Cards: A, B, C
Notes: 2, 5, 7, 9, 14

Lime House Inn

219 Elizabeth Street, 33040
(305) 296-2978

An "island within an island," this guest house for men is in the heart of the historic Old Town. It is the most private and friendly place to stay in Key West. Enjoy life in the old conch mansion or lounge in the pool or hot spa. All rooms have private bath, kitchenette, TV, air conditioning, and telephone. Situated just steps from the waterfront, two blocks off Duval Street where you will find shops and night life.

Hosts: Jim and Godfrey
Rooms: 7 (PB) $55-120
Continental Breakfast
Credit Cards: A, B, C
Notes: 5, 7, 9, 11, 14

Marquesa Hotel

600 Fleming Street, 33040
(305) 292-1919; (800) 869-4631

Exquisitely restored Victorian home—located in Old Towne, Key West—six blocks from Gulf of Mexico, three miles from the airport. All rooms with private bath, air-conditioning, remote-control cable TV, phone,

Colours Key West—The Guest Mansion

bathrobes, and security safe. Small gourmet restaurant, pool, concierge and turndown service with Godiva chocolates. AAA four diamond award.

Host: Carol Wightman
Rooms: 15 (PB) $105-275 seasonal
Full Breakfast
Credit Cards: A, B, C
Notes: 4, 5, 7, 8, 9, 10, 11, 12, 14

Merlinn Guest House

811 Simonton Street, 33040
(305) 296-3336

Lush tropical gardens, decks and pool in the heart of Old Town. Freshly baked breakfast served among exotic birds in the secluded garden. Evening cocktails and appetizers. 18 rooms and apartments with private baths, TV and air conditioning. Also handicapped accessible unit with private garden. Our staff can arrange your day on the water—snorkeling, fishing, sailing or playing. You'll never want to leave!

Host: Pat Hoffman
Rooms: 18 (PB) $59-120
Full Breakfast
Minimum stay holidays: 3 nights
Credit Cards: A, B, C
Notes: 2 (deposit only), 5, 6, 7, 8, 9, 11, 14

"The Palms" Guesthouse

820 White Street, 33040
(305) 294-3146; 1-800-558-9374

Located in the old part of town, the main house of The Palms was built in 1889. Secluded gardens surround a large swimming pool, and The Palms is within walking distance to beaches and Duval Street. Tennis courts are close by. All rooms have private baths, air conditioning, TV, and phone. Continental breakfast and some parking available.

Host: Terence Clarkson
Rooms: 19 (PB) $65-125
Continental Breakfast
Credit Cards: A, B
Notes: 5, 7, 8, 11

Papa's Hideaway

309 Louisa Street, 33040
No phone listed

Enjoy a secluded private getaway in lush tropical gardens. Lounge in your studio apartment with private bath, patio, kitchenette, air conditioning, and color cable TV. Take your home with you in our quaint two-bedroom cottage with one bath, full livingroom, dining room, kitchen, air conditioning, and cable TV. Swing or read on the wraparound porch, or sun on your private sun deck. Complimentary cappucino and pastries are served by our heated pool and Jacuzzi daily. Feel Papa Hemingway's inspiration within walking or biking distance to beaches, clubs, theaters, and restaurants.

Host: Sandy Islands
Rooms: $75-200
Continental Breakfast

Whispers Bed and Breakfast Inn

6 Pets welcome; 7 Smoking allowed; 8 Children welcome; 9 Social drinking allowed; 10 Tennis available; 11 Swimming available; 12 Golf available; 13 Skiing available; 14 May be booked through travel agents.

Credit Cards: None
Notes: 5, 7, 8, 9, 11, 14

Seascape

420 Olivia Street, 33040
(305) 296-7776

Listed on the National Register of Historic
Places, with heated pool-spa nestled under
crimson bougainvillaea, tropical garden, and
sun decks. All rooms feature private bath, air
conditioning, Bahama fan, color-cable television, queen-size bed. Compli-mentary wine
hour (in-season). In the heart of Old Town
only minutes to the Atlantic Ocean and the
Gulf of Mexico. Steps from the finest shops
and eating and drinking establishments.

Host: Alan Melnick
Rooms: 5 (PB) $64-104
Continental Breakfast
Credit Cards: A, B, C, D
Notes: 5, 7, 9, 10, 11, 12

Tropical Inn

812 Duval, 33040
(305) 294-9977

Listed on the National Register of Historic
Places, we are located in the heart of the
historic district. All rooms have private
baths, air-conditioning, fans, and radios,
and some have color TV and private sun
decks. Located one block from the
Hemingway House, Lighthouse Museum,
and just eight blocks from Sunses celebration, rooms are decorated with antique wicker furniture. Apartments can sleep two couples. The beach is just three blocks away.

Rooms: 7 (PB) $55
Credit Cards: A, B, C, D, E
Notes: 2, 6, 7, 8, 9

The Watson House

525 Simonton Street, 33040
(305) 294-6712; (800) 621-9405

The Watson House, circa 1860, is a distinctively furnished small inn/guest house in
the historic preservation district. Received
1986 award for excellence in rehabilitation
from Historical Florida Keys Preservation
Board. Swimming pool, heated Jacuzzi,
patio, decks, and gardens. All units have
their own distinct-style, private baths, color
TV, air conditioning, and telephone; larger
suites have fully equipped kitchens.
Privacy prevails; adults only; no pets.
Brochure available.

Hosts: Joe Beres and Ed Czaplicki
Suites: 3 (PB) $95-360
Continental Breakfast
Credit Cards: A, B, C
Notes: 5, 7, 9, 10, 11, 12, 14

Whispers
Bed and Breakfast Inn

409 William Street, 33040
(305) 294-5969

The owner-managers take great pride in
their service, hospitality, and the romance
of their historic 1866 inn. Each room is
unique and appointed with antiques.
Included in the room rate is a full gourmet
breakfast served in the tropical gardens.

Hosts: Les and Marilyn Tipton
Rooms: 6 (S3B) $69-125
Full Breakfast
Credit Cards: A, B, C
Notes: 5, 7 (limited), 9, 10, 11, 12

KISSIMMEE

Unicorn Inn

8 South Orlando Avenue, 32741
(407) 846-1200

Turn-of-the-century bed and breakfast.
Large rooms with private baths tastefully
decorated. Dining room with the English
flavor of brasses and hunt-scene oil paintings. Some antiques throughout the inn.
Suites available. The inn is just 15 minutes
from Disney World, Epcot, MGM
Universal studios.

NOTES: Credit cards accepted: A Master Card; B Visa; C American Express; D Discover Card; E Diner's
Club; F Other; 2 Personal Checks accepted; 3 Lunch available; 4 Dinner available; 5 Open all year;

Host: Janet Barnett
Rooms: 8 (PB) $55-65
Full Breakfast
Credit Cards: A, B
Notes: 2, 5, 7, 8, 9, 14

LAKE PARK

Classic Comfort #16

Open House Bed and Breakfast Registry
P. O. Box 3025, Palm Beach, 33480
(407) 842-5190

Located in suburban community seven miles north of West Palm Beach and five minutes from the beautiful ocean beaches of Singer Island, this comfortable bungalow offers a standard double bedroom, or a queen-size waterbed. You hosts serve freshly squeezed orange juice from citrus trees on the premises with your continental breakfast. Children over four welcome. Family rates available. $45.

LAKE WALES

Chalet Suzanne Country Inn and Restaurant

P. O. Drawer AC, 33859-9003
(813) 676-6011; (800) 288-6011

Discover Europe in the heart of Florida. This historic country inn is situated on 70 acres surrounded by orange groves. It has 30 charming guest rooms with private baths; award-winning dining overlooking Lake Suzanne. It is just 45 minutes southwest of the Orlando area.

Hosts: Carl and Vita Hinshaw
Rooms: 30 (PB) $95-185
Full Breakfast
Credit Cards: A, B, C, D, E
Notes: 2, 3, 4, 5, 6, 7, 8, 9, 10, 11, 12, 14

LAKE WORTH

College Park #5

Open House Bed and Breakfast Registry
P. O. Box 3025, Palm Beach, 33480
(407) 842-5190

Easy access to I-95. From the large, screened porch, relax and look out over the nicely landscaped lawn with beautiful shade trees. The cheery twin-bed guest room has a private bath. Full breakfast. $55.

LANTANA

Lagoon Setting #06

P. O. Box 3025, Palm Beach, 33480
(407) 842-5190

Twenty minutes south of Palm Beach International airport and west of I-95, this sprawling ranch home is secluded yet near good restaurants and ten minutes from the ocean. If you are traveling with family or friends, you will have a choice of double, king, or twin bedrooms. Children over five welcome. Family rates. Relax on the screened patio and by the pool. Continental breakfast. $55.

LOXAHATCHEE

Khaki Campbell Bed and Breakfast

P. O. Box 1352, 33470
(407) 790-0052

Charmingly furnished with nineteenth century English country antiques and equestrian art this bed and breakfast is located in Wellington, minutes from world-class polo and equestrian events, trap and skeet, sculling, sailing, swimming, water-skiing, fishing, golf, tennis, croquet, wild animal preserve, ocean beaches, restaurants, and shopping. Celebrities abound. Only 17 miles west of Palm Beach, 64 miles north of Miami. Continental breakfast, private baths, kitchen and laundry privileges. Boots polished, terriers welcome. Tours of equestrian facilities and antique districts.

6 Pets welcome; 7 Smoking allowed; 8 Children welcome; 9 Social drinking allowed; 10 Tennis available; 11 Swimming available; 12 Golf available; 13 Skiing available; 14 May be booked through travel agents.

Host: Joanna Thomas
Rooms: 2 (PB) $50-65
Continental Breakfast
Credit Cards: None
Notes: 2, 5, 6, 9, 10, 11, 12

MARATHON

Hopp-Inn Guest House

5 Man-O-War Drive, 33050
(305) 743-4118; FAX (305) 743-9220

Situated in the heart of the Florida Keys.
Every room has a water view. Charter fish-
ing on premises aboard the Sea Wolf.
Families welcome in villas.

Host: The Hopp family
Rooms: 5 (PB) $50-150
Villas: 4 (PB)
Full Breakfast
Credit Cards: A, B
Notes: 2 (for deposit), 5, 7 (limited), 8, 10, 11, 12

MIAMI

Miami River Inn

118 SW South River Drive, 33130
(305) 325-0045; (800) 468-3589

Enjoy a turn-of-the-century environment
overlooking Miami's vibrant riverfront and
downtown. Our 41 rooms, 38 of which
offer private baths, are individually decorated and furnished with antiques. All
rooms have Touch-tone phones, TV, and
central air conditioning and heat. Our pool
and Jacuzzi are surrounded by lush tropical
gardens. Complimentary breakfast is
served daily, and a glass of wine welomes
you. The lobby contains a library of historical publications about Miami and menus
from restaurants in the river district.

Rooms: 41 (38 PB; 2 SB) $65-120
Continental Breakfast
Credit Cards: A, B, C, D
Notes: 2, 5, 7, 8, 9, 11, 14

MICANOPY

Herlong Mansion

402 Northeast Cholokka Boulevard
P. O. Box 667, 32667
(904) 466-3322

"Micanopy is the prettiest town in Florida.
The Herlong Mansion is its crown jewel" -
Florida Trend, Nov. 1989. The brick Greek
Revival structure has four Corinthian
columns, ten fireplaces, six different types
of wood and is decorated in period
antiques. Built in 1845 and 1910, the two-
story house has six bedrooms, all with private baths, on two acres with moss-draped
oaks, pecans, dogwoods, and magnolias.

Host: H. C. (Sony) Howard, Jr.
Rooms: 6 (PB) $75-115
Full Breakfast Weekends
Continental Breakfast Sun.-Thurs.
Credit Cards: A, B
Notes: 2, 5, 8, 9, 14

Shady Oak
Bed and Breakfast

203 Cholokka Boulevard, 32667
(904) 466-3476

The Shady Oak stands majestically in the
center of the downtown business district in
historic MiCanopy. A marvelous canopy of
old live oaks, quiet shaded streets, and old
store fronts offer visitors a memorable connection to Florida's cultural past. This 19th-
century-style mansion features five beautiful
spacious suites, private porches, hot tub,
Florida room, and billiard parlor. Local
activities include antiquing, bicycling, canoeing, fishing, bird watching, and much more.

Host: Frank James
Rooms: 5 (PB) $75-125
Full Breakfast
Credit Cards: A, B, D
Notes: 2, 5, 7, 8, 9

NOTES: Credit cards accepted: A Master Card; B Visa; C American Express; D Discover Card; E Diner's
Club; F Other; 2 Personal Checks accepted; 3 Lunch available; 4 Dinner available; 5 Open all year;

NEW SMYRNA BEACH

Riverview Hotel

103 Flagler Avenue, 32169
(904) 428-5858

An elegant and historic hotel built in 1886.
Enjoy leisurely walks while shopping on
Flagler Avenue or sunbathe by the pool or
at the area's finest beach. You will be pampered with a complimentary continental
breakfast and newspaper delivered to your
private patio or balcony overlooking the
Intracoastal Waterway. Nightly turndown
service. Award-winning Riverview
Charlie's Restaurant.

Hosts: Jim and Christa Kelsey
Rooms: 18 (PB) $63-150
Continental Breakfast
Credit Cards: A, B, C, D, E
Notes: 2, 3, 4, 5, 7, 8, 9, 10, 11, 12, 14

ORLANDO

The Courtyard
at Lake Lucerne

211 North Lucerne Circle East, 32801
(407) 648-5188; (800) 444-5289

Victorian and Art Deco elegance in a tropical
setting in the heart of downtown Orlando.
Consisting of three separate buildings, each
with its own distinctive-style, surrounding a
luxuriously landscaped brick courtyard with
fountains. Complimentary bottle of wine on
arrival and expanded continental breakfast
each morning. Award-winning renovation in
beautiful surroundings, convenient to everything the area has to offer.

Hosts: Charles and Paula Meiner
Rooms: 22 (PB) $65-150
Expanded Continental Breakfast
Credit Cards: A, B, C
Notes: 2, 5, 7, 8, 9, 10, 14

Perri House
Bed and Breakfast Inn

10417 State Road 535, 32836
(407) 876-4830; (800) 780-4830

Perri House is a quiet, private, secluded
country estate conveniently located in the
backyard of the Walt Disney World Resort
area. Because of its outstanding location,
Perri House provides easy access to all that
Disney World and Orlando have to offer.
An upscale continental breakfast awaits you
each morning to start your day. The hosts
offer a unique blend of cordial hospitality,
comfort, and friendship to all their guests.

Host: Nick and Angi Perretti
Rooms: 4 (PB) $65-75
Upscale Continental Breakfast
Credit Cards: A, B, C, D
Notes: 2, 5, 8, 9, 10, 11, 12, 14

The Rio Pinar House

532 Pinar Drive, 32825
(407) 277-4903

A quiet, spacious, private home, furnished
with antiques, featuring a breakfast porch
overlooking a yard of trees and flowers.
Situated in a golf course community, convenient to the airport, downtown Church
Street Station, Disney World and Epcot, the
Space Center, and expressway exits.

Hosts: Delores and Vic Freudenburg
Rooms: 3 (PB) $50-55
Full Breakfast
Credit Cards: None
Notes: 2 (in advance), 5, 8, 9, 12

The Spencer Home
Bed and Breakfast

313 Spencer Street, 32809
(407) 855-5603

The suite with private entrance consists of
one or two bedrooms with a queen and
double bed and living room with queen-
sofa bed. TV, swimming pool, kitchen,
laundry are all available. Convention center
and most of Central Florida's attractions
are within 15 to 30 minutes away. Brochure
available.

Hosts: Neal and Eunice Schattauer
Rooms: 1-2 (PB) $50-100
Expanded Continental Breakfast

---

6 Pets welcome; 7 Smoking allowed; 8 Children welcome; 9 Social drinking allowed; 10 Tennis available; 11
Swimming available; 12 Golf available; 13 Skiing available; 14 May be booked through travel agents.

Minimum stay: 2 nights
Credit Cards: None
Notes: 5, 8, 9, 11

PALM BAY

Casa Del Sol

Country Estates, 232 Rheine Road Northwest, 32907
(407) 728-4676

An award-winning home on Florida's central east coast. Breakfast is served on the lanai, with breathtaking foliage. From here you can see a spaceship launched. Enjoy the luxury of a Roman tub. Minutes away from the space pad and all Disney attractions.

Host: Stanley Finkelstein
Rooms: 3 (1 PB; 2 SB) $55-125
Full Breakfast
Closed May 1-Oct. 31
Credit Cards: None
Notes: 2, 6, 8, 9, 10, 11, 12, 13, 14

PALM BEACH

Palm Beach Historic Inn

365 South County Road, 33480
(407) 832-4009

This beautifully restored historic landmark building has bright, tastefully furnished, comfortable rooms and suites, all of which offer private baths, air conditioning, telephones, and cable TV. Located in one of the most convenient spots in Palm Beach, Worth Avenue, sports, cultural, and boating activities, museums, the performing arts of every kind, spectacular shopping. Exquisite dining and unlimited recreational activities are within two blocks.

Hosts: Ruth and Franklin Frank
Rooms: 17 (PB) $65-150
Continental Breakfast
Credit Cards: A, B, C, D
Notes: 2, 5, 8, 9, 12, 14

PALM BEACH GARDENS

Heron Cay #17

Open House Bed and Breakfast Registry
P. O. Box 3025, Palm Beach, 33480
(407) 842-5190

Water, boats, sun, and fun describe this unique hideaway on two acres facing the Intracoastal Waterway. Explore the Private island or hop into the pool or hot tub. Weekly guests may enjoy a cruise on your host's 48-foot Sportsfisherman. Inside, relax by the stone fireplace in the Victorian parlor, or try your luck on the pinball machine in the game room. Guest rooms have either a king or double bed with balconies for a beautiful view of the inlet. Full breakfast; dinner served at extra charge. Resident dog and cats. $80-125.

PALM HARBOR

Bed and Breakfast of Tampa Bay

126 Old Oak Circle, 34683
(813) 785-2342

An Art Deco look invites guests to enjoy paintings, artifacts, and statues from all over the world. Two miles from the Suncoast white sand beaches, golf, tennis, boating, and fishing are all a short distance away. Ninety miles to Disney World and Seaworld. Busch Gardens, Adventureland, Dali Museums, and historic Tarpon Springs are all within a day's visit. Bus lines, shopping malls, ice skating, and fine restaurants nearby. AAA building for travel assitance within walking distance. A Jacuzzi and swimming pool are available for guests to use, and color TV and telephone are in every room.

Hosts: Vivian and David Grimm
Rooms: 4 (2 PB; 2 SB) $45-75
Full Breakfast
Credit Cards: None
Notes: 2, 5, 8, 11

NOTES: Credit cards accepted: A Master Card; B Visa; C American Express; D Discover Card; E Diner's Club; F Other; 2 Personal Checks accepted; 3 Lunch available; 4 Dinner available; 5 Open all year;

ST. AUGUSTINE

Carriage Way
Bed and Breakfast

70 Cuna Street, 32084
(904) 829-2467

An 1883 Victorian in the historic district, within walking distance of the waterfront, shops, restaurants, and historic sites. Complimentary cordials, newspaper, cookies, bicycles, and breakfast. The atmosphere here is leisurely and casual.

Hosts: Karen Burkley-Kovacik and Frank Kovacik
Rooms: 9 (PB) $49-99
Continental Breakfast
Credit Cards: A, B
Notes: 2, 3, 4, 5, 8, 9, 10, 11, 12, 14

Casa de la Paz

22 Avenida Menendez, 32084
(904) 829-2915

Mediterranean-style inn overlooking the Matanzas Bay in the historic district. Elegant furnishings and imported fine linens. From your room or from a second-story veranda, you will enjoy a view of Matanzas Bay. From the veranda an open stairway leads to a beautiful walled garden courtyard. The inn is central to all historic sites, fine restaurants, and miles of ocean beaches. Complimentary champagne and sherry, gourmet breakfast.

Host: Sandy Upchurch
Rooms: 6 (PB) $65-125
Full Breakfast
Credit Cards: A, B, C
Notes: 2, 5, 9, 10, 11, 12, 14

Casa de Solana
Bed and Breakfast Inn

21 Aviles Street, 32084
(904) 824-3555; (800) 771-3555

Built circa 1763, this inn has four antique-filled suites with cable TV, private bath, enclosed courtyard. Full breakfast is served in the formal dining room; a decanter of sherry is presented on arrival. The inn is downtown, with all the quaint shops, museums, restaurants, and horse and buggies to help you in your tour of St. Augustine, the nation's oldest city.

Hosts: Jim and Faye McMurry
Rooms: 4 (PB) $125-135
Full Breakfast
Minimum stay weekends and holidays: 2 nights
Credit Cards: A, B, C, D
Notes: 2, 5, 9

Castle Garden

15 Shenandoah Street, 32084
(904) 829-3839

Stay at the Castle and be treated like royalty! Relax and enjoy the peace and quiet of royal treatment at our newly restored 100-year-old castle of Moorish Revival design, where the only sound you'll hear hear is the occasional roar of a cannon shot from the old fort 200 yards to the south, the creak of the original solid wood floor, or the chirping of birds. The unusual coquina stone exterior is interesting to see, while the interior of this former Warden Castle Carriage House has been completely renovated and features two magnificent and romantic honeymoon suites with sunken bedrooms, in-

Casa de Solana Bed and Breakfast Inn

6 Pets welcome; 7 Smoking allowed; 8 Children welcome; 9 Social drinking allowed; 10 Tennis available; 11 Swimming available; 12 Golf available; 13 Skiing available; 14 May be booked through travel agents.

room Jacuzzis, and cathedral ceilings. Amenities include complimentary wine, chocolates, bikes, and fenced parking.

Hosts: Fredeen Welch and Bruce Kloeckner
Rooms: 6 (PB) $55-150
Full Breakfast
Credit Cards: A, B, C, D
Notes: 2, 3, 4, 5, 14

Cordova House

16 Cordova, 32084
(904) 825-0770

Once you've explored "the Nation's Oldest City," escape into the comfort of Cordova's antique- and craft-filled rooms. Enjoy the many shops, restaurants, and historic sites by carriage riding, walking, or bicycling. Complimentary wine, iced tea, evening desserts, cable, garden hot tub, and fresh flowers everywhere. Special packages and services available for honeymoons, birthdays, etc. Call for a detailed list. Escape into yesterday while creating tomorrow's memories.

Hosts: Carole and Hal Schroeder
Rooms: 5 (PB) $55-95
Full Breakfast
Credit Cards: A, B, C, E
Notes: 2, 5

The Kenwood Inn

38 Marine Street, 32084
(904) 824-2116

Local maps and early records show the inn was built between 1865 and 1885 and was functioning as a private boarding house as early as 1886. Situated in the historic district, the inn is within walking distance of many fine restaurants and all historic sights. One block from the Intracoastal Waterway, with its passing fishing trawlers, yachts at anchor, and the classic Bridge of Lions. Beautiful ocean beaches are just across the bridge.

Hosts: Mark Kerrianne and Caitlin Constant
Rooms: 12 (PB) $55-85
Continental Breakfast
Credit Cards: A, B, C

The Kenwood Inn

Notes: 2, 5, 9, 10, 11, 12

Old City House Inn and Restaurant

115 Cordova Street, 32084
(904) 826-0113

In the heart of town sits the Old City House, in a building that has been called a classic example of Colonial Revival architecture. Carefully restored in 1990 by its current owners, the premises include five bed-and-breakfast rooms and a full service five-star restaurant. It commands a view of some of the most beautiful, historic architecture in northeastern Florida. Queen-size beds, private baths, full breakfast.

Hosts: Bob and Alice Compton
Rooms: 5 (PB) $60-95 weekends and holidays; reduced weekdays
Full Breakfast
Credit Cards: A, B, C
Notes: 2, 3, 4, 5

Old Powder House Inn

38 Cordova Street, 32084
(904) 824-4149; (800) 447-4149

High ceilings, wraparound verandas, and elaborate woodwork distinguish this Victorian home built in 1899 on the site of an 18th-century Spanish powder magazine. Cordova Street is in the heart of the historic area with horse and buggies trotting right past the house. Restaurants, antique stores, and quaint shops are within easy walking distance. Full gourmet breakfast, high tea in the afternoon, and wine and hors d'oeuvres each day. Bicycles and tandems. In-ground Jacuzzi on premises. Parking.

Hosts: Michael and Constance Emerson
Rooms: 9 (PB) $59-98
Full Breakfast
Credit Cards: A, B
Notes: 2, 3, 4, 5, 9, 10, 11, 12, 14

St. Francis Inn

279 St. George Street, 32084
(904) 824-6068

The St. Francis Inn, situated in the historic district of St. Augustine, was built as a private home for a Spanish soldier in 1791. Originally known as the Garcia-Dummett House, it began operating as an inn in 1845. It is a Spanish Colonial structure with a private courtyard, fireplaces, balconies furnished with rocking chairs, and the modern amenity of a swimming pool. The inn has a wide variety of accommodations ranging from single rooms to two- and three-room suites to an entire cottage. The warmth and peacefulness of the inn itself, its location, and the kind of guests it attracts are all strong assets.

Host: Marie Register
Rooms: 14 (PB) $49-87
Continental Breakfast
Credit Cards: A, B
Notes: 2, 5, 9, 11, 14

Southern Wind

18 Cordova Street, 32084
No phone listed

Come stay with us and enjoy Southern Wind's gracious turn-of-the-century atmosphere. Built of coquina masonry with columns and pillars, the inn's personality is gracious elegance with an emphasis on casual relaxation. Southern Wind has retained all the original architectural charms, while also offering the contemporary comforts of central air, queen-size beds, and cable TV. Enjoy our buffet breakfast, afternoon tea, and complimentary wine. AAA approved.

Host: Jeannette and Dennis Dean
Rooms: (13 PB) $39-105
Full Breakfast
Credit Cards: A, B, C, D
Notes: 2, 5, 8, 9, 10, 11, 12, 14

Westcott House

146 Avenida Menendez, 32084
(904) 824-4301

One of St. Augustine's most elegant guest houses overlooking Matanzas Bay. Circa 1890, restored in 1983, in the historic area and within walking distance to historic sites. All rooms have private baths, king-size beds, cable television, private telephone, and are furnished in antiques. Year-round climate control. Complimentary bottle of wine upon arrival, snifter of brandy at bedtime for your pleasure. Situated one-half block from the city's yacht pier.

Hosts: Sherry and David Dennison
Rooms: 8 (PB) $95-150
Continental Breakfast
Credit Cards: A, B
Notes: 2, 5, 8, 9, 10, 11, 12, 14

Westcott House

ST. PETERSBURG

Bayboro House Bed and Breakfast

1719 Beach Drive Southeast, 33701
(813) 823-4955

Turn-of-the-century Queen Anne home furnished in antiques. Old-fashioned porch swing to enjoy sea gulls and sailboats on Old Tampa Bay. Minutes from the Dali Museum, Pier, Suncoast Dome, Bayfront Center, Al Lange Stadium. Many fine restaurants in the area. Personal apartment available on request.

Hosts: Gordon and Antonio Powers
Rooms: 4 (PB) $65-75
Continental Breakfast
Credit Cards: A, B
Notes: 2, 5, 7 (limited), 9, 10, 11, 12, 14

The Heritage Hotel

234 3rd Avenue North, 33701
(813) 822-4814; (800) 283-7829

The Heritage Hotel is downtown St. Petersburg's finest hotel, featuring gracious hospitality and southern charm. The Heritage Hotel combines the glamour and exuberance of the early 1920s architecture and furniture, with luxurious, comfortable rooms and suites. On site is the Heritage Grill, which combines excellent cuisine with one of Tampa Bay's finest art galleries.

Host: Nancy Link
Rooms: 70 (PB) $58-90
Continental Breakfast
Credit Cards: A, B, C, E
Notes: 2, 3, 4, 5, 7, 8, 9, 10 (close by), 11, 12
   (close by), 14

ST. PETERSBURG BEACH

Bernard's Swanhome

8690 Gulf Boulevard, 33706
(813) 360-5245

Casual, laid back, lazy Florida living. Fish off of overdock, sun on deck, lounge in spa, or wander one-half mile to milk-white sandy gulf beach. Kitchen and laundry privileges (seventh night free). Fishing poles, beach chairs, mats, and towels provided. Golf, tennis, major league sports, Dali Museum, Busch Gardens all nearby. Enjoy dancing, fabulous dining, and glorious sunsets nightly on the charming island. Smoking on patio only. Mrs. Bernard also operates a reservation service representing many beachfront homes.

Host: Mrs. "Danie" Bernard
Rooms: 3 (1 PB; 2 SB) $45-80
Continental Breakfast served
Full Self-serve Breakfast
Credit Cards: C (deposit only)
Notes: 5, 8, 9, 10, 11, 12, 13 (water), 14

Island's End

1 Pass-A-Grille Way, 33706
(813) 360-5023; FAX (813) 367-7890

Situated at the southernmost tip of St. Petersburg Beach, Island's End is a combination of the charming ambience of sand, sea, and sky creating a unique atmosphere of rustic charm among gray weathered cottages and natural wooded walkways. All cottages have modern kitchens and bathrooms (some with Jacuzzis). Furnishings are contemporary and extremely comfortable. Quality accommodations that enhance the ever-changing beauty and diversity of the waterfront are at the guests' disposal.

Hosts: Jone and Millard Gamble
Rooms: 6 (PB) $55-145
Continental Breakfast
Credit Cards: None
Notes: 2, 5, 7, 8, 9

SANIBEL ISLAND

Song of the Sea

863 East Gulf Drive, 33957
(813) 472-2220; (800) 231-1045

Song of the Sea is a picturesque Old World inn with whitewashed walls and red tile roofs, nestled among the palm trees and tropical foliage on the water's edge on Sanibel Island. Accommodations are furnished in the French country tradition with tile floors and flowers in every room. Sit by the pool and read a book, relax in the Jacuzzi, or take a long walk on the beach in search of shells. Daily maid service is provided.

Host: Patricia Slater
Rooms: 30 (PB) $95-253
Continental Breakfast
Credit Cards: None
Notes: 2, 5, 6, 7, 8, 9, 10, 11, 12, 14

STUART

The Homeplace Bed and Breakfast Inn

501 Akron Avenue, 34994
(407) 220-9148

The Homeplace, built in 1913 and restored in 1989, is truly a "find" on the Treasure Coast. Special individual attention, home-baked goodies at breakfast, pool and spa, rooms charmingly appointed with antiques, and quiet hospitality of an era much slower are earning this new inn a reputation as a romantic getaway. Stroll to fine restaurants and tandem bike through the historical area of old Stuart on the St. Lucie River.

Hosts: Jean Bell and Jim Smith
Rooms: 3 (PB) $60-85
Full Breakfast
Credit Cards: A, B
Notes: 2, 5, 9, 11

TALLAHASSEE

Cabot Lodge #1

2735 North Monroe Street, 32303
(904) 386-8880; (800) 432-0701 Florida
(800) 223-1964 U.S.

Charming southern-style lodge designed around a unique hospitable concept, offers you such home-like amenities as fireside cocktails, lending library, and old-fash-ioned back porch overlooking the pool. A generous continental breakfast buffet, complete with fresh fruit, pastries, croissants, and bagels.

Hosts: Ron Miller and Michele Ceska
Rooms: 160 (PB) $52-55
Continental Breakfast
Credit Cards: A, B, C, D, E
Notes: 2, 5, 7, 8, 9, 11, 12, 13

Governors Inn

209 South Adams Street, 32301
(904) 681-6855

The Governors Inn combines original woodwork, exposed beams, and brilliant skylights to create a French country environment. The 41 guest rooms and suites are furnished with antique armoires and English pub tables. No two rooms are alike. Some have French four-poster beds and framed prints. Others have loft bedrooms and fireplaces, spiral staircases, and clerestory windows. The Spessard Holland suite has a wet bar and vaulted ceilings. Conferences for up to 75 people can be arranged. One-half block from the state capitol.

Rooms: 41 (PB) $89-225
Continental Breakfast
Credit Cards: A, B, C, D, E
Notes: 5, 7, 8, 9, 14

TAMPA

B & B Suncoast Accommodations #1

8690 Gulf Boulevard
St. Petersburg Island, 33706
(813) 360-1753

The Homeplace Bed and Breakfast Inn

Walk to the Gulf of Mexico from this home. King-size bed, private bath. Waterfront with a dock, and outside tiki bar. Fantastic views from the second floor. Seventh night free. $75-85.

B & B Suncoast Accommodations #2

8690 Gulf Boulevard
St. Petersburg Island, 33706
(813) 360-1753

Rooftop sun decks, spa, dock, and fabulous sunsets characterize this bed and breakfast. Guest accommodations include queen bed, private bath, TV, phone, refrigerator, and microwave. See the dolphins swim by your breakfast table. Second room available for families. Seventh night free. $50-65.

B & B Suncoast Accommodations #3

8690 Gulf Boulevard
St. Petersburg Island, 33706
(813) 360-1753

Live bird aviary in an artist's home. Five minutes to the beach. Guest room includes king-size bed and a private bath. Second room available for families. Seventh night free. $50-65.

B & B Suncoast Accommodations #4

8690 Gulf Boulevard
St. Petersburg Island, 33706
(813) 360-1753

Bayfront home with a dock offers two guest rooms, both of which have private baths. Close to shopping, restaurants, etc. Seventh night free. $60-70.

B & B Suncoast Accommodations #5

8690 Gulf Boulevard
St. Petersburg Island, 33706
(813) 360-1753

Two queen rooms in a bayfront home with a pool and private baths is less than five minutes to the beach. Non-smoking, non-drinking home. Seventh night free. $75-85.

TARPON SPRINGS

East Lake Bed and Breakfast

421 Old East Lake Road, 34689
(813) 937-5487

Private home on two and one-half acres, situated on a quiet road along Lake Tarpon. Your hosts are retired business people who enjoy new friends and are well informed about the area. A full home-cooked breakfast is served. Brochure available.

Hosts: Marie and Dick Fiorito
Room: 1 (PB) $35-40
Full Breakfast
Credit Cards: None
Notes: 2, 5, 9, 10, 11, 12, 14

Governors Inn

Spring Bayou
Bed and Breakfast Inn

32 West Tarpon Avenue, 32689
(813) 938-9333

A large, elegant home built 1905 in center of historical district. Enjoy beautiful Spring Bayou, downtown antique shops, and area attractions of small Greek village. Excellent restaurants nearby, and short drive to the beach. Well-appointed rooms with antique furnishings and modern conveniences. Complimentary glass of wine and baby grand piano in lovely parlor, spacious wraparound front porch.

Hosts: Ron and Cher Morrick
Rooms: 5 (4 PB; 2 SB) $60-90
Expanded Continental Breakfast
Credit Cards: None
Notes: 2, 9, 10, 11, 12

TEQUESTA

County Line #18

Open House Bed and Breakfast Registry
P. O. Box 3025, Palm Beach, 33480
(407) 842-5190

Just north of Jupiter and 35 minutes from Palm Beach International Airport, this new home, designed for bed and breakfast travelers, is attractively situated on a residential cul-de-sac. The private sun decks of single, double, and family bedrooms overlook the pool and hot tub. Continental breakfast. $45 for a single, additional people $10 each.

VENICE

The Banyan House

519 South Harbor Drive, 34285
(813) 484-1385

Experience the Old World charm of one of Venice's historic Mediterranean homes, circa 1926, on Florida's Gulf Coast. Fully-equipped efficiencies are tastefully decorated, each with its own character. Large shaded courtyard with pool and Jacuzzi. Close to beaches, restaurants, golf, and fishing. Complimentary bicycles.

Hosts: Chuck and Susan McCormick
Rooms: 9 (7 PB; 2 SB) $49-89
Continental Breakfast
Credit Cards: None
Notes: 2, 5, 8 (over 12), 10, 11, 12

WELLINGTON

Polo Country #19

Open House Bed and Breakfast Registry
P. O. Box 3025, Palm Beach, 33480
(407) 842-5190

Antique buffs will love this charming home. It is embellished with nineteenth-century English pine and sporting art. You will be five minutes from the world-famous Palm Beach Polo grounds as well as the famous Florida Rowing Center at Lake Wellington. Other activities, such as the Palm Beach Trap and Skeet Club and the Winter Equestrian Festival, are open to guests. Your hostess may invite you to join her on a shopping tour of quality antique districts in the county. Children and pets welcome. Continental breakfast. $50-65.

WEST PALM BEACH

Cosmopolitan #20

Open House Bed and Breakfast Registry
P. O. Box 3025, Palm Beach, 33480
(407) 842-5190

Near Flagler Drive and the Intracoastal Waterway, this is an easy walk across the bridge to Palm Beach. Here, you may wine and dine in one of many renowned restaurants, and you can enjoy celebrity-watching from the sidewalk cafes. Convenient to shops, beach, and airport. King-size bedrooms, private bath, and continental breakfast. Resident dog and cat. $40-50.

6 Pets welcome; 7 Smoking allowed; 8 Children welcome; 9 Social drinking allowed; 10 Tennis available; 11 Swimming available; 12 Golf available; 13 Skiing available; 14 May be booked through travel agents.

Hibiscus House

501 30th Street, 33407
(407) 863-5633

Hibiscus House is in a charming historic neighborhood near the Intracoastal Waterway. This convenient location provides easy access to the ocean, Palm Beach airport, and the town of Palm Beach with its fabulous homes and shopping. Hibiscus House, built in 1922 by the mayor of West Palm Beach, offers elegant surroundings for your comfort and enjoyment both indoors and out. Period furniture and antiques abound in the principal rooms. Guest rooms are individually furnished to provide an intimate, relaxed atmosphere. Some rooms have private terraces overlooking the pool and all have private baths. A full breakfast is served in the dining room, by the pool, or in the gazebo overlooking the rose garden.

Host: Raleigh Hill
Rooms: 6 (PB) $65-85 Dec.-April;
$55-65 May-Nov.
Full Breakfast
Credit Cards: None
Notes: 2, 3, 5, 6, 7, 8, 9, 10, 11, 14

Old Northwood Historic District #21

Open House Bed and Breakfast Registry
P. O. Box 3025, Palm Beach, 33480
(407) 842-5190

Situated near the Intracoastal Waterway, several charming early century homes, restored to their original splendor, are featured in an annual Holiday Candlelight House Tour. Swimming pools available. Ten minutes to the beach and airport. Breakfast is special. Choice of accommodations, including unhosted, separate studio efficiencies with weekly or monthly rates. $55-90

The Royal Poinciana

521 36th Street, 33407
(407) 842-8433

Take a trip back in time and stay in this historic Spanish-style home once owned by Al Capone. Enjoy a gourmet breakfast served on a private sun deck overlooking beautiful gardens. Located near Henry Flagler's original road from St. Augustine to Key West and three minutes from Palm Beach, Flagler Museum, Trump's Mar-Lago Mansion, airport, and many other attractions. Minimum stay is two nights.

Hosts: Grove Taylor and Roxann Field
Rooms: 3 (PB) $75
Full Breakfast
Credit Cards: None
Notes: 2, 5, 6, 7, 8, 9

West Palm Beach Bed and Breakfast

419 Thirty-Second Street; P. O. Box 8581, 33407
(800) 736-4064

A cozy Key West-style cottage built in the 1930s with all the modern conveniences of today: private baths, air conditioning, paddle fans, cable TV. Your hosts have retained the charm of old Florida with white wicker furniture in a colorful Caribbean decor; sun by the lush tropical pool, ride complimentary bicycles, or just relax and kick off your sandals! Centrally situated in a historic district, just one block from the waterway, and minutes to the tropical waters of the Atlantic or Palm Beach.

Hosts: Dennis Keimel and Ron Seitz
Rooms: 2 plus cottage (PB) $55-75
Expanded Continental Breakfast
Credit Cards: None
Notes: 2, 5, 7, 8, 9, 10, 11, 12, 14

ZOLFO SPRINGS

Double M Ranch Bed and Breakfast

Route 1, P. O. Box 292, 33890
(813) 735-0266 (after 6 P.M.)

The Mathenys welcome you to their 4,500-acre working cattle and citrus ranch in the heart of agricutural Florida. There are numerous recreational opportunities nearby, including fishing, golfing, canoeing, and a state park. Your accommodations include approximately 100 square feet of space and your private entrance. A ranch tour is an option most guests enjoy taking.

If you want to see a part of Florida most tourists miss, come out to the ranch!

Hosts: Mary Jane and Charles Matheny
Rooms: 2 (1 PB; 1 SB) $55, plus tax
Continental Breakfast
Credit Cards: None

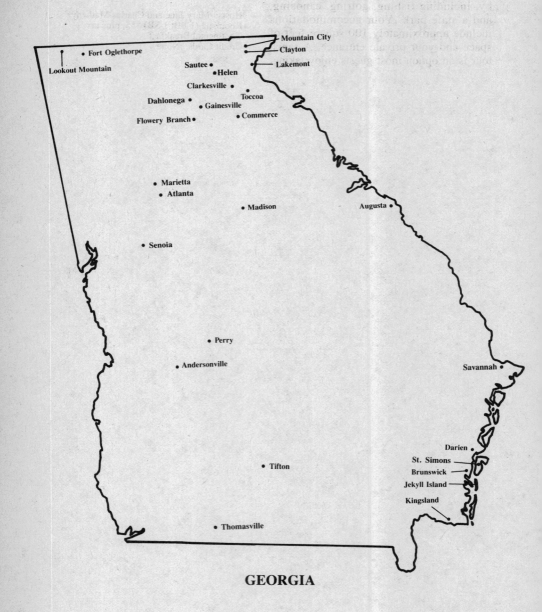

GEORGIA

Georgia

ANDERSONVILLE

A Place Away Cottage Bed and Breakfast

110 Oglethorpe Street, 31711
(912) 924-1044; (912) 924-2558

Charming country-style guest cottage in the quiet, peaceful, and historic Civil War village of Andersonville, Georgia, near the site of the Andersonville Confederate Prison. Easy walking distance to seven antique shops and three craft shops, Civil War museums, Oldtime Pioneer Farm, and restaurants. Three guest rooms with private baths, TV, coffee makers, telephone, front and back porch with rockers, golf practice area, tennis court. Expanded continental breakfast. Children welcome.

Hosts: Peggy, Fred, and Lee Sheppard
Rooms: 3 (PB) $35-50
Continental Plus Breakfast
Credit Cards: None
Notes: 2, 5, 7, 8, 9, 10

ATLANTA

Atlanta's Woodruff Inn

223 Ponce de Leon Avenue, 30308
(404) 875-9449

Southern hospitality and charm await you in this historic, beautifully restored bed and breakfast inn. Located in midtown Atlanta and convenient to everything. Lots of antiques. A full southern breakfast cooked by the on-site owners is a real treat.

Hosts: Joan and Douglas Jones
Rooms: 12 (8 PB; 4 SB) $65

Full Breakfast
Credit Cards: A, B, C
Notes: 2, 3, 5, 7 (limited), 8, 9, 10, 11, 12, 14

Bed & Breakfast Atlanta-TNN-GEORGIA

1801 Piedmont Avenue, Suite 208, 30324
(404) 875-0525; (404) 875-9672

Part of the Bed and Breakfast National Network, Bed and Breakfast Atlanta offers bed and breakfast not only in Georgia, but also in many other cities and states across the country. The members of this network adhere strictly to the standards set by TNN, such as getting to know the hosts personally, having an established cancellation and refund policy, and following a thorough inspection and approval process for all properties rented. This is because each member of the network is dedicated to ensuring your comfort, pleasure, and personal needs while you are staying at one of our "homes away from home."

Bed & Breakfast Atlanta D1

1801 Piedmont Avenue, Suite 208, 30324
(404) 875-0525

This traditional two-story house with swimming pool is located on 12 beautifully wooded acres in Druid Hills. Two guest rooms, each with queen bed, share one bath. One room has handmade quilts and an antique doll collection. The other provides a wonderful view of the pool, woods, and flowers. An expanded continental breakfast is served in the charming downstairs dining

NOTES: Credit cards accepted: A Master Card; B Visa; C American Express; D Discover Card; E Diner's Club; F Other; 2 Personal Checks accepted; 3 Lunch available; 4 Dinner available; 5 Open all year; 6 Pets welcome; 7 Smoking allowed; 8 Children welcome; 9 Social drinking allowed; 10 Tennis available; 11 Swimming available; 12 Golf available; 13 Skiing available; 14 May be booked through travel agents.

room. One of your hosts builds beautiful reproduction furniture; an impressive silver chest in the front entry is evidence of his skill. $52.

Bed & Breakfast Atlanta D2

1801 Piedmont Avenue, Suite 208, 30324
(404) 875-0525

Thirty-six-year-old Colonial brick home is in the heart of the Morningside, one of Atlanta's most desireable neighborhoods. There is a spacious bedroom with a queen-size bed and a bath with a shower. There are several sitting areas downstairs and a lovely outdoor deck overlooking a large walled yard. Guests may choose a continental or full breakfast, served in the sunlit dining room. Public transportation is excellent, and many resaurants, shops, and points of interest are within walking distance. No smoking. Resident dog and cat. $72.

Bed & Breakfast Atlanta E1

1801 Piedmont Avenue, Suite 208, 30324
(404) 875-0525

Fully renovated, spacious 1960s brick ranch-style home offers one sunny antique-furnished double with adjoining bath and one spacious and bright twin-bed room with private bath down the hall. A single-bed studio room with full view of the patio and garden is sometimes available. Host couple serves nutritious breakfasts featuring home-baked breads, and lively hospitality complete the picture as a bed and breakfast winner. Within walking distance of Emory University. Kosher dietary laws observed. No smoking. $48-56.

Bed & Breakfast Atlanta I1

1801 Piedmont Avenue, Suite 208, 30324
(404) 875-0525

This restored 1816 house was the honeymoon cottage for Robert Woodruff, the Coca-Cola magnate. The large livingroom displays a cherished Persian rug. Guest rooms include a private room and full bath downstairs—lace curtains, antique double iron bed.The upstairs suite has two bedrooms, a large sitting room with a built-in single bed, and a renovated full bath. One bedroom has an antique double sleigh bed, and the other has twin beds. High ceilings, heart-pine floors, wonderful old family furniture, and a gracious host welcome the guest. Relax along with the family cats on the screened porch overlooking an urban park. Continental or full breakfast. $60.

Bed & Breakfast Atlanta L1

1801 Peidmont Avenue NE, Suite 208, 30324
(404) 875-0525

This French Regency-style Victorian house circa 1872 was saved from demolition in 1990 and restored by the current owners. There are front and rear porches where breakfast is served when the weather permits, as well as a downstairs sitting room. Gourmet breakfast is served in the dining room, with careful attention given to low-fat ingredients and special dietary needs. Four guest rooms are available, one with king-size bed and three with queen-size beds, all with private baths. $76-100.

Bed & Breakfast Atlanta L1

1801 Peidmont Avenue NE, Suite 208, 30324
(404) 875-0525

An intimate bed and breakfast just one block off the square in Decatur, the house was built in 1937. There are two bedrooms for guests. The gourmet breakfasts include homemade breads, muffins, fresh fruit or fruit smoothies, freshly ground coffee, imported tea, and sweet, dark honey gathered from hives in the lower garden. There is a hot tub and a nearby pool available to guests. The city of Decatur is one of Atlanta's most historic and well maintained neighborhoods. It is less than six miles from downtown Atlanta and three miles from Emory University, the CDC, and the American Cancer Society.

Bed & Breakfast Atlanta M1

1801 Piedmont Avenue, Suite 208, 30324
(404) 875-0525

This early 1900s neighborhood is on the historic register and has special appeal for walkers and joggers. Nearby are the Woodruff Arts Center, High Museum, Botanical Gardens, Piedmont Park, and Colony Square with many appealing restaurants and shops. Public transit is excellent. Host couple resides in Dutch Colonial home with private cottage in rear. Bright, cheery, spacious unit has bedroom alcove with double bed and desk. The living-dining space has a double sleep sofa, chair, and breakfast table. New full bath and galley kitchen. Cable TV and phone available. Self-catered breakfast. No smoking. $80.

Bed & Breakfast Atlanta N1

1801 Peidmont Avenue NE, Suite 208, 30324
(404) 875-0525

This charming guest cottage is built on the site of a former peacock aviary in historic Druid Hills. The true post-and-beam timber frame cottage recalls the English Cotswolds. There is a livingroom, dining area, full kitchen, and a bath on the ground floor. The bedroom area with a double bed is in a large loft balcony with wrought iron railing overlooking the downstairs. Breakfast is stocked for self-catering. No smoking. Minium stay is 2 nights. $100.

Bed & Breakfast Atlanta S1

1801 Peidmont Avenue NE, Suite 208, 30324
(404) 875-0525

This authentic 1830s white two-story farmhouse was moved and carefully reassembled on this site in 1984. The house has porches on all sides. In the main house there is a terrace room with a private entry, king-size poster bed, antique furniture, a fireplace, and a large full bath. The carriage house has a suite with a large livingroom, dining room with a wet bar, undercounter refrig-

Beverly Hills Inn

6 Pets welcome; 7 Smoking allowed; 8 Children welcome; 9 Social drinking allowed; 10 Tennis available; 11 Swimming available; 12 Golf available; 13 Skiing available; 14 May be booked through travel agents.

erator, and microwave, and a large screen TV. The bedroom features a king-size canopied bed and more interesting aniques. The private bath has a shower only. There is a queen sleep sofa in the livingroom, and a Port-a-Crib are available.

Beverly Hills Inn

65 Sheridan Drive, 30305
(404) 233-8520

A charming city retreat located one-half block from public transportation, one and one-half miles from Lenox Square, and five minutes from the Atlanta Historical Society. Full kitchens, library, free parking, color TV, continental breakfast.

Host: Mit Amin
Rooms: 18 (PB) $65-120
Continental Breakfast
Credit Cards: A, B, C, E
Notes: 2, 5, 7, 8, 9, 10, 11, 12, 14

Woodruff Cottage

100 Waverly Way Northeast, 30307
(404) 688-9498

The honeymoon cottage of Robert Woodruff, Atlanta's famous anonymous donor and soft-drink magnate. Totally restored Victorian located in historic Inman Park. One block from the subway station, close to dining. Its 12-foot ceilings, heart-pine woodwork, fireplaces, antiques, screened porch, and private garden are yours to enjoy.

Host: Eleanor Matthews
Rooms: 3 (PB) $60-70
Full Breakfast
Credit Cards: A, B
Notes: 2 (deposit), 5, 8, 9, 10, 11, 12, 14

AUGUSTA

Into the Woods Bed and Breakfast

176 Longhorn Road, Hephzibah, 30815
(706) 554-1400

This house was built in the late 1800s in Waynesboro and relocated to Hephzibah,

fifteen minutes away. Relax in the Victorian palor, step out onto one of the porches, or pull up a rocker and have a cookie from the kitchen. All of the guest rooms have good firm beds. Guests can take a short drive to Augusta for for a lovely walk on the Riverwalk along the Savannah River, or visit the restaurants and shops.

Host: Mr. and Mrs. Robert L. Risser
Rooms: 4 (2 PB; 2 SB) $55-65
Full Country Breakfast
Credit Cards: A,B
Notes: 2, 5, 8, 12

The Partridge Inn

2110 Walton Way, 30904
(706) 737-8888; (800) 476-6888

The Partridge Inn is Augusta's National Historic Suite Inn, circa 1890, featuring 105 fully restored, oversized suites distinctively and traditionally furnished in a manner that reflects a grand and glorious past. Each suite is fully restored, offering the comforts of home with a livingroom, bedroom, and full kitchen, and most with open or private verandas. Our guests also enjoy a complimentary hot buffet each morning, complimentary beverage on arrival, 10 percent off VIP card for our dining room, full service restaurant, bar and grill, free valet service, meeting facilities, and an outdoor pool.

Rooms: 105 (PB) $65-105
Full Breakfast
Credit Cards: A, B, C
Notes: 2, 3, 4, 5, 6, 7, 8, 9, 11, 12 (off site), 14

BRUNSWICK

Brunswick Manor: An Historic Bed and Breakfast

825 Egmont Street, 31520
(912) 265-6889

Gracious hospitality in a coastal Deep South setting. Experience this concept of bed and breakfast accommodations, with canopied beds, thick towels, designer

---

NOTES: Credit cards accepted: A Master Card; B Visa; C American Express; D Discover Card; E Diner's Club; F Other; 2 Personal Checks accepted; 3 Lunch available; 4 Dinner available; 5 Open all year;

linens, and a wraparound veranda with an antique wicker swing. Enjoy a full gourmet breakfast served in a formal dining area and afternoon tea. Captain charters aboard *Alamar* also available.

Hosts: Claudia and Harry Trucanow
Rooms: 7 (5 PB; 2 SB) $55-85
Full Breakfast
Credit Card: F
Notes: 2, 5, 8

Rose Manor Guest House and Tea Room

1108 Richmond Street at Hanover Square, 31520
(912) 267-6369

This circa 1890 guest house is nestled among old southern trees and beautiful gardens. Charming bungalow cottage is elegantly restored and graciously furnished. Central location to the Golden Isles, marshes, and historic sites of the Georgia coast. Elegantly served breakfasts in the dining room and afternoon tea served by the garden pond. Evening refreshments are served in the Rose Parlor.

Host: Rachel Rose
Rooms: 4 (3 PB; 1 SB) $55-95
Full Breakfast
Credit Cards: None
Notes: 2, 5, 8, 9, 14

CLARKESVILLE

The Charm House Inn

108 North Washington Street, 30523
(706) 754-9347

This beautiful southern mansion, circa 1907, is listed in the National Register of Historic Homes. Large, cheerfully decorated rooms. Air conditioning and private baths. Elegant dining for guests by reservation 6:00 - 10:00 P.M. Thursday through Sunday. Enjoy golf, horseback riding, antiquing, sightseeing or just pass the time visiting with other guests on the veranda.

Hosts: Mary and Fred Newman
Rooms: 5 (PB)
Full Breakfast
Minimum stay holidays: 2 nights
Credit Cards: A, B
Notes: 2, 4, 5, 7, 9, 10, 11, 12

CLAYTON

English Manor Inns

P. O. Box 1605
U.S. Highway 76E, 30525
(800) 782-5780; FAX (404) 782-6183

Seven elegant inns on 7.2 acres of mountain garden park with 43 individually decorated rooms and ten suites with Jacuzzi tubs. One casual 17-bedroom lodge by Lake Rabun. All rooms have private bathrooms. Ideal for romantic getaways, family refreshers, corporate retreats. Gourmet and country breakfasts; wine and cheese at 5:00 p.m. Twenty-nine fireplaces, huge pool, 12-foot in-ground hot tub, near all recreation. Special events and mystery weekends. Epicurean catering at inns, exquisite amenities. Open all year for groups; open April 15-Dec. 1 for individuals. National Register of Historic Places.

Hosts: Susan and English Thornwell
Rooms: 70 (PB) $49-199
Full Breakfast
Credit Cards: A, B
Notes: 2, 3 and 4 (prior arrangement), 5, 6, 7, 8, 9, 10, 11, 12, 13, 14

COMMERCE

The Pittman House

103 Homer Street, 30529
(404) 335-3823

This house is a grand 1890 Colonial completely furnished with period antiques. Wraparound porch just waiting to be rocked on. Located in the northeastern Georgia foothills near many interesting places. One hour northeast of Atlanta just off I-85. Tennis, golf, fishing, antiquing, and watersports all nearby.

6 Pets welcome; 7 Smoking allowed; 8 Children welcome; 9 Social drinking allowed; 10 Tennis available; 11 Swimming available; 12 Golf available; 13 Skiing available; 14 May be booked through travel agents.

Hosts: Tom and Dot Tomberlin
Rooms: 4 (2 PB; 2 SB) $50-55
Full Breakfast
Credit Cards: A, B
Notes: 2, 5, 8, 10, 11, 12, 14

DAHLONEGA

Mountain Top Lodge at Dahlonega

Route 7, Box 150, 30533
(706) 864-5257

Share the magic of a secluded bed and breakfast inn surrounded by towering trees and spectacular views. Enjoy antique-filled rooms, cathedral-ceiling, great room, spa ciousdecks, heated outdoor spa, some rooms with fireplaces, whirlpool tubs, and porches. Generous country breakfast with homemade biscuits.

Host: David Middleton
Rooms: 11 (PB) $60.50-88.00
Deluxe Rooms: 2 (PB) $126-137.50
Full Breakfast
Minimum stay holidays: 2 nights
Credit Cards: A, B, C, D
Notes: 2, 5, 8 (over 11), 9, 14

The Smith House

202 South Chestatee, 30533
(706) 864-3566

Experience country hospitality in an 1884 inn. Old-time charm combined with new-fangled comforts. All rooms have TV and

The Smith House

private baths. Enjoy its famous family-style meals: three meats and nine to ten vegetables served daily.

Hosts: Fred, Shirley, Chris, and Freida Welch
Rooms: 16 (PB) $52-75
Continental Breakfast
Credit Cards: A, B, C, D
Closed Christmas Day
Notes: 3, 4, 5, 7, 8, 10, 11, 14

DARIEN

Open Gates Bed and Breakfast

P.O. Box 1526, 313095
(912) 437-6985

Explore untrammeled barrier islands and the Altamaha River Delta via a scenic byway one and one-half miles east of I-95. Open Gates was a timber baron's 1876 home; it has been featured on the cover of *Southern Homes* and in *Georgia Off the Beaten Path*. Family heirlooms, a superb library of coastal material, locally produced caviar, and hostess knowledgeable about Georgia's second oldest town and environment enhance your stay. Ecological and historical tours. Bicycles and canoeing. Sailing school nearby.

Host: Carolyn Hodges
Rooms: 4 (2 PB; 2 SB) $48-53
Full Breakfast
Credit Cards: None
Notes: 2, 5, 7 (restricted), 9, 11

FLOWERY BRANCH

Whitworth Inn

6593 McEver Road, 30542
(404) 967-2386; (706) 967-2386 after May 1992

Contemporary country inn on five wooded acres offers relaxing atmosphere, 11 uniquely decorated guest rooms, and two guest livingrooms with televisions. Full country breakfast served in large sunlit dining room. Meeting/party space available. Situated 30 minutes northeast of Atlanta at

NOTES: Credit cards accepted: A Master Card; B Visa; C American Express; D Discover Card; E Diner's Club; F Other; 2 Personal Checks accepted; 3 Lunch available; 4 Dinner available; 5 Open all year;

Lake Lanier. Nearby attractions and activities include boating, golf, beaches, and water parks. Close to Road Atlanta and Chateau Elan Winery/Golf Course. Easily accessible from major interstates. Three-diamond AAA rating.

Hosts: Ken and Chris Jonick
Rooms: 8 (PB) $55-65
Full Breakfast
Credit Cards: A, B
Notes: 2, 5, 8, 14

FORT OGLETHORPE

Captain's Quarters Bed and Breakfast

13 Barnhardt Circle, 30742
(706) 858-0624

Built in 1902, this home has been completely restored. Great attention has been paid to detail to retain the charm of yesterday and add the convenience of today. Located adjacent to Chickamauga-Chattanooga Military Park, and only twenty minutes from all the attractions in downtown Chattanooga, Tennessee, including the new Tennessee Aquarium, our quiet haven is convenient to many tourist attractions but restful when the day of sightseeing is done.

Host: Pam Humphrey and Ann Gilbert
Rooms: 4 (PB) $50-75
Full Breakfast
Credit Cards: A, B, C
Notes: 2, 5, 14

HAMILTON

Wedgwood Bed and Breakfast

P. O. Box 115, 31811
(706) 628-5659

Situated six miles south of Callaway Gardens. Beautiful 1850 home decorated in Wedgwood blue with white stenciling. Enjoy the piano in the livingroom, a classic movie on the VCR in the den, read in the library, swing on the screened porch, or doze in a hammock in the gazebo under pecan trees. Roosevelt's Little White House is nearby.

Host: Janice Neuffer
Rooms: 3 (PB) $55-70
Full Breakfast
Credit Cards: None
Notes: 2, 5, 9, 10, 11, 12, 14

HELEN

Chattahoochee Ridge Lodge

P. O. Box 175, 30545
(800) 476-8331

The lodge is a bird sanctuary in the woods above a waterfall, a mile from the center of Alpine Helen. The host will help guests plan great vacation days, like tours to gold mines, visits to craftsmen and historic sites, or Bob's Oompah band at the Edelweiss Restaurant. Five new pine-panelled, carpeted rooms, or suites with kitchens and fireplaces. All have private entrances and baths, TVs, air conditioning, phones, and refrigerators. Enjoy back-up solar heat and the large Jacuzzi.

Hosts: Bob and Mary Swift
Rooms: 5(PB) $40-60
Continental Breakfast
Credit Cards: A, B, C, D
Notes: 2, 5, 7, 8, 9, 10, 11, 12, 14

Habersham Hollow Country Inn and Cabins

Route 6, Box 6208, 30523
(706) 754-5147

Elegant country home nestled in the northeast Georgia mountains. Five minutes from Alpine Helen. Spacious rooms, a suite with a fireplace, sitting room, and its own covered porch for relaxing or dining alone. Relaxed, casual, friendly atmosphere. Cozy cabins with fireplaces located on the grounds where well-behaved children and pets are welcome.

6 Pets welcome; 7 Smoking allowed; 8 Children welcome; 9 Social drinking allowed; 10 Tennis available; 11 Swimming available; 12 Golf available; 13 Skiing available; 14 May be booked through travel agents.

Hosts: C. J. and Maryann Gibbons
Rooms: 4 (PB) $65-95
Full Breakfast
Credit Cards: A, B
Notes: 2, 5, 6, 7, 8, 9, 10, 11, 12, 13, 14

Hilltop Haus

Chattahoochee Street, Box 154, 30545
(404) 878-2388

Contemporary split-level overlooking Alpine
Helen and the Chattahoochee River. Near the-
foothills of the Smoky Mountains, six miles
from the Appalachian Trail. Rich wood paneling
and fireplaces create a homey atmosphere for the
traveler. Homemade biscuits and preserves.

Host: Ms. Frankie Tysor
Rooms: 5 (3 PB; 2 SB) $50-60
Full Breakfast
Credit Cards: A, B
Notes: 2, 5, 7, 8 (over 10), 9, 10, 11, 12, 13, 14

JEKYLL ISLAND

Jekyll Island
Bed and Breakfast Inn

117 West Gordon Street at Chatham Square, 31401
(912)238-0518; FAX (912) 233-2537

The Inn is a restored 1853 Federalist town
house in the historic district amid old mansions, museums, restaurants, churches, and
antique shops. Rooms are furnished with
antiques and quality reproductions. Palor
features museum quality Orientalia. Within
easy walking distance to most major attractions and River Street.

Hosts: Robert Mcalister and Pamela Gray
Rooms: 14(6PB;&SB) $33-84
Full Breakfast
Credit Cards: A, B, C, D
Notes: 2, 5, 7, 8, 9, 14

KINGSLAND

Historic Spencer House Inn

Osborne at Bryant Street, 31558
(912) 882-1872

A charming Victorian inn located in heart
of St. Mary's historic district features fourteen room filled with antiques and beautiful
reproductions. Enjoy the three verandas
overlooking the quiet streets of this historic
village. The Spencer House Inn is within
short driving distance to Georgia's Golden
Isles, Okefenokee Swamp, Amelia Island,
and Jacksonville, Florida.

Hosts: Tom and Janet Murray
Rooms: 14 (PB) $55-100
Continental Breakfast
Credit Cards: A, B
Notes: 2, 5, 8, 9, 12, 14

LAKEMONT

Lake Rabun Hotel

Lake Rabun Road, P. O. Box 10, 30552-0010
(404) 782-4946

An original mountain inn built in 1922. A
Rabun County landmark. Antique mountain furnishings, rustic, charming; huge
fieldstone fireplace in downstairs great
room. Has 16 rooms, shared baths.
Honeymoon suite with fireplace upstairs.
Third-generation guests now visit.

Host: Bill Pettys
Rooms: 16 (2 PB; 14 SB) $50-60
Continental Breakfast
Credit Cards: A, B
Notes: 2, 5, 7, 8, 9, 10, 11, 12, 13

LAVONIA

The Southern Trace
Inn and Restaurant

Highway 17, 30553
(404) 356-1033

This wonderful bed and breakfast, located in
the northeast Georgia foothills/lakes area, offers
16 beautifully decorated guest rooms. Guests
are provided gourmet dining nightly, continental breakfast, cable TV, lounge, room service,
plenty of parking, and telephone in each room.

NOTES: Credit cards accepted: A Master Card; B Visa; C American Express; D Discover Card; E Diner's
Club; F Other; 2 Personal Checks accepted; 3 Lunch available; 4 Dinner available; 5 Open all year;

Rooms: 16 (PB) $44
Continental Breakfast
Credit Cards: A, B
Notes: 2, 5, 7, 8, 9, 10, 11, 12, 13

LOOKOUT MOUNTAIN _____

Chanticleer Inn

1300 Mockingbird Lane, 37350
(706) 820-2015

Unique mountain stone buildings offer king, queen, double, and twin rooms, some of which have antiques and fireplaces. Suites, cable TV, and a pool are all available in a quiet atmosphere. Great for honeymoons, families, reunions, or weekends, only one block from Rock City Gardens, and 15 minutes away from the Tennessee Aquarium. AAA approved. Senior discounts. No pets.

Host: Gloria Horton
Rooms: 16 (PB and private entrances) $40-86
Continental Plus Breakfast
Credit Cards: A, B, C
Notes: 5, 7, 8, 9, 11

MADISON _____

The Brady Inn

250 North Second St, 30650
(706) 342-4400

The Stanley House

Two Victorian cottages linked together by an extended porch filled with rockers welcome you to this bed and breakfast. All rooms have private baths, heart-pine floors, and antiques. Come enjoy Southern hospitality and see "the town Sherman refused to burn."

Host: C. G. Rasch
Rooms: 6 (PB) $50-70 plus tax
Full Breakfast
Credit Cards: A, B
Notes: 2, 3, 4, 5, 6, 7, 8, 9, 10, 11, 12

MARIETTA _____

The Stanley House

236 Church Street, 30060
(404) 426-1881

Since 1895 the Stanley House has offered a delightful experience in Victorian elegance and charm. This beautiful four-story Queen Anne, decorated throughout with period antiques and wallpaper, was originally built for President Woodrow Wilson's Aunt Felie Woodrow. Historic Marietta Square, which is within walking distance, boasts antique stores, carriage rides, live theater, and many restaurants. Atlanta is just 20 minutes away. Hiking and Civil War buffs enjoy exploring Kennesaw Mountain nearby.

Host: Brigita Rowe
Rooms: 6 (PB) $75-85
Continental Breakfast
Credit Cards: A, B
Notes: 2, 5, 9, 14

MOUNTAIN CITY _____

The York House

P. O. Box 126, 30562
(404) 746-2068

A lovely 1896 bed and breakfast inn with a country flair and listed on the National Register of Historic Places. It is nestled among the beautiful north Georgia mountains and is close to recreational activities.

6 Pets welcome; 7 Smoking allowed; 8 Children welcome; 9 Social drinking allowed; 10 Tennis available; 11 Swimming available; 12 Golf available; 13 Skiing available; 14 May be booked through travel agents.

Completely renovated, the 13 guest rooms are decorated with period antiques and offer private baths and cable TV. Guests begin their day with a full continental breakfast served in their rooms on a silver tray. Situated between Clayton and Dillard one-quarter mile off Highway 441 on the York House Road.

Hosts: Tim and Kim Cook (owners); Phyllis and Jimmy Smith
Rooms: 13 (PB) $60
Continental Breakfast
Credit Cards: A, B
Notes: 2, 5, 7 (limited), 8, 9, 14

PERRY

Swift Street Inn

1204 Swift Street, 31069
(912) 987-3428

Step back 135 years to a time of southern charm, romance, and luxury. A gourmet breakfast, deluxe service, and spacious guest rooms, each with its own unique character and all filled with antiques, await you. Come experience the elegance and warm feeling of a small inn in a growing southern town. The

Ballastone Inn and Townhouse

hosts take pride in making your stay restful, pleasant, and memorable.

Hosts: Wayne and Jane Coward
Rooms: 4 (PB) $55-75
Full Breakfast
Credit Cards: A, B, C
Notes: 2, 5, 6, 12, 14

ST. SIMONS

Little St. Simons Island

P. O. Box 1078, 31522
(912) 638-7472

Privately owned, 10,000-acre barrier island retreat with six miles of pristine beaches. Comfortable accommodations, bountiful regional meals with hors d'oeuvres and wine, horseback riding, fishing, boating, canoeing, bird watching, naturalist expeditions. A unique experience in an unspoiled, natural environment.

Host: Debbie McIntyre
Rooms: 12 (10 PB; 2 SB) $300-400
Full Breakfast
Credit Cards: A, B, C
Open for individuals Mar.-May, Oct.-Nov.
Day trips and Full Island Rentals June-Sep.
Notes: 2, 3, 4, 7, 8 (over 5), 9, 11, 14

SAUTEE

The Stovall House

Route 1, Box 1476, 30571
(404) 878-3355

This 1837 farmhouse beckons you for a country experience in the historic Sautee Valley near Helen. The award-winning restoration and personal touches here will make you feel at home. Enjoy mountain views in all directions. The restaurant, recognized as one of the top 50 in Georgia, features regional cuisine with a fresh difference.

Host: Ham Schwartz
Rooms: 5 (PB) $70
Continental Breakfast
Credit Cards: A, B
Notes: 2, 4, 5, 7 (limited), 8, 9, 10, 11, 12

NOTES: Credit cards accepted: A Master Card; B Visa; C American Express; D Discover Card; E Diner's Club; F Other; 2 Personal Checks accepted; 3 Lunch available; 4 Dinner available; 5 Open all year;

SAVANNAH

Ballastone Inn and Townhouse

14 East Oglethorpe Avenue, 31401
(912) 236-1484; (800) 822-4553

A beautifully restored Victorian mansion dating from 1838 in the heart of the city's historic district, the Ballastone Inn is the epitome of gracious southern hospitality. The guest rooms reflect a distinct Victorian flavor. Added touches include flowers and fresh fruit, terry-cloth robes, fireplace, TV with VCR, some Jacuzzis. There is a beautifully landscaped courtyard and a full-service bar. In the mornings, a continental breakfast is served in your room, the parlor, or the courtyard. Sherry, coffee or tea, fruit, and pastries are available in the front parlor. Nightly turndown service includes robes, chocolates, and brandy. Recommended by The New York Times, Brides, Glamour, Atlantic, and Gourmet magazines.

Hosts: Richard Carlson and Tim Hargus
Rooms: 20 (PB) $95-175
Continental Breakfast
Credit Cards: A, B, C
Notes: 2, 5, 7, 9, 10, 11, 12, 13, 14

The Eliza Thompson House

The Eliza Thompson House

5 West Jones Street, 31401
(912) 236-3620; (800) 348-9378

Nestled in a tranquil residential neighborhood in the heart of the largest national historic district in the United States is the Eliza Thompson House, built in 1847. The main house contains 12 stately guest rooms, and the recent courtyard addition contains another 12 rooms. Enjoy the rich elegance of heart-pine floors and period furnishings and still have a phone and color television in a room, with your own private bath. A gracious continental breakfast, afternoon wine and cheese, and evening sherry are complimentary. The owners and long-time staff are always available to assist in dining suggestions, reservations, and travel arrangements.

Hosts: Lee and Terri Smith
Rooms: 25 (PB) $68-88
Continental Breakfast
Credit Cards: A, B, C
Notes: 2, 5, 7, 8, 9, 14

The Forsyth Park Inn

Foley House Inn

14 West Hull Street, 31401
(912) 232-6622

Rated by Vacations magazine as one of ten most romantic inns in the country. Built in 1896, the Foley House Inn represents a milestone in Savannah's historic preservation. Every evening, tea and wine are served in the elegant parlor, and every morning breakfast is served to you on a silver service in the privacy of your room or in the enclosed garden courtyard complete with Old World charm. Beautiful fountains, sunning decks, and an outdoor heated Jacuzzi.

Host: Susan Steinhauser
Rooms: 20 (PB) $85-165
Expanded Continental Breakfast
Credit Cards: A, B, C
Notes: 2, 5, 7, 8, 9, 14

The Forsyth Park Inn

102 West Hall Street, 31401
(912) 233-6800

Circa 1893 Queen Anne Victorian mansion with 16-foot ceilings, 14-foot doors. Ornate woodwork, floors, stairways, fireplaces, antiques. Whirlpool baths, courtyard cottage. Faces 73-acre park in large historic district. Complimentary wine, social hour; fine dining, tours, museum homes, river cruises, beaches all nearby.

Hosts: Virginia and Hal Sullivan
Rooms: 10 (PB) $82-161
Continental Breakfast
Credit Cards: A, B, C
Notes: 2 (deposit), 5, 7, 8, 9, 10, 11, 12, 14

The Haslam-Fort House

R.S.V.P. Savannah Bed and Breakfast
(800) 729-7787 Mon.-Fri. 9:30-5:30

Savannah's earliest bed and breakfast since 1979. This is an 1872 brick Victorian town house offering guests one entire suite of rooms consisting of a livingroom with fireplace, a king- and queen-size bedroom, private bath, and fully stocked country kitchen for self-serve breakfast. TV, VCR, phone. Guests have private entrances, off-street park ing, garden patio, and terraces. Handicapped accessible. Children and pets welcome. $95-165.

Jesse Mount House

209 West Jones Street, 31401
(912) 236-1774; (800) 347-1774

The Jesse Mount House, built in 1854, is in the historic district of Savannah. There are two three-bedroom suites accommodating from one to six people in a party. The house and suites have many rare antiques and reproductions. The garden suite has full kitchen and access to the walled rose garden. The upper suite has high, four-poster beds with canopies. Gilded harps are in the parlor and dining room, since your hostess is a concert harpist. Both suites have gas-log fireplaces, complimentary wine, fruit, and candy. Bicycles available.

Hosts: Howard Crawford and Lois Bannerman
Suites: 2-3 (PB) $95-195
Expanded Continental Breakfast
Credit Cards: None
Notes: 2, 5, 6 (limited), 7, 8, 9, 10, 11, 12, 14

Joan's on Jones Bed and Breakfast

17 West Jones Street, 31401
(912) 234-3863

In the heart of the historic district, two charming bed and breakfast suites in the garden level of this three-story Victorian private home. Each suite has a private entry, off-street parking, bedroom, sitting room, kitchen, bath, private phone, and cable TV. Note the original heart-pine floors, period furnishings, and Savannah grey brick walls. Innkeepers Joan and Gary Levy, former restaurateurs, live upstairs and invite you for a tour of their home if you are staying two nights or more.

Host: Joan Levy
Rooms: 2 suites (PB) $85-95
Continental Breakfast
Credit Cards: None
Notes: 2, 5, 6 (limited), 8, 9

Liberty Inn—1834

128 West Liberty Street, 31401
(912) 233-1007; (800) 637-1007

One- and two-bedroom suites with adjoining baths. Family room, sun deck, parking. Period/antique furnishings, phone, cable TV, VCRs, and movies. Reservations

NOTES: Credit cards accepted: A Master Card; B Visa; C American Express; D Discover Card; E Diner's Club; F Other; 2 Personal Checks accepted; 3 Lunch available; 4 Dinner available; 5 Open all year;

arranged for dining, carriage, bus tours. In the heart of Savannah's historic district.

Hosts: Frank and Janie Harris
Suites: 5 (PB) $95-140
Continental Breakfast
Credit Cards: A, B, C
Notes: 2, 5, 7, 8, 9, 14

Pulaski Square Inn

203 West Charlton Street, 31401
(800) 227-0650

This elegant home, built in 1853, is situated in Savannah's historic district, only a fifteen-minute walk from the Savannah River. It is completely restored with original wide-pine floors, chandeliers, and marble mantles. It is furnished with antiques and traditional furniture throughout. Modern luxury baths with gold-plated fixtures.

Hosts: Hilda and J. B. Smith
Rooms: 10 (8 PB; 2 SB) $48 plus
Continental Breakfast
Credit Cards: A, B, C
Notes: 2, 5, 7, 8, 9, 10, 11, 12, 14

Remshart-Brooks House

106 West Jones Street, 31401
(912) 234-6928

Enjoy casual southern hospitality at our historic Savannah home built in 1853. The guest accommodations are furnished with comfortable country antiques. Share the garden for your continental breakfast. Private off-street covered parking is free.

Host: Anne E. Barnett
Rooms: 1 suites (PB) $65 plus tax
Continental Breakfast
Credit Cards: None
Notes: 2, 5, 7, 9, 10,11, 12

R.S.V.P. Savannah B&B #01

(800) 729-7787 Mon.-Fri. 9:30-5:30

Situated in a historic Savannah district, this garden-level suite includes a livingroom, fireplace, sofa bed, kitchen, bedroom, full bath, and sun room. Enclosed garden and parking. No smoking. $85-95.

R.S.V.P. Savannah B&B #02

(800) 729-7787 Mon.-Fri. 9:30-5:30

An 1890s town house offers a second-floor bedroom with double bed and full private bath. Guests share the house with the host. Private parking. $55.

R.S.V.P. Savannah B&B #03

(800) 729-7787 Mon.-Fri. 9:30-5:30

A garden-level suite is complete with livingroom, fireplace, full kitchen, and dining area. The bedroom has twin beds and a private bath. Courtyard, private parking, resident cat. Two-week minimum stay. $250 weekly.

R.S.V.P. Savannah B&B #04

(800) 729-7787 Mon.-Fri. 9:30-5:30

This restored 1890 town house has two bedrooms, each with double bed and shared bath. Ideal for two couples or a family. $55-85.

R.S.V.P. Savannah B&B #05

(800) 729-7787 Mon.-Fri. 9:30-5:30

This is an 1853 inn with 22 rooms, each with either king or queen four-poster beds. Guests enjoy the beautiful courtyard and fountain in this historic district. $88-108.

R.S.V.P. Savannah B&B #06

(800) 729-7787 Mon.-Fri. 9:30-5:30

Located in Savannah's historic district, guest accommodations include a second-floor king-size bedroom with full private bath. No smoking. $85.

6 Pets welcome; 7 Smoking allowed; 8 Children welcome; 9 Social drinking allowed; 10 Tennis available; 11 Swimming available; 12 Golf available; 13 Skiing available; 14 May be booked through travel agents.

R.S.V.P. Savannah B&B #07
(800) 729-7787 Mon.-Fri. 9:30-5:30

This charming inn is in an 1845 restored warehouse. Twenty-eight rooms are available, with either single or queen beds. Evening refreshment and private parking. $96-115.

R.S.V.P. Savannah B&B #08
(800) 729-7787 Mon.-Fri. 9:30-5:30

A circa 1854 warehouse for tobacco, rice, or cotton has been converted into a spectacular 44-room inn. Rooms face the Savannah riverfront or park. Some rooms have balconies. $79-129.

R.S.V.P. Savannah B&B #09
(800) 729-7787 Mon.-Fri. 9:30-5:30

This 1893 Victorian brick mansion overlooks Chippewa Square. Elegant four-poster beds, Oriental carpets, working fireplaces, TV, VCR, films, and Jacuzzis are offered. Breakfast is served in your room. $85-175.

R.S.V.P. Savannah B&B #10
(800) 729-7787 Mon.-Fri. 9:30-5:30

This riverfront warehouse has been converted to full efficiency suites with kitchen, livingroom, and bedrooms. Ideal for families or two couples traveling together. Lovely river views. Ice cream and snacks are served at bedtime. $95-135.

R.S.V.P. Savannah B&B #11
(800) 729-7787 Mon.-Fri. 9:30-5:30

Situated in the historic district, this grand old city hotel has been beautifully restored and refurbished; 60 rooms with four-poster beds

R.S.V.P. Savannah B&B #12
(800) 729-7787 Mon.-Fri. 9:30-5:30

This charming garden-level suite, recently restored, offers private room and bath and elegant kitchen facilities. Courtyard access and parking. $75-85.

R.S.V.P. Savannah B&B #13
(800) 729-7787 Mon.-Fri. 9:30-5:30

This lavishly furnished two-bedroom, two-bath town house with balcony overlooking Tidal Creek, has its own dock. All amenities including washer/dryer. Weekly and monthly rates $500-1000.

R.S.V.P. Savannah B&B #14
(800) 729-7787 Mon.-Fri. 9:30-5:30

In Savannah's low country, this rustic two-story cabin with two bedrooms faces Tidal Creek and has a boat mooring. Peace and quiet are assured. Full amenities. Weekly or monthly rates $400-800.

SENOIA

The Culpepper House
35 Broad Street, 30276
(404) 599-8182

Treat yourself to a whimsical Victorian adventure in this restored home located in a picturesque country town just 30 minutes south of Atlanta's airport.

Host: Mary A. Brown
Rooms: 4 (1 PB; 3 SB) $50-60
Continental or Full Breakfast
Credit Cards: None
Notes: 2, 5, 7 (limited), 8 (infants or over 10), 9, 10, 12

The Veranda
252 Seavy Street, P. O. Box 177, 30276-0177
(404) 599-3095

NOTES: Credit cards accepted: A Master Card; B Visa; C American Express; D Discover Card; E Diner's Club; F Other; 2 Personal Checks accepted; 3 Lunch available; 4 Dinner available; 5 Open all year;

Beautifully restored spacious Victorian rooms in a 1907 hotel on the National Register of Historic Places. Just 30 miles south of Atlanta airport. Freshly prepared southern gourmet meals by reservation. Unusual gift shop featuring kaleidoscopes. Memorabilia and 1930 Wurlitzer player piano pipe organ. One room has a whirlpool bath; all have private baths and air conditioning.

Hosts: Jan and Bobby Boal
Rooms: 9 (PB) $80-100
Full Breakfast
Credit Cards: A, B, C
Notes: 2, 3*, 4, 5, 8*,10*, 12*, 14 (*with advance inquiry)

THOMASVILLE

Evans House Bed and Breakfast

725 South Hansell Street, 31792
(912) 226-1343; Ans (912) 226-0654
FAX (912) 226-0653

In the Parkfront Historical District, this restored Victorian home is directly across from 27-acre Paradise Park near fine downtown antique shops and dining. Featuring four bedrooms and four private baths. Full breakfast served in the country kitchen. Bikes and many other amenities.

Host: Lee Puskar
Rooms: 4 (PB) $50-85
Full Breakfast
Credit Cards: None
Notes: 2, 5, 8, 9, 14

TIFTON

Myon Bed and Breakfast

Tifton, 31794
(912) 382-0959

A turn-of-the-century grand hotel. Rooms furnished with antiques and collectibles. Enjoy the amenities of this fine old building situated in historic downtown Tifton. Antiques and specialty shops are close by for your shopping pleasure.

Host: Regenia Wells
Rooms: 6 (PB) $40 plus
Continental Breakfast
Credit Cards: A, B, C
Notes: 2, 3, 5, 7, 8, 9

TOCCOA

Simmons Bond Inn

130 West Tugalo, 30577
(404) 886-8411

This asymmetrical Victorian home on the National Register of Historic Places was built in 1903 and is filled with beautiful oak throughout the downstairs. A work of art in itself, it is decorated with antiques, collectibles, and art from around the world. Open to the public for lunch five days a week and Sunday dinner. It is close to Lake Hartwell and is the southeastern gateway into the north Georgia mountains.

Hosts: Joni and Don Ferguson
Rooms: 3 (PB) $48-59
Continental Breakfast
Credit Cards: A, B, C, D
Notes: 2, 3, 4, 5, 6, 7, 8, 9, 14

6 Pets welcome; 7 Smoking allowed; 8 Children welcome; 9 Social drinking allowed; 10 Tennis available; 11 Swimming available; 12 Golf available; 13 Skiing available; 14 May be booked through travel agents.

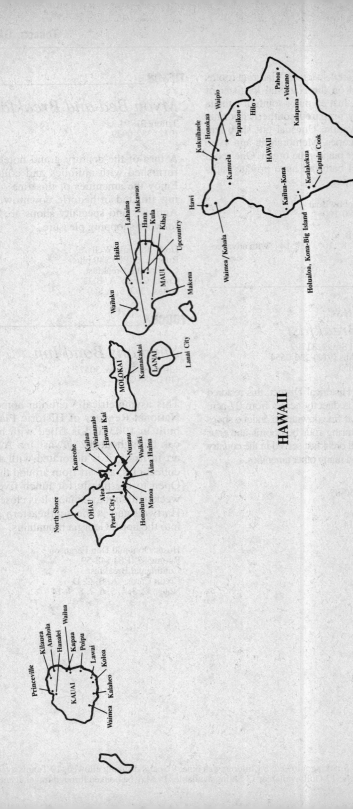

HAWAII

KAUAI

Princeville
Kilauea
Anahola
Hanalei
Wailua
Kapaa
Poipu
Lawai
Koloa
Waimea
Kalaheo

OHAU

North Shore
Kaneohe
Kailua
Waimanalo
Hawaii Kai
Nuuanu
Waikiki
Aina Haina
Manoa
Honolulu
Pearl City
Aiea

MOLOKAI

Kaunakakai

LANAI

Lanai City

MAUI

Wailuku
Haiku
Lahaina
Makawao
Hana
Kula
Kihei
Upcountry
Makena

HAWAII

Hawi
Kukuihaele
Honokaa
Waipio
Pahoa
Volcano
Papaikou
Hilo
Kalapana
Kamuela
Kailua-Kona
Keaukekua
Captain Cook
Waimea/Kohala
Keauhou, Kona-Big Island

Hawaii

Bed & Breakfast Hawaii H35

P. O. Box 449, Kapaa, 96746
(808) 822-7771

This bed and breakfast home is situated above the little town of Captain Cook. The accommodations offered are three bedrooms that share a bath. The home is an expanse of emerald lawn with many palms and exotic fruit trees. Guests are welcome to use the pool or watch TV. The hosts are helpful and interesting. $60.

Bed & Breakfast Hawaii H1

P. O. Box 449, Kapaa, 96746
(808) 822-7771

A large Hawaiian type house about two miles north of Hilo overlooking Hilo Bay, this home has a yard so private that if you decide to take a swim in the pool, only the birds will know. There are two bedrooms available to guests, each with a pair of twin beds, one which converts to a king-size bed, if desired. Not only is the yard beautifully landscaped around the pool, a lovely mile walk past the surfing beach meanders through a tropical forest. $55.

Bed & Breakfast Hawaii H1A

P. O. Box 449, Kapaa, 96746
(808) 822-7771

This host home is located right next door to host home H1, and guests are more than welcome to use the pool. The home is perched on the cliffs overlooking Hilo Bay and the Big Island's premier surfing spot. The house is small, and guests can choose a room with a private entrance and queen-size bed or a room with two twin beds. The bathroom between the two rooms is shared. Breakfast is served on the outdoor patio where guests can enjoy watching the sunrise, surfers, and ships. $45-55.

Bed & Breakfast Hawaii H2

P. O. Box 449, Kapaa, 96746
(808) 822-7771

Hale Paliku, which means "house against the cliff," is the name of this home originally built in the 1930s. Situated three blocks from downtown Hilo, guests share the TV, tape deck, microwave, and refrigerator. Two rooms with shared bath are available, one with ocean view and private balcony. Each room has down pillows, comforters, shuttered windows, and a table for two. Hosts live downstairs. $55-65.

Bed & Breakfast Hawaii H3

P. O. Box 449, Kapaa, 96746
(808) 822-7771

Relax on a grand scale in this large, modern, Hawaiian-style home surrounded by nearly four acres of parklike setting on an oceanfront bluff. With a spectacular view of Wailea Bay, this is the perfect spot for a

NOTES: Credit cards accepted: A Master Card; B Visa; C American Express; D Discover Card; E Diner's Club; F Other; 2 Personal Checks accepted; 3 Lunch available; 4 Dinner available; 5 Open all year; 6 Pets welcome; 7 Smoking allowed; 8 Children welcome; 9 Social drinking allowed; 10 Tennis available; 11 Swimming available; 12 Golf available; 13 Skiing available; 14 May be booked through travel agents.

peaceful haven. A tennis court and a municipal beach park are within walking distance, and the world-famous Akaka Falls is a short drive away. A spacious one-bedroom apartment includes bedroom, private bath, fully equipped kitchenette, and livingroom with cable TV, radio, piano, and day beds. Children over eight welcome. $75.

Bed & Breakfast Hawaii H3A

P. O. Box 449, Kapaa, 96746
(808) 822-7771

A charming little beachfront cottage surrounded by swaying coconut palms awaits guests. There is a nice beach and boat launch for guests to explore in a quiet, private setting. Guests can enjoy sitting out on the big lanai with ocean view or sitting on the rocks dangling their toes in the water while watching fishermen and sailboats. Two guest rooms with private bath. Resident dog. Two-night minimum stay. $75.

Bed & Breakfast Hawaii H4C

P. O. Box 449, Kapaa, 96746
(808) 822-7771

This bed and breakfast home is just three miles south of Hilo, near the zoo and equestrian center, on nine acres of parklike property. The home is in a secluded, private setting. Guests have a separate entrance to the cottage, which has light cooking facilities and a small glass fireplace. Breakfast supplies are provided. Three-night minimum stay. $75.

Bed & Breakfast Hawaii H5

P. O. Box 449, Kapaa, 96746
(808) 822-7771

A charming bed and breakfast host home that offers guests a view of Hilo Bay and Hilo town just ten minutes from the airport and 10 minutes to Richardson Beach. Guests are offered a choice of two rooms, both of which have private baths and ocean views. Breakfast is served in the breakfast nook or dining room, which is tastefully decorated with antiques. Smoking outside only. Children over 8 are welcome. $65.

Bed & Breakfast Hawaii H7

P. O. Box 449, Kapaa, 96746
(808) 822-7771

Right on a bluff overlooking the ocean, the home offers an oceanfront pool with Jacuzzi and a view of a popular surfing beach. Large, covered, comfortably furnished decks face the ocean where you can watch the whales and cruise ships. This modern home is just two miles from downtown Hilo but quiet and private. Three guest rooms with private baths are separated by a family room with TV, VCR, and a private entrance to the pool. The master suite is sometimes available. Minimum stay is three nights. $95.

Bed & Breakfast Hawaii H8

P. O. Box 449, Kapaa, 96746
(808) 822-7771

Paradise Place is the name of this accommodation on a rural acre just one-half mile from the ocean in Keaau. Accommodations are downstairs with a private entrance and consist of a two-room suite with a double bed in the bedroom, sofa sleeper in the livingroom, and private bath with a shower. This area also has a TV with VCR, microwave, small refrigerator, and table where host puts all the fixings for a leisurely breakfast served on a quiet landscaped patio. This area is a central location for a guest to explore the fresh lava flows and Volcano National Park. Seventh night is free. $50-55.

NOTES: Credit cards accepted: A Master Card; B Visa; C American Express; D Discover Card; E Diner's Club; F Other; 2 Personal Checks accepted; 3 Lunch available; 4 Dinner available; 5 Open all year;

Bed & Breakfast Hawaii H33

P. O. Box 449, Kapaa, 96746
(808) 822-7771

A rain forest retreat just south of Hilo is waiting next to an orchid nursery. Your hostess tends the orchids and boards horses on her property as well as accommodates bed and breakfast guests. A private studio complete with a king-size bed, private bath, and light cooking appliances (refrigerator, hot plate, and toaster oven). Guests are welcome to use the hot tub. This retreat is only thirty minutes away from Hilo and Volcano National Park. $45-60.

Bed & Breakfast Hawaii H42

P. O. Box 449, Kapaa, 96746
(808) 822-7771

Nestled in a tropical area in Pahoa, two studios can accommodate handicapped guests. Premises have a swimming pool, abundant fruit trees, flowers, and wild turkeys, pigs, and squabbling pigeons. The ranch unit has queen-size bed, private bath, air conditioning, TV, radio, private patio, and a refrigerator stocked with goodies. Hosts are former hoteliers on the main island and aim to please. Minimum stay is two nights. $65.

Bed & Breakfast Hawaii H45

P. O. Box 449, Kapaa, 96746
(808) 822-7771

Just between Hilo and Volcano, and twenty minutes from each. Guests are invited to stay with a charming hostess originally from England. An attractive two-story home with a portico and nicely landscaped grounds set in the rural area of Pahoa offers accommodations with twin beds and a private bath. Delicious breakfast is served in the dining room. Minimum stay is two nights. No smoking. $50.

Bed & Breakfast Hawaii H63

P. O. Box 449, Kapaa, 96746
(808) 822-7771

A detached studio apartment has a private bath and kitchenette. Hosts own an eight acre lot at 1,500-foot elevation above and three miles from Hawi. The view of the ocean is unobstructed, and access to the Alenuihaha Channel to Halaekala on Maui. The main house and the guest house are situated on the property. The guest house is furnished with a sofa bed and a double bed, color TV, and radio. Sliding glass doors overlook the view of the ocean. The kitchen is fully equipped for preparing all meals, and breakfast fixings are stocked in the refrigerator. Another studio attached to the main house has a separate entrance and private bath. $50-75.

Bed and Breakfast Honolulu (Statewide) KEGLS

3242 Kaohinani Drive, Honolulu, 96817
(808) 595-7533; (800) 288-4666

A five-minute walk to the center of Hilo, this home offers two guest rooms that share a bath. Livingroom for guests has TV, microwave, refrigerator, and ocean-mountain view. Breakfast is served on an enclosed porch. Smoking outside. Children over 12. From $45.

Bed and Breakfast Honolulu (Statewide) MILLS

3242 Kaohinani Drive, Honolulu, 96817
(808) 595-7533; (800) 288-4666

Large cedar home with four guest rooms (doubles and kings) just outside Hilo is within walking distance to shops and cafes. The king room has a private bath. All guest rooms have private lanais so that you can enjoy a tropical view and the stream that runs through the half-acre tropical setting.

6 Pets welcome; 7 Smoking allowed; 8 Children welcome; 9 Social drinking allowed; 10 Tennis available; 11 Swimming available; 12 Golf available; 13 Skiing available; 14 May be booked through travel agents.

Common room for guests has a TV, fireplace, and piano. Hearty breakfast served. Smoking outside. Children over 11. From $40.

Bed and Breakfast Honolulu (Statewide) MERCE

3242 Kaohinani Drive, Honolulu, 96817
(808) 595-7533; (800) 288-4666

Two guest rooms with private baths in a pretty country setting are five minutes outside Keaau and a twenty-minute drive to Hilo. Guests are welcome to use the spacious livingroom and enjoy the lovely views. Full breakfast is served. No small children. Hosts speak French and some Italian. From $40.

Bed and Breakfast Honolulu (Statewide) LANNA

3242 Kaohinani Drive, Honolulu, 96817
(808) 595-7533; (800) 288-4666

Two miles out of Hilo on a cliff overlooking Hilo Bay, this Hawaiian-type home has a private yard with a lovely pool. Two bedrooms are available. A full bath and a half bath are reserved for guests. The yard is beautifully landscaped, and there's also a charming tea house on the grounds. Children and smokers accepted. From $55.

Hale Kai-Bjornen

111 Honolii Pali, 96720
(808) 935-6330

A beautiful four-star bed and breakfast on the bluff facing the ocean, surfing beach, and Hilo Bay. Two miles from downtown Hilo, yet quiet and private. Hale Kai-Bjornen offers a swimming pool and Jacuzzi, large deck, and bar room. All rooms face the ocean and offer private baths and cable TV. Three miles away are Rainbow Falls and Botanical Gardens; nine miles away is Akaka Falls and thirty miles away are the volcanos and Waipo Valley. Your hostess and host are very friendly and ready to help direct you. Excellent restaurants nearby and guest cottages with kitchen facilities are also available. Minimum stay is three nights.

Hosts: Evonne Bjornen and Paw Tallett
Rooms: 5 (PB) $80-105
Full Deluxe Breakfast
Credit Cards: None
Notes: 2, 5, 7 (outside), 8 (over 12), 9, 11, 12, 14

HAWAII—HOLUALOA

Holualoa Inn

P. O. Box 222, 96725
(800) 392-1812; (808) 324-1121
FAX (808) 322-2472

An architectural masterpiece of cedar and eucalyptus flooring with a spectacular view of the Kona coast. Forty acres of coffee plantation and pastures surround this estate house for quiet seclusion, yet the art galleries of Holualoa are a short walk away and Kailua-Kona is a 15 minute drive down the mountain. Guests may enjoy a swim in the tiled pool, a game of billiards by the fireplace, or a legendary Kona sunset from the stone pool deck.

Host: Desmond Twigg-Smith
Rooms: 4 (PB) $100-150
Full Breakfast
Credit Cards: A, B, C
Notes: 2, 5, 9, 10, 11, 12, 14

HAWAII—HONOKAA

Bed & Breakfast Hawaii H11

P. O. Box 449, Kapaa, 96746
(808) 822-7771

The hostess of this large plantation estate enjoys having guests share its beauty and tranquility. With ocean views on three sides, the estate is built on an ocean point at the 1,200-foot level just outside of

Honokaa. The main house offers three guest accommodations; a large suite with fireplace, an adjoining bedroom, private lanai, and private bath; a queen room with private bath, 12-foot ceilings, and tongue-and-groove woodwork. There are also two cottages on the property. Lighted tennis courts, gazebo, macadamia orchard, fruit trees, and lush tropical flowers throughout the estate. $75-200.

Waipio Wayside Bed and Breakfast Inn

P. O. Box 840, 96727
(808) 775-0275; (800) 833-8849

Step back in time and experience the gracious hospitality of a 1938 sugar plantation home. Waipio Wayside Bed and Breakfast Inn has been renovated and decorated to preserve the charm and character of old Hawaii. It provides a relaxing and peaceful retreat, catering to those who wish to unwind in a warm and comfortable atmosphere. Guests are encouraged to stroll around the lush grounds enjoying beautiful tropical gardens, relax on the deck, or watch the sunset from the gazebo.

Host: Jacqueline Horne
Rooms: 5 (2 PB; 3 PB) $55-85
Full Breakfast
Credit Cards: A, B, E
Notes: 2, 5, 8, 9, 10, 11, 12, 14

HAWAII—KAILUA-KONA

Bed & Breakfast Hawaii H10

P. O. Box 449, Kapaa, 96746
(808) 822-7771

These warm-hearted hosts have a spacious home surrounded by tropical foliage about a five-minute drive from the ocean. The downstairs accommodation includes a private lanai with an ocean view and a separate entrance through glass doors to the bedroom. The room is large and has a minirefrigerator, a microwave, TV, and

phone. A tasty continental breakfast is served. No smoking. Two-night minimum stay. $65.

Bed & Breakfast Hawaii H13

P. O. Box 449, Kapaa, 96746
(808) 822-7771

A homey atmosphere with beauty. Two bedrooms can accommodate four traveling together. The private bath is between the two rooms. Conveniently situated on Highway 11 close to the new Keauhou Shopping Center and Kahaluu Beach, known for its fine snorkeling. No smoking. Two-night minimum stay. $50.

Bed & Breakfast Hawaii H15

P. O. Box 449, Kapaa, 96746
(808) 822-7771

In a large, homey residence on a hillside neighborhood of Kailua-Kona guests are offered a bedroom with queen bed and private bath. The view from the bedroom looks out over an exotic flower garden including gardenias, roses, night-blooming jasmine, and the expansive coastline of Kona. Fresh fruits from the garden are usually served in the sunny breakfast room or on the deck. The enthusiastic hosts devote their energies to their guests. Two-night minimum stay. $55.

Bed & Breakfast Hawaii H23

P. O. Box 449, Kapaa, 96746
(808) 822-7771

You are invited to share the magnificent panoramic view from this hillside home. Bed and breakfast guests can choose between the Hula Room, with queen-size bed and large, private lanai, and the Garden Room, with two twin beds. Both have TV, microwave, and small refrigerator. Smoking outside only. $50-55.

6 Pets welcome; 7 Smoking allowed; 8 Children welcome; 9 Social drinking allowed; 10 Tennis available; 11 Swimming available; 12 Golf available; 13 Skiing available; 14 May be booked through travel agents.

Bed & Breakfast Hawaii H26

P. O. Box 449, Kapaa, 96746
(808) 822-7771

Escape to the peaceful hillside of Hualalai Mountain overlooking the Kona coast. The interior of this lovely 2,500-square-foot home is meticulously furnished. The guest quarters are on the first level and have two bedrooms, with one bath and a kitchen and living area. There is a large deck for guests' exclusive use. Breakfast fixings are provided. Two-night minimum stay. $65.

Bed & Breakfast Hawaii H29

P. O. Box 449, Kapaa, 96746
(808) 822-7771

Guests can stay at this peaceful bed and breakfast just two miles from the middle of Kailua-Kona town and the ocean. A large covered lanai offers ocean views and comfortable seating for breakfast. The accommodation is furnished with twin beds, which can convert to a king-size bed, and a private bath. Your hosts are recently retired and enjoy serving breakfast and meeting new people. No smoking. $40-55.

Bed & Breakfast Hawaii H32A

P. O. Box 449, Kapaa, 96746
(808) 822-7771

Right on the beach in Kona is this luxurious and comfortable oceanfront home. Two rooms are available; one is oceanfront with a queen-size bed, and the other is ocean, view with a queen-size bed. Both have full private baths and a color TV. Hostess loves to play tennis and meet new people. No smoking. $70-90.

Bed & Breakfast Hawaii H34

P. O. Box 449, Kapaa, 96746
(808) 822-7771

Situated just 12 minutes from the airport and 15 minutes from Kailua Village in the cool Kaloko Mauka area is this beautiful new home on five acres. It offers an attractive separate apartment at garden level with two bedrooms, bath, and sitting room with TV and limited cooking facilities. Guests may choose to breakfast with their hosts or on their own. After a busy day of sports, shopping, or sightseeing, sit on the lanai high above the Kona coast and enjoy the magnificent sunset. Resident dog, cats, and llamas. Two-night minimum stay. No smoking. $75.

Bed & Breakfast Hawaii H44

P. O. Box 449, Kapaa, 96746
(808) 822-7771

A charming guest cottage awaits guests very near Kailua Bay and village. Relax in the private courtyard with a lovely garden view. Through sliding glass doors, the one-bedroom cottage offers a bedroom with queen-size bed and private bath, TV, VCR, and stereo. The kitchenette offers a full refrigerator, microwave, coffee pot, toaster oven, and blender. Great for a small family. Hosts have two children and welcome families with children. Beach equipment is available, and tennis courts are close by. Two-night minimum stay. $65; $350 weekly.

Bed & Breakfast Hawaii H46

P. O. Box 449, Kapaa, 96746
(808) 822-7771

Elegant, brand new, with an ocean view. Guests will enjoy this accommodation in Kona separate from the main house. One bedroom with a queen bed and full bathroom, plus a sitting area with TV, is decorated in off-white with rose-colored accents. There is also a dining area with a refrigerator and wet bar. Private deck. No smoking. Two-night minimum stay. $75.

Bed & Breakfast Hawaii H50

P. O. Box 449, Kapaa, 96746
(808) 822-7771

This bed and breakfast has a private entrance on the lower level of this beautiful, brand-new, two-story Art Deco home. Guests have a choice of two large bedrooms, with access to the gardens that offer a beautiful ocean view. A special aloha breakfast is served in the family room that is furnished with a piano, pool, and Ping-Pong tables, and big-screen TV. A great location for two couples traveling together. $50-80.

Bed & Breakfast Hawaii H59

P. O. Box 449, Kapaa, 96746
(808) 822-7771

Guests can experience one of the many breathtaking sunsets from this bed and breakfast overlooking the coastline just above Kona Village. Located on a three-acre estate, the accommodations for guests are private and self-contained. A separate apartment features one bedroom with a queen-size bed, livingroom with a fold-out sofa, private bath, kitchen, TV, private entrance, and lanai with a barbecue. A queen-size futon is also available. The building is designed like a dome with open beam ceilings. Smoking outside only, please. $65-85.

Bed & Breakfast Hawaii H60

P. O. Box 449, Kapaa, 96746
(808) 822-7771

For the traveller who enjoys the comforts of luxurious accommodations, this Kailua plantation house offers oceanfront and ocean-view suites, all of which have a private lanai that overlooks the ocean, spa, and pool. The house is elegantly decorated and air conditioned. Each of the five guest rooms is unique, and offers a variety of bed sizes, and one guest room has a whirlpool tub and bidet. All the rooms have a TV, telephone, small refrigerator, and daily maid service. $120-175

Bed and Breakfast Honolulu (Statewide) FREIS

242 Kaohinani Drive, Honolulu, 96817
(808) 595-7533; (800) 288-4666

Beautiful new two-story home overlooking the ocean with three large guest rooms (queen, king and twin beds). King room has a private bath; queen and twin rooms share a bath. Special Aloha breakfast is served in the family room, which is furnished with a piano, pool table, Ping Pong, big screen TV, wet bar, and refrigerator for drinks or snacks. Great for couples traveling together. No smoking. No children. From $50.

Hale Malia Bed and Breakfast

Go Native...Hawaii
P. O. Box 11418, Hilo, 96721
(800)662-8483

This magnificent island home by the ocean was built in the old plantation style. There is an oceanfront lanai that runs the length of the house on which breakfast is served. This wonderful bed and breakfast has Victorian decor, two guest rooms with in-suite baths, and queen-size beds. A beckoning sandy beach complements this Aloha accommodation. $70-90.

Kailua Plantation House

75-5948 Alii Dr.
Kailua-Kona, 96740
(800)329-3727

Kailua Plantation House is a tropical haven for travelers seeking Luxurious accommodations with the coziness of an oceanfront

6 Pets welcome; 7 Smoking allowed; 8 Children welcome; 9 Social drinking allowed; 10 Tennis available; 11 Swimming available; 12 Golf available; 13 Skiing available; 14 May be booked through travel agents.

bed and breakfast inn. Each individually decorated suite in this lovely mansion boasts a private lanai. Complete with its own outdoor dipping pool and spa, both overlooking the Pacific Ocean, Kailua Plantation House is an elegant lodging choice for island guests. Located less than 1 mile form the town of Kona, the inn is a short drive or walk from fine restaurants, shops, snorkeling, and diving establishments.

Host: Lisa J. Berger
Rooms: 5 (PB) $120-175
Continental Plus Breakfast
Credit Cards: A, B, C
Notes: 2, 5,

Luna Kai Bed and Breakfast

Go Native...Hawaii
P. O. Box 11418, Hilo, 96721
(800) 662-8483

Situated in popular Kailua-Kona, choice accommodations in either a self-contained cottage or delightful studio. The cottage is nestled in a tropical garden, is designer-decorated, and has king bed, private bath, and outside lanai. A studio is below the main house. A wonderful continental breakfast is served on a carpeted open lanai overlooking a 180-degree view of Kailua Bay and the Kona coastline. $75.

Mauna 'Ikini Bed and Breakfast

Go Native...Hawaii
P. O. Box 11418, Hilo, 96721
(800) 662-8483

Bed and breakfast in an almost new, two-story cedar home about three miles above Kailua town center. Guest quarters are situated on the lower level of the home. Accommodations include a two-bedroom apartment unit. Private bath, complete kitchen, and living area with a large deck. Hot tub for guests. Also color cable TV and radio. Continental breakfast. $55.

HAWAII—KAMUELA

Bed & Breakfast Hawaii H27A

P. O. Box 449, Kapaa, 96746
(808) 822-7771

The host and hostess have a 4,000-square-foot home and have used about 800 square feet of it for a completely separate apartment for guests. Guest quarters include a bedroom, private bath, and livingroom. There is also a sink and small refrigerator. The home borders a stream and has a 360-degree view of the Kohala Mountains, Pacific Ocean, and the famous Mauna Kea and Mauna Loa. Three-night minimum stay. $80-90.

Bed & Breakfast Hawaii H41

P. O. Box 449, Kapaa, 96746
(808) 822-7771

In the historic area of North Kohala just about seven miles from lush Pololu Valley and the rugged coastline of beautiful Hawaii, guests can enjoy the rural atmosphere and cooler climate. The home is set back from the road and is a modified A-frame. Accommodations include a self-contained studio under the main house with a separate entrance, limited kitchenette, private bath, and double bed. No smoking. Two-night minimum stay. $50.

Bed & Breakfast Hawaii H57

P. O. Box 449, Kapaa, 96746
(808) 822-7771

This newly built guest house with 1,900 square feet is located at the top of Knob Hill, and within walking distance to Kamuela. It offers beautiful views of twenty-five miles of coastline, Mauna Kea and Mauna Loa, and the accommodations border Parker Ranch. Two bedrooms, with queen and king beds, full bathroom, 300-square-foot deck, color TV, library, washer/dryer. Three night minimum stay. $125.

NOTES: Credit cards accepted: A Master Card; B Visa; C American Express; D Discover Card; E Diner's Club; F Other; 2 Personal Checks accepted; 3 Lunch available; 4 Dinner available; 5 Open all year;

Bed & Breakfast Hawaii H62

P. O. Box 449, Kapaa, 96746
(808) 822-7771

This bed and breakfast is part of Swiss chalet-style home just three and one-half miles from Kamuela and twelve minutes from Hapuna Beach. Accommodations consist of a two bedroom apartment, and each bedroom has a queen-size bed. Full bath, a livingroom with a fireplace, TV, and telephone included. Enjoy views of Mauna Kea and the ocean from the private sun deck.

Bed and Breakfast Honolulu (Statewide) BATEG

3242 Kaohinani Drive, Honolulu, 96817
(808) 595-7533; (800) 288-4666

Parker Ranch country. This Hawaiian missionary-style home is by a quiet, meandering stream. Completely private guest quarters contain bedroom, livingroom, light cooking facilities, and a full bath. Guests have a 360-degree view of famous Mauna Kea and Mauna Loa mountains and the blue Pacific. Hosts are widely traveled. He is a sailing enthusiast; and she spins, weaves, and does basketweaving. From $65.

Bed and Breakfast Honolulu (Statewide) DICKD

3242 Kaohinani Drive, Honolulu, 96817
(808) 595-7533; (800) 288-4666

This lovely bed and breakfast home is a three-mile country drive from Waimea. Two beautiful guest rooms (queen and double) and a lovely suite with private entrance and antique twin beds. Livingroom has fireplace and quiet music. Breakfast is served each morning. No children. Smoking outside only. $65.

Kamuela Inn

P. O. Box 1994, 96743
(808) 885-4243; FAX (808) 885-8857

Comfortable, cozy rooms and suites with private baths, with or without kitchenettes, all with color cable television. Continental breakfast served in a sunny lanai each morning. Situated in a quiet, peaceful setting near shops, parks, museums, and restaurants. Hawaii's white sand beaches, golfing, and valley and mountain tours are only minutes away.

Host: Carolyn Cascavilla
Rooms: 31 (PB) $54-165
Continental Breakfast
Credit Cards: A, B, C, D, E
Notes: 2, 5, 7, 8, 14

Morningstar Meadow

P. O. Box 2396, 96743
(808) 885-7674

Guests receive warm aloha with their choice of attentive service or considerate privacy at this gracious, upcountry home near famous Parker Ranch. Full gourmet breakfasts featuring fresh island products and produce offered with silver coffee pot service in bay-windowed room overlooking meadow where horses graze. Convenient to beaches, fine restaurants, waterfalls, myriad natural scenic attractions and trails. Golf, tennis, horseback riding, antiquing, polo, and rodeos nearby.

Host: Dee Dickson
Rooms: 3 (2 PB; 1 SB) $65-75, plus tax
Full Breakfast
Credit Cards: None
Notes: 2, 5, 9, 10, 11, 12, 13, 14

HAWAII—KEALAKEKUA

Bed & Breakfast Hawaii H28A

P. O. Box 449, Kapaa, 96746
(808) 822-7771

---

6 Pets welcome; 7 Smoking allowed; 8 Children welcome; 9 Social drinking allowed; 10 Tennis available; 11 Swimming available; 12 Golf available; 13 Skiing available; 14 May be booked through travel agents.

This bed and breakfast home is about thirty minutes from the airport at a 1,300-foot elevation overlooking the Pacific Ocean, Kailua-Kona, Kailua Bay, and the western slopes of Hualalai. The garden-level accommodations are large and offer a suite with two bedrooms, each with a queen-size bed, a livingroom with cable TV, full bathroom, and a large dressing table. The unit has a separate lanai and entrance. Breakfast is served upstairs on the host's lanai, which also provides beautiful views of the ocean and towns below. Minimum stay is two nights. $50-55.

Bed & Breakfast Hawaii H38

P. O. Box 449, Kapaa, 96746
(808) 822-7771

This is an unusual and beautifully designed home with hardwood floors, decks, and lots of windows with screens. This two-story home is just 200 yards from Napoopoo Bay, a great area for swimming and snorkeling. Downstairs, two separate bedrooms with private baths and queen-size beds share a sitting room with a covered deck that views the ocean. $75.

Bed & Breakfast Hawaii H52

P. O. Box 449, Kapaa, 96746
(808) 822-7771

This privately owned Hawaiian compound, which is fully contained on eight acres of lush tropical fruit trees, has a large rambling ranch house with an annex for guests. One room offers a queen-size bed, and the other offers two twin bed. A bathroom situated between the two rooms is shared. Cottages for families are also available. The grounds feature outdoor barbecue pit, tropical grass huts for picnics, sand volleyball court, tennis courts and a large pool. Host's lanai, where breakfast is served, has a spectacular view of the ocean. Two-night minimum stay. $65-100.

HAWAII—KOHALA

Bed and Breakfast Honolulu (Statewide) CHAPD

3242 Kaohinani Drive, Honolulu, 96817
(808) 595-7533; (800) 288-4666

At the tip of the Big Island in the old Hawaiian town of Hawi sits this complete, private downstairs unit. On three and one-half acres of pastoral land. Enjoy breakfast served on the lanai, and view Waimea ranch lands, horses, cows, and the blue Pacific. Private entrance and bath, refrigerator, coffee maker, TV, and twin beds. A swimming beach is three miles away. Hike to the king's birthplace or a sacred Heiau. Children over 12 welcome. Smokers accepted. From $50.

HAWAII—KONA

Bed and Breakfast Honolulu (Statewide) BOONW

3242 Kaohinani Drive, Honolulu, 96817
(808) 595-7533; (800) 288-4666

This home is on an expanse of emerald lawn with palms and exotic fruit trees. It is fenced along the road with head-high poinsettias and is surrounded by a wall of banana trees among groves of coffee and macadamias. Take a swim in the pool, play tennis nearby, or go to one of the nearby beaches. Three rooms share a bath. Generous continental breakfast includes homemade breads. Enjoy bicycling, Ping-Pong, or hiking with the hosts. Resident dog. From $55.

Bed and Breakfast Honolulu (Statewide) DEFAC

3242 Kaohinani Drive, Honolulu, 96817
(808) 595-7533; (800) 288-4666

NOTES: Credit cards accepted: A Master Card; B Visa; C American Express; D Discover Card; E Diner's Club; F Other; 2 Personal Checks accepted; 3 Lunch available; 4 Dinner available; 5 Open all year;

This Kona-style home is on the slopes above the City of Refuge. King bed, bath, and refrigerator for snacks are in the separate guest quarters on the ground level. Breakfast is served upstairs on the 50-foot lanai with a panoramic view of the ocean. Enjoy the cool, quiet, private half-acre of gardens. From $60.

Bed and Breakfast Honolulu (Statewide) RITZA

3242 Kaohinani Drive, Honolulu, 96817
(808) 595-7533; (800) 288-4666

This lovely home is situated on the slopes above the City of Refuge in Hanaunau. View of the ocean from the dining lanai and the hot tub. Hosts offer four rooms, two on the garden level with TV, VCR, refrigerator, microwave, and private bath and entrance. The room on the main level has a queen bed and shares a bath with the loft room. Rooms decorated with local art. From $55.

The Dragonfly Ranch: Tropical Fantasy Lodging

P. O. Box 675, 96726
(808) 328-9570; (800) 487-2159

The Dragonfly Ranch is located on the Big Island's sunny Kona Coast near playful dolphins and magical snorkeling. This peaceful country estate offers tropical fantasy lodging with the elegant simplicity of openness and privacy in a lush jungle setting. Each unique suite has an ocean view, private outdoor shower and indoor bathroom, cable TV/VCR, and food preparation areas. Ideal for reunions, weddings, and romantic honeymoons.

Host: Barbara Moore-Link and David Link
Rooms: 5 (3 PB; 2 SB) $50-140
Continental Breakfast
Credit Cards: A, B
Notes: 2, 5, 7(outside), 8, 9, 10, 11, 12, 13, 14

HAWAII—KUKUIHAELE

Bed and Breakfast Honolulu (Statewide) HUNTK

3242 Kaohinani Drive, Honolulu, 96817
(808) 595-7533; (800) 288-4666

Privacy! Your own home with a fantastic view in a small village above Waipio Valley. Walk 15 minutes to Waipio lookout, take a hiking adventure in the valley, or go horseback riding and come home to a hot tub. The home includes a livingroom with queen bed, futon upstairs, a fireplace, and kitchen. Watch the whales and the sunset. Listen to the year-round stream. Very romantic! Large screened porch. From $60.

HAWAII—PAHOA

Aloha Bed and Continental Breakfast

Go Native...Hawaii
P. O. Box 11418, Hilo, 96721
(800) 662-8483

Here in the rain forest near Volcanoes National Park is a new (1990) California country-style bed and breakfast, a designer's delight with open-beam ceilings and all-white interior. Guests may choose from an in-home self-contained studio (sleeps up to four) with private entrance and bath, queen bed, and refrigerator, or the lovely guest house, equally equipped, in the grand courtyard. There is even a splendid pool with fountain and footbath! $78.

Kalani Honua by the Sea

Ocean Road #137, 96778
(808) 965-7828; (800) 800-6886

Kalani Honua welcomes guests to a pleasant country retreat. Cozy lodges and cottages provide simple, comfortable accommodations on twenty secluded oceanfront,

---

6 Pets welcome; 7 Smoking allowed; 8 Children welcome; 9 Social drinking allowed; 10 Tennis available; 11 Swimming available; 12 Golf available; 13 Skiing available; 14 May be booked through travel agents.

landscaped acres of paradise on the Big Island. Delicious, healthful meals and a variety of educational and cultural programs. Individuals and groups (to 100) are welcome. Facilities for conferences, classes, sports, and spa relaxation. Near secluded beaches, snorkel tide-pools, warm springs, and natural steam baths.

Hosts: Richard Koob and Hillary Mayall
Rooms: 38 (12 PB; 26 SB) $20-80
Full Breakfast
Credit Cards: A, B, C, E, F
Notes: 3, 4, 5, 7 (limited), 8, 9, 10, 11, 12, 14

Kalani Honua by the Sea

HAWAII—VOLCANO

Bed & Breakfast Hawaii H51

P. O. Box 449, Kapaa, 96746
(808) 822-7771

Conveniently situated just two miles from Volcanoes National Park at 3,500-foot elevation. Helpful hosts offer a king-size bedroom with its own entrance and private bath. A futon can be put down for a third person. Great breakfasts are served every morning to get you off to a good start for exploring the park. $55.

Bed & Breakfast Hawaii H51A

P. O. Box 449, Kapaa, 96746
(808) 822-7771

Also available in H51 are three cottages. Guests check in with hosts and receive keys. The refrigerator and kitchen are stocked with breakfast foods more than ample for a week's stay. Choose from one of three cottages-The Dome, Grand Cedar, or Cedar One. All are plush and beautifully furnished with fireplaces, TV with VCR, and stereos. $85-125.

Bed and Breakfast Honolulu (Statewide) MORSG

3242 Kaohinani Drive, Honolulu, 96817
(808) 595-7533; (800) 288-4666

This historic home, circa 1889, is on a seven-acre estate. The drive is the original road from Volcano to Hilo. Volcanoes National Park (and eruptions), golf, hiking, museum, art, and helicopter tours are nearby. Rooms on each of the three floors have queen and single beds. All baths shared. The main livingroom has a fireplace, TV, Hawaiian library, and all the macadamia nuts you can eat. A cottage is available with three rooms, private entrance, and lanai. The studio has a fully equipped kitchen, TV, and phone. The host serves a full hearty breakfast from 6:00 to 9:00 a.m. Children and smokers welcome. Resident dog. From $35.

Kilauea Lodge

P. O. Box 116, 96785
(808) 967-7366; FAX (808) 967-7367

Charming mountain lodge situated one mile from Volcanoes National Park. Full service dining room with excellent wine list. Full breakfast readies guests for an active day of hiking and viewing the wonders of Pele, the volcano goddess. All private baths. Twelve rooms, six rooms with fireplace. Common area.

Rooms: 12 (PB) $85-125
Full Breakfast
Credit Cards: A, B
Notes: 2, 4, 5, 8, 9, 12

My Island Bed and Breakfast

P. O. Box 100, 96785
(808) 967-7216; FAX (808) 967-7719

Situated at a 3,800-foot elevation, this historic missionary home was built in 1886 and has a large botanical garden that blooms year-round. Five different rooms for singles, couples, or families. Host is an island-born native. Specially prepared maps and hiking guides to explore four different areas from this overnight spot. The specialty is a full, all-you-can-eat breakfast and all the macadamia nuts you can eat.

Hosts: Gordon and Joann Morse
Rooms: 5 (3 PB; 2 SB) $50-65
Full Breakfast
Credit Cards: None
Notes: 2, 5, 7, 8, 9, 14

Kilauea Lodge

HAWAII—WAIMEA

Bed & Breakfast Hawaii H43

P. O. Box 449, Kapaa, 96746
(808) 822-7771

Still the best kept secret on the Big Island, this area above Waimea (Kamuela) is very peaceful and rural. Situated in Hawi, this bed and breakfast is a large 89-year-old home set back in a secluded, rural atmosphere. The accommodations include two bedrooms with a private bath in between. The smaller of the two rooms offers a separate entrance and a double bed, and the other room is larger and can sleep three. No smoking. Children welcome. Outside pets. $45-$50.

HAWAII—WAIPIO

Bed & Breakfast Hawaii H22

P. O. Box 449, Kapaa, 96746
(808) 822-7771

Step back in time and experience the gracious hospitality of a 1938 sugar plantation home, renovated to preserve its character. Each bedroom is individually decorated with antique furniture, Chinese rugs, and exquisite hand-painted silk drapes. Breakfast includes pure Kona coffee and fine Stash teas. $85.

KAUAI—ANAHOLA

Bed & Breakfast Hawaii K67

P. O. Box 449, Kapaa, 96746
(808) 822-7771

Wake up in beautiful tropical surroundings at Anahola Beach abundant with flowers, fresh fruit, singing birds, and sounds of the ocean. Enjoy beautiful views and beach atmosphere in this bright studio with private yard and entrance, full bath, and breakfast facilities. The home is situated across the street from a beach great for swimming, snorkeling, boogie boarding, and wind surfing. Convenient to all Kauai attractions. Tropical continental breakfast fixings provided. Two-night minimum stay. $75.

Bed and Breakfast Honolulu (Statewide) SKAGJ

3242 Kaohinani Drive, Honolulu, 96817
(808) 595-7533; (800) 288-4666

On the beach for a peaceful vacation or a romantic honeymoon! Private studio with TV, laundry facilities, and ready for light cooking. Continental breakfast fixings are provided. Centrally situated for sightseeing and touring. The beach is reef-protected for swimming. Sun on the white sands, sit in your private yard and enjoy the tropical birds, flowers, trees, and the mountain view, or take a walk in the hills and valleys behind the home. Adults preferred. From $70.

KAUAI—HANALEI

Bed & Breakfast Hawaii K13

P. O. Box 449, Kapaa, 96746
(808) 822-7771

Your hosts' brand new and beautiful house is built on one and one-half acres. The community offers a 45-hole golf course, clubhouse, athletic club, tennis, swimming, and driving range just minutes away. Breakfast is served in the dining room or on the decks overlooking the Pacific. All rooms have private entrances, ceiling fans, refrigerators, and color TVs. Choose from three rooms—one a honeymoon suite with whirlpool tub, one a penthouse with whirlpool and balcony. Two-night minimum stay. $85-190.

Bed & Breakfast Hawaii K21

P. O. Box 449, Kapaa, 96746
(808) 822-7771

This hostess offers to share her beach house right on Anini Beach with visitors. She is a world traveler and has a natural affinity for travelers. Her home is halfway between Kilauea and Hanalei, and the room offered has a double bed, shared bath. There is large covered porch for relaxing and viewing the sunsets of the north shore. Two-night minimum stay. $40.

Bed & Breakfast Hawaii K32

P. O. Box 449, Kapaa, 96746
(808) 822-7771

This accommodation is a little backwards: the hosts live in the apartment above the garage while the guests stay in the main house. Just steps from the beach, a beautiful two-mile crescent-shaped bay surrounded by lush mountains and waterfalls. Two bedrooms share one and one-half baths, plus an outdoor shower for after the beach. The livingroom has open beam ceilings, wood floors, rattan furniture, cable TV, and a complete library. Five-night minimum stay. $100.

Bed & Breakfast Hawaii K45

P. O. Box 449, Kapaa, 96746
(808) 822-7771

This bed and breakfast accommodation is situated 100 yards from the gorgeous Hanalei Bay. Perfect for hiking, watersports, sightseeing, golf, sunbathing, or just long walks in a quaint, unpretentious town. Sunsets from the lanai are breathtaking. A two-story home with 1,000 square feet of deck surrounding the second floor and providing a partial ocean view and a mountain view of waterfalls. A continental breakfast of fresh island fruit, juice, and breads is served on the second-story lanai. $55-75.

Bed & Breakfast Hawaii K46

P. O. Box 449, Kapaa, 96746
(808) 822-7771

This spacious new country home and guest quarters offer comfort and a spectacular view of the Hanalei Valley. Enjoy the sunsets, the mountain waterfalls, and the peace of this special location. The guest bedroom has a king bed, a microwave, sink, refrigerator, and private bath. On five and one-half acres. Three-night minimum stay. $70.

Bed and Breakfast Honolulu (Statewide) BARNC

3242 Kaohinani Drive, Honolulu, 96817
(808) 595-7533; (800) 288-4666

NOTES: Credit cards accepted: A Master Card; B Visa; C American Express; D Discover Card; E Diner's Club; F Other; 2 Personal Checks accepted; 3 Lunch available; 4 Dinner available; 5 Open all year;

This lovely home has three units. The guest room with private bath and queen bed; a downstairs one-bedroom apartment with light cooking facilities, TV, private patio, and garden with ocean view; and the third-floor unit that sleeps four. View Hanalei Bay. Sunset and waterfall views are dramatic through the cathedral windows. Livingroom TV is available for guests. The beach is 100 yards away. Bright and airy with pine and wicker. Children over 12 welcome. Three-night minimum stay. From $70.

KAUAI—KALAHEO

Bed & Breakfast Hawaii K18A

P. O. Box 449, Kapaa, 96746
(808) 822-7771

A self-contained apartment awaits guests here in the hills of Kalaheo with a sweeping ocean view. This apartment offers a queen bed, a livingroom, private bath, and full kitchen. Only five minutes from the golf course and a 15-minute drive to Poipu Beach. Two-night minimum stay. $60.

Bed & Breakfast Hawaii K19

P. O. Box 449, Kapaa, 96746
(808) 822-7771

Three bedrooms open onto a swimming pool flanked by flowering hibiscus, gardenias, and bougainvillaeas in this home nestled in the hills of South Kauai. Out back, a second-story wooden porch overlooks sugar cane fields, jungle, and the National Botanical Gardens. It is only a 7- to 20-minute drive to beaches. All rooms have private baths, and one room is handicapped accessible. The hostess is proud of her breakfast that includes homemade bread and hot muffins, Hawaiian fruits, and Hawaiian coffee. No smoking. $55-75, seasonal.

Bed and Breakfast Hawaii K84

P. O. Box 449, Kapaa, 96746
(808) 822-7771

A serene landscape in Lawai is the setting for this separate one-room cottage set apart from the main house. Inside is a separate little kitchenette and private bath. The livingroom features a brand-new Serta queen size sofa-bed and a full-size futon. Hostess is an activities director, so she can give great sight seeing tips. $65-75.

Bed and Breakfast Hawaii K85

P. O. Box 449, Kapaa, 96746
(808) 822-7771

Mango Hills Cottage is situated on two and one-half acres in Kalaheo overlooking the ocean and many acres of coffee fields. The hostess is an interior designer, and her attention to details inside the cottage is apparent. The livingroom has a pull-out queen-size sofa bed, cable TV, and an adjoining full kitchen with counter seating. The bedroom has a mountain view and a queen-size bed with adjoining bath. Hosts invite you to swim in their pool or relax in a hammock under flowering trees. Minimum stay is three nights. $65.

Bed and Breakfast Honolulu (Statewide) GROWR

3242 Kaohinani Drive, Honolulu, 96817
(808) 595-7533; (800) 288-4666

Minutes away from major attractions in the countryside of Kalaheo on the garden island of Kauai are delightful, self-contained cottages. These unique units feature antique stained-glass leaded windows and all the comforts of home. Fully furnished, complete kitchens, TVs, and daily linen service. Ten minutes by car to the golden beaches of the sunny south shore of Poipu. Five minutes to Kukuiolono Golf Course.

---

6 Pets welcome; 7 Smoking allowed; 8 Children welcome; 9 Social drinking allowed; 10 Tennis available; 11 Swimming available; 12 Golf available; 13 Skiing available; 14 May be booked through travel agents.

Classic Vacation Cottages

2687 Onu Place, P. O. Box 901, Kalaheo, 96741
(808)332-9201

Minutes away from major attractions in the countryside of Kalaheo on the garden island of Kauai are delightful, self-contained cottages. These unique units feature antique stained-glass leaded windows and all the comforts of home. Fully furnished, complete kitchens, TVs, and daily linen service. Ten minutes by car to the golden beaches of the sunny south shore of Poipu. Five minutes to Kukuiolono Golf Course.

Hosts: Richard and Wynnis Grow
Cottages: 4 (pB) $55-65
Continental Breakfast
Credit Cards: None
Notes: 2, 5, 8, 9, 10, 11, 12, 14

South Shore Vista

Go Native...Hawaii
P. O. Box 11418, Hilo, 96721
(800) 662-8483

Centrally situated, South Shore Vista is ten minutes from the Poipu Beach resort area and ten minutes from beaches to the west. Accommodations include a bedroom with queen bed, private full bath, living area, and kitchenette. Beautifully decorated, this one-bedroom ohana has an ocean view and looks out toward the spectacular mountain scenery of Kauai's sunny south shore. Sleeps up to four. Children over four welcome. $75.

KAUAI—KAPAA

Bed and Breakfast Hawaii

P. O. Box 449, Kappa 96746
(808) 822-7771; (800) 733-1632
FAX (808) 822-2723

Private homes that offer bedroom with private bath, studios with their own entrance, or little cottages on the host's property all in out-of-the-way tropical settings with ocean and mountain views. Breakfasts include tropical fruits, Kona coffee, and banana breads, muffins, toast or homemade breads and juice usually served outside with tropical views. Accommodations can be found on every island of Hawaii (Big Island of Hawaii, Oahu, Kauai, Maui, Lanai, and Molokai) with friendly hosts. All homes personally inspected with high standards.

Contact: Evie Warner & Al Davis
Rates: $45-125

Bed & Breakfast Hawaii-TNN-HAWAII

P. O. Box 449, 96746
(808) 822-7771; (800) 733-1632

Part of the Bed and Breakfast National Network, Bed & Breakfast Hawaii offers bed and breakfast not only in Hawaii, but also in many other cities and states across the country. The members of this network adhere strictly to the standards set by TNN, such as getting to know the hosts personally, having an established cancellation and refund policy, and following a thorough inspection and approval process for all properties rented. This is because each member of the network is dedicated to ensuring your comfort, pleasure and personal needs while you are staying at one of our "homes away from home."

Bed & Breakfast Hawaii K1

P. O. Box 449, 96746
(808) 822-7771

A secluded oceanfront home on beautiful Anahola Bay where guests can enjoy a large studio apartment detached from the main house. Accommodations include queen-size bed and private bath with a garden shower, color cable TV, and a kitchenette. Breakfast fixings are provided for the first three days. Occasionally a honeymoon room with a deep Jacuzzi is available. Enjoy the oceanfront amenities and privacy of the property. Three-day minimum stay. Weekly rates. $85; $125 honeymoon room.

Bed & Breakfast Hawaii K3

P. O. Box 449, 96746
(808) 822-7771

Stay in a brand-new 600-square-foot, one-bedroom guest cottage nestled on the lush mountainside of Wailua Homesteads. Views of the wettest spot on earth can be seen from the deck. The kitchenette is great for preparing light meals and snacks and is stocked with breakfast fixing, for the first morning only. Private bath, color TV, and phone. No smoking. Children welcome. $70.

Bed & Breakfast Hawaii K3A

P. O. Box 449, 96746
(808) 822-7771

Cloud Nine Holiday is a spacious apartment that is completely private with its own entrance. It comes equipped with a color cable TV, a microwave, a small refrigerator, and all the breakfast fixings. The lanai overlooks a beautifully landscaped "bird of paradise" tropical garden perfect for romantic sunrise or sunset strolls. Situated near the beach and public tennis court. No smoking. $60-100.

Bed & Breakfast Hawaii K4

P. O. Box 449, 96746
(808) 822-7771

Enjoy traditional bed and breakfast in this lovely two-story cedar home. Guests have a choice of two rooms, each with their own private bath, queen-size bed, and TV. Each morning, wake up to the smell of fresh-baked bread and Kona coffee, which is served in the glassed-in lanai area that

offers views of Mt. Waialeale in the background. Five minutes to the beach. Smoking outside only. $40-45.

Bed & Breakfast Hawaii K6

P. O. Box 449, 96746
(808) 822-7771

These three fresh and comfortable accommodations overlook a horse pasture skirted by Opaekaa Stream. Waterfalls are often visible in the distance from the lanai. Private entrances open to all suites decorated in wicker and rattan. All rooms feature king- or queen-size beds, kitchen areas, and private baths. Smoking outside only. $50-100.

Bed & Breakfast Hawaii K7

P. O. Box 449, 96746
(808) 822-7771

On a quiet country road in the hills of Keapana Valley, your hostess offers guest rooms in a pastoral setting. Beautifully landscaped and architect-designed by the hostess herself, the property has panoramic views of the ocean and mountains. Three guest rooms, one with private bath, two with shared bath. A solar hot tub is available as well as a refrigerator. There is a spacious lanai with rattan furniture and hammocks in a tropical, nonsmoking, adult-only environment. Just five minutes from restaurants and beaches. $40-60.

Bed & Breakfast Hawaii K7A

P. O. Box 449, 96746
(808) 822-7771

A romantic, rustic, private cottage is nestled in a setting of ginger and hibiscus flowers under the shade of two huge monkey pod trees. This unique setting offers an outdoor hot- and cold-water shower off the bathroom surrounded by tropical foliage

6 Pets welcome; 7 Smoking allowed; 8 Children welcome; 9 Social drinking allowed; 10 Tennis available; 11 Swimming available; 12 Golf available; 13 Skiing available; 14 May be booked through travel agents.

for complete privacy. Perfect for a first or second honeymoon. No smoking. Three-night minimum stay preferred. $75; $450 weekly.

Bed & Breakfast Hawaii K16

P. O. Box 449, 96746
(808) 822-7771

Three rooms on the coconut coast of Kauai, just two blocks inland from the beach. Two rooms in the main house have private baths. A third room is separate from the main house. Enjoy breakfast with the hosts or choose do-it-yourself. All the rooms have hand-painted art done by the hostess. No smoking in rooms. $50.

Bed & Breakfast Hawaii K26A

P. O. Box 449, 96746
(808) 822-7771

Peace and quiet, mountain and ocean views, central location, and fabulous breakfast all characterize this home that offers guests one of two accommodations. A separate cottage with a livingroom/dining room and kitchen can comfortably sleep four and has a king- and queen-size bed. A downstairs one-bedroom apartment with a deck and private entrance offers a kitchenette with light cooking appliances. Minimum stay is three nights. No smoking. $85.

Bed & Breakfast Hawaii K33

P. O. Box 449, 96746
(808) 822-7771

Enjoy the "real Hawaii" in this home situated about eight miles north of Kapaa on Moloaa Beach. The little rustic cottage has a full kitchen, queen-size bed, and private bath. There is a cool spring that has been turned into a shower outside the cottage. Sometimes the host family has an old-fash-

ioned luau, and guests are welcome. Three-night minimum stay. $50.

Bed & Breakfast Hawaii K53

P. O. Box 449, 96746
(808) 822-7771

This lovely one-bedroom cottage overlooks several acres of what was once a nursery area for exotic tropical plants. Although the cottage is under the same roof as the main house, it offers private entrance and its own separate lanai where the hosts serve a continental breakfast each morning. Livingroom has color TV and cable with a VCR and stereo, and light meals can be prepared in the kitchenette or barbecue area. Bedroom has a queen-size bed, and the cottage has a full private bath. Children are welcome, and comfortable futons are available for extra bedding. $65.

Bed & Breakfast Hawaii K73

P. O. Box 449, 96746
(808) 822-7771

Enjoy a room and private bath in this rambling two-story Victorian home. Set against the backdrop of Sleeping Giant Mountain, two guest facilities are offered. One area is a screened lanai; upstairs there is a king-size bed with an adjoining private bath with sunken tub. For parties of three, a room on the east side of the house has queen-size bed and two twins with a bath across the hall. Good beaches are a five minute drive. No smoking. $45-60.

Bed & Breakfast Hawaii K76

P. O. Box 449, 96746
(808) 822-7771

Guests who stay here will find themselves living in a little valley where the hostess and her son, who lives next door, operate a plant nursery. Accommodations are just for two and include a bedroom with a king-size bed and a private bath. A coffee maker and small refrigerator are also provided. Breakfast can be enjoyed in the dining room or on the patio. Smoking permitted. Minimum stay is three nights. $55.

Bed & Breakfast Hawaii K78

P. O. Box 449, 96746
(808) 822-7771

This one-bedroom condo with an ocean view is not really a bed and breakfast, but since the hosts live nearby, breakfast can be arranged easily if desired. Queen-size bed in the bedroom and private bath, plus the livingroom can sleep two more on the double Murphy bed. Full kitchen and private lanai with an ocean view, and the beach is only a few steps away. Guests are welcome to the pool, Jacuzzi on premises, and restaurants and shops are within easy walking distance. $20 cleaning fee. Minimum stay is three nights. $72.

Bed & Breakfast Hawaii K79

P. O. Box 449, 96746
(808) 822-7771

Rainbow Valley is the name of this new home in the hills of Kapaa. Guests can enjoy an ocean view from the queen-size bedroom with shared bath. Amenities include refrigerator, color cable TV, and ceiling fan. Breakfast is served each morning on a large deck, and guests are encouraged to use outside grill, bicycles, beach mats, and chairs. $50-60.

Bed & Breakfast Hawaii K82

P. O. Box 449, 96746
(808) 822-7771

Hosts built an extra two-story house on their mountain view plateau property just for bed and breakfast guests. Accommoda-tions for guests are two separate units downstairs. One unit has a queen-size bed, private bath, living area with queen-size sofa bed, color TV, wet bar, refrigerator, and microwave. Another larger unit includes a bedroom with a pair of twin beds, spacious living area with a queen-size sofa bed, large private bath, color TV, wet bar, refrigerator, and microwave. Each area has its own lanai and entrance. Breakfast is served upstairs in the breakfast nook, and a gazebo with a sauna and Jacuzzi is on premises. $75-105.

Bed and Breakfast Honolulu (Statewide) LOWYT

3242 Kaohinani Drive, Honolulu, 96817
(808) 595-7533; (800) 288-4666

This private mountain bed and breakfast is behind Sleeping Giant Mountain on a love-ly landscaped half acre. The rooms have private baths with tubs and showers. Continental breakfast is served, and the fruit fresh off the trees surrounding the house. Well-lit off-street parking and five minutes to Wailua Bay. From $50.

Bed and Breakfast Honolulu (Statewide) SMITR

3242 Kaohinani Drive, Honolulu, 96817
(808) 595-7533; (800) 288-4666

Above Opaekaa Fall, a home located in the restored Wailua Homestead area offers two guest rooms. This plantation home is deco-rated in a country motif with antiques. One room has a king-size bed, and the other room has a queen and twins. Both have pri-vate baths, and the mountain and valley views from the porch are breathtaking. Hosts also offer two one-bedroom condos on the beach. Guests can enjoy the peaceful sounds of the Pacific from the lanais adjoining the condos, and the bedrooms have queen-size beds. Smoking outside only. $50 and up.

Kay Barker's Bed and Breakfast

P. O. Box 740, 96746
(808) 822-3073

The home is in a lovely garden setting, in a quiet rural area, with pastoral and mountain views. There is a large livingroom, TV room, extensive library, and lanai for you to enjoy. Brochures are available.

Host: Gordon Barker
Rooms: 5 (PB) $49.05-76.30
Continental Breakfast
Credit Cards: A, B
Notes: 2, 5, 7, 8, 9, 10, 11, 12, 14

Wailua Bed and Breakfast

Go Native...Hawaii
P. O. Box 11418, Hilo, 96721
(800) 662-8483

In a beautiful residential neighborhood, looking down upon lovely Wailua River. Attached to the main home are two complete studio units built of Koa wood. Impressive views from each apartment. Each unit has a small kitchen and full bath. There is also a charming courtyard. Continental breakfast. No smoking. $45-55.

KAUAI—KILAUEA

Bed & Breakfast Hawaii K31

P. O. Box 449, Kapaa, 96746
(808) 822-7771

A private, north shore of Kauai guest house is the perfect setting for getting away from it all. Accommodations include a light cooking area, full bath, queen bed, and a sitting area. Overlooking the beautiful Kilauea River and "rainbow valley," named for the brilliant rainbows that stretch from the lush recesses of the valley floor to the ocean. A private hiking trail takes you down to a secluded, semiprivate sandy beach. The main house has a pool available to guests. $115.

KAUAI—KOLOA

Gloria's Spouting Horn Bed and Breakfast

4464 Lawai Beach Road, 96756
(808) 742-6995

Oceanfront rooms are just steps from the surf, and hammocks under swaying palm trees overlook a secluded beach. This beachhouse is a restored plantation house nestled between the sea and acres of sugarcane. Walk to the Spouting Horn, the natural wonder a few houses away, or to Poipu Beach, where swimming and snorkeling are at their best year round. Extended tropical continental breakfast.

Hosts: Bob and Gloria Merkle
Rooms: 5 (PB) $55-125
Extended Continental Breakfast
Credit Cards: A, B
Notes: 2, 5, 9

Koloa Bed and Breakfast

Go Native...Hawaii
P. O. Box 11418, Hilo, 96721
(800) 662-8483

A delightful Japanese-hosted guest home in the countryside. Only two miles from Poipu Beach. Bedroom with private entrance, twin beds, refrigerator, TV, and small patio. Modest but comfortable accommodations. Lush tropical yard with stream. Continental breakfast. Three-night minimum stay. $35-40.

Poipu Bed and Breakfast Inn and Vacation Cottages

2720 Hoonani Road, Koloa, 96756
(808) 742-1146 Hawaii; (800) 552-0095

In Poipu, set amid almost one-half acre of lush tropical gardens and a short walk to the white sands of Poipu Beach, Kiahuna Tennis Club and pool (free to guests), restaurants, and shops. All rooms have garden views, private baths (some whirlpools), color cable TV/VCR, clock radios, ceiling fans; most have king beds. Also, four luxury suites with four-poster beds, sitting area, private lanai, and air conditioning. Two suites are handicapped accessible. The main plantation house was built in 1933 and exquisitely renovated. The cottages have kitchenettes, phones, and some have ocean views. Laundry facilities and guest kitchenette.

Hosts: Dotti Cichon and Audry Nokes
Rooms: 10; suites, cottages (PB) $65-225
Continental Breakfast
Credit Cards: A, B, C, E, F
Notes: 2, 5, 8, 9, 10, 11, 12, 14

KAUAI—LAWAI

Bed and Breakfast Honolulu (Statewide) SEYME

3242 Kaohinani Drive, Honolulu, 96817
(808) 595-7533; (800) 288-4666

Perched high in the hills of southern Kauai, overlooking the lush jungle, cane fields, and the Pacific, this bed and breakfast is an oasis of pampered comfort and privacy. With only three guest rooms and a studio apartment, this hillside inn looks out to the pool deck, filled with gardenia, bougainvillaea, ginger, and hibiscus. The hearty continental breakfast includes homemade breads and four or five tropical fruits. Vacationers receive personal attention from the gregarious proprietor who steers them to little-known restaurants, beaches, and scenic hideaways. Poipu beaches are only ten minutes away. Just five minutes to golf course, boutiques, and restaurants. Rental cars, helicopter tours, and horseback riding nearby. One room handicapped accessible. From $65.

Victoria Place
Bed and Breakfast

P. O. Box 930, 96765
(808) 332-9300

Perched high in the hills of southern Kauai, overlooking the lush jungle, the cane fields. and the Pacific, Victoria Place is an oasis of pampered comfort and privacy. With only three guest rooms and a studio apartment, the hillside inn looks out to the poolside deck, filled with gardenia, bougainvillaea, ginger, and hibiscus. The hearty continental breakfast includes homemade breads and four or five tropical fruits. Vacationers receive personal attention from the gregarious proprietor who steers them to little-known restaurants, beaches, and scenic hideaways. Poipu beaches are only ten minutes away. Just five minutes to golf course, boutiques, restaurants. Rental cars, helicopter tours, and horseback riding nearby. One room handicapped accessible.

Host: Edee Seymour
Rooms: 4 (PB) $65-95
Continental Breakfast
Credit Cards: None
Notes: 2, 5, 7 (outside), 9, 10, 11, 12, 14

KAUAI—LIHUE

Bed and Breakfast Honolulu (Statewide) ZAIML

3242 Kaohinani Drive, Honolulu, 96817
(808) 595-7533; (800) 288-4666

A lovely cottage only two minutes from the airport. It has a private entrance and tub/shower. There is a queen bed in the bedroom and a queen Hide-a-bed in the livingroom. TV, stereo/radio, even a piano. Twenty minutes to sunny Poipu beaches. Enjoy the barbecue pit. Breakfast fixings are provided. No children or smokers. From $60.

KAUAI—NORTHSHORE

Bed & Breakfast Hawaii K01

P. O. Box 449, Kapaa, 96746
(808) 822-7771

6 Pets welcome; 7 Smoking allowed; 8 Children welcome; 9 Social drinking allowed; 10 Tennis available; 11 Swimming available; 12 Golf available; 13 Skiing available; 14 May be booked through travel agents.

This suite is surrounded by what the hosts call "real Hawaii." The river that adjoins the property has been beautifully landscaped, has its own waterfalls, and is perfect for a swim. Two outdoor hot tubs, eight-person Jacuzzi, and massage are also available to guests. The accommodation is a private guest house with a loft bed, kitchen, and queen-size brass bed on the main level. Living area has a VCR and stereo CD/cassette player. Indoor and outdoor showers also available. $95-120.

Bed & Breakfast Hawaii K20

P. O. Box 449, Kapaa, 96746
(808) 822-7771

Heart Song Inn welcomes you to the magical healing beauty of Kauai. Two bedrooms with a private bath in the hall are offered for a group of one to four people. Breakfast is served out on the deck where the view of the valley is breathtaking. A lower deck offers a hot tub and a view of the Kilauea waterfalls. No smoking. Minimum stay is three nights. $65-115.

Bed & Breakfast Hawaii K28

P. O. Box 449, Kapaa, 96746
(808) 822-7771

Guests have the pleasure of staying at this new home at the river's edge in Kilauea. Guest accommodations are in separate wing with a private balcony overlooking the river. The bedroom has a queen-size bed, plus a fold-out sofa bed. A private full bath adjoins the room, plus small kitchen appliances for light cooking make this accommodation perfect for longer stays. $70.

Bed & Breakfast Hawaii K35

P. O. Box 449, Kapaa, 96746
(808) 822-7771

You are invited to come and enjoy this lush tropical paradise overlooking the Kilauea Valley. Your bedroom overlooks one of the most spectacular views of the island, and your room is newly remodeled with its own private entrance and bath. When you wake, step out onto your cedar deck and take in the view of the mountains, mist, and lush valley below, while smells of Kona coffee, baked goods, and fresh local fruits for your continental breakfast fill the air. Minimum stay is two nights. $65.

Bed & Breakfast Hawaii K39A

P. O. Box 449, Kapaa, 96746
(808) 822-7771

Located on the north shore of Kauai in Kalahiwai, hosts offer a room with a private entrance and adjoining bath. This home with three acres, horses, and golden retrievers, adjoins a 600-acre guava orchard. The accommodations are elegant, large, and sound-proofed, and include a king-size bed, double-head tiled shower, color TV and VCR, and a bay window that overlooks the grounds. Hosts encourage guests to explore the quiet, uninhabited grounds with waterfalls and streams that surround their lovely home. No smoking. Minimum stay is 3 nights. $70-80.

Bed & Breakfast Hawaii K45

P. O. Box 449, Kapaa, 96746
(808) 822-7771

This bed and breakfast accommodation is perfect for guests who enjoy hiking, water sports, sightseeing, golf at Princeville, sunbathing, or long walks in a quiet unpretentious Hawaiian-style town. The house is a stylish two-story home on grounds abundant with coconut, plumeria, and papaya trees, and the views from 1000-square-foot deck and the lanai are breathtaking. You will instantly feel at home in one of the rooms, which all feature queen-size beds

NOTES: Credit cards accepted: A Master Card; B Visa; C American Express; D Discover Card; E Diner's Club; F Other; 2 Personal Checks accepted; 3 Lunch available; 4 Dinner available; 5 Open all year;

and private baths. Continental breakfast of fresh fruit, juice, and warm breads is served each morning on the second-story lanai that views Mt. Waialeale. $55-75.

Bed & Breakfast Hawaii K481

P. O. Box 449, Kapaa, 96746
(808) 822-7771

You can spend your days looking for shells or snorkeling while staying in this small studio that is just a thirty-minute walk from the beach. The self-contained guest quarters include a king-size bed, wet bar with a refrigerator, small half bath, and private enclosed shower which has a view of the jungle. Minimum stay is two nights. $65.

Bed & Breakfast Hawaii K57

P. O. Box 449, Kapaa, 96746
(808) 822-7771

This little cottage is nestled in the trees behind the main house and is just a block to Tunnel Beach. Guest accommodations include a cozy living area with a double sofa bed, kitchenette stocked with breakfast foods, bathroom with an extra-large shower, and an upstairs bedroom with a queen-size bed. Minimum stay is three nights. $80.

Bed & Breakfast Hawaii K60

P. O. Box 449, Kapaa, 96746
(808) 822-7771

This brand-new, spacious accommodation is completely separate from the main house and a block from the beach. Sit out on your deck and enjoy the view of Bali Hai Mountain, or enjoy the ocean view with your breakfast in the dining area. Full kitchen, Jacuzzi tub, bedroom with queen-size bed and skylights make this guest area private and spacious. Livingroom also has a queen-size sofa bed for extra guests.

Another accommodation is a separate bedroom in the main house with its own private entrance, patio area, and unique private bath. Minimum stay is three nights. No smoking. $50-100.

Bed & Breakfast Hawaii K64

P. O. Box 449, Kapaa, 96746
(808) 822-7771

This private, handcrafted redwood cottage is carefully and comfortably equipped for any length of stay. It includes a kitchenette, a private full bath, queen-size bed in the bedroom, and a livingroom with a large futon couch. French doors open to deck that offers distant mountain, ocean and sunset views, and the area surrounding the cottage is full of thoroughbred horse farms and organic fruit, flower, and vegetable farms. No smoking inside. Children welcome. $75.

Bed & Breakfast Hawaii K74

P. O. Box 449, Kapaa, 96746
(808) 822-7771

A slightly rustic accommodation on a working farm is a great way to relax in Kauai. Hosts have added onto their barn by building a bedroom, efficiency kitchen, and private bath on the second-story. Comfortable king-size bed and double sofa bed furnish the room. Grounds have a pineapple patch and orchid greenhouse that guests are welcome to explore. Children are welcome. $65.

Bed & Breakfast Hawaii K81

P. O. Box 449, Kapaa, 96746
(808) 822-7771

This full apartment in Hanalei town is just 200 feet from the bay. Hostess lives in the upstairs half of a new two-story house across the street from the ocean. The whole downstairs portion of the house is for guests to enjoy. Guests have a private entrance, queen-size bed in the bedroom, private bath with tub and shower, fully equipped kitchen, and cozy livingroom. No breakfast is served here. Minimum stay is three nights. $90.

KAUAI—POIPU

Bed & Breakfast Hawaii K11A

P. O. Box 449, Kapaa, 96746
(808) 822-7771

Enjoy a luxury one-bedroom bed and breakfast with first-class accommodations on acres of gardens and tropical flowers just a five-minute walk to Poipu Beach. Guests have use of the main bedroom with king bed, color TV, sliding glass doors to the lanai, and private bath. A delicious breakfast is served on the lanai overlooking tropical gardens. Take advantage of the pool, tennis courts, and Jacuzzi on the condominium premises. Three-night minimum stay. $75-92.

Bed & Breakfast Hawaii K22

P. O. Box 449, Kapaa, 96746
(808) 822-7771

Bed and breakfast is available in this plantation house with two lovely rooms with private baths. Relax in the screened-in lanai or in the common livingroom. Tropical continental breakfast is served in the formal dining room or on the lanai. Two-night minimum is preferred. Smoking outside. $65-75.

Bed & Breakfast Hawaii K23

P. O. Box 449, Kapaa, 96746
(808) 822-7771

Right in Poipu and three blocks from Shipwreck Beach are two accommodations in one. The entire downstairs of this architect's home is devoted to bed and breakfast and has a suite and a bedroom available for guests. The suite offers a private bath with a queen-size bed and a sitting area with a queen-size sofa sleeper. The suite also has a kitchenette with a dishwasher, microwave, and refrigerator. The bedroom offers a queen-size bed, adjoining private bath and sliding glass doors to a sitting area. A walk-in closet has a small refrigerator for storing drinks. Breakfast is served each morning. Both rooms have TV. $65-85.

Bed & Breakfast Hawaii K24

P. O. Box 449, Kapaa, 96746
(808) 822-7771

Poipu Plantation is not really a bed and breakfast accommodation because twenty people can be accommodated in the small inn. Nine rooms feature a variety of bed sizes, face the garden or ocean, and have their own telephone lines. Two of the units are two-bedroom, two-bath suites. Guests are welcome to pick any fruit in season, and a barbecue, sunning area, and laundry facilities are available to guests. $75-125.

Bed & Breakfast Hawaii K25

P. O. Box 449, Kapaa, 96746
(808) 822-7771

This unhosted property is a two-bedroom condo at Makahuena. The condo has no ocean view, even though the complex is located on the oceanfront at Makahuena Point. Two bedrooms, two baths, fully equipped kitchen, TV, telephone, and swimming pool and tennis courts on premises make this a perfect spot for families. Walk along the cliffs to Shipwreck Point or down the street to Poipu Beach Park. No breakfast is served. $85.

NOTES: Credit cards accepted: A Master Card; B Visa; C American Express; D Discover Card; E Diner's Club; F Other; 2 Personal Checks accepted; 3 Lunch available; 4 Dinner available; 5 Open all year;

Bed & Breakfast Hawaii K29

P. O. Box 449, Kapaa, 96746
(808) 822-7771

Brand-new one-bedroom apartment over-looking the shore of Kauai is just minutes from the beach and centrally located in O'mao. Hosts have lived in Kauai over fifteen years and can share information about beaches, dining, and shopping. The apartment is upstairs through a private entrance and has a kitchen, telephone, cable TV, queen-size bed in the bedroom, private bath, and sofa bed in the livingroom. Guests can enjoy ocean view from their own private deck, and breakfast fixings are in the refrigerator. Smoking outside only. Minimum stay is three nights. $60.

Bed & Breakfast Hawaii K43

P. O. Box 449, Kapaa, 96746
(808) 822-7771

This bed and breakfast offers one of the most spectacular views of Kauai's South Shore and Poipu. The three suites offer you all the comforts of home with daily linen service, private bath, color TV, plush carpeting, private entrance, and continental breakfast. One suite offers a livingroom and a kitchenette. Home is very private but close to Garden Island. Kokee Mountain and Waimea Canyon are two of Kauai's "don't miss" attractions, and are only 20 miles west. $55-70.

Bed & Breakfast Hawaii K61

P. O. Box 449, Kapaa, 96746
(808) 822-7771

Enjoy a quiet, relaxing stay in lush surroundings on the South Shore of Kauai in a beautifully furnished room with a king-size bed, reading area, and breakfast nook with a coffee maker, small refrigerator, and microwave for light snacking. The bedroom is cool and airy with an adjoining private bath, and the home is within walking distance of the National Tropical Botanical Gardens. Your host is a third-generation-born Hawaiian. $65.

Bed & Breakfast Hawaii K71

P. O. Box 449, Kapaa, 96746
(808) 822-7771

Japanese decor is the theme for this 900-square-foot cottage in Poipu. Guests will enjoy the Shoji screen doors, as well as the miniature gardens at the entrance and in the bathroom. Sofa bed in the livingroom, kitchenette, and queen-size bed in the bedroom offer a guest plenty of living area. Although there is no ocean view, a five-minute walk will take you to the Poipu Beach Park. No breakfast is served at this accommodation. No smoking. Minimum stay is four nights. $100; $600 per week.

Bed & Breakfast Hawaii K75

P. O. Box 449, Kapaa, 96746
(808) 822-7771

Enjoy a relaxing stay practically oceanfront on Brennecke's Beach in Poipu. Your hostess offers one bedroom in her quaint two bedroom plantation cottage. A king-size bed and private adjoining bath with separate entrance and private lanai with ocean view is perfect for singles or couples. Your hostess prepares breakfast every morning and serves it either in her dining room or your lanai. A small refrigerator is provided to keep cold drinks. Minimum stay is two nights. $75-80.

Bed & Breakfast Hawaii K80

P. O. Box 449, Kapaa, 96746
(808) 822-7771

A new attraction in Poipu is a dinner show at the Stouffer Waiohai, and the host at this bed and breakfast helps direct the dinner

6 Pets welcome; 7 Smoking allowed; 8 Children welcome; 9 Social drinking allowed; 10 Tennis available; 11 Swimming available; 12 Golf available; 13 Skiing available; 14 May be booked through travel agents.

theater presentation. Guests are welcome to enjoy this entire home, provided they clean up after themselves. The guest room has a double bed with a private adjoining bathroom. Poipu Beach is about one-half mile from your host's home. $50-60.

Bed and Breakfast Honolulu (Statewide) NAKAS

3242 Kaohinani Drive, Honolulu, 96817
(808) 595-7533; (800) 288-4666

Centrally situated for sightseeing. The room has twin beds, private entrance and bath, a small refrigerator, TV, and a private patio. The tropical setting is complete with running stream. Three-night minimum stay. From $45.

Poipu Bed and Breakfast Inn and Vacation Cottages

2720 Hoonani Road, Koloa, 96756
(808) 742-1146 Hawaii; (800) 552-0095

In Poipu, set amid almost one-half acre of lush tropical gardens and a short walk to the white sands of Poipu Beach, Kiahuna Tennis Club and pool (free to guests), restaurants, and shops. All rooms have garden views, private baths (some whirlpools), color cable TV/VCR, clock radios, ceiling fans; most have king beds. Also, four luxury suites with four-poster beds, sitting area, private lanai, and air conditioning. Two suites are handicapped accessible. The main plantation house was built in 1933 and exquisitely renovated. The cottages have kitchenettes, phones, and some have ocean views. Laundry facilities and guest kitchenette.

Hosts: Dotti Cichon and Audry Nokes
Rooms: 10; suites, cottages (PB) $65-225
Continental Breakfast
Credit Cards: A, B, C, E, F
Notes: 2, 5, 8, 9, 10, 11, 12, 14

Poipu Oceanfront Inn Bed and Breakfast

2650 Hoonani Road, Koloa, 96756
(808) 742-9417; (800) 22POIPU

Oceanfront in Poipu Beach, only 150 feet away from the water and on one-half acre of exotic tropical gardens, this lovely bed and breakfast is only a short stroll from the sand of Poipu Beach, the Kiahuna Tennis Club and pool, shops, and restaurants. Each room or suite is like a cottage with a private lanai, kitchenette, tropical decor, ceiling fan, color cable TV, and most offer king-size beds. Our Dolphin Suite is especially nice for honeymooners with many extra amenities. Smoking outside only. A luxury beach oceanfront condominium and a rustic beach cottage are also available accommodations. Ask about our generous discounts for extended stays and our car rental rates.

Hosts: Elmer and Dotti Cichon and Audry Nokes
Units: suites, cottages, condo (PB) $60-195
Tropical Continental Breakfast
Credit Cards: A, B, C, E, F
Notes: 2, 5, 8, 9, 10, 11, 12, 14

KAUAI—PRINCEVILLE

Bed and Breakfast Honolulu (Statewide) DELOF

3242 Kaohinani Drive, Honolulu, 96817
(808) 595-7533; (800) 288-4666

This host offers one room in her two-bedroom condo. Guests have a private room and bath, and a continental breakfast is served. Take a short stroll down the path to a very private, lovely sandy beach. Enjoy peace and tranquility in paradise. From $55.

Hale 'Aha—Bed and Breakfast in Paradise

Box 3370, 96722
(808) 826-6733; (800) 826-6733

Newly built on one and one-half acres of golf resort property, this gracious home offers the serenity of 480 feet of fairway frontage overlooking the ocean and mountains of Kauai. Hale 'Aha hospitality also offers honeymoon privacy with separate decks and entrances. The 1000-square-foot fabulous Penthouse Suite has its own balcony, with open beams and 360-degree views (including "Bali Hai").

Hosts: Herb and Ruth Bockelman
Rooms: 4 (PB) $80-190
Continental Breakfast
Credit Cards: None
Notes: 2, 5, 10, 11, 12, 14

Hale Ho'o Maha Bed and Breakfast

Go Native...Hawaii
P. O. Box 11418, Hilo, 96721
(800) 662-8483

This bed and breakfast's name means "House of Rest'. It is located on Kauai's famous North Shore, a five minute drive from Lauai's most beautiful beaches and rivers. Panoramic view of the Kalalau mountain range and ocean can be seen from every window of the house. Guest accommodations include the Pineapple Room, with private entrance and full private bath and king-sized bed, and the Mango Room with a shared bath, cable TV, and double bed. $50-65.

KAUAI—WAILUA

Bed & Breakfast Hawaii K5B

P. O. Box 449, Kapaa, 96746
(808) 822-7771

Makana Inn offers two separate units. A one-bedroom guest cottage with private bath and light cooking facilities has a private lanai overlooking Mount Waialeale and green pastures. The apartment is downstairs in the main house and has a bedroom, sitting area, private bath, and kitchenette. A generous continental breakfast is stocked in your kitchen upon arrival. Three miles from beach, golf, tennis, shopping, and dining. Two-night minimum stay. $65-75.

Bed & Breakfast Hawaii K30

P. O. Box 449, Kapaa, 96746
(808) 822-7771

The Fern Grotto Inn is perfectly situated on the only private property in the middle of the Wailua River State Park. Breakfast is served on elegant English china in the Plantation Dining Room with its many windows providing a view of the Wailua River. Drift off to sleep in one of the three bedrooms on queen beds with designer sheets and comforter and piled high with white goose down pillows. European down/feather beds are provided for your added comfort and luxury. Elegant adjoining private bath. $70-100.

Bed & Breakfast Hawaii K36

P. O. Box 449, Kapaa, 96746
(808) 822-7771

Experience the magic of Kauai while staying in this A-frame cottage on the hosts' half-acre property in Wailua. Set back from the main home, there is plenty of privacy and space. A large deck fronts the cottage. Inside through French doors is an oversize all-glass family room. The kitchen is stocked with breakfast fixings. Two bedroom areas sleep up to four. Children welcome. Two-night minimum stay. $75.

Bed & Breakfast Hawaii K47

P. O. Box 449, Kapaa, 96746
(808) 822-7771

A spectacular 360-degree view of the ocean, Sleeping Giant, and Mount Waialeale can be seen from this bilevel cottage that sleeps up to six people. The bed-

6 Pets welcome; 7 Smoking allowed; 8 Children welcome; 9 Social drinking allowed; 10 Tennis available; 11 Swimming available; 12 Golf available; 13 Skiing available; 14 May be booked through travel agents.

room has a queen bed, and there is a queen-sofa bed in the livingroom. A private bath, livingroom, large screened-in lanai, and loft complete the accommodations. The hosts live in the main house. Children welcome. Baby equipment is available. Three-night minimum stay. $65.

Bed & Breakfast Hawaii K62

P. O. Box 449, Kapaa, 96746
(808) 822-7771

The Orchid Hut is a modern cottage situated on a bluff overlooking the north fork of the Wailua River. The front door opens into a sitting room with color TV and kitchenette. Dine at the outdoor table or just relax and enjoy the scenic view of nature and the meticulously landscaped tropical garden. Perfect for, couples and honeymooners, this beautifully furnished unit is just three minutes from the mouth of the Wailua River for water skiing, the beach, restaurants, and shopping. Nonsmoking adults only. Three-night minimum stay. $75.

Bed & Breakfast Hawaii K63

P. O. Box 449, Kapaa, 96746
(808) 822-7771

A private, cool, mountain bed and breakfast nestled behind Sleeping Giant Mountain. The entrance takes you into a cozy and comfortable recreation room with a fully equipped kitchen plus a fireplace. Three bedrooms have private adjoining baths. A continental breakfast is served at your wake-up time. Laundry service available. Enjoy fresh fruit right off the trees on a lovely, landscaped half acre. Situated on Kauai with a scenic drive past Opaeka'a Falls and only five minutes from Wailua Bay. $50.

Bed and Breakfast Honolulu (Statewide) MANTS

3242 Kaohinani Drive, Honolulu, 96817
(808) 595-7533; (800) 288-4666

This separate guest house is situated on the green pasturelands of Wailua. One bedroom with a queen bed, a livingroom with a queen Hide-a-bed, a private bath, and fully equipped kitchen. Enjoy the mountain view from your private deck. A similar unit for two is also available. Three miles to golf, shopping, beaches, and dining. From $60.

KAUAI—WAIMEA

Bed & Breakfast Hawaii K42

P. O. Box 449, Kapaa, 96746
(808) 822-7771

In the heart of old Waimea and within walking distance of the store, pier, restaurants, and shops, this home is perfect for those who want to hike the Waimea Canyon and explore Kokee State Park. There is a private entrance into the cozy bedroom, sitting area, and light cooking area. Private bath. A prepared continental breakfast is left in the refrigerator. Three-night minimum stay. $50.

LANAI—LANAI CITY

Bed & Breakfast Hawaii L1

P. O. Box 449, Kapaa, 96746
(808) 822-7771

Two of the bedrooms in this retired nurse's home are available for guests visiting the small, fairly remote island of Lanai. One room offers a double and single bed, while the other has a queen-size bed. There is a full and a half-bath shared by both hostess and guests. Both of the bedrooms are good-size and well-furnished. Hostess is an artist and has a fascinating collection of bottles and shells. $45-55.

NOTES: Credit cards accepted: A Master Card; B Visa; C American Express; D Discover Card; E Diner's Club; F Other; 2 Personal Checks accepted; 3 Lunch available; 4 Dinner available; 5 Open all year;

Bed and Breakfast Honolulu (Statewide) COLEP

3242 Kaohinani Drive, Honolulu, 96817
(808) 595-7533; (800) 288-4666

Two rooms are offered to guests in this bed and breakfast, one with a double bed and one with a pair of twins. Host provides coffee for guests, but no breakfast. Restaurants and convenience stores are nearby, and hostess' kitchen is available to guests for $5 a day. Smoking outside only. From $57.

Bed and Breakfast Honolulu (Statewide) GRAHLU

3242 Kaohinani Drive, Honolulu, 96817
(808) 595-7533; (800) 288-4666

The hostess is a long-time resident of Lanai and collects bottles, shells, and other curios. Some of her ancient Hawaiian artifacts are worthy of a museum. Two bedrooms are open to guests in this modest but very comfortable home. A full bath and a half-bath are shared. From $55.

MAUI—HAIKU

Bed and Breakfast Honolulu (Statewide) DOWNN

3242 Kaohinani Drive, Honolulu, 96817
(808) 595-7533; (800) 288-4666

Pleasant hosts offer a spacious one bedroom cottage in the heart of windsurfing country. Five minutes from Hookai Park, twenty minutes from the airport, and ten minutes from Paia, this ocean-view home has a quiet rural setting and an all-electric kitchen with washer/dryer, ice-maker, and garbage disposal. No children. From $55.

Haikuleana

555 Haiku Road, 96708
(808) 575 2890

Experience the real feelings of Aloha in an 1850s Hawaiian plantation. Set in agricultural district close to secluded waterfalls and beautiful beaches, Haikuleana is a convenient way station for visitors headed to Hana and the Haleakala Crater. Picturesque beaches, the world's best wind surfing, and golf courses are all nearby. The house is completely renovated, and you'll admire its high ceilings, plank floors, porch and lush Hawaiian gardens. The cool, tropical rooms are furnished with drapes, ticking comforters, wicker, and antiques.

Host: Frederick J. Fox, Jr.
Rooms: 4 (PB) $65-85
Full Breakfast
Credit Cards: None
Notes: 2, 5, 8, 9

Hamakualoa Bed and Breakfast

Go Native...Hawaii
P. O. Box 11418, Hilo, 96721
(800) 662-8483

A tea-house cottage in a peaceful, unspoiled environment on the lush north shore of Maui. Here in the center of a tropical jungle is a pleasant bed and breakfast with views of both the ocean and mighty Haleakala. The lovely cottage is tastefully furnished with antiques and Oriental rugs. Bedroom, livingroom, kitchenette, and screened lanai. A unique feature—requiring a bit of adventure—is the free-standing bathhouse and outhouse, both to modern standards. Continental breakfast. $65.

MAUI—HANA

Hana Plantation Houses

P. O. Box 489-AB, 96713
(808) 248-7248; (800) 657-7723 reservations only
  FAX (808) 248-8240

Imagine Jacuzzis indoors and out. Acres rich with ripe banana and papaya. Help yourself! Sparkling fresh waterfalls.

6 Pets welcome; 7 Smoking allowed; 8 Children welcome; 9 Social drinking allowed; 10 Tennis available; 11 Swimming available; 12 Golf available; 13 Skiing available; 14 May be booked through travel agents.

Explore Hamoa Beach, James Michener's favorite. Choose from a range of incredible options: a Japanese-style studio, a tiny studio inside a banyan tree, a solar-powered beach house. If a rejuvenating and thoroughly relaxing experience is your dream, your hosts will assist in any way to make it come true. Come to Hana Plantation Houses!

Hosts: Blair Shurtleff and Tom Nunn
Rooms: 12 (PB) $55-185
Coffee served
Credit Cards: A, B, E, F
Notes: 2, 5, 8, 9, 10, 11, 14

MAUI—KIHEI

Bed and Breakfast Hawaii M10

P. O. Box 449, Kapaa, 96746
(808) 822-7771

This unhosted one-bedroom condo on the ground floor of a small complex does not offer breakfast, but it is available for guests at an attractive rate. The condo is fully furnished, has all the appliances for cooking, including a dishwasher, color TV, and washer/dryer. There are two pools and a tennis court for guests to enjoy, and the unit could easily accommodate a family. A white sandy beach is across the street. $55.

Bed and Breakfast Hawaii M16

P. O. Box 449, Kapaa, 96746
(808) 822-7771

This a large home situated on the edge of of Ulapalakua Ranch is totally surrounded by decks. Breakfast is served on the upper deck, which provides a great place to whale-watch, and accommodations include two bedrooms decorated with Japanese antique furnishings. Both share a bath across the hall, and one has an ocean view, while the other views a tropical garden. A studio with a kitchenette, private entrance, and private bath, and a cottage with one

bedroom both offer more room and more privacy for families. $55-85.

Bed & Breakfast Hawaii M17

P. O. Box 449, Kapaa, 96746
(808) 822-7771

Tennis buffs could not ask for a better place to vacation than sunny Kihei, with courts available right outside their door. The accommodation is a full apartment with one bedroom, private bath, kitchenette, living/dining room, cable TV. The home has an ocean view and is a short drive to beaches, golf, and restaurants. Three-night minimum stay. $65-100.

Bed and Breakfast Hawaii M19

P. O. Box 449, Kapaa, 96746
(808) 822-7771

Two beautiful studio apartments for guests are three blocks away from the sunny beaches of Kihei. The ranch studio has a separate entrance, large bedroom with a queen bed, private bath, sitting room with a TV, full kitchen stocked with breakfast food, dining area, and a shared lanai where a barbecue is available to guests in both units. Laundry facilities are available. Minimum stay is three nights. Smoking outside only. $75.

Bed & Breakfast Hawaii M20

P. O. Box 449, Kapaa, 96746
(808) 822-7771

Guests have a choice of accommodations in the home of these busy hosts. A guest cottage can sleep four people comfortably, and includes a private deck, full kitchen, large room with a fold-out futon couch bed that also serves as the living area, and a full bath. The other accommodation is in the downstairs of the main house, has its own private entrance, kitchenette, bath, and queen-size bed. Breakfast foods are left in the units each morning for guests. Children over 12. Minimum stay is three nights. $75-120.

Bed & Breakfast Hawaii M28

P. O. Box 449, Kapaa, 96746
(808) 822-7771

Luxuriate in the privacy of one of three guest rooms in this large home. One accommodation is a suite with two bedrooms, queen-size beds, minikitchen, and one and one-half baths. A third bedroom has a king-size bed that can convert to twins, and a loft bed, private entrance, and private bath with a huge all-tile sunken tub. Minimum stay is three nights. $85-110.

Bed & Breakfast Hawaii M32

P. O. Box 449, Kapaa, 96746
(808) 822-7771

This beautiful home offers a bedroom with a private bath and private entrance off the deck. The room has a queen bed and color TV. Another single bedroom is next door. Breakfast is usually served on the lanai where guests can enjoy a view of a well-landscaped tropical garden. The hostess loves to treat her guests to some delicious breakfast treats. Three-night minimum stay. $55; $30 for additional room.

Bed & Breakfast Hawaii M32A

P. O. Box 449, Kapaa, 96746
(808) 822-7771

This accommodation is a large garden-level apartment with fully equipped kitchen and two bedrooms with one bath. Ideal for a small family. The unit has lots of windows that afford an excellent ocean view. The hostess serves breakfast on the lanai upstairs. One-week minimum stay. $80; $100 for four.

Bed & Breakfast Hawaii M38

P. O. Box 449, Kapaa, 96746
(808) 822-7771

This bed and breakfast accommodation offers two bedrooms on the second level of this oceanfront home. Each bedroom has a private entrance, private full bath, small refrigerator, color TV, and a queen-size bed. Breakfast is served downstairs, and guest rooms share a covered deck that overlooks the ocean and islands of Kahoolawe and Molokini. Minimum stay is two nights. No smoking. Children over 12. Resident dog. $70.

Bed & Breakfast Hawaii M62

P. O. Box 449, Kapaa, 96746
(808) 822-7771

Guests have their choice of a variety of accommodation at this large house. Queen-size beds are available, and private baths are in all accommodations. Breakfast is served on the deck, and the views are magnificent. No breakfast is included when you stay in the cottage. Smoking outside only. Minimum stay is two nights. $55-130.

Bed and Breakfast Honolulu (Statewide) SVENC

3242 Kaohinani Drive, Honolulu, 96817
(808) 595-7533; (800) 288-4666

This single-family Hawaiian-style pole home in Kihei offers a panoramic view of the ocean and the slopes of Haleakala from the lanai. It has two rooms on the ground floor—the hosts live upstairs. Cable TV, ceiling fan, twin beds or king, private bath, and a refrigerator for cold drinks. There are many shops and restaurants in Kihei, and the ocean is only a mile from the house. Two-bedroom cottage also available. From $90.

6 Pets welcome; 7 Smoking allowed; 8 Children welcome; 9 Social drinking allowed; 10 Tennis available; 11 Swimming available; 12 Golf available; 13 Skiing available; 14 May be booked through travel agents.

Bed and Breakfast Honolulu (Statewide) FEKEJ

3242 Kaohinani Drive, Honolulu, 96817
(808) 595-7533; (800) 288-4666

This large studio with private entrance and bath has light cooking facilities. Just six blocks to the beach. Full breakfast is served. Ocean view and wheelchair accessible. From $65.

Bed and Breakfast Honolulu (Statewide) LOWRP

3242 Kaohinani Drive, Honolulu, 96817
(808) 595-7533; (800) 288-4666

This hostess offers a studio with a queen bed, a cottage with a queen bed in the loft and a Hide-a-bed in the livingroom, and two rooms in her home that share a bath. Her home has an ocean view, and the islands of Lanai and Kahoolwe can be seen from her lanai. Five-minute drive to the beach, and a pool on premises. Breakfast is provided in the bed and breakfast room, and studio and cottage have light cooking facilities. From $55.

Bed and Breakfast Honolulu (Statewide) PISCB

3242 Kaohinani Drive, Honolulu, 96817
(808) 595-7533; (800) 288-4666

This studio is on the lower level of the host's home. The 600-square-foot unit has air conditioning, ceiling fan, washer/dryer, phone, cable TV, and full kitchen with dishwasher, stove, oven, and microwave. The garden patio has a barbecue and a wooden bench swing, and there are ocean and garden views. Less than one mile to beaches, shopping, and restaurants. A slightly smaller studio is also available. No smoking. From $65.

MAUI-KULA

Bed & Breakfast Hawaii M6

P. O. Box 449, Kapaa, 96746
(808) 822-7771

Kilohana bed and breakfast plantation style. Gather your own macadamia nuts, watch a melodious Chinese thrush build her nest, hike Haleakala. This spectacular home is situated at 3,300-foot elevation just a short walk to the Kula Botanical Gardens. There are four guest rooms available. Breakfast includes freshly ground Kona macadamia nut coffee, homemade whole-wheat toast or banana bread, and fresh fruit compote. Two-night minimum stay. $75.

Bed & Breakfast Hawaii M52

P. O. Box 449, Kapaa, 96746
(808) 822-7771

A lovely home with two rooms in Kula awaits guests. The master bedroom has a private adjoining bath. The second room shares the bath in the hall. Lovely landscaping and large decks with magnificent views can be enjoyed here. Breakfast is served in the dining area. $55.

Bed & Breakfast Hawaii M53

P. O. Box 449, Kapaa, 96746
(808) 822-7771

Enjoy an elegant and comfortable stay with charming, gracious hosts. Up on the slopes of the dormant volcano, Haleakala, guests can enjoy two separate bedrooms with private baths and separate entrances to the sunny courtyard where breakfast is served. The home is new and specially designed with a bed and breakfast in mind. About 30 minutes by car to the beaches and 40 minutes to the airport, this is truly a quiet, relaxing place to enjoy Maui. Three-night minimum stay. $57.

NOTES: Credit cards accepted: A Master Card; B Visa; C American Express; D Discover Card; E Diner's Club; F Other; 2 Personal Checks accepted; 3 Lunch available; 4 Dinner available; 5 Open all year;

Bloom Cottage
Bed and Breakfast

Rural Route 2, Box 229, 96790
(808) 878-1425

A romantic getaway situated one-third of
the way up Haleakala Crater. Spectacular
view, cool mountain climate, surrounded
by herb and flower gardens. There is an
antique Hawaiian quilt on four-poster bamboo bed, old wicker in breakfast nook,
original art on the walls. The two-bedroom
700-square-foot cottage has a fully stocked
kitchen, large livingroom with fireplace,
breakfast nook, bathroom. Hosts stock your
refrigerator; you fix your own breakfast.

Hosts: Herb and Lynne Horner
Cottage: $92.65
Continental Breakfast
Minimum stay: 2 nights
Credit Cards: None
Notes: 2, 5, 9, 14

MAUI—LAHAINA

Bed & Breakfast Hawaii M2A

P. O. Box 449, Kapaa, 96746
(808) 822-7771

Two different accommodations are offered
to suit your needs. There is a room with a
private bath in the main house with a window overlooking the ocean just steps away.
Easy access to the sea-wall through a private porch. Also an attached cottage,
Ohana House, just 50 feet from the ocean.
The cottage has a kitchenette and private
bath and entrance. The refrigerator will be
stocked with fresh fruit and juice. Two-
night minimum stay. $55-75.

Bed & Breakfast Hawaii M5

P. O. Box 449, Kapaa, 96746
(808) 822-7771

This guest house is a private home created
for those who appreciate a restful, relaxed
holiday. Every guest room offers you opti-
mum privacy with color TV, refrigerator,
ceiling fan, and air conditioning. All rooms
have private baths, and one includes a
Jacuzzi tub. The shared family room has a
VCR, and the livingroom has a 350-gallon
marine aquarium. A short walk to shops
and restaurants as well as the beach, or
relax beside the pool at the guest house.
$75-95.

Bed and Breakfast Honolulu
(Statewide) SWANT

3242 Kaohinani Drive, Honolulu, 96817
(808) 595-7533; (800) 288-4666

A place for relaxation! A cottage, plus
three guest rooms and a family suite. Most
offer private entrance, bath, TV, refrigerator, air conditioning, and lanai. One has a
Jacuzzi. Near old whaling village and
Kaanapali resort area. Quiet rooms and
generous continental breakfast. Decked
pool. Beach and picnic gear available.
Beach park is two blocks away. From $60.

Lahaina GuestHouse

Go Native...Hawaii
P. O. Box 11418, Hilo, 96721
(800) 662-8483

In the heart of Lahaina, only one block
from the beach, an elegant tropical-style
home with delightful, easy-living appointments. Offers five personalized guest
rooms, three with private baths, a spacious
family room, and a relaxing livingroom.
Full use of kitchenette stocked with
gourmet cooking utensils and spices.
Prepare your own snacks, picnics, or meals.
Continental breakfast is provided. From
$70.

6 Pets welcome; 7 Smoking allowed; 8 Children welcome; 9 Social drinking allowed; 10 Tennis available; 11
Swimming available; 12 Golf available; 13 Skiing available; 14 May be booked through travel agents.

Laha'Ole
Bed and Breakfast

Go Native...Hawaii
P. O. Box 11418, Hilo, 96721
(800) 662-8483

A wonderful oceanfront home in Lahaina right at the water's edge. Hosts offer one bedroom delightfully appointed with a queen-size day bed, TV, private bath, and ocean view. Accommodates two. Within walking distance of shops, restaurants, and entertainment. A delightful welcome awaits you in the tradition of aloha. Continental breakfast. $55.

Old Lahaina House

P. O. Box 10355, 96761
(808) 667-4663; FAX (808) 667-5615

A conveniently located, relaxing place to visit Maui invites you to enjoy the romantic, secluded ambience of a private pool in a tropical courtyard. We are only steps from a serene beach and convenient walking distance to dining and shopping in historic Lahaina Town, a culturally rich and diverse old whaling town. We can be your home away from home, your own special retreat, or your own intimate piece of paradise!

Hosts: John and Sherry Barbier
Rooms: 4 (2 PB; 1 SB) $60-95
Continental Breakfast
Credit Cards: A, B
Notes: 5, 8, 11, 12, 14

Plantation Inn

174 Lahainaluna Road, 96761
(808) 667-9225; (800) 433-6815

This unique country inn blends an elegant turn-of-the-century ambience with the amenities of the finest hotels. Home of Gerard's, a fine French restaurant, rated as one of Hawaii's top ten by *Who's Who in America's Restaurants*.

Host: Charles Robinson
Rooms: 18 (PB) $99-175
Continental Breakfast
Credit Cards: A, B, C, E
Notes: 2, 4, 5, 7, 9, 10, 11, 12, 14

MAUI—PAIA

Bed & Breakfast Hawaii M1

P. O. Box 449, Kapaa, 96746
(808) 822-7771

Million-dollar views of west Maui, the ocean, and two islands surround this house perched on top of a dormant volcano Hawaiians call the House of the Rising Sun. Breakfast is brought up each morning and served either on the private deck or in the room. The large studio has its own entrance, queen-size bed, wicker furniture, and private bath. There is a counter, sink, and refrigerator, so that picnic lunches can be prepared, but no cooking is possible. No smoking. Minimum stay is two nights. $75.

Bed & Breakfast Hawaii M4A

P. O. Box 449, Kapaa, 96746
(808) 822-7771

This charming inn was built in 1850 for Maui's first doctor who came with the pineapple cannery. Newly refurbished, it sits among nearly one and one-half acres of pineapple fields and pine trees. Located just 700 feet above sea level and just down the road from Hookipa Beach, this bed and breakfast includes full breakfast, twin or queen-size beds, and private baths in all rooms. Four rooms. Open from October through May. $80.

Bed & Breakfast Hawaii M12

P. O. Box 449, Kapaa, 96746
(808) 822-7771

Right on the beach and centrally situated for sightseeing all of Maui, this large plantation-style home is in an exclusive neigh-

NOTES: Credit cards accepted: A Master Card; B Visa; C American Express; D Discover Card; E Diner's Club; F Other; 2 Personal Checks accepted; 3 Lunch available; 4 Dinner available; 5 Open all year;

borhood adjacent to the Maui Country Club. It offers a large guest room with a private bath. There is no ocean view from the home, but a short walk will take you to a stretch of white, sandy beach good for walking. Usually the hosts' friendly dog will accompany you. No smoking inside. $70.

Huelo Point Flower Farm

Go Native...Hawaii
P. O. Box 11418, Hilo, 96721
(800) 662-8483

Bed and breakfast on a two-acre stunning oceanfront estate set high on the edge of a cliff overlooking Waipio Bay on Maui's rugged north shore. Only one-half hour from Kahului, this breathtaking site offers bed and breakfast in the marvelous gazebo with queen futon, wicker furnishings, color TV, small refrigerator, hot plate, and many other amenities. The cliffside views from the outside hot tub are unforgettable. $85.

MAUI—UPCOUNTRY

Bed & Breakfast Hawaii M7A

P. O. Box 449, Kapaa, 96746
(808) 822-7771

This newly remodeled home situated on one and one-half acres of upcountry ocean-view property can accommodate a family of three. The unit has a separate entrance and private bath. Count on fresh bread or rolls being served. No smoking. $45.

Bed & Breakfast Hawaii M9

P. O. Box 449, Kapaa, 96746
(808) 822-7771

A delightful bed and breakfast with an ocean view setting, this studio is attached to the host's home in a quiet and private setting. The accommodation offers a sepa-

rate entrance and is furnished with rattan furniture. Unit includes a double bed, private bath, ceramic tile floors, and a mini kitchen with a microwave, toaster, coffee maker, and refrigerator. Your host serves a delicious Aloha-style breakfast on the patio that has an exquisite ocean view. $55-65.

Bed & Breakfast Hawaii M15

P. O. Box 449, Kapaa, 96746
(808) 822-7771

For the free-spirited, this glass gazebo is perched on the cliff overlooking Waipio Bay on Huelo Point. Inside is fully carpeted with a futon on the floor; nicely appointed with a stereo, small refrigerator, and coffee maker. The half-bath is hidden behind all-glass sliding doors. The hot/cold shower is outside in the newly landscaped gardens, and the large cement patio includes a hot tub shared with the hosts who live in the main house. Hosts will rent the entire home when they are away. Three-night minimum stay. $85.

Bed & Breakfast Hawaii M18A

P. O. Box 449, Kapaa, 96746
(808) 822-7771

This accommodation in the Upcountry area is for guests who want a special experience and care little about the cost. As guests enter the home, they encounter a small interior stream and fish pond that is located in the living area. The bedroom uses glass to create an open feeling and adjoins a private bath that offers a view of the Kula landscape from the shower. Located above that room up a small circular staircase is the Moon Room. This room is made entirely of glass and has a bed that rotates 360 degrees. Guests breakfast by the stream that runs through the home and across a cantilevered deck. Hot tub available also. $75-95.

6 Pets welcome; 7 Smoking allowed; 8 Children welcome; 9 Social drinking allowed; 10 Tennis available; 11 Swimming available; 12 Golf available; 13 Skiing available; 14 May be booked through travel agents.

Bed & Breakfast Hawaii M26

P. O. Box 449, Kapaa, 96746
(808) 822-7771

Named Halemanu, which is Hawaiian for birdhouse, this home is perched 3,500 feet above the town of Kula and provides an awesome view of the island of Maui. The home is new and has lots of windows and decks. The guest room has its own private deck, private full bath, and queen-size bed. Breakfast is served in a sunny spot on the deck or in the dining area. $70.

Bed & Breakfast Hawaii M55

P. O. Box 449, Kapaa, 96746
(808) 822-7771

Real island-style living can be enjoyed while staying here, just five minutes from Hookipa, the windsurfing beach of Maui. Overlooking pineapple fields, this studio has a separate entrance and sun deck with tropical flowers and fruit trees. The artwork was done by a famous Maui artist. Three-night minimum stay. $55.

Bed & Breakfast Hawaii M56

P. O. Box 449, Kapaa, 96746
(808) 822-7771

This modern cedar chalet is built on about two acres on the beautiful green slopes of Haleakala crater near Makawao. The home is tastefully decorated, and offers two bedrooms, one with twin beds and one with a queen-size bed, that share a bath. A hearty breakfast is served. No children. No smoking. Minimum stay is three nights. $60.

Bed and Breakfast Honolulu (Statewide) BALDJ

3242 Kaohinani Drive, Honolulu, 96817
(808) 595-7533; (800) 288-4666

A bed and breakfast "inn" style. Two upstairs suites with shared bath. Furnished in antiques and collectibles. Guests have a livingroom with fireplace. A studio is also available. The sprawling grounds offer a panoramic view; a vineyard; macadamia nut, avocado, and loquat trees. Pick their fruit on a moment's whim. Buffet breakfast with fresh island fruit, tropical breads, Kona coffee, and exotic teas. From $65.

Bed and Breakfast Honolulu (Statewide) FOXF

3242 Kaohinani Drive, Honolulu, 96817
(808) 595-7533; (800) 288-4666

Located in the quiet country hillside at the base of Mt. Haleakala, this 100-year-old Hawaiian plantation house was recently renovated with antiques. This house has one and one-half acres of spacious lawn, with banana, mango, and poinciana trees. Breakfast includes fresh fruit, banana bread, and Kona coffee. The beach is two miles away, and the airport is twelve miles away. From $80.

Bed and Breakfast Honolulu (Statewide) HOPKJ

3242 Kaohinani Drive, Honolulu, 96817
(808) 595-7533; (800) 288-4666

Enjoy a panoramic view of Mount Haleakala and the ocean from two secluded acres. Two guest rooms with private entrance and bath: one with a king bed; one with twins. Eight minutes to windsurfing and beaches. The hostess enjoys talking about "her" island. From $60.

Bed and Breakfast Honolulu (Statewide) HORNH

3242 Kaohinani Drive, Honolulu, 96817
(808) 595-7533; (800) 288-4666

NOTES: Credit cards accepted: A Master Card; B Visa; C American Express; D Discover Card; E Diner's Club; F Other; 2 Personal Checks accepted; 3 Lunch available; 4 Dinner available; 5 Open all year;

This two-bedroom cottage is surrounded by herb and flower gardens. It contains a queen and twin room, livingroom with fireplace and TV, fully equipped kitchen, and breakfast nook. Watch a sunset from your private front porch. Smell the fresh-brewed Kona coffee, and enjoy homemade muffins, fresh fruit, and juice. No smoking. From $70.

Bed and Breakfast Honolulu (Statewide) POWEN

3242 Kaohinani Drive, Honolulu, 96817
(808) 595-7533; (800) 288-4666

Enjoy paradise in the cool Upcountry. A modern cedar chalet home in paniolo (cowboy) country. Two rooms share a bath. The host provides beach and picnic supplies—or warm clothing for trips to the Haleakala Crater. Enjoy a tropical setting from a comfortable lanai. From $55.

MAUI—WAILUKU

Bed & Breakfast Hawaii M14

P. O. Box 449, Kapaa, 96746
(808) 822-7771

This comfortable home is only a few minutes from the Kaului airport. Two bedrooms, each with private entrance and shared bath. Outdoor patio is shared and includes a pool. No children. No smoking. Two-night minimum stay. $50.

MOLOKAI—KAUNAKAKAI

Bed & Breakfast Hawaii MO2

P. O. Box 449, Kapaa, 96746
(808) 822-7771

This five-acre parklike property lies at the foot of Molokai's highest mountain. Surrounding the charming guest cottage is a variety of tropical foliage and flowering trees and shrubs. The cottage is fully furnished and includes everything you need to make yourself at home. Breakfast items are stocked in the kitchen area so that guests can eat when they please. There are many coves and beaches nearby, and hosts invite guests to use the lawn chairs, snorkel masks, and a good selection of Hawaiian records. Minimum stay is three nights. $60.

Bed & Breakfast Hawaii M04

P. O. Box 449, Kapaa, 96746
(808) 822-7771

This home is located only ten miles from the airport and three miles past the town of Kaunakakai. The deluxe quiet bedroom has a private bath, private entry, and a small lanai facing the east Molokai Mountains. The ocean is 35 steps away, and a swimming pool, snorkels, masks, and kayaks are available for those experienced in watersports. Continental breakfast is served each morning. $95.

Bed and Breakfast Honolulu (Statewide) LENNN

3242 Kaohinani Drive, Honolulu, 96817
(808) 595-7533; (800) 288-4666

This cedar home is next to a park in Kaunakakai. The host offers a continental breakfast on the deck overlooking the ocean toward Lanai. The deck has been said to have a million-dollar view. The guest room does not face the ocean. It has TV, double bed, couch, and private bath. It is 300 feet to the ocean (not a swimming beach), three miles to town, and 13 miles to a swimming beach. From $65.

Bed and Breakfast Honolulu (Statewide) NEWHJ

3242 Kaohinani Drive, Honolulu, 96817
(808) 595-7533; (800) 288-4666

6 Pets welcome; 7 Smoking allowed; 8 Children welcome; 9 Social drinking allowed; 10 Tennis available; 11 Swimming available; 12 Golf available; 13 Skiing available; 14 May be booked through travel agents.

Surrounded by the lush native plants of Molokai and an easy walk to the beach, Honomuni House offers a personal and unique Hawaiian holiday. The cottage is nestled in a tropical garden and lulled by the sound of the surf. Evidence of the early Hawaiians abounds in Honomuni Valley— ancient stonework, taro terraces, and house foundations. Breadfruit, bananas, mango, ginger, coffee, coconut, and guava plum still grow wild in the tropical forest. Prawns and native freshwater fish can be seen in nearby streams. Waterfalls and refreshing pools await the ambitious hiker. Full bath, plus outdoor Hawaiian shower. From $65.

Bed and Breakfast Honolulu (Statewide) PAUHA

3242 Kaohinani Drive, Honolulu, 96817
(808) 595-7533; (800) 288-4666

Pau Hana ("done work") and it's time to relax. This rustic, unspoiled, truly Hawaiian hideaway is a favorite of many islanders. The inn offers all the comforts of a full-service hotel with restaurant, bar, pool, daily room service, and a staff that welcomes all visitors with genuine warmth and aloha. It leaves no doubt that Molokai is the friendly island. Forty rooms, some along the ocean or facing the pool. Some with kitchenettes and some separate cottages. The oceanfront suite has a view spanning the spindrift surf of the Molokai channel and the lush islands of Lanai and Maui. Just 25 air-minutes from Honolulu, yet 30 years behind. From $49.

Bed and Breakfast Honolulu (Statewide) SWENYL

3242 Kaohinani Drive, Honolulu, 96817
(808) 595-7533; (800) 288-4666

Hosts are pleased to offer this one-bedroom cottage on the beach near good fishing and snorkeling. Bedroom has king or pair of twin beds, and the livingroom has a couch bed. The cottage is completely equipped, right down to the dishes, and offers privacy. A two-bedroom house on the beach is also available to accommodate large [parties. No breakfast is provided at either accommodation. From $55.

Bed and Breakfast Honolulu (Statewide) WRIGH

3242 Kaohinani Drive, Honolulu, 96817
(808) 595-7533; (800) 288-4666

Hale Kawaikapu ("house of sacred waters") has two rentals, totally separated. Eighteen miles to town, it is situated on a tropical garden estate of 250 acres stretching from sea to mountaintop. The spectacular seaward view of Maui and Kahoolawe is matched by the magnificent mountains and valleys. Reef protected for safe swimming, snorkeling, fishing, and wind surfing. Hike along a Jeep trail to the top of the mountain for a four-island view. The two-bedroom, two-bath home has a private lanai and is fully equipped. The A-frame has a lanai open to the gardens and ocean. Washer and dryer are included. Caretaker on grounds. $150 security deposit payable in advance. From $120.

Molokai Bed and Breakfast

Go Native...Hawaii
P. O. Box 11418, Hilo, 96721
(800) 662-8483

A cozy cottage with accommodations on the grounds of the main house. Only ten miles east of Kaunakakai and across from the Father Damien Church. Lovely setting with mountains in background and cascading waterfall. Features studio accommodations with cooking facilities, twin beds, bath, and make-your-own continental breakfast. Two adults maximum and three-night minimum stay. $50.

NOTES: Credit cards accepted: A Master Card; B Visa; C American Express; D Discover Card; E Diner's Club; F Other; 2 Personal Checks accepted; 3 Lunch available; 4 Dinner available; 5 Open all year;

OAHU—AILEA

Bed and Breakfast Honolulu (Statewide) NEESB

3242 Kaohinani Drive, Honolulu, 96817
(808) 595-7533; (800) 288-4666

This Oahu home is about two miles from Pearl Harbor and the Arizona Memorial. Two rooms are available. Kitchen privileges, laundry facilities, and color TV. The host loves Hawaii and enjoys sharing information with visitors. Children and smokers accepted. From $35.

OAHU—EAST HONOLULU

Bed & Breakfast Hawaii O40

P. O. Box 449, Kapaa, 96746
(808) 822-7771

This lovely condominium on the water is hosted by a single lady who knows quite a bit about Oahu and can give guests good recommendations on what to do and where to go. Situated close to Hanauma Bay, there are two single beds that can form a king bed. The room shares a bath in the hall. No smoking. $40.

Bed & Breakfast Hawaii O54

P. O. Box 449, Kapaa, 96746
(808) 822-7771

Spectacular bird's-eye views of Diamond Head and the entire Honolulu coastline can be seen from the deck of this little studio. The studio has its own private entrance, and sliding glass doors off the lanai open into an air conditioned bedroom with a king-size bed and a private bath. Your hosts stock the mini-fridge with breakfast fixings. Smoking outside only. Preferred minimum stay is three nights. $65.

Bed & Breakfast Hawaii O65

P. O. Box 449, Kapaa, 96746
(808) 822-7771

This artist's home is perfect for exploring Honolulu without being in the heart of Waikiki. Swim in the pool, and enjoy views of the ocean and Diamond Head. Accommodations include a two room suite with a full-size waterbed, private sitting room, and private bath. Breakfast is normally served poolside. Minimum stay is two nights. $70.

OAHU—HAWAII KAI

Bed & Breakfast Hawaii O19

P. O. Box 449, Kapaa, 96746
(808) 822-7771

The hosts, mother and daughter, are from England and combine Old World charm with New World aloha to make sure their guests have a good time. In this home there is a spacious, airy bedroom with private bath, color TV, and sliding door leading to the swimming pool. Breakfast is served in the dining room with the hosts. No smoking. Two-night minimum stay. $55.

Bed & Breakfast Hawaii O26

P. O. Box 449, Kapaa, 96746
(808) 822-7771

Stay in this beautiful home in the best part of town, and enjoy a spectacular ocean view from this hillside setting. The whole downstairs level of the house is devoted to bed and breakfast and accommodates up to six people. Sliding glass doors facing the ocean run the length of each room. No smoking. Two-night minimum stay. $50.

Bed & Breakfast Hawaii O40

P. O. Box 449, Kapaa, 96746
(808) 822-7771

This home is three blocks from the ocean in a quiet residential neighborhood. Handy to stores, the bus line, a beach park, restaurants, and tennis courts. Two roms available with shared bath. Hosts accept only one group at a time. Continental breakfast. Children welcome. Two-night minimum stay. $45.

Bed and Breakfast Honolulu (Statewide) ABEB

3242 Kaohinani Drive, Honolulu, 96817
(808) 595-7533; (800) 288-4666

The hosts came from England where bed and breakfast started. They have two guest rooms, one with private bath, TV, and refrigerator. The other has a TV and shared bath. The hearty continental breakfast is served in the dining room. On a bus line. Seven-minute drive to swimming beaches and Hanauma Bay. Enjoy the pool, or shop in the on-premises gallery of items collected from around the world. No smoking. Adults only. Two-night minimum stay. From $50.

Bed and Breakfast Honolulu (Statewide) BRUCB

3242 Kaohinani Drive, Honolulu, 96817
(808) 595-7533; (800) 288-4666

These hosts offer two renovated guest rooms with a shared bath. A queen-size bed is in one of the rooms, and a pair of twins that can convert to a king is in the other. Each room has a private entrance through a garden and patio area, TV, radio-alarm clock, ceiling fans, and small refrigerator. Guests are welcome to eat, sunbathe, or use the grill on the marina side of the house. Near Hanauma Bay, Sandy Beach, shopping, and restaurants. Nine miles to Waikiki, eleven miles to Ala Moana shopping center. Breakfast include if requested. From $55.

Bed and Breakfast Honolulu (Statewide) CRIPS

3242 Kaohinani Drive, Honolulu, 96817
(808) 595-7533; (800) 288-4666

On a high ridge, the bedrooms offer a beautiful view of the ocean and Koko Marina. They are large with private baths. Hanauma Bay, Oahu's best snorkeling beach, two shopping centers, and other tourist attractions, are a five-minute drive away. Coffee and doughnuts are served weekday mornings; a special breakfast is served on weekends. The comforts of home and more. From $55.

OAHU—HONOLULU

Bed & Breakfast Hawaii O22

P. O. Box 449, Kapaa, 96746
(808) 822-7771

Outstanding views characterize this home located on the edge of the beach and near local tourist attractions. Two upstairs suites with private baths and lanai are available for bed and breakfast guests. The Mauka Suite has an antique bed and a view of Diamond Head; the Makai Suite has two double beds and view of the garden. $75-100.

Bed & Breakfast Hawaii O30

P. O. Box 449, Kapaa, 96746
(808) 822-7771

This large family home is situated on the hillside of Manoa Valley. It is quiet, cool, and surrounded with birds. The guest room has a queen-size bed, futon, and shared bath. Breakfast is served in the dining room with a wraparound view of Waikiki, Honolulu, and Manoa Valley or on the spacious and sunny front deck. Close to bus stop. Smoking outside. $45.

NOTES: Credit cards accepted: A Master Card; B Visa; C American Express; D Discover Card; E Diner's Club; F Other; 2 Personal Checks accepted; 3 Lunch available; 4 Dinner available; 5 Open all year;

Bed & Breakfast Hawaii O52

P. O. Box 449, Kapaa, 96746
(808) 822-7771

This is not a true bed and breakfast, because no breakfast is served, but this cozy one-bedroom apartment await guests on a lush, landscaped residential hillside with nice views and mountain breezes. Guests walk around to the back of the house for a private entrance into the living area. Fully equipped kitchen, private full bath, and double bed in the bedroom provide guests with everything they need for a pleasant stay. $65.

Bed & Breakfast Hawaii O53

P. O. Box 449, Kapaa, 96746
(808) 822-7771

Built on a hillside about one-fifth of a mile from the University of Hawaii at Manoa, this home has two bed and breakfast rooms available for guests. Guests are encouraged to sit on the large deck and enjoy the city's skyline and ocean below. One room offers a queen-size bed and a private bath with a shower, and the other room offers extra-long twin beds and a private one-half bath connected to a shared shower. Smoking outside only. Children over ten years old. Minimum stay is three nights. $55-65.

Bed & Breakfast Hawaii O53A

P. O. Box 449, Kapaa, 96746
(808) 822-7771

The downstairs of this lovely home offers a peaceful, two-bedroom retreat ten minutes from Waikiki and Ala Moana Shopping Center. No breakfast is served here, but 1,150 square feet of living space provides a family with a perfect vacation accommodations. The sleeping porch area has a queen-size bed, and the two bedrooms have double beds. Area includes livingroom, dining room, fully equipped kitchen, and full bath.

Smoking outside only. Minimum stay is three nights. Discount for weekly stay. $95.

The Manoa Valley Inn

2001 Vancouver Drive, 96822
(800) 634-5115

An intimate country inn situated in lush Manoa Valley just two miles from Waikiki Beach. Furnished in antiques, each room is individually decorated to enhance its charm and personality. Continental breakfast buffet, wine and cheese served daily on the shady lanai.

Host: Lisa Hookano-Holly
Rooms: 8 (SB) $103.71-$191.05
Continental Breakfast
Credit Cards: A, B, C
Notes: 2, 5, 14

OAHU—KAILUA

Affordable Paradise Bed and Breakfast Reservations

362 Kailua Road, 96734
(808) 261-1693; (800) 925-9065
FAX (808) 261-7315

We are located on the Island of Oahu, and we serve all of the major Hawaiian islands. We represent bed and breakfast homes, private studios, one-bedroom suites, cottages, and entire homes. All of our accommodations are on private property, inspected and approved by us personally. We list over 300 hosts, with our daily rates starting at $40. Our guarantee is that if you are not satisfied, your deposit money will be refunded. Our experienced staff has been in the reservations service for over ten years and are eager to meet your travelling needs.

Akamai Bed and Breakfast

172 Kuumele Place, 96734
(808) 261-2227; (800) 642-5366

6 Pets welcome; 7 Smoking allowed; 8 Children welcome; 9 Social drinking allowed; 10 Tennis available; 11 Swimming available; 12 Golf available; 13 Skiing available; 14 May be booked through travel agents.

On a quiet and separate wing of this private home are two large, comfortably furnished studios, each with its own private entrance and bath. Each room is equipped with a cable TV and radio. The refrigerator is stocked with breakfast foods and condiments, and the kitchen has light-cooking appliances. Guests can enjoy the tropical setting of the lanai and pool. Laundry facilities available. Just three blocks from miles of Hawaii's most beautiful and uncrowded white sand beaches. Honolulu and Waikiki activities a short half-hour drive away.

Host: Diane Van Ryzin
Rooms: 2 (PB) $60
Full Breakfast
Credit Cards: None
Notes: 2, 3, 4, 5, 7, 8, 9, 10, 11, 12, 14

Bed & Breakfast Hawaii O6

P. O. Box 449, Kapaa, 96746
(808) 822-7771

A great location for enjoying Lanakai Beach, this accommodation in the downstairs area of a beautiful A-frame cedar home offers a kitchenette, dining area, living area, and bedroom with a queen-size bed and queen-size futon, and private full bath. Light cooking can be done in the kitchenette, and an extra futon for a child is also available. A nice breakfast of fruit, fresh croissants, and coffee is provided. Minimum stay is three nights. $85.

Bed & Breakfast Hawaii O8A

P. O. Box 449, Kapaa, 96746
(808) 822-7771

Within walking distance of Kailua Beach on the canal, this studio apartment is perfect for longer stays. The bedroom area has a queen bed, there is a kitchenette for light cooking, and the bathroom has a two-person Jacuzzi. Share the pool with the host family. The hostess enjoys interaction with guests. Five-night minimum stay. $65 daily; $395 weekly.

Bed & Breakfast Hawaii O9A

P. O. Box 449, Kapaa, 96746
(808) 822-7771

This delightful accommodation is just across the street from one of the most beautiful beaches in Hawaii. A fully furnished garden studio in a tropical setting includes a private lanai. The apartment is beautifully furnished and includes a queen-size bed and large bath. Enjoy breakfast on the private patio. Three-night minimum stay. $55.

Bed & Breakfast Hawaii O12

P. O. Box 449, Kapaa, 96746
(808) 822-7771

This accommodation allows guests to lounge by the swimming pool and enjoy a leisurely breakfast or sit in the hot tub after a day of sightseeing. One mile from Kailua Beach, this home gives guests their choice of two rooms with a shared bath between them. One room has a double bed, and the other has a twin bed. Guests are welcome to use the host's refrigerator to keep light snacks, and a crib is available. One-night stays have an extra $5 surcharge. $40-45.

Bed & Breakfast Hawaii O13A

P. O. Box 449, Kapaa, 96746
(808) 822-7771

Imagine waking up after a good night's sleep on a raised bamboo frame, all-cotton futon bed, and seeing the incredible blue waters and white sandy beach right outside your windows. This studio in Lanakai offers a private entrance, private bath, sitting area with a full ocean view, and wet bar. Minimum stay is three nights. $125.

Bed & Breakfast Hawaii O16

P. O. Box 449, Kapaa, 96746
(808) 822-7771

NOTES: Credit cards accepted: A Master Card; B Visa; C American Express; D Discover Card; E Diner's Club; F Other; 2 Personal Checks accepted; 3 Lunch available; 4 Dinner available; 5 Open all year;

A gracious home on a private access road one-half block from a safe swimming beach. There are two large bedrooms with adjoining bath. This is ideal for couples traveling together. Two covered lanais surrounded by tropical foliage and a separate refrigerator are for guests. A neighborhood shopping center and restaurants are within walking distance. Adults only. $65.

Bed & Breakfast Hawaii O17

P. O. Box 449, Kapaa 86746
(808) 822-7771

This contemporary home, a short five-minute drive from the beach, offers guests two bedrooms that share a bath. Breakfast is usually served on the lush and secluded lanai. Two-night minimum. $45.

Bed & Breakfast Hawaii O25

P. O. Box 449, Kapaa, 96746
(808) 822-7771

This delightful host home in Kailua offers two rooms, each with a private bath and air conditioning. Hosts have a beautiful garden with a covered patio and pool for guests to enjoy. Breakfast features something different and delicious every day. Guests have a bedroom with a queen-size bed that looks out toward the pool area. An additional bedroom with a queen-size bed is available for two couples travelling together. No smoking. Minimum stay is two nights. $65.

Bed & Breakfast Hawaii O27

P. O. Box 449, Kapaa 86746
(808) 822-7771

This home has easy access to the expansive Kailua Beach. The hosts offer an attractive studio apartment with a new screened-in lanai. The interior is furnished with twin beds and a loft. It has light kitchen facilities and an outdoor barbecue. Continental breakfast includes coffee, tea, fresh fruit, rolls, and juice. Resident pets. Three-night minimum stay. $60.

Bed & Breakfast Hawaii O31

P. O. Box 449, Kapaa, 96746
(808) 822-7771

An elegant oceanfront home opens in front on a large pool with Jacuzzi and in back opens to the ocean. The home is spacious and has comfortable areas for guests to relax after a day of sightseeing. Bedrooms have private bath and private entrance from the pool/courtyard area. Each is decorated with an antique and tropical mixture. A deluxe continental breakfast is served. $120.

Bed & Breakfast Hawaii O32

P. O. Box 449, Kapaa, 96746
(808) 822-7771

This bed and breakfast apartment is attached to the host's home, but has a private entrance and private porch with a two-person swing. The unit consists of a livingroom, bedroom with a queen-size bed, and a private full bath. The unit also has a microwave, refrigerator, toaster, coffee maker, TV, and radio. Kailua Beach is a five-minute drive. No breakfast is included in this accommodation. $55.

Bed & Breakfast Hawaii O42

P. O. Box 449, Kapaa, 96746
(808) 822-7771

A block away from Kailua Beach, guests have two newly remodeled bedrooms available with private baths, TV, microwave, and refrigerator, plus use of the swimming pool. Breakfast supplies for three days are stocked to use at your leisure. Three-night minimum stay. $50-60.

6 Pets welcome; 7 Smoking allowed; 8 Children welcome; 9 Social drinking allowed; 10 Tennis available; 11 Swimming available; 12 Golf available; 13 Skiing available; 14 May be booked through travel agents.

Bed & Breakfast Hawaii O44

P. O. Box 449, Kapaa, 96746
(808) 822-7771

Located one block from Kailua Beach, hosts offer three sets of accommodations. The first is a separate one-bedroom cottage with a complete kitchen, two double beds, color TV, and a private bath and patio area. The second accommodation is a studio attached to the house with a kitchenette, private bath, private patio, and private entrance. The third and newest studio can sleep only two in a double bed and also has a light kitchenette and color TV. Minimum stay is four nights. No breakfast is served. $55-75.

Bed & Breakfast Hawaii O57

P. O. Box 449, Kapaa, 96746
(808) 822-7771

Within walking distance from Kailua Beach is this two-bedroom apartment on the ground level of a two-story home. Two bedrooms, a private bath, and complete kitchenette. The livingroom is complete with TV and rattan furniture and has sliding glass doors to the patio and fenced yard. Perfect for a family of four. Smoking outside. $75; $100 for four.

Bed & Breakfast Hawaii O63

P. O. Box 449, Kapaa, 96746
(808) 822-7771

This complete studio cottage is separate from the main house and situated one block from Kailua Beach. It is well kept and nicely furnished with tropical rattan. The cottage sits on the edge of the swimming pool as well as an attractive gazebo. There is a queen bed, full bath, TV, table and chairs, light cooking area, and phone. Smokers accepted. No children. Five-night minimum stay. $65.

Bed and Breakfast Honolulu (Statewide) FINEV

3242 Kaohinani Drive, Honolulu, 96817
(808) 595-7533; (800) 288-4666

This attached studio is on the grounds of a windward Oahu estate. It has its own entrance, will sleep four, and has light cooking facilities. You're also welcome to use the pool. The host has lived on Oahu since shortly after World War II and is glad to provide tips about Oahu. The privacy of this location makes a car necessary. Children and smokers welcome. From $45.

Bed and Breakfast Honolulu (Statewide) WOODL

3242 Kaohinani Drive, Honolulu, 96817
(808) 595-7533; (800) 288-4666

This single-family home has two guest rooms. Bed and breakfast guests share a bath. Limited kitchen and refrigerator privileges. The host offers warm hospitality, maps, and a continental breakfast. Car not essential—bus is close by. Children and smokers accepted. From $45.

Bed and Breakfast Honolulu (Statewide) DIMOH

3242 Kaohinani Drive, Honolulu, 96817
(808) 595-7533; (800) 288-4666

This home is 50 yards from the beach, with private room and bath. Lovely patio and yard for your use. Breakfast on a covered lanai. A 10 percent discount for a two-week stay. Also, separate fully furnished private studio with private entrance and bath. No smoking. From $60.

Bed and Breakfast Honolulu (Statewide) ISAAC

3242 Kaohinani Drive, Honolulu, 96817
(808) 595-7533; (800) 288-4666

NOTES: Credit cards accepted: A Master Card; B Visa; C American Express; D Discover Card; E Diner's Club; F Other; 2 Personal Checks accepted; 3 Lunch available; 4 Dinner available; 5 Open all year;

Two hundred yards from the ocean, this accommodation has two bedrooms available for guests. One room has a pair of twin beds that can be made into a king, and the other room has a king-size bed. Both rooms have private entrances, private bath, microwave, coffee maker, and small refrigerator. Guests are welcome to use the pool, and breakfast is provided for the first three days of stay. Tropical gardens surround the pool and premises in a very private setting. No children under sixteen. From $50.

Bed and Breakfast Honolulu (Statewide) LOMBP

3242 Kaohinani Drive, Honolulu, 96817
(808) 595-7533; (800) 288-4666

Windward studio with kitchenette. Two single beds. Private entrance with small courtyard by pool. Poolside cabana room also has private entrance and bath. Deck with wet bar by pool. From $50.

Bed and Breakfast Honolulu (Statewide) PRICS

3242 Kaohinani Drive, Honolulu, 96817
(808) 595-7533; (800) 288-4666

Beautiful windward home; casual host. Two rooms with queen beds, TV, and refrigerator. For larger parties, a small twin room can be used. Guest rooms share a bath. Walk to the beach (five minutes); swim in the pool; enjoy the serenity of the view; stroll to the boat dock on the quiet canal running just beyond the landscaped lawn. Continental breakfast served. Smokers and children (over nine and swimmers) welcome. Resident cats. From $45.

Bed and Breakfast Honolulu (Statewide) SASAE

3242 Kaohinani Drive, Honolulu, 96817
(808) 595-7533; (800) 288-4666

One-bedroom detached cottage. A five-minute walk to Kailua Beach and adjacent to a cool, lush tropical park. Bedroom air conditioned, with king bed. Livingroom has twin beds. Small kitchen for light cooking. Furnished in white rattan. Phone, cable TV, radio available. Children welcome. From $65.

Kailua Bed and Breakfast

Go Native...Hawaii
P. O. Box 11418, Hilo, 96721
(800) 662-8483

Beautiful home with swimming pool beside a quiet stream and golf course, within walking distance of Kailua Beach Park. Two units available. One is master bedroom with private bath and separate entrance. The other is a lovely cottage featuring livingroom, bedroom, and kitchenette. Sleeps up to four. Large whirlpool bath. No smoking. Continental breakfast is served on the patio. $40-65.

Papaya Paradise

395 Auwinala Road, 96734
(808) 261-0316

Private, quiet, tropical and near all attractions. Swim in the 20- by 40-foot pool. Relax in the Jacuzzi. Stroll Kailua Beach. Enjoy a full breakfast on the lanai surrounded by Hawaiian plants, trees, and flowers with Mount Olomana in the background. Rooms with private bath, private entry, air conditioning, and TV. Tennis, golf, and all kinds of water sports nearby. Just 20 miles from Waikiki and the Honolulu airport.

Hosts: Bob and Jeanette Martz
Rooms: 2 (PB) $65-70
Full Breakfast
Credit Cards: None
Notes: 2, 5, 7, 8, 9, 10, 11, 12

6 Pets welcome; 7 Smoking allowed; 8 Children welcome; 9 Social drinking allowed; 10 Tennis available; 11 Swimming available; 12 Golf available; 13 Skiing available; 14 May be booked through travel agents.

OAHU—KANEOHE

Bed & Breakfast Hawaii O24

P. O. Box 449, Kapaa, 96746
(808) 822-7771

Wake up to the cool Kaneohe breeze as birds in the forest behind the guest cottage sing. Enjoy the large deck and your own private pool. Situated on a separate level from the hosts' residence, providing great privacy. The unit sleeps four comfortably, ideal for a family, and includes a kitchenette. Some of the finest beaches in Hawaii are on the windward side of Oahu, just a few minutes from this home. Two-night minimum stay. $55.

Bed & Breakfast Hawaii O56

P. O. Box 449, Kapaa, 96746
(808) 822-7771

This bed and breakfast is a luxuriously furnished private home with beautiful views of Kaneohe Bay from the livingroom, dining room, and swimming pool area. Your hosts offer two bedrooms, each of which has a private bath. One room offers twin beds with a bath across the hall, and the other room offers a double bed and has an adjoining bath. Ample, relaxed breakfasts are served each morning. Tea is served in the late afternoon. $50-55.

Bed and Breakfast Honolulu (Statewide) MUNRD

3242 Kaohinani Drive, Honolulu, 96817
(808) 595-7533; (800) 288-4666

This bed and breakfast overlooks Kanehoe Bay and the historic Heeia fish pond on windward Oahu. Furnished with antiques, this home is ideally located for exploring the windward and north shore, yet is only thirty minutes away from Waikiki, one block to the bus, and convenient to many restaurants and shops. Continental breakfast is served by the pool. One room has a double bed, and the other room has a pair of twins. Both have private baths. From $65.

Bed and Breakfast Honolulu (Statewide) RAYB

3242 Kaohinani Drive, Honolulu, 96817
(808) 595-7533; (800) 288-4666

Beautiful, quiet Japanese/Hawaiian home with pool. Windward Oahu. Two guest rooms with king beds and private garden baths with dressing rooms. A guest refrigerator by the pool cabana. Two miles to beach, shopping, and cafes. Watch TV in the den. Adults only. Smoking outside. Cheese and wine served poolside 5:00-6:00 P.M. Resident cats. From $65.

Windward Bed and Breakfast

Go Native...Hawaii
P. O. Box 11418, Hilo, 96721
(800) 662-8483

A spacious and delightful tropical home with continental ambience. Situated in the bedroom community of Kaneohe, it features two guest bedrooms with private baths. It is beautifully furnished with antiques and has a swimming pool and library. It overlooks Kaneohe Bay and ancient Heeia fish pond. Continental breakfast and afternoon tea are served. $45-55.

OAHU—LANIKAI

Bed and Breakfast Honolulu (Statewide) MAXEM

3242 Kaohinani Drive, Honolulu, 96817
(808) 595-7533; (800) 288-4666

Delightful, fully furnished, spacious garden

NOTES: Credit cards accepted: A Master Card; B Visa; C American Express; D Discover Card; E Diner's Club; F Other; 2 Personal Checks accepted; 3 Lunch available; 4 Dinner available; 5 Open all year;

studio. Beautiful swimming-wind-surfing beach across the street. Oriental rugs, comfortable chairs, TV, radio, queen and roll-away beds. Equipped for light cooking. Bright, airy, and very private. Has its own patio-garden area. Continental breakfast fixings are provided. Resident cat. Smoking outside. Adults only. From $60.

OAHU—MAKIKI

Bed and Breakfast Honolulu (Statewide) REEDN

3242 Kaohinani Drive, Honolulu, 96817
(808) 595-7533; (800) 288-4666

Comfortable guest room with twins or king-size bed is offered to guests by hosts that go out of their way to make their guests comfortable. The bath is shared with your hosts, and guests are welcome to use the kitchen and refrigerator. Home is located on a major bus line. $40-45.

OAHU—MANOA

Bed and Breakfast Honolulu (Statewide) CADEM

3242 Kaohinani Drive, Honolulu, 96817
(808) 595-7533; (800) 288-4666

University area, 15-minute drive to Waikiki beaches. Manoa Valley is blessed with passing showers and tradewinds. Host offers master bedroom with private bath, queen bed, and TV. Beautiful view of Diamond Head from the sun deck. Second room has twin beds and a half bath with shared shower. Continental breakfast. Resident cat. No smoking. Children welcome. $55.

Bed and Breakfast Honolulu (Statewide) SAURD

3242 Kaohinani Drive, Honolulu, 96817
(808) 595-7533; (800) 288-4666

Two bedroom condo offers a bedroom and private bath. Located on the slopes of Punchbowl, this condo overlooks downtown Honolulu and the Pacific Ocean. Learn about Hawaii from your Kama'aina host. Home is furnished with traditional Hawaiian rattan and old Hawaiian art. TV, laundry, and kitchen privileges. Near bus stop. From $50.

OAHU—NORTH SHORE

Bed & Breakfast Hawaii O46

P. O. Box 449, Kapaa, 96746
(808) 822-7771

A perfect spot on the ocean and one-half mile from the Polynesian Cultural Center, this home invites guests to enjoy a bedroom with a king-size bed and an additional bedroom with a twin bed. The bathroom is shared between the two rooms and has a tub and shower. Breakfast is prepared and waiting for you when you awake, and the hosts suggest dining by the beach. No Smoking. Preferred three-night minimum stay. $45-75.

Bed and Breakfast Honolulu (Statewide) FRASJ

3242 Kaohinani Drive, Honolulu, 96817
(808) 595-7533; (800) 288-4666

In a rural area on north shore and windward Oahu, two units nestled against the Ko'olau Mountains are a three-minute walk to the beach, shopping, or post office. Units have private baths, full cooking facilities, and ocean views. Host stocks the kitchen for a plentiful breakfast. Everything, including hibachi and picnic supplies, is provided. The upstairs unit has a private deck and an ocean view. From $60.

Bed and Breakfast Honolulu (Statewide) RICHN

3242 Kaohinani Drive, Honolulu, 96817
(808) 595-7533; (800) 288-4666

The warm, spunky hostess is a 45-year resident, an artist and author of a Hawaiian cookbook. She offers two large guest rooms. The master bedroom has a queen bed, air conditioning, and TV. The other room has twins beds and shared bath. Guests are welcome to watch the livingroom TV or enjoy the pool. Continental breakfast is served on the patio. Enjoy the serene view of the sweeping mountains and valleys. Five-minute drive to North Shore's famous beaches; 40 minutes to the airport. Much of "Old Hawaii" is here—like going back in time. From $65.

OAHU—NUUANU

Bed and Breakfast Honolulu (Statewide) HORNP

3242 Kaohinani Drive, Honolulu, 96817
(808) 595-7533; (800) 288-4666

Unhosted three-bedroom, one bath home in lush Nuuanu area. A 15- to 20-minute drive to airport or Waikiki; ten minutes to downtown. On bus line. Twin beds in one room; doubles in the others. Full kitchen. Refundable $250 security deposit. Four steps. Children and smokers accepted. No pets. From $80.

OAHU—PEARL CITY

Bed & Breakfast Hawaii O1A

P. O. Box 449, Kapaa, 96746
(808) 822-7771

This bed and breakfast home is situated just eight miles from Honolulu International Airport and offers an outstanding accommodation for its guests. The home is situated near the Pearl City Golf Course. The unit is a garden-level apartment with a separate entrance and private bath. A large pool is just outside the door. Children who know how to swim are welcome. $60.

OAHU—WAIKIKI

Bed and Breakfast Honolulu (Statewide) SHEAR

3242 Kaohinani Drive, Honolulu, 96817
(808) 595-7533; (800) 288-4666

Two blocks to beach, this tasteful condo has two guest rooms. The master bedroom has king bed and private bath. The other room has a king or two twin beds and a shared bath. View downtown Waikiki and the beach in the day, the beautiful stars and sunsets in the evening. Continental breakfast. An easy walk to shopping, restaurants, shows, and local tour agencies. Take a quiet stroll by the Ala Wai Canal. From $45.

Bed and Breakfast Honolulu (Statewide) WATTM

3242 Kaohinani Drive, Honolulu, 96817
(808) 595-7533; (800) 288-4666

This lovely penthouse is close to the beach. Three units with refrigerators, hot plates, air conditioning, and full baths. No food is provided, but facilities for light cooking are

---

NOTES: Credit cards accepted: A Master Card; B Visa; C American Express; D Discover Card; E Diner's Club; F Other; 2 Personal Checks accepted; 3 Lunch available; 4 Dinner available; 5 Open all year;

available. One unit has a private entrance, and the others enter from the hall. Parking by prearrangement. No smoking. From $65.

OAHU—WAIMANALO

Bed & Breakfast Hawaii O15A

P. O. Box 449, Kapaa, 96746
(808) 822-7771

Two separate accommodations are offered. The Mauka Suite has a large bedroom done in Polynesian-style and includes a small refrigerator, TV, and spacious bathroom. A private entrance opens to a fenced, secluded garden and lanai. Also, the elegant Ocean Suite with sleeping/livingroom, private bath, and separate entrance that opens to its own garden and lanai. Both units have access to a safe white-sand swimming beach. Breakfast is served each morning. Five-night minimum stay. $65-75.

Orchid Row Bed and Breakfast

Go Native...Hawaii
P. O. Box 11418, Hilo, 96721
(800) 662-8483

A charming hideaway bordered by the majestic Koolau Mountain Range at the footstep of Mount Olomana in the quiet countryside of Waimanalo (14 miles outside Waikiki). Situated on an orchid farm, this marvelous apartment-studio features a private bath, queen bed, cable TV, cozy kitchenette, and is perfectly decorated. Only minutes away from the best beaches on Oahu. Here is bed and breakfast with the peace and privacy of Old Hawaii. Continental breakfast. $65.

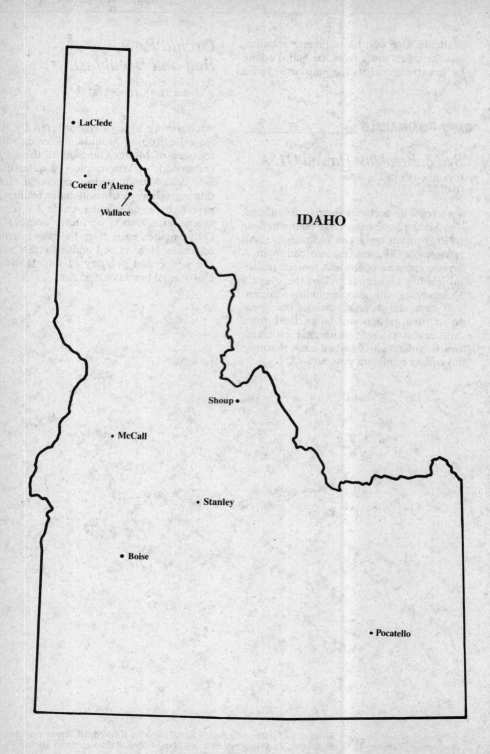

IDAHO

- LaClede
- Coeur d'Alene
- Wallace
- Shoup
- McCall
- Stanley
- Boise
- Pocatello

Idaho

BOISE

Idaho Heritage Inn

109 West Idaho, 83702
(208) 342-8066

This inn was a former governor's mansion and home to the late Senator Frank Church. Located in the historic Warm Springs District, the inn enjoys the convenience of natural geothermal water. It is surrounded by other distinguished turn-of-the-century homes, but it is also within walking distance of downtown, beautiful parks, museums, and Boise's famous Greenbelt river walkway. All rooms have been comfortably and charmingly appointed with private baths, period furniture, and crisp linens.

Hosts: Phyllis and Tom Lupher
Rooms: 5 (PB) $55-80
Continental Plus Breakfast
Credit Cards: A, B, C, D
Notes: 2, 5, 9, 14

COEUR D'ALENE

The Blackwell House

820 Sherman Avenue, 83814
(208) 664-0656

Located on Coeur d'Alene's main street, this stately home was built in 1904 by F.A. Blackwell as a wedding gift for his son. The guest rooms are decorated from quaint and cozy to spacious and elegant. All rates include full breakfast. Available by reservation for receptions, weddings, dinners, luncheons, and special parties. No children under twelve.

Host: Kathleen Sims
Rooms: 8 (6 PB; 2 SB) $75-119
Full Breakfast
Credit Cards: A, B, C, D
Notes: 2, 5, 7, 9

Cricket on the Hearth

1521 Lakeside Avenue, 83814
(208) 664-6926

Al and Karen Hutson have brought the beauty of Coeur d'Alene indoors and added a touch of country living, giving the inn an aura of "down home." The five guest rooms, three with private baths, are delightfully decorated to carry out a theme, setting the mood for a perfect getaway.

Hosts: Al and Karen Hutson
Rooms: 5 (3 PB; 2 SB) $45-75
Full Breakfast
Credit Cards: None
Notes: 2, 5, 9, 10, 11, 12, 13, 14

Idaho Heritage Inn

Greenbriar Inn

315 Wallace, 83814
(208) 667-9660

NOTES: Credit cards accepted: A Master Card; B Visa; C American Express; D Discover Card; E Diner's Club; F Other; 2 Personal Checks accepted; 3 Lunch available; 4 Dinner available; 5 Open all year; 6 Pets welcome; 7 Smoking allowed; 8 Children welcome; 9 Social drinking allowed; 10 Tennis available; 11 Swimming available; 12 Golf available; 13 Skiing available; 14 May be booked through travel agents.

Built in 1908, the Greenbriar is Coeur d'Alene's only nationally registered inn. Just four blocks from downtown and five blocks from the lake, the Greenbriar reflects the residential charm of years gone by. Surrounded by 40-foot-high maples, guests enjoy the spa outside, the wine and tea hour late in the afternoon, and a famous four-course gourmet breakfast in the morning.

Host: Kris McIlvenna
Rooms: 8 (4 PB; 4 SB) $55-85
Full Breakfast
Credit Cards: A, B, C, D
Notes: 2, 4, 5, 8, 9, 10, 11, 12, 13, 14

Inn the First Place

509 North 15th Street, 83814
(208) 667-3346

An ex-grocery store? Yes, but now a cozy home. Lots of books, artwork, magazines, and wonderful breakfasts ensure a delightful stay. Close to the freeway, downtown shopping, restaurants, and two swimming beaches. Two cats in residence. Reservations suggested.

Greenbriar Inn

Hosts: Tom and Lois Knox
Rooms: 3 (S2B) $40-50
Full Breakfast
Credit Cards: A, B
Notes: 2, 5, 9, 10, 11, 12, 13

Katie's Wild Rose Inn

E. 5150 Coeur d'Alene Lake Drive, 83814
(208) 765-9474; (800) 328-WISH

Bordered by tall pine trees and overlooking beautiful Lake Coeur d'Alene, Katie's Wild Rose Inn welcomes all who enjoy a cozy, quiet atmoshphere. An enjoyable breakfast may be served beside the wide windows or on the scenic deck. The guests will find relaxation in a game of pool or walk 1,000 yards down the road to a public dock and swimming area.

Hosts: Lee and Joisse Knowles
Rooms: 4 (2 PB; 2 SB) $55-85 plus 7% tax
Full Breakfast
Credit Cards: A, B, C
Notes: 2, 5

LACLEDE

River Birch Farm

P.O. Box 0280, 83841
(208) 263-3705

Imagine you are gazing from the parlor windows of a large turn-of-the-century home, and visualize a panoramic view of a wide river surrounded by meadows, forests, and mountains. Experience a fun-filled summer holiday swimming and canoeing from our dock facilities. Relax in our Jacuzzi. Capture the rich history of the area during a colorful autumn weekend. Spend a quiet winter evening relaxing by the fireplace after skiing. Look for spring wildflowers during a leisure vacation. Come stay for any occasion and enjoy the scenic serenity, friendly people, and special hospitality of northern Idaho.

Hosts: Charlie and Barbro Johnson
Rooms: 5 (SB) $65-75
Full Breakfast
Credit Card: F
Notes: 2, 4, 5, 9, 11, 12, 13, 14,

NOTES: Credit cards accepted: A Master Card; B Visa; C American Express; D Discover Card; E Diner's Club; F Other; 2 Personal Checks accepted; 3 Lunch available; 4 Dinner available; 5 Open all year;

MCCALL

Northwest Passage

P. O. Box 4208
201 Rio Vista Boulevard, 83638
(208) 634-5349

Originally built in 1938 for the crew of the film *Northwest Passage* starring Spencer Tracy, this beautiful pine lodge is nestled in tall ponderosa pines. Five guest rooms with private baths and a guest apartment that sleeps up to 12 with a kitchen, fireplace, and TV. Area activities: watersports on Payette Lake, fishing, snowmobiling, skiing, hunting, golf, tennis, mountain biking, and hiking. Groups of up to 22 welcome!

Hosts: Steve and Barbara Schott
Rooms: 5 plus apartment (PB) $50 and 125
Full Breakfast
Credit Cards: B, C, D
Notes: 2, 5, 6, 7, 8, 9, 11, 12, 13

POCATELLO

Holmes Retreat Bed and Breakfast

178 North Mink Creek Road, 83204
(208) 232-5518

This custom-designed, multilevel home with 15-foot vaulted ceiling and huge plants is nestled in the mountains beside scenic Mink Creek. Breakfast is served with crystal goblets from a silver tray. Dine on a deck in a garden with a fountain. Holmes Retreat is on six and one-half acres at the edge of the forest. A birdwatcher's paradise, April-June. 35 species seen from the grounds during one weekend. May through September many hummingbirds are at their feeders. Nature walk with printed guide. Mountain croquet, table games, popcorn, and videos. Turndown service complete with Teddy bear and mints. Scuba diving arranged.

Hosts: Shirley and Acel Holmes
Rooms: 2 (PB) $49-69
Full Breakfast

Credit Cards: A, B, C, E
Notes: 3, 4, 5, 8, 9, 12, 13, 14

SHOUP

Smith House Bed and Breakfast

49 Salmon River Road, 83469
(208) 394-2121; (800) 238-5915

Charming log cabin with all the comforts of home. Five distinctively furnished guest rooms with a large covered redwood deck and breathtaking view of the Salmon River. Complimentary beverages in addition to full country breakfast featuring homemade jams and fruit. Smoking outside only. Guest house includes kitchen, sleeps six (ideal for families).

Hosts: Aubrey and Marsha Smith
Rooms: 5 (1 PB; 4 SB) $35-54
Bed and Breakfast or Modified American Plan
Credit Cards: A, B
Notes: 2, 5, 6, 8, 9, 14

STANLEY

Idaho Rocky Mountain Ranch

HC 64, Box 9934, 83278
(208) 774-3544

One of Idaho's oldest and finest guest ranches, offering comfortably decorated lodge and cabin accommodations. Beautiful mountain vistas from your front porch. Delightful meals served by a friendly staff. Hiking, fishing, horseback riding, mountain biking, rafting, cross-country skiing, wildlife viewing, and much more, both on and off the ranch. Situated 50 miles north of Sun Valley on Highway 75. Brochure available; weekly rates available.

Hosts: Bill and Jeana Leavell
Rooms: 21 (PB) $80-110
Bed and Breakfast or Modified American Plan
Credit Cards: A, B
Closed April 15-May 31 and September 15-November 25
Notes: 2, 3, 4, 8, 9, 11, 13

6 Pets welcome; 7 Smoking allowed; 8 Children welcome; 9 Social drinking allowed; 10 Tennis available; 11 Swimming available; 12 Golf available; 13 Skiing available; 14 May be booked through travel agents.

WALLACE _____

The Jameson Hotel

304 Sixth Street, 83873
(208) 556-1554

Six antique-filled and renovated guest
rooms on the third floor of the Jameson
Hotel, Restaurant and Saloon. Nationally
recognized for its remodeling to represent a
turn-of-the-century hotel in this historical
mining town. Member of Idaho State
Historical Society as well as the National
Register of Historic Places. Swiming
canoeing, tubing, bicycling, skiing, snowmobiling, hiking, fishing, hunting, historical museums, and silver shops are readily
at hand.

Hosts: Mrs. Rose ("Rosie") Eaton and Mrs. Len
 Anthis
Rooms: 6 (SB) $50-65
Full Cold Breakfast
Credit Cards: A, B, C, D, E
Notes: 3, 4, 5, 7, 8, 9, 11, 12, 13, 14

Illinois

ATWOOD

Harshbarger Homestead

Rural Route 1, Box 110, 61913
(217) 578-2265

A casual, quiet, comfortable country home situated amid central Illinois prairie. Ten miles from a large Amish community. Many craft and antique shops. Visitors will enjoy beautiful herb and flower gardens, interesting coveys of collectibles throughout the house, and a 150-year-old log cabin displaying antiques with family history. Special playroom and sleeping quarters for children, but fun for all ages.

Hosts: Dale and Shirley Harshbarger
Rooms: 3 (S2B) $45
Continental Breakfast
Credit Cards: None
Notes: 2, 8, 9

BISHOP HILL

Holden's Guest House

East Main Street, 61419
(309) 927-3500

This restored 1869 farmstead is situated on one and one-half acres adjacent to your hosts and within blocks of the Bishop Hill historic district. Originally a commune, the village is a national landmark, offering five museums, restaurants, and over two dozen shops. It's truly a utopia on the prairie.

Hosts: Linda and Steve Holden
Suite: 1 (SB) $125
Rooms: 3 (1 PB; 2 SB) $50-60
Full Breakfast

Credit Cards: A, B
Notes: 2, 4, 5, 6, 7, 8, 9

CAIRO

B & B Midwest Reservations #02052

P.O. Box 95503, Hoffman Estates, 60195-0503
(800) 342-2632

This 120-year-old home sits on Millionaire's Boulevard in this historic town. The Ohio and Mississippi rivers converge at this point, making Cairo a peninsula overlooking Kentucky and Missouri. Civil War buffs will be in awe at the local history, antiques, and mementos from President Grant's stay in this town. The interior of the home has been completely restored and is filled with period antiques. The hostess can answer all your questions about the history of the area. All rooms have double beds. Private bath, $80; shared bath, $65-$70.

CARLYLE

Country Haus

1191 Franklin, 62231
(618) 594-8313

1890s Eastlake bed and breakfast. Country hospitality makes your stay in one of the four guest rooms, each with a private bath, a special memory. Family-style breakfast is served in the dining room, robes are provided for your trip to the Jacuzzi, a well-

6 Pets welcome; 7 Smoking allowed; 8 Children welcome; 9 Social drinking allowed; 10 Tennis available; 11 Swimming available; 12 Golf available; 13 Skiing available; 14 May be booked through travel agents.

ILLINOIS

stocked library and a family room with TV are here for you to enjoy. Only 55 miles east of St. Louis.

Hosts: Ron and Vickie Cook
Rooms: 4 (PB) $50-70
Full Breakfast
Credit Cards: A, B, C
Notes: 2, 5, 8, 10, 11, 12, 13 (water)

CARTHAGE

The Wright Farmhouse

Rural Route 3, 62321
(217) 357-2421

Comfortable, quiet rooms with period furnishings in a restored 19th-century home on a working farm. Country charm plus private baths, air conditioning, and private guest entrance. Nearby attractions include historic town square and courthouse and the scenic Mississippi River.

Hosts: John and Connie Wright
Rooms: 4 (PB) $26.50-37.10
Continental Breakfast
Credit Cards: A, B
Notes: 5, 8, 9, 10, 11, 12

CHAMPAIGN

Barb's Bed and Breakfast

606 South Russell, 61821
(217) 356-0376

This cozy cottage is situated in a quiet, attractive neighborhood with quick access to the University of Illinois. The comfortable guest rooms feature antiques, ceiling fans, and handmade quilts, and they share a parlor with a fireplace. Delicious breakfasts are served in the dining room. The twin cities and nearby communities offer a wide variety of things to see and do. Antique shops, theaters, museums, walking/biking trails, fishing lakes, swimming, and golf are all nearby.

Hosts: Barbara and Merle Eyestone
Rooms: 2 (SB) $45 plus tax
Hearty Continental Breakfast

Credit Cards: None
Notes: 2, 9, 10, 11, 12

The Golds Bed and Breakfast

Rural Route 3, Box 69, 61821
(217) 586-4345

Restored 1874 farmhouse with antique furnishings, just off I-74 west of Champaign, surrounded by farm fields. Antiques shopping, golfing, university, and parks nearby. Continental breakfast includes homemade coffee cake, muffins, jam, fresh fruit, and juice. Enjoy a cool beverage on the deck. Your hosts will strive to make your stay an enjoyable bed and breakfast experience. Call or write for a descriptive brochure.

Hosts: Rita and Bob Gold
Rooms: 3 (SB) $45
Continental Breakfast
Credit Cards: None
Notes: 2, 5, 9, 12, 14

The Golds

Grandma Joan's Homestay

2204 Brett Drive, 61821
(217) 356-5828

This comfortable contemporary home with two fireplaces, multilevel decks, Jacuzzi, screened-in porch, and collection of modern and folk art, is situated ten minutes

NOTES: Credit cards accepted: A Master Card; B Visa; C American Express; D Discover Card; E Diner's Club; F Other; 2 Personal Checks accepted; 3 Lunch available; 4 Dinner available; 5 Open all year; 6 Pets welcome; 7 Smoking allowed; 8 Children welcome; 9 Social drinking allowed; 10 Tennis available; 11 Swimming available; 12 Golf available; 13 Skiing available; 14 May be booked through travel agents.

from the University of Illinois. Grandma pampers you with cookies and milk at bedtime and a healthy breakfast. Let this be your home away from home.

Host: Joan Erickson
Rooms: 3 (1 PB; 2SB) $50
Full Breakfast
Credit Cards: None
Closed Dec. 20-Jan. 10
Notes: 2, 7, 9, 10, 11, 12, 14

CHICAGO

Annie's

Bed & Breakfast/Chicago, Inc.
P. O. Box 14088, 60614-0088
(312) 951-0085; FAX (312) 649-9243

This comfortable, completely furnished studio apartment has a fully equipped kitchen, queen-size bed and private bath. Close to some of Chicago's best restaurants and fine shopping. Air conditioning,TV. $75.

Bed & Breakfast/ Chicago, Inc. #2

P. O. Box 14088, 60614-0088
(312) 951-0085; FAX (312) 649-9243

This historic Kenwood home was recently restored by the architect/owner and her co-host who is a public television producer. Its Prairie-style architecture is wonderfully harmonized with antique furniture for an Old World European charm. $55 single and $65 double.

Bed & Breakfast/ Chicago, Inc. #3

P. O. Box 14088, 60614-0088
(312) 951-0085; FAX (312) 649-9243

This self-contained one-bedroom garden apartment is in a renovated frame building.

Recently decorated, it is furnished with a four-poster queen bed and sleeper sofa, and offers kitchen and private bath. There is a lovely garden for you to sit in and have your breakfast, weather permitting. Your host family lives upstairs; he is a TV reporter and she owns Bed and Breakfast/Chicago, Inc. $85.

Bed & Breakfast/ Chicago, Inc. #5

P. O. Box 14088, 60614-0088
(312) 951-0085; FAX (312) 649-9243

A traditionally furnished three-story townhouse offers an extra guest room with twin beds and a shared bath with host. Guests are welcome to enjoy the family room, fireplace, and other homey comforts provided. Your host has been with Bed and Breakfast/Chicago for over 5 years. Easily accessible to public transportation. Air conditioning, TV. $55 single; $65 double.

Bed & Breakfast/ Chicago, Inc. #8

P. O. Box 14088, 60614-0088
(312) 951-0085; FAX (312) 649-9243

This renovated Victorian brick building offers several possibilities. There are both guest rooms and self-contained apartments available. There is a twin guest room with a private bath available in the apartment of the owner. Other guest rooms include queen and double rooms with a shared bath. Guests also have access to livingroom and kitchen. This unit can also be rented as a self-contained two-bedroom apartment. The owner has just finished rehabbing a one bedroom unit with twins or a king bed, sleeper sofa in the livingroom, and a Jacuzzi bath. Air-conditioning and TV. $55 single; $65 double; $95 one-bedroom apartment; $135 two-bedroom apartment.

NOTES: Credit cards accepted: A Master Card; B Visa; C American Express; D Discover Card; E Diner's Club; F Other; 2 Personal Checks accepted; 3 Lunch available; 4 Dinner available; 5 Open all year;

Bed & Breakfast/Chicago, Inc. #9

P. O. Box 14088, 60614-0088
(312) 951-0085; FAX (312) 649-9243

This self-contained one-bedroom garden apartment has been recently decorated and offers a queen bed, bath, full kitchen, and a livingroom. Air conditioning, TV. No smoking. $85.

Bed & Breakfast/ Chicago, Inc. #12

P. O. Box 14088, 60614-0088
(312) 951-0085; FAX (312) 649-9243

A 60-year-old replica of a French chateau. The guest area is on the third floor and has a separate entrance. Two rooms, both with private baths, are available. Guests may use exercise room, full kitchen, and share a sitting room. Coffee, tea, and muffins. $65-75 single; $75-85 double.

Bed & Breakfast/ Chicago, Inc. #13

P. O. Box 14088, 60614-0088
(312) 951-0085; FAX (312) 649-9243

This turn-of-the-century townhouse is located a half a block from Lincoln Park. Two guest rooms, one with a single bed and one with twins or a king, share a bath in the 4th floor of the townhouse. Host is in public relations. No smoking. TV. $55 single; $65-75 double.

Bed & Breakfast/ Chicago, Inc. #14

P. O. Box 14088, 60614-0088
(312) 951-0085; FAX (312) 649-9243

Attractive single-family home offers two guest rooms on second floor. One has a double bed and the other has a single wicker bed. Shared bath if both guest rooms are rented. Lovely rooftop deck provides (weather permitting), a pleasant setting for continental breakfast and neighborhood watching. Your host is a sales engineer for his own company and your hostess is a retail sales manager. They have a dog. Air conditioning, TV. $65 single; $75 double.

Bed & Breakfast/ Chicago, Inc. #17

P. O. Box 14088, 60614-0088
(312) 951-0085; FAX (312) 649-9243

Relax and enjoy the modern comforts of this forty-year-old home renovated by an architect and brightly decorated in Southwest style. Downstairs guest room, located on same level as your hosts' bedroom, offers double bed and private bath (shower and tub). Upstairs guest room offers queen futon on frame, private attached bath with bathtub (handheld shower) and sitting area. Pleasant, outdoor deck off front of house offers excellent place for lounging. TV, air conditioning. Your hostess is in advertising/public relations and your host does research in cancer at Northwestern University Medical School. $55-65 single; $65-75 double.

Bed & Breakfast/ Chicago, Inc. #27

P. O. Box 14088, 60614-0088
(312) 951-0085; FAX (312) 649-9243

Located five miles from the Loop, on the border between the Gold Coast and Old Town, this self-contained apartment is in a renovated Victorian brick three-flat, occupied by your hosts. The apartment offers two bedrooms, two baths, fully equipped kitchen, fireplace, and washer/dryer. No breakfast. Air conditioning, TV. $150 daily; $2,000 monthly.

6 Pets welcome; 7 Smoking allowed; 8 Children welcome; 9 Social drinking allowed; 10 Tennis available; 11 Swimming available; 12 Golf available; 13 Skiing available; 14 May be booked through travel agents.

Bed & Breakfast/ Chicago, Inc. #29

P. O. Box 14088, 60614-0088
(312) 951-0085; FAX (312) 649-9243

This high-rise apartment offers a guest room in the spacious condominium of a public relation professional. The guest room in this stylish, contemporary home is furnished with a double bed and has a private bath. The building has a health club. Air conditioning, TV. $65-75.

Bed & Breakfast/ Chicago, Inc. #35

P. O. Box 14088, 60614-0088
(312) 951-0085; FAX (312) 649-9243

This centrally located accommodation is just two blocks from Northwestern University, Kendall College, and the Chicago "el" (elevated train). Only five minutes away, downtown Evanston and Lake Michigan are also easily accessible. This second-floor apartment offers two comfortable guest rooms, one with twin beds (placed together), and the other with a single bed. Enjoy a welcoming glass of sherry, assorted contemporary magazines, classical music, TV and VCR in a tastefully decorated environment. Terry bathrobes and other amenities add to the homey feeling. Shared bath. Continental breakfast consists of seasonal fruits or juices, and delectable scones, muffins, or croissants from Evanston's premier bakers. No smokers. $65 single; $75 double.

Bed & Breakfast/ Chicago, Inc. #37

P. O. Box 14088, 60614-0088
(312) 951-0085; FAX (312) 649-9243

Elegantly furnished country French home on 3/4 of an acre offers charm and sophistication, in a beautiful area just 10 blocks from Lake Michigan. This home has been written up in several local and city publications and features beautiful gardens, Olympic-size swimming pool, large game room with a 50-inch TV, marble entryway, and many antiques. Three guest rooms are offered: king bed with private hall bath, queen bed with private attached bath with Jacuzzi, and twin beds with private attached bath with Jacuzzi. Air conditioning, No smokers. Deluxe breakfast. $70-80 single; $80-90 double.

Bed & Breakfast/ Chicago, Inc. #41

P. O. Box 14088, 60614-0088
(312) 951-0085; FAX (312) 649-9243

This ground-floor, self-catering apartment in a two-flat building comes fully equipped for your short or long-term stay (three-night minimum), and consists of two bedrooms, one bath, livingroom, dining room, eat-in kitchen, porch, and private phone line. On a quiet residential street, it is close to public transportation in southeast Evanston. For short-term stays, continental breakfast is provided, and is self-serve. Your hosts, a retired professor and a teacher, live downstairs in their own apartments. $75 daily; $400 weekly; $900 monthly.

Bed & Breakfast/ Chicago, Inc. #43

P. O. Box 14088, 60614-0088
(312) 951-0085; FAX (312) 649-9243

This single-family home has just been rehabbed. Your host, who has traveled extensively and loves staying in bed and breakfast accommodations, lives in a coach house behind this accommodation. Offered are three guest rooms with private baths. Breakfast is self-serve from the kitchen. This is an ideal arrangement for groups traveling together or visitors in Chicago for an extended time who want to settle in and feel they've found a home away from home. Air conditioning, TV. $65-75; weekly and monthly rates are available.

Bed & Breakfast/ Chicago, Inc. #52

P. O. Box 14088, 60614-0088
(312) 951-0085; FAX (312) 649-9243

This three-story Victorian house on a beautiful residential street, studded with elm trees, is located one block west of Northwestern's campus and three blocks from the "el." Accommodations include one guest room with a double bed and another with twin beds. A private, unattached bath (no shower) is shared with other bed and breakfast guests. Your hosts, a family with two daughters, two cats, a cocker spaniel, and two guinea pigs, warmly welcome you to relax and watch TV in their first-floor livingroom. No smokers. $55 single; $65 double.

Bed & Breakfast/ Chicago, Inc. #54

P. O. Box 14088, 60614-0088
(312) 951-0085; FAX (312) 649-9243

Spacious, self-contained one-bedroom garden apartment, one block from St. Francis Hospital on Ridge, offers queen bed in bedroom plus a trundle bed in livingroom, kitchen, private bath/shower. Air conditioning. No smokers. Your hosts, an employee of the federal government and a vice president of education/training in health care, live on the premises in their own apartment. $75 daily.

Bed & Breakfast/ Chicago, Inc. #56

P. O. Box 14088, 60614-0088
(312) 951-0085; FAX (312) 649-9243

This Victorian home in Evanston's Lake Shore Historic District is conveniently situated one mile south of Northwestern University and a short walk from fine restaurants and public transportation. Featured in several local and national magazines, it is furnished with a blend of lovely antiques and art. One double room and one single room are available on the third floor. Shared bath when other guest room is occupied. A generous continental breakfast is provided. No smokers. Individuals or married couples only. $55 single; $65 double.

Bed & Breakfast/ Chicago, Inc. #64

P. O. Box 14088, 60614-0088
(312) 951-0085; FAX (312) 649-9243

This renovated mansion in prime Lincoln Park offers a double bedded guest room with a private, unattached bath. The Victorian home has been rehabbed to maintain the original feeling with antiques, wicker furniture, etc. Also available is a self-contained one-bedroom apartment on the third floor of the home. This unit is a large loft-like space with light wood floors, an island kitchen, and more contemporary furnishings. Guest room is $65 single; $75 double; apartment $125.

Bed & Breakfast/ Chicago, Inc. #71

P. O. Box 14088, 60614-0088
(312) 951-0085; FAX (312) 649-9243

This beautifully rehabbed Victorian Queen Anne, built in the late 1800s offers charm, original woodwork, hardwood floors, two fireplaces, and at the same time provides the best in modern comforts. The guest room offers a double bed, private hall bath, and sitting area. Air conditioning, TV. No smokers. $65 single; $75 double.

6 Pets welcome; 7 Smoking allowed; 8 Children welcome; 9 Social drinking allowed; 10 Tennis available; 11 Swimming available; 12 Golf available; 13 Skiing available; 14 May be booked through travel agents.

City View Inn

Bed and Breakfast/Chicago, Inc.
P. O. Box 14088, 60614-0088
(312) 951-0085; FAX (312) 649-9243

This lovely 22-room property was originally a private club. Located on the 40th floor of a building in the financial district, the rooms all have king-size beds and marble baths and gorgeous views. Included in the rate is use of the first-class health club located in the building. Parking, and continental breakfast. This is ideal for small group meetings. $105-155.

Hyde Park House

5210 South Kenwood Avenue, 60615
(312) 363-4595

This is a Victorian house with a veranda, porch swing, rear deck, two Steinways, attic greenhouse. Near the University of Chicago, Museum of Science and Industry, and 20 minutes from downtown by bus along the Lake Michigan shore. Also within walking distance are excellent sushi, Thai, Cantonese, Greek, Italian, and continental restaurants, gift shops, and art galleries.

Host: Irene Custer
Rooms: 3 (1 PB; 2 SB) $45-65
Continental Breakfast
Credit Cards: None
Notes: 2, 5, 7, 8, 9, 10, 11, 12, 13

River Plaza

Bed and Breakfast/Chicago, Inc.
P. O. Box 14088, 60614-0088
(312) 951-0085; FAX (312) 649-9243

These self-contained convertible studio apartments are among the most popular accommodations. Located in a high-rise building with a full grocery store, restaurants, health club with indoor/outdoor pool, and other amenities. Each apartment has a double or queen bed, sleeper sofa, complete kitchen, and a fabulous view of the skyline. You can walk to business appointments, shops on Michigan Avenue, the lakefront, the Merchandise Mart and the galleries of River North. Your "host" is Bed and Breakfast/Chicago. Coffee, tea, and muffins only. Air conditioning, TV. $95-125

COLLINSVILLE

Maggie's Bed and Breakfast

2102 North Keebler, 62234
(618) 344-8283

A rustic, wooded area surrounds Maggie's Bed and Breakfast, a historic former boarding house and mine superintendent's home. This beautiful, quiet country setting is just minutes from downtown St. Louis. Conveniently located near a hospital, good restaurants, and shopping areas, Maggie has tastefully furnished her home with exquisite antiques and art objects she has collected in her worldwide travels. Maggie's provides the ideal spot for one night or for several. Plenty of off-street parking available.

Host: Maggie Leyda
Rooms: 5 (1 PB; 4 SB) $35-50
Full Breakfast
Credit Cards: None
Notes: 2, 5, 6, 7, 8, 9, 10, 11, 12, 14

DUNLAP

Eagle's Nest

11125 North Trigger Road, 61525
(309) 243-7376

Country Georgian Colonial home, filled with interesting antiques and situated in a tranquil rural setting on two and one-half wooded acres. Swimming pool on premises; hiking, bicycling, cross-country skiing. Continental breakfast served on screened porch in nice weather. Rock Island hiking-biking trail, Jubilee College, Wildlife Prairie Park readily accessible. Ten minutes from Peoria.

NOTES: Credit cards accepted: A Master Card; B Visa; C American Express; D Discover Card; E Diner's Club; F Other; 2 Personal Checks accepted; 3 Lunch available; 4 Dinner available; 5 Open all year;

Hosts: John and Lou Ann Williams
Rooms: 2 (PB) $30-35
Continental Breakfast
Credit Cards: None
Notes: 2, 5, 8, 9, 10, 11, 12, 13

ELDRED

Hobson's Bluffdale

Rural Route 1, 62027
(217) 983-2854

Bluffdale lies at the east edge of the Illinois River Valley, 50 miles north of St. Louis, and is a complete vacation facility in itself. The centerpiece is a stone house built by Bill Hobson's great-great-grandfather in 1828. Guests stay in air-conditioned rooms and suites that combine modern comfort with a rustic setting. Added kitchen facilities feature Lindy's famous country cooking that brings guests back year after year and the dining room with a fireplace large enough to roast a whole deer make for homey indoor evenings. Activities include a heated swimming pool, hot tub, playground, pets, nature trails for hiking, horseback rides, hayrides, boat rides, campfire, and others.

Hosts: Bill and Lindy Hobson
Rooms: 9 (PB) $55
Full Breakfast
Credit Cards: A, B
Notes: 2, 3, 4, 8, 9, 11, 12, 14

ELIZABETH

Ridgeview
Bed and Breakfast

8833 South Massbach Road, 61028
(815) 598-3150

A 1921 country schoolhouse and former residence of author/ artist Thomas lockere overlooks ten miles of rich creek Valley. Three large, unique rooms and one loft suite, all with their own individual character, offer easy access to a Mississippi River town and other historic towns in the Galena/Jo Daviess County area. A great place to enjoy the outdoors and ride bikes on the hard top roads up the ridges. Romantic getaway packages available.

Host: Betty Valy
Rooms: 4 (PB) $60-89
Expanded Continental Breakfast
Credit Cards: A, B, C
Notes: 2, 5, 6 (call), 7 (limited), 8 (call), 9

Aldrich Guest House

GALENA

Aldrich Guest House

900 Third Street, 61036
(815) 777-3323

The Aldrich combines the elegance of the 19th century with the amenities of the 20th. Antique furnishings and period decor; central air conditioning; queen and twin beds; full gourmet breakfast. Double parlor with grand piano and screened-in porch available to guests. Historic Galena is within walking distance. Golf, swimming, and skiing are nearby.

Host: Judy Green
Rooms: 5 (3 PB; 2 SB) $65-95
Full Breakfast
Credit Cards: A, B, C, D
Notes: 2, 5, 7 (limited), 8 (over 5), 9, 10, 11, 12, 13, 14

Avery Guest House

606 South Prospect Street, 61036
(815) 777-3883

6 Pets welcome; 7 Smoking allowed; 8 Children welcome; 9 Social drinking allowed; 10 Tennis available; 11 Swimming available; 12 Golf available; 13 Skiing available; 14 May be booked through travel agents.

Situated within Galena's historic district, this pre-Civil War home is a short walk from antique shops and historic buildings. Enjoy the scenic view from the porch swing; feel free to play the piano or just visit. Breakfast is served in the sunny dining room with a bay window overlooking the Galena River valley.

Hosts: Flo and Roger Jensen
Rooms: 4 (S2B) $40-60
Expanded Continental Breakfast
Minimum stay weekends and holidays: 2 nights
Credit Cards: A, B
Notes: 2, 5, 8, 9, 10, 11, 12, 13

B & B Midwest Reservations #01012

P. O. Box 95503, Hoffman Estates, 60195-0503
(800) 342-2632

A beautiful farm home six miles south of Galena is overlooked by Chestnut Mountain. The original structure is 150 years old with additions built 75 and 25 years ago. The home, filled with antiques, offers three guest rooms. Queen waveless waterbed with private bath, queen brass bed with shared bath, and double brass bed with shared bath. Extended continental breakfast included. Easy drive to all Galena activities. $55-75

B & B Midwest Reservations #01059

P. O. Box 95503, Hoffman Estates, 60195-0503
(800) 342-2632

A pre-Civil War home built on the banks overlooking Galena's canal through town. Within walking distance of downtown Galena, this large, modest home offers four guest rooms all with queen beds sharing two full baths. One of the guest rooms has an additional twin bed available. Continental breakfast is included. Downtown Galena boasts of antique shops, craft shops, and fine restaurants. Riverboat

gambling is an easy drive nearby. $55-65. $10, additional adult; $5, child.

B & B Midwest Reservations #06059

P. O. Box 95503, Hoffman Estates, 60195-0503
(800) 342-2632

A restored farmhouse secluded in the hills near Galena. This inn has air conditioning, a large front porch, and beautiful views of the countryside. The Early American flavor is carried throughout the suite. Suite consists of king bed with Jacuzzi, loft and private porch at the farmhouse. Other freestanding locations in the Territories and Eagles Ridge include lovely homes with two bedrooms, one and -one-half or two baths, livingroom with fireplace. Can accommodate up to five people. A honeymoon or anniversary package including champagne, flowers, and breakfast in room is available. $195-315.

Bedford Guest House

11383 Route 20 West, 61036
(815) 777-2043

A charming Victorian farmhouse with four rooms, private baths, color TV, brass beds, outdoor sitting porch, antique furnishings, parklike setting one mile from historic Galena. Golf within walking distance. Nearby dog track and riverboat gambling. Call or write for price information.

Host: Linda Pluyon
Rooms: 4 (PB)
Continental Breakfast
Credit Cards: B, C
Notes: 2, 5, 7, 8, 9, 10, 11, 12, 13, 14

Belle Aire Mansion Guest House

11410 Route 20 West, 61036
(815) 777-0893

NOTES: Credit cards accepted: A Master Card; B Visa; C American Express; D Discover Card; E Diner's Club; F Other; 2 Personal Checks accepted; 3 Lunch available; 4 Dinner available; 5 Open all year;

Belle Aire Mansion is a pre-Civil War home set on 16 beautiful acres only minutes from historic Galena. The rooms are large and comfortable. Guests say, "It's just like visiting friends." The hosts say, "Welcome home—to our home."

Hosts: Jan and Lorraine Svec
Rooms: 4 (PB) $70.85-92.65
Minimum stay weekends April-Oct., holidays and
    special weekends: 2 nights
Credit Cards: A, B, C
Closed Christmas
Notes: 2, 8, 9, 11, 12, 13

Belle Aire Mansion

Brierwreath Manor Bed and Breakfast

216 North Bench Street, 61036
(815) 777-0608

Circa 1884 Queen Anne house with wraparound porch only one short block from historic Main Street. Cable TV, early morning coffee buffet, and full breakfast are only a few of the comforts you will experience. The manor has three large suites with sitting areas and private baths. Each is furnished with an eclectic blend of antiques and modern comforts. Special packages available.

Hosts: Mike and Lyn Cook
Suites: 3 (PB) $80
Full Breakfast
Credit Cards: None
Notes: 2, 5, 9

Colonial Guest House

1004 Park Avenue, 61036
(815) 777-0336

Red brick guest house with large white pillars, built in 1826. Guest rooms have private entrances, cable TV, all antique furnishings. Located one and one-half blocks from town. In the summer, breakfast is served on the porches.

Host: Mary C. Keller
Rooms: 3 and 3 suites (PB) $50-55
Continental Breakfast
Credit Cards: None
Notes: 2, 5, 6, 7 (limited), 8, 9, 10, 11, 12, 13, 14

The Country Gardens Guest House

1000 Third Street, 61036
(815) 777-3062

An 1858 brick home with large wicker-filled front porch. There are two guest rooms with new attached baths, and a 2-bed-room suite which shares a beautiful Victorian bath. Home has many antique furnishings, a Country-Victorian decor, and central air conditioning. Breakfast is served in the dining room. There is off-street parking, and it is a nice 4-block stroll to downtown Galena.

Hosts: Sandy and Dave Miller
Rooms: 4 (2 PB; 2 SB) $65-85
Hearty Continental Breakfast
Credit Cards: A, B
Notes: 2, 5, 7, 8, 9, 10, 11, 12, 13, 14

Craig Cottage

505 Dewey Avenue, 61036
(815) 777-1461

This restored two-story brick-and-limestone house sleeps two to five and is within walking distance of Galena's downtown. Enclosed porch, patio, grill, fireplace with wood supplied, washer/ dryer, color cable TV, phone, microwave, air conditioning, antique furnishings and decor. Coffee and wine are served every day. The inn over-

6 Pets welcome; 7 Smoking allowed; 8 Children welcome; 9 Social drinking allowed; 10 Tennis available; 11 Swimming available; 12 Golf available; 13 Skiing available; 14 May be booked through travel agents.

looks a wooded valley. Discounts for mid-week or multiple-night reservations are available. A very private and unique stay. Unhosted.

Hosts: Charles and Katherine Marsden; Mark Van Osdol
Cottage: (PB) $72-120
Credit Cards: A, B
Notes: 2, 5, 6, 7, 8, 9

Grandview Guest Home

113 South Prospect Street, 61036
(815) 777-1387; (800) 373-0732

A 120-year-old brick traditional on Quality Hill, overlooking the city and countryside. Victorian furnishings. Hearty continental breakfast featuring home-baked goods and European coffees. Two blocks from Main Street shops, museums, and restaurants.

Hosts: Harry and Marjorie Dugan
Rooms: 3 (1 PB; 2 SB) $60-75
Expanded Continental Breakfast
Credit Cards: A, B, C, D
Notes: 2, 5, 7, 8, 9, 10, 11, 12, 13, 14

Park Avenue Guest House

208 Park Avenue, 61036
(815) 777-1075; (800) 359-0743

An 1893 Queen Anne with "painted lady" original woodwork. Walk to town. Ample parking. Queen beds. Antique furniture. Shaded garden with gazebo. Wraparound screened porch. Central air conditioning, cable TV, and second parlor.

Host: Sharon Fallbacher
Rooms: 4 (PB) $50-95
Continental Breakfast
Credit Cards: A, B, D
Notes: 2, 5, 9, 11, 12, 13

Pine Hollow Inn

4700 North Council Hill, 61036
(815) 777-1071

Situated on a 110-acre Christmas tree farm one mile north of Galena. Helping make it one of the best are spacious rooms with fireplaces, skylights, private baths, and whirlpools, plus some superb scenery. Rooms at the inn are very large. Each is appointed with beautiful country furnishings. One of the unique qualities of the area is the peaceful solitude that is especially nice when enjoyed from the large porch surrounding the house.

Hosts: Larry and Sally Priske
Rooms: 5 (PB) $75-90
Continental Breakfast
Credit Cards: A, B
Notes: 2, 5, 9

Queen Anne Guest House

200 Park Avenue, 61036
(815) 777-3849

Restored 1891 Queen Anne Victorian nestled in a quiet residential neighborhood of historic Galena. Three romantically furnished rooms with private baths, claw foot tubs, ceiling fans, queen- and king-size beds, antiques, and period furnishings. Library, double parlors, wraparound porch, delicious breakfasts. Short stroll to antique shopping, museums, fine restaurants in historic downtown district. Minutes to skiing, golfing, riverboat excursions, and casino boats.

Hosts: Cary Mandelka and Kathleen Martin
Rooms: 3 (PB) $50-60
Expanded Continental Breakfast
Credit Cards: A, B
Notes: 2, 5, 9, 10, 11, 12, 13, 14

GOLCONDA

The Mansion of Golconda

515 Columbus, 62938
(618) 683-4400

Victorian elegance in a historical river town and richly appointed accommodations reflect a gracious lifestyle. Artfully combined with contemporary conveniences, this lovely bed and breakfast offers spacious rooms, luxurious linens, oversized towels, and special touches everywhere. A full service restaurant is on the main floor,

NOTES: Credit cards accepted: A Master Card; B Visa; C American Express; D Discover Card; E Diner's Club; F Other; 2 Personal Checks accepted; 3 Lunch available; 4 Dinner available; 5 Open all year;

limo pick-up for marina arrivals is available, and a full breakfast is served each morning on an enclosed porch or deck. Double Jacuzzi or oversized garden tub in one of the suites appeals to honeymooners or anniversary getaways. Located in the heart of the Shawnee National Forest, thirty miles from Paducah, Kentucky.

Hosts: Don and Marilyn Kunz
Rooms: 3 (PB) $75-90
Full Breakfast
Credit Cards: A, B, C, D, E
Notes: 2, 3, 4, 5, 9, 10, 11, 12, 14

Marilee's Guest House

Corner Washington and Monroe Streets
P. O. Box 88, 62938
(618) 683-2751

Very attractive bungalow, warmly furnished, comfortable; telephone, air conditioners, television, refrigerator, snacks, wood-burning fireplace, spacious rooms with open-beam ceilings. Situated near the beautiful Ohio River two blocks from the marina at Smithland Pool. Also, the deer capital of Illinois near the Shawnee National Forest. Deer hunting, bass fishing, wild turkey, quail country. Children welcome.

Host: Marilee Joiner
Rooms: 3 (1 PB; 2 SB) $45
Full Breakfast
Credit Cards: None
Notes: 2, 7, 8, 9, 13

GURNEE

B & B Midwest Reservations #02051

P. O. Box 95503, Hoffman Estates, 60195-0503
(800) 342-2632

This private home allows an entire lower-level floor for their guests. The bedroom offers a queen bed while living area provides a couch, fireplace, kitchenette, dining area, spa, and private bath. The home sits on a large lot where the guests may enjoy a small man-made lake for fishing or row-boating. Just minutes from The Pyramid House, Great America, skiing, or the Gurnee Mills Manufacturers' Discount Mall. $65.

B & B Midwest Reservations #10030

P. O. Box 95503, Hoffman Estates, 60195-0503
(800) 342-2632

"Wonderful" describes this cozy country farm home, 1/2 mile from Great America in Gurnee. Handmade quilts, feather comforters, and antiques throughout make staying in one of the three guest rooms a special experience. Accommodations in a large queen room with sitting area, queen four-poster bed with private bath; family two-room suite sleeping up to five. Separate cottage with double and twin with kitchenette. Short drive to discount mall and sports, or feed the llama and sheep. Extended continental breakfast included. $85-105.

B & B Midwest Reservations #12049

P. O. Box 95503, Hoffman Estates, 60195-0503
(800) 342-2632

This grand old red house, built in the early 1900s, features 44 windows throughout. Situated halfway between Chicago and Milwaukee, this location is convenient to Long Grove Village, Ravinia Park, Lamb's Farm, and more. Old-fashioned decor and a musical theme are woven together throughout this Victorian home. Three guest rooms share two full baths: two twin beds, a queen bed, and a king with private porch. Two rooms have private baths and double beds. Two rooms and a private bath are available as a suite. $40-110.

Sweet Basil Hill Farm Bed and Breakfast Inn

15937 West Washington Street, 60031
(708) 244-3333; (800) 228-HERB (4372)

Sitting atop a hill on seven and one-half wooded acres, Sweet Basil Hill Farm is midway between Chicago and Milwaukee. Sheep and llamas graze, paths offer summer walks or winter cross-country skiing. Herb gardens, lawn swing, hammock, picnic grove, and benches invite a more restful pace. The common room, with English pine antiques and fireplace, makes a cozy winter retreat. A generous breakfast and afternoon tea are served in the knotty pine breakfast room. Sweet Basil Hill Farm was featured in the August 1991 issue of *Country Home* magazine.

Hosts: Bob and Teri Jones
Rooms: 5 (PB) $85-115
Expanded Continental Breakfast
Credit Cards: A, B
Notes: 2, 5, 8, 9, 10, 11, 12, 13, 14

HINSDALE

B & B Midwest Reservations #19079

P. O. Box 95503, Hoffman Estates, 60195-0503
(800) 342-2632

Beautiful antique-filled home in affluent suburb featuring a suite with queen-size bed and an additional queen-size Hide-a-bed and lounge chair; Private bath with shower. A family room with fireplace and sun room are available for guests in addition to the wet bar. Desk and telephone within the room complete this wonderful setting. Close to downtown Chicago (by expressway or train), mall shopping, Brookfield Zoo, and the Western Open Golf Course. Rates include a continental breakfast. $75.

HIGHLAND

Phyllis' Bed and Breakfast

801 Ninth Street, 62249
(618) 654-4619

A remodeled bungalow about 100 years old, this bed and breakfast has a place for all seasons. A fireplace for winter wards off the cold, and a deck in the summer lets you watch the birds and squirrels. Just 25 minutes from St. Louis's many sights, Highland has a town square with antique shops, band concerts in the gazebo, and many festivals. There is plenty to do, or just enjoy a quiet, peaceful visit. We also have a gift shop on the premises.

Hosts: Bob and Phyllis Bible
Rooms: 4(PB) $50
Full Breakfast
Credit Cards: A, B
Notes: 2, 5, 8 (over 12), 10, 11, 12

LANARK

Standish House Bed and Breakfast

540 West Carrol Street, 61046
(815) 493-2307; (800) 468-2307

Traditional English bed and breakfast. Situated on Route 52, 120 miles west of Chicago. Relaxing small town atmosphere. Walking distance to business district and restaurants. Myles Standish heritage carried throughout with 18th-century English antiques, canopy beds, paintings, and decor. Dining room highlighted by antique portraits, rich, dark furniture, and formal chandelier. Full air conditioning. The owner, Norman Standish, is a direct descendant of Myles Standish.

Host: Eve Engles
Rooms: 5 (1 PB; 4 SB) $55-65
Full Breakfast
Credit Cards: A, B
Notes: 2, 5, 9, 12, 13

NOTES: Credit cards accepted: A Master Card; B Visa; C American Express; D Discover Card; E Diner's Club; F Other; 2 Personal Checks accepted; 3 Lunch available; 4 Dinner available; 5 Open all year;

MAEYSTOWN

Corner George Inn

P. O. Box 103, Corner of Main and Mill, 62256
(618) 458-6660; (800) 458-6020

A frontier Victorian structure built in 1884, the Maeystown Hotel and Saloon is now the Corner George Inn. Located 45 minutes south of St. Louis, the inn has five painstakingly restored, antique-filled guest rooms, two sitting rooms, a wine cellar, and an elegant ballroom. Maeystown is a quaint, 19th-century village with shops and a restaurant. Nearby are Fort de Chartres, Fort Kaskaskia, and the scenic bluff along the Mississippi.

Hosts: David and Marcia Braswell
Rooms: 5 (PB) $65-95
Full Breakfast
Credit Cards: A, B
Notes: 2, 5, 14

METAMORA

Stevenson House Bed and Breakfast

104 Walnut Street, 61548
(309) 367-2831

This 1858 Federal-style house is on the National Register of Historic Places and was the first home of Vice President Adlai Stevenson and his bride in 1866. Now restored and furnished with fine Victorian antiques, it is available as a bed and breakfast for guests. Relax in the warmth and charm of this house, stroll through the Victorian garden and patio, and then visit the many historical sights in the area. The Par-a-Dice Riverboat casino is thirteen miles away, and we have cruise packages available.

Hosts: Phil Fischer and Genny Downs
Rooms: 3 (SB) $55-69
Full Breakfast
Credit Cards: None
Notes: 2, 5

MOSSVILLE

Old Church House Inn Bed and Breakfast

1416 East Mossville Road, Box 295, 61552
(309) 579-2300

Situated five miles north of Peoria, this 1869 Colonial-style "church" welcomes you to the plush warmth of the Victorian era. Victorian antiques, period furnishings, pedestal sinks, thick robes, quilts, pillow chocolates, and queen feather beds. Enjoy fireside refreshments or take tea in the garden among colorful roses, perennials, and herbs. Bicycling and cross-country skiing on the Rock Island Trail are five minutes away; or indulge in shopping, dining, and Spirit of Peoria riverboat cruises.

Hosts: Dean and Holly Ramseyer
Rooms: 2 (1 PB; 2 SB) $65-85
Expanded Continental Breakfast
Credit Cards: A, B
Notes: 2, 5, 10, 11, 12, 13

MT. CARROLL

The Farm Bed and Breakfast

Route 1, Box 112, 61053
(815) 244-9885

The Farm has two beautifully decorated and spacious suites. They include fireplaces, private patios, comfortable sitting and dining areas, and various other amenities. The Barn Suite has its own double whirlpool, and just outside both units is a relaxing hot tub. With gently rolling hills and quiet surroundings, the Cottage and the Barn are perfect for a peaceful, intimate getaway for two.

Hosts: Herb and Betty Weinand
Rooms: 2 (PB) $75-89
Full Breakfast
Credit Cards: A, B
Notes: 2, 5, 7, 9

6 Pets welcome; 7 Smoking allowed; 8 Children welcome; 9 Social drinking allowed; 10 Tennis available; 11 Swimming available; 12 Golf available; 13 Skiing available; 14 May be booked through travel agents.

Prairie Path Guest House

Rural Route 3, Box 223, 61053
(815) 244-3462

This Victorian home was built in 1876 and is situated on 35 acres at the edge of a small, historic town. Country and Victorian rooms are available where guests are treated to warm hospitality and a full country breakfast of homemade specialties. Air conditioned. Unique quilt and antique shop on premises.

Hosts: DeLos and Fern Stadel
Rooms: 3 (1 PB; 2 SB) $50-60
Full Breakfast
Credit Cards: A, B
Notes: 2, 5, 12, 13

MT. MORRIS

B & B Midwest Reservations #16021

P. O. Box 95503, Hoffman Estates, 60195-0503
(800) 342-2632

This newly redecorated and refurbished country inn in Mt. Morris is located on nine wooded acres in the center of a public golf course. The inn is fully air conditioned and offers one- and two-bedroom suites, some with parlors, phones, color TVs, VCRs, mini-refrigerators, and microwave ovens. All six rooms have queen beds; some have private baths. Light continental breakfast included. $35-65.

NAPERVILLE

Harrison House Bed and Breakfast

26 North Eagle Street, 60540
(708) 420-1117

Harrison House Bed and Breakfast, circa 1911, is situated 25 miles west of Chicago in historic Naperville. Five antique-filled, air-conditioned guest rooms with private baths, one with Jacuzzi. Walk to downtown restaurants, historic sites, quaint shops, and Centennial Beach. Homemade chocolate chip cookies, fresh flowers, gourmet coffee, and scrumptious breakfast. Friendly atmosphere. Relax and be pampered.

Hosts: Lynn Harrison and Dawn Dau
Rooms: 5 (3 PB; 2 SB) $58-128
Full Breakfast
Credit Cards: A, B, C
Notes: 2, 5, 9, 10, 11, 12, 13, 14

NAUVOO

Mississippi Memories

Rural Route 1, Box 291, 62354
(217) 453-2771

Gracious lodging on the Mississippi riverbank. Elegantly served full homemade breakfasts, quiet wooded setting. Five minutes from restored Mormon city, "the Williamsburg of the Midwest." From two decks watch spectacular sunsets, abundant wildlife, and barges drifting by. Excellent geode hunting; air conditioning; fireplaces, piano, fruit and flowers in rooms. River boat gambling and cruising is only ten miles away.

Hosts: Marge and Dean Starr
Rooms: 5 (3 PB; 2 SB) $45 plus
Full Breakfast
Credit Cards: None
Notes: 2, 5, 8, 10, 11, 12, 13, 14

Parley Lane Bed and Breakfast

Rural Route 1, Box 220, 62354
(217) 453-2277

Secluded mid-1800 restored farmhouse. Peacefully situated on 80 acres of timber and pastures. Enjoy rooms furnished with antiques and wake up to a delightful continental breakfast. Stroll down Parley's wooded lane or ride complimentary bicycles into historical Nauvoo. Visit the winery, visitor centers, restaurants, antique shops, and many specialty shops. Let this home be your home and experience a memorable stay in rural Illinois.

Hosts: Garry and Ramona Myers
Rooms: 4 (1 PB; 3 SB) $35
Continental Breakfast
Credit Cards: A, B
Notes: 2, 5, 6, 7, 8, 10, 11, 12

OAKLAND

Inn on the Square

3 Montgomery, 61943
(217) 346-2289

This restored Colonial inn offers a potpourri of the "village experience." Antiques, flowers, gifts, and ladies' apparel shops all pique your curiosity. The tea room offers simple but luxurious luncheons. Golf, swimming, conservation park, Amish settlement, and Lincoln historical sites nearby.

Hosts: Caroline and Max Coon
Rooms: 4 (PB) $50
Full Breakfast
Credit Cards: A, B
Notes: 2, 3, 5, 7 (restricted), 8, 9, 10, 11, 12, 13

OAK PARK

B & B Midwest Reservations #15990

P. O. Box 95503, Hoffman Estates, 60195-0503
(800) 342-2632

Queen Anne Victorian home located in a prominent historic suburb of Chicago. The home, built in 1885, is air conditioned and accommodates guests in one room with a large queen-size bed, private bath, and Victorian-style antiques. A second room offers twin beds, private bath just steps from the room, and a private sitting room with TV. Enjoy breakfast in an elegant dining room or on the veranda when weather permits. Home is one block from Frank Lloyd Wright's home and studio. Just 20 minutes from Chicago. $55.

B & B Midwest Reservations #19111

P. O. Box 95503, Hoffman Estates, 60195-0503
(800) 342-2632

Truly for followers and admirers of Frank Lloyd Wright, this home is one of Mr. Wright's architectural creations. Furnished entirely with his signed pieces and in keeping with his choice of decor. Stay in one of three guest rooms, twin or double with shared bath for $100 per night, or king suite with private bath and sitting area for $150 per night. Enjoy a continental breakfast in the morning. The outdoor whirlpool in the summer or the large fireplace for the winter are available for guests' enjoyment. Two-night minimum is required.

Inn on the Square

Toad Hall

301 North Scoville Avenue, 60302
(708) 386-8623

A 1909 Colonial five miles from downtown Chicago in the Frank Lloyd Wright Historic District. Old World atmosphere and service. Antiques, Oriental rugs, Laura Ashley furnishings, telephones, TV, air conditioning. Walk to 25 Wright masterpieces, lovely shops, restaurants, public transportation.

---

6 Pets welcome; 7 Smoking allowed; 8 Children welcome; 9 Social drinking allowed; 10 Tennis available; 11 Swimming available; 12 Golf available; 13 Skiing available; 14 May be booked through travel agents.

Hosts: Cynthia and Jerry Mungerson
Rooms: 2 (PB) and 1 suite (PB) $55-65
Full Breakfast
Credit Cards: None
Notes: 2, 9, 10, 11, 12

Under the Ginko Tree Bed and Breakfast

300 North Kenilworth Avenue, 60302
(708) 524-2327; (800) 342-2632

The home is a magnificent Queen Anne Victorian built around 1890, air conditioned, with a wraparound front porch. It is situated one block from the Frank Lloyd Wright Home and Studio, and twenty minutes from downtown Chicago and all the museums and points of interest. Savor a light breakfast in the elegant dining room or bright, homey kitchen. When weather permits, enjoy your breakfast on the veranda.

Host: Gloria Onischuk
Rooms: 2 (PB) $55
Expanded Continental Breakfast
Credit Cards: A, C, D
Notes: 2, 5, 8, 14

OREGON

B & B Midwest Reservations #16059

P. O. Box 95503, Hoffman Estates, 60195-0503
(800) 342-2632

This 120-year-old Italianate country villa located in Oregon boasts 12 rooms and seven marble fireplaces, 11-foot ceilings, arched doorways, and antique Parisian wallpaper all adding to the charm. Rooms include a Victorian king with fireplace, private bath, and Jacuzzi, $165; two queen or king rooms with private bath and fireplaces, $110 each; three-room suite with double bed, queen bed, two half-baths, shower, and sitting room, $145 per night. Two-night minimum stay on weekends. Rates include an extensive gourmet break-

fast. Special packages and baskets available. Chocolate Fest, winter sports, Christmas tree farm, and river boat cruises available (in season).

PARIS

Tiara Manor Bed and Breakfast

403 West Court Street, 61944
(217) 465-1865; (800) 531-1865

Victorian elegance at its finest. Surround yourself in luxury as you cross the threshold of the largest Gothic mansion in downstate Illinois. Tiara Manor has been restored and meticulously decorated to represent the Civil War period with richly appointed rooms and attention to detail. This stately antebellum two-story is graced with fireplaces and lovely chandeliers. Oak and walnut ribbon parquet floors, period wallcoverings, and floor coverings. Museum quality antiques, tea room, and fine collectible shop available. There is also a formal Victorian garden with an 18-foot gazebo surrounded by century-old trees, flower beds, and fountains.

Hosts: Jo Marie and Richard Nowarita
Rooms: 4 (2 PB; 2 SB) $75-125
Full Breakfast
Credit Cards: A, B
Notes: 2, 8 (over 12), 9, 10, 11, 12

PEORIA—SEE ALSO DUNLAP

Wildlife Prairie Park

Rural Route 2, Taylor Road, 61615
(309) 676-7787

Rustic Cabin-on-the-Hill and renovated train cabooses set in the middle of 2,000 acres. Wildlife Prairie Park features animals native to Illinois in their natural habitats, which can be viewed from walking trails. Sunday brunch available April to October.

NOTES: Credit cards accepted: A Master Card; B Visa; C American Express; D Discover Card; E Diner's Club; F Other; 2 Personal Checks accepted; 3 Lunch available; 4 Dinner available; 5 Open all year;

Rooms: 6 (PB) $60-86
Continental Breakfast
Credit Cards: A, B
Closed December 14-March 14
Notes: 2, 3, 8

PLYMOUTH

Plymouth Rock Roost

201 West Summer, 62367
(309) 458-6444

This spacious Queen Anne Victorian home is located in historic Hancock County. Visit Nauvoo, Carthage, and Quincy while in the area. This gracious home is filled with antiques. Shop in the owner's antique shops, and enjoy the peace and quiet of small-town America.

Hosts: Ben Gentry and Joyce Steiner
Rooms: 3 (SB) $39
Full Breakfast
Credit Cards: A, B
Notes: 2, 5, 12

Victoria's

RANTOUL

Better 'N Grandma's Overniters

102 South Meyers Street, 61866
(217) 893-0469

This 110-year-old Victorian has a varied decor: Mexican hallway, a touch of country, and the Orient in other areas. At $10 per person per night, Better 'N Grandma's is an economical bed and breakfast in downtown Rantoul. Nearby is Chanute Air Force Base, with its air park. Fifteen miles to Champaign-Urbana and the University of Illinois.

Host: Janet Anderson
Rooms: 3 (SB) $20
Continental Breakfast
Credit Cards: None
Notes: 2, 5, 12

ROCKFORD

Victoria's

201 North Sixth Street, 61107
(815) 963-3232

Opulence, elegance, and generous hospitality await you in this turn-of-the-century mansion. Walk out the door and enter Victorian Village, 70 unique shops and eateries. Amenities: corporate telephone, cable TV, air conditioning, Jacuzzis. We specialize in weddings and banquets, and cater to the corporate traveler with weekday rates.

Hosts: Carol and Marty Lewis; Bekke Coulter
Rooms: 4 (PB) $69-169
Continental Breakfast
Credit Cards: A, B, D
Notes: 7, 9

ROCK ISLAND

Top o' the Morning

1505 Nineteenth Avenue, 61201
(309) 786-3513

6 Pets welcome; 7 Smoking allowed; 8 Children welcome; 9 Social drinking allowed; 10 Tennis available; 11 Swimming available; 12 Golf available; 13 Skiing available; 14 May be booked through travel agents.

Sam and Peggy welcome you to their brick mansion on the bluffs overlooking the Mississippi River. Fantastic view day or night. Three-acre wooded estate with winding drive, orchard, and gardens. Air-conditioned bedrooms, whirlpool tub, natural fireplaces.

Hosts: Sam and Peggy Doak
Rooms: 2 (PB) $50-60
Full Breakfast
Credit Cards: None
Notes: 2, 5, 7, 8, 9, 10, 11, 12, 13

SULLIVAN

The Little House on the Prairie

Rural Route 2 Patterson Road
P. O. Box 525, 61951
(217) 728-4727

A Victorian Queen Anne country homestead is surrounded by acres of woodlands, gardens, a swimming pool, and a pond. The little home was built in 1894 by Andrew Jackson Little, grandfather of the innkeeper. After forty years of involvement in the theater world, the host has opened his home to the public. The home is filled with antiques and theatrical memorabilia. Some of the bedrooms open onto a large sun room with a Jacuzzi, dining, and entertainment center.

Host: Guy S. Little, Jr.
Rooms: 4 (PB) $60
Full Breakfast
Credit Cards: None
Notes: 2, 7, 11, 12

SYCAMORE

Country Charm Inn

Route 2, Box 154, Quigley Road, 60178
(815) 895-5386

Understated elegance is the hallmark of this three-story country farm home. Pit fireplace, 2,000-book library, mini petting zoo, trick horse Champ, breakfast on the cozy front porch. Howard and Donna are former AFS hosts, and Donna, the oldest of 14 children, loves people.

Hosts: Howard and Donna Petersen
Rooms: 3 (PB) $35-60
Full Breakfast
Minimum stay holidays: 2 nights
Credit Cards: None
Notes: 2, 5, 8, 9, 10, 11, 12

TOLONO

Aunt Zelma's Country Guest House

1074 County Road 800 N, 61880
(217) 485-5101; (217) 485-8925

Situated near Champaign and the University of Illinois, just three miles from Willard Airport. This one-story country home is furnished with family antiques and quilts.

Host: Zelma Weibel
Rooms: 3 (1 PB; 2 SB) $42.40-47.70
Full Breakfast
Credit Cards: None
Notes: 2, 5, 8, 12

WENONA

Hart of Wenona

303 North Walnut, 61377
(815) 853-4778

Relax and enjoy the elegance of the past. Turn-of-the-century home with lovely stained glass, golden oak woodwork, wraparound veranda, and period antiques. Peace and quiet of a small town. Air conditioned.

Hosts: Henry and Beverly Hart
Rooms: 3 (SB) $40
Continental Breakfast
Credit Cards: D
Notes: 2, 5

WEST DUNDEE

B & B Midwest Reservations #08040

P. O. Box 95503, Hoffman Estates, 60195-0503
(800) 342-2632

NOTES: Credit cards accepted: A Master Card; B Visa; C American Express; D Discover Card; E Diner's Club; F Other; 2 Personal Checks accepted; 3 Lunch available; 4 Dinner available; 5 Open all year;

Step back into the early 1900's when you visit this newly renovated historical site in West Dundee. This mansion is filled with antiques and royal hospitality, and convenient shopping malls, interstate highways, and business districts are within a few minutes' drive. The six uniquely decorated rooms range from smaller country-style to formal Colonial doubles to a Victorian suite with a Jacuzzi. Several rooms have shared baths with Jacuzzis for guests. Accommo-dations include kings, queens, doubles, and twins. Central air conditioning. Designated smoking areas available. Extended continental breakfast included. $49-159.

Ironhenge Inn

Ironhedge Inn Bed and Breakfast

305 Oregon Avenue, 60118
(708) 426-7777

A 28-room romantic mansion sits amid formally landscaped grounds with a large gazebo beckoning guests to relax and enjoy afternoon tea. Once inside, time stands still as you experience Victorian ambience. Delight in the lavish honeymoon suite with king-size bed, oversized marble Jacuzzi for two, and complimentary breakfast in bed or served in the private breakfast room. Other rooms are uniquely decorated, each with its own theme and exuding a mood of pampered comfort.

Hosts: Sarah and Frank Hejhal
Rooms: 7 (2 PB; 3 SB) $49-159
Expanded Continental Breakfast
Credit Cards: A, B, C, D
Notes: 2, 5, 9, 14
Notes: 2, 5, 7, 8, 9, 14

WINNETKA

Chateau des Fleurs

552 Ridge Road, 60093
(312) 256-7272

Chateau des Fleurs is an elegant respite from the world that welcomes you with light, beauty, warmth, and lovely views of magnificent trees, gardens, and a swimming pool. A French country home filled with antiques, four fireplaces, 50-inch television, and a grand piano. Situated by a private road for jogging or walking, it is only four blocks from shops and restaurants and a 30-minute train ride to Chicago's Loop. Ten minutes from Northwestern University.

Host: Sally H. Ward
Rooms: 3 (PB) $80-90
Expanded Continental Breakfast
Minimum stay weekends and holidays: 2 nights
Credit Cards: A, B
Notes: 2, 5, 8 (over 11), 9, 10, 11, 12, 14

Chateau des Fleurs

Bristol • Middlebury • Shipshewana

Beverly Shores

Lagrange

Goshen

Mishawaka

Walkerton

Chesterton

Nappanee • Ligonier

Syracuse

Warsaw • Auburn

South Bend

Decatur

Huntington •

Rossville •

Attica •

Crawfordsville

Clinton •

Hagerstown •

Terre Haute •

Indianapolis •

Morgantown •

Connersville
Metamora

Nashville •

Madison •

West Baden •

Paoli •

Jasper •

Corydon •

Evansville •

Grandview •

INDIANA

Indiana

ATTICA

The Apple Inn

604 South Brady, 47918
(317) 762-6574

Step back into a time when the hostess's grandmother lived in this 1903 Colonial Revival home. Carolyn will guide you through four generations of antiques. Rest comfortably in one of five unique bedrooms: the Train Room, Sewing Room, Music Room, Toy Room, and Antique Doll Room. Sleep on down comforters and pillows. An expanded continental breakfast is served by candlelight on fine china. Stop and see this live-in museum. In Brady Street historic district.

Hosts: Carolyn Borst Carolson and Donald L. Martin
Rooms: 5 (1 PB; 4 S2B) $60-75
Expanded Continental Breakfast
Credit Cards: None
Notes: 2, 5, 10, 11, 12, 14

AUBURN

Yawn to Dawn Bed and Breakfast

211 West Fifth Street, 46706
(219) 925-2583

Relax in the friendly atmosphere of an early 1900s home. Three lovely bedrooms with a shared bath and a tasty continental breakfast with friendly conversation make for a pleasant stay. Within blocks is the famous Auburn, Cord & Duesenberg Museum, which draws people from all over the world to view over 160 classic cars.

Plenty of activities are within minutes, including golf, shopping malls, art museums, antique shops, and fine dining.

Hosts: Don and Shirley Quick
Rooms: 3 (3 SB) $45
Continental Breakfast
Credit Cards: None
Notes: 2, 5, 8

BEVERLY SHORES

Dunes Shore Inn

33 Lake Shore County Road, Box 807, 46301
(219) 879-9029

A casual bed and breakfast in secluded Beverly Shores is surrounded by the Indiana Dune National Lakeshore. Only one block to Lake Michigan, and one hour to Chicago. Miles of trails and beaches, spectacular sunrises and sunsets, and an everchanging lake await you.

Hosts: Rosemary and Fred Braun
Rooms: 12 (S4B) $45-55
Continental Breakfast
Minimum stay weekends and holidays: 2 nights
Credit Cards: A, B
Notes: 2, 5, 8, 9, 10, 11, 12, 13

BRISTOL

Tyler's Place

19562 State Road 120, 46507
(219) 848-7145

Adjoining a 27-hole golf course at the edge of Crystal Valley, Tyler's Place offers a pleasant view of the rolling course and plenty of warm Hoosier hospitality. The

NOTES: Credit cards accepted: A Master Card; B Visa; C American Express; D Discover Card; E Diner's Club; F Other; 2 Personal Checks accepted; 3 Lunch available; 4 Dinner available; 5 Open all year; 6 Pets welcome; 7 Smoking allowed; 8 Children welcome; 9 Social drinking allowed; 10 Tennis available; 11 Swimming available; 12 Golf available; 13 Skiing available; 14 May be booked through travel agents.

Common Room is decorated with an Amish flavor. Full breakfast is served in the sun room, and evenings are enjoyed in the back yard around the fire ring.

Hosts: Esther and Ron Tyler
Rooms: 2 (1 PB; 1 SB) $45
Full Breakfast
Credit Cards: None
Notes: 2, 5, 7 (outside) , 10, 11, 12, 13

Gray Goose Inn

CHESTERTON

Gray Goose Inn

350 Indian Boundary Road, 46304
(219) 926-5781

English-style country house situated on 100 wooded acres overlooking a private lake. Walking trails, paddle boat, rowboat, bikes are available for guests. Minutes from Dunes State and National Lake Shore parks; 50 minutes from Chicago.

Hosts: Tim Wilk and Chuck Ramsey
Rooms: 5 (PB) $65-85
Full Breakfast
Credit Cards: A, B, C, D
Notes: 2, 5, 7, 8 (over 11) , 9, 10, 11, 12, 13, 14

Indian Oak Resort

588 Indian Boundary, 46304
(219) 926-7413

Thirty-five miles southeast of Chicago on a lakeside, wooded parcel of land just off intersection I94/I49. Enjoy the health club, spa facilities, restaurants, meeting and conference space, hiking trails, and more. The Indian Oak Resort is the closest hotel to the wondrous Indiana Dunes State Park. Of course, an extensive continental breakfast is included.

Hosts: Cathy Chubb and Lori Wickham
Rooms: 100 (PB) $64-124
Continental Breakfast
Credit Cards: A, B, C, D
Notes: 2, 3, 4, 5, 6, 7, 8, 9, 11, 13 (XC) , 14

CLINTON

Pentreath House

424 Blackman Street, 47842-2007
(317) 832-2762

Relax in elegance in this 1926 mansion. Sit by the fireplace or on the porch, enjoy Clinton's Italian cuisine, or visit Parke County's famous covered bridges and state parks. Whether your trip is pleasure or business, you'll savor the atmosphere. Each guest room has its own character, and two have private baths. Close to Indiana State University, St. Mary-of-the-Woods College, and Rose Hulman Institute of Technology.

Hosts: Laura and Lou Savage
Rooms: 3 (2 PB; 1 SB) $45 and up
Expanded Continental Breakfast
Credit Cards: None
Notes: 5, 7, 8 (over 6) , 9, 12, 14

CONNERSVILLE

Maple Leaf Inn
Bed and Breakfast

831 North Grand Avenue, 47331
(317) 825-7099

The Maple Leaf Inn blends the old with the new, offering warm hospitality and boasting much of its original craftsmanship from the mid-1860s. Four bedrooms with private baths. Nearby are antique shops, two state parks, and an old canal town with unique shops.

Hosts: Karen and Gary Lanning
Rooms: 4 (PB) $45-55
Continental Breakfast
Credit Cards: A, B
Notes: 2, 5, 7, 8

CORYDON

Kintner House Inn

101 South Capitol Avenue, 47112
(812) 738-2020

Completely restored inn, circa 1873, a national historical landmark, with 15 rooms, each with private bath, furnished in Victorian and country antiques. Serves full breakfast. Also, three apartment suites adjacent to inn, completely furnished and decorated, that are ideal for families. Unique shops, fine restaurants, antique malls, horse-drawn carriage, and excursion train all within walking distance of the inn. Sports available. Rated AAA and Mobil. A hideaway for romantics. Weekend rates.

Host: Mary Jane Bridgwater
Rooms: 18 (PB) $39-89
Full Breakfast
Credit Cards: A, B, C, D, E
Notes: 2, 5, 8, 9, 10, 11, 12, 14

Maple Leaf Inn Bed and Breakfast

CRAWFORDSVILLE

Davis House

1010 West Wabash, 47933
(317) 364-0461

Davis House is a Victorian mansion built of bricks manufactured on the site and furnished with antique and country pieces. Guest rooms have private baths and telephones. A convenience center is available to guests. Crawfordsville has several museums, many antique shops, good restaurants.

Hosts: Jan and Dave Stearns
Rooms: 5 (PB) $50-60
Continental Breakfast
Credit Cards: A, B, C, D
Notes: 2, 5, 7, 8, 9, 10, 11, 12, 14

DECATUR

Cragwood Inn Bed and Breakfast

303 North Second Street, 46733
(219) 728-2000

Enjoy the ambience of the past and the conveniences of the present in this beautiful Queen Anne home, circa 1900. Magnificent woodwork and beveled leaded glass windows reflect the craftsmanship of a bygone era. Fireplaces in two rooms, several mystery dinners, and crafters' weekends are offered during the year. Chocolate lovers' weekends are held in March and October. Decatur, a delightful small town just south of Fort Wayne, has a large antique mall.

Hosts: George and Nancy Craig
Rooms: 5 (3 PB; 2 SB) $45-60
Full Breakfast (weekends); Hearty Continental
  (weekdays)
Credit Cards: A, B
Notes: 2, 5, 9, 10, 11, 12

EVANSVILLE

Brigadoon Bed and Breakfast

1201 SE Second Street, 47713
(812) 422-9635

Romantic white-frame Victorian with 1892 parquet floors, four fireplaces, and stained glass invites guests to enjoy ther rainbows cast every sunny morning in the lace-curtained parlor. Large, antique-furnished guest rooms are Scottish, English, Irish, and Welsh.

Host: Katelin Forbes
Rooms: 4 (2 PB; 2 SB) $45-50
Full Breakfast
Credit Cards: A, B, C
Notes: 2, 5, 6, 8, 9, 10, 11, 12, 14

GOSHEN

Business Bed and Beakfast

58885 County Road 115, 46526
(219) 875-8151

A pleasant alternative for the business traveler, minutes away from Elkhart, Indiana. The visitor to Business Bed and Breakfast will enjoy a private room and bath with a balcony view of the deep woods. There is a homelike, relaxing atmosphere, and the inn's features include a great room, suana, and DP GymPac. Take a walk along the riverbank. Healthy snacks and nutritions breakfasts are served.

Rooms: 4 (PB) $25 plus tax
Continental Breakfast
Credit Cards: None
Notes: 2, 5

The Checkerberry Inn

62644 County Road 37, 46526
(219) 642-4445

At the Checkerberry Inn you will find a unique atmosphere, different from anywhere else in the Midwest. Each individu-

ally decorated room has a breathtaking view of the unspoiled countryside. Outdoor pool, tennis court, and croquet green. Cycling, jogging, and walking area. Shopping and golf within 10 to 15 minutes.

Hosts: John and Susan Graff
Rooms: 12 (PB) $120-175
Continental Breakfast
Credit Cards: A, B, C
Closed January
Notes: 2, 3, 4, 8, 9, 10, 11, 12, 14

Timberidge

16801 State Road 4, 46526
(219) 533-7133

This Austrian chalet log home, nestled in the beauty of quiet woods, welcomes guests into a serene setting with a uniquely furnished suite with a private bath and private entrance. A continental breakfast is served in front of the large windows where the beauty of the countryside can be enjoyed. There is a walking path through the woods, and area attractions are nearby Amish and Mennonite communities.

Hosts: Edward and Donita Brookmyer
Rooms: 1 suite (PB) $55
Continental Breakfast
Credit Cards: None
Notes: 2, 8

GRANDVIEW

The River Belle

P. O. Box 669, 47615
(812) 649-2500; (800) 877-5165

Come to the River Belle for a little bit of southern charm in southern Indiana. Situated on the Ohio River; guests may choose from one of three accommodations: an 1866 white-painted brick steamboat style, an 1890 red-brick Italianate, or the "little house under the pecan tree"—an 1860 cottage with full kitchen. Guests may choose to walk along the river or sit quietly and watch the white squirrels play among

NOTES: Credit cards accepted: A Master Card; B Visa; C American Express; D Discover Card; E Diner's Club; F Other; 2 Personal Checks accepted; 3 Lunch available; 4 Dinner available; 5 Open all year;

the magnolias, pecan trees, and azaleas. Located within 20 miles of the Lincoln Boyhood National Memorial, Lincoln State Park, Lincoln drama, and Holiday World— the nation's oldest amusement park.

Hosts: Don and Pat Phillips
Rooms: 6 (2 PB; 4 SB) $45-65
Continental Breakfast
Credit Cards: A, B
Notes: 8

HAGERSTOWN

Teetor House

300 West Main Street, 47346
(317) 489-4422

Experience the comfort and charm of this elegant home with its inspiring history. Stroll its ten landscaped acres and explore the charming small town with quaint shops and excellent restaurants. Enjoy six golf courses, a large screened porch, a book by the fire, or the grand piano with player. Cable TV and a large pair of twins or king-size bed in each bedroom. Located in eastern Indiana five miles north of I- 70. Beer and wine available.

Hosts: Jack and JoAnne Warmoth
Rooms: 4 (PB) $82.50-99 plus tax
Full Breakfast
Credit Cards: A, B
Notes: 2, 5, 7 (limited) , 8, 9, 10, 11, 12, 14

HUNTINGTON

Purviance House Bed and Breakfast

326 South Jefferson, 46750
(219) 356-4218; (219) 356-9215

Freshly baked breads, a pot of coffee or tea, and fresh fruits welcome guests to a homey atmosphere with a TV, kitchen privileges, and well-stocked bookshelves. Comfy beds and tasty breakfasts add to the warm ambience of a lovingly restored 1859 Greek

Revival-Italianate home listed on the National Register of Historic Places. Features include a winding cherry staircase, parquet floors, ornate ceiling designs, four unique fireplaces, quilts, antiques, and period furnishings. Near lakes and nature trails.

Hosts: Bob and Jean Gernand
Rooms: 4 (2 PB; 2 SB) $40-55 plus tax
Full Breakfast
Credit Cards: None
Notes: 2, 5, 9, 10, 11, 12

Teetor House

INDIANAPOLIS

The Hoffman House Bed and Breakfast

545 East 11th Street, P. O. Box 906, 46206-0906
(317) 635-1701; FAX (317) 635-1701

The Hoffman House is a 1903 American Four square located in downtown Indianapolis. This bed and breakfast home-stay provides affordable elegance featuring oak dentil woodwork, oak hardwood floors, antiques, and period reproductions, as well as French Impressionist art prints. Two comfortable guest rooms are on the second floor. Rooms feature antique double beds with handmade quilts. A Continental plus breakfast is served on a lace tablecloth with blue and white china and cobalt blue glassware.

Host: Laura A. Arnold
Rooms: 2 (SB) $60-90
Continental Plus Breakfast
Credit Cards: A, B
Notes: 2, 8, 9, 14

6 Pets welcome; 7 Smoking allowed; 8 Children welcome; 9 Social drinking allowed; 10 Tennis available; 11 Swimming available; 12 Golf available; 13 Skiing available; 14 May be booked through travel agents.

JASPER

Artist's Studio Bed and Breakfast

429 West Haysville Road, 47546
(812) 695-4500

The Artist's Studio is home to watercolor artist Gail Roach. Regional paintings are displayed throughout the 1920s bungalow-style structure. Oak floors and woodwork are the most outstanding features of this beautiful inn, and bedrooms are furnished with period furniture. The Artist's Studio is located near Patoka Lake, Holiday World, Amish restaurants, and the Lincoln Outdoor Drama Center. Relax on the porch and watch the hummingbirds.

Host: Gail Roach
Rooms: 2 (1 PB; 1 SB) $40-45
Continental Breakfast
Credit Cards: None

KNIGHTSTOWN

Bed and Breakfast Midwest Reservations #12121

P.O. Box 95503, 60195-0503
(800) 342-2632

This historic country home located midway between Indianapolis and Richmond, Indiana, provides four rooms for guests with easy access to I-70. Guest rooms include king, queen with a fireplace, and queen and pair of twins, each of which has a private bath. This beautiful inn overlooks Hoosier farmland and a beautiful golf course that guests may use. A short drive to a quaint small town and four hours from Chicago, this home is in Antique Alley. Enjoy an extended continental breakfast before you begin your day's activities. Golf packages available.

LAGRANGE

The 1886 Inn

212 Factory Street, 46761
(219) 463-4227

The 1866 Inn bed and breakfast is filled with historical charm and elegance and glows with old-fashioned beauty in every room. Finest lodging area, yet affordable, this inn is ten minutes from Shipshewana Flea Market,

Hosts: Duane and Gloria Billman
Rooms: 4 (PB) $59
Expanded Continental Breakfast
Credit Cards: A, B
Notes: 2, 5

LIGONIER

Solomon Mier Manor

508 South Cavin Street, 46767
(219) 894-3668

This Italian/Queen Anne Renaissance home was built in 1899. It has four guest rooms completely furnished in antique furniture of the period. Each room has its own private bath. This home is situated on the edge of Ligonier's business district, which is in an area that has been placed on the National Register of Historic Places. It contains some of the grandest architecture to be seen. It is minutes away from the Shipshewana flea market, Nappanee Amish

Solomon Mier Manor

NOTES: Credit cards accepted: A Master Card; B Visa; C American Express; D Discover Card; E Diner's Club; F Other; 2 Personal Checks accepted; 3 Lunch available; 4 Dinner available; 5 Open all year;

Acres, Auburn-Cord Dusenburg Museum—Das Essenhause at Middlebury, and much more.

Hosts: Ron and Doris Blue
Rooms: 4 (PB) $45-55
Expanded Continental Breakfast
Credit Cards: A, B
Notes: 2, 5

MADISON

The Cliff House

122 Fairmont Drive, 47250
(812) 265-5272

The Cliff House is located high above historic downtown Madison overlooking the Ohio River. This 1885 Victorian-decorated home is filled with marble-topped tables, canopy beds, Haviland china, and many other period antiques. Guests enjoy sitting outside on the widow's walk watching the boats go up and down the river. Come step back into time.

Host: Joe Breitweiser
Rooms: 6 (PB) $75 plus tax
Continental Plus Breakfast
Credit Cards: A, B
Notes: 2, 5, 7 (restricted) , 8, 9, 10, 11, 12, 13, 14

METAMORA

The Thorpe House Country Inn

Clayborne Street, P. O. Box 36, 47030
(317) 647-5425; (317) 932-2365

Visit the Thorpe House in Metamora where the steam engine still brings passengers and the gristmill still grinds cornmeal. Spend a relaxing evening in this 1840 home, only one block from the historic Whitewater Canal. Homey, cozy rooms are tastefully furnished with antiques and country accessories. Enjoy a hearty breakfast before exploring over 100 shops in this quaint village. Public dining room. Special packages available. Between Indianapolis and Cincinnati.

Varns Guest House

Hosts: Mike and Jean Owens
Rooms: 5 (PB) $60-100
Full Breakfast
Credit Cards: A, B, D
Open April—mid-Dec.
Notes: 2, 3, 4, 6, 7, 8, 9, 14

MIDDLEBURY

Bee Hive Bed and Breakfast

Box 1191, 46540
(219) 825-5023

Come home to the farm. Enjoy country life, snuggle under a handmade quilt, and wake to the smell of freshly baked muffins. Located in the heart of Amish country. Enjoy the shops, flea markets, and antique stores in the area. Right off the Indiana Turnpike.

Hosts: Herb and Treva Swarm
Rooms: 4 (1 PB; 3 SB) $49.95-60
Full Breakfast
Credit Cards: A, B
Notes: 2, 5, 8, 10, 12, 13

Patchwork Quilt Country Inn

11748 Country Road 2, 46540
(219) 825-2417

6 Pets welcome; 7 Smoking allowed; 8 Children welcome; 9 Social drinking allowed; 10 Tennis available; 11 Swimming available; 12 Golf available; 13 Skiing available; 14 May be booked through travel agents.

Patchwork Quilt is a centennial farm which grows soybeans or corn. Restaurant is on the premises, and nine bedrooms are decorated in quaint country style.

Hosts: Maxine Zook and Susan Thomas
Rooms: 9 (6 PB; 3 SB) $51-95
Continental Breakfast
Credit Cards: A, B
Notes: 2, 3, 4, 5, 12

Varns Guest House

205 South Main Street, P. O. Box 125, 46540
(219) 825-9666

A circa 1898 house built by the innkeeper's great-grandparents, this home has been in the Varns family for over 90 years. Recently restored, it is in the heart of Amish country just three miles south of the Indiana toll road's Middlebury exit. There are five air-conditioned guest rooms, each with private bath and individually decorated and named after the hosts' ancestors. Relax on the wraparound porch or snuggle before a wood-burning fireplace in the parlor during cold weather. Area attractions include giant Shipshewana flea market, Amish communities, fine shops, and restaurants.

Hosts: Carl and Diane Eash
Rooms: 5 (PB) $65
Expanded Continental Breakfast
Credit Cards: A, B
Notes: 2, 5, 12

Windmill Hideaway Bed and Breakfast

11380 W. State Road 120, 46540
(219) 825-2939

You will find a Dutch windmill at the end of the driveway leading to the home, which is set in a wooded area. Nearby are beautiful Amish homes and the famous Shipshewana flea market, crafts, and shops. Carriage rides and dinner in an Amish home can be arranged. Hosts are never too busy to point out places of interest in the area and offer a basket of brochures for you to read.

Hosts: Ed and Pat Nelson
Rooms: 4 (SB) $50
Full Breakfast
Credit Cards: A, B
Notes: 2, 5, 12, 13

The Beiger Mansion Inn Fables Gallery, Inc.

MISHAWAKA

The Beiger Mansion Inn Fables Gallery, Inc.

317 Lincoln Way East, 46544
(219) 256-0365; (800) 437-0131
FAX (219) 259-2622

The 22,000-square-foot inn offers gracious accommodations for travelers who appreciate its blend of historic and cultural personality. The romance and nostalgia of the mansion appeal to travelers, whether on holiday or business trip. Listed on the National Register of Historic Places. Close to South Bend and Notre Dame. Gift and art gallery situated on main level. Gourmet dining weekends, lunch Tuesday-Saturday.

Hosts: Ron Montandon and Phil Robinson
Rooms: 8 (PB) $65-175
Full Breakfast
Credit Cards: A, B, C, E
Notes: 2, 3, 4, 5, 12

MORGANTOWN

The Rock House

380 West Washington Street, 46160
(812) 597-5100

NOTES: Credit cards accepted: A Master Card; B Visa; C American Express; D Discover Card; E Diner's Club; F Other; 2 Personal Checks accepted; 3 Lunch available; 4 Dinner available; 5 Open all year;

An 1894 Victorian built of concrete block, each block decorated with rocks, geodes, dice, doorknobs, dishes—even the skull of a wild boar! Visitors to Nashville/Brown County, Indiana University, and Lake Monroe are served a full breakfast before taking a "binocular" tour of the home's exterior (the only way to find all the embedded treasures).

Hosts: George and Donna Williams
Rooms: 6 (2 PB; 4 SB) $50-65
Full Breakfast
Credit Cards: A, B
Notes: 2, 5, 12, 13

NAPPANEE

Amish Acres
Bed and Breakfast
Reservation Service

1600 West Market Street, 46550
(800) 800-4942

Historic Amish Acres in Nappanee provides a unique bed and breakfast service that offers overnight accommodations in private, northern Indiana Amish country homes. Most accommodations are in two-story frame houses on large farms in Elkhart Country area. Most hosts are members of the Mennonite, German Baptist, and Old Order or conservative Amish faiths. Many Old Order homes do not have electricity and do not accept reservations for

The Rock House

Saturday or Sunday. Continental breakfast is served, although some offer full breakfast. $50.

Market Street
Bed and Breakfast

253 East Market Street, 46550
(800) 497-3791

The red-brick house on the corner nestled among the tall maples in Amish country, 45 minutes from Notre Dame campus, close to the Dunes and Lake Michigan recreation, art festivals; nationally famous flea market area. Home-baked cookies and picnic baskets overflowing with a delicious lunch for exploring the countryside. Back porch with wicker rockers for early risers to enjoy a quiet cup of coffee or tea before a full breakfast is served.

Host: Jean Janc
Rooms: 6 (4 PB; 2 SB) $40-65
Full Breakfast
Credit Cards: A, B
Notes: 2, 5

NASHVILLE

Allison House Inn

90 South Jefferson Street, 47448
(812) 988-0814

A yellow-and-white Victorian house built in 1883, completely remodeled in 1986 to encompass comfort and charm. This bed and breakfast located in the heart of Brown County's arts and crafts colony is conveniently situated and a traveler's delight.

Host: Tammy Galm
Rooms: 5 (PB) $85
Full Breakfast
Credit Cards: None
Notes: 2, 5

6 Pets welcome; 7 Smoking allowed; 8 Children welcome; 9 Social drinking allowed; 10 Tennis available; 11 Swimming available; 12 Golf available; 13 Skiing available; 14 May be booked through travel agents.

PAOLI

Braxtan House Inn Bed and Breakfast

210 North Gospel, 47454
(812) 723-4677

Braxtan House is a 21-room Queen Anne Victorian, lovingly restored and furnished in antiques. The inn overlooks the historic courthouse square and is near Paoli Peaks ski resort, Patoka Lake, and antique and craft shops in picturesque southern Indiana hill country.

Hosts: Terry and Brenda Cornwell
Rooms: 6 (PB) $42-63
Full Breakfast
Minimum stay holidays: 2 nights
Credit Cards: A, B, D (with surcharge)
Notes: 2, 5, 7, 8 (over 11) , 9, 10, 11, 12, 13

Braxtan House Inn Bed and Breakfast

ROSSVILLE

Country Lodging

Rural Route 1, Box 248, 46065
(317) 379-2796

A quiet place in thge country, this bed and breakfast is ten miles east of I-65 on Highway 26. Purdue University is fifteen miles away in Layfayette. This old home-stead has been remodeled. No TV. Just wake up to the birds singing. Christian community.

Host: Barbara Rogers
Rooms: 2 (1 PB; 1 SB) $40-50
Full Breakfast
Credit Cards: None
Notes: 2, 5, 8, 10, 12

SHIPSHEWANA

Green Meadow Ranch

790 West 450N, 46565
(219) 768-4221

You're a stranger only once at Green Meadow. Nestled in the center of Amish and Mennonite country, two miles from Shipshewana, home of the Amish-Mennonite Visitors Center, the Shipshewana auction, and many shops and attractions.

Hosts: Paul and Ruth Miller
Rooms: $50-60
Expanded Continental Breakfast
Credit Cards: A, B
Closed January and February
Notes: 2, 8, 11, 12

SOUTH BEND

The Book Inn

508 West Washington Street, 46601
(219) 288-1990

Second Empire home in downtown South Bend. Designers' showcase—every room beautifully decorated. Fresh flowers, silver, fine china, and candlelight. The hosts emphasize service for the business person as well as leisured guests. The inn also houses a quality used bookstore, and guests rooms include: the Louisa May Alcott, Jane Austen, and Charlotte Brontë rooms.

Hosts: Peggy and John Livingston
Rooms: 5 (PB) $75
Expanded Continental Breakfast
Credit Cards: A, B, C
Notes: 2, 5, 9, 14

NOTES: Credit cards accepted: A Master Card; B Visa; C American Express; D Discover Card; E Diner's Club; F Other; 2 Personal Checks accepted; 3 Lunch available; 4 Dinner available; 5 Open all year;

Queen Anne Inn

420 West Washington Street, 46601
(219) 234-5959

The Queen Anne Inn, an 1893 Victorian home listed on the historic register, is famous for the Frank Lloyd Wright bookcases and leaded glass. Antiques are used throughout the house. The inn is three blocks from downtown South Bend, near Notre Dame and Oliver House Museum. Relax and step back into the past.

Hosts: Bob and Pauline Medhurst
Rooms: 5 (PB) $65-95
Full Breakfast
Credit Cards: A, B, C
Notes: 2, 5, 7 (limited) , 8, 10, 11, 12, 13, 14

STORY

Story Inn

P. O. Box 64, Nashville, 47448
(812) 988-2273

Situated on the southern edge of the Brown County State Park, this historic Dodge City-style general store is now a country inn housing a critically acclaimed full-service restaurant. Overnight lodging is upstairs and in the surrounding village cottages. Rooms are furnished with period antiques, original artwork, fresh flowers, private baths, and air conditioning. Reservations required.

Hosts: Benjamin and Cyndi Schultz
Rooms: 17 (PB) $65-85
Full Breakfast
Credit Cards: A, B, C, D
Notes: 3, 4, 5, 8, 9, 10, 11, 12, 13

SYRACUSE

Anchor Inn
Bed and Breakfast

11007 North State Road 13, 46567
(219) 457-4714

Anchor Inn is a turn-of-the-century, two-story home filled with period furniture and antiques. Features of the home include: claw foot tub, pier mirror, transomed doorways, hardwood floors, and a large, inviting front porch that overlooks the greens of an 18-hole public golf course. Halfway between South Bend and Fort Wayne in Indiana's lake region and directly across the highway from Lake Wawasee (Indiana's largest natural lake) . Nearby attractions include Amish communities of Nappanee and Shipshewanna, several antique shops, flea markets, two live theater groups, stern-wheeler paddle boat rides, 101 lakes in Kosciusko County, and a 3,400-acre game preserve. Air conditioned for your comfort.

Hosts: Robert and Jean Kennedy
Rooms: 7 (5 PB; 2 SB) $50-65
Full Breakfast
Credit Cards: A, B, D
Notes: 2, 5

Story Inn

TERRE HAUTE

Deere Run Bed and Breakfast Home

6218 North 13th Street, 47805
(812) 466-3390

6 Pets welcome; 7 Smoking allowed; 8 Children welcome; 9 Social drinking allowed; 10 Tennis available; 11 Swimming available; 12 Golf available; 13 Skiing available; 14 May be booked through travel agents.

Country ranch-style home on a working farm is located just off US 41 north of Terre Haute and adjacent to the towpath of the old Wabash-Erie Canal. Home-grown products used in preparation of continental-plus breakfast as much as possible. Owners have international interests. Very nice county and state parks and other recreational activities are nearby. Many historical covered bridges in the area are interesting also.

Hosts: Dorothea and Robert Dunlap
Rooms: 3 (SB) $40
Expanded Continental Breakfast
Closed November 1-April 1
Credit Cards: None
Notes: 2

WALKERTON

Koontz House Bed and Breakfast

Rural Route 3, Box 592, 46574
(219) 586-7090

Come and enjoy the beautiful home Sam Koontz built on the western edge of 387-acre Koontz Lake around 1880. Large, airy bedrooms with color TV, air conditioning, swimming area, and boat dock. Lakeside restaurant, marina, boat rental, and antique shops within walking distance. Potato Creek State Park 12 miles, Plymouth 10 miles, LaPorte 20 miles, South Bend 23 miles.

Hosts: Les and Jan Davison
Rooms: 4 (SB) $40-60
Full Breakfast
Credit Cards: None
Notes: 2, 5, 7, 8, 9, 10, 11, 12, 13

WARSAW

Candlelight Inn

503 East Fort Wayne Street, 46580
(219) 267-2906; (800) 352-0640

The Candlelight Inn offers a gentle reminder of the past with the comforts and convenience of the present. In-room phones, TV, and private baths. Antiques

return you to the 1860s. Many lakes and antique shops provide great relaxation and sport. Close to Amish country.

Hosts: Bill and Debi Hambright
Rooms: 6 (PB) $57-67
Full Breakfast
Credit Cards: A, B, C
Notes: 2, 5, 8, 9, 10, 11, 12, 13 (XC), 14

White Hill Manor

2517 East Center Street, 46580
(219) 269-6933

Restored English Tudor mansion; hand-hewn oak beams and leaded glass windows. Eight elegant bedrooms with private baths, phones, TVs and air conditioning. Luxurious suite with spa bath. Breakfast served on dining porch furnished in wicker. Adjacent to Wagon Wheel Theatre and Restaurant. Lake recreation and wonderful antique shops nearby.

Host: Gladys Deloe
Rooms: 8 (PB) $75-112
Full Breakfast
Credit Cards: A, B, C
Notes: 2, 5, 8, 14

WEST BADEN—FRENCH LICK

E. B. Rhodes Bed and Breakfast

P. O. Box 7, Rhodes Avenue, 47469
(812) 936-7378

This first-edition home built in 1901 contains spacious rooms that have beautiful hand-carved woodwork. Two large porches, each equipped with rocking chairs, are great for relaxing and have breathtaking views. The area offers entertainment for all seasons. Take a ride on a steam locomotive, hike, fish, or swim at Patoka Lake or snow ski at Paoli Peaks. Antique shops everywhere.

Hosts: Tom and Tina Hilgediek
Rooms: 4 (PB) $30-45
Full Breakfast
Credit Cards: A, B
Notes: 2, 5, 8, 10, 11, 12, 13

NOTES: Credit cards accepted: A Master Card; B Visa; C American Express; D Discover Card; E Diner's Club; F Other; 2 Personal Checks accepted; 3 Lunch available; 4 Dinner available; 5 Open all year;

Iowa

AMANA COLONIES

Die Heimat Country Inn

Main Street, Homestead, 52236
(319) 622-3937

Die Heimat (German for "the home place")
has 19 rooms, all furnished with Amana
walnut and cherry furniture, private baths,
TVs, and air conditioning. Colony heirlooms and antiques are found throughout
the inn. Some rooms have Amana walnut
canopy beds. Nature trail, golf course,
wineries, woolen mills, and restaurants are
all nearby.

Hosts: Don and Sheila Janda
Rooms: 19 (PB) $36.95-65.95
Expanded Continental Breakfast
Credit Cards: A, B, D
Notes: 2, 5, 6, 7 (limited), 8, 9, 10, 11, 12, 13
    (XC), 14

Die Heimat Country Inn

ANAMOSA

The Shaw House

509 South Oak, 52205
(319) 462-4485

Enjoy a relaxing step back in time in this
three-story, 1866 Italianate mansion on a
hilltop overlooking scenery immortalized
in the paintings of native son Grant Wood.
Special rooms include porch with panoramic countryside view, two-room tower suite,
and ballroom. Located on a 45-acre farm
within easy walking distance of town. State
park, canoeing, antiques are nearby.

Hosts: Connie and Andy McKean
Rooms: 4 (3 PB; 1 SB) $35-50
Full Breakfast
Credit Cards: None
Notes: 2, 3, 4, 5, 8, 9, 10, 11, 12, 13, 14

ATLANTIC

Chestnut Charm Bed and Breakfast

1409 Chestnut Street, 50022
(712) 243-5652

The Shaw House

6 Pets welcome; 7 Smoking allowed; 8 Children welcome; 9 Social drinking allowed; 10 Tennis available; 11
Swimming available; 12 Golf available; 13 Skiing available; 14 May be booked through travel agents.

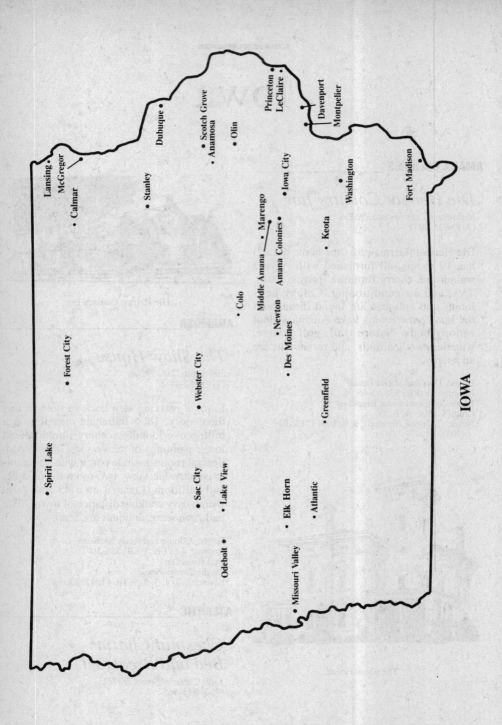

IOWA

Lansing•
McGregor•
Calmar•

Stanley•

Dubuque•

Scotch Grove•
Anamosa•

Olin•

Princeton•
LeClaire•

Davenport
Montpelier

Spirit Lake•

Forest City•

Webster City•

Colo•

Middle Amana•
Amana Colonies•
Newton•

Marengo•

Iowa City•

Washington•

Fort Madison•

Keota•

Des Moines•

Greenfield•

Sac City•
Lake View•

Elk Horn•

Atlantic•

Odebolt•

Missouri Valley•

Come and find the magic. Chestnut Charm is an enchanting 1898 Victorian mansion with serene surroundings. Experience beauty, pleasure, and fantasy with someone special or enjoy a wonderful respite in your busy travel schedule. Five elegant guest rooms, two sun rooms, and patio with fountain. Awaken to the aroma of gourmet coffee and home baking. A full breakfast of fruit juice, fresh fruit in season, eggs, meat, and a home-baked delight. Air conditioned. Come and be pampered in style.

Hosts: Bruce and Barbara Stensvad
Rooms: 5 (3 PB; 2 SB) $55-75
Full Breakfast
Credit Cards: A, B
Notes: 4, 5, 10, 11, 12, 14

CALMAR

Calmar Guesthouse

Rural Route 1, Box 206, 52132
(319) 562-3851

Newly remodeled Victorian home with many antiques, situated near Luther College and NITI Community College. Close to world-famous Bily Clocks in Spillville, Niagara Cave, Lake Meyer, and much more. Wake up to a fresh country breakfast. Air conditioned. Good variety of restaurants in the area.

Hosts: Art and Lucille Kruse
Rooms: 5 (1 PB; 4 SB) $35-45
Full Breakfast
Credit Cards: A, B
Notes: 2, 5, 7 (limited), 8, 9, 10, 11, 12, 13

COLO

Martha's Vineyard Bed and Breakfast

620 West Street, 50056
(515) 377-2586

Just fifteen minutes east of US 35, this bed and breakfast is a working farm on the edge of town. Homemade and homegrown food is served at meals, and your hostess is a retired home schooling teacher. This fourth-generation 1920 family home has been lovingly restored and is furnished with antiques and collectibles throughout. A wildlife area and an old-fashioned flower garden add quiet beauty. Open May through October.

Hosts: Narb and Martha Kash
Rooms: 2 (PB) $40-45 plus tax
Full Breakfast
Credit Cards: None
Notes: 2, 8, 9, 10, 11, 12, 14

DAVENPORT

River Oaks Inn

1234 East River Drive, 52803
(319) 326-2629

Built by local attorney Abner Davison in 1858, River Oaks Inn overlooks the Mississippi and has three acres of rolling lawn and garden with a large deck and historic gazebo. Inside, the guest rooms are spacious with private baths and are reminiscent of the gracious living of the period. A full breakfast is served in the formal dining room or on the deck, weather permitting.

Hosts: Mary Jo and Bill Pohl
Rooms: 5 (PB) $49-89
Full Breakfast
Credit Cards: A, B
Notes: 2, 5, 8, 9, 14

DES MOINES

Carter House Inn

640 20th Street, 50314
(515) 288-7850

Built in the late 1870s, this Italianate was moved from its original site in 1988 to save it from demolition. Located in the Sherman Hill Historic District, this bed and breakfast features original stenciling and faux marble fireplaces. Guest rooms have private baths with claw foot tubs. A full breakfast is served in the formal dining room.

NOTES: Credit cards accepted: A Master Card; B Visa; C American Express; D Discover Card; E Diner's Club; F Other; 2 Personal Checks accepted; 3 Lunch available; 4 Dinner available; 5 Open all year; 6 Pets welcome; 7 Smoking allowed; 8 Children welcome; 9 Social drinking allowed; 10 Tennis available; 11 Swimming available; 12 Golf available; 13 Skiing available; 14 May be booked through travel agents.

Richards House Bed and Breakfast

Host: Penny Schlitz
Rooms: 3 (PB) $50-60
Full Breakfast
Credit Cards: None
Notes: 2, 5, 14

DUBUQUE

The Hancock House

1105 Grove Terrace, 52001
(319) 557-8989

Perched on the bluffs of the mighty Mississippi, the Hancock House offers a panoramic view with old-fashioned elegance. Built in 1891 and restored to its original grandeur, all rooms are furnished in period antiques. Complimentary beverages are always available. Make yourself at home. Corporate rates available.

Hosts: Jim and Julie Gross
Rooms: 6 (3 PB; 3 SB) $55-110
Full Breakfast;
Credit Cards: A, B
Notes: 2, 5, 7 (restricted), 8, 9, 10, 11, 12, 13

Juniper Hill Farm

15325 Bupp Road, 52002
(319) 582-4405; (800) 572-1449

Beautiful country setting on 40 acres of woods with walking trails and a stocked pond. We are adjacent to Sundown Ski Area (the only bed and breakfast in Iowa where you can ski to the front door) ride to Heritage Bicycle Trail. Comfortably and restfully appointed with country atmosphere, some antiques. All rooms have private baths, one with whirlpool, and all rooms have access to an 8-foot-diameter hot tub.

Hosts: Ruth and Bill McEllhiney
Rooms: 3 (PB) $65-140
Full Country Breakfast
Credit Cards: A, B, D
Notes: 2, 5, 8, 9, 12, 13, 14

Mandolin Inn

199 Loras Boulevard, 52001
(319) 556-0069; (800) 524-7996

Tarry awhile amid Edwardian columns, beveled and stained-glass windows, parquet and mosaic floors. A perfect place to kindle and rekindle romance. Enjoy a sumptuous breakfast served to strains of Mozart in a magnificent dining room of oil wall paintings, floor-to-ceiling china cabinet, and Italian tile fireplace. Perfect for weddings, receptions, family reunions, and business meetings. Corporate rates available. Ideally located downtown. Checks and all major credit cards accepted.

Host: Jan Oswald
Rooms: 8 (4 PB; 4 SB) $65-125
Full Breakfast
Credit Cards: A, B, C, D
Notes: 2, 5, 8, 9, 10, 11, 12, 13, 14

Richards House Bed and Breakfast

1492 Locust Street, 52001
(319) 557-1492

Relax in this 1883 stick-style Victorian mansion with original interior, over 80 stained-glass windows, embossed wallcoverings, period furnishings, and more. Most rooms include working fireplaces, concealed TVs, and phones. A full breakfast is served in the formal dining room. Easy access with plenty of parking.

NOTES: Credit cards accepted: A Master Card; B Visa; C American Express; D Discover Card; E Diner's Club; F Other; 2 Personal Checks accepted; 3 Lunch available; 4 Dinner available; 5 Open all year;

Host: Michelle Delaney
Rooms: 5 (4 PB; 1 SB) $35-75
Full Breakfast
Credit Cards: A, B, C, D
Notes: 2, 5, 8, 9, 12, 13, 14

Kingsley Inn

ELK HORN

The Travelling Companion

4314 Main, 51531
(712) 764-8932

Delightful accommodations await you in this 1909 home in the peaceful Danish town of Elk Horn, Iowa, seven miles north of I-80. Elk Horn is located in the heart of the largest Danish settlement in the U.S. No more charming lodging could be found that offers so much to the traveler. Your room will contain the most comfortable furnishings available. The Ortgies chose the name, The Travelling Companion, from one of Hans Christian Andersen's fairy tales. Each guest room is named after a different fairy tale.

Host: Karolyn Ortgies
Rooms: 3 (SB) $45-50
Full Breakfast
Credit Cards: None
Notes: 2, 5, 8, 10, 11

FOREST CITY

1897 Victorian House Bed and Breakfast

306 South Clark, 50436
(515) 582-3613

The 1897 house is a Queen Anne style, furnished in period furniture, much of which is for sale. Air conditioning has been added, and the aroma of coffee and a four-course breakfast awakens you each morning of your stay. House is available for weddings, showers, dinners, teas, and weekend retreats.

Hosts: Richard and Doris Johnson
Rooms: 7 (3 PB; 4 SB) $40-60
Full Breakfast
Credit Cards: A, B
Notes: 2, 3, 4, 5

FORT MADISON

Kingsley Inn

707 Avenue H on Highway 61
(319) 372-7074; (800) 441-2327

Yesterday's charm and today's luxury describes this historic Victorian inn on the Mississippi River. Walk to the faithfully restored 1808 Old Fort Madison, Train Depot Museum, Steam Engine Park, unique shops, and galleries. Stately nineteenth-century residential district is nearby, and guests are a ten-minute drive to historic Nauvoo, Illinois, which has been called the "Williamburg of the Midwest," with forty restored 1840s shops and homes. Rooms have private baths, some of which are whirlpools. CATV, air conditioning, phones, sprinklers, and alarms. Elevator and FAX machine available.

Host: Myrna Reinhard
Rooms: 14 (PB) $65-105
Expanded Continental Breakfast
Credit Cards: A, B, C, D, E
Notes: 2, 5, 9, 14

6 Pets welcome; 7 Smoking allowed; 8 Children welcome; 9 Social drinking allowed; 10 Tennis available; 11 Swimming available; 12 Golf available; 13 Skiing available; 14 May be booked through travel agents.

GREENFIELD

The Wilson Home

Rural Route 1, Box 132, 50849
(515) 743-2031

A huge indoor pool nestled in the Iowa countryside makes this bed and breakfast one of the most unique in America. Each spacious guest room opens directly onto the pool deck areas that are beautifully furnished with wicker and wrought iron. A full breakfast is served in the adjacent 1918 antique-filled farm home. Perfect for honeymooners, hunters, vacationers, business or escape weekends!

Hosts: Wendy and Henry Wilson
Rooms: 2 (PB) $68-90
Full Breakfast
Credit Cards: None
Notes: 2, 6, 7 (limited), 8, 9, 10, 11, 12, 14

IOWA CITY

The Golden Haug

517 East Washington Street, 52240
(319) 338-6452

Elegance and whimsy decorate this 1920 arts and crafts house. Guests can retreat to one of four suites with in-room private bath or enjoy camaraderie of other guests. A full breakfast is served family style. Relax on the porch swing, munch on sweets from the candy bowl, soak in the whirlpool or birthday bath, and enjoy tasty evening dessert in air-conditioned comfort. Situated in the heart of Iowa City within a couple of blocks of the University of Iowa, eateries, and shopping.

Hosts: Nila Haug and Dennis Nowotny
Suites: 4 (PB) $65-90
Full Breakfast
Credit Cards: None
Notes: 2, 5, 8, 9, 14

Haverkamps' Linn Street Homestay

619 North Linn Street, 52245
(319) 337-4363

A large and comfortable 1908 Edwardian-style home filled with antiques and collectibles. Wonderful front porch with old-fashioned swing. Walking distance to University of Iowa campus and the downtown area. Only a short drive to the Amana Villages, Kalona, Hoover Museum in West Branch, and Cedar Rapids. One mile south of I-80 at Exit 244.

Hosts: Clarence and Dorothy Haverkamp
Rooms: 3 (SB) $30-40
Full Breakfast
Credit Cards: None
Notes: 2, 5, 8, 9, 10, 11, 12, 14

KEOTA

Elmhurst

305 County Line Road North, 52248
(515) 636-3001

This 1905 Victorian mansion retains much of its original grandeur: stained-glass and curved windows, circular solarium, parquet floors, beamed ceilings, marble fireplace mantels, ballroom, two grand stairways, leather wall coverings, and more. Golf course, swimming, and nature trail across the road.

Host: Marjie Schantz-Koehler
Rooms: 4 (SB) $36.40
Full Breakfast
Credit Cards: None
Notes: 2, 3, 4, 5, 7 (limited), 9, 10, 11, 12

LAKE VIEW

Armstrong Inn Bed and Breakfast

306 5th Street, 51450
(712) 657-2535

NOTES: Credit cards accepted: A Master Card; B Visa; C American Express; D Discover Card; E Diner's Club; F Other; 2 Personal Checks accepted; 3 Lunch available; 4 Dinner available; 5 Open all year;

Relax in this Lake View founders' Victorian home, located four blocks from beautiful, serene 100-acre Black Hawk Lake. The Armstrong Inn was built in 1886 and has three spacious bedrooms that will accommodate up to eight guests. Guests can enjoy antiques combined with modern comforts. Continental breakfast served with freshly ground coffee and herbal teas. Boating, fishing, hunting, and more to enjoy.

Hosts: Sandi and Jerry Glines
Rooms: 4 (3 PB; 1 SB) $45-65
Continental Breakfast
Credit Cards: A, B
Notes: 2, 3, 4, 5, 6, 8, 9, 11, 12, 14

LANSING

Lansing House

291 Front Street, Box 97, 51251
(319) 538-4263

Lansing House, a handsome riverfront home, is situated next to the picturesque Blackhawk Bridge and offers its guests an atmosphere of comfort and elegance—plus a picture-window view of the Great River. The area offers hikes in the woods and walks along the river. Rental boats are available for sightseeing and fishing in the backwaters.

Hosts: Chris and Margaret FitzGerald
Rooms: 2 (SB) $60
Full Breakfast
Credit Cards: None
Notes: 2, 5, 9, 10, 11, 12, 13

LE CLAIRE

Latimer Bed and Breakfast

127 North Second, P. O. Box 417, 52753
(319) 289-5747

A 1905 house that has been the home of the Latimer family since 1949. Warm and cozy large ten-room house, completely remodeled. Large porch with swing, and large

yard to wander in. Conveniently located to several local attractions. A riverboat departs daily for a two-day trip upriver. 20-minute drive for the *President* gambling boat, Buffalo Bill Museum one block away; Cody Homestead within ten miles. Quad-City Downs is a fifteen-minute drive. Other events in the Quad Cities area include the Bix Run and Hardee's Golf Classic.

Host: Darlene Nichols
Rooms: 4 (SB) $40 plus tax
Full Breakfast
Credit Cards: None
Notes: 2, 5, 7, 8, 9, 10, 11, 12

Mississippi Sunrise Bed and Breakfast

18950 Great River Road, 52753
(319) 332-9203

You'll be captivated by the superb panoramic view of the Mississippi River from the dining room, livingroom, enclosed porch, large deck, and bedroom. This lovely hillside brick home is surrounded by many trees, flowers, and birds on one acre of land. It is conveniently situated on Highway 67 near I-80. Nearby are casino boats, sightseeing river excursions, parks, museums, and the many special activities of the Quad Cities.

Hosts: Ted and Eloise Pfeiff
Rooms: 2 (SB) $40-50
Full Breakfast
Credit Cards: None
Notes: 2, 14

Mohr Haus

21710 Great River Road North, 52753
(319) 289-4503

Located in a century-old farmhouse overlooking the Mississippi River one-half mile north of LeClaire. The old is blended with the new to offer you a very enjoyable stay in air-conditioned comfort. Many points of interest within a 15 mile radius.

6 Pets welcome; 7 Smoking allowed; 8 Children welcome; 9 Social drinking allowed; 10 Tennis available; 11 Swimming available; 12 Golf available; 13 Skiing available; 14 May be booked through travel agents.

Hosts: Leona and Joe Mohr
Rooms: 3 (SB) $40
Continental Breakfast
Credit Cards: None
Closed: November 1 - May 27
Notes: 2, 9, 12

MARENGO

Loy's Bed and Breakfast

Rural Route 1, Box 82, 52301
I-80, Exit 216N
(319) 642-7787

Architecturally beautifull home on a large grain and hog farm. Recreation and facilities for all ages. Farm tour is available; located close to the Amana colonies, Iowa City, and many other interesting places. Gourmet breakfast with hot breads.

Hosts: Loy and Robert Walker
Rooms: 3 (1 PB; 2SB) $50-60, plus tax
Full Breakfast
Credit Cards: None
Notes: 2, 4, 5, 8, 9, 10, 11, 12, 14

MCGREGOR

Rivers Edge Bed and Breakfast

112 Main Street, 52157
(319) 873-3501

Beautiful river view, fully furnished kitchen, private baths, and patio. The second-story deck overlooks the river. Close to boating, fishing, hiking, hunting, skiing, golf.

Host: Rita Lange
Rooms: 3 (PB) $50
Continental Breakfast
Credit Cards: A, F
Notes: 2, 5, 8, 9, 10, 11, 12, 13

MIDDLE AMANA

Dusk to Dawn Bed and Breakfast

Box 124, 52307
(319) 622-3029

An invitation to relax in a peaceful, comfortable atmosphere, in a house decorated in beautiful Amana antiques. Located in historic Middle Amana. A touch of the past is accented with a greenhouse, spacious deck, and Jacuzzi.

Hosts: Bradley and Lynn Hahn
Rooms: 7 (PB) $43.05
Continental Breakfast
Credit Cards: A, B
Notes: 2, 5, 7, 8, 9, 12

MISSOURI VALLEY

Apple Orchard Inn

Rurual Route 3, Box 129, 51555
(712) 642-2418

Country home on a twenty-six-acre apple orchard situated on a hill overlooking the beautiful Boyer Valley. Gourmet cooking featuring fresh-ground wheat in homemade breads, and jellies. Comfortable rooms, a keeping room, and a Jacuzzi room. German and Spanish are spoken here.

Hosts: Dr. Electa and John Strub
Rooms: 3 (SB) $49-55
Full Breakfast
Credit Cards: A, B, C, D
Notes: 2, 3, 4, 5, 8, 10, 11, 12, 13, 14

MONTPELIER

Varners' Caboose Bed and Breakfast

204 East 2nd, P. O. Box 10, 52759
(319) 381-3652

Come stay in a real Rock Island Lines caboose. Set on its own track behind the hosts' house, the caboose is a self-contained unit, with bath, shower, and complete kitchen. It sleeps four, with a queen-size bed and two twins in the cupola. There is color TV, central air and heat, plus plenty of off-street parking. A fully prepared country breakfast is left in the caboose kitchen to be enjoyed by guests whenever they choose. Located on Route 22, halfway between Davenport and Muscatine, Iowa.

NOTES: Credit cards accepted: A Master Card; B Visa; C American Express; D Discover Card; E Diner's Club; F Other; 2 Personal Checks accepted; 3 Lunch available; 4 Dinner available; 5 Open all year;

Hosts: Bob and Nancy Varner
Room: 1 (PB) $55
Full Breakfast
Credit Cards: None
Notes: 2, 5, 8

NEWTON

La Corsette Maison Inn

629 First Avenue East, 50208
(515) 792-6833

Historic turn-of-the-century mission-style mansion. Charming French bedchambers; fireplaces; gourmet dining in a style of elegance. On I-80, 30 minutes from Des Moines. Close to horse track and Adventureland. Listed on the National Register of Historic Places.

Host: Kay Owen
Rooms: 5 (PB) $55-135
Full Breakfast
Credit Cards: C
Notes: 2, 4, 5, 6 (call), 7 (restricted), 8 (call), 9, 10, 11, 12, 14

ODEBOLT

Country Charm Tea Room and Bed and Breakfast

701 South Des Moines Street, 51458
(712) 668-4267

Staying at this inn is just like a visit to Granma's! This redecorated, two-story home is filled with antiques and period furnishings. Country Rose Bedroom and English Garden Bedroom share a bath with a claw foot tub. Wedding, anniversary, and hunting packages available, and tea room is open with reservations. Visit the herb gardens, knit shops, antique barn, museum, and pioneer home. Enjoy the peaceful memories a small town will give you.

Hosts: Richard and Shari Rohlf
Rooms: 2 (SB) $35-55
Full Breakfast
Credit Cards: None
Notes: 2, 3, 5, 8 (over 12), 10, 11, 12

La Corsette Maisin Inn

OLIN

LampPost Bed and Breakfastreet

101 East Cleveland Street, 52320
(319) 484-2925 evenings

A restored 1892 Victorian home located in the oldest town in Jones County, Iowa, which is famous for artist Grant Wood, painter of the "American Gothic." Enjoy the small town tranquility, a bit of the past, and hold onto a few precious mementoes with the antiques and wicker restoration shop available on site. Central air, golf, fishing, boat dock, and hunting close by.

Hosts: Vicki and Ronald Conley
Rooms: 3 (SB) $35-45
Full Breakfast
Credit Cards: None
Notes: 2, 3 (by reservation), 4 (by reservation), 5, 7, 8, 12

PRINCETON

The Woodlands

P. O. Box 127, 52768
(319) 289-3177; (319) 289-4661

A secluded woodland escape that can be as private or social as you wish. The Woodlands bed and breakfast is nestled among pines on 26 acres of forest and meadows in a private wildlife refuge. Guests delight in an elegant breakfast by the swimming pool or by a cozy fireplace while viewing the outdoor wildlife activity.

6 Pets welcome; 7 Smoking allowed; 8 Children welcome; 9 Social drinking allowed; 10 Tennis available; 11 Swimming available; 12 Golf available; 13 Skiing available; 14 May be booked through travel agents.

Boating and fishing on the Mississippi River, golfing, cross-country skiing, and hiking are available. A short drive to the Quad City metropolitan area, shopping, art galleries, museums, theater and sporting events.

Hosts: Betsy Wallace and E. Lindebraekke
Rooms: 3 (2 PB; 1 SB) $75-115
Full Breakfast
Credit Cards: A, B
Notes: 2, 3, 4, 5, 7 (limited), 8, 9, 10, 11, 12, 13, 14

SAC CITY

Brick Bungalow Bed and Breakfast

1012 Early Street, 50583
(712) 662-7302

A warm welcome greets you in this brick house in a quiet neighborhood. This is a solid 1930s house with beautiful dark oak woodwork and beams. Guests are invited to use all of the house and spacious backyard. Families are especially welcome. Guest rooms have golden pine paneling, separate baths, electric blankets, and central air. Refrigerator and coffee pots in every room.

Host: Phyllis Hartman
Rooms: 2 (PB) $35
Credit Cards: None
Notes: 2, 4, 5, 7(restricted), 8,10, 11, 12

SCOTCH GROVE

The Grove

Rural Route 1, 52331
(319) 465-3858

Have a mini vacation or an overnight at this peaceful rural working farm. Charming 135-year-old home. Hard-surface roads to within one-quarter of a mile. Big country breakfast featuring homemade rolls. Close to famous Grant Wood Country in Jones County.

Hosts: Robert and Ruth Zirkelbach
Rooms: 2 (SB) $26-36.40
Full Breakfast
Credit Cards: None
Notes: 2, 5, 6, 8, 9, 10, 11, 12

Hannah Marie Country Inn

SPENCER

Hannah Marie Country Inn

Rural Route 1, Highway 71 South, 51301
(712) 262-1286; (712) 332-7719

A lovingly restored farm home offering romantic country strolls, a good night's rest, and a hearty gourmet breakfast. Be pampered by private baths, air conditioning, afternoon tea; relax in a whirlpool or hot shower. Afternoon theme teas Tuesday to Saturday. Iowa Great Lakes 20 miles away.

Hosts: Mary and Dave Nichols
Rooms: 3 (PB) $52-62.40
Full Breakfast
Credit Cards: A, B, C
Closed Dec.-April
Notes: 2, 6 (in barn), 7 (limited), 8, 9 (limited), 10, 11, 12

SPIRIT LAKE

Moorland Country Inn

Box 7315, 51366
(507) 847-4707

Moorland is an English country estate built at the turn of the century. Much of the Moore family furnishings have been returned to the five-bedroom main house. Also on the estate is a three-bedroom carriage house and the gate house suite. Guests are treated to a formal breakfast served either in the main dining room or on the front sun porch.

Host: Kevin Joul
Rooms: 8 (PB) $70-110
Full Breakfast
Credit Cards: A, B
Notes: 2, 3, 5, 9, 11, 12, 13, 14

STANLEY

Sawtooth Hotel
West End of Ace of Diamonds, 83278

Stanley's first bed and breakfast. Warm western hospitality with an uninterrupted view of the Sawtooth Mountains, with their endless recreational opportunities. Enjoy world-famous sourdough pancakes and cinnamon rolls, country-style ham, sausage or bacon, fresh fruit, and other delights.

Hosts: Steve and Kathy Cole
Rooms: 8 (SB) $35-50
Full Breakfast
Credit Cards: A, B

STORM LAKE

The Parsonage
227 Lake Avenue, 50588
(712) 732-1736

On a quiet, tree-lined avenue, the Parsonage is just a stone's throw from Storm Lake's picturesque shoreline. The plush comfort of the inn's great room is a delightful place to congregate with new-found friends or to relax with a favorite book. The kitchen is a cheery place to visit, with fresh-from-the-oven delectables, fragrant teas, and friendly conversation abounding. And, at the end of the day's

activities, two inviting guest rooms offer welcome respite to the traveler.

Host: May Conde
Rooms: 2 (PB) $45-50
Full Breakfast
Credit Cards: A, B
Notes: 2, 4, 5, 8, 9

STRATFORD

Hook's Point Farmstead Country Inn
Rural Route 1, Box 222, 50249
(800) 383-7062

Big, red, turn-of-the-century home situated on 160-acre grain farm. One mile away are steeply wooded hills that border two rivers, one great for canoeing, the other for fishing. This is quiet country, excellent for long walks, bike rides, and backwoods picnics. Enter through the kitchen door and gather around the kitchen table for snacks. Three warmly furnished rooms with many amenities including feather beds and down comforters. Gourmet dining by reservation.

Hosts: Marvin and Mary Jo Johnson
Rooms: 3 (1 PB; 2 SB) $45-90
Full Breakfast
Credit Cards: None
Notes: 2, 3, 4, 5, 8, 9, 10, 11, 12, 14

WASHINGTON

Roses and Lace Bed and Breakfast
821 North 2nd Avenue, 52353
(319) 653-2462

Capture the ambience of Victorian living in this restored 1893 Queen Anne home that boasts Eastlake woodwork, beaded spandrells, pocket doors, and original chandeliers. All 11 rooms have antique furnishings. Relax in the parlor in front of a cozy fire in the winter, or enjoy a glass of lemonade on the inviting wraparound porch in the summer. Guests may use bicycles to

6 Pets welcome; 7 Smoking allowed; 8 Children welcome; 9 Social drinking allowed; 10 Tennis available; 11 Swimming available; 12 Golf available; 13 Skiing available; 14 May be booked through travel agents.

ride the Kewash Nature Trail. Enjoy the county's many antique shops.

Hosts: Milt and Judi Wildebuer
Rooms: 2 (PB) $45-50
Full Breakfast
Credit Cards: None
Notes: 2, 5, 8, 10, 11, 12, 13

WEBSTER CITY

Centennial Farm Bed and Breakfast

1091 220th Street, Rural Route 2, 50595
(515) 832-3050

Built in 1869, parts of the original homestead and barns have been incorporated into the air-conditioned farmhouse, which is situated among fields of corn and soybeans. Your hosts are fourth-generation farmers here, and Tom was born in the downstairs bedroom. Guests can see the farm operation and Tom's 1929 Model A Ford pickup. Located near golf, tennis, swimming, parks, antiques, and fine dining, just 22 miles west of I-35 at exit 142 or 144.

Hosts: Tom and Shirley Yungclas
Rooms: 2 (SB) $35
Full Breakfast
Credit Cards: None
Notes: 2, 5, 7, 8, 9, 10, 11, 12

Kansas

DOVER

Sage Inn

13553 SWK-4 Highway, P. O. Box 24, 66420
(913) 256-6336

On the National Register of Historic Places, the Sage Inn was built by pioneer Alfred Sage in the 1870s. The inn served as a hostelry to peddlers and cavalry crossing the plains of Kansas. It later served as a stagecoach stop at the turn of the century. The limestone inn has been totally restored to its original state: pine floors and plaster of Paris ceilings are just a small part of its charm. Furnished with a 20-year collection of antiques, including cast iron and brass beds.

Hosts: JoAnn and Victor Hepworth
Rooms: 3 (1 PB; 2 SB) $57-62
Continental Breakfast
Credit Cards: None
Notes: 2, 5

COLUMBUS

Meriwether House Bed and Breakfast

322 West Pine, 66725
(316) 429-2812

Visit the cottage on your next trip through southeast Kansas. Lovingly restored, this little green house on Pine Street is filled with antiques, lace, and accessories you may purchase to take home with you. Situated two hours from Tulsa, Oklahoma, Springfield and Kansas City, Missouri.

Hosts: Margaret Meriwether and Liz Simpson
Rooms: 7 (2 PB; 5 SB)
Continental Breakfast
Credit Cards: A, B, D
Notes: 2, 5, 8, 11, 12

HALSTEAD

Heritage Inn

300 Main Street, 67056
(316) 835-2118

Heritage Inn is an extraordinary 1922 bed and breakfast inn, located in the heart of Kansas. The moment you step through the doors of the Heritage Inn, you'll feel the comfort and relaxed charm of the 1920s, yet will enjoy the convenience of the 1990s.

Hosts: Jim and Gery Hartong
Rooms: 5 (PB) $29
Full Breakfast
Credit Cards: A, B
Notes: 2, 3, 4, 5, 7, 8, 9, 10, 11, 12, 14

HILL CITY

Pomeroy Inn Bed and Breakfast

224 West Main, 67642
(913) 674-2098

Located on Highway 24 one block east of stoplight, at the junction between Highway 283 and Highway 24, this old hotel is 106 years old, with yellow limestone walls, large lobby, and different decor for each room. Quiet and comfortable, you step inside and forget there is an outside world.

6 Pets welcome; 7 Smoking allowed; 8 Children welcome; 9 Social drinking allowed; 10 Tennis available; 11 Swimming available; 12 Golf available; 13 Skiing available; 14 May be booked through travel agents.

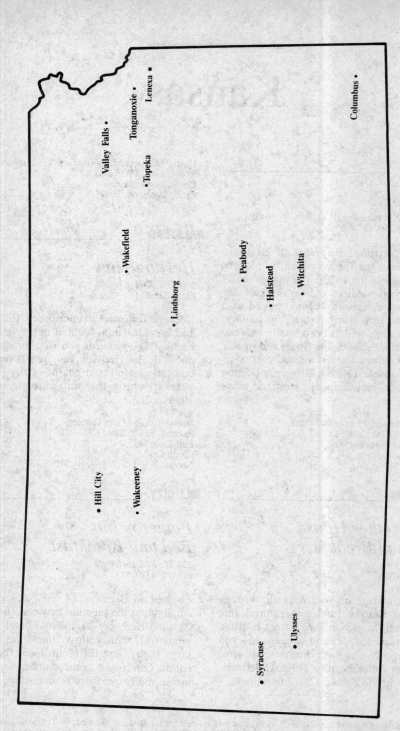

KANSAS

A large lobby is where guests can munch on homemade one-of-a-kind rolls and coffee, and the hotel is close to shopping and the school playground. Rooms all have TV, ceiling fans, and air conditioning.

Hosts: Don and Mary Worchester
Rooms: 9 (6 PB; 3 SB) $19.95-32
Continental Breakfast
Credit Cards: A, B, D, E
Notes: 2, 5, 7, 8, 9

KANSAS CITY - LENEXA

Bed and Breakfast Kansas City

P. O. Box 14781, 66285
(913) 888-3636

Forty Victorian turn-of-the-century contemporary homes and three inns for great getaways. Accommodations near County Club Plaza, Kansas City, Independence or adjacent historic towns. All sizes of beds, all but two with private bath. Some with fireplace, Jacuzzi, pools, hot tubs. Accommodations also available in the country. Full Breakfast. RSO Agent: Edwina Monroe. $40-125

LINDSBORG

Swedish Country Inn

112 West Lincoln Street, 67456
(913) 227-2985; (800) 231-0266 out of state

Lindsborg is a Swedish community in the center of Kansas. The inn is furnished in Swedish pine furniture, and beds have hand-quilted quilts. Full Scandinavian breakfast is served, and all rooms have private bath and TV. No smoking or pets. Near Bethany College, where Handel's *Messiah* is performed every Palm and Easter Sunday.

Host: Virginia Brunsell
Rooms: 19 (PB) $45-75
Full Breakfast

Credit Cards: A, B
Notes: 2, 5, 8, 10, 11, 12

NEWTON

Hawk House Bed and Breakfast

307 West Broadway, 67114
(316) 283-2045

In the heart of wheat country. A three-story Victorian home with massive oak staircase and spacious common rooms accented by oak floors and stained glass. Each guest room is fully furnished with antiques, linens, and appointments. Guests are surrounded with elegance and hospitality. Air conditioning.

Host: Norma Goering
Rooms: 4 (1 PB; 3 SB) $40-45
Full Breakfast
Credit Cards: A, B
Notse: 5, 10, 11, 12

PEABODY

Jones Sheep Farm Bed and Breakfast

Rural Route 2, Box 185, 66866
(316) 983-2815

Enjoy a turn-of-the-century home in a pastoral setting. Situated on a working sheep farm "at the end of the road," the house is furnished in 1930s style (no phone or TV). Quiet, private. Historic small town nearby.

Hosts: Gary and Marilyn Jones
Rooms: 2 (SB) $35
Credit Cards: None
Notes: 2, 5, 6, 10, 11, 12

SYRACUSE

Braddock Ames Bed and Breakfast

201 North Avenue B and Main Street, 67878
(316) 384-5218

NOTES: Credit cards accepted: A Master Card; B Visa; C American Express; D Discover Card; E Diner's Club; F Other; 2 Personal Checks accepted; 3 Lunch available; 4 Dinner available; 5 Open all year; 6 Pets welcome; 7 Smoking allowed; 8 Children welcome; 9 Social drinking allowed; 10 Tennis available; 11 Swimming available; 12 Golf available; 13 Skiing available; 14 May be booked through travel agents.

This senior-citizen residential hotel was built in 1933 and features four bed and breakfast rooms. Two large lobbies have been renovated and restored, and home-cooked food is served for breakfast, while dinner can be served if requested ahead of time. The sport of tanking on the Arkansas River originated here, and a ride can be arranged in advance. This area is renowned for the best pheasant hunting in the state.

Hosts: Dorothy Braddock Fouts and Mary Ruth
    Braddock Houdyshell
Rooms: 4 (PB) $35-55
Full or Continental Breakfast
Credit Cards: None
Notes: 2, 3, 4, 5, 12

TONGANOXIE

Almeda's Bed and Breakfast Inn

220 South Main Street, 66086
(913) 845-2295

In a picturesque small town made a historic site in 1983, the inn dates back to World War I. Sip a cup of coffee at the stone bar once used as a bus stop in 1930. In fact, this room was the inspiration for the play Bus Stop.

Hosts: Almeda and Richard Tinberg
Rooms: 7 (PB and SB) $40
Continental Breakfast
Credit Cards: None
Notes: 2, 5, 9, 11, 12

TOPEKA

Heritage House

3535 Southwest 6th Street, 66606
(913) 233-3800

A charming country inn, listed on the National Register of Historic Places, situated near the zoo, park, and museum. Thirteen tasteful designer-decorated rooms with private baths, telephones, and TVs.

The sun room/dining room is well known for its outstanding continental cuisine.

Hosts: Don and Betty Rich
Rooms: 13 (PB) $60-135
Full Breakfast
Credit Cards: A, B, C, D, E
Notes: 2, 3, 4, 5, 8, 9, 14

ULYSSES

Fort's Cedar View

1675 West Patterson, 67880
(316) 356-2570; (800) 328-2570

Fort's Cedar View is located in the heart of the world's largest natural-gas field. It is on the Santa Fe Trail, eight miles north of famed Wagon Bed Springs, the first source of water after crossing the Cimarron River west of Dodge City, which is eighty miles northeast.

Hosts: Lynda Fort
Rooms: 4 (1 PB, 3 SB) $25-35
Full Breakfast
Credit Cards: None
Notes: 2, 5, 7 (limited), 10, 11, 12

VALLEY FALLS

The Barn Bed and Breakfast Inn

Rural Route 2, Box 87, 66088
(913) 945-3225; (800) 869-7717

In the rolling hills of northeast Kansas you can sleep in a barn that is 100 years old. Supper is served the evening you arrive, along with homemade bread made from the wheat raised on the farm. Breakfast is served each morning. There's also an exercise room and indoor heated year-round pool for you to enjoy.

Hosts: Tom, Marcella, and Patricia Ryan
Rooms: 20 (PB) $54-72
Full Breakfast
Credit Cards: A, B, C, D
Notes: 2, 3, 4, 5, 8, 9, 10, 11, 12, 14

NOTES: Credit cards accepted: A Master Card; B Visa; C American Express; D Discover Card; E Diner's Club; F Other; 2 Personal Checks accepted; 3 Lunch available; 4 Dinner available; 5 Open all year;

WAKEENEY

Thistle Hill
Bed and Breakfast

Route 1, Box 93, 67672
(913) 743-2644

A comfortable, secluded, cedar farm home halfway between Kansas City and Denver along I-70. Experience farm life and visit Castle Rock. Self-guided prairie wildflower walks through a 60-acre prairie restoration project. Enjoy a hearty country breakfast by the fireplace or on the summer porch overlooking the herb garden.

Hosts: Dave and Mary Hendricks
Rooms: 3 (2 PB; 1 SB) $50
Full Breakfast
Credit Cards: None
Notes: 2, 5, 8, 9, 10, 11, 12

WAKEFIELD

Bed N Breakfast-
Still Country

206 6th Street, 67487
(913) 461-5596

Wakefield, population 900, is on Milford Lake (23 miles long) and is an excellent place for a getaway. In 1961, the host began inviting people to "Come, spend a spell, and share our home." Wakefield boasts an outstanding museum and arboretum, bird watching, nature trails, and unlisted corners (quilts, dolls, crafts, etc). The ultimate in peace and tranquility. Abilene is nearby. Prize-winning whole-wheat pancakes served for breakfast. Ten dollars deposit per room per night secures your room.

Host: Pearl Thurlow
Rooms: 2 (SB) $25-35
Full Breakfast
Credit Cards: None
Notes: 2, 5, 6, 7 (limited), 8, 10, 11

WICHITA

Inn at the Park

3751 East Douglas, 67218
(316) 652-0500

Elegant Old World charm and comfort in a completely renovated mansion. Twelve distinctive suites, ten in the main house and two in the carriage house. Some of the features are fireplaces, whirlpool bath, private courtyard, hot tub, and many spacious three-room suites. A preferred hideaway among people looking for a romantic retreat or convenient base of operation for corporate guests. The Inn at the Park was named one of the top ten outstanding new inns in the country by Inn Review newsletter in 1989.

Host: Rachel Howard
Rooms: 12 (PB) $75-135
Expanded Continental Breakfast
Credit Cards: A, B, C, D
Notes: 2, 3, 4, 5, 7 (limited), 8, 9, 10, 14

Inn at Willowbend

3939 Comotara, 67226
(316) 636-4032

This charming bed and breakfast was built in 1989 off the second fairway of a Tom Weiskopf-designed golf course. The inn has the charm and comfort of a bed and breakfast with the conveniences of a modern hotel. Our seven suites, nine king-size rooms, and six double/double rooms are named after famous golf courses. All have private baths, three telephones, TV, and VCR.

Hosts: Gary and Bernice Adamson
Rooms: 22 (PB) $69-160
Full Breakfast
Credit Cards: A, B, C, D, E, F
Notes: 2, 5, 7, 9, 11, 12, 14

Max Paul...an Inn

3910 East Kellogg, 67218
(316) 689-8101

---

6 Pets welcome; 7 Smoking allowed; 8 Children welcome; 9 Social drinking allowed; 10 Tennis available; 11 Swimming available; 12 Golf available; 13 Skiing available; 14 May be booked through travel agents.

Rooms are furnished with feather beds, European antiques, cable TV, and private baths. Executive suites have vaulted ceilings, wood-burning fireplaces, and features such as skylights and private balconies. There is a Jacuzzi/exercise room. Weekends, breakfast may be served in the room or in the garden. Centrally situated for the airport, downtown, shopping, and local attractions.

Host: Roberta Eaton
Rooms: 14 (PB) $70-125
Full Breakfast
Credit Cards: A, B, C, D, E
Closed Christmas Day
Notes: 2, 5, 7, 9, 10, 12

Kentucky

Lamplighter Inn

103 West Second Street, 41002
(606) 756-2603

The inn is the home of Lamplighter Mysteries, an overnight murder mystery event that includes reception, dinner, and a mystery to challenge your wits. Held any night for six or more couples. A second night may be included at a lower rate. Historic Augusta (settled 1795) offers ample opportunity for sports and relaxation. Swimming and tennis across the street at a public park is available. Bicycles are available to explore the town. Stroll shady streets lined with quaint houses steeped in history. Browse through Augusta's galleries, antique shops, and aging winery.

Host: Nancy Whithers
Rooms: 9 (PB) $55-75
Full Breakfast
Credit Cards: A, B
Notes: 2, 3, 4, 5, 8, 9, 10, 11, 14

Bruntwood Inn

714 North Third Street, 40004
(502) 348-8218

This 1830 antebellum mansion and adjacent cottage provide eight bedrooms furnished in antiques and lovely linens. The mansion, listed in the historic register, features dental molding, stained glass, ash floors, grand entrance foyer, and an ash and cherry staircase that spirals up three floors. A full plantation breakfast is included in your stay.

Hosts: Susan and Zyg Danielak
Rooms: 8 (6 PB; 2 SB) $55-75
Full Breakfast
Credit Cards: A, B, D
Notes: 2, 5, 8, 9, 14

The Historic Old Talbott Tavern and McLean House

Court Square, 40004
(502) 348-3494

Built in 1779, this is the oldest western stagecoach stop in America in continuous operation. Licensed under Patrick Henry over two centuries ago, the old stone tavern has been a silent witness to an amazing panorama of events and a unending parade of people, including Abraham Lincoln, Jesse James, Queen Marie of Rumania, King Louis Philippe, Daniel Boone, Gen. George Rogers Clark, John Fitch, Stephen Foster, and countless others.

Hosts: The Kelley Family
Rooms: 13 (11 PB; 2 SB) $50-69
Continental Breakfast
Credit Cards: A, B, C
Notes: 2, 3, 4, 7, 8, 9

Jailer's Inn

111 West Stephen Foster Avenue, 40004
(502) 348-5551

In 1819, Jailer's Inn was constructed for use as a jail until 1874 when it was turned into the jailer's residence. This complex was the oldest operating jail in the com-

---

6 Pets welcome; 7 Smoking allowed; 8 Children welcome; 9 Social drinking allowed; 10 Tennis available; 11 Swimming available; 12 Golf available; 13 Skiing available; 14 May be booked through travel agents.

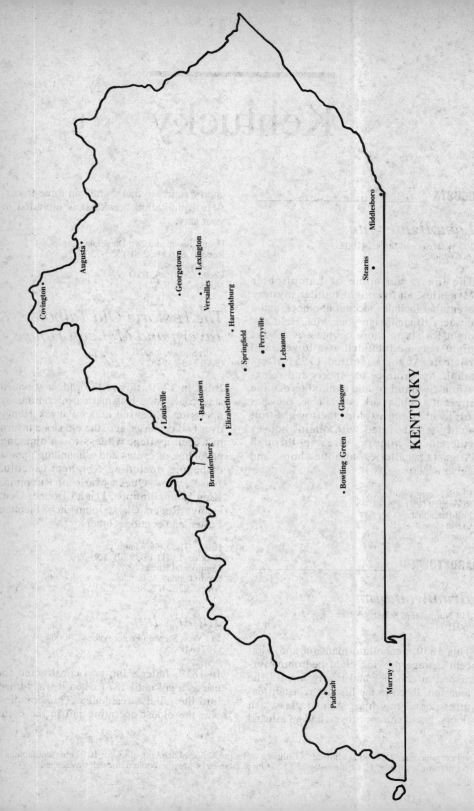

KENTUCKY

Middlesboro •

Stearns •

• Covington
Augusta •

• Georgetown
Versailles • • Lexington

Harrodsburg •

Louisville • Springfield •

Bardstown • Perryville •

Elizabethtown • Lebanon •

Brandenburg •

Bowling Green • • Glasgow

Murray •

Paducah •

monwealth of Kentucky until 1987. Large rooms, completely renovated and furnished with heirlooms and antiques. One room resembles a cell, with three of the original bunk beds; decorated in prison black and white, but color TV.

Hosts: Challen and Fran McCoy
Rooms: 5 (PB)
Continental Breakfast
Credit Cards: A, B, C, D
Closed January and February
Notes: 2, 9, 10, 11, 12, 14

The Mansion Bed and Breakfast

1003 North Third Street, 40004
(502) 348-2586

A beautiful Greek Revival mansion, circa 1851, on the National Register of Historic Places. Situated on over three acres of land, with magnificent trees and plantings, it reminds one of more genteel times. The Mansion is on the site where the first Confederate flag, the Stars and Bars, was raised in Kentucky for the first time. The rooms feature period antiques and hand-crocheted bedspreads, dust ruffles, and shams.

Hosts: Linda and Ken Anderson
Rooms: 3 (PB) $65-85
Full Breakfast
Credit Cards: A, B
Notes: 2, 5, 9

1790 House

110 East Broadway, 40004
(502) 348-7072

Located in the heart of the historic district, this early residence radiates the warmth and charm of the past. Two guest rooms feature fireplaces, and both have queen-size four-poster beds, mellow wood floors with area rugs, and are individually decorated with period antiques and quality reproductions. The brick patio overlooks lovely Colonial herb and perennial gardens. Central air conditioning.

Hosts: Linda and Ken Anderson
Rooms: 3 (PB) $65-85
Full Breakfast
Credit Cards: A, B
Notes: 2, 5,9

BEREA

Bluegrass Bed and Breakfast–Berea

Route 1, Box 263, Versailles, 40383
(606) 873-3208

Not every house can boast a 40-foot livingroom, but this one does. Three bedrooms from which to choose. This 1890 edge-of-town home puts you next to the world-famous Berea craftsmen who produce everything from pottery to fine furniture. For those who enjoy antiques, this house is a real treat. No smoking. $60.

BOWLING GREEN

Alpine Lodge

5310 Morgantown Road, 42101-8201
(502) 843-4846

Alpine Lodge is a Swiss chalet located on the outskirts of Bowling Green. There is a guest cottage, two suites that sleep up to six people, two bedrooms with private baths, and lots of flowers, gardens, and a nature trail with five deer stands. This cottage boasts a pool, gazebo, deck, and sceened-in porch. The honeymoon suite has a canopy bed, refrigerator, and private bath. The lodge serves a big country breakfast and is located near Mammoth Cave, Opryland USA, Horse Cave Theater, Steeplechase horse race track, Shakertown, and the Corvette plant.

Hosts: Dr. and Mrs. David Livingston
Rooms: 7 (3 PB; 4 SB) $40-150
Full Breakfast
Credit Cards: None
Notes: 2, 3, 4, 5, 6, 7, 8, 9, 11, 12, 14

NOTES: Credit cards accepted: A Master Card; B Visa; C American Express; D Discover Card; E Diner's Club; F Other; 2 Personal Checks accepted; 3 Lunch available; 4 Dinner available; 5 Open all year; 6 Pets welcome; 7 Smoking allowed; 8 Children welcome; 9 Social drinking allowed; 10 Tennis available; 11 Swimming available; 12 Golf available; 13 Skiing available; 14 May be booked through travel agents.

Walnut Lawn Bed and Breakfast

1800 Morgantown Road, 42101
(502) 781-7255

This is a restored Victorian house, part of
which was built in 1805. It is furnished
with family antiques of the period. Located
on a farm three miles from the center of
Bowling Green and just off Green River
Parkway and I-65. The place has been in
the family for 120 years. Walnut Lawn
requires reservations and serves a continental breakfast. No smoking.

BRANDENBURG

Doe Run Inn

500 Doe Run Hotel Road, 40108
(502) 422-2982

Owned by one of the fifth generation of
continuous family owners, this beautiful
historic inn, circa 1792, offers the best in
peace and quiet. Located in a parklike setting, with two-and-one-half-feet thick walls
and hand-hewn timbers. Abe Lincoln's
father worked on this building. Antique
furnishings are scattered throughout this
house, and prize-winning quilts can be
found in the gift shop. Secret recipes and a
bountiful smorgasbord make dining on the
screened-in porch above a babbling brook a
memorable experience. With only one TV
and one phone, a more desirable atmosphere to get back to the basics may not
exist. Hiking trails are nearby, and
Louisville is 40 minutes away.

Host: Van Smith
Rooms: 12; cabin that sleeps 6 (8 PB; 4 SB) $40-64
Full Breakfast
Credit Cards: A, B, D, E
Notes: 2, 3, 4, 5, 7, 8, 9, 12

COVINGTON

Amos Shinkle Townhouse Bed and Breakfast

215 Garrard Street, 41011
(606) 431-2118

This restored mansion, circa 1854, has won
several preservation awards. It features a
Greco-Italianate facade with a cast-iron fil-
igree porch. Inside there are lavish crown
moldings, Italianate mantels on the fireplaces, 16-foot ceilings, and Rococo
Revival chandeliers (Carnelius/Baker).
Guest rooms boast four-poster or massive
Victorian-style beds and period furnishings. Here southern hospitality is at its
finest. Just a 15-minute walk to downtown
Cincinnati, Ohio.

Hosts: Harry (Don) Nash and Bernie Moorman
Rooms: 7 (PB) $65-105 plus
Full Breakfast
Credit Cards: A, B, C, D, E
Notes: 2, 5, 7, 8, 9, 14

DAISY HILL

Bluegrass Bed and Breakfast

Route 1, Box 263, Versailles, 40383
(606) 873-3208

This stately brick home and extensive tree-
shaded grounds and horse farm have been
in the owner's family since 1812. It's a glorious combination of antique furnishings
and modern luxuries. A large downstairs
bedroom with elegantly canopied double
bed and private bath opens onto a brick
courtyard and lawn. A large upstairs bedroom with a king-size bed and private bath
overlooks the grounds including the family
cemetery dating from 1810. Another room
sharing a bath is available for family
groups. Air conditioned. $90.

DANVILLE

Bluegrass Bed and Breakfast

Route 1, Box 263, Versailles, 40383
(606) 873-3208

From its wraparound front porch to its spacious screened back porch overlooking the tree-shaded lawn this home offers turn-of-the-century charm and comfort. The upstairs guest suite has two large, corner bedrooms and one bath. Choose the twin-bed room or the double. Both rooms are rented only when families or, friends want to share the bath. Continental breakfast is served in the dining room or, weather permitting, on the screened porch. Air-conditioned. $45-60.

The Olde Bethlehem Acadamy Inn

ELIZABETHTOWN

The Olde Bethlehem Academy Inn

7051 St. John's Road, 42701
(502) 862-9003; (800) 662-5670

Once the stately home of Gov. John LaRue Helm and a girls' academy, the Olde Bethlehem Academy Inn offers five large bedrooms, all of which have private baths. Comfortably furnished with antiques, brass, and reproduction pieces. The rich history surrounding this lovely bed and breakfast enhances its beautifully restored setting,

and there are numerous areas for entertaining, including a second-floor chapel that is perfect for receptions, weddings, social gatherings, or a formal ball. A true testament to the 19th century, the Olde Bethlehem Academy Inn invites you to step back in time and enjoy the artifacts that remain from its significantly rich past.

Hosts: Mike and Jane Dooley
Rooms: 8 (5 PB; 3 SB); $45-75
Full Breakfast
Credit Cards: A, B
Notes: 2, 3, 4, 5, 6,,7, 8, 9, 14

GEORGETOWN

Breckinridge House (1820)

201 South Broadway, 40324
(502) 863-3163

This charming Georgian home was the residence of John C. Breckinridge, who ran against Abraham Lincoln for the presidency. After his defeat he became one of the leading Confederate generals. The two suites each have a bedroom, sitting room, kitchen, and bath and are furnished with antiques. Breakfast features homemade breads, pecan rolls, bacon and eggs, and fresh fruit.

Host: Annette Porter
Suites: 2 (PB) $65
Full Breakfast
Credit Cards: A, B
Notes: 2, 5, 6 (limited), 7, 9, 14

Log Cabin Bed and Breakfast

350 North Broadway, 40324
(502) 863-3514

Enjoy this Kentucky log cabin, circa 1809, with its shake roof, chinked logs, and period furnishings. Completely private. Two bedrooms, fireplace, fully equipped kitchen. Only five miles to Kentucky Horse Park and 12 miles north of Lexington. Children welcome.

Hosts: Clay and Janis McKnight
Cabin: (PB) $64
Expanded Continental Breakfast
Credit Cards: None
Notes: 2, 5, 6, 7, 8, 9, 10, 11, 12

Log House

Bluegrass Bed and Breakfast
Route 1, Box 263, Versailles, 40383
(606) 873-3208

This is a once-in-a-lifetime experience. A genuine log cabin from the days when Kentucky was the frontier. Handsomely restored and transformed into comfortabnle quarters that retain the charm. Two bedrooms, one very large. Livingroom with stone fireplace. Fully equipped kitchen large enough to eat in. Even a front porch for sitting and rocking. Twenty minutes from Lexington, 25 minutes from Keeneland Racecourse, and 15 minutes from the Kentucky Horse Park. Complete privacy. Air-conditioned. $75 for two, $105 for four.

GLASGOW

Four Seasons Country Inn

4107 Scottsville Road, 42141
(502) 678-1000

Charming Victorian-style inn built in 1989. All rooms have queen-size four-poster beds, private baths, remote-equipped TVs with cable. Continental breakfast served in inviting lobby with wood-burning fireplace. Some rooms open out to spacious deck or large front porch. Near Mammoth Cave National Park and Barren River Lake State Park.

Four Seasons Country Inn

Host: Henry Carter
Rooms: 17 (PB) $50-60
Continental Breakfast
Credit Cards: A, B, C, D, E
Notes: 2, 5, 7, 8, 9, 11, 12, 14

HARRODSBURG

Canaan Land Farm Bed and Breakfast

4355 Lexington Road, 40330
(606) 734-3984

This historic home, circa 1795, is located in central Kentucky and is a working sheep farm. Host is a shepherd/attorney, and hostess is a handspinner/artist. Lots of farm animals are on this bed and breakfast, and lambing seasons are in the spring and fall. Close to Shakertown, the airport, golf, and boating. Numerous antique shops are in the area. This wonderful getaway is peaceful and secluded. Full country breakfast is served each morning, and true southern hospitality characterizes your stay at this inn.

Hosts: Fred and Theo Bee
Rooms: 3 (PB) $60-75
Full Breakfast
Credit Cards: None
Notes: 5, 8, 9, 11, 14

Inn at Shaker Village of Pleasant Hill

3500 Lexington Road, 40330
(606) 734-5411

The Shaker Village of Pleasant Hill offers a one-of-a-kind guest experience. Its 80 guest rooms in buildings where Shakers once lived and worked are simply and beautifully furnished with Shaker-crafted furniture. A national historic landmark set on 2,700 acres of rolling bluegrass farmland, the village offers tours, daily exhibitions of Shaker crafts, and hearty country dining. Riverboat excursions from April through October.

NOTES: Credit cards accepted: A Master Card; B Visa; C American Express; D Discover Card; E Diner's Club; F Other; 2 Personal Checks accepted; 3 Lunch available; 4 Dinner available; 5 Open all year;

Host: Ann Voris
Rooms: 80 (PB) $55-100
Full and Continental Breakfast
Credit Cards: A, B
Notes: 2, 3, 4, 5, 7, 8

HENDERSON

The McCullagh House
Bed and Breakfast

304 South Main Street, 42420
(502) 836-0943

The McCullagh House, circa 1847, is listed
on the National Register of Historic Places.
This high-Victorian-style house blends
Greek Revival and Italianate design. In a
historic neighborhood, the inn has four
rooms filled with period antiques, high
ceilings, and a winding staircase. A
wrought iron fence frames the house. A
classic breakfast, served on Limoges china,
features homemade breads, fresh fruit, and
specially blended coffee and teas.

Hosts: Pamela and Michael Wolf
Rooms: 4 (2 PB; 2 SB) $55-65
Full Breakfast
Credit Cards: A, B

HOMEWOOD

Bluegrass
Bed and Breakfast

Route 1, Box 263, Versailles, 40383
(606) 873-3208

If your idea of luxury and romance
includes a four-poster bed in an old house
set in Kentucky's Bluegrass region this
farm is for you. Recently restored
Homewood invites you into a bedroom
with a fireplace, queen-size rice-carved
bed, and a private bath with tub and shower. Smoking permitted. Air-condtioned.
$75.

LAND O' GOSHEN

Bluegrass
Bed and Breakfast

Route 1, Box 263, Versailles, 40383
(606) 873-3208

If you've never stayed in a country bed and
breakfast with 18 rooms and breakfast eggs
fresh from the henhouse, here is your
chance. The grounds include stone walls, a
pond, flower and vegetable gardens, iron
gates, and a boxwood allee. Two rooms are
available one with double-bed and one
twin-bed. Both have fireplaces, private
baths, and are furnished with antiques. This
whole house illustrates a way of life virtually unkwnown in today's world. A stay
here is not to be missed. Air-conditioned.
Resident dogs and cats. $80.

LEBANON

Myrtledene

370 North Spalding Avenue, 40033
(502) 692-2223

Four rooms in the heart of Kentucky,
Myrteldene is a place to go back in time, to
slow down, to unwind. Make this gracious
Georgian home, built in 1833 and furnished
in period antiques, your headquarters as
you travel to area attractions. Come, stay a
while, and experience the rich heritage of
an area noted for its southern hospitality.

Host: Theresa Wheatley
Rooms: 4 (S2B) $60
Full Breakfast
Credit Cards: None
Notes: 2, 5, 7 (limited), 8, 9, 10, 11, 12, 14

6 Pets welcome; 7 Smoking allowed; 8 Children welcome; 9 Social drinking allowed; 10 Tennis available; 11
Swimming available; 12 Golf available; 13 Skiing available; 14 May be booked through travel agents.

LEXINGTON

Bed and Breakfast at Sills Inn-The Cottage

270 Montgomery Avenue, 40383
(800) 526-9801; (606) 252-3601
FAX (606) 873-4726

This bungalow cottage is within minutes of downtown, the University of Kentucky, and many other Lexington attractions. A short drive to Keeneland, Red Mile Race tracks, and the famous horse farm region, all rooms have private baths and use of the fully stocked guest kitchen.

Host: Tony Sills
Rooms: 2 (PB) $65
Full Breakfast
Credit Cards: A, B, C, D, E, F
Notes: 2, 5, 8, 9, 14

Lexington II

Bluegrass Bed and Breakfast
Route 1, Box 263, Versailles, 40383
(606) 873-3208

In the 1880s, Lexington's largest and finest homes were being built along Broadway, only blocks from the center of town. Today these houses are enjoying a rebirth as dedicated couples restore their glories. Your hosts offer a newly remodeled large air-conditioned bedroom with double bed, new private bath, and kitchenette. $54.

Lexington III

Bluegrass Bed and Breakfast
Route 1, Box 263, Versailles, 40383
(606) 873-3208

This is a lovely in-town house so surrounded by woods that you scarcely realize there are neighbors. Contemporary in style, its spacious feeling derives from its two-storied livingroom and generous use of glass. The guest room has twin mahogany four-posters and attached private bath. Also a king bedroom with a private bath. Fully air-conditioned. $54-58.

Lexington IV

Bluegrass Bed and Breakfast
Route 1, Box 263, Versailles, 40383
(606) 873-3208

Sycamore Ridge

NOTES: Credit cards accepted: A Master Card; B Visa; C American Express; D Discover Card; E Diner's Club; F Other; 2 Personal Checks accepted; 3 Lunch available; 4 Dinner available; 5 Open all year;

"French on the outside; English inside."
That is the way the owner describes her
stonecut house with walled garden and
graveled courtyard. Your accommodations
will be a sitting room/bedroom suite with
private bath and double bed. $60.

Sycamore Ridge

6855 Mount Horeb Road, 40511
(606) 231-7714

Nestled on a ridge in horse country, surrounded by sycamore trees, this unique
home affords guests a peaceful retreat with
a panoramic view of the Bluegrass.
Complimentary wine and cheese awaits
you. The gourmet breakfast includes items
such as freshly baked goods, fresh juice,
whole-wheat banana-pecan pancakes, and
an assortment of flavored coffee and teas.
Close to Kentucky Horse Park, downtown,
and the airport.

Hosts: Debbie and Jon Demos
Rooms: 3 (PB) $90
Full Breakfast
Credit Cards: None
Notes: 2, 5, 9, 10, 11, 12, 14

LOUISVILLE

Bed and Breakfast at Victoria House

P. O. Box 2756, 40201-2756
(502) 635-2551

This turn-of-the-century Victorian bed and
breakfast is located in the historic Old
Louisville district. Step through the doorway
into the romance of a bygone era. Full breakfast features homemade breads. Location is
central for the following sites: Kentucky
Center for the Arts, riverside events, Central
Park, University of Louisville, Speed
Museum, Churchill Downs, Freedom Hall,
many fine restaurants, and other beautiful
Louisville attractions. No children, no smoking. No pets. Hosts have pets (confined).
Deposit required.

Hosts: Eleanor and Jack Metcalf
Rooms: 4 (PB) $60-110
Full Breakfast
Credit Cards: None
Notes: 2, 9, 10

Cawain House

1436 St. James Court, 40208
(502) 636-1742

Georgian Revival home, circa 1895, is in
the historic district and features gas lights,
a fountain, and a common green. A bedroom, two baths, kitchen, dining, and
livingroom make up the guest accommodation., The home has been completely
restored. Swimming pool and tennis are
nearby; Churchill Downs is two miles,
downtown is one mile, and the airport is
ten minutes away. Old Louisville is unique
and fascinating to the antebellum home
lover.

Hosts: Walt Stern Jr. and Bruce Johnson
Rooms: 1 apartment (PB); $79
Credit Cards: None
Notes: 2, 5, 9, 10, 11

Kentucky Homes Bed and Breakfast Inc.

1219 South Fourth Avenue, 40208
(502) 635-7341

A reservation service for Louisville and
Kentucky offers approximately 85 rooms,
priced from $55-100.

Rooms: 85 approx. (PB) $55-100
Full and Continental Breakfast
Credit Cards: A, B, C
Notes: 2, 5, 8, 11, 14

The Victorian Secret Bed and Breakfast

1132 South First Street, 40203
(502) 581-1914

In historic old Louisville you will find a
three-story brick mansion appropriately
named the Victorian Secret Bed and
Breakfast. Its 14 rooms offer spacious

6 Pets welcome; 7 Smoking allowed; 8 Children welcome; 9 Social drinking allowed; 10 Tennis available; 11
Swimming available; 12 Golf available; 13 Skiing available; 14 May be booked through travel agents.

accommodations, high ceilings, 11 fireplaces, and original woodwork. Recently restored to its former elegance, the 110-year-old structure provides a peaceful setting for enjoying period furnishings and antiques.

Hosts: Nan and Steve Roosa
Rooms: 3 (1 PB; 2 SB) $53-58
Continental Breakfast
Credit Cards: None

MAYSVILLE

Bluegrass Bed and Breakfast

Route 1, Box 263, Versailles, 40383
(606) 873-3208

One of the most beautiful stretches of the Ohio River is at Maysville with its bridge and graceful bend in the river. You have spectacular, unobstructed views of it from the fourth (top) floor of a classic 1920s apartment house. A large corner guest room has a double bed, an alcove with daybed and private bath (tub, no shower). Weather permitting, enjoy your continental breakfast on the veranda that runs almost the length of the building. Elevator, air-conditioned. Additional double bedroom with bath is available. One hour from Cincinnati. $60.

MIDDLESBORO

The Ridge Runner

208 Arthur Heights, 40965
(606) 248-4299

Nestled in the Cumberland Mountains of southeastern Kentucky between Pine Mountain State Park and the Cumberland Gap National Park, this Victorian home, circa 1890, offers a spectacular view of the Cumberland Mountains. View the beautiful spring foliage from the sixty-foot porch, and enjoy the peace and quiet of yesteryear.

Relax and take in the tranquility of no TV or VCR; just enjoy nature and a croquet game.

Host: Susan Richards
Rooms: 4 (2 PB; 2 SB) $45-55
Full Breakfast
Credit Cards: A, B
Notes: 2, 5, 9

MIDWAY

Holly Hill

Bluegrass Bed and Breakfast
Route 1, Box 263, Versailles, 40383
(606) 873-3208

Holly Hill is a small country inn situated on a hill just outside downtown Midway, close enough to the antique shops yet with enough privacy for overnight guests to stroll the ground, the inn has become a favorite dining place for travelers and natives alike. Two rooms. $54.

Parrish Hill

Bluegrass Bed and Breakfast
Route 1, Box 263, Versailles, 40383
(606) 873-3208

A rare opportunity: spend the night in the guest house on a magnificent horse farm. The genuine charm of a log cabin combined with every convenience from air conditioning to a king bed. Cabin has large two-story livingroom with fireplace and wraparound porch. Bedroom has private bath with shower. Kitchen is fully equipped. Privacy is total, and from every window you'll see Thoroughbred horses in their pastures. $80.

Scottwood

Bluegrass Bed and Breakfast
Route 1, Box 263, Versailles, 40383
(606) 873-3208

An Early American jewel. Step back in time in this 1795 brick house sited on a lazy bend of the Elkhorn. Restored and furnished to absolute perfection, Scottwood will touch your heart if you love the beauty of the past. Choose a north wing room with a fireplace and private bath or the queen-size pencil post room. Both open onto a sitting room with fireplace and games table. There is also a sunlit guest cottage with deck overlooking the creek. No smoking. $90.

MURRAY

Diuguid House
Bed and Breakfast

603 Main Street, 42071
(502) 753-5470

This beautiful home, listed on the National Register of Historic Places, features a sweeping oak staircase, comfortable and spacious rooms, and a generous guest lounge area. This bed and breakfast is conveniently located in town near the university, lake area, and many antique shops. Full breakfast is included in the reasonable rates, and the area has the reputation for being a top rated retirement area.

Hosts: Karen and George Chapoman
Rooms: 3 (SB) $40
Full Breakfast
Credit Cards: A, B
Notes: 2, 5, 8, 14

OWENSBORO

Friendly Farms

5931 Highway 56, 42301
(502) 771-5590

Friendly Farms is a countryside cottage with two bedrooms, kitchenette, and sitting room plus tub/shower bath situated on a working farm across from a fishing pond stocked with ducks and geese. A wood-burning stove adds atmosphere. Indoor and outdoor tennis courts, Nautilus fitness training center, outdoor pool, horses, sauna, and walking paths. Located three miles west of the city, amid orchards and ponds, with a playground. Nearby restaurants. A full southern breakfast and snacks are furnished.

Host: Joan G. Ramey
Cottage: (PB) $60
Full Breakfast
Credit Cards: A, B
Notes: 2, 3, 4, 5, 6, 7, 8, 9, 10, 11

PADUCAH

Ehrhardt's
Bed and Breakfast

285 Springwell Lane, 42001
(502) 554-0644

This brick Colonial home is located just one mile off I-24, a highway noted for its lovely scenery. The hosts strive to make you feel at home in antique-filled bedrooms and a cozy den with a fireplace. Nearby are the beautiful Kentucky and Barkley lakes and the famous Land Between the Lakes area.

Hosts: Eileen and Phil; Ehrhardt
Rooms: 3 (SB) $30-35
Full Breakfast
Credit Cards: None
Notes: 2, 5, 8, 11, 12

Paducah Harbor Plaza
Bed and Breakfast

201 Broadway, 42001
(502) 442-2698

A warm, friendly atmosphere in the restored turn-of-the-century five-story bed and breakfast overlooking the Ohio River in downtown Paducah. Antiques abound, and the family antique quilt collection complements the New Quilters Museum built by the American Quilters Society, one block from the bed and breakfast. Paducah is known as Quilt City, USA. Museum, shops, and antique stores are accessible by a brick promenade along the river. Nostalgia is created with songs of the past played on a 1911 player piano. Sing-alongs are encouraged by the Harrises.

Hosts: Beverly and David Harris
Rooms: 4 (SB) $45-65
Expanded Continental Breakfast
Credit Cards: A, B, C
Notes: 2, 5

PERRYVILLE

Elmwood Inn

205 East Fourth Street, 40422
(606) 332-2400; (800) 765-2139

Civil War soldiers and American presidents have been hosted in the 150-year history of this gracious Greek Revival mansion. Browse the well-stocked library or enjoy afternoon tea in the English tea room. Recently restored guest suites include private baths and sitting rooms. This inn is a designated Kentucky landmark and is on the National Register of Historic Places. Close to Civil War battlefield and Shaker Village.

Hosts: Bruce and Shelly Richardson
Rooms: 2 (PB) $75-85
Full Breakfast
Credit Cards: A, B
Notes: 2, 5, 9

SPRINGFIELD

Maple Hill Manor

Route 3B, Box 20, 40069
(606) 336-3075

This circa 1851 brick Revival home with Italianate detail is a Kentucky landmark home on the National Register of Historic Places. It features thirteen and one-half-foot ceilings, ten-foot doors, a cherry spiral staircase, stenciling in the foyer, a large parlor, and formal dining room with fireplace, hardwood floors, and period furnishings. Seven bedrooms with private baths. Honeymoon accommodation has Jacuzzi, canopy bed, and private entrance.

Homemade dessert, and beverages in the evenings. No smoking.

Hosts: Bob and Kay Carroll
Rooms: 7 (PB) $60-80
Full Breakfast
Credit Cards: A, B
Notes: 2, 5, 8, 9, 14

STEARNS

The Marcum-Porter House

35 Hume Road, P.O. Box 369, 42647
(606) 376-2242

The Marcum-Porter House is on the National Register of Historic Places. It is in the heart of the Big South Fork area with its scenic beauty. The house is a company-built home and has retained its early 1900s charm. Accommodations include a bedroom with a private bath and three bedrooms with shared baths. Breakfast may include homemade bread, muffins, and casseroles.

Hosts: Sandra and Charles Porter; Patricia Porter-Newton
Rooms: 4 (1 PB; 3 SB) $55-65
Full Breakfast
Credit Cards: A, B
Notes: 2, 11, 12

VERSAILLES

Bed and Breakfast at Sills Inn

270 Montgomery Avenue, 40383
(606) 873-4478; (800) 526-9801
FAX (606) 873-4726

In the Lexington area. Restored Victorian inn located in historic downtown Versailles, just seven minutes west of the Lexington airport and the famous Keeneland race course. The state capital and beautiful bluegrass horse farm region are a few of many area attractions. All rooms have private baths and come with full gourmet breakfast. Ask about the Victorian suite with the double heart-shaped Jacuzzi.

NOTES: Credit cards accepted: A Master Card; B Visa; C American Express; D Discover Card; E Diner's Club; F Other; 2 Personal Checks accepted; 3 Lunch available; 4 Dinner available; 5 Open all year;

Bed and Breakfast at Sills Inn

Peacham

Bluegrass Bed and Breakfast
Route 1, Box 263, 40383
(606) 873-3208

Nine fireplaces typify the charm of this house built in 1829 from brick fired on the farm. Set amid ancient trees on a knoll one-half mile from the highway, this home is a quiet oasis bordered by horse farms. One second-floor room with twin beds and private bath. $60. Very private first-floor suite: living room, bedroom with queen-size canopy bed, air conditioning, and private bath. No smoking. $75.

Polly Place

Bluegrass Bed and Breakfast
Route 1, Box 263, 40383
(606) 873-3208

An artist's dream studio: beautiful, comfortable, yet with touches of whimsy. First level is one great room oriented around a huge fireplace. Above are open balconied bedrooms and bath with Jacuzzi. Studio rests on a shaded knoll on a 200-acre farm. Sleeps four comfortably. You have the entire house. Two-night minimum stay. $100-140.

Shepherd Place

US 60 and Heritage Road, 40383
(606) 873-7843

Marlin and Sylvia invite you to share their pre-Civil War home, built between 1820 and 1850. The house has windows that go all the way to the floor, crown moldings, hardwood floors, and large rooms with private baths, as well as a parlor and front porch swing for your relaxation. You may even want to stroll up to the barn and meet the resident ewes, or ride through the bluegrass horse farms.

Hosts: Marlin and Sylvia Yawn
Rooms: 2 (PB) $65 plus tax
Full Breakfast
Credit Cards: A, B
Notes: 2, 5

Springdale

Bluegrass Bed and Breakfast
Route 1, Box 263, 40383
(606) 873-3208

Nestled on a grassy slope above a stone springhouse, this fine old home is the perfect setting for those who want to experience quiet country living. The original dwelling, built about 1800, forms the nucleus of the airy brick home shaded by old trees. One air-conditioned bedroom has double bed and private bath. Another room is available for additional family or friends. Crib available. No smoking. $64.

Versailles I

Bluegrass Bed and Breakfast
Route 1, Box 263, 40383
(606) 873-3208

Enjoy all the comforts of home in this traditional 1990s brick house on a quiet residential street. Guests have upstairs to themselves. Choose the large Wicker Room with twin wicker beds and a seating area or the Cannonball Room, with antique cannonball double-bed and rocking chair. A connecting "shotgun" bathroom gives each room its own two-piece lavatory plus a tub/shower compartment in between. Air conditioned. $64.

Welcome Hall

Bluegrass Bed and Breakfast
Route 1, Box 263, 40383
(606) 873-3208

Built in 1792 when Kentucky was still the westernmost segment of Virginia, this handsome stone house and its grounds are a prime example of that period's self-sufficient country estate. Now devoted to blooded horses, as well as general farming, it provides a unique experience to its guests. Newly restored air-conditioned, two-room cabin with double four-poster. Light breakfast. Two-night minimum stay. $100.

Louisiana

BATON ROUGE

Southern Comfort Reservations LBR07

P. O. Box 13294, New Orleans, 70185-3294
(504) 861-0082; (800) 749-1928

This lovely bed and breakfast is a tree-shaded Victorian in a centrally located residential area. One upstairs bedroom furnished with comfortable antiques has a private bath, its own entrance, TV, and phone. Adjoining living area is available as a sitting room. Full breakfast. No smoking; children welcome. $45.

Southern Comfort Reservations LBR08

P. O. Box 13294, New Orleans, 70185-3294
(504) 861-0082; (800) 749-1928

Guest cottage with living/dining room, kitchen, bath, one bedroom, TV, phone. Sleeps four. FAX, copy machine, computer are available in host's home. Ideal for business people. $75.

CARENCRO

La Maison de Campagne, Lafayette

825 Kidder Road, 70520
(318) 896-6529

This Victorian home, circa 1900, is in a beautiful country setting with 200-year-old oak trees on nine acres. Come enjoy life the way it used to be. The inn offers private baths, antique-furnished rooms, a swimming pool, and three great Cajun restaurants and attractions five minutes away. A gourmet, full country Cajun breakfast is served with the hospitality of the award-winning chef/hostess. Enjoy early morning or late afternoon walks or just relax on the sweeping wraparound veranda or the upstairs balcony. You will want to come back again and again.

Hosts: Joeann and Fred McLemore
Rooms: 3 (PB) $72.10-75.10
Full Cajun Breakfast
Credit Cards: A, B
Notes: 2, 5, 11, 14

COVINGTON

Southern Comfort Reservations LCOV1

P. O. Box 13294, New Orleans, 70185-3294
(504) 861-0082; (800) 749-1928

This is a delightful nonworking farm situated 35 miles across Lake Pontchartrain north of New Orleans in the piney woods of St. Tammany Parish. Enjoy the landscaped gardens and dockside activities on the Tchefuncte River, including fishing and swimming. Comfortable guest cottage includes a livingroom with TV, full kitchen, twin, double, and king rooms, and one bath. Continental breakfast. $85.

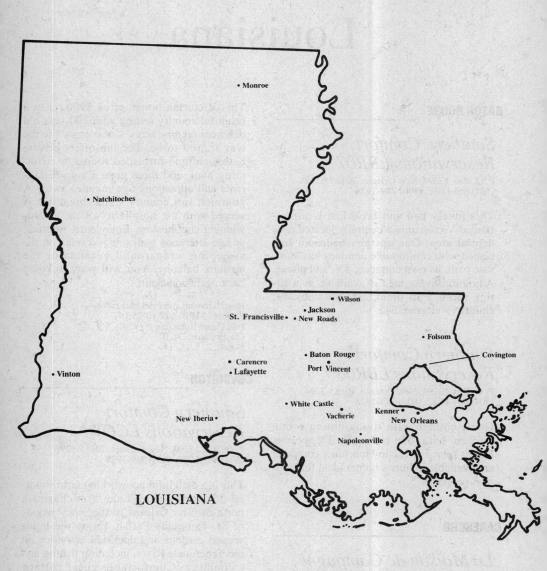

- Monroe

- Natchitoches

- Wilson
- Jackson
St. Francisville • • New Roads

- Folsom

Covington

- Carencro
- Lafayette

- Baton Rouge
Port Vincent

- Vinton

- White Castle
Kenner •
Vacherie
New Orleans

New Iberia •

Napoleonville

LOUISIANA

FOLSOM

Southern Comfort Reservations LFOL1

P. O. Box 13294, New Orleans, 70185-3294
(504) 861-0082; (800) 749-1928

Roomy country house with plenty of space. Enjoy the country quiet and the sandy beach on the beautiful Tchefuncte River. Three guest rooms and two baths. Advance reservations necessary. $60-80.

Southern Comfort Reservations LFOL2

P. O. Box 13294, New Orleans, 70185-3294
(504) 861-0082; (800) 749-1928

Secluded rustic retreat for total relaxation. Wood-burning stove, quilts, and country antiques fill this guest apartment, with a large great room, two bedrooms, bath, private drive and entrance, TV, and phone. One hour from downtown New Orleans. $85.

JACKSON

Milbank

102 Bank Street, 70748
(504) 634-5901

Milbank is a romantic antebellum mansion with irresistible charm, built in 1836. Today, as it was yesterday, Milbank presents an elegantly formal appearance derived from Greek Revival architecture. The house has twelve thirty-foot-high Doric columns on the exterior, and guest rooms are furnished with museum-quality antiques.

Host: M. Leroy Harvey, Jr.
Rooms: 4 (2 PB; 2 SB) $65-75
Full Breakfast
Credit Cards: A, B
Notes: 2, 5, 8, 9

Southern Comfort Reservations LJSN1

P. O. Box 13294, New Orleans, 70185-3294
(504) 861-0082; (800) 749-1928

Built in 1825-1836, this property on the national register has been a home, a bank, was occupied by Union troops, and is now totally restored. Bedroom and private bath on the first floor. One two-bedroom-and-bath suite on the second floor. Children welcome. Full breakfast; restricted smoking; 10 percent senior citizen discount. Picnic lunches and private sightseeing tours may be arranged. $65-130.

KENNER

Seven Oaks Plantation

2600 Gay Lynn Drive, 70065
(504) 888-8649

This 10,000-square-foot West Indies-style home overlooks the lake, is convenient to the airport, and is twenty minutes from the New Orleans French Quarter. Guest rooms open onto a large livingroom and onto twelve-foot galleries. A full plantation breakfast is served, and the entire home can be toured. Antiques and Mardi Gras memorabilia are found throughout. Seven Oaks offers southern hospitality and will make your visit full of warm, pleasant memories.

Host: Kay Andressen
Rooms: 2 (PB) $95
Full Breakfast
Credit Cards: A, B,
Notes: 2, 5, 8, 9

LAFAYETTE

Southern Comfort Reservations LLF01

P. O. Box 13294, New Orleans, 70185-3294
(504) 861-0082; (800) 749-1928

This authentic Acadian-raised mansion's Victorian carriage house is furnished with Louisana antiques. Breakfast is a Cajun feast served on a glassed-in porch overlooking the Old New Orleans-style courtyard, or in the dining room, with its original fireplace. In the evening, after-dinner drinks and chocolates are offered. Fishing and duck hunting trips or swamp tours can be arranged. Handicapped accessible. One double room, one queen room $85; suite $95-145.

Southern Comfort Reservations LFLO3

P. O. Box 13294, New Orleans, 70185-3294
(504) 861-0082; (800) 749-1928

Cajun Victorian home has three bedrooms, one twin, and two double beds, furnished with antiques. One has working fireplace and small Jacuzzi. Glassed-in porch has Victorian gingerbread; gazebo and swing in the yard. Full breakfast. $60.

MADISONVILLE

Southern Comfort Reservations LMA01

P. O. Box 13294, New Orleans, 70185-3294
(504) 861-0082; (800) 749-1928

This 100-year-old house is just seven miles from the 26-mile Lake Pontchartrain Causeway leading to New Orleans. Its big porches, wide hallways, high ceilings, and bright rooms provide a casual atmosphere. Just steps to the beautiful river, where you can enjoy crabbing, fishing, and many water sports. Three bedrooms, shared bath. Full breakfast may include crab omelets or popovers. $45.

METAIRIE

Metairie Meadows

141 Metairie Court, 70001
(504) 525-3983

Although the French Quarter is only minutes away, this home offers quiet, peaceful accommodations in a safe neighborhood. The bedrooms are large and opulent. One features an antique crown canopy bed, fireplace, balcony, private marble bath, elegance, and Old South charm. Continental breakfast and use of lovely patio. Stay and enjoy all of New Orleans, paddlewheelers on the Mississippi, plantations, the French Market, antique shops, restaurants, and Bourbon Street.

Host: Flo Cairo
Rooms: 3 (PB) $75-125
Continental Breakfast
Credit Cards: None

MONROE

Southern Comfort Reservations LMN01

P. O. Box 13294, New Orleans, 70185-3294
(504) 861-0082; (800) 749-1928

Situated 15 miles south of Monroe, this cottage is all that remains of a once-magnificent plantation. Its guest house has one spacious room with antique four-poster and a single sleigh bed, private bath. There's a cozy corner with reading lamp, TV, and VCR. Garconniere has one room with private bath, antiques, double bed. Full breakfast. $75.

NAPOLEONVILLE

Madewood Plantation House

4250 Highway 308, 70390
(504) 369-7151

A national historic landmark, Madewood is a stately Greek Revival mansion on Bayou Lafourche about 75 miles from New Orleans's French Quarter. Set on 20 acres in front of a working sugar cane plantation, Madewood is furnished with antiques. Bedrooms have canopied beds. Guests dine by candlelight, family style, after a wine and cheese party in the library. Featured in *Vogue*, *Country Home*, *Country Inns*, *Innsider*, the Los Angeles *Times*, BBC radio, and many more. In cottage, continental breakfast; in mansion, full breakfast, linner for two.

Hosts: Keith and Millie Marshall; Dave D'Aunoy
Rooms: 9 (PB) $90-165
Full or Continental Breakfast
Credit Cards: A, B, C
Closed major holidays
Notes: 2, 4, 5, 14

NATCHITOCHES

Breazeale House Bed and Breakfast

926 Washington Street, 71457
(318) 352-5630

Breazeale House was built for Congressman Phanor Breazeale in the late 1800s. It is within walking distance of the historic downtown district of Natchitoches. This Victorian house features 11 fireplaces, 12-foot ceilings, nine stained-glass windows, a set of servants' stairs, three balconies, eight bedrooms, and three floors with over 6,000 square feet of living space. President Taft slept here, and you can also see this house in *Steel Magnolias*.

Hosts: Willa and Jack Freeman
Rooms: 5 (2 PB; 3 SB) $50-75
Full Breakfast
Credit Cards: A, B
Notes: 2, 5, 8, 9, 11, 14

Martin's Roost

1735 1/2 Washington Street, 71457
(318) 352-9215

Comfortable contemporary home with country atmosphere. Patios, pool, deck with panoramic view of former Red River roadbed. Arts, crafts, plantation doll houses, and needlework. Home of background props filmed in *Steel Magnolias*. Gourmet breakfast; dinner du jour. Certified tour guide to enchanting history of oldest settlement in Louisana Purchase.

Hosts: Ronald and Vicki Martin
Rooms: 2 (PB) $55
Full Breakfast
Credit Cards: A, B
Notes: 2, 3, 4, 5, 7, 9, 11, 14

NEW IBERIA

Southern Comfort Reservations LNI02

P. O. Box 13294, New Orleans, 70185-3294
(504) 861-0082; (800) 749-1928

Contemporary home on three-acre estate overlooking Bayou Teche. Duck pond on the front lawn, unique house with glassed-in porch, large screened patio, and lighted tennis court combine to make your visit a delight. Two guest rooms, one with twins and one with queen bed, have bayou view and private baths and are connected by a large sitting room with TV and phone. Continental breakfast; no smoking; children welcome. $65.

NEW ORLEANS

A Hotel—The Frenchmen

417 Frenchmen Street, 70116
(504) 948-2166; (800) 831-1781

Two 1860s Creole town houses situated across from the old U.S. mint at Esplanade and Decatur. Each room is individually decorated and climate-controlled. Courtyard patio has pool and heated spa. Complimentary breakfast with daily changes in menu served in room or on the patio.

6 Pets welcome; 7 Smoking allowed; 8 Children welcome; 9 Social drinking allowed; 10 Tennis available; 11 Swimming available; 12 Golf available; 13 Skiing available; 14 May be booked through travel agents.

Host: Mark Soubie, Jr.
Rooms: 25 (PB) $84-124
Full Breakfast
Credit Cards: A, B, C
Notes: 2, 5, 7, 9, 11, 14

Antique Row Townhouse

Bed and Breakfast Inc.
1021 Moss Street, Box 52257, 70152-2257
(504) 488-4640; (800) 749-4640

In the heart of the antique shops of the French Quarter, the guest quarters are nestled in the courtyard of an 1850s town house. The second-floor accommodation has a private entrance, sitting room, bedroom, bath, and kitchenette. Self-serve continental breakfast is provided for guests to enjoy at their leisure. $100-175.

Architectural Gem

Bed and Breakfast, Inc.
1021 Moss Street, Box 52257, 70152-2257
(504) 488-4640; (800) 749-4640

Remaining true to the original design of this wonderful guest cottage has been of primary concern to the owners. They have overseen the renovation project from top to bottom, paying careful attention not to disturb the historic detail of this building. Thick exposed brick walls and three brick fireplaces, used in the 1830s as the kitchen facilities for the main house, reflect the authenticity of this historic restoration. Uniquely designed private baths adjoin each of the two cozy bedrooms. Self-serve continental breakfast is provided for guests to enjoy at their leisure. $75-150.

Beau Séjour Bed and Breakfast

1930 Napoleon Avenue, 70115
(504) 897-3746

This turn-of-the-century mansion is downtown on the Mardi Gras parade route and near the historic street car that carries guests to the French Quarter, convention center, Superdome, Aquarium, and Universities. Beau Séjour boasts a casual, tropical atmosphere with spacious rooms, queen-size beds, and antiques, embodying the charm and ambience of old New Orleans.

Hosts: Gilles and Kim Gagnon
Rooms: 5 (PB) $75-125
Continental Breakfast
Credit Cards: B
Notes: 5, 7, 8, 9, 14

Bougainvillea House

841 Bourbon Street, 70116
(504) 525-3983

Situated in the heart of the French Quarter, this 1820 house has been beautifully restored to its former elegance. Some rooms furnished with rare antiques, and all are richly decorated. One bedroom features a canopy bed, fireplace, and balcony. The courtyard and patio are contained within a privacy wall, and locked gates assure guests' security. The French Market, paddlewheelers on the Mississippi, antique shops, five-star restaurants, and music cafés on Bourbon Street are nearby.

Rooms: 3 (PB) $75-125
Continental Breakfast
Credit Cards: None

Bourbon Street Suite

Bed and Breakfast Inc.
1021 Moss Street, Box 52257, 70152-2257
(504) 488-4640; (800) 749-4640

Guests enjoy this private, first-floor suite opening onto world-famous Bourbon Street. The host is a New Orleans native and shares his vast knowledge of the special spots not to miss. One bedroom, private bath, continental breakfast. $75-100.

NOTES: Credit cards accepted: A Master Card; B Visa; C American Express; D Discover Card; E Diner's Club; F Other; 2 Personal Checks accepted; 3 Lunch available; 4 Dinner available; 5 Open all year;

Chartres Marigny Bed and Breakfast, Inc.

1021 Moss Street, Box 52257, 70152-2257
(504) 488-4640; (800) 749-4640

At the edge of the French Quarter sits this 1830s town house where the hosts are enjoying the painstaking restoration of the property. Ask your host for the renovation tour. Seeing the different phases of a renovation in progress is a mini course in the building and architectural styles of New Orleans. The charming guest cottage is tastefully furnished, has a private entrance, four-poster antique bed, bath and kitchenette. Self-serve continental breakfast is provided for guests to enjoy at their leisure. $75-100.

Club La Pension

115 Decatur Street, 70130
(504) 528-9254

The oldest existing structure on Canal Street, Club La Pension, circa 1821, is located in the historic French Quarter and offers Old World charm with all the modern conveniences and an ideal location. Café Giovanni, adjacent to the resort, serves award-winning international cuisine. Thirty lovely suites with fully equipped kitchens and oversized Jacuzzi tubs are furnished in antique-style French Provencial decor and decorated in soft natural colors. Relax and enjoy the rooftop patio observation deck, complete with personal Jacuzzi.

Host: John Santopadre, Sr.
Rooms: 30 (PB) $125-200
Continental Breakfast
Credit Cards: A, B, C
Notes: 3, 4, 5, 7, 8, 9

The Columns Hotel

3811 Saint Charles Avenue, 70115
(504) 899-9308; (800) 445-9308

One of the stateliest remaining examples of turn-of-the-century Louisiana architecture, the Columns Hotel offers a return to former elegance. Despite its elegance, the Columns is affordable and comfortable. Its 19 rooms range from the very simple to the very grand. Each features some small delight for the experienced traveler: unique fireplace, armoires, claw foot bathtubs. The dining room, Albertine's Tea Room, is one of the loveliest and most peaceful in New Orleans. Listed on the National Register of Historic Places. Featured in *Good Housekeeping*, *Elle*, the New York *Times*, "Good Morning, America," *Esquire*, and others.

Hosts: Claire and Jacques Creppél
Rooms: 19 (9 PB; 10 SB) $50-105
Continental Breakfast
Credit Cards: A, B, C
Notes: 2, 4, 5, 6, 7, 8, 9

The Cornstalk Hotel

915 Royal Street, 70116
(504) 523-1515

This early 1800s home is central to the sights, sounds, gourmet foods, and night life of old New Orleans. In perhaps the most distinctive and most photographed of

The Cornstalk Hotel

6 Pets welcome; 7 Smoking allowed; 8 Children welcome; 9 Social drinking allowed; 10 Tennis available; 11 Swimming available; 12 Golf available; 13 Skiing available; 14 May be booked through travel agents.

the small inns of the French Quarter, you will have a unique experience of Victorian charm in the Vieux Carré. Glowing crystal chandeliers, antique furnishings, stained-glass windows, fireplaces, Oriental rugs, canopy beds, and complimentary morning newspaper set the mood of quiet comfort during your stay.

Hosts: David and Debi Spencer
Rooms: 14 (PB) $75-135
Expanded Continental Breakfast
Credit Cards: A, B, C
Notes: 5

Creole Cottage

Bed & Breakfast Inc.
1021 Moss Street, Box 52257, 70152-2257
(504) 488-4640; (800) 749-4640

This quaint Creole cottage was built in 1902. The home is minutes away from major New Orleans attractions. The historic Saint Charles Avenue streetcar line makes the famous restaurants, jazz clubs, art galleries, and antique shops accessible. Two bedrooms; continental breakfast on silver service. $50-70.

Dauphine Street Suite

Bed & Breakfast Inc.
1021 Moss Street, Box 52257, 70152-2257
(504) 488-4640; (800) 749-4640

In the heart of the residential part of the French Quarter, this guest suite is nestled in the courtyard of an 1840s Creole cottage. The second-story suite is off the charming brick courtyard and has a private entrance, horse-hair double bed, and bath. Self-serve continental breakfast is provided. $75-100.

Dauzat House

337 Burgundy Street, 70130
(504) 524-2075

Dauzat House, snuggled cozily in the French Quarter, provides the personal attention and privacy that larger hotels cannot offer. Dauzat house, a four-star AAA, is a private compound with lush courtyards and pool that centers around suites with antiques, kitchenettes, balconies, wood-burning fireplaces, and a sunken tub. Staying here will be an experience that will bring you back again.

Host: Richard L. Nicolais
Suites: (PB) from $160
Credit Cards: None
Notes: 2, 5, 9, 14

Designer Guest Cottage

Bed and Breakfast Inc.
1021 Moss Street, Box 52257, 70152-2257
(504) 488-4640; (800) 749-4640

Originally the studio of a famous southern sculptor, the cottage displays his artistic creativity while preserving its historic past. A short streetcar ride to galleries, antiques, restaurants, and the French Quarter. One bedroom with private bath; continental breakfast. $95-135.

Galleried Home

Bed and Breakfast Inc.
1021 Moss Street, Box 52257, 70152-2257
(504) 488-4640; (800) 749-4640

Historians delight in this French Plantation-style home. The guest suite is just off the host's livingroom and opens onto the front balcony. The suite offers a sitting room, bedroom with four-poster double bed, and bath. The lush garden below provides a tropical approach. Lovely antiques; continental breakfast. $95-110.

Garden District Building

Bed and Breakfast Inc.
1021 Moss Street, Box 52257, 70152-2257
(504) 488-4640; (800) 749-4640

Conveniently located right on the streetcar line, a fun ride to downtown and the French Quarter is less than 15 minutes. You will be sharing the host's lovely condominium

NOTES: Credit cards accepted: A Master Card; B Visa; C American Express; D Discover Card; E Diner's Club; F Other; 2 Personal Checks accepted; 3 Lunch available; 4 Dinner available; 5 Open all year;

and will have access to the swimming pool. One bedroom with private bath; continental breakfast. $50-70.

Garden District Guest Suite

Bed and Breakfast Inc.
1021 Moss Street, Box 52257, 70152-2257
(504) 488-4640; (800) 749-4640

Three lovely antique twin beds grace a nicely decorated suite. Comfortably spacious with a livingroom and kitchen. Enjoy the special flavors of New Orleans-style cooking at the nearby famous bistros. Two bedrooms with private bath; continental breakfast supplies provided. $50-80.

Greek Revival Home

Bed and Breakfast Inc.
1021 Moss Street, Box 52257, 70152-2257
(504) 488-4640; (800) 749-4640

Nestled in a historic community just across the Mississippi River from the French Quarter, this imposing Greek Revival home offers guests a private apartment overlooking the swimming pool. Walk or drive to the free ferry for a brief romantic ride. One bedroom with private bath; continental breakfast. $50-80.

Grenoble House

329 Dauphine Street, 70112
(504) 522-1331

Grenoble House has seventeen suites, one- and two-bedroom accommodations that are fully equipped with a modern kitchen and offer unique amenities, such as a pool and and heated Jacuzzi, in one of the French Quarter's largest patios. The patio also features a covered barbecue/bar area and is available to guests for personal or business entertainment.

Host: Leslie Brewer
Rooms: 17 (PB) $110-320

Continental Breakfast
Credit Cards: A, B, C
Notes: 5, 7, 8, 11, 14

Guest Atelier in Town

Bed and Breakfast Inc.
1021 Moss Street, Box 52257, 70152-2257
(504) 488-4640; (800) 749-4640

Built around 1840, this Greek Revival Italianate building was once used as a town house. It currently houses several locally owned studios and art galleries and a private luxury bed and breakfast apartment. The French Quarter, Riverwalk, convention centers, and the streetcar are nearby. Two bedrooms with private bath; self-serve continental breakfast. $125-280.

Guest Suite in Greek Revival Cottage

Bed and Breakfast Inc.
1021 Moss Street, Box 52257, 70152-2257
(504) 488-4640; (800) 749-4640

Greek Revival cottage offers a well-appointed guest apartment with its own private entrance overlooking the swimming pool. Hosts have tastefully decorated their home. The streetcar ride to downtown is just ten minutes. A short walk takes you to other attractions. One bedroom with private bath; continental breakfast. $50-90.

Historic Blacksmith's Shop

Bed and Breakfast Inc.
1021 Moss Street, Box 52257, 70152-2257
(504) 488-4640; (800) 749-4640

Truly of national historic significance, this home's name dates back to 1775. Guests occupy a bedroom well appointed with antiques. The hosts are long-time French Quarter area residents who enjoy sharing their knowledge with guests. One bedroom with private bath; continental breakfast on fine china. $60-80.

6 Pets welcome; 7 Smoking allowed; 8 Children welcome; 9 Social drinking allowed; 10 Tennis available; 11 Swimming available; 12 Golf available; 13 Skiing available; 14 May be booked through travel agents.

Home Near Audubon Park

Bed and Breakfast Inc.
1021 Moss Street, Box 52257, 70152-2257
(504) 488-4640; (800) 749-4640

Guests can ride the streetcar to the interesting Riverbend with specialty shops and to French coffee houses, art galleries, antiques, famous restaurants, music clubs, and more. This 1950s brick home is set in a lovely historic neighborhood. One bedroom with hall bath; continental breakfast. $35-50.

Hotel Ste. Helene

508 Chartres, 70130
(504) 522-5014; (800) 348-3888

The Hotel Ste. Helene offers 16 custom-designed guest rooms, ideally situated in the heart of the French Quarter. A European atmosphere along with gracious hospitality greets you and continues throughout your visit. The courtyard's lush greenery and sparkling pool provide an inviting atmosphere for your continental breakfast served each morning. You will enjoy New World comfort and Old World charm with an attentive professional staff to help you make every minute of your visit memorable.

Rooms: 16 (PB) $98-135
Continental Breakfast
Credit Cards: A, B, C, D, E
Notes: 2, 5, 7, 8, 11, 14

Hotel St. Pierre

911 Burgundy Street, 70116
(504) 524-4401

A two-hundred-year-old inn where Creole-era buildings are located among secluded courtyards to create a restful oasis of swimming pools amid colorful tropical plantings and foliage. Complimentary continental breakfast and a champagne happy hour reflect the laid-back feeling so indigenous to the French Quarter location where history stirs at every corner.

Host: Mary Ann Grisby
Rooms: 70 (PB); $89-129
Continental Breakfast
Credit Cards: A, B, C, D, E
Notes: 2, 3, 4, 5, 6, 7, 8, 9, 11, 14

Jensen's Bed and Breakfast

1631 Seventh Street, 70115
(504) 897-1895

A 100-year-old Queen Anne Victorian, beautifully decorated with antiques, stained glass, 12-foot alcove ceilings, and cypress doors. Located across the street from the Garden District, an area famed for its lovely homes. The trolley is one block away and provides easy access to the French Quarter and Audubon Park and Zoo. All rooms are air conditioned.

Hosts: Shirley, Bruce, and Joni
Rooms: 4 (SB) $50-60
Continental Breakfast
Credit Cards: None
Notes: 2, 5, 8, 9, 10, 12

Lafitte Guest House

1003 Bourbon Street, 70116
(504) 581-2678; (800) 331-7971

This elegant French manor house, in the heart of the French Quarter, is meticulously restored to its original splendor and furnished in fine antiques and reproductions. Every modern convenience, including air conditioning, is provided for your comfort. Complimentary continental breakfast, wine, and hors d'oeuvres at cocktail hour, on-site parking, and a daily newspaper.

Host: Dr. Rovert Guyton
Rooms: 14 (PB) $79-165
Continental Breakfast
Credit Cards: A, B, C, D
Notes: 5, 7, 9, 14

La Maison Marigny

Bed and Breakfast Inc.
1021 Moss Street, Box 52257, 70152-2257
(504) 488-4640; (800) 749-4640

NOTES: Credit cards accepted: A Master Card; B Visa; C American Express; D Discover Card; E Diner's Club; F Other; 2 Personal Checks accepted; 3 Lunch available; 4 Dinner available; 5 Open all year;

Located in the French Quarter, this petite bed and breakfast inn was just completely renovated down to window dressings and dust ruffles. Each of the three guest rooms has a private entrance and modern bath. Enjoy a continental breakfast downstairs or outside in the traditional walled garden and patio. $75-100.

Lamothe House

621 Esplanade Avenue, 70116
(504) 947-1161

Elegantly restored Victorian mansion. All rooms have private baths, color TV, phones, and air conditioning. Some have high ceilings. Jackson Square, French Market, many jazz clubs, and fine restaurants just a stroll away.

Rooms: 20 (PB) $50 plus
Continental Breakfast
Credit Cards: A, B, C
Notes: 5, 9, 10, 12, 14

The Lanaux House

Bed and Breakfast Inc.
1021 Moss Street, Box 52257, 70152-2257
(504) 488-4640; (800) 749-4640

The historic Lanaux House was constructed in 1879 and has been restored by the hostess. A private entrance leads to the second-floor guest suite. Guests enjoy their own lovely livingroom, bedroom with antique brass double bed, bath, and kitchenette. Self-serve continental breakfast. $100-150.

La Petite Suite

Bed and Breakfast Inc.
1021 Moss Street, Box 52257, 70152-2257
(504) 488-4640; (800) 749-4640

This stylish guest suite, in the courtyard of an 1850s Creole cottage, offers the romance and history that is the ambience of New Orleans. The second-floor suite has a private entrance off the charmingly landscaped courtyard area. Once inside, guests enjoy the comfort of a four-poster bed, bath, and kitchenette. Continental breakfast. $75-100.

La Salle Hotel

1113 Canal Street, 70112
(800) 521-9450

Centrally situated in downtown New Orleans within one block of the French Quarter, famous restaurants, theaters, historic sites, exclusive shops, and major sporting events.

Host: Roland Bahan
Rooms: 57 (45 PB; 12 SB) $57-90
Continental Breakfast
Credit Cards: A, B, C, D, E, F
Notes: 5, 7, 8, 14

Le Garconiere Guest Suite

Bed and Breakfast Inc.
1021 Moss Street, Box 52257, 70152-2257
(504) 488-4640; (800) 749-4640

A charming couple welcomes guests to their historic home in the French Quarter. Antique shops, restaurants, and jazz clubs are just a short walk from this quiet neighborhood. Private, two-story guest cottage overlooking the tropical courtyard with a balcony and full kitchen. Experience the streetcar along the Mississippi River. Continental breakfast. $75-100.

Lincoln Ltd. #7

P. O. Box 3479, Meridian, Mississippi 39303
(601) 482-5483 information
(800) 633-MISS reservations

Lovely historic home furnished in antiques. Six beautifully appointed bedrooms with private baths. Situated conveniently close to the Garden District and public transportation. Continental breakfast served. $75-125.

6 Pets welcome; 7 Smoking allowed; 8 Children welcome; 9 Social drinking allowed; 10 Tennis available; 11 Swimming available; 12 Golf available; 13 Skiing available; 14 May be booked through travel agents.

Mazant Guest House

906 Mazant Street, 70117
(504) 944-2662

An informal, self-catering, modestly priced
and happy household situated only two
miles from the French Quarter. A small
kitchen is available to guests during their
stay, and we offer advice about restaurants
and the best places to hear local New
Orleans music.

Hosts: Lou Graff and Robyn Halvorsen
Rooms: 11 (4 PB; 7 SB) $18-55
Continental Breakfast
Notes: 2, 5, 6, 7, 8, 9, 10, 12

Mechlings 1860s Mansion Bed and Breakfast

2023 Esplanade Avenue, 70111
(504) 943-4131; (800) 725-4131

This 1860s historical mansion is located on
beautiful Esplanade Avenue. Experience
the ambience of the Victorian era; stroll
through the French Quarter or the city park;
public transportation is just outside the
door. Spacious, beautifully decorated
rooms all offer private baths, and complimentary breakfast is served on the veranda
or in the rooms. Original marble mantels,
gasoliers, slave quarters, cisterns, wine cellars, and a historical oak tree that spans 100
feet are available for guests to view. Guests
are welcome to tour this restored home.

Hosts: Keith and Claudine Mechling
Rooms: 6 (PB) $75-155
Full Breakfast
Credit Cards: A, B, C
Notes: 2, 3, 4, 5, 9, 14

Melrose Mansion

937 Esplanade Avenue, 70116
(504) 944-2255

The Melrose is an 1884 Victorian mansion
that has been completely restored to perfection. This opulent, galleried mansion features eight antique-filled guest rooms with
luxurious private baths, spacious heated
pool and tropical patio, whirlpools, wet
bars with refrigerators in the rooms.
Complimentary airport pick-up and delivery with house limousine, open bar at cocktail hour, and a full Creole breakfast. New
Orleans grandeur at its very finest.

Hosts: Melvin and Rosemary Jones
Rooms: 8 (PB) $195-395
Full Breakfast
Credit Cards: A, B, C
Notes: 2, 5, 9, 11, 14

New Orleans Bed and Breakfast-TNN-LOUISIANA

P. O. Box 8163, 70182
(504) 838-0071; FAX (504) 943-3417

Part of the Bed and Breakfast National
Network, Nrew Orleans Bed and Breakfast
offers bed and breakfast not only in
Louisiana, but also in many other cities and
states across the country. The members of
this network adhere strictly to the standards
set by TNN, such as getting to know the
hosts personally, having an established cancellation and refund policy, and following a
thorough inspection and approval process
for all properties rented. This is because

Melrose Mansion

each member of the network is dedicated to ensuring your comfort, pleasure, and personal needs while you are staying at one of our "homes away from home."

New Orleans Bed and Breakfast BD1

P. O. Box 8128, 70182
(504) 838-0071

Very friendly hosts have converted a commercial building into a comfortable, attractive home and offer two guest rooms with bath in between. Two other smaller rooms with double beds share a hall bath. Off-street parking is available. No smoking; no small children. $40-50.

New Orleans Bed and Breakfast CP1

P. O. Box 8128, 70182
(504) 838-0071

Situated in the historic district of the city and to the rear of an 1890 Creole cottage is a spacious efficiency apartment with double bed, double sofa bed, private bath, kitchenette, and private entrance. Walking distance to the Museum of Art, St. Louis Cemetery, plantation homes, and the beautiful 150-year-old oaks in City Park. Continental breakfast. $55-70.

New Orleans Bed and Breakfast CP2

P. O. Box 8128, 70182
(504) 838-0071

A comfortable one-bedroom apartment, completely private with twin beds and a fully furnished kitchen. A double sofa bed is in livingroom. Walk to activities in City Park or catch a bus at the corner to the French Quarter. No smoking. Continental breakfast. $55-70.

New Orleans Bed and Breakfast ER1

P. O. Box 8128, 70182
(504) 838-0071

Just beyond the French Quarter is a raised mid-1880s home with very congenial hosts (both artists of renown). They offer a full apartment with livingroom, bedroom, kitchen, and bath; lovely garden with mostly native plantings. Near bus. Continental breakfast. $55-70.

New Orleans Bed and Breakfast GE1

P. O. Box 8128, 70182
(504) 838-0071

On this tree-shaded boulevard, one large brick house has three bedrooms. The master bedroom is done in rose and black, has five tall windows, king bed, and private bath. Two other rooms share a bath. Continental breakfast. $55-70.

New Orleans Bed and Breakfast GE2

P. O. Box 8128, 70182
(504) 838-0071

A pretty garage apartment has double bed and a trundle bed in the living area; kitchen, bath, and loads of off-street parking. Continental breakfast. $55-70.

New Orleans Bed and Breakfast GE3

P. O. Box 8128, 70182
(504) 838-0071

Beautiful Spanish-style home, one bedroom with double bed, share bath with host family. A delightful kitchen where a continental breakfast is served. $55-70.

---

6 Pets welcome; 7 Smoking allowed; 8 Children welcome; 9 Social drinking allowed; 10 Tennis available; 11 Swimming available; 12 Golf available; 13 Skiing available; 14 May be booked through travel agents.

New Orleans Bed and Breakfast GE4

P. O. Box 8128, 70182
(504) 838-0071

Convenient home has two rooms, each with a private bath; one has a queen bed, the other a double bed. Both are clean, convenient, and have off-street parking. Continental breakfast. $55-70.

New Orleans Bed and Breakfast LK1

P. O. Box 8128, 70182
(504) 838-0071

A West Indies-style plantation home built from remains of a long-ago plantation mansion and filled with antiques, Mardi Gras mementoes, and giant Audubon prints. Two bedrooms, private baths, and breezeway on the second floor. On the levee, you can jog, ride bikes, or stroll hand-in-hand. A full plantation breakfast is served in the family dining room. Near the airport, 25 minutes by car to the French Quarter. $70 plus.

New Orleans Bed and Breakfast LV1

P. O. Box 8128, 70182
(504) 838-0071

One large, friendly home has two upstairs bedrooms with common den and independent bath. Great for family or two couples. Continental breakfast. $55-70.

New Orleans Bed and Breakfast LV2

P. O. Box 8128, 70182
(504) 838-0071

In a delightful lakeview subdivision, a cozy bungalow offers one bedroom with twin beds and private bath, private entrance, and off-street parking. The guest will find a restful den and lovely backyard garden. Continental breakfast. $55-70.

New Orleans Bed and Breakfast UP2

P. O. Box 8128, 70182
(504) 838-0071

This friendly, relaxed home has a cozy patio, spacious bedrooms, some with private bath, double or queen-size beds. Guests have use of kitchen facilities. The hostess is a licensed tour guide and speaks Spanish and French. Continental breakfast. $40-70.

New Orleans Bed and Breakfast UP4

P. O. Box 8128, 70182
(504) 838-0071

One moderately priced, luxurious home is near first-class restaurants. One bedroom with private bath. Hostess loves to travel. Continental breakfast. $70 plus.

New Orleans Bed and Breakfast UP6

P. O. Box 8128, 70182
(504) 838-0071

In a lovely uptown home with serene atmosphere is a large two-bedroom and bath suite, one with king bed and the other with a queen bed. Deluxe antiques, private entrance. Just steps away from St. Charles Avenue streetcar. Continental breakfast. $70 plus.

NOTES: Credit cards accepted: A Master Card; B Visa; C American Express; D Discover Card; E Diner's Club; F Other; 2 Personal Checks accepted; 3 Lunch available; 4 Dinner available; 5 Open all year;

New Orleans Bed and Breakfast UP7

P. O. Box 8128, 70182
(504) 838-0071

In a large two-story home with double gallery in front are two apartments. The second-floor apartment has twin beds in bedroom, sofa bed in livingroom, a full kitchen, private bath, 14-foot ceilings, and private entrance. Other apartment has two bedrooms (queen bed and single bed), also studio bed in livingroom, kitchen, and eating space. Close to bus. Continental breakfast. $55-70.

New Orleans Bed and Breakfast UP9

P. O. Box 8128, 70182
(504) 838-0071

In a nice location, a two-bedroom apartment has queen and single bed, plus a studio couch in livingroom; two full baths; kitchen and eating area. This can accommodate four people. Continental breakfast. $90.

New Orleans Bed and Breakfast UP10

P. O. Box 8128, 70182
(504) 838-0071

This renovated historic uptown residence was once a plantation home. It consists of five bedrooms, each with a private bath. Built in 1840, the house is furnished with antiques or reproductions of antiques, and all bedrooms have queen beds except one, which has a double Edwardian bed. Situated near the streetcar line and many fine restaurants. Continental breakfast. $70 plus.

New Orleans Guest House

1118 Ursulines Street, 70116
(504) 566-1177; (800) 562-1177

An 1848 Creole cottage with lush courtyard where a complimentary continental breakfast is served each morning. Private baths, free parking, tastefully decorated with antiques or contemporary furnishings, air conditioning, and TV. Three blocks to famous Bourbon Street.

Hosts: Ray and Alvin
Rooms: 14 (PB) $59-79
Continental Breakfast
Credit Cards: A, B, C
Notes: 5

The Orleans Cottage

Bed and Breakfast Inc.
1021 Moss Street, Box 52257, 70152-2257
(504) 488-4640; (800) 749-4640

Located in the French Quarter area, this 1890s historic Victorian cottage was recently renovated. One bedroom with private bath; continental breakfast. $75-110.

P.J. Holbrook's Olde Victorian Inn

914 North Rampart Street, 70116
(504) 522- 2446; (800) 725-2446

Once an 1800s bordello, this inn is located in the historic French Quarter. Recently restored, it is now New Orleans' most elegant guest house. Seven period guest rooms all have private baths, and most have fireplaces. Three also feature balconies. Beautiful courtyard for dining, and an elegant gathering room invites conversation. Specializes in honeymoons, anniversaries, and family reunions.

Hostess: P. J. Holbrook
Rooms: 7 (PB) $100-150
Full Breakfast
Credit Cards: A, B, C
Notes: 2, 5, 9, 14

6 Pets welcome; 7 Smoking allowed; 8 Children welcome; 9 Social drinking allowed; 10 Tennis available; 11 Swimming available; 12 Golf available; 13 Skiing available; 14 May be booked through travel agents.

The Prytania Inns

1415 Prytania Street, 70130
(504) 566-1515

Restored to its pre-Civil War glory and situated in the historic district, the inn
received the 1984 Commission Award.
Tender care, full gourmet breakfast. Patio,
slave quarters, 18 rooms with private baths,
most with kitchen facilities or microwave
and refrigerators. Five minutes to the
French Quarter and one-block walk to St.
Charles Avenue and the streetcar. Free
parking. Hosts speak German.

Hosts: Sally and Peter Schreiber
Rooms: 18 (PB) $35-55
Full Breakfast
Credit Cards: A, B, C, D, E, F
Notes: 5, 6, 7, 8

Prytania Street Suite

Bed and Breakfast Inc.
1021 Moss Street, Box 52257, 70152-2257
(504) 488-4640; (800) 749-4640

The designer of this 19th-century home
modeled it after an Austrian manse. Guests
enjoy a lovely apartment that includes two
bedrooms, full kitchen, one and one-half
baths. Just one block from the St. Charles
street car line, this suite is convenient to all.
Continental breakfast. $75-125.

Quaint Guest Cottages

Bed and Breakfast Inc.
1021 Moss Street, Box 52257, 70152-2257
(504) 488-4640; (800) 749-4640

A special place filled with romance.
Flavored with antiques and architectural
details, the cottages look onto a patio and
antique swing. The streetcar is downtown
at the French Quarter in just 15 minutes.
Guests enjoy antiques, famous bistros and
music nearby. Two cottages with private
baths; continental breakfast. $60-125.

Queen Anne Victorian Home

Bed and Breakfast Inc.
1021 Moss Street, Box 52257, 70152-2257
(504) 488-4640; (800) 749-4640

Recently renovated, this home, with its
original artwork and fabric-dressed walls,
shows the special touches of the hostess, an
interior designer. The Garden District mansions of the past are just steps away, as are
restaurants, antiques, and art galleries.
Three bedrooms with hall bath; continental
breakfast. $45-70.

Rue Dumaine

731 Dumaine Street, 70116
(504) 581-2802

Your private entranceway leads you
through a lush, secluded patio to your hideaway in the heart of the bustling French
Quarter. Built in 1824, this completely renovated slave quarters has every amenity,
including central air and heat, ceiling fans,
working fireplace, gaming table, piano, balcony, private bath, telephones, intercom,
kitchenette with microwave and refrigerator. Have the time of your life on Bourbon
Street just one-half block away and yet
sleep soundly in the quiet of your exclusive
retreat.

Host: Clydia Davenport
Room: 1 (PB) $90-150
Continental Breakfast
Credit Cards: None
Notes: 2 (in advance), 5, 9, 14

St. Charles Avenue Home

Bed and Breakfast Inc.
1021 Moss Street, Box 52257, 70152-2257
(504) 488-4640; (800) 749-4640

Hosts love sharing their enthusiasm for
New Orleans in a historic, homespun setting. Walking distance to the interesting
Riverbend area with its specialty shops,
coffee houses, and popular restaurants. The

NOTES: Credit cards accepted: A Master Card; B Visa; C American Express; D Discover Card; E Diner's
Club; F Other; 2 Personal Checks accepted; 3 Lunch available; 4 Dinner available; 5 Open all year;

host was born in this house that boasts some of the original antiques. Two bedrooms with hall bath; continental breakfast. $50-60.

Soniat House

1133 Chartres Street, 70116
(504) 522-0570; (800) 544-8808

Hidden in a quiet residential section of New Orleans' French Quarter, Soniat House was built in 1829 as a town home for the large family of Joseph Soniat Dufossat, a wealthy plantation owner. Typical of the period, the Creole house incorporates classic Greek Revival details. A wide carriageway entrance leads to a quiet and beautiful courtyard; galleries are framed by lace ironwork, and open spiral stairs lead to the two upper floors. All rooms are tastefully furnished with fine antiques, hand-carved bedsteads, and the work of contemporary New Orleans artists. The Soniat House was recognized as the French Quarter's best restoration on the 50th anniversary of the Vieux Carré Commission. Member of the National Historic hotels since 1990.

Hosts: Rodney and Frances Smith
Rooms: 24 (PB) $135-500
Continental Breakfast
Credit Cards: A, B, C
Notes: 2, 5, 7, 9, 14

Southern Comfort Reservations LNO01

P. O. Box 13294, New Orleans, 70185-3294
(504) 861-0082; (800) 749-1928

Carrollton Cottage near universities, parks, museums. Easy access to all highways, French Quarter, downtown. Hostess speaks fluent Spanish. No children; private bath, king or twin beds; continental breakfast. $45-50.

Southern Comfort Reservations LNO04

P. O. Box 13294, New Orleans, 70185-3294
(504) 861-0082; (800) 749-1928

Late 19th-century Italianate mansion in the lower Garden District with a central courtyard and balconies. Six rooms, private baths; four with nonworking fireplaces, all with TV. Continental breakfast. French and Spanish spoken. $75-135.

Southern Comfort Reservations LN005

P. O. Box 13294, 70185-3294
(504) 861-0082; (800) 749-1928

This house was built 148 years ago as a river boat captain's inn. It has been lovingly restored and now offers bed and breakfast with delightful hosts who have moved here from California. Since its restoration, the house has been filmed in two segments of *Unsolved Mysteries* TV Series. $95-105.

Terrell House Mansion

1441 Magazine Street, 70130
(504) 524-9859; (800) 878-9859

Terrell House was built in the Classical Revival style in 1858. Restored and opened as an inn in 1984, it has a large following of guests from around the country and abroad. The main mansion guest rooms feature balconies, galleries, and authentic furnishings. Each overlooks the courtyard. The original carriage house has been converted to four guest rooms, each furnished with period antiques and decorated with its own style. The lower Garden District is the oldest purely residential neighborhood outside the French Quarter. This is the real New Orleans.

Host: Frederick Nicaud
Rooms: 9 (PB) $65-110
Continental Breakfast

6 Pets welcome; 7 Smoking allowed; 8 Children welcome; 9 Social drinking allowed; 10 Tennis available; 11 Swimming available; 12 Golf available; 13 Skiing available; 14 May be booked through travel agents.

Credit Cards: A, B, C
Notes: 2, 5, 7, 9, 14

University Area Home

Bed and Breakfast Inc.
1021 Moss Street, Box 52257, 70152-2257
(504) 488-4640; (800) 749-4640

A welcoming couple provides a comfortable, homey flavor in this raised cottage. University campuses, restaurants, specialty shops, and music clubs are nearby. A pleasurable 40-minute streetcar ride will take you downtown. One bedroom with private bath; continental breakfast. $30-70.

The Uptown Home

Bed and Breakfast Inc.
1021 Moss Street, Box 52257, 70152-2257
(504) 488-4640; (800) 749-4640

Guests enjoy this residential neighborhood, with its shady trees and historic homes. Close to universities, restaurants, antique shops, art galleries, and the streetcar line, which can take you to many attractions. Each of the three bedrooms has a double bed and shared bath. Great for the budget-minded. Continental breakfast. $40-60.

Veranda

Bed and Breakfast Inc.
1021 Moss Street, Box 52257, 70152-2257
(504) 488-4640; (800) 749-4640

Enjoy a light, tropical atmosphere in this home, recently and lovingly renovated by the hosts. After an exciting day of sightseeing, guests relax on the wide front veranda. The guest bedrooms are apart from the family's sleeping rooms. Continental breakfast; close to downtown. $45-70.

Victorian Cottage

Bed and Breakfast Inc.
1021 Moss Street, Box 52257, 70152-2257
(504) 488-4640; (800) 749-4640

The host has lovingly restored this home. It offers peaceful, intimate guest rooms, comfortably furnished, and has a private bath and private entrance onto the patio. Nearby is the old French Market and Mississippi River Walk. Continental breakfast is served on the patio, which has a wet bar. $55-70.

Victorian Manse

Bread and Breakfast, Inc.
1021 Moss Street, P. O. Box 52257, 70152-2257
(504) 488-4640; (800) 749-4640

An authentic bejewelled crown and scepter, recalling Mardi Gras balls of the past, rest regally on the front parlor mantel of this beautifully restored 100-year-old Victorian home. Just around the corner from charming boutiques, delightful restaurants, and French coffee houses in the hub of the established Historic Uptown District. Designer-decorated guest bedroom and bath are on the second floor. Continental breakfast is served in the country kitchen. $60-70.

NEW ROADS

Lincoln Ltd. #38

P. O. Box 3479, Meridian, Mississippi 39303
(601) 482-5483 information
(800) 633-MISS reservations

This attractive Creole cottage is wonderful for a weekend getaway or a special fishing trip. Group accommodations by special request. The hostess is knowledgeable about the history of this Mississippi River town and can offer many ideas about special places to see (plantation homes, fishing, etc.). A continental breakfast is served each morning by the hostess/owner. Six guest rooms. $40.

NOTES: Credit cards accepted: A Master Card; B Visa; C American Express; D Discover Card; E Diner's Club; F Other; 2 Personal Checks accepted; 3 Lunch available; 4 Dinner available; 5 Open all year;

Pointe Coupee Bed and Breakfast

401 Richey Street, 70760
(504) 638-6254; (800) 832-7412

These two historic homes are located in the heart of plantation country. Hebert House, an 1898 Victorian, features private baths, footed tubs, fireplaces, antiques, wrap-around front porch. The Samson-Claiborne House, an 1835 Creole cottage, has suites with wood-burning fireplaces, private baths, and front and back galleries. Complimentary wine on arrival and full breakfast is served each morning. Candlelight dinners are served by request, and both houses are near the beautiful False River. Minutes from Baton Rouge and Cajun country, one and one-half hours from New Orleans.

Hosts: Al and Sidney Coffee
Rooms: 6 (PB) $55-75
Full Breakfast
Credit Cards: A, B
Notes: 2, 4, 5, 8, 9, 12, 13, 14

Southern Comfort Reservations LNR01

P. O. Box 13294, New Orleans, 70185-3294
(504) 861-0082; (800) 749-1928

Newly restored Victorian; seven bedrooms and baths with antiques and wicker; spacious porches. Experienced bed and breakfast hostess pampers guests with wake-up coffee and afternoon high tea. Near scenic Oxbow Lake and public boat launch. Good fishing, water sports, hiking. $65-80.

PORT VINCENT

Tree House in the Park

16520 Airport Road, Prairieville, 70769
(504) 622-2850; (504) 335-8942

A Cajun cabin in the swamp. Large bedrooms with Jacuzzi tub, queen waterbed, private hot tub on sun deck, heated pool on lower deck. Boat slip, fishing dock, double kayak float trip on Amite River. Three acres of ponds, bridges, cypress trees, ducks, and geese. Complimentary supper on arrival

Hosts: Fran and Julius Schmieder
Rooms: 2 (PB) $60-100
Full Breakfast
Credit Cards: A, B
Notes: 2, 4, 5, 9, 11, 14

ST. FRANCISVILLE

Barrow House

524 Royal Street, Box 1461, 70775
(504) 635-4791

Sip wine in a wicker rocker on the front porch while you enjoy the ambience of a quiet neighborhood of antebellum homes. Rooms are all furnished in antiques from 1840-1870. Gourmet candlelight dinners are available, as is breakfast in bed. A cassette walking tour of the historic district is included for guests.

Hosts: Shirley and Lyle Dittloff
Rooms: 3 (PB) $75-85
Suite: 1 (PB) $85-95
Continental Breakfast; Full Breakfast available
Credit Cards: None
Closed December 23-25
Notes: 2, 4, 5, 7, 8, 9, 12, 14

The Myrtles Plantation

Highway 61, 70775
(504) 635-6277

The Myrtles, situated in historic St. Francisville, is known as "America's most haunted house." This 20-room French Rococo mansion has elaborate plaster and ironwork throughout. Historic house tours and mystery tours; private parties welcome with reservations.

Hosts: Arlin Dease and Mark Willett
Rooms: 10 (PB) $75-130
Full Breakfast
Credit Cards: A, B, C
Notes: 2, 3, 4, 5, 8, 9, 12, 14

6 Pets welcome; 7 Smoking allowed; 8 Children welcome; 9 Social drinking allowed; 10 Tennis available; 11 Swimming available; 12 Golf available; 13 Skiing available; 14 May be booked through travel agents.

The St. Francisville Inn

118 North Commerce Street, 70775
(504) 635-6502

In the heart of Louisiana plantation country, the St. Francisville Inn has nine antique-furnished guest rooms opening onto a lovely New Orleans-style brick courtyard where guests may relax. The restored main house, circa 1880, has a restaurant, a sitting room for guests, porches, swings for rocking, and an original spectacular ceiling medallion with a Mardi Gras mask design. On the edge of the historic district.

Hosts: Florence and Dick Fillet
Rooms: 9 (PB) $42.90-64.90
Continental Breakfast
Credit Cards: A, B, C, D, E
Notes: 2, 3, 4, 5, 7, 8, 9, 11, 12, 14

The St. Francisville Inn

SHREVEPORT

Fairfield Place
Bed and Breakfast

2221 Fairfield Avenue, 71104
(318) 222-0048

Built before the turn of the century, Fairfield Place has been beautifully restored to bring you all the charm of a bygone era. Conveniently situated near downtown, I-20, the medical centers, and Louisiana Downs. Within walking distance of fine restaurants and unique shops. Breakfast includes rich Cajun coffee and freshly baked croissants, served in the privacy of your room, the balcony, porch, or courtyard.

Host: Jane Lipscomb
Rooms: 6 (PB) $65-145
Full Breakfast
Credit Cards: A, B, C
Notes: 2, 5, 9, 10, 11, 12

SLIDELL

Southern Comfort Reservations LSLD1

P. O. Box 13294, New Orleans, 70185-3294
(504) 861-0082; (800) 749-1928

A beautiful contemporary house with deck overlooking the Pearl River and docks for three boats. One guest room has a king bed and private bath; one has a queen bed with private bath. Your choice of breakfast. No smoking. $75-85.

Southern Comfort Reservations LSLD3

P. O. Box 13294, New Orleans, 70185-3294
(504) 861-0082; (800) 749-1928

Spacious 100-year-old Victorian on a four-acre plot full of azaleas and camellias, has five bedrooms with private baths, and antiques throughout. Guests enjoy several common areas and the glassed-in porch where breakfast is served. It is 35 miles on I-10 from New Orleans. $75-95; honeymoon or anniversary packages include champagne on arrival and breakfast in bed $125.

NOTES: Credit cards accepted: A Master Card; B Visa; C American Express; D Discover Card; E Diner's Club; F Other; 2 Personal Checks accepted; 3 Lunch available; 4 Dinner available; 5 Open all year;

VACHERIE

Oak Valley Restaurant and Inn

3645 LA Highway 18, 70090
(504) 265-2151

The guest cottages are in the residential quarters of the plantation, not far from the antebellum home. They were constructed from 1880 to 1890 and have recently been renovated to include such comforts as central heat and air conditioning and carpeting. The cottages are tastefully furnished and cheerfully decorated with the fresh charm of country living. The absence of TVs and telephones further enhances the peaceful setting. The restaurant on the grounds of the plantation has a gift shop and offers a daily menu representative of area Creole and Cajun specialities using recipes created in local kitchens.

Host: Donna Cortez
Cottages: 6 (PB) $75-100
Continental Breakfast
Credit Cards: A, B
Notes: 3, 5, 8, 14

VINTON

Old Lyons House

1335 Horridge Street, 70668
(318) 589-2903

Queen Anne Victorian in the downtown area of a small rural town, restored and furnished with antiques. The hosts will make you welcome and do everything possible to ensure that when you leave, you know the meaning of the words southern hospitality. Horse racing, fishing, swimming, canoeing, nature, old homes, and more are all within a few minutes' drive. Massage therapist and hot tub on premises.

Hosts: Danny Cooper and Ben Royal
Rooms: 2 (SB) $25-35
Full Breakfast
Credit Cards: None
Notes: 2, 4, 5, 7, 8, 9, 10, 11, 14

WHITE CASTLE

Nottoway Plantation Inn and Restaurant

P. O. Box 160, Louisiana Highway 1, 70788
(504) 545-2730

Nottoway, circa 1859, is a Greek Revival and Italianate mansion built for a wealthy sugar cane planter just before the Civil War. The home is situated beside the Mississippi River and surrounded by large oak and pecan trees. Guest rooms are also available in a restored 150-year-old overseer's cottage.

Hosts: Cindy Hidalgo and Faye Russell
Rooms: 13 (PB) $125-250
Full Breakfast
Credit Cards: A, B, C, D
Notes: 2, 3, 4, 5, 7 (restricted), 8, 9, 10, 11, 14

WILSON

Glencoe Plantation House

P. O. Box 178, 70789
(504) 629-5387; (800) 235-2695

Unusual castle-style Queen Anne Victorian Gothic house offers four inside guest rooms and eight cottage rooms. In the fabled Felicana Parishes, Glencoe House sits at the front of one thousand acres of parklike grounds. Bring your own gear and fish at one of the ponds. or play tennis and swim. This is a good area for sightseeing and bicycling. Elegant dining facilities are conveniently nearby.

Hosts: W. Jerome Westerfield, Jr. and Stirling Nagura
Rooms: 12 (PB) $65-85
Full Breakfast
Credit Cards: A, B
Notes: 2, 5, 8, 10, 11, 12, 14

6 Pets welcome; 7 Smoking allowed; 8 Children welcome; 9 Social drinking allowed; 10 Tennis available; 11 Swimming available; 12 Golf available; 13 Skiing available; 14 May be booked through travel agents.

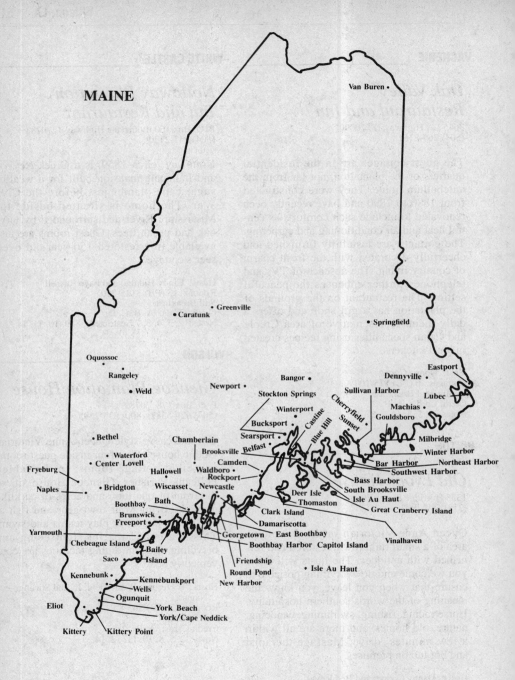

MAINE

Van Buren

Greenville

Caratunk

Springfield

Oquossoc

Rangeley

Weld

Newport   Bangor

Eastport

Dennyville

Stockton Springs   Sullivan Harbor   Lubec

Winterport   Cherryfield   Machias

Bethel   Bucksport   Castine   Sunset   Gouldsboro

Chamberlain   Searsport   Blue Hill   Milbridge

Waterford   Brooksville   Belfast   Winter Harbor

Center Lovell   Hallowell   Camden   Bar Harbor   Northeast Harbor

Fryeburg   Waldboro   Southwest Harbor

Naples   Bridgton   Rockport   Bass Harbor

Wiscasset   Newcastle   Deer Isle   South Brooksville

Boothbay   Isle Au Haut

Bath   Thomaston   Great Cranberry Island

Brunswick   Clark Island

Freeport   Damariscotta

Yarmouth   Georgetown   East Boothbay   Vinalhaven

Chebeague Island   Boothbay Harbor   Capitol Island

Saco   Bailey   Friendship   Isle Au Haut

Kennebunk   Island   Round Pond

Kennebunkport   New Harbor

Wells

Eliot   Ogunquit

York Beach

York/Cape Neddick

Kittery   Kittery Point

Maine

AUGUSTA

Maple Hill Farm Inn

Outlet Road, Rural Route 1, Box 1145, Hallowell, 04347
(207) 622-2708

Charming country inn. Quiet, relaxed elegance, away from all traffic, hearty country breakfast. Situated on more than 60 acres of unspoiled rural beauty. Central to Maine's lake regions, mountains, and coast. Near national historic district offering unique shopping, dining, and antiques. Rooms are tastefully furnished with antiques and overlook rolling meadows, woods and gardens; private suite with Jacuzzi available. Experience the freedom of open skies and country solitude for an intimate weekend, or as an alternative to everyday business accommodations, just minutes from the Maine Turnpike.

Hosts: Scott Cowger and Robert Audet
Rooms: 7 (4 PB; 3 SB) $50-75
Full Breakfast
Credit Cards: A, B
Notes: 2, 5, 6, 8, 9, 11, 12, 13

BAILEY ISLAND

Captain York House Bed and Breakfast

Route 24, P. O. Box 32, 04003
(207) 833-6224

Enjoy true island atmosphere on scenic Bailey Island, an unspoiled fishing village, accessible by car over the only cribstone bridge in the world. Near Brunswick, Freeport, Portland. Former sea captain's home tastefully restored to original charm, furnished with antiques. Informal, friendly atmosphere, eye-popping ocean views from every room. From the deck, enjoy sights of local lobstermen hauling traps and the most memorable sunsets on the coast. Nearby fine dining/summer nature cruise.

Hosts: Charles and Ingrid Di Vita
Rooms: 3 (1 PB; 2 SB) $55-75
Full Breakfast
Credit Cards: None
Notes: 2, 5, 9, 14

BANGOR

The Quality Inn-Phenix

20 Broad Street, West Market Square, 04401
(207) 947-3850

The Quality Inn-Phenix, a bed and breakfast on the National Register of Historic Places, circa 1873, has been tastefully decorated to offer the finest in historical charm, comfort, and quality in accommodations. We invite our guests to enjoy our elegant surroundings, warm, professional staff, and convenient location. Bangor's commercial and financial center, shops, restaurants, and cultural attractions are within walking distance of our inn. All rooms have heating/air conditioning, private bath, telephone, and television. Free parking.

Host: Kimberly M. Jurgiewich
Rooms: 37 (PB) $35-75
Continental Breakfast
Credit Cards: A, B, C, D, E
Notes: 5, 7, 8, 14

NOTES: Credit cards accepted: A Master Card; B Visa; C American Express; D Discover Card; E Diner's Club; F Other; 2 Personal Checks accepted; 3 Lunch available; 4 Dinner available; 5 Open all year; 6 Pets welcome; 7 Smoking allowed; 8 Children welcome; 9 Social drinking allowed; 10 Tennis available; 11 Swimming available; 12 Golf available; 13 Skiing available; 14 May be booked through travel agents.

BAR HARBOR

Black Friar Inn

10 Summer Street, 04609
(207) 288-5091

Comfortably restored and rebuilt Victorian
with antiques. Six guest rooms with queen
beds and private baths. Rates include full
breakfast, late afternoon refreshments, and
rainy-day teas. Easy access to Acadia
National Park. Short walk to waterfront,
shops, and restaurants. Ample parking.
Spring and fall salmon fishing trips with
Maine guide can be arranged. Two-night
minimum July 1 through mid-October.

Hosts: Barbara and Jim Kelly
Rooms: 6 (PB) $85-105
Full Breakfast
Credit Cards: A, B
Open May-Nov.
Notes: 2, 8 (over 11), 9, 10, 12, 14

Canterbury Cottage

12 Roberts Avenue, 04609
(207) 288-2112

Canterbury Cottage, a delightful Victorian
shingled structure built in 1900, is family
owned and operated. The cottage offers
guests a cozy and comfortable alternative
to the big inns. It is on a quiet side street a
short two-block walk to the many village
and harbor activities. Only five mintues
from Acadia National Park and the Nova
Scotia ferry terminal.

Hosts: Rick and Michele Suydam
Rooms: 4 (2 PB; 2 SB) $65-85
Expanded Continental Breakfast
Credit Cards: None
Notes: 2, 10, 11, 12

Castlemaine Inn

39 Holland Avenue, 04609
(207) 288-4563

Castlemaine Inn is nestled on a quiet side
street in the village of Bar Harbor, which is
surrounded by the magnificent Acadia

National Park. The rooms are well appointed, with canopy beds and fireplaces. A
delightful continental buffet-style breakfast
is served.

Hosts: Terence O'Connell and Norah O'Brien
Rooms: 13 (PB) $80-135 seasonal
Expanded Continental Breakfast
Credit Cards: A, B
Open May-Oct.
Notes: 2, 8 (over 13), 9, 10, 11, 12

Cleftstone Manor

92 Eden Street, 04609
(207) 288-4951

Cleftstone Manor is a distinguished 33-
room Victorian "cottage," set on a hill amid
formal gardens, offering gracious accommodations in one of nature's magnificent
meetings of land and sea, Mount Desert

Hearthside

Island. The manor offers cozy fireside chats, a library, games, a lavish continental breakfast buffet, and the peace of country living.

Hosts: Don and Pattie Reynolds
Rooms: 16 (PB) $90-175
Full Breakfast
Credit Cards: A, B, D
Closed Nov.-March
Notes: 2, 8 (over 7), 10, 11, 12, 13 (XC), 14

Hearthside

7 High Street, 04609
(207) 288-4533

Built at the turn of the century as the residence for Dr. George Hagerthy, Hearthside is now a cozy and comfortable bed and breakfast. Hearthside is conveniently situated on a quiet side street in Bar Harbor. All of the newly decorated rooms have queen-size beds and private baths; some have private porches and working fireplaces. Each morning a lavish breakfast buffet is served, and lemonade and homemade cookies are offered each afternoon. Off-season rates available.

Hosts: Susan and Barry Schwartz
Rooms: 9 (PB) $75-110
Full Breakfast
Credit Cards: A, B
Notes: 2, 5, 9

Holbrook House

74 Mount Desert Street, 04609
(207) 288-4970

A 19-room Victorian inn with chintz, lace, and flowers. Formal breakfast. Just a five-minute walk to the ocean, shops, and restaurants. One mile to Acadia National Park. Sun room, library, and parlor. Call/write for price information.

Hosts: Jack and Jean Ochtera
Rooms: 12 (PB)
Full Breakfast
Minimum stay: 2 nights
Credit Cards: A, B
Closed mid-Oct. through May 1
Notes: 2, 8 (over 7), 9, 10, 11, 12

Holbrook House

Manor House Inn

106 West Street, 04609
(207) 288-3759; (800) 437-0088

Enjoy an 1887 Victorian summer cottage listed on the National Register of Historic Places. Near Acadia National Park. Within walking distance of downtown Bar Harbor and waterfront. Enjoy the acre of landscaped grounds and gardens.

Host: Mac Noyes
Rooms: 14 (PB) $79-145
Continental Breakfast
Minimum stay July, August, and holidays: 2 nights
Credit Cards: A, B, C
Closed Nov. through mid-April
Notes: 2, 8 (over 8), 9, 10, 11, 12, 14

Manor House

The Maples Inn

16 Roberts Avenue, 04609
(207) 288-3443

6 Pets welcome; 7 Smoking allowed; 8 Children welcome; 9 Social drinking allowed; 10 Tennis available; 11 Swimming available; 12 Golf available; 13 Skiing available; 14 May be booked through travel agents.

Built in early 1900, the Maples Inn originally housed the wealthy summer visitors to Mount Desert Island. It is on a quiet, residential, tree-lined street. You'll be away from the traffic of Bar Harbor, yet within walking distance of attractive boutiques, intimate restaurants, and the surrounding sea. For the perfect romantic getaway, reserve the White Birch Suite, complete with a beautiful, working fireplace. Your palate will be treated to gourmet delights each morning in the bay-windowed dining room. Acadia National Park is minutes away.

Host: Susan Sinclair
Rooms: 6 (PB) $60-125 seasonal
Full or Continental Breakfast
Credit Cards: A, B, D
Notes: 2, 3 (picnic), 5, 9, 13

Mira Monte Inn

69 Mount Desert Street, 04609
(207)288-4263; (800) 553-5109

Built in 1864; graced by porches, balconies, bay windows, and several fireplaces. Antiques and period furnishings, king- or queen-size beds, private baths, cable TV, phones, all air conditioned.

Pachelbel Inn

Friendly, helpful staff. Breakfast buffet in formal dining room: fresh fruit, homemade breads, muffins, coffee. Afternoon refreshments. Quiet location in the heart of Bar Harbor on one and one-half-acre estate featuring exquisite gardens. Ample parking.

Host: Marian Burns
Rooms: 11 (PB) $90-150
Expanded Continental Breakfast
Credit Cards: A, B, C, F
Notes: 2, 7 (limited), 8, 9, 12, 14

Pachelbel Inn

20 Roberts Avenue, 04609
(207) 288-9655

Join Russell and Helene Fye, along with their children Russ and Samantha, in their comfortable Victorian home. Centrally situated in town. Easy walking to shops, restaurants, and the harbor. Five-minute drive to the Blue Nose Ferry Terminal and one mile to Acadia National Park. Smoking on front porch only. People remember the Fyes for their great breakfasts and warm hospitality. All children welcome.

Hosts: Russ and Helene Fye
Rooms: 6 (4 PB; 2 SB) $55-85
Full Breakfast
Credit Cards: A, B
Notes: 2, 5, 8

Stratford House Inn

45 Mount Desert Street 460-9
(207) 288-5189

Stratford House Inn features English Tudor architecture with a likeness to Queen Elizabeht's summer home. Beautiful bedrooms each one different. Easy walk to stores, restaurants, or waterfromt. Acadia National Park is close by with bearty and activities for all.

Hosts: Barbara and Norman Moulton
Rooms: 5 (3 PB; 2 SB) $70-135
Continental Breakfast
Minimum stay weekends and holidays: 2 nights
Credit Cards: A, B, C
Closed November -May
Notes: 2, 7, 8, 9, 10, 11, 12,

NOTES: Credit cards accepted: A Master Card; B Visa; C American Express; D Discover Card; E Diner's Club; F Other; 2 Personal Checks accepted; 3 Lunch available; 4 Dinner available; 5 Open all year;

Wayside Inn

11 Atlantic Avenue, 04609
(207) 288-5703; (800) 722-6671

A beautifully decorated early Victorian inn
offering private and semi-private rooms
with fireplaces. Full gourmet breakfast
served. On a quiet side street in historic
district within walking distance to all in
town activities. Open all year. Lower rates
available off-season.

Hosts: Steve and Sandi Straubel
Rooms: 8 (4 SB; 4 PB) $55-135
Full Breakfast
Credit Cards: A, B
Notes: 2 , 5, 8, 9, 10, 11, 12, 13, 14

BASS HARBOR

The Bass Harbor Inn

Shore Road, P. O. Box 326, 04653
(207) 244-5157

On beautiful Mount Desert Island, the Bass
Harbor Inn offers you a lovely harbor view
and choice of lodging ranging from rooms
with private or half-bath and fireplace, to
suite with full kitchen and bath. Write for
brochure.

Hosts: Alan and Barbara Graff
Rooms: 9 (PB and SB) $60-100
Continental Breakfast
Credit Cards: A, B
Notes: 2, 8

Pointy Head Inn

Route 102A, 04653
(207) 244-7261

Relax on the quiet side of Mount Desert
Island near Acadia National Park in an old
sea captain's home. On the shore of a picturesque harbor where schooners anchor
overnight. Haven for photographers and
artists. Minutes to lighthouse, trails, restaurants, stores.

Hosts: Doris and Warren Townsend
Rooms: 6 (2 PB; 4 SB) $50-65
Continental Breakfast

Credit Cards: None
Notes: 2, 8 (over 10), 9, 10, 11, 12

BATH

Elizabeth's Bed and Breakfast

360 Front Street, 04530
(207) 443-1146

Step into the warmth of yesteryear in a
beautiful old home overlooking the
Kennebec River. Choose from five guest
rooms furnished with country antiques, two
and one-half shared baths. Generous continental breakfast with home-baked breads.
Guest livingroom with TV; limited smoking. Feline assistant, Mr. T, in residence.

Host: Elizabeth Lindsay
Rooms: 5 (S2.5B) $40-60
Continental Breakfast
Credit Cards: None
Open April 15-Jan. 1
Notes: 2, 7 (limited), 8 (over 10), 9, 10, 11, 12, 14

Elizabeth's Bed and Breakfast

Fairhaven Inn at Bath

Rural Route 2, Box 85, 04530
(207) 443-4391

Where eagles soar, birds sing, and tidal
river meets meadow. This 1790 comfortable and quiet Colonial is renowned for its
breakfast and is the perfect mid-coast base

---

6 Pets welcome; 7 Smoking allowed; 8 Children welcome; 9 Social drinking allowed; 10 Tennis available; 11
Swimming available; 12 Golf available; 13 Skiing available; 14 May be booked through travel agents.

from which to enjoy all that Maine's coast offers. Hiking and cross-country skiing on property. Beaches and Maritime Museum nearby.

Hosts: George and Sallie Pollard
Rooms: 9 (PB and SB) $53.50-74.90
Full Breakfast
Credit Cards: A, B, C
Notes: 2, 5, 6 (limited), 7 (limited), 8, 9, 10, 11, 12, 13, 14

Glad II

60 Pearl Street, 04530
(207) 443-1191

A comfortable Victorian home, circa 1851, near the center of town and convenient to Maritime Museum, beaches, Freeport shopping, L. L. Bean, and Boothbay Harbor. The host and her four-legged concierge, Nicholas, love to welcome new friends.

Host: Gladys Lansky
Rooms: 2 (SB) $50 plus tax
Expanded Continental Breakfast
Minimum stay weekends and holidays: 2 nights
Credit Cards: A, B, C
Notes: 2, 5, 8 (over 12), 9, 10, 11, 12, 13, 14

BELFAST

Adaline Palmer House

7 Franklin Street, Corner of Cedar Street, 04915
(207) 338-5790

A warm welcome awaits you in this rambling Greek Revival Cape, circa 1850, close to harbor, shops, theaters, and restaurants. The home features tile and terra cotta fireplaces, detailed woodwork, pine floors,

a glass-enclosed breakfast porch, and spacious twin or queen bedrooms with private baths.

Hosts: Bob and Carol Lentilhon
Rooms: 3 (PB) $45
Full Breakfast
Credit Cards: None
Notes: 2, 9, 10, 11, 12

Bed and Breakfast Inns of New England ME-840

329 Lake Drive, Guilford, CT 06437
(800) 582-0853

This Greek Revival house was built around 1845 during Belfast's period of great architectural activity. Guests are welcome to use the beautiful formal livingroom with ornate tiled fireplace. Three large bedrooms with pine floors and a variety of bed sizes are available. All have private baths. There is a screened and glassed-in porch overlooking a garden where breakfast is usually served. Complimentary afternoon wine is served in the livingroom. No pets, but children over ten are welcome. No smoking. $45.

The Jeweled Turret Inn

16 Pearl Street, 04915
(207) 338-2304

Step back into a time when lace, elegant furnishings, and afternoon tea were an everyday necessity. The inn is named for the grand staircase that winds up the turret, lighted by stained- and leaded-glass panels with jewellike embellishments. Lots of woodwork, fireplaces, public rooms, and two verandas available for relaxation. Mornings welcome you with gourmet breakfasts, and afternoon tea is served with dessert. Situated in historic district; shops, restaurants, and waterfront close by.

Hosts: Carl and Cathy Heffentrager
Rooms: 7 (PB) $65-85
Full Breakfast
Credit Cards: None
Notes: 2, 5, 8, 9, 10, 11, 12, 13, 14

NOTES: Credit cards accepted: A Master Card; B Visa; C American Express; D Discover Card; E Diner's Club; F Other; 2 Personal Checks accepted; 3 Lunch available; 4 Dinner available; 5 Open all year;

BETHEL

The Chapman Inn

Box 206, 04217
(207) 824-2657

An 1865 Federal in a national historic district facing the village common. Friendly, homelike atmosphere; large, sunny rooms. Delicious breakfast features fresh fruits, muffins, and a variety of main courses. Private saunas, game room, color cable TV in sitting room. Dormitory accommodations also available.

Hosts: Sandra and George Wight; Doug and Robin
   Zinchuk
Rooms: 8 (4 PB; 4 SB) $55-75
Full Breakfast
Credit Cards: A, B, C
Notes: 2, 5, 6, 7, 8, 9, 10, 11, 12, 13, 14

The Chapman Inn

The Douglass Place

Star Route, Box 90, 04217
(207) 824-2229

A four-season, 19th-century, Early American/Victorian home situated between two major ski areas and the White Mountains of New Hampshire. Marvelous area for antiquing, summer sports, and hiking. Gardens and gazebo in summer; game room, cozy fireplace in winter.

Hosts: Dana and Barbara Douglass
Rooms: 4 (SB) $53.50
Continental Breakfast
Minimum stay weekends and holidays: 2 nights
Credit Cards: C
Closed Christmas and two weeks in April
Notes: 2, 6, 7, 8, 9, 10, 11, 12, 13

Sudbury Inn

Box 369, Main Street, 04217
(800) 395-7837 (SUDS)

Situated near Sunday River ski area, the inn has 18 rooms with private baths. Full breakfast; outstanding dining is available, as well as the famous Suds Pub, with entertainment on weekends. Area attractions include an 18-hole, 6,800-yard golf course, White Mountain National Forest, lakes, streams, and gorgeous landscapes.

Host: Jack Cronin
Rooms: 18 (PB) $50-90
Full Breakfast
Credit Cards: A, B, C
Notes: 2, 4, 5, 6, 8, 11, 12, 13

BLUE HILL

Blue Hill Farm Country Inn

Route 15, P. O. Box 437, 04614
(207) 374-5126

This old Maine farmhouse and barn sits on 48 acres at the foot of Blue Hill Mountain; nature trails, ponds, assorted ducks, geese, and goats surround the area. Spacious common areas are available for guests to use, and our location is two miles from the center of the village, close to a number of coastal villages, and less than one hour from Acadia National Park.

Hosts: Jim and Marcia Schatz
Rooms: 14 (7 PB; 7 SB) $68-78
Continental Plus Breakfast
Credit Cards: None
Notes: 2, 5

BOOTHBAY

Kenniston Hill Inn

Route 27, P. O. Box 125, 04537
(207) 633-2159; (800) 992-2915

A 1786 Georgian Colonial, ten rooms all with private baths, six working fireplaces, delicious full breakfast included. The inn is surrounded by large lawns, shady maples,

---

6 Pets welcome; 7 Smoking allowed; 8 Children welcome; 9 Social drinking allowed; 10 Tennis available; 11 Swimming available; 12 Golf available; 13 Skiing available; 14 May be booked through travel agents.

and gardens—a comfortable, historic inn close by to all things that make the Maine coast a very special and beautiful place to enjoy. The inn is open all year.

Hosts: David and Susan Straight
Rooms: 10 (PB) $65-95
Full Breakfast
Credit Cards: A, B
Notes: 2, 5, 14

Keniston Hill Inn

Seawitch

Route 27, Box 27, 04537
(207) 633-7804

All you deserve and more! Nestled in a secluded, wooded setting near Sherman Cove off Route 27, halfway between Route 1 and harbor activities. Gracious rooms with fireplaces, sitting areas, and full private baths afford a luxurious ambience amid fine antiques. Wine and appetizers welcome guests in the library. Bloody Mary fixings and the aroma of coffee greet guests in the morning, followed by an impressive breakfast. The Seawitch is a wickedly romantic retreat.

Hosts: Bill and Claire Hunt
Rooms: 3 (PB) $85-105
Full Breakfast
Credit Cards: None
Notes: 2, 5, 7, 9, 12

BOOTHBAY HARBOR

Admiral's Quarters Inn

105 Commercial Street, 04538
(207) 633-2474

Commanding a view of the harbor waterfront, this early sea captain's mansion offers charming accommodations with private baths, a blend of antiques and white wicker, color cable TV. Morning coffee and light fare in the dining room or on the deck overlooking the waterfront.

Host: Jean E. Duffy
Rooms: 10 (PB) $65-90
Continental Breakfast
Credit Cards: A, B
Notes: 2 (deposit), 5, 7, 8 (over 12), 9, 10, 11, 12, 14

Anchor Watch Bed and Breakfast

3 Eames Road, 04538
(207) 633-2284

With a shorefront location on a scenic, quiet lane, the Anchor Watch is just a short walk to town for shopping, dining, and boat trips. From the breakfast room you will see lobstermen hauling their traps, lighthouses flashing, and ducks feeding along the shore.

Hosts: Diane and Bob Campbell
Rooms: 4 (PB) $65-90
Full Breakfast
Credit Cards: A, B
Closed mid-Dec.-mid-Feb.
Notes: 2, 5, 9, 12, 14

The Atlantic Ark Inn

64 Atlantic Avenue, 04538
(207) 633-5690

An intimate bed and breakfast inn, offering lovely views of the harbor and only a five-minute stroll to town over a historic footbridge. This 100-year-old Maine home has been lovingly restored and tastefully furnished with antiques and Oriental rugs. Guest rooms are adorned with fresh flowers, floor-length drapes, queen-size poster beds, and private baths. Each morning a full breakfast features home-baked goods and a specially prepared entree for that day. Recommended by Stephen Birnbaum in *Good Housekeeping*, August 1990.

Host: Donna Piggott
Rooms: 5 (PB) $60-90
Full Breakfast
Credit Cards: A, B, C
Notes: 2, 9

Harbour Towne Inn

71 Townsend Avenue, 04538
(207) 633-4300

The finest bed and breakfast on the waterfront, a short stroll from the historic coastal village, with scenic harbor views and outside decks, in a quiet location on Boothbay Harbor, the boating capital of New England. Walk to fascinating shops, art galleries, restaurants, churches, library, dinner theaters, boat trips, fishing, and much more. All rooms have private baths in this refurbished Victorian town house that has been updated in traditional style. Also available is a luxury penthouse that will sleep six in absolute privacy. Reservations recommended. Special off-season getaway package. Open year-round, except for vacation periods in the winter.

Host: George Thomas
Rooms: 12 (PB) $40-175
Continental Breakfast
Credit Cards: A, B, C, D
Notes: 2, 7 (restricted), 9, 10, 11, 12, 13 (XC), 14

Hilltop Guest House

44 McKown Hill, 04538
(207) 633-2941

This home is only a three-minute walk to all activities: boat trips, restaurant, dinner theater, and shops, and has ample parking facilities, large porch, and a tree swing for the young and old. Family unit also available.

Hosts: Georgia Savory and Virginia Brewer
Rooms: 6 (2 PB; 4 SB) $34-46
Continental Breakfast
Credit Cards: None
Notes: 2, 5, 6, 7, 8, 9, 10, 11, 12, 14

The Howard House Motel Bed and Breakfast

Route 27, 04538
(207) 633-3933; (207) 633-6244

Each spacious room has a private bath, color cable TV, and its own balcony. Early American furnishings, high-beamed ceilings, and natural wood walls. Shopping, sightseeing, boating, island clam bakes, seal and whale watches, and fine restaurants are nearby. AAA and *Mobile Travel Guide* approved.

Hosts: Jim and Ginny Farrins
Rooms: 15 (PB) $46-79
Full Breakfast, seasonal
Credit Cards: None
Notes: 2, 5, 7 (limited), 8, 9, 10, 11, 12, 14

BRIDGTON

Tarry-A-While Bed and Breakfast Resort

Rural Delivery 2, Box 68
Highland Ridge Road, 04009
(207) 647-2522

On Highland Lake, with three sandy beaches in a protected cove. Schloss-Victorian house and gasthaus, more than 100 years old, serves a large buffet breakfast with a view of the lake. Cottages with four bed and breakfast units in each. Air conditioned, with individually controlled heat. Large recreation hall. Free canoes, rowboats, pedal boats, tennis, and bicycles. Water skis, wind surfers, sailboats, and small motors are available for rent. Clean, quiet lake. Three housekeeping units are also available. Swiss cuisine restaurant on premises.

Hosts: Hans and Barbara Jenni
Rooms: 34 (26 PB; 8 SB) $80-120
Full Buffet Breakfast
Credit Cards: None
Open June 6-Labor Day
Notes: 2, 4, 7, 8, 9, 10, 11, 12

---

6 Pets welcome; 7 Smoking allowed; 8 Children welcome; 9 Social drinking allowed; 10 Tennis available; 11 Swimming available; 12 Golf available; 13 Skiing available; 14 May be booked through travel agents.

BROOKSVILLE

Breezemere Farm Inn

Box 290, Breezemere Farm Road, 04617
(207) 326-8628

Picturesque 1850 farmhouse plus seven
cottages on 60 acres on Orcutt Harbor, East
Penobscot Bay. Spruce to smell, islands to
explore, water to sail, trails to hike, berries
to pick, mussels to rake. Bikes, beach,
boats. Bed sizes available include twins,
doubles, and queens. Full breakfast daily.
Open May through October. Free brochure.

Hosts: Joe and Linda Forest
Rooms: 7 (S4.5B) $65-95
Cottages: 7 (PB) $110-125
Full Breakfast
Credit Cards: A, B
Closed Nov. 1-April
Notes: 2, 8 (cottages), 9, 10, 11, 12, 14

BRUNSWICK

Bethel Point Bed and Breakfast

2387 Bethel Point Road, 04011
(207) 725-1115

Peaceful oceanside comfort in 150-year-old
home. Perfect view of ocean birds, seals,
and lobster boats. Opportunities for ocean
swimming and shoreline walks to explore
the local coast. An easy drive to the area's
focal points, such as Bowdoin College,
Popham Beach, L. L. Bean, and local
restaurants featuring seafood specialties.

Hosts: Peter and Betsy Packard
Rooms: 2 (SB) $60-70
Full or Continental Breakfast
Credit Cards: None
Notes: 2, 5, 8, 9, 11

The Samuel Newman House

7 South Street, 04011
(207) 729-6959

Adjoining the Bowdoin College campus,
this handsome Federal house was built in
1821 and is comfortably furnished in

antiques. Hearty continental breakfast
includes freshly baked muffins/pastry and
homemade granola. Brunswick is a culturally rich college town just ten-minutes
north of Freeport.

Host: Tom Holbrook
Rooms: 7 (SB) $42.80-58.85
Continental Breakfast
Credit Cards: A, B
Notes: 2, 5, 8, 9, 10, 11, 12, 13 (XC)

BUCKSPORT

The Old Parsonage Inn

P. O. Box 1577, 04416
(207) 469-6477

An 1809 Federal home, formerly the
Methodist parsonage, located one-half mile
from Route 1. Private guest entrance, winding staircase, and original architectural features. The third floor was a Masonic meeting hall. Short walk to restaurants and the
waterfront. Close to Fort Knox, Acadia
National Park, and Penobscot Bay.

Hosts: Brian and Judith Clough
Rooms: 3 (1 PB; 2 SB) $40-60
Full Breakfast
Credit Cards: A, B
Notes: 2, 8, 9, 10, 11, 12

The River Inn Bed and Breakfast

210 Main Street, P. O. Box 1657, 04416-1657
(207) 469-3783

Spacious old sea captain's home on the
Penobscot River in historic Bucksport.
Conveniently located at the northern tip of
Penobscot Bay, Bucksport offers easy
access to east and west bay tour areas.
Antiquing, auctions, crafts, golf, water, and
winter sports are some of the activities
available for guests. Public boat launch is
nearby, as are mooring rentals. Large deck
offers panoramic river views, and a rare
player grand piano will interest guests.
Breakfast features fruit plates. Children
over twelve. No smoking.

Host: The Stone family
Rooms: 3 (1 PB; 2 SB)
Full Breakfast
Credit Cards: None
Notes: 2, 5, 6, 9, 12, 13, 14

CAMDEN

Blackberry Inn

82 Elm Street, 04843
(207) 236-6060

Blackberry Inn is a restored Italianate
Victorian with large, spacious rooms decorated in period style, most with queen-size
beds and private bath. Some have
whirlpools, fireplaces, and cable TV. Stroll
to Camden's harbor and fine restaurants, or
relax in the comfortable parlors and enjoy
afternoon wine and cheese. Wonderful full
breakfast in the dining room or courtyard.
Featured in *Daughters of Painted Ladies:
America's Resplendent Victorians*. "A
delightful bed and breakfast," says the
Miami Herald.

Hosts: Vicki and Edward Doudera
Rooms: 8 (6 PB; 2 private half-baths) $53.50-107
Apartments: 2 (PB) $75-155
Full Breakfast
Credit Cards: A, B
Notes: 2, 5, 8, 9, 10, 11, 12, 13, 14

Blue Harbor House

Blue Harbor House, A Country Inn

67 Elm Street, 04843
(207) 236-3196; (800) 248-3196
FAX (207) 236-6523

Overlooking Mount Battie and within
walking distance of the village of Camden,
Blue Harbor House offers guests a casual
and comfortable country environment to
relax and enjoy the beauty that is coastal
Maine. Hearty breakfasts are served each
morning on the sun porch. Picnic lunches
and intimate candlelight dinners are available by reservation.

Hosts: Jody Schmoll and Dennis Hayden
Rooms: 10 (PB) $85-125
Full Breakfast
Credit Cards: A, B, C, F
Notes: 2, 3, 4, 5, 6 (limited), 7 (limited), 8, 9, 10,
11, 12, 13, 14

Camden Harbour Inn

83 Bayview Street, 04843
(207) 236-4200

This historic landmark inn with 22 rooms
offers spectacular panoramas of the harbor,
bay, and mountains. All rooms have private
baths and water views from either the
room, balcony, patio, or deck. Canopy beds
and fireplaces create a romantic ambience
in an elegant but casual country inn atmosphere. Enjoy the friendly service, excellent
lodging, food, and spirits that have made us
a favorite with travelers and diners for over
a century.

Hosts: Sal Vella and Patti Babij
Rooms: 22 (PB) $95-195 seasonal
Full or Continental Breakfast, seasonal
Credit Cards: A, B, C, D
Notes: 4, 5, 7, 9, 10, 11, 12, 13, 14

The Camden Maine Stay Inn

22 High Street, 04843
(207) 236-9636

A comfortable bed, a hearty breakfast, and
a friendly innkeeper will be found in this
old Colonial home. In Camden's historic
district, a short walk to harbor, shops,
restaurants, and state park. Recommended
by the *Miami Herald*, *Lewiston Journal*,
Watterville Sentinel, *Country Inns* and
Country Living magazines.

6 Pets welcome; 7 Smoking allowed; 8 Children welcome; 9 Social drinking allowed; 10 Tennis available; 11
Swimming available; 12 Golf available; 13 Skiing available; 14 May be booked through travel agents.

Hosts: Peter and Donny Smith; Diana Robson
Rooms: 8 (3 PB; 5 SB) $57 plus
Full Breakfast
Credit Cards: A, B
Notes: 2, 5, 8 (over 10), 9, 10, 11, 12, 13, 14

The Camden Mainstay Inn

Edgecombe-Coles House

HCR 60, P. O. Box 3010, 04843
(207) 236-2336; FAX (207) 236-6227

Edgecombe-Coles House is a classic Maine summer home on the quiet hillside with magnificent views of Penobscot Bay. Each room is furnished with country antiques and has a private bath. The generous breakfasts have been praised nationwide.

Hosts: Louise and Terry Price
Rooms: 6 (PB) $74-172
Full Breakfast
Credit Cards: A, B, C, E
Notes: 2, 5, 7, 8 (over 10), 9, 10, 11, 12, 13, 14

Goodspeed's Guest House

60(c) Mountain Street, Route 52, 04843
(207) 236-8077

An 1879 farmhouse with nine restored guest rooms. The interior decor features stained-glass windows and delightfully colored wallpapers set off the pine-plank floors. There are a number of antique clocks on display. Enjoy continental breakfast on the sunny deck. Quiet location, spacious grounds. Just five blocks from the village and harbor.

Hosts: Don and Linda Goodspeed
Rooms: 8 (1 PB; 7 SB) $72-85
Continental Breakfast
Credit Cards: None
Notes: 2, 5, 9, 10, 11, 13, 14

Hartstone Inn

41 Elm Street, 04843
(207) 236-4259

"In the heart of Camden, a stone's throw from the harbor." Large comfortable rooms all have private baths, some have fireplaces. A full gourmet breakfast and wonderful dinners by the fire. Featured in An Explorer's Guide to Maine and Inn Spots and Special Places.

Hosts: Sunny and Peter Simmons
Rooms: 8; 2 apartments (PB) $75-110 in-season;
    $55-85 off-season
Full Breakfast
Credit Cards: A, B, C, D
Notes: 2, 4 (by reservation), 5, 7, 8, 9, 10, 11, 12,
    13, 14

Hawthorn Inn

9 High Street, 04843
(207) 236-8842

An elegant family-run Victorian inn with harbor view, spacious grounds, large deck. Walk through the back garden to shops and restaurants. Full breakfast and afternoon tea served. Carriage house bedrooms with private Jacuzzi and balconies.

Hosts: Pauline and Bradford Staub
Rooms: 10; 2 apartments (PB) $70-225
Full Breakfast
Minimum stay July and Aug: 2 nights
Credit Cards: A, B
Notes: 2, 5, 8, 9, 10, 11, 12, 13, 14

Hartstone Inn

NOTES: Credit cards accepted: A Master Card; B Visa; C American Express; D Discover Card; E Diner's Club; F Other; 2 Personal Checks accepted; 3 Lunch available; 4 Dinner available; 5 Open all year;

The Swan House

49 Mountain Street, 04843
(207) 236-8275

This fine Victorian home dates from 1870 and has been renovated to offer six spacious guest rooms—all with private bath. Some offer private sitting areas as well. A creative and generous full breakfast is served each morning on the sun porch. Landscaped grounds and a gazebo are available for guests to enjoy. A Camden Hills State Park hiking trail starts right behind the inn. Located off busy Route 1, Swan House is a short walk to Camden's beautiful harbor, shops, and restaurants.

Host: Chrysanthe Soukas
Rooms: 6 (PB) $80-110
Full Breakfast
Credit Cards: A, B
Notes: 2, 8, 9, 10, 11, 12, 13, 14

Windward House

6 High Street, 04843
(207) 236-9656

A historic 1854 Greek Revival on stately High Street above picturesque Camden Harbor. Six tastefully appointed guest rooms are furnished with period antiques and have private baths. Several common rooms, gardens, full gourmet breakfast. Only a short walk to shops, restaurants, and the harbor.

Hosts: Jon and Mary Davis
Rooms: 6 (PB) $65-125
Full Breakfast
Credit Cards: A, B
Notes: 2, 5, 7 (outside), 9, 10, 11, 12, 13, 14

CAPITOL ISLAND

Albonegon Inn

Capitol Island, 04538
(207) 633-2521

Built in the 1880s, the Albonegon is one of the last old cottage-style inns. It is perched on the edge of the rocks and offers a delightful view of the Boothbay Harbor area and outer islands. It is a very quiet spot, four miles from downtown.

Hosts: Kim and Bob Peckham
Rooms: 15 (3 PB; 12 SB) $65-100
Continental Breakfast
Credit Cards: None
Notes: 2, 8, 10, 11

Albonegon Inn

CARATUNK

The Sterling Inn

P. O. Box 21, 04925
(800) 766-7238

The relaxed country atmosphere of this historic 175-year-old inn, with its hardwood floors, wood-burning stoves, down comforters, and cozy sitting rooms recalls the slower-paced days of a Maine sporting lodge at the turn of the century. Situated on 115 wooded acres on Wyman Lake. Complete packages available with whitewater rafting.

Host: Matthew Polstein
Rooms: 17 (S8B) $78
Continental Breakfast
Credit Cards: A, B
Notes: 2, 5, 9, 11

CASTINE

The Holiday House

Perkins Street, P. O. Box 215, 04421
(207) 326-4335

6 Pets welcome; 7 Smoking allowed; 8 Children welcome; 9 Social drinking allowed; 10 Tennis available; 11 Swimming available; 12 Golf available; 13 Skiing available; 14 May be booked through travel agents.

Oceanfront Edwardian mansion in undiscovered Castine. Guest rooms with private baths and spectacular ocean views. Expansive porches directly on the harbor for your afternoon enjoyment. Relax here to the sound of the waves and seabirds. Waterfront cottage available.

Hosts: Paul and Sara Brouillard
Rooms: 10 (8 PB; 2 SB) $95-115
Continental Breakfast
Credit Cards: A, B
Notes: 2, 6, 7, 8, 9, 10, 11, 12, 13 (XC)

The Manor

Battle Avenue, P. O. Box 276, 04421
(207) 326-4861

Romantic turn-of-the-century mansion in seacoast town. Spacious rooms with ocean views and fireplaces. Marble oyster bar, acclaimed dining, fine wines, cocktails, and intimate piano bar. Golf and tennis nearby. Housekeeping cottage available. Harbor tours and hike deserted shorelines. Near Acadia National Park.

Hosts: Paul and Sara Brouillard
Rooms: 14 (12 PB; 2 SB) $75-135
Continental Breakfast
Credit Cards: A, B
Notes: 2, 4, 5, 6, 7, 8, 9, 10, 11, 12, 13

CENTER LOVELL

Center Lovell Inn

Route 5, Box 261N, 04016
(207) 925-1575

Built in 1805, this house originally had two stories; a third was added in the mid-1800s. Center Lovell is situated in western Maine, within one-half hour of four ski areas. Great fishing, canoeing, hiking, and bird watching area, with miles of quiet, unspoiled forest to explore.

Hosts: Bill and Susie Mosca
Rooms: 13 (9 PB; 4 SB) $63-97.50
Full Breakfast
Credit Cards: A, B, C
Closed Oct. 30-May 1
Notes: 2, 3, 7, 8, 9, 10, 11, 12, 13, 14

Westways on Kezar Lake

Route 5, 04016
(207) 928-2663

Kezar Lake lies at the foothills of the White Mountains, with one-half mile of lakefront, swimming, canoeing, tennis, nature walks, playing fields, indoor rec room with Ping-Pong, billiards, bowling, and handball. Gourmet porch dining overlooking the lake. Westways staff will be here to greet you! Closed November and April.

Rooms: 7 (3 PB; 4 SB) $79-159 seasonal
Continental Breakfast
Credit Cards: A, B
Closed November and April
Notes: 2, 4, 8, 9, 10, 11

Center Lovell Inn

CHAMBERLAIN

Ocean Reefs on Long Cove

Route 32, 04541-3530
(207) 677-2386

Watch the waves break over the reefs, lobstermen hauling traps, or the shoreline between tides. Hike or bicycle roads along the rocky coast. Pemaquid Beach, Pemaquid lighthouse, Fort William Henry, and the boat to Monhegan Island are all within five miles.

Rooms: 4 (PB) $66
Continental Breakfast
Credit Cards: None
Closed Sept. 30-Memorial Day
Notes: 2, 7, 9, 10, 11, 12

NOTES: Credit cards accepted: A Master Card; B Visa; C American Express; D Discover Card; E Diner's Club; F Other; 2 Personal Checks accepted; 3 Lunch available; 4 Dinner available; 5 Open all year;

CHEBEAUGE ISLAND

Chebeague Island Inn

P. O. Box 492, 04017
(207) 846-5155; (207) 774-5891

Three-story inn high on a hill overlooking a golf course. The inn, circa 1926, offers no telephones or TV, but has a 117-foot-long wraparound porch. Full of antiques and art. Enjoy clean beaches; a great place for a family adventure. Baby-sitting service available. Access to island by ferry service only.

Hosts: Wendy and Kevin Bowden
Rooms: 21 (15 PB; 6 SB) $85-115
Full Breakfast
Credit Cards: All major
Open May-Oct.
Notes: 2, 3, 4, 8, 9, 11, 12, 14

CHERRYFIELD

Ricker House

Park Street, Box 256, 04622
(207) 546-2780

This comfortable 1802 Federal Colonial on the National Register of Historic Places borders the Narraguagus River and offers guests a central place for enjoying the many wonderful activities in Down East Maine including scenic coastal area, swimming, canoeing, hiking, and fishing.

Hosts: William and Jean Conway
Rooms: 3 (SB) $48.15-53.50
Full Breakfast
Credit Cards: None
Notes: 2, 5, 8, 9, 10, 11, 12, 13 (XC)

CLARK ISLAND

Craignair Inn

Clark Island Road, 04859
(207) 594-7644

Built in 1929 to house the stonecutters from the nearby quarries and now a gracious and cheery inn. Overlooking the water and off-shore islands, clam flats, tidal pools, lobster boats. Ten miles from Rockland, the Monhegan ferry, and Owls Head Light. Swim before dinner in the nearby deepwater quarry pool, or explore miles of coastal trails leading from the inn. Dinner served Monday through Saturday.

Hosts: Terry and Norman Smith
Rooms: 20 (8 PB; 12 SB) $57-87
Full Breakfast
Credit Cards: A, B, C, D
Notes: 2, 4, 6, 7, 8, 9, 10, 11, 12, 13, 14

DAMARISCOTTA

Brannon-Bunker Inn

HCR 64, Box 045X, 04543
(207) 563-5941

Intimate, relaxed country bed and breakfast in an 1820 Cape, 1880 converted barn, and 1900 carriage house. Seven rooms furnished in themes reflecting the charm of yesterday with the comforts of today. Ten minutes to lighthouse, fort, beach, antique and craft shopping. Antique shop on the premises.

Hosts: Jeanne and Joe Hovance
Rooms: 7 (4 PB; 3 SB) $48.15-64.20
Continental Breakfast
Credit Cards: A, B, C
Notes: 2, 5, 8, 9, 10, 11, 12, 13, 14

The Down Easter Inn

Bristol Road, Route 129/130, 04543
(207) 563-5332

A unique example of Greek Revival architecture, the Down Easter Inn is one mile from downtown Damariscotta, in the heart of the rocky coast of Maine. The Inn is fronted by a two-story porch with magnificent Corinthian columns. It is minutes from swimming, fishing, boating, and golf. Listed on the National Register of Historic Places, it features 22 rooms with private baths and televisions. Complimentary coffee and doughnuts served from 8:00-10:00 A.M.

Hosts: Robert and Mary Colquhoun
Rooms: 22 (PB) $58.50-75
Continental Breakfast
Credit Cards: A, B
Notes: 2, 7, 8, 9

DEER ISLE

The Inn at Ferry Landing

Rural Route 1, Box 163, Old Ferry Road, 04627
(207) 348-7760

Seaside retreat just a stone's throw from water's edge, where windjammers and waterfowl abound. Spacious antique-filled rooms offer magnifcent views. Sunbathe on the beach or deck, or relax in the shade of century-old oaks. Elaborate continental breakfast. Area renowned for its sailing waters, pristine harbors, artisans, and antique shops.

Hosts: Stephen and Donna Gormley
Rooms: 7 (PB) $80-95
Continental Breakfast
Credit Cards: None
Notes: 2, 8 (over 7), 9, 10, 11, 12

Laphroaig
Bed and Breakfast

P. O. Box 489, State Route 15, 04627
(207) 348-6088

Deer Isle's finest year-round accommodations. Treat yourself to bed and breakfast in this 1854 Greek Revival home in one of Maine's loveliest locales. Lighted private parking, flannel sheets in the cool weather, and a well-stocked library. Porch swing and rockers, garden benches, and flowers everywhere. Handmade afghans and many antiques. Elegant breakfasts for mature palates. Smoke-free, child-free atmosphere. Two-room suites with private baths. Enjoy the difference of Laphroaig! Brochure upon request.

Hosts: John and Andrea Maberry
Suites: 2 (PB) $79-93
Full Breakfast
Credit Cards: None
Notes: 2, 5, 9, 10, 11, 12, 14

DENNYSVILLE

Lincoln House Country Inn

Routes 1 and 86, 04628
(207) 726-3953

The centerpiece of northeastern coastal Maine. A lovingly restored Colonial on 95 acres bordering beautiful Cobsook Bay. Eagles, osprey, seals, whale watching. Choice accommodations. Rates include breakfast and dinner. Serves as a bed and breakfast only in the winter; reduced rates.

Hosts: Mary and Jerry Haggerty
Rooms: 10 (6 PB; 4 SB) $140-160
Full Breakfast
Credit Cards: A, B, C
Notes: 2, 4, 5, 7, 8 (over 10), 9, 10, 11, 13, 14

Lincoln House

EAST BOOTHBAY

Five Gables Inn

P. O. Box 75, Murray Hill Road, 04544
(207) 633-4551; (800) 451-5048

Five Gables Inn is a completely restored Victorian, circa 1865, located on Linekin Bay. All rooms have an ocean view and five have fireplaces. A gourmet breakfast is served in the large common room or on the spacious wraparound veranda.

Hosts: Ellen and Paul Morissette
Rooms: 15 (PB) $80-120
Full Breakfast
Minimum stay weekends: 2 nights; holidays: 3 nights
Credit Cards: A, B
Closed Nov. 16-May 15
Notes: 2, 8 (over 12), 9, 10, 11, 12

NOTES: Credit cards accepted: A Master Card; B Visa; C American Express; D Discover Card; E Diner's Club; F Other; 2 Personal Checks accepted; 3 Lunch available; 4 Dinner available; 5 Open all year;

Villa by the Sea

Van Horn and Shore Road, Ocean Point, 04544
(203) 633-2584

A 115-year-old summer home with 180-degree view of Gulf of Maine from the shoreline only 100 feet away. Five charming guest rooms with ocean view through floor-to-ceiling windows are warmly appointed with American antiques. Sunny mornings guests may breakfast on the east deck, and evenings enjoy sunsets on the west veranda. Tennis, beach, and hiking are possible on Ocean Point, while boat tours, live theater, and Down East shopping are available in nearby Boothbay Harbor.

Host: J. Irmischer
Rooms: 5 (S2B) $45-60
Continental Breakfast
Credit Cards: A, B
Open July and August to Labor Day
Notes: 2, 8, 9, 10, 11, 12, 14

EASTPORT

Todd House

1 Caper Avenue, 04631
(207) 853-7232

Todd House, circa 1775, on Todd's Head, is a large New England Cape with center chimney and an unusual front staircase. Panoramic views of Passamaquoddy Bay. Facilities in the large backyard are available for a relaxing cookout. Children and well-behaved pets are welcome. Handicapped access possible.

Host: Ruth McInnis
Rooms: 5 (2 PB; 3 SB) $45-80
Expanded Continental Breakfast
Credit Cards: None
Notes: 2, 5, 6, 8, 9, 10, 11, 14

Weston House

26 Boynton Street, 04631
(207) 853-2907

Built in 1810, this imposing Federal-style house overlooks Passamaquoddy Bay across to Campobello Island. Listed on the National Register of Historic Places; situated in a lovely Down East coastal village. Grounds include an expansive lawn suitable for croquet and a flower garden for quiet relaxation. Picnic lunches available.

Hosts: Jett and John Peterson
Room: $42.80-64.20
Full Breakfast
Credit Cards: None
Notes: 2, 3, 4, 5, 8, 9, 10

ELIOT

The Farmstead Bed and Breakfast

379 Goodwin Road, 03903
(207) 439-5033; (207) 748-3145

Come and step back in time and enjoy the hospitality that Farmstead offers its guests. Awake to the aroma of coffee, bacon/sausage, and blueberry pancakes on the griddle. Inspect the 1704 Cape and the "new" floor built in 1896. Explore the two and one-half acres, swing under the pear tree or have an early morning cup of coffee on the glider after your quiet restful night. All rooms have private bath, minirefrigerator, and microwave. Picnic facilities and gas grill available.

Hosts: Col. and Mrs. John Lippincott
Rooms: 9 (PB) $48
Full Breakfast
Credit Cards: A, B, D
Notes: 2, 5, 8, 14

FREEPORT

Atlantic Seal Bed and Breakfast

25 Main Street, P. O. Box 146, 04078
(207) 865-6112

Lovely harbor views year-round from each cozy bedroom of this 1850s Cape Cod home on Freeport Harbor. Antiques and nautical collections of seafaring family. Rooms feature sea breezes, fresh flowers, candlelight, thick towels, comfortable beds, homemade quilts, and down comforters. Shared and private baths, one with Jacuzzi. Down East hospitality, beverages by fireplace in old-fashioned parlor. Hearty sailor's breakfast, boat excursion discounts, five-minute drive to L. L. Bean and outlet stores. Resident dog and cat.

Hosts: Captain Thomas and Gaila Ring
Rooms: 3 (PB and SB) $55-125
Full Breakfast
Credit Cards: None
Notes: 2, 5, 8 (mature), 9, 10, 11, 12, 13 (XC), 14

The Bagley House

Rural Route 3, Box 269C, 04032
(207) 865-6566

Peace, tranquility, and history abound in this magnificent 1772 country home. Six acres of fields and woods invite nature lovers, hikers, berry pickers, and cross-country skiers. The kitchen's hand-hewn beams and enormous free-standing fireplace with beehive oven inspire mouthwatering breakfasts. A warm welcome awaits you.

Host: Sig Knudsen
Rooms: 5 (PB) $80-100
Full Breakfast
Credit Cards: A, B, C, D
Notes: 2, 5, 8, 9, 10, 11, 12, 13, 14

Captain Josiah Mitchell House (Nonsmoking Inn)

188 Main Street, 04032
(207) 865-3289

Famous, historic ship captain's home, circa 1779. The 1866 miraculous survival-at-sea story of Captain Mitchell of the ship Hornet is a classic. Mark Twain, then a young newspaperman, wrote about it. Restored more than 20 years ago by present owners, the house is filled with antiques. Beautiful grounds and only a five-minute walk to L. L. Bean. Eleventh year as an inn. Off-season (winter) rates available. No smoking.

Hosts: Alan and Loretta Bradley
Rooms: 6 (PB) $73-85
Full Breakfast
Credit Cards: A, B
Notes: 5, 9, 11, 12, 13, 14

Country at Heart Bed and Breakfast

37 Bow Street, 04032
(207) 865-0512

Enjoy staying in a cozy 1870 country home with handmade crafts, antiques, and reproduction furnishings. Choose one of the country-decorated rooms, the Shaker Quilt or Teddy Bear. A full breakfast is served on an eight-foot oak dining table. After breakfast, browse through Kim's Kraft Korner, a gift shop with country crafts and antiques. Park and walk to more than 100 outlet stores, restaurants, and L. L. Bean just two blocks away.

Hosts: Rogert and Kim Dubay
Rooms: 3 (1 PB; 2 SB) $55-75
Full Breakfast
Credit Cards: None
Notes: 2, 5, 8, 9, 12, 14

Harraseeket Inn

162 Main Street, 04032
(207) 865-9377

Luxury bed and breakfast inn two blocks north of L. L. Bean. Antiques, fireplaces, Jacuzzi, steam or standard bath, cable TV, air conditioning, tavern on premises. Afternoon tea served.

Hosts: Nancy and Paul Gray
Rooms: 54 (PB) $110-225
Full Breakfast
Credit Cards: A, B, C, D, E, F
Notes: 4, 5, 7, 8, 9, 10, 11, 12, 13 (XC)

The Isaac Randall House

5 Independence Drive, 04032
(207) 865-9295

Comfortable, charming, antique-furnished, air-conditioned rooms in an 1823 farmhouse. Oriental rugs and lovely old quilts.

NOTES: Credit cards accepted: A Master Card; B Visa; C American Express; D Discover Card; E Diner's Club; F Other; 2 Personal Checks accepted; 3 Lunch available; 4 Dinner available; 5 Open all year;

Situated on five wooded acres with a spring-fed pond. Just a few blocks from L. L. Bean and downtown Freeport. Hearty breakfasts and evening snacks. No smoking. Children and pets welcome.

Hosts: Cynba and Shannon Ryan
Rooms: 8 (6 PB; 2 SB) $60-120
Full Breakfast
Credit Cards: A, B, F
Notes: 2, 5, 6, 8, 9, 10, 11, 12, 13, 14 (off-season)

181 Main Street Bed and Breakfast

181 Main Street, 04032
(207) 865-1226

Comfortably elegant, antique-filled 1840 Cape. Just a five-minute walk to L. L. Bean and Freeport's luxury outlets. Hosts provide a renowned breakfast, New England hospitality, and information on all that Maine has to offer, on and off the beaten path. In-ground pool; ample parking. Featured in *Country Home* magazine. American Bed and Breakfast Association and AAA approved.

Rooms: 7 (PB) $75-95
Full Breakfast
Credit Cards: A, B
Notes: 2, 5, 9, 11, 12, 13 (XC), 14

Porter's Landing Bed and Breakfast

70 South Street, 04032
(207) 865-4488

Contemporary elegance and traditional New England charm in 1800s carriage house in Freeport's historic maritime district. Listed in National Register of Historic Places. Quiet, peaceful, country setting one mile from L. L. Bean. Large common room with working Count Rumford fireplace. Library in loft for quiet reading. Three cozy bedrooms—all with private baths—feature antiques, handmade quilts and fresh cut flowers. Full, hearty breakfast includes fresh fruits, homemade breads and muffins,

and specialties such as wild Maine blueberry pancakes, Belgian waffles and the Porter's Landing omelette, rated "excellent" by the American B&B Association.

Hosts: Peter and Barbara Guffin
Rooms: 3 (PB) $80-90
Full Breakfast
Credit Cards: A, B, F
Notes: 2, 9, 14

Country at Heart

White Cedar Inn

178 Main Street, 04032
(207) 865-9099

Quiet, historic inn just a short walk from Freeport's central outlet shopping district and L. L. Bean. Rooms are large, bright, and uncluttered. Quality reproductions and antiques throughout. Hearty breakfast is served in the sun room overlooking the town.

Hosts: Phil and Carla Kerber
Rooms: 6 (4 PB; 2 SB) $65-95
Full Breakfast
Credit Cards: A, B
Notes: 5, 9, 10, 12, 13, 14

FRIENDSHIP

The Outsiders' Inn Bed and Breakfast

Box 521A, Corner of Routes 97 and 220, 04547
(207) 832-5197

6 Pets welcome; 7 Smoking allowed; 8 Children welcome; 9 Social drinking allowed; 10 Tennis available; 11 Swimming available; 12 Golf available; 13 Skiing available; 14 May be booked through travel agents.

The Outsiders' Inn in the center of the village of Friendship, a short walk from the harbor, the home of historic Friendship Sloops and scores of lobster boats. This inn features five comfortable guest rooms with double beds, private, and semiprivate baths. Full breakfasts served daily. Friendship Sloop charters and dinners by prior arrangement also available. Country furnishings, delicious food, friendly folks. Come enjoy mid-coast Maine.

Hosts: Debbie and Bill Michaud
Rooms: 5 (1 PB; 4 SB) $45-55
Full Breakfast
Credit Cards: A, B
Notes: 2, 5, 8, 9

FRYEBURG

Admiral Peary House

9 Elm Street, 04037
(207) 935-3365

The home was once the residence of Arctic explorer Admiral Robert E. Peary. It has been lovingly restored for your comfort, with air-conditioned rooms and private bathrooms, country breakfast, billiards, and high tea. The clay tennis court is framed by spacious lawns and perennial gardens. Use one of the bicycles to explore the village and nearby sights of interest. Spend a few hours or a day canoeing and swimming the Saco River. Top it off with a leisurely soak in the outdoor spa. "We look forward to your visit and hope you'll enjoy the admiral's home as much as we do," say the hosts.

Hosts: Ed and Nancy Greenberg
Rooms: 4 (PB) $76-106
Full Breakfast
Credit Cards: A, B
Notes: 2, 5, 10, 11, 12, 13, 14

The Oxford House Inn

105 Main Street, 04037
(207) 935-3442

This stately turn-of-the-century inn has a gourmet restaurant on premises, with shopping, skiing, hiking, canoeing, tennis, and antiquing nearby. Open year-round, our comfortable, charming guest rooms are decorated with old-fashioned elegance, and some have mountain views. King, queen, double, and twin rooms are available, and a full gourmet breakfast is served in a a dining room with a view of the mountains. Dinner and room reservations required.

Hosts: John and Phyllis Morris
Rooms: 5 (PB) $65-85
Full Breakfast
Credit Cards: A, B, C, E
Notes: 4, 5, 8, 9, 10, 12, 13

GEORGETOWN

The Grey Havens

Box 308, 04548
(207) 371-2616; (517) 439-4115 (winter)

"All you can see is sea and sky," wrote one guidebook. Listed on the National Register of Historic Places as "the last 'shingle-style' hotel on the Maine coast." Turrets, veranda, 1904 interior. Peaceful and informal. Row to island sanctuary; walk long, quiet beaches; shop at L. L. Bean and other famous outlets.

Host: The Eberhart family
Rooms: 14 (11 PB; 3 SB) $90-150
Continental Breakfast
Credit Cards: None
Notes: 2, 4, 9, 11

GOULDSBORO

Bed and Breakfast Inns of New England ME-850

329 Lake Drive, Guilford, CT 06437
(800) 582-0853

The grounds of this bed and breakfast home border Jones Pond. Guests can enjoy swimming, fishing, and canoeing in warm

---

NOTES: Credit cards accepted: A Master Card; B Visa; C American Express; D Discover Card; E Diner's Club; F Other; 2 Personal Checks accepted; 3 Lunch available; 4 Dinner available; 5 Open all year;

months, and cross-country skiing, ice skating, and ice fishing in winter months. Artistic and photographic opportunities abound all year. Common rooms in this late Victorian home include a large dining room, a comfortable double parlor, and an inviting sun porch. Seven spacious bedrooms with shared baths are spread over three floors. Four of these rooms have ocean views and a fifth overlooks the pond. Resident pets, but no guest pets, please. Children are welcome. No smoking. $59-69.

Sunset House

HCR 60, Box 62, 04607
(207) 963-7156

This late-Victorian home is a traditional bed and breakfast with views of ocean and fresh water. Osprey, bald eagles, loons, and other wildlife can be observed in their natural environment. Schoodic Peninsula, considered the quiet side of Acadia National Park, is a short distance away.

Hosts: Carl and Kathy Johnson
Rooms: 7 (SB) $39-69
Full Breakfast
Credit Cards: A, B, D
Notes: 2, 5, 8 (over 10), 9, 11, 12, 13 (XC)

GREAT CRANBERRY ISLAND

The Red House

Main Road, 04625
(207) 244-5297

A charming shorefront saltwater farm with all the amenities of today. All rooms are newly decorated with traditional furnishings. A hearty American-style breakfast is included. Other meals are available. The island offers outstanding views of Acadia National Park. Whale watching, and sightseeing trips leave from nearby harbors. Separate kitchen available for guests.

Hosts: Dorothy and John Towns
Rooms: 6 (3 PB; 3 SB) $50-75, seasonal
Full Breakfast
Credit Cards: A, B
Notes: 2, 4, 9, 11

GREENVILLE

Greenville Inn

P. O. Box 1194, Norris Street, 04441
(207) 695-2206

This 1895-built Victorian lumber baron's mansion is situated on a hill overlooking Moosehead Lake and Squaw Mountain. A large, leaded-glass window decorated with a painted spruce tree is the focal point at the landing of the stairway. Gas lights, embossed wall coverings, carved fireplace mantels, and cherry and oak paneling grace the inn. In the elegantly appointed dining rooms, diners may savor fresh Maine seafood, glazed roast duckling, grilled chops, or steaks. Whether relaxing by a cozy fire or sipping cocktails on the veranda at sunset, the evening hours are most enjoyable.

Hosts: The Schnetzers
Rooms: 9 (7 PB; 2 SB) $65-90
Continental Breakfast
Credit Cards: A, B, D
Notes: 2, 4, 5, 7, 8, 9, 10, 11, 12, 13

Greenville Inn

Hillside Gardens

Blair Hill, P. O. Box 1189, 04441
(207) 695-3386

High on a hilltop overlooking 40 miles of beautiful Moosehead Lake and Squaw Mountains is a 100-year-old Victorian mansion with spacious rooms and private baths. Over 70 acres of land with trails for you to explore. "Like slipping back in time" to a more peaceful era.

Hosts: Mary and Marty Hughes
Rooms: 5 (4 PB; 1 SB) $65-95
Full Breakfast
Credit Cards: A, B
Notes: 2, 3, 4, 5, 7 (outside), 8 (over 12), 9, 10, 11, 12, 13, 14

The Sawyer House

P. O. Box 521, Lakeview Street, 04441
(207) 695-2369

The Sawyer House bed and breakfast overlooks Moosehead Lake, just a short walk to shops, restaurants, and local attractions. Relax, make yourself at home in the farmhouse, circa 1849. All rooms have king- or queen-size beds and private baths. Enjoy the view of Moosehead Lake from one of the outside porches, or relax in the parlor with cable TV.

Hosts: Pat and Hans Zieten
Rooms: 3 (PB) $55-65
Full Breakfast
Credit Cards: A, B, D
Notes: 2, 5, 10, 11, 12, 13

The Keepers House

ISLE AU HAUT

The Keepers House

Isle Au Haut, 04645
(207) 367-2261

Remote island lighthouse station in the undeveloped wilderness area of Acadia National Park. Guests arrive on the mail boat from Stonington. No phones, cars, TV, or crowds. Osprey, seal, deer, rugged trails, spectacular scenery, seclusion, and inspiration. Three elegant meals included in rate.

Hosts: Jeff and Judi Burke
Rooms: 6 (SB) $225, includes meals
Minimum stay July-Aug.: 2 nights
Credit Cards: None
Closed Nov. 1-April 30
Notes: 2, 3, 4, 8, 9, 11

KENNEBUNK

Arundel Meadows Inn

P. O. Box 1129, 04043
(207) 985-3770

This 165-year-old farmhouse two miles north on Route 1 from the center of Kennebunk, combines the charm of antiques and art with the comfort of seven individually decorated bedrooms with sitting areas—two are suites, three have fireplaces, some have cable television, and all have private bathrooms and summer air conditioning. Full homemade breakfasts and afternoon teas are prepared by co-owner Mark Bachelder, a professionally trained chef. The inn is open year-round.

Hosts: Mark Bachelder and Murray Yaeger
Rooms: 7 (PB) $75-125
Full Breakfast
Credit Cards: A, B
Notes: 2, 5, 9

Bed and Breakfast Inns of New England ME-810

329 Lake Drive, Guilford, CT 06437
(800) 582-0853

NOTES: Credit cards accepted: A Master Card; B Visa; C American Express; D Discover Card; E Diner's Club; F Other; 2 Personal Checks accepted; 3 Lunch available; 4 Dinner available; 5 Open all year;

Step back in time as you are welcomed to this 1756 farmhouse set on six acres of rolling hills. Common rooms, including a colonial kitchen, are furnished with period antiques, stenciled walls, pumpkin pine floors, and six fireplaces. Continental breakfast is served on the sun porch each morning. Three rooms with double beds are available, two included private bath and one has a fireplace. Resident pets, but no guest pets, please. Children over 14 are welcome. No smoking. $70.

English Meadows Inn

Rural Route 3, Box 141, 04043
(207) 967-5766

English Meadows is an 1860 Victorian farmhouse that has been operating as an inn for more than 80 years. It is a ten-minute stroll of the village of Kennebunkport, with its many unique shops, art galleries, and restaurants. English Meadows offers a friendly and comfortable place to visit.

Host: Charlie Doane
Rooms: 13 (9 PB; 4 SB) $65-90
Full Breakfast
Credit Cards: A, B
Notes: 2, 5, 8 (over 9), 10, 11, 12, 14

Lake Brook Guest House Bed and Breakfast

Lower Harbour Village
57 Western Avenue, 04043
(207) 967-4069

Charming rooms with paddle fans, fresh-cut flowers, great full breakfast. Lovely perennial garden. Rooms overlook a tidal marsh and brook. Lake Brook is situated only one-half mile from downtown Kennebunkport, with its shops, restaurants, galleries. Just over one mile to the beach.

Host: Carolyn A. McAdams
Rooms: 4 (3 PB; 1 SB) $69.55-85.60
Full Breakfast
Credit Cards: None
Notes: 2, 5, 9, 10, 11, 12, 13, 14

Sundial Inn

P. O. Box 1147
48 Beach Avenue, 04043
(207) 967-3850

Unique oceanfront inn furnished with turn-of-the-century Victorian antiques. Each of the 34 guest rooms has a private bath, phone, color TV, and air conditioning. Several rooms also offer ocean views and whirlpool baths. Visit Kennebunkport's art galleries and studios, museums, and gift shops. Go whale watching, deep-sea fishing, or hiking at the nearby wildlife refuge and estuary. Golf and tennis are nearby. Continental breakfast features muffins and coffee cakes.

Hosts: Larry and Pat Kenny
Rooms: 34 (PB) $60-148
Continental Breakfast
Credit Cards: A, B, C, E
Notes: 5, 7, 9, 10, 11, 12

Sundial Inn

KENNEBUNKPORT

Captain Fairfield Inn

P. O. Box 1308, 04046
(207) 967-4454

A gracious 1813 sea captain's mansion in Kennebunkport's historic district is only steps to the village green and harbor. A delightful walk to sandy beaches, Dock Square Marina, shops, and excellent restaurants. Situated on the corner or Pleasant and Green streets. Gracious and elegant, the bedrooms are beautifully decorated with antiques and period furnishings that lend an atmosphere of tranquility and charm. Several bedrooms have fireplaces, and guests are welcome to relax in the livingroom, study, or enjoy the tree-shaded grounds and gardens. You will awake to birdsong, fresh sea air, and the aroma of gourmet coffee. Come and enjoy a refreshing, comfortable, memorable stay with us!

Hosts: Bonnie and Dennis Tallagnon
Rooms: 9 (PB) $75-135
Full Breakfast
Credit Cards: A, B, C
Notes: 2, 5, 9, 10, 11, 12, 14

The Captain Lord Mansion

P. O. Box 800, 04046
(207) 967-3141; (800) 522-3141

The Captain Lord Mansion is an intimate 16-room luxury country inn, situated at the head of a sweeping lawn, overlooking the Kennebunk River. The inn is famous for its warm, friendly hospitality, attention to cleanliness, and hearty breakfasts served family-style in the big country kitchen.

Hosts: Bev Davis and Rick Litchfield
Rooms: 16 (PB)
Full Breakfast
Credit Cards: A, B, D
Notes: 2, 5, 9, 10, 11, 12

Cove House

South Main Street
Rural Route 3, Box 1615, 04046
(207) 967-3704

This cozy inn, an 18th-century Colonial with spacious rooms, is decorated in antiques. Full, hearty breakfast is served in the formal dining room. Short walk from village center and beach. Located in quiet area on Chick's Cove. Large yard offers views of water.

Host: The Jones family
Rooms: 3 (1 PB; 2 SB) $55-65
Full Breakfast
Credit Cards: A, B, C
Notes: 2, 5, 7, 8, 9, 10, 11, 12

1802 House

Locke Street, 04046
(207) 967-5632

1802 House is a 19th-century inn tucked away in a quiet section of the quaint seaside village of Kennebunkport. The inn is bounded by the Cape Arundel Golf Club, nestled along the fifteenth green, yet is only a ten-minute walk to bustling Dock Square. Each of the six guest rooms is furnished with antiques, all have private bathrooms, and two guest rooms offer working fireplaces. A full gourmet breakfast awaits you each morning.

Hosts: Ron and Carol Perry
Rooms: 6 (PB) $85-125
Full Breakfast
Credit Cards: A, B, C
Notes: 2, 4, 5, 9, 10, 11, 12, 14

The Green Heron Inn

P. O. Box 2578, Ocean Avenue, 04046
(207) 967-3315

Ten-room bed and breakfast offers the best breakfast in town, according to local folks. Each guest room is air conditioned and has cable TV. Homey, comfortable, and clean. Most guests return year after year, which adds to the charm and character of the inn.

Hosts: Charles and Elizabeth Reid
Rooms: 10 (PB) $60-85
Full Breakfast
Credit Cards: None
Notes: 2, 5 (limited in winter), 6 (prior arrangement), 7, 8, 9, 10, 11, 12

Inn on South Street

Box 478A, 04046
(207) 967-5151

Enjoy the comfortable elegance of this stately Greek Revival house located in Kennebunkport's historic district. There are three spacious, beautifully decorated guest rooms and one luxury apartment and suite. A sumptuous breakfast is served in the large country kitchen with views of the

NOTES: Credit cards accepted: A Master Card; B Visa; C American Express; D Discover Card; E Diner's Club; F Other; 2 Personal Checks accepted; 3 Lunch available; 4 Dinner available; 5 Open all year;

river and ocean. Restaurants, shops, and the water are a short walk away from the quiet street where the inn is located.

Hosts: Jacques and Eva Downs
Rooms: 4 (PB) $85-175
Full Breakfast
Credit Cards: A, B
Notes: 2, 5

The Kennebunkport Inn

One Dock Square, P. O. Box 111, 04046
(800) 248-2621

The Kennebunkport Inn was originally built by a sea captain in the late 1800s. Today it has 34 rooms with private baths and color TV. Situated in the center of town, just a skip from Dock Square, but set back from the hubbub. Near shops, the historic district. A small outdoor pool overlooks the river, and there is a turn-of-the-century bar with a piano bar on weekends.

Hosts: Rick and Martha Griffin
Rooms: 34 (PB) $54-155
Full Breakfast May-Oct; Continental off-season
Credit Cards: A, B, C
Notes: 4, 5, 11, 12, 14

Kilburn House

Chestnut Street, P. O. Box 1309, 04046
(207) 967-4762

Kilburn House is an 1890s Victorian home located one block from the center of downtown Kennebunkport, a colonial New England village with many fine restaurants, beaches, and shops. There are four guest rooms and a suite with two bedrooms.

Hosts: Samuel A. Minier and Muriel Friend
Rooms: 4 (2 PB; 2 SB) $60-75 plus tax
Suite: 1 (PB) $125 plus tax
Full Breakfast
Credit Cards: A, B, C
Notes: 2, 8, 9, 10, 11, 12, 14

Kylemere House

South Street, Box 1333, 04046
(207) 967-2780

Kylemere House, situated in a historic district, is a quiet haven just a minute's walk from the beach, shops, galleries, and restaurants. Come and relax in a friendly atmosphere in beautifully appointed rooms. Enjoy a Down East breakfast in the formal dining room overlooking the gardens.

Hosts: Bill and Mary Kyle
Rooms: 4 (PB) $70-115
Full Breakfast
Credit Cards: A, B, C
Closed Jan.-April
Notes: 2, 8 (over 10), 9, 10, 11, 12, 13, 14

Maine Stay
Inn and Cottages

Box 500 A, 04046
(207) 967-2117; (800) 950-2117

Elegant rooms and delightful garden cottages situated in the quiet surroundings

The Green Heron Inn

6 Pets welcome; 7 Smoking allowed; 8 Children welcome; 9 Social drinking allowed; 10 Tennis available; 11 Swimming available; 12 Golf available; 13 Skiing available; 14 May be booked through travel agents.

of Kennebunkport's historic district. Complimentary breakfast, afternoon tea, New England desserts. Color cable TV, private baths, fireplaces. Easy walking distance to restaurants, galleries, shops, and harbor. One mile to beach and golf.

Hosts: Linsay and Carol Copeland
Rooms: 17 (PB) $85-185
Full Breakfast
Credit Cards: A, B, C
Notes: 2, 5, 8, 9, 10, 11, 12, 13, 14

Old Fort Inn and Resort

Box M-30, 04046
(207) 967-5353; (800) 828-FORT

Discover the hospitality of a luxurious New England inn that combines all of yesterday's charm with today's conveniences, from the daily buffet breakfast to the comfort and privacy of antique-appointed rooms. Includes pool, tennis court, color TV, telephones, and a charming antique shop, all in a secluded setting.

Hosts: David and Sheila Aldrich
Rooms: 16 (PB) $98-225
Full Breakfast
Credit Cards: A, B, C, D
Closed mid-Dec.-mid-April
Notes: 2, 7, 9, 10, 11, 12, 14

KITTERY

Bed and Breakfast Inns of New England ME-805

329 Lake Drive, Guilford, CT 06437
(800) 582-0853

A romantic ambience and elegant antique furnishings await you at this 1890 Princess Anne Victorian bed and breakfast. Enjoy a full breakfast of gourmet coffees, omelettes, and pastries in the garden or on the sun deck. Six guest rooms are available with double and queen beds, shared and private baths. Resident pets, and guest pets are welcome. Children are welcome. No smoking. $79-100.

Maine Stay Inn

Enchanted Nights Bed and Breakfast

29 Wentworth Street, Route 103, 03904
(207) 439-1489

An 1890 Queen Anne Victorian centrally situated between Boston and Portland. Three minutes to dining and dancing in downtown Portsmouth, historic homes, scenic ocean drives, the renown Kittery outlet malls. Convenient day trips to lovely neighboring resorts. For the romantic at heart who delight in the subtle elegance of yesteryear; for those who are soothed by the whimsical charm of a French country inn. Gourmet coffee, omelettes, pastries.

Hosts: Nancy Bogenberger and Peter Lamandia
Rooms: 6 (5 PB; 1 SB) $35-95
Full Breakfast
Credit Cards: A, B, C
Notes: 2, 5, 6, 8, 9, 14

KITTERY POINT

Harbour Watch Bed and Breakfast

6 Follett Lane, 03905
(207) 439-3242

Colonial sea captain's house in same family since 1797. Wonderful view, quiet atmosphere. Within five miles to outlet shops, theaters, beaches, fabulous restaurants, whale-watching excursions, harbor cruises. Evening musicales with harpsichord and baroque instruments. Just an hour's drive from Boston.

Hosts: Marian and Robert Craig
Rooms: 4 (S2B) $65
Continental Breakfast
Minimum stay weekends and holidays: 2 nights
Credit Cards: None
Closed Nov.-April
Notes: 2, 9, 10, 11, 12

LUBEC

Breakers by the Bay

37 Washington, 04652
(207) 733-2487

One of the oldest houses in the 200-year-old town of Lubec, a small fishing village. Three blocks to Campobello Island, the home of Franklin D. Roosevelt. All rooms have hand-crocheted tablecloths and hand-quilted bedspreads. Five rooms have private decks for viewing the bay. All rooms that share a bath have their own washstands.

Host: E. M. Elg
Rooms: 5 (4 PB; 1 SB) $64.20
Full Breakfast
Credit Cards: None
Notes: 2, 12

MACHIAS

Clark Perry House

59 Court Street, 04654
(207) 255-8458

Lovely Victorian home built in 1868 and still in the family. Easy walking to shops, restaurants, churches, and historic sites. Large lawn for games and private patio for relaxation. Roque Bluffs State Park, Jasper Beach, and University of Maine at Machias nearby. Many nature trip opportunities. Enjoy local theater, chamber concerts, and the annual Blueberry Festival. Two spacious comfortable rooms; queen bed or twin beds. One small, cozy room with single bed. Shared bath. Full breakfast served. On the National Register of Historic Places.

Hosts: Robin and David Rier
Rooms: 2 (SB) $35-55
Full Breakfast
Credit Cards: A, B
Notse: 2, 5, 8, 10, 11, 12, 13

Old Fort Inn

MILBRIDGE

Bed and Breakfast Inns of New England ME-855

329 Lake Drive, Guilford, CT 06437
(800) 582-0853

This large Victorian has outstanding views of the bay and Narraguagus River. Common rooms include a sitting room, formal livingroom, dining room, and sun porch. This bed and breakfast is in a rural village with restaurants, light shopping, and an inexpensive movie theater a short walk from the doorstep. Full breakfast includes a bottomless cup of coffee or tea. Six guest rooms with a variety of bed sizes and shared and private baths are available. Children over 12 are welcome. No guest pets. Smoking outside only. $45-55.

NAPLES

The Augustus Bove House

Rural Route 1, Box 501, 04055
(207) 693-6365

You are always welcome at the historic 1850 Hotel Naples, on the corner of Routes 302 and 114. This restored bed and breakfast offers six spacious guest rooms with elegant yet homey furnishings, some with views of Long Lake, with shared or private bath. Walk to water, restaurants, recreation, and shops. Four-seasons area.

Hosts: David and Arlene Stetson
Rooms: 7 (3 PB; 4 SB) $39-85
Full Breakfast
Credit Cards: A, B, C, D
Notes: 2, 4 (off-season), 5, 6, 8, 9, 10, 11, 12, 13, 14

Inn at Long Lake

P. O. Box 806, 04055
(207) 693-6226

Enjoy romantic elegance and turn-of-the-century charm at the Inn at Long Lake, nestled amid the pines and waterways of the beautiful Sebago Lakes region. The inn has 16 restored rooms with TVs, air conditioners, and private baths. Situated one minute's walk from the Naples Causeway. Four-season activities and fine dining nearby. This three-diamond AAA facility is worth the trip. Midweek discounts available.

Hosts: Maynard and Irene Hincks
Rooms: 16 (PB) $63-100 seasonal
Expanded Continental Breakfast
Credit Cards: A, B, D
Notes: 2, 5, 8, 9, 11, 12, 13, 14

Lamb's Mill Inn

Box 676, Lamb's Mill Road, 04055
(207) 693-6253

A charming country inn in the foothills of Maine's western mountain and lake region. Romantic country atmosphere on 20 acres of fields and woods. Five rooms with private baths and full country breakfast. Hot tub. Near lakes, antique shops, skiing, canoeing.

Hosts: Laurel Tinkham and Sandra Long
Rooms: 5 (PB) $75-85
Full Breakfast
Credit Cards: None
Notes: 2, 4, 5, 9, 11, 12, 13

NEWCASTLE

The Captain's House Bed and Breakfast

P. O. Box 242, 19 River Road, 04553
(207) 563-1482

The Captain's House Bed and Breakfast is a Greek Revival home overlooking the Damariscotta River. On your arrival you will be overwhelmed with the river view, and inside you'll find the large, sunny rooms warm and inviting. Enjoy a leisurely walk to town for fine dining and carefree shopping. Homemade breads, blueberry pancakes, French toast, and farm-fresh eggs are served for a breakfast you'll never forget.

Hosts: Susan Rizzo and Joe Sullivan
Rooms: 5 (SB) $50-60
Full Breakfast
Credit Cards: None
Notes: 2, 5, 7, 8, 9, 10, 11, 12

Glidden House

Rural Route 1, Box 740, Glidden Street, 04553
(207) 563-1859

A lovely mansard-roof Victorian (Second Empire) overlooking the Damariscotta River. A memorable house that is attractively furnished, comfortable, and quiet. Excellent breakfast. Within walking distance of restaurants, shops, galleries, and historic sites.

Host: Doris E. Miller
Rooms: 3 (PB) $50-55
Full Breakfast

NOTES: Credit cards accepted: A Master Card; B Visa; C American Express; D Discover Card; E Diner's Club; F Other; 2 Personal Checks accepted; 3 Lunch available; 4 Dinner available; 5 Open all year;

Credit Cards: B
Notes: 2, 5, 7 (restricted), 8, 9, 10, 11, 12, 13 (XC)

The Markert House

Glidden Street, 04553
(207) 563-1309

Four rooms with two shared baths in a hillside 1900 Victorian overlooking the Damariscotta River. Your host is an artist, photographer, gourmet cook, and gardener. Reproduction Victorian veranda, antique furnishings, tasteful art gallery.

Host: William P. Markert
Rooms: 4 (S2B) $45-55
Full Breakfast
Credit Cards: A, B, C
Notes: 2, 5, 9, 12

Mill Pond Inn

Rural Free Delivery 1, Box 245, 04553
(207) 563-8014

Whimsical and cozy, this bed and breakfast in a 1780 home offers an excellent atmosphere to view the wonders of Maine's wildlife. The breakfast room has a view of the pond, complete with loons, otters, beavers, herons, a resident bald eagle, and breathtaking Maine wildflowers. A canoe can be paddled from the pond in the backyard directly into Damariscotta Lake (15.5 miles long), to within 20 feet of a bald eagle's nest! Also, Bobby is a registered Maine guide and guided fishing trips is another added feature to this lovely inn. Nestled in the little 1800s village of

Lamb's Mill Inn

Damariscotta Mills. Boothbay Harbor, Camden Hills, Pemaquid Lighthouse, Bath-Brunswick area, and the rugged coast of midcoast Maine await you.

Hosts: Bobby and Sherry Whear
Rooms: 6 (PB) $60-70
Full Breakfast
Credit Cards: None
Notes: 2, 5, 7, 8, 9, 10, 11, 12

The Newcastle Inn

River Road, 04553
(207) 563-5685

A romantic country inn on the Damariscotta River. All 15 rooms have private baths, most have river views, and some have canopy beds. Enjoy the changing tide while sitting on the glassed and screened sun porch. In the dining room, elegant four-star candlelight dinners and multicourse breakfasts are served. Featured in *Food and Wine.*

Hosts: Ted and Chris Sprague
Rooms: 15 (PB) $70-105
Full Breakfast
Credit Cards: A, B
Notes: 2, 4, 5, 14

NEW HARBOR

Gosnold Arms

HC 61, Box 161, Route 32, 04554
(207) 677-3727

On the harbor, the Gosnold Arms Inn and cottages, all with private baths, most with water view. A glassed-in dining room overlooking the water is open for breakfast and dinner. The Gosnold wharf and moorings accommodate cruising boats. Within a ten-mile radius are lakes, beaches, lobster pounds, historic sites, boat trips, golf, antiques, shops, and restaurants.

Host: The Phinney family
Rooms: 26 (PB) $89-115
Full Breakfast
Credit Cards: A, B
Notes: 2, 4, 8, 9, 11

6 Pets welcome; 7 Smoking allowed; 8 Children welcome; 9 Social drinking allowed; 10 Tennis available; 11 Swimming available; 12 Golf available; 13 Skiing available; 14 May be booked through travel agents.

NEWPORT

Lake Sebasticook Bed and Breakfast

P. O. Box 502, 8 Sebasticook Avenue, 04953
(207) 368-5507

Take a step back in history in this 1903 Victorian home situated on a quiet street. Relax on the second-floor sun porch or comfortable wraparound porch and enjoy the sounds of ducks and loons on Lake Sebasticook. Take a short walk to the lake park, or play tennis at the city park a block away. In the morning, savor a full country breakfast including homemade breads.

Hosts: Bob and Trudy Zothner
Rooms: 3 (S2B) $55
Full Breakfast
Credit Cards: None
Closed Nov.-May 1
Notes: 2, 10, 11, 12, 13

NORTHEAST HARBOR

Harbourside Inn

Northeast Harbor, 04662
(207) 276-3272

Peace and quiet, flower gardens at the edge of the forest, and woodland trails into Acadia National Park add to the delights of this genuine 1888 country inn. Spacious rooms and suites, all with private baths, many with king or queen beds. Beautiful antiques, working fireplaces in all first- and second-floor rooms. You can walk or drive into nearby Acadia National Park. Sailing, deep-sea fishing, carriage rides in the park. All rooms are nonsmoking. Reservations accepted for two nights or more.

Host: The Sweet family
Rooms: 11 plus 3 suites (PB) $85-210
Continental Breakfast
Credit Cards: None
Notes: 2, 10, 11, 12

OGUNQUIT

Beauport Inn

96 Shore Road, P. O. Box 1793, 03907
(207) 646-8680

A cozy nonsmoking bed and breakfast furnished with antiques offers four rooms, all of which have private baths. Pine-paneled livingroom with a fireplace and piano. Baked goods by the host. Antique shop on the premises.

Host: Dan Pender
Rooms: 4 (PB) $75-85
Continental Breakfast
Credit Cards: A, B, C
Closed January and February
Notes: 2, 8 (over 12), 9, 10, 11, 12

Gorges Grant Hotel

P. O. Box 2240, U.S. Route 1, 03907
(207) 646-7003

A modern inn of 56 luxury units with full-service restaurant and lounge. Heated indoor pool and Jacuzzi, heated outdoor pool, large patio/poolside area. A beautiful lobby featuring a fireplace and sitting areas. The restaurant, Raspberries, is open for breakfast and dinner. Bed and breakfast plan, Modified American Plan, and European packages are available. Ogunquit features one of the world's best beaches, a seacoast walkway called Marginal Way, and picturesque Perkins Cove. Nearby are President Bush's Kennebunkport home, and L. L. Bean. Rated three diamonds in AAA.

Hosts: Patty and Steve Farrar
Rooms: 56 (PB)
Full Breakfast
Credit Cards: A, B, C, D, E
Notes: 2, 3, 4, 7, 8, 9, 11

Hartwell House

118 Shore Road, P. O. Box 393, 03907
(207) 646-7210; (800) 235-8883

NOTES: Credit cards accepted: A Master Card; B Visa; C American Express; D Discover Card; E Diner's Club; F Other; 2 Personal Checks accepted; 3 Lunch available; 4 Dinner available; 5 Open all year;

In the tradition of fine European country inns, Hartwell House offers rooms and suites tastefully furnished with Early American and English antiques. A gourmet breakfast is served daily. Perkins Cove, Ogunquit Beach, and the Marginal Way are all within walking distance of the inn. Various seasonal package arrangements are available.

Hosts: Jim and Trisha Hartwell; Alec and Renée Adams
Rooms: 16 (PB) $80-175
Full Breakfast
Minimum stay weekends and holidays: 1-3 nights
Credit Cards: A, B, C
Notes: 2, 5, 8 (over 10), 9, 10, 11, 12, 14

The Morning Dove

30 Bourne Lane, Box 1940, 03907
(207) 646-3891

Elegant 1860s farmhouse featuring light, airy rooms with antiques, art, and European accents. Quiet location among spectacular gardens. Amenities include down comforters, air conditioning, welcoming wine, chocolates, and plush towels. Short stroll to the beaches, cove restaurants, and playhouse. Reservations appreciated.

Hosts: Peter and Eeta Sachon
Rooms: 8 (4 PB; 2 SB) $75-105
Expanded Continental Breakfast
Minimum stay in-season: 2 nights
Credit Cards: C, D
Closed Nov. 1-May 1
Notes: 2, 7, 8 (over 11), 9

OQUOSSOC

Oquossoc's Own Bed and Breakfast

Rangeley Avenue, P. O. Box 27, 04964
(207) 864-5584

Family home built in 1903 with 16 beds available in five guest rooms. On the snow machine trail for winter sports and just five minutes to golf. Within walking distance of tennis and two lakes. Large yard and porches for relaxing. The host has been in the bed and breakfast and catering business since 1980. Group rates available.

Host: Joanne Conner Koob
Rooms: 5 (1 PB; 4 SB) $30-55
Full Breakfast
Credit Cards: A, B
Notes: 2, 3, 4, 5, 7, 8, 9, 10, 12, 13

RANGELEY

Northwoods

P. O. Box 79, Main Street, 04970
(207) 864-2440

An historic 1912 home of rare charm and easy elegance, Northwoods is centrally located in Rangeley Village. With spacious rooms, a lakefront porch, expansive grounds, and private boat dock, Northwoods provides superb accommodations. Golf, tennis, water sports, hiking, and skiing are a few of the many activities offered by the region.

Host: Carol Scofield
Rooms: 4 (3 PB; 1 SB) $60-75
Full Breakfast
Credit Cards: None
Notes: 2, 9, 10, 11, 12, 13, 14

ROCKPORT

Sign of the Unicorn Guest House

P. O. Box 99, 191 Beauchamp Avenue, 04856
(207) 236-8789; (207) 236-4042

This is the seventeenth year as a bed and breakfast on a quiet lane overlooking Rockport Harbor. The beds, breakfasts, and

6 Pets welcome; 7 Smoking allowed; 8 Children welcome; 9 Social drinking allowed; 10 Tennis available; 11 Swimming available; 12 Golf available; 13 Skiing available; 14 May be booked through travel agents.

ambience are great. Near all sports, sailing, antiquing, wildlife, refuge hiking or biking, concerts, restaurants and lobster. Senior guests and long-stay rates. Pet accommodations are available at a nearby kennel. Groups can have as many as twelve people, and there are a variety of bed sizes available.

Hosts: Winnie and Howard Jones
Rooms: 5 (2 PB; 3 SB) $70-100, seasonal
Full Breakfast
Credit Cards: None
Notes: 2, 4, 5, 7(outside), 8, 9, 10, 11, 12, 13, 14

ROUND POND

The Briar Rose

Route 32, P. O. Box 27, 04564
(207) 529-5478

Escape to an unspoiled fishing village close to the Pemaquid lighthouse, beaches, Monhegan Island boat service, and other recreational facilities. The 150-year-old home faces Round Pond Harbor and offers large, airy rooms filled with comfortable antique furnishings and collectibles. Relax in the gardens, enjoy walks in the village, visit local antique shops, country stores, studios, and galleries. Older children welcome; reservations recommended.

Hosts: Anita and Fred Palsgrove
Rooms: 3 (1 PB; 2 SB) $50-65
Full Breakfast
Credit Cards: None
Notes: 2, 5, 8

The Carriage House Inn

SACO

Crown 'n' Anchor Inn

121 North Street, P. O. Box 228, 04072-0228
(207) 282-3829

This beautiful, two-story Greek Revival house was built circa 1827. The ornate Victorian furnishings, double parlors with twin mirrors, and boutiful country breakfast afford many memories for guests. All rooms at the inn are furnished with period antiques, many collectibles, and private facilities. Nearby attractions include the York Institute Museum, Thornton Academy, and the Dyer Library.

Hosts: John Barclay and Martha Forester
Rooms: 5 (PB) $65-85
Full Breakfast
Credit Cards: A, B
Notes: 2, 5, 6 (small), 8 (over 12), 9, 10, 11, 14

SEARSPORT

Brass Lantern Inn

Route 1, P. O. Box 407, 04974
(207) 584-0150

Nestled at the edge of the woods, this gracious Victorian Inn, circa 1850, overlooks Penobscot Bay. All of the comfortable guest rooms have private baths. Enjoy a hearty breakfast with friendly hospitality. Open all year, the Brass Lantern will be lit to welcome you!

Hosts: Pat Gatto; Dan and Lee Anne Lee
Rooms: 4 (PB) $65-70 seasonal
Continental Plus Breakfast
Credit Cards: A, B
Notes: 2, 5, 8, 14

The Carriage House Inn

Box 238, 04974
(207) 548-2289

Built in 1874, this classic Victorian has been beautifully maintained, and the large, cheerful rooms offer a restful night's stay. Located in the center of the "Antique

Capital of Maine," within walking distance of restaurants, flea markets, the museum, and oceanfront town park.

Hosts: Brad and Cathy Bradbury
Rooms: 4 (3 PB; 1 SB) $69.55
Continental Breakfast
Credit Cards: A, B, D
Closed March and April
Notes: 2, 8, 9, 10, 11, 12

Thurston House Bed and Breakfast Inn

8 Elm Street, P. O. Box 686, 04974
(207) 548-2213

Beautiful circa 1830 Colonial home with ell and carriage house. Built as a parsonage for Stephen Thurston, uncle of Winslow Homer, who visited often. Now you can visit in a casual environment. Quiet village setting is steps away from Penobscot Marine Museum, beach park on Penobscot Bay, restaurants, tavern, galleries, antiques, and more. Relax in one of four guest rooms, two with bay views, and enjoy the "forget about lunch" breakfasts.

Hosts: Carl and Beverly Eppig
Rooms: 4 (2 PB; 2 SB) $45-60
Full Breakfast
Credit Cards: None
Notes: 2, 5, 8, 9, 10, 11, 12, 13, 14

SOUTH BROOKSVILLE

Buck's Harbor Inn

P. O. Box 268, Steamboat Wharf Road, 04617
(207) 326-8660

Charming country inn on Buck's Harbor, Penobscot Bay, a famed yachting and boating center. Halfway between Acadia National Park/Bar Harbor and Camden on the west. Historic Deer Isle, Castine, Blue Hill are just a short drive away. Remote, beautiful, comfortable, Brooksville is just the way Maine should be experienced.

Hosts: Peter and Ann Ebeling
Rooms: 6 (SB) $60

Full Breakfast
Credit Cards: A, B
Notes: 2, 3, 4, 8, 9, 11, 12

SOUTHWEST HARBOR

Harbour Cottage Inn

P. O. Box 258, 04679-0258
(207) 244-5738

This elegant but informal inn is located in the heart of Acadia National Park. Private baths offer either whirlpools or steam showers and hair dryers. Harbor-facing guest rooms have individual heat and ceiling fans. Hikers, bikers, boaters, skiers, and tourists are welcome to enjoy the warm, friendly hospitality.

Hosts: Ann and Mike Pedreschi
Rooms: 8 (PB) $60-120
Full Breakfast
Credit Cards: A, B, C, D
Notes: 2, 5, 9, 10, 11, 12, 13, 14

Buck's Harbor Inn

Harbour Woods Lodging

P. O. Box 1214, 04679
(207) 244-5388

Relaxing, intimate bed and breakfast. Comfortable traditional furnishings accented with fresh flowers, family keepsakes, and candlelight. Spacious guest rooms with large private baths offer harbor and garden views. Full breakfast, served on fine china, made with the freshest ingredients and imaginatively prepared and presented. Situated at the edge of the village, sur-

6 Pets welcome; 7 Smoking allowed; 8 Children welcome; 9 Social drinking allowed; 10 Tennis available; 11 Swimming available; 12 Golf available; 13 Skiing available; 14 May be booked through travel agents.

rounded by Acadia National Park and the sparkling waters of one of Maine's most picturesque harbors. Special off-season packages. Cottages also available May through October.

Hosts: Margaret Eden and James Paviglionite
Rooms: 3 (PB) $55-105
Full Breakfast
Credit Cards: None
Notes: 2, 5, 9, 10, 11, 12, 13, 14

The Island House

Box 1006, 04679
(207) 244-5180

Relax in a gracious, restful seacoast home on the quiet side of the island. Island House favorites such as blueberry coffee cake and sausage/cheese casserole are served for breakfast. Charming, private loft apartment available. Acadia National Park is just a five-minute drive away. The house is across the street from the harbor, with swimming, sailing, biking, and hiking nearby.

Host: Ann Gill
Rooms: 5 (1 PB; 4 SB) $55-100
Full Breakfast
Credit Cards: None
Closed Jan. 1-Mar. 31
Notes: 2, 8 (over 12), 9, 10, 11, 12, 14

Island Watch Bed and Breakfast

Freeman Ridge Road, P. O. Box 1359, 04679
(207) 244-7229

Overlooking the harbor of Mount Desert Island and the village of Southwest Harbor, Island Watch sits atop Freeman Ridge on the quiet side of the island. The finest panoramic views, privacy, and comfoRoute Walk to Acadia National Park and the fishing village of Southwest Harbor. Some rooms have private baths.

Host: Maxine M. Clark
Rooms: 7 (4 PB; 3 SB) $65
Full Breakfast
Credit Cards: None
Notes: 5, 8 (over 11), 9, 10, 11, 12, 14

The Kingsleigh Inn

100 Main Street, Box 1426, 04679
(207) 244-5302

Situated in the heart of Acadia National Park overlooking the picturesque harbor is a romantic, intimate inn that will surround you with charm the moment you walk through the door. Many rooms enjoy spectacular harbor views, and all are tastefully decorated.

Hosts: Tom and Nancy Cerelli
Rooms: 8 (PB) $55-155
Full Breakfast
Credit Cards: A, B, C, D
Notes: 2, 5, 8 (over 12), 9

The Lambs Ear Inn

Clark Point Road, P. O. Box 30, 04679
(207) 244-9828

The inn is a stately old Maine house (circa 1857). Comfortable and serene, with a sparkling harbor view. Have sweet dreams on comfortable beds with crisp, fresh linens. Start your day with a memorable breakfast. Spend pleasant days here filled with salt air and sunshine. Please visit this special village in the heart of Mount Desert Island surrounded by Acadia National Park.

Hosts: George and Elizabeth Hoke
Rooms: 6 (PB) $65-125
Full Breakfast
Credit Cards: A, B
Notes: 2, 9, 10, 11, 12, 14

Lindenwood Inn

Clark Point Road, P. O. Box 1328, 04679
(207) 244-5335

This lovely sea captain's home overlooking the harbor on the quiet side of Acadia National Park offers a warm, cozy atmosphere and full breakfast. Explore Mount Desert Island, relax in the parlor, or play the harpsichord. Children over 6 welcome in cottage; over 12 in inn. Brochure available; open all year.

NOTES: Credit cards accepted: A Master Card; B Visa; C American Express; D Discover Card; E Diner's Club; F Other; 2 Personal Checks accepted; 3 Lunch available; 4 Dinner available; 5 Open all year;

Hosts: Gardiner and Marilyn Brower
Rooms: 7 (3 PB; 4 SB) $42.80-123.05
Cottage: 1 (PB) $80.25-112.35
Full Breakfast
Credit Cards: None
Notes: 2, 5, 8, 9, 10, 11, 12, 13, 14

Penury Hall

Main Street, Box 68, 04679
(207) 244-7102

On the quiet side of Mount Desert, 14 miles from Bar Harbor, is Penury Hall, where guests enjoy a breakfast of Eggs Benedict, blueberry pancakes, cinnamon waffles, or popovers. You're welcome to use the canoe or sail aboard Abaco Rage, a 21-foot daysailer. The sauna can relax you after a hard day of hiking or cross-country skiing.

Hosts: Toby and Gretchen Strong
Rooms: 3 (SB) $40-55
Full Breakfast
Credit Cards: None
Notes: 2, 5, 9, 10, 11, 12, 13

SPRINGFIELD

Old Farm Inn

P. O. Box 28, Rural Route 1, 04487
(207) 738-2730

This 1840 farmhouse is set on twelve acres of fields and woods. The inn has seven bedrooms with five partial baths. Bedrooms feature antique furniture, quilts, and original beamed ceilings. A lounge with TV and a porch with card tables is available for guests to enjoy. Eat in the dining room overlooking a pasture or in the kitchen by the fire. There are fields to walk, a barn to explore, and a horse to pet. Fishing, golf, public beach, and shopping are nearby.

Host: Marilyn Hamilton
Rooms: 7 (SB) $42.80
Full Breakfast
Credit Cards: None
Notes: 3, 4, 7, 8, 9

STOCKTON SPRINGS

The Hichborn Inn

Church Street, P. O. Box 115, 04981
(207) 567-4183

Come let us pamper you in relaxed Victorian elegance. This stately cupola-topped mansion was built in 1849 for shipbuilder N. G. Hichborn and is listed on the National Register of Historic Places. Visit the Penobscot Marine Museum, go treasure hunting in coastal Maine's best antiquing country and enjoy fine dining, all just minutes from the inn. A sumptuous breakfast, fireplaces, down comforters, and period furnishings will make your stay a memorable experience.

Hosts: Nancy and Bruce Suppes
Rooms: 4 (2 PB; 2 SB) $55-80
Full Breakfast
Credit Cards: D
Notes: 2, 5

SULLIVAN HARBOR

Islandview Inn

Route 1, Box 24, 04664
(207) 422-3031

Turn-of-the-century summer cottage is located just off Route 1, 15 minutes from Ellsworth and 35 minutes from Bar Harbor. Choose from seven guest rooms, five with private bath. Each room features original furniture and detailed restoration work, picturesque views of Frenchman's Bay and Mount Desert Island. Private beach and sailing are available.

Host: Evelyn Joost
Rooms: 7 (5 PB; 2 SB) $45-70
Full Breakfast
Credit Cards: A, B
Notes: 2, 8, 9, 10, 12

---

6 Pets welcome; 7 Smoking allowed; 8 Children welcome; 9 Social drinking allowed; 10 Tennis available; 11 Swimming available; 12 Golf available; 13 Skiing available; 14 May be booked through travel agents.

SUNSET

Goose Cove Lodge

Goose Cove Road, 04683
(207) 348-2508

Surrounded by 70 acres of nature trails and
one-half mile of ocean frontage with beaches. Cottages and rooms are rustic, with private baths, fireplaces, and sun decks overlooking the ocean. Modified American Plan
May 1 to mid-October; bed and breakfast
in the spring and fall. One-week minimum
stay in July and August.

Hosts: Joanne and Dom Parisi
Rooms: 10 (PB) $80-90
Cottages: 11 (PB) $90-100
Full Breakfast
Credit Cards: None
Closed Oct. 17
Notes: 2, 3, 4, 8, 9, 10, 11, 12

THOMASTON

Cap'n Frost's
Bed and Breakfast

241 West Main Street, 04861
(207) 354-8217

This 1840 Cape is furnished with country
antiques, some of which are for sale. If you
are visiting the mid-coast area, this is a
comfortable overnight stay, close to
Monhegan Island and a two-hour drive to
Acadia National Park. Reservations are
helpful.

Hosts: Arlene and Harold Frost
Rooms: 3 (1 PB; 2 SB) $40
Full Breakfast
Credit Cards: A, B
Notes: 2, 9

VAN BUREN

The Farrell-Michaud House

231 Main Street, 04785
(207) 868-5209

Situated in the scenic St. John Valley in
northern Maine, bordering Canada, this inn
was built in the mid-1800s. This restored
Victorian mansion is listed on the national
historic register. Meals are served in one of
three dining rooms separated by hand-
carved wooden arches. Decorative tin walls
and ceilings adorn several rooms.

Host: Sheila M. Cyr
Rooms: 4 (1 PB; 3 SB) $39-49
Continental Breakfast
Credit Cards: A, B
Notes: 2, 4, 5, 8, 11, 12, 13

VINALHAVEN

Bed and Breakfast Inns
of New England ME-830

329 Lake Drive, Guilford, CT 06437
(800) 582-0853

Stay at this comfortable, affordable bed and
breakfast in a fishing village by Carver's
Harbor. Explore uncrowded woodlands,
visit seaside nature preserves and parks,
and feast on Maine's freshest seafood
caught daily in the surrounding waters.
Each morning starts with a continental
breakfast and you can prepare a picnic in
the guest kitchen for the day's adventures.
Available are six guest rooms, all with
shared baths. Children over ten are welcome. Resident dog, no guest pets, please.
No smoking. $40-60.

Fox Island Inn

Carver Street, P. O. Box 451, 04863
(207) 863-2122

Discover the unspoiled coastal Maine
island of Vinalhaven. This comfortable,
affordable bed and breakfast is located in
the quaint fishing village nestled around
picturesque Carver's Harbor. Enjoy swimming in abandoned granite quarries and
exploring seaside nature preserves by foot
or bicycle. State-operated car ferry from
Rockland runs three times daily. Island
activities include flea markets, church suppers, and wonderful local restaurants.

NOTES: Credit cards accepted: A Master Card; B Visa; C American Express; D Discover Card; E Diner's
Club; F Other; 2 Personal Checks accepted; 3 Lunch available; 4 Dinner available; 5 Open all year;

Host: Gail Reinertsen
Rooms: 6 (SB) $40
Continental Breakfast
Credit Cards: None
Notes: 2, 9, 11

WALDOBORO

Bed and Breakfast Inns of New England ME-815

329 Lake Drive, Guilford, CT 06437
(800) 582-0853

This lovely 1830 inn is handsomely decorated with Victorian furnishings. There is a sun deck and shade garden with a hammock. The inn features a delicious full breakfast, and tea or sherry is served each afternoon. Five guest rooms include a variey of bed sizes and shared and private baths. Children over 12 are welcome. No guest pets. Smoking in designated areas only. $45-70.

Bed and Breakfast Inns of New England ME-816

329 Lake Drive, Guilford, CT 06437
(800) 582-0853

Built in 1905, this bed and breakfast features classic woodwork, tin ceilings, two fireplaces, and a large screened porch. Explore the flower and vegetable gardens or the gallery and gift shop in the barn. Coffee, tea, or hot chocolate is brought to your room upon awakening, and a full breakfast is served in the dining room. Special and vegetarian diets can be accommodated. Four guest room are available with shared and private baths, with a variety of bed sizes. Children welcome. No guest pets, please. No smoking. $55-65.

Broad Bay Inn and Gallery Bed and Breakfast

Box 607, 1014 Main Street, 04572
(207) 832-6668

Lovingly restored 1830 inn, handsomely appointed with Victorian furnishings, canopy beds, paintings, candlelight dinner by reservation only. Breakfast banquet feasts and afternoon tea or sherry on the deck. Established art gallery in the barn. Walk down to the river, to tennis, theater, antique shops. A short drive to the lighthouse, Audubon sanctuary, and fishing villages. Send for your free brochure.

Hosts: Jim and Libby Hopkins
Rooms: 5 (S3B) $35-70
Full Breakfast
Credit Cards: A, B
Closed Jan.
Notes: 2, 4, 7 (limited), 8 (over 10), 9, 10, 11, 12, 13, 14

The Roaring Lion

Box 756, 04572
(207) 832-4038

A 1905 Victorian home with tin ceilings; elegant woodwork throughout. The Roaring Lion caters to special diets and serves miso soup, sourdough bread, homemade jams and jellies. Hosts are well traveled and lived two years in West Africa. Their interests include books, gardening, art, and cooking. Gallery and giftshop on premises.

Hosts: Bill and Robin Branigan
Rooms: 4 (1 PB; 3 SB) $53.50-64.20
Full Breakfast
Credit Cards: None
Notes: 2, 5, 8, 10, 11, 12, 13, 14

WATERFORD

Lake House

Routes 35 and 37, 04088
(207) 583-4182; (800) 223-4182 outside ME

Lake House is one of 21 buildings in Waterford "Flat" listed on the national historic register. The inn was established in the 1790s. For much of the 19th century it served as the Maine Hygienic Institute for Ladies. From the 1890s to 1940, it was operated as a hotel.

6 Pets welcome; 7 Smoking allowed; 8 Children welcome; 9 Social drinking allowed; 10 Tennis available; 11 Swimming available; 12 Golf available; 13 Skiing available; 14 May be booked through travel agents.

Hosts: Michael and Suzanne Uhl-Myers
Rooms: 5 (PB) $69-125
Full Breakfast
Credit Cards: A, B
Notes: 2, 4, 5, 9, 11, 12, 13, 14

The Parsonage House Bed and Breakfast

Rice Road, P. O. Box 116, 04088
(207) 583-4115

The Parsonage House, built in 1870 as the Waterford Church, overlooks waterford Village, Keoka Lake, and Mount Tirem. Located in a four-season area, it provides many opportunities for outdoor enthusiasts. The Parsonage is a haven of peace and quiet. Double guest rooms or private suite available. A full breakfast is served on the screen porch or in the large farm kitchen beside a glowing wood stove.

Hosts: Joseph and Gail St. Hilaire
Rooms: 3 (1 PB; 2 SB) $50-75
Full Breakfast
Credit Cards: None
Notes: 2, 3, 5, 8, 11, 12, 13

The Waterford Inne

Box 149, 04088
(207) 583-4037

Escape to country quiet in an inn offering the elegance of a fine country home. Ten uniquely decorated guest rooms and carefully furnished common rooms provide a fine setting for four-star dining in historic Waterford. Near mountains and coastline; water and woodland activities nearby.

Hosts: Barbara and Rosalie Vanderzanden
Rooms: 10 (7 PB; 3 SB) $60-100
Full Breakfast
Credit Cards: C
Closed March and April
Notes: 2, 4, 6, 7, 8, 9, 11, 12, 13

WELD

Lake Webb House Bed and Breakfast

Route 142, P. O. Box 127, 04285
(207) 585-2479

An 1870s New Englander situated in western mountains of Maine offers comfortable country-casual accommodations and full country breakfast. Four-poster beds, braided rugs, and handmade quilts give a feeling of relaxation. Many hiking trails and Mount Blue State Park nearby. In winter, cross-country ski or snowmobile from door.

Hosts: Fred and Cheryl England
Rooms: 4 (SB) $45
Full Breakfast
Credit Cards: None
Notes: 2, 5, 7, 8, 9

WELLS

Purple Sandpiper Guest House

Rural Route 3, Box 226C, 04090
(207) 646-7990

The guest house is located on Route 1, minutes from the beach. Rooms are comfortably furnished with private baths, cable TV, and refrigerators. Continental breakfast includes freshly baked muffins and coffee cakes. Miniature golf, tennis, and restaurants are within walking distance.

Hosts: Paul and Sandi Goodwin
Rooms: 6 (PB) $36-67
Continental Breakfast
Credit Cards: A, B, C, D
Closed mid-Oct.-mid-May
Notes: 2, 7, 8, 9, 10, 11, 12, 14

WINTER HARBOR

Main Stay Inn

P. O. Box 459, 04693
(207) 963-5561

Restored Victorian home overlooking Henry's Cove. Housekeeping units with fireplaces. Walk to restaurants, post office. Enjoy breakfast at Chase's Restaurant. A quiet village within a mile of Acadia, hiking, biking, and local activities.

NOTES: Credit cards accepted: A Master Card; B Visa; C American Express; D Discover Card; E Diner's Club; F Other; 2 Personal Checks accepted; 3 Lunch available; 4 Dinner available; 5 Open all year;

Hosts: Pearl and Roger Barto
Rooms: 3 plus 2 units (PB) $45
Full Breakfast
Credit Cards: A, B
Notes: 2, 5, 7, 8, 11, 12

WINTERPORT

Colonial Winterport Inn

Main Street, Route 1A, P. O. Box 525, 04496
(207) 223-5307

This 1833 inn is full of warmth and hospitality. Decorated in antiques, the dining room is open to the public by reservation only. Cordon Bleu chef/owner is fully licensed. Centrally located to Blue Hill, Bar Harbor, and Camden, and twenty minutes to the Bangor airport.

Hosts: Duncan and Judie Mcnab
Rooms: 7 (PB) $50-65
Full Breakfast
Credit Cards: A, B, D
Notes: 2, 3, 4, 5, 6, 8, 9, 14

WISCASSET

The Squire Tarbox Inn

Rural Route 2, Box 620, 04578
(207) 882-7693

Clean, casual, comfortable, and all country, this is a handsome old farmhouse on a back road near mid-coast Maine harbors, beaches, antique shops, museums, and lobster shacks. The inn offers a proper balance of history, quiet country, good food, and relaxation. Serves a delicious fresh goat cheese by the fire before dinner. Known primarily for rural privacy and five-course dinners.

Hosts: Karen and Bill Mitman
Rooms: 11 (PB) $62-132
Expanded Continental Breakfast
Credit Cards: A, B, C, D
Notes: 2, 4, 7 (limited), 8 (over 14), 9, 14

YARMOUTH PORT

Old Yarmouth Inn

Route 6A, P. O. Box 626, 02675
(508) 362-3191; (800) 833-5125

The oldest inn on Cape Cod, built in 1696, is situated on historic Route 6A. Charming antique homes, inns, and antique shops along the road, as well as golf, swimming, and other activities.

Hosts: Karl Manchon and David Madison
Rooms: (PB) $90-110 in-season; $70-90 off-season
Full Breakfast
Credit Cards: A, B, C
Notes: 2, 4, 7, 9, 11, 12, 14

YORK

The Cape Neddick House

1300 Route 1, P. O. Box 70, 03902
(207) 363-2500

Situated in the historic coastal community of York, this 1800s Victorian farmhouse is central to beaches, boutiques, antique shops, wildlife sanctuaries, boat cruises, factory outlets, and historical and cultural opportunities to fill your days and evenings. Sleeping on antique high-back beds, snuggled under handmade quilts, you are assured of pleasant dreams. No alarm clock needed, as the fragrant smells of cinnamon popovers, apple almond tortes, or ham and apple biscuits drift by, gently waking you. Reason enough to return time and again.

Hosts: John and Dianne Goodwin
Rooms: 6 (1 PB; 5 SB) $55-70
Full Breakfast
Credit Cards: None
Notes: 2, 5, 7 (limited), 8, 9

Dockside Guest Quarters

Harris Island Road, Box 205, 03909
(207) 363-2868

6 Pets welcome; 7 Smoking allowed; 8 Children welcome; 9 Social drinking allowed; 10 Tennis available; 11 Swimming available; 12 Golf available; 13 Skiing available; 14 May be booked through travel agents.

The Dockside Guest Quarters is a small resort on a private peninsula in York Harbor. Panorama of ocean and harbor activities. Spacious grounds with privacy and relaxing atmosphere. Beaches, outlet shopping, and numerous scenic walks close by. Accommodations are in an early seacoast inn and modern, multiunit cottages. Full service marina, wedding facilities, and restaurant on site.

Host: The Lusty family
Rooms: 21 (19 PB; 2 SB) $55-129
Expanded Continental Breakfast
Minimum stay: 2 nights; holidays: 3 nights
Credit Cards: A, B
Closed Oct. 22-May 1
Notes: 2, 3, 4, 6, 7, 8, 9, 10, 11, 12, 14

Hutchins House

209 Organug Road, 03909
(207) 363-3058

Hutchins House is an elegant waterfront home overlooking the York River. The large rooms all have water views. The York Harbor beach is a delightful 20-minute walk along the river past historical landmarks, fishing, sailing, and lobster boats. From the dock, guests can fish or canoe up the river for a picnic. The riverview Jacuzzi is sensational. The neighboring country club offers golfing packages during spring and fall.

Host: Linda Hutchins
Rooms: 3 (PB) $75-85
Continental Breakfast
Credit Cards: None
Notes: 2, 3, 5, 9, 10, 11, 12

Scotland Bridge Inn

1 Scotland Bridge Road, 03909
(207) 363-4432

The Scotland Bridge Inn is a place as special as Maine itself. A perfect place to stay from May 1 to October 31. Relax in the livingroom or walk through the herbal English garden. Put your feet up on the veranda or back deck and watch the world go by. Full breakfast and afternoon tea are served.

Host: Sylvia S. B. Jansen
Rooms: 3 (1 PB; 3SB) $70- 90 plus tax
Full Breakfast
Credit Cards: A, B
Notes: 2, 8, 9, 10, 11, 12

YORK BEACH

Homestead Inn
Bed and Breakfast

8 South Main Street (Route 1A), 03910
(207) 363-8952

A converted 1905 summer boarding house, the inn is situated at Short Sands Beach. Individually decorated rooms have ocean views. Walk to beach, enjoy sunsets; visit local Nubble Lighthouse. Historic landmarks; fine restaurants. Relax, be pampered, and let the seashore entertain.

Hosts: Dan and Danielle Duffy
Rooms: 4 (S2B) $49-59
Continental Breakfast
Credit Cards: None
Notes: 2, 9, 10, 11, 12

YORK HARBOR

Bell Buoy
Bed and Breakfast

570 York Street, 03911
(207) 363-7264

At the Bell Buoy, there are no strangers, only friends who have not met. Open year-round and minutes from U.S. 95, Route 1, and the Kittery outlet malls. After a short walk to the beach, enjoy your afternoon tea served on the porch or the livingroom where cable TV is available. You will be served a full homemade breakfast in the dining room or on the porch, as desired.

Hosts: Wes and Kathie Cook
Rooms: 3 (1 PB; 2 SB) $55-80
Full Breakfast
Credit Cards: None
Notes: 2, 5, 7, 9

NOTES: Credit cards accepted: A Master Card; B Visa; C American Express; D Discover Card; E Diner's Club; F Other; 2 Personal Checks accepted; 3 Lunch available; 4 Dinner available; 5 Open all year;

Canterbury House

432 York Street, Box 881, 03911
(207) 363-3505

A lovely white Victorian overlooking unspoiled York Harbor, Canterbury House is within walking distance of the beach and other local attractions. Guests enjoy large hotel amenities while being pampered in a homey atmosphere. A scrumptious breakfast, served on fine Royal Albert china in either the dining room or, weather permitting, the scenic front porch, features hot muffins fresh from your hosts' own bakery.

Hosts: James T. Pappas and Jim S. Hager
Rooms: 7 (2 PB; 3 SB) $59-75
Continental and Full Breakfast
Minimum stay: 2 nights in-season
Credit Cards: A, B
Notes: 4, 5, 7, 8 (over 12), 9, 11, 14

York Harbor Inn

Box 573, Route 1A, 03911
(207) 363-5119; (800) 343-3869

Coastal country inn overlooking beautiful York Harbor, situated in an exclusive residential neighborhood. There are 32 air-conditioned rooms with antiques and ocean views, seven working fireplaces. Fine dining year-round. An English pub on the premises with entertainment. The beach is within walking distance; and boating, fishing, antique shops are all nearby.

Hosts: Joe, Jean, Garry, and Nancy Dominguez
Rooms: 32 (PB) $55-120
Continental Breakfast
Credit Cards: A, B, C
Notes: 2, 3, 4, 5, 7, 8, 9, 10, 11, 12, 14

6 Pets welcome; 7 Smoking allowed; 8 Children welcome; 9 Social drinking allowed; 10 Tennis available; 11 Swimming available; 12 Golf available; 13 Skiing available; 14 May be booked through travel agents.

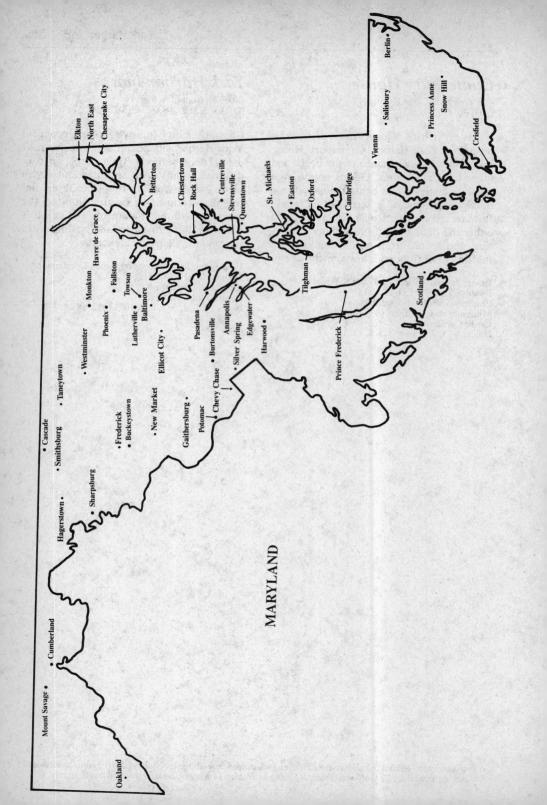

MARYLAND

Maryland

Amanda's Bed and Breakfast #112

1428 Park Avenue, 21217
(410) 225-0001; (410) 383-1274

Situated among beautiful trees on the cove of Severn River, this charming 1850 barn has been renovated with a taste of country, including antiques and old quilts. Historic Annapolis, US Naval Academy, and sailing schools are all nearby. Convenient snack bar. Children welcome. Continental breakfast or farm breakfast. One king with private half-bath; one double with private half-bath.

Amanda's Bed and Breakfast #139

1428 Park Avenue, 21217
(410) 225-0001; (410) 383-1274

Choose from five historic locations in downtown Annapolis that all accurately reflect early architecture. Some even include dining rooms, taverns, and conference space. Continental breakfast. $85-200.

Amanda's Bed and Breakfast #141

1428 Park Avenue, 21217
(410) 225-0001; (410) 383-1274

Nestled between the US Naval Academy and St. John's College, this beautifully decorated historic district town home features a private apartment suite with fireplace and ivy-covered courtyard. Another suite occupies the entire third floor of the main house. Continental breakfast. $140.

Amanda's Bed and Breakfast #163

1428 Park Avenue, 21217
(410) 225-0001; (410) 383-1274

Our ten-room bed and breakfast is on the main street in downtown Annapolis just steps away from the docks, shops, and historic buildings. As the inn is above a fantastic and famous deli, your meals may be chosen from a special bed and breakfast menu. One room (PB). Full breakfast. $65-75.

Amanda's Bed and Breakfast #182

1428 Park Avenue, 21217
(410) 225-0001; (410) 383-1274

Our beautiful, modern condo on the water looks out onto a marina. Location is just 15 minutes (3 miles) from downtown historic Annapolis. Continental breakfast. One queen bed. $81.

NOTES: Credit cards accepted: A Master Card; B Visa; C American Express; D Discover Card; E Diner's Club; F Other; 2 Personal Checks accepted; 3 Lunch available; 4 Dinner available; 5 Open all year; 6 Pets welcome; 7 Smoking allowed; 8 Children welcome; 9 Social drinking allowed; 10 Tennis available; 11 Swimming available; 12 Golf available; 13 Skiing available; 14 May be booked through travel agents.

Amanda's Bed and Breakfast #191

1428 Park Avenue, 21217
(410) 225-0001; (410) 383-1274

With pleasant Laura Ashley decor, this bright 1830s renovation is conveniently situated near the waters of East Port. Historic Annapolis docks and the Naval Academy are within walking distance. Added benefits include a view of the water, spacious parking, and water taxi. Four rooms (2 PB, 2 SB). Continental breakfast. $65-75.

Amanda's Bed and Breakfast #200

1428 Park Avenue, 21217
(410) 225-0001; (410) 383-1274

This fully furnished historic home is very close to the docks and the historic district of Annapolis. Feel free to walk to restaurants, shops, and the Naval Academy. Special features include modern kitchen, three working fireplaces, four bedrooms, three baths, TV, a washer/dryer, and central heat and air conditioning. Whole house rental. Sleeps 6-8. Self-catered breakfast. $300.

Amanda's Bed and Breakfast #218

1428 Park Avenue, 21217
(410) 225-0001; (410) 383-1274

Our three homes—Berman, Lauren, and Patterson House—are located in the heart of the historic district of Annapolis. You have a total of 20 guest rooms (SB) and two suites to choose from. Parlors, dining and meeting rooms are all lovingly furnished with beautiful antiques. $78-98.

Amanda's Bed and Breakfast #232

1428 Park Avenue, 21217
(410) 225-0001; (410) 383-1274

Across the street from the Naval Academy's Gate 3. Conveniently situated close to the docks, historic sites, shopping and restaurants. Reservations only for the entire house on a two-night minimum. Four bedrooms. Three baths. Self-catered breakfast. $300.

Amanda's Bed and Breakfast #258

1428 Park Avenue, 21217
(410) 225-0001; (410) 383-1274

A luxury 55-foot yacht on a lovely creek has every amenity. Put your worries to rest in the lounging area that adjoins the master stateroom. A spacious aft deck and fly bridge are also included for your enjoyment. Historic Annapolis city docks and restaurants are just minutes away with the help of a water taxi. Continental breakfast. Queen beds, $150. Twin beds, $125.

Amanda's Bed and Breakfast #259

1428 Park Avenue, 21217
(410) 225-0001; (410) 383-1274

This cozy cottage is just seven miles from Annapolis on two acres with a large garden, pool, and tennis courts surrounded by magnificent trees and a view towards the bay. A private deck faces the pool, and there are skylights and a loft upstairs. A boat is available for scenic tours. Private bath. Self-catered breakfast. $125.

NOTES: Credit cards accepted: A Master Card; B Visa; C American Express; D Discover Card; E Diner's Club; F Other; 2 Personal Checks accepted; 3 Lunch available; 4 Dinner available; 5 Open all year;

American Heritage Bed and Breakfast

108 Charles Road, 21401
(410) 280-1620

Built around 1862, this charming home is in the middle of the historic district of Annapolis. Within easy walking distance of the US Naval Academy, fine restaurants, and local attractions, this inn is filled with antiques and heirlooms that render a feeling of warmth and pleasant memories of the past. Wake to a full breakfast featuring family recipes, homemade breads, jellies, and jams. Enjoy a soothing massage, by appointment, at our bed and breakfast

Hosts: Bob and Adria Smith
Rooms: 2 (1 PB; 1 SB) $90-100
Full Breakfast
Credit Cards: None
Notes: 2, 5, 9

The Barn on Howard's Cove

500 Wilson Road, 21401
(301) 266-6840

Bed and breakfast in a restored 1850s barn on a secluded cove off the Severn River, three miles from the center of historic Annapolis, state capitol, and sailing center of the United States. Home of the US Naval Academy, with easy access to Washington, D.C., and Baltimore. Beautiful gardens, rural setting. Country decor with antiques and handmade quilts. Breakfast served on large deck overlooking river in the summer.

Hosts: Dr. and Mrs. Graham Gutsche
Rooms: 2 (SB) $60
Full Breakfast
Credit Cards: None
Notes: 2, 5, 8, 10, 11, 12, 14

The Charles Inn

74 Charles Street, 21401
(410) 268-1451

A gracious 1860s Civil War-era home with direct water access for water taxi (conve-nient to restaurants and city docks). Off-street parking available. Guests can relax in the four cozy guest rooms with featherbeds and down comforters. A full gourmet breakfast is served on three dining tables enhanced with fresh flowers on lace linen tablecloths with Lenox china and crystal.

Hosts: Paula and John Hartman
Rooms: 4 (2 PB; 2SB) $69-149
Full Breakfast
Credit Cards: A, B, C
Notes: 2, 5, 7, 8, 9, 14

Chez Amis Bed and Breakfast

85 East Street, 21401
(410) 263-6631

Renovated 70-year-old corner store offers three guest rooms combining yesteryear ambience with today's conveniences—central air conditioning, TVs, beverage centers. The 19th-century American antiques, original oak store counter, tin ceilings and Georgia pine floors blend with European art and South American artifacts in a setting of West Coast pastels. Centrally situated in historic district one block from city dock, state capital, and US Naval Academy. Enjoy romance and warm hospitality in America's sailing capital at "the Place of Friends."

Hosts: Tom and Valerie Smith
Rooms: 3 (PB) $75-90
Extended Continental Breakfast
Credit Cards: None
Notes: 2, 5, 8, 14

College House Suites

One College Avenue, 21401-1603
(410) 263-6124

This elegant brick town house, nestled between the US Naval Academy and St. John's College, features two suites: the Annapolitan Suite has a fireplace, Laura Ashley decor, and private entrance through the ivy-covered courtyard; the Colonial Suite has superb Oriental rugs, antiques, and views of naval academy parade grounds. Fresh flowers, bathrobes, toiletries, fruit baskets, and special chocolates enhance the romantic atmosphere. A "breakfast-out" option is available at a $20 rate reduction.

Hosts: Don and Jo Anne Wolfrey
Suites: 2 (PB) $150
Continental Breakfast
Minimum stay: 2 nights
Credit Cards: A, B
Notes: 5, 9, 14

Gibson Lodgings

Gibson's Lodgings

110 Prince George Street, 21401
(301) 268-5555

Historic twenty-room bed and breakfast inn with a new conference parlor for business and private gatherings. Group discount for six or more rooms Sundays through Thursdays. Located half a block from the city dock.

Hosts: Holly Perdue
Rooms: 20 (7PB; 13SB) $55-120
Continental Breakfast
Credit Cards: A, B, C
Notes: 2, 5, 7, 8, 9, 12, 14

Historic Inns of Annapolis

16 Church Circle, 21401
(410) 263-2641

Get a true sense of history within the lovely Inns of Annapolis. We offer 137 charming guest rooms with private baths, original antiques, a distinctive four-star restaurant, and the King of France lounge that features live jazz. Stroll along the waterfront, sail the bay, marvel at historic sights, and browse one-of-a kind shops. You'll discover why visitors have loved it here since the 1700s.

Host: Colleen Huther
Rooms: 137 (PB) $99
Continental Breakfast
Credit Cards: A, B, C, E
(301) 269-6232; (800) 736-4667 outside Maryland

Prince George Inn Bed and Breakfast

232 Prince George Street, 21401
(301) 263-6418

This Victorian town house in the historic district offers antique-filled guest rooms and immaculate baths. A charming parlor with fireplace, sunny breakfast porches, and lovely garden are for guests' enjoyment. Easy walk to nearby shops, restaurants, dock, and Naval Academy.

Hosts: Norma and Bill Grovermann
Rooms: 4 (2 PB; 2 SB) $78.75-89.25
Buffet Breakfast
Credit Cards: A, B, C
Notes: 2, 7, 8 (over 11), 9, 10, 12, 14

Riverwatch

145 Edgewater Drive, Edgewater, 21037
(410) 974-8152

From subtle sunrises to spectacular sunsets, Riverwatch offers guests luxurious accommodations and panoramic river views. Just minutes from historic Annapolis, this waterfront homestay bed and breakfast is exquisitely decorated in contemporary and oriental-style. Amenities include waterfront balconies, dockage for boaters, and ample off-street parking. Breakfast is served on the patio overlooking the river, or in the mirrored waterfront dining room.

Hosts: Karen Dennis and Donald Silawsky
Rooms: 2 (PB) $65-80, plus tax
Continental Plus Breakfast
Credit Cards: F
Notes: 2, 9, 10, 11, 12, 14

Shaw's Fancy Bed and Breakfast

161 Green Street, 21404
(301) 263-0320

Welcome to our 1902 Victorian Foursquare in the heart of the historic district. Midweek, business, or romantic getaway packages are available. Let us pamper you with terry robes, special soaps, and gourmet chocolates. Enjoy our front porch swing or garden hot tub.

Hosts: Lilith Ren and Jack House
Rooms: 3 (2 PB; 1 SB) $75-105
Full Breakfast
Credit Cards: None
Notes: 2, 5, 9, 14

The Traveller in Maryland-TNN-MARYLAND

P. O. Box 2277, 21404-2277
(410) 269-6232; FAX (410) 263-4841

Part of the Bed and Breakfast National Network, The Traveller in Maryland offers bed and breakfast not only in Maryland, but also in many other cities and states across the country. The members of this network adhere strictly to the standards set by TNN, such as getting to know the hosts personally, having an established cancellation and refund policy, and following a thorough inspection and approval process for all properties rented. This is because each member of the network is dedicated to ensuring your comfort, pleasure, and personal needs while you are staying at one of our "homes away from home."

The Traveller In Maryland # 105

P. O. Box 2277, 21404
(301) 269-6232

This ranch-style contemporary home is on a quiet residential street within walking distance of the Naval Academy football stadium and a hearty walk to the historic district and waterfront. The home was built by the owners and is comfortably furnished in contemporary pieces give it a real sense of home and relaxation. Guests are welcome to enjoy a livingroom and a den area with a TV, and an outdoor deck is a fine place to read a book or watch nature unfold. Two guest rooms are available. Continental breakfast. $50-55.

The Traveller In Maryland # 107

P. O. Box 2277, 21404
(301) 269-6232

This Victorian Italianate villa, circa 1864, is a charming piece of architecture situated in the middle of the historic district. A circular staircase greets guests in the entry hallway and flows up to the second floor guest room area. Furnished with period antiques and some reproductions, and numerous objects of art, this bed and breakfast has a livingroom with a baby grand piano and bay window with a nice view of the historic streets. The dining room overlooks the side gardens of the home. Three guest rooms are available. Full breakfast. No smoking. $50-80.

The Traveller In Maryland # 109

P. O. Box 2277, 21404
(301) 269-6232

6 Pets welcome; 7 Smoking allowed; 8 Children welcome; 9 Social drinking allowed; 10 Tennis available; 11 Swimming available; 12 Golf available; 13 Skiing available; 14 May be booked through travel agents.

This turn-of-the-century home is on Spa Creek and is easy walking distance to the hospital. Convenient to all attractions in the historic district, this large and gracious home is filled with antiques and family heirlooms. A warm second floor glassed-in sun porch is great for relaxing with an interesting book or magazine. The rear yard has a terrace where you can watch the sailboats quietly slip by on their way out to the bay. Two rooms available. Full breakfast. No smoking. $60-70.

The Traveller In Maryland # 111

P. O. Box 2277, 21404
(301) 269-6232

This three-story home in the historic district adjacent to St. John's College and the US Naval Academy was built in 1880 and is a comforting example of southwestern culture. Hardwood floors coupled with many art objects and paintings, all personally created by the owner, offer a nice contrast to the traditional lifestyle found just outside. Guests are encouraged to enjoy a quiet moment beside the koi pond on the brick patio or relax by the crisp fire in the livingroom on colder months. Three sets of accommodations are available. Continental plus breakfast. No smoking. $75-90.

The Traveller In Maryland # 113

P. O. Box 2277, 21404
(410) 269-6232

This two-story waterfront home is situated in a quiet community that has great views of the South River. You are sure to watch a lot of boating in this area, and this comfortable home invites you to make yourself at home. Three rooms available. Full breakfast. $55-65.

The Traveller In Maryland # 115

P. O. Box 2277, 21404
(301) 269-6232

From subtle sunrises to fiery sunsets, the views from this waterfront contemporary are spectacular. This three-story home is nicely furnished with antiques and contemporary pieces that have been carefully selected during the owner's trips abroad. A comfortable livingroom with a fireplace offers open views of the South River, and a large wooden deck opens onto the river, where a large hot tub and large swimming pool are available for guests. Two rooms, both of which have private baths, are available. Continental breakfast. No smoking. $65-75.

The Traveller In Maryland # 117

P. O. Box 2277, 21404
(301) 269-6232

This historic district town house offers the quiet and serenity of days of old, but remains only steps from the center of town. A two-story home comfortably furnished with family heirlooms and antiques is hosted by a couple knowledgeable and active in historic preservation. Two rooms are available. Full breakfast. Restricted smoking area. $70.

The Traveller In Maryland # 119

P. O. Box 2277, 21404
(301) 269-6232

This restored horse barn, circa 1860, is quietly nestled on a secluded cove off the Severn River. Just two miles from the historic district, this bed and breakfast invites you to relax in the country surroundings of

plank flooring and a stone fireplace. Added touches include handmade quilts, farm tools, and work pieces, and an outdoor deck is most inviting on a warm sunny day. Two bedrooms adjoin each other, and each room has a private half-bath. Full breakfast. No smoking. $55-60.

The Traveller In Maryland # 121

P. O. Box 2277, 21404
(301) 269-6232

This unhosted three-story home is centrally situated in the historic district, three blocks from the city dock and two blocks from the US Naval Academy. The home was built in the early 1900s and has a comfortable lived-in feeling. A rear brick patio surrounded by a ten-foot-high brick wall adds privacy. The first floor has a livingroom, dining room, and large rear kitchen; the second floor has two bedrooms, each with a double bed; and the third floor has a dormer room with a single bed. and window air conditioning. Three-night minimum. No smoking. $275.

The Traveller In Maryland # 123

P. O. Box 2277, 21404
(301) 269-6232

This contemporary town home in the historic district overlooks a creek. The home has eclectic furnishings, and there is a nice water view from the dining room and livingroom. A short walk from the dining and shopping districts, this home offers two guest rooms that share a hall bath. Restricted smoking. Continental breakfast. $60-65.

The Traveller In Maryland # 125

P. O. Box 2277, 21404
(301) 269-6232

This lovely two-story home is furnished with antiques and beautiful accessories. A five-minute drive from the historic district, this home offers three guest rooms on the second floor, a large formal livingroom and family room, screen porch, and in-ground swimming pool. Carefully hidden in a residential neighborhood, this home provides a feeling of the past in present-day, contemporary surroundings. Three rooms are available for guests. Full breakfast is served. No smoking. $50-80.

The Traveller In Maryland # 127

P. O. Box 2277, 21404
(301) 269-6232

On a quaint street in downtown Annapolis, three blocks from the city dock, this bed and breakfast is within walking distance to fine restaurants and shopping. Historical sites and tours, and the Naval Adademy are nearby. This Victorian home has comfortable accommodations, shared and private baths, a nicely furnished livingroom, and a brick patio in the rear yard. One guest room and one suite are available. Continental breakfast. No smoking. $60-95.

The Traveller In Maryland # 131

P. O. Box 2277, 21404
(301) 269-6232

This unique grey and white eight-sided home sits on a two-acre wooded lot 100 feet above the South River. As the name Dogwood Hills implies, the woods are full

6 Pets welcome; 7 Smoking allowed; 8 Children welcome; 9 Social drinking allowed; 10 Tennis available; 11 Swimming available; 12 Golf available; 13 Skiing available; 14 May be booked through travel agents.

of dogwood trees. The home is located in a quiet neighborhood called Southaven, but it is minutes from a major shopping center, downtown Annapolis, B.W.I. airport, and a half hour from Washington, D.C. Two spacious, second-floor bedrooms are available. Full breakfast is served. No smoking. $65-80.

The Traveller In Maryland # 133

P. O. Box 2277, 21404
(301) 269-6232

This contemporary town house offers the pleasures of home away from from home. Comfortable furnishings make this bed and breakfast home well-liked by travelers. Walking distance to several sailing schools and the historic district, or journey by water taxi to the city dock. Seafood restaurants and taverns are minutes away. Off-street parking is available and one upstairs guest room has twin beds and a private hall bath. Continental breakfast is served in this non-smoking environment. $55-60.

The Traveller In Maryland # 135

P. O. Box 2277, 21404
(301) 269-6232

This rambling country-style home sits on three acres of land in the outskirts of Annapolis. Eclectic furnishings blend well with the seasoned traveler. The livingroom and den have a TV. Outdoor deck is available. Annapolis is eight miles away, and Washington, D.C. is just 16 miles away. This is a great area for sightseeing. The double bedroom or twin bedroom have one and a half baths and both rooms have a shared bath option. Full breakfast is served in this non-smoking environment. $50-55.

The Traveller In Maryland # 139

P. O. Box 2277, 21404
(301) 269-6232

A recently renovated 70-year-old corner store features three guest rooms that combine yesteryear ambience (original tin ceiling and oak counter) with contemporary conveniences (coffee makers, TVs). Accommodations are decorated in West Coast pastels, turn-of-the-century furnishings, and art accents from Europe and South America. This central location is just two minutes from the city dock and Naval Academy. First floor Traveler's Room has a king-size bedroom with sofa (suitable for third person) and private bath en suite. Turn-of-the-century style on the second floor has a queen-size bedroom and bath in suite. Stage Coach Room offers double bed and a private hall bath. Extended continental breakfast is served. All rooms are non-smoking. $75-90.

The Traveller In Maryland # 141

P. O. Box 2277, 21404
(301) 269-6232

Historic Annapolis is just five minutes from this waterfront contemporary home. Guests can enjoy covered waterview deck or may visit with boat owners at the small dock nearby in the spring, summer, or fall. The house is furnished with a comfortable country feel. Large shade trees in the yard offer peaceful setting. The Blue Room has a double bed and private hall bath. The Cabin is a ground floor with large open room offering a livingroom with working fireplace and microwave. A third person can stay in the cabin. Private bath, air conditioning and private entrance are available. Full breakfast is served in this non-smoking environment. $65-90.

NOTES: Credit cards accepted: A Master Card; B Visa; C American Express; D Discover Card; E Diner's Club; F Other; 2 Personal Checks accepted; 3 Lunch available; 4 Dinner available; 5 Open all year;

The Traveller
In Maryland # 143

P. O. Box 2277, 21404
(301) 269-6232

Nestled quietly on the backwaters of the South River, this contemporary home is situated on a residential cul-de-sac. The home offers peace and quiet not always found at home. Guests are invited to enjoy the comfortable livingroom or the outdoor deck which overlooks the marshlands. Tastefully decorated with eclectic furnishings, the home's location is ideal for those taking sailing lessons as the marinas are just a short drive away. The historic district is just seven minutes by car. Our two rooms offer double or queen beds and both share a bath. Air conditioning and resident cat are included. Continental breakfast is served in this non-smoking environment. $60.

The Traveller
In Maryland # 145

P. O. Box 2277, 21404
(301) 269-6232

This contemporary home is nestled on the banks of the Church Creek, next to the South River. Quietness and serenity abound here. The gardens are landscaped for seclusion. Two of our water-view bedrooms, making up one entire level of the home, have queen beds, and a private livingroom is available. Guests are also invited to use the patio, garden, and family room. The historic district is just ten minutes away. Both rooms have a private or shared bath. Air conditioning and convenient parking are also available. Full breakfast is served in this non-smoking environment. $75.

The Traveller
In Maryland # 147

P. O. Box 2277, 21404
(301) 269-6232

Elegant multi-room suites are a part of this brick town home that is nestled between the US Naval Academy and St. John's College. The "Annapolitian" has a fireplace, Laura Ashley decor, and private entrance through the ivy-covered courtyard. The "Colonial" has superb orientals, antiques, and views of the Academy. Many personal touches and amenities have been added. A "breakfast out" option is available. Two-night minimum. A continental breakfast is served in this non-smoking environment. $120-175.

The Traveller
In Maryland # 149

P. O. Box 2277, 21404
(301) 269-6232

This restored foursquare home, built in 1908, offers distinctly appointed rooms with a mix of antiques. The third-floor suite has dormer ceilings, large sitting area, and whirlpool. The entry foyer with open stairway is flanked by crystal chandeliers and art work. The elegant common room has a working fireplace. Small groups are welcome. Amenities include queen-size beds, shared or private baths, fold-out sofa bed, off-street parking, air conditioning, wet bar setup in the common room, and full breakfast in this non-smoking environment. $75-120.

The Traveller
In Maryland # 151

P. O. Box 2277, 21404
(301) 269-6232

This restored pre-Revolutionary Georgian Colonial, built in 1747, has three beautifully decorated bedrooms each furnished with period reproductions. Sip coffee in one of the parlors or have breakfast on the brick patio surrounded by seasonal flowers. Walk out the back door to the harbor, US Naval

6 Pets welcome; 7 Smoking allowed; 8 Children welcome; 9 Social drinking allowed; 10 Tennis available; 11 Swimming available; 12 Golf available; 13 Skiing available; 14 May be booked through travel agents.

Academy, Main Street shopping and restaurants. Private bath, air conditioning, and resident cat, Muffin, are also included. Continental breakfast is served in this non-smoking environment. $85-90.

BALTIMORE

Admiral Fell Inn

888 South Broadway, 21231
(401) 522-7377; (800) 202-INNS
FAX (301) 522-0707

Situated on the waterfront, this charming historic inn has 38 guest rooms that are uniquely appointed with antiques and fine reproductions. The restaurant features New American cuisine and seafood specialities in an intimate atmosphere as well as light fare and spirits in the casual English-style pub. Specially catered meetings, receptions, and banquets up to 55 people are also available.

Host: Dominik Eckenstein
Rooms: 38 (PB) $89-155
Continental Breakfast
Credit Cards: A, B, C, D
Notes: 2, 3, 4, 5, 7, 8, 9, 11, 12, 14

Amanda's Bed and Breakfast #102

1428 Park Avenue, Annapolis, 21217
(410) 225-0001; (410) 383-1274

This beautifully restored four-story row house is decorated with antiques. You are only minutes away from the inner harbor, shopping, restaurants, and bars. Choose from four lovely guest rooms (2 double, 2 twin, all SB). Convenient to public transportation. Owners operate a card and gift shop on first floor. Continental breakfast. $65.

Amanda's Bed and Breakfast #104

1428 Park Avenue, Annapolis, 21217
(410) 225-0001; (410) 383-1274

This restored 1830 Federal town house is downtown in the historic Mt. Vernon district. It has a delightful courtyard and spacious guest rooms that are decorated with antiques and have different themes. Convenient parking. Four rooms (SB). Full breakfast. $65.

Amanda's Bed and Breakfast #108

1428 Park Avenue, Annapolis, 21217
(410) 225-0001; (410) 383-1274

In the suburbs just five minutes from the Baltimore Beltway and 20 minutes from the inner harbor, this quiet getaway is decorated with antiques, handmade furniture, and a garden. Owners are native Baltimoreans who love guests, cooking, and vegetable gardening. Full breakfast. One double. One twin. Swimming pool. $65.

Amanda's Bed and Breakfast #109

1428 Park Avenue, Annapolis, 21217
(410) 225-0001; (410) 383-1274

A colorful 18th-century community, Fells Point is the location for this wonderfully renovated urban inn at the water's edge. All 38 rooms (PB) are individually designed and decorated with antiques and period reproductions. Other attractions include an English pub and elegant dining room. $85-up.

Amanda's Bed and Breakfast #110

1428 Park Avenue, Annapolis, 21217
(410) 225-0001; (410) 383-1274

Tudor-style guest house, near Johns Hopkins University Homewood campus, is just minutes from the inner harbor, convention center, and stadium. Our residential neighborhood is bordered by two parks and a lake. Biking, fitness track, and public golf course are all within walking distance. Full breakfast. One queen. One twin (SB). $60-75.

Amanda's Bed and Breakfast #111

1428 Park Avenue, Annapolis, 21217
(410) 225-0001; (410) 383-1274

Federal-style town house offers two delightful guest rooms and is within walking distance of inner harbor. Convention center, other hotels, financial district, sports arena, Harbor Place, galleries, museums, theaters, and restaurants are all nearby. One double (SB). One twin (SB). $60.

Amanda's Bed and Breakfast #113

1428 Park Avenue, Annapolis, 21217
(410) 225-0001; (410) 383-1274

Federal Hill town home, just a short distance from the inner harbor and convention center, has a third-floor suite. Host will accommodate long-term at reasonable rates. Double (PB). $60.

Amanda's Bed and Breakfast #117

1428 Park Avenue, Annapolis, 21217
(410) 225-0001; (410) 383-1274

Restored 18th-century town house in historic Fells Point, a waterfront community that is full of unique shops and restaurants. Inner harbor is just one mile away either by walking, water taxi, or trolley. Full breakfast. Three double (PB). One twin (PB). $75-85.

Amanda's Bed and Breakfast #119

1428 Park Avenue, Annapolis, 21217
(410) 225-0001; (410) 383-1274

Elegant Victorian mansion is decorated with imported antiques and is in historic Mt. Vernon near antique row. All 15 rooms/suites offer private baths, kitchenettes, and meeting facilities. The inner harbor is just 10 blocks away and fine dining is nearby. Continental breakfast. $95-105.

Amanda's Bed and Breakfast #131

1428 Park Avenue, Annapolis, 21217
(410) 225-0001; (410) 383-1274

Downtown historic neighborhood town house is furnished with antiques and is on a quiet street facing a park. Public transportation, cultural center, and churches are all nearby. The guest room is a large suite with all the amenities. King with private kitchenette. Swimming pool/club privileges. $85.

Amanda's Bed and Breakfast #132

1428 Park Avenue, Annapolis, 21217
(410) 225-0001; (410) 383-1274

A romantic retreat in Baltimore's historic neighborhood of Fells Point, the oldest maritime area of the city. Just one mile from the inner harbor with water taxi service in the summer or other transportation options all year. Our roof deck overlooks the harbor. Full breakfast. $110-125.

Amanda's Bed and Breakfast #147

1428 Park Avenue, Annapolis, 21217
(410) 225-0001; (410) 383-1274

6 Pets welcome; 7 Smoking allowed; 8 Children welcome; 9 Social drinking allowed; 10 Tennis available; 11 Swimming available; 12 Golf available; 13 Skiing available; 14 May be booked through travel agents.

Californian charm and comfort offered at this historic bed and breakfast with romantic, airy, Roland Park Victorian-style. Tastefully decorated with deck, three wood, burning fireplaces, Jacuzzi, and skylights. Continental breakfast in gourmet kitchen overlooking woods. Nicely landscaped, rejuvenating setting. Two-night minimum. Double (PB)-$75. Master suite-$120.

Amanda's Bed and Breakfast #166

1428 Park Avenue, Annapolis, 21217
(410) 225-0001; (410) 383-1274

Urban inn and restaurant has European charm and warm hospitality. Each room has been tastefully appointed with rich Baltimorean artwork, antique furniture, and brass beds. The inn has a full restaurant and piano bar, lots of parking in lot next door, and free van service to inner harbor. Continental breakfast. $85 up.

Amanda's Bed and Breakfast #186

1428 Park Avenue, Annapolis, 21217
(410) 225-0001; (410) 383-1274

Restored Victorian town house nestled in the Union Square historic district and just minutes away from the inner harbor, convention center, and the new sports complex in Camden Station. The rooms (double, PB) are decorated with period furnishings. Full breakfast. $90.

Amanda's Bed and Breakfast #190

1428 Park Avenue, Annapolis, 21217
(410) 225-0001; (410) 383-1274

Charmingly historic, intimate waterfront retreat is located in Fells Point. This bed and breakfast is listed in the National Register of Historic Places. Includes English garden, marina, and period furnishings. Restaurants and shops are within walking distance and a water taxi is available from May to October. Completely smoke-free. Continental breakfast. All rooms have PB, some with water view. $150.

Amanda's Bed and Breakfast #195

1428 Park Avenue, Annapolis, 21217
(410) 225-0001; (410) 383-1274

An attractive Federal Hill row house, just a block and a half from the science center and inner harbor, within walking distance to sites, attractions, restaurants, and shopping. Water taxi is available for rides around harbor. The guest room has a queen-size bed (PB) and is bright and airy. Great breakfast. $75.

Amanda's Bed and Breakfast #197

1428 Park Avenue, Annapolis, 21217
(410) 225-0001; (410) 383-1274

The hostess speaks French, Italian, and Arabic at this Charles Village row house near Johns Hopkins University and the Baltimore Art Museum. The house is a showcase of modern Egyptian art. Great full breakfasts. Double (PB). $60.

Amanda's Bed and Breakfast #216

1428 Park Avenue, Annapolis, 21217
(410) 225-0001; (410) 383-1274

Beautiful restored town home in historic Federal Hill is furnished in antiques and Oriental rugs and is just six blocks from the inner harbor. Historic sites, shopping,

NOTES: Credit cards accepted: A Master Card; B Visa; C American Express; D Discover Card; E Diner's Club; F Other; 2 Personal Checks accepted; 3 Lunch available; 4 Dinner available; 5 Open all year;

restaurants, and public transportation are all close. Continental breakfast. Double (PB) and suite. $100.

Amanda's Bed and Breakfast #221

1428 Park Avenue, Annapolis, 21217
(410) 225-0001; (410) 383-1274

Experience a comfortable night's sleep on a queen-size brass bed. Enjoy the convenience and vitality of in-town living. A warmly welcoming 19th-century row house bed and breakfast in the heart of Federal Hill/Cross St. Market historic district. Great breakfast. One queen (SB). $70.

Amanda's Bed and Breakfast #225

1428 Park Avenue, Annapolis, 21217
(410) 225-0001; (410) 383-1274

In Charles Village near Johns Hopkins University. The decor spans a century of-styles from the Victorian to the contemporary. All rooms have brass fixtures, English soaps, amenities, hair dryers, alarm clocks, air conditioning and color TVs. Continental breakfast served to room. Double (PB). $69-129.

Amanda's Bed and Breakfast #226

1428 Park Avenue, Annapolis, 21217
(410) 225-0001; (410) 383-1274

Built in 1897, the official guest house of the city of Baltimore is comprised of three town houses in historic Mt. Vernon. Guests are treated to personalized service, private baths, ornate and unusual decor. Great location with guest parking. Continental breakfast. $100-125.

Amanda's Bed and Breakfast #265

1428 Park Avenue, Annapolis, 21217
(410) 225-0001; (410) 383-1274

This federal-style town house was built in 1982. Features include three stories, patio, garden in back, fireplace in den and living-room. Our Springer Spaniel, Rocky, loves people. Continental breakfast is served in the dining room. $65-75.

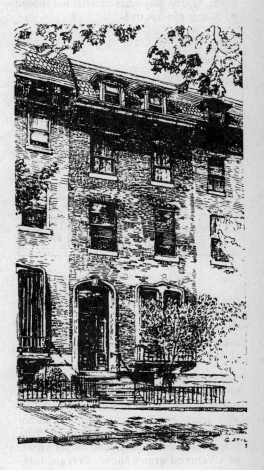

Betsy's Bed and Breakfast

---

6 Pets welcome; 7 Smoking allowed; 8 Children welcome; 9 Social drinking allowed; 10 Tennis available; 11 Swimming available; 12 Golf available; 13 Skiing available; 14 May be booked through travel agents.

Betsy's Bed and Breakfast

1428 Park Avenue, 21217-4230
(410) 383-1277

This four-story "petite" estate in downtown Bolton Hill is on a tree-lined street with white marble steps and brass rails. This spacious home features a hallway laid in alternating strips of oak and walnut, ceiling medallions, six marble mantles, and a center staircase that rises to meet a skylight. The expansive walls are hung with handsome brass rubbings and family heirloom quilts. Guests may relax in a hot tub shaded by a large pin oak tree.

Host: Betsy Grater
Rooms: 3 (PB) $75
Full Breakfast
Credit Cards: A, B, C, D
Notes: 2, 5, 8, 9, 11, 14

The Inn at Government House

Celie's Waterfront Bed and Breakfast

Historic Fell's Point, 1714 Thames Street, 21231
(301) 522-2323

Situated on Baltimore harbor. Ideal for business or pleasure. Seven air conditioned guest rooms, one wheelchair accessible, with access to a private garden and harbor view roof deck. Some with whirlpools, fireplaces, private balconies, and harbor views, in a relaxed atmosphere. Private telephones, marina, and conference space available. Minutes to Harbor Place, central business district, and Orioles Stadium by water taxi.

Host: Celie Ives
Rooms: 7 (PB) $85-140
Continental Breakfast
Credit Cards: A, B, C, D
Notes: 2, 5, 8 (over 10), 9, 14

The Inn at Government House

1125 North Calvert Street, 21202
(410) 539-0566; FAX (410) 539-0567

Managed by the Baltimore International Culinary College, this inn is in the historic Mt. Vernon District, one mile from the inner harbor. Victorian era home, elegant surroundings, complimentary continental breakfast, and parking. Afternoon tea and wine.

Hosts: Mariana Palicios and students
Rooms: 18 (PB) $100-120
Continental Breakfast
Credit Cards: A, B, C, E
Notes: 5, 7, 8, 9, 10, 11, 12

Mr. Mole Bed and Breakfast

1601 Bolton Street, 21217
(301) 728-1179

In the city on historic Bolton Hill amid quiet, tree-lined streets. An 1870s row house with 14-foot ceilings, marble fireplaces, and many antiques. Concert grand piano in music room. Suites, some with two bedrooms and sitting room. Attached garage parking with automatic door openers included. Walk to symphony, opera, and Metro. Close to Johns Hopkins University, University of Baltimore, University of Maryland Medical School, and the inner harbor, but without congestion. Handicapped accessible.

Hosts: Collin Clarke and Paul Bragaw
Rooms: 5 (PB) $75-125
Continental Breakfast
Credit Cards: A, B
Notes: 2, 5, 9

NOTES: Credit cards accepted: A Master Card; B Visa; C American Express; D Discover Card; E Diner's Club; F Other; 2 Personal Checks accepted; 3 Lunch available; 4 Dinner available; 5 Open all year;

Mulberry House

111 West Mulberry Street, 21201
(301) 576-0111

An 1830 town house in downtown
Baltimore with antiques, stained glass,
crystal and brass chandeliers, Oriental rugs,
Steinway grand piano, and fireplaces. Walk
to most points of interest, including Harbor
Place, the convention center, the aquarium,
all the best restaurants, and Oriole Park.
Air conditioned.

Hosts: Charlotte and Curt Jeschke
Rooms: 4 (S2B) $65
Full Breakfast
Credit Cards: None
Notes: 2, 5, 8 (over 16), 9, 14

Society Hill Hopkins

3404 Saint Paul Street, 21218
(301) 235-8600

A beautiful 26-room urban inn near Johns
Hopkins University and the Baltimore
Museum of Art. Only ten minutes from the
inner harbor. Conference space available.
Free parking, van service, local phone
calls. Styles of rooms and suites vary—
Federal, Art Deco, contemporary—some
with kitchenettes.

Hosts: Ken Settevering and Paula Rinker
Rooms: 26 (PB) $90-135
Expanded Continental Breakfast
Credit Cards: A, B, C, E
Notes: 2, 3, 4, 5, 7, 8, 9, 10, 12, 14

Society Hill Hotel

58 West Biddle Street, 21201
(410) 837-3630; (800) 676-3630

A delightful converted town house within
walking distance of the Meyerhoff
Symphony Hall and Lyric Opera House,
Antique Row, and the Light Rail System,
which takes you to Oriole Park at Camden
Yards. This fifteen-room inn offers the
exciting combination of a bed and breakfast
and an American country inn. Brass beds,
fresh flowers, rich Victorian furniture,
cable TV, breakfast served to your room.
The hotel has a bar and restaurant on the
premises, as well as a jazz piano bar.

Host: Kate Hopkins
Rooms: 15 (PB) $95-145
Continental Breakfast
Credit Cards: A, B, C, E
Notes: 2, 3, 4, 5, 7, 8, 9, 14

Mr. Mole Bed and Breakfast

The Traveller
In Maryland # 157

P. O. Box 2277, Annapolis, 21404
(301) 269-6232

Experience the charm and character of this
200-year-old town home located one-half
block from the waterfront of historic Fell's
Point. Recently restored, and great care was
taken to preserve much of the original
woodwork and fireplace mantels. Truly a
grand example of a bygone era. The waterfront, several restaurants and pubs are all
within walking distance. Trolley is available for a trip downtown. Amenities
include four guest rooms, two livingrooms,
and a private patio terrace. A continental
breakfast is served in this non-smoking
environment. $65-85.

6 Pets welcome; 7 Smoking allowed; 8 Children welcome; 9 Social drinking allowed; 10 Tennis available; 11
Swimming available; 12 Golf available; 13 Skiing available; 14 May be booked through travel agents.

The Traveller In Maryland # 159

P. O. Box 2277, Annapolis, 21404
(301) 269-6232

Originally an 1830 Federal town house, this home later took on an Italinate appearance with the addition of cornice work to the exterior. The complete restoration exemplifies leaded glass transoms and entrance fan windows. A modern bathroom and two beautiful bedrooms were created on each of the second and third floors. A delightful courtyard was created by the construction of a wall at the rear of the building. Amenities include sitting room with grand piano, fireplace, and banquet table with two chairs (1790) where a sumptuous, full breakfast is served. This is a non-smoking environment. $65.

The Traveller In Maryland # 163

P. O. Box 2277, Annapolis, 21404
(301) 269-6232

Situated in historic Bolton Hill, this grand 1870s house provides gracious accommodations for discriminating persons visiting Baltimore. The neighborhood is quiet, has tree-lined streets and warm, spacious, brick row houses. The home is decorated in a comfortable English-style with many 18th- and 19th-century antiques. On the first floor, the livingroom, breakfast room, and music room with 14-foot ceilings, bay windows, and marble fireplaces reflect the ambience of past times. A nine-foot concert grand piano is available for guests in the music room. Amenities include private baths, individual room decorations, air conditioning, phones, and on-site garage. A Dutch Continental breakfast is served in this non-smoking environment. $75-140.

The Traveller In Maryland # 165

P. O. Box 2277, Annapolis, 21404
(301) 269-6232

This majestic estate is quietly nestled on 45 acres of wooded land, offering the elegant lifestyle of the early 1900s. Guests will enjoy fireplaces, suites, Jacuzzis in bedrooms, gourmet breakfast, expansive porches, pool, tennis court, woodland trails and stream, and flower and herb gardens. Abundant history is associated with the house through its builder Alexander J. Cassatt, owner of the Pennsylvania Railroad and brother of Mary Cassatt, the American impressionist. Later it was owned by the Brewster family, descendants of Benjamin Franklin and important in government. In the 1950s it became the Koinonia Foundation, a predecessor of the Peace Corps. Amenities include double or king-size beds, private baths, some suites with separate livingroom and porches, family room, and library. This is a non-smoking environment. $115.

The Traveller In Maryland # 167

P. O. Box 2277, Annapolis, 21404
(301) 269-6232

This is a stately Federal period stone farmhouse situated on two acres with a pond near the historic mill town, Ellicott City. Continuing with the tradition of a lighted candle in each window, indicating the availability of rooms. The candles remain lighted as a nostalgic reminder of the inn's past. Off the center hall the parlor invites you to read and relax. In the winter months a fire in the fireplaces may encourage you to linger over a game of chess or checkers. Amenities include double and queen-size beds, parlor, and dining room. Continental breakfast is served in this non-smoking environment. $70-90.

The Traveller In Maryland # 169

P. O. Box 2277, 21404
(301) 269-6232

This small Victorian inn was built in 1827 in Baltimore's earliest fashionable residential area, the Mt. Vernon district. Each of the guest rooms are individually decorated,-styled with antiques throughout the house that have been lovingly hand-picked. The Victorian era wallpaper patterns and borders were custom designed for the guest rooms so that no two are alike. Rich Baltimore artworks grace the walls and even small details like porcelain doorknobs are much in evidence. Guest rooms are spacious; and fabrics, rich woods, brass accents and bouquets of flowers and plants all lend to a feeling of graciousness. Amenities include accessibility for handicapped, off-street parking, TV, and phones. Continental breakfast is served. Smoking is restricted. $80-140.

The Traveller In Maryland # 170

P. O. Box 2277, Annapolis, 21404
(301) 269-6232

Situated on a large working farm in the serene Piedmont countryside of Maryland, this Georgian-style country house has a Victorian addition and a hide-away guest house. The property is part of a 3,000-acre tract of land called Runnymeade Enlarged, patented prior to the American Revolution by Dr. Upton Scott. Enjoy the livingroom setting with a large fireplace, dining room, and wraparound porch with rocking chairs overlooking Bear Branch. Each room, with air conditioning, has a pleasant view of lawns, pastures, creeks, or woods. One suite has a private screened porch. One hundred yards across the wide and shaded lawn lies the guest house with two large bedrooms, a livingroom, and a kitchenette.

The guest house, with air conditioning, affords a comfortable and very private getaway. Full breakfast is served in this non-smoking environment. $55-100.

Twin Gates

Twin Gates Bed and Breakfast Inn

308 Morris Avenue, Historic Lutherville, 21093
(301) 252-3131; (800) 635-0370

Experience serene elegance in this Victorian mansion near the national aquarium, Harbor Place, and Maryland hunt country. Friendly hosts, wine and cheese, and gourmet breakfast.

Hosts: Gwen and Bob Vaughan
Rooms: 7 (3 PB; 4 SB) $85-95
Full Breakfast
Minimum stay weekends and holidays: 2 nights
Credit Cards: A, B, C
Notes: 2, 5, 9, 10, 12, 14

BERLIN

Atlantic Hotel Inn and Restaurant

2 North Main Street, 21811
(301) 641-3589

---

6 Pets welcome; 7 Smoking allowed; 8 Children welcome; 9 Social drinking allowed; 10 Tennis available; 11 Swimming available; 12 Golf available; 13 Skiing available; 14 May be booked through travel agents.

Restored Victorian hotel with 16 period-furnished rooms. A national register building in the historic district. Elegant dining and piano lounge on the premises. Situated eight miles west of Ocean City and Assateague Island National Seashore. Walk to nearby antique shops, gallery, and museum.

Host: Stephen T. Jacques
Rooms: 16 (PB) $55-125
Continental Breakfast
Credit Cards: A, B
Notes: 2, 3, 4, 5, 7, 8, 9, 10, 11, 12, 14

Merry Sherwood Plantation

8909 Worchester Highway, 21811
(410) 641-2112

Merry Sherwood Plantation, circa 1859, was listed on the National Register of Historic Places in 1991. A wonderful blend of Greek Revival, Classic Italianate, and Gothic architecture, this elegant 27 room mansion has Victorian-style, nine fireplaces, private baths, ballroom, 19 acres of 19th-century landscaping, and authentic period antiques. We are convenient to Ocean City and many historic and resort attractions.

Hosts: Kurk Burbage and Emily Farrand
Rooms: 8 (6 PB; 2 SB)
Full Breakfast
Credit Cards: A, B
Notes: 2, 5, 89, 10, 11, 12, 13, 14

The Traveller In Maryland # 171

P. O. Box 2277, Annapolis, 21404
(301) 269-6232

Built in 1895, this restored Victorian is located in the heart of Berlin's historic district. Antique shops and museums are within easy walking distance. Ocean City and Assateague National Seashore are just eight miles away. A four-star restaurant and piano lounge are on-site. $60-108.

BETTERTON

Amanda's Bed and Breakfast #162

1428 Park Avenue, Annapolis, 21217
(410) 225-0001; (410) 383-1274

The mouth of the Sassafras River and the headwaters of the Chesapeake Bay open up to this restored 1904 Victorian inn in the resort town of Betterton. Situated in the heart of goose and duck hunting country, this inn is one block from the beach, biking, boating, and wildlife refuges. Full breakfast. Seven rooms (PB and SB). $60-85.

Lantern Inn

115 Ericson Avenue, 21610
(410) 348-5809

A restored 1904 inn in a quiet town on Maryland's Eastern Shore. One and one-half blocks to a nice sand beach on Chesapeake Bay. Near historic Chestertown, hiking trails, three wildlife refuges. Miles of excellent hiking roads. Antiquing and good seafood restaurants abound.

Hosts: Ken and Ann Washburn
Rooms: 7 (2 PB; 5 SB) $65-80
Full Breakfast
Credit Cards: A, B, D
Notes: 2, 5, 9, 10, 11, 14

Merry Sherwood Plantation

BUCKEYSTOWN

The Inn at Buckeystown

3521 Buckeystown Pike, 21717
(301) 874-5755; (800) 272-1190

An award-winning full-service country inn, we occupy an 1897 Victorian mansion and an 1884 Gothic church in the heart of a village listed on the National Register of Historic Places. Period antiques and arts and crafts abound in this area. Opened in 1981, we are noted for food, hospitality, and luxury. Sixty to 70 percent of our guests are repeats, holidays and the changing seasons are celebrated with gusto, and meals are always special occasions.

Hosts: Daniel R. Pelz, Chase Barnett, Rebecca E. Shipman-Smith
Rooms: 7 (PB) $167-272
Full Breakfast and Dinner
Credit Cards: A, B, C
Notes: 2, 4, 5, 7, 9, 14

BURTONSVILLE

Amanda's Bed and Breakfast #176

1428 Park Avenue, Annapolis, 21217
(410) 225-0001; (410) 383-1274

The contemporary charm of the guest house features an airy living/dining area highlighted by a yellow pine interior, cathedral ceilings and an expansive picture window with a spectacular view. Join in the harmony of nature and hospitality. Two queen (PB). King suite (PB). $75-105.

The Traveller In Maryland # 189

P. O. Box 2277, 21404
(301) 269-6232

The contemporary charm of the guest house features an airy living/dining area highlighted by a yellow pine interior, cathedral ceilings and an expansive picture window offering an uninterrupted view of the natural surroundings. Guests can enjoy sunny mornings on the outdoor deck, afternoon tea in the greenhouse, or cool nights by the fireplace. Each of its two guest rooms has access to a private bath and is furnished with a unique sleep system that allows guests to achieve their own comfort level. Come enjoy life on a working horse farm and equestrian center, tour the 18th-century log cabin with herb and flower gardens—a local historic landmark, stroll along the miles of wooded trails bordering the Rocky Gorge reservoir, and get a glimpse of the deer, waterfowl and other natural wildlife occupying more than 1,000 acres of adjacent wooded watershed. Full breakfast is served in this non-smoking environment. $105.

CAMBRIDGE

Amanda's Bed and Breakfast #173

1428 Park Avenue, Annapolis, 21217
(410) 225-0001; (410) 383-1274

In the middle of 27 acres, this lovely old estate on Todd Creek has access to the Choptank River and a beautiful view towards Oxford. Features include a large pool room, grand piano, and a grand room with fireplace. Continental breakfast is served in a simulated "sidewalk cafe." Swimming pool. Three rooms (PB). $70-95.

Amanda's Bed and Breakfast #192

1428 Park Avenue, Annapolis, 21217
(410) 225-0001; (410) 383-1274

Three-story brick-and-clapboard with high ceilings, six fireplaces, mahogany stair rails and deep, old-fashioned window seats are

6 Pets welcome; 7 Smoking allowed; 8 Children welcome; 9 Social drinking allowed; 10 Tennis available; 11 Swimming available; 12 Golf available; 13 Skiing available; 14 May be booked through travel agents.

but a few of the features of this historic inn that faces the water. Other attractions include Palladian windows, Oriental rugs, and 18th-century reproductions. Fine seafood restaurants are nearby. Continental breakfast. Eight rooms (PB and SB). $90 and up.

Lodgecliffe

103 Choptank Terrace, 21613
(301) 228-1760

Relax at a country home just a mile from the city limits of Cambridge and the Eastern Shore of Chesapeake Bay. Bedrooms with twin beds facing the Choptank River only 50 feet away. One large room facing the driveway. Both are furnished with heirloom antiques. Large continental breakfasts served in dining room facing the river. Old Trinity Church, Blackwater Wildlife Refuge, other scenic places, and fine restaurants nearby.

Host: Sarah Richardson
Rooms: 2 (SB) $70
Continental Breakfast
Credit Cards: None
Notes: 2, 5, 6, 7, 8, 9, 12

Sarke Plantation Inn

6033 Todd Point Road, 21613
(410) 228-7020

An Eastern Shore waterfront property of 27 country acres with a spacious house that is furnished tastefully with many antiques. There is a large pool room with a regulation table, and the livingroom has a large fireplace, a good stereo system, and a grand piano for your enjoyment.

Host: Genevieve Finley
Rooms: 5 (3 PB; 2 SB) $50-90
Continental Breakfast
Credit Cards: A, B, C
Closed New Year's Eve
Notes: 2, 5, 6, 7, 8 (over 10), 9, 11

CASCADE

Amanda's Bed and Breakfast #261

1428 Park Avenue, Annapolis, 21217
(410) 225-0001; (410) 383-1274

Visit the Blue Ridge Summit and cascade, the undiscovered summer hideaway. Explore Gettysburg or Frederick, ski, or hike. This elegant 1900 manor house on the Mason Dixon line offers gracious old-fashioned porches, luxury, and beauty. Four rooms available. Fireplace. Jacuzzi. $95-115.

CENTREVILLE

Amanda's Bed and Breakfast #280

1428 Park Avenue, Annapolis, 21217
(410) 225-0001; (410) 383-1274

The Centerville Male Academy, built in 1804, is one of the oldest schoolhouses in the state of Maryland. It has been transformed into a charming bed and breakfast with 17th- and 18th-century antiques and paintings throughout. Two rooms available. Private baths. Continental Breakfast.

CHESAPEAKE CITY

Amanda's Bed and Breakfast #269

1428 Park Avenue, Annapolis, 21217
(410) 225-0001; (410) 383-1274

This large Victorian, built in 1868, is in the historic district and offers views of the canal from inside and outside the house. Architectural details are original, and the house is furnished with antiques. Shops and restaurants are within walking distance. Six rooms, all with private baths, are available. Continental breakfast. $85.

NOTES: Credit cards accepted: A Master Card; B Visa; C American Express; D Discover Card; E Diner's Club; F Other; 2 Personal Checks accepted; 3 Lunch available; 4 Dinner available; 5 Open all year;

Inn at the Canal

104 Bohemia Avenue, P. O. Box 187, 21915
(410) 885-5995

This elegant 1870 Victorian inn sits in the midst of the quaint historical district on the banks of the busy Chesapeake and Delaware Canal. Private baths, six antique-filled rooms, a full breakfast, and some of the best ocean-going and pleasure boat watching are all to be found at the inn.

Hosts: Mary and Al Ioppolo
Rooms: 6 (PB) $70-105
Full Breakfast
Credit Cards: A, B, C, D
Notes: 2, 5, 9, 14

CHESTERTOWN

Amanda's Bed and Breakfast #136

1428 Park Avenue, Annapolis, 21217
(410) 225-0001; (410) 383-1274

The inn sits on the Chester River, four miles below town. The original part of the house was built in the 1830s and was completely renovated prior to its opening as inn in 1985. Five acres of waterfront make up the grounds, and a marina offers deep-water slips. Five rooms, all with private baths, are available. Continental breakfast. $85-115.

Amanda's Bed and Breakfast #152

1428 Park Avenue, Annapolis, 21217
(410) 225-0001; (410) 383-1274

This large 1725 brick house is one-half mile from Colonial Chestertown on a small estate that has some interesting plantings, among them a century-old boxwood. The 1725 brick house features a unique spiral staircase rising from a large center hallway to the third floor. Two rooms with double beds and private baths are available. Full breakfast. $70.

Amanda's Bed and Breakfast #204

1428 Park Avenue, Annapolis, 21217
(410) 225-0001; (410) 383-1274

This Victorian inn was built in 1877 and is located in the heart of town. Restored to its original charm, the dining room and double parlor feature plaster moldings. Walk to historic Washington College and shops. Five rooms, all with private baths, are available. Continental breakfast. $75.

Amanda's Bed and Breakfast #205

1428 Park Avenue, Annapolis, 21217
(410) 225-0001; (410) 383-1274

This waterfront Georgian manor is situated at the mouth of the Fairlee Creek on Chesapeake Bay. Stroll through twelve acres of landscaped grounds, or enjoy a private sandy beach for swimming and rafting. Tennis courts, golf available, dinner available. 25 rooms. Private bath. $125.

The Inn at Mitchell House

Rural Delivery 2, Box 329, 21620
(301) 778-6500

Nestled on ten rolling acres, surrounded by woods and overlooking a pond, this historic manor house, built in 1743, greets you with warmth and affords a touch of tranquility. A mere half-mile from the Chesapeake, this six-bedroom inn, with parlors and numerous fireplaces, provides a casual, friendly atmosphere.

Hosts: Jim and Tracy Stone
Rooms: 5 (PB) $75-95
Full Breakfast
Credit Cards: A, B
Notes: 2, 4, 5, 7, 8, 9, 10, 11, 12

6 Pets welcome; 7 Smoking allowed; 8 Children welcome; 9 Social drinking allowed; 10 Tennis available; 11 Swimming available; 12 Golf available; 13 Skiing available; 14 May be booked through travel agents.

The River Inn at Rolph's Wharf

Route 1, Box 646, Rolph's Wharf Road, 21620
(410) 778-6347

The River Inn is an 1830s Victorian inn situated on the scenic Chester River just three miles south of Chestertown, Maryland. All guest rooms have private baths and a view of the river. Light breakfast is served with fresh squeezed orange juice, and a restaurant is on premises for lunch or dinner. We also have a boat ramp, ice, bait, and swimming. Our sandy beach is terrific!

Rooms: 6 (PB), $65-115
Continental Breakfast
Credit Cards: A, B, C
Notes: 2, 3, 4, 5, 7, 8, 9, 11

The White Swan Tavern

231 High Street, 21620
(301) 778-2300

The White Swan has been a landmark in Chestertown since pre-Revolutionary War days. A quiet, elegant place nestled on Maryland's Eastern Shore, with a history that goes back to before 1733, it was returned to its original purpose in 1978: "A comfortable tavern or Public House...situated in the center of business...with every attention given to render comfort and pleasure to such as favor it with their patronage."

Host: Mary Susan Maisel
Rooms: 6 (PB) $85-135
Continental Breakfast
Credit Cards: None
Notes: 2, 7, 8, 9, 10, 11, 12

Widow's Walk Inn

402 High Street, 21620
(301) 778-6455; (301) 778-6864

Restored Victorian home circa 1877 in the historic district. Elegant decorations throughout the home. In the heart of the Eastern Shore of Maryland, famous for crabs and geese. Only one and one-half hour from Washington, Baltimore, Philadelphia. Everyone's dream of old-time family warmth and charm.

Hosts: Don and Joanne Toft
Rooms: 5 (3 PB; 2 SB) $75-95
Continental Breakfast
Credit Cards: F
Notes: 2, 5, 9

CHEVY CHASE

Amanda's Bed and Breakfast #222

1428 Park Avenue, Annapolis, 21217
(410) 225-0001; (410) 383-1274

Charming beamed ceilings, and furnishings from around the world make the charming turn-of-the-century house and garden a perfect place to stay. The decor is an eclectic blend of country charm and foreign culture, and gracious hospitality makes this a relaxed setting while guests enjoy visiting the Washington area. Two rooms, one with a king bed and one with a double, offer private baths. Continental breakfast. $65.

Chevy Chase Bed and Breakfast

6815 Connecticut Avenue, 20815
(301) 656-5867

Enjoy gracious hospitality and the convenience of being close to the sights of Washington, D.C., in a charming beamed-ceiling, turn-of-the-century house and garden in historic Chevy Chase. Furnished with rare tapestries, Oriental rugs, and native crafts from around the world. Special breakfasts of homemade breads, jams, and coffee.

Host: S. C. Gotbaum
Rooms: Single (PB) $50-55; Double (PB) $60-65
Continental Breakfast
Credit Cards: None
Notes: 2, 5, 8, 10, 11, 12

NOTES: Credit cards accepted: A Master Card; B Visa; C American Express; D Discover Card; E Diner's Club; F Other; 2 Personal Checks accepted; 3 Lunch available; 4 Dinner available; 5 Open all year;

CRISFIELD

Amanda's Bed and Breakfast #256

1428 Park Avenue, Annapolis, 21217
(410) 225-0001; (410) 383-1274

The Southeastern Shore is low, flat, and sandy, covered with evergreens and fertile farmland. A region of the tidal creeks, vast wetlands, and wildlife refuges offers picturesque views along the Chesapeake. Two rooms share a bath, and continental breakfast is served. $50.

CUMBERLAND

Amanda's Bed and Breakfast #144

1428 Park Avenue, Annapolis, 21217
(410) 225-0001; (410) 383-1274

Family antiques, four Siamese cats, a screened-in porch, fireplaces in the family room and livingroom, a grand piano, and an antique black glass collection make your stay at this bed and breakfast interesting and fun. Located near historic sites, the Western Mountains, downtown, and steam locomotive. This bed and breakfast offers three guest rooms that share a bath. Full breakfast. $55.

Amanda's Bed and Breakfast #178

1428 Park Avenue, Annapolis, 21217
(410) 225-0001; (410) 383-1274

This 1820s Federal-style building offers a friendly parlor for guests to enjoy and a great TV/game room. Near the Alleghany Central Steam Railroad, the Cumberland Summer Theatre, the Cumberland Historic District, the History House Museum, and C&O Canal, this inn offers twelve guest rooms with both private and shared baths. Full breakfast. $70-80.

Inn at Walnut Bottom

120 Greene Street, 21502
(301) 777-0003

Traditional country inn bed and breakfast in the city of Cumberland, Maryland. Twelve guest rooms—suites, 2 parlors, TV room, private parking are all available to guests. Full breakfast served with overnight lodging. Arthur's Restaurant serves traditional country inn food made from scratch. 1815/1890 buildings, beautifully refurbished, furnished in antiques, and reproductions. Central air conditioning.

Host: Sharon Ennis Kazary
Rooms: 12 (7 PB; 5 SB) $60-85
Full Breakfast
Credit Cards: A, B, C, D
Notes: 3, 4, 5, 8, 14

EASTON

Amanda's Bed and Breakfast #118

1428 Park Avenue, Annapolis, 21217
(410) 225-0001; (410) 383-1274

This charming 1890 Victorian bed and breakfast is registered in the historic section of Easton, the Colonial capital of Maryland's Eastern Shore. Within walking distance of historical points of interest, restaurants, and antique shops, this inn has a wraparound porch offers seven guest rooms, all with private baths. Continental breakfast. $75-85.

Ashby 1663

27448 Ashby Drive, 21601
(410) 822-4235

This magnificent Colonial mansion is on the Miles River of Maryland's Eastern Shore. The estate features a heated swimming pool with a spa, lighted tennis court, exercise room with a tanning bed, canoe, jogging and bicycling path, volleyball, croquet, and badminton. The waterfront towns of Oxford and St. Michael's are within a few minutes' drive. Guests may secure their craft at the dock, which provides a six-foot MLW depth. Easton Airport is a five-minute drive for visitors arriving by air.

Hosts: Cliff Meredith and Jeanie Wagner
Rooms: 4 (PB) $250-575
Full Breakfast
Credit Cards: A, B
Notes: 2, 5, 9, 10, 12

The Bishop's House Bed and Breakfast

214 Goldsborough Street, P. O. Box 2217, 21601
(410) 820-7290

Circa 1880 Victorian in Easton's Historic District. Romantically furnished in period-style, accommodations include individually controlled air conditioning, working fireplaces, private off-street parking, secured overnight storage for bicycles, route maps for cycling in Talbot County, and hot, hearty breakfasts. Prearranged transportation to and from local marinas and Easton Airport provided at no extra charge. Spacious first-floor meeting rooms available for business meetings and private social functions.

Hosts: Diane M. Laird-Ippolito and john B. Ippololito
Rooms: 7 (2 PB; 5 SB) $75-120
Full Breakfast
Notes: 2, 5, 14

The McDaniel House

14 North Aurora Street, 21601
(410) 822-3704

Built circa 1890, the McDaniel House is a three-story, centrally air conditioned resi-

dence with a high octagonal tower and a large wraparound porch. The seven bedrooms are airy and attractive. Five have private baths. A substantial continental breakfast is served 8: 00-10: 00 A.M. Guests who have early business appointments may eat as early as they wish. Located within walking distance of theater, restaurants, and shops. There is off-street parking.

Hosts: Dan and Mary McWilliams
Rooms: 7 (5 PB; 2 SB) $55-75; $60-80 Fri.-Sat.
Expanded Continental Breakfast
Credit Cards: A, B, C
Notes: 2, 5, 8, 9, 14

EDGEWATER

Amanda's Bed and Breakfast #187

1428 Park Avenue, Annapolis, 21217
(410) 225-0001; (410) 383-1274

This contemporary waterfront home is ten minutes from Annapolis and can accommodate a group of four or six. Oriental and European antiques furnish this home, and guests have use of a private sitting room and terrace. Rowboat available for guests to use. Two rooms with private baths. Continental breakfast. $75.

Amanda's Bed and Breakfast #194

1428 Park Avenue, Annapolis, 21217
(410) 225-0001; (410) 383-1274

From subtle sunrises to fiery sunsets, the view from this riverfront, two-story house are spectacular! Furnished in contemporary and oriental themes. Guests are welcome to use the pool, hot tub, boat dock, and waterfront balcony. This bed and breakfast is a luxurious and serene retreat for visitors from Annapolis. Two rooms, both with private baths and one with a waterfront view, are available. Continental breakfast.

ELKTON

The Garden Cottage

234 Blair Shore Road, 21921
(410) 398-5566

In a setting with an early plantation house, including a 400-year-old sycamore, the garden cottage nestles at the edge of a meadow flanked by herb gardens and an old barn with gift shop. It has a sitting room with working fireplace, bedroom, and bath. Freshly ground coffee and herbal teas are offered with the full country breakfast. Longwood Gardens and Winterthur Museum are 50 minutes away. Historic Chesapeake City is seven minutes away.

Hosts: Bill and Ann Stubbs
Cottage: 1 (PB) $85
Full Breakfast
Credit Cards: A, B
Notes: 2, 5, 8, 9, 14

ELLICOTT CITY

Amanda's Bed and Breakfast #159

1428 Park Avenue, Annapolis, 21217
(410) 225-0001; (410) 383-1274

This early 19th-century stone farmhouse is minutes from the historic mill town, Ellicott City. It features a grand parlor with a fireplace and a music room that is decorated in antiques and reproduction pieces. Between Washington, DC, and Baltimore, and 45 minutes from Annapolis. Four rooms with both shared and private baths. Fireplace. $70-90.

The Wayside Inn

4344 Columbia Road, 21042
(410) 461-4636

The Wayside Inn is a stately Federal-period stone farmhouse situated on two acres with a pond, near the historic mill town of Ellicott City. The inn, built between 1800 and 1850, continues the tradition of a lighted candle in each window indicating availability of rooms. It has two suites with private baths; two rooms with working fireplaces, shared baths. Air conditioning, antiques, and reproduction pieces. Convenient to historic Ellicott City, Columbia, Baltimore. Short commute to Annapolis and Washington, DC.

Hosts: Margo and John Osantowski
Rooms: 4 (2 PB; 2 SB) $70-90
Continental Breakfast
Credit Cards: A, B, C
Notes: 14

FALLSTON

Amanda's Bed and Breakfast #174

1428 Park Avenue, Annapolis, 21217
(410) 225-0001; (410) 383-1274

In the heart of Maryland's "hunt" country on forty acres, this new Georgian-style house offers a pool and beautiful gardens for guests to enjoy. Wind down from a busy day by relaxing on our shady trellised patio overlooking the pond. Nice location for weddings. Five rooms available. Private and shared baths. Continental breakfast. $70-85.

FREDERICK

Amanda's Bed and Breakfast #106

1428 Park Avenue, Annapolis, 21217
(410) 225-0001; (410) 383-1274

This inn's 26-acre grounds include a picturesque garden and hen house. Each room offers a delightful 19th-century ambience, and all rooms have private baths and air conditioning. A stone fireplace, stained glass, windows, and skylights highlight the keeping room where guests can relax.

Three rooms, all of which have private baths, are available. Continental breakfast. $85.

Amanda's Bed and Breakfast #244

1428 Park Avenue, Annapolis, 21217
(410) 225-0001; (410) 383-1274

This historic three-story mansion is located in Frederick's courthouse square district. It features spacious rooms with elegant interior woodwork and a majestic winding staircase. Furnished with period antiques, this bed and breakfast offers six guest rooms, all with private baths. Continental breakfast. $90-125.

Middle Plantation Inn

9549 Liberty Road, 21701
(301) 898-7128

A rustic bed and breakfast built of stone and log. Drive through horse country to the village of Mount Pleasant. Several miles east of Frederick, on 26 acres. Each room has furnishings of antiques, with private bath, air conditioning, and TV. Nearby are antique shops, museums, and many historic attractions.

Hosts: Shirley and Dwight Mullican
Rooms: 3 (PB) $85-95
Continental Breakfast
Credit Cards: None
Notes: 2, 5, 8 (over 14), 9, 10, 11, 12, 14

Spring Bank, A Bed and Breakfast Inn

7945 Worman's Mill Road, 21701
(301) 694-0440

Built in 1880 and listed on the National Register of Historic Places, this 16-room country house is filled with antiques. Six spacious guest rooms, parlor with fireplace, and library of early books on Maryland history. Situated on ten acres of lawn, walking paths, and crop land. Frederick's charming historic district, with its excellent restaurants, is within a ten-minute drive.Whitetail and Ski Liberty are within a 40 minutes drive.

Hosts: Beverly and Ray Compton
Rooms: 6 (1 PB; 5 S2.5B) $70-85
Continental Breakfast
Credit Cards: A, B, C, D
Notes: 2, 5, 9, 10, 11, 12, 13 (within 40 minutes), 14

Turning Point Inn

3406 Urbana Pike, 21701
(301) 874-2421

Turning Point Inn is an 1910 Edwardian estate home with Georgian features. Less than an hour from the Washington, D.C., Baltimore, Gettysburg, and Antietam, this inn is situated for getaway weekends of sightseeing, shopping, antiquing, hiking, or exploring historic towns and battlefields.

Hosts: Charlie and Suzanne Seymour
Rooms: 5 (PB) $75-85
Full Breakfast
Credit Cards: A, B
Notes: 2, 3 (Tues.-Fri.), 4 (Tues.-Sun.), 5, 7 (limited), 8, 9, 10, 11, 12

GAITHERSBURG

Amanda's Bed and Breakfast #120

1428 Park Avenue, Annapolis, 21217
(410) 225-0001; (410) 383-1274

This is a comfortable luxury home in a planned community, with ample parking, a large screened-in porch, close proximity to restaurants and Washington, DC. Two rooms, both with private baths, are available for guests. Full breakfast. $60-100.

Gaithersburg Hospitality Bed and Breakfast

18908 Chimney Place, 20879
(301) 977-7377

In Montgomery Village near restaurants, shopping, and recreation, this luxury home is ideally situated in a residential neighborhood, offers all amenities, and is a thirty-minute ride to Washington, DC, via the car or Metro. It is conveniently near I-270 for a drive north to Harper's Ferry, Gettysburg, and Antietam. Hosts delight in catering to your travel needs with home cooking and spacious cozy comfort.

Hosts: Joe and Suzanne Danilowicz
Doubles: (PB) $50
Singles: (PB) $40
Full Breakfast
Credit Cards: None
Notes: 2, 8, 10, 11, 12, 14

The Traveller In Maryland # 183

P. O. Box 2277, Annapolis, 21404
(301) 269-6232

Two-story brick contemporary home near community lake. Residential streets provide quiet walks. Ten minutes to Metro stop. Restaurants nearby. Beautifully furnished, this bed and breakfast has two rooms with double beds and private baths. Full breakfast served. Screened porch overlooks nicely landscaped yards; TV, laundry facilities. Also, a large, sunny third room with twin beds. $55.

Beaver Creek House

HAGERSTOWN

Amanda's Bed and Breakfast #184

1428 Park Avenue, Annapolis, 21217
(410) 225-0001; (410) 383-1274

This 125-acre farm is set in a peaceful, quiet countryside five minutes from I-81 and I-70 and four miles from Hagerstown. Near Antietam, Harpers Ferry, C&O Canal, Gettysburg, bike trails, antique shops, outlet malls, and the Appalachian Trail, this bed and breakfast offers six rooms with both private and shared baths. Full breakfast. $55-75.

Beaver Creek House

Beaver Creek Road, 21740
(301) 787-4764

A turn-of-the-century country home filled with family antiques and memorabilia. Five guest rooms are available. A full country breakfast is served on the screened porch or elegantly decorated dining room. The parlor with fireplace is the setting for afternoon tea. A sitting room has reading material of local interest. Guests can enjoy a country garden with fishpond and fountain. Visiting historic sites, hiking, biking, golf, and antiquing are popular recreational pursuits.

Hosts: Don and Shirley Day
Rooms: 5 (3 PB; 2 SB) $75-85
Full Breakfast
Credit Cards: A, B
Notes: 2, 5, 9, 11, 12, 13, 14

Lewrene Farm Bed and Breakfast

Rural Delivery 3, Box 150
Downsville Pike, 21740
(301) 582-1735

6 Pets welcome; 7 Smoking allowed; 8 Children welcome; 9 Social drinking allowed; 10 Tennis available; 11 Swimming available; 12 Golf available; 13 Skiing available; 14 May be booked through travel agents.

Spacious colonial country farm home near I-70 and I-81. Large livingroom, fireplace, piano, antique family heirlooms. Deluxe bedrooms with canopy poster beds and other antique beds. Bedside snacks, shared and private baths, one of which has a whirlpool. Full breakfast. Home away from home for tourists, business people, families. Children welcome. Peacocks, old-fashioned swing, gazebo. Quilts for sale. Antietam battlefield, Harper's Ferry, C&O Canal, and antique malls nearby. Washington and Baltimore—70 miles away.

Hosts: Lewis and Irene Lehman
Rooms: 6 (3 PB; 3 SB) $50-80
Full Breakfast
Credit Cards: None
Notes: 2, 5, 8, 10, 11, 12, 13

HANOVER

Amanda's Bed and Breakfast #154

1428 Park Avenue, Annapolis, 21217
(410) 225-0001; (410) 383-1274

The "Woods of Love" is a large new house located in the woods. The front faces south and is a passive solar. The house has a sunken great room, huge kitchen, game room, greenhouse, a racquet ball court, and fruit trees. A one-room suite with a pair of twin beds and private bath is available. Full breakfast. $75.

HARWOOD

Amanda's Bed and Breakfast #151

1428 Park Avenue, Annapolis, 21217
(410) 225-0001; (410) 383-1274

An elegant early-19th-century manor house, circa 1840, is surrounded by lawns, terraced gardens, and shaded by towering

poplar, hickory, and maple trees on seven acres. Furnished with antiques and a blaze of color in the spring, with daffodils, irises, and forsythia, this bed and breakfast offers two rooms that share a bath. Continental breakfast. $60-65.

Amanda's Bed and Breakfast #158

1428 Park Avenue, Annapolis, 21217
(410) 225-0001; (410) 383-1274

This guest room has a balcony that overlooks a working farm. Ample parking area for a boat trailer or camper. Two rooms share a bath. Continental breakfast. $60.

HAVRE DE GRACE

Amanda's Bed and Breakfast #207

1428 Park Avenue, Annapolis, 21217
(410) 225-0001; (410) 383-1274

Turn-of-the-century charm and Victorian hospitality characterize this historic Victorian inn. Enjoy tastefully appointed rooms, fireplaces, and culinary delights. The inn is surrounded by historic sites and full-service marinas. Experience gracious Maryland living, Chesapeake Bay style. Eight rooms, all with private baths, are available. Full breakfast. $65-95.

LUTHERVILLE

Amanda's Bed and Breakfast #128

1428 Park Avenue, Annapolis, 21217
(410) 225-0001; (410) 383-1274

Serene elegance surrounds this romantic Victorian mansion. Each room is decorated in a different theme from the owner's

NOTES: Credit cards accepted: A Master Card; B Visa; C American Express; D Discover Card; E Diner's Club; F Other; 2 Personal Checks accepted; 3 Lunch available; 4 Dinner available; 5 Open all year;

favorite places. Charming and spacious with a lavish breakfast. Seven rooms, five with private baths; two share a bath. Full breakfast. $85-95.

MONKTON

Amanda's Bed and Breakfast #209

1428 Park Avenue, Annapolis, 21217
(410) 225-0001; (410) 383-1274

Warm hospitality and exceptional accommodations are offered on this working farm. Pond with fishing privileges (catch and throw back), bike and hike trails, and tubing on gunpowder river. Located near North Central Railroad, Ladew Gardens, and Amish Country. One room is offered to guests and it features a private bath. Continental breakfast. $85.

MT. SAVAGE

Amanda's Bed and Breakfast #243

1428 Park Avenue, Annapolis, 21217
(410) 225-0001; (410) 383-1274

This castle is a Gothic estate with Old World atmosphere. Guests enjoy themselves at this romantic hideaway with antique beauty and graceful style that complement the scenic Western Maryland Mountains setting. Six rooms with both shared and private baths are available. Full breakfast. $75-125.

NEW MARKET

National Pike Inn

9 West Main Street, Box 299, 21774
(301) 865-5055

The National Pike Inn offers four air conditioned guest rooms, each decorated in a different theme. Private baths are available, and our large Federal sitting room is available for guests to use. Our private enclosed courtyard is perfect for a quiet retreat outdoors. New Market, founded in 1793, offers over thirty specialized antique shops, all in historic homes along Main Street. An Old Fashioned General Store is everyone's favorite, and Mealey's, well known for dining excellence, is a few steps away.

Hosts: Tom and Terry Rimel
Rooms: 4 (2 PB; 2 SB) $75-100
Full Breakfast
Credit Cards: A, B
Notes: 2, 5, 8 (over 10), 10, 12, 13

Strawberry Inn

17 West Main Street, 21774
(301) 865-3318

A professionally run bed and breakfast serving our guests for 17 years. Innkeepers Jane and Ed are here to greet you and be sure your stay is a pleasant one. The 1837 restored Maryland farmhouse has five antique-furnished guest rooms, each with modern private bath. First floor has easy access for handicapped. Excellent dining at Mealey's across the street. On the grounds away from all inn activity is a restored log building with facilities for small business meetings. Send for brochure.

Hosts: Jane and Ed Rossig
Rooms: 5 (PB) $75-95
Continental Breakfast
Credit Cards: None
Notes: 2, 5, 7, 9, 10, 11, 12

NORTH EAST

Amanda's Bed and Breakfast #123

1428 Park Avenue, Annapolis, 21217
(410) 225-0001; (410) 383-1274

This bed and breakfast is really two houses; one was built for a miller, and the other one for a mill owner. Built in 1710, the house is furnished with antiques, and guests are welcome to relax in the parlor or stroll through the grounds close to Elk Neck State Park. Two rooms share a bath. Full breakfast. $65.

The Mill House Bed and Breakfast

102 Mill Lane, 21901
(410) 287-3532

The circa 1710 Mill House is furnished with antiques and waiting for your enjoyment. The extensive grounds include the mill ruins, a tidal marsh with a variety of wildflowers, and the lawn down to the North East Creek. North East has five antique shops and the Upper Bay Museum in the waterfront town park. A full breakfast with homemade hot breads is included.

Hosts: Lucia and Nick Demond
Rooms: 2 (SB) $55-65
Full Breakfast
Credit Cards: A, B
Notes: 2, 5, 9, 14

OAKLAND

The Oak and Apple Bed and Breakfast

208 North Second Street, 21550
(301) 334-9265

Built prior to 1920, this restored Colonial Revival sits on a beautiful large lawn with mature trees and includes a large, columned front porch, enclosed sun porch, livingroom with fireplace, and cozy music room with television. Awaken to a fresh continental breakfast served fireside in the dining room or on the sun porch. The quaint town of Oakland offers a wonderful small-town atmosphere, and Deep Creek Lake, Wisp Ski Resort, and state parks with

hiking, fishing, swimming, boating, and skiing are nearby.

Hosts: Jana and Ed Kight
Rooms: 4 (2 PB; 2 SB) $70
Continental Breakfast
Credit Cards: A, B
Notes: 2, 5, 9, 10, 11, 12, 13, 14

Red Run Inn

Route 5, Box 268, 21550
(301) 387-6606

Nestled in a natural wooded setting, Red Run overlooks the expansive blue waters of Deep Creek Lake. On 18 acres, with a large swimming pool, two tennis courts, cross-country ski trail, horseshoe pits, and dock facilities.

Host: Ruth M. Umbel
Rooms: 6 (PB) $65-100
Continental Breakfast
Credit Cards: A, B, C, D
Notes: 2, 3, 4, 5, 7, 8, 9, 10, 11, 12, 13, 14

OLNEY

Amanda's Bed and Breakfast #134

1428 Park Avenue, Annapolis, 21217
(410) 225-0001; (410) 383-1274

The quiet charm of this 170-acre thoroughbred horse ranch on a sprawling countryside twelve miles from Washington, DC, allows you to relax and enjoy pleasant walks, a swim, or just reading in the comfortable sitting room. An interesting stay for guests, this bed and breakfast offers nine rooms with both private and shared baths. Full breakfast. $60-85.

Thoroughbred Bed and Breakfast

16410 Batchellor's Forest Road, 20832
(301) 774-7649

NOTES: Credit cards accepted: A Master Card; B Visa; C American Express; D Discover Card; E Diner's Club; F Other; 2 Personal Checks accepted; 3 Lunch available; 4 Dinner available; 5 Open all year;

This is a beautiful 175-acre estate. Many fine racehorses were raised here. Full breakfast is served. In addition, there is a hot tub, swimming pool, pool table, and piano all available to guests. Guests may choose to stay in the main house or the quaint renovated 1900 farmhouse with whirlpool tubs. Just six miles from Metro and 12 miles from Washington, D.C.

Host: Helen M. Polinger
Rooms: 9 (3 PB; 6 SB) $60-85
Full Breakfast
Credit Cards: A, B
Notes: 2, 10, 11, 12, 14

The Traveller In Maryland # 191

P. O. Box 2277, Annapolis, 21404
(301) 269-6232

Nestled on seven acres of wooded land, this Georgian Colonial, parts of which date back to the early 20th century, offers a high degree of privacy and serenity. It is surrounded by large beech, oak, and hickory trees. Our four guest rooms are all decorated with antiques. A pond in the back and quiet gazebo offer a nice touch for a romantic getaway. Feel free to try the large indoor spa located in the solarium. A full breakfast is served in this non-smoking environment. $65-75.

OXFORD

Oxford Inn and Pope's Tavern

1 South Morris Street, 21654
(410) 226-5220

We welcome you to the historic seaport town of Oxford, Maryland, founded in 1683. The Inn offers a selection of clever, individually decorated rooms, as well as our three-star dining room where you can enjoy Chespeake Bay's famous seafood.

Stroll down one of the oldest streets in America and fill your sails with gusts of imagination.

Hosts: George, Susan, Rick and Sue Schmitt
Rooms: 11 (6 PB; 5 SB) $70-135
Continental Breakfast
Credit Cards: A, B
Notes: 2, 3, 4, 5, 7, 8, 9, 10, 12

1876 House

110 North Morris Street, P. O. Box 658, 21654
(410) 226-5496

A meticulously restored 19th-century Victorian home with ten-foot ceilings, wide-planked pine floors, Oriental carpeting, and Queen Anne reproduction furnishings. Decorated in the Williamsburg-style. Three guest accommodations in a quiet, relaxing atmosphere. A memorable breakfast in a formal dining room from 8: 00 to 9: 30 a.m. Oxford's only bed and breakfast—where guests come by choice, not by chance!

Hosts: Eleanor and Jerry Clark
Rooms: 3 (PB) $91-97
Expanded Continental Breakfast
Credit Cards: F
Notes: 2, 5, 7, 9, 10, 11, 12

PASADENA

Amanda's Bed and Breakfast #231

1428 Park Avenue, Annapolis, 21217
(410) 225-0001; (410) 383-1274

A lovely setting on the water, this waterfront community called Sunset Knoll is on 1 and 1/2 acres on the Magothy River about fifteen minutes from downtown Annapolis. Quiet and convenient to Annapolis, Washington DC, or Baltimore, two rooms, both of which have queen-size beds and private baths, are available for guests. Full breakfast. $85.

6 Pets welcome; 7 Smoking allowed; 8 Children welcome; 9 Social drinking allowed; 10 Tennis available; 11 Swimming available; 12 Golf available; 13 Skiing available; 14 May be booked through travel agents.

PHOENIX

Amanda's Bed and Breakfast #121

1428 Park Avenue, Annapolis, 21217
(410) 225-0001; (410) 383-1274

This unique post/beam home is set in the rolling countryside north of Baltimore. Comfortable rooms with antiques in a private wooded setting make this a special stay for guests. Continental breakfast. Private bath. $75.

POTOMAC

Amanda's Bed and Breakfast #198

1428 Park Avenue, Annapolis, 21217
(410) 225-0001; (410) 383-1274

Early American furnishings complement the charm of this forested, single-family dwelling located in Maryland's suburbs of Washington, D.C. Two rooms, both of which have a private bath, are available. Continental breakfast. $65.

PRINCE FREDERICK

Amanda's Bed and Breakfast #153

1428 Park Avenue, Annapolis, 21217
(410) 225-0001; (410) 383-1274

This century-old farmhouse with a wrap-around porch is in a country setting of fields, woods, and a view of the river. The private suite for guests includes a parlor and separate entrance. Located near Chesapeake Bay, Broomes Island, and Cypress Swamp. A full breakfast is served each morning. $60-70.

PRINCESS ANNE

Amanda's Bed and Breakfast #188

1428 Park Avenue, Annapolis, 21217
(410) 225-0001; (410) 383-1274

This authentically restored Federal-style home is on the National Historic Register and is on a 160-acre farm near the ocean and bay. Crabbing and oystering along a mile-long shoreline on the Manokin River is a popular activity for guests, and shallow draft boats are welcome. Four rooms, plus two cottages, are available for guests. Private baths. Full breakfast. $95-115.

Elmwood Bed and Breakfast

Locust Point Road, P. O. Box 220, 21853
(410) 651-1066

This historic manor house, circa 1770, has a wonderful setting on 160 acres of fields, woods, and lawn, with a mile of waterfront and a commanding view of of the Manokin River. The goal of the innkeepers is to surround their guests with the lifestyle of the nineteenth century.

Hosts: Helen and Steve Monick
Rooms: 4 (3 PB; 1 SB) $80-105
Full Breakfast
Credit Cards: A, B
Notes: 2, 5, 14

Elmwood Bed and Breakfast

QUEENSTOWN

Amanda's Bed and Breakfast #146

1428 Park Avenue, Annapolis, 21217
(410) 225-0001; (410) 383-1274

This bed and breakfast has been characterized as "an amazing hodge-podge of a converted telephone exchange merged with a private residence." Charming, comfortable, traditional, and conveniently located, this is a unique getaway specializing in relaxation, rejuvenation, and recreation. Your warm hospitable hosts offer five rooms with private baths for guests. Continental breakfast. $65.

Amanda's Bed and Breakfast #167

1428 Park Avenue, Annapolis, 21217
(410) 225-0001; (410) 383-1274

This bed and breakfast sits on a quiet harbor that becomes active in the afternoon with sail boats that come in for safe anchorage. Blue herons stalk the soft crabs along the creek bed. Breakfast is served overlooking the water, and we are close to outlet shopping, boating, and biking.

The House of Burgess'

Main Street, P. O. Box 269, 21658
(301) 827-6834; (301)827-7658

Charming, classic, traditional, and conveniently situated in small, quiet, Eastern Shore town. Warm, hospitable hosts. Central to Washington, D.C., Baltimore, Annapolis, Easton. Enjoy sights and sounds of Eastern Shore living while playing golf at Queenstown Harbor Golf Links; shop Chesapeake Village designer outlets, Queenstown Antique Center, The Pottery, and many more. Waterfront dining at numerous seafood restaurants. A unique getaway specializing in relaxation, rejuvenation, and repose!

Hosts: Pete and Helen Burgess
Rooms: 4 (PB) $65-70
Continental Breakfast
Credit Cards: None
Notes: 2, 5, 7, 8, 9, 10, 12, 14

The Traveller In Maryland # 173

P. O. Box 2277, Annapolis, 21404
(301) 269-6232

Located on Main Street in a quaint historic village, this home is conveniently accessible to Annapolis, Washington, Baltimore, Easton, Chestertown, and other areas of the Eastern Shore. Each of the four rooms is comfortably and tastefully decorated and includes private bath. A large family room is a spacious gathering place for guests to unwind and meet new acquaintances. It also opens onto the large screened porch overlooking flower gardens. Amenities include TV, reading/work area, off-set parking, and handicapped facilities. Continental breakfast is served in this non-smoking environment. $65-80.

The Traveller In Maryland # 175

P. O. Box 2277, Annapolis, 21404
(301) 269-6232

The "Cottage" is a gracious suite in a garden setting, with a spacious living-dining room with a view of your own fountain. Perhaps you would rather try the the "Carriage House" in its country setting. Awake refreshed to breakfst in the privacy of your own cottage. Ocean is easily accesible, and fishing, hunting, bird watching, biking, antique shopping, and Blackwater National Wildlife Refuge are nearby. No smoking please. $75-85. Weekly $450-517.

The Traveller In Maryland # 179

P. O. Box 2277, Annapolis, 21404
(301) 269-6232

Circa 1800, 50-acre waterfront farm offers the ultimate in peace and privacy. Comfortably restored Bay Hundred farmhouse and St. James Church (a property saved through historic preservation by the owners) offers the ambience and serenity of a waterman's retreat. Waterfowl and wildlife abound. Antiquing, boating, biking, bird watching, fine restaurants, and museums are but minutes away. Other features include French doors, deck, water views, private bath, marsh and creek. Continental breakfast is served in this non-smoking environment. $115.

The Traveller In Maryland # 181

P. O. Box 2277, Annapolis, 21404
(301) 269-6232

This charming Victorian home, circa 1890, is located in the center of the historic district of Easton. Easton is renowned as the Colonial capital of Maryland's Eastern Shore. The inn has a high octagonal tower, a hipped roof with dormers, both of which add some very interesting findings on the inside, and a southern wraparound porch for a relaxing afternoon or evening rest. Historic points and restaurants are within easy walking distance. Available for small meetings and seminars. Continental breakfast is served in this non-smoking environment. $60-70.

ROCK HALL

Amanda's Bed and Breakfast #203

1428 Park Avenue, Annapolis, 21217
(410) 225-0001; (410) 383-1274

This gracious waterfront manor house on 58.4 acres is one mile south of Rock Hall. Near the water, wildlife, and hunting, six rooms, all with private baths, are available in this quiet country setting. Continental breakfast. $75-145.

ST. MICHAELS

Amanda's Bed and Breakfast #245

1428 Park Avenue, Annapolis, 21217
(410) 225-0001; (410) 383-1274

This historic house, dating back to 1805 with period furnishings, working fireplaces, and four-poster canopy beds, is in an historic waterman's village on the Eastern Shore of the Chesapeake Bay. Within walking distance to shops, restaurants, and the museum, this inn offers seven rooms and one cottage with both private and shared baths. Continental breakfast. $55-85.

Kemp House Inn

412 Talbot Street, P. O. Box 637, 21663
(301) 745-2243

This fine Georgian home was built in 1805 by Col. Joseph Kemp, and Robert E. Lee was a guest here. Guests are welcomed into an atmosphere of eighteenth-century Maryland. Bedrooms have four-poster beds, some of which have trundle beds

NOTES: Credit cards accepted: A Master Card; B Visa; C American Express; D Discover Card; E Diner's Club; F Other; 2 Personal Checks accepted; 3 Lunch available; 4 Dinner available; 5 Open all year;

underneath. There are handmade quilts, old-fashioned tab curtains, nightshirts, and period furnishings, fireplaces, and candlelight. We are within walking distance of St. Michaels' quaint shops, antiques, restaurants, and the Chesapeake Bay Maritime Museum.

Hosts: Diane and Steve Cooper
Rooms: 8 (5 PB; 3 SB) $55-95
Continental Breakfast
Credit Cards: A, B, D
Notes: 2, 5, 7, 8, 9, 14

Parsonage Inn

210 North Talbot Street, Route 33, 21663
(301) 745-5519; (800) 234-5519

Late Victorian bed and breakfast, circa 1883, lavishly restored in 1985 with seven guest rooms, private baths, king or queen brass beds with Laura Ashley linens. Parlor and dining room in European tradition. Gourmet restaurant receiving rave reviews next door. Two blocks to Chesapeake Maritime Museum, shops, harbor. Fifteen percent off midweek for AARP or retired officers.

Hosts: David and Gina Hawkins
Rooms: 8 (PB) $82-108
Complete Gourmet Breakfast
Credit Cards: A, B
Notes: 2, 5, 8, 9, 10, 12

Two Swan Inn

Carpenter Street, 21663
(301) 745-2929

A comfortably restored 200-year-old country house on the harbor with old shade trees to the water's edge, quietly tucked away from the village two blocks away. Three rooms, each with view of the harbor, private bath, double occupancy, are attractively furnished in country antiques. There is a fireplace in the main livingroom and a small library. Breakfast is served before the fire or on the lawn. Enjoy the museum, shops, and local history.

Host: Mary Grimes
Rooms: 3 (PB) $100-115
Continental Breakfast
Credit Cards: A, B
Notes: 2, 5, 9, 10

Victoriana Inn

205 Cherry Street, P. O. Box 449, 21663
(301) 745-3368

The Victoriana Inn is on the harbor in the historic district of St. Michaels. From the porch view the famous Chesapeake Bay. The Maritime Museum is one-half block away. Shops and restaurants are all within walking distance. The house, built in 1883, offers gardens for quiet reflection in full view of the harbor. Decorated in period antique furniture. Air conditioning. Full country breakfast. Golden retriever named Vicki on premises.

Host: Janet Bernstein
Rooms: 5 (1 PB; 4 S2B) $95-135
Full Breakfast
Credit Cards: A, B
Notes: 2, 5, 7 (limited), 9, 10, 11, 12

Wades Point Inn on the Bay

P. O. Box 7, 21663
(301) 745-2500

On the Eastern Shore of Chesapeake Bay, this historic country inn is ideal for those seeking country serenity and bay splendor. The main hous, circa 1819, was built by a noted shipwright. From 1890 to the present the inn has provided a peaceful setting for relaxation and recreation such as fishing, crabbing, and a one-mile nature and jogging trail on 120 acres. Chesapeake Bay Maritime Museum, cruises, and sailing charters are nearby.

Hosts: Betsy and John Feiler
Rooms: 24 (14 PB; 10 SB) $65-165
Continental Breakfast
Credit Cards: A, B
Closed major winter holidays and Feb.
Notes: 2, 8, 9, 10, 11, 12

6 Pets welcome; 7 Smoking allowed; 8 Children welcome; 9 Social drinking allowed; 10 Tennis available; 11 Swimming available; 12 Golf available; 13 Skiing available; 14 May be booked through travel agents.

SALISBURY

Amanda's Bed and Breakfast #212

1428 Park Avenue, Annapolis, 21217
(410) 225-0001; (410) 383-1274

Retire to this Colonial home surrounded by five acres of red and white oak trees. Enjoy a breakfast overlooking a private lake. Beautifully decorated rooms with king, queen, or pair of twins share a bath. Continental breakfast. $65-85.

White Oak Inn

804 Spring Hill Road, Route 50W, 21801
(410) 742-4887

White Oak Inn is a warm, hospitable lakeside Colonial home nestled on five acres of lush trees and gardens. Enjoy the wildlife and beautiful sunsets. Breakfast overlooking the lake. A historic town of fine restaurants, antique shops, zoo, college, and nearby beaches. Cruise on the Paddle Queen. Mid-point to explore the Eastern Shore.

Host: Flo Davenport
Rooms: 4 (S2B) $60-65
Expanded Continental Breakfast
Credit Cards: A, B
Notes: 2, 5, 14

SCOTLAND

St. Michael's Manor Bed and Breakfast

St. Michael's Manor and Vineyard, 20687
(301) 872-4025

The land belongs to St. Michael's Manor (1805) and was originally patented to Leonard Calvert in 1637. The house, located on Long Neck Creek, is furnished with antiques. Boating, canoeing, bikes, swimming pool, and wine-tasting are available. Near Point Lookout State Park, Civil War monuments, and historic St. Mary's City.

Hosts: Joseph and Nancy Dick
Rooms: 4 (SB) $45-55
Full Breakfast
Credit Cards: None
Notes: 2, 5, 7 (limited), 8, 9, 10, 11

SHARPSBURG

Amanda's Bed and Breakfast #268

1428 Park Avenue, Annapolis, 21217
(410) 225-0001; (410) 383-1274

This inn sits amidst the hallowed ground of the Civil War's Antietam Battlefield. Furnishings of Victorian vintage define a gentler way of life, and the pastoral surroundings of the misty Blue Ridge Mountains can be seen from a wraparound porch. Four rooms have private baths. Continental breakfast. $105-125.

SILVER SPRING

Amanda's Bed and Breakfast #135

1428 Park Avenue, Annapolis, 21217
(410) 225-0001; (410) 383-1274

Close to the nation's capitol, this Cape Cod on a rolling hill in a forest of oak trees has a spacious livingroom with a piano, fireplace, and a hot tub that guests are welcome to use. Just eight miles from Washington, DC, and minutes from the Metro, this bed and breakfast offers three guest rooms with both private and shared baths. Continental breakfast. $65.

Amanda's Bed and Breakfast #281

1428 Park Avenue, Annapolis, 21217
(410) 225-0001; (410) 383-1274

This beige and brick Cape Cod is close to Washington, D.C. and a large park with trails for walking and biking. Minutes to the Metro with a large pool for guests to enjoy, this bed and breakfast offers two guest rooms that share a bath. Continental breakfast. $75.

Park Crest House

8101 Park Crest Drive, 20910
(301) 588-2845

This bed and breakfast is near downtown Washington, D.C. Ther is a suite of rooms that include a bathroom, dressing room, closet, and bedroom complete with king-size bed, color TV, and lounge chairs, and a room with a single bed and shared bath, and a room with twin beds and a shared bath. Kitchen and laundry facilities are available, and children and pets are welcome. Continental breakfast is served.

Hosts: Lowell and Rosemary Peterson
Rooms: Suite (1 PB; 2 SB) $65
Continental Breakfast
Notes: 2, 5, 6, 8, 10

The Traveller In Maryland # 185

P. O. Box 2277, Annapolis, 21404
(301) 269-6232

This English Tudor home, built of brick with a steep slate roof, sits alone on one acre of landscaped gardens including two patios that overlook the creek and woods. Location is inside the Beltway on Sligo Creek, and a Metro station is within a reasonable walk or a brief drive. The home is secluded among 50-foot beech and oak trees, with private bath and a nice view of the woods. Continental breakfast is served in this non-smoking environment. $65.

The Traveller In Maryland # 187

P. O. Box 2277, Annapolis, 21404
(301) 269-6232

The house is new Victorian-style with wraparound porches and decks for sitting or sunning. At the end of a residential street and backs up to a wooded area, it is so secluded that sometimes it is difficult to realize that Washington, DC, is only a few miles away. Amenities include livingroom, TV, fireplace, huge spa, and wooded overlook. Full breakfast is served in this non-smoking environment. $55-65.

SMITHSBURG

Blue Bear Bed and Breakfast

22052 Holiday Drive, 21783
(301) 824-2292

Country charm and warm, friendly hospitality await you at the Blue Bear. There are two beautifully decorated and air conditioned rooms with a shared bath. Enjoy a delicious breakfast of fresh fruits, breads and pastries, and quiche. Feel at home here.

Host: Ellen Panchula
Rooms: 2 (SB) $40-45
Continental Breakfast
Credit Cards: None
Notes: 2, 5, 8 (over 12), 10, 11, 12

SNOW HILL

Chanceford Hall Bed and Breakfast Inn

209 West Federal Street, 21863
(410) 632-2231

A 1759 Eastern Shore mansion impeccably restored. Listed in Smithsonian's Guide to Historic America. All private baths, canopy beds, Oriental rugs throughout. Ten working fireplaces, centrally air conditioned. Dinner by prior arrangement. Full breakfast served in formal dining room. Lap pool and bicycles. Ocean beaches 20 miles away. Canoe the famous Pocomoke River two blocks away. Complimentary wine and hors d'oeuvres. "When you require the finest."

6 Pets welcome; 7 Smoking allowed; 8 Children welcome; 9 Social drinking allowed; 10 Tennis available; 11 Swimming available; 12 Golf available; 13 Skiing available; 14 May be booked through travel agents.

Hosts: Michael and Thelma C. Driscoll
Rooms: 5 (PB) $100-115
Full Breakfast
Credit Cards: None
Notes: 2, 4, 5, 9, 10, 11, 12

SOLOMONS

Back Creek Inn

A and Calvert Streets, P. O. Box 520, 20688
(301) 326-2022

Lovely gardens and water surround this 1800s waterman's home. The view includes a lily pond and Back Creek, with pier and deep-water slips. Walking distance to Maritime Museum, fine shops, art gallery, restaurants, and antiques. Picnic baskets and bikes available. Choose the cottage for your honeymoon. A quiet and refreshing experience in a small waterfront town.

Hosts: Carol Szkotnicki and Lin Cochran
Rooms: 7 (4 PB; 3 SB) $65-100
Full and Continental Breakfast
Credit Cards: None
Closed Dec. 15-March 1
Notes: 2

STEVENSON

Amanda's Bed and Breakfast #115

1428 Park Avenue, Annapolis, 21217
(410) 225-0001; (410) 383-1274

Historic 45-acre estate offers elegant living. 1900-style fireplaces, Jacuzzi, gourmet breakfast, swimming pool, tennis, woodland trails and streams, flowers and herb gardens all make this majestic estate a special place to stay. Three guest rooms, all with private baths and fireplaces, are available. Full breakfast. $100-110.

STEVENSVILLE

Amanda's Bed and Breakfast #180

1428 Park Avenue, Annapolis, 21217
(410) 225-0001; (410) 383-1274

This historic manor is located on Kent Island on the Eastern Shore side of the Bay Bridge. This grand mansion, circa 1820, is on the Maryland Historic Register and is surrounded by 226 acres of land. A mile and a half from the waterfront with rooms decorated in Victorian style that will make your stay here memorable. Restaurant has a four-star rating. Continental breakfast.

TANEYTOWN

Amanda's Bed and Breakfast #161

1428 Park Avenue, Annapolis, 21217
(410) 225-0001; (410) 383-1274

This restored 1844 mansion sits on 24 acres, with clay tennis courts, croquet, gardens, a view of the Catoctin Mountains, and gourmet dinners provided with reservations. Winner of "Baltimore's Most Romantic Getaway," this inn offers six rooms, all with private baths and fireplaces. Full breakfast. $157.

Glenburn

3515 Runnymede Road, 21787
(301) 751-1187

Glenburn is a circa 1840 Georgian home with Victorian additions. Guest rooms overlook pasture, lawns, woods with creek. European and American antiques. Close to Gettysburg; 60 miles from Washington, D.C. Agricultural and recreational area with historic interest.

NOTES: Credit cards accepted: A Master Card; B Visa; C American Express; D Discover Card; E Diner's Club; F Other; 2 Personal Checks accepted; 3 Lunch available; 4 Dinner available; 5 Open all year;

Hosts: Robert and Elizabeth Neal
Rooms: 5 (3 PB; 2 SB) $65-100
Full Breakfast
Credit Cards: None
Notes: 2, 5, 7 (limited), 9, 10, 11, 12, 13

TILGHMAN

Amanda's Bed and Breakfast #255

1428 Park Avenue, Annapolis, 21217
(410) 225-0001; (410) 383-1274

Comfort, privacy, peace and quiet invite you to relax in the serenity at this bayside inn. Enjoy lighted tennis courts, swimming pool, baby grand piano, or the many area activities. An ideal setting for business meetings.

Sinclair House Bed and Breakfast

5718 Black Walnut Point Road, 21671
(410) 886-2147

The Sinclair House invites you to experience bed and breakfast at its best! On historic Tilghman Island, you'll discover unique antiques and nice restaurants. The dock is a short walk away where the skipjacks are moored. These vessels comprise one of the last commercial oyster sailing fleets in the world. The watermen still harvest their shellfish using traditional methods. The historical towns of St. Michaels', Oxford, and Easton are nearby

Host: Deenie Tyler
Rooms: 4 (2 PB; 2 SB) $40-60
Full Breakfast
Credit Cards: None
Notes: 2, 5, 6, 7, 8, 9, 10, 11, 12, 14

TOWSON

Amanda's Bed and Breakfast #103

1428 Park Avenue, Annapolis, 21217
(410) 225-0001; (410) 383-1274

This modern townhouse is in the woods near shopping and the downtown park and ride. Lower level with access to the patio, and tennis courts and outdoor swimming pool available. Continental breakfast. Seven rooms with both shared and private baths. $85-105.

VIENNA

Amanda's Bed and Breakfast #149

1428 Park Avenue, Annapolis, 21217
(410) 225-0001; (410) 383-1274

On the Nanticoke River in historic Vienna, this authentic Colonial tavern has been carefully restored. The Tavern House shares much of the history of the town, as it was built in 1706. Public tennis courts, boat ramp, and the blackwater wildlife refuge are nearby, and four rooms with a shared bath and fireplace are available for guests. Continental breakfast. $65-75.

Amanda's Bed and Breakfast #172

1428 Park Avenue, Annapolis, 21217
(410) 225-0001; (410) 383-1274

This Victorian inn built of brick in 1861 on the banks of the scenic Nanticoke River offers a view of the river from most rooms. The river is a refuge for waterfowl, osprey, eagles, and other birds and animals. House

6 Pets welcome; 7 Smoking allowed; 8 Children welcome; 9 Social drinking allowed; 10 Tennis available; 11 Swimming available; 12 Golf available; 13 Skiing available; 14 May be booked through travel agents.

maintains the original character and details. Four rooms with both shared and private baths are available. Continental breakfast. $65-85.

The Tavern House

Box 98, 21869
(301) 376-3347

A Colonial tavern on the Nanticoke River featuring the simple elegance of colonial living and special breakfasts that are a social occasion. A glimpse into Michener's Chesapeake for those who love Colonial homes, the peace of a small town, or watching osprey in flight.

Hosts: Harvey and Elise Altergott
Rooms: 4 (SB) $60-70
Full Breakfast
Credit Cards: A, B
Notes: 2, 5, 7, 8 (over 12), 9, 10, 12

WESTMINSTER

Amanda's Bed and Breakfast #142

1428 Park Avenue, Annapolis, 21217
(410) 225-0001; (410) 383-1274

This beautifully restored 1765 Georgian manor is located on 36 acres. A fireplace is in every room, and we are just two minutes from historic Westminster. Antiques, wineries, farm museum, Union Mills Homestead, Ski Liberty, and Wakefield Valley are all nearby. Full breakfast. $75-85.

Amanda's Bed and Breakfast #219

1428 Park Avenue, Annapolis, 21217
(410) 225-0001; (410) 383-1274

This Victorian inn is a former schoolhouse forty-five minutes from northwest Baltimore. All guest rooms have a queen-size bed and a Jacuzzi tub. Hearty breakfast buffet, and an athletic club available to guests, which includes, swimming, jogging, racquetball, and weight machines. Historic Union Hills Homestead and museums are all nearby. $110-155.

Westminster Inn

5 South Center Street, 21157
(410) 876-2893

Once a schoolhouse for kids of all ages, the Westminster Inn has been transformed into one of the most elegant bed and breakfast inns in Maryland. Designed to pamper, each of our thriteen rooms are beautifully decorated and offer a queen-size bed and Jacuzzi for your total comfort and relaxation. On-premise athletic club with indoor pool and running track, basketball, racquetball, weight room, lifecycle, and much more. Fine dining and outdoor courtyard with live entertainment.

Host: David S. Horner
Rooms: 13 (PB) $85-155
Full Breakfast-Sat & Sun only; Continental Breakfast-weekdays
Credit Cards: A, B, C, E
Notes: 2, 3, 4, 5, 7, 8, 9, 10, 11, 12, 13, 14

The Winchester Country Inn

430 South Bishop Street, 21157
(301) 876-7373

Built in the 1760s by the founder of Westminster, the inn is one of Carroll County's oldest buildings. Various recreational facilities and historic points of interest abound around the inn, which is centrally situated in Maryland. The refurbished interior makes this one of the most delightful country inns open to the public.

Hosts: Estella Williams and Mahlia Joyce
Rooms: 5 (3 PB; 2 SB) $65-75
Full Breakfast
Credit Cards: A, B
Notes: 2, 5, 7 (outside only), 8 (over 6), 9

NOTES: Credit cards accepted: A Master Card; B Visa; C American Express; D Discover Card; E Diner's Club; F Other; 2 Personal Checks accepted; 3 Lunch available; 4 Dinner available; 5 Open all year;

Massachusetts

Allen House Victorian Bed and Breakfast Inn

599 Main Street, 01002
(413) 253-5000

An authentic 1886 Queen Anne-style Victorian, this home features spacious bed chambers with private baths. Period antiques, decor, art, and wallcoverings are historically and accurately featured. In the heart of Amherst on three scenic acres and within walking distance to the Emily Dickinson House. Amherst College, the University of Massachusetts, fine galleries, museums, theatres, shops, and restaurants are nearby. Free busing throughout this five college area. A full formal breakfast is served. Brochure available. 1991 Historic Commission Award winner.

Bed and Breakfast Accommodations 120

984 Gloucester Place, Schenectady, New York 12309
(518) 370-4948

This in-town Victorian with wraparound veranda for outdoor relaxation is situated on a quiet, tree-lined street within walking distance to the college, university, and downtown. The decor is pristine and uncluttered, with shiny hardwood floors, lush green plants, fresh flowers, antique oak dressers and rocking chairs. The first-floor suite is actually a self-contained flat with bath and full kitchen. New second-floor guest quarters contain two bedrooms, shared bath, plus kitchen. Continental breakfast; children welcome. $60-85 one-night stay; $55-80.

Berkshire Bed and Breakfast Homes PV17

P. O. Box 211, Williamsburg, 01096
(413) 268-7244

This 1968 Garrison Colonial is decorated with traditional and antique furnishings. Twin beds and a semiprivate bath and parlor are available. Continental breakfast; no smoking; children welcome. $50-55.

Berkshire Bed and Breakfast Homes PV38

P. O. Box 211, Williamsburg, 01096
(413) 268-7244

An 1810 Colonial farmhouse on three acres. The common room and queen room with private bath are decorated with country and antique furnishings. Continental breakfast; no smoking; children over ten welcome. $60-65.

Bed and Breakfast Associates #IN185

P. O. Box 57166, Babson Park Branch
Boston, 02157-0166
(617) 449-5302; FAX (617) 449-5958

NOTES: Credit cards accepted: A Master Card; B Visa; C American Express; D Discover Card; E Diner's Club; F Other; 2 Personal Checks accepted; 3 Lunch available; 4 Dinner available; 5 Open all year; 6 Pets welcome; 7 Smoking allowed; 8 Children welcome; 9 Social drinking allowed; 10 Tennis available; 11 Swimming available; 12 Golf available; 13 Skiing available; 14 May be booked through travel agents.

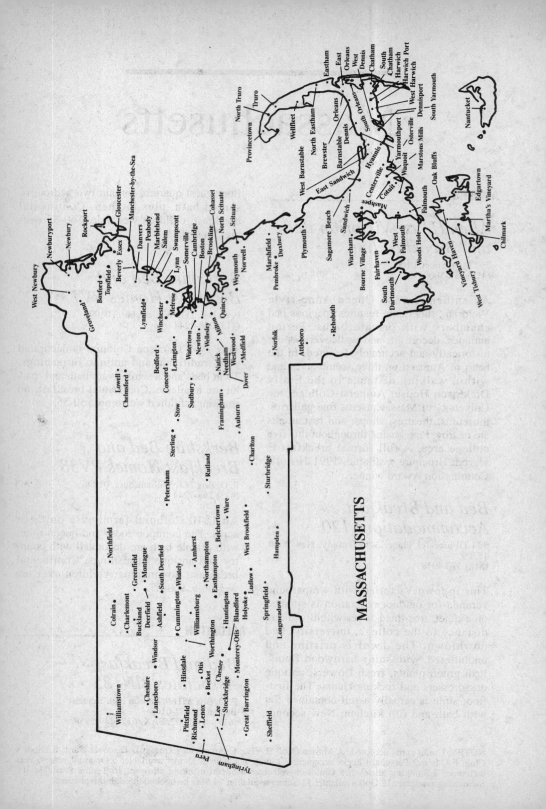

Convenient to Cambridge and to Route 195, this spacious Victorian home with fine traditional furnishings is set among large family homes in a quiet neighborhood just steps from Massachusetts Avenue buses to Harvard Square (15-minute ride). Guests are welcome to relax in a pretty upstairs sitting room, and they will enjoy the warm hospitality of this delightful host couple. Two guest rooms on the second floor share a bath. Generous continental breakfast; no toddlers, please. $55; family rates available.

ASHFIELD

Ashfield Inn

Main Street, Box 129, 01330
(413) 628-4571

An elegant Georgian mansion on more than nine acres of grounds boasting formal gardens, woods, and manicured lawns. Attractions include historic Deerfield Village, the Mohawk Trail, antique shopping, festivals, cross-country and downhill skiing, maple sugaring, foliage.

Hosts: Michael and Susan Brakefield
Rooms: 8 (S4B) $65-95
Credit Cards: A, B, C
Notes: 2, 3, 4, 5, 6, 8, 9, 10, 11, 12, 13

Bed and Breakfast/Inns of New England MA-1010

Guilford, CT 06437
(800) 532-0853

With its stately hilltop setting, this majestic Georgian-Colonial house with large porches is decorated in Victorian furnishings. The eight spacious rooms are named after local landmarks, with floral wall coverings, ruffle curtains, lacy sheets, period furniture, and loomed rugs. Each of the large bathrooms are shared by two rooms. A continental breakfast is served weekday mornings, and a full breakfast is served on weekends. Children welcome. $85.

ATTLEBORO

Bed and Breakfast Associates #CW875

P. O. Box 57166, Babson Park Branch
Boston, 02157-0166
(617) 449-5302; FAX (617) 449-5958

Nestled in a quiet country neighborhood, this Colonial reproduction home offers pleasant accommodations for guests attending concerts at Great Woods or visiting Wheaton College, both only ten minutes away. Providence is only a 15-minute drive. Two guest rooms on the second floor share a bath. Full breakfast; children welcome; no smoking. $55-65; family and monthly rates available.

The Col. Blackinton Inn

203 North Main Street, 02703
(508) 222-6022

The inn-between Boston and Providence is located on the Bungay River in the town of Attleboro, convenient to places of interest in southeastern New England and the commuter rail to Boston. The inn comprises two parlors, two dining rooms, foyer, and 16 guest rooms with a sunny garden terrace and the carriage house function room. Fully licensed, the inn caters small functions and meetings. Ideal location for business travelers visiting area firms and for pleasure travelers. National historic register property entirely renovated in 1985.

Host: Allana Schaefer
Rooms: 16 (11 PB; 5 SB) $52-72
Full Breakfast
Credit Cards: A, B, C, D, E
Notes: 2, 5, 8, 9, 12, 14

Emma C's Bed and Breakfast

18 French Farm Road, 02703
(508) 226-6365

6 Pets welcome; 7 Smoking allowed; 8 Children welcome; 9 Social drinking allowed; 10 Tennis available; 11 Swimming available; 12 Golf available; 13 Skiing available; 14 May be booked through travel agents.

Enjoy the warmth and hospitality of this country-Colonial home. Guest rooms feature antiques, quilts, flowers, air conditioning, and TVs. Enjoy breakfast by the pool in summer, or curl up by the wood stove in winter. Emma C's is situated in a wooded setting, less than one hour from Boston or Cape Cod and only minutes from Wheaton College in Norton, Brown University in Providence, Great Woods Performing Arts Center in Mansfield, and La Sallette Shrine in Attleboro.

Host: Caroline E. Logie
Rooms: 3 (1 PB; 2 SB) $55-70
Full Breakfast
Credit Cards: C
Notes: 2, 5, 6, 8, 9, 11, 12, 14

AUBURN

Capt. Samuel Eddy Bed and Breakfast Inn

609 Oxford Street South, 01501
(508) 832-5282

Come, step back in time to the warmth and charm of the 18th century in this 1765 inn. Antiques throughout, canopy beds, and common rooms with fireplaces. Breakfast is served in the sun room overlooking the herb gardens and pool area. Close to Sturbridge Village, 13 colleges, and Boston. Dinner is served by reservation.

Hosts: Jack and Carilyn O'Toole
Rooms: 5 (PB) $69-90
Full Breakfast
Credit Cards: A, B
Notes: 2, 3, 4 (by reservation), 5, 8, 9, 10, 11, 12, 14

BARNSTABLE (CAPE COD)

Ashley Manor

Box 856, 3660 Old Kings Highway, 02630
(508) 362-8044

Ashley Manor is a very special place, a gracious 1699 mansion on a two-acre estate in Cape Cod's historic district. Romantic rooms and suites feature private baths and fireplaces. Elegant public rooms with antiques, Oriental rugs. Delicious full breakfast in formal dining room or on terrace overlooking parklike grounds and new tennis court. Walk to the beach and village.

Hosts: Donald and Fay Bain
Rooms: 6 (PB) $100-165
Full Breakfast
Credit Cards: A, B, C, F
Notes: 2, 5, 7 (limited), 8 (over 14), 9, 10, 11, 12, 14

Bacon Barn Inn-Cape Cod

3400 Main Street, Box 621, 02630
(508) 362-5518

This Victorian country barn has been elegantly restored and was formerly part of the Bacon Estate. Charming large rooms with private baths are available, and antiques can be found throughout this beautiful home. A country breakfast is served on an enclosed porch filled with wicker furniture. In the off-season, enjoy breakfast in front of the warm cozy fire in the dining area. Within walking distance to the beach, harbor, whale watch, and many fine restaurants. A short drive to Hyannis. Strictly no smoking.

Hosts: Robert and Mary Giuffreda
Rooms: 3 (PB) $85-95
Continental Breakfast
Credit Cards: None
Notes: 2, 5, 9, 11, 12

Ashley Manor

Bed and Breakfast Cape Cod #27

P. O, Box 341, West Hyannisport, 02672-0341
(508) 775-2772; FAX (508) 775-2884

A few steps off Old King's Highway, this 1852 renovated Victorian home offers four rooms. Each room is complete with decorative wall coverings, period furnishings, and fresh flowers. All have private baths, and room #4 on the third floor is especially private, with a king-size bed. Perfect for honeymooners. Outside, a wraparound porch provides a place for relaxation after a day at the beach or shopping. $65-70.

Bed and Breakfast Cape Cod #35

P. O, Box 341, West Hyannisport, 02672-0341
(508) 775-2772; FAX (508) 775-2884

Not many bed and breakfast travelers have a chance to stay in a house built in 1635. This charming old building was part of the Cape Cod designer's tour of homes in 1989. The owner has two bedrooms used for bed and breakfast, with a king-size bed in one room and a pair of twins in the other. The rooms share one bath. The grounds are like a rural wooded setting with great trails for walking. A parlor is available on the first floor for guests to use. $60.

Bed and Breakfast Cape Cod #39

P. O, Box 341, West Hyannisport, 02672-0341
(508) 775-2772; FAX (508) 775-2884

Built two-hundred-and-eighty years ago by the founder of Barnstable, this Early American-style home has been painstakingly restored to the original design and decor of the early 1700s. Private baths, period antiques, and four-poster beds are featured in the three bedrooms. Two bedrooms have working fireplaces. A full country breakfast, cooked to order, is served in the common room each morning. $75-95.

Charles Hinckley House

Box 723, 02630
(508) 362-9924

Small, intimate country inn in historic Barnstable. Circa 1809 Federal gem listed on the National Register of Historic Places. Fireplace suites with private baths, four-poster beds, and English country breakfasts. A five-minute walk down a country lane to Cape Cod Bay; one and one-half miles to Barnstable harbor and all boating activities. Golf and tennis are within minutes; and museums, beaches, antique and craft shops are abundant.

Hosts: Les and Miya Patrick
Rooms: 4 (PB) $119-149
Full Breakfast
Credit Cards: None
Notes: 2, 3, 4, 5, 9, 10, 11, 12, 14

Cobb's Cove

Box 208, 02630
(508) 362-9356

This timbered Colonial manor overlooks Barnstable Village, the harbor, and Cape Cod Bay. Walk to the beach and whale-watch boat. All rooms have a full bath with whirlpool tub and toweling robes. Enjoy the keeping room, with its huge Count Rumford fireplace, and breakfast on the peaceful garden patio.

Hosts: Evelyn Chester and Henri-Jean
Rooms: 6 (PB) $139-169
Full Breakfast
Credit Cards: A, B
Notes: 2, 5, 7, 9, 10, 11, 12, 14

Thomas Huckins House

2701 Main Street, P. O. Box 515, 02630
(508) 362-6379

Sleep in canopy beds next to working fireplaces in this restored 1705 house.

6 Pets welcome; 7 Smoking allowed; 8 Children welcome; 9 Social drinking allowed; 10 Tennis available; 11 Swimming available; 12 Golf available; 13 Skiing available; 14 May be booked through travel agents.

Breakfast in the antique-filled keeping room; walk to the ocean and village through the historic district on the cape's picturesque and less-crowded north shore.

Hosts: Burt and Eleanor Eddy
Rooms: 3 (PB) $80-105
Suite: 1 (PB) $90-135
Deluxe Continental Breakfast
Credit Cards: A, B, C, D
Notes: 2, 5, 7, 8 (over 6), 9

Thomas Huckins House

BECKET

Tollgate Inn

Routes 8 and 20, 01223
(413) 243-0715

This restored authentic stagecoach inn, circa 1790, also served as a tollhouse. Five guest rooms, each with a private bath, are furnished with period pieces. The original ballroom with color TV is comfortably furnished for relaxing, as is the screened-in porch off the dining room. Close to all Berkshire attractions, such as Tanglewood, Jacob's Pillow, etc. Complimentary breakfast is served each morning. Gift shop is on premises.

Host: Betty Arnold
Rooms: 5 (PB) No price listed
Full Breakfast
Credit Cards: A, B
Notes: 2, 8

BEDFORD

Bed and Breakfast Folks

48 Springs Road, 01730
(617) 275-9025

Bed and Breakfast Folks offers tourists, business travelers, relocating personnel, or anyone visiting this area an opportunity to experience the warmth and friendliness of a private New England home. Choose from historic, contemporary, or farm homes. Learn about the charm and history of New England, and experience true hospitality. Near Concord, Lexington, and Boston. Close to lake region, skiing, fall foliage and much more. $40 plus. Monthly rates available.

BELCHERTOWN

Berkshire Bed and Breakfast Homes PV5

P. O. Box 211, Williamsburg, 01096
(413) 268-7244

Enjoy this 1839 Victorian in a small New England town. Two guest rooms, one with private bath, and livingroom are available to guests. Overlooks the town common. Continental breakfast; no smoking; children over 12 welcome. $30-60.

Berkshire Bed and Breakfast Homes PV8

P. O. Box 211, Williamsburg, 01096
(413) 268-7244

This 1989 modern contemporary home has a Scandinavian decor. There is a parlor, deck, and pool for guest use. Enjoy the British hospitality of the hosts. The guest room has twin beds and a private bath. Continental breakfast; smoking restricted; children welcome; resident pets. $65.

NOTES: Credit cards accepted: A Master Card; B Visa; C American Express; D Discover Card; E Diner's Club; F Other; 2 Personal Checks accepted; 3 Lunch available; 4 Dinner available; 5 Open all year;

Berkshire Bed and Breakfast Homes PV29

P. O. Box 211, Williamsburg, 01096
(413) 268-7244

This 1850 Federal-Greek Revival is on 13 acres. Two guest rooms share a bath and the parlor and den have antique furnishings. Full breakfast; no smoking; children welcome. $45-55.

Berkshire Bed and Breakfast Homes PV36

P. O. Box 211, Williamsburg, 01096
(413) 268-7244

Unhosted cottage built 175 years ago in Cape Cod-style. It sits on 25 acres of land with forest, beaver dams, mountain views, and small meandering river. The accommodations have a fully equipped kitchen, dining room, parlor, full bath, three bedrooms, wood-burning stove, gas grill, and picnic table. Full breakfast supplies; no smoking; children welcome. $85-150.

BEVERLY

Beverly Cove Bed and Breakfast

Bed and Breakfast Marblehead and North Shore
P. O, Box 35, Newtonville, 02160
(617) 964-1606; (800) 832-2632
FAX (617) 332-8572

Attractive, immaculate split-level, two-minute walk to private beach in quiet, prestigious area close to Endicott College. The hosts are English and enjoy entertaining in the best bed and breakfast tradition. Open year-round. Three guest rooms with shared bath. One room has working fireplace. All rooms have TV. Refrigerator for guests. Smoking permitted in common areas. Full breakfast. Children over eight welcome. Cat in residence. $55-65.

Lady Slippers Bed and Breakfast

Bed and Breakfast Marblehead and North Shore
P. O, Box 35, Newtonville, 02160
(617) 964-1606; (800)832-2632
FAX (617) 332-8572

Dutch-Colonial, antique-furnished attractive family home facing ocean. One or more teenage sons at home. The hostess is a retail merchandiser and is particularly interested in local history and politics. She speaks some Spanish and Hebrew. Four guest rooms available. No smoking. Continental breakfast. Children welcome. Dog in residence. Baby-sitting by prior arrangement. $45-75.

Next Door Inn Bed and Breakfast

Bed and Breakfast Marblehead and North Shore
P. O, Box 35, Newtonville, 02160
(617) 964-1606; (800) 832-2632

A beautifully decorated, cozy, Colonial-style home offers guests use of kitchen facilities, color TV in livingroom, enclosed sun porch, telephone, and off-street parking. There are three attractive guest rooms: a room with a queen-size bed and private bath, another room with a double bed and a fireplace, and a third room with a pair of twins. (Second and third rooms share a bath.) In hot weather, common areas have air conditioning, and the guest rooms have fans. Continental breakfast. No smoking. $50-75

BLANFORD

Berkshire Bed and Breakfast Homes SC5

P. O. Box 211, Williamsburg, 01096
(413) 268-7244

6 Pets welcome; 7 Smoking allowed; 8 Children welcome; 9 Social drinking allowed; 10 Tennis available; 11 Swimming available; 12 Golf available; 13 Skiing available; 14 May be booked through travel agents.

A 1768 central-chimney Colonial on six acres. Guest rooms share a bath, and all have Colonial furniture. Parlor with open fireplace and view of the woods. Full breakfast; no smoking; children welcome. $50-60.

BOSTON

A Bed and Breakfast Above the Rest #1

50 Boatswains Way, Suite 105, 02150
(617) 884-7748; (800) 677-2262

Credit goes to the architect-hostess for her professional renovation of this 100-year-old brick town house. The exterior is classic Beacon Hill. The interior, accented with contemporary paintings, is bright and youthful feeling. The two guest rooms are on the fourth floor and share a bath. The larger room has an Oriental rug, six large windows, and color TV, plus access to a roof deck. The smaller room is the picture of coziness, with windows nestled under the eaves and an inviting window seat. Continental breakfast.

A Bed and Breakfast Above the Rest #2

50 Boatswains Way, Suite 105, 02150
(617) 884-7748; (800) 677-2262

Built in 1869 in the opulent style of the time, this house has lavishly large rooms. Windows on the west side overlook the Charles; the east side view is of the Gothic Revival Church of the Advent. Each of the four guest rooms has a fireplace, high ceilings, original moldings, and antique furnishings. Two rooms are on the second floor; two are on the third. All have private baths. Full breakfast with homemade bread and granola.

A Bed and Breakfast Above the Rest #3

50 Boatswains Way, Suite 105, 02150
(617) 884-7748; (800) 677-2262

Built as a single-family home in 1894, this Victorian building was later used as a private retirement home. Extensively refurbished by its new owners, it is now an inviting inn, with spacious rooms, polished woodwork, and sparkling stained-glass windows. Guests are invited to make themselves at home on the main floor with two parlors, a sitting room with a TV, a sunny dining room, and a small kitchen. There are six guest rooms. Two rooms have private baths; four rooms share two baths. Continental breakfast.

A Bed and Breakfast Above the Rest #4

50 Boatswains Way, Suite 105, 02150
(617) 884-7748; (800) 677-2262

The Charles River Inn really is an old inn—about 100 years old. It was renovated three years ago and now offers 46 guest rooms, ranging from small singles to spacious suites. All rooms are air-conditioned and include TV, private phone, and daily maid service. Most rooms also have kitchenettes. A double parlor on the first floor serves as a reception and common area for guests. Continental breakfast.

A Bed and Breakfast Above the Rest #7

50 Boatswains Way, Suite 105, 02150
(617) 884-7748; (800) 677-2262

A handsomely restored brick warehouse is the setting for this roomy, open, and beautifully decorated condominium with exposed bricks and wooden beams. The hostess is a professional who used to co-manage a hotel in the White Mountains. She has furnished her home with Early American antiques. The guest room shares a bath with the hostess and has been designated a "single" room. Continental breakfast with delicious, freshly ground coffee.

A Bed and Breakfast Above the Rest #8

50 Boatswains Way, Suite 105, 02150
(617) 884-7748; (800) 677-2262

This contemporary condo is in one of the original waterfront condominium buildings. As a result, it has an excellent, unobstructed view of the harbor and its constant parade of boats. The guest room has a queen bed and private bath. The hostess is fluent in Greek and has two Shih Tzu dogs. Continental breakfast.

A Bed and Breakfast Above the Rest #9

50 Boatswains Way, Suite 105, 02150
(617) 884-7748; (800) 677-2262

This multiwindowed, 14th-floor condo has been converted into private accommodations for families or two couples traveling together. The view of Boston is spectacular. The building provides 24-hour concierge and laundry facilities. The air-conditioned, Victorian-furnished accommodations are unhosted, and the refrigerator is stocked with continental breakfast foods prior to each visit. There are two bedrooms, each with color TVs and charming prints on the walls.

A Bed and Breakfast Above the Rest #10

50 Boatswains Way, Suite 105, 02150
(617) 884-7748; (800) 677-2262

Guests who are afraid of heights may want to look elsewhere. You couldn't ask for a more exciting daytime view—the bustling, colorful harbor is always on the move. And at night the city, spread out around you, is absolutely breathtaking. The guest room in this hosted condominium is adorned with fresh flowers, handmade contemporary oak furniture, TV, VCR, and clock radio. Private bath. Self-serve continental breakfast.

A Bed and Breakfast Above the Rest #11

50 Boatswains Way, Suite 105, 02150
(617) 884-7748; (800) 677-2262

This unhosted condominium in the Beacon Hill area has amenities and creature comforts that make long stays a pleasure. The livingroom has a working fireplace, built-in bookshelves, and full-size sofa bed. The dining area has a greenhouse window overlooking the private patio. The fully equipped kitchen is stocked with continental breakfast supplies. Also, a TV, phone, iron, linens, washer, and dryer.

A Bed and Breakfast Above the Rest #12

50 Boatswains Way, Suite 105, 02150
(617) 884-7748; (800) 677-2262

This striking building in the Beacon Hill area dating from 1842 was designed by the architect Richard Upjohn. Originally a church and school, it was converted to a residence in 1960. Guests are welcome to share the livingroom to watch TV, read, or relax. The duplex apartment has central air conditioning. There are three guest rooms, although generally only two are rented. One has a private bath, country French furnishings, sponge-painted walls, and TV. Continental breakfast.

6 Pets welcome; 7 Smoking allowed; 8 Children welcome; 9 Social drinking allowed; 10 Tennis available; 11 Swimming available; 12 Golf available; 13 Skiing available; 14 May be booked through travel agents.

A Bed and Breakfast Above the Rest #13

50 Boatswains Way, Suite 105, 02150
(617) 884-7748; (800) 677-2262

There's always at least one "new" antique in this 1828 Federal town house; the hostess is an interior decorator who enjoys changing her furnishings to keep things interesting. There is a private livingroom with TV for guests. Breakfast is served in the dining room. There are three guest rooms with fresh flowers and private baths. Two have working fireplaces. Resident cat and dog. Continental breakfast.

A Bed and Breakfast Above the Rest #14

50 Boatswains Way, Suite 105, 02150
(617) 884-7748; (800) 677-2262

The Mount Vernon Houses are two historic Beacon Hill buildings typical of 1830s style of Boston brick town houses. They manage to be stately yet cozy. In all, there are 20 guest rooms. The high-ceilinged rooms are pleasant and homey and decorated in a 19th-century-style. Most rooms have private baths. A stair lift and automatic doors are available for people who need them. Self-serve continental breakfast.

A Bed and Breakfast Above the Rest #15

50 Boatswains Way, Suite 105, 02150
(617) 884-7748; (800) 677-2262

This third-floor, unhosted condominium is available for up to four people traveling together. The furnishings are casual and contemporary. The owners stock the refrigerator for guests. It has a fully equipped kitchen, full bath, livingroom with a foldout sofa, and bedroom. Near Symphony Hall.

A Bed and Breakfast Above the Rest #16

50 Boatswains Way, Suite 105, 02150
(617) 884-7748; (800) 677-2262

City Sights is a comfortable, air-conditioned condominium in a large, well-renovated building that was a candy factory in the 1900s. In the waterfront area near Boston Harbor. It is decorated with contemporary furnishings and many accessories. There are two guest bedrooms with private or shared bath, depending on whether the hostess is at home or whether both rooms are occupied. Continental breakfast.

A Bed and Breakfast Above the Rest #17

50 Boatswains Way, Suite 105, 02150
(617) 884-7748; (800) 677-2262

Built in the early- to mid-1900s, this white house with red trim and dormer windows is the recent purchase of an especially engaging retired couple. Guests shouldn't miss the chance to visit the Arboretum across the street. The home has a large back yard filled with 100-year-old trees. Inside the home, the cozy livingroom has an Oriental rug and a baby grand piano. The kitchen opens onto a porch, where guests may choose to have breakfast. There is one guest room. Full breakfast with homemade muffins.

A Bed and Breakfast Above the Rest #18

50 Boatswains Way, Suite 105, 02150
(617) 884-7748; (800) 677-2262

The rooms in this 1815 Federal-style town house are absolutely splendid. The resident hostess is an interior designer and caterer, and her graceful touch is evident everywhere. She speaks fluent French and some

Japanese. Both guest rooms are on the second floor. The larger room is romantic with a canopy bed and working fireplace. The smaller room overlooks the garden and shares a bath. Continental breakfast is served in the garden, weather permitting.

A Bed and Breakfast Above the Rest #19

50 Boatswains Way, Suite 105, 02150
(617) 884-7748; (800) 677-2262

The restoration of this antique-filled 1836 town house in downtown Boston was done with a careful hand and a discerning eye. Service at the Federal is hospitable, and the accommodations are stunning. There are two guest suites. The one on the second floor includes a bedroom, sitting room, and private bath. Also included are two fireplaces and formal furnishings. The third-floor suite also consists of a bedroom, sitting area, attached bath, and two fireplaces. Continental breakfast.

A Bed and Breakfast Above the Rest #20

50 Boatswains Way, Suite 105, 02150
(617) 884-7748; (800) 677-2262

Guests stay in a wonderful ground-floor studio in a 115-year-old house with a bow front and back. The town house, situated on a tranquil cul-de-sac, has a back yard with an oasis-like private garden. The guest apartment has a private rear entrance. Inside, there is a bath, kitchen, and one bedroom with a double and single bed. The walls are finished in rough pine, and the floor is real brick. The refrigerator is stocked with continental breakfast supplies.

A Bed and Breakfast Above the Rest #21

50 Boatswains Way, Suite 105, 02150
(617) 884-7748; (800) 677-2262

Featured in Country Inns, Yankee Magazine, and USA Today, the Terrace Townhouse deserves its high reputation. The restored 1870 home is in mint condition, its interior decorated as if by a turn-of-the-century Bostonian. The hostess, a graduate of La Varrennes in Paris, serves tea in the library and brings breakfast to guests' rooms on antique china and crystal. The four guest rooms have fresh flowers, private baths, and bathrobes. Full breakfast.

A Bed and Breakfast Above the Rest #22

50 Boatswains Way, Suite 105, 02150
(617) 884-7748; (800) 677-2262

Reservations for longer stays are preferred at the Victorian, a superbly restored 1870s brick town house in the Back Bay area. The guest room has a small sitting room, TV, marble fireplace, and private bath. The studio has a private entrance a few steps down from the main entrance and opens onto a garden. There is a full kitchen and bath, also a color TV, ceiling fan, and aquarium. The walls are exposed brick; the hardwood floors are covered with Oriental rugs. Self-serve continental breakfast for guests in the main house.

A Bed and Breakfast Above the Rest #23

50 Boatswains Way, Suite 105, 02150
(617) 884-7748; (800) 677-2262

Newbury House in the Back Bay area is a brick, Victorian home that has been converted into an eight-bedroom inn. The first floor has a handsome common area with a fireplace and elegant woodwork. Four rooms are on the second floor; the other four are on the third. Each floor has one shared bath. The antique furnishings are simple and tasteful. Continental breakfast.

A Bed and Breakfast Above the Rest #24

50 Boatswains Way, Suite 105, 02150
(617) 884-7748; (800) 677-2262

The inn is in a large, mixed-use building dating from 1903. The ground floor is home to the very popular Pizzeria Uno restaurant; the inn itself occupies the third through sixth floors. There are 160 guest rooms including several two- and three-room suites. Most rooms have private baths. The air-conditioned rooms are luxurious with mahogany furniture, carpeting, TVs, and phones. Continental breakfast.

A Bed and Breakfast Above the Rest #25

50 Boatswains Way, Suite 105, 02150
(617) 884-7748; (800) 677-2262

The St. Botolph is a sunny, nicely appointed condominium in a brownstone built in 1870 and renovated in 1980. The condo is air-conditioned and decorated with a mixture of antique and modern furnishings. The guest room has comfortable wicker furniture, a TV and radio, and shares a bath. Continental breakfast served in the parlor on weekends; self-serve on weekdays.

A Bed and Breakfast Above the Rest #27

50 Boatswains Way, Suite 105, 02150
(617) 884-7748; (800) 677-2262

Built as a family home in the 19th century and reconstructed to suit the needs of a 20th-century inn, the Allston is a family-owned bed and breakfast that is very popular with European visitors, students, travelers on extended stays, and any traveler on a budget. The inn has 24 guest rooms, many with kitchenettes. The rooms are clean, pleasant, and comfortable with TV and phone. In the Allston Station section. Continental breakfast served in the dining room between 8:00 and 10:00 A.M.

Architect's Home

Host Homes of Boston
P. O. Box 117, 02168
(617) 244-1308; FAX (617) 244-5156

Pleasant and private fourth-floor guest room with queen sofa bed, roof deck. Near Park Plaza and Tufts Medical Center. Air conditioning, private bath, TV, no smoking. $68.

Back Bay Condo

Host Homes of Boston
P. O, Box 117, 02168
(617) 244-1308; FAX (617) 244-5156

Comfy and casual home in the heart of elegant Back Bay offers a guest room with a queen bed, VCR, and Jacuzzi bath. Steps away from Copley Square, Hynes Convention Center, and Boston Common. $85.

Baileys Boston House

Host Homes of Boston
P. O. Box 117, Waban Branch, 02168
(617) 244-1308; FAX (617) 244-5156

This 1800 Victorian town house has guest parlor and European atmosphere. Of your hostess's eight guest rooms, she offers on the second floor two huge doubles (king/twins plus sofa beds) and two small singles. Luxury step-down two-person shower-bath. Buffet breakfast 7:30-10:00 A.M. Near Copely Place, Hynes Convention Center, Fenway Park. Air conditioning. $79.

NOTES: Credit cards accepted: A Master Card; B Visa; C American Express; D Discover Card; E Diner's Club; F Other; 2 Personal Checks accepted; 3 Lunch available; 4 Dinner available; 5 Open all year;

Beacon Hill Bed and Breakfast

27 Brimmer Street, 02108
(617) 523-7376

An 1869 spacious Victorian town house overlooking Charles River within an elegant historic neighborhood of brick sidewalks, gas lamps, and tree-lined streets. Boston's best location—two blocks from "Cheers," easy walk to Boston Common, Freedom Trail connecting historic sites, Quincy Market, downtown, Filene's Basement, convention center, subway, public garages, restaurants and shops. Elevator for luggage.

Host: Susan Butterworth
Rooms: 3 (PB) $95-120
Full Breakfast
Credit Cards: None
Notes: 5, 8 (over 10), 9, 14

Bed and Breakfast Afloat

Bed and Breakfast of Greater Boston and Cape Cod
P. O, Box 35, Newtonville, 02160
(617) 964-1606; (800) 832-2632
FAX (617) 322-8572

This completely refurbished yacht in Boston's waterfront district sleeps two to four and offers a galley kitchen stocked with breakfast food, livingroom with double sofa bed, air conditioning, color TV, separate bedroom with queen bed and private bath. By prior arrangement, hosts will cater private boatside parties or dinners. Available May 1-October 15. $140-180.

Bed and Breakfast Associates #M104

P. O. Box 57166, Babson Park Branch, 02157-0166
(617) 449-5302; FAX (617) 449-5958

Those seeking the charm of an old European hotel will enjoy staying in this prestigious private club with its elegant drawing room and small, gracious dining room. Convenient to Newbury Street shops,

historic sites, and the Hynes Convention Center. Four guest rooms, two with private baths. Continental breakfast; elevator service; children welcome. $66-107.

Bed and Breakfast Associates #M110

P. O. Box 57166, Babson Park Branch, 02157-0166
(617) 449-5302; FAX (617) 449-5958

Stay in the heart of Old Boston on Beacon Street near Copley Square, the Hynes Convention Center, the Charles River, and Boston University. This spacious, three-story town house is graced with high ceilings, rooms are comfortably furnished. Four rooms, one with private bath. Self-service continental breakfast; children welcome. $55-95.

Bed and Breakfast Associates #M126

P. O. Box 57166, Babson Park Branch, 02157-0166
(617) 449-5302; FAX (617) 449-5958

Situated just three blocks from the Public Garden, country antiques create a charming and comfortable atmosphere in this quiet Beacon Hill home. Stroll along nearby Charles Street and enjoy the fine antique shops, book stores, and cafes. Two guest rooms with private baths. Generous continental breakfast; children over ten welcome. $75-85.

Bed and Breakfast Associates #M127

P. O, Box 57166, 02157-0166
(617) 449-5302; FAX (617) 449-5958

A garden level suite in an impressive Beacon Hill townhouse features a pair of twin beds, cooking area, private bath, and antiuqes throughout. Three blocks to Boston Common and Freedom Trail. $88.

6 Pets welcome; 7 Smoking allowed; 8 Children welcome; 9 Social drinking allowed; 10 Tennis available; 11 Swimming available; 12 Golf available; 13 Skiing available; 14 May be booked through travel agents.

Bed and Breakfast Associates #M128

P. O. Box 57166, Babson Park Branch, 02157-0166
(617) 449-5302; FAX (617) 449-5958

This 1835 Federal town house has all its original architectural details. Guests enjoy the private use of the entire second floor that consists of a bedroom, sitting room, and bath. The two decorative fireplaces add a warm coziness to this peaceful urban retreat. Continental breakfast served in your room; children welcome; no smoking. $90.

Bed and Breakfast Associates #M131

P. O, Box 57166, 02157-0166
(617) 449-5302; FAX (617) 449-5958

In Boston's prestigious Beacon Hill and adjacent to the historic Massachusetts State House, this inn is a loving restoration of two attached 1830s townhouses. The fine period furnishings include four-poster and canopied beds, decorative fireplaces, and reproduction desks. New private baths throughout, and guests are always welcome to use the kitchen, the dining room, and the parlors. $85-99.

Bed and Breakfast Associates #M133

P. O. Box 57166, Babson Park Branch, 02157-0166
(617) 449-5302; FAX (617) 449-5958

Your fourth-floor guest room with cathedral ceiling and rooftop deck overlooks this quiet street behind the State House and near the Faneuil Hall Waterfront area. This special retreat awaits you atop an 1863 brick town house. Continental, self-serve breakfast; children welcome; no smoking. $95.

Bed and Breakfast Associates #M134

P. O, Box 57166, 02157-0166
(617) 449-5302; FAX (617) 449-5958

Adjacent to Hynes Convention Center, Prudential Center, and Sheraton Boston, this charming one-bedroom apartment is within an owner-occupied townhouse. The traditional decor and working fireplace provide a pleasant ambience, and the apartment includes a full kitchen, private bath, TV, and laundry. $90. Monthly rates also available.

Bed and Breakfast Associates #M136

P. O. Box 57166, 02157-0166
(617) 449-5302; FAX (617) 449-5958

This handsome 46-room mansion at the foot of Beacon Hill is within walking distance of many Boston attractions. Modern amenities have been incorporated into this careful restoration, and rooms include phone lines, private baths, color TVs, kitchenettes, and individual climate controls. Elevator and handicapped access is available. The gracious double parlor with working fireplace and period furnishings serves as the lobby, and reproduction furnishings create a warm and elegant atmosphere. Continental breakfast. Laundry and valet. $90-130.

Bed and Breakfast Associates #M137

P. O, Box 57166, 02157-0166
(617) 449-5302; FAX (617) 449-5958

Boston has only one Newbury Street, and it is THE street for art galleries, designer clothing boutiques, and fine window shopping. This twelve-room Newbury Street Inn puts all of this at your doorstep. Opened in 1991, this property is restored and offers warm, comfortable rooms with 19th-century reproductions. The front patio is a perfect spot for people watching; breakfast is served here when the weather permits. Selectively priced rooms are available on all four floors. Reserved parking in the rear ($10/day). Two blocks to Copley Square and Hynes Convention Center. $90-195.

Bed and Breakfast Associates #M240

P. O. Box 57166, Babson Park Branch, 02157-0166
(617) 449-5302; FAX (617) 449-5958

Lovely Victorian town house in the Back Bay just steps from the Prudential Center and Copley Place. This warm and hospitable couple offer their guests full use of their second floor with two charming guest rooms and a bath.They also offer a garden-level efficiency with a new kitchenette and private bath. Continental breakfast; children welcome; no smoking. $65-80.

Bed and Breakfast Associates #M306

P. O, Box 57166, 02157-0166
(617) 449-5302; FAX (617) 449-5958

In a 19th-century townhouse three blocks from Copley Square, guests enjoy the privacy and convenience of this newly decorated studio apartment with a Murphy double bed, futon couch, cooking nook, and private bath. $85.

Bed and Breakfast Associates #M308

P. O. Box 57166, Babson Park Branch, 02157-0166
(617) 449-5302; FAX (617) 449-5958

Housed just three blocks from the Boston Common and Copley Square, the charming hostess offers the privacy of a 500-square-foot garden-level suite in her renovated brownstone town house. Guests enjoy a sitting room, private patio, private bath, laundry, plus a large bedroom with queen and twin beds, color TV, stereo, refrigerator, and brick walls. Continental breakfast; children over 13 welcome. $78. Off-season monthly rates available.

Bed and Breakfast Associates #M309

P. O. Box 57166, Babson Park Branch, 02157-0166
(617) 449-5302; FAX (617) 449-5958

A fresh and newly renovated guest room awaits you in this classic Victorian town house near Copley Place. Your hostess is a retired secretary who enjoys gardening, music, and antiques, all of which are reflected in her inviting home. Her second floor is for guest use only and has a private guest room with private bath. Continental breakfast; children over six welcome. $75. Monthly rates available.

Bed and Breakfast Associates #M314

P. O, Box 57166, 02157-0166
(617) 449-5302; FAX (617) 449-5958

Attention to detail and gracious hospitality are the hallmark of this bed and breakfast. Selected as one of the 100 best bed and breakfast in the country, this 1863 townhouse is set in the historic district right next to Boston's famed Copley Square. Each impeccable guest room offers unique decorative features that include wide-pine floors, bow windows, marble fireplaces, queen-size brass beds, Chinese rugs, and private baths. Sumptuous breakfast served in the penthouse dining room. $97-110.

6 Pets welcome; 7 Smoking allowed; 8 Children welcome; 9 Social drinking allowed; 10 Tennis available; 11 Swimming available; 12 Golf available; 13 Skiing available; 14 May be booked through travel agents.

Bed and Breakfast Associates #M319

P. O. Box 57166, Babson Park Branch, 02157-0166
(617) 449-5302; FAX (617) 449-5958

This 19th-century brick town house is on a pretty, quiet street near Copley Square. Your hostess, an artist who also restores antique needlework, has tastefully blended her Victorian and contemporary furnishings. Two guest rooms, one with private bath. Continental breakfast; children over six welcome; no smoking. $65-78.

Bed and Breakfast Associates #M322

P. O, Box 57166, 02157-0166
(617) 449-5302; FAX (617) 449-5958

This congenial couple offers two lovely guest rooms (one queen and one double bed) with charming antique decor, private baths, and central air. Their beautifully restored Victorian bow-front townhouse is situated on a quiet street with private parking. $75.

Bed and Breakfast Associates #M324

P. O, Box 57166, 02157-0166
(617) 449-5302; FAX (617) 449-5958

This large family home in Boston's South End has reserved the fourth floor for guests. Located near Prudential Center with reserved parking ($10/day), two guest rooms, one with a queen bed, and one with a double bed plus a queen sleeper sofa, are available and share a bath. Buffet breakfast is served in the formal dining room. $75.

Bed and Breakfast Associates #M346

P. O, Box 57166, 02157-0166
(617) 449-5302; FAX (617) 449-5958

This newly restored brick bow-front townhouse has lovely traditional decor, spacious guest rooms, private baths, and period architectural details. Choose from a pair of twin, king, or double-size beds. This home is located on a quiet street three blocks from Copley Square, the John Hancock Tower, and many fine shops and restaurants. $95.

Bed and Breakfast Associates #M354

P. O, Box 57166, 02157-0166
(617) 449-5302; FAX (617) 449-5958

This garden level South End studio apartment has an attractive Danish contemporary decor, a queen platform bed, color TV, kitchenette, private bath, and library shelves. Parking is an additional $5. $85.

Bed and Breakfast Associates #M355

P. O. Box 57166, Babson Park Branch, 02157-0166
(617) 449-5302; FAX (617) 449-5958

A friendly young family welcomes you to their guest room with its Laura Ashley decor and sunlight through lace curtains. This renovated town house is situated three blocks from the Prudential Center. Enjoy your continental breakfast cafe-style by your private bay window. Semiprivate bath. Children welcome; no smoking. $75.

Bed and Breakfast Associates #M412

P. O. Box 57166, Babson Park Branch, 02157-0166
(617) 449-5302; FAX (617) 449-5958

The hostess and her daughter are pleased to welcome you to Boston in their waterfront condo with lovely decor. Master bedroom has desk and TV. Second bedroom has twin beds, shared bath, and a feminine decor.

NOTES: Credit cards accepted: A Master Card; B Visa; C American Express; D Discover Card; E Diner's Club; F Other; 2 Personal Checks accepted; 3 Lunch available; 4 Dinner available; 5 Open all year;

Enjoy a nice view of Boston Harbor from the balcony. Continental breakfast; children over 13 welcome; smoking limited. $80.

Bed and Breakfast Associates #M510

P. O. Box 57166, Babson Park Branch, 02157-0166
(617) 449-5302; FAX (617) 449-5958

A wonderful 12-room Victorian in the Jamaica Pond area near the Farber, Children's, and Brigham hospitals. Very large third-floor guest room provides privacy, and its furnishings include a desk and a sofa. A private bath and a full private kitchen adjoin. Drive ten minutes to downtown Boston. Self-serve continental breakfast; no smoking. $70; monthly rates available.

Bed and Breakfast Associates #M530

P. O. Box 57166, Babson Park Branch, 02157-0166
(617) 449-5302; FAX (617) 449-5958

A lovingly restored Victorian bed and breakfast set on a quiet street of large family homes in Boston's Dorchester neighborhood. It is just 20 minutes south of downtown by public transit, and you can reach the Kennedy Library and the Bayside Expo Center in just ten minutes. The home features exquisite woodwork, handsome architectural details, and stained glass. Guest facilities include four full baths (two private, two shared), two half-baths, a kitchenette for light cooking, laundry, and several gracious public rooms for guests. Self-serve continental breakfast; children welcome; smoking limited. $50-70; family rates and off-season monthly rates available.

Bed and Breakfast/Inns of New England MA-1007

329 Lake Drive, Guilford, CT 06437
(800) 582-0853

Built in 1894 by a prosperous Boston leather merchant, this late Victorian house was later converted to a retirement home, which it was for more than 70 years. The current owners extensively refurbished the house when they bought it. Spacious rooms, gleaming woodwork, and sparkling stained-glass windows give the house its character. Guests are invited to enjoy the parlor, oak-paneled sitting room with TV, sunny dining room, and breakfast kitchen. A substantial "help yourself" breakfast is provided each morning, and guests are welcome to use the kitchen for snacks or light meals. Six comfortable guest rooms, all with stained-glass windows. Two rooms have privage baths; the other four rooms share two additional bathrooms. $50-70.

Brick & Balcony

Host Homes of Boston
P. O, Box 117, 02168
(617) 244-1308; FAX (617) 244-5156

Situated in the shadow of the State House's golden dome, this typical 1863 brick town house is home to a friendly young family. The top (fourth) floor guest room is spacious and private with a queen-size bed, private bath, Jacuzzi tub, and private deck. Walk to Freedom Trail, Faneuil Hall, and theaters. $85-95.

Chandler Inn

26 Chandler at Berkeley, 02116
(617) 482-3450; (800) 842-3450

Boston's best value! Situated on the edge of the historic Back Bay. Walking distance to Newbury Street, Copley Place, shopping, theaters, and restaurants. In this small hotel

6 Pets welcome; 7 Smoking allowed; 8 Children welcome; 9 Social drinking allowed; 10 Tennis available; 11 Swimming available; 12 Golf available; 13 Skiing available; 14 May be booked through travel agents.

all rooms are equipped with private bath, television, direct-dial telephone, and air conditioning. Continental breakfast included.

Host: Susan Long
Rooms: 56 (PB) $69-84
Continental Breakfast
Credit Cards: A, B, C, D, E
Notes: 5, 7, 8, 9, 14

Coach House

Host Homes of Boston
P. O, Box 117, 02168
(617) 244-1308; FAX (617) 244-5156

Converted to a private home in 1890, the original structure of this bed and breakfast housed twelve coaches and staff. Here, on a quiet gas-lit street, your host family offers two well-appointed guest rooms on the second (single) and third (double) floors. Both rooms have private baths. Near Freedom Trail, hotels, restaurants, and "Cheers." Resident cats. $85-100.

Downtown Duplex

Host Homes of Boston, P. O. Box 117, 02168
(617) 244-1308; FAX (617) 244-5156

Boston's past and present meet here amid Faneuil Hall, waterfront, and downtown. Host's fifth- and sixth-floor walk-up has brick and beam decor, balcony, antiques. Guest room has double bed and skylights. Walk to Quincy Market, financial district, North End, and Freedom Trail. Air conditioning, TV, private bath, no smoking. $68.

The Lenox Hotel

710 Boylston Street, 02116
(617) 536-5300

The Lenox is a charming 222-room, turn-of-the-century hotel. It is intimate and traditional and offers gracious New England ambience, outstanding service, and excellent cuisine at remarkably reasonable rates.

The Lenox is the only hotel in a a major city that is listed in *Country Inns and Back Roads*. The Lenox specializes in personalized service.

Rooms: 222 (PB) $150-210
Full Breakfast-$9.50; Continental breakfast-$7.50
Credit Cards: A, B, C, D, E
Notes: None

Oasis Guest House

22 Edgerly Road, 02115-3007
(617) 267-2262; FAX (617) 267-1920

Two renovated Back Bay town houses in the heart of Boston on a quiet side street. Walk to historic sites, museums, shopping, and dining. Five-minute walk to Hynes Convention Center and Copley Square. Central air conditioning, telephones, color TVs, outdoor decks, continental breakfast, parking. Comfort, quality, convenience for much less than hotels. Call/write for more information.

Host: Joe Haley
Rooms: 16 (10 PB; 6 SB) $55-72
Continental Breakfast
Credit Cards: A, B, C
Notes: 5, 7, 9, 14

On the Avenue

Host Homes of Boston, P. O. Box 117, 02168
(617) 244-1308; FAX (617) 244-5156

Boston Common, Copley Place, convention hotels, subway are steps away from 19th-century ambience in private professional club. Dining room, guest parlor. Three spacious doubles have twin beds, phone, and private bath. Four small singles (one twin bed) share two baths. Roll-away, $20. Air conditioning, TV, elevator. $60-90.

On the Hill

Host Homes of Boston, P. O. Box 117, 02168
(617) 244-1308; FAX (617) 244-5156

This brick Federal town house (1790) on the Hill's loveliest street offers exceptional third-floor quarters—livingroom, bedroom, modern bath, kitchen, and dining room where breakfast is served. Near Freedom Trail, hotels, State House. Air conditioning, no smoking, TV. $85-95.

Proper Bostonian

Host Homes of Boston, P. O. Box 117, 02168
(617) 244-1308; FAX (617) 244-5156

Business people like this 1872 town house with authentic decor. Spacious third-floor guest room has twin beds, sitting area, small stocked kitchen where you make your own breakfast. Another twin room often available, if same party. Busy hosts offer privacy in best area. Four blocks to Copley Square, Hynes Convention Center. Near Boston Commons. Air conditioning, private bath, TV. $75.

Quincy Adams
Bed and Breakfast

P. O. Box 158, 02133
(617) 479-6215

Elegant turn-of-the-century home 15 minutes from downtown Boston. Fireplaces, canopy beds, and a Jacuzzi spa. Near restaurants, shopping, and the beach.

Host: Mary Lee Walsh
Rooms: 3 (PB) $60-80
Continental Breakfast weekdays; Full on weekends
Credit Cards: A, B
Notes: 2, 5

The South End Inn

Bed and Breakfast of Greater Boston and Cape Cod
P. O. Box 35, Newtonville, 02160
(617) 964-1606; (800) 832-2632
FAX (617) 332-8572

This small inn is situated in Boston's South End, a friendly neighborhood of professionals and renovated brownstones. Two blocks from train and bus stations, and the guest rooms are newly refurbished and feature private baths, TV, telephone, and air conditioning. Continental breakfast. Parking available. $74-84.

Victoriana

Host Homes of Boston
P. O, Box 117, 02168
(617) 244-1308; FAX (617) 244-5156

Host's 1860 Victorian home in historic neighborhood has a second floor guest room with a pair of twin beds and antiques. This home is on a quiet street near Copley Square, Convention Center, and Amtrak. $68.

BOURNE VILLAGE

Cape Cod Canalside
Bed and Breakfast

7 Coastal Way, 02532
(508) 759-6564

A "billion dollar view." Busiest canal in the world. View huge ships and graceful schooners. Entire first floor of new contemporary house for guests only. Private entrance. Total of seven rooms, kitchenette, refrigerator, barbecue, picnic table, fireplace, cable TV. Canal and bicycle path, free bikes, fishing, jogging. The canal is lighted at night. Located near Gulf Stream beaches, tennis, golf. AARP and military discount. Call for brochure.

Hosts: Terry and Paul Deasy
Rooms: 3 (1 PB; 2 SB) $40-90
Continental Breakfast
Credit Cards: None
Notes: 5, 9, 10, 11, 12, 14

BOXFORD

Day's End
Bed and Breakfast

Bed and Breakfast Marblehead and North Shore
P. O. Box 35, Newtonville, 02160

6 Pets welcome; 7 Smoking allowed; 8 Children welcome; 9 Social drinking allowed; 10 Tennis available; 11 Swimming available; 12 Golf available; 13 Skiing available; 14 May be booked through travel agents.

(617) 964-1606; (800) 832-2632
FAX (617) 332-8572

A beautiful architect-designed contemporary home in a country setting, with swimming pool and large grounds. The four guest rooms can be rented individually or as a separate entrance suite. In addition to the efficiency kitchenette and sitting room, the first-floor livingroom has facilities for entertaining, available for a fee. Open year-round. Continental breakfast. Children welcome. Smoking permitted on first floor. $55-70; weekly and monthly rates available.

BOYLSTON

Bed and Breakfast Associates #CW450

P. O. Box 57166, Babson Park Branch, 02157-0166
(617) 449-5302; FAX (617) 449-5958

This house is a restored barn overlooking a pool and tennis court with pastures beyond. The relaxed family will even provide a stall for your horse. Two guest rooms share a bath. Full breakfast; children welcome. $55; family rates available.

BREWSTER (CAPE COD)

Antique Inn and Cottage

Bed and Breakfast of Greater Boston and Cape Cod
P. O, Box 35, Newtonville, 02160
(617) 964-1606; (800) 832-2632
FAX (617) 332-8572

A completely restored 18th-century sea captain's house offers seven guest rooms, all with private baths, air conditioning, and antique furnishings. Award-winning gardens surround the house and full breakfast is served each morning. Children over 12 welcome. $82-108

Beacon Inn

1087 Beacon Street, 02146
(617) 566-0088

A turn-of-the-century town house has been converted into one of Brookline's most charming guest houses, Beacon Inn. The inn offers lobby fireplaces, large sunny rooms, and affordable prices. It is minutes from downtown Boston and the MBTA green lines. Boston's major hospitals and universities are easily accessible by public or private transportation. The area offers restaurants, shops, museums, theater, and other tourist attractions. The Beacon Inn looks forward to serving you.

Rooms: 24 (9 PB; 15 SB) $39-57
Continental Breakfast
Credit Cards: A, B, C
Notes: 7, 8, 9, 14

Beale House

Host Homes of Boston, P. O. Box 117, 02168
(617) 244-1308; FAX (617) 244-5156

This 1872 registered historic town house has been restored by hosts. The friendly family offers a small third-floor guest room with double bed (private bath on weekends). Resident cat. One block to Green Line-C. Near Boston College, Boston University, Back Bay, and restaurants. No smoking. $54.

A Bed and Breakfast Above the Rest #57

50 Boatswains Way, Suite 105, 02150
(617) 884-7748; (800) 677-2262

The hosts of this two-story, gambrel-roofed house have surrounded their home with color. It sits amid summer flowers, a rose garden, and a grape arbor. There are two guest bedrooms upstairs, sharing a bath. Downstairs there is a private apartment with a Pullman kitchen, color TV, and VCR. The private bath has a whirlpool. Full breakfast with homemade breads and fresh eggs is served in the formal dining room.

NOTES: Credit cards accepted: A Master Card; B Visa; C American Express; D Discover Card; E Diner's Club; F Other; 2 Personal Checks accepted; 3 Lunch available; 4 Dinner available; 5 Open all year;

Bed and Breakfast Associates #CC675

P. O. Box 57166, Babson Park Branch, 02157-0166
(617) 449-5302; FAX (617) 449-5958

A quiet neighborhood setting, abundant gardens, and an easy drive to the National Seashore await you at this cozy little bed and breakfast. You will enjoy a full country breakfast with eggs from chickens raised by the hosts. This sparkling fresh and charming home has two guest rooms that share a bath. Full breakfast; no smoking. $60. A two-room suite is available without breakfast ($450 weekly).

Bed and Breakfast Cape Cod #17

P. O, Box 341, West Hyannisport, 02672-0341
(508) 775-2772; FAX (508) 775-2884

Situated along the banks of Cape Cod Bay in historic Brewster is this 1750 sea captain's house. Six hundred yards from the house is a public beach where swimming and fishing are available. A continental breakfast on the patio with an ocean view is served each morning. Double or twin beds available. Golf, Nickerson State Park, and the village are less than a mile away. $65.

Bed and Breakfast Cape Cod #28

P. O, Box 341, West Hyannisport, 02672-0341
(508) 775-2772; FAX (508) 775-2884

This Cape Cod-style house was built in 1739. Today, this lovely old house retains its original appearance and is very well maintained. In a remote area, the birds and plants offer a natural wonderland for sitting or walking in the woods. A two-room suite with a sitting room, double bed, and private full bath is available, and a second guest room on the second floor is also available with a double bed and private bath. Continental breakfast. $85.

Bed and Breakfast Cape Cod #33

P. O, Box 341, West Hyannisport, 02672-0341
(508) 775-2772; FAX (508) 775-2884

Perched on a cliff fifty feet above the waters of a beautiful freshwater pond sits a ranch home with two private bath/bedroom suites. On the ground floor, a room with a king-size bed, large sitting area, and a lake view is also available. The hosts serve a continental breakfast in a lovely, bright dining room, and guests are encouraged to use the parlor. Bring your swim suit and fishing pole, and be prepared to relax in this private setting on the beach. $75.

Bed and Breakfast Cape Cod #41

P. O, Box 341, West Hyannisport, 02672-0341
(508) 775-2772; FAX (508) 775-2884

In an antique village, this lovely home was rebuilt in 1973 and has all amenities, including air conditioning, TV, and traditional decor. A short walk takes you to shops, bay beaches, and other points of interest. A large second floor private bath/ bedroom has a king-size bed, and four other rooms with either double or queen-size beds are also available. Big gourmet breakfast served each morning. $65-105.

The Beechcroft Inn

1360 Main Street, 02631
(508) 896-9534

This 140-year-old New England inn is nestled among stately beech trees in a quiet historical section of Cape Cod. Central to beaches, golf shops, play houses, etc. This casually elegant inn, decorated with a cozy flair, has a warmth that is irresistably inviting and somehow familiar. The hosts look forward to enjoying your company as guests in their home. Off season rates available.

6 Pets welcome; 7 Smoking allowed; 8 Children welcome; 9 Social drinking allowed; 10 Tennis available; 11 Swimming available; 12 Golf available; 13 Skiing available; 14 May be booked through travel agents.

Hosts: The DeReveres
Rooms: 10 (PB) $65-95
Full Breakfast
Credit Cards: A, B, C
Notes: 2, 4, 5, 7, 9

Captain Freeman Inn

Captain Freeman Inn

15 Breakwater Road, 02631
(508) 896-7481

Charming old sea captain's mansion offers luxury suites with balcony, private spa, fireplace, canopy bed, TV, air conditioning. Spacious rooms with canopy beds and private baths and rooms with shared bath. Enjoy the wraparound porch, outdoor pool, bikes, and full breakfast. Centrally situated on Cape Cod's historic north side, close to beaches, restaurants, and shopping.

Host: Carol Covitz
Rooms: 12 (9 PB; 3 SB) $50-185
Full Breakfast
Credit Cards: A, B, C
Notes: 2, 5, 8 (over 11), 9, 10, 11, 12, 14

Isaiah Clark House and Rose Cottage

1187 Main Street, 02631
(508) 896-2223

Built in 1780, this inn was once the mansion of a famous sea captain and is set on five acres of landscaped gardens. All guests enjoy a full American breakfast served on a deck overlooking the gardens. Many guest rooms have working fireplaces; all are air conditioned. Host was formerly trained as a Swiss hotelier. Special welcome for honeymooners.

Host: Charles Phillipe DiCesare
Rooms: 12 (8 PB; 4 SB) $68-110
Full Breakfast
Credit Cards: A, B, C
Notes: 5, 7 (limited), 8, 9, 10, 11, 12, 14

Old Sea Pines Inn

2553 Main Street, 02631
(508) 896-6114

Lovely turn-of-the-century mansion, once the Sea Pines School of Charm and Personality for Young Women, now a newly renovated and redecorated country inn. Furnished with antiques, some of the

Old Sea Pines

NOTES: Credit cards accepted: A Master Card; B Visa; C American Express; D Discover Card; E Diner's Club; F Other; 2 Personal Checks accepted; 3 Lunch available; 4 Dinner available; 5 Open all year;

rooms have working fireplaces. Situated on three and one-half acres of land, with a wraparound porch looking out over the lawn, trees, and flowers. Complimentary beverage on arrival.

Hosts: Stephen and Michele Rowan
Rooms: 16 (PB) $45-90
Full Breakfast
Credit Cards: A, B, C, E
Notes: 2, 5, 8 (over 8), 10, 11, 12, 14

Quail Hollow

Orleans Bed and Breakfast Associates
P. O. Box 1312, Orleans, 02653
(508) 255-3824; (800) 541-6226

Spacious grounds surround this charming 18th-century Cape farmhouse between two ponds. Second-floor bedroom has a queen-size bed and private bath with shower. A single room is available for another family member. Both rooms have water view. Breakfast is served on large screened porch. Canoe to lakeside beach for swimming, or walk there in ten minutes. $70.

The Skep Garden

Orleans Bed and Breakfast Associates
P. O. Box 1312, Orleans, 02653
(508) 255-3824; (800) 541-6226

Ideally situated for exploring the unique charms of historic Route 6A with its many antique shops. You can enjoy a good night's sleep in quiet surroundings off the beaten path. Two upstairs bedrooms—one with double bed, the other with two twins. Bath is shared. Nice sitting room downstairs. A five-minute walk to bike trail, Nickerson State Park, and private bay beach. $55.

Stonybrook

Orleans Bed and Breakfast Associates
P. O. Box 1312, Orleans, 02653
(508) 255-3824; (800) 541-6226

A pre-1776 restored Colonial house in a storybook setting next to the old grist mill and famous Stony Brook Herring Run. Private entrance to upstairs large double room with fireplace, sitting room, small modern kitchenette, and private bath. Suite has TV and air conditioning. Attractive sitting area outside overlooks the mill pond. $60.

BROOKLINE

A Bed and Breakfast Above the Rest #BR7

50 Boatswains Way, Suite 105
Boston, 02150
(617) 884-7748; (800) 677-2262

This two-family residence is perfect for people who prefer a relaxed and informal atmosphere. Guests stay on the second floor. The yard is spacious, and there is a large open back porch. The home is well-decorated and nicely furnished. There is a pleasant livingroom with a fireplace and piano. The guest room has a private bath, writing desk, and an Oriental rug. Continental breakfast.

A Bed and Breakfast Above the Rest #BR8

50 Boatswains Way, Suite 105, 02150
(617) 884-7748; (800) 677-2262

Overlooking the Putterham Golf Course, the Chestnut Hill Ranch is a traditional home in one of the nicest areas of greater Boston. The hostess and has been doing bed and breakfast for five years. There are two guest rooms that share a bath. A crib is available for a nominal charge. Full breakfast.

6 Pets welcome; 7 Smoking allowed; 8 Children welcome; 9 Social drinking allowed; 10 Tennis available; 11 Swimming available; 12 Golf available; 13 Skiing available; 14 May be booked through travel agents.

A Bed and Breakfast Above the Rest #14

50 Boatswains Way, Suite 105, 02150
(617) 884-7748; (800) 677-2262

The Perch is a smartly appointed duplex condo with wonderful views. Each floor has a balcony with French doors and graceful, cascading flowers. The interior has contemporary decor with a fireplace and wood trim. The hostess genuinely appreciates her bed and breakfast guests and has received standing invitations to the homes of some European guests. The guest room shares one and one-half baths with the hostess. Overlooking Fisher Hill. Continental breakfast.

A Bed and Breakfast Above the Rest #28

50 Boatswains Way, Suite 105, 02150
(617) 884-7748; (800) 677-2262

Situated in a charming cul-de-sac, the Parsonage is indeed home to an Episcopal minister—and a court stenographer. The atmosphere at this Victorian-era brick town house is friendly and casual. The two guest bedrooms are on the third floor and share a bath. A crib and roll-away cot are available. Continental breakfast.

A Bed and Breakfast Above the Rest #29

50 Boatswains Way, Suite 105, 02150
(617) 884-7748; (800) 677-2262

Guests stay in a private apartment on the lower level of the town house. A comfortable sitting area with TV overlooks a garden in the rear. Furnishings tend toward the antique, with new hardwood floors everywhere except in the carpeted bedroom. There is a brand new bath and tiny kitchen. Breakfast supplies are provided.

A Bed and Breakfast Above the Rest #31

50 Boatswains Way, Suite 105, 02150
(617) 884-7748; (800) 677-2262

A very large first-floor apartment in a small and charming three-story brownstone apartment building near Washington Square. The hostess is an impressionistic painter, and her oils are hung throughout the house. Guests are invited to make themselves at home in the enormous livingroom with TV and stereo. The guest room has charming old furnishings, a single bed, and a private bath. A large fan keeps the room cool in the summer. Continental breakfast.

A Bed and Breakfast Above the Rest #32

50 Boatswains Way, Suite 105, 02150
(617) 884-7748; (800) 677-2262

Listed in the National Register of Historic Places, this English Brick is truly unique. Three attached town houses with sharply peaked dormers are spanned across the front by a wide balcony. The main entrance is on this balcony. Inside, the house is furnished with pieces from around the world. There are two guest rooms that share one and one-half bath. The host speaks fluent Spanish. Long-term stays are welcome. Continental breakfast.

A Bed and Breakfast Above the Rest #33

50 Boatswains Way, Suite 105, 02150
(617) 884-7748; (800) 677-2262

This single-family home, a white stucco Cape, is hosted by an active and amiable married couple. There are two large guest rooms. One is a combination bedroom/sitting room with TV and convertible couch. The two rooms share a bath. Cribs are available. Within walking distance of vari-

---

NOTES: Credit cards accepted: A Master Card; B Visa; C American Express; D Discover Card; E Diner's Club; F Other; 2 Personal Checks accepted; 3 Lunch available; 4 Dinner available; 5 Open all year;

ous restaurants. Full breakfast is served on an enclosed porch that overlooks the garden.

A Bed and Breakfast Above the Rest #34

50 Boatswains Way, Suite 105, 02150
(617) 884-7748; (800) 677-2262

A two-story family home built in 1874, the Italianate Victorian occupies a spacious corner lot across the street from a park. The hostess devotes her busy days to bed and breakfast. Traditional furnishings include some antiques, and large windows add to the overall feeling of roominess. Two guest rooms, one with private bath; one shares a bath with the hosts. Children welcome. Continental breakfast.

A Bed and Breakfast Above the Rest #35

50 Boatswains Way, Suite 105, 02150
(617) 884-7748; (800) 677-2262

This 100-year-old Queen Anne-style Victorian has turrets, bay windows, and a lovely circular porch. The two third-floor guest rooms are prettily decorated with chintz, lace, and white wicker furniture. Both share a bath. Continental breakfast.

A Bed and Breakfast Above the Rest #36

50 Boatswains Way, Suite 105, 02150
(617) 884-7748; (800) 677-2262

This Second Empire-style, clapboard mansard home was built in 1871 by its architect namesake, William Wood. Reflecting the history of the house, the decor includes lovely muted wall colors and period antiques. The common room is filled with maps and information on the greater Boston area. There are three guest

rooms on the second floor. One has a private bath. Two rooms are air-conditioned. Continental breakfast.

A Bed and Breakfast Above the Rest #37

50 Boatswains Way, Suite 105, 03250
(617) 884-7748; (800) 677-2262

Blake Road bed and breakfast is a handsome brick home nicely set on a corner lot. There are three guest rooms, one on the second floor, and the other on the third floor. A full bath on the second floor is for guests. All rooms are carpeted and have desks and TVs. Continental breakfast.

A Bed and Breakfast Above the Rest #38

50 Boatswains Way, Suite 105, 02150
(617) 884-7748; (800) 677-2262

Guests from as far away as the Soviet Union have stayed in this well-preserved home built in 1899. The three-story house sits on a small hill with a view of the Back Bay area. It has three porches, original light fixtures, and original woodwork and hardwood floors. The dining room still has its original wallpaper. There are seven guest rooms (because of zoning, only two can be occupied at one time). Many have fireplaces and private baths. All rooms have TVs and alarm clocks. Full breakfast served from 8:00-8:30 A.M.

A Bed and Breakfast Above the Rest #39

50 Boatswains Way, Suite 105, 02150
(617) 884-7748; (800) 677-2262

There's a wonderful view from the livingroom of this charming home. Two Siamese cats share Top o' the Hill with the gourmet caterer-hostess. There are two guest rooms, and a third bedroom is sometimes available. One has a private bath. Near Boston College. Full breakfast, including homemade breads.

A Bed and Breakfast Above the Rest #40

50 Boatswains Way, Suite 105, 02150
(617) 884-7748; (800) 677-2262

The Steams family, Boston merchants, built this elegant Victorian mansion in 1903. Today it has been restored to capture its original spirit. Oak paneling, leaded-glass windows, and a grand staircase hearken back to an earlier time. Continental breakfast is served in the large first-floor common room. There are 12 guest rooms, all furnished with distinctive antiques, designer curtains, and bed coverings. Most rooms have private baths. In the Coolidge Corner area.

A Bed and Breakfast Above the Rest #41

50 Boatswains Way, Suite 105, 02150
(617) 884-7748; (800) 677-2262

This cheery first-floor apartment has a beautiful screened front porch for summertime relaxing and two fireplaces to keep things cozy in the winter. The hostess is a gourmet cook. Two guest rooms, one with a mahogany, four-poster Queen Anne bed, share a bath. Full breakfast is served on weekends, self-serve on weekdays. Close to restaurants and shops.

Bed and Breakfast Associates #M605

P. O. Box 57166, Babson Park Branch, 02157-0166
(617) 449-5302; FAX (617) 449-5958

An active family invites you to their stately home for a minimum of four nights. Across from a lovely park, the home offers a serene setting in a fine neighborhood just steps from public transportation and a short walk from Boston University. The guest room is pretty and includes a coffee maker, refrigerator, and dining table. Self-serve continental breakfast; children welcome; no smoking. $75; monthly rates available.

Bed and Breakfast Associates #M610

P. O. Box 57166, Babson Park Branch, 02157-0166
(617) 449-5302; FAX (617) 449-5958

This quiet Brookline Hills neighborhood is convenient to the Longwood Medical area as well as the "T" to central Boston. The guest suite is a large room featuring a fully stocked kitchenette, private bath, dining table, and sofa. Continental breakfast; children welcome; no smoking. $70.

Bed and Breakfast Associates #M617

P. O. Box 57166, Babson Park Branch, 02157-0166
(617) 449-5302; FAX (617) 449-5958

Just three blocks from Commonwealth Avenue, near Boston University, this Victorian bed and breakfast is a haven for guests visiting both Boston and Cambridge. The restful decor is enhanced by the 19th-century American antiques throughout the house. Three second-floor guest rooms with shared bath. Full breakfast; children welcome; smoking outside. $55-70; monthly rates available.

Beech Tree Inn

83 Longwood Avenue, 02146
(617) 277-1620; (800) 544-9660

The Beech Tree Inn is a turn-of-the-century Victorian private home that has been converted to a bed and breakfast. Each room is individually decorated, some with fireplaces, and they vary in size and decor. A continental breakfast is served, and a fully equipped kitchen is available. The inn is within walking distance of many shops, restaurants, and world-renowned medical centers; and internationally famous academic institutions are only a few blocks away. The nearby subway will take you into downtown Boston in 12 minutes. A pleasant interlude for a night, a weekend, or even a week.

Hosts: Kathrine Anderson and Bette Allen
Rooms: 9 (3 PB; 6 SB) $52.65-58.14
Continental Breakfast
Credit Cards: None
Notes: 2, 5, 6, 7, 8

Briarwood

Host Homes of Boston, P. O. Box 117, 02168
(617) 244-1308; FAX (617) 244-5156

Historic 1875 landmark home combines Early American antiques with modern amenities. Exceptional first-floor guest wing with private entrance, queen bed, two twins, skylights, alcove with dining table, and light cooking facilities. Second-floor guest room with double bed. Guests prepare own breakfast in room. One block to Boston College campus. Three blocks to Green Line-D. Air conditioning; TV; no smoking. $68-75.

Greater Boston Hospitality

P. O. Box 1142, 02146
(617) 277-5430

Situated throughout the greater Boston area, this reservation service has Federal, Colonial, and Georgian private homes, unhosted apartments, and small, intimate inns in the Back Bay, Beacon Hill, Waterfront areas, as well as Brookline, Cambridge, and suburbs. Many include parking; many are on the subway system; all include breakfast.

Coordinator: Lauren Simonelli
Rooms: 180 (120 PB; 60 SB) $50-150
Continental Breakfast
Credit Cards: A, B, C
Notes: 2, 5, 8, 9, 10, 11, 12, 14

Heath House

Host Homes of Boston, P. O. Box 117, 02168
(617) 244-1308; FAX (617) 244-5156

Country atmosphere close to city in classic Colonial on rolling lawn. English hostess offers two second-floor guest rooms (queen with air conditioning and twins). Children welcome. Near Pine Manor, Boston College, Longwood medical area. Boston five miles. Green Line-D one-half mile. No smoking. $61-68.

The Pleasant Pheasant

Host Homes of Boston, P. O. Box 117, 02168
(617) 244-1308; FAX (617) 244-5156

Here's that old-inn feeling in a Colonial on two secluded acres. Hosts and children share spacious home and kids' equipment. Two guest rooms: second floor has double and twin, private bath; lower floor has queen sofa bed and twin. Children welcome. Near Boston College, Pine Manor, Longwood Medical Center. Boston five miles. Green Line-D one-half mile. $54-68.

Sarah's Loft

Host Homes of Boston, P. O. Box 117, 02168
(617) 244-1308; FAX (617) 244-5156

Bright and spacious third-floor suite with private entrance. Guest quarters include queen bedroom and smaller room with queen sofa bed. Also, a large living area with skylights, stereo, dining table (where breakfast is served), refrigerator, microwave, and extra sofa bed. Children are welcome. Green Line-C, village two blocks. Fenway Park, Boston one mile. Air conditioning, crib, private bath, TV, no smoking. $71.

6 Pets welcome; 7 Smoking allowed; 8 Children welcome; 9 Social drinking allowed; 10 Tennis available; 11 Swimming available; 12 Golf available; 13 Skiing available; 14 May be booked through travel agents.

Studio Apartment

Host Homes of Boston, P. O. Box 117, 02168
(617) 244-1308; FAX (617) 244-5156

Colonial home (1620 Salem house replica)
on quiet cul-de-sac offers above-ground
basement room with double bed, sofa, galley kitchen, patio, and private entrance.
Choice of breakfast on tray or self-serve.
Five blocks to Green Line-C. Ten minutes
to Copley Square. TV, no smoking, private
bath. $68.

Town and Country

Host Homes of Boston, P. O. Box 117, 02168
(617) 244-1308; FAX (617) 244-5156

Elegant 1916 French Riviera-style home in
Boston's estate area has walled garden,
skyline view. Spacious second-floor guest
room (king or twin beds) with fireplace.
Near Museum of Fine Arts, Longwood
medical area, Boston College, Boston
University, Back Bay. Green Line-D one
mile. Boston one-half mile. Private bath, no
smoking. $68.

BROOKLINE HILLS

The Treehouse

Host Homes of Boston, P. O. Box 117, 02168
(617) 244-1308; FAX (617) 244-5156

Meg's modern town house with traditional
decor has a sweeping view from the glass-
walled livingroom and deck. Two second
floor guest rooms (double and twins). Also,
in season, a king room with air conditioning and private bath. Two Siamese cats.
Near Back Bay, Boston College, Boston
University. Ten minutes to Hynes
Convention Center via Green Line-C and D
three blocks. Private bath, TV, no smoking.
$57-75.

BROOKLINE VILLAGE

Historic Row

Host Homes of Boston, P. O. Box 117, 02168
(617) 244-1308; FAX (617) 244-5156

The National Register of Historic Places
lists this 1928 Williamsburg attached
house. Three large second-floor guest
rooms (two queens and twins) each with
color TV. Resident cat and dog. Near
Boston College, Boston University,
Longwood Medical center. Green Line-D
three blocks. 10 minutes to Back Bay and
convention center. TV, shared bath, no
smoking. $57.

BUCKLAND

1797 House

Upper Street-Clarlemont Road, 01338
(413) 625-2975

This 18th-century home is located in a
peaceful rural area, yet is convenient to
many attractions and all points in New
England. Large rooms, private baths, down
quilts, and a lovely screened porch insure
your comfort. A modicum of civilization in
an increasingly uncivilized world.

Host: Janet Turley
Rooms: 3 (PB) $60-75
Full Breakfast
Credit Cards: None
Closed Dec.
Notes: 10, 12, 13

CAMBRIDGE

A Bed and Breakfast Above the Rest #42

50 Boatswains Way, Suite 105, Boston, 02150
(617) 884-7748; (800) 677-2262

Hardwood floors, Oriental rugs, window
boxes, and plants add wonderful color to
this airy third-floor home in a typical

Cambridge row house. TV and VCR in the sitting room. There is one guest room with a shared bath. A ten-minute walk to Harvard Square. Continental breakfast with freshly baked muffins and excellent French-roast coffee.

A Bed and Breakfast Above the Rest #43

50 Boatswains Way, Suite 105, Boston, 02150
(617) 884-7748; (800) 677-2262

Samuel Fay, a prominent citizen and influential probate judge, built this home for his family in 1805. Today the Federal-style house is listed in the National Register of Historic Places. There is one large, air-conditioned guest room with a cathedral ceiling and wide-pine floor. The entrance to this room is private, as is the guest bath. Guests are treated to fresh fruit and flowers in their room. Within walking distance of restaurants, shops, and services. Continental breakfast supplies are provided.

A Bed and Breakfast Above the Rest #48

50 Boatswains Way, Suite 105, Boston, 02150
(617) 884-7748; (800) 677-2262

Though built in the last century, this Victorian duplex has been remodeled by a contemporary designer who added a tree-shaded deck and a glass wall in the kitchen. There are two guest rooms that share a bath. Situated on a quiet tree-lined street, just a 12-minute walk to Harvard Square. Continental breakfast includes homemade bread.

A Bed and Breakfast Above the Rest #49

50 Boatswains Way, Suite 105, Boston, 02150
(617) 884-7748; (800) 677-2262

Cambridge House, featured on TV by the BBC and "Evening Magazine," is a classic Colonial Revival home dating from 1892. The interior has been thoughtfully designer-decorated to reflect its original style. There are 12 guest rooms with a variety of bed sizes. Generally baths are shared, though a few are private. Full gourmet breakfast. In the Porter Square area.

Bed and Breakfast Associates #M804

P. O. Box 57166, Babson Park Branch
Boston, 02157-0166
(617) 449-5302; FAX (617) 449-5958

Near Harvard Yard, this impeccable Philadelphia-style Victorian, circa 1890, is situated on a quiet street among the finest homes in Cambridge. Your two-room suite features a spacious sitting room with sleeper sofa, fireplace, writing table, TV, and balcony. Continental breakfast; children welcome; no smoking. $85-100.

Bed and Breakfast Associates #M817

P. O. Box 57166, Babson Park Branch
Boston, 02157-0166
(617) 449-5302; FAX (617) 449-5958

Situated on the northern perimeter of Harvard, this Victorian offers comfort and convenience. Between them, your host couple speak Italian, French, Spanish, German, Russian, Mandarin, Cantonese, and Japanese. Three guest rooms, one with private bath, on the second floor. Generous continental breakfast; children welcome. $58-70; monthly rates available.

Bed and Breakfast Associates #M875

P. O. Box 57166, Babson Park Branch
Boston, 02157-0166
(617) 449-5302; FAX (617) 449-5958

6 Pets welcome; 7 Smoking allowed; 8 Children welcome; 9 Social drinking allowed; 10 Tennis available; 11 Swimming available; 12 Golf available; 13 Skiing available; 14 May be booked through travel agents.

A large home set in a quiet neighborhood adjacent to jogging paths. Just a 20-minute walk from Harvard Square, this home features skylights, sliding doors to deck, many plants, antiques, playroom, and a fenced yard. Three guest rooms with private baths. Full and imaginative breakfast; children welcome. $55; family and monthly rates available.

Bed and Breakfast Associates #M885

P. O. Box 57166, Babson Park Branch
Boston, 02157-0166
(617) 449-5302; FAX (617) 449-5958

Your congenial hostess, a Boston attorney, shares her cozy Greek Revival home (circa 1853) just outside Harvard Square. Her decor is accented by a refreshing mix of country antiques and her quiet urban neighborhood provides a convenient setting for activities in Boston or Cambridge. Two second-floor guest rooms share a bath. Full breakfast upon request; children welcome; no smoking. $75; family and monthly rates available.

Bed and Breakfast Associates #M930

P. O. Box 57166, Babson Park Branch
Boston, 02157-0166
(617) 449-5302; FAX (617) 449-5958

A spectacular decorator-furnished bed and breakfast inn in North Cambridge. Each room has a built-in vanity with sink and color TV. Full breakfast is served in the formal Victorian dining room, and guests are invited to relax in one of the gracious parlors. A lovely carriage house and a nearby guest house have also been restored and are offered as bed and breakfast accommodations. Shared baths; children over six welcome; smoking on porch only. $85-150.

Blue Hawthorne

Host Homes of Boston
P. O. Box 117, Boston, 02168
(617) 244-1308; FAX (617) 244-5156

This 100-year-old Victorian home off Brattle Street is a quiet oasis near bustling Harvard Square. Your host offers two first-floor guest rooms (queen and twins) with private baths, phone, and TV. Shady side garden. Three blocks to the square, Red Line, Charles Hotel, restaurants, and shops. Air conditioning, TV. No smoking. $75

Cambridge Suite

Host Homes of Boston
P. O. Box 117, Boston, 02168
(617) 244-1308; FAX (617) 244-5156

This large home (1855) is on a quiet road only three blocks from bustling Harvard Square. The first-floor guest suite has a queen bedroom, sitting room with sofa, desk. Breakfast served in the dining room. Near William James Hall and law school. Red Line three blocks. Air conditioning. No smoking. $81.

Near Harvard Square

Host Homes of Boston
P. O. Box 117, Boston, 02168
(617) 244-1308; FAX (617) 244-5156

Just a seven-minute walk to the square, Harvard Yard, Brattle Street, and Red Line. Quiet. Shady location. European decor. Coffee ground fresh for breakfast. Private first-floor guest room with double bed. Air conditioning, TV, shared bath. $68.

True Victorian

Host Homes of Boston
P. O. Box 117, Boston, 02168
(617) 244-1308; FAX (617) 244-5156

Host's Victorian jewel sits on a quiet hill near Massachusetts Avenue between

NOTES: Credit cards accepted: A Master Card; B Visa; C American Express; D Discover Card; E Diner's Club; F Other; 2 Personal Checks accepted; 3 Lunch available; 4 Dinner available; 5 Open all year;

Harvard and Porter squares. Three second-floor guest rooms—two with double bed, TV, and desk; king room. Only two rooms booked at a time. Shared family bath. Hearty breakfast in sunny kitchen, often self-serve on weekdays. Red Line and train at Porter Square three blocks. TV. No smoking. $61.

CENTERVILLE

Bed and Breakfast Cape Cod #23

P. O, Box 341, West Hyannisport, 02672-0341
(508) 775-2772; FAX (508) 775-2884

Formerly the home of Cardinal Spellman, this elegant 1830s mansion with grounds designed by Frederick Law Olmstead has been restored in the Victorian splendor of a past era. It offers suites or rooms, all with private baths, a full gourmet breakfast, and a short walk to Craigville Beach. Hyannis is five minutes away. No children. $85-185.

Bed and Breakfast Cape Cod #43

P. O, Box 341, West Hyannisport, 02672-0341
(508) 775-2772; FAX (508) 775-2884

This quiet bed and breakfast overlooks Lake Wequaquet, the largest fresh water lake on Cap Cod. The second floor has been set aside for guests, featurng two rooms that share a bath. A first-floor room offers a king-size bed and a private bath. Continental breakfast. $55-65.

Bed and Breakfast Cape Cod #52

P. O, Box 341, West Hyannisport, 02672-0341
(508) 775-2772; FAX (508) 775-2884

This property has been featured in *Country Magazine* and is on the National Register of Historic Places. It offers three guest rooms, all with private baths and air conditioning. Full country breakfast served in the dining room. Children over twelve welcome. $70-85.

Bed and Breakfast/Inns of New England MA-1045

329 Lake Drive, Guilford, CT 06437
(800) 582-0853

This inn offers the warmth and luxury of a Victorian home in the romantic ambience of an earlier time. Guest rooms have hardwoor floors of cherry, maple, and oak, Oriental carpets, and antiques. Privacy is assured, for this 100-year-old home was designed so that no two guest rooms share the same wall. Five suites with private bath (two more with a shared bath), fireplaces, cathedral ceilings, roof deck, and a private library make this inn unique. $125-185. Garden cottage with full bed, wraparound porch, and private bath: $105.

Carver House

638 Main Street, 02632
(508) 775-9414

Flowers decorate a picket fence in front of the Carver House. The inn, situated one-half mile from Craigville Beach, has three rooms with twin beds and TV; two rooms have sinks. Carver House is centrally situated for golf, biking, tennis, and the island ferries.

Hosts: Marguerite and Harold MacNeely
Rooms: 3 (SB) $45
Continental Breakfast
Credit Cards: None
Notes: 5, 7

---

6 Pets welcome; 7 Smoking allowed; 8 Children welcome; 9 Social drinking allowed; 10 Tennis available; 11 Swimming available; 12 Golf available; 13 Skiing available; 14 May be booked through travel agents.

Copper Beech Inn

497 Main Street, 02632
(508) 771-5488

Built in 1830 by an intercoastal ship captain, this charmingly restored house is now in the National Register of Historic Places. It stands amid tall trees, including the largest European beech tree on Cape Cod. Interior features include a parlor and a common room for guest use. Walk to Craigville Beach, one of the ten best beaches in the United States. Hyannis, the population center of the Cape where the ferry to Nantucket and Martha's Vineyard is boarded, is four miles away. Air-conditioned.

Host: Joyce Diehl
Rooms: 3 (PB) $80-85
Full Breakfast
Minimum stay May 25-Oct. 10 2 nights
Credit Cards: A, B, C, D
Notes: 2, 5, 7 (limited), 8 (over 11), 9, 10, 11, 12

Long Dell Inn

436 South Main Street, 02632
(508) 775-2750

One of Centerville's finest inns, an 1850 sea captain's home. Enjoy a country Victorian atmosphere, delightfully romantic. In cooler months, relax before the fire in the livingroom. Off-street parking.

Copper Beech Inn

Hosts: Joy and Roy Swayze
Rooms: 6 plus apartment (PB) $75-90
Full Breakfast
Credit Cards: None
Notes: 2, 5, 8, 9, 10, 11, 12, 14

CHARLEMONT

Forest Way Farm

Jacksonville Stage Road, 01337
(413) 337-8321

This carefully restored, circa 1812, mountaintop country inn reflects the ambience of rural New England. Family heirlooms, nicely decorated rooms, and farm breakfasts with homemade fixings and grits make your stay an unforgettable experience.

Hosts: Jimmie and Paul Snyder
Rooms: 3 (S2.5B) $45-65
Full Breakfast
Minimum stay holidays: 2 nights
Credit Cards: C
Notes: 2, 5, 7, 12, 13, 14

CHARLTON

The Prindle House Bed and Breakfast

71 Prindle Hill Road, 01507
(508) 248-3134

The Prindle House is a charming and warm 1734 country farmhouse with majestic views of Prindle Pond and surrounding countryside. Enjoy your breakfast by one of six fireplaces or on the comfortable porch. Nearby there is Old Sturbridge Village, the famous Brimfield fleamarkets, museums, many specialty and antique shops, fishing, golfing, and cross-country skiing.

Hosts: Richard and Roberta DeLeo
Rooms: 3 (SB) $45-50
Continental Breakfast
Credit Cards: None
Notes: 2, 5, 8, 9, 12

NOTES: Credit cards accepted: A Master Card; B Visa; C American Express; D Discover Card; E Diner's Club; F Other; 2 Personal Checks accepted; 3 Lunch available; 4 Dinner available; 5 Open all year;

CHATHAM

Bed and Breakfast Associates #CC475

P. O. Box 57166, Babson Park Branch
Boston, 02157-0166
(617) 449-5302; FAX (617) 449-5958

Your hostess invites you to share her sprawling Cape-style home with its Early American decor. This wooded setting is perfect for country walks. Nearby is the village of Chatham, renowned for its treasure trove of galleries, shops, ice cream parlors, and restaurants in a gracious old-fashioned seaside setting. Three guest rooms, some with private baths, and a studio apartment. Continental breakfast; children welcome; no smoking. No breakfast served for apartment. $68-93.

Bed and Breakfast Cape Cod #12

P. O, Box 341, West Hyannisport, 02672-0341
(508) 775-2772; FAX (508) 775-2884

This reproduction of an Early American Cape Cod Home offers a first-floor room with a private bath, queen-size bed; the second floor offers two rooms with double beds. (These rooms are never rented separately, so they share a "private" bath.) Continental breakfast. A short walk to the village, fish pier, and the beach. $65.

Bed and Breakfast Cape Cod #48

P. O, Box 341, West Hyannisport, 02672-0341
(508) 775-2772; FAX (508) 775-2884

This eighteen-room country inn was built in the 1830s and painstakingly restored in 1989. All guest rooms are air conditioned, have private baths, and are filled with antiques and tasteful accents. Continental

breakfast is served from 8:30-10:00 and cocktails are served in the Schooner Tavern on the premises. $102-145.

Bed and Breakfast Cape Cod #78

P. O, Box 341, West Hyannisport, 02672-0341
(508) 775-2772; FAX (508) 775-2884

Built in 1985, this lovely host home offers a second-floor suite that has a large bedroom with a double bed and a pair of twins, sitting area, TV, and private bath with a shower. A generous continental breakfast with homemade breads and muffins is served in the country room or patio, and the home is half mile from town and 3/4 mile from the harbor. $55-65.

Bed and Breakfast Cape Cod #79

P. O, Box 341, West Hyannisport, 02672-0341
(508) 775-2772; FAX (508) 775-2884

This large contemporary home built in 1981 offers a large first-floor suite with a private entrance. Two rooms have double beds and share a bath, and another room with a pair of twin beds shares another bath. Ocean beaches are a half mile away and village shops are two miles. This is a great spot for families or two couples. No smoking. $60.

The Bradford Inn and Motel

26 Cross Street
P. O. Box 750, 02633
(508) 945-1030; (800) CHATHAM

The Bradford Inn and Motel is a unique complex of 25 rooms situated in the quaint seaside village of Chatham. It is within the historic district, a short stroll from charming shops, theaters, concerts, restaurants,

---

6 Pets welcome; 7 Smoking allowed; 8 Children welcome; 9 Social drinking allowed; 10 Tennis available; 11 Swimming available; 12 Golf available; 13 Skiing available; 14 May be booked through travel agents.

beach, golf, and tennis. Yet the accommodations are in a secluded area away from the hustle of the village proper.

Hosts: William and Audrey Gray
Rooms: 25 (PB) $80-175
Full Breakfast
Credit Cards: A, B, C, D
Notes: 2, 4, 5, 7, 8 (over 8), 9, 10, 11, 12, 14

Chatham Town House Inn

Chatham Town House Inn

11 Library Lane, 02633
(508) 945-2180; (800) 242-2180

This 1881 sea captain's mansion is a rare blend of the old and new and is situated on a grassy knoll in the heart of Chatham. Twenty-two rooms, two fireplaced cottages, air conditioning, telephones, minifridge, TV, HBO, and NESN; some rooms also offer canopy beds and private balconies. Swimming pool and spa. Breakfast buffet included and served in our Two Turtles dining room. Within walking distance of all major activities and beaches. No smoking.

Hosts: Russell and Svea Peterson
Rooms: 24 (PB) $98-175
Continental Breakfast; Full Breakfast available
Credit Cards: All major
Notes: 2, 3, 5, 9, 10, 11, 12, 13, 14

Classic Cape Bed and Breakfast

Bed and Breakfast Greater Boston and Cape Cod
P. O. Box 35, Newtonville, 02160
(617) 964-1606; (800) 832-2632
FAX (617) 332-8572

Classic Cape Cod-style home in a quiet area within walking distance of the historic Chatham village center. The spacious guest room is on the second floor, separate from the hosts. It includes one double and two twin beds and a sitting area. Private bath. Generous continental breakfast. No smoking; children over 12 welcome. $70 in-season; $65 off-season.

Cranberry Inn at Chatham

359 Main Street, 02633
(508) 945-9232; (800) 332-4667

Chatham's oldest inn, completely renovated. Conveniently situated in the heart of the historic village district within steps of shopping, dining, and beautiful beaches. Each of the 18 guest rooms is individually appointed and furnished with antiques and reproductions. All private baths; rooms with fireplaces, balconies, and wet bars available. Spacious, deluxe suite available with fireplace and loft. Hospitable hosts and staff. Homemade continental breakfast served daily.

Hosts: Peggy DeHan and Richard Morris
Rooms: 18 (PB) $85-160
Continental Breakfast
Credit Cards: A, B, C
Notes: 2, 8 (over 12), 9, 11, 12, 14

Cranberry Inn at Chatham

The Cyrus Kent House Inn

63 Cross Street, 02633
(800) 338-5368

Comfortably elegant, the inn is an award-winning restoration of a 19th-century sea captain's mansion. Rooms are large, bright, and airy, furnished with antiques. Private baths, telephone, television. Conveniently situated on a quiet lane in the quaint seaside village of Chatham, a historic district. Excellent restaurants and beaches are within steps.

Hosts: Jim and Vena Johnstone, Jodie Dorman
Rooms: 10 (PB) $90-145
Continental Breakfast
Credit Cards: A, B, C
Closed Jan.-March
Notes: 2, 5, 7, 8 (over 12), 9, 10, 11, 12

Moses Nickerson House Inn

364 Old Harbor Road, 02633
(508) 945-5859

Quiet, elegant, romantic. Built in 1839 by whaling captain Moses Nickerson, this small inn has seven individually decorated guest rooms featuring canopy beds, fireplaces, Oriental rugs. Glass-enclosed breakfast room. Walk to the quaint village of Chatham with its fine shops, galleries, and restaurants or turn right at the end of the driveway and walk to the beach or fishing pier.

The Cyrus Kent House Inn

Moses Nickerson House Inn

Hosts: Elsie and Carl Piccola
Rooms: 7 (PB) $70-149
Full Breakfast
Credit Cards: A, B, C
Notes: 2, 5, 9, 14

Olde Nantucket House

Orleans Bed and Breakfast Associates
P. O. Box 1312, Orleans, 02653
(508) 255-3824; (800) 541-6226

Once a Nantucket sea captain's home, this Greek Revival-style house was "floated" to Cape Cod and moved to its current site in the mid-1800s. Five guest rooms are comfortably and tastefully furnished with antiques. All rooms have private baths. Short, pretty walk to the beach and convenient to dining and shopping in Chatham and Harwich Port. $62-75.

Salt Marsh House

Orleans Bed and Breakfast Associates
P. O. Box 1312, Orleans, 02653
(508) 255-3824; (800) 541-6226

Fresh breezes ruffle the white curtains in this pristine house to give you a real feeling of being at the seaside. Only a two-minute walk to Nantucket Sound beach with sailboat and windsurfer rentals and snack bar. Three rooms on second floor; one spacious king with private bath; two twin rooms with large shared bath. Buffet-style breakfast. $55-65.

6 Pets welcome; 7 Smoking allowed; 8 Children welcome; 9 Social drinking allowed; 10 Tennis available; 11 Swimming available; 12 Golf available; 13 Skiing available; 14 May be booked through travel agents.

Scrabbletown

Orleans Bed and Breakfast Associates
P. O. Box 1312, Orleans, 02653
(508) 255-3824; (800) 541-6226

Graced with window boxes, this mansard-roof Civil War era house is in the old Chatham village, within earshot of surf, close to Lighthouse Beach and its dramatic "breakthrough." Short walk to town center noted for its shops and Friday night band concerts. Guests share bath with shower and two bedrooms each have sinks. Ample off-street parking. Skipper, a friendly dog, greets you. $55.

The Sleepy Whale

Orleans Bed and Breakfast Associates
P. O. Box 1312, Orleans, 02653
(508) 255-3824; (800) 541-6226

A separate entrance brings you into a huge high-ceilinged family room with many windows giving country views. Your own spacious deck for sunning and relaxing. Private bath, wet bar with refrigerator, color TV. New double day bed for comfortable sleeping plus a convertible couch. Breakfast served by sociable hosts on your deck or in country kitchen. Only .4-mile walk to the warm waters of Nantucket Sound. $70.

CHESHIRE

Berkshire Bed and Breakfast Homes NC6

P. O. Box 211, Williamsburg, 01096
(413) 268-7244

An 1817 Mansard-style home on 12 acres with wraparound porch. Guest rooms with private and semiprivate baths and parlor are furnished in Victorian and country-style. Full breakfast; children welcome. $40-85.

CHESTER

Berkshire Bed and Breakfast Homes SC3

P. O. Box 211, Williamsburg, 01096
(413) 268-7244

This unhosted 1990 Colonial-style home is on 168 acres. It is furnished with country and Colonial decor. There is a parlor with a TV, a fully equipped kitchen with microwave, bath with shower, a double bed, and four adult-size bunk beds. All air conditioned. Continental breakfast; no smoking; children welcome. $65-125

Breakfast at Tiasquam

CHILMARK, MARTHA'S VINEYARD

Breakfast at Tiasquam

Rural Route 1, Box 296, 02535
(508) 645-3685

Breakfast at Tiasquam is set among the farms, ponds, woodlands, and rolling pastures of Martha's Vineyard, on the peak of a hill, well off the beaten path. Just minutes away is one of the most beautiful beaches on the entire East Coast, Lucy Vincent. Delicious full country breakfast; beautifully decorated, smoke-free house; attention paid to craftsmanship, privacy, comfort, and quiet. Breakfast at Tiasquam will make your stay on Martha's Vineyard truly unforgettable.

NOTES: Credit cards accepted: A Master Card; B Visa; C American Express; D Discover Card; E Diner's Club; F Other; 2 Personal Checks accepted; 3 Lunch available; 4 Dinner available; 5 Open all year;

Host: Ron Crowe
Rooms: 8 (2 PB; 6 SB) $75-175
Full Breakfast
Credit Cards: None
Notes: 2, 5, 8, 9, 10, 11, 12, 14

COHASSET

Actor's Row

90 Howard Gleason Road, 02025
(617) 383-1093

Spectacular harborside home, circa 1840, is situated on three acres of manicured grounds and furnished with wonderful antiques. A large veranda overlooks the harbor, and several common rooms are open for guests to use. Three bedrooms have fireplaces, all rooms have either harbor views or pool views. Twenty miles south of Boston in the picturesque seaside town of Cohasset.

Host: Mary Tubbett
Rooms: 5 (PB) $85-125
Continental Breakfast
Credit Cards: None
Notes: 5, 9, 10, 11, 14

Bed and Breakfast Cape Cod #81

P. O. Box 341, West Hyannisport, 02672-0341
(508) 775-2772; FAX (508) 775-2884

Enjoy the beautiful harbor, take a swim in the on-premises pool, or play a game of tennis on the host's court. This charming bed and breakfast in a most picturesque village south of Boston, offers five bedrooms with private baths. Continental breakfast. Forty minutes to Boston by watercraft or bus. No children under 12. $85-125.

COLRAIN

Maple Shade Bed and Breakfast

469 Nelson Road, 01340
(413) 624-3931

Enjoy the peaceful and quiet 18th-century farmhouse in the shade of giant 100-year-old maple trees. Set on 80 acres of fields and woodland in picturesque Colrain. Just six and one-half miles from the I-91, Route 2 intersection in Greenfield. Nearby are historic Deerfield, glacial pot holes, bridge of flowers, covered bridges, Northfield Mountain Recreation Center, skiing, and the Mohawk Trail.

Hosts: Audrey and Freda
Rooms: 3 (SB) $35
Continental Breakfast
Credit Cards: None
Notes: 2, 5, 6, 8, 9

CONCORD

Anderson-Wheeler Homestead

154 Fitchburg Turnpike, 01742
(508) 369-3756

An 1890 Victorian with wraparound veranda, tastefully decorated with antiques, accentuated with window seats and fireplaces. A popular area for canoeing, birdwatching, and cross-country skiing. Rural, but convenient to two restaurants and a grocery store. Only three miles from historic Concord center, Walden Pond, and the Audubon Center.

Hosts: David and Charlotte Anderson
Rooms: 5 (2 PB; 3 SB) $60-80
Expanded Continental Breakfast
Credit Cards: A, B, C, E
Notes: 2, 5, 7 (limited), 8, 9, 10, 11, 12, 13 (XC), 14

Bed and Breakfast/Inns of New England MA-1009

329 Lake Drive, Guilford, CT 06437
(800) 582-0853

This 1775 center-chimney Colonial has hand-hewn beams, gunstock posts, handsome six-over-six windows, and 18th-century paneling or molding. Guest rooms have double beds and queen beds; all have private bathrooms, direct-dial telephone, color TV, and individual climate control. The inn is two miles from Walden Pond and within a one-minute walk from the Concord Fitness Center, where you can stretch, swim, and sauna as a guest of the inn. No smoking. No pets. $65-75.

Colonel Roger Brown

1694 Main Street, 01742
(508) 369-9119; (800) 292-1369

This 1775 Colonial home is on the historic register and situated close to the Concord and Lexington historic districts, 15 miles west of Boston and Cambridge. Five rooms with air conditioning, private baths, TV, and telephones. Continental breakfast and complimentary beverages at all times.

Host: Kate Williams
Rooms: 5 (PB) $65-75
Continental Breakfast
Credit Cards: A, B, C, D
Notes: 2, 5, 8 (over 12), 9, 10, 11, 12, 13, 14

Hawthorne Inn

464 Lexington Road, 01742
(508) 369-5610

Built circa 1870 on land once owned by Ralph Waldo Emerson, Nathaniel Hawthorne, and the Alcotts. Situated alongside the "battle road" of 1775 and within walking distance of authors' homes, battle sites, and Walden Pond. Furnished with antiques, handmade quilts, original artwork, Japanese prints, and sculpture.

Hosts: G. Burch and M. Mudry
Rooms: 7 (PB) $75-150
Continental Breakfast
Credit Cards: None
Notes: 2, 5, 7 (limited), 8, 9, 10, 11, 12, 13 (XC), 14

1775 Colonial Inn

Bed and Breakfast Greater Boston and Cape Cod
P. O. Box 35, Newtonville, 02160
(617) 964-1606; (800) 832-2632
FAX (617) 332-8572

Just 20 miles west of Boston with easy access to main highways, this meticulously restored Colonial inn offers five guest rooms, all with private baths, color TV, air conditioning, and telephones. Hearty continental buffet breakfast is served in the mornings, and afternoon tea or sherry is served by the fireplace in the two-hundred-year-old sitting room. Fitness club facilities only a short walk from the inn. $65-75.

COTUIT

A Bed and Breakfast Above the Rest #60

50 Boatswains Way, Suite 105
Boston, 02150
(617) 884-7748; (800) 677-2262

The hostess has decorated this 18th-century home with antique furnishings and Oriental rugs. Downstairs, guests will find a private sitting room where they can read, watch TV, use the phone, or socialize with other guests. Upstairs, there are three guest rooms sharing two baths. Within walking distance of boat launch, golf, tennis, and the library. Continental breakfast.

Salty Dog Inn

451 Main Street, 02635
(508) 428-5228

A restored Victorian home in a quaint Cape Cod village near Hyannis, Falmouth, Island boats, dining, and theater. Warm water beaches, antique and crafts shopping nearby. Complimentary bikes and picnic tables. Private suite with a canopy bed, or rooms with shared bath. Brochure available. Minimum stay on Labor Day or Memorial Day is two nights.

Hosts: Lynn and Jerry Goldstein
Rooms: 4 (1 PB; 3 SB) $55-75
Continental Plus Breakfast
Credit Cards: A, B
Notes: 8 (over 12), 10, 11, 12, 14

NOTES: Credit cards accepted: A Master Card; B Visa; C American Express; D Discover Card; E Diner's Club; F Other; 2 Personal Checks accepted; 3 Lunch available; 4 Dinner available; 5 Open all year;

CUMMAQUID

Bed and Breakfast Cape Cod #61

P. O, Box 341, West Hyannisport, 02672-0341
(508) 775-2772; FAX (508) 775-2884

Just east of Barnstable, this house built in 1950 is a typical Cape Cod-style home with several acres of manicured grounds. Three rooms with private baths are available for guests. Hostess serves a full country breakfast with a Scandinavian flair. Hyannis and the ferry to Nantucket or Martha's Vineyard is four miles away. No smoking; no children. $65-90.

CUMMINGTON

Cumworth Farm

Rural Route 1, Box 110, Route 112, 01026
(413) 634-5529

A 200-year-old house with a sugar house and blueberry and raspberry fields on the premises. Pick your own berries in season. The farm raises sheep and is close to Tanglewood, Smith College, the William Cullen Bryant Homestead, cross-country skiing, and hiking trails.

Hosts: Ed and Mary McColgan
Rooms: 6 (SB) $58
Full Breakfast
Credit Cards: None
Notes: 2, 5, 8, 9, 10, 11, 12, 13, 14

Hidden Brook

South Street in Plainfield, 01026
(413) 634-5653

Private country carriage-shed studio with deck and well-stocked kitchenette for breakfast at your leisure. Light arrival supper of homemade bread and soup or salad included. Refreshing, romantic escape in the Berkshire Hills for a family or honeymooners, with miles of country roads and trails to hike, bike, or ski lined with gnarled old maples, jewelwood, trillium, and many other wildflowers. Children welcome. Call for a brochure with map.

Hosts: Harold Hofreiter and Jody Kerssenbrock
Apartment: 1 (PB) $60
Full or Continental Breakfast and light Dinner
Credit Cards: None
Notes: 2, 4, 5, 7 (outside), 8, 9, 11, 13

Windfields Farm

Windsor Bush Road
Rural Route 1, Box 170, 01026
(413) 684-3786

Secluded, Federal homestead on a dirt road amid fields and forests. Guests have their own entrance, book-lined livingroom, fireplace, piano, dining room. Family antiques, paintings, flowers. Windfields' organic produce, eggs, maple syrup, raspberries, wild blueberries enrich the hearty breakfasts. Near Tanglewood and six colleges.

Hosts: Carolyn and Arnold Westwood
Rooms: 2 (SB) $45-60
Full Breakfast
Credit Cards: None
Closed March and April
Notes: 2, 8 (over 12), 9, 11, 13

DANVERS

The Antique Sleigh Bed and Breakfast

Bed and Breakfast Marblehead and North Shore
P. O, Box 35, Newtonville, 02160
(617) 964-1606; (800) 832-2632
FAX (617) 244-5156

A beautiful 1854 federal landmark Colonial home with beamed ceilings in a historic district with many other antique Colonial and Greek Revival homes, many with large gardens. It is one-half mile from Route 1 and is very close to Route 95, the highway leading to New Hampshire, Maine, and Vermont. A delicious full breakfast is served on pewter. Open year-round. Three guest rooms, all with shared baths and air conditioning. Swimming pool. Children

welcome. Baby-sitting by prior arrangement. Smoking in the family room. Cat in
residence. $65-75.

Bed and Breakfast Associates #CN150

P. O. Box 57166, Babson Park Branch
Boston, 02157-0166
(617) 449-5302; FAX (617) 449-5958

This immaculate 200-year-old house has
beamed ceilings, beehive fireplaces, a lovely in-ground pool, and private guest quarters. Your hostess serves a luscious homemade breakfast on antique pewter. Two
guest rooms on the second floor share a
bath. Full breakfast; children welcome;
smoking downstairs only. $65; family rates
available.

DENNIS

Bed and Breakfast Cape Cod #4

P. O, Box 341, West Hyannisport, 02672-0341
(508) 775-2772; FAX (508) 775-2884

Restored several years ago with Victorian
antiques, this lovely home is now an elegant bed and breakfast, offering three guest
rooms with private baths. Twin or double
beds are available, and the village shops,
restaurants, and summer theater are within
walking distance. Breakfast is served from
8:00-10:00 A.M. and is full of house specialties. No smoking; no children. $65-95.

Bed and Breakfast Cape Cod #68

P. O, Box 341, West Hyannisport, 02672-0341
(508) 775-2772; FAX (508) 775-2884

This 1880 sea captain's home is built on
two acres of land on the banks of Scargo
Lake. This twenty-one-room mansion

Isaiah Hall

offers two guest rooms, one with a pair of
twins, and one with a queen-size bed. Both
have private baths, and the queen-size
room has a sitting room and a private bath.
Continental breakfast is served from 7:00-
11:00 A.M. in the enclosed porch or patio.
No children under 12. $65-98.

The Four Chimneys Inn

946 Main Street, 02638
(508) 385-6317

A comfortable, spacious 1881 Victorian
home with lovely gardens, situated on historic Route 6A across from Scargo Lake.
Short walk to Cape Cod Bay, the playhouse, Fine Arts Museum, restaurants,
shops. Golf, tennis, bike trails within two
miles. Central to all of Cape Cod.

Hosts: Christina Jervant and Diane Robinson
Rooms: 9 (7 PB; 2 SB) $45-95
Expanded Continental Breakfast
Credit Cards: A, B, C, D
Closed Nov.-Mar.
Notes: 2, 7, 8 (over 8), 9, 11, 12, 14

Isaiah Hall Bed and Breakfast Inn

152 Whig Street, 02638
(508) 385-9928; (800) 736-0160

Enjoy country ambience and hospitality in the heart of Cape Cod. Lovely 1857 farmhouse tucked away on a quiet historic sidestreet, within walking distance of the beach and village shops, restaurants, museums, cinema, and playhouse. Nearby bike trails, tennis, and golf. Comfortably appointed with antiques and Orientals. Excellent central location for day trips.

Host: Marie Brophy
Rooms: 11 (10 PB; 1 SB) $55-99
Expanded Continental Breakfast
Credit Cards: A, B, C
Closed mid-Oct.-April 1
Notes: 2, 7, 8 (over 7), 9, 10, 11, 12, 14

DENNISPORT

The Rose Petal Bed and Breakfast

152 Sea Street, Box 974, 02639
(508) 398-8470

Lovely accommodations and complete homemade breakfast in an attractively restored 1872 historic home in the heart of Cape Cod. Walk to beach, shops, dining, or relax in the guest parlor or beautifully landscaped yard. Just a short drive to the ferries to Nantucket and Martha's Vineyard. Enjoy the diverse recreation, beautiful scenery, and interesting history of Cape Cod. Brochures are available. Reservations preferred.

Hosts: Dan and Gayle Kelly
Rooms: 4 (SB) $40-55
Full Breakfast
Minimum stay holidays: 2 nights
Credit Cards: A, B
Notes: 2, 5, 7 (limited), 8, 9, 10, 11, 12, 14

DOVER

1802 House

Locke Street, 04046
(207) 967-5632

On Cape Arundel Golf Course, 1802 House provides peace and quiet, yet is within walking distance of Dock Square. A pleasant cozy interlude that you will long remember is the legacy of the 1802 House.

Hosts: Ron and Carol Perry
Rooms: 6 (PB) $75-125
Full Breakfast
Credit Cards: A, B, C
Notes: 2, 5, 9, 10, 11, 12, 13, 14

EAST FALMOUTH

Bed and Breakfast Cape Cod #44

P. O, Box 341, West Hyannisport, 02672-0341
(508) 775-2772; FAX (508) 775-2884

This picturesque modern home on Cape Cod features cathedral ceilings, glass walls, and a magnificent waterview of Waquoit Bay. A large solarium with antique wicker furniture and a spa can accommodate up to six people. Another room offers a king-size bed and shares a bath with third room that has a double and single bed. No smoking. Children over 12. $85.

EASTHAM

Bed and Breakfast Cape Cod #72

P. O, Box 341, West Hyannisport, 02672-0341
(508) 775-2772; FAX (508) 775-2884

This sixty-year-old beach home is built in the heart of what is now Cape Cod National Seashore Park. Enter from a private entrance to a livingroom with TV, library, and sitting area. Two bedrooms, one with a queen and one with a pair of twins, share the suite's bath. Casual eclectic decor adds to the relaxed-style of this popular beach setting. Continental breakfast from 7:30-9:30. Ocean view. No smoking. $90.

6 Pets welcome; 7 Smoking allowed; 8 Children welcome; 9 Social drinking allowed; 10 Tennis available; 11 Swimming available; 12 Golf available; 13 Skiing available; 14 May be booked through travel agents.

Bed and Breakfast/Inns of New England MA 1050

329 Lake Drive, Guilford, CT 06437
(800) 582-0853

A traditional two-story home located in the secluded area on the shore of Great Pond. There is a 1927 Chickering Grand Piano in the music room. The large master bedroom and bath on the second floor has a queen-size bed and color TV. A second large bedroom with pond view has twin beds. A private bathroom is directly across from the bedroom. A continental breakfast is served on the deck or in the dining room. No children; no smoking; no pets. $75-80.

Bread and Roses

Orleans Bed and Breakfast Associates
P. O. Box 1312, Orleans, 02653
(508) 255-3824; (800) 541-6226

Cozy, sunlit, modern suite. Two bedrooms with skylights, one double and one twin, separated by reading area with color TV. Bath has stall shower. Access to clean, freshwater pond for swimming and canoeing. Breakfast served in dining area or on sunny deck off music room. Artistic, musical hosts and an enchanting Shih Tzu named Muffie will add to your pleasure. Ideal for those traveling with children. $55.

The Over Look Inn

Route 6, Box 771, 02642
(508) 255-1886; (800) 356-1121

Situated on the beautiful outer cape, across from Cape Cod National Seashore. Full breakfast, afternoon tea served. Victorian billiard room, library, parlor, porches. Near biking, hiking, fine dining. Scottish hospitality.

Hosts: Ian and Nan Aitchison
Rooms: 8 (PB) $70-125
Full Breakfast
Credit Cards: A, B, C
Notes: 2, 5, 7 (limited), 8 (over 12), 9, 10, 11, 12, 14

The Quilted Pineapple

Orleans Bed and Breakfast Associates
P. O. Box 1312, Orleans, 02653
(508) 255-3824; (800) 541-6226

Half-Cape country house in wooded area has charm, comfort, and convenience. First-floor suite with king bed and sitting area. Second-floor guest room has double bed. Guests share modern bathroom. Loveable springer spaniel in residence. Breakfast served in an interesting country kitchen. Near National Seashore Visitor Center, bike path, and ocean beaches. $50-60.

Soft Winds

Orleans Bed and Breakfast Associates
P. O. Box 1312, Orleans, 02653
(508) 255-3824; (800) 541-6226

Staying here is like having your own comfortable apartment. Private guest wing with livingroom, kitchen, bath, bedroom, and your own deck. Cable TV with HBO. Continental breakfast foods are on hand. Situated on bike path, convenient to beaches and ponds. $70.

Spindrift

Orleans Bed and Breakfast Associates
P. O. Box 1312, Orleans, 02653
(508) 255-3824; (800) 541-6226

Delightful wing of old house just five-minute walk to Coast Guard Beach. Near bike path. Private entrance into library/sitting room with windows facing ocean. Queen or twin room with private bath. Patio. Interesting hosts offer privacy or great hospitality as you wish. Breakfast served on dishes made by your host, a potter who maintains a shop in Orleans. $80; $140 for both rooms.

NOTES: Credit cards accepted: A Master Card; B Visa; C American Express; D Discover Card; E Diner's Club; F Other; 2 Personal Checks accepted; 3 Lunch available; 4 Dinner available; 5 Open all year;

Summertime

Orleans Bed and Breakfast Associates
P. O. Box 1312, Orleans, 02653
(508) 255-3824; (800) 541-6226

Darling Cape Cod house 100 feet from
lovely beach on Cape Cod Bay. This is a
light, softly decorated, restful environment.
On the second floor a charming twin bedroom with a sleeper sofa and an adjoining
double bedroom share bath. TV available
in livingroom and a wide deck for breakfast
or relaxing. This is a good location for a
family vacation. Convenient to National
Seashore. $60.

Sylvanus Knowles House

Orleans Bed and Breakfast Associates
P. O. Box 1312, Orleans, 02653
(508) 255-3824; (800) 541-6226

Magnificent views of Nauset Marsh and
leisurely walks on historic Fort Hill surround this impeccably restored 1838 Greek
Revival farmhouse. The original house
contains two guest rooms furnished with
fine antiques. The romantic Emma suite
has a private library/sitting room, bedroom
with lace-canopied bed, and elegant bathroom featuring an oversize tub and window
seat. Upstairs, a quaint, airy double room,
Lucille, has its own private bath, hall, and
dressing room. Breakfast served in elegant
dining room. $65-85.

Tory Hill

Orleans Bed and Breakfast Associates
P. O. Box 1312, Orleans, 02653
(508) 255-3824; (800) 541-6226

An old Cape house with a private entrance
into separate guest wing. Twin sitting room
with vanity and refrigerator. Full private
bath. Guests are invited to share the adjoining family room and lovely patio with
hosts. Owners have a specialized antique
business in an adjacent barn, and everything reflects their lively interest. Walk to

the ice cream parlor from here! It is three-
fourths mile to Bay Beach and two miles
to the ocean. $65.

EASTHAMPTON

Berkshire Bed and Breakfast Homes PV35

P. O. Box 211, Williamsburg, 01096
(413) 268-7244

This 1902 Victorian on three-fourths acre
has a view of the Connecticut River and
Mount Tom. One guest room with private
bath, two share a bath. Full breakfast; no
smoking; children over eight. $50-65.

EAST ORLEANS

Bed and Breakfast Cape Cod #25

P. O, Box 341, West Hyannisport, 02672-0341
(508) 775-2772; FAX (508) 775-2884

This Cape Cod-style house offers a second-
floor suite with a pair of twin beds that
convert to a king, private bath separate sitting room with studio couch and twin pull-
out. The village is one mile away, and the
host will pick up and drop off guests at
Nauset Beach. Continental breakfast. No
smoking. $65.

Bed and Breakfast Cape Cod #73

P. O, Box 341, West Hyannisport, 02672-0341
(508) 775-2772; FAX (508) 775-2884

This very special Colonial-style house
offers two suites. The honeymoon suite
offers queen-size bed, Jacuzzi for two, skylights, private entrance, and Victorian
decor. A second suite has a double four
poster bed, a sitting room with a fireplace,

and a private entrance. Full breakfast is served each morning. Harbor is one hundred yards away. Children over seven. $120-150.

Bed and Breakfast/Inns of New England MA 1048

329 Lake Drive, Guilford, CT 06437
(800) 582-0853

A restored sea captain's home that offers travelers the charm of old-style New England lodging with all the conveniences the modern guest has learned to expect. Some of the rooms have ocean views, and the master suite has a working fireplace. A complimentary breakfast that might consist of tasty carrot and blueberry muffins, homemade breads, cinnamon toast, English muffins, coffee, tea, and hot chocolate is served. Children over 12 welcome; smoking restricted; no pets. $50-100.

The Farmhouse

163 Beach Road, 02653
(508) 255-6654

This 19th-century farmhouse has been carefully restored and furnished to provide a unique blend of country life in a seashore setting. Short walk to Nauset Beach, close to sailing, golf, tennis, bike trails, theater, fishing, shopping, museums, and surfing. Some ocean-view rooms. Breakfast is served on an ocean-view deck.

Ship's Knees Inn

Hosts: The Standishes
Rooms: 8 (4 PB; 4 SB) $32-95
Expanded Continental Breakfast
Credit Cards: A, B
Notes: 2, 5, 7 (limited), 8, 14

Nauset House Inn

143 Beach Road, Box 774, 02643
(508) 255-2195

The Nauset House Inn is a place where the gentle amenities of life are still observed, a place where sea and shore, orchard and field all combine to create a perfect setting for tranquil relaxation. The Nauset House Inn is ideally situated near one of the world's great ocean beaches, yet is close to antique and craft shops, restaurants, art galleries, scenic paths, and remote places for sunning, swimming, and picnicking.

Hosts: Diane and Al Johnson, Cindy and John Vessella
Rooms: 14 (8 PB; 6 SB) $64-104
Full Breakfast; Continental available for lesser rate
Credit Cards: A, B
Closed Nov. 1-March 31
Notes: 2, 7 (limited), 9, 10, 11, 12

The Red Geranium

Orleans Bed and Breakfast Associates
P. O. Box 1312, Orleans, 02653
(508) 255-3824; (800) 541-6226

You will feel the warmth of home in this lovely country Cape. Comfortable bedrooms decorated with heirloom treasures. Large bath. Cozy sitting room. Guest wing has separate entrance, livingroom, complete kitchen, and romantic bedroom with queen-size bed, private bath. All guest rooms have individually controlled air conditioning and cable TV. Breakfast, a social event, is served buffet-style for all guests in Colonial dining room. A graceful gazebo by the pond is ideal for picnics. $70-90.

Ship's Knees Inn

186 Beach Road, P. O. Box 756, 02643
(508) 255-1312

NOTES: Credit cards accepted: A Master Card; B Visa; C American Express; D Discover Card; E Diner's Club; F Other; 2 Personal Checks accepted; 3 Lunch available; 4 Dinner available; 5 Open all year;

A 170-year-old restored sea captain's home; rooms individually appointed with their own colonial color schemes and authentic antiques. Only a short walk to popular sand-dunes of Nauset Beach. Swimming pool and tennis on premises. Also available three miles away, overlooking Orleans Cove, are an efficiency and two heated cottages.

Rooms: 21 (8 PB; 13 SB) $40-100
Continental Breakfast
Credit Cards: A, B
Notes: 2, 5, 7, 8 (over 12), 9, 10, 11, 12, 14

EAST SANDWICH

Spring Garden

578 Route 6A, P. O. Box 867, 02537
(508) 888-0710

Charming country inn. Tranquil, panoramic views of salt marsh and Tidal Creek from deck or patio. Color cable TV, air conditioning, room phones, refrigerators, efficiences, one suite, pool, or walk to private beach. Free generous continental breakfast. All rooms individually decorated with pillow shams, comforters, dust ruffles, and decorator sheets. Beamed ceilings. No minimum stay. Central to entire Cape, Boston, and Newport.

Hosts: Marvin and Judith Gluckman
Rooms: 11 (PB) $37-62
Continental Breakfast
Credit Cards: A, B, C, D
Notes: 2, 7, 8, 9, 10, 11, 12, 14

EDGARTOWN, MARTHA'S VINEYARD

The Arbor

222 Upper Main Street, P. O. Box 1228, 02539
(508) 627-8137

This turn-of-the-century home was originally built on the adjoining island of Chappaquiddick and moved by barge to its present location. A short stroll to village shops, fine restaurants, and the bustling activity of Edgartown Harbor, The Arbor is

filled with the fragrance of fresh flowers. Peggy will gladly direct you to the walking trails, unspoiled beaches, fishing, and all the delights of Martha's Vineyard.

Host: Peggy Hall
Rooms: 10 (8 PB; 2 SB) $55-125, seasonal rates apply
Continental Breakfast
Credit Cards: A, B
Notes: 2, 9, 10, 11, 12, 14

Ashley Inn

P. O. Box 650, 129 Main Street, 02539
(508) 627-9655

Situated among spacious lawns, gardens, and apple trees, the Ashley Inn offers an attractive 1860s captain's home with country charm. Conveniently situated on Edgartown's historic Main Street, the inn is a leisurely stroll from shops, beaches, and fine foods. Each room has been individually decorated. Join us for continental breakfast and relax in our hammocks. We hope to make your visit to Martha's Vineyard a memorable one.

Hosts: Jude Cortese and Fred Hurley
Rooms: 10 (8 PB; 2 SB) $65-175
Continental Breakfast
Credit Cards: A, B
Notes: 2, 5, 7, 9, 14

Bed and Breakfast Nantucket/ Martha's Vineyard #204

P. O. Box 341, West Hyannisport, 02672-0341
(508) 775-2772; FAX (508) 775-2884

This 1840s sea captain's house offers eleven rooms with private baths, some with fireplaces. The decor is Victorian, and a continental breakfast is served each morning. Transportation to the beach is right outside your door, and a short walk takes you to the village shops and restaurants. No children under 12. $65-175.

Captain Dexter House of Edgartown

35 Pease's Point Way, Box 2798, 02539
(508) 627-7289

Built in 1840, this historic inn offers you a memorable vacation, retreat, or reunion. From its white clapboard siding to its garden swing to its immense flower garden, our home is traditional New England. Add canopy beds, working fireplaces, home-baked breads/muffins, outstanding hospitality—and you're bound to feel special. Just a short stroll to town and the harbor.

Host: Tenneé Casaccio
Rooms: 11 (PB) $65-165
Continental Breakfast
Credit Cards: A, B, C, E
Notes: 2, 7, 9, 14

The Charlotte Inn

27 South Summer Street, 02539
(508) 627-4751

Fine English antiques and fireplaces in a romantic garden setting with private courtyards and porches. Has 24 impeccably maintained and individually decorated guest rooms. Attention to detail is the Charlotte Inn's trademark. Walking distance to shops, beaches, tennis, and sailing. Excellent French restaurant called l'Étoile in the inn. Serves dinner and Sunday brunch. *Mobil Travel Guide* four-star rating. Voted one of two "Country House Hotels" of the year—*Andrew Harper's Hideaway Report*.

Hosts: Gery and Paula Conover
Rooms: 24 (PB) $85-350
Continental Breakfast; Full available
Credit Cards: A, B, C
Notes: 2, 4, 5, 7, 9, 10, 11, 12

Colonial Inn of Martha's Vineyard

38 North Water Street, P. O. Box 68, 02539
(508) 627-4711

In the heart of historic Edgartown overlooking the harbor, sits the Colonial Inn. It offers 42 newly renovated and lovingly refurbished rooms, all with heat, air conditioning, color TV, telephone, and private bath. Continental breakfast is served daily in the solarium and garden courtyard. Affordable luxury.

Host: Linda Malcouranne
Rooms: 42 (PB) $50-185
Continental Breakfast
Credit Cards: A, B, C
Closed Jan.-March
Notes: 2, 3, 4, 7, 8, 9, 10, 11, 12, 14

The Edgartown Inn

56 North Water Street, 02539
(508) 627-4794

Historic inn built in 1798 as the home for whaling Captain Worth. Early guests included Daniel Webster, Nathaniel

Governor Bradford Inn

NOTES: Credit cards accepted: A Master Card; B Visa; C American Express; D Discover Card; E Diner's Club; F Other; 2 Personal Checks accepted; 3 Lunch available; 4 Dinner available; 5 Open all year;

Hawthorne, and Charles Summer. Later, John Kennedy stayed here as a young senator. Completely restored over the last 150 years, today it is filled with antiques. Convenient to beaches, harbor, and restaurants. Famous for breakfast, including homemade breads and cakes.

Hosts: Liliane and Earle Radford
Rooms: 20 (16 PB; 4 SB) $85-145
Full and Continental Breakfast
Credit Cards: None
Notes: 2, 9, 10, 11, 12

Governor Bradford Inn

128 Main Street, Box 239, 02539
(508) 627-9510

The atmosphere at this restored 1865 Edgartown home is one of casual elegance. Guests can walk to the many shops and restaurants in Edgartown, bicycle to beaches, or simply relax. Freshly baked treats are served at breakfast and afternoon tea. All guest rooms have private baths and are decorated with a mixture of antiques and reproductions.

Hosts: Ray and Brenda Raffurty
Rooms: 16 (PB) $60-195
Full Breakfast
Credit Cards: A, B, C
Notes: 2, 4, 5, 7, 9, 10, 11, 12, 14

Jonathan Munroe House

100 Main Street, 02539
(508) 627-5536

Not too far from the center of town, this is a private home that has been converted to receive guests. Six quaint, homey rooms share two full upstairs baths.

Host: Margaret M. Patch
Rooms: 6 (SB) $85 and up.
Credit Cards: None
Notes: 7, 8, 9, 14

Point Way Inn

Box 128, 02539
(508) 627-8633

This delightful country inn provides a warm, relaxed retreat with working fireplaces in 11 rooms. Tea and scones are provided in the winter; in the summer, lemonade and oatmeal cookies are served in the gazebo overlooking the croquet court and gardens. Complimentary courtesy car available.

Hosts: Linda and Ben Smith
Rooms: 15 (PB) $70-205
Continental Breakfast
Minimum stay holidays: 2 nights
Credit Cards: A, B, C
Notes: 2, 5, 7, 8, 9, 10, 11, 12, 14

EGREMONT

American Country Collection 138

4 Greenwood Lane, Delmar, NY 12054
(518) 439-7001

This 1700s Victorian rural farm is on 500 acres of rolling hills, woods, and fields. It is furnished with antiques and Oriental rugs. There are four guest rooms, one with a private bath. Tanglewood, Norman Rockwell Museum, Berkshire Festival, and skiing are all within fifteen minutes. There is an in-ground pool available for guest use, Full breakfast; smoking outdoors; children over 10 welcome; resident dog. $55-75.

Berkshire Bed and Breakfast Homes SC8

P. O. Box 211, Williamsburg, 01096
(413) 268-7244

An 1803 country farmhouse on three acres. Guest rooms with private baths and parlor are furnished with antiques. Air-conditioned. Full breakfast; no smoking; children over 16 welcome. $75-100.

ESSEX

George Fuller House

148 Main Street, 01929
(508) 768-7766

This handsome Federal home has much of
the original paneling and woodwork.
Private baths, air conditioning, TVs, and
phones in all rooms. Two rooms with fireplaces. A country breakfast with such specialties as French toast drizzled with
brandied lemon butter are served. Cruise or
take lessons on inn's 30-foot sailboat with
the innkeeper, a licensed captain.

Hosts: Cindy and Bob Cameron
Rooms: 6 (PB) $60-100
Full Breakfast
Credit Cards: A, B, C, D
Notes: 2, 5, 8, 9, 14

FAIRHAVEN

Edgewater Bed and Breakfast

2 Oxford Street, 02719
(508) 997-5512

A gracious waterfront house situated in the
early shipbuilding area of historic
Fairhaven. Spectacular views of neighboring New Bedford Harbor so close to the
water you'll think you're on a boat.

Capt. Tom Lawrence House

Convenient to historic areas, beaches, factory outlets, ferries to Martha's Vineyard
and Cuttyhunk; five minutes from I-195.
Five rooms, each with private bath (two
with fireplace and sitting room).

Host: Kathy Reed
Rooms: 5 (PB) $45-65
Continental Breakfast
Credit Cards: A, B, C
Notes: 2, 5, 7, 8, 9, 10, 11, 12, 14

FALMOUTH

Bed and Breakfast Cape Cod #10

P. O. Box 341, West Hyannisport, 02672-0341
(508) 775-2772; FAX (508) 775-2884

This beachfront ranch-style house faces a
beautiful saltwater inlet that offers private
beach, quiet walks, fishing from the host's
property, sailing, and clamming. Two
rooms with double beds have private baths
and are furnished with antiques. Full country breakfast. Children over 12. $85.

Bed and Breakfast Cape Cod #38

P. O. Box 341, West Hyannisport, 02672-0341
(508) 775-2772; FAX (508) 775-2884

Built in 1880, this home on the road to
Woods Hole has been restored comfortably, offering four guest rooms with private
baths. You will enjoy a full breakfast
served in the dining room, and a nice parlor
for reading or relaxing is also available.
The village shops in Falmouth are a mile
away, and the ferry is one and one half
miles. No smoking. Children over seven.
$60-80.

Capt. Tom Lawrence House

75 Locust Street, 02540
(508) 540-1445

NOTES: Credit cards accepted: A Master Card; B Visa; C American Express; D Discover Card; E Diner's
Club; F Other; 2 Personal Checks accepted; 3 Lunch available; 4 Dinner available; 5 Open all year;

Beautiful 1861 Victorian, former whaling captain's residence in the historic village of Falmouth. Comfortable, spacious corner guest rooms. Firm beds—some with canopies. Steinway piano and working fireplace. Gourmet breakfast consists of fresh fruit, breads, pancakes made from freshly ground organic grain, and a variety of other delicious specialties. German spoken.

Rooms: 6 (PB) $70-99
Full Breakfast
Minimum stay: 2 nights
Credit Cards: A, B
Notes: 2, 5, 7 (limited), 8 (over 12), 9, 11, 12

Gladstone Inn

219 Grand Avenue South, 02540
(508) 548-9851

An oceanfront Victorian inn overlooking Martha's Vineyard. Established in 1910. Light, airy guest rooms have period furniture and their own wash stations. Buffet breakfast is served on the glassed-in porch that also provides a cozy place to read, watch cable TV, or relax. Refrigerators, bikes, and gas grill are provided for guests to use.

Hosts: Jim and Gayle Carroll
Rooms: 16 (1 PB; 15 SB) $52-75
Full Breakfast
Credit Cards: None
Closed Oct. 15-May 15
Notes: 2, 7, 8 (over 11), 9, 10, 11, 12

Grafton Inn

261 Grand Avenue South, 02540
(508) 540-8688; FAX (508) 540-1861

Oceanfront Victorian inn with miles of beautiful beach and breathtaking views of Martha's Vineyard. Sumptuous breakfasts are served on a lovely enclosed porch. Private baths, airy, comfortable rooms furnished with period antiques, thoughtful amenities. Picnic lunches and bicycles are available, as is ample parking. Short walk to restaurant, shops, and ferry. Ask about off-season rates and package plans.

Hosts: Liz and Rudy Cvitan
Rooms: 11 (PB) $65-110
Full Breakfast
Credit Cards: A, B, C
Notes: 2, 5, 9, 10, 11, 12, 14

The Moorings Lodge

207 Grand Avenue South, 02540
(508) 540-2370

Enjoy homemade breads for buffet breakfast served on a large glassed-in porch with lovely ocean view. This charming old sea captain's home with large airy rooms overlooks Vineyard Sound and Martha's Vineyard Island. Opposite a good family beach and within a short walk to good restaurants and the island ferry.

Hosts: Ernie and Shirley Benard
Rooms: 8 (6 PB; 2 SB) $50-70
Expanded Continental Breakfast
Credit Cards: A, B
Notes: 2, 7 (restricted), 9, 10, 11, 12

Mostly Hall
Bed and Breakfast Inn

27 Main Street, 02540
(508) 548-3786; (800) 682-0565

Romantic 1849 southern plantation-style Cape Cod home with wraparound veranda and widow's walk. Set back from the road on an acre of beautiful gardens with a gazebo. Close to restaurants, shops, beaches, island ferries. Spacious corner rooms with queen-size canopy beds, central air conditioning, gourmet breakfast, bicycles, private baths.

Grafton Inn

6 Pets welcome; 7 Smoking allowed; 8 Children welcome; 9 Social drinking allowed; 10 Tennis available; 11 Swimming available; 12 Golf available; 13 Skiing available; 14 May be booked through travel agents.

Hosts: Caroline and Jim Lloyd
Rooms: 6 (PB) $80-105
Full Breakfast
Minimum stay Memorial Day-Columbus Day 2 nights
Credit Cards: A, B
Closed Jan.-mid Feb.
Notes: 2, 8 (over 15), 9, 10, 11, 12

Mostly Hall

The Palmer House Inn

81 Palmer Avenue, 02540-2857
(508) 548-1230; (800) 472-2632

Turn-of-the-century Victorian bed and breakfast in the historic district. Antique furnishings return you to the romance of a bygone era. Full gourmet breakfast featuring pain perdue, Belgian waffles, Finnish pancakes. Close to island ferries, beaches, shops. Bicycles available.

Hosts: Ken and Joanne Baker
Rooms: 8 (PB) $75-115
Full Breakfast
Credit Cards: A, B, C, D, E
Notes: 2, 5, 8 (over 12), 10, 11, 12, 14

Peacock's "Inn on the Sound"

Box 201, 313 Grand Avenue, 02541
(508) 457-9666

Oceanfront bed and breakfast with ten spacious guest rooms, most with spectacular ocean views, all with private baths, several with fireplaces. Full gourmet breakfast served each morning with homemade pastries and coffee cakes, fresh fruit, juices, and specialty entrees. Minutes' walk to beach and to Martha's Vineyard Island ferry. Near museums and galleries, shops, and restaurants, bike path, golf, and tennis. Day trips: whale watching, Plymouth Rock, Woods Hole Oceanographic Institute. Packages.

Hosts: Bud and Phyllis Peacock
Rooms: 10 (PB) $75-115
Full Breakfast
Credit Cards: A, B, C, D, E
Notes: 2, 5, 7, 9, 10, 11, 12

Village Green Inn

40 West Main Street, 02540
(508) 548-5621

Gracious old Victorian, ideally situated on historic Village Green. Walk to fine shops and restaurants, bike to beaches, tennis, and the picturesque bike path to Woods Hole. Enjoy 19th-century charm and warm hospitality in elegant surroundings. Four lovely guest rooms and one romantic suite all have private baths. Discount rates from November to May.

Hosts: Linda and Don Long
Rooms: 5 (PB) $75-110
Full Breakfast
Credit Cards: A, B, C
Notes: 2, 5, 7 (outside), 8 (over 16), 9, 10, 11, 12

Palmer House Inn

Woods Hole Passage

186 Woods Hole Road, 02540
(508) 548-9575

Woods Hole Passage is a magical, quiet
retreat, a charming old house surrounded
by blueberries and raspberries, and sheltered by old trees, where the excitement
and beauty of Cape Cod is only minutes
away from your door. The rooms are elegant, soft and spacious, all with private
baths. In the morning you can catch the sun
with breakfast beside a huge multipaned
window, or invigorate yourself by breakfast
on the patio overlooking the grounds, or in
the garden.

Host: Christina Mozo
Rooms: 5 (PB) $65-85
Full Breakfast
Credit Cards: A, B
Notes: 2, 5, 8, 9, 11

FRAMINGHAM

Bed and Breakfast Associates #CW625

P. O. Box 57166, Babson Park Branch
Boston, 02157-0166
(617) 449-5302; FAX (617) 449-5958

This is an idyllic country setting at the end
of a private road, yet a short walk to
Framingham Centre shops and public transportation. The home was once a barn. The
contemporary restoration was completed
just over 20 years ago but the weathered
siding has the rich hues of age. Exit your
first-floor suite via French doors to acres of
open land. The guest room has a cathedral
ceiling and an attached sitting area. Full
breakfast; children welcome. $68; monthly
rates available.

GAY HEAD

Duck Inn

Box 160, 02535
(508) 645-9018

A 200-year-old, five-bedroom farmhouse
on eight and one-half acres just a short
walk to the beach. Ocean views in most
rooms. Watch the sunset over the cliffs and
ocean. Fireplaces, decks, piano, hot tub,
masseuse, gourmet health breakfasts.
Casual and eclectic antique setting. Open
year-round with off-season rates.

Host: Elise LeBovit
Rooms: 5 (1 PB; 4 SB) $65-175
Full Breakfast
Credit Cards: A, B, C
Notes: 2, 5, 7, 8, 9, 11

GLOUCESTER

Bed and Breakfast Associates #NS500

P. O. Box 57166, Babson Park Branch
Boston, 02157-0166
(617) 449-5302; FAX (617) 449-5958

Just steps from the Atlantic, this white
frame house in the little village of
Lanesville (five miles from Gloucester and
Rockport) offers three guest rooms with a
shared bath and a separate cottage. Your
hostess is an energetic woman who has
done much of the interior renovation of her
attractive New England-style home.
Continental breakfast; children over ten
welcome; no smoking. $60; family and
winter rates available.

Bed and Breakfast Associates #NS505

P. O. Box 57166, Babson Park Branch
Boston, 02157-0166
(617) 449-5302; FAX (617) 449-5958

Originally an 1898 Victorian "cottage," this
splendid seaside retreat has been completely
updated and redecorated. It is situated on
the banks of the Annisquam River, and
guests may enjoy watching boats passing
from each of the guest rooms, the inviting
decks, or the gardens below. There is also a
private swimming beach. These three beau-

6 Pets welcome; 7 Smoking allowed; 8 Children welcome; 9 Social drinking allowed; 10 Tennis available; 11
Swimming available; 12 Golf available; 13 Skiing available; 14 May be booked through travel agents.

tifully decorated rooms share two full baths. Continental breakfast; children over 12 welcome. $55-75; family rates available.

Bed and Breakfast Cape Cod #30

P. O, Box 341, West Hyannisport, 02672-0341
(508) 775-2772; FAX (508) 775-2884

This 1899 restoration is the perfect place to watch ships sail by. Decorated with both Victorian and traditional themes, this home offers four carpeted guest rooms that have twin, double, or queen-size beds and share two full baths. All have a view of the water, and each morning a continental breakfast is served in the dining area or the one-hundred-foot wraparound porch. $65-75.

Fermata Bed and Breakfast

Bed and Breakfast Marblehead and North Shore
P. O, Box 35, Newtonville, 02160
(617) 964-1606; (800) 832-2632
FAX (617) 332-8572

In the exclusive Bass Rocks area with an ocean view, this attractive architect-designed cottage is a short block from a beautiful sandy beach. The guest room has its own staircase, providing added privacy. Continental breakfast. The hostess has two sons at home. Children welcome. Smoking permitted. Two cats in residence. Open year-round. $55-65.

Four-Bedroom Oceanfront Cottage

Bed and Breakfast Marblehead and North Shore
P. O, Box 35, Newtonville, 02160
(617) 964-1606; (800) 832-2632
FAX (617) 332-8572

Oceanfront cottage in spectacular location, with lawn sloping down to rocky shoreline. Four bedrooms. Full kitchen with dish-

washer, washer, and dryer. Large porch facing ocean. Available Sept. 15-Oct. 30. $950/week.

Good Harbor Guest House

Bed and Breakfast Marblehead and North Shore
P. O, Box 35, Newtonville, 02160
(617) 964-1606; (800) 832-2632
FAX (617) 332-8572

This large three-story shingle wood frame offers a variety of accommodations, all newly decorated. The Good Harbor Beach is only one hundred yards away, and shops, restaurants, and art galleries are nearby. Resident dog. Restricted smoking. Children welcome. $45-90.

Oceanfront Cottage

Bed and Breakfast Marblehead and North Shore
P. O, Box 35, Newtonville, 02160
(617) 964-1606; (800) 832-2632
FAX (617) 332-8572

Small one-bedroom oceanfront cottage in spectacular location, with lawn sloping down to rocky shoreline. Small kitchen, livingroom, and private bath with shower only. Full breakfast in refrigerator which guests prepare themselves. Children welcome. Smoking permitted. No pets. Open mid-May to end of October. $90.

GREAT BARRINGTON

Arrawood Bed and Breakfast

105 Taconic Avenue, 01230
(413) 528-5868

A charming Victorian residence near Tanglewood, two ski basins, and many Berkshire Mountain tourist attractions. Arrawood offers comfortable, large guest rooms, all tastefully furnished. It has a large guest parlor with a fireplace, a beautiful covered front porch, and a charming, sunny dining room where a full country breakfast is served by candlelight and music.

Hosts: Marilyn and Bill Newmark
Rooms: 4 (2 PB; 2 SB) $50-85
Full Breakfast
Credit Cards: None
Notes: 2, 5, 8, 11, 12, 13, 14

Bed and Breakfast Accommodations 053

984 Gloucester Place
Schenectady, New York 12309
(518) 370-4948

This classic hilltop farmhouse was designed for visitors in 1907 and features wraparound porches with panoramic views of the Berkshire Hills. The dairy barn, renovated in 1987, dates from the 1820s. The main house has five bedrooms decorated with Laura Ashley prints, antique furniture, art, and an extensive book collection. The dairy barn has a hayloft renovation containing two air-conditioned luxury suites with private baths. Guests choose from an extensive country menu for breakfast at any time they wish. Children over 16 welcome. No smoking. $65-135; $15-20 surcharge for in-season weekends, one-night stays.

Bed and Breakfast/Inns of New England MA 1020

329 Lake Drive, Guilford, CT 06437
(800) 582-0853

A circa 1800 farmhouse built by the Indians early in the last century. It has been added to over the years until it assumed its present rambling shape. There are five brightly furnished guest rooms, each with its own private bath. Bathrobes are found in the bedroom closets for the guests to use. All bedrooms are air-conditioned and eequipped with telephones and clock radios.

Berkshire Bed and Breakfast Homes SC12

P. O. Box 211, Williamsburg, 01096
(413) 268-7244

An 1898 Victorian on one-half acre. Victorian and antique furnishings in parlor and guest rooms. Private and semiprivate baths. Located in residential neighborhood. Continental breakfast; no smoking; children welcome. $80-95 summer; $60-80 winter.

Coffing-Bostwick House

98 Division Street, 01230
(413) 528-4511

Unique, historic Greek Revival home (1825). Spacious, well-appointed guest rooms. Cozy parlor with TV; commodious library-livingroom; elegant mahogany-paneled dining room; all with fireplaces. Lavish, homemade full breakfasts with fresh produce and fruits. Relaxed, informal atmosphere. Four acres with lovely river to stroll. Convenient to art galleries, Berkshire ski areas, theaters, antique shops, Tanglewood, and fine dining. Midweek discounts; special weekly packages.

Hosts: Diana and William Harwood
Rooms: 6 (2 PB; 4 SB) $60-95
Full Breakfast
Credit Cards: None
Notes: 2, 5, 8, 9

Covered Bridge 1GBMA

P. O. Box 447A, Norfolk, CT 06058
(203) 542- 5944

Charming Victorian farmhouse in a rural setting. A full breakfast is served in the dining room. There are three large rooms, each with private bath, cable TV, and air conditioning. Two of the rooms have queen beds, and one has twins. A barn on the grounds has also been converted into a two-bedroom cottage. $85-110.

6 Pets welcome; 7 Smoking allowed; 8 Children welcome; 9 Social drinking allowed; 10 Tennis available; 11 Swimming available; 12 Golf available; 13 Skiing available; 14 May be booked through travel agents.

Covered Bridge 2GBMA

P. O. Box 447A, Norfolk, CT 06058
(203) 542-5944

A 1907 farmhouse set on 16 acres offers a
lovely retreat. There is a large, formal parlor available for guest use, and a full breakfast is served in the country kitchen. In the
main house there are six guest rooms with
double and twin beds that share three baths.
The hayloft of the dairy barn has been converted into a charming two bedroom, two
bath apartment. $75-85; $115-300 dairy
barn.

Elling's Bed and Breakfast Guest House

Rural Route 3, Box 6, 250 Maple Avenue, 01230
(413) 528-4103

Our 1742 homestead is the second oldest
lived-in house in Great Barrington. Six
attractive guest rooms, four of which offer
private baths and two of which share a
bath, are available for guests and are air
conditioned. Lawns, gardens, scenic views,
and porches, and fireplaces in the guest
parlor and dining room highlight a guest's
stay at this lovely old home. An abundant
continental breakfast is served in the dining
room where guests are served each morning. Guests have been coming here since
1972. Near all attractions, winter sports,
and restaurants.

Hosts: Jo and Ray Elling
Rooms: 67 (2 PB; 4 SB) $55-85
Continental Breakfast
Credit Cards: None
Notes: 2, 5, 10, 11, 12, 13

Littlejohn Manor

1 Newsboy Monument Lane, 01230
(413) 528-2882

Victorian charm recaptured in this uniquely
personable home. Antiques grace four
warmly furnished, air-conditioned guest
rooms—one with fireplace. Guest parlor
with color TV and fireplace. Full English
breakfast and afternoon tea. Set on spacious, landscaped grounds with extensive
herb and flower beds. Scenic views. Close
to major ski areas and Berkshire attractions.

Hosts: Herbert Littlejohn, Jr. and Paul A. DuFour
Rooms: 4 (SB) $60-85
Full Breakfast
Credit Cards: None
Notes: 2, 5, 7 (limited), 9, 10, 11, 12, 13

Nutmeg Bed and Breakfast Agency #346

P. O. Box 1117, West Hartford, CT 06107
(203) 236-6698

A newly restored Victorian of the 1890s,
with lovely old maples and a wraparound
front porch. Secluded yet within walking
distance to shops, theaters, and restaurants.
The three lovely guest rooms with private

Round Hill Farm

and semiprivate baths have bay windows and antiques. Close to Stockbridge, Tanglewood, and major ski areas. A full breakfast with home-baked bread is included. Children welcome; no smoking.

Round Hill Farm

17 Round Hill Road, 01230
(413) 528-3366

Haven for nonsmokers, a delightful 19th-century hilltop horse farm overlooking 300 spectacular acres, glorious panorama of the Berkshires. Tended fields, trails, and trout stream. Tanglewood and Norman Rockwell. 2.6 miles from Routes 7 and 23. No smoking. Please call for our brochure.

Hosts: Thomas and Margaret Whitfield
Rooms: 8 (3 PB; 5 SB) $65-150
Full Breakfast
Credit Cards: A, B, C
Horses welcome
Notes: 2, 5, 6 (horses), 8 (over 16), 9, 10, 11, 12, 13, 14

Seekonk Pines Inn

142 Seekonk Cross Road, 01230
(413) 528-4192; (800) 292-4192

This restored 1830s homestead, set amid lovely flower and vegetable gardens, offers a large guest livingroom with a fireplace and grand piano. A full country breakfast is different every day, and special diets can be accommodated. Convenient to Tanglewood and other cultural events, museums, shops, golf, and hiking. Features antique quilts, stencilling, original artwork, gardens, picnic tables, in-ground pool, and guest pantry. Seen in the *Boston Globe*, *Philadelphia Inquirer*, *Los Angeles Times*, and the August 1991 issue of *Country Inns* magazine.

Hosts: Linda and Chris Best
Rooms: 6 (40PB; 2 SB) $65-95
Full Breakfast
Credit Cards: A, B, C
Notes: 2, 5, 8, 9, 10, 11, 12, 13

Thornewood Inn

453 Stockbridge Road, 01230
(413) 528-3828

Antiques and mahogany furniture allow the ten guest rooms to be comfortable and elegant. All guest rooms have private baths, air conditioning, and include a full breakfast. Centrally situated in the Berkshires, minutes away from area attractions. There is a full service dining room with an intimate atmosphere and a library-style taproom for a more casual evening. Live entertainment on weekends.

Hosts: Terry and David Thorne
Rooms: 10 (PB) $65-155
Full Breakfast
Credit Cards: A, B, C, D
Notes: 2, 4, 5, 8 (over 12), 9, 11, 13

The Turning Point Inn

3 Lake Buel Road, 01230
(413) 528-4777

An 18th-century former stagecoach inn. Full, delicious breakfast. Featured in *The New York Times*, *Boston Globe*, *Los Angeles Times*. Adjacent to Butternut Ski Basin; near Tanglewood and all Berkshire attractions. Hiking, cross-country ski trails. Sitting rooms with fireplaces, piano, cable TV. Groups and families welcome.

Hosts: The Yosts
Rooms: 8 (6 PB; 2 SB) $80-100
Full Breakfast
Credit Cards: A, B, C
Notes: 2, 5, 8, 9, 10, 11, 12, 13, 14

GREENFIELD—SEE ALSO COLRAIN

Hitchcock House

15 Congress Street, 01301
(413) 774-7452

This 1881 Victorian gem is minutes away from nine well-known schools and colleges, tennis courts, golfing, hiking trails, skiing, rafting, Historic Old Deerfield, museums, and fabulous foliage in the fall. Shopping areas and restaurants are close by. A sumptuous breakfast and tastefully decorated rooms are trademarks of genial hospitality the Hitchcock House shares with its guests.

Hosts: Betty and Peter Gott
Rooms: 7 (SB) $50-100
Full or Continental Breakfast
Credit Cards: A, B
Notes: 2, 5, 6, 7, 8, 9, 10, 11, 12, 13, 14

GROVELAND

Seven Acre Farm Bed and Breakfast

Bed and Breakfast Marblehead and North Shore
P. O, Box 35, Newtonville, 02160
(617) 964-1606; (800) 832-2632
FAX (617) 332-8572

A charming country farmhouse, built in 1987, offers three guest rooms. Enjoy the peace and tranquility of quiet walks through the seven acres of land that was once an herb farm. This bed and breakfast is furnished with antiques and has beautiful wood floors, Oriental rugs, atrium, skylights, and a cozy wood-burning stove. Three guest rooms share one and one half baths. Easy access to highways leading to Maine, New Hampshire, and Vermont. Generous continental breakfast. No smoking. Children welcome. $55-75.

HAMILTON

The Dudley Pickman House

Bed and Breakfast Marblehead and North Shore
P. O, Box 35, Newtonville, 02160
(617) 964-1606; (800) 832-2632
FAX (617) 332-8572

A large gracious 1720s Colonial on one acre of land with herb and vegetable gardens. This home is two miles away from Crane's Beach. Three guest rooms, all with private baths, are included, and two guest rooms have working fireplaces. Generous continental breakfast included. Children welcome. Laundry facilities available. $55-75.

HAMPDEN

Berkshire Bed and Breakfast Homes GS11

P. O. Box 211, Williamsburg, 01096
(413) 268-7244

A 1987 Cape Cod-style home on 35 acres. Guest rooms with semiprivate baths have contemporary and antique furnishings. Parlor and den for guest use. Continental breakfast; children welcome. $70.

HARWICH

Bed and Breakfast Cape Cod #7

P. O, Box 341, West Hyannisport, 02672-0341
(508) 775-2772; FAX (508) 775-2884

This Cape-style home is one hundred yards from a freshwater pond and offers two bedrooms, one with a double bed and the other a pair of twins. The bath is shared, and a full breakfast served in the dining room features home baked specialties. The pond is available for swimming or fishing, and the beach is close to this pleasant accommodation. No smoking. Children over eight. $60.

Bed and Breakfast/Inns of New England MA 1047

329 Lake Drive, Guilford, CT 06437
(800) 582-0853

Set on one and one-half acres with flower and vegetable gardens, the main house was built in 1835. A contemporary wing has since been added. Upstairs there are twin beds with a shared bath. Downstairs there is a king-size bed with private bath and entrance. This room boasts five windows and is especially delightful in the summer. An extra small room with a twin bed for a third guest is available, with a shared bath. A continental breakfast is served each morning. No children; no smoking; resident cat. $30-50.

Freshwater Whale

Orleans Bed and Breakfast Associates
P. O. Box 1312, Orleans, 02653
(508) 255-3824; (800) 541-6226

Charming antique-filled cottage has view from every room of large, clear lake excellent for swimming. Two bedrooms, one king, one twin. Private bath. Lower-level guest family room with fireplace and TV opens to patio surrounded by exquisite old-fashioned garden and sandy beach. Canoe and beach towels provided. Five minutes to ocean beach, bike path, golf, and tennis. $70.

The Larches

97 Chatham Road, 02645
(508) 432-0150

This 1835 Greek Revival with contemporary wing offers a downstairs room with a king-size bed, private bath, private entrance, adjoining common room with color TV, and an upstairs room with twin beds that share a bath with the owner. A flower and vegetable garden is here for guests to enjoy. This peaceful country setting is only 1 and 1/4 miles from the beach. Many art galleries are nearby, as well as bike trails. We are midway on Cape Cod.

Host: Dr. Edwin O. Hook
Rooms: 2 (1 PB; 1 SB) $50-60
Continental Breakfast
Credit Cards: None
Notes: 2, 5, 9

Serendipity

Orleans Bed and Breakfast Associates
P. O. Box 1312, Orleans, 02653
(508) 255-3824; (800) 541-6226

Peace and quiet "on golden pond." Spacious deck overlooking private, sandy beach. Upstairs king bedroom with TV, full bath, lovely water view. Downstairs large room with sliders for private entrance from patio, king-size bed, TV, full bath. Adjacent single room on each floor for another family member ($30). Very private. Minutes to ocean, tennis, and golf. $60.

HARWICH PORT

A Bed and Breakfast Above the Rest #52

50 Boatswains Way, Suite 105
Boston, 02150
(617) 884-7748; (800) 677-2262

Originally a summer residence, the spacious Drangea House has been converted by its retired owners into a comfortable year-round home. June through November, guests can stay either in the main home or the adjacent cottage. In the main house, the second-floor guest room has a private deck with ocean view and a private bath. Full or continental breakfast is served in the patio overlooking the garden. The cottage has two bedrooms, kitchen, private bath, and sitting room with working fireplace. No breakfast is served in the cottage.

Bed and Breakfast Associates #CC360

P. O. Box 57166, Babson Park Branch
Boston, 02157-0166
(617) 449-5302; FAX (617) 449-5958

This luxurious Victorian mansion provides an unforgettable setting for a romantic getaway. You can stay in one of five richly appointed guest rooms with fine period fur-

6 Pets welcome; 7 Smoking allowed; 8 Children welcome; 9 Social drinking allowed; 10 Tennis available; 11 Swimming available; 12 Golf available; 13 Skiing available; 14 May be booked through travel agents.

nishings, lovely new baths, and modern amenities. You will savor the full gourmet breakfasts and the afternoon hors d'oeuvres in the gracious parlor. Lawn games are provided, as is a guest recreation room. Stroll over to the quaint shopping area and to the nearby beach on Nantucket Sound. Full gourmet breakfast; no children. $155-170 in season (July and August).

Bed and Breakfast Associates #CC370

P. O. Box 57166, Babson Park Branch
Boston, 02157-0166
(617) 449-5302; FAX (617) 449-5958

White wicker rocking chairs and hanging geraniums on the wraparound porch beck-on you to this Victorian home situated one-third mile from the sandy beach. There are five guest rooms with brass beds, fine period furnishings, and pleasing pastel wallpapers. Shops and restaurants are within easy walking distance. Continental breakfast. $95; family and monthly rates available.

Bed and Breakfast Associates #CC371

P. O. Box 57166, Babson Park Branch
Boston, 02157-0166
(617) 449-5302; FAX (617) 449-5958

Your hosts offer excellent family accommodations in the relaxed atmosphere of this guest house. All rooms are thoughtfully furnished, spacious, and breezy. A continental breakfast is served in the dining room, while an outdoor pool awaits just beyond. The beach is less than one-half mile. Children welcome. $75; $125 family guest room for four; off-season rates available.

Bed and Breakfast Cape Cod #13

P. O, Box 341, West Hyannisport, 02672-0341
(508) 775-2772; FAX (508) 775-2884

This Dutch-style Colonial has served as small inn for thirty years and is on a private beach on the Nantucket Sound. The house features a large sun porch, livingroom with fireplace, and a large dining area. A variety of rooms, all of which offer private baths and have queen and king-size beds, are available. Two apartments with separate entrances are also available. No children. $85-125.

Bed and Breakfast Cape Cod #56

P. O, Box 341, West Hyannisport, 02672-0341
(508) 775-2772; FAX (508) 775-2884

This restored 1860s Country Victorian home is very close to Bank Street Beach, village shops, fine restaurants, and two public golf courses. There are two bedrooms available with a shared bath, one with twin beds and the other with a double bed. Ideal private quarters for a couple with two children or two couples traveling together. Fresh fruit, hot breads, brewed coffee/tea, and cereals included. $65.

Captain's Quarters

85 Bank Street, 02642
(800) 992-6550

A romantic 1850s Victorian with a classic wraparound porch, nostalgic gingerbread trim, and a graceful curving front stairway. Our guest rooms have private baths, quen brass beds with eyelet lace-trimmed sheets, lace curtains, and comfortable reading chairs. Just a three-minute walk into town and a five-minute walk to an ocean beach. Experience Cape Cod in a relaxed and friendly atmosphere.

Hosts: Ed and Susan Kenney
Rooms: 5 (PB) $65-95
Continental Breakfast
Credit Cards: A, B, C
Notes: 2, 5, 9, 10, 11, 12, 14

Country Inn

86 Sisson Road, 02646
(508) 432-2769; (800) 231-1722

An inn of New England tradition set on six
country acres. Newly restored guest rooms
with color TVs, air conditioning, and
romantic bedding offer a perfect setting for
a getaway or vacation. Some rooms offer
fireplaces. Cozy fireside dining in the fall
and winter, and a varied menu features the
freshest of native seafood and the finest of
meats and poultry. Tennis courts, an in-
ground swimming pool, and walk-to-beach
parking provided free of charge (parking is
one mile away.)

Hosts: Kathleen and David Van Gelder
Rooms: 7 (PB) $75-125
Continental Plus Breakfast
Credit Cards: A, B, C
Notes: 2, 4, 5, 7, 9, 10, 11, 14

Dunscroft-by-the-Sea

24 Pilgrim Road, 02646
(508) 432-0810

Beautiful, private, mile-long beach on
Nantucket Sound. Romantic inn in an
exclusive, quiet residential area. In-town
walk to quaint shops, art galleries, and
restaurants. The king and queen bed chambers, each with in-room private bath, greet
you by way of candlelight, double plump
pillows, eyelet, ruffles, and lace—a romantic interlude by Alyce and Laura Ashley.
Full breakfast. Enchanted fireplaced cottage sleeps three.

Hosts: Alyce and Wally Cunningham
Rooms: 8 plus cottage (PB) $75-175
Full Breakfast
Credit Cards: A, B, C
Notes: 2, 5, 8 (over 12), 9, 14

Harbor Breeze and Bayberry Shores

326 Lower Country Road, 02646
(800) 272-4343

Two distinct walk-to-beach bed and breakfasts offering a choice of country casual or
traditional homestay settings in the beautiful coastal town of Harwich Port—the best
central location for touring Cape Cod.
Hearty continental breakfast with homemade baked goods, family suites, TVs,
refrigerators, pool, tennis, some air conditioning and private entrances. Efficiency
suite with fireplace also available.

Rooms: 12 (PB) $50-125
Continental Breakfast
Credit Cards: A, B, C
Notes: 2, 5, 7, 8, 9, 10, 11, 12, 14

HINSDALE

Berkshire Bed and Breakfast Homes NC7

P. O. Box 211, Williamsburg, 01096
(413) 268-7244

A 100-year-old, remodeled Colonial home
on ten acres. Guest room with private bath
has private entrance. Parlor and deck available to guests. Full breakfast; children welcome. $65-70.

Berkshire Bed and Breakfast Homes NC10

P. O. Box 211, Williamsburg, 01096
(413) 268-7244

This 1770 central-hall Colonial on six acres
has antique and country furnishings
throughout guest rooms with shared bath.
One room with private bath; three with a
shared bath. Parlor and glass porch for
guest use. Full breakfast; no smoking; children welcome. $55-70.

HOLYOKE

Yankee Pedlar Inn

1866 Northampton Street, 01040
(413) 532-9494

This New England inn with guest accommodations and restaurant is in western Massachusetts, in the scenic Connecticut River Valley. Fall foliage is breathtaking, and antiquing is excellent. Skiing, golf, tennis, water slides, and other sports facilities are nearby. Museums and Old Deerfield are some historical points of interest. Close to many educational institutions.

Hosts: Lawrence Audette, John Symasko, and
  Roddy Cameron, Jr.
Singles: 30 (PB) $55-65
Doubles: 16 (PB) $65-75
Continental Breakfast
Credit Cards: A, B, C, D, E

HUNTINGTON

Berkshire Bed and Breakfast Homes PV27

P. O. Box 211, Williamsburg, 01096
(413) 268-7244

At this 1920 split-level Colonial on four acres guest rooms have semiprivate bath and share a parlor with TV. Country furnishings throughout. Continental breakfast; children welcome. $45-55.

HYANNIS

Elegance By-The-Sea

162 Sea Street, 02601
(508) 775-3595

Romantic 1880 Queen Anne Victorian home furnished with antiques in the European-style. Guest rooms offer canopy beds or antique French Louis XV beds. Walk to beaches, restaurants, island ferries. Great as a base for visiting all of Cape Cod. Many common areas available to guests: porch, breakfast greenhouse room, formal dining room with separate tables, fireplace, and parlor with TV and piano.

Hosts: Clark and Mary Boydston
Rooms: 6 (PB) $60-90

Full Breakfast
Credit Cards: A, B, C
Closed January
Notes: 2, 8 (over 16), 9, 10, 11, 12

The Inn on Sea Street

358 Sea Street, 02601
(508) 775-8030

A small, elegant 1849 Victorian inn with fireplace, just steps from the beach. Antiques, canopy beds. Persian rugs and objets d'art abound in this unpretentious, hospitable atmosphere where no detail has been overlooked to assure your comfort. A full breakfast of home-baked delights and fruit is served at individual tables set with the hosts' finest silver, china, crystal, and fresh flowers. One-night stays welcome.

Rooms: 9 (7 PB; 2 SB) $70-90
Full Breakfast
Credit Cards: A, B, C, D
Notes: 2, 9, 10, 11, 12

Sea Breeze Inn

397 Sea Street, 02601
(508) 771-7213

Sea Breeze is a Cape Cod-style building three-minute walk from the beach. Its 14 rooms have private baths, and some have water views. A continental breakfast is served each morning. Restaurants, ferries to Nantucket and Martha's Vineyard, shopping, tennis, and entertainment are within a 20-minute walk from the Sea Breeze.

Host: Patricia Battle
Rooms: 14 (PB) $45-85
Expanded Continental Breakfast
Credit Cards: A, B, C
Notes: 2 (in advance), 5, 7, 8, 9, 14

HYANNISPORT

Bed and Breakfast Cape Cod #32

P. O. Box 341, West Hyannisport, 02672-0341
(508) 775-2772; FAX (508) 775-2884

NOTES: Credit cards accepted: A Master Card; B Visa; C American Express; D Discover Card; E Diner's Club; F Other; 2 Personal Checks accepted; 3 Lunch available; 4 Dinner available; 5 Open all year;

This two-hundred-year-old Colonial-style house is one mile from the center of town, five blocks from the Kennedy compound, two blocks from the ferry to Martha's Vineyard or Nantucket, and less than a mile away from great beaches. One bedroom with a double bed shares a tub and shower with a bedroom that has a pair of twin beds. A continental breakfast is served each morning, and guests are welcome to use the parlor for relaxing. Children over 12. $55.

The Simmons Homestead Inn

288 Scudder Avenue, 02647
(508) 778-4999

An 1820 sea captain's estate that is now one of the nicest inns on Cape Cod. In the country, yet only one-half mile from Hyannis. A very pleasant inn with large porches and huge common rooms, the perfect home base for enjoying the Cape.

Host: Bill Putman
Rooms: 10 (PB) $100-130
Full Breakfast
Credit Cards: A, B, C
Notes: 2, 5, 7, 9, 10, 11, 12

LANESBORO

Bascom Lodge

P. O. Box 1652, 01237
(413) 743-1591

A rustic stone-and-wood lodge on the summit of Mount Greylock on the Great Appalachian Trail. Enjoy a hearty breakfast and dinner, bunk-style dormitory or private accommodations, 100-mile views to Vermont and New York, and traditional mountain hospitality. Close to Williamstown Theatre Festival, Tanglewood, Jacob's Pillow Dance Festival, fishing, boating, biking, and hiking. Or stay in and put your feet up by the fire.

Host: Appalachian Mountain Club
Rooms: 8 (SB) $60 private; $28 bunk or dorm
Full Breakfast

Credit Cards: A, B
Closed mid-Oct.-mid-May
Notes: 2, 3, 4, 8, 9

Berkshire Bed and Breakfast Homes NC1

P. O. Box 211, Williamsburg, 01096
(413) 268-7244

A 200-year-old Colonial farmhouse at the foot of Mount Greylock. Working sheep farm and bakery on premises. Guest rooms with shared bath and sitting room are furnished with country charm. Continental breakfast; children welcome. $45-60.

Berkshire Bed and Breakfast Homes NC9

P. O. Box 211, Williamsburg, 01096
(413) 268-7244

Late 1800s Colonial farmhouse on three acres. This home was once a turkey farm and has a view of Mount Greylock. Guest rooms with semiprivate baths and parlor have country furnishings. Full breakfast; no smoking; children over eight welcome. $70-80.

LEE

Applegate

279 West Park Street, 01238
(413) 243-4451

A circular driveway leads to this pillared Georgian Colonial home set on six peaceful acres. Applegate is special in every way, with canopy beds, antiques, fireplaces, pool, and manicured gardens. Its mood is warm, hospitable, and relaxed. Enjoy complimentary wine and cheese in the libraried livingroom, complete with a baby grand piano. Near Norman Rockwell museum and Tanglewood in the heart of the Berkshires.

6 Pets welcome; 7 Smoking allowed; 8 Children welcome; 9 Social drinking allowed; 10 Tennis available; 11 Swimming available; 12 Golf available; 13 Skiing available; 14 May be booked through travel agents.

Hosts: Nancy Begbie-Cannata and Richard Cannata
Rooms: 6 (PB) $85-190
Expanded Continental Breakfast
Credit Cards: A, B
Notes: 2, 5, 7 (restricted), 8 (over 12), 9, 10, 11, 12, 13

Berkshire Bed and Breakfast Homes SC11

P. O. Box 211, Williamsburg, 01096
(413) 268-7244

1780 Garrison Colonial on four acres features antique and formal furnishings, TV room, porch, and patio. This home offers one bedroom with a queen-size bed and private bath, and two other bedrooms that share a bath and have double beds. No smoking. $75-100.

Berkshire Bed and Breakfast Homes SC21

P. O. Box 211, Williamsburg, 01096
(413) 268-7244

1989 Colonial on 1.3 acres offers three rooms with a variety of bed sizes and choice of either private or semi-private bath. The home is furnished in antiques, with a parlor for guest use, and golf and tennis nearby. No smoking. Children over 12 welcome. $80-95.

Haus Andreas

Stockbridge Road, 01238
(413) 243-3298

Completely restored Colonial mansion with heated pool, tennis, lawn sports, bicycle, air conditioning. Fireplaces in some rooms. Library, piano, TV room, guest pantry.

Hosts: Gerhard and Lilliane Schmid
Rooms: 8 (PB) $50-225
Continental Plus Breakfast
Credit Cards: A, B
Notes: 2, 5, 7, 8 (over 10), 9, 10, 11, 12, 13

LENOX

The American Country Collection 154

4 Greenwood Lane, Delmar, NY 12054
(518) 439-7001

A Berkshire tradition since 1780, this gracious country home has 14 guest rooms, three with a Jacuzzi and private porch, two with a fireplace, and all with private baths. Rooms are cozy and comfortable. The 72-foot swimming pool is available for guest use. A full breakfast is served daily. Children over 12 welcome; smoking permitted. $65-170.

Bed and Breakfast Accommodations 063

984 Gloucester Place, Schenectady, New York 12309
(518) 370-4948

This elegant 11-bedroom inn is in the heart of a vibrant Berkshire community. Meticulously restored and on the National Register of Historic Places, this home features large rooms and six fireplaces. Each room has been tastefully furnished to please even the most discriminating traveler. Seven rooms have private baths, two share a bath, and the carriage house has two private suites. Full breakfast includes muffins, omelets, pancakes, French toast, and more. $65-150 off-season; $85-185 in-season (6/25-10/31).

Birchwood Inn

7 Hubbard Street, 01240
(413) 637-2600; (800) 524-1646

Drive through the village of Lenox, and at the end of the street stands the historic Birchwood Inn. The first town meeting was held here in 1767. Elegant and beautifully restored, the inn is know for its hospitality

Blantyre

throughout the region. Enjoy antiques, fire-places, library, and wonderful porch. Cultural activities include the Boston Symphony at Tanglewood and performing arts. There is marvelous fall foliage, hiking, and biking. Full breakfast with international specialities daily.

Hosts: Joan, Dick, and Dan Toner
Rooms: 12 (10 PB; 2 SB) $50-190
Full Breakfast
Credit Cards: A, B
Notes: 2, 5, 9, 10, 11, 12, 13

Blantyre

East Street, P. O. Box 995, 01240
(413) 637-3556 mid-May-early Nov.
(413) 298-3806 winter

A gracious country house/hotel surrounded by 85 acres of grounds. The hotel has a European atmosphere and exceptional cuisine. Offers tennis, croquet, and swimming as its leisure acitivites.

Host: Roderick Anderson
Rooms: 23 (PB) $150-525
Continental Breakfast; Full available
Credit Cards: A, B, C, E
Notes: 2, 3, 4, 7, 10, 11, 12, 14

Brook Farm Inn

15 Hawthorne Street, 01240
(413) 637-3013

There is poetry here. Large library, poets on tape. Near Tanglewood (Boston Symphony), theater, ballet, shops. Pool,

gardens, fireplaces. Cross-country and downhill skiing close by in the winter. Relax and enjoy.

Hosts: Joe and Anne Miller
Rooms: 12 (PB) $70-165
Buffet Breakfast and Afternoon Tea
Credit Cards: A, B
Notes: 2, 5, 7 (limited), 8 (over 14), 9, 10, 11, 12, 13

Cornell Inn

197 Main Street, 01240
(413) 637-0562

Warm and friendly full service 1880 Victorian inn with fireplaces, antique furnishings, private baths. The carriage house has been converted to four modern suites with fireplaces, kitchens, Jacuzzi tubs. There is a tavern, as well. Central to all downhill skiing and free cross-country skiing.

Cornell Inn

6 Pets welcome; 7 Smoking allowed; 8 Children welcome; 9 Social drinking allowed; 10 Tennis available; 11 Swimming available; 12 Golf available; 13 Skiing available; 14 May be booked through travel agents.

Host: Davis A. Rolland
Rooms: 17 (PB) $50-250
Expanded Continental Breakfast
Credit Cards: A, B, C, D
Notes: 2, 4, 5, 7, 9, 10, 11, 12, 13, 14

Covered Bridge

P. O. Box 447, Norfolk, CT 06058
(203) 542-5944

This historic Colonial within walking distance of the center of town is very convenient to the Berkshires. There is a sitting room for guest use and a large wraparound porch to enjoy in the summer. There are seven guestrooms, two with private baths and five with shared baths. $65-100.

The Gables Inn

103 Walker Street, 01240
(413) 637-3416

Former home of novelist Edith Wharton. Queen Anne-style with period furnishings, pool, tennis, fireplaces, and theme rooms.

Host: Frank Newton
Rooms: 18 (16 PB; 2 SB) $60-195
Continental Breakfast
Credit Cards: A, B, D
Notes: 2, 5, 7, 10, 11, 12, 13

Garden Gables Inn

141 Main Street, P. O. Box 52, 01240
(413) 637-0193

The Gables Inn

A charming 200-year-old gabled inn situated in the historic center of Lenox on five wooded acres dotted with gardens, maples, and fruit trees. A 72-foot outdoor swimming pool, fireplaces, Jacuzzi. Minutes away from Tanglewood and other attractions. Good skiing in winter. Reasonable rates with breakfast included.

Hosts: Mario and Lynn Mekinda
Rooms: 12 (PB) $60-145
Expanded Continental Breakfast
Credit Cards: A, B
Notes: 2, 5, 9, 10, 11, 12, 13, 14

Gateways Inn and Restaurant

71 Walker Street, 01240
(413) 637-2532

Stay and dine in this elegantly restored inn located in the heart of Lenox. Close to Tanglewood and many other cultural attractions. Mobil four-star rated restaurant.

Host: Vito Perulli
Rooms: 9 (PB) $85-295
Continental Breakfast
Minimum stay summer weekends: 3 nights
Credit Cards: A, B, C, D, E
Notes: 2, 3, 4, 5, 9, 10, 12, 13

Walker House Inn

74 Walker Street, 01240
(413) 637-1271; (800) 235-3098

This historic Federal mansion was constructed in 1804 and offers eight spacious rooms, all named for composers and furnished with antiques. Some offer canopy beds and fireplaces, and a large parlor with a grand piano and games, well-stocked library with seven-foot-wide screen where good films, operas, plays, and special television programs can be enjoyed. The dining room offers two large sociable tables where complimentary breakfast and afternoon tea is served. Two verandas, one open and another closed, are available for admiring the landscaped grounds. Walker House is within walking distance to several good restaurants, shops, and galleries.

NOTES: Credit cards accepted: A Master Card; B Visa; C American Express; D Discover Card; E Diner's Club; F Other; 2 Personal Checks accepted; 3 Lunch available; 4 Dinner available; 5 Open all year;

Hosts: Peggy and Richard Houdek
Rooms: 8 (PB) $50-160
Continental Plus Breakfast
Credit Cards: None
Notes: 2, 5, 6, 8 (over12), 9, 10, 11, 12, 13,

Whistlers' Inn

5 Greenwood Street, 01240
(413) 637-0975

Historic 1820 Tudor mansion on seven acres of woodland just three blocks from the town center. Antique-filled home has eight fireplaces, English library, baronial dining room, and Louis XVI music room with Steinway and chandeliers. Full breakfast, afternoon sherry/tea.

Hosts: Joan and Richard Mears
Room: 11 (PB) $80-190
Full Breakfast
Credit Cards: A, B, C
Notes: 2, 5, 13, 14

LEXINGTON

Halewood House

2 Larchmont Lane, 02173
(617) 862-5404

A quiant New England home with clean, attractive, well-appointed rooms. Modern bath. Excellent food. Relaxing atmosphere. traditional New England Cape home. Walking distance to the town center and historical sights. Convenient to I-95.

Host: Carol Halewood
Rooms: 2 (SB) $60
Expanded Continental Breakfast
Credit Cards: None
Notes: 2, 5, 9, 10, 11, 12

Peacock House

Host Homes of Boston
P. O. Box 117, Boston, 02168
(617) 244-1308; FAX (617) 244-5156

In a quiet wooded setting one mile from historic Battle Green, hosts' 1960 split-level has open airy feeling. Guest room with king bed, private bath, and three-room suite (twins, single, and den with private bath). Children welcome. Resident dog. $61.

LOWELL

Bed and Breakfast Associates #CN300

P. O. Box 57166, Babson Park Branch
Boston, 02157-0166
(617) 449-5302; FAX (617) 449-5958

This beautiful Victorian home with its wraparound porch and stained glass is meticulously maintained and is graced by many authentic architectural details and tasteful period furnishings. Two guest rooms on the second floor share a bath. Expanded continental breakfast; children welcome; no smoking. $50-55; family rates available.

Sherman-Berry House

163 Dartmouth Street, 01851-2425
(508) 459-4760; FAX (508) 459-4760

The "very Victorian" Sherman-Berry House will let you experience a bygone era in a fine 1893 restored Queen Anne home. Porches, player piano, antiques, stained glass, peace and quiet. This home, located in a National Historic District, is part of a walking tour, a great walk before breakfast. The elegant breakfast may include French toast sandwich, Irish oatmeal, and Alaska reindeer sausage. (Hosts spent many years in Alaska).

Host: Susan Scott
Rooms: 2 (SB) $50-60
Full Breakfast
Credit Cards: None
Notes: 2, 5, 8, 9, 14

LUDLOW

Misty Meadows, Ltd.

467 Fuller Street, 01056
(413) 583-8103

6 Pets welcome; 7 Smoking allowed; 8 Children welcome; 9 Social drinking allowed; 10 Tennis available; 11 Swimming available; 12 Golf available; 13 Skiing available; 14 May be booked through travel agents.

One of Ludlow's oldest houses (200-year-old) with 85 acres on which to wander. A country scenic atmosphere on a working farm raising "Scottish Highlanders." Brook fishing, scenic patio overlooking Minechaug Mountain Range. Screened cabana with in-ground pool. An area with a lot of history and many historical sites less than one-half hour away.

Host: Donna Belle Haluch
Rooms: 2 (SB) $30-40
Continental Breakfast
Credit Cards: None
Notes: 2, 5, 6, 7, 8, 9, 10, 11, 12, 13

LYNNFIELD

Willow Tree Farm Bed and Breakfast

Bed and Breakfast Marblehead and North Shore
P. O, Box 35, Newtonville, 02160
(617) 964-1606; (800) 832-2632
FAX (617) 332-8572

Antique house circa 1802 features cozy single and double bedrooms with both shared and private baths. A hearty breakfast is served in the post-and-beam dining room that overlooks the gardens, farmstead and wooded preserve. Easy access to other North Shore towns and tourist attractions. Extended stays welcome at special rates. $55-70.

MANCHESTER-BY-THE-SEA

Federal Revival Colonial

Bed and Breakfast Marblehead and North Shore
P. O, Box 35, Newtonville, 02160
(617) 964-1606; (800) 832-2632
FAX (617) 332-8572

This cozy Colonial home is furnished with antiques and features a magnificent English garden where breakfast is served in good weather. It offers one guest room on the second floor with a shared bath. This home is one block from the harbor and one mile from Singing Beach. Gourmet breakfast includes fresh homemade jams. Children over 12 welcome. Resident cats. No smoking. $55-65.

MARBLEHEAD

Bed and Breakfast Associates #NS255

P. O. Box 57166, Babson Park Branch
Boston, 02157-0166
(617) 449-5302; FAX (617) 449-5958

Guests enjoy the privacy of this third-floor suite with its own entry. Situated a few blocks from Marblehead Harbor and its quaint village, this Colonial home was built in 1752. Steep stairs lead to the large guest suite with a living area and limited cooking facilities. Elegant continental breakfast; children welcome; no smoking. $65; off-season monthly rates available.

Bed and Breakfast Associates #NS261

P. O. Box 57166, Babson Park Branch
Boston, 02157-0166
(617) 449-5302; FAX (617) 449-5958

Just two blocks to beaches, antique shops and restaurants, this restored Federal property offers beamed cathedral ceilings and a cozy, charming decor. Two guest rooms on the second floor share a bath. Continental breakfast; children welcome; no smoking. $75-80.

Bed and Breakfast Associates #NS262

P. O. Box 57166, Babson Park Branch
Boston, 02157-0166
(617) 449-5302; FAX (617) 449-5958

This friendly couple offers two guest rooms in their charming multilevel hillside home.

NOTES: Credit cards accepted: A Master Card; B Visa; C American Express; D Discover Card; E Diner's Club; F Other; 2 Personal Checks accepted; 3 Lunch available; 4 Dinner available; 5 Open all year;

Both rooms overlook Marblehead Harbor. Two guest rooms share a bath. Generous continental breakfast; children welcome. $68; family rates available.

The Cobbler's Perch

Bed and Breakfast Marblehead and North Shore
P. O, Box 35, Newtonville, 02160
(617) 964-1606; (800) 832-2632
FAX (617) 332-8572

Built in 1894 as a home and shop for a local shoemaker, this historic house still has its original floor boards. It is within walking distance to Old Town, the Lee Mansion, and good shops and restaurants. Guest accommodations include a kitchen and livingroom with phone and and color TV on the first floor, and a bedroom with an adjoining bath on the second. Minimum stay is two nights. $100.

1890 Marblehead Victorian

Bed and Breakfast Marblehead and North Shore
P. O, Box 35, Newtonville, 02160
(617) 964-1606; (800) 832-2632
FAX (617) 332-8572

This gracious Victorian, with its wainscot foyer and stairwell, offers three beautifully decorated guest rooms (two with queen beds, and the other with a pair of twins), that share a bath in the hall. An extra half-bath is available on the first floor, and a separate guest cottage that sleeps two to four people has a private bath. A wonderful breakfast, featuring home-baked breads, muffins, and granola cereal, is served in the breakfast room, or the gardens, weather permitting. Close to beaches and Old Town Marblehead. Children welcome. Smoking outside only. $75-100.

The Harbor Light Inn

58 Washington Street, 01945
(617) 631-2186

Premier inn one block from the harbor, with rooms featuring air conditioning, TV, private baths, and working fireplaces. Two rooms have double Jacuzzis and sun decks. Beautiful 18th-century period mahogany furniture.

Hosts: Peter and Suzanne Conway
Rooms: 12 (PB) $75-110; $145-175 suites
Continental Breakfast
Credit Cards: A, B, C
Notes: 2, 5, 7, 8, 9, 10, 11, 12

Harborside House

23 Gregory Street, 01945
(617) 631-1032

This handsome 1850 home in the historic district overlooks Marblehead Harbor. Enjoy water views from a fireplaced parlor, period dining room, third-story sun deck, and summer breakfast porch. Walk to historic sights, excellent restaurants, and unique shops. Resident cat. Hostess is a professional dressmaker and nationally ranked competitive swimmer.

Host: Susan Livingston
Rooms: 2 (SB) $70-75
Expanded Continental Breakfast
Credit Cards: None
Notes: 2, 5, 8 (over 10), 10, 11

The Nesting Place

16 Village Street, 01945
(617) 631-6655

This charming 19th-century home is conveniently located in historic Marblehead, and within walking distance of the renowned harbor, beaches, historic homes, galleries, eateries, shops, and famous parks. A relaxing, refreshing home away from home. Two comfortably furnished guest rooms feature a healthful breakfast, outdoor hot tub, and smoke-free environment will be found at The Nesting Place. One half hour from Boston, or one hour from New Hampshire. Day trips by car or bicycle are possible.

6 Pets welcome; 7 Smoking allowed; 8 Children welcome; 9 Social drinking allowed; 10 Tennis available; 11 Swimming available; 12 Golf available; 13 Skiing available; 14 May be booked through travel agents.

Host: Louise Hirshberg
Rooms: 2 (SB) $55-65, seasonal rates available
Semi-full Breakfast
Credit Cards: None

Pleasant Manor Inn

264 Pleasant Street, 01945
(617) 631-5843

Pleasant Manor, a fine example of classic
Victorian architecture, was built in 1872
and has been a charming inn since 1923.
On the bus line 14 miles north of Boston
and two miles from Salem. Beaches,
restaurants, shops, and historic points of
interest are easily accessible from this convenient location. Some features include private baths, TVs, VCRs, air conditioning,
tennis court, off-street parking, and immaculate accommodations. Welcome to one of
the most beautiful towns in the country.

Hosts: Takami and Richard Phelan
Rooms: 12 (PB) $65-75
Continental Breakfast
Credit Cards: None
Notes: 2, 5, 7, 8, 9, 10, 14

Spray Cliff on the Ocean

25 Spray Avenue, 01945
(508) 744-8924; (800) 626-1530

Spray Cliff on the Ocean is a marvelous
Old English Tudor mansion set high above
the Atlantic with views that extend forever.
Six rooms with private baths, some with
fireplaces, some with ocean views.
Continental breakfast. Steps from a sandy
beach.

Hosts: Richard and Diane Pabick
Rooms: 6 (PB) $95-200
Continental Breakfast
Credit Cards: A, B, C, D, E, F
Notes: 2, 5, 7, 8, 9, 10, 11, 12, 13 (XC), 14

State Street Pilot House

Bed and Breakfast Marblehead and North Shore
P. O, Box 35, Newtonville, 02160
(617) 964-1606; (800) 832-2632
FAX (617) 332-8572

Attractively restored and situated among
Old Town's quaint antique and gift shops,
this historic inn was originally the home of
John Adams. The inn offers two comfortable guest rooms, both with private baths,
and is close to Marblehead's famous harbor
and many good restaurants. No smoking.
Children over 12 welcome. $85.

Stillpoint

27 Gregory Street, 01945
(617) 631-2433

Nicely appointed 1840s house is open all
year, graciously landscaped, and filled with
antiques, fireplace, piano, books, no TV, and
quiet, refreshing ambience. Three spacious
bedrooms share two full baths (the option of
a private bath is available), and a hearty,
healthy continental breakfast is served in the
morning on the deck overlooking
Marblehead Harbor in good weather. Within
walking distance to shops, restaurants,
beaches, and public transportation. Twenty
minutes north of Boston, near Logan airport,
and an hour south of Maine/ New Hampshire
border. Trips to Concord, Lexington
Sturbridge Village shopping outlets, and
New Hampshire ski slopes are feasible.

Host: Sarah Lincoln-Harrison
Rooms: 3 (2SB) $70-90
Hearty Continental Breakfast
Credit Cards: A, B
Notes: 2, 5, 10, 11, 13

Tidecrest Bed and Breakfast

Bed and Breakfast Marblehead and North Shore
P. O, Box 35, Newtonville, 02160
(617) 964-1606; (800) 832-2632
FAX (617) 332-8572

Minutes by car to Old Town, this
Mediterranean-style villa with spectacular
view of the ocean offers two accommodations, both with private baths and ocean
views. Breakfast is served on a large sun
porch overlooking the ocean. Open weekends only, Memorial Day through
Columbus Day. Children over 6 welcome.
No smoking. $100-150.

NOTES: Credit cards accepted: A Master Card; B Visa; C American Express; D Discover Card; E Diner's
Club; F Other; 2 Personal Checks accepted; 3 Lunch available; 4 Dinner available; 5 Open all year;

Victorian Rose Bed and Breakfast

72 Prospect Street, 01945
(617) 631-4306; (800) 225-4306

Built at the turn of the century, the Victorian Rose welcomes you to its Victorian wainscot foyer and stairwell. You will fancy spacious bedrooms with high ceilings, brass or antique beds, in a rose accented decor. Share the family room, where you can play billiards or relax with an intriguing book. You will also find that the Victorian Rose is at the edge of Marblehead's historic Old Town, featuring many historic sights and close to its renowned picturesque harbor.

Hosts: Robert and Denise Campbell
Rooms: 4 (1 PB; 3 SB) $65-95
Continental Breakfast
Credit Cards: A, B
Notes: 2, 8, 9, 10, 11, 14

Victorian Rose

MARSHFIELD

Bed and Breakfast Associates #SS350

P. O. Box 57166, Babson Park Branch
Boston, 02157-0166
(617) 449-5302; FAX (617) 449-5958

What enthusiasm and hospitality this retired couple bring to hosting! Their New England farm-style home is one block from Marshfield Beach. Built in 1875, it is furnished with warmth and charm; guests will find this bed and breakfast a welcoming retreat. Three guest rooms with private baths. Full breakfast; children welcome; no smoking. $60-70; family rates available.

Bed and Breakfast Cape Cod #77

P. O, Box 341, West Hyannisport, 02672-0341
(508) 775-2772; FAX (508) 775-2884

This two-story home facing the water has two rooms for bed and breakfast, one with a double bed and the other has a pair of twin beds. The bath is shared, and the breakfast is continental, served between 8:00-9:30 AM. Convenient to the bus to Boston. Children over 12 welcome. $60.

Island Retreat

Be Our Guest Bed and Breakfast
P. O, Box 1333, Plymouth, 02362
(617) 837-9867

This lovely custom-built home is at the point of a small island overlooking salt marshes and the North River. Enjoy beautiful view from the decks and a dock at the back of the home. The east wing of the home offers three guest rooms with a shared bath. All tastefully decorated, there is a room with a pair of twin beds, a room with a single, and a room with a double. Continental breakfast is served on the deck, weather permitting. Children welcome. $75.

The Little Inn

Be Our Guest Bed and Breakfast
P. O, Box 1333, Plymouth, 02362
(617) 837-9867

This two-hundred-year-old Federal Colonial offers three guest rooms furnished in antiques with queen, double, and a pair of twin beds, and private and shared baths. Less than one mile to the beach, the inn is set on a scenic road centrally and conveniently located to Boston, Plymouth Center, and the Mid-Cape. Full breakfast is served in the fireplaced dining room. No smoking. Children welcome. $40-60.

Oceanside

Be Our Guest Bed and Breakfast
P. O, Box 1333, Plymouth, 02362
(617) 837-9867

Just step out the door and cross the street to a long stretch of sandy beach and the Atlantic Ocean. Set on a cliff above the water, this charming beach house offers two guest rooms that share a common bath. One room has a pair of twin beds and the other has a double bed. A full breakfast is served in the dining room. Resident dogs. $40-60.

Woodlands

Be Our Guest Bed and Breakfast
P. O, Box 1333, Plymouth, 02362
(617) 837-9867

This lovely Cape is hidden in the woods and surrounded by lush gardens with a scenic ocean view. Guests should be "animal friendly," as the hosts have chickens, sheep, and a pony. One guest room is available offering a queen-size bed and private bath. A full breakfast is served, and garden tours are avilable upon request. $75.

MARSTONS MILLS

Bed and Breakfast Cape Cod #34

P. O, Box 341, West Hyannisport, 02672-0341
(508) 775-2772; FAX (508) 775-2884

Built in 1986 in a quiet residential neighborhood, this ranch-style house has all the extras one could ask for. One room has queen-size bed, private deck, and private entrance, and another room has a queen-size bed and semi-private bath. The beach is two miles away and the ferry to Martha's Vineyard or Nantucket is three miles away. Children over 12 welcome. No smoking. $65-75.

Bed and Breakfast Cape Cod #58

P. O, Box 341, West Hyannisport, 02672-0341
(508) 775-2772; FAX (508) 775-2884

Built in 1790, this beautiful Colonial-style inn sits on three acres of rolling hillside and overlooks a freshwater pond. A working fireplace and country furnishings create a warm, comfortable atmosphere in the first-floor parlor, and a porch with white wicker furniture and fresh floral arrangements looks out onto a swimming pool. A small suite, a carriage house, and three guest rooms offer special appeal. Children over 12. $65-98.

MASHPEE

Coogan's Bluff

Host Homes of Boston
P. O, Box 117, Boston, 02168
(617) 244-1308; FAX (617) 244-5156

In the resort area of New Seabury, this host's airy and bright deck house is laden with antiques. Three guest rooms offer private baths; and a swimming pool, patio, and deck that overlooks the golf course and ocean are available for guests to enjoy. Short drive to Hyannis for ferry to Martha's Vineyard or Nantucket, and a short walk to the beach or village. $85-101.

MEDFIELD

Bed and Breakfast Associates #CW835

P. O. Box 57166, Babson Park Branch
Boston, 02157-0166
(617) 449-5302; FAX (617) 449-5958

Situated six miles from I-95 and just off Route 109, this pleasant split-level home is in a residential neighborhood just 45 minutes from Boston. The charming host couple are well traveled and will provide the hospitality that you and they have come to expect from bed and breakfast hosts. Two guest rooms, one with a private half-bath. Full breakfast; children welcome. $55; family and monthly rates available.

MEDFORD

Bed and Breakfast Associates #IN210

P. O. Box 57166, Babson Park Branch
Boston, 02157-0166
(617) 449-5302; FAX (617) 449-5958

Just 20 minutes from Concord and Lexington, 15 minutes from Boston, and one and one-half miles from Tufts University. This young family offers a charming third-floor guest room with antique quilt and brass bed in their large Victorian home. Bath is shared with resident graduate student. Continental breakfast; children welcome. French, Arabic, Spanish, Italian spoken. $55; monthly rates available.

Bed and Breakfast Associates #IN220

P. O. Box 57166, Babson Park Branch
Boston, 02157-0166
(617) 449-5302; FAX (617) 449-5958

This grand home near Tufts University has three gracious porches and an irresistible appeal. Your host, a retired food service manager, is dedicated to hospitality. One guest room is quite large and features an antique reproduction double bed and a large bay window plus an attached porch with cheerful white wicker furniture. Shared bath; continental breakfast; children welcome. $50-65; family rates available.

MELROSE

My Melrose Bed and Breakfast

12 Hopkins Street, 02176
(617) 665-1826

Situated near some of the most beautiful coastline and country in the US, you will marvel at the variety of early American history available. Melrose is situated adjacent to three major highways, and I-95 and I-93 provide access to all major attractions from the mountains and crystal clear lakes of Maine and New Hampshire to the vacation mecca of Cape Cod. Two bedrooms share a bath, and a complimentary homemade breakfast features a fresh fruit cup, muffins, bread, cereal, juice, coffee, and tea.

Hosts:George and Lucy Farr
Rooms: 2 (SB) $65
Continental Breakfast
Credit Cards: None
Notes: 2, 7, 8, 9, 10, 11, 12, 14

MILTON

Historic Country House

Host Homes of Boston
P. O, Box 117, Boston, 02168
(617) 244-1308; FAX (617) 244-5156

This 1780 country home restored by architect/owners blends heirlooms and modern amenities for a special stay. Second-floor guest room offers a pair of twin beds, and the grounds offer a swimming pool and a barn. Located near I-93, Route 128, and I-95. $44-51.

6 Pets welcome; 7 Smoking allowed; 8 Children welcome; 9 Social drinking allowed; 10 Tennis available; 11 Swimming available; 12 Golf available; 13 Skiing available; 14 May be booked through travel agents.

MONTAGUE

Berkshire Bed and Breakfast Homes PV34

P. O. Box 211, Williamsburg, 01096
(413) 268-7244

An 1851 country Victorian on two acres offers two guest rooms with semiprivate bath, parlor, and den, all furnished with antiques. Full breakfast; children over 12 welcome. $55-60.

NAHANT

A Bed and Breakfast Above the Rest #50

50 Boatswains Way, Suite 105
Boston, 02150
(617) 884-7748; (800) 677-2262

A private entrance leads into your own home away from home. This ground-floor apartment has everything you need to be really comfortable. The apartment includes two bedrooms, a sitting room, a full kitchen overlooking a glassed-in sun porch, and a private bath with an antique tub and separate shower. One of the bedrooms has a water bed. The hostess provides fresh towels and sets the table with china and crystal every day. Continental breakfast is served.

NANTUCKET

A Bed and Breakfast Above the Rest #63

50 Boatswains Way, Suite 105
Boston, 02150
(617) 884-7748; (800) 677-2262

You would be hard-pressed to find a more authentically Nantucket home. The recently retired hostess grew up on the island and has traced her home as far back as 1792.

The home is full of antiques. There are two guest rooms on the second floor. The rooms, with ships' beams in the corners, have lovely quilts and braided rugs. Two minutes from Main Street. Continental breakfast.

A Bed and Breakfast Above the Rest #64

50 Boatswains Way, Suite 105
Boston, 02150
(617) 884-7748; (800) 677-2262

Bright and cheery. The large dining room table is always set for guests to share. There are four guest rooms sharing three baths. One block from Town Hall, Steamship Wharf, and the Jared Coffin House. An easy walk to the beach, restaurants, shops, and museums. Continental breakfast. Guests are advised not to bring cars as parking is difficult on the island.

Bed and Breakfast Nantucket/ Martha's Vineyard #102

P. O. Box 341, West Hyannisport, 02672-0341
(508) 775-2772; FAX (508) 775-2884

This sixteen-room bed and breakfast is located close to the harbor in the village. From the widow's walk on the third floor, there is panoramic view of the Nantucket harbor. All guest rooms have private baths, and two suites are also available. Breakfast is served in the large dining room on the first floor. No smoking. Children over 12 welcome. $80-130.

Bed and Breakfast Nantucket/ Martha's Vineyard #104

P. O. Box 341, West Hyannisport, 02672-0341
(508) 775-2772; FAX (508) 775-2884

A few steps from Main Street in the village, this 1830 Greek Revival-style home

---

NOTES: Credit cards accepted: A Master Card; B Visa; C American Express; D Discover Card; E Diner's Club; F Other; 2 Personal Checks accepted; 3 Lunch available; 4 Dinner available; 5 Open all year;

offers two bedrooms and a separate cottage for bed and breakfast. Each room has a private bath and king-size bed, and continental breakfast is served in the dining room. A porch, lovely gardens, and convenience to the village are several of the amenities this home offers. $75-100.

Cliff Lodge/Stilldock Apartments

The Carlisle House Inn

26 North Water Street, 02554
(508) 228-0720

Built in 1765, the Carlisle House has been a quality inn for more than 100 years. Situated just off the center of town, the inn has been carefully restored. Hand-stenciled wallpapers, working fireplaces, inlaid pine paneling, wide-board floor, rich Oriental carpets.

Hosts: Peter and Suzanne Conway
Rooms: 14 (8 PB; 6 SB) $125
Minimum stay: 2 nights
Continental Breakfast
Credit Cards: A, B, C
Notes: 2, 5, 7, 8 (over 10), 9, 14

The Centerboard Guest House

8 Chester Street, 02554
(508) 228-9696

"Possibly the most elegant and certainly the most romantic of Nantucket's small inns" —*Inn Spots and Special Places in New*

England, 1989 edition. A newly restored Victorian guest house close to historic cobblestone Main Street and the beach. Most noteworthy is the handsome suite with Jacuzzi and fireplace.

Hosts: Marcia Wasserman and Reggie Reid
Rooms: 6 (PB) $85-225
Continental Breakfast
Credit Cards: A, B, C
Notes: 2, 5, 7, 11, 12, 14

Cliff Lodge/Stilldock Apartments

9 Cliff Road, 02554
(508) 228-9480

Enjoy bed and breakfast accommodations in a 1771 sea captain's home. Overlooking scenic Nantucket town and harbor, a short walk from the many fine restaurants, art galleries, and shops on Main Street. Beautiful English country decor. Seen in Country Homes magazine, August 1988. Cocktail snack served at 5:00 P.M. The Stilldock Apartments include one- and two-bedroom apartments overlooking North Wharf. You will enjoy a patio, a deck, stocked kitchens, and cable TV. Weekly rates.

Host: Geraldine Miller
Rooms: 12 (PB) $50-150
Continental Breakfast
Credit Cards: A, B, C
Notes: 2, 5, 7, 8 (over 10), 9, 11

Cobblestone Inn

5 Ash Street, 02554
(508) 228-1987

This 1725 home is located on a quiet street in Nantucket's historic district, just a few minutes' walk from the steamboat wharf, museums, shops, and restaurants. Guests can walk to nearby beaches or explore others by taking a bike path. Relax in the yard, sun porch, and livingroom.

Hosts: Robin Hammer-Yankow and Keith Yankow
Rooms: 5 (PB) $50-130
Continental Breakfast

6 Pets welcome; 7 Smoking allowed; 8 Children welcome; 9 Social drinking allowed; 10 Tennis available; 11 Swimming available; 12 Golf available; 13 Skiing available; 14 May be booked through travel agents.

Credit Cards: A, B
Notes: 2, 5, 8, 9, 10, 11, 12

Eighteen Garden Street Inn

Eighteen Gardner Street Inn

18 Gardner Street, 02554
(508) 228-1155

You are warmly welcomed to the circa
1835 home of Captain Robert Joy. Built
from the wealth of the whaling era, your
island home includes amenities such as
fireplaced bedrooms, canopy bed, private
baths, and spacious common rooms for the
leisure hours of your stay. Whether you
choose the cozy Garden Room or a deluxe
suite, you'll be attended by a courteous
staff serving a full Nantucket breakfast and
assisting you with all your holiday enjoyment.

Hosts: Roger and Mary Schmidt
Rooms: 17 (PB) $65-185
Full Breakfast
Credit Cards: A, B
Notes: 2, 5, 8, 9, 10, 11, 12, 13, 14

The Fairway

9 Fair Street, 02554
(508) 228-9467

Enjoy complete privacy or become part of
the family. It's your choice at the Fairway.
This stately home in the historic district is
run by a Nantucket native. It has a large
yard and offers a homemade continental
breakfast daily in the formal dining room.
A private latticed porch allows guests to
watch the world go by. Golfers are especially welcome.

Host: Lee Holmes
Rooms: 2 (PB) $50-100
Continental Breakfast
Credit Cards: A, B
Notes: 2, 7, 8, 9, 10, 11, 12

Four Chimneys Inn

38 Orange Street, 02554
(508) 228-1912

A 155-year-old sea captain's mansion with
canopy beds, ten fireplaces, harbor views,
fine antiques, and porches. In the historic
district. Continental breakfast is served in
your room; cocktail snack at 5:00 P.M.

Host: Bernadette Mannix
Rooms: 10 (PB) $115-175
Continental Breakfast
Credit Cards: A, B, C
Closed Dec. 15-April 15
Notes: 7, 9, 10, 11, 12

Grieder Guest House

43 Orange Street, P. O. Box 333, 02554
(508) 228-1399

Four Chimneys Inn

NOTES: Credit cards accepted: A Master Card; B Visa; C American Express; D Discover Card; E Diner's
Club; F Other; 2 Personal Checks accepted; 3 Lunch available; 4 Dinner available; 5 Open all year;

The house was built in the early 1700s on the "street of whaling captains." Rooms with four-poster beds, antiques, exposed beams made from ships' knees. Only several minutes' walk from Main Street. Parking permits and refrigerators provided. Large off-street yard.

Hosts: Ruth and Bill Grieder
Rooms: 2 (SB) $55-80
Continental Breakfast
Credit Cards: None
Notes: 2, 7, 8 (over 3), 9, 10, 11, 12

House of Seven Gables

32 Cliff Road, 02554
(508) 228-4706

Situated in the historic district of Nantucket. A continental breakfast is served in your room. Most rooms in this 100-year-old Victorian have a view of Nantucket Sound.

Hosts: Suzanne and Ed Walton
Rooms: 10 (8 PB; 2 SB) $40-140
Continental Breakfast
Credit Cards: A, B, C
Notes: 2, 5, 7, 8 (over 10), 9, 10, 11, 12

La Petite Maison

132 Main Street, 02554
(508) 228-9242

An owner-managed European inn quietly located five minutes' walk from the center of town. Breakfast with homemade baked goods and stimulating conversation. Warmth and hospitality abound.

Host: Holli Martin
Rooms: 12 (PB) $55-95
Suite: 1 (PB) $150-200
Apartment: $150-200
Continental Breakfast
Credit Cards: A, B
Closed Dec. 10-April 30
Notes: 7, 8 (over 10), 9, 10, 11, 12

The Martin House Inn

61 Centre Street, P. O. Box 743, 02554
(508) 228-0678

In a stately 1803 mariner's home in the Nantucket district, a romantic sojourn awaits you. A glowing fire in our spacious livingroom/dining room is the perfect place to read and relax. Large airy guest rooms with authentic period pieces and four-poster beds and a lovely yard and veranda for peaceful, summer afternoons make sure you have a memorable stay. A large breakfast featuring homemade breads and muffins, fresh fruits, and granola is served in the dining room.

Hosts: Ceci and Channing Moore
Rooms: 13 (9 PB; 4 SB) $135
Continental Breakfast
Credit Cards: A, B, C
Notes: 2, 5, 8, 9

House of Seven Gables

Parker Guest House

4 East Chestnut, 02554
(508) 228-4625; (800) 248- 4625

A small, cozy guest house in the heart of Nantucket Town near the ferry terminals, our bed and breakfast offers rooms with private baths, queen-size or twin beds, coffee maker, cable TV, and air conditioning. Parker Guest House is just a short walk to every point of interest in Nantucket Town. The innkeepers host a wine and cheese party for their guests every Wednesday and Saturday.

6 Pets welcome; 7 Smoking allowed; 8 Children welcome; 9 Social drinking allowed; 10 Tennis available; 11 Swimming available; 12 Golf available; 13 Skiing available; 14 May be booked through travel agents.

Hosts: Ben and Beverly Parker
Rooms: 6 (PB) $65-115
Continental Breakfast
Credit Cards: A, B, C
Notes: 2, 5, 8, 9, 10, 11, 12, 14

76 Main Street

76 Main Street, 02554
(508) 228-2533

All the quiet and subtle beauty of
Nantucket is yours to explore while you
make yourself comfortable in our 1883
Victorian home in the historic district, on
elm-shaded and cobblestoned Main Street.
The hosts are dedicated to your enjoyment
of the island and look forward to accommodating you.

Host: Shirley Peters
Rooms: 18 (PB) $115-135
Continental Breakfast
Credit Cards: A, B, C
Notes: 2, 5, 8, 9, 10, 11, 12, 14

Stumble Inne

109 Orange Street, 02554
(508) 228-4482

The Stumble Inne and Starbuck House are
on historic Orange Street, a pleasant ten-
minute walk to Main Street town center for
shops and restaurants. The Stumble Inne
has seven double and queen rooms, all with
cable TV, and most with bar refrigerators.
Some rooms are air conditioned. Our
Starbuck House, right across the street, has
six double rooms. All rooms in both buildings feature period antiques and Laura
Ashley decor.

Hosts: Mary Kay and Mal Condon
Rooms: 13 (11 PB; 2 SB) $45-130
Continental Breakfast
Credit Cards: A, B, C
Notes: 2, 5, 7, 8, 9, 11, 12, 14

Tuckernuck Inn

60 Unions Street, 02554
(508) 228-4886; (800) 228-4886

Tuckernuck Inn is named for the small
island just one mile off Nantucket's westernmost tip. Tuckernuck is an Indian word
meaning "a loaf of bread." The inn is
Colonial in decor and quite comfortable.
Amenities include a large back lawn for
relaxing and a rooftop widow's walk deck
overlooking Nantucket Harbor. Fine dining
is offered throughout October at our in-
house restaurant, "Bounty." Personal attention for each guest is our primary objective,
and many of our guests return year after

Tuckernuck Inn

NOTES: Credit cards accepted: A Master Card; B Visa; C American Express; D Discover Card; E Diner's
Club; F Other; 2 Personal Checks accepted; 3 Lunch available; 4 Dinner available; 5 Open all year;

year. Tuckernuck Inn is recommended by AAA and *Mobil Travel Guide.*

Host: Ken Parker
Rooms: 16, plus 1 suite (PB) $80-130, seasonal
rates apply
Continental Breakfast
Credit Cards: A, B, C
Notes: 2, 3, 4, 5, 8, 9, 10, 11, 12, 14

Union Street Inn

7 Union Street, 02554
(508) 228-9222; (800) 225-5116

Circa 1770, this bed and breakfast is in the heart of the historic district. An easy walk to the ferry, fine restaurants, quaint shops, and beaches. Continental breakfast is served on a landscaped patio. Twelve spacious rooms with private baths, and some with canopy beds, are available.

Host: Marilyn Music
Rooms: 12 (PB) $55-150
Continental Breakfast
Credit Cards: None
Notes: 2, 5, 14

The Woodbox Inn

29 Fair Street, 02554
(508) 228-0587

Nantucket's oldest inn, built in 1709 is one and one-half blocks from the center of town. The Woodbox offers three double rooms and six suites with working fireplaces, all with private bath. Candlelight gourmet dinner available.

Host: Dexter Tutein
Rooms: 9 (PB) $115-180
Full Breakfast
Credit Cards: None
Closed mid-Oct.-June 1
Notes: 2, 4, 7, 8, 9, 10, 11, 12, 14

NATICK

Bed and Breakfast Associates #IW575

P. O. Box 57166, Babson Park Branch
Boston, 02157-0166
(617) 449-5302; FAX (617) 449-5958

Situated on the Natick/Wellesley line, and a short stroll from the beautiful Wellesley College campus, you will find this small, pleasant Cape-style home. Your hostess is a self-employed musician, organist, and choir director. One guest room with private bath. Children over eight welcome; continental breakfast; no smoking. $50.

NEEDHAM

Bed and Breakfast Associates #IW635

P. O. Box 57166, Babson Park Branch,
Boston, 02157-0166
(617) 449-5302; Fax (617) 449-5948

Your hostess is director of human resources at a local college and offers a large, tastefully decorated guest room in her immaculate suburban home, just 25 minutes from Boston. Private bath; continental breakfast; children welcome; no smoking. $55.

The Thistle Bed and Breakfast

Host Homes of Boston
P. O. Box 117, Boston, 02168
(617) 244-1308; FAX (617) 244-5156

Typical, cozy Cape Cod on a quiet street has a fireplaced livingroom for guests and two second-floor guest rooms with doubles or twins and private and shared baths. A few blocks from Route 128/ I-95, and you can walk to the train. $44-61.

NEWBURY

Dolan Antique Colonial

Bed and Breakfast Marblehead and North Shore
P. O. Box 35, Newtonville, 02160
(617) 964-1606; (800) 832-2632
FAX (617) 332-8572

6 Pets welcome; 7 Smoking allowed; 8 Children welcome; 9 Social drinking allowed; 10 Tennis available; 11 Swimming available; 12 Golf available; 13 Skiing available; 14 May be booked through travel agents.

This restored Colonial farmhouse is surrounded by five acres of fields and perennial gardens. Convenient to beaches, downtown Newburyport, and Maudsley State Park, the bed and breakfast offers one large, sunny guest room with a double and single bed, private bath, skylights, and color TV. Guests may relax in the family room or screened porch, and continental breakfast offers home-baked goodies. $45-55.

NEWBURYPORT

Bed and Breakfast/Inns of New England MA 1000

329 Lake Drive, Guilford, CT 06437
(800) 582-0853

Built in 1806 by Captain William Hoyt, this estate typifies the three-story square style of the Federal period. Among its many fine architectural features are cornices, mantles, balustrades, and a graceful hanging staircase. There are summer and winter porches, a formal front parlor, and library. Many special events are offered throughout the year, including weekend murder mysteries, fashion shows, weddings, and corporate conferences. Just a five-minute walk from downtown Newburyport, a seaport area. There are nine guest rooms on the inn's three floors, all furnished in antiques and some with canopied beds. Children 12 and older welcome. $50-77.

Morrill Place Inn

209 High Street, 01950
(508) 462-2808

This gracious 1806 Federal sea captain's mansion is in Historic New England's seaport. Enjoy our cozy library, elegant dining room, formal music parlor, and our summer and winter porches. Each of our nine guest rooms is appointed with fine antiques, canopy four poster, or sleigh beds.

Host: Rose Ann Hunter
Rooms: 9 (3 PB; 6 SB) $60-90
Continental Breakfast
Credit Cards: None
Notes: 2, 5, 6, 9, 14

Newburyport Federal Bed and Breakfast

Bed and Breakfast Marblehead and North Shore
P. O. Box 35, Newtonville, 02160
(617) 964-1606; (800) 832-2632
FAX (617) 332-8572

Attractive 1803 Federal mansion is located close to Market Square and is filled with antiques. The Inn features six beautiful guest rooms, all with private baths and air conditioning. A generous continental breakfast is served in the sunny garden room, and afternoon tea is served in front of the magnificent Samuel McIntyre fireplace. $95-125.

The Windsor House in Newburyport

38 Federal Street, 01950
(508) 462-3778

Built as a wedding present, this 18th-century Federal mansion offers a rare blend of Yankee hospitality and the English tradition of bed and breakfast. Designed as a residence/ship's chandlery, the inn's spacious rooms recall the spirit of an English country house. Situated in a historic seaport near a wildlife refuge. Whale watching, museums, theater, and antiques. Rates include afternoon tea, English cooked breakfast, tax, and service. Evening meal available November to May.

Hosts: Judith and John Harris
Rooms: 6 (3 PB; 3 SB) $75-115
Full Breakfast
Credit Cards: A, B, D
Notes: 2, 4, 5, 6, 8, 10, 11, 12, 13, 14

NOTES: Credit cards accepted: A Master Card; B Visa; C American Express; D Discover Card; E Diner's Club; F Other; 2 Personal Checks accepted; 3 Lunch available; 4 Dinner available; 5 Open all year;

NEWTON

Alderwood

Host Homes of Boston
P. O. Box 117, Boston, 02168
(617) 244-1308; FAX (617) 244-5156

Guests migrate to the gourmet kitchen in this 1930 Colonial. Second floor guest room has twin beds. "Pumpkin" the cat lives here. Children welcome. Quiet road near Boston College Law campus. One mile to Green Line-D. 10 minutes drive to Boston. Private bath, TV. $68.

Beazie's on the Charles

Host Homes of Boston
P. O. Box 117, Boston, 02168
(617) 244-1308; FAX (617) 244-5156; FAX (617) 244-5156

In a sylvan setting along the Charles River, this Colonial is replete with Early Americana. Breakfast is served in the "Sturbridge" dining room. A second-floor guest room with view of river and woods. Also, single room if same party. Five blocks to village, Green Line-D, air conditioning, private bath, TV. No smoking. $68.

A Bed and Breakfast Above the Rest #44

50 Boatswains Way, Suite 105
Boston, 02150
(617) 884-7748; (800) 677-2262

An M.D. and an MIT administrator are your hosts in this perfectly restored, 60-year-old home. The host speaks fluent Japanese and German. The two handsome guest rooms with single beds are situated on the second floor. They share a bath and private hallway. Longer stays are preferred. Full breakfast.

A Bed and Breakfast Above the Rest #45

50 Boatswains Way, Suite 105
Boston, 02150
(617) 884-7748; (800) 677-2262

This large and extremely comfortable home was designed and built by the hostess's architect husband. It is beautifully decorated and thoughtfully landscaped with grounds visible through many picture windows and a glassed-in porch. There is one guest room overlooking the garden with a mahogany double bed and private bath. The room has a country feel, with pretty patterned wallpaper and a hooked rug. Full breakfast.

Bed and Breakfast Associates #IW265

P. O. Box 57166, Babson Park Branch
Boston, 02157-0166
(617) 449-5302; FAX (617) 449-5958

Your host, a lovely lady, will proudly show you the distinctive interior and spectacular landscaping of the ranch-style home that her architect husband designed. Large windows afford delightful views of the seasonal splendor. This is one of Boston's best suburban neighborhoods. One guest room with private bath and a single den rented with guest room. Full breakfast; children over ten welcome; no smoking. $50-80.

Bed and Breakfast Associates #IW270

P. O. Box 57166, Babson Park Branch
Boston, 02157-0166
(617) 449-5302; FAX (617) 449-5958

Situated on one acre in a neighborhood little changed since the 1890s, this grand home, furnished with 18th- and 19th-century antiques, is only 15 minutes from downtown Boston via the Massachusetts Pike.

6 Pets welcome; 7 Smoking allowed; 8 Children welcome; 9 Social drinking allowed; 10 Tennis available; 11 Swimming available; 12 Golf available; 13 Skiing available; 14 May be booked through travel agents.

The dining room is graced with a beautiful fireplace as are both guest rooms. Full breakfast; children welcome; no smoking. $65; family rates available.

Bed and Breakfast Associates #IW277

P. O. Box 57166, Babson Park Branch
Boston, 02157-0166
(617) 449-5302; FAX (617) 449-5958

In a pretty Waban Village neighborhood, this large, cheerful house is the home of an active young family. Their spacious guest rooms are newly redecorated. Three rooms, one with private bath. Kids will enjoy a large playroom and outdoor play yard. Full breakfast; children welcome; no smoking. $55-65; family rates available.

Bed and Breakfast Associates #IW281

P. O. Box 57166, Babson Park Branch
Boston, 02157-0166
(617) 449-5302; FAX (617) 449-5958

Gorgeous 1912 Georgian Colonial on large lot in historic neighborhood. This delightful young family offers a wonderfully decorated corner room with sitting area and TV. A charming room is also available on the third floor with bath facilities on the second floor. Rented to same party only. Generous continental breakfast; children welcome; no smoking. $65-75.

Breamore by the Pike

Host Homes of Boston
P. O. Box 117, Boston, 02168
(617) 244-1308; FAX (617) 244-5156

Large, authentic Victorian home (1898) offers double and twin rooms. Both, if same party. This retired educator and vegetable gardener bakes fruit breads for breakfast. Three blocks to restaurants,

express bus (11 minutes to Boston). Easy drive to airport, Cambridge. Air conditioning, private bath. No smoking. $61-112.

The Carriage House

Bed and Breakfast Greater Boston & Cape Cod
P. O. Box 35, Newtonville, 02160
(617) 964-1606; (800) 832-2632
FAX (617) 332-8572

A charming, renovated private studio in a suburb just west of Boston. The first level has comfortable sitting area; second level has fully equipped kitchenette, private bath, sitting area with a comfortable double futon, two couches, wood-burning stove, color TV, air conditioning, and phone. Rate includes breakfast provided by host and self-served by guest. Weather permitting, guests may use the host's barbecue and back yard deck. Easy access by car or public transportation to Boston/Cambridge. Short walk to village shopping area with movie theater. Special rates for extended stays. $75.

Crescent Avenue Bed and Breakfast

Bed and Breakfast Greater Boston and Cape Cod
P. O. Box 35, Newtonville, 02160
(617) 964-1606; (800) 832-2632
FAX (617) 332-8572

In a lovely suburb just west of Boston with easy access to Boston/Cambridge, this gracious twelve-room Greek Revival circa late 1800s has a pool and lovely gardens. Two guest rooms with a private bath and separate entrance are available, and a generous continental breakfast is served in the dining room or the screened porch. No smoking. $75-90.

The Evergreens

Host Homes of Boston
P. O. Box 117, Boston, 02168
(617) 244-1308; FAX (617) 244-5156

NOTES: Credit cards accepted: A Master Card; B Visa; C American Express; D Discover Card; E Diner's Club; F Other; 2 Personal Checks accepted; 3 Lunch available; 4 Dinner available; 5 Open all year;

Older Colonial is filled with host's pottery and Mexican art collection. Two second-floor guest rooms share bath. Cozy screened porch. Five minutes walk to Boston College or Green Line-B to Boston University, Back Bay and Downtown. Air conditioning, shared bath. $46-57.

Meadowbrook Run

Host Homes of Boston
P. O. Box 117, Boston, 02168
(617) 244-1308; FAX (617) 244-5156

Your hosts offer old-fashioned hospitality in their contemporary home on a quiet road. Enjoy a game of billiards in the den. First-floor guest room. Resident cat. Village, Green Line-D one mile. Near Boston College. Boston seven miles. Air conditioning, TV, private bath. $54.

Rockledge

Host Homes of Boston
P. O. Box 117, Boston, 02168
(617) 244-1308; FAX (617) 244-5156

Stately 1882 Victorian in prime location. Cordial hosts offer bright, spacious rooms, antiques, trees, gardens. Three second-floor guest rooms, but only two booked at a time. Ceiling fans. Second-floor guest parlor. Resident cat. Two blocks to lake, village, and subway. Older children welcome. Shared bath, TV. No smoking. $57.

The Suite at Chestnut Hill

Bed and Breakfast Greater Boston and Cape Cod
P. O. Box 35, Newtonville, 02160
(617) 964-1606; (800) 832-2632
FAX (617) 332-8572

This gorgeous furnished efficiency, situated in a neighborhood of very beautiful homes, offers easy access by public trans-portation to Boston/Cambridge. Efficiency has a kitchen area, full bath, color TV, phone, air conditioning separate dining, and sitting areas, and a queen bed. Self-catered breakfast provided. $90.

NEWTON CENTRE

A Bed and Breakfast Above the Rest #46

50 Boatswains Way, Suite 105
Boston, 02150
(617) 884-7748; (800) 677-2262

This stately brick Georgian-style house is an excellent choice for guests accustomed to an upscale lifestyle. Built in 1933 and substantially expanded in 1945, the home is elegantly appointed with Oriental rugs, chandeliers, china, crystal, and luxurious linens. On the third floor are two large and comfortable guest rooms that share a bath. Each has a double bed, TV, radio, clock, hardwood floors and high ceilings. One and one-half from Boston College. Continental breakfast on weekdays; full breakfast on weekends.

Mount Pleasant

Bed and Breakfast Greater Boston and Cape Cod
P. O. Box 35, Newtonville, 02160
(617) 964-1606; (800) 832-2632
FAX (617) 332-8572

This beautiful large New England farm, built in 1820 and set back from the road to maintain a quiet atmosphere, offers a blend of the old and new. One charming guest room with a double bed shares a bath. Breakfast is included and is served in the sunny kitchen or more formal dining room. Conveniently located near public transportation, and you are close to area colleges, shopping, and restaurants. $61-68.

6 Pets welcome; 7 Smoking allowed; 8 Children welcome; 9 Social drinking allowed; 10 Tennis available; 11 Swimming available; 12 Golf available; 13 Skiing available; 14 May be booked through travel agents.

NEWTON CORNER

The Berry Patch

Bed and Breakfast Greater Boston and Cape Cod
P. O. Box 35, Newtonville, 02160
(617) 964-1606; (800) 832-2632
FAX (617) 332-8572

This three-story brick Colonial offers easy access to Boston/Cambridge by car or public transporation. The main guest room has a queen bed and private bath, and a second guest room has a pair of twins with a shared bath. Host serves a wonderful breakfast that features natural foods and home-baked goodies, and in July, fresh berries from the back yard berry patch. No smoking. Children over 12 welcome. $55-70.

NORFOLK

Bed and Breakfast Associates #CW825

P. O. Box 57166, Babson Park Branch
Boston, 02157-0166
(617) 449-5302; FAX (617) 449-5958

Guests enter a world of tranquility as they approach this 36-acre sprawling country retreat. Located 40 minutes from downtown Boston by car or commuter rail, the original part of this house was built in 1661 with additions in 1733. Guests enjoy swimming in the year-round, heated indoor pool, walking, cross-country skiing, or relaxing before the fire. Two guest rooms with private bath. One has a fireplace, the other has a waterbed. Full breakfast upon request; children welcome; smoking limited. $65-75.

NORTHAMPTON (FLORENCE)

The Knoll

230 North Main Street, 01060
(413) 584-8164

The Knoll is situated on 17 acres overlooking farmland and forest. It is in town and yet in a rural setting with an acre of lawn and large circular driveway. This is the five-college area of western Massachusetts: Smith, Amherst, Mount Holyoke, the University of Massachusetts, and Hampshire.

Host: Mrs. Lee Lesko
Rooms: 3 (SB) $40-50 Full Breakfast
Credit Cards: None
Notes: 2, 5, 10, 11, 12, 13

NORTH EASTHAM

Bed & Breakfast/Inns of New England MA-1051

329 Lake Drive, Guilford, CT 06437
(800) 582-0853

This house, a half-Cape with saltbox addition, is decorated with quilts and collectibles. In a quiet neighborhood less than a mile from Cape Cod National Seashore Visitor's Center, it is minutes from bay beaches, fresh water ponds, and two ocean beaches. Two guest rooms are available, both with shared baths. The first floor room has a king bed, and the upstairs room has a double bed. No smoking. House dog; no guest pets. $50-60.

NORTH FALMOUTH

Bed and Breakfast Cape Cod #51

P. O. Box 341, West Hyannisport, 02672-0341
(508) 775-2772; FAX (508) 775-2884

Built in 1793, this Cape Cod Colonial was expanded and fully restored to its original condition and appearance some years ago. Primitive Early American decor and antiques fill this antique dealer's home. Two guest rooms each have a private bath, double canopy beds, fireplaces, and a sitting area where the hostess serves breakfast. $85.

NOTES: Credit cards accepted: A Master Card; B Visa; C American Express; D Discover Card; E Diner's Club; F Other; 2 Personal Checks accepted; 3 Lunch available; 4 Dinner available; 5 Open all year;

NORTHFIELD

Berkshire Bed and Breakfast Homes PV14

P. O. Box 211, Williamsburg, 01096
(413) 268-7244

This 1890 Colonial home on two acres has country and Colonial furnishings. There is a parlor for guests' use, and a gift and craft shop on the premises. There are two guest rooms, one with a king-size bed and one with a queen-size bed. Both have private baths. Full breakfast. No smoking. Children welcome. Resident pets. $55-65.

Centennial House Bed and Breakfast

94 Main Street, 01360
(413) 498-5921

In its eleven years as a bed and breakfast, this lovely old Colonial, built in 1811, has hosted guests from throughout the country and the world. Located in one of New England's lovely villages and near the fine independent school, Northfield Mount Hermon, Centennial House looks forward to welcoming you.

Host: Marguerite Linsert Lentz
Rooms: 5 (2 PB; 3 SB) $60-70
Hearty Continental Breakfast
Credit Cards: A, B
Notes: 2, 5, 10, 11, 12, 13

NORTH SCITUATE

Rasberry Ink

748 Country Way, 02060
(617) 545-6629

Coastal Scituate is 350 years old, 25 miles southeast of Boston, midway between Boston and Plymouth. It was the home of Thomas Lawson, a copper king in the 1900s. His estate is close by. Rasberry Ink is an early Victorian farmhouse furnished in lace

and antiques, located in the village. Antique shops nearby; ocean and historic sites.

Hosts: Fran Honkonen and Carol Hoban
Rooms: 2 (SB) $65
Continental Breakfast
Credit Cards: None
Notes: 2, 10, 11, 12, 13 (XC)

NORTH TRURO

The Summer House

Pond Road, 02652
(508) 487-2077

The Summer House is a Greek Revival with five tastefully decorated rooms located five miles from Provincetown, Massachusetts. A short walk to the Bay beach, and the ocean beach is a mile down the road. The Highland Links golf course is also a mile away.

Host: Diana Worthington
Rooms: 5 (SB) $60
Continental Breakfast
Credit Cards: A, B
Notes: 2, 7, 9, 10, 11, 12

NORWELL

Bed and Breakfast Associates #SS330

P. O. Box 57166, Babson Park Branch
Boston, 02157-0166
(617) 449-5302; FAX (617) 449-5958

Situated in the pretty suburban town of Norwell, this country home was built in 1810. The house features beamed ceilings, Oriental rugs, and antiques. Three guest rooms share a bath. Full breakfast; children welcome; no smoking. $63.

OAK BLUFFS, MARTHA'S VINEYARD

Admiral Benbow Inn

520 New York Avenue, Box 2488, 02567
(508) 693-6825

6 Pets welcome; 7 Smoking allowed; 8 Children welcome; 9 Social drinking allowed; 10 Tennis available; 11 Swimming available; 12 Golf available; 13 Skiing available; 14 May be booked through travel agents.

A charming, turn-of-the-century home, the Admiral Benbow has been restored to its former grandeur. The inn offers comfortable, non-smoking rooms with private baths, period furnishings, and personal attention.

Rooms: 7 (PB) $40-130, seasonal rates apply
Full Breakfast
Credit Cards: A, B, C
Notes: 2, 5, 8, 9, 10, 11, 12

Arend's Samoset on the Sound

Box 847, 02557
(508) 693-5148

Charming Victorian beach house, built in 1873 on the waterfront. A five-minute walk to the ferries, shops, restaurants, parks, tennis, bike rentals, and more. The house offers a livingroom, piano nook, dining room, sun porch, open porch, widow's walk, and an unobstructed view of the sunrise over Martha's Vineyard Sound.

Hosts: Valgerd and Stanley Arend
Rooms: 8 (3 PB; 5 SB) $65-125
Continental Breakfast
Credit Cards: A, B, C
Closed Columbus Day-Memorial Day
Notes: 2 (deposit), 7, 8, 9, 10, 11, 12, 14

The Beach House Bed and Breakfast

Corner of Seaview and Pennacook Avenue, 02557
(508) 693-3955

A newly renovated 1890s house directly across from large, sandy swimming beach. Friendly, helpful, and relaxed atmosphere. Rooms have brass queen-size beds, ceiling fans, and TV. Close to town, shops, restaurants, ferries, shuttle bus, and tours; moped, car, bike, and boat rentals. Oak Bluffs is a magnificent town for strollers and photographers with its many-hued gingerbread cottages. It is also home to the Flying Horses, the nation's oldest carousel.

Hosts: Pamela, Calvin, and Justin Zaiko
Rooms: 9 (PB) $60-125 (winter rates $50)
Continental Breakfast
Credit Cards: A, B, C, D
Notes: 2, 5, 7, 9, 10, 11, 12, 14

Bed and Breakfast Nantucket/ Martha's Vineyard #201

P. O. Box 341, West Hyannisport, 02672-0341
(508) 775-2772; FAX (508) 775-2884

This 1872 Victorian cottage has six bedrooms for bed and breakfast and is one city block from the beaches. Bedrooms with private baths and king or double beds are available. Continental breakfast is served from 8:00-10:00 AM. Public tennis and public transportation to other parts of the island are two blocks away. $75-125.

The Dockside Inn

Circuit Avenue Extension, P. O. Box 1206, 02557
(508) 693-1066

A candy-colored Victorian inn on the lively Oak Bluffs harborfront, this bed and breakfast features spacious porches where you can watch the boats, ferries, and world go by. Twenty comfortable rooms and kitchen suites all feature private baths, air conditioning, cable TV, and queen beds. You are steps to the ferries, beaches, transportation, and restaurants. Extended stay discounts.

Host: Leo P. Connery
Rooms: 15 double, 5 suites (PB) $95-160
Continental Breakfast
Credit Cards: A, B, D
Notes: 2, 7, 8, 9, 10, 11, 12, 14

The Nashua House

P. O. Box 803, 02557
(508) 693-0043

For a holiday on Martha's Vineyard on a budget, clean rooms and continental breakfast in July and August. Shared baths, steps

---

NOTES: Credit cards accepted: A Master Card; B Visa; C American Express; D Discover Card; E Diner's Club; F Other; 2 Personal Checks accepted; 3 Lunch available; 4 Dinner available; 5 Open all year;

to the beach, ferries, harbor, shuttle buses, laundry, grocery, post office, bike rentals, restaurants, movies, the historic ginger-bread campgrounds, and antique carousel by the sea.

Hosts: Harry and son
Rooms: 15 (SB) $25-65
Continental Breakfast
Credit Cards: A, B, C
Closed Oct.-April
Notes: 8 (over 10), 10, 11, 12

The Oak House

Seaview Avenue, Box 299 AB, 02557
(508) 693-4187

Enjoy a romantic Victorian seaside holiday. Elegant oak interior in restored 1876 summer home of Governor Claflin. Furnished with antiques; most rooms have ocean view. Wide porches and stained-glass sun porch. Daily maid service; afternoon tea; lovely beach; walk to ferry and downtown.

Host: Betsi Convery-Luce
Rooms: 10 (PB) $110-160
Two-room Suite: (PB) $220
Continental Breakfast
Credit Cards: A, B, D
Closed Oct. 16-May 10
Notes: 2, 7, 8 (over 9), 9, 10, 11, 12, 14

Pequot House

19 Pequot Avenue, P. O. Box 1146, 02557
(508) 693-5087

A small, friendly inn, situated amid Victorian gingerbread cottages. The Pequot has been hosting summer guests for over 75 years. It is one block from the ocean beaches and a five minute walk from downtown dining and shopping establishments. Public transportation and ferries are also conveniently close. You will find accommodations clean and comfortable, staff eager to make your stay a memorable one.

Host: Peter Martell
Rooms: 25 (PB) $70-110
Continental Breakfast
Credit Cards: A, B, C
Notes: 2, 7, 8, 9, 10, 11, 12, 14

The Wesley House

P. O. Box 2370, 1 Lake Avenue, 02557
(508) 693-6611

A beautiful Victorian inn overlooking Oak Bluffs Harbor is just a few minutes walk to shops, beaches, fine restaurants, and enter-tainment. Relax on the large porch in one of the many rocking chairs, or visit with friends in the elegant lobby. The conve-nience of the location remains unsurpassed to explore the islands of beauty and diversi-ty. Please visit us and experience the old-fashioned hospitality. The courteous staff will make your stay relaxing and memo-rable.

Host: Lynda Martell
Rooms: 82 (62 PB; 20 SB) $50-150
Continental Breakfast
Credit Cards: A, B, C, E
Notes: 2, 7, 8, 9, 10, 11, 12, 14

ORLEANS

Academy Place

Orleans Bed and Breakfast Associates
P. O. Box 1312, 02653
(508) 255-3824; (800) 541-6226

A quaint Cape Cod home with comfortable beds awaits you. This 1752 house has many antique charms, post-and-beam construc-tion, wide-pine boards, and period antiques. On the edge of Orleans' shopping district, all the downtown's retail stores and restau-rants are a short walk. Atlantic Ocean and Cape Cod Bay beaches only two and one-half miles. $50-70.

Arey's Pond Relais

Orleans Bed and Breakfast Associates
P. O. Box 1312, 02653
(508) 255-3824; (800) 541-6226

A very special house filled with warmth, a myriad of delightful details, and intriguing collections. Flower-filled patio serves as private entrance to guest rooms. Queen bed

6 Pets welcome; 7 Smoking allowed; 8 Children welcome; 9 Social drinking allowed; 10 Tennis available; 11 Swimming available; 12 Golf available; 13 Skiing available; 14 May be booked through travel agents.

with white wicker headboard invites rest. Private bath, small guest refrigerator. Adjacent queen room can accommodate your children or other people traveling with you. Breakfast is served on deck overlooking Arey's Pond. $70.

Bed and Breakfast Cape Cod #8

P. O. Box 341, West Hyannisport, 02672-0341
(508) 775-2772; FAX (508) 775-2884

This dramatic contemporary home is built on high ground and overlooks five acres of wooded land. The large deck is next to an in-ground pool. Interior features include a soaring cathedral ceiling, Oriental carpets, wood-burning fireplaces, and sprial staircase. Bedrooms have queen-size beds and private baths, and Nauset Beach is two miles away. A cottage is also available. Full breakfast. No smoking. No children. $90.

Bed and Breakfast Cape Cod #69

P. O. Box 341, West Hyannisport, 02672-0341
(508) 775-2772; FAX (508) 775-2884

Built in 1840, this Greek Revival house offers four guest accommodations in the heart of Orlean's historic district. All rooms have private baths and are well appointed. A generous continental breakfast is served each morning from 7:00-10:00, and full breakfast is available upon request. Children over 12. $65-85.

The 1840 House

Orleans Bed and Breakfast Associates
P. O. Box 1312, 02653
(508) 255-3824; (800) 541-6226

An 1840 Greek Revival situated in a residential neighborhood within walking dis-

tance of town center, restaurants, galleries, and the Academy of Performing Arts. One twin room, one double room, each with private bath. Sitting room with TV. Breakfast served on fine china. Roll-away bed available ($30). $65.

The Farmhouse

163 Beach Road, 02653
(508) 255-6654

This 19th-century farmouse has been carefully restored and furnished to provide a unique blend of country life in a seashore setting. Short walk to Nauset Beach, close to sailing, golf, tennis, bike trails, theater, fishing, shopping, museums, and surfing. Some ocean-view rooms. Breakfast is served on an ocean-view deck.

Hosts: The Standishes
Rooms: 8 (4 PB; 4 SB) $32-95
Expanded Continental Breakfast
Credit Cards: A, B
Notes: 2, 5, 7 (limited), 8, 14

Gray Gables

Orleans Bed and Breakfast Associates
P. O. Box 1312, , 02653
(508) 255-3824; (800) 541-6226

An enormous old elm shades a secluded yard with lawn furniture set out for your pleasure. A private entrance leads to guest wing of a fine old house with plenty of charm and wonderfully warm hosts. Comfortably spacious twin or king guest room, refrigerator, TV, and air conditioning. Bath has huge tiled shower. Breakfast served on Limoges china in your room at 8:30 A.M. or will be set out for you. Resident dog. $65.

Hilltop

Orleans Bed and Breakfast Associates
P. O. Box 1312, 02653
(508) 255-3824; (800) 541-6226

NOTES: Credit cards accepted: A Master Card; B Visa; C American Express; D Discover Card; E Diner's Club; F Other; 2 Personal Checks accepted; 3 Lunch available; 4 Dinner available; 5 Open all year;

Overlooking Baker's Pond, this sparkling new Cape Cod home offers two comfortable bedrooms with adjoining bath, each room freshly furnished. Swim in clear freshwater with private sandy beach. Walk to nearby Nickerson State Park's trails and ponds. Generous continental breakfast served on sunny spacious deck. Families welcome. $60.

Maison de La Mer

Orleans Bed and Breakfast Associates
P. O. Box 1312, 02653
(508) 255-3824; (800) 541-6226

Attractively decorated contemporary country home on Cape Cod Bay, a short, pretty walk to Skaket Beach. Spacious first-floor twin room with private bath. Second-floor bedroom has water view, queen bed, and private bath with whirlpool tub. Guests are encouraged to use livingroom with front entrance. Sunny dining area overlooks seaside garden or enjoy an alfresco meal on the deck. $70-80.

Morningside

Orleans Bed and Breakfast Associates
P. O. Box 1312, 02653
(508) 255-3824; (800) 541-6226

Waterfront suite with private entrance in gracious home overlooking Nauset Harbor and the Atlantic. Private beach. Huge room with king bed and sitting area faces the ocean. Private bath. Superb is the only word for it. $90.

Sweet Retreat

Orleans Bed and Breakfast Associates
P. O. Box 1312, 02653
(508) 255-3824; (800) 541-6226

A delightful in-town studio. Outside stairs lead to a private deck with view of attractive garden. Enter into kitchenette area with breakfast table. A step down into bedroom

with queen bed and private bath. Host owns a beautiful patisserie and catering business. Count on good things for your breakfast. Bike to beaches and walk to village. $75.

Taffrail

Orleans Bed and Breakfast Associates
P. O. Box 1312, 02653
(508) 255-3824; (800) 541-6226

Located in one of the choicest areas of Orleans and owned by delightful couple. Separate entrance leads upstairs to large room overlooking Nauset Harbor and the Atlantic. Double bed, private bath, and small kitchenette. Living/sitting area with fireplace and TV. Breakfast available in your own private guest quarters or on main house patio facing the ocean. Just a short walk to saltwater beach. $85.

Winterwell

Orleans Bed and Breakfast Associates
P. O. Box 1312, 02653
(508) 255-3824; (800) 541-6226

Restored 19th-century Cape Cod farmhouse, a short stroll to Skaket Beach yet close to town and bike path, offers two comfortable accommodations. The main house offers a first-floor guest room with separate entrance and private bath. Main livingroom for occasional reading and TV. A spacious guest wing with separate entrance has bedroom with private bath, sitting room, and kitchen-dining area. All guests enjoy breakfast on enclosed porch overlooking large private yard with busy bird feeder. $60-80.

OSTERVILLE

Bed and Breakfast Cape Cod #59

P. O. Box 341, West Hyannisport, 02672-0341
(508) 775-2772; FAX (508) 775-2884

6 Pets welcome; 7 Smoking allowed; 8 Children welcome; 9 Social drinking allowed; 10 Tennis available; 11 Swimming available; 12 Golf available; 13 Skiing available; 14 May be booked through travel agents.

Imagine the quintessential New England village, and you have found Osterville. This ten-year-old spacious Colonial house offers three guest accommodations, two with double beds and the other has a pair of twin beds. One room has a private bath, and the other two share a bath. No smoking. $65.

Bed and Breakfast Cape Cod #65

P. O. Box 341, West Hyannisport, 02672-0341
(508) 775-2772; FAX (508) 775-2884

This house built in 1730 was at one time the town's first library. Two upstairs bedrooms share a bath; one room has a double bed and the other room has a pair of twin beds. Only one party at a time accepted. This beautifully restored home is owned by a surgeon's wife and has lovely private gardens. Short walk to the village and the beach. No smoking. $65.

OTIS

Berkshire Bed and Breakfast Homes SC6

P. O. Box 211, Williamsburg, 01096
(413) 268-7244

A 100-year-old country farmhouse on 15 acres. Antique furnishings throughout parlor and guest rooms with king and queen bveds and semiprivate baths. Attic room available with private bath. Full breakfast; no smoking; children over ten welcome. $75-135.

PEABODY

1660 Antique Colonial

Bed and Breakfast Marblehead and North Shore
P. O. Box 35, Newtonville, 02160
(617) 964-1606; (800) 832-2632
FAX (617) 332-8572

This beautifully restored historic home provides you with comfortable accommodations in a home listed on the National Register of Historic Places. Furnished with wonderful antiques, the two guest suites each have a sitting room, private bath, fireplace, and air conditioning. Breakfast is served in the country kitchen, sun room, or terrace. By prior arrangement, the host will prepare dinner. No smoking. $75-90.

PEMBROKE

Serenity

Be Our Guest Bed and Breakfast
P. O. Box 1333, Plymouth, 02362
(617) 837-9867

This beautiful circa 1700 antique Cape is completely restored and decorated with many fine antiques and artwork. There is one guest room with a fireplace, double bed, and private bath. Outside there are many beautiful plantings and trees around the corral that houses two horses. A full breakfast is served in either the dining room or the screened porch. No smoking. $40-60.

PERU

Bed and Breakfast Accommodations 069

984 Gloucester Place, Schenectady, New York 12309
(518) 370-4948

Built in 1830 as the town parsonage, this private homestay features the original wide-plank floors and floor-to-ceiling windows that look out onto old stone walls and 13 acres of woods. Guests dine in a sun room with bay windows and French doors that lead onto a patio. The decor is French country, and the home is furnished with antiques and colorful Waverly and Laura Ashley chintz fabrics. Three excellent cross-country centers and one downhill ski area are within an eight-mile radius. Two bedrooms with private baths. No smoking. $55; $60 6/1-10/31.

Berkshire Bed and Breakfast Homes NC8

P. O. Box 211, Williamsburg, 01096
(413) 268-7244

1815 Federal-style home on the historic register is on 13 acres. Guest rooms with private and semiprivate baths share a sun room and patio. Continental breakfast; no smoking; children over 13 welcome. $55-65.

Berkshire Bed and Breakfast Homes NC13

P. O. Box 211, Williamsburg, 01096
(413) 268-7244

A 1970 Garrison-style apartment on 160 acres of land. Country and colonial furnishings. The apartment contains sitting room with TV, kitchenette, full bath, queen and twin rooms. Pond on premises and lots of hiking. Continental breakfast supplies; children welcome. $50-95.

Chalet d'Alicia

East Windsor Road, 01235
(413) 655-8292

This Swiss chalet-style home offers a private, casual atmosphere. Set in the Berkshire Mountains, it overlooks the beautiful countryside. Fresh homemade breads and muffins round out the full country breakfasts. Four resident cats and one dog make everyone welcome. Tanglewood, Jacob's Pillow, Williamstown Theater, and lots of cross-country skiing are nearby.

Hosts: Alice and Richard Halvorsen
Rooms: 3 (1 PB; 2 SB) $55

Full Breakfast
Credit Cards: None
Notes: 2, 5, 6 (inquire), 7, 8, 9, 10, 11, 12, 13

PETERSHAM

Winterwood at Petersham

North Main Street, 01366
(508) 724-8885

An elegant 16-room Greek Revival mansion built in 1842, situated just off the common of a classic New England town. The inn boasts numerous fireplaces and several porches for relaxing. Cocktails available. On the National Register of Historic Places.

Hosts: Jean and Robert Day
Rooms: 5 (PB) $63.42-84.56
Continental Breakfast
Credit Cards: A, B, C
Notes: 2, 5, 7, 8, 9, 12, 13, 14

PITTSFIELD

Country Hearts Bed 'N' Breakfast

52 Broad Street, 01201
(413) 499-3201

Centrally situated, Country Hearts is easily accessible to all Berkshire attractions. Nestled on a quiet residential street well known for its collection of beautifully restored "aristocrats," this lovely "painted lady" is waiting to open her doors to you.

Hosts: Jan and Steve Foose
Rooms: 3 (1 PB; 2 SB) $40-75
Continental Breakfast
Credit Cards: A, B
Notes: 2, 5, 8, 9, 10, 11, 12, 13

PLYMOUTH

A Bed and Breakfast Above the Rest #54

50 Boatswains Way, Suite 105, Boston, 02150
(617) 884-7748; (800) 677-2262

6 Pets welcome; 7 Smoking allowed; 8 Children welcome; 9 Social drinking allowed; 10 Tennis available; 11 Swimming available; 12 Golf available; 13 Skiing available; 14 May be booked through travel agents.

The parklike yard is only one of the nice things about Morton Park Place. Guests are invited to make themselves at home in three delightful common areas. The dining room, where continental breakfast is served, is also always available to guests. There are four guest rooms that share two baths. They can be rented as suites.

A Bed and Breakfast Above the Rest #56

50 Boatswains Way, Suite 105, Boston, 02150
(617) 884-7748; (800) 677-2262

This graciously refurbished home is located in a very picturesque setting and lends itself perfectly to bed and breakfast. In fair weather, there is a delightful deck to breakfast on. There are two guest rooms. One has a private attached bath. Continental breakfast.

Brookside Farm

Be Our Guest Bed and Breakfast, Ltd.
P. O. Box 1333, 02362
(617) 837-9867

This lovely contemporary home is located on nine acres that provide privacy. A guest room with twin beds is beautifully decorated with hand stenciling. A full breakfast is served in a true country kitchen. Walk through the meticulously groomed gardens that surround a running stream. Easy access to Plymouth (15 minutes), and Boston (50 minutes). No smoking. $45.

Center Street Bed and Breakfast

Be Our Guest Bed and Breakfast, Ltd.
P. O. Box 1333, 02362
(617) 837-9867

This historic Colonial, built in 1735, has many period features throughout the house. Minutes off the highway and five miles to Plymouth Center. Two adjoining guest rooms, each with a double bed, share a bath. Beautifully decorated, these rooms will make you feel right at home. A full breakfast is served. Ideal for families and parties traveling together. $50.

Country Living

Be Our Guest Bed and Breakfast, Ltd.
P. O. Box 1333, 02362
(617) 837-9867

Only a 20-minute drive from Boston, this lovely 136-year-old farmhouse is accessible from the highway for easy travel to Plymouth Center in 20 minutes and the Cape in 45 minutes. A twin guest room shares a bath with the hosts. Beautifully decorated, this cozy country retreat has displays of the host's talent for flower arranging throughout. Full breakfast is served. Many fine restaurants nearby. $50.

Foxglove Cottage

Be Our Guest Bed and Breakfast
P. O. Box 1333, Plymouth, 02362
(617) 837-9867

Situated less than a mile from Plymouth Plantation, this lovely Cape circa 1820 has been carefully restored. Two guest rooms share a common bath and are decorated in Laura Ashley and Waverly prints. One room offers a double bed and another room offers a pair of twins. A full breakfast is served on the deck overlooking acres of conservation land. $65.

The Little Inn

Be Our Guest Bed and Breakfast, Ltd.
P. O. Box 1333, 02362
(617) 837-9867

This 200-year-old Federal Colonial offers three guest rooms. A white-wicker room has a queen bed and private bath. The brass room has an antique double bed and shares

NOTES: Credit cards accepted: A Master Card; B Visa; C American Express; D Discover Card; E Diner's Club; F Other; 2 Personal Checks accepted; 3 Lunch available; 4 Dinner available; 5 Open all year;

a bath with an adjoining room, furnished with twin mahogany sleigh beds. Built in 1785, the home has fireplaces throughout and many antique furnishings. Close to the beach, the Little Inn is set on a scenic road 40 minutes south of Boston and 20 minutes north of Plymouth Center. The mid-Cape is less than an hour's drive. A full breakfast is served in the fireplaced dining room. No smoking. Children welcome. $60.

Main Street Bed and Breakfast

Be Our Guest Bed and Breakfast, Ltd.
P. O. Box 1333, 02362
(617) 837-9867

Equally close to Boston and Plymouth, this beautiful contemporary home offers a quiet escape from their hustle and bustle. Enjoy a guest suite with a loft bedroom and queen bed, private bath with Jacuzzi, and living area that opens out to a deck. Your host, a gourmet cook, offers a hearty full breakfast. Close to shopping and restaurants. $60.

Marshview

Be Our Guest Bed and Breakfast, Ltd.
P. O. Box 1333, 02362
(617) 837-9867

This Cape-style home offers beautiful views of the marshland. Only 40 minutes south of Boston and 25 mintues north of Plymouth, the location is ideal for seeing both. A guest wing offers two guest rooms. The rooms share one and one-half baths and a sitting room with a TV. A private entrance opens out to a large deck overlooking the marsh. A full breakfast is served on the deck, weather permitting. Ideal for families. $50.

PROVINCETOWN

Bed and B'fast

44 Commercial Street, 02657
(508) 487-9555

In the quiet west end of Provincetown, this true bed and breakfast contains private-bath rooms and shared-bath rooms. A suite with harbor views and a private deck is available, as are fully equipped apartments. The apartments and suites have TV/ VCRs, microwave ovens, and refrigerators. Open all year, and special serenity seasonal rates are available.

Hosts: John Fitzgerald and Jack Kosko
Rooms: 7 (4 PB; 3 SB) $40-130, seasonal rates apply
Full Breakfast
Credit Cards: A, B
Notes: 5, 7, 14

Bradford Gardens Inn

178 Bradford Street, 02657
(508) 487-1616

1820 Colonial country inn with rooms offering fireplaces, ceiling fans and antiques. Fireplaced cottages set in the beautiful gardens. All units have private baths. One block from the ocean and a five-minute stroll to town center for shopping, fine dining, art galleries, and whale watching.

Host: Susan Culligan
Rooms: 8 (PB); 9 cottages (PB) $69-175
Full Breakfast
Credit Cards: A, B, C
Notes: 2, 7, 10, 11, 12, 14

Elephant Walk Inn

156 Bradford Street, 02657
(508) 487-2543

A romantic Edwardian inn near Provincetown's center. The spacious, well-appointed rooms offer an eclectic mixture of antique furnishings and decorations. All have private bath, color TV, and refrigerator. Enjoy our large sun deck or lounge with your morning coffee.

Host: Len Paoletti
Doubles: 8 (PB) $45-82
Type of Beds: 6 Double; 3 Queen; 1 King
Continental Breakfast
Closed November-Mid-April
Credit Cards: A, B, C
Notes: 2 (for deposit), 7, 8 (off-season), 9, 10, 11

The Fairbanks Inn

90 Bradford Street, 02657
(508) 487-0386

The Fairbanks Inn is a lovingly restored, 200-year-old ship captain's house filled with a collection of art, antiques, and reproduction furnishings. Rooms have four-poster or canopy beds, Oriental rugs, wide-plank pine floors. Some have working fireplaces. In the summer, a continental breakfast is served on the glass-enclosed porch that overlooks the patio and private gardens.

Host: Adam Erenberg
Rooms: 14 (10 PB; 4 SB) $48-90
Continental Breakfast
Credit Cards: A, B, C, D
Notes: 5, 7, 9, 10, 11, 12, 14

Gabriel's

104 Bradford Street, 02657
(508) 487-3232; FAX (508) 487-1605

Apartments and guest rooms in the heart of Provincetown, our accommodations are are distinctive, charming, and immaculate. Open year-round; in-room phones, cable TV, VCR, library, hot tub, garden patio, sun decks, homemade breakfast, parking, housekeeping, fully equipped kitchens, common room with a fireplace.

Hosts: Gabriel Brooks and Pam Parmaigian
Rooms: 20 (16 PB; 4 SB) 50-110
Credit Cards: A, B
Notes: 2, 5, 6, 7, 8, 9, 10, 11, 12, 14

Lamplighter Inn

26 Bradford Street, 02657
(508) 487-2529

Sea captain's home, commanding 50-mile vistas of the ocean and Cape Cod. Centrally situated in Provincetown, close to shopping, museums, whale watches, beaches, restaurants, shows, and tours. Clean, airy rooms and suites with private baths await your arrival for a memorable stay at the Lamplighter on old Cape Cod.

Hosts: Michael R. Novik and Joseph I. Czarnecki
Rooms: 10 (8 PB; 2 SB) $40-130
Continental Breakfast
Credit Cards: A, B, C
Notes: 2, 5, 7, 9, 10, 11, 12, 14

Land's End Inn

22 Commercial Street, 02657
(508) 487-0706

High atop Gull Hill, Land's End Inn overlooks Provincetown and all of Cape Cod Bay. Large, airy, comfortably furnished livingrooms, a large front porch, and lovely antique-filled bedrooms provide relaxation and visual pleasure to guests.

Host: David Schoolman
Rooms: 15 (11 PB; 4 SB) $76-220
Continental Breakfast
Credit Cards: None
Notes: 2, 5, 7, 8 (infants or over 12), 9, 10, 11, 12, 14

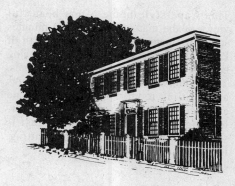

The Fairbanks Inn

Rose and Crown Guest House

Rose and Crown Guest House

158 Commercial Street, 02657
(508) 487-3332

The Rose and Crown is a classic Georgian "square rigger" built in the 1780s. The guest house sits behind an ornate iron fence, and a ship's figurehead greets visitors from her post above the paneled front door. During restoration, wide floorboards were uncovered and pegged posts and beams exposed. An appealing clutter of Victorian antiques and artwork fills every nook and cranny.

Host: Sam Hardee
Rooms: 8 (5 PB; 2 SB) $45-100
Continental Breakfast
Credit Cards: A, B, E
Notes: 5, 7, 14

Six Webster Place

6 Webster Place, 02657
(508) 487-2266

A restored 1750s bed and breakfast on a quiet lane in the heart of Provincetown, our bed and breakfast is one block from the Town Hall and Commercial Street and 200 yards from the bay beaches. All rooms have period furnishings, most offer working fireplaces, and most have private baths.

A delicious continental breakfast is served each morning; and in the off-season, we serve tea or a glass of wine by a roaring fire in the afternoon. Open all year.

Host: Gary Reinhardt
Rooms: 6 (4 PB; 2 SB) $35-75, seasonal rates apply
Continental Breakfast
Credit Cards: A, B, C, D
Notes: 2, 5, 6, 7, 8, 9, 14

Watership Inn

7 Winthrop Street, 02657
(508) 487-0094

Rustic 1820 sea captain's home, with Colonial rooms, private baths, and spacious lobby. Open year-round, serving continental breakfast daily. Parking is available, and a five-minute walk gets you to the beach or to the center of town.

Hosts: Jim Foss and Bob Marcotte
Rooms: 17 (15 PB; 2 SB) $45-83
Continental Breakfast
Credit Cards: A, B, C
Notes: 5, 7, 9

Watership Inn

White Wind Inn

174 Commercial Street, 02657
(508) 487-1526

A white Victorian, circa 1845, across the street from the beach and a five-minute walk from almost everything. Continental breakfast in season. Write or call for brochure.

6 Pets welcome; 7 Smoking allowed; 8 Children welcome; 9 Social drinking allowed; 10 Tennis available; 11 Swimming available; 12 Golf available; 13 Skiing available; 14 May be booked through travel agents.

Host: Russell Dusablon
Rooms: 12 (10 PB; 2 SB) $45-110
Continental Breakfast in-season
Credit Cards: A, B, C
Notes: 5, 6 (inquire), 7, 8, 10

Perryville Inn

QUINCY

Quincy Adams Bed and Breakfast

Host Homes of Boston
P. O. Box 117, Boston, 02168
(617) 244-1308; FAX (617) 244-5156

This elegant turn-of-the-century home near
the ocean has fireplaces, canopy beds, and
a den with a TV and hot tub. There are
three guest rooms; two have queen-size
beds and the third-floor maid's quarters has
a double. Near Bayside Expo Center,
restaurants, and historic mansions. Boston
is 15 minutes away, and the Red Line is
one block away. $68-75.

REHOBOTH

Gilbert's Bed and Breakfast

30 Spring Street, 02769
(508) 252-6416; (800) 828-6821

A 150-year-old New England Cape home
with authentic hardware, wood floors, and
windows. Situated on 100-acre tree farm
only 12 miles east of Providence, Rhode

Island. Guests may enjoy in-ground pool,
hiking and pony cart rides, delicious full
country breakfasts.

Hosts: Jeanne and Peter Gilbert
Rooms: 3 (SB) $45-50
Full Breakfast
Credit Cards: None
Notes: 2, 5, 6 (horses $15/night), 8, 9, 11, 14

Perryville Inn

157 Perryville Road, 02769
(508) 252-9239

This 19th-century restored Victorian on the
National Register of Historic Places is on
four and one-half wooded acres with a
quiet brook, mill pond, stone walls, and
shaded paths. Bicycles are available for
guests, including a tandem. The inn overlooks an 18-hole public golf course. All
rooms are furnished with antiques and
accented with colorful handmade quilts.
Nearby you will find antique stores, museums, Great Woods Performing Arts Center,
fine seafood restaurants, and an old-fashioned New England clambake. Arrange for
a horse-drawn hayride or a hot-air-balloon
ride. Within one hour of Boston, Plymouth,
Newport, and Mystic.

Hosts: Tom and Betsey Charnecki
Rooms: 5 (3 PB; 2 SB) $50-85
Continental Breakfast
Credit Cards: A, B, C, D
Notes: 2, 5, 8, 9, 10, 11, 12, 14

RICHMOND

Berkshire Bed and Breakfast Homes SC17

P. O. Box 211, Williamsburg, 01096
(413) 268-7244

A Geodesic-style home built by the owners. This dome-shaped home is on three
rural acrees and is furnished with country
collectibles. There is a king-size bed and a
private bath. A Hide-a-bed is also available. Continental breakfast. No smoking.
Children welcome. $65.

NOTES: Credit cards accepted: A Master Card; B Visa; C American Express; D Discover Card; E Diner's
Club; F Other; 2 Personal Checks accepted; 3 Lunch available; 4 Dinner available; 5 Open all year;

Middlerise
Bed and Breakfast

State Road, 01254-0017
(413) 698-2687

A charming country home six miles from Tanglewood in the heart of the Berkshires. Quiet, private, and congenial, with a guest livingroom. Convenient to all winter and summer activities.

Hosts: Carol and Carter White
Rooms: 3 (1 PB; 2 SB) $75-85
Continental Breakfast
Credit Cards: None
Cl;osed November 15- January 31
Notes: 2, 6 (call), 7, 8 (call), 9, 10, 11, 12, 13

ROCKPORT

Bed and Breakfast
Associates #NS557

P. O. Box 57166, Babson Park Branch
Boston, 02157-0166
(617) 449-5302; FAX (617) 449-5958

Overlooking Ipswich Bay, this charming older home is furnished with fine New England treasures and offers wonderful views of Folly Cove. Nearby swimming beaches, courtesy bicycles, and reasonably priced picnic baskets are offered. You will also enjoy its proximity to the state park and to the local shops, galleries, and restaurants. Three guest rooms, one with private bath. Full breakfast; no infants please; smoking limited. $55-75; family rates available.

Bed & Breakfast/Inns of
New England MA-1005

329 Lake Drive, Guilford, CT 06437
(800) 5882-0853

An intimate, welcoming guest house open year-round, situated only one block from Main Street and the T-Wharf, which is full of shops, galleries, and restaurants. Leave your car and walk to everything. A spacious sun deck is reserved for guests. Television, games, magazines, and books are available. Guests have use of their own refrigerator. Seven rooms are available. Children welcome. No smoking. House cat; no guest pets. $58-70.

Bed & Breakfast/Inns of
New England MA-1006

329 Lake Drive, Guilford, CT 06437
(800) 582-0853

A small, centrally located inn limited to non-smokers, this 1987 facility is within a five-minute walk from Rockport's art galleries, Headlands beach, restaurants, and shops. Three ground-floor larger-than-average rooms with private bathrooms are available with king or queen beds; all three have private bathrooms. All rooms have controlled air conditioning and heat, cable TV, refrigerators, and microwaves. No children. No smoking. No pets. $85 (June 12 to September 14); $80 off season.

The Inn on Cove Hill

37 Mount Pleasant Street, 01966
(508) 546-2701

A friendly atmosphere with the option of privacy, this painstakingly restored 200-year-old Federal home is two blocks from the harbor and shops. Meticulously appointed, cozy bedrooms are furnished with antiques, and some have canopy beds. Wake up to the delicious aroma of hot muffins, and enjoy a continental breakfast at our umbrella tables in the Pump Garden. The fresh sea air is preserved in our non-smoking facility.

Hosts: John and Marjorie Pratt
Rooms: 11 (9 PB; 2 SB) $47-95
Continental Breakfast
Credit Cards: None
Notes: 2, 9, 11, 12

6 Pets welcome; 7 Smoking allowed; 8 Children welcome; 9 Social drinking allowed; 10 Tennis available; 11 Swimming available; 12 Golf available; 13 Skiing available; 14 May be booked through travel agents.

Lantana House

22 Broadway, 01966
(508) 546-3535

An in-town Victorian guest house open year-round in the historic district of Rockport, a classic, picturesque, seacoast village. A one- to five-minute walk takes you to the beaches, art galleries, restaurants, and gift shops. Rockport is an artists' haven.

Host: Cynthia Sewell
Rooms: 7 (5 PB; 2 SB) $60-70
Continental Breakfast
Credit Cards: None
Notes: 2, 5, 7 (restricted), 8, 9, 10, 11, 12
Notes: 2, 9, 10, 11, 12, 14

Mooringstone for Nonsmokers

12 Norwood Avenue, 01966
(508) 546-2479

We have added a ground-floor wing to our home for guests to enjoy. Each room has comfortable beds, air conditioning, cable TV, refrigerator, microwave, parking, etc. Breakfast includes delicious homemade muffins and breads. Park and walk to the beach, restaurants, shops, art galleries, and picturesque headlands, or take day trips to the many special places in this area. Ask about our "RST no B" plan. No room tax.

Hosts: David and Mary Knowlton
Rooms: 3 (PB) $73-83
Expanded Continental Breakfast
Credit Cards: A, B, C
Notes: 2, 9, 10, 11, 12, 14

Seacrest Inn

Old Farm Inn

291 Granite Street, Route 127, 01966
(508) 546-3237

A charming 1799 creaky-floored farmhouse overflows with colorful quilts and country antiques. The cheerful, comfortable guest rooms all have private baths and TV, and most have small refrigerators. The housekeeping cottage is also available. The peaceful setting includes five acres of lawns, meadows, trees, and gardens, and is surrounded by a beautiful oceanfront state park with woodland paths to the rocky coastline. Minutes away is downtown Rockport where you can enjoy unusual shops and art galleries, excellent seafood dining, whale watching trips, and sandy beaches. Minimum stay on weekends is two nights; holidays, three nights.

Hosts: The Balzarini family
Rooms: 9 (PB) $68-108
Expanded Continental Breakfast
Credit Cards: A, B, C
Notes: 2, 7(limited), 8, 9, 10, 11, 12, 14

Peg Leg Inn and Restaurant

2 King Street, 01966
(800) 346-2352

The original charm of colonial New England in five Early American homes on the edge of the sea at Front Beach. Oceanview rooms with traditional appointments of the gracious past, plus all the comforts of today. A short stroll into downtown Rockport. Garden restaurant is famous for fresh local seafood and Yankee specialties.

Rooms: 33 (PB) $60-105
Continental Breakfast
Credit Cards: A, B
Notes: 2, 3, 4, 7, 8, 14

Seacrest Manor

131 Marmion Way, 01966
(508) 546-2211

Decidedly small, intentionally quiet. Gracious hospitality in luxurious surroundings with magnificent views overlooking woods and sea. Spacious grounds, lovely gardens, ample parking. Famous full breakfast and afternoon tea included. No pets. Not recommended for children. Fresh flowers, free daily paper, mints, and turndown. Mobil-rated three stars; AAA-rated three diamonds. Only an hour north of Boston by car or train.

Hosts: Leighton T. Saville and Dwight B. MacCormack
Rooms: 8 (6 PB; 2 SB) $84-104
Full Breakfast
Credit Cards: None
Closed: December to March
Notes: 2, 7 (limited), 11, 12

The Seafarer

Be Our Guest Bed and Breakfast, Ltd.
P. O. Box 1333, Plymouth, 02362
(617) 837-9867

Just 45 minutes north of Boston in the quaint seaside community of Rockport, this lovely bed and breakfast offers six guest rooms. Each room is unique, and each has an ocean view. Some rooms are equipped with kitchenettes, all have TVs and refrigerators. An apartment is also available on a weekly basis. A lovely continental breakfast is served on the deck overlooking the bay. Within walking distance of the village and the beach. $60-80.

Seaward Inn and Cottages

62 Marmion Way, 01966
(508) 546-3471

Quietly tucked away on Boston's rocky north shore, this grand old oceanfront estate offers the perfect respite for weary travelers. Elegant oceanfront dining, expansive grounds and beautiful gardens, active bird sanctuary, putting green, private cottages with fireplaces, spectacular ocean views at every turn, and impeccable service are only the beginning. Short stroll to downtown Rockport (300-year-old fishing village and art colony), shops and boutiques, and wide sandy beaches.

Hosts: Anne and Roger Cameron
Rooms: 38 (PB) $85-125
Full Breakfast
Credit Cards: None
Notes: 2, 4, 7, 8, 9, 11, 12, 14

Seven South Street—The Inn

7 South Street, 01966
(508) 546-6708

Built in 1750, the inn has a friendly, informal atmosphere in a quiet setting, with gardens, deck, and pool. An ample continental breakfast is served each morning, after which the guest is free to explore the art galleries and shops within walking distance of the inn.

Host: Aileen Lamson
Rooms: 6 (3 PB; 3 SB) $68-78
Continental Breakfast
Credit Cards: None
Notes: 2, 7, 9, 10, 11, 12

SAGAMORE BEACH

Bed and Breakfast Cape Cod #19

P. O. Box 341, West Hyannisport, 02672-0341
(508) 775-2772; FAX (508) 775-2884

Perched on a cliff fifty feet above Cape Cod Bay, this contemporary home built in 1987 features two suites for guests. The honeymoon suite has a Jacuzzi overlooking the ocean, private bath, king-size bed, and Laura Ashley bed coverings. The second suite has a queen-size bed, ocean view, and adjoining room with a pair of twin beds. A ground-floor basement suite offers a parlor with a fireplace, two sleeping rooms, one with a king-size bed and the other with twin beds and small kitchen. $65-100.

Bed and Breakfast of Sagamore Beach

One Hawes Road, 02562
(508) 888-1559

6 Pets welcome; 7 Smoking allowed; 8 Children welcome; 9 Social drinking allowed; 10 Tennis available; 11 Swimming available; 12 Golf available; 13 Skiing available; 14 May be booked through travel agents.

A private, peaceful home overlooking Cape Cod Bay, just 60 miles from Provincetown or Boston. Relax in front of the fireplace or on the large porches and decks that surround the house. Walk for miles on the quiet, sandy beach. Home has been featured in *Bon Appetit* and *Better Homes and Gardens*.

Host: John F. Carafoli
Rooms: 3 (SB) $85
Continental Breakfast
Credit Cards: None
Notes: 2, 5, 9, 10, 11, 12, 14

SALEM

Amelia Payson House

16 Winter Street, 01970
(508) 744-8304

Built in 1845, this fine example of Greek Revival architecture is located in the heart of Salem's historic district. Guest rooms are furnished with canopy or brass beds and antiques. A five-minute stroll to downtown shopping, historic houses, museums, Pickering Wharf's waterfront dining, and train station.

Hosts: Ada and Donald Roberts
Rooms: 4 (PB) $75-85
Continental Breakfast
Credit Cards: A, B, C
Notes: 5, 8 (over 12), 9, 10, 11, 12

Coach House Inn

284 Lafayette Street, 01970
(508) 744-4092; (800) 688-8689

Return to the elegance of an earlier time. Enjoy the intimacy of a small European-type hotel. Cozy, comfortable rooms with private baths retain the charm of this Victorian mansion. Complimentary continental breakfast. Air conditioning, off-street parking. Only 16 miles from Boston.

Host: Patricia Kessler
Rooms: 11 (9 PB; 2 SB) $74-86
Continental Breakfast
Credit Cards: A, B, C
Notes: 5, 7, 8, 9, 10, 11, 12, 13, 14

Essex Street Bed and Breakfast

Bed and Breakfast Marblehead and North Shore
P. O. Box 35, Newtonville, 02160
(617) 964-1606; (800) 832-2632
FAX (617) 332-8572

This turn-of-the-century wood frame house is in the McIntyre historic district of Salem. The hosts have lovingly labored to restore their home to its former elegance and charm. One guest room with private bath, separate entrance, and air conditioning is available. Continental breakfast is served. No smoking. Children welcome. $75-85.

The Inn on the Green

Bed and Breakfast Marblehead and North Shore
P. O. Box 35, Newtonville, 02160
(617) 964-1606; (800) 832-2632
FAX (617) 332-8572

In the heart of Salem, this inn is close to many tourist attractions, historic sites, and world-famous museums. The inn is Greek Revival-style, built in 1846 as a private residence for a naval officer. It has been completely restored with modern amenities added. Six guest rooms all have a private bath and color TV. Breakfast is served in a cozy, sun-filled room overlooking Washington Square. Children welcome. Smoking area provided. $65-80.

The Salem Inn

7 Summer Street, 01970
(508) 741-0680; (800) 446-2995

Elegantly restored 1834 Federal town house, in the heart of Salem's historic district, has 21 luxuriously appointed rooms with private baths and some working fireplaces. Direct-dial phones, cable TVs, and air conditioning. Hearty continental breakfast and lovely rose garden. "Go Fish" Seafood Emporium. Jacuzzi suites available.

NOTES: Credit cards accepted: A Master Card; B Visa; C American Express; D Discover Card; E Diner's Club; F Other; 2 Personal Checks accepted; 3 Lunch available; 4 Dinner available; 5 Open all year;

Hosts: Richard and Diane Pabich
Rooms: 21 (PB) $85-125
Continental Breakfast
Credit Cards: A, B, C, D, E, F
Notes: 2, 3, 4, 5, 7, 8, 9, 10, 11, 12, 13 (XC), 14

The Schoolhouse Bed and Breakfast

Bed and Breakfast Marblehead and North Shore
P. O. Box 35, Newtonville, 02160
(617) 964-1606; (800) 832-2632
FAX (617) 332-8572

A beautifully decorated home in a turn-of-the-century school converted to a condominium, featuring skylights and cathedral ceilings. This bed and breakfast is a short walk from the Salem commuter rail station. One guest room with private bath and TV. Continental breakfast. Attractive livingroom with TV and designated parking. Air conditioning. No smoking. Children welcome if over five or infants. No pets. $65-75.

Stephen Daniels House

1 Daniels Street, 01970
(508) 744-5709

Built by a sea captain in 1667 and enlarged in 1756, the house is beautifully restored and furnished with antiques. Wood-burning fireplaces in the bedrooms with charming canopy beds. Continental breakfast is served before two huge fireplaces. Walk to all points of interest in Salem.

Host: Catherine Gill
Rooms: 5 (3 PB; 2 SB) $50-95
Continental Breakfast
Credit Cards: C
Notes: 2, 5, 6, 7, 8, 9, 10, 11, 12, 13, 14

The Suite at the Tannet Woods House

Bed and Breakfast Marblehead and North Shore
P. O. Box 35, Newtonville, 02632
(617) 964-1606; (800) 832-2632
FAX (617) 332-8572

Built in 1799, the Tannet Woods House was originally a four-room carpenter shop. The guest area includes a completely furnished three-room suite with modern kitchen and bath, color TV, sun deck, separate guest entrance, and parking. It has heat and air conditioning for year-round comfort. The hosts provide a generous supply of breakfast foods, self-prepared by the guest. Easy access by computer rail to Boston and other North Shore locations. Sleeps up to three adults. Children welcome. Restricted smoking. $85-100.

SANDWICH

Bay Beach Bed and Breakfast

1-3 Bay Beach Lane, Box 151, 02563
(508) 888-8813

Luxury beachfront bed and breakfast with super amenities in a romantic setting overlooking Cape Cod Bay. Three spacious guest rooms with decks and ocean views, plus a honeymoon suite with a king-size bed and Jacuzzi are available for guests to choose. A two-fireplaced livingroom and an exercise room with a Lifecycle and Stairmaster are also for guests to enjoy. A full continental breakfast is served each morning. All rooms have air conditioning, telephones, cable TV, refrigerators, and compact disk players. AAA Four Diamond Inn. No smoking. Adults only.

Hosts: Emily and Reale Lemieux
Rooms: 3 (PB) $125-175
Continental Breakfast
Credit Cards: None
Notes: 2, 10, 11, 12, 14

Bed and Breakfast Cape Cod #1

P. O. Box 341, West Hyannisport, 02672-0341
(508) 775-2772; FAX (508) 775-2884

6 Pets welcome; 7 Smoking allowed; 8 Children welcome; 9 Social drinking allowed; 10 Tennis available; 11 Swimming available; 12 Golf available; 13 Skiing available; 14 May be booked through travel agents.

This elegant Victorian-style house was built in 1849 and meticulously restored in 1987. The five guest rooms have private baths and are furnished with antiques. The first-floor common rooms for dining and reading are available for guest use. A continental breakfast is served each morning in the dining room. Convenient to many fine restaurants, Heritage Plantation, Sandwich Glass Museum, and the beach. No children under 12. $65-110.

Bed and Breakfast Cape Cod #22

P. O. Box 341, West Hyannisport, 02672-0341
(508) 775-2772; FAX (508) 775-2884

This elegant Victorian-style house in the heart of Sandwich has six bedrooms, most of which offer private baths. In the center of the oldest village on Cape Cod, this inn is within walking distance of fine restaurants, beaches, trails, museums, and parks. A continental breakfast is served in the large dining room. No smoking. Children over six welcome. $50-85.

Bed and Breakfast Cape Cod #31

P. O. Box 341, West Hyannisport, 02672-0341
(508) 775-2772; FAX (508) 775-2884

The design of this 1699 built home reflects the charm of early America. Three bedrooms with private baths are furnished with antiques or furniture with an Early American design. Across the street from a saltwater marsh full of birds, this bed and breakfast is short walk to many restaurants and shops. A continental breakfast is served in a keeping room with a beehive oven. No smoking. Children over 12 welcome. $65-75.

Bed and Breakfast Cape Cod #55

P. O. Box 341, West Hyannisport, 02672-0341
(508) 775-2772; FAX (508) 775-2884

This beautiful contemporary home overlooks the Cape Cod Canal. Three spacious guest rooms offer private baths, ocean views, TV, refrigerators, phones, and special touches that enhance any holiday stay. One bedroom has a whirlpool tub for two and a king-size bed. A continental breakfast is served each morning from 8:00-10:30 A.M. in the guest's room, on the deck, or in the dining area. No smoking. No children. $100-175.

Bed & Breakfast/Inns of New England MA-1040

329 Lake Drive, Guilford, CT 06437
(800) 582-0853

This 1829 clapboard house reflects the interests of the innkeepers, who have furnished it with Early American pieces and with treasures they have collected from the Orient and the American Southwest. Guests are invited to play the piano, read a book, or play a game in the den. The six guest rooms, four with private baths, are individually painted and stenciled in bright colors; each has a special personality. Furnishings include canopy, spindle, sleigh, and four-poster beds; one room has a fireplace, and another has a claw-foot tub. $50-85 (in season); $50-75 (off season).

Capt. Ezra Nye House

152 Main Street, 02563
(508) 888-6142; (800) 388-2278

Comfort and warmth, amid antique-filled rooms, some with fireplaces and canopies, make your stay a treat in this 1829 Federal home. Museums, lake, restaurants within a block. Featured in *Glamour* and *Innsider* magazines. "Thank you for opening your hearts and your home to us. . . You have made our first trip to Cape Cod a memorable one!"

Hosts: Elaine and Harry Dickson
Rooms: 7 (4 PB; 2 SB) $55-90
Suite: 1(PB)
Full Breakfast
Credit Cards: A, B, C, D
Notes: 2, 5, 8 (over 5), 9, 10, 11, 12, 14

Isaiah Jones Homestead

Dan'l Webster Inn

149 Main Street, 02563
(508) 888-3622

This historic four star inn features 47 beautifully appointed rooms, including nine suites, some with canopy beds, working fireplaces, whirlpool tubs. On-premises restaurant offers three Colonial dining rooms, including the glassed conservatory, specializing in fresh native seafood and choice meats with an award-winning wine list. Manicured gardens and gazebo, outdoor pool, and gift shop on premises,. Many historical sites and ocean nearby. Handicapped accessible. Open year-round, except Christmas Day.

Host: The Cantania family
Rooms: 47 (PB) $95-165
Full Breakfast
Credit Cards: A, B, C, D, E
Notes: 2, 3, 4, 5, 7, 8, 9, 11, 12

Dillingham House

71 Main Street, 02563
(508) 833-0065

Built circa 1650, the Dillingham House is one of the oldest in the country. It offers its guests an interesting historical experience while providing a quiet and comfortable natural environment off the beaten path. Sandwich has many historical attractions, as well as quiet beaches for relaxation and a scenic waterfront nearby.

Host: Kathy Kenney
Rooms: 4 (2 PB; 2 SB) $65-75
Continental Breakfast
Credit Cards: None
Notes: 2, 5, 6 (small), 7, 8 (over 12), 9, 11, 12

Isaiah Jones Homestead

165 Main Street, 02563
(508) 888-9115

An intimate Victorian bed and breakfast inn with beautiful antiques, fresh flowers, and candlelight awaits guests. Homemade, freshly baked breakfast and afternoon tea is served daily. Most points of interest are within walking distance. "Superior in every respect a trip into the past." Minimum stay in–season and holidays is 2 nights.

Host: Shirley Jones Sutton
Rooms: 5 (PB) $72-121
Continental Breakfast
Credit Cards: A, B, C, D
Notes: 2, 10, 11, 12, 14

Seth Pope House
1699 Bed and Breakfast

110 Tupper Road, 02563
(508) 888-5916

This historic village Colonial inn is set on a tree-filled acre overlooking the salt marsh. Within walking distance from shops, museums, and fine restaurants and a short drive to the beach and marina. There are three antique-furnished spacious rooms with private baths. Wide-board floors, gunstock

6 Pets welcome; 7 Smoking allowed; 8 Children welcome; 9 Social drinking allowed; 10 Tennis available; 11 Swimming available; 12 Golf available; 13 Skiing available; 14 May be booked through travel agents.

posts, exposed beams, and fireplaces add to the 17th-century character of this fine old home. An extended continental breakfast is served in the keeping room by candlelight.

Hosts: Beverly and John Dobel
Rooms: 3 (PB) $55 (off season); $75 (in season)
Extended Continental Breakfast
Credit Cards: None
Notes: 2, 5, 8 (over 10), 9, 10, 11, 12, 14

The Summer House

158 Main Street, 02563
(508) 888-4991

Elegant circa 1835 Greek Revival bed and breakfast featured in Country Living magazine, in the heart of historic Sandwich Village, Cape Cod's oldest town (settled 1637). Antiques, hand-stitched quilts, fireplaces, flowers, large sunny rooms, English-style gardens. Close to dining, museums, shops, pond and gristmill, boardwalk to beach. Bountiful breakfast, elegantly served. Afternoon tea in the garden included.

Hosts: David and Kay Merrell
Rooms: 5 (1 PB; 4 SB) $50-75
Full Breakfast
Credit Cards: A, B, C, D
Notes: 2, 5, 8 (over 5), 9, 10, 11, 12, 14

SCITUATE

The Allen House

18 Allen Place, 02066
(617) 545-8221

Sleep comfortably and quietly in a gracious, gabled Victorian merchant's home overlooking an unspoiled New England fishing town and harbor. Only an hour's drive south of Boston. Then wake to classical music and gourmet cuisine. Your hosts are English, professional caterers, and cat lovers. On every sunny, warm day expect a full breakfast—and sometimes afternoon tea—on the porch overlooking the harbor.

Hosts: Christine and Iain Gilmour
Rooms: 4 (2 PB; 2 SB) $59-119

Full Breakfast
Credit Cards: A, B, C
Notes: 2, 5, 9, 14

Bed and Breakfast Associates #SS250

P. O. Box 57166, Babson Park Branch
Boston, 02157-0166
(617) 449-5302; FAX (617) 449-5958

Situated just one mile from the ocean, this pretty home affords visitors to the South Shore the opportunity to relax and enjoy nearby tennis, yacht club, pool, and clam digging. Your hosts are active tennis players. Two guest rooms, one with private bath. Full breakfast on weekends; children welcome; no smoking. $50-55; family and monthly rates available.

The Summer House

Bed and Breakfast Associates #SS260

P. O. Box 57166, Babson Park Branch
Boston, 02157-0166
(617) 449-5302; FAX (617) 449-5958

Offered by a gourmet caterer and her husband, this circa 1905 home is a scant two-minute walk from Scituate Harbor. They have lovingly remodeled their fine bed and breakfast and filled it with period furniture, classical music, and English-style hospitality. You will surely make yourself comfortable in the cheerful parlor, indulge in the fabulous gourmet breakfast (or ask for a low-cal or "happy heart" diet), relax before the Edwardian fireplace, or gaze out at the yachts in the bustling harbor. A short stroll brings you to local shops and seafood restaurants. Three guest rooms, two with private baths. Full breakfast; children over 16 welcome; no smoking. $75.

Bed and Breakfast Cape Cod #64

P. O. Box 341, West Hyannisport, 02672-0341
(508) 775-2772; FAX (508) 775-2884

Ocean views and English elegance characterize this 1905 Victorian-style inn. Four guest rooms feature queen or double-size beds and water views; two rooms have a private bath and two other rooms share a bath. Your English hosts serve a full gourmet breakfast in the morning, and afternoon tea at 5:00 each day. Breakfast is served in the Victorian dining room or on a porch overlooking the harbor. No smoking. No children. $100-175.

Harborside

Be Our Guest Bed and Breakfast
P. O. Box 1333, Plymouth, 02362
(617) 837-9867

Commanding an ocean views from every angle. This contemporary-style beach house overlooks the open ocean on one side and pictuersque Scituate Harbor on the other. One air-conditioned guest room and a private bath. Continental breakfast is served. Resident dog. $45-65.

Sycamore

Be Our Guest Bed and Breakfast, Ltd.
P. O. Box 1333, 02362
(617) 837-9867

Conveniently situated between Boston and Plymouth, this ranch-style home is within walking distance to the harbor. Beautifully decorated with a blend of contemporary and antiques. A lovely lace-filled guest room with a queen bed, private bath, and deck. A second twin room, again decorated beautifully, shares a bath with your hosts. A full breakfast is served. Walk to shops and restaurants. $50.

SEARSPORT

Homeport Inn

Box 647, EAst Main Street, Route 1, 04974
(207) 548-2259

Homeport, listed on the National Register of Historic Places, is a fine example of a New England sea captain's mansion situated on beautiful landscaped grounds, with flower gardens and pond that extend to the ocean. This elegant home is furnished with family heirlooms and antiques. There are ten guest rooms, six with private baths. A Victorian cottage is also available. A visit offers a rare opportunity to vacation or be an overnight guest in a warm, homey, hospitable atmosphere without the customary traveler's commercialism.

Hosts: Edith and George Johnson
Rooms: 10 (6 PB; 4 SB) $55-75
Cottage: $450
Full Breakfast
Credit Cards: A, B, C, D, F
Notes: 2, 5, 7 (limited), 8, 9, 10, 11, 12, 13, 14

SHEFFIELD

Berkshire Bed and Breakfast Homes SC19

P. O. Box 211, Williamsburg, 01096
(413) 268-7244

An 1815 Colonial on five acres. Formal furnishings. Parlor, screened-in porch, and in-ground pool for guests. One king room with private bath; other rooms share a bath. Full breakfast; children over 16 welcome. $85-150. Closed Nov-May.

6 Pets welcome; 7 Smoking allowed; 8 Children welcome; 9 Social drinking allowed; 10 Tennis available; 11 Swimming available; 12 Golf available; 13 Skiing available; 14 May be booked through travel agents.

Covered Bridge 1SHMA

P. O. Box 447A, Norfolk, CT 06058
(203) 542-5944

This charming log home, commanding a sweeping view of the Berkshires, is the perfect spot for an idyllic pastoral retreat. A horse grazes nearby, and it's a short walk across the fields to the swimming pond. A full breakfast is served in the kitchen or on the porch. The host, an actress, has traveled extensively and is also well informed about area activities. There are two double guest rooms that share a bath. $85.

Covered Bridge 2SHMA

P. O. Box 447A, Norfolk, CT 06058
(203) 542-5944

This 1771 Colonial set in the village of Sheffield is surrounded by antique shops and close to Tanglewood. There are several common rooms for guests to enjoy as well as a tree-shaded terrace. A full breakfast is served in the dining room. The guest rooms are decorated with antiques. Three rooms share a bath, and one room has a private bath. $80-90.

A Unique Bed and Breakfast Inn

Box 729, 01257
(413) 229-3363

A most relaxing bed and breakfast. Cozy, attractively furnished and decorated. Central air conditioning. Lounge/dining room with fireplace. Full buffet country breakfast. Only 20 minutes to Tanglewood Music Festival; 15 to Lime Rock; 10 to skiing. Hand-ironed percale sheets, fresh flowers in rooms. Antique shops galore.

Host: May Stendardi
Rooms: 3 (PB) $95-110
Full Breakfast
Minimum stay weekends and holidays: 2-3
Credit Cards: A, B (for reservations only)
Notes: 5, 8 (over 14), 9, 10, 11, 12, 13

SOMERVILLE

Spreadby's

Host Homes of Boston
P. O. Box 117, Boston, 02168
(617) 244-1308; FAX (617) 244-5156

Spotless new home sits on a hill near Tufts' main campus. Second-floor guest room. Breakfast in glass-walled dining room or on deck. Resident dog. Close to Cambridge and Arlington. One block to bus. Private bath; TV; no smoking. $57.

SOUTH CHATHAM

Bed and Breakfast Cape Cod #60

P. O. Box 341, West Hyannisport, 02672-0341
(508) 775-2772; FAX (508) 775-2884

This two-story garrison Colonial home offers three guest rooms. One room has a king-size bed, private bath, and an extra twin bed. Two other rooms share a bath and both have a pair of twin beds. Two-tenths of a mile from the Nantucket Sound, this is an ideal location for beach lovers. No smoking. Children over 5. $55-65.

Ye Olde Nantucket House

2647 Main Street, P. O. Box 468, 02659
(508) 432-5641

Once a Nantucket sea captain's home, this Greek Revival-style house was "floated" to Cape Cod in 1867 and moved to its present site. Five guest rooms are comfortably and tastefully furnished with antiques. All rooms have private baths. A short, pretty walk to the beach (the warm Nantucket Sound), and convenient to dining and shopping in Chatham and Harwich Port.

Hosts: Norm Anderton and Cory
Rooms: 5 (PB) $63-76
Full Breakfast

NOTES: Credit cards accepted: A Master Card; B Visa; C American Express; D Discover Card; E Diner's Club; F Other; 2 Personal Checks accepted; 3 Lunch available; 4 Dinner available; 5 Open all year;

Credit Cards: A, B
Notes: 2, 5, 7 (limited), 8 (over 8), 9, 10, 11, 12, 14

SOUTH DARTMOUTH

Salt Marsh Farm

322 Smith Neck Road, 02748
(508) 992-0980

A 1780 Federal farmhouse with narrow stairs and working fireplaces, antiques, interesting library of local and natural history. Situated on 90-acre nature preserve with trails, stone walls, organic gardens, laying hens. Bikes available. Scenic coastal community convenient to Martha's Vineyard ferry and day trips to Plymouth, Cape Cod, Newport, Mystic, Boston, Nantucket. New Bedford Whaling Museum, historic waterfront, beaches are nearby.

Hosts: Larry and Sally Brownell
Rooms: 2 (PB) $60-80
Full Breakfast
Credit Cards: A, B
Notes: 2, 5, 8, 9

SOUTH DEERFIELD

Berkshire Bed and Breakfast Homes SC30

P. O. Box 211, Williamsburg, 01096
(413) 268-7244

This 1910 Georgian Colonial is situated on eleven acres. Furnished with formal and classical furnishings, this bed and breakfast offers a suite with a queen bed, adjoining room with a double bed, and private bath. Two double bedrooms are also available and share a bath. No smoking. Full breakfast. Children over 12 welcome. $50-75.

Breakfast Homes PV30

P. O. Box 211, Williamsburg, 01096
(413) 268-7244

This 1910 Georgian Colonial on 11 acres has formal and classic furnishings, sun room with TV, formal livingroom, and in-ground pool for guest use. A suite with queen bed and adjoining double with private bath. Two other rooms share a bath. Full breakfast. Children over 12 welcome. $65-125.

Bed & Breakfast/Inns of New England MA-1015

329 Lake Drive, Guilford, CT 06437
(800) 582-0853

This old country house is in the heart of a historical and cultural area and is set on the site of the Bloody Brook Massacre of 1675. Furnished with period antiques, it is just four miles from historic Deerfield and ten minutes from the five college area. Three air-conditioned guest rooms, one with a private bath, are available. Children age ten and over are welcome. No smoking. No pets. $70-85 (in season); $40-65 (off season).

Berkshire Bed and Deerfield Bed and Breakfast

The Yellow Gabled House
307 North Main Street, 01373
(413) 665-4922

This old country house is situated in the heart of a historic and cultural area and is the site of the Bloody Brook Massacre in 1675. Furnished with period antiques, it promises a comfortable stay with the ambience and personal attention unique to New England. Convenient to the five-college area, prep schools, and historic Deerfield. Easily accessible to splendid back-roading. Situated one mile from the crossroads of I-91, Route 116, and Routes 5 and 10. Air-conditioned. Carriage rides can be arranged.

6 Pets welcome; 7 Smoking allowed; 8 Children welcome; 9 Social drinking allowed; 10 Tennis available; 11 Swimming available; 12 Golf available; 13 Skiing available; 14 May be booked through travel agents.

Host: Edna Julia Stahelek
Rooms: 3 (PB) $55-75
Full Breakfast
Minimum stay holidays: 2 nights
Credit Cards: None
Notes: 2, 5, 8 (over 9), 9, 10, 11, 12, 13, 14

SOUTH ORLEANS

Bed and Breakfast Cape Cod #37

P. O. Box 341, West Hyannisport, 02672-0341
(508) 775-2772; FAX (508) 775-2884

The Atlantic Ocean is directly in front of this circa 1780 home that offers three bedrooms with private baths and choice of a king, queen, or twin beds. Enjoy the full breakfast served each morning before walking out to the beach or the host's boathouse on the water. Children over five. $75-90.

Bed and Breakfast Cape Cod #80

P. O. Box 341, West Hyannisport, 02672-0341
(508) 775-2772; FAX (508) 775-2884

On high ground above Pleasant Bay, this 1973 Cape Cod-style home offers three bedrooms. One is a large room with a queen-size bed and private bath, and the other two share a bath and have a queen-size or a pair of twins. This lovely home is convenient to both Chatham and Orleans shops and restaurants. The deck is great for relaxing after spending the day at the beach. No smoking. $55-70.

Hillbourne House

Route 28, #654 , 02662
(508) 255-0780

This charming bed and breakfast was built in 1798, and during the Civil War, was part of the Underground Railroad. A circular hiding place is still in evidence beneath the trap door in the Common Room. We offer a magnificent view of Pleasant Bay and the great dunes of Outer Beach on the Atlantic. Convenient to all Cape activities. Private beach and dock.

Host: Barbara Hayes
Rooms: 8 (PB) $50-80, seasonal rates apply
Full Breakfast-off season; Deluxe Continental Full
   breakfast-in-season
Credit Cards: None
Notes: 2, 9, 11, 12

SOUTH YARMOUTH

Bed and Breakfast Cape Cod #2

P. O. Box 341, West Hyannisport, 02672-0341
(508) 775-2772; FAX (508) 775-2884

This 1820s sea captain, house is restored and in immaculate condition. Three bright, airy rooms with Victorian decor are available for guests. One room has a private bath, and the other two rooms share a bath. Walk to the beach, and a short distance to restaurants and shops. The hostess serves a continental breakfast in the dining room each morning. A carriage house is also available for guests. No smoking. Children over 12 welcome. $60-70.

SPRINGFIELD

Berkshire Bed and Breakfast Homes GS6

P. O. Box 211, Williamsburg, 01096
(413) 268-7244

An 1896 Greek Revival on one-fourth acre. Colonial and antique furnishings in guest rooms with shared baths and parlor. Porch is also available to guests. View of the local park. Continental breakfast; no smoking; children welcome. $45-75.

NOTES: Credit cards accepted: A Master Card; B Visa; C American Express; D Discover Card; E Diner's Club; F Other; 2 Personal Checks accepted; 3 Lunch available; 4 Dinner available; 5 Open all year;

STERLING

Sterling Orchards' Bed and Breakfast

60 Kendall Hill Road, 01564-1455
(508) 422-6595; (508) 422-6170

Built in 1740, this Colonial home features many original details such as the twelve-foot center chimney, Indian shutters, and wide-pine floors. Situated in a working apple orchard. A full breakfast is served in solarium overlooking lawns and gardens. Afternoon tea is also served on screen porch. No smoking in entire house. Closed January to March. Exit 6 from I-190.

Hosts: Robert and Shirley P. Smiley
Rooms: 2 (PB) $65-85
Full Breakfast
Credit Cards: None
Closed Jan.-Mar.
Notes: 2, 4, 10, 11, 12, 13 (day and night), 14

STOCKBRIDGE

Berkshire Bed and Breakfast Homes SC7

P. O. Box 211, Williamsburg, 01096
(413) 268-7244

This 1880 Colonial is decorated with antique and country furnishings. There is a parlor and a den with a TV and refrigerator for guest use. All rooms are air-conditioned. A room with a king-size bed has a private bath. A room with a double bed shares a bath with a room that has twin beds. Full breakfast. No smoking. Children over twelve welcome. $90-150.

Berkshire Bed and Breakfast Homes SC9

P. O. Box 211, Williamsburg, 01096
(413) 268-7244

An 1865 Federal-style home on three acres with antique-furnished guest rooms, private baths, and canopy beds. Swimming pool, patio and parlor for guests. Full breakfast; no smoking. $90 winter (continental breakfast); $150 summer.

The Inn at Stockbridge

Route 7, Box 618, 01262
(413) 298-3337

An elegant Georgian Colonial set on 12 acres. Each room is individually decorated with antiques and reproductions. Eight rooms, each with private bath, five with king beds. A scrumptious full breakfast is served in a formal dining room setting. In-ground pool. Complimentary wine and cheese. Near Tanglewood, Rockwell Museum, and all Berkshire attractions.

Hosts: Lee and Don Weitz
Rooms: 8 (PB) $75-170
Full Breakfast
Credit Cards: A, B, C
Notes: 2, 5, 7 (limited), 8 (over 12), 9, 10, 11, 12, 13, 14

Merrell Tavern Inn

Merrell Tavern Inn

Route 102, Main Street, South Lee, 01260
(800) 243-1794

---

6 Pets welcome; 7 Smoking allowed; 8 Children welcome; 9 Social drinking allowed; 10 Tennis available; 11 Swimming available; 12 Golf available; 13 Skiing available; 14 May be booked through travel agents.

This 200-year-old brick stagecoach inn situated in a small New England village along the banks of the Housatonic River is listed on the National Register of Historic Places. Rooms with fireplaces, canopy beds, and antique furnishings. Full breakfast is served in the original tavern room. One mile to Norman Rockwell's beloved Stockbridge.

Hosts: Charles and Faith Reynolds
Rooms: 9 (PB) $55-140
Full Breakfast
Credit Cards: A, B, C
Notes: 5, 8, 9, 10, 11, 12, 13, 14

STOW

Amerscot House

61 West Acton Road, 01775
(508) 897-0666

Convenient to Boston and historic Concord, this charming 1734 Colonial farmhouse offers the warmth and hospitality of the past. Come home from a day of business or vacationing to a welcoming fire in the hearth. Visit historic sites, golf on any one of four top-flight courses, canoe, hike, or pick apples at neighboring orchards.

Host: Doreen Gibson
Rooms: 3 (PB) $80-95
Full Breakfast
Credit Cards: A, B, C
Notes: 2, 5, 10, 12

Bed and Breakfast Associates #CW325

P. O. Box 57166, Batson Park Branch,
    Boston, 02157-0166
(617) 449-5302; FAX (617) 449-5958

Authentic Colonial farmhouse circa 1734 features romantic guest rooms. Honeymoon suite has a sitting room, Jacuzzi in the bath, queen-size canopy bed. All guest rooms have hand-made quilts, decorative fireplaces, and antique furnishings. $80-95.

STURBRIDGE

Berkshire Bed and Breakfast Homes ST2

P. O. Box 211, Williamsburg, 01096
(413) 268-7244

This contemporary home built in 1986 sits on two and one-half acres and is furnished in antiques. There is a parlor and a ground-floor atrium with a sitting area for guests, a TV, and access to the landscaped lawns. There are two bedrooms, one with a double bed and one with twin beds, and a semiprivate bath. Continental breakfast is served. No smoking. Children over ten welcome. $65.

Berkshire Bed and Breakfast Homes ST3

P. O. Box 211, Williamsburg, 01096
(413) 268-7244

A 1971 Dutch Colonial on one acre. One guest room with private bath; others share a bath. Country and antique furnishings throughout. High English tea by reservation only. Full breakfast; no smoking; children welcome. $65-75.

Bethany Bed and Breakfast

Bed and Breakfast Marblehead and North Shore
P. O. Box 35, Newtonville, 02160
(617) 964-1606; (800) 832-2632
FAX (617) 332-8572

An attractive Cape Cod-style home with livingroom and off-road parking. Less than an hour from the Berkshires, Boston, and Hartford. Four guest rooms, two with private bath. Full breakfast. Children welcome. Cat in residence. Guest pets by prior arrangement. Smoking on porch only. $65-75.

NOTES: Credit cards accepted: A Master Card; B Visa; C American Express; D Discover Card; E Diner's Club; F Other; 2 Personal Checks accepted; 3 Lunch available; 4 Dinner available; 5 Open all year;

1880 Inn

14 Pleasant Street, 012082
(413) 967-7847

Relax in yesterday's charm. This twelve-room Colonial is complete with six fireplaces, rustic beams, and hardwood floors. Breakfast may be served on the porch or in the dining room. Enjoy afternoon tea before the cozy fireplace.

Hosts: Margaret and Stan Skutnik
Rooms: 3; $50-65
Full Breakfast
Credit Cards: None
Notes: 2, 5, 8, 9, 10, 11, 12, 14

Sturbridge Country Inn

530 Main Street, 01566
(508) 347-5503

A historic 1840s inn custom-decorated with Colonial bedrooms. Each room features fireplace and private whirlpool tub. Situated less than a mile from Old Sturbridge village. Walking distance to restaurants and antique shops.

Host: Kevin MacConnell
Rooms: 9 (PB) $69-135
Continental Breakfast
Credit Cards: A, B, C, D
Notes: 2, 5, 7, 8, 9, 10, 11, 12, 13, 14

SUDBURY

Carousel House

Host Homes of Boston
P. O. Box 117, Boston, 02168
(617) 244-1308; FAX (617) 244-2700

This countryside estate, isolated on a hilltop near Concord offers three guest rooms with outstanding amenities. Second-floor Victorian and Green rooms have queen beds, Jacuzzi, and shower baths, and the third-floor Rose room has a pair of twin beds and a shower bath. Grounds include a private golf course and swimming pool, and antique carousel horses artfully blend with traditional decor to make this a special place to stay. No smoking. $95.

Checkerberry Corner Bed and Breakfast

5 Checkerberry Circle, 01776
(508) 443-8660

Situated in a quiet residential neighborhood only a short drive to Longfellow's Wayside Inn, the Old North Bridge, the Alcott, Emerson, Hawthorne, and Thoreau houses. Boston's Freedom Trail, Quincy markets, and other attractions are easily reached within 40 minutes.

Hosts: Stu and Irene MacDonald
Rooms: 3 (SB) $55-65
Full Breakfast
Credit Cards: None
Notes: 2, 5, 8, 9, 14

Sudbury Bed and Breakfast

3 Drum Lane, 01776
(508) 443-2860

A large Garrison Colonial home with traditional furnishings situated on a quiet tree-studded acre. A continental breakfast is served, with homemade muffins and rolls. Close to Boston, Lexington, and Concord. An abundance of outdoor recreation and historical sights nearby. Friendly hospitality for the New England visitor.

Hosts: Don and Nancy Somers
Rooms: 2 (S1.5B) $55-65
Continental Breakfast
Credit Cards: None
Notes: 2, 5, 8, 9, 11, 12

SWAMPSCOTT

A Bed and Breakfast Above the Rest #51

50 Boatswains Way, Suite 105
Boston, 02150
(617) 884-7748; (800) 677-2262

The Marshall House is an impeccably refurbished country home with three guest rooms. Each room has a double bed, TV, and refrigerator, and all share a bath. Located three doors from the Atlantic Ocean. Continental breakfast.

6 Pets welcome; 7 Smoking allowed; 8 Children welcome; 9 Social drinking allowed; 10 Tennis available; 11 Swimming available; 12 Golf available; 13 Skiing available; 14 May be booked through travel agents.

Bed and Breakfast Associates #NS200

P. O. Box 57166, Babson Park Branch
Boston, 02157-0166
(617) 449-5302; FAX (617) 449-5958

Just two and one-half blocks to a sandy beach. This hostess collects antiques, refinishes furniture, and enjoys quilting. As a tour escort around New England, she has a wealth of information to share with her guests. Her small Colonial home in a quiet neighborhood is neat and clean. Three guest rooms share a bath. Full breakfast; children over 12 welcome; no smoking. $50-60; family and monthly rates available.

Harborview Victorian

Bed and Breakfast Marblehead and North Shore
P. O. Box 35, Newtonville, 02160
(617) 964-1606; (800) 832-2632
FAX (617) 332-8572

This lovely Victorian offers a marvelous view of the ocean. Four guest rooms share two baths, and two of the rooms have ocean views. Each room has a color TV, and a guest refrigerator and phone are provided in the guest hallway. Five-minute walk to bus or train for easy access to Boston, Salem, or Marblehead. Hosts will also provide airport pickup by prior arrangement. Children over six welcome. Smoking in restricted areas. $65-75.

Oak Shores Bed and Breakfast

64 Fuller Avenue, 01907
(617) 599-7677

This 60-year-old Dutch Colonial is on Boston's lovely North Shore. Rooms are filled with fine restored furniture. Sleep in the comfort of old brass and iron beds, relax in the private garden, or stroll the two blocks to the beach. Near public transportation.

Host: Marjorie L. McClung
Rooms: 2 (SB) $60
Continental Breakfast
Credit Cards: None
Closed Dec. 2-Mar. 31
Notes: 8 (over 8), 10, 11

Ocean View

Host Homes of Boston
P. O. Box 117, Boston, 02168
(617) 244-1308; FAX (617) 244-5156

Built on a land grant from the king of England, this sprawling country-style Victorian has the best ocean view in town. Down the hill are fine restaurants, shops, beaches, and the bus to Boston, and two lovely second-floor guest rooms, one with a queen bed and the other a double bed, are available. Fireplaced kitchen, and ground and deck with a view add to the amenities this bed and breakfast offers. No smoking. Children welcome. $75-85.

Oceanview Bed and Breakfast

Bed and Breakfast Marblehead and North Shore
P. O. Box 35, Newtonville, 02160
(617) 964-1606; (800) 832-2632
Fax (617) 332-8572

This beautiful Queen Anne Victorian is set high on a hilltop and has sweeping views of Swampscott Harbor and the ocean. Two beautifully decorated guest rooms share a bath, and a studio apartment is also available. Three levels of outside decking enable guests to take full advantage of the lovely gardens and outside ocean views. The sunny country kitchen with a fireplace is filled with wonderful aromas of herbs and natural foods cooked by the host. Children welcome. Smoking permitted on outside decks. $80-100.

NOTES: Credit cards accepted: A Master Card; B Visa; C American Express; D Discover Card; E Diner's Club; F Other; 2 Personal Checks accepted; 3 Lunch available; 4 Dinner available; 5 Open all year;

TOPSFIELD

The Wild Berry
Bed and Breakfast

Bed and Breakfast Marblehead and North Shore
P. O. Box 35, Newtonville, 02160
(617) 964-1606; (800) 832-2632
FAX (617) 332-8572

A Greek Revival home with all the modern amenities in an area of large properties. This bed and breakfast is close to Hood's Pond, where guests may swim. In winter, guests may use cross-country ski trails behind the house. Livingroom with large stone fireplace and TV. Two guest rooms, one with private bath. Full breakfast. Children welcome. Pets in residence. Guest pets by prior arrangement. Smoking on porch only. $60-85.

TRURO

Bed and Breakfast Cape Cod #9

P. O. Box 341, West Hyannisport, 02672-0341
(508) 775-2772; FAX (508) 775-2884

This two-hundred-year-old home, built by the founder of Truro, overlooks the Pamet River. Two guest rooms, one with a double and the other, a pair of twins, offer private baths, and lush growth and natural beauty add to the overall feeling of this rural setting. Continental breakfast. Children oevr 15. $65.

Edgewood Farm

Orleans Bed and Breakfast Associates
P. O. Box 1312, Orleans, 02653
(508) 255-3824; (800) 541-6226

This is authentic rural Truro. Private lane leads to a typical old Cape house and long low cottage. Surrounded by meadows, it has a trail up Great Hill that overlooks the Atlantic Ocean. The cottage offers two bright studios, each with private bath; one with fireplace and kitchenette, the other with a nice sun room opening onto extensive lawns. There is also one double room with bath on the second floor of the main house. Breakfast is served in the dining room. $65-70.

Parker House

P. O. Box 1111, 02666
(508) 349-3358

The Parker House is an 1820 classic full-Cape nestled into the side of Truro Center between the Cobb Memorial Library and the Blacksmith Shop Restaurant. Clean ocean and bay beaches two miles to east or west. Many art galleries and restaurants in Provincetown and Wellfleet ten minutes away by car. Golf, tennis, sailing, whale watches nearby. The Cape Cod National Seashore and Audubon Sanctuary offer many trails and guided walks. The Parker House offers haven to a limited number of guests who can rest and read or enjoy the many activities nearby.

Host: Stephen Williams
Rooms: 2 (SB) $55
Continental Breakfast
Credit Cards: None
Notes: 2, 5, 9, 10, 11, 12

TYRINGHAM

The Golden Goose

Main Road, 01264
(413) 243-3008

Small, friendly 1800 country inn nestled in Tyringham Valley in the Berkshires. Victorian antiques, sitting rooms with fireplaces, homemade breakfast fare. Within one-half hour are Tanglewood, Stockbridge, Jacob's Pillow, Hancock Shaker Village, the Norman Rockwell Museum, Berkshire Theater Festival, skiing, golf, tennis. The inn is one mile off the

---

6 Pets welcome; 7 Smoking allowed; 8 Children welcome; 9 Social drinking allowed; 10 Tennis available; 11 Swimming available; 12 Golf available; 13 Skiing available; 14 May be booked through travel agents.

Appalachian Trail. Near Butternut, Otis, Jiminy Peak, and Catamount ski slopes.

Hosts: Lilja and Joe Rizzo
Rooms: 6 (4 PB; 2 SB) $60-110
Expanded Continental Breakfast
Credit Cards: C
Notes: 2, 5, 7, 8 (in apartment), 9, 10, 11, 12, 13, 14

The Golden Goose

VINEYARD HAVEN, MARTHA'S VINEYARD _

Bed and Breakfast Associates #IW300

P. O. Box 57166, Babson Park Branch
Boston, 02157-0166
(617) 449-5302; FAX (617) 449-5958

Your friendly hostess will welcome you to her charming little house with a white picket fence and a screened porch. It is situated in a neighborhood of manicured lawns just one and one-half miles from I-95, which circles Greater Boston. Two guest rooms on the second floor share a bath. Full breakfast upon request; children welcome. $55; family rates available.

Bed and Breakfast Nantucket/Martha's Vineyard #205

P. O. Box 341, West Hyannisport, 02672-0341
(508) 775-2771' FAX (508) 775-2884

This home was built nearly 100 years ago as a private home. Later it was used for 40 years as a guest house. It was restored several years ago, and the present owner uses 8 rooms for bed and breakfast. Each room has a private bath, and all are clean and bright with tasteful decor. The continental breakfast is served in a comon room where guests meet and greet one another. Walk to all Vineyard Haven shops, stores, and restaurants. Bike rental available on the premises. $75-150.

Captain Dexter House of Vineyard Haven

100 Main Street, P. O. Box 2457, 02568
(508) 693-6564

Built in 1843 as the home of sea captain Rodolphas Dexter, the Captain Dexter House of Vineyard Haven has a country colonial atmosphere and is elegantly furnished with period antiques, original fireplaces, and canopy beds. Enjoy a delicious home-baked continental breakfast and evening apértif. Walk to ferry, beach, shops, and restaurants.

Hosts: Jim and Tenée Casaccio
Rooms: 8 (PB) $55-165
Continental Breakfast
Credit Cards: A, B, C
Notes: 2, 5, 7, 9, 10, 11, 12, 14

Hanover House

10 Edgartown Road; P. O. Box 2107, 02568
(508) 693-1066; (800) 339-1066 (MA)

Recommended by The New York Times, the Hanover House is a large old inn that has been fully renovated, offering guests modern conveniences while still retaining the quaintness and personalized hospitality of the lovely old inns of yesteryear. The guest rooms are beautiful, and all feature private baths, color cable TV, queen-size or double beds, air conditioning, and individual heat controls. Continental Breakfast is served on the lovely sun porch May

NOTES: Credit cards accepted: A Master Card; B Visa; C American Express; D Discover Card; E Diner's Club; F Other; 2 Personal Checks accepted; 3 Lunch available; 4 Dinner available; 5 Open all year;

through October. Gas grills and picnic tables are provided for guests. The inn is within walking distance of the ferry and the town of Vineyard Haven.

Host: Barbara N. Hanover
Rooms: 16 (PB) $45-145
Continental Breakfast
Credit Cards: A, B, C
Notes: 2, 5, 7, 8, 14

Hanover House

High Haven House

P. O. Box 289, 02568
(508) 693-9204; (800) 232-9204

On the island of Martha's Vineyard, a short walk from the shops and ferry. Pool, hot tub. Beautiful beaches and nature trails are nearby, as well as fishing and boating. Third night free off-season.

Hosts: Joe and Kathleen Schreck
Rooms: 11 (4 PB; 7 SB) $65-120
Continental Breakfast
Credit Cards: A, B, C
Notes: 2, 5, 7, 8, 9, 10, 11, 12, 14

Lothrop Merry House

Owen Park, Box 1939, 02568
(508) 693-1646

The Merry House, built in the 1790s, overlooks Vineyard Haven Harbor, has a private beach, expansive lawn, flower-bordered terrace. Most rooms have ocean view and fireplace. All are furnished with antiques and fresh flowers. Complimentary canoe and sunfish for guests' use. Sailing also available on 54-foot ketch Laissez Faire. Close to ferry and shops. Open year-round.

Hosts: John and Mary Clarke
Rooms: 7 (4 PB; 3 SB) $60-150
Continental Breakfast
Credit Cards: A, B
Notes: 2 (for deposit), 5, 7, 8, 9, 10, 11, 12, 14

Martha's Vineyard and Nantucket Reservations

Lagoon Pond Road, P. O. Box 1322, 02568
(508) 693-7200

Why spend hours dialing long-distance to find the ideal bed and breakfast inn, hotel, hotel cottage, condominium, or guest house? Call us to select from over 150 listings, and book your reservation–all of which can be done with one phone call. Established in 1977, we are the Island's oldest and largest reservation service. We accommodate individual and corporate reservation needs. Open year round.

Thorncroft Inn

Box 1022, 278 Main Street, 02568
(508) 693-3333

Lothrop Merry House

6 Pets welcome; 7 Smoking allowed; 8 Children welcome; 9 Social drinking allowed; 10 Tennis available; 11 Swimming available; 12 Golf available; 13 Skiing available; 14 May be booked through travel agents.

Thirteen antique-appointed rooms in two restored buildings. Private baths, working fireplaces, air conditioning, two-person Jacuzzis or private hot tub. Fine dining. Romantic and intimate. Four-diamond rating from AAA. Named one of the top inns in the country by *Glamour* magazine, September 1990. Located on three and one-half landscaped acres in an exclusive residential neighborhood, 150 yards from the ocean.

Hosts: Karl and Lynn Buder
Rooms: 13 (PB) $99-299
Full Breakfast
Minimum stay weekends and holidays in-season: 3 nights
Credit Cards: A, B, C, F
Notes: 2, 4, 5, 9, 14

Twin Oaks Inn

8 Edgartown Road, P. O. Box 1767, 02568
(508) 693-8633

This cozy turn-of-the-century farmhouse is decorated with antiques, romantic floral prints, and pastel colors. Walking distance to the ferry, town, shopping, recreation. Four rooms share full baths in the main house, and a one-bedroom apartment with a fireplace and sun room is also available. Nightly and weekly rates are available. Off-season rates. Open year round.

Host: Doris L. Stewart
Rooms: 4 (SB) $75-95; apartment-$160; in season
Continental Breakfast
Credit Cards: A, B
Notes: 2, 5, 8, 9, 10, 11, 12, 14

WAQUOIT

Mariners Cove Bed and Breakfast

Host Homes of Boston
P. O. Box 117, Boston, 02168
(617) 244-1308; FAX (617) 244-5156

Contemporary on the water, with glass walls, cathedral ceilings, view of Vineyard Sound. Two second-floor guest rooms with decks. Passive solarium, bubbling spa. Children over 11 welcome. Near Falmouth and Hyannis. Summer only. Shared bath; private beach; no smoking. $85; weekly $550.

WARE

Berkshire Bed and Breakfast Homes PV22

P. O. Box 211, Williamsburg, 01096
(413) 268-7244

This 1880 Colonial with colonial furnishings offers five guest rooms sharing baths and a parlor. Full breakfast; no smoking; children welcome. $50-75.

Berkshire Bed and Breakfast Homes PV33

P. O. Box 211, Williamsburg, 01096
(413) 268-7244

A 1910 Colonial Revival on one acre. Guest rooms share a bath and parlor with piano and fireplace. Antique furnishings. Continental breakfast; children over six welcome. $45-55.

The Wildwood Inn

121 Church Street, 01082
(413) 967-7798

A homey, welcoming 1880 Victorian furnished in American primitive antiques, handmade heirloom and new quilts, and early cradles greets guests as they drive up a maple canopied street with stately Victorian homes. Laze in the hammock, swing, or rock on the wraparound front porch. Try a jigsaw puzzle or board game. Play croquet, frisbee, or sit under the fir trees to read. Wander in the 110 acre park. Canoe, bike, or ski nearby. An easy drive to the five college area, Old Sturbridge, and Deerfield, the basketball hall of fame. Our motto is "the NO-LUNCH breakfast"!

NOTES: Credit cards accepted: A Master Card; B Visa; C American Express; D Discover Card; E Diner's Club; F Other; 2 Personal Checks accepted; 3 Lunch available; 4 Dinner available; 5 Open all year;

Hosts: Fraidell Fenster and Richard Watson
Rooms: 7 (PB) $38-74
Full sit-down Breakfast
Credit Cards: C
Notes: 2, 5, 8 (over 6), 9, 10, 11, 12, 13, 14

WAREHAM

Mulberry Bed and Breakfast

2257 High Street, 02571
(508) 295-0684

This lovely Cape Cod-style home, circa 1840, was originally occupied by Sampson the blacksmith. Purchased by the owner's grandfather in 1892 and used as a general store in the historic section of Wareham, the home offers seven trunk white mulberry trees that provide shade, birdwatching, berries for jam, a tranquil setting, and the name for your cozy home away from home. Furnished with family antiques and heirlooms. The hostess and her two cats welcome you. Convenient to historic Plymouth, Boston, New Bedford, Fall River, and Newport.

Host: Frances A. Murphy
Rooms: 3 (SB) $45-55
Hearty Continental Breakfast
Credit Cards: C
Notes: 2, 5, 8 (over 10), 9

WATERTOWN

Bed and Breakfast Associates #IW130

P. O. Box 57166, Babson Park Branch
Boston, 02157-0166
(617) 449-5302; FAX (617) 449-5958

This Victorian home, built in the 1890s, has many architectural features including parquet floors, curved walls and windows, spacious rooms, and a sunny front porch. Guests enjoy a lovely room with a desk and TV plus a second-floor sitting room. Continental breakfast; children over ten welcome; no smoking. $55; monthly rates available.

WELLESLEY

Bed and Breakfast Associates #IW545

P. O. Box 57166, Babson Park Branch
Boston, 02157-0166
(617) 449-5302; FAX (617) 449-5958

This striking home in a rural setting features a light and airy guest room with double bed and private attached bath. Turret staircase leads to this second-floor room and the third-floor den. Generous continental breakfast; children over ten welcome; no smoking. $75-95; weekly and monthly rates available.

Washington Place

Host Homes of Boston
P. O. Box 117, Boston, 02168
(617) 244-1308; FAX (617) 244-5156; GSC (617) 244-5156

A warm welcome awaits you in this 1920 Colonial near the village. Your hostess offers two second-floor guest rooms and parlor with books, TV, stereo. Route 128 one mile. Boston 12 miles. Seven minute walk to commuter train weekdays. Shared bath; no smoking. $57.

WELLFLEET

Deep Denes

Orleans Bed and Breakfast Associates
P. O. Box 1312, Orleans, 02653
(508) 255-3824; (800) 541-6226

Overlooking the great Atlantic, set in unusual gardens, with lots of glass to take advantage of the views, this house offers peace and enrichment. Talented hosts. Serene double room, adjacent sitting room with fireplace, and private bath. Japanese garden, close to beach. $70.

6 Pets welcome; 7 Smoking allowed; 8 Children welcome; 9 Social drinking allowed; 10 Tennis available; 11 Swimming available; 12 Golf available; 13 Skiing available; 14 May be booked through travel agents.

A Different Drummer

Orleans Bed and Breakfast Associates
P. O. Box 1312, Orleans, 02653
(508) 255-3824; (800) 541-6226

A spacious multilevel home on a hill over-looking secluded Drummer's Cove. Four-minute walk to Bay beach. Ocean only one mile away. Enjoy sun deck, a screened-in porch, and light-filled living/dining area. On a separate level two bedrooms, one with twin beds and the other a queen, share a cedar-lined bath and adjacent TV and reading room. Hostess is a cellist with the Cape Cod Symphony, and avid gardener. $60.

Inn at Duck Creeke

Box 364, 02667
(508) 349-9333

Five-acre complex with duck pond and salt marsh. Two outstanding restaurants. Within walking distance of Wellfleet and within the Cape Cod National Seashore. Antique shops, fine art galleries, ocean and bay beaches, fresh-water ponds, cycling, and boating.

Hosts: Robert Morrill and Judith Pihl
Rooms: 25 (17 PB; 8 SB) $60-90
Continental Breakfast
Credit Cards: A, B, C
Closed Oct. 15-May 15
Notes: 4, 7, 8, 9, 10, 11, 12

Inn at Duck Creeke

Owl's Nest

Orleans Bed and Breakfast Associates
P. O. Box 1312, Orleans, 02653
(508) 255-3824; (800) 541-6226

Peace and quiet surround this Gothic contemporary home situated on six acres known as Owl Woods. A charming cathedral-ceilinged livingroom and dining room, filled with antiques and collectibles, are yours to enjoy. Upstairs a skylighted sitting area separates two bedrooms that share a large bath. Continental breakfast served inside or on 40-foot deck overlooking gardens and woods. Walk to bay beach or ride to ocean or pond for swimming. $60.

WEST BARNSTABLE

Honeysuckle Hill

591 Main Street, 02668
(508) 362-8414; (800) 441-8418
EMA (800) 696-1397

Charming country inn near the dunes of Sandy Neck Beach. Full country breakfast and afternoon tea. Feather beds, down comforters, and homemade cookies at bedside. English toiletries and terry-cloth robes in private baths. Wraparound screen porch filled with wicker and a large great room for games and large-screen TV watching make this a perfect spot for any season.

Host: Barbara Rosenthal
Rooms: 3 (PB) $75-105
Full Breakfast
Minimum stay on seasonal weekends and holidays: 2 nights
Credit Cards: A, B, C, D
Notes: 2, 5, 7, 8 (over 12), 9, 10 ,11, 12, 14

WEST BROOKFIELD

Berkshire Bed and Breakfast Homes ST6

P. O. Box 211, Williamsburg, 01096
(413) 268-7244

Honeysuckle Hill

This 1880 Victorian is furnished in country and Victorian style. There is a parlor for guest use. One double bedroom and one queen bedroom are available, and both have private baths and air conditioning. Continental breakfast. No smoking. Children welcome. Resident pets. $55-65.

WEST DENNIS

Bed and Breakfast Cape Cod #15

P. O. Box 341, West Hyannisport, 02672-0341
(508) 775-2772; FAX (508) 775-2884

On the warm waters of Nantucket Sound is this 62-year-old beach home that has been restored into a seven-bedroom private bath and breakfast accommodation. From all rooms there is an ocean or pond view. The carefully maintained house has a breakfast room overlooking a deck that leads to the 100 yards of private sandy beach. A kitchen on the ground floor is available for guests to cook and eat on the beach. All equipment is available. Convenient to many shops and restaurants, only minutes away from Hyannis. $60-80.

WEST FALMOUTH

Sjoholm Inn Bed and Breakfast

17 Chase Road, P. O. Box 430, 02574
(508) 540-5706

An 1850s farmhouse located in the peaceful countryside of West Falmouth, Sjoholm is close to warm water ocean beaches, golf, cycling trails, fine dining, and summer theatre. Fifteen rooms, with both private and shared baths, are decorated in charming country decor, and reasonably priced. Our hearty buffet-style breakfast is served each morning and included in your room rate. 10% discount for senior citizens and stays over four nights. Children five and over welcomed if supervised. A comfortable, quiet, homey place to stay!

Host: Barbara Eck
Rooms: 15 (7 PB; 8 SB) $55-85
Full Breakfast
Credit Cards: None
Notes: 2, 5, 7, 8, 9

6 Pets welcome; 7 Smoking allowed; 8 Children welcome; 9 Social drinking allowed; 10 Tennis available; 11 Swimming available; 12 Golf available; 13 Skiing available; 14 May be booked through travel agents.

WEST HARWICH

Bed and Breakfast Associates #CC330

P. O. Box 57166, Babson Park Branch
Boston, 02157-0166
(617) 449-5302; FAX (617) 449-5958

Victorian ambience and a generous full Irish breakfast await you in this comfortable and welcoming bed and breakfast. Enjoy a swim in the pool accompanied by afternoon hors d'oeuvres or chat with your gregarious hosts before the blazing livingroom fireplace. One mile to the beach, 12 miles to Hyannis. Six guest rooms with private baths. Full breakfast; children over ten welcome. $90.

Bed and Breakfast Cape Cod #16

P. O. Box 341, West Hyannisport, 02672-0341
(508) 775-2772; FAX (508) 775-2884

This thirty-five-year-old ranch-style home is three blocks from the warm waters of Nantucket Sound. There is one wing set aside for bed and breakfast. The first-floor bedroom has a queen-size bed, private bath, large sitting area, color TV, Oriental carpets, and a small refrigerator for guest use. A marvelous full breakfast is served from 8:00 to 9:30 A.M. Shopping and restaurants are convenient. No smoking. No children. $70.

Bed and Breakfast Cape Cod #26

P. O. Box 341, West Hyannisport, 02672-0341
(508) 775-2772; FAX (508) 775-2884

This six-guest-room inn was originally built as a sea captain's home in the 1820s. It features pine-board floors and an original-style "captain's stairs" leading to the second floor. A large pool for guest use is next to the main house. There are six bed-rooms with private baths, and some of the suites adjacent to the pool will accommodate up to four persons. A full country breakfast is served in a dining area overlooking the pool. $60-100.

Cape Cod's Lion's Head Inn

186 Belmont Road, P. O. Box 444, 02671
(508) 432-7766; (800) 321-3155

The Lion's Head Inn is a former sea captain's home dating from the 1820s. Recently renovated, it combines the charm of yesteryear with modern amenities. Walk to Nantucket Sound Beach, fine restaurants, and shops. Golf, biking, tennis nearby. Full candlelight breakfast in terrace room overlooking pool and patio. Off-season rates available.

Hosts: Fred, Deborah, and Ricky Denton
Rooms: 6 (PB) $90-130
Full Breakfast
Credit Cards: A, B
Minimum stay July and August: 2 nights
Notes: 2, 5, 7, 8 (by arrangement), 9, 10, 11, 12, 14

Cape Cod Sunny Pines Bed and Breakfast Inn and Claddagh Tavern

77 Main Street, P. O. Box 667, 02671
(508) 432-9628; (800) 356-9628 reservations

Irish hospitality in a Victorian ambience. Eight suites with air conditioning, TV, paddle fans, and designer linens and lace. Pool, Jacuzzi, picnic grounds, and garden walk to Nantucket Sound. Seven miles from Chatham, ten miles from Hyannis. Gourmet Irish candlelight breakfast served family-style. Centrally located on the Cape's south side for day trips to Provincetown, Boston, and Plymouth. Fully licensed Irish pub with full menu specializing in homemade food. Irish music and instruments on hand. Sing alongs encouraged.

Hosts: Jack and Eileen Connell
Rooms: 8 (PB) $75-100
Full Gourmet Breakfast

Credit Cards: A, B, C, D
Notes: 2, 3, 4, 5, 7 (limited), 9, 11, 12, 14

WEST NEWTON

The Carriage House

Bed and Breakfast Greater Boston and Cape Cod
P. O. Box 35, Newtonville, 02160
(617) 964-1601; (800) 832-2632
FAX (617) 332-8572

A charming, renovated privat studio in sub-urb just west of Boston. Easy access by car of public transportation to Boston/

WEST STOCKBRIDGE

Bed and Breakfast Accommodations 109

984 Gloucester Place, Schenectady, New York 12309
(518) 370-4948

Built in 1830 and recently renovated, this immaculate home boasts shiny hardwood floors, lace curtains, oak dining table, and artwork by the host's father. Guests are welcome to use the livingroom, dining room, or front porch for relaxation and con-versation. Four guest rooms, two with pri-vate baths. Just miles from Tanglewood. Children over ten welcome; no smoking. $75-100 in-season; $50-65 off-season (Nov. 1-June 30).

Berkshire Bed and Breakfast Homes SC10

P. O. Box 211, Williamsburg, 01096
(413) 268-7244

A 1982 contemporary on five acres. Modern antique touches throughout the guest rooms, with private and semiprivate baths. Family room, formal livingroom, and deck with view of Berkshire Hills. Full breakfast; no smoking; children over ten welcome. $80-85.

Berkshire Bed and Breakfast Homes SC15

P. O. Box 211, Williamsburg, 01096
(413) 268-7244

An 1830 Colonial on one-half acre. The parlor and porch are available for guest use. The hosts teach yoga and relaxation and cater to health-conscious guests. A double room has a private bath, and two queen bedrooms and a double bedroom have shared baths. Full breakfast. No smoking. Children welcome. $75-100.

WEST TISBURY, MARTHA'S VINEYARD

The Bayberry Inn

Old Courthouse Road; P. O. Box 654, 02575
(508) 693-1984

The Bayberry Inn is on a quiet country lane, surrounded by meadows with horses. It is a short drive to a beautiful, secluded beach. Canopy beds with romantic linens, flowers, and antiques furnish the guest rooms. Memorable breakfasts of Belgian waffles with fresh blueberry sauce or "Dream Boats" (everyone's favorite) are served on the terrace or before the fireplace.

Host: Rosalie Powell
Rooms: 5 (3 PB; 2 SB) $95-130
Full Breakfast
Credit Cards: A, B
Notes: 2, 5, 8 (over 12), 9, 10, 11, 12

WESTWOOD

Bed and Breakfast Associates #IW725

P. O. Box 57166, Babson Park Branch
Boston, 02157-0166
(617) 449-5302; FAX (617) 449-5958

This country house and barn are graced by an inviting brick patio with a large in-ground pool. The first floor has been redesigned to provide a view of the

6 Pets welcome; 7 Smoking allowed; 8 Children welcome; 9 Social drinking allowed; 10 Tennis available; 11 Swimming available; 12 Golf available; 13 Skiing available; 14 May be booked through travel agents.

grounds through walls of glass. Three guest rooms on the second floor share a bath. A Boston tour guide, this hostess claims there is a "friendly ghost" in the house. Full breakfast; children welcome. $55; family rates available.

Bed and Breakfast Associates #IW726

P. O. Box 57166, Babson Park Branch
Boston, 02157-0166
(617) 449-5302; FAX (617) 449-5958

This private hideaway is a converted schoolhouse. Your party of five can enjoy the two-story apartment with two bedrooms, two full baths, a kitchen, dining area, livingroom, and deck. Sleeping space includes an antique double bed, two twins that can be made up as a king, and one single. Full breakfast; children welcome; no smoking. $150 for four adults; $120 for family of four.

Bed and Breakfast Associates #IW750

P. O. Box 57166, Babson Park Branch
Boston, 02157-0166
(617) 449-5302; FAX (617) 449-5958

This retired couple enjoys greeting guests in their large comfortable home located just one mile from I-95 in this lovely suburban town. Their private yard features an in-ground pool for your pleasure. Three guest rooms, one with private bath. Full breakfast upon request; children welcome. $45-55; family and monthly rates available.

Woods Abloom

Host Homes of Boston
P. O. Box 117, Boston, 02168
(617) 244-1308; FAX (617) 244-5156

A tree grows through the roof of this 1958 redwood contemporary in the woods.

Stunning blend of antiques, modern art, pottery and porcelain collection. Stone walls and sculptured patio. Both rooms available to same party. Twelve miles southwest of Boston near I-95/128. Air conditioning; private bath; TV; no smoking. $68.

WHATELY

Berkshire Bed and Breakfast Homes PV21

P. O. Box 211, Williamsburg, 01096
(413) 268-7244

An 1870 sprawling farmhouse on 50 acres. Guest rooms with semiprivate baths and a parlor are available. Antique furnishings. Berry picking nearby. Full breakfast; no smoking; children over ten welcome. $50-85.

WILLIAMSBURG

Berkshire Bed and Breakfast Homes PV2

P. O. Box 211, 01096
(413) 268-7244

This 100-year-old Victorian on one acre is a short walk to town center. Guest rooms share a bath and private sitting room. Two-night minimum stay in winter. Full breakfast; children over eight welcome. $45-55.

Berkshire Bed and Breakfast Homes PV3

P. O. Box 211, 01096
(413) 268-7244

A 200-year-old restored farmhouse on 27 acres. Guest rooms furnished with antique and brass share a bath. A porch and sitting room are offered to guests. Full breakfast; no smoking; children welcome. $45-60; plus $5 surcharge for one-night stay.

NOTES: Credit cards accepted: A Master Card; B Visa; C American Express; D Discover Card; E Diner's Club; F Other; 2 Personal Checks accepted; 3 Lunch available; 4 Dinner available; 5 Open all year;

Berkshire Bed and Breakfast Homes PV18

P. O. Box 211, 01096
(413) 268-7244

This 1864 restored Victorian town house is a short walk to town center. Guest rooms share a bath and livingroom with fireplace. Full breakfast; children welcome. $45-50.

WILLIAMSTOWN

The American Country Collection 167

4 Greenwood Lane, Delmar, NY 12054
(518) 439-7001

Accommodations in this newly renovated facility on 350 acres in the Berkshires include cozy rooms with private bath, one-, two-, and three-bedroom suites with livingroom and fireplace, kitchen, and bedroom with queen-size bed, and secluded fully equipped cottages with one, two, or three bedrooms, each with a fireplace. Heated pool. All are air-conditioned, with phone and color TV. Children under 16 are welcome and stay free. Pets permitted in cottages. Continental breakfast. Smoking permitted. No resident pets, although there may be guests traveling with pets. $78-188.

Bed and Breakfast Accommodations 022

984 Gloucester Place, Schenectady, New York 12309
(518) 370-4948

Set on a knoll with a tri-state view of the mountains and valleys, this home and the surrounding 52-acre farm is the perfect complement to a busy vacation. Swim, row, or fish for trout in the stocked pond. Walk or cross-country ski the five kilometers of trails. Visit the chicks, pigs, cows, and oxen in the barn and pasture. Each of the three guest rooms is furnished with country treasures, oak antique beds, and marble-topped dressers. Breakfast is served in the dining room or on the porch. $60.

Bed and Breakfast Accommodations 029

984 Gloucester Place, Schenectady, New York 12309
(518) 370-4948

This 600-acre dairy farm and 200-year-old farmhouse are in the valley with a pond to swim, fish, or just feast on the beautiful tri-state view. The property is adjacent to the Appalachian Trail. Cross-country ski; make your own trails through open fields and wood roads in the mountains. Two guest rooms share a bath with the hosts. Breakfast is served on antique china and may be enjoyed on the porch on a nice summer day. $45.

Berkshire Bed and Breakfast Homes NC4

P. O. Box 211, Williamsburg, 01096
(413) 268-7244

A 1870 country farmhouse on 127 acres. Guest rooms with private and semiprivate baths and sitting room have country and natural-wood furnishings. Gazebo is available to guests. Continental breakfast; children over six welcome. $60-85.

Berkshire Bed and Breakfast Homes NC11

P. O. Box 211, Williamsburg, 01096
(413) 268-7244

At this 200-year-old farmhouse on a 600-acre dairy farm, guests share a bath and enjoy antique furnishings. Scenic farmland and view of fields and mountains. Farm tour, swimming pond, and bass fishing. Continental breakfast; no smoking; children over six welcome. $45-50.

Steep Acres Farm Bed and Breakfast

520 White Oaks Road, 01267
(413) 458-3774

Situated two miles from Williams College and the Williamstown Theatre Festival. A country home on a high knoll with spectacular views of the Berkshire Hills and Vermont's Green Mountains. Trout and swimming pond welcome guests on this working farm's 52 acres adjacent to both the Appalachian and Long trails. Short distance to Tanglewood and Jacob's Pillow.

Hosts: Mary and Marvin Gangemi
Rooms: 4 (SB) $40-60
Full Breakfast
Credit Cards: None
Notes: 2, 5, 9, 10, 11, 12, 13

Upland Meadow House

1249 Northwest Hill Road, 01267
(413) 458-3990

Situated on the slope of the Taconic Range, this contemporary house provides a panoramic view. With 160 acres of field and woods, privacy and quiet are assured. Williams College woods offers opportunities for hiking and cross-country skiing.

Hosts: Pam and Alfred Whitmas
Doubles: 2 (SB) $60
Types of Beds: 1 Twin; 1 Double
Full Breakfast
Credit Cards: None
Notes: 2, 5, 10, 11, 12, 13

WINCHESTER

Bed and Breakfast Associates #IN600

P. O. Box 57166, Babson Park Branch
Boston, 02157-0166
(617) 449-5302; FAX (617) 449-5958

Set in a residential area near the center of this peaceful old New England village, this home is just 15 minutes by car or train from Boston. A large, older home, hosted by a warm and welcoming couple. Two guest rooms share a bath and are rented to one party only. Full breakfast; children welcome. $40-55; family and monthly rates available.

WINDSOR

Warren Hill

255 High Street Hill, 01270
(413) 684-1402

A country mountain road leads to this newly built contemporary home. A private entryway leads guests to a livingroom, kitchen, full bath, one double bedroom and one king-size bedroom with a skylight. Enjoy the privacy of the surrounding woods on the spacious deck or relax in your private quarters.

Hosts: Tim and Kathy Cooper
Rooms: 2 (1 PB; 1 SB) $60-80
Full Breakfast
Credit Cards: None
Notes: 2, 5, 8, 9, 10, 11, 12, 13

WOODS HOLE

The Marlborough

320 Wood Hole Road, 02543
(508) 548-6218

The Marlborough is an intimate Cape Cod cottage of five guest rooms individually decorated with antiques and collectibles, each with private bath and air conditioning. The spacious wooded grounds include a pool and paddle tennis court. Private beach one mile away with lifeguard and free parking; one and one-half miles to the Martha's Vineyard ferry; easy day trips to Boston, Newport, Plymouth, Provincetown, and Nantucket. Delightful breakfast.

NOTES: Credit cards accepted: A Master Card; B Visa; C American Express; D Discover Card; E Diner's Club; F Other; 2 Personal Checks accepted; 3 Lunch available; 4 Dinner available; 5 Open all year;

Host: Diana Smith
Rooms: 5 (PB) $85-105
Full Breakfast
Credit Cards: A, B
Notes: 2, 3, 5, 9

WORTHINGTON

A Bed and Breakfast Above the Rest #59

50 Boatswains Way, Suite 105
Boston, 02150
(617) 884-7748; (800) 677-2262

The name of this delightful home says it all, "Country Antique." Three guest rooms share a full bath that has been renovated but still has its claw foot tub. Full breakfast is served either in the plant-filled dining room, or on the glass-enclosed porch overlooking a picturesque field that changes with the seasons. Situated only five minutes from the Berkshires, Tanglewood, and "the best cross-country skiing and lessons ever."

Berkshire Bed and Breakfast Homes PV20

P. O. Box 211, Williamsburg, 01096
(413) 268-7244

This 1780 Colonial is furnished with antiques, Oriental rugs, five fireplaces, and wide-pine floors. Rooms with private baths and parlor are available. Full breakfast; no smoking; children over four welcome. $90.

Country Cricket Village Inn

Route 112, Huntington Road, 01098
(413) 238-5366

The Colonial-style inn is on 23 acres near the town common of a lovely New England village. The inn has five country bedrooms, each with private bath. Each room has a distinctive quality of its own and is furnished with complementary antiques. A

common room has been provided for gathering, visiting, reading, viewing television, or enjoying the fireplace. The dining room offers a full breakfast with Belgian waffles and pure Worthington maple syrup.

Hosts: Jacquie and Don Bridgeman
Rooms: 5 (PB) $80 plus breakfast
Full Breakfast
Credit Cards: A, B, C, D
Notes: 2, 3, 4, 5, 7 (limited), 8 (over 11), 9, 11, 12, 13, 14

Hill Gallery

HC 65, Box 96, 01098
(413) 238-5914

Sitauted on a mountaintop in the Hampshire Hills on 25 acres. Enjoy relaxed country living in an owner-built contemporary home with art gallery, fireplaces, and swimming pool. Self-contained cottage also available.

Hosts: Ellen and Walter Korzec
Rooms: 2 (PB) $60
Full Breakfast
Minimum stay holidays: 2 nights
Credit Cards: None
Notes: 2, 5, 8 (over 5), 9, 10, 11, 12, 13

Inn Yesterday

Huntington Road, 01098
(413) 238-5529

In 1877 this restored Greek Revival home was known as Frissell's Inn. Today, Inn Yesterday welcomes guests with many amenities of the past, including antiques throughout. In nice weather, a full country breakfast is served in the porch sun room.

Hosts: Janet and Robert Osborne
Rooms: 3 (SB) $60
Full Breakfast
Credit Cards: None
Notes: 2, 5, 7 (limited), 8 (over 5), 9, 10, 11, 12, 13

Nutmeg Bed and Breakfast Agency #347

P. O. Box 1117, West Hartford, CT 06107
(203) 236-6698

6 Pets welcome; 7 Smoking allowed; 8 Children welcome; 9 Social drinking allowed; 10 Tennis available; 11 Swimming available; 12 Golf available; 13 Skiing available; 14 May be booked through travel agents.

This Colonial-style full service country inn is on 23 wooded acres near the town common of a lovely New England village. The five spacious guest rooms each have private baths and are furnished with antiques. A common room for guests has a fireplace and TV. The dining room offers a full breakfast, as well as lunch and candlelight dinners. Picnic baskets and "breakfast in bed" are available. Hunting, fishing, golfing, swimming, and cross-country skiing are nearby. A lovely country crafts gift and antique shop is on the premises. Children over 12 are welcome. Smoking restricted.

YARMOUTH PORT

Bed and Breakfast Cape Cod #11

P. O. Box 341, West Hyannisport, 02672-0341
(508) 775-2772; FAX (508) 775-2884

This host home has an adjacent carriage house built with a second-floor suite expressly for bed and breakfast guests. It is spacious and air-conditioned and has a sitting area with a couch, chairs, TV, and refrigerator stocked with beverages. There is a king-size bed or twin beds. A pull-out is available for a third person. No smoking. No children under twelve. $110.

Bed and Breakfast Cape Cod #40

P. O. Box 341, West Hyannisport, 02672-0341
(508) 775-2772; FAX (508) 775-2884

Built 210 years ago, this unique Cape house has all the character of the past reflected in its antiques and Early American decor. A double bedroom and a twin bedroom share a bath. The full continental breakfast is served on the patio or in the keeping room in front of a fireplace with a beehive oven. Walk to a fresh water beach or to the salt water bay beaches.

Restaurants and shops are a short walk from this antique house. $60.

Bed and Breakfast Cape Cod #71

P. O. Box 341, West Hyannisport, 02672-0341
(508) 775-2772; FAX (508) 775-2884

This Cape Cod-style house built in 1800 has three bedrooms with private baths, one with a queen-size bed, one with a double, and one with twin beds. A parlor with a TV is available for guests. Enjoy a nice continental breakfast. Walk to the fresh water pond or to the beach nearby, or simply relax on the pleasant grounds. $55-80

Bed and Breakfast Cape Cod #75

P. O. Box 341, West Hyannisport, 02672-0341
(508) 775-2772; FAX (508) 2884

An authentic 1830 Greek Revival host home with two bedrooms. One has a double bed and the other twins. The house was restored by the owners several years ago. There is a Jacuzzi on the ground floor in an atrium porch. This enclosed porch is comfortable for enjoying the full breakfast served by the hosts. The house is one mile from a lake and one and one-half miles from the ocean. No smoking. No children under ten. $75.

The Colonial House Inn

Route 6A, 277 Main Street, 02675
(508) 362-4348; (800) 999-3416

This registered historic landmark has antique-appointed guest rooms, private baths, and air conditioning. It features gracious hospitality, Old World charm, and traditional New England cuisine. Full liquor license, fine wines, and an indoor heated swimming pool. Lovely grounds,

NOTES: Credit cards accepted: A Master Card; B Visa; C American Express; D Discover Card; E Diner's Club; F Other; 2 Personal Checks accepted; 3 Lunch available; 4 Dinner available; 5 Open all year;

large deck, reading room, television room, and Victorian livingroom. Close to nature trails, golf, tennis, antique shops, beaches, and shopping, space for wedding receptions and other functions, up to 135 people.

Rooms: 21 (PB) $50-85
Continental Breakfast
Credit Cards: A, B, C, D
Notes: 2, 3, 4, 5, 6, 7, 8, 9, 10, 11, 12, 13, 14

Liberty Hill Inn on Cape Cod

77 Main Street, 02675
(508) 362-3976; (800) 821-3977

Elegant, attractive, romantic. Large rooms beautifully furnished with Early American pieces. Free maps to Cape Cod and 38 golf courses. Built as a luxurious private home in 1825, it is now a charming bed and breakfast inn providing a unique experience to the discriminating traveler who seeks only the finest in service and hospitality. Walk to restaurants, shops, conservation areas.

Hosts: Jack and Beth Flanagan
Rooms: 5 (PB) $75-125
Full Breakfast
Credit Cards: A, B, C
Notes: 2, 3, 4, 5, 7, 8, 9, 10, 11, 12, 14

Olde Captain's Inn

101 Main Street, 02675
(508) 362-4496

Charming restored captain's home, situated in the historic district. Fine lodgings and superb continental breakfast. Cable TV. The inn has a truly friendly, elegant atmosphere. Walk to shops and restaurants. Stay two nights and your third night is free.

Hosts: Betsy O'Connor and Sven Tilly
Rooms: 3 (SB) $60-75
Continental Breakfast
Credit Cards: None
Notes: 2, 5, 7, 9, 10, 11, 12

The Village Inn

92 Main Street, Route 6A, P. O. Box 1, 02675
(508) 362-3182

This charming sea captain's home built in 1795 has been an inn since 1946. Noted for cordial hospitality and comfortable rooms with private bath. Public rooms, screened porch, and shaded lawn. The inn is within easy walking distance of Cape Cod Bay, excellent restaurants, and antique shops.

Hosts: Mac and Esther Hickey
Rooms: 10 (8 PB; 2 SB) $40-85
Contintental Breakfast; Full Breakfast á la carte
Credit Cards: A, B
Notes: 2, 5, 6, 8, 9, 10, 11, 12, 14

Wedgewood Inn

83 Main Street, 02675
(508) 362-5157

Situated in the historic area of Cape Cod, the inn is in the National Register of Historic Places and has been featured in Country Inns of America. Near beaches, art galleries, antique shops, golfing, boating, and fine restaurants. Fireplaces and private screened porches.

Host: Milton Graham
Rooms: 6 (PB) $105-145
Full Breakfast
Credit Cards: A, B, C, E
Notes: 2, 5, 7 (restricted), 8 (over 10), 9, 10, 11, 12, 14

Wedgewood Inn

---

6 Pets welcome; 7 Smoking allowed; 8 Children welcome; 9 Social drinking allowed; 10 Tennis available; 11 Swimming available; 12 Golf available; 13 Skiing available; 14 May be booked through travel agents.

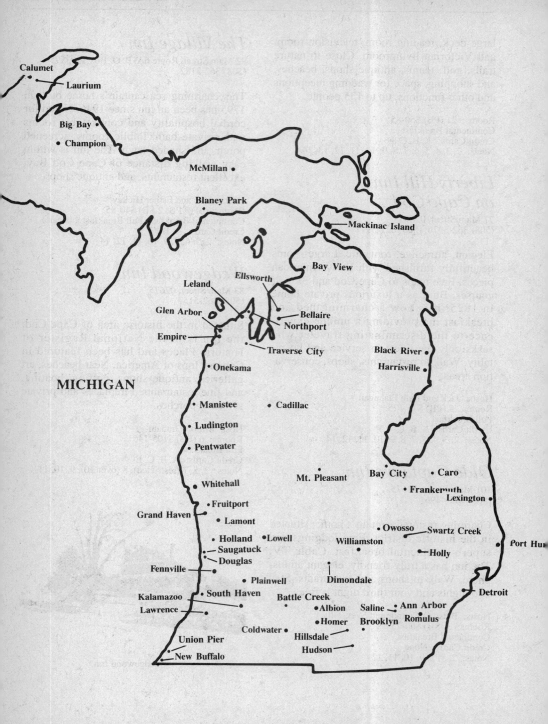

MICHIGAN

Calumet
Laurium

Big Bay
Champion

McMillan

Blaney Park

Mackinac Island

Bay View

Leland
Ellsworth
Bellaire
Northport

Glen Arbor

Empire

Traverse City

Black River
Harrisville

Onekama

Manistee
Cadillac

Ludington

Pentwater

Mt. Pleasant
Bay City
Caro

Frankenmuth
Lexington

Whitehall

Fruitport

Grand Haven
Lamont

Owosso
Swartz Creek

Holland
Lowell
Williamston
Holly

Saugatuck
Port Hu

Douglas

Fennville
Dimondale

Plainwell
Detroit

Kalamazoo
South Haven
Battle Creek
Saline
Ann Arbor

Lawrence
Albion
Brooklyn
Romulus

Homer

Coldwater
Hillsdale

Union Pier
Hudson

New Buffalo

Michigan

ALBION

Smith-White House Bed and Breakfast

401 East Porter Street, 49224
(517) 629-2220

Just one block from the Albion College campus, this 1867 Victorian home is furnished with antiques, handcrafted country pieces, and many original light fixtures. Oak woodwork and wood floors add charm to this Queen Anne home with air conditioning, phone, and color TV. Located midpoint between Chicago and Detroit just off I-94.

Hosts: Margaret Smith and Jill White
Rooms: 4 (3 SB) $48-65
Full Breakfast
Credit Cards: A, B
Notes: 2, 5, 6, 7, 8, 9, 10, 11, 12, 13

ANN ARBOR—SEE ALSO SALINE

Bed and Breakfast on Campus

921 East Huron, 48104
(313) 994-9100

Bed and Breakfast on Campus is housed in a unique contemporary building across the street from the University of Michigan campus and five university theaters. It is within walking distance to the hospital and Ann Arbor's cosmopolitan downtown area with diverse restaurants and theaters. It has a spacious common area and three elegantly furnished guest rooms with private baths. A full gourmet breakfast is served. Covered parking is provided at the main entrance.

Host: Viriginia Mikola
Rooms: 3 (3 PB) $55-75
Full Gourmet Breakfast
Credit Cards: A, B
Notes: 2, 3, 4, 5, 7 (on deck), 9, 10, 11, 12, 13, 14

The Urban Retreat

2759 Canterbury Road, 48104
(313) 971-8110

Comfortable 1950s ranch home on a quiet, tree-lined street, minutes from downtown and the University of Michigan campus. Rooms are furnished with antiques, old-fashioned wallpapers, and stained glass. Stretch your legs along the paths of the adjacent County Farm Park, 127 acres of meadowland. The Retreat has been designated a back yard wildlife habitat by the National Wildlife Federation.

Hosts: Andre Rosalik and Gloria Krys
Rooms: 2 (SB) $50
Full Breakfast
Credit Cards: None
Notes: 2, 5, 7, 9, 10, 11, 12, 13, 14

BATTLE CREEK

The Old Lamp-Lighter's

276 Capital Avenue NE, 49017
(616) 963-2603

Features of this magnificent Arts and Crafts-style home include: fifteen-inch-thick walls, clear clay French tile roof, porch roofs and house gutters of copper, quarry tile porch floor. The two-floor foyer

NOTES: Credit cards accepted: A Master Card; B Visa; C American Express; D Discover Card; E Diner's Club; F Other; 2 Personal Checks accepted; 3 Lunch available; 4 Dinner available; 5 Open all year; 6 Pets welcome; 7 Smoking allowed; 8 Children welcome; 9 Social drinking allowed; 10 Tennis available; 11 Swimming available; 12 Golf available; 13 Skiing available; 14 May be booked through travel agents.

features the original stenciled canvas with its background restored, an elegant open oak staircase, and a large stained-glass window on the west wall. The library features a fireplace flanked by shelves covered with leaded-glass doors depicting Aladdin's lamp. Close to the Y Center, Bailey Park, Kellogg Community College, McCamly Place, Civic Theatre, Kellogg Center Arena and Auditorium, shops, restaurants, and the linear parkway for walks and jogging.

Hosts: Perry and Joyce Warner
Rooms: 7 (PB)
Full Breakfast
Credit Cards: A, B, C, D
Notes: 2, 5, 8, 10, 12, 13 (XC), 14

BAY CITY

Stonehedge Inn Bed and Breakfast

924 Center Avenue (M-25), 48708
(517) 894-4342

Built by a lumber baron, this 1889 English Tudor home is indeed an elegant journey into the past. Original features include nine fireplaces, stained-glass windows, speaking tubes, and even a warming oven. Its magnificent open foyer with its grand oak staircase leads to eight bedrooms. Ideal for small weddings, parties, meetings. Corporate rates Sunday-Thursday.

Hosts: Ruth Koerber and John Kleekamp
Rooms: 7 (S3B) $60-85
Continental Plus Breakfast
Credit Cards: A, B, C, D
Notes: 2, 5, 7 (limited), 8, 9, 14

BAY VIEW

Terrace Inn

216 Fairview, Bay View; P.O. Box 266, Petoskey, 49770
(616) 347-2410; (800) 530-9898

The Terrace Inn, a late Victorian hotel built in 1911 and restored in 1987, retains the charm of the early 20th century. Solid wood paneling graces the lobby and dining room. Each of the 44 guest rooms is furnished in original period furniture and has its own private bath. There are no television sets or telephones in the rooms. In summer, guests may relax on the spacious front porch overlooking historic Bay View and in winter enjoy a book or a board game in front of the fireplace. The Terrace Inn is on the east side of Petoskey, near Little Traverse Bay.

Hosts: Patrick and Mary Lou Barbour
Rooms: 44 (PB) $42-96
Continental Breakfast
Credit Cards: A, B, C
Notes: 2, 4, 5, 7, 8, 10, 11, 12, 13, 14

BELLAIRE

Grass River Bed and Breakfast

5615 Grass River Road, 49615
(616) 533-6041

Situated 30 miles north of Traverse City, this home offers modern comfort in a natural environment. It is tucked in the woods of Antrim County on a chain of lakes, and the house is located just steps from its dock on the Grass River. Frequently visited by a variety of wildlife. Soothe your aches and pains away in the hot tub or relax in the glass sun room. Many activities and two ski resorts are just a few miles away.

Hosts: Harriett and Susan Beach
Rooms: 3 (PB) $85-95
Full Breakfast
Credit Cards: A, B
Notes: 2, 5, 9, 11, 12, 13,

BIG BAY

Big Bay Point Lighthouse

3 Lighthouse Road, 49808
(906) 345-9957

A registered working lighthouse. Boasts one-haf mile of Lake Superior shore, 50 wooded acres, groomed trails, 60-foot tower, five-acre lawn, mountain views.

Safari tours to waterfalls within the Huron Mountains, artisan center, hiking, skiing, and water sports.

Host: Linda Gamble
Rooms: 7 (5 PB, 2 SB) $95-165
Continental Breakfast
Credit Cards: None
Notes: 2, 5, 9, 10, 11, 13, 14

BLACK RIVER

Silver Creek Lodge Bed and Breakfast

4361 U.S. 23 South, 48721
(517) 471-2198

Spacious lodge and craft shop nestled on sixty tranquil acres that adjoin 5,200 acres of beautiful national forest. Step out the door and enjoy nature trails for hiking or cross-country skiing. Pick wild mushrooms or berries in season. View deer, turkey, and all forms of wildlife in a woodland setting where nature flourishes. No smoking. No pets.

Hosts: Gladys and Larry Farlow
Rooms: 4 (SB) $45-55
Full Breakfast
Credit Cards: None
Notes: 2, 5, 8

BLANEY PARK

Celibeth House

Blaney Park Road, Route 1, Box 58A, 49836
(906) 283-3409

The Celibeth House, built in 1895, offers eight lovely rooms. Each room is spacious, clean, and tastefully furnished. Guests may also enjoy the cozy livingroom, a guest reading room, enclosed quaint porch, and a lovely back porch overlooking 86 acres.

Host: Elsa Strom
Rooms: 8 (6 PB; 2 SB) $40-50
Continental Breakfast
Credit Cards: A, B, D
Open May 1-Dec. 1; by reservation only Dec. 1-
May
Notes: 2, 8, 9, 10, 13, 14

BROOKLYN

The Chicago Street Inn

219 Chicago Street, 49230
(517) 592-3888

An 1880s Queen Anne Victorian, in the heart of the Irish Hills. Furnished with family and area antiques. Antiquing, hiking, biking, swimming, shops, museums, and more are available. Area of quaint villages.

Hosts: Karen and Bill Kerr
Rooms: 4 (PB) $55-65
Full Breakfast
Expanded Continental Breakfast
Credit Cards: A, B
Notes: 2, 5, 7, 9, 10, 11, 12, 14

Dewey Lake Manor

11811 Laird Road, 49230
(517) 467-7122

This century-old house sits atop a knoll overlooking Dewey Lake in the Irish Hills of southern Michigan. Four guest rooms feature comfortable, country Victorian decor. A glass-enclosed porch facing the lake provides a pleasant place to enjoy breakfast or just to relax in the summertime. The common rooms include a parlor with piano and a sitting room. In summer enjoy croquet, volleyball, and picnics by the lake. In winter, ice skate or cross-country ski.

Host: The Phillips family
Rooms: 4 (PB) $50-65
Expanded Continental Breakfast
Credit Cards: A, B
Notes: 2, 5, 9, 11, 12, 14

CADILLAC

The Essenmacher's Bed and Breakfast

204 Locust Lane, 49601
(616) 775-3828

Waterfront home boasts spectacular sunsets over Lake Mitchell. Romantic beach bonfires under starry skies. There is a queen-size bed in each lakeside guest room. In the morning, a hearty continental breakfast is served in the common room, or lighter fare is served in bedroom. Well-decorated home within walking distance of bowling, golfing, shopping, and restaurants. Cross-country skiing and snowmobiling are at your doorstep. Downhill skiing minutes away. Guided boat tours available for nominal charge.

Hosts: Doug and Vickie Essenmacher
Rooms: 2 (PB) $55
Continental Breakfast
Credit Cards: A, B
Notes: 2, 5, 8, 10, 11, 12, 13

Hermann's European Hotel

214 North Mitchell Street, 49601
(616) 775-2101; (800) 354-1523

Upstairs from a three-star European cafe. Seven unique rooms that reflect European tastes but have all the American comforts. Large continental breakfast served to your room with the daily paper. Affordable summer rates; corporate rates available.

Host: Hermann J. Suhs
Rooms: 7 (PB) $50-85
Continental Breakfast
Credit Cards: A, B
Notes: 2, 3, 4, 5, 7 (limited), 8, 9, 10, 11, 12, 13, 14

CALUMET

Calumet House

1159 Calumet Avenue, P.O. Box 126, 49913
(906) 337-1936

The Calumet House is on the scenic, historic Keweenaw Peninsula. The house was built by the Calumet and Hecla Mining Company, circa 1895. It features original woodwork and antique furniture. Breakfast is served in the formal dining room, which has the original butler's pantry. Near Michigan Technological University and Suomi College.

Hosts: George and Rose Chivses
Rooms: 2 (SB) $25-30
Full Breakfast
Credit Cards: None
Notes: 2, 5, 9, 10, 11, 12, 13

CARO

Garden Gate Bed and Breakfast

315 Pearl Street, 48723
(517) 673-4823

Built with charm in the Cape Cod Colonial-style, Garden Gate Bed and Breakfast is a new home designed with its guests in mind. Antiques adorn every corner of its rooms. In a quiet residential area of Caro. In summer, the yard is full of flowers and shrubs, including a large planting of New England wildflowers. On cool evenings, guests can warm up by the fireplace that adds rustic charm to the livingroom.

Hosts: Jim and Evelyn White
Rooms: 4 (PB) $50 plus
Full Breakfast
Credit Cards: A, B
Notes: 2, 4, 5, 7 (limited), 8, 9, 10, 11, 12, 13 (XC)

CHAMPION

Michigamme Lake Lodge

P.O. Box 97, 49814
(906) 339-4400; (800) 358-0058

Experience the exclusive two-story grand lodge situated on the shore of Lake Michigamme and listed on the national and state registers of historical places. Built in 1934 of log construction and surrounded by birch trees, flower gardens, and the Peshkee River. All rooms are decorated with some original antiques. Breakfast is served on the sun porch or the dining room overlooking the lake. Sandy beach, swimming, canoeing, fishing, biking, hiking, and guide service available. Gifts and antique shopping on the premises. Package rates available.

NOTES: Credit cards accepted: A Master Card; B Visa; C American Express; D Discover Card; E Diner's Club; F Other; 2 Personal Checks accepted; 3 Lunch available; 4 Dinner available; 5 Open all year;

Hosts: Linda A. Stabile
Rooms: 9 (3 PB; 6 SB) $59-125
Full and Continental Breakfast
Credit Cards; A, B
Notes: 2, 5, 8, 11

COLDWATER

Batavia Inn

1824 West Chicago Road, US 12, 49036
(517) 278-5146

This 1872 Italianate country inn with original massive woodwork and high ceilings offers a restful charm. Seasonal decorations are a speciality, and an in-ground pool is available for guests to enjoy in the summer. Guests are pampered with evening turn-down and gourmet breakfast. Antique and discount shopping nearby. Recreation and acres of wildlife trails nearby.

Host: E. Fred Marquardt
Rooms: 5 (PB) $59-99
Full Breakfast
Credit Cards: None
Notes: 2, 5, 11

Chicago Pike Inn

215 East Chicago Street, 49036
(517) 279-8744

Turn-of-the-century renovated Colonial mansion adorned with antiques from the Victorian era. Six guest rooms with private baths, individually decorated for your pleasure and comfort. Formal dining room, library, and reception room featuring sweeping cherry staircase, parquet floors, and stained-glass window. Full country breakfast and seasonal refreshments served. Come and enjoy the restfulness of the inn.

Host: Rebecca Schultz
Rooms: 6 (PB) $75-130
Full Breakfast
Credit Cards: A, B, C
Notes: 2, 5, 7 (limited), 8 (over 12)

DETROIT

The Blanche House Inn

506 Parkview, 48214
(313) 822-7090

The Blanche House Inn and The Castle were built at the turn of the century and have been lovingly restored to their former elegance. They are decorated with post-Victorian antiques and each room has its own style. All guest rooms are equipped with private, free cable TV, phone, and bath or shower. Three rooms have hot tubs. Located just three and one-half miles from downtown Detroit and close to shopping in the suburbs.

Hosts: Mary-Jean and Sean Shannon
Rooms: 14 (PB) $60-120
Full Breakfast
Credit Cards: A, B, C, D
Notes: 2, 5, 8, 9, 14

DIMONDALE

Bannick's Bed and Breakfast

4608 Michigan Road, 48821
(517) 646-0224

Large ranch-style home features attractive decor throughout with stained-glass entrances. Almost three rural acres offer a quiet escape from the fast pace of the workaday world. Situated on a main highway (M99) five miles from Lansing and close neighbor to Michigan State University.

Hosts: Pat and Jim Bannick
Rooms: 2 (SB) $25-35
Full Breakfast
Credit Cards: None
Notes: 5, 8, 11, 12, 13

6 Pets welcome; 7 Smoking allowed; 8 Children welcome; 9 Social drinking allowed; 10 Tennis available; 11 Swimming available; 12 Golf available; 13 Skiing available; 14 May be booked through travel agents.

ELLSWORTH

The House on the Hill

Box 206, 49729
(616) 588-6304

A Victorian farmhouse near a quiet village overlooking the beautiful Chain of Lakes in the resort region of northern Michigan with year-round recreation and great dining. Antiquing, winery tours, and Mackinac Island are nearby. The five guest rooms are furnished with period antiques, queen-size beds, and all modern amenities. Share a delicious Texas breakfast with your hosts.

Hosts: Julie and Buster Arnim
Rooms: 5 (PB) $95-105
Full Breakfast
Credit Cards: A, B
Notes: 2, 8, 9, 10, 11, 12, 13

The House on the Hill

EMPIRE

Empire House Bed and Breakfast

11015 La Core, P.O. Box 203, 49630
(616) 326-5524

This 19th-century farmhouse is located in the beautiful Sleeping Bear Dunes Lakeshore area. Four rooms with outside entrances are available for guests, and guests are welcome to use the large screened porch. A quiet, homey atmosphere, fresh-ground coffee, and wonderful extended continental breakfast make this bed and breakfast worth visiting. Close to the beaches of Lake Michigan, golfing, tennis, hiking trails in the summer, and skiing trails in the winter.

Hosts: Harry and Rosemary Friend
Rooms: 4 (1 PB; 3 SB) $46.80
Continental Plus Breakfast
Credit Cards: None
Notes: 2, 5, 10, 11, 12, 13

FENNVILLE

Heritage Manor Inn

2253 Blue Star Highway, 49408
(616) 543-4384

Country hospitality is served daily in this lovely English manor and town houses. Enjoy homemade country breakfast, Jacuzzi, fireplace suites, indoor pool and whirlpool, volleyball, basketball, and canoeing with picnic lunch. Hiking and horseback riding nearby. Near Saugatuck and Lake Michigan. Ideal for family reunions and holiday retreats. Specializing in honeymoons and anniversaries.

Hosts: Ken and Ione
Rooms: 14; 3 town houses (PB) $65-130
Full Breakfast
Credit Cards: A, B, D
Notes: 2, 5, 7, 8, 9, 11, 12

Hidden Pond Bed and Breakfast

5975 128th Avenue, 49408
(616) 561-2491

Hidden Pond Bed and Breakfast is a quiet retreat set on 28 acres. Full gourmet breakfast included. Sunny breakfast porch, fireplace, library, and 60-foot deck for guests' exclusive use. Behind the house is a ravine with a pond, the perfect spot to relax and watch the wildlife. This lovely retreat is near the beaches of Lake Michigan, the boutiques of Saugatuck, and the winery and cider mill in Fennville.

Hosts: Larry and Priscilla Fuerst
Rooms: 2 (PB) $80-110
Full Breakfast

NOTES: Credit cards accepted: A Master Card; B Visa; C American Express; D Discover Card; E Diner's Club; F Other; 2 Personal Checks accepted; 3 Lunch available; 4 Dinner available; 5 Open all year;

Credit Cards: None
Notes: 2, 5, 9, 10, 11, 12, 13, 14

The Kingsley House

626 West Main Street, 49408
(616) 561-6425

An elegant Victorian inn on the edge of
Fennville, near Saugatuck, Holland, and
South Haven. The five guest rooms with
private baths are decorated in Victorian elegance. Honeymoon suite with Jacuzzi and
fireplace. Beaches, shopping, fine dining,
and a playhouse theater nearby. The
Allegan State Forest, with miles of nature
trails, is enjoyable to explore. Bicycles and
horse and buggy rides to the lake or winery
available. Country lover's delight. Featured
in *Innsider* magazine, *Great Lakes
Getaway*. Chosen Top 50 Inn in America
by *Inn Times*.

Hosts: David and Shirley Witt
Rooms: 6 (PB) $50-125
Full Breakfast
Credit Cards: A, B
Notes: 2, 3, 5, 9, 10, 11, 12, 13, 14

FRANKENMUTH

Bed and Breakfast at The Pines

327 Ardussi Street, 48734
(517) 652-9019

Frankenmuth, a Bavarian village, is
Michigan's number-one tourist attraction.
This ranch-style home is within walking
distance of tourist areas and famous restaurants. Bedrooms tastefully decorated with
heirloom quilts, antique accents, and ceiling fans. Enjoy homemade breads and rolls.
Beverage recipes shared. No smoking or
drinking.

Hosts: Richard and Donna Hodge
Rooms: 3 (1 PB; 2 SB) $37.80
Expanded Continental Breakfast
Credit Cards: None
Notes: 2, 5, 6, 8

The Kingsley House

FRUITPORT

Village Park Bed and Breakfast

60 West Park Street, 49415
(616) 865-6289

Overlooking the welcoming waters of
Spring Lake and Village Park where you
can picnic, play tennis, or use the boat
launch to enjoy Spring Lake with access to
Lake Michigan. Relaxing common area
with fireplace, decks. Historic setting of
mineral springs health resort. Tradition
continues with "Wellness Weekend" special package including complimentary massage, use of exercise facility, programs on
stress management, and creative visualiza-
tion. Serving Grand Haven and Muskegon
areas; Hoffmaster Park and Gillette Sand
Dune Nature Center nearby.

Hosts: John and Virginia Hewett
Rooms: 6 (PB) $50-65 (excluding special pack-
ages)
Full Breakfast
Credit Cards: A, B
Notes: 2, 5, 8, 10, 13, 14

6 Pets welcome; 7 Smoking allowed; 8 Children welcome; 9 Social drinking allowed; 10 Tennis available; 11
Swimming available; 12 Golf available; 13 Skiing available; 14 May be booked through travel agents.

GLEN ARBOR

Sylvan Inn

6680 Western Avenue, 49636
(616) 334-4333

The Sylvan Inn is a beautifully decorated historic landmark building situated in the heart of the Sleeping Bear Dunes National Lakeshore. Its easy access to Lake Michigan and other inland lakes makes a stay at the Sylvan Inn a unique experience.

Hosts: Jenny and Bill Olson
Rooms: 14 (7 PB; 7 SB) $60-110
Continental Breakfast
Credit Cards: A, B
Closed November, March, and April
Notes: 2, 8 (over 7), 9, 10, 11, 12, 13, 14

Sylvan Inn

GRAND HAVEN

Bouden House Inn Bed and Breakfast

301 South Fifth Street, 49417
(616) 846-3538

Built in 1874, this Victorian-style inn is located in the heart of Grand Haven within walking distance to shopping, restaurants, beach, and the boardwalk. Some rooms have fireplaces and balconies. Great kitchen and two common rooms are available for guests to use. Full homemade breakfast served in the beautiful dining room.

Hosts: Corrie and Berend Snoeyer
Rooms: 5 (PB) $55-85
Full Breakfast
Credit Cards: A, B, C
Notes: 2, 5, 8, 9, 10, 12, 13, 14

Harbor House Inn

114 South Harbor Drive, 49417
(800) 841-0610

Built in 1987, this luxurious Victorian-style inn overlooks Grand Haven's historic Lake Michigan harbor and the musical fountain. Fifteen rooms with air conditioning are available, all of which offer a private bath, and many of which have fireplaces and whirlpool bath tubs. Common rooms for meeting include library and gathering room, and the beach, shops, and restaurants are only a short walk away. Homemade breakfast buffet.

Hosts: Jim and Joyce Cole
Rooms: 15 (PB) $85-125
Continental Plus Breakfast
Credit Cards: A, B
Notes: 2, 5, 9, 11, 12, 13

Seascape Bed and Breakfast

20009 Breton, Spring Lake, 49456
(616) 842-8409

On private Lake Michigan beach, scenic lakefront rooms. Relax and enjoy the warm hospitality and cozy "country living" ambience of this nautical lakeshore home. Full country breakfast served in gathering room with fieldstone fireplace or on large wraparound deck. Both offer panoramic view of Grand Haven Harbor. Quiet residential setting. Stroll or cross-country ski through dune preserve. A charming retreat for all seasons.

Host: Susan Meyer
Rooms: 3 (PB) $75-90
Full Breakfast
Credit Cards: A, B
Notes: 2, 5, 9, 10, 11, 12, 13, 14
222 Fountain Northeast, 49503
(616) 458-6621

HARRISVILLE

Widow's Watch Bed and Breakfast

401 Lake Street, P.O. Box 245, 48740
(517) 724-5465

This romantic Victorian home built in 1866 by lumber baron George Colwell overlooks picturesque Harrisville Harbor on Michigan's unspoiled northeast coast. Shaded by century-old maples, a wrap-around porch lined with wicker furniture is a perfect place to enjoy summer breezes from Lake Huron. The four bedrooms are decorated in an antique country decor, and shopping, movie theaters and local restaurants are a leisurely walk to town.

Hosts: Bill and Becky Olson
Rooms: 4 (S3B) $52-65
Full Breakfast
Credit Cards: None
Notes: 2, 5, 6, 9, 11, 12, 13

HILLSDALE

Shadowlawn Manor Bed and Breakfast

84 Union Street, 49242-1332
(517) 437-2367

A brick Victorian built in 1863, this bed and breakfast has lots of gingerbread trim, spacious entrance hall, and a small iron fireplace that extends into the parlor providing warm oven heat for the area. Rooms are in various period-styles, including Victorian, turn-of-the-century, 1920s, and rattan and white wicker bedrooms. Five blocks from Hillsdale College and three blocks from downtown.

Host: Art Young
Rooms: 5 (2 PB; 4 SB) $50-60
Continental Plus Breakfast
Credit Cards: A, B
Notes: 2, 5, 9, 11, 12, 14

HOLLAND

Dutch Colonial Inn

560 Central Avenue, 49423
(616) 396-3664

An award-winning Dutch Colonial inn built in 1928 features elegant decor with 1930s furnishings and lovely heirloom antiques. All guest rooms have tiled private baths, some with whirlpool tub for two. Honeymoon suite available for that "special getaway." Attractions include excellent shopping, Hope College, bike paths, ski trails, and Michigan's finest beaches. Business people welcome; corporate rates available. Air conditioning. Open all year with special Christmas touches. Dutch hospitality at its finest.

Hosts: Bob and Pat Elenbaas
Rooms: 5 (PB) $60-125
Full Breakfast
Credit Cards: A, B, C, D
Notes: 2, 5, 10, 11, 12

McIntyre Bed and Breakfast

13 East 13th Street, 49423
(616) 392-9886

This lovely spacious older remodeled and modernized home was built in 1906. Three sunny, nicely decorated rooms offer very good beds and air conditioning. Family antiques are throughout the house, and there is ample off-street aprking. We give our guests lots of tender, loving care and hearty continental breakfast served in our dining room. Open all year. Near Hope College and downtown. No smoking, no pets, no children under five years old.

Hosts: Russ and Betty Jane McIntyre
Rooms: 3 (1 PB; 2 SB) $50
Continental Breakfast
Credit Cards: None
Notes: 2, 5, 8 (over 5)

The Parsonage

6 East 24th Street, 49423
(616) 396-1316

---

6 Pets welcome; 7 Smoking allowed; 8 Children welcome; 9 Social drinking allowed; 10 Tennis available; 11 Swimming available; 12 Golf available; 13 Skiing available; 14 May be booked through travel agents.

Experience a true European-style bed and breakfast near Hope College. Enjoy the peaceful elegance of the home built in 1908 as the parsonage for one of Holland's early churches. The inside glows with the warmth of rich oak woodwork, and leaded glass windows and authentic antique furnishings are found throughout. Two cozy sitting rooms, a summer porch, patio garden, and country kitchen with fireplace are available for guests to enjoy. Lake Michigan beaches, fine dining, art, theater, shopping, and golf are nearby. Five minutes to the convention center and Tulip City airport for business traveler's convenience. AAA approved.

Host: Bonnie Verwys
Rooms: 4 (2 PB; 2 SB) $65-90
Full Breakfast
Credit Cards: None
Notes: 2, 8 (over 10), 9, 10, 11, 12, 14

The Side Porch

HOLLY

The Side Porch Bed and Breakfast

120 College Street, 48442
(313) 634-0740

In Holly, known as the Village of Festivals, you are invited to enjoy this lovely 1800s Italianate-style home. The delightful guest rooms are tastefully decorated with antiques, collectibles, and fresh flowers. The home is within a pleasurable walking

distance of the village, where guests may enjoy quaint shops, antiquing, and gourmet dining. Guests also enjoy a continental-plus breakfast after coffee in their room.

Hosts: Sally and Dave Eyberse
Rooms: 2 (PB) $55-65
Expanded Continental Breakfast
Credit Cards: A, B
Closed Feb. 28-April 1
Notes: 9, 11, 12, 13

HOMER

Grist Mill Inn

310 East Main, 49245
(517) 568-4063

A late Victorian home in the heart of Michigan's antique country only a few minutes away from Marshall, the Williamsburg capital of the Midwest, and Allen, the self-styled antiques capital of Michigan. Featured in *The Great Country Inns of America Cookbook,* the inn is noted for its exceptional food and creative decorating. The newest addition, "Memories," has facilities for a series of workshops emphasizing quick and easy gourmet cooking and decorative arts.

Host: Judith Krupka
Rooms: 9 (PB) $55-95
Full Breakfast (weekends); Continental (weekdays)
Credit Cards: None
Notes: 2, 4, 5, 9, 12, 14

HUDSON

Baker Hill Bed and Breakfast

119 Tiger Drive, 49247
(517) 448-8536

Baker Hill was built in 1859 by one of historic Hudson's most prominent citizens. The home was a part of the Underground Railway. Country charm and hospitality prevail in this quiet and private setting. Hot tub, bicycles, swimming, walking, hiking, fishing, tennis, fine dining, antiques, and specialty shops are available. Eighteen

NOTES: Credit cards accepted: A Master Card; B Visa; C American Express; D Discover Card; E Diner's Club; F Other; 2 Personal Checks accepted; 3 Lunch available; 4 Dinner available; 5 Open all year;

miles to Michigan's International Speedway. Located eleven miles north of the Michigan-Ohio line, one block off I-27.

Hosts: Doug and Shirley Sprague
Rooms: 3 (SB) $45-60
Continental Plus Breakfast
Credit Cards: None
Notes: 2, 5, 6, 8, 9, 10, 11, 12

Sutton's Weed Farm Bed and Breakfast

18736 Quaker Road, 49247
(517) 547-6302; (800) VAN FARM

Visiting this seven-gable Victorian farmhouse, built in 1873, is like going back to Grandma's. Filled with family antiques. Situated on 180 acres of woods, trails, wildlife, birds, etc. Ancient maple trees are still tapped for syrup to be enjoyed at the breakfast table. Good restaurants nearby.

Hosts: Jack and Barb Sutton
Rooms: 4 (SB) $65
Full Breakfast
Credit Cards: A
Notes: 2, 5, 8, 9, 10, 11, 12, 14

KALAMAZOO

Stuart Avenue Inn

Bed and Breakfast
237 Stuart Avenue, 49007
(616) 342-0230

A full-service inn in two meticulously restored Victorian buildings in a registered historic district. Beautiful antiques and hand-printed wallpapers combine with modern amenities. Features more than an acre of gardens. Evening meals available on request. Near downtown, Western Michigan University, Kalamazoo College; 45 minutes from Lake Michigan. Ideal for business and pleasure travelers.

Hosts: The Casteels
Rooms: 16 (PB) $55-120
Continental Breakfast
Credit Cards: A, B, C, D, E
Notes: 2, 4, 5, 8, 9, 10, 11, 12, 13, 14

LAMONT

The Stagecoach Stop Bed and Breakfast

0-4819 Leonard Road West, P.O. Box 18, 49430
(616) 677-3940

The quaint and charming Grand River village of Lamont is the setting of this restored 1850s Gothic Revival home. Furnished with antiques and country primitives and once a stop for stagecoaches making trips between Grand Rapid, and Grand Haven, this bed and breakfast is just three minutes south off I-96. Crib available. Twenty-minute drive to both Grand Haven and Grand Rapids.

Hosts: Gene and Marcia Ashby
Rooms: 3 (1 PB; 2 SB) $55-65
Full Breakfast
Credit Cards; A, B
Notes: 2, 5, 8, 10, 11, 12, 13

LANESBORO

Historic Scanlan House Bed and Breakfast

708 Parkway Avenue South, 55949
(507) 467-2158; (800) 944-2158

An 1889 Victorian home on the National Register of Historic Places. Five large bedroom suites furnished with antiques. Original ornate wodwork and beautiful stained-glass windows. Three fireplaces and rooms with private and shared baths also whirlpool suites. Situated six blocks from te Root River, with canoeing, fishing, and tubing, and the 38-mile paved Root River Trail for biking, hiking, walking, rollerblading, and cross-country skiing. Tennis courts. An exquisite bed and breakfast. You will have the feeling of home. Complimentary champagne and chocolates. All rates include a famous five-course breakfast. Seen in the *Chicago Tribune* and the *Minneapolis Star Tribune*.

---

6 Pets welcome; 7 Smoking allowed; 8 Children welcome; 9 Social drinking allowed; 10 Tennis available; 11 Swimming available; 12 Golf available; 13 Skiing available; 14 May be booked through travel agents.

Hosts: The Mensings
Rooms: (3 PG; 2 SB) $55-125
Full Breakfast
Credit Cards: A, B, C
Notes: 2, 5, 8, 9, 10, 11, 12, 13, 14

LAURIUM

Laurium Manor Inn

320 Tamarack Street, 49913-2141
(906) 337-2549

Opulent 1905 mansion situated in the middle of Keweenaw Peninsula with 42 rooms in 13,000-square-feet of accommodations. Some unique features include hand-painted murals; embossed and gilded elephant hide and leather wall coverings; hand-carved oak fireplaces and staircases; built-in wall-size oak, tile, and marble ice box; gilded tile and marble fireplaces; and 1,000-square-feet of tiled porch. Activities and attractions available are skiing, snowmobiling, scuba diving, cycling, antiques, autumn colors, and ghost towns.

Hosts: Julie and Dave Sprenger
Rooms: 10 (8 PB; 2 SB) $39-99
Continental Breakfast
Credit Cards: A, B
Notes: 2, 5, 8, 9, 10, 12, 13, 14

LAWRENCE

Oak Cove Resort

58881 46th Street, 49064
(616) 674-8228

Historic lodge and cottages nestled in woods overlooking a beautiful lake in Michigan wine country. Rowboats, canoes, paddleboats, golf, heated pool, trails, games, bicycles, winery tour, scenic wine train, and flea market nearby. Meal plan and full package available. Turn-of-the-century lodge.

Hosts: Susan and Bob Wojcik
Rooms: 14 (7 PB; 7 SB) $85 plus tax
Full Breakfast
Credit Cards: None
Closed mid-Sept.-Memorial Day
Notes: 2, 3, 4, 8, 9, 10, 11, 12, 14

LELAND

Manitou Manor

Bed and Breakfast
P.O. Box 864, 49654
(616) 256-7712

Early 1900s farmhouse renovated throughout. Surrounded by cherry orchards and woods. A large livingroom with fireplace, sun porch, and formal dining room with traditional furnishings. Large guest rooms with queen-size beds and private baths. Country breakfast serving products indigenous to Leelanau County. Near Lake Michigan, Lake Leelanau, and Sleeping Bear Dunes National Lakeshore Park.

Hosts: Penny and Walt Mace
Rooms: 4 (PB) $85-90
Full Breakfast
Credit Cards: A, B
Notes: 2, 5, 9, 10, 11, 12, 13, 14

LEXINGTON

Centennial Bed and Breakfast

5774 Main Street, 48450
(313) 359-8762

Centennial is a warm and inviting home. Furnished in traditional styles, the house is bright and cheerful. You will enjoy a great night's sleep in the historically furnished bedrooms and wake to freshly brewed coffee and a homemade breakfast. Fresh fruits from the garden and orchard are served. A stay at Centennial is always special, and great pleasure is taken in sharing with you a piece of the romantic past. Come and unwind.

Hosts: Dilla and Dan Miller
Rooms: 4 (2 PB; 2 SB) $50-55
Full Breakfast
Credit Cards: None
Notes: 2, 5, 9, 10, 11, 12

NOTES: Credit cards accepted: A Master Card; B Visa; C American Express; D Discover Card; E Diner's Club; F Other; 2 Personal Checks accepted; 3 Lunch available; 4 Dinner available; 5 Open all year;

LOWELL

McGee Homestead

2534 Alden Nash Northeast, 49331
(616) 897-8142

Come to the country! Beautiful 110-year-old brick farmhouse surrounded by orchards and next to a golf course. Spacious guest rooms, livingroom with fireplace, and a small kitchen for your convenience. Enjoy rural Michigan in a true country farmhouse just like Grandma's.

Hosts: Bill and Ardie Barber
Rooms: 4 (PB) $33-48
Full Breakfast
Credit Cards: A, B
Notes: 2, 8, 9, 12

LUDINGTON

The Inn at Ludington

701 East Ludington Avenue, 49431
(616) 845-7055

Elegant accommodations in an 1889 Queen Anne Victorian mansion, appointed with treasured antiques and cherished collectibles. Fireplace rooms, bridal suite, and family suite. Situated "on the avenue" close to shopping, fine dining, and miles of Lake Michigan's sandy beach. Early morning coffee and homemade muffins in the parlor are followed by a sumptuous breakfast in the dining room. Enjoy custom-made getaway weekends all year—fishing, golfing, and diving packages—and a Dickens Christmas weekend in December. Dinner by prior arrangement.

Host: Diane Shields
Rooms: 6 (PB) $60-85
Full Breakfast
Credit Cards: A, B, C
Notes: 2, 3, 4, 5, 7 (limited), 8, 9, 10, 11, 12, 13, 14

The Ludington House 1878 Victorian Bed and Breakfast

501 East Ludington Avenue, 49431
(616) 845-7769; (800) 827-7869

With the car ferry, beaches, parks, marinas, fishing, hunting, and cross-country and downhill skiing only minutes away, this bed and breakfast specializes in service. Picnic baskets and bicycles are available for your use. Bridal suite is decorated in peach and cream colors with an Italian marble fireplace to accent the room. Group retreats and rates, corporate rates, conference facilities, and meeting rooms available.

Hosts: Patti and Bill Cunningham
Rooms: 9 (7 PB; 2 SB) $55-80
Full Breakfast
Credit Cards; A, B, C
Notes: 2, 5, 7 (limited), 8, 9, 10, 11, 12 13, 14

MACKINAC ISLAND

Cloghaun

P. O. Box 203, 49757
(906) 847-3885

Cloghaun, a large Victorian home built in 1884, is close to shops, restaurants, and ferry lines. The name *Cloghaun* is Gaelic and means "land of little stones." Built by Thomas and Bridgett Donnelly to house their large Irish family, the Cloghaun represents the elegance and ambience of a bygone era. The house is still owned by their descendants and has undergone recent renovations to bring it back to its original elegance.

Cloghaun

---

6 Pets welcome; 7 Smoking allowed; 8 Children welcome; 9 Social drinking allowed; 10 Tennis available; 11 Swimming available; 12 Golf available; 13 Skiing available; 14 May be booked through travel agents.

Hosts: James and Dorothy Bond
Rooms: 8 (6 PB; 2 SB) $50-95
Continental Breakfast
Credit Cards: None
Notes: 2, 8, 9, 10, 11, 12

Haan's 1830 Inn

Box 123, 49757
(906) 847-6244

Lovely restored Greek Revival home furnished with antiques and decorated from the period. In a quiet neighborhood three blocks from historic fort and 19th-century downtown. Dining room has 12-foot harvest table for breakfast of home-baked cakes and breads, plus cereals and fruit. A short ferry ride brings you to this historic and beautiful island. Sightseeing, bicycling, horseback riding, fine dining, tennis, golf, shopping nearby. Or sit on three porches and watch the horse-drawn carriages go by. Winter address: 1134 Geneva Street, Lake Geneva, Wisconsin 53147. Winter phone: (414) 248-9244.

Hosts: Nicholas and Nancy Haan; Vernon and Joy Haan
Rooms: 7 (5 PB; 2 SB) $75-105
Expanded Continental Breakfast
Credit Cards: None
Notes: 2, 8, 9, 10, 12
Notes: 2, 8, 12

MANISTEE

1879 E.E. Douville House

111 Pine Street, 49660
(616) 723-8654

Victorian home with ornate hand-carved woodwork, interior shutters, a soaring staircase, and elaborate archways with original pocket doors. Ceiling fans in every room. Lake Michigan beaches, fishing, golf, skiing, and historic buildings are nearby.

Hosts: Barbara and Bill Johnson
Rooms: 3 (SB) $40-45
Continental Breakfast
Credit Cards: None
Notes: 2, 5, 9, 10, 11, 12, 13

Inn Wick-a-te-wah

3813 Lakeshore Drive, 49660
(616) 889-4396

Enjoy the spectacular sunsets and beautiful views of Portage Lake and Lake Michigan channel in a quiet, relaxing setting. Lakeside living with swimming, sailing, fishing, nearby golf and shopping. The inn has light, airy bedrooms with unusual period furnishings. Enjoy breakfast and lounging on the decks, screen porch, sun parlor with wood-burning stove, or livingroom with fireplace.

Hosts: Len and Marge Carlson
Rooms: 4 (1 PB; 3 SB) $50-70
Full Breakfast
Credit Cards: A, B
Closed Jan. 2-Mar. 31
Notes: 2, 8, 9, 10, 11, 12, 13, 14

MARQUETTE

Michigamme Lake Lodge

2403 U.S. 41 West, 49855
(906) 225-1393; (906) 339-4400

A historic landmark, this two-story grand lodge is situated on the shore of Lake Michigamme. Log construction built in 1934, surrounded by birch trees, flower gardens, and the Peshekee River. Large room to gather in with a two-and-one-half-story fireplace. All rooms decorated have down quilts. Gift and antique shop on property. Situated 30 miles west of Marquette. Sandy beach, swimming, fishing, hiking trails, biking, and guided historical tour of the area available.

Host: Linda Stubile
Rooms: 9 (3 PB; 6 SB) $100-125
Full Breakfast
Credit Cards: A, B
Notes: 2, 8, 11

MCMILLAN

Helmer House Inn

Rural Route 3, County Road 417, 49853
(906) 586-6119

NOTES: Credit cards accepted: A Master Card; B Visa; C American Express; D Discover Card; E Diner's Club; F Other; 2 Personal Checks accepted; 3 Lunch available; 4 Dinner available; 5 Open all year;

Designated a Michigan historical site, built in the late 1800s as a mission for early settlers. Original and antique furnishings adorn this beautifully restored bed and breakfast. Nestled between two lakes with access to Big Manistique Lake by Helmer Creek. Five guest rooms, a common parlor, and a lovely dining room invite guests to enjoy their stay. Specializes in home-cooked meals, including Helmer's shrimp, frog legs, grilled breast of chicken, and whitefish dinners. Lunch and dinner seasonal.

Hosts: Guy and Imogene Teed
Rooms: 5 (SB) $36-55
Full Breakfast
Credit Cards; A, B
Notes: 2, 3, 4, 7, 8, 11, 12, 14

MT. PLEASANT

Country Chalet

723 South Meridian Road, 48858
(517) 772-9259

Enjoy peaceful times at the Country Chalet, a comfortable, Bavarian-style home. Its 18 acres of rolling pasture, ponds, and woods are playgrounds to wild animals and birds to provide memorable moments. Awake to delightful sounds of nature, smell Carolyn's freshly baked goodies, and delight in the scrumptious breakfast buffet. Feel free to share your unique experiences in travel, family, education, and future plans.

Hosts: Ron and Carolyn Lutz
Rooms: 3 (SB) $49-59
Full Breakfast
Credit Cards: None
Notes: 5, 7 (limited), 8, 9

NEW BUFFALO

Sans Souci Euro Inn

19265 South Lakeside Road, 49117
(616) 756-3141; FAX (616) 756-5511

A lushly landscaped estate one-third encompassed by Lake Sans Souci and other water bodies. Sans Souci means "without care or worries." Classic European design characterizes each interior in two- and three-bedroom homes and suites. Individual air control, all king beds, private baths, whirlpools, fireplaces, TV, VCR, phones, audio systems, microwave, and refrigerator offer modern comfort. Six guest rooms, two suites, also two- or three-bedroom homes for a party of four or more. Nature and waterfowl become your neighbor where the sun rises over Lake Sans Souci and sets over Lake Michigan.

Hosts: Angelika Siewert and family
Rooms: 8 (PB) $95-160
Full Breakfast
Credit Cards: A, B, C
Notes: 2, 5, 7 (limited), 8, 9, 11, 13, 14

NORTHPORT

Wood How

15311 East Camp Road
(616) 386-7194

Enjoy the cabin-peaceful atmosphere of an environment that offers a unique experience in a return to a more quiet, relaxed time. Wood How is an authentic log lodge located in a secluded 10 acres of hardwood forest at the tip of the Leelanau Peninsula in beautiful northern Michigan.

Hosts: Kay and Charley Peak
Doubles: 3 (PB) $75
Full Breakfast
Credit Cards: None
May 15 - Oct. 15
Notes: 2, 7, 9

ONEKAMA

Lake Breeze House

5089 Main Street, 49675-0301
(616) 889-4969

6 Pets welcome; 7 Smoking allowed; 8 Children welcome; 9 Social drinking allowed; 10 Tennis available; 11 Swimming available; 12 Golf available; 13 Skiing available; 14 May be booked through travel agents.

Two-story frame house overlooking Portage Lake, where guests share the family bath, livingroom, and breakfast room. Each room has its own special charm of family antiques. Come relax and enjoy the back porch and the sounds of the babbling creek with your full breakfast. Reservations and deposit required.

Hosts: Bill and Donna Erickson
Rooms: 3 (SB) $55-65
Full Breakfast
Credit Cards: None
Notes: 2, 10, 11, 12, 13

OWOSSO

R&R Farm-Ranch

308 East Hibbard Road, 48867
(517) 723-3232; (517) 723-2553

A newly remodeled farmhouse from the early 1900s, the Rossman's ranch sits on 150 acres overlooking the Maple River Valley. Rossman's large concrete circular drive and white board fences lead to stables of horses and cattle. Guests may use the family parlor, game room, and fireplace or stroll about the gardens and pastures along the river. Breakfast is served in the dining room or outside on the deck. Children and pets are welcome. No smoking.

Hosts: Carl and Jeanne Rossman
Rooms: 2 (SB) $35-45
Continental Breakfast
Credit Cards: None
Notes: 2, 5, 6, 8, 13 (XC)
(616) 843-1888

PENTWATER

Historic Nickerson Inn

262 West Lowell, Box 109, 49449
(616) 869-6731

Since 1914, historic Nickerson Inn and Restaurant has been a place of hospitality for the business or vacation guest. Ten guest rooms all with private bath and air conditioning. One block away, you will find the beaches of Lake Michigan and Pentwater Lake. The small village of Pentwater has quaint shops, three marinas, and dunes of the state park.

Hosts: Harry and Gretchen Shiparski
Rooms: 10 (PB) $65-95
Full Breakfast
Credit Cards: A, B, C, D
Notes: 2, 4, 5, 8 (over 12), 9, 10, 11, 12, 13, 14

Pentwater Inn

180 East Lowell, Box 98, 49449
(616) 869-5909

Charming 1880s home full of antiques, quilts, and teddy bears. Walking distance to town, beautiful Lake Michigan beach, charter boats, and international shopping. Cross-country skiing just outside the village. Cable TV, game table, and hot tub. Weekly rates.

Hosts: Sue and Dick Hand
Rooms: 5 (SB) $50-60
Full Breakfast
Credit Cards: A, B
Notes: 2, 5, 8 (over 10), 9, 10, 11, 12, 13

PLAINWELL

The 1882 John Crispe House Bed and Breakfast

404 East Bridge Street, 49080
(616) 685-1293

Museum quality Victorian elegance and elaborate original gaslight fixtures and plaster moldings complement this home's fine Victorian furnishings. Situated between Kalamazoo and Grand Rapids and within walking distance of some of Michigan's finest gourmet dining and antique districts, the two-and one-half-acre parklike grounds on the banks of the Kalamazoo River offer a relaxing atmosphere for guests to enjoy.

Host: Ormand J. Lefever
Rooms: 5 (3 PB; 2 SB) $55-95
Full Breakfast
Credit Cards: A, B
Notes: 2, 5, 10, 12, 13

NOTES: Credit cards accepted: A Master Card; B Visa; C American Express; D Discover Card; E Diner's Club; F Other; 2 Personal Checks accepted; 3 Lunch available; 4 Dinner available; 5 Open all year;

PORT HURON

The Victorian Inn

1229 Seventh Street, 48060
(313) 984-1437

Fine dining and guest rooms in an authentically restored Victorian. One hour north of metropolitan Detroit, this fine inn has a timeless ambience matched by its classic, creative cuisine, gracious service, and thoughtful wine list. All food and beverages are prepared with utmost attention to detail. Cozy pub on the lower level.

Hosts: Lewand Lynne Secory; Ed and Vicki
   Peterson
Rooms: 4 (2 PB; 2 SB) $55-65
Continental Breakfast
Credit Cards: A, B, C, D, E, F
Notes: 2, 3, 4, 5, 7, 9, 10, 11, 12, 13

ROMULUS

Country Lane Bed and Breakfast

32285 Sibley Road, 48174
(313) 753-4586

Modern Cape Cod-style farmhouse on a twenty-acre farm has ample off-street parking. A full country-style breakfast is served featuring homemade specialties. Large, comfortable rooms with TV and air conditioning invite guests to settle in, and wooded trails and picnic facilities are nearby. Five minutes from Detroit, Metro airport, 20 minutes to Detroit, Ann Arbor, Windsor, and the Henry Ford Museum/Greenfield Village. Package specials available.

Hosts: J. and V. LaRoy
Rooms: 2 (SB) $40-45
Full Breakfast
Credit Cards: None
Notes: 2, 5, 8, 9, 12, 14

SALINE

The Homestead Bed and Breakfast

9279 Macon Road, 48176
(313) 429-9625

You will feel at home in this traditional bed and breakfast, which is truly a very comfortable place, mixing country and Victorian elegance. On a 50-acre farm, just minutes from downtown Ann Arbor and Ypsilanti, 30 minutes from Greenfield Village, the 1851 brick farmhouse is filled with both antique furnishings and peace. Walk or cross-country ski, read, or just relax. Tennis and golf close by. Wine and cheese served 5:00 to 7:00 p.m.

Host: Shirley Grossman
Rooms: 6 (1 PB; 5 SB) $50-65
Full Breakfast
Credit Cards: A, B, C, E
Notes: 2, 5, 7, 9, 13, 14

SAUGATUCK

Maplewood Hotel

728 Butler Street, P.O. Box 1059, 49453
(616) 857-1771

The Maplewood Hotel architecture is unmistakably Greek Revival. Some rooms have fireplaces and double Jacuzzi tubs. Other areas include a library, dining room, lounge, sun room, screened porch, and lap pool. Situated in downtown Saugatuck, within walking distance to all shops and restaurants.

Hosts: Catherine L. Simon and Sam Burnell
Rooms: 15 (PB) $65-155
Full Breakfast; Sunday Brunch
Credit Cards: A, B, C
Notes: 2, 5, 8, 9, 10, 11, 12, 13, 14

The Park House

888 Holland Street, 49453
(616) 857-4535

6 Pets welcome; 7 Smoking allowed; 8 Children welcome; 9 Social drinking allowed; 10 Tennis available; 11 Swimming available; 12 Golf available; 13 Skiing available; 14 May be booked through travel agents.

Saugatuck's oldest residence (1857) hosted Susan B. Anthony. Summer guests enjoy Lake Michigan, short walks to town, and air conditioning. Winter guests relax fireside with Jimmy the dog curled at their feet. Tulip Festival, Victorian Christmas, Grand Escapes are favorites.

Hosts: Lynda and Joe Petty
Rooms: 8 (PB) $79.50-169.60
Continental Breakfast
Credit cards: A, B, D
Notes: 2, 5, 7 (limited), 9, 10, 12, 13, 14

The Red Dog Bed and Breakfast

132 Mason Street, 49453
(616) 857-8851

At this comfortable place in the heart of Saugatuck, you are steps away from shopping, restaurants, art galleries, marinas, and all the year-round activities that have made this harbor village the "Cape Cod of the Midwest." Built in 1879, the Red Dog features a mix of contemporary and antique furnishings. No minimum stay requirement on weekends. Children welcome.

Hosts: Daniel Indurante, Kristine Richter, Gary Kott
Rooms: 7 (5 PB: 2 SB) $55-80
Continental Breakfast
Credit Cards: A, B, D
Notes: 2, 5, 8, 9, 10, 11, 12, 13, 14

Rosemont Inn

Rosemont Inn

83 Lakeshore Drive, Douglas; P. O. Box 214, 49453
(616) 857-2637

This Victorian home, built in 1886, offers 14 delightful rooms, each with private bath and air conditioning. Nine rooms feature gas fireplaces. Four common rooms, two with fireplaces. There is a heated pool. Public beach on Lake Michigan across the street. Unique shopping, charter fishing, golfing, and cross-country skiing are nearby.

Hosts: Joseph and Marilyn Sajdak
Rooms: 14 (PB) $55-105
Continental Breakfast
Minimum stay weekends May 1-Oct. 31: 2 nights
Credit Cards: A, B, D
Notes: 2, 5, 8, 9, 10, 11, 12, 13

Sherwood Forest Bed and Breakfast

938 Center Street, Douglas; P.O. Box 315, 49453
(616) 857-1246

Surrounded by woods, this beautiful Victorian-style house was built in the 1890s. Each of the five bedrooms has a private bathroom and queen-size bed, which adds twentieth-century comforts to the traditionally furnished rooms. There is a heated swimming pool and patio, and the eastern shore of Lake Michigan and a public beach are one-half block away.

Hosts: Keith and Susan Sharak
Rooms: 5 (PB) $75-105
Continental Breakfast
Credit Cards: A, B
Notes: 2, 5, 8, 10, 11, 12, 13, 14

Twin Gables Country Inn

900 Lake Street, 49453
(616) 857-4346

Built in 1865, this state historic inn is rich in history, having undergone several changes of function. Recently restored, it features 14 charming guest rooms with private baths and antiques. Swimming pool, indoor hot tub, air conditioning, fireplace.

NOTES: Credit cards accepted: A Master Card; B Visa; C American Express; D Discover Card; E Diner's Club; F Other; 2 Personal Checks accepted; 3 Lunch available; 4 Dinner available; 5 Open all year;

Hosts: Michael and Denise Simcik
Rooms: 14 (PB) $44-99.34
Continental Breakfast
Minimum stay weekends: 2 nights; holidays: 3
  nights
Credit Cards: A, B
Notes: 2, 5, 8 (over 5), 9, 10, 11, 12, 13

SAULT ST. MARIE

The Water Street Inn

140 East Water Street, 49783
(906) 632-1900; (800) 236-1904

This restored 1900's Queen Anne home is
graced by Tiffany windows, orginal woodwork, and Italian marble fireplaces. The
guestrooms are individually decorated with
lovely antiques and have private baths.
Guests may relax in the parlor, on the wrap
around porch, or in the gazebo that overlooks St. Mary's River. The inn is just one
and one-half blocks from Soo Locks and is
within walking distance of restaurants and
other tourist attractions.

Hosts: Phylis and Greg Walker
Rooms: 4 (PB) $70-85
Continental Breakfast
Credit Cards: A, B
Notes: 2, 7, 12, 13

SOUTH HAVEN

A Country Place

Bed and Breakfast
Route 5, Box 43, North Shore Drive, 49090
(616) 637-5523

Our traditional homestay bed and breakfast
is an 1860's Greek Revival situated on five
and one-half acres of woodland, two miles
from the center of town and one block to
Lake Michigan beach. The English country
theme throughout is created by the use of
pretty prints, floral arrangements, and
antique furnishings. The cozy common area
features a wood-burning fireplace and
entertainment center. Warm days are

enjoyed on the spacious deck or gazebo.
Leisurely breakfasts feature home-baked
goodies and lots of fresh fruit.

Hosts: Art and Lee Niffenegger
Rooms: 5 (PB) $65-75
Full Breakfast
Credit Cards: A, B
Notes: 2, 5, 9, 14

Ross House

Bed and Breakfast
229 Michigan Avenue, 49090
(616) 637-2256

The historic Ross House was built in 1886
by lumber tycoon Volney Ross. It sits on a
quiet tree-lined street on the south side of
the Black River. Lake Michigan public
beaches, downtown shopping area, Kal-
Haven Trail, and many fine restaurants are
only blocks away.

Hosts: Cathy Hormann and Brad Wilcox
Rooms: 7 (1 PB; 6 S3B) $45-55
Full Breakfast (weekends)
Credit Cards: None
Notes: 2, 5, 9, 10, 11, 12, 13 (XC)

Yelton Manor

140 North Shore Drive, 49090
(616) 637-5220

An elegant, gracious Victorian miniman-
sion on the sandy shore of beautiful Lake
Michigan. Eleven gorgeous rooms, all with
private bath, some with Jacuzzis. Plentiful
common areas, two salons with fireplaces,
cozy wing chairs, floral carpets, four-poster
beds, lovely antiques, a wicker porch
retreat, and a pampering staff set the tone
for relaxation and romance. Enjoy wonderful breakfasts, day-long treats, and evening
hors d'oeuvres. You will never want to
leave!

Hosts: Elaine and Rob
Rooms: 11 (PB) $95-180
Full Breakfast
Credit Cards: A, B, C
Notes: 2, 5, 9, 11, 13

6 Pets welcome; 7 Smoking allowed; 8 Children welcome; 9 Social drinking allowed; 10 Tennis available; 11
Swimming available; 12 Golf available; 13 Skiing available; 14 May be booked through travel agents.

STURGIS

Christmere House Inn

110 Pleasant, 49091
(616) 651-8303; (800) 874-1882

Lovely Queen Anne house, perfect for the romantic who enjoys fine food and special weekends, as well as the business traveler. Wonderful features are five fireplaces, stained-glass windows, and rooms of lovely antiques. Nice drive from Detroit and Chicago in the heart of Amish country. Private baths and hot tubs.

Host: Janette Parr Johns
Rooms: 14 (PB) $62-85
Full Breakfast
Credit Cards: A, B
Notes: 2, 3, 4, 5, 8, 9, 10, 11, 12, 14

SWARTZ CREEK

Pink Palace Farms Bed and Breakfast

6095 Baldwin Road, 48473
(313) 655-4076

This estate is a working dairy farm on the National Register of Historic Places. The house, built in 1888, is furnished with many antiques. It is surrounded by 300 acres of fields, streams, and wooded lots. There is a small spring-fed lake for picnics and fishing. The barns and silos are nearby. It is all for your access and enjoyment. It is also near Flint for city activities.

Hosts: Blaine and Jeannette Pinkston
Rooms: 3 (1 PB; 2 SB) $39.50-45
Full Breakfast
Credit Cards: None
Notes: 2, 8, 9, 10, 11, 12, 13, 14

TRAVERSE CITY

Cider Ho.use

5515 Barney Road, 49684
(616) 947-2833

The emphasis here is on the simple, warm country life, as you awake to the smell of apple blossoms in the spring and juicy apples in the fall. Relax and enjoy cider or homemade Scottish shortbread and tea on the front porch of this contemporary inn overlooking an orchard. Or relax in front of the fireplace in winter.

Hosts: Ron and Nan Tennant
Rooms: 5 (PB) $65-75
Full Breakfast
Credit Cards: None
Closed Thanksgiving and Christmas Day
Notes: 2, 5, 9, 10, 11, 12, 13, 14

The Victoriana 1898

622 Washington Street, 49684
(616) 929-1009

Touch a bit of history and feel a welcoming warmth that will be long remembered when you stay at this classic Victorian treasure. Magnificently crafted with tiled fireplaces, bubble-glass windows, fretwork, oak staircase, gazebo, and two-story carriage house. Located in a quiet historic district close to West Grand Traverse Bay and downtown. Very special breakfasts. Featured in "Lodgings We Like," *Midwest Living*.

Hosts: Flo and Bob Schermerhorn
Rooms: 3 (PB) $55-70
Full Breakfast
Credit Cards: A, B
Notes: 2, 5, 14

Warwickshire Inn

5037 Barney Road, 49684
(616) 946-7176

This stunning turn-of-the-century gem sits on a hill next to an antique shop just minutes from downtown Traverse City. Famous for its family-style breakfast elegantly served on fine Wedgewood china and sterling silver in a dining room overlooking rolling hills. Air conditioning. Private baths.

Host: Dan Warwick
Rooms: 2 (PB) $55-65
Full Breakfast
Credit Cards: A, B
Notes: 2, 5, 9, 14

NOTES: Credit cards accepted: A Master Card; B Visa; C American Express; D Discover Card; E Diner's Club; F Other; 2 Personal Checks accepted; 3 Lunch available; 4 Dinner available; 5 Open all year;

UNION PIER

The Inn at Union Pier

9708 Berrien Street, P.O. Box 222, 49129
(616) 469-4700

An elegantly refurbished inn blending bare-foot informality with all the comforts of a well-appointed country home. Enjoy the gardens and courtyard. Lake Michigan is across the street. Most rooms have porches or balconies and Swedish fireplaces. Relax in the sauna or outdoor hot tub. Linger over the hearty homemade breakfasts. The Veronda room accommodates meetings, Featured in *Brides, Midwest Living, Travel and Leisure* and *Chicago* magazines.

Hosts: Madeleine and Bill Reinke; Libby Johnston
Rooms: 15 (PB) $95-140
Full Breakfast
Credit Cards: A, B, D
Notes: 2, 5, 7, 9, 10, 11, 12, 13

The Inn at Union Pier

Pine Garth Inn and Cottages

15790 Lakeshore Road, P.O. Box 347, 49129
(616) 469-1642

The Pine Garth Inn and Cottages is nestled on the shores of Lake Michigan in a heavily wooded area of summer houses within the village of Union Pier. Steps and spacious decks lead to 200 feet of private sugar-sand beach. The inn is completely renovated and designer-decorated with walls of windows overlooking the lake.

Also available are five cottages with kitchens, fireplaces, hot tubs and a private walkway and decks to the beach.

Hosts: Russ and Paula Bulin; Sandy Marske
Rooms: 7 (PB) $105-140
Cottages: $195-225
Full Breakfast (Inn only)
Credit Cards: A, B, C
Notes: 2, 5, 8 (cottages), 9, 10, 11, 12, 13, 14

WHITEHALL

The Timekeepers Inn

303 Mears Avenue, 49461
(616) 894-5169; FAX (616) 893-2528

Beautiful century-old home with screened porch, spacious rooms furnished with antiques. Warm, comfortable, quiet atmosphere year-round. Two blocks from shops and restaurants, one block from White Lake, directly across from Fine Arts Summer Playhouse. Also features clock shop specializing in antique clock restoration.

Hosts: Michael and Marjie Bronsink
Rooms: 4 (PB) $60
Expanded Continental Breakfast
Credit Cards: A, B, C, D
Notes: 2, 5, 9, 10, 11, 12, 13

WILLIAMSTON

Williamston Bed and Breakfast

3169 South Williamstown Road, 48895
(517) 655-1061

Your hosts welcome you to the comfort and charm of country living, while having easy access to Lansing, Michigan State University, and many small towns known for antique shops and artisans. Try to do everything, or do nothing at all—you will thoroughly enjoy the ambience of this early 1900s homestead.

Hosts: Colleen and Bob Stone
Rooms: 3 (2 SB) $43-50
Continental Plus Breakfast
Credit Cards: A, B

6 Pets welcome; 7 Smoking allowed; 8 Children welcome; 9 Social drinking allowed; 10 Tennis available; 11 Swimming available; 12 Golf available; 13 Skiing available; 14 May be booked through travel agents.

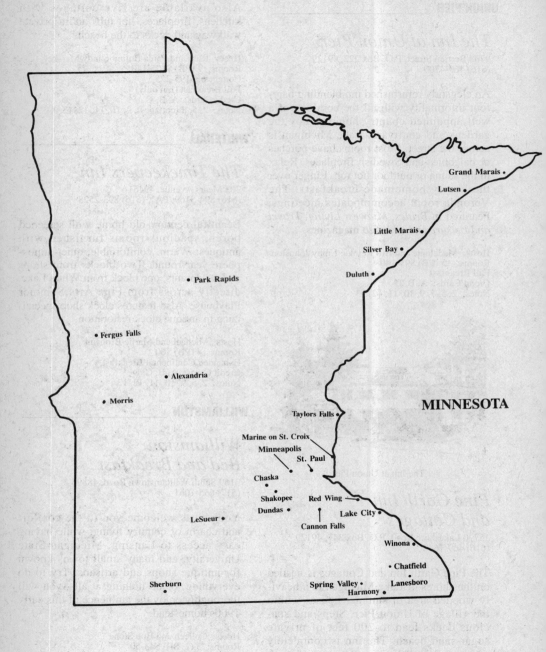

Grand Marais •

Lutsen •

Little Marais •

Silver Bay •

Duluth •

Park Rapids •

MINNESOTA

Fergus Falls •

• Alexandria

• Morris

Taylors Falls •

Marine on St. Croix •

Minneapolis •

St. Paul •

Chaska •

Shakopee •   Red Wing —

Dundas •   Lake City •

LeSueur •   Winona •

Cannon Falls •

• Chatfield

Spring Valley •   Lanesboro •

Sherburn •   Harmony •

Minnesota

ALEXANDRIA

Carrington House Bed and Breakfast

Route 5, Box 88, 56308
(612) 846-7400

Single-level home built in 1911, with 200 feet of lakeshore along Lake Carlos. Quiet, informal elegance, antiques, and wicker. Two acres of lawn, trees, and lakeside patio area for your enjoyment. The six-foot fireplace in the livingroom and the wood-burning stove on the lakeside sun room offer cozy warmth and relaxation on crisp fall nights and sparkling snowy days. Private baths. Separate honeymoon cottage with queen bed and double whirlpool tub.

Host: Joan Pease
Rooms: 5 (PB) $55-90
Full Breakfast
Credit Cards: A, B
Notes: 2, 5, 7, 9, 10, 11, 12, 13, 14

CANNON FALLS

Quill and Quilt

615 West Hoffman Street, 55009
(507) 263-5507; (800) 488-3849

Colonial Revival house (1897). Oak woodwork and spacious, airy common areas. Decorated with delicate wallpapers, Early American stenciling, antiques, and handmade quilts. Four guest rooms. Private baths. One suite with double whirlpool. Full breakfast, evening sweet. Near biking, hiking, skiing, and antiquing. Midweek rates; gift certificates.

Hosts: Denise Anderson and David Karpinski
Rooms: 4 (PB) $45-105
Full Breakfast
Credit Cards: A, B
Notes: 2, 5, 7 (limited), 9, 10, 11, 12, 13, 14

CHASKA

Bluff Creek Inn

1161 Bluff Creek Drive, 55318
(612) 445-2735

Antique-filled country farmhouse, circa 1860, and Hollyhock Cottage are set on the bluffs of the Minnesota River surrounded by wildflowers, fields, and forests. Five romantic guest rooms, all of which have private water closets, are available for guests, and a gourmet three-course breakfast is served in the morning. Close to dinner theaters, gambling casino, race track, and arboretum. Renaissance Festival and many hiking, biking, and cross-country trails.

Hosts: Ann and Gary Delaney
Rooms: 5 (PB) $65-150
Full Breakfast
Credit Cards: A, B
Notes: 2, 5, 9

CHATFIELD

Lunds' Guest House

500 Winona Street, 55923
(507) 867-4003

Charming 1920 bungalow furnished with 1920s and 1930s furniture. Quaint kitchen, dining room, livingroom with fireplace, TV, old electric organ. Large screened

NOTES: Credit cards accepted: A Master Card; B Visa; C American Express; D Discover Card; E Diner's Club; F Other; 2 Personal Checks accepted; 3 Lunch available; 4 Dinner available; 5 Open all year; 6 Pets welcome; 7 Smoking allowed; 8 Children welcome; 9 Social drinking allowed; 10 Tennis available; 11 Swimming available; 12 Golf available; 13 Skiing available; 14 May be booked through travel agents.

front porch and small screened back porch. A quiet escape just 20 miles from Rochester and 100 miles from Minneapolis. Four rooms with 3 1/2 baths are available, or the entire house.

Hosts: Shelby and Marion Lund
Rooms: 4 (PB) $55-65 plus tax
Continental Breakfast
Credit Cards: A, B
Notes: 2, 5, 7 (outside), 8, 9, 10, 11, 12, 13

DULUTH

Barnum House Bed and Breakfast

2211 East Third Street, 55812
(218) 724-5434; (800) 879-5437

An elegant haven in Duluth's historic East End. Built in 1910, it is surrounded by stately mansions of historic and architectural significance. Situated on a quiet cul-de-sac with wooded ravine and brook. Refreshing retreat for those seeking history, quality, and luxury. Museum-quality antiques throughout, king/queen antique bedrooms with fireplaces, verandas, and private baths. Barnum House provides breakfasts that are as distinctive as the guests. Whatever the season, indulge in a delicious full breakfast with fresh fruit, muffins and breads, main entree, and gourmet coffee or tea.

Hosts: Dorothy and Dick Humes; Susan Watt
Rooms: 5 (PB) $95-115
Full Breakfast
Credit Cards: A, B
Notes: 2, 5, 13

DUNDAS

Martin Oaks Bed and Breakfast

107 First Street, 55019
(507) 645-4644

A Victorian Italianate home near the Cannon River, built in 1869, has been restored and is furnished throughout with antiques. Elegant breakfasts and check-in teas accompanied by storytelling. Golf, hiking, biking, swimming, fishing, antiques, and bookstore browsing nearby.

Hosts: Marie and Frank Gery
Rooms: 3 (SB) $65
Full Breakfast
Credit Cards: A, B
Notes: 2, 4, 5, 9, 10, 11, 12, 13

FERGUS FALLS

Bakketopp Hus

Rural Route 2, Box 187 A (Long Lake), 56537
(218) 739-2915

Contemporary rustic lake home ten minutes from I-94. Waterbed, spa, fireplace, skylight, vaulted ceilings with use of natural woods and windows to create a feeling of spaciousness. Country French canopy decks on the lakeside and flower garden patio. Furnished with antiques. State park nearby, as well as nature, ski, snowmobile, and hiking trails. Antiques, restaurants, golf, and other recreation nearby. A relaxed retreat surrounded by woods and a hilltop view of the lake and woods.

Hosts: Judy and Dennis Nims
Rooms: 3 (1 PB; 2 SB) $55-85
Full Breakfast
Credit Cards: None
Notes: 2, 5, 8, 9, 10, 11, 12, 13

GRAND MARAIS

Pincushion Mountain Bed and Breakfast

220 Gunflint Trail, 55604
(218) 387-1276; (800) 542-1226

This quiet, secluded bed and breakfast sits on a ridge of Minnesota's Sawtooth Mountains overlooking the north shore of Lake Superior 1,000 feet below. New, country decor. Superior hiking trail, mountain biking, and cross-country ski trails are

NOTES: Credit cards accepted: A Master Card; B Visa; C American Express; D Discover Card; E Diner's Club; F Other; 2 Personal Checks accepted; 3 Lunch available; 4 Dinner available; 5 Open all year;

at its doorstep. Twenty minutes from Boundary Waters Canoe Area entry point; three miles from Grand Marais.

Hosts: Scott and Mary Beattie
Rooms: 4 (4 PB) $75-90
Full Breakfast
Credit Cards: A, B
Closed April
Notes: 2, 8 (over 12), 9, 10, 11, 12, 13, 14

HARMONY

Michel Farm Vacations

45 Main Avenue North, Route 1, Box 914, 55939
(507) 886-5392

Three country homes in beautiful historic Bluff Country of southeastern Minnesota: #1-Contemporary house nestled on hillside overlooking wooded valley and adjacent to Root River and state hiking/biking trail (one bedroom, shared bath); #2-Comfortable vacation home next to historic church in tiny rural village. Walking distance to Upper Iowa River (three bedrooms with one and one-half baths); #3-Cottage situated in area's Amish community offering complete privacy to enjoy wooded view, grazing cattle, and Amish buggies passing (two bedrooms, shared bath).

Rooms: 6 (SB) $40-50
Continental Breakfast at #1; additional $5/person at others for Full Breakast
Credit Cards: A, B

LAKE CITY

Evergreen Knoll Acres Bed and Breakfast

Rural Route 1, Box 145, 55041
(612) 345-2257

This bed and breakfast is on a 160-acre dairy farm with 75 milk cows. It is 8.5 miles southwest of Lake City and 35 miles north of Rochester. Nearby Lake Pepin provides fishing, sailing, and waterskiing. The large, German-style country home was built in 1919 and is furnished with antiques, country crafts, air conditioning, and a fireplace. A four-bedroom guest cottage is available, situated in a secluded area. Plenty of room for hiking, cross-country skiing and biking. Open year-round.

Hosts: Paul and Bev Meyer
Rooms: 3 (SB) $45-99
Full Breakfast
Credit Cards: None
Notes: 2, 5, 8, 9, 10, 11, 12, 13

A Victorian Bed and Breakfast

Red Gables Inn

403 North High Street, 55041
(612) 345-2605

Red Gables Inn is in a quiet residential section of Lake City, home of the largest small-boat marina on the Mississippi. This red Victorian was built in 1865 and displays a mixture of Italianate and Greek Revival architecture. Formal Victorian antiques are in the parlor and dining room, while the guest rooms have floral wallpapers and antique Victorian painted iron and brass beds. In early evening, guests are served beverages.

Hosts: Mary and Doug DeRoos
Rooms: 9 (5 PB; 4 SB) $58-75
Full Breakfast
Credit Cards: A, B
Closed: Thanksgiving Day and Christmas Day
Notes: 2, 5, 8 (over 12), 9, 10, 11, 12, 13, 14

The Victorian Bed and Breakfast

620 South High Street, 55041
(612) 345-2167

An 1896 Victorian home where each room has a lake view. Carved woodwork, stained-glass windows, antique music boxes and furnishings. Mayo Clinic 35 miles; Minneapolis-St. Paul 65 miles. Breakfast is served in your air-conditioned room or the formal dining room. Enjoy afternoon tea.

Hosts: Joel and Sandra Grettenberg
Rooms: 3 (1 PB; 2 private half-baths) $55-75
Expanded Continental Breakfast
Credit Cards: None
Notes: 2, 5, 8 (over 10), 9, 10, 11, 12, 13, 14

LANESBORO

Carrolton Country Inn

Rural Route 2, Box 139, 55949
(507) 467-2257

Carrolton Country Inn is nestled among hills in an open valley near Lanesboro in southeastern Minnesota historic bluff country. Situated on the Root River and Trail for hiking, biking, cross-country skiing, fishing, and canoeing year-round. This private guest home with Victorian accents has accommodations for bed and breakfast, whole-house rental, and family reunions. Amish farms nearby. Ask for free brochure.

Hosts: Charles and Gloria Ruen
Rooms: 4 (2 PB; 2 SB) $55-85
Full Breakfast
Credit Cards: A, B
Notes: 2, 3, 4, 5, 8, 9, 10, 11, 12, 13

Historic Scanlan House Bed and Breakfast

708 Parkway Avenue South, 55949
(507) 467-2158; (800) 944-2158

An 1889 Victorian home on the National Register of Historic Places. Five large bedroom suites furnished with antiques. Original ornate wodwork and beautiful stained-glass windows. Three fireplaces and rooms with private and shared baths also whirlpool suites. Situated six blocks from te Root River, with canoeing, fishing,

and tubing, and the 38-mile paved Root River Trail for biking, hiking, walking, rollerblading, and cross-country skiing. Tennis courts. An exquisite bed and breakfast. You will have the feeling of home. Complimentary champagne and chocolates. All rates include a famous five-course breakfast. Seen in the *Chicago Tribune* and the *Minneapolis Star Tribune*.

Hosts: The Mensings
Rooms: (3 PG; 2 SB) $55-125
Full Breakfast
Credit Cards: A, B, C
Notes: 2, 5, 8, 9, 10, 11, 12, 13, 14

LESUEUR

The Cosgrove Bed and Breakfast

228 South Second Street, 56058
(612) 665-2763

Located in the heart of the beautiful Minnesota River Valley, the Cosgrove is a gracious Colonial Revival home with four period rooms, two with fireplace. A full breakfast is served in the formal wood-paneled dining room. This is a National Register home.

Host: Pam Quist
Doubles: 4 (4 SB) $65
Full Breakfast
Credit Cards: None
Notes: 2, 5, 7, 9, 10, 11, 12

LITTLE MARAIS

Stone Hearth Inn Bed and Breakfast

1118 Highway 61 East, 55614
(218) 226-3020

An 1889 homestead nestled on the shore of Lake Superior offers comfortable elegance. All guest rooms have Old World antiques and private baths. Enjoy four seasons of activities while you are treated to relaxed hospitality and North Shore serenity. Enjoy the cozy stone fireplace or the covered

NOTES: Credit cards accepted: A Master Card; B Visa; C American Express; D Discover Card; E Diner's Club; F Other; 2 Personal Checks accepted; 3 Lunch available; 4 Dinner available; 5 Open all year;

front porch. Breakfast of regional cuisine is served in the lakeside dining room. Hike from this bed and breakfast to another bed and breakfast along the Superior hiking trail. Also near downhill and cross-country skiing, golf, and mountain biking.

Hosts: Charlie and Susan Michels
Rooms: 7 (PB) $75-124
Full Breakfast
Credit Cards: A, B, C
Notes: 2, 3, 4, 5, 9, 10, 12, 13

LUTSEN

Lindgren's Bed and Breakfast

County Road 35, P.O. Box 56, 55612-0056
(218) 663-7450

A 1920s log home in Superior National Forest on walkable shoreline of Lake Superior. Knotty cedar interior decorated with trophies of bear, moose, timber wolf, wild turkey, and fox. Massive stone fireplaces, Finnish sauna, whirlpool, baby grand piano, color TV/VCR. In center of area known for skiing, golfing, stream and lake fishing, skyride, mountain biking, snowmobiling, horseback riding, alpine slide, Superior Hiking Trail, and near Boundary Waters Canoe Area entry point. Spacious manicured grounds. One-half mile off Highway 61 on the Lake Superior Circle Tour.

Hosts: Bob and Shirley Lindgren
Rooms: 4 (4 PB) $80-110
Full Breakfast
Credit Cards: A, B
Notes: 2, 5, 7, 9, 10, 11, 12, 13, 14

MARINE ON ST. CROIX

Asa Parker House

17500 St. Croix Trail North, 55047
(612) 433-5248

The Asa Parker House is a restored lumberman's home, sitting high on a hill overlooking the beautiful St. Croix Valley and the historic village of Marine on St. Croix. Four charming, flower filled bedrooms, all of which have private baths, period antiques, and English fabrics and wallpapers, are available for guests. A wicker-filled porch, gazebo, tennis court, and marina with canoes are available for guests to enjoy. Cross-country skiing and bike trails are in the adjacent state park. Scrumptious breakfast awarded four stars. Midweek rates available.

Host: Marjorie Bush
Rooms: 5 (PB) $99-135
Full Breakfast
Credit Cards: A, B
Notes: 2, 5, 9, 10, 11, 12, 13, 14

Brasie House

MINNEAPOLIS

Brasie House

2321 Colfax Avenue South, P.O. Box 300041, 55403
(612) 377-5946

A gracious alternative combining the ambience of a European bed and breakfast with convenience to all the Twin Cities have to offer. Antiques, fireplaces, resident cats, unique and comfortable bedrooms in a 1913 Craftsman-style home. Convenient to downtown, uptown, theaters, museums, Warehouse District, business and interstate to St. Paul and other metro-area attractions. Walk to the lakes, interesting restaurants, and shopping.

Hosts: Gatos and Mari Griffin
Rooms: 3 (SB) $60-75
Continental Breakfast
Credit Cards: A, B, C,
Notes: 2 (with credit card), 5

Evelo's Bed and Breakfast

2301 Bryant Avenue South, 55405
(612) 374-9656

This 1897 house is located in the Lowry Hill East neighborhood and has a well-preserved Victorian interior. The three guest rooms are on the third floor, each furnished in period furniture. The entire first floor is done in original dark oak millwork. A small refrigerator, coffee maker, phone, and television are available for guest use. The bed and breakfast is within walking distance of downtown, Lake of the Isles, Upton shopping area, Walker Art Center, Guthrie Theatre, and the Minneapolis Art Institute. Established in 1979, it was featured in Innsider magazine (June 1989).

Hosts: David and Sheryl Evelo
Rooms: 3 (SB) $50
Full Breakfast
Credit Cards: A, B, C
Notes: 2, 5, 8, 9

Nan's Bed and Breakfast

2304 Fremont Avenue South, 55405
(612) 377-5118

Comfortable urban 1890s Victorian family home with guest rooms furnished in antiques. Friendly, outgoing hosts will help you find your way around town. Near downtown, lakes, theaters, galleries, restaurants, and shopping. One block from buses.

Hosts: Nan and Jim Zosel
Rooms: 3 (SB) $45-50
Full Breakfast
Credit Cards: C
Notes: 2, 5, 6, 7, 8, 11, 12

MORRIS

The American House

410 East Third Street, 56267
(612) 589-4054

Victorian home decorated with antiques and country charm. Ride the tandem bike on scenic trails. Within walking distance of area restaurants and shops. Situated one block from the University of Minnesota, Morris campus.

Host: Karen Berget
Rooms: 3 (SB) $35-44
Full Breakfast
Credit Cards: A, B
Notes: 2, 5, 8, 9, 10, 11, 12, 14

PARK RAPIDS

Dickson Viking Huss Bed and Breakfast

202 East Fourth Street, 56470
(218) 732-8089

Aunt Helen invites you to her charming contemporary home with vaulted ceiling and fireplace in her livingroom that features a watercolor exhibit. Big continental breakfast. Bicycle or cross-country ski the Heartland Trail. Visit Itasca Park, the source of the Mississippi. Unique shops and restaurants. State inspected.

Host: Helen K. Dickson
Rooms: 3 (1 PB; 2 SB) $29.50-41.50
Expanded Continental Breakfast
Credit Cards: A, B
Notes: 2, 5, 7 (limited), 9, 10, 11, 12, 13 (XC)

RED WING

St. James Hotel

406 Main Street, 55066
(612) 388-2846; (800) 252-1875

Experience cozy, intimate, warm hospitality in a beautifully restored hotel. Stay in one of 60 elegantly decorated rooms and pamper yourself with complimentary champagne, turn-down service, and morning coffee, tea, or hot chocolate delivered to your room. Dine in the Veranda Cafe or Port of Red Wing restaurant, or relax in Jimmy's Pub on the fifth floor. Also offered are eleven unique shops and a warm, friendly shopping atmosphere.

Host: Gene Foster
Rooms: 60 (PB) $90-135
Credit Cards: A, B, C, D, E
Notes: 2, 3, 4, 5, 7, 8, 9, 14

ST. PAUL

Chatsworth Bed and Breakfast

984 Ashland Avenue, 55104
(612) 227-4288

Elegantly furnished Victorian home in a quiet residential neighborhood. Fifteen minutes from the airport. Near governor's mansion and numerous restaurants and shops. Easy access to downtown St. Paul and Minneapolis. Two rooms with double whirlpool baths. Licensed; no smoking.

Hosts: Donna and Earl Gustafson
Rooms: 5 (3 PB; 2 SB) $63.90-106.50
Expanded Continental Breakfast

Credit Cards: None
Notes: 2, 5, 8, 9, 10, 11, 12, 13

The Rose Bed and Breakfast

2129 Larpenteur Avenue West, 55113
(612) 642-9417

This 1925 English Tudor is situated on a large wooded setting between a historic farm museum and a golf course in the center of the Twin Cities metro area and is next to the University of Minnesota, St. Paul campus. Fresh flowers, private tennis court, cross-country skiing, art and books, privacy and/or conversation. Full, wonderful breakfasts accommodating personal dietary preferences.

Hosts: Carol Kindschi and Larry Greenberg
Suites: 2 (PB) $65-75
Full Breakfast
Credit Cards: A, B
Notes: 2, 5, 9, 10, 11, 12, 13

University Club of St. Paul

420 Summit Avenue, 55102
(612) 222-1751

Circa 1912. Established to enhance literary, cultural, and social activities for the well-educated, this Tudor Revival club is modeled after the Cambridge and Oxford clubs in London. Fine English antiques and oil

University Club of St. Paul

6 Pets welcome; 7 Smoking allowed; 8 Children welcome; 9 Social drinking allowed; 10 Tennis available; 11 Swimming available; 12 Golf available; 13 Skiing available; 14 May be booked through travel agents.

paintings of English landscapes decorate the interiors. In the Grill Bar, F. Scott Fitzgerald's initials can be found carved beside those of other club members. There are a library, dining room, fireside room, conference room, and a fitness center. TV available.

Host: John Rupp
Rooms: 5 (PB) $45-85
Credit Cards: A, B, D
Notes: 2, 3, 4, 5, 7 (limited), 8, 9, 10, 11, 12, 13

SHAKOPEE

Valley Manor Bed and Breakfast

314 South Scott Street, 55379
(612) 496-2936

Built in 1880 for Shakopee's founding father Col. Horace Straite, Valley Manor's spacious Victorian styling offers comfortable and relaxing home away from home. Located close to Shakopee's exciting attractions, such as the mystic Lake Casino, Valley Fair Amusement Park, Murphy's Landing, Raceway Park, and Minnesota River Bike trails. We feature a full family-style breakfast and free use of bikes.

Hosts: Allen and Lisa Brakemeier
Rooms: 5 (S3B) $55-65
Full Breakfast
Credit Cards: A, B
Notes: 2, 5, 7, 8, 9, 12, 14

SHERBURN

Four Columns Inn

Route 2, Box 75, 56171
(507) 764-8861

Built in 1884 as a stagecoach stop, this lovingly remodeled inn again welcomes travellers. Four antique-filled bedrooms, claw foot tubs, and working fireplaces welcome you. A library, circular stairway, living-room with a grand piano, music room with a jukebox and player piano, and a sun room

with a sauna make your stay memorable. A hideaway bridal suite with access to a roof deck with a super view of the countryside is perfect for honeymooners, and full breakfast is served in the formal dining room, balcony, or gazebo.

Hosts: Norman and Pennie Kittleson
Rooms: 4 (2 PB; 2 SB) $50-70
Full Breakfast
Credit Cards: None
Notes: 2, 5, 6

SILVER BAY

The Inn at Palisade

384 Highway 61 East, 55614
(218) 226-3505

Cozy, rambler style on Lake Superior. Four guest rooms, one suite with kitchen, fireplace. Handmade quilts, antiques. Bay windows overlooking lake. Private entrance. Full breakfast in dining room. Easy access to 300-foot beach. Adjoins Tettegouche State Park.

Hosts: Bob and Mary Barnett
Rooms: 5 (PB) $65-80
Full Breakfast
Credit Cards: A, B
Notes: 2, 10, 12

SPRING VALLEY

Chase's

508 North Huron Avenue, 55975
(507) 346-2850

It's life in the slow lane at this Second Empire mansion. It's flowers, birds, stars, and exploring this unglaciated area. Step back in time with a tour: Amish, Laura Ingalls Wilder, or caves. Enjoy the trails, trout streams, and bike trail.

Hosts: Bob and Jeannine Chase
Rooms: 5 (PB) $60-75
Full Breakfast
Credit Cards: A, B, D
Closed Dec.-Feb.
Notes: 2, 8, 9, 10, 11, 12, 13

NOTES: Credit cards accepted: A Master Card; B Visa; C American Express; D Discover Card; E Diner's Club; F Other; 2 Personal Checks accepted; 3 Lunch available; 4 Dinner available; 5 Open all year;

TAYLORS FALLS

The Old Jail Company

100 Government Road, Box 203, 55084
(612) 465-3112

The historic Taylors Falls Jail Guesthouse
and the Cave and Playhouse suites in the
Schottmuller Saloon building next door
overlook the St. Croix River Valley, just a
few yards from Interstate Park, with its
ancient glacial potholes and dramatic black
rock cliffs. Swim, fish, rent canoes, hike,
enjoy riverboat cruises, antiques, potteries,
and much more.

Hosts: Julie and Al Kunz
Rooms: 3 (PB) $60-110
Expanded Continental Breakfast
Credit Cards: None
Notes: 2, 5, 7, 9, 10, 11, 12, 13

WINONA

Carriage House Bed and Breakfast

420 Main Street, 55987
(507) 452-8256

Indulge yourself at Winona's Carriage
House Bed and Breakfast. Stay in one of
the beautifully decorated rooms, each with
its own special charm. Built in 1870, the
Carriage House is on the Mississippi River.
Enjoy a wonderful breakfast, free tandem
bikes, and old-fashioned river town hospitality.

Hosts: Deb and Don Salyards
Rooms: 4 (2 PB; 2 SB) $60-85
Expanded Continental Breakfast
Credit Cards: A, B
Notes: 2, 5, 9, 10, 11, 12, 13, 14

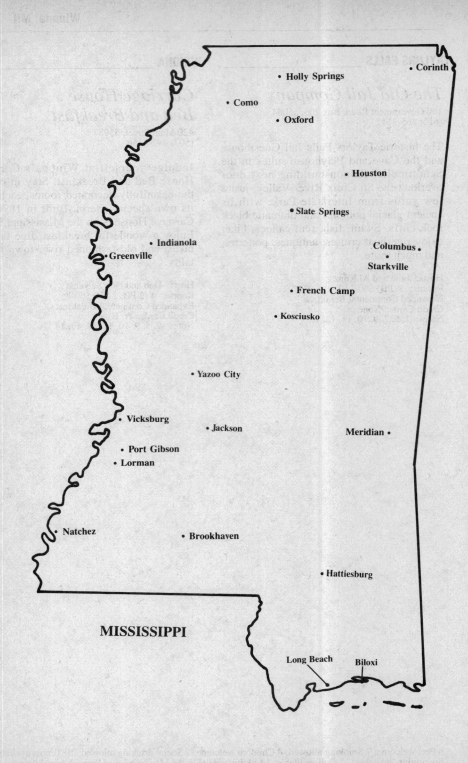

- Corinth
- Holly Springs
- Como
- Oxford
- Houston
- Slate Springs
- Indianola
- Columbus
- Greenville
- Starkville
- French Camp
- Kosciusko
- Yazoo City
- Vicksburg
- Jackson
- Meridian
- Port Gibson
- Lorman
- Natchez
- Brookhaven
- Hattiesburg

MISSISSIPPI

Long Beach   Biloxi

Mississippi

BROOKHAVEN

Lincoln Ltd. #1

P. O. Box 3479, Meridian, 39303
(601) 482-5483 information
(800) 633-MISS reservations
FAX (601) 693-7447

A beautiful 19th-century home completely restored and furnished in the Victorian style with antiques. The host is well known as a decorator and architectural designer. There are four large bedrooms, each with private bath. Dinner is available by special arrangement and reservation. A full breakfast is served. Three guest rooms. $95-110.

COLUMBUS

Lincoln Ltd. #5

P. O. Box 3479, Meridian, 39303
(601) 482-5483 information
(800) 633-MISS reservations
FAX (601) 693-7447

This is a Federal-style house and the oldest brick house in Columbus. It was built in 1828, the same year Andrew Jackson was elected president. The house has been completely restored and is furnished with antiques of the period. Three bedrooms, each with private baths. Full breakfast is included. $75.

Lincoln Ltd. #71

P. O. Box 3479, Meridian, 39303
(601) 482-5483 information
(800) 633-MISS reservations
FAX (601) 693-7447

Enjoy this Italian villa-style home built in 1848 and owned by the family of the original builders. Furnished in period antiques and on the National Register of Historic Places. A full southern breakfast is served. Four guest rooms with private baths. $75.

COMO

Lincoln Ltd. #49

P. O. Box 3479, Meridian, 39303
(601) 482-5483 information
(800) 633-MISS reservations
FAX (601) 693-7447

An attractive guest cottage in a delightful small Mississippi town right on I-55 between Memphis and Jackson. There are also accommodations in the main house. A continental breakfast in the guest cottage, full breakfast in the main house. Two guest rooms. One guest cottage. $60.

CORINTH

The Generals' Quarters

924 Fillmore, P. O. Box 1505, 38834
(601) 286-3325

Circa 1870s. Situated in the historic district of the old Civil War village of Corinth. Near Battery Robinett and site of Fort Williams. Only 22 miles from Shiloh National Military Park and 15 miles from the Tennessee-Tombigbee Waterway. Five rooms with private baths. Full southern breakfast.

NOTES: Credit cards accepted: A Master Card; B Visa; C American Express; D Discover Card; E Diner's Club; F Other; 2 Personal Checks accepted; 3 Lunch available; 4 Dinner available; 5 Open all year; 6 Pets welcome; 7 Smoking allowed; 8 Children welcome; 9 Social drinking allowed; 10 Tennis available; 11 Swimming available; 12 Golf available; 13 Skiing available; 14 May be booked through travel agents.

Host: J. L. Aldridge
Rooms: 5 (PB) $70
Full Breakfast
Credit Cards: A, B, C, E, F
Notes: 2, 4, 5, 7, 8, 9, 14

Lincoln Ltd. #37

P. O. Box 3479, Meridian, 39303
(601) 482-5483 information
(800) 633-MISS reservations
FAX (601) 693-7447

A beautiful Victorian home, completely furnished with antiques. Convenient to Memphis, Tennessee, and Shiloh National Park, a Civil War battlefield. A full southern breakfast is served to guests. Lunch and dinner are also available. Four guest rooms. $70.

Lincoln Ltd. #75

P. O. Box 3479, Meridian, 39303
(601) 482-5483 information
(800) 633-MISS reservations
FAX (601) 693-7447

Circa 1869, this southern-style Colonial house is situated on two acres of oak and dogwood in the city of Corinth. Your host is a native of Oxford, England, and he and his wife are very knowledgeable about the area. Enjoy the original pine floors and walls of two-inch-thick planks. A continental breakfast is served on the back veranda as you relax in antique wicker furniture. Four guest rooms available. $55-70.

FRENCH CAMP

Lincoln Ltd. #59

P. O. Box 3479, Meridian, 39303
(601) 482-5483 information
(800) 633-MISS reservations
FAX (601) 693-7447

Enjoy the spacious view of forest and wildlife from the wide windows of this two-story log home. Built with chinked log walls, the home was reconstructed from

two log cabins more than 100 years old. Awake to a traditional country breakfast and air scented with cypress and sweet pine. The hosts share their historic home with southern hospitality and their personal collection of antique tables, books, and quilts. Four guest rooms with private baths. $53.

GREENVILLE

Lincoln Ltd. #48

P. O. Box 3479, Meridian, 39303
(601) 482-5483 information
(800) 633-MISS reservations
FAX (601) 693-7447

This antebellum mansion, circa 1856, is one of the finest examples of Italianate architecture in Mississippi. It is situated on historic Lake Washington and is listed on the National Register of Historic Places. On the River Road just south of Greenville, this lovely home has been restored and decorated with antiques and the personal collections of its owners. The home is surrounded by several acres of beautiful river land. Sit on the front porch and enjoy a lake view, or stroll the grounds, then settle in to a room beautifully decorated for your comfort. The hosts are Mississippians interested in tourism within their state and in their community and will direct you to all the special things to do in the Mississippi Delta. Four guest rooms with private baths. $75-85.

HOLLY SPRINGS

Hamilton Place

105 East Mason Avenue, 38635
(601) 252-4368

Antebellum home built in 1838 and listed on the national register. All rooms furnished in antiques. There is an antique shop in the carriage house, seasonal pool, and year-round hot tub for guests to enjoy. Museum, art gallery, and other historic homes are within walking distance.

Hosts: Linda and Jack Stubbs
Rooms: 4 (PB) $75
Continental Breakfast
Credit Cards: A, B
Notes: 2, 5, 7, 8, 9, 10, 11, 14

Lincoln Ltd. #8

P. O. Box 3479, Meridian, 39303
(601) 482-5483 information
(800) 633-MISS reservations
FAX (601) 693-7447

Lovely home furnished with heirloom antiques. Also an antique shop adjoining. Young executive hosts have completely restored this home themselves. Full breakfast is served. Three guest rooms with private baths. $55-65.

HOUSTON

Lincoln Ltd. #39

P. O. Box 3479, Meridian, 39303
(601) 482-5483 information
(800) 633-MISS reservations
FAX (601) 693-7447

This Victorian home, completely renovated, is a comfortable stop for travelers on business or pleasure in this small Mississippi town. Just one block from the town square, there are five pleasant bedrooms, all with private bath and TV. Guests can relax and socialize in the downstairs sitting room. A full southern breakfast is served. $40-45.

INDIANOLA

Lincoln Ltd. #9

P. O. Box 3479, Meridian, 39303
(601) 482-5483 information
(800) 633-MISS reservations
FAX (601) 693-7447

Enjoy a full breakfast of country ham and homemade biscuits at this extremely attractive two-story home in the heart of the Mississippi Delta. The hosts, known for their hospitality, will take guests on a tour of the area pointing out crops in season and directing them to well-known area restaurants. One guest room. $50.

JACKSON

Lincoln Ltd. #50

P. O. Box 3479, Meridian, 39303
(601) 482-5483 information
(800) 633-MISS reservations
FAX (601) 693-7447

Circa 1888. Step through the door and step back across 100 years into a graceful world of sparkling chandeliers and finely crafted furnishings in this 19th-century home. Mere moments away from the city's central business and government districts. Convenient to many of Jackson's finest shopping, dining, and entertainment opportunities. The bedrooms are individually decorated, each accompanied by a fully modern private bath. Eleven guest rooms. $80-155.

Millsaps Buie House

628 North State Street, 39202
(601) 352-0221

The historic Millsaps Buie House is the epitome of the finest in southern hospitality and elegance catering to the discriminating taste of the corporate traveler during the week and the leisure traveler on the weekend. Though the inn has only 11 rooms, the dedicated staff prides itself in providing the personal service found in a first-class hotel. Services available to guests upon request include FAX capabilities, computer dataport, personal laundry, and concierge service.

6 Pets welcome; 7 Smoking allowed; 8 Children welcome; 9 Social drinking allowed; 10 Tennis available; 11 Swimming available; 12 Golf available; 13 Skiing available; 14 May be booked through travel agents.

Host: Judy Fenter
Rooms: 11 (PB) $80-155
Full Breakfast
Credit Cards: A, B, C, D, E
Notes: 2, 5, 9, 14

Millsaps Buie House

KOSCIUSKO

Lincoln Ltd. #63

P. O. Box 3479, Meridian, 39303
(601) 482-5483 information
(800) 633-MISS reservations
FAX (601) 693-7447

One of the finest examples of Queen Anne architecture, this historic inn stands as a visual example of the lifestyle and culture of 1884. Four lovely bedrooms, furnished with antiques. Lunch and dinner are available by reservation. Breakfast included. $75.

LONG BEACH

Lincoln Ltd. #53

P. O. Box 3479, Meridian, 39303
(601) 482-5483 information
(800) 633-MISS reservations
FAX (601) 693-7447

Three-story raised French cottage one and one-half miles south of I-10 at Long Beach on 11 acres of live oaks and magnolias. Features antiques, six fireplaces, and a 64-foot front porch with swings. Gardens,

campsites, and cabins are under development. Expanded continental breakfast is served. Four guest rooms with private baths. $54-64.

Red Creek Colonial Inn

7416 Red Creek Road, 39560
(601) 452-3080 information; (800) 729-9670 reservations

This three-story, raised French cottage is situated on eleven acres of live oaks and magnolias. The sixty-four-foot porch and six fireplaces add to the relaxing atmosphere of this circa 1899 brick and cypress home. English, French, Victorian, and country antiques, and workable wooden radios and a Victrola are for guests' use. The inn is located just a half mile south of I-10 off Exit 28 and about five miles from Beach Highway 90, via Menge Avenue and Red Creek Road in Pass Christian. Biloxi is about twenty minutes, and New Orleans is about an hour away.

Hosts: Keith and Michelle Franks
Rooms: 7 (5 PB; 2 SB) $49-69
Continental Plus Breakfast
Credit Cards: None
Closed: Jan. - Feb.
Notes: 2, 5, 9, 10, 11, 12, 13 ,14

LORMAN

Rosswood Plantation

Route 552, 39096
(601) 437-4215

An authentic antebellum mansion, close to Natchez and Vicksburg, offering luxury, comfort, charm, and hospitality on a serene country estate. Once a cotton plantation, Rosswood now grows Christmas trees. Ideal for honeymoons. A Mississippi landmark, national register, AAA recommended.

Hosts: Jean and Walt Hylander
Rooms: 4 (PB) $95
Full Breakfast
Credit Cards: A, B

NOTES: Credit cards accepted: A Master Card; B Visa; C American Express; D Discover Card; E Diner's Club; F Other; 2 Personal Checks accepted; 3 Lunch available; 4 Dinner available; 5 Open all year;

Closed: Jan.-Feb.
Notes: 2, 7, 8, 9, 11, 14

MERIDIAN

Lincoln Ltd. #13

P. O. Box 3479, 39303
(601) 482-5483 information
(800) 633-MISS reservations
FAX (601) 693-7447

Restored Victorian home filled with antiques and situated on ten wooded acres within the city limits. Hostess is a noted gourmet cook and by special arrangement will prepare dinner for an additional charge. Full breakfast included. One guest room. $60-65.

Lincoln Ltd. #16

P. O. Box 3479, 39303
(601) 482-5483 information
(800) 633-MISS reservations
FAX (601) 693-7447

A charming guest suite in a home situated in one of Meridian's historic neighborhoods. Bedroom, bath, living area decorated in antiques. Kitchen privileges. Private entrance. Continental breakfast. $55-65; weekly and monthly rates available.

Rosswood Plantation

Lincoln Ltd. #18

P. O. Box 3479, 39303
(601) 482-5483 information
(800) 633-MISS reservations
FAX (601) 693-7447

In one of Meridian's loveliest neighborhoods, this home is set among flowering shrubs and dogwood trees. The host and hostess have always been active in civic and cultural activities, both locally and within the state. Attractively furnished, two bedrooms with shared bath (for family or four people traveling together, only) or a double room with private bath. Full Mississippi breakfast. $55-70.

Lincoln Ltd. #58

P. O. Box 3479, Meridian, 39303
(601) 482-5483 information
(800) 633-MISS reservations
FAX (601) 693-7447

A contemporary inn convenient to I-59 and I-20 with 100 beautiful, spacious guest rooms. Meeting space for up to 60 people. Continental breakfast is served. Swimming pool and whirlpool on premises. $39-45; weekly and monthly rates available.

NATCHEZ

The Burn

712 North Union Street, 39120
(601) 442-1344; (800) 654-8859

Circa 1834, three-story mansion especially noted for its semispiral stairway, unique gardens, and exquisite collection of antiques. Overnight guests are pampered with a seated plantation breakfast, tour of the home, and use of the swimming pool. Owner occupied. Member of Independent Innkeepers Association.

Host: Loveta Byrne
Rooms: 6 (PB) $75-125
Full Breakfast
Credit Cards: A, B, C, D, E
Notes: 2, 5, 7, 9, 10, 11, 12, 14

6 Pets welcome; 7 Smoking allowed; 8 Children welcome; 9 Social drinking allowed; 10 Tennis available; 11 Swimming available; 12 Golf available; 13 Skiing available; 14 May be booked through travel agents.

The Burn

Lincoln Ltd. #19

P. O. Box 3479, Meridian, 39303
(601) 482-5483 information
(800) 633-MISS reservations
FAX (601) 693-7447

Circa 1832. This three-story mansion's outstanding architectural feature is the semi-eliptical stairway. Horses once trod where a collection of priceless furnishings and fine paintings now reside. Listed on the National Register of Historic Places. Full breakfast served. Swimming pool on premises. Ten guest rooms. $70-125.

Lincoln Ltd. #20

P. O. Box 3479, Meridian, 39303
(601) 482-5483 information
(800) 633-MISS reservations
FAX (601) 693-7447

Dating from 1774-1789 and surrounded by old-fashioned gardens, this home was once the home of a Spanish governor. In keeping with the period of the house, it is charmingly furnished with family heirlooms and other rare antiques. Formerly the home of Mr. and Mrs. J. Balfour Miller. The late Mrs. Miller was the originator of the Natchez Pilgrimage. Listed on the National Register of Historic Places. Full breakfast served. Four guest rooms. $85-105.

Lincoln Ltd. #21

P. O. Box 3479, Meridian, 39303
(601) 482-5483 information
(800) 633-MISS reservations
FAX (601) 693-7447

Circa 1790. Once the home of Thomas B. Reed, first elected U.S. senator from Mississippi, this architectural gem of the Federal period has been occupied since 1849 by the Conner family and its descendants. Listed on the National Register of Historic Places. Full breakfast served. Seven guest rooms. $75-110.

Lincoln Ltd. #22

P. O. Box 3479, Meridian, 39303
(601) 482-5483 information
(800) 633-MISS reservations
FAX (601) 693-7447

Circa 1818. The former home of General John A. Quitman, an early Mississippi governor of Mexican War fame. This antebellum home contains many original Quitman pieces. Listed on the national register. Fourteen guest rooms; suite available. $85-160.

Lincoln Ltd. #29

P. O. Box 3479, Meridian, 39303
(601) 482-5483 information
(800) 633-MISS reservations
FAX (601) 693-7447

Sleep in a canopied bed or stretch out in a hammock at this historic home hosted by a person who can tell you all you want to know about Natchez, past and present. A full plantation breakfast is served on the sunny porch. Five guest rooms. $75-100.

Lincoln Ltd. #30

P. O. Box 3479, Meridian, 39303
(601) 482-5483 information
(800) 633-MISS reservations
FAX (601) 693-7447

NOTES: Credit cards accepted: A Master Card; B Visa; C American Express; D Discover Card; E Diner's Club; F Other; 2 Personal Checks accepted; 3 Lunch available; 4 Dinner available; 5 Open all year;

An outstanding historical home with a panoramic view of the Mississippi River. Furnished with an impressive collection of antiques, including the works of John Belter and P. Mallard. Welcoming beverage, tour of the home, and a large plantation-style breakfast are included. Five guest rooms. $70.

Lincoln Ltd. #44

P. O. Box 3479, Meridian, 39303
(601) 482-5483 information
(800) 633-MISS reservations
FAX (601) 693-7447

This home, which is listed on the National Register of Historic Places, was built in 1858. It is situated on a bluff overlooking the Mississippi River, which can be seen from all of the bedrooms. The home is beautifully decorated in period antiques, and all bedrooms feature tester beds. The original second story was removed during the Civil War by Union forces to prevent its being used to signal Confederate troops. The second story was rebuilt in 1903. Full breakfast is served. Three guest rooms. $75-110.

Lincoln Ltd. #45

P. O. Box 3479, Meridian, 39303
(601) 482-5483 information
(800) 633-MISS reservations
FAX (601) 693-7447

Planters Cottage, built in 1836, is situated on a 500-acre working plantation 13 miles south of Natchez. Owned by descendants of the builders, it was restored in 1986 and retains some original furniture and documents. It is one of the oldest farms in Mississippi and is on the National Register of Historic Places. Pastures and ponds surround the house and provide a peaceful, relaxing setting. Three guest rooms. $90-125.

Lincoln Ltd. #46

P. O. Box 3479, Meridian, 39303
(601) 482-5483 information
(800) 633-MISS reservations
FAX (601) 693-7447

One of the finest examples of early southern Plantation-style architecture, this lovely home is situated on a promontory overlooking the Mississippi River. Abounding in history, the antique-filled rooms offer the guest a time to relax and enjoy the very room where Jefferson Davis was married in 1845. All 13 bedrooms are spacious. Private baths available. Full breakfast is served. $105-135.

Lincoln Ltd. #69

P. O. Box 3479, Meridian, 39303
(601) 482-5483 information
(800) 633-MISS reservations
FAX (601) 693-7447

Once owned by the last territorial governor and the first U.S. governor of Mississippi, this home was built in 1794 and is situated in the heart of Natchez. Many of the rooms have original 18th-century paneling and are furnished in period antiques. Enjoy the formal drawing room and eat your full plantation breakfast in the elegant dining room or cozy breakfast room. Five guest rooms and one suite available. $75-110.

Lincoln Ltd. #70

P. O. Box 3479, Meridian, 39303
(601) 482-5483 information
(800) 633-MISS reservations
FAX (601) 693-7447

Circa 1853. This beautiful Plantation, which is still inhabited by the descendants of the original builders, is on 150 acres of land. Most of the original family antiques still decorate the home. Stay in one of the "Dependencies" and enjoy your full southern breakfast in the main house. Two guest rooms. $90.

---

6 Pets welcome; 7 Smoking allowed; 8 Children welcome; 9 Social drinking allowed; 10 Tennis available; 11 Swimming available; 12 Golf available; 13 Skiing available; 14 May be booked through travel agents.

Linden

1 Linden Place, 39120
(601) 445-5472

Linden sits on seven landscaped acres and has been in the present owner's family for six generations. It is a Federal-style house furnished in antiques and many heirlooms. All seven bedrooms have four-poster beds and other antiques of the Federal period. The front doorway was copied in *Gone With the Wind*. Early morning coffee, a full southern plantation breakfast, and a tour of the house are included in the price of a room. Linden is on the famous spring and fall pilgrimages, quality rated by Mobile Guide and three-diamond rated by AAA. The owner welcomes her guests and gives the tour of the home herself.

Host: Jeanette S. Feltus
Rooms: 7 (PB) $90 plus tax
Full Breakfast
Credit Cards: None
Notes: 2, 5, 7, 8 (over 10), 9, 10, 11, 12, 14

Mount Repose

Natchez Pilgrimage Tours, Canal Street Depot, 39120
(601) 446-6631

Mount Repose is a typical southern planter's home, complete with spacious rooms and fine antiques throughout. Identical galleries on the first and second stories span the width of the main facade, both of which provide outstanding views of the giant, moss-draped oak and magnolia trees which canopy the beautiful grounds. The home was built in 1824, and since that time, descendants of the builder have maintained their ancestral home.

Hosts: Family members
Rooms: 3 (PB) $110-125
Full Breakfast
Credit Cards: A, B, C
Notes: 2, 5, 8, 9, 14

Oakland Plantation

1124 Lower Woodville Road, 39120
(601) 445-5101; (800) 824-0355

This charming retreat is about eight miles south of Natchez, with 360 acres of pastures, nature trails, fishing ponds, and a tennis court. The guest house dates back to 1785, and guests to this estate include Andrew Jackson and his future wife, Rachel Robards. Come for the peace and quiet, and relax in an eighteenth-century atmosphere.

Hosts: Andy and Jeanie Peabody
Rooms: 3 (2 PB; 1 SB) $55-65
Full Breakfast
Credit Cards: A, B
Notes: 2, 5, 8, 9, 10, 14

Sweet Olive Tree Manor

700 Orleans Street, 39120
(601) 442-1401

Breakfast in Victorian splendor when you stay at this mansion furnished in antiques and antique reproductions of the Victorian period. A full breakfast is served in the formal dining room with fine crystal, silver, and china. Wine and cheese and teas are served in the early evening. Children over fourteen years old are welcome. No smoking. No pets. Location is three blocks from downtown Natchez in the historic district and within walking distance of several antebellum homes which are on the Natchez Pilgrimage tour. Stay at Sweet Olive Tree Manor, where southern hospitality becomes a reality in historic Natchez, Mississippi.

Hosts: Judee McKenna-Brown and Peggy McKenna
Rooms: 4 (2 PB; 1 SB) $80-115
Full Breakfast
Credit Cards: None
Notes: 2, 5, 8 (over 14), 14

Weymouth Hall Inn

One Cemetery Road, 39120
(601) 445-2304

Located on the bluff overlooking the mighty Mississippi River, Weymouth Hall stands alone, with its unequaled scenic view. Guests can relax on recessed porches in the late afternoon while delighting in the panoramic view of the river. The outstanding home is completely furnished with an impressive collection of period antiques.

Host: Gene Weber
Rooms: 5 (PB) $80-85
Full Breakfast
Credit Cards: None
Closed January
Notes: 2, 7 (outside), 9, 14

OXFORD

Lincoln Ltd. #23

P. O. Box 3479, Meridian, 39303
(601) 482-5483 information
(800) 633-MISS reservations
FAX (601) 693-7447

Built in 1838, this lovely antebellum home is made entirely of native timber and is on the National Register of Historic Places. Treasures abound here. "It's a homey museum/showplace," says the hostess. In an attic, 150 years of fashion are displayed on mannequins. Guests can enjoy cakes that are still warm and have a full breakfast on the balcony on warm spring mornings. Conveniently situated close to the University of Mississippi and the William Faulkner home. Downstairs filled with antiques. Four guest rooms. $55-70.

PORT GIBSON

Lincoln Ltd. #26

P. O. Box 3479, Meridian, 39303
(601) 482-5483 information
(800) 633-MISS reservations
FAX (601) 693-7447

Enjoy a night in one of the South's most beautiful antebellum mansions. On the National Register of Historic Places, this home is furnished with family heirlooms. Visitors will step back in history to an era of gracious living. Includes a full southern-style breakfast and a tour of the home. Eleven guest rooms. $85.

Lincoln Ltd. #66

P. O. Box 3479, Meridian, 39303
(601) 482-5483 information
(800) 633-MISS reservations
FAX (601) 693-7447

Circa 1832. This late Federal-style home is noted for its beautiful three-story curved show-off stairway. Once owned by Judge Harry T. Ellet, who drew up the secession paper for the Confederacy. Enjoy one of five guest rooms beautifully decorated or one large suite complete with Jacuzzi. Listed on the National Register of Historic Places. Full southern breakfast. $75-95.

Oak Square Plantation

1207 Church Street, 39150
(601) 437-4350; (800) 729-0240

In the town Gen. U. S. Grant said was "too beautiful to burn," this antebellum mansion features heirloom antiques and canopied beds. On the National Register of Historic Places. Four-diamond rated by AAA.

Hosts: Mr. and Mrs. William Lum
Rooms: 10 (PB) $75-95
Full Breakfast
Credit Cards: A, B, C, D
Notes: 2, 5, 8, 9, 14

SLATE SPRINGS

Lincoln Ltd. #65

P. O. Box 3479, Meridian, 39303
(601) 482-5483 information
(800) 633-MISS reservations
FAX (601) 693-7447

Circa 1890. This lovely old farmhouse with curved staircase has been lovingly restored to its present beauty with half-tester Victorian beds and heirloom antiques. Walk the 150-acre farm with its beautiful wild flowers, colorful birds, and trees. Enjoy a full southern breakfast and a full-course dinner included in the price. Three guest rooms with private baths. $95.

6 Pets welcome; 7 Smoking allowed; 8 Children welcome; 9 Social drinking allowed; 10 Tennis available; 11 Swimming available; 12 Golf available; 13 Skiing available; 14 May be booked through travel agents.

STARKVILLE

Lincoln Ltd. #56

P. O. Box 3479, Meridian, 39303
(601) 482-5483 information
(800) 633-MISS reservations
FAX (601) 693-7447

A unique place to stay, combining the history of a 200-year-old hand-hewn square logged cabin with the convenience of today. Situated in the middle of 35 acres overlooking a small lake and nestled in a grove of cedars. The executive suite is on the second floor and has a large sun deck on which to relax and enjoy the scenery as you overlook the lake. You will find a large livingroom, separate bedroom with fireplace and a four-poster bed, and a kitchen. A complimentary beverage will greet you upon arrival and a continental breakfast with freshly ground coffee will be provided. $65.

Lincoln Ltd. #60

P. O. Box 3479, Meridian, 39303
(601) 482-5483 information
(800) 633-MISS reservations
FAX (601) 693-7447

This special country home is in a wonderful setting, on a 15-acre Christmas tree farm complete with cows and horses. The private suite is on the second floor, and you can enjoy a living/kitchen area and a bedroom with private bath. It can sleep up to four people. A continental breakfast is provided. Convenient to Mississippi State University, only 15 minutes away. $55-75.

VICKSBURG

Annabelle

501 Speed street, 39180
(601) 634-8564; (800) 634-8564

Overnight memories can be yours in this elegant two-story Victorian inn located in Leinston's Landing, the historic Garden District of Vicksburg. Furnished in period antiques, Annabelle, the home of the Mayers, offers four guest rooms with king- and queen-size beds, private baths, twelve-foot ceilings, and beautiful Vieux Carré patio surrounded by sculptured gardens. Your delicious southern breakfast is served in the formal dining room. No children, pets, smoking.

Hosts: Carolyn and George Mayer
Rooms: 4 (PB) $65-85
Full Breakfast
Credit Cards: A, B

Cedar Grove Mansion-Inn

2200 Washington Street, 39180
(800) 862-1300; (800) 448-2820 in Mississippi

Straight out of *Gone With the Wind* is this 1840 magnificently furnished inn with its four acres of gardens and its fountains, courtyards, gas lights, four-poster beds, period antiques. Pool, Jacuzzi, and the terrace have a view of the Mississippi River. Chosen by the book *Escape in Style* as one of the most romantic inns in the world. Four-diamond rated by AAA and a national historic property.

Rooms: 18 (PB) $85-150
Full Breakfast
Credit Cards: A, B, C
Notes: 2, 5, 7 (limited), 8 (over 5), 9, 10, 11, 12, 14

Lincoln Ltd. #27

P. O. Box 3479, Meridian, 39303
(601) 482-5483 information
(800) 633-MISS reservations
FAX (601) 693-7447

True southern hospitality in this Federal-style home. Here history combines with every modern amenity, including a hot tub and a swimming pool. Step back in time as you sleep in an antique-filled bedroom and enjoy a full plantation-style breakfast in the formal dining room. A tour of the home and a welcoming beverage are included. There are 11 guest rooms. $75-115.

NOTES: Credit cards accepted: A Master Card; B Visa; C American Express; D Discover Card; E Diner's Club; F Other; 2 Personal Checks accepted; 3 Lunch available; 4 Dinner available; 5 Open all year;

Lincoln Ltd. #32

P. O. Box 3479, Meridian, 39303
(601) 482-5483 information
(800) 633-MISS reservations
FAX (601) 693-7447

Situated on six landscaped acres, this outstanding home designed in the Federal style boasts exquisite milled woodwork, sterling silver door knobs, French bronze chandeliers, and a lonely ghost—all echoes of the past. Three lovely guest rooms all furnished in antiques: a Mallard bed, a Heppelwhite tester, or a plantation-style room are yours to enjoy. A tour of the home, a plantation breakfast and mint juleps included. $85.

Lincoln Ltd. #35

P. O. Box 3479, Meridian, 39303
(601) 482-5483 information
(800) 633-MISS reservations
FAX (601) 693-7447

Circa 1873. This home was built as a wedding present from father to daughter. It is an interesting mixture of Victorian and Greek Revival architectural styles. All bedrooms are furnished with antiques and have private baths. Some rooms are available with fireplace and television. Enjoy a spectacular view of the Mississippi River and valley from a rocking chair on the front gallery. Full plantation breakfast is included. Listed on the National Register of Historic Places. Six guest rooms. $75-130.

Lincoln Ltd. #36

P. O. Box 3479, Meridian, 39303
(601) 482-5483 information
(800) 633-MISS reservations
FAX (601) 693-7447

Lavish antebellum mansion built between 1840 and 1858 as a wedding present from a wealthy businessman to his bride. Gone With the Wind elegance that you won't soon forget. Exquisitely furnished with many original antiques. Enjoy the beautiful formal gardens, gazebos, and fountains. Relax in the courtyard. Pool and spa available. Listed on the National Register of Historic Places. Its 17 guest rooms have private baths. $75-140.

Lincoln Ltd. #41

P. O. Box 3479, Meridian, 39303
(601) 482-5483 information
(800) 633-MISS reservations
FAX (601) 693-7447

Elegant antebellum mansion, circa 1856, situated in Vicksburg's historic district. It is the best example of Palladian architecture found in Mississippi. Used as a hospital during the Civil War, it was shelled during the siege of Vicksburg. Listed on the National Register of Historic Places. A welcoming beverage, tour of the home, and full breakfast are included. Eight guest rooms. $85-140.

The Vicksburg

801 Clay Street, 39180
(601) 636-4146; (800) 844-4146

Relive the golden days of the Hill City, when cotton was king and this Mississippi River port was bustling. Built in 1928 as a 200-room, 11-story hotel, the Vicksburg was completely renovated in 1983 into 56 residential suites and guest rooms. It is within easy walking distance of the historic district, major shopping, and antebellum mansions. It houses the internationally acclaimed Old Southern Tea Room and is listed on the National Register of Historic Places.

Hosts: Carolyn and George Mayer
Rooms: 2 and 3 suites (PB) $65-85
Full Breakfast
Credit Cards: A, B, C, D, E
Notes: 3, 4, 5, 7, 8, 9, 14

YAZOO CITY

Lincoln Ltd. #70

P. O. Box 3479, Meridian, 39303
(601) 482-5483 information
(800) 633-MISS reservations
FAX (601) 693-7447

Twenty miles from Yazoo City. Step back into history and walk among azaleas and spectacular day lilies. This manager's plantation home, built in 1860, has four bedrooms and tastefully decorated with period antiques offers an intriguing oasis of privacy for those who wish to get away from the rush of life. Relax in two gazebos and absorb nature's sounds and aromas or slip away to a cozy sitting room upstairs and enjoy a panoramic view of the entire front garden. A full plantation evening meal and breakfast are included. $90-110.

Missouri

ARROW ROCK

Borgman's Bed and Breakfast

706 Van Buren, 65320
(816) 837-3350

We invite you to experience the historic town of Arrow Rock in the warmth of our century-old home. Choose one of four spacious guest rooms that share three baths, and relax in the sitting room or porch. Wind up the old Victrola for a song, choose a game or puzzle, browse through a book, or just sit for a spell and listen to the sounds of Arrow Rock. In the morning you will enjoy Helen's family-style breakfast of freshly baked bread, juice or fruit, and coffee and tea.

Host: Kathy and Helen Borgman
Rooms: 4 (S3B) $45-50
Continental Plus Breakfast
Credit Cards: None
Notes: 2, 5, 8

BOLIVAR

Ozark Mountain Country Bed and Breakfast 247

Box 295, Branson, 65616
(800) 321-8594

Our lodge is located on 90 acres of Ozark woods between Bolivar and Humansville. Venture the outdoors on nature trails, fishing or at swimming ponds. Our lodge is open all year. Other features include a courtyard with picnic table, game table, piano, livingroom, TV/VCR/video library, and country breakfast. Three doubles with private bath. Two rooms with shared bath. $35-45.

BONNE TERRE

The Mansion Hill Country Inn

651 Oak Street, 63628
(314) 731-5003 reservations
(314) 358-5311 dinner reservations
FAX (314) 895-3160

Built as a retreat residence for St. Joseph Lead Company presidents in 1909 by company carpenters, the Mansion Hill Country Inn is Missouri's only true country inn. The estate is situated atop the foothills of the Ozark Mountains on 132 acres with a 45-mile view of surrounding villages and countryside. Huge fireplace in great room. Three blocks from world famous Bonne Terre Mine. Scuba diving available.

Hosts: Catherine and Douglas Goergens
Rooms: 5 (2 PB; 3 SB) $80
Continental Breakfast
Credit Cards: A, B, D
Notes: 3 (Sat.), 4, 5, 7 (limited), 8, 9, 12, 14

The 1909 Depot

Oak and Allen Streets, 63628
(314) 731-5003; FAX (314) 895-3160

A three-story turreted 1909 Victorian train depot, completely restored by its owners, Doug and Cathy Goergens. Careful attention has been paid to retaining the train

NOTES: Credit cards accepted: A Master Card; B Visa; C American Express; D Discover Card; E Diner's Club; F Other; 2 Personal Checks accepted; 3 Lunch available; 4 Dinner available; 5 Open all year; 6 Pets welcome; 7 Smoking allowed; 8 Children welcome; 9 Social drinking allowed; 10 Tennis available; 11 Swimming available; 12 Golf available; 13 Skiing available; 14 May be booked through travel agents.

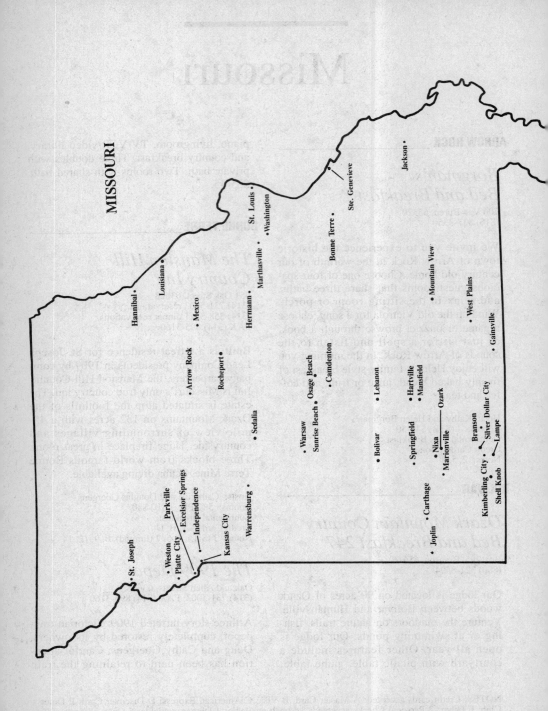

MISSOURI

- St. Joseph
- Weston
- Platte City
- Parkville
- Excelsior Springs
- Independence
- Kansas City
- Warrensburg
- Sedalia
- Arrow Rock
- Rocheport
- Hannibal
- Louisiana
- Mexico
- Marthasville
- Hermann
- St. Louis
- Washington
- Ste. Genevieve
- Bonne Terre
- Jackson
- Warsaw
- Sunrise Beach
- Osage Beach
- Camdenton
- Mountain View
- West Plains
- Gainsville
- Bolivar
- Lebanon
- Hartville
- Mansfield
- Springfield
- Ozark
- Nixa
- Marionville
- Branson
- Silver Dollar City
- Kimberling City
- Lampe
- Shell Knob
- Joplin
- Carthage

motif as evidenced by the authentic railroad antiques and memorabilia which Doug and Cathy have spent countless hours collecting. The second floor has five large suites, each with private bathroom. Also, two converted rail cars on a siding next to the depot offer unique accommodations.

Hosts: Doug and Cathy Goergens
Rooms: 7 (PB) $80-120
Continental Breakfast
Credit Cards: A, B, D
Notes: 3 (Sat.), 4, 5, 7 (limited), 9, 12, 14

BRANSON

The Branson Hotel Bed and Breakfast Inn

214 West Main, 65616
(417) 335-6104

The Branson Hotel is truly Branson's elegant little hotel. History, romance, and elegance await you at this historical inn that has provided memories since 1903. Enjoy one of nine beautiful guest rooms, all of which have full private baths. Antique decor, king- and queen-size beds, and cable TV. Two large verandas overlook downtown Branson. Full gourmet breakfast in a glass-enclosed breakfast room. AAA/Mobile Guide recommended.

Hosts: Teri Murquia and Lois Simmons
Rooms: 9 (PB) $75-95
Full Breakfast
Credit Cards: None
Notes: 2, 5, 9, 14

The Branson Hotel

The Branson House Bed and Breakfast Inn

120 Fourth Street, 65616
(417) 334-0959

Bed and breakfast in an authentic country home. Early 1900s charm with antique decor. Seven pleasant guest rooms, each with its own private bath. Enjoy complimentary sherry in a huge, comfortable parlor with 150-year-old pump organ. Fireplace. At bedtime, help yourself to cookies and milk in the country kitchen. A specially prepared breakfast is served in the dining room or on the veranda overlooking old downtown Branson and Lake Taneycomo. Near all Branson attractions. A short stroll to shops, eateries, and antiques. AAA/Mobil Guide recommended.

Host: Opal Kelly
Rooms: 7 (PB) $60-75
Full Breakfast
Credit Cards: None
Notes: 2, 7 (outside), 9, 10, 11, 12, 14

Country Gardens

Lakeshore Drive, Box 2202, 65616
(417) 334-8564; (800) 727-0723

A lakefront home in the heart of country music and the Ozark Mountains. Branson is a beautiful family vacation area and offers the greatest number of country music shows in the world as well as theme parks. Country Gardens contains three beautiful rooms, each done in a different style. All have private entrances, private baths, and access to whirlpool area. One has a private spa in the room; great for honeymooners. Full breakfast can include the trout you catch from the lake. Join the Country Gardens for a relaxing, memorable retreat.

Hosts: Bob and Pat Cameron
Rooms: 3 (PB) $75-95
Full Breakfast
Credit Cards: A, B, D
Notes: 2, 5, 7, 9, 11, 14

6 Pets welcome; 7 Smoking allowed; 8 Children welcome; 9 Social drinking allowed; 10 Tennis available; 11 Swimming available; 12 Golf available; 13 Skiing available; 14 May be booked through travel agents.

Josie's Bed and Breakfast

Indian Point Road, HCR. 1, Box 1104, 65616
(417) 338-2978; (800) 289-4125

Peaceful getaway on the shore of Table
Rock Lake. Three hundred feet of lakefront
is yours to enjoy. Contemporary home with
15-foot-high stone fireplace and cathedral
ceilings. Fresh flowers, china, stained
glass. Honeymoon-anniversary suite has
private entrance, patio, kitchenette, fireplace, living area, queen-size bed,
whirlpool for two. All units feature unique
decor and furnishings. Porch with
panoramic view. Near marina and Silver
Dollar City. Easy access to country music
shows.

Hosts: Bill and JoAnne Coats
Rooms: 3 (PB) $50-95 plus tax
Full Breakfast
Credit Cards: A, B
Notes: 2, 5, 8, 9, 11, 12, 14

Ozark Mountain Country Bed and Breakfast 103

Box 295, 65616
(800) 321-8594

"On a clear day you can see forever" from
this high bluff overlooking Lake
Taneycomo. Three miles south of Branson.
The lakeview guest room has TV, private
bath, and entrance from deck. A smaller
room is also available with TV. School-age
children welcome. Picnic table and grill
available for guests. Full breakfast with
choice of entrées. Smoking only on the
deck. $50-85.

Ozark Mountain Country Bed and Breakfast 107

Box 295, 65616
(800) 321-8594

Two blocks from Table Rock Lake with
easy access to Silver Dollar City, Table
Rock Dam, and state park. Easy access to
shows. Two guest areas available with
color TV, private bath, and private
entrance. Sitting area, game table, refrigerator, cable TV. Special breakfast on weekends. No smoking. $60-80.

Ozark Mountain Country Bed and Breakfast 112

Box 295, 65616
(800) 321-8594

Delightful retreat across Lake Taneycomo
from Branson. Swimming pool available.
Three lakeview guest areas with private
entrances. Fishing docks, rental boats, and
picnic table with charcoal grill available.
Smoking permitted. Full breakfast.
Secluded outdoor spa. The Dogwood apartment has whirlpool bath and kitchenette.
The Rose Suite has a Jacuzzi, refrigerator,
and microwave. No children. $70-90.

Ozark Mountain Country Bed and Breakfast 124

Box 295, 65616
(800) 321-8594

This bed and breakfast offers easy access to
Silver Dollar City and shows. Private
entrance, bath with shower, sitting area,
and patio. Marvelous view of the valley
and Ozark Mountains. Full breakfast
upstairs in dining room. Continental breakfast served in guest area. No smoking.
Children welcome. $45.

Ozark Mountain Country Bed and Breakfast 125

Box 295, 65616
(800) 321-8594

Six lakeview suites with private baths, private entrances, complete kitchenettes, and
patio/deck. Color TV, air conditioning.
Hearty continental breakfast. Rental boats

NOTES: Credit cards accepted: A Master Card; B Visa; C American Express; D Discover Card; E Diner's
Club; F Other; 2 Personal Checks accepted; 3 Lunch available; 4 Dinner available; 5 Open all year;

available. Private dock. Group discounts available as well as discounts after the third night. $78-95.

Ozark Mountain Country Bed and Breakfast 127

Box 295, 65616
(800) 321-8594

Just one and one-half miles from Branson, this bed and breakfast offers a swimming pool and hot tub to rest your worries. Some of your fringe benefits include a large country breakfast, country Victorian furnishings, and available cottage. Other amenities include snacks, high chair and baby bed. Smoking OK in common areas. King bed and TV in Rose Room; TV, queen bed in Paisley Room. $50-65.

Ozark Mountain Country Bed and Breakfast 132

Box 295, 65616
(800) 321-8594

Seven miles southwest of Branson on a bluff above Lake Taneycomo, this private suite has easy access to attractions. Features includesitting area, king bed, sleeper sofa, TV, and full breakfast delivered to your suite. Open weekends only from November to May. $70.

Ozark Mountain Country Bed and Breakfast 134

Box 295, 65616
(800) 321-8594

Try this famous early 1900s restored and decorated hotel in the historic district. Features include hearty breakfast in formal dining room, nine guest areas, antiques and collectibles. Available April through December. $70-95.

Ozark Mountain Country Bed and Breakfast 135

Box 295, 65616
(800) 321-8594

This private cottage is located five miles south of Branson and has complete kitchen, sitting area, and antiques. Other features include day bed, double bed, and both with shower. Infants allowed. Full breakfast in cottage. No smoking. Open all year. $50-55.

Ozark Mountain Country Bed and Breakfast 136

Box 295, 65616
(800) 321-8594

This contemporary A-frame private cottage in located six miles southeast of Branson. Your attractions are close by, and the windows from floor to roof overlook the lake. Features include queen bed, full kitchen, great room, TV, dining area overlooking lake, and continental breakfast delivered to your cottage. Open all year. $55.

Ozark Mountain Country Bed and Breakfast 139

Box 295, 65616
(800) 321-8594

Two-room suite has easy access to local attractions. The hostess is an interior designer. Other features include double bed, private hall bath, hearty breakfast, sitting area with love seats and TV. No smoking. $55.

Ozark Mountain Country Bed and Breakfast 140

Box 295, 65616
(800) 321-8594

6 Pets welcome; 7 Smoking allowed; 8 Children welcome; 9 Social drinking allowed; 10 Tennis available; 11 Swimming available; 12 Golf available; 13 Skiing available; 14 May be booked through travel agents.

These elegant contemporary guest rooms are above Lake Taneycomo with easy access to attractions. Rooms have sitting areas, lake views, private baths, king and queen beds, cable TV, private hot tub, kitchenette; two rooms with fireplace, and pinball. The meeting/conference room is ideal for large families or groups. Smoke-free environment. $70-80.

BRIGHTON

Ozark Mountain Country Bed and Breakfast 204

Box 295, Branson, 65616
(800) 321-8594

This private guest cottage is 15 miles north of Springfield. The cottage features a hand-made hickory bedstead, fireplace, sitting room, and kitchenette. Guests can enjoy the wildlife sanctuary and stocked pond. They may also fish, hike, pet animals, and relax. Well-behaved children and pets welcome. $70-75.

CAMDENTON

Ramblewood Bed and Breakfast

402 Panoramic Drive, 65020
(314) 346-3410 after 5:00 p.m.

This inviting cottage nestles in a grove of oak and dogwood trees. The decor is traditional, touched with Victorian. You will be welcomed with tea or lemonade and home-made goodies. Your breakfast is special, beginning with a beautiful fruit plate, followed by tempting dishes and breads. You are minutes from the lake, state park, fine restaurants, music shows, and shops.

Host: Mary E. Massey
Rooms: 2 (SB) $45
Full Breakfast
Credit Cards: None
Notes: 2, 5, 9, 10, 11, 12

Ozark Mountain Country Bed and Breakfast 203

Box 295, Branson, 65616
(800) 321-8594

This guest house is 50 feet from Lake of the Ozarks. The master suite has adjoining bath. Another room shares a hall bath. Adults only. Smoking only on decks. Hearty continental breakfast. $55.

Ozark Mountain Country Bed and Breakfast 207

Box 295, Branson, 65616
(800) 321-8594

The two guest rooms come with a full hearty breakfast served in the dining room or on the shady deck. King and queen bed with shared bath or private bath option. Smoking on deck. Available all year. $45-80.

Ozark Mountain Country Bed and Breakfast 239

Box 295, Branson, 65616
(800) 321-8594

Two contemporary suites are located on Lake of the Ozarks, each able to sleep six. Boat slip is available, dining room, private entrances, extra meals arranged on request. Three-night minimum stay and open all year. $100.

CARTHAGE

Brewer's Maple Lane Farm Bed and Breakfast

Rural Route 1, 64836
(417) 358-6312

On the National Register of Historic Places, with 20 rooms filled with family heirlooms, this 240-acre farm is ideal for hunting, fishing, or a family vacation. There is a barnyard of animals, a playground for kids, and a 22-acre lake for fishermen. Hiking, picnic area, and game rooms are also available. Nearby are historic places and art museums.

Hosts: Arch and Renee Brewer
Rooms: 4 (SB) $45
Continental Breakfast
Credit Cards: None
Notes: 2, 5, 8

Leggett House

1106 Grand, 64836
(417) 358-0683

A Victorian stone house; beautiful woodwork throughout; large, airy rooms in period decor. Full breakfast served in formal dining room. Central air conditioning, off-street parking, elevator, big porch equipped with swing. Near downtown historic square and all local points of interest.

Hosts: Nolan and Nancy Henry
Rooms: 5 (1 PB; 4 SB) $45
Full Breakfast
Credit Cards: A, B
Notes: 2, 5, 7

Ozark Mountain Country Bed and Breakfast 209

Box 295, Branson, 65616
(800) 321-8594

This 676-acre farm is eight miles northeast of Carthage. The four-story mansion, built between 1900 and 1904, contains 22 guest rooms filled with family heirloom antiques. Four guest rooms on the second floor. Continental breakfast. Pool and Ping-Pong tables. Tour of the home and grounds. $55.

Ozark Mountain Country Bed and Breakfast 227

Box 295, Branson, 65616
(800) 321-8594

This 1890s mansion filled with antiques permits its guests to return to the Victorian era. Five elegant guest rooms, each uniquely furnished. Private bath. Hearty homemade breakfast. $50-90.

Crescent Lake Manor

EXCELSIOR SPRINGS

Crescent Lake Manor

1261 St. Louis Avenue, 64024
(816) 637-2958

Your retreat from reality! This charming three-story brick mansion, situated on 21 acres, offers hospitality and a visit into the past. It was built during the turn of the century and is surrounded by a moat. A large swimming pool and walking trail are available for your relaxation. Banquet, meeting, and reception areas are available. Rates start at $60.

Host: Mary Elizabeth Leake
Rooms: 4 (SB) $60
Full Breakfast
Credit Cards: B
Notes: 2, 3, 4, 5,7 (restricted), 9, 10, 11, 12, 14

GAINESVILLE

Ozark Mountain Country Bed and Breakfast 225

Box 295, Branson, 65616
(800) 321-8594

6 Pets welcome; 7 Smoking allowed; 8 Children welcome; 9 Social drinking allowed; 10 Tennis available; 11 Swimming available; 12 Golf available; 13 Skiing available; 14 May be booked through travel agents.

This 10,000-square-foot Colonial-style mansion overlooks a private lake. Four guest rooms with four full baths. Country breakfast. Adults only. Guests can enjoy an indoor swimming pool and Jacuzzi spa as well as a game room with pool table and Ping-Pong table. Smoking only in pool room. $55.

HANNIBAL

Fifth Street Mansion

213 South Fifth Street, 63401
(314) 221-0445

Historic 1858 Italianate home of lifelong friends of Mark Twain combines Victorian charm with contemporary comforts. Period furnishings, original fireplaces, stained glass, and old-fashioned hospitality abound. Walk to historic sites, shops, restaurants. Inquire about special weekends.

Hosts: Donalene and Mike Andreotti
Rooms: 7 (PB) $60-90
Full Breakfast
Credit Cards: A, B, C, D
Notes: 2, 5, 7 (restricted), 8, 9, 10, 11, 12, 14

Garth Woodside Mansion

Rural Route 1, 63401
(314) 221-2789

Garth Woodside Mansion

You'll be surrounded by Victorian splendor in this 1871 home that once hosted Mark Twain. Stroll the 39 acres or fish in the pond. Enjoy pampered elegance with afternoon tea and nightshirts for you to wear. Chosen "One of the Ten Best Inns in the Midwest."

Hosts: Irv and Diane Feinberg
Rooms: 8 (PB) $58-90
Full Breakfast
Minimum stay holidays: 2 nights
Credit Cards: A, B
Notes: 2, 5, 7 (limited), 8 (over 12), 9, 10, 12

HERMANN

Alice's Wharf Street Bed and Breakfast

206 Wharf Street, 65041
(314) 486-5785

Private first-floor apartment in former Wiedersprecker-Eitzen store constructed in 1840. This building, built of native red brick, has had a long history. At one time it was the Masonic Hall, later it was headquarters for supplies for river boats on the Missouri River. In the early 1970s the Leo Jacobsons bought and restored this charming old building that overlooks the Missouri River, Gasconade County Court House, and Missouri River Bridge.

Host: Alice A. Jacobson
Suite: 1 (PB) $55
Full Breakfast
Credit Cards: None
Notes: 2, 5, 8, 9, 11, 12

Birk's Gasthaus

700 Goethe Street, 65041
(314) 486-2911

Romantic Victorian mansion. Two weekends a month you can be Agatha Christie and try to solve the mystery of the month.

Hosts: Elmer and Gloria Birk
Rooms: 9 (7 PB; 2 SB) $51.21-83.49
Full Breakfast
Credit Cards: A, B, C, D

NOTES: Credit cards accepted: A Master Card; B Visa; C American Express; D Discover Card; E Diner's Club; F Other; 2 Personal Checks accepted; 3 Lunch available; 4 Dinner available; 5 Open all year;

Closed Dec. 24-Jan. 31
Notes: 2, 7 (limited), 8 (over 16), 9, 10, 11, 12, 14

Mollye C's
Bed and Breakfast

120 East Third Street, 65041
(314) 486-3783

Capture the spirit of Missouri wine country in a quaint four-story German home, circa 1850. A stay in this restored vaulted, stone-and-brick wine cellar is a unique and romantic experience. An adjoining suite features antique quilts and country decor. Also available is an apartment-size suite ideal for an extended stay. All rooms have private entrances, telephones, and cable TV.

Host: Mollye C. Cooper
Rooms: 3 (PB) $75-85
Full Breakfast
Credit Cards: A, B
Notes: 2, 5, 9, 10, 11, 12

Ozark Mountain Country
Bed and Breakfast 232

Box 295, Branson, 65616
(800) 321-8594

The two rooms are located near Hermann, and children are welcome. Features include sitting area for guest, TV/VCR, deck overlooking lake and quaint village, and queen waterbed for one room. Children under two stay for free. Three guest rooms. $45-90.

INDEPENDENCE

Woodstock Inn
Bed and Breakfast

1212 West Lexington, 64050
(816) 833-2233

Situated in the heart of historic Independence, close to the Truman Library and home, historic mansions, sports stadiums, theme parks, and denominational cen-

ters of the Latter Day Saints. Eleven guest rooms, each with private bath, air conditioning, tasteful furnishings. Two suites are handicapped accessible. Excellent food, private parking, personalized touring directions.

Hosts: Mona and Ben Crosby
Rooms: 11 (PB) $45-65
Full Breakfast
Credit Cards: A, B, C
Notes: 2, 5, 8, 9, 10, 11, 12, 14

INDIAN POINT AREA

Ozark Mountain Country
Bed and Breakfast 116

Box 295, Branson, 65616
(800) 321-8594

This home on Indian Point, two miles from Silver Dollar City, is on Table Rock Lake. The home offers a large, carpeted, air-conditioned guest area that is great for families. Private entrance, patio overlooking the lake, large boat dock. Guests may secure a rental boat at dock; public launch is less than a mile from the home. The guest area has a queen bed, sitting area, adjoining bath. Another small bedroom has a double bed. Full breakfast. Children welcome; no smoking. From $50.

Ozark Mountain Country
Bed and Breakfast 117

Box 295, Branson, 65616
(800) 321-8594

This home offers a peaceful lakefront getaway three miles from Silver Dollar City. Amenities include full breakfast, private baths, king and queen beds, TV, view of Table Rock Lake, exclusive use of great room, private entrance, fireplace, whirlpool. Children are welcome. Open all year, and discounts are available January and February. $50-90.

---

6 Pets welcome; 7 Smoking allowed; 8 Children welcome; 9 Social drinking allowed; 10 Tennis available; 11 Swimming available; 12 Golf available; 13 Skiing available; 14 May be booked through travel agents.

Ozark Mountain Country Bed and Breakfast 126

Box 295, Branson, 65616
(800) 321-8594

This contemporary home near Silver Dollar City has a view of Table Rock Lake. Two guest rooms with private baths. Full gourmet breakfast with homemade breads. Children welcome; smoking permitted only on screened porch. $50-75.

JACKSON

Trisha's Bed and Breakfast

203 Bellevue, 63755
(314) 243-7427

Enjoy a gourmet breakfast by candlelight in a 1905 Victorian home in a traditional small town. Tastefully decorated antique bedrooms take you back to yesteryear, yet you will enjoy comfortable amenities at reasonable prices. A vintage steam train operates on weekends only three blocks away. Innkeepers impersonate Bonnie and Clyde, Minnie Pearl, and other colorful characters aboard the train. Come try hospitality, southeast Missouri-style.

Hosts: Gus and Trisha Wischmann
Rooms: 4 (3 PB; 1 SB) $65-75
Full Breakfast

Doanleigh Wallagh Inn

Credit Cards: A, B
Notes: 2, 4, 5, 8, 10, 11, 12, 14

JOPLIN

Ozark Mountain Country Bed and Breakfast 245

Box 295, Branson, 65616
(800) 321-8594

Ten guest rooms are available in this 1898 Victorian mansion in the historic district. Amenities include private baths (claw foot tubs and pedestal sinks), antiques throughout, hearty breakfast, and restaurant-style room service. King and queen beds with elegant decor. $50-75.

Visages

327 North Jackson, 64801
(417) 624-1397

Visages, built in 1898, is named for the faces on exterior masonry walls and family portraits inside. Its beauty is achieved through artistry and ingenuity, not money. Marge and Bill, retired teachers, find guests fascinating and enjoy serving a typical mid-American breakfast.

Hosts: Bill and Marge Meeker
Rooms: 3 (1 PB; 2 SB) $30-60
Full Breakfast
Credit Cards: A, B, C
Notes: 2, 5, 8, 9, 10, 11, 12

KANSAS CITY

Doanleigh Wallagh Inn

217 East 37th Street, 64111
(816) 753-2667

A turn-of-the-century mansion minutes from Crown Center, Country Club Plaza, and Westport. Antiques, telephone, and cable television with movie channels in each room. Also available for parties, weddings, and conferences. Hosts will help plan sightseeing and make restaurant reservations.

NOTES: Credit cards accepted: A Master Card; B Visa; C American Express; D Discover Card; E Diner's Club; F Other; 2 Personal Checks accepted; 3 Lunch available; 4 Dinner available; 5 Open all year;

Hosts: Carolyn and Edward Litchfield
Rooms: 5 (PB) $80-110
Full Breakfast
Credit Cards: A, B, C
Notes: 2, 5, 7 (limited), 8, 9, 10, 12, 14

Hotel Savoy

219 West 9th Street, 64105
(816) 842-3575

Hotel Savoy is one of the finest European bed and breakfast hotel in the United States. Built in 1888, it offers the opportunity to drift back into time in suites filled with antiques and Victorian decor. Breakfast consists of more than 32 items such as lobster bisque, salmon and caviar, medallions of beef, or even oysters Rockefeller. Situated in the heart of Kansas City's historic garment district. A very romantic getaway.

Host: Sean Byrnes
Rooms: 110 (PB) $79-120
Full Breakfast
Credit Cards: A, B, C, D, E, F
Notes: 2, 3, 4, 5, 6, 7, 8, 9, 14

Milford House

3605 Gillham Road, 64111
(816) 753-1269

Milford House is a three-story red brick home combining Queen Anne and Dutch Colonial architecture, situated conveniently

Hotel Savoy

between the Plaza and Crown Center. The guest rooms are reached by climbing the 100-year-old spiral staircase and are furnished with antiques. Each guest room is equipped with cable TV. The livingroom is dominated by a 70-square-foot stained-glass window which is a copy of a Tiffany landscape. The house is centrally heated and air-conditioned and breakfast is a real eye-opener.

Hosts: Ian and Pat Mills
Rooms: 4 (PB) $70
Full Breakfast
Credit Cards: A, B, C
Notes: 2, 5, 9, 10, 14

Pridewell

600 West 50th Street, 64112
(816) 931-1642

A fine Tudor residence situated in a residential area on the site of the Civil War battle of Westport. Near the Nelson Art Gallery; University of Missouri, Kansas City; Missouri Repertory Theatre; Rockhurst College. Adjacent to County Club Plaza shopping district, including several four-star restaurants, public transportation, public tennis courts, and park.

Hosts: Edwin and Louann White
Rooms: 2 (1 PB; 1 SB) $65-70
Full Breakfast
Credit Cards: None
Notes: 2, 5, 8, 9, 14

Southmoreland on the Plaza

116 East 46th Street, 64112
(816) 531-7979

A two-time winner of "Top Bed and Breakfasts in the United States," and awarded "Outstanding Achievement in Preservations" by the Association of American Inns and "Most Romantic New Urban Inn" by *Romantic Hideaways* newsletter, this classic New England Colonial located between Country Club Plaza and the Nelson-Atkins Museum of Art has elegant bed and breakfast atmosphere with

6 Pets welcome; 7 Smoking allowed; 8 Children welcome; 9 Social drinking allowed; 10 Tennis available; 11 Swimming available; 12 Golf available; 13 Skiing available; 14 May be booked through travel agents.

small hotel amenities. Many rooms offer private decks or fireplaces. Special services designed for business travelers. Sport and dining privileges at a nearby historic private club.

Hosts: Penni Johnson and Susan Moehl
Rooms: 12 (PB) $105-125 plus tax
Full Breakfast
Credit Cards: A, B, C
Notes: 2, 5, 9, 14

KIMBERLING CITY AREA

Ozark Mountain Country Bed and Breakfast 102-A

Box 295, Branson, 65616
(800) 321-8594

This charming log home is four miles south of Kimberling City. Full breakfast is served. Two guest rooms available. The room in the loft is decorated with antiques. Downstairs guest bath includes tub and shower. Smoking only on deck. No pre-teenagers. $50-90.

Ozark Mountain Country Bed and Breakfast 102-B

Box 295, Branson, 65616
(800) 321-8594

A log cabin with double bed plus sleeper sofa is at your disposal. There is also a sleeping loft for children, and you are entitled to a full breakfast. Open April through November. $50.

Ozark Mountain Country Bed and Breakfast 102-C

Box 295, Branson, 65616
(800) 321-8594

Gingerbread-style log cabin has queen bed, kitchenette, sleeping loft for three, Franklin stove, and continental breakfast is self-serve. Open all year. $60.

Ozark Mountain Country Bed and Breakfast 111

Box 295, Branson, 65616
(800) 321-8594

Victorian furnishings and unique decor adorn this house located near Kimberling City. Amenities include private entrance, bath with shower, king bed, sitting area, cable TV, lake view deck, and gourmet breakfast. No smoking. Open all year. $50-65.

Southmoreland on the Plaza

Ozark Mountain Country Bed and Breakfast 137

Box 295, Branson, 65616
(800) 321-8594

Located near a golf course in Kimberling City, this bed and breakfast offers private entrances, private baths, deck, sitting area, TV/VCR, full breakfast, queen and double beds. Not suitable for children. No smoking. Available all year. $60-125.

LAKE TANEYCOMO

Ozark Mountain Country Bed and Breakfast 114

Box 295, Branson, 65616
(800) 321-8594

NOTES: Credit cards accepted: A Master Card; B Visa; C American Express; D Discover Card; E Diner's Club; F Other; 2 Personal Checks accepted; 3 Lunch available; 4 Dinner available; 5 Open all year;

Your suite overlooks Lake Taneycomo and valley. Features include private entrance, full breakfast, cable TV, great room, queen bed, sleeper sofa, and private bath. Families would love it. Weekends only September through May. $55.

Ozark Mountain Country Bed and Breakfast 133

Box 295, Branson, 65616
(800) 321-8594

Lake Taneycomo is practically on the doorstep of this new rustic cedar home. Some of the features include private entrance, private bath, TV, king and queen bed, whirlpool tub, king bed, kitchenettes, sleeper sofa, dining area and great room in lake cabin. No smoking. $60-75.

LAMPE

Ozark Mountain Country Bed and Breakfast 105

Box 295, Branson, 65616
(800) 321-8594

A contemporary home with spectacular lake view, this elegant retreat offers two guest rooms, each with double bed and bath. Guests have exclusive use of TV, game room, pool table, wet bar, lakeside patio, and refrigerator. School-age children welcome. Hearty country breakfast served. $55-75.

Ozark Mountain Country Bed and Breakfast 121

Box 295, Branson, 65616
(800) 321-8594

You can get a special country breakfast at this farm home built in 1890 near Lampe. Features include king bed, private entrance,

bath/hot tub, garden room, family suite, hiking trails, and deck. Children are welcome. Available all year. $45-65.

LEBANON

Ozark Mountain Country Bed and Breakfast 246

Box 295, Branson, 65616
(800) 321-8594

This spacious contemporary/country home is just three miles from Lebanon. You can be treated to a full breakfast, have a private bath, queen bed, sleeper sofa. Well-behaved children are welcome. Smoking is permitted. $50.

LOUISIANA

The Orthwein Mansion

2000 West Georgia Street, 63353
(314) 754-5449; (314) 965-4328

In Louisiana, Missouri, a Mississippi River town, enjoy bed and breakfast in an imposing baronial mansion. Polished wood, stained-glass windows, tapestried walls, and hand-painted canvas ceilings offer you a charming Old World setting in the serenity you deserve. Featured in *Midwest Living* and *St. Louis* Magazine.

Hosts: Clarence and Dottie Brown
Rooms: 3 (1 PB; 2 SB) $70-90
Continental Breakfast
Credit Cards: None
Notes: 2, 5, 7, 9, 12

MANSFIELD

Ozark Mountain Country Bed and Breakfast 233

Box 295, Branson, 65616
(800) 321-8594

This quaint bungalow with country Victorian decor and antiques is located near the Laura Ingalls Wilder home. Children are welcome, and a hearty country breakfast is served. No smoking. $35-45.

Ozark Mountain Country Bed and Breakfast 234

Box 295, Branson, 65616
(800) 321-8594

A stone's throw from the Wilder home, this contemporary-style home offers hiking trails, picnic area, fishing ponds, optional picnics and dinners, great room with cathedral ceiling, fireplace, games, and TV. Open all year. Delicious breakfasts. $60.

MARIONVILLE

Ozark Mountain Country Bed and Breakfast 210

Box 295, Branson, 65616
(800) 321-8594

This 1896 Victorian mansion, situated 21 miles southwest of Springfield, has been completely restored with antiques and stained glass. You can watch rare white squirrels romp here. Hearty country breakfast. Five guest rooms. Well-behaved children are welcome. Winter rates and group rates available. Specials for wedding/honeymoon combination. Resident dog. Smoking in common areas. $45-75.

MARTHASVILLE

Gramma's House Bed and Breakfast

1105 Highway D, 63357
(314) 433-2675

Recall the good memories of your gramma's house when you stay in this 150-year-old farmhouse. Nearby attractions are the historic Daniel Boone Home, antique shopping, wineries, and the Katy hiking and biking trail. Gramma's House has three guest rooms plus the Old Smokehouse Cottage, which is a perfect cozy atmosphere for a romantic couple.

Hosts: Judy and Jim Jones
Rooms: 4 (2 PB; 2 SB) $50-75
Full Breakfast
Credit Cards: A, B
Notes: 2, 5, 7, 8, 9, 14

MEXICO

Hylas House Inn

811 South Jefferson, 65265
(314) 581-2011

A gracious and elegant bed and breakfast experience. Italianate architecture, magnificent staircase, moulded scroll work on staircase, moulded scroll work on staircase, windows with leaded glass, white carpeting, and deep cherry wood. Four bedrooms. Three shared bathrooms. Suite with parlor and lounging balcony with chairs. Cable remote TV in three rooms with telephones. Rooms color-coordinated. Gourmet full breakfast includes freshly ground coffee, fresh muffins, and fresh fruits. Museum and antique stores within a ten-minute walk. Spacious lawns and flower beds.

Hosts: Tom and Linda Hylas
Rooms: 4 (1 PB; 3 SB) $45-95
Full Breakfast
Credit Cards: A, B,
Notes: 2, 5, 7, 9, 10, 12, 14

MOUNTAIN VIEW

Ozark Mountain Country Bed and Breakfast 237

Box 295, Branson, 65616
(800) 321-8594

Mark Twain National Forrest and streams are near this rambling country home with parklike grounds. Relax in the gazebo, on the deck, in the spa or pool. A hearty country breakfast is served. We offer specials for wedding/honeymoon combo. Open all year. Children over ten are welcome. Group rates and winter rates are also available. $75.

NIXA

Ozark Mountain Country Bed and Breakfast 211

Box 295, Branson, 65616
(800) 321-8594

This charming country home four miles south of Springfield is filled with antiques. Full country breakfast is served on antique china. Resident dogs and cats. No smoking or pre-teenagers. Whirlpool tub. One room has a queen canopy bed with adjoining bath and sitting room. $40-95.

OSAGE BEACH

Ozark Mountain Country Bed and Breakfast 208

Box 295, Branson, 65616
(800) 321-8594

This beach house provides three guest rooms. One has private entrance to private area, sitting area with TV, and kitchenette. Other two share adjoining baths and private patio. Children welcome. Smoking permitted. Continental breakfast in guest area. Boat dock for guest use. $80.

Ozark Mountain Country Bed and Breakfast 228

Box 295, Branson, 65616
(800) 321-8594

Contemporary lakeside home features sitting area with fireplace. On the lower level, there is a guest room with queen-size bed and private bath with shower. On the main level, there are two guest rooms which share a hall bath with tub. Hearty breakfast. Smoking only on decks. $60.

Ozark Mountain Country Bed and Breakfast 238

Box 295, Branson, 65616
(800) 321-8594

Exclusive use of contemporary two-bedroom home. Features include full kitchen, continental breakfast, boat dock for guest use with space for boat, king/queen bed, and children are welcome. Sleeps 12-16 persons. Available March through November. $100-250.

Ozark Mountain Country Bed and Breakfast 246

Box 295, Branson, 65616
(800) 321-8594

A private suite overlooking Lake of the Ozarks is available with guest sitting area and hearty breakfast. Adults only and no smoking. Available May through October. $60.

OZARK

Ozark Mountain Country Bed and Breakfast 236

Box 295, Branson, 65616
(800) 321-8594

This rustic home built by Amish craftsmen is located 12 miles from Ozark and 20 miles from Springfield. Wooded surroundings include a view of Mark Twain National Forest. Feel free to relax in spa on

6 Pets welcome; 7 Smoking allowed; 8 Children welcome; 9 Social drinking allowed; 10 Tennis available; 11 Swimming available; 12 Golf available; 13 Skiing available; 14 May be booked through travel agents.

the deck at the end of each day or bring a book to cuddle up with next to the fireplace. Other features include queen bed, TV, huge bath tub and shower, antiques, upstairs loft room and dressing area. Expect a bountiful breakfast. $50-85.

PARKVILLE-KANSAS CITY

Down to Earth Lifestyles Bed and Breakfast

12500 North Crooked Road, 64152
(816) 891-1018

Unique getaway haven offering the best of midwestern country and city living. Indoor heated pool, plus 86 acres with farm animals, fishing ponds, wildlife, walking, and jogging areas. Full special-order breakfast served at place and time of guest's choice.

Hosts: Lola and Bill Coons
Rooms: 4 (PB) $59-69
Full Breakfast
Credit Cards: None
Notes: 2, 5, 7, 8, 9, 10, 11, 12, 13, 14

Ozark Mountain Country Bed and Breakfast 245

Box 295, Branson, 65616
(800) 321-8594

This unique bed and breakfast is actually an earth shelter home on a farm near Kansas City. There are fish in the pond, and be sure to bring your swim suit for the heated indoor pool. Other amenities include patio, picnic table, lounge, quilts, antiques, great room, fireplace, piano, guest entrance, and parking. A full breakfast is served in this smoke-free environment. $55-75.

PLATTE CITY

Basswood Country Bed and Breakfast

15880 Interurban Road, 64079
(816) 431-5556

Come stay where the rich and famous relaxed and played in the 1940s and 1950s! Most beautiful secluded, wooded, private lakefront accommodations in entire Kansas City area. Try the Truman, Bing Crosby, or Rudy Vallee suites, the 1935, the Mother-in-law cottage, or country French suites.

Hosts: Don and Betty Soper
Rooms: 7 (PB) $58-125
Cottage: 1 (PB) $93
Continental Breakfast
Minimum stay holidays: 2 nights
Credit Cards: A, B
Notes: 2, 5, 7, 8 (over 7), 9, 11, 12, 13, 14

ROCHEPORT-COLUMBIA

School House Bed and Breakfast

Third and Clark Streets, 65279
(314) 698-2022

The School House is a three-story brick school building with 13-foot ceilings, black slate chalkboards, and a number nine cast-iron school bell on the front lawn. It is a magical setting for reliving fond school memories or for just getting away. Each of the eight guest rooms is uniquely furnished with beautiful but unassuming antiques. A delicious breakfast is prepared in the turn-of-the-century second-floor classroom. Antique shops and a pottery shop; a riverview walking and bicycling corridor; a local winery, cafe, and bistro are all in this historic river town listed on the National Register of Historic Places.

NOTES: Credit cards accepted: A Master Card; B Visa; C American Express; D Discover Card; E Diner's Club; F Other; 2 Personal Checks accepted; 3 Lunch available; 4 Dinner available; 5 Open all year;

Hosts: Vicki and John Ott
Rooms: 8 (6 PB; 2 SB) $60-100
Full Breakfast
Credit Cards: A, B
Notes: 2, 5, 8, 9, 14

STE. GENEVIEVE

The Creole House
Bed and Breakfast

339 St. Mary's Road, 63670
(314) 883-7171; (800) 275-6041

This French Creole-style house on 2.5 acres is set within the city limits of Missouri's oldest town. Amenities include spacious rooms with attached sitting rooms, fireplaces, a Jacuzzi bath tub. Relax on breezy galleries and enjoy a view of the *grand champ* "big field." Hospitality hour is every afternoon, and full gourmet breakfasts are delicious; shops, restaurants, and historic French Colonial homes are a short walk away. Open all year.

Hosts: Royce and Marge Wilhauk
Rooms: 4 (2 PB; 2 SB) $68-98
Full Breakfast
Credit Cards: A, B
Notes: 2, 5, 6 (call), 7 (limited), 8, 9, 11, 12

Inn Ste. Gemme Beauvais

78 North Main, 63670
(314) 883-5744

This inn is the oldest continuously operating inn in Missouri. Located in the historic district of the oldest permanet settlement west of the Mississippi, you can choose from seven guest rooms furnished with antiques. A three-course breakfast is served in the elegant Victorian livingroom, and all historic buildings are within walking distance. Lunch is served daily, and dinner is served by special arrangement.

Host: Janet Joggerst
Rooms: 12 (10 PB; 2 SB) $40-65
Full Breakfast
Credit Cards: None
Notes: 2, 3, 5, 7, 8, 9, 10, 11, 12

ST. LOUIS

The Coachlight
Bed and Breakfast

P.O. Box 8095, 63156
(314) 367-5870

Three-story turn-of-the-century brick home situated in the historic central West End. Furnishings include fine antiques, Laura Ashley fabrics, down comforters, antique quilts, mahogany four-poster bed, brass bed, white wicker furniture. Within walking distance of historic mansions, sidewalk cafes, unique shops, and galleries. Next to forest park, art museum, zoo. Minutes from the Arch and riverfront.

Hosts: Susan and Chuck Sundermeyer
Rooms: 3 (PB) $65-80
Full Breakfast
Credit Cards: A, B, C
Notes: 2, 5, 7 (limited), 8 (over 3), 9, 10, 12, 14

Lafayette House

2156 Lafayette Avenue, 63104
(314) 772-4429

An 1876 brick Queen Anne mansion in the center of things to do in St. Louis. Furnished with antiques but with modern conveniences. Extensive library, many interesting collections. Complimentary soda, cheese, crackers. Train, plane, and bus pick-up for a small fee. Four cats in residence.

Lafayette House

Hosts: Sarah and Jack Milligan
Rooms: 4 (1 PB; 3 SB) $50-75
Suite: 1 (PB) sleeps 6-8
Full Breakfast
Minimum stay in suite: 2 nights
Credit Cards: A, B
Notes: 2, 5, 6 (prior arrangement), 7 (limited), 8, 9,
  10, 11, 12, 13, 14

Ozark Mountain Country Bed and Breakfast 241

Box 295, Branson, 65616
(800) 321-8594

This large two-story suburban home is complete with antiques, collectibles, homemade breads and breakfast cakes. You have three rooms to choose from. $35-45.

Ozark Mountain Country Bed and Breakfast 242

Box 295, Branson, 65616
(800) 321-8594

Located on the bluffs of the Mississippi River, this French Colonial home was built circa 1790. Completely and authentically restored, features include a spacious solarium, antiques, quilts, dining room with working fireplace, private and shared baths, homemade breads and continental breakfast. Children are welcome, especially if they want to meet the resident cat. $45-60.

Ozark Mountain Country Bed and Breakfast 243

Box 295, Branson, 65616
(800) 321-8594

In the historic district of St. Charles, this 1840 inn is quaintly furnished with old quilts and late 1800s antiques. You have six guest rooms to choose from (four have private showers and entrances). Two rooms include shared bath with claw foot tub and shower. Children over ten welcome. No smoking. $50-75.

The Winter House

3522 Arsenal Street, 63118
(314) 664-4399

Ten-room Victorian built in 1897 features pressed-tin ceiling in lower bedroom and a suite with balcony and decorative fireplace on second floor. Breakfast is served in the dining room using crystal and antique Wedgewood china and always includes freshly squeezed orange juice. Tea and live piano music are available by reservation. Fruit, candy, and fresh flowers are provided in bedrooms. Nearby attractions include a Victorian walking park on the National Register and the Missouri Botanical Garden. Within four miles are the Arch, Busch Baseball Stadium, the new Science Center, zoo, symphony, and Union Station. Walk to fine dining. Reservations required.

Hosts: Sarah and Kendall Winter
Room: 1 (PB) $55
Suite: 1 (PB) $70
Expanded Continental Breakfast
Credit Cards: A, B, C, D, E
Notes: 2, 5, 8, 9, 10, 11, 12, 14

SEDALIA

Ozark Mountain Country Bed and Breakfast 244

Box 295, Branson, 65616
(800) 321-8594

This 1900s home on a farm, located near Sedalia, is decorated with antiques. Your pets can be accommodated or meet the resident dogs, if you like. Expect a hearty breakfast to start your day. $48-55.

SHELL KNOB

Ozark Mountain Country Bed and Breakfast 128

Box 295, Branson, 65616
(800) 321-8594

NOTES: Credit cards accepted: A Master Card; B Visa; C American Express; D Discover Card; E Diner's Club; F Other; 2 Personal Checks accepted; 3 Lunch available; 4 Dinner available; 5 Open all year;

Located 28 miles to Eureka Springs and 28 miles to Silver Dollar City, this bed and breakfast has a deck that overlooks Table Rock Lake. Water activities include a pool, rowboat, swimming area in the lake, and complimentary cruises on the lake. Other features include private entrance, private bath, kitchenette, hot tub on deck, sitting area, queen beds, and children are welcome. Open all year. $40-70.

Ozark Mountain Country Bed and Breakfast 129

Box 295, Branson, 65616
(800) 321-8594

This private suite is one-half block from Table Rock Lake near Shell Knob. At your disposal is a complete kitchen, dining area, sitting area and queen sleeper sofa. Open all year. $60.

Ozark Mountain Country Bed and Breakfast 130

Box 295, Branson, 65616
(800) 321-8594

Boat rides on Table Rock Lake with this contemporary bed and breakfast located two blocks away from the lake. Other features include exclusive guest sitting room, queen or double bed, fireplace, TV, and hearty breakfast. Open all year. $45-48.

SILVER DOLLAR CITY

Ozark Mountain Country Bed and Breakfast 119

Box 295, Branson, 65616
(800) 321-8594

Contemporary lake-view home four miles from Silver Dollar City. Near Highway 265. Special gourmet breakfast. Hostess operated a catering service for 18 years. Smoking permitted in common areas only. Private bath. Adults only. Two guest rooms with TV and air conditioning. $50-70.

Ozark Mountain Country Bed and Breakfast 122

Box 295, Branson, 65616
(800) 321-8594

This private guest cottage, built in the 1920s and recently refurbished, is situated one-half mile from Silver Dollar City on Highway 76. Great for special occasions. Bath with pedestal tub and separate shower. Dining area with ceiling fan, equipped kitchenette. Hearty continental breakfast in cottage. Air conditioning, private patio. Adults only. $60-80.

SPRINGFIELD

Mansion at Elfindale

1701 South Fort, 65807
(417) 831-5400

The Mansion, built in the 1800s, features ornate fireplaces, stained-glass windows, and unique architecturally designed rooms. It offers 13 suites, all of which have private baths, and a full breakfast served in the dining room and prepared by an English chef. Weddings, banquets, or even small business meetings can be accommodated at the Mansion. Come relive the past in Missouri's largest bed and breakfast.

Host: Paula Gibson
Rooms: 13 (PB) $70-125
Full Breakfast
Credit Cards: A, B, C, D
Notes: 2, 3, 5, 14

Ozark Mountain Country Bed and Breakfast 205

Box 295, Branson, 65616
(800) 321-8594

6 Pets welcome; 7 Smoking allowed; 8 Children welcome; 9 Social drinking allowed; 10 Tennis available; 11 Swimming available; 12 Golf available; 13 Skiing available; 14 May be booked through travel agents.

Colonial-style home with antiques situated in a quiet, rural area in southeast Springfield. Three guest rooms available. Two rooms upstairs share a hall bath. The private suite has a sitting room with TV and fireplace, and a kitchen. Full breakfast in formal dining room. Airport pickup can be arranged. Two resident Yorkshire terriers. All guests can enjoy a Jacuzzi spa and exercise/game room. $40-70.

Ozark Mountain Country Bed and Breakfast 206

Box 295, Branson, 65616
(800) 321-8594

Take a step back in time! This 1894 mansion situated in Springfield's historic district has been redecorated with antiques and stained glass. The gathering room has a fireplace and game table. Seven distinctive guest rooms. Full gourmet breakfast. Weekday special, Sunday through Thursday. Children over eight welcome. Smoking only on veranda. $65-110.

SUNRISE BEACH

Ozark Mountain Country Bed and Breakfast 235

Box 295, Branson, 65616
(800) 321-8594

This elegant home is on the quiet side of Lake of the Ozarks with a spectacular view. Amenities include fresh flowers, swimming/fishing dock, gas grill, sitting area, spa, and a gourmet breakfast served overlooking the lake. Fishing trips, candlelight dinners, and cruiser excursions can be arranged to Tantara Resort. Also available is dinner at nearby Amish settlement. Open all year. $75-95.

TABLE ROCK LAKE

Ozark Mountain Country Bed and Breakfast 106

Box 295, Branson, 65616
(800) 321-8594

This bed and breakfast is located one and one-quarter miles from a marina and swimming area, and just up the hill from Table Rock Lake. Features include private baths, livingroom, TV, and sleeper sofa. A continental breakfast is served in this smoke-free environment. $35-45.

Ozark Mountain Country Bed and Breakfast 116

Box 295, Branson, 65616
(800) 321-8594

Located on Indian Point and two miles from Silver Dollar City, this bed and breakfast offers two lake view suites, private entrances, private baths, boat launch, full breakfast, homemade breads, air conditioning, view of the lake, queen bed, TV, sleeper sofa, and whirlpool. No smoking and open all year. $55-65.

WARRENSBURG

Cedarcroft Farm

Route 3, 431 SE "Y" Highway, 64093
(816) 747-5728; (800) 368-4944

Cedarcroft Farm offers old-fashioned country hospitality, country quiet, and country cooking in an antique-filled 1867 family farmhouse. Guests may explore the 80 acres of secluded woods, meadows, and streams, and enjoy a full country breakfast. Civil War re-enactor hosts demonstrate 1860s soldiers' life. Horseback riding and bike trails nearby.

NOTES: Credit cards accepted: A Master Card; B Visa; C American Express; D Discover Card; E Diner's Club; F Other; 2 Personal Checks accepted; 3 Lunch available; 4 Dinner available; 5 Open all year;

Hosts: Sandra and Bill Wayne
Rooms: 2 (SB) $43-50
Full Breakfast
Credit Cards: A, B, D
Notes: 2, 4, 5, 7 (limited), 8, 9, 11, 12, 14

WASHINGTON

Washington House Bed and Breakfast

3 Lafayette Street, 63090
(314) 239-2417; (314) 239-9834

Washington House, built circa 1837, is situated in a National Historic District. This authentically restored inn on the Missouri River features river views, canopy beds, antiques, complimentary wine, and full breakfast. Washington House is situated in the heart of Missouri's wine country, only 45 minutes west of St. Louis.

Hosts: Chuck and Kathy Davis
Rooms: 4 (PB) $55-75
Full Breakfast
Credit Cards: None
Notes: 2, 5, 8, 9, 10, 11, 12, 14

WEST PLAINS

Ozark Mountain Country Bed and Breakfast 212

Box 295, Branson, 65616
(800) 321-8594

This farm welcomes pets and has a stable for horses. Double beds with hall bath. Resident cat. Weekends only. $35-60.

Ozark Mountain Country Bed and Breakfast 219

Box 295, Branson, 65616
(800) 321-8594

This 100-year-old Colonial-style home offers many antiques, a library, and a gazebo. Three guest rooms share two hall baths with tub and shower. $32.50-55.

6 Pets welcome; 7 Smoking allowed; 8 Children welcome; 9 Social drinking allowed; 10 Tennis available; 11 Swimming available; 12 Golf available; 13 Skiing available; 14 May be booked through travel agents.

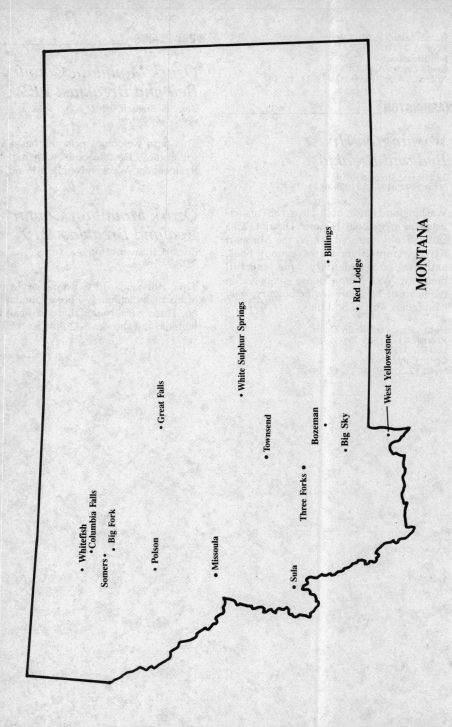

MONTANA

• Billings

• Red Lodge

• White Sulphur Springs

• Great Falls

• Townsend

West Yellowstone

• Big Sky

Bozeman

• Three Forks

Sula •

• Whitefish
• Columbia Falls
Somers • • Big Fork

• Polson

• Missoula

Montana

Burggraf's Countrylane Bed 'n Breakfast on Swan Lake

Rainbow Drive, 59911
(406) 837-4608; (800) 525-3344

Log home on seven acres beside Swan Lake with panoramic view, only 45 minutes from Glacier National Park. All-you-can-eat breakfast. Complimentary bottle of wine with fruit and cheese tray upon arrival. Guest refrigerator, Jacuzzi/whirlpool tub. All rooms with TVs.

Hosts: Natalie and R. J. Burggraf
Rooms: 5 (PB) $75
Full Breakfast
Credit Cards: A, B
Notes: 2, 3, 5, 8, 9, 11, 12, 13

Gustin Orchard

East Lake Shore, 59911
(406) 983-3329

Bordered by majestic pines and halted only by the shores of the whimsical giant of Flathead Lake, the ten-acre mountainside working cherry orchard greets its guests with two different themes of vacation residence. The fully restored and equipped lakeside log cottage blends its early decor with romantic seclusion, while the in-home room, with large bays, is set amid rock gardens and ponds. All accommodations have private bath, fireplace, barbecue, and patios.

Host: Carol Gustin
Rooms: 2 (PB) $75-115
Full Breakfast (room); Continental Breakfast (log cottage)
Credit Cards: None
Notes: 2, 6, 7, 8, 9, 10, 11, 12, 13, 14

O'Duachain Country Inn

675 Ferndale Drive, 59911
(406) 837-6851

Luxurious log lodging with full gourmet breakfast. Situated on five acres of landscaped solitude. Walking trails, ponds, and wildlife. One-day junkets include Glacier National Park, Flathead and Swan lakes and valleys, Jewel Basin hiking, National Bison Range. Golf, swimming, boating, and skiing areas abound.

Hosts: Margot and Tom Doohan
Rooms: 5 (2 PB; 3 SB) $65-85
Full Breakfast
Credit Cards: A, B, C
Notes: 2, 5, 8, 9, 10, 11, 12, 13

Lone Mountain Ranch

Box 160069, 59716
(406) 995-4644

Comfortable ranch cabin accommodations nestled in a secluded valley. Horseback riding, Yellowstone National Park interpretive trips, Orvis-endorsed fly-fishing program, kids' activities, nature hikes in summer. Cross-country skiing, sleigh-ride dinners in winter. Nationally acclaimed cuisine in the spectacular new dining lodge. All meals are included in the weekly rate.

NOTES: Credit cards accepted: A Master Card; B Visa; C American Express; D Discover Card; E Diner's Club; F Other; 2 Personal Checks accepted; 3 Lunch available; 4 Dinner available; 5 Open all year; 6 Pets welcome; 7 Smoking allowed; 8 Children welcome; 9 Social drinking allowed; 10 Tennis available; 11 Swimming available; 12 Golf available; 13 Skiing available; 14 May be booked through travel agents.

Hosts: Bob and Vivian Schaap
Cabins: 23 (PB) $900-1140/week
Full Breakfast
Credit Cards: A, B, D
Notes: 2, 3, 4, 8, 9, 10, 12, 13, 14

Hosts: Richard and Patricia Crowle
Rooms: 3 (1 PB; 2 SB) $40-65
Full Breakfast
Credit Cards: A, B
Notes: 2, 5, 9, 13, 14

BILLINGS

Feather Cove Inn

5530 Vermilion Road, 59105
(406) 373-5679; (800) 735-1695

A spacious cedar-sided ranch-style home on five acres overlooking the beautiful Vermilion River Valley. A two-acre private lake is stocked with large-mouth bass. One mile to Yellowstone River and 15 minutes to Pompeys Pillar Monument. One hour to Big Horn Battlefield. Amenities abound with garden hot tub, bicycle and paddle boat rentals, hay and sleigh rides, romantic candlelight dinners. Full, delicious breakfast served daily. Honeymoon Suite with one veranda and private outdoor breakfast available.

Hosts: Larry and Kathy Gantz
Rooms: 4 (1 PB; 3 SB) $46-60
Full Breakfast
Credit Cards: A, B, D
Notes: 2, 3, 4, 5, 7 (restricted), 8, 9, 11, 12, 13, 14

BOZEMAN

Sun House Bed and Breakfast

9986 Happy Acres West, 59715
(406) 587-3651

Sun House is a quiet country retreat five miles south of Bozeman. This large solar home features a garden solarium, breakfast room, deluxe creekside setting, nature trails, and spectacular mountain views. Sun House is two miles from Hyalite Canyon Recreation area; 25 miles from two ski areas and three blue-ribbon trout streams; and 90 miles north of Yellowstone National Park.

Torch and Toes Bed and Breakfast

309 South Third Avenue, 59715
(406) 586-7285; (800) 446-2138

Set back from the street, it looks much as it did when it was built in 1906. A tall, trim brick-and-frame house in the Colonial Revival-style. There are just enough lace curtains and turn-of-the-century furniture to remind one that this is a house with a past. Smells of blueberry muffins, coddled eggs, and fresh fruit will entice you to breakfast in the oak-paneled dining room with the wood-burning fireplace.

Hosts: Ronald and Judy Hess
Rooms: 4 (2 PB; 2 SB) $50-55
Full Breakfast
Credit Cards: A, B
Notes: 2, 5, 8, 9, 13, 14

Torch and Toes

NOTES: Credit cards accepted: A Master Card; B Visa; C American Express; D Discover Card; E Diner's Club; F Other; 2 Personal Checks accepted; 3 Lunch available; 4 Dinner available; 5 Open all year;

Voss Inn Bed and Breakfast

319 South Wilson, 59715
(406) 587-0982

Magnificently restored Victorian inn in the historic district with elegant guest rooms with private baths. A delightful gourmet breakfast is served in the privacy of your room. Bozeman is 90 miles north of Yellowstone Park, near skiing, fishing, hiking, snowmobiling. Guided day trips are conducted into Yellowstone and the surrounding area by your host.

Hosts: Bruce and Frankee Muller
Rooms: 6 (PB) $55-70
Full Breakfast
Credit Cards: A, B
Notes: 2, 5, 8 (over 5), 9, 10, 11, 12, 14

Voss Inn

COLUMBIA FALLS

Mountain Timbers Lodge

5385 Rabe Road, 59912
(406) 387-5830

Serene wilderness lodge situated in the Rocky Mountains with all the modern amenities. Just one mile outside Glacier National Park, which has the "most abundant wildlife in the lower forty-eight states" (*National Geographic* magazine). Enjoy incredible views into the heart of Glacier National Park. Six tastefully furnished rooms, with private and shared baths. This lodge is built out of 450-year-old tamarack logs. Enjoy downhill and cross-country skiing and then soak in the Jacuzzi. The tenth largest ski area in the country only 25 miles from the lodge.

Hosts: Dane and Bonnie McNabb
Rooms: 7 (2 PB; 5 SB) $50-85
Full Breakfast
Credit Cards: A, B
Notes: 2, 5, 8, 9, 12, 13, 14

GREAT FALLS

The Chalet Bed and Breakfast Inn

1204 Fourth Avenue North, 59401
(406) 452-9001

Built in 1909, this former governor's home retains the grace and charm of an earlier age while providing modern comforts. Guest rooms range from quaint and cozy to spacious and elegant. Help yourself to refreshments in the butler's pantry. Breakfast features local products. Violin-making classes available. Conveniently situated across from the C.M. Russell Museum on the way to Glacier and Yellowstone national parks.

Hosts: Margie and Dave Anderson
Rooms: 5 (2 PB; 3 SB) $35-60
Full Breakfast
Credit Cards: C, D
Notes: 2, 3, 4, 5, 7, 8, 9, 10, 11, 12, 13, 14

The Sarah Bed and Breakfast Inn

626 4th Avenue North, 59401
(406) 452-5906

You will experience the simple elegance and quaint character of this grand Victorian mansion. You will enjoy a full gourmet breakfast served each morning in the wainscoted dining room. The front porch is a very enjoyable area. In the heart of the historical area of Great Falls, within walking distance of the famous C.M. Russel

Museum and Gibson Park. Also available is a suite that has two bedrooms, living-room, and a private bath.

Hosts: Paul and Lynne Stubbs
Rooms: 6 (2 PB; 3 SB) $50-110
Full Breakfast
Credit Cards: None
Notes: 2, 5, 8, 14

MISSOULA

Goldsmith's Inn

809 E. Front Street, 59801
(406) 721-6732

This beautiful 1911 brick home is situated on the banks of the Clark Fork River, only four blocks from downtown Missoula. You can enjoy your breakfast in the dining room which captures an unparalleled view of the Bitterfoot Mountain and the sparkles of the Clark Fork River as it glistens in the morning sun. Formerly the home for several University of Montana presidents.

Hosts: Jean and Richard Goldsmith
Rooms: 7 (PB) $65-75
Full Breakfast
Credit Cards: A, B, C, E
Notes: 2, 3, 5, 8, 9, 10, 12, 13, 14

POLSON

Ruth's Bed and Breakfast

802 Seventh Avenue West, 59860
(406) 883-2460

There are two guest rooms with portable bathroom facilities and one room in this home. Bath and shower are shared. Each room has a comfortable double bed, TV, and sofa that can be used for an extra bed. Each room will accommodate four people.

Host: Ruth Hunter
Rooms: 3 (SB) $28
Full Breakfast
Credit Cards: None
Notes: 2, 5, 8, 9, 10, 11, 12

RED LODGE

Willows Inn

224 South Platt Avenue, 59068
(406) 446-3913

Spectacular mountain scenery surrounds this delightful turn-of-the-century inn. Discover the charm of yesteryear in the warm and cheery atmosphere of this beautiful Victorian home. Five individually decorated rooms with brass and iron and four-poster beds await your pleasure. Delicious home-baked pastries and afternoon refreshments. Close to skiing, hiking, golfing, fishing, and Yellowstone Park. Video movies, books, games, and large sun deck. Two storybook cottages with kitchen and laundry in country decor also available.

Host: Elven Boggio
Rooms: 5 (3 PB; 2 SB) $45-60
Expanded Continental Breakfast
Credit Cards: A, B, D
Notes: 2, 5, 8, 9, 11, 12, 13, 14

SOMERS

Osprey Inn
Bed and Breakfast

P. O. Box 133, 59911
(406) 886-2002; FAX (406) 886-2002

The Osprey Inn is on the shore of Flathead Lake. There is a private pebble beach, boat dock, and hot tub. Experience a morning row in a single scull while watching the sun rise over the Mission Mountains. Stay in a real log "honeymoon cabin." A guest lounge has a fireplace, player piano, library, and cable TV. Enjoy boating, canoeing, swimming, fishing, bird watching, the evening campfire, and fresh mountain air. Only one hour from Glacier National Park.

NOTES: Credit cards accepted: A Master Card; B Visa; C American Express; D Discover Card; E Diner's Club; F Other; 2 Personal Checks accepted; 3 Lunch available; 4 Dinner available; 5 Open all year;

Hosts: Sharon and Wayne Finney
Rooms: 4 plus log cabin (3 PB; 2S SB) $78-88.40
Full Breakfast
Credit Cards: A, B, C
Closed Oct. 15-Dec. 15 and Jan. 15-May 15
Notes: 9, 11, 12, 13, 14

SULA

Camp Creek Inn Bed and Breakfast Guest Ranch

7674 Highway 93 South, 59871
(406) 821-3508

Visit this 1920s ranch that is referred to as a "stage stop." Guided horseback rides are available in the summer. Stalls are also available for guests' horses. Over 100 miles of Bitterfoot Forest trails surrounding the ranch with direct access to the Continental Divide trail system. Winter and spring ski packages are obtainable for Lost Trail Powder Mountain that is only nine miles away. Two comfortable cabins, each with kitchen, also provide complete, old-fashioned western hospitality.

Host: Sandy Skorupa
Rooms: 3 (2 PB; 1 SB) $40-65
Full Breakfast
Credit Cards: None
Notes: 2, 3 (summer/fall), 4 (summer/fall), 5, 8, 9,
   13, 14

THREE FORKS

Sacajawea Inn

P. O. Box 648, 5 North Main, 59752
(406) 285-6515

The hotel was founded in 1910 by John Quincy Adams to serve the travelers of the Milwaukee Railroad and named after Sacajawea, who guided the expeditions of Lewis and Clark in the Three Forks area. Located on the route between Yellowstone and Glacier National Parks and within easy access of hiking, skiing, fishing, hunting, and golf. Graced with rocking chairs, a large veranda welcomes you to a spacious lobby, fine dining, and comfortable nostalgic rooms.

Host: Jane & Smith Roedel
Rooms: 33 (PB) $55-85
Continental Breakfast
Credit Cards: A, B, D
Notes: 3 (summer), 4, 5, 6 (call first), 8, 9, 12, 14

TOWNSEND

Hidden Hollow Ranch

211 Flynn Lane, 59644
(406) 266-3580

Hidden Hollow Ranch offers you 11,000 acres to wander on. Other features include a ranch/farm with meadows, mountains, creeks, fields with hay, grain, livestock, and beautiful gardens. If you are looking for a large farmhouse with that "homey" atmosphere decorated with antiques, then you just found it.

Host: Rose Flynn
Rooms: 4 (1 PB; 3 SB) $40-65
Full Breakfast
Credit Cards: None
Notes: 2, 3, 4, 8, 11, 12

WEST YELLOWSTONE

Sportsman's High

750 Deer Street, 59758
(406) 646-7865; (800) 272-4227

This spacious country-style home with wraparound porch is nestled on three acres of aspen and pines. Spectacular views await guests' arrival, only eight miles from the west entrance of Yellowstone Park. The moment you enter the front door, you are treated like a friend. All five antique-filled rooms are lovingly decorated with country colors and fabrics. Feather pillows, terry-cloth robes, and hot tub are just some of the amenities you will enjoy.

Hosts: Diana and Gary Baxter
Rooms: 5 (PB) $75-85 in-season; $65-75 off-
   season
Full Breakfast
Credit Cards: A, B
Notes: 2, 5, 13, 14

6 Pets welcome; 7 Smoking allowed; 8 Children welcome; 9 Social drinking allowed; 10 Tennis available; 11 Swimming available; 12 Golf available; 13 Skiing available; 14 May be booked through travel agents.

WHITEFISH

Castle Bed and Breakfast

900 South Baker, 59937
(406) 862-1257

Enjoy one of three comfortable guest
rooms in this home that is listed on the
National Register of Historic Places. The
Castle has unusual architecture and charm.
Breakfasts are hearty and tempting and
include homemade breads and freshly
ground gourmet coffee to compliment the
feature menu of the day. The Castle is nine
miles from the Big Mountain Ski Resort
and 25 miles from Glacier National Park.

Hosts: Jim and Pat Egan
Rooms: 3 (1 PB; 2 SB) $63-98
Full Breakfast
Credit Cards: A, B, D
Notes: 2, 9, 10, 11, 12, 13

Kandahar Lodge

Box 1659, 59937
(406) 862-6098

Kandahar is a beautiful 50-room mountain
lodge in an alpine setting at Big Mountain
Ski Resort village area, five miles above
the town of Whitefish. You will enjoy personal service and hospitality in a rustic yet
elegant setting. There are a variety of summer activities, and you can ski to the back
door during winter. There are two indoor
sauna-Jacuzzi spa areas as well as an excellent cafe.

Hosts: Buck and Mary Pat Love
Rooms: 50 (PB) $68-98
Continental Breakfast
Credit Cards: A, B, C, D
Notes: 2, 4, 7, 8, 9, 10, 11, 12, 13, 14

WHITE SULPHUR SPRINGS

The Columns

19 East Wright Street, P.O. Box 611, 59645
(406) 547-3666

Recently renovated red brick 1882 private
home with an eclectic blend of yesterday's
charm and today's comfort in the middle of
cow country. Big Sky hospitality at its best.
Delicious ranch-style breakfasts.

Host: Dale N. McAfee
Rooms: 3 (1 PB; 2 SB) $35-50
Full Breakfast
Credit Cards: A, B
Notes: 2, 5, 8 (over 6), 9, 11, 12, 13, 14

Nebraska

BARTLEY

Pheasant Hill Farm

HCR 68, Box 12, 69020
(308) 692-3278

Enjoy the good life on this southwest Nebraska farm. Unique family experience. In-season hunting for dove, quail, pheasant, deer. Fish, swim, boat on area lakes. Thirty-minutes to world-class golf, shopping, and entertainment. Relax on a porch with ten-mile vistas. Enjoy country cooking.

Hosts: Max and Dona Nelms
Rooms: 5 (2 PB; 3 SB) $55
Full Breakfast
Credit Cards: None
Notes: 2, 3, 4, 5, 7, 8, 9, 14

DIXON

The George's

Rural Route 1, Box 50, 68732
(402) 584-2625

Enjoy friendly country hospitality and hearty breakfasts featuring homemade jellies and jams. This is an opportunity to see a modern farm operation, some chickens and other farm animals. Stay in an air-conditioned, spacious farm home. Pheasant hunting in season and bird watching anytime. Just 35 miles west of Sioux City, Iowa; Ponca State Park and Wayne State College is within 20 miles.

Hosts: Harold and Marie George
Rooms: 4 (SB) $35-40
Full Breakfast
Credit Cards: None
Notes: 2, 3 (prior arrangements), 4 (prior arrangements), 5, 6, 7 (outside), 8, 9, 14

GOTHENBURG

Swede Hospitality Bed and Breakfast

1617 Avenue A, 69138
(308) 537-2680

This reservation service provides unique experiences in Nebraska. You can stay on a Nebraska farm or ranch, or you can choose to enjoy the peace and quiet of a home in a beautiful small town. Contact: Merle or Linda Block.

GRAND ISLAND

Kirschke House

1124 West Third Street, 68801
(308) 381-6851

Enjoy and experience yesterday today! A 1902 Victorian home decorated in period furnishings and antiques. A wooden hot tub adds to the Old World charm in the lantern-lit brick wash house.

Host: Lois Hank
Rooms: 4 (SB) $50
Full Breakfast
Credit Cards: A, B
Notes: 2, 5, 9, 14

6 Pets welcome; 7 Smoking allowed; 8 Children welcome; 9 Social drinking allowed; 10 Tennis available; 11 Swimming available; 12 Golf available; 13 Skiing available; 14 May be booked through travel agents.

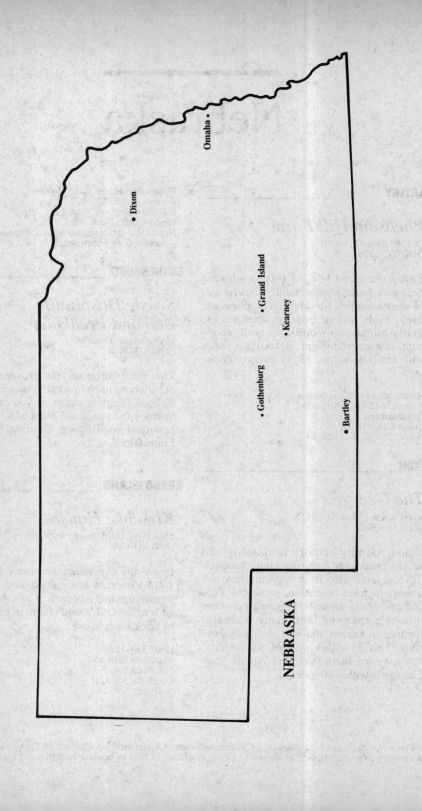

NEBRASKA

Omaha •

Dixon •

Grand Island •

Kearney •

Gothenburg •

Bartley •

KEARNEY

The George W. Frank, Jr., House

621 West 27th Street, 68847
(308) 237-7545

Built in 1884, this Queen Anne shingle-style home is packed with history. A night's stay will transport you to a time when the luxuries of peaceful quiet and soft comfort were abundant. Fall in love with the leaded-glass windows, spacious rooms, and beautifully carved wood details. Included is a continental breakfast served in the family dining room on heirloom dishes.

Hosts: Ted and Sylvia Asay
Rooms: 2 (SB) $45
Continental Breakfast; Full Breakfast upon request
Credit Cards: None
Notes: 2, 5, 8, 14

OMAHA

The Jones's

1617 South 90th Street, 68124
(402) 397-0721

Large private residence with deck and gazebo in the back. Fresh homemade cinnamon rolls are served for breakfast. Horseracing nearby in summer as well as several golf courses and Boys Town.

Hosts: Don and Theo Jones
Rooms: 3 (1 PB; 2 SB) $25
Continental Breakfast
Credit Cards: None
Notes: 2, 5, 6, 7, 8, 9, 10, 12

The Offutt House

140 North 39th Street, 68131
(402) 553-0951

This comfortable mansion, built in 1894, is in the section of large homes built around the same time by Omaha's most wealthy residents. Rooms are comfortably spacious and furnished with antiques. Some feature fireplaces. The house is near downtown Omaha and the historic Old Market area, which offers many beautiful shops and excellent restaurants. Reservations, please.

Host: Jeannie K. Swoboda
Rooms: 7 (5 PB; 2 SB) $45-75
Continental Breakfast
Credit Cards: A, B, C
Notes: 2, 5, 7, 8, 9, 10, 11, 12, 14

The Offutt House

NOTES: Credit cards accepted: A Master Card; B Visa; C American Express; D Discover Card; E Diner's Club; F Other; 2 Personal Checks accepted; 3 Lunch available; 4 Dinner available; 5 Open all year; 6 Pets welcome; 7 Smoking allowed; 8 Children welcome; 9 Social drinking allowed; 10 Tennis available; 11 Swimming available; 12 Golf available; 13 Skiing available; 14 May be booked through travel agents.

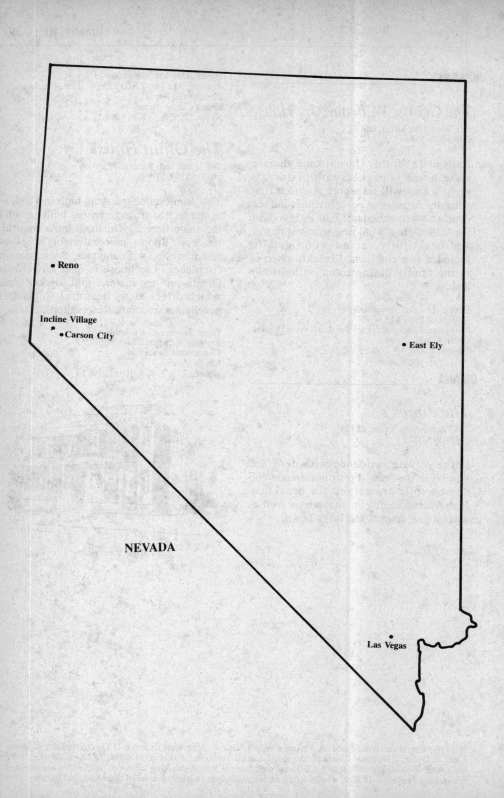

Reno

Incline Village

Carson City

East Ely

NEVADA

Las Vegas

Nevada

CARSON CITY, WASHOE VALLEY

Deer Run Ranch
Bed and Breakfast

5440 Eastlake Boulevard, 89704
(702) 882-3643

Western ambience in a unique architect-designed ranch house on spacious grounds, situated between Reno and Carson City and just minutes from Lake Tahoe and Virginia City. Pond with boat for summer, skating in winter. Above-ground pool and lots of privacy on 200 acres.

Hosts: David and Muffy Vhay
Rooms: 2 (PB) $75-85
Full Breakfast
Credit Cards: A, B
Notes: 2, 5, 9, 11, 13

EAST ELY

Steptoe Valley Inn

P.O. Box 151110, 220 E. 11th Street, 89315-1110
(702) 289-8687

Elegantly reconstructed in 1990 from the Ely City Grocery of 1907, this new inn is one-half block from the Nevada Northern Railway Museum with its weekend train excursions, and 70 miles from the Great Basin National Park. Its individually decorated guest rooms are on the second floor and have private balconies with views of the mountains and valley or gazebo and rose garden. Guests have use of the veranda, Victorian living/dining room, and library.

Hosts: Jan and Norman Lindley
Rooms: 5 (PB) $73.15-79.63
Full Breakfast
Credit Cards: A, B, C
Notes: 2, 10, 12, 14

INCLINE VILLAGE

Haus Bavaria

P.O. Box 3308, 89450
(702) 831-6122; (800) GO-TAHOE

Haus Bavaria is a European-style guest house, built in 1980. Each of the five upstairs guest rooms opens onto a balcony, offering a view of the surrounding mountains, while the livingroom, with its rustic wood paneling and collection of German bric-a-brac, retains the Alpine charm set in place by the original owners. Breakfast, served daily in the cozy dining room downstairs, includes freshly baked goods, seasonal fruits and juices, freshly ground coffee and a selection of teas.

Host: Bick Hewitt
Rooms: 5 (PB) $70-90
Full Breakfast
Credit Cards: A, B, C
Notes: 2, 5, 9, 10, 11, 12, 13, 14

Deer Run Ranch

LAS VEGAS

Mi Casa Su Casa #334

P.O. Box 950, Tempe, Arizona 85280-0950
(602) 990-0682; (800) 456-0682

This large 1950 home with a southwestern-style exterior is located in an established quiet neighborhood within two miles of the Strip. Hostess is an interior designer and has been an interior designer for hotels. Antiques are blended into the other lovely furnishings throughout this bed and breakfast. Two guest rooms with two hall baths are available. Bicycles are also on hand for guests to use. Prefer two-night minimum on the weekends. Full breakfast. Smoking outside only. $40-50.

RENO

Bed and Breakfast: South Reno

136 Andrew Lane, 89511
(702) 849-0772

Situated just off Highway 395 in South Reno, 12 miles from the airport. The decor is Early American, which includes poster-queen beds and beamed ceilings. Landscaped lawns, patios, and decks surround a heated swimming pool. Facing the bed and breakfast are ranch lands, Mount Rose, and Slide Mountain for hiking, sleigh riding, and downhill skiing. Visit Lake Tahoe, Virginia City, or the many Reno casinos. Open all year.

Hosts: Caroline S. Walters and Robert McNeill
Rooms: 3 (1 PB; 2 SB) $54-64
Full Breakfast
Credit Cards: C
Notes: 2, 5, 7, 8, 9, 10, 11, 12, 13, 14

NOTES: Credit cards accepted: A Master Card; B Visa; C American Express; D Discover Card; E Diner's Club; F Other; 2 Personal Checks accepted; 3 Lunch available; 4 Dinner available; 5 Open all year;

New Hampshire

ANDOVER

Andover Arms Guest House

P. O. Box 256, 03216
(603) 735-5953

This 150-year-old country Victorian offers four guest rooms that share one and one-half baths. A suite with a private bath is also available. Close to skiing, golf, swimming, tennis, hiking, snowmobiling, and use of all the sitting rooms and porches. Decorated with antiques. Fireplaces.

Host: Michelle Kettwig
Rooms: 4 (S1.5B) $50
Continental Breakfast
Credit Cards: F
Notes: 2, 5, 8, 9, 10, 11, 12, 13, 14

The English House

Box 162, 03216
(603) 735-5987

This home has been renovated and furnished to re-create an English country house. Afternoon tea, as well as a notable breakfast, is served to all guests. All breads, muffins, cakes, jams, jellies, and marmalades are homemade.

Hosts: Gillian and Ken Smith
Rooms: 7 (PB) $54-75
Full Breakfast
Minimum stay for foliage weekends and holidays:
   2 nights
Credit Cards: A, B
Closed one week in mid-March
Notes: 2, 5, 8 (over 7), 9, 10, 11, 12, 13, 14

New Hampshire Bed and Breakfast NH 306

329 Lake Drive, Guilford, CT 06437
(800) 582-0853

This turn-of-the-century house built in 1906, was constructed with many fine features of that era, particularly hardwood floors, paneling, and large rooms. It was fully renovated in 1986 and decorated and furnished in the style of an English country home. Afternoon tea and evening sherry are served each day by your hosts. Guests are welcome to use the well- furnished sitting room. Breakfast menus are the choice of the chef, and each morning, you will awaken to freshly baked breads or muffins, which are always accompanied by fruits in season, homemade cereal, and dishes of distinction. Each of the seven well-appointed bedrooms offers private bath, a lovely view, and the homey touches of caring hosts. Children over eight welcome. No smoking. $55-75.

BARTLETT

The Country Inn at Bartlett

Route 302, P. O. Box 327, 03812
(603) 374-2353

A bed and breakfast inn for hikers, skiers, and outdoor lovers in the White Mountains of New Hampshire. Inn and cottage rooms, fireplaces, hearty breakfasts, outdoor hot

---

6 Pets welcome; 7 Smoking allowed; 8 Children welcome; 9 Social drinking allowed; 10 Tennis available; 11 Swimming available; 12 Golf available; 13 Skiing available; 14 May be booked through travel agents.

NEW HAMPSHIRE

Jefferson
Shelburne
Whitefield

Bethlehem
Lisbon
Franconia
Sugarhill
Haverhill
Easton
Jackson
Lincoln
Glen
Bartlett Intervale
North Woodstock North Conway
Waterville Valley
West Thornton Conway
Eaton Center
Campton Madison
Lyme Rumney Chocorua
Wentworth Plymouth Tamworth
Holderness

Enfield Ossipee
Meredith Center Harbor
Wolfeboro
West Springfield Wakefield

Laconia
Winnisquam
Andover Tilton
New London Sunapee Franklin
North Sutton
Claremont Newbury
Bradford

Dover
Henniker Northwood

Hillsboro

Portsmouth
Stratham Rye
Munsonville New Hampton
New Boston Hampton
Marlborough Hampstead
Temple
Jaffrey Londonderry
Fitzwilliam Greenfield
Rindge

New Ipswich

tub. The warmth and friendly atmosphere of this inn are here for you to enjoy. Come stay at the Country Inn!

Host: Mark Dindorf
Rooms: 16 (10 PB; 6 SB) $28-48 per person
Full Breakfast
Credit Cards: A, B, C
Notes: 2, 5, 6, 8, 9, 10, 11, 12, 13, 14

The Notchland Inn

Hart's Location, 03812
(603) 374-6131

A traditional country inn where hospitality hasn't been forgotten. There are 11 guest rooms, all with working fireplaces and private baths. Gourmet dining, spectacular mountain views, hiking, cross-country skiing, and swimming are offered at this secluded mountain estate.

Hosts: John and Pat Bernardin
Rooms: 11 (PB) $47.50-83/person
Full Breakfast and Dinner
Credit Cards: A, B, C
Notes: 2, 4, 5, 10, 11, 12, 13, 14

BETHLEHEM

The American Country Collection 164

4 Greenwood Lane, Delmar, NY 12054
(518) 439-7001

The Bells

Carefully restored over seven years, this bed and breakfast has carefully tended wood moldings and is furnished with antiques. In-ground pool and outdoor heated Jacuzzi are available to guests. Another room has a private half-bath. The suite, which sleeps two to four people, has a private bath. Queen and double beds. Full breakfast. Children welcome. Smoking permitted. $65-80.

The Bells

Strawberry Hill Street, 03574
(603) 869-2647

Situated in town, within walking distance of restaurants, antique shops, golf, and tennis; all White Mountain attractions close by. Unusual Victorian house named for the scores of bells hanging from the eaves. Inside, gracious suites and the romantic room-with-a-view cupola are furnished with four generations of heirlooms and mementos.

Hosts: Bill and Louise Sims
Rooms: 4 (PB) $65-90
Full Breakfast
Minimum stay some holidays
Credit Cards: A, B, C
Notes: 2, 5, 7, 8, 9, 10, 11, 12, 13, 14

The Mulburn Inn

Main Street, 03574
(603) 869-3389

A sprawling summer estate built in 1913 as a family retreat on the Woolworth estate. Spacious, elegant rooms, stained-glass windows, and even an elevator are maintained in gracious style. Situated in the heart of the White Mountains, minutes from Franconia Notch and the Mount Washington Valley attractions.

Hosts: Bob and Cheryl Burns; Moe and Linda Mulkigian
Rooms: 7 (PB) $55-85
Full Breakfast
Credit Cards: A, B, C, D
Notes: 2, 5, 8, 9, 10, 11, 12, 13, 14

NOTES: Credit cards accepted: A Master Card; B Visa; C American Express; D Discover Card; E Diner's Club; F Other; 2 Personal Checks accepted; 3 Lunch available; 4 Dinner available; 5 Open all year; 6 Pets welcome; 7 Smoking allowed; 8 Children welcome; 9 Social drinking allowed; 10 Tennis available; 11 Swimming available; 12 Golf available; 13 Skiing available; 14 May be booked through travel agents.

New Hampshire Bed and Breakfast NH 135

329 Lake Drive, Guilford, CT 06437
(800) 582-0853

Built circa 1892, this large Victorian "cottage" is a wonderful example of Victorian ingenuity. Trimmed like a pagoda with bells and dragons and complete with veranda and comfortable rocking chairs, this bed and breakfast has been cited by many home and travel magazines. Each guest room has the welcoming warmth of overstuffed easy chairs, touches of lace and wicker, firm mattresses, and soft, fluffy towels. Throughout the house, family heirlooms and memorabilia mix with pleasing surprises. Relax with morning coffee in your room and enjoy a full breakfast that varies from day to day. Seasonal beverages, sherry, and afternoon tea are always available. Four guest rooms with private baths. Two suites and one guest cottage. $50-70.

BRADFORD

The Bradford Inn

Main Street, 03221
(603) 938-5309

The Bradford Inn, a restored 1898 small country hotel, features comfortable lodging and J. Albert's Restaurant, which serves exceptional New England cuisine. Fireplaces, large parlors, wide halls, with antiques and personal mementos. Four-season activity area.

Hosts: Connie and Tom Mazol
Rooms: 12 (PB) $59-79
Full Breakfast
Credit Cards: A, B, C, D, E
Notes: 2, 4, 5, 6, 7, 8, 9, 10, 11, 12, 13, 14

Mountain Lake Inn

P. O. Box 443, 03221
(603) 938-2136; (800) 662-6005

A true New England country inn, built in 1760 on the shores of Massaseusm Lake. The private sandy beach provides summer enjoyment. In winter, guests snowshoe on 167 acres. The inn is tastefully decorated with antiques and period furniture, and the country cuisine will please the most delicate palate. Peace and tranquility abound.

Hosts: Carol and Phil Fullerton
Rooms: 9 (PB) $75-85
Full Breakfast
Credit Cards: A, B, D
Notes: 2, 4, 5, 7, 8, 9, 10, 11, 12, 13, 14

CAMPTON

New Hampshire Bed and Breakfast NH 116

329 Lake Drive, Guilford, CT 06437
(800) 582-0853

Situated just minutes from I-93, the Waterville Valley four-season resort area, the Franconia Notch State Park, and Plymouth. This large, white clapboard farmhouse has gables, a farmer's porch, and a warm hearth. You can enjoy the recreational activities in the White Mountains: hiking the marked Appalachian Mountain Club trails, bicycling, snowmobiling, swimming, picnicking, and an excellent selection of alpine and cross-country skiing. The large lawns feature volleyball and croquet sets. Guests are welcome to use the large country livingroom with fireplace, color cable TV with VCR, games, puzzles, and books. Enjoy a full breakfast and generous seasonal snacks. Eight guest rooms with private baths, three with shared bath. Children welcome. No smoking, please. $40-70.

Mountain-Fare Inn

Mad River Road, P. O. Box 553, 03223
(603) 726-4283

NOTES: Credit cards accepted: A Master Card; B Visa; C American Express; D Discover Card; E Diner's Club; F Other; 2 Personal Checks accepted; 3 Lunch available; 4 Dinner available; 5 Open all year;

The Mountain-Fare Inn is a comfortable, friendly home two hours from Boston, fifteen minutes from Waterville Valley Resort, twenty minutes from Franconia Notch. The White Mountains offer a peaceful retreat as well as New England's most alluring sports and recreation possibilities. The hosts make this vitality and excitement available to you.

Hosts: Susan and Nick Preston
Rooms: 8 (5 PB; 3 SB) $48-70
Full Breakfast
Credit Cards: None
Notes: 2, 5, 8, 9, 10, 11, 12, 13, 14

Osgood Inn

P. O. Box 419, 03223
(603) 726-3543

The hosts welcome you year-round to their warm and gracious village home with four spacious rooms featuring handmade quilts and lovely views. Located close to skiing, hiking, golf, shopping, and tourist attractions. Full country breakfast is served in the morning, and afternoon tea is served every day. Charming common room with fireplace, serene gardens, and back porch are available for guests to enjoy. Housekeeping two bedroom suite available in the Annex. Minutes from I-93.

Hosts: Dexter and Pat Osgood
Rooms: 4 (SB) $50
Full Breakfast
Credit Cards: None
Notes: 2, 5, 7 (limited), 8, 9, 12, 13

CAMPTON VILLAGE

The Campton Inn

Rural Route 2, P. O. Box 12, 03223
(603) 726-4449

In 1836 The Campton Inn was built on Main Street, the same year Campton Village was built. A boarding house and inn since 1880, this classic farmhouse still has its original pine floors, wood stove, screened-in porch, piano, separate TV and

game room, and the finest in New England hospitality. A full country breakfast is served, and because we are located in the heart of the White Mountains, skiing, swimming, biking, hiking, and other recreations can be found at every corner.

Hosts: Peter and Robbin Adams
Rooms: 5 (1 PB; 4 SB) $50-60
Full Breakfast
Credit Cards: None
Notes: 2, 5, 8, 9, 10, 11, 12, 13, 14

CENTER HARBOR

New Hampshire Bed and Breakfast NH 215

329 Lake Drive, Guilford, CT 06437
(800) 582-0853

Situated on 75 beautiful acres on Long Island in the center of Lake Winnipesaukee (connected by bridge). The house was built in the 1830s and was established as an inn in 1874. It is now run by a descendant of the original family. Guests enjoy the 75 acres of lawns, fields, and woods which run to the water's edge, either of two private beaches, the lakeside picnic area, and the large livingroom with fieldstone fireplace. A hearty country breakfast is served in the dining room. Children welcome. No smoking; no pets. Open from the end of June through September. $45 for single; $50 for double.

New Hampshire Bed and Breakfast NH 218

329 Lake Drive, Guilford, CT 06437
(800) 582-0853

Just five-minutes from the center of a pleasant village, you can enjoy the amenities of this contemporary ranch-style home, yet be surrounded by tall pine trees, singing birds, and a peaceful, wooded setting. You can sunbathe or swim at the town beach, take a breakfast cruise on Lake

Winnipesaukee, or treat yourself at any of the fine craft, antique, and retail shops. Don't miss the region's most expansive quilt shop. Guests enjoy the use of a large screened porch, a livingroom with fieldstone fireplace, or the den with ample books, magazines, and TV. A continental breakfast is served each morning in the dining room. No smoking. No pets. Children welcome. $55-60.

Red Hill Inn

Rural Free Delivery 1, Box 99M, 03226
(603) 279-7001

Restored country estate on 60 acres overlooking Squam Lake and the White Mountains. Twenty-one rooms, each with private bath, many with fireplace and Jacuzzi. Country gourmet restaurant serving all meals; entertainment in the Runabout Lounge. Cross-country skiing (and rentals) on property. Two hours north of Boston.

Hosts: Rick Miller and Don Leavitt
Rooms: 21 (PB) $65-125
Full Breakfast
Credit Cards: A, B, C, D, E
Notes: 2, 3, 4, 5, 7, 8, 9, 10, 11, 12, 13, 14

CHOCORUA

New Hampshire Bed and Breakfast NH 107

329 Lake Drive, Guilford, CT 06437
(800) 582-0853

Situated 20-minutes south of North Conway, this spacious hilltop Colonial is on 22 acres of woodlands with majestic views of Mount Chocorua and Ossipee Lake. Relax beside the fire in the livingroom with a good book, play board games, watch TV, or strike up a tune on the piano. Sit on the screened porch to enjoy breathtaking views and the fresh mountain air. Work up an appetite for Bernice's hearty country breakfast out on the clay

tennis court. Horseshoes, badminton, croquet, and nature walks on premises. Enjoy hiking, boating, swimming, antiquing, auctions, summer theater, and restaurants. Three guest rooms with shared baths. All rooms have spectacular mountain views, hand-stenciled walls, and antique furnishings. A private guest house with fireplace, large deck, kitchen, wood-burning stove, and bedding for four guests is also available. Open May through October. $50-75.

CLAREMONT

Goddard Mansion Bed and Breakfast

25 Hillstead Road, 03743
(603) 543-0603; (800) 736-0603

Delightful early 1900s English manor-style 18-room mansion on seven acres with panoramic mountain view. Expansive porches and tea house. Eight uniquely decorated guest rooms await. A full continental, natural food breakfast starts each day. Four-season activities nearby, including historical sites, antique shops, and excellent restaurants. Smoke-free atmosphere.

Hosts: Frank and Debbie Albee
Rooms: 8 (2 PB; 6 SB) $65-95
Full Breakfast
Credit Cards: A, B, D, E, F
Notes: 2, 5, 8, 9, 10, 12, 13

CONWAY

Darby Field Inn

Bald Hill Road, 03818
(603) 447-2181; (800) 426-4147

A charming, out-of-the-way country inn that offers excellent dining, a cozy atmosphere, and spectacular mountain views. There are an outdoor pool, cross-country ski trails, and a staff that is both friendly and courteous. Reservations recommended. Rate includes breakfast, tax, and gratuity.

NOTES: Credit cards accepted: A Master Card; B Visa; C American Express; D Discover Card; E Diner's Club; F Other; 2 Personal Checks accepted; 3 Lunch available; 4 Dinner available; 5 Open all year;

Hosts: Marc and Maria Donaldson
Rooms: 16 (12 PB; 4 SB) $120
Full Breakfast
Minimum stay weekends: 2 nights; holidays: 2-3
  nights
Credit Cards: A, B, C
Notes: 2, 4, 5, 7, 8 (2 to 12), 9, 10, 11, 12, 13, 14

Merrill Farm Resort

Rural Free Delivery, Box 151, 03860
(603) 447-3866; (800) 445-1017

Cozy rooms in the main house, all with private baths. Efficiency cottages and spacious loft units with fireplaces. Some non-smoking rooms. Outdoor pool, canoes on the river, in-room whirlpools, conference facilities. All rooms have cable TV and phones. Relaxed, informal setting (age 17 and under free). Tax-free outlet shopping in a summer and winter recreation area. Three-diamond AAA rating.

Hosts: Lee and Christine Gregory
Rooms: 60 (PB) $39-139 seasonal
Expanded Continental Breakfast
Credit Cards: A, B, C, D, E
Notes: 5, 7, 8, 9, 10, 11, 12, 13, 14

Valley Manner Bed and Breakfast

Bed and Breakfast Marblehead and North Shore
P. O. Box 35, Newtonville, Massachusetts 02160
(617) 964-1606; (800) 832-2632 outside MA

This Victorian bed and breakfast, only steps from a traditional covered bridge, provides real New England hospitality for couples and families. The antique pump organ is a feature in the livingroom, where guests may relax and plan their dinner venue or the activities for the following day, with the help and advice of their host. Baby-sitting is available by prior arrangement. Four guest rooms, two with private baths. Many seasonal sports and activities are available. Full breakfast on weekends; continental on weekdays. $65.

DOVER

New Hampshire Bed and Breakfast NH 410

329 Lake Drive, Guilford, CT 06437
(800) 582-0853

The charming 100-year-old Queen Anne Victorian offers a special experience for a traveler who wants more than the ordinary. A turned oak staircase and fretwork welcome guests to the turn-of-the-century era. Relax on the tree-shaded porch or enjoy the livingroom in all seasons. Located in the seacoast area, convenient to UNH, Portsmouth, Durham, and Maine. Two guest rooms furnished with antiques and a double bed share a full bath. Children over four welcome. No smoking. $45-50.

New Hampshire Bed and Breakfast NH 412

329 Lake Drive, Guilford, CT 06437
(800) 582-0853

A large Victorian country home dating from the mid-19th century, this farm offers comfortable, spacious guest rooms in a unique rural setting. The inn is set among rolling fields with nature trails along the Cacheco River. Guests are welcome to use the antique-filled formal parlor and library. There are horseshoe pits and a volleyball net. Swimming, cross-country skiing, golf, and snowmobiling are available nearby. A full, home-cooked breakfast is complemented by fresh fruits and juices, homemade muffins, breads, scones, and fresh brewed coffee, all served with a touch of Scottish hospitality. Located near New Hampshire's seacoast and mountains, near Spaulding Turnpike. Downtown Dover is two miles away and Portsmouth is fifteen-minutes away. Five guest rooms share two antique baths and are furnished with antiques. No smoking. Children welcome. $45-65.

---

6 Pets welcome; 7 Smoking allowed; 8 Children welcome; 9 Social drinking allowed; 10 Tennis available; 11 Swimming available; 12 Golf available; 13 Skiing available; 14 May be booked through travel agents.

EASTON

New Hampshire Bed and Breakfast NH 105

329 Lake Drive, Guilford, CT 06437
(800) 582-0853

In a beautiful meadow setting, only ten-min-utes from Franconia Notch, an unadorned, restored Victorian farmhouse. Built in 1887, it was considered haunted by some in the 1940s. You will appreciate the decorative painting, stenciling, and glazing. A full breakfast is served in the common room. Minutes from hiking and cross-country ski-ing on the Appalachian Trail. A day's trip to the attractions of the White Mountains, the Connecticut River valley, and Vermont. Five guest rooms with shared baths. Children welcome. No smoking. Dog in res-idence. No guest pets permitted. $40-60.

EATON CENTER

The Inn at Crystal Lake

Route 153, Box 12, 03832
(603) 447-2120; (800) 343-7336

Unwind in a restored 1884 inn in a quiet, scenic corner of the Mount Washington valley. Eleven guest rooms have Victorian antiques and private baths. There's a parlor, TV-den/library, and cocktail lounge for your enjoyment. Swim, fish, sail, canoe, ski, skate, outlet shop, or just relax! Modified American Plan available.

Hosts: Walter and Jacqueline Spink
Rooms: 11 (PB) $60-110
Full Breakfast
Credit Cards: A, B, C
Notes: 2, 4, 5, 7 (limited), 8, 9, 10, 11, 12, 13, 14

ENFIELD

Boulder Cottage

Rural Route 1, Box 257, Crystal Lake Road, 03748
(603) 632-7355

A spacious turn-of-the-century home facing beautiful Crystal Lake, in the Dartmouth-Sunapee region, 13 miles south of Lebanon. Wake up to the breezes of the lake; enjoy a swim, a canoe or boat ride; or take a quiet walk along the shore of the lake. A full New England breakfast is served. Special rates for children and three-night stays.

Hosts: Barbara and Harry Reed
Rooms: 3 (1 PB; 2 SB) $50-55
Full Breakfast
Credit Cards: None
Notes: 2, 8, 9, 10, 11, 12, 14

FITZWILLIAM

Fitzwilliam Inn

Route 119, On the Common, 03447
(603) 585-9000

An inn since 1796, the Fitzwilliam Inn is situated on one of the most picturesque town commons in New England. Two spa-cious parlors and a baby grand piano remind you of visiting Gramma's. Breakfast, lunch, and dinner are served. Fireside dining in winter. Five miles of cross-country ski trails available. Five miles from Mount Monadnock. Antique shops abound. This is a home away from home!

Host: Barbara Wallace
Rooms: 28 (15 PB; 13 SB) $40-60
Full Breakfast
Credit Cards: A, B, C, E
Notes: 2, 3, 4, 5, 7, 8, 9, 11, 13

FRANCONIA

Blanche's B&B

351 Easton Valley Road, 03580
(603) 823-7061

A sunny, century-old farmhouse, restored to a former glory it probably never had. Quiet, pastoral setting with views of the Kinsman Ridge. In the English bed and breakfast tradition, offering cotton linens,

---

NOTES: Credit cards accepted: A Master Card; B Visa; C American Express; D Discover Card; E Diner's Club; F Other; 2 Personal Checks accepted; 3 Lunch available; 4 Dinner available; 5 Open all year;

down comforters, comfortable beds, and a great breakfast which might include fresh fruit salad, spinach omelet, or blueberry pancakes (with pure maple syrup) and homemade muffins. Decorative painting throughout; working studio featuring unusual handmade floorcloths. Ask about the live folk music.

Hosts: Brenda Shannon and John Vail
Rooms: 5 (SB) $60
Full Breakfast
Credit Cards: A, B, C
Notes: 2, 4 (to groups), 5, 8, 9, 10, 11, 12, 13, 14

Bungay Jar
Bed and Breakfast

P. O. Box 15, Easton Valley Road, 03580
(603) 823-7775

Secluded woodlands with spectacular mountain views, brook, and gardens make memorable this home built from an 18th-century barn. King or queen suites, private balconies, skylights, six-foot soaking tub, sauna, canopy bed. Two-story common area with fireplace for reading, music, and talk. Mountain gaze in the morning sun while breakfasting outside in summer. Small in scale, intimate. Hosts are a landscape architect and a patent attorney, and their young son.

Hosts: Kate Kerivan and Lee Strimbeck
Rooms: 6 (4 PB; 2 SB) $60-110
Full Breakfast
Credit Cards: A, B, C
Notes: 2, 5, 8, 9, 10, 11, 12, 13, 14

Franconia Inn

Easton Road, 03580
(603) 823-5542; (800) 473-5299

A charming inn situated on 107 acres in the Easton valley, affording breathtaking views of the White Mountains. The inn's 34 rooms are decorated simply, yet beautifully. Elegant American cuisine highlights the inn's quiet country sophistication. Children welcome. On Route 116.

Host: The Morris family
Rooms: 34 (30 PB; 4 SB) $75-110
Full Breakfast
Credit Cards: A, B, C
Closed April 1-May 15
Notes: 2, 4, 7, 8, 9, 10, 11, 12, 13, 14

Franconia Inn

Lovetts' Inn
by Lafayette Brook

Route 18, Profile Road, 03580
(603) 823-7761; (800) 356-3802

Lovetts' Inn is a sophisticated country inn and bed and breakfast that emphasizes excellent food and service. Situated at the head of Franconia Notch, it affords a great opportunity for sightseeing, hiking, walking, and photo trips. The area abounds with things to do: antiquing, summer theater, and exploring the unique trails and gorges in the notch. Cross-country ski trails are on premises, and downhill skiing is available on nearby Cannon Mountain. Reserve early.

Hosts: Anthony and Sharon Avrutine
Rooms: 30 (22 PB; 8 SB) $40-146
Full Breakfast
Credit Cards: A, B, C
Notes: 2, 4, 5, 6 (limited), 8, 9, 10, 11, 12, 13 (XC), 14

FRANKLIN

Webster Lake Inn

108 Webster Avenue, 03235
(603) 934-4050

6 Pets welcome; 7 Smoking allowed; 8 Children welcome; 9 Social drinking allowed; 10 Tennis available; 11 Swimming available; 12 Golf available; 13 Skiing available; 14 May be booked through travel agents.

Cozy country inn authentically modeled after a Swiss chalet overlooking Webster Lake. Situated off Route 93 at Exit 17. Three fireplaces. Area attractions include five ski areas within 30-minutes of inn. Resident dog and two cats. Families welcome.

Host: H. McCue
Rooms: 8 (2 PB; 6 SB) $35-65
Full Breakfast
Credit Cards: None
Notes: 2, 5, 7, 8, 9, 11, 12, 13

GLEN

The Bernerhof Inn

P. O. Box 240, 03838
(603) 383-4414; (800) 548-8007

An elegant white Victorian set in the foothills of the White Mountains, the Bernerhof remains true to its European tradition. A Taste of the Mountains Cooking School, the inn's dining table, offers a changing menu of middle European favorites, while popular tap room offers lighter fare. Several rooms boast extra-large hot tubs for true relaxation.

Hosts: Ted and Sharon Wroblewski
Rooms: 9 (2 suites) $90-140
Full Breakfast
Credit Cards: A, B, C
Notes: 2, 3, 4, 5, 7 (restricted), 8, 9, 10, 11, 12, 13, 14

Covered Bridge House

P. O. Box 358, 03838
(800) 232-9109

Unique from the charming Colonial decor to the location next to covered bridge, you are just two-minutes away from Attiash where in winter you can enjoy some of the best skiing in the east. In summer, cool off in the Saco River at the private beach.

Hosts: The Letoile Family
Rooms: 5 (3 PB; 2 SB) $40-60
Full Breakfast
Credit Cards: A, B
Notes: 2, 5, 7, 8, 11

GREENFIELD

Greenfield Bed and Breakfast Inn

Box 400, 03047
(603) 547-6327

A romantic Victorian mansion on three acres of lawn in the Monadnock Mountain valley between Keene and Nashua. Enjoy the relaxing mountain view from the spacious veranda. Breakfast is served with crystal, china, and Mozart Very close to skiing, swimming, hiking, tennis, golf, biking, and bargain antique shopping. A favorite of Mr. and Mrs. Bob Hope and honeymooners of all ages. Senior citizen discount. Mountain view meeting room.

Hosts: Vic and Barbara Mangini
Rooms: 9 (5 PB; 4 SB) $49-69
Two vacation apartments: each sleeps up to six
Full Breakfast
Credit Cards: A, B
Notes: 2, 5, 6 (limited), 7 (limited), 8 (limited), 9, 10, 11, 12, 13, 14

HAMPSTEAD

New Hampshire Bed and Breakfast NH 605

329 Lake Drive, Guilford, CT 06437
(800) 582-0853

Built by the Ordway family in 1850, this Greek Renaissance Italianate rests on gentle acreage on Main Street in Hampstead. This bed and breakfast boasts three stairways, five chimneys, hardwood floors with Oriental rugs, working wood stoves, and fireplaces. An expanded continental breakfast is served on the weekdays, and a full, hot, hearty breakfast is served in the formal dining room on weekends. Complimentary wine will greet you on arrival, and the cookie jar is always full. Five-minutes to Sunset Lake, and one-half hour from both Manchester and Nashua. Four sets of accommodations are available. Children welcome. No smoking. $60-90.

NOTES: Credit cards accepted: A Master Card; B Visa; C American Express; D Discover Card; E Diner's Club; F Other; 2 Personal Checks accepted; 3 Lunch available; 4 Dinner available; 5 Open all year;

Stillmeadow Bed and Breakfast at Hampstead

P. O. Box 565, 545 Main Street, 03841
(603) 329-8381

Historic home built in 1850 with five chimneys and three staircases. Set on rolling meadow adjacent to professional croquet courts. Single, double, and suites, each with private bath. Families welcome; children's playroom and fenced-in play yard available. Private livingroom and dining room for guests. Honeymoon suite with sitting room. Cookie jar is always full! Easy commute to Manchester, New Hampshire, and Boston, Massachusetts.

Hosts: Lori and Randy Offord
Rooms: 4 (PB) $60-90
Full Breakfast
Credit Cards: C
Notes: 2, 5, 8, 9, 10, 11, 12, 13

HAMPTON

The Curtis Field House

735 Exeter Road, 03842
(603) 929-0082

This restored Cape is situated on five country acres on Route 27-E or 101-C, three miles from the center of Exeter, seven miles from the ocean, and fifty miles from Boston. Historic Portsmouth and Durham are nearby. A full breakfast is served. The large bedrooms with private baths and air conditioning are decorated with antiques and many lovely reproductions crafted by a descendant of Darby Field.

Hosts: Mary and Daniel Houston
Rooms: 3 (2 PB; 1 SB) $65
Full Breakfast
Credit Cards: A, B
Closed Dec.-March
Notes: 2, 9, 10, 11, 12

New Hampshire Bed and Breakfast NH 421

329 Lake Drive, Guilford, CT 06437
(800) 582-0853

This restored custom Cape is on five country acres, just over the Exeter line. The large sunny rooms are furnished with many antiques and lovely reproductions that are crafted by a descendent of Darby Field. Enjoy fresh fruit in your air-conditioned guest room and comfortable cozy livingroom, or enjoy the breeze on the porch. A full country breakfast is served each morning. Three quiet rooms, two of which have private bath, and one of which shares a bath, are air conditioned and furnished with antiques. Limited smoking. No small children. $65.

The Oceanside

365 Ocean Boulevard, 03842
(603) 926-3542

The Oceanside overlooks the Atlantic Ocean and its beautiful sandy beaches. Each of the ten rooms is tastefully and individually decorated, many with period antiques and all with private baths. The intimate cafe is open for breakfast during July and August and features homemade bread and pastries. At other times a complimentary continental breakfast is available. This gracious inn is in a less congested part of Hampton Beach within easy walking distance of restaurants, shops, and other attractions.

Hosts: Skip and Debbie Windemiller
Rooms: 10 (PB) $80-108
Continental Breakfast
Credit Cards: A, B, C, D
Closed mid-Oct.—mid-May
Notes: 8 (limited), 9, 10, 11, 12

The Roy Family Bed and Breakfast

473 Ocean Boulevard, 03842
(603) 926-7893; (800) 235-2897

Oceanfront accommodations in an immaculate New England home on the shores of the Atlantic. The house is decorated in a mix of traditional, Victorian, and casual

6 Pets welcome; 7 Smoking allowed; 8 Children welcome; 9 Social drinking allowed; 10 Tennis available; 11 Swimming available; 12 Golf available; 13 Skiing available; 14 May be booked through travel agents.

pieces. Choose from two spacious sun decks to enjoy the sun and ocean views. On rainy days, relax in the cozy TV room overlooking Hampton Beach, or venture off to one of many nearby discount outlet malls and points of historical interest. Your host can provide picnic lunches or special dinners with advance reservations. The sandy beach is one and one-half miles long and includes boardwalk shops, boutiques, and restaurants.

Host: Matt Roy
Rooms: 6 (SB) $45-70
Continental Breakfast
Credit Cards: A, B, D
Notes: 2, 4, 5, 7, 8 (over 11), 9, 10, 11, 12, 13, 14

The Victorian Inn at Hampton

430 High Street, 03842
(603) 929-1437

Comfort and elegance await you in this charming century-old guest house. A short walk to sandy beaches and close to good restaurants, factory outlet shopping, theater, art events, and antiquing. Enjoy a large country breakfast in the glassed-in morning room with white wicker furniture and lace. Sit and relax on porches overlooking a picturesque gazebo and gardens. Six rooms are available, all of which have individual personalities and warm furnishings.

Hosts: Linda Lamson and Leo LeBlanc
Rooms: 6 (3 PB; 3 SB) $55-90
Full Breakfast
Credit Cards: A, B
Notes: 2, 5, 8 (over 11), 9, 10, 11, 12, 13, 14

HAVERHILL

Haverhill Inn

Route 10, 03765
(603) 989-5961

This gracious 1810 Colonial home is located in the Haverhill Cornet Historic District. Enjoy hikes in the nearby White Mountains, take walks along country lanes, converse in the parlor, or choose a book and settle in by the fire. Four rooms, all of which have private baths and working fireplaces, are available.

Hosts: Stephen Campbell and Anne Baird
Rooms: 4 (PB) $75
Full Breakfast
Credit Cards: None
Notes: 2, 9, 10, 13

HENNIKER

Henniker House Bed and Breakfast

2 Ramsdell Road, Box 191, 03242
(603) 428-3198

Henniker House, a 19th-century Victorian home with wraparound porches, is bracketed by huge pine trees. The solarium/breakfast room overlooks the Contoocook River; the 50-foot deck overhangs the water. Henniker is the site of New England College, in the heart of antiquing, hosts a fiber studio, arts and crafts, quilting, summer music festivals, theater, and symphony. Camping, fishing, skiing, boating, golfing, wind surfing, sailing are all available, or just relax in this little village.

Host: Bertina Williams
Rooms: 4 (2 PB; 2 SB) $55-65
Full Breakfast
Credit Cards: A, B
Notes: 2, 5, 8, 9, 10, 11, 12, 13, 14

HILLSBORO

New Hampshire Bed and Breakfast NH 511

329 Lake Drive, Guilford, CT 06437
(800) 582-0853

This home is a passive-solar Cape with open concept downstairs. Full southern exposure allows you year-round enjoyment of the all-glass breakfast room and patio, which features scenic views of fields, woods, and birds. A full breakfast of bacon and eggs, or waffles, sausage, muffins, and fruits is served. Walk to Gleason Falls and the stone arch bridge, or enjoy the brook and swimming hole nearby. Resident cat. No children. Smoking permitted. $50.

HOLDERNESS

The Inn on Golden Pond

Route 3, 03245
(603) 968-7269

An 1879 Colonial home situated on 55 wooded acres. Bright and cheerful sitting, breakfast, and game rooms. Close to major ski areas. Nearby is Squam Lake, the setting for the film On Golden Pond.

Host: Bill Webb
Rooms: 9 (PB) $90-135
Full Breakfast
Minimum stay holidays
Credit Cards: A, B, C
Notes: 2, 5, 8 (over 12), 9, 10, 11, 12, 13, 14

INTERVALE

Wildflowers Guest House

Route 16, 03845
(603) 356-2224

Return to the simplicity and elegance of yesteryear. With an ideal location and gracefully decorated rooms, this small 1878 Victorian inn specializes in comfort and convenience for the modern-day traveler.

The Inn at Jackson

From the cheery dining rrom with fireplace to the porch rockers overlooking the award-winning gardens, Wildflowers will be a welcoming respite on your journey.

Hosts: Dean Franke and Eileen Davies
Rooms: 6 (2 PB; 4 SB) $51.84-99.36
Continental Breakfast
Credit Cards: A, B
Closed Nov.-April
Notes: 2, 7, 8, 9, 10, 11, 12, 13

JACKSON

Dana Place Inn

Box L, Pinkham Notch, 03846
(603) 383-6822; (800) 537-9276

Century-old inn situated at the base of Mount Washington on 300 acres along the Ellis River. Dana Place features cozy rooms, fine dining, indoor heated pool, river swimming, Jacuzzi, tennis, hiking, walking trails, fishing, and cross-country skiing on the premises. Golf, outlet shopping, and downhill skiing nearby.

Hosts: Harris and Mary Lou Levine
Room: 33 (29 PB; 4 SB) $85-125
Full Breakfast
Credit Cards: A, B, C, D
Notes: 2, 3, 4, 5, 6, 7, 8, 9, 10, 11, 12, 13, 14

Ellis River House

Route 16, Box 656, 03846
(603) 383-9339; (800) 233-8309

A traditional bed and breakfast that boasts fine lodging and superb country dining in a turn-of-the-century farmhouse overlooking the spectacular Ellis River. Jacuzzi, antiques, minutes to all area attractions. Cross-country skiing from the door. Trout fishing on premises. Enjoy hiking, canoeing, and outlet shopping.

Hosts: Barry and Barbara Lubao
Rooms: 5 (SB) $47.20-141.60
Cottage: 1 (PB)
Suite: 1 (PB)
Full Breakfast
Credit Cards: A, B, C
Notes: 2, 4, 5, 6 (call), 8, 9, 10, 11, 12, 13, 14

---

6 Pets welcome; 7 Smoking allowed; 8 Children welcome; 9 Social drinking allowed; 10 Tennis available; 11 Swimming available; 12 Golf available; 13 Skiing available; 14 May be booked through travel agents.

The Inn at Jackson

P. O. Box H, Thornhill Road, 03846
(603) 383-4321; (800) 289-8600

You'll find this inn on a knoll overlooking
the peaceful village of Jackson. In summer,
you can enjoy golf, swimming, tennis, fishing, or just a walk on a quiet mountain trail.
In winter, enjoy cross-country skiing,
Alpine skiing, sleigh rides, or relax by the
cozy fireplace. Spacious guest rooms offer
a relaxing atmosphere.

Hosts: R. and Lori Tradewell
Rooms: 8 (PB) $56-78
Full Breakfast
Minimum stay weekends and holidays: 2 nights
Credit Cards: A, B, C, D
Notes: 2, 5, 7, 8, 9, 10, 11, 12, 13, 14

Nestlebrook Farm

Dinsmore Road, 03846
(603) 383-9443

Escape into a Victorian past on a 65-acre
estate. Seven elegant guest rooms, all of
which have two-person Jacuzzis and some
of which have parlor stoves, canopy beds,
and fireplaces, are also available. Intimate
pub, antiques, and fireplace gazebo.
Horsedrawn sleighs, trolley rides, horseback riding, mountain bikes, rowboats,
fishing, and Victorian pool. Savor the
romance and step back in time at Nestle-
brook Farm, a gingerbread country inn.

Hosts: Robert and Nancy Cyr
Rooms: 7 (PB) $140-250
Full Breakfast
Credit Cards: A, B, C
Notes: 2, 4, 9, 11, 12, 13, 14

New Hampshire
Bed and Breakfast NH 109

329 Lake Drive, Guilford, CT 06437
(800) 582-0853

Situated on a birch-covered hill looking
towards Mount Washington, this brand-
new house has opened recently as a bed
and breakfast to rave reviews. The home
offers 18th-century antiques, textiles, and
folk art, handmade quilts, designer sheets,
fresh flowers, fruit baskets, and terry-cloth
robes. The full gourmet breakfast served
on English bone china features sticky buns,
shortbread, and fudge. Afternoon tea is
served. The livingroom has a fireplace, TV,
and VCR. The deck, hammock, and flower
gardens provide splendid mountain views.
Three guest rooms with private baths. One
room has a private Jacuzzi tub and private
deck looking towards Mount Washington.
No smoking; no pets. Children over ten
welcome. $50-95.

The Village House

P. O. Box 359, Route 16A, 03846
(603) 383-6666

Just over the covered bridge is this charming Colonial inn with wraparound porch
facing the mountains. In summer, enjoy
tennis, swimming, and Jacuzzi on premises,
riding, golfing, hiking, canoeing, and fine
dining nearby. In winter visitors ski from
the door of the house onto the 157 kilometers of cross-country trails. Downhill skiing
is available at four major nearby mountains. Sleigh rides, ice skating, and snowshoeing are also available.

Host: Robin Crocker
Rooms: 10 (8 PB; 2 SB) $40-100
Continental Breakfast; Full Breakfast in ski season
Credit Cards: A, B, D
Notes: 2, 5, 7, 8, 9, 10, 11, 12, 13, 14

JAFFREY

Benjamin Prescott Inn

Route 124 East, 03452
(603) 532-6637

Come discover the charm of the past and
the comforts of the present within a classic
Greek Revival home furnished with
antiques. Ten charming guest rooms, each
of which has its own private bath, are available for guests, and a full breakfast of

---

NOTES: Credit cards accepted: A Master Card; B Visa; C American Express; D Discover Card; E Diner's
Club; F Other; 2 Personal Checks accepted; 3 Lunch available; 4 Dinner available; 5 Open all year;

hearty country fare is served each morning. Relax and enjoy the surrounding dairy farm, walk the stonewall lined lane, shop, climb Mt. Monadnock, visit local artisans, and eat in excellent restaurants.

Hosts: Jan and Barry Millor
Rooms: 10 (PB) $60-130
Full Breakfast i
Credit Cards: A, B, C
Notes: 2, 5, 8 (over 7), 9, 10, 11, 12, 13, 14

The Galway House Bed and Breakfast

247 Old Peterborough Road, 03452
(603) 532-8083

A traditional bed and breakfast operated like those in the Old Country. A great way to get to know the area and its people. Set on a quiet woodland road in the heart of the Monadnock region, the Currier and Ives corner of New Hampshire, this bed and breakfast makes an excellent point from which to enjoy the many attractions of this four-season area.

Hosts: Joe and Marie Manning
Rooms: 2 (SB) $50
Full Breakfast
Credit Cards: None
Notes: 2, 7 (restricted), 8, 9, 10, 11, 12, 13

Lilac Hill Acres Bed and Breakfast

5 Ingalls Road, 03452
(603) 532-7278

Five-star service in a beautiful 1840 home overlooking beautiful 115-acre Gilmore Pond. Surrounded by mountains. Hiking, skiing, summer playhouses, antiquing, and dining close by. Hearty breakfast served in the morning.

Hosts: Frank and Ellen McNeill
Rooms: 5 (2 PB; 3 SB) $50-70
Full Breakfast
Credit Cards: None
Closed Christmas-New Year's and Easter
Notes: 2, 8 (over 13), 9, 10, 11, 12, 13, 14

Woodbound Inn

Woodbound Road, 03452
(603) 532-8341; (800) 688-7770

The Monadnock Region's finest full-service country inn and resort. Enjoy a romantic dinner for two in the charming dining room or bring a group of up to 150 to party or meet in the spacious banquet facilities. This year-round resort features a par 3 golf course, tennis, cross-country skiing, hiking, and private lakefront beach. Last but not least is the incredible view of Mount Monadnock.

Host: Jim Collins
Rooms: 40 (36 PB; 4 SB) $75-100
Full Breakfast
Credit Cards: A, B, C
Notes: 3, 4, 5, 6, 7, 8, 9, 10, 11, 12, 13, 14

JEFFERSON

Applebrook Bed and Breakfast

Route 115A, 03583-0178
(603) 586-7713; (800) 545-6504

Taste the midsummer raspberries while enjoying panoramic mountain views from this old Victorian farmhouse. Bike, hike, fish, ski, go antiquing, or just relax in the sitting room by the goldfish pool. Near Santa's Village and Six Gun City. Dormitory rooms available in addition to private guest rooms. Brochure available.

Hosts: Sandra J. Conley and Martin M. Kelly
Rooms: 10 (4 PB; 6 SB) $46-60
Dorm Rooms: $20/person
Full Breakfast
Credit Cards: A, B, D
Notes: 2, 4, 5, 6, 8, 9, 11, 12, 13, 14

The Jefferson Inn

Route 2, Rural Free Delivery 1, Box 68A, 03583
(603) 586-7998; (800) 729-7908

Situated among the White Mountains National Forest, the Jefferson Inn offers a 360-degree view. With Mount Washington nearby, the inn is an ideal location for hiking, cross-country and downhill skiing. Six golf courses nearby. Afternoon tea is served. Swimming pond. Two family suites available and a large family room

Hosts: Greg Brown and Bertie Koelewijn
Rooms: 13 (13 PB) $50-120
Full Breakfast
Minimum stay weekends and holidays: 2 nights
Credit Cards: A, B, C, D
Closed November and April
Notes: 2, 8, 9, 10, 11, 12, 13, 14

New Hampshire Bed and Breakfast NH 125

329 Lake Drive, Guilford, CT 06437
(800) 582-0853

Built in 1896, this charming Victorian is nestled among the White Mountain National Forest and enjoys 360-degree mountain views. Look across the Jefferson Meadows to Franconia Notch, Mount Washington, and the northern Presidential Range. See Mount Star King and Waumbek in back of the inn. Each room is furnished with period antiques and has a character of its own, such as the Victorian and Shaker rooms. Daily afternoon tea is served in the common room. The inn is ideally situated for hiking, golf, biking, fishing, canoeing, swimming, antiquing, alpine and Nordic skiing, skating, and snowshoeing. Right in town are Santa's Village and Six Gun City attractions. Ten guest rooms, five with private bath. A two-room suite with private bath accommodates families. Children welcome. No smoking; no pets. $55-82.

LACONIA

New Hampshire Bed and Breakfast NH 235

329 Lake Drive, Guilford, CT 06437
(800) 582-0853

Four blocks from downtown Laconia, this large Victorian home, built in 1903, offers guests a formal livingroom with fireplace and piano; a den with books, games, and TV; a carpeted front porch with comfortable wicker and cane rockers; and a magnificent two-story solar greenhouse addition with wood-burning stove and tables for board games and puzzles. A full breakfast is served in the formal dining room and there are tea and beverages for afternoon snacks. Two guest rooms with shared bath. Children ages 3-16 are welcome. No smoking in the bedrooms; no pets. $45-50.

New Hampshire Bed and Breakfast NH 237

329 Lake Drive, Guilford, CT 06437
(800) 582-0853

Spacious contemporary home on Lake Winnisquam with spectacular views of lake and mountains. Swimming, canoeing, fishing, and sunbathing on premises. Ten-minutes to Lake Winnipesaukee attractions and Laconia's downtown area of shops and fine restaurants; 20-minutes to Gunstock Ski area; 30-minutes to White Mountains National Forest. Guests enjoy the great outdoors, the livingroom, and the large fieldstone fireplace in the dining area. A continental breakfast is served each morning. Two guest rooms with private bath. Upstairs suite offers an antique double canopy bed, cable TV, refrigerator, and wet bar, a private sitting area, and a balcony-porch overlooking the lake and mountains. Children welcome. $60-85.

New Hampshire Bed and Breakfast NH 238

329 Lake Drive, Guilford, CT 06437
(800) 582-0853

In the local native American tongue, *Winnisquam* means "smiling water." One

---

NOTES: Credit cards accepted: A Master Card; B Visa; C American Express; D Discover Card; E Diner's Club; F Other; 2 Personal Checks accepted; 3 Lunch available; 4 Dinner available; 5 Open all year;

cannot help but smile at this beautiful setting. The serenity of the lake, mountains, and surrounding woodlands lifts one's spirit. This recently built contemporary was expertly designed and finished by your host. All of the wood finish is native oak and pine milled from trees where the house now stands. There is a two-story solarium greenhouse overlooking the lake that serves as a wonderful place to read or have a snack. Two sitting rooms have TVs, books, and board games; guests are welcome to use the canoe or sunfish sailboat. Breakfast is an expanded continental, and three freshly decorated guest rooms are available. Resident dog, but no guest pets please. Children welcome. No smoking. $85-130.

Tin Whistle Inn

1047 Union Avenue, 03246
(603) 528-4185

Enjoy gracious hospitality at this charmning post-Victorian home. Fireplaced livingroom, leaded-glass windows, oak woodwork. Comfortable, spacious bedrooms. View memorable sunsets from the large veranda overlooking Paugus Bay. Minutes to Lake Winnipesaukee attractions and winter skiing facilities. Full, no-need-for-lunch breakfasts.

Host: Maureen Blazok
Rooms: 4 (PB) $45-60 plus tax
Full Breakfast
Credit Cards: A, B, C, D, F
Closed November
Notes: 2, 6, 7 (restricted), 8, 9, 10, 11, 12, 13, 14

LINCOLN

Red Sleigh Inn

Pollard Road, P. O. Box 562, 03251
(603) 745-8517

Family-run inn with mountain views. Just off the scenic Kancamagus Highway. One mile to Loon Mountains. Waterville, Cannon, and Bretton Woods nearby. Many summer attractions and superb fall foliage. Shopping, dining, and theater are minutes away. Hiking, swimming, golf, and train rides.

Hosts: Bill and Loretta
Rooms: 7 (1 PB; 6 SB) $55-65
Full Breakfast
Credit Cards: A, B
Notes: 2, 5, 11, 12, 13, 14

LISBON

Ammonoosuc Inn

Bishop Road, 03585
(603) 838-6118

Nestled in a quaint valley of New Hampshire is this charming country inn overlooking the Ammonoosuc River. Recently renovated, this 100-year-old farmhouse offers guests golf on premises, along with nearby hiking, biking, and fishing. Relax with a good book on the wraparound front porch. Dinner in the dining room is complemented by homemade breads and desserts. Top all of this off with warm hospitality and you have chosen the perfect getaway.

Hosts: Stephen and Laura Bromley
Rooms: 9 (PB) $50-85
Continental Breakfast
Credit Cards: A, B, C, D
Notes: 2, 4, 6 (call), 7 (limited), 8, 9, 11, 12, 14

LONDONDERRY

New Hampshire Bed and Breakfast NH615

329 Lake Drive, Guilford, CT 06437
(800) 582-0853

This large Colonial bed and breakfast home specializes in meeting the needs of family vacationers or business travelers. Just minutes from I-93 in a quiet New Hampshire town, relax in the great room or enjoy the comforts of the fireplace in the family room. Sing songs around a piano in the formal livingroom. Enjoy a breeze on the all-

6 Pets welcome; 7 Smoking allowed; 8 Children welcome; 9 Social drinking allowed; 10 Tennis available; 11 Swimming available; 12 Golf available; 13 Skiing available; 14 May be booked through travel agents.

season porch. Take a dip in the pool, play horseshoes, or barbecue your evening meal. Continental breakfast is served each morning. Two guest rooms share a bath. Infants and children over ten are welcome. No smoking. $45-50.

LYME

Dowd's Country Inn

5 Main Street, 03768
(603) 795-4712; FAX (603) 795-4220

Dowd's Country Inn is a picture perfect white Colonial built in the 1780s set on six acres with a tranquil pond frequented by ducks and resident turtles. Guests can enjoy afternoon tea with flaky scones and a homemade country breakfast served in the sun porch and the dining room. Twenty-three guest rooms offer their own private baths, and Dartmouth College, biking and hiking trails, and snowmobiling are all close by.

Hosts: Mickey and Tami Dowd
Rooms: 23 (PB) $55-110
Full Breakfast
Credit Cards: A, B, D, E
Notes: 2, 4, 5, 8, 9, 10, 11, 12, 13

Loch Lyme Lodge

Rural Free Delivery 278, Route 10, 03768
(603) 795-2141

Loch Lyme Lodge has been hosting guests since 1924. From May through September, the 25 cabins and rooms in the main lodge are open for the enjoyment of summer vacationers. During the fall and winter months, the main lodge, a farmhouse built in 1784, is open. Children are welcome at any season, and the emphasis is always on comfortable, informal hospitality.

Hosts: Paul and Judy Barker
Rooms: 4 (SB) $24-36/person
Full Breakfast
Credit Cards: None
Notes: 2, 3 (summer), 4 (summer), 5, 6 (summer), 8, 9, 10, 11, 12, 13

The Lyme Inn

On the Common, 03768
(603) 795-2222

"The kind of New England inn you always hoped to find." Situated in the heart of the Connecticut River Valley, the Lyme Inn offers Old World hospitality to the traveler. Rooms are furnished in authentic style, complete with four-poster beds, hooked rugs, and samplers. A master chef makes the restaurant a notable place to eat, and the cozy tavern is inviting.

Hosts: Fred and Judy Siemons
Rooms: 14 (12 PB; 2 SB) $65-105
Full Breakfast
Credit Cards: A, B, C
Notes: 2, 4, 5, 7, 9, 10, 11

MADISON

New Hampshire Bed and Breakfast NH 110

329 Lake Drive, Guilford, CT 06437
(800) 582-0853

In a peaceful farm and ranch town on 70 acres of fields and woods, this comfortable farmhouse bed and breakfast is only 15-minutes from the Conways and the Scenic Kancamagus Highway. Guests may enjoy the country kitchen with fireplace and the guest parlor, furnished with antiques. The spacious grounds offer scenic trails for walking, cross-country skiing, and wagon or sleigh rides. A full breakfast is served in the dining room. Children welcome. No smoking in bedrooms. No pets. $35 for single; $55 for double.

MARLBOROUGH

Peep-Willow Farm

51 Bixby Street, 03455
(603) 876-3807

Peep-Willow Farm is a working Thoroughbred horse farm that also caters to humans.

NOTES: Credit cards accepted: A Master Card; B Visa; C American Express; D Discover Card; E Diner's Club; F Other; 2 Personal Checks accepted; 3 Lunch available; 4 Dinner available; 5 Open all year;

Situated on 20 acres with a view all the way to the Connecticut River valley. Guests are welcome to help with chores or watch the young horses frolic in the fields, but there is no riding. Flexibility and serenity are the key ingredients to enjoying your stay.

Host: Noel Aderer
Rooms: 3 (SB) $27.50-45
Full Breakfast
Credit Cards: None
Notes: 2, 5, 6 (by arrangement), 8, 9, 13 (XC), 14

Thatcher Hill Inn

Thatcher Hill Road, 03455
(603) 876-3361

A rambling, revitalized 1794 country home on 60 acres of rolling meadows and woodlands in New Hampshire's quiet, uncrowded, and remarkably beautiful Monadnock Region, "the heart of New England." Antique-filled, immaculate, comfortable rooms. Private baths. Wheelchair access. Leisurely buffet breakfasts. Enjoy nearby villages, back roads, ponds and streams, covered bridges, state parks, antique shops, maple syrup, fall foliage, and cross-country skiing. No smoking.

Hosts: Marge and Cal Gage
Rooms: 7 (PB) $68-88
Full Breakfast
Credit Cards: A, B
Notes: 2

MEREDITH

New Hampshire Bed and Breakfast NH 211

329 Lake Drive, Guilford, CT 06437
(800) 582-0853

On the shore of Lake Winnipesaukee, four miles from the center of town, sits this beautiful turn-of-the-century home. Enjoy swimming, boating, canoeing, and badminton outside. Inside, relax on the screened porch or in front of the fireplace in the livingroom, overlooking the Ossipee Mountains and Lake Winnipesaukee. In town, you'll find shops, galleries, antiques, and restaurants. In the Lakes Region, you can enjoy such attractions as scenic train and boat rides, amusement centers, golf, tennis, and boat rentals. Full breakfast is served on the porch or on the 80-foot deck. Three guest rooms with shared bath. Children welcome; smoking outdoors; pets accepted. Open May, June, September, October. $55.

New Hampshire Bed and Breakfast NH 212

329 Lake Drive, Guilford, CT 06437
(800) 582-0853

The closest bed and breakfast to Meredith Bay village. Just a short stroll to the Marketplace of shops, galleries, restaurants, and Lake Winnispesaukee. Situated on a quiet residential lane, it guarantees peaceful days and nights, yet you are central to all activities of the Lakes Region. Minutes away from Winnispesaukee Scenic Railroad, the M.S. Mt. Washington cruise ship, Analee's Dolls Gift Shop and Museum, and Weirs Beach. Inside the inn, you'll enjoy an Early American ambience of fluffy quilts, hand-stenciled walls and floors, antique furnishings, and a romantic brick fireplace in the guest parlor. A continental breakfast is served in the dining room. Evening snacks feature seasonal beverages and freshly baked delights. Five guest rooms, two with private bath. Children welcome. No smoking. Small pets permitted. $50-65.

MUNSONVILLE

New Hampshire Bed and Breakfast NH 505

329 Lake Drive, Guilford, CT 06437
(800) 582-0853

6 Pets welcome; 7 Smoking allowed; 8 Children welcome; 9 Social drinking allowed; 10 Tennis available; 11 Swimming available; 12 Golf available; 13 Skiing available; 14 May be booked through travel agents.

This 200-year-old house was used to house the workers from the mill across the road. The mill produced cotton and woolen fabrics, and later became the Colony Mill Chair Company. Although the mill is no longer standing, the house stands near Granite Lake. This is a natural, spring-fed, sandy bottom, 212 acre lake that accommodates swimming, fishing, and boating. A full country breakfast is served each morning, and handmade quilts, afghans, stencils, and teddy bears adorn each guest room. Five rooms share two full bathrooms. Children Smoking. No smoking. $35-45.

NEW BOSTON

Colburn Homestead Bed and Breakfast

280 Colburn Road (off Route 136), 03070
(603) 487-5250

This Colonial farmhouse in a country setting is seventy miles from Boston, twenty miles from Manchester, and near many shopping and recreational facilities. Swimming pool available in-season. TVs in all the rooms. Christmas shop with gifts and crafts open year round.

Hosts: Olive and Robert Colburn
Rooms: 3 (SB) $50-65
Full Breakfast
Credit Cards: A, B
Notes: 2, 5, 7, 8, 11

NEWBURY

The 1806 House

Route 103 Traffic Circle, P. O. Box 54, 03277
(603) 763-4969

In the unspoiled New Hampshire countryside, the 1806 House has recently been restored to its current condition, with beamed ceilings, wide plank floors, and a charming livingroom complete with candlelight, cozy couches, wing chairs, and a

wood-burning stove. Every guest room has been tastefully and individually decorated with period furnishings and modern conveniences. A special gourmet breakfast is served every morning, complete with fine china, candlelight, and a Pavarotti aria. A perfect getaway, where Mount Sunapee is your backyard, gourmet restaurants abound, skiing, hiking, boating, and swimming are just steps across the road.

Hosts: Lane and Gene Bellman
Rooms: 6 (4 PB; 2 SB) $79-99
Full Breakfast
Credit Cards: A, B
Notes: 2, 5, 8, 9, 11, 12, 13, 14

NEW HAMPTON

New Hampshire Bed and Breakfast NH 240

329 Lake Drive, Guilford, CT 06437
(800) 582-0853

This 150-year-old antique-filled home with a converted barn is in the heart of the Lakes Region. Common rooms include the livingroom with a fireplace, den with TV and Nordic Track, and a pool room with pool table, piano, and stereo system. A hearty full breakfast is served, and wine will be offered, candy will be in your room, and fruit is always on the table. New Hampton, home to the co-ed prep school by the same name, is an easy stroll from the inn. Four rooms are available. No smoking. Children are welcome. $40-60.

NEW IPSWICH

The Inn at New Ipswich

Porter Hill Road, P. O. Box 208, 03071
(603) 878-3711

Relax awhile in a graceful 1790 home amid fruit trees and stone walls. Cozy fireplaces, front-porch rockers, and large comfortable guest rooms furnished country-style. All rooms have private baths. Scrumptious hearthside breakfasts (with fresh eggs from the premises). Situated in the Monadnock region of New Hampshire. Hiking, band concerts, antique auctions, maple sugaring, apple picking, unsurpassed autumn color, cross-country and downhill skiing. No smoking. Children over eight welcome.

Hosts: Ginny and Steve Bankuti
Rooms: 5 (PB) $60
Suite: 1 (PB) $95 sleeps 4
Full Breakfast
Credit Cards: A, B
Notes: 2, 5, 8 (over 8), 9, 13

New Hampshire Bed and Breakfast NH 545

329 Lake Drive, Guilford, CT 06437
(800) 582-0853

Built in 1790, this lovely farmhouse still possesses its early American charm. A classic red barn adjoins the house, and the grounds are bordered by stone walls, gardens, and fruit trees. In summer, guests may enjoy the fresh air on a screen porch full of white wicker furniture. In cooler seasons, guests may play Scrabble by the fire in the parlor or choose a book from the library. Breakfast is served in the keeping room by a crackling fire, and the inn is within short driving distance from a myriad of activities in the Monadnock area. Five guest rooms, two of which share a bath and three of which offer private baths, are available. Resident dog. Children over seven welcome. No smoking. $45-60.

NEW LONDON

Pleasant Lake Inn

125 Pleasant Street, P. O. Box 1030A, 03257
(603) 526-6271

Descending 500 feet from Main Street, you will find Pleasant Lake Inn on the shore of Pleasant Lake with Mount Kearsarge as its backdrop. All rooms have been renovated, have private baths, and are furnished with antiques. Five acres of woods, pastures, and gardens surround the inn. Hiking trails nearby. The lake provides swimming and fishing in summer; skiing and skating are equally popular in winter. Video available.

Hosts: Margaret and Grant Rich
Rooms: 11 (PB) $75-90
Full Breakfast
Credit Cards: A, B
Notes: 2, 4, 5, 7, 8, 9, 10, 11, 12, 13, 14

Pleaasant Lake Inn

NORTH CONWAY—SEE ALSO INTERVALE

The Buttonwood Inn

Box 1817 AD, 03860
(800) 258-2625

Built in the 1820s as a farmhouse, the inn is tucked away on Mount Surprise, where it is quiet and secluded, yet only two miles to the village and excellent dining and shopping. Minutes to Mount Washington, skiing (cross-country from the inn door), hiking, fishing, and canoeing. Enjoy the outdoor pool.

Hosts: Ann and Hugh Begley
Rooms: 9 (PB and SB) $25-50/person
Full Breakfast
Credit Cards: A, B, C
Notes: 2, 3 (winter), 4 (winter), 5, 7, 8, 9, 10, 11, 12, 13, 14

6 Pets welcome; 7 Smoking allowed; 8 Children welcome; 9 Social drinking allowed; 10 Tennis available; 11 Swimming available; 12 Golf available; 13 Skiing available; 14 May be booked through travel agents.

The Center Chimney-1787

P. O. Box 1220, River Road, 03860
(603) 356-6788

One of the earliest houses in North Conway is now a cozy, affordable bed and breakfast. Just off Main Street and the Saco River (swim, fish, and canoe). Walk to shops, restaurants, summer theater, free ice skating and cross-country skiing. Rock and ice climbing on nearby Cathedral Ledge.

Host: Farley Ames Whitley
Rooms: 4 (SB) $44-55
Continental Breakfast
Credit Cards: None
Notes: 2, 5, 7, 8, 9, 10, 11, 12, 13, 14

Cranmore Mt. Lodge

Box 1194, Kearsarge Road, 03860
(603) 356-2044; (800) 356-3596

Cranmore Mt. Lodge, a historic New England country inn, is the perfect place to unwind. The atmosphere is homey, and the accommodations and reasonable rates are ideal for families and groups. Formerly owned by Babe Ruth's daughter and visited by him many times. Hiking, rock climbing, skiing, kayaking, canoeing, bicycling, tennis, golf, riding, summer theater, and fine restaurants are just some of the area's attractions.

Hosts: Dennis and Judy Helfand
Rooms: 20 (16 PB; 4 SB) $67-99
Full Breakfast
Credit Cards: A, B, C, D
Notes: 2, 4, 5, 7, 8, 9, 10, 11, 12, 13

Nereledge Inn

River Road, P. O. Box 547, 03860
(603) 356-2831

Small 1787 comfortable, casual bed and breakfast with English-style pub (with darts and draft beer). Close to all outdoor activities: hiking, fishing, climbing, canoeing, golfing, and skiing. Walk to village or to river. Reasonable rates include country breakfast with warm apple pie. No smoking.

Hosts: Valerie and Dave Halpin
Rooms: 9 (4 PB; 5 SB) $59-85
Full Breakfast
Credit Cards: A, B, C
Notes: 2, 5, 8, 10, 11, 12, 13

New Hampshire Bed and Breakfast NH 108

329 Lake Drive, Guilford, CT 06437
(800) 582-0853

This restored country inn, built 215 years ago, features brass beds, skylights, antique rockers, fresh flowers, chocolates, and bath salts. Complimentary wine and cheese are served in front of the fireplace in the common room each afternoon. A hearty New England breakfast is served every morning. The upstairs reading room offers magnificent views of the Moat Mountains. Discount passes to the Cranmore Recreation Center (saunas, swimming, racquet sports) and local restaurants. One mile from Mount Cranmore ski area and two miles from downtown North Conway. Has 18 guest rooms, most with private bath. Children welcome. Smoking in common room only; no pets. $74-104.

Peacock Inn

P. O. Box 1012, 03860
(603) 356-9041; (800) 328-9041

Recapture romance in this intimate country inn in the heart of the White Mountains near the quaint village of North Conway. Guests have access to Cranmore Recreation Center for indoor swimming, aerobics, tennis, climbing wall, and saunas. Has received AAA three-diamond rating.

Hosts: Claire and Larry Jackson
Rooms: 15 (14 PB; 1 SB) $84-118
Full Breakfast
Credit Cards: A, B, C
Notes: 2, 5, 7, 8, 9, 10, 11, 12, 13, 14

Scottish Lion Inn and Restaurant

Route 16, Main Street, 03860-1527
(603) 356-6381

NOTES: Credit cards accepted: A Master Card; B Visa; C American Express; D Discover Card; E Diner's Club; F Other; 2 Personal Checks accepted; 3 Lunch available; 4 Dinner available; 5 Open all year;

At the Scottish Lion you'll find country inn atmosphere with splendid cuisine and comfortable accommodations. All seven rooms have private baths. Five have clan names with corresponding decor. The pride of the Lion is its unique and varied menu of American and Scottish favorites. The inn has the largest selection of single malts and Scotches in New Hampshire, and it is the only inn in New England to serve 100 percent Kona coffee.

Hosts: Chef Michael and Janet Procopio
Rooms: 7 (PB) $49.95-99 (tax and tip included)
Full Breakfast
Credit Cards: A, B, C, D
Notes: 3, 4, 5, 7, 8, 9, 13

The 1785 Inn

Route 16 at the Scenic Vista, 03860
(603) 356-9025; (800) 421-1785

The 1785 Inn offers romantic accommodations, spectacular views of Mount Washington, and award-winning dining. In the spring and summer there are nature walks, hikes, swimming pool, fishing, and lawn games. In the fall it has the best views of foliage anywhere. In the winter there are 60 kilometers of cross-country trails, with downhill skiing only two miles away.

Hosts: Becky and Charlie Mallar
Rooms: 17 (12 PB; 5 SB) $60-115
Full Breakfast
Credit Cards: A, B, C, D, E, F
Notes: 2, 4, 5, 7, 8, 9, 10, 11, 12, 13, 14

The Stonehurst Manor

Route 16, 03860
(603) 356-3113; (800) 525-9100

Rustically elegant 19th-century country manor constructed from locally quarried granite, finished with a forest of hand-carved oak, and accented with museum-quality leaded- and stained-glass windows and doors. This turn-of-the-century manor also has a 20th-century hot tub. The dining rooms and porches feature formal and casual dining that is unequaled in the valley, with guests returning year after year to enjoy the American- and European-style cuisine. Rates include breakfast and dinner.

Host: Peter Rattay
Rooms: 24 (22 PB; 2 SB) $96-166
Credit Cards: A, B, C
Notes: 4, 5, 7, 8, 9, 10, 11, 12, 13, 14

Sunny Side Inn

Seavey Street, 03860
(603) 356-6239

The Stonehurst Manor

6 Pets welcome; 7 Smoking allowed; 8 Children welcome; 9 Social drinking allowed; 10 Tennis available; 11 Swimming available; 12 Golf available; 13 Skiing available; 14 May be booked through travel agents.

A casual, affordable country inn in a restored 1850s farmhouse. Short walk to North Conway village and its many shops and restaurants. Enjoy mountain views from the flower-trimmed porches in summer, or relax by the fireplace in winter.

Hosts: Chris and Marylee Uggerholt
Rooms: 10 (2 PB; 8 SB) $45-65
Full Breakfast
Credit Cards: A, B
Notes: 2, 5

Wyatt House Country Inn

Main Street, Route 16, P. O. Box 777, 03860
(603) 356-7977; (800) 527-7978

Experience the charm of an elegant country Victorian inn with panoramic mountain and river views. Six guest rooms are uniquely decorated and furnished with antiques. A candlelit gourmet multi-entree breakfast is served on English Wedgewood and Irish lace. Stroll from the backyard to the Saco River for swimming or fishing. Early morning coffee and muffins are served in the handsome study, as well as afternoon tea and cakes. Village location, and minutes to downhill and cross-country skiing. Tax-free outlet shopping. Smoking limited to Victorian wraparound porch and grounds. Fresh flowers and fruits and cookie baskets in every room; turndown service at night.

Hosts: Bill and Arlene Strickland
Rooms: 6 (4 PB; 2 SB) $58-90
Full Breakfast
Credit Cards: A, B, D
Notes: 2, 3, 5, 7 (limited), 8 (over 12), 9, 11, 13, 14

NORTH SUTTON

Follansbee Inn

P. O. Box 92, 03260
(603) 927-4221; (800) 626-4221

An authentic 1840 New England inn with white clapboard and green trim. Situated on peaceful Kezar Lake, with an old-fashioned porch, comfortable sitting rooms with fire-places, and charming antique furnishings. Nestled in a small country village but convenient to all area activities (4 miles south of New London and 95 miles north of Boston). Private pier with rowboat, canoe, paddle boat, and windsurfer for guests. Beautiful walk around the lake during all seasons. No smoking.

Hosts: Dick and Sandy Reilein
Rooms: 23 (11 PB; 12 SB) $70-90
Full Breakfast
Credit Cards: A, B
Closed parts of Nov. and April
Notes: 2, 4, 8 (over 10), 9, 10, 11, 12, 13, 14

NORTHWOOD

The Aviary

P. O. Box 268, 03261
(603) 942-7755

This secluded, owner-designed lakeside home can accommodate up to six guests in gracious surroundings. Birds and small wildlife are in abundance. Guests may enjoy the deck, private beach, screened porch, lawn games, and other year-round outside activities. The den has a TV, and the livingroom is well stocked with books and games to enjoy by the fireplace. The Aviary is just-minutes away from Northwood's famous antique alley. Accommodations by reservation only.

Hosts: Tad and Georgette Comstock
Rooms: 3 (2 PB; 1 SB) $55-60
Full Breakfast
Credit Cards: None
Notes: 2, 5, 9, 11

New Hampshire Bed and Breakfast NH 621

329 Lake Drive, Guilford, CT 06437
(800) 582-0853

This authentic 18th-century New England Colonial home is on sixty acres in a country setting. Enjoy the character of old beams, original fireplaces, early paneling, and wide-board floors. A full breakfast is served in the keeping room in front of the fireplace. Fields and woods surround the property, and horses graze in the pastures. A short walk down a country lane brings you to a private beach on Jenness Pond, where guests are welcome to swim. Three guest rooms furnished with antiques share a bath. Concord is one-half hour away. Two resident dogs. No smoking. Children welcome. $45-55.

NORTH WOODSTOCK

New Hampshire Bed and Breakfast NH 117

329 Lake Drive, Guilford, CT 06437
(800) 582-0853

This 80-year-old inn offers seven personally decorated guest rooms and family suites, each with views of the gardens, Mooselake River, or the south ridge of Loon Mountain. The livingroom has a fireplace, TV, and games. The spacious front porch is a favorite among guests. Breakfast in the dining room includes apple or cranberry-walnut pancakes with pure New England maple syrup and jugs of freshly ground café au lait. You may also choose a continental breakfast in bed. Close to many parks and resort areas. Children welcome. Smoking limited; no pets. $40-95 seasonal.

Woodstock Inn

80 Main Street, 03262
(603) 745-3951; (800) 321-3985

Personal service, comfortable accommodations, and excellent dining ensure a pleasant stay, whether you are skiing, hiking, vacationing with the family, or just relaxing. The Main House is a 100-year-old Victorian home with six guest rooms that are individually decorated, accented with antiques, and share three full hall bathrooms. The Woodstock Inn Riverside,

overlooking the Pemigewasset River, has been renovated into 11 guest rooms all with private bathrooms. All 17 rooms have color TV, air conditioning, and telephones. Two dining rooms offering pub-style and fine dining are open seven days. Lounge provides entertainment on weekends.

Hosts: Scott and Eileen Rice
Rooms: 17 (11 PB; 6 SB) $40-89
Full Breakfast
Credit Cards: A, B, C, D
Notes: 2, 3, 4, 5, 7, 8, 9, 10, 11, 12, 13, 14

OSSIPEE

Acorn Lodge

Duncan Lake, Box 144, 03864
(603) 539-2151

Once President Grover Cleveland's summer fishing camp, Acorn Lodge overlooks tranquil Duncan Lake. Breakfast is served on the veranda. Then you may wish to fish from the dock or use the rowboat or canoe. Enjoy a cool swim from the sandy beach or play lawn games. Close to Wolfeboro, summer theater, golf. Bicycle available.

Hosts: Julie and Ray Terry
Rooms: 6 (PB) $46
Continental Breakfast
Minimum stay: 2 nights
Credit Cards: A, B
Closed Oct. 15-May 15
Notes: 2, 7, 8, 9, 10, 11, 12, 13 (XC)

PLYMOUTH

Crab Apple Inn

Rural Route 4, Box 1955, 03264
(603) 536-4476

This inn is an 1835 brick Federal situated beside a brook at the foot of Tenney Mountain. The grounds are complemented by an English garden and brick courtyard. Situated at the gateway to the White Mountains.

Hosts: Harry and Maria Dunham
Rooms: 4-5 (PB) $75-85

Full Breakfast
Credit Cards: A, B, C
Notes: 2, 5, 7, 8 (over 10), 9, 10, 11, 12, 13

PORTSMOUTH

The Bow Street Inn

121 Bow Street, 03801
(603) 431-7760

An attractive alternative for any seacoast tourist, the Bow Street Inn is also irresistible lodging for the traveling professional and visitor. Situated on the Piscataqua River, in downtown Portsmouth, the inn's newly decorated and furnished rooms offer spectacular river views, rooftop views of Portsmouth, telephone, full bath, and color TV. Guests can also enjoy the sitting room and complimentary continental breakfast. The Bow Street Theatre is on the premises. You can walk across the city's classic liftbridge into Maine or enjoy the flower gardens at Prescott Park just blocks away. Other local attractions include ten restaurants within three blocks and access to waterfront decks and marina.

Hosts: Joe and Jann Bova
Rooms: 10 (PB)
Expanded Continental Breakfast
Credit Cards: A, B
Notes: 2, 5, 9, 14

RINDGE

Grassy Pond House

Rindge, 03461
(603) 899-5166; (603) 899-5167

An 1831 homestead nestled among 150 forested acres, overlooking water and gardens. Convenient to main roads, restaurants, antique marts, weekly local auctions, theater, music, and craft fairs. Hike the Grand Monadnock; ski cross-country and downhill. A retreat for all seasons.

Hosts: Carmen Linares and Bob Multer
Rooms: 4 (2 PB; 2 SB) $40-65

Full Breakfast
Minimum stay during foliage: 2 nights
Credit Cards: None
Notes: 2, 5, 9, 10, 11, 12, 13, 14

RUMNEY

New Hampshire Bed and Breakfast NH 248

329 Lake Drive, Guilford, CT 06437
(800) 582-0853

This 1790 Early American farmhouse and attached ell sits on 125 acres of beautiful fields and woodland, with views of the White Mountains. Gardens, a real sugar house, and a barn all add to the peaceful country setting. Guests will enjoy private sitting areas, games, books, and the full country breakfast in the dining room of the main house. Hiking, walking, or cross-country ski trails are available throughout the property. The sugar house is in opertaion during March and April of every year. Three guest rooms are available. Resident dog. Children welcome. No smoking. $55-75.

RYE

Rock Ledge Manor Bed and Breakfast

1413 Ocean Boulevard, Route 1A, 03870
(603) 431-1413

Gracious traditional seaside manor home (1840-1880) with wraparound porch. All rooms have ocean view. Six-minutes to historic Portsmouth; 20-minutes to University of New Hampshire; 15-minutes to Hampton; within one-half hour to southern Maine's seacoast attractions. No smoking.

Hosts: Norman and Janice Marineau
Rooms: 4 (2 PB; 2 SB) $65-80
Full Breakfast
Credit Cards: None
Notes: 2, 5, 8 (over 10), 9

NOTES: Credit cards accepted: A Master Card; B Visa; C American Express; D Discover Card; E Diner's Club; F Other; 2 Personal Checks accepted; 3 Lunch available; 4 Dinner available; 5 Open all year;

SHELBURNE

New Hampshire Bed and Breakfast NH 140

329 Lake Drive, Guilford, CT 06437
(800) 582-0853

A stone's throw away from the Maine state line and just minutes east of Gorham, this large, restored farmhouse welcomes you to enjoy the peaceful atmosphere of the White Mountains. Two miles to the Appalachian Trail; 15-minutes to alpine, Nordic, and cross-country skiing, golf, snowmobiling, and hiking; 30-minutes to Mount Washington Auto Road. A full country breakfast is just one of the many personal touches offered by your hosts. Cheese and crackers and fresh flowers are daily enjoyments. Three guest rooms with shared bath. No children; no pets. Smoking permitted. $40 for single; $50 for double.

STARK VILLAGE

New Hampshire Bed and Breakfast NH 130

329 Lake Drive, Guilford, CT 06437
(800) 582-0853

Situated in historic Stark Village on the banks of the Upper Ammonoosuc River, this large, rambling white farmhouse has been restored and updated to offer guests a large livingroom with TV and fireplace, a country kitchen with antique wood stove, and a dining room where wonderful breakfasts are served. The inn borders the White Mountains National Forest, and is three miles from the Nash Stream Valley Wilderness Area known for some of the best hunting and fishing in New Hampshire. Hiking, swimming, canoeing, bicycling, picnicking, hunting, fishing, cross-country skiing, snowmobiling, and skating are all available. Three guest rooms with private baths. Children welcome. No pets; no smoking. $45.

STRATHAM

New Hampshire Bed and Breakfast NH 430

329 Lake Drive, Guilford, CT 06437
(800) 582-0853

Just a short drive from UNH and Portsmouth, this large garrison in a quiet evergreen setting is a perfect location for those who enjoy a busy day's activities and quiet evenings. The large livingroom and dining room have lovely stenciling and handmade braided rugs done by the hostess. Relax and enjoy the cool summer breezes from the lovely shaded back yard, which is perfect for a do-it-yourself barbecue. Enjoy the garden, deck, woods, and pond. A full breakfast is served each morning, and guests are welcome to use the kitchen. Located in New Hampshire's seacoast region. Two guest rooms share a bath. Children welcome. Smoking limited. $35-45.

SUGAR HILL

The Hilltop Inn

Sugar Hill Road, Box 9, 03585
(603) 823-5695; (800) 551-3084

An 1895 Victorian inn in the small village of Sugar Hill, which is in the heart of the White Mountains near Franconia Notch. Peaceful and homey, filled with antiques, lots of porches, and a deck for sunsets and bird watching. Comfortable beds, with handmade quilts and large country breakfasts. The Victorian dining room offers memorable fine dining. All rooms have private baths. AAA three diamonds.

Hosts: Meri and Mike Hern
Rooms: 6 (PB) $60-110
Full Breakfast
Minimum stay holidays and fall foliage: 2 nights
Credit Cards: A, B, C, D
Notes: 2, 4, 5, 6, 7 (limited), 8, 9, 10, 11, 12, 13

6 Pets welcome; 7 Smoking allowed; 8 Children welcome; 9 Social drinking allowed; 10 Tennis available; 11 Swimming available; 12 Golf available; 13 Skiing available; 14 May be booked through travel agents.

Inn at Skunk Hollow

Route 117, Main Street, P. O. Box 581, 03585
(603) 823-8532; (800) 551-3084

In the heart of the White Mountains, the
Inn at Skunk Hollow will welcome you
home after a day's adventure. The best
winter skiing, shopping, hiking, and every
summer activity imaginable. Warm your
hands and feet by the fireplace when it's
cold or bask in the sun on the deck. Every
season is a joy. Three generations of the
Williams family make their home your
home.

Hosts: Bill and Lee Williams
Rooms: 4 (2 PB; 2 SB) $45-75
Full Breakfast
Credit Cards: A, B
Notes: 2, 5, 9, 14

New Hampshire Bed and Breakfast NH 133

329 Lake Drive, Guilford, CT 06437
(800) 582-0853

Located on the eastern slope of Sugar Hill
overlooking Franconia Notch, Mount
Washington and the Presidential Range.
Relax on the porch in a comfortable rocker
and enjoy views of expansive fields with a
backdrop of Mount Washington's snow-
capped peak.The surrounding White
Mountains region offers year-round recreation and activities, and an on-site tennis
court and nearby golf course are available
for guests to use. A full country breakfast is
served each morning, and three guest
rooms, all of which offer private baths, are
available. Centrally located within a short
drive to Franconia Notch State Park, the
Robert Frost Homestead, Cannon Mountain
Ski Area, and the New England Ski
Museum. Resident dog. Children welcome.
No smoking. $65-80.

SUNAPEE

Journey's End Bed and Breakfast

485 Edgemont Road, Route 103B, 03782
(603) 763-4849

Nestled in the heart of the lovely Lake
Sunapee-Dartmouth area, this bed and
breakfast offers cozy and comfortable lodging in an 18th-century farmhouse. Within
minutes, lakes and mountains provide
recreational activities year-round. The inn
offers a delicious breakfast, which is surpassed only by the warmth and hospitality
of your hosts.

Hosts: Tom and Mary McCormack
Rooms: 4 (2 PB; 2 SB) $45 single; $50 double
Full Breakfast
Credit Cards: A, B
Notes: 2, 5, 8, 9, 10, 11, 12, 13, 14

New Hampshire Bed and Breakfast NH 302

329 Lake Drive, Guilford, CT 06437
(800) 582-0853

Nestled in the heart of New Hampshire's
Lake Sunapee region, this 18th-century
farmhouse sits on six country acres. This
bed and breakfast prides itself on warm
hospitality, cleanliness, and a hearty homemade breakfast served in a room that overlooks the pond. Fun awaits in the game
room where you will find a pool table, a
variety of board games, or a good book or
movie. During the winter months, savor the
comfort of a crackling fire with a complimentary cup of hot soup or stew. Four
guest rooms share two baths. Smoking is
allowed downstairs only. Resident dog.
Children over six welcome. $40-50.

Seven Hearths Inn

Old Route 11, 26 Seven Hearths Lane, 03782
(603) 763-5657; (800) 237-2464

Seven Hearths is at the center of a year-round resort area within minutes of Sunapee Harbor with its marina and the state park's beach and ski area. The area also offers several golf courses, tennis, horseback riding, and boat excursions. Some of the guest rooms have fireplaces, and all are air-conditioned. Enjoy cocktails in the Hearth Room and gourmet candle-light dining. On-site pool and full liquor license.

Host: Laraine Pedrero
Rooms: 10 (PB) $88-138
Full Breakfast
Minimum Stay Weekends: 2 nights
Credit Cards: A, B
Notes: 2,4, 5, 7, 8, 9, 10, 11, 12, 13, 14

SUTTON MILLS

The Quilt House

Bed and Breakfast Marblehead and North Shore
P. O. Box 35, Newtonville, Massachusetts 02160
(617) 964-1606; (800) 832-2632 outside MA

This is one of the prettiest bed and break-fasts in the area. It is a 130-year-old Victorian country house overlooking a quaint village. The hostess runs workshops on quilting, and there are many fine quilts throughout the house. Three guest rooms on the second floor share two baths. Situated ten-minutes away from summer theater, excellent restaurants, fine shopping, and antiquing. Delicious full breakfast; children welcome; no smoking. $45-55.

TAMWORTH

New Hampshire Bed and Breakfast NH 100

329 Lake Drive, Guilford, CT 06437
(800) 582-0853

Situated in the center of historic Tamworth Village, this 18th-century Colonial dates back to 1785 and is furnished with period

antiques. Exposed beams, wainscoting, stenciled floors, gunstock posts, and fire-places exude the charm you hope to find in a country inn. The inn is only a stone's throw from the Swift River for trout fishing; a stroll to summer theater; minutes from AMC hiking trails; and a short drive to North Conway and Mount Washington valley areas. Breakfast is a hearty affair served on antique china in the dining room. Four guest rooms, one with private bath. Children 12 and older welcome. Smoking permitted. No pets. $50-85.

TEMPLE

Birchwood Inn

Route 45, 03084
(603) 878-3285

A cozy family-run inn on the National Register. Elegant dining in small dining rooms with candlelight and Rufus Porter murals on the walls. Guest rooms are filled with antiques, and homemade quilts are on the beds.

Hosts: Judy and Bill Wolfe
Doubles: 7 (5PB; 2 SB) $70
Full Breakfast
Credit Cards: None
Closed 2 weeks in April and 1 in Nov.
Notes: 2, 7, 8 (over 10), 9, 10, 11, 12, 13

TILTON

Black Swan Inn

308 West Main Street, 03276
(603) 286-4524

An 1880 restored Victorian situated in the lakes region on four acres overlooking the Winnipesaukee River. Exceptional mahogany and oak woodwork and stained-glass windows. Two screened porches and formal gardens for guests' enjoyment. Refrigerators and sodas available for guests.

Hosts: Janet and Bob Foster
Rooms: 7 (3 PB; 4 SB) $55-65
Full Breakfast
Credit Cards: A, B, C, D, F
Closed March
Notes: 2, 7, 8 (over 11), 9, 10, 11, 12, 13, 14

WAKEFIELD

The Wakefield Inn

Rural Route 1, Box 2185, 03872
(603) 522-8272; (800) 245-0841

Situated within the historic district of
Wakefield Corner. Early travelers arrived
by stagecoach. The majestic mountains and
cool, blue lakes offer unlimited outdoor
activities. Or just relax and enjoy the ambience of days gone by.

Hosts: Lou and Harry Sisson
Rooms: 7 (PB) $65
Full Breakfast
Minimum stay holidays: 2 nights
Credit Cards: A, B
Notes: 2, 4, 5, 8 (over 10), 9, 12, 13 (XC)

WATERVILLE VALLEY

The Snowy Owl Inn

Box 407, 13215
(603) 236-8383

Rustic country inn in picturesque Waterville
Valley. Eighty rooms, some with Jacuzzis
and wet bars. Indoor and outdoor pools,
saunas, reading porch, and six lobbies with
fireplaces. Complimentary wine and cheese
party every afternoon, plus free admission
to a nearby sports center; golf, tennis, and
boating are available nearby.

Host: Tor Brunvand
Rooms: 80 (PB) $49-129
Continental Breakfast
Credit Cards: A, B, C, D, E
Notes: 2, 5, 7, 8, 10, 11, 13, 14

WENTWORTH

Hilltop Acres

East Side and Buffalo Road, 03282
(603) 764-5896

Treat yourself to this peaceful country
retreat; large pine-paneled recreation room
with fireplace, piano, games, and cable TV.
Spacious grounds surrounded by pine forest with natural brook; lawn games; peaceful atmosphere. Rooms with private baths;
housekeeping cottages. Near White
Mountains and lakes region attractions.

Host: Marie A. Kauk
Rooms: 4 (PB) $60
Cottages: 2 (PB) $75
Expanded Continental Breakfast
Credit Cards: A, B
Notes: 2, 5, 8, 9

Mountain Laurel Inn

Route 25 at 25A, 03282
(603) 764-9600; (800) 338-9986

Step back into the 19th century at the
Mountain Laurel Inn. This 1840 Colonial
was built by the prominent Webster family
and has emanated elegant hospitality for
150 years. Your romantically appointed
rooms are distinctive and comfortable, and
your leisurely breakfast in the dining room
will energize you for your day's activities
in New Hampshire. Minutes away from the
famous Kancamagus Highway, the
Appalachian Trail, major ski areas, excellent fishing, cycling routes, and New
Hampshire lakes.

Host: Don LaBrie
Rooms: 5 (3 PB; 2 SB) $65-75
Full Breakfast
Credit Cards: A, B
Notes: 2, 5, 9

New Hampshire
Bed and Breakfast NH 120

329 Lake Drive, Guilford, CT 06437
(800) 582-0853

This charming home, built in the early
1880s, is within an easy drive of both the
Lakes Region and Franconia Notch, where
you can enjoy outdoor sports, shops, crafts
and art galleries, theater, and fine restaurants. Wentworth offers three natural swim-

---

NOTES: Credit cards accepted: A Master Card; B Visa; C American Express; D Discover Card; E Diner's
Club; F Other; 2 Personal Checks accepted; 3 Lunch available; 4 Dinner available; 5 Open all year;

ming holes, many hiking trails, fishing streams, and antique shops. The home itself is furnished with antiques. The pine-paneled recreation room is complete with an antique piano, games, an extensive library, and cable TV. Continental breakfast and afternoon teas are served. Six guest rooms, four with private bath. Two housekeeping cottages with kitchen unit, private livingroom with fireplace, and screened porch available. Children welcome. No smoking; no pets. $60.

WEST SPRINGFIELD

New Hampshire Bed and Breakfast NH 310

329 Lake Drive, Guilford, CT 06437
(800) 582-0853

This lovely manor inn offers spacious terraces that overlook rolling fields, unspoiled wood and mountain vistas, privacy, and cozy elegance combined with antiques that remind you of England's elegant country inns. A winding staircase, imposing two-story livingroom, and an upstairs "Caesar's Balcony" are but a few of the architectural details that make this a grand country manor. Eight expansive and elegant guest accommodations with modern amenities and private baths offer gracious elegance and luxury. Modified American Plan includes evening appetizers and wine, a four-course dinner, and a full country breakfast. Bed and breakfast only is $20 less per person. No appropriate facilities are available for small children. Smoking is in designated areas only. $80-120.

WEST THORNTON

Amber Lights Inn Bed and Breakfast

Route 3, 03223
(603) 726-4077

Newest bed and breakfast in the White Mountains. Lovingly restored 1815 Colonial offering a sumptuous six-course breakfast, homemade bread and muffins like Gramma made, queen-size country beds with handmade quilts, and meticulously clean guest rooms. Private and semiprivate baths, Hannah Adams dining room with fireplace, guest library, and garden rooms. Hors d'oeuvres served nightly. Conveniently situated between Loon Mountain and Waterville Valley. Close to all White Mountain attractions. No pets. No smoking.

Hosts: Paul Sears and Carola Warnsman
Rooms: 5 (1 PB; 4 SB) $55-75
Full Breakfast
Credit Cards: A, B, D
Notes: 2, 3, 5, 8, 9, 10, 11, 12, 13, 14

WHITEFIELD

New Hampshire Bed and Breakfast NH 102

329 Lake Drive, Guilford, CT 06437
(800) 582-0853

One mile down a quaint winding road, surrounded by stone walls and 32 acres of forest and fields, this Victorian home, circa 1860, offers a fireside sitting room, a private library with TV and VCR movies, and a wraparound porch with outside seating. Horseshoes, volleyball, croquet, and weekend barbecues offered. Twenty-minutes to White Mountains; fishing and swimming on Burns Pond; white-water rafting and canoeing on the Connecticut River. Your choice of breakfast plans. Six guest rooms with shared bath and one two-room suite with kitchenette and balcony. Children welcome. No smoking in bedrooms; no pets. $30-60.

WINNISQUAM

Tall Pines Inn

Old Route 3, Box 327, 03289
(800) 722-6870

6 Pets welcome; 7 Smoking allowed; 8 Children welcome; 9 Social drinking allowed; 10 Tennis available; 11 Swimming available; 12 Golf available; 13 Skiing available; 14 May be booked through travel agents.

A four seasons destination on Lake Winnisquam. Spectacular lake and mountain views; boat rental and sandy beach only yards away. Winter skiing within minutes of the inn's wood stove. Special dinners by reservation.

Hosts: Kent and Kate Kern
Rooms: 3 (1 PB; 2 SB) $48-70
Full Breakfast
Minimum stay weekends and holidays: 2 nights
Credit Cards: A, B
Notes: 2, 4, 5, 7 (limited), 9, 10, 11, 12, 13, 14

WOLFEBORO

Tuc' Me Inn

68 North Main Street, P. O. Box 657, 03894
(603) 569-5702

This circa 1850 Colonial/Federal is within walking distance of the quaint village of Wolfeboro, on the eastern shore of Lake Winnipesaukee, the oldest summer resort in America. Plan to spend several days here and enjoy scenic drives, country stores, museums, authentic taverns, fine restaurants, golf, tennis, horseback riding, cross-country and downhill skiing, along with a cruise on the M.S. Mt. Washington. The inn's new owners invite you to share high tea in the Victorian garden room, and relax in the music room and parlor. After a restful evening, wake up to a full gourmet breakfast in the elegant dining room.

Hosts: Ernie, Terry, and Tina Foutz; Idabel Evans
Rooms: 8 (3 PB; 5 SB) $50-150
Full Breakfast
Credit Cards: A, B
Notes: 2, 5, 8, 9, 10, 11, 12, 13, 14

The Wolfeboro Inn

44 North Main Street, 03894
(603) 569-3016; (800) 451-2389

Situated on Lake Winnipesaukee, in the oldest summer resort town in America. With 43 guest rooms, private beach, and two restaurants, the Wolfeboro Inn combines the decor and ambience of an authentic 1812 New England inn with the quality service of a AAA four-diamond hotel.

Host: Dale Sampson
Rooms: 43 (PB) $76-197
Continental Breakfast
Credit Cards: A, B, C, D, E
Notes: 2, 3, 4, 5, 7, 8, 9, 10, 11, 12, 13 (XC), 14

New Jersey

AVON-BY-THE-SEA

The Sands
Bed and Breakfast Inn

42 Sylvania Avenue, 07717
(908) 776-8386

The Sands is located in a small Victorian town just seven houses from the nicest beach on the Jersey shore. The inn radiates warmth and hospitality. Each of the nine rooms has a paddle fan, and many has sinks and refrigerators. Spend an afternoon on the beautiful white sandy beach, which is just steps away. A lovely breakfast is served each morning in the family dining room or on the porch. A stay at the inn will make you feel relaxed and refreshed.

Host: Ana Suchecki
Rooms: 9 (SB) $50-70
Full Breakfast
Credit Cards: A, B
Notes: 2, 11, 12

Cashelmara Inn

22 Lakeside Avenue, 07717
(908) 776-8727

Oceanside/lakefront Victorian inn where you can enjoy views of the Atlantic from your bed. Room decorated in beautiful Victorian antiques, and a wicker-filled veranda overlooking the ocean make your stay memorable. A suite with a fireplace is also available. Only 55 minutes from New York City and one hour from Philadelphia.

Host: Martin J. Mulligan
Rooms: 14 (PB) $80-157
Full Breakfast

Minimum stay summer weekends: 3 nights; holidays: 4 nights
Credit Cards: A, B, C
Notes: 2, 5, 8, 9, 10, 11, 12

BARNEGAT

The Dynasty

Pebble Beach, 248 Edison Road, 08005
(609) 698-1566

A quiet, bayside, air-conditioned home on a peninsula with dock space. Breakfast is served around an award-winning pool amid beautiful foliage. Enjoy a picturesque view of the sunset and wildlife reserve, the warmth of a designer's fireplace, and the ultimate in antiques collected from around the world. Just minutes to the world's largest playground, Atlantic City.

Host: Stanley Finkelstein
Rooms: 3 (1 PB; 2 SB) $56-125
Full Breakfast
Closed November 1-April 31
Credit Cards: None
Notes: 2, 8, 9, 10, 11, 12, 13, 14

BAY HEAD

Conover's Bay Head Inn

646 Main Avenue, 08742
(908) 892-4664

The 12 romantic, antique-filled bedrooms have views of the ocean, bay, marina, or gardens. The aroma of inn-baked biscuits, muffins, or coffee cake will awaken you each morning. The full breakfast may feature a savory egg casserole, French toast, or a special blueberry pancake. Enjoy a large

NOTES: Credit cards accepted: A Master Card; B Visa; C American Express; D Discover Card; E Diner's Club; F Other; 2 Personal Checks accepted; 3 Lunch available; 4 Dinner available; 5 Open all year; 6 Pets welcome; 7 Smoking allowed; 8 Children welcome; 9 Social drinking allowed; 10 Tennis available; 11 Swimming available; 12 Golf available; 13 Skiing available; 14 May be booked through travel agents.

Hope • Stanhope

Denville •

Lyndhurst •

Stewartsville •

Flemington •

Princeton •

Avon-by-the-Sea

Stockton •

Belmar
Spring Lake
Sea Girt
Bay Head

Barnegat •

Beach Haven •

Longport •
Woodbine •
Ocean City •

North Wildwood •

NEW JERSEY

collection of original art or swim at the private ocean beaches. Collect seashells and sea glass. Walk to Twilight Lake and feed the ducks or relax in the garden.

Hosts: Carl and Beverly Conover
Rooms: 12 (PB) $75-165
Full Breakfast
Credit Cards: A, B, C
Notes: 2, 5, 9, 10, 11, 12

BEACH HAVEN

Bayberry Barque Bed and Breakfast

117 Centre Street, 08008
(609) 492-5216

Circa 1890, this Victorian bed and breakfast is in Beach Haven's historic district on Long Beach Island. Beautiful, romantic, antique-filled rooms compliment the cool ocean beaches. Lounge on the wraparound porch, or enjoy the 18 miles of white sand beach. Visit unique shops, museums, summer playhouse, great restaurants and night life, all within walking distance. Guests enjoy a cold buffet breakfast and a wine and cheese party on summer Saturday nights. Experience the Jersey shore with its warm hospitality.

Host: Patricia Miller
Rooms: 9 (2 PB; 7 SB) $60-115
Expanded Continental Breakfast
Credit Cards: A, B, C
Notes: 2, 5, 8, 9, 10, 11, 12

Victoria Guest House

126 Amber Street, 08008
(609) 492-4154

Step back to the charm of the late 19th century. The gracious guest houses offer the warmth of a friendly atmosphere and the refreshment of a home away from home in the heart of beautiful Long Beach Island. Guests are only four houses from the beach and steps away from the heated pool. Bicycle, beach chairs, and badges are avail-

able. An expanded continental breakfast is served every morning, and lemonade and iced tea are offered in the late afternoon.

Hosts: Marilyn and Leonard Miller
Rooms: 17 (16 PB; 1 SB) $85-130
Expanded Continental Breakfast
Credit Cards: None
Notes: 2, 9, 10, 11, 12

BELMAR

The Seaflower Bed and Breakfast Inn

110 Ninth Avenue, 07719
(908) 681-6006

This Dutch Colonial home was built in 1907. Now with private baths, the flower-and-light-filled rooms make a perfect seashore getaway. Beach and boardwalk are one-half block away for sunning or moonlight strolls. Enjoy all the activities ocean and bay provide, great seafood, historic sites, and amusements.

Hosts: Pat O'Keefe and Knute Iwaszko
Rooms: 7 (5 PB; 2 SB) $55-90
Full Breakfast
Credit Cards: C
Notes: 2, 5, 7 (limited), 8 (over 10), 9, 10, 11, 12, 14

CAPE MAY

The Abbey

Columbia Avenue and Gurney Street, 08204
(609) 884-4506

The Abbey consists of two restored Victorian buildings originally in the John McCreary family in the heart of Cape May's historic district. All rooms are furnished with period Victorian antiques and have private baths. On-site or remote parking; beach chairs included. Afternoon tea served.

Hosts: Jay and Marianne Schatz
Rooms: 14 (PB) $90-185
Continental (summer) and Full (spring and fall) Breakfast

NOTES: Credit cards accepted: A Master Card; B Visa; C American Express; D Discover Card; E Diner's Club; F Other; 2 Personal Checks accepted; 3 Lunch available; 4 Dinner available; 5 Open all year; 6 Pets welcome; 7 Smoking allowed; 8 Children welcome; 9 Social drinking allowed; 10 Tennis available; 11 Swimming available; 12 Golf available; 13 Skiing available; 14 May be booked through travel agents.

Minimum stay June 15-September 30 and major
  holidays: 3-4 nights
Closed mid-December-March
Credit Cards: A, B
Notes: 2 (deposit), 8 (over 12), 9, 10, 11, 12

The Albert Stevens Inn

127 Myrtle Avenue, 08204
(609) 884-4717

Built in 1889 by Dr. Albert G. Stevens for
his bride, Bessie, this Queen Anne
Victorian home offers its guests a warm,
restful visit. Just three blocks from the
beach and shopping. A two-course hot
breakfast is served each morning with a
relaxing tea in the afternoon.

Hosts: Curt and Diane Diviney Rangen
Rooms: 7 (PB) $65-135
Full Breakfast
Credit Cards: A, B
Notes: 2, 4 (off-season), 5, 7 (veranda), 9, 10, 11,
  12, 14

Amanda's
Bed and Breakfast #168

1428 Park Avenue, Annaplois, MD, 21217
(410) 225-0001; (410) 383-1274

Built in 1840 and enlarged in 1900, this
Victorian mansion retains the ambience
and grandeur of the era. Enjoy elegance
and comfort, period reproduction wallpa-

Bedford Inn

pers, and the original furnishings of the
Wilbraham family. Heated swimming pool
available to guests. Seven accommodations, all with private baths. Full breakfast.
$85-145

Barnard-Good House

238 Perry Street, 08204
(609) 884-5381

The Barnard-Good House is known for its
breakfasts, which were selected as number
one by *New Jersey Monthly* magazine. The
hosts continue to make them even better.
Breakfast consists of four courses, all
gourmet and homemade. This purple house
caters to happiness and comfort. All rooms
have private baths and air conditioning.

Hosts: Nan and Tom Hawkins
Rooms: 5 (PB) $94.16-126.26
Full Breakfast
Minimum stay weekdays and weekends in-season:
  3 nights; holidays in-season: 4 nights
Credit Cards: A, B (for deposit only)
Closed November15-March 15
Notes: 2, 7 (restricted), 9, 10, 11, 12

Bedford Inn

805 Stockton Avenue, 08204
(609) 884-4158

Restored Italianate Victorian inn with an
unusual double staircase to the third floor.
Full-width first- and second-floor verandas
have comfortable wicker furniture and old-
fashioned porch rockers. Dining room and
parlor with fireplace. Full breakfast and
afternoon tea. All rooms have private baths
and are air conditioned. Honeymoon suites
available. Central location. On-site parking.

Hosts: Cindy and Al Schmucker
Rooms: 11 (PB) $85-140
Full Breakfast
Credit Cards: A, B, C
Notes: 2, 7, 8 (over 6), 9, 10, 11, 12

The Brass Bed Inn

719 Columbia Avenue, 08204
(609) 884-8075

NOTES: Credit cards accepted: A Master Card; B Visa; C American Express; D Discover Card; E Diner's
Club; F Other; 2 Personal Checks accepted; 3 Lunch available; 4 Dinner available; 5 Open all year;

The restored rooms in this 1872 house boast a fine collection of 19th-century brass beds, antiques, lace curtains, and period wall coverings. Bountiful, multi-course breakfasts are served year-round by the hearth. Tea and refreshments are served in the afternoon. Two blocks to beaches. All rooms are air conditioned. Special Christmas tour and lodging.

Hosts: John and Donna Dunwoody
Rooms: 8 (6 PB; 2 SB) $65-135
Full Breakfast
Credit Cards: A, B
Closed Thanksgiving and Christmas Day
Notes: 2, 5, 9 (moderate), 10, 11, 12, 14

Captain Mey's Inn

202 Ocean Street, 08204
(609) 884-7793

The Dutch heritage is evident, from the Persian rugs on table tops to Delft blue china to European antiques. You will marvel at the Eastlake paneling in the dining room, leaded-glass bay window, and the recently restored fireplace. The full country breakfast consists of homemade breads, cakes, egg dishes, meats, cheeses from Holland, fresh fruit, and jelly. The meal is served by candlelight with classical music. Cape May offers a beach, shops, fine restaurants, bicycling, walking and trolley tours, bird-watching, boating, fishing, and gaslit street.

Host: Milly LaCanfora
Rooms: 9 (6 PB; 3 SB) $75-155 in-season; $65-120 off-season
Full Breakfast
Credit Cards: A, B
Notes: 5, 8, 9

Chalfonte Hotel

301 Howard Street, 08204
(609) 884-8409

A rustic 1876 Victorian summer hotel with verandas, rocking chairs, and delicious southern fare. It is relaxing and comfortable. Inquire about workshops, children's programs, classical and jazz concerts, historic programs, tours, and special discounts. Breakfast and dinner are included in the daily rate. Bar service.

Hosts: Anne LeDuc and Judy Bartella
Rooms: 72 (11 PB; 61 SB) $90-150
Full Breakfast
Credit Cards: A, B
Closed November-April
Notes: 2, 4, 7 (limited), 8, 9, 10, 11, 12, 14

Chalfonte Hotel

6 Pets welcome; 7 Smoking allowed; 8 Children welcome; 9 Social drinking allowed; 10 Tennis available; 11 Swimming available; 12 Golf available; 13 Skiing available; 14 May be booked through travel agents.

Cliveden Inn

709 Columbia Avenue, 08204
(609) 884-4516

Enjoy the Cliveden's comfortable and
attractive accommodations. All rooms are
spacious and cozy, with period furniture.
Centrally situated on Cape May's popular
Columbia Avenue in the historic district.
Two blocks from the beach and within easy
walking distance to the Victorian Mall and
fine restaurants. Afternoon tea and continental plus breakfast.

Hosts: Sue and Al De Rosa
Rooms: 10 (8 PB; 2 SB) $75-90
Expanded Continental Breakfast
Credit Cards: A, B, C
Closed November- mid-April
Notes: 2, 7 (restricted), 8, 9, 10, 11, 12

Colvmns by the Sea

1513 Beach Drive, 08204
(609) 884-2228

Elegant Victorian mansion overlooking the
ocean in a historic landmark village. Large,
airy rooms are decorated with antiques.
Gourmet breakfast and snacks, complimentary bikes, hot tub, beach towels, and
badges. Relaxing, enjoyable retreat for history buffs, bird-watchers, and seashore
lovers. Great restaurants nearby.

Colvmns by the Sea

Duke of Windsor

Hosts: Barry and Cathy Rein
Rooms: 11 (PB) $95-155
Full Breakfast
Minimum stay summer weekends and holidays: 3
  nights
Credit Cards: None
Notes: 2, 7 (limited), 8 (over 12), 9, 10, 11, 12

Duke of Windsor
Bed and Breakfast Inn

817 Washington Street, 08204
(609) 884-1355

Queen Anne Victorian house with a 45-foot
tower, built in 1896 and restored with period furnishings. Foyer with three-story,
carved-oak open staircase, fireplace. Sitting
room, parlor with fireplace, library, dining
room. Beach tags, hot and cold outdoor
showers, and off-street parking are available.

Hosts: Bruce and Fran Prichard
Rooms: 10 (8 PB; 2 SB) $75-125
Full Breakfast
Credit Cards: A, B
Notes: 2, 8 (over 12), 9, 10, 11, 12

NOTES: Credit cards accepted: A Master Card; B Visa; C American Express; D Discover Card; E Diner's
Club; F Other; 2 Personal Checks accepted; 3 Lunch available; 4 Dinner available; 5 Open all year;

Mainstay Inn and Cottage

The Gingerbread House

28 Gurney Street, 08204
(609) 884-0211

The Gingerbread House is one of eight original Stockton Row cottages, Victorian summer homes built for families from Philadelphia and Virginia. The inn is elegantly restored with period antiques and original watercolors. Enjoy the well-appointed guest rooms, listen to classical music by the fire in the parlor, or enjoy the ocean breezes on the wicker-filled front porches. Centrally situated, it is within a short walk to Cape May's fine restaurants and shops.

Hosts: Fred and Joan Echevarria
Rooms: 6 (3 PB; 3 SB) $85-145
Full Breakfast
Credit Cards: A, B
Notes: 2, 5, 7, 8, 9, 10, 11, 12

The Humphrey Hughes House

29 Ocean Street, 08204
(609) 884-4428

Nestled in the heart of Cape May's historic section is one of its most authentically restored inns—perhaps the most spacious and gracious of them all. Until 1980 it was the Hughes family home; while the house is filled with magnificent antiques, it still feels more like a home than a museum.

Hosts: Lorraine and Terry Schmidt
Rooms: 7 (PB) $85-120
Suites: 3

Full Breakfast
Minimum stay weekends and holidays
Credit Cards: A, B
Notes: 5, 10, 11, 12

Mainstay Inn and Cottage

635 Columbia Avenue, 08204
(609) 884-8690

"The jewel of them all has got to be the Mainstay," says *The Washington Post*. Twelve large, comfortable, antique-filled rooms with private baths. Three parlors, spacious gardens, breakfast/tea daily. This former gentlemen's gambling house offers history, romance, and hospitality. Near shops, restaurants, historic attractions, and beaches.

Hosts: Tom and Sue Carroll
Rooms: 12 (PB) $85-145
Full Breakfast
Credit Cards: None
Notes: 2, 9, 10, 11

The Manse
Bed and Breakfast

510 Hughes Street, 08204
(609) 884-0116

The Manse is an elegant turn-of-the-century home ideally located in the midst of the historical district of Cape May. It boasts spacious rooms, natural floors, Persian rugs, lace curtains, antiques, and unsurpassed hospitality. Breakfast is a special occasion with homemade specialties served

The Manse Bed and Breakfast

6 Pets welcome; 7 Smoking allowed; 8 Children welcome; 9 Social drinking allowed; 10 Tennis available; 11 Swimming available; 12 Golf available; 13 Skiing available; 14 May be booked through travel agents.

in a formal dining room or on the veranda. One block from the mall or one and one-half miles to the ocean.

Hosts: Nate and Dorothy Marcus
Rooms: 6 (4 PB; 2 SB) $75-125
Full Breakfast
Credit Cards: None
Notes: 2, 8, 9, 10, 11, 12, 14

The Mission Inn

1117 New Jersey Avenue, 08204
(609) 884-8380; (800) 800-8380

A touch of California on the East Coast. A latticed open pergola or dining room for breakfast and enclosed porch offer relaxing ambience, with the beach and surf one-half block away. Spacious guest rooms contain king- and queen-size beds. Hollywood stars and Broadway show people stayed here. Restore yourself in this historic inn. All parking on-site. All baths private. Continental breakfast.

Hosts: Diane Fischer and Judith DeOrio
Rooms: 6 (4 PB; 2 SB) $60-135
Continental Breakfast
Credit Cards: A, B
Notes: 2, 7 (outside), 9, 10, 12, 14

Perry Street Inn

29 Perry Street 08204
(609) 884-4590

Enter the Perry Street Inn Victorian guest house from the porch overlooking the Atlantic Ocean. You are in the front parlor. To your right, you will find a sitting room and a dining room. There are ten bedrooms on the two floors above. The entire house is decorated in period furniture. It is situated in the prime historic district of a national landmark city, one-half block to the beach and Victorian mall. A small modern motel is part of the property. There is free parking.

Hosts: John and Cynthia Curtis
Rooms: 10 (7 PB; 3 SB) $45-110
Full Breakfast
Credit Cards: A, B, C
Notes: 2, 3, 5, 9, 10, 11, 12, 14

Poor Richard's Inn

17 Jackson Street, 08204
(609) 884-3536

Run by two expatriate New York artists since 1977 and lovingly restored over time, Poor Richard's has been growing into its own personality, one where the hosts are helpful and knowledgeable but insistent on being unobtrusive; one where the personal touches of the present and the furnishings and architecture of the past ask more to be lived in than admired.

Hosts: Richard and Harriett Samuelson
Rooms: 9 (4 PB; 5 SB) $39-112
Continental Breakfast
Credit Cards: A, B
Closed January 2-February 12
Notes: 2, 3, 4, 6, 7, 8, 9, 10, 11, 12

The Queen Victoria

102 Ocean Street, 08204
(609) 884-8702

The Wells family welcomes you as friends and treats you royally with unpretentious service and attention to detail. Three restored buildings, furnished with antiques, are in the center of the historic district. Nationally recognized for its special Christmas.

Hosts: Dane and Joan Wells
Rooms: 17 and 7 suites (PB) $55-205 plus tax
Full Breakfast
Credit Cards: A, B
Notes: 2, 5, 8, 9, 10, 11, 12

The Sand Castle

829 Stockton Avenue, 08204
(609) 884-5451

This 1873 Carpenter Gothic cottage is situated in the nation's oldest seashore resort. The decor is a blend of country and Victorian, creating a charming, cozy, informal atmosphere. Settle into a rocker on the wraparound veranda and savor the ocean views and the salty sea breezes. Just a stroll from many unique shops and restaurants.

NOTES: Credit cards accepted: A Master Card; B Visa; C American Express; D Discover Card; E Diner's Club; F Other; 2 Personal Checks accepted; 3 Lunch available; 4 Dinner available; 5 Open all year;

Hosts: Tracie and Daniel Spinosa
Rooms: 10 (4 PB; 6 SB) $65-125
Continental Breakfast
Credit Cards: A, B
Notes: 2, 5, 8, 9, 11, 12

Sea Holly
Bed and Breakfast Inn

815 Stockton Avenue, 08204
(609) 884-6294

This bed and breakfast is comfortably Victorian with antique beds and bureaus. The parlor is Eastlake, and you will find small antiques and collectibles throughout the house. Famous for Christy's cooking, all breakfasts are full sit-down affairs year-round. The inn offers two suites and some ocean-view rooms. Anniversary and birthday specials and holiday packages are available.

Hosts: Christy and Chris Igoe
Rooms: 8 (PB) $85-180
Full Breakfast
Credit Cards: A, B, C
Notes: 2, 5, 9, 10, 11, 12

The Victorian Lace Inn

901 Stockton Avenue, 08204
(609) 884-1772

Come back to an unhurried era in this spacious Victorian home built in 1869. During spring and fall, it is a bed and breakfast, and in the summer, the suites rent by the week. Front suites have ocean views, one with a fireplace in the bedroom. Wonderful wraparound porch filled with wicker. Adorable cottage. Lovely Victorian furnishings. Wicker, lace, pastel colors, and hosts who love their job! No extra charge for a friendly chat!

Hosts: Joe and Helen Fox
Suites: 3 and 1 cottage (PB) $85-140
Full Breakfast
Credit Cards: None
Notes: 2, 8, 9, 10, 11, 12, 14

The Victorian Rose

715 Columbia Avenue, 08204
(609) 884-2497

A delightful experience awaits you at the Victorian Rose. For over 120 years, this guest house has served as host to Cape May visitors. Today, the Victorian Rose offers gracious hospitality of years gone by. The restored parlor and dining room allow guests to linger in times past. The wide veranda allows guests to savor the ocean breeze from their favorite rocker. Eight well-appointed guest rooms, deluxe suites with fully equipped kitchens, and a cottage that sleeps four are available for guests.

Hosts: Robert and Linda Mullock
Rooms: 10 (8 PB; 2 SB) $80-130
Full Breakfast
Credit Cards: None
Notes: 2, 7, 9, 12

White Dove Cottage

619 Hughes Street, 08204
(609) 884-0613

This elegant little bed and breakfast, circa 1866, is located in the center of the historical district on a quiet tree-lined gaslit street. Five rooms plus one suite offer cheerful accommodations for guests, and bicycle rental, golf course, ocean and beach are all nearby. Tea and snacks are served every afternoon, and a full breakfast starts out your day. AAA, ABBA, PAII, and NJBBA approved.

Host: Frank Smith
Rooms: 6 (PB) $75-125
Full Breakfast
Credit Cards: None
Notes: 2, 5, 8 (over 8)

Windward House

24 Jackson Street, 08204
(609) 884-3368

Edwardian shingle-style cottage one-half block to beach and Victorian Mall. Completely decorated in elegant antiques plus vintage collectibles, paintings, and clothing. All rooms have private baths, minirefrigerators, sitting areas, ceiling fans, and air conditioners. Some have TV. Three

---

6 Pets welcome; 7 Smoking allowed; 8 Children welcome; 9 Social drinking allowed; 10 Tennis available; 11 Swimming available; 12 Golf available; 13 Skiing available; 14 May be booked through travel agents.

sun and shade porches, plus three common rooms. Stained and leaded glass abound throughout. Afternoon tea served.

Hosts: Sandy and Owen Miller
Rooms: 8 (PB) $90-135
Full Breakfast
Minimum stay weekends: 2-3 nights; holidays: 4 nights
Credit Cards: A, B
Notes: 2, 5, 7, 8 (over 12), 9, 10, 11, 12

The Wooden Rabbit

609 Hughes Street, 08204
(609) 884-7293

Situated on one of the prettiest streets in Cape May, the Wooden Rabbit is nestled in the heart of the historic district, surrounded by Victorian cottages, cool, shady trees, and brick walkways. Two blocks from beautiful sandy beaches, one block from Cape May's quaint shopping mall, and within easy walking distance of fine restaurants. Each guest room is air conditioned, has a private bath, TV, and comfortably sleeps two to four persons. The Wooden Rabbit is also the home of the hosts, comfortable and casual folks, who look forward to sharing their home with you. Decor is country and relaxed. No smoking. Children welcome.

Hosts: Greg and Debby Burow
Rooms: 3 (PB) $85-165
Full Breakfast
Credit Cards: A, B
Notes: 2, 5, 8, 9, 10, 11

Woodleigh House

808 Washington Street, 08204
(609) 884-7123

Victorian, but informal. Centrally situated, with off-street parking, beach bikes, comfortable parlor, courtyard, and gardens. Walk to everything: marvelous restaurants, sights galore, nearby nature preserve, dinner theater, craft and antique shows.

Hosts: Jan and Buddy Wood
Roooms: 4 (PB) $80-120
Expanded Continental Breakfast

Credit Cards: A, B
Notes: 2, 5, 8 (over 5), 10, 11, 12

DENVILLE

Lakeside Bed and Breakfast

11 Sunset Trail, 07834
(201) 625-5129

Just off I-80, midway between Manhattan and the Poconos, is this modern two-story home with private guest quarters on the first floor. There is a lovely view of the bay leading to Indian Lake. Guest room has a double bed; family room has color TV; private bath. Rowboat and beach passes for guests. Explore unspoiled towns and points of interest off the tourist trail.

Hosts: Annette and Al Bergins
Room: 1 (PB) $50
Full Breakfast
Credit Cards: None
Notes: 2, 5, 9, 10, 11

EAST BRUNSWICK

Amanda's Bed and Breakfast #273

1428 Park Avenue, Annapolis, MD 21217
(410) 225-0001; (410) 383-1274

Enjoy a charming and comfortable bed and breakfast experience in this spacious Cape Cod-style home nestled in the privacy of the East Brunswick suburbs. Sumptuous breakfasts served on the screened-in patio. Three guest rooms share a bath. $60

FLEMINGTON

Jerica Hill— A Bed and Breakfast Inn

96 Broad Street, 08822
(908) 782-8234

Be warmly welcomed at this gracious country inn located in the historic town of

Flemington. Spacious, sunny guest rooms, livingroom with a fireplace, and a wicker-filled screen porch invite you to relax. Champagne hot-air balloon flights are arranged, as well as country picnic and winery tours. A delightful continental plus breakfast is served, afternoon refreshments are available, and you can have a rental bicycle delivered to the inn. Corporate and midweek rates available. Featured in *Country Inns Bed and Breakfast* and *Mid-Atlantic Country*.

Host: Judith S. Studer
Rooms: 5 (PB) $60-95 plus tax
Expanded Continental Breakfast
Credit Cards: A, B, C
Notes: 2, 5, 9, 10, 11, 12, 14

HOPE

The Inn at Millrace Pond

Route 519, P.O. Box 359, 07844
(908) 459-4884

A gracious country inn restored to Colonial grandeur situated along Beaver Brook in historic Hope. Seventeen individually decorated guest rooms, each with private bath and modern amenities. Scenic location offers hiking, canoeing, tennis, golf, Waterloo Village, craft fairs, wineries, and antique shows. Grist Mill Dining Room open daily and for Sunday brunch. Three stars from Mobil guide. Three diamonds from AAA.

Hosts: Gloria B. Carrigan and Richard Gooding
Rooms: 17 (PB) $85-130
Expanded Continental Breakfast
Credit Cards: A, B, C
Notes: 4, 5, 7, 8, 9, 10, 12, 14

LONGPORT

Winchester House

1 South 24th Avenue, 08403
(609) 822-0623

Situated in a quiet residential seashore community overlooking Great Egg Harbor

Bay. All rooms are spacious, air-conditioned, with private baths, cable TV, radio, and daily maid service. Atlantic City casinos and the boardwalk are less than five miles away. Tennis, golf, swimming, boating, fishing, and great restaurants are nearby.

Hosts: Jim and Mary Jane Kelly
Rooms: 14 (PB) $70-75
Credit Cards: A, B
Closed September 20-May 20
Notes: 2, 7, 8, 9, 10, 11, 12, 14

LYNDHURST

The Jeremiah J. Yereance House

410 Riverside Avenue, 07071
(201) 438-9457

This 1841 house, a state and national landmark, is five minutes from the Meadowlands complex and 20 minutes from New York City. The guest rooms in the south wing include a front parlor with fireplace, a central hall, and a small but comfortable bedroom that adjoins the parlor and private bath. The north wing includes a common parlor with three bedrooms that share a bath.

Hosts: Evelyn and Frank Pezzolla
Rooms: 4 (1 PB; 3 SB) $55-75
Continental Breakfast
Credit Cards: C
Notes: 2, 5, 8 (over 12), 9, 10

NORTH WILDWOOD

Candlelight Inn

2310 Central Avenue, 08260
(609) 522-6200

"There is a quaint haven for those in a vintage romantic mood," wrote the *Philadelphia Inquirer* (July 1988). The Candlelight Inn is a beautifully restored bed and breakfast built at the turn of the century by Leaming Rice. This Queen Anne Victorian structure served as the family home for many years until it was pur-

6 Pets welcome; 7 Smoking allowed; 8 Children welcome; 9 Social drinking allowed; 10 Tennis available; 11 Swimming available; 12 Golf available; 13 Skiing available; 14 May be booked through travel agents.

chased by its present innkeepers in 1985. Within minutes of Cape May and Atlantic City. Special touches and personalized service abound.

Hosts: Paul DiFilippo and Diane Buscham
Rooms: 9 (7 PB; 2 SB) $55-150
Full Breakfast
Credit Cards: A, B, C, D
Notes: 2, 5, 9, 10, 11, 12, 14

OCEAN CITY

Beach End Inn

815 Plymouth Place, 08226
(609) 398-1016

At this inn on a quiet street in the heart of town, guests are steps from the beach, boardwalk, and music pier. Six distinctly decorated and themed guest rooms featuring Victorian antiques are available, and common areas include the front deck, parlor room, fireplaces, and breakfast room. All guests receive complimentary beach tags during the summer. monthly murder mystery affairs are fun. Minutes from Atlantic City. Bicycling, fishing, golf, and historical attractions are at hand.

Host: Len Cipkins
Rooms: 6 (1 PB; 5 SB) $40-70
Full Breakfast
Credit Cards: A, B
Notes: 2, 5, 8, 9, 10, 11, 12

The Enterprise Bed and Breakfast

1020 Central Avenue, 08226
(609) 398-1698

Create a special memory. Linger over stuffed French toast, luscious eggs Benedict, or fresh blueberry pancakes. Relax in a porch rocking chair. Plan the day's adventures together. Explore the beach and boardwalk, the quaint shops. Gingerbread trim, pink hearts, and white doves create "a little bit of country at the shore."

Hosts: Steve and Patty Hydock
Rooms: 9 (7 PB; 2 SB) $55-85
Full Breakfast
Credit Cards: A, B
Notes: 2, 5, 7, 9, 10, 11, 12, 14

New Brighton Inn

519 Fifth Street, 08226
(609) 399-2829

Magnificently restored 1800s seaside Queen Anne-style Victorian. Premises comfortably furnished with antiques throughout. Breakfast on sun porch. A romantic, relaxing, charming hideaway close to the beach, boardwalk, tennis courts, restaurants, and fine shops.

Hosts: Daniel and Donna Hand
Rooms: 4 (2 PB; 2 SB) $55-75
Full Breakfast
Credit Cards: A, B, C
Notes: 2 (NJ), 5, 8 (over 10), 10, 11, 12

New Brighton Inn

OCEAN GROVE

Cordova

26 Webb Avenue, 07756
(908) 774-3084; (212) 751-9577

The Cordova is a century-old Victorian situated in a lovely, historic beach community with Old World charm. It's only one and one-half blocks from the white sand beach and wooden boardwalk. Selected by New

Jersey magazine as "one of the seven best places on the Jersey Shore." Family atmosphere. Many former presidents (Wilson, Cleveland, Roosevelt) have slept in Ocean Grove and spoken at the 7,000-seat Great Auditorium, the largest wooden structure in the United States.

Host: Doris Chernik
Rooms: 15 (SB) $35-60
Expanded Continental Breakfast
Credit Cards: None
Closed Labor Day-Memorial Day
Notes: 2, 8, 9, 10, 11, 14

PRINCETON

Bed and Breakfast of Princeton

P. O. Box 571, 08542
(609) 924-3189; FAX (609) 921-6271

This service offers a variety of homestay accommodations in several local private residences. A few homes are within walking distance to the town center, while others are more convenient to public transportation or a few minutes away by automobile. Some homes do not allow smoking. Some baths are shared. Rates, which begin at $40 for single and $50 for a double occupancy, include a continental breakfast.

SEA GIRT

Holly Harbor Guest House

112 Baltimore Boulevard, 08750
(908) 449-9731; (800) 348-6999 outside New Jersey

Sea Girt is a quiet residential town 60 miles south of New York City on the Jersey shore. Gracious cedar-shingled house is bordered by holly trees and has a spacious front porch. Only one block from the beach.

Hosts: Bill and Kim Walsh
Rooms: 12 (SB) $75-100
Full Breakfast
Credit Cards: A, B, C
Notes: 2, 5, 8, 9, 10, 11, 12

Ashling Cottage

SPRING LAKE

Ashling Cottage

106 Sussex Avenue, 07762
(908) 449-3553

Under sentinel sycamores since 1877 in a storybook setting, Ashling Cottage, a Victorian seaside inn, has long served as a portal to an earlier time. A block from the ocean and just one-half block from a freshwater lake.

Hosts: Goodi and Jack Stewart
Rooms: 10 (8 PB; 2 SB) $60-135
Full breakfast
Credit Cards: None
Closed January-March
Notes: 2, 7 (limited), 8 (over 12), 9, 10, 11, 12

The Chateau

500 Warren Avenue, 07762
(908) 974-2000

The house may be 101 years old, but it's brand-new inside: air conditioning, color cable TV, HBO, phones, refrigerators. Suites and parlors have livingrooms, wet bars, paddle fans. Some have fireplaces and facilities for FAX machines and personal computers. VCRs, private porches, and balconies.

Host: Scott Smith
Rooms: (PB) $44-96
Suites: (PB) $70-142
Continental Breakfast
Credit Cards: A, B, C
Notes: 2, 5, 7, 8, 9, 10, 11, 12, 14

6 Pets welcome; 7 Smoking allowed; 8 Children welcome; 9 Social drinking allowed; 10 Tennis available; 11 Swimming available; 12 Golf available; 13 Skiing available; 14 May be booked through travel agents.

Johnson House Inn

25 Tuttle Avenue, 07762
(201) 449-1860

A family-style ambience awaits you just one-half block from the beach. Come relax on the spacious wraparound porch with wicker chairs and rockers. Family suites available.

Host: Helen Gomboa; Hellin and Joe Desiderio
Rooms: 16 (14 PB; 2 SB) $75
Continental Plus Breakfast
Credit Cards: None
Notes: 2, 5, 8, 9, 10, 11, 12

Normandy Inn

Normandy Inn

21 Tuttle Avenue, 07762
(908) 449-7172

Less than a block from the ocean, this 1888 Italianate villa has been authentically restored inside and out. Antique-filled guest rooms and parlors invite you to step back in time to 19th-century elegance. The wide front porch with wicker furniture invites quiet conversation and cool breezes at sunset. A hearty country breakfast awaits you in the morning. Explore the wide, tree-lined streets, turn-of-the-century estates, quaint shops, and boutiques. Golf, tennis, horseback riding, and historic villages are nearby.

Hosts: Michael and Susan Ingino
Rooms: 17 (PB) $77-146; seasonal suite (PB)
  $164-205
Full Breakfast
Minimum stay March-November weekends: 2 nights; holidays: 3 nights; July and August weekends: 4 nights; July and August midweek: 2 nights
Credit Cards: A, B, C
Notes: 2, 5, 7, 8, 9, 10, 11, 12, 14

STANHOPE

Whistling Swan Inn

110 Main Street, P. O. Box 791, 07874
(201) 347-6369

The inn is northwest New Jersey's finest Victorian bed and breakfast, situated just off I-80 only 45 minutes west of the George Washington Bridge. Near Waterloo Village, International Trade Zone, skiing, antiques, shops, restaurants. "For those with more refined nesting instincts."

Hosts: Paula Williams and Joe Mulay
Rooms: 10 (PB) $65-95
Full Breakfast
Credit Cards: A, B, C, D
Notes: 2, 5, 8 (over 12), 9, 10, 11, 12, 13, 14

STEWARTSVILLE

The Stewart Inn

P.O. Box 571, Rural Route 1, South Main Street, 08886
(908) 479-6060

This 1770s stone manor home is set amidst 16 acres of lawns, gardens, woods, streams, and pasture. The swimming pool, trout stream, barns, and outbuildings (not to mention the farm animals) create a relaxed pastoral setting. Close to Flemington, Clinton, Hope, and Lambertville; Bucks County and Delaware River attractions of Pennsylvania are close by also. The weekender will find relaxation and romance; the business person will experience what being away from home should be.

Hosts: Brian and Lynne McGarry
Rooms: 7 (6 PB; 1 SB) $85-135
Full Breakfast
Credit Cards: A, B
Notes: 2, 5, 9, 10, 11, 12, 13, 14

NOTES: Credit cards accepted: A Master Card; B Visa; C American Express; D Discover Card; E Diner's Club; F Other; 2 Personal Checks accepted; 3 Lunch available; 4 Dinner available; 5 Open all year;

STOCKTON

The Stockton Inn, "Colligan's"

Main and Bridge Street, 08559
(609) 397-1250

Built in 1710, this inn was the inspiration
for the Rodgers and Hart song "There's a
Small Hotel (With a Wishing Well)."
Distinctive suites and rooms, many with
fireplaces. American/Continental cuisine
served fireside. In season, dine in the garden with its waterfalls and trout pond.
Three miles from galleries, theaters, and
antiquing in Lambertville-New Hope.

Hosts: Andrew McDermott and Bruce Monti
Rooms: 11 (PB) $60-145
Continental Breakfast
Credit Cards: A, B, C
Closed Christmas
Notes: 3, 4, 5, 7, 9, 10, 12, 13

Woolverton Inn

6 Woolverton Road, 08559
(609) 397-0802

A 10-acre estate with formal gardens, stately trees, and an elegant stone Victorian
manor house. Its 13 antique-filled rooms
offer privacy with convenient access to
many activities. The inn offers croquet,
horseshoes, or bicycling. Museums, shopping, antiques, water sports, and golf are
nearby.

Host: Louise Warsaw
Rooms: 13 (3 PB; 10 SB) $66-135
Full Breakfast
Credit Cards: A, B
Notes: 2, 5, 9, 10, 11, 12, 14

WOODBINE

Henry Ludlam Inn

Cape May Country, 1336 Route 47, 08270
(609) 861-5847

This circa 1760 home, voted "Best of the
Shore 1991," offers enchanting rooms,
scrumptious gourmet breakfasts, bedroom
fireplaces, fireside picnic baskets, and six-
course gourmet dinners Saturday nights
October-May. Guests invest in memories
here.

Hosts: Ann and Marty Thurlow
Rooms: 5 (3 PB; 2 SB) $75-95
Full Breakfast
Credit Cards: A, B, C
Notes: 2, 4, 5, 9, 10, 11, 12

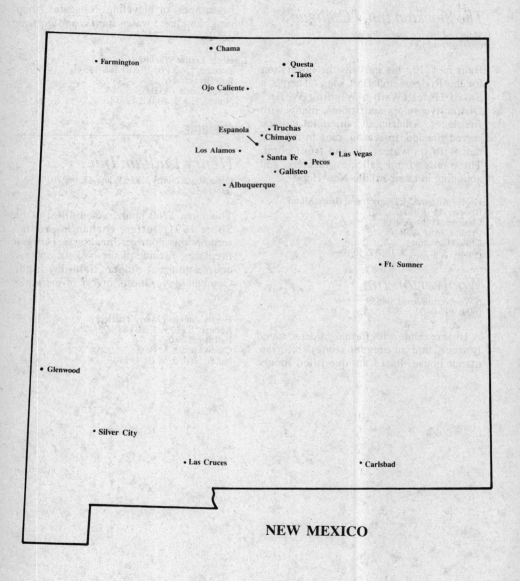

- Chama

- Farmington

- Questa
- Taos

Ojo Caliente •

Espanola • Truchas
• Chimayo

Los Alamos •   • Santa Fe • Las Vegas
• Pecos
• Galisteo

• Albuquerque

• Ft. Sumner

• Glenwood

• Silver City

• Las Cruces   • Carlsbad

NEW MEXICO

New Mexico

Adobe and Roses

1011 Ortega Northwest, 87114
(505) 898-0654

An adobe hacienda on two acres in Albuquerque's North Valley, featuring a casually elegant and spacious suite with private entrance, fireplace, piano, kitchen, big windows overlooking the gardens and horse pasture. Also a two-bedroom, two-bath adobe guest house. A quiet, romantic place to visit.

Host: Dorothy Morse
Rooms: 2 (1 PB; 1 SB) $50-105
Full Breakfast
Credit Cards: None
Notes: 2, 5, 6, 8, 9, 10, 12, 13

B&B of New Mexico #402

P. O. Box 2805, Santa Fe, 87504
(505) 982-3332

Beautiful and large single-story adobe home with 18-inch thick walls, brick floors, and viga ceilings. Very private. Surrounded by alfalfa fields, yet close to Albuquerque. Private bath in both rooms. $60.

B&B of New Mexico #404

P. O. Box 2805, Santa Fe, 87504
(505) 982-3332

This dramatic pueblo-style home has magnificent mountain views and spectacular sunsets. A generous continental breakfast with freshly ground coffee is served in your room, on the patio, or in the dining area. One room with the king bed has a private deck and bath outside door. Twin beds in other room with private bath across livingroom. $55-60.

Casa de Placitas

Bed and Breakfast Rocky Mountains
906 South Pearl Street, Denver , Colorado 80209
(303) 744-8415; (800) 733-8415

Enjoy this uniquely styled passive solar adobe home with breathtaking views of the Sandia Mountains. A king bedroom features traditional southwestern viga ceilings, brick floors, a wood-burning stove, and private Mexican-tiled bath. A separate studio guest house is also available. A wonderful place for a getaway. Pets and children over 12 welcome. Smoking in guest house only. Moderate rates.

Casas de Suenos
Bed and Breakfast Inn

310 Rio Grande Boulevard Southwest, 87104
(505) 247-4560; (800) CHAT W/US

Fresh flower arrangements, blooming gardens, and hospitality. Adjoining Albuquerque's famous Old Town, with museums, theater, fine dining (and fast food), galleries, shops, parks, nature trails, and zoo. Excellent gourmet breakfast beautifully presented. All aspects absolutely first rate. World-famous architecture combined with superb location and southwestern hospitality. Like Old Mexico and Santa

NOTES: Credit cards accepted: A Master Card; B Visa; C American Express; D Discover Card; E Diner's Club; F Other; 2 Personal Checks accepted; 3 Lunch available; 4 Dinner available; 5 Open all year; 6 Pets welcome; 7 Smoking allowed; 8 Children welcome; 9 Social drinking allowed; 10 Tennis available; 11 Swimming available; 12 Golf available; 13 Skiing available; 14 May be booked through travel agents.

Fe, which is only one hour away by car and is an unforgettable day trip. Several Indian pueblos, the beautiful hot springs, ancient ruins, unusual geological formations, high desert, mountain peaks, the panoramic Valle Grande volcanic crater and mountain villages, and artists' communities in every direction. Travel information is provided. Featured on the TV program "America's Great Bed and Breakfast Inns" on the Discovery Channel.

Hosts: Jennifer Kutrer, Mari Penshurst-Gersten, and Kelli Williams
Rooms: 12 casitas (PB) $65-200
Full Breakfast
Credit Cards: A, B, C
Notes: 2, 5, 9, 10, 11, 12, 13, 14

The Corner House

Bed and Breakfast Rocky Mountains
906 South Pearl Street, 80209
(303) 744-8415; (800) 733-8415

Surrounded by fruit trees in the front and back yards and a sprawling garden on the side, The Corner House brings a taste of the country to this convenient city location. Nearby attractions include the Sandia Mountains, the Sandia Peak Tramway/Ski Area, Old Town, and the zoo. Great for tourists and business travelers alike. Resident house dog and two overly friendly yard dogs. Minutes away from many excellent restaurants, shopping, municipal tennis, golf, and swimming. Three rooms—one private bath, two shared, choice of room with king bed, one with antique twin beds or one with single bed. Stone fireplace in comfortable family room, cable TV and VCR, games; baby bed available. Full breakfast served on Italian della Robia pottery. No smoking. No pets. Budget rates.

Las Palomas Valley Bed and Breakfast

2303 Candelaria Road NW, 87107
(505) 345-7228

One of Albuquerque's most beautiful historic adobe estates, this lovely inn is situated on three glorious acres of lawns, gardens, and orchards. Outdoor hot tub, tennis court, croquet, and bike trails complement the uniquely furnished suites. All rooms have king-size beds, antique furnishings, private bathrooms and lounges, splendid views, and fireplaces. The chef makes fresh breads daily. Full English breakfast is served in the lovely dining room or on the lawns.

Hosts: Lori and Andrew Caldwell
Rooms: 10 (PB) $65-95
Full Breakfast
Credit Cards: A, B
Notes: 2, 5, 6, 7 (limited), 8, 9, 10, 11, 12, 13, 14

Maggie's Raspberry Ranch

9817 Eldridge Road NW, 87114
(505) 897-1523

This modern family home in Albuquerque's North Valley near the Rio Grande River has a heated pool, lots of flowers, a berry patch, and fruits trees (Maggie makes all the jams and jellies served). There also is a cozy sitting area where you can watch the geese, chickens, ducks, fish, rabbits, and Callie the cat. Hot air balloons drift overhead at breakfast time.

Host: Maggie Lilley
Rooms: 3 (1 PB; 2 SB) $55-75
Full Breakfast
Credit Cards: None
Notes: 2, 5, 6, 8, 11

Mi Casa Su Casa #1800

P. O. Box 950, Tempe, Arizona 85280-0950
(602) 990-0682; (800) 456-0682

Twenty minutes from downtown Albuquerque, your hostess welcomes you to this nice southwestern-style home in a quiet, residential neighborhood. Surrounded by fruit trees in the front and back with a large vegetable garden in the corner side yard, this bed and breakfast brings a taste of the country to a convenient city location.

NOTES: Credit cards accepted: A Master Card; B Visa; C American Express; D Discover Card; E Diner's Club; F Other; 2 Personal Checks accepted; 3 Lunch available; 4 Dinner available; 5 Open all year;

Three sets of accommodations are available. Full breakfast is served. $30-55.

Old Town Bed and Breakfast

707 17th Street NW, 87104
(505) 764-9144

Old Town Bed and Breakfast is an adobe home situated on a beautiful, quiet street just two blocks from historic Old Town Plaza, the museums, and a lovely park. The second floor guest room has a queen-size bed, private bath and entrance, provides views of the mountains and tree-lined neighborhood streets. The spacious first-floor guest room has a king-size bed, kiva fireplaces, private entrance, and shared bath with a Jacuzzi. Additional sleeping accommodations in adjacent sitting room. Redwood hot tub in secluded garden setting. Generous continental breakfast. Caring hospitality.

Host: Nancy Hoffman
Rooms: 2 (1 PB; 1 SB) $60-75
Continental Breakfast
Credit Cards: None
Notes: 2, 5

Sarabande

5637 Rio Grande Boulevard NW, 87107
(505) 345-4923

Luxurious rooms, private flower-filled courtyards, private baths, attention to individual preferences, lap pool, and spa to help you relax and enjoy real enchantment and blue skies.

Hosts: Betty Vickers and Margaret Magnussen
Rooms: 3 (PB) $75-90
Full Breakfast
Credit Cards: A, B
Notes: 2, 5, 9, 10, 11, 12, 13

W. E. Mauger Estate

701 Roma Avenue NW, 87102
(505) 242-8755

This wonderful 1897 Queen Anne Victorian is on the National Registsr of Historic Places and has eight unique accommodations with private baths, full breakfast, and afternoon refreshments. Within walking distance of Old Town, museums, zoo, Indian Center, shops and restaurants. The beautiful front porch is furnished in wicker. Other features include indoor and outdoor dining rooms. Elegant, gracious, and affordable, this showplace is a must see.

Hosts: Chuck Silver and Brian Miller
Rooms: 8 (PB) $59-99
Full Breakfast
Credit Cards: A, B, C, E, F
Notes: 2, 5, 6, 8, 9, 14

The Windmill Ranch

6400 Coors Boulevard NW, 87120
(505) 898-6864

Windmill Ranch is an old southwestern hacienda sitting amid ancient elms next to the Rio Grande. Tree-lined paths along the river provide beautiful scenery for those who wish to jog, bicycle, or simply enjoy a peaceful nature walk. With the mesa at your back and the Sandia Mountains in your eyes, you're only a stone's throw from the famous Indian petroglyphs, Albuquerque's Old Town, and Santa Fe.

Hosts: Margaret and Bob Cover
Rooms: 4 (PB) $65-95
Full Breakfast
Credit Cards: A, B
Notes: 2, 5, 9

CARLSBAD

B&B of New Mexico #507

P. O. Box 2805, Santa Fe, 87504
(505) 982-3332

The main house and casita of this bed and breakfast were built in 1929. The exterior is stucco and the roof has a red-tile look in keeping with the Spanish style. There is a

6 Pets welcome; 7 Smoking allowed; 8 Children welcome; 9 Social drinking allowed; 10 Tennis available; 11 Swimming available; 12 Golf available; 13 Skiing available; 14 May be booked through travel agents.

waist-high stone wall surrounding the property, giving it a private feeling. There is a courtyard dotted with patio furniture. It is a short walk to downtown, and 30 minutes to Carlsbad Caverns. Four guest rooms with shared or private bath. $45-65.

CHAMA

B&B of New Mexico #250

P. O. Box 2805, Santa Fe, 87504
(505) 982-3332

This remote, fully modern cottage offers an unobstructed view of the Brazos Cliff located in the foothills of the San Juan Mountains. Your only visitors will be the deer and the elk. Only seven miles from Chama and Cumbres/Toltec Railroad. You can either cook your meal or have pizza and sandwiches delivered. After your meal, take a hike or fish in the trout pond. Twin or double. $90-120.

Casa de Martinez

Bed and Breakfast Rocky Mountains
906 South Pearl Street, Denver, Colorado 80209
(303) 744-8415; (800)733-8415

History and charm abound just a few minutes south of Chama in northern New Mexico near the Colorado border. This adobe dwelling dates back to 1869. Located in the village of Brazos, the inn has a wonderful view of the El Choro waterfall. One suite and six double rooms are available, three with private baths and four with a shared bath. Full breakfast. Moderate rates.

Evans-Jones Inn Bed and Breakfast

311 Terrace Avenue, P. O. Box 887, 87520
(505) 756-2908

Directly opposite America's longest and highest historic steam railroad. Choose a train package which includes meals, lodging, and train ticket. Train season: Memorial Day through mid-October. Winter offers tranquility for the cross-country skier with fireplace in the common room, hot cider, and two-person whirlpool. Each room is comfortable and tastefully furnished.

Host: Sara Jayne Cole
Rooms: 5 (3 PB; 2 SB) $55-85
Full Breakfast
Credit Cards: A, B, C
Notes: 2, 3, 4, 5, 8, 9, 13, 14

Jones House Bed and Breakfast

Bed and Breakfast Rocky Mountains
906 South Pearl Street, 80209
(303) 744-8415; (800) 733-88415

Enjoy the friendly, comfortable atmosphere of this Tudor-style home. Across from the Cumbres-Toltec Scenic Railroad, this inn is a train buff's dream with a library full of books and videos about trains. In the winter you can cross country ski at Cumbres Pass or relax in an oversized chair in the living room by the fire. In the Chama Historic Dictrict, it is within walking distance to Chama River and Sargent Wildlife Preserve. Early morning coffee and fine soaps provided. In the summer, a lovely yard offers benches, a picnic table, and grill; in the winter, enjoy the fireplace, hot cider, and a snack after skiing. Full breakfast with home-baked muffins and breads, served between 7:00 and 9:00 A.M. No smoking in the house. No pets, but a dogsitter can be arranged. Children over 6 welcome. Moderate rates.

CHIMAYO

Casa Escondida

P. O. Box 142, 87522
(505) 351-4805

On the high road from Sante Fe to Taos, one of the most beautiful rides in New Mexico, a serene, rural Spanish Colonial sits on six acres of land. Year-round panoramic views of breathtaking beauty will stimulate your creativity. The house has gentle soul, and five bedrooms furnished with American arts and crafts antiques are available for your stay. This is a perfect getaway.

Hosts: Irenka Taurels and Babette Landan
Rooms: 5(PB) $60-100
Credit Cards: A, B
Notes: 2, 4, 5, 9

La Posada de Chimayo

Box 463, 87522
(505) 351-4605

A cozy, comfortable adobe inn in a traditional northern New Mexico village famous for its tradition of fine Spanish weaving and its beautiful old church, El Santuario. Thirty miles north of Santa Fe on the high road to Taos.

Host: Sue Farrington
Rooms: 2 and 1 suite (PB) $85-110
Full Breakfast
Minimum stay holidays: 2-4 nights
Credit Cards: A, B
Notes: 2, 5, 6 (call), 8 (over 12), 9

ESPANOLA

B&B of New Mexico #260

P. O. Box 2805, Santa Fe, 87504
(505) 982-3332

This simple, elegant adobe casita is nestled in the pine cliffs of northern New Mexico. It is filled with local handmade crafts and furniture. High-beamed ceiling, Talavera tile, pine floors, and a fireplace in the bedroom. The sleeping arrangements can be either a king bed or two twin beds. Situated near Española, halfway between Santa Fe and Taos. It is a short walk from the Chama River. The casita is detached from the main house to afford privacy. No kitchen. Full breakfast. $70.

Casa Del Rio

P. O. Box 92, 87532
(505) 753-2035

Casa Del Rio is a traditional adobe bed and breakfast set amid the pink cliffs of northern New Mexico on twelve acres of land along the Chama River and within a half hour of Sante Fe, Taos, and Los Alamos. Furnished in authentic southwestern style with hand-carved furniture and crafts. Viga and Latilla ceilings and Talavara tile add to its charm. There are Arabian horses and fine wool sheep on the premises, and a tray of wake-up coffee is delivered to your room each morning.

Hosts: Eileen and Mel Vigil
Rooms: 2 (PB) $75-95
Full Breakfast
Credit Cards: A, B (to hold reservation only)
Notes: 2, 5, 9, 14

Inn of La Mesilla

Bed and Breakfast Rocky Mountains
906 South Pearl Street, 80209
(303) 744-8415; (800) 733-8415

A newly constructed adobe pueblo-style home with southwestern decor throughout. Spectacular views of the Jemez Mountains add to the atmosphere. Conveniently situated between Santa Fe, Los Alamos, and Taos; 18 miles from Santa Fe Opera; in the vicinity of five Indian pueblos. King and queen beds and private baths available; Mexican and Spanish tile throughout; living room with fireplace, cable TV, library; afternoon refreshments 4:00 to 6:00 P.M. A full breakfast is served. The hosts are a retired doctor and his wife. Smoking outside only. No pets (accommodations are close by). No children. Moderate to luxury rates.

FARMINGTON

B&B of New Mexico #601

P. O. Box 2805, Santa Fe, 87504
(505) 982-3332

6 Pets welcome; 7 Smoking allowed; 8 Children welcome; 9 Social drinking allowed; 10 Tennis available; 11 Swimming available; 12 Golf available; 13 Skiing available; 14 May be booked through travel agents.

A traditional northern New Mexico adobe situated on the cliffside confluence of the San Juan and La Plata rivers on the outskirts of Farmington, this newly constructed bed and breakfast suite includes bedroom with queen bed, livingroom/dining room with two twin day beds, bathroom with Mexican tile shower, kitchen, and hot tub. $65-80.

FORT SUMNER/TAIBAN

B&B of New Mexico #301

P. O. Box 2805, Santa Fe, 87504
(505) 982-3332

This small guest house, near Fort Sumner beside the ghost town of Taiban, is truly the Little House on the Prairie. It is in the middle of Billy the Kid country. It has two bedrooms that can accommodate up to four people in the same party who share a bath. It is filled with antiques. Guided tours are available at night or on weekends. With advance notice and $10 per person, the host will grill lamb for dinner. $60.

GALISTEO

The Galisteo Inn

HC 75, Box 4, 87540
(505) 982-1506

Visit this 240-year-old adobe hacienda in the beautiful countryside of northern New Mexico, 23 miles southeast of Santa Fe. Enjoy the hot tub, sauna, pool, bicycles, and horseback riding. The dinners feature creative southwestern cuisine, nightly except for Monday and Tuesday. Reservations required for accommodations and dining.

Hosts: Joanna Kaufman and Wayne Aarniokoski
Rooms: 12 (8 PB; 4 SB) $90-165
Continental Breakfast
Credit Cards: A, B, D
Notes: 2, 3, 4, 9, 10, 11, 14

GLENWOOD

Los Olmos Guest Ranch

U.S. 180 and Catwalk Road, P. O. Box 127, 88039
(505) 539-2311

A quiet country inn situated in a narrow valley amidst a bulky mountain range. Located in a popular outdoor recreation area; hiking, birding, and fishing abound. Guest recreation room is situated in the main building, and guest accommodations are in individual stone cottages with private baths. A swimming pool, spa, bicycles, and horseback riding are all available. Modified American plan (dinner and breakfast included).

Hosts: Brigitte and Leonard Leth
Rooms: 13 (PB) $65-80
Full Breakfast
Credit Cards: A, B, C
Notes: 2, 4, 7, 8, 9, 11

LAS CRUCES

B&B of New Mexico #506

P. O. Box 2805, Santa Fe, 87504
(505) 982-3332

Just 11 miles from Las Cruces at the foot of the Organ Mountains. Surrounded by U.S. government land, the area is quiet and beautiful. Horse boarding is available and you can take your horse for a ride in the mountains. Owners speak German, French, Greek, Spanish, Arabic, and understand Italian. The home has a pool for guests. Two guest rooms are available: one has two twin beds and a private bath; the other has an atrium door that opens onto the deck surrounding the pool, double bed, private bath, and kitchenette. $50-60.

Hilltop Hacienda

2520 Westmoreland Road, 88001
(505) 382-3556

NOTES: Credit cards accepted: A Master Card; B Visa; C American Express; D Discover Card; E Diner's Club; F Other; 2 Personal Checks accepted; 3 Lunch available; 4 Dinner available; 5 Open all year;

Discover the magic of the Southwest with spectacular desert, mountain, and city views on these 20 beautiful acres. This unique adobe home with patios, verandas, and old beam ceilings is a secluded retreat which has attracted many artists and writers. Three comfortable rooms decorated with family antiques and southwestern flavor. Minutes from downtown and famous Old Mesilla. Personal service and many amenities.

Hosts: Bob and Teddi Peters
Rooms: 3 (SB) $55
Full Breakfast
Credit Cards: None
Notes: 2, 5, 9

Lundeen Inn of the Arts

618 South Alameda Boulevard, 88005
(505) 526-3327

For those who appreciate meaningful living, the Inn of the Arts is definitely the place to start. The inn, along with the Linda Lundeen Art Gallery, is housed in a century-old adobe hacienda. Fifteen guest rooms, all of which have private bath, gazebos, patios, and cozy alcoves, are representative of a southwestern artist, and some rooms have kiva fireplaces. Furnishings combine English and American antiques with traditional Mexican white walls and red brick floors. While staying at the inn, you can visit one of the many nearby attractions. The inn also schedules Indian dancing, southwestern archtectural seminars, and pottery making. A popular location for wedding ceremonies and honeymoon retreats.

Hosts: Jerry and Linda Lundeen
Rooms: 15 (PB) $45-85
Full Breakfast weekends; Continental weekdays
Credit Cards: A, B, C, D
Notes: 2, 5, 9, 10, 11, 12, 14

LAS VEGAS

Plaza Hotel

230 Old Town Plaza, 87701
(505) 425-3591

Built in 1882, the Plaza Hotel has been welcoming visitors to Las Vegas for over 110 years. The Italianate bracketed building houses a full-service restaurant, the Landmark Grill, and a lounge, Byron T's, which is named after a resident ghost. The charming guest rooms have Victorian appointments and modern amenities, which provide a delightful stay for business or pleasure traveler. Considered the finest restaurant in Las Vegas, the Landmark Grill serves breakfast, lunch, and dinner and is open 365 days a year.

Hoss: Wid Slick
Rooms: 38 (PB) $55-85
Full Breakfast
Credit Cards: A, B, C, D
Notes: 3, 4, 5, 6, 7, 8, 9, 12, 13, 14

LOS ALAMOS

Casa del Rey

305 Rover Street, 87544
(505) 672-9401

Quiet residential area, friendly atmosphere. Situated in White Rock, minutes from Los Alamos and 40 minutes from Santa Fe. Excellent recreational facilities and restaurants nearby. The area is rich in Indian and Spanish history. Breakfast features homemade granola and breads served on the sun porch overlooking flower gardens, with views of the mountains.

Host: Virginia King
Rooms: 2 (SB) $30
Expanded Continental Breakfast
Credit Cards: None
Notes: 2, 5, 8 (over 7), 9, 10, 11, 12, 13

OJO CALIENTE

The Inn at Ojo

11 Route 414, P. O. Box 215, 87549
(505) 583-2428

Relaxing, small country inn at the edge of the high desert, close to the rhythms of nature. Six cozy, private rooms surround-

6 Pets welcome; 7 Smoking allowed; 8 Children welcome; 9 Social drinking allowed; 10 Tennis available; 11 Swimming available; 12 Golf available; 13 Skiing available; 14 May be booked through travel agents.

ing a half-acre shaded courtyard abuzz with hummingbirds in summer. Delicious natural breakfasts and desserts. Shiatsu massage, hiking, mountain biking, and horseback riding available. Walking distance to historic hot springs. Close to Indian pueblos and rafting in the Rio Grande Gorge. Close to Taos and Santa Fe.

Hosts: Rob Dorival and K. C. Kennedy
Rooms: 6 (PB) $44-54
Full Breakfast
Credit Cards: A, B, C, D, E
Notes: 2, 4 (groups of 8 or more), 8 (over 4)

PECOS

B&B of New Mexico #290

P. O. Box 2805, Santa Fe, 87504
(505) 982-3332

This historic three-bedroom log cabin, situated six miles above Pecos toward Cowels on State Road 63, is probably the most photographed in the canyon. Sitting on a natural rock foundation right on the river, and only 25 minutes from Santa Fe, it offers beautiful scenic trails, trout fishing at your doorstep, and a chance to reflect while sitting on the outdoor patio surrounded by the Sangre de Cristo Mountains. Continental breakfast. One bedroom has a fireplace and half-bath. A full bath is across the hall. The other bedroom has a queen bed and a single bed with a full bath. $70.

QUESTA

B&B of New Mexico #210

P. O. Box 2805, Santa Fe, 87504
(505) 982-3332

Large, cozy, rustic log home is waiting for you at the base of the Sangre de Cristo Mountains with three bedrooms, two baths, hot tub and sauna. Area is quiet and restful with close access to Rio Grande. Wild river

hiking, wilderness area, three major ski resorts, much wildlife, and shopping in Taos are all at your disposal. Continental breakfast, southwestern style. Rooms are queen, double, and single. $40-60.

RAMAH

Mi Casa Su Casa #1805

P. O. Box 950, Tempe, Arizona, 85280-0950
(602) 990-0682; (800) 456-0682

Enjoy warmhearted hospitality on this working cattle ranch owned by rancher and writer Evon Vogt. Built in 1915 of rocks from the nearby Anasazi Indian ruins, this typical old farmhouse has wood floors, Navajo rugs, large enclosed gardens, and big elm trees. Two bedrooms, both of which have Navajo rugs and original works of art, lead off from the large central livingroom. No smoking. No pets. Full breakfast. $44.36-58.09.

RATON

The Red Violet Inn

Bed and Breakfast Rocky Mountains
906 South Pearl Street, Denver , Colorado 80209
(303) 744-8415; (800) 733-8415

Located on the Santa Fe trail, this stately red brick Victorian home was built in 1902. Furnished with many wonderful antiques, including a collection of pitchers, bowls, chamber pots, and plates. Guests can choose between four rooms, two with private baths. Fresh flowers, candy, fruit, cookies, and decanter of sherry greet you; tea and coffee trays are always available. Box lunches to go and extra meals are available with advance notice and additional cost. Full breakfast. Children require prior approval. Moderate rates.

NOTES: Credit cards accepted: A Master Card; B Visa; C American Express; D Discover Card; E Diner's Club; F Other; 2 Personal Checks accepted; 3 Lunch available; 4 Dinner available; 5 Open all year;

SANTA FE

Adobe Abode

202 Chapelle, 87501
(505) 983-3133

Just three blocks from the plaza, this is a historic adobe home restored into an inviting and intimate European-style bed and breakfast inn. Decorated with flair and authentic southwestern charm. Two delightful guest rooms (queen four-poster or double brass bed) in the main house sharing a 30-foot livingroom with fireplace, cable TV. Complimentary sherry, fruit, and cookies. Also available is a detached guest house in pure Santa Fe style with private entrance, twin beds, and landscaped patio.

Host: Pat Harbour
Rooms: 3 (PB) $90-110
Full Breakfast
Credit Cards: A, B, D
Notes: 2, 5, 7, 8, 9, 14

Alexander's Inn

529 East Palace, 87501
(505) 986-1431

For a cozy, romantic stay in Santa Fe, come to a bed and breakfast featuring the best of American country charm. Situated in a lovely residential neighborhood on the town's historic east side, the inn is within walking distance of the downtown plaza and Canyon Road. Afternoon tea and homemade cookies are served.

Hosts: Carolyn Delecluse and Mary Jo Schneider
Rooms: 6 (4 PB; 2 SB) $70-140
Expanded Continental Breakfast
Credit Cards: A, B
Notes: 2, 5, 8 (over 5), 9, 10, 11, 12, 13, 14

B&B of New Mexico #102

P. O. Box 2805, 87504
(505) 982-3332

Your own adobe casita. Ideally situated in a quiet historic neighborhood, short walk to plaza, surrounded by shops, restaurants, and galleries. Three separate casitas can accommodate between two to six people per casita. All the casitas have equipped kitchens and telephones. The first is elegant, newly restored, remodeled and decorated. High-beamed ceilings, plastered walls, pine and tile floors, air-conditioned, and a front courtyard. Two bedrooms. The second is in the back part of the first casita and also has high beamed ceilings, pine and tile floors. The third is a separate house with pine floors and Mexican tile. Large, well-equipped kitchen, livingroom and dining room, and two bedrooms. $85-$165.

B&B of New Mexico #104

P. O. Box 2805, 87504
(505) 982-3332

Large, two-story home with Spanish-tile roof in the Sangre de Cristo Mountains. Master bedroom has king-size bed, fireplace, sitting area, refrigerator, and private bath with room for a roll-away bed if needed. Second bedroom has queen bed and shares bath across the hall with twin bedroom. Home has pool table for guest use and an outside dog. No smoking. $50-60.

B&B of New Mexico #105

P. O. Box 2805, 87504
(505) 982-3332

Beautiful two-story home less than one mile from the plaza. Large downstairs bedroom with queen bed, refrigerator, lots of closet space, private bath and shower. Upstairs room has twin bed, walls covered with watercolors, private three-quarter bath. Breakfast upstairs in dining room with view of hills filled with piñon trees. Livingroom has views of Sangre de Cristo Mountains, beamed ceiling, and kiva fireplace. Spanish tile in kitchen and hallways. No smoking. $50-70.

6 Pets welcome; 7 Smoking allowed; 8 Children welcome; 9 Social drinking allowed; 10 Tennis available; 11 Swimming available; 12 Golf available; 13 Skiing available; 14 May be booked through travel agents.

B&B of New Mexico #107

P. O. Box 2805, 87504
(505) 982-3332

Pure Santa Fe! This new adobe-style home has high-beam and rough-sawn ceilings throughout, with foot-thick walls, saltillo-tile floors, Mexican tile in baths and kitchen, kiva fireplace, and vigas in the livingroom. One-half block to historic Canyon Road, one mile to the plaza. Both rooms are on the second floor and have private baths. One room has its own private portal and small refrigerator. The other has its own private sitting room with twin bed. No smoking. $75 for two in either room; $90 for three in suite.

B&B of New Mexico #108

P. O. Box 2805, 87504
(505) 982-3332

Small, cozy adobe home two blocks from Canyon Road and five blocks from downtown plaza. Kiva fireplace in livingroom, enclosed courtyard in front. Door from guest room opens onto back garden area. Host very knowledgeable about activities in Santa Fe. Private full bath down the hall and king-size bed. No smoking. $70.

B&B of New Mexico #110

P. O. Box 2805, 87504
(505) 982-3332

Beautiful pueblo-style home in the foothills of the Sangre de Cristo Mountains. Gorgeous sunsets and views of the city lights at night. Jogging trails behind the house. Very quiet except for the sounds of nature. Only 15 minutes to ski basin, 10 minutes to the plaza. Patio for sunning; livingroom and dining room have high-beamed ceiling with fireplace. Master bedroom has king bed, dressing area, walk-in closet, private bath, and views of the foothills. Smaller bedroom has twin beds, large closet, and private bath. Cat in residence. No smoking. $65-80.

B&B of New Mexico #119

P. O. Box 2805, 87504
(505) 982-3332

From 1867 to 1890 this lovely old adobe was the Santa Fe Meat and Livestock Headquarters. Situated in the heart of the historic district five blocks from the plaza and one block south of Canyon Road. Parts of the home are believed to date prior to 1846. All of the outside and some of the inside walls are made of adobe, in some cases 30 inches thick; the ceiling of the livingroom has six inches of dirt on top in spite of the pitched roof. There is a parlor grand piano in the home that guests can use. The bunkhouse can sleep four in two queen beds sharing a bath (same party). Queen bed, private bath, and private library in the main house. No smoking. $80.

B&B of New Mexico #120

P. O. Box 2805, 87504
(505) 982-3332

This adobe casita has viga ceilings, separate bedroom, small livingroom with double sleeper/sofa, full bath, and kitchenette. Located approximately one and one-half miles from the plaza. $70-$80.

B&B of New Mexico #127

P. O. Box 2805, 87504
(505) 982-3332

Beautiful, spacious adobe-style home in fashionable northeast Santa Fe, only one and one-fourth miles from downtown. Situated on a ridge above the city, this home offers a lovely view, spectacular sunsets, and walled back yard. Extensive decks provide summertime relaxation and privacy. Kiva fireplace and beamed ceiling in the den offer winter comfort. Glass-enclosed hot tub feels great at the end of a long day. King bed with private bath. Twin beds with private bath next to main room. Breakfast features a variety of homemade breads served in the elegant dining room. No smoking. $65-75.

B&B of New Mexico #128

P. O. Box 2805, 87504
(505) 982-3332

This is a delightful home on the east side, one-half block to Canyon Road and walking distance to town. It has hardwood floors and some antiques. Enjoy breakfast on its cheerful sun porch. Cable TV is available. There are two rooms to choose from. One is a master bedroom with a private bath and queen bed; the other has a full-size bed with private three-quarter bath. $75.

B&B of New Mexico #133

P. O. Box 2805, 87504
(505) 982-3332

Very private 150-year-old adobe casita plaqued by the Historic Santa Fe Foundation in the historic Bario De Analco near the oldest church. Entrance to private casita is framed by a giant wisteria. Sitting room with Taos day bed and pigskin furniture features kiva fireplace, vigas, flagstone and pine floor. Bedroom has Taos-style queen bed, McMillan bureau, and Spanish chair. Fully furnished kitchen with Mexican tile, full bath, southwestern art throughout. Courtyard and garden are adorned with apple, catalpa, and sumac trees. $95.

B&B of New Mexico #134

P. O. Box 2805, 87504
(505) 982-3332

In-town, country living, guest house apartment at a private residence. Fully furnished, this attractive space offers a Posturepedic king-size bed, tub and shower, livingroom with fireplace, equipped kitchen, TV, outside cooking facilities, and phone. A cozy spot for all seasons. Located three and one-half miles south of the plaza with off-street parking. Santa Fe's private clubs are just six miles away. $60-100.

B&B of New Mexico #139

P. O. Box 2805, 87504
(505) 982-3332

This home begins with the hostess' music space and ends with the host's painting area. The bedroom corridor gives a warm welcome to visitors. The queen bedroom is a comfortable size and overlooks the garden; the single bedroom, though smaller, enjoys spaciousness of a mountain view and a wall of books to tempt a guest tired from tourist activities. Cat and dog are also on the premises. Both rooms share same bath. $50-65.

B&B of New Mexico #142

P. O. Box 2805, 87504
(505) 982-3332

Romantic guest suite in the heart of Santa Fe's historic eastside. This adobe residence is at the end of a narrow lane, secluded and quiet, surrounded by rock walls, coyote fence, and adobe walls, yet minutes to Canyon Road, galleries, shops, and restaurants. Features include sun-filled bedroom, queen four-poster bed, kiva fireplace, vigas, clerestory windows so you can watch the stars. Also available are a cozy sitting room, and cable TV, with both rooms opening onto patio. $75.

6 Pets welcome; 7 Smoking allowed; 8 Children welcome; 9 Social drinking allowed; 10 Tennis available; 11 Swimming available; 12 Golf available; 13 Skiing available; 14 May be booked through travel agents.

B&B of New Mexico #143

P. O. Box 2805, 87504
(505) 982-3332

This attractive casita, located about one and one-fourth miles from the plaza, is furnished with handcrafted furniture by a leading furniture maker in the Santa Fe tradition. Queen and twin beds available with full kitchen and small dining room. $75-85.

B&B of New Mexico #145

P. O. Box 2805, 87504
(505) 982-3332

Decorated in Santa Fe style, this casita has a fully equipped kitchenette, TV, stereo, microwave, and king bed with convertible sofa. It only takes minutes to get to the Plaza, Santa Fe Ski Basin, and Ten Thousand Waves (a Japanese bath house). $70-80.

Canyon Road Casitas

652 Canyon Road, 87501
(505) 988-5888; (800) 279-0755

Situated in the historic district behind a walled private courtyard garden on Santa Fe's famous Canyon Road. Built around 1887, the accommodations include a suite with dining room, kitchen, and two separate beds. Fine amenities include duvets, down pillows, imported linens, custom toiletries, Pima cotton towels, guest robes, French-roast coffee, with complimentary wine and cheese upon check-in. The finest in southwestern decor, including kiva fireplace, hand-carved beds, vigas, latillas, original art, and hand-tiled private baths. Award-winning.

Host: Trisha Ambrose
Rooms: 2 (PB) $85-169
Continental Breakfast
Credit Cards: A, B, C, D, E
Notes: 2, 5, 8, 9, 14

Casa Contenta

Bed and Breakfast Rocky Mountains
906 South Pearl Street, Denver , Colorado 80209
(303) 744-8415; (800) 733-8415

Great care has been taken with this 100-year-old adobe guest house to make it a very private hideaway that is Santa Fe warm and cozy. Prints from local artists, cactus plants, Mexican rugs and glasses, ceramic lamps, and a garden add to the southwestern charm. No pets. Well-mannered children welcome. Moderate to luxury rates.

Don Gaspar Compound

617 Don Gaspar, 87501
(505) 986-8664

The Don Gaspar Compound, a blend of Adobe and Mission styles, was built in 1912 in Santa Fe's historic district. The main house and five suites, each with kitchens, overlook the walled orchard, flower gardens and fountain —an oasis in the high desert. Each suite has complimentary fruits, cereals, juices, coffee, and tea with many restaurants and shops just a short walk away.

Hosts: Joy Thrun; Shirley and David Alford
Rooms: 8 (PB)
Continental Breakfast
Credit Cards: None
Notes: 2, 3, 4 (occasionally), 5, 8, 9, 14

Dunshee's

986 Acequia Madre, 87501
(505) 982-0988

A romantic adobe getaway in the historic east side, about a mile from the plaza. Your suite includes a livingroom and bedroom with kiva fireplaces, antiques, folk art, fresh flowers, homemade cookies, refrigerator, private bath, and patio. Gourmet breakfast.

Host: Susan Dunshee
Room: 1 (PB) $88-99

NOTES: Credit cards accepted: A Master Card; B Visa; C American Express; D Discover Card; E Diner's Club; F Other; 2 Personal Checks accepted; 3 Lunch available; 4 Dinner available; 5 Open all year;

Full Breakfast
Minimum stay weekends and holidays: 2 nights
Credit Cards: A, B
Closed Christmas
Notes: 2, 8, 9

El Paradero

220 West Manhattan, 87501
(505) 988-1177

Just a short walk from the busy plaza, this 200-year-old Spanish farmhouse was restored as a charming southwestern inn. Enjoy a full gourmet breakfast, caring service, and a relaxed, friendly atmosphere. The inn offers lots of common space and a patio for afternoon tea and snacks.

Hosts: Thom Allen and Onida MacGregor
Rooms: 14 (10 PB; 4 SB) $40-125
Full Breakfast
Credit Cards: None
Notes: 2, 5, 6, 8 (over 4), 9, 10, 11, 12, 13, 14

Grant Corner Inn

Grant Corner Inn

122 Grant Avenue, 87501
(505) 983-6678

An exquisite Colonial manor home in downtown Santa Fe with an ideal location just two blocks from the historic plaza, the inn nestles among intriguing shops, restaurants, and galleries. Each room is appointed with antiques and treasures from around the world: quilts, brass and four-poster beds, armoires, and art. Private phones, cable TV, and ceiling fans. Wine is served in the evening.

Hosts: Louise Stewart and Pat Walter
Rooms: 15 (8 PB; 7 SB) $55-130
Full Breakfast
Credit Cards: A, B
Closed January
Notes: 2, 7, 8, 10, 11, 12, 13

Inn on the Alameda

303 East Alameda, 87501
(505) 984-2121; (800) 289-2122

An enchanting small hotel in Old Santa Fe, the Inn on the Alamada offers a personal, intimate atmosphere with convenience and privacy. Each of the 47 guest rooms and suites is individually designed with southwestern decor, and some offer private patios or balconies and kiva fireplaces. Each day begins with a gourmet breakfast buffet of fresh pastries and fruits. The inn is just steps away from the historic plaza and Canyon Road. Relax after a day of touring with a book from the lobby library, refreshment in the Agoyo Room Lounge, or in a Jacuzzi under the Santa Fe sky.

Host: David Oberstein
Rooms: 47 (PB) $155-330
Continental Breakfast Buffet
Credit Cards: A, B, C, D, E, F
Notes: 5, 7, 8, 9, 10, 11, 12, 13, 14

Inn of the Animal Tracks

707 Paseo de Peralta, 87501
(505) 988-1546

Inn of the Animal Tracks is a whimsical, warm bed and breakfast inn located three blocks east of the Santa Fe plaza. The best homemade full breakfast and only afternoon tea in Santa Fe will send you home full and happy. Three sweet cats and one loving dog are part of the staff. The rooms boast vigas, handmade furniture, feather mattresses and comforters, TV, clock radios, and private baths.

6 Pets welcome; 7 Smoking allowed; 8 Children welcome; 9 Social drinking allowed; 10 Tennis available; 11 Swimming available; 12 Golf available; 13 Skiing available; 14 May be booked through travel agents.

Host: Dawn Martin
Rooms: 5 (PB) $85-110
Full Breakfast
Credit Cards: A, B, C, D
Notes: 2, 3, 5, 8, 9, 10, 11, 12, 13, 14

Mi Casa Su Casa #335

P. O. Box 950, Tempe, Arizona 85280-0950
(602) 990-0682; (800) 456-0682

Secluded and quiet, this 76-year-old adobe estate is on a narrow lane in the heart of the historic eastside of Santa Fe. Surrounded by rock walls, a coyote fence, and old gates, it is minutes from Canyon Road art galleries, shops, and restaurants, the plaza, and museums. Your host is a retired writer for a major newspaper, and the guest wing is a lovely L-shaped accommodation with a kiva fireplace, private bath, mini-fridge, coffee maker, telephone, and daily maid service. Minimum stay is two nights. No children. Continental plus breakfast. $70.

Pueblo Bonito
Bed and Breakfast Inn

Bed and Breakfast Rocky Mountains
906 South Pearl Street, Denver , Colorado 80209
(303) 744-8415; (800) 733-8415

Now secluded behind its thick adobe walls, Pueblo Bonito was an estate with its own stable and landscaped grounds built around the turn of the century. Newly renovated, it still boasts beautiful private courtyards, foot-thick adobe walls, shady gardens, and adobe archways to the street. Pueblo Bonito is a one-of-a-kind experience in traditional New Mexican living. Continental plus breakfast. No smoking. Fifteen casitas available. Moderate-luxury rates.

Spacious Adobe

Bed and Breakfast Texas Style
4224 West Red Bird Lane, Dallas, Texas 75237
(214) 298-8586

This bed and breakfast home is in fashionable northeast Santa Fe and hosted by a gracious couple who wish to show their guests the city. Relax in either of the two guest rooms and in front of the fireplace in the sitting room. Enjoy the complimentary beverages on arrival as well as Mexican omelettes for breakfast. Lavish gardens and deck invite sun soaking and contemplation. $65-75.

Territorial Inn

215 Washington Avenue, 87501
(505) 989-7737

Elegantly remodeled, 100-year-old home just one block north of historic plaza. Eleven rooms, some with fireplaces, cable TV, and telephones. Hot tub in rose garden. Continental-plus breakfast, afternoon treats, and brandy turn-down. Personal service is the hallmark of the hostess.

Host: Lela McFerrin
Rooms: 11 (8 PB; 3 SB) $70-140
Expanded Continental Breakfast
Credit Cards: A, B, D
Notes: 2, 5, 10, 11, 12, 13, 14

Victoria's

Bed and Breakfast Rocky Mountains
906 South Pearl Street, Denver, Colorado 80209
(303) 744-8415; (800) 733-8415

Come to Santa Fe and enjoy one of three little adobe apartments nestled together on a quiet little road near the plaza. Each has a private bedroom, separate entrance and fully equipped kitchen. Small adobe has a queen sofa sleeper and twin beds. The medium-size adobe has two twin beds in a bedroom and a queen sofa sleeper in the livingroom. The largest adobe has a double bed in the bedroom and two queen sofa sleepers, one in the living room and the other in the den. Freshly brewed coffee is provided. Minimum stay is three nights. Smoking and pets permitted. Moderate rates.

SILVER CITY

Bear Mountain Guest Ranch

Box 1163, 88062
(505) 538-2538

Two-story ranch house, two cottages, five-bedroom house available for guests. Elevation 6,250 feet; air conditioning unnecessary. Piñon-juniper area. Ranch features home cooking, Lodge and Learn programs (six days, five nights), tours for bird watching, wild plant identification, ghost towns, archaeological sites, and prehistoric primitive pottery workshops. Rate includes breakfast, sack lunch, and dinner.

Host: Myra B. McCormick
Rooms: 15 (PB) $114
All meals included
Credit Cards: None
Notes: 2, 3, 4, 5, 6, 7 (limited), 8, 9, 10, 11, 12, 14

Hummingbird Inn Bed and Breakfast

206 West 6th Street, 88061
(505) 388-3606

Listed on the National Register of Historic Places and located in the heart of the Main Street area, Hummingbird Inn, circa 1870, provides homey suites with full baths (claw foot tubs and all), and kitchenettes. Up to six family members may stay in either the Pueblo Suite or the Cottage Suite at no extra cost. Families are welcomed, with a crib and little girl's canopy bed included in the Cottage Suite. The quaint ranching and mining town of Silver City is home to the inn, and the area is an outdoor enthusiast's paradise, with millions of acres of national forestlands and wilderness areas a short drive away.

Host: Linda Luccro
Rooms: 2 (PB) $60
Full Breakfast
Credit Cards: A, B, C, F
Notes: 2 (NM only), 5, 6 (call), 7, 8, 10, 11, 12, 14

TAOS

American Artists Gallery House

P. O. Box 584, 87571
(505) 758-4446; (800) 532-2041

Charming southwestern hacienda filled with artwork by American artists. Gourmet breakfasts, adobe fireplaces, private baths, outdoor hot tub, and gardens. Magnificent view of mountains. Minutes from art galleries, museums, restaurants, St. Francis Assisi Church, and ski valley.

Hosts: Judie and Elliot Framan
Rooms: 6 (PB) $65-95
Full Breakfast
Credit Cards: A, B
Notes: 2, 5, 8, 9, 10, 11, 12, 13, 14

Hummingbird Inn

B&B of New Mexico #207

P. O. Box 2805, Santa Fe, 87504
(505) 982-3332

In an open meadow a short walk to Taos Plaza, 5 minutes from Taos Pueblo, and 25 minutes from Taos Ski Valley, this bed and breakfast offers the Vigil Suite with two large bedrooms, private livingroom, kiva fireplace in livingroom, private entrance, open beam ceilings, and split bath with Spanish tile throughout. The Truchas Suite has a large bedroom with queen bed, sculpted adobe walls, kiva fireplace with bancos and sitting area, private entrance, viga and latilla ceiling, and private bath with Spanish tile. Vigil Suite $85; Truchas Suite $75.

B&B of New Mexico #209

P. O. Box 2805, Santa Fe, 87504
(505) 982-3332

This two-story house on a quiet corner is available near the plaza. Rooms are huge with private baths on opposite sides of house; one upstairs and one downstairs. The livingroom offers a stone fireplace. There is artwork throughout the house. $85-95.

The Brooks Street Inn

119 Brooks Street, Box 4954, 87571
(505) 758-1489

Selected as one of the ten best inns of North America for 1988 by Country Inns magazine. The atmosphere is casual and fun. Just a short walk from the plaza. The rambling main house and charming guest house feature fireplaces, reading nooks, and private baths.

Hosts: Susan Stevens and John Testore
Rooms: 6 (PB) 81.58-104.97
Full Breakfast
Credit Cards: A, B, C
Notes: 2, 5, 8 (over 15), 9, 13, 14

Casa Europa

Bed and Breakfast Rocky Mountains
906 South Pearl Street, Denver , Colorado 80209
(303) 744-8415; (800) 733-8415

Come to Taos and enjoy an elegant blend of European tradition and southwestern architecture. The golden adobe structure is built around a center courtyard filled with colorful flowers and a soothing, trickling fountain. Originally built by the Spanish

almost 200 years ago, the inn has been beautifully renovated. Six guest rooms are available. Gourmet breakfast is served in the dining room. No pets. Moderate-luxury rates.

El Rincon
Bed and Breakfast

114 Kit Carson, 87571
(505) 758-4874

A special bed and breakfast in a historic adobe home, conveniently nestled in the heart of Taos. It boasts a fine art collection distributed throughout. In the summer, breakfast is served on a flower-filled patio. In the winter, it is served near a blazing adobe fireplace. Breakfast is served early to those headed for Taos's fine ski areas. Most rooms have fireplaces, some have refrigerators and VCRs. Hot tub or Jacuzzi available. A lovely blend of old and new.

Hosts: Nina C. Meyers and Paul C. Castillo
Rooms: 12 (PB) $45-125
Continental Breakfast
Credit Cards: A, B, C
Notes: 2, 5, 6, 7, 8, 9, 13, 14

Hacienda del Sol

P. O. Box 177, 87571
(505) 758-0287

A 180-year-old historic, charming, quiet adobe with fireplaces, viga ceilings, and surrounded by century-old trees. Guest rooms have down comforters, carefully selected furnishings, and fine art. Enjoy an unobstructed view of Taos mountains from the deck of the outdorr hot tub. Generous breakfasts are served by a crackling fire in the winter, or on the patio in the summer. Chosen by *USA Weekend* as one of America's ten most romantic inns. Located one mile north of Taos plaza.

Hosts: John and Marcine Landon
Rooms: 7 (5 PB; 2 SB) $55-115
Continental Plus Breakfast
Credit Cards: None
Notes: 2, 5, 8, 9, 10, 11, 12, 13, 14

NOTES: Credit cards accepted: A Master Card; B Visa; C American Express; D Discover Card; E Diner's Club; F Other; 2 Personal Checks accepted; 3 Lunch available; 4 Dinner available; 5 Open all year;

Harrison's Bed and Breakfast

P. O. Box 242, 87571
(505) 758-2630

A bit off the beaten path, at Harrison's Bed and Breakfast you can find the Taos that remains hidden to many visitors. This large adobe home is situated in a rural setting just two and one-half miles from the Taos plaza and is convenient to the Taos Ski Valley and other local attractions. The view is grand, the rooms are attractive, the beds are comfortable, and the breakfasts are delicious.

Hosts: Jean and Bob Harrison
Rooms: 2 (PB) $50
Full Breakfast
Credit Cards: None
Notes: 2, 5, 8, 9, 10, 13, 14

La Posada de Taos

309 Juanita Lane, Box 1118, 87571
(505) 758-8164

La Posada de Taos, located two and one-half blocks from the Taos plaza, was created out of a turn-of-the-century home in the historic district. Soothing adobe walls lead guests to a Japanese garden, then into a vaulted-ceiling foyer and livingroom centered around a traditional adobe fireplace. French doors in the dining room outline the mountains as guests savor a hearty breakfast. The hospitality is highly personal and will bring you back to Taos again.

Host: Sue Smoot
Rooms: 5 (PB) $65-95
Full Breakfast
Minimum stay May-October weekends: 2 nights;
   holidays: 3 nights
Credit Cards: None

Orinda

Box 4551, Valverde Street, 87571
(505) 758-8581

Surrounded by open meadows and towering elm trees, Orinda is a dramatic adobe estate that combines spectacular views, and country privacy, with walking distance to

Taos Plaza. Enjoy a spacious two-bedroom suite with livingroom or a distinctive one-bedroom suite. Each has a kiva fireplace, Mexican-tiled bath, and private entrance. Healthy breakfasts are served in the huge, art-filled sunroom.

Hosts: Dave and Karol Dondero
Rooms: 3 (1 PB; 2 SB) $75-95
Continental Breakfast
Credit Cards: A, B
Notes: 2, 5, 8, 9, 13, 14

Salsa del Salto Bed and Breakfast

P. O. Box 1468, 87529
(505) 776-2422

Designed by world-renowned architect Antoine Predock, this beautiful home offers six guest rooms, each of which reflect the southwestern earth tones and pastel colors. All are decorated to tend to the guest's every need, with king-size beds, down comforters, furniture specially designed by local artisans for Salsa del Salto, and original paintings by Taos artists throughout the inn. As an added treat, all rooms have spectacular views of the mountains and mesas. Breakfast is a gourmet's delight. Hot tub, heated pool, and private tennis court.

Hosts: Dadou Mayer and Mary Hockett
Rooms: 6 (PB) $85-160
Full Breakfast
Credit Cards: A, B, D
Notes: 2, 5, 9, 10, 11, 13, 14

Stewart House Gallery and Inn

P. O. Box 2326, 87571; (505) 776-2913
FAX (505) 758-1399

Storybook house built by an artist as his home and studio. Each room is constructed from materials that are described as reclaimed parts of history. Bedrooms have private baths; many have private patios and fireplaces. A large outdoor hot tub has magnificent sunset views, as well as mountain views. Hearty breakfasts are served in

---

6 Pets welcome; 7 Smoking allowed; 8 Children welcome; 9 Social drinking allowed; 10 Tennis available; 11 Swimming available; 12 Golf available; 13 Skiing available; 14 May be booked through travel agents.

the art gallery/common area. Rooms are filled with original artwork. Selected for the 1991 and 1992 editions of *America's Wonderful Little Hotels and Inns.* Converted into an inn in 1989 by owner Mildred Cheek.

Hosts: Mildred and Don Cheek
Rooms: 6 (PB) $75-120
Full Breakfast
Credit Cards: A, B
Notes: 2, 5, 9, 10, 11, 12, 13, 14

TRUCHAS _____

Rancho Arriba

Box 338, 87578
(505) 689-2374

A European-style bed and breakfast with an informal and tranquil atmosphere, this traditional adobe hacienda is situated on a historic Spanish land grant. Spectacular mountain view in every direction, amid colonial villages featuring traditional arts and architecture. Adobe churches, hand weaving, wood carving, and quilting.

Host: Curtiss Frank
Rooms: 4 (SB) $35-55
Full Breakfast
Credit Cards: B
Notes: 2, 4, 5, 7 (outside), 8, 9, 13

New York

The American Country Collection 097

4 Greenwood Lane, Delmar, 12054
(518) 439-7001

This elegant turn-of-the-century Victorian home is conveniently situated on the bus route and just a few minute's drive from all major area colleges, state buildings, and attractions. Four guest rooms, two with shared baths. All rooms have telephones and air conditioning. Children over 12 welcome. Continental breakfast. Guests can use the TV in the livingroom. Off-street parking is provided. $49-64.

The American Country Collection 110

4 Greenwood Lane, Delmar, 12054
(518) 439-7001

City convenience combined with quiet residential living makes this suburban ranch home an ideal location. Just one block from the bus line. In summer months, a hearty continental breakfast is served on the screened porch. There's a redwood deck for sunning and a livingroom with a fireplace. Two guest bedrooms with shared bath, usually rented to only one traveling party. Children welcome. $40-50; $70 for two persons taking both rooms.

The American Country Collection 111

4 Greenwood Lane, Delmar, 12054
(518)489-7001

Once a residence for Albany's earliest extended families, this Victorian bed and breakfast also served as a tavern and grocery store. Situated in the shadow of the Empire State Plaza. Twelve guest rooms with private baths, air conditioning, color cable TV, and phone. Children welcome. Smoking permitted. Cat in residence. $95-145.

The American Country Collection 142

4 Greenwood Lane, Delmar, 12054
(518) 439-7001

Restored in 1991 as a private bed and breakfast inn, this in-town brownstone is registered as a historic landmark with the Historic Albany Foundation. Completed in 1881, it represents one of the earliest examples of a private building in Albany built in the Neo-Classical style of architecture. Seven rooms on the second floor offer double and single beds, and one suite with two double beds features a working fireplace and refrigerators. All rooms offer a private bath, except for two rooms that have one twin bed a piece and share a hall bath. Breakfast includes bread and muffins, seasonal fresh fruit, cereal, juices and beverages, including gourmet tea and coffee. No pets. Childen welcome. Smoking permitted. $49-95.

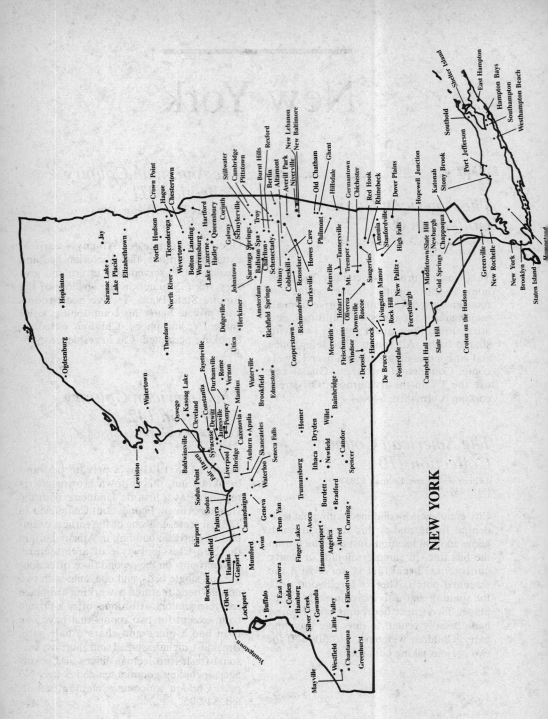

NEW YORK

ALFRED

Saxon Inn

One Park Street, 14802
(607) 871-2600

Twenty elegantly appointed guest rooms
and six suites with wood-burning marble
fireplaces. Richly furnished in deluxe cherry woods with a Colonial-style. European
breakfast is served in the fireside hospitality room. Smoke-free rooms available;
handicapped accessible.

Host: Dawn M. Schirmer
Rooms: 26 (PB) $75-79
Continental Breakfast
Credit Cards: A, B, C, D, E
Notes: 2, 5, 7, 8, 9, 10, 11, 14

ALTAMONT

The American Country Collection 020

4 Greenwood Lane, Delmar, 12054
(518) 439-7001

A renovation in 1910 added the large front
pillars on the veranda to give the house its
southern Colonial flavor, but this impressive home on the site of the first town
meeting of Guilderland was actually built
in 1765. It first served as a tavern and is
now on the state and national historic registers. It is at the base of the Helderburg
Mountains on six acres of grounds. Four
guest rooms with shared baths. Pets in residence. Children welcome. Crib available.
Smoking in common rooms on first floor.
$50-75, seasonal.

The American Country Collection 045

4 Greenwood Lane, Delmar, 12054
(518) 439-7001

This 75-year-old refurbished Colonial is
just 20 miles from the State Capitol. It is
situated on 15 acres of well-groomed
lawns, old shade trees, a swimming pool,
barns, patio, and orchards. Business travelers find this location offers convenient
access to both Albany and Schenectady.
One third-floor suite has two bedrooms,
livingroom, and private bath. One single
room on the second floor shares the bath
with the owner. Pets in residence. Children
welcome. Smoking outdoors only. $35-50.

AMENIA

Covered Bridge 2AMNY

P. O. Box 447 A, Norfolk, Connecticut 06058
(203) 542-5944

Contemporary home set on three acres has
been tastefully decorated with antiques and
paintings from the owner's gallery. A full
breakfast is served in the dining room. The
house has central air conditioning. There
are four guest rooms, two of which share a
bath. Double, twin, queen and king beds
are available. $75-95 for rooms, or the
house can be rented on a weekly basis.

Troutbeck

Leedsville Road, 12501
(914) 373-9681

Troutbeck is a world-class country inn with
a regional four-star rating for its cuisine.
Indoor (covered and heated) and outdoor
pools, tennis courts, 442 acres, and a reputation for relaxed, attentive service. Just
over two hours hours from midtown New
York City. Open only on weekends. Room
rate includes all meals and open bar from
Friday evening to Sunday at 2:00 P.M.

Host: Jim Flaherty
Rooms: 34 (PB) $575-790
Full Breakfast Saturday; Continental on Sunday
Credit Cards: C
Notes: 2, 3, 4, 5, 7, 8 (over 12), 9, 10, 11, 12, 13

NOTES: Credit cards accepted: A Master Card; B Visa; C American Express; D Discover Card; E Diner's
Club; F Other; 2 Personal Checks accepted; 3 Lunch available; 4 Dinner available; 5 Open all year; 6 Pets
welcome; 7 Smoking allowed; 8 Children welcome; 9 Social drinking allowed; 10 Tennis available; 11
Swimming available; 12 Golf available; 13 Skiing available; 14 May be booked through travel agents.

The American Country Collection 118

4 Greenwood Lane, Delmar, 122054
(518) 439-7001

The guest rooms in this brick Federal Colonial have wide-pine floors, fireplaces, and are decorated with a mix of antiques, country furniture, and treasures found in the home. The history of the house is preserved in photos and mementos displayed throughout the home. Guests are treated to afternoon tea served in the English tradition with light pastries and sweet cakes. Three guest rooms with shared bath. Parakeet in residence. Children welcome. Crib available. No smoking. $35.

ANGELICA

Rainbow Hospitality A100

466 Amherst Street, Buffalo, 14207
(716) 874-8797

An 1886 Victorian mansion decorated in antiques, with crystal chandeliers, parquet floors, carved woodwork, and stained-glass windows. Each room has a private bath, and four of the rooms have fireplaces. Suites available for families or groups of hunters, fishermen, or sports enthusiasts. Hosts cater small wedding receptions, business luncheons, meetings, and family reunions. Set on 130 acres of forested land, which is available for hiking and hunting. Easily accessible from New Jersey, Pennsylvania, Buffalo, Rochester, and Canada. $55-65.

APULIA

Elaine's Bed and Breakfast Reservation Service

4987 Kingston Road, Elbridge, 13060
(315) 689-2082

Thirty minutes south of Syracuse near Route 80, this quaint old farmhouse offers three guest rooms, two queen-size beds, and a view of the hills. Full breakfast. Near ski areas.

AUBURN

Elaine's Bed and Breakfast and Inn Reservation Service

4987 Kingston Road, Elbridge, 13060
(315) 689-2082

Situated on Lake Owasco, this magnificent 1910 Adirondack cottage-lodge features spacious rooms, excellent craftmanship throughout, solid wood paneling, and built-ins. Each room has picture windows overlooking the lake and double French doors opening onto a large screened porch filled with antique wicker and hung with plants. Each room has private half-bath and shares a full bath. Fireplaces in bedrooms. The livingroom has a large fieldstone fireplace and an ever-changing view of the entire lake. Breakfasts are varied, with homemade hot casseroles, muffins, fruit, juice, coffee, and cold cereal. No smoking. No children under 12. No pets. No credit cards. Winter rate, $65; after May 1, $75.

Elaine's Bed and Breakfast Reservation Service

4987 Kingston Road, Elbridge, 13060
(315) 689-2082

Restored Victorian in the city, beautifully decorated with antiques and wicker. Five guest rooms, some with private baths. Full bourmet breakfast.

The Irish Rose Bed and Breakfast

102 South Street, 13021
(315) 255-0196

NOTES: Credit cards accepted: A Master Card; B Visa; C American Express; D Discover Card; E Diner's Club; F Other; 2 Personal Checks accepted; 3 Lunch available; 4 Dinner available; 5 Open all year;

Victorian elegance, witty Irish hospitality. Beautiful Queen Anne Victorian mansion on the National Register of Historic Places with lots of attention to details: fresh flowers, homemade candies in room, snack on arrival, gourmet breakfast, homemade baked goods. Gardens, porch swing, deck, in-ground pool, four fireplaces. Close to all upstate New York attractions; skiing, boating. Situated in the historic district.

Hosts: The Fitzpatricks and son Kevin
Rooms: 5 (2 PB; 3 SB) $55-110
Full Breakfast
Credit Cards: A, B, D
Notes: 2, 3, 5, 8, 9, 10, 11, 12, 13, 14

AVERILL PARK

The American Country Collection 015

4 Greenwood Lane, Delmar, 12054
(518) 439-7001

This 1830 Colonial is in the center of this little village and houses a restaurant that specializes in continental cuisine. Twelve guest rooms with private baths, individually controlled heating and air conditioning. There is a swimming pool outdoors. A buffet-style breakfast is served in the common room, with a homey atmosphere. Children over six welcome. No pets. Smoking permitted. $65-80.

Ananas Hus Bed and Breakfast

Route 3, Box 301, 12018
(518) 766-5035

The Tomlinsons' hillside ranch home, situated in West Stephentown on 30 acres, offers a panoramic view of the Hudson River Valley, with its natural beauty, and tranquility. Patio dining in summer and the warmth of a fireplace in winter. Skiing and culture abound in nearby western Massachusetts and the capitol district of New York state.

Hosts: Thelma and Clyde Tomlinson
Rooms: 3 (SB) $45-60
Full Breakfast
Credit Cards: C
Closed Christmas Day
Notes: 2, 5, 8 (over 12), 9, 11, 12, 13

AVOCA

Patchwork Peace Bed and Breakfast

4279 Waterbury Hill, 14809
(607) 566-2443

Enjoy the sights, sounds, and smells of a real farm. Visit dairy cows and calves. Observe the patchwork of fields in different hues of greens and golds. Take a delightful walk. This 1920 farmhouse with natural floors and woodwork and light, airy bedrooms affords a gentle night's sleep nestled in sun-dried linens. Heirloom quilts throughout. Incredibly quiet. Country breakfast with hosts. Spend a night or a week. Special weekly rates.

Hosts: Bill and Betty Mitchell
Rooms: 3 (1 PB; 2 SB) $35-60
Full Breakfast
Credit Cards: None
Notes: 2, 5, 8, 9, 13

AVON

Mulligan Farm Bed and Breakfast

5403 Barber Road, 14414
(716) 226-6412

Comfortable country atmosphere and rural hospitality await guests. A working dairy farm where guests are welcome to wander through the tranquil pastures and visit the milking parlor. The house, barns, and farm are all listed on the National Register of Historic Places. The 1840s home is an outstanding example of Greek Revival architecture. An ample home-cooked breakfast is served.

6 Pets welcome; 7 Smoking allowed; 8 Children welcome; 9 Social drinking allowed; 10 Tennis available; 11 Swimming available; 12 Golf available; 13 Skiing available; 14 May be booked through travel agents.

Hosts: Lesa and Jeff Mulligan
Rooms: 4 (2 PB; 2 SB) $50
Full Breakfast
Credit Cards: None
Notes: 2, 5, 8, 11, 12, 14

BAINBRIDGE

Berry Hill Farm

Rural Delivery 1, Box 128, 13733
(607) 967-8745

A friendly, informal atmosphere. Sunrises, sunsets, stargazing, fresh air, views. Restored 1820s farmhouse on a hilltop surrounded by vegetable and flower gardens. On its 180 acres you can hike, swim, birdwatch, pick berries, skate, cross-country ski, or just sit on the wraparound porch and watch the nature parade. The rooms are furnished with comfortable antiques, and a scrumptious country breakfast is served. A ten-minute drive takes you to restaurants, golf, tennis, auctions, and antique centers.

Hosts: Jean Fowler and Cecilio Rios
Rooms: 3 (1 PB; 2 SB) $55-65
Full Breakfast
Credit Cards: A, B
Notes: 2, 5, 7, 8, 9, 11, 12, 13

BALDWINSVILLE

Elaine's Bed and Breakfast and Inn Reservation Service

4987 Kingston Road, Elbridge, 13060
(315) 689-2082

Spacious, historic Colonial in the village. The home was built around 1845 and, in keeping with its character, is decorated with many antiques and collectibles. Four guest rooms available, some with private bath and working fireplace. The house is on two acres high on a hill, a short walk to stores and the picturesque Seneca River.

BALLSTON SPA

The American Country Collection 009

4 Greenwood Lane, Delmar, 12054
(518) 439-7001

This renovated Second Empire Victorian is once again the focal point of the historic district of this tiny village. The home is divided into two segments. The rear bed and breakfast section has a private entrance, guest livingroom with fireplace, dining room, kitchen, and porch for afternoon refreshments. The second floor has three guest rooms and a bath. Rooms in this section are ideal for family gatherings and groups of four-to-six traveling together. Smoking outdoors only. No pets. Children over 11 welcome. Younger children permitted when entire bed and breakfast section is rented to one party. $65-110 rooms, seasonal; $150-175 for suite.

The American Country Collection 119

4 Greenwood Lane, Delmar, 12054
(518) 439-7001

This working farm and girls' summer riding academy is situated on 100 acres of rolling meadows and scenic farmland. Riding lessons are available on the indoor riding arena. A heated swimming pool on the premises is available for guest use. The three guest bedrooms, one with private bath, have air conditioning. There is also a full apartment on the lower level during off-season. No smoking. Children welcome. Crib available, but guests should bring crib linens. Dogs and cats indoors; horses, ducks, geese, goats on the farm. $70-95 July-August; $50-65 Sept.-June.

NOTES: Credit cards accepted: A Master Card; B Visa; C American Express; D Discover Card; E Diner's Club; F Other; 2 Personal Checks accepted; 3 Lunch available; 4 Dinner available; 5 Open all year;

The American Country Collection 133

4 Greenwood Lane, Delmar, 12054
(518) 439-7001

Part of a modern home set back from the road on 2.9 acres, this self-contained three-room efficiency apartment is only 15-20 minutes from Saratoga. A fully furnished livingroom is the first thing you enter when you step through your private entrance, and the kitchen, which is within view of the livingroom, is fully equipped. The bedroom and full bath are off the hall. An abundant continental breakfast is self-catered. The bedroom has queen-size bed, and a fold-out queen-size sofa is in the livingroom. $55-95, seasonal.

BERLIN

The Sedgwick Inn

Route 22, 12022
(518) 658-2334

A historic colonial inn situated on 12 acres in the scenic Taconic Valley, beautifully furnished with antiques. The inn is close to the Williamstown Theater, the Tanglewood Festival, other Berkshire attractions, and both downhill and cross-country skiing. There is a renowned restaurant and a small motel unit behind the main house.

Hosts: Robert and Edith Evans
Rooms: 10 (PB) $65-85
Suite: 1 (PB) $100
Full Breakfast
Credit Cards: A, B, C, E
Notes: 2, 3, 4, 5, 6 (motel only), 7, 8 (motel only), 9, 10, 11, 13, 14

BOLTON LANDING

The American Country Collection 056

4 Greenwood Lane, Delmar, 12054
(518) 439-7001

This 11-room farmhouse was built in 1926 as the caretaker's cottage for a large estate on Millionaire's Row along the west side of Lake George. Two second-floor rooms with shared bath. Third second-floor room has a private bath. Cottage (May to October) has private bath, refrigerator and full breakfast. Children over four welcome. Pets in residence. Swimming, fishing and ice fishing, skating, parasailing, boating are available. Just 20-25 miles to Fort Ticonderoga and Great Escape Amusement Park. $45-55 double; $60 cottage.

The Sedgwick Inn

BROCKPORT

Rainbow Hospitality B100

466 Amherst Street, Buffalo, 14207
(716) 874-8797

An 1850 Greek Revival historic landmark and recipient of the Gold Medallion Award in 1991. Nestled among sycamore, maple, and blue spruce trees in the historic district of Clarkson. Hand-painted lead glass foyer panels, ten-foot ceilings, large windows, and three working fireplaces all combine to welcome bed and breakfast travelers for a special time and fond memories. $50-60.

BROOKFIELD

Gates Hill Homestead

P. O. Box 96, Dugway Road, 13314
(315) 899-5837

A quiet, secluded pioneer-type farmstead, cleared, designed, and built by owners. Unusual saltbox open-beamed construction with massive central fireplace, wide-plank flooring, stenciling, candle chandeliers. Air-conditioned, delicious full breakfasts. Selected in 1987 by Frommer's Guide to Bed & Breakfast in North America as one of the 100 best. Optional entertainment: 70-minute, four-horse stagecoach tour of "the Eternal Hills," followed by elegant country dinner, all home-cooking, by reservation.

Hosts: Charlie and Donna Tanney
Rooms: 3 (2 PB; 1 SB) $49-69
Full Breakfast
Credit Cards: A, B
Notes: 2, 4, 5, 7, 8, 13

BROOKLYN

Bed and Breakfast on the Park

113 Prospect Park West, 11215
(718) 499-6115

This lovely 1892 limestone Victorian four-story inn is fully renovated and decorated in period antiques, Oriental rugs, stained-glass windows, and original paintings. Guests enjoy the ambience of gracious living from the turn of the century. Original mantels and woodwork with modern amenities. Situated in Booklyn just two miles from Manhattan; one-half mile from the Brooklyn Museum and Botanic Gardens; two blocks from shopping and restaurants. Guests keep coming back to this charming Big Apple inn.

Host: Liana Paolella
Rooms: 6 (4 PB; 2 SB) $100-175
Full Breakfast
Credit Cards: A, B
Notes: 2, 5, 7 (limited), 8, 9, 14

Brooklyn Bed and Breakfast

128 Kent Street, 11222
(718) 383-3026

The "3 Bs" is a New York landmark historic 1867 brownstone, formerly the elegant home of one of New York's early shipping magnates. In the Greenpoint section along the East River, just minutes to the heart of Manhattan. It is here that some of the finest ships in the country were built, including the famed Monitor. Six bedrooms available with TV, air conditioning, and continental breakfast.

Host: Donald Kurz-Fiedeke
Rooms: 6 (2 PB; 4 SB) $65-80
Continental Breakfast
Credit Cards: None
Notes: 2, 5, 14

BUFFALO

Bryant House

236 Bryant Street, 14222
(716) 885-1540

Stay in a charming Victorian house, a pleasant and reasonable alternative to commercial accommodations. Five minutes to downtown and the Canadian border: convenient to theaters, boutiques, excellent restaurants, and Niagara Falls. A delicious continental breakfast is served in the formal dining room or on the multilevel deck, weather permitting. Brochure on request.

Hosts: John and June Nolan
Rooms: 3 (PB) $50-60
Continental Breakfast
Credit Cards: None
Notes: 2 (deposit only), 5, 8, 9, 14

Rainbow Hospitality B701

466 Amherst Street, 14207
(716) 874-8797; (800) 373-8797

This gracious 100-year-old Queen Anne Victorian mansion is minutes from Buffalo's downtown-in-renaissance and cultural events. Near colleges, a major hos-

NOTES: Credit cards accepted: A Master Card; B Visa; C American Express; D Discover Card; E Diner's Club; F Other; 2 Personal Checks accepted; 3 Lunch available; 4 Dinner available; 5 Open all year;

pital, Allentown antique shops, Elmwood Avenue restaurants and boutiques. Niagara Falls is only 20 minutes away. Your hosts offer four beautifully restored rooms, each representative of Buffalo's cultural history. Superb breakfast and pleasant surroundings.

Warnick's Village Bed and Breakfast

328 Wardman Road, 14217
(716) 875-5860

The hosts welcome you to their three-story wood-frame home on a residential tree-lined street just north of the city of Buffalo. Bedrooms are furnished with antiques, and fluffy robes are provided for your comfort. The home is situated just minutes from his-

Bryant House

torical Allentown, antique shops, Albright-Knox Art Gallery, the Buffalo waterfront, and many fine restaraunts. Wake up to the aroma of freshly ground coffee, locally made sausage, homemade muffins, and fresh fruit.

Hosts: Connie and Fred Warnick
Rooms: 2 (SB) $40
Full Breakfast
Credit Cards: None
Notes: 5, 7 (limited), 8, 9

BURDETT

The Red House Country Inn

Finger Lakes National Forest Picnic Area Road,
   14818
(607) 546-8566

The only residence within the 13,000-plus acre Finger Lake National Forest, with 28 miles of hiking and cross-country trails. Near Watkins Glen Gorge, wineries, swimming beach. The house is a restored 1840s farmstead with beautifully appointed rooms, a pool, and five acres of lawns and gardens. Large breakfast; guest kitchen. Goats and champion Samoyed dogs on the property.

Hosts: Joan Martin and Sandy Schmanke
Rooms: 5 (S4B) $60-85
Full Breakfast
Credit Cards: A, B, C, D
Closed Thanksgiving and Christmas
Notes: 2, 5, 8 (over 12), 9, 11, 13, 14

BURNT HILLS

The American Country Collection 114

4 Greenwood Lane, Delmar, 12054
(518) 439-7001

The oldest part of this home was built in 1796. The main house, a brick center-hall Colonial, was completed about 150 years ago. The home is surrounded by trees and old-fashioned flower gardens that abut a 12-acre apple orchard. Two guest rooms

6 Pets welcome; 7 Smoking allowed; 8 Children welcome; 9 Social drinking allowed; 10 Tennis available; 11 Swimming available; 12 Golf available; 13 Skiing available; 14 May be booked through travel agents.

with private baths. Smoking limited to sitting room and outdoors. Children school-age and over welcome. No pets in residence, but may accept guest pet (charge $10). $65; $80 during Jazz Festival and August racing.

CAMBRIDGE

The American Country Collection 010

4 Greenwood Lane, Delmar, 12054
(518) 439-7001

The main house dates from 1896-1903 and features stained-glass windows, ceiling murals, and an Otis brass cage elevator. The carriage house offers a variety of eight suites, each with one to three bedrooms, livingroom, refrigerator, color TV, and private bath. Smoking permitted. Children welcome. Playpen available; no crib. No pets. $55.

Maple Ridge Inn

Rural Delivery 1, Box 391C, 12816
(518) 677-3674

Grand large Victorian mansion furnished in fine antiques. All rooms have private baths. In country surroundings, twenty-five minutes from Saratoga Springs and ten from the Vermont border.

Host: Ken Riney
Rooms: 4 (PB) $75-495
Continental Breakfast
Credit Cards: None
Notes: 2, 4, 5, 8, 9, 10, 11, 12, 13, 14

CAMILLUS

The American Country Collection 168

4 Greenwood Lane, Delmar, 12054
(518) 439-7001

Italianate Colonial inn in a suburban/rural area, completely furnished with antiques and period pieces. Fully restored in 1980, there is also an attached full-service restaurant and pub serving lunch and dinner. Six rooms, all with private bath, air conditioning, and TV. Two of the rooms have a Jacuzzi. Continental breakfast. Children welcome. $60-99.

Maple Ridge Inn

CAMPBELL HALL

Tara Farm Bed and Breakfast

Rural Delivery 2, Box 290, 10916
(914) 294-6482

Tara Farm is a minifarm situated about 70 miles north of New York City in the Hudson Valley at the foot of the Catskill Mountains. It is operated by Fred and Meghan Hughes, who formerly were innkeepers in England. The farm consists of a menagerie of horses, dogs, cats, goats, ducks, geese, and hens. Pets and children are welcome. Nearby points of interest include West Point Military Academy, Sugarloaf craft village, the Hall of Fame of the Trotter.

Hosts: Fred and Meghan Hughes
Rooms: 2 (PB) $50-60
Full Breakfast
Credit Cards: None
Notes: 2, 3, 4, 5, 6, 7, 8, 9, 12, 13, 14

NOTES: Credit cards accepted: A Master Card; B Visa; C American Express; D Discover Card; E Diner's Club; F Other; 2 Personal Checks accepted; 3 Lunch available; 4 Dinner available; 5 Open all year;

CANAAN

Berkshire B&B Homes NY 4

P.O. Box 211, Williamsburg, MA, 01096
(413) 268-7244

An 1806 Federal-style home on one-half acre. Victorian and Federal furnishings. Parlor for guest use. Three double, two twin, and two single rooms with shared baths. Full breakfast. Children over five welcome. Animals in residence. Specified smoking area. $50-70.

Covered Bridge

P. O. Box 447, Norfolk, CT 06058
(203) 542-5944

This 1806 Federal Colonial set on more than three acres is on the National Register of Historic Places and has been an inn for 185 years. There is a sitting area with a TV and VCR, two dining rooms, where a full breakfast is served, and a large porch for guest use. Seven guest rooms with air conditioning and individual heat controls share three full baths. $65-85

CANANDAIGUA

The Acorn

4508 Route 64 South, Bristol Center, 14424
(716) 229-2834; (716) 398-9910

A 1795 stagecoach inn sensitively renovated to preserve the warmth and charm of yesteryear, furnished with 18th- and 19th-century antiques. The sound-proofed, centrally air-conditioned guest rooms feature canopy beds, luxury bedding and linens, comfortable sitting areas, and private baths. Relax before a cheery fire in the book-lined Common Room or in the seclusion of the private gardens. Warm hospitality, attention to guests' comfort, and a hearty country breakfast await the discerning traveler.

Hosts: Joan and Louis Clark
Rooms: 4 (PB) $75-125
Full Breakfast
Credit Cards: A, B
Notes: 2, 5, 6, 9, 11, 12, 13, 14

Nottingham Lodge Bed and Breakfast

5741 Bristol Valley Road, 14424
(716) 374-5355

Rural and mountainous, situated on Route 64 across from Bristol Mountain Ski Center. This English Tudor lodge has a common room two stories high, with balcony overlooking ski mountain, barnwood walls, and a cobblestone fireplace. Casual elegance. Three guest rooms with private baths; full breakfast. Ski packages are available. Bicycle tours available May through October.

Hosts: Bonnie and Bill Robinson
Rooms: 3 (1 PB; 2 SB) $55
Full Breakfast
Credit Cards: A, B, D
Notes: 2, 5, 8, 12, 13

Oliver Phelps Country Inn

252 North Main Street, 14424
(716) 396-1650

An historic bed and breakfast in the heart of beautiful Canandaigua. This Federal-style home built in the 1800s is decorated in country charm. Each guest room has a private bath. Guests are treated to a full breakfast featuring fresh-from-the-oven muffins, breads, and sticky buns.

Hosts: John and Joanne Sciarratta
Rooms: 4 (PB) $70-95
Full Breakfast
Credit Cards: A, B
Notes: 2, 5, 8 (6 and over), 9, 10, 11, 12, 13

CANDOR

Edge of Thyme Bed and Breakfast

6 Main Street, 13743
(607) 659-5155

6 Pets welcome; 7 Smoking allowed; 8 Children welcome; 9 Social drinking allowed; 10 Tennis available; 11 Swimming available; 12 Golf available; 13 Skiing available; 14 May be booked through travel agents.

Turn-of-the-century Georgian house with antiques, porch with leaded-glass windows, comfortable atmosphere, and outdoor gardens with pergola. Central to the Finger Lakes, Cornell University, Ithaca College, Watkins Glen, wineries, and Corning Glass.

Hosts: Eva Mae and Frank Musgrave
Rooms: 7 (2 PB; 5 SB) $50-70
Full Breakfast
Credit Cards: A, B
Notes: 2, 5, 8, 9, 12, 13 (XC), 14

CAZENOVIA

The American Country Collection 162

4 Greenwood Lane, Delmar, 12054
(518) 439-7001

Peaceful, quiet retreat directly on the shore of Lake Cazenovia. Unique, modern home furnished with antiques and collectibles from owner's world travels. Large livingroom with fireplace. Swimming at lake shore and rowboat available. First-floor room with queen bed, private deck and bath. On second floor, one room with a queen bed and private bath, and one room with a single bed and shared bath. Continental breakfast in dining room or on outside patio. Smoking permitted. Handicapped access. Children are welcome. One dog in residence. $50-80.

Brae Loch Inn

5 Albany Street, US Route 20, 13035
(315) 655-3431

The twelve quiet rooms in this inn are on the second floor of the Brae Loch. They feature the old-time charm of antiques, classic luxury of Stickley furniture, and the modern comfort of some king-size beds in selected rooms. All rooms have private baths, and these rooms are so handsome and so reasonably priced you'll want to visit over and over again.

Hosts: J im and Val Barr
Rooms: 15 (13 PB; 2 SB) $75-125
Continental Breakfast
Credit Cards: A, B, C
Notes: 2, 4, 5, 7, 8, 9, 10, 11, 12, 13, 14

Elaine's Bed and Breakfast Reservation Service

4987 Kingston Road, Elbridge, 13060
(315) 689-2082

In the country near Cazenovia, this Greek Revival farmhouse offers a two-bedroom apartment with a private bath, and a master bedroom in the main house with a queen-size waterbed. Two-night minimum. Breakfast is served in the main dining room.

Heart of Cazenovia

111 Lincklaen Street, 13035
(315) 655-8661

Nestled in Cazenovia on a quiet tree-lined street just three blocks from unique shops, country inns, restaurants, and scenic Cazenovia's Lake Lorenzo's historical mansion. This stately 1888 Victorian home offers three guest rooms with private baths, private dining, and private livingroom for a quiet, relaxing atmosphere.

Host: Catherine Crosby
Rooms: 3 (SB) $60-80
Full Breakfast
Credit Cards: None
Notes: 2, 6, 8

CHAPPAQUA

Crabtree's Kittle House

11 Kittle Road, 10514
(914) 666-8044

Built in 1790, Crabtree's Kittle House maintains a distinctive blend of country-style and comfort. Only 20 miles from New York City, the inn is also a comfortable base from which to explore Van Cortlandt and Philipsburg manors, Sunnyside, and

Pocantico Hills. Not to be missed are the dinner specialties of the house, including roasted baby pheasant, fillet of red snapper with mint and basil, and an award-winning wine list. Live jazz and dancing Thursday through Saturday.

Hosts: John and Dick Crabtree
Rooms: 11, $75-85
Continental Breakfast
Credit Cards: A, B, C, D, E, F
Notes: 2, 3, 4, 5, 7, 8, 9

CHARLTON

The American Country Collection 087

4 Greenwood Lane, Delmar, 12054
(518) 439-7001

A sense of history prevails throughout this pre-Revolutionary War estate set on 100 acres just a few miles west of Saratoga. One guest room on the first floor has wide-plank pine walls, built-in bookcases, cannonball bed, and comfortable sitting area. A second-floor master suite has a canopy bed and adjacent nursery. Both rooms have private bath. Children welcome. Smoking permitted. $65; $85 Jazz Festival, July-Labor Day.

CHAUTAUQUA LAKE—GREENHURST

Plumbush

Route 33, P. O. Box 864, Chatauqua, 14722
(716) 789-5309

Newly restored, circa 1865, Italian villa one a hilltop surrounded by 125 acres. Just one mile from Chautauqua Institution. Bluebirds and wildlife abound. Bicycles available; cross-country ski trail. Sunny rooms, wicker, antiques, and a touch of elegant charm. As seen in *Victorian Homes,* Summer 1991, *Innsider* magazine, May/June 1990 and *Victoria* magazine, August 1989.

Hosts: George and Sandy Green
Rooms: 4 (PB) $70-85
Expanded Continental Breakfast
Credit Cards: A, B

CHERRY PLAIN

Berkshire B&B Homes NY 3

P. O. Box 211, Williamsburg, MA, 01096
(413) 268-7244

A 1790 Federal-style home surrounded by acres of woodlands and ponds. Swimming pond, trout stream, and hiking on ten acres. Both full breakfast and gourmet dinner served. Three double bedrooms with private baths. No smoking. Children over nine welcome. Animals in residence. $110.

Covered Bridge 1CPNY

P. O. Box 447 A, Norfolk, CT, 06058
(203) 542-5944

This 1790 Colonial, nestled in the New York Berkshires, is secluded yet minutes from Tanglewood and summer theaters. Hiking trails, cross-country skiing, and a pond for fishing and skating are available on the grounds. Enjoy a full breakfast and dinner, both made with natural foods. The four guest rooms, two with antique canopy beds, have private baths. The rate, including dinner, is $110.

CHESTERTOWN

The Balsam House

Friends Lake, 12817
(518) 494-2828; (518) 494-4431

A Victorian nestled in the Adirondacks, this home offers twenty spacious guest rooms that are appointed with antiques, wicker, Oriental carpets, a spiral staircase in the honeymoon suite, and private baths for complete comfort. The "wine spectator" wine list complements an award-winning

6 Pets welcome; 7 Smoking allowed; 8 Children welcome; 9 Social drinking allowed; 10 Tennis available; 11 Swimming available; 12 Golf available; 13 Skiing available; 14 May be booked through travel agents.

French country cuisine dining room known as Le Papillon; the 1892 Grill is true Adirondack dining with a cherished view. The inn's beach also has canoes, paddleboats, motorized fishing boats, a gazebo, docks, and a screened-in bungalow. Mountain bikes, bountiful trails, skiing, and warm hospitality are what you'll find when you stay here.

Hosts: Bruce Robbins, Jr., and Helen Edmark
Rooms: 20 (PB) $65-105
Continental and Full Breakfast
Credit Cards: A, B, C, E, F
Notes: 2, 3, 4, 5, 7, 8, 9, 10, 11, 12, 13, 14

Friends Lake Inn

Friends Lake Road, 12817
(518) 494-4751

Situated in the Adirondacks, overlooking Friends Lake, the fully restored 18th-century inn is 20 minutes north of Lake George, with Gore Mountain Ski Center only 15 minutes away. Breakfast and gourmet dinner are served daily accompanied by an award-winning wine list. Mountain bike, swimming, hiking, and cross-country skiing facilities are on the inn's beautiful grounds.

Hosts: Sharon and Greg Taylor
Rooms: 10 (PB) $65-160
Full Breakfast
Credit Cards: A, B
Notes: 2, 4, 5, 7, 8, 9, 10, 11, 12, 13, 14

CHICHESTER

Maplewood Bed and Breakfast

c/o Nancy Parsons
6 Park Road, 12416
(914) 688-5433

A lovely Colonial home in the heart of the Catskill Mountains, 12 miles from Hunter or Belleayre Mountain for skiing; close to fishing, tubing, antiquing, and hiking; 20 minutes to Woodstock. Single, double canopy, queen, and king bedrooms share

two bathrooms. Each room has a different view of the mountains. Beautiful porch, gardens, and in-ground pool. A full breakfast.

Hosts: Nancy and Albert Parsons
Rooms: 4 (S2B) $55
Full Breakfast
Credit Cards: None
Notes: 2, 5, 8, 10, 11, 12, 13

CLARKSVILLE

The American Country Collection 008

4 Greenwood Lane, Delmar, 12054
(518) 439-7001

Dream away in your canopy bed in this antique-filled, historic 1760 Dutch farmhouse just 15 miles from downtown Albany. Take a walk on the wooded ten acres that include two streams and an old graveyard begun in 1806. The second floor contains one two-bedroom suite with a wood-burning stove and air conditioning. Summer guests can use the in-ground swimming pool. Smoking permitted in common rooms only. Children welcome, but children under eight are restricted from pool area. $60.

CLEVELAND

Elaine's Bed and Breakfast and Inn Reservation Service

4987 Kingston Road, Elbridge, 13060
(315) 689-2082

On the north shore of Oneida Lake, you will find this circa 1820 white Colonial built by an early industrial baron. It has 6,000 square feet of living space. An open porch welcomes you with antique wicker and a hammock. From the wide center hall, there is a large playroom with billiard table, jukebox, many musical instruments, and the owner's collection of prizes from showing his many antique automobiles. The family room features a large TV, stereo, and beautiful stained-glass leaded window behind the bar. All rooms have working fireplaces and private baths. There is a formal livingroom full of antiques, a large cheery dining room with a player piano and more than 1,000 rolls. As this is a musical inn, there is an organ and a nickelodeon. No pets. No smoking. No children under 16. $50-75.

COLDEN

Back of the Beyond

7233 Lower East Hill Road, 14033
(716) 652-0427

A charming country miniestate situated in the Boston Hills and ski area of western New York; 25 miles from Buffalo and 50 from Niagara Falls. Accommodations are a separate chalet with three bedrooms, one and one-half baths, fully furnished kitchen, dining/livingroom, piano, pool table, and fireplace. Stroll through the organic herb, flower, and vegetable gardens; swim in the pond; or hike the woods. Cross-country ski trails on the premises; commercial downhill slopes are only one mile away.

Hosts: Bill and Shash Georgi
Rooms: 3 (S1.5B) $60
Full Breakfast
Credit Cards: None
Notes: 2, 5, 8, 9, 10, 11, 12, 13, 14

COLD SPRING

Hudson House

2 Main Street, 10516
(914) 265-9355

Hudson House, a lovely country inn built in 1832, has all the warmth and charm of times past. Situated on the banks of the historic Hudson River, it is conveniently situated just 50 miles north of New York City. Its 13 quaintly decorated rooms, all with private bath, provide a tranquil respite for guests. A continental menu featuring superbly prepared seasonal American foods complements the Hudson House experience. A sumptuous buffet brunch is served every Sunday from 11:20 A.M. until 3:00 P.M.

Hosts: Robert Contiguglia and Kathleen Dennison
Rooms: 13 (PB) $70-200
Continental Breakfast Weekdays; Full Breakfast Weekends
Credit Cards: A, B, C, D
Notes: 2, 3, 4, 5, 6, 7, 8, 9, 12, 14

CONSTANTIA

Elaine's Bed and Breakfast Reservation Service

4987 Kingston Road, Elbridge, 13060
(315) 689-2082

Large, cozy, and warm farmhouse overlooks Oneida Lake. Three guest rooms and bath upstairs, and two rooms with a bath downstairs. Next to restaurant. All freshly remodeled and cheery.

COOPERSTOWN

The American Country Collection 014

4 Greenwood Lane, Delmar, 12054
(518) 439-7001

This Victorian cottage and restored barn are situated on 14 acres of meadows and hills. The barn features three first-floor rooms with private baths. The house has a two-bedroom suite and guest bath on the second floor. Wicker, timeless antiques, old photos, ceiling fans, and green plants tie each room to the past. Guests are welcome to sit by the fire in the common room. Children welcome. Smoking outdoors only. Two-night minimum on weekends, holidays, major festival activities. $75.

The American Country Collection 128

4 Greenwood Lane, Delmar, 12054
(518) 439-7001

Enjoy this rural farmhouse set on 7.5 acres just outside of historic Cooperstown. Surrounded by a pond, sugar bush, hills and meadows, this inn offers travelers a parlor room for relaxing or reading, an air-conditioned breakfast room, and an adjoining room with TV. Three bedrooms are available for guests. One room has a private bath, and the other two rooms share a full hall bath. Smoking outdoors only. Full country breakfast. Children over five welcome. Resident cat. $45-55.

Ängelholm

14 Elm Street, Box 705, 13326
(607) 547-2483; FAX (607) 547-2309

Leave your cars and care behind and wander the lovely streets, parks, museums, and shops of Cooperstown's historic homes. Only a four-minute walk to Main Street and the Baseball Hall of Fame. A hearty continental breakfast is served in the formal dining room and is a marvelous way to start a happy day of exploring the Leatherstocking Country, which is rich in history, scenic drives, recreation, antiques shops, and colleges.

Hosts: Jan and Fred Reynolds
Rooms: 4 (2 PB; 2 SB) $70-90
Full Breakfast
Credit Cards: A, B
Notes: 2, 5, 8, 9, 10, 11, 12

Creekside Bed and Breakfast

Rural Delivery 1, Box 206, 13326
(607) 547-8203

"A personal favorite," wrote American Express's *Travel & Leisure*. This nationally renowned bed and breakfast offers beautiful surroundings in an elegant atmosphere. Its elegant Colonial features, bridal chamber, honeymoon cottage, and penthouse suite are ideal for honeymooners, reunions, or romantic escapes. Hosts are founders of and performers with Glimmerglass Opera. Four guest rooms all have queen-size beds, private bath, TV/HBO. Five minutes to Baseball Hall of Fame.

Hosts: Gwen and Fred Ermlich
Rooms: 4 (PB) $65-99
Full Breakfast
Credit Cards: A, B, C
Notes: 2, 5, 8, 9, 10, 11, 12, 13, 14

The Inn at Brook Willow

Rural Delivery 2, Box 514, 13326
(607) 547-9700

An 1885 Victorian country home on 14 acres with a fine collection of antiques in the main house and three guest rooms in the "reborn barn." Fresh fruit, garden flowers, and a bountiful breakfast await each guest. Two fireplaces, fields, and meadows relax the traveler. Five minutes to the Baseball Hall of Fame and Otsego Lake.

Hosts: Joan and Jack Grimes
Rooms: (PB) $55-75 (single rate upon request)
Minimum stay weekends and holidays: 2 nights
Full Breakfast
Credit Cards: None
Notes: 2, 5, 8, 9, 10, 11, 12, 13

The Inn at Cooperstown

16 Chestnut Street, 13326
(607) 547-5756

The Inn at Cooperstown, built in 1874, continues to provide genuine hospitality within walking distance of all of Cooperstown's attractions. The 17 guest rooms, each with private bath, are simply decorated with the guests' well-being in mind. Enjoy the comfortable beds and the large, thirsty towels. Relax in a rocking chair on the sweeping veranda shaded by 100-year-old maples or in front of the cozy fireplace in the sitting room. Off-street parking is available.

NOTES: Credit cards accepted: A Master Card; B Visa; C American Express; D Discover Card; E Diner's Club; F Other; 2 Personal Checks accepted; 3 Lunch available; 4 Dinner available; 5 Open all year;

Host: Michael Jerome
Rooms: 17 (PB) $80-95
Continental Breakfast
Credit Cards: A, B, C, D, E
Notes: 2, 5, 9, 14

Serendipity Bed and Breakfast

Rural Route 2, Box 1050, 13326
(607) 547-2106

Serendipity is a contemporary home, designed by a student of Frank Lloyd Wright, that offers a friendly, casual atmosphere, and panoramic views of Otsego Lake in a quiet, serene setting with your own private entrance and deck. Rates include queen-size bed and a low-cholesterol breakfast, while you enjoy the romantic, natural beauty of the surrounding woods and lake.

Host: Vera A. Talevi
Room: 1 (PB) $75-95
Low Cholesterol Breakfast
Credit Cards: None
Notes: 2, 9, 11, 12

The Inn at Cooperstown

CORINTH

The American Country Collection #151

4 Greenwood Lane, Delmar, 12054
(518) 439-7001

You are graciously invited to share a most unusual country inn at the gateway to the Adiriondacks, only minutes away from the villages of Saratoga Springs, Lake George, and Lake Luzerne. Five rooms, all with private baths, and an access ramp for handicapped guests is available. Saratoga, the racetracks, Skidmore College, and SPAC are all within an easy drive. Breakfast features a fresh fruit platter, juice selection, muffins with jam, Belgian waffles with cinnamon apples or strawberry blend, coffee and tea. $50-99.

CORNING

DeLevan House

188 DeLevan Avenue, 14830
(607) 962-2347

Southern Colonial with homelike hospitality. Overlooking Corning. Quiet surroundings, outstanding accommodations, complimentary cool drink served on the beautiful screened porch. Free pick-up from and delivery to airport.

Host: Mary M. DePumpo
Rooms: 3 (1 PB; 2 SB) $70.85-81.75
Full Breakfast
Credit Cards: None
Notes: 2, 5, 7, 8 (over 12), 9, 11, 12

1865 White Birch Bed and Breakfast

69 East First Street, 14830
(607) 962-6355

Imagine a friendly, warm atmosphere in an 1865 Victorian setting. Cozy rooms await guests; both private and shared baths. Awake to the tantalizing aromas of a full home-baked breakfast. Walk to museums, historic Market Street, and the Corning Glass Center. Experience it all at the White Birch.

Hosts: Kathy and Joe Donahue
Rooms: 4 (2 PB; 2 SB) $50-85

6 Pets welcome; 7 Smoking allowed; 8 Children welcome; 9 Social drinking allowed; 10 Tennis available; 11 Swimming available; 12 Golf available; 13 Skiing available; 14 May be booked through travel agents.

Full Breakfast
Credit Cards: A, B, C (deposit)
Notes: 2, 5, 7 (limited), 8, 9, 12, 13 (XC)

CROTON-ON-HUDSON

Alexander Hamilton House

49 Van Wyck Street, 10520
(914) 271-6737

An 1889 Victorian home overlooking the
Hudson with in-ground pool and antique
furniture. Four rooms share two baths. The
first-floor suite has queen bed, private bath,
and sitting room with fireplace. The Bridal
Chamber has king bed, fireplace, private
bath with Jacuzzi, and skylights. An executive apartment with private bath, full
kitchen, and private entrance is also available. Convenient to West Point and White
Plains (12 miles) and New York City (30
miles).

Host: Barbara Notarius
Rooms: 7 (3 PB; 4 SB) $65-250
Full Breakfast
Credit Cards: A, B, C
Notes: 2, 5, 8, 9, 11, 14

The American Country Collection 157

4 Greenwood Lane, Delmar, 12054
(518) 439-7001

Perfect for vacations, business travel, and
romantic getaways, this stately Victorian
home, circa 1889, is nestled on a cliff
above the Hudson River, only a short walk
from the picturesque village of Croton-on-
Hudson. Luxurious without being ornate,
this bed and breakfast offers two suites,
each with a private bath and fireplace, four
rooms on the second floor that share two
hall baths, and a third-floor suite with a
whirlpool. Breakfast offers juice, deep-dish
pancakes, stuffed French toast or eggs, coffee, or tea. Smoking outside only. Train
station is within close proximity. Children
welcome. Resident dog. $65-250.

CROWN POINT

The American Country Collection 095

4 Greenwood Lane, Delmar, 12054
(518) 370-4948

It took three years for a team of Italian
craftsmen to complete this 18-room
Victorian mansion, circa 1887, situated on
five and one-half acres in the center of this
small town. Carved woodwork, doors, and
stair railing from oak, cherry, mahogany,
and walnut grace the home. Two of the five
guest rooms have private baths. In winter,
breakfast is served in front of the fireplace
in the dining room. Fort Ticonderoga and
Fort Crown Point are nearby. Children welcome. $45-90.

DE BRUCE

De Bruce Country Inn on the Willowemoc

De Bruce Road, 12758
(914) 439-3900

In a spectacular 1,000-acre natural setting
within the Catskill forests overlooking the
Willowemoc trout stream, the inn offers
turn-of-the-century charm and hospitality.
Terrace dining, wooded trails, wildlife,
pool, sauna, fitness and health center, fresh
air, and mountain water.

Hosts: Ron and Marilyn
Rooms: 15 (PB) from $70/person
Full Breakfast and Dinner
Credit Cards: C
December 15-April 1 by special arrangement
Notes: 2 (deposit only), 4, 6 (call), 7, 8, 9, 10, 11, 12, 13

DELMAR

The American Country Colletion 166

4 Greenwood Lane, 12054
(518) 439-7001

NOTES: Credit cards accepted: A Master Card; B Visa; C American Express; D Discover Card; E Diner's
Club; F Other; 2 Personal Checks accepted; 3 Lunch available; 4 Dinner available; 5 Open all year;

Completely restored 1800s farmhouse and barn on three tree-shaded acres. Decorated in a country motif and appointed with solid cherry furnishings. Four rooms with queen, double, or single beds. Shared bath. Full breakfast. Children welcome. Resident barn cat. Smoking in common rooms. $40-50.

DEPOSIT

The White Pillars Inn

82 Second Street, 13754
(607) 467-4191

The White Pillars Inn is "the perfect place to do nothing at all. . .but eat." For breakfast, try the French Toast Sampler, a baked apple in pastry served in a warm caramel sauce, or any one of seven overstuffed omelettes. Dining is truly an experience, with seafood and decadent desserts being the specialty. Magnificent floral arrangements, soothing sounds of soft jazz, and a bottomless cookie jar are just a few of the unexpected pleasures you'll find. The lavishly furnished inn evokes romance and privacy and kick-off-your-shoes relaxation amid elegant surroundings.

Host: Ms. Najla R. Aswad
Rooms: 5 (3 PB; 2 SB) $65-110
Full Breakfast
Credit Cards: A, B, C, D, E, F
Notes: 2, 3, 4, 5, 8, 9, 10, 11, 12, 13, 14

The White Pillars Inn

DEWITT

Elaine's Bed and Breakfast Reservation Service 1

4987 Kingston Road, Elbridge, 13060
(315) 689-2082

Near Shoppington, this fine, older Colonial is warmly furnished with some antiques. A large front guest room has an antique double bed, and a den with a sofa sleeper is available if neccessary for family.

Elaine's Bed and Breakfast Reservation Service 2

4987 Kingston Road, Elbridge, 13060
(315) 689-2082

This three-year-old two-story contemporary is in a great area of newer homes. A guest room has a super-firm bed, TV, and phone. A second room is available if necessary. Air conditioned.

Elaine's Bed and Breakfast Reservation Service-3

4987 Kingston Road, Elbridge, 13060
(315) 689-2082

This executive Colonial is only two miles from Syracuse University. Two nice guest rooms with one double bed each. Trundle bed available also.

DOLGEVILLE

Adrianna Bed and Breakfast

44 Stewart Street, 13329
(315) 429-3249

Adrianna is situated just off the New York Thruway at Exit 29A, amid glorious views of the Adirondack foothills. Just a short ride to Cooperstown, Saratoga, Syracuse, and Utica areas. A most cozy and hospitable bed and breakfast.

6 Pets welcome; 7 Smoking allowed; 8 Children welcome; 9 Social drinking allowed; 10 Tennis available; 11 Swimming available; 12 Golf available; 13 Skiing available; 14 May be booked through travel agents.

Host: Adrianna Naizby
Rooms: 3 (1 PB; 2 SB) $50
Full Breakfast
Minimum stay weekends and holidays: 2 nights
Credit Cards: A, B
Closed Christmas Eve & Day
Notes: 2, 5, 7, 13

Covered Bridge 1DPNY

P. O. Box 447 A, Norfolk, CT, 06058
(203) 542-5944

Genuine old farmhouse with a large sitting porch on which to relax and admire the views of the Connecticut hills. Enjoy a full farm breakfast in the sunny dining room or on the porch. Four beautifully appointed guest rooms, one with private bath, are decorated with the owner's collection of antique linens. There are three doubles and one room with twin beds. There is also a pool for guests to enjoy. $65-95.

DOVER

Nutmeg B&B Agency 311

P. O. Box 1117, West Hartford, CT 06107
(203) 236-6698

Tucked just over the border from Kent, Connecticut, is this charming "Eyebrow" Colonial built in 1850. Guests can use the livingroom with TV, warm up by the wood-burning stove, lounge on the large front porch complete with wicker furniture, and enjoy the pool. All four guest rooms are on the second floor. Three rooms share a bath. The room with a private bath has a handsome double sleigh bed. All rooms have spectacular views of the surrounding countryside, a foliage lover's delight. Full breakfast. Children welcome. Pets in residence.

DOVER PLAINS

The Mill Farm Inn

66 Cricket Hill Road, 12522
(914) 832-9198

This 1850 rambling Colonial makes you feel a welcomed guest. Enjoy panoramic views from the large sitting porch. The home is decorated with antique furniture and linens. The setting is real country, yet only one and one-half hours north of New York City near the Connecticut line. Married couples only, please.

Host: Margery Mill
Rooms: 4 (1 PB; 3 SB) $50-90
Full Breakfast
Closed Feb. and Mar.
Credit Cards: None
Notes:2, 9, 10, 11, 12, 13

DOWNSVILLE

Adams' Antique Farm House B&B and Store

Upper Main Street, P. O. Box 18, 13755
(607) 363-2757

A 100-year-old farmhouse on an acre of land with babbling brook and giant maple trees in the Catskill Mountains. Full of antiques and beautifully decorated; gourmet breakfasts (crepes and omelettes); homemade muffins and brownies; afternoon sweets and evening drink. Lots of things to do in the area: fishing, hunting, canoeing, swimming, antiquing, or just sitting on the front porch.

Hosts: Harry and Nancy Adams
Rooms: 3 (1 PB; 2 SB) $50
Full Breakfast
Credit Cards: None
Notes: 2, 3, 4, 11, 12, 14

DRYDEN

Serendipity Bed and Breakfast

15 North Street (Route 13), P. O. Box 29, 13053
(607) 844-9589; FAX (607) 844-8311

An 1834 village home, cheerfully furnished with antiques, brass queen beds, stained-glass windows. A full country breakfast

NOTES: Credit cards accepted: A Master Card; B Visa; C American Express; D Discover Card; E Diner's Club; F Other; 2 Personal Checks accepted; 3 Lunch available; 4 Dinner available; 5 Open all year;

starts your day. Afternoon and evening snacks, as well as amenities for the bath, complement the hospitality. Near Ithaca College, Cornell University, and Greek Peak ski area in the heart of the Finger Lakes. Corporate/midweek discounts apply.

Host: Kaaren W. Hoback
Rooms: 3 (S2B) $65-85
Full Breakfast
Credit Cards: A, B, D, F
Notes: 2, 3, 4, 5, 7, 8, 9, 10, 11, 12, 13, 14

Margaret Thacher's Spruce Haven Bed and Breakfast

9 James Street, Box 119, 13053
(607) 844-8052

This log home surrounded by tall spruce trees gives you the feeling of being in the woods while you enjoy the advantages of the village. On a quiet street, this warm and friendly home is within 12 miles of Ithaca, Cortland, lakes, golf, skiing, colleges, museums. Restaurants nearby. One night's deposit holds reservations.

Host: Margaret Thatcher Brownell
Rooms: 2 (SB) prices on request
Full Breakfast
Credit Cards: None
Notes: 2, 5, 8, 10, 11, 12, 13

Sarah's Dream

49 West Main Street, 13053
(607) 844-4321

A place to be coddled. On the National Register of Historic Places, this 1828 homestead, furnished with antiques, is subtly elegant without being pretentious. The beds and breakfasts will make you sigh. Convenient to Ithaca, Cornell, wineries, and the Finger Lakes. All rooms are air-conditioned; one with a fireplace.

Hosts: Judi Williams and Ken Morusty
Rooms: 4 (PB) $40-85
Suites: 2 (SB)
Full Breakfast
Credit Cards: A, B, C, D, E
Notes: 2, 5, 8 (over 10), 9, 10, 11, 12, 13, 14

DURHAMVILLE

The American Country Collection 166

4 Greenwood Lane, Delmar, 12054
(518) 439-7001

Completely restored 1800s farmhouse and barn on three tree-shaded acres. Decorated in a country motif and furnished with solid cherry furnishings. Four rooms with queen, double, or single beds and shared baths. Full breakfast; children welcome. Resident barn cat. Smoking in common rooms. $40-50.

Elaine's Bed and Breakfast and Inn Reservation Service

4987 Kingston Road, Elbridge, 13060
(315) 689-2082

This stately old farm Colonial sits on its own quiet three acres in the country yet has easy access to all activities in the Oneida Valley: Sylvan Beach, Verona Beach, fishing, boating, Vernon Downs, antique shops on Route 20, historic Fort Stanwix in Rome, Charlestown outlet shopping in Utica, and several nearby colleges. The interior is brand-new and carpeted throughout. Four guest rooms share two full baths and have individual heat control. TV/VCR in livingroom. Check in is after 5:00 P.M. during the week as owner works in Rome. Mastercard and Visa. Children under five free. $45-65.

EAST AURORA

Rainbow Hospitality EA789

466 Amherst Street, Buffalo, 14207
(716) 874-8797

Rural splendor awaits you in this spacious contemporary situated on more than 100 acres with trails, creek, in-ground pool, and

6 Pets welcome; 7 Smoking allowed; 8 Children welcome; 9 Social drinking allowed; 10 Tennis available; 11 Swimming available; 12 Golf available; 13 Skiing available; 14 May be booked through travel agents.

relaxation. Three spacious rooms include a master suite with private Jacuzzi. Vivacious hosts have built their custom home to capture the quiet ambience of lush, green countryside combined with city-side convenience. Minutes from the quaint village of East Aurora, 20 minutes from downtown Buffalo, and 50 minutes from Niagara Falls. $50-125.

EAST HAMPTON

Mill House Inn

33 North Main Street, 11937
(516) 324-9766

A 1790 Colonial situated in "America's most beautiful village." Open all year so you can enjoy lemonade while overlooking the Old Hook windmill or a restful nap in the back yard hammock. In the off-season, enjoy hot cider by the fireplace or a brisk walk to the beach.

Hosts: Barbara and Kevin Flynn
Rooms: 8 (6 PB; 2 SB) $75-155
Full Breakfast
Credit Cards: A, B, C
Notes: 2, 5, 8 (over 11), 10, 11, 12

EDMESTON

Elaine's Bed and Breakfast Reservation Service

4987 Kingston Road, Elbridge, 13060
(315) 689-2082

Six varied guest rooms, two baths, above a fine restaurant. Great location in a tiny village.

ELIZABETHTOWN

The American Country Collection 072

4 Greenwood Lane, Delmar, 12054
(518) 439-7001

This bed and breakfast, circa 1775, was a sawmill, a "dine and dance," a resident summer art school and home of Wayman Adams, and since 1972, a summer residence for student classical musicians. It is situated on two and one-half acres bordered on two sides by the Bouquet River, a favorite fishing and swimming hole for the locals. Five guest rooms available, some with private bath. In summer, breakfast is served on the covered stone patio that overlooks the grounds. Small cottages also available. Well-behaved children welcome. Resident pets. $66-78.

ELLICOTTVILLE

Ilex Inn

P. O. Box 1585, 6416 East Washington Street, 14731
(716) 699-2002

An old, completely remodeled and restored Victorian with a full porch and period decor. A livingroom with movies, an upper livingroom with games and reading, and snacks served at night are touches that make your stay pleasant. A full buffet breakfast is served in the morning, and a gift shop is on premises. Golf packages, skiing packages, and free passes to the local fitness center.

Hosts: John and Bonnie Cady
Rooms: 5 (PB) $75-125
Full Breakfast
Credit Cards: A, B
Notes: 2, 5, 8, 9, 10, 11, 12, 13, 14

FAIR HAVEN

Brown's Village Inn Bed and Breakfast

Box 378, Stafford Street, 13064
(315) 947-5817

Traveling the Seaway Trail? For old-fashioned hospitality and a warm welcome, stop by and enjoy quality accommodations

NOTES: Credit cards accepted: A Master Card; B Visa; C American Express; D Discover Card; E Diner's Club; F Other; 2 Personal Checks accepted; 3 Lunch available; 4 Dinner available; 5 Open all year;

in a quiet and relaxing atmosphere. Minutes to shops, restaurants, and beach. Guest cottage and antique shop on premises.

Host: Sally Brown
Rooms: 5 (1 PB; 4 SB) $50-65
Continental Breakfast
Credit Cards: A, B, D
Notes: 2, 5, 8, 9, 14

FAYETTEVILLE

Elaine's Bed and Breakfast Reservation Service

4987 Kingston Road, Elbridge, 13060
(315) 689-2082

Executive Cape has a lovely guest room and private bath on the first floor with a queen-size bed. Double room upstairs shares a bath with the hostess.

FINGER LAKES

Conesus Lake Bed and Breakfast

2388 East Lake Road, 14435
(716) 346-6526

Situated lakeside on beautiful Conesus Lake. Relaxing atmosphere includes large private dock; picnic facilities; and free use of canoe, paddleboat, rowboat, and overnight docking with mooring whips. Each attractive bedroom has cable TV and private balcony. Two bathrooms available, one with double whirlpool tub. Near Excellent restaurants. Weekly discount. Reservations suggested.

Hosts: Dale and Virginia Esse
Rooms: 2 (SB) $60
Full Breakfast
Credit Cards: A, B, D
Notes: 2, 5, 9, 11, 12

FLEISCHMANNS

The American Country Collection 161

4 Greenwood Lane, Delmar, 12054
(518) 439-7001

The inn, a sports enthusiast's delight, is in the high peaks of the Catskill Mountains. Eight rooms, five with private baths and three that share a bath, are available. Private efficiency cottages are also available. Breakfast consists of juice, fruit in season, eggs Florentine or Dutch pancakes, cinnamon muffins, and coffee or tea. $65-85.

FORESTBURGH

Inn at Lake Joseph

400 St. Joseph Road, 12777
(914) 791-9506

A quiet, secluded 125-year-old Queen Anne mansion surrounded by 2,000 acres of wildlife preserve and forest, with a 250-acre private lake. Once the vacation estate of Cardinals Hayes and Spellman, the house now offers swimming, boating, fishing, tennis, cross-country skiing, and more on the premises. Both breakfast and dinner are included in the daily rate.

Host: Ivan Weinger
Rooms: 9 (PB) $108-198
Full Breakfast and Dinner
Credit Cards: A, B, C
Notes: 2, 3, 4, 5, 7, 8, 9, 10, 11, 12, 13, 14

FOSTERDALE

Fosterdale Heights House

205 Mueller Road, 12726
(914) 482-3369

Historic 1840 bed and breakfast on a Catskill mountaintop overlooks the scenic

6 Pets welcome; 7 Smoking allowed; 8 Children welcome; 9 Social drinking allowed; 10 Tennis available; 11 Swimming available; 12 Golf available; 13 Skiing available; 14 May be booked through travel agents.

Delaware River Valley. A Victorian parlor with a grand piano, billiards, library, 20 acres of grounds, a pond, and a Christmas tree farm are surrounded by woodland. Canoeing and horseback riding are nearby, and a bountiful country breakfast is served each morning. Make new friends, or just relax alone together. A cool mountain breeze in the summer, exquisite fall foliage, warm and cozy by the stove in winter, and the mountain mist in the spring truly makes this a bed and breakfast for all seasons. Minimum stay: 2 nights.

Host: Roy Singer
Rooms: 12 (3 PB; 9 SB) $52-103
Full Breakfast
Credit Cards: A, B
Notes: 2, 4, 5, 7, 9, 10, 11, 12, 13

GALWAY

The American Country Collection 049

4 Greenwood Lane, Delmar, 12054
(518) 439-7001

This was a stagecoach stop and tavern run by General E. Stimpson in the late 1700s. Local tradition indicates that it was a stopover for Generals George Washington and Lafayette. In the 1960s, it housed famous and wealthy visitors to Saratoga Springs. This center-hall Colonial is situated on three acres of tree-shaded lawns. The three guest rooms have private baths and Colonial decor, including some four-poster beds, comfortable chairs, and fresh flowers. Guests may use the in-ground pool. Smoking permitted in common areas only. Well-behaved children welcome. Pets in residence. $55 Nov.-May; $75 pool season; $95 Jazz Festival and Saratoga racing season (Aug.). A fully furnished cottage with bed loft, TV, wood-burning stove, and kitchen is available for weekly and monthly rental.

The American Country Collection 150

4 Greenwood Lane, Delmar, 12054
(518) 439-7001

Come and enjoy the gracious hospitality of your host and hostess in this traditional Irish farmhouse set on a high knoll with views of both the Adirondack Mountains and the Green Mountains of Vermont. Two air-conditioned guest rooms can be booked individually or as a family suite. One room is furnished with a Shaker four-poster bed, cherry dresser, antique rocker and fold-out sofa bed, and the second room has a brass bed, antique oak dresser, and easy chair. Breakfast is served when the guest wishes, children are welcome, and a crib and baby-sitting are available. $50-90, seasonal.

GASPORT

Rainbow Hospitality G200

466 Amherst Street, Buffalo, 14207
(716) 874-8797

Charming, intimate country cottage nestled in Niagara's fruit belt. Furnished with antiques, this Cape Cod embraces a comfortable-style and timeless good taste. Convenient to Lockport, Olcott, Niagara Falls, and Buffalo. You'll feel right at home with your friendly proprietress, a traveled professional and an award-winning kite maker. A country breakfast featuring freshly baked scones and seasonal fruits will be served on the spacious deck or family dining room. Double or twin accommodations available. $50.

GENEVA

Elaine's Bed and Breakfast and Inn Reservation Service

4987 Kingston Road, Elbridge, 13060
(315) 689-2082

A freshly decorated, comfortable, clean, and convenient brick Federalist house offers first-floor room with private bath and double bed or larger second-floor room with queen bed and shared bath. Master suite with two twins and one twin in large dressing room with private bath may be available. Near historic Main Street, colleges, Cornell Experimental Agriculture Center, State Park on Seneca Lake. $50-75.

99 William Street

99 William Street, 14456
(315) 789-1273

99 William Street is a pre-Civil War home that lends itself to gracious hospitality in these modern hectic times. In Geneva, New York, in the heart of the Finger Lakes region, deep in history and rich with natural beauty, the inn is within a day's drive to wineries, state parks, and lakes, as well as Rochester, Ithaca, and Syracuse. Offered are two bedrooms with private baths and the privacy that you expect and require.

Hosts: Christopher M. Lang and David B. Gallipeau
Rooms: 2 (PB) $65
Continental or Full Breakfast
Credit Cards: None
Notes: 2, 5, 9

GERMANTOWN

The American Country Collection 102

4 Greenwood Lane, Delmar, 12054
(518) 439-7001

Built by Peter Rockefeller around 1807, this center-hall Colonial was a roadside tavern and dance hall, then a fox farm until World War II. It features post-and-beam construction, oak-pinned rafters, hand-hewn timbers, and poured-glass windows. Four guest rooms, all with private baths, have air conditioning. Children over nine welcome. Smoking permitted on the first floor only. No pets. Full country breakfast. $70.

The American Country Collection 113

4 Greenwood Lane, Delmar, 12054
(518) 439-7001

Wonderful views of the Catskill Mountains and the Hudson Valley can be had from this 18-year-old home. The guest quarters include two bedrooms and a private bath. There is a family room with fireplace, piano, and TV. Breakfast is served on the porch or in the dining room. Guests are welcome to use the in-ground swimming pool. Smoking outdoors only. Children welcome. Crib available. No pets. Full breakfast on weekends; continental breakfast Tuesday through Thursday. $60 (Nov.1-May 30); $65 (June 1-Oct. 31).

GHENT

The American Country Collection 082

4 Greenwood Lane, Delmar, 12054
(518) 439-7001

This early 19th-century farmhouse is situated on ten scenic acres of open fields, perfect for walking and picnicking. There is also a private one-acre pond for fishing and paddleboating and a miniature horse farm. The guest room on the second floor is air-conditioned and has a TV and private bath. The two-room suite on the third floor is air-conditioned and has a TV. Smoking outdoors only. Children welcome. Dog in residence. $60-70.

GOWANDA

The Teepee

Rural Delivery 1, Box 543, 14070
(716) 532-2168

This bed and breakfast is operated by Seneca Indians on the Cattaraugus Indian

Reservation near Gowanda. Tours of the reservation and the Amish community nearby are available.

Hosts: Maxwell and Phyllis Lay
Rooms: 3 (SB) $35 single; $45 double
Full Breakfast
Credit Cards: None
Notes: 2, 5, 6, 7, 8, 9, 10, 11, 12

GREENFIELD

The American Country Collection 112

4 Greenwood Lane, Delmar, 12054
(518) 439-7001

It was an inn for British officers during the War of 1812, then a stagecoach stop in the 1820s before serving as part of the Underground Railroad before the Civil War. A rich sense of history is enhanced by Oriental rugs and fine antiques from Europe and the Middle and Far East. Five guest rooms, three with private baths. One room has a Jacuzzi. Smoking outdoors and on the patio. Children over 11 welcome. Pets in residence. $60-125, seasonal.

GREENHURST

Spindletop Bed and Breakfast

Polo Drive off East Avenue, 14742
(716) 484-2070

Enjoy your days and nights in this elegantly casual lakefront estate with docking for your boat and secluded, heated in-ground pool. Expanded continental breakfast, a bottle of local wines, and nibblers are yours each day. Visit famed Chautauqua Institution and prowl the antique shops, galleries, and Amish areas for a treasure. Come and be pampered.

Hosts: Lee and Don Spindler
Rooms: 4 (PB) $55-70
Expanded Continental Breakfast

Credit Cards: A, B, C
Notes: 2, 5, 7 (1st floor), 8, 9, 10, 11, 12, 13, 14

GREENVILLE

The American Country Collection 146

4 Greenwood Lane, Delmar, 12054
(518) 439-7001

Warm and inviting hospitality, accompanied by all the amenities, await guests at this bed and breakfasts on 245 acres at the foot of the Catskill Mountains. All rooms are comfortably furnished and offer private baths. A honeymoon cottage is available also. One hundred rooms are above the main reception area, in two large cottages, and three homes, all on the resort property. Children over 13 welcome. Smoking permitted. Full breakfast. Open May through October 15. $50-70.

Greenville Arms

Rural Delivery 1, Box 2, 12083
(518) 966-5219

An historic Victorian inn in the Hudson River Valley, featuring 18 unique guest rooms, 6 acres of lush lawns, gardens, shade trees, and a 50-foot pool. Golf and tennis nearby. Catskill Mountain sightseeing and hiking. Original art, antiques, and

Greenville Arms

fireplaces add warmth and grace to the dining rooms where guests enjoy famous country breakfasts. Elegant country dining in the Vanderbilt Room on weekends. Open June 1 through December 1.

Hosts: Eliot and Letitia Dalton
Rooms: 18 (13 PB; 5 SB) $75-120
Full Breakfast
Credit Cards: A, B
Notes: 2, 4, 8, 9, 11, 12, 14

HADLEY

The American Country Collection 135

4 Greenwood Lane, Delmar, 12054
(518) 439-7001

Built in the late 1800s and purchased in 1988 by the present owners, this restored Victorian country inn is in the southern Adirondacks ideally situated within easy driving distance to Saratoga, Glens Falls, and Lake George. Five distinctive guest rooms, all with private baths, are individually decorated and named and offer their own special amenities. Private dinners and breakfasts can be arranged in the three larger rooms. A gourmet breakfast served each morning may include Grand Marnier French toast or eggs Anthony, home-baked muffins, juice, coffee, or tea. Packages available. $80-140, seasonal.

Saratoga Rose

4870 Rockwell Street, 12835
(518) 696-2861; (800) 942-5025

Romantic Victorian inn in southern Adirondacks near Saratoga Springs and Lake George. Swimming, boating, outlet shopping, skiing, rafting, antiquing, golf and tennis. Comfortable rooms with private baths. Fireplace room and room with private outside deck and Jacuzzi. Full gourmet breakfast included. Packages available. The candlelit restaurant offers specialties prepared by chef-owner Anthony Merlino.

Saratoga Rose

Hosts: Anthony and Nancy Merlino
Rooms: 4 (PB) $65-130
Full Breakfast
Credit Cards: A, B, C, D
Notes: 2, 3, 4, 5, 9, 10, 11, 12, 13, 14

HAGUE

The American Country Collection 137

4 Greenwood Lane, Delmar, 12054
(518) 439-7001

Rustic elegance with an Adirondack feel and 400 sandy beachfront feet directly on the shore of the Lake George describes the atmosphere of this bed and breakfast. Perfect as a romantic getaway or for families, there are eight cabins that can accommodate up to four people and offer their own private bath. Five rooms in the lodge are also available, and there are two rooms that have one single and one double bed and share a bath. A full country breakfast is served at the guest's convenience. Children are welcome. $36-233, seasonal.

HAMBURG

Missert's Bed and Breakfast

66 Highland Avenue, 14075
(716) 649-5830

This three-story wooden frame house in a quiet residential neighborhood is designed for company, with its large livingroom and fireplace. The house is filled with hanging plants and paintings, is ten minutes from Lake Erie, and Hamburg's community playground is one block away. Your hostess enjoys local acclaim for her full breakfasts that include apricot muffins and mouth-watering coffee cakes fresh from the oven. Only 10 minutes to Rich Stadium, 25 minutes to downtown Buffalo or ski slopes, 45 minutes to Niagara Falls. Baby-sitting is available.

Hosts: Tom and Betty Missert
Rooms: 3 (SB) $35-45
Full Breakfast
Credit Cards: C
Notes: 2, 5, 6, 7, 8, 9, 10, 12, 13

HAMLIN

Sandy Creek Manor House

1960 Redman Road, 14464-9635
(716) 964-7528

Feather pillows, Amish quilts, and quiet nights lull you at this peaceful retreat. The 1910 English tudor is on six wooded acres with several perennial gardens beckoning you to "stop and smell the roses." Trout, bass, and salmon fish in the backyard. The antique player piano is reminiscent of grandma's house. One-half hour to Rochester, one and a half hours to Niagara Falls along the Seaway Trail.

Hosts: Shirley Hollink and James Krempasky
Rooms: 3 (SB) $40-60
Full Breakfast
Credit Cards: None
Notes: 2, 5, 6, 9, 14

HAMMONDSPORT

Blushing Rosé Bed and Breakfast

11 William Street, 14840
(607) 569-3402; (607) 569-3483

The Blushing Rosé has served as a pleasant hideaway for honeymooners, anniversary celebrators, and romantic trysters alike. Whether you spend your day driving, hiking, biking, or just relaxing, this is the ideal haven in which to end your day and a great place to start your day with a copious specialty breakfast. The village has shopping, dining, and great walking. Keuka Lake is just a few doors away; wineries are nearby, as is the Corning Glass and Watkins Glen.

Hosts: The Laufersweilers
Rooms: 4 (PB) $65-85
Full Breakfast; Early Continental Breakfast
Credit Cards: None
Notes: 2, 5, 9, 10, 11, 12, 13

Gone With the Wind on Keaka Lake

453 West Lake Road, Branchport, 14418
(607) 868-4603

The name paints the picture of this 1887 stone Victorian. Fourteen acres on a slight rise overlook a quiet lake cove adorned by an inviting gazebo. Feel the magic of total relaxation and peace of mind, enjoying the solarium hot tub, nature trails, three fireplaces, and delectable breakfasts. Private beach and dock.

Hosts: Linda and Robert Lewis
Rooms: 5 (SB) $65-95
Full Breakfast
Credit Cards: None
Notes: 2, 5, 10, 11, 12, 13

J. S. Hubbs Bed and Breakfast

17 Sheather Street, P. O. Box 366, 14840
(607) 569-2440; (607) 569-3629

Come and relax in this family home. This historic Greek Revival (inkbottle house) was built in 1840 and has been in the family for almost 100 years. It offers a suite, single, and double rooms with two private

---

NOTES: Credit cards accepted: A Master Card; B Visa; C American Express; D Discover Card; E Diner's Club; F Other; 2 Personal Checks accepted; 3 Lunch available; 4 Dinner available; 5 Open all year;

baths and two half-baths. Situated one-half block from Keuka Lake and the village square. Full breakfast.

Hosts: Walter, Linda, and John Carl
Rooms: 4 (1 PB; 3 SB) $62
Full Breakfast
Credit Cards: A, B
Notes: 5, 11

Pleasant Valley Bed and Breakfast

8323 Germania Road, 14840
(607) 569-3472

Spend a night or more in a lovely old Victorian home situated in the beautiful Finger Lakes country. There are many places of interest in the immediate area: Corning Glass Works, Thoroughbred racing, fine wineries, and the shops of the enchanting village of Hammondsport are within walking distance.

Host: Jeanne
Rooms: 3 (S2B) $55
Full Breakfast
Credit Cards: None
Notes: 2, 5, 7, 9, 11, 12

HAMPTON BAYS

House on the Water

Box 106, 11946
(516) 728-3560

Ranch house with two acres of garden on Shinnecock Bay. Quiet location. One mile to village, train, and bus. Seven miles to Southampton and Westhampton. Two miles to ocean beaches. Bicycles, windsurfers, pedal boat, barbecue, beach lounges, and umbrellas. German, Spanish, and French spoken. Kitchen facilities

Host: Mrs. Ute Lamber
Rooms: 2 (PB) $75-95
Full Breakfast
Minimum stay weekdays: 2 nights; weekends: 3 nights; holidays: 4 nights
Credit Cards: None
Closed Nov. 1-May 1
Notes: 2, 9, 10, 11, 12, 14

HANCOCK

The Cranberry Inn

38 West Main Street, 13783
(607) 637-2788

Built in 1894, this stately, turn-of-the-century Victorian is enveloped by the glorious Upper Catskill Mountains, the famous Delaware River, and a great front porch. Inside, enjoy antique and deco design, adorned in fine woodwork and old-style architecture. The inn offers warmth, charm, and hospitality. Come fish and canoe the rivers, bicycle and hike the miles of country roads, or shop for antiques. Seasonal packages available.

Hosts: Lorene and George Bang
Rooms: 4 (2 PB; 2 SB) $50-70
Full Breakfast
Credit Cards: A, B, D
Notes: 2, 3, 4, 5, 7, 8, 9, 11, 12, 13

Sunrise Inn Bed and Breakfast

Rural Delivery 1, Box 232B, Walton, 13856
(607) 865-7254

At this 19th-century farmhouse nestled in the Catskills, you will enjoy homey comfort, country tranquility, a gazebo, wraparound porch, library, and wood-burning stove. Awaken to the aroma of homemade soda bread. Browse through a quaint antique shop. Pets in residence. No smoking.

Hosts: Jim and Adele Toth
Rooms: 3 (1 PB; 2 SB) $36.40-58
Continental Breakfast
Credit Cards: None
Notes: 5, 8, 9, 12

HARTFORD

The American Country Collection 160

4 Greenwood Lane, Delmar, 12054
(518) 439-7001

6 Pets welcome; 7 Smoking allowed; 8 Children welcome; 9 Social drinking allowed; 10 Tennis available; 11 Swimming available; 12 Golf available; 13 Skiing available; 14 May be booked through travel agents.

Within a short drive of both Saratoga Springs and Lake George, this historic Colonial tavern offers a relaxed country atmosphere in a quiet, rural setting. A history buff's delight, this restored home was built in 1802 and "remodeled" in 1878. Two second-floor rooms and one first-floor room are available for guests and offer both private and shared baths. A bountiful, full breakfast is served each morning in the dining room and includes juices and cereals, homemade rolls, breads, and muffins, eggs, bacon or sausage, and coffee and tea. $25-50.

HARTSDALE

Bed and Breakfast U.S.A., Ltd. 328

Old Sheffield Road, South Egremont, MA, 01258
(413) 528-2113

An 1896 central-hall Victorian home with wonderful antique colonial decor. This home on a hillside acre with a country atmosphere is a 15-minute walk to the Hartsdale train station, a five-minute drive to White Plains and the revamped County Center, with easy access to New York City by bus or train. There is a fireplace in the home. TV and laundry facilities are available. Situated on the bus line, and pickup is available. There are 20 restaurants within one mile. Accommodations include three guest rooms, two with private bath. Full breakfast. Smoking permitted. Children welcome. No pets. $40-55; $250-330 weekly.

HEMPSTEAD—GARDEN CITY LINE

Country Life Bed and Breakfast

237 Cathedral Avenue, 11550
(516) 292-9219

Gracious old Dutch Colonial, near airports, beaches, train to Manhattan. Decorated with antiques and reproductions, the home has been featured on two house tours. Each room has air conditioning, color TV, and special charm: hand-crocheted spreads, marble-top antique dresser, teddy bears, or other animals. Sightseeing, beaches, three universities nearby. Breakfast is served in a sunny, plant-filled room and consists of caramel French toast, puff pancakes, and homemade granola.

Hosts: Richard and Wendy Duvall
Rooms: 4 (PB) $60-95
Full Breakfast
Credit Cards: A, B
Notes: 2 (deposit only), 4, 5, 8, 9, 10, 12, 14

Duvall Bed and Breakfast

237 Cathedral Avenue, 11550
(516) 292-9219

Charming old Dutch Colonial near airports, railroad to New York City (40 minutes), beaches, Adelphi and Hofstra universities, Nassau Coliseum. Furnished with antiques; rooms have air conditioning and color TV. On-premises parking, complimentary wine. Many nearby tourist attractions.

Hosts: Richard and Wendy Duvall
Rooms: 4 (2 PB; 2 SB) $60-75
Full Breakfast
Minimum stay weekends: 2 nights; holidays: 3 nights
Credit Cards: A, B
Notes: 2 (deposit only), 4, 5, 8, 9, 12

HERKIMER

Bellinger Woods Bed and Breakfast

611 West German Street, 13350
(315) 866-2770

Circa 1860 Victorian welcomes you with charm, comfort, and cordiality to the heart of Leatherstocking country. Situated in the village of Herkimer, nestled along the Mohawk River, it has been carefully restored and furnished with antiques and traditional pieces. Visit historic sites, antique stores, and gift shops nearby. Six miles from Herkimer diamond mines and 40 minutes from Cooperstown Baseball Hall of Fame. Recently given a three rating by the American Bed and Breakfast Association.

Hosts: Barbara and Paul Mielcarski
Rooms: 3 (2 PB; 1 SB) $35-55
Full Breakfast
Credit Cards: A, B
Notes: 2, 5, 8, 9, 10, 11, 12

Bellinger Woods

HIGH FALLS

Locktender Cottage

Route 213, 12440
(914) 687-7700

Step back in time at a Victorian guest house for a romantic getaway in a charming canal town. Dine in a national historic landmark, the Depuy Canal House Restaurant, serving culinary treats from regional and international sources. One and one-half hours north of New York City in the Catskill foothills. Choice of fireplace or Jacuzzi suite.

Host: John Novi
Rooms: 2 (PB) $85-110
Continental Breakfast
Credit Cards: All Major
Notes: 2, 4, 7, 8, 9, 10, 11, 12, 13, 14

HILLSDALE

The American Country Collection 106

4 Greenwood Lane, Delmar, 12054
(518) 439-7001

This inn is surrounded by 100 acres of meadows, woodlands, and an ancient cemetery. Built as a farmhouse around 1830, it was formerly the parsonage to the old church next door, then an inn with a somewhat dubious reputation during Prohibition. Four guest rooms, two with private baths. Smoking outdoors only. Breakfast is served on the screened porch or in the candlelit dining room. Children over 11 welcome. Two cats in residence. $90-95; two-night minimum stay on in-season weekends; three-night minimum stay on holiday weekends.

Berkshire B&B Homes NY 6

P. O. Box 211, Williamsburg, MA 01096
(413) 268-7244

An 1830 Colonial on one acre. Antique and Victorian furnishings. Parlor and den with TV for guest use. View of fields. One queen with private bath; two double bedrooms and one single. Full breakfast. No smoking. Children of all ages welcome. $50-95.

HOBART

Breezy Acres Farm Bed and Breakfast

Rural Delivery 1, Box 191, 13788
(607) 538-9338

"Better than home" reads one entry in the guest book. That's because your hosts strive for excellence in every area. Individually decorated rooms, each with private, squeaky-clean bath. Bountiful,

6 Pets welcome; 7 Smoking allowed; 8 Children welcome; 9 Social drinking allowed; 10 Tennis available; 11 Swimming available; 12 Golf available; 13 Skiing available; 14 May be booked through travel agents.

homemade breakfast. Folders with menus, clippings about local events and activities. Spa, fireplace, pond for fishing and swimming, hunting, 300 acres for hiking, deck surrounded by beautiful flower gardens, shady porch for relaxing.

Hosts: Joyce and David Barber
Rooms: 3 (PB) $50-60
Full Breakfast
Credit Cards: A, B
Notes: 2, 5, 9, 10, 11, 12, 13

HOMER

David Harum House

80 South Main Street, 13077
(607) 749-3548

Well-known Federal house, circa 1815, situated in the historic district. An 11-by-34-foot foyer with beautiful spiral staircase. David Harum memorabilia on display. One-half mile from I-81.

Hosts: Ed and Connie Stone
Rooms: 2 (PB) $45-55
Full Breakfast
Credit Cards: None
Notes: 2, 5, 8, 9, 10, 11, 12, 13

HOOSICK FALLS

The American Country Collection 068

4 Greenwood Lane, Delmar, 12054
(518) 439-7001

Beginning as a stagecoach inn in 1843, then as a stop for the Underground Railroad, this bed and breakfast is just ten minutes from Bennington, Vermont, and in the center of beautiful Grandma Moses country. Six second-floor guest rooms, one with private bath. There's a sitting room with cable TV and an inviting hot tub and sauna. Smoking outdoors only. Children welcome. Well-behaved pets permitted occasionally. $50-65.

HOPEWELL JUNCTION

Covered Bridge 1HJNY

P. O. Box 447 A, Norfolk, CT 06058
(203) 542-5944

This 1841 Georgian Colonial built for a prominent Dutch silversmith is set on six acres which include lovely perennial gardens and a pool. The house has six fireplaces with double livingrooms that are adorned with large, imported crystal chandeliers and a fabulous sun room that overlooks the grounds. The common rooms and the four guest rooms are all beautifully decorated with antiques, some of which the owners collected when they lived in France. A full country breakfast is served by the hostess, who attended the Culinary Institute of America. $85-140.

HOWE'S CAVE

The American Country Collection 058

4 Greenwood Lane, Delmar, 12054
(518) 439-7001

Conveniently situated just three miles from I-88, this 150-year-old Greek Revival home rests high on a hill overlooking the scenic valley and tiny hamlet of Barnerville. Three guest rooms with private baths. Each room is uniquely decorated. Smoking in the kitchen and outdoors. Children over 11 welcome. Cross-country ski at Howe Caverns. Pets in residence. Two night minimum stay. $55.

ITHACA

Geneva On The Lake

1001 Lochland Road, P. O. Box 929, Geneva, 14456
(315) 789-7190; (800) 3GENEVA

NOTES: Credit cards accepted: A Master Card; B Visa; C American Express; D Discover Card; E Diner's Club; F Other; 2 Personal Checks accepted; 3 Lunch available; 4 Dinner available; 5 Open all year;

Geneva On The Lake is an elegant, small resort on Seneca Lake in the Finger Lakes wine district. An Italian Renaissance villa offering luxurious suites overlooking a furnished terrace, formal gardens, pool, and lake. "The food is extraordinarily good," writes *Bon Appetit*. Friendly, attentive staff. Awarded AAA four diamonds for the tenth consecutive year. Suite rates include continental breakfast; complimentary bottle of wine, fresh fruit, and flowers on arrival; a wine and cheese party on Friday even-ings; and a daily copy of *The New York Times* is provided.

Host: Norbert H. Schnickel, Jr.
Suites: 29 (PB) $148-338
Continental and Full Breakfast
Minimum stay weekends: 2 if Sat. (May 15-Oct. 31)
Credit Cards: A, B, C, D
Notes: 2, 4 (weekends only), 5, 7, 8, 9, 10, 11, 12, 14

Hanshaw House Bed and Breakfast

15 Sapsucker Woods Road, 14850
(607) 273-8034

Framed by a white picket fence, this 1830s farmhouse is comfortable and elegant. Nestled serenely overlooking a pond and woods, rooms are furnished with antiques and colorful chintzes in a country English decor. Birds and wildlife complete the view. Scrumptious breakfasts are served in a cozy dining room. Guests are invited to enjoy gardens and the patio in warmer weather. Private baths, goose-down comforters and pillows, air conditioning make this a pleasant place to stay. Conveniently located near colleges, state parks, skiing, fine restaurants, and vineyards.

Host: Helen Scoones
Rooms: 4 (PB) $65-110
Full Breakfast
Credit Cards: A, B, C
Notes: 2, 5, 8, 9, 10, 11, 12, 13

La Tourelle

1150 Danby Road, 14850
(607) 273-2734; FAX (607) 273-4821
(800) 765-1492 Reservations

Rated highly by AAA and Mobil travel guides, La Tourelle is the perfect blend of Old World charm and contemporary comfort. Situated next to L'Auberge du Cochon Rouge restaurant, the beautifully appointed guest rooms are reminiscent of the delightful country hotels of Europe, each with private bath, air conditioning, TV, and telephone. Choose one of the king- or queen-bed rooms or indulge in the Fireplace Suite or romantically exciting Tower Room.

Host: Leslie Leonard
Rooms: 35 (PB) $87-135
Continental Breakfast
Credit Cards: A, B, C
Notes: 5, 6, 7, 8, 9, 10, 13, 14

Log Country Inn

Box 581, 14851
(607) 589-4771; (800) 274-4771

Enjoy the rustic charm of a log house at the edge of a 7,000-acre state forest. Modern accommodation in the spirit of international hospitality. European country breakfast, afternoon tea. Hiking, skiing, and sauna. Convenient to Ithaca College, Cornell, Corning Glass, wineries, and antique shopping.

Host: Wanda Grunberg
Rooms: 3 (1 PB; 2 SB) $45-65
Full Breakfast
Credit Cards: A, B
Notes: 2, 4, 5, 6, 7, 8, 10, 11, 13

Peirce House Bed and Breakfast

218 South Albany Street, 14850
(607) 273-0824

Ithaca's only downtown bed and breakfast, this turn-of-the-century residence was built by Willard Peirce in a-style befitting a proper Victorian family. The home features period furniture, fireplace, stained glass, fine woodwork, Oriental rugs, whirlpool baths, air conditioning. Just three blocks to shops, galleries, restaurants, music, and movies. One mile to Cornell, Ithaca

6 Pets welcome; 7 Smoking allowed; 8 Children welcome; 9 Social drinking allowed; 10 Tennis available; 11 Swimming available; 12 Golf available; 13 Skiing available; 14 May be booked through travel agents.

College, Cayuga Lake. Gourmet coffees, fruit, and home-baked goods. Special weekday rates.

Hosts: Cathy Emilian and Joe Daley
Rooms: 4 (2 PB; 2 SB) $70-100
Full Breakfast
Credit Cards: A, B, C
Notes: 2, 5, 9, 10, 11, 12, 13

Peregrine House Victorian Inn

140 College Avenue, 14850
(607) 272-0919

An 1874 brick home with sloping lawns and pretty gardens, just three blocks from Cornell University. Down pillows, fine linens, and air-conditioned bedrooms with Victorian decor. In the center of Ithaca, one mile from Cayuga Lake, with its boating, swimming, summer theater, and wineries. Wonderful breakfasts, free snacks.

Hosts: Nancy Falconer and Susan Vance
Rooms: 8 (PB) $69-99
Full Breakfast
Credit Cards: A, B
Notes: 2, 5, 7, 8 (over 8), 9, 10, 11, 12, 13, 14

Rose Inn

Route 34 North, Box 6576, 14851-6576
(607) 533-7905; FAX (607) 533-4202

An elegant 1840s Italianate mansion on 20 landscaped acres. Fabulous circular staircase of Honduran mahogany. Prix fixe dinner served with advance reservations. Close to Cornell University. Twice selected by Uncle Ben's as one of Ten Best Inns in America. Mobil four-star rated; AAA, four diamonds.

Hosts: Sherry and Charles Rosemann
Rooms: 15 (PB) $100-160
Suites: $175
Full Breakfast
Credit Cards: A, B
Notes: 2, 4, 5, 8 (over 12), 9, 10, 11, 12, 13, 14

A Slice of Home

178 North Main Street, Spencer, 14883
(607) 589-6073

A 150-year-old farmhouse on 12 acres is just twenty minutes from Ithaca, Elmira, and Watkins Glen. Guest rooms are in a private wing of the house, which gives the quarters an old-fashioned atmosphere tuned in to complete privacy and relaxation. Hearty weekend breakfasts are designed so you'll skip lunch; weekday breakfasts are special culinary delights. Hundreds of acres are available for hiking and skiing. Open all year.

Host: Bea Brownwell
Rooms: 4 (1 PB; 1 SB) $35-75
Full or Continental Breakfast
Credit Cards: None
Notes: 2, 5, 13, 14

JAMESVILLE

Elaine's Bed and Breakfast and Inn Reservation Service

4987 Kingston Road, Elbridge, 13060
(315) 689-2082

Country atmosphere. High on a hill, with a view for 35 miles, including three lakes, this owner-designed contemporary home offers the ultimate in peace and quiet, though only 15 minutes from downtown Syracuse or the university. Unique solarium full of plants and casual seating; rear deck with picnic table offers marvelous view. Two guest rooms share skylighted bath. House is ideal for a small family. Two dogs in residence. $40-55.

High Meadows Bed and Breakfast

3740 Eager Road, 13078
(315) 492-3517

Country hospitality only 12 miles south of Syracuse. Situated high in the hills with a 40-mile view. Enjoy a plant-filled solarium, fireplace, or a quiet country walk. A healthy continental breakfast awaits you. The hosts are eager to serve you and make your stay a pleasant one.

NOTES: Credit cards accepted: A Master Card; B Visa; C American Express; D Discover Card; E Diner's Club; F Other; 2 Personal Checks accepted; 3 Lunch available; 4 Dinner available; 5 Open all year;

Hosts: Alex and Nancy Mentz
Rooms: 2 (1 PB; 2 SB) $35-50
Continental Breakfast
Credit Cards: None
Notes: 2, 4, 5, 8, 14

JAY

The Book and Blanket Bed and Breakfast

P. O. Box 164, Route 9N, 12941-9998
(518) 946-8323

This charming, 100-year-old Greek Revival is nestled in the quaint hamlet of Jay, just seven miles to Whiteface Mountain and less than twenty minutes to Lake Placid. View of the Covered Bridge, and fishing and swimming in the AuSable River. The livingroom features an extra large fireplace, and an extra large porch is available for guests to enjoy. A booklover's dream, three guest rooms honor Jane Austen, F. Scott Fitzgerald, and Jack London, with their works well represented. Borrowers and browsers welcome. Full breakfast.

Hosts: Kathy, Fred, and Daisy the Basset Hound
Rooms: 3 (1 PB; 2 SB) $45-65
Full Breakfast
Credit Cards: None
Notes: 2, 5, 9, 13

JOHNSTOWN

The American Country Collection 099

4 Greenwood Lane, Delmar, 12054
(518) 439-7001

This 100-year-old in-town home is situated on one-half acre of manicured lawns, vegetable and flower gardens, with an above-ground swimming pool. Two guest rooms, one bath shared with owners. Rooms are normally rented to one party traveling together. The bedrooms have lots of natural light and cross ventilation. There's a TV in the livingroom and den. No smoking in

bedrooms. No pets. Children over two welcome. $40.

KASOAG LAKE

Elaine's Bed and Breakfast and Inn Reservation Service

4987 Kingston Road, Elbridge, 13060
(315) 689-2082

About ten miles east of Pulaski, Route 11, and Route 81. Sportsmen's paradise. A quiet, rustic getaway retreat in the country convenient to Lake Ontario, 45 minutes to Syracuse or Watertown; easy drive to Salmon River. Great for snowmobilers and fishermen, this bed and breakfast features efficiencies sleeping up to six. Handicapped accessible, plenty of parking, porches, outdoor fireplace, and very moderate rates. Each unit has a full kitchen with microwave and fixings for continental breakfasts. No credit cards. $22/person per night. Minimum four people.

KATONAH

The American Country Collection 128

4 Greenwood Lane, Delmar, 12054
(518) 439-7001

Dream away in this 16th-century Dutch Colonial farmhouse situated on 4 acres of woods, gardens, and maple sugar bush. A short climb up four steps brings guests to the master bedroom, which has a brass bed, free-standing fireplace, and private, hand-painted Portuguese tile bath. A small study with a desk and library connects to the bedroom and a common room. The third floor has two more bedrooms that share a bath. Across the street is a lovely pond for trout fishing or swimming. A full breakfast is served each morning. No smoking. $50-75.

6 Pets welcome; 7 Smoking allowed; 8 Children welcome; 9 Social drinking allowed; 10 Tennis available; 11 Swimming available; 12 Golf available; 13 Skiing available; 14 May be booked through travel agents.

LAKE GEORGE

House on the Hill

Route 28, Box 248, Warrensburg, 12885
(518) 623-9390; (800) 221-9390

The bed and breakfast romantic fling. An unforgettable experience for lovers. Nurture that special relationship. Coffee and freshly baked goodies in your room followed by a full sumptuous breakfast in the wraparound sunroom overlooking 176 acres. Air conditioning, satellite TV/VCR. Two-night minimum stay. Special packages available.

Hosts: Joe and Lynn Rubino
Rooms: 4 (1 PB; 3 SB) $85-95
Full breakfast
Credit Cards: A, B
Notes: 2, 3, 4, 5, 8 (by arrangement), 9, 10, 11, 12, 13, 14

LAKE LUZERNE

The American Country Collection 159

4 Greenwood Lane, Delmar, 12054
(518) 439-7001

Imagine stepping back 100 years into a grand Victorian summer in Lake Luzerne. Carefully restored by the present owners, this inn has a genuinely warm, comfortable atmosphere characterized by a lot of personal service and attention. Ten rooms, with either a double or queen-size bed, offer private baths, and two of the rooms have an additional single bed. Breakfast is served on a large sun porch each morning, and consists of fruit, cakes, granola, waffles, French toast, crepes, omelets, sausage and homefries, coffee or tea. $70-140, seasonal.

The Lamplight Inn Bed and Breakfast

2129 Lake Avenue, Box 70, 12846
(518) 696-5294

Award-winning 1992 "Inn of the Year." Romantic 1890 Victorian estate nestled in the Adirondacks across from a crystal clear lake. Mountain view rooms with fireplaces, and memorable breakfast served on the picturesque sun porch.

Hosts: Gene and Linda Merlino
Rooms: 10 (PB) $70-140
Full Breakfast
Credit Cards: A, B, C
Notes: 2, 3, 5, 7 (restricted), 8 (over 12), 9, 10, 11, 12, 13, 14

LAKE PLACID

Blackberry Inn

59 Sentinel Road, 12946
(518) 523-3419

This Colonial built in 1915 is situated one mile from the center of the village on Route 73. Five guest rooms offer country flair. Convenient to all major Olympic sites; surrounded by the Adirondack Parks. Nearby recreation includes skiing, skating, hiking, golf, and fishing. Home-baked breakfasts.

Hosts: Bill and Gail Billerman
Rooms: 5 (SB) $45-65
Full Breakfast
Credit Cards: None
Notes: 2, 5, 7, 8, 9, 10, 11, 12, 13

Highland House Inn

3 Highland Place, 12946
(518) 523-2377

Peaceful central location in the village of Lake Placid. Each room is equally appealing, all having been recently redecorated. Enjoy the hot tub on the deck amidst the trees. The full breakfast includes special blueberry pancakes. Fully efficient country cottage also available adjacent to inn.

Hosts: Teddy and Cathy Blazer
Rooms: 7 (PB) $55-75
Cottage: $80-105
Full Breakfast
Credit Cards: A, B
Notes: 2, 5, 7, 8, 9, 10, 11, 12, 13, 14

NOTES: Credit cards accepted: A Master Card; B Visa; C American Express; D Discover Card; E Diner's Club; F Other; 2 Personal Checks accepted; 3 Lunch available; 4 Dinner available; 5 Open all year;

Interlaken Inn and Restaurant

15 Interlaken Avenue, 12946
(518) 523-3180

A Victorian inn in the heart of Lake Placid
featuring a gourmet restaurant and 12
uniquely decorated rooms. The inn has tin
ceilings, a cozy fireplace in the livingroom,
lots of lace and charm. Nearby you can
enjoy golf, skiing, or any of the pleasures
of the Adirondacks.

Hosts: Roy and Carol Johnson
Rooms: 12 (PB) $100-160/couple, Modified
 American Plan
Full Breakfast
Credit Cards: A, B, C
Closed Nov. and April
Notes: 2, 4, 7, 8 (over 5), 9, 10, 11, 12, 13, 14

South Meadow Farm and Lodge

HCR 1 Box 44, Cascade Road, 12946
(518) 523-9369; (800) 523-9369

Small working farm on 75 acres, bordered
by state land in the heart of the Adirondack
High Peaks. Ski out the back door onto
Olympic cross-country trails. Family-style
lodging with full, hearty meals. Come join
us all year and share our lodge, our view,
and our Adirondack hospitality.

Hosts: Tony and Nancy Corwin
Rooms: 5 (SB) $70-90
Full Breakfast
Credit Cards: A, B, C
Notes: 2, 3, 4, 5, 8, 9, 13, 14

Stagecoach Inn

370 Old Military Road, 12946
(518) 523-9474

Built in 1833, this inn was the original stagecoach stop for travelers to the Adirondacks.
In fact, Verplank Colvin stayed here when he
conducted the survey of the Adirondacks in
1873. The interior of the inn is in original
condition, with wainscoting floor to ceiling
and birch-log trim. Modern baths.

Interlaker Inn and Restaurant

Host: Lyn Witte
Rooms: 9 (5 PB; 4 SB) $55-80
Full Breakfast
Credit Cards: None
Notes: 2, 5, 7, 8, 9, 10, 11, 12, 13, 14

LEWISTON

The Cameo Inn

4710 Lower River Road, Route 18F, 14092
(716) 754-2075; (716) 745-3034

This stately Queen Anne Victorian commands a majestic view of the lower
Niagara River and Canadian shoreline.
Lovingly furnished with period antiques
and family heirlooms, the Cameo will
charm you with its quiet elegance. Here
you can enjoy the ambience of days past in
a peaceful setting far from the bustle of
everyday life. Three guest rooms with private or shared baths are available, as well
as a three-room private suite which overlooks the river.

Hosts: Greg and Carolyn Fisher
Rooms: 4 (2 PB; 2 SB) $65-99
Full Breakfast
Credit Cards: A, B
Notes: 2, 5, 9, 14
(716) 874-8797

Rainbow Hospitality L600

466 Amherst Street, Buffalo, 14207
(716) 874-8797

6 Pets welcome; 7 Smoking allowed; 8 Children welcome; 9 Social drinking allowed; 10 Tennis available; 11
Swimming available; 12 Golf available; 13 Skiing available; 14 May be booked through travel agents.

Private guest cottage minutes from the village of Lewiston. Young hosts greet guests with knowledge of the area and warm hospitality. Completely furnished cottage is ideal for the perfect getaway. Queen-size bed, privacy, cozy. $65-75.

LITTLE VALLEY

The Napoli Log Homestead
Rural Delivery #2, Box 301, 14755
(716) 938-6755; (716) 358-3926

This cedar log cedar home was built in 1988. It is furnished with Early American pieces handed down from five generations. Two rooms share a bath, and one room upstairs has a private bath. There is a cozy Victorian sitting room upstairs. The full breakfast of waffles and sausage, served with pure maple syrup or bacon and eggs, is included in the room rate. A convenient twenty minutes from Holiday Valley, Cockaigne, Allegheny State Park, Chautauqua Lake, and Amish settlement.

Hosts: Dean and Annette Waite
Rooms: 3 (1 PB; 2 SB) $40-50
Full Breakfast
Credit Cards: None
Notes: 2, 5, 6, 8

LIVERPOOL

Elaine's Bed and Breakfast and Inn Reservation Service
4987 Kingston Road, Elbridge, 13060
(315) 689-2082

Victorian house filled with country charm and antiques. A 100-year-old, three-story house overlooking the Yacht Club on Onondaga Lake. Conveniently situated next to antique and craft center. Walk everywhere: restaurants, shops, library, prize-winning Johnson Park, grocery, just one-half block to Onondaga Lake Park. Only five minutes from NYS Thruway (I-

90), Exit 38, and only five minutes to downtown Syracuse. One large guest room with a four-poster bed and bay window alcove with table and chairs for private morning coffee before going downstairs to a full country breakfast. The room is fresh, bright, and beautifully decorated. Another guest room features a maple and pine antique bed with matching chests and collections of powder boxes and dresser jars. These rooms share a lovely modern tub and shower bath. Smoking in designated areas. Ideal for a party of four. $45-65.

LIVINGSTON MANOR

Lanza's Country Inn
Rural Delivery 2, Box 446, 12758
(914) 439-5070

Catskill Mountain outdoor enjoyment: rivers, streams, lakes, woods, mountains, country roads, and quaint villages. Comfortable antique-filled rooms; great food. Invigorating, relaxing, with friendly personal service. You'll love the "Covered Bridge Country."

Host: Dick Lanza
Rooms: 8 (PB) $72-84
Full Breakfast
Credit Cards: A, B, C, F
Notes: 2, 4, 5, 7, 8, 9, 10, 11, 12, 13

LOCKPORT

Chestnut Ridge Inn
7205 Chestnut Ridge Road, 14094
(716) 439-9124

An 1826 Federal mansion with eight acres of gardens and lawns, circular staircase, library, fireplaces, and antique furniture. On the historic Niagara frontier, within minutes of Niagara Falls, Canada, and Fort Niagara. Country auctions, lush fruit farms, fairs, summer theaters. Holidays are special occasions.

Hosts: Frank and Lucy Cervoni
Rooms: 2 (PB) $70-75
Suite: 1 (PB) $75-95
Full Breakfast
Credit Cards: C
Notes: 2, 3, 4, 5, 8, 9, 10, 11, 12, 13, 14

MANLIUS

Elaine's Bed and Breakfast Reservation Service

4987 Kingston Road, Elbridge, 13060
(315) 689-2082

Whole unhosted village house available during school vacations. Bright and freshly decorated.

MARSHALL

Marshall House

5 Hill Street, 28753
(704) 649-9205; (800) 562-9258

Built in 1903, the inn overlooks the peaceful town of Marshall and the waters of the French Broad River. The house is a 20-room country inn, decorated with fancy chandeliers, antiques, and pictures. It has been entered in the National Register of Historic Places under the name of the James H. White House.

Host: Ruth Boyland
Rooms: 9 (2 PB; 7 SB) $35-70
Continental Breakfast
Credit Cards: A, B, C, D, E
Notes: 3, 4, 5, 6, 7, 8, 9, 11, 12, 13, 14

MAYVILLE

The Village Inn

111 South Erie Street, Route 394, 14757
(716) 753-3583

Spend restful nights in a turn-of-the-century Victorian near the shores of lakes Chautauqua and Erie. The home is furnished with antiques and trimmed in wood-

work crafted by European artisans. Near the Chautauqua shops, wineries, swimming, golf, biking, arts and crafts, hang gliding, and skiing.

Host: Dean Hanby
Rooms: 3 (SB) $50
Full Breakfast
Credit Cards: C
Notes: 2, 5, 7, 8, 9, 10, 11, 12, 13, 14

MEREDITH

The Nutmeg Inn

80 Pease Road, 03253
(603) 279-8811

A restored 1763 stagecoach inn. Country decorated rooms with handmade quilts and crafts. Some rooms with fireplaces for added romance. Spend the day enjoying swimming, boating, fishing, skiing, antiquing. As the sun sets, relax in our graciously appointed parlor. On-site pool, central air-conditioning.

Hosts: Bo and Shirley Lawrence
Rooms: 11 (9 PB; 2 SB)$ 65-85
Full Breakfast
Credit Cards: A, B, C, D
Notes: 5, 8, 9, 10, 11, 12, 13, 14

MIDDLETOWN

The American Country Collection 064

4 Greenwood Lane, Delmar, 12054
(518) 439-7001

This circa 1850 farmhouse was once part of the Underground Railroad. All seasons are exciting in this scenic area, with events ranging from antique shows, craft fairs, fall festivals, holiday celebrations, canoeing, and winery tours. Three second-floor guest rooms plus two suites, two shared baths, and extra first-floor bath. Rooms are furnished with country quilts, ruffles, lace, eyelet, and antique furnishings. There is a game room with billiard table, exercise

6 Pets welcome; 7 Smoking allowed; 8 Children welcome; 9 Social drinking allowed; 10 Tennis available; 11 Swimming available; 12 Golf available; 13 Skiing available; 14 May be booked through travel agents.

equipment, and a Jacuzzi. Smoking in designated areas. Pets in residence. Children welcome. $75-80.

MT. TREMPER

Mt. Tremper Inn

Box 51, Route 212and Wittenberg Road, 12457
(914) 688-5329

Victorian hospitality and elegant antiques await you in this 23-room mansion built in 1850 in the Catskill Mountains. Large parlor with fireplace, library/game room, classical music at breakfast. Outdoor dining in season. Near Woodstock, all ski slopes, historic Kingston, and Rhinebeck.

Host: Lou Caselli
Rooms: 12 (2 PB; 10 SB) $60-90
Full Breakfast
Credit Cards: A, B
Notes: 5, 7 (limited), 9, 10, 11, 13, 14

Mt. Tremper Inn

MUMFORD

Genesee Country Inn

948 George Street, Box 340, 14511-0340
(716) 538-2500; FAX (716) 538-4565

Historic stone mill on eight quiet acres of woods and waterfalls. Lovingly restored, with all timely conveniences, individually decorated guest rooms. Tea and full breakfast. Nearby is Genesee Museum, fine restaurants, Letchworth State Park, Rochester; Niagara Falls is one hour away. Trout fishing. Chosen by *Country Inn* magazine as one of the 1990-91 best inns in the USA. AAA approved.

Rooms: 9 (PB) $80-115
Full Breakfast and Tea
Credit Cards: A, B, E
Notes: 2, 5, 7, 9, 11, 12, 13, 14

NEW BALTIMORE

The American Country Collection 089

4 Greenwood Lane, Delmar, 12054
(518) 439-7001

Originally a farmhouse in the early 1800s, this Victorian home was enlarged during the 1860s in Italianate style. Three guest rooms with private baths. One room has a working fireplace and air conditioning. The livingroom has a piano and fireplace; the library has a TV and Victorian gas stove. Breakfast is served in front of the fire in the kitchen, in the dining room, or on the porch or terrace. It's an easy walk to the historic hamlet with its marina, old mill stream, and early cemetary. Smoking permitted. Children accepted occasionally. $65-75.

NEWBERG

The American Country Collection 156

4 Greenwood Lane, Delmar, 12054
(518) 439-7001

Come and visit this fully restored Queen Anne Victorian mansion listed on the National Register of Historic Places, in the heart of the historic district. Enjoy your full breakfast served either in front of a twelve-foot ceiling grand parlor fireplace with a crackling fire, or on a cabana-like sun porch with panoramic views of the majestic

Hudson River and mountains. Both guest rooms are on the second floor, are furnished with antiques, and share a common bath. Two apartments for long or short term rental are also available. $55-65.

Bed and Breakfast U.S.A., Ltd. 211

Old Sheffield Road, South Egremont, MA 01258
(413) 528-2113

An authentic, restored Red Caboose. It features built-in twin beds, with an additional twin over the bathroom. Small kitchen and sitting area. Beautiful landscaping near the in-ground pool overlooking the Hudson River. Only 13 miles to West Point and 40 minutes to Hyde Park. Private entrance. Unique accommodations. Continental breakfast. Pets in residence. Guest pets permitted. Children over 12 welcome. Smoking permitted. $90.

NEW FIELD

Decker Pond Inn

1076 Elmira Road 14867
(607) 273-7133

An elegant inn on ten acres, this home is within minutes of state parks, wineries, colleges, downtown, and restaurants. The antique-filled bedrooms have air conditioning and private baths, and our two-room suite offers a fireplace. There are wonderful hiking trails and swimming in the Robert Treman State Park that borders our property, and fishing is allowed in our bass-stocked pond. The Inn is AAA approved and offers corporate rates to business people.

Host: Diane Carroll Carney
Rooms: 4 (PB) $65-125
Full Breakfast
Credit Cards: A, B, C, D
Notes: 2, 5, 9, 14

NEW LEBANON

The American Country Collection 132

4 Greenwood Lane, Delmar, 12054
(518) 439-7001

This historic Colonial was built in 1797 for a preacher and his family. Nestled on 18 acres just outside of town, this country inn is convenient to Lenox, the Berkshires, the Capital District, and major ski areas. There is a suite on the first floor with a feather mattress, day bed with a trundle, and a private bath, and three rooms on the second floor share a bath. Rooms are light and airy with homemade quilts and period Colonial furniture. A full country breakfast is served each morning. Smoking outside only. $35-75, seasonal.

Covered Bridge

P. O. Box 447, Norfolk, CT 06058
(203) 542-5944

This 1797 Colonial farmhouse set on 18 acres offers a quiet country retreat but is close to all of the activities offered in the Berkshires. Guests may relax beside the fireplace in the livingroom, or enjoy the beautiful front porch with a view of the Taconic Hills. A full country breakfast is served in the dining room. There is a first-floor suite with a private bath and three guest rooms on the second floor that share a bath. $60-75.

Elaine's Bed and Breakfast and Inn Reservation Service

4987 Kingston Road, Elbridge, 13060
(315) 689-2082

A cozy home filled with antiques, this rambling farmhouse on 50 acres lies in the heart of Shaker country. It has wide-plank floors, five delightful guest rooms, and

6 Pets welcome; 7 Smoking allowed; 8 Children welcome; 9 Social drinking allowed; 10 Tennis available; 11 Swimming available; 12 Golf available; 13 Skiing available; 14 May be booked through travel agents.

three baths. The original house dates back to 1836. Share the relaxed country atmosphere with other interesting guests, a dog, and the cat family. Children and pets are welcome. A spacious new three-room contemporary apartment in an adjacent building is available. Moderate.

NEW PALTZ

The American Country Collection 116

4 Greenwood Lane, Delmar, 12054
(518) 439-7001

Rejuvenating one's mind and body can be as simple as strolling through the apple, pear, and quince orchards on a warm summer day, or as fascinating as a session on stress management and holistic health offered by the host. Four guest rooms, two private baths, two shared baths. One room has a double Murphy bed, working fireplace, air conditioning, and private bath. All rooms have air conditioning. A healthful gourmet breakfast is served in the light and airy country kitchen. Smoking in guest rooms and outdoors. Children welcome. No pets. $70-90; children under seven free.

The American Country Collection 117

4 Greenwood Lane, Delmar, 12054
(518) 439-7001

Plan your day from the rambling lemonade porch of this immaculate Queen Anne Victorian in this tiny village near the Shawangunk Mountains. Three guest rooms, one with private bath. Guests in the master bedroom have a view of the solarium and the gardens from their indoor balcony. Smoking outdoors only. Children over ten welcome. Two cats in residence. $70-80.

Nana's

54 Old Ford Road, 12561
(914) 255-5678

Comfortable country home on 20 acres with spacious lawns, woods, trails, cross-country skiing, horseback riding, hiking in mountains, and rock climbing. House is furnished with antiques. Country breakfast from large menu. Deer, racoons, red fox, possum, and bunnies on the property. Hunters are not welcome.

Host: Kathleen Maloney
Rooms: 2 (SB) $50
Full Breakfast
Credit Cards: None
Notes: 2, 5, 8, 10, 11, 12, 13

NEW ROCHELLE

The American Country Collection 152

4 Greenwood Lane, Delmar, 12054
(518) 439-7001

Set in a quiet suburban community, this gracious English Tudor sits on one-third acre of manicured lawn and shrubs and is surrounded by other homes which are some of the finest examples of Norman Tudor architecture in the Northeast. A large elm tree, one of the few that survived the great Dutch Elm disease, highlights the muted charm of this picturesque location not far from New York City and the Long Island Sound beaches. One third-floor room, which is air-conditioned in the summer, offers a king-size bed and private hall bath. A continental plus breakfast is served in the morning. Children over 10 welcome. No smoking. $75.

Rose Hill Guest House

44 Rose Hill Avenue, 10804
(914) 632-6464

The hostess at this beautiful, intimate French Normandy home is a real estate

---

NOTES: Credit cards accepted: A Master Card; B Visa; C American Express; D Discover Card; E Diner's Club; F Other; 2 Personal Checks accepted; 3 Lunch available; 4 Dinner available; 5 Open all year;

agent and bridge Life Master. Weather permitting, enjoy breakfast on the flower patio or in the chandeliered library/dining room. Thirty minutes to Manhattan by train or car. Safe parking behind house.

Host: Marilou Mayetta
Rooms: 2 (SB) $48.50-64.65
Deluxe Continental Breakfast
Minimum stay holidays: 2 nights
Credit Cards: None
Notes: 2, 5, 6, 7, 8, 9, 14

NEW YORK

Aaah! Bed and Breakfast #1, Ltd. ALD-1

P. O. Box 200, 10108-0200
(212) 246-4000; (800) 776-4001
FAX (212) 265-4346

Quintessential bed and breakfast on a quiet, tree-lined street. This five-story brownstone family home is the prettiest bed and breakfast accommodation of 176 listed by Aaah! Private apartment on the first floor is available for two to four people. Good quality antiques throughout the house. Your hostess makes a sumptuous continental breakfast starting at 7:30 A.M. and serves it on sterling silver flatware and good quality dishes by the fireplace in the breakfast room. Victorian sitting room with piano. Smoking permitted. $80-100.

Aaah! Bed and Breakfast #1, Ltd. BALD45-1

P. O. Box 200, 10108-0200
(212) 246-4000; (800) 776-4001
FAX (212) 265-4346

Brownstone on a tree-lined street just opposite London Terrace. Second-floor studio walkup. The apartment has original ornate ceiling moldings. Three windows facing north fill the apartment with plenty of natural light. Round dining table and fold-out day bed are the major pieces of furniture. Many accent pieces make this studio with Pullman kitchen a very homey place. Continental breakfast. $80-100.

Aaah! Bed and Breakfast #1, Ltd. BRUE45-1

P. O. Box 200, 10108-0200
(212) 246-4000; (800) 776-4001
FAX (212) 265-4346

Simple studio in a mid-rise building with elevator and doorman. Japanese hostess keeps apartment spotlessly clean. The location is ideal for Javitz Center conventioneers, as the free bus goes to the front door of the Days Inn directly across the street. Excellent midtown location with mass transit buses at the door and subway stops within a block. Smoking permitted. Continental breakfast. TV, stereo, laundry service, and air conditioning. $80.

Aaah! Bed and Breakfast #1, Ltd. BUC-1

P. O. Box 200, 10108-0200
(212) 246-4000; (800) 776-4001
FAX (212) 265-4346

Tastefully appointed duplex apartment (two levels) with guest room and private entrance in a low-rise building. Very bright and sunny apartment with skylights. Spiral staircase goes up to the guest room that overlooks the livingroom equipped with a fire mantel. This apartment is in the heart of the theater district and is accessible to all major transportation. The hostess is a German-born language interpreter who is friendly and hospitable. Continental breakfast. TV, stereo, air conditioning, and laundry service. Smoking permitted. Hosted. $60-80.

---

6 Pets welcome; 7 Smoking allowed; 8 Children welcome; 9 Social drinking allowed; 10 Tennis available; 11 Swimming available; 12 Golf available; 13 Skiing available; 14 May be booked through travel agents.

Aaah! Bed and Breakfast #1, Ltd. CHA

P. O. Box 200, 10108-0200
(212) 246-4000; (800) 776-4001
FAX (212) 265-4346

West Side midtown two-bedroom apartment in a fourth-floor walkup that has been redone. New floors, walls, doors, appliances, windows, and sleeping for as many as eight. Continental breakfast. TV, air conditioning, and dishwasher. Unhosted. $160/night.

Aaah! Bed and Breakfast #1, Ltd. DAVI

P. O. Box 200, 10108-0200
(212) 246-4000; (800) 776-4001
FAX (212) 265-4346

If guests are looking for romantic and charming surroundings, this studio apartment, filled with walls covered with miniature busts and other art, is suggested frequently. Its courtyard with trellises, trees, and a carriage house make it hard to to realize it is on restaurant row in New York City. Continental breakfast. Unhosted. $80-100.

Aaah! Bed and Breakfast #1, Ltd. DOS

P. O. Box 200, 10108-0200
(212) 246-4000; (800) 776-4001
FAX (212) 265-4346

Studio apartment in mid-rise building with elevator and intercom at the door. Two blocks south of Washington Square on the corner of Washington and Bleeker streets. The interior is contemporary in design and features a glass-top round dining room table. There is a small balcony. Nicely equipped with color TV, stereo, air conditioning, and dishwasher. Continental breakfast. Unhosted. $80-100.

Aaah! Bed and Breakfast #1, Ltd. DUNB32-CC1

P. O. Box 200, 10108-0200
(212) 246-4000; (800) 776-4001
FAX (212) 265-4346

A gracious parlor-floor one-bedroom unit in a brownstone on 35th Street featuring 14-foot ceilings, a modern kitchen, tasteful furnishings, cable/color TV/VCR, air conditioning, and fireplace. Continental breakfast. Smoking permitted. Must be 18 or older. Unhosted. $120.

Aaah! Bed and Breakfast #1, Ltd. DUNB32-CIV

P. O. Box 200, 10108-0200
(212) 246-4000; (800) 776-4001
FAX (212) 265-4346

The Louisa May at East 35th Street is a third-floor, one-bedroom apartment in an old brownstone. This tree-shaded apartment has cable TV/VCR, air conditioning, and carpeting. The kitchen is fully equipped. Continental breakfast. Smoking permitted. Must be 18 or older. Unhosted. $85.

Aaah! Bed and Breakfast #1, Ltd. EIN

P. O. Box 200, 10108-0200
(212) 246-4000; (800) 776-4001
FAX (212) 265-4346

West Village. Two-bedroom loft space on ground floor. Every window looks out into a yard or garden. The building is more than 100 years old and is in one of the oldest sections of the city. Originally a farm occupied this site. The building is pointed out on the Smithsonian walking tour. TV/VCR, stereo, air conditioning, microwave, and dishwasher. Continental breakfast. Smoking permitted. Must be 16 or older.

NOTES: Credit cards accepted: A Master Card; B Visa; C American Express; D Discover Card; E Diner's Club; F Other; 2 Personal Checks accepted; 3 Lunch available; 4 Dinner available; 5 Open all year;

Aaah! Bed and Breakfast #1, Ltd. ROGER

P. O. Box 200, 10108-0200
(212) 246-4000; (800) 776-400
FAX (212) 265-4346

This apartment is a second-floor walkup on the Upper East Side on East 92nd Street. The neighborhood is an expensive one. The apartment is both aesthetic and functional. It is obvious that no expense was spared in making this home. TV/VCR, stereo, air conditioning, microwave, dishwasher, and laundry service. Continental breakfast. Smoking permitted. Unhosted. $75-100.

Aaah! Bed and Breakfast #1, Ltd. SALLY

P. O. Box 200, 10108-0200
(212) 246-4000; (800) 776-4001
FAX (212) 265-4346

Perfect Upper East Side location for all the shops and museums in the area. The apartment is equipped with one and one-half baths and has spectacular views overlooking both Central Park and the East River. Potted plants and trees abound in the livingroom, which offers a possibility of three different sleeping arrangements. There is a full-service health club with pool. Parking $22. TV/VCR, stereo, air conditioning, dishwasher, maid service, laundry service, and elevator. Continental breakfast. Smoking permitted. Hosted. $60-80.

Ariel

Bed and Breakfast Network of New York
134 West 32nd Street, Suite 602, 10001
(212) 645-8134

Lovely room with a unique jeweled canopy bed. The room is furnished in a Victorian-style and has a private bath and telephone. Midtown, West Side, near Broadway theaters, Carnegie Hall, Lincoln Center, and Central Park. $90 doubles only.

Bed and Breakfast (& Books)

35 West 92nd Street, 10025
(212) 865-8740

Sample listings: Beautifully renovated town house on quiet tree-lined street near Central Park offers one double-bed room with private bath. Convenient to museums, theaters, shopping, and all transportation. Children welcome in loft areas. $70 for one; $80 for two; $115 for three. Working artist's loft in the heart of Soho has comfortable twin-bed room, sitting area, and bath en-suite. Convenient to Soho galleries, shops, and restaurants. Sofa opens to sleep two. $85 for one; $92.50 for two; $120 for three.

Host: Judith Goldberg
Rooms: 50 (45 PB; 5 SB) $70-90
Continental Breakfast
Credit Cards: None
Notes: 5, 14

Bed and Breakfast U.S.A., Ltd. 37

Old Sheffield Road, South Egremont, MA, 01258
(413) 528-2113

Three large studio apartments in a historic landmark townhouse on Riverside Drive (between 75th and 76th) in Manhattan. Romantically decorated with antiques, queen beds, comfortable sofas, dining areas, TVs, and kitchenettes. Monogrammed terry-cloth robes are provided in the oversize baths. The guest apartments give total privacy with the advantage of hosts nearby. Easy access to all public transportation. Walking distance to Lincoln Center and Columbus Avenue shops and eateries. Continental breakfast. No pets. Children welcome. No smoking. $110-120.

---

6 Pets welcome; 7 Smoking allowed; 8 Children welcome; 9 Social drinking allowed; 10 Tennis available; 11 Swimming available; 12 Golf available; 13 Skiing available; 14 May be booked through travel agents.

Bed and Breakfast U.S.A., Ltd. 266

Old Sheffield Road, South Egremont, MA, 01258
(413) 528-2113

Directly across the river from Manhattan's Lower East Side, this bed and breakfast was formerly the home of one of New York's shipbuilders. In Greenpoint's harbor the Monitor was built. It is one of the grand houses of the Civil War period. Today homes in this area have been designated landmarks by the New York Landmarks Preservation Commission. Air conditioning, high ceilings, large windows, and color TV. Continental breakfast delivered to your room. Major subway and bus lines are at the corner. It is 20 minutes to Manhattan. There are five guest rooms, two with private bath. Children over 12 welcome. Smoking permitted. Dog in residence. No guest pets accepted. $65-80. Weekly rates available.

Charlotte's

Bed and Breakfast Network of New York
134 West 32nd Street, Suite 602, 10001
(212) 645-8134

Six unhosted apartments in a 100-year-old brownstone in midtown on the East Side. Accommodations range from modest, small one-bedroom at $75 to a palatial parlor-floor apartment with 14-foot ceilings, fireplace, modern kitchen, cable TV, air conditioning, and tasteful furnishings. $75-180.

Community Church Off Park Bed and Breakfast

61 Irving Place #4D, 10003
(212) 228-4645

Offered are five private, fully furnished, comfortable one-bedroom apartments and a studio apartment in a turn-of-the-century brownstone building on East 35th Street in the lovely Eastside Murray Hill neighborhood. Near the Empire State Building, Grand Central, Penn State, and 5th Avenue shopping. Stocked kitchens, private baths, cable TV, answering machines, and many personal touches. Convenient to all transportation. Minimum stay is three nights.

Host: C. McPherson
Rooms: 6 apartments (PB) $75-125
Continental Breakfast
Credit Cards: F
Notes: 5, 6 (additional $5), 7, 8, 9

Eileen S.

Bed and Breakfast Network of New York
134 West 32nd Street, Suite 602, 10001
(212) 645-8134

Doorman building on West 96th Street on the 17th floor, this bed and breakfast overlooks Central Park and reservoir. Private bath, queen-size bed. Two resident cats. No smoking. $60-80.

Florence N.

Bed and Breakfast Network of New York
134 West 32nd Street, Suite 602, 10001
(212) 645-8134

Doorman building on 86th Street, this accommodation offers a river view, a large room with a pair of twins, TV, air conditioning, and private bath. $60-90.

Guida

Bed and Breakfast Network of New York
134 West 32nd Street, Suite 602, 10001
(212) 645-8134

This lovely townhouse with a garden on East 62nd Street is furnished with antiques, paintings, and rugs. Four working fireplaces, beautiful furniture, two rooms available, one with a pair of twins, and the other a queen-size bed. TV, private bath, air conditioning. $90.

Judie H.

Bed and Breakfast Network of New York
134 West 32nd Street, Suite 602, 10001
(212) 645-8134

Doorman building on West 22nd Street on
the fifteenth floor, this accommodation has
a great view, private bath, TV, air conditioning, phone in room. No smoking. $60-
90.

Julius

Bed and Breakfast Network of New York
134 West 32nd Street, Suite 602, 10001
(212) 645-8134

Doorman building on East 86th Street on
the 21st floor, this bed and breakfast has a
great view, private bath, TV, air conditioning, laundry, access to a health club. $60-
90.

Marjorie

Bed and Breakfast Network of New York
134 West 32nd Street, Suite 602, 10001
(212) 645-8134

Doorman building on East 69th Street, this
accommodation offers a private bath, air
conditioning, laundry, king-size bed. No
smoking. $60-90.

Serge

Bed and Breakfast Network of New York
134 West 32nd Street, Suite 602, 10001
(212) 645-8134

In Greenwich Village, this 1840s townhouse is one-half block from Washington
Square park, and offers guests an entire
parlor floor. Fifteen-foot ceilings, access to
the backyard and garden, art from all over
the world, double bed, double sofa bed in
the livingroom, air conditioning, ceiling
fans, and laundry. Host lives downstairs.
$130-150.

Steve H.

Bed and Breakfast Network of New York
134 West 32nd Street, Suite 602, 10001
(212) 645-8134

This building with a doorman is on Central
Park South on the seventeenth floor.
Beautiful furnished room, air conditioning,
cable TV, laundry, queen-size bed. $60-90.

Urban Ventures, Inc.
BER003

P. O. Box 426, 10024
(212) 594-5650; FAX (212) 947-9320

A take-off-your-shoes apartment that will
please. Soft, white carpets, huge closets,
queen bed, and two cats. Doorman, elevator building right behind the Essex Hotel.
Compare prices! $80-130.

Urban Ventures, Inc.
BRE000

P. O. Box 426, 10024
(212) 594-5650; FAX (212) 947-9320

The lucky new owners of this apartment
have created a breathtakingly beautiful
home. Two bedrooms, a queen and double,
with private baths. Built-in mahogany closets, a terrace, garden, and delightful extras
to discover. At East 29th off 3rd Avenue.
$190-194.

Urban Ventures, Inc.
FAB111

P. O. Box 426, 10024
(212) 594-5650; FAX (212) 947-9320

An 1840 home in all its elegance. Original
brick, fireplace, two baths, on a landmark
street. A place to write home about! On
West 22nd between 8th and 9th avenues.
$115.

---

6 Pets welcome; 7 Smoking allowed; 8 Children welcome; 9 Social drinking allowed; 10 Tennis available; 11
Swimming available; 12 Golf available; 13 Skiing available; 14 May be booked through travel agents.

Urban Ventures, Inc. HOW100

P. O. Box 426, 10024
(212) 594-5650; FAX (212) 947-9320

The sun sets on your balcony about the same time as the theater lights sparkle on. Your room with private bath is in an apartment filled with theater memorabilia. The building has an exercise room with a sauna and a tiled roof garden. First class! West 55th Street and 8th Avenue. $75 single; $90 double; $115 as apartment.

Urban Ventures, Inc. KIR100

P. O. Box 426, 10024
(212) 594-5650; FAX (212) 947-9320

Bed and breakfast on the 15th floor at 38th and Lexington gives you views of penthouses. Very nice! Light, airy, twin-bed room in a fashionable building. $90 double; $125 as apartment.

Urban Ventures, Inc. MAU003

P. O. Box 426, 10024
(212) 594-5650; FAX (212) 947-9320

Sitting on top of the world with Central Park and Lincoln Center at your feet. Open air concerts float up to your 27th-floor window. Wonderful Irish host. On West 62nd street. $90-115.

NIAGARA FALLS

Rainbow Hospitality NF200

466 Amherst Street, Buffalo, 14207
(716) 874-8797

Step back in time to the grandeur of yesteryear in this cross-gabled Queen Anne Victorian home. Built in 1906, this beautifully restored home boasts original light fixtures, oak woodwork and wainscoting, stained-glass windows, many family antiques, and friendly hospitality. Situated in the heart of the city of Niagara Falls, bus service and fine dining are within walking distance. Ample off-street parking. Full breakfast. No smoking. $60-70.

NIVERVILLE

The American Country Collection 079

4 Greenwood Lane, Delmar, 12054
(518) 439-7001

Beautifully preserved gingerbread and an old oak door with Venetian glass inserts detail this Italianate private home built in 1870. Two second-floor guest rooms share one bath. Normally rented to one party traveling together. Breakfast is served in either the elegant dining room with its original faux fireplace and crystal chandelier, or in the new solarium overlooking the garden. No smoking. Adults only. No pets. $60 (Nov. 1-May 1); $70 (May 2-Oct. 31).

NORTH HUDSON

Pine Tree Inn Bed and Breakfast

Route 9, 12855
(518) 532-9255

Small, century-old classic Adirondack inn. Full breakfast served, featuring homemade breads, in the dining room with its original tin ceiling. Period furniture decorates the country-comfortable rooms. Centrally situated for year-round activities.

Hosts: Peter and Patricia Schoch
Rooms: 5 (SB) $35-55
Minimum stay holidays: 2-3 nights
Credit Cards: None

NOTES: Credit cards accepted: A Master Card; B Visa; C American Express; D Discover Card; E Diner's Club; F Other; 2 Personal Checks accepted; 3 Lunch available; 4 Dinner available; 5 Open all year;

Notes: 2, 4 (winter only), 5, 7, 8 (over 6), 9, 10, 11, 12, 13

NORTH RIVER

Highwinds Inn

Barton Mines Road, P. O. Box 70, 12856
(518) 251-3760

Situated at an elevation of 2,500 feet on 1,600 acres of land in the middle of a garnet mine. All guest rooms and the dining area have a spectacular view to the west. On the property there is mountain biking, canoeing, hiking to several peaks and ponds, garnet mine tours, gardens, cross-country ski touring, and guided summer and winter mid-week trips available. Nearby spring rafting on the Hudson; Lake George; Octoberfest.

Host: Kim Repscha
Rooms: 4 (PB) $35/person
Full Breakfast
Credit Cards: A, B
Closed Nov. and Apr.
Notes: 2, 3 (picnic), 4, 8 (over 12), 9, 10, 11, 12, 13, 14

NYACK

Bed and Breakfast U.S.A., Ltd. 157

Old Sheffield Road, South Egremont, MA, 01258
(413) 528-2113

This former carriage house has been entirely rebuilt and renovated in Art Deco-style. Set among elaborate gardens and terraces, it is a separate guest cottage with lots of glass, a quarry-stone floor, built-in Jacuzzi, wrought iron spiral staircase to sleeping loft with a queen bed, wet bar, cable TV, and air conditioning. Fabulous getaway. Privacy, but close to the little town of Nyack, antique shops, and fine restaurants. Gourmet breakfast is self-serve. Smoking permitted. No children. Dog in residence. Guest pets permitted. $125.

OGDENSBURG

Maple Hill Country Inn

Riverside Drive, Box 21, 13669
(315) 383-3961

Charming Cape Cod home situated amid fifty-year-old maples overlooking the beautiful St. Lawrence River. Decorated with antiques and wicker. Open all year, with special winter packages available.

Host: Marilyn Jones
Rooms: 4 (SB) $40-65
Full Breakfast
Credit Cards: None
Notes: 2, 4, 5, 6, 8, 9, 12, 13

OLCOTT

Bayside Guest House

1572 Lockport Olcott Road
(State Road 78), 14126-0034
(716) 778-7767

Overlooking the harbor and marina, near Lake Ontario, this country-style Victorian home offers fishermen and travelers a comfortable, relaxed stay. Antiques and collectibles furnish this guest house. Great fishing and a county park within walking distance. Plenty of restaurants. One-half hour from Niagara Falls, one hour from Buffalo.

Bayside guest house

---

6 Pets welcome; 7 Smoking allowed; 8 Children welcome; 9 Social drinking allowed; 10 Tennis available; 11 Swimming available; 12 Golf available; 13 Skiing available; 14 May be booked through travel agents.

Host: Jane M. Voelpel
Rooms: 5 (SB) $30
Continental Breakfast
Credit Cards: None
Notes: 2, 5, 6, 8, 9, 10, 12

OLD CHATHAM

The American Country Collection 037

4 Greenwood Lane, Delmar, 12054
(518) 439-7001

Wildflowers and birds, stone walls, and lawns beckon the guest to sit back and enjoy a simpler life-style in this 175-year-old Greek Revival private home on one-half acre. The home features a collection of antiques from the late 1700s that has been handed down from generation to generation. One second-floor guest room with private hall bath. Breakfast can be served on the patio in nice weather. Smoking limited to first floor. Adults only. No pets. $40.

OLIVEREA

Slide Mountain Forest House

805 Oliverea Road, 12410
(914) 254-5365; (914) 254-4269

Nestled in the Catskill Mountains State Park, this inn offers the flavor and charm of the old country. Come and enjoy the beautiful country setting, superb lodging, fine dining, and chalet rentals. Having run this bed and breakfast for over 55 years, the hosts strive to give you a pleasant and enjoyable stay. German and continental cuisine, a bar and lounge, pool, tennis, hiking, fishing, antiquing, and more are available for your pleasure.

Hosts: Ursula and Ralph Combe
Rooms: 21 (17 PB; 4 SB) $50-60, American Plan
   or Modified American Plan available

Full Breakfast
Credit Cards: A, B
Notes: 2, 3, 4, 5 (chalets only), 7, 8, 9, 10, 11, 12, 13

OSWEGO

The Chestnut Grove Inn

Rural Delivery #7, Box 10, 13126
(315) 342-2547

A 150-year-old three-story Victorian Mansard-style home. Near SUNY, Oswego, Lake Ontario, Community living-room with TV, VCR, piano, and telephone. All 5 guest rooms have private baths. Full breakfast is served, other meals catered by appointment. Private dining room and meeting facilities. Antiques, air conditioning, box lunches. Airport transportation available.

Hosts: Frank and Kathy Casella
Rooms: 5 (PB) $35-47.50
Full Breakfast
Credit Cards: A, B
Notes: 2, 3, 4, 5, 6, 7, 8

PALENVILLE

The American Country Collection 031

4 Greenwood Lane, Delmar, 12054
(518) 439-7001

This large old Victorian with wraparound porch is nestled along the creek by the scenic mountain road that leads to Tannersville. Leaf peepers, creek swimmers, waterfall seekers, hikers, and nature lovers will find this area exciting. One first-floor guest room with double bed and private bath. Four second-floor rooms share two baths. The livingroom has a fireplace, TV, and piano. Smoking limited. Children welcome. Pets in residence. Full breakfast. $40-60.

NOTES: Credit cards accepted: A Master Card; B Visa; C American Express; D Discover Card; E Diner's Club; F Other; 2 Personal Checks accepted; 3 Lunch available; 4 Dinner available; 5 Open all year;

Bed and Breakfast U.S.A., Ltd. 21

Old Sheffield Road, South Egremont, MA, 01258
(413) 528-2113

A turn-of-the-century Queen Anne Victorian with large rooms. Distance is 18 miles to Woodstock, 10 miles to Hunter Mountain, 2 miles to horseback riding, 5 miles to Catskill Game Farm and North Lake, 8 miles to cross-country skiing, and a short walk to swimming or golf. Accommodations include a ground-floor suite with private entrance, private bath with whirlpool, fireplace and a ladder to the loft; a room with a double bed and private bath; two other rooms with shared bath. Full breakfast. No pets. No smoking. Children over four welcome. $55-125.

The Kenmore Country Bed and Breakfast

Malden Avenue, 12463
(518) 678-3494

This quaint country home, was built in the late 1800s and is nestled at the bottom of Hunter Mountain. Spend the night in one of the three cozy bedrooms. Enjoy the day relaxing in the large livingroom or screened-in porch. Close to many attractions. Cottage rental also available, but breakfast is not included.

Hosts: John and Lauren Hanzl
Rooms: 3 (1 PB; 2 SB) $45-55
Full Breakfast
Credit Cards: None
Notes: 5, 6 (cottage only), 7 (limited), 8

Palenville House

Junction Routes 23A and 32A, P. O. Box 465, 12463
(518) 678-5649

Palenville House is a magnificent turn-of-the-century Victorian home. It is named for the quaint hamlet in the Catskill Mountains where it is situated. This ideal location is within minutes of North Lake State Park, hiking trails, canoeing, horseback riding, Hunter Mountain Ski Bowl, Ski Windham, and much more. A suite is available.

Hosts: Jim Poretta and Jim Forster
Rooms: 5 (3 PB; 2 SB) $60-125
Full Breakfast
Credit Cards: None
Notes: 2, 5, 8, 9, 12, 13, 14

PALMYRA

Canaltown Bed and Breakfast

119 Canandaigua Street, 14522
(315) 597-5553

Savor a delicious country breakfast in this 1850s Greek Revival home. Situated close to antique stores and local museums. One hundred yards to the Erie Canal Hiking Trail; canoe rentals nearby.

Hosts: Robert and Barbara Leisten
Rooms: 2 (SB) $52.50
Full Breakfast
Credit Cards: C
Notes: 2, 5, 8, 9, 13, 14

PENNFIELD

Strawberry Castle

1883 Penfield Road, 14526
(716) 385-3266

In suburban Rochester, this 1875 landmark Victorian Italianate Villa combines the historic charm of yesteryear with the pleasures of a private luxury pool and patio on three acres of grounds. Brass or Empire beds in large, air-conditioned rooms. Fine restaurants and golf courses nearby. Turn this trip into a special memory.

Hosts: Cynthia and Charles Whited
Rooms: 3 (PB) $75-95
Continental Breakfast
Credit Cards: A, B, C, D
Notes: 2, 5, 7, 9, 11, 14

---

6 Pets welcome; 7 Smoking allowed; 8 Children welcome; 9 Social drinking allowed; 10 Tennis available; 11 Swimming available; 12 Golf available; 13 Skiing available; 14 May be booked through travel agents.

PENN YAN

The Wagener Estate Bed and Breakfast

351 Elm Street, 14527
(315) 536-4591

Centrally situated in the Finger Lakes, this bed and breakfast is in an historic 1796 home furnished with antiques and nestled on four acres. Hospitality, country charm, comfort, and an elegant breakfast await you.

Hosts: Norm and Evie Worth
Rooms: 4 (2 PB; 2 SB) $60-70
Full Breakfast
Credit Cards: A, B, C
Closed Jan.
Notes: 2, 8, 9, 10, 11, 12

PHILMONT

The American Country Collection 066

4 Greenwood Lane, Delmar, 12054
(518) 439-7001

Set back from the country road, this spacious lodge-style bed and breakfast is enveloped in eight acres of woods but is just one mile from the Taconic Parkway and 30 minutes from Tanglewood, Massachusetts. Four guest rooms, two with private baths. The two rooms on the second floor can be rented as a unit with private livingroom, refrigerator and sink alcove, private bath, and private entrance. Smoking in designated areas. Children welcome. Full breakfast served in the kitchen, livingroom, sun room, or decks or patio in summer. $55-65; suite $150.

PITTSTOWN

Maggie Towne's Bed and Breakfast

Rural Delivery 2, Box 82, Valley Falls, 12185
(518) 663-8369; (518) 686-7331

An old Colonial situated amid beautiful lawns and trees 14 miles east of Troy on NY Route 7. Enjoy tea or wine before the fireplace in the family room. Use the music room or read on the screened porch. Your hostess will prepare lunch for you to take on tour or enjoy at the house. It's 20 miles to historic Bennington, Vermont, and 30 to Saratoga Springs.

Host: Maggie Towne
Rooms: 3 (SB) $35-45
Full Breakfast
Credit Cards: None
Notes: 2, 5, 8, 9, 10, 11, 12, 13

POMPEY

Elaine's Bed and Breakfast and Inn Reservation Service

4987 Kingston Road, Elbridge, 13060
(315) 689-2082

Close to Cazenovia. Nestled on the edge of Old Cherry Valley Turnpike, this early 1800s center-hall Colonial is nicely furnished with antiques. It has two bedrooms available with a private bath and entrance. The master suite with queen-size waterbed and private bath may be available with a two-night minimum stay. A perfect place for a family to visit or a couple to get away to the quiet countryside. Fresh flowers, hot coffee, wine, and cheese. A full country breakfast is served, including heart-shaped waffles and pure maple syrup. Conveniently situated to Syracuse, Colgate University, ski areas, antique row, shopping, and swimming. Plenty to do for a week!

Elaine's Bed and Breakfast Reservation Service

4987 Kingston Road, Elbridge, 13060
(315) 689-2082

Charming, well-furnished, sparkling ranch flat on two acres with a view of a sculpture garden. Guests may have the entire main floor. Two double bedrooms. Master bedroom opens to another room with a sleeper sofa for a family suite. One and one-half baths. Southeast of Syracuse in the country.

PORT JEFFERSON

Compass Rose Bed and Breakfast

415 West Broadway, 11777
(516) 474-1111

Dating from the 1820s, this home and barn of a ship's captain are situated above the busy harbor of Port Jefferson with its ferry to Connecticut. Beautiful Port Jefferson is a restored whaling village with unique shops and fine restaurants. Although modernized with new baths and central air conditioning, the home is decorated with antiques and country furnishings. Breakfast specialties of homemade breads, jams, freshly ground coffee, teas, and cereals are served each morning in the Rose Parlor.

Host: Kathleen Burk
Rooms: 4 (2 PB; 2 SB) $58-125
Continental Breakfast
Credit Cards: A, B, C
Notes: 2, 5, 7, 8, 9, 10, 11, 12, 14

PURLING

Shepherd's Croft

Mountain Avenue, Box 263, 12470
(518) 622-9504

Nestled in the Catskill Mountains with all the modern conveniences. Wonderful vistas, streams, and waterfalls nearby; swimming, skiing, golf, and more. Approximately 100 miles from New York City, 50 from Albany, but a world away from the noise and commotion.

Rooms: 11 (6 PB; 5 SB) $40-50
Continental Breakfast
Credit Cards: A, B
Notes: 2, 5, 8, 9, 13, 14

QUEENSBURY

The American Country Collection 126

4 Greenwood Lane, Delmar, 12054
(518) 439-7001

Original gingerbread accents this 100-year-old farmhouse on a working berry farm. There's a comfortable country feeling here with family furnishings and mementos, patchwork quilts, and oak furnishings. Two guest rooms with private baths. One room has a whirlpool tub. Excellent location for outlet shopping, hot air balloon festival, Great Escape Amusement Park, and Lake George. Smoking outdoors only. Children over six welcome. Cat in residence. $50-65.

Crislip's Bed and Breakfast

Rural Delivery 1, Box 57, Ridge Road, 12804
(518) 793-6869

Situated just minutes from Saratoga Springs and Lake George, this landmark Federal home provides spacious accommodations, complete with period antiques, four-poster beds, and down comforters. The country breakfast menu features buttermilk pancakes, scrambled eggs, and sausages. Your hosts invite you to relax on the porches and enjoy the mountain view of Vermont.

Hosts: Ned and Joyce Crislip
Rooms: 3 (PB) $55-75
Full Breakfast
Credit Cards: A, B, C
Notes: 2, 5, 8, 9, 10, 11, 12, 13

RED HOOK

The American Country Collection 115

4 Greenwood Lane, Delmar, 12054
(518) 439-7001

---

6 Pets welcome; 7 Smoking allowed; 8 Children welcome; 9 Social drinking allowed; 10 Tennis available; 11 Swimming available; 12 Golf available; 13 Skiing available; 14 May be booked through travel agents.

This home, built in 1821 in the Federal-style and restored in 1988, offers a ground-level suite with private entrance and bath, non-working fireplace, antique table and chairs, microwave, coffee maker, and small refrigerator. Smoking outdoors only. Children welcome. Port-a-crib available. No pets. Breakfast, made with only the freshest organic ingredients, is served at the table in front of the two deep-silled windows that look out to two acres of trees, vegetable, and flower gardens. $85.

REXFORD

The American Country Collection 042

4 Greenwood Lane, Delmar, 12054
(518) 439-7001

This Queen Anne Victorian manor house had a humble beginning in 1763 as a cabin, grew to a farmhouse in the early 19th century, and in 1883 took on its present elegant form. Three air-conditioned guest rooms, one with private bath. One suite on the second floor has two bedrooms, a sitting room with TV, and a private bath. Two first-floor rooms with TV and private entrances. An English country buffet breakfast is served in the dining room or on the terrace. The Mohawk River, a yacht club, two golf courses, and a bicycle path are within walking distance. Smoking permitted, with consideration for other guests. Children welcome. Two dogs in residence. $65-125, seasonal.

The American Country Collection 123

4 Greenwood Lane, Delmar, 12054
(518) 439-7001

An idyllic landscape of rolling hills, grassy fields, woodlands, and flowers surrounds this private suite set 800 feet back from a cul-de-sac on seven country acres. The suite includes a private bath, kitchenette, and separate entrance. No smoking. Children school age and over welcome. No pets. Arrangements for guest dog may be made occasionally. Fixings for breakfast provided in kitchenette for leisurely breakfast at guests' convenience. $65; $85 during August; $200 weekly; $500 monthly.

RHINEBECK

The American Country Collection 060

4 Greenwood Lane, Delmar, 12054
(518) 439-7001

Two years ago, skilled local craftsmen painstakingly restored this 1860 Victorian in the heart of this historic village, filled with antique and specialty shops, art galleries, and fine restaurants. The Aerodrome and Roosevelt and Vanderbilt mansions are just a short drive away. A gourmet breakfast is served at small tables in the fireplace oak dining room. Five guest rooms with private baths. One room has a working fireplace. Guests may choose from brass, canopy, or carved Victorian beds. Smoking limited to parlor. Children over 16 welcome. No pets. $175-275.

Sepascot Farms

301 Route 308, A-2, 12572
(914) 876-5840

This Victorian bed and breakfast is on a retired dairy farm complete with red barns, in historic Rhinebeck. The rooms are furnished with fourth-generation family heirlooms. There are two charming guest rooms, one with a queen-size bed and the other, a pair of twin beds. A separate breakfast/sitting room is provided solely for guest use. Farm-fresh full breakfasts are served each morning. Lawn sports, nature walks, cross-country skiing, and jogging are available. Member of the Rhinebeck Chamber of Commerce.

Host: Susan Kelly
Rooms: 2 (SB) $50
Full Breakfast
Credit Cards: A, B
Notes: 2, 5, 8 (over 12), 13

Village Victorian Inn

31 Center Street, 12572
(914) 876-8345

A seductive retreat filled with antiques, canopy beds, fine linens, and laces. Situated in the heart of historic Rhinebeck Village and close to fine dining, historic mansions, the Hudson River, and antiquing.

Hosts: Judy and Richard Kohler
Rooms: 7 (PB) $175-250
Full Breakfast
Credit Cards: A, B, C
Notes: 2, 5, 10, 11, 12, 13, 14

Village Victorian Inn

RICHFIELD SPRINGS

Country Spread Bed and Breakfast

23 Prospect Street, P. O. Box 1863, 13439
(315) 858-1870

Built in 1893 and situated within the village limits directly on New York State Route 28. Convenient to many central

Leatherstocking attractions, including antiquing, Coopers- town, opera, swimming, and boating. Guest rooms have a country decorated flair. Breakfast offers many delicious choices from Karen's kitchen. Families welcome. The hosts have two children. A casual respite with genuine and sincere hospitality. Rated and approved by the American Bed and Breakfast Association.

Hosts: Karen and Bruce Watson
Rooms: 2 (PB) $50-75
Full Breakfast
Credit Cards: A, B
Notes: 2, 5, 8, 9, 10, 11, 12, 14

RICHMONDVILLE

The American Country Collection 125

4 Greenwood Lane, Delmar, 12054
(518) 439-7001

This renovated Federal-style home is situated on 23 acres of scenic pastures and pines. Three guest rooms have private baths and shared baths. There is a large livingroom with fireplace, light and airy dining room, and a deck. Special treats include fresh fruit at night and gifts at breakfast table on holidays. Smoking permitted. Resident dog. Guest pets accepted with $15 deposit. Children welcome. Crib available. $50-60.

ROCHESTER

Rainbow Hospitality R200

466 Amherst Street, Buffalo, 14207
(716) 874-8797

Delightful hideaway guest house/cabin. Completely furnished with queen-size bed, livingroom with fireplace, private bath, and full kitchen. The main house offers guests a choice of two bedrooms with shared bath. The home is artistically decorated with

6 Pets welcome; 7 Smoking allowed; 8 Children welcome; 9 Social drinking allowed; 10 Tennis available; 11 Swimming available; 12 Golf available; 13 Skiing available; 14 May be booked through travel agents.

barn beams and antiques, situated on a quiet five acres of trees and wildlife. Ten minutes from I-90 and only 20 minutes from downtown Rochester. Great location for honeymoons and getaway weekends! $75-95.

ROCK HILL

Erehwon Retreat

28 Lord Road, 12775
(914) 794-3972

Enjoy a unique, wholistic bed and breakfast experience in Sullivan County's Catskill Mountains, two hours from New York City. Breakfast includes, but is not limited to, freshly baked breads, preserves, honeys, buckwheat kasha, pancakes, pure maple syrup, and freshly made juices. Massage, aroma therapy, Jacuzzi on premises. Hike, swim, ski, play tennis, or just hang out. Many other attractions nearby, and the home is filled with antiques.

Host: Murietta Lee
Rooms: 4 (3 SB) $50-100
Full Breakfast
Credit Cards: A, B, C, D, E
Notes: 2, 3, 4, 5, 10, 11, 12, 13, 14

ROCKPORT

Woods-Edge

151 Bluhm Road, 14450
(716) 223-8877

Woods-Edge is nestled among fragrant pines and wildlife only 20 minutes from downtown Rochester, near Exit 45 of I-90. Hideaway cabin is a romantically decorated private lodge with a large fireplace, queen bed, full kitchen, and private bath. Woods-Edge main house has two additional bedrooms with private baths. Rooms have wonderful old country pine against white walls and barn beams. Full breakfast is included. Children welcome; smoking restricted; no pets.

Host: Betty Kinsman
Rooms: 3 (1 PB; 2 SB) $50-95
Full Breakfast
Credit Cards: None
Notes: 2, 5, 8, 9, 10, 12, 13, 14

ROME

Elaine's Bed and Breakfast and Inn Reservation Service

4987 Kingston Road, Elbridge, 13060
(315) 689-2082

On six acres near state Thruway, this 1840 Cape saltbox is warmly furnished with many antiques and crafts made by the hostess. Full country breakfast of your choice. Suite features double bed, sitting area, and private bath. Two other rooms with one double bed each share main bath. Cot available. Perfect stop-off from Route 90 about halfway between Boston and Toronto. $45-60.

Elaine's Bed and Breakfast Reservation Service

4987 Kingston Road, Elbridge, 13060
(315) 689-2082

This brick Victorian farmhouse built in 1857 features complete antique furnishings. Three guest rooms are upstairs; one room offers a double and single bed. Near Griffiss Air Force Base. Pool, 40 acres, gardens, hiking trails, cross-country skiing. Near downhill skiing area. Resident dog and cat.

The Little Schoolhouse

6905 Dix Road, 13440
(315) 336-4474

A warm and welcoming 1840 Colonial saltbox situated on six private, quiet acres. Furnished in Early American with handcrafts throughout. Quick access to I-90, airport, and recreational facilities. Near

NOTES: Credit cards accepted: A Master Card; B Visa; C American Express; D Discover Card; E Diner's Club; F Other; 2 Personal Checks accepted; 3 Lunch available; 4 Dinner available; 5 Open all year;

Hamilton College. Enjoy breakfast in the summer kitchen or cozy dining room with homemade pastries and jellies always on the menu. Then take a tour to the Little Schoolhouse in the back yard, authentically furnished for the period 1900-1920. Come and make yourselves at home.

Host: Beverly Zingerline
Rooms: 3 (1 PB; 2 SB) $50-60
Full Breakfast
Credit Cards: A, B
Notes: 2, 5, 8, 12, 14

Maplecrest Bed and Breakfast

6480 Williams Road, 13440
(315) 337-0070

Maplecrest is a modern split-level home three miles northwest of historic Rome, featuring a large twin-bed room with private bath and a double and single with shared bath. Complete breakfast served in the dining room overlooking a spacious deck and flower garden. The thruway traveler can reach Maplecrest from Exits 32 or 33, since it is situated off Route 26 North. Within two miles of the Griffiss Air Force Base.

Host: Diane Saladino
Rooms: 3 (1 PB; 2 SB) $50-55
Full Breakfast
Credit Cards: None
Notes: 2, 5, 8, 9, 11, 12, 13, 14

ROOSEVELT ISLAND

Aaah! Bed and Breakfast #1, Ltd. BRI

P. O. Box 200, New York, 10108
(212) 246-4000; (800) 776-4001
FAX (212) 265-4346

Roosevelt Island, one of the safest places in Manhattan, is conveniently situated by tram across the East River just three and one-half minutes from midtown Manhattan. The island is filled with parks and beautiful promenades. Excellent views of Manhattan.

The apartment itself is a duplex in a high-rise building with a doorman. It is tastefully and eclectically furnished in contemporary and antiques. The master bedroom has a private bath and air conditioning. TV/VCR, laundry service, elevator. Continental breakfast is served. Hosted. $60-75.

ROSCOE

Huff House

Rural Delivery 2, 12776
(914) 482-4579

Enjoy 188 acres of secluded mountain beauty just 2 hours from New York City. Trout pond, heated pool, golf, and tennis available. Hosting the Roland Stafford Golf School. Outstanding dining in our new glass-walled dining room. Excellent wine cellar.

Hosts: Joseph and Joanne Forness
Rooms: 24 (PB) $105-120
Full Breakfast
Credit Cards: A, B, C
Closed Nov.-April
Notes: 2, 3, 4, 6 (restricted), 7, 8, 9, 10, 11, 12, 14

SARANAC LAKE

Elaine's Bed and Breakfast Reservation Service

4987 Kingston Road, Elbridge, 13060
(315) 689-2082

In the Adirondacks near Lake Placid are three bed and breakfasts. One rustic ranch has three double bed guest rooms; a stately old Colonial offers two large guest rooms; an updated Victorian has two guest rooms.

SARATOGA SPRINGS

Adelphi Hotel

365 Broadway, 12866
(518) 587-4688

6 Pets welcome; 7 Smoking allowed; 8 Children welcome; 9 Social drinking allowed; 10 Tennis available; 11 Swimming available; 12 Golf available; 13 Skiing available; 14 May be booked through travel agents.

Built in 1877 during the opulent Saratoga Victorian era, the Adelphi offers rooms that are lavishly and individually decorated, from rich curtain treatments and wallpapers to the antique furnishings and artwork. Each room has been modernized with a private full bath, air conditioning, direct dial phones, and cable TV. The charming Cafe Adelphi, with its lush garden courtyard, is a popular gathering place for cocktails, supper, or coffee and dessert.

Hosts: Gregg Siefker and Sheila Parkert
Rooms: 34 (PB) $65-290
Continental Breakfast
Credit Cards: A, B, C
Notes: 2, 4, 7, 9

The American Country Collection 086

4 Greenwood Lane, Delmar, 12054
(518) 439-7001

This private condominium offers contemporary conveniences in the setting of an historic former church. Two rooms are available, one furnished with an antique cherry chest and table that has been in the owner's family for years, and a second room with a private bath and two single beds with its own phone lines, is available on a short- or long-term basis. The new private bath has a Jacuzzi tub, and a balcony adjacent to the bedroom and livingroom overlooks a garden and is a perfect setting for breakfast. Another nonhosted condo with air conditioning, full kitchen, and livingroom, that sleeps two, is also available. Closed August. $65-95, seasonal.

The American Country Collection 105

4 Greenwood Lane, Delmar, 12054
(518) 439-7001

The friendly atmosphere of this working organic farm is a delight for children and adults. The Victorian farmhouse and barns have been restored to offer seven air-conditioned guest rooms, three with private baths. One room has two double beds, private bath, TV, wood-burning stove, and private deck. A gourmet is served in the Florida room amid flowering plants and the hot tub/Jacuzzi. The Saratoga Performing Arts Center and racetrack are two miles away. Smoking permitted. Children welcome. $100.

The American Country Collection 107

4 Greenwood Lane, Delmar, 12054
(518) 439-7001

This cozy, restored Victorian cottage with gingerbread millwork was probably the caretaker's home for one of the nearby mansions on North Broadway. It is conveniently situated within walking distance of the downtown shops and Skidmore College. Two guest rooms share one bath with the owner. Rooms are comfortable and immaculately clean. No smoking. Cat in residence. Children welcome. $55; $105 during jazz, racing season, college weekends.

The American Country Collection 136

4 Greenwood Lane, Delmar, 12054
(518) 439-7001

This "minisuite" in a 140-year-old historic Federal period brick home in town, offers a private second floor apartment/suite that includes a sitting room, refrigerator, appliances, screened-in porch, color TV, and antique furnishings. Its spacious front porch with wicker furniture and flower boxes invite guests to sit and enjoy the beauty of an evening sunset or a refreshing glass of lemonade. A continental plus breakfast and a daily newspaper is delivered to your door each morning, and two 10-speed bikes are available to guests. $100.

The American Country Collection 139

4 Greenwood Lane, Delmar, 12054
(518) 439-7001

This in-town historic home is only three blocks from the Saratoga Racetrack. Built in 1868 by a Civil War captain, it offers a front porch with white wicker furniture and a porch rocker, and a side lawn with a patio, a picnic table, and an outdoor grill. Furnishings include a mix of antiques, floral print wallpaper, lace curtains, and fresh and dried arrangments. One first-floor room with a queen bed and shared bath, one-second floor room with queen and single beds and a private bath, two second-floor rooms with double beds and shared bath, and one second-floor room with a single bed, private side porch, and a shared bath. Continental breakfast. $75-120.

The American Country Collection 141

4 Greenwood Lane, Delmar, 12054
(518) 439-7001

Capture the peace and charm of Saratoga in this warm and inviting 100-year-old Queen Anne-style home restored to its original elegance by its owners. Across the street from the Saratoga Racetrack, this bed and breakfast is minutes from the harness track and the Saratoga Performing Arts Center. Three rooms share one large bath with a double sink and vanity; two rooms have double beds; and a third room has two single beds. Bedrooms are light and airy, and all three rooms are air-conditioned in the summer. Full breakfast. $65-110, seasonal.

The American Country Collection 153

4 Greenwood Lane, Delmar, 12054
(518) 439-7001

Just five miles from Saratoga, this four-year-old contemporary home is set in an exclusive wooded setting across from a private country club. Two guest rooms on the second floor, one with two twin beds and the other with one double bed, share a connecting bath. Each room has its own alcove with sink, vanity, and walk-in closet. Another guest room on the first floor has a queen-size bed, and a private bath with a Jacuzzi. The livingroom has a TV/VCR, fireplace, and two extra-large sofas, and a rear screened-in porch can be used anytime in summer for reading or just relaxing. Breakfast is continental plus. $65-95.

The Clarion Inn at Saratoga

231 Broadway, 12866
(518) 583-1890

A turn-of-the-century, fully restored historic Inn in the heart of Saratoga, offering delightful atmosphere and cozy surroundings. One may enjoy the intimate cocktail lounge and sample a special selection offered nightly in the Victorian appointed dining room, complete with a fireplace. Oversized rooms echo the Victorian era, and many overlook an English garden. Nearby are many quaint shops and boutiques, as well as outlet malls. Also close by is the world-famous Saratoga Thoroughbred track and historic mineral baths.

Host: David Cykoski
Rooms: 38 (PB) $39-300
Full Breakfast, summer; Continental, winter
Credit Cards: A, B, C, D, E, F
Notes: 2, 4, 5, 7, 8, 9, 14

The Inn on Bacon Hill

P. O. Box 1462, 12866
(518) 695-3693

6 Pets welcome; 7 Smoking allowed; 8 Children welcome; 9 Social drinking allowed; 10 Tennis available; 11 Swimming available; 12 Golf available; 13 Skiing available; 14 May be booked through travel agents.

A peaceful alternative where you come as a stranger and leave as friends, just 10 minutes east of Saratoga Springs. The 1862 Victorian is situated in a quiet, pastoral setting with four air-conditioned bedrooms. Enjoy beautiful gardens and gazebo, explore country lanes, or relax in comfortable guest parlor with an extensive library. Baby grand piano adorns a Victorian parlor suite. Innkeeping courses offered. Full country breakfasts included.

Host: Andrea Collins-Breslin
Rooms: 4 (PB) $60-130
Full Breakfast
Credit Cards: A, B
Notes: 2, 5, 9, 10, 11, 12, 13, 14

Six Sisters
Bed and Breakfast

149 Union Avenue, 12866
(518) 583-1173

This beautifully appointed 1880 Victorian is on a historic, flower-laden boulevard in the heart of Saratoga Springs. Luxurious, immaculate rooms and suites offer king-size beds, private baths, and air conditioning. Antiques, Oriental carpets, hardwood

The Westchester House

floors, and Italian marble create a resplendent decor. The inn is close to Skidmore College, Convention Center, the racetracks, SPAC, downtown, museums, spa, antiques, and restaurants. SPAC discounts. The owner is a native of Saratoga eager to share local information. Recommended by *Gourmet*.

Hosts: Kate Benton and Steve Ramirez
Rooms: 4 (PB) $45-65
Full Breakfast
Credit Cards: None
Notes: 2, 5, 8 (over 10), 9, 13

The Westchester House

102 Lincoln Avenue, Box 944, 12866
(518) 587-7613

This gracious 1885 Queen Anne Victorian inn features elaborate chestnut moldings, antique furnishings, and up-to-date comforts. Enjoy the extensive library or play the baby grand piano. The charm and excitement, museums and racetracks, boutiques and restaurants of historic Saratoga are an easy walk from the Westchester House. After a busy day of sampling the delights of Saratoga, relax on the wraparound porch, in the old-fashioned gardens, or the double Victorian parlors, and enjoy a refreshing glass of lemonade.

Hosts: Bob and Stephanie Melvin
Rooms: 7 (PB) $70-125
Continental Breakfast
Minimum Stay Weekends and Holidays: 2 nights
Credit Cards: A, B, C
Notes: 2, 5, 8 (over 12), 9, 10, 11, 12, 13, 14

SAUGERTIES

Bed by the Stream

7531 George Sickle Road, Route 212, 12477
(914) 246-2979

This beautiful five-acre farm is a streamside property. Seven miles from Woodstock, and three miles from the New York State Thruway (Exit 20), the farm offers two lovely rooms, one with a mountain

NOTES: Credit cards accepted: A Master Card; B Visa; C American Express; D Discover Card; E Diner's Club; F Other; 2 Personal Checks accepted; 3 Lunch available; 4 Dinner available; 5 Open all year;

view, and the other, a view of the stream. A swimming pool is available for guests to use.

Host: Odette Reinhardt
Rooms: 2 (PB) $70
Full Breakfast
Credit Cards: None
Notes: 2, 5, 8, 9, 10, 11, 12, 13

SCHENECTADY

The American Country Collection 043

4 Greenwood Lane, Delmar, 12054
(518) 439-7001

This bed and breakfast, formerly a tavern, is in the heart of the city's historic Stockade district. The entire house can be rented for overnight lodging, weddings, or long-term stays. Three second-floor guest rooms, each with a TV, share one and one-half baths. One has a working fireplace, and two are air-conditioned. The luxurious bath has a Jacuzzi and a separate shower. Breakfast is served in the dining room or in the breakfast room that looks out into the gardens and terrace. Within walking distance to theaters, shopping, restaurants, bike trail, train station, and Union College. Smoking limited. Children welcome. No pets. $85; $90 May-October.

SCHUYLERVILLE—SEE ALSO SARATOGA SPRINGS

The American Country Collection 124

4 Greenwood Lane, Delmar, 12054
(518) 439-7001

Built in 1770, this home is in the midst of an apple orchard on an elevation overlooking the Hudson River. The mantel holds cannonballs that American troops fired at the house when it served as a hospital for British and Hessian troops during the Revolutionary War. In the main house, there are three guest rooms with shared bath. The Apple Cottage offers one bedroom, one and one-half baths, livingroom with fireplace, kitchen, and sitting area with fireplace. The Island Cottage offers two bedrooms, bath, loft, livingroom/kitchen with fireplace, and screened porch. Smoking in common areas only. Children welcome in the Island Cottage. They are welcome at the main house and Apple Cottage when the pool is not open. Pets in residence. Full or continental breakfast offered. $65-85 main house; $125-175 Apple Cottage; $90-125 Island Cottage. Rates depend on season.

SENECA FALLS

Locustwood Country Inn

3563 Route 89, 13148
(315) 549-7132

In the heart of the Finger Lakes, the Locustwood Inn is one of the oldest in Seneca County. Constructed of early brick, the inn still has huge beams, wide-plank floors, and five fireplaces that were familiar to an era long past. Guests are welcome to stroll the grounds, view the herbs and flowers, visit with the animals, or while away the hours in our hammock for two under the pines.

Host: Robert Hill
Rooms: 3 (S2B) $50-70
Full Breakfast
Credit Cards: F
Notes: 2, 5, 8, 9, 12, 14

SHELTER ISLAND

Belle Crest Inn

163 North Ferry Road, 11965
(516) 749-2041

Spacious Dutch Colonial in a lovely garden setting, convenient to Dering Harbor. All guest rooms are furnished in Early

6 Pets welcome; 7 Smoking allowed; 8 Children welcome; 9 Social drinking allowed; 10 Tennis available; 11 Swimming available; 12 Golf available; 13 Skiing available; 14 May be booked through travel agents.

American collectibles and antiques. Romantic guest rooms, some with private baths, canopy beds, air conditioning, and TV. A full breakfast is served in the dining room.

Hosts: Yvonne and Henry Loinig
Rooms: 8 (4 PB; 4 SB) $45-125
Full Breakfast
Credit Cards: A, B
Notes: 2, 4, 5, 7, 8, 9, 10, 11, 12, 13, 14

SILVER CREEK

Grape Country Manor

Old Main Road, 14136
(716) 934-3532

This bed and breakfast is situated in the heart of the Concord Grape Region on the shore of Lake Erie, midway between Erie, Pennsylvania, and Buffalo, New York. Just five minutes from the New York State Thruway, it is also close to wineries, ski resorts, antique shops, and Lakes Erie and Chautauqua. Guests are welcome year-round in the quiet, comfortable, 65-year-old restored farmhouse. Situated on 12 acres of expansive lawn, flowers, trees, and woods, the hosts offer country living surrounded by antiques, art collections, and history.

Hosts: Burt and Jean Rae Valvo
Rooms: 3 (S2.5B) $65
Continental Breakfast
Credit Cards: None
Notes: 2, 5, 7, 8, 9, 11, 12, 13

SKANEATELES

Cozy Cottage

4987 Kingston Road, Elbridge, 13060
(315) 689-2082 after 10:00 A.M.

Just four miles outside of a Finger Lakes village on a quiet country road, this remodeled ranch house has two comfortable guest rooms sharing one and one-half baths with the hostess. Smoke-free environment. Bask in the sun, hike or bike. Enjoy flowers, birds, the orchard, and pick berries. Visit the village, stroll the scenic streets, browse in galleries and boutiques, take a cruise, launch your boat, and enjoy fine restaurants. Antique shops nearby. Syracuse just 20 minutes, Auburn just 15 minutes drive.

Host: Elaine Samuels
Rooms:2 (SB) $40-50
Continental Breakfast
Credit Cards: None
Notes: 2, 5, 6, 9, 11, 12, 13, 14

Elaine's Bed and Breakfast and Inn Reservation Service

4987 Kingston Road, Elbridge, 13060
(315) 689-2082

Cute, clean, comfortable, convenient, cozy, congenial, casual country atmosphere in a newly remodeled ranch on five acres. Adults preferred. Two modest guest rooms, each with a firm double bed, share a new bathroom. The hostess can direct you to almost any place in Onondaga County including Syracuse (12 miles), Auburn (9 miles), Skaneateles Village (4 miles). No smoking. Resident cat. $40-50.

Elaine's Bed and Breakfast Reservation Service

4987 Kingston Road, Elbridge, 13060
(315) 689-2082

Elaine's offers three bed and breakfasts in this gorgeous historic village on the eastern shore of Finger Lakes. An executive ranch freshly remodelled and redecorated offers an antique-furnished guest room with a double iron bed and private bath. A sleeper sofa in the den can take two or more guests, and lakes, stores, restaurants and cruise boats are within walking distance. Another freshly decorated ranch-style home offers two guest rooms with good double beds that share one and one-half baths. A Queen Anne on Main Street offers two rooms full of antiques; one room has a pair of twin beds, and the other offers a full-size bed.

SLATE HILL

The Ridgebury Inn and Hunt Club

Rural Delivery 1, Box 342, 10973
(914) 355-4868

A 1730s farmhouse with lots of English country charm, this is a place to relax and enjoy the sights and sounds of Mother Nature. Evening activities include a 54-inch TV and VCR, movies or parlor games, or afternoons may find you playing croquet or hiking our 87 acres of fields, streams, and woods. Perhaps you are an early morning riser and would enjoy a wonderful ride in our hot air balloon or a full gourmet breakfast.

Hosts: Bob and Jan Yonelunas
Rooms: 5 (1 PB; 4 SB) $75-90
Full Breakfast
Credit Cards: A, B, C, E
Notes: 3, 4, 5, 7 (limited), 8, 9, 10, 11, 12, 13, 14

SODUS

Maxwell Creek Inn, Inc.

7563 Lake Road, 14551
(315) 483-2222

An 1840 cobblestone house decorated in antiques, with two sitting rooms, one with a player piano. The rural setting offers apple blossoms in May; boating, swimming, sailing, golf in summer; apple picking and fall foliage; skiing in winter. Charter fishing from April to October.

The Old Post House Inn

Separate stone cottage sleeps four to six. Tennis and stream fishing (early spring and late fall) on premises.

Hosts: Joseph and Edythe Ann Long
Rooms: 8 (1 PB; 7 SB) $50-75
Full Breakfast
Credit Cards: A, B, D
Notes: 2, 5, 7, 8, 9, 10, 11, 12, 13, 14

SODUS POINT

Carriage House Inn

8375 Wickman Boulevard, 14555
(315) 483-2100; (800) 292-2990 reservations

This Victorian house or stone carriage house overlooks the historic lighthouse and Lake Ontario with beach access. Eight rooms feature private baths; a suite and efficiency is also available. All include full breakfast. Situated on four acres in a quiet, residential area.

Host: James DenDecker
Room: 8 (PB) $60
Full Breakfast
Credit Cards: A, B, C
Notes: 5, 7, 9, 10, 11, 12, 13

SOUTHAMPTON

The Old Post House Inn

136 Main Street, 11968
(516) 283-1717

The Old Post House, a small, charming country inn, was built in 1684 and is listed on the National Register of Historic Places. All rooms have private baths and air conditioning. Continental breakfast is included. Close to boutiques and Saks Fifth Avenue.

Hosts: Cecile and Ed Courville
Rooms: 7 (PB) $80-170
Continental Breakfast
Credit Cards: A, B, C
Notes: 3, 4, 5, 7, 8 (over 12), 9, 10, 11, 12, 14

Village Latch Inn

101 Hill Street, 11968
(516) 283-2160

6 Pets welcome; 7 Smoking allowed; 8 Children welcome; 9 Social drinking allowed; 10 Tennis available; 11 Swimming available; 12 Golf available; 13 Skiing available; 14 May be booked through travel agents.

Village Latch Inn is known internationally for its charming ambience. A 37-room mansion on five acres, right in town, within walking distance of the famous Jobs Lane boutiques. Swimming and tennis; all rooms have private bath. Rent your own mansion for group celebrations, corporate outings, and weddings.

Hosts: Marta and Martin White
Rooms: 70 (PB) $79-175
Continental Breakfast
Minimum stay weekends: 2 nights
Credit Cards: A, C, D, E
Notes: 2, 3, 5, 6, 7, 9, 10, 11, 12, 14

SOUTHOLD

Goose Creek Guesthouse

1475 Waterview Drive, 11971
(516) 765-3356

Goose Creek Guesthouse is a quiet Civil War-era bed and breakfast home nestled in the woods on the south side of Goose Creek. A country breakfast is served, featuring all homemade foods: granola, whole wheat or cornmeal pancakes, the specialty apple rings, jams, jellies, and freshly baked bread. Farm-fresh eggs and homegrown or local fruits and vegetables are used. A continental breakfast is available if guests prefer.

Host: Mary Mooney-Getoff
Rooms: 4 (SB) $70-75
Full Breakfast
Credit Cards: None
Notes: 2 (deposit only), 5, 6, 8, 9, 14

STANFORDVILLE

Lakehouse Inn on Golden Pond

Shelley Hill Road 12581
(914) 266-8093

The most enchanting lakefront sanctuary in the Hudson River Valley, the inn offers swimming, fishing, boating, suites with private Jacuzzi tubs for two, wood-burning fireplaces, private decks, and stunning views of the lakes and woods. Gourmet breakfasts and afternoon appetizers. A unique private inn where you are free to enjoy a special time in splendid circumstances. Just 90 minutes from Manhattan.

Hosts: Judy and Rick Kohler
Rooms: 8 (PB) $175-350
Full Breakfast
Credit Cards: A, B, C
Notes: 2, 5, 10, 11, 12, 13, 14

STATEN ISLAND

Victorian Bed and Breakfast of Staten Island

92 Taylor Street, 10310
(718) 273-9861

This fine Italianate mansion dating back to 1846 is located on the North Shore of Staten Island and twelve minutes to the Staten Island Ferry. The original Victorian decor of 1860 includes magnificent chandeliers, mirrors, and many pieces of furniture original to the house. There are marble fireplaces in every room. Bedrooms are large, and a modern bathroom is close. Beds are high quality, and a full breakfast is served in the formal dining room at a huge round, hand-carved table. Manhattan can be reached by car in 35 minutes via the Bayonne Bridge, and the Newark Airport is a close 35 minutes as well.

Host: Danuta Gorlach
Rooms: 3 (1 PB 2 SB) $45-65
Full Breakfast
Credit Cards: C
Notes: 2, 5, 8, 13, 14

STILLWATER

The American Country Collection 005

4 Greenwood Lane, Delmar, 12054
(518) 439-7001

This is a quiet retreat on 100 acres of rolling countryside, complete with mountain vistas. The circa 1800 barn has been transformed into an exquisite home. It is conveniently between Saratoga Lake and Saratoga National Historical Park. Two rooms and two second-floor suites, each with private bath. Breakfast is served in the dining room or on the deck overlooking the countryside. Smoking outdoors only. Children over nine welcome. Dog in residence. Sept. 1-June 30: suites $75 and rooms $65; July to two days before racing season: suites $95 and rooms $85; August (racing)/Jazz Fest/ Christmas-New Year's: suites $105 and rooms $95 (three-night minimum stay).

STONY BROOK

Three Village Inn

150 Main Street, 11790
(516) 751-0555

The Three Village Inn is in a unique location, offering historic colonial charm with magnificent views of Stony Brook Harbor on Long Island Sound. The inn offers the finest in food, service, and hospitality. The dining rooms are open daily; weekend live music in the tap room. The inn's 27 guest rooms are in the original 1751 inn and in the country cottages. All rooms have private bath, phone, and cable TV.

Hosts: Jim and Louis Miaritis
Rooms: 27 (PB) $85-110
Full Breakfast
Credit Cards: A, B, C
Closed Christmas
Notes: 3, 4, 5, 8, 9, 10, 11, 12, 14

SYRACUSE—SEE ALSO JAMESVILLE

Bed and Breakfast Wellington

707 Danforth Street, 13208
(800) 724-5006

This historic 1914 brick and stucco Tudor-style home designed by prolific Arts and Crafts architect, Ward Wellington Ward, considered one of the most interesting landmarks in Syracuse. The home contains rich wood interiors, ample interior glass, tiled fireplaces, arched foyer, and cozy porches. Antiques are everywhere, and the rooms and suites are spacious. The location is central to downtown medical centers, Carousel Center, Armory Square, and universities. A wide variety of ethnic restaurants is within walking distance.

Hosts: Wendy Wilber and Ray Borg
Rooms: 5 (PB) $55-95
Full and Expanded Continental Breakfast
Credit Cards: A, B, C
Notes: 2, 5, 8 (over 12), 9, 10, 12, 13

Elaine's Bed and Breakfast and Inn Reservation Service

4987 Kingston Road, Elbridge, 13060
(315) 689-2082

Convenient to Syracuse University and LeMoyne College, this delightful knotty pine basement apartment can sleep two and has a completely furnished eat-in kitchen and attractive shower-bath with many built-ins. The living-bedroom includes color TV, desk, easy chairs, game table, and much more. Patio and yard. Quiet dead-end street with a great view. Use of laundry for long-term guest. $65-75; long-term rates available.

Elaine's Bed and Breakfast Reservation Service-1

4987 Kingston Road, Elbridge, 13060
(315) 689-2082

This spacious Tudor built in 1920 offers three beautifully decorated guest rooms. An Art Deco room features a queen-size bed and private bath. A Victorian room has a double bed and shares a spacious vintage bath with a more traditional room that has a pair of twin beds, a sitting area, and TV.

---

6 Pets welcome; 7 Smoking allowed; 8 Children welcome; 9 Social drinking allowed; 10 Tennis available; 11 Swimming available; 12 Golf available; 13 Skiing available; 14 May be booked through travel agents.

Elaine's Bed and Breakfast Reservation Service-2

4987 Kingston Road, Elbridge, 13060
(315) 689-2082

Situated in the Eastside area near LeMoyne College and Syracuse University, this cute, customized Cape Cod has a newly redecorated first floor-guest room with a double bed, handmade chest, rocker, window seat, and private bath. An adjacent TV den can be a second guest room with a sofa bed. Both rooms are in a separate rear wing of the house.

Elaine's Bed and Breakfast Reservation Service-3

4987 Kingston Road, Elbridge, 13060
(315) 689-2082

This charming Cape Cod is only 16 blocks from Syracuse University and features two well furnished guest rooms, each with a double bed.

Elaine's Bed and Breakfast Reservation Service-4

4987 Kingston Road, Elbridge, 13060
(315) 689-2082

This Eastside area duplex offers four guest rooms, two with double beds and two with single beds. All rooms share one hall bath. Decorated with Mexican artifacts, plants, and lace curtains.

Elaine's Bed and Breakfast Reservation Service-5

4987 Kingston Road, Elbridge, 13060
(315) 689-2082

In the southwestern corner of the city, this newer executive Colonial offers roomy double antique bedroom with two dressers, new rugs, and a private bath. A second guest room has a double bed. A swimming pool is on premises, and tennis courts are close by. On the bus line.

Elaine's Bed and Breakfast Reservation Service-6

4987 Kingston Road, Elbridge, 13060
(315) 689-2082

Situated on the western edge of the city, this three-year-young, contemporary Cape is set on three acres. The guest area is on the second floor. One room has twin beds, and one has a double bed; both share a bath. Peaceful, quiet setting, yet quite handy to shopping, state fair, zoo, restaurants, Onodaga Community College, highways, and Syracuse University.

Elaine's Bed and Breakfast Reservation Service-7

4987 Kingston Road, Elbridge, 13060
(315) 689-2082

This wonderful large brick house has decor of many periods. Top floor features an executive or honeymoon suite with a king-size canopy bed, Jacuzzi, complete kitchen under an L-shaped mahogany bar, lovely sitting area with wood stove, skylight, round table, and leather chairs. A private marble bath, garage, and fresh flowers are only a few of the amenities you'll find in this home. Three rooms on the second and first floors are furnished with antiques, and all offer private baths. Guest kitchen is stocked with snack foods, and breakfast is always served on beautiful china.

TANNERSVILLE

The Kennedy House

P. O. Box 770, 12485
(518) 589-6082

NOTES: Credit cards accepted: A Master Card; B Visa; C American Express; D Discover Card; E Diner's Club; F Other; 2 Personal Checks accepted; 3 Lunch available; 4 Dinner available; 5 Open all year;

This historic, antique-filled bed and breakfast is situated in the heart of the northern Catskill Mountains. All rooms feature private baths, and there is a spacious lounge with a fireplace, cable TV, and VCR. Hearty continental breakfast is served in the morning, and antique and gift shops are on premises. Walk to shops, restaurants, and night spots. Minutes to the Hunter and Windham mountains. Long-stay discounts available.

Host: Donna Kennedy
Rooms: 4 (PB) $50-70
Expanded Continental Breakfast
Credit Cards: None
Notes: 2, 5, 7, 9, 11, 12, 13, 14

THENDARA

Moose River House Bed and Breakfast

12 Birch Street, P. O. Box 184, 13472
(315) 369-3104; (800) 241-6188

Back in the 19th century, Moose River House was accessible only by the Fawn, a tiny side-wheeler that steamed upstream from Minnehaha, where New York's only wooden train rails terminated. Today, there are several routes to this northern Adirondack Inn. However you choose to arrive, you won't want to leave. From cross-country and downhill skiing in the winter to hiking, horseback riding, and canoeing in the summer, the recreational options are vast. The adjacent town of Old Forge has a wealth of shops, restaurants, and recreational fun.

Host: Frederick J. Fox
Rooms: 5 (3 PB; 2 SB) $55-85
Full Breakfast
Credit Cards: None
Notes: 2, 5, 8, 9

TICONDEROGA

The American Country Collection 046

4 Greenwood Lane, Delmar, 12054
(518) 439-7001

This 52-acre farm offers year-round activities: sleigh rides and cross-country skiing in winter, horsedrawn wagon rides in summer. Canoeing, fishing, and swimming are nearby. Three double-bed rooms on the second floor share a bath. The entire house is furnished with family antiques and treasures. Smoking outdoors only. Well-behaved children welcome. $40-50.

TROY

The American Country Collection 158

4 Greenwood Lane, Delmar, 12054
(518) 439-7001

This unique Victorian farmhouse, circa 1849 is situated above Troy and set back 300 feet from the road with a long circular drive. It is near Rensselaer Polytechnical Institute, the Emma Willard School, Russell Sage College, and the Hudson Valley Community College. Four second-floor guest rooms share two full baths, and full country breakfast is served each morning. Smoking is allowed in designated areas only. $40-50.

TRUMANSBURG

Westwind Bed and Breakfast

1662 Taughannock Boulevard , 14886
(607) 387-3377

Gracious hospitality and casual elegance await you at Westwind Bed and Breakfast, a stately 1870 country Victorian home situated on the hillside above Cayuga Lake. One-half mile south of Taughannock Falls State Park on Route 89. Convenient to Cornell University and marina, golf courses, and museums. Shopping and restaurants in abundance. Westwind Bed and Breakfast is on the Cayuga Wine Trail.

Host: Sharon R. Scott
Rooms: 4 (SB) $55-75

6 Pets welcome; 7 Smoking allowed; 8 Children welcome; 9 Social drinking allowed; 10 Tennis available; 11 Swimming available; 12 Golf available; 13 Skiing available; 14 May be booked through travel agents.

Full Breakfast
Credit Cards: A, B
Notes: 2, 5, 9, 11, 12, 13

TULLY-VESPER

Elaine's Bed and Breakfast and Inn Reservation Service

4987 Kingston Road, Elbridge, 13060
(315) 689-2082

Just four scenic miles from Route 81, this owner-built raised ranch offers two double rooms plus a master bedroom suite with private bath. Full country breakfast. Close to Song Mountain downhill skiing, 20 minutes from Syracuse, Cortland, and Auburn in a quiet country setting with view of rolling hills. Guests may relax in front of a cozy fire in the Pennsylvania bluestone fireplace.

Elaine's Bed and Breakfast Reservation Service

4987 Kingston Road, Elbridge, 13060
(315) 689-2082

Twenty minutes south of Syracuse off Route 81, this custom-built ranch offers three guest rooms. The master bedroom has a private bath, and the owners ask for a two-night minimum for this room. Two rooms with a double bed in each share a bath. Full country breakfast. Close to ski areas. 25 minutes to Skaneateles.

UTICA

The Iris Stonehouse Bed and Breakfast

16 Derbyshire Place, 13501-4706
(315) 732-6720; (800) 446-1456

In town, close to everything, this stately stone house with leaded-glass windows, listed on the National Register of Historic Places. A separate guest sitting room, and guest rooms with private and and shared baths. Full breakfast from the daily menu, central air, located three miles from I-90, Exit 31 (NYS Thruway), one block off Genesee Street, three blocks from the North/South arterial and Routes 5, 8, and 12. No smoking. Member of ABBA with three-crown ratings. Visa and MasterCard accepted.

Hosts: Shirley and Roy Kilgore
Rooms: 3 (1 PB; 2 SB) $45-60
Full Breakfast
Credit Cards: A, B
Notes: 2, 5, 14

VERNON

Elaine's Bed and Breakfast and Inn Reservation Service

4987 Kingston Road, Elbridge, 13060
(315) 689-2082

A marvelous sprawling Victorian-Italianate manor house atop a knoll on seven acres. Filled with antiques, this home has been featured in several local history books and is a must-see for architectural and history buffs. There are five guest rooms. Children and well-behaved pets welcome. No smoking in bedrooms. $60-70.

WARRENSBURG

The American Country Collection 067

4 Greenwood Lane, Delmar, 12054
(518) 439-7001

This 1850 Greek Revival inn has a new guest house featuring ten rooms and a Jacuzzi in a plant-filled solarium. The inn is in the center of an old-fashioned Adirondack village that features bandstand concerts in the summer. The inn itself has a public restaurant, a cozy fireplace tavern, and a common room with TV. Ten rooms

NOTES: Credit cards accepted: A Master Card; B Visa; C American Express; D Discover Card; E Diner's Club; F Other; 2 Personal Checks accepted; 3 Lunch available; 4 Dinner available; 5 Open all year;

with private baths, air conditioning, fireplace, queen, king, or two twin beds. Handicapped access. Smoking permitted with consideration for nonsmokers. No pets. Children over 11 welcome. $60-70; $85-95 (July and Aug.). Minimum stay of two nights on holiday weekends and on July and August weekends.

Country Road Lodge

HCR 1, Box 227, Hickory Hill Road, 12885
(518) 623-2207

With a view of the Adirondack Mountain and the Hudson River, and minutes from Lake George, the lodge has offered seclusion and casual comfort since 1974. Homemade bread, hiking, skiing, horseshoes, badminton, books, board games. Fine restaurants and antiquing nearby.

Hosts: Steve and Sandi Parisi
Rooms: 4 (2 PB; 2 SB) $52-65
Full Breakfast
Credit Cards: None
Notes: 2, 5, 7, 9, 10, 11, 12, 13, 14

The Merrill Magee House

2 Hudson Street, 12885
(518) 623-2449

From the inviting wicker chairs on porch to the elegant candlelit dining rooms, the inn offers the romance of a visit to a country estate. Guest rooms abound with 19th-century charm and 20th-century comforts. Guests can relax in the inn's secluded gardens, enjoy the outdoor pool, or shop for antiques in the village. Situated in the Adirondack Park, all outdoor activities are minutes away.

Hosts: Ken and Florence Carrington
Rooms: 10, plus 1 suite (PB) $85-105
Full Breakfast
Credit Cards: A, B, C, D, E
Notes: 2, 3, 4, 5, 7, 8, 9, 10, 11, 12, 13, 14

White House Lodge

53 Main Street, 12885
(518) 623-3640

An 1847 Victorian in the heart of the Adirondacks. The home is furnished with many antiques. Only five minutes to Lake George Village, historic Fort William Henry, and Great Escape Amusement Park. Walk to restaurants, antique shops, and shopping areas. Enjoy the comfort of the air-conditioned TV lounge or rock on the front porch. Only 20 minutes to Gore Mountain Ski Lodge and the Adirondack Balloon Festival. Smoking in TV lounge only.

Hosts: James and Ruth Gibson
Rooms: 3 (SB) $85
Continental Breakfast
Credit Cards: A, B
Notes: 5, 7 (restricted), 8 (over 7), 10, 11, 12, 13, 14

WATERLOO

General Dobbin Bed and Breakfast

0089 Packwood Road, 13165
(315) 789-0580

This bed and breakfast was built in a country setting of meadows and woods in 1823. Tennis court and antique shop on the premises. Five miles to Seneca Lake and Geneva. Suite with private bath and room with private bath. Situated three and one-half miles south of Thruway Exit 42, off Route 14, within three miles of Routes 5 and 20.

Host: Betty Waldman
Rooms: 2 (PB) $55-65
Full Breakfast
Credit Cards: None
Notes: 2, 5, 9, 10, 11, 12, 13

WATERTOWN

Starbuck House

253 Clinton Street, 13601
(315) 788-7324

This 17-room Italianate mansion is a haven for business travelers, a delight for tourists

---

6 Pets welcome; 7 Smoking allowed; 8 Children welcome; 9 Social drinking allowed; 10 Tennis available; 11 Swimming available; 12 Golf available; 13 Skiing available; 14 May be booked through travel agents.

from all across the country, Canada, and Europe. Completed in 1864 for state senator James F. Starbuck, the home retains original architectural features, gilded valances, gas chandeliers, marble fireplace, cornices, and so much more. A full gourmet breakfast is served daily in an elegant dining room. In-room phones; air conditioning. Handicapped accessible.

Host: Marsha Eger Saal and Gary Saal
Rooms: 5 (3 PB; 2 SB) $70-80
Full Breakfast
Credit Cards: A, B, C
Notes: 2, 5, 9, 10, 11, 12, 13, 14

WATERVILLE

Bed and Breakfast of Waterville

211 White Street, 13480
(315) 841-8295

This Victorian home in a historic area is close to Utica, Hamilton College, Colgate University, antique shops. One block from Route 12 and one mile from Route 20. Accommodations include a triple with private bath, triple and double rooms with shared bath. Experienced, enthusiastic hosts are a retired utility manager and a quilt maker.

Hosts: Carol and Stanley Sambora
Rooms: 3 (1 PB; 2 SB) $35-65
Full Breakfast
Credit Cards: A, B
Notes: 2, 5, 8, 9, 10, 12, 13

WATKINS GLEN

Clarke House Bed and Breakfast

102 Durland Place, 14891
(607) 535-7965; (800) 223-5707

Charming English Tudor home circa 1920 in the lovely village of Watkins Glen. Walk to the famous gorge, restaurants, and activities at Seneca Lake. Short drive to Watkins

Glen International Raceway, famous wineries, and Corning Glass. Immaculate bedrooms feature antique decor and a choice of twin, double, or queen-size beds. Hearty breakfast graciously served by the hosts in our formal dining room. Guest livingroom with fireplace. Central air conditioning.

Hosts: Jack and Carolyn Clarke
Rooms: 4 (2 PB; 2 SB) $55-65
Full Breakfast
Credit Cards: None
Notes: 2, 5, 9

WESTFIELD

William Seward Inn

Rural Delivery 2, South Portage Road, 14787
(716) 326-4151

Formerly the home of Lincoln's secretary of state, this 1821 Greek Revival mansion features ten rooms with period antiques and private baths. Comfortable elegance close to Westfield's wineries and national antique center. Minutes from the world-famous Chautauqua Institution and both downhill and cross-country skiing.

WESTHAMPTON BEACH

1880 House

2 Seafield Lane, 11978
(800) 346-3290

This 100-year-old country retreat is only 90 minutes from Manhattan on Westhampton Beach's exclusive Seafield Lane. A swimming pool and tennis court are on the premises, and it's only a short walk to the beach. The Hamptons offer numerous outstanding restaurants and shops. Indoor tennis is available locally, as is a health spa at Montauk Point.

Host: Elsie Pardee Collins
Rooms: 2 (PB) $100-200 (suites)
Full Breakfast
Minimum stay: 2 nights
Credit Cards: C
Notes: 2, 5, 9, 10, 11

NOTES: Credit cards accepted: A Master Card; B Visa; C American Express; D Discover Card; E Diner's Club; F Other; 2 Personal Checks accepted; 3 Lunch available; 4 Dinner available; 5 Open all year;

WEVERTOWN

Mountainaire Adventures

Route 28, Box A, 12886
(800) 950-2194; (800) 950-2194

Renovated private lodge and deluxe three-bedroom chalet in the Adirondack Park, near Lake George and Gore Mountain Ski Center. Jacuzzi, sauna, beer and wine, bikes, and canoes. Custom adventure trips, such as white-water rafting and camping are available. Ideal for private meetings or romantic getaways!

Host: Douglas Cole
Rooms: 8 (6 PB; 2 SB) $64.50-80.25
Full Breakfast
Credit Cards: A, B
Notes: 2, 4, 5, 6, 7, 8, 9, 10, 11, 12, 13, 14

WILLET

Woven Waters

HC 73, Box 193E, Cincinnatus Lake, 13863
(607) 656-8672

A beautifully renovated 100-year-old barn on the shores of a lovely private lake in south central New York. The rustic interior is accented with antiques and imported laces. Relax in the large comfortable livingroom with beamed cathedral ceiling and massive stone fireplace or on one of the porches overlooking the lake (one open, one enclosed).

Hosts: Erika and John
Rooms: 4 (SB) $58
Full Breakfast
Credit Cards: A, B, D
Notes: 5, 9, 13, 14

WINDSOR

Country Haven Bed and Breakfast

Rural Delivery 4, Box 4408, Garrett Road, 13865
(607) 655-1204

A restored 1800s farmhouse in a quiet country setting on 350 acres. A haven for today's weary traveler and a weekend get-away. Country Haven is also home to a craft shop and log home sales office. Situated one mile from Route 17, Exit 78 east, 12 miles east of Binghamton, and 7 miles from Route 81.

Hosts: Rita and Doug Saunders
Rooms: 4 (1 PB; 3 SB) $45-55
Full Breakfast
Credit Cards: None
Notes: 2

YOUNGSTOWN

Rainbow Hospitality Y110

466 Amherst Street, Buffalo, 14207
(716) 874-8797

This large villa overlooks the Niagara River and Canada. The home, surrounded by scenic grounds, is just 5 to 15 minutes from Niagara Falls. Huge rooms with fire-places for relaxing after a day of sightseeing or theater events. Private/shared baths and either a porch or patio adjacent to each room. $65-150.s

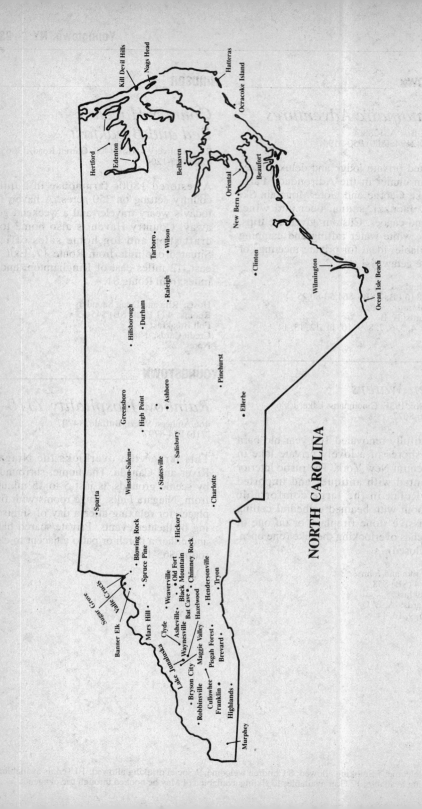

NORTH CAROLINA

Kill Devil Hills
Nags Head
Hatteras
Ocracoke Island

Hertford
Edenton
Belhaven
Oriental
Beaufort

New Bern

Clinton

Wilmington

Ocean Isle Beach

Hillsborough
Durham
Tarboro
Wilson
Raleigh

Greensboro
High Point
Ashboro
Salisbury
Pinehurst
Ellerbe

Winston-Salem
Statesville
Charlotte

Sparta
Blowing Rock
Spruce Pine
Old Fort
Black Mountain
Chimney Rock
Hickory
Hendersonville
Tryon

Banner Elk
Valle Crucis
Sugar Grove
Mars Hill
Clyde
Weaverville
Asheville
Bat Cave
Waynesville
Maggie Valley
Hazelwood
Pisgah Forest
Brevard
Lake Junaluska
Bryson City
Cullowhee
Robbinsville
Franklin
Highlands
Murphey

North Carolina

The Doctor's Inn

716 South Park Street, 27203
(919) 625-4916; (919) 625-4822

The Doctor's Inn is a home filled with antiques. It offers its guests the utmost in personal accommodations. Amenities include a gourmet breakfast served on fine china and silver, fresh flowers, terry-cloth robes and slippers, homemade "goodies," and a refrigerator stocked with soft drinks, juices, and ice cream parfaits. Nearby are 42 potteries and the North Carolina Zoo.

Hosts: Marion and Beth Griffin
Rooms: 2 (1 PB; 1 SB) $50-65
Full Breakfast
Credit Cards: None
Notes: 2, 5, 7, 8, 9, 10

ASHEVILLE

Aberdeen Inn

64 Linden Avenue, 28801
(704) 254-9336

A 1908 Colonial with a wraparound porch for summer eating and rocking. Antiques, working fireplace, books, and a large sun room for winter dining. Private grounds with century-old trees. You are six blocks to downtown and three miles to the Biltmore Estate. Welcome!

Host: Eleanor Smith
Rooms: 5 (PB) $65-80
Full Breakfast
Credit Cards: A, B
Notes: 2, 5, 7 (limited), 8 (over 12), 9, 14

Albemarle Inn

86 Edgemont Road, 28801
(704) 255-0027

A distinguished Greek Revival mansion with exquisite carved oak staircase, balcony, paneling, and high ceilings. Located in beautiful residential area. On the National Register of Historic Places. Eleven spacious and comfortable guest rooms with television, telephones, air conditioning, and private baths with claw foot tubs, and showers. Delicious full breakfast served in the dining room or on the sun porch. Unmatched hospitality.

Hosts: Dick and Kathy Hemes
Rooms: 11 (PB) $75-110
Full Breakfast
Credit Cards: A, B
Notes: 2, 5, 8 (over 13), 9, 10, 11, 12, 14

Applewood Manor

62 Cumberland Circle, 28801
(704) 254-2244

A fine, turn-of-the-century Colonial Revival manor set on two acres of rolling lawn and woods in Asheville's historic Montford District. Conveniently located within 15 minutes of the finest restaurants, antique shops and attractions, including the Biltmore Estate. Amenities include private baths, queen beds, fireplaces, balconies, full gourmet breakfasts and afternoon tea. Bikes, badminton, croquet and complimentary fitness club passes are available.

Hosts: Maryanne Young and Susan Poole
Rooms: 4 and guest cottage (PB) $75-100
Full Breakfast

NOTES: Credit cards accepted: A Master Card; B Visa; C American Express; D Discover Card; E Diner's Club; F Other; 2 Personal Checks accepted; 3 Lunch available; 4 Dinner available; 5 Open all year; 6 Pets welcome; 7 Smoking allowed; 8 Children welcome; 9 Social drinking allowed; 10 Tennis available; 11 Swimming available; 12 Golf available; 13 Skiing available; 14 May be booked through travel agents.

Credit Cards: A, B, D
Notes: 2, 5, 9, 10, 11, 14

The Black Walnut Bed and Breakfast Inn

288 Montford Avenue, 28801
(704) 254-3878

The Black Walnut is a turn-of-the-century shingle-style home in the heart of the Montford Historic District just minutes from downtown Asheville and the Biltmore Estate. The inn is decorated with a blend of antiques and traditional furniture. Amenities include large guest rooms with fireplace and TV, full breakfast featuring homemade breads and preserves, welcoming refreshments, use of all common areas, the grand piano, and air conditioning. Supervised children are welcome.

Hosts: Jeanette Syprzak
Rooms: 4 (PB) $55-95
Full Breakfast
Credit Cards: A, B, D
Closed Dec. 1-March 31
Notes: 2, 5, 8, 9, 10, 11, 12, 14

Blake House Inn

150 Royal Pines Drive, 28704
(704) 684-1847

Built in 1847, Blake House Inn is one of the area's finest surviving examples of French Gothic architecture. The house served as a field hospital for Confederate armies still active in western North Carolina near the close of the war. The Blake House offers spacious bedrooms, all elegantly decorated with country antiques and family heirlooms. Full breakfast. Minutes to Biltmore Estate, the Blue Ridge Parkway, and other area attractions. Fireside dining Wednesday through Saturday and brunch on Sunday.

Hosts: Bob, Eloise, and Pati Roesler
Rooms: 5 (PB) $65-85
Full Breakfast
Credit Cards: A, B
Notes: 2, 3, 4, 5, 8 (over 12), 10, 11, 12, 13

Cairn Brae

217 Patton Mountain Road, 28804
(704) 252-9219

Cairn Brae is situated in the mountains above Asheville. Very private, on three acres of woods, but only 12 minutes from downtown. Guests have private entrance to livingroom with fireplace. Complimentary snacks are served on the terrace overlooking Beaverdam Valley. Beautiful views. Woodsy trails. Quiet and secluded.

Hosts: Milli and Ed Adams
Rooms: 3 (PB) $75-85
Full Breakfast
Credit Cards: A, B
Closed Dec. 1-March 31
Notes: 2, 8 (over 6), 9, 10, 11, 12, 14

Carolina Bed and Breakfast

177 Cumberland Avenue, 28801
(704) 254-3608

Comfortable turn-of-the-century home on an acre of beautiful gardens in the historic Montford district. Charming guest rooms, four with fireplaces, have antiques and collectibles, as well as private baths. Convenient to downtown shopping, galleries, restaurants, and the Biltmore Estate. A quiet, relaxing getaway in the heart of the city.

Hosts: Sam, Karin, and Regina Fain
Rooms: 5 (PB) $75-85
Full Breakfast
Credit Cards: A, B
Notes: 2, 5, 7 (limited), 8 (over 12), 9, 10, 12, 14

Cedar Crest Victorian Inn

674 Biltmore Avenue, 28803
(704) 252-1389

An 1890 Queen Anne mansion listed on the National Register of Historic Places. Lavish interior features carved oak paneling, ornate glasswork, authentic Victorian decor with period antiques, and romantic guest rooms. Croquet pitch, fireplaces, and English gardens. Situated one-quarter mile from the entrance to the Biltmore Estate and four miles from the Blue Ridge Parkway.

Hosts: Jack and Barbara McEwan
Rooms: 13 (9 PB; 4 SB) $65-120
Expanded Continental Breakfast
Credit Cards: A, B, C, D
Notes: 2, 5, 7 (limited), 8 (over 12), 9, 10, 12, 14

The Colby House

230 Pearson Drive, 28801
(704) 253-5644; (800) 982-2118

This elegant and charming Dutch-Tudor house in the Montford Historic District is known as special place. There are beautiful gardens, an outdoor porch, and inviting fireplaces. The home has four guest rooms, each with individual decor, queen beds, and private baths. A full breakfast is varied daily. Southern hospitality abounds in the host's personal attention to every guest's needs.

Hosts: Everett and Ann Colby
Rooms: 4 (PB) $75-95
Full Breakfast
Credit Cards: A, B, C, D
Notes: 2, 5, 9, 10, 11, 12, 13, 14

Corner Oak Manor

53 Saint Dunstans Road, 28803
(704) 253-3525

This lovely English Tudor home is just minutes away from the famed Biltmore Estate and Gardens. Antiques, handmade wreaths, weavings, and stitchery complement the restored elegance of this home. Breakfast specialties include orange French toast, blueberry-ricotta pancakes, or four-cheese herb quiche. A livingroom with fireplace and baby grand piano, and outdoor deck with Jacuzzi are among the gracious amenities.

Hosts: Karen and Andy Spradley
Rooms: 4 (PB) $80-100
Full Breakfast
Credit Cards: A, B, C, D
Notes: 2, 3, 5, 8, 9, 14

Flint Street Inns

100 and 116 Flint Street, 28801
(704) 253-6723

Two lovely old homes on an acre lot with century-old trees. Comfortable walking distance to town. Guest rooms, furnished with antiques and collectibles, have air conditioning, and some have fireplaces. The inns provide wine, bicycles, and restaurant menus. Breakfast is full southern-style, featuring home-baked breads and iron-skillet biscuits.

Hosts: Rick, Lynne, and Marion Vogel
Rooms: 8 (PB) $80
Full Breakfast
Credit Cards: A, B, C, D
Notes: 2, 5, 7 (limited), 14

The Inn on Montford

296 Montford Avenue, 28801
(704) 254-9569

A turn-of-the-century Arts and Crafts home by Asheville's most famous architect. Filled with light, it is a perfect setting for the owner's fine collection of antiques, porcelains, and Oriental rugs. Fireplaces in all rooms, whirlpools in several, a wide front porch, boxwood garden with a fountain behind the house. Located in the Montford Historic District, close to downtown and a 10-minute drive from the Biltmore Estate.

Hosts: Ripley Hotch and Owen Sullivan
Rooms: 4 (PB) $90-120
Full Breakfast
Credit Cards: A, B, C
Notes: 2, 5, 12, 13, 14

The Old Reynolds Mansion

100 Reynolds Heights, 28804
(704) 254-0496

Bed and breakfast in an antebellum mansion listed on the National Register of Historic Places. Beautifully restored with furnishings from a bygone era. In a country setting with acres of trees, mountain views from all rooms. Wood-burning fireplaces, two-story verandas, and pool.

Hosts: Fred and Helen Faber
Rooms: 10 (8 PB; 2 SB) $45-90

6 Pets welcome; 7 Smoking allowed; 8 Children welcome; 9 Social drinking allowed; 10 Tennis available; 11 Swimming available; 12 Golf available; 13 Skiing available; 14 May be booked through travel agents.

Continental Breakfast
Minimum stay weekends and holidays: 2 nights
Credit Cards: None
Open weekends only Jan.-March
Notes: 2, 7, 8 (over 11), 9, 10, 11, 12

Reed House

119 Dodge Street, 28803
(704) 274-1604

Come stay in this comfortable Victorian home built in 1892. Near Biltmore Estate. There are working fireplaces in every room. Breakfast, featuring homemade low-sodium muffins, is served on the wrap-around porch. Relaxing rocking chairs everywhere. Furnished in period decor. On the National Register of Historic Places.

Host: Marge Turcot
Rooms: 3 (1 PB; 2 SB) $50-70
Continental Breakfast
Credit Cards: A, B
Closed Nov. 1-May 1
Notes: 2, 7, 8, 9, 10, 11, 12

Richmond Hill Inn

87 Richmond Hill Drive, 28806
(800) 545-9238

Historic Victorian mansion built in 1889 overlooking the Blue Ridge Mountains and the Asheville skyline. Listed on the National Register of Historic Places.

Richmond Hill Inn

Magnificently restored mansion elegantly furnished with antiques. Features 21 guest rooms, all with private bath and many with a fireplace. Fine dining in gourmet restaurant with mountain view. Croquet lawn and extensive library. Situated close to the Blue Ridge Parkway and Biltmore Estate.

Host: Susan Michel
Rooms: 21 (PB) $95-235
Full Breakfast
Credit Cards: A, B, C
Notes: 2, 3, 4, 5, 7 (restricted), 8, 9, 14

The Wright Inn and Carriage House

235 Pearson Drive, 28801
(704) 251-0789; (800) 552-5724

The Old Renolds Mansion

NOTES: Credit cards accepted: A Master Card; B Visa; C American Express; D Discover Card; E Diner's Club; F Other; 2 Personal Checks accepted; 3 Lunch available; 4 Dinner available; 5 Open all year;

Elegantly restored Queen Anne Victorian inn in the Montford historic district. The main house offers eight guest rooms with phones and cable TV. One suite, one guest room, parlor, and drawing room all have fireplaces. Full breakfast served in the formal dining room. A three-bedroom carriage house with two baths is also available, breakfast not included.

Rooms: 9 (PB) $75-110
Full Breakfast
Credit Cards: A, B
Notes: 2, 5, 9

BANNER ELK

Archer's Inn

Route 2, Box 56-A, Surface Road 184, 28604
(704) 898-9004

Archer's Inn is perched on the side of Beech Mountain (the highest city in the eastern United States), with a beautiful view of the Elk River Valley and surrounding mountains. All rooms have fireplaces and private baths, most have a porch or deck. Just two miles to skiing and close to the Blue Ridge Parkway and Grandfather Mountain. Carriage rides available.

Hosts: Joe and Bonny Archer
Rooms: 14 (PB) $45-95
Full Breakfast
Credit Cards: A, B
Notes: 2 (for deposits), 4 (seasonally), 5, 7 (limited), 8, 9, 10, 12, 13

The Banner Elk Inn Bed and Breakfast

Route 3, P. O. Box 1953, 28604
(704) 898-6223

A charming, historic, cozy inn filled with antiques collected from around the world, original tapestries, and artworks. Originally built as a church in 1912, then converted to the Shawneehaw Inn in the 1920s, it was recently renovated with a stunning decor - a bright pink exterior, deep green interior theme, fresh new wallpapers. Elegant gourmet full breakfasts are provided by your host, Beverly Lait, who lived abroad many years with the foreign service. The inn is located within the mountain village resort of Banner Elk, on Highway 194 North, but in a pastoral setting. Close to major attractions such as Grandfather Mountain, Linville Falls, the Blue Ridge Parkway, Valle Crucis, golf courses, Beech and Sugar ski resorts. There are several very fine restaurants nearby. No smoking.

Host: Beverly Lait
Rooms: 4 (2 PB; 2 SB) $60-90
Full Breakfast
Credit Cards: A, B
Notes: 2 (for deposits), 5, 6 (call), 8, 9, 12, 13

BAT CAVE

Stonehearth Inn

P. O. Box 242, 28710
(800) 535-6647

A gentle reminder of days and nights at Grandma's house, enjoying Grandma's cooking or napping in the swing by the river. Chimney Rock Park, Biltmore House, Lake Lure, downtown Hendersonville, the Blue Ridge Parkway, and various other attractions are a short drive away. Breakfast includes home-baked breads, fruit, juice, and beverage. Dining room open to public for lunches and dinners.

Hosts: John and Susie Simmons
Rooms: 4 (PB) $45 plus tax
Continental Breakfast
Credit Cards: A, B
Notes: 2, 3, 4, 7, 8, 9, 11

BEAUFORT

The Cedars Inn

305 Front Street, 28516
(919) 728-7036

This lovingly restored 18th-century inn offers 12 elegantly appointed rooms with private baths and fireplaces. The dining room boasts the finest cuisine on the

Carolina coast. Daily tours of historic Beaufort and the Outer Banks are available in season. Special weekly rate for Sunday night through Friday morning, including breakfast.

Hosts: Bill and Pat Kwaak
Rooms: 12 (PB) $81-136
Full Breakfast
Minimum stay in-season weekends: 2 nights; holidays: 3 nights
Credit Cards: A, B
Notes: 2, 4, 5, 7, 8, 9, 10, 11, 12

Delamar Inn

217 Turner Street, 28516
(919) 728-4300

Enjoy the Scottish hospitality of this Civil War home in the heart of Beaufort's historic district. The inn offers three guest rooms with antique furnishings and private bath. After a delightful breakfast, enjoy a stroll to the waterfront, specialty shops, or historic sites. Borrow the hosts' bicycles or beach chairs, and when you return, you'll find soft drinks, cookies, and a smile waiting for you. The hosts are pleased to have been selected for Beaufort's 1991 historic homes tour.

Hosts: Philip and Kay
Rooms: 3 (PB) $49-82
Expanded Continental Breakfast
Credit Cards: A, B
Notes: 2, 5, 7 (restricted), 8 (over 10), 9

Pecan Tree Inn

116 Queen Street, 28516
(919) 728-6733

Relive history in the historic town of Beaufort, the third oldest city in North Carolina. At the Pecan Tree Inn, you are only a few blocks from wonderful restaurants and quaint shops. There are seven air-conditioned guest rooms, all with private baths. The bridal suite features a Jacuzzi tub for two and a king-size canopy bed. You will enjoy Susan's freshly baked, homemade muffins, cakes, and breads along with choice of fruit, cereal, and beverages for breakfast. Beaufort's historic district is a leisurely walk from the Inn.

Hosts: Susan and Joe Johnson
Rooms: 7 (PB) $65-115
Expanded Continental Breakfast
Credit Cards: A, B
Notes: 2, 5, 8 (over 12), 9, 10, 11, 12, 14

BELHAVEN

Pungo River Inn

105 Riverview Street, 27810
(919) 943-2117

Pungo River Inn is found in the quaint town of Belhaven on the peaceful Pungo River. Your hostess invites you to relax in an atmosphere of southern hospitality. Belhaven is 25 miles from Swan Quarter ferry taking you to Ocracoke Island and the Outer Banks of North Carolina. Whether traveling on 264 east to the coast or 264 west to the capital, plan a stay at Pungo River Inn and enjoy a southern breakfast featuring Fran's Oat and Honey Loaf. Afternoon beverages are served in the courtyard.

Host: Fran Johnson
Rooms: 3 (1 PB; 2 SB) $50
Full Breakfast
Credit Cards: A, B
Notes: 5, 7, 8, 9

River Forest Manor and Marina

600 East Main Street, 27810
(919) 943-2151

An elegant mansion situated on the Pungo River. Besides being a wonderful country inn with leaded cut-glass windows and crystal chandeliers, River Forest Manor is also a fully equipped marina. The famous smorgasbord is served nightly during the season, with dinner from a menu the rest of the year. Bar and lounge are open year-round. The grand old manor offers a carefully preserved feeling of Victorian times. Hot tub available for wonderful relaxation.

NOTES: Credit cards accepted: A Master Card; B Visa; C American Express; D Discover Card; E Diner's Club; F Other; 2 Personal Checks accepted; 3 Lunch available; 4 Dinner available; 5 Open all year;

Hosts: Melba G. Smith and Axson Smith, Jr.
Rooms: 12 (PB) $40-75
Continental Breakfast
Credit Cards: A, B, C
Notes: 3, 4, 5, 7, 9, 10, 11, 12

River Forest Manor

BLACK MOUNTAIN

Bed and Breakfast Over Yonder

Route 1, Box 269, North Fork Road, 28711
(704) 669-6762

This comfortable old mountain home, furnished with antiques, has views of mountains and the surrounding woods from its landscaped decks and terrace. Secluded on 40 acres, it is two miles from I-40 and Black Mountain, which has antique and craft shopping. Close to the Blue Ridge Parkway and Asheville's Biltmore Estate. The breakfast specialty is fresh mountain brown trout.

Host: Wilhelmina Headley
Rooms: 5 (PB) $42.20-64.80
Full Breakfast
Credit Cards: None

Closed Dec.-May 14
Notes: 2, 7 (limited), 8, 9, 10, 11, 12, 14

Black Mountain Inn

718 West Old Highway. 70, 28711
(704) 669-6528

Discover a peaceful retreat for body and soul. Built at the turn of the century, this lovingly restored inn is cloaked in a long and colorful history. Once a studio and haven for artists, this small and intimate inn embraces its guests with long forgotten hospitality and charm. With seven comfortable guest rooms, each decorated with casual country decor, and with private bath.

Host: June Bergern Colbert
Rooms: 7 (PB) $60-65
Full Breakfast
Credit Cards: None
Notes: 2, 9, 10, 11, 12, 14

BLOWING ROCK

Hound Ears Club and Lodge

P.O. Box 188, 28605
(704) 963-4321

Luxury four-star resort in the heart of the Blue Ridge Mountains. Amenities include golf, tennis, swimming, fishing, and snow skiing, as well as excellent dining in the clubhouse. The 28 guest rooms are all centrally situated and entitle guests and club members to exclusive use of the facilities. Long-term and seasonal rentals available.

Host: Lillian Smith
Rooms: 28 (PB) $110-140/person with two people
    per room
Full Breakfast Modified American Plan
Credit Cards: A, B, C
Notes: 3, 4, 5, 8, 9, 10, 11, 12, 13, 14

Ragged Garden Inn and Restaurant

Box 1927, Sunset Drive, 28605
(704) 295-9703

6 Pets welcome; 7 Smoking allowed; 8 Children welcome; 9 Social drinking allowed; 10 Tennis available; 11 Swimming available; 12 Golf available; 13 Skiing available; 14 May be booked through travel agents.

Ragged Garden, built at the turn of the century as a summer home, is surrounded by terraced rose gardens, dogwoods, azaleas, and rhododendrons. The building has a stone-columned entrance, and its exterior is covered with chestnut bark slabs. It has an unusual slate and stone staircase. The restaurant has pre-blight chestnut paneling. The guest rooms are cozy with comforters and papered walls with contrasting trim. The open-air porch is used for breakfast and dinner, overlooking the garden. Chef/owner Joe Villani serves gourmet northern Italian cuisine.

Hosts: Joe and Joyce Villani
Rooms: 9 (PB) $50-110
Full Breakfast
Credit Cards: A, B, C
Notes: 2, 4, 7, 9, 10, 11, 12, 13

BREVARD

The Inn at Brevard

410 East Main Street, 28712
(704) 884-2105

Listed on the National Register of Historic Places, this inn hosted a reunion dinner for Stonewall Jackson's troops in 1911. Beautifully restored in 1984 with a European flavor throughout. Just minutes from Brevard Music Center, Blue Ridge Parkway, and Pisgah National Forest.

Hosts: Eileen and Bertrand Bourget
Rooms: 15 (14 PB; 1 SB) $59-95
Full Breakfast
Credit Cards: A, B
Notes: 2, 4, 5, 9, 10, 12

The Red House Inn

412 West Probart Street, 28712
(704) 884-9349

The Red House was built in 1851 and has been lovingly restored and furnished in turn-of-the-century period antiques. Ideally situated in the Blue Ridge Mountains, for the wonderful Brevard Music Center performances every night during the summer.

Hosts: Lynne Ong and Mary MacGillycuddy
Rooms: 6 (PB and SB) $43-57
Full Breakfast
Credit Cards: None
Closed November 30-April 1
Notes: 2, 9, 11, 12, 14

BRYSON CITY

Folkestone Inn

767 West Deep Creek Road, 28713
(704) 488-2730

Enjoy the romance of an Old World inn, the charm and nostalgia of the long-forgotten lifestyle of gracious country living. The inn is situated in the Great Smoky Mountains, in Swain County, which is 86 percent parkland. You may hike, fish, sail, raft, or horseback ride.

Hosts: Norma and Peter Joyce
Rooms: 9 (PB) $59-79
Full Breakfast
Credit Cards: None
Notes: 2, 4, 5, 10, 11

Fryemont Inn

Box 459, 28713
(704) 488-2159

Overlooking Great Smoky Mountains National Park. All rooms have private bath. Dinner and breakfast are included in the daily rate, and the inn is on the National Register of Historic Places. Featured in Bon Appetit.

Hosts: Sue and George Brown
Rooms: 39 (PB) $85-155
Full Breakfast
Credit Cards: A, B
Closed Nov.—mid-April
Notes: 2, 3, 4, 7, 8, 9, 11

Randolph House Inn

Fryemont Road, P.O. Box 816, 28713
(704) 488-3472

This mansion, built in 1895 of the finest timber in the Smokies, is listed on the National Register of Historic Places. The inn is on a mountain shelf overlooking the

The Homeplace

quaint town of Bryson City. Six guest rooms, three with private bath, are furnished with original furnishings, some dating back to 1850. Area attractions include Asheville, Blue Ridge Parkway, Great Smoky Mountains National Park, Fontana Lake, a Cherokee Indian reservation, whitewater activities, and excursion train rides. Gourmet dinners are available. Open mid-April through October. 10 percent discounts for AAA, senior citizens, and travel agents.

Hosts: Bill and Ruth Randolph Adams
Rooms: 6 (3 PB; 3 SB) $70-120
Full Breakfast
Credit Cards: A, B, C
Closed Nov.—mid-April
Notes: 2, 4, 7, 8, 9, 14

CHARLOTTE

The Homeplace

5901 Sardis Road, 28270
(704) 365-1936

Restored 1902 country Victorian on two and one-half acres with garden gazebo and wraparound porch. Victorian elegance and old-fashioned charm with a full home-cooked breakfast. A quiet setting and unique experience for the traveler, business executive, or connoisseur of fine older homes.

Hosts: Peggy and Frank Dearien
Rooms: 3 (PB) $83

Full Breakfast
Credit Cards: A, B, C
Notes: 2, 5, 14

McElhinney House

10533 Fairway Ridge Road, 28277
(704) 846-0783

McElhinney House is located in a quiet area of southeast Charlotte. A host speaking French, Italian, German, or English welcomes American and international guests. A lounge area, cable TV, laundry facilities, and barbecue grill are available to guests. Close to I-77 and I-85 and the attractions of Charlotte and northern South Carolina. Six golf courses and Carowinds theme park are minutes away.

Hosts: Mary and Jim McElhinney
Rooms: 2 (PB) $55-65
Continental Breakfast
Credit Cards: A, B
Notes: 2, 7, 8, 9, 12

CHIMNEY ROCK VILLAGE

The Dogwood Inn

P. O. Box 70, Highway 64-74, 28720
(704) 625-4403

A charming white two-story country bed and breakfast. Come enjoy the five porches that grace this wonderful early 1900s inn on the banks of the peaceful Rocky Broad River. Massive Chimney Rock Mountain can be seen from any of the porches. A full country breakfast is served each morning at

The Dogwood Inn

6 Pets welcome; 7 Smoking allowed; 8 Children welcome; 9 Social drinking allowed; 10 Tennis available; 11 Swimming available; 12 Golf available; 13 Skiing available; 14 May be booked through travel agents.

a huge handmade oak table. Children over 12 are welcome. Come rest a while. The river is calling you.

Hosts: Christine and Mark Piper
Rooms: 10 (2 PB; 8 SB) $50-60
Full Breakfast
Credit Cards: A, B, C, D, F
Notes: 2, 5, 7, 8 (over 12), 9, 10, 11, 12, 13, 14

CLINTON

The Shield House

216 Sampson Street, 28328
(919) 592-2634; (800) 462-9817 reservations

This plantation-style house is reminiscent of *Gone With the Wind* and is listed in the National Register of Historic Places. This spectacular Classic Revival home has many dramatic features, including four dominating Corinthian fluted columns surrounding the entrance and 12 Ionic columns on the porches. A large foyer with enclosed columns outlines a grand central-flight staircase. Spacious bedrooms are decorated with period antiques and comfortable seating arrangements. A parlor and lounging area are available.

Hosts: Juanita McLamb and Anita Green
Rooms: 6 (PB) $45-60
Continental Breakfast
Credit Cards: A, B, D
Notes: 2, 5, 7 (limited), 8 (prior arrangements), 9, 10, 12, 14

CLYDE

Windsong: A Mountain Inn

120 Ferguson Ridge, 28721
(704) 627-6111

Enjoy a secluded, romantic interlude at this contemporary log inn high in the breathtaking Smoky Mountains. Though the inn is small and intimate, the rooms are large and bright, with high-beamed ceilings, pine log walls, and Mexican tile floors. Each room has a fireplace, oversize tub, separate shower, and private deck or patio. Guest

lounge with billiards and wet bar. Full breakfast included. On 25 acres, with pool, tennis, hiking, and lovable llamas.Newly added is a separate two-bedroom log suite with full kitchen and the Pond House. Near Maggie Valley. Closed in January.

Hosts: Donna and Gale Livengood
Rooms: 5 (PB) $90-95
Full Breakfast
Credit Cards: A, B
Closed January
Notes: 2, 9, 10, 11, 12, 14

CULLOWHEE

Cullowhee Bed and Breakfast

150 Ledbetter Road, 28723
(704) 293-5447

Situated on a hillside among pines, oaks, and maples, this bed and breakfast offers the relaxing atmosphere of an immaculate country home and a beautiful view of the mountains. All bedrooms are comfortably furnished with queen- or king-size beds. The coffee pot starts at dawn for early risers, and a special treat awaits you at breakfast with full country fare and hot muffins.

Hosts: Charles and Janet Moore
Rooms: 3 (1 PB; 2 SB) $50-60
Full Breakfast
Credit Cards: None
Notes: 2, 5

DURHAM

Arrowhead Inn

106 Mason Road, 27712
(919) 477-8430

This restored 1775 manor house on four rural acres offers homey hospitality in an atmosphere that evokes colonial Carolina. But along with 18th-century architecture, decor, and furnishings, Arrowhead Inn features contemporary comfort, sparkling housekeeping, and bounteous home-cooked

---

NOTES: Credit cards accepted: A Master Card; B Visa; C American Express; D Discover Card; E Diner's Club; F Other; 2 Personal Checks accepted; 3 Lunch available; 4 Dinner available; 5 Open all year;

breakfasts. Open all year. Written up in *Food and Wine*, *USA Today*, and many metro newspapers.

Hosts: Jerry, Barbara, and Cathy Ryan
Rooms: 8 (6 PB; 2 SB) $72.15-144.30
Full Breakfast
Credit Cards: A, B, C, E
Notes: 2, 5, 7, 8, 9, 10, 11, 12, 14

Arrowhead Inn

The Blooming Garden Inn

513 Holloway Street, 27701
(919) 687-0801

An unexpected use of color transforms this restored 1892 Queen Anne-style home into a cozy, pleasant retreat in downtown historic Durham. Exquisite antiques, stained glass, and craft/art treasures from around the world add to your visiting pleasure. In addition to three guest rooms, two spacious luxury suites with Jacuzzis for two are available.

Hosts: Dolly and Frank Pokrass
Rooms: 5 (PB) $140
Full Breakfast
Credit Cards: A, B, C
Notes: 2, 5, 8, 9, 14

EDENTON

The Lords Proprietors' Inn

300 North Broad Street, 27932
(919) 482-3641

Establishing a reputation for the finest accommodations in North Carolina, the inn offers 20 elegantly appointed rooms with private baths and spacious parlors for gathering for afternoon tea by the fire. Inquire about special weekend programs that include dinner and tour.

Hosts: Arch, Jane, and Martha Edwards
Rooms: 20 (PB) $80-120
Full Breakfast
Credit Cards: None
Notes: 2, 5, 7 (restricted), 8, 9, 10, 11, 12

The Trestle House Inn

Route 4, Box 370, 27932
(919) 482-2282

South of Albemarle's colonial capital, off Route 32 and Soundside Road. Luxurious, immaculate accommodations include private baths, HBO, exercise room with steam bath, game room with billiards and shuffleboard, sun deck, private 15-acre fishing lake. Overlooks a 60-acre wildlife preserve.

Hosts: Willie and Carol Brothers
Rooms: 4 (PB) $60
Full Breakfast
Credit Cards: A, B, C
Notes: 2, 5, 7 (limited), 8, 9, 10, 11, 12, 14

ELLERBE

Ellerbe Springs Inn

Route 1, Box 179C, 28338
(919) 652-5600

Ellerbe Springs Inn is a beautiful, historic resort nestled in nearly 50 acres of rolling hills and lush greenery. Established in 1857, the pre-Civil War manor has been completely renovated and redecorated as of 1988. Each of the 14 charming guest rooms features antique furniture and oriental carpets. Private bathrooms and color cable TV are also available. Enjoy delectable southern cooking in the gracious first-floor dining room, open seven days serving breakfast, lunch, and dinner. It's an easy drive from Charlotte, Greensboro, Raleigh, and

Myrtle Beach. Family owned and operated. Listed in the National Register of Historic Places.

Host: Beth Cadieu-Diaz
Rooms: 14 (PB) $54-74
Full Breakfast
Credit Cards: A, B, C
Notes: 2, 3, 4, 5, 7, 8, 9, 14

FRANKLIN

Buttonwood Inn

190 Georgia Road, 28734
(704) 369-8985

A quaint, small mountain inn awaits those who prefer a cozy country atmosphere. Before hiking, golfing, gem mining, or horseback riding, enjoy a breakfast of puffy scrambled eggs and apple sausage ring or eggs Benedict, Dutch babies, blintz soufflé, strawberry omelet, or stuffed French toast.

Host: Liz Oehser
Rooms: 4 (2 PB; 2 SB) $54.50-65.40
Full Breakfast
Credit Cards: None
Closed Dec.-March
Notes: 2, 9, 10, 11, 12

The Franklin Terrace

67 Harrison Avenue, 28734
(704) 524-7907; (800) 633-2431

The Franklin Terrace, built as a school in 1887, is listed in the National Register of Historic Places. Wide porches and large guest rooms filled with period antiques will carry you to a time gone by, when southern hospitality was at its best. Antiques, crafts, and gifts are for sale on the main floor. Within walking distance of Franklin's famous gem shops, clothing boutiques, and fine restaurants.

Hosts: Ed and Helen Henson
Rooms: 9 (PB) $48-65
Full Breakfast
Credit Cards: A, B
Open April 1-Nov. 15
Notes: 2, 7, 8, 9, 10, 11, 12, 14

GREENSBORO

The Greenwich Inn

111 West Washington Street, 27401
(919) 272-3474

Situated in central city. Guest rooms are furnished in 18th-century furniture yet offer all modern conveniences. Some rooms have four-poster beds; all rooms have private bath, TV hidden in armoire, telephone, and refrigerator. Laundry service is available daily. Wine and cheese are served in the evening. Soda and snack machines are on the first floor in the main lobby. Ice is furnished upon request.

Host: Emily Moorefield
Rooms: 23 (PB) $75-85
Continental Breakfast
Credit Cards: A, B, C, E
Notes: 5, 7, 8, 9, 14

Greenwood

205 North Park Drive, 27401
(919) 274-6350

Enjoy the warm hospitality of this 1910 home in the park in the historic district of Greensboro. Three minutes from downtown; three miles from I-85 and I-40. Air conditioning, two fireplaces in livingrooms, swimming pool, TV room, guest kitchen. Hearty continental breakfast is served.

Host: Jo Anne Green
Rooms: 3 plus suite (PB) $64-95
Expanded Continental Breakfast
Minimum stay Southern Furniture Market: 3 nights
Credit Cards: A, B, C
Notes: 2, 5, 7, 8 (over 4), 9, 10, 11, 12, 14

HATTERAS

Outer Banks
Bed and Breakfast

P. O. Box 610, Eagle Pass Road, 27943
(919) 986-2776

Taste life as it used to be in this quaint and charming old fishing village house. Cozy

---

NOTES: Credit cards accepted: A Master Card; B Visa; C American Express; D Discover Card; E Diner's Club; F Other; 2 Personal Checks accepted; 3 Lunch available; 4 Dinner available; 5 Open all year;

bedrooms, early morning coffee trays in your room, and an incredible breakfast start off a day of exploring the miles of unpopulated beaches of the Cape Hatteras National Seashore. Complete your day with a fabulous fresh seafood dinner at any of the local restaurants. Near marinas, golf course, and small airport.

Host: The Phoenix family
Rooms: 3 (SB) $60-65
Full Breakfast
Credit Cards: A, B, D
Notes: 2, 7 (limited), 8, 9, 11, 12

HAZELWOOD

Belle Meade Inn

P. O. Box 1319, Waynesville, 28786
(704)456-3234

This Craftsman-style elegant home from yesteryear features chestnut woodwork in the formal rooms and a large fieldstone fireplace. An interesting and eye-appealing blend of antique and traditional furnishings, the inn is near the Great Smoky Mountains National Park and Ashville. Amenities include central air conditioning and distinctive full breakfast. Golf, hiking, rafting, and the Biltmore House are nearby.

Rooms: 4 (PB) $50-55
Full Breakfast
Credit Cards: A, B, D
Notes: 9, 12, 13, 14

HENDERSONVILLE

Claddagh Inn

755 North Main Street, 28792
(704) 697-7778; (800) 225-4700

The Claddagh Inn is situated in downtown Hendersonville, just two blocks from the beautiful Main Street Shopping Promenade. The inn has undergone extensive remodeling. The guest rooms have private bath, telephone, and air conditioning. TV available. Guests awake to a delicious full coun-

try breakfast. AAA approved. Listed on the National Register of Historic Places.

Hosts: Vickie and Dennis Pacilio
Rooms: 14 (PB) $63-89
Full Breakfast
Credit Cards: A, B, C, D
Notes: 2, 5, 7, 8, 9, 10, 11, 12, 14

The Waverly Inn

783 North Main Street, 28792
(704) 693-9193; (800) 537-8195

Listed in the National Register of Historic Places, this is the oldest surviving inn in Hendersonville. The recently renovated inn has something for everyone, including claw foot tubs and king and queen four-poster canopy beds. Convenient to restaurants, shopping, Biltmore Estate, Carl Sandburg home, Blue Ridge Parkway, and Flat Rock Playhouse. AAA approved.

Hosts: John and Diane Sheiry
Rooms: 15 (PB) $65-89
Full Breakfast
Credit Cards: A, B, C, D
Notes: 2, 5, 7, 8, 9, 10, 11, 12, 14

HERTFORD

Gingerbread Inn and Bakery, Inc.

103 South Church Street, 27944
(919) 426-5809

This beautifully restored turn-of-the-century home is on the local historic tour and boasts a wraparound porch with paired columns. The comfortably furnished rooms are spacious, with queen- or king-size beds and plush carpeting. All rooms are centrally air-conditioned and have color cable TV. The aroma of freshly baked gingerbread from the bakery entices you during your stay, and you are offered a gingerbread boy or girl for your ride home.

Host: Jenny Harnisch
Rooms: 3 (PB) $47.70
Full Breakfast
Credit Cards: A, B
Notes: 2, 5, 8, 9, 12

6 Pets welcome; 7 Smoking allowed; 8 Children welcome; 9 Social drinking allowed; 10 Tennis available; 11 Swimming available; 12 Golf available; 13 Skiing available; 14 May be booked through travel agents.

HICKORY

Hickory Bed and Breakfast

464 7th Street, Southwest, 28602
(704) 324-0548; (800) 654-2961

This 1908 two-story Georgian-style house that sits on one and one-half acres surrounded by various trees and flowers offers a true a home away from home. Sit in the parlor or curl up with a good book or play a game in the library. You can sit by the pool and enjoy iced tea or lemonade with something freshly baked from the oven. Relax on the screened porch. The house is decorated with a country theme. A full country breakfast is offered.

Hosts: Bob and Suzanne Ellis
Rooms: 4 (4 PB) $55
Full Breakfast
Credit Cards: None
Notes: 2, 5, 10, 11, 12, 13

HIGHLANDS

Colonial Pines Inn

Route 1, Box 22B, 28741
(704) 526-2060

A quiet country guest house with lovely mountain view. Comfortably furnished with antiques and many fine accessories. One-half mile from Highlands's fine dining and shopping area. Full breakfast includes egg dishes, homemade breads, fresh fruit, coffee, and juice. A separate two-bedroom guest house with kitchen is great for small families.

Hosts: Chris and Donny Alley
Rooms: 6 (PB) $60-85
Guest House: $70
Full Breakfast
Credit Cards: A, B
Notes: 2, 5, 8, 9, 10, 11, 12, 13

The Laurels: Freda's Bed and Breakfast

Route 2, Box 102, 28741
(704) 526-2091

The Laurels, a unique bed and breakfast, is situated in historic Horse Cove, two and one-half miles outside of Highlands. It is on seven acres. The half-acre pond is stocked with rainbow trout. Come in the afternoon and have an English tea. Two cozy fireplaces warm the cool evenings. The large English country breakfast features fresh fruit, bacon, ham, and eggs any way you want them. The hosts grind their own whole-wheat flour and make crunchy toast. No smoking.

Hosts: Warren and Freda Lorenz
Rooms: 4 (PB) $50-60
Full Breakfast
Credit Cards: None
Notes: 2, 9

Long House Bed and Breakfast

Highway 64E, P. O. Box 207B, 28741
(704) 526-4394; (800) 833-0020

Long House Bed and Breakfast offers a comfortable retreat in the scenic mountains of western North Carolina. Any time of the year guests can enjoy the beauty and charm of this quaint town and the scenic wonders of the Nantahala National Forest. The rustic mountain bed and breakfast offers country charm and warm hospitality. A hearty breakfast is served family-style and is usually the highlight of everyone's visit.

Hosts: Lynn and Valerie Long
Rooms: 4 (PB) $55-85
Full Breakfast
Credit Cards: A, B
Notes: 2, 5, 8, 9

HIGH POINT

The Premier Bed and Breakfast

1001 Johnson Street, 27262
(919) 889-8349

Enjoy a glass of wine by the fireplace or on the front porch. Relax by candlelight in a

NOTES: Credit cards accepted: A Master Card; B Visa; C American Express; D Discover Card; E Diner's Club; F Other; 2 Personal Checks accepted; 3 Lunch available; 4 Dinner available; 5 Open all year;

bubble bath. Mingle with folks from all over. Awaken to the smell of a magnificent breakfast. Shop for furniture conveniently. Whether you're traveling for business or pleasure, this bed and breakfast provides the perfect mix.

Host: Peggy Burcham
Rooms: 6 (PB) $60-125
Full Breakfast
Credit Cards: A, B, C
Notes: 2, 4, 5, 7 (limited), 8, 9, 10, 12

HILLSBOROUGH

The Colonial Inn

153 West King Street, 28211
(919) 732-2461

A charming old country inn in historic Hillsborough, the Colonial Inn has served guests continuously since 1759, among them Lord Cornwallis and Aaron Burr. A short distance from Chapel Hill, Durham, and Duke University. Convenient to I-85 and I-40. Famous for southern cooking and homelike comfort. Great antique shopping nearby.

Hosts: Carlton and Sara McKee
Rooms: 8 (6 PB; 2 SB) $55-65
Full Breakfast
Credit Cards: A, B
Notes: 2, 3, 4, 5, 7, 8, 9, 14

KILL DEVIL HILLS

Ye Olde Cherokee Inn

500 North Virginia Dare Trail, 27948
(919) 441-6127

This large beach house with cypress-wood interior is five hundred feet from ocean beach. Quiet and restful. Ideal for relaxing and romance. Close to fine restaurants, golf, hang gliding, scuba diving, wind surfing, deep-sea fishing, and shopping. Be as active or inactive as you wish.

Hosts: Bob and Phyllis Combs
Rooms: 6 (PB) $55-85
Continental Breakfast
Minimum stay holidays: 3 nights

Credit Cards: A, B, C
Closed: Oct.-Apr.
Notes: 2, 9, 10, 11, 12

LAKE JUNALUSKA

Providence Lodge

207 Atkins Loop, 28745
(704) 456-6486

Providence Lodge is situated near the Blue Ridge Parkway and is an easy drive from the Cherokee Indian Reservation, Great Smoky Mountains National Park, or the Biltmore Estate in Asheville. Rustic, with period furniture, comfortable beds, claw foot tubs, and big porches. Delicious family-style meals feature the best in country cooking.

Hosts: Ben and Wilma Cato
Rooms: 16 (8 PB; 8 SB) $60-75
Credit Cards: None
Closed Sept.-May
Notes: 2, 4, 8, 9, 10, 11, 12

The Colonial Inn

LAKE TOXAWAY

The Greystone Inn

Greystone Lane, 28747
(704) 966-4700

The Greystone Inn, an early 1900s restored Swiss revival-style mansion, is listed on the National Register of Historic Places. Golf and tennis, swimming, boating, and fishing on the largest private lake in North Carolina.

6 Pets welcome; 7 Smoking allowed; 8 Children welcome; 9 Social drinking allowed; 10 Tennis available; 11 Swimming available; 12 Golf available; 13 Skiing available; 14 May be booked through travel agents.

Hosts: Tim and Boo Boo Lovelace
Rooms: 33 (PB) $125-165/persdon
Full or Continental Breakfast
Credit Cards: A, B, C
Closed Jan.-Mar.
Notes: 2, 4, 7, 8, 9, 10, 11, 12, 14

MAGGIE VALLEY

Smokey Shadows Lodge

P. O. Box 444, 28751
(704) 926-0001

This secluded log lodge and one adjacent
cottage sit on a stone bluff at 4,500 feet,
one and one-half miles up a winding road
from Maggie Valley and one and one-half
miles from Cataloochee ski slopes. It is
made of native stone and great hand-hewn
logs from an old gristmill. Country and
antique furnishings, bowls of fresh apples
and flowers, cheerful quilts, and curtains
blend beautifully with the stone and log
walls and log-beamed ceilings. Private
baths, oil heat, and large closets are things
you won't miss here. The 100-year-old log
cabin with fireplace sleeps 6; the lodge up
to 31, plus 9 more in the "stable dorm," a
favorite for the younger set. Also available
for guests is a new log cabin with kitchen.

Hosts: Bud and Ginger Shinn
Rooms: 12 (PB) $60, seasonal
Continental Breakfast
Credit Cards: A, B
Notes: 2, 3, 4, 5, 6, 8, 9, 10, 12, 13, 14

MARS HILL

Baird House, Ltd.

41 South Main Street, 28754
(704) 689-5722

Five guest rooms—two with a working
fireplace, two with private bath—are featured in an old brick, antique-filled bed and
breakfast inn that once was the grandest
house in this pastoral corner of the western
North Carolina mountains. Eighteen miles
north of Asheville.

Host: Yvette Wessel
Rooms: 5 (2 PB; 3 SB) $42.40-53
Full Breakfast
Credit Cards: C
Closed December
Notes: 2, 7, 8, 9, 10, 11, 12, 13, 14

MOUNT AIRY

Pine Ridge Inn

2893 West Pine Street, 27030
(919) 789-5034

Built in 1948, this southern mansion offers
private bedroom suites, swimming pool
with sun deck, large indoor hot tub, and
exercise room. Lunch and dinner available
Tuesday through Saturday.

Hosts: Ellen and Manford Haxton
Rooms: 6 (PB) $60-100
Full or Continental Breakfast
Credit Cards: A, B, C
Notes: 2, 3, 4, 5, 7, 8, 9, 10, 11, 12, 14

MURPHY

Hill Top House

104 Campbell Street, 28906
(704) 837-8661

Hill Top House is a step back into a turn-
of-the-century home. Built around 1902,
the house has been modernized only in the
kitchen and plumbing. Each room has been
tastefully decorated in period pieces and
antiques. A full breakfast featuring homemade breads is served in the spacious dining room, and the hosts gladly cater to individual diet needs. Three rooms are available for reservations, all with queen or twin
beds.

Hosts: Don and Jacqueline Heinze
Rooms: 3 (1 PB; 2 SB) $45-50
Full Breakfast
Credit Cards: None
Notes: 2, 5, 8, 9, 10, 12

NOTES: Credit cards accepted: A Master Card; B Visa; C American Express; D Discover Card; E Diner's
Club; F Other; 2 Personal Checks accepted; 3 Lunch available; 4 Dinner available; 5 Open all year;

Huntington Hall Bed and Breakfast

500 Valley River Avenue, 28906
(704) 837-9567; (800) 824-6189

Ginger-peach crepes, English ivy, and low stone walls await you. Five guest rooms with private baths. Wonderful breakfasts served on the sun porch overlooked by 100-year-old maple trees. This former mayor's home is warm and comfortable. Circa 1881. Here in the mountains of western North Carolina, you can hike, whitewater raft, ride the Great Smoky Mountains Railway, visit the John C. Campbell Folk School, or just relax on the porch and smell the mountain breeze.

Hosts: Bob and Katie DeLong
Rooms: 5 (PB) $49-65
Full Breakfast
Credit Cards: A, B, C, D, E
Notes: 2, 5, 7, 8, 9, 10, 11, 12, 14

NAGS HEAD

First Colony Inn

6720 South Virginia Dare Trail, 27959
(919) 441-2343; (800) 368-9390 reservations

Enjoy Southern hospitality in this historic inn with direct access to the beach and views of the ocean and sound. Convenient to all historic and natural attractions.

The Aerie

Decorated with antiques. Efficiencies, wet bars, luxury baths, Jacuzzis, wonderful porches with rockers and hammocks, pool, and library.

Hosts: Richard and Camille Lawrence
Rooms: 26 (PB) $60-230, seasonal
Continental Breakfast
Credit Cards: A, B, D
Notes: 2, 4, 5, 8, 9, 10, 11, 12, 14

NEW BERN

The Aerie

509 Pollock Street, 28560
(919) 636-5553

A Victorian inn one block from Tryon Palace. Individually decorated rooms are furnished with antiques and reproductions; sitting room with player piano. Bicycles are available for guests who want to tour New Bern's historic district.

Hosts: Rick and Lois Cleveland
Rooms: 7 (PB) $85
Full Breakfast
Credit Cards: A, B, C
Notes: 2, 5, 7, 8, 9, 12, 14

Harmony House Inn

215 Pollock Street, 28560
(919) 636-3810

This circa 1850 Greek Revival inn provides comfortable elegance in the historic district. Unusual spaciousness, antiques, a guest parlor, rocking chairs and swings on the front porch, and a parking area add to guests' enjoyment. Near Tryon Palace, restaurants, and shops.

Hosts: A. E. and Diane Hansen
Rooms: 9 (PB) $80
Full Breakfast
Credit Cards: A, B, C
Notes: 2, 5, 8, 9, 10, 12, 14

Kings Arms Inn

212 Pollock Street, 28560
(919) 638-4409

6 Pets welcome; 7 Smoking allowed; 8 Children welcome; 9 Social drinking allowed; 10 Tennis available; 11 Swimming available; 12 Golf available; 13 Skiing available; 14 May be booked through travel agents.

The King's Arms Inn, named for an old New Bern tavern reputed to have hosted members of the First Continental Congress, upholds a heritage of hospitality and graciousness as New Bern's "first and foremost" in bed and breakfast accommodations. Spacious rooms with comfortable four-poster, canopy, or brass beds; fireplaces; private baths; and elegant decor harbor travelers who want to escape the present and steep themselves in colonial history. Home-baked breakfasts include banana or zucchini bread; blueberry, lemon ginger, apple streusel, or sweet potato muffins; Smithfield ham and biscuits; fresh fruit; juice; and cinnamon coffee or tea— all delivered to your room with the morning paper.

Hosts: David and Diana Parks
Rooms: 9 (PB) $59-79
Expanded Continental Breakfast
Credit Cards: A, B, C
Notes: 2, 5, 8, 9, 10, 11, 12, 14

New Berne House Inn

709 Broad Street, 28560
(800) 842-7688

Listed on the National Register of Historic Places and situated one block from Tryon Palace, New Berne House offers the charm and ambience of English country house decor. Guest rooms all have private baths, some with claw foot tubs and pedestal sinks. Antique beds piled with pillows; crisp eyelet sheets; fireplaces in some rooms. The inn is noted for its fine breakfasts, including southern specialties such as pralines'n'cream waffles and peach French toast. The library features an interesting collection of books, and the Rose Parlor boasts a baby grand piano.

Hosts: Marcia Drum and Howard Bronson
Rooms: 7 (PB) $65-85
Full Breakfast
Credit Cards: A, B, C
Notes: 2, 5, 9, 10, 11, 12, 14

OCEAN ISLE BEACH

The Winds-Clarion Carriage House Inn

310 East First Street, 28469
(800) 334-3581 (US and Canada)

This delightful inn, surrounded by palm trees and lush subtropical landscaping, is on the oceanfront on an island beach just 20 minutes from North Myrtle Beach, South Carolina. The Winds features oceanfront two- and three-room suites and studios with full kitchens or kitchenettes and seaside balconies. Amenities include daily housekeeping, a heated pool, whirlpool, sauna, beach volleyball, fitness room, rental bicycles, sailboats, golf on 70 courses, and free tennis on the island. There are several restaurants on the island and nearby Myrtle Beach offers many more.

Hosts: Miller and Helen Pope
Rooms: 73 (PB) $49-160
Continental Breakfast
Credit Cards: A, B, C, D, E
Notes: 5, 7, 8, 9, 10, 11, 12, 14

OCRACOKE ISLAND

Oscar's House

Route 12, Box 206, 27960
(919) 928-1311

Oscar's House offers friendly accommodations in a comfortable 1940s home on Ocracoke Island. The home is one block from the harbor and one mile from the Atlantic Ocean, within easy walking distance of shops, restaurants, and historic sites. The full breakfast is healthy, and special diets are accommodated.

Host: Ann Ehringhaus
Rooms: 4 (1 PB; 3 SB) $42-57
Full Breakfast
Credit Cards: A, B
Closed Nov.-early April
Notes: 2, 7 (restricted), 8 (over 3), 9, 11

NOTES: Credit cards accepted: A Master Card; B Visa; C American Express; D Discover Card; E Diner's Club; F Other; 2 Personal Checks accepted; 3 Lunch available; 4 Dinner available; 5 Open all year;

OLD FORT

The Inn at Old Fort

P. O. Box 1116, 28762
(704) 606-9384

Two-story Gothic Revival-style Victorian cottage, circa 1880. Located on more than 3.5 acres overlooking the historic small town of Old Fort. Features rooms furnished with antiques; warm, friendly conversation; front-porch rockers; terraced lawn and gardens; and extended continental breakfast featuring freshly baked breads and fresh fruits.

Hosts: Chuck and Debbie Aldridge
Rooms: 5 (3 PB; 2SB) $40-50
Expanded Continental Breakfast
Credit Cards: None
Notes: 2, 5, 7, (outside), 8, 9, 10, 11, 12, 14

ORIENTAL

The Cartwright House Bed and Breakast

Box 310, Church Street, 28571
(919) 249-1337

A charming turn-of-the-century, completely restored Victorian inn in a quaint fishing village tucked on the banks of the widest river in North America, the Neuse. Sailing charters, bicycles, croquet, porch swings and rockers, English gardens, art galleries, great restaurants, and no traffic lights. Elegant furnishings include canopied queen beds, cable TV, private baths. Gourmet breakfasts and champagne receptions.

Hosts: Patricia and Tom Davis
Rooms: 5 (4 PB; 1 SB) $70-85
Full Breakfast
Credit Cards: A, B
Notes: 2, 3, 4, 5, 7, 9, 10, 11, 12

The Tar Heel Inn

Box 176, 28571
(919) 249-1078

Oriental, a quiet fishing village on the Neuse River and the Pamlico Sound, is known as the sailing capital of North Carolina. This quaint, circa 1890, inn has been restored to capture the feeling of an old English country inn with comfortable common rooms. The patios and gardens are yours to enjoy, and you can even borrow bikes to pedal around town. Excellent restaurants and shops, sailing, golf, tennis, and fishing are within walking or biking distance.

Hosts: Dave and Patti Nelson
Rooms: 8 (PB) $55-75
Full Breakfast
Credit Cards: A, B
Closed Dec.-Feb.
Notes: 2, 8, 9, 10, 11, 12, 14

PINEHURST

Magnolia Inn

P. O. Box 818, 28374
(919) 295-6900; (800) 526-5562

The Magnolia Inn was built in 1896 and was completely renovated and refurbished with Victorian furnishings and accessories in 1989. Situated in the heart of the village of Pinehurst, the inn offers golf packages as well as use of other area amenities. Easy access to shopping, dining, and walking tours of historic Pinehurst.

Hosts: Jan and Ned
Rooms: 13 (PB) $95 plus
Full Breakfast
Credit Cards: A, B, C
Notes: 2, 4, 5, 10, 11, 12, 14

PISGAH FOREST

The Pines Country Inn

719 Hart Road, 28768
(704) 877-3131

The Pines Country Inn is situated in the Blue Ridge Mountains overlooking a beautiful valley. Truly a country inn, where guests are treated like family at Grandma's

---

6 Pets welcome; 7 Smoking allowed; 8 Children welcome; 9 Social drinking allowed; 10 Tennis available; 11 Swimming available; 12 Golf available; 13 Skiing available; 14 May be booked through travel agents.

house. Available by day, week, or month. Situated between Brevard and Hendersonville.

Hosts: Tom and Mary McEntire
Rooms: 18 (16 PB; 2 SB) $58-68
Full Breakfast
Credit Cards: None
Notes: 2, 4, 8, 9, 12

RALEIGH

The Oakwood Inn

411 North Bloodworth Street, 27604
(919) 832-9712

The Oakwood Inn is an 1871 Victorian listed on the National Register of Historic Places and situated in a downtown historic district. Its Victorian heritage is seen in the carefully restored decor, period architecture, and interesting details.

Host: Terri L. Jones
Rooms: 6 (PB) $60-100
Full Breakfast
Credit Cards: A, B, C, D
Notes: 2, 5, 8 (over 10), 9, 14

ROBBINSVILLE

Blue Boar Lodge

200 Santeetlah Road, 28771
(704) 479-8126

Secluded mountain retreat cooled by mountain breezes. Hiking, fishing, hunting, bird watching, and canoeing are all very close by. Rustic but modern house. Meals served family-style on the lazy Susan table. Situated away from all city traffic, ten miles northwest of Robbinsville. Quiet and peaceful. Rate includes breakfast and dinner.

Hosts: Roy and Kathy Wilson
Rooms: 7 (PB) $90
Full Breakfast and Dinner
Credit Cards: A, B
Open April 1—mid-Oct.
Notes: 4, 7

SALISBURY

The 1868 Stewart-Marsh House

220 South Ellis Street, 28144
(704) 633-6841

Gracious 1868 Federal-style home on a quiet tree-lined street in the West Square historic district. Cozy pine-paneled library, screened porch with wicker, spacious guest rooms with air conditioning, antiques, heart pine floors. Delicious breakfast with home-baked muffins and breads plus entree. Warm, friendly, southern hospitality. Historic sights, antebellum homes, shopping, and restaurants are within walking distance. Guided tours available. Easy access to I-85.

Hosts: Gerry and Chuck Webster
Rooms: 2 (PB) $50-55
Expanded Continental Breakfast
Credit Cards: A, B
Notes: 2, 5, 7 (limited), 8 (over 6), 9, 10, 12, 14

Rowan Oak House

208 South Fulton Street, 28144
(704) 633-2086; (800) 786-0437

Romantic and lavish describes this Queen Anne Victorian mansion: wraparound porch, rocking chairs, elaborate woodwork, stained glass, and original fixtures. Bedrooms are enormous with air conditioning, English and American antiques, fruit, and flowers. One room has Jacuzzi and working fireplace. Your full gourmet breakfast will be served with silver, crystal, and Queen Louise china. Located in the heart of the historic district, one mile from I-85, Exit 76B.

Hosts: Bill and Ruth Ann Coffey
Rooms: 4 (2 PB; 2 SB) $65-95
Full Breakfast
Credit Cards: A, B, D
Notes: 2, 5, 7 (limited), 8 (over 10), 9, 10, 11, 12, 14

NOTES: Credit cards accepted: A Master Card; B Visa; C American Express; D Discover Card; E Diner's Club; F Other; 2 Personal Checks accepted; 3 Lunch available; 4 Dinner available; 5 Open all year;

SPARTA

Turby-villa

Highway 18 North, Star Route 1, Box 48, 28675
(919) 372-8490

The Turby-villa is situated on 20 acres of beautiful mountain farmland. Breakfast is selected from a menu and served on a glassed-in porch with a beautiful view of the mountains. The bed and breakfast is ten miles from the Blue Ridge Parkway, which is maintained by the National Park Service, on Highway 18 N, two miles from Sparta.

Host: Maybelline Turbiville
Rooms: 3 (PB) $52.50
Full Breakfast
Credit Cards: None
Notes: 2, 5, 7, 8, 9, 10, 12

SPRUCE PINE

Ansley/Richmond Inn

101 Pine Avenue, 28777
(704) 765-6993

This lovely half-century-old "country elegant" inn, specializing in pampering guests, is nestled into the hills overlooking the town of Spruce Pine and the Blue Ridge Parkway just four miles to the south. Centrally situated for hiking, crafts, skiing, golf, and gem mining, the inn has seven luxurious rooms, all with private baths, and serves a full breakfast each morning and a complimentary glass of wine in the evening.

Hosts: Bill Ansley and Lenore Boucher
Rooms: 7 (PB) $55-75
Full Breakfast
Credit Cards: A, B
Notes: 2, 5, 8, 9, 10, 11, 12, 13, 14

The Fairway Inn Bed and Breakfast

110 Henry Lane, 28777
(704) 765-4917

Beautiful country home with a scenic view. Situated on Highway 226, three miles north of the Blue Ridge Parkway. Six guest rooms, each with private bath. Gourmet breakfast. Wine and cheese in the afternoon. Restaurants nearby.

Hosts: Margaret and John P. Stevens
Rooms: 6 (PB) $65-75
Full Breakfast
Credit Cards: A, B
Closed Jan.-March
Notes: 2, 7, 8, 9, 10, 12, 13, 14

STATESVILLE

Cedar Hill Farm Bed and Breakfast

Route 1, Box 492, 28677
(704) 873-4332

An 1840 farmhouse and private cottage on a 32-acre sheep farm in the rolling hills of North Carolina. Antique furnishings, air conditioning, color cable TV, and phones in rooms. After your full country breakfast, swim, play badminton, or relax in a porch rocker or hammock. For a busier day, visit two lovely towns with historic districts, Old Salem, or two large cities in a 45-mile radius. Convenient to restaurants, shopping, and three interstate highways.

Hosts: Jim and Brenda Vernon
Rooms: 2 (PB) $50-70
Full Breakfast
Credit Cards: A, B
Notes: 2, 5, 7 (limited), 8, 9, 11, 14

Madelyn's Bed and Breakfast

514 Carroll Street, 28677
(704) 872-3973

Fresh flowers and homemade cookies await your arrival at Statesville's first bed and breakfast. It is a charming 1940s brick home filled with unique collections of family antiques, Raggedy Anns, iron dogs, and bottles. There are three lovely bedrooms with private baths. Each has a different size bed to suit any traveler's needs. A full gourmet breakfast includes a choice of juice, fresh or baked fruit, bread, and entree. The house has central air conditioning. No smoking.

Hosts: Madelyn and John Hill
Rooms: 3 (PB) $55-65
Full Breakfast
Credit Cards: A, B
Notes: 2, 5, 9, 10, 12, 14

SUGAR GROVE

Rivendell Lodge

P. O. Box 211, 28679
(704) 297-1685

Secluded mountainside setting overlooking Watauga River rapids. Easy trail to the river. Guests have seen deer, beavers, rabbits, chipmunks, red-tailed hawks, herons, and hummingbirds on or near the property. Each guest room has down comforters and mountain views. Spacious great room with fireplace and library; multilevel decks and picnic/grill facilities outside. Twenty-five miles from the Blue Ridge Parkway (Blowing Rock exit).

Hosts: Sarah and Loren Williams
Rooms: 4 (2 PB; 2 SB) $60
Full Breakfast
Credit Cards: None
Notes: 2, 5, 9, 12, 13, 14

TARBORO

Little Warren

304 East Park Avenue, 27886
(919) 823-1314

Large, gracious Edwardian family home, renovated and modernized, in a quiet neighborhood in the historic district. Deeply set wraparound front porch overlooks the town common, which is one of two originally chartered commons remaining in the United States. Antiques available.

Hosts: Patsy and Tom Miller
Rooms: 3 (PB) $68.90
Continental and Full Breakfast
Credit Cards: A, B, C
Notes: 2, 5, 7, 8 (over 6), 9, 10

TRYON

Fox Trot Inn

800 Lynn Road, Route 108, P. O. Box 1561, 28782
(704) 859-9706

An elegant retreat that is situated on eight wooded acres in the heart of Tryon. This large, graciously proportioned inn features four bedrooms, two of which are suites. All rooms have private baths. Wine and hors d'oeuvres each evening. Air conditioning. Heated swimming pool. Also available is a fully furnished guest house with hanging deck, mountain view, and cable TV. Guests may use the inn's pool.

Hosts: Mimi Colby and Betty Daugherty
Rooms: 4 (PB) $60-85
House: (PB) $350-450 weekly; monthly rates available.
Full Breakfast
Credit Cards: None
Closed Dec. 15-March 14
Notes: 2, 7, 9, 10, 11, 12

Pine Crest Inn

Pine Crest Inn

200 Pine Crest Lane, 28782
(704) 859-9135; (800) 633-3001

The Pine Crest Inn is nestled in the foothills of the Blue Ridge Mountains. Listed on the National Register of Historic Places, the inn has 30 private rooms, suites,

---

NOTES: Credit cards accepted: A Master Card; B Visa; C American Express; D Discover Card; E Diner's Club; F Other; 2 Personal Checks accepted; 3 Lunch available; 4 Dinner available; 5 Open all year;

or cottages. The gourmet restaurant, fireplaces, wide porches, and beautiful grounds create a casual elegance and relaxing atmosphere. Nearby attractions include the Blue Ridge Parkway and the famous Biltmore Estate and Gardens.

Hosts: Jeremy and Jennifer Wainwright
Rooms: 30 (PB) $95-130
Continental Breakfast
Credit Cards: A, B
Notes: 2, 4, 5, 7, 8, 9, 10, 11, 12, 14

Stone Hedge Inn

Box 366, 28782
(704) 859-9114

Grand old estate on 28 acres at the base of Tryon Mountain. Lodging in the main building, cottage, and guest house. Private baths, TV, antiques, and wonderful views. Some rooms have kitchens and some have fireplaces. A full breakfast is served in the dining room by the picture windows. The restaurant features fine continental cuisine.

Hosts: Ray and Anneliese Weingartner
Rooms: 6 (PB) $65-85
Full Breakfast
Credit Cards: A, B
Notes: 2, 4, 5, 7, 8 (over 6), 9, 10, 11, 12, 14

VALLE CRUCIS

Mast Farm Inn

Box 704, 28691
(704) 963-5857

Recently restored 12-room inn on the National Register of Historic Places. Vegetables and berries for the dining room are grown on the 18-acre farm situated in North Carolina's high country near the Blue Ridge Parkway. Country cooking with a gourmet touch. Golf, hiking, swimming, fishing, and skiing are nearby. Breakfast and dinner are included.

Hosts: Sibyl and Francis Pressly
Rooms: 12 (10 PB; 2 SB) $75-150 Modified
    American Plan
Expanded Continental Breakfast
Credit Cards: A, B
Closed March 6-April 25 and Nov. 6-Dec. 26
Notes: 2, 4, 9, 10, 11, 12, 13

WAYNESVILLE

Grandview Lodge

809 Valley View Circle Road, 28786
(704) 456-5212; (800) 255-7826

Mast Farm Inn

6 Pets welcome; 7 Smoking allowed; 8 Children welcome; 9 Social drinking allowed; 10 Tennis available; 11 Swimming available; 12 Golf available; 13 Skiing available; 14 May be booked through travel agents.

A country inn in the western North Carolina mountains; open all year. Southern home cooking, with breakfast featuring homemade breads, jams, and jellies. Dinner includes fresh vegetables, freshly baked breads, and desserts. Meals, served family-style, are included in the rates. Private bath and cable TV.

Hosts: Stan and Linda Arnold
Rooms: 15 (PB) $95-110
Full Breakfast
Credit Cards: None
Notes: 2, 4 (included), 5, 7, 8, 9, 10, 11, 12, 13, 14

Hallcrest Inn

299 Halltop Circle, 28786
(704) 456-6457; (800) 334-6457

The homelike atmosphere here encourages a relaxing stay at this 1880s farmhouse on a mountaintop. Southern-style meals are served around large, lazy susan tables. All rooms have private baths. There's a beautiful view from the front porch, where rocking chairs await you. The daily rate includes both breakfast and dinner.

Hosts: Martin and Tesa Burson; David and
    Catherine Mitchell
Rooms: 12 (PB) $65-75
Full Breakfast
Credit Cards: A, B
Closed Dec.-April
Notes: 2, 3 (by arrangement), 4, 7, 8, 9 (restricted),
    10, 11, 12, 14

Haywood Street House

409 South Haywood Street, 28786
(704) 456-9831

A turn-of-the-century home graced with antiques. Relax on the veranda and enjoy a panoramic view of the mountains. Walk to Main Street, restaurants, antique shops, churches, and library. Within 15 minutes to one-hour drive of the Blue Ridge Parkway, Smoky Mountains, white water rafting, horseback riding, and much more.

Hosts: Chris and Lynn Sylvester
Rooms: 4 (S2B) $45-50
Continental Breakfast

Credit Cards: None
Notes: 2, 5, 8 (over 10), 9, 10, 11, 12, 13, 14

Heath Lodge

900 Dolan Road, 28786
(704) 456-3333; (800) 432-8499

A nostalgic 22 room country inn built of native stone and timber. Situated on six and one-half wooded mountain acres. Rooms have wide porches, rockers, and color cable TV. Meal plans inclusive of bountiful breakfasts and country gourmet dinners are available with your room. AAA and Mobil rated.

Hosts: Rovert and Cindy Zinser
Rooms: 20 and 2 suites (PB) $54-84
Continental Breakfast; Full Breakfast available
Credit Cards: A, B
Notes: 2, 4, 5, 7, 8, 9, 10, 11, 12, 13, 14

The Palmer House

108 Pigeon Street, 28786
(704) 456-7521

Built before the turn-of-the-century, the Palmer House is one of the last of Waynesville's once numerous tourist homes. Within one block of Main Street. Relaxing environment, beautiful mountains, and good food. A home away from home.

Hosts: Jeff Minick and Kris Gillet
Rooms: 7 (PB) $50-60
Full Breakfast
Credit Cards: A, B, C, D
Notes: 2, 5, 8, 9, 10, 11, 12, 13

The Way Inn

299 South Main Street, 28786
(704) 456-3788

Nestled in the breathtaking glory of the Great Smoky Mountains stands an impressive example of the true South. The Way Inn, a carefully restored Victorian residence, welcomes both bed and breakfast travelers and dinner guests to the elegance of the late 19th century. Situated in scenic Waynesville, the Way Inn combines the

NOTES: Credit cards accepted: A Master Card; B Visa; C American Express; D Discover Card; E Diner's Club; F Other; 2 Personal Checks accepted; 3 Lunch available; 4 Dinner available; 5 Open all year;

conveniences of modern accommodations with southern tradition to make your mountain vacation a memorable experience.

Host: Barbara Rhoads
Rooms: 9 (4 PB; 5 SB) $45-55
Full Breakfast
Credit Cards: A, B
Notes: 2, 4, 7, 8, 9, 10, 11, 12, 13

WEAVERVILLE

Dry Ridge Inn

26 Brown Street, 28787
(704) 658-3899

Large, comfortable farmhouse, circa 1849, furnished with many antiques and handmade quilts. The hosts try to keep their home in the manner of the time it was built: no TV, but plenty of books, games, and good conversation.

Hosts: Paul and Mary Lou Gibson
Rooms: 5 (PB) $60
Full Breakfast
Minimum stay fall weekends and holidays: 2 nights
Credit Cards: A, B
Notes: 2, 5, 8, 9, 12, 13

WILMINGTON

Anderson Guest House

520 Orange Street, 28401
(919) 343-8128

An 1851 Italianate town house with separate guest quarters overlooking the private garden. Furnished with antiques, ceiling fans, and working fireplaces. Drinks on arrival. A delightful gourmet breakfast is served.

Hosts: Landon and Connie Anderson
Rooms: 2 (PB) $50-65
Full Breakfast
Credit Cards: None
Notes: 2, 5, 6, 7 (limited), 8, 9, 10, 11, 12

Catherine's Inn on Orange

410 Orange Street, 28401
(800) 476-0723

Experience the warm, gracious hospitality of this restored home built in 1875. Charming rooms furnished with antiques and reproductions in historical downtown Wilmington. Relax by the pond after a tasty breakfast. Antiques, shopping, art galleries are all within walking distance along Cape Fear River. Sandy beaches and golf courses are just minutes away by car. Complimentary refreshments are served on arrival and bedside liqueur completes a day at Catherine's Inn.

Hosts: Catherine and Walter Ackiss
Rooms: 3 (PB) $60-70
Full Breakfast
Credit Cards: A, B,
Notes: 2, 5, 9, 10, 11, 12, 14

The Five Star Guest House

14 North Seventh Street, 28401
(919) 763-7581

The Five Star Guest House was built in 1908 and is just minutes from beaches, restaurants, shops, and galleries. It features spacious bedrooms furnished with antiques and private baths with deep claw foot tubs. Listed with AAA.

THe Five Star Guest House

6 Pets welcome; 7 Smoking allowed; 8 Children welcome; 9 Social drinking allowed; 10 Tennis available; 11 Swimming available; 12 Golf available; 13 Skiing available; 14 May be booked through travel agents.

Hosts: Ray Higgins and Jim Long
Rooms: 3 (PB) $55-80
Full Breakfast
Credit Cards: A, B, C
Notes: 2, 5, 8 (over 12), 9, 10, 11, 12, 14

Market Street Bed and Breakfast

1704 Market Street, 28403
(919) 763-5442; (800) 242-5442

Built in 1917, this elegant Georgian-style brick house is on the National Register of Historic Places but has modern conveniences including central air conditioning and off-street parking. It is on more than an acre of land in the Mansion District, on U.S. Highways 17 and 74, only a few miles from several beaches. A large side porch is available for rocking and relaxing.

Hosts: Jo Anne and Bob Jarrett
Rooms: 3 (PB) $65-80
Full Breakfast
Credit Cards: A, B
Notes: 2, 5, 9, 10, 11, 12

The Worth House

412 South Third Street, 24801
(919) 762-8562

Elegantly restored Victorian inn located in historic Wilmington. Five spacious guest rooms/suites all with private bath and fireplace. Antiques, hardwood floors, fresh flowers, and romance surround you. Gourmet breakfast served in the privacy of your room, in the formal dining room, on the veranda, or in the garden.

Hosts: Sharon and Dale Smith
Rooms: 5 (PB) $75-95
Full Breakfast
Credit Cards: A, B
Notes: 2, 5, 8 (over 8), 14

WILSON

Miss Betty's Bed and Breakfast Inn

600 West Nash Street, 27893-3045
(919) 243-4447; (800) 258-2058 reservations only

Situated in the downtown historic district, this inn is comprised of two beautifully restored homes. The Davis-Whitehead-Harriss house, circa 1858 and on the National Register of Historic Places, and the adjacent Riley House, circa 1800, recapture the elegance and style of a bygone era. Wilson, the "Antique Capital of North Carolina," with its four golf courses, numerous tennis courts, and Olympic-size pool, is also stategically located midway between Maine and Florida on I-95.

Hosts: Betty and Fred Spitz
Rooms: 8 (PB) $60-70
Full Breakfast
Credit Cards: A, B, C, D
Notes: 2, 5, 7, 9, 10, 11, 12, 14

WINSTON-SALEM

Colonel Ludlow Inn

Summit and West Fifth, 27101
(919) 777-1887

Two adjacent houses from the late 1800s listed on the National Register of Historic Places have been converted into a luxurious inn. The unique guest rooms (each with private deluxe bath and most with two-person whirlpool tubs) are furnished with beautiful period antiques. All rooms have phone, stereo with tapes, cable TV/VCR (free movies), mini refrigerator, and coffee/tea maker. Some rooms have fireplaces. Gourmet restaurants, cafes, shops, and parks are within easy walking distance.

Host: Ken Land
Rooms: 12 (PB) $68-119
Full Breakfast
Credit Cards: A, B, C, D
Notes: 2, 5, 7, 9, 10, 11, 12, 14

Lady Anne's Victorian Bed and Breakfast

612 Summit Street, 27101
(919) 724-1074

Warm southern hospitality surrounds you in this 1890 historic Victorian. An aura of romance touches every suite and room, all of which are individually decorated with period antiques and treasures, while skillfully including modern luxuries, such as private baths, whirlpools, balconies, porches, HBO/ cable TV, stereo with music and tapes, and telephones. An evening dessert/ tea tray and a delicious full breakfast are served on fine china and lace. Ideally situated near downtown attractions, performances, restaurants, and shops. Near Old Salem Historic Village.

Host: Shelley Kirley
Rooms: 5 (3 PB; 2 SB) $45-95
Full Breakfast
Credit Cards: None
Notes: 2, 5, 9, 10, 12, 14

Mickle House
Bed and Breakfast

927 West Fifth Street, 27101
(919) 722-9045

Step back in time to a quaint 1892 Victorian cottage. A gracious welcome, lovely antiques, restful canopy over poster beds, and a delicious breakfast served in the spacious dining room or on the brick patio. The old-fashioned rocking chairs and swing on the porch and the boxwood gardens offer you a respite from all cares. Located in the picturesque National

Historic District of West End. It is only five minutes from Old Salem, the Medical Center, and the downtown/ convention center. Walk to fine restaurants, parks, shops, the Ys, churches, and library. Golfing, tennis, and swimming nearby.

Host: Barbara Garrison
Rooms: 2 (1 PB; 1 SB) $45-65
Full Breakfast
Credit Cards: A, B
Notes: 2, 5, 9, 14

Wachovia
Bed and Breakfast, Inc.

513 Wachovia Street, 27101
(919) 777-0332

Lovely rose and white Victorian cottage on a quiet street, within walking distance of city center, Old Salem Historia, antique shops, and gourmet restaurants. A European-style bed and breakfast. Flexible check-in/check-out. No rigid breakfast schedule. Expanded continental breakfast—all you can eat. Complimentary wine. No smoking. No credit cards.

Host: Carol Royals
Rooms: 6 (3 PB; 3 SB) $45-55
Expanded Continental Breakfast
Credit Cards: None
Notes: 2, 5, 8, 9

6 Pets welcome; 7 Smoking allowed; 8 Children welcome; 9 Social drinking allowed; 10 Tennis available; 11 Swimming available; 12 Golf available; 13 Skiing available; 14 May be booked through travel agents.

Lidgerwood

McClusky

Wing

Dickinson

NORTH DAKOTA

North Dakota

DICKINSON

Joyce's Home Away from Home Bed and Breakfast

1561 First Avenue East, 58601
(701) 227-1524

Large all-white brick ranch-style home with Spanish arches was built in the 1980s. Situated right off I-94, just minutes from shopping malls. Exercise room and large family room with a fireplace, cable TV, and VCR available for guests to use. This home is filled with lots of handmade furniture and paintings done by Joyce's husband and daughter. Lots of parking in front of the house on a quiet street. Play park located next door. Tourist attraction town of Medora only one-half hour away.

Host: Joyce Scott
Rooms: 4 (1 PB; 3 SB) $25-65
Continental Plus Breakfast
Credit Cards: None
Notes: 2, 5, 7, 9, 10, 11, 12

LIDGERWOOD

Kaler Bed and Breakfast

Route 2, P. O. Box 151, 58053
(701) 538-4848

Enjoy country living on this 640-acre small grain farm situated in the pheasant heartland. This older farmhouse has five beautiful bedrooms upstairs. A delicious full breakfast is served, and children are most welcome.

Hosts: Mark and Dorothy Kaler
Rooms: 5 (SB) $25-30
Full Breakfast
Credit Cards: None
Notes: 2, 5, 7, 8, 9, 10, 11, 12

MCCLUSKY

Midstate Bed and Breakfast

Route 3, P.O. Box 28, 58463
(701) 363-2520

Country peace and quiet prevail at this easy-to-find location alongside Highway 200. This newer home is located on a working grain and livestock farm. The house features a private entrance to a complete lower level where guests stay. As a guest, your bedroom, bath, large TV lounge with fireplace, and kitchenette provide you with everything you need. Hunting parties up to six may use next-door quarters with special rates. Over 4,500 acres available for guests only who want to experience excellent hunting of upland game, water fowl, and deer.Breakfast is served in a lovely plant-filled atrium.

Hosts: Grace and Allen Faul
Rooms: 6 (2 PB; 4 SB) $30.
Continental and Full Breakfast
Credit Cards: None
Notes: 2, 5, 6 (call), 8, 10, 11

WING

Eva's Bed and Breakfast

HC1, P.O. Box 10, 58494
(701) 943-2461

NOTES: Credit cards accepted: A Master Card; B Visa; C American Express; D Discover Card; E Diner's Club; F Other; 2 Personal Checks accepted; 3 Lunch available; 4 Dinner available; 5 Open all year; 6 Pets welcome; 7 Smoking allowed; 8 Children welcome; 9 Social drinking allowed; 10 Tennis available; 11 Swimming available; 12 Golf available; 13 Skiing available; 14 May be booked through travel agents.

Your hosts are retired farmers who built a new house in 1983. Two bedrooms for guests share a bath, large family room, fireplace, and library. A full breakfast is served, and a tour of the farm is available upon request. Good hiking to Haystack Butte one milea away. Mitchel Lake recreation is four miles away, and a toy museum withhandmade piece quilts, and stuffed toys are all within five miles. Open all year.

Hosts: Harold and Eva Williams
Rooms: 2 (2 SB) $25
Full Breakfast
Credit Cards: None
Notes: 2, 3, 4, 5, 8

Ohio

AKRON

Portage House

601 Copley Road, 44320
(216) 535-1952

A large, gracious Tudor home in Akron on the ancient portage route between the Cuyahoga and Tuscarawas rivers. Five second-floor rooms and two baths, large livingroom. Breakfast is served in the formal dining room or at the large center island in the modern kitchen. Homemade breads and jams. The host and her late husband, a retired physics professor, opened the house in 1982.

Host: Jeanne Pinnick
Rooms: 5 (1 PB; 4 SB) $32
Full Breakfast
Credit Cards: None
Closed Dec. and Jan.
Notes: 2, 6, 7 (limited), 8, 9, 10, 11, 12, 13

ALBANY

The Albany House

9 Clinton Street, 45710
(614) 698-6311

Enjoy today's comfort in yesterday's atmosphere at The Albany House, a charming 150-year-old bed and breakfast in the village of Albany, seven miles west of Athens and Ohio University. A historic house featuring antiques, quilts, Oriental rugs and family heirlooms plus the modern amentities of air-conditioning, indoor pool and guest living room with television and VCR. Resident cat. Afternoon or evening beverages.

Hosts: Sarah and Ted Hutchins
Rooms: 7 (4 PB; 3 SB) $50-75
Continental Breakfast
Credit Cards: None
Notes: 2, 5, 7, 9, 10, 11, 12, 14

ASHTABULA

Michael Cahill Bed and Breakfast

1106 Walnut Boulevard, 44004
(216) 964-8449

Large 1887 stick-style Victorian home on the National Register of Historic Places. It is a short walk to Lake Erie beach, marine museum, and charter boat fishing. This bed and breakfast overlooks the center of the harbor historic district. Large parlors, open porches, and convenience kitchen for guests. Ten minutes from I-90.

Hosts: Paul and Pat Goode
Rooms: 4 (2 PB; 2 SB) $45-50
Full Breakfast
Credit Cards: None
Notes: 2, 5, 7, 8, 9, 10, 11, 12

AVON

A French Creek House

37511 Detroit Road, 44011
(216) 934-5195

June and Jack Kearney welcome you to their 104-year-old farmhouse in the heart of Lorain County. Guests may choose from a large bedroom with two antique brass beds or a smaller room with a queen-size canopy bed. Breakfast includes blueberry pancakes with locally made syrup and is enjoyed in

---

6 Pets welcome; 7 Smoking allowed; 8 Children welcome; 9 Social drinking allowed; 10 Tennis available; 11 Swimming available; 12 Golf available; 13 Skiing available; 14 May be booked through travel agents.

OHIO

the privacy of your own room or in the dining room downstairs. The Kearneys invite you to relax with a drink in the cozy sitting room beside the wood-burning fireplace. Lorain County is a haven for antique lovers, with more than 14 shops in Avon. Three public golf courses are within a five-minute drive, and activities in Westlake, Sheffield Lake, and Cleveland are close by.

Hosts: June and Jack Kearney
Rooms: 2 (SB) $50-55
Full Breakfast
Credit Cards: None
Notes: 2, 5, 9, 12

BELLEFONTAINE

Whitmore House

3985 State Route 47 West, 43311
(513) 592-4290

This Victorian home on four acres of lawn and gardens offers four antique-filled bedrooms. Relax in the library, stroll in the gardens, or enjoy an evening sunset from the porch or spacious deck. Not only do you enjoy a breakfast buffet but, with prior arrangements, a lavish dinner can be served. A brief escape to a more leisured life!

Hosts: Carey and Sandra Musser
Rooms: 3 (SB) $45-60
Full Breakfast
Credit Cards: None
Notes: 2, 3, 4, 5, 8

BELLVILLE

The Frederick Fitting House

72 Fitting Avenue, 44813
(419) 886-2863

An 1863 Victorian home in a quaint country village between Columbus and Cleveland. Gourmet breakfast served in hand-stenciled dining room, garden gazebo, or country kitchen. Near Mohican and Malabar Farm state parks, downhill and cross-country skiing, canoeing, Kenyon and Wooster colleges.

Hosts: Ramon and Suzanne Wilson
Rooms: 3 (PB) $44-66
Full Breakfast
Credit Cards: None
Closed Thanksgiving and Christmas
Notes: 2, 4, 7, 8 (over 7), 9, 10, 11, 12, 13

CENTERVILLE

Yesterday Bed and Breakfast

39 South Main Street, 45458
(513) 433-0785; (800) 225-0485

Ten miles south of the center of Dayton, in the heart of the Centerville historic district, the house adjoins a group of fine antique shops and is near restaurants and two museums. The Lavender and Old Lace Shop features fine bath products and vintage linens. The house was built in 1882 and is tastefully furnished with antiques. Within easy driving distance of the Air Force Museum in Dayton, Kings Island Amusement Park, historic Lebanon and Waynesville, a major antique center. The University of Dayton, Wright State University, and downtown Dayton are 15 to 20 minutes away. Discount for stay of three or more nights.

Host: Barbara
Rooms: 3 (PB) $60-70
Expanded Continental Breakfast
Credit Cards: None
Notes: 2, 8 (over 12), 9

The Frederick Fitting House

NOTES: Credit cards accepted: A Master Card; B Visa; C American Express; D Discover Card; E Diner's Club; F Other; 2 Personal Checks accepted; 3 Lunch available; 4 Dinner available; 5 Open all year; 6 Pets welcome; 7 Smoking allowed; 8 Children welcome; 9 Social drinking allowed; 10 Tennis available; 11 Swimming available; 12 Golf available; 13 Skiing available; 14 May be booked through travel agents.

CHAGRIN FALLS

Inn of Chagrin Falls

87 West Street, 44022
(216) 247-1200

Formerly Crane's Canary Cottage, this
handsome Western Reserve building, circa
1927, has been transformed into a distinctive village inn. Fifteen exquisite rooms,
with luxurious private baths, have been
tastefully decorated to reflect the grace and
charm of Victorian elegance. Attached to
the inn is Gamekeeper's Tavern, where
guests enjoy casual, sophisticated dining
amid warm woods and crackling fireplaces,
or a spacious outdoor patio colored by
large market umbrellas.

Host: Mary Beth O'Donnel
Rooms: 15 (PB) $95-175
Continental Breakfast
Credit Cards: A, B, C
Notes: 2, 3, 4, 5, 9

CHARDON

Bass Lake Inn

426 South Street, 44024
(216) 285-3100

Twelve tasefully decorated rooms provide
guests with a queen-size bed, TV, gas log
fireplace, kitchenette with refrigerator,
microwave and coffee maker, relaxing

Jacuzzi, and spectacular view of the lake
and golf course. Adjacent to the inn is Bass
Lake Tavern, where guests can enjoy comfortable dining at the fireside; or al fresco.

Host: Walter Zmijewski
Rooms: 12 (PB)
Continental Breakfast
Credit Cards: A, B, C
Notes: 2, 3, 4, 5, 7, 9, 12, 13

CHARM

Charm Countryview Inn

P. O. Box 100, 44617
(216) 893-3003

The Charm Countryview Inn, in Holmes
County, is in the heart of Ohio's Amish
country. Owned and operated by the Abe
Mast family, the inn offers a beautiful view
and fresh country air. Each of the 15 lovely
rooms features air conditioning, private
bath, queen-size beds, and authentic oak
furniture. Prices include a full Amish
breakfast. Inquire about the meeting room.

Hosts: Paul and Naomi Miller
Rooms: 15 (PB) $65-92.50
Full Breakfast; Continental Sunday
Credit Cards: A, B
Notes: 2, 5, 8

CHILLICOTHE

The Greenhouse Bed and Breakfast

47 East 5th Street, 45601
(614) 775-5313

The Greenhouse Bed and Breakfast is more
than another home listed in the National
Register of Historic Places. It's a step back
to the quiet elegance of the lavish Victorian
era. The home was built with a profusion of
varied elements in 1894. The lower level of
the home contains the greenhouse. It offers
large, quiet, comfortable rooms to those
who appreciate the warmth and charm of
the Queen Anne style of architecture and
furnishings. Full breakfast served in the

NOTES: Credit cards accepted: A Master Card; B Visa; C American Express; D Discover Card; E Diner's
Club; F Other; 2 Personal Checks accepted; 3 Lunch available; 4 Dinner available; 5 Open all year;

formal cherry dining room. Situated in the historic district close to downtown Chillicothe.

Hosts: Tom and Dee Shoemaker
Rooms: 4 (3 PB; 1 SB) $50-60
Full Breakfast
Credit Cards: None
Notes: 2, 5, 8, 9

CINCINNATI

Prospect Hill Bed and Breakfast

408 Boal Street, 45210
(513) 421-4408

Nestled into a wooded hillside, this Italianate Victorian town house was built in 1867 on Prospect Hill, Cincinnati's first suburb and now a national historic district. The bed and breakfast has been restored, keeping original woodwork, doors, hardware, and light fixtures. Each room is furnished with period antiques and offers fireplaces, skeleton keys, and spectacular views. Prospect Hill overlooks downtown and is only a 15-minute walk to Fountain Square or the Ohio River.

Host: Gary Hackney
Rooms: 3 (1 PB; 2 SB) $69-79
Full Breakfast
Credit Cards: A, B
Notes: 2, 5, 9, 14

CLEVELAND

Notre Maison

Private Lodgings, Inc. A-1
P. O. Box 18590, 44118
(216) 249-0400

A lovely French chateau not far from the university hospitals and museums. Two guest rooms with private bath or a carriage house with private bath are available. $65-75.

Private Lodgings, Inc.

P. O. Box 18590, 44118
(216) 249-0400

A variety of accommodations including houses and apartments for rent in the greater Cleveland area. They are near the Cleveland Clinic, Case Western Reserve University, major museums and galleries, Metro park system, downtown Cleveland business district, and some are near or on Lake Erie. No credit cards. $45-125.

COLUMBUS

50 Lincoln - A Very Small Hotel

50 East Lincoln Street, 43215
(614) 291-5056

This small hotel is situated in the art district adjacent to downtown Columbus, the convention center, and the Ohio State University. Nine guest rooms, each with queen-size bed and private full bath. A restored 19th-century Italianate brick building with a beautiful garden. Walk to Columbus's finest dining and shopping. 50 Lincoln is especially attractive to business travelers.

Hosts: Jack and Zoe Johnstone
Innkeeper: Kris Miesel
Rooms: 9 (PB) $99-149
Full Breakfast
Credit Cards: A, B, C
Notes: 2, 5, 7, 9, 14

COSHOCTON

1890 Bed and Breakfast

663 North Whitewoman Street
Roscoe Village, 43812
(614) 622-1890

Spend a romantic getaway in a Victorian bed and breakfast in the heart of historic Roscoe Village. The home is furnished

6 Pets welcome; 7 Smoking allowed; 8 Children welcome; 9 Social drinking allowed; 10 Tennis available; 11 Swimming available; 12 Golf available; 13 Skiing available; 14 May be booked through travel agents.

with antiques and features a delightful fireplace. Restaurants, museums, and exclusive shops are within walking distance of the bed and breakfast.

Hosts: Curt and Debbi Crouso
Rooms: 4 (PB) $60-70
Expanded Continental Breakfast
Credit Cards: A, B, C, D
Notes: 2, 5, 9, 12

DANVILLE

The White Oak Inn

29683 Walhonding Road, 43014
(614) 599-6107

This turn-of-the-century farmhouse in a rolling wooded countryside features antiques and hand-stitched quilts. Guests read, play board games, or socialize in the common room with a fireplace, or relax on the 50-foot-long front porch. An outdoor enthusiast's haven. Three rooms have fireplaces. Near the world's largest Amish population and historic Roscoe Village.

Hosts: Joyce and Jim Acton
Rooms: 10 (PB) $50-100
Full Breakfast weekends; Continental weekdays
Credit Cards: A, B
Notes: 2, 4, 5, 9, 10, 11, 12, 14

DAYTON

Price's Steamboat House

6 Josie Street, 45403
(513) 223-2444

Built in 1852, Victorianized in 1889, the mansion was completely restored in an eleven-year effort that was culminated in 1986. This twenty-two room house has been furnished with antiques, Oriental rugs, handsome woodwork, and rounded front porches on the first and second levels, with a widow's walk on the third floor. Rocking chairs, elegant bedrooms, piano in the parlor, and an extensive library make this an extra special place to stay, and visitors are close to Arcade Square, U.S. Air Force Museum, "Blue Jacket," Dayton Art Institute, Paul Lawrence Dunbar's home, University of Dayton, and Wright State University.

Hosts: Ron and Ruth Price
Rooms: 3 (PB) $69
Full Breakfast
Credit Cards: None
Notes: 2, 5, 9, 10

DEGRAFF

Rollicking Hills

2 Rollicking Hills Lane, 43318
(513) 585-5161

This is a 160-acre farm in scenic hills. The homestead began as an Indian trading post in the late 1700s on a path that became the county stagecoach road. Remodeling in 1825 and an eight-room addition by the host's grandfather in 1865 are part of the home's five-generation history. Hiking, horseback riding, a natural peat bog left by a glacier, farm animals including llamas. Lake well stocked with blue gill and large-mouth bass. Canoe to a bullfrog chorus. Spartan in-ground pool, cross-country skiing, beech-maple climax woods. No smoking. No alcohol or drugs. No pets.

Hosts: Suzanne and Robert Smithers and family
Rooms: 4 (1 PB; 3 SB) $28-50
Full Breakfast
Credit Cards: None
Notes: 2, 3, 4, 5, 8

DELLROY

Pleasant Journey Inn

4247 Roswell Road Southwest, 44620
(216) 735-2987

Less than two hours from Cleveland, Pittsburgh, and Columbus. A 14-room Victorian mansion situated on 12 acres, including stream, gardens, and gently sloping hills in the Atwood Lake area. Seven marble fireplaces, a curved staircase of gleaming walnut, an oil chandelier, antiques and crafts collected locally add to the inn's gracious atmosphere. The inn has a quiet, rural feeling yet is within a short drive to horseback riding, golf, fishing, swimming, boating, and Amish country visits.

Hosts: Jim and Marie Etterman
Rooms: 4 (1 PB; 3 SB) $50-65
Expanded Continental Breakfast
Credit Cards: A, B
Notes: 2, 5, 9, 10, 11, 12, 13, 14

Whispering Pines Bed and Breakfast

P. O. Box 340, 44620
(216) 735-2824

Come to this 1880 Victorian home overlooking Atwood Lake. Filled with elegant antiques of the period, each guest room has a breathtaking view of the lake and a private bath. One room has a wood-burning fireplace. A scrumptious breakfast served on the enclosed porch makes this a perfect romantic getaway. The pontoon is available for rental. Golf, boating, and sweetheart packages are also available.

Hosts: Bill and Linda Horn
Rooms: 3 (PB) $70-85
Full Breakfast
Credit Cards: None
Notes: 2, 5, 9, 11, 12

EAST FULTONHAM

Hill View Acres

7320 Old Town Road, 43735
(614) 849-2728

Situated ten miles southwest of Zanesville off U.S. 22 W. Spacious home on 21 acres with pond. Enjoy the pool, year-round spa, or relax in the family room by the fireplace. Country cooking is a specialty. The area is popular for antiquing, pottery, and outdoor activities.

Hosts: Jim and Dawn Graham
Rooms: 2 (SB) $35-40 (5% discount for cash)
Full Breakfast

Credit Cards: A, B
Notes: 2, 3, 4, 5, 7, 8, 9, 10, 11, 12

FINDLAY

Wildflower Farm Bed and Breakfast

13178 TR 45, 45840
(419) 424-1151

Rock on the front porch and enjoy the beautiful view of the countryside in this 130-year-old farmhouse. Pet and feed the farm animals, play lawn croquet, wander through a quarter acre of wildflowers, or borrow a bicycle and ride through the country. Warm hospitality awaits you inside this country decorated home. Breakfast includes homemade breads and muffins, cereals, yogurts, coffee, tea, and juice. Nearby are Ohio's largest antique shops, parks, swimming, canoeing, tennis, fishing, craft shops, and Ghost Town.

Hosts: Dennis and Amy Kubly
Rooms: 2 (PB) $50-60
Continental Breakfast
Credit Cards: A, B, C
Notes: 2, 5, 8

GENEVA-ON-THE-LAKE

The Otto Court Bed and Breakfast

5653 Lake Road, 44041
(216) 466-8668

Hotel and cottage complex overlooking Lake Erie. Within walking distance of the famous Geneva-on-the-Lake amusement center, Geneva State Park and Marina, and the Old Firehouse Winery. Conveniently situated near the historic Ashtabula Harbor area and 13 covered bridges.

Host: C. Joyce Otto
Rooms: 12 (8 PB; 4 SB) $32-45
Full Breakfast
Minimum stay weekends and holidays: 2 nights
Credit Cards: A, B
Notes: 2, 4, 5, 7, 8, 9, 10, 11, 12

6 Pets welcome; 7 Smoking allowed; 8 Children welcome; 9 Social drinking allowed; 10 Tennis available; 11 Swimming available; 12 Golf available; 13 Skiing available; 14 May be booked through travel agents.

GRANVILLE

Buxton Inn—1812

313 East Broadway, 43023
(614) 587-0001

Quiet elegance and cozy charm describe Buxton Inn's four guest rooms, all authentically furnished in period antiques. Twin, double and queen beds are available. There are five dining rooms, a tavern, and wine cellar. The adjacent Warner House—1815 houses eleven period rooms. Breakfast, lunch, and dinner are available daily.

Hosts: Orville and Audrey Orr
Rooms: 15 (PB) $59.95-87.20
Continental Breakfast
Credit Cards: A, B, C, E, F
Notes: 2, 3, 4, 5, 7, 8, 9, 10, 11, 12

The Follett Wright House

403 East Broadway, 43023
(614) 587-0941

Built in 1860 and listed on the National Register of Historic Places, this gracious bed and breakfast overlooks the historic village of Granville. Within walking distance of Dennison University, shopping, and restaurants. Breakfast consists of homemade Danish rolls and other delicious specialties.

Hosts: Kirsten and Jurgen Pape
Rooms: 2 (PB) $50
Full Breakfast
None: None
Notes: 2, 5, 6, 8, 9, 10, 11, 12

HANOVERTON

The Spread Eagle Tavern

10150 Plymouth Street, P. O. Box 277, 44423
(216) 223-1583

The Spread Eagle Tavern is an artfully restored Federal-style three-story historic brick inn that features a gourmet restaurant, a unique rathskeller, seven dining rooms,

and six guest rooms for overnight lodging. All rooms are tastefully decorated with antiques that give insight into Ohio's canal period history. Listed on the National Register of Historic Places. Quiet, romantic, and unique.

Hosts: Peter and Jean Johnson
Rooms: 6 (4 PB; 2 SB) $75-125
Continental Breakfast
Credit Cards: A, B, D
Notes: 3, 4, 5, 7, 8, 9, 12

HIRAM

The Lily Ponds

6720 Route 82, 44234
(216) 569-3222

Spacious lovely home in a quiet country setting surrounded by woods and ponds. It's a five-minute walk to Hiram College campus; 15-minute drive to Sea World, Geauga Lake, and Aurora Farms; 45 minutes to Cleveland, Akron, and Youngstown. Charming rooms with private baths. The owner is a world traveler.

Host: Marilane Spencer
Rooms: 2 (PB) $50-60
Full Breakfast
Credit Cards: None
Notes: 2, 5, 8, 9, 10, 11, 12, 13, 14

The Spread Eagle Tavern

HURON

Captain Montague's Guest House

229 Center Street, 44839
(419) 433-4756

A memorable step back in time. Private baths, air conditioning, swimming pool surrounded by lattice-fenced gardens. Adjacent gazebo with white wicker furniture; parlor with fireplace and player piano. Five to ten minutes from well-known golf courses, estuaries, Cedar Point, and outlet mall. Walking distance to Lake Erie and restaurants.

Hosts: Shirley and Bob Reynolds
Rooms: 6 (PB) $68-85
Expanded Continental Breakfast
Minimum stay weekends (Memorial Day-Labor Day): 2 nights
Credit Cards: None
Closed Dec.15-Feb. 15
Notes: 2, 9, 10, 11, 12, 13 (XC)

KELLEYS ISLAND

Sweet Valley Inn

P. O. Box 733, 43438
(419) 746-2750

A stay at the Sweet Valley Inn completes a delightful visit to Kelleys Island. This 2,800-acre island situated in Lake Erie is the only United States island designated a national historic district. Circa 1892, this pretty yellow Victorian has been renovated to display its beautiful woodwork, stained glass, four working fireplaces, and original kitchen wood-burning stove. Breakfast is served overlooking the rolling lawn and beautiful gardens. A special feature: horse-drawn carriage rides. Winter information available upon request.

Hosts: Bev and Paul Johnson
Rooms: 4 (SB) $75
Full Breakfast
Credit Cards: A, B
Notes: 2, 4 (winter), 5, 7, 8 (over 8), 9, 11, 13

LAKESIDE

Poor Richards Inn

317 Maple Avenue, 43440
(419) 798-5405

Poor Richards is an unpretentious, family-oriented retreat where vacationers may relax while exploring the area's many attractions. The inn was originally opened as a summer hotel in 1885. There are Ben Franklin portraits and aphorisms prominently displayed throughout. The inn is decorated with a lot of greenery, wicker furniture, and magazines from the 1940s and 1950s to sustain the "step back in time" mood. Complimentary breakfast is served, plus guests may prepare other meals in the communal kitchen. Alcoholic beverages are not permitted. There is a reading lounge on the second floor, and a large first-floor lounge with a piano and table games.

Hosts: Tom and Jean Kern
Rooms: 28 (8 PB; 20 SB) $20-40
Continental Breakfast
Credit Cards: None
Notes: 2, 7, 8, 10, 11, 12, 14

LEBANON

Burl Manor

230 South Mechanic Street, 45036
(513) 932-1266

Travel back in time to the early 1800s with a visit to Burl Manor, a bed and breakfast in the historic district of Lebanon, Ohio. The restored manor holds much of its original charm and grandeur, and is furnished throughout with fine antiques, of solid cherry, mahogany, and walnut pieces from the 1800s. Burl Manor is located within walking distance of downtown Lebanon and Ohio's best selection of antique stores and mills.

Hosts: John and Ruth Ann Ware
Rooms: 3 (PB) $60
Continental weekdays
Credit Cards: None
Notes: 2, 5, 8, 10, 12

6 Pets welcome; 7 Smoking allowed; 8 Children welcome; 9 Social drinking allowed; 10 Tennis available; 11 Swimming available; 12 Golf available; 13 Skiing available; 14 May be booked through travel agents.

LEXINGTON

White Fence Inn

8842 Denman Road, 44904
(419) 884-2356

A breathtaking country retreat situated on
73 acres, with gardens, apple orchard,
grapevines, fishing pond, and fields.
Breakfast is delectable and includes homemade granola, homemade jams, grape
juice, pastries, and farm-fresh eggs. Dine in
the large country dining room or out on the
porch. Two large sitting rooms with fireplaces, games, TV, and spectacular views
from every window. Special wedding or
anniversary baskets available and dessert
bar Saturday nights for all guests, in season. The largest guest room boasts a king-
size four-poster bed, cathedral wood ceiling, sunken tub, fireplace, and private deck.

Hosts: Bill and Ellen Hiser
Rooms: 6 (4 PB; 2 SB) $60-105
Full Breakfast
Credit Cards: None
Notes: 2, 5, 6, 8, 9, 10, 12, 13, 14

LOGAN

Critter Ridge

15459 State Route 328, 43138
(614) 385-4941

This modern ranch offers a guest room
with a shared bath on the main floor or a
private lower-level apartment that is completely furnished, with a private bath. Walk
through majestic white pine woods, or simply enjoy the panoramic view. Full breakfast.

Hosts: Dan and Judy Clark
Rooms: 3 (1 PB; 2 SB) $30-45
Full Breakfast
Credit Cards: None
Notes: 2, 5, 7, 8, 9, 14

LOUDONVILLE

Blackfork Inn

303 North Water Street, Box 149, 44842
(419) 994-3252

Victorian town house in small-town setting
providing an elegant getaway and a place
for pampered relaxation. Nearby are two
state parks with swimming, boating, scenic
trails, and the world's largest settlement of
Old Order Amish, with down-home cooking and cottage industries: quiltmaking,
cabinetry, clock and doll making. The inn
has two Victorian parlors for guests. Fresh
raspberries for breakfast from the inn's
back yard gardens.

Hosts: Sue and Al Gorisek
Rooms: 6 (PB) $65-75
Continental Breakfast

MALONE

Kilborn Manor

59 Milwaukee Street, 12953
(518) 483-4891

Named after the congressman who owned
this stately and elegantly appointed Greek
Revival 1820 home, the Kilborn Manor is
nestled on three and one-half acres in the
northern Adirondacks. Malone boasts an
irresistibly challenging and scenic 36-hole
golf complex, trout fishing, and an impressive array of downhill and cross-country
skiing, bicycling and hiking trails. Enjoy
antiquing, browsing through the congressman's library, or visiting next door's House
of History.

Hosts: Paul and Suzanne Hogan
Continental Breakfast
Credit Cards: None
Notes: 2, 5, 8, 10, 11, 12

NOTES: Credit cards accepted: A Master Card; B Visa; C American Express; D Discover Card; E Diner's
Club; F Other; 2 Personal Checks accepted; 3 Lunch available; 4 Dinner available; 5 Open all year;

MARBLEHEAD

Old Stone House on the Lake

133 Clemons Street, 43440
(419) 798-5922

The shoreline of Lake Erie's western basin. Overlooks Kelleys Island and is situated between the Kelleys ferry and the Marblehead lighthouse. Patio on the water, library sitting room with cable TV and games. Craft and gift shop in summer kitchen. Shopping, sightseeing, marinas, and restaurants are all nearby. Seasonal executive fishing-charter service available.

Host: Pat Whiteford Parks
Rooms: 13 (1 PB; 12 SB) $55-85
Expanded Continental Breakfast
Credit Cards: A, B, D
Notes: 2, 5, 7, 9, 10, 11, 12, 14

MARIETTA

House of Seven Porches

331 Fifth Street, 45750
(614) 373-1767

Step into the past at this southern-style home, circa 1835. Spacious rooms are enhanced by family antiques. Dolls, teddy bears, old toys, and vintage clothing are cherished. The garden level reveals a dignified dining room and cozy kitchen. "The Little House under the Stairs" charms children and the young at heart. On a street of grand old homes, this lovely bed and breakfast looks onto an ancient Indian mound, and the porches allow visitors to enjoy expansive views of the terraced grounds.

Host: Jeane Kelsa
Rooms: 3 (2 PB; 1 SB) $40-50
Continental Breakfast
Credit Cards: None
Notes: 2, 5, 6, 8, 9, 10, 11, 12

MARION

Olde Town Manor

245 St. James Street, 43302
(614) 382-2402

This elegant stone home is on a beautiful acre of land on a quiet street in Marion's historic district. Enjoy a quiet setting in the gazebo, or relax while reading from more than 1,000 books available in the library. A leisurely stroll will take you to the home of President Warren G. Harding and the Harding Memorial. A quiet, relaxed, and elegant atmosphere for your stay. Awarded the 1990 Marion Beautification Award for Most Attractive Building.

Host: Mary Louisa Rimbach
Rooms: 4 (PB) $55-65
Full Breakfast
Credit Cards: A, B, D
Notes: 2, 5, 7 (limited), 8 (over 12), 10, 12

MARTIN'S FERRY

Mulberry Inn Bed and Breakfast

53 North 4th Street, 43935
(614) 633-6058

This Victorian house built in 1868 by Dr. Ong features four period rooms with antiques, paintings, and quilts. Guests have a beautiful parlor to relax in, and a private dining room in which to enjoy the sumptuous continental plus breakfast. Visit the oldest organized settlement in Ohio and Walnut Grove Cemetery (in which lies Betty Zane, who saved Fort Henry in the last battle of the Revolutionary War). This bed and breakfast is within walking distance of the Ohio River, museums, and shops. Wheeling, West Virginia, is five minutes away, where you can visit Oglebay Park, Festival of Lights, Jamboree USA, dog races, many golf courses, and ice skating. The inn is air-conditioned in the summer and has a beautiful wood-burning fireplace in the parlor.

Hosts: Shirley and Charlie Probst
Rooms: 4 (2 PB; 2 SB) $30-40
Expanded Continental Breakfast
Credit Cards: D
Notes: 2, 5, 7, 9

MILLERSBURG

Kaufman's Bed and Breakfast

9905 State Route 39, 44654
(216) 674-4123

Welcome to an Amish-Mennonite home in scenic Holmes County. Enjoy the comfort of a modern brick ranch home, quiet country atmosphere convenient to the heart of the world's largest Amish community. Only a short drive to the many quilt, craft, and furniture shops featuring handmade items. Nearby is the Mohican River, canoeing, horseback riding, cheese factories. Nonsmoking rooms. Large family room with Ping-Pong table and fireplace.

Hosts: Reuben and Elva Kaufman
Rooms: 3 (1 PB; 2 SB) $45-57
Full Breakfast
Credit Cards: None
Notes: 2, 5, 8

MORROW

Country Manor Bed and Breakfast

6315 Zoar Road, 45152
(513) 899-2440

Country Manor sits on a quiet 55 acres overlooking a valley, yet is conveniently situated in an area of southern Ohio that features Kings Island Amusement Park, Jack Nicklaus Golf Course, and Lebanon Raceway. Large, comfortable rooms feature 1868 elegance with modern conveniences. Twin, double, and king beds are available.

Hosts: Rhea Hughes and Bobby Salyers
Rooms: 3 (1 PB; 2 SB) $40-65 plus tax
Full Breakfast

Credit Cards: None
Closed Dec. 1-Jan. 31
Notes: 2, 6 (outdoor facilities), 8 (over 12), 9, 10, 11, 12

MOUNT VERNON

The Russell-Cooper House

115 E. Gambler Street, 43050
(614) 397-8638

Ohio's only four-time national award winning bed and breakfast inn! History lives in this National Register Inn, and all around Mount Vernon, Ohio—"America's Hometown." Grand and comfortable, The Russell-Cooper House will refresh your spirit, ease your mind, stimulate your curiosity, and generally warm the cockles of your heart. Private baths, full delicious candlelit breakfasts, and a friendly "welcome home" will make your visit a memory you will always cherish.

Hosts: Maureen and Tim Tyler
Rooms: 6 (PB) $75
Full Breakfast
Credit Cards: A, B, C
Notes: 2, 3 (within walking distance), 4 walking distance), 5, 7, 8 (over 12), 9, 10, 11, 12, 13, 14

NEW RICHMOND

Hollyhock

1610 Altman Road, 45157
(513) 553-6585

Hollyhock is a working sheep farm in a small community 25 miles from Cincinnati. Close to cultural attractions (symphony, opera, ballet, art museums), sporting events (Jack Nicklaus Golf Center, Vineyards Country Club, Riverfront Stadium and the Reds, Riverfront Coliseum and the Bengals), and the Ohio River with excellent marinas and boating facilities. Hollyhock is a pleasing mixture of country and suburban, nestled in hundreds of acres of productive farmland, yet within one-half hour of Cincinnati. The peace and tranquility are inspiring. Full gourmet breakfast.

NOTES: Credit cards accepted: A Master Card; B Visa; C American Express; D Discover Card; E Diner's Club; F Other; 2 Personal Checks accepted; 3 Lunch available; 4 Dinner available; 5 Open all year;

Host: Evelyn Cutter
Rooms: 1 queen suite (PB) 1 double (SB) $75
Full Breakfast
Credit Cards: None
Notes: 2, 3, 4, 5, 6 (outside), 7, 8, 9, 10, 11, 12, 14

NORTH RIDGEVILLE

St. George House

33941 Lorain Road, 44039
(216) 327-9354

Situated at the "Crossroads of the Nation," near the shores of Lake Erie, midway between two great cities (Cleveland and Lorain). Fish, frogs, and ducks inhabit a lush, one-acre lake. An aviary may be viewed through French doors. Grade A accommodations at modest prices. Wheelchair accessible. Ten minutes from Cleveland's Hopkins International Airport. Off three interstate highways.

Hosts: Helen Bernardine and Muriel Dodd
Rooms: 4 (1 PB; 3 SB) $45-65
Continental Breakfast
Minimum stay: 2 nights
Credit Cards: None
Notes: 2, 5, 6, 7, 8, 9, 11, 12, 13

OLD WASHINGTON

Zane Trace Bed and Breakfast

P. O. Box 115, 225 Old National Road, 43768
(614) 489-5970

Brick Victorian built in 1859. In-ground swimming pool, extra-large rooms, beautiful woodwork, high ceilings, antique furnishings. The quaint, quiet village of Old Washington is seven miles east of Cambridge, Exit 186 off I-70. Write for your free brochure.

Host: Ruth Wade-Wilson
Rooms: 4 (SB) $40-65
Continental Breakfast
Credit Cards: None
Closed November 15-April 15
Notes: 2, 7, 8 (over 10), 9, 11, 12

ORRVILLE

Grandma's House Bed and Breakfast

5598 Chippewa Road, 44667
(216) 682-5112

Peace and quiet prevail on this 1860s farm home with comfortable beds, antiques, and handmade quilts. Situated in the heart of Wayne County's rolling farmland, planted in alternating strips of corn, soybeans, and wheat. Several hiking trails meander through the large woods on the hill. Hickory rockers grace the front porch for relaxing. Just a few minutes from Amish country.

Hosts: Marilyn and Dave Farver
Rooms: 4 (2 PB; 2 SB) $45
Continental Breakfast
Credit Cards: None
Notes: 2, 5, 8, 9

OXFORD

The Duck Pond

6391 Morning Sun Road
State Road 732 North, 45056
(513) 523-8914

An 1863 Civil War farmhouse on five and one-half acres. Furnished in country antiques and collectibles. Full country-style breakfast, including such specialties as Hawaiian French toast, German pancakes, and cheese blintzes. Three miles north of Miami University, two miles south of Hueston Woods State Park with golf, nature trails, boating, swimming, and fishing. Enjoy antiquing in Fairhaven on weekends, seven miles north, and in several other nearby towns during the week.

Hosts: Don and Toni Kohlstedt
Rooms: 4 (3 SB; 1PB) $50-65
Full Breakfast
Credit Cards: None
Closed Christmas
Notes: 2, 5, 9, 11, 12

6 Pets welcome; 7 Smoking allowed; 8 Children welcome; 9 Social drinking allowed; 10 Tennis available; 11 Swimming available; 12 Golf available; 13 Skiing available; 14 May be booked through travel agents.

PAINESVILLE

Rider's Inn Bed and Breakfast

792 Mentor Avenue, 44077
(216) 354-8200

This historic Colonial stagecoach inn built in 1812 is one mile west of downtown Painesville on Route 20. Choose from ten guest rooms, each with private bath, air conditioning, queen-size beds, and fine antique furnishings that are for sale. Area attractions include Lake Erie College, Fairport Harbor, Grand River Winery, Indian Museum, golf, tennis, horseback riding, water sports, and Amish country tours. Continental breakfast in bed available. A full-service restaurant and separate English pub offer additional meals and a Sunday stagecoach brunch. A second-floor ballroom offers facilities for meetings and social functions.

Hosts: Elaine Crane and daughter Courtney
Rooms: 9 (8 PB; 1 SB) $55-95
Full Breakfast (no eggs)
Credit Cards: A, B, C, D, E
Notes: 2, 3, 4, 5, 6, 7, 8, 9, 10, 12, 14

PENINSULA

Tolle House

1856 Main Street, 44264
(216) 657-2900

Restored Victorian house, extensively decorated and furnished by hosts. Private parlor for guests, with TV, games, easy chairs. Porches with swings and rockers. Full country breakfast; five o'clock tea. Historic village has shops, antiques, old stone sidewalks. Surrounded by national park. Bike, hike, fish, golf, ski, explore. Peaceful yesteryear atmosphere.

Hosts: Ina and Jerry Tolle
Rooms: 3 (SB) $45-60
Full Breakfast
Credit Cards: A, B
Notes: 2, 5, 7, 8 (over 10), 9, 10, 11, 12, 13

POLAND

Inn at the Green

500 South Main Street, 44514
(216) 757-4688

A classically proportioned Victorian town house on the south end of the green in preserved Connecticut Western Reserve Village. Featuring large moldings, 12-foot ceilings, five Italian marble fireplaces, original poplar floors, and interior-shuttered windows.

Hosts: Ginny and Steve Meloy
Rooms: 4 (PB) $45-50
Continental Breakfast
Credit Cards: A, B
Notes: 2, 5, 7, 8 (over 7), 9, 14

Inn at the Green

PUT-IN-BAY

Maple Cottage Bed and Breakfast

571 Catawba Avenue, 43456
(419) 285-4144

This Victorian farmhouse has been an island guesthouse for over 100 years. Its location is only two blocks from the downtown area. Resort shopping, a winery, Perry's victory, and Peace Memorial, plus good restaurants, are all within a five-minute drive. Your hosts invite you to visit their newly remodeled home designed for your comfort and relaxation. Recall the past and embrace the future by visiting Maple Cottage while "putting an island in your life."

Hosts: John and Carla Rayman
Rooms: 7 (SB) $75-95
Continental Breakfast
Credit Cards: A, B
Notes: 2, 5, 8, 9

RIPLEY

The Signal House

234 North Front Street, 45167
(513) 392-1640

Share historic charm and hospitality while visiting this 1830s home on the scenic Ohio River. View spectacular sunrises from three porches or elegant parlors. Enjoy spacious rooms furnished with family antiques. The area offers antiques and craft shops, restaurants, winery, herb farms, covered bridges, history (early pioneers and the Underground Railroad), and lots of friendly people. Pickup provided from local marinas.

Hosts: Vic and Betsy Billingsley
Rooms: 2 (2 SB) $58-68
Full Breakfast
Credit Cards: None
Notes: 2, 5, 7 (limited), 9, 10, 12, 14

SANDUSKY

The Big Oak

2501 South Campbell Street, 44870
(419) 626-6821

This 1879 Victorian farmhouse is furnished with antiques and family heirlooms. Enjoy the family great room or relax by the warmth of the Franklin fireplace. Jim and Jeanne enjoy gardening and play pinochle. Guests are treated like members of the family. Enjoy the patio and gardens. Visit Cedar Point and local museums. Cruise on Lake Erie to Put-in-Bay and Kelley's Island. Visit Edison's birthplace. Golfing, swimming, shopping, dining, and entertainment nearby.

Hosts: Jim and Jeanne Ryan
Rooms: 3 (SB) $40-50
Full Breakfast
Credit Cards: B
Notes: 2, 5, 8

1890 Queen Anne Bed and Breakfast

714 Wayne Street, 44870-3507
(419) 626-0391

A family home for three years, the hosts now enjoy sharing their home and community with you. Three bedrooms furnished with family antiques and a lovely porch overlooking gardens and patio for breakfast in the warm months make your stay here unforgettable. Close to ferries for Cedar Point and Lake Erie Islands.

Hosts: Joan and Robert Kromer
Rooms: 3 (2 PB; 1 SB) $65-70
Continental
Credit Cards: A, B
Notes: 2, 5

The Red Gables Bed and Breakfast

421 Wayne Street, 44870
(419) 625-1189

A lovely old Tudor Revival home furnished in 1907, the Red Gables is located in the historic Old Plat District. Guests are welcomed into the great room, which features a massive fireplace and a large bay window where breakfast is served. The home features many interesting architectural details, including lots of oak woodwork. The Red Gables is decorated in an eclectic style from Oriental artifacts in the great room to flowered chintz in the bedrooms. The rooms are filled with handmade slipcovers, curtains, and comforters made by the innkeeper, who is a semiretired costumemaker. The guest rooms are light and airy and have easy access to a wicker-filled sitting area with a refrigerator, coffee maker, and tea kettle. Guests have said, "It's like going to Grandma's house!"

6 Pets welcome; 7 Smoking allowed; 8 Children welcome; 9 Social drinking allowed; 10 Tennis available; 11 Swimming available; 12 Golf available; 13 Skiing available; 14 May be booked through travel agents.

Host: Jo Ellen Cuthbertson
Rooms: 4 (2 PB; 2 SB) $50-75
Continental Plus
Credit Cards: A, B
Closed January
Notes: 2, 8, 9

Wagner's 1844 Inn

230 East Washington Street, 44870
(419) 626-1726

Elegantly restored, antique-filled Victorian home. Built in 1844 and listed on the National Register of Historic Places. Features a Victorian parlor with antique Steinway piano, livingroom with wood-burning fireplace, billiard room, screened porch, and enclosed courtyard. Bedrooms are air-conditioned. Situated in downtown Sandusky within walking distance of parks, historic buildings, antique shops, museums, and ferries to Cedar Point and Lake Erie islands.

Hosts: Walt and Barb Wagner
Rooms: 3 (PB) $50-75
Expanded Continental Breakfast
Credit Cards: A, B, D
Notes: 5, 9, 10, 11, 12

SHARON CENTER

Hart and Mather Guest House

1343 Sharon Copley Road, P. O. Box 93, 44274
(216) 239-2801; (800) 352-2584

This 1840s home and the Sharon Center Circle where it sits are both on the National Register of Historic Places. Furnished with both traditonal antiques and reproductions, Hart and Mather offers two guest rooms with private baths, one suite with an adjoining room, fireplace, private bath. All rooms have color TV with VCR, and basic cable. Common livingroom with fireplace is available for guests' use, and a delicious breakfast comes from the in-house bakery. Conference rooms available. Gift shop, bakery, and dining room open to the public.

Hosts: Thomas and Sally Thompson
Rooms: 3 (PB) $85-135

Full Breakfast
Credit Cards: A, B, C, D
Notes: 2, 3, 7, 14

SMITHVILLE

The Smithville Bed and Breakfast

171 West Main Street, P. O. Box 142, 44677
(216) 669-3333, (800) 869-6425

Turn-of-the-century simple elegance. Enjoy breakfast in a solid cherry dining room. Breakfast features homegrown blueberry specialties. Your ideal stopping place while visiting the College of Wooster or Amish country. Three-room cottage suites available with special rates for weekly, monthly, and yearly options. Famous restaurants are nearby, as well as gift, craft, and antique shops. Conveniently situated on State Road 85 northeast of Wooster.

Hosts: Jim and Lori Kubik
Rooms: 5 (3 PB; 2 SB) $42-62
Full Breakfast
Credit Cards: A, B
Notes: 2, 5, 8

SOUTH AMHERST

Birch Way Villa

111 White Birch Way, 44001
(216) 986-2090

Birch Way Villa is in a 30-acre wooded lot with a 10-acre spring-fed lake and tennis court. The hostess is a gourmet cook and serves excellent meals. Children are welcome. The home is fully air-conditioned, and many recreational facilities and historic sites are nearby. Tennis lessons and fishing in the summer.

Hosts: Simon and Marjorie Isaac
Rooms: 3 (S1.5B) $45
Full Breakfast
Credit Cards: None
Closed Nov. 21-26; Dec. 23-Jan. 2
Notes: 2, 3, 4, 7 (limited), 8, 10, 11, 12, 13, 14

NOTES: Credit cards accepted: A Master Card; B Visa; C American Express; D Discover Card; E Diner's Club; F Other; 2 Personal Checks accepted; 3 Lunch available; 4 Dinner available; 5 Open all year;

SOUTH BLOOMINGTON

Steep Woods

24830 State Route 56, 43152
(614) 332-6084

This new log home on a wooded hillside is located in the beautiful Hocking Hills, 60 miles southeast of Columbus. Nearby is the Hocking State Park with its famous recessed caves, waterfalls, and unusual rock formations. Available in the area are hiking, swimming, canoeing, fishing, horseback riding, and the Hocking Valley Scenic Railroad.

Hosts: Barbara and Brad Holt
Rooms: 2 (SB) $35
Full Breakfast
Credit Cards: None
Notes: 2, 5, 7, 9

SUGARCREEK

Bed and Breakfast Barn

County Road 70, P. O. Box 454, 44681
(216) 852-BEDS (2337)

Come and enjoy the rustic surroundings of the Bed and Breakfast Barn. There are twelve rooms with private baths, and two rooms that share a big bath. Also in the barn, a large livingroom, dining room, and sitting room are available for your leisure. Wood decking surrounds the barn, which overlooks Sugarcreek and Alpine Meadows. A gift shop is located in the basement of the barn. Craft shows bi-monthly. Situated in Sugarcreek, the Little Switzerland of Ohio and the hub of Amish country.

Hosts: Thomas Agler and Jacqueline Schall
Rooms: 14 (12 PB; 2 SB) $55-65
Full Breakfast
Credit Cards: A, B
Notes: 2, 5, 6, 7, 8, 9, 12

TIPP CITY

Willow Tree Inn

1900 West Street, Route 571, 45371
(513) 667-2957

Restored 1830 Federal manor home with four fireplaces. Each room is a suite. Pond, ducks, original 1830 barn on the premises, working springhouse and smokehouse, beautiful gardens. Just minutes north of Dayton in a quiet location with attentive personal service.

Hosts: Tom and Peggy Nordquist
Rooms: 4 (1 PB; 3 SB) $45-65
Full Breakfast
Credit Cards: A, B
Notes: 2, 5, 7 (restricted), 8 (over 8), 9, 10, 11, 12

TOLEDO

Mansion View Inn Bed and Breakfast

2035 Collingwood Boulevard, 43630
(419) 244-5676

Mansion View Inn is in the historic Old West End, near downtown, the Toledo Museum of Art, and the Toledo Zoological Gardens. On the National Register of Historic Places, this 104-year-old mansion was built in the Queen Anne style. Each guest room is a showcase of art, antiques, and fanciful color.

Hosts: Matt Jasin, Tam Gagen, and Tim Oller
Rooms: 4 (PB) $55-75
Full Breakfast
Credit Cards: A, B
Notes: 2, 5, 8, 9, 10, 11

TROY

Allen Villa Bed and Breakfast

434 South Market Street, 45373
(513) 335-1181

---

6 Pets welcome; 7 Smoking allowed; 8 Children welcome; 9 Social drinking allowed; 10 Tennis available; 11 Swimming available; 12 Golf available; 13 Skiing available; 14 May be booked through travel agents.

This bed and breakfast has seven fireplaces and is decorated in period antiques. Each room has a private bath, TV, telephone, and central air conditioning. Both king and queen beds are available. There is a self-serve snack bar for your evening pleasure, and a bountiful breakfast is served on the 15-foot antique dining room table that seats 12 guests.

Hosts: Robert and June Smith
Rooms: 4 (PB) $45-65
Full Breakfast
Credit Cards: A, B, C
Notes: 2, 5, 7, 8, 9, 10, 11, 12, 14

Allen Villa

URBANA

At Home in Urbana

301 Scioto Street, 43078-2129
(513) 653-8595; (800) 800-0970

At Home in Urbana is a restored 1842 home in a National Register historic district at the center of the Simon Kenton Historical Corridir along US Route 36. Guest rooms on the second and third floors await the traveler who wishes to step back in history among period pieces and family antiques. The historic, residential, and business districts, quaint shops, restaurants, movie theaters, and county library that contains genealogical records from 1805 are within easy walking distance.

Hosts: Grant and Shirley Ingersoll
Rooms: 3 (1 PB; 2 SB) $50-60
Full Breakfast
Credit Cards: A, B, C
Notes: 2, 4 (by reservation only), 5, 8 (over 12),
12, 13

WALNUT CREEK

Troyer's Country View Bed and Breakfast Inn

P. O. Box 91, 44687
(216) 893-3284

Troyer's Country View Bed and Breakfast combines small country town convenience with authentic country atmosphere. In the heart of Amish country, this charming four-suite house is within walking distance of Der Dutchman restaurant, bakery, candy store, gift shops, and Amish museum. The 18th-century home has been remodeled, with each suite having its own private entrance from one of three decks. In your suite's private kitchen area, you will find the refrigerator and cupboard shelves stocked with food, dishes, and utensils for your country breakfast, which you assemble at your leisure and enjoy indoors or on the panoramic deck outside. The suites also have Amish-crafted double extra long, or queen beds. Cable TV and air conditioning. Beautiful view.

Hosts: Owen and Sue Troyer
Rooms: 4 (PB) $65-80; $60 (Jan. and Feb. winter rate only with reservation)
Full Breakfast
Credit Cards: A, B
Notes: 2, 5, 7 (limited)

WAVERLY

Governor's Lodge

171 Gregg Road, 45690
(614) 947-2266

Governor's Lodge is a place like no other. Imagine a beautiful, shimmering lake, an iridescent sunset, and a quiet calm. A friendly atmosphere in an eight-room bed and breakfast that is open year round and situated in Lake White describes this bed and breakfast. Magnificent views can be enjoyed from every room. An affiliate of Bristol Village Retirement Community, it offers a meeting room and group rates for gatherings using the whole lodge.

Hosts: David and Jeannie James
Rooms: 8 (PB) $50-62
Continental Breakfast
Credit Cards: A, B
Notes: 2, 5, 7, 8

WEST ALEXANDRIA

Twin Creek Country Bed and Breakfast

5353 Enterprise Road, 45381
(513) 787-3990; (513) 787-4264; (513) 787-3279

This 1830s farmhouse has been remodeled to offer a quiet getaway. The entire house, upper or lower level, or an individual room is available. There are three bedrooms, two bathrooms, furnished kitchen, and a living-room. The owners live 100 yards away. Guests can roam 170 acres which include 50 acres of woods. Restaurants, deli foods, and antique shops are a short distance away. Local catering available. Suitable for two families at once.

Hosts: Dr. Mark and Carolyn Ulrich
Rooms: 3 (1 PB; 2 SB) $59-79
Expanded Continental Breakfast
Credit Cards: A, B
Notes: 2, 5, 8

WEST LIBERTY

Liberty House Bed and Breakfast

208 North Detroit Street, U.S. Route 68, 43357
(513) 465-1101; (800) 437-8109

West Liberty is a scenic rural village offering a blend of past and present. It is nestled in the Mad River Valley, which the Shawnee Indians called Mac-a-cheek,

meaning "Smiling Valley." Built in the early 1900s, Liberty House has patterned oak floors and woodwork, Oriental rugs, antiques, spacious air-conditioned rooms with private baths. The rooms are bedecked with beautiful linens, old and new quilts. Homemade breads are part of the sumptuous breakfasts and candlelight dinners. Reservations required.

Hosts: Sue and Russ Peterson
Rooms: 2 (PB) $50
Full Breakfast
Credit Cards: None
Notes: 2, 4, 5, 13

WEST MILTON

Locust Lane Farm Bed and Breakfast

5590 Kessler Cowlesville Road, 45383
(513) 698-4743

Delightful Cape Cod home in a rural setting. Air-conditioned bedrooms. Relax in the library or in front of the fireplace. Full breakfast served on the screened porch in the summer. Browse through antique shops, enjoy the nature center, golf, or canoeing.

Hosts: Ruth and Don Shoup
Rooms: 2 (1 PB; 1 SB) $40-50
Full Breakfast
Credit Cards: None
Notes: 2, 5, 8, 10, 12

WESTERVILLE

Priscilla's Bed and Breakfast

5 South West Street, 43081
(614) 882-3910

Priscilla's 1854 home is surrounded by one-half acre of white picket fence. Lovely perennial gardens, bird feeders, and bird-baths accompany the one-time log cabin in the historic setting adjacent to Otterbein College. Borrow bicycles, cook on the patio, enjoy the water garden and adjoining Alum Creek Park. Leisurely browse

6 Pets welcome; 7 Smoking allowed; 8 Children welcome; 9 Social drinking allowed; 10 Tennis available; 11 Swimming available; 12 Golf available; 13 Skiing available; 14 May be booked through travel agents.

through 35 shops. At the rear of the house, Priscilla operates a miniature/dollhouse shop. Two miles north of Columbus. Free airport pickup is available.

Host: Priscilla H. Curtiss
Rooms: 3 (1 PB; 2 SB) $45-55 plus tax
Continental Breakfast
Notes: 6 (prior arrangements), 7 (limited), 8 (limited), 9

WOOSTER

Howey House Bed and Breakfast

340 North Bever Street, 44691
(216) 264-8231

This 142-year-old Victorian Gothic Revival home is situated on Route 30 between Canton and Mansfield. The house has been restored, and each room is furnished with antiques. Howey House is located near the College of Wooster, Ohio Research and Development Center, and Amish country. Several fine restaurants and downtown Wooster are within walking distance.

Host: Jo Howey
Rooms: 4 (1 PB; 3 SB) $36-45
Continental Breakfast
Credit Cards: None
Notes: 2, 5

WORTHINGTON

A.M. House Bed and Breakfast

556 High Street, 43085
(614) 885-5580; (614) 885-5579

A restored turn-of-the-century Queen Anne home in the heart of Old Worthington, within walking distance of shops, restaurants, and New England-style village green. A.M. House has easy access to Columbus events and walking paths along the Olentangy River. Varied breakfast menus with special dietary needs considered. Enjoy porches and yard, TV in parlor. Discount for longer stay. Smoke- and pet-free environment.

Hosts: Doug and Lee Buford; Colin and Robin Buford Wigney
Rooms: 4 (2 PB; 2 SB) $60-70
Full Breakfast
Credit Cards: A, B
Notes: 2, 5, 10, 11, 12

The Worthington Inn

649 High Street, 43085
(614) 885-2600

Historical inn, built in 1831 and refurbished in 1983 and 1990. Ohio's second oldest inn. Four-star Mobil rating. Has 26 exquisitely appointed hotel suites furnished with stunning period antiques. Highly acclaimed restaurant featuring regional American cuisine. Banquet facilities accommodating 150 guests. Stay includes continental breakfast and champagne turndown. Details large and small taken care of professionaly and personally. One mile south of I-270 at the corner of High and New England.

Host: Shirley Black
Rooms: 26 (PB) $105-170
Continental Breakfast
Credit Cards: A, B, C, D, E
Notes: 3, 4, 5, 7, 8, 9, 14

ZOAR

The Weaving Haus

Box 605, Southwest corner of 5th and Main, 44697
(216) 874-3318

Built in 1825 by German separatists for the purpose of weaving flax and wool for their fabrics.There are four levels to Weaving Haus, one being a vaulted fruit cellar. Each of the two guest rooms has a half bath and shares a shower. Convenient for strolling around the village and exploring other historic buildings. Just minutes from the Football Hall of Fame and Atwood Lake.

Hosts: Dan and Nancy Luther
Rooms: 2 (SB) $50-60
Full Breakfast
Credit Cards: A, B
Notes: 2, 5, 10, 12

NOTES: Credit cards accepted: A Master Card; B Visa; C American Express; D Discover Card; E Diner's Club; F Other; 2 Personal Checks accepted; 3 Lunch available; 4 Dinner available; 5 Open all year;

Oklahoma

CLAREMORE

Country Inn
Bed and Breakfast

Route 3, Box 1925, 74017
(918) 342-1894

Leland and Kay invite you to their country retreat. Stay in charming barn-style guest quarters, separate from the main house. Enjoy the swimming pool, relax under a big shade tree with a cool drink, or take a country walk. A delightful continental breakfast is provided. Also, visit the on-premises quilt and craft shop. Nearby are J. M. Davis Gun Museum, Will Rogers Memorial, and horse racing at Will Rogers Downs during August and September.

Hosts: Leland and Kay Jenkins
Rooms: 2 (PB) $47
Suite: 1 (PB) $59
Full Breakfast

Credit Cards: None
Notes: 2, 5, 9, 11

EDMOND

The Arcadian Inn
Bed and Breakfast

328 East First Street, 73034
(405) 348-6347

This historical home of Dr. Ruhl welcomes you to enjoy peaceful surroundings and Oklahoma hospitality. Grand wraparound front porch beckons you to an old-fashioned, intimate retreat. Special guest rooms fulfill your dreams of yesterday.`Enjoy Edmond, Oklahoma City, and Guthrie attractions.

Host: Martha Hall
Rooms: 5 (PB) $45-105
Full Breakfast
Credit Cards: A, B
Notes: 2, 4 (by reservation), 5, 12

Harrison House

6 Pets welcome; 7 Smoking allowed; 8 Children welcome; 9 Social drinking allowed; 10 Tennis available; 11 Swimming available; 12 Golf available; 13 Skiing available; 14 May be booked through travel agents.

OKLAHOMA

Oklahoma

- Claremore

- Guthrie
- Edmond
- Oklahoma City

GUTHRIE

Harrison House Inn

124 West Harrison, 73044
(405) 282-1000

Thirty-five rooms furnished in Victorian style with antiques and quilts. All have private baths. Central heat and air. Situated next door to the theater in central downtown Guthrie. Featured in Glamour, Innsider, and Southern Living.

Host: Phyllis Murray
Rooms: 35 (PB) $55-85
Expanded Continental Breakfast
Credit Cards: A, B, C, D, E
Notes: 2, 5, 6, 7, 8, 9, 10, 11, 12, 14

OKLAHOMA CITY

Country House Bed and Breakfast

10101 Oakview Road, 73165
(405) 794-4008

A quiet country getaway on five acres is perfect for a weekend or longer. Some of the furnishings in the home include 19th-century antiques, heirloom quilts, 1817 grandfather clock, and country collectibles. One mile from water sports and riding stables at Lake Draper. You can start your day with a full, homemade breakfast served on antique Spode china in the dining room, or on the balcony. Spacious rooms and bathrooms, and TVs in the rooms upon request. Guests are pampered and will find fresh fruit, Godiva chocolates, and sparkling drinks in their rooms.

Hosts: Dee and Nancy Ann Curnutt
Rooms: 3 (PB) $45-55
Full Breakfast
Credit Cards: None
Notes: 2, 3, 4, 5, 6 (outside), 7, 8, 9, 14

Flora's Bed and Breakfast

2312 Northwest 46th, 73112
(405) 840-3157

Located in a quiet neighborhood, the home is furnished with antiques and collectibles and includes an elevator. Guests may relax in front of the large wood-burning fireplace, or enjoy the outdoors on a 1,500-square-foot balcony. There is covered parking, and your hosts enjoy square dancing. Easy access to Cowboy Hall of Fame, Remington Park Race Track, Omniplex, and other points of interest. Many good eating places in the vicinity.

Hosts: Newton W. and Joann Flora
Rooms: 2 (PB) $40-45
Continental Breakfast
Credit Cards: None
Notes: 2, 5, 7, 8 (over 7), 9, 14

The Grandison Inn

1841 Northwest 15th, 73106
(405) 521-0011

This country Victorian, circa 1896, has all of its original stained glass and brass lighting fixtures. The private suite covers the entire third floor. Honeymoon and anniversary packages are available, as well as breakfast in bed and other room services. Enjoy the beautiful gazebo among fruit trees and gardens, relax on the rocker-lined front porch, or just spend time in the Victorian parlor. Convenient to downtown and I-35 and I-40.

Hosts: Claudia and Bob Wright
Rooms: 5 (PB) $45-125
Expanded Continental Breakfast
Credit Cards: A, B, C
Notes: 2, 3, 4, 5, 6, 7, 9, 14

Willow Way

27 Oakwood Drive, 73121-5410
(405) 427-2133

Willow Way is a wooded town retreat in country English Tudor style with antique decor and genuine charm. The two-story stone den, with vaulted ceiling and picture window, is the guests' favorite place for breakfast. Safe and comfortable with off-street parking. Quiet, situated near nature,

NOTES: Credit cards accepted: A Master Card; B Visa; C American Express; D Discover Card; E Diner's Club; F Other; 2 Personal Checks accepted; 3 Lunch available; 4 Dinner available; 5 Open all year; 6 Pets welcome; 7 Smoking allowed; 8 Children welcome; 9 Social drinking allowed; 10 Tennis available; 11 Swimming available; 12 Golf available; 13 Skiing available; 14 May be booked through travel agents.

the race track, Cowboy Hall of Fame, and other area attractions. Three rooms with two private baths. Full breakfast; occasions and dinner by arrangement.

Hosts: Johnita and Lionel Turner
Rooms: 3 (2 PB; 1 SB) $50-80
Full Breakfast
Credit Cards: A, B
Notes: 2, 3, 4, 5, 8, 9, 12

Oregon

Adams Cottage Bed and Breakfast

737 Siskiyou Boulevard, 97520
(800) 345-2570

Less than five blocks to theaters and shopping. This historic 1900 vernacular/Victorian home offers four uniquely decorated guest rooms featuring air conditioning, queen beds, private bath, wet bar, private patio/balcony, and large social areas. A delicious full breakfast awaits you each morning. Beautiful garden areas and mountain views add to your enjoyment for an extended vacation, honeymoon stay, or romantic weekend. Adams Cottage offers the ultimate Ashland experience.

Host: Jeff vonHauf
Rooms: 4 (PB) $59-105 seasonal
Full Breakfast
Credit Cards: None
Notes: 2, 5, 8, 9, 10, 11, 12, 13, 14

Ashland's Victory House

271 Beach Street, 97520
(503) 488-4428

Celebrate the 1940s in this charming Tudor with eclectic furnishings and decor of that period. Three cozy bedrooms with private baths and an informal atmosphere make this a comfortable place to stay. Enjoy the USO den with a jukebox, piano, classical movies, and memorabilia. Soak in FDR's Hot Springs Spa on the deck. Play backyard croquet. Enjoy nutritious and award-winning breakfasts. Ashland offers Oregon Shakepeare Festival, art, music, and boutique shopping. The Rogue River and nearby mountains provide quality rafting, fishing, and skiing.

Host: Dale Swire
Rooms: 3 (PB) $59-75
Full Breakfast
Credit Cards: None
Notes: 2, 5, 9, 10, 11, 12, 13, 14

Buckhorn Springs

2200 Buckhorn Springs Road, 97520
(503) 488-2200

Buckhorn Springs invites you to enjoy modern-day comfort amidst the charms of yesteryear at this century-old mineral spring resort. Lodging is in period-decorated guest rooms, creekside cabins. Nestled in a wooded glen, this National Register of Historic Places district is a twelve-mile picturesque drive from Ashland. Beautiful organic gardens supply the restaurant with the freshest of ingredients prepared with a

Hershey House

---

6 Pets welcome; 7 Smoking allowed; 8 Children welcome; 9 Social drinking allowed; 10 Tennis available; 11 Swimming available; 12 Golf available; 13 Skiing available; 14 May be booked through travel agents.

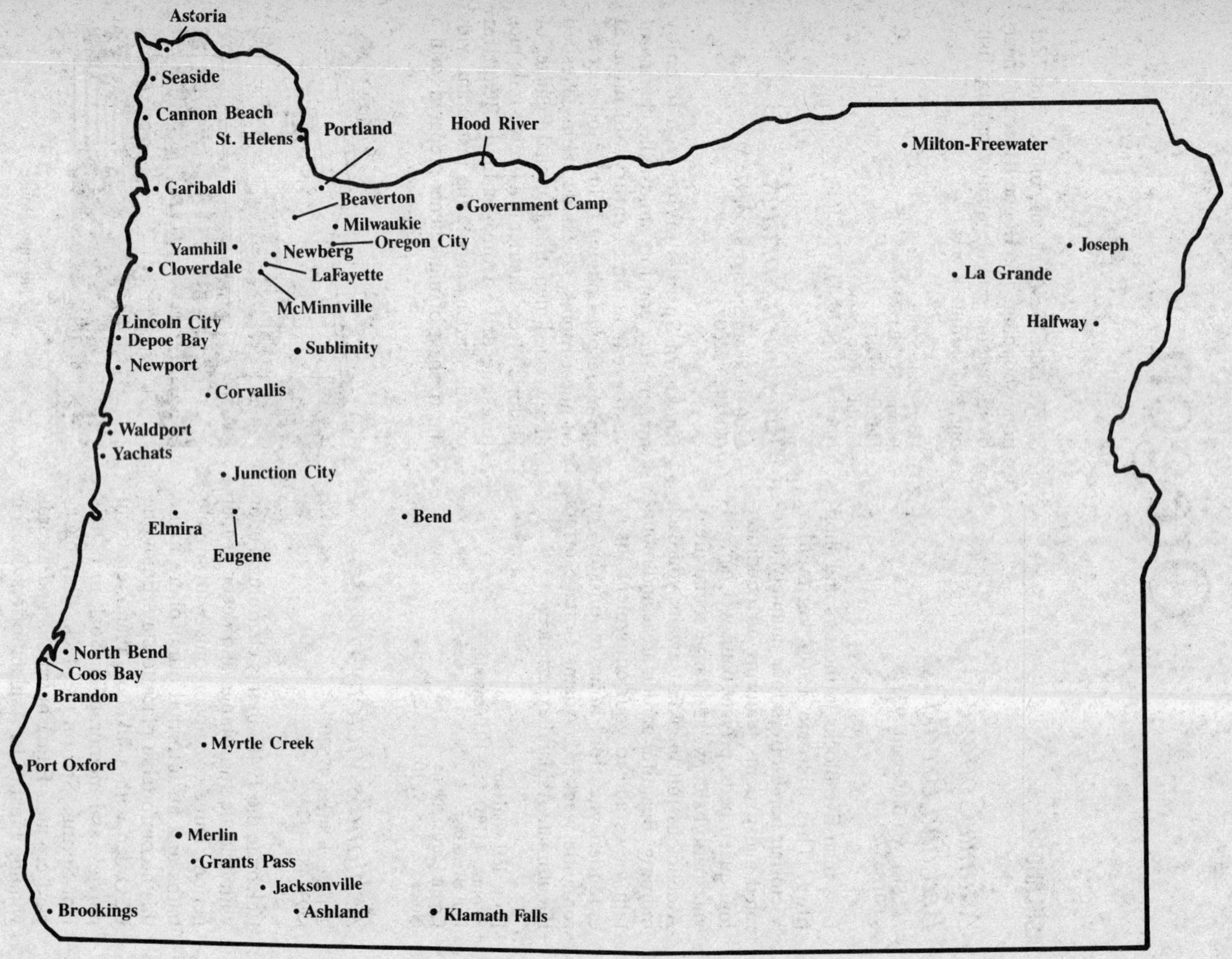

Joseph

Milton-Freewater

La Grande

Halfway

Hood River

Government Camp

Portland

Beaverton

Milwaukie

Oregon City

Newberg

LaFayette

McMinnville

Sublimity

Bend

St. Helens

Cannon Beach

Garibaldi

Yamhill

Cloverdale

Corvallis

Junction City

Astoria

Seaside

Lincoln City

Depoe Bay

Newport

Waldport

Yachats

Elmira

Eugene

Myrtle Creek

North Bend

Coos Bay

Brandon

Port Oxford

Merlin

Grants Pass

Jacksonville

Ashland

Klamath Falls

Brookings

gourmet flourish. Sunday brunch is served on the deck.

Hosts: Bruce and Leslie Sargent; Chris Fowler
Rooms: 8 (6 PB; 2 SB) $55-150
Cabins: 5
Full Breakfast
Credit Cards: A, B, D
Notes: 2, 3 (box), 4, 8, 14

Country Willows

1313 Clay Street, 97520
(503) 488-1590

A quiet, relaxing hideaway on five white-fenced acres with a beautiful view of the Siskiyou Mountains. This 1905 home was elegantly rebuilt with your comfort in mind. Enjoy a full breakfast on the porch or relax by the pool and spa. All rooms have private baths and air conditioning.

Hosts: Bill and Barabara Huntley
Suite: 1 (PB) $80-145, off-season rates available
Full Breakfast
Credit Cards: A, B
Notes: 2, 5, 9, 10, 11, 12, 13, 14

Cowslip's Belle

159 North Main Street, 97520
(503) 488-2901

The Cowslip's Belle has cozy down comforters and teddy bears to snuggle into, the softest white linens to touch your skin, foam baths to linger in, scrumptious breakfasts to savor, and homemade smooth, creamy chocolate truffles to melt in your mouth. Just three blocks to restaurants, shops, and theaters, this 1913 craftsman bungalow and carriage house is nestled in Ashland's historic district. Voted one of the top 50 bed and breakfasts in the country by *Inn Times*. Four rooms with private baths and entrances. Special winter rates November 1 through February 12.

Hosts: Jon and Carmen Reinhardt
Rooms: 4 (PB) $65-105
Full Breakfast
Credit Cards: A, B
Notes: 2, 5, 9, 10, 11, 12, 13, 14

Hersey House

451 North Main Street, 97520
(503) 482-4563

Gracious living in an elegantly restored Victorian with a colorful English country garden. Also a separate bungalow for families or groups that sleeps two to six. Sumptuous breakfasts. Central air conditioning. Walk to plaza and three Shakespeare theaters. Nearby, you will find white water rafting on the Rogue and Klamath rivers, Crater Lake National Park, Britt Music Festival, Jacksonville National Historic District, and Oregon wineries.

Hosts: Gail Orell and Lynn Savage
Rooms: 4 (PB) $94-104
Bungalow: 1 (PB) $120-180
Full and Continental Breakfast
Credit Cards: A, B
Notes: 2, 9, 10, 11, 12, 13, 14

The Iris Inn

59 Manzanita Street, 97520
(503) 488-2286

A 1905 Victorian furnished with antiques. Elegant breakfasts feature eggs Benedict and cheese-baked eggs. Mountain views, quiet neighborhood. Near the Oregon Shakespeare Theater and the Rogue River for rafting. A bungalow is also available for families; it sleeps two-six, and self-catered continental breakfast is provided.

Host: Vicki Lamb
Rooms: 5 (1 PB; 4 SB) $80-90
Full Breakfast
Credit Cards: A, B, D
Notes: 2, 5, 8 (over 6), 10, 11, 12, 13

The Morical House

668 North Main Street, 97520
(503) 482-2254

A superbly restored 1880s farmhouse on one and one-half acres of beautifully landscaped grounds, the Morical House offers 18th-centrury hospitality with 20th century comfort. Five gracious, air conditioned guest rooms, a bountiful breakfast menu that changes daily, afternoon refreshments, a putting green, unobstructed view of the Rouge Valley, and Cascade Mountains.

Hosts: Pat and Peter Dahl
Rooms: 5 (PB) $85-115 seasonal
Full Breakfast
Credit Cards: A, B
Closed Jan. 15-30
Notes: 2, 8 (over 12), 10, 11, 12, 13, 14

Mount Ashland Inn

550 Mount Ashland Road, 97520
(503) 482-8707

Situated on the crest of the Siskiyou Mountains, this beautiful handcrafted log inn commands spectacular mountain views, including 14,200-foot Mount Shasta. Hand carvings, Oriental rugs, and antiques provide an atmosphere of comfortable elegance. Guests enjoy the sunny deck and large stone fireplace. Hiking and skiing at the door.

Hosts: Jerry and Elaine Shanafelt
Rooms: 5 (PB) $85-130
Full Breakfast
Credit Cards: A, B
Notes: 2, 5, 8 (over 9), 9, 10, 12, 13, 14

Neil Creek House

341 Mowetza Drive, 97520
(503) 482-6443

A country retreat with European charm and elegance, set in a five-acre paradise, with swimming pool, duck pond, lively creek, and forest. Spacious rooms, antiques, queen-size beds, private patio, private baths, and air conditioning. Gourmet breakfast by the creek. Afternoon refreshments served in the creekside gazebo. Guest livingroom with stone fireplace and cathedral ceiling.

Hosts: Paul and Gayle Negro
Rooms: 2 (PB) $85-100
Full Breakfast
Credit Cards: None
Notes: 2, 5, 9, 11, 12

Pinehurst Inn at Jenny Creek

17250 Highway 66, 97520
(503) 488-1002

Offering the finest dining and lodging, this handsomely restored 1920s roadhouse is situated in a mountain setting on the banks of Jenny Creek, 23 miles east of Ashland (home of the world-famous Shakespeare Festival). Each room is decorated with antique furniture and custom-made quilts. All meals are prepared from fresh foods and served in the elegant dining room. Hiking trails and trout fishing nearby. Airstrip nearby. No smoking.

Host: Delia Smith
Rooms: 4 (PB) $75-95
Suites: 2 (PB)
Full Breakfast
Credit Cards: A, B
Notes: 2, 4, 5, 9 (beer and wine only)

The Queen Anne Bed and Breakfast

125 North Main Street, 97520
(503) 482-0220

This elegant 1880 Victorian home is furnished with antiques and vintage quilts. Over one-fourth acre of splendid rose gardens and an exquisite English flower garden with a waterfall gazebo and spacious deck. Two blocks away from the Shakespeare theaters and downtown. Full country breakfasts served in the morning.

Host: Elaine Martens
Rooms: 3 (PB) $75-110 seasonal
Full Breakfast
Credit Cards: None
Notes: 2, 5, 13

Redwing

115 N. Main Street, 97520
(503) 482-1807

This 1911 Craftsman-style home, with its original lighting fixtures and beautiful woodwork, is nestled in Ashland's charm-

NOTES: Credit cards accepted: A Master Card; B Visa; C American Express; D Discover Card; E Diner's Club; F Other; 2 Personal Checks accepted; 3 Lunch available; 4 Dinner available; 5 Open all year;

ing historic district. Each guest room enjoys its own distinctive intimacy and private bath. You can relax on the front porch swing and view the Cascade Mountains or walk two blocks to Lithia Park, shops or the nationally acclaimed Shakespearean Festival. In addition, downhill and cross country skiing, river rafting, salmon and steelhead fishing are all nearby.

Hosts: Mike and Judi Cook
Rooms: 3 (PB) $90
Full Breakfast
Credit Cards: None
Notes: 2, 5, 13

Romeo Inn

295 Idaho Street, 97520
(503) 488-0884

Mobil gives this inn a three-star rating. A quiet, elegant, lovely Cape Cod amid pines, with a valley view. Four spacious rooms with central air conditioning. Some rooms have fireplaces. Two luxurious suites with fireplaces; one has a whirlpool tub. There's a spa and pool, beautiful gardens, and gourmet breakfast. Walk to the Oregon Shakespeare theaters and town.

Hosts: Margaret and Bruce Halverson
Rooms: 6 (PB) $105-175
Full Breakfast
Credit Cards: A, B
Notes: 2, 5, 9, 10, 11, 12, 13, 14

Treon's Country Homestay

1819 Colestin Road, 97520
(503) 482-0746

Refresh your spirit in the tall pine forest. Nine acres with stream and pond offer swimming, hiking, croquet, horseshoes, and barbecue. Spacious guest area includes three bedrooms, plus common room with fireplace, recreation room with pool table, kitchen, and exercise room. Hearty country breakfasts. Ideal for families and small groups.

Hosts: Donna and Francis Treon
Rooms: 3 (1 PB; 2 SB) $65

Full Breakfast
Credit Cards: None
Notes: 2, 5, 8, 9, 11, 13, 14

The Wood's House Bed and Breakfast Inn

333 North Main Street, 97520
(503) 488-1598; (800) 435-8260

Located in the historic district of Ashland four blocks from the Shakespearean theaters, 100-acre Lithia Park, restaurants, and shops, this 1908 Craftsman-style home offers six sunny and spacious guest rooms. Simple furnishings of warm woods, antique furniture, fine linens, watercolors, Oriental carpets, laces, leather books, and private label amenities invite guests to relax in this comfortable, yet elegant, home. The one-half-acre terraced English gardens provide many areas for guests to relax, read, and socialize. Golfing, swimming, hiking, biking, rafting, hot air ballooning nearby.

Hosts: Françoise and Lester Roddy
Rooms: 6 (PB) $65-105
Full Breakfast
Credit Cards: A, B
Notes: 2, 5, 8, 9, 14

ASTORIA

Columbia River Inn Bed and Breakfast

1681 Franklin Avenue, 97103
(503) 325-5044

A five-star Victorian charmer. You'll note an elegant "Painted Lady" when you enter the Columbia River Inn Bed and Breakfast, built in the late 1870s. Nearby you will find the Columbia River Maritime Museum and Captain George Flavel House. The ocean is five miles away. Full breakfast and a gift shop on the premises; river view; off-street parking.

Host: Karen N. Nelson
Rooms: 5 (PB) $65-80 seasonal
Full Breakfast
Minimum stay summer and holidays: 2 nights

6 Pets welcome; 7 Smoking allowed; 8 Children welcome; 9 Social drinking allowed; 10 Tennis available; 11 Swimming available; 12 Golf available; 13 Skiing available; 14 May be booked through travel agents.

Credit Cards: A, B
Closed two days for Thanksgiving and Christmas
Notes: 2, 5, 8, 9

Columbia River Inn

Franklin Street Station Bed and Breakfast

1140 Franklin Street, 97103
(503) 325-4314

A Victorian home built in 1900 by ship-builder Ferdinand Fisher. Five rooms (two rooms are suites); two have views of the Columbia River. All rooms have queen beds and private baths. Full breakfast is served each morning. Ornate craftsmanship throughout the home expresses the rich history of Astoria. Three-star rating in Northwest Best Places. Close to downtown and within walking distance of museums.

Hosts: Jim and Renee Caldwell
Rooms: 5 (PB) $50-85
Full Breakfast
Credit Cards: A, B
Notes: 2, 5, 8, 9, 10, 11, 12, 14

Grandview Bed and Breakfast

1574 Grand Avenue, 97103
(503) 325-5555; (800) 488-3250

Wonderful views of the Columbia River; close to the best maritime museum on the West Coast and other museums, churches, and Victorian homes. Tour domestic and foreign ships in port. Light, airy, three-story Victorian with hardwood floors.

Host: Charleen Maxwell
Rooms: 3 (PB) $39-88 plus tax
Suites: 3 (2 bedrooms, PB) $79-102 plus tax
Expanded Continental Breakfast
Credit Cards: A, B, D
Notes: 2, 5, 8 (over 10), 10, 11, 12, 14

BANDON

Lighthouse Bed and Breakfast

650 Jetty Road, Box 24, 97411
(503) 347-9316

Contemporary home situated on the beach across from the historic Bandon lighthouse. Unequaled jetty, lighthouse, and ocean views. Walk to Old Town, shops, galleries, and fine restaurants. In-room Jacuzzi available; fireplace, wood stove. A quiet, peaceful setting.

Hosts: Bruce and Linda Sisson
Rooms: 4 (PB) $80-115
Expanded Continental Breakfast
Credit Cards: A, B
Notes: 2, 5, 8 (over 12), 9, 10, 12, 14

Sea Star Guesthouse

370 First Street, 97411
(503) 347-9632

This guest house is a comfortable, romantic coastal getaway with European ambience. It is situated on the harbor and provides harbor, river, and ocean views. The shops, galleries, theater, and other sights of Old Town are just a stroll away. The newly decorated rooms offer a warm, private retreat. Some rooms have skylights and open-beam ceilings; all have decks. Prices include wine and breakfast served from the menu of Sea Star's own charming bistro.

Hosts: David and Monica Jennings
Rooms: 4 (PB) $50-90
Full Breakfast
Credit Cards: A, B, C
Notes: 3, 4, 5, 8, 9, 12

NOTES: Credit cards accepted: A Master Card; B Visa; C American Express; D Discover Card; E Diner's Club; F Other; 2 Personal Checks accepted; 3 Lunch available; 4 Dinner available; 5 Open all year;

BEAVERTON

The Yankee Tinker Bed and Breakfast

5480 Southwest 183rd Avenue, 97007
(503) 649-0932

Suburban convenience close to Washington County wineries, farms, orchards, as well as high-tech Sunset Corridor. Ten miles west of Portland, midway between the coast and the mountains. Wind surf, fish, boat, or canoe on Hagg Lake, or canoe the lazy Tualatin River. Canoe available. Private yard and gardens, deck with hot tub. Washington County wines offered between 4:00 and 6:00 P.M. Comfortable rooms furnished with family heirlooms, antiques, cozy quilts, and garden flowers. Acclaimed breakfast often includes Yankee tradition of pie.

Hosts: Jan and Ralph Wadleigh
Rooms: 3 (2 PB; 1 SB) $55-65
Full Breakfast
Credit Cards: A, B, C, E
Notes: 2, 5, 9, 14

BEND

Farewell Bend Bed and Breakfast

29 Northwest Greeley, 97701
(503) 382-4374

Restored 70-year-old Dutch Colonial house. Four blocks from downtown shopping, restaurants, and Drake Park on the Deschutes River. In winter, ski Mount Bachelor. In summer, golf, whitewater rafting, fishing, and hiking. Complimentary wine or sherry. King beds, down comforters, handmade quilts, and terry-cloth robes.

Host: M. Lorene Bateman
Rooms: 3 (PB) $55-75
Full Breakfast
Credit Cards: A, B, C
Notes: 2, 5, 12, 13

Gazebo Bed and Breakfast

21679 Obsidian Avenue, 97702
(503) 389-7202

Enjoy friendly hospitality and a relaxed atmosphere in a spacious home that the owner designed and built. Antique furnishings. "Inn the country, close to town." Beautiful mountain view. The area offers opportunities for hiking, biking, skiing, fishing, rock climbing, rafting, sightseeing, golf, dining, shopping, swimming, and more. A full breakfast is served at your convenience.

Hosts: Gale and Helen Estergreen
Rooms: 2 (SB) $45
Full Breakfast
Credit Cards: None
Notes: 2, 5, 8, 11, 12, 13

Juniper Acres

65220 Smokey Ridge Road, 97701
(503) 389-2193

This hand-crafted log home is on 9 wooded acres overlooking 7 mountain peaks. Each guest room has a private bath. A delicious full breakfast is served outside on the sun deck in the summer season. Shopping, skiing, golfing and many other outdoor activities are nearby.

Hosts: Vern and Della Bjerk
Rooms: 2 (PB) $65
Full Breakfast
Credit Cards: None
Notes: 2, 5, 12, 13, 14

Lara House Bed and Breakfast

640 Northwest Congress, 97701
(503) 388-4064

This magnificent historic home overlooking Drake Park and Mirror Pond invites guests to relax in a cozy livingroom with fireplace, TV, reading/game area. Sun room with a view of the park and sprawling manicured grounds is a nice place to sit and reflect. Guests can choose between four uniquely decorated suites with sitting area and private baths. There is also a two-bedroom suite with a private bath as well. Full gourmet breakfast is served each morning, and you are close to skiing, fishing, hiking, rafting, and cycling. No smoking. Children welcome. Featured in *NW Best Places*.

Hosts: Doug and Bobbye Boger
Rooms: 5 (PB) $55-95
Full Breakfast
Credit Cards: A, B, C
Notes: 2, 3, 4, 5, 8, 9; 10, 11, 12, 13

BROOKINGS

Chetco River Inn

21202 High Prairie Road, 97415
(503) 469-8128
(800) 327-2688 Pelican Bay Travel

Relax in the peaceful seclusion of 35 private forested acres. Only a short distance from the seacoast town of Brookings. The inn is small, so guest numbers are limited. Surrounded on three sides by the lovely Chetco River, the inn may use alternative energy, but it will offer you all the modern conveniences. Delicious big meals. River fishing, swimming, hiking horseshoes, darts, croquet, and badminton for diversions.

Host: Sandra Brugger
Rooms: 4 (3 PB; 1 SB) $85
Full Breakfast
Credit Cards: A, B
Notes: 2, 4, 5, 7 (outside), 9, 11 (river)

Holmes Sea Cove Bed and Breakfast

17350 Holmes Drive, 97415
(503) 469-3025

A delightful seacoast hideaway with a spectacular ocean view, private guest entrances, and a tasty continental breakfast served to your room. Enjoy beachcombing and whale watching.

Hosts: Jack and Lorene Holmes
Rooms: 3 (PB) $80-95
Expanded Continental Breakfast

Credit Cards: A, B
Notes: 2, 5, 7 (limited), 9, 10, 11

The Ward House Bed and Breakfast

Box 86, 97415
(503) 469-5557

A 1917 vintage home built in the Craftsman-style architecture by William Ward. Restored and furnished with antiques and treasures, this home has a happy, warm feeling that makes guests feel right at home. Large parlor, hot tub/sauna, spacious bedrooms upstairs. Ocean view; just a few blocks from the river and harbor. Gourmet breakfast, including Norwegian waffles.

Hosts: Jim and Margie
Rooms: 3 (PB) $65-75
Full Breakfast
Credit Cards: A, B
Notes: 2, 5, 8 (over 12), 9, 10, 11, 14

CANNON BEACH

Grey Whale Inn and Gallery

P. O. Box 965, 164 Kenai Street, 97110
(503) 436-2848

Just 300 feet to miles of Oregon's most beautiful white sandy beach. This small, quiet inn offers five romantic rooms with fresh flowers, down comforters, and original art. Enjoy Bruce's homemade nut breads and jams, explore Cannon Beach shops and galleries, and peek into Elaine's art studio and gallery. All this and whale watching too!

Hosts: Bruce and Elaine Simon
Rooms: 5 (PB) $70-125
Continental Breakfast
Minimum stay weekends and holidays: 2 nights
Credit Cards: A, B
Notes: 2, 5, 11, 14

Tern Inn

3663 South Hemlock, Box 952, 97110
(503) 436-1528

NOTES: Credit cards accepted: A Master Card; B Visa; C American Express; D Discover Card; E Diner's Club; F Other; 2 Personal Checks accepted; 3 Lunch available; 4 Dinner available; 5 Open all year;

European-style bed and breakfast with an ocean view. Light goose-down quilts for year-round comfort, private bath, and color TV. Fresh, home-baked goods are served, including vegetarian and low-cholesterol foods. Rooms are suitable for up to four adults or may be combined for seven adults. Special off-season and weekly rates; gift certificates; 6 percent lodging tax.

Hosts: Chris and Enken Friedrichsen
Rooms: 2 (PB) $75-95 plus tax
Full Breakfast
Minimum stay Memorial Day-Labor Day: 2-3 nights
Credit Cards: None
Notes: 2, 9, 10, 11, 12, 14

CARVER

Kipling Rock Farm

17000 SE Highway 224, 97015
(503) 658-5056

Fish, hike, raft, and swim! One exceptional guest room ensures a place to renew the senses. Your large guest room has a fireplace, antiques, flowers, private bath, own entrance, and sitting room, complete with a small refrigerator. Seven rural acres at edge of the Clackamas River, 16 miles from downtown Portland, and 40 minutes to Mt. Hood. Full breakfast.

Host: Kris Tabor
Room: 1 (PB) $75
Full Breakfast
Credit Cards: None
Notes: 2, 5, 8, 9, 11 (seasonal), 13

CLOVERDALE

Sandlake Country Inn

8505 Galloway Road, 97112
(503) 965-6745

A private, peaceful place for making marriage memories on the awesome Oregon coast. A shipwreck-timbered farmhouse built in 1894; old roses, private garden spa, and honeymoon suite (four rooms). The cottage has fireplace, Jacuzzi tub for two, and kitchen. Full breakfasts, bicycles, and croquet amid an exuberant country garden. One mile to the beach. "Togetherness Baskets" available. Wheelchair accessible.

Hosts: Margo and Charles Underwood
Rooms: 4 (PB) $65-100
Full Breakfast
Credit Cards: A, B
Notes: 2, 3, 4, 14

COOS BAY

Blackberry Inn Bed and Breakfast

843 Central, 97420
(503) 267-6951

Situated on the southern Oregon coast, this charming bed and breakfast offers the elegant atmosphere of an old Victorian home. Since the inn is separate from the hosts' residence, guests can enjoy the hospitality but have privacy, too. A quick walk takes you to several restaurants, stores, a theater, an art museum, and the city park, with its lovely Japanese gardens, tennis courts, and picnic areas.

Hosts: John and Louise Duncan
Rooms: 4 (3 PB; 1 SB) $35-50
Continental Breakfast
Credit Cards: A, B
Notes: 2, 5, 8, 9, 10, 11, 12

Sandlake Country Inn

CORVALLIS

Huntington Manor

3555 Northwest Harrison Boulevard, 97330
(503) 753-3735

Huntington Manor is a beautiful, 65-year-old Williamsburg Colonial that has been completely refurbished and is elegantly furnished with American and European antiques. Guest rooms feature down comforters and color TV, phones, and air conditioning.

Host: Ann Sink
Rooms: 3 (PB) $55
Full Breakfast
Credit Cards: A, B, C, D
Notes: 2, 5, 8 (over 12), 9, 10, 11, 12, 14

Shady Maple Farm Bed and Breakfast

27183 Bundy Road, 97333
(503) 847-5992; (800) 821-4129

Shady Maple Farm offers a peaceful, relaxed atmosphere on 48 parklike acres along the banks of the Willamette River. You'll find a charming 1912 farmhouse, bunkhouse, flower gardens, rolling lawns, and tennis court. A hearty breakfast of orchard fruits, farm-fresh eggs, and homemade specialties is served fireside in the library/dining room with a view of grazing cattle or sheep. Guests are offered a variety

Channel House

of indoor and outdoor games, stereo, VCR, piano, guest refrigerator, picnic area, and barbecue.

Host: Carol May
Rooms: 3 (1 PB; 2 SB) $55-75
Full Breakfast
Credit Cards: A, B
Notes: 2, 5, 6, 7, 8, 9, 10, 11, 14; (restrictions on 6, 7, 8, 9)

DEPOE BAY

Channel House Bed and Breakfast Inn

35 Ellingson Street, 97341
(503) 765-2140

Dramatically perched on the ocean and at the entrance to Oregon's Depoe Bay is the Channel House Inn. Watch ocean storms and spouting whales from one of ten ocean-front rooms or from the privacy of your own whirlpool. Deep sea fishing, fireplaces, and lots of sea air!

Host: Vicki Mix
Rooms: 12 (PB) $55-200
Full Breakfast
Credit Cards: A, B
Notes: 2, 5, 7, 8, 9, 10, 11, 12, 14

Gracie's Landing

235 Bayview Avenue, P. O. Box 29, 97341
(503) 765-2322; (800) 228-0448 reservations

This Oregon coast inn, in Cape Cod style, is charming and relaxing. Parlor with baby grand piano; dining room with teas and coffees and homemade cookies available; and library/game room with fireplace. Fireplaces and whirlpool bathtubs lend romance to the rooms. Ocean fishing and whale watching tours add adventure. All rooms have TV/VCR, telephone, and "fishing village" view of the harbor. Receptions, retreats, reunions. Hors d'oeuvres, luncheons, or culinary extravaganzas can be arranged.

Hosts: Dale and LaRona ("Lee") Hoehne
Rooms: 13 (PB) $75-100

NOTES: Credit cards accepted: A Master Card; B Visa; C American Express; D Discover Card; E Diner's Club; F Other; 2 Personal Checks accepted; 3 Lunch available; 4 Dinner available; 5 Open all year;

Full Breakfast
Credit Cards: A, B, C, D, E
Notes: 2, 5, 7, 9, 10, 12

ELMIRA

McGillivray's Log Home Bed and Breakfast

88680 Evers Road, 97437
(503) 935-3564

West of Eugene, Oregon, you will find the best of yesterday with the comforts of today. Situated on five wooded acres, this airconditioned home has wheelchair access. The hearty breakfasts are often prepared on an antique wood-burning cook stove.

Host: Evelyn R. McGillivray
Rooms: 2 (PB) $40-70
Full Breakfast
Credit Cards: A, B
Notes: 2, 5, 8, 9

EUGENE

Kjaer's House in the Woods

814 Lorane Highway, 97405
(503) 343-3234

A 1910 Craftsman-style home in a peaceful setting on a quiet, countrylike road ideal for walking, jogging, hiking, deer and bird watching. Antiques, Oriental carpets, fireplace, square grand piano available for guests. "Urban convenience/suburban tranquility."

Hosts: George and Eunice Kjaer
Rooms: 2 (SB) $40-65
Full Breakfast
Credit Cards: None
Closed Dec. 22-Jan. 3
Notes: 2, 5, 8 (under 2 or over 12), 9, 10, 11, 12, 13, 14

The Lyon and the Lambe Inn

988 Lawrence at Tenth, 97401
(503) 683-3160

In the heart of Eugene, in a quiet 1920s neighborhood, this newly built inn has spacious, luxurious rooms, each with large private bathroom. Memorable gourmet breakfasts are served at your convenience. Amenities include "Betthupferl," Perrier, fresh-cut flowers, fine soaps and shampoos, and the famous tub room with whirlpool bath, music, and lotions, plus potions galore. Five languages spoken. The ultimate bed and breakfast for sophisticated inn-goers.

Hosts: Barbara and Henri Brod
Rooms: 4 (PB) $60-83
Full Breakfast
Credit Cards: A, B
Notes: 2, 4, 5, 6, 7, 9, 12, 13, 14

GARIBALDI

Gracy Manor

119 East Driftwood, P. O. Box 220, 97118
(503) 322-3369

Gracy Manor is quiet and secluded. It has a scenic view of the bay and hillside. Minutes away from chartered fishing boats, beaches, and golfing. Bedrooms are beautifully decorated with ruffled curtains, each furnished in the past and present. Queen beds and TV in each room. Guests share bathroom. No smoking. Full complimentary breakfast.

Host: Dorothy Gracy
Rooms: 3 (SB) $50
Full Breakfast
Credit Cards: None
Notes: 2, 5, 9, 12, 14

Hill Top House Bed and Breakfast

617 Holly Avenue, P. O. Box 145, 97118
(503) 322-3221

This beautiful three-story home offers a fantastic ocean view, private bathrooms, garden spa, full breakfast, and warm welcoming atmosphere. Close to great beaches, golf, tennis, fishing, and hiking.

6 Pets welcome; 7 Smoking allowed; 8 Children welcome; 9 Social drinking allowed; 10 Tennis available; 11 Swimming available; 12 Golf available; 13 Skiing available; 14 May be booked through travel agents.

Hosts: Don and Shuzz Hedrick
Rooms: 3 (PB) $62-84
Full Breakfast
Closed December and January
Credit Cards: A, B
Notes: 2, 8, 9, 12

GOVERNMENT CAMP

Falcon's Crest Inn

P. O. Box 185, 87287 Government Camp Loop
  Highway, 97028
(503) 272-3403; (800) 624-7384

Elegance "Mount Hood-style" features three
rooms and two suites with private baths.
Individually decorated with family heirlooms, in-room telephones, bed turndown
service, morning refreshment tray, complimentary après-activity snacks. A full breakfast is served in the morning. Located in the
heart of a year-round recreation area, skiing,
hiking, fishing, and horseback riding are all
nearby. Corporate, private and mystery parties are a specialty. Winter weekends. Fine
evening dining and spirits available.

Hosts: Melody and Bob Johnson
Rooms: 5 (PB) $85-139
Full Breakfast
Credit Cards: A, B, C
Notes: 2, 4, 5, 9, 11, 12, 13, 14

GRANTS PASS

AHLF House
Bed and Breakfast

762 NW Sixth Street, 97526
(503) 474-1374

1902 Queen Anne Victorian, architecturally interesting. Largest historic residence in
Grants Pass. Furnished with lovely antiques
this beautifully appointed home offers travelers pleasing accommodations. Featured
on the walking tour of National Historic
Buildings. A Victorian evening, with music
and refreshments, is special.

Hosts: Herbert and Betty Buskirk, Rosemary
  Althaus
Rooms: 3 (SB) $65
Full Breakfast
Credit Cards: None
Notes: 2, 5

Clemens House
Bed and Breakfast Inn

612 Northwest Third Street, 97526
(503) 476-5564

Down-home hospitality is plentiful and
makes you feel at ease in the elegant surroundings of this historic home. Antiques
and family treasures are found throughout.
Guest rooms have private baths, queen
beds, and air conditioning. One suite is
extra spacious and has a small kitchenette,
while another has a fireplace and can be
made into a two-bedroom suite when the
adjoining bedroom is included. The full
breakfast is sure to please.

Hosts: Gerry and Maureen Clark
Rooms: 3 (PB) $60-70
Full Breakfast
Credit Cards: A, B
Notes: 2, 5, 8, 9, 12, 14

Lawnridge House

1304 NW Lawnridge, 97526
(503) 476-8518

Restored, antique-furnished 1909 Craftsman, shaded by 200-year-olds. Beamed ilil-
ngs, fireplace, VCR in guest livingroom.
One suite features queen canopy bed, balcony, closeted 'fridge full of goodies, TV,
air conditioned, phone, sitting room, and
bath. A second contains handmade
canopied king bed, bay windows, TV, air
conditioning, phone, private bath. A third
room offers a queen bed, bay windows,
TV. Dark wood floors, Oriental rugs, Full
NW regional breakfasts.

Host: Barbara Head
Rooms: 3 (2 PB; 1 SB) $45-70
Full Breakfast

NOTES: Credit cards accepted: A Master Card; B Visa; C American Express; D Discover Card; E Diner's
Club; F Other; 2 Personal Checks accepted; 3 Lunch available; 4 Dinner available; 5 Open all year;

Credit Cards: None
Notes: 2, 5, 8, 9, 11, 12, 14

Morrison's Rogue River Lodge

8500 Galice Road, Merlin, 97532
(503) 476-3825; (800) 826-1963

This beautiful river lodge is on the banks of the famous Rogue River in southern Oregon. Enjoy gourmet and country cuisine. Facilities include a pool, tennis, hot tub, putting green, TV, phone, air conditioning, and Fax. The lodge is famous for Steelhead fishing in the fall, and whitewater rafting trips on the "wild" section of the Rogue River. River trips are multiday, camp, or lodge trips. Hiking and photo opportunities.

Hosts: B. A. and Elaine Hanten
Rooms: 13 (PB) $80-120
Full Breakfast
Credit Cards: A, B, C
Notes: 2, 3, 4, 7, 8, 9, 10, 11, 14

The Washington Inn

1002 Washington Boulevard, 97526
(503) 476-1131

The Washington Inn is a charming Victorian listed on the National Register of Historic Places. Each guest room is named for one of the Thompsons' three children and offers individual charms. Linda's is a suite with fireplace, queen bed, private bath, and balcony; Pattie's Parlor is a red room with fireplace and large private bath with claw foot tub; Sally's Sunny View overlooks the mountains, has a canopy bed, and is decorated in delicate pink. Many interesting shops and restaurants are within easy walking distance. Fishing, rafting, and jet-boat rides can be enjoyed on the Rogue River.

Hosts: Maryan and Bill Thompson
Rooms: 3 (2 PB; 1 SB) $40-65
Full Breakfast
Credit Cards: A, B, C
Notes: 2, 5, 8, 9, 10, 12, 13, 14

HALFWAY

Birch Leaf Farm Bed and Breakfast: A Country House

Rural Route 1, Box 91, 97834
(503) 742-2990

Alpine lakes, fishing, whitewater rafting, birding, and cross-country skiing are included in the Hells Canyon National Recreation Area. This lovely historic home on a 42-acre farm has sweeping mountain views. A baby grand piano is available. Breakfast includes fresh eggs from the farm, local honey, and baked goods. Relax on the veranda and look out on the orchards and pastures. Full ranch breakfast that includes fresh eggs, fruits, and jams.

Hosts: Dave and Maryellen Olson
Rooms: 5 (1 PB; 4 SB) $55-65
Full Breakfast
Credit Cards: A, B
Notes: 2, 5, 6, 9, 11, 13, 14

HOOD RIVER

Brown's Bed and Breakfast

3000 Reed Road, 97031
(503) 386-1545

This house is a functioning farmhouse built in the early 1930s and remodeled in 1985. It has a modern kitchen where the large farm-style breakfasts are prepared, a new bathroom that is shared by the two bedrooms. One bedroom has twin beds and overlooks beautiful Mount Hood, the other bedroom has a double bed and overlooks the orchard. Nestled in the forest and at the end of the road; the only noise you hear is that of birds chirping. There are nature trails for either hiking or jogging.

Hosts: Al and Marian Brown
Rooms: 2 (SB) $60
Full Breakfast
Credit Cards: A, B
Notes: 2, 8, 11, 12, 13

6 Pets welcome; 7 Smoking allowed; 8 Children welcome; 9 Social drinking allowed; 10 Tennis available; 11 Swimming available; 12 Golf available; 13 Skiing available; 14 May be booked through travel agents.

Columbia Gorge Hotel

4000 Westcliff Drive, 97031
(503) 386-5566; (800) 345-1921

The Columbia Gorge Hotel is famous for its spectacular setting above the Columbia River, with sweeping vistas of Mt. Hood and 206-foot Wah Gwin Gwin Falls.

Host: Lynn L. LaFountaine
Rooms: 42 (PB) $175-225
Full Breakfast
Credit Cards: A, B, C, D, E

Lincoln Street Lodging

1344 Lincoln Street, 97031
(503) 386-6166

This two-bedroom suite with queen-size beds offers a kitchenette, private entrance, and a view of the mountain and marina. Air conditioned; all linens and breakfast fixings are provided. Off-street parking; a locked storage area near the staircase is perfect for storing your spare luggage. In a quiet neighborhood near the river and windsurfing; mountain biking in Columbia Gorge National Scenic Area, one-half mile from downtown, with easy freeway access and train station nearby. Portland's International Airport is one hour away, and year-round skiing on Mount Hood, one hour away.

Reames House 1868

Hosts: Paul and Linda Keir
Suite: 1 (PB) $60
Continental Breakfast
Credit Cards: None
Notes: 2, 8, 9, 10, 12, 13, 14

JACKSONVILLE

Jacksonville Inn

175 East California Street, 97530
(503) 899-1900

Jacksonville Inn offers eight air-conditioned rooms furnished with restored antiques and a historic honeymoon cottage furnished with everything imaginable. A lovely breakfast is provided. An award-winning dinner house featuring gourmet dining and more than 700 wines is in the 1861 vintage building.

Hosts: Jerry and Linda Evans
Rooms: 9 (PB) $80-175
Full Breakfast
Credit Cards: A, B, C, D, E
Notes: 2, 3, 4, 5, 8, 9, 10, 11, 12, 13, 14

Orth House Bed and Breakfast

105 West Main Street, P. O. Box 1437, 97530
(503) 899-8665

Situated in the historic corridor of Jacksonville, this house was built in 1880 and is listed on the historic register. Featured on TV and in magazines for its unique restoration with hidden electronic wizardry. One block from Britt Music Pavilion, 16 miles to ski slopes. Senior discount rates.

Hosts: The Jays
Rooms: 3 (PB) $95-175
Continental and Full Breakfast
Credit Cards: None
Notes: 2, 5, 12, 13, 14

Reames House 1868

540 East California Street, P. O. Box 128, 97530
(503) 899-1868

NOTES: Credit cards accepted: A Master Card; B Visa; C American Express; D Discover Card; E Diner's Club; F Other; 2 Personal Checks accepted; 3 Lunch available; 4 Dinner available; 5 Open all year;

Built by one of Jacksonville's early sheriffs and prosperous merchants, this inn is on the National Register of Historic Places. Victorian elegance—lace, climbing roses, and potpourri. Surrounded by spacious lawns and beautiful perennial gardens. Four guest rooms with period decor, two with private bath, share a bright sitting room furnished with white wicker, plants, and twining rose stenciling. Breakfast dishes include Oregon's bounty of fruits, berries, and home-baked goods. Three blocks from the center of town.

Hosts: George and Charlotte Harrington-Winsley
Rooms: 4 (2 PB; 2 SB) $70-90
Full Breakfast
Credit Cards: None
Notes: 2, 5, 9, 10, 11, 12, 13, 14

JOSEPH

Chandlers' Bed, Bread and Trail Inn

700 South Main Street, P. O. Box 639, 97846
(503) 432-9765

Chandlers' Bed, Bread and Trail Inn offers farm-style comfort at the foot of the Wallowa Mountains and provides a snug summer or winter home base for guests to visit local galleries and art casting foundries, the Eagle Cap Wilderness, and Hells Canyon National Recreation Area, or other seasonal activities in northeast Oregon's Switzerland of America.

Hosts: Jim and Ethel Chandler
Rooms: 5 (SB) $50
Full Breakfast
Credit Cards: A, B
Notes: 2, 5, 9, 11, 12, 13

JUNCTION CITY

Black Bart Bed and Breakfast

94125 Love Lake Road, 97448
(503) 998-1904

The Black Bart Bed and Breakfast, an 1880s farmhouse, is completely remodeled and air-conditioned. It is filled with antiques, old-fashioned charm and hospitality. Surrounded by stately maples, redwoods, and flower gardens. Guests are welcome to enjoy the parlor, read the books, stroll around the flower gardens, jog or bicycle in the country, relax in the garden room or in the privacy of their rooms. Smoking outside only. Situated 15 minutes north of Eugene.

Hosts: Don and Irma Mode
Rooms: 3 (2 PB; 1 SB) $50-70
Full Breakfast
Credit Cards: A, B, C
Notes: 2, 5, 9, 10, 11

Chandlers'

KLAMATH FALLS

Thompson's Bed and Breakfast

1420 Wild Plum Court, 97601
(503) 882-7938

Rooms with views overlooking Klamath Lake and beautiful sunsets are next door to Moore Park, with its marina, tennis courts, picnic areas, bald eagles, deer, hiking trails, and other wildlife. One hour to Crater Lake. Four rooms and three baths available. King-size beds, private entrance, and use of the family room. Full breakfast.

Host: Mary J. Thompson
Rooms: 4 (3 PB; 1 SB) $50-65
Full Breakfast
Credit Cards: None
Notes: 2, 5, 8, 9, 14

6 Pets welcome; 7 Smoking allowed; 8 Children welcome; 9 Social drinking allowed; 10 Tennis available; 11 Swimming available; 12 Golf available; 13 Skiing available; 14 May be booked through travel agents.

LAFAYETTE

Kelty Estate Bed and Breakfast

675 Third Street, P. O. Box 817, 97127
(503) 864-3740

Built in 1872 in historic Lafayette, this early Colonial-style home is on the National Register of Historic Places. Situated in the heart of Oregon Wine Country, Kelty House is ideally situated to visit the entire Willamette Valley. After enjoying a full or continental breakfast featuring Oregon-grown products, you may stroll across the street to browse at the antique mall, visit the county museum or one of the many nearby wineries. Less than an hour's drive to the state Capitol, Salem, or to the many attractions of Portland. Within two hours' drive of scenic Mount Hood, the Columbia River Gorge, or the colorful Oregon coast.

Hosts: Ron and JoAnn Ross
Rooms: 2 (PB) $55-65
Full and Continental Breakfast
Credit Cards: None
Notes: 2, 5, 8, 9, 12

LA GRANDE

Pitcher Inn Bed and Breakfast

608 "N" Avenue, 97850
(503) 963-9152

Your host and hostess lay out the welcome mat for you at their recently remodeled Georgian home. The Pitchers have redecorated their 1925 home to give it its original feel. The homey dining room with oak floor and table welcomes you in the morning for a full breakfast. Four guest rooms are available, and each room mingles a touch of romance with a different color theme and accents of roses, bows, and pitchers. Guests are welcome to enjoy the privacy of their room or join others downstairs in the livingroom. No smoking. Children over 12.

Hosts: Carl and Deanna Pitcher
Rooms: 4 (1 PB; 3 SB) $55-95
Full Breakfast
Closed January 2-15
Credit Cards: A, B
Notes: 2, 5, 8 (over 12), 10, 12, 13, 14

Stange Manor Bed and Breakfast

1612 Walnut Street, 97850
(503) 963-2400

Open the doors of this elegant old mansion and find yourself surrounded by warm hospitality and the graciousness of the 1920s. Built by lumber baron August Stang, this Georgian Colonial home is situated in the beautiful Grande Ronde Valley of northeastern Oregon, one mile from I-84. Afternoon wine and sumptuous breakfast served.

Hosts: Pat and Marjorie McClure
Rooms: 5 (PB) $60-70
Full Breakfast
Credit Cards: A, B
Notes: 2, 5, 9, 10, 11, 12, 13

LINCOLN CITY

Brey House Ocean View Bed and Breakfast Inn

3725 Northwest Keel Avenue, 97367
(503) 994-7123

This three-story Cape Cod-style house has a nautical theme that shows throughout the home. Across the street from the ocean, you are a short walk to shops and restaurants. queen-size beds are in all the rooms, and guests can use a hot tub under the stars. Close to sea lion caves, the world's smallest harbor. Lincoln City is also the kite capital of the world. Enjoy watching the ocean while eating a fantastic breakfast served by your hosts.

Hosts: Milt and Shirley Brey
Rooms: 4 (2 PB; 2 SB) $60
Full Breakfast
Credit Cards: None

NOTES: Credit cards accepted: A Master Card; B Visa; C American Express; D Discover Card; E Diner's Club; F Other; 2 Personal Checks accepted; 3 Lunch available; 4 Dinner available; 5 Open all year;

The Rustic Inn

2313 Northeast Holmes Road, 97367
(503) 994-5111

The Rustic Inn is right off Highway 101 and is one-half mile from the ocean. It has a large front porch, spacious back deck in a private garden setting. Each room has a personality of its own and the Romance of Roses room has a Jacuzzi tub for two. Awake to the aroma of coffee brewing and bread baking. Lincoln City offers many tourist attractions to make your stay enjoyable.

Hosts: Evelyn and Lloyd Bloomberg
Rooms: 3 (PB) $40-70
Full Breakfast
Credit Cards: A, B
Notes: 2, 5, 8 (over 12), 9, 12

McMINNVILLE

Steiger Haus

360 Wilson Street, 97128
(503) 472-0821

An architecturally delightful classic inn with Old World character and a lovely wooded garden setting. Within walking distance to Linfield College. Downtown restaurants and shops, regional wine trips, and northwest Oregon day trips inspire countless return visits. The *Inn Times*, 1991, named it as the number two inn in America. It is listed in *Northwest Best Places*. Member, Oregon Lodging Association, Oregon B&B Guide, and PAII. No smoking or pets.

Hosts: Doris and Lynn Steiger
Rooms: 5 (PB) $60-75
Full Breakfast
Credit Cards: A, B
Notes: 2, 8 (over 10)

Youngberg Hill Farm Bed and Breakfast/Vineyard

10660 Youngberg Hill Road, 97128
(503) 472-2727

One of Oregon's loveliest bed and breakfast inns. A farm, forest, and wine lover's paradise. Comfortable rooms (two with fireplaces) offer spectacular valley and mountain views, private baths, and central air. Sitting room, breakfast room, and covered porches. Hearty, healthful Austrian farm breakfasts. Hiking trails, abundant wildlife, March lambing, and vineyard. Winelover's wine cellar. Minutes from premiere wineries. Sumptuous dinners by prearrangement. Conference facilities. Three stars. Listed in *Northwest Best Places*.

Hosts: Eve and Norman Barnett and family
Rooms: 5 (PB) $65-75
Full Breakfast
Credit Cards: A, B, C
Closed mid-Jan.-Valentine's eve
Notes: 2, 3, 4, 5, 9, 14

MILTON-FREEWATER

Birch Tree Manor

615 South Main Street, 97862
(503) 938-6455

A handsome brick home surrounded by birch trees that offers guests pleasant, personable accommodations. Situated at the foot of the Blue Mountains in eastern Oregon, where travelers can experience year-round outdoor activities. Full breakfast with local fruit and berries, along with homemade breads and pastries.

Hosts: Ken and Priscilla Dauble
Rooms: 3 (1 PB; 2 SB) $35-45
Full Breakfast
Minimum stay holidays: 2 nights
Credit Cards: A, B
Notes: 2, 5, 8, 10, 11, 12, 13, 14

MILWAUKIE

Historic Broetje House

3101 Southeast Courtney, 97222
(503) 659-8860

6 Pets welcome; 7 Smoking allowed; 8 Children welcome; 9 Social drinking allowed; 10 Tennis available; 11 Swimming available; 12 Golf available; 13 Skiing available; 14 May be booked through travel agents.

An 1890 Queen Anne estate with 40-foot water tower nestled in quiet residential area 15 minutes from downtown Portland. Approximately two acres of lovely gardens, gazebo, and 100-year-old redwood trees. House and grounds used for weddings and receptions. Antique-filled rooms and country decor lend a warm, cozy atmosphere. Close to shopping and restaurants.

Hosts: Lorraine Hubbard and Lois Bain
Rooms: 3 (1 PB; 2 SB) $45-85
Full Breakfast
Credit Cards: A, B, C
Notes: 2, 5, 6, 8, 9, 10, 11, 12, 14

MYRTLE CREEK

Sonka's Sheep Station Inn

901 Northwest Chadwick Lane, 97457
(503) 863-5168

The Sonka Ranch covers 400 acres along the picturesque South Umpqua River. This working ranch raises purebred Dorset sheep and markets fat lambs from 800 commercial ewes. Depending on the time of the year, guests can share ranch activities such as lambing, shearing, and haying. The working border collies always give demonstrations. Enjoy rural relaxing or visit local points of interest. More than just a bed and breakfast, this inn promises a memorable stay.

Hosts: Louis and Evelyn Sonka
Rooms: 4 (3 PB; 1 SB) $50-60
Full Breakfast
Credit Cards: A, B
Closed Christmas holidays
Notes: 2, 8, 9, 14

NEWBERG

Secluded Bed and Breakfast

19719 Northeast Williamson Road, 97132
(503) 538-2635

Secluded beautiful country home situated on ten acres. The ideal retreat in the woods for hiking, country walks, and observing wildlife. Ten minutes' drive to several wineries; about one hour to the coast. Breakfast is a special occasion. Many antiques in the home. Situated near George Fox College and Linfield College.

Hosts: Durell and Del Belanger
Rooms: 2 (1 PB; 1 SB) $40-50
Full Breakfast
Credit Cards: None
Notes: 2, 5, 8, 10, 11, 12, 14

Spring Creek Llama Ranch and Bed and Breakfast

14700 Northeast Spring Creek Lane, 97132
(503) 538-5717

Discover total seclusion in the midst of 24 acres of rolling pasture and forest. This family-run farm features a llama breeding operation. Friendly llamas and contented barn cats love visitors. Guests may choose to walk wooded paths, experience farm life firsthand, or just relax. Comfortable guest rooms offer private baths, and full breakfast is tailored to guests' tastes and schedules. Air conditioned. Situated in the wine country of Yamhill County, only 35 minutes from downtown Portland.

Hosts: Dave and Melinda VanBossuyt
Rooms: 2 (PB) $50-65
Full Breakfast
Credit Cards: None
Notes: 2, 5, 8, 14

NEWPORT

Ocean House Bed and Breakfast

4920 NW Woody Way, 97365
(503) 265-6158; (503) 265-7779

Ocean House at the beautiful agate beach has guest rooms that overlook gardens and the surf. A private trail leads to beach and tide pool, and nearby attractions include the lighthouse, aquarium, marine science center, and bay front with restaurants and galleries. Storm and whale watching lure winter guests, and the spacious great room is just the place to gather. Morning coffee for early birds is followed by breakfast in the sun room.

Hosts: Bob and Bette Garrard
Rooms: 4 (PB) $65-100
Full Breakfast
Credit Cards: A, B
Notes: 2, 5, 9, 12

Sylvia Beach Hotel

267 Northwest Cliff, 97365
(503) 265-5428

Oceanfront bed and breakfast for book lovers. Each room is named after a different author and decorated individually. Some have fireplaces. Hot spiced wine is served in the library at 10:00 P.M. Dinner served nightly. Not suitable for young children. No smoking.

Hosts: Goody Cable and Sally Ford
Rooms: 20 (PB) $50-120
Full Breakfast
Credit Cards: A, B, C
Notes: 2, 4, 5, 9

NORTH BEND

Highlands Bed and Breakfast

608 Ridge Road, 97459
(503) 756-0300

Unbelievable panoramic views from this tranquil 3,000-square-foot cedar home on six secluded acres. Guests have a separate ground-floor entrance to their own family room with wood-burning stove, completely equipped kitchen, two beautifully appointed bedrooms (one with whirlpool tub), and a romantic spa on secluded deck. Private phones, satellite TV/VCR. Full breakfast served on expansive deck.

Hosts: Jim and Marilyn Dow
Rooms: 2 (PB) $65-70
Full Breakfast
Credit Cards: A, B
Notes: 2, 5, 7 (on deck), 8 (over 10), 9, 10, 11, 12, 14

OREGON CITY

Inn of the Oregon Trail

416 South McLoughlin, 97045
(503) 656-2089

A Gothic Revival-style home built in 1867 by E. B. Fellows, a ship's captain on the Willamette River. Three tastefully appointed guest rooms on the third floor overlook landscaped gardens. An additional room on the bottom fkoor offers a private entrance, bath, fireplace, and wet bar. The main floor houses the Fellows House Restaurant, open to the public Monday-Friday, 11:00 A.M.-3:00 P.M. Private dinners for inn guests are available with prior notice. Discover historic Oregon City, the end of the Oregon Trail. Just nine miles east of Portland on 99 East.

Hosts: Mary and Tom DeHaven
Rooms: 4 (PB) $47.50-77.50
Full Breakfast
Credit Cards: A, B
Notes: 2, 3, 4, 5, 9

Jagger House Bed and Breakfast

512 Sixth Street, 97045
(503) 657-7820

Furnished with antiques and reproductions, this carefully restored 1880 house has many special touches, including a garden gazebo, handmade folk art, the house jigsaw puzzle, and privacy. Oregon City, 12 miles south of Portland, is the official end of the Oregon Trail, with five museums within two blocks of the inn. The innkeeper is an old house fanatic and is very knowledgeable of local history and local walking tours.

Host: Claire Met
Rooms: 3 (1 PB; 2 SB) $55-60
Full Breakfast
Credit Cards: A, B
Notes: 2, 5, 10, 11, 12, 13, 14

PORTLAND

General Hooker's Bed and Breakfast

125 Southwest Hooker, 97201
(503) 222-4435; (800) 745-4135
FAX (503) 222-4435

Superbly located in a quiet historic district within walking distance of downtown, General Hooker's is a casually elegant Victorian town house that combines the best of two centuries: the mellow charm of family heirlooms from the 19th century, and the comfort and convenience of the 20th century. Eclectic in ambience, the house features a restrained use of Victorian detail, an interesting collection of northwestern art (some done by artists in the host's family), comfortable, tasteful furniture, and the music of Bach and Vivaldi playing throughout. Knowledgable host is a fourth-generation Portlander and a charter member of Oregon's B&B Guild. Sociable Abyssinian cat in residence. Wine and beer sold on premises.

Host: Lori Hall
Rooms: 4 (1 PB; 3 SB) $70-105
Expanded Continental Breakfast
Minimum stay holidays: 2 nights
Credit Cards: A, B, C
Notes: 2, 5, 8 (over 10), 9

General Hooker's

John Palmer House

4314 North Mississippi Avenue, 97217
(503) 284-5893

Forty-five minutes from Columbia Gorge, Mount Hood, and wine country. One hour from the Pacific Ocean. This beautiful, historic Victorian can be your home away from home. Award-winning decor; gourmet chef. Your hosts delight in providing the extraordinary. Dinner available. Wine sold on premises.

Hosts: Mary and Richard Sauter
Rooms: 7 (2 PB; 5 SB) $112.65
Full Breakfast
Credit Cards: A, B (6% service charge), C, D
Notes: 2, 4 (with notice), 5, 8, 9, 14

Pittock Acres Bed and Breakfast

103 NW Pittock Avenue, 97210
(503) 226-1163

This lovely eighteen-year-old contemporary with traditional, Victorian, and country furnishings is located on a quiet country lane just five minutes from downtown Portland and within easy access to historic Pittock Mansion. From the mansion grounds, walk beautiful forested trails to the zoo, Hoyt Arboretum, Washington Park, and the beautiful Japanese and rose gardens. Bus service is close by, as are fine restaurants, art galleries, and all major attractions and transportation.

Hosts: Linda and Richard Matson
Rooms: 3 (2 PB; 1 SB) $60-70 plus tax
Full Breakfast
Credit Cards: A, B, C, D
Notes: 2, 5, 8 (over 13), 14

Portland Guest House

1720 Northeast Fifteenth Street, 97212
(503) 282-1402

Portland's most convenient address. A Victorian jewel in the historic Irvington neighborhood, this guest house is the closest bed and breakfast to the convention center, Coliseum, Lloyd Center, public transit, including MAX line. Exquisite accommodations: great beds, vintage linens, private phones, a spacious suite, and luscious breakfasts. Stroll through herb, vegetable, and flower gardens. No smoking. Excellent value.

Host: Susan Gisvold
Rooms: 4 (2 PB; 2 SB) $40-60
Family Suite: 1 (PB) $75-95
Full Breakfast
Credit Cards: A, B, C
Notes: 2, 5, 9, 10, 14

Portland's White House

1814 NE 22nd Avenue, 97212
(503)287-7131

This elegant historic landmark house, with its stately Greek columns, carriage house, fountains and circular driveway, has been restored to its former splendor. You will easily see why this mansion is referred to as the White House. The impressive entry foyer with its original handpainted garden murals and oak inlaid floors greets you as you enter, and on the second floor the feeling of old-fashioned romantic elegance is carried through the six guest rooms.

Hosts: Larry and Mary Hough
Rooms: 6 (PB) $88-104
Full Breakfast
Credit Cards: A, B
Notes: 2, 5, 14

PORT ORFORD

Home by the Sea Bed and Breakfast

P. O. Box 606, 97465-0606
(503) 332-2855; FAX (503) 332-7585

The hosts built their contemporary wood home on a spit of land overlooking a stretch of Oregon coast that takes your breath away. Queen-size Oregon myrtle wood beds and cable TV are featured in both accommodations, which make ideal quarters for two couples traveling together.

It's a short walk to restaurants, public beaches, historic Battle Rock Park, and the town's harbor. Amenities include a dramatic ocean view, direct beach access, smoke-free environment, full breakfast, laundry privileges, cable TV, and phone jacks in the rooms. No pets. No children. Brochure available.

Hosts: Alan and Brenda Mitchell
Rooms: 2 (PB) $60-70
Full Breakfast
Credit Cards: A, B
Notes: 2, 5, 9, 10, 12

ST HELEN'S

Hopkins House Bed and Breakfast

105 South First Street, 97051
(503) 397-4676

This restored 1905 Dutch Colonial in historic Olde Towne offers you the waterfront and quaint shops only two blocks away. Fishing, boating, public golf course, tennis, and a small airport are within six miles. Enjoy the fireplace in the parlor and the player piano in the dining room. Midway between mountain skiing and beautiful Oregon beaches, you are just 50 minutes from Portland, Oregon, and across the Columbia River from Washington State.

Host: Evelyn Neal Hopkins
Rooms: 3 (1 PB; 2 SB) $40-60
Full Breakfast
Credit Cards: None
Notes: 2, 5, 7 (outside), 8, 9, 10, 11, 12, 13, 14

SEASIDE

Gaston's Beachside Bed and Breakfast

921 South Prom, 97138-5415
(503) 738-8320

On the promenade, with panoramic views of the Pacific Ocean, this gracious 1940 home is decorated with country antiques.

6 Pets welcome; 7 Smoking allowed; 8 Children welcome; 9 Social drinking allowed; 10 Tennis available; 11 Swimming available; 12 Golf available; 13 Skiing available; 14 May be booked through travel agents.

Just four blocks from downtown with the beach just outside your door, enjoy watching the ocean in the summer or the winter storms from a large livingroom in front of a fireplace. If you have family or just want more privacy and a private bath, we suggest you rent both rooms for $65 ($80 for four people). Seaside is a destination resort community.

Host: Helen Gaston
Rooms: 2 (SB) $40-65
Full Breakfast
Credit Cards: None
Notes: 2, 5, 8, 9, 11, 12, 14

Gilbert Inn
Bed and Breakfast

341 Beach Drive, 97138
(503) 738-9770

The Gilbert Inn, Seaside's only Queen Anne Victorian, was built in the late 1800s. Today the inn features ten guest rooms, all with private baths, plush carpeting, antiques, and down quilts. The past has been left intact and modern comforts have been added. The house features 1892 natural fir tongue- and-groove ceilings and walls on the first two floors. The parlor features a large fireplace and is filled with flowery country French furniture and antiques. The Gilbert Inn is a wonderful escape to the past and you can walk to everything—one block from the ocean and one block to Broadway.

Hosts: Dick and Carole Rees
Rooms: 10 (PB) $65-80
Full Breakfast
Credit Cards: A, B, D
Closed January
Notes: 2, 8, 9

Riverside Inn
Bed and Breakfast

430 South Holladay Drive, 97138
(503) 738-8254; (800) 826-6151

A charming country-style inn situated on the Necanicum River in Seaside, on Oregon's beautiful north coast. All private baths and separate entrances give each room or suite the privacy and seclusion of a small, quaint hotel. Spectacular garden deck overlooks the river. Featured twice on TV's "P.M. Magazine" and listed in Northwest Best Places every year since

Gilbert Inn

1984. One of the most popular inns on the north Oregon coast. Now in its thirteenth year. Member of Oregon Bed and Breaakfast Guild.

Hosts: Sharon and Ken Ward
Rooms: 11 (PB) $45-85
Full Breakfast
Credit Cards: A, B, D
Notes: 2, 5, 8, 9,

SUBLIMITY

Silver Mountain
Bed and Breakfast

4672 Drift Creek Road SE, 97385
(503) 769-7127

This is a working farm located in the Cascade foothills near Salem. A one-half hour drive from mountains, the coast, and Portland; a five-minute drive to Silver Falls State Park for biking, picnicking, biking, and horseback riding. Stay in the modernized "barn" with a Jacuzzi, sauna, pool table, Ping Pong, TV, fireplace, and kitchen. Fishing, hiking, white-water rafting, and float trips available on the nearby Santiam River. Join in the farm chores or enjoy some solitude. Closed November through February.

Hosts: Jim and Shirley Heater
Rooms: 2 (SB) $30-50
Full Breakfast
Credit Cards: None
Notes: 2, 3, 4, 8, 10, 11, 12

WALDPORT

Cliff House

Adahi Street-Yaquina John Point, Box 436, 97394
(503) 563-2506

Each room is uniquely decorated with antiques, chandeliers, carpeting, remote control color TV; all have private cedar baths and balconies. Elegant lodging coupled with magnificent panoramic ocean view. Deep-sea fishing, river fishing, crabbing, golf club (one-half mile), croquet. Horseback riding close by; massage by appointment.

Hosts: Gabrielle Duvall and Debra J. Novgrod
Rooms: 5 (PB) $95-225
Full Breakfast
Minimum stay weekends: 2 nights; holidays: 3 nights
Credit Cards: A, B
Closed Oct. 15-March 31
Notes: 2, 4, 9, 10, 11, 12, 14

YACHATS

Ziggurat

95330 Highway 101, P. O. Box 757, 97498
(503) 547-3925

Ziggurat means "terraced pyramid," and this one is a spectacular, contemporary, four-story sculpture by the sea. Guests have the privacy of the entire first floor, with a sauna, solarium, and library/livingroom. There are glass-enclosed decks on the second floor for ocean viewing, where superb food is served. Dunes, parks, and coastal activities are nearby.

Hosts: Mary Lou Cavendish and Irv Tebor
Rooms: 3 (PB) $85-125
Full Breakfast
Credit Cards: None
Closed Christmas and February
Notes: 2, 8 (over 14), 9, 14

YAMHILL

Flying M Ranch

23029 Northwest Flying M Road, 97148
(503) 662-3222; FAX (503) 662-3202

The bounty of Yamhill County's wine country joins with the coastal mountains to harbor the Flying M's spectacular log lodge. Delectable cuisine, year-round horseback riding, limitless outdoor activities. Full-service restaurant, lounge, airstrip, gift shop, primitive camping, fishing, and dancing on Friday and Saturday evenings.

Hosts: Bryce and Barbara Mitchell
Rooms: 35 (PB) $50-150
Full Breakfast
Credit Cards: A, B, C, E
Notes: 2, 3, 4, 5, 6, 7, 8, 9, 10, 11, 14

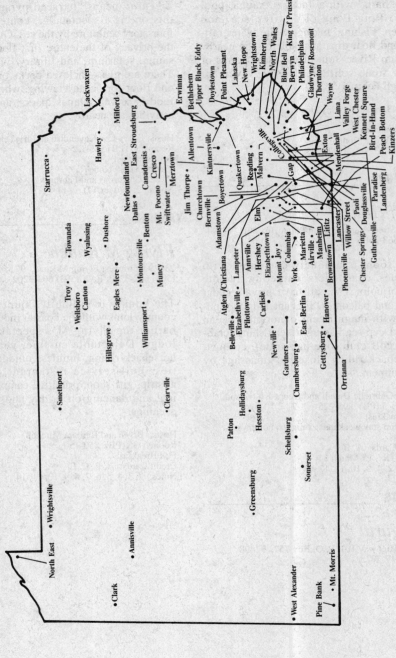

PENNSYLVANIA

Pennsylvania

ADAMSTOWN

Adamstown Inn

62 W. Main Street, 19501
(215) 484-0800; (800) 594-4808

Experience the simple elegance of the
Adamstown Inn, a Victorian bed and
breakfast resplendent with leaded-glass
windows and door, magnificent chestnut
woodwork, and Oriental rugs. All four
guest rooms are decorated with family heirlooms, handmade quilts, lace curtains, fresh
flowers, and many distinctive touches that
make your stay special. The accommodations range from antique to king-size beds.
All rooms have private baths (two rooms
feature two-person Jacuzzis). The
Adamstown Inn is in the heart of the
antique district and only minutes from the
Reading Outlet Centers and Lancaster.
Come experience the joy and magic of yesteryear.

Hosts: Tom and Wanda Berman
Rooms: 4 (PB) $65-105
Expanded Continental Breakfast
Credit Cards: A, B
Notes: 2, 5, 7 (limited), 8 (over 12), 9, 10, 11, 12,
14

Spring House

AIRVILLE

Spring House

Muddy Creek Forks, 17302
(717) 927-6906

Built in 1798 of fieldstone, the house is
named for the pure spring it protects in the
tranquil pre-Revolutionary War river valley
village. Lovingly restored to stenciled
whitewashed walls, furnished with antiques
and art, the inn offers full breakfast of local
specialties, wine by the fire or on the front
porch, Amish-made cheese, and caring hospitality. Horseback riding, wineries, hiking,
and trout fishing in immediate area. Near
Amish community.

Host: Ray Constance Hearne
Rooms: 5 (3 PB; 2 SB) $52-85

NOTES: Credit cards accepted: A Master Card; B Visa; C American Express; D Discover Card; E Diner's
Club; F Other; 2 Personal Checks accepted; 3 Lunch available; 4 Dinner available; 5 Open all year; 6 Pets
welcome; 7 Smoking allowed; 8 Children welcome; 9 Social drinking allowed; 10 Tennis available; 11
Swimming available; 12 Golf available; 13 Skiing available; 14 May be booked through travel agents.

Full Breakfast
Minimum stay weekends and holidays: 2 nights
Credit Cards: None
Notes: 2, 5, 8, 9, 11, 12, 14

ALLENTOWN

Coachaus—The City Inn

107-111 North Eighth Street, 18101
(215) 821-4854; (800) 762-8680
FAX (215) 821-6862

Five gracious, century-old, lovingly restored brownstones provide a center-city oasis from which to explore antique shops, historic sites, museums, fine dining, golf, hiking, skiing, and professional theater. The rooms, apartments, and town houses all have a unique charm and are fully equipped with the finest amenities for your relaxation.

Host: Barbara Kocher
Rooms: 24 (PB) $75-155
Full Breakfast
Credit Cards: A, B, C, D, E
Notes: 2, 5, 7, 8, 9, 10, 11, 12, 13, 14

ANNVILLE

Hershey Bed and Breakfast Reservation Service

P. O. Box 208, Hershey, 17033-0208
(717) 533-2928

Victorian mansion built in 1860, 10 miles from Hershey, 18 miles from Harrisburg, and 2 miles from Indiantown Gap. All queen-size beds in ten guest rooms. Four of the rooms can accommodate four people. Children welcome. Full breakfast. Air conditioning, private bath. No smoking. $50-70.

Swatara Creek Inn

Box 692, Rural Delivery 2, 17003
(717) 865-3259

An 1860 Victorian mansion in a country setting near Hershey and featuring nine rooms with private baths, air conditioning, queen-size canopy beds, and a full breakfast served in the dining room. Sitting room and gift shop on the first floor. Restaurant within walking distance. Near Amish and outlet shops and Renaissance Faire at Mount Hope Winery. No pets; no smoking.

Rooms: 9 (PB) $50-70
Full Breakfast
Credit Cards: A, B, C, D
Notes: 2, 5, 8, 9, 10, 11, 12, 14

ARDMORE

Ardmore Bon Vivant

Bed and Breakfast of Philadelphia
1616 Walnut Street, Suite 1120, Philadelphia, 19103
(215) 735-1917; (800) 220-1917
FAX (215) 735-1905

This attractively decorated suburban home is on a tree-lined street and offers second-floor sitting room with TV and wicker furniture for guest relaxation. All rooms have private baths. $50-60.

ATGLEN

Glen-Run Valley View Farm

Rural Delivery 1, Box 69, 19310
(215) 593-5656

Swatara Creek Inn

A charming old farm, neatly furnished in the heart of Pennsylvania Dutch country. Three rooms tucked away for guests to enjoy. Wonderful farm breakfast. The coffee pot is always hot. Many things to see and do in Amish country: Longwood Gardens, Hershey Chocolate Factory, Outlets City, all within 15 miles. Wake up to a rooster crowing and many farm activities. No smoking.

Hosts: Harold and Hanna Stoltzfus
Rooms: 3 (1 PB; 2 SB) $50
Full Breakfast
Credit Cards: None
Notes: 2, 5, 6, 10, 12, 14

Highland View Bed and Breakfast

Highland Road, P. O. Box 154C, 19310
(215) 593-5066

Highland View is surrounded by farmlands. Guests get a warm welcome staying with this Mennonite couple in this ranch-style home. A full breakfast is served in a brightly lit sun room. The village of Intercourse, shopping outlets, Longwood gardens, and many family style restaurants are within fifteen to twenty minutes away. King- and queen-size beds are available. Rooms are air-conditioned.

Hosts: Sam and Cora Umble
Rooms: 2 (SB) $40-45
Full Breakfast
Credit Cards: None
Notes: 2, 4, 5, 8, 12

AUDUBON

Bonny Blue Farm— 1750 Farmhouse

Bed and Breakfast of Valley Forge #0800
P. O. Box 1151, Valley Forge, 19481-1151
(215) 783-7838; (800) 344-0123

Situated on three acres of woodland and gardens, this stone farmhouse was built around 1750 on part of a William Penn land grant. Enjoy the warmth and hospitality of this Colonial home with an outdoor hot tub set near a four-square garden with roses, lavender, Medieval Elizabethean, and biblical gardens. Minutes from Valley Forge, one-half hour to Lancaster and Brandywine. Three guest rooms, three baths, one room with a king-size waterbed. $65-85.

BELLVILLE

Hickory Grove Bed and Breakfast

Rural Delivery 1, Box 281, 17004
(717) 935-5289

Charming country style in the heart of Amish country describes this bed and breakfast, which is only 30 minutes from Penn State. Other nearby attractions include state parks, the Big Valley Auction and Flea Market, crafts, antiques, gift and quilt shops, plus a craft shop on the premises. Enjoy the flower and vegetable gardens, swing under the grape arbor, picnic on the patio. Homemade muffins and fruit cobbler made from fresh berries raised at Hickory Grove grace the breakfast table. Private entrance, fireplace, family room.

Hosts: Caleb and Bertha Peachey
Rooms: 5 (1 PB; 4 SB) $40-45
Expanded Continental Breakfast
Credit Cards: None
Notes: 2, 5, 8

BERNVILLE

Sunday's Mill Farm Bed and Breakfast

Rural Delivery 2, P. O. Box 419, 19506
(215) 488-7821

In 1723, German settlers came to this beautiful site in Western Berks County. The property is listed on the National Register of Historic Places as part of the Historic

District. A convenient 12 miles from Reading, the outlet capital of the world, this bed and breakfast is now a twenty-three-acre farm. Guests may tour the 1820s stone grist mill and the 1850 house, which is furnished with antiques and original paintings. Fishing is available at the pond and nearby creek.

Hosts: Sally and Len Blumberg
Rooms: 5 (1 PB; 4 SB) $45-60
Full Breakfast
Credit Cards: None
Notes: 2, 5, 7 (outside), 8, 9, 11, 12, 13, 14

BERWYN

Bed and Breakfast Connections #00243

P. O. Box 21, Devon, 19333
(215) 687-3565; (800) 448-3619 (outside PA)

This charming 1770 fieldstone farmhouse is in the picturesque countryside of Main Line Philadelphia near area universities, the Brandywine Valley, and Valley Forge park. Two second-floor guest rooms with a shared bath are in the old part of the home. Each room has a four-poster canopied queen-size bed. Also available on the second floor is a large room with views of the pastures, canopied king-size bed, and private attached bath. A delicious breakfast is served in the breakfast nook. A turnout shed and pasture are available for a guest's horse. Resident dog. No smoking. $85-110.

C. 1770 Country Farmhouse

Bed and Breakfast of Valley Forge # 0501
P. O. Box 1151, Valley Forge, 19481-1151
(215) 783-7838; (800) 344-0123

This farmhouse features beamed ceilings, hand-stenciled walls, antique country furnishings, samplers, and local quilts. The oldest part is a restored 1770 tenant house. Set on five acres, there are pastoral views from every room. Your guest room may have a canopy bed and fireplace, or a pri-

vate stairway to the cozy den with fireplace. A hearty country breakfast will be served in a brick-floored sun room overlooking the gardens. Minutes from tennis and swimming. Resident Pomeranian. Three guest rooms with private bath. $85-110.

Greystone Manor

Hilltop Privacy

Bed and Breakfast of Valley Forge #1912
P. O. Box 1151, Valley Forge, 19481-1151
(215) 783-7838; (800) 344-0123

This home is situated in a quiet wooded area. The guest quarters occupy the entire downstairs and include two bedrooms, family room with fireplace, hot tub solarium, and bar area with private entrance off the gardens. Other amenities include cable TV, refrigerator, phone, air conditioning, laundry facilities, use of the kitchen, and a breathtaking setting. Ingredients for breakfast are provided; self-serve at your leisure. Basic French and Dutch spoken. Weekly and monthly rates upon request.

BIRD-IN-HAND

Greystone Manor Bed and Breakfast

2658 Old Philadelphia Pike, Box 270, 17505
(717) 393-4233

NOTES: Credit cards accepted: A Master Card; B Visa; C American Express; D Discover Card; E Diner's Club; F Other; 2 Personal Checks accepted; 3 Lunch available; 4 Dinner available; 5 Open all year;

Greystone Manor is a lovely old French Victorian mansion and carriage house with Victorian furnishings, decorative windows and doors. Surrounded by Amish farms. Minutes from Lancaster, Intercourse, Strasburg, outlet malls, farmers' market, and local craft shops. Quilt shop in mansion basement.

Hosts: Sally and Ed Davis
Rooms: 13 (PB) $55-90
Continental Breakfast
Credit Cards: A, B
Notes: 2, 5, 7 (limited), 8, 9, 10, 12, 14

The Village Inn of Bird-in-Hand

Box 253, 2695 Old Philadelphia Pike, 17505
(717) 293-8369

The historic Village Inn of Bird-in-Hand was originally built in 1834. The innkeepers reside in the inn and provide you with the finest hospitality. It is situated in the heart of the Pennsylvania Dutch country. Each morning a continental breakfast including fresh fruits, pastries, and cereals is served. All guests enjoy free use of the indoor and outdoor swimming pools and tennis courts within walking distance. A complimentary tour of the surrounding Amish farmlands is offered daily, except Sunday.

Hosts: Richmond and Janice Young
Rooms: 11 (PB) $65-139
Continental Breakfast
Credit Cards: A, B, C, D
Notes: 2, 5, 7, 8, 10 ,11

BLUE BELL

Stoney Creek

Bed and Breakfast of Valley Forge #1905
P. O. Box 1151, Valley Forge, 19481-1151
(215) 783-7838; (800) 344-0123

Guest quarters are reached through a private entrance from a garden walkway and have a fully equipped kitchen, cozy parlor, bedroom, and bath. Breakfast foods are provided in your kitchen. Enjoy 15 acres with bank barn, springhouse, orchard, stream, and swimming pool. Lots of room to roam, relax, and enjoy! $75. Weekly and monthly rates available.

The Enchanted Cottage

BOYERTOWN

The Enchanted Cottage

South Benfield Road, Box 337
Rural Delivery 4, 19512
(215) 845-8845

You'll be the only guests in this rustic, romantic, one and one-half story Cotswold-like stone cottage nestled among rolling, wooded acres. Gourmet breakfasts are served in the main house beside the garden or before a blazing fire. Fine restaurant within walking distance. Close to historic sites, country auctions, Amish area, antiques, retail outlets, and flea markets. With fresh flowers and complimentary wine and cheese, this bed and breakfast offers an informal but gracious lifestyle in a storybook atmosphere.

Hosts: Peg and Richard Groff
Room: 1 (PB) $80
Full Breakfast
Credit Cards: None
Notes: 2, 3, 4, 5, 7, 9, 10, 12, 13, 14

6 Pets welcome; 7 Smoking allowed; 8 Children welcome; 9 Social drinking allowed; 10 Tennis available; 11 Swimming available; 12 Golf available; 13 Skiing available; 14 May be booked through travel agents.

Indian Mountain Inn

buildings, gardens, paths, and trails, each season is special at this bed and breakfast. Well-appointed rooms offer canopied king-size beds, queens, doubles, twins, and suites, five large country baths with showers. All rooms have TV, and most have private baths. A full country breakfast with homemade breads, muffins, croissants, and other goodies is served each morning. Concierge services are offered, and arrangements can be made for local activities. $75-110.

BRACKNEY

Indian Mountain Inn

Rural Delivery 1, Box 68, Tripp Lake Road, 18812
(800) 435-3362

Built in 1890, the inn is sequestered in over 3,500 acres of scenic wilderness, with five miles of trails for hiking and cross-country skiing. Specializing in authentic country cuisine prepared by the chef, a graduate of the Culinary College in Washington, D.C. Accommodations include a gourmet breakfast. Hot tub, ice skating, and theme weekend are part of the amenities; golf, antiques, fishing, and downhill skiing are all nearby. Discover the undiscovered endless mountains, just 12 miles south of Binghamton, New York.

Hosts: Nancy and Dan Strnatka
Rooms: 10 (8 PB; 2 SB) $65-75
Full Breakfast
Credit Cards: A, B
Notes: 3, 4, 5, 6 (call), 7 (limited), 8, 9, 12, 13, 14

BRANDYWINE

Bed and Breakfast Connections #00358

P. O. Box 21, Devon, 19333
(215) 687-3565; (800) 448-3619 (outside PA)

Discover this tucked-away, quietly elegant manor house near the heart of the Brandywine Valley. With 36 acres, historic

BROGUE

Bed and Breakfast Collections #00311

P. O. Box 21, Devon, 19333
(215) 687-3565; (800) 448-3619 (outside PA)

Lovingly restored, this late 1800s six-room guest house is nestled in the woods beside a meandering stream. Relax on the screen porch, and take in the beauty and serenity of this magnificent Susquehanna River estate that once was the home of Benjamin Franklin's grandson. Fish in the stream, swim in the old-fashioned swimming hole, bike or jog on the country roads, or wander through the grist mill that is being restored. Fine restaurants and a winery are nearby. Lancaster County attractions are within an easy drive. This is an ideal spot for business meetings with phone and FAX available. $95.

BROWNSVILLE

Pineapple Inn Bed and Breakfast

50 Main Street, 17508
(717) 656-0566

Candlewick Inn Bed and Breakfast was built in 1840. The rooms have tall poster canopy beds with private baths. The inn is furnished with antiques. It retains the original wide-pine flooring, and three fireplaces. An antique shop is on premises. The hosts will be more than glad to share their knowledge of Amish country antique shops and local history with their guests.

Hosts: Mary and Bernie Peters
Rooms: 2 (PB) $65-75
Full Breakfast
Credit Cards: A, B
Notes: 5, 7 (outside), 8 , 9

BUCKS COUNTY

Mill Creek Farm

Bed and Breakfast of Philadelphia
1616 Walnut Street, Suite 1120, Philadelphia, 19103
(215) 735-1917; (800) 220-1917
FAX (215) 735-1905

Situated on fourteen beautiful acres in Bucks County, your host raises Thoroughbred horses on this classical Colonial farmstead. Them original part of the stone house was built in 1750, and the second section was added before 1800. Three guest rooms, all with private baths, are available. A full breakfast is served each morning. Children welcome. No smoking. $115-125.

1819 Farmhouse

Bed and Breakfast of Philadelphia
1616 Walnut Street, Suite 1120, Philadelphia, 19103
(215) 735-1917; (800) 220-1917
FAX (215) 735-1905

Step through the door of this Bucks County farmhouse and go back a century in time. Country crafts and antique farm implements, five fireplaces, and a Franklin stove, wide-plank floors and trestle tables all seduce you into believing you have been lost in time. The two bedrooms on the second floor share a bath, and feature working fireplaces for cool nights and four-poster beds. Breakfasts are a treat and could include such Pennsylvania specialities as shoofly pie or homemade scrapple. Children welcome. Smoking allowed. Pets allowed for an extra charge. $75-85.

Upper Black Eddy B&B

Bed and Breakfast of Valley Forge #1302
P. O. Box 1151, Valley Forge, 19481-1151
(215) 783-7838; (800) 344-0123

Welcome to peace and serenity in this 1820 farm house situated on 26 acres surrounded by hundreds of acres of wildlife preserve. Within minutes of the finest restaurants along the delaware, and just twenty minutes to New Hope. Three antique-filled guest rooms. $115-135.

CANADENSIS

Brookview Manor Bed and Breakfast Inn

Rural Route 1, Box 365, 18325
(717) 595-2451

Situated on four picturesque acres in the Pocono Mountains, Brookview Manor offers eight guest rooms and suites uniquely appointed with country and antique furnishings. Enjoy the wraparound porch, hiking trails, fishing, and nearby skiing, golf, tennis, boating, and antiquing. A delicious full breakfast, afternoon refreshments, and warm hospitality are all included.

Hosts: Lee and Nancie Cabana
Rooms: 8 (6 PB; 2 SB) $65-145
Full Breakfast
Credit Cards: A, B, C, D
Notes: 2, 5, 8 (over 12), 9, 10, 11, 12, 13, 14

Dreamy Acres

Box 7, 18325
(717) 595-7115

Dreamy Acres is situated in the heart of the Pocono Mountains vacationland on three acres of land with a stream flowing into a small pond. The house is 500 feet back from the highway, giving a pleasing, quiet atmosphere.

Hosts: Esther and Bill Pickett
Rooms: 6 (4 PB; 2 SB) $34-50
Continental Breakfast (May-October)

---

6 Pets welcome; 7 Smoking allowed; 8 Children welcome; 9 Social drinking allowed; 10 Tennis available; 11 Swimming available; 12 Golf available; 13 Skiing available; 14 May be booked through travel agents.

Minimum stay weekends: 2 nights; holidays: 3 nights
Credit Cards: None
Closed Christmas
Notes: 2, 7, 8, 9, 10, 11, 12, 13

The Pine Knob Inn

P. O. Box 295, 18325
(717) 595-2532

Step back into yesteryear. Experience the
atmosphere of years gone by in this 1840s
inn situated on 6.5 acres abounding with
antiques and art. Enjoy gourmet dining.
Wine and spirits available. Guests gather
on the veranda on summer evenings or by
the fireplace after a day on the slopes.
Daily rate includes breakfast and dinner.
Perfect place for a wedding.

Hosts: Dick and Charlotte Dornich
Rooms: 27 (21 PB; 6 SB) $145
Full Breakfast
Credit Cards: A, B
Notes: 2, 4, 5, 7, 8 (over 5), 9, 10, 11, 12, 13

Pump House Inn

Skytop Road, 18325
(717) 595-7501

High in the Poconos, the Pump House Inn
dates from 1842. Antiques, books, and distinctive furnishings grace this friendly
country inn. Sophisticated dining is the
mainstay at the Pump House, where the
chef emphasizes French continental cuisine.

Host: John Keeney
Rooms: 6 (2 PB; 4 SB) $65-100
Continental Breakfast
Credit Cards: A, B, E, F
Notes: 2, 4, 5, 7, 8, 9, 10, 11, 12, 13, 14

CANTON

Mm-m Good

Rural Delivery 1, Box 71, 17724
(717) 673-8153

Located in the center of the endless mountains of Pennsylvania, this large bed and
breakfast has a large lawn with picnic
tables under sugar maple trees. In the
morning the host serves a full breakfast of
your choice, including homemade muffins
and rolls.

Hosts: Melvin and Irene Good
Rooms: 3 (SB) $23.50
Full Breakfast
Credit Cards: None
Notes: 2, 5, 8

CARLISLE

Line Limousin Farmhouse Bed and Breakfast

2070 Ritner Highway, 17013
(717) 243-1281

This 110-acre homestead has an eleven-
room brick and stone home. It is only one
and one-half miles from Exit 12 of I-81 and
within close proximity to Dickinson
College and many fine restaurants. Carlisle
Fairgrounds, home of many fine automobile shows, are nearby. Furnishings inside
the inn include antiques and a player piano
that guests will enjoy pumping. Hosts raise
Limousin beef cattle, and guests may play
croquet, bocce ball, or drive golf balls on
two of the golf courses that border the
farm. No smoking.

Hosts: Robert and Joan Line
Rooms: 4 (2 PB; 2 SB) $45-55
Full Breakfast
Credit Cards: None
Notes: 2, 5, 8, 9, 12

CHALFONT

Bed and Breakfast Connections #00356

P. O. Box 21, 19333
(215) 687-3565; (800) 448-3619

Nestled in beautiful central Bucks County,
this inn offers comfortable lodging on more
than four handsomely landscaped acres.
Thoughtful improvements by each succes-
sive owner have enhanced the property to

its present state. Each room is tastefully furnished with period pieces reflecting a warm and relaxing atmosphere. There is a cozy fireplace to enjoy in the winter, and a patio and swimming pool to enjoy in the summer. Sleep in the luxury of a queen-size spindle-post bed, or choose the cozy twin-bed room. Private and semi-private baths. A full gourmet breakfast is served in the dining room. $65-95.

CHAMBERSBURG

Falling Spring Inn

1838 Falling Spring Road, 17201
(717) 267-3654

Enjoy country life in a mid-19th-century Pennsylvania stone farmhouse. Falling Spring Inn is conveniently situated two miles south off Exit 6 of I-81 and Route 30 in Chambersburg. The inn takes its name from the Falling Spring, a nationally renowned freshwater trout stream that moves slowly through inn property. The stream, a large pond, lawns, meadows, and wooded areas make for a pleasant overnight stay.

Hosts: Adin and Janet L. Frey
Rooms: 5 (PB) $49-69
Full Breakfast
Credit Cards: A, B
Notes: 2, 5, 8

CHESTER SPRINGS

Bed and Breakfast Collections #00216

P. O. Box 21, Devon, 19333
(215) 687-3565; (800) 448-3619 (outside PA)

Complimentary wine or sparkling water await you upon your arrival at this lovely 1830s farmhouse with classic mid-century features. Two spacious guest rooms share a hall bath. While visiting, you are invited to jog or walk a meandering trail or relax by

the stream on this quiet ten-acre country retreat. A continental-plus breakfast is served in the dining room in front of the original fireplace and beehive oven. No smoking. Resident cat. $65.

Springdale Farm

Bed and Breakfast of Valley Forge #1302
P. O. Box 1151, Valley Forge, 19481-1151
(215) 783-7838; (800) 344-0123

A circa 1840 farmhouse on ten acres of lawns and woods perfect for biking, jogging, hiking, or just appreciating. Good location for Longwood Gardens and Brandywine area. An expanded continental breakfast is served in the formal dining room, with random width flooring, fireplace, and beehive oven. You may choose to stay in the Blue Room with a reading corner and windows on three sides, or Grandmother's Room with Early American pine furniture and rope bed. Enjoy fireplaces, porches, barbecue, patio, and chairs by the stream. $65-75.

CHRISTIANA

Winding Glen Farm Guest House

107 Noble Road, 17509
(215) 593-5535

Winding Glen is a dairy farm situated in a beautiful valley. The house is 250 years old with 16-inch-thick stone walls. Watch the cows being milked, walk to the covered bridge, visit Amish shops nearby, see handmade quilts, or just relax on the front porch. You are welcome to worship in a Mennonite church on Sunday morning.

Host: Minnie B. Metzler
Rooms: 5 (SB) $35
Full Breakfast
Credit Cards: None
Notes: 2, 5, 8, 12

CHURCHTOWN

The Foreman House Bed and Breakfast

2129 Main Street, 17555
(215) 445-6713; FAX (215) 445-8229

The Foreman House is a turn-of-the-century home furnished with antiques and decorated with quilts and local artwork. There is a large livingroom with a piano and fireplace and a side porch that guests are welcome to use. The back yard offers a view of Amish farms, and there is a lawn swing and picnic table for relaxing and enjoying the view.

Hosts: Jacqueline and Stephen Mitrani
Rooms: 2 (1 PB; 1 SB) $55-65 plus tax
Continental Breakfast
Credit Cards: None
Notes: 5, 8 (over 10), 9, 10, 11, 12

The Inn at Twin Linden

2029 Main Street, 17555
(215) 445-7619

This bed and breakfast is a perfect getaway in Pennsylvania Dutch Country. Elegant restored historic estate with six guest rooms, private baths, queen-size canopy beds, air conditioning, unsurpassed gourmet breakfast, and outdoor Jacuzzi. Situated on two acres of beautifully landscaped grounds and Amish farm views, it serves a renowned candlelight dinner on the weekends. Intimate romantic setting with wicker-filled porches and private gardens. Afternoon tea and sherry included.

Hosts: Bob and Donna Leahy
Rooms: 6 (PB) $79-106
Full Breakfast
Credit Cards: A, B, C, D
Notes: 2, 4 (weekends), 5, 9

CLARK

Tara — A Country Inn

3665 Valley View Road, 16113
(412) 962-3535; (800) 782-2803

Based on the movie *Gone With the Wind*, Tara recreates the grace and grandeur of the Old South. Its 27 guest rooms are all lovingly named and themed after characters from the movie or the Civil War era. All have fireplaces and sitting areas; many have Jacuzzis. There are three distinctive dining rooms. Ashley's serves a seven-course gourmet meal; Stonewall's Tavern specializes in steak, veal, and seafood; and the Old South Restaurant offers a family-style feast.

Hosts: Donna and Jim Winner
Rooms: 27 (PB) $198-318
Full and Continental Breakfast
Credit Cards: A, B, C, D
Notes: 2, 3, 4, 5, 7 (limited), 9, 11, 12

CLEARVILLE

Conifer Ridge Farm

Rural Route 2, Box 202A, 15535
(814) 784-3342

A beautiful, contemporary, passive solar home with a rustic exterior and an interior of exceptional design beauty. The 125-acre farm features a wading stream, a lake for swimming, fishing, boating, woodlands and mountains for hiking, Christmas trees, and grazing cattle. The Granary is a cabin that sleeps four. Day trips to Bedford Village, Raystown Lake, country auctions, and historic Bedford.

Rooms: 2 (1 PB; 1 SB) $45
Cabin: 1 (PB) $30
Full Breakfast
Credit Cards: None
Notes: 2, 4, 5, 6 (restricted), 7 (limited), 8, 11, 12, 13

COLLEGEVILLE

Fircroft

Bed and Breakfast of Valley Forge #1305
P. O. Box 1151, Valley Forge, 19481-1151
(215) 783-7838; (800) 344-0123

Near Ursinas College. In 1838, this spacious Federal-style home with wraparound porch was built around the original 1769 homestead. The country kitchen has beamed ceiling and stained glass. A full country breakfast is served in the large formal dining room. Guest quarters are private and appealing. The bath has a flowered pedestal sink with gold fixtures and a claw foot tub. $65.

Victorian Elegance

Bed and Breakfast of Valley Forge #1904
P. O. Box 1151, Valley Forge, 19481-1151
(215) 783-7838; (800) 344-0123

Skilled European and American craftsmen fashioned this 22-room Victorian mansion in 1897. Stained glass and fireplaces abound. A three-story winding chestnut staircase leads to the air-conditioned guest rooms, that offer such touches as marble lavatory, ornate medicine cabinet, and built-in armoire of exotic woods. A full breakfast is served in the dining room. This elegant mansion is renowned for year-round house tours, weddings both in the mansion and in the gardens, small corporate meetings, dinners in the dining room, and the perfect setting for wedding pictures. Six guest rooms, each with private bath. $65-75.

COLUMBIA

The Columbian

360 Chestnut Street, 17512
(717) 684-5869; (800) 422-5869 Reservations

This restored turn-of-the-century mansion is a splendid example of Colonial Revival architecture, complete with unique wraparound sun porches, ornate stained-glass window, and magnificent tiered staircase. Decorated with antiques in Victorian or country style, large air-conditioned rooms offer queen-size beds and private baths.

The hearty country breakfast consists of a variety of fresh fruit, hot main dishes, and homemade breads.

Hosts: Linda and John Straitiff
Rooms: 5 (PB) $60-80
Full Breakfast
Credit Cards: A, B, C, D
Notes: 2, 5, 9

CONFLUENCE

RiveRest Bed and Breakfast

Rural Delivery 1, Box 130F, 15424
(814) 395-3771

This country home is on the banks of Laurel Hill Creek in an ideal setting for a short visit or an extended vacation. Located near Youghiogheny River, where white water, kayaking, canoeing, and rafting are popular activities, and also near bike trails, Frank Lloyd Wright's Falling Water, ski resorts in Seven Springs and Hidden Valley, hiking, fishing, hunting. Four spacious bedrooms, a large wraparound porch, kitchen facilities, common room, and full breakfast.

Host: John Enos
Rooms: 4 (1 PB; 3 SB) $39
Full Breakfast
Credit Cards: None
Notes: 2, 5, 8, 9

COOKSBURG

Clarion River Lodge

River Road-Cook Forest, 16217
(800) 648-6743

Nestled in northwestern Pennsylvania's great forest beside the gentle Clarion River, the 20-room Clarion River Lodge, featuring one of the finest dining rooms in western Pennsylvania, is a great place for romantic getaways. Chef-prepared entrees are complemented with a fine wine list. All rooms have private bath, air conditioning, and TV. Spectacular natural setting. Great canoeing and hiking. AAA three-diamonds.

6 Pets welcome; 7 Smoking allowed; 8 Children welcome; 9 Social drinking allowed; 10 Tennis available; 11 Swimming available; 12 Golf available; 13 Skiing available; 14 May be booked through travel agents.

Host: Ellen O'Day
Rooms: 20 (PB) $79-109
Continental Breakfast
Credit Cards; A, B, C
Notes: 3, 4, 5, 7, 9, 11, 14

Gateway Lodge and Cabins

Route 36, Box 125, 16217
(814) 744-8017

Experience gracious hospitality at a rustic authentic log cabin country inn that has been designated as one of the top ten inns in the USA. Located in William Penn's forest primeval, it offers family cabins, private bungalows, and an antique-filled lodge that is open all year. Indoor heated pool, sauna, tea-time, and planned activities available for lodge and bungalow guests. On-premise gift shop and restaurant. Activities abound. Call or write for a free brochure.

Hosts: Joe and Linda Burney
Rooms: 16 (11 PBl 5 SB) $55-164
Full Breakfast
Credit Cards: A, B, C
Notes: 2, 3, 4, 5, 7, 8 (over 8), 9, 10, 11, 12, 13

CRANESVILLE

Zion's Hill

9023 Miller Road at Carriage Hill Farm, 16410
(814) 774-2971

This historical 1830 Colonial-style mansion is situated on a knoll surrounded by majestic maples, a small orchard, and a variety of flowers. As a working farm, it has a variety of farm animals and a bird sanctuary on site. The five guest rooms are furnished with beautiful antiques. Near Lake Erie, Presque Isle and Pymatuning state parks.

Host: John and Kathy Byrne
Rooms: 5 (3 PB; 2 SB) $40-70
Continental Breakfast
Credit Cards; None
Notes: 2 (advance reservation), 5, 8, 9, 13 (XC) 14

CRESCO

LaAnna Guest House

Rural Delivery 2, Box 1051, 18326
(717) 676-4225

Built in the 1870s, this Victorian home welcomes guests with large rooms that are furnished in Empire and Victorian antiques. Situated in a quiet mountain village with waterfalls, mountain views, and outdoor activities.

Hosts: Kay Swingle and Julie Wilson
Rooms: 2 (SB) $25-30
Continental Breakfast
Credit Cards: None
Notes: 2, 5, 7, 8, 9, 10, 11, 12, 13 (XC), 14

DALLAS

Ponda-Rowland Bed and Breakfast Inn and Farm Vacations

Rural Route. 1 Box 349, 18612
(717) 639-3245

Large, scenic farm in the mountains. Farm animals. This 30-acre wildlife refuge offers ponds, hiking, canoeing, swimming, cross-country skiing, ice skating. State park, game land, fishing, horseback riding, antiquing, restaurants, downhill skiing, county fairs nearby. Museum-quality country antiques. Circa 1850 timberframe (post-and-beam) double plank construction. Large stone fireplace. Satellite TV. Awarded Gold Seal of Approval by Bed and Breakfast Worldwide. Featured in

LaAnna Guest House

B&B/Unique Inns of Pennsylvania. Member of ABBA and PAII.

Hosts: Jeanette and Clifford Rowland
Rooms: 3 (PB) $60-80
Full Breakfast
Credit Cards: A, B
Notes: 2, 5, 8, 9, 11, 13, 14

DONEGAL

Mountain View Bed and Breakfast

Mountain View Road, 15628
(412) 593-6349

Historic 1850s farmhouse and barn with guest rooms has been furnished with 18th- and early 19th-century American furniture. Spectacular views of the nearby mountains, and close proximity to Fallingwater, hiking, skiing, rafting, and mountain resorts. Antique shop on premesis.

Hosts: Jerry and Lesley O'Leary
Rooms: 6 (3 PB; 3 SB) $75-125
Full Breakfast
Credit Cards: A, B, C, D, E
Notes: 2, 5, 9, 13

DOUGLASSVILLE

Yellow House Hotel

Rural Delivery 2, Box 170, 19518
(215) 689-9410

Situated in the scenic Oley Valley, close to Reading, the outlet capital of the world, this bed and breakfast was built in 1801 and offers five rooms with private baths and antique furnishings. Its dining rooms are open daily for lunch and dinner.

Hosts: Carl Brown and Jack Rahn
Rooms: 5 (PB) $50
Continental Breakfast
Credit Cards: A, B, C, E
Notes: 2, 3, 4, 5, 7, 9

DOYLESTOWN

The Butler's House

Bed and Breakfast of Valley Forge #1906
P. O. Box 1151 Valley Forge, 19481-1151
(215) 783-7838; (800) 344-0123

The original owners came to the unsettled wilderness of Bucks County in 1720 and built a stone dwelling to which a main formal house was added in 1840. A magnificent walk-in fireplace greets arriving guests. After a full day, guests can relax next to a fire in the livingroom or library. The country kitchen has rustic stone walls, beehive oven, and hand-hewn beams. Seven guest rooms, all with private bath. $95-100.

Highland Farms

70 East Road, 18901
(215) 340-1354

The famous country estate of lyricist Oscar Hammerstein, this bed and breakfast is situated on five acres, with a stone home, carriage house, and wine cellar all built in 1740. A sixty-foot pool, tennis, video library, four-course breakfast, and afternoon refreshments are part of the amenities offered. Listed on the National Register of Historic Places, the beautifully decorated rooms that are all named after Hammerstein's Broadway musicals. Featured on CBS radio, ABC news, "Jeopardy" gameshow, and *Gourmet* magazine.

Hosts: Mary and John Schnitzer
Rooms: 4 (2 PB; 2 SB) $85-150
Full Breakfast
Credit Cards: A, B, C
Notes: 2, 5, 7, 10, 11, 12, 13, 14

Ye Olde Inn

Bed and Breakfast of Valley Forge #0803
P. O. Box 1151, Valley Forge, 19481-1151
(215) 783-7838; (800) 344-0123

6 Pets welcome; 7 Smoking allowed; 8 Children welcome; 9 Social drinking allowed; 10 Tennis available; 11 Swimming available; 12 Golf available; 13 Skiing available; 14 May be booked through travel agents.

This pre-Revolutionary War farmhouse built of fieldstone and stucco is set on eight wooded acres in historic Bucks County. A wonderful stone fireplace in the lobby greets guests with warmth. Fifteen guest rooms, all with private bath.

DUSHORE

Cherry Mills Lodge

Rural Route 1, Route 87 South, 18614
(717) 928-8978

Situated in the scenic Endless Mountains near two beautiful state parks, covered bridges, and many waterfalls, this bed and breakfast offers relaxation. The lodge welcomes you year-round. Relax with reading, fishing at the creek, and taking country walks in the beautiful valley, once an 1800s logging village. There is mountain biking, hiking, nearby cross-country skiing, tobogganing, hunting, swimming, canoeing, golfing, and antiquing. Visit the Victorian town of Eagles Mere.

Hosts: Florence and Julio
Rooms: 8 (1 PB; 7 SB) $57-75
Full Breakfast
Credit Cards: A, B
Notes: 2, 3, 4, 5, 7, 8, 9, 10, 11, 12, 13

EAGLES MERE

Eagles Mere Inn

Mary and Sullivan Avenues, 17731
(717) 525-3273; (800) 426-3273

This 1887 country inn with old-fashioned hospitality and outstanding food features a hearty breakfast and a five-course gourmet dinner included in your room rates. Called the "Last Unspoiled Resort," it offers the ultimate stress relief, peace and quiet, crystal clear mountaintop lake, swimming and boating, incredible waterfalls, hiking trails and vistas, trout fishing, golf, tennis, cross-country skiing, tobogganing, antique shops, winetasting weekends, and more. Featured

as a special vacation spot in *Mid-Atlantic, Washingtonian,* and numerous travel articles.

Hosts: Susan and Peter Glaubitz
Rooms: 15 (PB) $118-175
Full Breakfast
Credit Cards: A, B
Notes: 2, 4 (included), 5, 7(limited), 8, 9, 10, 11, 12, 13 14

Eagles Mere Inn

Shady Lane: A Bed and Breakfast Inn

Allegheny Avenue, P. O. Box 314, 17731
(717) 525-3394

A picturesque mountaintop resort close to excellent hiking, swimming, and fishing. In a quiet Victorian town high in the Endless Mountains, the charming seven-bedroom inn offers all the conveniences and amenities of a home away from home. Explore the laurel path that surrounds the crystal-clear lake. Take a step back in time to the Eagles Mere gaslight era village shops. In winter, enjoy the famous Eagles Mere toboggan slide or some of the finest cross-country skiing. Mystery weekends.

Hosts: Pat and Dennis Dougherty
Rooms: 8 (PB) $65-100
Full Breakfast
Credit Cards: None
Notes: 2, 5, 7, 8, 9, 10, 11, 12, 13, 14

NOTES: Credit cards accepted: A Master Card; B Visa; C American Express; D Discover Card; E Diner's Club; F Other; 2 Personal Checks accepted; 3 Lunch available; 4 Dinner available; 5 Open all year;

EAST BERLIN

Bechtel Mansion Inn

400 West King Street, 17316
(717) 259-7760; (800) 331-1108

Magnificently restored Victorian mansion with quality period furnishings and hand-made quilts. Perfect setting for honey-moons and special occasions. Guest rooms are air-conditioned, with private baths. The mansion is on the western frontier of the Pennsylvania Dutch country. Excellent restaurants, golf courses, and antiques near-by. Convenient to York, Gettysburg, and Lancaster County. Situated in a national historic district approximately 100 miles from both Washington, D.C., and Philadelphia. Skiing just 18 miles away.

Hosts: Ruth Spangler; Charles and Mariam Bechtel
Rooms: 7 (PB) $82.50-110
Suites: 2 (PB) $125-135
Expanded Continental Breakfast
Minimum stay October weekends and holidays: 2
 nights
Credit Cards: A, B, C, D
Notes: 2, 5, 7 (limited), 8, 9, 10, 12, 13, 14

Bechtel Mansion Inn

EAST STROUDSBURG

Red Rock Inn

Cherry Lane Road, Rural Delivery 7, Box 7703,
 18301
(717) 421-4976

A cozy comfortable, homey place, Red Rock offers a relaxing atmosphere at rea-sonable prices. Over 100 years old, it is a family-oriented, casual bed and breakfast in the heart of the Poconos and close to all major sports and attractions. Red Rock is perfect for families, individuals, and groups. An outdoor pool, volleyball, bas-ketball, shuffleboard, and small recreation hall are on the premises. Red Rock Inn is not fancy, just fun.

Hosts: Jenny and Bruce Collier; Tiffany Buoni
Rooms: 10 (1 PB; 9 SB) $40-50
Full Breakfast
Credit Cards: A, B
Notes: 2, 4 (for groups), 5, 7, 8, 9, 11, 12, 13

ELIZABETHTOWN

Hershey Bed and Breakfast Reservation Service

P. O. Box 208, Hershey, 17033-0208
(717) 533-2928

A luxurious getaway at a beautiful country estate home. Hobby farm with horses, Angus cattle, two fishing ponds, tennis court. Health room with hot tub. Full breakfast. Eight rooms with private bath. $60-85.

West Ridge Guest House

1285 West Ridge Road, 17022
(717) 367-7783

Tucked midway between Harrisburg and Lancaster, this European-type manor can be found four miles off Route 283 at Rheems-Elizabethtown Exit. Nine guest rooms, four in the main house and five in a separate guest house, which offers com-plete privacy. Private baths. Each room decorated to reflect a different historical style. Exercise room with hot tub, large social room, and dining area. Fish in one of two ponds, or travel 20 to 40 minutes to local attractions, such as Hershey Park, Lancaster County Amish farms, outlet

6 Pets welcome; 7 Smoking allowed; 8 Children welcome; 9 Social drinking allowed; 10 Tennis available; 11 Swimming available; 12 Golf available; 13 Skiing available; 14 May be booked through travel agents.

shopping, Masonic homes, or Gettysburg, Full breakfast. No smoking. Handicapped accessible.

Host: Alice P. Heisey
Rooms: 9 (PB) $60-85
Full Breakfast
Credit Cards: A, B, C
Notes: 2, 5, 8, 9, 10, 14

ELIZABETHVILLE

Inn at Elizabethville

30 West Main Street, 17023
(717) 362-3476

Situated in the heart of central Pennsylvania, the Inn at Elizabethville serves business and leisure travelers to northern Dauphin County. Built in 1883 and furnished in Mission Oak/Arts and Crafts style, the inn has seven guest rooms with private baths. Convenient to superb hiking, fishing, hunting, golfing, and country auctions. A conference room, FAX, phone, and copy service cater to business clients.

Hosts: Beth and Jim Facinelli
Rooms: 7 (PB)
Continental Breakfast
Credit Cards: A, B
Notes: 2, 5, 8, 9, 11, 12, 14

ELM

Elm Country Inn

Box 37, 17521
(717) 664-3623; (800) 245-0532

Situated in a small country village in beautiful Lancaster County, this inn is near the Amish country. The house was built in 1860 and has been refurbished, keeping most of the old character intact. Hosts are knowledgeable about the area and will help guests plan their sightseeing.

Hosts: Berry and Melvin Meck
Rooms: 2 (1 PB; 1 SB) $45-55
Full Breakfast
Credit Cards: A, B
Notes: 5, 8, 9, 10, 11, 12, 14

EPHRATA

Clearview Farm Bed and Breakfast

355 Clearview Road, 17522
(717) 733-6333

A beautiful limestone farmhouse built in 1814, this bed and breakfast overlooks a large pond with a pair of swans. Beautifully restored and lovingly redecorated, it is surrounded by a well-kept lawn on 200 acres of peaceful farm land. A touch of elegance in Pennsylvania Dutch Country, it was featured in *Country Decorating Ideas*.

The 1777 House at Doneckers

Hosts: Glenn and Mildred Wissler
Rooms: 5 (3 PB; 2 SB) $59-89
Full Breakfast
Credit Cards: A, B
Notes: 2, 5, 9, 10, 12

The Guesthouse and the 1777 House at Doneckers

318-324 North State Street, 17522
(717) 733-8696

Experience Doneckers' warm hospitality in the picturesque setting of historic Lancaster County. Elegant country rooms and suites appointed in fine antiques, hand-stenciled walls, designer linens. Some rooms retain original Victorian inlaid wood floors and stained-glass windows, plus added luxuries of fireplaces and Jacuzzis. The Doneckers' community also includes upscale fashion stores for the family and the home, a gourmet French restaurant, a complex of 40 art/craft/quilt galleries, and a farmers' market of local produce and specialties.

Host: H. William Donecker
Rooms: 31 (29 PB; 2 SB) $59-175
Continental Breakfast
Credit Cards: A, B, C, D, E, F
Closed Christmas Day
Notes: 2, 3, 4, 5, 7, 8, 10, 11, 12, 14

Hackman's Country Inn Bed and Breakfast

140 Hackman Road, 17522
(717) 733-3498

Hackman's Country Inn is an 1857 farmhouse on a 90-acre working farm in Lancaster County. Shaded lawns and a porch provide a peaceful retreat on a hot summer day. The inn features spacious, air-conditioned rooms with bubble-glass windows and patchwork quilts. Breakfast is served in the keeping room by the walk-in fireplace. Shop the nearby antique malls and outlets. Tour beautiful Amish country. Dinner can be arranged with a River Brethren family.

Host: Kathryn H. Hackman
Rooms: 4 (2 PB; 2 SB) $60-70
Continental Breakfast
Credit Cards: A, B
Notes: 2, 5, 8, 9

The Historic Smithton Inn

900 West Main Street, 17522
(717) 733-6094

A romantic 1763 stone inn with fireplaces in every room, canopy beds, easy chairs, quilts, candles, down pillows, nightshirts,. flowers, chamber music, and feather beds. Parlor, library, and gardens for guests to enjoy. Lancaster County is an antique and

crafts area settled by the Pennsylvania Dutch, Mennonite, and Amish peoples.

Host: Dorothy Graybill
Rooms: 8 (PB) $65-115
Full Breakfast
Credit Cards: A, B, C
Notes: 2, 5, 6, 8, 9, 10, 11, 12

ERWINNA

Evermay-on-the-Delaware

River Road, 18920
(215) 294-9100

Lodging in manor house and carriage house. Liquor license. Parlor with fireplace. A significant, distinguished country retreat situated on 25 acres of gardens, woodland paths, and pastures between the Delaware River and Canal. Dinner served Friday, Saturday, Sunday, and holidays.

Hosts: Ron Strouse and Fred Cresson
Rooms: 16 (PB) $85-155
Expanded Continental Breakfast
Minimum stay weekends: 2 nights
Credit Cards: A, B
Closed December 24
Notes: 2, 4, 5, 7, 8 (over 12), 9, 14

Golden Pheasant Inn

River Road, 18920
(215) 294-9595

This 1857 fieldstone inn is situated between the Delaware River and the Pennsylvania Canal. Six intimate guest rooms feature four-poster, queen-size canopy beds. Three romantic dining rooms, including a candlelit greenhouse overlooking the canal. Masterful classical French cuisine by chef/owner Michel Faure. Extensive wine selections. Dinner served Tuesday through Sunday.

Hosts: Michel and Barbara Faure
Rooms: 6 (PB) $110-135
Continental Breakfast
Minimum stay weekends: 2 nights; holidays: 3 nights
Credit Cards: A, B, E
Notes: 2, 4, 5, 6, 9

---

6 Pets welcome; 7 Smoking allowed; 8 Children welcome; 9 Social drinking allowed; 10 Tennis available; 11 Swimming available; 12 Golf available; 13 Skiing available; 14 May be booked through travel agents.

EXTON

Duling Kurtz House & Country Inn

146 South Whitford Road, 19341
(215) 524-1830

Charming 1830s stone house and barn, elegantly furnished with period reproduction furniture. Fifteen guest rooms, including four suites, all with private baths. Fine restaurant serves lunch Monday through Friday and dinner all week.

Rooms: 15 (PB) $49.95
Continental Breakfast
Credit Cards: A, B, C, D, E
Notes: 3, 4, 5, 7, 8, 9, 10, 12, 14

GAP

Fassitt Mansion

6051 Old Philadelphia Pike, 17527
(717) 442-3139

Situated in the rolling hills of Pennsylvania Dutch country, this restored 1845 country home combines charm with modern conveniences. Beautifully appointed rooms with locally made, hand-stitched Amish quilts. In winter, snuggle under down comforters and enjoy the glow of one of six fireplaces. A full country breakfast is served in the cheerful dining room or on the front porch.

Hosts: Tara and Ed Golish
Rooms: 4 (2 PB; 2 SB) $60-85 (subject to change)
Full Breakfast
Credit Cards: A, B
Notes: 5, 7 (outside)

GERMANTOWN

Bed and Breakfast Connections #00331

P. O. Box 21, Devon, 19333
(215) 687-3565; (800) 448-3619

Circa 1885, this home offers several fascinations: its history, its antique furnishings, and its well-traveled host who lovingly cares for it. Two second-floor guest rooms with connecting baths are available; one offers a single canopied bed, and the other, a pair of twin beds. Each has been tastefully appointed and reflects the overall elegance of the home. The location of this home is ideal for a visit to historic Germantown or the interesting shops of Chestnut Hill. No smoking. Resident dog. $25-35.

"Ka Bob"

Bed and Breakfast of Philadelphia
1616 Walnut Street, Suite 1120, Philadelphia, 19103
(215) 735-1917; (800) 220-1917
FAX (215) 735-1905

This rambling house in a beautiful secluded property is located near Fairmont Park. Wood paneling, six large fireplaces, and large bedrooms reflect Civil War suburbia. King, twins, or double bed. $40-50.

GETTYSBURG

Amanda's Bed and Breakfast #125

1428 Park Avenue, Annapolis, MD 21217
(301) 225-0001; (301) 383-1274

Situated on Oak Ridge, this restored Colonial offers a splendid view of the town. Enjoy the charm of a by-gone era with the comforts of home-cooked breakfasts, cozy quilts, and country antiques. Rooms are decorated with Civil War accents. Nine rooms have private and shared baths. $79-99.

Amanda's Bed and Breakfast #214

1428 Park Avenue, Annapolis, MD 21217
(301) 225-0001; (301) 383-1274

NOTES: Credit cards accepted: A Master Card; B Visa; C American Express; D Discover Card; E Diner's Club; F Other; 2 Personal Checks accepted; 3 Lunch available; 4 Dinner available; 5 Open all year;

Split-level house five minutes from historic Gettysburg. Antiques, quiet setting, excellent breakfast. Two rooms share a bath. $50

The Brafferton Inn

44 York Street, 17325
(717) 337-3423

This 1786 stone home is listed on the National Register of Historic Places. Enjoy the colonial antiques, stenciled decor, and full breakfast served near a primitive mural. Experience Gettysburg in the first house built in town. Featured in the February 1988 issue of Country Living magazine.

The Brafferton Inn

Hosts: Mimi and Jim Agard
Rooms: 10 (6 PB; 4 SB) $55-95
Full Breakfast
Credit Cards: A, B
Notes: 2, 4, 5, 7 (limited), 8 (over 7), 9, 10, 11, 12, 13, 14

Goose Chase
Bed and Breakfast

200 Blueberry Road, Gardners, 17324
(717) 528-8877

A restored 18th-century stone home on 25 tranquil acres among vast apple orchards. Air-conditioned for summer comfort, it is handsomely furnished with handmade quilts, folk art, and carefully chosen American antiques. Wide-plank floors, Oriental rugs, stenciled walls, and deep-silled windows add to the charming atmosphere. Full breakfast is always served and afternoon refreshments are graciously offered. Summer swimming pool and walking trails are on the property. Just 15 minutes from Gettysburg Battlefield.

Host: Marsha Lucidi
Rooms: 5 (3 PB; 2 SB) $69-89
Full Breakfast
Credit Cards: A, B
Notes: 2, 5, 9, 11, 12, 13

Keystone Inn

231 Hanover Street, 17325
(717) 337-3888

Keystone Inn is a large late-Victorian brick house filled with lots of natural woodwork. The guest rooms are bright, cheerful, and air-conditioned. The soft pastels and ruffles give you a warm welcome. Each room has a reading nook and writing desk. Relax with a book in Aunt Weasie's Library. Choose a breakfast from the full menu to suit your mood.

Hosts: Wilmer and Doris Martin
Rooms: 4 (2 PB; 2 SB) $59-75
Full Breakfast
Credit Cards: A, B
Notes: 2, 5, 8, 10, 11, 12, 13

The Old Appleford Inn

218 Carlisle Street, 17325
(717) 337-1711

This elegant three-story Victorian mansion, built in 1867, has 12 antique-filled guest rooms, each with private bath and air-conditioning. The livingroom features high ceilings, baby grand piano, and complimentary sherry. The Lincoln Library features many unique collections, books, and

6 Pets welcome; 7 Smoking allowed; 8 Children welcome; 9 Social drinking allowed; 10 Tennis available; 11 Swimming available; 12 Golf available; 13 Skiing available; 14 May be booked through travel agents.

solitude. There's a plant-filled sun room with white wicker and afternoon beverages. The apple-stenciled dining room is where the sumptuous breakfasts are served. Surrounded by history, this inn is on the Historic Pathway. Antiquing and sports nearby. Gettysburg College within walking distance. New carriage house offers accommodations for honeymooners.

Hosts: Maribeth and Frank Skradski
Rooms: 12 (PB) $78-88
Full Breakfast
Credit Cards: A, B, C
Notes: 2, 5, 8 (over 14), 9, 14

GETTYSBURG BATTLEFIELD

The Doubleday Inn

104 Doubleday Avenue, 17325
(717) 334-9119

Situated directly on the Gettysburg Battlefield, this Colonial inn is beautifully restored with Civil War furnishings, comfortable antiques, and central air conditioning. Enjoy afternoon tea and hors d'oeuvres and, in the morning, a candlelight country breakfast. Available to guests is a Civil War library with more than 600 volumes devoted exclusively to the Battle of Gettysburg. On selected evenings, participate in a discussion with a Civil War historian who brings the battle alive with accurate accounts, authentic memorabilia, and weaponry.

Hosts: Joan and Sal Chandon; Olga Krossick
Rooms: 9 (5 PB; 4 SB) $74-100
Full Breakfast
Credit Cards: A, B,
Notes: 2, 3, 5, 9, 11, 12, 13, 14

GLADWYNE

Glad Haven

Bed and Breakfast of Valley Forge #0202
P. O. Box 1151, Valley Forge, 19481-1151
(215) 783-7838; (800) 344-0123
FAX (215) 783-7783

This spacious, air-conditioned Cape Cod Colonial home is situated on a large wooded lot. Fine furnishings, collectibles, art, and expanses of windows all contribute to the sunlit, cheerful atmosphere. The gourmet country breakfasts may be served in the formal dining room with its collection of blue glass, or in the sun room with its wicker and foliage. The adjoining terrace, gardens, lawn, reflecting pool and fountain enhance the feeling of privacy and rest. Four guest rooms with private baths. $55.

Gladwyn Invitation

Bed and Breakfast of Philadelphia
1616 Walnut Street, Suite 1120, Philadelphia, 19103
(215) 735-1917; (800) 220-1917
FAX (215) 735-1905

This comfortable ranch-style suburban home with nice sun porch and gardens offers a room with a double bed and private bath, and a room with a single bed and a shared bath. Host and hostess are widely traveled medical professionals. $40-60.

GREENSBURG

Huntland Farm Bed and Breakfast

Rural Delivery 9, Box 21, 15601
(412) 834-8483

The 100-acre Huntland Farm is three miles northeast of Greensburg, a convenient halfway stop between the East coast and the Midwest. From Pennsylvania Turnpike, exit at New Stanton (east) or Monroeville (west). Circa 1848 house in scenic, historical Laurel Highlands of western Pennsylvania. Four corner bedrooms, two shared baths. Living areas furnished with antiques. Good restaurants and antique shops nearby. Full country breakfast.

NOTES: Credit cards accepted: A Master Card; B Visa; C American Express; D Discover Card; E Diner's Club; F Other; 2 Personal Checks accepted; 3 Lunch available; 4 Dinner available; 5 Open all year;

Hosts: Robert and Elizabeth Weidlein
Rooms: 4 (SB) $50-70
Full Breakfast
Credit Cards: C
Notes: 2, 5, 7, 9, 14

GULPH MILLS

Red Barn Bed and Breakfast

Bed and Breakfast of Valley Forge #0306
P. O. Box 1151, Valley Forge, 19481-1151
(215) 783-7838; (800) 344-0123

A home made from a barn, this fabulous,
luxury barn offers an atmosphere of quiet
taste to highlight your visit to this historic
area. All guest rooms are located off the
spacious entrance hall. A full breakfast is
served in the parlor or in the great room
with a fireplace and antiques. In warm
weather, lounge or dine on the upper deck
overlooking the enclosed stone paddock,
the rolling green hills and pond. Close to
Valley Forge, Philadelphia. An easy drive
to Brandywine and Amish areas. Three
guest rooms, each with a private bath. $85-
95.

GUTHRIESVILLE

Burns 1805 Bed and Breakfast

Bed and Breakfast of Valley Forge #1502
P. O. Box 1151, Valley Forge, 19481-1151
(215) 783-7838; (800) 344-0123

Lovely example of an early 19th-century
Pennsylvania farmhouse overlooking a
panoramic view of farm and woodland. It
has been on Chester County day tours for
many years. Share the special warmth and
serenity of this lovely old house. Walk
about on eight acres of hill, meadow, and
hedgerow, or just enjoy the views from the
porch. Close to the Amish/Lancaster area,
and the Brandywine Longwood Garden
area. Two guest rooms, each with a private
bath. $45-75.

HALLAM

Bed and Breakfast Connections #00360

P. O. Box 21, Devon, 19333
(215) 687-3565; (800) 448-3619

After enjoying the attractions of York
County, retreat to the quiet elegance of this
lovely 1836 Colonial home appointed with
a blend of antiques and authentic reproductions. On arrival, chat with your host in the
comfortable livingroom to learn the history
of the house, and then discover three tastefully decorated second-floor rooms, each
with its own unique charm and decor.
These three rooms share two full baths. A
full gourmet breakfast, including dessert, is
served in the large country dining room.
Your host will gladly help you plan trips in
the area, whether you choose to go to York
County, Amish country, Baltimore's inner
harbor, or Gettysburg. Resident cat and
smoker. $60.

HANOVER

Beechmont Inn

315 Broadway, 17331
(800) 553-7009

An elegant 1834 Federal period inn with
seven guest rooms, private baths, fireplaces, air conditioning, afternoon refreshments, and gourmet breakfast. One large
suite has a private whirlpool tub, canopy
bed, and fireplace. Gettysburg Battlefield,
Lake Marburg, golf and great antiquing
nearby. Convenient location for visits to
Hershey, York, or Lancaster. Weekend
packages and romantic honeymoon or
anniversary packages offered. Picnic baskets available. Great area for biking and
hiking. AAA and Mobil approved.

Hosts: Terry and Monna Hormel
Doubles: 7 (PB) $70-125
Full Breakfast

---

6 Pets welcome; 7 Smoking allowed; 8 Children welcome; 9 Social drinking allowed; 10 Tennis available; 11
Swimming available; 12 Golf available; 13 Skiing available; 14 May be booked through travel agents.

Credit Cards: A, B, C
Notes: 2, 5, 7 (limited), 8 (over 12), 9, 10, 11, 12,
13 (XC), 14

HARRISBURG

Hershey Bed and Breakfast Reservation Service #1

P. O. Box 208, Hershey, 17033-0208
(717) 533-2928

A comfortable home offering three bed and
breakfast rooms with shared bath. Pool in
yard. Air conditioning, full breakfast.
Smokers allowed. $55.

HAWLEY

Academy Street Bed and Breakfast

528 Academy Street, 18428
(717) 226-3430; (201) 316-8148 winter

Outstanding historic 1863 Italianate
Victorian built by Civil War hero, the first
sheriff of Wayne County. Near the largest

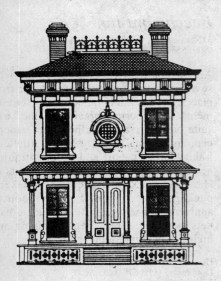

Academy Street Bed and Breakfast

and most beautiful recreational lake in the
state, with all activities. Convenient to I-84.
Lovely furnished inn; full gourmet breakfast and afternoon tea. Air-conditioned
rooms. Cable television.

Host: Judith Lazan
Rooms: 7 (3 PB; 4 SB) $65-75
Full Breakfast
Credit Cards: A, B
Closed November-April
Notes: 7, 9, 10, 11, 12

The Settlers Inn

4 Main Street, 18428
(717) 226-2993

A grand Tudor-style hotel beside the park
in the village of Hawley. Near Lake
Wallenpaupack and many recreational
activities. Pleasant dining featuring a creative regional menu, which Philadelphia
magazine describes "as surely the best in
the Poconos." Enjoy specialty shopping,
antiquing, museums, and summer theaters.

Hosts: Grant and Jeanne Genzlinger
Rooms: 18 (PB) $70-80
Full Breakfast
Credit Cards: A, B, C
Notes: 2, 3, 4, 5, 7, 8, 9, 10, 11, 12, 13, 14

HERSHEY

Hershey Bed and Breakfast Reservation Service #1

P. O. Box 208, 17033-0208
(717) 533-2928

Lovely home near the Hershey Medical
Center. One guest room with private bath
and choice of full or continental breakfast.
Air conditioning. Dog in residence. No
smoking. $50.

Hershey Bed and Breakfast Reservation Service #2

P. O. Box 208, 17033-0208
(717) 533-2928

NOTES: Credit cards accepted: A Master Card; B Visa; C American Express; D Discover Card; E Diner's
Club; F Other; 2 Personal Checks accepted; 3 Lunch available; 4 Dinner available; 5 Open all year;

A former Milton Hershey Boys School, this large brick home is convenient to Hershey museums, park, rose gardens, Chocolate World, sports arena and stadium, theater, and outdoor recreations. Twelve guest rooms, one room with private bath, three shared bathrooms on the second level and one on the first floor. Continental breakfast. Resident cat. Handicapped-accessible. Air conditioning. No smoking. $54-59. Children $5 with parents in same room. Extra adults $10.

Hershey Bed and Breakfast Reservation Service #3

P. O. Box 208, 17033-0208
(717) 533-2928

A log home dating from the 1700s on a lovely horse farm. Country roads for walking and biking, and fields and woods for hiking. One guest room with private half-bath and sitting room. Continental breakfast. Resident pets; no smoking. $65. Children over six $10 additional charge.

Hershey Bed and Breakfast Reservation Service #4

P. O. Box 208, 17033-0208
(717) 533-2928

Countryside home offers one guest room with king bed and private bath. Resident cat. Full breakfast on weekends, continental during the week. Air conditioning. No smoking. $55.

Hershey Bed and Breakfast Reservation Service #5

P. O. Box 208, 17033-0208
(717) 533-2928

Home near Hershey Motor Lodge offers three guest rooms with shared bath, plus a new suite with a private bath. Full breakfast. Children welcome. $55-75

Pinehurst Inn Bed and Breakfast

50 Northeast Drive, 17033
(717) 533-2603

Spacious brick home surrounded by lawns and countryside. There is a warm, welcoming, many-windowed livingroom or a large porch with an old-fashioned porch swing for outdoor relaxation. All this within walking distance of all Hershey attractions: Hershey Museum and Rose Gardens, Hershey Park, Chocolate World, and many golf courses. Less than one hour's drive to Lancaster and Gettysburg. Each room welcomes you with a queen-size bed and a Hershey Kiss on each pillow.

Host: Phyllis Long
Rooms: 14 (1 PB; 13 SB) $42-54
Full Breakfast
Credit Cards: A, B
Notes: 2, 5, 8, 11, 12

Union Canal House Country Inn and Restaurant

107 South Hanover Street. 17033
(717) 566-0054

One of the first buildings in what is now the village of Union Deposit, in the 1700s Ye Old Canal House was filled with soldiers from the French and Indian and Revolutionary wars. The inn offers nine rooms, each with private bath and color TV. Tastefully decorated in Pennsylvania Colonial style. One room, considered the penthouse suite, includes a livingroom, bedroom, full kitchen, and Jacuzzi. Conveniently situated near all Hershey attractions.

Hosts: Mr. Whitney Simmons and Mr. Sterl
   Simmons
Rooms: 9 (PB) $55-75 seasonal
Full Breakfast
Credit Cards: A, B, C, E, F
Notes; 2, 4, 5, 8, 9

6 Pets welcome; 7 Smoking allowed; 8 Children welcome; 9 Social drinking allowed; 10 Tennis available; 11 Swimming available; 12 Golf available; 13 Skiing available; 14 May be booked through travel agents.

HESSTON

Aunt Susie's Country Vacations

Rural Delivery 1, Box 225, 16647
(814) 658-3638

Experience country living in a warm, friendly atmosphere in a Victorian parsonage or a renovated country store and post office. All rooms are nicely furnished with antiques and oil paintings. Raystown Lake is nearby for recreation; boating, swimming, and fishing are within three miles. Bring your family to the country.

Host: John Wilson
Rooms: 8 (2 PB; 6 SB) $45-50
Expanded Continental Breakfast
Credit Cards: None
Notes: 2, 5, 8, 9, 10, 11, 12

HILLSGROVE

The Tannery House

Box 99, Route 87, 18619
(717) 924-3505

Situated in picturesque Sullivan County, in the village of Hillsgrove, this country home has an old-fashioned wraparound porch. Summer breakfasts are served in the gazebo. Furnishings are antiques and collectibles, and there is a Victorian parlor with player piano. The house is surrounded by a state forest where you can enjoy cross-country skiing, hunting, fly-fishing, canoeing, and hiking. The house is suitable for groups of 12 to 16 people.

Hosts: Linda and Dennis Renninger
Singles: 3 (SB) $20.67
Rooms: 4 (1 PB; 3 SB) $41.34-53
Continental Breakfast
Credit Cards: A, B (surcharge)
Notes: 2 (2 weeks in advance), 5, 7 (limited), 8, 9, 13 (XC)

HOLLIDAYSBURG

Hoenstine's Bed and Breakfast

418 Montgomery Street, 16648
(814) 695-0632

Antique lover's dream in an elegant 1839 town house in downtown registered historic Hollidaysburg. Next door to private historical and genealogical library. Extended continental breakfast includes fresh fruits, cold cereals, juice. Ask about children and pets. Near antique shops, parks in beautiful section of Pennsylvania. Protected by attack cats and standard poodle.

Host: Barbara Hoenstine
Rooms: 3 (1 PB; 2 SB) $50-60
Expanded Continental Breakfast
Credit Cards: A, B
Notes: 2, 5, 9, 10, 11, 12, 13

HUNTINGDON VALLEY

Bed and Breakfast Collections #00338

P. O. Box 21, Devon, 19333
(215) 687-3565; (800) 448-3619 (outside PA)

This fantasy cottage is an ideal spot for a quiet retreat from the hubbub of Philadelphia, yet just 30 minutes away. The combination greenhouse and potting shed shares a broad expanse of lawn with the main house. It is bordered on one side by a grape arbor and on the other side by a swimming pool. The in-room refrigerator is stocked with wine, cheese, and soft drinks, as well as all that is needed to fix your own hearty continental breakfast. Enjoy a fruit basket on your arrival. There is air conditioning in the warm weather and a fireplace for the cooler months. Horseback riding, tennis courts, and jogging trails nearby. No smoking. $85.

NOTES: Credit cards accepted: A Master Card; B Visa; C American Express; D Discover Card; E Diner's Club; F Other; 2 Personal Checks accepted; 3 Lunch available; 4 Dinner available; 5 Open all year;

JENKINSTOWN

Jenkinstown Victorian

Bed and Breakfast of Philadelphia
1616 Walnut Street, Suite 1120, Philadelphia,
   19103
(215) 735-1917; (800) 220-1917
FAX (215) 735-1905

Just off Jenkinstown's main throughfare on
a quiet street sits this statuesque stone
Victorian home. From the large porch, you
walk through double ruby-glass doors into
a large foyer with a staircase that ascends
all the way to the second-floor bedroom,
which has a double bed, recliner/rocker,
TV/AC radio, private bath, sitting room
with two sofas, comfortable chairs, and
reading lamps. Children over six welcome.
No smoking. $40-50.

JIM THORPE

The Harry Packer Mansion

Packer Hill, P. O. Box 458, 18229
(717) 325-8566

This 1874 Second Empire mansion features
original appointments and Victorian decor.
Completely restored for tours, bed and
breakfast, fabulous mystery weekends, and
a host of other activities. The adjoining carriage house is decorated in a hunt motif.

Hosts: Bob and Patricia Handwerk
Rooms: 13 (8 PB; 5 SB) $75-110
Full Breakfast
Credit Cards: A, B
Notes: 2, 5, 9, 10, 11, 12, 13, 14

The Inn at Jim Thorpe

4 Broadway, 18229
(717) 325-2599; FAX (717) 325-9145

The Inn at Jim Thorpe rests in a lovely setting in the heart of historic Jim Thorpe. The
elegant, restored guest rooms are complete
with private baths, remote cable TV, and
air conditioning. While in town, take a his-

toric walking tour of Millionaire's Row;
shop in fifty quaint shops and galleries; go
mountain biking on the Northeast's best
trails; raft then turbulent LeHigh River. It's
all right outside the inn's door.

Host: David Drury
Rooms: 22 (PB) $65-125
Continental Breakfast
Credit Cards: A, B, C, D, E
Notes: 3, 4, 5, 7 (limited), 8, 11, 12, 13, 14

The Harry Packer Mansion

KANE

Kane Manor
Bed and Breakfast

230 Clay Street, 16735
(814) 837-6522

We are one of the best-kept secrets in the
Alleghenies. Come and discover for yourself the feeling of being surrounded by the
Allegheny National Forest. Step inside the
inn and you will find yourself surrounded
by history. All ten guest rooms are decorated differently, and all have their own personality. Enjoy hiking, boating, swimming,
golfing and cross-country skiing. Gathering
Room, Gift Shoppe, and Cellar Pub.
Inquire about the mystery clue weekends

6 Pets welcome; 7 Smoking allowed; 8 Children welcome; 9 Social drinking allowed; 10 Tennis available; 11
Swimming available; 12 Golf available; 13 Skiing available; 14 May be booked through travel agents.

Hosts: Dusty Byham, Helen Johnson and Carol Benson
Rooms: 10 (6 PB; 4 SB) $79-89
Continental Breakfast Weekdays; Full on weekends
Credit Cards: A, B, C, D
Notes: 2, 5, 7, 8, 9, 10, 11, 12, 13, 14

Kane Manor

KENNETT SQUARE

B&B of Chester County:
A Reservation Service

P. O. Box 825, 19348
(215) 444-1367

We are a reservation service that offers fine
accommodations in the Brandywine
Valley, an area that includes Pennsylvania
and northern Delaware. Local attractions
include Longwood Gardens, Winterthur,
Brandywine River Museum of Chadd's
Ford, Hagley Museum, Nemours, Valley
Forge, Pennsylvania Dutch country, and
the sights of Philadelphia and Wilmington,
Delaware.

Owner: Doris Passante
Forty guest homes (85% PB; 15% SB) $45 and up
Continental and Full Breakfast
Notes: 2. 5. 7. 8. 9, 10, 11, 12

Meadow Spring Farm

201 East Street Road, 19348
(215) 444-3903

The hosts of this 1836 farmhouse on a
working farm with animals invite guests to
participate in gathering eggs for breakfast.

The house is filled with family antiques,
Amish quilts, fine linens, and a doll collection including Santas and cows. The hosts
will prepare a gourmet breakfast for guests
before they start their day touring the area.
Guests are welcome to enjoy the pool, hot
tub, game room and solarium. This bed and
breakfast has been featured in *Country
Inns,* New York *Times*, and the Washington
Channel 7.

Hosts: Anne Hicks and Debbie Axelrod
Rooms: 7 (5 PB; 2 SB) $55-75
Full Breakfast
Credit Cards: None
Notes: 2, 5, 7, 8, 9, 11, 14

Round Hill
Bed and Breakfast

Bed and Breakfast of Valley Forge #1200
P. O. Box 1151, Valley Forge, 19481-1151
(215) 783-7838; (800) 344-0123

Enjoy the charm of nature on five acres of
wooded land that boasts a pond and a
stream. Watch Canadian geese, Mallard
ducks, and domestic ducks raise their
young and wander the property. This hillside ranch offers privacy and hospitality;
choose either the Burgundy Room with a
pencil post canopy bed or the Forest Room
with Victorian furniture. Enjoy a hearty
country breakfast with homemade preserves. Located in the heart of Brandywine
Valley. Two guest rooms. $75.

KIMBERTON

The Amsterdam

Bed and Breakfast of Valley Forge #2201
P. O. Box 1151, Valley Forge, 19481-1151
(215) 783-7838; (800) 344-0123

This Dutch-style farmhouse was built in
1860 and grew into a rambling home that
has been lovingly restored. The
Netherlands influence is evident in the
decor, food, and hospitality. A full
European breakfast is served. The

king/twin suite has a private entrance, deck, sitting room with access to a Jacuzzi. The queen rooms also share a sitting room. Enjoy the terrace, Jacuzzi, and Japanese gardens. $65-75.

KING OF PRUSSIA

Tranquil Haven

Bed and Breakfast of Valley Forge #0201
P. O. Box 1151, Valley Forge, 19481-1151
(215) 783-7838; (800) 344-0123

This home is set in a peaceful, heavily wooded neighborhood and is decorated with both antique and modern furnishings. Sitting room with fireplace and color cable TV, laundry facilities, and in-ground pool. Gourmet breakfasts are served in the dining room or on the spacious screened porch overlooking the garden. Some French spoken. Two cats in residence. Three guest rooms with private baths. $45-60.

KINTNERSVILLE

The Bucksville House

Rooute 412 and Buck Drive
Rural Delivery 2, Box 146, 18930
(215) 847-8948

Country charm and a friendly atmosphere await the guests at this 1795 Bucks County registered historical landmark. Offering beautifully decorated rooms with many quilts, baskets, antiques and handmade reproductions. Enjoy the six fireplaces, air conditioning, gazebo, herb garden, and courtyard. Near New Hope, Peddler's Village and Nockamixon State Park.

Hosts: Barbara and Joe Szollosi
Rooms: 5 (PB) $85-125
Full Breakfast
Credit Cards: A, B, C, D
Notes: 2, 5, 9

KINZERS

Sycamore Haven Farm

35 South Kinzer Road, 17535
(717) 442-4901

This dairy farm is 15 miles east of Lancaster, right in Pennsylvania Dutch country. The rooms are newly papered and painted, and there is a porch in the back of the house with a lovely swing. There is also a balcony with lounge chairs. Forty dairy cows are milked morning and evening. The children will really enjoy the many kittens and pet sheep, who like a lot of attention.

Hosts: Charles and Janet Groff
Rooms: 3 (SB) $30
Continental Breakfast
Credit Cards: None
Notes: 2, 5, 6, 8, 10

LACKAWAXEN

Roebling Inn on the Delaware

Scenic Drive, P. O. Box 31, 18435
(717) 685-7900

Featured in New York magazine, this classic inn is located on the majestic upper Delaware River, near historic sites. With surrounding mountains, this is a great place to unwind. Old World charm plus private baths. TV, air conditioning, queen beds. Canoeing, hiking, rafting, fishing, tennis, and skiing nearby. Midweek specials.

Hosts: Donald and JoAnn Jahn
Rooms: 5 (PB) $49-85
Full Breakfast
Minimum stay holidays: 2 or 3 nights
Credit Cards: A, B, C
Closed Christmas
Notes: 2, 5, 7 (restricted), 8, 9, 10, 11, 12, 13, 14

LAHASKA

The Golden Plough Inn

Route 202 and Street Road, 18931
(215) 794-4000; (215) 794-4003 (group sales)
FAX (215) 794-4001

6 Pets welcome; 7 Smoking allowed; 8 Children welcome; 9 Social drinking allowed; 10 Tennis available; 11 Swimming available; 12 Golf available; 13 Skiing available; 14 May be booked through travel agents.

Each of the 60 elegant guest rooms reflects the charm of the 18th-century American country style: cherry wood, exquisite fabrics, balconies, fireplaces. All rooms have private bath, Jacuzzis, dressing area, refrigerator, air conditioning, TV. Adjacent to Peddler's Village, six restaurants, 70 specialty shops, entertainment. Award-winning gardens, seasonal country festivals, antiques, and New Hope galleries nearby. Washington's Crossing, vineyards, Bucks County museums, and the canals along the Delaware River are handy. Seasonal packages available.

Hosts: Earl and Donna Jamison; Robert Cassidy
Rooms: 60 (PB) $95-250
Continental Plus Breakfast
Credit Cards: A, B, C, D, E
Notes: 2, 3, 4, 5, 7, 8, 9, 10, 11, 12, 13, 14

The Golden Plough Inn

LAMPETER

Bed and Breakfast:
The Manor Inn

830 Village Road, Route 741, P. O. Box 416, 17537
(717) 464-9564

This cozy farmhouse is just minutes away from Lancaster's historic sights and attractions, such as Dutch Wonderland and the Strasburg Railroad. Guests delight in Mary

Lou's delicious breakfasts, which feature gourmet treats such as eggs Mornay, crepes or strata, apple cobbler, and homemade jams and breads. A swim in the pool or a nap under one of the many shade trees is the perfect way to cap a day of touring.

Hosts: Mary Lou Paolini and Jackie Curtis
Rooms: 5 (2 PB; 3 SB) $55
Full Breakfast
Credit Cards: A, B
Notes: 2, 3, 4, 5, 8, 10, 11, 12

LANCASTER

The Apple Bin Inn

2835 Willow Street Pike, Willow Street, 17584
(717) 464-5881; (800) 338-4296

A village bed and breakfast, the Apple Bin Inn offers distinctive colonial charm with a country touch. Built in the 1860s, this home established its roots in the mainstream of southern Lancaster County. Drive through the beautiful countryside, learn of the Amish, browse antique and craft shops and outlets. Comfortable guest rooms feature pencil-post beds, quilts, wing chairs, love seats, cable TV, and air conditioning. Full breakfast is served.

Hosts: Barry and Debbie Hershey
Rooms: 4 (2 PB; 2 SB) $55-70
Full Breakfast
Credit Cards: A, B, C
Notes: 2, 3, 5, 8 (over 7), 9, 10, 12

The Apple Bin

Buona Notte
Bed and Breakfast

2020 Marietta Avenue, 17603
(717) 295-2597

Turn-of-the-century home with large, comfortable rooms, wraparound porch, large back yard, and picnic table. Hershey Park, Gettysburg area, and Pennsylvania Dutch country are all nearby. Breakfast includes homemade breads, muffins, coffee cakes, and jams. French and Italian are spoken here. Franklin and Marshall College is two miles away.

Hosts: Joe and Anna Predoti
Rooms: 3 (1 PB; 2 SB) $45-50
Continental Breakfast
Credit Cards: None
Notes: 5, 8, 10, 12

Candlelite Inn

2574 Lincoln Highway East, Ronks, 17572
(717) 299-6005

Surrounded by Amish farmlands, this 1920s farmhouse offers four clean, quiet guest rooms, sitting room with TV, central air/heat, phone, and country breakfast. Two rooms have private half-baths. Full baths are shared. It is close to all attractions. There is also an antiques and collectibles shop on the premises.

Host: David W. Simpson
Rooms: 4 (SB) $55-65
Full Breakfast
Credit Cards: A, B, D

Hershey Bed and Breakfast
Reservation Service #1

P. O. Box 208, Hershey, 17033-0208
(717) 533-2928

Country farmhouse, circa 1817, situated on a working dairy farm near Hershey, Lancaster, and Harrisburg at Exit 20. Two guest rooms with shared bath, plus a cottage that sleeps four with private bath. Full breakfast. No smoking. $55.

Hershey Bed and Breakfast
Reservation Service #2

P. O. Box 208, Hershey, 17033-0208
(717) 533-2928

Farmhouse inn, circa 1738, nestled on 12 acres of farmland in Lancaster County. Situated just off Route 283 between Lancaster and Harrisburg. Three guest rooms with private or shared bath. Continental breakfast. Resident cat. No smoking. $75-95.

Hershey Bed and Breakfast
Reservation Service #3

P. O. Box 208, Hershey, 17033-0208
(717) 533-2928

Historic Civil War brick house situated near Routes 30 and 501. Seven guest rooms, including family suites, with private or shared bath. Continental breakfast. No smoking. $75-85; $95 for family of four with private bath.

John Hayes House

Bed and Breakfast of Philadelphia
1616 Walnut Street, Suite 1120, Philadelphia, 19103
(215) 735-1917; (800) 220-1917
FAX (215) 735-1905

The John Hayes House is a working dairy farm surrounded by Amish farms. The house was built from bricks used as a ballast in ships arriving from England in the late 1700s. There are three large comfortable bedrooms on the second floor which share a bath. All bedrooms are air conditioned and a color TV is available. Breakfast is served in the sunny, antique-filled dining room only steps away from a genuine country kitchen with a lovely fireplace. Being a working farm, there are plenty of cows, cats, and dogs, and you are only 20 minutes from Amish country, 25 minutes from Brandywine River area, and

6 Pets welcome; 7 Smoking allowed; 8 Children welcome; 9 Social drinking allowed; 10 Tennis available; 11 Swimming available; 12 Golf available; 13 Skiing available; 14 May be booked through travel agents.

your hostess will arrange for horseback riding if you give advance notice. No pets. Children over 12 welcome. Smoking outside only. $50-60.

The King's Cottage, A Bed and Breakfast Inn

1049 East King Street, 17602
(800) 747-8717

Traditionally styled elegance, modern comfort, and warm hospitality in Amish country. King and queen beds, private baths, gourmet breakfasts, and personal service create a friendly atmosphere at this award-winning Spanish-style mansion. Relax by the fire and enjoy afternoon tea in the library while chatting with innkeepers about directions to restaurants or attractions. Special Amish dinners or personal tours arranged. Near farmers' markets, Gettysburg, and Hershey. On the National Register of Historic Places. AAA- and Mobil-listed excellent.

Hosts: Karen and Jim Owens
Rooms: 7 (PB) $75-115
Full Breakfast
Credit Cards: A, B, D
Notes: 2, 5, 9, 10, 11, 12, 14

The King's Cottage

Lincoln Haus Inn Bed and Breakfast

1687 Lincoln Highway East, 17602
(717) 392-9412

Centrally situated in Lancaster County. A suburban home, built in 1915, with distinctive hip roofs. Front porch for sitting and double lawn swings for relaxing. Inside are natural oak woodwork and gleaming hardwood floors. Antique furniture and rugs are throughout the house. Mary, a member of the Old Order Amish church, serves a full breakfast family-style in her shining, homey dining room. Her specialty is to be a great hostess.

Host: Mary K. Zook
Rooms: 5 plus apartment (PB) $43-70
Full Breakfast
Credit Cards: None
Notes: 2, 5, 8, 14

Meadowview Guest House

2169 New Holland Pike, Route 23, 17601
(717) 299-4017

Located in the heart of the Pennsylvania Dutch area, close to historic sites, antiques, farmers' and flea markets, and excellent restaurants. Large air-conditioned rooms, guest kitchen with coffee and tea. To help you enjoy the beautiful county, personalized maps are provided.

Host: Ed and Sheila Christie
Rooms: 3 (1 PB; 2 SB) $25-40
Continental Breakfast
Credit Cards: None
Closed December 1-March 14
Notes: 2, 5, 8 (over 6), 9, 10, 11, 12

Mennonite Farm

Bed and Breakfast of Philadelphia
1616 Walnut Street, Suite 1120, Philadelphia, 19103
(215) 735-1917; (800) 220-1917
FAX (215) 735-1905

This is a simple, cozy farm owned by two remarkable likable people who go out of their way to make their guests atnhome. Hannah's farm breakfasts are enormous, and what guests say about their visit here incidcate that it is a very special s place. Two second floor guest rooms, one of which has a double bed and the other a twin bed, share a bath with a tub and shower. Children welcome. No smoking. Pets-$5 additional charge. $40-50.

New Life Homestead Bed and Breakfast

1400 East King Street, 17602
(717) 396-8928

Traditional Lancaster County brick home built in 1912, operated by a Mennonite family. Natural chestnut trim, antiques, and family heirlooms. Centrally situated, minutes to farms, Amish markets, and attractions. Full breakfast and evening treats. Tours and meals in Amish homes arranged. Rooms have private bath.

Hosts: Carol and Bill Giersch
Rooms: 4 (2 PB; 2 SB) $50-70
Full Breakfast
Credit Cards: None
Notes: 5, 8, 14

O'Flaherty's Dingeldein House

1105 East King Street, 17602
(717) 293-1723

O'Flaherty's Dingeldein House is the former residence of the Armstrong family of the floor tile fortune. Since its original construction in 1912, portions have been added, and other owners have included the Leath family, founders of the Strasburg Railroad Museum. Each of the air-conditioned guest rooms has been individually decorated and has a unique personality. Available are several common areas with fireplaces, a spacious porch, and beautiful landscaped gardens.

Hosts: Jack and Sue Flatley
Rooms: 4 (2 PB; 2 SB) $60-70
Full Breakfast
Credit Cards: A, B, D
Notes: 2, 5, 8

Patchwork Inn

2319 Old Philadelphia Pike, 17602
(717) 293-9078; (800) 584-5776

Patchwork Inn is a 19th-century farmhouse furnished throughout with antique oak. The inn is decorated with over 60 new and antique quilts from all parts of the USA. The queen-size beds are covered with handmade quilts, and other private collections include 25 old telephones and an extensive Delft china collection. Reading material abounds, and bike storage and routes are available. Patchwork Inn is east of Lancaster across the street from a working Amish farm.

Hosts: Lee and Anne Martin
Rooms: 4 (2 PB; 2 SB) $55-75
Full Breakfast
Credit Cards: A, B, D
Notes: 2, 5, 9

Sunny Acres

Bed and Breakfast of Philadelphia
1616 Walnut Street, Suite 1120, Philadelphia, 19103
(215) 735-1917; (800) 220-1917
FAX (215) 735-1905

This country home is in a peaceful setting surrounded by Amish farms. A comfortable ranch house with a large sun room to enjoy your full breakfast. There are two guest rooms on the ground level that share a bath. The location is ideal for touring Pennsylvania Dutch Country, 20 minutes from Lancaster, 12 minutes from Longwood Gardens and Winterthur. A special attraction for golfing is the eighteen-hole golf course at Moccasin Run only one mile away. $45-55.

The Walkabout Inn

837 Village Road, Lampeter, 17537
(717) 464-0707

The Walkabout Inn is an authentic British-style bed and breakfast in the heart of the Amish country, convenient to all major attractions. The house is a 22-room brick 1925 Mennonite farmhouse with wraparound porches. Australian-born Richard and his wife, Maggie, serve a full five-course candlelight breakfast. Guest rooms have private baths, canopy and/or queen-size beds, antiques, and cable television. Restaurant guides and coupons are available. Ask about the $99 mid-week specials which include an Amish dinner and tour. Anniversary/honeymoon specials available.

Hosts: Richard and Margaret Mason
Rooms: 5 (PB) $79-99
Full Breakfast
Credit Cards: A, B, C
Notes: 2, 4, 5, 8, 9, 10, 11, 12, 14

Witmer's Tavern—Historic 1725 Inn

2014 Old Philadelphia Pike, 17602
(717) 299-5305

Lancaster's only pre-Revolutionary War inn still lodging travelers. Restored to the simple, authentic, pioneer style that was familiar to European immigrants who joined the Conestoga wagon trains being provisioned at the inn for the western and southern treks into the wilderness areas. Fresh flowers, working fireplaces, antique quilts, and antiques in all the romantic rooms. Pandora's Antique Shop in-house. Bird-in-Hand and Intercourse villages, other antique shops, and auctions just beyond. Valley Forge, Hershey, Gettysburg, Winterthur, Chadds Ford, New Hope, all within three-fourths to one and one-half hour's drive. On the National Register of Historic Places and a national landmark.

Host: Brant Hartung
Rooms: 7 (2 PB; 5 SB) $60-90
Continental Breakfast
Credit Cards: None
Notes: 2, 5, 7, 8, 9, 10, 11, 12, 13, 14

Ye Olde Bank Bed and Breakfast

29 North Prince Street, 17603
(717) 393-7774

In the heart of downtown Lancaster within walking distance of the Farmers' Market, the Fulton Theatre, and a variety of shops and restaurants. Enjoy the delightful continental plus breakfast, downy robes, and relaxing in your own private bath.

Host: Nina Balgar
Rooms: 2 (PB) $75-105
Expanded Continental Breakfast
Credit Cards: None
Notes: 2, 5, 8, 9 14

Witmer's Tavern

LANDENBERG

Cornerstone Bed and Breakfast

Rural Delivery 1, Box 155, 19350
(215) 274-2143

To understand history is to live it. Charming 18th-century country inn with canopy beds, fireplaces in bedrooms, private baths, and antiques galore situated minutes from Brandywine Valley museums and gardens: Longwood, Winterthur, Hagley.

Hosts: Linda and Marty
Rooms: 5 (PB) $75-130

NOTES: Credit cards accepted: A Master Card; B Visa; C American Express; D Discover Card; E Diner's Club; F Other; 2 Personal Checks accepted; 3 Lunch available; 4 Dinner available; 5 Open all year;

Full Breakfast
Credit Cards: A, B, C
Notes: 2, 5, 8, 9, 11, 12

LIMA

Amanda's Bed and Breakfast #279

1428 Park Avenue, Annapolis, MD 21217
(301) 225-0001; (301) 383-1274

This bed and breakfast is a large 19th-century country manor house. Built in 1856, it has been on the National Register of Historic Places since 1971. More than three-fourths of the land is covered with luxuriant growth. Eight guest rooms, all with private baths, are available. $85-125.

Hamanassett

P. O. Box 129, 19037
(215) 459-3000

Private estate with secluded historic 19th-century country manor house on 36 acres of woodlands, gardens, fields and trails; near the beautiful Penna/Del's Brandywine Valley attractions: Longwood Gardens, Winterthur, Hagley, Nemours. Enjoy an elegantly quiet weekend getaway. The rooms have king, queen, double, or twin beds, television, and private baths.

Host: Evelene H. Dohan
Rooms: 8 (6 PB; 2 SB) $90-110
Full Breakfast
Credit Cards: None
Notes: 2, 5, 7 (limited), 9, 10, 12, 14

LITITZ

Spahr's Century Farm Bed and Breakfast

192 Green Acre Road, 17543
(717) 627-2185

This Lancaster County farm has been in the Spahr family since 1855. Antique shops and candy and pretzel factories are in nearby Lititz. Biking, walking, and peace and quiet surround this charming bed and breakfast.

Host: Naomi Spahr
Rooms: 4 (1 PB; 3 SB) $45-55
Continental Plus Breakfast
Credit Cards: None
Notes: 2

Swiss Woods Bed and Breakfast

500 Blantz Road, 17543
(717) 627-3358; (800) 594-8018

A visit to Swiss Woods, nestled on the edge of the woods overlooking Speedwell Forge Lake, is reminiscent of a trip to one of Switzerland's guest houses. Situated in beautiful Lancaster County, home of the Pennsylvania Dutch, Swiss Woods was designed with comfort and atmosphere in mind. The gardens are landscaped with flowering perennials and annuals. Enjoy breakfast in the Ankerstube, dominated by a sandstone fireplace with lots of natural woodwork and large, sunny windows. The rooms feature queen beds and private baths (two with whirlpool baths), patios, or balconies.

Hosts: Debrah and Werner Mosimann
Rooms: 7 (PB) $70-105
Full Breakfast
Credit Cards: A, B, D
Notes: 2, 5, 8, 9, 14

MALVERN

Eaglesmere

Bed and Breakfast of Valley Forge, #0702
P. O. Box 1151, Valley Forge, 19481-1151
(215) 783-7838; (800) 344-0123

This 21-sided contemporary home is nestled on a wooded cul-de-sac. It boasts three cathedral ceilings, exposed beams, and walls of windows overlooking Great Valley and Valley Forge Mountain. A gourmet breakfast is served in the dining room or on one of four decks. The enormous lower level contains the guest quarters. Preheated beds, bath gels, bathroom toe warmers, and thick terry-cloth robes are provided for your pleasure. Two guest rooms with private bath. $75/

The Great Valley House of Valley Forge

110 Swedesford Road, Rural Delivery 3, 19355
(215) 644-6759

This historical 1690 stone farmhouse has rooms filled with antiques and hand-stenciled walls. Located on four acres with swimming pool and walking trails for guests, this old farmhouse is ideal for a quiet getaway. A full breakfast is served in the pre-revolutionary kitchen in front of a 14-foot walk-in fireplace. Just a short drive from Philadelphia, Lancaster, and Brandywine Valley. The Great Valley House has been featured in the Philadelphia Inquirer and Washington Post.

Rooms: 3 (2 PB; 1 SB) $65-80
Full Breakfast
Credit Cards: None
Notes: 2, 3, 5, 7, 8, 9, 11, 14

MANHEIM

Herr Farmhouse Inn

2256 Huber Driver, 17545
(717) 653-9852

Historic stone farmhouse, circa 1738, on 11.5 scenic acres of farmland. The inn has been tastefully restored, retaining original pine floors, moldings, and six working fireplaces. The perfect retreat, with Lancaster County attractions and fine restaurants nearby.

Host: Barry Herr
Rooms: 4 (2 PB; 2 SB) $70-95 plus tax
Expanded Continental Breakfast
Credit Cards: A, B
Notes: 2, 5, 7 (limited), 8 (over 12), 9

Manheim Manor

140 South Charlotte Street, 17545
(717) 664-4168

Experience Victorian hospitality in this 1856 historic home. Magnificent chestnut wood; Laura Ashley decor; bountiful breakfast, plus cordials, mints, and toffee. Rooms have air conditioning, color cable TV, and refrigerators. On bikers' loop, with bicycles available. Ask about Amish dinners, buggy rides, romantic winter sleigh rides. Convenient to all major Amish-area attractions.

Hosts: Alfred and Alice Avella
Rooms: 6 (PB) $80-100
Full Breakfast
Credit Cards: None
Notes: 2, 5, 9, 10, 11, 12, 14

Rose Manor Bed and Breakfast

124 South Linden Street, 17545
(717) 664-4932

This lovely bed and breakfast is surrounded by Pennsylvania Dutch country attractions. The perfect location for relaxation. Retire among romantic Victorian antiques, hand-carved furniture, and draped beds. Breakfast, chosen from a menu, is served at the guest's convenience.

Hosts: Don and Carol Bryant
Rooms: 4 (PB) $70-90
Full Breakfast
Credit Cards: A, B
Notes: 2, 5, 8 (over 9), 9, 10, 11, 12, 13, 14

Stone Haus Farm

360 South Esbenshade Road, 17545
(717) 653-5819

Located in the country, this cozy bed and breakfast offers a relaxing environment for guests. Close to Lancaster Amish country, Hershey, Gettysburg, and a popular Mennonite restaurant. Guests are welcome to join hosts during Mennonite church service.

NOTES: Credit cards accepted: A Master Card; B Visa; C American Express; D Discover Card; E Diner's Club; F Other; 2 Personal Checks accepted; 3 Lunch available; 4 Dinner available; 5 Open all year;

Hosts: Henry and Irene Shenk
Rooms: 6 (SB) $29-34
Full Breakfast
Credit Cards: None
Notes: 2, 5, 8, 10

MARIETTA

The River Inn

258 West Front Street, 17547
(717) 426-2290

Restored home, circa 1790, situated in National Historic District of Marietta. Centrally located, along Susquehanna River, near Lancaster, York, and Hershey attractions. Decorated with antiques and reproductions, this home offers three cozy guest rooms. When weather permits, breakfast is served on the screened porch. In the winter, warm your body with the six fireplaces located through out the home. Enjoy the herb and flower gardens. Owner can provide guided boat fishing on river. Air conditioning, cable TV.

Hosts: Joyce and Bob Heiserman
Rooms: 3 (PB) $60-70
Full Breakfast
Credit Cards: A, B, D
Notes: 2, 5, 9, 14

Vogt Farm Bed and Breakfast

1225 Colebrook Road, 17547
(717) 653-4810

Vogt Farm guests are treated like friends by the hosts of this bed and breakfast. The guest rooms are decorated with antiques and other family treasures. Guests are welcome to enjoy the fireplace in the livingroom, cozy porches, and air conditioning. Breakfast is served at 8:30 weekdays, and 8:00 on Sunday in the large farm kitchen. Air-conditioned, spacious yard, three porches, animals.

Rooms: 3 (SB) $55
Full Breakfast
Credit Cards: A, B, C, D
Notes: 2, 5, 8, 12

MENDENHALL

Fairville Inn

Kennett Pike, Route 52, P. O. Box 219, 19357
(215) 388-5900

This elegant country house is on beautiful grounds in the heart of the Brandywine Valley chateau country. Situated right between Winterthur, Longwood Gardens, and the Brandywine River Museum, it offers fifteen wonderful guest rooms, all of which have modern conveniences. Many rooms have a canopy bed, fireplace, and deck, and all rooms are graced with fresh flowers. Afternoon tea and a lovely continental breakfast served daily. Many historic taverns and restaurants for dinner are nearby.

Hosts: Ole and Patricia Retlev
Rooms: 15 (PB) $100-165
Continental Breakfast
Credit Cards: A, B, C, D
Notes: 2, 5, 7, 8, 9

MERTZTOWN

Blair Creek Inn and Lodging

P. O. Box 20, Rural Delivery 2, 19539
(215) 682-6700

This Mobil four-star-rated restaurant offers lodging, breakfast, and dinners Wednesday through Saturday. Sunday brunch is served. Set on four and one-half acres of beautiful lawn and gardens, the inn also caters to weddings, receptions, business affairs, and private parties.

Hosts: Dr. and Mrs. Joseph A. Miller
Rooms: 2 (PB) $90-125
Continental Breakfast (Mon.-Sat.); Full Brunch
 (Sun.)
Credit Cards: A, B
Notes: 2, 4, 9

---

6 Pets welcome; 7 Smoking allowed; 8 Children welcome; 9 Social drinking allowed; 10 Tennis available; 11 Swimming available; 12 Golf available; 13 Skiing available; 14 May be booked through travel agents.

Longswamp
Bed and Breakfast

Rural Delivery 2, Box 26, 19539
(215) 682-6197

This 200-year-old home, furnished with
antiques and every comfort, is set in gorgeous countryside, yet is close to Reading,
Kutztown, Allentown, and Amish country.
Delicious, bountiful breakfasts draw raves
from guests.

Hosts: Elsa and Dean Dimick
Rooms: 10 (6 PB; 4 SB) $63-79.50
Full Breakfast
Credit Cards: A, B
Notes: 2, 5, 8, 9, 10, 11, 12, 13

MIDDLETOWN

Hershey Bed and Breakfast
Reservation Service

P. O. Box 208, Hershey, 17033-0208
(717) 533-2928

Gracious home set on nine acres of land
with a deck facing the woods. Ten minutes
from Hershey Park and local attractions.
Two guest bedrooms with shared bath. Full
breakfast. No smoking. $50.

MILFORD

Black Walnut
Bed and Breakfast Inn

Rural Delivery 2, Box 9285, 18337
(717) 296-6322

Tudor-style stone house with historic marble fireplace and 12 charming guest rooms
with antiques and brass beds. A 160-acre
estate, it is quiet and peaceful and conveniently situated near horseback riding,
antiquing, golf, skiing, rafting, and canoeing on the Delaware River. Serving the
finest cuisine and cocktails in a beautiful
country setting overlooking a five-acre lake
just outside of Milford.

Host: Stewart and Effie Schneider
Rooms: 12 (8 PB; 4 SB) $60-100
Full Breakfast
Credit Cards: A, B, C
Notes: 2, 3, 4, 5, 9, 11, 12, 13

Cliff Park
Inn and Golf Course

Rural Route 4, Box 7200, 18337-9708
(717) 296-6491; (800) 225-6535 (outside PA)

Historic country inn surrounded by
long-established golf course with cliffs
overlooking the Delaware River. Inn and
restaurant rated three stars by Mobil Guide.
Fine dining. Modified American Plan or
bed and breakfast plan available. Golf
school. Inn/golf packages. Cross-country
skiing in winter. Golf and ski equipment
rentals. Conferences. Country weddings.
Ninety minutes from New York City.
Brochures by FAX.

Hosts: The Buchanan family
Rooms: 18 (PB) $85-135
Full Breakfast
Credit Cards: A, B, C, D, E
Notes: 2, 3, 4, 5, 7, 8, 9, 12, 13, 14

Cliff Park Inn

MONTGOMERY COUNTY

Blue Bell Artist's Roots

Bed and Breakfast of Philadelphia
1616 Walnut Street, Suite 1120, Philadelphia, 19103
(215) 735-1917; (800) 220-1917
FAX (215) 735-1905

NOTES: Credit cards accepted: A Master Card; B Visa; C American Express; D Discover Card; E Diner's
Club; F Other; 2 Personal Checks accepted; 3 Lunch available; 4 Dinner available; 5 Open all year;

Stately brick posts guard the driveway of this solid, turn-of-the-century home. Inside you will find a cozy, clean country atmosphere. The hostess invites you to share her hospitality, comfortable home, and, in the summer, the swimming pool and spacious grounds. One guest room is on the second floor and offers twin beds and a private bath. Children are welcome. Smoking is allowed. $30-40.

Shirl's Shed

Bed and Breakfast of Philadelphia
1616 Walnut Street, Suite 1120, Philadelphia, 19103
(215) 735-1917; (800) 220-1917
FAX (215) 735-1905

Tucked away in a corner of this large, forest-rimmed back lawn of a comfortable suburban home is a small cottage with an attached greenhouse. The room includes a queen-size bed and private bath that is a greenhouse, walled and curtained with white boards and ruffled green calico for privacy, but open to the sun and moon and treetop vistas. Firewood is provided for the stove, and a generous breakfast basket filled with a continental assortment is left at your doorstep to enjoy on your own schedule. Children welcome. Smoking allowed. $85

MONTOURSVILLE

The Carriage House at Stonegate

Rural Delivery 1, Box 11 A, 17754
(717) 433-4340

Nestled in the lower Loyalsock Creek Valley, on one of the oldest farms in the valley, the Carriage House offers its guests a unique concept in the bed and breakfast world. President Herbert Hoover was a descendent of the original settlers of the farm. The converted carriage house pro-

vides visitors with total privacy and 1,400 square feet of space on two floors. The Carriage House is furnished in antiques and period reproductions. There are two bedrooms and a bath upstairs, with a fully equipped kitchen, half-bath, and living/dining area downstairs.

Hosts: Harold and Dena Mesaris
Rooms: 2 (SB) $50
Continental Breakfast
Credit Cards: None
Notes: 2, 5, 6, 7, 8, 9, 10, 11, 12, 13, 14

MOUNT AIRY

Bed and Breakfast Connections #00321

P. O. Box 21, Devon, 19333
(215) 687-3565; (800) 448-3619 (outside PA)

This 12-room stone home features Scandanavian decor and carved woodwork. The quaint shops and restaurants of Chestnut Hill are only a short walk away. Accommodations in this turn-of-the-century Victorian are on the third floor. Hand-stenciled walls, handwoven fabrics, and lace curtains make it an inviting home away from home. On weekends, a full gourmet breakfast is served and afternoon tea is available in the parlor. A continental-plus breakfast is provided during the week. No smoking. Resident cats. $50-60.

"Eyrie"

Bed and Breakfast of Philadelphia
1616 Walnut Street, Suite 1120, Philadelphia, 19103
(215) 735-1917; (800) 220-1917
FAX (215) 735-1905

This historically certified town house was built circa 1900 and is furnished in Victorian style with many antiques. On the third floor there is a room with a double bed and shared bath, and on the fourth floor there is a double bed with a shared bath,

6 Pets welcome; 7 Smoking allowed; 8 Children welcome; 9 Social drinking allowed; 10 Tennis available; 11 Swimming available; 12 Golf available; 13 Skiing available; 14 May be booked through travel agents.

and a room with a pair of twins and a shared bath. $50-65.

Cedar Hill Farm

Mt. Airy Home

Bed and Breakfast of Philadelphia
1616 Walnut Street, Suite 1120, Philadelphia, 19103
(215) 735-1917; (800) 220-1917
FAX (215) 735-1905

This spacious suburban home is set high above the street in a lovely garden. Conveniently located and a three-minute walk from commuter rail and bus. There is a queen-size bed with a private bath, a pair of twins with a shared bath, and a double bed with a shared bath. $40-50.

MOUNT JOY

Cedar Hill Farm

305 Longenecker Road, 17552
(717) 653-4655

This 1817 stone farmhouse sits in a quiet area overlooking a stream. The charming bedrooms have private baths and are centrally air-conditioned. The farm is situated near Amish farms and Hershey. Other attractions are nearby farmers' markets, antique shops, and interesting country villages.

Hosts: Russel and Gladys Swarr
Rooms: 4 (PB) $60-65
Expanded Continental Breakfast
Credit Cards: A, B, C, D
Notes: 2, 5, 8, 9, 10, 11, 12

MOUNT MORRIS

High Places Ranch Camp

P. O. Box 97, 15349
(412) 324-2770

Located at Mount Morris, between Waynesburg, Pennsylvania, and Morgantown, West Virginia. Offered are primitive camping on the Warrior Indian Trail, horseback riding, farm pets, hiking, hay and carriage rides, winter sledding, cross-country skiing, and hunting are a few of the activities guests will enjoy. Also available at Cheat Lake near Morgantown is a private three-bedroom, two-bath modern mobile home.

Host: JoAnn Moon
Rooms: 4 (1 PB; 3 SB) $25-150
Continental Breakfast
Credit Cards: None
Notes: 2, 5, 6, 7, 8

MOUNT POCONO

Farmhouse Bed and Breakfast

HCR 1, Box 6 B, 18344
(717) 839-0796

"Where the Honor of Our House is Hospitality." An 1850 homestead on six manicured acres. Separate cottage and two suites in house, all with fireplace. Farm-style breakfast complete with original country recipes prepared by your host, a professional chef. Enjoy bedtime snacks freshly baked each day. Antiques adorn each room, with cleanliness being the order of the day. Accommodations have private baths, queen beds, TV, phones, and air conditioning. No smoking.

NOTES: Credit cards accepted: A Master Card; B Visa; C American Express; D Discover Card; E Diner's Club; F Other; 2 Personal Checks accepted; 3 Lunch available; 4 Dinner available; 5 Open all year;

Hosts: Jack and Donna Asure
Rooms: 3 (PB) $75-95
Full Breakfast
Credit Cards: A, B, D
Notes: 5, 9, 10, 11, 12, 13

MUNCY

The Bodine House

307 South Main Street, 17756
(717) 546-8949

Built in 1805 and situated in the National
Historic District of Muncy, the Bodine
House offers guests the opportunity to
enjoy the atmosphere of an earlier age. The
comfortable rooms are furnished with
antiques, and candlelight is used in the
livingroom by the fireplace, where guests
enjoy refreshments. Three blocks from
town center, movies, restaurants, library,
and shops.

Hosts: David and Marie Louise Smith
Rooms: 4 (3 PB; 1 SB) $50-75
Full Breakfast
Credit Cards: A, B, C
Notes: 2, 5, 8 (over 6), 9, 10, 11, 12, 13, 14

The Bodine House

NEW CUMBERLAND

Hershey Bed and Breakfast Reservation Service

P. O. Box 208, Hershey, 17033-0208
(717) 533-2928

An 11-room limestone farmhouse that sits
on three acres high on a hill overlooking
Yellow Breeches Creek. Legend has it that
this house was part of the Underground
Railroad. Each guest room has a double
bed and comfortable seating with good
lighting. One room has a private bath; two
rooms share a bath. Two rooms have large
porches to enjoy in good weather. Antique
furnishings throughout. Full breakfast.
$65-70; $15/additional person.

NEWFOUNDLAND

White Cloud

Rural Delivery 1, Box 215, 18445
(717) 676-3162

This is a meatless, natural foods inn and
restaurant with 45 acres of woodland, tennis court, pool, library, and meditation
room. Situated three miles south of
Newfoundland on Route 447. Specialties
are peace, quiet, and good food.

Hosts: George and Judy Wilkinson
Rooms: 20 (7 PB; 13 SB) $34.25-63.50
Full Breakfast
Credit Cards: A, B
Notes: 2, 3, 4, 5, 6, 8, 9, 10, 11, 12, 13, 14

NEW HOPE—SEE ALSO WRIGHTSTOWN

Aaron Burr House

80 West Bridge Street, 18938
(215) 862-2343

This vintage village Victorian inn sits atop
a residential tree-lined street in New
Hope's historic district. Named for the U.S.
vice president who sought a safe haven in

---

6 Pets welcome; 7 Smoking allowed; 8 Children welcome; 9 Social drinking allowed; 10 Tennis available; 11
Swimming available; 12 Golf available; 13 Skiing available; 14 May be booked through travel agents.

Bucks County in 1804, Aaron Burr House offers today's business and pleasure travelers similar refuge.

Hosts: Nadine and Carl Glassman
Rooms: 6 (PB)
Expanded Continental Breakfast
Minimum stay weekends: 2 nights; holidays: 3
  nights
Credit Cards: C
Notes: 2, 5, 8, 9, 10, 11, 12, 13, 14

Backstreet Inn of New Hope

144 Old York Road, 18938
(215) 862-9571

The Backstreet Inn of New Hope offers the comfort and serenity of a small inn in the town of New Hope, Bucks County. It is situated in a quiet, tucked-away street, yet within walking distance of the center of town.

Hosts: Bob Puccio and John Hein
Rooms: 7 (PB) $95-175
Full Breakfast
Minimum stay weekends: 2 nights; holidays:
  3 nights
Credit Cards: A, B, C, D
Notes: 2, 5, 7, 8, 10, 11, 12, 13, 14

Backstreet Inn of New Hope

Bucks County Inn

Bed and Breakfast of Valley Forge #2301
P. O. Box 1151, Valley Forge, 19481-1151
(215) 783-7838; (800) 344-0123

This inn was constructed in 1870 with a flourish of later Victorian architectural features including a cruciform floor plan, deep eaves, projecting two-story bay window, a wraparound veranda with scrolled brackets, porte-cochère, and a gazebo on which guests can enjoy breakfast. Tradition states that General Alexander and Lord Sterling were quartered in an earlier structure on whose foundation the inn was built just prior to the momentous Battle of Trenton in December 1776. Five guest rooms with private bath. $90-120.

Centre Bridge Inn

River Road, 18938
(215) 862-9139

A romantic country inn overlooking the Delaware River in historic Bucks County, featuring canopy beds and river views. Fine restaurant serving French continental cuisine and spirits in an Old World-style dining room with fireplace, or alfresco dining in season.

Host: Stephen R. Dugan
Rooms: 9 (PB) $80-125
Continental Breakfast
Minimum stay weekends: 2 nights; holidays: 3
  nights
Credit Cards: A, B, C
Notes: 2, 4, 5, 7, 8 (over 8), 9, 10, 11, 12, 14

Holly Hedge Estate Bed and Breakfast

6987 Upper York Road, 18938
(215) 862-3136

Relax and enjoy the warm, friendly atmosphere at this 200-year-old country estate set back from the road on 20 acres of beautiful gardens. Swimming, tennis, private baths, catering facilities, and corporate meetings and retreats are some of the amenities offered. Some rooms have fireplaces, and you are minutes from New Hope and Lambertville. Shopping, antiquing, and Delaware River activities are close by. Closed Christmas.

NOTES: Credit cards accepted: A Master Card; B Visa; C American Express; D Discover Card; E Diner's Club; F Other; 2 Personal Checks accepted; 3 Lunch available; 4 Dinner available; 5 Open all year;

Hosts: Joe and Amy Luccaro
Rooms: 14 (PB) $75-150
Full Breakfast
Credit Cards: A, B, C
Notes: 2, 5, 6, 7 (limited), 8, 10, 11, 14

Hotel du Village

North River Road, 18938
(215) 862-9911

Intimate country dining and lodging on spacious grounds. Outdoor pool, two tennis courts on property. Delightful restaurant with fireplaces and outdoor terrace for use in season. Chef owned and operated. Rooms decorated with country furnishings. Continental breakfast includes juice, fruit, and assorted pastries. Conference space available.

Hosts: Barbara and Omar Arbani
Rooms: 19 (PB) $85-105
Expanded Continental Breakfast
Credit Cards: C, E
Notes: 2, 4, 5, 7, 8 (weekdays), 9, 10, 11

Oak Farm Bed and Breakfast

Bed and Breakfast of Valley Forge #1901
P. O. Box 1151, Valley Forge, 19481-1151
(215) 783-7838; (800) 344-0123

This traditional 18th-century farmhouse is situated in the heart of Bucks County on ten wooded acres. Open-beamed ceilings and Oriental carpets throughout the 14 rooms contribute to its rustic charm and elegance. After a full day, guests can relax in the redwood hot tub, or on cool days relax by the fire. Breakfast can be enjoyed in the dining room or on the lovely sun porch.

Tattersall Inn

Box 569, 18950
(215) 297-8233

Overlooking a river village, this manor house dates to the 18th century and features broad porches for relaxation and a walk-in

fireplace for cool evenings. Breakfast in the dining room, in your room, or on the veranda. Enjoy the antique-furnished rooms and collection of vintage phonographs. Close to New Hope.

Hosts: Gerry and Herb Moss
Rooms: 6 (PB) $75-95
Continental Breakfast
Credit Cards: A, B, C, D
Notes: 2, 5, 7 (limited), 8, 9, 10, 11, 14

Wedgwood Inn of New Hope

111 West Bridge Street, 18938
(215) 862-2570

Voted Inn of the Year by readers of inn guidebooks, this historic inn, on two acres of landscaped grounds, is steps from the village center. Antiques, fresh flowers, and Wedgwood china are the rule at the inn, where guests are treated like royalty. AAA three diamonds.

Hosts: Carl A. Glassman and Nadine Silnutzer
Rooms: 12 (10 PB; 2 SB) $70-160
Expanded Continental Breakfast
Credit Cards: C
Notes: 2, 5, 8, 9, 10, 11, 12, 13, 14

Tattersall Inn

The Whitehall Inn

Rural Delivery 2, Box 250, 18938
(215) 598-9745

Experience a 1794 estate with fireplaces in rooms, heirloom sterling, European crystal and china. Afternoon high tea, chamber

6 Pets welcome; 7 Smoking allowed; 8 Children welcome; 9 Social drinking allowed; 10 Tennis available; 11 Swimming available; 12 Golf available; 13 Skiing available; 14 May be booked through travel agents.

music, velour robes, chocolate truffles. Swimming pool on premises, dressage horses, roses, and the legendary four-course candlelight breakfast featured in Bon Appetit, Gourmet, and Food and Wine.

Hosts: Mike and Suella Wass
Rooms: 6 (4 PB; 2 SB) $120-170
Full Breakfast
Minimum stay weekends: 2 nights; holidays: 3 nights
Credit Cards: A, B, C, D, E, F
Notes: 2, 5, 8 (over 12), 9, 10, 11, 12, 13, 14 (weekdays)

NEW MILFORD

Hilltop House and Country House

69 Beaver Meadow Road, 18834
(717) 434-2360

A clean, comfortable hideaway sleeps six or more in any of the four seasons for quiet restfulness or active outdoor adventure. Just bring your toothbrush! Located on a 300-acre farm with skiing at Elk Mountain, fishing, hunting, hiking, TV, and reading.

Hosts: Carol and Bill Guild
Rooms: 3 (SB) $75-175
Credit Cards: None
Notes: 2, 5, 10, 11, 12, 13, 14

NEWTON

Upper Black Eddy Bed and Breakfast

Bed and Breakfast of Valley Forge, #0102
P. O. Box 1151, Valley Forge, 19481-1151
(215) 783-7838; (800) 344-0123

Welcome to peace and security in this 1820s farmhouse on 26 acres surrounded by hundreds of acres of wildlife preserve. Situated within minutes of the finest restaurants along the Delaware River and just 20 minutes to New Hope. Three antique-filled guest rooms. $115-135.

NEWVILLE

Nature's Nook Farm

740 Shed Road, 17241
(717) 776-5619

Nature's Nook Farm is a 96-acre working dairy farm in a quiet, peaceful setting along the Blue Mountains. Warm Mennonite hospitality and clean, comfortable lodging await you. Enjoy freshly brewed garden tea. Homemade cinnamon rolls, muffins, or coffee cake a specialty. Close to Colonel Denning State Park with hiking trails, swimming, and fishing. Two hours to Lancaster, one hour to Harrisburg, one and one-half hours to Gettysburg and Hershey. Wheelchair accessible.

Hosts: Don and Lois Leatherman
Room: 1 (PB) $40
Continental Breakfast
Credit Cards: None
Notes: 2, 5, 8, 10, 11, 12

NORTH EAST

Brown's Village Inn

51 East Main Street, 16428
(814) 725-5522

This Federal-style home, built in 1832, once served as a stagecoach stop and a station for the Underground Railroad. Today, after an extensive renovation, the house appears much as it did just after the Civil War. The inn is filled with nostalgia that will take visitors back in time: a fluffy eiderdown, an old armoire like the one you used to hide in at Grandma's house, and a banister that makes even the most prim yearn for that forbidden slide. Rebecca and her staff prepare fresh, delicious fare for you each morning. The beautifully restored village of North East will capture your heart, and all of the rooms have private baths and air conditioning.

Hosts: Ruth and Bill Brown
Rooms: 4 (PB) $65
Continental Plus Breakfast
Credit Cards: A, B
Notes: 2, 3, 4, 5, 8, 9

NOTES: Credit cards accepted: A Master Card; B Visa; C American Express; D Discover Card; E Diner's Club; F Other; 2 Personal Checks accepted; 3 Lunch available; 4 Dinner available; 5 Open all year;

NORTH WALES

Joseph Ambler Inn

1005 Horsham Road, 19454
(215) 362-7500

As guests make their approach up the long, winding drive, they are at once struck by the peaceful, historic setting of this fine country inn. Nestled on 12 acres of picturesque lawns and gardens, the inn features 28 delightful guest rooms in three buildings, with an outstanding Colonial restaurant located in the Pennsylvania fieldstone barn. The guest rooms are furnished with antiques and reproductions, and each has a private bath, telephone, air conditioning, and TV. Meeting and conference facilities are available for up to fifty people. Banquets, parties, and weddings may be held for up to 120 people.

Hosts: Steve and Terry Kratz
Rooms: 28 (PB) $95-140
Full Breakfast
Credit Cards: A, B, C, D, E
Notes: 2, 4, 5, 7, 8, 9, 10, 11, 12, 14

OAKS

Benjamin's 1833 House

Bed and Breakfast of Valley Forge #0904
P. O. Box 1151, Valley Forge, 19481-1151
(215) 783-7838; (800) 344-0123

This is an on-going restoration of a Federal-style, pointed stone farmhouse built in 1833. Highlights include five fireplaces, some of which work, original woodwork, stenciling, and antique furnishings. Breakfast is served in the keeping room in front of a working "walk-in" fireplace. Fragrances from the herb garden are an aromatic delight in spring and summer. Located in a small suburb close to Valley Forge, Amish country, and an easy drive to the Brandywine area. Two guest rooms. $75-85.

ORRTANNA

Hickory Bridge Farm

96 Hickory Bridge Road, 17353
(717) 642-5261

Situated at the edge of the mountains just eight miles west of Gettysburg. Country cottages in a quiet, wooded area by a pure mountain stream. Dinners are offered Friday, Saturday, and Sunday in a restored barn furnished with fine antiques. Family-owned and operated for 15 years. Reservations appreciated.

Hosts: Dr. and Mrs. James Hammett; Mary Lynn
and Robert Martin
Rooms: 4 (PB) $45-85
Full Breakfast
Credit Cards: A, B
Notes: 2, 4, 5, 7, 8, 9, 11, 12, 13

OXFORD

Hershey's Log House Bed and Breakfast

15225 Limestone Road, 19363
(215) 932-9257

Chester County quiet country farm. Wooded area, away from city and traffic noises. Midway between Lancaster (Amish country), Philadelphia, and Wilmington. Visit gardens, museums, battlefields. Rooms have air conditioning, television and telephone for guests' convenience. Family room is also available. Picnic area, hiking, bicycling. No smoking.

Hosts: E. E. and Arlene Hershey
Rooms: $45
Full Breakfast
Notes: 2, 5, 8, 10, 11, 12, 14

PALMYRA

Hershey Bed and Breakfast Reservation Service

P. O. Box 208, Hershey, 17033-0208
(717) 533-2928

---

6 Pets welcome; 7 Smoking allowed; 8 Children welcome; 9 Social drinking allowed; 10 Tennis available; 11 Swimming available; 12 Golf available; 13 Skiing available; 14 May be booked through travel agents.

Situated on the edge of town surrounded by one acre of country pleasures is this circa 1825 Georgian-style farmhouse. A warm "down home" atmosphere prevails throughout, offering simple hospitality and comfort away from the hustle and bustle of the city. Our six air-conditioned rooms offer private baths and cozy informal comfort. A full breakfast is served from 8:00 to 9:30, and afternoon or early evening refreshments provide a relaxing break from the day's activities. $65.

PAOLI

The General's Inn

Bed and Breakfast of Valley Forge #0701
P. O. Box 1151, Valley Forge, 19481-1151
(215) 783-7838; (800) 344-0123

This inn has been in service since 1745. It is authentically restored and furnished; and air-conditioned. Eight complete suites, three with fireplaces and one with Jacuzzi. The first floor is an upscale restaurant and lounge open to the public for lunch and dinner. A continental breakfast is served in the dining room. No pets; no children under 12. $85-135.

The Great Valley House

Bed and Breakfast of Valley Forge #0203
P. O. Box 1151, Valley Forge, 19481-1151
(215) 783-7838; (800) 344-0123

Situated on four acres, this 15-room stone farmhouse, built in 1692, is the second oldest in the state. It is one of the 100 oldest in the country. The original flooring, exposed beams, hand-wrought hinges, and fireplaces add to the charm. An English breakfast is served in front of the walk-in fireplace in the kitchen. Each of the three guest rooms is hand-stenciled, accented with handmade quilts, air-conditioned, furnished with antiques, TV, and radio. Refrigerator, coffee pot, and microwave are provided for guests. Swimming pool. $70-80.

PARADISE

Maple Lane Guest House

505 Paradise Lane, 17562
(717) 687-7479

In the heart of Amish country in Lancaster County, you will find this working dairy farm with winding stream and woodland. Clean, comfortable, air-conditioned rooms have TV, canopy and poster beds, handmade quilts, wall stenciling, and antiques. Close to all the Pennsylvania Dutch attractions such as farmers' markets, outlets, historic sites, and excellent restaurants. See the dairy in operation.

Hosts: Edwin and Marion Rohrer
Rooms: 4 (2 PB; 2 SB) $45-55
Expanded Continental Breakfast
Minimum stay weekends and holidays: 2 nights
Credit Cards: None
Notes: 2, 5, 8, 10, 12

PATTON

Nationality House

209 Magee Avenue, 16668
(814) 674-2225

Guest rooms decorated with international artifacts: Egyptian, Chinese, Spanish, African, Italian, nautical, American Indian. Decorator linens. Remote color TV in rooms. German livingroom, French sitting room, Oriental dining room, Polynesian patio, Grecian gardens. First day huge country breakfast; each day after, gourmet breakfast. All with crystal, silver, china, and linens. In ten wooded acres. Relaxing. Reduced rates for two days and more. Weekly rates available. Distinctively different. The goal is to pamper, with an emphasis on privacy. Reservations advised. Well-behaved children only. Smoking restricted to dining room and enclosed patio. Located 18 miles northwest of Altoona on Route 36.

Host: Loretta Albright
Rooms: 7 (SB) $50-90

NOTES: Credit cards accepted: A Master Card; B Visa; C American Express; D Discover Card; E Diner's Club; F Other; 2 Personal Checks accepted; 3 Lunch available; 4 Dinner available; 5 Open all year;

Pleasant Grove Farm

Full Breakfast
Credit Cards: None
Open May 1-October 31
Notes: 2, 3 (advance notice), 4 (advance notice),
7 (restricted), 8, 9

PEACH BOTTOM

Pleasant Grove Farm

368 Pilottown Road, 17563
(717) 548-3100

Come and enjoy this large, 177-year-old
Federal-style home, at one time a country
store and post office. Century Farm Award.
Watch the cows being milked or feed the
pigs. Full country breakfast by candlelight.

Hosts: Charles and Labertha Tindall
Rooms: 4 (SB) $37.10-42.40
Full Breakfast
Minimum stay weekdays and weekends: 2 nights;
holidays: 3 nights
Credit Cards: None
Notes: 2, 5, 8, 11, 12

PHILADELPHIA

B 'n B at 19th Street

All About Town-B&B in Philadelphia #1205
P. O. Box 1151, Valley Forge, 19481-1151
(215) 783-7838; (800) 344-0123

A recently restored 145-year-old town
house situated just south of Rittenhouse
Square. In good weather, breakfast is
served in the minigarden or on the private
deck of the third-floor suite. Afternoon tea
and scones or a glass of wine can be
enjoyed. Films on the VCR and popcorn in
the parlor. A 20-minute walk to the
Academy of Music, the Curtis Institute of
Music, the University of the Arts, the Civil
War and Rosenbach Rare Book museums
and theaters. $65-85.

Bed and Breakfast Accommodations Downtown Philadelphia

728 Manning Street, 19106
(215) 923-7349

This three-story Colonial town house is
located on a quiet street 2.5 blocks from
Independence Hall. Decorated in Queen
Anne style, this home offers two guest
rooms for your comfort. Televisions, ceiling fans, central air and heat, and intercoms
are in each room.

Host: Margaret Poxon
Rooms: 2 (SB) $60-65
Full Breakfast
Credit Cards: None
Notes: 5, 9, 14

6 Pets welcome; 7 Smoking allowed; 8 Children welcome; 9 Social drinking allowed; 10 Tennis available; 11
Swimming available; 12 Golf available; 13 Skiing available; 14 May be booked through travel agents.

Bed and Breakfast Connections #00108

P. O. Box 21, Devon, 19333
(215) 687-3565; (800) 448-3619 (outside PA)

This charming town house is located just off Rittenhouse Square on a lovely city street. The focal point of it magnificently appointed guest rooms is the massive walnut antique double bed beautifully adorned with a Marsailles spread. Select a book, make a cup of hot tea from the electric kettle, and curl up on the Hide-a-bed sofa to rest from the day's activities. All the comforts of home are yours, including a small refrigerator tucked behind closet doors. Private adjoining bath. Private entrance. Gourmet continental breakfast. No smoking. Resident cats. $70-75.

Bed and Breakfast Connections #00111

P. O. Box 21, Devon, 19333
(215) 687-3565; (800) 448-3619

This historic registered row home provides generous third-floor guest quarters and is conveniently located to the University of Pennsylvania, Drexel University, the Civic Center, and Children's Hospital. At one end of the third floor, you will find a bedroom which can accommodate a family with its two twin beds and a double. The sitting room is located at the opposite end of the hall and is perfect for relaxing in front of the TV or curling up with a book. Private bath. Laundry facilities and refrigerator space are available. $45-55.

Bed and Breakfast Connections #00114

P. O. Box 21, Devon, 19333
(215) 687-3565; (800) 448-3619 (outside PA)

This 1811 historic registered town house was purchased as a shell and has been interestingly renovated and decorated to retain much of its original charm. Its Society Hill address is right in the hub of historic Phildelphia, and close by are the attractions of New Market Square and South Street. The original "tight winder" stairs lead to the third-floor guest room that is tastefully, yet simply, furnished. One large room has a fireplace, settee, and double bed with a private adjoining bath, and a second room with a double and private adjoining bath is available also. A full breakfast is served in the kitchen where the original exposed beams add to the warmth and charm of the home. No smoking. $50-60.

Bed and Breakfast Connections #00122

P. O. Box 21, Devon, 19333
(215) 687-3565; (800) 448-3619 (outside PA)

Complete third-floor privacy awaits the guest in this town house located on Antique Row within walking distance of the historic district. Simply, yet tastefully, furnished, this guest room is bright and inviting with double bed accommodations, TV, and phone. Sliding glass doors lead to a deck where you can relax and enjoy the city skyline and the beauty of the patio gardens below. With a private adjoining bath and full breakfast, this accommodation could not be more perfect for the business traveler or the long term guest. $45-55.

Bed and Breakfast Connections #00147

P. O. Box 21, Devon, 19333
(215) 687-3565; (800) 448-3619 (outside PA)

Built between 1805 and 1810 and redone after the Civil War in Federalist style, this charming Society Hill town house saw further renovation when its current owners bought it as a shell some twenty years ago.

NOTES: Credit cards accepted: A Master Card; B Visa; C American Express; D Discover Card; E Diner's Club; F Other; 2 Personal Checks accepted; 3 Lunch available; 4 Dinner available; 5 Open all year;

Your creative host has done much of the renovation himself, finding unusual artifacts in old churches and homes in the city that have created a unique and inviting atmosphere. The second-floor bedroom offers a color TV, phone jack, and individual thermostat with a private hall bath. On the third floor there are two more rooms, one with a trundle bed and a queen-size bed and the other with a double bed. All rooms have an individual thermostat, TV, and private bath. Continental breakfast is served in the pleasant kitchen in the winter or on the partio in the warm months. Two-night minimum stay on weekends. $75-80.

Bed and Breakfast Connections #00152

P. O. Box 21, Devon, 19333
(215) 687-3565; (800) 448-3619 (outside PA)

A comfortably furnished room provides pleasant accommodations in a friendly homestyle atmosphere at a surprisingly affordable price. This row house, on a quaint historic registered residential block is located within walking distance of the University of Pennsylvania, Children's Hospital, and the Civic Center. The historic sites and museums of Center City are just ten minutes away and easily accessible with public transportation. The spacious third-floor room includes an antique oak double bed and armoire. A private hall bath with an old-fashioned tub and shower is available. Full breakfast. $45-55.

Bed and Breakfast Connections #00156

P. O. Box 21, Devon, 19333
(215) 687-3565; (800) 448-3619 (outside PA)

Conveniently located two blocks from the Italian Market and two blocks from Antique Row, this home offers private third-floor accommodations. The double

bedded guest room furnished with antiques and collectibles has a sitting room and a private attached bath. A large collection of books is available for you to enjoy during your stay, and your hosts are fluent in Portugese and French and have a deep interest in music. Breakfast is a hearty continental with delicious pasteries, fresh fruit, and coffees and teas from nearby bakeries and markets. No smoking. $45-55.

Bed and Breakfast of Philadelphia-TNN-PENN-SYLVANIA

1616 Walnut Street, Suite 1120, 19103
(800) 220-1917; (215) 735- 1917; FAX (215) 735-
   1905

Part of the Bed and Breakfast National Network, Bed and Breakfast of Philadelphia offers bed and breakfast not only in Pennsylvania but also in many other cities and states across the country. The members of this network adhere strictly to the standards set by TNN, such as getting to know the hosts personally, having an established cancellation and refund policy, and following a thorough inspection and approval process for all properties rented. This is because each member of the network is dedicated to ensuring your comfort, pleasure, and personal needs while you are staying at one of our "homes away from home."

Chestnut Hill Bed and Breakfast

All About Town-B&B in Philadelphia #1907
P. O. Box 1151,Valley Forge, 19481-1151
(215) 783-7838; (800) 344-0123

This home is a lovely renovated old stone schoolhouse. The atmosphere exudes the warmth and welcome of a cozy fire on a cold day. Its location in the historic area of Chestnut Hill in Philadelphia reminds one of the early days of this great nation. $65.

---

6 Pets welcome; 7 Smoking allowed; 8 Children welcome; 9 Social drinking allowed; 10 Tennis available; 11 Swimming available; 12 Golf available; 13 Skiing available; 14 May be booked through travel agents.

City Guesthouse

All About Town-B&B in Philadelphia #0603
P. O. Box 1151, Valley Forge, 19481-1151
(215) 783-7838; (800) 344-0123

This charming guest house (built in 1750) is family owned and operated. The inn features a large, walled colonial herb and rose garden, and the cooking here is known for the use of fresh herbs. Breakfast is served in the garden. Tea or wine and cheese are served each afternoon. The city guest house is historically certified, and the interiors have been carefully preserved. Carriage rides to Philadelphia's historic district can be arranged. Seven blocks to the major historic sites, Penn's Landing, and one block off South Street with its many shops, restaurants, and night life. Four blocks to the Italian market. $70-105.

Country Inn the City

All About Town-B&B in Philadelphia #0206
P. O. Box 1151, Valley Forge, 19481-1151
(215) 783-7838; (800) 344-0123
FAX (215) 783-7783

This 12-room country inn in the historic area of Philadelphia is a restored, circa 1769, guest house within Independence National Historic Park. All rooms are individually decorated and have private baths, telephones, TV, and period furniture. An enclosed parking garage is next door. Continental breakfast is served weekdays and a full breakfast on weekends. Walk to restaurants and the major historic sites in Philadelphia . $95-140.

Cromwell House

Bed and Breakfast of Philadelphia
1616 Walnut Street, Suite 1120, 19103
(215) 735-1917; (800) 220-1917
FAX (215) 735-1905

The Cromwell House is an 1850 Victorian town house on "Architect's Row" in the Art Museum section of the city. The guest quarters, on the air-conditioned third floor, are a self-contained suite with private bath. It is furnished in the Queen Anne style with matching walnut twin beds and dressers. A writing desk is provided for those addicted to writing postcards to the folks back home. The full English breakfast may be served in the sunny kitchen greenhouse, or in the city garden. $55-65.

Germantown Bed and Breakfast

5925 Wayne Avenue, 19144
(215) 848-1375

Your 1900s oak bedroom in a 100-year-old house has cable TV and a private bath. This is a homestay with a family with four children. Twenty minutes to Independence Hall; walk to other historic sites and restaurants.

Hosts: Molly and Jeff Smith
Room: 1 (PB) $40-45
Continental Breakfast
Credit Cards: None
Notes: 2, 5, 8, 9, 12, 14

Historic Philadelphia Bed and Breakfast

All About Town-B&B in Philadelphia #2203
P. O. Box 1151, Valley Forge, 19481-1151
(215) 783-7838; (800) 344-0123

This circa 1811 certified historic home is situated near Society Hill. Guests have access to the city while also enjoying a historic atmosphere. Two guest rooms with private bath. Very comfortable. $65-70.

Logan Square Townhouse

Bed and Breakfast of Philadelphia
1616 Walnut Street, Suite 1120, 19103
(215) 735-1917; (800) 220-1917
FAX (215) 735-1905

This town house is located near the Franklin Institute, Museum of Natural History, and the Moore College of Art. The third-floor bedrooms share the bathroom and its old-fashioned claw foot tub with the hosts. One room offers a double bed and air conditioning for the summer nights. The other has a single bed and is fan-cooled. $32-42.

Marietta's Bed and Breakfast

All About Town-B&B in Philadelphia #1401
P. O. Box 1151, Valley Forge, 19481-1151
(215) 783-7838; (800) 344-0123

This turn-of-the-century elegant town house has high ceilings and is furnished throughout with antiques and artwork. Ideally situated for access to Center City, Rittenhouse Square, and an elegant shopping area. Good restaurants abound. $75-80.

Modern Antique

Bed and Breakfast of Philadelphia
1616 Walnut Street, Suite 1120, 19103
(215) 735-1917; (800) 220-1917
FAX (215) 735-1905

This attractive, spacious 19th-century town house is in the Society Hill section of Philadelphia. It is within walking distance of Independence Hall and the historic area of Philadelphia. The livingroom opens onto the south-facing city patio/garden. The three bedrooms are spacious, comfortable, and air conditioned. A full breakfast is served and low cholesterol diets can be accommodated. $65-80.

New Market Surprise

Bed and Breakfast of Philadelphia
1616 Walnut Street, Suite 1120, 19103
(215) 735-1917; (800) 220-1917
FAX (215) 735-1905

This historic 1811 Philadelphia brick town house was transformed from a dilapidated shell into a comfortable, attractive home with a modern interior. The two air-condi-

tioned bedrooms on the second floor are simply furnished with a double bed in each room, private baths, and television. There is a working fireplace on the third floor for guests' enjoyment. A full breakfast is served to guests willing to rise early on weekdays, and a more leisurely hour on weekends. $60-65.

Olde City Inn

Bed and Breakfast of Philadelphia
1616 Walnut Street, Suite 1120, 19103
(215) 735-1917; (800) 220-1917
FAX (215) 735-1905

This lovely inn in Olde City Philadelphia overlooks Penns Landing on the Delaware River on a historic street. The bed and breakfast inn offers elegance in a distinguished setting. Each of the 20 rooms is designed to cater to the guests' comfort and features exquisite furnishings and modern amenities. The Premium rooms have fireplaces and Jacuzzi tubs. The suite consists of two spacious bedrooms and parlor with fireplace and a private kitchen. $150-200.

Rittenhouse Highrise

All About Town-B&B in Philadelphia #0100
P. O. Box 1151, Valley Forge, 19481-1151
(215) 783-7838; (800) 344-0123

This apartment is in a magnificent highrise that encompasses a spectacular view of Philadelphia from the 30th floor. Nearby cultural attractions include historic Philadelphia, Fairmount Park, legitimate theaters, museums, and the Academy of Music. $55 for single room with private bath; $75 for queen room with private bath Sun.-Thurs. and $85 Fri.-Sat.

Rodman Renaissance

Bed and Breakfast of Philadelphia
1616 Walnut Street, Suite 1120, 19103
(215) 735-1917; (800) 220-1917
FAX (215) 735-1905

6 Pets welcome; 7 Smoking allowed; 8 Children welcome; 9 Social drinking allowed; 10 Tennis available; 11 Swimming available; 12 Golf available; 13 Skiing available; 14 May be booked through travel agents.

This hostess will provide you with a warm welcome to her 90-year-old town house which has been lovingly restored and furnished with selected antiques suggesting the ambience of an earlier era. This three-story home offers a livingroom with fireplace, dining area, and kitchen on the first floor. On the third floor is a cozy, secluded double bedroom with adjacent, private powder room. $35-50.

Shippen Way Inn

418 Bainbridge Street, 19147
(215) 627-7266: (800) 245-4873

The inn, originally built in 1750, is a cozy family owned and operated bed and breakfast in the historical area of Center City Philadelphia. Each room has been individually decorated with antique furniture. Within walking distance to Independence Hall. Near public transportation.

Hosts: Ann Foringer and Raymond Rhule
Rooms: 9 (PB) $70-105
Continental Plus Breakfast
Credit Cards: A, B, C
Notes: 2, 5, 7 (limited), 8, 9, 14

Society Hill
Bed and Breakfast

All About Town-B&B in Philadelphia #0104
P. O. Box 1151, Valley Forge, 19481-1151
(215) 783-7838; (800) 344-0123

This townhouse was built about 1805 and renovated in the Federal style during the post-Civil War era. Three guest rooms with individual thermostat control for heat and air conditioning, and TV. Full breakfast.

During warm weather, breakfast may be served on the patio. One and one-half blocks to Independence Hall. If your stay is over a Saturday night, there is a two-night minimum. $80.

The Spite House

All About Town-B&B in Philadelphia #0801
P. O. Box 1151, Valley Forge, 19481-1151
(215) 783-7838; (800) 344-0123

This historically certified home is associated with the Museum Council of Philadelphia and Delaware Valley, and the Historical Society of Pennsylvania. This is one of the "spite houses," so called because it was built, according to legend, with its back to its neighbors. Full breakfast served. The first floor houses the kitchen, with its Victorian oak oval table and wash stand. The second level features the parlor with grand piano and dining room and butler's pantry with original soapstone sink and dumbwaiter. In Mount Airy amid the Lutheran Seminary, Spring Garden College, and the Coombs College of Music. Near train station. $60-70.

Spruce Garden
Bed and Breakfast

All About Town-B&B in Philadelphia #0205
P. O. Box 1151, Valley Forge, 19481-1151
(215) 783-7838; (800) 344-0123

Guest quarters are a private first-floor suite in an 1840 town house ideally situated in Center City Philadelphia. A full breakfast is served in the second-floor dining area. The guest suite consists of two bedrooms, two bathrooms, and a sitting room for reading, TV, cards or sipping sherry. If both rooms are rented at the same time, the occupants must be relatives or good friends, as you must pass through one bedroom to get out or enter the other. $60-70.

NOTES: Credit cards accepted: A Master Card; B Visa; C American Express; D Discover Card; E Diner's Club; F Other; 2 Personal Checks accepted; 3 Lunch available; 4 Dinner available; 5 Open all year;

Steele Away
Bed and Breakfast

7151 Boyer Street, 19119
(215) 242-0722

This spacious 1902 stone Victorian home reflects your host's interests in art, textiles, architecture, and Scandinavian furnishings. Handwoven textiles accent the airy, hand-stenciled guest quarters, which include a private kitchen. Situated in the city's historic Mount Airy neighborhood (15 minutes from Center City), fine restaurants, shops, galleries, and public transportation are within blocks. Your hosts are happy to help you plan over breakfasts of homemade pastries and fruit cobblers.

Host: Diane Steele
Rooms: 2 (SB) $65
Full Breakfast
Minimum stay weekends: 2 nights; holidays: 3
  nights
Credit Cards: None
Notes: 2, 5, 8 (over 6), 9

The Thomas Bond House

The Thomas Bond House
Bed and Breakfast

129 South Second Street, 19106
(215) 923-8523; (800) 845-BOND

A restored, Early American, c. 1769, guest house located within Independence National Historic Park. The 12 guest rooms rooms are individually decorated and have private baths, telephones, and period furnishings. Parking is available in the public parking garage adjacent to the Thomas Bond House.

Hosts: Jerry and Lisa Dunn
Rooms: 12 (PB) $80-150
Continental Plus Breakfast
Credit Cards: A, B, C, E
Notes: 2, 5, 7, 8, 9, 11, 14

Trade Winds
Bed and Breakfast

All About Town-B&B in Philadelphia #0101
P. O. Box 1151, Valley Forge, 19481-1151
(215) 783-7838; (800) 344-0123

This historically certified town house was built in 1790. Two third-floor guest rooms are elegantly appointed with collectibles and Old World antiques. Each room has color cable TV, phone, central air conditioning, and the twin room has a refrigerator. A full breakfast is served on the French Empire table in the dining area. For special occasions, you may consider a very large second-floor guest room with antique brass bed, fireplace, color cable TV, phone, private bath, air conditioning. Situated on the Washington Square/Society Hill border. Six blocks to Independence Hall and one block to South Street. Public tennis courts across the street. $65-70 for rooms; $100 for suite.

Trinity Bed and Breakfast

All About Town-B&B in Philadelphia #2101
P. O. Box 1151, Valley Forge, 19481-1151
(215) 783-7838; (800) 344-0123

This home is one of four located in a small court in the lovely and quiet Rittenhouse Square section within the bustle of the city. Guests have access to all the attractions of the city and still enjoy a private retreat after a day of sightseeing. $75-85.

6 Pets welcome; 7 Smoking allowed; 8 Children welcome; 9 Social drinking allowed; 10 Tennis available; 11 Swimming available; 12 Golf available; 13 Skiing available; 14 May be booked through travel agents.

Victoria Galerie

Bed and Breakfast of Philadelphia
1616 Walnut Street, Suite 1120, 19103
(215) 735-1917; (800) 220-1917
FAX (215) 735-1905

In one of center city Philadelphia's most desirable neighborhoods, with its high ceilings and large windows, Victoria Galerie reflects a bygone era. You feel transported back to the 19th century as you climb the winding stairs to your private quarters. The large room is furnished with an antique Victorian headboard and inlaid-walnut closets and includes a private bath. $75.

Washington Square Bed and Breakfast

All About Town-B&B in Philadelphia #1601
P. O. Box 1151, Valley Forge, 19481-1151
(215) 783-7838; (800) 344-0123

Built in the 1830s, this three-story Colonial townhouse is situated on one of Society Hill's narrow, cobblestone streets just blocks from Independence Hall. A wisteria-covered patio with a bubbling fountain welcomes guests in the summer. In the winter, a Franklin stove in the guests' parlor warms them. $60-65.

PHOENIXVILLE

Manor House

Bed and Breakfast of Valley Forge #0301
P. O. Box 1151, Valley Forge, 19481-1151
(215) 783-7838; (800) 344-0123

Built in 1928 by a British executive, this English Tudor home stands on a lovely sycamore-lined street. It boasts a massive slate roof and original red oak flooring and stairway. The spacious livingroom and cozy den both have fireplaces. Gourmet breakfasts are served in the formal dining room or on the brick-floored screened porch overlooking the garden.

Complimentary bedtime beverage and snack in the room. Five guest rooms with private bath. $45-70.

Cole's Log Cabin

Tinker Hill Bed and Breakfast

Bed and Breakfast of Valley Forge #0210
P. O. Box 1151, Valley Forge, 19481-1151
(215) 783-7838; (800) 344-0123

This contemporary house on two and one-half acres is in a private, wooded area. Two-story glass-walled livingroom. Guest rooms are separated from the suite and overlook the woods. Hot tub on the deck, swimming pool. Full breakfast. $60-65.

PINE BANK

Cole's Log Cabin Bed and Breakfast

Rural Delivery 1, Box 98, 15341
(412) 451-8521

The Log Cabin Bed and Breakfast is made up of two Colonial log homes, circa 1820s, joined to form one large house. The bed and breakfast is in the extreme southwestern part of Pennsylvania, in a very rural farming area. Major activities are hiking, bird-watching, antiquing, and relaxing. There is now a secluded, fully equipped lodge available for families or groups.

NOTES: Credit cards accepted: A Master Card; B Visa; C American Express; D Discover Card; E Diner's Club; F Other; 2 Personal Checks accepted; 3 Lunch available; 4 Dinner available; 5 Open all year;

Hosts: Jane and Terry R. Cole
Rooms: 3 (1 PB; 2 SB) $50
Continental Breakfast
Credit Cards: None
Notes: 2, 5, 7, 8, 9, 11, 12, 14

POCONO MOUNTAINS

Nearbrook Bed and Breakfast

Rural Delivery 1, Box 630, Canadensis, 18325
(717) 595-3152

Meander through rock garden paths and enjoy the roses, woods, and stream at Nearbrook. A hearty breakfast is served on the outdoor porch. The hosts will join you for morning conversation to help you find trails for good hiking and to describe other areas of interest. A contagious informality encourages guests to play the upright piano and enjoy the many games. Restaurant menus, maps, and art lessons are available.

Hosts: Barbara and Dick Robinson
Rooms: 3 (1 PB; 2 SB) $45
Full Breakfast
Credit Cards: None
Notes: 2, 5, 8, 10, 11, 12, 13

Victoria Ann's Bed and Breakfast

Bed and Breakfast of Valley Forge #1502
P. O. Box 1151, Valley Forge, 19481-1151
(215) 783-7838; (800) 344-0123

Built in 1860 on Millionaire's Row. Once you step inside, you feel as if you have stepped back into time with all the delightful charms of antiques, lace, and elegant chandeliers of day gone by. Enjoy an air of leisurely 19th-century opulence, beautiful Victorian porches, garden terraces, and spacious rooms. Close to white-water rafting, swimming, walking, hunting, good restaurants, winter sports, and walking. $85-145.

QUAKERTOWN

Sign of the Sorrel Horse

243 Old Bethlehem Road, 18951
(215) 536-4651

Built in 1749 of stone, near Lake Nockamixon in Bucks County, as a stagecoach stop. Secluded on five manicured acres. A gracious country inn with five antique-filled rooms, each with private bath. Includes sherry and fruits in the common area and fine gourmet dining. Swimming pool. Garden weddings are a speciality. Near New Hope's Peddler's Village. Received food and wine DiRona award 1992. AAA three-star rated.

Hosts: Monique Gaumont-Lanvin and Jon Atkin
Rooms: 5 (PB) $85-125
Continental Breakfast
Credit Cards: A, B, C
Notes: 4, 9, 11, 13

RADNOR

Bed and Breakfast Connections #00220

P. O. Box 21, Devon, 19333
(215) 687-3565; (800) 448-3619 (outside PA)

This home-within-a-barn offers privacy, a refreshing night's sleep, and a delicious breakfast. The two-story entrance hall and stairway welcome you to this 19th- century bank barn and its exposed post-and-beam construction. One room has a king bed, private bath, and dining area. Another room has twin beds and private bath. Both rooms have refrigerators. Breakfast is served in your room or in the great room with fireplace surrounded by English antiques and Japanese prints. Close to Gulph Creek, near the Schuylkill Expressway, Valley Forge/King of Prussia, and 20 minutes from downtown Philadelphia. No smoking. Resident cat. $80-90

Main Line Estate

Bed and Breakfast of Valley Forge #2601
P. O. Box 1151, Valley Forge, 19481-1151
(215) 783-7838; (800) 344-0123

This expansive English Tudor, built in 1969, is surrounded by three and one-half acres of original grounds belonging to two estates owned by the brothers who made a local German beer. The spacious guest rooms can be reached privately by a back staircase. A full breakfast is served in the country French kitchen. Greenhouse, swimming pool, cabana, and tennis court. Washer/dryer, baby equipment, and cable TV available. $70.

READING

Hunter House

118 South Fifth Street, 19602
(215) 374-6608

Situated in historic downtown, this elegant 1846 restoration offers spacious rooms/suites with private baths, kitchens, TV, and air conditioning. Convenient to Reading's outlets, commercial centers, antique markets, Amish country, and more. A casual and friendly atmosphere amid period furnishings and antiques creates a unique and sheltered urban experience. Fine restaurants within walking distance. Business travelers welcome.

Hosts: Norma and Ray Staron
Rooms: 4 (2 PB; 2 SB) $60-75
Full Breakfast
Credit Cards: A, B
Notes: 2, 5, 7 (limited), 8, 9, 10, 11, 12, 13

The Inn in Reading

Bed and Breakfast of Valley Forge #0903
P. O. Box 1151, Valley Forge, 19481-1151
(215) 783-7838; (800) 344-0123

This mansion and carriage house were built in the late 1800s and are beautifully preserved examples of Victorian elegance.

Original leaded glass, ornate plaster, paneled and carved woods are part of the architectural style. Hors d'oeuvres and sherry served in the afternoon. Four guest rooms, all with private bath. $130-160.

Reading Bed and Breakfast

Bed and Breakfast of Valley Forge #0806
P. O. Box 1151, Valley Forge, 19481-1151
(215) 783-7838; (800) 344-0123

This bed and breakfast is a fine combination of the time-honored European tradition of the English bed and breakfast, the French hostelry, and the Italian pensione, all in one. It offers the warmth and friendliness of a private home coupled with the furnishings and privacy required to maintain a comfortable and relaxed atmosphere. Two guest rooms, one with private bath. $60-70.

ROSEMONT

Conestoga Bed and Breakfast

Bed and Breakfast of Valley Forge #1802
P. O. Box 1151, Valley Forge, 19481-1151
(215) 783-7838; (800) 344-0123

The hosts of this bed and breakfast inherited the home they were raised in. Guests have the privilege of the entire house. The interior of this 1890 home has been restored and furnished. Fully equipped kitchen, living- room, dining room, sun room, two bedrooms, and bath. TV, on-site parking, grill, furnished patio. The kitchen is stocked with breakfast foods. $100 nightly; $1,200 monthly.

SCHELLSBURG

Bedford's Covered Bridge Inn

RD #1, Box 196, 15559
(814) 733-4093

NOTES: Credit cards accepted: A Master Card; B Visa; C American Express; D Discover Card; E Diner's Club; F Other; 2 Personal Checks accepted; 3 Lunch available; 4 Dinner available; 5 Open all year;

Delightful countryside accommodations in a historic home near a covered bridge afford guests full breakfasts and private baths amid a picturebook setting. Hiking, biking, antiquing, fishing, bird watching, and cross-country skiing are available from the door. Old Bedford Village, Blue Knoll ski resort, Shawnee State Park, Coral Caverns, and many covered bridges are nearby. Eight miles from Exit 11, I-76.

Rooms: 2 (PB) $65
Full Breakfast
Credit Cards: A, B, C, D
Notes: 2, 5, 8 (over 12), 9, 10, 11, 12, 13, 14

SCHWENKSVILLE

Highpoint Victoriana

Bed and Breakfast of Valley Forge #1908
P. O. Box 1151, Valley Forge, 19481-1151
(215) 783-7838; (800) 344-0123

Dutch Colonial Victorian five-acre farmette consists of a barn with vintage cars and fields that serve as a Christmas tree farm. The house has been carefully restored and modernized in authentic keeping with the Victorian atmosphere. It is filled with lovely antiques. Enjoy a lovely wraparound porch to cool you in the summer, and a wood-burning stove to warm you in the winter. Four guest rooms. $50-70.

Bedford's Covered Bridge Inn

SELINSGROVE

The Blue Lion Inn

350 South Market Street, 17870
(717) 374-2929

Experience a night in an authentic plantation home over 150 years old. Located in the heart of the Susquehanna Valley, known for its antique shops, farmers's markets, picturesque landscapes, and beautiful fall foliage. Antique furnishings, gourmet breakfast and warm and friendly hospitality add to the atmosphere. A few blocks from Susquehanna University, and convenient to Bucknell University in Lewisburg.

Hosts: Kent and Marilyn Thomson
Rooms: 4 (PB) $52.50-62.50
Full Breakfast
Credit Cards: A, B, C
Notes: 2, 8, 9

SMETHPORT

Blackberry Inn Bed and Breakfast

820 West Main Street, 16749-1039
(814) 887-7777

A Victorian home built in 1881 and restored in 1988-89. Breakfast is served when guests want to wake up. Parlor with a TV, guest phone, and two large open porches. Friendly small-town atmosphere, near Kinzua Bridge State Park and the Allegheny National Forest. Wonderful area for hiking, biking, fishing, fall foliage tours, festivals, or just relaxing.

Hosts: Marilyn and Arnie Bolin
Rooms: 5 (S2B) $42-47
Full Breakfast
Credit Cards: None
Notes: 2, 5, 8, 11, 12

SMOKETOWN

Homestead Lodging

184 East Brook Road, 17576
(717) 393-6927

6 Pets welcome; 7 Smoking allowed; 8 Children welcome; 9 Social drinking allowed; 10 Tennis available; 11 Swimming available; 12 Golf available; 13 Skiing available; 14 May be booked through travel agents.

Come to our beautiful Lancaster County setting, where you hear the clippity-clop of Amish buggies go by and can experience the sights and freshness of our farmlands. Our clean country rooms provide a homey atmosphere, and an Amish farm is adjacent to our property. There is a large grassy area and a creek to enjoy. We are located within walking distance of restaurants and within minutes of farmers' markets, quilt, antiques and craft shops, outlets, auctions, and museums.

Hosts: Robert and Lori Kepiro
Rooms: 5 (PB) $28-49
Continental Breakfast
Credit Cards: A, B
Notes: 2, 5, 7, 8, 9, 10, 11, 12

SOMERSET

Bayberry Bed and Breakfast

611 North Center Avenue, Route 601, 15501
(814) 445-8471

A romantic, friendly, comfortable inn that pays attention to detail, offering all non-smoking rooms with private baths. Homemade baked goods served at a lovely table for two. Near Exit 10 of the Pennsylvania Turnpike. Close to Seven Springs and Hidden Valley resorts, Frank Lloyd Wright's Falling Water, Ohiopyle white-water rafting, state parks, antique shops, and outlet malls.

Host: Marilyn Lohr
Rooms: 11 (PB) $45-55
Expanded Continental Breakfast
Credit Cards: A, B, C, D
Notes: 2, 5, 8 (over 11), 9, 10, 11, 12, 13, 14

The Heart of Somerset

130 West Union Street, 15501
(814) 445-6782

A beautifully refurbished home built circa 1839. Antiques fill every room, and the wooden oak floors have been returned to their original beauty. Edison electric light fixtures grace the lower level, and each

room is decorated differently, with eyelet comforters and pillow shams to enhance that romantic feeling of the Victorian era. The Heart is a most restful getaway in the beautiful Laurel Highlands ski and biking country.

Hosts: Phyllis and Hank Vogt
Rooms: 6 (4 PB; 2 SB) $35-85
Continental Plus Breakfast
Credit Cards: A, B, C, D
Notes: 2, 5, 9, 12, 13

STARLIGHT

The Inn at Starlight Lake

Box 27, 18461
(717) 798-2519

A classic country inn since 1909 on a clear lake in the rolling hills of northeast Pennsylvania, with activities for all seasons, from swimming to cross-country skiing. Near the Delaware River for canoeing and fishing. Excellent food and spirits, convivial atmosphere.

Hosts: Jack and Judy McMahon
Rooms: 26 (20 PB; 6 SB) $110-140 Modified
                            American Plan
Full Breakfast
Credit Cards: A, B
Closed first two weeks of April
Notes: 2, 3, 4, 7 (limited), 8, 9, 10, 11, 12, 13, 14

STARRUCCA

The Nethercott Inn

1 Main Street, 18462
(717) 727-2211

A lovely Victorian home built around 1893, nestled in the Endless Mountains in the quaint borough of Starrucca. Downhill and cross-country skiing, snowmobiling, hunting, and fishing.

Hosts: Ned and Ginny Nethercott
Rooms: 5 (PB) $65
Expanded Continental Breakfast
Credit Cards: A, B, C, D
Notes: 2, 5, 8, 9, 12, 13

STRAFFORD

Stratford Village Home

Bed and Breakfast of Philadelphia
1616 Walnut Street, Suite 1120, Philadelphia,
19103
(215) 735-1917; (800) 220-1917
FAX (215) 735-1905

Comfortable, attractive, Colonial-style sur-
burban home with a pristine interior.
Summer breakfasts under a yellow umbrella in the garden. Double bed with private
bath available. $35-45.

SWIFTWATER

The Britannia Country Inn

P. O. Box 8, Upper Swiftwater Road, 18370
(717) 839-7243

A charming Colonial 170-year-old inn with
cottages set in twelve acres with all lawn
sports and a pool. New British owners
bring you a "Taste of England in the Heart
of the Poconos" serving British favorites
and afternoon teas. Some rooms have been
renovated in Laura Ashley style, and some
cottages with fireplaced are available. Full
breakfast included; dinner available.
Smallest bar in the Poconos.

Hosts: Bob and Joan Matthews; Barry and Mary
    Webster
Rooms: 21 (PB) $60-90
Full Breakfast
Credit Cards: A, B, C, E
Notes: 4, 5, 6, 7, 8, 10, 11

Holiday Glen

Bush Road, Box 96, 18370
(717) 839-7015

Secluded and peaceful country resort on 17
acres run by two Scottish sisters. Seven cottages and two A-frames with free-standing
fireplaces, small refrigerators, color cable
TV, queen-size beds. Wooded trails, pond,
and stream; minutes away from horseback
riding, shopping, and restaurants.

Hosts: Sarah and Marie McGinn
Rooms: 9 (PB) $75.50-89.50
Full Breakfast
Credit Cards: A, B
Notes: 5, 7, 8, 11

THORNTON

Pace One Restaurant and Country Inn

Box 108, 19373
(215) 459-3702

Pace One is a renovated 250-year-old stone
barn with rooms on the upper three levels.
The ground floor is a restaurant and bar.
Beautiful hand-hewn wood beams, old
wood floors, and deep-set windows estab-
lish a charming rustic atmosphere.

Host: Ted Pace
Rooms: 7 (PB) $65-85
Continental Breakfast
Credit Cards: A, B, C, E
Notes: 2, 3, 4, 5, 7, 8, 9, 10, 11, 12

TOWANDA

Victorian Guest House

118 York Avenue, 18848
(717) 265-6972

A charming Victorian guest house, circa
1897, complete with tower rooms, arched
windows, and wraparound porches.
High-ceilinged guest rooms are furnished

Victorian Guest House

6 Pets welcome; 7 Smoking allowed; 8 Children welcome; 9 Social drinking allowed; 10 Tennis available; 11
Swimming available; 12 Golf available; 13 Skiing available; 14 May be booked through travel agents.

in Victorian and turn-of-the-century antiques. Guests are welcome to share the parlor.

Hosts: Tom and Nancy Taylor
Rooms: 12 (9 PB; 3 SB) $45-60
Continental Breakfast
Credit Cards: A, B, C, E
Notes: 2, 5, 7, 8

TROY

Silver Oak Leaf Bed and Breakfast

196 Canton Street, 16947
(717) 297-4315; (800) 326-9824

Silver Oak Leaf Bed and Breakfast is in the heart of the Endless Mountains. The house is a 90-year-old Victorian that has great charm. There is a great deal to do and see: antiques, auctions, fishing, hunting, or just relaxing. Gourmet breakfasts; wine served in the evening.

Hosts: Steve and June Bahr
Rooms: 4 (1 PB; 3SB) $40-45
Full Breakfast
Credit Cards: None
Notes: 2, 5, 9, 10, 11, 12, 13

UPPER BLACK EDDY

The Bridgeton House on the Delaware

P. O. Box 167, River Road, 18972
(215) 982-5856

Bucks County's only riverfront bed and breakfast. French doors, private balconies, river views, morning mist, canopy beds, fireplaces, rocking chairs, fresh flowers, gourmet breakfast, afternoon tea. Circa 1836 structure furnished with antiques. Luxurious penthouse with marble bathroom, fireplace, and nonstop view. Featured in New York Times, New York magazine, Philadelphia magazine, and Washington Post.

Rooms: 8 and 2 suites (PB) $65-175
Full Breakfast
Credit Cards: None
Notes: 2, 4, 5, 9, 10, 11, 12, 13

VALLEY FORGE

Bed and Breakfast Connections #00201

P. O. Box 21, Devon, 1933
(215) 687-3565; (800) 448-3619 (outside PA)

Enjoy the charm of this historical home convenient to the Valley Forge area. The original part of the house was built sometime before 1700, and two additions, each more than 200 years old, were constructed in the traditional Colonial style. Two third-floor rooms offer guests spacious privacy and the convenience of a small refrigerator, microwave, and telephone on the landing. A large, inviting second-floor room has an antique double bed and a sitting area with a camelback, queen-size sofa bed. All rooms have private or semi-private baths. A full English-style breakfast is served in the oldest part of the house in front of the fireplace with its huge mantle and eight-foot-wide hearth. Resident dog and smoker. $55-75.

Country Charm

Bed and Breakfast of Valley Forge #1203
P. O. Box 1151, 19481-1151
(215) 783-7838; (800) 344-0123

This Colonial farmhouse is on three acres of an original William Penn land grant, and dates from the 1700s. The outbuildings include a smokehouse, springhouse, and outhouse. The home is cozy, comfortable, and furnished in traditional country style appropriate to the home's age, complete with antiques, quilts, and hand stenciling. A full breakfast is served in the cheerful dining room. $60-65.

NOTES: Credit cards accepted: A Master Card; B Visa; C American Express; D Discover Card; E Diner's Club; F Other; 2 Personal Checks accepted; 3 Lunch available; 4 Dinner available; 5 Open all year;

Deep Well Farm

Bed and Breakfast of Valley Forge #0804
P. O. Box 1151, 19481-1151
(215) 783-7838; (800) 344-0123

This 18th-century fieldstone farmhouse has 16-inch-thick-walls and exposed beams overhead. Originally it was part of Gen. Anthony Wayne's estate. The two and one-half acres accommodate a horse barn and a pond where geese gather. The bedrooms are spacious and comfortable, cooled by ceiling fans. A full breakfast is served in the country dining room or kitchen. A parrot and two horses reside. One mile to Valley Forge Park; one-half mile to Valley Forge Music Fair. $60-70.

Deer Run

Bed and Breakfast of Philadelphia
1616 Walnut Street, Suite 1120, Philadelphia, 19103
(215) 735-1917; (800) 220-1917
FAX (215) 735-1905

Deer Run is an original farmhouse dating back to the 1880s. The home appears on survey maps from the 1740s and is an original William Penn land grant property. The two guest rooms are decorated in period style. One has its original fireplace, pine random-width floors, and an original "rope" cannonball bed with a feather down mattress, and air conditioning. The second bedroom is decorated in Laura Ashley prints, and furniture includes an iron-and-brass bed, and an oak dresser with an interesting French provincial sideboard/long chest. The two rooms share a bath. Children over 12 welcome. Limited smoking. $70-80.

French Provincial

Bed and Breakfast of Valley Forge #1304
P. O. Box 1151, 19481-1151
(215) 783-7838; (800) 344-0123

This air-conditioned Colonial sits on three acres of wooded land adjoining Valley Forge Park. Paths lead from this property to the park. A continental breakfast is served in the glass-enclosed solar sun deck overlooking the pagoda trellis and lawns where deer often visit. Guests are welcome to use the family room with fireplace, TV, and piano. One guest room has a private entrance. Friendly dog in residence. $65-70.

Great Valley House

Bed and Breakfast of Philadelphia
1616 Walnut Street, Suite 1120, Philadelphia, 19103
(215) 735-1917; (800) 220-1917
FAX (215) 735-1905

The title documents for this beautiful old stone house trace back to a grant from William Penn in 1681. This stone farmhouse has fifteen rooms, which was built in three phases, and the latest phase was completed over 200 years ago. Two guest rooms on the third floor are air-conditioned for summer comfort. Both rooms have private baths. A full country breakfast is served before a warming fire in the 1690 kitchen or on the terrace under ancient trees in summer. Children welcome. Queen and double beds are available. $80-85.

Oak Haven

Bed and Breakfast of Philadelphia
1616 Walnut Street, Suite 1120, Philadelpia, 19103
(215) 735-1917; (800) 220-1917
FAX (215) 735-1905

Oak Haven is a 1791 white southern Colonial set in a large yard with its own stream and cottage with Valley Forge National Park as a nearby neighbor. Close to King of Prussia, you are convenient to local attractions such as the Devon Horse Show. Three third-floor guest rooms are available with a variety of beds. Children over ten years old welcome. No smoking. $60-80.

Valley Forge Garden Spot

Bed and Breakfast of Philadelphia
1616 Walnut Street, Suite 1120, Philadelphia, 19103
(215) 735-1917; (800) 220-1917
FAX (215) 735-1905

Lush greenery greets your eyes if your arrival is in spring or summer. This two-story Colonial-style house is nestled on a hillside bordered by flowering shrubs and trees. Your hostess is a college professor and knowledgeable about many cultural and human service organizations. Breakfast is your preference. Three rooms, one with a pair of twin beds and a private bath, another with a pair of twin beds and shared bath, and a third with one single bed and shared bath. Children welcome. No smoking. $30-60.

Valley Forge Mt. Bed and Breakfast

Box 562, 19481
(215) 783-7838; (800) 344-0123
FAX (215) 783-7783

George Washington had headquarters here. Centrally situated between Philadelphia, Lancaster County, Reading outlets, and Brandywine Valley. French Colonial on three wooded acres adjacent to Valley Forge Park. Air conditioning, complimentary breakfast, guest room telephone, TV, VCR, computer, printer, FAX, two fireplaces. Bridle and hiking trail. Finest shopping, antiquing, restaurants, cross-country skiing, horseback riding, golf within minutes. California king and single/sitting room with private bath. Double/sitting room with private bath.

Host: Carolyn Williams
Rooms: 2 (PB) $45-65
Full Breakfast
Credit Cards: A, B, C, E
Notes: 2, 3, 5, 6, 7 (limited), 8, 9, 10, 11, 12, 13, 14

VILLANOVA

English Regency

Bed and Breakfast of Valley Forge #1903
P. O. Box 1151, Valley Forge, 19481-1151
(215) 783-7838; (800) 344-0123

This home, featured on house tours, is situated on one and one-half acres in an elegant, quiet, wooded area. It is furnished with antiques, art, and Oriental rugs. The guest room is beautifully appointed and includes a graceful canopy bed and leather wing chair. Weekdays, breakfast is self-serve continental. On weekends, a full breakfast is served. Central air conditioning. $70-75.

WASHINGTON CROSSING

Woodhill Farms Inn

150 Glenwood Drive, 18977
(215) 493-1974

Woodhill Farms Inn is nestled on ten wooded acres in historic Washington Crossing, Bucks County. The beautiful six-bedroom lodge offers quiet seclusion, private baths, color TV, air conditioning, indoor garden and a delicious breakfast.

Hosts: John and Donna Behun
Rooms: 6 (PB) $81-118.80
Continental Breakfast weekdays; full on weekends
Credit Cards: A, B
Notes: 2, 5, 7 (limited), 8 (under 1 or over 6), 10, 12, 14

WAYNE

Fox Knoll

Bed and Breakfast of Valley Forge #0904
P. O. Box 1151, Valley Forge, 19481-1151
(215) 783-7838; (800) 344-0123

Completely private accommodations in this 12-room old stone Colonial filled with antiques and country comfort. The guest entrance leads from the terrace to a spacious and charming room with areas for eating, sitting, and sleeping. The kitchenette is fully equipped and stocked for your breakfast, or join your hosts in the country dining room. The stone terrace with grill and umbrella are for your use. Other amenities include a large stone fireplace, TV, and stereo. A cheerful bedroom with sitting room in the main house is also available. $75-100.

Woodwinds

Bed and Breakfast of Valley Forge #1309
P. O. Box 1151, Valley Forge, 19481-1151
(215) 783-7838; (800) 344-0123

This newly remodeled home sits on two acres on a quiet, wooded street, surrounded by gardens, lawns, and trees. The light, comfortable guest room is up a short, private flight of stairs separated from your hosts' quarters. A continental breakfast is served in the formal dining room or on the terrace. Just one-half block from the main line train station and the Paoli local to Philadelphia. $55-65.

WELLSBORO

Kaltenbach's Bed and Breakfast Inn

Rural Delivery 6, Box 106 A, Kelsey Street
Stony Fork Road, 16901
(717) 724-4954; (800) 722-4954

Nestled on 72 beautiful acres, Kaltenbach's bed and breakfast features a view of the countryside unequaled in north central Pennsylvania. All-you-can-eat country style breakfasts featuring homemade jellies, jams, and blueberry muffins. Spacious guest rooms with queen- and king-size beds. Accommodations for 32 guests. Cable TV in rooms, phones available. Honeymoon suites with tub for two. Hiking, bicycling, horseback riding, picnicking in summer. In winter, cross-coun-

try skiing and snowmobiling are nearby. Golf packages are available. Pena Grand Canyon. Year-round service.

Host: Lee Kaltenbach
Rooms: 11 (4 PB; 7 SB) $50-100
Full Breakfast
Credit Cards: A, B
Notes: 2, 3, 4, 5, 8, 9, 10, 11, 12, 13, 14

WEST ALEXANDER

Saint's Rest Bed and Breakfast

77 Main Street, P. O. Box 15, 15376
(412) 484-7950

Earl and Myrna invite you to visit their beautiful gingerbread-style Victorian home located one minute from Interstate 70 east or west. Fifteen minutes from Oglebay Park, Jamboree USA, and Wheeling Downs dog track. Saint's West stands on Old National Road. Fresh flowers, homemade muffins, a welcome-in drink, and good beds are just some of the guests' comments about this friendly home away from home.

Hosts: Myrna and Earl Lewis
Rooms: 2 (PB) $60 plus tax
Continental Plus Breakfast
Credit Cards: None
Notes: 2, 5, 8, 9

Saint's Rest

WEST CHESTER

The Bankhouse Bed and Breakfast

875 Hillsdale Road, 19382
(215) 344-7388

An 18th-century "bankhouse" nestled in a quiet country setting with view of pond and horse farm. Rooms charmingly decorated with country antiques and stenciling. Offers a great deal of privacy, with private entrance, porch, sitting room/library, and air conditioning. Near Longwood Gardens, Brandywine River Museum, and Winterthur. Easy drive to Valley Forge, Lancaster, and Philadelphia. Canoeing, horseback riding, biking, walking/jogging trails offered in the area. Also, luscious country breakfast and afternoon snacks.

Hosts: Diana and Michael Bove
Rooms: 2 (1 PB; 1SB) $65-85
Full Breakfast
Credit Cards: None
Notes: 2, 5, 9, 12, 13

Bed and Breakfast Connections #00352

P. O. Box 21, Devon, 19333
(215) 687-3565; (800) 448-3619 (outside PA)

Picture a majestic 1850 farmhouse with a wraparound porch sitting atop the highest point in beautiful Chester County. The original landowner was the founder of West Chester, and since then it has been the site of an Arabian horse farm and the summer home of a wealthy family who owned the house for ninety-five years before they sold it to your hosts. Four guest rooms are available; two suites offer a private bath, and two rooms on the second floor share a hall bath. A full farm-style breakfast is served each morning, and you are invited to join your hostess for tea in the grand entry room in front of the crackling fire. Attractions, such as Longwood Gardens, Winterthur, and the historic Brandywine Valley, are within a short drive. $100-135.

Bingham House

All About the Brandywine Valley B&B #0204
P. O. Box 1151, Valley Forge, 19481-1151
(215) 783-7838; (800) 344-0123
FAX (215) 783-7783

This modern farmhouse situated on property deeded from William Penn is furnished with Early American furnishings and antiques collected and inherited over the years. In West Chester, one-half hour to Brandywine Valley, Valley Forge, and Amish country, as well as all businesses along the Route 202 corridor from King of Prussia to Wilmington. Guests have access to refrigerator, microwave, grill, washer/dryer, phone, TV, and VCR. $55-65.

The Crooked Windsor

409 South Church Street, 19382
(215) 692-4896

Charming Victorian home centrally situated in West Chester and completely furnished with fine antiques. Full breakfast served. Tea time or refreshments for those who so desire. Also, pool and garden in season. Points of interest within easy driving distance.

Host: Winifred Rupp
Rooms: 4 (SB) $65
Full Breakfast
Credit Cards: None
Notes: 2, 5, 8, 9, 11

Hamanassett

Bed and Breakfast of Philadelphia
1616 Walnut Street, Suite 1120, Philadelphia, 19103
(215) 735-1917; (800) 220-1917
FAX (215) 735-1905

This elegant manor house of a gentle country estate is tucked away on 36 acres of the Bradywine Valley. There are eight well-appointed rooms, all with private baths. When the cold winds blow, guests can relax before the large Federal fireplace in the grand livingroom, and a library with over 2,000 volumes is available for guests to enjoy. Children over 12 welcome. Smoking outdoors only. $80-210.

Pheasant Hollow

Bed and Breakfast of Philadelphia
1616 Walnut Street, Suite 1120, Philadelphia, 19103
(215) 735-1917; (800) 220-1917
FAX (215) 735-1905

This rural homestead of the 1800s sits quietly and majestically in the hills of Chester County. Set on three wooded acres, amidst neighboring horse farms, the first-floor guest rooms share a bath and are well-appointed with antiques and working fireplaces. A full country breakfast will satisfy your appetite for the better part of the day. Children are welcome. No smoking. $55-75.

West Chester Victorian Home

Bed and Breakfast of Philadelphia
1616 Walnut Street, Suite 1120, 19103
(215) 735-1917; (800) 220-1917
FAX (215) 735-1905

Situated on a knoll curved round by a country road, this gracious, former summer home is sheltered by ancient trees. It, and its equally gracious host, welcome the traveler to rooms with high ceilings and tall windows, warm breezes in the summer, and a crackling fire in the winter. The Atrium is on ground level just off the pool, with its queen-size double beds and private bath. A guest room with two twin beds, private bath, and fireplace is on the second floor. A third floor offers two rooms with double beds, one with a pair of twins; and both share a bath. Children welcome. Smoking allowed. $40-60.

WILLIAMSPORT

The Reighard House

1323 East Third Street, 17701
(717) 326-3593; FAX (717) 323-4734

Built in 1905, the house is stone and brick. It boasts a formal parlor, music room with grand piano, library, formal oak-paneled dining room, and a cheery breakfast room with wood-burning stove. Up the open oak staircase are six bedrooms, each with private bath, color TV, phone, carpeting, and air conditioning. The old-fashioned front porch is perfect for rocking and relaxing.

Hosts: Bill and Sue Reighard
Rooms: 6 (PB) $58-78
Full Breakfast
Credit Cards: A, B, C, E, F
Notes: 2, 5, 7, 8, 9, 10, 11, 12, 13, 14

WILLOW STREET

Green Gables Bed and Breakfast

2532 Willow Street Pike, 17584
(717) 464-5546

Situated three miles south of Lancaster, on Route 222 N, Green Gables Bed and Breakfast is a 1907 Victorian home with original oak woodwork and stained-glass windows. Be a guest while visiting and touring Lancaster County.

Hosts: Karen and Mike Chiodo
Rooms: 3 (SB) $50
Expanded Continental Breakfast
Credit Cards: None
Notes: 2, 5, 8, 10, 11, 12

WRIGHTSTOWN

Hollileif Bed and Breakfast Establishment

677 Durham Road (Route 413), 18940
(215) 598-3100

6 Pets welcome; 7 Smoking allowed; 8 Children welcome; 9 Social drinking allowed; 10 Tennis available; 11 Swimming available; 12 Golf available; 13 Skiing available; 14 May be booked through travel agents.

An 18th-century farmhouse on five and one-half acres of Bucks County countryside with romantic ambience, gourmet breakfasts, fireplaces, central air conditioning, and private baths. Gracious service is combined with attention to detail. Each guest room is beautifully appointed with antiques and country furnishings. Enjoy afternoon refreshments by the fireside or on the arbor-covered patio. Relax in a hammock in the meadow overlooking a peaceful stream. View a vibrant sunset and wildlife. Close to New Hope.

Hosts: Ellen and Richard Butkus
Rooms: 5 (PB) $75-120
Full Breakfast
Credit Cards: A, B, C
Notes: 2, 5, 9, 14

WRIGHTSVILLE

1854 House

811 Grand Manor Drive, 17368
(717) 252-4643' (800) 722-6395

Located between Lancaster and York, this authentically restored brick home is on 22 easily accessible acres. There are three guest rooms with antiques, air conditioning, and private baths. Enjoy a full gourmet breakfast and then escape by relaxing on the porches, touring the property, or using the spring-fed pond.

Hosts: Roger and Amelia Healey
Rooms: 3 (PB) $60-70 plus tax
Full Breakfast
Credit Cards: A, B
Notes: 2, 3, 4, 5, 9, 11, 12, 13

Roundtop Bed and Breakfast

6995 Roundtop Lane, 17368
(717) 252-3169

Romantic century-old stone home high above the Susquehanna River. Over 100 acres of woodlands and hiking trails and magnificent views of five counties and the river from every window in the winter. Full gourmet breakfast served from the Culinary Institute of America by the chef/manager. Observation deck on the roof is eye level with hawks, bald eagles, and many other birds of the area.

Hosts: Jodi and Tyler Sloan
Rooms: 6 (1 PB; 5 SB) $50-75
Full Breakfast
Credit Cards: A, B
Notes: 2, 5, 7, 8, 9

WYALUSING

Wyalusing Hotel

111 Main Street, 18853
(717) 746-1204; FAX (717) 746-1247

A Victorian atmosphere awaits you at the historic Wyalusing Hotel, situated along the shores of the upper Susquehanna River amid some of Pennsylvania's breathtaking Endless Mountains scenery. The hotel enjoys a wide reputation for fine food and warm hospitality. The dining room offers a full menu of traditional recipes, along with a sure-to-please wine list. Informal dining is available in the large country barroom.

Hosts: Terry and Barb Keeney
Rooms: 10 (PB) $50-75
Continental Breakfast
Credit Cards: A, B, D, E, F
Notes: 2, 3, 4, 5, 7, 8, 9, 10, 12

Wyalusing Hotel

YORK

Amanda's Bed and Breakfast #105

1428 Park Avenue, Annapolis, MD 21217
(301) 225-0001; (301) 383-1274

This 1836 restored brick Colonial is on
three acres of manicured lawns with trees,
shrubs, and flowers. This farmhouse with a
fireplace has an antique shop on the
premises. Three guest rooms with two
shared baths. Twenty minutes from
Lancaster and a little more than one hour
from Baltimore. $60.

Briarwold Bed and Breakfast

Rural Delivery 24, Box 469, 17406
(717) 252-4619

Large, circa 1836, Colonial brick house,
sitting in the middle of three acres of manicured lawn and many large trees. The three
large bedrooms are furnished with country
antiques, as are the other rooms of the
house. Air conditioning.

Host: Marion Bischoff
Rooms: 3 (SB) $60
Full Breakfast
Credit Cards: A, B
Notes: 2, 5, 7, 8, 9, 12, 13, 14

Smyser-Bair House Bed and Breakfast

30 South Beaver Street, 17401
(717) 854-3411

A magnificent 12-room Italianate town
house in the historic district, this home is
rich in architectural detail and contains
stained-glass windows, pier mirrors, and
ceiling medallions. There are three antique-
filled guest rooms and a two-room suite.
Enjoy the warm hospitality, walk to the
farmers' market, historic sites, and antique
shops. Eight blocks to the York Fairgrounds; near Lancaster and Gettysburg.

Hosts: The King family
Rooms: 4 (1 PB; 3 SB) $60-80
Full Breakfast
Credit Cards: A, B
Notes: 2, 5, 8, 9, 12, 13, 14

Smyser-Bair House

RHODE ISLAND

Providence

Bristol

Wickford/North Kingston •

• Wyoming

Kingston •

South Kingstown-Wakefield •

Narragansett

Green Hill

Charlestown

Block Island

Rhode Island

ASHAWAY

Nutmeg B&B Agency #514

P. O. Box 1117, West Hartford, Connecticut 06107
(203) 236-6698

Set on a knoll, this Colonial home is surrounded by trees and has a large yard, two
patios, a screen house, and a pool. The
three guest rooms share one bath on the
second floor. There is a TV in the
livingroom for guest use. A roll-away bed
is available. The home is convenient to
Mystic as well as the Coast Guard
Academy, the University of Rhode Island,
Newport, and Brown University.
Continental breakfast. Smoking in designated areas. Children under 6 welcome.
Pets in residence.

BLOCK ISLAND

The Adrian

Old Town Road, 02807
(401) 466-2693

This grand Victorian is now listed on the
National Register of Historic Places. Cool,
quiet location with scenic ocean views
from lawns, porches, and decks, and five
minutes drive to the Atlantic Ocean and
Old Harbor Village. Each of the ten rooms
is furnished with antiques and has a private
bath. Homemade continental breakfast is
included.

Host: Douglas Langdon
Rooms: 10 (PB) $75-175
Continental Breakfast

Credit Cards: None
Notes: 2, 8, 9

Atlantic Inn

P. O. Box 188, 02807
(401) 466-5883

The Atlantic, with its sweeping panorama
of Block Island's pristine coastline and
view of the distant mainland, offers an
exceptional opportunity to relax. Uncrowded beaches, warm atmosphere, imaginative menus create an unforgettable vacation.

Hosts: Patricia Vincent and Barbara Belniak
Rooms: 21 (PB) $100-165
Continental Breakfast
Minimum stay weekdays: 2 nights; holidays:
 3 nights
Credit Cards: A, B, C
Closed Dec. - March
Notes: 2, 4, 7, 8, 9, 10, 11

The Blue Dory Inn

Box 488, 02807
(401) 466-5891

The Victorian age is alive and well at the
Blue Dory. Situated on Crescent Beach,
this delightful year-round inn offers an
opportunity to revisit a period of time that
has long since gone by. The inn is filled
with antiques and turn-of-the-century
decor, yet has all the modern comforts.

Hosts: Ann and Ed Loedy
Rooms: 14 (PB) $55-245
Expanded Continental Breakfast
Credit Cards: A, B, C, F
Notes: 2, 5, 8, 9, 10, 11, 14

NOTES: Credit cards accepted: A Master Card; B Visa; C American Express; D Discover Card; E Diner's
Club; F Other; 2 Personal Checks accepted; 3 Lunch available; 4 Dinner available; 5 Open all year; 6 Pets
welcome; 7 Smoking allowed; 8 Children welcome; 9 Social drinking allowed; 10 Tennis available; 11
Swimming available; 12 Golf available; 13 Skiing available; 14 May be booked through travel agents.

Harborside Inn

Water Street, 02807
(401) 466-5504

Escape from the 20th-century stress and
strain to Victorian-style peace and tranquility at Harborside Inn. As you sail into Old
Harbor, you are welcomed by a harbor-
view terrace decorated with window boxes
ablaze with fresh red geraniums. Ideally
located on Water Street, it's a pleasant
stroll to the stretching beaches, quaint
shops, and breathtaking bluffs. At the day's
end, visit the festive sidewalk restaurant/
bar, and enjoy cocktails, dinner, and the
harborside hospitality.

Host: Christopher Sereno
Rooms: 35 (22 PB; 13 SB) $65-145
Full Breakfast
Credit Cards: A, B, C
Notes: 2, 3, 4, 7, 8, 9

Hotel Manisses

Spring Street, 02807
(401) 466-2421; (401) 466-2063

On Block Island, a scenic vacation spot,
biking, beaches, sailing, and just relaxing
are right at hand. The Hotel Manisses is a
restored Victorian inn with period furnishings. The restaurant serves all fresh seafood
and flaming coffees. Open all year. There
is also a petting zoo with five llamas,
Indian runner ducks, black swans, Sicilian
donkeys, Nubian, Pygmy, and fainting
goats.

Hosts: The Abrams family
Rooms: 17 (PB) $65-300
Full Breakfast
Credit Cards: A, B, C
Notes: 2, 4, 5, 7, 8 (over 10), 9, 10, 11, 14

The Inn at Old Harbour

Water Street, 02807
No phone

The Inn at Old Harbour is in the heart of
Block Island's historic district. Built in
1882 with extraordinary gingerbread trim
and magnificent Victorian styling. Listed
on the National Register of Historic Places,
the inn has ten newly renovated, individually decorated rooms, all appointed with
period furnishings. The ferry landing,
shops, restaurants, and beaches are within
walking distance.

Hosts: Barbara and Kevin Butler
Rooms: 10 (6 PB; 4 SB) $65-145
Continental Breakfast
Credit Cards: A, B, C
Notes: 2, 3, 7, 9, 10, 11

The New Shoreham House Inn

Water Street, P. O. Box 160, 02807
(401) 466-2651

Complete with resident ghost and crooked
stairs, New Shoreham House, circa 1890,
maintains a fresh, newly papered and painted Victorian seaside charm. A deck faces
out to sea. Most rooms overlook the
Atlantic Ocean. Block Island is great for
cycling. Walking trails are numerous and
the beaches are great. There are many fine
restaurants and shops.

Hosts: Kathy and Bob Schleimer
Rooms: 15 (SB) $35-115
Full Breakfast
Credit Cards: A, B, C
Notes: 2, 5, 8

Rose Farm Inn

Roslyn Road, Box 3, 02807
(401) 466-2021

Hotel Manisses

NOTES: Credit cards accepted: A Master Card; B Visa; C American Express; D Discover Card; E Diner's
Club; F Other; 2 Personal Checks accepted; 3 Lunch available; 4 Dinner available; 5 Open all year;

Sea and country setting, convenient to downtown and beaches. Comfortable rooms with ocean view, furnished with antiques, queen or king beds. Great stone porch and sun deck cooled by sea breezes. Light buffet breakfast is served on the porch.

Hosts: Robert and Judith Rose
Rooms: 10 (8 PB; 2 SB) $85-150
Continental Breakfast
Credit Cards: A, B, C
Closed Nov.-April
Notes: 2, 7, 8 (over 12), 9, 10, 11, 14

1661 Inn and Guest House

Spring Street, 02807
(401) 466-2421; (401) 466-2063

The 1661 Inn has nine guest rooms, all with private baths, and is open May 14 through November 10. The guest house has ten rooms, five with private baths, and is open April to November. Full breakfast is served, and children are welcome. There is a petting zoo with three llamas, Sicilian donkeys, Nubian, Pygmy, and fainting goats.

Hosts: Joan and Justin Abrams; Steve and Rita Draper
Rooms: 19 (14 PB; 5 SB) $65-300
Full Breakfast
Credit Cards: A, B, C
Notes: 2, 3, 4, 5 (guest house), 7, 8, 9, 10, 11, 14

The White House

Spring Street, 02807
(401) 466-2653

Large island manor house with six bedrooms and two baths. French Provencial antique furnishings. Notable collection of presidential autographs and documents. Full breakfast. All kinds of in-house services and amenities.

Host: V. M. Connolly
Rooms: 2 (SB) $50-120 seasonal
Full Breakfast
Credit Cards: A, B, C
Notes: 2, 5, 6, 7, 9, 10, 11

BRISTOL

Rockwell House Inn

610 Hope Street, 02809
(401) 253-0040

Federal-style home built in 1809 is located in the heart of the historic Waterfront District. Large and inviting guest rooms with king-size beds and fireplaces are available for guests, and a casual yet elegant decor with stenciling throughout adds to the house's charm. Breakfast is served on the porch or in the garden, and afternoon tea and sherry are served by the fire. Two rooms with private baths and two rooms with a shared bath are available. Antiquing, museums, boating, tennis, and golf are nearby.

Hosts: Debra and Steve Krohn
Rooms: 4 (2 PB; 2 SB) $55-90
Continental Breakfast
Credit Cards: A, B, C, D, E, F
Notes: 2, 5, 9, 10, 11, 12, 14

CHARLESTOWN

One Willow by the Sea

1 Willow Road, 02813
(401) 364-0802

Enjoy hospitality year-round in a peaceful, rural home. South County shoreline community. Guest comfort is a priority. Wake to birds, sunshine, and sea breezes. Delicious gourmet breakfast is often served on the sun deck. Explore the miles of beautiful sandy beaches, salt ponds, wildlife refuges. Restaurants, theaters, live music, antique shows, craft fairs, historic New England, and Narragansett Indian landmarks nearby. Providence, Newport, Block Island, and Mystic are a short drive. Host speaks French.

Host: Denise Dillon Fuge
Rooms: 4 (SB) $45 off-season, $55 in-season
Full Breakfast
Credit Cards: None
Notes: 2, 5, 8, 10, 11, 12, 14

GREEN HILL

Fairfield-By-The-Sea Bed and Breakfast

527 Green Hill Beach Road, 02879-6215
(401) 789-4717

An artist's contemporary home in a secluded country area 20 miles east of Mystic and 25 miles west of Newport. Day trips to Plymouth and Block Island. Biking and birding are favorite pastimes. Large fireplace and good library for guests. Fine restaurants abound. An informal and relaxed atmosphere.

Host: Jeanne Lewis
Rooms: 2 (SB) $45-60
Expanded Continental Breakfast
Minimum stay summer weekends: 2 nights; holidays: 3 nights
Credit Cards: C
Notes: 2, 5, 7, 8, 9, 10, 11, 12, 13

HOPKINTON

Nutmeg B&B Agency #515

P. O. Box 1117, West Hartford, Connecticut 06107
(203) 236-6698

History lovers will enjoy this classic 18th-century Colonial listed on the National Register of Historic Places. The house has massive chestnut hand-hewn beams, original pine-plank floors, five fireplaces, and two sitting/reading rooms. There are five guest rooms, two with private baths. Full breakfast. Smoking in designated areas. Children over ten welcome.

KINGSTON

Hedgerow Bed and Breakfast

P. O. Box 1586, 02881
(401) 783-2671

Lovely Colonial in Kingston, one-half mile from the University of Rhode Island campus. Handy for trips to Newport, Block Island, and the Rhode Island beaches, Mystic aquarium and seaport. Happy hour and full breakfast are included. Beautiful gardens and a tennis court on the premises for guests to enjoy.

Hosts: Ann and Jim Ross
Rooms: 4 (SB) $55-60 plus tax
Full Breakfast
Credit Cards: None
Notes: 2, 5, 8, 9, 10, 11, 12, 14

MIDDLETOWN

Lindsey's Guest House

6 James Street, 02840
(401) 846-9386

One mile to Newport's famous mansions, Cliff Walk, Tennis Hall of Fame. Lindsey's is a split-level home with large yard, deck, and off-street parking. Ten-minute walk to beaches and Norman Bird Sanctuary.

Hosts: Anne and Dave
Rooms: 3 (1 PB; 2 SB) $40-70
Continental Breakfast
Credit Cards: A, B
Notes: 2, 5, 8, 9, 10, 11, 12, 14

NARRAGANSETT

Bed and Breakfast Inns of New England RI-905

329 Lake Drive, Guilford, 06437
(800) 582-0853

Enjoy the elegance of a circa 1884 oceanfront Victorian summer estate on the National Register of Historic Places. Overlooking the ocean and set on two acres, guests may explore the grounds, play croquet, sunbathe or swim on the ocean beach, and relax on the sun porch or patio. The eight guest rooms have a variety of bed sizes, are furnished with antiques and collectibles, and many have ocean views. All rooms have private baths. Children over ten are welcome. Resident dog, but no guest pets, please. No smoking. $60-125, seasonal.

NOTES: Credit cards accepted: A Master Card; B Visa; C American Express; D Discover Card; E Diner's Club; F Other; 2 Personal Checks accepted; 3 Lunch available; 4 Dinner available; 5 Open all year;

House of Snee

191 Ocean Road, 02882
(401) 783-9494

Turn-of-the-century Dutch Colonial with a magnificent view from the front porch, within easy walking distance of the beach. Breakfast is served in the family dining room daily. There's a guest reading room on the second floor and a TV in the livingroom. The house has five fireplaces.

Host: Mildred A. Snee
Rooms: 3 (1 PB; 2 SB) $50-65
Full Breakfast
Credit Cards: None
Notes: 2, 5, 9, 10, 11, 12

House of Snee

Ilverthorpe Cottage

41 Robinson Street, 02882
(401) 789-2392

Lacy touches, hand-carved moldings, stenciled walls are found throughout this 1896 Victorian "cottage." A convenient three blocks from the beach. Travel to Newport for a day of mansion touring, sailing, and shopping, or take the ferry to nearby Block Island. Whatever your pleasure, you'll enjoy the sumptuous gourmet breakfast each morning.

Hosts: Jill, Chris and John Webb
Rooms: 4 (2 PB; 2 SB) $70-75
Full Breakfast
Credit Cards: None
Notes: 2, 7 (restricted), 8, 9, 10, 11, 12, 14

Murphy's B&B

43 South Pier Road, 02882
(401) 789-1824

Charming 1894 Victorian restored with care by the owners is situated on a tree-lined street one block from the ocean, which makes this a perfect base for enjoying our beautiful beaches, historic Newport and Providence, Block Island, the area's many antique shops, art galleries, and fine restaurants. Known for gracious ambience and fabulous breakfasts.

Hosts: Kevin and Martha Murphy
Rooms: 3 (SB) $50-80
Full Breakfast
Credit Cards: None
Notes: 3, 4, 7 (outside), 8(over 10), 9, 10, 11, 12

The 1900 House
Bed and Breakfast

59 Kingstown Road, 02882
(401) 789-7971

From the 1900 House, a Victorian home, it is a leisurely walk to Narragansett Beach, pier shops, fine dining, and the theater. It is a brief ride to Newport, Providence, University of Rhode Island. Mystic Seaport and the Theater-by-the-Sea. After a day in the salt air, you will be lulled to sleep by the sounds of the sea in your antique and lace surroundings. Double bedrooms, shared bath. Full gourmet breakfast.

Hosts: Bill and Sandra Panzeri
Rooms: 3 (1 PB; 2 SB) $50-65
Full Breakfast
Credit Cards: None

The Richards

144 Gibson Avenue, 02882
(401) 789-7746

Gracious accommodations in an 1884 historic manse. Relax by the fire in the library or your guest room with fireplace. Enjoy a leisurely full breakfast with homemade muffins, strudels, blintzes. Nancy's special touches will spoil you—down comforters,

6 Pets welcome; 7 Smoking allowed; 8 Children welcome; 9 Social drinking allowed; 10 Tennis available; 11 Swimming available; 12 Golf available; 13 Skiing available; 14 May be booked through travel agents.

canopy beds, flowers from the gardens.

Hosts: Steven and Nancy Richards
Rooms: 4 (2 PB; 2 SB) $55-85
Full Breakfast
Minimum stay weekends: 2 nights; holidays: 3
  nights
Credit Cards: None
Notes: 2, 5, 8 (over 12), 9

Seafield Cottage

110 Boon Street, 02882
(401) 783-2432

A 17-room, 100-year-old Cape Anne furnished with lace and full of charming ambience. Bedrooms with canopy beds, down
comforters and pillows, swooner couch.
Semi-private baths. Continental breakfast
includes unlimited freshly ground imported
coffee, juice, fruit compote, and Belgian
waffles, Scotch scones, or coffee cake. One
block from the ocean; 15 minutes from
Newport.

Hosts: Carl and Anne Cottle
Rooms: 3 (S2B) $40 plus tax
Continental Breakfast
Credit Cards: None
Notes: 2, 5, 7, 9

NEWPORT

Admiral Benbow Inn

93 Pelham Street, 02840
(401) 846-4256; (800) 343-2863
FAX (401) 846-4289

This treasure on the island is Newport's
best kept secret when it comes to lodging.
Built by Captain Littlefield in 1855 as an
inn and carefully renovated, the owners
have preserved the black marble fireplaces,
arched windows, and high celings and
added canopy and brass beds, duvets, and
charm. Several rooms overlook the waterfront, and one third-floor room has a
sweeping view of the Newport Harbor.
Each room has its own private bath, telephone, and air conditioner, and complimentary breakfast is served homestyle next to
our warm woodstove.

Host: Jane Berriman
Rooms: 15 (PB) $55-120, seasonal
Continental Breakfast
Credit Cards: A, B, C, E
Notes: 5, 7, 9, 14

Admiral Farragut Inn

31 Clarke Street, 02840
(401) 846-4256; (800) 343-2863
FAX (401) 846-4289

Welcome to a most unique Colonial inn.
Everywhere amid our guest rooms, keeping
room, foyer and halls there are fresh inter-
pretations of Colonial themes and bits of
whimsy to make your stay a delight. The
inn was built in 1702, remodeled in 1755,
and restored to its present condition in
1987. We have furnished the inn with
handmade Shaker-style pencil-post beds,
English antiques, handmade spreads and
drapes, fluffy duvets, and even added lace
to our sheets and pillow cases. We have not
forgotten the modern conveniences of a private bath, telephone, and air conditioning
in each room, and complimentary breakfast
is served homestyle in our keeping room.

Host: Jane Berriman
Rooms: 10 (PB) $45-120
Full Breakfast
Credit Cards: A, B, C, E
Notes: 2, 5, 7, 9, 14

The Admiral Fitzroy Inn

398 Thames Street, 02840
(401) 848-8000; (800) 343-2863
FAX (401) 846-4289

This inn is located in the heart of Newport's yachting district, central to all that
Newport has to offer. The inn is decorated
in its own distinctive style, artfully con-
ceived, and a showcase for fine craftsmanship. Sleigh and brass beds, lace linens and
plush duvets are part of each room's individual decor, and each room has glazed finished walls, hand-painted with pleasing
designs and crisp flower motifs. Hidden
away within our handmade Swedish cupboards, you will find a TV with cable, a
small refrigerator, electric tea kettle, and

fixings. Also, in each room, there is a private bath with a tub, telephone, heat and cool controls, and a hair dryer. Complimentary full breakfast can be enjoyed downstairs or in your own room or on our deck overlooking Newport Harbor.

Host: Jane Berriman
Rooms: 18 (PB) $65-150
Full and Continental Breakfast
Credit Cards: A, B, C , E
Notes: 2, 5, 7, 8, 9, 14

Anna's Victorian Connection

5 Fowler Avenue, 02840
(401) 849-2489

This is a reservation service for Rhode Island and southeast Massachusetts. Office hours are from 9 A.M.-9 P.M. daily (8 A.M.-10 P.M. during the summer). We are members of the B&B: TNN (The National Network). All homes, inns, apartments, and houses have been inspected. Call to select the bed and breakfast accommodation that best suits your needs.

Host: Susan C. White
Rooms: 300 plus (PB and SB) $35-250
Continental and Full Breakfast
Credit Cards: A, B, C, E, F

Bed and Breakfast of Rhode Island

38 Bellvue Avenue, P. O. Box 3291, 02840
(401) 849-1298

Bed and Breakfast of Rhode Island is a reservation service that serves all of Rhode Island, including Block Island and southeastern Massachusetts. Our 120 bed and breakfasts range from the small one-room homestays to the large 19-room inns. In season rates apply May through October with rates from $55-95 for shared baths and $95-225 for private baths. Off-season rates apply November-April. Rooms with shared baths are $45-75 and rooms with private baths are $60-115.

Rooms: 400 (PB and SB) $55-225

Full and Continental Breakfast
Credit Cards: A, B, C
Notes: 2, 5, 6, 8, 9, 10, 11

Bellevue House

14 Catherine Street, 02840
(401) 847-1828

Built in 1774, Bellevue House was converted into the first summer hotel in Newport in 1828. Situated on top of Historic Hill, off the famous Bellevue Avenue, three blocks from the harbor. The house retains a combination of ideal location, colonial history, nautical atmosphere, and Victorian charm.

Hosts: Joan and Vic Farmer
Rooms: 8 (6 PB; 2 SB) $65-100, plus tax
Continental Breakfast
Credit Cards: None
Closed Nov.-April
Notes: 2, 8 (over 12), 9, 10, 11, 12, 14

Brinley Victorian Inn

23 Brinley Street, 02840
(401) 849-7645

Romantic all year long, the inn becomes a Victorian Christmas dream come true. Comfortable antiques and fresh flowers fill every room. Friendly, unpretentious service and attention to detail will make this inn your haven in Newport. Park and walk everywhere. AAA approved.

Host: Peter Carlisle
Rooms: 17 (13 PB; 4 SB) $55-130
Continental Breakfast
Minimum stay weekends: 2 nights; holidays: 3 nights
Credit Cards: A, B, D
Notes: 2, 5, 7, 8 (over 12), 9, 10, 11, 12, 14

Cliffside Inn

2 Seaview Avenue, 02840
(401) 847-1811

Perfect site on a quiet, tree-lined street removed from the hubbub of downtown, yet just one block from Cliff Walk (the city's famous seaside walking trail), two blocks from the beach, and a short stroll

6 Pets welcome; 7 Smoking allowed; 8 Children welcome; 9 Social drinking allowed; 10 Tennis available; 11 Swimming available; 12 Golf available; 13 Skiing available; 14 May be booked through travel agents.

from the Newport mansions. Built in 1880 as a summer getaway for Gov. Thomas Swann of Maryland, the cottage became the site of Saint George's School in 1897. The inn was later owned by well-known Newport artist Beatrice Turner. Guest bedrooms have private bath. Conference facilities available.

Hosts: Annette and Norbert Mede
Rooms: 12 (PB) $115-225
Full Breakfast
Credit Cards: A, B, C, D, E
Notes: 2, 5, 14

Cliffside Inn

Cliff View Guest House

4 Cliff Terrace, 02840
(401) 846-0885

This two-story Victorian with an ocean view from two porches sits on a quiet dead-end street that leads to the famous Cliff Walk, which is a three-mile path bordering the ocean. A five-minute walk to the beach, ten-to-fifteen-minute walk to the wharf area, this ten-room house has four guest rooms. Two rooms share a bath and have a view of the ocean. The other two rooms have private baths. Located five houses uphill from the cliffs.

Hosts: Pauline and John Shea
Rooms: 4 (2 PB; 2 SB) $55-65
Continental Breakfast
Credit Cards: A, B
Note: 2

Commodore Perry Inn

348 Thames Street, 02840
(401) 848-8000; (800) 343-2863

FAX (401) 846-4289

The Commodore Perry Inn atop the Ark Restaurant on Thames Street is Newport's European pension. Located on the third floor, some rooms have rooftop views of the harbor. All rooms have private baths, telephones, cable TV, air conditioning, small refrigerator, electric tea kettle, and the fixings. We named our inn after a native Newporter who opened up trade with Japan in 1854, commanding his first fleet of Black Ships. Our decor is Japanese, and our hall mural depicts Commodore Perry entering Eno Harbor in Tokyo.

Host: Jane Berriman
Rooms: 8 (PB) $45-95
Self-eater Breakfast
Credit Cards: A, B, C, E
Notes: 5, 7, 8, 9, 14

The Francis Malbone House

392 Thames Street, 02840
(401) 846-0392

This historic inn was built in 1760 for Colonel Francis Malbone, who made his fortune as a shipping merchant. The design of the house is attributed to Peter Harrison, the architect responsible for Touro Synagogue and the Redwood Library. You will enjoy the comfortable elegance of the Francis Malbone House, which is proudly listed on the National Register of Historic Places. The inn offers a downtown harbor location, private baths, full breakfast, fireplaces, corporate packages, and gracious rooms and gardens for elegant entertaining.

Host: Jim Maher
Rooms: 9 (PB) $90-225
Full Breakfast
Credit Cards: A, B, C
Notes: 2 , 5, 9, 14

Halidon Hill Guest House

Halidon Avenue, 02840
(401) 847-8318

Modern, spacious rooms, ample on-site parking, in-ground pool, and deck area.

NOTES: Credit cards accepted: A Master Card; B Visa; C American Express; D Discover Card; E Diner's Club; F Other; 2 Personal Checks accepted; 3 Lunch available; 4 Dinner available; 5 Open all year;

Just minutes from beaches, shopping areas, local restaurants, and mansions.

Host: Helen Burke
Rooms: 4 (2 PB; 2 SB) $55-150
Continental Breakfast
Credit Cards: A, B, C
Notes: 2, 5, 7, 8, 9, 11, 14

Harborside Inn

Christie's Landing, 02840
(401) 846-6600; (800) 421-3454

The Harborside Inn blends the charm of colonial Newport with the hustle and bustle of Newport's active waterfront. Each suite provides a view of the harbor and features a wet bar, refrigerator, cable TV, sleeping loft, and balcony. A short walk to quaint specialty shops, colonial homes and churches, restaurants, and antique shops.

Host: Mary Comforti
Rooms: 14 (PB) $55-190
Continental Breakfast
Credit Cards: A, B, C, E
Notes: 2, 5, 7, 8, 9, 10, 11, 12

The Inn at Newport Beach

Memorial Boulevard, 02840
(401) 846-0310; (800) 786-0310

The Inn at Newport Beach offers spectacular views of the Atlantic Ocean and the famous Cliff Walk. Each of the 49 guest rooms is unique in its distinctive homestyle decor and comfort. Accommodations feature cable TV with HBO, private bath, individual heat and air conditioning. The Newport Beach Club Restaurant serves lunch and dinner with an exceptional Sunday brunch. Continental breakfast included in the rate.

Host: Cathy Morrison
Rooms: 49 (PB) $49-165
Expanded Continental Breakfast
Credit Cards: A, B, C, D, E
Notes: 3, 4, 5, 7, 8, 9, 10, 11, 12, 14

The Inn at Old Beach

19 Old Beach Road, 02840
(401) 849-3479

Once the gracious Victorian home of an affluent physician and commodore, the Inn at Old Beach is now an elegant bed and breakfast inn. Built in 1879, it is centrally situated in one of Newport's most prestigious areas. The fabled mansions, Cliff Walk, beache and historic harbor are all close by. Each of the charming guest rooms has a private bath. Several have fireplaces.

Hosts: Cynthia and Luke Murray
Rooms: 5 (PB) $75-125
Continental Breakfast
Credit Cards: A, B, C
Notes: 2, 5, 9

Harborside Inn

6 Pets welcome; 7 Smoking allowed; 8 Children welcome; 9 Social drinking allowed; 10 Tennis available; 11 Swimming available; 12 Golf available; 13 Skiing available; 14 May be booked through travel agents.

Inntowne Inn

6 Mary Street, 02840
(401) 846-9200; FAX (401) 846-1534

An elegant Colonial inn located in the heart
of downtown Newport offers four-poster
beds, canopies, and a rooftop deck, which
is a perfect place to unwind. Use of health
club and pool within walking distance.
Afternoon tea and continental breakfast
served daily. Located one mile from the
Newport mansions. Take harbor cruises,
shop for antiques, or just enjoy the bustle
of the harbor.

Host: Carmella Gardner
Rooms: 26 (PB) $90-250
Continental Breakfast
Credit Cards: A, B, C
Notes: 5, 7, 10, 11, 14

Jenkins Guest House

206 South Rhode Island Avenue, 02840
(401) 847-6801

This home was built on a quiet side street
in a residential area of Newport when the
hosts married. A three-minute walk to the
beach; 15 to downtown; 10 to mansions.
Yachting activities, boutiques, and shopping. Plenty of parking on grounds.

Hosts: David and Sally Jenkins
Rooms: 2 (SB) $60
Continental Breakfast
Credit Cards: None
Open April 1-Nov. 1
Notes: 2, 8, 9, 10, 11, 12

La Forge Cottage

96 Pelham Street, 02840
(401) 847-4400

La Forge Cottage is a Victorian bed and
breakfast in the heart of Newport's Historic
Hill area. Close to beaches and downtown.
All rooms have private baths, TV, phone,
air conditioning, refrigerators, and full
breakfast room service. French and German
spoken. Reservations suggested.

Hosts: Louis and Margot Droual
Rooms: 6 (PB) $67.20-106.40
Suites: 4 (PB) $106.40-140
Full Breakfast
Minimum stay weekends: 2 nights; holidays: 3
  nights
Credit Cards: A, B, C, D
Notes: 2, 5, 7, 8, 9, 10, 11, 12, 14

The Melville House

39 Clark Street, 02840
(401) 847-0640

Step back into the past and stay at a
Colonial inn, built circa 1750, "where the
past is present." The Melville House is on
the National Register of Historic Places and
is in the heart of Newport's historic district.
Walk around the corner to the Brick
Market and the wharves. Enjoy a leisurely
homemade breakfast in the morning, and
join the hosts for complimentary sherry
before dinner. Off-street parking.

Hosts: Rita and Sam Rogers
Rooms: 7 (5 PB; 2 SB) $40-100
Expanded Continental Breakfast
Credit Cards: A, B, C
Notes: 2, 7, 8 (over 12), 9, 10, 11, 12, 14

Melville House

Mill Street Inn

75 Mill Street, 02840
(401) 849-9500

This luxury all-suite hotel is sure to please
guests with an award-winning interior in a
renovated national historic landmark mill.
Town houses have spectacular views from
private decks, and parking is available.

Walk to the harbor, restaurants, and shops. All suites have queen-size beds in the bedroom and queen-size sofa sleepers in the livingroom, plus the added charm of old beams and exposed bricks from the old mill. Many packages available throughout the year.

Hosts: Paula and Robert Briskin
Suites: 23 (PB) $75-250
Continental Breakfast
Credit Cards: A, B, C, E
Notes: 5, 6, 7, 8, 9, 14

Pilgrim House Inn

123 Spring Street, 02840
(401) 846-0040; (800) 525-8373

This Victorian inn, with its comforts and elegance, is two blocks from the harbor in the midst of the historic district. A livingroom with fireplace, immaculate rooms, and wonderful atmosphere await you. Breakfast on the deck overlooking Newport's harbor. Just outside the door are the mansions, shops, and restaurants.

Hosts: Pam and Bruce Bayuk
Rooms: 10 (8 PB; 2 SB) $49.50-137.50
Continental Breakfast
Credit Cards: A, B
Closed January
Notes: 2, 8 (over 12), 9, 10, 11, 12, 14

Polly's Place

349 Valley Road, Route 214, 02840
(401) 847-2160

A quiet retreat one mile from Newport's harbor, historic homes, and sandy beaches. Polly is a longtime Newport resident willing to give helpful advice to travelers interested in the area. Rooms are large, clean, and very attractive. Breakfast is served in the dining room with a lovely view of wildlife and birds of the area. Polly also offers a one-bedroom apartment that is available by the week and completely equipped for reasonable rates. This bed and breakfast has been inspected and approved.

Host: Polly Canning
Rooms: 4 plus apt. (1 PB; 4 SB) $80
Full Breakfast
Credit Cards: None
Notes: 2, 9, 10, 11, 12, 14

Spring Street Inn

353 Spring Street, 02840
(401) 847-4767

An Empire Victorian, circa 1858, with seven double rooms and one apartment, all with private baths. Guest sitting room. Walk to all Newport highlights. Off-street parking; free bus nearby. Harbor view suite with balcony sleeps two to four people. Extensive full breakfast.

Host: Parvine Latimore
Rooms: 6 (PB) $50-115
Full Breakfast
Credit Cards: A, B
Notes: 2, 3, 4, 5, 8 (over 11), 9, 10, 14

Villa Liberté

22 Liberty Street, 02840
(401) 846-7444

Enjoy quiet and private luxury with contemporary European decor in the heart of Newport. Deluxe suites, queen rooms, and suites with kitchens are designed with hues of seafoam green and peach. Dramatic black and white tile baths feature pedestal sinks and arched alcoves. The Villa's ideal location is just a walk from the mansions, Newport's beaches, brick marketplace, and the wharf area. All accommodations have private baths, air conditioning, TV, and phone. Complimentary continental breakfast is served on the sun deck.

Host: Leigh Anne Mosco
Rooms: 15 (PB) $59-125
Continental Breakfast
Credit Cards: A, B
Notes: 7, 8

The Willows

8 Willow Street, 02840
(401) 846-5486

In the historic section of Newport, the Willows pampers you with secluded gardens, solid brass canopy beds, fresh flowers in rooms, mints on pillows, champagne glasses and silver ice bucket, lights on dim. Breakfast in bed on bone china and silver service. Three blocks from downtown and the waterfront.

Host: Patricia Murphy
Rooms: 5 (PB) $88-135
Continental Breakfast
Credit Cards: None
Closed Jan.
Notes: 2, 7 (limited), 9, 10, 11, 12, 14

NORTH KINGSTOWN

The John Updike House

19 Pleasant Street, 02852
(401) 294-4905

Built in 1745, this elegant Georgian has retained its beauty and charm for nearly two and one-half centuries. It continues to be the only bed and breakfast on the west passage of Narragansett Bay, overlooking the bay and Wickford Harbor, and can be used as your base, since it is an easy day trips to Newport, Block Island, South Shore beaches, Providence, Cape Cod. A private sandy beach is avialable for your pleasure. Accommodations vary depending on the needs of the customers: two rooms with common room; a suite of two bedrooms and common room; an apartment that includes suite and full private kitchen.

Hosts: Mary Anne and Bill Sabo
Rooms: Variable $75-150
Expanded Continental Breakfast
Credit Cards: A, B
Notes: 2, 5, 7, 8, 9, 11

PROVIDENCE

Old Court Bed and Breakfast

144 Benefit Street, 02903
(401) 757-2002

In the heart of Providence historic Benefit Street area, you'll find the Old Court, where tradition is combined with contemporary standards of luxury. The Old Court was built in 1863 and reflects early Victorian styles. In rooms that overlook downtown Providence and Brown University, you'll feel as if you've entered a more gracious era.

Host: Robert Shields
Rooms: 11 (PB) $75-160
Continental Breakfast
Credit Cards: A, B, C
Notes: 2, 5, 7, 14

State House Inn

43 Jewett Street, 02908
(401) 785-1235

In the center of a quiet and quaint neighborhood, the State House Inn is a 100-year-old building newly restored and renovated into a country bed and breakfast. Situated minutes from downtown Providence and the many local colleges and universities. The inn brings country living to the big city.

Hosts: Frank and Monica Hopton
Rooms: 10 (PB) $75-105
Full Breakfast
Credit Cards: A, B, C
Notes: 5, 8, 9, 14

SNUG HARBOR

"Almost Heaven" in Snug Harbor

49 West Street, Wakefield, 02879
(401) 783-9272

Situated around the corner from Rhode Island's beautiful saltwater beaches, marinas, and famous seafood restaurants, "Almost Heaven" offers the traveler easy access to everything. Newport is 30 minutes away; Mystic, 40 minutes; fishing, swimming, summer theater nearby. Peaceful and quiet. Accommodations are ideal for a family of four or two couples.

NOTES: Credit cards accepted: A Master Card; B Visa; C American Express; D Discover Card; E Diner's Club; F Other; 2 Personal Checks accepted; 3 Lunch available; 4 Dinner available; 5 Open all year;

Host: Deloris Simpson
Rooms: 2 (SB) $45-60
Full Breakfast
Credit Cards: None
Notes: 2, 5, 7 (on deck), 8, 9, 10, 11, 12

SOUTH KINGSTOWN

Admiral Dewey Inn

668 Matunuck Beach Drive, 02879
(401) 783-2090; (401) 783-8298

Nestled in the small beach village of
Matunuck, this Victorian bed and breakfast
first opened for guests in 1898. Now on the
National Historic Register of Historic
Places, the Admiral Dewey has been completely restored and is decorated entirely
with Victoriana. There are rockers on the
wraparound porch and a large breakfast
room with tiled fireplace. Near the
Theatre-by-the-Sea, the Trustom Pond
Wildlife Refuge, Matunuck and Moonstone
beaches, and antique shops. Shuttle service
to the Block Island ferry and local airports.
Polish and French spoken.

Hosts: Joan and Hardy LeBel
Rooms: 10 (8 PB; 2 SB) $80-120
Continental Breakfast
Credit Cards: A, B
Notes: 2, 5, 9, 10, 11, 12

The Gardener House

629 Main Street, 02879
(401) 789-1250

This Federal 1818 home was featured in
Country Interiors in 1992. Immaculate
rooms filled with antiques, private baths off
each bedroom, gourmet breakfast served in
the dining room, music, and candlelight set
the mood for a memorable stay. Garden
flowers and two acres of gardens and
woodlands surround a huge pool and add
an ambience of beauty. This historic area is
near the University of Rhode Island,
Theatre-by-the-Sea, beaches, fishing, Block
Island, Newport, Mystic whaling village,
bird and wildlife sanctuary, special restaurants, and superb scenery.

Hosts: Will and Nan Gardner
Rooms: 3 (PB) $65-85
Full Breakfast
Credit Cards: None
Notes: 2, 5, 8, 9, 11

Larchwood Inn

521 Main Street, 02879
(401) 783-5454

The Larchwood Inn is a family-run country
inn that has kept pace with the 20th century
without sacrificing its rural beauty. Holly
House, located across the front lawn from
the main inn, offers additional lodging.
Most rooms have private baths, and all
guests are encouraged to use the services of
the main inn, which includes three restaurants (all of which serve three meals daily)
and a cocktail lounge (with lunch and
happy hour daily, and live music on the
weekends). Near beaches, boating, hiking,
horseback and bike riding, and skiing.
Breakfast not included in rates.

Host: Francis Browning
Rooms: 20 (12 PB; 8 SB) $40-80
Credit Cards: A, B, C, D, E
Notes: 2, 3, 4, 5, 6, 7, 8, 9, 14

WESTERLY

Grandview Bed and Breakfast

212 Shore Road, 02891
(401) 596-6384

Stately turn-of-the-century home with
splendid ocean view. Hearty continental
breakfast served on cheery breakfast porch.
Large comfortable livingroom with stone
fireplace. Walk to tennis and golf. A short
drive to beaches, Mystic Seaport, Newport
mansions, and Watch Hill shopping.

Host: Pat Grande
Rooms: 12 (2 PB; 10 SB) $55-85
Continental Breakfast
Credit Cards: A, B, C
Notes: 2, 5, 8, 14

---

6 Pets welcome; 7 Smoking allowed; 8 Children welcome; 9 Social drinking allowed; 10 Tennis available; 11
Swimming available; 12 Golf available; 13 Skiing available; 14 May be booked through travel agents.

Nutmeg B&B Agency #504

P. O. Box 1117, West Hartford, Connecticut 06107
(203) 236-6698

Savor the splendid views from the wrap-around stone porch of this turn-of- the-century bed and breakfast. There are 12 guest rooms, two with private baths. The home has a large family room equipped with a player piano, cable TV, games, and variety of reading material. Pick-up available from local train station or airport. If you love the beach, this home is a perfect base for enjoying the five Rhode Island beaches nearby. Only minutes from Mystic, Connecticut. Continental breakfast. Limited Smoking. Children welcome. Pets in residence.

Nutmeg B&B Agency #505

P. O. Box 1117, West Hartford, Connecticut 06107
(203) 236-6698

Overlooking the park is this newly renovated classic Greek Revival home in the historic district. There are three rooms for bed and breakfast guests. They share one and one-half baths and a den. The den has comfortable chairs, cable TV, and plenty to read, making it perfect for winding down after a day of golf or swimming. Continental breakfast. Children welcome. Smoking in designated areas.

Nutmeg B&B Agency #507

P. O. Box 1117, West Hartford, Connecticut 06107
(203) 236-6698

Situated five minutes from the beach, this renovated 1920 summer home is by a salt-water pond that looks out to the ocean. Originally a working farm, it provides the perfect quiet getaway. One guest room has two double beds, many windows, and a private bath with shower. The second guest room has a canopy double bed, private deck with a view of the water, and a private bath with a tub. For the family getaway, there are also two summer cottages available, one with three bedrooms and the other with six. Continental breakfast. No smoking. Children welcome. Pets in residence.

The Villa

190 Shore Road, 02891
(401) 596-1054; (800) 722-9240

Open year-round, The Villa is a deluxe bed and breakfast located at the crossroads of Westerly and Watch Hill, and just minutes from Rhode Island's pristine shore line. This large, gracious home is on one and one-half landcaped acres, surrounded by beautiful gardens and spacious lawns. Indulge yourself with the fireplace and Jacuzzi suites, outdoor hot tub, and designer pool. The Villa is a perfect romantic destination.

Host: Jerry Maiorano
Rooms: 7 (5 PB; 2 SB) $45-125
Continental Plus Breakfast
Credit Cards: A, B, C
Notes: 5, 6, 7, 9, 11, 14

Woody Hill Bed and Breakfast

330 Woody Hill Road, 02891
(401) 322-0452

Your hostess, a high school English teacher, invites you to share her reproduction Colonial home, with antiques and gardens. You may snuggle under quilts, relax on the porch swing, visit nearby Newport and Mystic, or swim in the pool or at beautiful ocean beaches. Westerly has it all!

Host: Dr. Ellen L. Madison
Rooms: 3 (1 PB; 2 SB) $60-80
Full Breakfast
Credit Cards: None
Closed one week in Feb.
Notes: 2, 5, 8, 9, 10, 11, 12,

NOTES: Credit cards accepted: A Master Card; B Visa; C American Express; D Discover Card; E Diner's Club; F Other; 2 Personal Checks accepted; 3 Lunch available; 4 Dinner available; 5 Open all year;

WICKFORD

Meadowland Bed and Breakfast Ltd.

765 Old Baptist Road, 02852
(401) 294-4168

Built in 1835, Victorian Meadowland served as a roadhouse for travelers. Today, share a picturesque fireplaced livingroom and six graciously appointed guest rooms. Join us for golf, scuba diving, mystery or Ladies' Getaway weekends set in the ambience of days gone by. Located minutes from the historic village of Wickford.

Host: Linda Savorone
Rooms: 6 (SB) $65
Full Breakfast
Credit Cards: None
Notes: 2, 5, 8, 10, 11, 12

WYOMING

The Cookie Jar Bed and Breakfast

64 Kingstown Road, 02898
(401) 539-2680

The heart of this home, the livingroom, was built in 1732 as a blacksmith's shop. The original ceiling, handhewn beams, and granite walls remain today. The country property includes a barn, a swimming pool, 50 fruit trees, grapevines, a flower garden, and an acre of grass. The hosts offer friendly homestyle living just a short drive from the beaches, the University of Rhode Isalnd, Mystic, and Providence.

Hosts: Dick and Madelein Sohl
Rooms: 3 (1 PB; 2 SB) $60
Full Breakfast
Credit Cards: A, B
Notes: 2, 5, 8, 9, 11, 12, 14

6 Pets welcome; 7 Smoking allowed; 8 Children welcome; 9 Social drinking allowed; 10 Tennis available; 11 Swimming available; 12 Golf available; 13 Skiing available; 14 May be booked through travel agents.

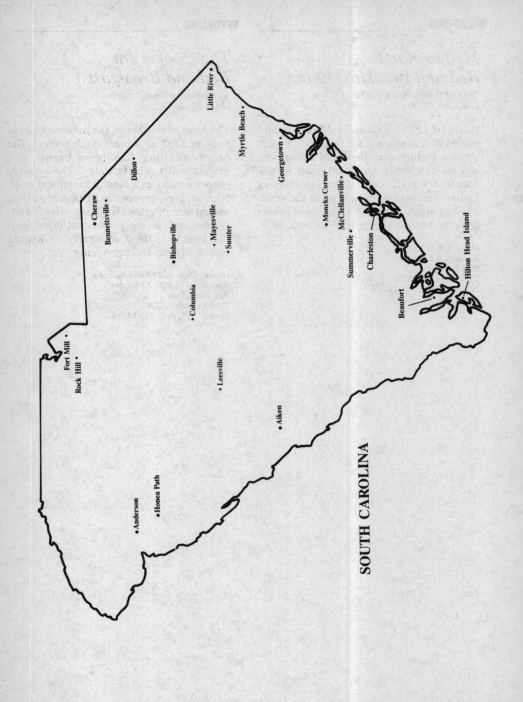

Little River •

Myrtle Beach •

Georgetown •

Dillon •

• Moncks Corner

McClellanville •

• Cheraw

Bennettsville •

• Mayesville

• Bishopville

• Sumter

Summerville •

Charleston •

Hilton Head Island

Beaufort

Fort Mill •

Rock Hill •

• Leesville

• Columbia

• Aiken

Anderson •

• Honea Path

SOUTH CAROLINA

South Carolina

AIKEN

Holley Inn

235 Richland Avenue, 29801
(803) 648-4265

This beautiful hotel was built in 1929. All rooms offer private baths, TV, and phones. A pool is on premises, and a courtyard and lounge are available for guests to use. Within walking distance of quaint shops and restaurants, and the inn is located in the center of downtown. Guests can golf at several private golf courses where host is a member.

Host: T. E. Holley
Rooms: 35 (PB) $40-54
Continental Breakfast
Credit Cards: A, B, C, D, E
Notes: 2, 3, 4, 5, 6, 7, 8, 9, 10, 11, 12, 14

The Willcox Inn

100 Colleton Avenue, 29801
(803) 649-1377; (800) 368-1047

Beautiful, spacious rooms that have been occupied by Winston Churchill, President Roosevelt, and Elizabeth Arden. Our dining room is known for its fine cuisine, including pheasant in whiskey sauce, rack of lamb, etc. Beautiful town with a lot to offer: golf, polo matches, antique shopping, and more.

Host: John Moore
Rooms: 30 (PB) $78-113
Full Breakfast
Credit Cards: A, B, C, E
Notes: 3, 4, 5, 7, 8, 9, 10, 12, 14

ANDERSON

Evergreen Inn

1103 South Main Street, 29621
(803) 225-1109

Two historic mansions on the national register, with on-premises restaurant. The inn has seven guest rooms, six baths, and eight fireplaces; there is also a honeymoon suite done in pink and rose velvet with satin and lace. Twenty minutes away from three lakes, each with over 1,000 miles of shoreline and public parks. Antique shops and the downtown area are within walking distance. Located halfway between Charlotte and Atlanta, the inn is an excellent stopping place for a quiet dinner and enjoyable stay.

Hosts: Peter and Myrna Ryter
Rooms: 7 (6 PB; 1 SB) $65
Continental Breakfast
Credit Cards: A, B, C, E
Notes: 2, 4, 5, 7, 9, 10, 11, 12

BEAUFORT

Bay Street Inn

601 Bay Street, 29902
(803) 524-7720

Serene in its command of the S curve of the Beaufort River, the house has remained a haven of hospitality for two centuries. On the national register, within the historic district, site of the filming of the movie *The Prince of Tides*, noted in *Family Circle* magazine for its cuisine, the inn personifies the best of the Old and New South. Columned elegance forever in its prime.

NOTES: Credit cards accepted: A Master Card; B Visa; C American Express; D Discover Card; E Diner's Club; F Other; 2 Personal Checks accepted; 3 Lunch available; 4 Dinner available; 5 Open all year; 6 Pets welcome; 7 Smoking allowed; 8 Children welcome; 9 Social drinking allowed; 10 Tennis available; 11 Swimming available; 12 Golf available; 13 Skiing available; 14 May be booked through travel agents.

Host: Gene Roe
Rooms: 5 (PB) $80-95
Full Breakfast
Credit Cards: A, B
Notes: 2, 5, 6, 7, 8, 9, 10, 11, 12, 14

Bay Street Inn

The Rhett House Inn

1009 Craven Street, 29902
(803) 524-9030

All the guest rooms have been created for
your comfort and convenience. They are
authentically furnished with homespun
quilts and freshly cut flowers, adding to
their warmth and individuality. The inn
beautifully re-creates the feeling of the Old
South. You'll fall in love with the warmth
and graciousness of an earlier way of life.
In-room massages are available. Television
and jacuzzi are also available to help you
relax before retiring to a bed that has been
turned down for you. FAX available.
Phones in rooms. Barbara Streisand and
Nick Nolte have stayed in this inn. A picnic
lunch is available with a 24-hour notice
and dinner by reservation.

Hosts: Marianne and Steve Harrison
Rooms: 10 (PB) $85.60 - 192.60
Full Breakfast
Minimum stay weekends and holidays: 2 nights
Credit Cards: A, B
Notes: 2, 5, 8 (over 5), 9, 10, 11, 12, 14

Two Suns Inn
Bed and Breakfast

1705 Bay Street, 29902
(803) 522-1122; FAX (803) 522-1122

A prince of an inn in an antebellum
brigadoon. Southern charm abounds historic Beaufort, the film site for *Prince of
Tides,* and informal elegance characterizes
this 1917 grand home right on the bay.
Visit the quaint downtown, enjoy a carriage
ride, or bicycle through the historic waterfront community. Relax in this newly
restored home, complete with Carrol's
weavings, period decor, collectibles, full
handicapped facilities, and business amenities.

Hosts: Carrol and Ron Kay
Rooms: 5 (PB) $79-99
Full Breakfast
Credit Cards: A, B, C
Notes: 2, 5, 9, 10, 11, 12, 14

BENNETTSVILLE

The Breeden House Inn

404 East Main Street, 29512
(803) 479-3665

Built in 1886 as a wedding present for the
original owner's bride, the romantic
Breeden House is a beautifully restored
Southern mansion on two acres that include
a carriage house. Listed on the National
Register of Historic Places, the inn is 20
minutes off I-95; a great halfway point
between Florida and New York. A haven
for antique lovers. Pool, goldfish pond, and
cable TV. Indoor and outdoor sitting areas
including a wraparound front porch, rockers, swings. The comfortable surroundings
will capture your interest and inspire your
imagination. Near museums and antique
shops.

Hosts: Wesley and Bonnie Park
Rooms: 7 (PB) $50-55
Full Breakfast
Credit Cards: A, B, D
Notes: 2, 5, 11, 14

NOTES: Credit cards accepted: A Master Card; B Visa; C American Express; D Discover Card; E Diner's
Club; F Other; 2 Personal Checks accepted; 3 Lunch available; 4 Dinner available; 5 Open all year;

BISHOPVILLE

Law Street Inn

200 South Main Street, P. O. Box 814, 29010
(803) 484-5639; (800) 253-5474
FAX (803) 484-6678

Law Street Inn is in a small southern town
with a relaxed atmosphere. Convenient to
I-20 and 30 minutes from I-95, halfway
between New York and Florida. The Greek
Revival circa 1834 inn is furnished in
antiques and reproductions, and is on the
National Register of Historic Places. The
owner is a professional interior designer.
Cities such as Camden, Charleston,
Columbia, Myrtle Beach, and Sumter are
all accessible within a two-hour or less
drive.

Hosts: Robert and Jerry Law
Rooms: 5 (2 PB; 3 SB) $40-70
Full and Continental Breakfast
Credit Cards: None
Notes: 2, 5, 10, 11, 12, 14

CHARLESTON

Ann Harper's Bed and Breakfast

56 Smith Street, 29401
(803) 723-3947

This circa 1870 home is situated in
Charleston's historic district. Two rooms
with connecting bath and sitting area with
TV. The owner is a retired medical technol-
ogist and enjoys serving a full breakfast.

Host: Ann D. Harper
Rooms: 2 (PB) $60-70
Full Breakfast
Minimum stay: 2 nights
Credit Cards: None
Notes: 2, 5, 7 (limited), 8 (over 10), 9, 10, 11, 12

The Battery Carriage House Inn

20 South Battery, 29401
(800) 775-5575

This 1843 mansion on Charleston's famous
Battery waterfront park offers southern
comfort with European elegance. Eleven
discreetly renovated rooms are available in
the carriage house overlooking private gardens. Four rooms have steam baths, three
offer whirlpool tubs. Business phone system, FAX, and Xerox. Friendly and professional staff. Elegant continental breakfast.
Amenities include cable TV, fluffy robes,
and towels. Escape the ordinary.

Host: Katharine Hastie
Rooms: 11 (PB) $79-159
Continental Breakfast
Credit Cards: A, B, C
Notes: 2, 9, 14

The Belvedere

40 Rutledge Avenue, 29401
(803) 722-0973

A beautiful mansion built in 1900 with a
Colonial exterior and a Georgian interior.
Situated in the downtown historic section,
on Colonial Lake, within short walking distance of all historical points of interest,
restaurants, and shopping. Guests use public areas and piazzas in this romantic, beautifully restored and furnished mansion.

Hosts: David S. Spell and Rick Zender
Rooms: 3 (PB) $95-110
Continental Breakfast
Credit Cards: None
Closed Dec. 1-Feb. 15
Notes: 2, 9, 10, 11, 12, 14

Brasington House Bed and Breakfast

328 East Bay Street, 29401
(803) 722-1274

Elegant accommodations in a splendidly
restored Greek Revival Charleston single
house furnished with antiques. Centrally
located in Charleston's beautiful historic
district, four lovely, well-appointed guest
rooms with central heat and air conditioning include private baths, telephones, cable
TV, and tea making services. King, queen,

and twin beds are available. Included is a bountiful family-style restaurant, wine and cheese served in the livingroom, liqueurs and chocolates available in the evening, and off-street parking.

Host: Dalton K. Brasinton
Rooms: 4 (PB) $89-98
Full Breakfast
Credit Cards: A, B
Notes: 2, 5, 9

Brasington House

Cannonboro Inn Bed and Breakfast

184 Ashley Avenue, 29403
(803) 723-8572

The Cannonboro Inn lies at the heart of a section of Charleston's historic district. This circa 1850 historical single house shares Ashley Avenue with the antebellum Lucas and Weckinburg mansions and former U.S./Confederate arsenal grounds. Shaded by crepe myrtles and palmettos, guests enjoy a full breakfast served in a formal dining room or on a columned piazza overlooking a Low Country garden. The parlor welcomes guests to visit, read, or play games; complimentary sherry served in the afternoon and complimentary bicycles provided for touring.

Hosts: Sally and Bud Allen
Rooms: 6 (PB) $69-98
Full Breakfast
Credit Cards: None
Notes: 2, 5, 9, 10, 11, 12, 14

Charleston Society Bed and Breakfast A1

84 Murray Boulevard, 29401
(803) 723-4948

Situated on South Market Street in the heart of the Old Market area. One bedroom with fireplace, double bed, private bath, private entrance, air-conditioning, heat, TV. Recently decorated in reproduction period furniture. Within walking distance of restaurants, shops, and other major points of interest. Continental breakfast. $85.

Charleston Society Bed and Breakfast A2

84 Murray Boulevard, 29401
(803) 723-4948

Situated on Meeting Street, this lovely carriage house has a private entrance, livingroom with fireplace, and full kitchen on the first floor. Upstairs, there are two bedrooms (one with double, one with twins) and two baths. Air conditioning, heat, TV. Within walking distance of restaurants, shops, and other major points of interest. Continental breakfast. $100 per couple; $200 for four people.

Charleston Society Bed and Breakfast A3

84 Murray Boulevard, 29401
(803) 723-4948

Situated on Orange Street, this bed and breakfast offers a private entrance, bedroom with twin beds, and private bath with shower. Air conditioning, heat, TV. Within

NOTES: Credit cards accepted: A Master Card; B Visa; C American Express; D Discover Card; E Diner's Club; F Other; 2 Personal Checks accepted; 3 Lunch available; 4 Dinner available; 5 Open all year;

walking distance of restaurants, shops, and other major points of interest. Continental breakfast. $90.

Charleston Society Bed and Breakfast A4

84 Murray Boulevard, 29401
(803) 723-4948

Situated on Legare Street, this carriage house provides a private entrance, livingroom, toaster oven, and refrigerator, one bedroom with twin beds, bath with shower, patio, and garden. Continental breakfast. Air conditioning, heat, TV. Within walking distance of restaurants, shops, and other major points of interest. $95.

Charleston Society Bed and Breakfast B1

84 Murray Boulevard, 29401
(803) 723-4948

Situated on Legare Street, this private home offers one large bedroom with four-poster Rice bed and a private bath. Air conditioning, heat, TV. Within walking distance of all major points of interest. Continental breakfast. $85.

Charleston Society Bed and Breakfast B2

84 Murray Boulevard, 29401
(803) 723-4948

Situated on Church Street, this private home offers third-floor accommodations consisting of one large bedroom with twin beds and private bath. Air conditioning, heat, TV. Within walking distance of all major points of interest. Continental breakfast. $100.

Charleston Society Bed and Breakfast B3

84 Murray Boulevard, 29401
(803) 723-4948

Situated on Tradd Street, this private home offers two bedrooms on the third floor. One has twin beds; one has double beds. Private bath. Air conditioning, heat, TV. Within walking distance of all major points of interest. Continental breakfast. $70; $110 for both rooms.

Charleston Society Bed and Breakfast B4

84 Murray Boulevard, 29401
(803) 723-4948

Situated on East Battery, this historic home has a beautiful view of Charleston Harbor. Pool. Two bedrooms with double beds. Air conditioning, heat, TV. Within walking distance of all major points of interest. Continental breakfast. $100.

Colonial Lake Bed and Breakfast

32 Rutledge Avenue, 29401
(803) 722-6476

Two suites in restored 1850 Victorian residence overlooking Colonial Lake in the historic district. Both spacious, beautifully decorated suites have sitting room, bath, queen-size beds, family antiques, and private entrances through the wicker-furnished piazza and formal garden. Elegant but comfortable with personal attention and true hospitality.

Hosts: Ann and Bill Wagner
Rooms: 2 (PB) $80-110
Full Breakfast
Credit Cards: A, B
Notes: 2, 5

6 Pets welcome; 7 Smoking allowed; 8 Children welcome; 9 Social drinking allowed; 10 Tennis available; 11 Swimming available; 12 Golf available; 13 Skiing available; 14 May be booked through travel agents.

Country Victorian

Coosaw Plantation

P. O. Box 160, 29402
(803) 577-0021; (803) 723-6516 (evenings)

Waterfront plantation located right on St. Helen's Sound and the Coosaw River. *Prince of Tides* views and setting. Stay in a small cottage and enjoy swimming, tennis, canoeing, fishing, and country walks. Cottage has two bedrooms, small kichen, livingroom, and full bath.

Host: The Sanford family
Cottage: 1 (PB) $125
Continental Breakfast
Credit Cards: None
Notes: 2, 5, 6, 7, 8, 9, 10, 11, 14

Country Victorian Bed and Breakfast

105 Tradd Street, 29401-2422
(803) 577-0682

Rooms have private entrances and contain antique iron and brass beds, old quilts, oak and wicker antique furniture, and braided rugs over the heart-of-pine floors. Homemade cookies will be waiting. The house, built in 1820, is within walking distance of restaurants, antique shops, churches, art galleries, museums, and all points of historicalinterest. Parking and bicycles are available. Many extras.

Host: Diane Deardurff Weed
Rooms: 2 (PB) $65-85
Expanded Continental Breakfast
Credit Cards: None
Notes: 2, 5, 8, 9, 10, 11, 12, 14

1837 Bed and Breakfast and Tea Room

126 Wentworth Street, 29401
(803) 723-7166

Accommodations in a wealthy cotton planter's home and brick carriage house, now owned by two artists. Centrally situated in the historic district, within walking distance of boat tours, Old Market, antique shops, restaurants, and main attractions. Full gourmet breakfast is served in the formal dining room. Visit with others while enjoying such specialities as sauage pie, eggs Benedict, ham omelettes, and home-baked breads (lemon, apple spice, banana, and cinnamon swirl). Afternoon tea is served. Verandas, rockers and southern hospitality.

Hosts: Sherri Weaver and Richard Dunn
Rooms: 8 (PB) $55-95
Full Breakfast
Credit Cards: A, B, C
Notes: 2, 5, 7 (veranda only), 9, 10

Elliot House Inn

78 Queen Street, 29401
(800) 729-1855

Twenty-six beautifully appointed guest rooms graced with elegant period-style furniture and Oriental rugs. Secluded courtyard with heated jacuzzi for year-round enjoyment. Within walking distance of fine restaurants, horse-drawn carriage tours, and the best shopping. Wine and tea service every afternoon.

Rooms: 26 (PB) $100-130
Contiental Breakfast
Credit Cards: A, B, C
Notes: 2, 5, 7, 8, 9

NOTES: Credit cards accepted: A Master Card; B Visa; C American Express; D Discover Card; E Diner's Club; F Other; 2 Personal Checks accepted; 3 Lunch available; 4 Dinner available; 5 Open all year;

The Hayne House

30 King Street, 29401
(803) 577-2633

The Hayne House, circa 1755, is located in the heart of the Charleston historic district one block from the Battery which overlooks the Charleston Harbor and Fort Sumter, a treasury of good books, art, and antiques provides guests all they need to step back in time. No TV. Parlor grand in livingroom, sherry on the piano, fireplaces throughout, Charleston garden with eating area, rockers, swing, jogging, back porch. Smoking allowed.

Rooms: 5 (3 PB; 2 SB) $45-88
Continental Breakfast
Credit Cards: None

Historic Charleston Bed and Breakfast

43 Legare Street, 29401
(803) 722-6606

A reservation service for private historic homes, carriage houses, mansions, plantations in or near Charleston. This port city is one of the most historical in the United States, with many cultural activities offered. All bed and breakfasts offered have private baths, TV, air-conditioning. Many have lovely gardens, patios, or porches. Most locations are within walking distance of restaurants, shops, museums, and other historic sites. Beaches are ten miles away.

Host: Charlotte Fairey
Rooms: 70 (PB) $60-140
Continental and Full Breakfast
Credit Cards: A, B, C
Notes: 2, 5, 7, 8, 9, 10, 11, 12

John Rutledge House Inn

116 Broad Street, 29401
(803) 723-7999; (800) 476-9741

This national landmark was built in 1763 by John Rutledge, co-author and signer of the U.S. Constitution. Large rooms and suites in the main and carriage houses offer the ambience of historic Charleston. Rates include wine and sherry upon arrival, turndown service with brandy and chocolate, and breakfast with newspaper delivered to your room. Free parking. AAA four diamonds. Historic Hotels of America.

Rooms: 19 (PB) $105-250
Continental Breakfast
Credit Cards: A, B, C
Notes: 5, 7, 8, 9, 10, 12, 14

King George Inn and Guests

32 George Street, 29401
(803) 723-9339

The King George Inn is a 200-year-old (circa 1790s) historic house in the downtown historic district. The inn is a Federal-style home with a Greek Revival parapet-style roofline. There are four stories in all, with three levels of lovely Charleston porches. All rooms have fireplaces, either Federal or plain Gothic Revival, ten-foot ceilings and six-foot windows. All rooms have original lovely wide-planked hardwood floors, original eight-foot oak doors, old furnishings and many antiques. One-minute walk to King Street shopping and restaurants and a five-minute walk to the Historic Market. Maps and brochures of historic sights and dining information is available. On-site parking. Come visit the past!

Hosts: Jean, B. J., Lynn, and Mike
Rooms: 8 (PB) $60-85
Continental Breakfast, seasonal
Credit Cards: A, B
Notes: 2, 5, 6 (limited), 7 (porches), 8, 9, 10, 11, 12, 13 (water)

Kings Courtyard Inn

198 King Street, 29401
(803) 723-7000; (800) 845-0688

Kings Courtyard Inn, circa 1853, is in the heart of the antique and historic district. Convenient to attractions, shops, and restaurants. Rate includes continental breakfast and newspaper, wine and sherry served in the lobby. Turndown service with chocolate and brandy. Free parking. AAA four diamonds. Historic Hotels of America. Double, king, queen beds and suites are available.

Host: Laura Fox
Rooms: 44 (PB) $140
Continental Breakfast
Credit Cards: A, B, C
Notes: 2, 5, 7, 8, 9, 10, 11, 12, 14

King's Inn

136 Tradd Street, 29401
(803) 577-3683

Situated in the heart of the historic district, this private home includes two bed and breakfast units with separate entrances. The waterfront, antique shops, and house museums are minutes away. The entire historic area can be covered on foot. Enjoy blooming gardens and magnificent house tours in April, the international arts festival—Spoleto—in May, and warm beaches in June. Your hostess is a registered tour guide for Charleston.

Host: Hazel King
Rooms: 2 (PB) $85-100
Continental Breakfast
Credit Cards: None
Notes: 2, 5, 7, 8, 9

The Kitchen House

126 Tradd Street, 29401
(803) 577-6362

In the heart of the historic district, the Kitchen House is a completely restored 18th-century dwelling designed to accommodate from one to four people in total luxury. Centered around its four original fireplaces, the house consists of a living-room, dining area, and full kitchen on the first floor; two bedrooms and a bath on the second floor. A walled garden with patio and colonial herb garden are your vistas. Concierge service provided.

Host: Lois Evans
Rooms: 3 (1 PB; 2 SB) $90-150
Full Breakfast

Credit Cards: A, B
Notes: 2, 5, 7, 8, 9, 14

Maison Du Pré

317 East Bay Street, 29401
(803) 723-8691; (800) 844-INNS

Three restored Charleston "single houses" and two carriage houses constitute Maison Du Pré, originally built in 1804. The inn features period furniture and antiques and is ideally situated in the historic Ansonborough district. Complimentary continental breakfast and a Low Country tea party are served. "Maison Du Pré, with its faded stucco, pink brick, and gray shutters is one of the city's best-looking small inns"—The New York Times.

Hosts: Lucille, Bob, and Mark Mulholland
Rooms: 15 (PB) $98-200
Continental Breakfast
Credit Cards: A, B, C
Notes: 2, 5, 8, 9, 10, 11, 12

Rutledge Victorian Inn

Rutledge Victorian Inn

114 Rutledge Avenue, 29401
(803) 722-7551

A century-old Italianate-style, Victorian house in Charleston's downtown historic district. The house is quaint but elegant: a beautiful round decorative porch, 12-foot ceilings, eight- to ten-foot doors and windows, fireplaces everywhere! Private or shared baths are modern. Air conditioning and TV. 10- to 20-minutes walk to all tours and historic sites. Help with tours. Come and "set a spell" on an old rocker and feel the history around you.

Hosts: Jean, Lynn, B. J., and Mike
Rooms: 7-10 (5 PB; 5 SB) $45-90, seasonal
Continental Breakfast
Credit Cards: A, B
Notes: 2, 5, 6 (restricted), 7 (porches), 8, 9, 10, 11, 12

1730 Bed and Breakfast

69 Church Street, 29401
(803) 722-2263

Situated within Charleston's original walled city, the Capers-Motte house is a magnificent pre-Revolutionary Georgian mansion noted for its architectural detail and listed on the National Register of Historic Places. Its spacious second-story drawing room, with original cypress paneling and outstanding Adam mantels, is among the most handsome in the city. The house is in the heart of the finest residential sections, yet it is easy walking distance to antique shops and the better restaurants in town.

Hosts: Jessica and Keith Marshall
Rooms: 4 (PB) $85-100
Full Breakfast
Credit Cards: A, B
Notes: 2, 5, 9, 10, 11, 12

Two Meeting Street Inn

2 Meeting Street, 29401
(803) 723-7322

"The Belle of Charleston's bed and breakfasts." This Queen Anne Victorian mansion, circa 1890-1892, has welcomed guests for more than half a century. Situated in the historic district overlooking the Battery, the inn charms its visitors with exquisite Tiffany windows, canopy beds, Oriental rugs, and English antiques. The day starts with freshly baked muffins served in the oak-covered courtyard and ends with evening sherry on the wraparound piazza. The epitome of southern hospitality and turn-of-the-century luxury.

Hosts: Pete and Jean Spell
Rooms: 9 (PB) $85-150
Continental Breakfast
Minimum stay weekends and holidays: 2 nights
Credit Cards: None
Notes: 2, 5

1730 Bed and Breakfast

Victoria House Inn

208 King Street, 29401
(803) 720-2944; (800) 933-5464

Built in 1889, this Romanesque-style building has 16 elegantly renovated guest rooms. Modern amenties are provided in every room, including a stocked refrigerator. Guests receive evening turndown service, wine and sherry served in the lobby; continental breakfast and newspaper delivered to the room each morning. Free on-site parking. AAA four diamonds.

Host: Larry Spelts
Rooms: 16 (PB) $90-150 seasonal
Continental Breakfast
Credit Cards: A, B
Notes: 5, 7, 8, 9, 10, 12, 14

---

6 Pets welcome; 7 Smoking allowed; 8 Children welcome; 9 Social drinking allowed; 10 Tennis available; 11 Swimming available; 12 Golf available; 13 Skiing available; 14 May be booked through travel agents.

Villa de La Fontaine Bed and Breakfast

138 Wentworth Street, 29401
(803) 577-7709

Villa de La Fontaine is a columned Greek Revival mansion in the heart of the historic district. It was built in 1838 and boasts a three-quarter-acre garden with fountain and terraces. It has been restored to impeccable condition and furnished with museum-quality furniture and accessories. Your hosts are retired A.S.I.D. interior designers and have decorated the rooms with 18th-century American antiques. Several of the rooms feature canopy beds. Breakfast is prepared by a master chef who prides himself on serving a different menu every day. Off-street parking.

Hosts: William Fontaine and Aubrey Hancock
Rooms: 4 (PB) $85-100
Suites: 2 (PB) $165
Full Breakfast
Minimum stay weekends: 2 nights; holidays: 3 nights
Credit Cards: A, B, C
Notes: 2, 5, 8 (over 11), 9, 10, 11, 12, 14

CHERAW

501 Kershaw Bed and Breakfast

501 Kershaw Street, 29520
(803) 537-7733

Enjoy southern hospitality at an antebellum home listed on the National Register of Historic Places. Built in 1845, it offers a spacious bedroom complete with a fireplace and antique furnishings, as well as a private beach and dressing room. Guests may enjoy a continental or full breaakfast in bed, in the formal dining room, or in the sun room. Visit local historical sites, gardens, and antique shops in the "prettiest town in Dixie."

Hosts: Kay and Larry Spears
Room: 1 (PB) $55-65
Full Breakfast

Credit Cards: None
Notes: 2, 5, 7, 8, 9, 10, 11, 12

COLUMBIA

Claussen's Inn

2003 Greene Street, 29205
(803) 765-0440; (800) 622-3382

Restored bakery, circa 1928, listed on the National Register of Historic Places and situated within walking distance of shopping, restaurants, and entertainment. Luxurious rooms with private baths, outdoor Jacuzzi, and four-poster beds. Rates include a continental breakfast delivered to the room, complimentary wine and sherry, turndown service with chocolates and brandy, and a newspaper.

Host: Dan O. Vance
Rooms: 29 (PB) $80-110
Continental Breakfast
Credit Cards: A, B, C
Notes: 5, 7, 8, 9, 10, 12, 14

DILLON

Magnolia Inn Bed and Breakfast

601 East Main Street, Highway 9, 29536
(803) 774-0679

Southern hospitality abounds as you enter the Magnolia Inn's magnificent foyer. Relax and make yourself at home in the "duck" library or Victorian parlor. Mornings are filled with the savory aromas of breads, pastries, pecan-apple pancakes, breakfast casseroles, fresh fruits, coffee, or tea. Breakfast is served in the formal dining room or on the second-floor summer porch. Four guest rooms are available—the Azalea, the Camellia, the Dogwood, and the Wysteria. The Magnolia Inn is easily accessible from I-95.

Hosts: Jim and Pam Lannoo
Rooms: 4 (3 PB; 1 SB) $35-50
Full Breakfast
Credit Cards: A, B
Notes: 2, 5, 8, 9

NOTES: Credit cards accepted: A Master Card; B Visa; C American Express; D Discover Card; E Diner's Club; F Other; 2 Personal Checks accepted; 3 Lunch available; 4 Dinner available; 5 Open all year;

FORT MILL

Pleasant Valley Bed and Breakfast Inn

P. O. Box 446, 29715
(803) 547-7551

Nestled in the beautiful Old English
District, the inn is in the wooded, peaceful
countryside. Built in 1874, it has been
restored and furnished with some antiques.
Each guest room has its own bath and TV.
After breakfast, take a stroll in the shade of
100-year-old oaks. Equipped with facilities
for the disabled. The house is convenient to
Carowinds Theme Park, Rock Hill,
Lancaster, South Carolina, and Charlotte,
North Carolina. Ten percent senior citizen
discount. Close to Heritage, U.S.A.

Hosts: Mr. and Mrs. Bob Lawrence
Rooms: 5 (PB) $45
Continental Breakfast
Credit Cards: None
Closed Dec. 15-Jan. 1
Notes: 2, 8, 10, 11, 12, 14

GEORGETOWN

Ashfield Manor

3030 South Island Road, 29440
(803) 546-0464

A comfortably elegant country setting in
the style of an old plantation, Ashfield
Manor is situated within easy reach of historic Georgetown, Myrtle Beach, and
Charleston. The area offers an abundance
in seafood at waterfront restaurants. Area
activities include golf, tennis, plantation
and historic tours, deep-sea fishing, shopping, and beaches. Ashfield guests enjoy a
private entrance and parlor, Charleston rice
beds, and individual remote TVs. Breakfast
is served in your room, the parlor, or on the
57-foot screened porch overlooking the
lake.

Hosts: Dave and Carol Ashenfelder
Rooms: 4 (SB) $45-65

Continental Breakfast
Credit Cards: A, B, C, D, E
Notes: 2, 5, 8, 10, 11, 12

Five Thirty Prince Street Bed and Breakfast

530 Prince Street, 29440
(803) 527-1114

Innovatively decorated, light, airy
75-year-old home nestled in a charming
circa 1725 historic district. High ceilings,
antiques, original art, large front porch with
fans, upstairs deck, fans, seven fireplaces,
full gourmet breakfasts. Stroll to shops,
restaurants, and the Harborwalk. Short
drive to nearby beaches, golf and
Brookgreen Gardens. Boat, tram, and walking tours available. Enjoy the Low
Country's finest. One hour to Charleston
and Myrtle Beach.

Host: Nancy Bazemore
Rooms: 2 (PB) $60
Full Breakfast
Credit Cards: None
Notes: 2, 5, 6, 7, 8, 9, 10, 11, 12, 14

1790 House

630 Highmarket Street, 29440
(803) 546-4821

Meticulously restored, this 200-year-old
plantation-style inn is in the heart of historic Georgetown. Spacious, luxurious
rooms with fireplaces and central air and
heat. Stay in the the Rice Planters Room,
the beautiful honeymoon cottage with
Jacuzzi tub, or one of the other lovely
rooms. Walk to shops, restaurants, and historic sights. Just a short dirve to Myrtle
Beach and Grand Strand—a golfer's paradise.

Hosts: John and Patricia Wiley
Rooms: 6 (PB) $60-180
Full Breakfast
Credit Cards: A, B
Notes: 2, 5, 9, 10, 12, 14

The Shaw House

8 Cypress Court, 29440
(803) 546-9663

Lovely view overlooking Willowbank Marsh; wonderful bird watching. Many antiques throughout the house; rocking chairs on porch. Within walking distance of the historical district and many wonderful restaurants. Fresh fruits and southern breakfast. One-hour drive to Myrtle Beach or Charleston.

Hosts: Mary and Joe Shaw
Rooms: 3 (PB) $50
Full Breakfast
Credit Cards: None
Notes: 2, 5, 7, 8, 9, 10, 11, 12, 14

ShipWright's

11 Cypress Court, 29440
(803) 527-4475

Serving tourists and boaters, with transportation from intracoastal waterways. Quiet, spacious with a tasteful decor of heirlooms and antiques. Experience the breathtaking view of the Avenue of Live Oaks and the Alive marshes of the Black River while rocking on the large porch or gazing out the great room window. Taste Grandma Eicher's pancakes, freshly ground coffee, and fresh fruit. Guests say, "I feel like I just visited my best friend."

Hosts: Leatrice and Curtis Wright
Rooms: 2 (PB) $50
Full Breakfast
Credit Cards: None
Notes: 2, 5, 7, 8, 9, 11, 12

HILTON HEAD ISLAND

Ambiance

8 Wren Drive, 29928
(803) 671-4981

Marny welcomes you to sunny Hilton Head Island. Her cypress home, nestled in subtropical surroundings, is in Sea Pines Plantation. Ambiance reflects the hostess's

interior decorating business by the same name. All the amenities of Hilton Head are offered in a contemporary, congenial atmosphere. The climate is favorable year-round for all sports. Ambiance is across the street from a beautiful beach and the Atlantic Ocean.

Host: Marny Kridel Daubenspeck
Rooms: 2 (PB) $65-75
Continental Breakfast
Credit Cards: None
Notes: 2, 5, 7, 8 (over 12), 9, 10, 11, 12

HONEA PATH

Sugarfoot Castle's Bed and Breakfast

211 South Main Street, 29654
(803) 369-6565

Enormous trees umbrella this 19th-century brick Victorian home. Fresh flowers grace the 14-foot thick walled rooms furnished with family heirlooms. Enjoy the livingroom's interesting collection or the library's comfy chairs, TV, VCR, books, fireplace, desk, and game table. Upon rising, guests will find coffee outside their doors, followed by breakfast of fresh fruit, cereal, hot breads, and beverages served in the dining room by candlelight. Rock away the world's cares on the screened porch overlooking peaceful gardens.

Hosts: Cecil and Gale Evans
Rooms: 3 (SB) $44-48
Continental Plus Breakfast
Credit Cards: A, B
Notes: 2, 5, 8 (over 10), 9, 10, 11, 12

Able House Inn

LEESVILLE

Able House Inn

244 West Church Street, 29072
(803) 532-2763

Chateau estate, ten miles from I-20 on
Route 1, 30 minutes from Columbia.
Choose from five guest rooms, each with
private bath. Livingroom, sun room, swimming pool, and patio are available to
guests. Fresh popcorn and soft drinks each
evening.

Hosts: Annabelle and Jack Wright
Rooms: 5 (PB) $45-55
Continental Breakfast
Credit Cards: A, B
Notes: 2, 5, 7 (limited), 8, 9, 11, 12

LITTLE RIVER

Stella's Guest Home

P. O. Box 564, Highway 17, 29566
(803) 249-1871

Sometimes something different can be best,
and if you are planning a trip to South Carolina's Grand Strand, we invite you to stay
with Stella. All of the guest rooms and
suites are charmingly, tastefully, and luxuriously decorated and offer private baths,
entrances, and color cable TV. You will
find Stella's Guest Home to be genuinely
convivial and welcoming. We consider
each guest a visiting friend and take a personal interest in their enjoyment of our
home.

Hosts: Mr. and Mrs. Lamb
Suites: 3 (PB) $30-50
Credit Cards: None
Notes: 5, 12

MAYESVILLE

Windsong

Route 1, Box 300, 29104
(803) 453-5004; (800) 453-5004

Situated in open farmland, this large house
has balconies, porches, and an open fireplace in the large den. Private entrance. A
quail hunting preserve is operated by your
host. An excellent place to stop over,
whether you're traveling north or south.

Hosts: Lynda and Billy Dabbs
Rooms: 2 (PB) $45-50
Full Breakfast
Credit Cards: None
Notes: 2, 4, 5, 7, 8, 9

Windsong

MCCLELLANVILLE

Laurel Hill Plantation

8913 North Highway 17, P. O. Box 190, 29458
(803) 887-3708

Laurel Hill faces the Intracoastal Waterway
and the Atlantic Ocean. Porches provide a
scenic view of marshes and creeks. The
house is furnished in country and primitive
antiques that reflect the Low Country
lifestyle. Thirty miles north of Charleston,
60 miles south of Myrtle Beach.

Hosts: Jackie and Lee Morrison
Rooms: 4 (PB) $75
Full Breakfast
Credit Cards: None
Notes: 2, 5, 9, 14

6 Pets welcome; 7 Smoking allowed; 8 Children welcome; 9 Social drinking allowed; 10 Tennis available; 11
Swimming available; 12 Golf available; 13 Skiing available; 14 May be booked through travel agents.

MONCKS CORNER

Rice Hope Plantation Inn

206 Rice Hope Drive, 29461
(803) 761-4832

Set among live oaks on a bluff overlooking
the Cooper River, Rice Hope Plantation has
been a popular gathering place for over 200
years. This large, rambling house and old
formal gardens are a quiet setting for a
great getaway. Bird watching, bass fishing,
and nearby Francis Marion National Forest,
Strawberry Chapel, circa 1725, and Mepkin
Abbey will make a stay at Rice Hope one
to remember.

Host: Doris Kasprak
Rooms: 4 (PB) $60
Continental Breakfast
Credit Cards: A, B
Notes: 3, 4, 5, 6, 10

MOUNT PLEASANT

Guilds Inn

101 Pitt Street, 29464
(803) 881-0510

A six-room inn. All rooms have private
bath with whirlpool tubs. Situated in a historic neighborhood four miles from historical Charleston, and four miles from the
beaches of Sullivan's Island and Isle of
Palms.

Hosts: Guild and Joyce Hollowell
Rooms: 6 (PB) $60-100
Continental Breakfast
Credit Cards: A, B, C
Notes: 2, 3, 4, 5, 7, 8, 9, 10

MYRTLE BEACH

Serendipity

407 71st Avenue North, 29577
(803) 449-5268

Award-winning Mission-style inn, one and
one-half blocks from the beach. Pool,
Jacuzzi, shuffleboard, Ping-Pong. Near 70
golf courses, tennis, pier, and deep-sea
fishing. Air conditioning, color TV, refrigerator, private baths in all rooms. Historical
Charleston 90 miles; great shopping, and
restaurants are nearby.

Hosts: Cos and Ellen Ficarra
Rooms: 2 (PB) $50-68
Efficiencies: 4 (PB) $62-75
Suites: 4 (PB) $70-87
Expanded Continental Breakfast
Credit Cards: A, B, C
Closed Dec.-Jan.
Notes: 7, 8, 9, 10, 11, 12, 14

ROCK HILL

East Main Guest House

600 East Main Street, 29730
(803) 366-1161

Situated in the downtown historic district,
this Craftsman-style bungalow has been
completely renovated and beautifully decorated. Guest rooms include private baths,
fireplaces, queen-size beds. The Honeymoon Suite has a canopy bed and a
whirlpool tub. A sitting/game room is provided, and breakfast is served in the beautifully appointed dining room.

Hosts: Jerry and Melba Peterson
Rooms: 3 (PB) $59-79
Continental Breakfast
Credit Cards: A, B
Notes: 2, 5, 9, 12, 14

SUMMERVILLE

Bed and Breakfast of Summerville

304 South Hampton Street, 29483
(803) 871-5275

Slaves' quarters of a restored 1865 house
on the National Register of Historic Places
in a quiet setting. Weather permitting,
breakfast can be served in the greenhouse,
gazebo, by the pool, or self-prepared from
a stocked refrigerator. Phone, TV, kitch-

enette, bath with shower, and bikes are available. Winter monthly rental by reservation.

Hosts: Dusty and Emmagene Rhodes
Room: 1 (PB) $45-50
Continental Breakfast
Credit Cards: None
Notes: 2, 5, 7, 8 (over 11), 9, 10, 11, 12

SUMTER

Sumter Bed and Breakfast

6 Park Avenue, 29150
(803) 773-2903

Charming 1896 home, facing lush green, quiet park in the historic district. Large front porch. Spacious guest rooms upstairs with fireplaces, antiques, and private entrance. HBO, FAX, and library with ancient artifacts. Tours, tennis, and 15 golf courses available. Breakfast includes fresh juice, fruits, freshly baked pastries, and homemade granola.

Hosts: Bob and Merilyn Carnes
Rooms: 4 (2 PB; 2 SB) $45-55
Continental Plus Breakfast
Credit Cards: A, B
Notes: 2, 5, 9, 10, 12

SOUTH DAKOTA

• Webster

• Gettysburg

• Canova

Vermillion

• Rapid City
• Hill City
• Custer

• Wall

South Dakota

CANOVA

Skoglund Farm

Route 1, Box 45, 57321
(605) 247-3445

Enjoy yourself on the prairie: cattle, fowl, peacocks, horses, home-cooked evening meal, and full breakfast. Visit nearby attractions: Little House on the Prairie, Corn Palace, Doll House, Prairie Village, or just relax, hike, and enjoy a family farm. Rate includes evening meal and breakfast: $30 for adults; $20 for teens; $15 for children; children five and under free.

Hosts: Alden and Delores Skoglund
Rooms: 5 (SB) $30
Full Breakfast
Credit Cards: None
Notes: 2, 3, 4, 5, 6, 7, 8, 9, 10, 11, 12, 14

CUSTER

Custer Mansion Bed and Breakfast

35 Centennial Drive, 57730
(605) 673-3333

Historic 1891 Victorian Gothic home features country charm and western hospitality with clean, quiet, comfortable accommodations and home-cooked full breakfast. Central to all Black Hills attractions, such as Mount Rushmore. Recommended by Bon Appetit and G.M.C. Friends magazines.

Hosts: Mill and Carole Seaman
Rooms: 6 (2 PB; 2 SB) $35-75

Full Breakfast
Credit Cards: None
Notes: 2, 5, 8, 10, 12, 13, 14

GETTYSBURG

Harer Lodge Bed and Breakfast

Rural Route 1, P. O. Box 87A, 57442
(605) 765-2167

Set in a prairie where buffalo once roamed, this modern cedar lodge has a miniature golf course, miniature horses, farm animals, five lovely guest rooms, all of which have private baths, a recreation room that all guests are welcome to use, a reading, fresh flowers in every room, and tea and cookies when you arrive. A teepee made by a native American indian is available for our young campers, and a separate honeymoion cottage done in romantic whispy white with an oversized Jacuzzi set in the floor is available for our newlyweds. The honeymoon suite has sliding glass doors leading from the bathroom to a small private garden, comlplete with a porchg swing and lots of privacy. Lunch and beverage

Custer Mansion

NOTES: Credit cards accepted: A Master Card; B Visa; C American Express; D Discover Card; E Diner's Club; F Other; 2 Personal Checks accepted; 3 Lunch available; 4 Dinner available; 5 Open all year; 6 Pets welcome; 7 Smoking allowed; 8 Children welcome; 9 Social drinking allowed; 10 Tennis available; 11 Swimming available; 12 Golf available; 13 Skiing available; 14 May be booked through travel agents.

served by candlelight, and breakfast is served in the cottage. Country stiore with crafts and antiquyes and a sweet shop is in a restored on premises.

Hosts: Norma and Don harer
Rooms: 5 , plus honeymoon cottage (PB) $35 (SB) $30
Full Breakfast
Credit Cards: None
Notes: 2, ,3, 4, 5, 6, 9, 11, 12

HILL CITY

Bed and Breakfast Heart of the Hills

517 Main Street, 57745
(605) 574-2704

Within walking distance of the 1880 train, gift shops, and restaurants. Mount Rushmore and the Crazy Horse Memorial are just minutes away. Queen bed, large sitting room with a studio couch that makes into a double bed, private bath, private entrance. Breakfast is served on the deck by the fountain or in the dining room.

Hosts: Carol Ball and Wes Shafer
Rooms: 2 (PB) $40-45
Full Breakfast
Credit Cards: None
Notes: 2, 5, 7, 8, 9, 10, 11, 12

OKATON

Bunkhouse

HCR 74, Box 16, 57562
(605) 669-2529

On your way to Mount Rushmore, relax at this working cattle ranch away from Interstate 90. Milk the cow, gather eggs, and pet the kittens. Children and pets can enjoy running in lots of prairie. Visit the Badlands, Black Hills, Oahe Dam, and the famous Pioneer Auto Museum. Guide service available.

Hosts: Mel and Clarice Roghair
Rooms: 2 (SB) $35
Full Breakfast

Credit Cards: None
Notes: 2, 3, 4, 5, 6, 8, 14

RAPID CITY

Abend Haus Cottage and Audrie's Cranbury Corner Bed and Breakfast

Rural Route 8, Box 2400, 57702
(605) 342-7788

The Black Hills "inn place. " Ultimate in charm and Old World hospitality, this country home and five acres of estate is surrounded by thousands of acres of national forest 30 miles from Mount Rushmore and 7 miles from Rapid City. Each quiet, comfortable room, suite, and cottage has a private entrance, bath, hot tub, patio, cable TV, and refrigerator. Trout fishing, biking, hiking on property. Full breakfast served.

Hosts: Hank and Audry Kuhnhauser
Rooms: 6 (PB) $78-85
Full Breakfast
Credit Cards: None
Notes: 2, 5, 9, 10, 11, 12

Black Forest Inn Bed and Breakfast Lodge

HC 33, Box 3123, 57702
(605) 574-2000; (800) 888-1607

The beautiful main lodge has ten guest rooms and outdoor Jacuzzi, while the great room features a large stone fireplace and picture windows framing the beauty of the outdoors. Situated in the heart of the Black Hills, near lakes, golf, hiking, swimming, and fishing. One-half hour from Mount Rushmore, Deadwood, and other historic sites. A delicious full breakfast is served each morning.

Hosts: Bruce and Polly Ashland
Rooms: 10 (8 PB; 2 SB) $57.20-78
Full Breakfast
Credit Cards: A, B, C
Notes: 2, 5, 8, 9, 11, 12, 13

NOTES: Credit cards accepted: A Master Card; B Visa; C American Express; D Discover Card; E Diner's Club; F Other; 2 Personal Checks accepted; 3 Lunch available; 4 Dinner available; 5 Open all year;

The Carriage House

721 West Boulevard, 57701
(605) 343-6415

The stately, three-story pillared Colonial house is on a historic, tree-lined boulevard of Rapid City. The English country decor creates an ambience of elegance, refinement, and relaxed charm. Gourmet breakfasts are served in the formal dining room. Scenic Mount Rushmore is only 26 miles away.

Hosts: Betty and Joel King
Rooms: 5 (2 PB; 3 SB) $59-89
Full Breakfast
Credit Cards: A, B
Notes: 2, 5, 9, 10, 11, 12, 13

Willow Springs Cabins

HCR 39, Box 108, 57702
(605) 342-3665

Private one room log cabin located in the beautiful Black Hills National Forest. Secluded setting offers privacy like no other retreat. Each cabin is charmingly decorated with many extras and antique treasures. Breakfast is wonderful, featuring freshly ground coffee, juices, baked goods, and egg dishes served in the privacy of the cabin. Hiking, swimming, and fishing abound. Chosen by *Country Living* magazine, October 1991.

Hosts: Joyce and Russell Payton
Cabins: 2 (PB) $70-87
Full Breakfast
Credit Cards: None
Notes: 2, 5, 8, 9, 14

SENECA

Rainbow Lodge

Box 81, Rural Route 1, 57473
(605) 436-6795

Rustic lodge on the quiet, serene South Dakota prairie. Family and spiritual flavor. Private meditation areas. Lovely landscaped lakefront. Situated near the Missouri River, golfing, swimming, museums, Cathedral on the Prairie. Enjoy home-cooked country breakfast prepared on a wood-burning stove. Lunch or dinner available upon request. Reservations only.

Hosts: Ralph and Claire Ann Wheeler
Rooms: 3 (1 PB; 2 SB) $25-35
Full Breakfast
Credit Cards: None
Notes: 2, 3, 4, 5, 8

VERMILLION

The Goebel House Bed and Breakfast

102 Franklin, 57069
(605) 624-6691

A friendly old home built in 1916 and furnished with antiques and collectibles. Vermillion is home of the nationally known Shrine of Music and the University of South Dakota. Four bedrooms grace the upper chambers and have both private and shared bath. Each room is individually decorated with furniture and mementos of the past.

Hosts: Don and Pat Goebel
Rooms: 4 (2 PB; 2 SB) $45
Full Breakfast
Credit Cards: None
Notes: 2, 5, 9, 10, 11, 12

WEBSTER

Lakeside Farm Bed and Breakfast

Rural Route 2, Box 52, 57274
(605) 486-4430

You are invited to sample a bit of country life at Lakeside Farm. Feel free to explore the grove, barns, and pastures or just relax with a cup of tea in the farmhouse. Accommodations for four to five guests on the second floor. The second-floor bathroom and shower serve both guest rooms. Children welcome. Situated in northeastern

6 Pets welcome; 7 Smoking allowed; 8 Children welcome; 9 Social drinking allowed; 10 Tennis available; 11 Swimming available; 12 Golf available; 13 Skiing available; 14 May be booked through travel agents.

South Dakota with museums featuring pioneer and Native American culture. Fort Sisseton nearby. No smoking or alcoholic beverages.

Hosts: Glenn and Joy Hagen
Rooms: 2 (SB) $35
Full Breakfast
Credit Cards: None
Notes: 2, 5, 8, 12

Tennessee

ASHLAND CITY

Birdsong Country Inn Bed and Breakfast

1306 Highway 49 West at Sycamore Mill, 37015
(615) 792-4005; (615) 320-7914

Built in 1920 by the Cheek family of the Maxwell House coffee fame, this rambling cedar lodge is listed on the National Register of Historic Places. An extensive collection of art and antiques brings the spacious rooms to life. Each one offers its own delights, from the large and sunny guest room with an adjoining bath to the masterful, yet cozy, Great Room to the screened-in front porch that overlooks sweeping lawns and Sycamore Valley. Natural surroundings provide beautiful ways to relax. Stroll in the woods along the creek; soak in the heated spa on the flagtone patrio; enjoy a good book, a nap, or your own company in hammocks under stately trees. Golf, tennis, and swimming are just across the valley, and Nashville is twenty minutes away, where you can enjoy the music, shopping, and restaurants of Music City.

Hosts: Anne and Brooks Parker
Rooms: 3 (PB) $80-100
Continental Plus Breakfast
Credit Cards: A, B, C
Notes: 2, 5, 6, 7, 8, 9, 10, 11, 12, 14

BROWNSVILLE

Peach Tree Inn

1551 Skeet Road, 38012
(901) 772-5680

A bed and breakfast with a country setting, offering private, comfortable accommodations. In-house catering services available for luncheons, dinners, office parties, and wedding receptions. A swimming pool is on the premises. Peach Tree Inn is on the outskirts of Brownsville, two miles off I-40 at Exit 56, only 56 miles from Memphis and 25 miles from Jackson. Visit Brownsville's historic homes district, historic College Hill, Hatchie National Wildlife Refuge, and the scenic Hatchie River.

Hosts: Elving and Evelyn Anderson
Rooms: 4 (PB) $45-55
Continental Breakfast
Credit Cards: A, B
Notes: 5, 11, 14

Alford House

CHATTANOOGA

Alford House

Alfred Hill Drive, Route 4, 37419
(615) 821-7625

In a quiet setting on the side of Lookout Mountain, one and one-half miles off I-24, this 17-room traditional home has antique decor. Coffee is served at wake-up. Breakfast may be served in the dining room

6 Pets welcome; 7 Smoking allowed; 8 Children welcome; 9 Social drinking allowed; 10 Tennis available; 11 Swimming available; 12 Golf available; 13 Skiing available; 14 May be booked through travel agents.

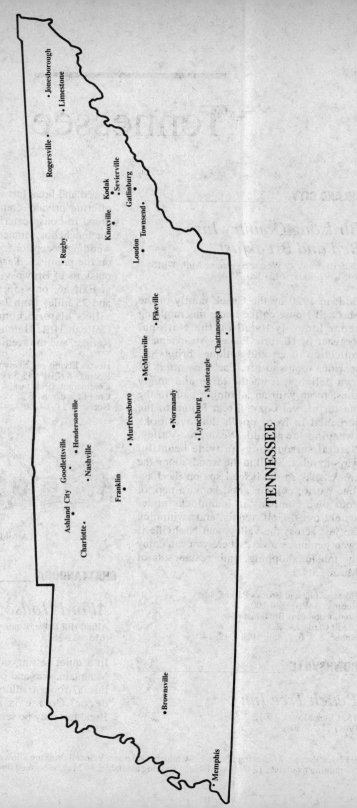

TENNESSEE

Jonesborough •
• Limestone

Rogersville •

Kodak
Knoxville • Sevierville
• Gatlinburg
Rugby • Loudon •
Townsend •

Pikeville •

McMinnville •
Normandy •
Lynchburg • Monteagle •
Chattanooga

Murfreesboro •

Goodlettsville
Ashland City • Hendersonville •
• Nashville

Charlotte • Franklin •

Brownsville •

Memphis •

or in the gazebo. Ten minutes from downtown and most attractions. There is a fireplace and piano in the livingroom and an antique shop on the premises. Antique glass basket collection on display. Mountain trails begin across the road.

Host: Rhoda Alford
Rooms: 3 (SB) $45-55
Full Breakfast
Credit Cards: None
Notes: 2, 5, 8, 14

DANDRIDGE

Mill Dale Farm Bed and Breakfast

140 Mill Dale Road, 37725
(615) 397-3470; (800) 767-3471

This nineteenth-century farmhouse is in Tennessee's second oldest town. Three beautifully decorated guest rooms, all with private baths, are available to guests. The house is furnished with antiques, and the common rooms and kitchen have large stone fireplaces. Located one mile off I-40 with easy access to Gatlinburg, Pigeon Forge, and the Great Smoky Mountains. A delicious country breakfast is served daily.

Hosts: Lucy C. and Hood Franklin
Rooms: 3 (PB) $65 plus tax
Full Breakfast
Credit Cards: None
Notes: 2, 5, 8, 10, 11, 12

Sugar Fork Bed and Breakfast

743 Garrett Road, 37725
(615) 397-7327; (800) 487-5634

Guests will appreciate the tranquil setting of Sugar Fork Bed and Breakfast, situated on Douglas Lake in the foothills of the Great Smoky Mountains. Private access and floating dock. Enjoy warm-weather water sports and fishing year-round. Fireplace in common room, guest kitchenette, wraparound deck, swings, and park bench by the lake. A hearty breakfast is served family-style in the dining room or, weather permitting, on the deck.

Hosts: Mary and Sam Price
Rooms: 3 (2 PB; 1 SB) $55-65
Full Breakfast
Credit Cards: A, B
Notes: 2, 5, 7, 8, 9

Sweet Basil and Thyme

P. O. Box 1132, 102 West Meeting Street, 37725
(800) 227-7128

This historically registered Victorian home built circa 1830 is surrounded by rose gardens and furnished with antiques while reflecting the ambience of the past. A full gourmet breakfast is served, possibly in the garden, weather permitting. Dinner is available with advance reservations. Relax in the parlor or library, or simply stroll among the gardens. We are conviently located within easy driving distance to Gatlinburg, Dollywood, Great Smoky Mountain National Park, and the University of Tennessee. Smoking is not allowed in the guest rooms.

Hosts: Dolores and Bill Pudifin
Rooms: 3 (1 PB; 2 SB) $50-65
Full Breakfast
Credit Cards: None
Notes: 2, 3, 4, 5, 7, 8, 9, 12, 13

FLAT CREEK

Bottle Hollow Lodge

111 Gobbler Ridge Road, 37160
(615) 695-5253

Nestled high in the rolling hills of Middle Tennessee, Bottle Hollow Lodge occupies 68 acres of beautiful countryside and magnificent views. The ultimate in peace, quiet, and solitude, this inn is just minutes from Lynchburg's Jack Daniel's Distillery and the Tennessee Walking Horse National Celebration in Shelbyville. Bottle Hollow Lodge, with its inviting rockers on the front porch and plush sofas in front of the large stone fireplace, will add to your enjoyment of activities in the area.

Hosts: Pat and Jim Whiteside
Rooms: 5 (PB) $85-150
Full Breakfast
Credit Cards: A, B
Notes: 2, 3 (on request), 4 (on request), 5, 9, 12, 14

FRANKLIN

Carothers House Bed and Breakfast

4301 South Carothers Road, 37064
(615) 794-4437; (800) 327-8492

This cheerful log home in a wooded setting is minutes from Nashville. Civil War historic area, antique stores, Galleria mall, unique restaurants, and limousine service. Two enclosed lofts and two suites, all of which have private baths. Private outdoor spa available. Relaxing porch, stone fireplace. Full business amenities. One mile from I-65 at the Franklin exit. Many historical buildings and activities. Wedding arrangements. Host is a Tour Tennessee promotion member.

Host: John Reitmeier
Rooms: 4 (PB) $68-108
Full Breakfast
Credit Cards: A, B
Notes: 3, 4, 5, 8, 9, 14

GATLINBURG

Buckhorn Inn

2140 Tudor Mountain Road, 37738
(615) 436-4668

A unique country inn offering peaceful seclusion with the feeling and tradition of early Gatlinburg. Established in 1938, Buckhorn Inn was built on a hillside facing magnificent views of Mount Leconte and includes 35 acres of woodland, meadows, and quiet walkways. Located just six miles northeast of Gatlinburg near the Greenbriar entrance to the Great Smoky Mountains.

Carothers House

Host: John and Connie Burns
Rooms: 12 (PB) $95-250
Full Breakfast
Credit Cards: A, B
Closed over Christmas
Notes: 2, 4, 5, 7 (restricted), 9, 10, 11, 12, 13

Eight Gables

219 North Mountain Trail, 37738
(615) 430-3344

Guests of this new bed and breakfast are welcomed by a peaceful mountain setting. Located near the Trolley stop, it features a unique design and decor. Comfort is assured in the ten spacious guest rooms, each individually decorated with its own theme and style. Each first-floor guest room has its private entrance, and all of the second-floor guest rooms are graced with cathedral ceilings and arched windows. There is a "gathering room" for relaxing, a lounge for viewing TV, and an outdoor spa. The breakfast buffet varies from day to day. Picnic lunches are available at an extra charge.

Host: Helen W. Smith
Rooms: 10 (PB) $89-110
Full Breakfast
Credit Cards: A, B
Notes:2, 5, 9, 12, 13, 14

7th Heaven Log Home Inn

3944 Castle Road, 37738
(615) 430-5000; (800) 248-2923

NOTES: Credit cards accepted: A Master Card; B Visa; C American Express; D Discover Card; E Diner's Club; F Other; 2 Personal Checks accepted; 3 Lunch available; 4 Dinner available; 5 Open all year;

On the seventh green of a golf resort, but you don't have to play golf to enjoy sitting on the deck or in the log gazebo Jacuuzzi overlooking the creek, a quiet pond, and the beautiful, lush golf course. Gaze at ehe wonnders of the great Smoky Mountains National Park just across the road. Fully equipped guest kitchen, large game room with pool tables, and stone fireplace. Close to Dollywood, craft, antique, and outlet shopping.

Host: Ginger and Paul Wolcott
Rooms: 4 (PB) $59-89
Full Breakfast
Credit Cards: A, B
Notes: 2, 4, 5, 7, 9, 10, 11, 12, 13, 14

GOODLETTSVILLE

Woodshire Bed and Breakfast

600 Woodshire Drive, 37072
(615) 859-7369

Family antiques, homemade preserves, southern hospitality—all these just 15-20 minutes from Nashville's universities, museums, Parthenon, Opryland, and many country music attractions. Private entrance, use of screened porch, continental breakfast. Country atmosphere with urban conveniences. A mid-1800s reconstructed log cabin is also available.

Hosts: John and Beverly Grayson
Rooms: 2 (PB) $50
Log Cabin: $70
Continental Breakfast
Credit Cards: None
Notes: 2, 8, 14

HENDERSONVILLE

Monthaven

1154 Main Street West, 37075
(615) 824-6319

On the National Register of Historic Places, Monthaven offers both a heritage of nearly 200 years and a 75-acre estate for the enjoyment of visitors to Nashville and Middle Tennessee. The main house served as a field hospital during the Civil War. Log cabin, built in 1938 from 200-year-old timber, is available.

Hosts: Hugh Waddell, Lisa Neideffer, and Lee Owens
Rooms: 3 (PB) $75
Log Cabin: (PB) $85
Suite: $75
Expanded Continental Breakfast
Credit Cards: Major
Notes: 2, 3, 4, 5, 6, 7, 8, 9, 10, 11, 12, 14

JOELTON

Hachland Hill Inns (The Vineyard)

5396 Rawlings Road, 37080
(615) 876-0647

The Vineyard is ideal for corporate meetings. There are sleeping accommodations for up to forty people, and the facilities feature a honeymoon suite (the Clarksville location is ideal for honeymooners), meeting room, and break areas. This bed and breakfast is perfect for the traveler looking for an inn furnished with southern antiques and serving southern plantation-style cooking at its best. All three meals available (Both Clarksville and Joelton locations handled by the Joelton office.) Joelton is part of Metropolitan Nashville.

Hosts: Joe and Phila Hach
Rooms: 12 (PB) $84.50
Cottage: $131.50 (includes breakfast and dinner)
Full and Continental Breakfast
Credit Cards: A, B, C
Notes: 2, 3, 4, 5, 7, 8, 9, 12

JONESBOROUGH

Jonesborough Bed and Breakfast

100 Woodrow Avenue, P. O. Box 722, 37659
(615) 753-9223

This beautifully restored home was built in 1848 and is in Jonesborough's historic district. All restaurants and shops are within easy walking distance. To make your visit memorable, you will find robes, high beds, antique furnishings, fireplaces, large porch with rocking chairs, secluded terrace, air-conditioning, and a delightful breakfast.

Host: Tobie Bledsoe
Rooms: 4 (SB) $50
Full Breakfast
Credit Cards: None
Notes: 2, 5, 8, 9

Jonesborough

KNOXVILLE

Langskomen

1212 Nighthawk Lane, 37923
(615) 693-3797

You are cordially invited to experience the Old World hospitality of Langskomen, a country bed and breakfast three miles from I-75/I-40, just west of Knoxville. Langskomen is convenient to many of the TVA lakes, the Smoky Mountains, the University of Tennessee, cultural events, and art festivals. A wide selection of restaurants is nearby. Bedrooms are comfortably furnished with antiques. Advance reservations are required.

Hosts: Bill and Jan Groenier
Rooms: 2 (SB) $50
Full Breakfast
Credit Cards: None
Notes: 2, 5

Mitchell's

1031 West Park Drive, 37909
(615) 690-1488

This bed and breakfast offers a comfortable room in a private home in a pleasant tree-shaded neighborhood near fine shops and restaurants. Parking at a private entrance, double bed, small TV, refrigerator, and microwave; rollaway bed and crib available. It is 45 minutes to the Smoky Mountains, 25 minutes to Oak Ridge, one and one-half miles to I-75/I-40, and 8 miles to downtown Knoxville.

Host: Mary M. Mitchell
Rooms: 1 (PB) $40
Continental Breakfast
Credit Cards: None .
Notes: 2, 5, 6, 7, 8, 9

KODAK

Grandma's House

P. O. Box 445, 37764
(615) 933-3512; (800) 676-3512

Situated at the base of the Great Smoky Mountains in Dumplin Valley, this two-story Colonial-style house combines antique charm with modern-day comfort. Three guest rooms, each with a private bath, are decorated in antiques and country themes. Hosts are both native East Tennesseans with lots of down-home friendliness. A loosen-your-belt breakfast is served, and snacks are always on hand.

Grandma's House

NOTES: Credit cards accepted: A Master Card; B Visa; C American Express; D Discover Card; E Diner's Club; F Other; 2 Personal Checks accepted; 3 Lunch available; 4 Dinner available; 5 Open all year;

Hosts: Charlie and Hilda Hickman
Rooms: 3 (PB) $65
Full Breakfast
Credit Cards: A, B

LIMESTONE

Snapp Inn
Bed and Breakfast

Route 3, Box 102, 1990 Davy Crockett Road,
  37681
(615) 257-2482

Your hosts will welcome you into this gracious 1815 Federal home furnished with
antiques and set in farm country. Enjoy the
mountain view from the full back porch or
play a game of pool or horseshoes. Close to
Davy Crockett Birthplace Park; 15-minute
drive to historic Jonesborough or
Greeneville. Third person in room at no
extra charge.

Hosts: Dan and Ruth Dorgan
Rooms: 2 (PB) $40-50
Full Breakfast
Credit Cards: None
Notes: 2, 5, 6, 8 (one child only), 9, 11, 12, 14

LOUDON

The Mason Place
Bed and Breakfast

600 Commerce Street, 37774
(615) 458-3921

The Mason Place, nestled in a quaint Civil
War setting along the Tennessee River, is a
lovely, impeccably restored plantation
home, circa 1865. Tastefully decorated
throughout with comfortable period
antiques, original chandeliers, delightful
feather beds, and ten working fireplaces.
Three acres of lawn and gardens, Gecian
swimming pool, gazebo, and wisteria-covered arbor. Overflowing with charm and
character, the Mason Place is near Knoxville, Smoky Mountains, I-75, and I-40.

Hosts: Bob and Donna Siewert
Rooms: 5 (PB) $88

Full Breakfast
Credit Cards: None
Notes: 2, 5, 9, 10, 11, 12

LYNCHBURG

County Line
Bed and Breakfast

Route 6, Box 126, Shelbyville, 37160
(615) 759-4639

Two-story house locatd on a horse farm
four and one-half miles from Jack Daniel
Distillery and Lynchburg Square. Relaxed
country atmosphere. Continental breakfast.
Brochure available; reservations encouraged.

Hosts: Harriet and Jim Rothfeldt
Rooms: 3 (1 PB; 2 SB) $38-40
Continental Breakfast
Credit Cards: A, B
Notes: 2, 5, 7, 9

Lynchburg
Bed and Breakfast

P. O. Box 34, 37352
(615) 759-7158

This nineteenth-century home is located
within walking distance of the Jack
Daniel's Distillery. Each spacious room
feaures carefully selected antiques.
Formerly the home of the first Moore
County sheriff (1877).

Snapp Inn

Host: Virginia Tipps
Rooms: 2 (PB) $38-45
Continental Breakfast
Credit Cards: A, B
Notes: 5, 7, 9, 10, 12, 14

MCMINNVILLE

Falcon Manor Bed and Breakfast

Faulkner Springs Road, 37110
(615) 668-4444

"Where elegance and history go hand in hand" describes this 1896 Victorian mansion, which is listed on the National Register of Historic Places and filled with period antiques. Experience the friendly warmth of this fine old house. Rock on the peaceful gingerbread veranda, shaded by giant trees. Located half-way between Nashville and Chattanooga off I-24 and one and one-half hours from Opryland and Rock City, 1 hour from the Jack Daniel's distillery, 30 minutes from four state parks. McMinnville is known as the "nursery capital of the world" and home of America's second largest cave. Opens May 1993.

Host: George and Charlien McGlothin
Rooms: 5 (2 PB; 3 SB) $60
Generous Continental Breakfast
Credit Cards: A, B
Notes:2, 5, 8 (over 12), 14

MEMPHIS

B&B in Memphis #D-0302

P. O. Box 41621, 38174-1621
(901) 726-5920; FAX (901) 725-0194

Gracious southern living on the mighty Mississippi epitomizes this open and airy garden condo beautifully decorated with antiques and Orientals. Two guest rooms, each with its own private bath, continental breakfast served in full view of the river, and a thoroughly engaging southern hostess all trake you back to a more gentle time of grace and elegance. The Wonders Series world class exhibitions are within walking distance; great jazz and blues on famous Beale Street. Smoke outside only, please. $115.

B&B in Memphis #D-0303

P. O. Box 41621, 38174-1621
(901) 726-5920; FAX (901) 725-0194

Magnificent sunsets. Romantic riverboats and city lights from a private balcony of this gorgeous unhosted condominium on the river. Spacious livingroom, dining room seating six, bedroom with king bed, Jacuzzi, fully equipped kitchen with microwave. Private indoor parking, indoor and outdoor pools, spa, sauna, tennis courts, racquetball courts, 24-hour security. Five-night minimum stay. Smoking on the balcony only. $110-125. Weekly and monthly rates .

B&B in Memphis #D-7369

P. O. Box 41621, 38174-1621
(901) 726-5920; FAX (901) 725-0194

Retreat to a nearby Arkansas working farm and southern mansion just thirty minutes from downtown Memphis. Tour the farm and cotton gins, enjoy complimentary tea on the veranda each evening and country breakfast each morning. Poke around antique shops and eat some of the best catfish you've ever had in nearby smaller towns. Take a jaunt into Memphis for night life, or bring a book and just put your feet up. Three handsome guest rooms, two guest baths in the upostairs wing, TV in rooms. Resident dog. $85

B&B in Memphis #E-1706

P. O. Box 41621, 38174-1621
(901) 726-5920; FAX (901) 725-0194

Leave your cares and retreat to this beautiful private suite in elegant east location.

NOTES: Credit cards accepted: A Master Card; B Visa; C American Express; D Discover Card; E Diner's Club; F Other; 2 Personal Checks accepted; 3 Lunch available; 4 Dinner available; 5 Open all year;

Bright and cheery library opens to your bedroom, with four-poster double bed and private bath with Jacuzzi. Hosted. Dogs in residence. $73.61.

B&B in Memphis #G-1900

P. O. Box 41621, 38174-1621
(901) 726-5920; FAX (901) 725-0194

This friendly host couple travels extensively in bed and breakfasts. You will enjoy breakfast on the screened porch in fashionable Germantown. Spacious guest room with antique pineapple twin beds, private bath, and use of office area for business travelers. Privacy, comfort, and congeniality for only $62.29.

B&B in Memphis #G-1903

P. O. Box 41621, 38174-1621
(901) 726-5920; FAX 901-725-0194

Delicious mauves and grays decorate this beautifully furnished condo in Germantown. Livingroom (queen sleeper), dining/work area, fully equipped kitchen, one bedroom (double bed), full bath with shower. Cable TV. Private covered parking, laundry room, pool and tennis courts. Unhosted. Five-night minimum stay. $79. Weekly and monthly rates available.

B&B in Memphis #M-0400

P. O. Box 41621, 38174-1621
(901) 726-5920; FAX (901) 725-0194

Say good-bye to expensive hotel rates and living out of a suitcase. If you have to be away from your loved ones, this is the next best thing. Charming studio apartment in award-winning midtown high-rise offers large livingroom with Stearnes and Foster double sleeper, dining/work area, sleeping alcove (twin bed), full bath with shower, fully equipped kitchen with microwave, and ample closet space. Cable TV, VCR,

and one complimentary video. FAX and secretarial services available. Unhosted. Minimums may apply. $75. Weekly and monthly rates available.

B&B in Memphis #M-0404

P. O. Box 41621, 38174-1621
(901) 726-5920; FAX (901) 725-0194

Enjoy gracious hospitality that would make even Martha Stewart ask for entertaining tips. Exceptionally interesting host couple opens their beautiful home to you! Two upstairs guest rooms with private guest bath. Quiet and elegant midtown neighborhood conveniently situated to all areas of the city. Visit Dixon Gallery and Gardens; the majestic Orpheum Theatre for Broadway hits, opera and ballet; Memphis Brooks Museum of Art; and Beale Street for hot jazz and blues. No smoking. $73.28.

B&B in Memphis #M-1106

P. O. Box 41621, 38174-1621
(901) 726-5920; FAX (901) 725-0194

If a charming suite with antiques and Oriental rugs is your cup of tea, then here it is. In excellent Memphis State University area, you will enjoy private entrance, spacious livingroom with queen sleeper, bedroom with twin beds, newly decorated shower, excellent closets, and wet bar. Cable TV, off-street parking, convenient to everything. No smoking. Hosted. $62.01-84.56.

B&B in Memphis #M-1200

P. O. Box 41621, 38174-1621
(901) 726-5920; FAX (901) 725-0194

Lovely gardens, lush trees, and scampering squirrels are all right in the heart of the city. Professionally decorated host home in the historic Hein Park near Rhodes College and the zoo. Choice of upstairs suite (double and single beds) with shower and wet bar, or downstairs guest room with king-size bed, cable TV, VCR, and private bath. Popular hostess teaches English at a local college and travels extensively. $67.95.

B&B in Memphis #M-1203

P. O. Box 41621, 38174-1621
(901) 726-5920; FAX (901) 725-0194

Stately home surrounded by towering old trees and lovely gardens near Rhodes College and the zoo. Enjoy this interesting couple's family antiques and flair for entertaining. Choose either elegant queen-size canopy or antique twin guest rooms with private bath in the hallway. Pool. Aristocratic alley cat in residence. $62.29.

Lowenstein-Long House

217 North Waldran, 381095
(901) 527-7174

This beautifully restored Victorian mansion near downtown is listed on the National Register of Historic Places. Convenient to all major attractions, such as the Mississippi River, Graceland, Beale Street, the Memphis Zoo, Brooks Museum, and the Victorian Village. Free off-street parking.

Host: Samantha Long
Rooms: 4 (PB) $60-90
Continental Plus Breakfast
Credit Cards: A, B, C
Notes: 2, 5, 7(limited), 8, 9 14 (limited)

MONTEAGLE

Adams Edgeworth Inn

Box 340, Monteagle Assembly, 37356
(615) 924-2669

A friendly ten-room 1896 mountain inn in the Monteagle Assembly National Historic District, the southern Chautauqua. Enjoy rope hammocks, wicker rockers, and gingerbread porches; delve into plentiful books and magazines by the cheerful library fire; or experience the refreshing waterfalls and pools along the many nearby trails. The University of the South at Sewanee is six miles away.

Hosts: Wendy and David Adams
Rooms: 9 (PB) $65-85
Expanded Continental Breakfast
Credit Cards: A, B
Notes: 2, 5, 7, 8 (call), 9, 10, 11, 12, 14

Adams Edgeworth Inn

North Gate Lodge

P. O. Box 858, Monteagle Assembly, 37356
(615) 924-2799

The bright blue awning of this 1890s boarding house welcomes you to warm hospitality and sumptuous breakfasts. Purchased and renovated in 1984 by Nancy and Henry Crais, this inn is open year-round. Experience the cool mountain air of the Cumberland Plateau; participate in the summer Chatauqua program; and explore the vistas, waterfalls, caves, and hiking trails in the area. Become a part of the changing seasons of summer activities, fall mountain colors, mist and snow of winter, and the brilliance of spring flowers.

Hosts: Nancy and Henry Crais
Rooms: 7 (PB) $60
Full Breakfast
Credit Cards: None
Notes: 2, 5, 8, 10, 11, 12, 14

Clardy's Guest House

MURFREESBORO

Clardy's Guest House

435 East Main Street, 37130
(615) 893-6030

Situated in the historic district, this 20-room Victorian Romanesque home is filled with antiques and features ornate woodwork and fireplaces. An eight-by-eight-foot stained-glass window overlooks the magnificent staircase. The area has much to offer history buffs and antique shoppers. Thirty miles from Nashville, just two miles off I-24.

Hosts: Robert and Barbara Deaton
Rooms: 4 (2 PB; 2 SB) $35-45
Continental Breakfast
Credit Cards: None
Notes: 2, 5, 7, 8, 9, 10, 11, 12

NASHVILLE—SEE ALSO GOODLETTSVILLE, HENDERSONVILLE, AND JOELTON

Bed and Breakfast Hospitality, Tennessee

P. O. Box 110227, 37222-0227
Reservations: (800) 678-3625 (TN) and (800) 458-2421 (U.S.) Information: (615) 331-5244; FAX (615) 833-7701

Accommodations in private homes or inns convenient to local points of interest. Continental breakfast served each morning. Guests fill out a questionnaire upon request

for reservations. Then a compatible host is carefully selected to assure a pleasant experience for both the guest and the host. Accommodations in such cities as Nashville, Gatlinburg, Memphis, Lynchburg, Knoxville, Chattanooga, Jackson, and Columbia.

NORMANDY

Parish Patch Farm and Inn

625 Cortner Road, 37360
(615) 857-3017

Relax in the view of smoky blue hills, meadows, and corn fields on a 300-acre working farm along the Duck River. The inn features cherry-and-walnut paneled library and great room with fireplaces. Elegant country dining is featured at the inn or in the restaurant at Cortner Mill, built in 1845. Located one hour south of Nashville, it is convenient to Opryland, Jack Daniel's and George Dickel's distilleries, Normandy Lake, and Tennessee Walking Horse stables. Enjoy hiking, fishing, canoeing, bicycling, bird watching, antique shopping, or a Patch picnic. The 55-person conference center is fully equipped. Pool, antique furnishings, color TV, kennel, and stable.

Hosts: David and Claudia Hazelwood
Rooms: 20 (16 PB; 4 SB) $60-110
Full Breakfast
Credit Cards: A, B
Notes: 2, 3, 4, 5, 6, 7, 8, 9, 11, 12

Parish Patch Farm and Inn

6 Pets welcome; 7 Smoking allowed; 8 Children welcome; 9 Social drinking allowed; 10 Tennis available; 11 Swimming available; 12 Golf available; 13 Skiing available; 14 May be booked through travel agents.

PIKEVILLE

Fall Creek Falls Bed and Breakfast

P. O. Box 309, Route 3, 37367
(615) 881-5494

Enjoy the country atmosphere of an English manor home on 40 acres of rolling hillside one mile from the nationally acclaimed Fall Creek Falls Resort Park. Beautiful upstairs accommodations have a common sitting area with TV. Lodging includes a full breakfast served in a cozy country kitchen, an elegant dining room, or a sunny Florida room with a magnificent view. Assistance with touring, dining, and shopping information. Off-season rates.

Hosts: Doug and Rita Pruett
Rooms: 8 (6 PB; 2 SB) $50-75
Full Breakfast
Credit Cards: A
Notes: 2, 5, 10, 11, 12

RED BOILING SPRINGS

Armour's Red Boiling Springs Hotel

Route 2, Box 1, 37150
(615)-699-2180

This historical hotel, built in 1924 and listed on the National Register of Historic

Hale Springs Inn

Places, offers 26 rooms, all of which have private baths and a full-size bed or pair of twins. Traditional mineral baths. Three meals a day, if desired. The building is currently being renovated, keeping the 1920s style as much as possible. Accommodations for group retreats, wedding receptions, and family reunions.

Hosts: Brenda and Bobbie Thomas
Rooms: 26 (PB) $20-60 (includes three meals)
Full Breakfast
Credit Cards: None
Notes: 2, 3, 4, 5, 7, 8, 9

ROGERSVILLE

Hale Springs Inn

110 West Main Street, 37857
(615) 272-5171

This elegant, three-story Federal brick building built in 1824 is the oldest continuously run inn in Tennessee. Beautifully furnished with antiques from the period. Some of the rooms feature four-poster canopy beds, and all rooms have working fireplaces. Air conditioning. Bring your own wine. Candlelight dining.

Host: Ed Pace
Rooms: 9 (PB) $45-75
Continental Breakfast
Credit Cards: A, B, C
Notes: 4, 5, 7, 8, 9, 10, 11, 12

RUGBY

Grey Gables Bed 'n' Breakfast

Highway 52, P. O. Box 5252, 37733
(615) 628-5252

Situated one mile west of the 1880s English village, this bed and breakfast offers visitors the best of its Victorian English and Tennessee pioneer heritage. Eight guest rooms, with both private and shared baths, are available, and guests are invited to enjoy an elegant evening meal, hearty country breakfast, and two porches

NOTES: Credit cards accepted: A Master Card; B Visa; C American Express; D Discover Card; E Diner's Club; F Other; 2 Personal Checks accepted; 3 Lunch available; 4 Dinner available; 5 Open all year;

with white wicker and rustic rockers. Canoe rental and shuttle; access to golf, swimming, hiking, and cycling; and horses boarded. Private luncheons, teas, dinners, receptions, conferences, retreats, and group functions by reservation. No pets, restricted smoking. Adults preferred.

Hosts: Bill and Linda Brooks Jones
Rooms: 8 (4 PB; 4 SB) $90 (includes breakfast
    and dinner)
Full Breakfast
Credit Cards: A, B
Notes: 2, 3, 4, 5, 7 (limited), 9, 11, 12, 14

Newbury House at Historic Rugby

P. O. Box 8, Highway 52, 37733
(615) 628-2441; (615) 628-2430

Newbury House was the Rugby colony's first boarding house, starting in 1880. Sash and pulley cords on the windows reveal an 1879 patent date. Board and batten siding, a lovely front porch, mansard roof, and dormer windows are all hallmarks of this beautifully restored, Victorian-furnished bed and breakfast. Newbury House lodged both visitors and incoming settlers to British author Thomas Hughes's utopian colony. In a nationally registered village with historic building tours, museum stores, specialty restaurant, and river gorge hiking trails.

Richmont Inn

Host: Historic Rugby, Inc.
Rooms: 5 (3 PB; 2 SB) $50-70
Full Breakfast
Credit Cards: A, B
Notes: 2, 3, 4, 5, 7, 9, 11, 12

SEVIERVILLE

Blue Mountain Mist Country Inn

1811 Pullen Road, 37862
(615) 428-2335

This inn is a new Victorian-style farmhouse with a big wraparound porch overlooking rolling hills, with the Great Smoky Mountains as a backdrop. Furnished with country antiques, Grandmother's quilts, and old photographs, this inn provides a homey atmosphere. Just minutes from the Great Smoky Mountains National Park, Gatlinburg, and Dollywood.

Hosts: Norman and Sarah Ball
Rooms: 12 (PB) $79-115
Cottages: 5 (PB) $125
Full Breakfast
Credit Cards: A, B
Notes: 2, 5

Milk and Honey Country Hideaway

2803 Old Country Way, 37862
(615) 428-4858

Near Gatlinburg and Pigeon Forge, this charming two-story cedar home has six bedrooms, each furnished with antiques and decorated in country Victorian. The parlor, which has a large stone fireplace, usually filled with aromas of freshly baked desserts coming from Cathy's kitchen. The surrounding area has much to offer in the unparalleled beauty of the Great Smoky Mountains National Park. Off-season rates and group discounts available.

Hosts: Gary and Cathey McFarland
Rooms: 6 (4 PB; 2 SB) $65-97
Full Breakfast
Credit Cards: A, B
Notes: 2, 5, 12, 13, 14

6 Pets welcome; 7 Smoking allowed; 8 Children welcome; 9 Social drinking allowed; 10 Tennis available; 11 Swimming available; 12 Golf available; 13 Skiing available; 14 May be booked through travel agents.

TOWNSEND

Richmont Inn

220 Winterberry Lane, 37882
(615) 448-6751

Located on the "peaceful side of the Smokies," this Apopalachian barn is beautifully furnished with eighteenth-century antiques and French paintings. Breathtaking mountain views, graciously appointed rooms with sitting areas, wood-burning fireplaces, spa tubs for two, and balconies. French and Swiss cuisine are served at breakfast with flavored coffees, and gourmet desserts by candlelight in the venings are just some of our specialities. The Smoky Mountains, arts/crafts shops, historic Cades Cove, and golfing are all nearby. "A special place for couples."

Hosts: Susan and Jim Hind
Rooms: 10 (PB) $85-130
Full Breakfast
Credit Cards: None
Notes: 2, 5, 12

Smoky Bear Lodge

160 Bear Lodge Drive, 37882
(615) 448-6442; (800) 48-SMOKY (outside TN)

Situated in the foothills of the Smokies and constructed of logs, Smoky Bear Lodge offers spacious guest rooms, pool, hot tub, conference facility, and cabins. Specializes in church groups. Ideal for families, business retreats, and tourists to the area. Near Smoky Mountain passion play, Tuckaleechee Caverns, Cades Cove, horseback riding, tubing, hiking, golfing.

Hosts: Gary and Sandy Plummer
Rooms: 11 (PB) $55-85
Full Breakfast
Credit Cards: A, B, C
Notes: 2, 5, 8, 11, 12, 13, 14

WARTRACE

Ledford Mill

Route 2, Box 152, 37183
(615) 455-2546

A private hideaway where you are the only guests in this cozy, open suite with kitchenette. Spend the night in a 19th-century grist mill, listening to the waterfalls and murmuring waters of Shippmans Creek.

Hosts: Norma and Bill Rigler
Room: 1 (PB) $60
Continental Breakfast
Credit Cards: A, B, C
Notes: 2, 5, 6, 7, 8, 9

Texas

Bolin's Prairie House Bed and Breakfast

508 Mulberry, 79601
(915) 675-5855

Nestled in the heart of Abilene is a 1902 home furnished with antiques and modern luxuries combined to create a homelike, warm atmosphere. Downstairs, you find high ceilings, hardwood floors, and a wood-burning stove. Upstairs are four unique bedrooms (Love, Joy, Peace, Patience), each beautifully decorated. Breakfast of special baked egg dishes, fruit, and homemade bread is served in the dining room that is decorated with a collection of cobalt glass and blue and white china.

Hosts: Sam and Ginny Bolin
Rooms: 4 (SB) $40-50
Full Breakfast
Credit Cards: A, B, C, E
Notes: 2, 5

The Prairie House

Bed and Breakfast Texas Style
4224 West Red Bird Lane, Dallas, 75237
(214) 298-8586

Nestled in the heart of the city is this Prairie-style red brick that was built in 1928. There are three guest rooms upstairs, one hall bath with tub and shower. Breakfast will be a full gourmet treat of eggs, meat, homemade muffins, and breads, jams and jellies, juice, and coffee or tea. $45-50.

Windchimes

Bed and Breakfast Texas Style
4224 West Red Bird Lane, Dallas, 75237
(214) 298-8586

Near Eagle Lake and Columbus, this private retreat in the countryside is a perfect location for couples seeking privacy and serenity. There are a large private lake and two separate guest areas, each with private bath. The Crown Room offers two queen beds, double dresser, color TV, and private bath. The Garden Room has two bedrooms with twin beds, a bath with shower, sitting room, and small kitchen. Walking, fishing, biking, wildflower trekking are possible activities. $75.

Parkview House

1311 South Jefferson, 79101
(806) 373-9464

This turn-of-the-century Prairie Victorian situated in the heart of the Texas Panhandle has been lovingly restored by the present owners to capture its original charm. Furnished with antiques and comfortably updated, it has a large family TV room and parlor for reading or listening to music. Convenient to a park, biking, jogging, hiking, and the prize-winning musical drama *Texas* in Palo Duro State Park. Near the Panhandle Historical Museum and Lake Meredith.

NOTES: Credit cards accepted: A Master Card; B Visa; C American Express; D Discover Card; E Diner's Club; F Other; 2 Personal Checks accepted; 3 Lunch available; 4 Dinner available; 5 Open all year; 6 Pets welcome; 7 Smoking allowed; 8 Children welcome; 9 Social drinking allowed; 10 Tennis available; 11 Swimming available; 12 Golf available; 13 Skiing available; 14 May be booked through travel agents.

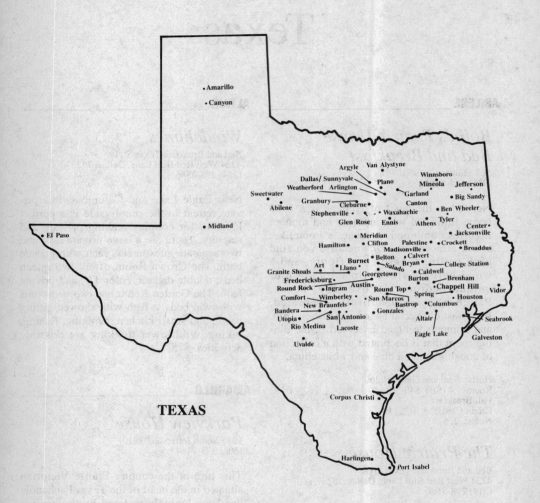

Amarillo

Canyon

Sweetwater

Abilene

Midland

El Paso

Argyle   Van Alystyne
Dallas/ Sunnyvale   Plano   Winnsboro
Weatherford Arlington   Mineola   Jefferson
Granbury   Cleburne   Garland   Big Sandy
Stephenville   Waxahachie   Ben Wheeler
Glen Rose   Ennis   Athens   Tyler
Center
Meridian   Jacksonville
Hamilton   Clifton   Palestine   Crockett
Madisonville   Calvert   Broaddus
Art   Belton   Bryan   College Station
Granite Shoals   Llano   Salado   Caldwell
Georgetown   Burton   Brenham
Fredericksburg   Burton   Chappell Hill
Round Rock   Ingram Austin   Round Top   Spring   Vidor
Comfort   Wimberley   San Marcos   Houston
Bandera   New Braunfels   Bastrop   Columbus
Utopia   San Antonio   Gonzales   Altair   Seabrook
Rio Medina   Lacoste   Eagle Lake   Galveston

Corpus Christi

TEXAS

Harlingen

Port Isabel

Hosts: Nabil and Carol Dia
Rooms: 4 (2 PB; 2 SB) $50-60
Suite: 1 (PB) $75
Expanded Continental Breakfast
Credit Cards: A, B
Notes: 2, 5, 8 (by prior arrangement), 9, 10, 14

Parkview House

ARGYLE

Country Cottage

Bed and Breakfast Texas Style
4224 West Red Bird Lane, Dallas, 75237
(214) 298-8586

A charming guest house awaits couples or
a small family that wishes to experience
ranch life. Just 45 minutes north of Dallas,
near Lake Lewisville, this three-room
house offers a queen bed, full bath, a sofa
sleeper in the livingroom, TV, fireplace,
and stocked kitchen. Many walking trails
on the 200 acres of ground. $65.

ARLINGTON

Meadow Brook

Bed and Breakfast Texas Style
4224 West Red Bird Lane, Dallas, 75237
(214) 298-8586

Right next to a golf course, convenient to
both Dallas and Fort Worth, near the
Texas Ranger Stadium, the University of
Texas, Six Flags Over Texas amusement
park, this bed and breakfast has one guest
room with a Murphy bed and private bath
in a wing of the house that offers complete
privacy. An expanded continental breakfast, including homemade muffins, is
served. No smoking. Dogs in residence.
$48.

ART

Hasse House

7 miles east of Mason, on Highway 29, 76820
(915) 347-6463

The Hasse House is listed on the National
Register of Historic Places and has been
featured on various TV programs. Other
than hunting season, the 320-acre Hasse
Ranch invites guests to explore its grounds,
using the two-mile hiking path. The house
has two bedrooms, two baths, a dining area,
livingroom, and modern kitchen with
microwave, dishwasher, and washer/dryer.
Furnished with antiques. Central heat/ air.
Rents as one unit.

Host: Laverne Lee
Whole House: $65
Continental Breakfast
Credit Cards: None
Notes: 2, 5, 7, 8, 9

ATHENS

New York Texas Cheesecake

Bed and Breakfast Texas Style
4224 West Red Bird Lane, Dallas, 75237
(214) 298-8586

This wonderful two-story farmhouse overlooks about 25 acres of peaceful meadow
and a well-stocked bass lake. The new inn
has four upstairs guest bedrooms; two bedrooms have private baths, and two bedrooms share a hall bath. The host is famous
for her New York Texas Cheesecake,
which is offered to all who come through
the door. The inn provides a library, formal

6 Pets welcome; 7 Smoking allowed; 8 Children welcome; 9 Social drinking allowed; 10 Tennis available; 11
Swimming available; 12 Golf available; 13 Skiing available; 14 May be booked through travel agents.

dining room, wonderful veranda with big rocking chairs, and rooms filled with antiques that are for sale. Breakfast will be a bonanza of ham or sausage, buttered new potatoes, and eggs with mushroom-and-onion sauce. Children and pets are welcome. Smokers are welcome to smoke on the porch. $79.

Porches

Bed and Breakfast Texas Style
4224 West Red Bird Lane, Dallas, 75237
(214) 298-8586

This fine old log and stone farm home, circa 1910, has been completely restored by the grandson of the original owners. The live oak in the back yard is reportedly 800 years old. The home offers two large porches, a hot tub, two upstairs guest rooms with adjoining bath. Breakfast will be a full Texas treat, with eggs, meat, biscuits, gravy, grits, or guests' choice. Convenient for Canton Trades Day and the Black-eyed Pea Festival. $85.

AUSTIN

Bad Griesbach Bed and Breakfast

1006 East 50th Street, 78751
(512) 452-1004

Family hospitality awaits the traveler in this European-style bed and breakfast. There are seven cozy bedrooms, five with a private bath. Enjoy a full home-style breakfast and snacks throughout the day. Near the airport; also a five-minute drive from downtown, the lake, and campus area. Nearby public tranportation. Smoking is allowed in the smoking room. Special weekly and monthly rates available.

Hosts: Ruth and Jospeh Brown
Rooms: 7 (5 PB; 2 SB) $49
Full Breakfast
Credit Cards: A, B, C, D
Notes: 2, 5, 7 (limited), 8, 14

The Brook House Bed and Breakfast

609 West 33rd, 78705
(512) 459-0534

The Brook House is a 1920s Texas classic that has been lovingly restored to its present country charm. High ceilings, large windows, antique-filled rooms, and relaxed atmosphere provide a cozy retreat from the busy world. Guests enjoy a full breakfast served outside on the greenery-lined veranda, weather permitting. The backyard boasts a large tin-roofed gazebo, herb and flower garden, and room to roam or relax with a good book. Five charming guest rooms for guests to choose, from delightfully airy and light to enchantingly romantic; cozy livingroom features TV/VCR and a fireplace.

Hosts: Maggie and Gary Guseman
Rooms: 5 (PB) $55-99
Full Breakfast
Credit Cards: A, B, C, D, E

Burnet Country Garden Bed and Breakfast

1200 West 22 1/2, 78705
(512) 477-9639

This lovely two-story 1936 home has beautiful oak hardwood floors, antiques, and lace. Gourmet breakfast served in the country garden or dining room. Enjoy the deck under a large Texas oak tree. Country charm in the heart of Austin. Midweek business rates available.

Hosts: Kay Jackson and Claudean Schultz
Rooms: 4 (2 PB; 2 SB)
Full Breakfast
Credit Cards: A, B, C
Notes: 2, 5, 9

NOTES: Credit cards accepted: A Master Card; B Visa; C American Express; D Discover Card; E Diner's Club; F Other; 2 Personal Checks accepted; 3 Lunch available; 4 Dinner available; 5 Open all year;

Carrington's Bluff

Carrington's Bluff Bed and Breakfast

1900 David Street, 78705
(512) 479-0638

Carrington's Bluff is in the heart of Austin on an acre of tree-covered bluff. Built in 1877, this historic Texas farmhouse has been transformed into an English country bed and breakfast. Antique-filled rooms, handmade quilts, and the sweet smell of potpourri await you. Breakfast begins with gourmet coffee, fresh fruit, and homemade granola served on fine English china. Homemade muffins and breads and a house specialty ensure you won't go away hungry.

Hosts: Gwen and David Fullbrook
Rooms: 5 (3 PB; 2 SB) $60-75
Full Breakfast
Credit Cards: A, B, C, E, F
Notes: 2, 5, 8, 9, 14

Cliffside Guesthouse

Bed and Breakfast Texas Style
4224 West Red Bird Lane, Dallas, 75237
(214) 298-8586

The beautiful view and the large greenbelt area keep folks coming back to this cozy guest house with kitchenette. High above Barton Springs Creek, there is a queen Hide-a-bed and private bath. Breakfast goodies are placed in the small refrigerator for guests to prepare at their leisure. Smoking is permitted outside only. Two-night minimum stay. $65.

LaPrelle Place Bed and Breakfast

Bed and Breakfast Texas Style
4224 West Red Bird Lane, Dallas, 75237
(214) 298-8586

Discover the magic of Austin's past while experiencing the beauty of the present in this premier home just south of the Colorado River. The four upstairs guest rooms, each with private bath, offer Victorian decor. Guests may use the hot tub and deck overlooking the garden. Continental breakfast is served in the formal dining room downstairs or on request in the common area upstairs that overlooks the garden. $49-69.

6 Pets welcome; 7 Smoking allowed; 8 Children welcome; 9 Social drinking allowed; 10 Tennis available; 11 Swimming available; 12 Golf available; 13 Skiing available; 14 May be booked through travel agents.

The McCallum House

613 West 32nd Street, 78705
(512) 451-6744

The historic McCallum House, an Austin landmark with a Texas historical marker, is ten blocks north of the University of Texas-Austin and 20 blocks north of the Texas capitol and downtown. All rooms and suites have private baths, period Victorian furnishings, extension phones, kitchen facilities, sitting areas, and color TVs. Four have private porches. Owner-occupant innkeepers are your hosts. Easy access to state capitol, LBJ Library, Highland Lakes, Zilker Park, Mount Bonnell, and lots more. Two-night minimum stay on weekends.

Hosts: Nancy and Roger Danley
Rooms: 5 (PB) $65-95
Full Breakfast
Credit Cards: None (Reservations held with
    Visa/MC)
Notes: 2, 5, 9, 10, 11, 12

Peaceful Hill
Bed and Breakfast

10817 Ranch Road 2222, 78730-1102
(512) 338-1817

The only country inn in the Austin area located on ranch land high in the beautiful rolling hills. This native stone sixteen-year-old home overlooks the hills and lights of the city's skyline. Only fifteen minutes from Austin and five minutes from Lake Travis and Oasis, the inn is only two miles from the River Place Country Club where you can swim, play tennis, or play golf on the 18-hole golf course that Tom Kite designed. On a cold winter night enjoy a cheery, roaring fire in the spacious living room, sipping coffee and hot chocolate and playing games; on a warm spring day sit on the south porch overlooking downtown Austin and watching cows, calves, and horses in a field.

Host: Mrs. Peninnah Thurmond
Rooms: 2 (PB) $65
Full Breakfast

Credit Cards: A, B, C
Notes: 2, 5, 6 (limited), 7, 8, 9, 10, 11, 12

Southard-House

908 Blanco Street, 78703
(512) 474-4731

Charming 1890 Greek Revival home situated in a quiet neighborhood 12 blocks from the capitol and two from the unique West End shopping district. Restaurants are within a safe walking distance of 4 to 15 minutes. The Treaty Oak suite provides all the amenities. Recently opened two blocks away in another 1890 home is the Peppermint Inn, with one elegant, luxurious suite, with complimentary continental breakfast basket available upon request.

Hosts: Jerry and Rejina Southard
Rooms: 4 (PB) $59-74
Suites: 2 (PB) $129-159
Full Breakfast weekends; Continental weekdays
Credit Cards: A, B, C, D, E
Notes: 2, 5, 7, 8, 9, 10, 11, 14

Tarrytown

Bed and Breakfast Texas Style
4224 West Red Bird Lane, Dallas, 75237
(214) 298-8586

This private residence in an older, affluent area of the city is perfect for business men and women who need to be near the heart of the city. The guest bedroom has a double bed and private bath. The home has many lovely antiques as well as contemporary furnishings. Breakfast will be continental, served in the cozy breakfast nook. No smoking. Cat in residence. $60.

Zilker Park

Bed and Breakfast Texas Style
4224 West Red Bird Lane, Dallas, 75237
(214) 298-8586

The guest room at this private home has a double bed with a private bath right in the room and a sofa if children are along. There is a pool out back and the home sits on a hill. The capitol may be seen at night when the dome is lighted. Breakfast may be eggs Benedict or scrambled, homemade muffins, orange juice, coffee, or milk. No smoking. $45.

BANDERA

Dixie Dude Ranch

Bed and Breakfast Hosts of San Antonio
166 Rockhill, San Antonio, 78209
(512) 824-8036

"Your home on the range" is situated in the beautiful Texas Hill Country. The special package includes an afternoon hayride upon arrival, great home-cooked dinner, comfortable cottage lodging, full country breakfast, and a morning horseback trail ride, all for one modest daily price. Large pool, lounge with fireplace, and dining room in headquarters. Hike the 800 acres of the William Wallace Whitley family or just relax and enjoy the scenery. Open seven days a week during the summer. $85 per person.

The Horseshoe Inn

Bed and Breakfast Hosts of San Antonio
166 Rockhill, San Antonio, 78209
(512) 824-8036

The Horseshoe Inn is an early "no-frills" motel that has been converted into a real western bed and breakfast. Seven rooms with an assortment of bed sizes, along with private baths, black-and-white-TVs, and clock radios. Breakfast is cooked to order in the adjoining cafe; early morning coffee will be brought to your room. $65.

BASTROP

The Historic Pfeiffer House

1802 Main Street, 78602
(512) 321-2100

The Pfeiffer House is one of Bastrop's 25 Texas Historical Homes and is listed on the National Register of Historic Places. Each room is tastefully decorated with antiques, offering guests relaxation free from television and telephone. A full breakfast is served formally in the dining room. The three upstairs bedrooms are charmingly decorated to give each room a warm, welcome feeling. Two porches invite guests to "sit a spell" and relax.

Host: Marilyn C. Whites
Rooms: 3 (SB) $55
Full Breakfast
Credit Cards: None
Notes: 2, 5, 10, 11, 12

BELTON

The Belle of Belton

Bed and Breakfast Texas Style
4224 West Red Bird Lane, Dallas, 75237
(214) 298-8586

A beautiful antebellum home right in town with five bedrooms to charm and pamper guests. The rooms are named after the four seasons: Spring, with twin four-poster beds and claw foot tub across the hall; Summer, with king bed, white wicker furniture and shared bath; Fall, with brass bed, rocking chairs in the triple window, and private bath with shower; Winter, with a corner cupola where poinsettias are displayed, queen bed, and private bath. Continental breakfast includes quiche or croissants, fresh fruit, and specially blended coffees or teas. $40-50.

BEN WHEELER

The Arc Ridge Guest Ranch

Bed and Breakfast Texas Style
4224 West Red Bird Lane, Dallas, 75237
(214) 298-8586

This 600-acre ranch in east Texas near Canton and Tyler has its own lake. The

6 Pets welcome; 7 Smoking allowed; 8 Children welcome; 9 Social drinking allowed; 10 Tennis available; 11 Swimming available; 12 Golf available; 13 Skiing available; 14 May be booked through travel agents.

guest house has two bedrooms, livingroom, complete kitchen, and shower. Fishing and paddleboats are available. No hunters allowed in this environmentally protected area. Breakfast will be left in the refrigerator for guests to prepare themselves. Family rates will be considered. $65/night; $250/week.

Wild Briar: The Country Farm at Edom

P. O. Box 21, 75754
(903) 852-3975

Located in the beautiful countryside of East Texas, Wild Briar is a favorite inn for relaxation, good food, and elegant surroundings. The 6,000-square-foot inn reflects the owners' travels in England, Scotland, and Wales, and it is decorated to reflect these special places. Each room is named for a special inn or village, using antiques and period furnishings. A dining room seats twenty; a breakfast room seats sixteen. The inn has twenty-three acres of grounds, and is a frequent site for weddings and family gatherings. Located seventeen miles from Canton and Tyler.

Hosts: Max and Mary Scott
Rooms: 6 (PB) $100
Full Breakfast and Full Dinner
Credit Cards: None
Notes: 2, 4, 5, 7 (limited)

BIG SANDY

Annie's Bed and Breakfast

Bed and Breakfast Texas Style
4224 West Red Bird Lane, Dallas, 75237
(214) 298-8586

Take a step back in time at this fascinating inn that has 13 bedrooms, each with small refrigerator for soft drinks and fruit. Breakfast is served in Annie's Tea Room, a historical home that has been converted into a charming restaurant. Tyler is only 10-15 minutes away; Jefferson is one and

one-half hours away. Call early since rooms are booked far in advance. No smoking. $115-173.

BRENHAM

Captain Clay Home Bed and Breakfast

Route 5, P. O. Box 149, 77833
(713) 622-6744

This early Texas home, circa 1852, is located on a hilltop overlooking beautiful rolling countryside in historic Independence, Texas. Enjoy the peaceful porches watching miniature horses frolic in the pastures, or a walk to the creek, a visit to the nearby Antique Rose Emporium. Air conditioning for summer and a big, cozy fireplace for winter make this bed and breakfast a place to stay for all seasons.

Host: Thelma Zwiener
Rooms: 4 (2 PB; 2 SB) $50-65
Full Breakfast
Credit Cards: None
Notes: 2, 5, 7, 8, 9

BROADDUS

Sam Rayburn Bed and Breakfast: The Cole House

Woodvillage Addition., Route 1, P. O. Box 258, 75929
(409) 872-3666

In the piney woods of the Angelina National Forest is a peaceful little getaway located on Sam Rayburn Lake. Not a traditional bed and breakfast, this is a cozy little guest house that will sleep nine adults. The setting would delight Thoreau himself, with peaceful waters of the lake and tall, shady oaks and pine trees, and absolute seclusion. Thirty years of antique collections fill this five-room cottage on the lake. Fully central air conditioning. All-electric kitchen. Everything is furnished for a peaceful, relaxing stay.

Hosts: Gene and Jean Cole
Cottage: 2 (SB) $55
Continental Breakfast
Credit Cards: None
Notes: 2, 5, 7, 9, 11, 13 (water-skiing), 14

BRYAN

Creekway

Bed and Breakfast Texas Style
4224 West Red Bird Lane, Dallas, 75237
(214) 298-8586

A contemporary home right in the middle
of town, just ten minutes from Texas A&M
University. Three guest rooms share a bath.
Continental breakfast consists of sausage
kolaches (Czech), fresh fruit platter, cereal
assortment, coffee or tea. Cats in residence.
Smoking permitted outside only. $50.

BURNET

Airy Mount

Bed and Breakfast Texas Style
4224 West Red Bird Lane, Dallas, 75237
(214) 298-8586

Built in 1884, this fine old stone barn was
named appropriately by General Johnson
because of the constant breeze on the hill
above Burnet. Airy Mount has two bedrooms upstairs that are named after General
Johnson and his wife Josephine. The bedrooms are decorated with plaid taffeta comforters, an old trunk, library desk, memorabilia reminiscent of the Civil War, an old
sewing machine, and a picture of the
General and his wife. Both bedrooms have
private baths. Enjoy a full Texas breakfast
with meat, eggs, fresh fruit, beverage,
homemade muffins or breads. $65.

Rocky Rest
Bed and Breakfast

404 South Water Street, 78611
(512) 756-2600

Rocky Rest is a two-story rock house built
by Adam R. Johnson in 1860. Situated in
Burnet, the heart of the Texas Hill Country.
In the area you can enjoy boating, fishing,
water skiing, and hunting. Burnet is 90
miles north of San Antonio and 40 miles
northwest of Austin. Enjoy wildflowers in
the spring and perhps the breathtaking sight
of a bald eagle.

Host: Fannie Shepperd
Rooms: 3 (1 PB; 2 SB) $55-60
Full Breakfast
Credit Cards: None
Closed Dec.
Notes: 2, 3 (upon request), 4 (upon request), 6, 8,
9, 11, 12, 14

BURTON

Long Point Inn

Route 1, P. O. Box 86-A, 77835
(409) 289-3171

Texas hospitality on a 175-acre cattle ranch
describes this bed and breakfast. Situated
on one of the officially designated scenic
highways of Texas, the historic La Bahia
Road, which was one of the Bluebonnet
trails of Washington County, the inn is in
the county voted by readers of *Texas
Highways* as the most scenic county in
Texas for spring flowers. A luxury home
copied inside and out from Old World
chalets and featured as the "Prettiest Place
in the Country" in *Farm and Ranch Living,*
June 1988.

Hosts: Bill and Jeannine Neinast
Rooms: 3 (2 PB; 1 SB) $83.25-94.35

Long Point Inn

Full Breakfast
Credit Cards: C
Notes: 2, 5, 8, 9

CALDWELL _____

The Alexander House

Bed and Breakfast Texas Style
4224 West Red Bird Lane, Dallas, 75237
(214) 298-8586

This Southern Colonial home is 20 minutes from the home of the Texas Aggies, College Station. The 140-year-old mansion offers one guest bedroom with private bath and old pedestal sink. Since this is the Kolache Capital of Texas, breakfast will be an assortment of sausages and fruit kolaches as well as juice and coffee or tea. No smoking. $85.

Texas Star

Bed and Breakfast Texas Style
4224 West Red Bird Lane, Dallas, 75237
(214) 298-8586

This large two-story ranch home located five miles south of Caldwell is surrounded by huge oak trees which shade the three porches and patios. The Texas Star has three guest rooms, one with a private bath and two share a bath. Breakfast will consist of bacon, eggs, toast, juice, fruit, ground coffees, and herbal tea. Complimentary "mimosas" of champagne and orange juice will be offered. $75-93.

CALVERT _____

Our House

Bed and Breakfast Texas Style
4224 West Red Bird Lane, Dallas, 75237
(214) 298-8586

The town of Calvert is a gem, with almost all the buildings on the National Register of Historic Places. This home offers five guest rooms and two baths in the hall. Breakfast

will be a gourmet treat, with Belgian waffles, ham and cheese omelettes, fresh fruit, and beverage. Children welcome. The location is convenient to Bryan-College Station and the Aggie events. No smoking. $65.

CANTON _____

Heavenly Acres

Bed and Breakfast Texas Style
4224 West Red Bird Lane, Dallas, 75237
(214) 298-8586

This wonderful hideaway is just ten miles from Canton and seven miles from Mabank. There is a rustic cabin with a complete kitchen, twin beds, and a queen sleeper sofa. The front porch overlooks the lake and picnic table, and benches are there for guests to enjoy. Inside the home, there is a Victorian guest room with two beds, a sitting area, and private bath. $65 for cabin; $75 for Victorian room.

Pasture Prime

Bed and Breakfast Texas Style
4224 West Red Bird Lane, Dallas, 75237
(214) 298-8586

This 150-acre farm has a six-acre lake that is stocked for anyone who wishes to wet a line. The home has three guest bedrooms. The one downstairs room has twin beds and a private bath. The two upstairs bedrooms have a double bed and share one hall bath. Dinner is served with advance notice. $60-75.

CANYON _____

Hudspeth House

1905 Fourth Avenue, 79015
(806) 655-9800

This historic bed and breakfast is only 12 minutes from Palo Duro Canyon, home of

NOTES: Credit cards accepted: A Master Card; B Visa; C American Express; D Discover Card; E Diner's Club; F Other; 2 Personal Checks accepted; 3 Lunch available; 4 Dinner available; 5 Open all year;

the famous *Texas* musical drama. The facilities offer beautiful accommodations, gourmet breakfasts, and a health spa. Take a stroll to the Panhandle Plains Museum or just relax and enjoy the warm hospitality.

Hosts: Dave and Sally Haynie
Rooms: 8 (5 PB; 3 SB) $45-110
Full Breakfast
Credit Cards: A, B
Notes: 2, 3 & 4 (by reservation), 5, 8, 9, 12, 14

CARTHAGE

Best Little Horse House

Bed and Breakfast Texas Style
4224 West Red Bird Lane, Dallas, 75237
(214) 298-8586

Completely renovated, this carraige house was originally a stable which the host had moved to the beautiful spot surrounded by tall pines. Collectibles and fine antiques are attractively displayed in this getaway cottage. Breakfast may be delivered to the cottage in the morning or guests are invited into the main home for an exquisite meal. $75.

Pine Colony Inn

CENTER

Pine Colony Inn

500 Shelbyville Street, 75935
(409) 598-7700

Situated in a quiet east Texas town, this inn sits just west of the Sabine River which runs between Texas and Louisiana. Only a few miles from Toledo Bend, it is a popular spot for bass fishing. Group gatherings welcome.

Hosts: Regina Wright and Marcille Hughes
Rooms: 12 (8 PB; 4 SB) $27-55
Full Breakfast
Credit Cards: A, B
Notes: 2, 5, 8, 9, 10, 11, 12

CHAPPELL HILL

The Browning Plantation

Bed and Breakfast Texas Style
4224 West Red Bird Lane, Dallas, 75237
(214) 298-8586

Experience the romantic Old South in the only working plantation in Texas that also is a bed and breakfast. One hour from Houston you will find this getaway, which offers four bedrooms filled with authentic antiques. There are two baths on the third floor, one for men and one for women. Breakfast, which is served in the large dining room, consists of egg-and-sausage casserole, grits, fresh fruit, coffee, and juice. Pool and hammocks available. $75-150.

Stagecoach Inn

Main at Chestnut, P. O. Box 339, 77426
(409) 836-9515

The inn, built in 1850 by Jacob and Mary Haller, the founders of Chappell Hill, was a favorite stopping place for many noted Texans traveling from Houston to Austin or Waco over the first stagecoach line organized in Texas in 1841 by Smith and Jones. The inn, listed on the National Register of Historic Places, is a 14-room Greek Revival structure with six fireplaces. A country breakfast is served.

Hosts: Elizabeth and Harvin Moore
Rooms: 6 (5 PB; 1 SB) $90
Full Breakfast
Credit Cards: None
Notes: 2

6 Pets welcome; 7 Smoking allowed; 8 Children welcome; 9 Social drinking allowed; 10 Tennis available; 11 Swimming available; 12 Golf available; 13 Skiing available; 14 May be booked through travel agents.

CLEBURNE

Anglin Queen Anne

Bed and Breakfast Texas Style
4224 West Red Bird Lane, Dallas, 75237
(214) 298-8586

Fine architecture, a magnificent collection of antiques, and genuine hospitality make a stay in this inn a memorable experience. There are five guest rooms, three with private baths. The bridal suite upstairs has two rooms: The sitting area has a working fireplace, and the bedroom has a double bed with matched bird's eye maple furniture including armoire and wash stand. Four other rooms available. A full breakfast is served in the formal dining room or the big kitchen. The inn may be reserved for corporate meetings, weddings, teas, and other social events. Handicap access. No smoking. No pets. $59-99 for rooms; $149 for bridal suite.

CLIFTON

The Sweetheart Cottage

Bed and Breakfast Texas Style
4224 West Red Bird Lane, Dallas, 75237
(214) 298-8586

A historical home once damaged in a tornado and now restored for a perfect weekend getaway. A loft room has a king bed, and a pull-out sofa is available downstairs. Country breakfast fare is left in the complete kitchen for the guests to prepare. No smoking. Two-night minimum stay required. $70.

COLLEGE STATION

Aggieland

Bed and Breakfast Texas Style
4224 West Red Bird Lane, Dallas, 75237
(214) 298-8586

This private home offers one guest room with private bath. It is within walking distance of Texas A&M University and is available for all year. Breakfast will be full Texas-style, with homemade bread or muffins, eggs, meat, juice or fruit, and beverage. Smoking outside only. $50.

Country Gardens

Bed and Breakfast Texas Style
4224 West Red Bird Lane, Dallas, 75237
(214) 298-8586

A sense of peace and tranquility will descend on you as you enter this little country hide-away located on four acres. Stroll through the wooded glen with a fruit orchard, grape vines, berry patches, and enjoy the birds and wildflowers. The hosts will prepare a delicious breakfast consisting of wheat pancakes or homemade bread, coffee, tea, or milk, and fruit in season.

COLUMBUS

The Gant Guest House

Bed and Breakfast Texas Style
4224 West Red Bird Lane, Dallas, 75237
(214) 298-8586

This typical German cottage has authentic stenciled walls that have been reproduced for the Smithsonian Institution. There are two bedrooms completely furnished with lovely antiques, armoires, iron beds, and washstands. Breakfast here is do-it-yourself. There is one bath for two bedrooms. The house is one block from the main section of town, which has many historical homes.

Raumonda

Bed and Breakfast Texas Style
4224 West Red Bird Lane, Dallas, 75237
(214) 298-8586

NOTES: Credit cards accepted: A Master Card; B Visa; C American Express; D Discover Card; E Diner's Club; F Other; 2 Personal Checks accepted; 3 Lunch available; 4 Dinner available; 5 Open all year;

This large, two-story antebellum home (circa 1887) has been beautifully and carefully restored to better than original condition. It now has air-conditioning, ceiling fans, and a private bath in every room. The enhanced continental breakfast buffet arranged on the gallery overlooking the pool and garden may be enjoyed by visitors from other bed and breakfasts. $80.

The Comfort Common

COMFORT

The Comfort Common

818 High Street, P. O. Box 539, 78013
(512) 995-3030

Historic limestone hotel, circa 1880, listed on the National Register of Historic Places. Rooms and suites are furnished with antiques. The downstairs of the hotel features numerous shops filled with American antiques. Your stay at the Comfort Common will put you in the heart of Texas Hill Country with Fredericksburg, Kerrville, Boerne, Bandera, and San Antonio, all a brief 15 to 30 minutes away. Fiesta Texas theme park is only 20 minutes away.

Hosts: Jim Lord and Bobbie Dent
Rooms: 6 (PB) $45-85
Continental Breakfast
Credit Cards: A, B, C, D
Notes: 2, 5, 9

Idlewilde Lodge Bed & Breakfast

Bed and Breakfast Hosts of San Antonio
166 Rockhill, 78209
(512) 824-8036

This bed and breakfast was originally a girl's camp for 60 years. The present owners have restored and modernized the lodge and cabins with every comfort in mind. Tennis courts, swimming pool, hiking trail and the Guadalupe River for rafting are all available for small or large groups to enjoy. A home-style breakfast is served in the main lodge or provided in your cottage. Pets are welcome. $76.30-97.50.

CORPUS CHRISTI

Bay Breeze

Sand Dollar Hospitality
3605 Mendenhall, 78415
(512) 853-1222

This "Texas Colonial" home is truely charming. There are two guest rooms with private baths. One guest room has hunter decor, and the other is decorated with family heirlooms. Guests are invited to enjoy the porch swing while relaxing or socializing. A full breakfast is served to guests. $72.

Coral Sea

Sand Dollar Hospitality
3605 Mendenhall, 78415
(512) 853-1222

The indoor hot tub and plant-filled covered patio are the outstanding features of this attractive host home. The newly added guest quarters in the rear of the home have trundle beds, private bath, and private entrance. $54-60.

Dolphin

Sand Dollar Hospitality
3605 Mendenhall, 78415
(512) 853-1222

This lovely home is in a fine neighborhood and offers two bedrooms and a shared bath to guests. One bedroom has a queen bed; the other has a double. Breakfast, served to your room or in the formal dining room on the family's good china, is sure to include the house specialty: fresh strawberry crepes in season. No smoking. $54-60.

Driftwood

Sand Dollar Hospitality
3605 Mendenhall, 78415
(512) 853-1222

A great place for families or small groups. Near the bay, the Naval Air Station, and Corpus Christi State University, this home offers four spacious second-floor bedrooms that share a lounge area with refrigerator and TV. There are three full baths upstairs. A patio hot tub is available. A public golf course and fishing pier are nearby. Children welcome. Bus service nearby. No pets. Smoking on patio only. $54-60.

Harbor House

Sand Dollar Hospitality
3605 Mendenhall, 78415
(512) 853-1222

Guests quickly feel welcome in this gracious old Colonial house on a tree-lined street near Corpus Christi Bay. The hosts' Early American antiques and collectibles complement the fine architectural detail of a spacious family home. The large guest bedroom is on the second floor. Guests are served breakfast in the dining room while seated on hundred-year old deacon benches at a harvest table. No smoking inside house, please. $72-75.

Meadow View

Sand Dollar Hospitality
3605 Mendenhall, 78415
(512) 853-1222

This contemporary one-story brick home is across from a well maintained city park just two minutes from Padre Island Drive, which leads to Padre Island and gulf beaches. The guest bedroom is decorated with southwestern touches with a queen-size bed and private bath. Continental breakfast is served during the week and full breakfast on weekends. $51-54.

Nancy's Place

Sand Dollar Hospitality
3605 Mendenhall, 78415
(512) 853-1222

This comfortable contemporary brick home offers a private suite with a private entrance; it can accommodate up to three guests traveling together. The suite has a bedroom with a king-size bed and an adjoining sitting room with a day bed, TV, table, chairs, and small refrigerator. Guests are invited to enjoy the outdoor spa on a prearranged basis. No pets or smoking indoors please. $54-66.

Padre Islander

Sand Dollar Hospitality
3605 Mendenhall, 78415
(512) 853-1222

Leasing arrangements can also be made for this furnished resort condominium on Padre Island close to the gulf beaches. This efficiency condo offers a queen Murphy bed (folds into the wall) and a queen sofa bed. Amenities include a heated indoor pool and spa, outdoor pool, shuffleboard, game room, boat docking slips. Provisions for breakfast are supplied by the owner with stays of two or more nights. No small children. No pets. Available for rental April through September. $59.

NOTES: Credit cards accepted: A Master Card; B Visa; C American Express; D Discover Card; E Diner's Club; F Other; 2 Personal Checks accepted; 3 Lunch available; 4 Dinner available; 5 Open all year;

Sand Piper

Sand Dollar Hospitality
3605 Mendenhall, 78415
(512) 853-1222

You'll feel at home in this attractive brick home on a quiet street in one of the city's nicer neighborhoods. There are two bedrooms available: one with a king bed and private bath; one with a double bed. Weather permitting, breakfast may be served on the lovely, plant-filled, covered patio. $51-54.

Seagull

Sand Dollar Hospitality
3605 Mendenhall, 78415
(512) 853-1222

The New England and Old World decor add to the charm and homey atmosphere of this host home. When you are done sightseeing or have had enough of the beach and sun, feel free to turn on the TV or curl up in one of the oversized chairs in the living room. There are two guest rooms available with a shared bath. $51-54.

Sea Oats

Sand Dollar Hospitality
3605 Mendenhall, 78415
(512) 853-1222

Grandmother's house revisited! You'll love this newly remodeled 1920s bungalow with its beautiful hardwood floors and down-home furnishings. The large guest bedroom has its own private entrance and private bath. Two-night minimum on weekends. $60.

Sunset Retreat

Sand Dollar Hospitality
3605 Mendenhall, 78415
(512) 853-1222

Private suite on lower floor with private entrance, front and rear. Includes bedroom with king bed, spacious separate livin-groom with sleeper sofa, bath, and TV. Two bedrooms upstairs have shared bath. Covered patio and dock on the water just outside your suite. Sunning deck on roof. Off-street parking. Breakfast, served in your suite, patio, or in the sun room, includes freshly baked breads, muffins, quiche, cinnamon rolls, fruit, juice, and tea. No pets. $68-100.

Tarpon

Sand Dollar Hospitality
3605 Mendenhall, 78415
(512) 853-1222

This two-story brick home is in one of Corpus Christi's finest residential neighborhoods. The three guest bedrooms have private baths. The largest has a king-size brass bed and a sitting area, as well as a balcony overlooking the beautifully landscaped back yard. Full breakfast is served to guests. Older children welcome. $54-60

CROCKETT

The Arledge House

Bed and Breakfast Texas Style
4224 West Red Bird Lane, Dallas, 75237
(214) 298-8586

This wonderful historic two-story home built in 1895 is on a spacious corner lot and is surrounded by large pecan trees. The bedrooms have king-size beds and private baths, televisions and collectible items from the hosts' family. For breakfast the hosts will prepare a Mexican buffet or homemade cinnamon rolls with fresh fruit and coffee. $85.

DALLAS

Artist's Haven

Bed and Breakfast Texas Style
4224 West Red Bird Lane, 75237
(214) 298-8586

6 Pets welcome; 7 Smoking allowed; 8 Children welcome; 9 Social drinking allowed; 10 Tennis available; 11 Swimming available; 12 Golf available; 13 Skiing available; 14 May be booked through travel agents.

This private home offers two upstairs guest rooms with shared bath. Each room has two twin beds and lovely amenities. Breakfast is continental-plus, with fruit, pastries, and beverages. Cat in residence. No smoking. Children are welcome. $60.

Bed and Breakfast Texas Style

4224 West Red Bird Lane, 75237
(214) 298-8586, (214) 298-5433

We represent over 125 bed and breakfasts across Texas that we have personally inspected. Ranches, farms, historic mansions, country inns, private cottages, and lakeside getaways are some of the settings we offer. We have inns near major universities in Austin, Dallas, Houston, and San Antonio. Our Host Home Directory describes each place; it is $5.

The Cloisters

Bed and Breakfast Texas Style
4224 West Red Bird Lane, 75237
(214) 298-8586

This lovely home is one block from White Rock Lake in a secluded area of Dallas. There are two guest rooms, each with a private bath. Both rooms have double beds, one with an antique Mexican headboard that is a conversation piece. Breakfast will be lots of protein, eggs, and/or blueberry pancakes. A bicycle is available for riding around the lake. No smoking. $75.

Coral Cove

Bed and Breakfast Texas Style
4224 West Red Bird Lane, 75237
(214) 298-8586

Spacious home near Olla Podrida and Richardson has three bedrooms. One is a sitting room combination with private bath and cable TV. The other two share a bath

and can accommodate families or couples traveling together. A welcoming glass of iced tea or cup of hot coffee is served upon arrival. Breakfast is full or continental, your choice. Smoking permitted. Cats in residence. $50.

East Dallas

Bed and Breakfast Texas Style
4224 West Red Bird Lane, 75237
(214) 298-8586

An exciting blend of fine artwork and California modern furnishings is in this home situated near museums, downtown, Cotton Bowl and Fair Park, and Market Center. Bus line is one-half block away. Pool for summer guests and fireplace for winter coziness. Continental breakfast is served on the patio in nice weather. Double bed with private bath. Smoking permitted. $50.

Executive Condo

Bed and Breakfast Texas Style
4224 West Red Bird Lane, 75237
(214) 298-8586

This completely furnished condo in North Dallas is within walking distance of the Valley View shopping mall and five minutes from Galleria Mall. Visitors to this condo will be met by the owners and given a key. Breakfast fixings are left in the kitchen and guests may use the facility to prepare other meals as well. Murphy bed; TV is available. Bath is full and private. No children. A pool and hot tub are available in the apartment complex. Smokers welcome. $60.

Fan Room

Bed and Breakfast Texas Style
4224 West Red Bird Lane, 75237
(214) 298-8586

NOTES: Credit cards accepted: A Master Card; B Visa; C American Express; D Discover Card; E Diner's Club; F Other; 2 Personal Checks accepted; 3 Lunch available; 4 Dinner available; 5 Open all year;

The antique fan displayed in this lovely twin bedroom is the focal point and was the start of a large collection of fans. The home is near Prestonwood, Marshall Fields, and the Galleria Mall. Southfork Ranch is a 15-minute drive north. A full country breakfast includes jalapeño muffins for first-time Texas visitors. There is a second bedroom near the kitchen with a double bed and private bath. $50.

Hotel St. Germain

2516 Maple Avenue, 75201
(214) 871-2516

Hotel St. Germain is an elegant European style full service hotel furnished in turn-of-the century French antiques. A renovated mansion built in 1906, it has fourteen-foot ceilings, crystal chandeliers, ormolu mirrors, and Aubusson taspestries. The seven guest suites have fireplaces, canopied beds, and black-and-white tiled bathrooms, and they overlook a walled New Orleans-style courtyard. There is 24-hour concierge service. Prime location near shops restaurants, and galleries. Haute cuisine served in the dining room.

Host: Clair Heymann
Suites: 7 (PB) $200-600
Continental Breakfast
Credit Cards: A, B, C, E
Notes: 2, 4, 5, 7, 9, 11, 14

Iris Canopy

Bed and Breakfast Texas Style
4224 West Red Bird Lane, 75237
(214) 298-8586

This home with a historical marker offers a lovely double bedroom featuring iris coverlet, canopy, and prints on the wall. Many antiques in this large, two-story red-brick, Prairie-style home. Private bath, no shower. Convenient to the public bus line, Convention Center, and arts district. $75.

North Dallas Guesthouse

Bed and Breakfast Texas Style
4224 West Red Bird Lane, 75237
(214) 298-8586

Centrally situated and convenient to the Valley View and Galleria malls is this unhosted guest house with double bed, private bath, small kitchen, and sitting area. Private entrance and off-street parking. Breakfast fixings are left in the refrigerator for guests to warm up in the microwave. TV, phone, and pool. One-half block to the bus line. No smoking; no children. $50.

Hotel St. Germain

Pilgrim's Rest

Bed and Breakfast Texas Style
4224 West Red Bird Lane, 75237
(214) 298-8586

Situated just 10 minutes from DFW airport, this home offers two bedrooms with an adjoining hall bath. Antiques have been used in decorating, many of them restored by the hosts. The hosts enjoy cooking for their guests. No smokers. No children. $45-50.

Province

Bed and Breakfast Texas Style
4224 West Red Bird Lane, 75237
(214) 298-8586

This private home offers a double bed and private bath. The hosts are health food enthusiasts and will serve fresh carrot juice to those who desire to try it. The conventional fare of toast, coffee, and fresh fruit is served as well. It is 25 minutes to downtown Dallas, the Market, and Convention Center. Two blocks to the public bus line. No smoking; no children. $50.

The Rose

Bed and Breakfast Texas Style
4224 West Red Bird Lane, 75237
(214) 298-8586

This historical home was built in 1901 and has three guest bedrooms, each with a private bath. Guests are treated to special breakfasts on the weekends, continental during the week. Children over 12 welcome. Smoking permitted. $85.

The Royal Suite

Bed and Breakfast Texas Style
4224 West Red Bird Lane, 75237
(214) 298-8586

Located just north of downtown and Love Field, this suite is located in the home of an energetic host who offers her guest room to bed and breakfast guests. The suite has a double-size bed, private bath, television, and phone. The host will prepare a full gourmet breakfast of homemade cinnamon rolls, fresh fruit, or eggs Benedict, juice, and coffee. $70.

Serendipity

Bed and Breakfast Texas Style
4224 West Red Bird Lane, 75237
(214) 298-8586

This bed and breakfast resembles an English countryside home. It was built in 1925 and has been completely renovated. Situated near White Rock Lake, the Lakewood Shopping Center, and many restaurants, it offers one bedroom with queen bed and private bath. Breakfast features a special egg and potato dish that is a family tradition. No smoking. $50.

Tudor Mansion

Bed and Breakfast Texas Style
4224 West Red Bird Lane, 75237
(903) 298-8586

Built in 1933 in an exclusive neighborhood in the shadow of downtown, this Tudor-style mansion offers queen bed and private bath. A full gourmet breakfast of either cheddar on toast, Texas-style creamed eggs with jalapeño, or fresh vegetable omelet is served. The bus line is three blocks away. Spanish and French are spoken. Three miles from downtown. Close to public golf course. $70.

White Rock Lake

Bed and Breakfast Texas Style
4224 West Red Bird Lane, 75237
(214) 298-8586

An upstairs bedroom with double bed and private bath right in the room is available at this location. There also is a twin bedroom, which makes the inn a great location for families with children. Breakfast consists of dry or cooked cereals, bread of rolls, fresh fruit, and beverage. Cat in residence. $45.

EAGLE LAKE _____

Eagle Hill Retreat

Bed and Breakfast Texas Style
4224 West Red Bird Lane, Dallas, 75237
(214) 298-8586

A historical mansion, circa 1936, and adjoining estate, situated an hour and 15 minutes from Houston and an hour and 30 minutes from San Antonio, offers an Olympic-size pool, wet and dry saunas, lighted tennis courts, two guest houses, and six bedrooms upstairs in the main home. Most rooms have two double beds and private baths, but the bridal suite has a large four-poster king bed and fireplace. The guest houses have three bedrooms each and

NOTES: Credit cards accepted: A Master Card; B Visa; C American Express; D Discover Card; E Diner's Club; F Other; 2 Personal Checks accepted; 3 Lunch available; 4 Dinner available; 5 Open all year;

shared baths. Breakfast is served in the large dining room and is full Texas-style buffet. Nearby national wildlife refuge protects the Attwater's prairie chicken, which has been on the endangered species list. Children are welcome. Smoking is permitted in designated areas. $85 rooms in main house; $65 for guest house; $150 for bridal suite.

Sunset Heights

EL PASO

Mexican Retreat
Bed and Breakfast Texas Style
4224 West Red Bird Lane, Dallas, 75237
(214) 298-8586

This cozy bed and breakfast contains museum quality artifacts, masks, and musical instruments of interest. Guests wishing to go into Mexico will be gladly escorted by the host to her favorite shopping markets and restaurants. The bedroom is furnished in antiques, and the breakfast will be typical Mexican fare. Resident cat. $40-50.

Sunset Heights Bed and Breakfast Inn
717 West Yandell Avenue, 79902
(915) 544-1743; (800) 767-8513
FAX (915) 544-5119

National historic home offers restored Victorian elegance. Built in 1905, architectural details feature Tiffany doors, windows, chandeliers, stained glass windows. Elegance surrounds you inside and out. Palm trees, pool with Jacuzzi. All rooms have an individual motif. Marble baths and balcony baths. Antiques. Security. Catering to the carriage trade. Mature adults will appreciate gourmet French and continental foods. Breakfast is five to eight courses. Dinner is eight to twelve courses. Reservations required.

Hosts: R. Barnett and R. Martinez
Rooms: 6 (PB) $70-165
Full Breakfast
Credit Cards: A, B, C
Notes: 2, 3, 4, 5, 9, 11, 14

ENNIS

Raphael House
500 West Ennis Avenue, 75119
(214) 875-1555

Six exquisite bedrooms with private baths set in a beautifully restored 1906 Neoclassical mansion appointed with original antiques, rich wall coverings, and luxurious fabrics. Amenities include oversize beds with down comforters and pillows, claw foot tub with scented soaps and bubble baths, afternoon refreshments, and turndown service. Located in a National Register historic district just 35 minutes from Dallas and 15 minutes from Waxa-hachie and the Superconducting Super Collider campus.

Raphael House

6 Pets welcome; 7 Smoking allowed; 8 Children welcome; 9 Social drinking allowed; 10 Tennis available; 11 Swimming available; 12 Golf available; 13 Skiing available; 14 May be booked through travel agents.

Host: Dana Cody
Rooms: 6 (PB) $65-88
Full Breakfast
Credit Cards: A, B, C, E
Notes: 2, 3, 4, 5, 9, 10, 11, 12, 14

FREDERICKSBURG

The Cottage

415B Plum Street, 77979
(512) 552-2800

The Cottage is located three blocks from
Main Street and is built of native rock from
the Fredricksburg area and matches the
host's home. It is a completely private
facility which allows you to come and go
as you please and caters to those who do
not care for communal breakfasts. You are
provided a private driveway, kitchen,
livingroom, bedroom, and bath, and there is
an attached deck for outside dining if you
choose. You have a color TV with cable,
HBO, and the Movie Channel. The kitchen
contains a four-burner gas stove, a refrigerator, and a microwave oven. The Cottage is
for non-smokers only.

Hosts: Diane and Weldon Weeks
Rooms: One Cottage $55
Self-catered Breakfast
Credit Cards: None
Notes: 2, 5, 9

Country Cottage Inn

405 East Main Street, 78624
(512) 997-8549

Fredricksburg's two most historic homes
(the Chester Nimitz Birthplace and Kiehne
House) form this inn. Thick limestone
walls, handcut beams and woodwork, and
mellow stone fireplaces are in both homes.
Both are on the National Register of
Historic Places. Enjoy complimentary
wine, large continental breakfasts, king-
size beds, old fans, room refrigerators,
microwaves, bathrobes, giant whirlpool
tubs, tubside candles, and wood-burning
fireplaces.

Host: Ms. Jeffrey Webb
Rooms: 7 (PB) $70-105
Continental Plus Breakfast
Credit Cards: A, B
Notes: 2, 5, 8, 9, 10, 11, 12

Haus Wilhelmina

407 Cora Street, 78624
(512) 997-3997

Turn-of-the-century German kindergarten
redone into a delightful and elegant home
featuring Minna's collectibles from around
the world and treasured local antiques.
Only a few short blocks from the
Hauptstrasse Shopping District downtown,
the home is surrounded by giant pecan
trees and flower gardens. There are two
guest rooms with double beds with a connected, shared bathroom. Another bedroom
is available with a single bed and private
bath. One of the first bed and breakfasts in
Texas, Minna is noted for her photo-oppor-
tunities, full and hearty German breakfasts
served under a glistening chandelier or in
the Garten Terrasse outside, and her shining hospitality. No pets, no children under
18, no smoking. Credit cards taken through
reservation service.

Hosts: Minna Knopp
Rooms: 3 (1 PB; 2 SB) $70
Full Breakfast
Credit Cards: A, B (through reservation service)
Notes: 2, 5, 9, 11, 12, 14

Inn on the Creek

107 North Washington, 78624
(512) 997-9585

This beautiful, historic limestone home is
located on Town Creek, across from the
Nimitz Museum complex, and is shaded by
one of Fredricksburg's oldest and largest
live oak trees. Today the home retains its
character with original wood floors, twelve-
foot ceilings, and Victorian lace-covered
canopy beds. The entire home is sophisticated country Victorian decor at its best.
The antiques and family heirlooms give you
a glimpse of the past and complement the
understated grandeur of this fine home.

NOTES: Credit cards accepted: A Master Card; B Visa; C American Express; D Discover Card; E Diner's
Club; F Other; 2 Personal Checks accepted; 3 Lunch available; 4 Dinner available; 5 Open all year;

Host: Dianne Hauerland
Rooms: 6 (3 PB; 3 SB) $75-85
Continental Plus Breakfast
Credit Cards: A, B
Notes: 2, 5, 8, 9, 14

J Bar K Ranch Bed and Breakfast

HC-10, Box 53-A, 78624
(512) 669-2471

Relax and enjoy your visit to a Texas Hill Country ranch in this large German rock home with antiques and a historic marker. Enjoy a full country breakfast, native wildlife, Texas hospitality, and a tour of the ranch. Next to a small, active country church. Situated just 15 minutes northwest of Fredericksburg, with its German heritage and architecture, many quaint shops, and excellent restaurants.

Hosts: Kermit and Naomi Kothe
Rooms: 4 (3 PB; 1 SB) $65 (extra person $20)
Full Breakfast
Credit Cards: A, B (surcharge)
Notes: 2, 5, 7, 8, 9

J Bar K Ranch

Kneipp Guesthaus

Route 1, Box 249C, 78624
(512) 997-3164

This warm, rustic bed and breakfast welcomes you to enjoy the breathtaking views from the two guest rooms. In the Aubry room, the queen bed, twin bed, desk, sitting area and view of the peach orchard and verdant meadows offer a place for relaxation. Often white-tail deer can be seen playing in the fields and nibbling at the peaches. The Dylan room looks out to massive oak trees and serene pastures. Both rooms are decorated with antique and handmade furniture. Guests are always welcome in the very open living areas with cathedral ceiling and wood-burning fireplace. Being a traditional bed and breakfast, a hearty, full breakfast is served in the downstairs dining area. Special diets are respected.

Host: Judy Kaiser Gold
Rooms: 2 (SB) $70-75
Full Breakfast
Credit Cards: Some accepted for prepayment
Notes: 2

Landhaus Bed and Breakfast

P. O. Box Drawer E, 78624
(512) 997-4916

This bed and breakfast is a charming 1883 restored guest house on 40 acres in the heart of Texas Hill Country, approximately eight minutes northeast of Fredericksburg on Rural Route 1631. There are four bedrooms, one large bath with shower tub, modern kitchen, den, and livingroom. The house has central heat and air, two cast-iron wood-burning stoves, a microwave oven, dishwasher, TV and telephone. Hiking, jogging, biking, fishing permitted. Not far from Lyndon Baines Johnson Ranch and Boyhood Home, Nimitz Museum, Enchanted Rock, and many other historic sites, shopping, and excellent restaurants. No smoking.

Hosts: Monty and Maria McDonald
Rooms: 4 (SB) $95
Full Breakfast (self-serve)
Credit Cards: None
Notes: 2, 5, 8 (under 1 and over 13), 9, 14

Magnolia House

101 East Hackberry, 78624
(512) 997-0306

Built circa 1925 and restored in 1991, this inn exudes southern hospitality in a grand and gracious manner. Outside, magnolias and a bubbling fishpond/waterfall set a soothing mood. Inside, beautiful living-room, game room, and formal dining room provide areas for guests to mingle. Four romantic rooms and two beautiful suites have been thoughtfully planned, appointed with antiques and original paintings by the owner. Southern-style, seven-course breakfast and complimentary wine, cap a memorable experience.

Host: Geri Lilly
Rooms: 6 (4 PB; 2 SB) $68-98
Full Breakfast
Credit Cards: A, B, C
Notes: 2, 5, 7, 9, 14

Schmidt Barn

231 West Main Street, 78624
(512) 997-5612

This guest house bed and breakfast is a renovated 130-year-old rock barn situated one and one-half miles from historic Fredericksburg, next door to the hosts' home. A loft bedroom with queen bed overlooks the livingroom below. Small kitchen and bath. All decorated in antiques. Featured in *Country Living* and *Travel & Leisure*.

Hosts: Charles and Loretta Schmidt
Room: 1 (PB) $70
Expanded Continental Breakfast
Credit Cards: A, B, D
Notes: 2, 5, 7, 8, 9, 14

GALVESTON

The Gilded Thistle

1805 Broadway, 77550
(409) 763-0194; (800) 654-9380

The Guilded Thistle is a wonderland of down-home elegance and service. Guests are pampered with an evening wine, fruit, and cheese tray, and morning freshly ground coffee and juice tray, all of which are left at your door. Many other amenities are provided as well.

Host: Helen Hanemann, owner
Rooms: 3 (1 PB; 2 SB) $135-145
Full Breakfast
Credit Cards: A, B
Notes: 2, 5, 8, 9

Hazlewood House

1127 Church Street, P. O. Box 1326, 77550
(409) 762-1668

Romantic Victorian home with three rooms to choose from with private baths, and a Jacuzzi suite. Antique furnishings, Oriental carpets, and fine tapestries throughout. Wine and cheese on arrival; morning coffee and a hearty continental breakfast are served on fine china, crystal, and silver. Near the beach, historical tours, musicals, museums, and trolley.

Host: Pat Hazelwood
Rooms: 3 (PB) $55-125
Continental Breakfast
Credit Cards: A, B
Notes: 2, 5, 9, 10, 11, 12, 13, 14

The Queen Anne Bed and Breakfast

1915 Sealy Avenue, 77550-2312
(409) 763-7088; (800) 472-0930

This home is a four-story Queen Anne Victorian built in 1905. Stained-glass windows, beautiful floors, large rooms, pocket doors, twelve-foot ceilings with transom doors, beautifully redecorated in 1991. Walk to historic shopping district, restaurants, 1886 opera house, museums, and the historic homes district. A short drive to the beach. A visit to Queen Anne is to be anticipated, relished, and remembered.

Hosts: John McWilliams and Earl French
Rooms: 4 (SB) $85-125
Full Breakfast
Credit Cards: A, B
Notes: 2, 5, 9

Trube Castle Inn

1627 Sealy Avenue, 77550
(800) 662-9647

NOTES: Credit cards accepted: A Master Card; B Visa; C American Express; D Discover Card; E Diner's Club; F Other; 2 Personal Checks accepted; 3 Lunch available; 4 Dinner available; 5 Open all year;

This remarkable castle, built in 1890, has been completely restored and is listed on the National Register of Historic Places. Offering just two exclusive suites, this 27-room mansion is furnished throughout with period antiques. Accommodations include private baths, porches, stereo systems, television, and in-room refrigerators. Within walking distance to historic Strand and beaches, "Texas' most beautiful Victorian home" replicates the Danish royal castle of the period and offers guests a unique opportunity to sample 1890s wealth and extravagance.

Host: Nonette O'Donnell
Rooms: 2 suites (PB) $100-200
Full Breakfast
Credit Cards: A, B, C
Notes: 2, 5, 7 (limited), 9, 10, 11, 12, 14

Trube Castle Inn

The Victorian Inn

511 Seventeenth Street, 77550
(409) 762-3235

Massive Italian villa built in 1899. Spacious guest rooms are romantically decorated with king beds and antiques. The four rooms on the second floor have balconies. Third-floor suite has a private bath and two bedrooms. The inn is within walking distance of historic Strand: restaurants, shops, boats. Less than one mile to the beach.

Hosts: Janice and Bob Hellbusch
Rooms: 6 (2 PB; 4 SB) $80-150
Continental Breakfast
Credit Cards: A, B, C
Notes: 2, 5, 7 (limited), 8 (over 12), 9, 10, 11, 12, 13, 14

GARLAND

Catnip Creek

Bed and Breakfast Texas Style
4224 West Red Bird Lane, Dallas, 75237
(214) 298-8586

Right on Spring Creek, the hot tub on the deck overlooks the wooded creek. The guest bedroom has a queen bed, private bath, and private entrance. Breakfast consists of granola and cinnamon-raisin biscuits or other homemade muffins or breads. Weekend guests are treated to a healthy quiche or pancakes. Herbal teas and special blended coffees are offered. Bicycles are provided. Just 30 minutes from downtown Dallas and very near Hypermart, the newest tourist attraction of the metroplex; 15 minutes to Southfork Ranch. $45.

The Victorian Inn

GEORGETOWN

Page House

Bed and Breakfast Texas Style
4224 West Red Bird Lane, Dallas, 75237
(214) 298-8586

This Queen Anne-style house, perched on top of a grassy knoll overlooking the banks of the South San Gabriel River, was built in

1903. Guests have a choice of four bedrooms, three upstairs and one downstairs, all with private baths. Lovely family treasures and antiques are thoughout the home. Many items in the rooms may be purchased. The Tea Room, known for its delicious lunches, will be used for breakfast by guests. Enjoy the Dinner Theatre located in the barn at the back of the property. Smokers are welcome to smoke outside. $70.

GLEN ROSE

Inn on the River

205 Southwest Barnard Street, 76043
(817) 897-2101

This 1919 inn on the Paluxy River near the town square is a designated Historic Texas Landmark. The 19 rooms and three suites are individually designed, and all have private baths. The Great Blue Heron Meeting House was added in 1990. This area of Texas is noted for its scenic hills, rivers, Dinosaur Valley State Park, Fossil Rim Wildlife Conservation Center, and Texas Amphitheatre.

Hosts: Nancy and Michael Rosenthal
Rooms: 22 (PB) $80-140
Full Breakfast
Credit Cards: A, B, C, D
Notes: 2, 5, 9, 10, 11, 12, 14

GONZALES

Saint James Inn

Bed and Breakfast Hosts of San Antonio
166 Rockhill, San Antonio, 78209
(512) 824-8036

This inn is a Greek Revival home built in 1914. One hour from San Antonio, Austin, and Victoria, it has three rooms. For breakfast, enjoy fruit, fresh pastries, homemade jams, juices, and other surprises with freshly brewed coffee or tea. Each room is unique, with antiques and fresh flowers;

and there are porches on which to enjoy the breeze, church bells, and birds. No smoking. No pets. Children over 12 only. $65.

GRANBURY

The Doyle House

Bed and Breakfast Texas Style
4224 West Red Bird Lane, Dallas, 75237
(214) 298-8586

A lovely estate one block from the downtown square. There is a pool cottage near the lake with a queen bed, sleeper sofa, private bath, and nice bar. The carriage house next to the weight and exercise room has a sitting area, small kitchen, and bedroom. The master suite in the main house has a king bed, bath with Jacuzzi, and lots of American antiques. Breakfast is taken to the carriage house and pool cottage in a basket and consists of sweet rolls, muffins, preserves, juice, and coffee. $65 for carriage house; $85 for pool cottage; $100 for master suite.

Nutt House Hotel

Town Square, 76048
(817) 573-5612

The inn was constructed in 1880 as a grocery store owned by two brothers, Jesse and Jacob Nutt. It was enlarged to accommodate stagecoach passengers. The building's walls are made of limestone, and many of its original furnishings are still in use, including antique iron beds and ceiling fans. The restaurant is famous for its regional cooking, hot-water cornbread, and pecan cobbler. The Nutt House Hotel also has a log cabin on a wooded waterfront lot one block from the square.

Host: Sam Overpeck
Rooms: 15 (6 PB; 9 SB) $39-49
Suites: $75-85
Log Cabin: $75
Continental Breakfast
Credit Cards: A, B, C
Notes: 2, 3 (except Monday); 4 (Friday, Saturday), 5, 8

NOTES: Credit cards accepted: A Master Card; B Visa; C American Express; D Discover Card; E Diner's Club; F Other; 2 Personal Checks accepted; 3 Lunch available; 4 Dinner available; 5 Open all year;

The Pecan Plantation

Bed and Breakfast Texas Style
4224 West Red Bird Lane, Dallas, 75237
(214) 298-8586

This fine, large home has a golf course, tennis, swimming, and country club dining. Guests may use all services. The bedroom has twin beds, private bath in the room, new upbeat decor, and many fine amenities. Guests may use the hot tub on the enclosed porch. Breakfast will be full western-style with omelets or scrambled eggs. Cat in residence. Smoking permitted. $50.

GRANITE SHOALS

La Casita

Bed and Breakfast Texas Style
4224 West Red Bird Lane, Dallas, 75237
(214) 298-8586

This charming private guest house is very rustic Texan and is filled with aeronautical items from the host's Navy career. A menu of 14 breakfast entrees is left for guests each day; it may be served in the guest house by request or in the main house. $60 plus tax.

HAMILTON

Crooked Chimney

Bed and Breakfast Texas Style
4224 West Red Bird Lane, Dallas, 75237
(214) 298-8586

This wonderful unhosted cottage is next door to the Crooked Chimney Antique Shop, which actually has a crooked chimney. The cottage has central heat and air, king bed, bath, and lovely sitting room/kitchen. The spacious ranch home across the way has three guest bedrooms. Breakfast will be served either in the gazebo or the pleasant nook overlooking the English garden, and will be an expanded with continental homemade jams and jellies. Children welcome. $40 rooms in the house; $50 for cottage.

HARLINGEN

The Ross Haus

Bed and Breakfast Texas Style
4224 West Red Bird Lane, Dallas, 75237
(214) 298-8586

A distinctive green bubble awning sets the four-unit apartment complex apart from the surrounding residences. Each unit has a large livingroom, full kitchen with microwave, bedroom with double bed, and bath. A basket of goodies will be left in the kitchen for overnight guests. Weekly and monthly rentals available. About 40 miles away, you will find the beach, South Padre National Seashore, and shopping in Mexico. $65 daily; $245 weekly; $500 monthly.

HELIOTES

The Herb Farm

Bed and Breakfast Hosts of San Antonio
166 Rockhill, 78209
(512) 824-8036

Situated only 25 minutes northwest of San Antonio on 15 acres nestled in the Grey Forest of the Texas Hill Country. The Herb Farm is an 1850s rock wall house built over a natural spring. A spacious courtyard overlooks the swimming pool, and the Honeymoon Villa is set apart from the main house for overnight stays in rustic charm; featured is an antique double iron bed, fireplace, and large private bath. $95.

HOUSTON

The Angel's Nest

Bed and Breakfast Texas Style
4224 West Red Bird Lane. Dallas. 75237
(214) 298-8586

The "angels" who live at this bed and breakfast are an artist and engineer. She paints and decorates, and he has a collection of antique trains. Bicycles are available for nearby touring. $40-50 plus tax.

Durham House Bed and Breakfast

921 Heights Boulevard, 77008
(713) 868-4654

Durham House is a faithfully restored Queen Anne Victorian on the National Register of Historic Places. Situated in central Houston, just ten minutes from downtown, Durham House is convenient for business travelers and tourists. Guests may use the back yard gazebo, the player piano, the screened back porch. Walk and jog on the boulevard.

Host: Marguerite Swanson
Rooms: 5 (4 PB; 1 SB) $60-75
Full Breakfast
Credit Cards: A, B, C
Notes: 2, 5, 8, 10, 11, 12, 14

The Highlander

607 Highland Street, 77009
(713) 861-6110

A tranquil oasis only five minutes from downtown. Choose from luxurious rooms or whimsical delights. The gracious hospitality includes afternoon tea, bedside snacks, and a lovely full breakfast. Long-time residents of Houston, your hosts can assist you in planning your visit. Only one block to metro bus, near both I-45N and I-10W, this location is convenient to everything. Here southern charm and Christian hospitality combine to make your memories beautiful.

Hosts: Arlen and Georgie McIrvin
Rooms: 4 (2 PB; 2 SB) $60-75
Full Breakfast
Credit Cards: A, B, C, D
Notes: 2, 5, 8, 14

Patrician Bed and Breakfast Inn

1200 Southmore Avenue, 77004-5826
(713) 523-1114

There will always be fresh flowers and a full breakfast at this 1919 three-story Colonial Revival mansion. Queen beds and private baths. Several rooms have adjoining sitting rooms, and some baths have claw foot tubs and shower contraptions. Between downtown Houston and the Texas Medical Center. Walk to Houston Zoological Gardens, Hermann Park, and the Museum of Fine Arts. Excellent dining nearby.

Host: Pat Thomas
Rooms: 5 (PB) $65-85
Full Breakfast
Credit Cards: A, B, C, E
Notes: 2, 5, 9, 10, 12, 14

Robin's Nest

4104 Greeley, 77006
(713) 528-5821

History, comfort, convenience, and taste make your stay at Robin's Nest memorable. The rooms are spacious and airy, furnished in eclectic Victorian. The atmosphere is relaxed and easy. Situated in a vibrant neighborhood in the inner city, among Houston's five major museums, downtown, theater district, medical center, and major sporting events. No fussing over you, but you know you are special as a guest at Robin's Nest.

Host: Robin Smith
Rooms: 2 (SB) $50-60
Full Breakfast
Credit Cards: None
Notes: 2, 5, 9, 10, 11, 12, 14

Sara's Bed and Breakfast Inn

941 Heights Boulevard, 77008
(713) 868-1130; (800) 593-1130

This Queen Anne Victorian is in Houston Heights, a neighborhood of historic homes, many of which are on the National Register of Historic Places. Each bedroom is uniquely furnished, having either single, double, queen, or king beds. The balcony suite consists of two bedrooms, two baths, kitchen, living area, and a fine view overlooking the deck. The sights and sounds of downtown are only four miles away.

Hosts: Donna and Tillman Arledge
Rooms: 12 (3 PB; 9 SB) $50-120
Continental Breakfast
Credit Cards: A, B, C, D, E, F
Notes: 2, 5, 8, 9, 10, 11, 12, 14

Sara's Bed and Breakfast

INGRAM

Guadalupe Retreat

Bed and Breakfast Texas Style
4224 West Red Bird Lane, Dallas, 75237
(214) 298-8586

Swimming, tubing, or canoeing in the river is the fun and excitement at this bed and breakfast near Kerrville and about one hour from San Antonio. The mansion has a complete apartment with kitchen, two bed-

rooms, and bath. A delicious breakfast of blueberry muffins and poppy seed bread with a fruit plate, eggs, and bacon will be the fare. Smoking permitted. Children welcome. $65.

JACKSONVILLE

English Hearth

Bed and Breakfast Texas Style
4224 West Red Bird Lane, Dallas, 75237
(214) 298-8586

Right in Jacksonville, this Tudor mansion was built by a local lumber baron in the 1920s. Amenities include a 200-year-old grandfather clock, an olive wood dining room set, and other fine antiques. There are three guest bedrooms. The honeymoon suite has a private bath right in the room. Two bedrooms upstairs share a hall bath. Breakfast will be a full Texas-style one, with biscuits or croissants, eggs, choice of meats, fresh fruit or juice, and coffee. $65-85.

JEFFERSON

Gone With The Wind Bed and Breakfast

412 Soda Street, 75657
(903) 665-8783; (903) 665-8824

Built in 1851, this antebellum Greek Revival one-story frame house is the fifth oldest home in Jefferson. Listed on the Texas Register of Historic Places, it is furnished with a scattering of antiques and reproductions. The lovely front porch is furnished for interesting conversation with other guests and the host and hostess. Four oversized bedrooms offer high ceilings, ceiling fans, coffee service, and private baths with showers. Each room has a separate entrance, and Scarlett's Room has a working fireplace. A full country-style breakfast is furnished each morning.

---

6 Pets welcome; 7 Smoking allowed; 8 Children welcome; 9 Social drinking allowed; 10 Tennis available; 11 Swimming available; 12 Golf available; 13 Skiing available; 14 May be booked through travel agents.

Hosts: Phillis and Ramon Gonzalez
Rooms: 4 (3 PB; 1 SB) $85 plus tax
Full Country Breakfast
Credit Cards: None
Notes: 2, 3, 4, 5, 9, 14

McKay House
Bed and Breakfast Inn

306 East Delta Street, 75657
(903) 665-7322; (903) 348-1929 (Dallas)

Jefferson is a riverport town from the frontier days of the Republic of Texas. It has historical mule-drawn tours, 30 antique shops, boat rides on the river, and a narrow-gauge train. The McKay House, a recently restored 1851 Greek Revival cottage, offers period furnishings, cool lemonade, porch swings, fireplaces, and a full gentleman's breakfast. Hospitality abounds, and Victorian nightclothes are provided.

Owner: Peggy Taylor
Innkeeper: Alma Anne Parker
Rooms: 7 (PB) $70-125
Full Breakfast
Credit Cards: A, B
Notes: 2, 5, 9, 12, 14

Pride House

409 Broadway, 75657
(903) 665-2675

The oldest and first bed and breakfast in the state of Texas, Pride House offers ten rooms, all with private baths and are furnished with inherited family Victorian antiques. Large, sunny breakfast room that is also used for small business conferences is where a full breakfast, made from Ruth's famous recipes, is served. Temperature is maintained by central heat and air, and the morning sun shines through original stained-glass windows of this 1888 Victorian mansion. King and queen beds. Telephones and TVs by request.

Host: Ruthmary Jordan
Rooms: 10 (PB) $65-100
Full Breakfast

Credit Cards: A, B
Notes: 2, 5, 7, 8, 9, 14

Rowell House

301 South Alley Street, 75657
(903) 665-2634

Sip a glass of lemonade while enjoying the front porch rocking chairs of this historic residence in the historic district. This 1858 home is within walking distance of major attactions. Gourmet breakfasts and afternoon refreshments. Guest rooms have king or queen bed, TV, and coffee maker. Required two-night stay on holidays and weekends.

Hosts: Collie and Brooks Parker
Rooms: 2 (PB) $65-75
Full Breakfast
Credit Cards: A, B
Notes: 2, 5, 8, 9, 14

JOHNSON CITY

Hoppe's Guest House

Bed and Breakfast Hosts of San Antonio
166 Rockhill, San Antonio, 78209
(512) 824-8036

This charming, turn-of-the-century restoration in a quiet neighborhood provides two bedrooms, one with a queen-size bed and the other with a double bed. The rooms share a bath. $55.

Wise Manor

312 Houston Street, 75657
(214) 665-2386

A gem of a Victorian home that looks as if it has just stepped out of a fairy tale. The little two-story cottage is painted in salmon tones with crisp, white gingerbread trim. Surrounded by large pecan trees, it peers out from behind a wrought-iron fence. It is furnished in Victorian pieces with marble-top tables and ruffled curtains at the windows. Antique white bedspreads and folded appliqued quilts adorn the ornate walnut beds.

NOTES: Credit cards accepted: A Master Card; B Visa; C American Express; D Discover Card; E Diner's Club; F Other; 2 Personal Checks accepted; 3 Lunch available; 4 Dinner available; 5 Open all year;

Host: Katherine Ramsay Wise
Rooms: 3 (2 PB; 1 SB) $30-55
Credit Cards: A, B
Notes: 2, 5, 7, 8, 9

LA COSTE

Swan and Railway Inn

Bed and Breakfast Texas Style
4224 West Red Bird Lane, Dallas, 75237
(214) 298-8586

At one time it was known as the City Hotel
and had only three guest bedrooms. It now
has five, three with private bath. A separate
historical building that has been added
behind the new pool contains a therapeutic
hot tub, a Scandinavian sauna, exercise
equipment, and room for aerobics classes.
Breakfast may be yogurt and granola or
bran muffins, fruit, and herb teas. About
18-20 minutes from San Antonio; 10 from
Sea World. La Coste was a French settlement, and nearby Castroville has German
roots. $55-65.

LAREDO

The Allen House Bed & Breakfast

Bed and Breakfast Hosts of San Antonio
166 Rockhill, San Antonio, 78209
(512) 824-8036

Only a five-minute drive from Mexico, this
beautifully decorated bed and breakfast is
furnished with family heirlooms, antiques,
and treasured collectibles. There are four
guest rooms, two with private baths and
two sharing a bath. Guests are encouraged
to make themselves at home in the sitting
room and the parlor with a baby grand
piano. The breakfast menu varies but
always includes homemade breads, an
abundance of fresh fruit, and homemade
granola. $50-95.

Fraser House

Bed and Breakfast Texas Style
4224 West Red Bird Lane, Dallas, 75237
(214) 298-8586

Enjoy the four upstairs guest bedrooms of
this 1900 solid granite house located in the
middle of town. The bedrooms have private
baths with claw foot tubs, a sleigh bed, a
Jenny Lind bed, and iron beds. A ham and
quiche breakfast along with complimentary
mimosas will be served. $55-65.

MADISONVILLE

Ranch 102

Bed and Breakfast Texas Style
4224 West Red Bird Lane, Dallas, 75237
(214) 298-8586

This charming log home was built by the
hosts as a getaway home about eight years
ago. Ranch 102 is heated by a Ben Franklin
stove which produces ample heat for the
loft and three rooms downstairs. The full,
well-stocked kitchen includes a microwave.
Television, VCR, and lots of movies are
provided for guests. Guests are invited to
fish in the seven-acre lake and to walk
around the farm. The hosts will serve a full
breakfst. $95.

MARBLE FALLS

La Casita

1908 Redwood Drive, 78654
(512) 598-6443

Nestled 50 feet behind the main house, this
private cottage is rustic and Texan on the
outside yet thoroughly modern inside.
Native Texan hosts can suggest parks,
wineries, and river cruises. However, relaxing and bird watching in a country setting
are the main attractions here. Guests

choose their entree with a full breakfast. Laundry facilities available. Brochure available.

Hosts: Joanne and Roger Scarborough
Rooms: 1 (PB) $60
Full Breakfast
Credit Cards: None
Notes: 2, 5, 8, 9, 11, 12, 14

MERIDIAN

The Hastings House

Bed and Breakfast Texas Style
4224 West Red Bird Lane, Dallas, 75237
(214) 298-8586

This charming older home is on a farm near Meridian, just south of Fort Worth and Dallas. Not far from Lake Whitney. The farmhouse is about 60 years old and has a large front porch, three bedrooms, livingroom, breakfast nook, and kitchen. There is a large bath. Breakfast is left in the refrigerator for guests to prepare. Local attractions include the Safari in nearby Clifton, the Dinosaur Tracks Park in Glenrose, and the pageant The Promise in Glenrose on weekends. $65.

MINEOLA

Munzesheimer Manor

202 North Newsom, 75773
(903) 569-6634

This 1898 Victorian is a short walk to downtown shopping with antiques, boutiques, restored buildings, and friendly people. Totally restored in 1987, this home welcomes you to take a very special trip into the past. Complete with central heat and air, seven fireplaces, and a wraparound porch. Furnished with antiques. Fresh flowers, Victorian nightshirts, sparkling cider, and turndown service are but a few of the amenities. Near First Monday/Trade Days in Canton, area parks and lakes, theater and music parlor concerts.

Hosts: Bob and Sherry Murray
Rooms: 7 (PB) $65-90
Full Breakfast
Credit Cards: A, B, D, E
Notes: 2, 5,10, 12, 14

NEW BRAUNFELS

Lillian B's Bed and Breakfast

322 Lakeview Terrace, 78130
(512) 629-0750

Enjoy Victorian elegance while experiencing wonderful weather, sparkling-clean spring-fed rivers, antique shops, and wonderful German atmosphere. Two beautifully appointed bedrooms with private baths in this 1889 Victorian cottage, just 20 minutes from San Antonio.

Hosts: John and Betty Paine
Rooms: 2 (PB) $60
Continental Breakfast
Credit Cards: None
Notes: 2, 5, 10, 11, 12

Danville School and Historic Waldrip Haus

1620 Hueco Springs Loop Road, 78132
(512) 625-8372; (800) 299-8372

This secluded 43-acre ranch is five minutes from the Guadalupe and Comal rivers, Gruene Historical District, Schlitterbahn, and New Braunfels. Genuine friendship and hospitality are yours with a delightful stay in two fully restored pioneer buildings with fireplace and wood burning stove. All rooms have private baths. In a shaded yard, a pet deer may eat from your hand and the resident champion registered bloodhound will try to get acquainted with you.

Hosts: Margy Waldrip and Darrell Waldrip
Rooms: 7 (7 PB; 1 SB with whirlpool) $79-105
Full Breakfast
Credit Cards: A, B, C, D
Notes: 2, 5, 8, 9

NOTES: Credit cards accepted: A Master Card; B Visa; C American Express; D Discover Card; E Diner's Club; F Other; 2 Personal Checks accepted; 3 Lunch available; 4 Dinner available; 5 Open all year;

PALESTINE

Grandma's House

Bed and Breakfast Texas Style
4224 West Red Bird Lane, Dallas, 75237
(214) 298-8586

Nestled in the heart of east Texas is a country Christmas tree farm with a guest house furnished with twin beds and private bath. Relax on the front porch, stroll among the Christmas trees, or ride a paddleboat around the pond. Hearty breakfast of homemade bread, jellies, fresh farm eggs, quail, and gravy. Convenient to antique shopping, historical sites, spring dogwood trails, and fall foliage. Just 30 minutes to the East Texas Historical Train Ride at Palestine or Rusk, Canton's First Monday Trades Day, and Athens Black-eyed Pea Jamboree. $50.

The Sunday House

Bed and Breakfast Texas Style
4224 West Red Bird Lane, Dallas, 75237
(214) 298-8586

A charming duplex with two bedrooms, large parlor, full kitchen, and shared hall bath is a classic brick residence near downtown. Near the historic Texas Steam Train and the Dogwood Trails in spring, Palestine is a quaint town filled with many historic homes. A continental breakfast is left in the kitchen for guests to prepare, or they may drive to the Christmas Tree Farm about 12 miles away and partake of the full Texas country breakfast. $50.

PLANO

Los Rios

Bed and Breakfast Texas Style
4224 West Red Bird Lane, Dallas, 75237
(214) 298-8586

Exclusive residential area in east Plano, the hot-air balloon capital of Texas. One bedroom has lovely cherry furniture, double bed, and private bath. A second room has twin beds. Three miles to Southfork Ranch. Tennis courts and golf course nearby. Full breakfast is served. No smoking. $50.

PORT ARANSAS

Harbor View Bed and Breakfast

Sand Dollar Hospitality
3605 Mendenhall, Corpus Christi, 78415
(512) 853-1222

This three-story Mediteranean-style home on the Port Aransas Municipal Harbor offers three large bedrooms with private baths and a third-floor suite. On each of the three levels the decks and balconies afford a beautiful, unobstructed view of the harbor. The inn is within convenient walking distance of restaurants, shops, charter boats, and fishing operations. On-site mooring facilities are available for craft up to 50 feet in length. $70-75.

PORT ISABEL

Yacht Club Hotel and Restaurant

700 Yturria Street, 78578
(512) 943-1301

Since 1926, the Yacht Club Hotel and Restaurant has provided its guests with fine dining in the casual atmosphere of the 1920s and 1930s. There are 24 cozy rooms that overlook the harbor. Come fish, beachcomb, and visit Mexico, or relax and sip margaritas on the veranda. The award-winning chef serves fresh seafood, steaks, and pasta.

Host: Lynn Speter
Rooms: 24 (PB) $30-69
Continental Breakfast
Credit Cards: A, B, C, E
Notes: 4, 5, 8, 9, 11, 14

---

6 Pets welcome; 7 Smoking allowed; 8 Children welcome; 9 Social drinking allowed; 10 Tennis available; 11 Swimming available; 12 Golf available; 13 Skiing available; 14 May be booked through travel agents.

RIO MEDINA

Haby Settlement Inn

Bed and Breakfast Hosts of San Antonio
166 Rockhill, San Antonio, 78209
(512) 824-8036

Cottage in beautiful rural setting lovingly restored has one bedroom, bath, livingroom with sleeper sofa, dining room, and kitchen. Adults only. $65.

ROUND ROCK

St. Charles
Bed and Breakfast

Bed and Breakfast Texas Style
4224 West Red Bird Lane, Dallas, 75237
(214) 298-8586

Once a mercantile store and the Brushy Creek post office, this 1854 historic building was restored by the owners. Filled with antiques, this carriage house provides a romantic setting for guests. Enjoy the mock fireplace, armoire, handmade quilt, claw foot tub, and many other collectibles. Breakfast will be a gourmet treat that can be enjoyed in the carriage house or in the main house. Children are welcome. $70.

ROUND TOP

Broomfields

Route 1, Box 30, 78954
(409) 249-3706; FAX (713) 493-9159

Country retreat five miles from Round Top on 40 acres of meadowland with wooded tracts and stocked pond. Historic restorations, classical music, and semiannual antique shows nearby. Spectacular displays of wildflowers in spring and foliage in fall. An 1800s Texas-vernacular modern home built with 100-year-old barn beams and furnished with selected European and American antiques. Comfortable, well-appointed rooms and baths. Suppers and picnic lunches may be booked in advance.

Hosts: Julia and Bill Bishop
Rooms: 3 (1 PB; 2 SB) $60-90
Full Breakfast
Credit Cards: None
Notes: 2, 3, 4, 5, 9, 10, 12

SALADO

Halley House
Bed and Breakfast

North Main Street, 76571
(817) 947-1000

Come join your hosts for a relaxing retreat away from that corporate world, hustle and bustle of traffic and tension. The beds are superb, and the breakfast is one you will talk about for years to come. All rooms are appointed with the cozy antiques of this 1860s Greek Revival home built and owned by the Hally family many years ago. A gathering room is available for those special occasions, seating up to 150 people.

Hosts: Larry and Cathy Sands
Rooms: 7 (PB) $70-105
Full Breakfast
Credit Cards: A, B, D
Notes: 2, 5, 10, 11, 12

SAN ANTONIO

Alan's Guest House

Bed and Breakfast Hosts of San Antonio
166 Rockhill, 78209
(512) 824-8036

Located in the King William area, Alan's Guest House has all the modern conveniences. Loft bedroom with twin beds, downstairs bedroom with double bed and private bath. Sofa bed in livingroom and full kitchen with continental breakfast provided. Original portion of home was built in 1871. Two bicycles are available. $70-100.

NOTES: Credit cards accepted: A Master Card; B Visa; C American Express; D Discover Card; E Diner's Club; F Other; 2 Personal Checks accepted; 3 Lunch available; 4 Dinner available; 5 Open all year;

Beauregard House Bed and Breakfast

Bed and Breakfast Hosts of San Antonio
166 Rockhill, 78209
(512) 824-8036

Charming Victorian home built in 1910, with hardwood floors and period furnishings. Two downstairs rooms with queen beds share a bath. One of these rooms has a separate kitchen and private entrance. The upstairs room has twin beds and a private bath. Breakfast is served in the dining room, tree-shaded back yard deck, or spacious front porch. Laundry facilities available. $60-75.

Beckman Inn and Carriage House

222 E. Guenther Street, 78204
(210) 229-1449

This charming Victorian is in the heart of San Antonio in the King William district. The beautiful wraparound porch welcomes guests to this cozy home. Guest rooms are colorfully decorated featuring antique Victorian queen-size beds and private baths. Stroll leisurely on the scenic river walk or ride the trolley to enjoy all of the festivities.

Hosts: Betty Jo and Don Schwartz
Rooms: 5 (PB) $80-120
Gourmet Continental Breakfast
Credit Cards: A, B
Notes: 2, 5

Bed and Breakfast Hosts of San Antonio #6

166 Rockhill, 78209
(512) 824-8036

This restored turn-of-the-century Victorian offers an upstairs bedroom with queen bed and adjoining private bath. A second upstairs bedroom has a double bed and private hallway bath. Each bedroom opens onto its own charming private porch. Continental breakfast is served in the dining room or on the porch. One-half block from Ten Cent Trolley and VIA bus that take you to the Alamo, River Walk, the Old Market, and many other downtown attractions. $60.

Bed and Breakfast Hosts of San Antonio C

166 Rockhill, 78209
(512) 824-8036

New, modern upstairs guest house in Cross Mountain Ranch subdivision in the northwest hills on more than two acres. The main house is Hill Country style white rock and cedar. Outdoor spa. Livingroom, bedroom, kitchen, dinette, full bath. One double bed, day bed, and trundle. Central heat and air-conditioning. Airport transportation may be arranged. Children welcome. Pets permitted outside. Breakfast provided in guest quarters. $60.

Bed and Breakfast Hosts of San Antonio E

166 Rockhill, 78209
(512) 824-8036

Attractively furnished upstairs apartment near Trinity University with TV, stereo, telephone, and ample parking. One bedroom with four-poster, canopy bed; twin beds in dining/sitting area. Full bath. Linens and towels provided. The fully equipped kitchen is stocked with continental breakfast treats for guests to prepare at any time. Centrally situated in a prestigious neighborhood, yet only three doors to shopping center and VIA bus to downtown in minutes. Older children welcome. Call for current rates.

6 Pets welcome; 7 Smoking allowed; 8 Children welcome; 9 Social drinking allowed; 10 Tennis available; 11 Swimming available; 12 Golf available; 13 Skiing available; 14 May be booked through travel agents.

Bed and Breakfast on the River

Bed and Breakfast Hosts of San Antonio
166 Rockhill, 78209
(512) 824-8036

Restored Victorian right on the river in downtown. All rooms feature queen beds and private baths. Some rooms have adjoining sitting room overlooking the river. Special continental breakfast is provided. The host, Dr. Zucht, is a licensed hot-air balloon pilot who can arrange for charter flight for guests or anyone visiting San Antonio. $99.

The Belle of Monte Vista

505 Belknap Place, 78212
(512) 732-4006

J. Riely Gordon designed this Queen Anne-style Victorian as a model house. Built in 1890 with limestone, the house has been beautifully restored and is located in the elegant Monte Vista historic district. Inside, you'll find eight fireplaces, stained-glass windows, a hand-carved oak staircase, and Victorian furnishings. Mary Lou and Jim serve a full southern breakfast and are happy to help you plan your day.

Hosts: Mary Lou and Kim Davis
Rooms: 5 (4S2B) $50 plus tax
Full Breakfast
Credit Cards: F
Notes: 2, 5, 8, 9

Beauregard House Bed and Breakfast

Bed and Breakfast Hosts of San Antonio
166 Rockhill, 78209
(512) 824-8036

This charming Victorian home was built in 1910 with hardwood floors and furnishings appropriate to the ear. Downstairs room has queen bed, private bath and entrance. The two upstairs guest rooms have king beds and private baths. Breakfast is served in the dining room, on the tree-shaded backyard deck, or on the spacious front porch - whichever the guest preferred. $60-75.

The Bonner Garden

Bed and Breakfast Hosts of San Antonio
166 Rockhill, 78209
(512) 824-8036

This bed and breakfast is a large Italian-style villa in the Monte Vista area. Stroll in the garden, relax on the rooftop, or swim in the beautiful pool surrounded by flowers and shrubs in full bloom. Three guest rooms with private bath in the main house and a private detached studio. This was the home of Mary Bonner, renowned artist. Call for current rates.

Bullis House Inn

621 Pierce Street, P. O. Box 8059, 78208
(512) 223-9426

Lovely, historic, white-columned mansion with wide veranda, swimming pool, spacious guest rooms with fireplaces. Downstairs parlors have decorative 14-foot plaster ceilings, marble fireplaces, lovely patterned wood floors, and more. Weekend and honeymoon packages available.

Hosts: Steve and Alma Cross
Rooms: 8 (2 PB; 6 SB) $36-69
Continental Breakfast
Credit Cards: A, B, C, D
Notes: 5, 7, 8, 9, 10, 11, 14

Buttercup Bed and Breakfast

Bed and Breakfast Hosts of San Antonio
166 Rockhill, 78209
(512) 824-8036

Spacious guest cottage centrally situated on one acre in a quiet Alamo Heights neighborhood. Two blocks to shopping center, VIA bus to downtown in minutes. Airport transportation provided. Landscaped

---

NOTES: Credit cards accepted: A Master Card; B Visa; C American Express; D Discover Card; E Diner's Club; F Other; 2 Personal Checks accepted; 3 Lunch available; 4 Dinner available; 5 Open all year;

grounds and extensive playground equipment make this home ideal for children of all ages. Private cottage consists of one bedroom with twin beds and adjoining bath, second bedroom with double bed and sitting area. Private bath in hallway. Hosts provide a special breakfast in the cottage kitchen for guests to serve themselves. Guests may use the kitchen and game room with pool table. No smoking. $115.

Chabot Reed House

403 Madison, 78204
(512) 223-8697

The Chabot Reed House is an 1876 Victorian house located one block from the Riverwalk in the King William Historical District in downtown San Antonio. A special treat is staying in the Carriage House where two guest suites are located. Luxurious, yet comfortable; bold and colorful with an appropriate sense of history and sophistication. Private and romantic, the Carriage House is situated on the lovely landscaped grounds to the side of the main house. Guests are welcomed in the manor house as well.

Hosts: Sister and Peter Reed
Rooms: 5 (4 PB; 1 SB) $95-105
Full Breakfast
Credit Cards: None
Notes: 2, 5, 8 (over 12), 9, 14

Cross Mountain Ranch

Bed and Breakfast Hosts of San Antonio
166 Rockhill, 78209
(512) 824-8036

This modern upstairs guest house in the northwest hills of San Antonio set on 2.2 acres land provides a livingroom, bedroom, kitchen, dinette, and full bath. Central heat and air conditioning. Children are welcome. Pets permitted outside. $60.

Doddie Furrh's

Bed and Breakfast Hosts of San Antonio
166 Rockhill, 78209
(512) 824-8036

This attractive upstairs apartment near Trinity University is furnished with a brass bed in bedroom, sofa bed in the livingroom, and twin bed in dining-sitting area, plus TV, stero, telephone, and ample parking. Older children are welcome. Maid service weekly; two-night minimum. $60. Weekly rate: $250.

Falling Pines Inn

300 West French Place, 78212
(512) 733-1998

Falling Pines is in the Monte Vista Historic District one mile north of downtown San Antonio. Construction of the home began in 1911 under the direction of famed architect Atlee Ayres. Pine trees, not native to San Antonio, tower over the mansion on a one-acre parklike setting. Of brick and limestone construction, a green tiled roof, and shuttered windows enhance a magnificent limestone archway entry and veranda on the front facade. The guest rooms are on the second level. The entire third floor is the Persian Suite which commands a grand view of downtown San Antonio.

Hosts: Grace and Bob Daubert
Rooms: 4 (PB) $75-105
Full Breakfast
Credit Cards: A, B, C
Notes: 2, 5, 8, 9, 10, 12, 14

The Gatlin House

Bed and Breakfast Hosts of San Antonio
166 Rockhill, 78209
(512) 824-8036

This beautifully restored turn-of-the-century Victorian home is furnished with lovely antiques. The first upstairs bedroom has a queen bed and adjoining private bath; the second has a double bed and private hall-

---

6 Pets welcome; 7 Smoking allowed; 8 Children welcome; 9 Social drinking allowed; 10 Tennis available; 11 Swimming available; 12 Golf available; 13 Skiing available; 14 May be booked through travel agents.

way bath. Each bedroom opens onto its own private porch. Continental breakfast. One-half block from Ten Cent Trolley and VIA bus. $60.

Linden House

Bed and Breakfast Hosts of San Antonio
166 Rockhill, 78209
(512) 824-8036

Twelve blocks north of downtown, this house was built in 1902 by Judge Linden, a colorful character with a peg leg who rode posse with the best of them to pursue notorious criminals and bandits in South Texas. The present owners offer four second-floor bedrooms, each with adjacent private bath. A generous continental breakfast is served in the coffee room. TV is available. Airport transportaiton. Convenient to downtown, only two blocks from the Ten Cent Trolley to downtown. No smoking. Older children welcome. $60.

Naegelin Bed and Breakfast

Bed and Breakfast Hosts of San Antonio
166 Rockhill, 78209
(512) 824-8036

Situated in the La Vaca historic district of San Antonio adjacent to all downtown attractions, this Colonial brick home with Corinthian columns was built in 1910 and carefully restored and furnished in Victorian style. A special continental breakfast is served in the dining room. Four guest rooms, one with private bath. $55-70.

Norton Brackenridge House

230 Madison, 78204
(512) 271-3442

This is an 80-year-old fully restored home in the King William historic district, the oldest historic district in Texas. It is a two-story house with Corinthian columns, and verandas on the front and back. It is decorated with Victorian antiques and has private entrances and baths, central air and heat, fans in all rooms. A full gourmet breakfast is served on the veranda or in the dining room.

Host: Nancy Cole
Rooms: 5 (PB) $75-95
Full Breakfast
Credit Cards: A, B, C, D
Notes: 2, 5, 7 (on verondas only), 14

Nunez Home

Bed and Breakfast Hosts of San Antonio
166 Rockhill,　78209
(512) 824-8036

The Nunez Home is near all downtown San Antonio attractions. Our European guests have been very appreciative of this charming couple's knowledge of San Antonio and enjoy being welcomed as true friends into their restored family Victorian Home. They have an upstairs bedroom with a double bed and a single bed with a private bath in the hallway. Airport transportation upon request. $35-45.

The Ogé House on the Riverwalk

209 Washington Street, 78204
(800) 242-2770; FAX (512) 226-5812

Step back to an era of elegance and romance in this historic antebellum mansion shaded by massive pecans and oaks, graciously situated on one and one-half landscaped acres along the banks of the famous San Antonio Riverwalk. The inn, beautifully decorated with antiques, has large verandas with antiques and a grand foyer. All rooms have either queen or king beds, private baths, air conditioning, telephones, and televisions. Dining, entertainment, convention centers, trolley, and the Alamo are steps away.

Hosts: Patrick and Sharrie Magatagan
Rooms: 10 (PB) $115-185
Continental Breakfast
Credit Cards: A, B, C
Notes: 2, 5, 7 (outside), 9, 14

Romantic Hideaway

Bed and Breakfast Texas Style
4224 West Red Bird Lane, Dallas, 75237
(214) 298-8586

In a secluded area just 20-30 minutes west
of San Antonio in the Hill Country lies this
separate apartment that is perfect for a getaway from the city. There are three beds, a
double and two singles, and a private bath.
Breakfast fixings are left in the refrigerator
in the well-stocked kitchen. The hosts will
escort guests to Sea World and get them
discount fares. Smoking outside only. Pets
welcome but must be restrained as there are
dogs in residence. Children are welcome if
families want to take advantage of this special offer. $60 nightly; $250 weekly.

Sartor House

217 King William, 78204
(512) 227-5770

This 1880 stone house is near downtown
Riverwalk in a residential historic district.
Antiques, magic swing on a fifty-foot,
magnolia-shaded front porch. Suite with a
kitchenette sleeps four. Good library and
piano, TV, and telephone. Superb breakfasts concocted of southern, historic,
Mexican, and western recipes. Low cal or
low cholesterol diets accommodated.
Consideration for extended stays, corporate
rates, senior citizens. Off-street parking.

Host: Julia Cauthorn
Rooms: 2 (PB) $95-120
Full Breakfast
Credit Cards: None

Sharecropper's Cabin

Bed and Breakfast Hosts of San Antonio
166 Rockhill, 78209
(512) 824-8036

One of the earliest stone structures built in
San Antonio, Sharecropper's Cabin has
been carefully restored. The one guest
room has an iron double bed and a fireplace
opening; the private bath has a footed tub
and shower. Six blocks from the River
Walk, one block from the Ten Cent Trolley.
Infants are welcome. No smoking. $80.

Summit Haus I and II

Bed and Breakfast Hosts of San Antonio
166 Rockhill, 78209
(512) 824-8036

These two renovated 1920s residences–side
by side–are in the historic Monte Vista
area. The main residence provides a suite
with king-size bed and a full bath, with a
double bed in the adjoining sun room. The
cottage has two large bedrooms, one with a
king-size bed and the other with a double
bed. Summit Haus I is furnished with
German Biedermier antiques, crystal,
linens, porcelains, and antique Persian and
Turkish rugs. Summit Haus II is furnished
with French and English antiques. $70.

Terrell Castle
Bed and Breakfast

Bed and Breakfast Hosts of San Antonio
166 Rockhill, 78209
(512) 824-8036

Terrell Castle was built in 1894 as the residence of Edwin Holland Terrell, who
served as ambassador to Belgium in the
early 1890s. A full breakfast is served in
the dining room. No charge for children
under six. A variety of rooms and suites
are available on the second and third floors
of this mansion, which was inspired by the
beauty of the castles and chateaux of
Europe. $70-100 plus tax.

6 Pets welcome; 7 Smoking allowed; 8 Children welcome; 9 Social drinking allowed; 10 Tennis available; 11
Swimming available; 12 Golf available; 13 Skiing available; 14 May be booked through travel agents.

Vintage Lace

Bed and Breakfast Hosts of San Antonio
166 Rockhill, 78209
(512) 824-8036

This exceptional home in the historic district has wood-burning fireplaces, a circular front veranda, and authentic period furniture throughout. Catering is avaialble for parties, weddings, and receptions. The Victorian Suite has an attached sitting room with a twin bed. The McCarthy Room has a four-poster bed and access to front and back verandas. Room: $85. Suite: $105.

SAN MARCOS

Crystal River Inn

326 West Hopkins Street, 78666
(512) 396-3739

Romantic, luxurious Victorian mansion that captures the matchless spirit of the Texas Hill Country. Close to headwaters of crystal-clear San Marcos River. Antiques, fireplaces, and fresh flowers adorn the rooms. Wicker-strewn veranda and fountain courtyard offer hours of peaceful rest and relaxation. Enjoy sumptuous brunches including gourmet items such as stuffed French toast and bananas Foster crepes.

Hosts: Mike and Cathy Dillon
Rooms: 12 (10 PB; 2 SB) $50-100
Full Breakfast
Credit Cards: A, B, C, E, F
Notes: 2, 5, 9, 11, 12, 14

SEABROOK

High Tide

Bed and Breakfast Texas Style
4224 West Red Bird Lane, Dallas, 75237
(214) 298-8586

Right on Galveston Bay at the channel where shrimp boats and ocean liners go in and out, this Cape Cod-style cottage is available for families or romantic get-aways. It will sleep seven to nine people with two bedrooms downstairs, each with a private bath. A loft room upstairs with two double beds and a twin bed has a half-bath. A large deck with chairs is perfect for sunning and watching birds and boats. Continental breakfast. $65.

SPRING

McLachlan Farm Bed and Breakfast

P. O. Box 538, 24907 Hardy Road, 77383
(713) 350-2400

The McLachlan family homestead, built in 1911, was restored and enlarged in 1989 by the great-granddaughter, and her husband, of the original McLachlan family who settled the land in 1862. Set back among huge sycamore and pecan trees, it is a quiet oasis that returns you to a time when life was simpler. Visitors can sit on the porch, walk in the woods, or visit Old Town Spring where there are over 100 shops to enjoy.

Hosts: Jim and Joycelyn (McLachlan) Clairmonte
Rooms: 4 (2 PB; 2 SB) $65-75
Full Breakfast
Credit Cards: None
Notes: 2, 5, 14

Crystal River Inn

NOTES: Credit cards accepted: A Master Card; B Visa; C American Express; D Discover Card; E Diner's Club; F Other; 2 Personal Checks accepted; 3 Lunch available; 4 Dinner available; 5 Open all year;

STEPHENVILLE

The Oxford House

563 North Graham Street, 76401
(817) 965-6885

Stephenville is in the northern tip of the beautiful Texas Hill Country. Situated on Highway 67 west of Lake Granbury and east of Proctor Lake. Tarleton State University is in town. Only 30 minutes from Fossil Rim Wildlife Preserve and Dinosaur Valley. The Oxford House was built in 1898 by Judge W. J. Oxford, Sr., and the completely restored, two-story Victorian, presently owned by the grandson of the judge, has antique furnishings. Enjoy a quiet atmosphere and country breakfast. Shopping within walking distance.

Hosts: Bill and Paula Oxford
Rooms: 5 (4 PB; 1 SB) $65-72
Full Breakfast
Credit Cards: A, B
Notes: 2, 4, 5, 7 (limited), 8 (over 10), 9, 11, 12, 14

SUNNYVALE-MESQUITE

The Durant Star Inn

Bed and Breakfast Texas Style
4224 West Red Bird Lane, Dallas, 75237
(214) 298-8586

Antique cars is the theme of this country inn near Dallas. The owner has a fleet of Durant and Star cars that he has restored over the years, and he will be happy to show guests around his museum. The inn is on ten acres of wooded land, with a pond right outside the back door. There are five bedrooms, three upstairs and two downstairs. Three baths are for guest use only. A full breakfast is served in the restored dining room. The spacious downstairs is perfect for corporate seminars, weddings, even family reunions. Children welcome. Smoking limited. $65-75.

The Oxford House

SWEETWATER

The Special Place

Bed and Breakfast Texas Style
4224 West Red Bird Lane, Dallas, 75237
(214) 298-8586

This charming place was a wedding present to a couple in 1916 and continues to stand as a beautiful monument to people in love. There are three guest bedrooms, a nice parlor, and a formal dining room. Guests have the entire house to themselves unless other folks are also visiting. There are two bathrooms. Breakfast is prepared by the hosts and consists of homemade sausage, eggs with picante, fried potatoes, homemade bread, juice, and coffee. $65.

TYLER

Mary's Attic
Bed and Breakfast

413 South College, 75702
(903) 592-5181; FAX (903) 592-3846

A two-bedroom, two-bath 1920 bungalow restored and furnished with English and American antiques on the brick streets in the historical part of Tyler. The continental breakfast features homemade sweet rolls and breads. Refrigerator stocked with complimentary cold drinks, juice, and fresh fruit tray. No smoking. No pets. No children.

Rooms: 2 (PB) $65
Continental Breakfast
Credit Cards: A, B, D
Notes: 2, 5

Rosevine Inn
Bed and Breakfast

415 South Vine, 75702
(903) 592-2221

Rosevine Inn is in the historical Brick Street Shoppes area of Tyler. There are several shops within walking distance and a lovely courtyard with fountain and fireplace. There is also an outdoor hot tub for your enjoyment. Refreshments are served in the late afternoon, and a delectable breakfast awaits you in the morning. Your hosts welcome you to Tyler, the Rose Capital of the World.

Hosts: Bert and Rebecca Powell
Rooms: 4 (PB) $65-75
Full Breakfast
Credit Cards: A, B, C, E
Notes: 2, 5, 8 (over 12), 9, 10, 12, 14

Vintage Farm Home

Bed and Breakfast Texas Style
4224 West Red Bird Lane, Dallas, 75237
(214) 298-8586

This newly renovated, circa 1836-1864 home, once an original dogtrot plantation home, sits in the piney woods of East Texas. Catch the morning sun or evening breeze on the large veranda where rocking charis and a swing invite relaxation. Take a stroll through the trails during dogwood season or fall foliage. The guest room has a king-size bed and private bath. Breakfast is served downstairs in the cozy nook. $75-85.

UTOPIA

Blue Bird Hill
Bed and Breakfast

P. O. Box 206, 78884
(512) 966-3525; (512) 966-2320

The Blue Bird Hill Bed and Breakfast is an early Texas German-style house on a 250-acre ranch with a spring-fed stream. Partake in bird watching, wildlife photography, hiking, river swimming, and rock hunting in a country setting. Relax on a deck, in a hot tub, or in front of a romantic fire. Storytelling. Magnificent fall foliage.

Hosts: B. and Roger Garrison
Rooms: 3 (PB) $65-75
Full Breakfast
Credit Cards: None
Notes: 2, 5, 8, 9, 10, 11

Bluebird Hill Ranch

Bed and Breakfast Texas Style
4224 West Red Bird Lane, Dallas, 75237
(214) 298-8586

A private cabin on a creek in a secluded corner of this 260-acre ranch home is now available for guests. Breakfast will be left in the refrigerator in the complete kitchen. The cabin will accommodate six people. Near Garner State Park and the Frio River, one hour to San Antonio. Two-night minimum stay. Smoking outside. $65.

UVALDE

Casa de Leona
Bed and Breakfast

P. O. Box 1829, 1149 Pearsall Road, 78802
(512) 278-8550

Spanish hacienda on 17 acres of wilderness at Fort Inge historical site on Leona River. Relaxing fountains and a gazebo on the

---

NOTES: Credit cards accepted: A Master Card; B Visa; C American Express; D Discover Card; E Diner's Club; F Other; 2 Personal Checks accepted; 3 Lunch available; 4 Dinner available; 5 Open all year;

river. Also a sun deck. Ideal for weddings, receptions, honeymoons, or small business meetings. All amenities available.

Hosts: Carolyn and Ben Durr
Rooms: 6 (4 PB; 2 SB) $55-76
Full Breakfast
Credit Cards: None
Notes: 2, 5, 9

VAN ALYSTYNE

The Durning House

Bed and Breakfast Texas Style
4224 West Red Bird Lane, Dallas, 75237
(214) 298-8586

Historical home that was an antique shop in the past and is now a bed and breakfast with two guest rooms. The owners will welcome guests and then leave them with complete privacy. Breakfast is homemade cinnamon rolls, juice, and coffee. The room upstairs has a double bed and a small rocking cradle at the foot of the bed. The downstairs room has an antique headboard almost to the ceiling and a double bed. One bath with claw foot tub. Comfortable parlor and dining area downstairs. The hosts will only rent to one couple at a time unless it is a family or two couples traveling together so the bath will be private. $60 one couple; $80 two couples.

VIDOR

Poppa Bear's House

Bed and Breakfast Texas Style
4224 West Red Bird Lane, Dallas, 75237
(214) 298-8586

A warm and loving home near the Louisiana border and Beaumont. Teddy bears are displayed throughout the home. There is a pool for summer fun, fireplace for cozy visiting in winter. Breakfast will be Czech kolaches, homemade cinnamon rolls, juice or fruit, and coffee or tea. Visit the downs in Louisiana or the beach just

south of Beaumont. Two rooms have queen beds, one with private bath. There is one room with a double. No smoking. Children welcome. $55.

WAXAHACHIE

Bonnynook

Bed and Breakfast Texas Style
4224 West Red Bird Lane, Dallas, 75237
(214) 298-8586

This bed and breakfast is in the historical district of the picturesque town of Waxahachie. There are three bedrooms upstairs with private baths. All rooms have double beds with antique headboards. One bed is a lovely sleigh bed. Jacuzzi tub. A Pennsylvania Dutch breakfast including shoofly pie and crepes will be served in the formal dining room. Scarborough Fair is popular in the spring. $70.

Millie's Victorian

Bed and Breakfast Texas Style
4224 West Red Bird Lane, Dallas, 75237
(214) 298-8586

This beautiful Queen Anne-style mansion filled with antiques has a guest bedroom downstairs with a private entrance and a private bath with a claw foot bath tub. Enjoy a full beakfast in the dining room. Another gest area is a private gingerbread cottage located behind the main home. Breakfast will be left in the kitchen of the private cottage. Non-smokers please. $75-150.

WIMBERLEY

Blair House

#1 Spoke Hill, Route #1, Box 122, 78676
(512) 847-8828

The Blair House is nestled on 85 beautiful acres of Texas Hill Country close to San

---

6 Pets welcome; 7 Smoking allowed; 8 Children welcome; 9 Social drinking allowed; 10 Tennis available; 11 Swimming available; 12 Golf available; 13 Skiing available; 14 May be booked through travel agents.

Antonio and Austin. This lovely limestone house has a tile roof, verandas, patios, decks, and hammocks and is ideal for romantic getaways, weddings, small groups, seminars, and rest and relaxation. Enjoy meticulous service, delectable cuisine (dinner is available) and ultimate comfort, as well as a library of great books, CDs, and movies, and a gallery of fine art.

Hostess: Jonnie Stansbury
Rooms: 5 (PB) $85-125
Full Breakfast
Credit Cards: None
Notes: 2, 3, 4, 5, 8, 9, 10, 11, 12

Coleman Canyon Ranch

Bed and Breakfast of Wimberley
P. O. Box 589, 78676
(512) 847-9666; (512) 847-2837

Relax on the front porch swing or hike over this Hill Country ranch, find fossils in the creek bed, or watch deer from the rear deck. Two bedrooms, two baths, livingroom, dining room, kitchen, and library. Four miles north of Wimberley Square. Full breakfast included. Two-night minimum stay holiday and market day weekends. Smoking outdoors only. No pets. Special dietary requirements can be met with advance notice. $100.

Dancing Water Inn

Bed and Breakfast of Wimberley
P. O. Box 589, 78676
(512) 847-9666; (512) 847-2837

Step into a magical, relaxing environment of lush, green meadows painted with wildflowers. Experience the pure blue waters of Jacobs Well. Two native stone homes have been transformed to offer primitive folk art, handcrafted furniture, and exquisite textiles. Four private bedrooms, four fireplaces, four baths, conference room, hot tub, massage therapy by appointment. A full kitchen provides a bountiful breakfast. Gourmet candlelight dinner by reservation.

Swimming, hiking, biking, tennis, golf, sailing, water skiing, horseback riding nearby. $65. Group rates available.

Delafield's Delight

Bed and Breakfast of Wimberley
P. O. Box 589, 78676
(512) 847-9666; (512) 847-2837

This one-bedroom home, located in Eagle Rock, has a large bedroom with a double bed and a trundle bed that sleeps two. Private bath and full kitchen. Relax in front of the wood-burning fireplace. Swimming, paddle boats, horseback riding, fishing, and golf are available nearby. Cook out on an old stone fireplace. $60.

The Homestead Bed and Breakfast

Bed and Breakfast of Wimberley
P. O. Box 589, 78676
(512) 847-9666; (512) 847-2837

The Homestead guest cottages are located directly on Cypress Creek, which is 6 miles long and fed from Jacob's Well. An abundance of wildlife lives in the area. The cottages can accommodate up to 8 adults and are complete with full kitchens, telephone, cable, fireplace, microwave, air-conditioning, heat, and reading material. Continental breakfast is provided. From $55.

J. R. Dobie House

Bed and Breakfast of Wimberley
P. O. Box 589, 78676
(512) 847-9666; (512) 847-2837

This restored, historical cottage is furnished with comfortable antiques: 1890s charm combined with 1990s comfort. Enjoy the wood-burning fireplace with the wood provided by the hosts. Cable TV, telephone, full kitchen, private bath, central air and heat, and picnic facilities are provided. $85.

NOTES: Credit cards accepted: A Master Card; B Visa; C American Express; D Discover Card; E Diner's Club; F Other; 2 Personal Checks accepted; 3 Lunch available; 4 Dinner available; 5 Open all year;

Mountaintop Villa

Bed and Breakfast of Wimberley
P. O. Box 589, 78676
(512) 847-9666; (512) 847-2837

Hilltop home with breathtaking views, indoor swimming pool, 225 square feet of decks on seven and one-half acre of beautiful Texas Hill Country. The house has more than 3,000 square feet and sleeps six people. $125 nightly Sun.-Thurs.; $150 nightly Fri.-Sat.; $800 weekly.

Old Oaks Ranch Bed and Breakfast

P. O. Box 912, 78676
(512) 847-9374

This bed and breakfast offers the warmth of the Texas Hill Country and the delight of well-prepared continental and full breakfasts. There are three unique cottages here: the Chicken House, with one bedroom; the Storehouse, with two bedrooms; and the Barn, with a queen bed and sitting room. Furnished in comfortable antiques and bent willow, Old Oaks is the perfect escape from the hectic pace of the city.

Hosts: Susan and Bill Holt
Rooms: 4 (2 PB; 2 SB) $60-75
Expanded Continental or Full Breakfast
Credit Cards: A, B
Notes: 2, 5, 9, 10, 12, 14

Singing Cypress Gardens Bed and Breakfast

Bed and Breakfast of Wimberley
P. O. Box 589, 78676
(512) 847-9666; (512) 847-2837

This private estate is at the end of Mill Race Lane on Cypress Creek among trees and 600 feet of rolling creek property. Guests enjoy hand-laid rock steps into the creek and the picnic area. You will enjoy the view of 2,000-year-old cypress trees with beautiful Blue Hole Dam and waterfall just off to the left. Linens and kitchen items provided. Continental breakfast and wine are provided in the evening so you won't be disturbed in the morning. Seven guest rooms, some with child and pet restrictions. $65-150.

Wide Horizon

Bed and Breakfast of Wimberley
P. O. Box 589, 78676
(512) 847-9666; (512) 847-2837

Located on Ranch Road 12, south of the Blanco River, this bi-level home offers two very private accommodations, each with private entrance and private bath. The Southwest Suite has a wet bar, color TV, and king-size bed. The Antique Suite has a private sitting room with a Hide-a-couch and a large bedroom with antique double beds. Relax on the large deck that spans the width of the house. No smokers or pets please. $85.

WINNSBORO

Thee Hubbell House

307 West Elm Street, 75494
(903) 342-5629

Thee Hubbell House bed and breakfast is located in beautiful northeast Texas just 90 miles east of Dallas on a two-acre estate with a 104-year-old Colonial two-story with five bedrooms and suites, all of which offer private baths. Common areas include two verandas, gallery, patio, parlor, garden room, and three dining rooms. Accessible to two lakes, six golf courses, and five antique/arts and crafts shopping malls. Southern hospitality at its best.

Hosts: Dan and Laurel Hubbell
Rooms: 5 (PB) $65-150
Full Breakfast
Credit Cards: A, B, C, D, E, F
Notes: 2, 4, 5, 9, 10, 11, 12, 14

---

6 Pets welcome; 7 Smoking allowed; 8 Children welcome; 9 Social drinking allowed; 10 Tennis available; 11 Swimming available; 12 Golf available; 13 Skiing available; 14 May be booked through travel agents.

UTAH

- Salt Lake City
- Park City
- Midway
- Nephi
- Mount Pleasant
- Ephraim
- Moab
- Monroe
- Duck Creek
- Glendale
- St. George
- Kanab

Utah

CEDAR CITY

Paxman Summer House

Bed and Breakfast Rocky Mountains
906 South Pearl Street, Denver, Colorado 80209
(303) 744-8415; (800) 733-8415

The Paxman Summer House is a turn-of-the-century Victorian on a quiet street two blocks from the Shakespeare Festival. Tastefully decorated with antiques. A short drive to Cedar Mountain, Brian Head Ski Resort, Zion National Park, and Bryce Canyon National Park. Local golf course, pool, and tennis courts are nearby. The four rooms all have private baths. Smoking permitted outside.

DUCK CREEK

Meadeau View Lodge

P. O. Box 356, Cedar City, 84720
(801) 682-2495

Situated in the triangle reaching from Cedar Breaks to Bryce Canyon to Zion Park. Hiking, fishing, bicycling, snowmobiling, cross-country skiing, or just relaxing. Quiet, homey atmosphere. Nine rooms with private baths. Families welcome. Dinner by advance reservation. Twenty-nine miles east of Cedar City on Highway 14; ten miles west of Highway 89.

Hosts: Val and Harris Torbenson
Rooms: 9 (PB) $50-60
Full Breakfast
Credit Cards: A, B
Notes: 2, 3, 4, 5, 6, 7 (limited), 8, 9, 13, 14

EPHRAIM

Ephraim Homestead Bed and Breakfast

135 West 100 North (43-2), 84627
(801) 283-6367

Reminiscent of homesteads from the pioneer settlement period, Ephraim Homestead offers private lodging in either an 1860s log cabin or an 1880s Victorian cottage. Both are furnished with antiques and surrounded with beautiful old-fashioned gardens. A large country breakfast is cooked on a century-old cookstove and served privately to guests in their own overnight cottage. Also, a delicious nighttime treat is provided. Children of all ages are welcome. Truly a unique and memorable experience.

Hosts: Sherron and McKay Andreasen
Cottages: 2 (PB) $50-75 ($15 more, October-March)
Full Breakfast
Credit Cards: None
Notes: 2, 5, 8, 10, 11, 12, 13 (cross-country)

GLENDALE

Smith Hotel

Highway 89, P. O. Box 106, 84729
(801) 648-2156

Historic hotel built in 1927 by descendants of Mormon settlers in the town of Glendale. Has western charm; screened porch overlooking the hills of southern Utah's beautiful Long Valley. Close to the scenic wonders of Zion, Bryce, and Grand

NOTES: Credit cards accepted: A Master Card; B Visa; C American Express; D Discover Card; E Diner's Club; F Other; 2 Personal Checks accepted; 3 Lunch available; 4 Dinner available; 5 Open all year; 6 Pets welcome; 7 Smoking allowed; 8 Children welcome; 9 Social drinking allowed; 10 Tennis available; 11 Swimming available; 12 Golf available; 13 Skiing available; 14 May be booked through travel agents.

Canyon national parks and the recreational facilities of Lake Powell. All rooms have private baths. Late 1800s private family cemetery on property. No smoking rooms available.

Host: Shirley Phelan
Rooms: 7 (PB) $40-55
Continental Breakfast
Credit Cards: A, B
Notes: 2, 9

KANAB

Miss Sophie's Bed and Breakfast

30 North 200 West, 84741
(801) 644-5952

A restored 1800s home with an in-town location. Guest rooms have private bath and are furnished with antiques and queen-size beds. Kanab, hub to many parks, is called Little Hollywood for its western movie production past. Warm days and cool evenings due to 5,000-foot elevation. Fall foliage in mid to late October.

Hosts: Ronald and Aprile Barden
Rooms: 4 (PB) $44
Full Breakfast
Credit Cards: A, B
Open May-Oct.
Notes: 9, 12, 14

MIDWAY

Schneitter Family Hotel at the Homestead Resort

700 North Homestead Drive, 84049
(801) 654-1102; (800) 327-7220

The original Schneitter Family Hotel at the historic Homestead Resort. Eight Victorian rooms individually appointed with antiques, linens, and special amenities. Adjacent solarium and whirlpool. The AAA four-diamond resort offers golf, swimming, horseback riding, tennis, elegant dining, sleigh rides, cross-country ski-ing, snowmobiling, and complete meeting facilities. Restricted smoking.

Host: Britt Mathwich
Rooms: 8 (PB) $85-99
Continental Breakfast
Credit Cards: A, B, C
Notes: 2, 3, 4, 5, 7 (limited), 8, 9, 10, 11, 12, 13, 14

MOAB

Canyon Country Bed and Breakfast

590 North 500 West, 84532
(801) 259-5262

Enjoy the casual atmosphere of this ranch-style home while you experience the magic of canyon country. This home is in a quiet residential setting where guests awake to a medley of birds singing and the smell of fresh country air. A warm southwestern decor, freshly cut flowers in your room, a mint on your pillow, a large yard with patio, barbecue, hot tub, comfortable livingroom, and a travel library are all elements that combine to provide a home away from home atmosphere.

Hosts: Jeanne Lambla and Robert Grupp
Rooms: 5 (4 PB; 1 SB) $58-70
Full Breakfast
Credit Cards: A, B, C, D
Notes: 2, 5, 14

Castle Valley Inn

CVSR Box 2602, 424 Amber Lane, 84532
(801) 259-6012

Castle Valley Inn offers guests sophisticated comfort in the rugged canyonlands of southeast Utah. Its 11 acres of orchards, lawns, and fields feature 360-degree redrock-to-mountaintop views. Visitors enjoy the outdoor Grandview hot tub. The inn offers full meal service to registered guests, with a complete gourmet breakfast included in room rates. No TV; VCR's and film library available. Close to Arches and Canyonlands national parks. Five minutes to Colorado River Canyon.

NOTES: Credit cards accepted: A Master Card; B Visa; C American Express; D Discover Card; E Diner's Club; F Other; 2 Personal Checks accepted; 3 Lunch available; 4 Dinner available; 5 Open all year;

Hosts: Eric and Lynn Thomson
Rooms: 8 (PB) $49-82
Full Breakfast
Credit Cards: A, B
Notes: 2, 3, 4, 5, 12, 14

Whitmore Mansion

MONROE

Petersons
Bed and Breakfast

Box 142, 84754-0142
(801) 527-4830; (800) 336-BNNB

This bed and breakfast is located halfway between Denver and Los Angeles. One guest room has a king-size feather bed, private entrance, bath, refrigerator stocked with cold drinks, and color cable television. The suite has twin beds and a double bed. Near five national parks and four national forests. Three blocks to restaurant.

Hosts: Mary Ann Peterson
Rooms: 3 (2 PB; 1 SB) $45-60
Full Breakfast
Credit Cards: None
Notes: 4, 8, 10, 11, 12, 14

MT. PLEASANT

The Mansion House
Bed and Breakfast Inn

298 South State Street, #13, 84647
(801) 462-3031

The town of Mt. Pleasant, in the heart of rural Utah, was given its name because of the pleasant, open views of the surrounding countryside. The Mansion House was built in 1897 by a prominent sheepman and features a carved oak staircase, hand-painted ceiling, and stained-glass windows.

Hosts: Denis and Terri Andelin
Rooms: 4 (PB) $39-49
Full Breakfast
Credit Cards: A, B
Notes: 2, 5, 9, 11, 13 (cross-country)

NEPHI

The Whitmore Mansion
Bed and Breakfast Inn

110 South Main Street, 84648
(801) 623-2047

This Queen Anne Victorian mansion, built in 1898, represents the warmth and charm of days past. A visit to the mansion is truly a memorable experience. Easy access from I-15; just 85 miles south of Salt Lake City.

Hosts: Bob and Dorothy Gliske
Rooms: 6 (PB) $49.05-70.85
Full Breakfast
Credit Cards: A, B
Notes: 2, 4, 5, 8, 9, 11, 12, 14

PARK CITY

The Old Miners' Lodge

615 Woodside Avenue, Box 2639, 84060
(801) 645-8068; (800) 648-8068

A restored 1893 miners' boarding house in the national historic district of Park City, with ten individually decorated rooms filled with antiques and older pieces. Close to historic Main Street, with the Park City ski area in its back yard, the lodge is "more like staying with friends than at a hotel!" A non-smoking inn.

Hosts: Hugh Daniels, Jeff Sadowsky, Susan
    Wynne
Rooms: 10 (PB) $45-180
Full Breakfast

6 Pets welcome; 7 Smoking allowed; 8 Children welcome; 9 Social drinking allowed; 10 Tennis available; 11 Swimming available; 12 Golf available; 13 Skiing available; 14 May be booked through travel agents.

Minimum stay Christmas: 4-6 nights; US Film: 4
nights; Art: 2 nights
Credit Cards: A, B, C, D
Notes: 2, 5, 8, 9, 10, 11, 12, 13, 14

Snowed Inn

Bed and Breakfast Rocky Mountains
906 South Pearl Street, Denver, Colorado, 80209
(303) 744-8415; (800) 733-8415

Beautiful surroundings, comfort, and
Victorian elegance describe this 10-room
country inn located outside of Park City.
Each room offers a private bath with a
soaking tub, as well as color TV. This is an
excellent location for family reunions, weddings, receptions, and business functions.
Continental breakfast. No pets. Moderate-
luxury rates.

Washington School Inn

P. O. Box 536, 84060
(801) 649-3800; (800) 824-1672

Historical restoration of an old schoolhouse, decorated with modified Victorian.
Hot tub and sauna on the property.
Situated in downtown historic Park City,
close to Salt Lake area airport (45 minutes)
and some of the best skiing in the world.

Hosts: Nancy Beaufait and Delphine Covington
Rooms: 15 (PB) $75-225
Full Breakfast; Continental in summer
Credit Cards: A, B, C, D, F
Notes: 5, 8 (over 12), 9, 10, 11, 12, 13, 14

SAINT GEORGE

Greene Gate Village

76 West Tabernacle Street, 84770
(801) 628-6999; (800) 350-6999

Eight comfortable homes, all dating back to
the time of the pioneers, each lovingly
restored with attention to detail. Greene
Gate Village can cater parties, receptions,
conventions, and family reunions. Close to
Zion, Bryce, and Grand Canyon national

parks. Nine golf courses and skiing in the
area. Mild climate year-round.

Hosts: Mark and Barbara Greene
Rooms: 13 (PB) $40-85
Full Breakfast
Credit Cards: A, B, C
Notes: 2, 3, 4 (Thurs.-Sat.), 5, 8, 9, 10, 11, 12, 13,
14

Seven Wives Inn

217 North 100 West, 84770
(801) 628-3737; (800) 484-1084 code 0165

The inn consists of two adjacent pioneer
adobe homes with massive hand-grained
moldings framing windows and doors.
Bedrooms are furnished in period antiques
and handmade quilts. Some rooms have
fireplaces; one has a whirlpool tub.
Swimming pool on premises.

Hosts: Donna and Jay Curtis; Alison and Jon
Bowcutt
Rooms: 12 (PB) $45-100
Full Breakfast
Credit Cards: A, B, C, E
Notes: 2, 5, 8, 9, 10, 11, 12, 14

Seven Wives Inn

SALT LAKE CITY

Brigham Street Inn

1135 East South Temple, 84102
(801) 364-4461; FAX (801) 521-3201

Brigham Street Inn is a Victorian mansion
built in 1898, done in both traditional and
contemporary design. Minutes away from

NOTES: Credit cards accepted: A Master Card; B Visa; C American Express; D Discover Card; E Diner's
Club; F Other; 2 Personal Checks accepted; 3 Lunch available; 4 Dinner available; 5 Open all year;

Temple Square, downtown, and the University of Utah. Also minutes away from all outdoor activities: hiking, skiing, tennis, and golf.

Hosts: John and Nancy Pace
Rooms: 9 (PB) $75-149
Continental Breakfast
Credit Cards: A, B, C
Notes: 2, 5, 7, 8, 9, 10, 11, 12, 14

The National Historic Bed and Breakfast

Bed and Breakfast Rocky Mountains
906 South Pearl Street, Denver, Colorado 80209
(303) 744-8415; (800) 733-8415

This lovely 100-year-old home is one of the few original Perkins edition structures in the area. Only a twenty-five-minute drive from some of the most beautiful canyons in the Wasatch Range, there are many state parks with well-maintained hiking trails close by, not to mention great skiing. Full gourmet breakfast. No smoking. Moderate-luxury rates.

Peery Hotel

Bed and Breakfast Rocky Mountains
906 South Pearl Street, Denver, Colorado 80209
(303) 744-8415; (800) 733-8415

Enjoy and relax at this hotel in downtown Salt Lake City. The Peery offers a unique blend of elegance and the architectural atmosphere of a bygone era. Within walking distance to the Mormon Temple, seven theaters, 25 restaurants, clubs, and taverns. No pets. Continental-plus breakfast. Moderate-luxury, seasonal rates.

Saltair Bed and Breakfast

Bed and Breakfast Rocky Mountains
906 South Pearl Street, Denver, Colorado 80209
(303) 744-8415;(800) 733-8415

Sunny, cozy, and restful! You'll feel right at home in the warmth of this historic five-bedroom manor house. The handsome antiques, fine woodwork, and unique light fixtures give a turn-of-the-century appeal. Large cut-glass windows let in sunlight from the east and west, keeping parlor and rooms bright all day. Brass and oak beds covered with Amish quilts add to restful nights. Full breakfast. No smoking. No pets. Well-mannered children only. Moderate rates.

The Spruces Bed and Breakfast

Bed and Breakfast Rocky Mountains
906 South Pearl Street, Denver, Colorado 80209
(303) 744-8415; (800) 733-8415

Built in 1903, this bed and breakfast is surrounded by a quarterhorse breeding and training farm. There is an abundance of wildlife in the area, as well as shopping, restaurants, and ski resorts. The inn has four suites with folk art and Southwestern touches. Continental-plus breakfast. No smoking. No pets. Moderate rates.

6 Pets welcome; 7 Smoking allowed; 8 Children welcome; 9 Social drinking allowed; 10 Tennis available; 11 Swimming available; 12 Golf available; 13 Skiing available; 14 May be booked through travel agents.

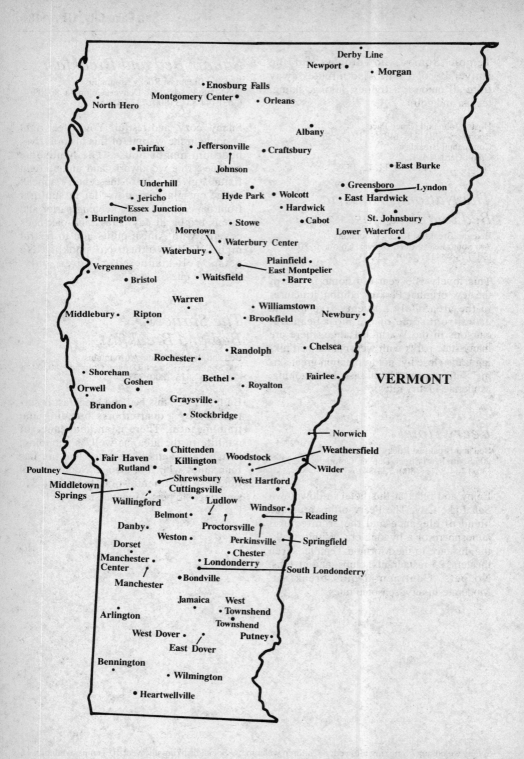

Vermont

ALBURG

Thomas Mott
Bed and Breakfast

Blue Rock Road, Route 2, P. O. Box 149B, 05440
(802) 796-3736; (800) 348-0843

Open all year and hosted by Patrick J.
Schallert, Sr., this completely restored 1838
farmhouse offers four rooms, all with private baths, which overlook Lake Champlain. A full view of the Green mountains
can be enjoyed from this beautifully
restored bed and breakfast, and you are less
than one hour to Burlington and the island
of montreal. Lake activities for all seasons;
Sno-Springers & Vast; game room with
bumper pool and darts. Approved AAA,
AB&BA Yankee management; National
B&B Association. Complimentary Ben and
Jerry's ice cream. Lawn games and R&R.

Host: Patrick J. Schallert, Sr.
Rooms: 4 (PB) $50-70
Full Breakfast
Credit Cards: A, B
Notes: 2, 3, 4, 5, 8 (over 6), 9, 10, 11, 12, 13, 14

ARLINGTON

The Arlington Inn

Historic Route 7A, 05250
(802) 375-6532; (800) 443-9442

An elegant Victorian with antique-filled
guest room in one of Vermont's finest
Greek Revival mansions invites you to
relax and savor award-winning American
cuisine. Enjoy the old-fashioned hospitality
by romantic candlelight surrounded by
lovely antiques. Gourmet menu selections
made with the finest, freshest ingredients,
complemented by an outstanding wine list
will begin a memorable tradition. "One of
Vermont's Special Places."

Hosts: Sandy and Bob Ellis
Rooms: 13 (PB) $60-150
Continental Breakfast
Minimum stay weekends: 2 nights; holidays: 3 nights
Credit Cards: A, B, C, D, E
Notes: 2, 4, 5, 8, 9, 10, 11, 12, 13, 14

The Evergreen Inn

Sandgate Road, Box 2480, 05250
(802) 375-2272

Old-fashioned Colonial country inn in the
Green River Valley and Green Mountains.
Off the beaten path, casual, relaxed atmosphere. Family owned and operated for
more than 50 years. Close to art centers,
summer theaters, antiques, auctions, fairs,
golf courses. Home cooking and baking.

Host: Mathilda Kenny
Rooms: 19 (PB and SB) $50-60
Full Breakfast
Credit Cards: None
Closed Oct. 15-May 15
Notes: 2, 3 (July and Aug.), 4, 6, 7, 8, 9, 10, 11, 12

The Arlington Inn

NOTES: Credit cards accepted: A Master Card; B Visa; C American Express; D Discover Card; E Diner's
Club; F Other; 2 Personal Checks accepted; 3 Lunch available; 4 Dinner available; 5 Open all year; 6 Pets
welcome; 7 Smoking allowed; 8 Children welcome; 9 Social drinking allowed; 10 Tennis available; 11
Swimming available; 12 Golf available; 13 Skiing available; 14 May be booked through travel agents.

Hill Farm Inn

Hill Farm Inn

Rural Route 2, Box 2015, 05250
(802) 375-2269; (800) 882-2545

Visit one of Vermont's original farmsteads
that has also been an inn since 1905. Stay
in a 1790 or 1830 farmhouse and enjoy
hearty home cooking and homegrown vegetables, plus a jar of homemade jam to take
home. Nestled at the foot of Mount
Equinox and surrounded by 50 acres of
farmland with the Battenkill River bordering the lower pasture.

Hosts: George and Joanne Hardy
Rooms: 13 (8 PB; 5 SB) $60-95
Full Breakfast
Minimum stay weekends: 2 nights; holidays: 3 nights
Credit Cards: A, B, C, D
Notes: 2, 4, 5, 7 (limited), 8, 9, 10, 11, 12, 13, 14

Ira Allen House

Rural Delivery 2 Box 2485, 05250
(802) 362-2284

Vermont State Historic Site, home of Ira
Allen (Ethan's brother, who lived here with
him). Norman Rockwell Museum, Robert
Todd Lincoln's Hildene, hiking, canoeing,
biking, skiing, and antiques. Enjoy the
unique experience of a relaxing stay at this
historic inn on the Battenkill River along
with a bountiful home-cooked breakfast.

Hosts: Rowland and Sally Bryant
Rooms: 9 (4 PB; 5 SB) $55-70
Full Breakfast
Credit Cards: A, B, C
Notes: 2, 4 (Sat. in winter), 8 (over 10), 9, 10, 11, 12, 13

West Mountain Inn

West Mountain Road, 05250
(802) 375-6516

Nestled on a mountainside, this century-
old, seven-gable inn invites guests to discover its many treasures. Distinctively decorated guest rooms, comfortable common
areas, 150 woodland acres with wildflowers, a bird sanctuary, and llamas provide
space to relax and rejuvenate the body and
spirit. Miles of wilderness ski or hiking
trails and the Battenkill River provide seasonal outdoor activities. A hearty breakfast
and a savory country dinner in front of an
open hearth complement your stay.

Hosts: Wes and Mary Ann Carlson
Rooms: 15 (PB) $152-179 Modified American
    Plan
Full Breakfast
Credit Cards: A, B, C, D
Notes: 2, 4, 5, 7 (limited), 8, 9, 10, 11, 12, 13, 14

Willow Bed and Breakfast

Route 7A, 05250
(802) 375-9773

A picturesque 1850 Vermont farmhouse
decorated with early American antiques is
nestled on the banks of the Battenkill River
with a magnificent view of the mountains.
Come and let us share a "touch of vermont"
with you.

The Ira Allen House

Host: Jean Pansell
Rooms: 3 (1 PB; 2 SB) $50-60
Full Breakfast
Credit Cards: None
Notes: 2, 5

The Leslie Place

BARRE

Woodruff House

13 East Street, 05641
(802) 476-7745; (802) 479-9381

Large Victorian 1883 home situated on a
quiet park close to downtown shops and
restaurants. Barre is the Granite Center of
the World. Great scenery, fantastic fall
foliage. Halfway between Boston and
Montreal, off I-89. Like coming home to
Grandma's.

Hosts: Robert and Terry Somaini and Katie
Rooms: 2 (PB) $55-65
Full Breakfast
Credit Cards: None
Notes: 2, 5, 8 (over 11), 12, 13

BELLOWS FALLS

The Schoolhouse Inn

Bed and Breakfast Marblehead and North Shore
P. O. Box 35, Newtonville, MA 02160
(617) 964-1606; (800) 832-2632
FAX (617) 332-8572

Situated in the scenic countryside of the
Connecticut River Valley, this country inn
was formerly a schoolhouse for almost a
century before its renovation to a residence.
The common room has original wide floorboards and a magnificent stone fireplace
There are five guest rooms, sharing three
baths. Each room is beautifully decorated
and has a goose-down comforter for cold
nights. A full country breakfast is served on
weekends, continental mid-week. $60-75,
seasonal.

BELMONT

The Leslie Place

P. O. Box 62, 05730
(802) 259-2903; (800) 352-7439

Peacefully set on 100 acres near Weston,
this restored 1840 farmhouse is close to
major ski areas, restaurants, theater, and
shops. Surrounded by mountain views and
meadows, guests will find comfortably spacious rooms creating a welcome retreat.

Host: Mary K. Gorman
Rooms: 4 (PB) $55-65
Full Breakfast
Credit Cards: A, B
Notes: 2, 5, 8, 9, 10, 11, 12, 13

BENNINGTON

The American Country Collection #041

4 Greenwood Lane, Delmar, NY 12054
(518) 439-7001

This carefully landscaped Victorian has a
stream on the back property and a large
front porch for rocking. There's a
wood-burning stove on the brick hearth in
the first-floor common room. Braided rugs
cover wide-plank pine floors. Six guest
rooms, two with private baths. Full
gourmet breakfast includes pancakes,
French toast, eggs, Belgian waffles,

6 Pets welcome; 7 Smoking allowed; 8 Children welcome; 9 Social drinking allowed; 10 Tennis available; 11
Swimming available; 12 Golf available; 13 Skiing available; 14 May be booked through travel agents.

blintzes or quiche. Smoking outdoors only. Children over 11 welcome. $60-90, seasonal.

Molly Stark Inn

1067 East Main Street, 05201
(800) 356-3076

A true country inn with an intimate atmosphere, this 1890 Victorian home is located on the main road through a historic town in southwestern Vermont and welcomes visitors year-round. Decorated and tastefully furnished with antiques, country collectibles, braided rugs on gleaming hardwood floors, and patchwork quilts on the beds. guests are invited to use the wraparound front porch with rocking chairs, and the den and parlor with wood-burning stoves are most inviting on those cool Vermont nights. Clean, affordable, no smoking. Champagne dinner packages available, too.

Host: Reed Fendler
Rooms: 6 (2 PB; 4 SB) $60-80
Full Breakfast
Credit Cards: A, B, C, D
Notes: 2, 4, 5, 8, 9, 14

Greenhurst Inn

BETHEL

Greenhurst Inn

Rural Delivery 2, Box 60, 05032-9404
(802) 234-9474

Queen Anne Victorian mansion listed on the National Register of Historic Places.

Situated in central Vermont near I-89, halfway between Boston and Montreal. Mints on the pillows, Perrier in the rooms, and a library of 3,000 volumes that was featured in The New York Times, March 3, 1991.

Host: Lyle Wolf
Rooms: 13 (7 PB; 6 SB) $50-95
Continental Breakfast
Credit Cards: A, B, D
Notes: 2, 5, 6 (dogs only), 7, 8, 9, 11, 12, 13, 14

BONDVILLE

Alpenrose Inn

Winhall Hollow Road, 05340
(802) 297-2750

Small country inn on a quiet road. All rooms are furnished with antiques, some with canopy beds. Cozy lounge with large fireplace. Free tennis to house guests, golf, horseback riding, and fishing are within minutes. Near ski lifts and the Appalachian Trail.

Host: Rosemarie Strine
Rooms: 7 (PB) $75-98
Full Breakfast
Credit Cards: A, B, C
Notes: 2, 7 (limited), 9, 10, 11, 12, 13

BRANDON

The Brandon Inn

On the Village Green, 05733
(802) 247-5766

Restored 1786 inn on the village green in Brandon, a typical Vermont village. Individually decorated guest rooms have private baths. Relax in the beautifully appointed, spacious public rooms or around the large, secluded pool. Fine dining, outside terrace. Chef owned and operated.

Hosts: Sarah and Louis Pattis
Rooms: 28 (PB) $90-125
Full Breakfast
Minimum stay some weekends: 2 nights
Credit Cards: A, B, C
Notes: 2, 3, 4, 5, 7, 8, 9, 10, 12, 13, 14

NOTES: Credit cards accepted: A Master Card; B Visa; C American Express; D Discover Card; E Diner's Club; F Other; 2 Personal Checks accepted; 3 Lunch available; 4 Dinner available; 5 Open all year;

Churchill House Inn

Rural Route 3, Box 3265, 05733
(802) 247-3078

This charming, century-old country inn at
the edge of the Green Mountain National
Forest is everything a country inn should
be. A blend of original furnishings, antique
pieces, modern bedding, and private baths
provides a homelike and comfortable
atmosphere. Dine by candlelight around the
old oak table, enjoying homemade soups,
breads, and desserts that accompany cre-
atively prepared entrees. Excellent hiking,
biking, fishing, and cross-country skiing
await just outside the door. Sauna and outdoor pool.

Hosts: The Jackson family
Rooms: 8 (PB) $140-170 Modified American Plan
Full Breakfast
Credit Cards: A, B
Notes: 2, 3, 4, 8 (over 5), 9, 11, 12, 13, 14

The Brandon Inn

BRISTOL

Long Run Inn

Rural Delivery 1, Box 560, 05443
(802) 453-3233

Antique-filled country inn built in 1799
near the base of Mount Abraham in
Lincoln. A wraparound rocking-chair
porch overlooks a peaceful trout stream.

Various cuisines are represented in menus
developed and prepared by the innkeepers.
Cross-country skiing, fishing, swimming,
and hiking available. Close to Middlebury
and Burlington attractions.

Hosts: Mike and Bev Conway
Rooms: 8 (SB) $66-76
Full Breakfast
Credit Cards: None
Closed mid-March to mid-May; Nov.-Dec. 30
Notes: 2, 4, 7 (limited), 8 (over 10); 9, 10, 11, 13

BROOKFIELD

Green Trails Country Inn

By the Floating Bridge, 05036
(802) 276-3412; (800) 243-3412

Cozy, relaxing, informal, like going home
to Grandma's. Home-cooked meals at
hearthside, guest rooms decorated with
quilts and antiques. Hiking and biking, with
vistas. In winter, enjoy horse-drawn sleigh
rides, cross-country skiing (34 km. tracked
trails), and fireside friendship. "The epitome of a country inn"—NBC's "Today."
Bed and breakfast or Modifed American
Plan available.

Hosts: Pat and Peter Simpson
Rooms: 15 (9 PB; 6 SB) $68-80
Credit Cards: A, B
Closed April
Notes: 2, 4, 8, 9, 10, 11, 12, 13, 14

BURLINGTON

The American Country Collection #073

4 Greenwood Lane, Delmar, NY 12054
(518) 439-7001

You'll find this turn-of-the-century farmhouse down a country lane on ten acres of
locust and maple trees, gardens, woods,
and pastures. Pillars and three porches
emphasize the Victorian structure. Guests
have a private entrance via a large porch
with rockers. Guest refrigerator, dining
room, and livingroom with fireplace, TV,

6 Pets welcome; 7 Smoking allowed; 8 Children welcome; 9 Social drinking allowed; 10 Tennis available; 11
Swimming available; 12 Golf available; 13 Skiing available; 14 May be booked through travel agents.

VCR, stereo, and pool table. Three immaculate guest rooms are furnished with antiques. Two share a bath. Smoking in the livingroom only. Children over 16 welcome. $70-85.

Creamery Bed and Breakfast

Howden Cottage Bed and Breakfast

32 North Champlain Street, 05401
(802) 864-7198

Howden Cottage offers cozy lodging and warm hospitality in the home of a local artist. Located in downtown Burlington, the house is convenient to shopping, Lake Champlain, movies, night spots, churches, and some of Burlington's best restaurants.

Host: Bruce Howden
Rooms: 2 (SB) $35-45
Continental Breakfast
Credit Cards: A, B
Notes: 5, 9, 10, 11, 12

CABOT

Creamery Bed and Breakfast

P. O. Box 187, 05647
(802) 563-2819

Our spacious and comfortable home is picturesquely set only a mile from the Cabot Creamery. You may walk the country roads, enjoy ponds and waterfalls, drive to Burke Mountain or Stowe for skiing, or just relax. Enjoy our full, homemade breakfast, featuring Finnish pancakes, muffins, and more. We offer special rates for stays of more than two nights.

Host: Dan Lloyd
Rooms: 4 (2 PB; 2 SB) $45-60
Full Breakfast
Credit Cards: None
Notes: 2, 4, 5, 8, 9, 13

CHELSEA

Shire Inn

8 Main Street, 05038
(802) 685-3031

An 1832 historic brick Federal, "Very Vermont" inn. Eighteenth-century accommodations with twentieth-century bathrooms. Small and intimate; some rooms have working fireplaces. Chef-owned and operated, with five-course dining available. Centrally situated: 30 miles north of Woodstock/Queeche; 34 miles to Hanover and Dartmouth; 30 miles south of Montpelier.

Hosts: James and Mary Lee Papa
Rooms: 6 (PB) $65-95
Full Breakfast
Minimum stay weekends and holidays: 2 nights
Credit Cards: A, B
Notes: 2, 4, 5, 8 (over 6), 9, 10, 11, 13

Shire Inn

NOTES: Credit cards accepted: A Master Card; B Visa; C American Express; D Discover Card; E Diner's Club; F Other; 2 Personal Checks accepted; 3 Lunch available; 4 Dinner available; 5 Open all year;

CHESTER

The "Chester House"

P. O. Box 708, Main Street, 05143
(802) 875-2205

A village bed and breakfast inn of extraordinary charm and hospitality. Located on the village green, the home was built in 1780 and is in the National Register of Historic Places. Easy access to skiing, hiking, cycling, antiquing, golf, and just enjoying the beautiful Green Mountains of Vermont. AAA approved.

Hosts: Irene and Norm Wright
Rooms: 4 (PB) $50-75
Full Breakfast
Credit Cards: None
Notes: 2, 5, 9, 10, 11, 12, 13, 14

Greenleaf Inn

Depot Street, Box 188, 05143
(802) 875-3171

Lovely 1880's home, now a comfortable village inn facing an expansive lawn. Just five charming rooms, each with private bath. Art gallery on premises features Vermont scenes—browse or buy. Walk to antiques, village green attractions. Bicycle tourists welcome. Full breakfast in the sunny dining room.

Hosts: Elizabeth and Dan Duffield
Rooms: 5 (PB) $65-70
Full Breakfast
Credit Cards: A, B
Notes: 2, 5, 7, 8 (over 6), 9, 10, 11, 12, 13, 14

Henry Farm Inn

P. O. Box 646, Green Mountain Turnpike, 05143
(802) 875-2674

The Henry Farm Inn provides the beauty of Vermont with old-time simplicity. Nestled on 50 acres of rolling hills and meadows, assuring peace and quiet. Spacious rooms, private baths, country sitting rooms, kitchen, and sunny dining room guarantee a feeling of home. Come visit for a day or more.

Host: J. Bowman
Rooms: 7 (PB) $50-90
Full Breakfast
Credit Cards: A, B
Notes: 2, 5, 7 (limited), 8, 9, 14

The Hugging Bear Inn and Shoppe

Main Street, 05143
(802) 875-2412

Bed, breakfast, and bears. Charming Victorian home on the village green. The shop has over 3,500 bears, and guests may "adopt" a bear for the night as long as he's back to work in the shop by nine the next morning. Puppet show often performed at breakfast; breakfast music provided by an 1890 music box. Two lovable cats in residence. A magical place to visit!

Hosts: The Thomases
Rooms: 6 (PB) $75-95
Full Breakfast
Minimum stay weekends: 2 nights; holidays: 2-3 nights
Credit Cards: A, B, C, D
Notes: 2, 5, 6, 8, 9, 10, 11, 12, 13

The Inn at Long Last

Main Street, P. O. Box 589, 05143
(802) 875-2444

A warm and welcoming inn where all the rooms have individual themes, where the decor is highly personal, and where the staff hospitality is exceptional. Gardens, tennis courts, food, and theme weekends that draw raves. Modified American Plan meals.

Host: Jack Coleman
Rooms: 30 (25 PB; 5 SB) $160
Full Breakfast
Credit Cards: A, B
Notes: 2, 4, 8, 9, 10, 12, 13, 14

The Stone Hearth Inn

Route 11 West, 05143
(802) 875-2525

Built in 1810, the Stone Hearth Inn is widely known for its old-fashioned, informal

6 Pets welcome; 7 Smoking allowed; 8 Children welcome; 9 Social drinking allowed; 10 Tennis available; 11 Swimming available; 12 Golf available; 13 Skiing available; 14 May be booked through travel agents.

Finchingfield Farm

hospitality. All of the guest rooms retain the romance of the period with antique furnishings, exposed beams and wide pine floors. Fully licensed pub, dining room, library, and recreation room with whirlpool spa. Gift shop.

Host: Janet and Don Strohmeyer
Rooms: 10 (PB) $40-95
Full Breakfast
Credit Cards: A, B, D
Notes: 2, 4, 5, 7, 8, 9, 10, 11, 12, 13, 14

CHITTENDEN

Mountain Top Inn

Mountain Top Road, 05737
(802) 483-2311; (800) 445-2100

Nestled amid the picturesque Green Mountains of central Vermont and secluded on a 1,000-acre estate, Mountain Top Inn commands a spectacular view of the lake and surrounding mountains. This warm New England country inn is steeped in the area's finest tradition and has been referred to as "Vermont's best kept secret." Fine dining and recreational facilities, including boating, sailing, windsurfing, canoeing, lake and fly fishing, trapshooting, horseback riding, golf school, 5-hole par-3 golf course, putting green, tennis, mountain biking, heated pool, cross-country skiing (110 km.), ice skating, horse-drawn sleigh rides, and winter horseback riding are available on premises.

Host: William Wolfe
Rooms: 33 (PB) $118-260
Full Breakfast
Credit Cards: A, B, C
Notes: 2, 3, 4, 5, 7, 8, 9, 10, 11, 12, 13, 14

CRAFTSBURY

Finchingfield Farm Bed and Breakfast

Rural Route 1, P. O. Box 1195,
East craftsbury Road, 05826
(802) 586-7763

This elegant, turn-of-the-century country house is set in the tranquil, picturesque village of East craftsbury. Guest facilities include a library, cozy sitting room, four large, bright bedrooms with two private baths, down comforters, and English-style antique furniture. decor and service is distinctively British.

Hosts: Janet and Bob Meyer
Rooms: 4 (2 PB; 2 SB) $60-75
Full Breakfast
Credit Cards: A, B
Notes: 2, 5, 8, 11, 12, 13, 14

CUTTINGSVILLE—SEE ALSO SHREWSBURY

Maple Crest Farm

Lincoln Hill Road, Box 120, 05738
(802) 492-3367

NOTES: Credit cards accepted: A Master Card; B Visa; C American Express; D Discover Card; E Diner's Club; F Other; 2 Personal Checks accepted; 3 Lunch available; 4 Dinner available; 5 Open all year;

Situated high in the Green Mountains, ten miles south of Rutland and twelve miles north of Ludlow, this 1808 27-room historic home has been lovingly preserved for five generations. Cross-country skiing and hiking are offered on the farm. Close to major ski areas, Rutland, and places of historic interest. A real taste of true old Vermont hospitality. Maple syrup made on premises. This year marks 22 years of business for this bed and breakfast home.

Hosts: William and Donna Smith
Rooms: 6 (1 PB; 5 SB) $50
Full Breakfast
Credit Cards: None
Closed Jan. and Feb.
Notes: 2, 7, 9, 10, 11, 12, 13, 14

DANBY

Bed and Breakfast Inns of New England VT 710

329 Lake Drive, Guilford, CT 06437
(800) 582-0853

Vermont's first millionaire built a gracious Victorian mansion and carriage house in 1891 for his new bride. Today the mansion and carriage house have been carefully renovated, appointed with modern conveniences, and furnished lovingly with antiques. Guests are welcome to enjoy the extensive common areas with library, fireplace, TV room, and swimming pool. Hot or cold drinks, games, and storage for skis and bicycles are available. The inn is within easy driving distance of many Vermont attractions and ski areas. Seventeen guest rooms are comfortably decorated with Victorian wallpaper and curtains, and furnished with antiques. Private and shared baths. Children welcome. Smoking in common areas only. Resident cat, but no guest pets, please. $54-84.

Quails Nest Bed and Breakfast Inn

Box 221, 05739
(802) 293-5099

Nestled in a quiet mountain village, the inn offers its guests friendly conversation around the fireplace, rooms filled with cozy quilts and antiques, tips about local attractions, and a hearty home-cooked breakfast in the morning.

Hosts: Anharad and Chip Edson
Rooms: 5 (3 PB; 2 SB) $60-75
Full Breakfast
Credit Cards: A, B
Notes: 2, 5, 7, 8 (over 6), 9, 10, 11, 12, 13

Silas Griffith Inn

South Main Street, 05739
(802) 293-5567

Built in 1891 by Vermont's first millionaire, now a lovingly restored Victorian mansion and carriage house. Relax in antique-filled guest rooms with spectacular Green Mountain views. Dinner available.

Hosts: Paul and Lois Dansereau
Rooms: 17 (14 PB; 3 SB) $69-86
Full Breakfast
Minimum stay holidays: 2 nights
Credit Cards: A, B, C
Notes: 2, 4, 5, 7 (limited), 8, 9, 11, 14

DERBY LINE

Derby Village Inn

46 Main Street, 05830
(802) 873-3604

A charming old Victorian mansion situated in the quiet village of Derby Line. Five charming rooms, each with private bath. Nestled within walking distance of the Canadian border and the world's only international library and opera house. The nearby countryside offers year-round recreation: downhill and cross-country skiing, water sports, cycling, fishing, hiking, golf, snowmobiling, sleigh rides, antiquing, and most of all, peace and tranquility.

Hosts: Tom and Phyllis Moreau
Rooms: 5 (PB) $50-60
Full Breakfast
Credit Cards: A, B, D
Notes: 2, 5, 8, 9

DORSET

The Little Lodge at Dorset

Route 30, Box 673, 05251
(802) 867-4040

This delightful old house sits on a hillside overlooking a pond and mountains beyond and surrounded by wildflowers, white birch, and pines. Quilts, stenciling, wide floorboards, and antiques add to this appealing inn. Barnboard den with fireplace, wet bar, refrigerator, TV, games, puzzles, and books. Screened porch. Unusual toasted homemade breads, Vermont cheese, and crackers offered. Coffee, tea, and hot chocolate always available. Hiking, biking, fishing, boating, swimming, tennis, golf, and skiing nearby. Some rooms are air-conditioned.

Hosts: Allan and Nancy Norris
Rooms: 5 (PB) $80-100
Expanded Continental Breakfast
Credit Cards: C, D
Notes: 2, 8, 9, 10, 11, 12, 13, 14

EAST BURKE

Lanier's Hilltop Bed and Breakfast

Highway 19, P. O. Box 103, 05832
(802) 626-9637

The hosts decided to open their home to travelers because this area in Vermont is one of the nicest quaint areas still around. Less than one mile from Burke mountain, which is great for hiking in the summer and skiing in the winter. The vast snowmobile trails start at the bottom of the driveway, and great fishing and beautiful lakes are nearby. It is a modern split-level home on a hill with panoramic views, situated on four acres. Twenty-by-forty-foot in-gound pool is available for guests to use, as are the outside patios, gazebos, perennial gardens, and a rambling brook on property. Five miles off I-91.

Hosts: Marilyn and Lionel Lanier
Rooms: 3 (1 PB; 2 SB) $50-60
Full Breakfast
Credit Cards: A, B
Notes: 2, 5, 8, 9, 11, 12, 13

The Nutmegger Bed and Breakfast

P. O. Box 73, mountain Road, 05832
(802) 626-5205

Located in the tiny hamlet of East Burke, we are barely one-half a mile from the lower base lodge of burke mountain Ski Area. Less than one mile to excellent cross-country trails. Spectacular fall foliage. Rooms offer a quiet, informal rest in a warm and homey setting.

Host: Lucille Ventres
Rooms: 2 (SB) $40-45
Continental Breakfast
Credit Cards: A, B
Notes: 2, 5, 7, 8, 9, 13

The Village Inn of East Burke

Route 114, P. O. Box 186, 05832
(802) 626-3161

This warm, comfortable village home is convenient to restaurants, country store, post office, and laundromat. Guests can enjoy a warm fire in the winter, and the cooling back-yard stream in the summer. Hearty continental breakfast is served to guests' rooms. Comfortable sitting room with shelves full of books; games and television. Great getaway for bikers and skiers.

Hosts: Lorraine and George Willy
Rooms: 3 (PB)
Continental Breakfast
Credit Cards: A, B
Notes: 2, 5, 6, 7, 8, 9, 11, 12, 13

EAST DOVER

Cooper Hill Inn

Cooper Hill Road, Box 146, 05341
(802) 348-6333

Informal and cozy hilltop inn with "one of
the most spectacular mountain panoramas
in all New England." Quiet country-road
location. Hearty home-cooked meals are a
tradition here. Double rooms and family
suites all feature private baths. Dinner and
breakfast included in the daily rate.

Hosts: Pat and Marilyn Hunt
Rooms: 7 (PB) $80-110 Modified American Plan
Suites: 3 (PB) $95-159 Modified American Plan
Full Breakfast
Credit Cards: None
Closed for one week in April and Nov.
Notes: 2, 4, 7, 8, 9, 10, 11, 12, 13, 14

EAST HARDWICK

Brick House Guests

Box 128, 2 Brick House Road, 05836
(802) 472-5512

Federal brick house with comfortable
Victorian furnishings, sitting on the edge of
a small village with open farmland and
woods nearby. Beautiful gardens, perennial
flowers, and herb nursery. The area is
unspoiled, hilly, and rural. Nearby you'll
find tennis and golf, horseback riding,
swimming in clear lakes, canoeing, and
good local restaurants.

Hosts: Thomas and Judith Kane
Rooms: 3 (1 PB; 2 SB) $50-65
Full Breakfast
Credit Cards: A, B
Closed Dec. 24-26
Notes: 2, 5, 6, 7, 8, 9, 10, 11, 12, 13 (XC)

EAST SPRINGFIELD

Cherry Tree Hill Bed and Breakfast

Cherry Tree Hill Road, 05651
(802) 223-0549

Completely restored Dutch roof farmhouse
offers luxurious accommodations in a
country setting. Panoramic views of the
Green mountains can be seen from all
angles of this beautiful bed and breakfast,
and you are just minutes from the state capital. relax in the heated pool with a Jacuzzi,
or enjoy a crackling fire in our Count
Rumford fireplace. Breakfast is served in
the greenhouse among fragrant herbs and
cascading water. Sheep, horses, fields, and
meadows cover the 55-acre setting. Private
guest house with full kitchen also available.

Hosts: Cheryl Potter and Kevin Rice
Rooms: 6, plus guest house (2 PB; 4 SB) $60-100
Full Breakfast
Credit Cards: None
Notes: 2, 8 (over 10), 11, 13

Berkson Farms

ENOSBURG FALLS

Berkson Farms

Rural Delivery 1, Route 108, 05450
(802) 933-2522

6 Pets welcome; 7 Smoking allowed; 8 Children welcome; 9 Social drinking allowed; 10 Tennis available; 11
Swimming available; 12 Golf available; 13 Skiing available; 14 May be booked through travel agents.

Homey, relaxed atmosphere in a century-old restored farmhouse situated on a 600-acre working dairy farm, surrounded by a large variety of animals and all the simple, wonderful joys of nature and life itself. Warm hospitality and country home cooking.

Hosts: Terry and Susan Spoonire
Rooms: 4 (1 PB; 3 SB) $54-64.80
Full Breakfast
Credit Cards: None
Notes: 2, 3, 4, 5, 6, 7, 8, 9, 10, 11, 12, 13

The Inn at Buck Hollow Farm

ESSEX JUNCTION

The Inn at Essex

70 Essex Way, 05452
(802) 878-1100; (800) 727-4295

The Inn at Essex is a 97-room hotel that is just starting its third year of operation. It has also received the AAA Four Diamond Award for Quality for the third year as well. All of the rooms are individually decorated, and thirty have wood-burning fireplaces. It is located just outside of Burlington between Lake Champlain and the beautiful Green Mountains. One of the more outstanding features is the food. All of the inn's restaurants are operated under the watchful eye of New England Culinary Institute. With over 100 cooks in the kitchen, you can imagine the creations that they can come up with. The inn is within twenty minutes of five golf courses, five ski areas, beaches, boating, craft shows, museums, canoeing, tennis, and swimming.

Also offered is complimentary airport transportation.

Hosts: Jim and Judi Lamberti
Rooms: 97 (PB) $69-165
Continental Breakfast
Credit Cards: A, B, C, D, E, F
Notes: 2, 3, 4, 5, 7, 8, 9, 10, 11, 12, 13, 14

FAIRFAX

The American Country Collection #149

The Willows, 4 Greenwood Lane, Delmar, NY, 12054
(518) 439-7001

Imagine yourself in a comletely renovated New England carriage house in the year 1790, and begin your jouney through this completely renovated inn with original exposed beams and wood-burning stove. Four rooms are available for guests. Two rooms on the second floor share a bath, and two rooms on the first floor share another bath and a Jacuzzi tub. Snacks, wine, beer, and soft drinks are available to guests, and a fax machine, Macintosh computer, copier, and antique and gift shop are on premises. In the spring, enjoy watching maple syrup being made. Breakfast is served from 8:00-9:00 a.m. $45-75.

The Inn at Buck Hollow Farm

Rural Route 1, Box 680, 05454
(802) 849-2400

The Inn at Buck Hollow Farm is a small country inn nestled on 400 spectacular acres. It features canopy beds, beamed ceilings, sun room with fireplace, and antique decor. The guests enjoy a heated pool, Jacuzzi, cross-country skiing, and an antique shop. With Burlington's famed marketplace and major ski resorts only minutes away, the Inn at Buck Hollow Farm is truly a four-season retreat.

NOTES: Credit cards accepted: A Master Card; B Visa; C American Express; D Discover Card; E Diner's Club; F Other; 2 Personal Checks accepted; 3 Lunch available; 4 Dinner available; 5 Open all year;

Hosts: Dody Young and Brad Schwartz
Rooms: 4 (SB) $55-75
Full Breakfast
Credit Cards: A, B
Notes: 2, 5, 8, 9, 11, 13, 14

FAIR HAVEN

Maplewood Inn and Antiques

Route 22A South, 05743
(802) 265-8039; (800) 253-7729 (outside VT)

This beautifully restored 1843 Greek Revival inn has exquisitely appointed rooms, suites, and common areas that include a TV room with fireplace, BYOB tavern, gathering room with books and games furnished in various period styles and antiques. Parlor with complimentary cordial bar. Many extras: near lakes, shops, and restaurants. Bike rental on site.

Hosts: Cindy and Doug Baird
Rooms: 5 (PB) $70-95
Continental Plus Breakfast
Credit Cards: A, B, C
Notes: 2, 5, 7, 8 (over 5, call), 9, 10, 11, 12, 13, 14

Vermont Marble Inn

12 West Park Place, 05743
(800) 535-2814

A dream come true for the innkeepers and you. A nationally historic 125-year-old marble mansion restored to a fare-thee-well. This romantic inn is endowed with many working fireplaces, a wraparound porch, gourmet cuisine, and unrivaled hos-

Maplewood Inn

pitality. In 1991 alone, the inn was voted one of America's ten best, rated with four diamonds by AAA, and received the Inn of the Year, 1992 award from *Inn Review*.

Hosts: Bea and Richard Taube; Shirley Stein
Rooms: 12 (PB) $140-195
Full Breakfast
Credit Cards: A, B, C
Notes: 4, 7, 9, 14

FAIRLEE

Silver Maple Lodge

Route 5, 05045
(802) 333-4326; (800) 666-1946

Historic bed and breakfast country inn. Cozy rooms with antiques or knotty pine cottages. Enjoy beach, boating, fishing, and swimming at Lake Morey, one mile away. Golf, tennis, skiing, and hot-air balloon rides nearby. Dartmouth College is 17 miles away. Walk to restaurant.

Hosts: Scott and Sharon Wright
Rooms: 14 (12 PB; 2 SB) $44-64
Continental Breakfast
Minimum stay holidays: 2 nights
Credit Cards: A, B, C
Closed Christmas Eve
Notes: 2, 5, 7, 8, 9, 10, 11, 12, 13, 14

FAYSTON

Mad River Barn

Route 17, Box 88, 05673
(802) 496-3310

This Vermont country lodge offers spacious rooms with private baths. A stone fireplace, game room with a 36-inch shuffleboard, outdoor pool, meadows, flower gardens, large sportsman's breakfast. Hiking, biking, and shopping are only a few of the many amenities you will enjoy here.

Hosts: The Pratts
Rooms: 15 (PB) $45-65
Full Breakfast
Credit Cards: A, B, C
Notes: 2, 5, 7, 8, 10, 11, 12, 13, 14

6 Pets welcome; 7 Smoking allowed; 8 Children welcome; 9 Social drinking allowed; 10 Tennis available; 11 Swimming available; 12 Golf available; 13 Skiing available; 14 May be booked through travel agents.

Highland Lodge

GAYESVILLE

Cobble House Inn

Box 49, 05746
(802) 234-5458

The inn sits secluded on a hilltop overlooking the Green Mountains. The White River flows along the boundary, offering swimming and fishing. Each room is decorated in antiques and country furnishings, and there is a dining room that features northern Italian cuisine prepared by the chef/owners. Complimentary afternoon hors d'oeuvres are served. Dinner is available by reservation. A host of sports including biking, swimming, tubing, skiing, and golf are available to help work off the day's meals.

Hosts: Beau and Phil Benson
Rooms: 6 (PB) $80-100
Full Breakfast
Credit Cards: A, B, C
Notes: 3, 4, 5, 8, 9, 11, 12, 13

GOSHEN

Blueberry Hill Inn

Rural Free Delivery 3, 05733
(802) 247-6735

Nestled on the mountainside is a blueberry-colored farmhouse built in 1813 and pres-

ently known as Blueberry Hill Inn. In winter, it serves as a ski touring center, and at other times, a place to get away from it all. Noted for its genuine hospitality and sumptuous meals, Blueberry Hill leaves you with a most unforgettable experience. The inn, filled with antiques, is bordered by grassy fields, a spring-fed pond, and countless perennial flower and herb gardens.

Host: Sharon Coleman
Rooms: 12 (PB) $76-110 Modified American Plan
Continental Breakfast
Credit Cards: A, B,
Notes: 2, 4, 5, 8, 9, 11, 13, 14

GREENSBORO

Highland Lodge

Caspian Lake, Rural Route 1, Box 1290, 05841
(802) 533-2647

The Highland Lodge is in Vermont's least seen yet most beautiful region. It graces a hillside covered in wildflowers overlooking crystal-clear Caspian Lake and the mountains beyond. Swim in the summer at the private beach. Forty miles of Vermont's best ski-touring in the winter. Meals are imaginative. Breakfast and dinner are included in the rate. The white 1860s farmhouse has a large Queen Anne porch, the perfect place to enjoy the view. Secluded, pristine area off the beaten path. Free summer kid's program. A rare find.

Hosts: David, Wilhelmina and Alex Smith
Rooms: 11 (PB) $150-190 Modified American Plan
Cottages: 10 (PB)
Full Breakfast
Credit Cards: A, B
Notes: 2, 3, 4, 8, 9, 10, 11, 12, 13

HARDWICK

Somerset House Bed and Breakfast

24 Highland Avenue, 05843
(802) 472-5484

NOTES: Credit cards accepted: A Master Card; B Visa; C American Express; D Discover Card; E Diner's Club; F Other; 2 Personal Checks accepted; 3 Lunch available; 4 Dinner available; 5 Open all year;

This comfortable, elegant 1894 home is on a maple-lined street within short walking distance of the village center. The warm sitting room with antiques, piano, and fireplace offers peace, quiet, and privacy. Enjoy a rocking chair on the porch or wander in the "hidden" perennial garden. A full, healthy, delicious breakfast is served in the dining room. Situated near beautiful lakes, rivers, and mountains.

Hosts: Ruth and David Gaillard
Rooms: 4 (SB) $60-75
Full Breakfast
Credit Cards: A, B
Notes: 2, 5, 8, 9, 10, 11, 12, 13

Somerset House

HARTLAND

The American Country Collection #163

4 Greenwood Lane, Delmar, NY 12054
(518) 439-7001

Modern home in a rural farm setting. Guests have the privacy of the entire first floor, including private entrance, if desired.

Mostly new and modern furnishings. Continental breakfast. Two rooms, one with twin beds and one with a double bed; each has a private bath. Resident cat. Children welcome. No smoking. $55-65.

HEARTWELLVILLE

Berkshire B&B Homes VT 2

P. O. Box 211, Williamsburg, MA 01096
(413) 268-7244

A 1783 Colonial on 18 acres. Country furnishings. Parlor and den for guest use. View of the Green Mountains. Three double bedrooms with shared bath. Full breakfast. No smoking. Children over 12 welcome. Pets in residence. $55-75.

HYDE PARK

Bed and Breakfast Inns of New England VT 725

329 Lake Drive, Guilford, CT 06437
(800) 582-0853

Situated in the lovely Lamoille River Valley on a hill overlooking the magnificent Green Mountains, this inn offers a special opportunity to enjoy a true Vermont experience. Set in four acres of woodland and central to Vermont's all-season vacation country, you can choose from any number of activities: skiing, fishing, hiking, biking, canoeing, tennis, golf, auctions, and antique shopping. The inn is only ten minutes from Stowe, one hour from Burlington Airport, and two hours from Montreal. A full gourmet breakfast is included, and dinners are available. Four tastefully decorated guest rooms, a colonial dining room, a Federalist-style livingroom, and a comfortable library full of video tapes and books are available to guests. Private and shared baths. Children over nine welcome. No smoking. $50-125.

6 Pets welcome; 7 Smoking allowed; 8 Children welcome; 9 Social drinking allowed; 10 Tennis available; 11 Swimming available; 12 Golf available; 13 Skiing available; 14 May be booked through travel agents.

Fitch Hill Inn

Rural Free Delivery Box 1879, Fitch Hill Road,
05655
(802) 888-5941

Affordable elegance on a hilltop overlooking Vermont's highest mountain in the beautiful Lamoille River Valley, ten miles north of famous Stowe, the historic Fitch Hill Inn, circa 1795, offers four tastefully antique-decorated rooms, all of which have views. There are four common livingroom areas and over 200 video movies for guests to enjoy. Ungroomed cross-country ski trails begin on the property, and there are also nature trails to explore. A full gourmet breakfast is served, and dinners are available at a modest price. Packages available.

Host: Richard A. Pugliese
Rooms: 4 (SB) $50-60
Full Breakfast
Credit Cards: A, B
Notes: 2, 4, 5, 9, 13, 14

JACKSONVILLE

The American Country Collection #165

4 Greenwood Lane, Delmar, NY 12054
(518) 439-7001

Victorian country home built in 1840. Queen Anne Colonial furnishings. Dining room with fireplace, livingroom, and sitting room with TV. Swimming pool available for guests' use. Three guest rooms with private and shared baths. Full breakfast. Children welcome. Smoking outside. $45-65.

JAMAICA

Three Mountain Inn

P. O. Box 180 A, 05343
(802) 874-4140

Small, romantic 1780's authentic country inn. Fine food and comfortable rooms.

Situated in a historic village, just four blocks to hiking in the state park and cross-country skiing. Ten minutes to Stratton. The innkeepers plan special day trips with detailed local maps of the area. Special midweek rates. Honeymoon suites available.

Hosts: Charles and Elaine Murray
Rooms: 16 (14 PB; 2 SB) $75-100 Bed and
    Breakfast; $90-180 Modified American Plan
Full Breakfast
Credit Cards: C
Notes: 2, 4, 9, 11, 13, 14

JEFFERSONVILLE

Mannsview Inn

Rural Route 2, Box 4319, Route 108 South, 05464
(802) 644-8321; (800) 937-6266 reservations

Mannsview Inn, circa 1875, is a colonial-style home with a Victorian flair. Completely restored, it offers queen-size, high-poster beds, a library, parlor, fireplace, cable TV, and home-cooked breads and muffins with a full breakfast. Located at the base of Mount Mansfield in the heart of Vermont's number-one resort area, you are surrounded by breathtaking mountain views, pastures, and trout streams. Located on the premises you will also find a 10,000-square-foot antique center, canoe touring; skiing, hiking, and canoeing packages available.

Hosts: Bette and Kelley Mann
Rooms: 6 (2 PB; 4 SB) $50-60
Full Breakfast
Credit Cards: A, B, C
Notes: 2, 3, 5, 8, 9, 10, 11, 13, 14

JERICHO

Henry M. Field House Bed and Breakfast

Rural Route 2, P. O. Box 395, 05465
(802) 899-3984

Henry M. Field House is located near skiing, cycling, hiking, swimming, and golf.

NOTES: Credit cards accepted: A Master Card; B Visa; C American Express; D Discover Card; E Diner's Club; F Other; 2 Personal Checks accepted; 3 Lunch available; 4 Dinner available; 5 Open all year;

The house is convenient to Burlington area colleges and shops. The Italianate Victorian was built in 1875 and features tall ceilings, wood floors, etched glass, and period decor including antiques and covered lighting. vegetable crepes with a mushroom sauce, banana French toast, and a variety of home-baked items are specialties of the house. Children are welcome, but must be in another rented room.

Hosts: Mary Beth and Terrence Horan
Rooms: 3 (PB) $60-70
Full Breakfast
Credit Cards: A, B
Notes: 2, 5, 9, 10, 11, 12, 13

Henry M. Field House

Homeplace

Rural Route 2, Box 367, 05465
(802) 899-4694

Homeplace is a lovely house set in the woods. It is a quiet place with beautiful gardens, a relaxing atmosphere, and space either to be on your own or join in with the family.

Host: Mariot Huessy
Rooms: 3 (1 PB; 2 SB) $50
Full Breakfast

Credit Cards: None
Notes: 2, 5, 8, 11, 12, 13

JOHNSON

The Homestead Bed and Breakfast

Rural Route 2, Box 623, 05656
(802) 635-7354

The quiet beauty of Vermont's countryside surrounds this c. 1830 brick Colonial farmhouse. A hearty breakfast starts guests on their way to enjoying the many activities offered in the area: canoeing, hiking, fishing, biking, antiquing, skiing.

Hosts: Erwin and Ella May Speer
Rooms: 4 (SB) $40-50
Full Breakfast
Credit Cards: A, B
Notes: 2, 3, 4, 5, 8, 10, 11, 12, 13

KILLINGTON

Grey Bonnet Inn

Route 100 North, 05751
(802) 775-2537; (800) 342-2086

Romantic, antique-filled moutain inn on 25 acres with indoor and outdoor pools, whirlpool, sauna, game and exercise rooms. Library and cozy pub. Relax in front of the fire in the livingroom. All rooms have private bath, color TV, phone. Award-winning dining, piano entertainment, ski movies. Cross-country skiing out the back door. AAA three-diamond and Mobil three-star rated.

Hosts: Barbara and Bill Flohr
Rooms: 40 (PB) $54-125
Full Breakfast
Credit Cards: A, B, C
Closed April 15-June 1; Oct. 22-Thanksgiving
Notes: 2, 4, 7, 8, 9, 10, 11, 12, 13, 14

The Inn at Long Trail

Route 4, Sherburne Pass, Box 267, 05751
(802) 775-7181; (800) 325-2540

6 Pets welcome; 7 Smoking allowed; 8 Children welcome; 9 Social drinking allowed; 10 Tennis available; 11 Swimming available; 12 Golf available; 13 Skiing available; 14 May be booked through travel agents.

Historic country inn, high in the ski country of Vermont, situated at the jucntion of the historic Appalachian and Long trails, for excellent hiking in the mountains. Irish pub, wood-paneled public rooms, and fireplace suites. Hot tub. Ideal for hiking and skiing.

Host: The McGrath family
Rooms: 26 (PB) Seasonal rates
Minimum stay weekends: 2 nights; holidays: 3
 nights
Full Breakfast
Credit Cards: A, B
Closed April 15-June 30
Notes: 2, 4, 7, 8, 9, 10, 11, 12, 13, 14

The Vermont Inn

Mountain Meadows Lodge

Thundering Brook Road, Rural Route 1
Box 4080, 05751
(802) 775-1010

Would you like a nice place on a lake in the mountains of Vermont? Mountain Meadows is a friendly country inn in a beautiful lakeside setting, with homestyle cooking, a swimming pool, hiking, boating, and fishing. Scenic aerial gondola, alpine slide, tennis, golf, an excellent playhouse, and many attractions are nearby. Or just sit back and enjoy Vermont scenery.

Host: The Stevens family
Rooms: 18 (15 PB; 3 SB) $39-78
Modified American Plan also available
Full Breakfast
Credit Cards: A, B
Closed April 1-June 1; Oct. 15-Nov. 20
Notes: 2, 4, 8, 9, 10, 11, 12, 13, 14

The Vermont Inn

Route 4, 05751
(802) 775-0708; (800) 541-7795

A small country inn built as a farmhouse in 1840. Country charm, warm atmosphere, and gourmet dining in a five-acre mountain setting. Dining room, open to public, has a three-diamond rating from AAA, and is the winner of the Korbel Champagne fine dining award. Package plans are available.

Hosts: Susan and Judd Levy
Rooms: 17 (13 PB; 4 SB) $90-190 Modified
 American Plan
Full Breakfast
Minimum stay weekends: 2 nights
Credit Cards: A, B, C
Closed April 15-May 25
Notes: 2, 4, 7, 8 (over 6), 9, 10, 11, 12, 13, 14

LONDONDERRY

The Highland House

Route 100, 05148
(802) 824-3019

This 1842 inn, with swimming pool and tennis court set on 32 acres, offers 17 rooms, 15 with private bath. Classic candlelight dining, with homemade soups, breads, and desserts. Within minutes of skiing, hiking, horseback riding, golf, shopping, and points of interest.

Hosts: Mike and Laurie Gayda
Rooms: 17 (15 PB; 2 SB) $63-93
Full Breakfast
Minimum stay weekends: 2 nights; holidays: 3
 nights
Credit Cards: A, B, C
Closed one week in Nov., three in April
Notes: 2, 4, 7, 8 (over 5), 9, 10, 11, 12, 13

Swiss Inn

Route 11, Rural Route 1, P. O. Box 140, 05148
(802) 824-3442; (800) 847-9477

The swiss Inn is situated in the heart of the Green mountains with spectacular views of the surrounding area. Our cozy, comfortable rooms all feature cable color TV, telephones, and private baths. Full Vermont

NOTES: Credit cards accepted: A Master Card; B Visa; C American Express; D Discover Card; E Diner's Club; F Other; 2 Personal Checks accepted; 3 Lunch available; 4 Dinner available; 5 Open all year;

breakfast is served daily. Two fireside sitting rooms, game room, and library are available for guests to enjoy. Restaurant on premises featuring Swiss specialties. Both downhill and cross-country skiing nearby in the winter. Shopping, antiques, golf, summer theatre, and fall foliage at its best.

Hosts: Joe and Pat Donahue
Rooms: 18 (PB) $45-85
Full Breakfast
Credit Cards: A, B, C
Notes: 2, 4, 5, 7, 8, 9, 10, 11, 12 13, 14

The Village Inn at Landgrove

215 Landgrove Road, 05148
(802) 824-6673

This warm renovated farstead was featured in Country Inns and Back Roads. Rooms, meals, pool, tennis courts, pitch-and-putt golf. Families are welcome.

Hosts: Kathy and Jay Snyder
Rooms: 20 (16 PB; 4 SB) $65-85
Full Breakfast
Credit Cards: A, B, C, D
Closed April 1-May 26 and Oct. 30-Dec. 15
Notes: 2, 4, 7 (limited), 8, 9, 10, 11, 12, 13, 14

LOWER WATERFORD

Rabbit Hill Inn

Route 18, 05848
(802) 76-BUNNY; (802) 748-5168

You are invited home to a New England classic established 1795. Set on 15 acres

Rabbit Hill Inn

above the Connecticut River, the inn is a hideaway in a tiny historic district. This romantic inn is award winning and features antiques, many canopy beds, fireplaces. The exceptional detail, cuisine, decor, and service have been featured by both national and international media. Guests enjoy a sense of fantasy, whimsy, and charm.

Hosts: John and Maureen Magee
Rooms: 18 (PB) $78-150
Full Breakfast
Credit Cards: A, B
Notes: 2, 4, 5, 9, 11, 12, 13, 14

LUDLOW

The American Country Collection #134

4 Greenwood Lane, Delmar, NY, 12054
(518) 439-7001

Rumor has it that this was a major stop on the Underground Railroad before the Civil War and among the first structures ever built in Ludlow. Renovated in 1989 by its present owners, this 19th-century inn pampers guests with a delightful continental breakfast, afternoon tea, and evening fruit and wine. The cozy accommodations feature six guest rooms, each with its own special accent of country decor and lace curtains, private bath, and stunning views of Okemo Mountain. Breakfast is served from 8:00-9:00 A.M. $80-150, seasonal.

The Andrie Rose Inn

13 Pleasant Street, 05149
(802) 228-4846; (800) 223-4846

Elegant circa 1829 country village inn at the base of Okemo Ski Resort. Enjoy fireside cocktails with complimentary hors d'oeuvres. Lavishly appointed, antique-filled guest rooms, all with private baths, fine linens, and down comforters. Some rooms boast whirlpool tubs and skylights. Indulge yourself in one of the luxury suites featuring marble fireplaces, canopy beds,

6 Pets welcome; 7 Smoking allowed; 8 Children welcome; 9 Social drinking allowed; 10 Tennis available; 11 Swimming available; 12 Golf available; 13 Skiing available; 14 May be booked through travel agents.

and oversize whirlpool tubs. Family suites also avaialble. Savor delectable breakfasts and epicurean dinners. Use inn bikes to tour back roads. Minutes from lakes, theaters, golf, tennis, hiking, downhill and cross-country skiing.

Hosts: Rick and Carolyn Bentzinger
Rooms: 10 (PB) $95-115
Suites: $185-250
Full Breakfast
Credit Cards: A, B, C
Notes: 2, 4 (weekends and holidays), 5, 9, 10, 11, 12, 13, 14

The Andrie Rose Inn

Black River Inn

100 Main Street, 05149
(802) 228-5585

A charming 1835 country inn, on the bank of the Black River at the town green. Ten antique furnished guest rooms, eight with private baths. A variety of antique beds with down comforters and feather pillows, including a 1794 walnut four-poster that Abraham Lincoln slept in. Full country breakfast, fireside cocktails, intimate dinners in a candlelit dining room. Near downhill and cross-country skiing, golf, hiking, bicycle rentals, swimming, and fishing.

Hosts: Rick and Cheryl DelMastro
Rooms: 10 (8 PB; 2 SB) $105-115
Full Breakfast
Credit Cards: A, B, C
Notes: 2, 4, 5, 7, 9, 12, 13, 14

The Combes Family Inn

Rural Free Delivery 1, Box 275, 05149
(802) 228-8799

Bring your family home to visit The Combes Family Inn. Situated on a quiet country back road with 50 acres of meadows to explore. Luke, reported to be the friendliest Lab around, shares the farm with lots of equally friendly cats, dogs, innkeepers, and guests. Homey atmosphere and country cooking.

Hosts: Ruth and Bill Combes
Rooms: 11 (PB) $78-90
Full Breakfast
Minimum stay fall and winter weekends: 2 nights; holidays: 4 nights
Credit Cards: A, B, C, D
Closed April 15-May 15
Notes: 2, 4, 6, 7, 8, 9, 10, 11, 12, 13, 14

Echo Lake Inn

P. O. Box 154, 05149
(800) 356-6844

Year-round country inn and resort built in 1840. One of six inns in Vermont originally built as an inn. Situated in beautiful lakes region, minutes to ski areas and golf. On premises: tennis, pool, boating, fishing. Full breakfast and dinner, porch dining. Cocktail lounge, tavern, game room, steam bath, gift shops. Desserts homemade by Kathy. Menu according to season: homemade pasta, venison and other game dishes, always fresh fish. Close to many points of interest such as the birthplace of President Coolidge and cheese factory. On Route 100, five miles north of Ludlow.

Echo Lake Inn

NOTES: Credit cards accepted: A Master Card; B Visa; C American Express; D Discover Card; E Diner's Club; F Other; 2 Personal Checks accepted; 3 Lunch available; 4 Dinner available; 5 Open all year;

Hosts: Phil and Kathy Cocco
Rooms: 26 (12 PB; 14 SB) $90-120
Full Breakfast
Credit Cards: A, B
Notes: 2, 3, 4, 5, 7, 8, 9, 10, 11, 12, 13, 14

The Governor's Inn

86 Main Street, 05149
(802) 228-8830

An extraordinary reputation for excellence
surrounds this premier, eight-guest-room
Victorian country house. Snuggle in a century-old brass four-poster, wake up to a
wonderful full gourmet breakfast. Enjoy
Vermont all day, then come home to
Mozart, afternoon tea, and a crackling fire.
Gather for hors d'oeuvres and a six-course
dinner. Sip brandy in the late evening.
Judged one of the nation's ten best inns for
the second year. Rates include breakfast,
tea, and dinner. Mobil four-star rated.

Hosts: Charlie and Deedy Marble
Rooms: 8 (PB) $130-140
Full Breakfast
Credit Cards: A, B
Notes: 2, 3 (picnic basket), 4, 5, 9, 10, 11, 12, 13, 14

LYNDON

Branch Brook
Bed and Breakfast

South Wheelock Road, P. O. Box 143, 05849
(802) 626-8316

Restored 1850 house in northeast Vermont.
An attractive livingroom, dining room, and
library are available for guest use.
Conveniently situated one-half mile off I-
91 at exit 23. Burke Mountain Ski area is
eight miles for both downhill and cross-
country skiing. Hiking, biking, and swimming available. A complete breakfast prepared on an English AGA cooker is served
in the dining room.

Hosts: Ted and Ann Tolman
Rooms: 5 (3 PB; 2 SB) $55-70
Full Breakfast
Credit Cards: A, B
Notes: 2, 5, 8, 9, 12, 13

MANCHESTER

The American Country Collection #080

4 Greenwood Lane, Delmar, NY 12054
(518) 439-7001

You'll find tranquility in this 1890 tenant
farmer's house on a five-acre plot at the
foot of the Green Mountains and bordered
by a babbling brook. Two cozy guest
rooms are decorated in country pastels and
prints. Each room has a magnificent view
and a private bath. Guests may enjoy tea on
the deck by the brook, by the wood-burning
stove in the dining room, or by the fireplace in the livingroom. Continental breakfast can be served in the dining room or on
the deck. Smoking permitted, but not in the
guest rooms. Children over 12 welcome.
Dog in residence. $60.

Birch Hill Inn

P. O. Box 346, 05254
(802) 362-2761

Quiet country inn away from busy streets.
Panoramic views, swimming pool, trout
pond, and walking trails on premises. Golf,
antiquing, biking, tennis, and hiking nearby. Selected for The Inkeepers Register.

Hosts: Jim and Pat Lee
Rooms: 6 (PB) $100-110
Full Breakfast
Credit Cards: A, B
Closed Nov.1-Dec. 26; April 5-Memorial Day
Notes: 2, 4, 7 (limited), 10, 11, 12, 13, 14

1811 House

Box 39, 05254
(802) 362-1811

This classic Vermont inn offers you the
warmth and comfort of your own home.
Built in the 1770's, the house has operated
as an inn since 1811 except for one brief
period when it was the residence of
Abraham Lincoln's granddaughter.All

6 Pets welcome; 7 Smoking allowed; 8 Children welcome; 9 Social drinking allowed; 10 Tennis available; 11
Swimming available; 12 Golf available; 13 Skiing available; 14 May be booked through travel agents.

guest rooms have private baths; some have fireplaces, Oriental rugs, fine paintings, and canopy beds. The more than three acres of lawn contain flower gardens and trout pond and offer an exceptional view of the Green Mountains. Walk to golf and tennis, near skiing, fishing, canoeing, and all sports.

Hosts: Marnie and Bruce Duff
Rooms: 14 (PB) $110-180
Full Breakfast
Credit Cards: A, B, C
Notes: 2, 5, 7 (limited), 8 (over 16), 9, 10, 11, 12, 13, 14

The Inn at Manchester

Box 41, 05254
(802) 362-1793

Beautifully restored turn-of-the-century Victorian set on four acres in the picture-book village of Manchester. Elegant rooms with bay windows, brass beds, antiques, and an extensive art collection. Luscious full country breakfast. Secluded pool, skiing, shops, theater in the area. Come for peace, pancakes, and pampering.

Hosts: Stan and Harriet Rosenberg
Rooms: 20 (13 PB; 7 SB) $65-130
Full Breakfast
Credit Cards: A, B, C, D
Notes: 2, 5, 7 (limited), 8 (over 8), 9, 10, 11, 12, 13, 14

MANCHESTER CENTER

Brook-N-Hearth Inn

State Route 11 and 30, Box 508, 05255
(802) 362-3605

Homey Colonial-style inn one mile east on U.S. 7 on Routes 11 and 30. Features full breakfast, cozy rooms, private baths, family suite, cable TV, lounge, BYOB, recreation rooms, outdoor heated swimming pool, and walking trails by brook.

Hosts: Larry and Terry Greene
Rooms: 3 (PB) $50-80
Full Breakfast
Minimum stay holidays: 2 nights
Credit Cards: A, B, C, D
Closed early Nov. and early May
Notes: 2, 7, 8, 9, 10, 11, 12, 13

The Inn at Ormsby Hill

Historic Route 7A, Rural Route 2,
P. O. Box 3264, 05255
(802) 362-1163

This splendid, restored manor house is located on two and one-half acres overlooking Green mountain. Listed on Vermont's Register of Historic Places, the inn offers five guest rooms, all of which have private baths, four with fireplaces, and four with whirlpools. Rates include full breakfast. many excellent places for lunch and dinner nearby. Manchester is a four-season resort community with a full assortment of sports and cultural activities.

Hosts: Nancy and Don Burd
Rooms: 5 (PB) $85-155
Full Breakfast
Credit Cards: A, B, C
Notes: 2, 9, 10, 11, 12, 13, 14

Manchester Highlands Inn

Box 1754 AD, Highland Avenue, 05255
(802) 362-4565

Discover Manchester's best-kept secret, a graceful Queen Anne Victorian inn on a hilltop overlooking town. Front porch with rocking chairs, large outdoor pool, game room, and pub with stone fireplace. Rooms individually decorated with feather beds, down comforters, and lace curtains. Gourmet country breakfast and afternoon snacks are served.

Hosts: Robert and Patricia Eichorn
Rooms: 15 (12 PB; 3 SB) $80-110
Full Breakfast
Credit Cards: A, B, C, D
Notes: 2, 5, 7 (limited), 8, 9, 10, 11, 12, 13, 14

River Meadow Farm

P. O. Box 822, 05255
(802) 362-1602

Secluded farm, with beautiful views, situated at the end of a country lane with a remodeled farmhouse built just prior to 1800. Five guest bedrooms sharing two and one-half baths, large country kitchen with a fireplace and adjoining screen/ glassed-in porch, pleasant dining room, livingroom with baby grand, den with TV. Seventy acres to hike or cross-country ski, bordered by famous Battenkill River.

Host: Patricia J. Dupree
Rooms: 5 (SB) $25/person
Full Breakfast
Credit Cards: None
Notes: 2, 5, 8, 9

MANCHESTER VILLAGE

The Reluctant Panther Inn

West Road, P. O. Box 678, 05254
(800) 822-2331

Relax and forget the world in individually decorated, quiet guest rooms or suites. All rooms offer a private bath, phones, air conditioning, cable TV, and some have wood-burning fireplaces and Jacuzzis. Enjoy a laugh with the innkeepers at the Panther Bar or the tree-shaded patio, and relish in an extrodinary candlelight dinner at the award-winning restaurant. House guests enjoy priority for fireplace or solarium tables.

Hosts: Maye and Robert Bachofen

Rooms: 16 (PB) $160-280
Full Breakfast
Credit Cards: A, B, C
Notes: 2, 4, 5, 9, 10, 11, 12, 13, 14

MIDDLEBURY

The Annex

Route 125, 05740
(802) 388-3233

This 1830 Greek Revival home was originally built as an annex to the Bob Newhart "Stratford Inn." The annex features four rooms with private bath and two that share a bath. The decor is a blend of country, antiques, and handmade quilts. A warm and homey atmosphere welcomes guests.

Host: T. D. Hutchins
Rooms: 6 (4 PB; 2 SB) $50-75
Continental Breakfast
Credit Cards: None
Notes: 2, 5, 8, 9, 10, 11, 12, 13

Brookside Meadows Country Bed and Breakfast

Rural Delivery 3, Box 2460, 05753-8751
(802) 388-6429; (800) 442-9887 reservations

Attractive and comfortable home in rural setting just two and one-half miles from village center. All rooms have private baths. Two-bedroom suite has livingroom and wood stove. Spacious lawns and perennial gardens. Best downhill and cross-country skiing. Many excellent restaurants in town. Near Shelburne Museum. Quiet rest and relaxation at foot of Green Mountains.

Brookside Meadows Country Bed and Breakfast

6 Pets welcome; 7 Smoking allowed; 8 Children welcome; 9 Social drinking allowed; 10 Tennis available; 11 Swimming available; 12 Golf available; 13 Skiing available; 14 May be booked through travel agents.

Hosts: Linda and Roger Cole
Rooms: 3 (PB) $81-91.80
Suite: $145.80-156.60
Full or Continental Breakfast
Credit Cards: A, B
Notes: 2, 5, 8 (over 5), 9, 10, 12, 13

The Middlebury Inn

Courthouse Square, 05753
(802) 388-4961; (800) 842-4666

Elegantly restored 1827 village inn situated
in the historic district of a lovely college
town. Guest rooms have private baths, telephone, color TV. Formal or informal dining; afternoon tea served daily. Museums,
unique shops, historic sites to explore.
Swimming, golf, hiking, boating, downhill
and cross- country skiing are nearby.
Special packages are available.

Hosts: Frank and Jane Emanuel
Rooms: 75 (PB) $88-144
Credit Cards: A, B, C, D
Notes: 2, 3, 4, 5, 6 (restricted), 7, 8, 9, 10, 11, 12,
13, 14

19th Century Farmhouse

Bed and Breakfast Marblehead and North Shore
P. O. Box 35, Newtonville, MA 02160
(617) 964-1606; (800) 832-2632
FAX (617) 332-8572

Built in 1879, this beautiful country farmhouse is situated off a quiet country road on
20 acres of meadowland, surrounded by
spacious lawns and lovely gardens. There
are two beautifully decorated guest rooms
and a two-bedroom suite that sleeps up to
four. All rooms have private baths. Full
country breakfast in the morning and complimentary wine and cheese in the
evenings. This bed and breakfast is close to
Middlebury College, many wonderful
tourist attractions, and downhill and cross-
country skiing areas. Resident dog and cat.
No smoking. Children over eight welcome.
Open all year. Two-night minimum stay.
$80-150.

A Point of View

Rural Delivery 3, P. O. Box 2675, 05753
(802) 388-7205

This country bed and breakfast near
Middlebury, with fantastic views of the
valley and Green Mountains, offers excellent beds in comfortable air-conditioned
rooms. The livingroom with large cable TV
and game room with a pool table is available for guests. This is a warm, friendly
atmosphere where each guest is treated special. hostess prides herself on serving a full
vermont-style breakfast featuring seasonal
fruits and generous entrees. Area attractions include the Morgan Horse Farm,
museums, crafts center, skiing, and golf.

Host: Marie Highter
Rooms: 2 (1 PB; 1 SB) $45-50
Full Breakfast
Credit Cards: None
Notes: 2, 5, 7 (limited), 8, 9, 10, 12, 13

The Middlebury Inn

Swift House Inn

Route 7, 05753
(802) 388-9925

A warm and gracious Federal-style estate with window seats overlooking the formal gardens, fireplaces in ten of the rooms, and whirlpool tubs. Relax in the cozy pub room and then enjoy award-winning cuisine in the elegant cherry-paneled dining room. Walking distance to shopping and Middlebury College; just a short drive to skiing, golf, and swimming.

Hosts: John and Andrea Nelson
Rooms: 20 (PB) $85-150
Continental Breakfast
Credit Cards: A, B, C, D
Notes: 2, 4, 5, 7, 8, 9, 10, 11, 12, 13, 14

MIDDLETOWN SPRINGS

The American Country Collection #147

4 Greenwood Lane, Delmar, NY 12054
(518) 439-7001

There is a treat waiting for you as you step back 100 years in time to an age of elegance in this rural New England village. Listed on the National Register of Historic Places, this historic home is filled with antiques and a large music box collection. You are near Lake St. Catherine for boating and picnicking, and fishermen will love the trout that can be caught in a stream that borders the porperty. Six guest rooms are available, all with private baths, and a continental plus breakfast is served daily. Dinner is also available. $55-65.

Middletown Springs Inn

Box 1068, 05757
(802) 235-2198

Relax and enjoy the gracious elegance of a Victorian mansion overlooking the village green in this historic resort spa. Listed on the National Register of historic places, this inn features ten guest rooms furnished with antiques. Experience rural vermont and an exceptional country inn.

Hosts: Jayne and Eugene Ashley
Rooms: 10 (PB) $60-125
Full Breakfast
Credit Cards: A, B
Notes: 2, 4, 5, 7 (limited), 8 (over 6), 9, 10, 11, 12, 13 (XC), 14

MONTGOMERY CENTER

The Inn on Trout River

P. O. Box 76, The Main Street, 05471
(802) 326-4391; (800) 338-7049

Surrounded by magnificent mountain ranges in a quaint "Currier and Ives" style village, this 100-year-old country Victorian inn features private baths, queen-size beds, down comforters, feather pillows, flannel sheets, cozy fireplaces, antiques, gourmet dining, a pub, and game room. Close by summer and winter sports, covered bridges, and shopping. A full menu at breakfast is always included. AAA-approved Historic Country Inn.

Hosts: Michael and Lee Forman
Rooms: 10 (PB) $80-103
Full Breakfast
Credit Cards: A, B
Notes: 2, 4, 5, 7, 8, 9, 10, 11, 12, 13, 14

Phineas Swann Bed and Breakfast

Main Street, Box 344, 05471
(802) 326-4306

A charming Victorian home with a country flavor, Phineas Swann has an enclosed porch and lots of gingerbread trim. Three large, cozy guest rooms. The nearby Green Mountains and Jay Peak provide plenty of hiking, skiing, and biking. Within walking distance to shops and restaurants. Awake to a hearty candlelight breakfast.

Hosts: Maureen and Frank Kane
Rooms: 4 (1 PB; 3 SB) $55-65
Full Breakfast

Credit Cards: A, B
Notes: 2, 5, 8, 9, 13

MORETOWN

Camel's Hump View

P. O. Box 720, 05660
(802) 496-3614

Camel's Hump View is a unique old-style Country inn dating back to 1831, with the Mad River to the east and Camel's Hump Mountain to the west. Warm yourself by the glowing fire in the winter, or enjoy cattle grazing in the fields during the summer. The inn can accommodate 16 guests and serves hearty country meals from our gardens. Skiing, golfing, fishing, horseback riding, and hiking are all available.

Hosts: Jerry and Wilma Maynard
Rooms: 8 (1 PB; 7 SB) $50-60
Full Breakfast
Credit Cards: None
Notes: 2, 4, 5, 9, 11, 12, 13, 14

Camel's Hump View

MORGAN

Hunts Hideaway

Route 111, 05872
(802) 895-4432; (802) 334-8322

Contemporary split-level on 100 acres: brook, pond, in-ground pool. Situated in Morgan, six miles from I-91, near the Canadian border. Three guest rooms with double bed and shared bath. Guests may use kitchen and laundry facilities. Lake Seymour is two miles away; 18-hole golf courses at Newport and Orleans; jogging, bicycling, skiing at Jay Peak and Burke Mountain, antiquing, bird-watching, fishing.

Host: Pat Hunt
Rooms: 3 (SB) $35
Full Breakfast
Credit Cards: None
Notes: 2, 5, 6, 7, 8, 9, 10, 11, 12, 13

Seymour Lake Lodge

Route 1, P. O. Box 61, 05853
(800) 828-7760

Seymour Lake Lodge overlooks beautiful Lake Seymour. It is in a quiet country setting where relaxation and nature abound. From the spacious front porch to the large livingroom, comfort and friendliness can be found. The hosts always try to please and will provide food for special dietary needs.

Hosts: Dave and Sue Benware
Rooms: 6 (2 PB; 4 SB) $80-100
Full Breakfast
Credit Cards: A, B
Notes: 2, 3, 4, 5, 7, 8, 9, 11, 12, 13

NEWBURY

A Century Past

Box 186, Route 5, 05051
(802) 866-3358

A charming, historic house dating back to 1790, nestled in the tranquility of a quaint Vermont village. A cozy sitting room with fireplace; chat with newfound friends or curl up with a good book. Wake up to freshly baked muffins, hot coffee or tea, great French toast—all served in a comfortable dining room. Activities include walking, biking, and canoeing.

Host: Patricia Smith
Rooms: 4 (S2B) $55
Full Breakfast
Credit Cards: A, B
Closed Christmas
Notes: 2, 8 (over 12), 9, 10, 11, 12, 13

NOTES: Credit cards accepted: A Master Card; B Visa; C American Express; D Discover Card; E Diner's Club; F Other; 2 Personal Checks accepted; 3 Lunch available; 4 Dinner available; 5 Open all year;

NEWPORT

The American Country Collection #148

4 Greenwood Lane, Delmar, NY 12054
(518) 439-7001

With views of Lake Memphremogog, this charming Cape Cod set on a hillside in northeastern Vermont affords travelers of every taste a secluded retreat. Two second-floor rooms share one bath. One room has a double bed, one single bed, and a feather bed. The second room has a sofa that folds out into a double bed. (The second room is only rented to travelers who are with those in the first party.) Breakfast of juice, fresh blueberry pancakes, sausage or bacon, homemade corn muffins, coffee or tea fills you up for most of the day. $50.

Mrs. Winfield's Non-Smokers' Bed and Breakfast

7 Herrick Street, 05855
(802) 334-6624

This hillside retreat with a view of Lake Memphremagog is run by a writer and world traveler formerly with the Metropolitan opera and American Museum of Natural History. This charmed spot is close to all seasonal sports. farm-fresh breakfasts are served at the whim of the weather in either a lake-view dining room, on the sun deck, or before the fireplace. Two upstairs bedrooms, one of which is air-conditioned, offer private baths and cable TV. hostess is a genial lady with a lively appreciation for life.

Host: Carol L. Winfield
Rooms: 2 (PB) $50-65
Full Breakfast
Credit Cards: None
Notes: 2, 5, 8, 9, 10, 11, 12, 13, 14

NORTHFIELD

The Woodland

Bed and Breakfast Marblehead and North Shore
P. O. Box 35, Newtonville, MA 02160
(617) 964-1606; (800) 832-2632
FAX (617) 332-8572

Built in 1990 in a mix of traditional and contemporary design, this inn is situated in a secluded mountain woodland. There are five beautifully decorated guest rooms, three with private baths. A full country breakfast is included. The village of Northfield and Norwich University are less than five miles away. Warren, the Mad River Valley, Montpelier, Barre, and Randolph are all within twenty miles. Children over 12 welcome. Closed March and April. $60-85. Entire inn available for rent at $500 a day.

NORTH HERO

The American Country Collection #047

4 Greenwood Lane, Delmar, NY 12054
(518) 439-7001

A quiet, secluded estate on 50 acres with one-half mile of private lakefront on Lake Champlain. The four rooms in the annex are for bed and breakfast guests only during winter and spring. Nineteen additional rooms in the motel are available during summer and fall. All rooms have private baths. Some have air conditioning. Children welcome. Guests pets permitted for a $10 charge. Smoking is permitted, but smoke-free rooms are available. No smoking in the restaurant. $57.50-89, seasonal.

Charlie's Northland Lodge

Rural Route 1, Box 88, U.S. Route 2, 05474
(802) 372-8822

---

6 Pets welcome; 7 Smoking allowed; 8 Children welcome; 9 Social drinking allowed; 10 Tennis available; 11 Swimming available; 12 Golf available; 13 Skiing available; 14 May be booked through travel agents.

Early 1800s guest house in a quiet village setting on North Hero Island overlooking Lake Champlian. Three guest rooms furnished with country antiques share a modern bath, private entrance and livingroom. A place to fish, sail, canoe, bike, or just plain relax. In winter, you may ice fish, even cross-country ski the meadows.

Hosts: Dorice and Charlie Clark
Rooms: 3 (SB) $40-50
Continental Breakfast
Credit Cards: A, B
Notes: 2, 5, 8, 9, 11, 12, 13

NORWICH

The Norwich Inn

Main Street, P. O. Box 908, 05055
(802) 649-1143

A 200-year-old tradition. The Norwich Inn originally opened as a stagecoach stop in 1797, giving this classic New England inn a heritage of hospitality unmatched in these parts. Each of the 22 guest rooms has a private bath, telephone, and color TV. Situated one mile from Dartmouth College, just off I-91 and I-89, the inn is known for its exceptional restaurant, open for breakfast, lunch, dinner, and Sunday brunch. Catered functions and weddings are welcome.

Host: Sally A. Johnson
Rooms: 22 (PB) $54-99
Full and Continental Breakfast
Credit Cards: A, B, C
Notes: 2, 3, 4, 5, 6, 7, 8, 9, 10, 11, 12, 13, 14

ORLEANS

Valley House Inn

4 Memorial Square, 05860
(802) 754-6665

One-quarter mile from Exit 26 off I-91. An 1800s country inn in the center of the Northeast Kingdom's lakes region. One mile from top 18-hole golf course. Easy access to scenic hiking, biking, hunting,

and ice, lake, and river fishing. Skiing at Jay Peak and Burke Mountain just 30 minutes away. Cocktail lounge on premises.

Hosts: David and Louise Bolduc
Rooms: 22 (PB) $35-60
Full Breakfast
Credit Cards: A, B, C, D
Notes: 2, 3, 4, 5, 7, 8, 9, 11, 12, 13, 14

ORWELL

Historic Brookside Farms

Route 22A, 05760
(802) 948-2727

In 1989, the farms celebrated their 200th anniversary. This 300-acre estate with its Greek Revival mansion offers rooms furnished with antiques, which, as part of the antique shop, are for sale. On the premises are cross-country skiing, hiking, boating, and fishing; golf and tennis are nearby.

Rooms: 8 (4 PB; 4 SB) $65-152
Full Breakfast
Credit Cards: None
Notes: 2, 3, 4, 5, 7, 8, 9, 13, 14

PERKINSVILLE

The Inn at Weathersfield

Route 106, Box 165, 05151
(802) 263-9217

An 18th-century stagecoach stop offering bedrooms with private baths, most with working fireplaces. The inn serves American nouvelle cuisine dinners, has a full bar and extensive wine cellar, and features live piano music nightly. Dinner, high tea, and full breakfast are included in the room rate. On the 21-acre premises are a pond, an outdoor recreation area, horse-drawn sleigh or carriage rides, box stall and paddock facilities. An indoor recreation room features a sauna, aerobics equipment, and a pool table. Nearby are alpine and cross-country skiing, golf, tennis, hiking, and many points of interest.

NOTES: Credit cards accepted: A Master Card; B Visa; C American Express; D Discover Card; E Diner's Club; F Other; 2 Personal Checks accepted; 3 Lunch available; 4 Dinner available; 5 Open all year;

Hosts: Mary Louise and Ron Thorburn
Rooms: 12 (PB) $175-205 Modified American
    Plan
Full Breakfast
Credit Cards: A, B, C, D, E, F
Notes: 2, 4, 5, 6 (prior permission), 7, 8 (over 7), 9,
    10, 11, 12, 13, 14

PLAINFIELD

Yankees' Northview Bed and Breakfast

Rural Delivery 2, Box 1000, 05667
(802) 454-7191

Roomy Colonial situated on a quiet country
road in picturesque Calais. Antique-filled
rooms, quilts, stenciled walls, sitting room
with fireplace. Enjoy your breakfast on the
garden patio with mountain views.
Museums, antiques, quaking bog, and year-
round recreation are nearby. Cross-country
skiing. Picnic area with fireplace for guest
use.

Hosts: Joani and Glenn Yankee
Rooms: 3 (SB) $40-50
Full Breakfast
Credit Cards: None
Notes: 2, 5, 8, 9, 10, 11, 12, 13 (XC)

POULTNEY

Bed and Breakfast Inns of New England VT 712

329 Lake Drive, Guilford, CT 06437
(800) 582-0853

This bed and breakfast is a 100-year-old
beautifullly restored Queen Anne
Victorian. A wraparound porch and tower
make this inn distinctive. Three guest
rooms welcome guests with brass beds,
antique oak, stenciling, and gorgeous
views. An expanded continental breakfast
is served each morning, and all guests
receive a loaf of "parting bread" when they
leave. Lake St. Catherine is only three
miles away, and five ski areas are within
twenty miles. Private and shared baths.

Children over eight are welcome. Smoking
permitted. Resident dog and cats, but no
guest pets, please. $55-60.

Lake Saint Catherine Inn

Cones Point Road, 05764
(802) 287-9347; (800) 626-LSCI (reservations)

Rural country resort on crystal-clear Lake
Saint Catherine. Relaxation and wholesome
dining. Families welcome. AAA and Mobil
Travel Guide approved. Rates include free
use of aluminum boats, canoes, paddleboats, and sailboats. Breakfast, dinner, and
all gratuities are included in the daily rate.

Hosts: Patricia and Raymond Endlich
Rooms: 35 (PB) $124-164
Full Breakfast and Dinner
Credit Cards: None
Open mid-May to mid-Oct.
Notes: 2, 4, 7, 8, 9, 10, 11, 12, 14

The Stonebridge Inn

Route 30, 05764
(802) 287-9849

The Stonebridge Inn occupies Poultney's
most opulent building, sitting on a knoll
overlooking Main Street, and is listed in the
National Register of Historic Places.
Inside, the design reflects the Victorian era,
using bold colors in the common rooms
and soft florals, antiques, and down comforters in the guest rooms. A three-course
European breakfast is prepared by the hostess and served in the dining room. The
entire downstairs is open for guests' enjoyment.

The Stonebridge Inn

6 Pets welcome; 7 Smoking allowed; 8 Children welcome; 9 Social drinking allowed; 10 Tennis available; 11
Swimming available; 12 Golf available; 13 Skiing available; 14 May be booked through travel agents.

Host: Gail R. McGrath
Rooms: 5 (2 PB; 3 SB) $64-84
Full Breakfast
Credit Cards: A, B
Notes: 2, 5, 8, 9, 10, 11, 12, 13

PROCTORSVILLE

The Golden Stage Inn

Box 218, 05153
(802) 226-7744

The tradition of hospitality continues in this 200-year-old stagecoach stop. The warmth of grandmother's quilts, antiques, greenery, favorite books, and a blazing fire comfort you while Marcel prepares silken sauces and Kirsten bakes delectable chocolate desserts. The pool and gardens provide summertime delights, and the cookie jar is always full.

Hosts: Kirsten Murphy and Marcel Perret
Rooms: 10 (6 PB; 4 SB) $135-155
Full Breakfast
Credit Cards: A, B
Closed April and Nov.
Notes: 2, 4, 7, 8 (over 8), 9, 10, 11, 12, 13, 14

PUTNEY

Hickory Ridge House

Rural Route 3, Box 1410, 05346
(802) 387-5709

Gracious 1808 Federal brick manor surrounded by rolling fields and woods on a quiet country road near Putney village. Six working fireplaces (four in bedrooms), original tamarack wide-board floors, antique furnishings throughout, perennial gardens. Area offers fine crafts and music, antiques, hiking, cross-country skiing, boating, and swimming. Two miles from I-91 and the Connecticut River. Handicapped accessible.

Hosts: Jacquie Walker and Steve Anderson
Rooms: 7 (3 PB; 4 SB) $45-80
Full Breakfast
Credit Cards: A, B
Notes: 2, 5, 8, 9, 11, 13

RANDOLPH

Placidia Farm Bed and Breakfast

Rural Delivery 1, Box 275
(802) 728-9883

Six miles north of Randolph on 81 acres with mountain views, pond, and brook. Hand- hewn log home with private apartment for bed and breakfast guests. Deck for enjoying the view. TV, stereo, books, and games.

Host: Viola A. Frost
Apartment: 1 (PB) $75-80
Full Breakfast
Credit Cards: None
Notes: 2, 5, 8, 9, 10, 11, 12, 13

READING

The Peeping Cow Bed and Breakfast

Route 106, P. O. Box 178, 05062
(802) 484-5036; FAX (802) 484-9558

Circa 1820 farmhouse in pastoral stone-walled setting. Antiques, fireplace, goose down comforters, mellow old pine floors with handmade nails. A no-TV bed and breakfast where one can wallow in peace. Winter is the hiss and crackle of the fire, and watching snowfflakes drift to the ground. Summer showers drum on metal roof and adorn the meadow with rainbows. Featured in Christie's (fine art auctioneers) fund-raising gala. Quilts sold on premises.

Hosts: Anne R. (Nancy) and Frank Lynch
Rooms: 4 (2 PB; 2 SB) $60-80
Continental Breakfast
Credit Cards: None
Notes: 2, 5, 9, 11, 12, 13

RIPTON

The Chipman Inn

Route 125, 05766
(802) 388-2390

NOTES: Credit cards accepted: A Master Card; B Visa; C American Express; D Discover Card; E Diner's Club; F Other; 2 Personal Checks accepted; 3 Lunch available; 4 Dinner available; 5 Open all year;

A traditional Vermont inn built in 1828, situated in the Green Mountain National Forest. Fine food, wine, and spirits for guests. Nine rooms, all with private bath. Fully licensed bar and large fireplace.

Hosts: Joyce Henderson and Bill Pierce
Rooms: 9 (PB) $80-108
Full Breakfast
Credit Cards: A, B, C
Closed Nov. 15-Dec. 26; Apr. 1-May 15
Notes: 2, 4, 7, 8 (over 12), 9, 12, 13

ROCHESTER

Harvey's Mountain View Inn

Rochester North Hollow, 05767
(802) 767-4273

One of eleven choices by Family Circle (September 26, 1989) under farm and ranch categories, "Family Resorts of the Year." Accommodates 20 visitors. Heated swimming pool, duck/trout pond, special animal area at the inn. Farm one mile across the valley view. Fireplace room, modern bedrooms, many antiques, hayrides, picnics, pony rides. Chalet rental is also available, but meals are not included. Family rates available.

Hosts: Don and Maggie Harvey
Rooms: 10 (4 PB; 6 SB) $90-104
Chalet: $450 weekly
Full Breakfast and Dinner
Credit Cards: None
Notes: 2, 3, 4, 5, 6 (chalet only), 7 (limited), 8, 9, 10, 11, 12, 13

ROYALTON

Fox Stand Inn

Route 14, 05068
(802) 763-8437

Built in 1818 as a stagecoach stop. The dining room and tavern are open to the public and offer fresh seafood, choice meats, and international creations. The inn's second floor has five comfortably furnished guest rooms. Swimming, canoeing, tubing, bicycling, hiking, or fishing are readily at hand.

Hosts: Jean and Gary Curbery
Rooms: 5 (SB) $50-60
Full Breakfast
Credit Cards: A, B
Notes: 2, 4, 5, 7, 8, 9, 10, 11, 12, 13, 14

RUTLAND

The Inn at Rutland

70 North Main Street, 05701
(802) 773-0575

The inn is a beautiful restored 1890s mansion filled with unique period details. This Victorian bed and breakfast has eleven old-fashioned comfortable guest rooms with updated private baths, TVs, and phones. Guests are sure to enjoy our cozy, fireplaced common rooms after a busy day of sightseeing or skiing. A delicious continental breakfast and afternoon snack is included. Near Killington and pico ski areas. Corporate and off-season rates. No smoking.

Hosts: Amber and Mark Quinn
Rooms: 11 (PB) $65-150
Continental Breakfast
Credit Cards: A, B, C, D
Notes: 2, 5, 8 (over ten), 9, 10, 11, 12, 13

Fox Stand Inn

ST. JOHNSBURY

Echo Ledge Farm Inn

P. O. Box 77, East, 05838
(802) 748-4750; FAX (802) 748-1640

6 Pets welcome; 7 Smoking allowed; 8 Children welcome; 9 Social drinking allowed; 10 Tennis available; 11 Swimming available; 12 Golf available; 13 Skiing available; 14 May be booked through travel agents.

The Inn at Rutland

A charming Colonial farmhouse, circa 1793, with six bedrooms and private baths located in the center of the Northeast Kingdom. There is a field, river, greenhouse, gardens, and a big red barn to enjoy. Afternoon tea is served. Relax indoors with old books and magazines, or classic films on TV/VCR. Convenient to winter and summer activities. Everyone enjoys the hearty farm breakfasts. Recommended by National Geographic Traveler.

Hosts: Dorothy and Fred Herman
Rooms: 6 (5 PB; 1 SB) $45-67
Full Breakfast
Credit Cards: A, B
Notes: 5, 10, 11, 12, 13

SHOREHAM VILLAGE

Shoreham Inn and Country Store

P. O. Box 182, 05770
(802) 897-5861; (800) 255-5081

On the Village Green close to the college town of Middlebury and Fort Ticonderoga, this family-run inn, circa 1790, offers good food, great location, and excellent lodging. Close to all seasons' activities in Vermont! Call or write for free activities map and travel directions.

Hosts: Cleo and Fred Alter
Rooms: 11 (SB) $70
Full Breakfast
Credit Cards: None
Closed Nov.
Notes: 2, 4, 7 (limited), 8, 9, 10, 11, 12, 13, 14

SHREWSBURY

Buckmaster Inn

Rural Route 1, Box 118, Lincoln Hill Road, 05738
(802) 492-3485

Historic country inn that was originally a stagecoach stop stands on a knoll overlooking a typical red barn scene and picturesque valley. The charm of a center hall, grand staircase, and wide-pine floors show off family antiques. Wood-burning fireplaces, a library, huge porches, dining room, and country kitchen with wood-burning stove are special favorites of guests. Near ski areas, eight miles southeast of Rutland, near Cuttingsville.

Hosts: Sam and Grace Husselman
Rooms: 4 (2 PB; 2 SB) $50-65
Full Breakfast
Credit Cards: 2, 5, 8, 10, 11, 12, 13

SOUTH LONDONDERRY

The Londonderry Inn

Route 100, Box 301-70, 05155
(802) 824-5226

An 1826 homestead that has been welcoming guests for nearly 50 years. Special family accommodations. Huge livingroom, billiards, and Ping-Pong rooms, and cozy tavern. Well-known dining room with dinner menu that changes nightly.

Hosts: Jim and Jean Cavanagh
Rooms: 23 (18 PB; 5 SB) $33-82
Expanded Continental Breakfast

Shoreham Inn

NOTES: Credit cards accepted: A Master Card; B Visa; C American Express; D Discover Card; E Diner's Club; F Other; 2 Personal Checks accepted; 3 Lunch available; 4 Dinner available; 5 Open all year;

Credit Cards: None
Notes: 2, 4, 5, 7, 8, 9, 10, 11, 12, 13, 14

SOUTH STRAFFORD

The American Country Collection #078

4 Greenwood Lane, Delmar, NY 12059
(518) 439-7001

The large red barn serves as a backdrop to the striking white Colonial Cape with black shutters built in 1850. There's a trout stream across the road with an inviting swimming hole. The flagstone fireplace is the focal point of the livingroom, which also has a piano, couches, and plants. The two second-floor guest rooms have wide-pine floors and original Shaker-style doors and share a bath. There is a half-bath on the first floor. Smoking in common rooms only. Children welcome. Pets in residence. $60.

SPRINGFIELD

Hartness House Inn

30 Orchard Street, 05156
(802) 885-2115

This beautiful 1903 inn is listed on the national Register of historic Places. once the home of governor James Hartness, this home invites you to step back in time to a setting of gracious living, with carved beams, majestic fireplaces, and a grand staircase leading up to ten beautifully decorated rooms. You can also choose from 33 modern rooms in the annex. Enjoy swimming, tennis, gracious dining, and a unique feature: a 1910 tracking telescope and a small underground museum reached via a 240-foot tunnel.

Host: Eileen Gennette-Coughlin
Rooms: 43 (PB) $70-115
Full Breakfast
Credit Cards: A, B, C
Notes: 2, 3, 4, 5, 6, 7, 8, 9, 10, 11, 14

STOCKBRIDGE

The Wild Berry Inn

Route 100, 05772
(802) 746-8141

Unwind in this homey 1780 post-and-beam farmhouse. Situated on Route 100, the Skier's Highway and a scenic bike route. Wake up to a full country breakfast and enjoy late afternoon refreshments. Relax by the beautiful weatherworn sugar house or try activities such as hiking, fishing, swimming, picnicking, golf, antiquing, downhill and cross-country skiing, all nearby. At day's end, warm yourself at fireside.

Hosts: Barbara Havelka and Janet Heider
Rooms: 5 (3 PB; 2 SB) $60-125 seasonal
Suite: 1
Full Breakfast
Credit Cards: A, B, C
Notes: 2, 5, 8, 9, 11, 12, 13

STOWE

The American Country Collection #074

4 Greenwood Lane, Delmar, NY 12054
(518) 439-7001

Drive over the wood bridge that crosses the brook and up the long drive to the white Colonial set admi tall pine trees. The inn operates as a bed and breakfast from spring until the end of autumn. For the remainder of the year, the Modified American Plan is honored. The five guest rooms are large and sleep three or four people. Four rooms have private baths. Guests may use the livingroom/lounge with stone fireplace, game room, and workshop, where guests repair and sharpen skis. Easy access to antiquing, biking, hiking, canoeing, and leaf peeking. Smoking permitted. Continental breakfast is offered. $48-108, seasonal.

---

6 Pets welcome; 7 Smoking allowed; 8 Children welcome; 9 Social drinking allowed; 10 Tennis available; 11 Swimming available; 12 Golf available; 13 Skiing available; 14 May be booked through travel agents.

The American Country Collection #091

4 Greenwood Lane, Delmar, NY 12054
(518) 439-7001

Contemporary alpine-style private home nestled into the side of the Worcester Mountain Range just six miles from Stowe. The second floor is entirely for guests' use. The two guest rooms share a bath. One room may be rented with private bath. Breakfast is served in the elegant country kitchen in front of the wood-burning stove. No smoking; couples only. $65; $75-95 during foliage, with a two-night minimum stay.

Andersen Lodge— An Austrian Inn

3430 Mountain Road, 05672
(802) 253-7336; (800) 336-7336

A small, friendly Tyrolean inn in a quiet setting. Heated swimming pool, tennis court, livingrooms with fireplaces, TV, and air conditioning. Near a major ski area, 18-hole golf course, riding, hiking, fishing. Recreational path close by. Sauna and Jacuzzi.

Hosts: Dietmar and Trude Heiss
Rooms: 78 (PB) $78-98
Full Breakfast
Credit Cards: A, B, C
Closed April 10-June 1; Oct. 25-Dec. 10
Notes: 2, 4, 9, 10, 12, 13

Butternut Inn at Stowe

2309 Mountain Road, 05672
(800) 3BU-TTER

Award-winning inn on eight acres of beautifully landscaped grounds alongside a mountain stream. Cottage gardens, pool, antiques, afternoon tea, collectibles. All rooms have private baths. Close to sleigh rides, downhill and cross- country skiing, summer hiking, golf, tennis, horseback riding. Written as one of the "best bed and breakfasts in the northeast" by Skiing magazine. Honeymoon and anniversary packages available. Enjoy real "Texas" hospitality in Vermont. No smoking.

Hosts: Jim and Deborah Wimberly
Rooms: 18 (PB) $90-140
Full Breakfast
Credit Cards: A, B
Notes: 9, 10, 11, 12, 13, 14

Edson Hill Manor

1500 Edson Hill Road, 05672
(800) 621-0284

Romantic, secluded restaurant and country inn on 225 acres, minutes from the village of Stowe and Mount Mansfield. Most rooms are furnished with four-poster canopy beds, fireplaces, and sitting room areas. Newly redecorated dining room features innovative American cuisine. Riding stables and forty kilometers of cross-country ski trails on site.

Hosts: Jane and Eric Lande
Rooms: 26 (PB) $70-209
Full Breakfast
Credit Cards: A, B, C, D
Notes: 2, 3, 4, 5, 8, 9, 11, 13, 14

The Gables Inn

Mountain Road, Rural Route 1, Box 570, 05672
(802) 253-7730

Classic country inn with 13 beautifully appointed rooms in an 1860's farmhouse. New carriage house suites have queen beds, fireplaces, Jacuzzis, and TV. Outdoor hot tub and pool, sitting room and den. Hearty country breakfasts and candlelight family-style dinners. Minutes from seasonal attractions and Stowe village. Smoke-free bedrooms and dining room.

Hosts: Sol and Lynn Baumrind
Rooms: 17 (PB) $75-115 summer; $110-180
   Modified American Plan winter
Full Breakfast
Credit Cards: A, B, C
Notes: 2, 4 (winter), 5, 8, 9, 10, 11, 12, 13, 14

NOTES: Credit cards accepted: A Master Card; B Visa; C American Express; D Discover Card; E Diner's Club; F Other; 2 Personal Checks accepted; 3 Lunch available; 4 Dinner available; 5 Open all year;

Green Mountain Inn

Green Mountain Inn

Main Street, P. O. Box 60, 05672
(802) 253-7301; (800) 445-6629 (U.S. and eastern
  Canada)

Beautifully renovated 1833 country inn
listed on the National Register of Historic
Places and a member of Historic Hotels of
America. There are 54 antique-furnished
rooms, cozy sitting areas, two restaurants
and bars, full-service health club, beauty
salon, and shops. Situated in the heart of
Stowe Village close to area attractions:
alpine and Nordic skiing, hiking, biking,
tennis, golf, horseback riding, antiquing.
AAA and Mobil approved.

Host: Gameroff family
Rooms: 54 (PB) $80-190
Full Breakfast (additional charge)
Credit Cards: A, B, C
Notes: 2, 3, 4, 5, 6, 7, 8, 9, 11, 12, 13, 14

Guest House Christel Horman

4583 Mountain Road, 05672
(802) 253-4846; (800) 821-7891

Small, cozy bed and breakfast with eight
large double rooms with full private baths.
Guest livingroom with color TV, VCR,
hearthstone fireplace, and many books and
magazines. Rates include a full country
breakfast. One and one-half miles to downhill and cross-country skiing. Ski week rate
available.

Hosts: Christel and Jim Horman
Rooms: 8 (PB) $56-60
Full Breakfast
Credit Cards: A, B
Notes: 2, 5, 7, 8 (over 10), 9, 10, 11, 12, 13, 14

The Inn at the Brass Lantern

717 Maple Street, 05672
(802) 253-2229; (800) 729-2980

A traditional Vermont bed and breakfast
country inn in the heart of Stowe. Award-
winning restoration of an 1810 farmhouse
and carriage barn overlooking Mount
Mansfield, Vermont's most prominent
mountain. The inn features period antiques,
air conditioning, handmade quilts, planked
floors and private baths. Some rooms have
fireplaces and most have views. An intimate inn for house guests only. AAA three-
diamond inn. Special packages include
honeymoon, gourmet dining out, skiing,
golf, air travel, sleigh and surrey rides, and
more.

Hosts: Dustin and Andy Aldrich
Rooms: 9 (PB) $65-125
Full Breakfast
Credit Cards: A, B, C
Notes: 2, 5, 9, 10, 11, 12, 13, 14

Logwood Inn and Chalets

199 Edson Hill Road, 05672
(802) 253-7354; (800) 426-6697

6 Pets welcome; 7 Smoking allowed; 8 Children welcome; 9 Social drinking allowed; 10 Tennis available; 11
Swimming available; 12 Golf available; 13 Skiing available; 14 May be booked through travel agents.

Handsome main lodge offers eighteen guest rooms and two fully equipped chalets. Large, quiet livingroom with a massive fieldstone fireplace, and a TV room, swimming pool, and tennis are amenities guests are welcome to use. Five private acres with trees and flowers in abundance, and many bedrooms have private balconies. Situated near golf course, riding, biking, and restaurants.

Hosts: Melanie and Sam Kerr
Rooms: 26 (20 PB; 6 SB) $55-65
Full Breakfast
Credit Cards: A, B
Notes: 2, 5, 7, 8, 9, 10, 11, 14

The Raspberry Patch

606 Randolph Road, 05672
(802) 253-4145; (800) 624-0639

Country elegance, breathtaking views, and a warm, cheery welcome invite you to enjoy the peaceful, friendly atmosphere. Rooms are beautifully decorated with down comforters and antiques. A great breakfast is served when you want it, until 10:30 a.m. Sitting room with TV, games, and fireplace. Air conditioning. Minutes to restaurants.

Host: Linda V. Jones
Rooms: 4 (PB) $50-100
Full Breakfast
Credit Cards: A, B
Notes: 2, 5, 6, 7, 8, 9, 10, 11, 12, 13, 14

Scandinavia Inn

3576 Mountain Road, 05672
(802) 253-8555

Home of the Trolls! You can enjoy Troll ambience as a result of Mother, Father, and young Yorg's arrival from Norway. Since that great day, more relatives have arrived and are taking residence in each of the inn's rooms. They are busy working magic and bringing good luck to all guests. New troll stories have been known to originate from the porch while gazing at the moon and stars. You need to experience this troll magic and fairytale excitement personally. Words cannot express these feelings.

Hosts: Jan and Ed Griffiths
Rooms: 18 (PB) $55-90
Full Breakfast
Credit Cards: A, B, C
Notes: 2, 8, 11

The Siebeness

3681 Mountain Road, 05672
(802) 253-8942; (800) 426-9001

A warm welcome awaits you at this charming country inn. Antiques, private baths, homemade quilts, air conditioning. Fireplace lounge, BYOB bar, hot tub, pool with beautiful mountain views. Famous for outstanding food. Near skiing and golf. Packages available.

The Siebeness

Hosts: Nils and Sue Andersen
Rooms: 10 (PB) $60-95
Full Breakfast
Credit Cards: A, B, C, D, E
Notes: 2, 4 (winter), 5, 7, 8, 9, 10, 11, 12, 13, 14

Ski Inn

Route 108, 05672
(802) 253-4050

This comfortable inn, noted for good food and good conversation, is a great gathering place for interesting people. Guests enjoy themselves and one another. Nearest lodge to all Stowe ski lifts with miles of cross-country trails at the door. Cool and quiet in the summer.

Host: Harriet Heyer
Rooms: 10 (5 PB; 5 SB) $20-25/person
Continental Breakfast; Full Breakfast in Winter
Minimum stay holidays: 2-3 nights
Credit Cards: C
Notes: 2, 4 (winter), 5, 7, 8, 9, 10, 11, 12, 13, 14

Stowe-Bound Lodge

673 South Main Street, 05672
(802) 253-4515

A small guest house on a sheep farm in the beautiful Green Mountains. Downhill and cross-country skiing in the winter. Hiking and biking in summer. Meals are plentiful. Anyone desiring to change fast pace of city life for some relaxation and slower pace of country life will find Stowe, sometimes called the Ski Capital of the East, a refreshing change. Why not be Stowe-bound?

Hosts: Dick and Erika Brackenbury
Rooms: 12 (4 PB; 8 SB) $40-80
Full Breakfast
Credit Cards: None
Notes: 2, 5, 6, 7, 8, 9, 14

Timberholm Inn

452 Cottage Club Road, 05672
(802) 253-7603; (800) 753-7603

Nestled in a quiet location in the woods, this ten-room bed and breakfast is friendly, cozy, and comfortable. A large, airy common room has a fieldstone fireplace. Enjoy

mountain views from the deck. Guests are also invited to enjoy the outdoor hot tub. Two-bedroom suites are ideal for families. Near skiing, golf, hiking, tennis, and bike trails. Feast on a Vermont country buffet breakfast.

Hosts: Kay and Richard Hildebrand
Rooms: 10 (PB) $60-100
Full Breakfast
Credit Cards: A, B
Notes: 2, 5, 7, 8, 9, 10, 11, 12, 13, 14

Ye Old England Inne

Mountain Road, Box 320 B, 05672
(802) 253-7558; (800) 477-3771

As filmed in "Lifestyles of the Rich and Famous." Laura Ashley rooms and cottages, four-posters, fireplaces, and Jacuzzis. Classic English luxury amid beams, brass, copper, and stone, plus Mr. Pickwick's Polo Pub with rare ales, malts, cognacs, and vintage ports. Copperfields for superb gourmet cuisine. AAA three-diamonds and Mobil rated.

Hosts: Christopher and Linda Francis
Rooms: 18 (PB) $69-125
Cottages: 3 (PB)
Full Breakfast
Minimum stay weekends: 2 nights
Credit Cards: A, B
Notes: 2, 3, 4, 5, 6, 7, 8, 9, 10, 11, 12, 13, 14

TOWNSHEND

Townshend Country Inn

Rural Route 1, P. O. Box 3100, Route 30, 05353
(802) 365-4141

This inn was originally a farmhouse built in 1775 and has recently undergone major renovations. The dining rooms and lounge have working fieldstone fireplaces and are decorated in the traditional New England motif that includes white ash paneling and unique stencils. The cuisine is centered around hearty New England dishes such as seafood, veal, beef, duck, and many other specialties. Although the inn stresses attention to detail in service, as well as in our

6 Pets welcome; 7 Smoking allowed; 8 Children welcome; 9 Social drinking allowed; 10 Tennis available; 11 Swimming available; 12 Golf available; 13 Skiing available; 14 May be booked through travel agents.

kitchen, the atmosphere is one of casual dress, comfortable dining, and New England hospitality.

Hosts: Joseph and Donna Peters
Rooms: 3 (SB) $55-65
Continental Breakfast
Credit Cards: A, B, D
Notes: 2, 4, 8, 9

UNDERHILL

Sinclair Towers
Bed and Breakfast Inn

Rural Route 2, P. O. Box 35, 05489
(802) 899-2234; (800) 433-4658

A showcase of builder Edward Sinclair's craftsmanship, this 1890 Victorian, fully restored in 1989, has been described as "a study in architectural styles, incorporating a little bit of everything." Features include towers, gables, turrets, colored glass, and an intricately carved fretwork valance across the livingroom and stairway. Located halfway between Burlington and Smuggler's Notch. Barbecue and picnic areas. Handicap bathroom.

Hosts: Al and Bette Royce
Rooms: 6 (PB) $55-70
Full Breakfast
Credit Cards: A, B
Notes: 2, 5, 10, 11, 12, 13, 14

VERGENNES

Emerson's Guest House

82 Main Street, 05491
(802) 877-3293

Experience fine Vermont hospitality in this 1850 Victorian home surounded by spacious lawns, flower and vegetable gardens. Relax in the gracious living quarters or on the porch. Enjoy the full breakfast which includes homemade breads, muffins, jams, and jellies. Visit nearby Shelburne Museum, Morgan Horse Farm, and Kennedy Brothers Marketplace. Area reacreation includes fishing, boating, canoeing, hiking, and bicycling.

Hosts: Pat and John Emerson
Rooms: 5 (1 PB; 4 SB) $40-65
Full Breakfast
Credit Cards: None
Notes: 2, 5, 8, 10, 11, 12

Strong House Inn

82 West Main Street, 05491
(802) 877-3337

Comfortable, elegant lodging in an 1834 Federal-style home listed on the National Register of Historic Places. Perfectly located in the heart of the Lake champlain Valley with fine views of the Green Mountains and Adirondack ranges, the area offers some of the finest cycling in vermont. Nearby lake, hiking, golf, and Shelburne. The inn offers eight rooms, five with private baths and three with working fireplaces. A full country breakfast is included, and dinner is available on request.

Host: Mary Bargiel
Rooms: 8 (5 PB; 3 SB) $55-130
Full Breakfast
Credit Cards: A, B, C
Notes: 2, 3, 4, 5, 8, 9, 11, 12, 13, 14

WAITSFIELD

Hyde Away

Rural Route 1, Box 65, 05673
(802) 496-2322; (800) 777-4933

One of the oldest, circa 1820, and most comfortable inns in the valley. Centrally situated less than five minutes from Sugarbush, Mad River Glen, Mount Ellen, historic Waitsfield, the Long and Catamount trails. Full public restaurant and rustic tavern; hearty country meals. Families and children are welcome. Hiking, biking, swimming, fishing, tennis, and golf nearby. Mountain bike touring center.

NOTES: Credit cards accepted: A Master Card; B Visa; C American Express; D Discover Card; E Diner's Club; F Other; 2 Personal Checks accepted; 3 Lunch available; 4 Dinner available; 5 Open all year;

Host: Bruce Hyde
Rooms: 16 (4 PB; 12 SB) $60-70
Full Breakfast
Credit Cards: A, B, C
Notes: 2, 4, 5, 7, 8, 9, 10, 11, 12, 13, 14

Lareau Farm Country Inn

Box 563, Route 100, 05673
(802) 496-4949

Nestled in an open meadow beside the Mad
River, this 1832 Greek Revival farmhouse
is only minutes from skiing, shopping, dining, soaring, and golf. Sleigh rides,
cross-country skiing, and swimming on the
premises. When you come, you feel at
home and relaxed. Hospitality is the inn's
specialty. "One of the top 50 inns in
America"—The Inn Times.

Hosts: Dan and Susan Easley
Rooms: 14 (10 PB; 4 SB) $75-110
Full Breakfast
Credit Cards: A, B
Notes: 2, 5, 8, 11

Mad River Barn

Route 17, Box 88, 05673
(802) 496-3551

Mad River Barn preserves the rich, warm
atmosphere of a 1940s ski lodge. The Barn
houses a large game room, a lounge with a
fireplace and full bar, a restaurant, and
many comfortable, deep chairs. The pine-
paneled guest rooms are usually large and
nicely furnished. The beds have quilts
made by the hostess. The Annex is a small
farmhouse dating from 1820. It has been
remodeled to provide deluxe rooms, each
with a sauna, TV, and kitchenette. Up the
road is Mad River Glen, a favorite spot for
cross-country and downhill skiers. Other
year-round activities include local theater,
horseback riding, and gliding.

Hosts: Betsy Pratt
Rooms: 15 (PB) $50-75, seasonal
Full Breakfast
Credit Cards: A, B, C
Notes: 2, 5, 7, 8, 11, 12, 13, 14

Millbrook Inn

Route 17, Rural Free Delivery, Box 62, 05673
(802) 496-2405

Relax in the friendly, unhurried atmosphere
of this cozy 1850;s inn. Seven guest rooms
are decorated with hand stenciling, antique
bedsteads, and handmade quilts. Breakfast
and dinner included in the daily rate. Dine
in the romantic, small restaurant that features hand-rolled pasta, fresh fish, veal,
shrimp, and homemade desserts from the
varied menu.

Hosts: Joan and Thom Gorman
Rooms: 7 (4 PB; 3 SB) $50-130
Full Breakfast
Minimum stay weekends: 2 nights; holidays: 3
    nights
Credit Cards: A, B, C, E
Closed April 10-June 10; Oct. 25-Thanksgiving
Notes: 2, 4, 6 (summer only, prior arrangement) 7,
    8 (over 10), 9, 10, 11,12, 13

Mountain View Inn

Rural Free Delivery, Box 69, Route 17, 05673
(802) 496-2426

Mountain View Inn, a small country inn,
circa 1826, has seven guest rooms, each
with private bath, accommodating two people. The rooms are decorated wtih stenciling, quilts, braided rugs, and antique furniture. Meals are served family style around
an antique harvest table. Good fellowship
is enjoyed around the wood-burning fireplace in the livingroom.

Mountain View Inn

---

6 Pets welcome; 7 Smoking allowed; 8 Children welcome; 9 Social drinking allowed; 10 Tennis available; 11
Swimming available; 12 Golf available; 13 Skiing available; 14 May be booked through travel agents.

Hosts: Fred and Susan Spencer
Rooms: 7 (PB) $64.80-75.60
Full Breakfast
Minimum stay weekends: 2 nights
Credit Cards: None
Notes: 2, 4, 5, 7 (restricted), 8, 9, 10, 11, 12, 13, 14

Newtons' 1824 House Inn

Route 100, Box 159, 05673
(802) 496-7555

Enjoy relaxed elegance in a perfect country setting. Six guest rooms, all with private baths. Classical music, Oriental rugs, fireplaces, sun porch. Gourmet breakfast with breakfast souffles and freshly squeezed orange juice. Stroll on 52 acres on the Mad River. Even a private swimming hole! Featured in the Los Angeles Times, Glamour magazine and Travel & Leisure.

Hosts: Nick and Joyce Newton
Rooms: 6 (PB) $75-105
Full Breakfast
Credit Cards: A, B, C
Notes: 2, 5, 8, 9, 10, 11, 12, 13, 14

White Rocks Inn

The Waitsfield Inn

Route 100, P. O. Box 969, 05673
(802) 496-3979

This gracious 1820s restored colonial inn is located in the heart of the beautiful Mad River Valley. The inn offers spectacular skiing minutes away from Sugarbush and wonderful hiking, shopping, antiquing, and much more. Relax in one of the fourteen rooms, all of which are beautifully appointed with antiques, quilted beds, and private baths. Enjoy a full breakfast and let our "Innspired" staff make your stay a memorable one.

Host: David Reardon
Rooms: 14 (PB) $50-100
Full Breakfast
Credit Cards: A, B, C
Notes: 2, 4, 5, 8, 9, 12, 13

WALLINGFORD

The American Country Collection #055

4 Greenwood Lane, Delmar, NY 12054
(518) 439-7001

This restored 1840 Colonial farmhouse listed on the National Register of Historic Places is situated on 20 acres of pastures and woods. The Gothic-style barn, a Vermont landmark, is often painted by artists. Swimming, fishing, canoeing on the premises; golf, tennis, and horseback riding nearby. Five guest rooms, all with private baths. No smoking. Children over ten welcome. Pets in residence. $65-85. Rates slightly higher during foliage season. Two-night minimum stay during foliage season.

White Rocks Inn

Rural Route 1, Box 297, 05773
(802) 446-2077

Circa 1840s farmhouse inn, listed on the National Register of Historic Places, beautifully furnished with antiques, Oriental rugs, canopy beds. All rooms have private baths. Charming cottage with slate roof and cupola. Cathedral ceiling in living area, loft bedroom, whirlpool bath, kitchenette, and deck overlooking pastures. Close to four major ski areas, hiking, horseback riding, canoeing, summer theater, and good restaurants. No smoking.

Hosts: June and Alfred Matthews
Rooms: 5 (PB) $60-95
Cottage: (PB) $130
Full Breakfast
Minimum stay weekends: 2 nights; holidays: 2-3 nights
Credit Cards: A, B, C
Closed November
Notes: 2 (deposit), 8 (over 10), 9, 10, 11, 12, 13

Sugartree Inn

WARREN

Beaver Pond Farm Inn

Rural Delivery Box 306, Golf Course Road, 05674
(802) 583-2861

Beaver Pond Farm is an elegantly restored Vermont farmhouse situated on a quiet country meadow with spectacular views of the nearby Green Mountains. It is adjacent to the Sugarbush Golf Course and 40 km. of groomed cross-country ski trails. One mile from downhill trails of Sugarbush. Hearty breakfasts, snacks, hors d'oeuvres, and setups. Prix fixe dinners are available three times a week during winter season. Package plans are available, including skiing in winter and golf in summer.

Hosts: Bob and Betty Hansen
Rooms: 6 (4 PB; 2 SB) $32-65

Full Breakfast
Credit Cards: A, B, C
Closed April 10-May 25
Notes: 2, 4, 7, 8 (over 6), 9, 10, 11, 12, 13, 14

Sugartree Inn

Rural Route Box 38, 05674
(802) 583-3211; (800) 666-8907

An intimate mountainside country inn featuring handmade quilts atop canopy, brass, and antique beds. Oil lamps, original art, antiques, stained glass, and country curtains. Full country breakfast. Enchanting gazebo amid myriad flowers in summer, blazing foliage in fall, and downhill skiing in winter.

Hosts: Howard and Janice Chapman
Rooms: 10 (PB) $75-120
Full Breakfast
Minimum stay holidays: 2 nights
Credit Cards: A, B, C, D
Closed the last two weeks in April
Notes: 2, 7, 8 (over 6), 9, 10, 11, 12, 13, 14

West Hill House Bed and Breakfast

West Hill Road, Rural Route 1
P. O. Box 292, 05674
(802) 496-7162

Location, location, location! Just one mile from Sugarbush Ski/Summer Resort, Cross-Country Center, golf course, restaurants, and activities galore, yet still off the beaten path, West Hill House boasts both country charm and idyllic setting. An intimate, restored farmhouse, circa 1862, offers quiet privacy, gorgeous mountain views, cozy guest rooms, fireplace, BYOB wet bar, and a spacious porch with rockers. Mornings bring sounds of soft music and a hearty, delicious breakfast. Relaxed, friendly and affordable.

Hosts: Nina and Bob Heyd
Rooms: 4 (2 PB; 2 SB) $60-85
Full Breakfast
Credit Cards: A, B
Notes: 2, 3 (picnic), 4 (groups), 5, 8 (over 9), 9, 10, 11, 12, 13, 14

---

6 Pets welcome; 7 Smoking allowed; 8 Children welcome; 9 Social drinking allowed; 10 Tennis available; 11 Swimming available; 12 Golf available; 13 Skiing available; 14 May be booked through travel agents.

Grünberg Haus Bed and Breakfast

WATERBURY

The American Country Collection #039

4 Greenwood Lane, Delmar, NY 12054
(518) 439-7001

This 1790 Cape Cod was once a stagecoach stop and is now a haven for modern-day travelers seeking country comfort and hospitality. The six guest rooms are filled with country antiques. One room has a working fireplace. Two have private baths. The inn has a library, livingroom, dining room, large porch, and country kitchen, where a full breakfast is served at the long trestle table next to the brick hearth overlooking the Green Mountains. Smoking in common areas only. Children over six welcome. $65-110, seasonal. Three-night minimum stay over holiday weekends.

Bed and Breakfast Inns of New England VT 717

329 Lake Drive, Guilford, CT 06437
(800) 582-0853

Come enjoy the wonderful comfort at this restored 1832 farmhouse. The front porch, furnished with wicker chairs and flowers, is an inviting spot to relax, watch the sun go down, or enjoy a glass of wine. The sunny common rooms are large but cozy. Each of the six guest rooms has a private bath and individually controlled heat and air conditioning. A full breakfast of homemade sweetbreads, muffins, raspberry and blueberry pancakes, eggs, juices, and coffee is served each morning. The neighborhood offers downhill and cross-country skiing, snowmobile rides, and the inn's big screen television and VCR. Children over six are welcome. No guest pets, please. No smoking. $65-89.

Bed and Breakfast Inns of New England VT 718

329 Lake Drive, Guilford, CT 06437
(800) 582-0853

This three-story Austrian chalet is a classic example of Tyrolean architecture, complete with intricately carved balconies. The stenciled booths in the BYOB pub are perfect for a game of backgammon or checkers, and the adjacent Austrian dining room is set for memorable, musical breakfasts. Ten second-floor guest rooms overflow with antiques, comforters, and quilts. Each room opens to a balcony that surrounds the bed and breakfast and provides relaxing views of the Green Mountains. Private and shared baths. Children of all ages welcome. Two resident cats, but no guest pets, please. No smoking. $35-65.

Grünberg Haus Bed and Breakfast

Rural Route 2, Box 1595, Route 100 S, 05676
(802) 244-7726; (800) 800-7760

Hand-built Austrian chalet secluded in a mountainside forest. Year-round fireplace, BYOB pub, sauna, jacuzzi, tennis court, hiking, and cross-country ski trails and chickens. Guest rooms open onto a balcony wiht dramatic views of the mountains. Memorable, musical breakfasts such as ricotta-stuffed French toast, maple-poached pears, pumpkin apple streusel muffins. Innkeepers entertain at fireside grand piano. Minutes from Stowe and Sugarbush ski areas in Ben & Jerry Ice Cream's hometown. An environmentally responsible inn.

Hosts: Christopher Sellers and Mark Frohman
Rooms: 10 (5 PB; 5 SB) $55-70
Full Breakfast
Credit Cards: A, B, C, D, F
Notes: 2, 3, 4, 5, 8, 9, 10, 11, 12, 13, 14

Inn at Blush Hill

Blush Hill Road, Box 1266, 05676
(802) 244-7529; (800) 736-7522

A circa 1790 restored Cape on five acres with beautiful mountain views. The inn has four fireplaces, a large sitting room, and lots of antiques. It is lsituated across from a golf course, and all summer sports are nearby. Enjoy skiing at Stowe, Sugarbush, and Bolton Valley, only minutes away. Packages available.

Hosts: Gary and Pam Gosselin
Rooms: 6 (2 PB; 4 SB) $50-110
Full Breakfast
Credit Cards: A, B, C, D, F
Notes: 2, 5, 8, 9, 10, 11, 12, 13, 14

Thatcher Brook Inn

Thatcher Brook Inn

Rural Delivery 2, Box 62, Route 100 North, 05676
(802) 244-5911; (800) 292-5911

A faithfully restored Victorian mansion on the Vermont Register of Historic Buildings.

The guest rooms all have private baths; some have fireplaces, and others whirlpool tubs. Enjoy the gourmet restaurant and Baileys Fireside Tavern. Near Ben and Jerry's ice cream factory, Cold Hollow Cider Mill, and Shelburne Museum.

Hosts: Kelly and Peter Varty
Rooms: 24 (PB) $75-160
Expanded Continental Breakfast
Credit Cards: A, B, C, D, E
Notes: 2, 4, 5, 7 (limited), 8, 9, 10, 11, 12, 13, 14

WATERBURY CENTER

The Black Locust Inn

Rural Route 1, Box 715, 05677
(800) 366-5592

Circa 1832 farmhouse set on a hill graced with black locust trees and looking to the Green Mountains and Camel's Hump. Antiques, old beds, lace curtains, Laura Ashley wallpapers, and Oriental rugs on polished hardwood floors. In the large livingroom there are movies, books, music, games, and magazines. Wine and cheese are served in the afternoon. Comfort, wonderful breakfasts, and a relaxed atmosphere are the inn's number one amenities.

Hosts: Anita and George Gajdos
Rooms: 6 (PB) $65-100
Full Breakfast
Credit Cards: A, B, D
Notes: 2, 5, 9, 10, 11, 12, 13, 14

WEATHERSFIELD

The American Country Collection #076

4 Greenwood Lane, Delmar, NY 12054
(518) 370-4948

This gracious inn was once a farmhouse that served as a stagecoach stop, part of the Underground Railroad, and a summer estate. Ten guest rooms and two suites, all with private baths. Most rooms have working fireplaces. Handicapped accessible. Guests can relax in the conservatory or

6 Pets welcome; 7 Smoking allowed; 8 Children welcome; 9 Social drinking allowed; 10 Tennis available; 11 Swimming available; 12 Golf available; 13 Skiing available; 14 May be booked through travel agents.

work out in the exercise room complete with Finnish sauna and pool table. A four-course breakfast begins the day. English high tea is served each afternoon, and a gourmet dinner is prepared each evening. Smoking in designated areas. Well-behaved children over eight welcome. $175 for a double; $200 for a suite. These rates include breakfast, tea, and dinner. Two-night minimum stay on weekends; three nights on holidays.

The Inn at Weathersfield

Route 106, Box 165, 05151
(802) 263-9217; (800) 477-4828 Reservations

An 18th-century stagecoach stop offering bedrooms with private baths, most with working fireplaces. The inn serves American nouvelle cuisine dinners, has a full bar and extensive wine cellar, and features live piano music nightly. Dinner, high tea, and full breakfast are included in the room rate. On the 21-acre premises are a pond, an outdoor recreation area, horse-drawn sleigh or carriage rides, box stall, and paddock facilities. An indoor recreation room features a sauna, aerobics equipment, and a pool table. Nearby are alpine and cross-country skiing, golf, tennis, hiking, and many points of interest.

Hosts: Mary Louise and Ron Thorburn
Rooms: 12 (PB) $175-205
Full Breakfast
Credit Cards: A, B, C, D, E
Notes: 2, 4, 5, 6 (prior permission), 7, 8 (over 7), 9, 10, 11, 12, 13, 14

WEST DOVER

Austin Hill Inn

Route 100, 05356
(802) 464-5281; (800) 332-RELAX

Guests are invited to experience a less complicated world where one can leave behind the pressures of life with timeless relaxation. Each guest room is refreshingly different. Austin Hill offers fireplace in common rooms, peace at poolside, afternoon tea and wine list selections, and wonderfully prepared home-cooked meals. All recreational activities and shopping are within minutes, even though the inn is tucked away at the edge of the Green Mountains.

Host: Robbie Sweeney
Rooms: 12 (PB) $72-125
Full Breakfast
Credit Cards: A, B, C
Notes: 2, 4 (weekends), 5, 10, 11, 12, 13

Deerhill Inn and Restaurant

Valleyview Road, Box 136, 05356-0136
(802) 464-3100

A gracious English country house with mountain views, candlelight dining, superb cuisine, spacious sitting rooms, fine English and American antiques, afternoon tea, licensed lounge, private baths, some rooms with canopy beds, lovely grounds, swimming pool, tennis court. Located in Mount Snow area. Alpine and Nordic skiing, mountain biking, two champion golf courses, golf school, walking, fishing, boating, antiquing, shopping, craft fairs, Marlboro Music Festival, and just plain relaxing.

Hosts: Robert and Joan Ritchie
Rooms: 17 (15 PB; 2 SB) $99-130
Full Breakfast
Credit Cards: A, B, C, E
Open Thanksgiving-Mar. 31; Memorial Day-Oct.
Notes: 2, 4, 8 (8 and over), 9, 10, 11, 12, 13, 14

West Dover Inn

P. O. Box 506, Route 100, 05356
(802) 464-5207

Historic old inn, circa 1846, located in the foothills of the Green Mountains. Elegant rooms, all with private baths, and luxurious fireplace suites with whirlpool tubs. Full complimentary breakfast. Elegant dining in the Capstone Restaurant, featuring tableside cooking, extensive wine list. Full bar and lounge. Minutes to golf, skiing, tennis, and swimming. AAA three-diamond rated.

Hosts: Don and Madeline Mitchell
Rooms: 10 (PB) $75-195
Full Breakfast
Credit Cards: A, B, C
Notes: 2, 4, 7, 8 (over 8), 9, 10, 11, 12, 13, 14

WEST HARTFORD

The Half Penny Inn

Handy Road, P. O. Box 84, 05084
(802) 295-6082

You probably think that the last thing Vermont needs is another cutesy bed and breakfast. We agree! That's why we don't boast about Laura Ashley prints, Oriental rugs, rare art, or cable TV by the whirlpool. As a matter of fact, we had little to do with the Half Penny. Our ancestors provided the furniture; the Hazen family created the farm in 1775; Mother Nature had a hand in creating the mountain, the pond, and the White River Valley; the Appalachian Mountain Club built the hiking trail; and the town highway department grades our road. The Half Penny is a peaceful retreat away from all the traffic on busy Route 4, yet only twenty minutes from Woodstock, Hanover, Quechee, and west Hartford. All we do is open the door and say, "Welcome! It's yours to enjoy."

Hosts: Gretchen and Bob Fairweather
Rooms: 5 (PB) $90-125
Full Breakfast
Credit Cards: None
Notes: 2, 5, 9, 10, 11, 12, 13, 14

WESTON

1830 Inn on the Green

Route 100, 05161
(802) 824-6789

Colonial building built in 1830 as a blacksmith/wheelwright shop, situated in the center of town overlooking the delightful village green. Parlor with fireplace, slate terrace overlooking the gardens and pond.

Furnished with traditional and family antiques.

Hosts: Sandy and Dave Granger
Rooms: 4 (PB) $60-80
Full Breakfast
Credit Cards: A, B
Notes: 2, 5, 9, 10, 11, 12, 13, 14

The Wilder Homestead Inn

The Wilder Homestead Inn and 1827 Craft Shoppe

Rural Route 1, Box 106 D, 05161
(802) 824-8172

An 1827 brick home listed on the National Register of Historic Places.Walk to shops, museums, summer theater. Crackling fires in common rooms, canopy beds, down comforters. Rooms have original Moses Eaton stenciling and are furnished with antiques and reproductions. Weston Priory nearby.

Hosts: Peggy and Roy Varner
Rooms: 7 (5 PB; 2 SB) $60-95
Full Breakfast
Minimum stay weekends: 2 nights; holidays: 2-3
  nights
Credit Cards: A, B
Notes: 2, 5, 8 (over 6), 9, 10, 11, 12, 13, 14

WEST RUTLAND

The American Country Collection #081

4 Greenwood Lane, Delmar, NY 12054
(518) 439-7001

---

6 Pets welcome; 7 Smoking allowed; 8 Children welcome; 9 Social drinking allowed; 10 Tennis available; 11 Swimming available; 12 Golf available; 13 Skiing available; 14 May be booked through travel agents.

The inn is surrounded by three acres of green pastures, sugar maple forests, and mountains. In winter there is skiing at nearby Killington and Pico ski areas. Seven guest rooms, all with private baths. Three rooms on the first floor, four on the second floor. Elegant four-course dinners and hearty breakfasts are served in two intimate dining rooms. Smoking in common areas only. Children over 11 welcome. Resident dogs. $75-135. Modified American Plan also available. Three-night minimum stay most holidays.

WEST TOWNSHEND

The American Country Collection #093

4 Greenwood Lane, Delmar, NY 12054
(518) 439-7001

Steeped in history, this farmhouse, built in 1773, is reputed to be the oldest standing house in West River Valley. There are several out-buildings and a duck pond on five acres. Three guest rooms with private baths offer such amenities as handmade crafts and quilts, fresh towels, sweets in the bed-chambers, and a tour of the small but historic property. Near covered bridges, flea markets, auctions, antiquing, factory outlet shopping, hiking, boating, fishing, swimming, and canoeing. Smoking limited to porch and outdoors. Children welcome. Cat in residence. Choice of full or continental breakfast. $55-60.

Windham Hill Inn

Rural Route 1, Box 44, 05359
(802) 874-4080

Circa 1825 farmhouse and barn situated at the end of a dirt road high in the mountains on 160 acres. Spectacular views, hiking trails, cross-country skiing. Summer out-door programs and concerts in the white barn. Fifteen guest chambers recently updated and redecorated (king and queen beds) some with hand-made solid cherry canopy beds. Hosts have an old-fashioned shoe collection. Wonderful candlelit dinners with six courses on fine china and antique silverware. Warm, caring innkeepers. A true country experience; judged one of the ten best inns in the nation. No smoking.

Hosts: Ken and Linda Busteed
Rooms: 15 (PB) $160-180 Modified American
  Plan
Full Breakfast
Credit Cards: A, B, C
Closed April 1-May 15; Nov. 1-Thanksgiving
Notes: 2

WILDER

New Hampshire Bed and Breakfast NH 320

329 Lake Drive, Guilford, CT 06437
(800) 582-0853

This 180-year-old residence was opened as a bed and breakfast inn in 1987. Situated on two acres with handsome red barns and lovely old trees, the former dairy farm belonged to a prominent local citizen who entertained guests such as President and Mrs. Coolidge and Amelia Earhart. A large formal livingroom with beamed ceililng and curved oak staircase has a wood-burning stove to ward off the chill on cold nights. In warmer weather, French doors open to a lovely private stone terrace bordered by flowers. Guests meet around the table for an elaborate continental breakfast in the cheerful dining room. There are five guest rooms, all comfortably furnished with antiques and tastefully decorated. A variety of bed sizes is available, and rooms have both private and shared baths. Children welcome. Smoking limited. Two resident dogs, but no guest pets, please. $100-130.

NOTES: Credit cards accepted: A Master Card; B Visa; C American Express; D Discover Card; E Diner's Club; F Other; 2 Personal Checks accepted; 3 Lunch available; 4 Dinner available; 5 Open all year;

Stonecrest Farm Bed and Breakfast

119 Christian Street, P. O. Box 509, 05088
(802) 295-2600

Founded in 1810, this former dairy farm still boasts red barns and spacious grounds in a country setting, but is close to everything. Located just three and one-half miles from Dartmouth College, Stonecrest welcomes parents and alumni, plus hikers, bikers, skiers, and visitors from near and far. there are five elegant guest rooms, three with private baths and antique furnishings throughout. Breakfast offers fresh fruit and homemade scones, and muffins and breads in the dining rooms where Calvin Coolidge was once a guest. Write for details about the Inn to Inn canoe trip.

Host: Gail Sanderson
Rooms: 5 (3 PB; 2 SB) $90-100
Continental Breakfast
Credit Cards: A, B
Notes: 2, 5, 9, 10, 11, 12, 13, 14

WILLIAMSTOWN

The Autumn Crest Inn

Rural Free Delivery 1, Box 1540, 05679
(802) 433-6627

The Autumn Crest Inn is a fully restored farmstead over 180 years old, nestled on 46 lush acres of fields and forest overlooking the spectacular Williamstown Valley. Enjoy a cozy fireplaced livingroom and sleigh rides in the winter, and in summer, relax on the wraparound front porch. Outstanding dinners by candlelight in the world-class setting. A robust breakfast is served each morning. This is a true country inn.

Rooms: 18 (PB) $88-138
Full Breakfast
Credit Cards: A, B, C
Notes: 2, 4, 5, 10, 11, 12, 13, 14

WILMINGTON

The Inn at Quail Run

HCR 63, P. O. Box 28, Smith Road, 05363
(802) 464-3362; (800) 34ESCAPE

Enjoy pristine mountain views, comfortable large rooms, a full country breakfast, and après ski snacks. Located on a quiet country road away from traffic. The entire inn is non-smoking. In winter, enjoy cross-country trails, and in summer, enjoy the heated pool and clay tennis courts. Amenities include large sauna, TV room, library, exercise room, game room, and antique store. A charming and romantic getaway.

Hosts: Tom, Marie, and Molly Martin
Rooms: 15 (14 PB; 1 SB) $80-125
Full Breakfast
Credit Cards: A, B
Notes: 2, 5, 8, 9 10, 11, 12, 13, 14

Misty Mountain Lodge

Stowe Hill Road, Box 114, 05363
(802) 464-3961

A small family inn built in 1803, with a beautiful view of the Green Mountains. The lodge can accommodate 20 people. Home-cooked meals are prepared by the owners. The cozy livingroom has a large fireplace where guests gather to visit, read, or join in a hearty sing-along with your hosts. Summer walking trails. Close to several major southern Vermont ski areas and Marlboro Music for summer enjoyment.

Hosts: Buzz and Elizabeth Cole
Rooms: 9 (SB) $44-60
Full Breakfast
Credit Cards: None
Notes: 2, 4, 5, 7, 8, 9, 12, 13

Nordic Hills Lodge

179 Coldbrook Road, 05363
(800) 326-5130

6 Pets welcome; 7 Smoking allowed; 8 Children welcome; 9 Social drinking allowed; 10 Tennis available; 11 Swimming available; 12 Golf available; 13 Skiing available; 14 May be booked through travel agents.

Let yourself be spoiled at Nordic Hills, where one of the family members will serve you a choice-of-menu breakfast to start your day. This lodge offers the nostalgia of a country inn with the relaxing qualities of modern amenities including a Jacuzzi, sauna, outdoor pool, game room, and in-room TV. For the more active, skiing, championship golf, tennis, and horseback riding are within minutes. Two-diamond AAA rating.

Hosts: George and Sandy Molner; Marianne
   Coppola
Rooms: 27 (PB) $50-130
Full Breakfast
Credit Cards: A, B, C, D, E
Notes: 2, 4 (winter), 7, 8, 9, 10, 11, 12, 13, 14

Nutmeg Inn

Route 9 West (Molly Stark Trail), 05363
(802) 464-3351

For Vermont country elegance at its finest, a country inn just as you've always imagined a Vermont country inn to be. A 1770s farmhouse, carriage house, and barn combined. AAA three-diamond rated. Air-conditioned guest rooms, fireplace suites, all with private baths. Full country breakfast served daily. Nearby golf, swimming, tennis, downhill and cross-country skiing. BYOB bar and afternoon tea.

Hosts: Del and Charlotte Lawrence
Rooms: 10 (PB) $75-155
Suites: 3 (PB) $120-190
Full Breakfast
Credit Cards: A, B
Notes: 2, 5, 7 (limited), 8, 9, 10, 11, 12, 13

Nutmeg Inn

The Red Shutter Inn

Route 9 West, P. O. Box 636, 05363
(802) 464-3768; (800) 845-7548

This 1894 nine-room Colonial inn with fireplace suites sits on a hillside within walking distance of the town of Wilmington. Tucked behind the inn is the renovated carriage house with four rooms, one a two-room fireplace suite with a two-person whirlpool bath. A renowned restaurant with candlelight dining (alfresco dining on an awning-covered porch in the summertime). Championship golf (golf packages), skiing, hiking, boating, and antiquing are minutes away. Experience the congenial atmosphere of country inn life.

Hosts: Max and Carolyn Hopkins
Rooms: 9 (PB) $80-155
Full Breakfast
Credit Cards: A, B
Notes: 2, 4, 7, 8 (over 11), 9, 10, 11, 12, 13

Trail's End—A Country Inn

Smith Road, 05363
(802) 464-2727

Tucked along a country road, Trail's End offers traditional New England hospitality in a secluded, tranquil setting. The inn provides a warm, cozy atmosphere with a mix of antiques and family pieces. The rooms vary in size and have been decorated with oak dressers, brass headboards, and fluffy comforters.

Hosts: Bill and Mary Kilburn
Rooms: 14 (PB) $85-150
Full Breakfast
Credit Cards: A, B
Closed mid-April - mid-May
Notes: 2, 7, 8, 9, 10, 11, 12, 13

WINDSOR

Juniper Hill Inn

Rural Route 1, Box 79, 05089
(802) 674-5273

NOTES: Credit cards accepted: A Master Card; B Visa; C American Express; D Discover Card; E Diner's Club; F Other; 2 Personal Checks accepted; 3 Lunch available; 4 Dinner available; 5 Open all year;

Pamper yourself in this elegant but informal inn with antique-furnished guest rooms, all with private baths and some with working fireplaces. Sumptuous candlelight dinners and hearty full breakfasts are served. Cool off in the outdoor pool or visit antique shops, covered bridges, museums, and craft shops. Only 20 minutes to Woodstock and Quechee in Vermont and Hanover, New Hampshire. A perfectly romantic inn.

Hosts: Jim and Krisha Pennino
Rooms: 15 (PB) $80-120
Full Breakfast
Credit Cards: A, B, D
Closed Nov. 1-Dec. 15; mid-March-April 30
Notes: 2, 4, 9, 10, 11, 12, 13, 14

WOLCOTT VILLAGE

The American Country Collection #130

4 Greenwood Lane, Delmar, NY 12054
(518) 439-7001

Situated 12 miles north of Stowe, this Greek Revival-style three-bedroom inn is bordered by the LaMoille River and offers guests authentically appointed rooms and spacious bed chambers. Guest rooms are decorated according to themes, and breakfast features fresh fruit, cereal, French toast or baked eggs, scones or hot muffins, locally made preserves, coffee or tea. $41-59, seasonal.

Golden Maple Inn

Route 15, 05680-0035
(802) 888-6614

A delightful country inn nestled alongside northern Vermont's Lamoille River offers large common rooms and spacious bed chambers appointed with comfortable antiques and cozy down comforters. Scrumptious breakfasts are served in the victorian dining room. Canoe, fish, hike, bike, and cross-country ski right from the inn. Located near Fisher Covered Railroad Bridge, Bread and Puppet Museum, Cabot Creamery, Stowe, and craftsbury villages.

Hosts: Dick and Jo Wall
Rooms: 3 (1-PB; 2-SB) $54-68
Full Breakfast
Credit Cards: A, B, C, D
Notes: 2, 4, 5, 9, 13, 14

WOODSTOCK

Applebutter Inn

Happy Valley Road, 05091
(802) 457-4158

The Applebutter Inn is a restored Federal house, built in 1854, with six guest rooms, situated in Taftsville, a historic hamlet of Woodstock. European-style bed and breakfast that combines country elegance, warm hospitality, and personal attention. Fine linens and down comforters on comfortable beds. Formal parlor and a sitting room with fireplace induce ultimate relaxation. A hearty, natural foods breakfast starts your day with exuberance.

Hosts: Andrew and Beverlee Cook
Rooms: 6 (2 PB; 4 SB) $60-80
Full Breakfast
Credit Cards: A, B
Notes: 2, 5, 8, 9, 10, 11, 12, 13, 14

Canterbury House

43 Pleasant Street, 05091
(802) 457-3077

A 100-year-old village home just east of the village green. This bed and breakfast, furnished with authentic Victorian antiques, has seven rooms with private baths. Livingroom with TV and stereo. Within walking distance of shops and restaurants. Full breakfast in dining room. Guest rooms have air conditioning and fresh flowers. Bicycles provided summer and fall.

Hosts: The Houghs
Rooms: 7 (PB) $75-125
Full Breakfast
Credit Cards: A, B,
Notes: 2, 5, 8, 9, 10, 11, 12, 13, 14

The Charleston House

21 Pleasant Street, 05091
(802) 457-3843

This circa 1835 Greek Revival home has been authentically restored. Listed in the National Register of Historic Places. Furnished with antiques combined with a hospitality reminiscent of a family homecoming. Situated in the picturesque village of Woodstock, "one of the most beautiful villages in America."

Hosts: Barb and Bill Hough
Rooms: 7 (PB) $100-135
Full Breakfast
Credit Cards: A, B
Notes: 2, 5, 8 (over 9), 9, 10, 11, 12, 13, 14

Virginia

Summerfield Inn

101 West Valley Street, 24210
(703) 628-5905

Summerfield Inn is in the Abingdon historic district, just two blocks from the world-famous Barter Theatre. Near the Appalachian Trail, Mount Rogers National Recreation Area, South Holston Lake, the Blue Ridge Parkway, Virginia Creeper Trail, excellent restaurants, and marvelous shops. Just off I-81 at Exit 8.

Hosts: Champe and Don Hyatt
Rooms: 4 (PB) $55-75
Continental Breakfast
Credit Cards: A, B
Notes: 2, 7 (limited), 8 (over 12), 9, 10, 12

ALEXANDRIA

Amanda's Bed and Breakfast #183

1428 Park Avenue, Annapolis, MD 21217
(410) 225-0001; (410) 383-1274

Historic old town Alexandria. Four blocks to stores, restaurants, and historic sites. One room with double bed and private bath. Continental breakfast. $85.

The Little House

719 Gibbon Street, 22314
(703) 548-9654

The entire antique-filled, two-bedroom Victorian town house is rented to guests. A

The Little House

Jacuzzi, washer and dryer, and stocked kitchen are available. Privacy is assured, but should guests need help with reservations or sightseeing, the off-premises manager will provide these services.

Host: Jean Hughes
Rooms: 2 (PB) $200
Self-serve Refrigerator
Credit Cards: None
Notes: 2, 5, 6, 7, 8, 9

Princely Bed and Breakfast, Ltd.

819 Prince Street, 22314
(703) 683-2159

6 Pets welcome; 7 Smoking allowed; 8 Children welcome; 9 Social drinking allowed; 10 Tennis available; 11 Swimming available; 12 Golf available; 13 Skiing available; 14 May be booked through travel agents.

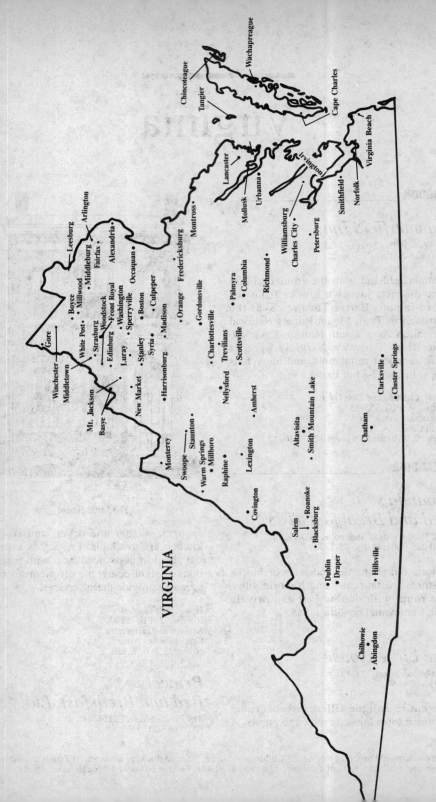

Thirty-three historic (1750-1875) homes in Old Town, Alexandria. Most homes are furnished with antiques, many of which are museum quality. Walk to all restaurants, shops, and monuments. Metro subway is a fast fifteen minutes to the White House and frequents ten major universities within ten miles. Mount Vernon is seven miles away. Accommodations range from $75-90.

Host: J. M. Ansimann
Rooms: 37 available homes; $75 and up
Continental Breakfast
Credit Cards: None
Notes: 2, 5, 7, 8, 9, 10, 12

ALTAVISTA

Castle to Country House

1010 Main Street, 24517
(804) 369-4911

Three luxurious, beautifully furnished guest rooms with access to a large living-room with a fireplace, formal dining room, sitting room with color TV and VCR, and a sun porch. All rooms are equipped with color cable television, telephones, king- and queen-size beds, and private baths. Central heat and air conditioning. Guests may choose either a continental or a full country breakfast. Whether you are traveling on business or vacationing for a week or a weekend, you are welcome.

Host: Christine Critchley
Rooms: 3 (PB) $50-60
Full Breakfast
Credit Cards: C, D
Notes: 2, 4, 5

AMHERST

Dulwich Manor Bed and Breakfast

Route 5, Box 173 A, 24521
(804) 946-7207

Gracious country lodging in an elegant English-style manor house with views of the Blue Ridge Mountains. Six beautifully appointed bed chambers with fireplaces; windowseats or whirlpool tub; canopy, brass, and antique beds. Enjoy the hot tub in the Victorian gazebo. Surrounded by 85 acres of natural beauty at the end of a country lane. A perfect romantic getaway convenient to Washington, Richmond, Charlottesville, and Lynchburg. Sumptuous country breakfast.

Hosts: Bob and Judy Reilly
Rooms: 6 (4 PB; 2 SB) $65-85
Full Breakfast
Credit Cards: None
Notes: 2, 5, 7, 8, 9, 14

ARLINGTON

Amanda's Bed and Breakfast #189

1428 Park Avenue, Annapolis, MD 21217
(410) 225-0001; (410) 383-1274

Victorian built in 1899. All exterior gingerbread is original except for the gable trim. Period antiques and lovely decor. Metro is one block away. One room with double bed and private half-bath. Continental breakfast. $75.

Crystal Bed and Breakfast

2620 South Fern Street, 22202
(703) 548-7652

Charming bed and breakfast furnished with country antiques close to Washington, D.C. Handmade quilts on queen beds. Large continental breakfast served weekdays, full country breakfast on weekends. Hostess is native Washingtonian with lots of suggestions. Lovely gardens in which to relax at day's end.

Host: Susan Swain
Rooms: 2 (SB) $60
Continental Breakfast weekdays; Full weekends
Credit Cards: A, B
Notes: 2, 5, 7, 8, 9, 10, 14

NOTES: Credit cards accepted: A Master Card; B Visa; C American Express; D Discover Card; E Diner's Club; F Other; 2 Personal Checks accepted; 3 Lunch available; 4 Dinner available; 5 Open all year; 6 Pets welcome; 7 Smoking allowed; 8 Children welcome; 9 Social drinking allowed; 10 Tennis available; 11 Swimming available; 12 Golf available; 13 Skiing available; 14 May be booked through travel agents.

Memory House

6404 North Washington Boulevard, 22205
(703) 534-4607

Charming, ornate 1899 Victorian fully restored with period antiques, wall stenciling, prize-winning handicrafts, and collectibles. Relax on front porch wicker or in double parlors. Tasty continental-plus breakfast. Conveniently situated for touring Washington, D.C. One block from the subway; three blocks from I-66 (Exit 69). Share in the old-fashioned comfort and friendship of Memory House. Smoking outside only.

Hosts: John and Marlys McGrath
Rooms: 2 (1 PB; 1 SB) $70
Expanded Continental Breakfast
Credit Cards: None
Notes: 2, 5, 14

Memory House

BASYE

Sky Chalet Country Inn and Restaurant

Route 263 West, P. O. Box 300, 22810
(703) 856-2147

This romantic hideaway in the Shenandoah Valley boasts spectacular breathtaking panoramic mountain and valley views. Welcoming weary travelers since 1937, Sky Chalet has rustic, homey, comfortable rooms, some of which have fireplaces, and all of which have private baths. Enjoy mountaintop dining with the open stone

fireplace, homemade breads, desserts, and "Valley" applebutter. The cozy, cedar pub has more views, a fireplace, and charm. Architecture and setting often compared to Switzerland.

Hosts: Mona and Ken Seay
Rooms: 8 (PB) $49-75
Continental Breakfast
Credit Cards: A, B
Notes: 2, 4, 5, 6, 7, 8, 9, 10, 11, 12, 13, 14

BLACKSBURG

L'Arche Farm Bed and Breakfast

1867 Mount Tabor Road, 24060
(703) 951-1808

Situated on five pastoral acres in close proximity to the educational, recreational, and historic attractions of southwest Virginia, L'Arche Farm Bed and Breakfast is a charming 1790 farmhouse. Spacious rooms traditionally decorated with antiques and handmade quilts have private baths. Delicious full farm breakfast featuring freshly gathered eggs from the farm, homemade breads, cakes, jams, jellies, and farm-fresh entrees. Good food and gracious hospitality on a country farm.

Host: Vera G. Good
Rooms: 4 (PB) $70
Full Breakfast
Credit Cards: None
Notes: 2, 5

Per Diem Bed and Breakfast

401 Clay Street Southwest, 24060
(703) 953-2604; (800) 272-4707

Located one block from Virginia Tech's campus and a five-minute walk to the stadium, Coliseum, and downtown Blacksburg, this lovely bed and breakfast offers two guest houses with fully equipped kitchens and comfortable living areas that are connected to the main house by a large covered porch. Antiques, Appalachian crafts and quilts, oriental rugs, and original art are

NOTES: Credit cards accepted: A Master Card; B Visa; C American Express; D Discover Card; E Diner's Club; F Other; 2 Personal Checks accepted; 3 Lunch available; 4 Dinner available; 5 Open all year;

featured. A beautifully landscaped court-yard includes a large heated swimming pool, patios, decks, and gardens. The guest houses are equipped with cable TV, phones, and air conditioning.

Host: Jo Pat Huggins
Rooms: 6 (4 PB; 2 SB) $65-75
Full Breakfast
Credit Cards: A, B
Notes: 2, 5, 9, 10, 11, 12, 14

Sycamore Tree
Bed and Breakfast Inn

P. O. Box 10937, 24062-0937
(703) 381-1597

Your dream of a romantic, luxurious vacation is on a picturesque mountain meadow in a custom-built bed and breakfast where you'll be pampered, enjoy wildlife from the porches, and sip tea by the fire. You can hike over 126 acres or meditate by the porch. The six guest rooms have private baths and central heat and air. Nearby are excellent restaurants, antique shops, golf courses, swimming, and university activities. Come be a part of the magic of the mountains.

Hosts: Charles and Gilda Caines
Rooms: 6 (PB) $85-110
Full Breakfast
Credit Cards: A, B
Notes: 2, 5, 8 (over 12), 14

BOSTON

Thistle Hill
Bed and Breakfast

Route 1, P. O. Box 291, 22713
(703) 987-9142

Situated on a hillside on the morning side of the Blue Ridge Mountains, Thistle Hill offers modern amenities in a rural parklike setting. Two cottages, one with a fireplace, and the main house are cozily decorated with antiques and collectibles. Relax in the hot tub, or wander through the lawns and woods. Enjoy afternoon tea in the gazebo and a hearty, savory breakfast in the morning. Picnics and candlelight dinners by arrangement.

Hosts: Charles and Marianne Wilson
Rooms: 4 (PB) $85-135
Full Breakfast
Credit Cards: A, B, C, D
Notes: 2, 3, 4, 5, 8, 9, 14

BOYCE

The River House

Route 2, Box 135, 22620
(703) 837-1476; FAX (703) 837-2399

A rural getaway on the Shenandoah River, built in 1780 and 1820. Convenient to scenic, historic, and recreational areas, the house offers special features and programs for house parties, small workshops, and family reunions. Accommodations are available for small, two- or three-day business conferences and executive retreats during the week. Relaxing, book-filled bed/sitting rooms have fireplaces, air conditioning, and private baths.

Host: Cornelia S. Niemann
Rooms: 5 (PB) $75-95
Full Breakfast/Brunch
Credit Cards: A, B
Notes: 2, 3 (prior arrangement), 4 (prior arrangement), 5, 7, 8, 9, 10, 11, 12, 14

CAPE CHARLES

Amanda's
Bed and Breakfast #122

1428 Park Avenue, Annapolis, MD 21217
(410) 225-0001; (410) 383-1274

Lovely, quiet, rural setting along the Chesapeake Bay featuring unspoiled land, abundant wildlife, game birds, miles of private beach, and nature's most fabulous sunsets. This two-story brick home has a great view of the bay and is decorated with antiques, reproductions, and collectibles. Three rooms with private baths. Full breakfast. $75-85.

6 Pets welcome; 7 Smoking allowed; 8 Children welcome; 9 Social drinking allowed; 10 Tennis available; 11 Swimming available; 12 Golf available; 13 Skiing available; 14 May be booked through travel agents.

Amanda's Bed and Breakfast #224

1428 Park Avenue, Annapolis, MD 21217
(410) 225-0001; (410) 383-1274

A picturesque country retreat with seventeen acres of private beaches for quiet leisure. Chartered fishing boats leave from the nearby village daily. Complimentary wine and cheese while watching the sunset. Six rooms with private and shared baths. Full breakfast. $60-75.

Amanda's Bed and Breakfast #138

1428 Park Avenue, Annapolis, MD 21217
(410) 225-0001; (410) 383-1274

Restored 1910 Colonial Revival. Just steps from a public beach on the bay. Enjoy and relax on one of the proches, sample the cool breezes off the bay, or bike through the historic town. Set your own pace and explore. Four guest rooms and one cottage. Full breakfast. $65-75.

Bed and Breakfast of Tidewater Virginia

P. O. Box 6226, Norfolk, 23508
(804) 627-1983

Nottingham Ridge

Located just two houses from the beach in a town designated as a "historic district," this 1910 house has been lovingly restored by its owners. There are French, English, and American antiques throughout with an antique brass bed in one room and a four-poster bed in another guest room. Four guest rooms are available. Full breakfast and afternoon tea served. $60-70.

Nottingham Ridge Bed and Breakfast

P. O. Box 97-B, 23310
(804) 331-1010

This lovely home reflects the beauty and charm of Virginia's historical Eastern Shore. Private secluded beach on the Chesapeake Bay bordered by tall trees, sand dunes, and abundant wildlife. Breakfast on the porch watching boats and birds or spectacular sunsets. Cooler times are spent in the den by a crackling fire. Biking, fishing, tennis, golf, running, bird-watching, crabbing, swimming, and sight-seeing are among the guests' favorite past-times. Visitors to Nottingham Ridge can look forward to an informal and relaxed atmosphere with emphasis on the small details that create a memorable stay.

Host: Bonnie Nottingham
Rooms: 3 (PB) $65-85
Full Breakfast
Credit Cards: None
Notes: 2, 5, 7 (restricted), 8 (over 8), 9, 10, 11, 12, 14

Pickett's Harbor

P. O. Box 97 AA, 23310
(804) 331-2212

Nestled in pines and dogwoods in a back yard of 27 acres in secluded and marvelous wide beach for guests, seagulls, pelicans, and herons. A Colonial home (big house, little house, and kitchen) with cupboards, doors, and floors made from old barn rafters. Fireplaces, antiques, and reproductions. All rooms and the porch face the

---

NOTES: Credit cards accepted: A Master Card; B Visa; C American Express; D Discover Card; E Diner's Club; F Other; 2 Personal Checks accepted; 3 Lunch available; 4 Dinner available; 5 Open all year;

Chesapeake Bay. Country breakfast served overlooking the bay. Late afternoon beverage served. Central air.

Hosts: Sara and Cooke Goffigon
Rooms: 6 (2 PB; 4 SB) $65-110
Full Breakfast
Credit Cards: None
Notes: 2, 5, 8, 10, 11, 12, 14

CASTLETON

Blue Knoll Farm

Route 1, Box 141, 22716
(703) 937-5234

This lovingly restored 19th-century farmhouse is located in the foothills of the Blue Ridge Mountains. The original house was built before the Civil War. Four guest rooms with private baths are open to guests. Blue Knoll provides a charming rural retreat minutes from the Inn at Little Washington—a renowned 5-star restaurant —and other fine dining establishments. Near Shenandoah National Park and Skyline Drive.

Hosts: Gil and Mary Carlson
Rooms: 4 (PB) $95-125
Full Breakfast
Credit Cards: A, B
Notes: 2, 5, 9

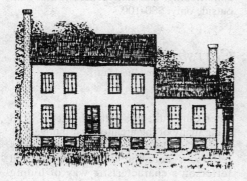

Pickett's Harbor

CHARLOTTESVILLE

Afton House

Guesthouses Bed and Breakfast
P. O. Box 5737, 22905
(804) 979-7264

A mountain retreat with panoramic views east to valleys and hills, this spacious home is on the old road up the mountain pass. There are four bedrooms, mostly furnished with antiques. One has a private adjoining bath, and three share two hall baths. Full breakfast is served. Antique shop on the premises and others in the village. $75-80.

Alderman House

Guesthouses Bed and Breakfast
P. O. Box 5737, 22905
(804) 979-7264

This large, formal Georgian home is authentic in style and elegant in decor. It was built by the widow of the first president of the University of Virginia in the early 1900s and is about one mile from the university. Breakfast is served with true southern hospitality. Guests may choose a room with a four-poster bed or one with twin beds, each with adjoining private bath. Air-conditioning. No smoking in the house. $72-80

Auburn Hill

Guesthouses Bed and Breakfast
P. O. Box 5737, 22905
(804) 979-7264

An antebellum cottage situated on a scenic farm that was part of the original Jefferson plantation. The main house was built by Jefferson for one of his overseers. It is convenient to Monticello and Ash Lawn, just six miles east of the city. The cottage has a sitting room with fireplace, bedroom with four-poster queen bed, and connecting bath and shower. Guests may use the pool in summer. Scenic trails, walks, and views. Air conditioning. No smoking. Supplies provided for guests to prepare breakfast. $100-125. Weekly rates available.

Balla Machree

Guesthouses Bed and Breakfast
P. O. Box 5737, 22905
(804) 979-7264

A deluxe separate suite in a contemporary home, this superb lakefront location offers complete privacy for guests. The suite is ten miles west of Charlottesville and overlooks a 250-acre lake with excellent fishing. The cozy quarters have a private entrance, large brick fireplace, and comfortable bedroom with iron frame double bed and private adjoining bath. Tennis is available on new courts, but please bring proper shoes. Golf, riding, hiking, fishing, and canoeing are nearby. Continental breakfast supplies left in the suite for guests to prepare. Air conditioning. $100-125.

Belleview

Guesthouses Bed and Breakfast
P. O. Box 5737, 22905
(804) 979-7264

A contemporary frame guest cottage offering complete privacy to guests. Situated five miles west of Charlottesville, in the Farmington Hunt country, these lovely quarters include livingroom with fireplace, Pullman kitchen, two bedrooms (one with twin beds, one with double tester bed) and full bath. A flagstone terrace off the livingroom offers privacy and mountain views. Air conditioning. Supplies provided for guests to prepare breakfast. $125-200.

Bollingwood

Guesthouses Bed and Breakfast
P. O. Box 5737, 22905
(804) 979-7264

A lovely home in a convenient neighborhood with a private "city" garden featured on the spring 1988 Friendly Garden Tour, this guest house is within walking distance of the University of Virginia, restaurants, and shops. One guest room with twin canopy beds has a hall bath. The second room has a double canopy bed, a three-quarter bed, and an adjacent bath. Air conditioning. $68-80.

Boxwood Lane Farm

Guesthouses Bed and Breakfast
P. O. Box 5737, 22905
(804) 979-7264

Virginia country living at its best describes this lovely bed and breakfast. A boxwood-lined path leads to the gracious front door of this 19th-century manor house just 15 miles south of Charlottesville and 15 miles from the Blue Ridge Parkway. There is a fine collection of contemporary paintings in this tastefully appointed home of a designer and an architect. This home has lovely surroundings, country walks past gardens with ponds and unusual plantings, and a pool is available for summer enjoyment. There are two large guest rooms, one with a queen-size bed and the other a double bed. Both rooms offer private baths, air conditioning, and full breakfast. Smoking outside only. $80-100.

Carrsbrook

Guesthouses Bed and Breakfast
Box 5737, 22905
(804) 979-7264

Peter Carr built this estate home in 1798 using many of the architectural innovations of his uncle and guardian, Thomas Jefferson, including 15-foot ceilings and Jefferson's characteristic way of hiding stairways. Private entrance to the suite is from a large patio overlooking a formal boxwood garden with the deepest hand-dug well in Albermarle County.

NOTES: Credit cards accepted: A Master Card; B Visa; C American Express; D Discover Card; E Diner's Club; F Other; 2 Personal Checks accepted; 3 Lunch available; 4 Dinner available; 5 Open all year;

Downstairs is the sitting room with a pull-out sofa, adjacent bath, and small refrigerator. Upstairs is a bedroom with a king-size bed. Listed on the National Register of Historic Places. Air conditioning. No smoking. $68-100.

Chathill

Guesthouses Bed and Breakfast
P. O. Box 5737, 22905
(804) 979-7264

A delightful country house in a rural setting only a few minutes' drive from Charlottesville and the University of Virginia. Accommodations consist of a large paneled room with fireplace and sofa bed in the sitting area, a queen bed, and adjoining bath. During the summer, visitors can enjoy the swimming pool and the informal gardens. No smoking in the house. Air conditioning. $80-100. .

Clifton—The Country Inn

Route 9, Box 412, 22901
(804) 971-1800

A Virginia historic landmark, Clifton is among the few remaining large plantation properties in Albermarle County. On 45 secluded acres with walking trails, private lake, small pool, tennis courts, and croquet pitch. All rooms feature wood-burning fireplaces, private baths, large sitting areas, canopy or four-poster beds. Five minutes to Charlottesville.

Host: Sue Putalik
Rooms: 9 (PB) $115-165
Full Breakfast
Credit Cards: A,B
Notes: 2, 4 (by arrangement), 5, 8, 9, 10, 11, 12, 13, 14

Clover Green Farm

Guesthouses Bed and Breakfast
P. O. Box 5737, 22905
(804) 979-7264

This farm is situated in beautiful rolling country in the foothills of the Blue Ridge Mountains. Guests are welcome to sit by the fire in the livingroom or enjoy the spectacular views from the sun room. The first-floor guest room with double bed is a large, sunny room furnished with Victorian family pieces. It has an adjoining bath with a shower stall. Smokers welcome. $68-100.

Coleman Cottage

Guesthouses Bed and Breakfast
P. O. Box 5737, 22905
(804) 979-7264

A late 19th-century servant's house, situated on Seven Oaks Farm, an antebellum estate 15 miles west of Charlottesville. Sitting below Afton Mountain, it offers guests splendid mountain views and spacious grounds. The cottage has three bedrooms (two with double, one with twin), living and dining rooms, kitchen, bath, and two porches. Convenient to Wintergreen ski resort 20 miles away. Air conditioning. Supplies provided for guests to prepare breakfast. $150-200.

Copps Hill Farm

Guesthouses Bed and Breakfast
P. O. Box 5737, 22905
(804) 979-7264

This ranch home is set on a small horse farm seven miles northwest of Charlottesville. Guests may enter through private lower-level entrance, where they have the seclusion of their own suite, a family room with TV and sofa bed, two bedrooms with adjoining bath. A full farm-style breakfast is served in the dining room or on the sun porch overlooking rolling pastures. Air conditioning. $68-80.

Cottage Grove

Guesthouses Bed and Breakfast
P. O. Box 5737, 22905
(804) 979-7264

6 Pets welcome; 7 Smoking allowed; 8 Children welcome; 9 Social drinking allowed; 10 Tennis available; 11 Swimming available; 12 Golf available; 13 Skiing available; 14 May be booked through travel agents.

This quaint country cottage offers beautiful views from two porches. The cozy guest room has an antique double bed and private hall bath. Another bedroom with a queen bed and private adjacent bath is available for a minimum of two nights. No smoking. $60-80.

Cross Creek

Guesthouses Bed and Breakfast
P. O. Box 5737, 22905
(804) 979-7264

A spectacular wood, stone, and glass "cottage" on a hilltop nine miles west of Charlottesville, Cross Creek is a perennial favorite. The livingroom, dining room, half-bath, and kitchen are built around a massive central stone fireplace. A deck provides a wonderful wooded view. Two bedrooms (one double, one king) are on the lower level with a full bath across the hall. Air conditioning. Supplies provided for guests to prepare breakfast. $125-200.

Farmington Heights

Guesthouses Bed and Breakfast
P. O. Box 5737, 22905
(804) 979-7264

Gracious living just off the Farmington Country Club back nine. This lovely home has wonderful views of pastures and hills. One guest room has a queen bed and adjoining bath; a second room has twin beds and private adjoining bath. This second room has a two-night minimum stay. In warmer weather, guests may enjoy the pool. Air conditioning. $72-100.

Fox View

Guesthouses Bed and Breakfast
P. O. Box 5737, 22905
(804) 979-7264

This traditional-style home has spectacular views of hills, fields, and mountains. The

guest facilities consist of a separate unit upstairs with a large sitting room, double bedroom with adjoining bath, and a room with twin beds sharing a second larger bathroom. Extra cots available. Air conditioning. $60-80.

Garth Cottage

Guesthouses Bed and Breakfast
P. O. Box 5737, 22905
(804) 979-7264

This charming guest cottage, previously the kitchen for the main house, is on a beautiful road in Virginia. The cottage has a whirlpool in the modern bath, bedroom with queen bed, and queen pull-out sofa in the large, comfortable livingroom. There are two TVs, kitchen, and dining nook. The huge working fireplace has the original cranes used for cooking. Enjoy beautiful mountain views. Air conditioning. Supplies provided for guests to prepare breakfast. $125-200.

Goose Call

Guesthouses Bed and Breakfast
P. O. Box 5737, 22905
(804) 979-7264

Gracious living in the woods 20 minutes northwest of Charlottesville. This tasteful home offers a guest wing off the family room and kitchen with two bedrooms with twin beds and a bath. There is an additional room on the lower level with twin beds and a private bath. Air conditioning. $60-80.

Indian Springs

Guesthouses Bed and Breakfast
P. O. Box 5737, 22905
(804) 979-7264

This new cottage with a rustic feel is in a lovely wooded setting on a private lake. The lake is stocked and has a small dock for fishing, basking in the sun, or swimming at your own risk. There is a large main room with a king bed, a sitting area with a queen sofa bed, dining area, kitchen, and bath. This cottage has complete privacy. TV, air conditioning. Supplies are provided for guests to prepare breakfast. $125-200.

Ingleside

Guesthouses Bed and Breakfast
P. O. Box 5737, 22905
(804) 979-7264

A farm that has been in the same family for several generations, Ingleside lies on 1,250 acres of rolling pasture backed by steep, wooded mountains. The house was built around 1840 of bricks made from the farm's red clay. Accommodations consist of a large, antique-furnished room with double bed, fireplace, and adjacent bath. A tennis court is available for guest use. Air conditioning. $68-80.

Ingwood

Guesthouses Bed and Breakfast
P. O. Box 5737, 22905
(804) 979-7264

In a lovely villa on six wooded acres in one of Charlottesville's most prestigious neighborhoods, Ingwood is an elegant, separate-level suite with its own drive and private entrance. The bedroom is appointed with antiques, queen bed, and adjoining bath. The sitting room includes a fireplace, Pullman kitchen, and sofa for an extra person. A second bedroom with twin beds and private bath is also available. Sliding glass doors open to a secluded terrace with a view of the woods. Air conditioning. Breakfast supplies are left in the suite for guests to prepare. $80-100.

The Inn at the Crossroads

Route 2, Box 6, North Garden, 22959
(804) 979-6452

Built in 1820 as a tavern on the historic James River Turnpike, the inn continues its long tradition, offering a quiet respite for the weary traveler. A four-story brick building with a long front porch, it is situated on five acres overlooking pastures and the foothills of the Blue Ridge Mountains and is convenient to Monticello and Charlottesville, as well as the James River and Skyline Drive.

Host: Lynn L. Neville
Rooms: 5 (SB) $59-69
Full Breakfast
Credit Cards: A, B
Notes: 2, 4, 5, 9, 13, 14

The Inn at Monticello

Guesthouses Bed and Breakfast
P. O. Box 5737, 22905
(804) 979-7264

A charming country inn on "Constitution Route," two miles from Monticello and Michie Tavern. There are five guest rooms furnished with antiques, two with fireplaces, and all with private baths. Common areas and porches abound. One porch overlooks lovely grounds. Carter's Mountain and a willow pond nearby. Full breakfast is served. No smoking or pets. Air conditioning. $115-125.

Keswick Victorian

Guesthouses Bed and Breakfast
P. O. Box 5737, 22905
(804) 979-7264

Lovely new home in the Victorian style built in beautiful Keswick hunt country. The guest quarters offer complete privacy in a large room with cathedral ceiling and furnished with many Victorian pieces. An old quilt hangs behind the brass double bed. There is a private entrance from a lovely deck overlooking the woods and garden. There is an adjoining full bath and a pullman kitchen where breakfast supplies will be left for you. No smoking. Air conditioning. $72-100.

6 Pets welcome; 7 Smoking allowed; 8 Children welcome; 9 Social drinking allowed; 10 Tennis available; 11 Swimming available; 12 Golf available; 13 Skiing available; 14 May be booked through travel agents.

Longhouse

Guesthouses Bed and Breakfast
P. O. Box 5737, 22905
(804) 979-7264

Built sometime between 1812 and 1845 to serve as stagecoach tavern, this two-story gray clapboard house twenty minutes west of Charlottesville blends stateliness of outline with a snug interior decor, and warm, friendly hospitality. The guest wing offers a large room with a double bed, a smaller room with a double bed, and a private bath. Guest quarters also include a private entrance. There is a creek on premises for wading. No smoking in the house. Air conditioning. $60-80.

Maho-Nayama

Guesthouses Bed and Breakfast
P. O. Box 5737, 22905
(804) 979-7264

Attention to detail is evident in the landscaping and furnishings of this beautiful Japanese-style home. The large master bedroom has a king bed with custom furnishings. The master bath has a sunken tub. Two rooms with double beds share a connecting bath. A private tennis court is available with advance notice and a service fee. Maho-Nayama is in a rural wooded area six miles northeast of town. Air conditioning. $80-100.

Meadow Run

Guesthouses Bed and Breakfast
P. O. Box 5737, 22905
(804) 979-7264

Enjoy relaxed rural living in this new Contemporary/Classical home six miles west of Charlottesville. Guest rooms have either a double bed or twin beds and share a bath. Guests are welcome to browse in the boat lover's library, play the grand piano, or lounge in the livingroom. Many windows offer bucolic vistas of the Southwest Range. Fireplaces in the kitchen and livingroom add to the homey, friendly feel of Meadow Run. Air conditioning. $68-80.

Meander Inn

Guesthouses Bed and Breakfast
P. O. Box 5737, 22905
(804) 979-7264

A 75-year-old Victorian farmhouse on 50 acres of pasture and woods skirted by hiking trails and traversed by the Rockfish River. The inn offers five queen or twin bedrooms, some with private bath. A full country breakfast is served. Guests may enjoy the hot tub, wood-burning stove, player piano, deck, or front porch. Wintergreen Resort and Stoney Creek golf and tennis facilities are available to guests. Smoking permitted outdoors only. Air conditioning. $60-80.

Millstream

Guesthouses Bed and Breakfast
P. O. Box 5737, 22905
(804) 979-7264

A lovely, large house about 20 minutes north of Charlottesville up a long driveway lined with old box bushes. The house, with a brick English basement, was built before the Civil War and enlarged in 1866. There are two guest rooms, each with private bath. Guests may enjoy the fireplace in the library or the mountain views from the livingroom. A full breakfast is served in the kitchen, which has hand-hewn exposed beams. No smoking. Air conditioning. $72-100.

Northfields

Guesthouses Bed and Breakfast
P. O. Box 5737, 22905
(804) 979-7264

This gracious home is on the northern edge of Charlottesville. The guest room is furnished with twin beds and has a TV, private bath, and air conditioning. There is another bedroom available with a double four-poster bed and private hall bath. A full gourmet breakfast is served. No smoking. $60-68.

North Garden

Guesthouses Bed and Breakfast
P. O. Box 5737, 22905
(804) 979-7264

This 110-year-old restored farmhouse is on a small farm with a pastoral setting and beautiful views. The guest room has three large windows, bright cheery colors, and private bath. Go hiking, enjoy the scenery, or just sit! Only 20 minutes to Charlottesville; 30 to Wintergreen. This farmhouse is ideal for families, as additional bedrooms are usually available for children. $68-80.

Park Street Victorian

Guesthouses Bed and Breakfast
P. O. Box 5737, 22905
(804) 979-7264

This late Victorian mansion is one of the largest homes in the downtown historical district. Surrounded by a large lawn and gardens, this accommodation offers a two-room suite with fireplace. Antique furnishings feature a stately high-back double bed. Private bath with shower adjoins the guest room. A continental breakfast is served in a beautiful formal dining room. Air conditioning. $80-100.

Piney Mountain

Guesthouses Bed and Breakfast
P. O. Box 5737, 22905
(804) 979-7264

This contemporary home on the side of a mountain is in a wooded setting with spec-tacular views of valley and mountain. There are several levels of deck, a hot tub, and pool. The lower-level suite has a sitting room with fireplace and two bedrooms with queen beds sharing a bath. On the main level, there is a queen room with a private hall bath. Upstairs is a room with twin beds and an adjoining bath. Guests may choose a continental or full breakfast. No smoking. Children over 12 welcome. $68-100.

Polaris Farm

Guesthouses Bed and Breakfast
P. O. Box 5737, 22905
(804) 979-7264

In the middle of rolling farm land dotted with horses and cattle, this architect-designed brick home offers guests an atmosphere of casual elegance. The accommodations consist of a ground floor room with twin beds and adjoining bath and two upstairs rooms with twin beds and shared bath. There are gardens and terraces where one can view the Blue Ridge Mountains; a spring-fed pond for swimming, boating, and fishing; and miles of trails for walking or horseback riding (mounts available at nearby stables). Air conditioning. $68-100.

Recoletta

Guesthouses Bed and Breakfast
P. O. Box 5737, 22905
(804) 979-7264

Recoletta is an older Mediterranean-style house built with flair and imagination. The red tile roof, walled gardens with fountain, and artistic design create the impression of a secluded Italian villa within walking distance of the University of Virginia, shopping, and restaurants. Many of the antique furnishings are from Central America and Europe. The charming guest room has a beautiful brass double bed and a private hall bath with shower. Air conditioning. $68-80.

6 Pets welcome; 7 Smoking allowed; 8 Children welcome; 9 Social drinking allowed; 10 Tennis available; 11 Swimming available; 12 Golf available; 13 Skiing available; 14 May be booked through travel agents.

The Rectory

Guesthouses Bed and Breakfast
P. O. Box 5737, 22905
(804) 979-7264

This charming home in a small village five miles west of Charlottesville was a church rectory. It is furnished in lovely antiques and has an English garden in the back. The guest room overlooking the formal rose garden has its own entrance, twin beds, and adjoining full bath. Air conditioning. No smoking.$68-80.

Silver Thatch Inn

Robin Hill

Guesthouses Bed and Breakfast
P. O. Box 5737, 22905
(804) 979-7264

A brick cottage on a lovely estate with boxwood gardens, Robin Hill consists of two bedrooms (one with twins, one with queen), parlor with fireplace and pull-out double sofa bed, full kitchen, and bath. A llama lives on the property. Children welcome. Arrival between noon and 7:00 p.m. Air conditioning. Supplies provided for guests to prepare breakfast. $125-200.

Rolling Acres Farm

Guesthouses Bed and Breakfast
P. O. Box 5737, 22905
(804) 979-7264

A lovely brick Colonial home in a wooded setting on a small farm, this guest house has two bedrooms with a hall bath upstairs. One room has a double bed and the other has twin beds. The house is furnished with many Victorian pieces. No smoking. Air conditioning. $60-80.

Silver Thatch Inn

3001 Hollymead Drive, 22901
(804) 978-4686

Silver Thatch Inn is a rambling white clapboard home that dates from 1780. With three dining rooms and seven guest rooms, it is a sophisticated retreat on the outskirts of Charlottesville. Silver Thatch's modern American cuisine uses the freshest of ingredients, and all sauces are prepared with fruits and vegetables. The menu features grilled meats, poultry, and game in season, and there are always vegetarian selections. The inn provides a wonderful respite for the sophisticated traveler who enjoys fine food and a quiet, caring atmosphere.

Hosts: Vince and Rita Scoffone
Rooms: 7 (PB) $105-125
Expanded Continental Breakfast
Credit Cards: A, B
Notes: 2, 4, 5, 8, 9, 10, 11

Stadium

Guesthouses Bed and Breakfast
P. O. Box 5737, 22905
(804) 979-7264

Located within walking distance of Scott Stadium, this one-story brick house offers convenience for university visitors. Guest accommodations consist of a double-bed room furnished with antiques and an adjacent private bath. This hostess is a Charlottsville native. Air conditioned. $60-72.

NOTES: Credit cards accepted: A Master Card; B Visa; C American Express; D Discover Card; E Diner's Club; F Other; 2 Personal Checks accepted; 3 Lunch available; 4 Dinner available; 5 Open all year;

Sunnyfields

Guesthouses Bed and Breakfast
P. O. Box 5737, 22905
(804) 979-7264

Sunnyfields is between Monticello and Ash Lawn. Opened for Garden Week in Virginia in 1981, it once operated as a dairy farm and vineyard. The main house has been modified several times, with the last major addition being in 1880. The original slave quarters are still standing nearby. The two guest rooms are large and airy and each has a fireplace. One has twin beds, the other a double. They share a hall bath. A swimming pool is available in the summer. $80-100.

Sunset Hill Country Inn

Guesthouses Bed and Breakfast
P. O. Box 5737, 22905
(804) 979-7264

A grand old house built below Wintergreen Mountain offers sweeping views and rooms furnished with period pieces. All nine guest rooms have private baths, some with Jacuzzis, some with private entrance and porches. Many activities nearby, including ballooning. Sumptuous continental breakfast. No smoking in the house. Air conditioning. $95-115.

Timberlake

Guesthouses Bed and Breakfast
P. O. Box 5737, 22905
(804) 979-7264

Timberlake is a large white clapboard house built in the 1920s as a summer retreat in the countryside near Ivy, west of Charlottesville. The large porch and beautiful gardens provide a wonderful place to stop and enjoy life passing by. A large guest room offers a double bed and private adjoining bath with shower. Other rooms are available for larger groups and families on special weekends. $60-80.

Tunlaw

Guesthouses Bed and Breakfast
P. O. Box 5737, 22905
(804) 979-7264

This modest cottage is hidden away on a side street near the University of Virginia. The guest room has a double bed and private adjoining bath with shower. A continental breakfast with delicious homemade breads is served. No air conditioning. $52-60.

200 South Street Inn

200 South Street, 22901
(804) 979-0200

Lovely restored inn, garden terrace, sweeping veranda, located in historic downtown Charlottesville, with English and Belgian antiques, six Jacuzzi tubs, eleven fireplaces, canopy and four-poster beds. Continental breakfast and afternoon tea (with wine) and canapes. Near Monticello, Ash Law, and University of Virginia.

Hosts: Brendan Clancy
Rooms: 20 (PB) $98-185
Continental Breakfast
Credit Cards: A, B, C
Notes: 2, 4, 5, 7, 8, 9 10, 11, 12, 13, 14

Upland Manor

Guesthouses Bed and Breakfast
P. O. Box 5737, 22905
(804) 979-7264

A grand old house built below Wintergreen Mountain has sweeping views of the surrounding countryside. The central part of the house was built in 1860 with additions from 1884 to 1907. Its gracious rooms are furnished with period pieces, and all nine guest rooms have private baths, some have Jacuzzis, and some offer a private entrance and porches. Many activities nearby including balooning. Sumptuous continental breakfast. No smoking in the house, please. Air conditioning $95-115.

6 Pets welcome; 7 Smoking allowed; 8 Children welcome; 9 Social drinking allowed; 10 Tennis available; 11 Swimming available; 12 Golf available; 13 Skiing available; 14 May be booked through travel agents.

Upstairs Slave Quarters

Guesthouses Bed and Breakfast
P. O. Box 5737, 22905
(804) 979-7264

A fascinating place to stay if you want interesting decor with the privacy of your own entrance. There is a harmonious mixture of antiques and art objects. The guest suite consists of a sitting room with a fireplace and two bedrooms (king and single) with bath (tub only). A couch in the sitting room opens to a double bed for extra guests. Adjacent to the University of Virginia and fraternity row, it is especially convenient for university guests. Air conditioning. $80-100.

Wayside

Guesthouses Bed and Breakfast
P. O. Box 5737, 22905
(804) 979-7264

A one-story brick Colonial furnished in Early American antiques, this well-kept home is on an elegant private street near the University of Virginia. Guests may use a single or a double room with hall bath, or a twin room with adjoining bath and private entrance. Two-night minimum stay for the twin room. Air conditioning and ceiling fans. $60-80.

Westbury

Guesthouses Bed and Breakfast
P. O. Box 5737, 22905
(804) 979-7264

Built around 1820, this antebellum plantation home is a beautiful reminder of what country living and sourthern hospitality are all about. Once a carriage stop between the James River and the Shenedoah Valley, Westbury now returns to the old tradition of welcoming travelers. Located in Batesville, a tiny community southwest of Charlottesville with a genuine country store, Westbury is only twenty minutes

from Skyline Drive and the Appalachian Trail. A comfortable double four-poster bed awaits you in the guest room. Private hall bath. No air conditioning. $60-72.

Winston

Guesthouses Bed and Breakfast
P. O. Box 5737, 22905
(804) 979-7264

This quaint Cape Cod brick home is on a quiet side street in an academic neighborhood near the University of Virginia. The private upstairs guest room offers twin beds and an adjoining bath. A home-style breakfast is served. Air conditioning. $52-60.

Winton on Pantops

Guesthouses Bed and Breakfast
P. O. Box 5737, 22905
(804) 979-7264

A brick Colonial east of town on Pantops Mountain overlooking the city of Charlottesville. The home offers two double bedrooms. One room also has a single bed, and both rooms share a hall bath. Full breakfast is served. There are resident cats. No air connditioning. $52-60.

Woodstock Hall

Guesthouses Bed and Breakfast
P. O. Box 5737, 22905
(804) 979-7264

A few miles west of Charlottesville, Woodstock was built about 1757 and 1808 and served as an 18th-century inn. Now listed as a Virginia landmark and with the National Register of Historic Places, the inn has been restored and furnished with period pieces. Four guest rooms are available, each with private bath and fireplace. Afternoon tea and a full breakfast are served. Guests may use the Federal parlor, keeping room, and patio. No smoking in the house. $95-130.

NOTES: Credit cards accepted: A Master Card; B Visa; C American Express; D Discover Card; E Diner's Club; F Other; 2 Personal Checks accepted; 3 Lunch available; 4 Dinner available; 5 Open all year;

House of Laird

CHATHAM

House of Laird
Bed and Breakfast

335 South Main Street, P. O. Box 1131, 24531
(804) 432-2523

A small-town setting where the amenities
of a less-hurried time are still preserved.
Century-old Greek Revival is in a grove of
200-year-old oaks. Professionally, lovingly
restored and decorated, all rooms have private baths, fireplaces, and canopied beds.
Antiques, Oriental rugs, imported moldings
and fabrics. Full breakfast on period china
and silver. Afternoon tea. Complimentary
wine and snack bar. Central heat/air.
Heated towels. Monitored security system.
Guest centered. Historic hospitality.

The Garden and the Sea Inn

Hosts: Mr. and Mrs. Ed Laird
Rooms: 4 (PB) $40-80
Full Breakfast
Credit Cards: A, B
Notes: 2, 5, 9, 14

CHILHOWIE

Clarkcrest
Bed and Breakfast

Star Route, Box 60, 24319
(703) 646-3707; (703) 646-3737

Clarkcrest is a solid brick farmhouse built
in the early 1800s with handmade brick. It
is located 1.4 miles south of I-81 on nine
acres of pastureland with barns.

Hosts: Doug and Mary Clark
Rooms: 4 (2 PB; 2 SB) $55-70
Continental Breakfast
Credit Cards: A, B
Notes: 2, 7, 12

CHINCOTEAGUE

The Garden and the Sea Inn

Virginia Eastern Shore, Route 710
New Church, 23415
(804) 824-0672

Elegant European-style country inn with
fine dining in a French-style gourmet
restaurant. Near beautiful beach and
wildlife refuge at Chincoteague and
Assateague islands. Large, luxurious
rooms, beautifully designed, with spacious
private baths. Fine Victorian detail, stained
glass, antiques, Oriental rugs, bay windows, skylights. Hearty continental breakfast and afternoon tea. Monthly chamber
music dinner concerts. Romantic Interlude
Package. Just 20 minutes to a beautiful
white sand beach/ocean and to tennis and
golf.

Hosts: Victoria Olian and Jack Betz
Rooms: 6 (PB) $75-115
Continental Breakfast
Credit Cards: A, B, C, D, E, F
Notes: 2, 4, 7 (public areas), 8, 9, 10, 11, 12, 14

6 Pets welcome; 7 Smoking allowed; 8 Children welcome; 9 Social drinking allowed; 10 Tennis available; 11
Swimming available; 12 Golf available; 13 Skiing available; 14 May be booked through travel agents.

The Little Traveller Inn

The Little Traveller Inn

112 North Main Street, 23336
(804) 336-5436

Gracious and romantic, this antebellum, beautifully furnished home is filled with Federal-style antiques. A garden sitting room with a fireplace opening onto a private brick courtyard with a fountain and rose garden is inviting to sit in, and all rooms are air-conditioned. Delicious homemade breakfast and afternoon tea specialties. Four minutes from Chincoteague Wildlife Refuge (with over 300 species), and a beautiful beach. Bicycling, hiking, swimming, antiquing, and canoeing close by. Ideal for small weddings, parties, and meetings.

Hosts: Charles D. Kalmykow and Carol W. Rogers
Rooms: 8 (3 PB; 5 SB) $65-105
Full Breakfast
Credit Cards: A, B
Notes: 2, 5, 9, 11, 14

Miss Molly's Inn

113 North Main Street, 23336
(804) 336-6686

A charming Victorian inn on the bay two miles from Chincoteague National Wildlife Refuge and Assateague National Seashore. All rooms are air-conditioned and furnished with period antiques. Room rate incudes full breakfast and a traditional English afternoon tea. Marguerite Henry stayed here while writing Misty of Chincoteague.

Hosts: Barbara and David Wiedenheft
Rooms: 7 (5 PB; 2 SB) $59-115
Full Breakfast
Credit Cards: None
Closed: January 1-February 12
Notes: 2, 8 (over 10), 9, 10, 11, 12, 14

Miss Molly's Inn

NOTES: Credit cards accepted: A Master Card; B Visa; C American Express; D Discover Card; E Diner's Club; F Other; 2 Personal Checks accepted; 3 Lunch available; 4 Dinner available; 5 Open all year;

The Watson House

4240 North Main Street, 23336
(804) 336-1564

The Watson House has been tastefully restored with Victorian charm. Nestled in the heart of Chincoteague, the house is within walking distance of shops and restaurants. Each room has been comfortably decorated, including air conditioning, private baths, and antiques. A full, hearty breakfast and afternoon tea are served in the dining room or on the screened porch. Enjoy free use of bicycles to tour the island. Assateague National Wildlife Refuge is two minutes away, offering nature trails, surf, and Chincoteague's famous wild ponies.

Hosts: David and Jo Anne Snead; Tom and Jacque
    Derrickson
Rooms: 6 (PB) $55-99
Full Breakfast
Credit Cards: A, B
Notes: 2, 7 (limited), 8 (10 and over), 9, 10, 11, 12, 13

The Watson House

Year of the Horse Inn

600 South Main Street, 23336
(804) 336-3221

Three guest rooms with private bath and balcony, right on the water, plus a two-bedroom apartment that sleeps six. One-hundred-foot pier for fishing or crabbing. Situated just ten minutes from the ocean beach, wildlife refuge, and wild ponies of Chincoteague.

Host: Carlton Bond
Rooms: 5 (PB) $70-90
Continental Breakfast
Credit Cards: A, B
Closed December and January
Notes: 2, 7, 8, 9, 10, 11, 12, 14

CLARKSVILLE

Needmoor Inn

801 Virginia Avenue, P. O. Box 629, 23927
(804) 374-2866

Needmoor Inn, circa 1889, a Victorian bed and breakfast in the heart of the beautiful Kerr Lake country, stands amid one and one-fourth acres of stately shade and fruit trees and a large herb garden. Enjoy comfortable antiques, private baths, gourmet breakfasts, complimentary bicycles, and therapeutic massage. Area activities include all water sports, excellent bass fishing, Occoneechee State Park, and Prestwould Plantation.

Hosts: Lucy and Buddy Hairston
Rooms: 3 (PB) $45-65
Full Breakfast
Credit Cards: None
Notes: 2, 5, 8, 9, 10, 11, 12

CLUSTER SPRINGS

Oak Grove Plantation

P. O. Box 45, 24535
(804) 575-7137

Operated from May to September 20 by the descendants of the family who built the house in 1820. Full country breakfast in the Victorian dining room. Hiking, biking, and over 400 acres of grounds. Near Buggs Island for swimming, boating, and historic Danville. In one of their midweek packages, hosts lead children's activities while parents relax. One hour north of Raleigh-Durham.

Host: Mary Pickett Craddock
Rooms: 2 (SB) $45
Full Breakfast
Credit Cards: None
Notes: 2, 4, 8, 9, 11, 14

---

6 Pets welcome; 7 Smoking allowed; 8 Children welcome; 9 Social drinking allowed; 10 Tennis available; 11 Swimming available; 12 Golf available; 13 Skiing available; 14 May be booked through travel agents.

COLUMBIA

Upper Byrd Farm Bed and Breakfast

6452 River Road West, 23038
(804) 842-2240

A turn-of-the-century farmhouse nestled in the Virginia countryside on 26 acres overlooking the James River. Enjoy fishing or tubing. Canoe rentals available. Visit Ashlawn and Monticello plantations. See the states' Capitol or simply relax by the fire, surrounded by antiques and original art from around the world. Breakfast is special.

Hosts: Ivona Kaz-Jespen and Maya Laurinaitis
Rooms: 4 (SB) $70
Full Breakfast
Credit Cards: None
Notes: 2, 5, 11, 14

Fountain Hall

COVINGTON

Milton Hall Bed and Breakfast Inn

207 Thorny Lane, 24426
(703) 965-0196

Milton Hall Bed and Breakfast Inn is an Virginia Historic Landmark, listed on the National Register of Historic Places. This country manor house built by English nobility in 1874, is located on 44 acres adjoining the George Washington National Forest and one mile from I-64, Exit 10. Spacious rooms are decorated in the style of the period and furnished with a combination of antiques, period reproductions, and unique pieces collected from various locations across the USA and overseas. Guest rooms feature queen-size beds, private baths, and sitting areas. All guest rooms, as well as common rooms, have fireplaces for your enjoyment.

Hosts: John and Vera Eckert
Rooms: 6 (PB) $75-140
Full Breakfast
Credit Cards: A, B
Notes: 2, 3, 4, 5, 6, 7, 8, 9, 14

CULPEPER

Fountain Hall Bed and Breakfast

609 South East Street, 22701-3222
(703) 825-8200; (800) 476-2944

Built in 1859, this grand bed and breakfast is within walking distance of historic downtown Culpeper. The inn is furnished with antiques and warmly welcomes business and leisure travelers. It offers one twin, two double, and three queen-size beds, and area activities and attractions include wineries, historic battlefields, antique shops, Skyline Drive, tennis, swimming, golf, and more. No smoking.

Hosts: Steve, Kathi, and Leah-Marie Walker
Rooms: 5 (PB) $50-115
Expanded Continental Breakfast
Credit Cards: A, B, C, D
Notes: 2, 5, 8 (supervised), 9, 10, 11, 12, 13, 14

DRAPER

Claytor Lake Homestead Inn

P. O. Box 7, 24324
(703) 980-6777; (800) 676-LAKE

NOTES: Credit cards accepted: A Master Card; B Visa; C American Express; D Discover Card; E Diner's Club; F Other; 2 Personal Checks accepted; 3 Lunch available; 4 Dinner available; 5 Open all year;

The inn is on the shores of Claytor Lake. Guests are greeted on the wraparound porch, then tour the 1800s farmhouse, with its antiques, reproductions, and items from the old Hotel Roanoke. A gourmet country breakfast served in the dining room with lake view features homemade muffins, Virginia ham, homemade sausage, or other southern foods. Swim or sun on the private beach. Boats, too! Blue Ridge Parkway, historic Newbern, and antique mall nearby.

Hosts: Judy and Don Taylor
Rooms: 5 (1 PB; 4 SB) $60-65
Full Breakfast
Credit Cards: A, B
Notes: 2, 5, 11, 14

DUBLIN

Bell's Bed and Breakfast

P. O. Box 405, 13 Giles Avenue, 24084
(703) 674-6331; (800) 437-0575

Situated in the beautiful New River Valley of southwestern Virginia, convenient to Radford University, Virginia Tech, New River Community College, Claytor Lake State Park, the historic Newbern community. Brick turn-of-the century Victorian home on large, shady lawn. Available to guests downstairs are livingroom, wide porch, parlor with fireplace, and a formal dining room where breakfast is served. Upstairs are five guest rooms, four with fireplaces, private or shared baths, a sun porch, sitting room, and kitchen. Hosts conversant in German, Spanish, and French, in addition to English.

Hosts: Helga and David Bell
Rooms: 5 (1 PB; 4 S3B) $45-65
Full Breakfast
Credit Cards: A, B
Notes: 2, 7 (limited), 8 (over 6), 9

EDINBURG

Mary's Country Inn

218 South Main Street, Route 2, Box 4, 22824
(703) 984-8286

This Victorian inn is situated in the heart of the Shenandoah Valley on the edge of town next to Stoney Creek and the Edinburg Mill restaurant. Close to a vineyard, antique shops, hiking, fishing, caverns, and other points of interest. The inn is reminiscent of Grandma's country home, with a full breakfast buffet.

Hosts: Mary and Jim Clark
Rooms: 5 (3 PB; 2 SB) $60-95
Full Breakfast
Credit Cards: A, B
Closed January
Notes: 2, 7 (limited), 8, 9, 12, 13, 14

Mary's Country Inn

FAIRFAX

The Bailiwick Inn

4023 Chain Bridge Road, 22030
(703) 691-2266; (800) 366-7666

In the heart of the historic city of Fairfax, 15 miles west of the nation's capital. George Mason University is just down the street, and Mount Vernon and Civil War battlefields are nearby. On the National Register of Historic Places. Fourteen rooms with queen-size feather beds and private baths, fireplaces, Jacuzzis, bridal suite. Afternoon tea. Candlelight dinner served by reservation. Small meetings and weddings.

Hosts: Anne and Ray Smith
Rooms: 14 (PB) $105-225

6 Pets welcome; 7 Smoking allowed; 8 Children welcome; 9 Social drinking allowed; 10 Tennis available; 11 Swimming available; 12 Golf available; 13 Skiing available; 14 May be booked through travel agents.

Full Breakfast
Credit Cards: A, B, C
Notes: 2, 4, 5, 8, 9, 10, 11, 12, 14

FRANKTOWN

Amanda's Bed and Breakfast #150

1428 Park Avenue, Annapolis, MD 21217
(410) 225-0001; (410) 383-1274

This charming 1895 Victorian home is in a setting of old maples, loblolly, white pines, dogwood, magnolia, and azaleas. The library is filled with volumes of books, many of them historical. Guests may also use the piano. Afternoon tea is served. Three rooms with private baths. Full breakfast. $65-75.

FREDERICKSBURG

Kenmore Inn

1200 Princess Anne Street, 22401
(703) 371-7622

Elegant inn built in the late 1700s. On the historical walking tour, near shops and the river. Grand dining and a relaxing pub for your enjoyment. Serving lunch and dinner daily.

La Vista Plantaion

Hosts: Ed and Alice Bannan
Rooms: 13 (PB) $85-150
Continental Breakfast
Credit Cards: A, B, C
Notes: 2, 3, 4, 5, 7, 9, 10, 11, 12, 14

The Spooner House

La Vista Plantation

4420 Guinea Station Road, 22408
(703) 898-8444

This lovely 1838 Classical Revival home is just outside historic Fredricksburg. On ten quiet acres, the grounds present a fine balance of mature trees, flowers, shrubs, and farm fields. The pond is stocked with bass. Choose from a spacious apartment that sleeps six with a kitchen and a fireplace or a formal room with a king mahogany rice-carved four-poster bed, fireplace, and Empire furniture. Homemade jams and farm-fresh eggs for breakfast.

Hosts: Michele and Edward Schiesser
Rooms: 2 (PB) $85
Full Breakfast
Credit Cards: A, B
Notes: 2, 5, 8, 9, 14

Richard Johnston Inn

711 Caroline Street, 22401
(703) 899-7606

In the downtown historic district, near many antique shops, a Civil War battlefield, and the homes of George Washington and Robert E. Lee. Close to Amtrak and hiking.

Hosts: Dennis and Libby Gowin
Rooms: 7 and 3 suites (PB) $60-130
Continental Breakfast
Credit Cards: A, B, C
Notes: 2, 5, 14

The Spooner House Bed and Breakfast

1300 Caroline Street, 22401
(703) 371-1267

A lovely two-room suite with private bath and private entrance in a 1794 Federal-style home within Fredericksburg's National Historic District. Breakfast served with a morning newspaper at the guests' convenience in their private quarters. Complimentary tour of the Rising Sun Tavern located next door to the Spooner House. Within walking distance of attractions, museums, restaurants, Amtrak, and shopping.

Hosts: Peggy and John Roethel
Rooms: 1 suite (PB) $70
Continental Breakfast
Credit Cards: None
Notes: 2, 5, 9

FRONT ROYAL

Chester House

43 Chester Street, 22630
(703) 635-3937; (800) 621-0441

A stately Georgian mansion with extensive formal gardens on two acres in Front Royal's historic district. Quiet, relaxed atmosphere in elegant surroundings, often described as an oasis in the heart of town. Easy walking distance to antique and gift shops and historic attractions; and a short drive to Skyline Caverns, Skyline Drive, Shenandoah River, golf, tennis, hiking, skiing, horseback riding, fine wineries, and excellent restaurants.

Hosts: Bill and Ann Wilson
Rooms: 6 (1 PB; 5 SB) $55-95
Continental Plus Breakfast
Credit Cards: A, B, C
Notes: 2, 5, 9, 10, 11, 12, 13, 14

Constant Spring Inn

413 South Royal Avenue, 22630
(703) 635-7010; FAX (703) 635-8217

The Constant Spring Inn is a combination of a warm country inn with the privacy, comfort, and convenience of a small hotel. Hilltop park-like setting, delightful views. All guest rooms have television, air conditioning, and private baths. To add to the enjoyment of this cozy inn, guests can also enjoy the fireplaces, cardroom, fitness studio, sports courts, lawn games, parlors, and bicycles. Nearby golf, horseback riding, canoeing, and vineyard tours.

Hosts: Charles and Mary Ann Wood
Rooms: 9 (PB) $58-95
Full Breakfast
Credit Cards: A, B
Notes: 2, 5, 8, 9, 10, 12, 13, 14

Sleepy Hollow Farm

GORDONSVILLE

Sleepy Hollow Farm

Route 3, Box 43, 22942
(703) 832-5555

This is a two-story, 18th-century farmhouse with flower and herb gardens, a pond, gazebo, and restored slave cottage.

6 Pets welcome; 7 Smoking allowed; 8 Children welcome; 9 Social drinking allowed; 10 Tennis available; 11 Swimming available; 12 Golf available; 13 Skiing available; 14 May be booked through travel agents.

Antiques and other lovely objects fill the rooms. Located near Montpelier in Orange Country's western historic district, amid cattle and horse farms.

Hosts: Beverley Allison and Dorsey Allison
   Comer
Rooms: 6 (PB) $60-95
Full Breakfast
Credit Cards: A, B
Notes: 2, 3 (by arrangement), 4 (by arrangement), 5, 6 (by invitation), 7, 8, 9, 10, 11, 12, 14

GORE

Rainbow's End

Route 1, Box 335, 22637
(703) 858-2808

Enjoy your stay at this comfortable country home on Timber Ridge in the Appalachian Mountains. Nearby Winchester provides quaint shops, historic attractions, antiquing, and fairs. The area provides hiking, fishing, and hunting in season. Every season has much to offer in this quiet apple country.

Hosts: Thom and Eleanor McKay
Rooms: 2 (SB) $45
Continental Breakfast
Credit Cards: None
Notes: 2, 5, 9

HARRISONBURG

Kingsway Bed and Breakfast

3581 Singers Glen Road, 22801
(703) 867-9696

Enjoy a view of the mountains from this modern country home in the beautiful Shenandoah Valley. The residence reveals the carpentry and homemaking skills of the hosts, who enjoy people and meeting their needs. Many house plants and outdoor flowers plus the in-ground pool make your stay restful and refreshing. Skyline Drive, caverns, historic sights, antique shops, and flea markets are nearby.

Hosts: Verna and Chester Leaman
Rooms: 2 (PB) $50-55 plus tax
Continental Plus Breakfast
Credit Cards: None
Notes: 2, 5, 6, 8, 11, 12, 13

HILLSVILLE

Bray's Manor Bed and Breakfast Inn

Route 3, Box 210, 24343
(703) 728-7901

This turn-of-the-century home is conveniently situated on U.S. 58, three and one-half miles east of I-77 at Exit 14. Rambling porch offers sitting, sipping, chatting, and cool breezes spring through fall. The parlor and sitting rooms provide TV, VCR, books, and cards before a warm fire in season. Croquet and badminton on the lawn. Convenient to Blue Ridge Parkway, crafts, golf, and tennis. Queen or twin beds, private or shared baths. Full country breakfast served anytime between 7:00 and 10:00 A.M. at your convenience.

Hosts: Dick and Helen Bray
Rooms: 4 (2 PB; 2 SB) $40-50
Full Breakfast
Credit Cards: A, B, D
Notes: 2, 5, 8, 9, 10, 12

IRVINGTON

Bed and Breakfast of Tidewater Virginia

P. O. Box 6226, Norfolk, 23508
(804) 627-1983

Originally a 19th-century boarding school, this is now an inn with nine guest rooms and assorted livingrooms, dining rooms, and screened porches. There is something for everyone here: side trips to historic houses, mainly Stratford Hall, for history buffs, and numerous activities for sports enthusiasts. A special country breakfast is served. Most rooms offer private baths. $50-65.

NOTES: Credit cards accepted: A Master Card; B Visa; C American Express; D Discover Card; E Diner's Club; F Other; 2 Personal Checks accepted; 3 Lunch available; 4 Dinner available; 5 Open all year;

King Carter Inn

King Carter Drive, 22480
(804) 438-6053

Victorian inn in the historic Northern Neck
of Virginia. Bicycles for use of guests;
golf, sailing, and fishing are nearby. Many
fine restaurants in the area.

Hosts: Marilyn Taylor
Rooms: 8 (4 PB; 4SB) $62.70-67.93
Full Breakfast
Credit Cards: None
Notes: 2, 5, 6, 7, 8, 9, 10, 12, 14

IVY

Nicola Log Cabin

Guesthouses Bed and Breakfast
P. O. Box 5737, Charlottesville, 22905
(804) 979-7264

This romantic, 200-year-old log cabin, situated on a 150-acre farm in historic Ivy
eight miles west of Charlottesville, has
spectacular views of the Blue Ridge
Mountains. The one-room cabin has a double bed, sleeper sofa, a new bath with
shower, microwave, refrigerator, and
wood-burning stove. Children's playset and
tennis court available. Supplies provided
for guests to prepare breakfast. $100-150.

LANCASTER

Holly Point

Route 3, Box 410, 22503
(804) 462-7759

Besides the many historical sites in the
area, Holly Point has 120 acres of pine forest and looks out on a lovely view of the
Rappahannock River. There are many land
and water activities: hiking, biking, swimming, boating, water skiing, fishing, and
crabbing.

Host: Mary Chilton Graham
Rooms: 4 (1 PB; 3 SB) $30-40
Continental Breakfast

Credit Cards: None
Closed November 1st-May 1st
Notes: 2, 6, 7, 8, 9, 11

LEESBURG

Fleetwood Farm Bed and Breakfast

Route 1, Box 306-A, 22075
(703) 327-4325

Beautiful 1745 plantation manor house, a
Virginia Historic Landmark on the
National Register of Historic Places.
Fireplaces, air conditioning, private baths
(one with large Jacuzzi), cookout facilities,
horseshoes, croquet, canoe, fishing equipment, and riding stables nearby. Lovely
gardens. Near Middleburg, Manassas
Battlefield, Harpers Ferry, and Wolftrap,
40 miles to Washington, D.C.

Hosts: Bill and Carol Chamberlain
Rooms: 2 (PB) $95-120
Full Breakfast
Credit Cards: None
Notes: 2, 5, 7 (outside), 8 (over 12), 9, 10, 11, 12,
  14

Norris House Inn

108 Loudoun Street, Southwest, 22075
(703) 777-1806

Elegant accommodations in the heart of
historic Leesburg. Six guest rooms all furnished with antiques, two with working

Fleetwood Farm

6 Pets welcome; 7 Smoking allowed; 8 Children welcome; 9 Social drinking allowed; 10 Tennis available; 11
Swimming available; 12 Golf available; 13 Skiing available; 14 May be booked through travel agents.

fireplaces. Full country breakfast served by candlelight. Perfect for romantic getaways, small meetings, and weddings. Featured in *Better Homes and Gardens*.

Rooms: 6 (SB) $80-130
Full Breakfast
Credit Cards: A, B
Notes; 2, 5, 9, 14

LEXINGTON—SEE ALSO RAPHINE

Historic Country Inns of Lexington

11 North Main Street, 24450
(703) 463-2044

Historic Country Inns of Lexington consists of three beautifully restored historic homes: Alexander-Withrow House and McCampbell Inn in the historic district, and Maple Hall, six miles north of Lexington, offering elegant lodging, intimate dining, fireplaces, fishing, swimming, tennis, historic touring, hiking, shopping, and relaxing. Wedding parties, honeymooners, small conferences, and family reunions, as well as travelers, enjoy the facilities. Come discover Lexington.

Owners: Peter M. Meredith Family
Innkeeper: Don Fredenburg
Rooms: 43 (PB) $85-120
Expanded Continental Breakfast
Credit Cards: A, B, D
Notes: 2, 4, 5, 7 (limited), 8, 9, 10, 11, 14

Llewellyn Lodge at Lexington

603 South Main Street, 24450
(703) 463-3235; (800) 882-1145

A warm and friendly atmosphere awaits guests at this lovely brick Colonial. Upon arrival, they are welcomed with refreshments. A hearty gourmet breakfast is served that includes omelets, Belgian waffles, sausage, bacon, and homemade muffins. The decor combines traditional and antique furnishings. Within walking distance of the Lee Chapel, Stonewall Jackson House, Washington and Lee University, and Virginia Military Institute.

Hosts: Ellen and John Roberts
Rooms: 6 (PB) $60-80
Full Breakfast
Credit Cards: A, B, C
Notes: 2, 5, 7, 8, 9, 10, 11, 14

LINCOLN

Springdale Country Inn

Lincoln, 22078
(703) 338-1832; (800) 388-1832

Restored historic landmark 45 miles west of Washington, D.C. This inn is on six acres of secluded terrain with bubbling brooks, walking bridges, and terraced gardens. Full meal service available to groups; breakfast is included in room price. Fully air conditioned.

Host: Nancy Fones
Rooms: 9 (3 PB; 6 SB) $95-125
Full Breakfast
Credit Cards: A, B, D, E
Notes: 2, 5, 8, 14

LOCUSTVILLE

Amanda's Bed and Breakfast #143

1428 Park Avenue, Annapolis, MD 21217
(410) 225-0001; (410) 383-1274

This 18th-century Colonial is near Wachapreague and just one mile from the ocean. Quiet and comfortable. Water sports nearby. One room with double bed and private bath. Continental breakfast. $68.

LURAY

Shenandoah River Roost

Route 3, Box 566, 22835
(703) 743-3467

Country log home facing the Shenandoah River. Three miles from famous Luray Caverns, ten minutes from Skyline Drive, fishing, swimming, tubing, and hiking. Close to two golf courses and horseback riding. No smoking.

Hosts: Gerry and Rubin McNab
Rooms: 2 (SB) $60
Full Breakfast
Credit Cards: None
Closed November 1st-May 1st
Notes: 2, 8 (over 12), 9, 10, 11, 12

LYNCHBURG

Langhorne Manor

313 Washington Street, 24504-4619
(804) 846-4667

Share the comforts, delights, and heritage of this home, a 27-room antebellum mansion built circa 1850. The spacious bedrooms and suites feature massive antiques, family heirlooms, private baths, and central air conditioning. Enjoy hearty homemade breakfasts with freshly ground coffee, then stroll around the architecturally magnificent historic neighborhood of Diamond Hill. Call about the "feel better" weekends of aerobic walks, biking, massage, and herbal cooking.

Host: Jaynee Acevedo
Rooms: 4 (PB) $70-95
Full Breakfast
Credit Cards: A, B, C
Notes: 2, 4, 5, 9

The Madison House Bed and Breakfast

413 Madison Street, 24504
(804) 528-1503

Lynchburg's finest Victorian bed and breakfast (1880) boasts a magnificent, authentic interior decor. Spacious, elegantly appointed guest rooms graced with antiques, private baths, plush robes and linens. Full breakfast served on antique limoges and Wedgewood china; fresh-perked cinnamon coffee and afternoon high

tea included. Central air, telephones, off street parking. Near colleges, Appomattox, Poplar Forest, fine restaurants.

Hosts: Irene and Dale Smith
Rooms: 3 and 1 suite (PB) $70-95
Full Breakfast
Credit Cards: A, B
Notes: 2, 5, 9, 10, 11, 12, 14

MADISON

Laurel Run

Guesthouses Bed and Breakfast
P. O. Box 5737, Charlottesville, 22905
(804) 979-7264

A recently built cottage in the woods of Madison County, 30 miles north of Charlottesville. This private cabin offers a great room, kitchen, dining area, and two bedrooms on the first floor. The loft has a double bed and cot. The broad, screened porch offers views of fields, stream, and woods. Hiking, fishing, and riding are available in nearby Shenandoah National Park. Breakfast supplies are included for the first morning of your stay. $60-100.

MADISON HEIGHTS

Winridge

Route 1, Box 362, 24572
(804) 384-7220

Come and share this grand southern Colonial home on a 14-acre country estate with views of the mountains. Enjoy the birds, flowers, and shade trees. Relax on the large, inviting porches. Warm, casual atmosphere. Hot, hearty breakfasts are served in the dining room. Families welcome. Close to Blue Ridge Parkway and Lynchburg.

Hosts: LoisAnn and Ed Pfister
Rooms: 3 (1 PB; 2 SB) $49-69
Full Breakfast
Credit Cards: None
Notes: 2, 5, 8, 10, 12, 13, 14

---

6 Pets welcome; 7 Smoking allowed; 8 Children welcome; 9 Social drinking allowed; 10 Tennis available; 11 Swimming available; 12 Golf available; 13 Skiing available; 14 May be booked through travel agents.

MIDDLEBURG

Amanda's Bed and Breakfast #126

1428 Park Avenue, Annapolis, MD 21217
(410) 225-0001; (410) 383-1274

Federal home, circa 1824, with high ceilings, seven working fireplaces, and a private garden. Three dining rooms, all with fireplaces and quiet music. Four guest rooms with private baths. A romantic retreat in Virginia's horse country. Continental breakfast. $125-225.

Welbourne

Middleburg, 22117
(703) 687-3201

A seven-generation, antebellum plantation home in the middle of Virginia's fox-hunting country. On a 600-acre working farm. Full southern breakfasts, working fireplaces, cottages. On the National Register of Historic Places.

Hosts: Nat and Sherry Morison
Rooms: 10 (PB) $64-96
Full Breakfast
Credit Cards: None
Notes: 2, 5, 6, 7, 8, 9

MIDDLETOWN

The Wayside Inn

7783 Main Street, 22657
(703) 869-1797

Hearty colonial dishes are the trademark of the Wayside Inn, nestled in the Shenandoah Valley. Its history is as rich as its traditional food. Originally built in 1797 as Wilkinson's Inn, it served early travelers through the Shenandoah even before a road was cut for stagecoaches. The chef has done historical research to produce his special Jeffersonian dishes. Three meals served daily.

Rooms: 24 (PB) $70-125 American Plan
Full Breakfast
Credit Cards: None
Notes: 3, 4

MILLBORO

Fort Lewis Lodge

HCR 3, Box 21A, 24460
(703) 925-2314

Mountain forests teeming with deer and wild turkey; glistening river runs cool and clear. These are the gifts nature bestowed on Fort Lewis. The lodge's large gathering room and 12 guest rooms with wildlife art and handcrafted furniture are cozy and downright comfortable. For dinner and breakfast you'll feast on meals of homemade everything in a magnificently restored 19th-century grist mill.

Hosts: John and Caryl Cowden
Rooms: 12 (10 PB; 2 SB) $120-130 Modified
   American Plan
Full Breakfast
Credit Cards: A, B
Notes: 2, 3, 4, 8, 9, 11, 12, 14

MILLWOOD

Brookside Bed and Breakfast

Brookside, 22646
(703) 837-1780

Located in Virginia hunt country, Brookside was built in 1780. This bed and breakfast features authentic canopy beds with feather ticks and down comforters,

Fort Lewis Lodge

Highland Inn

working fireplaces, and private baths in each room. Also available is the Tool House with a fireplace and screened porch. Brookside is fully airconditioned. A full breakfast is served to guests. Antique shops, vineyards, excellent restaurants, and outdoor activities abound.

Hosts: Gary and Carol Konkel
Rooms: 4 (PB) $110-140
Full Breakfast
Credit Cards: A, B
Notes: 2, 5, 9, 12, 14

MOLLUSK

Greenvale Manor

Route 354, Box 70, 22517
(804) 462-5995

An 1840 waterfront plantation house on 13 acres, situated on the Rappahannock River, with private beach, dock, pool, spacious

The Inn at Montross

lawns, large, antique-filled rooms with private baths and air conditioning. Enjoy sunsets and sweeping water views from the veranda and relax in a tranquil setting.

Hosts: Pam and Walt Smith
Rooms: 6 (PB) $65-100
Cottage: 1 (PB)
Full Breakfast
Credit Cards: None
Notes: 2, 5, 7, 9, 10, 11, 12

MONTEREY

Highland Inn

Main Street, 24465
(703) 468-2143

Classic Victorian inn listed on the National Register of Historic Places. Tranquil location in the picturesque village of Monterey, nestled in the foothills of the Allegheny Mountains. There are 17 individually decorated rooms furnished with antiques and collectibles, each with private bath. Full-service dining room offers continental cuisine for dinner Wednesday through Saturday and Sunday brunch. Antiquing, hiking, fishing, golf, and mineral baths are nearby.

Hosts: Michael Strand and Cynthia Peel
Rooms: 17 (PB) $45-64
Continental Breakfast
Credit Cards: A, B
Notes: 2, 4, 5, 7, 8, 9, 11, 12, 14

MONTROSS

The Inn at Montross

Courthouse Square, 22520
(804) 493-9097; (800) 321-0979

On the site of a 17th-century tavern, this house has been in continuous use for more than 300 years. Guest rooms feature four-poster beds (some with canopies) and antiques. A restaurant featuring fine dining, pub room, and English tavern are on the premises. Historic area near Washington's birthplace and Stratford Hall.

6 Pets welcome; 7 Smoking allowed; 8 Children welcome; 9 Social drinking allowed; 10 Tennis available; 11 Swimming available; 12 Golf available; 13 Skiing available; 14 May be booked through travel agents.

Hosts: Eileen and Michael Longman
Rooms: 6 (PB) $65-125
Continental Breakfast
Credit Cards: A, B, C, D
Notes: 2, 3, 4, 5, 6, 7, 9, 10, 11, 12, 14

MOUNT JACKSON

Amanda's Bed and Breakfast #181

1428 Park Avenue, Annapolis, MD 21217
(410) 225-0001; (410) 383-1274

An 1830 Colonial homestead on seven acres overlooking the George Washington Mountains. Some bedrooms have wood-burning fireplaces, and the antique furniture is for sale. Pool on premises. Area activities include craft fairs, hiking, fishing, tennis, and horseback riding. Five rooms with private baths. Two guest cottages. Full breakfast. $65-85.

The Widow Kip's Shenandoah Inn

Route 1, Box 117, 22842
(703) 477-2400

A stately 1830 Colonial on seven rural acres in the Shenandoah Vallley overlooking the mountains. Friendly rooms filled with family photographs, bric-a-brac, and antiques (all for sale). Each bedroom has a working fireplace, canopy, sleigh or Lincoln bed. Two cozy cottages are also available. Pool on premises; nearby battle-

A Touch of Country

fields to explore, caverns, canoeing, hiking, or downhill skiing. Bicycles, picnics, grill available.

Host: Betty Luse
Rooms: 7 (PB) $65-85
Full Breakfast
Minimum stay holidays: 2 nights
Credit Cards: A, B
Notes: 2, 5, 6, 10, 11, 12, 13

NELLYSFORD

Acorn Inn Bed and Breakfast

P. O. Box 431, 22958
(804) 361-9357

European-style inn with Dutch cyclist and American artist as hosts to guests. Ten cozy guest rooms in a renovated horse stable. The renovated stable has a center lounge with Finnish soapstone fireplace, striking photographs and woodcut prints, and artistic, friendly, contemporary atmosphere. There is also a charming cottage available to guests. Delicious homemade breads and fruit cobbler are also available for guests' enjoyment. Close to Wintergreen Ski/Golf Resort, Blue Ridge Parkway, Appalachian Trail, and waterfalls.

Hosts: Kathy and Martin Versluys
Rooms: 10 (SB) $47
Cottage: 1 (PB) $85
Expanded Continental Breakfast
Credit Cards: A, B
Notes: 2, 5, 8, 12, 13

The Meander Inn at Penny Lane Farm

Routes 612 and 613, P. O. Box 443, 22958
(804) 361-1121

Lovely Victorian farmhouse nestled on 50 acres along the Rockfish River in the Blue Ridge foothills. Thirty miles south of Wintergreen and central Virginia wineries. The hosts invite guests to enjoy this special place, a refreshing change of pace. After winetasting, hiking, fishing, or golf at near-

---

NOTES: Credit cards accepted: A Master Card; B Visa; C American Express; D Discover Card; E Diner's Club; F Other; 2 Personal Checks accepted; 3 Lunch available; 4 Dinner available; 5 Open all year;

by championship courses, relax under the stars in the outdoor hot tub or in front of the wood-burning stove. Five cozy rooms with fresh flowers, bathrobes, and spectacular views. Full gourmet breakfast with farm-fresh eggs.

Hosts: Kathy and Rick Cornelius
Rooms: 5 (PB) $65-90
Full Breakfast
Credit Cards: A, B
Notes: 2, 5, 9, 10, 11, 12, 13, 14

NEWCHURCH

Amanda's Bed and Breakfast #210

1428 Park Avenue, Annapolis, MD 21217
(410) 225-0001; (410) 383-1274

This historic country inn offers elegant lodging and gourmet dining in the tradition of a small French inn. Near Chincoteague and Assateague National Seashore and Wildlife Refuge. Only a 15-minute drive to one of the most beautiful beaches on the eastern shore. Two guest rooms. Continental breakfast. $165.

NEW MARKET

A Touch of Country

9329 Congress Street, 22844
(703) 740-8030

Come relax at this restored 1870s home where a warm, friendly, atmosphere awaits you. Daydream on the porch swings or stroll through town, with its antique shops, gift shops, and restaurants. Rest in one of six bedrooms decorated with a country flavor. In the morning enjoy a down-home country breakfast. Near caverns and battlefields.

Hosts: Jean Schoellig and Dawn Kason
Rooms: 6 (PB) $60-70
Full Breakfast
Credit Cards: A, B
Notes: 2, 5, 8 (over 12), 9, 10, 11, 12, 13, 14

NORFOLK

Bed and Breakfast of Tidewater Virginia

P. O. Box 6226, 23508
(804) 627-1983

This bed and breakfast is a spacious third-generation home on a tree-lined street in old Ghent where your world-traveled hostess grew up. A short drive to Old Dominion University, Chrysler Museum, medical complex, and the Norfolk Naval Base. Rooms have four-poster beds, and a private porch overlooks an enchanting patio and garden offering privacy and tranquility. Two guest rooms are available; one offers a private bath. Full breakfast. $55-65.

Bed and Breakfast of Tidewater Virginia

P. O. Box 6226, 23508
(804) 627-1983

Near I-64, this contemporary house features a solarium and an open kitchen in the middle of the house. Comfortable and unique, this bed and breakfast features two rooms, one with twin beds and the other a double. Both rooms offer a private bath. Full breakfast. $55-65.

Bed and Breakfast of Tidewater Virginia Reservation Service

P. O. Box 6226, 23508
(804) 627-1983

Norfolk boasts the world's largest naval base, the famed Chrysler Museum, and MacArthur Memorial. It is a cultural hub in which top-rated opera, symphony, and stage productions abound. There are miles of scenic beaches to explore on the Chesapeake Bay and the Atlantic Ocean.

6 Pets welcome; 7 Smoking allowed; 8 Children welcome; 9 Social drinking allowed; 10 Tennis available; 11 Swimming available; 12 Golf available; 13 Skiing available; 14 May be booked through travel agents.

Old Dominion University, Eastern Virginia Medical School, and Virginia Weslyan College are conveniently located. Town and beach homes, inns and apartments are available. Now offering Bed and Breakfast Dockside. Charters available. $55-150.

Page House Inn

323 Fairfax Avenue, 23507
(804) 625-5033

Elegant accommodations in the heart of the Ghent historic district. Built in 1899 by Herman L. Page, a prominent real estate developer, as his personal residence, the Page House Inn is a three-story Georgian Revival, in-town mansion made of brick laid in the Flemish bond pattern. Accommodations have been professionally decorated, each with a distinct personality. Amenities include fireplaces, whirlpool baths, claw foot tubs, canopy beds, and fabulous gourmet breakfast served with freshly made espresso and cappuccino. Within walking distance of most of Norfolk's cultural attractions, fine restaurants, the downtown financial district, and the local medical center.

Host: Stephanie DiBelardino
Rooms: 4 (PB) $75-105
Suites: 2 (PB) $125-135
Continental Plus Breakfast
Credit Cards: None
Notes: 2, 5, 9, 14

OCCOQUAN

Rockledge Mansion

410 Mill Street, 22125
(703) 690-3377

National historic landmark built in 1758, this stone house is less than a mile from I-95 and is 30 minutes to Washington, D.C. Working fireplaces, antiques, oversized Jacuzzis, and kitchenette. Walk to the river, shops, art galleries, restaurants. Very quiet and private on two acres in the center of town. No meals on premises.

Hosts: Joy and Ron Houghton
Suites: 3 (PB) $75-120
Continental Breakfast at a Local Cafe
Credit Cards: None
Notes: 2, 5, 8, 9, 10, 11, 12, 14

ORANGE

Hidden Inn

249 Caroline Street, 22960
(703) 672-3625

A romantic Victorian featuring ten guest rooms, each with private bath. Jacuzzi tubs, working fireplaces, and private verandas are available. Wicker and rocking chairs on the wraparound verandas; handmade quilts and canopy beds enhance the Victorian flavor. Full country breakfast, afternoon tea, and gourmet dinners are served. Situated minutes from Monticello, Montpelier, and Virginia wineries.

Hosts: Ray and Barbara Lonick
Rooms: 10 (PB) $69-159
Full Breakfast
Credit Cards: A, B
Notes: 2, 4, 5, 8, 9, 10, 14

The Holladay House

155 West Main Street, 22960
(703) 672-4893

The Holladay House, circa 1830, is a restored Federal-style home that has been in the Holladay family since 1899. The large, comfortable rooms are furnished with family pieces and each one features its own sitting area. Breakfast is normally served to guests in their own rooms. Surrounded by a residential neighborhood on three sides, the Holladay House is located two blocks from the center of the historic town of Orange and just 90 minutes from Richmond or Washington, D.C.

Hosts: Pete and Phebe Holladay
Rooms: 6 (4 PB; 2 SB) $75-120
Full Breakfast
Credit Cards: A, B
Notes: 2, 5, 7 (limited), 8, 9

NOTES: Credit cards accepted: A Master Card; B Visa; C American Express; D Discover Card; E Diner's Club; F Other; 2 Personal Checks accepted; 3 Lunch available; 4 Dinner available; 5 Open all year;

PALMYRA

Palmer Country Manor

Route 2, Box 1390, 22963
(804) 589-1300

Palmer Country Manor is a gracious 1830s
estate situated on 180 wooded acres and
gently rolling meadows. The private cottages offer a living area with a sofa and
fireplace, color TV, king or queen
four-poster beds, full bath and shower, and
private outdoor wood decks. Activities
include swimming in the estate's pool, fishing, river rafting, hiking, ballooning, local
sightseeing as well as wineries. Fine dining
in the manor house. Approximately 35
minutes from downtown Charlottesville.
Call or write for a free brochure.

Hosts: Gregory and Kathleen Palmer
Rooms: 12 (10 PB; 2 SB) $80-125
Full Breakfast
Credit Cards: A, B, C, E
Notes: 2, 3, 4, 5, 6, 7, 8, 9, 11, 12, 14

PETERSBURG

Mayfield Inn

3348 West Washington Street, 23804
(804) 733-0866; (804) 861-6775

Mayfield Inn is a 1750 manor house listed
on the National Register of Historic Places.
It was authentically restored in 1986. Guest
accommodations are luxuriously appointed
with Oriental carpets, pine floors, antiques,
period reproductions, and private baths.
Situated on four acres of grounds, with a
40-foot outdoor swimming pool.

Hosts: Jamie and Dot Caudle
Rooms: 4 (PB) $65-90
Full Breakfast
Credit Cards: A, B
Notes: 2, 5, 7, 8, 9, 10, 11, 12, 14

PRATTS

Colvin Hall
Bed and Breakfast

HCR 03, Box 30G (Route 230 East), 22731
(703) 948-6211

Relaxation and romance await you at this
1870 country retreat on seven and one-half
acres. It offers working fireplaces and firewood, air conditioning, swimming, and
warm hospitality. Close to antique/craft
shops, Skyline Drive, Montpelier, hiking,
and wineries. Rooms include a queen
canopy bed with fireplace and private bath,
king bed with firelace and private bath, and
twin beds with shared bath. Located in the
central Virginia Piedmont between Charlottesville and Culpepper. Enjoy a true
breakfast experience.

Host: Sue and Dave Rossell
Rooms: 3 (2 PB; 1 SB) $60-85
Full Breakfast
Credit Cards: A, B
Notes: 2, 5, 9, 11, 13

RAPHINE

Oak Spring Farm
and Vineyard

Route 1, Box 356, 24472
(703) 377-2398

Newly restored 1826 plantation house on
40 acres filled with antiques, family treasures, and other items reflecting 26 years of
worldwide military service. There are modern conveniences on this working farm and
vineyard. Three rooms available, all with
private baths. You can expect spectacular
views, woods to walk in, exotic animals in
the pasture, along with peace and quiet, all
convenient to I-81 and I-64 halfway
between historic Lexington and Staunton.

Hosts: Pat and Jim Tichenor
Rooms: 3 (PB) $55-65

6 Pets welcome; 7 Smoking allowed; 8 Children welcome; 9 Social drinking allowed; 10 Tennis available; 11
Swimming available; 12 Golf available; 13 Skiing available; 14 May be booked through travel agents.

Expanded Continental Breakfast
Credit Cards: A, B
Notes: 2, 5, 9, 11, 12, 13

RICHMOND

Abbie Hill
Bed and Breakfast

P. O. Box 4503, 23220
(804) 355-5855; FAX (804) 353-4656

Elegant 1910 Federal town house in
Richmond's most prestigious historic district, near museums and other historic
attractions. Walk to wonderful neighborhood restaurants, shopping, and churches.
Be spoiled in beautiful, newly decorated
rooms done in period style with family
antiques and chintzes. Rooms have fireplaces and huge modern baths with
old-fashioned charm. Full breakfasts served
by your hosts will prepare you for days of
exploration and fun in this beautiful, historic city. TV, FAX, laundry facilities
available. No smoking.

Hosts: Barbara and Bill Fleming
Rooms: 4 (PB) $55-95
Suite: 1 (PB) $150
Full Breakfast
Credit Cards: A, B
Notes: 2, 5, 9, 14

Amanda's
Bed and Breakfast #271

1428 Park Avenue, Annapolis, MD 21217
(410) 225-0001; (410) 383-1274

Antiques, family heirlooms, and working
fireplaces await you at this bed and breakfast. Situated in the historic Church Hill
District. Beautiful period furniture, canopied beds, large armoires, crystal chandeliers, and hospitality that will make your
stay most pleasant. Five rooms with private
and shared baths. Full breakfast. $75-160.

Bensonhouse of
Williamsburg, Virginia

2036 Monument, 23220
(804) 353-6900

Representing seven carefully selected private homes, inns, and cottages located in
close proximity to Colonial Williamsburg.
Selections include a beautiful reproduction
of an 18th-century Connecticut tavern, with
a queen bed in the bedroom, private bath,
and fireplace. There are also two charming
Colonial cottages, with queen beds in the
bedrooms, private baths (one has a Jacuzzi)
and one of these cottages has a fireplace.

Rooms: 7 (PB) $60-125
Continental Plus Breakfast
Credit Cards: A, B
Notes: 2, 5, 8, 9, 14

The Emmanuel Hutzler
House

2036 Monument Avenue, 23220
(804) 355-4885

Abbie Hill

This large Italian Renaissance-style inn has been totally renovated in the past three years and offers leaded-glass windows, coffered ceilings, and natural mahogany raised paneling throughout the downstairs, as well as a large livingroom with a marble fireplace for guests' enjoyment. There are four guest rooms on the second floor, each with private bath. The suite has a four-poster queen bed, love seat, and wing chair. The two queen rooms have a sitting area and private baths. The largest room has a marble fireplace, four-poster mahogany bed, antique sofa, dresser, and a private bath with shower and Jacuzzi tub.

Hosts: Lyn M. Benson and John E. Richardson
Rooms: 4 (PB) $89-135
Full Breakfast
Credit Cards: A, B, C
Notes: 2, 5, 9, 14

West-Bocock House

1107 Grove Avenue, 23220
(804) 358-6174

Circa 1817 historic house in the heart of Richmond offers elegant guest rooms with private baths, French linens, fresh flowers, full breakfast, and off-street parking. Convenient to museums, historic sites, restaurants, shopping, and Capitol Square. The Wests invite you to sample true southern hospitality.

Hosts: Jim and Billie Rees West
Rooms: 3 (PB) $65-75
Full Breakfast
Credit Cards: None
Notes: 2, 5, 7, 8, 9, 14

The William Catlin House

2304 East Broad Street, 23223
(804) 780-3746

Antiques, family heirlooms, and working fireplaces await you at the William Catlin House. Situated in the historic district of Church Hill, the house was built in 1845. The luxury of bedroom fireplaces, goose down pillows, and sherry and mints

promises a restful night. Each morning a delicious full breakfast and endless pots of coffee or tea await you in the elegant dining room. While here, be sure to visit nearby historic sites and King's Dominion.

Hosts: Robert and Josephine Martin
Rooms: 5 (3 PB; 2 SB) $70-89.50
Full Breakfast
Credit Cards: A, B
Notes: 2, 5, 7, 8, 9, 14

ROANOKE—SEE ALSO SMITH MOUNTAIN LAKE

The Manor at Taylor's Store

Route 1, Box 533, Wirtz, 24184
(703) 721-3951

Explore this secluded, historic 120-acre estate conveniently situated near Smith Mountain Lake, Roanoke, and the Blue Ridge Parkway. The manor has six guest suites with extraordinary antiques and Oriental rugs. Guests enjoy all luxury amenities, including central air conditioning, hot tub, fireplaces, private porches, billiard room, exercise room, guest kitchen, movies, and six private, spring-fed ponds for swimming, fishing, and canoeing. A lovely gazebo overlooks the ponds for picnics. A full "heart healthy" gourmet breakfast is served in the dining room with panoramic views of the countryside.

Hosts: Lee and Mary Lunn Tucker
Rooms: 6 (4 PB; 2 SB) $65-90
Cottage: 1 (PB)
Full Breakfast
Credit Cards: A, B
Notes: 2, 3, 5, 7 (cottage), 8, 9, 10, 11, 12, 13, 14

The Mary Bladon House

381 Washington Avenue Southwest, 24016
(703) 344-5361

A lovely 1890s Victorian house in the historic Old Southwest neighborhood. Spacious rooms, tastefully decorated with crafts and period antiques to capture the charm of a time when elegant comfort was a way of life. A step back in time for the young and the young at heart.

Hosts: Bill and Sheri Bestpitch
Rooms: 2 (PB) $75
Suite: 1 (PB) $110
Full Breakfast
Credit Cards: A, B
Notes: 2, 3, 4, 5, 8, 9, 10, 11, 12, 14

SALEM

The Old Manse

530 East Main Street, 24153
(703) 389-3921

The Old Manse occupies land once owned by Andrew Lewis, Revolutionary War general. The antebellum home is furnished with antiques and has air conditioning. You can enjoy a leisurely, home-cooked, full southern breakfast. The Old Manse offers a sitting room and parlor for visiting or watching TV. Nearby are Roanoke and Hollins colleges, farmers' market, Salem Civic Center, tennis courts, exercise trail and park, antique malls, and shops.

Host: Charlotte Griffith
Rooms: 3 (SB) $40
Full Breakfast
Credit Cards: None
Notes: 2, 5, 8, 10

SANDBRIDGE

Bed and Breakfast of Tidewater Virginia

P. O. Box 6226, Norfolk, 23508
(804) 627-1983

A delightful suite on the first floor of the builder/owner's home offers a combination livingroom-bedroom with a queen-size bed and a queen-size sleeper sofa. Across the street from the Atlantic Ocean, which guests can enjoy from a picture window and the rear door, a lovely flower and herb garden can be explored and enjoyed. Guest room has a private entrance. Hostess pro-

High Meadows—Virginia's Vineyard Inn

vides beach chairs and a bicycle for guests to use. Private bath and refrigerator. Continental breakfast. $85, plus $5 per child.

SCOTTSVILLE

Chester

Guesthouses Bed and Breakfast
P. O. Box 5737, 22905
(804) 979-7264

This charming large country home in Scottsville, 25 minutes south of Charlottsville, was built in 1825 through 1875; lots of history and beautiful trees are on the grounds. Five guest rooms make this a great retreat for a large group, or come with a smaller group and meet fellow guests. Accommodations have bed sizes from a twin to a queen, and the house is furnished with an interesting and eclectic collection of pieces from the owner's travels. Several porches provide a pleasant place to sit at night. Full breakfast is served in the morning, and dinner is available by reservation. $80-100.

High Meadows— Virginia's Vineyard Inn

Route 4, Box 6, Route 20 South, 24590
(804) 286-2218

NOTES: Credit cards accepted: A Master Card; B Visa; C American Express; D Discover Card; E Diner's Club; F Other; 2 Personal Checks accepted; 3 Lunch available; 4 Dinner available; 5 Open all year;

Enchanting 19th-century European-style auberge with tastefully appointed, spacious guest rooms, private baths, period antiques. Two-room suites available. Several common rooms, fireplaces, and tranquility. Pastoral setting on 50 acres. Privacy, relaxing walks, gourmet picnics. Virginia wine tasting and romantic candlelight dining nightly. Virginia Architectural Landmark. National Register of Historic Places.

Hosts: Peter, Sushka, and Mary Jae Abbitt
Rooms: 12 (PB) $90.52-172.42
Full Breakfast
Minimum stay weekends and holidays: 2 nights
Credit Cards: A, B
Closed December 24-25
Notes: 2, 4, 6, 8, 9, 10, 11, 13, 14

The Prodigal

Guesthouses Bed and Breakfast
P. O. Box 5737, 22905
(804) 979-7264

On the site of an old summer kitchen, this cottage sits behind a farmhouse built around 1830. It features a large fireplace, sleeper sofa, Pullman kitchen, and full bath downstairs, and a room with a double bed upstairs. Fish in the pond, swim nearby in the Hardware River swimming hole, or rent a tube or canoe on the James River. You can even bring your horse. There are extra stalls and wooded trails. Air conditioning. Supplies provided for guests to prepare breakfast. $80-125.

SMITHFIELD

Isle of Wight Inn

1607 South Church Street, 23430
(804) 357-3176

Luxurious Colonial bed and breakfast inn situated in a delightful historic river port town. Several suites with fireplaces and Jacuzzis. Antique shop featuring tallcase clocks and period furniture. More than 60 old homes in town dating from 1750. Just 30 minutes and a ferry ride from Williamsburg and Jamestown; less than an hour from James River plantations, Norfolk, Hampton, and Virginia Beach.

Hosts: The Harts and the Earls
Rooms: 10 (PB) $49-79
Full Breakfast
Credit Cards: A, B, C, D
Notes: 2, 5, 7, 8, 9, 10, 11, 12, 14

SMITH MOUNTAIN LAKE

Holland-Duncan House

Route 5, Box 681, 24121
(703) 721-8510

Historic 1820 Blue Ridge plantation home on 28 acres with a log summer kitchen and smokehouse renovated with large fireplaces for guests. Two lovely rooms in the Federal house are tastefully furnished with antiques. Central to all recreation at beautiful Smith Mountain Lake.

Hosts: Kathryn and Clint Shay
Rooms: 4 (2 PB; 2 SB) $45-75
Full Breakfast
Credit Cards: A, B
Closed December and January
Notes: 2, 8, 10, 11, 12, 13, 14

SPERRYVILLE

The Conyers House

Route 707, Box 157, 22740
(703) 987-8025; FAX (703) 987-8709

Nestled in the foothills of the Blue Ridge Mountains, the Conyers House is in the middle of Virginia's most beautiful Hunt Country. The hostess is an avid fox hunter who will encourage you to ride cross country. The host collects old cars and is an old film buff. An elegant candlelight fireside seven-course dinner may be ordered at extra charge. Innkeeping seminars are offered for those thinking of becoming hosts.

Rooms: 8 (PB) $90-195
Full Breakfast
Credit Cards: None
Notes: 2, 4, 5, 6 (call), 8 (weekdays), 9, 10, 11, 12, 13

STANLEY

Jordan Hollow Farm Inn

Route 2, Box 375, 22851
(703) 778-2209; (703) 778-2285

A restored Colonial horse farm featuring 21
rooms with private baths, several with fireplaces and whirlpool baths; one suite.
Full-service restaurant and pub. Horseback
riding, English and western. In the
Shenandoah Valley just ten miles from
Skyline Drive and six miles from Luray
Caverns. Box lunches and full dinner provided in addition to a full breakfast.

Hosts: Jetze and Marley Beers
Rooms: 21 (PB) $78-130 Modified American Plan
Full Breakfast
Credit Cards: A, B, D, E
Notes: 2, 3, 4, 5, 6, 7, 8, 9, 10, 11, 12, 13, 14

STAUNTON

Ashton Country House

1205 Middlebrook Road, 24401
(703) 885-7819

The Ashton Country House, circa 1860, is
a Greek Revival brick home located on
twenty peaceful acres at the outskirts of
Staunton. Each of the four spacious guest
rooms features a private bath and a queen
or double bed. Mornings begin with a
hearty breakfast which is often accompanied by live piano music. Convenient to
historic attractions and fine restaurants.

Hosts: Sheila Kennedy and Stanley Polanski
Rooms: 4 (PB) $65-80
Full Breakfast
Credit Cards: None
Notes: 2, 5

Frederick House

Frederick and New Streets, P. O. Box 1387, 24401
(703) 885-4220; (800) 334-5575

A small hotel and tea room in the European
tradition. Large, comfortable room or
suites, private baths, cable TV, air condi-

tioning, telephones, and antique furnishings. Across from Mary Baldwin College.
Convenient to fine restaurants, shopping,
museums, and the Blue Ridge Mountains.

Hosts: Joe and Evy Harman
Rooms: 14 (PB) $45-110
Credit Cards: A, B, C, D, E
Notes: 2, 3, 4, 5, 8, 9, 10, 11, 12, 13, 14

Jordan Hollow Farm Inn

Kenwood

235 East Beverley Street, 24401
(703) 886-0524

Spacious, restored 1910 Colonial Revival
brick home adjacent to Woodrow Wilson
Birthplace and Museum. Filled with period
furniture and antiques, Kenwood offers
comfortable accommodations in a relaxed
atmosphere. Two miles west of the I-81
and I-64 intersection, near the Museum of
American Frontier Culture, Skyline Drive,
Blue Ridge Parkway, Statler Brothers
Museum, Monticello. Four guest rooms
with queen beds, private baths, air conditioning, full breakfast.

Hosts: Liz and Ed Kennedy
Rooms: 4 (2 PB; 2 SB) $55-65
Full Breakfast
Credit Cards: A, B
Notes: 2, 5, 8, 9

The Sampson Eagon Inn

238 East Beverley Street, 24401
(703) 886-8200

NOTES: Credit cards accepted: A Master Card; B Visa; C American Express; D Discover Card; E Diner's
Club; F Other; 2 Personal Checks accepted; 3 Lunch available; 4 Dinner available; 5 Open all year;

Situated in the Virginia historic landmark district of Gospel Hill, this gracious, circa 1840, town residence has been thoughtfully restored and transformed into a unique inn offering affordable luxury and personal service in an intimate, inviting atmosphere. Each elegant, spacious, air-conditioned room and suite features private bath, sitting area, canopy queen bed, and antique furnishings. Adjacent to the Woodrow Wilson Birthplace and Mary Baldwin College, the inn is within two blocks of downtown dining and attractions.

Hosts: Laura and Frank Mattingly
Rooms: 4 (PB) $75-90
Full Breakfast
Credit Cards: None
Notes: 2, 5, 9, 14

Thornrose House at Gypsy Hill

531 Thornrose Avenue, 24401
(703) 885-7026

A wraparound veranda and Greek colonnades distinguish this turn-of-the-century Georgian residence. Family antiques, a grand piano, and fireplaces create an elegant, restful atmosphere. Breakfast specialties served in a formal dining room energize you for sight-seeing in the beautiful Shenandoah Valley. Located at a 300-acre park with golf, tennis, swimming, and trails. Other attractions include include Woodrow Wilson's birthplace, the Museum of American Frontier Culture, and the nearby Skyline Drive and Blue Ridge Parkway.

The Sampson Eagon Inn

Hosts: Suzanne and Otis Huston
Rooms: 5 (PB) $50-65
Full Breakfast
Credit Cards: None
Notes: 2, 5, 8, 9, 10, 11, 12, 13

STRASBURG

The Strasburg

201 South Holliday Street, 22601
(703) 465-9191

A charming Victorian restoration, all rooms furnished in period antiques. Situated in Strasburg, the Antique Capital of Virginia. Each room has air conditioning, private bath, and phone. Most have TV. Jacuzzi. Suites available. Private dining room for meetings, conferences, and family dinners. Excellent food and quaint bed and breakfast. Hiking, canoeing, theater, Skyline Drive, antiquing, horseback riding, swimming, and biking nearby.

Host: Gary Rutherford
Rooms: 27 (PB) $69-149
Continental Breakfast
Credit Cards: A, B, C, E
Notes: 3, 4, 5, 6 (call), 7, 8, 9, 10, 11, 12, 13, 14

SWOOPE

Lambsgate Bed and Breakfast

Route 1, Box 63, 24479
(703) 337-6929

Six miles west of Staunton on Routes 254 and 833. Restored 1816 farmhouse and working sheep farm in the historic Shenandoah Valley. Relaxing country setting with hiking and biking nearby. Central for visiting historic sites, national park, and forests.

Hosts: Dan and Elizabeth Fannon
Rooms: 3 (SB) $47.03
Full Breakfast
Minimum stay July 4: 2 nighs
Credit Cards: None
Notes: 2, 5, 8, 9

6 Pets welcome; 7 Smoking allowed; 8 Children welcome; 9 Social drinking allowed; 10 Tennis available; 11 Swimming available; 12 Golf available; 13 Skiing available; 14 May be booked through travel agents.

SYRIA

Graves' Mountain Lodge

Route 670, 22743
(703) 923-4231

This peaceful lodge is located in the shadow of Blue Ridge Mountains next to the Shenandoah National Park on a large cattle and fruit farm. Guests enjoy three meals a day while getting rest and relaxation during their visit. Trout stream and farm ponds are available for fishing. Hiking trails and horseback riding are also available for guests' enjoyment. Open mid-March through November.

Hosts: Rachel and Jim Graves
Rooms: 45 plus cabins and cottages (45 PB; 7 SB)
  $50-75, per person American Plan
Full Breakfast
Credit Cards: A, B
Notes: 2, 3, 4, 6, 7, 9, 10, 11

TANGIER

Sunset Inn

Box 156, 23440
(804) 891-2535

The Soft Crab Capital of the nation, Tangier is a romantic destination for those who would see a largely unspoiled fishing village with quaint narrow streets. The inn offers nine rooms. All have air conditioning and private bath. There is a deck and cable TV. Guests enjoy a wonderful view of the bay. Situated one-half block from the beach. A continental breakfast is served.

Hosts: Grace and Jim Brown
Rooms: 9 (PB) $60
Continental Breakfast
Credit Cards: None
Notes: 2, 5, 8, 9, 11

TREVILIANS

Prospect Hill

Route 3, Box 430, 23093
(703) 967-0844; (800) 277-0844

Prospect Hill is a 1732 plantation just 15 miles east of Charlottesville. Lodgings in the manor house and renovated outbuildings feature working fireplaces, Jacuzzis, and breakfast in bed. Candlelight dinners are served every evening by reservation.

Host: The Sheehan family
Rooms: 13 (PB) $120-200
Full Breakfast
Credit Cards: A, B
Closed December 24 and 25
Notes: 2, 4, 5, 7, 8, 14

URBANNA

Bed and Breakfast of Tidewater Virginia

P. O. Box 6226, Norfolk, 23508
(804) 627-1983

Located on Virginia's Middle Peninsula between the York River and the Rappahannock, this country waterfront inn offers peace and seclusion. The inn faces the Rappahannock, which is two miles wide at this point. The nearby town of Urbana hosts Virginia's annual Oyster Festival and also boasts an award-winning restaurant. Six guest rooms available, some with private baths. $65-75.

VIRGINIA BEACH

Angie's Guest Cottage

302 24th Street, 23451
(804) 428-4690

Situated in the heart of the resort area, one block from the ocean. Large beach house

Angie's Guest Cottage

that guests describe as "cute, clean, comfortable, and convenient." All rooms are air-conditioned; some have small refrigerators and private entrances. Breakfast is served on the front porch, and there is also a sun deck, barbecue pit, and picnic tables.

Host: Barbara G. Yates
Rooms: 6 (1 PB; 5 SB) $48.18-67.89
Expanded Continental Breakfast
Minimum stay in season: 2 nights
Credit Cards: None
Closed October 1-April 1
Notes: 8, 9, 10, 11, 12

Barclay Cottage

400 16th Street, 23451
(804) 422-1956

Casual sophistication for adults, in a warm, historic, innlike atmosphere. Located two blocks from the beach and in the heart of the Virginia Beach recreational area, the Barclay Cottage has been decorated in turn-of-the-century style and antique furniture. The hosts welcome guests to the Barclay Cottage where their theme is, We go where our dreams take us.

Hosts: Peter and Claire
Rooms: 6 (3 PB; 3 SB) $65-80 (May-October)
Full Breakfast
Credit Cards: A, B
Notes: 9, 10, 11, 12, 14

Bed and Breakfast of Tidewater Virginia

P. O. Box 6226, Norfolk, 23508
(804) 627-1983

Casual sophistication for adults in a warm, historic, inn-like atmosphere describes this delightful turn-of-the-century cottage, which is two blocks from the beach and fishing pier. Six rooms, two with private baths, are available. Full breakfast. $65-80.

The Picket Fence

209 43rd Street, 23451
(804) 428-8861

The furnishings in this comfortable Colonial home glow with the patina of loving care. The beach is just one block away, and beach chairs and umbrellas are provided for your comfort. Near the new Marine Science Museum. One room, one suite, and one guest cottage are available.

Host: Kathleen J. Hall
Room: 1 (PB) $50-75 (May-October 15)
Suite: 1 (SB)
Cottage: 1 (PB)
Full Breakfast
Credit Cards: None
Notes: 2, 5, 9, 10, 11, 12

WACHAPREAGUE

Amanda's Bed and Breakfast #267

1428 Park Avenue, Annapolis, MD 21217
(410) 225-0001; (410) 383-1274

Lovely Victorian, circa 1875, in a quaint fishing village. Four bedrooms, two full baths, contempoary kitchen, livingroom, dining room, fireplace, central heat and air, and cable TV and stereo. Self-catered breakfast. Whole house rental. $500/week.

The Burton House

11 Brooklyn Street, 23480
(804) 787-4560

6 Pets welcome; 7 Smoking allowed; 8 Children welcome; 9 Social drinking allowed; 10 Tennis available; 11 Swimming available; 12 Golf available; 13 Skiing available; 14 May be booked through travel agents.

The Burton House

The Burton House bed and breakfast is composed of two side-by-side Victorian houses located in a seaside fishing village. Both are fully air conditioned when needed. Guests can enjoy biking, birding, and boating. Bikes are provided and rental boats are available. Generous country breakfast and afternoon tea or coffee. Quiet, affordable elegance. Cabins are also available. Marina is very close; guests should feel free to bring their own boats.

Hosts: Pat, Tom, and Mike Hart
Rooms: 10 (PB) $65-75 plus tax
Cabins: 4 (PB) $40-50 plus tax
Full Breakfast
Credit Cards: A, B
Notes: 2, 5, 7 (porches), 8 (over 12), 10, 11, 12, 14

WARM SPRINGS

Meadow Lane Lodge

Route 1, Box 110, 24484
(703) 839-5959

A little jewel of a country inn, set in meadows and mountains on a 1600-acre estate. Surrounded by bountiful resources for tennis, golf, swimming, riding, trout fishing, bird watching, botanizing, hiking, walking, and creative loafing. Wake to the sounds of roosters crowing in the barn and the smells of what will be a memorable breakfast.

Hosts: Philip and Catherine Hirsh
Rooms: 11 (PB) $90-130
Full Breakfast
Credit Cards: A, B, C
Notes: 2, 3, 5, 6 (call), 7 (limited), 8, 9, 10, 11, 12, 13

WASHINGTON

Caledonia Farm

Route 1, Box 2080, Flint Hill, 22627
(703) 675-3693

Beautifully restored 1812 stone home and romantic guest house on farm adjacent to Shenandoah National Park. This historic landmark listed on the National Register of Historic Places offers splendor for all seasons in Virginia's Blue Ridge Mountains. Skyline Drive, wineries, caves, historic sites, superb dining. Fireplaces, air conditioning, bicycles. Only 68 miles to Washington, D.C.

Host: Phil Irwin
Rooms: 2 plus suite (1 PB; 2 SB) $70-100
Full Breakfast
Credit Cards: A, B (for confirmation only)
Notes: 2, 3, 4 (by reservation), 5, 8 (over 12), 9, 10, 11, 12, 13, 14

The Foster-Harris House

Main Street, Box 333, 22747
(703) 675-3757

A charming country Victorian in a tiny historic village just 65 miles from Washington, D.C. World-acclaimed five-star restaurant three blocks away. Antiques, fresh flowers, outstanding views of the Blue Ridge Mountains. Fireplace stoves in some rooms. Near Skyline Drive and Luray Caverns. Fully air-conditioned.

Host: Phyllis Marriott
Rooms: 4 (3 PB; 1 SB) $74.90-133.75
Full Breakfast
Credit Cards: A, B
Notes: 2, 4 (by reservation), 5, 6, 7, 8, 9, 10, 11, 12, 14

Heritage House

P. O. Box 427, 22747
(703) 675-3207

NOTES: Credit cards accepted: A Master Card; B Visa; C American Express; D Discover Card; E Diner's Club; F Other; 2 Personal Checks accepted; 3 Lunch available; 4 Dinner available; 5 Open all year;

This 1837 manor house is located in Little Washington, a picturesque village originally surveyed by George Washington. Guests are invited to enjoy heirloom antiques, international collectibles, gourmet breakfasts, and gorgeous panoramic views. Central to fine dining, antiquing, hiking, horseback riding, historic attractions, wineries, and the joys of Skyline Drive and the Shenandoah National Park.

Hosts: Jean and Frank Scott
Rooms: 4 (PB) $95-125
Full Breakfast
Credit Cards: A, B
Notes: 2, 5, 9, 10, 12, 14

WHITE POST

L'Auberge Provençale

P. O. Box 119, 22663
(703) 837-1375; FAX (703) 837-2004

Elegant overnight accommodations, with romantic dining and the breakfast of one's dreams. L'Auberge Provençale offers the perfect getaway for pleasure or business. Superb French cuisine moderne is created by Master Chef Alain. Chosen by the James Beard Foundation Great Country Inn Series; four-diamond rating. L'Auberge Provençale has re-created an inn of the South of France. Country charm, city sophistication—"Where great expectations are quietly met."

Hosts: Alain and Celeste Borel
Rooms: 10 (PB) $115-200
Full Breakfast
Credit Cards: A, B, C, E
Notes: 2, 4, 7, 8 (over 10), 9, 10, 11, 12, 13, 14

WILLIAMSBURG

Applewood Colonial

605 Richmond Road, 23185
(804) 229-0205; (800) 899-2753

Circa 1921, this Flemish-bond brick home was built during the restoration of Colonial Williamsburg. The inn's parlor is decorated in Colonial style and features dentil crown molding. A crystal chandelier hangs above the dining table where breakfast is served. The Colonel Vaughn Suite boasts a private entrance, a fireplace, and a queen-size canopy bed.

Host: Fred Strout
Rooms: 4 (PB) $70-100
Expanded Continental Breakfast
Credit Cards: A, B
Notes: 2, 5, 8, 14

Amanda's Bed and Breakfast #253

1428 Park Avenue, Annapolis, MD 21217
(410) 225-0001; (410) 383-1274

This Flemish bond brick home was one of the first homes built on Richmond Road after the restoration of Colonial Williamsburg began in the late 1920s. The house features 18th-century decor, and the owner's apple collection is evident throughout. Four rooms with private baths. Continental plus breakfast. $65-95.

The Cedars

616 Jamestown Road, 23185
(804) 229-3591

The Cedars is a short walk from Colonial Willamsburg and across the street from the College of William and Mary. The guest home is attractively furnished in Colonial style, with beautiful 18th-century reproductions and traditional antiques. The beds are canopy or four-poster, graced with handmade quilts. This is Williamsburg's oldest and largest bed and breakfast, serving a continental breakfast and afternoon tea. There is a sitting room with a fireplace and glassed-in sun porch. The Cedars is air-conditioned. A separate country cottage accommodates six people.

---

6 Pets welcome; 7 Smoking allowed; 8 Children welcome; 9 Social drinking allowed; 10 Tennis available; 11 Swimming available; 12 Golf available; 13 Skiing available; 14 May be booked through travel agents.

Host: Deborah Howard
Rooms: 9 (7 PB; 2 SB) plus cottage (PB)
Continental Breakfast
Credit Cards: A, B
Notes: 2, 5, 8, 9, 14

Colonial Capital

Colonial Capital Bed and Breakfast

501 Richmond Road, 23185
(804) 229-0233; (800) 776-0570

Situated only three blocks from the historic
area, this charming Colonial Revival, circa
1926, home and its gracious hosts welcome
you. Enjoy spring gardens, summer festivities, autumn colors, and colonial
Christmastide. Antique furnishings blend
charm and elegance from the large parlor
with wood-burning fireplace to the airy
guest rooms, each with canopy bed and private bath. Full breakfast with a gourmet
touch and afternoon tea and wine. ABC
licensed, bikes, and free off-street parking.

Hosts: Barbara and Phil Craig
Rooms: 5 (PB) $90-125
Full Breakfast
Credit Cards: A, B
Notes: 2, 5, 7, 8 (over 6), 9, 10, 12, 14

Erika's Cottage

706 Richmond Road, 23185
(804) 229-6421

This cozy country Cape Cod looks as
though it jumped off the pages of *Country
Living* magazine with its unique country
antiques, stenciled walls, and canopy beds.
A full country breakfast is served each
morning. Central air. Ten-minute walk to
restored area. Complimentary bikes. No
smoking.

Hosts: Erika and Walter Gerber
Rooms: 2 (PB) $85
Full Breakfast
Credit Cards: A, B
Notes: 2, 5, 8, 9, 14

For Cant Hill Guest Home

4 Canterbury Lane, 23185
(804) 229-6623

This home is only six to eight blocks from
the restored area of Williamsburg, yet very
secluded and quiet in a lovely wooded setting overlooking a lake that joins the
College of William and Mary campus. The
rooms are beautifully decorated, and the
hosts are happy to make dinner reservations
for you and provide helpful information on
the many area attractions.

Hosts: Martha and Hugh Easler
Rooms: 2 (PB) $55
Continental Breakfast
Credit Cards: None
Notes: 2, 5, 8 (over 9), 9, 10, 11, 12

Fox Grape

701 Monumental Avenue, 23185
(804) 229-6914; (800) 292-3699

Warm hospitality awaits you just a
seven-minute walk north of Virginia's
restored colonial capital. Furnishings
include counted cross-stitch, antiques,
stained glass, stenciled walls, duck decoys,
and a cup plate collection. Pat enjoys doing
counted cross-stitch. Bob carves walking
sticks and makes stained-glass windows.

NOTES: Credit cards accepted: A Master Card; B Visa; C American Express; D Discover Card; E Diner's
Club; F Other; 2 Personal Checks accepted; 3 Lunch available; 4 Dinner available; 5 Open all year;

Hosts: Bob and Pat Orendorff
Rooms: 4 (PB) $78
Continental Breakfast
Credit Cards: A, B
Notes: 2, 5, 7, 8, 9, 10, 11, 12, 14

Governor's Trace

303 Capitol Landing Road, 23185
(804) 229-7552

Rekindle romance. Think about an intimate breakfast for two, served in your room at the closest bed and breakfast to Colonial Williamsburg. Governor's Trace, a lovely old Georgian brick home, lets you step into history just one door away. Candlelit, antique-furnished, spacious rooms offer choice of tall, four-poster, king-size bed with fireplace or full Colonial-style canopy bed, with screened porch, each with private bath.

Hosts: Sue and Dick Lake
Rooms: 2 (PB) $85-115
Expanded Continental Breakfast
Credit Cards: A, B
Notes: 2, 5, 9, 14

Hite's Bed and Breakfast

704 Monumental Avenue, 23185
(804) 229-4814

This attractive Cape Cod is located just a seven-minute walk from Colonial Williamsburg. Guests can relax in large rooms, cleverly furnished with collectibles and antiques. Each guest room has a television, telephone, radio, coffee maker, and a charming sitting area which makes breakfast a private affair. Guests are invited to smoke in the designated smoking area.

Hosts: Mr. and Mrs. James Hite
Rooms: 3 (1 PB; 2 SB) $50-65
Contiental Plus Breakfast
Credit Cards: None
Notes: 2, 5, 8, 12

Indian Springs Bed and Breakfast

330 Indian Springs Road, 23185
(804) 220-0726

Located in a quiet, wooded setting in downtown Williamsburg, Indian Springs offers a delightful retreat for guests after a day of sightseeing. Guests are invited to browse in the library or enjoy a board game on the veranda. A hearty breakfast is always on the menu. Suites are available.

Hosts: Kelly and Paul Supplee
Rooms: 4 (PB) $63-85
Full Breakfast
Credit Cards: None
Notes: 2, 5, 8

Legacy of Williamsburg Tavern

930 Jamestown Road, 23185
(800) WMB-GSBB (962-4722)

The Tavern is of true 18th-century tradition. Once guests cross the brick entry way, they begin a journey over the threshold and into another place in time. Canopy beds, private baths, six fireplaces, bathrobes, bikes, billiards and a full breakfast are all available for guests' enjoyment. Great location for walkers.

Hosts: Mary Anne and Ed Lucas
Rooms: 4 (PB) $80-125
Full Breakfast
Credit Cards: A, B, F
Notes: 2, 5, 9, 10, 11, 12, 14

Liberty Rose

1022 Jamestown Road, 23185
(804) 253-1260

Liberty Rose offers guests enchanting decor and delightful hospitality when visiting this bed and breakfast. This is a wonderful old Williamsburg home showcased on wooded hilltops near historic area. Liberty Rose is for lovers of exquisite queen beds, claw foot bathtubs, marble showers, papered walls, 18th-century country French and Victorian antiques, fireplaces, chocolate chip cookies, in-room television and VCR, and a big, scrumptious breakfast.

Hosts: Brad and Sandi Hirz
Rooms: 4 (PB) $100-155
Full Breakfast
Credit Cards: A, B
Notes: 2, 5, 10, 12, 14

Newport House

710 South Henry Street, 23185-4113
(804) 229-1775

Newport House was designed in 1756 by Peter Harrison. It is furnished totally in the period, including four-poster canopy beds. Each room has a private bathroom. The full breakfast includes authentic colonial-period recipes. Situated only afive-minutes walk from the historic area (as close as you can get). Your host is a former museum director and author of many books on colonial history. Enjoy colonial dancing in the ballroom every Tuesday evening.

Hosts: John and Cathy Millar
Rooms: 2 (PB) $95-105
Full Breakfast
Credit Cards: None
Notes: 2, 5, 8, 12, 14

Newport House

Piney Grove at Southall's Plantation

P. O. Box 1359, Charles City, 23187-1359
(804) 829-2480

Piney Grove is 20 miles west of Williamsburg in the James River plantation country, among working farms, country stores, and historic churches. The elegant accommodations at this National Register of Historic Places property are in two restored antebellum homes (1800 and 1857). Guests are welcomed to enjoy the parlor-library, pool, nature trail, farm animals, or a game of croquet or badminton. Upon arrival, guests are served mint juleps and Virginia wine.

Hosts: Brian, Joan, and Joseph Gordineer
Rooms: 5 (PB) $125-150
Full Breakfast
Credit Cards: None
Notes: 2, 5, 8, 9, 11, 12, 14

The Travel Tree 9

P. O. Box 838, 23187
(804) 253-1571

Treat your family to an elegant two-bedroom suite near Busch Gardens while you enjoy all that Williamsburg has to offer. The convenience of your own bath, breakfast nook, sitting area, and private entrance assures you the privacy you seek. Four miles from the restored area. No smoking. $75.

The Travel Tree 10

P. O. Box 838, 23187
(804) 253-1571

Rest safe and secure tucked under the eaves of a one-and-one-half-story cottage in a charming wooded setting. Sleep upstairs in a queen-size brass bed; relax downstairs in

NOTES: Credit cards accepted: A Master Card; B Visa; C American Express; D Discover Card; E Diner's Club; F Other; 2 Personal Checks accepted; 3 Lunch available; 4 Dinner available; 5 Open all year;

the sitting room with Pullman kitchen. With sofa bed downstairs, accommodates four. One and one half baths. One mile from the restored area. No smoking. $115.

The Travel Tree 133

P. O. Box 838, 23187
(804) 253-1571

Luxuriate in your home away from home in a spacious room complete with king-size bed, dining alcove, private bath, and private entrance. Or enjoy a pleasant twin-bed room, furnished with Oriental accents and adjacent private bath. Three miles from the restored area. No smoking. $50-70.

The Travel Tree 139

P. O. Box 838, 23187
(804) 253-1571

Relax in an airy, inviting room with private entrance, private bath, kitchenette, and patio doors leading to the lawn. Or choose the gracious suite furnished with 18th- and 19th-century antiques, a four-poster double bed, sitting area with fireplace, breakfast room, and private bath. One mile from the restored area. Roll-away bed available. No smoking. $65-90.

The Travel Tree 501

P. O. Box 838, 23187
(804) 253-1571

Bike the lovely streets of Williamsburg, returning in time for afternoon tea or wine in the parlor. Choose from five rooms, each charmingly furnished in Colonial style, with canopy or four-poster beds and private baths. Family suite available. Four blocks from the restored area. Smoking in the parlor only. $90.

The Travel Tree 517

P. O. Box 838, 23187
(804) 253-1571

Unwind in a charming Colonial Revival home with your choice: the cozy Country Room with a pair of twins or king-size bed, or the Victorian Room with an antique double bed. Each room has an adjacent private bath. Four blocks from the restored area. No smoking. $65.

The Travel Tree 605

P. O. Box 838, 23187
(804) 253-1571

Walk to the historic area after starting the day with the companionship of fellow guests at breakfast. The lovely guest rooms, each in Colonial decor, will charm you, from the first-floor suite with fireplace to the quaint third-floor dormered room. All have queen beds and private baths. Five blocks from the restored area. No smoking. $65-95.

The Travel Tree 706

P. O. Box 838, 23187
(804) 253-1571

Enjoy the country Colonial ambience of stenciled walls and interesting small antiques. Sleep under lacy canopies in the double or queen dormered rooms with private baths. Adjacent sitting area serves both rooms. Seven blocks from restored area. No smoking. $85.

The Travel Tree 710

P. O. Box 838, 23187
(804) 253-1571

Savor the Colonial atmosphere in a replica of an 18th-century home. Each bedroom is

6 Pets welcome; 7 Smoking allowed; 8 Children welcome; 9 Social drinking allowed; 10 Tennis available; 11 Swimming available; 12 Golf available; 13 Skiing available; 14 May be booked through travel agents.

furnished with both a queen and a twin canopy bed and has a private bath. Breakfast is served in the formal downstairs dining room. Five blocks from the restored area. No smoking. $100.

Williamsburg Sampler

War Hill Inn

4560 Long Hill Road, 23188
(804) 565-0248

This replica of an 18th-century home sits on a 32-acre farm three miles off Route 60. Close to Colonial Williamsburg, the College of William and Mary, Busch Gardens, shopping outlets. Seven antique-furnished guest rooms with private baths. Cable television is available.

Hosts: Shirley, Bill, Cherie, and Will Lee
Rooms: 7 plus 2 suites (PB) $65-85
Cottage: 1 (PB) $95
Full Breakfast
Credit Cards: A, B, C
Notes: 2, 5, 8, 9, 14

Williamsburg Sampler Bed and Breakfast

922 Jamestown Road, 23185
(804) 253-0398; (800) 722-1169

This bed and breakfast is an elegant plantation-style, six-bedroom brick Colonial, richly furnished with antiques, pewter, and samplers. Internationally known as a favorite for honeymoons, anniversaries, or romantic getaways. The hosts return guests to an era when hospitality was a matter of pride and fine living was an art. Lovely rooms with four-poster king/queen-size beds plus private baths. Skip-lunch breakfast. Close to all major attractions. Personalized gift certificates available. AAA rated three-diamonds.

Hosts: Helen and Ike Sisane
Rooms: 4 (PB) $85-100
Full Breakfast
Credit Cards: A, B
Notes: 2, 5, 9, 10, 11, 12, 14

WILLIS WHARF

Amanda's Bed and Breakfast #145

1428 Park Avenue, Annapolis, MD 21217
(410) 225-0001; (410) 383-1274

Eighty-year-old country farmhouse with wraparound porch and gazebo by a stream. Near freshwater pond, bird watching, photographic scenes, and guided tours. Amenities include outside swings, hammock, play gym, and bicycles. Relaxed family atmosphere. Four rooms with shared and private baths. Full breakfast. $60-75.

WINTERGREEN

Upland Manor

Route 1, Box 375, Nellysford, 22958
(804) 361-1101; (800) 562-8072

Between the Blue Ridge Mountains and Charlottesville, Upland Manor offers a relaxing getaway to enjoy scenic and historical areas, or nearby activities of golfing, swimming, canoeing, horseback riding and skiing. Beautifully restored to its original grandeur, Upland Manor offers luxurious rooms and romantic suites with private

NOTES: Credit cards accepted: A Master Card; B Visa; C American Express; D Discover Card; E Diner's Club; F Other; 2 Personal Checks accepted; 3 Lunch available; 4 Dinner available; 5 Open all year;

bathrooms and gracious furnishings to recall wonderful memories of yesteryear. Awaken to the delightful fragrance of home-baked breads and fresh ground coffee. AAA, three diamonds; AB&BA, three crowns.

Hosts: Stan and Karen Pugh
Rooms: 10 (PB) $95-115
Expanded Continental Breakfast
Credit Cards: A, B
Notes: 2, 5, 8 (over 12), 9, 10, 11, 12, 13, 14

Azalea House

WOODSTOCK

Azalea House

551 South Main Street, 22664
(703) 459-3500

The Azalea House dates back 100 years when it was built in the Victorian tradition and used as a church manse. The guest rooms are pleasing and comfortable, with antique furnishings and mountain views. Situated in the rolling hills of the Shenandoah Valley near fine restaurants, vineyards, shops, caverns, Civil War sites, hiking, and fishing. A great place to relax!

Hosts: Margaret and Price McDonald
Rooms: 3 (1 PB; 2 SB) $45-55
Full Breakfast
Credit Cards: A, B, C
Notes: 2, 5, 12, 13

Country Fare

402 North Main Street, 22664
(703) 459-4828

A small, cozy country inn where old-fashioned hospitality has not gone out of style. Carefully restored and preserved, wide-pine floorboards upstairs, original doors and hardware with hand-stenciled walls. Relax and unwind in one of the three bedroooms tastefully furnished with a comfortable blend of family antiques and country collectibles, with touches of greenery throughout. Original house built in 1772 with an addition in 1840. It served as a hospital between 1861 and 1864. A stay will surprise and delight you.

Host: Bette Hallgren
Rooms: 3 (1 PB; 2 SB) $45-65
Expanded Continental Breakfast
Credit Cards: B
Notes: 2, 5, 8, 9

The Inn at Narrow Passage

U.S. 11 South, 22664
(703) 459-8000

Historic log inn with five acres on the Shenandoah River. Colonial-style rooms, most with private baths and working fireplaces. Once the site of Indian attacks and Stonewall Jackson's headquarters, the inn is now a cozy spot in winter with large fireplaces in the common living and dining rooms. In spring and summer, fishing and

The Inn at Narrow Passage

6 Pets welcome; 7 Smoking allowed; 8 Children welcome; 9 Social drinking allowed; 10 Tennis available; 11 Swimming available; 12 Golf available; 13 Skiing available; 14 May be booked through travel agents.

rafting are at the back door. Fall brings the foliage festivals and hiking in the national forest a few miles away. Nearby are vineyards, caverns, historic sites, and fine restaurants. Washington, D.C., is 90 miles away.

Hosts: Ellen and Ed Markel
Rooms: 12 (10 PB; 2 SB) $55-90
Full Breakfast
Credit Cards: A, B
Notes: 2, 5, 8, 9, 10, 11, 12, 13, 14

Washington

ABERDEEN

Pacific B&B Agency A B-1

701 Northwest 60th Street, Seattle, 98107
(206) 784-0539

A grand house built in 1908 by a million-aire lumber baron. Totally restored and saved from the wrecker's ball, it now offers you a delightful bed and breakfast experience. Eight bedrooms, five with private baths. The atmosphere is relaxed, and the breakfasts are legendary. Enjoy the golf course and tennis courts next to the inn and the hot tub and sauna. Fifteen minutes from ocean beaches and the best whale watching from March to May. $55-85.

ANACORTES

Albatross Bed and Breakfast

5708 Kingsway West, 98221
(206) 293-0677

Across from the Skyline Marina, our 1927 Cape Cod-style home with a large viewing deck offers king- and queen-size beds, and all rooms feature a private bath. Skyline Marina offers charter boats, a deli, and fine dining. Nearby are the Washington Park and ferries to the San Juan Islands and Victoria, B.C. Free transportation to and from the ferries and Anacortes airport. AAA approved.

Hosts: Cecil and Marilyn Short
Rooms: 4 (PB) $60-75
Full Breakfast
Credit Cards: A, B, D
Notes: 2, 5, 12, 14

Anacortes

Pacific Bed and Breakfast Agency
701 Northwest 60th Street, Seattle, 98107
(206) 784-0539

This restored Victorian turn-of-the-century home features fine antiques, Oriental carpets, a library, colorful flower gardens, three fireplaces, and an outdoor hot tub. Views of Puget Sound can be seen from two rooms and the shared bathrooms. Intimate in size with warm hospitality. $60-105.

Channel House

Channel House Bed and Breakfast

2902 Oakes Avenue, 98221
(206) 293-9382

A classic island home built in 1902, the Channel House offers large, comfortable rooms, two with fireplaces, and lovely water and island views. The outdoor hot tub is a treat after a busy day of hiking or

6 Pets welcome; 7 Smoking allowed; 8 Children welcome; 9 Social drinking allowed; 10 Tennis available; 11 Swimming available; 12 Golf available; 13 Skiing available; 14 May be booked through travel agents.

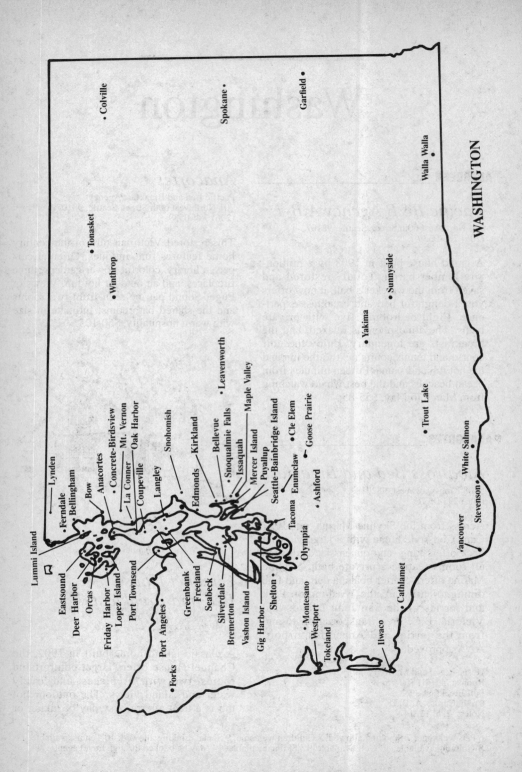

biking on the islands. Pat's oatmeal-raisin cookies are baked fresh every day. Anacortes is the beginning of the San Juan Island and Sydney, British Columbia, ferry routes and a center for chartering sail and power boats for wonderful vacation trips.

Hosts: Dennis and Patricia McIntyre
Rooms: 6 (4 PB; 2 SB) $69-95
Full Breakfast
Credit Cards: A, B, D
Notes: 2, 5, 8 (over 12), 9, 10, 11, 12, 14

Dutch Treat House

1220 31st Street, 98221
(206) 293-8154

Dutch Treat House offers comfortable, attractively furnished, large, bright corner rooms and tastefully prepared breakfasts. Ideally located and surrounded by some of the finest fishing and boating waters anywhere. Vistors enjoy many nearby attractions such as San Juan Island, Victoria and the Olympic Peninsula.

Hosts: Mike and Melanie Coyne
Rooms: 5 (SB) $40-55
Full Breakfast
Credit Cards: A, B
Notes: 2, 5, 8, 9, 10, 11, 12, 14

Hasty Pudding House Bed and Breakfast

1312 8th Street, 98221
(206) 293-5773; (800) 368-5588

Celebrate romance in our delightful 1913 heritage home. A wonderful example of Craftsman-style archtitecture, our home is filled with Victorian antiques, fresh flowers, window seats, and wonderful private rooms, all with turn-of-the-century charm and comfort you'll enjoy. You will snuggle in king, queen, and twin top-of-the-line beds that your grandmother would envy. Melinda's luscious breakfasts and table setting will begin your Anacortes adventure each day of your stay.

Hosts: Mikel and Melinda Hasty
Rooms: 4 (1 PB; 3 SB) $55-75, plus tax

Full Breakfast
Credit Cards: A, B, C, D
Notes: 2, 5, 9, 10, 11, 12, 13, 14

Sunset Beach Bed and Breakfast

100 Sunset Beach, 98221
(206) 293-5428

On the exciting Rosario Strait overlooking seven San Juan isalnds, this bed and breakfast invites you to enjoy the water scenery that includes water birds, deer, fishing boats, and more. Take a stroll and enjoy the scenic view of the Olympic Mountains, or amble down the beach. Close to the ferry, marina, and excellent restaurants, and adjacent to Washington Park. Full breakfasts, queen-size beds, and private bath. Hot tub on request.

Hosts: Joann and Hal Harber
Rooms: 3 (1 PB; 2 SB) $69
Full Breakfast
Credit Cards: A, B
Notes: 2, 5, 8, 9, 10, 11, 12, 14

ANDERSON ISLAND

The Inn at Burg's Landing

8808 Villa Beach Road, 98303
(206) 884-9185

Catch the ferry from Steilacoom to stay at this contemporary log homestead built in 1987. It offers spectacular views of Mt. Rainier, Puget Sound, and the Cascade Mountains and is ten miles south of Tacoma off I-5. Choose from three guest rooms, including the master bedroom with a queen-size "log" bed with a skylight above, and private whirlpool bath. The inn has a private beach. Collect seashells and agates, swim in two freshwater lakes nearby, or enjoy a game of tennis or golf. Tour the island by bicycle or on foot, and watch for sailboats and deer. Hot tub. Full breakfast. Families welcome. No smoking.

Hosts: Ken and Annie Burg
Rooms: 3 (2 PB; 1 SB) $65-90

NOTES: Credit cards accepted: A Master Card; B Visa; C American Express; D Discover Card; E Diner's Club; F Other; 2 Personal Checks accepted; 3 Lunch available; 4 Dinner available; 5 Open all year; 6 Pets welcome; 7 Smoking allowed; 8 Children welcome; 9 Social drinking allowed; 10 Tennis available; 11 Swimming available; 12 Golf available; 13 Skiing available; 14 May be booked through travel agents.

Full Breakfast
Credit Cards: A, B, C
Notes: 2, 5, 8, 9, 10, 11, 12, 13

ASHFORD

Growly Bear Bed and Breakfast

37311 State Road 706, 98304
(206) 569-2339

Experience a bit of history and enjoy your mountain stay at a rustic homestead house built in 1890. Secluded location near Mount Rainier National Park. Listen to Goat Creek just outside your window; indulge in fresh pastries from the Sweet Peaks Bakery.

Host: Susan Jenny
Rooms: 2 (1 PB; 1 SB) $50-80
Full Breakfast
Credit Cards: A, B, C
Notes: 2, 5, 7 (limited), 13, 14

Jasmer's Guesthaus Bed and Breafast

30005 State Road 706 E, 98304
(206) 569-2682

Jasmer's Guesthaus is a perfect balance of pampering and privacy! A love nest! Upstairs is an all-wood interior, angled ceilings, king-size bed, wood stove, and antiques. Downstairs, a heartwarming bubble bath/shower, and kitchen. The cabin on Big Creek has a complete kitchen, bath, two bedrooms, wood stove, deer, bird feeders, a seasonal hot tub, and a perfect setting of restful solitude. Come! See! Smell! Relax among the noble works of nature. Near Mount Rainier National Park and open all year.

Hosts: Tanna and Luke Osterhaus
Rooms: 2, plus 5 cabins (PB) $65-125
Continental Breakfast
Credit Cards: A, B
Notes: 2, 5, 9, 13, 14

Mountain Meadows Inn

28912 State Road 706 East, 98304
(206) 569-2788

Gracious hospitality, unique, quiet country atmosphere. Relax while absorbing nature's colors and sounds from the full porch overlooking the pond. Evening campfires. Nearby Mount Rainier National Park offers all-season recreation. Model trains are on display. Listed as "Northwest Best Places."

Host: Chad Darrah
Rooms: 5 (PB) $93.08
Full Breakfast
Minimum stay holidays: 2 nights
Credit Cards: A, B
Notes: 2, 5, 7 (limited), 8 (over 10), 9, 12, 13, 14

Growly Bear

BAINBRIDGE ISLAND

Bombay House

8490 Beck Road, 98110
(206) 842-3926; (800) 598-3926

The Bombay House is a spectacular 35-minute ferry ride from downtown Seattle. The house was built in 1907 and sits high on a hillside in the country overlooking Rich Passage. Widow's walk; rustic, rough-cedar gazebo; masses of gardens exploding with seasonal color. Watch the ferry pass and see the lights of Bremerton in the distance. Just a few blocks from the beach, a country theater, and fine dining. A great spot for the Seattle business traveler or vacationer.

NOTES: Credit cards accepted: A Master Card; B Visa; C American Express; D Discover Card; E Diner's Club; F Other; 2 Personal Checks accepted; 3 Lunch available; 4 Dinner available; 5 Open all year;

Hosts: Bunny Cameron and Roger Kanchuk
Rooms: 5 (3 PB; 2 SB) $55-95
Continental Breakfast
Credit Cards: A, B, C
Notes: 2, 5, 9, 10, 11, 12, 14

Pacific B&B Agency Bainbridge Island-1

701 Northwest 60th Street, Seattle, 98107
(206) 784-0539

This special country inn invites you to sit on the wraparound porch, enjoy the beautiful flower gardens, the gazebo, or snuggle up by the crackling fire in the fireplace. Your stay here will renew and refresh your spirits. Built for a ship's captain, this lovely bed and breakfast offers nice views over the water, three bedrooms with private baths, and two bedrooms that share a bath. Legendary country breakfast. $65-95.

Pacific B&B Agency Bainbridge Island -2

701 Northwest 60th Street, Seattle, 98107
(206) 784-0539

This Bainbridge accommodation is on a beautifully landscaped acre enclosed by a forest on both sides. You can relax on comfortable wicker furniture and look out at the rose garden after a day of sightseeing or exploration. Perfect for honeymooners and couples. The cookie jar here is always deep, a new snack is served on the table next to the sofa every day, and the bedroom has a queen-size bed with a wonderful new mattress and a private bath. $85.

Pacific B&B Agency Bainbridge Island-3

701 Northwest 60th Street, Seattle, 98107
(206) 784-0539

In this traditional, but not overly formal bed and breakfast, you can relax in a brand-new English-shingled cottage. Two large private rooms are only a short stroll from the beach. Both rooms have queen-size beds, private baths, large windows, telephones, and TV. Near the quaint towns of Rolling Bay and Winslow. $75.

BELLEVUE

Bellevue Bed and Breakfast

830-100th Avenue, Southeast, 98004
(206) 453-1048

This hilltop bed and breakfast offers mountain and city views. Private suite or single rooms, with private baths and entrances, are available. Full breakfast with gourmet coffee is served. Cable TV. In Seattle 's Best Places.

Host: Cyrus and Carol Garnett
Rooms: 2 (PB) $55 per room
Full Breakfast
Credit Cards: A, B
Notes: 2, 3, 4, 5, 11, 12, 13, 14

Petersen Bed and Breakfast

10228 SE Eighth, 98004
(206) 454-9334

Petersen bed and breakfast is in a well-established neighborhood five minutes from the Bellevue Shopping Square and 20 minutes from Seattle. It offers two rooms, one with a queen waterbed, and a spa on the deck off the atrium kitchen. Home-style breakfast.

Hosts: Eunice and Carl Petersen
Rooms: 2 (SB) $50-55
Full Breakfast
Credit Cards: None
Notes: 2, 5, 7 (outside), 8

BELLINGHAM

Bellingham

Pacific Bed and Breakfast Agency
701 Northwest 60th Street, Seattle, 98107
(206) 784-0539

6 Pets welcome; 7 Smoking allowed; 8 Children welcome; 9 Social drinking allowed; 10 Tennis available; 11 Swimming available; 12 Golf available; 13 Skiing available; 14 May be booked through travel agents.

Decorated with stained glass and etchings crafted by the hostess, this restored Victorian overlooking the bay is a great getaway spot. The two guest rooms have private baths. The hosts will be more than happy to give advice to sightseers if needed. Guests are assured a warm, friendly welcome at this bed and breakfast. $42-57.

The Castle
Bed and Breakfast

1103 Fifteenth Street, 98225
(206) 676-0974

This 102-year-old house overlooks the San Juan Islands, Bellingham Bay, and historic Fairhaven in America's fourth corner, northwestern Washington. Gorgeous scenery, boating, hiking, skiing, special shopping areas, and restaurants. Close to Alaska ferry and Western Washington University. Collections of early electric lamps, castle furnishings. Highly unusual castle atmosphere and healthful food.

Hosts: Larry and Gloria Harriman
Rooms: 3 (1 PB; 2 SB) $45-95
Full Breakfast
Credit Cards: A, B
Notes: 2, 5, 9, 10, 11, 12, 13, 14

Farmstay Near Bellingham

Pacific Bed and Breakfast Agency
701 Northwest 60th Street, Seattle, 98107
(206) 784-0539

This modern home is situated on a 100-acre working dairy farm that was homesteaded in 1892. The two guests rooms have double beds and share a bath. Take a walk along the nature trails with wildlife, around the lake, or try out the seven golf courses that are nearby. $50.

North Garden Inn

1014 North Garden, 98225
(206) 671-7828

North Garden Inn is an 1897 Queen Anne Victorian on the national register. Many of the guest rooms have splendid views of Bellingham Bay. The inn features two studio grand pianos in performance condition and is situated close to shopping, fine dining, and Western Washington University.

Hosts: Frank and Barbara De Freytas
Rooms: 8-10 (6 PB; 4 SB) $52.82-68.60
Full Breakfast
Credit Cards: A, B
Notes: 2, 5, 8, 9, 14

Schnauzer Crossing

4421 Lakeway Drive, 98226
(206) 733-0055; (206) 734-2808

Schnauzer Crossing is a luxury bed and breakfast between Seattle and Vancouver, British Columbia. Enjoy this destination bed and breakfast, with its lakeside ambience, outdoor hot tub, and its master suite with fireplace and Jacuzzi tub. There is also a new cottage. Sail in the San Juan Islands or climb 10,000-foot Mount Baker. Experience Washington State!

Hosts: Vermont and Donna McAllister
Rooms: 2 (PB) $100-175
Full Breakfast
Credit Cards: A, B
Notes: 2, 5, 7 (outdoors), 8, 9

Sunrise Bay
Bed and Breakfast

2141 North Shore Road, 98226
(206) 647-0376

This romantic getaway offers a luxury cottage for your relaxation. On Lake Whatcom, with scenic views. The hosts offer private baths, TV/ VCR, private phones, heated pool, outdoor hot tub, and canoeing, all available for your use and pleasure. Enjoy a delicious, tantalizing breakfast. Families are welcome.

Host: Karen and Jom Moren
Rooms: 2 (SB) $80
Full Breakfast
Credit Cards: A, B
Notes: 2, 5, 8, 11

NOTES: Credit cards accepted: A Master Card; B Visa; C American Express; D Discover Card; E Diner's Club; F Other; 2 Personal Checks accepted; 3 Lunch available; 4 Dinner available; 5 Open all year;

Willcox House

BOW

Benson Farmstead

1009 Avon-Allen Road, 98232
(206) 757-0528

The Benson Farmstead is a 1914 restored seventeen-room farmhouse filled with antiques, quilts, and a cozy decor. It is surrounded by flower gardens and farmland and is just off I-5 near LaConner, Burlington, Chuckanot Drive, and the tulip fields. Jerry and Sharon are third-generation Skagit Valley farmers and are friendly hosts who serve dessert and coffee in the evening and a full country breakfast.

Hosts: Jerry and Sharon Benson
Rooms: 4 (2 PB; 2 SB) $65-75
Full Breakfast
Credit Cards: B
Notes: 2, 5, 6 (outside), 7 (outside), 8, 9, 10, 11, 12, 13

BREMERTON

Willcox House

2390 Tekiu Road, Northwest, 98312
(206) 830-4492

Overlooking Hood Canal and the Olympic Mountains is a place where time rests. Life is paced by the slow, steady hand of nature. It is quiet enough to hear the birds sing. Deer amble through the gardens. Saltwater beaches and good books wait for quiet companions. Willcox House is an elegant 10,000-square-foot mansion built in 1936 with landscaped grounds, private pier, and

beach. Five guest rooms, all with private baths and magnificent views of Hood Canal and Olympic Mountains.

Hosts: Cecilia and Philip Hughes
Rooms: 5 (PB) $100-165
Full Breakfast
Credit Cards: A, B
Notes: 2, 3, 4, 5, 9, 14

CAMANO ISLAND

Willcox House Bed and Breakfast

1462 Larkspur Lane, 98292
(206) 629-4746

Built in 1985, this two-story house with a wraparound covered porch is furnished with family antiques and named for an early 1900s children's illustrator, Jessie Willcox Smith. The rooms overlook the Puget Sound where snow geese and trumpet swans migrate each fall. Mount Baker looms in the distance. Gourmet breakfasts are served in a peaceful country setting on an island one hour north of Seattle connected by bridge to the mainland, close to picturesque towns.

Host: Phyllis Watkins
Rooms: 4 (1 PB; 3 SB) $55-65
Full Breakfast
Credit Cards: None
Notes: 2, 5, 8, 9, 10, 11, 12, 13

CATHLAMET

The Gallery Bed and Breakfast at Little Cape Horn

4 Little Cape Horn, 98612
(206) 425-7395

Large contemporary home with picture windows overlooking the majestic Columbia River ship channel. Private bath. Fishing, wind surfing, and pleasant walking; deer, bald eagles, hummingbirds, hawks, and water birds. Beautiful mature

6 Pets welcome; 7 Smoking allowed; 8 Children welcome; 9 Social drinking allowed; 10 Tennis available; 11 Swimming available; 12 Golf available; 13 Skiing available; 14 May be booked through travel agents.

cedar and fir trees; very restful surroundings. Friendly hosts enjoy guests. Two cats and Labrador retriever will greet you.

Hosts: Carolyn and Eric Feasey
Rooms: 4 (2 PB; 2 SB) $60-70 depending on breakfast
Full or Continental Breakfast
Credit Cards: C
Note: 2, 5, 8 (over 10), 14

CLE ELUM

The Moore House Country Bed and Breakfast

526 Marie Street, Box 629, 98943
(509) 674-5939; (800) 22 TWAIN

The Moore House offers nine bright and airy rooms in a renovated railroad-crew hotel recently placed on the historic register. Accommodations range from economical to exquisite, including two real cabooses. They each capture the essence of the bygone era of railroading. Old print wallpaper, oak antiques, and artifacts combine with the peaceful language of nature to create an ideal romantic interlude. Adjacent to Iron Horse Trail State Park.

Hosts: Eric and Cindy Sherwood
Rooms: 11 (6 PB; 5 SB) $45-105
Full Breakfast
Minimum stay winter weekends & holidays: 2 nights
Credit Cards: A, B, C
Notes: 2, 5, 8, 9, 12, 13, 14

CONCRETE-BIRDSVIEW

Cascade Mountain Inn

3840 Pioneer Lane, 98237
(206) 826-4333; (800) 826-0015

The inn is close to the Skagit River, Baker Lake, and the North Cascades National Park, just off Highway 20 in a pastoral setting. Easy access to hiking, fishing, and sight-seeing in one of the nation's most scenic mountain areas. Full cooked country breakfast. AAA rated three diamonds.

Hosts: Ingrid and Gerhard Meyer
Rooms: 6 (PB) $89-95
Full Breakfast
Credit Cards: A, B
Notes: 2, 5, 8 (over 10), 9, 14

COUPEVILLE

The Colonial Crockett Farm Bed and Breakfast Inn

1012 S. Fort Casey Road, 98239
(206) 678-3711

The inn offers 135 years of Victorian/Edwardian serenity in the farm-quiet island setting with pastoral and marine views. Period antiques enhance three large bed/sitting rooms and two smaller bedrooms, all with private baths. Common areas include an oak-panelled library, a wicker-furnished solarium, and a dining room featuring individual tables. Full hot breakfast is served each morning, and the owners live in a separate apartment. This 1855 Victorian farmhouse is on the National Register of Historic Places. Extensive grounds, walkways, and flowerbeds. No smoking.

Hosts: Robert and Beulah Whitlow
Rooms: 5 (PB) $65-95
Full Breakfast
Credit Cards: A, B
Notes: 2, 5, 8 (over 14), 14

The Colonial Crockett Farm

DEER HARBOR

Palmer's Chart House

Box 51, 98243
(206) 376-4231

The first bed and breakfast on Orcas Island (since 1975) with a magnificent water view. The 33-foot private yacht Amante is available for a minimal fee with Skipper Don. Low-key, private, personal attention makes this bed and breakfast unique and attractive. Well-traveled hosts speak Spanish.

Hosts: Majean and Donald Palmer
Rooms: 2 (PB) $45-60
Full Breakfast
Credit Cards: None
Notes: 2, 4 (by arrangement), 5, 8 (over 10), 9, 10, 11, 12, 14

EASTSOUND, ORCAS ISLAND

Kangaroo House

Box 334, 98245
(206) 376-2175

Restful 1907 home on Orcas Island, gem of the San Juans. Period furnishings, extensive lawns, and flower gardens. Gourmet breakfasts. Walk to village shops, galleries, and restaurants. Panoramic view of the islands from Moran State Park.

Hosts: Jan and Mike Russillo
Rooms: 5 (2 PB; 3 SB) $65-100
Full Breakfast
Credit Cards: A, B
Notes: 2, 5, 8, 9, 10, 11, 12

Outlook Inn on Orcas Island

P. O.Box 210, Main Street, 98245
(206) 376-2200; FAX (206) 376-2256

This remodeled turn-of-the-century country inn is on the gem of the San Juan Islands in Washington State. Rustic Victoriana with English and American antiques can be found throughout the house; handcrafted beds, marble-topped dresser, and period memorabilia are scattered through this lovely bed and breakfast. A conference room is available for banquets or will seat 75 people theater-style. A world class chef cooks your meals. Rooms are clean and

comfortable, with colors inspired by the sea and influenced by nature. Gardens and ponds are available for guests to enjoy, and we offer a convenient central location. Get reservations early; we are extremely popular.

Host: Carol Cheney
Rooms: 29 (11 PB; 18 SB) $35-94
Full Breakfast- winter and off-season; dining room for breakfast and dinner open during the season
Credit Cards: None
Notes: None

Turtleback Farm Inn

Route 1, Box 650 (Crow Valley Road), 98243
9206) 376-4914

This meticulously restored farmhouse has been described as a "marvel of bed and breakfastmanship decorated with country finesse and a sophisticated sense of the right antiques." Seven bedrooms with private baths. Award-winning breakfasts.

Hosts: William and Susan Fletcher
Rooms: 7 (PB) $65-150
Full Breakfast
Credit Cards: A, B
Notes: 2, 5, 9, 10, 11 (nearby), 12, 14

EDMONDS

Harrison House

210 Sunset Avenue, 98020
(206) 776-4748

New waterfront home with sweeping view of Puget Sound and the Olympic Mountains. Many fine restaurants within walking distance. Your spacious room has a private bath, private deck, TV, wet bar, telephone, and king-size bed. University of Washington is nearby.

Hosts: Jody and Harve Harrison
Rooms: 2 (PB) $40-55
Continental Breakfast
Credit Cards: None
Notes: 2, 5, 9, 10, 11, 12, 13

---

6 Pets welcome; 7 Smoking allowed; 8 Children welcome; 9 Social drinking allowed; 10 Tennis available; 11 Swimming available; 12 Golf available; 13 Skiing available; 14 May be booked through travel agents.

ENUMCLAW

Stillmeadow bed and Breakfast

46225 284th Avenue, S.E., 98022
(206) 825-6381

In Enumclaw, "the gateway to mount Rainier," this 1940s Tudor farmhouse sits on five tranquil acres and a rushing creek. Two charming rooms, both of which have private baths, a generous continental breakfast, books, and music are all available for your rest and relaxation. Thirty minutes to Crystal mountain and Mount Rainier for skiing and hiking. Scenic bicycling and golfing nearby.

Hosts: Miles and Sue Nelson
Rooms: 2 (PB) $50-60
Continental Breakfast
Credit Cards: None
Notes: 2, 5, 10, 11, 12, 13

Anderson House

FERNDALE

Anderson House Bed and Breakfast

2140 Main Street, P. O. Box 1547, 98248-1547
(206) 384-3450

Whatcom County's most famous inn. Dave and Kelly Anderson have restored this landmark to its original 1897 charm. All rooms tastefully decorated in 1890s motif.

If this is your first bed and breakfast experience, Anderson House is a perfect choice. Guests from 43 states and 25 countries have left words of praise. Stay where the book authors stay!

Hosts: Dave and Kelly Anderson
Rooms: 4 (PB) $49-79
Full Breakfast
Credit Cards: A, B, C
Notes: 2, 5, 9, 10, 12, 13

Slater Heritage House Bed and Breakfast

1371 West Axton Road, 98248
(206) 384-4273

Come and spend a night in another era! This completely restored Victorian home is less than one mile off I-5. Close to the largest shopping mall in the Pacific Northwest, guests have easy access to mountains, water, or golfing. Only 12 miles from Canada. We offer four lovely bedrooms with queen-size beds and private baths. You will find an atmosphere of nostalgia and comfort. A full country breakfast is included in your room rate.

Host: Rickie Prink
Rooms: 4 (PB) $52-65
Full Breakfast
Credit Cards: A, B, C, E
Notes: 2, 5

FORKS

Misty Valley Inn Bed and Breakfast

P. O.Box 2239, Rural Route 1, Box 5407, 98331
(206) 374-9389

This 6000-square-foot stone and cedar home is nestled on a ridge in the rain forest and offers a magnificent view of Sol Duc River Valley. Antique furniture and collectibles are set off by rubbed natural woods and unusual lighting. Individualized wake-up and breakfast service times. A three-course breakfast is served bedside, in the main dining room, or on the decks. Afternoon tea service and evening pastry treats. Queen-size brass beds with custom linens.

Hosts: Rachel and Jim Bennett
Rooms: 4 (1 PB; 3 SB) $50-65
Full Breakfast
Credit Cards: A, B
Notes: 5, 9

FREELAND

Cliff House

5440 Windmill Road, 98249
(206) 321-1566

On Whidbey Island, a setting so unique there is nothing anywhere quite like Cliff House. In a private world of luxury, this stunning home is yours alone. Secluded in a forest on the edge of Puget Sound, the views are breathtaking. Stone fireplace, spa, miles of driftwood beach. King-size feather bed, gourmet kitchen. Also The Snug and Enchanting Seacliff cottage.

Hosts: Peggy Moore and Walter O'Toole
Rooms: 2 (PB) $155-310
Expanded Continental Breakfast
Minimum stay: 2 nights
Credit Cards: None
Notes: 2, 5, 9, 12

FRIDAY HARBOR

Hillside House Bed and Breakfast

365 Carter Avenue, 98250
(206) 378-4730

This large contemporary home, set among pines and firs on an acre of land, overlooks pastures, the harbor entrance, ferries, and Mount Baker. Less than a mile (an easy walk) from downtown, seven distinctive rooms offer private and/or shared baths, cozy window seats, and a variety of sleeping arrangements. The Eagle's Nest, a very special third-floor retreat, offers every amenity. Full breakfast. Liquid refresh-

ments and ice always available. Children over 10. No pets. Group rates.

Hosts: Richard and Catherine Robinson
Rooms: 7 (3 PB; 4 SB) $75-125
Full Breakfast
Credit Cards: A, B, C
Notes: 2, 5, 7 (outside only), 8 (over 10), 10, 11, 12, 14

States Inn

2039 West Valley Road, 98250
(206) 378-6240

This nine-bedroom inn is rated three diamonds by AAA. It is a completely restored and modernized farmhouse on 44 acres in a quiet, pastoral setting. Each room is decorated with the flavor of the state for which it is named. Additionally, one has a fireplace, and one room is equipped for the handicapped. The sun room offers an overlook of the nearby creek and distant hills while you are enjoying your early morning coffee.

Hosts: Dan and Judy Conniff
Rooms: 9 (PNB) $80-110
Full Breakfast
Credit Cards: A, B
Notes: 2, 5, 7, 8, 9, 14

States Inn

6 Pets welcome; 7 Smoking allowed; 8 Children welcome; 9 Social drinking allowed; 10 Tennis available; 11 Swimming available; 12 Golf available; 13 Skiing available; 14 May be booked through travel agents.

Wharfside Bed and Breakfast: on Board the "Jacquelyn"

P. O. Box 1212, 98250
(206) 378-5661

A romantic winter retreat or challenging summer adventure—aboard the *Jacquelyn*, the West Coast's original, floating bed and breakfast. This elegantly restored 60-foot traditional sailing vessel offers two spacious, private guest staterooms with with private half-baths, a main salon replete with antiques, art and artifacts, as well as a wood-burning stove for cozy evenings. Bask on deck, while enjoying a sumptuous and hearty breakfast. Take a spin in the rowing gig or book a fishing charter.

Hosts: Clyde and Bette Rice
Rooms: 2 (SB) $75-80
Full Breakfast
Credit Cards: A, B
Notes: 2, 5, 6, 8, 9, 10, 11, 12

GARFIELD

Garfield

Pacific Bed and Breakfast Agency
701 Northwest 60th Street, Seattle, 98107
(206) 784-0539

This beautiful guest home was built as a Classical Revival house in 1898 and offers two guestrooms, one with a double bed and the other with two twin beds. There is a large shared bathroom with a huge claw-foot soaking tub. Breakfast might include juices, flapjacks with local organic red wheat, homemade jams, maple syrup, home-baked breads and other delights prepared on an old-fashioned wood-burning stove. $60.

GIG HARBOR

Orchard

Pacific Bed and Breakfast Agency
701 Northwest 60th Street, Seattle, 98107
(206) 784-0539

This lovely bed and breakfast was built in 1984 on three acres of rural land between Gig Harbor and Bremerton, ninety minutes from Seattle. The large guest room features a double bed and a private bath, and welcomes you to relax in the two-person whirlpool tub. Views of Mount Rainier can be seen from the living and dining rooms. What a perfect spot for a quiet country getaway! $60-75.

GLENWOOD

Flying L Ranch

25 Flying L Lane, 98619
(509) 364-3488

Built in 1945 by the Lloyds and operated as a bed and breakfast since 1960. On 160 beautiful acres with trails, wildflowers, wildlife, pond; in a tranquil secluded valley at the base of 12,276-foot Mt Adams. Intimate lodge, guest house with views, fireplaces, common kitchens, cabins, and spa Restaurants nearby.

Hosts: Darvel and Ilse Lloyd
Rooms: 13 (9 PB; 4 SB) $55-85
Full Breakfast
Credit Cards: A, B, C, E
Notes: 2, 4 (groups only), 5, 6 (cabins only), 7 (limited), 8, 9, 12 (nearby), 13 (XC), 14
Minimum stay required on certain weekends and holidays

GOOSE PRAIRIE

The Hopkinson House Bed and Breakfast

8391 Bumping River Road, 98929
(509) 453-9431

Goose Prairie is situated at 3,200 feet in the Cascade Mountain Range. Surrounded by the William O. Douglas wilderness area. A comfortable, spacious, and private bed and breakfast. Private entrance and decks that extend to river's edge. Write for information or reservations.

NOTES: Credit cards accepted: A Master Card; B Visa; C American Express; D Discover Card; E Diner's Club; F Other; 2 Personal Checks accepted; 3 Lunch available; 4 Dinner available; 5 Open all year;

Host: Martha Jean Hopkinson
Rooms: 2 (1 PB; 1 SB) $60
Full Breakfast
Credit Cards: C
Notes: 2, 3, 4, 5, 9, 13

GREENBANK

Guest House Cottages

835 East Christenson Road, 98253
(206) 678-3115

A couple's romantic retreat, this AAA four diamond-rated bed and breakfast hideaway offers storybook cottages in cozy settings on 25 acres. Fireplaces, VCRs, in-room Jacuzzis, kitchens, feather beds, country antiques, and wildlife pond are all amenities guests can enjoy. Pool, spa, peace, and pampering. Voted "Best place to Kiss in the Northwest". Near the winery. No smoking, no pets, no children.

Hosts: Don and Mary Jane Creger
Rooms: 6 (PB) $135-185
Expanded Continental Breakfast
Minimum stay weekends: 2 nights; holidays: 2-3 nights
Credit Cards: A, B, C, D
Notes: 2, 5, 9, 11, 14

HOOD CANAL

Hood Canal Waterfront Victorian

Pacific Bed and Breakfast Agency
701 Northwest 60th Street, Seattle, 98107
(206) 784-0539

This bed and breakfast offers three guest rooms, a charming atmosphere of genteel living, and sloping grounds leading to the beach. Enjoy a homecooked breakfast and a relaxed friendly environment just right for getaways. $55-65.

Waterfront Hood Canal

Pacific Bed and Breakfast Agency
701 Northwest 60th Street, Seattle, 98107
(206) 784-0539

This cozy bed and breakfast offers guests total privacy. There are two bedrooms, one with queen bed and the other with a double bed; both share a bath. A wall of windows allows guests to take in the ever-changing view. Guests can snuggle up in front of the tall stone fireplace or take the elevator to a private beach where oysters can be gathered. Hosts are not on location to serve breakfast; the full kitchen will have everything that is needed. $125+.

Waterfront Hood Canal Cottage

Pacific Bed and Breakfast Agency
701 Northwest 60th Street, Seattle, 98107
(206) 784-0539

Guests can enjoy this private waterfront hideaway in an atmosphere of serenity; the sunsets are magnificent. The cottage and the two guest rooms are decorated in a quaint fashion with antiques, ruffles, and collectible memorabilia. The honeymoon cottage features its own hot tub and deck. A delicious light breakfast is brought to guests rooms in the morning for private dining. $75-115.

Waterfront Mansion Hood Canal

Pacific Bed and Breakfast Agency
701 Northwest 60th Street, Seattle, 98107
(206) 784-0539

Experience the grandeur of a bygone time and the opulence of the rich and famous in the 1930s at this premier bed and breakfast inn. Built in 1936, this inn is on several acres of waterfront property and features a combination of Art Deco, the architecture of Northern China, seasoned with Northwestern flair. There are five guest rooms with private baths, towel warmers, clothes steamers, down comforters, and hair dryers. $90-145.

6 Pets welcome; 7 Smoking allowed; 8 Children welcome; 9 Social drinking allowed; 10 Tennis available; 11 Swimming available; 12 Golf available; 13 Skiing available; 14 May be booked through travel agents.

HOQUIAM

Pacific B&B Agency HO-1

701 Northwest 60th Street, Seattle, 98107
(206) 784-0539

A historic 20-room mansion is offered to
you on the southern tip of the Olympic
Peninsula only two hours from Seattle and
minutes to the Pacific Ocean. The mansion
is filled with a fascinating array of
antiques. Five bedrooms with queen beds
share three baths. A full and delicious
breakfast is served in the large, formal dining room. Recommended by the Los
Angeles Times. $55-65.

ILWACO

Inn at Ilwaco

120 Williams Street NE, 98624-0922
(206) 642-8686

The inn, a 1928 New England/Georgian-
style church lovingly transformed into a
gracious bed and breakfast with a 120-seat
wedding chapel/playhouse. Cozy guest
rooms nestled under eaves and dormers.
Generous and informal parlor with library.
Eclectically furnished, some old, some
new, some antiques and country touches.
Occupies hillside site overlooking historic
port town where the Columbia River meets
the ocean. Nearby are 28 miles of sandy
beach, working lighthouses, museums, and
three nationally acclaimed restaurants.

Host: Laurie Blancher
Rooms: 9 (7 PB; 2 SB) $55-75
Full Breakfast
Credit Cards: A, B
Notes: 2, 5, 8, 9, 10, 11, 12, 14

ISSAQUAH

Issaquah

Pacific Bed and Breakfast Agency
701 Northwest 60th Street, Seattle, 98107
(206) 784-0539

This lovely log inn is located in peaceful
seclusion, nestled in woods filled with
evergreens. With a gazebo in back, this getaway is perfect for family gatherings and
small weddings. Hosts offer four guest
rooms, two with private baths, for their visitors. Comfortable brass queen beds, cozy
wall coverings, country charm, and
antiques all add to the wonderful feeling of
being made welcome and treasured. $60.

Wildflower Bed and Breakfast Inn

25237 Souptheast Issaquah-Fall City Road, 98027
(206) 392-1196

Quiet country charm in a small, delightful
suburb of Seattle. Two-story log home nestled in acres of evergreens offers the comfort of spacious rooms, antique furnishings,
home-cooked breakfasts. Nearby are
Gilman Shopping Village, a small theater,
and excellent restaurants. Close to state and
county recreational parks; 35 minutes from
skiing.

Host: Laureita Caldwell
Rooms: 4 (2 PB; 2 SB) $55
Full Breakfast
Credit Cards: None
Notes: 2, 5, 10, 11, 12, 13, 14

KIRKLAND

Shumway Mansion

11410 99th Place Northeast, 98033
(206) 823-2303

Overlook Lake Washington from this
award-winning, 23-room mansion dating
from 1909. Seven individually decorated
guest rooms with private baths. Variety-
filled breakfast. Complimentary use of athletic club. Short distance to all forms of
shopping; 20 minutes to downtown Seattle.
Water and snow recreation close at hand.

Hosts: Richard and Salli Harris
Rooms: 7 (PB) $65-95

NOTES: Credit cards accepted: A Master Card; B Visa; C American Express; D Discover Card; E Diner's
Club; F Other; 2 Personal Checks accepted; 3 Lunch available; 4 Dinner available; 5 Open all year;

Full Breakfast
Credit Cards: A, B, C
Notes: 2, 5, 8 (over 12), 9, 10, 11, 14

The Rainbow Room

LA CONNER

Heather House

505 Maple Street, 98257
(206) 466-4675

Three-bedroom, two-bath Cape Cod home in downtown La Conner. Easy walk to shopping and dining. Hosts live next door, so guests can enjoy freedom and privacy. View of farm, Cascade Mountains, and Mount Baker. Halfway between Seattle and Vancouver, British Columbia. Near ferry to the San Juan Islands.

Hosts: Wayne and Bev Everton
Rooms: 3 (SB) $50-70
Continental Breakfast
Credit Cards: A, B
Notes: 2, 5, 9, 10, 11, 12, 14

Pacific B&B Agency - LA-1

701 Northwest 60th Street, Seattle, 98107
(206) 784-0539

This charming house was built in 1979 as a replica circa 1900 home. Three guest rooms are featured in this home where guests have total privacy since the host is next door and not in the guest house. The host will come over to prepare breakfast for guests in the mornings. Enjoy the lovely views over the fields, meadows, and mountains. $50-75.

Pacific B&B Agency - LA-2

701 Northwest 60th Street, Seattle, 98107
(206) 784-0539

Guests can relax and enjoy themselves in this beautiful Victorian-style country inn. The hosts offer ten guest rooms with private baths, telephone, television, and some with fireplaces and wonderful views. The honeymoon suite features a Jacuzzi. Guests are invited to enjoy the outdoor hot tub. $55-150.

The Rainbow Inn

P. O.Box 15, 98257
(206) 466-4578

This beautifully restored 1908 farmhouse is located one half mile from the historic fishing village of La Conner, with panoramic views of the rich Skagit Valley farmlands, the Cascade Mountain Range, and Mount Baker. There are eight guest rooms with private or shared baths, and a deck with a gazebo and hot tub. A hearty gourmet breakfast is served, featuring fresh, locally grown produce.

Hosts: Sharon Briggs and Ron Johnson
Rooms: 8 (5 PNB; 3 SB) $75-95
Full Breakfast
Credit Cards: A, B
Notes: 2, 5, 9, 12, 13

LANGLEY

Country Cottage of Langley

215 Sixth Street, 98260
(206) 221-8709

6 Pets welcome; 7 Smoking allowed; 8 Children welcome; 9 Social drinking allowed; 10 Tennis available; 11 Swimming available; 12 Golf available; 13 Skiing available; 14 May be booked through travel agents.

Lovely country setting in Langely-by-the-Sea. Sweeping water and mountain views stroll to town, beach or relax in Old World charm with modern comforts. Restored farmhouse and separate guest cottage. Guests are provided a great breakfast.

Hosts: Bob and Mary Decelles
Rooms: 4 (PB) $80
Full Breakfast
Credit Cards: A, B
Notes: 2, 5, 9,

Pine River Ranch

Eagles Nest Inn

3236 East Saratoga, 98260
(206) 321-5331

The inn's rural setting on Whidbey Island offers a sweeping view of Saratoga Passage and Mount Baker. Casual elegance abounds. Relax and enjoy the wood stove, spa, library, and bottomless chocolate chip cookie jar. Canoeing available. Write or call for brochure.

Hosts: Nancy and Dale Bowman
Rooms: 4 (PB) $85-105
Full Breakfast
Minimum stay holiday weekends: 2 nights
Credit Cards: A, B
Notes: 2, 5, 10, 14

Log Castle

3273 East Saratoga Road, 98260
(206) 321-5483

Situated on Whidbey Island, 30 miles north of Seattle. Log lodge on secluded beach. Big stone fireplace, turret bedrooms, panoramic views of Puget Sound and the Cascade Mountains. Norma's breakfast is a legend. Watch for bald eagles and Orca whales from the widow's walk.

Hosts: Senator Jack and Norma Metcalf
Rooms: 4 (PB) $77.50-97.50
Full Breakfast
Minimum stay holidays: 2 nights
Credit Cards: A, B, D
Notes: 2, 5, 8 (over 11), 10

Lone Lake Cottages and Breakfast

5206 South Bayview Road, 98260
(206) 321-5325

Whidbey's Shangri-la. Enjoy privacy in the waterfront cottages or in a sternwheel houseboat. All are decorated with touches of the Orient. View, fireplace, kitchen, TV/VCR, Jacuzzi, canoes, fishing, and bicycles.

Host: Dolores Meeks
Rooms: 3 (PB) $110
Expanded Continental Breakfast
Credit Cards: None
Notes: 2, 5, 9, 10, 11, 12

The Whidbey Inn

106 Fiorst Street, P. O.Box 156, 98260
(206) 221-7115

Perched on a bluff, this bed and breakfast offers a dramatic view of the Saratoga Passage Waterway, the Cascade Mountains, and Camano Island from each room. When you arrive, your hosts will greet you warmly, and encourage you to take a moment and relax over a glass of sherry and an appetizer. Each of our romantic rooms is decorated with antiques and offers a private bath with English amenities and Swiss chocolates on the pillows. The Whidbey Inn is a perfect setting for romance.

Host: Gretchen Bower
Rooms: 6 (PB) $95-145
Full Breakfast
Credit Cards: A, B, C
Notes: 2, 5

NOTES: Credit cards accepted: A Master Card; B Visa; C American Express; D Discover Card; E Diner's Club; F Other; 2 Personal Checks accepted; 3 Lunch available; 4 Dinner available; 5 Open all year;

LEAVENWORTH

All Seasons River Inn Bed and Breakfast

8751 Icicle Road, 98826
(509) 548-1425

Put the phone and the world on hold, and come relax in this peaceful setting at the base of the Cascade Mountains. Nestled in evergreens overlooking the Wenatchee River, all rooms are spacious with antique decor, private baths, and riverfront decks. In the evening, enjoy a scrumptious dessert in our guest livingroom or upstairs TV room, play one of several games in our game room, or listen to the relaxing sounds of the waters below the decks. Awaken to the hearty breakfasts that guests say lasts them all day. Enjoy hiking, biking, rafting, cross-country skiing, or fishing, all within a mile from our home. Once you have been our guests, you'll want to return again and again.

Hosts: Cathy and Jeff Falconer
Rooms: 5 (PB) $90-115
Full Breakfast
Credit Cards: A, B
Notes: 2, 5, 9, 13, 14

Leavenworth

Pacific Bed and Breakfast Agency
701 Northwest 60th Street, Seattle, 98107
(206) 784-0539

This peaceful country inn is located in a town that has taken on a Bavarian atmosphere with German stores, shops, restaurants, and flowers everywhere. Enjoy the wonderful views, hot tub, pool, and the continental breakfast. Some rooms have private baths. $55-85.

Pine River Ranch

19668 Highway 207, 98826
(509) 763-3959

An exceptional inn, perfect for special getaways or family retreats, the Pine River Ranch offers spacious, beautifully decorated rooms that will pamper you with wood stoves, decks, and sunny sitting areas. A deluxe suite offers romantic seclusion with a claw foot tub, wet bar, breakfast nook, and entertainment center. Private cottages are ideal for families. Fabulous food, hot tubs, stream fishing, private ski trails, and lots of friendly farm animals are but a few of the features on premises. In the Lake Wenatchee Area, a 200-acre valley with a million-dollar view.

Hosts: Mary Ann and Michael Zenk
Rooms: 3, plus guest cottages (PB) $75-125
Full Breakfast
Credit Cards: A, B
Notes: 2, 5, 7, 8, 9, 10, 11, 12, 13, 14

Run of the River Bed and Breakfast

9308 East Leavenworth Road
P. O. Box 285, 98826
(509) 548-7171; (800) 288-6491

Run of the River, a log bed and breakfast inn on the Icicle River, is surrounded by a wildlife and bird refuge. All rooms have hand-hewn log furniture, high cathedral pine ceilings, and private baths. From the decks, enjoy the Cascade view.

Hosts: Monty and Karen Turner
Rooms: 5 (PB) $90-145
Full Breakfast
Credit Cards: A, B, C
Notes: 2, 5, 9, 10, 11, 12, 13, 14

LONG BEACH

Pacific B&B Agency LB-1

701 Northwest 60th Street, Seattle, 98107
(206) 784-0539

A three- to four-hour drive will take you to this lovely but often undiscovered spot of the state where the Columbia River meets the Pacific Ocean. The best beachcombing, clam digging, salmon fishing, and relaxation can be found here. This historic inn offers 12 rooms that are furnished in antiques as a reminder of a gentler time. Five rooms have private baths. $60-145.

LOPEZ ISLAND

Edenwild Inn

Box 271, 98261
(206) 468-3238

This elegant country inn in Lopez Village within walking distance of shops and restaurants offers seven large, comfortable guest rooms, each of which has its own private bath, some with fireplaces, and some with water or garden views. We have facilities for children and a room designed for the handicapped. Included with your room is a full family-style breakfast served in our dining room or in your room upon request, and an afternoon apertif. If you have any allergies or diet restrictions, just let us know. We hope to make your stay a pleasant one. For the comfort of our guests, we are a non-smoking establishment. Ferry landing, sea plane, or airport pickup is available.

Host: Sue Aran
Rooms: 7 (PB) $100-140
Full Breakfast
Credit Cards: A, B
Notes: 2, 3, 4, 5, 8, 9, 12, 14

Inn at Swifts Bay

Route 2, Box 3402, 98261
(206) 468-3636

On Lopez Island, in the San Juans of Washington State, the Inn at Swifts Bay is situated on three wooded acres. Five guest rooms, three with private bath. Fireplaces in common areas, hot tub on deck, private beach, award-winning breakfasts. A designated 3-star Northwest Best Place, AAA, Mobil.

Hosts: Robert Herrmann and Christopher Brandmeir
Rooms: 5 (3 PB; 2 SB) $75-125
Full Breakfast

Credit Cards: A, B, C, D
Notes: 2, 5, 9, 10, 11, 12, 14

MacKaye Harbor Inn

Route 1, Box 1940, 98261
(206) 468-2253

The ideal beachfront getaway. Lopez's only bed and breakfast on a low-bank sandy beach, perfect for beach-combing, kayaking, rowing, and biking. This 1927 Victorian home has been painstakingly restored. Guests are pampered in comfortable elegance. Eagles, deer, seals, and otters frequent this Cape Cod of the Northwest. Commendations from Sunset, Pacific Northwest magazine, the Los Angeles Times, and Northwest Best Places.

Hosts: Mike and Robin Bergstrom
Rooms: 5 (1 PB; 4 SB) $69-105
Full Breakfast
Credit Cards: A, B
Notes: 2, 5, 9, 12, 14

Pacific B&B Agency LI-1

701 Northwest 60th Street, Seattle, 98107
(206) 784-0539

At the first stop by the ferry, relax at this Victorian waterfront inn with lovely antiques, a restaurant on the premises, and all the charm of a tranquil setting. Grand sunsets, sandy beaches, tidal pools, and beachcombing. Watching the eagles and other wildlife will keep you busy. Bring your kayak, bicycles, windsurfing, or fishing gear. Five guest rooms, one with private bath. $55-75.

LUMMI ISLAND

West Shore Farm Bed and Breakfast

2781 West Shore Drive, 98262
(206) 758-2600

Unique octagonal owner-built home with 180-degree view of islands, passing boats, sunsets, eagles, seals, and Canadian mountains on the northern horizon. The quiet natural beach, farm animals, garden, orchard with resident poultry, stock of books, maps, bicycles, and natural gourmet food are rejuvenating.

Hosts: Carl and Polly Hanson
Rooms: 2 (PB) $80
Full Breakfast
Credit Cards: A, B
Notes: 2, 4, 5, 8, 9

The Willows Inn

2579 West Shore Drive, 98262
(206) 758- 2620

Established in 1911 by Victoria's grandparents, The Willows is an island landmark. On the sunset side of the island, it boasts a private beach and a spectacular view of the San Juan Islands. Noted for its fine dining and award-winning gardens, The Willows is a most peaceful and romantic destination. Ten minutes from I-5 near Bellingham and a seven-minute ferry ride brings you to our quiet little island.

Hosts: Victoria and Gary
Rooms: 7 (5 PB; 2 SB) $95-135
Full Breakfast
Credit Cards: A, B
Notes: 2, 4, 9, 11

LYNDEN

Dutch Village Inn

655 Front Street, 98264
(206) 354-4440

We are a unique hotel built under a windmill in the charming Dutch community. Each room is indivdually decorated in antiques and is representative of a Dutch Province. Complimentary breakfasts are included with your stay.

Hosts: Kim, Elaine, and Deena
Rooms: 6 (PB) $65-95
Full Breakfast Monday-Saturday; Expanded
    Continental on Sunday
Credit Cards: A, B
Notes: 2, 3, 5, 8, 9, 12, 13, 14

MAPLE VALLEY

Maple Valley Bed and Breakfast

20020 SE 228, 98038
(206) 432-1409

Welcome to this warm cedar home in the wooded Northwest. Spacious grounds, wildlife pond, and fine feathered friends. Experience the "Good Morning" rooster, hootenanny pancakes, "hot babies," and gracious family hospitality. Crest Airpark is just minutes away. Be special; be a guest at Maple Valley.

Hosts: Jayne and Clarke Hurlbut
Rooms: 2 (SB) $50-60
Full Breakfast
Credit Cards: None
Notes: 2, 5, 8, 9, 10, 11, 12, 13, 14

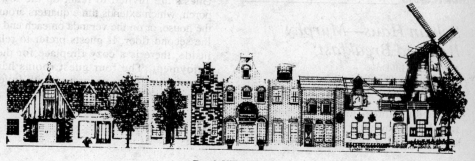

Dutch Village Inn

6 Pets welcome; 7 Smoking allowed; 8 Children welcome; 9 Social drinking allowed; 10 Tennis available; 11 Swimming available; 12 Golf available; 13 Skiing available; 14 May be booked through travel agents.

MERCER ISLAND

Mercer Island Bed and Breakfast

P. O. Box 924, 98040
(206) 232-2345

Just ten minutes from downtown Seattle across a floating bridge in an area of executive homes, this wondrous vintage cottage on Lake Washington awaits you. Furnished in early country Americana it has two bedrooms, livingroom, kitchen, and bath. Complete with TV and telephone. Rolling lawns to the water's edge invite swimming or lazy days.

Host: Jean Knight
Rooms: 2 (SB) $65-100
Full Breakfast
Credit Cards: A, B, C, D
Notes: 2, 5, 8, 9, 11, 14

Pacific B&B Agency MI-2

701 Northwest 60th Street, Seattle, 98107
(206) 784-0539

A spacious contemporary home with special features. The livingroom will surprise you with two grand pianos and an organ. Several rooms with various bed sizes. Have your home-cooked gourmet breakfast on the sunny patio or around the inviting round dining room table. Listed in Seattle's Best Places. $65 and up.

MONTESANO

Sylvan Haus—Murphy Bed and Breakfast

417 Wilder Hill Drive
P. O. Box 416, 98563
(206) 249-3453

A gracious, three-story family home surrounded by towering evergreens at the top of Wilder Hill Drive. Watch the changing seasons while breakfasting at the old round oak dining table. Grays Harbor, Sea-Tac Airport, Olympic Peninsula, Lake Quinalt Rain Forest; 30 minutes to ocean beaches.

Hosts: Mike and JoAnne Murphy
Rooms: 3 (1 PB; 2 SB) $50
Full Breakfast
Credit Cards: None
Notes: 2, 5, 8 (over 14), 11, 12

MOUNT RAINIER AREA

Country Inn

Pacific Bed and Breakfast Agency
701 Northwest 60th Street, Seattle, 98107
(206) 784-0539

Originally built in 1912, this inn was restored in 1984 and features eleven guest rooms with queen beds. The hand-made quilts, antiques, tiffany lamps, and stained-glass windows all add to the comfort of this bed and breakfast. There is also a critically acclaimed restaurant that serves delicious food in a relaxed, genteel fashion by a big stone fireplace. $65-105.

Georgian Mansion Near Mt. Rainier

Pacific Bed and Breakfast Agency
701 Northwest 60th Street, Seattle, 98107
(206) 784-0539

This wonderful 1903 Georgian mansion is in a delightful setting against a backdrop of giant evergreens which strech into the sky. Guests are invited to relax on the lower porch, which extends three quarters around the house, or on the veranda on each end of the second floor. If guests prefer to relax inside, there is a cozy fireplace for their enjoyment. The four guest rooms have been individually decorated with lovely antiques. $65-80.

NOTES: Credit cards accepted: A Master Card; B Visa; C American Express; D Discover Card; E Diner's Club; F Other; 2 Personal Checks accepted; 3 Lunch available; 4 Dinner available; 5 Open all year;

MT. VERNON

Ridgeway Bed and Breakfast

1292 McLean Road, 98273
(206) 428-8068

A 1928 yellow brick Dutch Colonial farmhouse built on the "Ridgeway" from the historic waterfront town of LaConner. Situated in the heart of the rich Skagit Valley where daffodils, tulips, and iris fields paint the landscape. The large windows in our home offer an airy and open feeling with a view of the mountains and farm fields in every direction. Homemade desserts served by the fireplace. Wake up to coffee, tea, or hot chocolate to sharpen your appetite for our hearty farm breakfast. Quiet, smoke-free guest rooms with queen or king beds. An orchard, flowers, and two acres of lawn are here for your enjoyment. Come home to the farm and let us pamper you.

Hosts: Louise and John Kelley
Rooms: 5 (2 PB; 3 SB) $70-90
Full Breakfast
Credit Cards: A, B, C
Notes: 5

The White Swan Guest House

1388 Moore Road, 98273
(206) 445-6805

The White Swan is a "storybook" farmhouse six miles from the historic waterfront town of La Conner. Fine restaurants, great antiquing, and interesting shops in Washington's favorite artist community. Just one hour north of Seattle and 90 miles south of Vancouver. Separate honeymoon cottage.

Host: Peter Goldfarb
Rooms: 4 (1 PB; 3 S2B) $70-100
Continental Breakfast
Credit Cards: A, B
Notes: 2, 5, 8, 9

OAK HARBOR

Maranatha Sea Horse Bed and Breakfast

4487 North Moran Beach Lane, 98277
(206) 679-2075

A spacious beach home decorated with comfortable antiques, our home invites you to step back from the lawn and walk for miles exploring the beach to Deception Pass State Park. Inside, enjoy a spectacular view of Olympic Mountain, shipping lanes, and islands, while we serve your delicious homemade breakfast. Relax in a big hot tub and enjoy an incredible sunset. Snuggle by the fire and watch 52-inch TV/VCR with Surround Sound, or enjoy our pool table, volleyball court, and horseback riding. We also offer a modern beach cabin that sleeps six. Children are welcome.

Hosts: Rosemary and Ragnor Gustafson
Rooms: 3 (1 PB; 2 SB) $59-75
Full Breakfast
Credit Cards: A, B, C
Notes: 2, 5, 11, 12, 13

OCEAN SHORES

Pacific B&B Agency Ocean Shores-1

701 Northwest 60th Street, Seattle, 98107
(206) 784-0539

A bed and breakfast inn located right on the ocean offers five bedrooms, all of which feature private baths. Enjoy your full breakfast in the dining room overlooking the everchanging scenery of the water and the seagulls. Take a dip in the hot tub after a long walk on the beach. Hospitality is the word here, and your hostess will see to it that you have a fine stay. $50-70.

6 Pets welcome; 7 Smoking allowed; 8 Children welcome; 9 Social drinking allowed; 10 Tennis available; 11 Swimming available; 12 Golf available; 13 Skiing available; 14 May be booked through travel agents.

OLYMPIA

Harbinger Inn

1136 East Bay Drive, 98506
(206) 754-0389

Completely restored national historic landmark. View of East Bay marina, Capitol,
and Olympic Mountains. Ideally situated
for boating, bicycling, jogging, fine dining,
and business ventures. A Northwest Best
Place.

Hosts: Marisa and Terrell Williams
Rooms: 4 (1 PB; 3 SB) $60-85
Continental Breakfast
Credit Cards: A, B, C
Notes: 2, 5, 8 (over 12), 9

Puget View Guesthouse

7924 61st Avenue, Northeast, 98506
(206) 459-1676

Classic Puget Sound. Quaint waterfront
guest cottage suite that sleeps four, on the
shore of Puget Sound next to host's
home. Expansive marine-mountain view.
Breakfast is served privately in the cottage.
Great honeymoon/romantic retreat. Near
Tolmie State Park, five minutes off I-5, just
north of downtown Olympia.

Hosts: The Yunkers
Cottage: 1 (PB) $72
Expanded Continental Breakfast
Credit Cards: A, B
Notes: 2, 7, 8, 9, 11

OLYMPIC

Pacific B&B Agency Olympic-1

701 Northwest 60th Street, Seattle, 98107
(206) 784-0539

With an unobstructed view over the water,
this private two-bedroom cottage with double and twin beds invites you to linger.

Right next door to a state park, you can rent
a boat and enjoy the lovely water, or relax
in the privacy of the cottage, nicely furnished and decorated in country-style.
Breakfast will be served to you in the
morning on a tray, to eat outside or in,
depending on the weather. Minimum of
two nights on the weekends. $85.

OLYMPIC PENINSULA

Pacific B&B Agency Olympic Peninsula-1

701 Northwest 60th Street, Seattle, 98107
(206) 784-0539

This is where we offer you a splendid historic lodge. Majestically situated in a picturesque setting with the finest views ever
offered from a lodge, the gravel lobby of
this home with its imposing stone fireplaces gives a quiet elegance and charm of
yesteryear. Cocktails by the fire, an elegant
dinner in the restaurant, and a refreshing
dip in an indoor pool all add up to great
vacation experience. European-style bath in
the lodge. Two-night minimum on weekends. $55-100.

ORCAS

Pacific B&B Agency OI-1

701 Northwest 60th Street, Seattle, 98107
(206) 784-0539

A large two-story log inn welcomes you
with seven bedrooms, all with private
baths. Most of the rooms have views of the
water. Rustic and comfortable, this inn is
newly built and has a restaurant on the
premises. Breakfast will be delivered to
you in a basket to enjoy in the privacy of
your room. $65-75, winter rates available.

NOTES: Credit cards accepted: A Master Card; B Visa; C American Express; D Discover Card; E Diner's
Club; F Other; 2 Personal Checks accepted; 3 Lunch available; 4 Dinner available; 5 Open all year;

PORT ANGELES

Anniken's Bed and Breakfast

214 East Whidbey Avenue, 98362
(206) 457-6177

Enjoy a wonderful view of the harbor and
the mountains of Olympic National Park
from our Scandinavian-style home, decorated in blues, whites, and wood tones. Two
comfortable double-bedded rooms share a
bath and enjoy a lofty sitting room. High,
light, and homey characterizes our guest
quarters. Anniken's is just five minutes
from Victoria ferries or the Park Visitor
Center. Our homemade breakfast always
includes fresh fruit and gourmet coffee.

Hosts: Robert and Ann Kennedy
Rooms: 2 (SB) $50-60
Full Breakfast
Credit Cards: A, B
Notes: 2, 5

Pacific B&B Agency Port Angeles-1

701 Northwest 60th Street, Seattle, 98107
(206) 784-0539

Uniquely European in style, this comfortable and magnificent English-style Tudor
house was built in 1910 and restored to
serve as an inn. Five guest rooms with a
view of the water are available. Full breakfast. Wonderful antiques are throughout
this lovely old house. Two-night minimum
on weekends. Two blocks to downtown
and restaurants. $55-85.

Tudor Inn

1108 South Oak, 98362
(206) 452-3138

Situated between the mountains and the
sea, this half-timbered Tudor home was
built by an Englishman in 1910 and has
been tastefully restored and furnished with
European antiques and an English garden.
Tea is served in the lounge or the library.

Hosts: Jane and Jerry Glass
Rooms: 5 (1 PB; 4 S2B) $55-85
Full Breakfast
Minimum stay weekends & holidays: 2
Credit Cards: A, B
Notes: 2, 5, 8 (over 10), 9, 10, 11, 12, 13, 14

Tudor Inn

PORT TOWNSEND

Ann Starrett Mansion Victorian Bed & Breakfast Inn

744 Clay Street, 98368
(206) 385-3205; (800) 321-0644

Situated on a bluff overlooking the
Olympic Mountains, the Cascades, Puget
Sound, and historic Port Townsend. The
house is renowned for its Victorian architecture, free-hanging staircase, frescoed
domed ceiling with a solar calendar, and
sumptuous breakfasts.

Hosts: Edel and Bob Sokol
Rooms: .$65-125
Full Breakfast
Credit Cards: A, B, C, D
Notes: 2, 5, 9, 10, 11, 12, 14

The Bishop Victorian Guest Suites

714 Washington Street, 98368
(206) 385-6122; 1-800-824-4738

6 Pets welcome; 7 Smoking allowed; 8 Children welcome; 9 Social drinking allowed; 10 Tennis available; 11
Swimming available; 12 Golf available; 13 Skiing available; 14 May be booked through travel agents.

Built by William Bishop in 1890, the three-story Bishop Block Building is a fine example of the award-winning downtown restoration for which Port Townsend is famous. A short climb upstairs and the unsuspecting visitor is transported into Victorian grace and comfort. Each suite is furnished with vintage pieces that reflect the grandeur and charm of a bygone era. Views range from Mount Baker in the Cascade Mountains and the rugged peaks of the Olympics to the waters of Port Townsend Bay and Admiralty Inlet. The downtown location means convenient access to the towns, shops, sites, and restaurants.

Hosts: Lloyd W and Marlene M. Cahoon
Rooms: 13 (PB) $68-89, seasonal rates apply
Continental Breakfast
Credit Cards: A, B, C
Notes: 2, 5, 6, 7, 8, 14

1892 Castle

Pacific Bed and Breakfast Agency
701 Northwest 60th Street, Seattle, 98107
(206) 784-0539

The castle sits on a hill with commanding marina views. It features rooms with private baths and Victorian decor, and lovely gardens. The landmark mansion is on the National Register of Historic Places and was totally restored in 1973. Enjoy splendid luxury while you are in Port Townsend. Continental breakfast. $75-150.

The Grand Dame

Pacific Bed and Breakfast Agency
701 Northwest 60th Street, Seattle, 98107
(206) 784-0539

The most photographed house in Port Townsend, this great Victorian was built in 1889 by a wealthy contractor for his wife as a wedding present. It features a spiral freestanding staircase that is one of the finest in existence. Special frescoes in the dome will delight you. Most of the rooms on the second floor have a wonderful view of the water and the mountains. Five bedrooms on the second floor, and four bedrooms on the carriage level. Healthful breakfast is served on fine china. $60, shared bath. $70-135, private bath.

Heritage House

305 Pierce Street, 98368-8131
(206) 386-6800

Featuring the finest collection of Victorian antiques on the Olympic Peninsula, this national historic landmark, circa 1880, offers spectacular water and mountain views from atop the bluff. Warm hospitality and comfort, and marvelous breakfasts, too.

Hosts: Pat and Jim Broughton; Carolyn and Bob Ellis
Rooms: 6 (4 PB; 2 SB) $55-89
Full Breakfast
Credit Cards: A, B, C, D
Notes: 2, 5, 8 (over 11), 9, 10, 11, 12, 14

Holly Hill House Bed and Breakfast

611 Polk, 98368
(206) 385-5619

Built in 1872, this home was a private residence until 1988. Well-preserved and graciously furnished, it feels like home. Queen size-beds in four rooms, and a king-size bed in the suite ensure your comfort. Views of Admiralty Inlet and the Cascades can be enjoyed from many windows of this lovely home. All rooms have a large private bath, and a bountiful full breakfast is served. In historic Uptown, six block from downtown.

Hosts: Bill or Laurie Medlicott
Rooms: 5 (PB) $76-130
Full Breakfast
Credit Cards: A, B, C, D
Notes: 2, 5, 9

The James House

1238 Washington Street, 98368
(206) 385-1238

NOTES: Credit cards accepted: A Master Card; B Visa; C American Express; D Discover Card; E Diner's Club; F Other; 2 Personal Checks accepted; 3 Lunch available; 4 Dinner available; 5 Open all year;

The first bed and breakfast in the Northwest, the James House is situated on the bluff overlooking this charming Victorian seaport town. With unobstructed views of Puget Sound, Mt., the Olympic and Cascade Mountain ranges, the James House offers twelve rooms, including a cottage and a lovely two-bedroom suite. Full breakfast and lovely gardens are a few of the amenities of this beautiful inn.

Hosts: Carol McGough and Anne Tieman
Rooms: 12 (4 PB; 8 SB) $65-135
Full Breakfast
Credit Cards: A, B
Notes: 2, 5

The Lincoln Inn

538 Lincoln Street, 98368
(206) 385-6677

An 1888 historic inn situated in the West Coast's famous Victorian seaport of Port Townsend. Antique-filled rooms, water views, private baths, full sumptuous breakfast, and gourmet dining available at night.

Hosts: Robert and Joan Allen
Rooms: 3 (PB) $70-80
Full Breakfast
Credit Cards: A, B
Notes: 2 (in advance), 4, 5, 9, 10, 12, 14

Lizzie's Victorian Bed and Breakfast

731 Pierce Street, 98368
(206) 385-4168

An 1888 Victorian mansion within walking distance of shops and restaurants. The inn is decorated in antiques and some original wallpaper. Parlors are comfortable retreats for reading or conversation. Gateway to the Olympic Mountains, San Juan Islands, and Victoria.

Hosts: Bill and Patti Wickline
Rooms: 8 (5 PB; 3 SB) $50-89
Full Breakfast
Credit Cards: A, B, D
Notes: 2, 5, 8 (over 10), 9, 10, 11, 12

Manresa Castle

Seventh and Sheridan, P. O. Box 564, 98368
(206) 385-5750; (800) 732-1281 (WA only)

This historic landmark, listed on the National Register of Historic Places, now houses 40 Victorian-style guest rooms, an elegant dining room, and an Edwardian-style lounge. Set atop Castle Hill, almost all rooms, including the dining room and lounge, have spectacular views of the town, harbor, marina, and/or Olympic Mountains. The guest rooms offer private baths, direct dial phones, TV, and continental breakfast.

Hosts: Lena and Vernon Humber
Rooms: 40 (PB) $64-175
Continental Breakfast
Credit Cards: A, B
Notes: 4, 5, 7, 8, 9, 10, 11, 12, 14

The Palace Hotel

1004 Water Street, 98368
(206) 385-0773; (800) 962-0741 (Washington only)

The Palace Hotel, on Water Street, is in the heart of Port Townsend's historic district. Excellent in-house restaurant, close to galleries and shops, it offers convenient off-street parking and is within blocks of ferry and bus services. Accommodations range from Continental-style bedrooms with a shared bath to multi-room suites with kitchens and luxurious private baths. Your stay at the Palace includes a complimentary continental breakfast, served at 9:00 A.M. All rooms have cable TV, coffee, and tea. Many non-smoking rooms are available, and children are welcome.

Rooms: 15 (12 PB; 3 SB) $54-95, off-season discounts in winter
Continental Breakfast
Credit Cards: A, B, C, D
Notes: 2, 3, 4, 5, 8, 9, 10, 11, 12, 13

Quimper Inn

1306 Franklin Street, 98368
(206) 385-1060

This 1886 mansion in the historic uptown district offers lovely water and mountain views. Four comfortable bedrooms, plus a two-room suite with a sitting room and bath. Antique period furniture, lots of books, and two porches for relaxation. Walking to historic downtown with its many shops and restaurants. A wonderful breakfast is served.

Hosts: Ron and Sue Ramage
Rooms: 5 (3 PB; 2 SB) $65-120
Full Breakfast
Credit Cards: A, B
Notes: 2, 5, 9, 10, 12

A Rose Cottage

13120 Clay Street, 98368
(206) 385-6944

Recently restored, this 130-year-old home is located in a Victorian seaport. Each guest room has its own distinctive style (country, Oriental, Victorian, and European). Two rooms have whirlpool tubs, and all rooms have either ocean or mountain views. Enjoy the Victorian parlor and dining room. Relax in an inviting cottage-style garden, a beautiful spot for weddings and parties.

Host: Jo Reynolds
Rooms: 4 (PB) $70-95
Deluxe Continental Breakfast
Credit Cards: A, B
Notes: 2, 5, 9, 10, 12,

Sequiem Victorian

Pacific Bed and Breakfast Agency
701 Northwest 60th Street, Seattle, 98107
(206) 784-0539

A fine bed and breakfast inn, one-half mile from the beach, on Dungeness Spit, a quiet, peaceful area, yet only minutes from Port Townsend, Port Angeles, or the Victoria ferry. Remember that this area is the "Banana Belt" of the region, with less rainfall. Your favorite beverage and morning paper will be delivered to your door in the morning. A full breakfast will be served downstairs. Four bedrooms, two that share a bath, and two that offer private baths, are available. $55-85.

Quimper Inn

Trenholm House

2037 Haines, 98368
(206) 385-6059

Step back in time and enjoy the warmth and comfort of an 1890 Victorian farmhouse inn. Built by shipbuilder Howard Trenholm, the house has been maintained in almost original condition and is furnished in country antiques. The aroma of freshly brewed coffee will awaken your senses as a gourmet breakfast is being prepared especially for you. What a great way to greet the day!

Hosts: Michael and Patrice Kelly
Rooms: 6 (2 PB; 4 SB) $59-89
Full Breakfast
Credit Cards: A, B
Notes: 2, 5, 9, 10, 11, 12, 14

POULSBO

Pacific B&B Agency PO-1

701 Northwest 60th Street, Seattle, 98107
(206) 784-0539

A lovely contemporary Northwest home offers two bedrooms with one bath, a library with TV and VCR, pool table, a kitchenette with self-catered breakfast, private entrance. On 200 feet of waterfront. Visit the Bainbridge Island Winery, the Suquamish Museum, and downtown Seattle, only 12 minutes away. $45-55.

NOTES: Credit cards accepted: A Master Card; B Visa; C American Express; D Discover Card; E Diner's Club; F Other; 2 Personal Checks accepted; 3 Lunch available; 4 Dinner available; 5 Open all year;

PUGET SOUND INLET

Pacific B&B Agency Puget Sound Inlet-1

701 Northwest 60th Street, Seattle, 98107
(206) 784-0539

On the water, we offer a delightful Victorian farmhouse with a rolling lawn down to the water's edge. Furnished with antiques and three bedrooms to choose from, this is a favorite of weekenders. A great breakfast is served in the morning. Shared bath. $60-75.

PUYALLUP

Hart's Tayberry House Bed and Breakfast

7406 80th Street East, 98371
(206) 848-4594

Tayberry's bed and breakfast is a Victorian House, with stained-glass, open stairway, and tin ceiling in the kitchen. The romantic atmosphere sweeps you back to an age of charm and history. Old-fashioned hospitality welcomes the crowd-weary traveler with a cheerful room, bath, and breakfast. Owners share rich history and places of interest with guests.

Hosts: Sandy Hart-Hammer; Ray and Donna Hart
Rooms: 3 (1 PB; 2 SB) $40-60
Full Breakfast
Credit Cards: None
Notes: 2, 5, 8 (over 12), 9, 10, 12

SAN JUAN ISLANDS

Friday Harbor

Pacific Bed and Breakfast Agency
701 Northwest 60th Street, Seattle, 98107
(206) 784-0539

This is a floating inn, a restored 60-foot wooden sailboat which offers guests two staterooms, one with a queen bed and pri-vate bath, the other with a double bed, two bunk beds, and shared bath. The hosts will provide a full seaman's breakfast that might be served on the deck in fair weather or in front of a roaring fire in the parlor. Have a totally different experience here! $85.

Orcas Island Country Inn

Pacific Bed and Breakfast Agency
701 Northwest 60th Street, Seattle, 98107
(206) 784-0539

This is a beautiful country inn nestled in a valley with fine views of meadows and mountains. The inn offers eight guest rooms, all with private baths with claw foot tubs, and antique furnishings. Guests can enjoy a gourmet breakfast in a charming, elegant atmosphere. $65-135.

Waterfront Country Inn

Pacific Bed and Breakfast Agency
701 Northwest 60th Street, Seattle, 98107
(206) 784-0539

Built before 1888, this inn used to serve as a meeting place for the townspeople, barber shop, general store, post office, and jail. Now as a popular getaway. It offers guest rooms with and without private baths, hand-carved beds, marble-topped dressers, and a collection of period memorabilia. No pets please. $60-84.

SEABECK

Summer Song

Box 82, 98380
(206) 830-5089

The majestic Olympic Mountains reflecting on Hood Canal provide a quiet, spectacular setting for this private waterfront cottage with its gentle touch of country comfort. The cottage will accommodate up to four

6 Pets welcome; 7 Smoking allowed; 8 Children welcome; 9 Social drinking allowed; 10 Tennis available; 11 Swimming available; 12 Golf available; 13 Skiing available; 14 May be booked through travel agents.

guests and features a bedroom, livingroom, kitchen, bath, fireplace, TV, and VCR. A perfect place to relax, swim, boat, fish, or hike.

Hosts: Ron and Sharon Barney
Cottage: 1 (PB) $69
Full Breakfast
Credit Cards: A, B
Notes: 2, 5, 7, 9, 11, 14

SEATTLE

Beech Tree Manor

1405 Queen Anne Avenue, North, 98109
(206) 281-7037

Wood panelling, English wallpaper, and matching fabrics create the ambience of an English country home. decorated with original art, Oriental rugs, and antique beds. Antique linen shop on premises. Your innkeeper is a chef.

Host: Virginia Cucoro
Rooms: 6 (3 PB; 3 SB) $55-75
Full Breakfast
Credit Cards: A, B
Notes: 2, 5, 6, 8, 14

Bellevue Place
Bread and Breakfast

1111 Bellevue Place East, 98102
(206) 325 9253

Bellevue Place is in the Landmark District of Capitol Hill. Our 1905 "story book" house with leaded glass and Victorian charm is close to Broadway restaurants and stores, Volunteer Park, and a twenty-minute walk to downtown Seattle. Parking is available.

Hosts: Gunner Johnson and Joseph C. Pruett
Rooms: 3 (SB) $75-85
Expanded Continental Breakfast
Credit Cards: A, B, C
Notes: 5, 14

Broadway Guest House

959 Broadway East, 98102
(206) 329-1864

One of Seattle's gracious mansions within two blocks of the Broadway shopping district. The Broadway Guest House is in the Harvard-Belmont historical district. Guest rooms have private baths. Grand staircase, turn-of-the-century library; breakfast in the formal dining room.

Host: H. Lee Vennes
Rooms: 3 (PB) $85-95
Expanded Continental Breakfast
Credit Cards: C
Notes: 2, 5, 9, 14

Capital Hill House

2215 East Prospect, 98112
(206) 322-1752

Elegantly furnished traditional brick house on a tree-lined street in an exclusive residential neighborhood. Near the University of Washington, Seattle Art Museum, Seattle Center, and central city. Three hours from Canada. Excellent public transportation. Enjoy a delicious full breakfast in the formal dining room. Hostess has traveled extensively in Europe, Canada, the United States, and Mexico.

Host: Mary A. Wolf
Rooms: 3 (1 PB; 2 SB) $55
Full Breakfast
Credit Cards: None
Notes: 2, 5, 8, 9, 10, 11, 12, 14

Chambered Nautilus

5005 22nd Avenue Northeast, 98105
(206) 522-2536

Seattle's finest, a gracious 1915 Georgian Colonial nestled high on a hill. This famous hospitable inn is furnished with a mixture of American and English antiques and reproductions, Persian rugs, a grand piano, and a 2,000-plus volume library. It offers national award-winning breakfasts, plus excellent access to Seattle's fine restaurants, theaters, shopping, public transportation, bike and jogging trails, tennis, and golf, and the nearby University of Washington campus.

NOTES: Credit cards accepted: A Master Card; B Visa; C American Express; D Discover Card; E Diner's Club; F Other; 2 Personal Checks accepted; 3 Lunch available; 4 Dinner available; 5 Open all year;

Hosts: Bunny and Bill Hagemeyer
Rooms: 6 (4 PB; 2 SB) $69-95
Full Breakfast
Credit Cards: A, B, C, E, F
Notes: 2, 5, 9, 10, 11, 12, 14

Chambered Nautilus

Chelsea Station
Bed and Breakfast Inn

4915 Linden Avenue North, 98103
(206) 547-6077

For a quiet, comfortable, and private accommodation, nothing beats Chelsea Station. With Seattle's rose gardens at the doorstep, you can breathe in the restorative calm. Walk Greenlake's exceptional wooded pathways, then try a soothing cup of tea or a nap in the afternoon. That's the style at Chelsea Station, and you're welcome to enjoy it. Member Washington Bed and Breakfast Guild.

Hosts: Dick and Marylou Jones
Rooms: 5 (PB) $59-94
Full Breakfast
Minimum stay holidays: 3 nights
Credit Cards: A, B, C, D, E, F
Notes: 2, 5, 8 (over 11), 9, 10, 11, 12, 14

Continental Inn

955 10th Avenue East on Capitol Hill, 08102
(206) 324-9511

Classic brick within two blocks of Volunteer Park and exciting Broadway restaurants, boutiques, and theaters. A five-minute bus to the City Center or University District. Each of the large guest rooms is decorated in colors and the atmosphere of a different city (Copenhagen, Paris, Madrid, Casablanca), queen or twin beds, color TVs, and Jacuzzi. Extensive original art collection includes antiques/artifacts from the innkeeper's travels. Breakfast is served by candlelight. Enjoy the warmth and comfort and the continental experience.

Hosts: Martha and Jean Dunn
Rooms: 4 (1 PB; 4 SB) $55-95
Full Breakfast
Credit Cards: A, B
Notes: 2, 5,7, 9, 14

The Downtown Hotel

Pacific Bed and Breakfast
701 Northwest 60th Street, 98107
(206) 784-0539

Built in 1928 and recently remodeled, this lovely European-style hotel offers you comfortable room with double or twin beds. Walk to the waterfront, scores of fine restaurants, Pike Place Market, the Kingdome, Amtrak station, and the convention center. Many of the original fixtures, such as the mahogany door and tiling, were left. Personal service, friendly staff, and professional help is at your beck and call. Continental breakfast. Parking available. $60.

Gaslight Inn

1727 15th Avenue, 98122
(206) 325-3654

This beautifully restored turn-of-the-century home is on Capitol Hill in downtown Seattle. Oak panelling, fireplaces, decks, and a heated in-gound pool makes the Gaslight a very special place for the guests, whether they are visiting for pleasure or business.

Host: Steve Bennett
Rooms: 9 (6 PB; 3 SB) $58-89
Continental Breakfast
Credit Cards: A, B, C
Notes: 2, 5, 7, 11

6 Pets welcome; 7 Smoking allowed; 8 Children welcome; 9 Social drinking allowed; 10 Tennis available; 11 Swimming available; 12 Golf available; 13 Skiing available; 14 May be booked through travel agents.

Mildred's Bed and Breakfast

1202 Fifteenth Avenue East, 98112
(206) 325-6072

A traditional 1890 Victorian gem in an elegant style. Old-fashioned hospitality awaits. Red carpets, lace curtains, fireplace, grand piano, and wraparound porch. Across the street is the Seattle Art Museum, Flower Conservatory, and historic 44-acre Volunteer Park. Electric trolley at the front door. Minutes to city center, freeways, and all points of interest.

Host: Mildred Sarver
Rooms: 3 (SB) $55-65
Full Breakfast
Credit Cards: A, B, C
Notes: 2, 5, 8, 9, 10, 11, 12, 14

Mildred's Bed and Breakfast

Pacific B&B Agency BA-1

701 Northwest 60th Street, 98107
(206) 784-0539

Here is the private apartment with everything: private entrance, livingroom with TV, phone, private bath, queen bed, equipped kitchen. Maid service, chocolates on your pillow, fresh flowers, and a warm welcome. One block to bus lines and a 15-minute ride to downtown. Close to University of Washington area. $45.

Pacific B&B Agency BA-2

701 Northwest 60th Street, 98107
(206) 784-0539

All the comforts of home can be found in this two-bedroom cottage in a quiet neighborhood. One bedroom features a 1925 antique bedroom set, and the second room offers twin beds. The cottage sleeps up to six, and is comfortably furnished with brass and oak accents. Close to Greenlake, the university, parks, the zoo, beaches, marinas, shops, and restaurants. Children welcome. No smoking. $75, monthly rates available.

Pacific B&B Agency BA-3

701 Northwest 60th Street, 98107
(206) 784-0539

While viewing Shilshole Bay, the marina, Puget Sound, and the Olympic Mountains, guests enjoy fine breakfasts served on the deck. Guest room features a queen bed and private half bath. Six miles from downtown on a bus line. Two resident dogs. $50-55.

Pacific B&B Agency BA-4

701 Northwest 60th Street, 98107
(206) 784-0539

A brand-new home, Northwest-style, offers a private suite of two rooms with sliding glass doors to a private patio. Private bath, queen bed. Kitchenette with breakfast supplies provided. Occasionally breakfast is served upstairs in the dining room. Close to Greenlake and restaurants. $55.

Pacific B&B Agency BA-5

701 Northwest 60th Street, 98107
(206) 784-0539

For families or business groups, nothing compares to the comfort of your own house. You may take over the whole house,

NOTES: Credit cards accepted: A Master Card; B Visa; C American Express; D Discover Card; E Diner's Club; F Other; 2 Personal Checks accepted; 3 Lunch available; 4 Dinner available; 5 Open all year;

or just rent one room, but you will always receive great value staying here. Close to Greenlake, shops and restaurants, and just minutes from downtown via the freeway. Two bedrooms are available, but sleeping accommodations can be made for up to ten guests. No smoking. No pets. Free off-street parking. $45.

Pacific B&B Agency BA-6

701 Northwest 60th Street, 98107
(206) 784-0539

For family or business groups nothing compares to the comfort of your own home. Rent the whole guest house or just one room for a great value. Close to Greenlake, shops, and restaurants, and minutes to downtown. Two bedrooms can sleep up to ten. Children welcome. Fully equipped kitchen with staple foods galore. Two TVs, two VCRs, movies, playthings for kids, and many other surprises. No smoking. $45 and up.

Pacific B&B Agency BE-1

701 Northwest 60th Street, 98107
(206) 784-0539

This large family home on Beacon Hill was built in 1910 with fine woodwork, beamed ceilings, built-ins, a tiled fireplace in the parlor, huge windows, and decks that take advantage of the wonderful views of Elliott Bay, the Olympic Mountains, and the skyline. Four guest rooms and two large bathrooms are offered. Fine antiques, Navajo weavings, and artwork from Latin American countries will delight you. At breakfast time, enjoy the specialties of this inn: Mexican and Latin American dishes, or American, if you desire. $35-45 and up.

Pacific B&B Agency Bellevue-1

701 Northwest 60th Street, 98107
(206) 784-0539

This wonderful contemporary home offers a private suite with two bedrooms, a living-room, one full bath, and a private entrance. Have your full breakfast served upstairs in the dining room. You are also welcome to use the hot tub in the back. An urban oasis at its finest. One mile from the center of Bellevue, this guest home will be a comfortable retreat after a day of sightseeing or business. $50-55.

Pacific B&B Agency Bellevue-2

701 Northwest 60th Street, 98107
(206) 784-0539

Hospitable retired hosts offer you two bedrooms, with a livingroom, private bath, kitchenette, private entrance, and a tasty breakfast. Handy location. Fine views of the lake. $50-55.

Pacific B&B Agency CH-2

701 Northwest 60th Street, 98107
(206) 784-0539

Here is a true Victorian built in 1890 with stained-glass windows, fine period furniture, original woodwork, and an ambience that is unequaled. The hostess makes everyone feel right at home. All the little touches that provide that special bed and breakfast experience are here. Breakfasts are legendary. $60-65.

Pacific B&B Agency CH-4

701 Northwest 60th Street, 98107
(206) 784-0539

An elegantly furnished traditional brick house with a lovely garden and covered patio is on a tree-lined street in an exclusive, residential neighborhood. Within a few minutes from the University of Washington, downtown, theaters, shopping, and the convention center. On the bus

---

6 Pets welcome; 7 Smoking allowed; 8 Children welcome; 9 Social drinking allowed; 10 Tennis available; 11 Swimming available; 12 Golf available; 13 Skiing available; 14 May be booked through travel agents.

lines. Breakfast is served in the formal dining room. Children welcome.

Pacific B&B Agency CH-5

701 Northwest 60th Street, 98107
(206) 784-0539

A large turn-of-the-century home that looks like a castle has been lovingly restored. The location is handy to everything in the city, only 12 blocks from downtown. The guest rooms are on the first floor and have private baths. The library with a wonderful window seat is all yours to lounge, read, watch TV, or sit and plan your day's activities. $40-45; $10 surcharge for one-night stays.

Pacific B&B Agency CH-6

701 Northwest 60th Street, 98107
(206) 784-0539

A spacious Victorian greets its visitors with warm hospitality. From the second floor you will have a great view of the city, the Space Needle, the Sound, and the Olympic Mountains. Walk to restaurants, shops, action on Broadway, and art museum. Two guest rooms share a bath. Home-cooked breakfast served in the dining room by an experienced hostess. Some Spanish, Norwegian, and Indonesian spoken. $40-75.

Pacific B&B Agency CH-8

701 Northwest 60th Street, 98107
(206) 784-0539

This grand house was built in 1912 for the astonishing sum of $100,000. It has 14,000 square feet and features a ballroom, a billiard room, several huge public rooms, and an impressive entry hall. The second-floor guest rooms feature antiques, Old World charm, original tile baths with pedestal sinks and showers. There are five grand

pianos in the house. Continental breakfast is served in the formal dining room. Within walking distance of shops, restaurants, parks, and gardens. $65-125.

Pacific B&B Agency CH-10

701 Northwest 60th Street, 98107
(206) 784-0539

A gracious brick building the Georgian style welcomes you in a convenient location on Capitol Hill. Walk to restaurants, bus lines, a fine city park, and other attractions. Spacious rooms on the first floor with sitting areas and queen beds. Enjoy your breakfast on the patio or in the dining room. $55-75.

Pacific B&B Agency CH-12

701 Northwest 60th Street, 98107
(206) 784-0539

Private entrance, private bath, double bedroom, all in this wonderful brick home. You may have as much privacy as you want. Self-catered breakfast is in the refrigerator. Visiting relatives love this spot, because of its convenience to the city, 10 to 15 minutes to downtown, or the buslines. The hosts are young professionals, most interested in making your stay as pleasant as possible. So close to the University of Washington, you could even walk there. A fine garden is available for guests to enjoy. $50-60.

Pacific B&B Agency CH-14

701 Northwest 60th Street, 98107
(206) 784-0539

Near Broadway on Capitol Hill where you can walk to restaurants, shops, and bus lines. This fine old house is kept in the style of its time, and the antiques compliment the house. Your full breakfast will be served on heirloom china and silverware. Two guest rooms share a bath. $45-55.

NOTES: Credit cards accepted: A Master Card; B Visa; C American Express; D Discover Card; E Diner's Club; F Other; 2 Personal Checks accepted; 3 Lunch available; 4 Dinner available; 5 Open all year;

Pacific B&B Agency MAG-2

701 Northwest 60th Street, 98107
(206) 784-0539

Two miles northwest of downtown, we offer a quiet street and a private bedroom with a double bed, a single bed and a private bath. Full breakfast is served, and you have a lovely view of Seattle from the patio where your breakfast is served. $50-70.

Pacific B&B Agency QA-1

701 Northwest 60th Street, 98107
(206) 784-0539

A beautiful professional facility in an impressively restored building with a comfortable, relaxed atmosphere. You'll wish you could stay longer to enjoy the proximity to downtown, the fine antiques, the window seat, the wicker furniture, and great breakfasts that are served in the formal dining room. Four bedrooms, some with private baths. $65-75.

Pacific B&B Agency QA-3

701 Northwest 60th Street, 98107
(206) 784-0539

An elegant 1928 brick Colonial surrounded by formal English gardens with lovely views of the city, the Sound, and the mountains. The atmosphere is enhanced by fine antiques collected in Europe. Three bedrooms, one with a private bath. Walk to the Seattle Center or be downtown in minutes by bus. During the week, a generous self-serve breakfast; on weekends a hearty home-cooked breakfast in the formal dining room. Children welcome. $60.

Pacific B&B Agency QA-6

701 Northwest 60th Street, 98107
(206) 784-0539

On lower Queen Anne, only two blocks from the Seattle Center and all the restaurants and shops there, we offer you delightful alternatives to motels. Stay in these fine studio apartments, with queen-size beds, TV, phones, and kitchenettes. $45-50.

Pacific B&B Agency QA-10

701 Northwest 60th Street, 98107
(206) 784-0539

In a private home atmosphere, you'll enjoy a cozy one-bedroom suite on the second floor, private entrance, phone, TV, full kitchen, on a busline. See the downtown skyscrapers from the bedroom windows and enjoy a lovely view of Capitol Hill. A second suite is on the garden level, with a private entrance, full bath, and kitchen. No breakfast is served. No smoking. $45-50.

Pacific B&B Agency QA-12

701 Northwest 60th Street, 98107
(206) 784-0539

If there ever was the ultimate lodging for travelers, this must be it. The setting is Queen Anne Hill, the most desirable location in the city. Private suite with private bath, a European kitchen, private entrance, TV, phone, queen bed, and security system. The large deck lets you drink in the great view of Puget Sound and the Olympic Mountains. Ideal for honeymooners, business travelers, and visiting relatives. $75.

Pacific Bed and Breakfast Agency-TNN-WASHINGTON

701 Northwest 60th Street, 98107
(206) 784-0539

Part of the Bed and Breakfast National Network, Pacific Bed and Breakfast Agency offers bed and breakfast not only

6 Pets welcome; 7 Smoking allowed; 8 Children welcome; 9 Social drinking allowed; 10 Tennis available; 11 Swimming available; 12 Golf available; 13 Skiing available; 14 May be booked through travel agents.

in Washington, but also in many other cities and states across the country. The members of this network adhere strictly to the standards set by TNN, such as getting to know the hosts personally, having an established cancellation and refund policy, and following a thorough inspection and approval process for all properties rented. This is because each member of the network is dedicated to ensuring your comfort, pleasure, and personal needs while you are staying at one of these "homes away from home."

Pacific B&B Agency UD-3

701 Northwest 60th Street, 98107
(206) 784-0539

A greenbelt with a creek through the adjacent property sets the tone for this stunning, architecturally designed, traditional home. Skylights, bright and airy, a sun deck, two double bedrooms, each of which is individually decorated, one of which has a full bath, and a private livingroom all add up to a great bed and breakfast experience. Add a home-cooked breakfast with great flair, and you will never want to leave. $55-75.

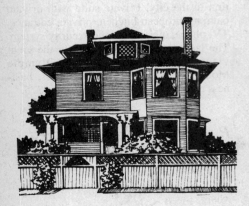

Prince of Wales

Prince of Wales Bed and Breakfast

133 13th Avenue East, 98102
(206) 325-9692

Well situated for the business and convention traveler. Within walking distance of or a short bus ride to downtown Seattle and the Washington State Convention and Trade Center. A charming turn-of-the-century bed and breakfast on scenic Capitol Hill. Rooms include a romantic attic hideaway with private deck and panoramic view of the city skyline, Puget Sound, and Olympic Mountains. Restaurants and shops nearby. Great breakfasts! No smoking.

Hosts: Naomi Reed and Bert Brun
Rooms: 4 (2 PB; 2 SB) $55-80
Full Breakfast
Credit Cards: A, B
Notes: 2, 5, 9, 14

Salisbury House

750 Sixteenth Avenue East, 98112
(206) 328-8682

An elegant turn-of-the-century home on Capitol Hill, just minutes from Seattle's cultural and business activities. Gracious guest rooms with private baths. A well-stocked library and wraparound porch invite relaxation. In a historic neighborhood with parks, shops, and restaurants.

Hosts: Mary and Cathryn Wiese
Rooms: 4 (PB) $74-88
Full Breakfast
Credit Cards: A, B, E
Notes: 2, 5, 8 (over 12), 9, 10, 11, 12, 14

Shafer-Baillie Mansion Bed and Breakfast

907 14th Avenue East, 98112
(206) 322-4654; FAX (206) 329-4654

A quiet and livable atmosphere, Shafer-Baillie Mansion is the largest estate on historic Millionaire's Row on Seattle's Capitol Hill. We have recently undergone a facelift, and you'll enjoy new luxury services and surroundings that are second to none. We are entirely smokeless, but smoking is allowed on porches and balconies. A TV and refrigerator are in every room, and a gourmet continental breakfast are served between 8:30 and 9:30 A.M. with your morning newpaper. We offer eleven suites, most with private baths.

Host: Erv Olssen
Rooms: 13 (10 PB; 3 SB) $55.10-115
Continental Breakfast
Credit Cards: A, B, C
Notes: 2, 5, 8, 9, 10, 14

Tugboat Challenger

Tugboat Challenger

1001 Fairview Avenue North, 98109
(206) 340-1201

Restored 1944 tugboat in downtown Seattle. Carpeted, granite fireplace; laundry. Refrigerators, TV, phone, VCR, sinks, sprinkler system, private entrance for each room. Restaurants, bars, classic and modern sail boats, power boats, row boats, and kayak rentals. Featured in *Travel & Leisure, Cosmopolitan*, and many major papers.

Host: Jerry Brown
Full Breakfast
Minimum Stay Winter Weekends and Holidays: 2 nights
Credit Cards: A, B, C, E
Notes: 2, 5, 9, 14

Villa Heidelberg

4845 45th Avenue Southwest, 98116
(206) 938-3658

Historical 1909 vintage country home in the heart of West Seattle, 10 minutes to downtown, and 20 minutes to airport. Leaded glass, beamed ceilings, fireplaces, wraparound porch, lovely gardens, view of Puget Sound and Olympic Mountain. Elegant breakfast.

Hosts: Barbara, John, and David Thompson
Rooms: 4 (SB) $55-75
Full Breakfast
Credit Cards: C
Notes: 2, 5

Wallingford

Pacific Bed and Breakfast Agency
701 Northwest 60th Street, Seattle, 98107
(206) 784-0539

Private suite with a queen-size bed, private entrance, livingroom, and kitchen in a private home, which is on the busline. You will be only a short three miles from the downtown core of the city and conveniently near the University of Washington and the people-oriented University District. This home is ideal for longer stays for the person who is looking for comfortable private lodgings. $45-50.

Williams House Bed and Breakfast

1505 Fourth Avenue North, 98109
(206) 285-0810

A family bed and breakfast in an Edwardian home with much of the original woodwork and original gaslight fixtures. Decorated with antiques, most guest rooms have views of Seattle, the mountains, or the water. A sunny enclosed porch is shared by all. Close to downtown, the Space Needle, public market. Public transportation available.

6 Pets welcome; 7 Smoking allowed; 8 Children welcome; 9 Social drinking allowed; 10 Tennis available; 11 Swimming available; 12 Golf available; 13 Skiing available; 14 May be booked through travel agents.

Hosts: Williams family, owners
Rooms: 5 (2 PB; 3 SB) $65-90
Full Breakfast
Credit Cards: A, B, C, E
Notes: 2, 5, 7 (porches), 8 (by prior arrangement),
10, 11, 12

SEQUIM

Groveland Cottage

4861 Sequim-Dungeness Way, 98382
(206) 683-3565

This historic inn is five miles north of
Sequim. Ideally located to tour the
Olympic penisula, guests can enjoy beach
walks, golfing, fishing, biking, and sightseeing within minutes. Five rooms are
available to choose from, and private baths
and king-size beds are also available.
Coffee or tea and the morning newspaper
delivered to each door prior to a tasty,
gourmet, but health-conscious breakfast
served in the dining room.

Host: Simone Nichols
Rooms: 5 (3 PB; 2 SB) $65-85
Full Breakfast
Credit Cards: A, B, D
Notes: 2, 3, 9, 12, 14

Margie's Inn on the Bay

120 Forrest Road, 98382
(206) 683-7011

A spacious, contemporary ranch home on
beautiful Sequim Bay. Margie's is
Sequim's only waterfront bed and breakfast. This bed and breakfast offers five
well-appointed rooms, each with its own
distinctive personality and private bath.
King, queen, double, and twin beds are
available. Mount Baker, Sequim Bay, and
the Strait of Juan de Fuca are all part of the
panorama waiting to greet you from the
guest rooms. Rear patios and breakfast
room. Relax in the large TV room.

Hosts: Margie and Don Vorhies
Rooms: 6 (PB) $66-125
Full Breakfast
Credit Cards: A, B
Notes: 2, 5, 8 (over 12), 9, 10, 11, 12, 13

SHELTON

Pacific B&B Agency Shelton-1

701 Northwest 60th Street, Seattle, 98107
(206) 784-0539

This old farmhouse offers you special hospitality. A huge stone fireplace and beamed
ceilings in this farmhouse on 140 acres of
working cattle ranch. Ever had the desire to
go back to Mother Nature? Stay here and
be only thirty miles from Bremerton and on
an inlet on Puget Sound. Stroll around the
ranch and watch blue herons, eagles, and
Canadian geese that visit these marshes. A
creek runs by, and you can often see otters,
beavers, and salmon. $55.

Twin River Ranch Bed and Breakfast

5730 Highway #3, 98584
(206) 426-1043

Splendid 1918 manor house is located on
the Olympic Peninsula. Stone fireplace,
antiques, granny rooms tucked under the
eaves overlooking the garden and stream.
Black Angus cattle graze on 140 acres of
pasture surrounded by old growth trees.
Puget Sound laps the marsh and gulls, blue
heron, and eagles circle overhead in season.
By advance reservation only.

Hosts: Phlorence and Ted Tohde
Rooms: 2 (SB) $50
Full Country Breakfast
Credit Cards: A, B
Notes: 12, 14

SILVERDALE

Seabreeze Beach Cottage

16609 Olympic View Road Northwest, 98383
(206) 692-4648

Challenged by lapping waves at high tide,
this private retreat will awaken your five

Seabreeze Beach Cottage

senses with the smell of salty air, a taste of fresh oysters and clams, views of the Olympic Mountains, the exhilaration of sun, surf, and sand. Spa at water's edge.

Host: Dennis Fulton
Rooms: 2 (PB) $119-149
Continental Breakfast
Credit Cards: A, B
Notes: 2, 5, 6, 8, 9, 11, 12, 14

SNOHOMISH

Countryman Bed and Breakfast

119 Cedar Street, 98290
(206) 568-9622

An 1896 landmark Queen Anne Victorian near 250 antique shops. Library, art gallery, private parking, private airport nearby. Free limousine tour of the historic district offered.

Hosts: Larry and Sandy Countryman
Rooms: 3 (PB) $65
Full Breakfast
Credit Cards: A, B, C, D
Notes: 2, 5, 6, 8, 10, 11, 12, 14

Pacific B&B Agency Sno-1

701 Northwest 60th Street, Seattle, 98107
(206) 784-0539

This beautifully restored Victorian country estate was built in 1884. Crowning the crest of a hill overlooking Snohomish, with a panoramic view of the Cascades, Mount Rainier, and the Olympics, the accommodation offers a quiet serenity and relaxed atmosphere. Guests are encouraged to linger in the sun-filled parlors, stroll the beautiful gardens, or just relax and swim in the heated pool. Guest rooms are tastefully decorated with antiques, handmade quilts, and unique beds. $55-65.

SNOQUALMIE FALLS

The Old Honey Farm Country Inn

8910 384th Avenue SE, 98065
(206) 888-9399

Lovely ten-room New England-style country inn. Beautiful rural setting with Cascade Mountain view. Gracious dining open to the public for breakfast, lunch, and dinner. Service bar. Snoqualmie Falls, historic railroad, herb farm, shopping, golf, and hiking nearby. No smoking.

Hosts: Conrad, Mary Jean, and Marilyn Potter
Rooms: 10 (PB) $75-125
Full Breakfast

6 Pets welcome; 7 Smoking allowed; 8 Children welcome; 9 Social drinking allowed; 10 Tennis available; 11 Swimming available; 12 Golf available; 13 Skiing available; 14 May be booked through travel agents.

Credit Cards: A, B, D
Notes: 2 (in advance), 5, 8 (over 14), 9, 12, 13

Snoqualmie Falls

Pacific Bed and Breakfast Agency
701 Northwest 60th Street, Seattle, 98107
(206) 784-0539

Located at the side of the spectacular Falls, this new inn offers guests unequaled comfort, privacy, and style in each of the 90-plus rooms. Curl up in front of the wood-burning fireplace or relax in a personal spa. Each room has a private bath. A library, country store, and fine restaurant await guests. Hiking, biking, skiing, golfing, wineries, and fishing are nearby. $150-450.

SPOKANE

Hillside House

1729 East 18th, 99203
(509) 535-1893 day; (509) 534-1426 night

Charming guest house, built in the 1930s and added on to several times, offers country decor and exquisite hospitality. On a quiet residential street on a hillside overlooking the city and mountains. Hosts love to cook and share their knowledge of the community.

Hosts: Jo Ann and Bud
Rooms: 2 (SB) $50-55
Full Breakfast
Credit Cards: A, B
Notes: 2, 5

Marianna Stoltz House

East 427 Indiana, 99207
(509) 483-4316

American four-square classic historic home is situated five minutes from downtown Spokane. Furnished with antiques, old quilts, and lace, we offer a wraparound veranda, sitting room, and parlor, which provide relaxation and privacy. King, queen, or single beds, with private or semi-private baths, air conditioning and TV. A tantalizing, unique, and hearty breakfast is preapred fresh every day. Close to the Opera House, Convention Center, and Riverfront Park.

Host: Phyllis Magune
Rooms: 4 (2 PB; 2 SB) $59
Full Breakfast
Credit Cards: A, B, C
Notes: 2, 5, 8 (over 12), 9, 14

Spokane Bed and Breakfast Reservation Service

East 627 25th, 99203
(509) 624-3776

This reservation service covers Washington, northern Idaho, and British Columbia. Included are Colonial, authentic Victorian, and spacious contemporary homes. They are situated just blocks from city center activities, on a mountaintop, at lakeside, or at a winter ski resort. This service will assist you in finding the bed and breakfast specifically suited to your tastes and needs.

Coordinator: Pat Conley
Rooms: 90 (40 PB; 50 SB) $45-68
Full or Continental Breakfast
Credit Cards: A, B, C
Notes: 2, 5, 8, 9, 11, 12, 13, 14

Spokane

Pacific Bed and Breakfast Agency
701 Northwest 60th Street, Seattle, 98107
(206) 784-0539

Enjoy this fine, restored 1891 Victorian featuring hand-carved woodwork, tin ceilings, and an open, curved staircase. A cheerful fire in the parlor will warm guests in the winter, while the wraparound porch is a nice place to relax on a warm day. Period furniture decorates the guest rooms, and a wonderful home-cooked breakfast is served in the mornings. The host will gladly assist and advise sightseers. $45-55.

NOTES: Credit cards accepted: A Master Card; B Visa; C American Express; D Discover Card; E Diner's Club; F Other; 2 Personal Checks accepted; 3 Lunch available; 4 Dinner available; 5 Open all year;

Spokane-2

Pacific Bed and Breakfast Agency
701 Northwest 60th Street, Seattle, 98107
(206) 784-0539

Located in an attractive suburb, this bed and breakfast offers guests a quiet, relaxing place to unwind and enjoy. This home features a livingroom-bedroom combination, queen-size bed, private bath, television, and a private deck overlooking a picturesque garden. A gourmet breakfast is served with the morning news. Golf course and shops are nearby. $45-55.

Marianna Stoltz House

STEVENSON

Evergreen Inn
Bed and Breakfast

P. O. Box 608, 333 Vancouver Avenue, 98648
(509) 427-4303

Tucked into the heart of the scenic Columbia River Gorge, this turn-of-the-century home provides a cozy, comfortable base of operations for a get-away-from-it-all stay. Each cheerful room has a queen-size bed, antique and replica furnishings,

and its own sink. The hosts provide full gourmet breakfast, plus other meals with reservations. Within easy walk of wind-surfing sites. Smoking allowed outside only.

Hosts: Mark and Bethany Waters
Rooms: 3 (SB) $45
Full Breakfast
Credit Cards: A, B
Notes: 2, 3, 4, 5, 8, 9, 14

SUNNYSIDE

Sunnyside Inn
Bed and Breakfast

800 East Edison Avenue, 98944
(509) 839-5557

Eight luxurious rooms all with private baths. King- and queen-size beds, phones, and cable TV. Seven rooms have double Jacuzzi tubs. Situated in the heart of Washington wine country with over 20 wineries and tasting rooms.

Hosts: Karen and Donavon Vlieger
Rooms: 8 (PB) $45-75
Full Breakfast
Credit Cards: A, B, C
Notes: 3, 4, 5, 8, 9, 10, 11, 12

TACOMA

Cottage in the Woods

Pacific Bed and Breakfast Agency
701 Northwest 60th Street, Seattle, 98107
(206) 784-0539

Situated on fifteen forested acreas, this hidden cottage will be equally suitable for long or short stays, honeymoons, anniversaries, or getaways. Overlooking a salmon stream and next to a golf course, it affords guests total privacy. Hosts live on the property and are available to assist guests with sightseeing plans, but will honor the privacy guests seek. One room has a freestanding fireplace on a hearth, brass bed, and kitchenette where breakfast is self-catered. $65.

6 Pets welcome; 7 Smoking allowed; 8 Children welcome; 9 Social drinking allowed; 10 Tennis available; 11 Swimming available; 12 Golf available; 13 Skiing available; 14 May be booked through travel agents.

Keenan House

2610 North Warner, 98407
(206) 752-0702

The Keenan House offers you clean, attractively decorated rooms and a full breakfast, featuring freshly baked breads and rolls. Just seven blocks from the University of Puget Sound, ten minutes by car from Point Defiance Park and Vashon Island ferry and one and one-half hour from Paradise Resort at Mount Rainier.

Host: Lenore Keenan
Rooms: 6 (2 PB; 4 SB) $45-55
Full Breakfast
Credit Cards: None
Notes: 2, 5, 8, 9, 14

Tacoma Tudor

Pacific Bed and Breakfast Agency
701 Northwest 60th Street, Seattle, 98107
(206) 784-0539

This cozy bed and breakfast is located next door to the Victorian Guesthouse. Enjoy friendly hospitality and comfort in this home with country-style decor. Guests should allow themselves to be pampered here. $45-55.

Victorian Guesthouse

Pacific Bed and Breakfast Agency
701 Northwest 60th Street, Seattle, 98107
(206) 784-0539

This lovely guesthouse is located near the university on a tree-lined street, away from busyness of downtown. Mt. Rainier and Commencement Bay are nearby. While relaxing in the parlor, the innkeeper can help guests with sightseeing plans. The Guesthouse offers clean, comfortable guest rooms furnished with country antiques. $40-50.

TOKELAND

Tokeland Hotel

100 Hotel Road, 98590
(206) 267-7006

A national historic landmark, the Tokeland Hotel is on a peninsula bordering Washington's Willapa Bay and the Pacific Ocean.

Host: Erin Radke
Rooms: 18 (SB) $43.50-95
Credit Cards: A, B, C, D
Notes: 2, 3, 4, 5, 6, 7 (limited), 8, 9, 11, 14

TONASKET

Orchard Country Inn

P. O.Box 634, 1st and Antwine, 98855
(509) 486-1923

This elegant 1920 orchard house is located in the small, quiet town of Tonasket, which overlooks the Okanogan River Valley. Located where Highway 20 (North Cascade Highway), and Highway 97 (twenty miles to the Canadian border) intersect. Great fishing, hunting, skiing, hiking, biking, etc. Great breakfast and the best coffee in town.

Hosts: Joy and John Barnhart
Rooms: 2 (PB) $46
Full Breakfast
Credit Cards: A, B
Notes: 2, 5, 8, 9, 10, 11, 12, 13

TROUT LAKE

Mio Amore Pensione

P. O. Box 208, 53 Little Mountain Road, 98650
(509) 395-2264

Secluded in Trout Lake Valley, at the base of Mount Adams, sits Mio Amore Pensione, a European-style bed and breakfast/restaurant. Tom and Jill Westbrook distinctively decorated each of their four rooms with memorabilia from around the world. Having apprenticed in Italy for five years, Tom prepares gourmet northern Italian cuisine every evening. Mio Amore offers the perfect year-round getaway, whether you enjoy the multitude of outdoor activities or simply relaxing in the spa overlooking Trout Creek.

Hosts: Tom and Jill Westbrook
Rooms: 4 (1 PB; 3 SB) $50-135
Full Breakfast
Credit Cards: A, B
Notes: 2, 4, 5, 10, 11, 12, 13, 14

VANCOUVER

Kola House Bed and Breakfast
P. O.Box 646, 98624
(206) 642-2819

This beautiful home, built in 1919, offers a view of the bay and Astoria. Suite has a fireplace and sauna. Pool table and hot tub available for guests to enjoy. TVs are in every room, and fishing grounds, museums, and shopping are within walking distance. This is a quiet town, but close to the beach and activities in Long Beach. Four rooms sleep two, and the suite with a Hide-a-bed sleeps three. Guest house sleeps five. Roll-away beds and Hide-a-beds are available to accommodate groups.

Host: Linda Luokkala
Rooms: 5 (PB) $65-75
Full Breakfast
Credit Cards: A, B
Notes: 2, 5, 9, 12

VASHON ISLAND

Vashon Island
Pacific Bed and Breakfast Agency
701 Northwest 60th Street, Seattle, 98107
(206) 784-0539

This wonderful guest house is located on a lovely island. There is a private suite in the loft of a traditionally styled barn separate from the main residence of the innkeepers, which affords guests total privacy. Guests will find this hideaway equipped with everything needed for relaxing, including VCR and microwave oven. Just a short walk to the beach. This is a great place for celebrating an anniversary or a well-deserved rest and relaxation weekend. $85.

WALLA WALLA

Green Gables Inn
922 Bonsella, 99362
(509) 525-5501

This award-winning mansion is located in a neighborhood of historic homes one block from the Whitman College campus. Green Gables Inn offers five spacious bedrooms with private bathrooms and a separate carriage house apartment. The main floor of the 1909 house, with its beamed ceilings, original woodwork, and two fireplaces, is a comfortable place where guests can relax. Delicious full breakfasts are served in the dining room, and local attractions and downtown Walla Walla are within walking distance.

Hosts: Jim and Margaret Buchan
Rooms: 7 (PB) $65-90
Full Breakfast
Credit Cards: A, B, D
Notes: 2, 5, 9

WESTPORT

Pacific B&B Agency WE-1
701 Northwest 60th Street, Seattle, 98107
(206) 784-0539

A small, lovely town on the ocean where the salmon fishing is the greatest. If you are not into fishing, there are many other activities you will enjoy. Stay in this historic mansion situated on eight acres two blocks from the ocean with the peacefulness you desire. Choose from five bedrooms, all

6 Pets welcome; 7 Smoking allowed; 8 Children welcome; 9 Social drinking allowed; 10 Tennis available; 11 Swimming available; 12 Golf available; 13 Skiing available; 14 May be booked through travel agents.

with private baths, with lace curtains, antiques, and fine period furnishings. Don't forget to take a long soak in the large hot tub on the grand cedar deck under the gazebo. Also enjoy the barbecue and picnic areas, badminton, volleyball, and horseshoes. $45-65.

WHIDBEY ISLAND

Oak Harbor

Pacific Bed and Breakfast Agency
701 Northwest 60th Street, Seattle, 98107
(206) 784-0539

At this bed and breakfast guests can enjoy a fresh complete Northwest breakfast, including salmon or mussels prepared in the hostess' sunlit kitchen. Spend the day searching out the treasures of Whidbey Island and spend the evening refreshing in the hot tub while enjoying the outside view. The hosts offer three wonderful, cozy guest rooms to guests when they are ready to retire for the evening. $65-95.

The Victorian Bed and Breakfast

602 North Main, P. O. Box 761, Coupeville, 98239
(206) 678-5305

The Jenne family home, now the Victorian Bed and Breakfast, proudly provides gracious accommodations throughout the year to Whidbey Island visitors. Guests at the Victorian may choose from either of the charming upstairs bedrooms with private baths, and queen beds, or they may hideaway in the guest cottage.

Host: Dolores Fresh
Rooms: 3 (PB) $80-100
Full Breakfast
Credit Cards: A, B
Notes: 2, 5, 8 (cottage only), 9, 14

Whidbey-3

Pacific Bed and Breakfast Agency
701 Northwest 60th Street, Seattle, 98107
(206) 784-0539

Situated on a quiet cove along wooded shores, this turn-of-the-centry country inn offers guests the charm and comfort of rooms and cottages. Some guest rooms are furnished with antiques. The cottages with kitchenettes are suitable for family getaways. Guests are invited to enjoy the charm of the big stone fireplace in the parlor and the breathtaking views over the water. $55-95.

Whidbey-4

Pacific Bed and Breakfast Agency
701 Northwest 60th Street, Seattle, 98107
(206) 784-0539

This new and splendidly built waterfront inn offers a great getaway location. All rooms have lanais, queen beds, whirlpool bath for two, wood-burning fireplaces, and are beautifully decorated. Restaurant with award-winning cuisine is located on the premises. $135+.

Whidbey-5

Pacific Bed and Breakfast Agency
701 Northwest 60th Street, Seattle, 98107
(206) 784-0539

This bed and breakfast is a spacious, modern beach home decorated with comfortable homey antiques, including a beautiful diamond-tufted leather love seat with matching wing-backed chairs. Guests can sit back, enjoy a warm, crackling fire, watch the 52-inch television, or enjoy a game of pool. The breathtaking view of the Olympic Mountains, Puget Sound, and the San Juan Islands will encourage guests to linger and sip freshly ground coffee while savoring the view. $65-95.

WHITE SALMON

Llama Ranch Bed and Breakfast

1980 Highway 141, 98672
(509) 395-2786

Situated between two snow-capped mountains, we offer hands-on experience with llamas, including guided llama walks through the woods. Get better acquainted with these beautuiful, intelligent animals. Queen-size beds with spectacular views in any direction, refreshing waterfalls, and natural lava bridges. Nearby activities include white-water rafting, golfing, plane trips over Mount St. Helens, fishing, hunting, hiking, cave exploration, huckleberry picking. Cross-country skiing and snowmobiling in the winter. Close to nice restaurants.

Hosts: Jerry and Rebeka Stone
Rooms: 7 (2 PB; 5 SB) $55-75
Full Breakfast
Credit Cards: A, B, D
Notes: 2, 5, 8, 9, 14

WINTHROP

Dommann's Bed and Breakfast

716 Highway 20, 98862
(509) 996-2484; (800) 423-0040

Our antique-filled guest rooms are located on the banks of the Northern River. We offer a recreation room, piano, outdoor hot tub overlooking the river, and no smoking. The valley is a recreation paradise for photography, seasonal hunting, fishing, hiking, camping, and skiing. Eight lakes within six to eight miles, we are right at the foot of the Cascade Mountains.

Hosts: Hank and Jean Dommann
Rooms: 2 (1 PB; 1 SB) $50
Continental Breakfast
Credit Cards: None
Notes: 2, 5, 9, 10, 11, 12, 13

YAKIMA

'37 House

4002 Englewood Avenue, 98908
(509) 965-5537

An inn of extraordinary elegance, the '37 House was built in 1937 by one of Yakima's first fruit-growing families. The warm and gracious atmosphere invites guests of all ages to sit by one of three large hearth fireplaces or roam the two and one-half acres that surround the house with extensive gardens. With a total of 7,500 square feet, the '37 House offers a variety of overnight accommodations, each room offering its own special charm. And everywhere you can find those special touches of the 1930s—roomy walk-in closets, window seats tucked under sloping eaves, built-in desks with los of cubby holes, shuttered windowpanes, and full-tiled baths. Dessert before bed is included in every overnight stay.

Host: Beatrice McKinney
Rooms: 6 (PB) $65-120
Full Breakfast
Credit Cards: A, B, C
Notes: 2, 5, 10, 14

Yakima

Pacific Bed and Breakfast Agency
701 Northwest 60th Street, Seattle, 98107
(206) 784-0539

This stately English Tudor mansion was built in 1929 and is surrounded by beautiful grounds, formal hedges, a variety of trees, flowers, and a garden pool. Each room is furnished with antiques from the early 1800s and has a color television. The bridal suite features a king-size bed, private bath, bar with refrigerator, microwave oven, and a bottle of champagne. $65-125.

---

6 Pets welcome; 7 Smoking allowed; 8 Children welcome; 9 Social drinking allowed; 10 Tennis available; 11 Swimming available; 12 Golf available; 13 Skiing available; 14 May be booked through travel agents.

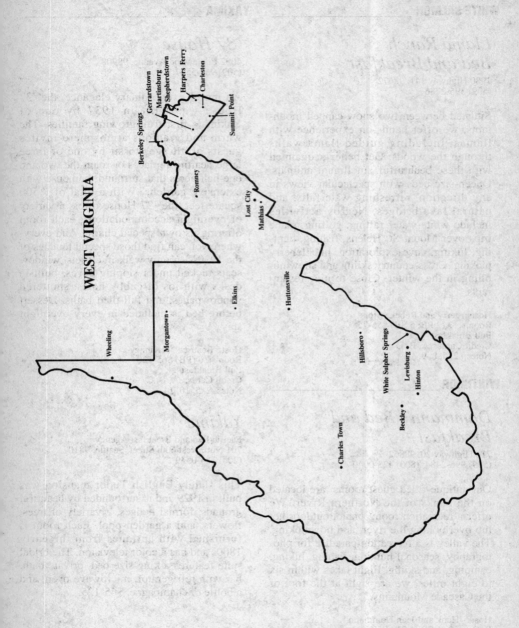

WEST VIRGINIA

Wheeling

Morgantown

Berkeley Springs
Gerrardstown
Martinsburg
Shepherdstown
Harpers Ferry
Charleston
Summit Point

Romney

Lost City
Mathias

Elkins

Huttonsville

Charles Town

Hillsboro
White Sulpher Springs
Lewisburg
Beckley
Hinton

West Virginia

BECKLEY

Prosperity Farmhouse Bed and Breakfast

Box 393, Prosperity, 25909
(304) 255-4245

This bed and breakfast is situated in rural West Virginia; however, it is just six miles from Beckley, which offers all the attractions of a small city of 20,000. The hosts work the 80-acre farm by raising cattle, chickens, horses, a huge garden, feed corn, and hay. The building itself is not part of the house; it sits 30 feet behind it. Upstairs includes a bedroom that sleeps four. Downstairs there is a great room with kitchenette, bath, and dining area that sleeps two. Near white-water rafting, Winterplace Ski Resort, state parks, New River Gorge, theater.

Hosts: John and Tara Wooton
Rooms: 2 (SB)
Full Breakfast
Credit Cards: None
Notes: 2, 7, 8, 9, 10, 11, 12, 13

The Country Inn

BERKELEY SPRINGS

The Country Inn

207 South Washington Street, 25411
(304) 258-2210; (800) 822-6630
FAX (304) 258-3986

Just over the mountain, the inn offers distinctive accommodations, seventy rooms, an art gallery, a lounge, gift shop, air conditioning, color cable TV, no-smoking rooms, handicapped facilities, room service, and complimentary afternoon tea. Enjoy superb dining in one of two dining rooms, serving breakfast, lunch, and dinner. Table-side cooking, live entertainment on Saturaday nights. Conference center for up to 60 people. Renaissance Spa, featuring whirlpool mineral baths, facials, massages, manicures, pedicures, and waxing.

Rooms: 70 (59 PB; 11 SB) $35-145
Full and Continental Breakfast
Credit Cards: A, B, C, D, E
Notes: 2, 3, 4, 5, 7, 8, 9, 10, 11, 12, 13, 14

Folkestone Bed and Breakfast

Route 2, Box 404, 25411
(304) 258-3743

English Tudor home built in 1930 on ten acres of wooded ground. Dogwood, azalea, rhododendron, and oak trees on grounds. Upstairs accommodations feature two bedrooms, sitting room, and bath. Separate loft apartment with private entrance, deck, and bath. The 18-hole Robert Jones golf course is ten miles away. State-operated bath house is two miles away.

NOTES: Credit cards accepted: A Master Card; B Visa; C American Express; D Discover Card; E Diner's Club; F Other; 2 Personal Checks accepted; 3 Lunch available; 4 Dinner available; 5 Open all year; 6 Pets welcome; 7 Smoking allowed; 8 Children welcome; 9 Social drinking allowed; 10 Tennis available; 11 Swimming available; 12 Golf available; 13 Skiing available; 14 May be booked through travel agents.

Host: Hettie Hawvermale
Rooms: 2 (PB) $50-70
Full Breakfast
Credit Cards: None
Notes: 2, 5, 7, 9, 12

BRAMWELL

Three Oaks and a Quilt

Box 84, 24715
(304) 248-8316

Visitors to historic Bramwell come to view a unique town of mansions built by bituminous coal operators in the early 1900s. Three Oaks and a Quilt is a delightfully relaxing Victorian experience. Quilts are artfully displayed; a Whig Rose hangs on the front porch wall. Reservations, please.

Host: B. J. Kahle
Rooms: 3 (PB and SB) $55
Full Breakfast
Credit Cards: None
Notes: 2, 5, 7 (limited), 8 (over 11), 9, 10, 11, 12

CHARLESTON

The Brass Pineapple

1611 Virginia Street East, P. O. Box 5253, 25311
(304) 344-0748

This cozy old home is in Charleston's historic district within sight of the capitol dome. The house has been carefully restored to its original grandeur, with antiques and period reproductions throughout. Guest rooms are all furnished in different styles, so that the returning travelers can enjoy new surroundings. All rooms are air-conditioned, with phones and color TV. Bus and trolly are nearby. Airport and train station pickup can be arranged.

Host: Virginia Pepper
Rooms: 4 (PB) $60-75
Full Breakfast
Credit Cards: A, B
Notes: 2, 7 (limited), 8, 9, 14

CHARLES TOWN

The Carriage Inn

417 East Washington Street, 25414
(304) 728-8003

Each of the five bedrooms is large and airy, with its own private bath and queen canopy bed, and four of the rooms have working fireplaces. Charles Town is the home of the Charles Town races, the Jefferson Country Museum, Old Opera House, and the site of the John Brown gallows. The inn is eight miles from Harpers Ferry.

Hosts: Bob and Virginia Kaetzel
Rooms: 5 (PB) $65-95
Full Breakfast
Credit Cards: A, B
Notes: 2, 5, 9, 10, 11, 12

Cottonwood Inn

Route 2, Box 61-S
Kabletown Road and Mill Lane, 25414
(304) 725-3371

The Cottonwood Inn offers bed and breakfast accommodations in a restored Georgian farmhouse (circa 1800). The inn is on Bullskin Run in the historic Shenandoah Valley, near Harpers Ferry and Charles Town, and is furnished in antiques and period reproductions. Fireplaces in the dining room, parlor/library, and one guest room. You are invited to enjoy the inn's peaceful, secluded acres, memorable country breakfasts, and warm hospitality.

The Cottonwood Inn

NOTES: Credit cards accepted: A Master Card; B Visa; C American Express; D Discover Card; E Diner's Club; F Other; 2 Personal Checks accepted; 3 Lunch available; 4 Dinner available; 5 Open all year;

Hosts: Colin and Eleanor Simpson
Rooms: 7 (PB) $75-105, seasonal
Full Breakfast
Credit Cards: A, B, C
Notes: 2, 5, 7, 8, 9, 10, 11, 12, 13 (XC), 14

Gilbert House
Bed and Breakfast

P.O. Box 1104, 25414
(304) 725-0637

Near Harpers Ferry and Antietam
Battlefield. Experience a touch of class in
the country. Enjoy the magnificent stone
house, circa 1760, listed on the national
register, offering outstanding hospitality.
Spacious and romantic rooms with working
fireplaces and air conditioning. Bridal
Suite has curtains around bed, claw foot
tub, champagne. The house is filled with
European treasures, many from royal families. In the Middleway historic district, an
area of unsurpassed countryside and historic sites. Local activities include opera
house, horse/auto races, shooting clubs,
rafting, outlet shopping. Village ghost.

Hosts: Jean and Bernie Heiler
Rooms: 3 (PB) $70-150
Full Breakfast
Credit Cards: A, B, C
Notes: 2, 5, 10, 11, 12, 14

ELKINS

The Retreat at Buffalo Run

214 Harpertown Road, 26241
(304) 636-2960

Ideal location for exploring mountains,
forests, and rivers of West Virginia.
Secluded setting near Davis and Elkins
College and Summer Augusta Festival, one
mile from downtown Elkins, and ten minutes from commuter airport. Turn-of-the-
century home on five acres with tall oaks,
hemlock rhododendron groves, flower and
vegetable gardens. Six comfortable guest
rooms and three and one-half baths. Hearty
breakfast with homemade goods.

The Retreat at Buffalo Ran

Hosts: Kathleen, Bertha, and Earl Rhoad
Rooms: 6 (SB) $48
Expanded Continental Breakfast
Credit Cards: None
Notes: 2, 5, 8, 9, 10, 11, 12, 13

Tunnel Mountain
Bed and Breakfast

Route 1, Box 59-1, 26241
(304) 636-1684

This charming, three-story fieldstone home
is nestled on the side of Tunnel Mountain
on five private, wooded acres, surrounded
by scenic mountains, lush forests, and
sparkling rivers. The interior is finished in
pine and rare wormy chestnut woodwork.
Tastefully decorated throughout with
antiques, collectibles, and crafts, it extends
a warm and friendly atmosphere to guests.

Hosts: Anne and Paul Beardslee
Rooms: 3 (PB) $45-55
Full Breakfast
Credit Cards: None
Notes: 2, 5, 7, 9, 10, 11, 12, 13

GERRARDSTOWN

Gerrardstown's
Prospect Hill Farm

Box 135, 25420
(304) 229-3346

6 Pets welcome; 7 Smoking allowed; 8 Children welcome; 9 Social drinking allowed; 10 Tennis available; 11
Swimming available; 12 Golf available; 13 Skiing available; 14 May be booked through travel agents.

Gerrardstown's Prospect Hill is a Georgian mansion set on 225 acres and listed on the National Register of Historic Places. Once a well-to-do gentleman's home, it has a permanent Franklin fireplace, antiques, and a hall mural depicting life in the early republic. Guests may choose one of the beautifully appointed rooms in the main house or the former slave quarters, where rooms are complete with country kitchen and fireplace. There is much to do on this working farm near Harpers Ferry, Martinsburg, and Winchester.

Hosts: Charles and Hazel Hudock
Rooms and Cottage: (PB) $85-95
Full Breakfast
Credit Cards: A, B
Notes: 2, 5, 7, 8 (in cottage), 9, 10, 11, 12

HARPERS FERRY

Fillmore Street Bed and Breakfast

Fillmore Street, 25425
(410) 321-5634; (304) 535-2619

With a clear mountain view, this antique furnished Victorian home is known for its hospitality, service, and gourmet breakfast. Private accommodations and baths, in-room television, air conditioning, complimentary sherry and tea, and a blazing fire on cool mornings.

Hosts: Alden and James Addy
Rooms: 2 (PB) $65-72
Full Breakfast
Credit Cards: None
Closed Thanksgiving, Christmas, and New Year's Day
Notes: 2, 7, 8 (over 12), 9

HILLSBORO

The Current Bed and Breakfast

HC 64, Box 135, 24946
(304) 653-4722

This restored 1904 farmhouse rests in a high river valley surrounded by the Allegheny Mountains. Nearby the Greenbrier River Trail, Cranberry Wilderness, and many state and national forests and parks offer solitude and abundant wildlife. A cozy, relaxed atmosphere prevails. Antiques, quilts, and outdoor hot tub.

Hosts: Leslee McCarty and John Walkup
Rooms: 5 (1 PB; 4 SB) $50-75
Full Breakfast
Credit Cards: A, B
Notes: 2, 5, 8, 9, 12

Gerrardstown's Prospect Hill Farm

HINTON

Sunset

413 1/2 Sixth Avenue, 25951
(304) 466-3740

A unique and memorable setting/service. One full cabin, separate from innkeeper's home, with porch overlooking New River in woods above historic Hinton. Kitchen (breakfast foods and treats provided, special requests honored), bath, private entrance. Situated near Bluestone and Pipestem state parks off I-77 or I-64; sports and hunting facilities close by; blocks from Amtrak depot. Open year-round. A private cabin for a luxurious country experience in the bed and breakfast tradition. Reservations required.

Host: Jane Duffield
Cabin: 1 (PB)

NOTES: Credit cards accepted: A Master Card; B Visa; C American Express; D Discover Card; E Diner's Club; F Other; 2 Personal Checks accepted; 3 Lunch available; 4 Dinner available; 5 Open all year;

Full Breakfast (self-serve)
Credit Cards: None
Notes: 2, 5, 8, 9

HUTTONSVILLE

Hutton House

General Delivery, P. O. Box 88, 26273
(304) 335-6701

Enjoy the relaxed atmosphere of this historically registered and antique-filled Queen Anne Victorian. Guest rooms are individually styled, and each guest has his/her own personal favorite. Breakfast varies from gourmet to hearty. Sometimes it is served at a specific time, while at other times it is served at your leisure. Children can play games on the lawn. You can lose yourself in the beauty of the Laurel Mountains from the wraparound porch.

Hosts: Dean Ahren and Loretta Murray
Rooms: 7 (3 PB; 4 SB) $55-85
Full Breakfast
Credit Cards: A, B
Notes: 2, 3, 4, 5, 8, 9, 12, 13, 14

LEWISBURG

Lynn's Inn Bed and Breakfast

Route 4, Box 40, 24901
(304) 645-2003

A comfortable home in a farm setting with full country breakfast. Downtown historic Lewisburg is 3 miles away; the state fair is 4.5 miles away; and the Greenbriar Hotel is 10 miles away. Within easy driving distance to some of the best hiking, fishing, hunting, golf, spelunking, white-water and skiing places in the East.

Host: Richard and Lynn McLaughlin
Rooms: 3 (PB) $45-60
Full Breakfast
Credit Cards: A, B
Notes: 2, 5, 9, 10, 11, 12, 13, 14

LOST CITY

Kathleen's

P. O. Box 83, 26810
(304) 897-6787

A completely renovated 19th-century farmhouse. The amenities here include three full baths, central heat and air, outside deck, patio, and wraparound front porch. Located on a hill that provides an excellent view of the Lost River Valley and surrounding mountains, it caters to couples and families. Special family extended-stay rates available. Located near the George Washington National Forest and Lost River State Park.

Host: Kathleen Funkhouser
Rooms: 3 (1 PB; 2 SB) $65-80
Full Breakfast
Credit Cards: None
Notes: 2, 8, 9

MARTINSBURG

Amanda's Bed and Breakfast #282

1428 Park Avenue, Annapolis, MD 21217
(410) 225-0001; (410) 383-1274

Restored 19th-century Federal-style stone farmhouse surrounded by acres of rolling pasture and woods. Seven-foot windows provide lots of cheery light and give each room a remarkable view. Visit nearby Harpers Ferry, Antietam Battlefield, and more. Three guest rooms with private and shared baths. Full breakfast. $85-100.

Aspen Hall Inn

405 Boyd Avenue, 25401
(304) 263-4385

A majestic 18th-century limestone mansion situated on a four-acre estate in a pleasant West Virginia village. Its spacious high-ceilinged rooms are furnished with an accumulation of centuries past. The bedchambers have canopy beds and private baths. Tea is served on the terrace on summer afternoons or in the parlor in cooler weather. The country breakfast is a delicious surprise each morning here where hospitality is a matter of pride and calories are ignored.

Hosts: Gordon and Lou Anne Claucherty
Rooms: 4 (PB) $95-110
Full Breakfast
Credit Cards: A, B
Notes: 2, 5, 9, 10, 11, 12, 14

Boydville, The Inn at Martinsburg

601 South Queen Street, 25401
(304) 263-1448

1812 stone plantation mansion in 14-acre private park, once part of the Lord Fairfax Grant. Original wallpaper and woodwork. High ceilings, great porch with rockers. National Register of Historic Places. Built by Gen. Elisha Boyd, War of 1812 hero. Retreat for Stonewall Jackson and Henry Clay. Just off I-81, one and one-half hours from Washington, D.C., in the heart of Civil War Country.

Hosts: LaRue Frye, Bob Beege, Carolyn Snyder, Pete Bailey
Rooms: 6 (PB) $100-125
Expanded Continental Breakfast
Credit Cards: A, B
Notes: 2, 5, 9, 10, 11, 12, 13, 14

MATHIAS

Valley View Farm

Route 1, Box 467, 26812
(304) 897-5229

National Geographic Society's *America's Great Hideaways* calls Valley View Farm "your home away from home." This cattle and sheep farm of 250 acres specializes in excellent food and friendly hosts. Near Lost River State Park, horseback riding, and other recreation in season. Craft shops.

Host: Edna Shipe
Rooms: 4 (SB) $40
Full Breakfast
Credit Cards: None
Notes: 2, 4, 5, 6, 7, 8, 9, 10, 11

MORGANTOWN

Chestnut Ridge School

1000 Stewartstown Road, 26503
(304) 598-2262

A restored 1920s elementary school welcomes you with warm hospitality. It is surrounded by outstanding scenic attractions and recreational areas. Come back to school, and enjoy personal attention, special muffins, and beautiful sunsets.

Hosts: Sam and Nancy Bonasso
Rooms: 4 (PB) $52.32-58.86
Continental Breakfast
Minimum stay football weekends: 2 nights
Credit Cards: None
Notes: 2, 5, 8, 9, 10, 11, 12

ROMNEY

Hampshire House 1884

165 North Grafton Street, 26757
(304) 822-7171

Completely renovated 1884 brick home. Period furniture, fireplaces, air conditioning, quiet. Private baths and garden. The charm of the 1880s with the comforts of today in a sleepy small town on the beautiful south branch of the Potomac River. Therapeutic massage available. No smoking.

Hosts: Jane and Scott Simmons
Rooms: 4 (PB) $60-80
Full Breakfast
Credit Cards: A, B, C, D, E
Notes: 2, 4, 5, 9, 14

SHEPHERDSTOWN

The Little Inn

Corner German and Princess Streets, 25443
(304) 876-2208

NOTES: Credit cards accepted: A Master Card; B Visa; C American Express; D Discover Card; E Diner's Club; F Other; 2 Personal Checks accepted; 3 Lunch available; 4 Dinner available; 5 Open all year;

The Little Inn consists of two rooms, each with private bath. Continental breakfast is served daily (optional full breakfast Sunday). Decor is a combination of antique and art deco. The inn is close to Civil War battlefields at Antietam, Harpers Ferry, and Gettysburg. There is Thoroughbred horse racing at Charles Town. Also, the Blue Ridge Outlet in Martinsburg is only minutes away. Approximately one and one-half hours from Washington, D.C., and Baltimore.

Host: Kevin Connell
Rooms: 2 (PB) $75-85
Continental Breakfast
Credit Cards: A, B, E
Notes: 3, 4, 5, 9

Stonebrake Cottage

P. O. Box 1612, Shepherd Grade Road, 25443
(304) 876-6607

Stonebrake Cottage offers a private getaway near historic Shepherdstown on a 145-acre farm. The Victorian cottage is furnished with antiques, has a fully equipped kitchen, two bathrooms, three bedrooms, and central air. It is within minutes of the C&O Canal Tow Path, Harpers Ferry, Antietam Battlefields, Blue Ridge outlet center, and the Charles Town race track. Golfing and horseback riding are available nearby. Discount available for one-week stays.

Host: Anne Small
Rooms: 3 (2 PB; 1 SB) $80-90
Full Breakfast
Credit Cards: A, B
Notes: 2, 5, 8, 9, 12, 14

Thomas Shepherd Inn

Box 1162, 25443
(304) 876-3715

Small, charming inn in a quaint, historic Civil War town that offers that special hospitality of the past. Guests find fresh flowers at their bedsides, fluffy towels and special soaps in their baths, complimentary beverage by the fireside, memorable breakfasts. Bicycles, picnics available.

Host: Margaret Perry
Rooms: 6 (PB) $75-95
Full Breakfast
Credit Cards: A, B, C, D
Notes: 2, 5, 7 (limited), 8 (over 12), 9, 10, 12

SUMMIT POINT

Amanda's Bed and Breakfast #114

1428 Park Avenue, Annapolis, MD 21217
(410) 225-0001; (410) 383-1274

In the quaint village of Summit Point near Harpers Ferry. Decorated with cheery mixture of old and new. Old-fashioned hospi-

Thomas Shepherd Inn

6 Pets welcome; 7 Smoking allowed; 8 Children welcome; 9 Social drinking allowed; 10 Tennis available; 11 Swimming available; 12 Golf available; 13 Skiing available; 14 May be booked through travel agents.

tality for the crowd-weary traveler. Many activities in the area, including hiking, bicycling, and sightseeing. Two rooms with private baths. Continental breakfast. $65.

Countryside

P. O. Box 57, 25446
(304) 725-2614

Countryside is in a charming village near historic Harpers Ferry and is decorated with items old and new: quilts, baskets, books, and collectibles. Guests are welcomed with a cheerful room, bath, and breakfast amid lovely rural scenery.

Hosts: Lisa and Daniel Hileman
Rooms: 2 (PB) $53-68.90
Continental Breakfast
Credit Cards: A, B
Notes: 2, 5

WHEELING _____

Stratford Springs

355 Oglebay Drive, 26003
(304) 233-5100; (800) 521-8435

This historic inn is nestled on 30 acres of rolling wooded hills in the Mountain State's historic Ohio Valley, ten minutes from I-70. Elegant large rooms and suites, casual to fine dining, unique gift shops, swimming, tennis, golf, and athletic center. Adjacent to Oglebay Park and near other points of interest.

Host: Deanne Wines
Rooms: 6 (PB) $95-150
Continental Breakfast
Credit Cards: A, B, C
Notes: 2, 3, 4, 5, 7, 8, 9, 10, 11, 12, 13, 14

Yesterday's Ltd.

827 Main Street, 26003
(304) 232-0864

Victorian decor is an awesome delight for those who think more is best, but here in Wheeling where high is the ceiling, you'll discover a wonderful rest. Off-street park-

ing, and shops within walking, with the "alarming" you'll find breakfast charming. See antiques galore when you pass through the door. So after many a mile, please stop here a while.

Hosts: Bill and Nancy Fields
Rooms: 10 (7 PB; 3 SB) $60-120
Full Breakfast
Credit Cards: A, B
Notes: 2, 3, 4, 8, 9, 10, 11, 12, 14

WHITE SULPHUR SPRINGS _____

The James Wylie House Bed and Breakfast

208 East Main Street, 24986
(304) 536-9444

Located in a circa 1819 Georgian Colonial house, this bed and breakfast is located in a small-town setting ten blocks from the Greenbriar Resort and nine blocks from historic Lewisburg. Large, spacious rooms offer comfort in this historical home. A family suite and log cabin guest house offer accommodations as well. The Wylie House has been given excellent reviews in a national golf magazine, Mid-Atlantic Country magazine, and state-wide newspapers.

Hosts: Cheryl and Joe Griffith
Rooms: 4 (PB) $65-120
Full Breakfast
Credit Cards: A, B, C
Notes: 2, 5, 8, 9

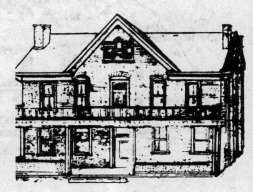

The James Wylie House

Wisconsin

ALBANY

Albany Guest House

405 South Mill Street, 53502
(608) 862-3636

Enjoy a restored, spacious block house in the heart of South Central Wisconsin's Swiss communities. Swing or rock amongst the flowers on the front porch or stroll through the two acres of lawn and gardens. Bike, hike, or ski the Sugar River Trail; canoe, tube, or fish the river; or light the fireplace in the master bedroom and relax. Visit the huge farmers' market on the state capitol square only 30 miles north, or discover the nearby virgin prairie.

Hosts: Bob and Sally Braem
Rooms: 4 (2 PB; 2 SB) $45-65
Full Breakfast
Credit Cards: None
Notes: 2, 5, 8, 11, 12, 13

ALMA

The Gallery House

215 North Main Street, 54610
(608) 685-4975

A traditional bed and breakfast in a historic 1861 mercantile building. Three guest rooms, full breakfast. John Runions' water-color gallery and the Spice Shop, with herbs, spices, teas, and gifts.

Hosts: John and Joan Runions
Rooms: 3 (1 PB; 2 SB)
Full Breakfast
Credit Cards: None
Notes: 2, 5, 9, 10, 11, 12

APPLETON

The Queen Anne Bed and Breakfast

837 East College Avenue, 54911
(414) 739-7966

This three-story Queen Anne-style home has lovely oak trim, oak and maple floors, exquisite beveled and stained-glass windows, and fine period antique furnishings. Guests can enjoy the enchanting first-floor Victorian retreat with private bath. Air-conditioned sleeping rooms with queen beds. Gracious hosts invite guests to relax and enjoy the nostalgia of times gone by. Within walking distance of Lawrence University. Visit Houdini collection and world's first hydroelectrically lit home.

Hosts: Susan and Larry Bogenschutz
Rooms: 3 (1 PB; 2 SB) $60-85
Full Breakfast Weekends; Continental Weekdays
Credit Cards: None
Notes: 2, 5, 8, 11, 12, 13

The Queen Anne

6 Pets welcome; 7 Smoking allowed; 8 Children welcome; 9 Social drinking allowed; 10 Tennis available; 11 Swimming available; 12 Golf available; 13 Skiing available; 14 May be booked through travel agents.

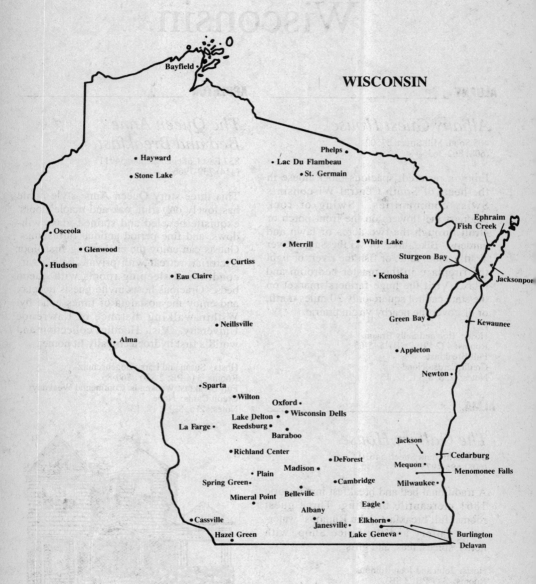

WISCONSIN

Bayfield

Phelps
• Lac Du Flambeau
• St. Germain

Hayward
Stone Lake

Osceola
Glenwood
Hudson
Curtiss
Eau Claire

Merrill
White Lake

Ephraim
Fish Creek

Sturgeon Bay

Jacksonport

Kenosha

Green Bay

Kewaunee

Neillsville

Alma

Newton

Appleton

Sparta
Wilton
Oxford
Wisconsin Dells
Lake Delton
La Farge   Reedsburg
Baraboo

Richland Center
DeForest

Jackson
Cedarburg
Mequon
Menomonee Falls

Madison
Plain
Spring Green
Cambridge
Milwaukee
Belleville
Mineral Point
Albany   Eagle
Cassville
Janesville   Elkhorn
Hazel Green   Lake Geneva   Burlington
Delavan

BARABOO

Frantiques Showplace

704 Ash Street, 53913
(608) 356-5273

This unique 25-room mansion was featured on *PM Magazine* as unbelievable. Fran conducts personal tours of her home as part of the bed and breakfast experience. There are over 40 sets of dishes; a children's section; a ladies' section with all periods of women's attire—hats, shoes, and beaded hand bags; a men's section; music area with pump organ, electric baby grand player piano; a Chinese section; 1950s room; black, red, and green rooms. Guests may choose between the Cinema Suite or the Oak and Brass Room.

Hosts: Bud and Fran Kelly
Rooms: 2 (PB) $60-70
Full Breakfast
Credit Cards: None
Notes: 2, 5, 8, 10, 11, 12, 13

BAYFIELD

Cooper Hill House

33 South 6th Street, P. O. Box 1288, 54814
(715) 779-5060

The Cooper Hill House offers guests quiet, comfortable lodging in an 1888 historic home in Bayfield. This bed and breakfast has four rooms with private baths, central air, and antique and heirloom furnishings. In the winter, snuggle under down comforters. Cross-country or downhill skiing at Mount Ashwabay is complimentary with a two-night minimum stay during ski season. Gift certificates are available.

Hosts: Julie and Larry MacDonald
Rooms: 4 (PB) $60-75
Continental Breakfast
Credit Cards: A, B
Notes: 2, 5, 8 (limited), 9, 10, 11, 12, 13

Old Rittenhouse Inn

Box 584, 54814
(715) 779-5111

The inn is a beautiful Victorian mansion built in 1890 overlooking Lake Superior. Guest rooms are furnished with antiques and working fireplaces. Dinner, offered nightly by reservation, features fine formal service. Double Jacuzzis.

Hosts: Jerry and Mary Phillips
Roosm: 20 (PB) $79-179
Continental Breakfast (full available at extra charge)
Minimum stay May-October weekends: 2 nights
Credit Cards: A, B
Notes: 2, 5, 8, 9, 10, 11, 12, 13

BELLEVILLE

Abendruh Bed and Breakfast Swiss Style

7019 Gehin Road, 53508
(608) 424-3808

Abendruh stands for peaceful and relaxing lodging. Guest rooms are large, uniquely decorated, cool and relaxing in the summer, and warm and cozy in the winter. Take a leisurely walk or sit by a crackling fire. Enjoy Swiss and Norwegian settlements in neighboring villages. Visit many cultural events in the capital city of Wisconsin. Shopping, biking, and cross-country ski trails and parks are nearby. Featured as exceptional bed and breakfast in Wisconsin, January 1992.

Host: Mathilde Jaggi
Rooms: 3 (2 PB; 1 SB) $45-55
Expanded Continental Breakfast
Credit Cards: None
Notes: 2, 5, 10, 11, 12, 13, 14

BURLINGTON

Hillcrest Bed and Breakfast

540 Storle Avenue, 53105
(414) 763-4706

A turn-of-the-century historic estate sitting high on a hill offering a spectacular view of the rivers and lake below. Enjoy four acres of lovely flower gardens and woods—a secluded and serene setting just a short walk to restaurants and shopping. This Edwardian home has been meticulously restored and features mahogany and walnut woodwork, maple floors, and bevelled glass windows. It is beautifully decorated with period antiques. Lakes, hiking, biking, skiing, nearby.

Hosts: Dick and Karen Granholm
Rooms: 3 (1 PB; 2 SB) $50-75
Full Breakfast
Credit Cards: A, B
Notes: 2, 5, 9, 11, 12, 13

CAMBRIDGE-ROCKDALE

The Night Heron Bed, Books and Breakfast

315 East Water Street, 53523
(608) 423-4141

Romantic getaway nestled among flowering crab trees in a parklike setting across from the beautiful Koshkonong River. This bed and breakfast features three enchanting guest rooms, an umbrella terrace, hot tub, fireplace, and Art Deco interior. Full Wisconsin breakfast is served on weekends. Bikes are available for bikers; hiking trails, cross-country skiing, and swimming are nearby. Only two miles from Cambridge.

Hosts: Pamela Schorr and John Lehman
Rooms: 3 (1 PB; 2 SB) $45-65
Full Breakfast Weekends and Continental Breakfst
   Weekdays
Credit Cards: None
Notes: 2, 5, 9, 11, 12, 13, 14

CASSVILLE

The Geiger House

401 Denniston Street, 53806
(608) 725-5419

Built in 1855 on land purchased from Nelson Dewey, Wisconsin's first governor, this Greek Revival home offers three spacious guest rooms with primitive antiques and homespun charm. Nelson Dewey State Park and Stonefield Historic Village are nearby. Homemade jams, jellies, breads, and juices compliment the full breakfast.

Hosts: Marcus and Penny Neal
Rooms: 3 (SB) $50
Full Breakfast
Credit Cards: A, B
Notes: 2, 5

CEDARBURG

Stagecoach Inn

West 61 North 520, Washington Avenue, 53012
(414) 375-0208

The Stagecoach Inn is a historic, restored 1853 stone building of Greek Revival style. Its 13 cozy rooms offer stenciled walls and Laura Ashley comforters, central air conditioning, and private baths. Suites with large whirlpool baths are available. Situated in the heart of historic Cedarburg, the inn also features an on-premises pub with a 100-year-old bar and a chocolate shop.

Hosts: Liz and Brook Brown
Rooms: 13 (PB) $65-95
Continental Breakfast
Credit Cards: A, B, C
Notes: 2, 5, 9, 10, 11, 12, 13, 14

The Washington House Inn

West 62 North, 573 Washington Avenue, 53012
(414) 375-3550; (800) 554-4717

Built in 1884 and listed on the National Registry, the Washington House Inn is situated in the heart of the Cedarburg historic district. Rooms feature antique furnishings, whirlpool baths, fireplaces. Walking distance to Cedar Creek Settlement antique shops and fine dining.

Host: Wendy Porterfield
Rooms: 29 (PB) $61.95-145.95

NOTES: Credit cards accepted: A Master Card; B Visa; C American Express; D Discover Card; E Diner's Club; F Other; 2 Personal Checks accepted; 3 Lunch available; 4 Dinner available; 5 Open all year;

Continental Breakfast
Credit Cards: A, B, C, D, E, F
Notes: 2, 5, 7, 8, 9, 10, 11, 12, 13

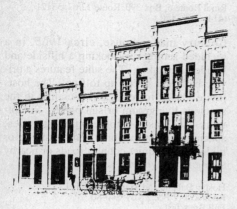

The Washington House Inn

CURTISS

Thompson's Inn

County Highway E, P. O. Box 128, 54422
(715) 223-6041

The Thompson's Inn is a large, restored
Victorian home filled with antiques and
collectibles. Dale's novelty room contains
toy trains, collector steins, and 285 cookie
jars. The guest rooms with bath and sitting
room are on the upper level. A large back
yard filled with trees and flower gardens
can be enjoyed from an old-fashioned
porch. There is also a large guest room
with full bath on the lower level. Nearby
attractions include Chequamegon National
Forest, Medford, Rib Mountain ski area,
the High Ground War Memorial, Amish
settlements. In the heart of Wisconsin's
dairyland.

Hosts: Arla and Dale Thompson
Rooms: 4 (1 PB; 3 SB) $35-45
Full Breakfast
Credit Cards: None
Notes: 2, 5, 7 (limited), 9, 12, 13

DE FOREST

Circle B Bed and Breakfast

3804 Vinburn Road, 53532
(608) 846-3481

Enjoy a relaxed stay in the country on a
160-acre farm with livestock. This neat,
well-kept home and yard offer a beautiful
view of sunrises and sunsets. Enjoy the
wonderful antique decor. Madison, Wisconsin Dells, parks, and golf are nearby.

Host: Donna Buchner
Rooms: 3 (1 PB; 2 SB) $55-75
Full Breakfast
Credit Cards: F
Notes: 2, 5, 8 (limited), 12, 13

DELAVAN

Allyn Mansion Inn

511 East Walworth Avenue, 53115
(414) 728-9090

This meticulously restored 1885 National
Register mansion situated in Wisconsin's
Southern Gateways Region offers an
authentic Victorian setting. Guests are
encouraged to enjoy the whole house with
its spacious rooms and fine antique furnishings. Read by one of the ten marble fireplaces, play the grand piano, peruse the
collections of Victoriana, have a good soak
in a copper bathtub, or swap stories with
the hosts on restoration or antiquing.

Hosts: Joe Johnson and Ron Markwell
Rooms: 8 (S6B) $40-85
Full Breakfast
Credit Cards: A, B
Notes: 2, 5, 9, 10, 11, 12, 13, 14 (weekdays only)

EAGLE

Eagle Centre House

W370 S9590 Highway 67, 53119
(414) 363-4700

A replicated 1846 Greek Revival stagecoach inn decorated with antiques on 16

6 Pets welcome; 7 Smoking allowed; 8 Children welcome; 9 Social drinking allowed; 10 Tennis available; 11 Swimming available; 12 Golf available; 13 Skiing available; 14 May be booked through travel agents.

secluded acres in the southern Kettle Morraine Forest. Five large chambers with private baths; two with whirlpools. Near "Old World Wisconsin," the state of Wisconsin's Outdoor Living History Museum. Ski, bike, hike, shop, golf, swim, fish, or horseback ride.

Hosts: Riene Wells (Herriges) and Dean Herriges
Rooms: 5 (PB) $69-115
Full Breakfast
Credit Cards: A, B, C
Notes: 2, 5, 9, 11, 12, 13

Eagle Centre House

EAU CLAIRE

Fanny Hill Inn and Dinner Theatre

3919 Crescent Avenue, 54703
(715) 836-8184; (800) 292-8026

Located on a bluff overlooking the Chippewa River Valley, Fanny Hill is the perfect setting to "get away from it all." Each of the seven guest rooms has a private bath and is tastefully decorated with antiques and curiosities. The unique combination of scenic beauty, gracious fine dining, hilarious live theatre, and warm Victorian atmosphere will make guests' stay a pleasure.

Host: Larry Barr
Rooms: 7 (PB) $69-139
Continental Breakfast
Credit Cards: A, B, C, D
Notes: 2, 4, 5, 9

ELKHORN

Ye Olde Manor House

Rural Route 5, Box 390, Route 12/67, 53121
(414) 742-2450

Country manor house, circa 1905, in a secluded setting overlooking a hillside and Lauderdale Lakes. The suite features a private bath and sleeps up to five. The hosts invite guests to relax and socialize in the spacious livingroom or sun porch. Sumptuous breakfast of home-baked goodies; special diets are honored. Enjoy hiking or biking on the quiet country roads or nearby skiing in the winter.

Hosts: Babette and Marvin Henschel
Rooms: 4 (2 PB; 2 SB) $40-80
Full Breakfast
Credit Cards: A, B, C, D
Notes: 2, 5, 8, 11, 12, 13, 14

EPHRAIM

Eagle Harbor Inn

9914 Water Street, Box 72, 54211
(414) 854-2121

Nestled in the heart of historic Ephraim, Eagle Harbor is a gracious, antique-filled country inn. Centrally situated, across from the lake, and close to the boat ramp, golf course, park, beach, and cross-country ski trails.

Hosts: Ronald and Barbara Schultz
Rooms: 9 (PB) $67-98
Full Breakfast
Credit Cards: A, B
Notes: 2, 5, 9, 10, 11, 12, 13, 14

Hillside Hotel

9980 Highway 42, 54211
(414) 854-2417

This beautifully restored country Victorian bed and breakfast overlooks the Eagle Harbor on Green Bay. Well known for full speciality breakfasts and gourmet dining, the inn features hand-restored original fur-

NOTES: Credit cards accepted: A Master Card; B Visa; C American Express; D Discover Card; E Diner's Club; F Other; 2 Personal Checks accepted; 3 Lunch available; 4 Dinner available; 5 Open all year;

nishings, a 96-foot veranda with a spectacular view, and a large private beach. There are also two cottages available.

Rooms: 12 (SB) $71
Full Breakfast
Credit Cards: A, B, C, D
Notes: 4, 5, 8, 11, 12

FISH CREEK

Thorp House Inn

Box 490, 54212
(414) 868-2444

Find history and charm with a view of the bay on a quiet wooded street in the heart of Fish Creek. Gracious antique-filled guest rooms feature private baths (one with whirlpool), air conditioning, guest library, fireplace, parlor, and delicious home-baked breakfast. Cottages feature wood-burning fireplaces, country antiques, kitchens, decks, and full baths (one with whirlpool).

Hosts: Christine and Sverre Falck-Pedersen
Rooms: 4 (PB) $70-115
Continental Breakfast
Credit Cards: None
Notes: 2, 5, 9, 10, 11, 12, 13

Thorp House Inn

GREEN BAY

Stonewood Haus

P. O. Box 10201, 54307
(414) 499-3786

Minutes from downtown Green Bay and airport, lovely Stonewood Haus is nestled on nine acres of woods, meadows, and rippling Trout Creek. Exquisitely unique, combining Old World charm with modern comforts. Relax on the patio, curl up in front of the fireplace, or enjoy the many scenic views. Individually decorated guest rooms, cozy down comforters. Across from the Brown County Golf Course. Full breakfast. Air conditioning. Corporate rates available.

Host: JoAnn Naumann King
Rooms: 5 (1 PB; 4 S3B) $59-89
Full or Continental Breakfast
Credit Cards: A, B, D
Notes: 2, 5, 9, 12, 13, 14

HAYWARD

The Open Window Bed and Breakfast

Rural Route 4, Box 4550, 54843
(715) 462-3033

Guests are welcome in this beautiful home on Big Round Lake, nine miles east of Hayward. This getaway offers a level, sandy, and private beach 65 feet from the front door. There are three guest rooms, one with king-size bed, private bath, and balcony overlooking the lake. Guests will enjoy the large breakfast that is served on a butcher block table.

Hosts: Lori and Ed Wielgot
Rooms: 3 (1 PB; 2 SB) $55-70
Full Breakfast
Credit Cards: None
Notes: 2, 5, 7, 8, 11, 12, 13

6 Pets welcome; 7 Smoking allowed; 8 Children welcome; 9 Social drinking allowed; 10 Tennis available; 11 Swimming available; 12 Golf available; 13 Skiing available; 14 May be booked through travel agents.

HAZEL GREEN

Wisconsin House Stage Coach Inn

2105 Main Street, 53811
(608) 854-2233

The inn is a historic, country-furnished bed and breakfast. Built in 1846 as a stagecoach inn, it now offers six guest rooms and two guest suites. Located 10 minutes from Galena, 12 minutes from Dubuque, and 15 minutes from Platteville. The inn is convenient to all the attractions of the tri-state area.

Hosts: Ken and Pat Disch
Rooms: 8 (6 PB; 2 SB) $40-85
Full Breakfast
Credit Cards: A, B
Notes: 2, 3, 4, 5, 8, 9, 14

Phipps Inn

HUDSON

Jefferson-Day House

1109 3rd Street, 54016
(715) 386-7111

This 1857 home offers antique collections, air-conditioned rooms, double whirlpools, gas fireplaces, and three-course fireside breakfasts. The pleasing decor and friendly atmosphere will relax you, while the near-

by St. Croix River, Octagon House Museum, and Phipps Theatre for the Arts will bring you enjoyment.

Hosts: Sharon and Wally Miller
Rooms: 4 (2 PB; 2 SB) $79-149
Full Breakfast weekends; Continental weekdays
Credit Cards: None
Notes: 2, 5, 8 (over 9), 9, 11, 12, 13, 14

Phipps Inn

1005 Third Street, 54016
(715) 386-0800

Described as the "Grand Dame" of Queen Anne houses in historic Hudson, this 1884 Victorian mansion offers authentic furnishings and cozy suites, some with fireplaces and whirlpools. Guests enjoy three parlors, two porches, a baby grand piano, and lavish and leisurely breakfasts in bed or served in the elegant dining room. Only 30 minutes from Minneapolis/St. Paul. A romantic retreat.

Host: Cyndi and John Berglund
Rooms: 6 (PB) $79-159
Full Breakfast weekends; Continental weekdays
Credit Cards: A, B
Notes: 2, 5, 9, 11, 12, 13, 14

JANESVILLE

Jackson Street Inn Bed and Breakfast

210 South Jackson Street, 53545
(608) 754-7250

Comfortable Victorian air-conditioned home. Leaded-glass windows and cushioned window seats in the spacious, cheerful sleeping rooms. Sitting room with books, games, magazines, and menus from nearby restaurants. Marble fireplace, intricate oak paneling, coffered ceilings in the dining and TV rooms. Rotary International Gardens, golf and trails. Near I-90 on Highway 11. Off-street parking. Rated unusually good value by *Mobil Travel Guide*. Close to Rotary International.

NOTES: Credit cards accepted: A Master Card; B Visa; C American Express; D Discover Card; E Diner's Club; F Other; 2 Personal Checks accepted; 3 Lunch available; 4 Dinner available; 5 Open all year;

Hosts: Ilah and Bob Sessler
Rooms: 4 (2 PB; 2 SB) $45-65
Full Breakfast
Credit Cards: A, B, C
Notse: 2, 5, 7, 8, 9, 10, 11, 12, 13 (XC), 14

Jackson Street Inn

KENOSHA

The Manor House

6536 Third Avenue, 53143
(414) 658-0014

Romantic, breathtaking stately brick
Georgian mansion overlooking Lake
Michigan in the heart of Kenosha's
lakeshore historic district. Listed on the
National Register of Historic Places.
Furnished with carefully selected antiques
and surrounded by beautifully landscaped
grounds. Midway between Chicago and
Milwaukee. Meeting rooms available.
Weekday discounts and corporate rates.

Hosts: Janice and Cecil Nichols
Rooms: 4 (PB) $99.90-144.30
Continental Breakfast
Credit Cards: A, B, C
Notes: 2, 5, 10, 11, 12, 13, 14

KEWAUNEE

The "Gables"

821 Dodge Street, 54216
(414) 388-0220

Relax and be pampered is the motto for
guests. Cuddle up in one of five individual-

ly decorated rooms in this 22-room historical Queen Anne Victorian home. Or enjoy
conversation with your hosts around the
fireplace. Wake to the smell of a full
Wisconsin foods breakfast. Stroll along
scenic Lake Michigan's shoreline. Enjoy
one of Wisconsin's oldest port cities. Only
20 minutes to famous Door County.

Hosts: Penny and Earl Dunbar
Rooms: 5 (1 PB; 4 SB) $60-65
Full Breakfast
Credit Cards: C
Notes: 2, 5, 8, 10, 11, 12, 13

LAC DU FLAMBEAU

Ty-Bach

3104 Simpson Lane, 54538
(715) 588-7851

For a relaxing getaway anytime of the year,
share this modern home on the shore of a
tranquil northwoods lake with 80 acres of
woods to explore. Guest quarters include a
large living area and a deck overlooking
"Golden Pond." Visit the area attractions:
the cranberry marshes, the Native
American Museum and pow-wows, professional theater, wilderness cruises, and
more. Guests are pampered with delicious
country breakfasts served at flexible times.

Hosts: Kermit and Janet Bekkum
Rooms: 2 (PB) $50-60
Full Breakfast
Credit Cards: None
Notes: 2, 5, 6, 9, 11, 13

LA FARGE

Trillium

Route 2, Box 121, 54639
(608) 625-4492

Your own private cottage situated on this
farm amid 85 acres of fields and woods,
near a tree-lined brook. Situated in a thriving Amish farming community just 35
miles southeast of La Crosse.

6 Pets welcome; 7 Smoking allowed; 8 Children welcome; 9 Social drinking allowed; 10 Tennis available; 11
Swimming available; 12 Golf available; 13 Skiing available; 14 May be booked through travel agents.

Host: Rosanne Boyett
Cottage: 1 (PB) $65-70
Full Breakfast
Children under 12 stay without charge
Credit Cards: None
Notes: 2, 5, 7, 8, 9, 10, 11, 12, 13

LAKE DELTON

The Swallow's Nest Bed and Breakfast

141 Sarrington, P. O. Box 418, 53940
(608) 254-6900

This new home in a secluded setting is situated one mile off I-90 and I-94. Choose from four guest rooms, each with private bath. The home features monastery windows, two-story atrium with skylights, library with fireplace, and decks with bird's-eye view of the lake. A photography studio and gallery are on the premises. Area attractions include Wisconsin Dells, Devil's Lake and Mirror Lake state parks. Downhill and cross-country skiing. Circus World Museum, antique shops, and fine restaurants nearby.

Hosts: Rod and Mary Ann Stemo
Rooms: 4 (PB) $55-65
Full Breakfast
Credit Cards: A, B
Notes: 2, 5, 11, 12, 13

LAKE GENEVA

Eleven Gables Inn on the Lake

493 Wrigley Drive, 53147
(414) 248-8393

Nestled in evergreens amid giant oaks in the Edgewater Historical District, this quaint lakeside Carpenter's Gothic bed and breakfast offers romantic bedrooms, bridal chamber, and two- or three-bedroom family "Country Cottages." Fireplaces, private baths, televisions, VCR, down comforters, wet bars, balconies, courtyards, lake views, and private pier are all part of the amenities

that guests enjoy. Bikes are available for rental. Fine dining, boutique shopping, and entertainment are within walking distance.

Host: A. Milliette
Rooms: 12 (PB) $89-145
Full Breakfast
Credit Cards: A, B, C
Notes: 5, 6, 7, 8, 9, 10, 11, 12, 13, 14

Elizabethian Inn

463 Wrigley Drive, 53147
(414) 248-9131

The inn, on the lakefront of Lake Geneva, has its own pier for swimming, sunbathing, boating, and fishing. Enjoy the comfortable, warm atmosphere of an old New England inn with high poster beds, beautiful old quilts, and antique furniture.

Host: Elizabeth Farrell
Rooms: 10 (PB) $85-95
Full Breakfast
Minimum stay weekends and holidays: 2
Credit Cards: A, B
Notes: 2, 5, 8 (over 12), 9, 10, 11, 12, 13

The French Country Inn on the Lake

Highway 50 West, Route 4, Box 690, 53147
(414) 245-5220

Historic European inn with modern amenities. All guest rooms, decorated in French country, feature a private bath with whirlpool tub, fireplaces, and lakeshore balcony. Afternoon tea and full breakfast are included. Ideal for anniversaries, special occasions, or romantic getaways. The restaurant and cocktail lounge overlook the lake. Call for current rates.

Rooms: 24 (PB)
Full Breakfast
Credit Cards: A, B
Notes: 2, 5, 11

T. C. Smith Inn Historic Bed and Breakfast

865 Main Street, 53147
(414) 248-1097

NOTES: Credit cards accepted: A Master Card; B Visa; C American Express; D Discover Card; E Diner's Club; F Other; 2 Personal Checks accepted; 3 Lunch available; 4 Dinner available; 5 Open all year;

Experience and recapture the majesty of 19th-century ambience at the downtown T. C. Smith Inn (circa 1845) complete with oriental carpets, fine period antiques, and European paintings. Traditional to the grand Victorian era, the inn offers four elegant, spacious, and bright guest chambers with a lake view and romantic surroundings. Buffet breakfast is served in the Grand Parlor under a Tiffany chandelier before the marble fireplace hearth. A garden and waterfall in the midst of new classic statues grace the large courtyard.

Host: The Marks Family
Rooms: 4 (S2B) $45-165 seasonal
Buffet Breakfast
Credit Cards: A, B, C, D
Notes: 2, 5, 6, 7, 8, 9, 10, 11, 12, 13, 14

MADISON

Annie's Bed and Breakfast

2117 Sheridan Drive, 53704
(608) 244-2224

When you want the world to go away, come to Annie's Bed and Breakfast. This quiet little inn on Warner Park offers a beautiful view and deluxe accommodations. Enjoy the romantic gazebo surrounded by butterfly gardens, the lily pond by the terrace for morning coffee, followed by a sumptuous breakfast. The guest rooms are cozy with antiques, gorgeous quilts, and down comforters. Double Jacuzzi is available. Convenient to everything.

Hosts: Anne and Larry Stuart
Suites (2 rooms each): 2 (PB) $75-95
Full Breakfast
Credit Cards: A, B, C, D
Notes: 2, 5, 9, 10, 11, 13

The Collins House

704 East Gorham Street, 53703
(608) 255-4230

On the shores of Lake Mendota in downtown Madison, this restored home of the Prairie school of architecture is listed on the National Register of Historic Places.

Hosts: Barb and Mike Pratzel
Rooms: 5 (PB) $66.08-110.88
Full Breakfast weekends: Continental weekdays
Minimum stay holidays: 2 nights
Credit Cards: A, B
Notes: 2, 5, 6 (limited), 7 (limited), 8, 9 (limited), 10, 11, 12, 13

Mansion Hill Inn

424 North Pinckney Street, 53703
(608) 255-3999; (800) 798-9070

Eleven luxurious rooms, each with private bath. Whirlpool tubs, fireplaces, stereo systems, remote cable television, and minibars. Private wine cellar. VCRs and access to athletic club available on request. Refreshments served daily in the parlor.

Host: Polly Elder
Rooms: 11 (PB) $112-280
Continental Breakfast
Credit Cards: A, B, C
Notes: 2, 4 (with notice), 5, 7, 9, 14

Plough Inn Bed and Breakfast

3402 Monroe Street, 53711
(608) 238-2981

The Plough Inn, listed on the National Register of Historic Places, has been a Madison landmark since the mid-1800s. A handsome Greek Revival building nestled among mature trees on a large lot across from the University of Wisconsin Arboretum, the inn provides the feeling of country charm within an urban, university community. The Arborview guest room has whirlpool bath and fireplace. Studio has skylights, study, and whirlpool.

Hosts: Katherine Naherny and Roger Ganser
Rooms: 4 (PB) $59-94
Full Breakfast Weekends; Continental Weekdays
Credit Cards: A, B
Notes: 2, 5, 9, 10, 12, 13

---

6 Pets welcome; 7 Smoking allowed; 8 Children welcome; 9 Social drinking allowed; 10 Tennis available; 11 Swimming available; 12 Golf available; 13 Skiing available; 14 May be booked through travel agents.

MENOMONEE FALLS

Dorshel's Bed and Breakfast Guest House

W140 N7616 Lilly Road, 53051
(414) 255-7866

Contemporary home decorated with beautiful antiques and situated in a lovely wooded residential area. Enjoy breakfast on a screened-in porch or in the formal dining room. Play a game of pool or watch the wildlife feast at special feeders. Two fireplaces offer cozy warmth. Only 20 minutes from Milwaukee. Full continental breakfast always includes Wisconsin's finest cheese, fresh fruits of the season, and special breads and pastries.

Hosts: Dorothy and Sheldon Waggoner
Rooms: 3 (2 PB; 1 SB) $45-50
Expanded Continental Breakfast
Credit Cards: None
Notes: 2, 5, 7, 9, 12, 13

MERRILL

Candlewick Inn

700 West Main Street, 54452
(715) 536-7744

The ambience of yesteryear is truly reflected in this classic Victorian Prairie-style home built by a lumber baron in the early 1880s. Recently restored to its original elegance, this four-season inn radiates all the warmth and charm of the Victorian era. It includes fine antiques, handmade quilts, oak and mahogany woodwork, collectibles, and gift shop, all combining to create a romantic masterpiece. Conveniently situated in a historic district of Merrill, the inn provides easy access to shops, museums, antiques, and restaurants.

Host: Dan Staniak
Rooms: 5 (3 PB; 2 SB) $50-95
Full Breakfast
Credit Cards: A, B
Notes: 2, 5, 10, 11, 12, 13, 14

MILWAUKEE

Marie's Bed and Breakfast

346 East Wilson Street, 53207
(414) 483-1512

Handsome 1896 Victorian home in historic Bay View district. Six minutes from downtown and seven minutes from the airport. Furnished with heirlooms, collectibles, and original artwork. Full breakfast served in the Fan Room or the garden. Off-street parking provided. Central air conditioning. Please write or call for a brochure.

Host: Marie M. Mahan
Rooms: 4 (S2B) $55-65
Full Breakfast
Credit Cards: A, B
Notes: 2, 5, 8, 9, 10, 11, 12

Ogden House

2237 North Lake Drive, 53202
(414) 272-2740

Situated just two blocks from Lake Michigan and one mile north of downtown, Ogden House is in the historic district of Milwaukee's early mansions. It offers the charm of fireplaces, high canopy beds, and old-fashioned hospitality. The hosts will make you feel at home.

Hosts: Mary Jane and John Moss
Rooms: 2 (PB) $79.13-89.68
Expanded Continental Breakfast
Credit Cards: None
Notes: 2, 5, 7, 9, 14

MINERAL POINT

Duke House

618 Maiden Street, 53565
(608) 987-2821

An 1870 Federal house furnished with hardwood floors, Oriental rugs, four-poster or canopy beds, wingback chairs, tie-back curtains. A perfect blend of antiques and reproduction furniture. Evening social hour

---

NOTES: Credit cards accepted: A Master Card; B Visa; C American Express; D Discover Card; E Diner's Club; F Other; 2 Personal Checks accepted; 3 Lunch available; 4 Dinner available; 5 Open all year;

and a full breakfast that always includes homemade coffee cake, muffins, tea biscuits, and scones.

Hosts: Tom and Darlene Duke
Rooms: 2 (SB) $45-55
Full Breakfast
Credit Cards: A, B
Notes: 2, 5, 9, 10, 11, 12, 13

Knudson Guest House

415 Ridge Street, 53565
(608) 987-2733

Enjoy a relaxed stay with old-fashioned hospitality amidst antique-filled rooms furnished for your comfort with a television in each guest room in this restored 1920 brick home. Antique stores and specialty shops are within walking distance. The House on the Rock, Governor Dodge State Park, and Spring Green are just a short drive away.

Hosts: Ag and Jim Knudson
Rooms: 3 (1 PB; 2 SB) $49-55.95
Full Breakfast
Credit Cards: None
Notes: 2, 5, 8, 9, 13

NEILLSVILLE

Bluebell Inn

122 Hewett Street, 54456
(715) 743-2929

Guests will experience warm hospitality in a friendly little city. This 1891 home with original woodwork, antiques, central air, and fireplace offers guests a wonderful stay. Relax in the parlor or library with collections of old records, magazines, and books. Full country breakfast is served to guests. After breakfast, explore the hilly streets, lovely parks, nearby Amish country, Wisconsin Vietnam Veterans Memorial, museums, and other nearby attractions.

Host: Jeanne Reuter
Rooms: 3 (1 PB; 2 SB) $40-45
Full Breakfast
Credit Cards: A, B
Notes: 2, 5, 8, 9, 10, 11, 12, 13

NEWTON

Rambling Hills Tree Farm

8825 Willever Lane, 53063
(414) 726-4388

Enjoy the serenity of country living in a comfortable modern home with panoramic views of 50 acres of rolling hills, small fishing lake, swimming pond, marsh, meadows, and woods with a network of trails and boardwalks to hike or ski. Three miles from Lake Michigan.

Hosts: Pete and Judie Stuntz
Rooms: 3 (SB) $42
Full Breakfast
Credit Cards: None
Notes: 2, 5, 7, 8, 9, 11, 13

OSCEOLA

St. Croix River Inn

305 River Street, 54020
(715) 294-4248

A meticulously restored 80-year-old stone home nestled in one of the region's finest recreational areas. Ski at Wild Mountain or Trollhaugen. Canoe or fish in the lovely St. Croix River. Then relax in your suite, some with fireplaces, all with Jacuzzi whirlpool baths.

Host: Ben Johnson and Bev Johnson
Rooms: 7 (PB) $100-200
Full Breakfast
Credit Cards: A, B, C
Notes: 2, 5, 7 (limited), 9, 10, 11, 12, 13, 14

OXFORD

Halfway House Bed and Breakfast

Route 2, Box 80, 53952
(608) 586-5489

The Halfway House was a stopping place for travelers on an old logging road and has been called Halfway House since the

Halfway House

1800's. In a quiet, rural setting with a large lawn, flower beds, birds, and game. The hosts, a veterinarian and his wife, have traveled to Africa and Europe. Skiing within 25 miles.

Hosts: Dr. J. A. and Geneviere Hines
Rooms: 4 (SB) $29.40 - 44.10
Full Breakfast
Credit Cards: None
Notes: 2, 5, 9, 12

PHELPS

Limberlost Inn

2483 Highway 17, 54554
(715) 545-2685

Modern log home with rustic northwoods charm surrounded by acres of national forest and lakes. Relax on the porch swing, in the hammock, or in the sauna before retiring to the comfort of down pillows and handmade quilts. Enjoy the screened porch, decks, or VCR and movie collection in the livingroom. Full breakfast is served in front of the fieldstone fireplace in the dining room.

Hosts: Bill and Phoebe McElroy
Rooms: 2 (SB) $55 plus tax
Full Breakfast
Credit Cards: None
Notes: 2, 5, 9, 11, 12, 13

PLAIN

Bettinger House Bed and Breakfast

Highway 23, 53577
(608) 546-2951

This 1904 brick home, once owned by the host's grandmother, who was a midwife, is located near the world famous House on a Rock, Frank Lloyd Wright's Taliesin, and the American Players Theatre. A home-cooked full breakfast is served every morning.

Hosts: Marie and Jim Neider
Rooms: 6 (2 PB; 4 SB) $45-55
Full Breakfast
Credit Cards: A, B
Notes: 2, 5, 7, 8, 9, 10, 11, 12, 13, 14

The Kraemer House Bed and Breakfast Inn

1190 Spruce Street, 53577
(608) 546-3161

You are invited to come and feel pampered in this very comfortable, traditional bed and breakfast home. Wake-up coffee is served with freshly baked cookies. The four guest rooms are lovely and bright with fresh flowers for accent. Retire to the smell

NOTES: Credit cards accepted: A Master Card; B Visa; C American Express; D Discover Card; E Diner's Club; F Other; 2 Personal Checks accepted; 3 Lunch available; 4 Dinner available; 5 Open all year;

and feel of sun-dried fine cotton sheets. Situated in a small village nestled among the rolling hills that some say reminds them of southern Germany. Near House on the Rock, American Players Theatre, Frank Lloyd Wright's home.

Hosts: Duane and Gwen Kraemer
Rooms: 4 (1 PB; 3 SB) $52-71.25
Full Breakfast
Credit Cards: None
Notes: 2, 5, 8, 10, 11, 12, 13, 14

PLYMOUTH

52 Stafford, An Irish Guest House

52 Stafford Street, 53073
(414) 893-0552

Listed on the National Register of Historic Places, this inn has 20 rooms, 17 of which have whirlpool baths and cable TV. 52 Stafford features one of the most beautiful pubs in America, which serves lunch on Saturday and dinner seven nights a week. There are 35,000 acres of public recreation land nearby; cross-country skiing, hiking, biking, sports fishing, boating, swimming, golfing. Crystal-clear lakes and beautiful fall colors.

Hosts: Rip and Christine O'Dwanny
Rooms: 20 (PB) $69-99
Continental Breakfast Weekdays; Full Weekends
Credit Cards: A, B, C, D, E
Notes: 2, 3, 4, 5, 6, 7, 8, 9, 10, 11, 12, 13, 14

PRINCETON

The Gray Lion Inn Bed and Breakfast

115 Harvard Street, 54968
(414) 295-4101

Just like Grandma's house—complete with bedtime snacks, always-full cookie jar, and a warm welcome! Classic Victorian in picturesque Central Wisconsin with spacious heirloom-filled rooms (all non-smoking).

Enjoy hearty, extra-full breakfast featuring homemade bakery and offering "health-conscious" menu options. Experience Green Lake Country—antiques, golf, water sports, scenic byways, fine restaurants, and shops—all within 20 minutes.

Hosts: Don, Mabel, and Deby Gray
Rooms: 5 (4 PB; 1 SB) $45-60
Full Breakfast
Credit Cards: None
Notes: 2, 5, 8, 9, 12

Lochnaiar Inn

1121 Lake Avenue, 53403
(414) 633-3300

Lochnaiar Inn, one of the finest inns in the Mid-West, sits majestically atop a bluff overlooking Lake Michigan. Inside and out, from the copper-clad shingled roof to the six fireplaces, Lochnaiar displays warmth and elegance. Each of the eight guest rooms has its own personality. Guests may relax in deep empress or whirlpool tubs for one or two. They may enjoy books, games, or companionship of other guests in the main salon and library.

Hosts: Dawn and Christy Weisbrod
Rooms: 8 (PB) $80-165
Full Breakfast
Credit Cards: A, B, C, D
Notes: 2, 5, 9, 10, 11, 12, 13

REEDSBURG

Parkview Bed and Breakfast

211 North Park Street, 53959
(608) 524-4333

Located in Reedsburg's historical district, this 1895 Queen Anne Victorian home has fish ponds, windmill, and playhouse enhancing the grounds. The three guest rooms overlook City Park. Discover the original woodwork and hardware, tray ceilings, suitor's window, and built-in buffet inside this cozy home. Wisconsin Dells, Baraboo, and Spring Green are nearby.

6 Pets welcome; 7 Smoking allowed; 8 Children welcome; 9 Social drinking allowed; 10 Tennis available; 11 Swimming available; 12 Golf available; 13 Skiing available; 14 May be booked through travel agents.

Hosts: Tom and Donna Hofmann
Rooms: 3 (SB) $55
Full Breakfast
Credit Cards: A, B, C
Notes: 2, 5, 8, 9

RICHLAND CENTER

The Mansion

323 South Church Street, 53581
(608) 647-2808

This 19-room brick mansion was built in the early 1900s by a lumberman. Situated just around the corner from Frank Lloyd Wright Warehouse/Museum in this city of Wright's birth. Quarter-sawn oak wood-work and parquet floors of oak, walnut, and maple. Quietly elegant, but affordable. Air-conditioned, but no TV.

Hosts: Beth Caulkins and Harvey Glanzer
Rooms: 5 (S2B) $25-55
Expanded Continental Breakfast
Credit Cards: None
Notes: 2, 5, 6 (inquire), 7, 8 (over 12), 10, 11, 13
  (XC)

ST. GERMAIN

St. Germain Bed and Breakfast Resort

6255 Highway 70 East, P. O. Box 6, 54558
(715) 479-8007

Indoor heated pool—Jacuzzi spa to relax. Full breakfast with homemade muffins or cinnamon rolls. Walk to choice of three excellent supper clubs. Play volleyball, ten-nis, croquet, or hoops. Adjacent to 19,000 acres of national forest for hiking and bik-ing. Pedal boats/bike rentals. On main snowmobile trail. Snowmobile rentals and personal snowmobile tours available. Nine cross-country trails nearby. Four uniquely decorated rooms. Great room with TV, VCR, fireplace, and games. Modified American Plan optional.

Hosts: Ron and Joyce
Rooms: 4 (SB) $55-70

Full Breakfast
Credit Cards: A, B
Notes: 2, 4, 5, 7, 8, 9, 10,11, 12, 13, 14

SPARTA

Just-N-Trails Bed and Breakfast/Farm Vacation

Route 1, Box 274, 54656
(608) 269-4522; (800) 488-4521

A bed and breakfast specializing in recre-ation, relaxation, and romance. Separate buildings: The Woodshed with two bed-rooms, whirlpool in atrium, and fireplace. The Granary, a perfect playhouse for two, whirlpool, and fireplace. Little House on the Prairie log cabin with whirlpool and fireplace. Five rooms in 1920 farmhouse on active dairy farm. Laura Ashley linens. Three-course breakfasts.

Hosts: Donna and Don Justin
Rooms: 8 (7 PB; 1 SB) $65-195
Full Breakfast
Credit Cards: A, B
Notes: 2, 5, 8, 13, 14

SPRING GREEN

Hill Street Bed and Breakfast

353 Hill Street, 53588

At the Hill Street Bed and Breakfast guests will find airy rooms and Victorian splen-dor. A parcel of the homestead of Thomas Hill, Sr., who arrived from Lancaster, England, in 1887. Frank Lloyd Wright's Taliesin, House on the Rock, Tower Hill State Park, Wisconsin River, American Players Theatre, biking, cross-country ski-ing, golf, canoeing, and fishing are avail-able or nearby.

Rooms: 7 (5 PB; 2 SB) $50-70
Full Breakfast
Credit Cards: A, B
Notes: 2, 5, 10, 11, 12, 13

NOTES: Credit cards accepted: A Master Card; B Visa; C American Express; D Discover Card; E Diner's Club; F Other; 2 Personal Checks accepted; 3 Lunch available; 4 Dinner available; 5 Open all year;

STEVENS POINT

Dreams of Yesteryear Bed and Breakfast

1100 Brawley Street, 54481
(715) 341-4525

Designed by J. H. Jeffers, this bed and breakfast was built in 1901 and is lavish in Victorian detail. Period furniture is evident throughout. The hosts love to visit with guests and talk about their cozy home and its furnishings. The home is listed on the National Register of Historic Places and its restoration was featured in Victorian Homes magazine.

Hosts: Bonnie and Bill Maher
Rooms: 4 (2 PB; 2 SB) $55-75
Full Breakfast
Credit Cards: A, B, D
Notes: 2, 5, 7 (limited), 8 (over 12), 9, 10, 11, 12, 13, 14

Victorian Swan on Water

1716 Water Street, 54481
(715) 345-0595

Explore this romantic, historic house at the gateway to Wisconsin vacationland. Cozy nooks, fireplace, bountiful breakfasts in the plant-filled sun room. There is also a TV room, and meeting rooms are available. River walkways, forest preserves, bird trails, scenic cross-country ski trails, golf, and tennis nearby. Air-conditioned.

Host: Joan Ouellette
Rooms: 4 (PB) $45-65
Full Breakfast
Credit Cards: A, B, C, D
Notes: 2, 5, 9, 10, 12, 13, 14

STONE LAKE

The Lake House

P.O. Box 177, 54843
(715) 865-2811

The Lake House offers three comfortable guest rooms, either single or double, one with a private bath. Two rooms offer a lake view and one has a treetop view. All are decorated in a pleasant country decor and open to a sitting area. The large room sleeps four. Relax in the sun room or in the sitting room in front of the fireplace. Groomed cross-country ski trails, golf, and antique shops are nearby. Take a swim, fish, or paddle around the clear, spring-fed lake or bike quiet country roads.

Hosts: Betty and Turk Debus
Rooms: 3 (1 PB; 2 SB) $40-55
Full Breakfast
Credit Cards: None
Notes: 2, 5, 8 (prior arrangement), 11, 12, 13

Dreams of Yesteryear

STURGEON BAY

The Gray Goose Bed and Breakfast

4258 Bay Shore Drive, 54235
(414) 743-9100

Enjoy warm hospitality in this Civil War home in Door County. Authentic antique furnishings. Four large, comfortable rooms share two baths. Guest sitting room with a water/sunset view to remember. Beautiful dining room. Full porch with wicker and swing. Quiet, wooded site north of town. Brochure and gift certificates available.

Hosts: Jack and Jessie Burkhardt
Rooms: 4 (S2B) $60-75
Full Breakfast
Minimum stay holidays: 2 nights
Credit Cards: A, B, C
Notes: 2, 5, 7, 8 (over 16), 9, 10, 11, 12, 13, 14

6 Pets welcome; 7 Smoking allowed; 8 Children welcome; 9 Social drinking allowed; 10 Tennis available; 11 Swimming available; 12 Golf available; 13 Skiing available; 14 May be booked through travel agents.

The Gray Goose

The Scofield House
Bed and Breakfast

908 Michigan Street, P. O. Box 761, 54235
(414) 743-7727

Described as "Door County's most elegant
bed and breakfast." Authentic bed and
breakfast in turn-of-the-century restored
Victorian Queen Anne house, circa 1902.
Prominent home of Sturgeon Bay Mayor
Bert Scofield. Very ornate interior with
inlaid floors and ornamented woodwork.
Six guest rooms, each with private bath.
Some with double whirlpool, fireplaces,
color TV/cable, VCR/stereo. Free movie
library. High Victorian decor throughout
with fine antiques. Air conditioned. Full
gourmet breakfast and afternoon complimentary sweet treats and teas. Call or write
for brochure.

Hosts: Bill and Fran Cecil
Rooms: 5 (PB) $65-175
Full Breakfast
Credit Cards: None
Notes: 2, 5, 9, 10, 11, 12, 13

White Lace Inn

16 North 5th Avenue, 54235
(414) 743-1105

The White Lace Inn is a romantic getaway
featuring three restored turn-of-the-century
homes surrounding lovely gardens and a
gazebo. The 15 wonderfully inviting guest
rooms are furnished in antiques with four-
poster and Victorian beds, in-room fireplaces in some rooms, and double
whirlpool tubs in others.

Hosts: Bonnie and Dennis Statz
Rooms: 15 (PB) $66-148
Continental Breakfast
Credit Cards: A, B, C
Notes: 2, 5, 9, 10, 11, 12, 13

WHITE LAKE

Wolf River Lodge

Highway 55, one-fourth mile north of Highway 64,
54491
(715) 882-2182

A historic country inn. Comfortable log
building. Handmade quilts and braided rugs
add warmth to the eight antique-filled guest
rooms. Full breakfast, restaurant, and pub.
Overlooks Wolf River. Serene, rustic,
wooded campground adjoins. White-water
rafting, canoeing, fishing, hunting, and
cross-country skiing. Equipment rental
available.

Hosts: Joe and Joan Jesse
Rooms: 8 (2 PB; 6 SB) $40-120
Full Breakfast
Credit Cards: A, B
Notes: 2, 3, 4, 5, 6 (limited), 7 (limited), 8, 9, 13,
    14

WHITEWATER

The Greene House Country
Inn and Guitar Gallery

Route 2, Box 214, Highway 12, 53190
(414) 495-8771; (800) 468-1959 outside Wisconsin

Put your feet up and relax in an authentic
1848 farmhouse or enjoy 100-plus miles of
hiking, biking, and horseback riding trails.
Superb cross-country skiing, antiquing,
outdoor music theater. Quiet, rural countryside 15 minutes north of Lake Geneva; a
two-hour drive to Chicago, and a one-hour
drive to Milwaukee and Madison. Group
bookings and weddings available.

NOTES: Credit cards accepted: A Master Card; B Visa; C American Express; D Discover Card; E Diner's
Club; F Other; 2 Personal Checks accepted; 3 Lunch available; 4 Dinner available; 5 Open all year;

White Lace Inn

Hosts: Lynn and Mayner Greene
Rooms: 7 (SB) $49-79
Full Breakfast
Credit Cards: A, B, C, D
Notes: 2, 3, 4, 5, 8, 9, 10, 11, 12, 13, 14

WILTON

Pahl's Bed and Breakfast

608 Railroad Street, P.O. Box 245, 54670
(608) 435-6434

At the midpoint of the Elroy-Sparta bicycle
trail, comfortable sleeping accommodations
and hearty breakfasts are at this bed and
breakfast for its guests. The hosts are more
than happy to accommodate special diets.
Amish communities, Wildcat Mountain
State Park, and Kickapoo are nearby.

Hosts: Carroll and Evelyn Pahl
Rooms: 4 (1 PB; 3 SB) $45-55
Full Breakfast
Credit Cards: A, B
Notes: 2, 5, 8, 11, 13

WISCONSIN DELLS

Bennett House

825 Oak Street, 53965
(608) 254-2500

Relax and enjoy romantic guest rooms and
fireside breakfasts at the Bennett House.
Picture celebrating your special occasion in
this gracious Victorian 1863 home that is
on the National Register of Historic Places.
Antiquing, eagles, greyhound racing, five
state parks, and river scenic tours are nearby.

Hosts: Gail and Rich Obermeyer
Rooms: 3 (1 PB; 2 SB) $65-85
Full Breakfast
Credit Cards: None
Notes: 2, 5, 9, 10, 11, 12, 13, 14

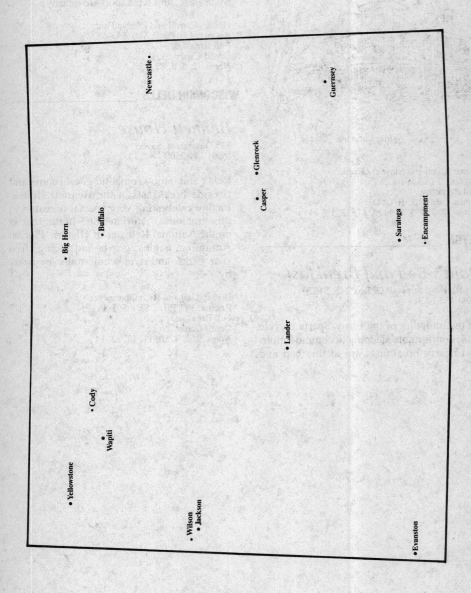

WYOMING

Wyoming

BIG HORN

Spahn's Bighorn Mountain Bed and Breakfast

Box 579, 82833
(307) 674-8150

Towering log home and secluded guest cabins on the mountainside in whispering pines. Borders one million acres of public forest with deer and moose. Gracious mountain breakfast served on the deck with binoculars to enjoy the 100-mile view. Owner was a Yellowstone Ranger. Just 15 minutes from Sheridan and I-90.

Hosts: Ron and Bobbie Spahn
Rooms: 4 (PB) $45-90
Full Breakfast
Credit Cards: A, B
Notes: 4, 5, 6 (call), 8, 9, 13 (XC)

BUFFALO

South Fork Inn

Box 854, 82834
(307) 684-9609

Located in the Big Horn National Forest, South Fork Inn is a rustic mountain lodge. There are ten guest cabins and a main lodge with a dining room and game room. Activities include horseback riding, fishing, hiking, biking, skiing, and many others.

Hosts: Ken and Patty Reid
Rooms: 10 (3 PB; 7 SB) $25-45
Full Breakfast
Credit Cards: None
Notes: 2, 3, 4, 6, 7, 8, 13

CASPER

Durbin Street Inn Bed and Breakfast

843 South Durbin Street, 82601
(307) 577-5774

Whether you are traveling for business or pleasure, you will feel right at home at the Durbin Street Inn. The 75-year-old house is furnished mostly in antiques and tastefully decorated to provide a warm, relaxed atmosphere. Full breakfast is included, and other meals are available. Food is plentiful and very good. Located in the "Big Tree" area within an easy walk of downtown Casper.

Hosts: Don and Sherry Frigon
Rooms: 4 (SB) $47.70-63.60
Full Breakfast
Credit Cards: A, B, C, D, E
Notes: 3, 4, 5, 7 (limited), 9, 11, 12, 13, 14

NOTES: Credit cards accepted: A Master Card; B Visa; C American Express; D Discover Card; E Diner's Club; F Other; 2 Personal Checks accepted; 3 Lunch available; 4 Dinner available; 5 Open all year; 6 Pets welcome; 7 Smoking allowed; 8 Children welcome; 9 Social drinking allowed; 10 Tennis available; 11 Swimming available; 12 Golf available; 13 Skiing available; 14 May be booked through travel agents.

CHEYENNE

Drummond's Ranch Recreation Bed and Breakfast

399 Happy Jack Road, Route 210, 82007
(307) 634-6042

Quiet, tranquil retreat conveniently situated between Cheyenne and Laramie in the Laramie Range, the scenic by-pass for I-80. Adjacent to state park and five miles to national forest; fishing, hiking, rock climbing, cross-country skiing. Bring your horse or mountain bicycle and train at 7,500 feet. Boarding for horses and family pets. Just get away from cars and crowds. Outdoor hot tub. Added touches: Flowers in room, terry-cloth robes for guests during stay; beverages, fresh fruit, and homemade snacks always available. No smoking, please. Reservations required.

Hosts: Kent and Taydie Drummond
Rooms: 3 (1 PB; 2 SB) $60-70
Full Breakfast
Credit Cards: None
Notes: 2, 3 & 4 (advance notice), 6, 8, 9, 13 (XC), 14

Howdy Pardner

P. O. Box 20972, Billings, MT 59104-0972
(406) 259-7993

Western atmosphere with a big Wyoming Welcome! Rural setting with view of mountains to the west. Comfortable modern rustic home on 10 country acres close to the junction of I-25 North/South and I-80 East/West. Near antelope, deer, and elk hunting, plus fishing. Five miles to Old West Museum and annual Frontier Days Daddy of 'Em All Rodeo at Frontier Park during the last full week in July.

Hosts: Jan and Don Peterson
Rooms: 3 (SB) $50
Full Breakfast
Credit Cards: A, B, C
Notes: 2, 5, 6, 7, 8, 9, 10, 11, 12, 13, 14

CODY

Hunter Peak Ranch

Box 1731, Painter Route, 82414
(307) 587-3711

Hunter Peak Ranch, at 6,700-foot elevation, is located in the Shoshone National Forest, with access to North Absaroka and Beartooth Wilderness Areas and Yellowstone. Come enjoy the area's photographic opportunities, hiking, horseback riding, and pack trips.

Hosts: Louis and Shelley Cary
Rooms: 8 (PB) $50
Full Breakfast
Minimum stay: 3 nights
Credit Cards: C
Closed December 15-May 15
Notes: 2 (deposit), 3, 4, 6, 7, 8, 9, 11, 14

The Lockhart Inn Bed and Breakfast

109 West Yellowstone Avenue, 82414
(307) 587-6074

The historical home of famous Cody author Caroline Lockhart. Built in the 1890s and refurbished from 1985 to 1991. Seven guest rooms, all with private baths, are decorated in turn-of-the-century style with modern conveniences. Enjoy breakfast in the dining area where coffee, tea, cider, and brandy are always available. Wood-burning stove in parlor with piano. Within walking distance of Buffalo Bill Historical Center, Cody Nite Rodeo, Old Trail Town, and river rafting.

Host: Cindy Baldwin
Rooms: 7 (PB) $55-75
Full Breakfast
Credit Cards: A, B, D, E
Notes: 2, 3, 5, 8, 9, 10, 11, 12, 13, 14

ENCAMPMENT

Lorraine's Bed and Breakfast Homestay

1016 Lomax, P. O. Box 685, 82325
(307) 327-5200

NOTES: Credit cards accepted: A Master Card; B Visa; C American Express; D Discover Card; E Diner's Club; F Other; 2 Personal Checks accepted; 3 Lunch available; 4 Dinner available; 5 Open all year;

Handcrafted lodge pole pine home. Nestled in the Medicine Bow Range Mountains in the historic town of Encampment. Wildlife abounds in the high country and may be seen in the open sagebrush, high mountain areas, and rugged hills. The recreation room is filled with wildlife mounts. It has a pool table, TV, fireplace, piano, and a relaxing atmosphere.

Host: Lorraine Knotwell
Rooms: 4 (S2B) $42
Full Breakfast
Credit Cards: A, B
Notes: 2, 5, 6, 8, 9, 10

Platt's Rustic Mountain Lodge

Star Route 49, 823325
(307) 327-5539

A peaceful mountain view and wholesome country atmosphere with lots of western hospitality, horseback riding, pack trips, fishing, hiking, rock hounding; fully guided tours available to ranch recreational activities and scenic mountain areas. Enjoy the flora and fauna, historic trails, and old mining camps, plus snowmobiling and cross-country skiing in the winter. By reservation only. Fishing cabin rentals available.

Hosts: Mayvon and Ron Platt
Rooms: 3 (SB) $35
Continental or Full Breakfast
Minimum stay: 2 nights
Credit Cards: None
Closed Thanksgiving and Christmas
Notes: 5, 6, 8, 9, 13

EVANSTON

Pine Gables Bed and Breakfast Inn

P. O. Box 1049, Center Street, 82930
(307) 789-2069

The 1883 restored Eastlake-style mansion has four guest rooms with private baths on the second floor. Rooms are furnished with 1880s-style furniture, and the antiques are original; there are no reproductions. A continental breakfast is served upstairs on an antique buffet each morning at 7:00 A.M. Evanston is located on I-80, 75 miles east of Salt Lake City, a convenient stop for travelers to Yellowstone Park. AAA approved.

Hosts: Arthur and Jessie Monroe
Rooms: 4 (PB) $36.50
Continental Breakfast
Credit Cards: A, B, C
Notes: 5, 7, 8, 9, 14

GLENROCK

Hotel Higgins

416 West Birch, 82637
(307) 436-9212; (800) 458-0144

A grand old hotel in its heyday (1916), the Hotel Higgins has been restored to its original grandeur, using original pieces of furniture and many collectibles. The hotel is listed on the National Register of Historic Places and has hosted regionally famous people from the early 1900s to present-day governors, senators, and congressmen. A full gourmet breakfast is served in sunny, private dining areas. The hotel boasts the award-winning Paisley Shawl Restaurant.

Hosts: Jack and Margaret Doll
Rooms: 8 (PB)
Full Breakfast
Credit Cards: A, B, C, E
Notes: 2, 3, 4, 5, 7, 8, 9, 10, 11, 12, 13, 14

GUERNSEY

Annette's Whitehouse

P. O. Box 31, 82214
(307) 836-2148

Annette's Whitehouse is in an area where there are many historical sites. Beautiful Lake Guernsey State Park, golfing, swimming, and fishing. The Platte River runs alongside the city, and nearby are three restaurants. Located on the way to Yellowstone in wonderful Wyoming. Two bedrooms share a bath.

6 Pets welcome; 7 Smoking allowed; 8 Children welcome; 9 Social drinking allowed; 10 Tennis available; 11 Swimming available; 12 Golf available; 13 Skiing available; 14 May be booked through travel agents.

Host: Annette Dombeck
Rooms: 2 (SB) $30
Full and Continental Breakfast
Credit Cards: None
Notes: 2, 5, 6, 8, 9, 10, 11, 12

JACKSON

The Wildflower Inn

P. O. Box 3724, 83001
(307) 733-4710

The Wildflower Inn

A lovely log home with five sunny guest rooms, this bed and breakfast is situated on three acres of land only five minutes from the Jackson Hole Ski Area, ten minutes from the town of Jackson, and thirty minutes to Grand Teton.

Hosts: Ken and Sherrie Jern
Rooms: 5 (PB) $110-130
Full Breakfast
Credit Cards: A, B
Notes: 2, 5, 8, 9, 10, 11, 12, 13

LANDER

Country Fare Bed and Breakfast

904 Main Street, 82520
(307) 332-5906

Country Fare is an adventure in old-fashioned charm. Enjoy the delicious English breakfasts, antique-filled bedrooms, and warm hospitality. Lander is the sports enthusiast's dream: hunting, fishing, hiking, snow sports, and more. On direct route to Yellowstone. Open May through October.

Hosts: A. R. and Mary Ann Hoyt
Rooms: 2 (SB) $50 plus tax
Full Breakfast
Credit Cards: A, B
Notes: 2, 5, 9, 10, 11, 12, 13, 14

LARAMIE

Annie Moore's Guest House

819 University Avenue, 82070
(307) 721-4177

Restored Queen Anne home with six individually decorated guest rooms, four with sinks. Large, sunny, common livingrooms, second-story sun deck. Across the street from the University of Wyoming; two blocks from the Laramie Plains Museum; six blocks from downtown shops, galleries, and restaurants. Just 15 minutes from skiing, camping, biking, and fishing in uncrowded wilderness areas.

Hosts: Ann Acuff and Joe Bundy
Rooms: 6 (SB) $50-60
Continental Breakfast
Credit Cards: A, B, C, D
Notes: 2, 5, 9, 14

NEWCASTLE

4W Ranch Recreation

1162 Lynch Road, 82701
(307) 746-2815

Looking for the unbeaten path? Spend a few days on this working cattle ranch with 20,000 acres of diversified rangeland to explore at your leisure. Rates include three meals a day.

Hosts: Bob and Jean Harshbarger
Rooms: 2 (SB) $60-100 American Plan
Full Breakfast
Credit Cards: B
Notes: 2, 3, 4, 5, 7, 8, 9

SARATOGA

Hotel Wolf

Box 1298, 82331
(307) 326-5525

NOTES: Credit cards accepted: A Master Card; B Visa; C American Express; D Discover Card; E Diner's Club; F Other; 2 Personal Checks accepted; 3 Lunch available; 4 Dinner available; 5 Open all year;

The Hotel Wolf, built in 1893, served as a stagecoach stop. During its early years, the hotel was the hub of the community and noted for its fine food and convivial atmosphere. The same holds true today. The dining room is acclaimed as one of the finest in the region. Nearby is a mineral hot springs.

Hosts: Doug and Kathleen Campbell
Rooms: 10 (6 PB; 4 SB) $21-35
Suite: 1 (PB) $75
Continental Breakfast
Credit Cards: A, B, C, E
Notes: 2, 3, 4, 5, 7, 8, 9, 10, 11, 12

WAPITI

Trout Creek Inn

Yellowstone U.S. Highway 14, 82414
(307) 587-6288

Imagine basking in the morning sunshine, a sumptuous breakfast on a lawn table, scenic mountains all around (unless you prefer privacy in your deluxe room). Located in the valley Theodore Roosevelt called the "world's most scenic." Private trout fishing, swimming, horseback riding, picture taking. Four kitchenettes available: accessible to the handicapped. Trout Creek Inn is part of a ranch.

Hosts: Bert and Norma Sowerwine
Rooms: 21 (PB) $56-88
Full Breakfast
Credit Cards: A, B, C, D
Notes: 5, 6, 7, 8, 9 11, 13, 14 (without commission)

WILSON

Teton Tree House

Box 550, 83014
(307) 733-3233

Helpful longtime mountain and river guides offer a special four-story, open-beam home on a forested mountainside. Large, rustic, but elegant rooms have exceptional views of the Jackson Hole Valley and mountains beyond. Generous, tasty, healthy, low-cholesterol breakfasts.

Hosts: Chris and Denny Becker
Rooms: 5 (PB) $90.95-123.05
Full Breakfast
Credit Cards: A, B, D
Notes: 5, 8 (no infants), 9, 10, 11, 12, 13, 14

Teton View
Bed and Breakfast

2136 Coyote Loop, Box 652, 83014
(307) 733-7954

Rooms all have mountain views, cozy country decor, own entrance, private deck overlooking Teton Mountain range, and comfortable lounge area with books and refrigerator. Convenient location to Yellowstone and Grand Teton national parks.

Hosts: John and Jo Engelhart
Rooms: 3 (1 PB; 2 SB) $48.15-96.95
Full Breakfast
Credit Cards: A, B
Notes: 2, 5, 6, 8, 9, 10, 11, 12, 13, 14

YELLOWSTONE-EAST

Elephant Head Lodge

Yellowstone U.S. Highway 14, 16, 20, 82450
(307) 587-3980

Historic Elephant Head Lodge, situated just 11 miles east of Yellowstone National Park, is an ideal base for touring the park and Cody. Even though it is small (and affordable), it has everything: riding, hiking, fishing, tubing, Western movies, warm hospitality, and wonderful food. Your family will make memories that will last a lifetime. Call or write.

Hosts: Phil, Gretchen, and Nicole Lamb
Rooms: 11 (PB) $50-65
Full Breakfast
Credit Cards: A, B, C
Notes: 2, 3, 4, 6, 7, 8, 9, 13, 14

6 Pets welcome; 7 Smoking allowed; 8 Children welcome; 9 Social drinking allowed; 10 Tennis available; 11 Swimming available; 12 Golf available; 13 Skiing available; 14 May be booked through travel agents.

Canada
Puerto Rico
Virgin Islands

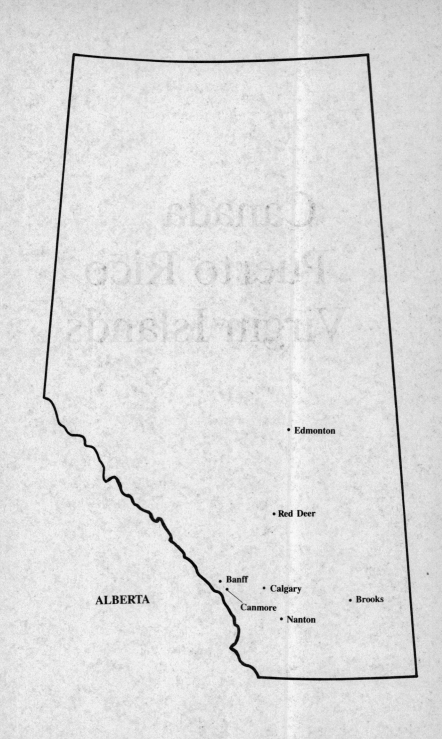

ALBERTA

• Edmonton

• Red Deer

• Banff   • Calgary
              Canmore   • Brooks
           • Nanton

Alberta

Brewster's Kananaskis Guest Ranch

Box 964, T0L 0C0
(403) 673-3737; FAX (403) 762-3953

The original Brewster Homestead offers cabin and chalet accommodations featuring antique furnishings, cedar interiors, and private showers/baths. On the shores of the Bow River, the guest ranch also has a licensed dining room and cocktail lounge, whirlpool, trail riding, and western barbecues. Golfing, white-water rafting, hiking, and mountain biking opportunities also available. Just 45 minutes west of Calgary; 30 minutes east of Banff.

Hosts: The Brewster Family
Rooms: 29 (PB) $88
Full Breakfast
Credit Cards: A, B
Notes: 3, 4, 7, 8, 9, 11, 12, 14

BROOKS

Alberta Bed and Breakfast 3

P. O. Box 15477, MPO,
Vancouver, BC, V6B 5B2
(604) 944-1793

A country inn offering four double rooms, each with private bath, air-conditioned throughout. A full country breakfast is served in the solarium. The "Gathering Room" with fireplace is for guests' use. Pets are welcome to stay in the heated kennels. Sportsmen have on-site facilities for cleaning their catch, with freezer storage.

CALGARY

Alberta Bed and Breakfast 1

P. O. Box 15477, MPO,
Vancouver, BC, V6B 5B2
(604) 944-1793

Older home built in 1902 offers three very large guest rooms with shared bath. Within walking distance to downtown Calgary, numerous restaurants, and fashionable Mount Royal Village Fort boutique shopping. Minutes away from LRT for transportation to Stampede Grounds and the annual Calgary Exhibition and Stampede.

CANMORE

Cougar Creek Inn

P. O. Box 1162, T0L 0M0
(403) 678-4751

Quiet, rustic cedar chalet with mountain views in every direction. Grounds border on Cougar Creek and back onto land reserve area. There is hiking out your back door with wildlife often spotted. Hostess is an outdoor enthusiast with a strong love for mountains; she can assist your plans for local hiking, skiing, canoeing, mountain biking, and back-packing. Barbecue, bonfire pit, private entrance. Fireplace, sitting room with TV, games, private dining and serving area, sauna.

Host: Patricia Doucette
Rooms: 4 (S2B) $55-60 Canadian
Full Breakfast

NOTES: Credit cards accepted: A Master Card; B Visa; C American Express; D Discover Card; E Diner's Club; F Other; 2 Personal Checks accepted; 3 Lunch available; 4 Dinner available; 5 Open all year; 6 Pets welcome; 7 Smoking allowed; 8 Children welcome; 9 Social drinking allowed; 10 Tennis available; 11 Swimming available; 12 Golf available; 13 Skiing available; 14 May be booked through travel agents.

Credit Cards: None
Notes: 2 (for deposit), 3, 5, 8, 9, 10, 11, 12, 13

Haus Alpenrose

629 9th Street, P.O. Box 723, T0L 0M0
(403) 678-4134

Haus Alpenrose is a small, rustic lodge in the town of Canmore, the very heart of the Canadian Rockies. The Alpenrose is built in a Bavarian chalet style, with a recreational lodge for the outdoor enthusiast. It offers rooms for two to four people, with private or shared bathrooms, kitchen access, and a large lounge. Hosts speak German and French. The Alpenrose is also home to the Canadian School of Mountaineering, where hiking and climbing trips and courses are offered in the summer, cross-country skiing and ice-climbing instruction in the winter. Close to Banff National Park, Kananaskis Provincial Park, and Assiniboine Provincial Park.

Hosts: Ottmar and Ulrike Setzer
Rooms: 9 (4 PB; 5 SB) $55-65, seasonal
Full Breakfast
Credit Cards: A, B
Notes: 5, 8, 9, 10, 11, 12, 13, 14

EDMONTON

Alberta
Bed and Breakfast 2

P. O. Box 15477, MPO,
Vancouver, BC, V6B 5B2
(604) 944-1793

Home is within walking distance to West Edmonton Mall. Sauna, hot tub, and deck available for guests. Two spacious double and one single bedroom with a shared bath.

Chez Suzanne Bed and Breakfast

18603, 68 Avenue, T5T 2M8
(403) 487-2071

The hosts sincerely like people and love to hear their travel stories! Relax and enjoy the privacy of one entire level of their home. Unwind by the fireplace with books, games, TV, or VCR movies. There is a refrigerator and beverage station for your convenience. Three bedrooms are available, and families are welcome. Laundry facilities or airport pick-ups are also available at slight cost. Neighborhood restaurants offer a pleasant stroll and Wiedmonton Mall and Jasper Highway are five minutes away. The hosts will go over maps and directions with you and, if you wish, suggest the best routes or attractions. "Prince," the cat, will also be delighted to make your acquaintance.

Hosts: Suzanne and Paul Croteau
Rooms: 3 (1 PB; 2 SB) $45-50
Full or Continental Breakfast
Credit Cards: None
Notes: 2, 4, 5, 8, 9

NANTON

Alberta B&B 5

P. O. Box 15477, MP0
Vancouver, BC, V6B 5B2
(604) 944-1793

A small ranch in the beautiful foothills of the Canadian Rockies. The hosts keep cattle, horses, and sheep. Two guest rooms and shared bath. Horseback riding is available, as well as fishing in nearby lake and mountain streams.

Timber Ridge Homestead

P.O. Box 94, T0L IR0
(403) 646-5683 (summer); (403) 646-2480 (winter)

Timber Ridge Homestead is a rustic establishment in the beautiful foothills of ranching country about 70 miles southwest of Calgary. There are good, quiet horses to help you explore the abundant wildflowers, wildlife, and wonderful views of the Rockies. Good, plain cooking, if you want it.

NOTES: Credit cards accepted: A Master Card; B Visa; C American Express; D Discover Card; E Diner's Club; F Other; 2 Personal Checks accepted; 3 Lunch available; 4 Dinner available; 5 Open all year;

Hosts: Bridget Jones and family
Rooms: 3 (SB) $25 Canadian
Full Breakfast
Credit Cards: None
Notes: 2, 3, 4, 8, 9

Situated approximately midway between Edmonton and Calgary, this home offers a bungalow with upstairs guest room, downstairs guest room with adjacent sitting room, and one guest bath.

RED DEER

Alberta Bed and Breakfast 6

P. O. Box 15477, MP0,
Vancouver, BC, V6B 5B2
(604) 944-1793

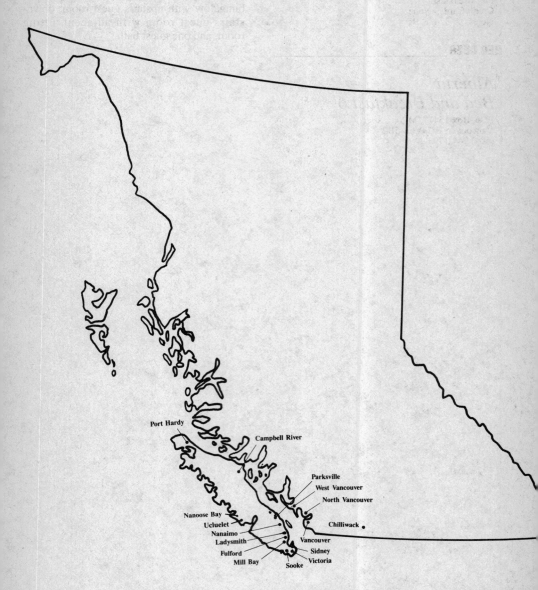

BRITISH COLUMBIA

British Columbia

BRENTWOOD BAY

Brentwood Bay Bed and Breakfast

7247 West Saanich Road, Box 403, V0S 1A0
(604) 652-2012

A homey heritage house, circa 1912 , this bed and breakfast is outside the city, yet close enough to pop in and come back each evening for a restful sleep and a hearty three-course breakfast for those staying in the suite. Home cooking, with whole-wheat breads, fresh fruit cobblers, juices, and jams, brings guests back again after eight years of welcoming them from all over the world. There is so much to see and do that a two-night stay is recommended, and a relaxing week is a delightful way to discover the area. Victoria is 20 miles away; Butchart Gardens and Butterfly World are down in the village.

Host: Evelyn Hardy
Rooms: 7 (4 PB; 3 SB) $65-135
Full or Continental Breakfast
Credit Cards: None
Notes: 2, 5, 8, 9, 14

CAMPBELL RIVER

The Grey Mouse

All Seasons Bed and Breakfast Agency
P. O. Box 5511, Station "B," Victoria, V8R 6S4
(604) 655-7173

Welcoming seaside home on sandy beach. Sport court for tennis, volleyball, basketball, and shuffleboard. Hot tub. Nature trails and golf course in immediate area,

and beachcombing on the doorstep. Nordic and alpine skiing 45 minutes away. Full breakfast served in the dining room. $55.

CHILLIWACK

Charterre Bed and Breakfast

45360 Hodgins Avenue, V2P 1P5
(604) 795-0088

Bright, beautiful Victorian rooms are available in an 1885 heritage farmhouse. Close to shopping, hospital, fairgrounds, and sports facilities. There is golf, swimming, sailing, hiking, and skiing in the immediate area.

Hosts: Lorne and Iris Gehman
Rooms: 4 (SB) $55
Full Breakfast
Credit Cards: None
Notes: 2, 5, 9

FULFORD HARBOR

Weston Lake Inn Bed and Breakfast

813 Beaver Point Road, Rural Route 1, V0S 1C0
(604) 653-4311

Nestled on a knoll of flowering trees and shrubs overlooking beautiful Weston Lake, this exquisite country bed and breakfast is a serene adult getaway. Down quilts, fresh bouquets, a fireside lounge, hot tub, wonderful breakfasts, and warm hospitality. Recommended in *Northwest Best Places*, the Vancouver *Sun*, and the Seattle *Times*.

NOTES: Credit cards accepted: A Master Card; B Visa; C American Express; D Discover Card; E Diner's Club; F Other; 2 Personal Checks accepted; 3 Lunch available; 4 Dinner available; 5 Open all year; 6 Pets welcome; 7 Smoking allowed; 8 Children welcome; 9 Social drinking allowed; 10 Tennis available; 11 Swimming available; 12 Golf available; 13 Skiing available; 14 May be booked through travel agents.

Salt Spring Island, near Victoria, has a mild climate, exceptional beauty, and a large population of artists and artisans.

Hosts: Susan Evans, Ted Harrison, and Brian Clarkson
Rooms: 3 (PB) $80-100
Full Breakfast
Credit Cards: A, B
Notes: 2, 5, 9, 10, 11, 12, 14

LADYSMITH

Manana Lodge and Marina

4760 Brenton Page Road, Rural Route 1, V0R 2E0
(604)245-2312

On a secluded bay in Ladysmith Harbour. Facilities include waterfront licensed dining room, gift shop, boat rentals, moorage, gas, ice, bait, groceries, laundry, and tidal water swimming. The accommodations consist of guest rooms and one-bedroom cabins. Enjoy complimentary use of canoe and mountain bikes. Reservations are recommended. 14-day cancellation policy.

Hosts: Jim and Ruth Bangay; Don and Gail Kanelakos
Rooms: 6 (4 PB; 2 SB) $55-85
Full Breakfast
Credit Cards: A, B
Notes: 4, 5, 8, 14

MILL BAY

Pine Lodge Farm Bed and Breakfast

3191 Mutter Road, V0R 2P0
(604) 743-4083

A charming pine lodge built on a 30-acre farm overlooking ocean and islands. Walking trails, farm animals, and deer and magnificent arbutus trees add to the paradiselike setting. Antique-filled lodge with stained-glass windows features cozy bedrooms with private bathrooms, furnished with beautiful antiques. Enjoy a full breakfast with homemade jams, and then browse

through a spectacular collection of antiques. Featured in *Country Living* and on CBS television.

Hosts: Cliff and Barbara Clarke
Rooms: 8 (PB) $65-95
Full Breakfast
Credit Cards: A, B
Notes: 2, 5, 9, 14

NANAIMO

Carey House

All Seasons Bed and Breakfast Agency
P. O. Box 5511, Station "B," Victoria, V8R 6S4
(604) 655-7173

Wonderful Scottish hospitality close to downtown ferry, bus terminal, and historic Hudson's Bay Bastion and museum. Offers a suite with queen bed, kitchenette, recreation room with TV, private bath and entrance. Also, one double and one single room sharing a bath. $30-55.

NANOOSE BAY

The Lookout at Schooner Cove

3381 Dolphin Drive, V0R 2R0
(604) 468-9796

Situated halfway between Victoria and Tolfino, this cedar home is set in tall evergreens with a 180-degree view of the Georgia Strait and the majestic mountains beyond. Relax on the wraparound deck in this little bit of heaven and enjoy the passing boats, Alaskan cruise ships, eagles, and whales. Fairwinds Golf Course, Schooner Cove Marina and Resort are within one-half mile. Hearty breakfast is served on the deck when you want it.

Hosts: Marj and Herb Wilkie
Rooms: 3 (2 PB; 1 SB) $50-70
Full Breakfast
Credit Cards: None
Notes: 8 (over 10), 9, 10, 11, 12, 13, 14

NOTES: Credit cards accepted: A Master Card; B Visa; C American Express; D Discover Card; E Diner's Club; F Other; 2 Personal Checks accepted; 3 Lunch available; 4 Dinner available; 5 Open all year;

Somerville's By The Sea

All Seasons Bed and Breakfast Agency
P. O. Box 5511, Station "B," Victoria, V8R 6S4
(604) 655-7173

Beautiful contemporary home on the Strait of Georgia. Explore the tidal pools below the separate suite that contains a queen bedroom, sitting room with TV, private bath, deck, and entrance. Two single sofabeds complete the scene. Another suite is also available. There is a wood-burning fireplace where guests can cook up a steak or a salmon. Horseback riding nearby, as is Fairwinds Golf Course and Schooner Cove Marina. Enjoy a melt-in-your-mouth breakfast. $75-85.

NORTH VANCOUVER

Helen's Bed and Breakfast

302 East 5th Street, V7L 1L9
(604) 985-4869

Welcome to this old Victorian home, its charm and comfort enhanced by antiques, wonderful views, and color cable TV in each room. Five blocks to the Pacific; 20 minutes to the Horseshoe Bay ferries to Victoria; minutes to Grouse Mountain Sky Ride, Whistler Ski Resort, restaurants, and shopping. Gourmet breakfast served in elegant dining room. Ten percent senior discount; 10 percent discount from November-April. Member of the North Vancouver Chamber of Commerce.

Host: Helen Boire
Rooms: 3 (1 PB; 2 SB) $65 plus
Full Breakfast
Credit Cards: B
Closed Christmas
Notes: 2, 5, 7, 8, 9, 10, 11, 12, 13

Laburnam Cottage Bed and Breakfast

1388 Terrace Avenue, V7R 1B4
(604) 988-4877

Set on one-half acre of award-winning English garden, nestled against a forest, yet only fifteen minutes from downtown Vancou-ver. Each of the upstairs guest rooms in the main house has its own decor, featuring delicate wallpapers, stunning antiques, and invitingly warm colors complemented by magnificent garden views. Breakfasts are jolly occasions in the big farmhouse-style kitchen near the cozy Aga cookers where all enjoy a full three- or four-course meal.

Hosts: Delphine and Margot Masterton
Rooms: 3, plus 2 cottages (PB) $95-125
Full Breakfast
Credit Cards: None

Old English Bed and Breakfast Registry

P. O. Box 86818, V7L 4L3
(604) 986-5069; FAX (604) 986-8810

The Old English Bed and Breakfast Registry is a professional reservation service. We represent 45 bed and breakfast homes in the Greater Vancouver area, as well as Victoria and Vancouver Island. Each home has been personally inspected and will provide you with a friendly, hospitable, and relaxing stay in our area. Let us know what you require, and we will do our utmost to please you. All prices include breakfast and free parking. Visa and MasterCard accepted. Open all year. $65 and up.

Old English Bed and Breakfast 1

P. O. Box 86818, V7L 4L3
(604) 986-5069

This deluxe accommodation includes a one-bedroom suite located on beachfront property just 40 minutes from downtown Vancouver. The decor is romantic to the last detail, including a fireplace. You have the ocean at your doorstep and the moun-

6 Pets welcome; 7 Smoking allowed; 8 Children welcome; 9 Social drinking allowed; 10 Tennis available; 11 Swimming available; 12 Golf available; 13 Skiing available; 14 May be booked through travel agents.

tains at your back. Breakfast is served by Elisabeth in the dining room that overlooks the ocean. You can catch the train to Whistler Mountain or Lillooet in the heart of B.C. right outside your door. $105.

Old English Bed and Breakfast 2

P. O. Box 86818, V7L 4L3
(604) 986-5069

Jane pampers you year round in your own private garden suite in North Vancouver. Tastefully decorated with fine antiques, the suite is very cozy and romantic. It is complete to every detail, including fireplace, TV, stereo, and private patio. Prepare yourself for the memorable gourmet breakfast that awaits you each morning in this first-class accommodation. Close to beaches and mountains and only 20 minutes to downtown Vancouver. Children welcome. $85.

Old English Bed and Breakfast 3

P. O. Box 86818, V7L 4L3
(604) 986-5069

This gracious home with a Victorian air is located on a quiet tree-lined street in the lovely Kerrisdale area of Vancouver. Your queen-sized bedroom has a private four-piece bathroom. There is a small sitting room with a fireplace adjoining your bedroom. Your hostess Lydele will serve you breakfast in the intimacy of your own room, on the sun deck, or in the dining room. Just 12 minutes from the airport and downtown Vancouver. Bus service is nearby. $65.

Old English Bed and Breakfast 4

P. O. Box 86818, V7L 4L3
(604) 986-5069

This North Vancouver Bed and Breakfast is charm plus. You have your own ground-level studio suite with queen bed, potbelly fireplace, TV, and patio. Beautifully decorated in old country style. Barb, your hostess, will leave food for you to prepare at your convenience, or you are invited to enjoy breakfast with the family. 15 minutes to downtown. $65.

Old English Bed and Breakfast 5

P. O. Box 86818, V7L 4L3
(604) 986-5069

You will receive the royal treatment at Giselle's Bed and Breakfast in North Vancouver. This Bed and Breakfast is nestled on a very large lot that has natural, parklike setting. Accommodations consist of three rooms, one with private bath and large Jacuzzi tub. Each room is equipped with TV and telephone. Giselle will bring you coffee and the morning paper to start your day before breakfast is served. $65-75.

Pacific Bed and Breakfast Agency NVAN-1

701 Northwest 60th Street, Seattle, WA, 98107
(206) 784-0539

One acre of seclusion a short ten-minute ride over the Lions Gate Bridge from downtown. At the end of a dead end street with a creek running through the award-winning English gardens and a fountain. This Tudor house is furnished with antiques with a distinctly British influence and offers you a queen room with private bath, a twin room with shared bath, and two private cottages. Breakfast is served in the oversized kitchen around a big table and will surely include some special surprises and a different elegant setting every morning. German and French spoken. $85-105 Canadian.

NOTES: Credit cards accepted: A Master Card; B Visa; C American Express; D Discover Card; E Diner's Club; F Other; 2 Personal Checks accepted; 3 Lunch available; 4 Dinner available; 5 Open all year;

The Platt's Bed and Breakfast

4393 Quinton Place, V7R 4A8
(604) 987-4100

Just 15 to 20 minutes to the heart of town and famous Stanley Park. Close to the Capilano suspension bridge, fish hatchery, and the Cleveland Dam. Quiet parklike area, ideal for cycling. Homemade bread and jams featured at breakfast.

Hosts: Nancy and Elwood Platt
Rooms: 2 (PB) $50 US
Full Breakfast
Credit Cards: None
Notes: 2, 5, 8 (over 10), 9, 10, 11, 12

Sue's Victorian Guest House

152 East 3rd, V7L 1E6
(604) 985-1523

This lovely, restored 1904 nonsmoking home is just four blocks from the harbor, seabus terminal, and Quay market. Centrally located for restaurants, shops, and transportation. The decor is ideal for those who appreciate that loving-hand touch, Victorian soaker baths (no sharers), and are happy to remove outdoor shoes at the door to help maintain cleanliness. Each

Sue's Victorian Guest House

room is individually keyed and offers a TV, phone, fan and video player. Minimum stay is three nights in busy seasons; long-term stays encouraged. Two resident cats.

Host: Sue Chalmers
Rooms: 3 (1 PB; 2 SB) $55-60
Continental Breakfast
Credit Cards: None
Notes: 2 (deposit only)

PARKSVILLE

Loon Watch

All Seasons Bed and Breakfast Agency
P. O. Box 5511, Station "B," Victoria, V8R 6S4
(604) 655-7173

A gracious welcome awaits on Columbia Beach, close to Parksville or Qualicum. Fishermen will delight in local salmon fishing. Beachcomb or visit the many local artists and craftspeople. Cathedral Grove with its 500-year-old trees is a treat. Watch ships going up the Inside Passage to Alaska as you lie in your bed or relax on your private deck. Full breakfast. $45-55.

PORT HARDY

Audrey's Bed and Breakfast

All Seasons Bed and Breakfast Agency
P. O. Box 5511, Station "B," Victoria, V8R 6S4
(604) 655-7173

The Island Highway ends at the sea, and Port Hardy is the southern terminus of Prince Rupert Ferry. From this tasteful home you can enjoy a sea view to the Mainland Glacier 150 miles away. Charter bus service to ferry available. Full or continental breakfast. $35-50.

SIDNEY

Ease-Mate

All Seasons Bed and Breakfast Agency
P. O. Box 5511, Station "B," Victoria, V8R 6S4
(604) 655-7173

6 Pets welcome; 7 Smoking allowed; 8 Children welcome; 9 Social drinking allowed; 10 Tennis available; 11 Swimming available; 12 Golf available; 13 Skiing available; 14 May be booked through travel agents.

Welcoming contemporary home in Cape Cod-style with extensive grounds, home to a well-known West Coast artist. Furnished in antique pine. One very large bedroom with bath and Hide-a-bed is ideal for two or more. Close to Butchart Gardens and Washington State ferries. Only 20 minutes to Victoria. Full breakfast. $75.

Ocean Wilderness

Graham's Cedar House Bed and Breakfast

1825 Lands End Road, V8L 3X9
(604) 655-3699; FAX (604) 655-1422

Spectacular West Coast home on acreage where tall trees and magnificent ferns surround the house. Relish the peace and quiet, walk among the trees, or to the beach. Enjoy either the romantic executive suite or a one- or two-bedroom apartment for up to six people. All rooms feature a private bath, private entrance, patio, deck, and TV. Breakfast is served at your convenience. Close to Butchart Gardens, Victoria, marinas, USA and Canadian ferries.

Hosts: Dennis and Kay Graham
Rooms: 3 (PB) $65-85
Full Breakfast
Credit Cards: B
Notes: 2, 5, 9, 10, 12, 14

Orchard House

All Seasons Bed and Breakfast Agency
P. O. Box 5511, Station "B," Victoria, V8R 6S4
(604) 655-7173

Original farmhouse owned by the family who helped develop Sidney. Built in the early 1900s, it retains original features while offering total comfort. A five-minute walk to the ferry, and within walking distance of beach, tennis, shops, and restaurants. Full breakfast served in the panelled dining room. $65.

Seaside

All Seasons Bed and Breakfast Agency
P. O. Box 5511, Station "B," Victoria, V8R 6S4
(604) 655-7173

Unsurpassed accommodation in contemporary house on the water's edge overlooking tidal pools, ocean, and mountains beyond. Watch for sea lions and passing grey whales. Only one suite in this splendid setting consisting of bedroom with private bath, sitting room with sofa beds, and private patio leading to the large swimming pool. Close to parks, bird sanctuaries, and Olympic golf club. A relaxed, restful retreat. Minimum stay of two nights. $120.

SOOKE

Ocean Wilderness

109 West Coast Road, Rural Route 2, V0S 1N0
(604) 646-2116

Romantic hideaway on the west coast of Vancouver Island, 30 miles from Victoria. Relax in the hot tub and watch the moonlight on the ocean! On five acres with oceanfront and private beach. Private entrances, patios, and large, luxurious rooms furnished with canopied beds and antiques. Watch the whales, sea lions, and eagles. Explore hiking trails and beaches. A bird watcher's paradise.

NOTES: Credit cards accepted: A Master Card; B Visa; C American Express; D Discover Card; E Diner's Club; F Other; 2 Personal Checks accepted; 3 Lunch available; 4 Dinner available; 5 Open all year;

Host: Marion Paine
Rooms: 7 (PB) $75-150 US
Full Breakfast
Credit Cards: A, B
Notes: 2, 4 (by arrangement), 5, 6 (by arrangement), 8 (by arrangement) 9, 12, 14

UCLUELET

Burley's

1078 Helen Road, Box 550, V0R 3A0
(604) 726-4444

A waterfront home on a small island at the harbor mouth, offering single, double, and queen, water or regular beds, and TV in friendly Ucluelet. Enjoy the open ocean, sandy beaches, lighthouse lookout, nature walks, charter fishing, diving, fisherman's wharves,whale watching and sightseeing cruises, or later, the exhilarating winter storms. A view from every window. No pets; no smoking. Adult oriented. French spoken.

Hosts: Ron Burley and Micheline Riley
Rooms: 6 (S4B) $40-50
Full Breakfast
Credit Cards: A, B
Notes: 5, 10, 11, 12

VANCOUVER

Diana's Luxury Bed and Breakfast

1019 East 38 Avenue, V5W 1J4
(604) 321-2855

This bed and breakfast is ten minutes from the airport and ten minutes from downtown Vancouver. Open all year, it is close to shopping, restaurants, Stanley Park, Whistler ski area, and theaters. Guest accommodations include four guest rooms with shared bath, common livingroom with TV; a honeymoon suite with private bath, TV, Jacuzzi, and phone; and a self-contained one-bedroom apartment. Reservations with a one-night deposit required.

Hosts: Diana and Danny
Rooms: 6 (2 PB; 4 SB) $60 US
Full Breakfast
Credit Cards: A, B
Notes: 5 , 7, 8, 9, 10, 11, 12, 13, 14

Kenya Court Guest House

2230 Cornwall Avenue, V6K 1B5
(604) 738-7085

Ocean-view suites on the waterfront, in a gracious heritage building minutes from downtown Vancouver. Across the street are tennis courts, a large heated saltwater pool, and walking and jogging paths along the water's edge. It's an easy walk to Granville Island, the planetarium, and interesting shops and restaurants. All the suites are large and tastefully furnished. Breakfast is served in a glass solarium with a spectacular view of English Bay.

Host: D. M. Williams
Suites: 4 (PB) $85-105
Full Breakfast
Credit Cards: F
Notes: 2, 5, 9, 10, 11

Pacific Bed and Breakfast Agency VAN-1

701 Northwest 60th Street, Seattle, WA, 98107
(206) 784-0539

A gracious 1920 Colonial that offers guests two bedrooms, one with two twin beds, one with a double bed, and a shared bathroom. Enjoy the sun deck, garden, den, and private breakfast room. Take a walk down the quiet tree-lined street or take the bus to the many attractions in the area. The host is a long-time resident and is available to assist guests with sightseeing plans. $50-55 U.S.

Pacific Bed and Breakfast Agency VAN-2

701 Northwest 60th Street, Seattle, WA, 98107
(206) 784-0539

6 Pets welcome; 7 Smoking allowed; 8 Children welcome; 9 Social drinking allowed; 10 Tennis available; 11 Swimming available; 12 Golf available; 13 Skiing available; 14 May be booked through travel agents.

With a view of Kitsilano Beach, the North Shore Mountains, English Bay, and downtown Vancouver, this guest house is in the best location for a peaceful, cozy getaway. This guest house features large, tastefully decorated rooms with king, queen, or twin beds, and private entrances. Breakfast may consist of gourmet coffees, juices, fruits, croissants, fresh breads, cereal, or for the hearty eaters eggs and bacon, served in a glass-enclosed solarium. $65-100 Can-adian.

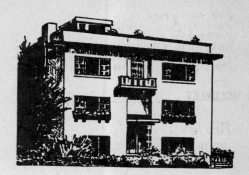

Kenya Court Guest House

Pacific Bed and Breakfast Agency VAN-3

701 Northwest 60th Street, Seattle, WA, 98107
(206) 784-0539

This Tudor house is furnished with antiques with a distinctly British influence and offers guests a guest room with a queen-size bed with a private bath, or one with twin and double beds, as well as two private cottages. Breakfast is served in the oversized kitchen and will include some special suprises and a different elegant setting every morning. Grouse Mountain and other attractions are nearby. $65-75 Canadian.

Pacific Bed and Breakfast Agency VAN-4

701 Northwest 60th Street, Seattle, WA, 98107
(206) 784-0539

This cozy country heritage guest home features three private rooms with sitting area, cable TV, and private bath. Enjoy the full farm breakfasts in the morning and take a dip in the large outdoor heated pool or soak in the whirlpool. $40-55 U.S.

Peloquin's Bed and Breakfast

Town & Country Bed and Breakfast in B.C.
P. O. Box 74542, 2803 West Fourth Avenue, V6K 1K2
(604) 731-5942

This comfortable, newly decorated home is in a quiet, central neighborhood. Your hospitable hosts speak French and Ukranian, and enjoy sharing helpful information on the city. Close to restaurants, shops, parks, major bus lines. Two guest rooms. Full breakfast. $60.

Pillow and Porridge

Town & Country Bed and Breakfast in B.C.
P. O. Box 74542, 2803 West Fourth Avenue, V6K 1K2
(604) 731-5942

Rest and relax in your home away from home. You have a choice of three lock and keyed bedrooms, each with a unique character. Antiques and collectibles from around the world are found throughout the house. A hearty breakfast featuring pancakes, eggs cooked any style, cereals, fresh fruits and juices, muffins, and wild oat porridge topped with fruit, nuts, sunflower seeds and brown sugar. In the City Hall Heritage area.

Town & Country Bed and Breakfast in British Columbia

P. O. Box 74542, 2803 West Fourth Avenue, V6K 1K2
(604) 731-5942

NOTES: Credit cards accepted: A Master Card; B Visa; C American Express; D Discover Card; E Diner's Club; F Other; 2 Personal Checks accepted; 3 Lunch available; 4 Dinner available; 5 Open all year;

We offer bed and breakfast homes in residential areas of Vancouver and Victoria, and our listings include some small inns. A few of our listings have waterfront or special views. Private and shared baths available. Homes have from one to three guest rooms. Some character homes, some West Coast-style homes, or town house accommodations.

The West End Guest House

1362 Hard Street, V6E 1G2
(604) 681-2889; FAX (604) 688-8812

This heritage house was constructed in 1906 and was occupied by one of the city's first photographers. Today, the West End Guest House offers the informal ambience of a fine country inn, the amenities of a small luxury hotel, and the excitement of its surroundings, such as shopping on Robson Street, a walk in Stanley Park, a peak at the zoo, possibly a splash at the Whale Show, or a romantic gaze at a sunset on English Bay. Rooms include a bathroom, TV, telephone, off-street parking, bathrobes and slippers, full breakfast, use of two bikes, and a sun deck with wicker furniture where on a hot summer day iced tea is served. Sherry is provided year round in front of the fireplace.

Rooms: 7 (PB) $95-175
Full Breakfast
Credit Cards: A, B, C, D
Notes: 2, 5, 10, 11, 12, 13

VICTORIA

Arundel Manor

All Seasons Bed and Breakfast Agency
P. O. Box 5511, Station "B," V8R 6S4
(604) 655-7173

Gracious heritage home on one-half acre of lawns and gardens, a short drive from city centre. The property slopes to an inlet. Superb sunset views. Full breakfast served in the handsome dining room, or on the veranda. All rooms have private baths. Two rooms have balconies overlooking the water. Special gatherings or small weddings can be arranged. Honeymoons are special. $90-95.

Arundel Manor

Battery Street Guest House

670 Battery Street, V8V 1E5
(604) 385-4632

This newly renovated guest house, built in 1898, offers bright, comfortable rooms centrally located within walking distance to downtown. The bed and breakfast is only one block from Beacon Hill Park and Victoria's scenic marina. A full, hearty breakfast is served by your Dutch hostess. No smoking.

Host: Pamela Verduyn
Rooms: 6 (2 PB; 4 SB) $60-75
Full Breakfast
Credit Cards: None
Notes: 2, 5, 8

Bowden House

All Seasons Bed and Breakfast Agency
P. O. Box 5511, Station "B," V8R 6S4
(604) 655-7173

Built in 1913, this quiet, comfortable character home has been personally restored by the owners. It has high ceilings and the relaxed charm and ambience of the traditional Bed and Breakfast. Wake up to the aroma of fresh coffee and a hearty English breakfast. Stroll through Banfield Park overlooking the Seilerk Water. Guest rooms share bathrooms. $45-60.

Camellia House

All Seasons Bed and Breakfast Agency
P. O. Box 5511, Station "B," V8R 6S4
(604) 655-7173

Tucked away in a quiet residential area close to Oak Bay Village shopping, recreation centre, and ocean walks. Camellia House offers a relaxing atmosphere, original 1913 charm, and convenient access to downtown. $45-55.

Garden City Bed and Breakfast

660 Jones Terrace, V8Z 2L7
(604) 479-9999; (604) 479-1986

For the ultimate in relaxation, as well as areas for discovery and excitement, it's Vancouver Island. Many carefully chosen and varied accommodations will provide city convenience, country cottage, or heritage with antiques. Or try the smaller nearby islands–Quadra, Gabriola, Saturna, Mayne, or Saltspring. One call to Doreen, and you will receive careful, personal attention at no fee to you, and total satisfaction according to your requests.

Hanging Baskets

All Seasons Bed and Breakfast Agency
P. O. Box 5511, Station "B," V8R 6S4
(604) 655-7173

Nicely decorated, cozy home in parklike setting five minutes to Butchart Gardens. Ideal for those wanting quiet slumber, comfort, and charm. Close to Mill Bay ferry and Brentwood Bay. Golf courses nearby. Full breakfast. $50-60.

Holly House

All Seasons Bed and Breakfast Agency
P. O. Box 5511, Station "B," V8R 6S4
(604) 655-7173

A tasteful contemporary home close to airport, ferries, and aviation museum. Take a morning jog or a leisurely walk through the nearby stand of trees, or enjoy a dip in the private swimming pool. Hearty breakfasts. Children welcome. $49-65.

Huckleberry Inn

All Seasons Bed and Breakfast Agency
P. O. Box 5511, Station "B," V8R 6S4
(604) 655-7173

One of the jewels of the Victorian era built by a famous architect. Located in an area of tall trees, winding road, and mansion houses only a few minutes from downtown or Oak Bay Village. Buffet breakfast is served in the dining room. A warm, friendly atmosphere. French spoken. $75-115.

The Little Garden Bed and Breakfast

5373 Patricia Bay Highway, V8Y 1S9
(604) 658-8404

This hobby farm is centrally located overlooking Elk Lake only ten kilometers (6 miles) from downtown Victoria. Four character rooms offer all the charm of the country with antique furnishings, guest rooms with lake and garden views, comfortable parlor, and full country-style breakfast. Convenient to ferries, airport, downtown, and Butchart Gardens.

Hosts: Paul and Elizabeth Gregory
Rooms: 4 (1 PB; 3 SB) $50-75
Full Breakfast
Credit Cards: A, B
Notes: 2, 5, 8, 9, 11, 12, 14

Mikkers

All Seasons Bed and Breakfast Agency
P. O. Box 5511, Station "B," V8R 6S4
(604) 655-7173

Spacious new home overlooking quiet farmland with a great view of Mount

Baker. Island View Beach is just a short drive away. One room with Jacuzzi, one with fireplace. Dutch and German spoken. $45-60.

Our Home on the Hill Bed and Breakfast

546 Delora Drive, V9C 3R8
(604) 474-4507

A warm welcome, as well as peace and quiet, awaits you just twenty minutes from downtown Victoria. Enjoy the shady seclusion of the yard, relax amid the yesteryear charm of the antique-accented home, stroll along the ocean just moments away, or take a dip in the sheltered hot tub. Each upstairs bedroom has a double bed and shares a bath. A guest sitting room is available. Your hearty breakfast includes special homemade jams, fresh muffins, and a hot entree.

Hosts: Grace and Arnie Holman
Rooms: 3 (1 PB; 2 SB) $55
Full Breakfast
Credit Cards: None
Notes: 2, 5, 8, 10, 11, 12, 14

Pacific Bed and Breakfast Agency VIC-A

701 Northwest 60th Street, Seattle, WA, 98107
(206) 784-0539

A turn-of-the-century home one block to the beach and a grand beach walk. It offers three bedrooms, one with a private bath and fireplace, favorite with honeymooners. The spacious livingroom and dining room welcome you to sit back and relax with your German hostess. She will fix you a memorable breakfast. Discover the wonderful Beacon Hill Park close by. On a bus line. $60-75 Canadian.

Pacific Bed and Breakfast Agency VIC-B

701 NW 60th Street, Seattle, WA, 98107
(206) 784-0539

An elegant, refined small inn with ten bedrooms. Two blocks to the harbor and within walking distance of everything. All rooms have private baths and decks. The breakfasts are either served to you in the dining room or in your own room. Ideal for your honeymoon, anniversary, or that special weekend. Unequalled comfort and charm with original art by the premier artists of Victoria. $100-160 Canadian.

Pacific Bed and Breakfast Agency VIC-C

701 Northwest 60th Street, Seattle, WA, 98107
(206) 784-0539

Cordova Bay. Here is luxury at a modest cost. This lodge features oversized rooms with private baths, refrigerators, and TV. Some rooms have kitchenettes. This residential area is 15 minutes from Victoria and close to Butchart Gardens, airport, and ferries. A delicious full breakfast is served. Golfing, skiing, water skiing, fresh and salt water fishing, swimming, and walking are just some of the activities waiting for you. $55-75 Canadian.

Pacific Bed and Breakfast Agency VIC-D

701 Northwest 60th Street, Seattle, WA, 98107
(206) 784-0539

Lakefront mansion. Turn-of-the-century mansion on 17 acres with frontage on a large lake. Built by prominent architect Samuel McClure, this special guest home features waterfront garden paths to enjoy

6 Pets welcome; 7 Smoking allowed; 8 Children welcome; 9 Social drinking allowed; 10 Tennis available; 11 Swimming available; 12 Golf available; 13 Skiing available; 14 May be booked through travel agents.

while watching the graceful swans. Tennis court and billiard room with a magnificent antique table. Visit the famous Forest Open Air Museum. Three distinctively decorated guest rooms share a bath. $95-120 Canadian.

Pacific Bed and Breakfast Agency VIC-E

701 Northwest 60th Street, Seattle, WA, 98107
(206) 784-0539

A truly fine mansion reflecting the Edwardian Tudor Revival style popular in British Columbia in the early years of the century. Minutes away from the inner harbor and the many attractions of Victoria. Most of the 14 rooms have ocean views, and others have a garden view. All suites are self-contained with private baths and full kitchens. Breakfast supplies are stocked in each refrigerator. $75-135 Canadian.

Pacific Bed and Breakfast Agency VIC-F

701 Northwest 60th Street, Seattle, WA, 98107
(206) 784-0539

An exceptional house located on half an acre overlooking Portage Inlet. This house is three miles from the inner harbor and is furnished with antiques. Many views are available in this guest home featuring five bedrooms. Two rooms have private balconies, and all rooms have private baths. A sumptuous gourmet breakfast is provided to start your day's activities. $80-100 Canadian.

Pacific Bed and Breakfast Agency VIC-2

701 Northwest 60th Street, Seattle, WA, 98107
(206) 784-0539

The hostess of this wonderful bed and breakfast is dedicated to her guests and shows this dedication in everything she does for you, from the welcome drink to the delicious breakfasts. This two-story house, built in 1885, features a high ceiling, fireplaces, charm, and fine antiques. One room has a private bath, the others share a bath. Your breakfast will be served on fine china in the formal dining room. $65-100.

Pacific Bed and Breakfast Agency VIC-4

701 Northwest 60th Street, Seattle, WA, 98107
(206) 784-0539

This guest home was built in 1899. It is now restored and offers three bedrooms with shared bath. Antiques fill the house and complement the original woodwork fireplaces, floors, and fittings. A memorable, full breakfast changes from day to day. $70-80 Canadian.

Park Royale House

All Seasons Bed and Breakfast Agency
P. O. Box 5511, Station "B," V8R 6S4
(604) 655-7173

Exquisitely furnished contemporary West Coast home set in an English country lane. Bright sunny rooms with private baths. The suite offers queen bed, fireplace, sun deck with water glimpses, and exercise equipment. A short stroll to nearby historic pub and restaurant. Heartfelt welcome awaits you here. Full breakfast. $75.

Prior House

All Seasons Bed and Breakfast Agency
P. O. Box 5511, Station "B," V8R 6S4
(604) 655-7173

Elegant English mansion built in 1912 for the King's representative in British Columbia. Enjoy the relaxed ambience of

NOTES: Credit cards accepted: A Master Card; B Visa; C American Express; D Discover Card; E Diner's Club; F Other; 2 Personal Checks accepted; 3 Lunch available; 4 Dinner available; 5 Open all year;

days gone by. Canopied beds, down comforters, down comforters, private baths, and working fireplaces in every room. Breakfast is served in the panelled dining room overlooking the large garden terrace. Afternoon tea in the parlor. $110-190.

Rose Cottage

3059 Washington Avenue, V9A 1P7
(604) 381-5985

Rose Cottage is a large, attractive 1912 Victorian-style home located on a quiet street. Robert and Shelley work very hard to create a warm, fun, and informal atmosphere with lots of sharing between guests and hosts. Shelley serves a four-course breakfast that sustains one all morning. Robert has sailed and traveled extensively; he loves stimulating conversation over breakfast or on the porch watching a sunset. Their information about the area will guide you to the best of Victoria.

Hosts: Robert and Shelley Bishop
Rooms: 3 (S2B) $55-75 Canadian
Full Breakfast
Credit Cards: A, B
Notes: 2, 5, 8, 9, 11, 12, 14

Shirewood

All Seasons Bed and Breakfast Agency
P. O. Box 5511, Station "B," V8R 6S4
(604) 655-7173

Rose Cottage

Large English Tudor home nestled on four acres with space to roam and relax. Discover bed and breakfast in a little bit of Olde England. Two suites with private entrances, each with large bed/sitting rooms. Resident dog and cat. $55-80.

Sigrid's Bed and Breakfast

Town & Country Bed and Breakfast in B.C.
P. O. Box 74542, 2803 West Fourth Avenue, V6K 1K2
(604) 731-5942

This modern home, directly across from the beach and park, has a magnificent view of sea and mountains. German is a second language. Bus stops in front; 15 minutes to downtown, and ten minutes to UBC. Swimming, sailing, tennis, and Jericho Nature Park are all five minutes away. Two guest rooms. Breakfast is served from 7:30 to 9:30 A.M. $65-75.

Sunnymeade House Inn

1002 Fenn Avenue, V8Y 1P3
(604) 658-1414

Take the scenic route into Victoria and discover this inn on a winding country road by the sea. The Thompsons designed, built, and decorated the custom-finished English country-style house. Nancy, a former professional cook, will prepare a choice breakfast for you. You'll be steps away from the beach, there is a lovely new golf course and restaurant just a block from the house, and the village shops and great little restaurants are within walking distance. Come and join Jack and Nancy for their sixth season at Sunnymeade.

Hosts: Jack and Nancy Thompson
Rooms: 6 (2 PB; 4 SB) $69-109
Full or Continental Breakfast
Credit Cards: A, B
Notes: 2, 5, 9, 10, 12, 14

Top O' Triangle Mountain

3442 Karger Terrace, V9C 3K5
(604) 478-7853; FAX (604) 478-2245

6 Pets welcome; 7 Smoking allowed; 8 Children welcome; 9 Social drinking allowed; 10 Tennis available; 11 Swimming available; 12 Golf available; 13 Skiing available; 14 May be booked through travel agents.

Spacious, solid, cedar home overlooking Victoria, Juan de Fuca Strait, and Olympic Mountains in Washington. Enjoy fresh air, quiet, comfortable rooms, hearty breakfasts, friendly hosts. Close to golf courses, swimming, parks, just 22 minutes to the heart of Victoria. A peaceful retreat!

Hosts: Henry and Pat Hansen
Rooms: 3 (PB) $60-85 Canadian
Full Breakfast
Credit Cards: A, B
Notes: 5, 7 (limited), 8, 11, 12, 14

Wellington Bed and Breakfast

66 Wellington Avenue, V8V 4H5
(604) 383-5976

Situated just one-half block from the scenic Pacific Ocean bordered by a panoramic walkway, three blocks from beautiful Beacon Hill Park, this 1912 inn offers you a taste of true Victorian hospitality. All rooms have private baths, walk-in closets, large windows, king or queen beds, and are wonderfully appointed. The quiet, tree-lined street allows for the most restful sleep, and the breakfasts are a delight.

Hosts: Inge and Sue Ranzinger
Rooms: 3 (PB) $60-75 US
Full Breakfast
Credit Cards: A
Notes: 2, 5, 9, 10, 11, 12, 14

WEST VANCOUVER

Beachside Bed and Breakfast

4208 Evergreen Avenue, V7V 1H1
(604) 922-7773; (800) 563-3311
FAX (604) 926-8073

Stay in a quiet, beautiful, waterfront home in one of the finest areas in Vancouver. A lovely beach is at the doorstep. Minutes from downtown, Stanley Park, Horseshoe Bay ferries, and North Shore attractions. Its southern exposure affords a panoramic view of the city, harbor, and Alaska Cruise ships. A hearty home-baked breakfast is served in the seaside dining room. Close to fishing, sailing, wilderness hiking, skiing, antiques, shopping, and excellent restaurants.

Hosts: Gordon and Joan Gibbs
Rooms: 3 (PB) $95-150 Canadian
Full Breakfast
Credit Cards: A, B
Notes: 2, 5, 9, 10, 11, 12, 13, 14

Beachside Bed and Breakfast Agency

4208 Evergreen Avenue, V7V 1H1
(604) 922-7773; (800) 563-3311
FAX (604) 926-8073

We offer warm, Canadian hospitality in pleasant, well-maintained, tastefully decorated homes. Rooms have good quality beds and private baths. Full breakfast is served by environmentally conscious hosts. No smoking. Close to amenities. We inspect to maintain our uncompromising standards. We offer superior quality that you can count on. Don't settle for less than Beachside's "Standard of Excellence." You'll come to expect those touches that make your vacation memorable. Deposit required. Cancellation notice 14 days in advance. Visa and MasterCard accepted.

Beachside

NOTES: Credit cards accepted: A Master Card; B Visa; C American Express; D Discover Card; E Diner's Club; F Other; 2 Personal Checks accepted; 3 Lunch available; 4 Dinner available; 5 Open all year;

Manitoba

BOISSEVAIN

Dueck's Cedar Chalet

Box 362, R0K 0E0
(204) 534-6019

Situated three-fourths of a mile north of the town of Boissevain, Cedar Chalet offers accommodations with complete privacy, including Jacuzzi, color TV, refrigerator, and coffee percolator. Also offered is a motor home, which is air-conditioned, fully equipped to sleep six, and allows you to sightsee in the area for $50 plus 12 cents a mile. Car rental is also available. Extra meals by prearrangement. English, German, and some French spoken. Boissevain is the home of the Canadian Turtle Derby. The chalet is near the golf course and offers a heated outdoor swimming pool, playground, Turtle Mountain Provincial Park, lake fishing, nature trails, horseback riding, and the International Peace Gardens.

Hosts: Hilda and Henry Dueck
Rooms: 2-4 (SB) $40-50
Full Breakfast
Credit Cards: None
Notes: 2, 5, 6, 8, 11, 12, 13, 14

BRANDON

Casa Maley Bed and Breakfast

1605 Victoria Avenue, R7A 1C1
(204) 728-0812

For a unique family atmosphere and display of genuine hospitality, stay at this European-style, three-story Tudor house. Built in 1912 of red brick, the home has been designated a Heritage sight. There are many antiques and antique furnishings. For breakfast you have a choice of the host's specialties—mouth-watering French toast, delicious omelets, fluffy pancakes.

Host: W. J. Shwaluk
Rooms: (PB) $40
Full Breakfast
Credit Cards: B
Notes: 2, 3, 4, 5, 8, 9, 10, 11, 12, 13

RICHER

Geppetto

Bed and Breakfast of Manitoba
93 Healy Crescent, Winnipeg, R2N 2S2
(204) 256-6151

Enjoy your stay in a quiet and attractive modern home with country-style hospitality. Outdoor activities include bird-watching, horseshoes, fishing in stocked trout pond, 27-hole golfing. 45 minutes from Falcon Lake Beach; 25 minutes from Steinbach shopping center and Mennonite Heritage Village. $45.

THOMPSON

Anna's Bed and Breakfast

Bed and Breakfast of Manitoba
93 Healy Crescent, Winnipeg, R2N 2S2
(204) 256-6151

Open all year, Anna and Robert invite you to share their comfortable home and warm Dutch hospitality. Pickup at airport and train station. Completely private quarters and private bath. Come and enjoy the heart of the north! $30-45.

6 Pets welcome; 7 Smoking allowed; 8 Children welcome; 9 Social drinking allowed; 10 Tennis available; 11 Swimming available; 12 Golf available; 13 Skiing available; 14 May be booked through travel agents.

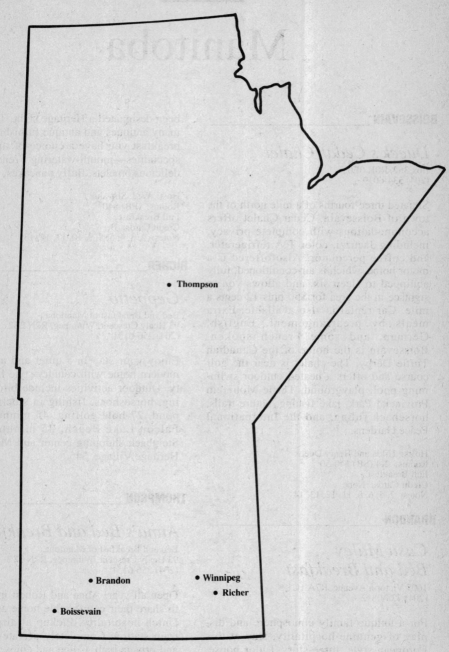

Thompson

Brandon   **Winnipeg**

          Richer

Boissevain

MANITOBA

WINNIPEG

Alego

Bed and Breakfast of Manitoba
93 Healy Crescent, R2N 2S2
(204) 256-6151

Walk in Fraser's Grove Park along the Red
River. Frequent bus service, restaurants,
and shopping nearby. Convenient to Bird's
Hill Park, Rainbow Stage, beaches, and
museums. Full breakfast. $30-40.

Bannerman East

Bed and Breakfast of Manitoba
93 Healy Crescent, R2N 2S2
(204) 256-6151

Come and enjoy this lovely Georgian
home, evening tea, quiet walks in St. Johns
Park or along the Red River. Close to
Seven Oaks Museum, planetarium, concert
hall, and Rainbow Stage. $40.

Belanger

Bed and Breakfast of Manitoba
93 Healy Crescent, R2N 2S2
(204) 256-6151

Enjoy the relaxing atmosphere in this special home built in 1900. Sitting room adjacent to guest bedroom. Can accommodate a
family of four. $40.

Bright Oaks
Bed and Breakfast

137 Woodlawn Avenue, R2M 2P5
(204) 256-9789

Guests can relax in comfortable, spacious
bedrooms, play a tune on the grand piano,
or swing in a hammock in the back yard.
The four-level split home with many
antique furnishings is located on a half-acre
of landscaped grounds near the river and
the university restaurants, with quick and
easy access to St. Boniface and downtown
attractions. A full breakfast can be enjoyed
on the patio overlooking the gardens.

Hosts: Francis and Anya Lobreau
Rooms: 3 (1 PB; 2 SB) $40-45
Full Breakfast
Credit Cards: None
Notes: None

Drenker

Bed and Breakfast of Manitoba
93 Healy Crescent, R2N 2S2
(204) 256-6151

Enjoy a private and pleasant stay in this
quiet, neat home. Located in old St.
Boniface, it is within a short walking distance of the Forks, the St. Boniface
Hospital, and downtown. Near museum,
Manitoba Theatre Centre, concert hall, and
paddlewheel boats. $45.

Ellie

Bed and Breakfast of Manitoba
93 Healy Crescent, R2N 2S2
(204) 256-6151

This downtown accommodation in a peaceful neighborhood is near good bus service,
two major hospitals, the zoo, convention
center, concert hall, museums, theatre centre, planetarium, the Forks, bus depot, and
Via Rail. $45-47.

Fillion

Bed and Breakfast of Manitoba
93 Healy Crescent, R2N 2S2
(204) 256-6151

Located in a nice community setting close
to the Trans-Canada Highway city route.
Nearby attractions include the mint, St.
Vital Mall, Fun Mountain Waterslide,
Tinkertown, outdoor pool, and bicycle
path. $40.

6 Pets welcome; 7 Smoking allowed; 8 Children welcome; 9 Social drinking allowed; 10 Tennis available; 11
Swimming available; 12 Golf available; 13 Skiing available; 14 May be booked through travel agents.

Hawchuk

Bed and Breakfast of Manitoba
93 Healy Crescent, R2N 2S2
(204) 256-6151

Located on the banks of the Red River, this beautiful Tudor home has English gardens and a riverbank walkway. Top off the day with a paddlewheel boat dinner cruise. English, German, and French spoken. For an additional charge, a full-course dinner is available. $69.

Hillman

Bed and Breakfast of Manitoba
93 Healy Crescent, R2N 2S2
(204) 256-6151

Cozy private sitting room, full breakfast of your choice. Located downtown, close to bus route, airport, Polo Park, planetarium, concert hall, and theatre centre. $45.

Irish

Bed and Breakfast of Manitoba
93 Healy Crescent, R2N 2S2
(204) 256-6151

This beautifully furnished home is the place for quiet, private, and relaxed stays. Come and enjoy well-travelled hosts and educational conversation. Located near the racetracks, good restaurants, Grace Hospital, and shopping. $30-40.

Johnson

Bed and Breakfast of Manitoba
93 Healy Crescent, R2N 2S2
(204) 256-6151

Located in a quiet residential area with a very private yard for sunbathing. Private kitchen available. near two public swimming pools, Assiniboia Downs Racetrack, shopping centres. and Living Prairie Museum. Children welcome. $40.

Narvey

Bed and Breakfast of Manitoba
93 Healy Crescent, R2N 2S2
(204) 256-6151

This quiet, attractive, comfortable home in the River Heights area offers a family room, garden, and good hospitality. Excellent bus service, city wide. Close to downtown, Assinboine Park and Zoo, the Forks, Grant Park, and Polo Park shopping malls. $32-42

Paulley

Bed and Breakfast of Manitoba
93 Healy Crescent, R2N 2S2
(204) 256-6151

Quiet, comfortable, and relaxing, and within walking distance of the Convention Center, Manitoba Archives, tourist bureau, shopping, direct bus route to the Via Rail, the historic Forks site, and three hospitals. One block south of the Trans-Canadian Highway. $30-40.

Preweda

Bed and Breakfast of Manitoba
93 Healy Crescent, R2N 2S2
(204) 256-6151

Enjoy complete privacy in lower level with a spacious and attractive sitting lounge. Excellent transit service and public library. Quick access to the Mint, the Forks, downtown, Osborne Village, and St. Boniface Hospital. $45.

Ronald

Bed and Breakfast of Manitoba
93 Healy Crescent, R2N 2S2
(204) 256-6151

Our home is spacious, luxurious, quiet, and on the banks of the Assiniboine River. Enjoy a lovely evening walk, bird watching, tennis, and game room. Close to

NOTES: Credit cards accepted: A Master Card; B Visa; C American Express; D Discover Card; E Diner's Club; F Other; 2 Personal Checks accepted; 3 Lunch available; 4 Dinner available; 5 Open all year;

Assiniboia Downs Racetrack, city parks, Unicity Mall, winter cross-country skiing. the specialty is home-baked bread. $40.

Ryz

Bed and Breakfast of Manitoba
93 Healy Crescent, R2N 2S2
(204) 256-6151

These amiable hosts will provide you with hospitality you enjoy. A cozy home in a beautiful neighborhood of Wildwood Park is perfect for evening walks, bicycling, and golfing. Quick access to the University of Manitoba, the University of Winnipeg, Osborne Village, Crescent Park, downtown Winnipeg Convention Center.

Selci

Bed and Breakfast of Manitoba
93 Healy Crescent, R2N 2S2
(204) 256-6151

Very private facilities in this private home can accommodate a family of four. A warm welcome to guests, and quick access to the Trans-Canada Highway. $30-40.

Siemens

Bed and Breakfast of Manitoba
93 Healy Crescent, R2N 2S2
(204) 256-6151

Warm hospitality and quiet relaxation! Can accommodate a family of five. Close to the express bus route, Unicity Mall, Assiniboina Downs, shopping, restaurants, and recreation. $38-40.

Tidmarsh

Bed and Breakfast of Manitoba
93 Healy Crescent, R2N 2S2
(204) 256-6151

This attractive older home is located in the quiet, tree-lined River Heights area. Guest sitting room on mezzanine floor with tea and coffee making facilities. Choose your breakfast from an ample menu. Close to Polo Park shopping centre, the Forks, and casino. Enjoy the English-style hospitality. $40-42.

Zonneveld

Bed and Breakfast of Manitoba
93 Healy Crescent, R2N 2S2
(204) 256-6151

Enjoy a relaxed atmosphere in this unique three-story home with a beautiful oak interior. Excellent transit service, near downtown, will pick up at the airport. Quick access to the Forks, zoo, hospital, and Dainavert museum. $30-40.

6 Pets welcome; 7 Smoking allowed; 8 Children welcome; 9 Social drinking allowed; 10 Tennis available; 11 Swimming available; 12 Golf available; 13 Skiing available; 14 May be booked through travel agents.

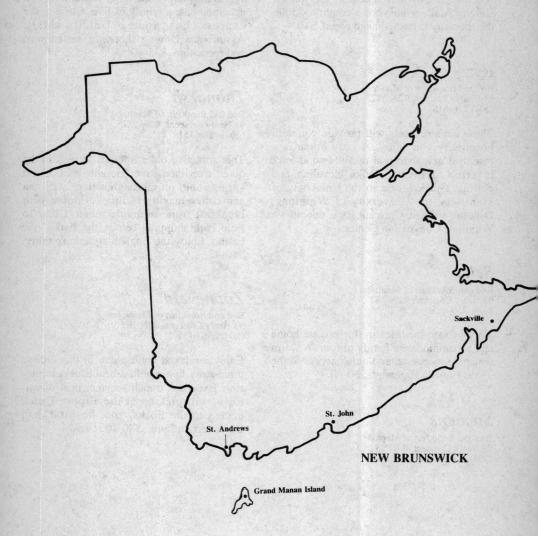

Sackville

St. John

St. Andrews

Grand Manan Island

NEW BRUNSWICK

New Brunswick

GRAND MANAN ISLAND

Shorecrest Lodge

North Head, E0G 2M0
(506) 662-3216

A Victorian country inn located on a unique island blessed with an abundance of wildflowers, whales, and birds. The sweeping veranda overlooks flower beds and the sea. Catch-of-the-day dinner specials are fresh from the Bay of Fundy and served with locally grown herbs and vegetables.

Hosts: Andrew and Cynthia Normandeau
Rooms: 16 (2 PB; 14 SB) $50-60 Canadian
Buffet Breakfast
Credit Cards: B
Notes: 2, 3, 4, 7, 8, 9, 10, 11, 12

SACKVILLE

The Different Drummer

P.O. Box 188, 82 West Main Street, E0A 3C0
(506) 536-1291

Welcome to the Different Drummer Bed and Breakfast. Here you can enjoy the comforts and conveniences of modern living in a restful and homey atmosphere. Attractive bedrooms are furnished much as they would have been at the turn of the century, and they all have private baths. In the large parlor and adjacent sun room, guests can chat, browse through a well-stocked library, watch color TV, or just relax. A continental breakfast is served each morning; enjoy home-baked bread, muffins, local honey, freshly ground coffee, and berries in season.

Hosts: Georgette and Richard Hanrahan
Rooms: 8 (PB) $48-51
Expanded Continental Breakfast
Credit Cards: A, B
Notes: 5, 8, 9, 10, 11, 12, 13

ST. ANDREWS

Pansy Patch

59 Carleton Street, E0G 2X0
(506) 529-3834

A turreted 80-year-old house is a combination bookshop (used and rare), antique shop, and bed and breakfast. All rooms are furnished in antiques, paintings, and prints, and all overlook the Bay of Fundy. Evening meals feature the freshest fish and vegetables, and home-baked rolls and breads. This should be a destination, rather than a one-night stay, in order to enjoy the comely gardens and village. Host also caters to special diets.

Host: Kathleen Lazare
Rooms: 4 (S2B) $75 (Canadian)
Full Breakfast
Credit Cards: A, B, C
Notes: 2, 4, 9, 10, 11, 12, 14

The Different Drummer

NOTES: Credit cards accepted: A Master Card; B Visa; C American Express; D Discover Card; E Diner's Club; F Other; 2 Personal Checks accepted; 3 Lunch available; 4 Dinner available; 5 Open all year; 6 Pets welcome; 7 Smoking allowed; 8 Children welcome; 9 Social drinking allowed; 10 Tennis available; 11 Swimming available; 12 Golf available; 13 Skiing available; 14 May be booked through travel agents.

Rossmount

Rural Route 2, E0G 2X0
(506) 529-3351

The inn is a three-story manor house with 16 rooms, all distinctive and spacious. Furnished with antiques from all over the world, each room includes its own private bath, and there is a choice of bed sizes. The inn dining room has been awarded four stars from AAA.

Hosts: Lynde Chambers and Lorne McCullough
Rooms: 16 (PB) $85-95
Continental Breakfast
Credit Cards: A, B
Notes: 2, 4, 6, 7 (limited), 8, 9, 10, 11, 12, 14

SAINT JOHN

The Quaco Inn

Beach Street, St. Martins, E0G 2T0
(506) 833-4772

The Quaco Inn is a Victorian inn consisting of seven lovely rooms (two suites), named after sea captains of the area. St. Martins of the 1800s. Enjoy breakfast in the unhurried dining room with an atmosphere of warmth and personal attention. Antiques from the 1800s are throughout the inn, and bay windows have lovely views of the Bay of Fundy. Like a visit to Grandmother's.

Host: M. Jackson
Rooms: 7 (PB) $60-90
Full Breakfast
Credit Cards: A, B
Notes: 4, 5, 9, 11, 14

NOTES: Credit cards accepted: A Master Card; B Visa; C American Express; D Discover Card; E Diner's Club; F Other; 2 Personal Checks accepted; 3 Lunch available; 4 Dinner available; 5 Open all year;

Nova Scotia

AMHERST

Amherst Shore Country Inn

Rural Route 2, B4H 3X9
(902) 667-4800

Not far from Amherst, the Amherst Shore Country Inn offers a quiet seaside escape from your busy lifestyle. With comfortable accommodations in private rooms, suites, or cottages and country-style gourmet meals, you'll find this renovated century-old farmhouse the perfect place to escape from it all and relax. The ocean is a two-minute walk from your room, and the private beach is 600 feet long, and safe for all ages.

Hosts: Donna and Jim Laceby
Rooms: 4 , plus one cottage (PB) $69-99
Full Breakfast ($5 each)
Credit Cards: A, B
Notes: 4 (by reservation), 9, 11, 14

ANNAPOLIS ROYAL

The Poplars
Bed and Breakfast

124 Victorian Street, Box 277, B0S 1A0
(902) 532-7936

This restored Victorian home is situated in the heart of Canada's oldest permanent European settlement. A Registered Heritage site, it is shaded by huge 300-year-old poplars. Color cable TV in the family room, evening coffee and conversation. Two blocks from other amenities.

Host: Iris Williams
Rooms: 9 (6 PB; 3 SB) $35-50 plus tax
Continental Breakfast
Credit Cards: B
Notes: 5, 8, 9

CHESTER

Mecklenburgh Inn

78 Queen Street, B0J 1J0
(902) 275-4638

A welcoming bed and breakfast in the heart of Chester, renowned seaside village/resort area. Rooms are spacious and comfortably appointed. Gourmet breakfasts are served around the big dining table before a crackling wood fire. The perfect home base from which to explore the area, browse the shops, or relax after a sail on the bay or a round of golf.

Host: Sue Fraser
Rooms: 4 (S2B) $55-60
Full Breakfast
Credit Cards: B
Notes: 2, 3, 6, 8, 9, 10, 11, 12, 14

LOUISBOURG

Greta Cross
Bed and Breakfast

81 Pepperell Street, B0A IM0
(902) 733-2833

An older home situated off Main Street on a hill overlooking the harbor and the Fortress of Louisbourg. In a quiet area, it offers guests kitchen privileges and a babysitting service is also available. Home-

---

6 Pets welcome; 7 Smoking allowed; 8 Children welcome; 9 Social drinking allowed; 10 Tennis available; 11 Swimming available; 12 Golf available; 13 Skiing available; 14 May be booked through travel agents.

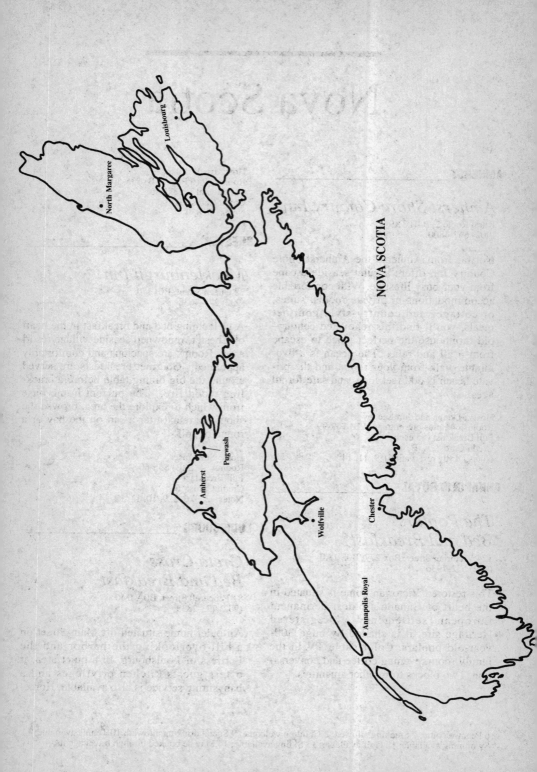

baked breads, muffins, oatcakes, and jams are provided for breakfast, and a snack is served on arrival if desired.

Hostess: Greta Cross
Rooms: 3 (SB) $35-40
Full Breakfast
Credit Cards: C
Notes: 2, 6, 8, 9, 10, 11

NORTH MARGAREE

Heart of Hart's Tourist Home, Ltd.

Northeast Magaree, Box 21, B0E 2H0
(902) 248-2765

This home is situated near the famous Margaree Salmon River on fifty acres. The house is furnished with antiques and colonial glass. The home's second floor has fine, comfortably furnished guest rooms with two shared baths. A TV is located in the lounge, along with lots of reading material. Swimming, canoeing, bicycling, hiking, or fishing are readily at hand. The home is conveniently situated for day trips to Cabot Trail or to various museums in the area.

Host: Mary Hart
Rooms: 5 (S2B) $45
Full Breakfast
Credit Cards: None
Notes: 2, 7, 8, 9

PUGWASH

The Blue Heron Inn

P. O. Box 405, Route 6, Durham Street, B0K 1L0
(902) 243-2900; (902) 243-2516 (off-season)

Five tastefully restored rooms in the village of Pugwash, close to warm-water beaches, craft shops, an 18-hole golf course, and tennis courts. In-season is June 10 through Labor Day.

Hosts: Bonnie Bond and John Caraberis
Rooms: 5 (2 PB; 3 SB) $42-54
Continental Breakfast
Credit Cards: B
Notes: 2, 8

SMITH'S COVE

Harbourview Inn

P. O. Box 39, 25 Harbourview Road, B0S 1S0
(902) 245-5686

A turn-of-the-century village inn overlooking the tidal waters of the beautiful Annapolis Basin, the inn is furnished in Victorian country fashion and has welcomed summer guests since the 1890s. Harbourview offers you a freshwater pool, tennis court, and an ocean beach for clamming, rock hounding, and viewing the world's most dramatic tides. Meals are served daily in a fully licensed dining room. Fresh local seafoods are featured.

Hosts: Mona and Phillip Webb
Rooms: 12 (PB) $55-75 (Canadian)
Full Breakfast
Credit Cards: A, B
Notes: 2, 4, 7, 8, 9, 10, 11, 12, 14

WOLFVILLE

Blomidon Inn

127 Main Street, P. O. Box 839, B0P 1X0
(902) 542-2291; FAX (902) 542-7461

Operated by hosts Jim and Donna Laceby, the Blomidon Inn has a reputation for elegant accommodation and gracious country cuisine—a reputation that extends beyond the province of Nova Scotia. This 19th-century sea captain's mansion is situated on four acres of terraces and spaded lawns in the heart of Wolfville. The inn is open year round and features 26 guest rooms, all of which offer private baths. For your business needs, it boasts two handsome meeting rooms with seating up to 35, which is great for meetings, seminars, or retreats.

Hosts: Jim and Donna Laceby
Rooms: 26 (PB) $69-119
Continental Breakfast
Credit Cards: A, B
Notes: 3, 4, 5, 10, 14

NOTES: Credit cards accepted: A Master Card; B Visa; C American Express; D Discover Card; E Diner's Club; F Other; 2 Personal Checks accepted; 3 Lunch available; 4 Dinner available; 5 Open all year; 6 Pets welcome; 7 Smoking allowed; 8 Children welcome; 9 Social drinking allowed; 10 Tennis available; 11 Swimming available; 12 Golf available; 13 Skiing available; 14 May be booked through travel agents.

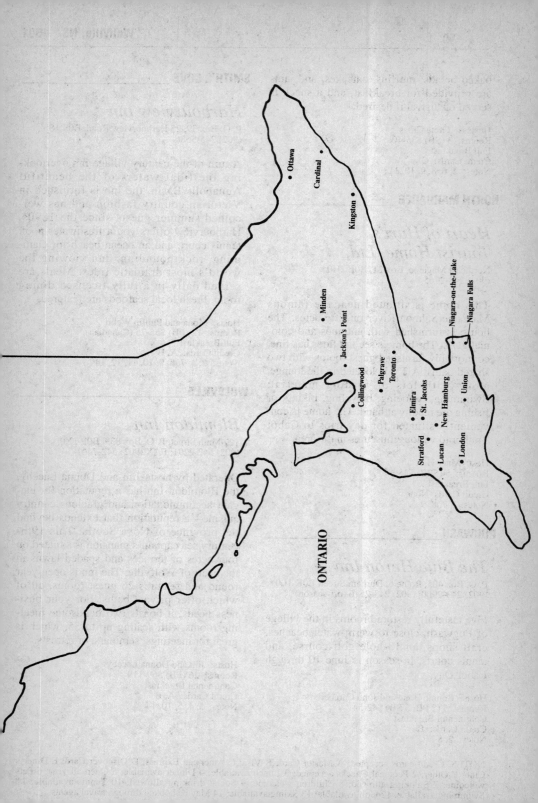

Ontario

ARVA

Robon's Rolling Ridge Farm

Rural Route 1, N0M 1C0
(519) 666-0896; FAX (509) 666-0896

Unwind in this big old country home ten
miles northwest of London and five miles
west of Arva. Three double bedrooms
offered, one with a private two-piece bath.
Air-conditioned. A warm welcome awaits
you. See the maple syrup making and products. Use of swimming pool.

Hosts: Everett and Joyce Robson
Rooms: 3 (1 PB; 2 SB) $25-35
Full Breakfast
Credit Cards: None
Notes: 5, 11

BRACEBRIDGE

Century House
Bed and Breakfast

155 Dill Street, P1L 1E5
(705) 645-9903

The hosts invite you to their charming, air-
conditioned, restored century-old home in
the province's premier recreational lake
district, a two-hour drive fom Toronto.
Sandy's breakfasts are creative and generous. Waffles with local maple syrup are a
specialty. Century House is close to shopping, beaches, and many craft studios and
galleries. Enjoy the sparkling lakes, fall
colors, studio tours, and winter cross-country skiing. An aloof cat and a friendly dog
are residents here.

Hosts: Norman Yan and Sandy Yudin-Yan
Rooms: 3 (SB) $45-50 Canadian
Full Breakfast
Credit Cards: None
Notes: 2, 5, 7 (restricted), 8, 10, 11, 12, 13

CARDINAL

Roduner Farm

Rural Route1, K0E 1E0
(613) 657-4830

To their active dairy farm, the hosts have
been welcoming guests for many years.
Children like to gather the eggs and
observe the milking. Two bikes are available to explore the surroundings. Relax on
the shaded lawn or in our comfortable
home. Close to Upper Canada Village,
Thousand Islands, or the locks at Iroquois.
Only a one-hour drive to Ottawa.
Schweizerdeutsh and a little French are
spoken.

Hosts: Walter and Margareta Roduner
Rooms: 2 (1 PB; 1 SB) $35
Full Breakfast
Credit Cards: None
Notes: 2, 4 (reservations only), 5, 6, 7, 8, 9, 11, 12,
   13

COLLINGWOOD

Beild House Inn

64 Third Street, L9Y 1K5
(705) 444-1522

This turn-of-the-century home has been
meticulously converted into an elegant
country inn. It features a five-course breakfast of your choice and a selection of hot

NOTES: Credit cards accepted: A Master Card; B Visa; C American Express; D Discover Card; E Diner's
Club; F Other; 2 Personal Checks accepted; 3 Lunch available; 4 Dinner available; 5 Open all year; 6 Pets
welcome; 7 Smoking allowed; 8 Children welcome; 9 Social drinking allowed; 10 Tennis available; 11
Swimming available; 12 Golf available; 13 Skiing available; 14 May be booked through travel agents.

Beild House Inn

and cold hors d'oeuvres offered each evening. Marvelous five-course gourmet dinners are also available. Discover the beauty of Georgian Bay and the Blue Mountains at Beild House Inn.

Hosts: Bill and Stephanie Barclay
Rooms: 17 (7 PB; 10 SB) $65-125
Full Breakfast
Credit Cards: A, B
Notes: 2, 3 (picnic), 4, 5, 6, 7, 8, 9, 10, 11, 12, 13, 14

ELMIRA

Teddy Bear Bed and Breakfast Inn

Rural Route 1, N3B 2Z1
(519) 660-2379

Relax and enjoy the hospitality of this gracious and elegant inn, enhanced with Canadiana and quilts. In the Old Order Mennonite countryside close to St. Jacobs, Kitchener-Waterloo's markets, museums, Stratford, Elora, Fergus, and Guelph. Spacious deluxe bedrooms, private or shared bathrooms, TV lounge, craft shop. Cross-country skiing, golf, boating, hiking, tours, and much more are nearby. Sumptuous continental breakfast, or full breakfast on request. Seminar and private dining facilities are available.

Hosts: Vivian and Gerrie Smith
Rooms: 3 (1 PB; 2 SB) $45-65

Continental or Full Breakfast
Credit Cards: A, B
Notes: 2, 4, 5, 8

JACKSON'S POINT

The Briars

55 Hedge Road, L0E IL0
(416) 722-3271; (800) 465-2376
FAX (416) 722-9698

Experience another world at The Briar's Inn and Country Club, located on the shore of Lake Sincoe. The unique Briar's 200-acre property, including its original landscape and lovingly preserved buildings, has been nurtured by the Sibbald family for over five generations. One hour north of Toronto, we are a five star resort.

Teddy Bear Inn

NOTES: Credit cards accepted: A Master Card; B Visa; C American Express; D Discover Card; E Diner's Club; F Other; 2 Personal Checks accepted; 3 Lunch available; 4 Dinner available; 5 Open all year;

KINGSTON

Barr

Kingston & Area B&B 77
P.O. Box 37, K7L 4V6
(613) 542-0214 24 hours

Come and enjoy this older red brick house that has 12 rooms in gorgeous solid oak and a beautifully landscaped, fenced courtyard. One floor has two large bedrooms and a full bath. A spacious twin room is also available. Guests are invited to enjoy the TV lounge and the sun room. Nonsmoking. May-November; off-season by arural routeangement. $37-51.

Baywinds

Kingston & Area B&B 93
P.O. Box 37, K7L 4V6
(613) 542-0214   24 hours

This spacious, air-conditioned, side-split home has a beautiful view of Lake Ontario at Collins Bay and is just 15 minutes from Kingston. Close to fine restaurants, shopping, and historical attractions with parks, picnic areas, and swimming. Two guest rooms with private baths. Children are welcome. $53.

Best

Kingston & Area B&B 31
P.O. Box 37, K7L 4V6
(613) 542-0214 24 hours

From the farm property that dates back to 1858, we have made the stable into this garden home. University and hospitals. A bus route at a nearby corner enables one to get to any area in Kingston. One double room and private bath. Nonsmokers. $42-53.

Burt

Kingston & Area B&B 65
P.O. Box 37, K7L 4V6
(613) 542-0214 24 hours

This B&B is a spacious split-level home is situated on a large tree-filled lot with lawns and gardens. Convenient parking available in the triple driveway. Located in a quiet residential neighborhood less than five minutes from the Olympic Harbor and ten minutes from downtown Kingston and the city hall. Residents of Kingston enjoy a variety of interests including gardening, bridge, tennis, golf, and crafts. $42-56.

Charmant

Kingston & Area B&B 100
P.O. Box 37, K7L 4V6
(613) 542-0214 24 hours

A spacious two-story farm home is a landmark. It was built between 1879 and 1890 by the grandson of a United Empire Loyalist. Its distinctive Cape Cod blue color and white shutters make it easy to identify. It is located on an 1.6 acres backing on Big Creek, just a short drive to the Bay of Quinte, Hay Bay, and Picton. Two guest rooms and a full, hearty breakfast in the morning. $49-51.

Debruyn

Kingston & Area B&B 80
P.O. Box 37, K7L 4V6
(613) 542-0214 24 hours

A two-story red brick home is near a fresh water spring that empties into Upper Rideau Lake. There are three guest rooms: one with twin beds, one with a king bed, and one with a queen bed. Within five miles are public beaches, golf courses, marked nature trails, several lakes, restaurants, and antique shops. $40.

6 Pets welcome; 7 Smoking allowed; 8 Children welcome; 9 Social drinking allowed; 10 Tennis available; 11 Swimming available; 12 Golf available; 13 Skiing available; 14 May be booked through travel agents.

Deschenes

Kingston & Area B&B 94
P.O. Box 37, K7L 4V6
(613) 542-0214 24 hours

The spacious, elevated bungalow backs on a park affording quiet and privacy. There is queen room with a private bath and two single rooms with a shared bath. Heated in-ground pool. English and French spoken. $37-54.

Fisher

Kingston & Area B&B 14
P.O. Box 37, K7L 4V6
(613) 542-0214 24 hours

A beautiful limestone house is part of an early 19th-century row. Renovated and restored, we are still captivated by its warmth and elegance. Within walking distance of the downtown with its interesting stores, restaurants, and boutiques, Queen's University, the hospitals, beautiful parks and the waterfront. Nonsmokers. $37-51.

Gormley

Kingston & Area B&B 21
P.O. Box 37, K7L 4V6
(613) 542-0214 24 hours

This lovely old 1853 brick house on King Street is a cool retreat in summer. You are invited to find comfort in this home amidst a blend of old and new decor. Only a few blocks from the downtown, boat cruises, and several museums. There are two rooms with shared baths. $37-48.

Hodges

Kingston & Area B&B 76
P.O. Box 37, K7L 4V6
(613) 542-0214 24 hours

This bed and breakfast in a charming red brick home in the village of Cataraqui is accessible from Highway 401 or from downtown Kingston. There are two spacious bedrooms that share a bath. A traditional breakfast is served, or enjoy fresh English scones with Devonshire cream and homemade strawberural routey jam. $37-48.

Keyes

Kingston & Area B&B 57
P.O. Box 37, K7L 4V6
(613) 542-0214 24 hours

From the deck of this spacious home that overlooks the St. Lawrence River, come and enjoy watching the freighters and pleasure craft passing on the seaway. There are three double rooms. On warm summer evenings, cool breezes off the river promote restful sleep. Within walking distance of a park and swimming area. A relatively short drive to Upper Canada Village, the Seaway locks, golf courses, a bird sanctuary, the city of Ottawa. $37-48.

MacLachlan

Kingston & Area B&B 1
P.O. Box 37, K7L 4V6
(613) 542-0214 24 hours

A Cape Cod-style house with a spacious addition, situated on a large lot in a delightful area called Greenville Park. All guest rooms have cross ventilation. Two full bathrooms for guests' use. The large dining room overlooks a beautiful garden. Bus routes and several restaurants are close by. $37-51.

McNeill-Knowles

Kingston & Area B&B 99
P.O. Box 37, K7L 4V6
(613) 542-0214 24 hours

After a busy day in Kingston, we'll welcome you to the shady maples and spacious lawns of our century limestone home. Relax over breakfast on the front porch, in

NOTES: Credit cards accepted: A Master Card; B Visa; C American Express; D Discover Card; E Diner's Club; F Other; 2 Personal Checks accepted; 3 Lunch available; 4 Dinner available; 5 Open all year;

the kitchen, or in your own eating area. Visit nearby country fairs, auctions, and sand beaches. Also, experience the local tea house, bakery, and the excellent cross-country ski trails and skating arena. Children welcome. $37-51.

Meserve

Kingston & Area B&B 86
P.O. Box 37, K7L 4V6
(613) 542-0214 24 hours

This bed and breakfast is surrounded by open fields. It is just west of the Loyalist Parkway Gates within easy access to Kingston's historical environs, eateries, and shopping. Excellent fishing, swimming, or hiking trails nearby. There are double and twin rooms. Breakfast can be served in the coffee room, in the dining room, or on the sun porch. $48-51.

North

Kingston & Area B&B 68
P.O. Box 37, K7L 4V6
(613) 542-0214 24 hours

The "North Nook" is situated in a quiet, wooded area, a short walk to the Olympic Harbour and St. Lawrence College, a bit farther to Queen's. This air-conditioned home has two double rooms and a single room with shared baths. During July and August, there is a self-contained suite on a lower level, excellent for families. $37-60.

O'Brien

Kingston & Area B&B 85
P.O. Box 37, K7L 4V6
(613) 542-0214 24 hours

This spacious Colonial brick home that backs onto a park is bright and cheerful. Only ten minutes from downtown by car, and minutes from theatres, boat cruises, St. Lawrence College, and Queen's University.

There are three rooms, each with ceiling fan. Full breakfast; children welcome. $37-51.

Richard

Kingston & Area B&B 90
P.O. Box 37, K7L 4V6
(613) 542-0214 24 hours

This lovely century frame home is on a quiet street close to Queen's University, minutes from downtown and waterfront parks. There is a double and a twin room with shared bath and a TV room. Full breakfast is served in the cozy country kitchen. Nonsmokers. $48-51.

Rideau En Ville

Kingston & Area B&B 98
P.O. Box 37, K7L 4V6
(613) 542-0214 24 hours

A century-old brick/stone house, furnished with early Canadian antiques, welcomes you to beautiful, historic downtown Kingston. Located three blocks from the Thousand Islands tour boats, theatres, the market, entertainment, and restaurants. There are two rooms. Rental bicycles available. $37-49.

Roberts

Kingston & Area B&B 66
P.O. Box 37, K7L 4V6
(613) 542-0214 24 hours

Easily located, this bed and breakfast is 19 kilometers north of Kingston on a main road in the historic Sydenham area. This charming 100-year-old limestone converted schoolhouse is in a farming area and near two beautiful lakes, good for boating, swimming, and fishing. There is a twin room with a private bath. Large garden and trees. Black currant jam, and wheat germ muffins are the specialty. French is spoken. $40-50.

6 Pets welcome; 7 Smoking allowed; 8 Children welcome; 9 Social drinking allowed; 10 Tennis available; 11 Swimming available; 12 Golf available; 13 Skiing available; 14 May be booked through travel agents.

Rochon

Kingston & Area B&B 96
P.O. Box 37, K7L 4V6
(613) 542-0214 24 hours

This new, air-conditioned French-Canadian style home is a short drive from downtown Kingston, close to Old Fort Henry, Royal Military College, a short walk to Rideau Marina, and to a waterfront park. There is a double-bed room with ample room for a crib or cot, also a large twin room. A full bath includes a Jacuzzi for guests' use. English and French are spoken. Nonsmokers. $37-51.

Thomson

Kingston & Area B&B 32
P.O. Box 37, K7L 4V6
(613) 542-0214 24 hours

A limestone house, built in the early 1860s, is situated on a hill on the north shore of Lake Sydenham. Bring a bathing suit (sand beach), or a fishing rod. Great area for history buffs, antique hunters, sightseers and skiers. There are three rooms. Nonsmokers. English and French spoken. $37-51.

Troughton

Kingston & Area B&B 84
P.O. Box 37, K7L 4V6
(613) 542-0214 24 hours

This bed and breakfast is a newly renovated, traditional three-story brick home (circa 1911) is on a quiet residential street. It is one block from Queen's University, three blocks from Lake Ontario. An easy walk to downtown Kingston. There are three rooms, and a generous, delicious, old-fashioned breakfast. $48-51.

Van Horne

Kingston & Area B&B 20
P.O. Box 37, K7L 4V6
(613) 542-0214 24 hours

A spacious farmhouse, surural routeounded by trees, is back from the road. 14 kilometers from Kingston and Gananoque and you can readily reach such attractions as Fort Henry, boat cruises, golf courses, the MacLachlan Woodworking Museum, and Grass Creek Park. There are two double rooms and a single room. Adjoining the house on ground-floor level is a complete air-conditioned apartment, equipped with stove and refrigerator. $37-60.

Wellington House

Kingston & Area B&B 72
P.O. Box 37, K7L 4V6
(613) 542-0214 24 hours

A three-story brick house with a limestone foundation was built in 1925. Within walking distance of restaurants, shopping, Queen's University, two hospitals, and Lake Ontario. There are three bedrooms and a cot. Full breakfast served in the dining room or on a back patio. $48-51.

Westenberg

Kingston & Area B&B 78
P.O. Box 37, K7L 4V6
(613) 542-0214 24 hours

A solidly built 1840 limestone house is nestled deep in a wooded lot. There are four rooms, and a suite is also available for a couple or a family. Wake up to a Dutch-Canadian breakfast. $37-56.

LONDON

Annigan's

194 Elmwood Avenue East, N6C 1K2
(519) 439-9196

Owned by an interior designer, this turn-of-the-century house, featuring a turural routeet, fireplace, and fine architectural details, offers double and twin bedrooms, full bath, powder room, TV, and smoking lounge. Downtown, Grand Theatre, University of Western Ontario, bus routes, antique stores close by. $40-55.

Chiron House

398 Piccadilly Street, N6A 1S7
(519) 673-6878

Recall the comfort and elegance of an earlier time in this turn-of-the-century home, lovingly maintained and furnished in period style with modern amenities discreetly added. Within walking distance of theatre, restaurants, and shopping. Convenient to University of Western Ontario and airport. Suite with whirlpool available. $44-55.

Clermont Place

679 Clermont Avenue, N5X 1N3
(519) 672-0767

Air-conditioned home in a parklike setting, recreational facilities nearby. Close to Highways 22 and 126 in northeast London. Each room has a double bed, one with a water bed. Gourmet meals served by a cozy fireside are available upon request. $35-45.

Cosy Corners

87 Askin Street, N6C 1E5
(519) 673-4598

This 1871 Victorian-style home is in the core area of London. It has been lovingly restored to maintain the warm glow of wood and stained glass. There are two bedrooms, a kitchenette, and a bathroom. English and French are spoken. Full breakfast is served. $35-40; children under 10, $10.

Dillon's Place

56 Gerural routeard Street, N6C 4C7
(519) 439-9666

This peaceful 1917 home in Old South has comfortable people and a large, friendly Labrador dog. The second floor has three attractive rooms and a full bath. Central air for summer comfort, fireplace for cozy winter evenings. Nonsmoking guests are welcome, and nutritious breakfasts are served. $25-35.

Eileen's

433 Hyde Park Road, N6H 3R9
(519) 471-1107

Comfortable Cape Cod home on a treed acre. One double, one twin, and one single bedroom. Five minutes to Thames Valley Golf Course and Springbank Park. Ten minutes to downtown, theaters, shopping, and University of Western Ontario. Bus service. Lots of parking. Use of swimming pool. Central air conditioning. $25-40.

Ferndale West

53 Longbow Road, N6G 1Y5
(519) 471-8038

Elegant modernized home in northwest London. Extra-large bedrooms, one with two-piece en suite plus sofa and chair. Queen and twin beds and central air. Very close to university and ten minutes from downtown. Cross-country skiing and nature walk at the bottom of the street. Swimming pool. $32-47.

Hilltop

82 Compton Crescent, N6C 4G1
(519) 681-7841

Modern air-conditioned home located on quiet crescent in South London with easy access to Highway 401 and downtown. Twin/double room with private bath. Dining room overlooks the city and outdoor pool that is available to guests. Nonsmoking adults. $30-50.

6 Pets welcome; 7 Smoking allowed; 8 Children welcome; 9 Social drinking allowed; 10 Tennis available; 11 Swimming available; 12 Golf available; 13 Skiing available; 14 May be booked through travel agents.

Lambert House

231 Cathcart Street, N6C 3M8
(519) 672-8996

Quiet, turn-of-the-century, air-conditioned home in the heart of Old South London is close to downtown, parks, golf, and six antique shops. Guests are served welcome snacks. Breakfast is served daily from 8:00 A.M.-9:00 A.M. Afternoon tea, and champagne with breakfast, on weekends only. Gift shop. No smoking please. $30-45.

McLellan Place

651 Baseline Road East, N6C 2R2
(519) 686-3590

Lovely air-conditioned home on south edge of city west of Baseline and Wellington. Minutes from Storybook Gardens, miniature golf, waterslides, and Thames Valley Trail. Three large bedrooms, two baths, TV available. Nonsmoking. On bus route. $30-40; Children under 10, $10.

Overdale

2 Normandy Gardens, N6H 4A9
(519) 641-0236

Quiet, air-conditioned home in mature residential West London. Near parks and golf courses. Easily accessible to University of Western Ontario and downtown by bus or car. Rooms include one with three-piece en suite. $32-50 Canadian.

The Rose House

526 Dufferin Avenue, N6B 2A2
(519) 433-9978

Welcome to a fine, air-conditioned old home on a beautiful, tree-lined street, in an area of downtown historic, century-old homes. Easy access to the University of Western Ontario, all hospitals, shopping, and all types of recreation and entertain-

ment. Parking. No smoking. Reservations recommended.

Hosts: Betty and Douglas Rose
Rooms: 3 (1 PB; 2 SB) $35-50
Full Breakfast
Credit Cards: None
Notes: 5, 9, 10, 11, 12, 13

Serena's Place

720 Headley Drive, N6H 3V6
(519) 471-6228

Air-conditioned home in prestigious residential area of West London. Three bedrooms and full bath. Sun room for relaxation. Near Springbank and Thames Valley golf course. Ten minutes from Theatre London. Bus service at the door. $25-40.

Trillium

71 Trillium Crescent, N5Y 4T3
(519) 453-3801

Restful, modern, air-conditioned home offers two guest rooms—one with queen-size bed, one with twin beds—on a quiet crescent just off Highway 156. Close to University of Western Ontario, hospitals, airport, Fanshawe College, golf course, bus routes, and shopping. No smoking, please. Home-cooked meals on request. $30-45.

LUCAN

Hindhope

Rural Route 2, N0M 2J0
(519) 227-4514

Century-old country home on Middlesex County Road 22 offering two bedrooms. One mile north of Highway 7, one and one-half miles south of Highway 4, 20 minutes from London. 30-minute drive to Lake Huron and Grand Bend, 60 miles from Sarnia. Children and pets welcome. No smoking in bedrooms. Other meals on request. $25-30.

NOTES: Credit cards accepted: A Master Card; B Visa; C American Express; D Discover Card; E Diner's Club; F Other; 2 Personal Checks accepted; 3 Lunch available; 4 Dinner available; 5 Open all year;

MINDEN

The Stone House

Rural Route 2, K0M 2K0
(705) 286-1250

This primitive-style stone house is situated
in secluded, mature woods. Restful atmosphere with large fireplace, antiques, handmade quilts, rugs, and country charm.
Laundry facilities available, and coffee and
tea are always on tap. Choice of bed sizes.
Swimming and boating in lake or river
within one mile. Just two hours from
Toronto.

Host: Phyllis Howarth
Rooms: 2 (SB) $40-50
Cabin, Apartment, Trailer
Continental Breakfast
Credit Cards: None
Open July 1-August 31
Notes: 8, 9, 11

NEW HAMBURG

The Waterlot

17 Huron Street, N0B 2G0
(519) 662-2020

The Waterlot opened in the fall of 1974,
and from the onset it has been committed to
quality of ambience and service. Two large
and comfortably appointed rooms share a
memorable marbled shower, bidet, water
closet, wet vanity, and sitting area. The inn
is one of Ontario's finest dining establishments. This bed and breakfast offers quality and service in a memorable lodging.

Rooms: 3 (1 PB; 2 SB) $65-85
Continental Breakfast
Credit Cards: A, B, C
Notes: 2, 3, 4, 5, 9, 10, 11, 12, 13

NIAGARA FALLS

Gretna Green

5077 River Road, L2E 3G7
(416) 357-2081

This tourist home offers bright, comfortable rooms with en suite bathrooms; all
guest rooms are air-conditioned and have
TV. Families are welcome. This is like "a
home away from home" where you'll be
treated to a full, home-cooked breakfast
which includes homemade muffins, scones,
jams, and jellies. Niagara has much to offer
tourists—the falls, Skylow Tower, IMAX
Theatre, the Floral Clock, the Rose
Gardens, and museums. Bike rentals available.

Hosts: Stan and Marg Gardiner
Rooms: 4 (PB) $45-55, seasonal
Full Breakfast
Credit Cards: None
Notes: 5, 7 (limited), 8, 9, 12

NIAGARA-ON-THE-LAKE

Hiebert's Guest House

P.O. Box 1371, 275 John Street West, L0S 1J0
(416) 468-3687

Enjoy a peaceful setting in a quaint, historic town twenty minutes north of Niagara
Falls, Ontario. Attend the Shaw Festival
Theatre, browse through the many shops,
or relax at the waterfront. Guest rooms
offer queen and twin beds. Warm hospitality in air-conditioned comfort. Come and be
our guests! Brochure available.

Hosts: Otto and Marlene Hiebert
Rooms: 3 (PB) $55-85
Full Breakfast
Credit Cards: None
Notes: 2, 5, 8, 10, 11, 12

The Kiely House Heritage Inn

209 Queen Street, Box 1642, L05 1S0
(416) 468-4588

A historic home built in 1832 on one acre
of beautiful gardens, this lovely home is
furnished with antiques and decorated in
period style. Many rooms have fireplaces,
verandas, or porches. All rooms en suite.
Guest parlor, Victorian breakfast room, and
bicycles available at no extra charge.

Within a few minutes walk to theaters, stores, and restaurants. Ample parking.

Hosts: Heather and Ray Pettit
Rooms: 13 (PB) $55-168, seasonal
Continental Plus Breakfast
Credit Cards: A, B, C
Notes: 5, 7, 9, 10, 11, 12, 14

OTTAWA

Albert House

478 Albert Street, K1R 5B5
(613) 236-4479; (800) 267-1982

Gracious Victorian home built in 1875 by noted Canadian architect. Each room is individually decorated and has private facilities, telephone, television, and air conditioning. Guest lounge with fireplace. Famous Albert House breakfast. Parking is available, but within walking distance to most attractions. There are two large but friendly dogs in the house.

Hosts: Cathy and John Delroy
Rooms: 17 (PB) $68-90
Full Breakfast
Credit Cards: A, B, C, E
Notes: 5, 7, 9, 14

Australis Guest House

35 Marlborough Avenue, K1N 8E6
(613) 235-8461

This guest house is the oldest established and still operating bed and breakfast in Ottawa. Located on a quiet, tree-lined street one block from the Rideau River, with its ducks and swans, and Strathcona Park, it is a 20-minute walk to the Parliament buildings. The home boasts leaded windows, fireplaces, oak floors, and unique eight-foot stained-glass windows. The spacious rooms, including a suite with private bathroom, feature many collectibles from different parts of the world. The hearty, delicious breakfasts, with homebaked breads and pastries, help you start the day right. Multiple winner of the Ottawa Hospitality Award and recommended by Newsweek.

Hosts: Brian and Carol Waters
Rooms: 3 (1 PB; 2 SB) $40-58
Full Breakfast
Credit Cards: None
Notes: 2, 5, 7, 8, 10, 11, 12, 13

Beatrice Lyon Guest House

479 Slater Street, K1R 5C2
(613) 236-3904

This is an old-fashioned family home surural routeounded by large trees. The place is within walking distance of the Parliament buildings, the Museum of Man, the National Archives, Byward Market, Rideau Canal, and Hull, Quebec. Children are welcome, and babysitting can be arural routeanged. Members of the Downtown Bed & Breakfast Association.

Host: Beatrice Lyon
Rooms: 3 (S2B) $45
Full Breakfast
Credit Cards: None
Notes: 2, 5, 7, 8, 9

Australis Guest House

Cartier House Inn

46 Cartier Street, K2P 1J3
(613) 236 INNS (4667)

Cartier House Inn, Ottawa's first fine accommodations, offers ten guest rooms and suites with Jacuzzis and complimentary breakfast. All rooms are equipped with queen-size beds. Within walking distance to downtown Ottawa, Parliament buildings, the National Gallery, National Arts Centre, Rideau Center, and Rideau Canal. Quiet, tranquil accommodations.

Host: Barbara LaFlamme
Rooms: 10 (PB) $94-134 Canadian
Continental Breakfast
Credit Cards: A, B, C, E, F
Notes: 2, 5, 7 (limited), 8 (over 7), 9, 10, 11, 12, 13, 14

Constance House Bed and Breakfast

62 Sweetland Avenue, K1N 7T6
(613) 235-8888

Constance House is a restored award-winning Victorian house (1895) where you are invited to find comfort in its modest scale and antique details, all in a nonsmoking, air-conditioned environment. Parking, too! Close to Parliament Hill, National Art Gallery, and the Byward Market area with its great restaurants and shops.

Host: Esther M. Peterson
Rooms: 4 (1 PB; 3 SB) $54-88
Full or Continental Breakfast
Credit Cards: A, B, C, E, F
Notes: 2, 5, 8, 9

Constance House

Gasthaus Switzerland Inn

89 Daly Avenue, K1N 6E6
(613) 237-0335; FAX (613) 594-3327
(800) 267-8788 Canada and Northeast US

Charming, affordable accommodation. All rooms feature comfortable, cozy Swiss-style beds covered with handmade duvets; air-conditioned, smoke-free; with telephone and TV. Traditional Swiss hospitality in the heart of Canada's capital! Recommended by CAA, AAA, and Tourism of Ontario.

Hosts: Josef and Sabina Sauter
Rooms: 25 (21 PB; 4 SB) $64-88
Full Breakfast
Credit Cards: A, B
Notes: 5, 9, 10, 11, 12, 13

Gwen's Guest Home

2071 Riverside Drive, K1H 7X2
(613) 737-4129

This 93-year-old home sits opposite a winding parkland bordering the Rideau River and Ottawa's famous bicycle path. A secluded garden provides a relaxed country setting, and a ten-minute drive brings you to Parliament Hill and major attractions. Public transportation is at the front door. Antique Canadian furniture, stained glass, handcrafted pottery, native Indian art, and textiles from host's loom create an atmosphere of gracious comfort.

Host: Gwen Goulding
Rooms: 3 (SB) $55-59 Canadian
Full Breakfast
Credit Cards: A, B
Notes: 2, 5, 7, 8, 9, 11, 14

Haydon House

18 The Driveway, K2P 1C6
(613) 230-2697

Haydon House is a completely renovated and modernized Victorian-era mansion that offers rest and comfort. It is air-conditioned, has a private outdoor portico sitting area, spacious bedrooms, and modern facilities, embellished with traditional Canadian pine decor. Haydon House is nestled in a tranquil residential area beside the historic and picturesque Rideau Canal and scenic parkway. All important points of interest, such as the Parliament buildings, museums,

6 Pets welcome; 7 Smoking allowed; 8 Children welcome; 9 Social drinking allowed; 10 Tennis available; 11 Swimming available; 12 Golf available; 13 Skiing available; 14 May be booked through travel agents.
6 Pets welcome; 7 Smoking allowed; 8 Children welcome; 9 Social drinking allowed; 10 Tennis available; 11

and National Art Gallery, are within a short and easy walk.

Host: Mary Haydon
Rooms: 3 (1 PB; 2 SB) $65
Continental Breakfast
Credit Cards: None
Notes: 2, 5, 7, 8, 9

O'Connor House Bed and Breakfast

172 O'Connor Street, K2P 1T5
(613) 236-4221; (800) 236-4232 eastern Canada

Located in the center of downtown Ottawa, the O'Connor House is a short walk to the Parliament buildings, Rideau Canal, National Gallery, and Byward Market. The pleasant staff is happy to tell you about Ottawa's attractions. Internationally renowned, the O'Connor House offers clean, quiet rooms with air conditioning, telephones, and an exceptional full-course breakfast. Complimentary beverages and snacks are available in the guest lounge by the fireplace. Full parking, bicycles, ice skates, and FAX services are available for guests.

Host: Ron Chiarelli
Rooms: 34 (16 PB; 18 SB) $49-77 US
Full Breakfast
Credit Cards: A, B, C, E, F
Notes: 2, 5, 8, 9, 10, 12, 13, 14

Rideau View Inn

177 Frank Street, K2P 0X4
(613) 236-9309; FAX (613) 231-6842

This inn is a large Edwardian home with seven well-appointed guest rooms furnished in that period. Though located on a quiet street, it is within easy walking distance of all major attractions, shops, and fine restaurants. Guests are encouraged to enjoy the home, take a stroll along the famous Rideau Canal, or play tennis on nearby public courts. A hearty breakfast is provided each morning to help you on your way.

O'Connor House

Host: George Hartsgrove
Rooms: 7 (SB) $58-66
Full Breakfast
Credit Cards: A, B, C, F
Notes: 5, 8, 10, 13, 14

PALGRAVE

Country Host

Rural Route 1, L0N 1P0
(519) 941-7633

Country Host reservation service was organized in 1980 and represents fine guest homes in some of Ontario's most picturesque areas. Tucked away in the countryside, and a few in villages, these homes continue the European tradition of lodging in comfortable privacy at reasonable cost. Country Host homes have particular appeal to Bruce Trail hikers, naturalists, bicyclists, bird watchers, and nature lovers. Rates range from $35-40 for singles and $45-60 for doubles. A hearty breakfast is included, and family rates are available. Plan early.

ST. JACOBS

Jakobstettel Guest House, Inc.

16 Isabella Street, N0B 2N0
(519) 664-2208; FAX (519) 664-1326

NOTES: Credit cards accepted: A Master Card; B Visa; C American Express; D Discover Card; E Diner's Club; F Other; 2 Personal Checks accepted; 3 Lunch available; 4 Dinner available; 5 Open all year;

Turn-of-the-century estate Victorian home, completely renovated. Has 12 individually decorated guest rooms with private baths. Library, lounge for all guests, and open kitchen all day and evening for coffee, tea, juice, and cookies. Outdoor pool, tennis court, horseshoe pits, bikes, and walking trail. Within a few blocks of over 80 retail shops, this is a shopper's delight.

Host: Elle Burbacher
Rooms: 12 (PB) $105-150
Continental Breakfast
Credit Cards: A, B, C
Notes: 2, 5, 10, 11

SOUTH GILLIES

Unicorn Inn and Restaurant
Rural Route 1, P0T 2V0
(807) 475-4200

An intimate and widely acclaimed serendipity of country-elegant accommodations and superb dining. Restaurant rated among the top 35 nationally by *Where to Eat in Canada '90*. Nestled in the heart of a hidden rural valley, 30 minutes from Thunder Bay in northwest Ontario, on 640 spectacular acres of fields, forests, and mountains. Bright, cozy rooms with oak floors and handcrafted pine furniture; exquisite honeymoon cottage with bay windows and view.

Hosts: David and Arlan Nobel
Rooms: 4 (1 PB; 3 SB) $59-89 Canadian
Full Breakfast
Credit Cards: A, B, E, F
Notes: 2, 4, 5, 8, 9, 14

STRATFORD

Burnside Guest Home
139 William Street, N5A 4X9
(519) 271-7076

Burnside is a turn-of-the-century home on the north shore of Lake Victoria, the site of the first Stratford logging mill and, later, a brick factory, built by family ancestors

from Perthshire, Scotland. Burnside features many family heirlooms and antiques, and is centrally air conditioned. The rooms have been recently redecorated in light, airy, and cheery colors. The beds and mattresses are very comfortable, each with its own Mennonite hand-crafted quilt. Relax in the gardens overlooking the Avon River on hand-crafted furniture amidst the rose, herb, and annual herbaceous flower gardens. A full, nutritious breakfast, with home-baked muffins, jams, and jellies, awaits guests in the morning. Caters to singles.

Host: Lester J. Wilker
Rooms: 5 (SB) $35-60
Full or Continental Breakfast
Credit Cards: A
Notes: 2, 5, 8, 9, 10, 11, 12, 13

TORONTO

Bed and Breakfast Guest Homes-TNN-ONTARIO
153 Huron Street, M5T 2B6
(416) 977-6841; FAX (416) 598-4562

Part of the Bed and Breakfast National Network, Bed and Breakfast Guest Homes offers bed and breakfast not only in Ontario, but also in many other cities and provinces across the country. The members of this network adhere strictly to the standards set by TNN, such as getting to know the hosts personally, having an established cancellation and refund policy, and following a thorough inspection and approval process for all properties rented. This is because each member of the network is dedicated to ensuring your comfort, pleasure, and personal needs while you are staying at one of our "homes away from home."

Burken Guest House
322 Palmerston Boulevard, M6G 2N6
(416) 920-7842; FAX (416) 960-9529

6 Pets welcome; 7 Smoking allowed; 8 Children welcome; 9 Social drinking allowed; 10 Tennis available; 11 Swimming available; 12 Golf available; 13 Skiing available; 14 May be booked through travel agents.

Burken Guest House

Splendidly situated in a charming residential neighborhood adjacent to downtown. Eight tastefully appointed rooms with wash basins, private phones, and ceiling fans; shared baths. European-style atmosphere. Limited free parking on premises; public transportation nearby. Friendly, capable service.

Hosts: Burke and Ken
Rooms: 8 (SB) $60-65
Continental Breakfast
Credit Cards: A, B
Notes: 5, 8, 9, 14

Downtown Toronto Association of B&B Guesthouses

P.O. Box 190, Station B, M5T 2W1
(416) 977-6841; Fax (416) 598-4562

Quality, charm and location are the three main elements in Susan Oppenheim's B&B network. All hosts are active in the arts and/or the hospitality industry. Locations are within 30 minutes of the Eaton Centre on 24-hour public transit lines. Brochures and maps are supplied, and taxi service is easily arural routeanged to your door. All rooms are nonsmoking. $50-70 for two; $10 additional for private bath; $5 additional for air-conditioning; $10 surcharge for one-night stays.

Oppenheim's

153 Huron Street, M5T 2B6
(416) 598- 4562

Since 1980, Oppenheim's has consistently been featured in the media and won the Tourism Superhero award from the Convention Bureau in 1991. The house has a 400-square-foot kitchen, where breakfast is served, featuring all home-cooking and fresh produce only. The location is halfway between the museum and gallery, and within walking distance to most attractions. No extra charge for parking or tax. Two queens, one double bed, and two single beds. French and English spoken, some Spanish. House is 105 years old.

Host: Susan Oppenheim
Rooms: 5 (SB) $45-60
Full Breakfast
Credit Cards: None
Notes: 5, 8

Toronto Bed and Breakfast

Box 269, 253 College Street, M5T 1R5
(416) 588-8800; (416) 916-3676
FAX (416) 964-1756

A professional bed & breakfast reservation service for quality bed and breakfast accommodations throughout metropolitan Toronto. Canada's longest running urban bed and breakfast service (11 years). Advance reservation recommended. Free brochure upon request.

Coordinators: Larural routey Page and Michael
  Coyne
Homes: 20; $51-85 Canadian
Full or Continental Breakfast
Credit Cards: A, B, E
Notes: 5, 7, 8, 9, 14

NOTES: Credit cards accepted: A Master Card; B Visa; C American Express; D Discover Card; E Diner's Club; F Other; 2 Personal Checks accepted; 3 Lunch available; 4 Dinner available; 5 Open all year;

UNION

Great Lakes Farms Guest House

Rural Route 1, N0L 2L0
(519) 633-2390; (519) 631-2171
FAX (519) 631-3852

Great Lakes Farms

This century-old home is situated amid apple trees on a 150-acre farm. Rent one room, or rent the whole house for a night, a weekend, or longer. Enjoy TV, a pool table, whirlpool, continental breakfast, and the warmth of this country retreat located just five minutes from Port Stanley.

Hosts: Bob and Marge Thomas
Rooms: 3 (SB) $40-50
Continental Breakfast
Credit Cards: None
Notes: 2, 5, 8, 9, 11, 12, 13, 14

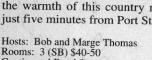

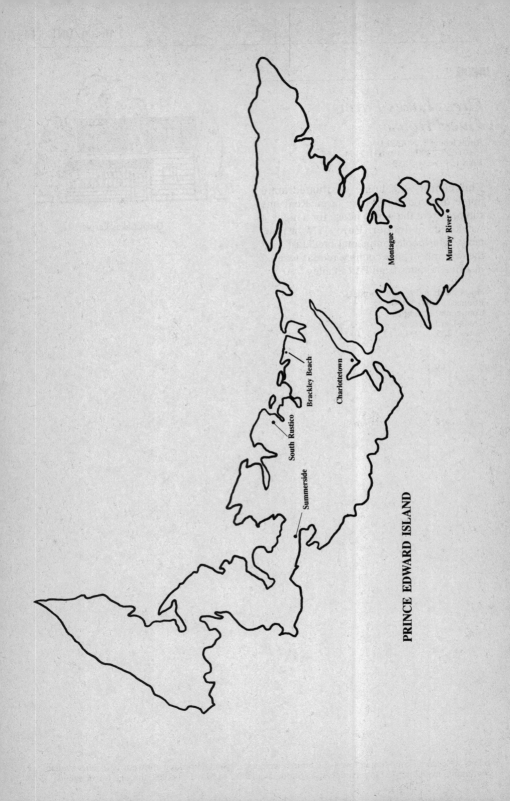

PRINCE EDWARD ISLAND

Murray River

Montague

Charlottetown

Brackley Beach

South Rustico

Summerside

Prince Edward Island

BRACKLEY BEACH

Shaw's Hotel

Brackley Beach, C0A 2H0
(902) 672-2022

Great-grandfather Shaw opened the hotel as an inn in 1860. The fourth generation of Shaws continues to provide a relaxing country lodging on this fair isle. Each of the 22 rooms is decorated individually in island style. The original farmhouse is now a suite with a large sitting room, fireplace, and antique furniture. Of the 18 charming cottages surrounding the inn, some have as many as four bedrooms. Many have fireplaces. The Sunday buffet is legendary, and the desserts are outrageous. The beach is a short walk down a rose-bordered lane. Many activities include cycling, sailing, and windsurfing. No telephones or noise pollution.

Hosts: Robbie and Pam Shaw
Rooms: 22 (9 PB; 13 SB) $100-145
Full Breakfast
Credit Cards: A, B, C
Notes: 2, 3, 4, 7, 8, 9, 11, 12, 14

CHARLOTTETOWN

"Just Folks" Bed and Breakfast

Rural Route 5, C1A 7J8
(902) 569-2089

This 103-year-old home on Route 215 is nine kilometers east of Charlottetown. A quiet location, large grounds, use of a picnic table and barbecue, and four bedrooms are available for guests. One bedroom has a

Shaw's Hotel

double and two singles, a second bedroom offers a double bed with one single, and the third and fourth bedrooms offer double beds. Cots and cribs are available. One bathroom with a shower and tub, and one bathroom with a shower are shared by guests. Complimentary tea and coffee. Children and well-trained pets welcome. Open May 1-October 15. Three-star rating.

Host: Marguerite Wood
Rooms: 4 (S2B) $30-35
Full or Continental Breakfast
Credit Cards: None
Notes: 6, 8

MONTAGUE

Partridge's Bed and Breakfast

Panmure Island, Rural Route 2, C0A 1R0
(902) 838-4687

NOTES: Credit cards accepted: A Master Card; B Visa; C American Express; D Discover Card; E Diner's Club; F Other; 2 Personal Checks accepted; 3 Lunch available; 4 Dinner available; 5 Open all year; 6 Pets welcome; 7 Smoking allowed; 8 Children welcome; 9 Social drinking allowed; 10 Tennis available; 11 Swimming available; 12 Golf available; 13 Skiing available; 14 May be booked through travel agents.

Partridge's Bed and Breakfast is near Panmure Island Provincial Park, where lifeguards patrol one of the most beautiful beaches on Prince Edward Island. One house has three bedrooms with private baths and is wheelchair accessible. The other house has two bedrooms with shared bath and another bedroom with private bath. Seal cruises, plays, tennis, golf, and horseback riding within 20 miles. Canoe, rowboat, and bicycles free for guests. Laundry and kitchen for guests.

Host: Gertrude Partridge
Rooms: 7 (5 PB; 2 SB) $40-50
Full Breakfast
Credit Cards: B
Notes: 2, 5, 6, 8, 9, 14

MURRAY RIVER

Bayberry Cliff Inn Bed and Breakfast

Rural Route 4, Little Sands, C0A 1W0
(902) 962-3395

Situated on the edge of a 40-foot cliff, the inn consists of two converted post-and-beam barns decorated with antiques and marine art. Stairs to the shore allow for swimming, innertubing, snorkeling, and beachcombing. Seal boat tours and bird watching tours nearby, as well as fine restaurants and craft shops. A honeymoon suite with private bath is available.

Hosts: Nancy and Don Perkins
Rooms: 8 (3 PB; 5 SB) $35-65
Full Breakfast
Credit Cards: A, B
Closed October 1-May 1
Notes: 2, 8, 9, 11

SOUTH RUSTICO

Barachois Inn

P. O. Box 1022, Charlottetown, C1A 7M4
(902) 963-2194

The Barachois Inn is located on the Church Road, Route 243, in South Rustico only six kilometers from both of Prince Edward Island's national parks. The inn is a 15-room Victorian home that is in a beautiful and historic community that boasts a museum and the oldest Catholic church on the island. The inn has been totally restored to its former graciousness with antiques in every room and beautiful artwork by island artists. Enjoy a view of Winter Bay that is only a hop, skip, and a jump from the inn and is great for shore walks.

Hosts: Judy and Gary MacDonald
Rooms: 4 (PB) $75-95 plus tax
Full Breakfast
Credit Cards: None
Notes: 2, 8, 9, 11, 12

Barachois Inn

SUMMERSIDE

The Arbor Inn

380 MacEwen Road, C1N 4X8
(902) 436-6847

Royalty Suite contains a canopy bed, Jacuzzi bath, and private entrance. Peppermint Suite has private bath, canopy bed. Housekeeping apartment accommodates four and has a fully equipped kitchen, private bath, and entrance. The elegant Rose and Lavender rooms share a Jacuzzi bath. The basic Cedar and Pine rooms share a shower. Private kitchen and common room for guests. Patio and barbecue available. Restaurants, shopping, golf, swimming are all nearby.

NOTES: Credit cards accepted: A Master Card; B Visa; C American Express; D Discover Card; E Diner's Club; F Other; 2 Personal Checks accepted; 3 Lunch available; 4 Dinner available; 5 Open all year;

Hosts: JoAnn and Ian Doughart
Rooms: 7 (3 PB; 4 SB) $35-85
Continental Breakfast
Credit Cards: A, B
Notes: 5 (Royalty Suite only), 8, 9, 12

Silver Fox Inn

61 Granville Street, C1N 2Z3
(902) 436-4033

For over a century proud owners have carefully preserved the beauty of the spacious rooms with their fireplaces and fine woodwork. Combining modern comfort with the cherished past, the Silver Fox Inn offers accommodations for 12 guests. Its six bedrooms, each with private bath, feature period furnishings.

Silver Fox Inn

Host: Julie Simmons
Rooms: 6 (PB) $60-70
Continental Breakfast
Credit Cards: A, B, C
Notes: 5, 9, 10, 11, 12, 13, 14

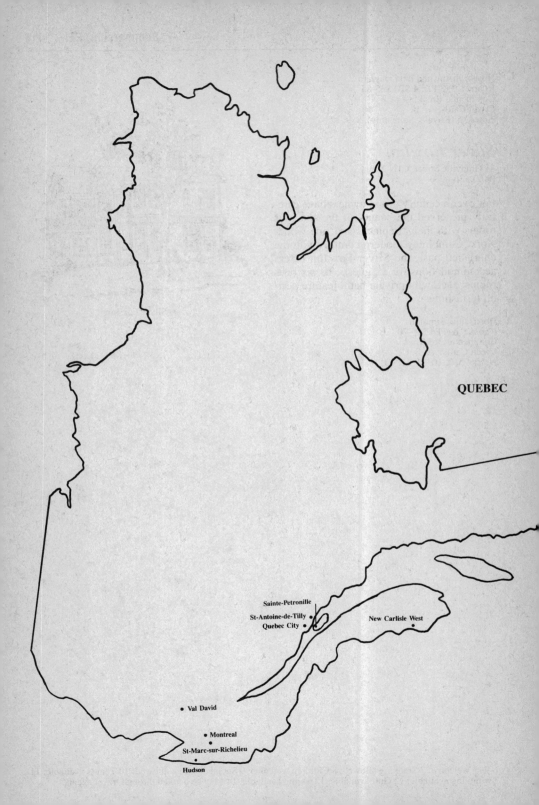

QUEBEC

Sainte-Petronille
St-Antoine-de-Tilly •
Quebec City •

New Carlisle West
•

• Val David

• Montreal
St-Marc-sur-Richelieu
•
Hudson

Quebec

Auberge Willow Place Inn

208 Main Road, J0P 1H0
(514) 458-7006; FAX (514) 458-4615

Forty-five minutes from the heart of
Montreal, on the peaceful Lake of Two
Mountains, the Willow Place Inn is in a
world of quiet roads and majestic trees. The
atmosphere at The Willows is indeed
unique, and is a great place to make your
headquarters. Guest rooms at the inn are
tastefully decorated in a style reminiscent
of the inn's historic beginnings and include
fully equipped bathrooms. Five rooms are
located in a separate building and share two
bathrooms.

Host: Luci Thifault
Rooms: 14 (9 PB; 5 SB) $65-85
Continental Breakfast
Credit Cards: A, B, C, F
Notes: 3, 4, 5, 7, 8, 9

MONTREAL

A B&B Downtown Network 1

3458 Laval Avenue, H2X 3C8
(514) 289-9749; FAX (514) 287-7386

Downtown, turn-of-the-century home. This
restored Victorian home features a marble
fireplace, original hardwood floors, and a
skylight. Your host offers two charmingly
decorated double rooms, and Grandma's
quilt in the winter. You can bird watch on
the balcony or have a challenging game of
Trivial Pursuit in the evening. Full breakfast. $35-55 Canadian.

A B&B Downtown Network 2

3458 Laval Avenue, H2X 3C8
(514) 289-9749; FAX (514) 287-7386

Be in the heart of everything! The big bay
window of Bob's 90-year-old restored
home overlooks the city's most historic
park. Original woodwork and detail add to
the charm of this nine-room home, where a
double and triple are offered. The neighborhood is famous for is excellent "bring
your own wine" restaurants, and your host
knows them all. Full breakfast. $35-75
Canadian.

A B&B Downtown Network 3

3458 Laval Avenue, H2X 3C8
(514) 289-9749; FAX (514) 287-7386

Downtown double off Sherbrooke Street.
This antique-filled apartment on
Drummond Street is tastefully decorated
and only two minutes to the Museum of
Fine Arts and all shopping. Mount Royal
Park is nearby, and McGill University is
just two blocks. Your hosts will pamper
you with a gourmet breakfast and invite
you to join them for a sherry in the
evening. One double room, shared bath.
$55 Canadian.

A B&B Downtown Network 4

3458 Laval Avenue, H2X 3C8
(514) 289-9749; FAX (514) 287-7386

Downtown, in the heart of the Latin
Quarter. Enjoy the superb location of this

NOTES: Credit cards accepted: A Master Card; B Visa; C American Express; D Discover Card; E Diner's
Club; F Other; 2 Personal Checks accepted; 3 Lunch available; 4 Dinner available; 5 Open all year; 6 Pets
welcome; 7 Smoking allowed; 8 Children welcome; 9 Social drinking allowed; 10 Tennis available; 11
Swimming available; 12 Golf available; 13 Skiing available; 14 May be booked through travel agents.

restored traditional Québecoise home. Your host, active in the restaurant business, offers two sunlit doubles and one triple with a bay window opening onto a typical Montreal scene. The privacy of this tastefully furnished home is perfect for first or second honeymoons. Shared bath, full breakfast. $55-75 Canadian.

A B&B Downtown Network 6

3458 Laval Avenue, H2X 3C8
(514) 289-9749; FAX (514) 287-7386

When traveling to Quebec City, stop at this landmark home built in 1671, facing the beautiful St. Lawrence River. Your hostess, a blue-ribbon chef, offers guests a memorable breakfast featuring "Quiche Floriane." For an unforgettable stay, you are invited to experience thee warmth and hospitality of a typical Québecoise home. Two enchanting doubles. Full breakfast. $55 Canadian.

A B&B Downtown Network 7

3458 Laval Avenue, H2X 3C8
(514) 289-9749; FAX (514) 287-7386

This Old Montreal landmark offers eight guest rooms and one suite. Decorated with a combination of antiques and contemporary pieces, the guest rooms are spacious and air-conditioned. All have private baths in marble, some with Jacuzzi. In winter, snuggle before a crackling fire with a good book. Within strolling distance of Notre Dame church, fine restaurants, shops, and museums. Enjoy the richness of Montreal's heritage. Full gourmet breakfast. $75-95 Canadian.

Armor Inn

151 Sherbrooke Est, H2X 1C7
(514) 285-0140

The Armor Inn is a small hotel with a typical European character. Situated in the heart of Montreal, it offers its guests a warm family atmosphere. Ideally located close to Métro, St. Denis and Prince-Arthur streets. A 15-minute walk to Old Montreal, the Palais of Congress, and numerous underground shopping centers.

Host: Annick Morvan
Rooms: 15 (7 PB; 8 SB) $35-59
Continental Breakfast
Credit Cards: A, B
Notes: 5, 7, 8, 14

Auberge de la Fontaine

1301 East Rachel Street, H2J 2K1
(514) 597-0166

You will be warmly welcomed in this charming bed and breakfast inn, located in front of Parc la Fontaine, an 84-acre park close to the downtown area. The 21 air-conditioned rooms and suites, some with whirlpool bath, others with terrace or balcony, are beautiful, comfortable, and will make you feel at home. Take this opportunity to discover the exclusive shops, restaurants, and art galleries of the Plateau Mont-Royal, typical of French Montreal.

Hosts: Céline Boudreau and Jean Lamothe
Rooms: 21 (PB) $105-175 Canadian
Continental Breakfast
Credit Cards: A, B, C, F
Notes: 5, 7, 8, 14

Bed and Breakfast à Montréal

P. O. Box 575, Snowdon Station, H3X 3T8
(514) 738-9410

Our bed and breakfasts are located in the finest private homes and condo apartments, carefully selected for their comfort, cleanliness, and convenient locations downtown or just minutes away. Many are within walking distance of Old Montreal and the Convention Centre. All of our hosts are fluent in English. They'll enhance your visit with their suggestions, their outgoing personalities, and their delicious breakfasts. Stay long enough to visit Old Montreal, the lively Italian Quarter, the Underground City, Botanical Gardens, Mount Royal Park, and St. Joseph's Oratory, among other sights. Coordinator: Marian Kahn.

Brigette's Bed and Breakfast

Bed and Breakfast à Montréal
P. O. Box 575, Snowdon Station, H3X 3T8
(514) 738-9410

Brigette's love of art and antiques is obvious in her fabulous three-story townhouse. Fireplace, cozy livingroom, and view of the city's most historic park all add to the charm of this home. One double with brass bed, duvet, antique pieces, and your own bathroom. Experience the nearby "bring your own wine" restaurants. $50-70 Canadian.

Carole's Bed and Breakfast

Bed and Breakfast à Montréal
P. O. Box 575, Snowdon Station, H3X 3T8
(514) 738-9410

Stay in Carole's delightful, plant-filled townhouse featuring a grand piano played by her musician daughter. Relax in the master bedroom with a king-size bed. Enjoy browsing in the nearby antique shops and at the Atwater Market. $50-70 Canadian.

Jacqueline's Bed and Breakfast

Bed and Breakfast à Montréal
P. O. Box 575, Snowdon Station, H3X 3T8
(514) 738-9410

This magnificent four-story home is less than ten minutes from tourist attractions. One guest room with queen bed and private bath is on the second floor; several single rooms are on the third. Off-street parking is available. No smoking please. Dog in residence. $30-70 Canadian.

Lillian's Bed and Breakfast

Bed and Breakfast à Montréal
P. O. Box 575, Snowdon Station, H3X 3T8
(514) 738-9410

Lillian's large Georgian home with double rooms and one single room is filled with fine objects and a wonderful collection of Canadian art. Formerly a travel agent, she now lets the world come to her. St. Joseph's Oratory highlights the skyline in this chic neighborhood. $35-70 Canadian.

Manoir Ambrose

3422 Stanley Street, H3A 1R8
(514) 288-6922; FAX (514) 288-5757

Situated on the quiet and restful slope of beautiful Mont-Royal, within walking distance of Montreal's restaurants, theaters, shopping districts, metro system.

Host: Lucie Seguin
Rooms: 22 (17 PB; 5 SB) $50-90
Continental Breakfast
Credit Cards: A, B
Notes: 5, 6, 7, 8, 14

Martha's Bed and Breakfast

Bed and Breakfast à Montréal
P. O. Box 575, Snowdon Station, H3X 3T8
(514) 738-9410

From Martha's house walk to Montreal's hockey arena, the Forum, or the city's most elegant shopping complex, Westmount Square. Stenciled glass windows, original woodwork and detail, and smart period furnishings are just some of the features of this B&B. $50-70 Canadian.

NEW CARLISLE WEST

Bay View Farm

Box 21, 337 Main Highway, Route 132, G0C 1Z0
(418) 752-2725; (418) 752-6718

6 Pets welcome; 7 Smoking allowed; 8 Children welcome; 9 Social drinking allowed; 10 Tennis available; 11 Swimming available; 12 Golf available; 13 Skiing available; 14 May be booked through travel agents.

Bay View Farm

Located on Route 132 between New Carlisle and Bonaventure on the rugged and beautiful Baie de Chaleur coastline of Quebec's Gaspé Peninsula. Seaside accommodations include five comfortable guest rooms. Full country breakfast is made from fresh farm and garden produce. Additional light meals by arrangement. Handicrafts on display. August Bay View Folk Festival, museums, historic sites, Fauvel Golf Course, beaches, lighthouse, hiking, bird watching. Breathtakingly beautiful panoramic seascapes. Tranquil and restful environment.

Host: Helen Sawyer
Rooms: 5 (1 PB; 4 SB) $35
Full Breakfast
Credit Cards: None
Notes: 3, 4, 5, 8, 10, 11, 12, 13

QUEBEC CITY

Au Manoir Ste. Geneviève

13 Avenue Sainte Geneviève, G1R 4A7
(418) 694-1666; FAX (418) 694-1666

Enjoy your stay in a Victorian stone mansion furnished with antiques. Conveniently situated across from Governor's Park. View of Chateau Frontenac and St. Lawrence River. Next door to U.S. consulate. Recommended by AAA and New York *Times*. Modern facilities. Some efficiencies.

Host: Marguerite Corriveau
Rooms: 10 (PB) $85-100
Credit Cards: A, B
Notes: 5, 7, 8, 14

Au Petit Hotel

3 Ruelle des Ursulines, G1R 3Y6
(418) 694-0965; FAX (418) 692-4320

Located in the heart of Old Quebec, Au Petit Hotel offers quiet surroundings with a warm and hospitable atmosphere, such as the Ursulines convent, the Citadel, and the Chateau Frontenac. Discriminating gourmets will have no trouble finding neighborhood restaurants, smart boutiques, and all kinds of entertainment.

Host: The Tim Family
Rooms: 15 (PB) $45-70
Continental Breakfast
Credit Cards: A, B, C
Notes: 5, 7, 8

Bed and Breakfast Bonjour Québec

3765 Boulevard Monaco, G1P 3J3
(418) 527-1465

The first reservation service organization of Quebec represents 11 homes that were carefully selected to make your visit a genuine French experience. The Grande-Allee is reminiscent of the Champs Elysée in Paris. Historic sites, the St. Lawrence River, charming restaurants, and shops are wtihin easy reach of every bed and breakfast. From May to October. $45-95 (Canadian). Contact Denise and Raymond Blanchet for more information and city map with directions.

Gîte-Québec

3729, Avenue Le Corbusier
Sainte-Foy, G1W 4R8
(418) 651-1860

Gîte-Québec Bed & Breakfast arranges accommodations in private homes offering comfortable rooms, a complete breakfast,

---

NOTES: Credit cards accepted: A Master Card; B Visa; C American Express; D Discover Card; E Diner's Club; F Other; 2 Personal Checks accepted; 3 Lunch available; 4 Dinner available; 5 Open all year;

and warm hospitality. All listings have been personally inspected for their comfort and cleanliness. All are convenient to the city's attractions through excellent public transportation. $60-70 Canadian with a $15 deposit per person required. Call or write for a brochure and reservation form.

Le Chateau de Pierre

17 Avenue Sainte Genevieve, G1R 4A8
(418) 694-0429

This old English mansion is located in the heart of this historical city. Very comfortable rooms have private baths and are nicely decorated. Near all historical activities. Open all year.

Hosts: Richard and Lily Couturier
Rooms: 16 (PB) $65-105 Canadian
Continental Breakfast
Credit Cards: A, B
Notes: 2, 5, 7, 8

Maison Marie Rollet

81 Rue Sainte Anne, G1R 3X4
(418) 694-9271

A small hotel of ten rooms, La Maison Marie Rollet was built in 1876 by the Ursuline Sisters. The first floor of the small hotel has dark paneling, a fireplace, and stained glass. Two rooms have a working fireplace, and most have air conditioning. On the third floor, a terrace overlooks the gardens of the Ursuline's convent school.

Host: Fernaud Blouin
Rooms: 10 (PB) $55-90
No Breakfast
Credit Cards: B
Notes: 5, 7, 8, 9, 10, 11, 12, 14

ST-ANTOINE-DE-TILLY

Auberge Manoir de Tilly

3854 Chemin de Tilly, G0S 2C0
(418) 886-2407

Manoir de Tilly dates from 1786 and is an authentic manor built by one of the king's representatives. The chef offers a highly praised cuisine where regional farm and sea products are lovingly prepared for guests. In 1990, a 32-room pavilion was added, as well as a health center and conference facilities. The rooms are lovingly decorated and offer calm and tranquility. The manor is only a few kilometers from historic Quebec City. Golfing and tennis courts nearby.

Host: Jocelyne Gagnon
Rooms: 32 (PB)
Full Breakfast
Credit Cards: A, B, C
Notes: 4, 5, 7, 8, 9, 10, 11, 12, 14

SAINTE-PÉTRONILLE

Auberge la Goéliche Inn

22 Chemin du Quai, G0A 4C0
(418) 828-2248; FAX (418) 692-1742

Overhanging the St. Lawrence River, this castlelike inn offers a breathtaking view of Quebec City, a 15-minute drive away. It is also close to famous Mont Ste. Anne ski center. Its 24 rooms are warmly decorated in rustic French-Canadian style. Outdoor swimming pool. English and continental breakfasts. Guided tours of historic surroundings available.

Hosts: Janet Duplain, Andrée Marchand, and Alain Turgeon
Rooms: 24 (16 PB; 8 SB) $80-130
Full or Continental Breakfast
Credit Cards: A, B
Notes: 3, 4, 5, 7, 8, 9, 10, 11, 12, 13, 14

ST-MARC-SUR-RICHELIEU

Auberge Handfield

555 Richelieu, J0L 2E0
(514) 584-2226; FAX (514) 584-3650

The Handfield Inn is a family business that stresses genuine hospitality. In 1984, major

6 Pets welcome; 7 Smoking allowed; 8 Children welcome; 9 Social drinking allowed; 10 Tennis available; 11 Swimming available; 12 Golf available; 13 Skiing available; 14 May be booked through travel agents.

renovations enabled the inn to maintain efficiency and comfort without sacrificing the originality of this home, which was built more than 160 years ago. A new health club was added in 1991.

Host: Conrad Handfield
Rooms: 53 (PB) $55-145
Continental Breakfast
Credit Cards: A, B, C, D, E, F
Notes: 3, 4, 5, 7, 8, 9, 10, 11, 12, 13

Hostellerie les Trois Tilleuls

290 Rue Richelieu, J0L 2E0
(514) 584-2231

The Hostellerie les Trois Tilleuls is a charming inn on the banks of the Richelieu River, a short 30 minutes from Montreal. The 24 rooms with balconies overlook the Richelieu River. The dining room features authentic French cuisine with an extensive wine list of exceptional vintages.

Host: Michel Aubriot
Rooms: 24 (PB) $84-145 Canadian
Full Breakfast
Credit Cards: A, B, C, D, E
Notes: 3, 4, 5, 7, 8, 9, 10, 11, 12, 13

VAL DAVID

Auberge Charme de Suisse

1459 Rue Merette, J0T 2N0
(819) 322-3434

This inn has beautiful and quiet surroundings and is in the midst of various activities: golf, skiing, swimming, and much more. Each room has a private bath and balcony. Your host is from Switzerland. Inquire for directions.

Host: Alfred Giger
Rooms: 10 (PB) $65-85
Full Breakfast
Credit Cards: A, B
Notes: 4, 5, 7, 8, 11, 12, 13, 14

NOTES: Credit cards accepted: A Master Card; B Visa; C American Express; D Discover Card; E Diner's Club; F Other; 2 Personal Checks accepted; 3 Lunch available; 4 Dinner available; 5 Open all year;

Puerto Rico

CEIBA

Ceiba Country Inn

P. O. Box 1067, 00635
(809) 885-0471

In the hills on the East Coast, in a pastoral setting with a view of the sea. Quiet, serene atmosphere with a cozy cocktail lounge. Centrally located for trips to El Yunque, Luquillo, San Juan, Vieques, Culebra, and St. Thomas.

Hosts: Don Bingham and Nicki Treat
Rooms: 9 (PB) $55
Continental Breakfast
Credit Cards: A, B, C, D, E
Notes: 3, 5, 7, 8, 9, 14

Ceiba Country Inn

CONADO

Aloe Inn on the Beach

1125 Seaview Street, 00907
(809) 725-5313

Situated in the heart of the tourist zone, the Aloe Inn is right on the beach. Four of the rooms have a spectacular ocean view, and all are air conditioned. Also offered is one efficency unit at a slightly higher cost. The inn is a short walk from restaurants, hotels, casinos, and boutiques.

Hosts: Eileen and Julio Bran
Rooms: 9 (8 PB; 1 SB) $55-85
Continental Breakfast
Credit Cards: A, B
Notes: 5, 8, 9, 11

ISLA VERDE

The Duffys' Inn

9 Isla Verde Road, 00979
(809) 726-1415; (800) 221-3917

The Duffys', established in 1947 from an old Spanish hacienda with lush tropical plants in the courtyard, is open 24 hours. A full menu restaurant operates from 7:30 A.M. through midnight. Across the street from the ocean and near the airport. Casinos, golf, tennis, water sports, and other dining facilities are nearby. Comfortable rooms include air conditioning, ceiling fans, cable TV, and phones.

Host: Madeline Weihe
Rooms: 10 (PB) $55-75
Full Breakfast
Credit Cards: A, B, C
Notes: 3, 4, 5, 7, 8, 9, 14

MARICAO

La Hacienda Juanita

Road 105 KM 23.5, Box 777, 00606
(809) 838-2550

Built 160 years ago as the main lodge of a coffee plantation, this bed and breakfast offers exuberant tropical vegetation and

PUERTO RICO

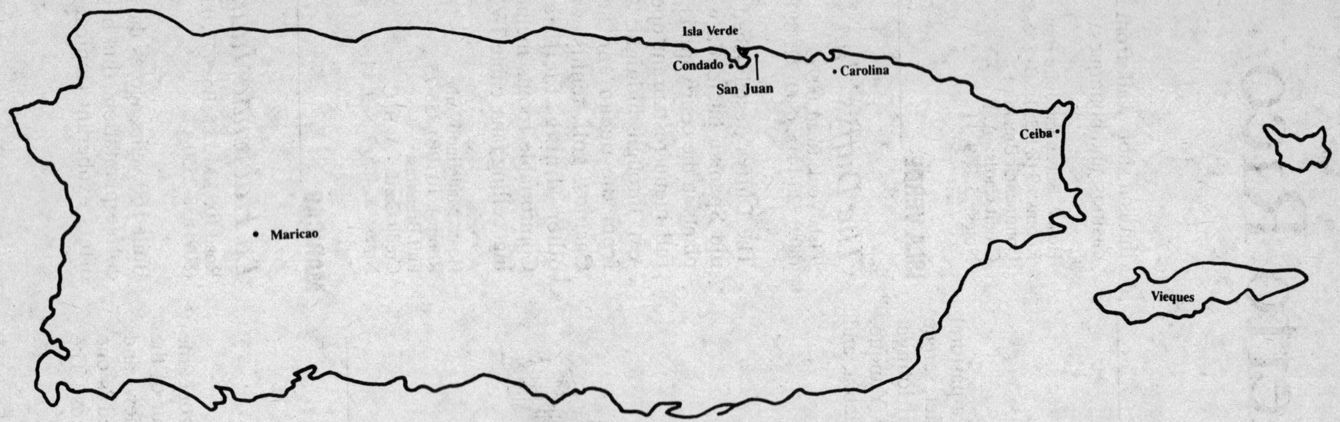

Vieques

Ceiba

Carolina

Isla Verde

Condado

San Juan

Maricao

verdant views of the mountains. Caressed by scents of orange, grapefruit, and guava and kissed by the brightened starlight of the mountain elevation. Songs of tropical birds, and the wide verandas, complete with wicker furniture and rocking chairs, invite lazy siestas.

Hosts: Cynthia and Luis Rivera-Lugo
Rooms: 21 (PB) $75
Full Breakfast
Credit Cards: A, B, C
Notes: 2, 3, 4, 5, 7, 8, 9, 10, 11

El Canario Inn

SAN JUAN

El Canario Inn

1317 Ashford Avenue, Condado, 00907
(809) 722-3861; (800) 223-0888

San Juan's most historic and unique bed and breakfast. All 25 guest rooms are air-conditioned, with private bath, telephone, and cable TV. Beautiful tropical patio areas for relaxation. Only one block to beautiful Condado Beach, casinos, boutiques, and many fine restaurants. El Canario is perhaps the best deal for your vacation dollar in the Caribbean.

Hosts: Jude and Keith Olson
Rooms: 25 (PB) $65-85
Continental Breakfast
Credit Cards: A, B, C, D, E
Notes: 5, 7, 8, 9, 14

VIEQUES

Esperanza Beach Club and Marina

P. O. Box 1569, 00765
(809) 741-8675; FAX (809) 741-1313

A special place still remains far removed from the hectic pace of everyday life. This twenty-room inn is located on the southern side of the picturesque island of Vieques, sixteen miles off the eastern coast of Puerto Rico. A stroll through lovely gardens takes you directly to the tropical, aquamarine waters of the Caribbean Sea. You can kayak, row, swim, snorkel, fish, scuba, windsurf, or sail in yhe beautiful bay. Some rooms are large enough for a family of four.

Hosts: Rosita Haeussler and Tito Ruiz
Rooms: 20 (PB) $76-96
Continental Breakfast
Credit Cards: A, B, C
Notes: 2, 3, 4, 5, 6, 7, 8, 9, 10, 11, 12, 14

NOTES: Credit cards accepted: A Master Card; B Visa; C American Express; D Discover Card; E Diner's Club; F Other; 2 Personal Checks accepted; 3 Lunch available; 4 Dinner available; 5 Open all year; 6 Pets welcome; 7 Smoking allowed; 8 Children welcome; 9 Social drinking allowed; 10 Tennis available; 11 Swimming available; 12 Golf available; 13 Skiing available; 14 May be booked through travel agents.

Virgin Islands

ST. CROIX

Pink Fancy Inn

27 Prince Street, 00820
(809) 773-8460; (800) 524-2045
FAX (809) 773-6448

A small, uniquely private inn located in downtown Christiansted in St. Croix, this historic landmark was built in 1780 and 1880 and completely remodeled in 1990. You will find a pool, courtyard, garden, hardwood floors, air conditioning, plus a ceiling fan, a large room, and friendly and helpful staff. Room rates include continental breakfast, a complimentary bar open 24 hours, and walking distance to restaurants and duty-free shopping. Arrangements made for watersports, an island tour, and wedding and honeymoon packages.

Host: Jens Thomsen
Rooms: 12 (PB) $75-125
Continental Plus Breakfast
Credit Cards: A, B, C
Notes: 5, 7, 8, 9, 10 (by arrangement), 11, 12 (by arrangement), 14

ST. THOMAS

The American Country Collection #001

4 Greenwood Lane, Delmar, New York 12054
(518) 439-7001

This small bed and breakfast hotel is representative of Spanish Colonial architecture, 800 feet above Charlotte Amalie, the capital of the Virgin Islands. Minisuites and rooms with air conditioning and private baths are available. Suites also have cabl TV. A full service restaurant is on premis es, and a continental breakfast and a poo with a snack bar are available for guests t enjoy. Smoking permitted. Free transporta tion to Magens Bay Beach daily. $60-13 seasonal.

The American Country Collection #002

4 Greenwood Lane, Delmar, New York 12054
(518) 439-7001

This bed and breakfast is located in tov and offers rooms and family suites wi kitchenette, air conditioning, TV, ar phone in your room. Minutes from sho ping and restaurants. Dinner is available guests, and a full breakfast is serve Double beds in the rooms, and four doub beds in the suites. No pets. Smokir allowed. $60-120 seasonal.

The American Country Collection #003

4 Greenwood Lane, Delmar, New York, 12054
(518) 439-7001

This upscale bed and breakfast overloo the Charlotte Amalie Harbor. Listed on t National Register of Historic Homes, th Caribbean-style home is a short walk fr town and offers eight rooms, all of whi have air conditioning, TV, and phon Continental breakfast. A full-servi restaurant is on premises for dinner, an

NOTES: Credit cards accepted: A Master Card; B Visa; C American Express; D Discover Card; E Diner's Club; F Other; 2 Personal Checks accepted; 3 Lunch available; 4 Dinner available; 5 Open all year;

pool is available to guests. Smoking permitted. No pets. $90-215, seasonal.

The American Country Collection #004

4 Greenwood Lane, Delmar, New York, 12054
(518) 439-7001

Spacious and luxurious guest rooms, all with either king- or queen-size beds, cable TV, ceiling fans, air conditioning, and private bath, are what you'll find in this lovely bed and breakfast. A large, luxurious pool overlooks Charlotte Amalie Harbor, continental breakfast is served daily, and a gourmet restaurant serving continental cuisine with West Indian flair is on premises. Piano lounge with outdoor terrace for dancing. No pets. Smoking permitted. $95-190, seasonal.

Danish Chalet Inn

P. O. Box 4319, 00803
(809) 774-5764; (800) 635-1531
FAX (809) 777-4886

Family-operated 13-room inn overlooking beautiful Charlotte Amalie Harbor with cool harbor and mountain breezes. Ten minutes from airport and five-minute walk to center of town for duty-free shopping, fine restaurants, and waterfront activities; 15 minutes to world-famous beaches. In-room phones, sun deck, Jacuzzi, honor bar, free beach towels, and welcoming beverage. Congenial family atmosphere. Dinner restaurant two minutes away. Minimart and laundromat one block away.

Hosts: Frank and Mary Davis
Rooms: 13 (5 PB; 8 SB) $60-95
Continental Breakfast
Credit Cards: A, B
Notes: 5, 7, 8, 9, 10, 11, 12, 14

Galleon House

Box 6577, 00804
(809) 774-6952; (800) 524-2052

Lovely 14-room small hotel in a historic district, one block from town. Fantastic harbor view. Warm, hospitable inn with delightful home-cooked breakfast. Freshwater pool, easy walk to shopping and restaurants. Air-conditioned rooms with private balconies, cable TV, telephones, and guest refrigerators. Write or call for color brochure.

Host: John Slone
Rooms: 14 (12 PB; 2 SB) $49-119
Expanded Continental Breakfast
Credit Cards: A, B, C
Notes: 5, 7, 8, 9, 11, 12, 14

Island View Guest House

P. O. Box 1903, 00803
(809) 774-4270; (800) 524-2023

A charming 15-room guest house is available to visitors at affordable rates. Located midway between the airport and Charlotte Amalie on Crown Mountain, Island View is 545 feet above and overlooks the harbor. Complimentary continental breakfast, pool, and daily maid service. King, queen, or twin accommodations. Dinner and fine dining available. Honeymoon packages.

Hosts: Norman Leader and Barbara Cooper
Rooms: 15 (13 PB; 2 SB) $45-95
Continental or Full Breakfast
Credit Cards: A, B, C
Notes: 3, 4, 5, 7, 9, 11, 14

6 Pets welcome; 7 Smoking allowed; 8 Children welcome; 9 Social drinking allowed; 10 Tennis available; 11 Swimming available; 12 Golf available; 13 Skiing available; 14 May be booked through travel agents.

Bed and Breakfast
Reccomendation Form

As *The Annual Directory of American Bed & Breakfasts* gains approval from the traveling public, more and more bed and breakfasts are asking to be included on our mailing list. If you know of another bed and breakfast who may not be on our list, give them a great business-boosting opportunity by providing us with the following information:

B&B Name _____

Address _____

City _____State _____Zip Code _____

Telephone _____

Name of Hosts _____

B&B Name _____

Address _____

City _____State _____Zip Code _____

Telephone _____

Name of Hosts _____

B&B Name _____

Address _____

City _____State _____Zip Code _____

Telephone _____

Name of Hosts _____

Please send this form to:
The Annual Directory of American Bed & Breakfasts
513 Third Avenue South
Nashville, TN 37210